汉英大词典

Chinese-English Dictionary

主　编: 王瑞晴　王宇欣

副主编: 刘淑慧　周丽锦　李宝芬

编　委: 王宇欣　刘淑慧　周丽锦　王树国
王宏丽　白国芳　毕军贤　姜国霞
贾振堂　刘传清　高　琨　高　峰

外文出版社
FOREIGN LANGUAGES PRESS

图书在版编目（CIP）数据

汉英大词典／王瑞晴主编.
北京：外文出版社，2005
ISBN 7-119-04050-2

Ⅰ. 汉... Ⅱ. 王... Ⅲ. ①英语－词典②词典－汉、英
Ⅳ. H316

中国版本图书馆CIP数据核字(2005)第049530号

外文出版社网址：
http://www.flp.com.cn
外文出版社电子信箱：
info@flp.com.cn
sales@flp.com.cn

汉英大词典
主　　编　王瑞晴　王宇欣

责任编辑　刘承忠　曾惠杰
封面设计　小雨工作室
印刷监制　张国祥
出版发行　外文出版社
社　　址　北京市百万庄大街24号　　邮政编码　100037
电　　话　（010）68996177
　　　　　（010）68329514/68327211（推广发行部）
印　　刷　北京飞达印刷有限责任公司
经　　销　新华书店/外文书店
开　　本　大32开　　字　　数　2500千字
印　　数　00001—16000册　　印　　张　38
版　　次　2006年第1版第1次印刷
装　　别　精
书　　号　ISBN 7-119-04050-2
定　　价　48.00元

Contents 目录

Preface 前言

近年来，随着经济的全球化和信息技术的广泛普及，多领域的国际交流日益频繁，人们对于汉英工具书的需求也大幅度增加。

为了满足大中学生、专业技术人员、英语爱好者以及学习汉语的外国朋友的需要，我们在总结了近年来研究成果的基础上，参考了大量的国内外出版的相关工具书和报刊资料，编写了这本新世纪版《汉英大词典》。本词典收录的词和词条，均是最常见的汉字和最常见的表达方式，另有附录十余种，基本上可以满足不同文化程度的读者日常学习的需要。

在选词方面，本词典注重突出以下几个特点：

1. 内容新颖。以求新为宗旨，对出现及广泛承认和使用的词语，尽量收录。由于时代的发展，汉语也出现了不少新词汇，比如彩信、非典型性肺炎、禽流感、充值卡等。

2. 收词广泛。随着各学科的相互渗透，传媒的发展和知识的普及，只在大型的专业工具书中才出现的一些高科技词汇也收录其中，比如全球通(Global System for Mobile Communications)；网上冲浪(Surf the Internet)；生态足迹(Ecological Footprint)；非典型性肺炎(Sever Acute Respiratory syndrome)等等。

3. 词义准确。力争英语释义切合汉语原意。对于英文中没有直接对应的汉语解释，先写出词条，然后给出比较完整的解释。

4. 实用性强。我们参考了很多权威词典，收集了大量的词组、成语、谚语、俚语和习语等。汉语中的某些口语表达方式往往被认为难登大雅之堂而不被其他汉英辞书收录，本词典在口语方面进行了选择收录，以满足不同读者的需要。

在本词典的成书过程中，参考了许多权威辞书和资料，在此表示感谢。

该词典力求新颖，丰富，准确，实用性强。然而，精益求精永无止境，其中的缺憾之处也在所难免，希望广大读者和有关专家多提宝贵意见，以便再版时使之更加完善。

编　者

Explanatory Notes 凡例

一、本词典所收录条目分为单字条目和多字条目。前者用4号书宋排印，后者用小6号书宋排印。

二、单字条目按《现代汉语词典》中汉语拼音字母顺序排列。同音异调的汉字按声调顺序排列。单字条目用汉语拼音字母注音。正文前为读者编写的“汉语拼音索引”，供读者查字时使用。

三、多字条目按第一个字排列在单字条目后。同一单字条目后的多字条目不止一条时，按第二个字的汉语拼音字母的顺序排列。第二个字为同音字时按其笔画顺序排列；第二个字相同时按第三个字排列，依次类推。为节省篇幅，多字条目不标注拼音。但有些多字词条有不同的读音，则标注拼音，以示区别。

四、条目一般采用对应的英语释义。单字若无独立义项，则在拼音后直接排多字条目；若有两个或两个以上的英语释义时，分立义项，在词目的右上角注1,2,3…等数码标出顺序。

五、多字条目的不同义项，意思相距较远者用①②③等分立，相距较近者用分号“;”隔开。

六、条目释义、例证或其译文中，如果有限定性或补充性说明，可省略部分或可替换部分，或有关用法、语法特征等英语说明用圆括号“( )”括出。

七、条目释义后，根据需要收入词句作为例证。例证前加冒号“:”。例证中的本条目用代词号“~”表示。例证的英文译文不止一个时，例证与例证之间用斜线号“/”隔开。

Abbreviations 略语表

[讽]讽刺
[迷]迷信
[粗]粗语
[俚]俚语
[喻]比喻
[谑]戏谑
[谚]谚语
[俗]俗语
[贬]贬义
[旧]旧语
[古]古语
[谦]谦词
[方]方言
[书]书面
[口]口语
[俗]俗语
[量]量词
[象]象声词

【心】心理学
【军】军事
【戏】戏剧
【体】体育
【语】语言学
【宗】宗教
【微】微生物
【经】经济
【律】法律
【音】音乐
【美】美术
【哲】哲学
【逻】逻辑学
【解】解剖学
【商】商业
【摄】摄影
【考】考古
【林】林业
【油】石油工业;石油化工
【测】测绘;测量
【数】数学

【工】工业
【印】印刷
【天】天文学
【化】化学
【生化】生物化学
【水】水利
【生理】生理
【气】气象学
【统】统计
【地】地质
【机】机械工程
【交】交通运输
【农】农业
【医】医学
【药】药物;药物学
【中医】中医
【植】植物学
【影】影视
【冶】冶金
【纺】纺织工业
【矿】矿业;矿物学
【物】物理学
【建】建筑工程
【生】生物
【电】电工;电信;电子
【史】历史
【航】航天;航空;航海

说明:(1)略语用于注明词源、修饰色彩、学科等;
(2)有些以本表略语为基础构成的略语,不再收入本表。
(3)未经略语、意义自明的,也不收入本表。如:【会计】等。

A

A

ā

阿 [方] ① a prefix used before pet names, monosyllabic surnames, or numbers denoting order of seniority in a family, to form terms of endearment: ~宝 *A Bao* ②a prefix used before kinship terms: ~爸 *dad*; *pop*; *pa*
see also ē

【阿比让】Abidjan, capital of Cote d'Ivoire (formerly Ivory Coast)

【阿比西尼亚】Abyssinia (now called Ethiopia): ~人 *Abyssinian*

【阿波罗】Apollo, Greek and Roman god of the sun

【阿波罗飞船】【航】Apollo (spaceship)

【阿波罗计划】【航】Apollo programme (moon-landing programme launched by NASA of the US in the 1960's and 1970's)

【阿布扎比】Abu Dhabi, capital of the United Arab Emirates

【阿尔巴尼亚】Albania: ~人 *Albanian* / ~语 *Albanian*

【阿尔卑斯山】the Alps

【阿尔及尔】Algiers, capital of Algeria

【阿尔及利亚】Algeria: ~人 *Algerian*

【阿尔泰山】Altai Mountains

【阿飞】teddy boy; beatnik; hippie (hippy); a youth given to rowdy behaviour and queer dress

【阿富汗】Afghanistan: ~人 *Afghan*

【阿根廷】Argentina: ~人 *Argentine*

【阿訇】*ahung*; imam (the officiating priest of a mosque)

【阿基米德】Archimedes (c. 287-212 BC), Greek mathematician and inventor of many devices such as the helical screw: ~原理 *Archimedes' principle*

【阿克拉】Accra, capital of Ghana

【阿拉伯】Arab; Arabia

【阿拉伯半岛】Arabian Peninsula; Arabia

【阿拉伯国家】Arab state; Arab country

【阿拉伯国家联盟】League of Arab States; Arab League

【阿拉伯联合酋长国】United Arab Emirates (UAE)

【阿拉伯人】Arab; Arabian: 那个~坚持说他没有见过那只骆驼。*The Arabian insisted that he had never seen the camel.*

【阿拉伯石油输出国组织】Organization of Arab Petroleum Exporting Countries (OAPEC)

【阿拉伯树胶】【化】Arabic gum; gum acacia

【阿拉伯数字】Arabic numerals: 请用文字和~写出这个数。*Write the number in words and in figures, please.*

【阿拉伯也门共和国】Yemen Arab Republic

【阿拉伯字母】Arabic alphabet

【阿拉法特】Yasser Arafat (1929-2004), Palestinian leader

【阿拉木图】Alma-Ata, former capital of Kazakhstan

【阿拉斯加】Alaska: ~半岛 *Alaska Peninsula*

【阿门】amen

【阿婆】granny; grandma: ~告诉我不要把手弄脏了。*Granny told me not to get my hands dirty.*

【阿姨】① mother's sister; aunt; auntie: ~刚去美国。*Aunt has just left for America.* /那个临终的妇女把她小儿子托付给~。*The dying woman commended her little child to her aunt.* ② term of address for a woman of one's parents generation: 刘~看起来很漂亮。*Auntie Liu looks very pretty.*

啊 express surprise or admiration: ~,这地方多美啊! *Oh, what a beautiful place!* / ~,这水真甜啊! *Ah, the water is really sweet!* /可爱的孩子们在牧场上跳来跳去,这是一幅多么恬静而又生气勃勃的景象~。*What a quiet but lively scene; the lovely children frisked about in the pastures.*

á

啊 express for an answer or ask for something to be repeated: ~,你说什么? *Pardon?* / ~,是啦。我来了。*Ah, yes. I'm coming.*

ǎ

啊 express surprise: ~? 你怎么啦? *Gosh, what's the matter with you?* /那个孩子长得多快~! *How quickly the child is growing.*

à

啊 express sudden realization: ~,原来是你! *Ah, so it's you.* / ~,那么你们下星期要出发了。*So you're going to start next week, eh?*

ɑ

啊 ① express admiration: 多好的天气~! *What a nice day!* ② express confirmation: 你不能去

A

那儿～。*You can't go there.* ③ express doubt：你现在忙～？*Are you busy now?* ④ indicate a short pause to draw attention to what is to be said next ⑤ used after things enumerated

āi

哎 ① convey surprise or dissatisfaction：～！是你啊！*Oh, it's you!* ② express a reminder or warning：～小心点！*Hey, be careful.*

【哎呀】① express surprise ② express complaints or impatience：～，你怎么又迟到了？*Ah, why do you come late again?*

【哎哟】express apology or mild surprise：～，下雨了。*Ah, it's raining.* /～，真烫。*Ouch! It's hot.*

哀 ① grieved；sorrowful ② mourning；condolences：致～ *express one's condolences* ③ pity；compassion

【哀兵必胜】an army burning with indignation is bound to win

【哀愁】unhappy；sorrowful；sad：母亲死的那一天，他无限～。*It was a sad day for him when his mother died.*

【哀辞】a formal expression of sorrow or mourning, often in rhyme；elegy

【哀悼】grieve over sb's death；lament sb's death：为某人父亲的逝世向他表示～ *condole with sb on the death of his father* /工人们～乔，记住了他的英名。*The workers mourned Joe and remembered his name.* /举国上下～他们敬爱的领导人。*The whole nation mourned the death of their much-loved leader.*

【哀告】implore；supplicate；beg piteously

【哀歌】① mournful song；elegy：～是曲调忧郁悲哀的音乐作品。*A composition is melancholy or pensive in tone.* ② croon plaintively

【哀号】cry piteously；bemoan；wail：为某人的不幸而～ *wail (over) one's misfortunes*

【哀叫】cry sadly；whine：狗低声～，意思是想和我们一起出去。*The dog whined to go out with us.*

【哀矜】feel compassion for；sympathize；commiserate

【哀怜】feel compassion for；pity

【哀鸣】whine plaintively；wail：她仿佛听到那只鸟在树丛中～。*She seemed to hear the bird wailing in the trees.* /狗在低声～。*The dog was whining softly.*

【哀凄】sad；mournful

【哀泣】sob：那个婴儿的～声渐趋沉寂。*The baby's sobs gradually died down.*

【哀求】entreat；implore；plead piteously：～某人怜悯 *entreat sb piteously for mercy*；*supplicate sb for mercy* /～的眼光 *an imploring glance*

【哀伤】distressed；sad；grieved and heartbroken：她依然在为她死去的丈夫～。*She is still grieving for her dead husband.* /母亲为她孩子的病感到～。*The mother was distressed by her baby's illness.*

【哀思】sad memories (of the deceased)；grief；sorrow：寄托～ *give expression to one's grief over sb's death*

【哀叹】sigh in sorrow；bewail；lament：～自己运气不好 *bewail one's failure* /王室家族成员～贵族社会的消失。*The royal members lamented the passing of aristocratic society.*

【哀恸】mourn；grief；deep sorrow：她的～是无法用语言形容的。*Words could not describe how sad she was.*

【哀婉】sad and moving；pathetic

【哀怨】sad；plaintive

【哀乐】funeral music；dirge：奏～ *play funeral music*；*play a lament*

埃[1] dust：空气中有尘～。*There is dust in the air.*

埃[2] 【物】angstrom (A)

【埃菲尔铁塔】Eiffel Tower

【埃及】Egypt：～人 *Egyptian* /～在非洲，首都是开罗。*Egypt is in Africa; it's capital is Cairo.*

【埃塞俄比亚】Ethiopia：～人 *Ethiopian*

挨 ① one after another；next to：那两座房子紧～着。*The two houses are next to each other.*
see also ɑ́i

【挨次】take turns；in turn；one by one；one after another

【挨个儿】by turns；one by one；in turn：要求男孩子们～回答问题。*The boys were asked to answer the questions in turn.*

【挨户】go from door to door；go from house to house：战士们挨门～搜查敌人。*The soldiers carried out a house-to-house to search the enemies.*

【挨近】be near to；get close to：～房子的地方附近有些树。*There are some trees near the house.*

【挨靠】① lean against；lean on：～在桌子上 *lean on the desk* /那小孩～在母亲身边。*The child nestled up to its mother.* ② depend on

【挨着】be close to：学校～医院。*The school is close to the hospital.*

唉 ① sound indicating response：——小王，快点儿！——～，来了！— *Hurry up, Xiaowang.* — *Yes, just coming.* ② express sadness, weariness；regret or disappointment：～！我早告诉过你了！*Ah! I told you so!*
see also ɑ̀i

【唉声叹气】sigh in despair；moan and groan：不要受了一点挫折就～。*Don't moan and groan because of a little setback.*

ɑ́i

挨 ① suffer；endure：同学们～了雨淋，回家时都已浑身湿透。*The students were caught in the rain and came home saturated.* ② struggle to pull through hard times；drag out ③ delay；put off see also āi

【挨呲儿】[书] get a scolding or a dressing-down

【挨打】cop it; get a thrashing; take a beating; come under attack

【挨斗】be denounced; be struggled against

【挨饿】famish; hunger: 他在～。*He is suffering from hunger.* /她们都下了决心，宁愿死也不愿～。*They are all resolved rather to die than to famish.*

【挨批】be criticized; be denounced

【挨整】be in for criticism and denunciation

皑 [书] pure white; snow white

【皑皑】[书] (of snow, frost, etc.) pure white

癌 cancer; carcinoma: 胃～ *cancer of the stomach; stomach cancer* /肝～ *live cancer* /食道～ *cancer of the esophagus* /皮肤～ *cancer of the skin; skin cancer* /肺～ *lung cancer* /子宫～ *cancer of the uterus* /骨～ *cancer in the bones* /乳腺～ *breast cancer* /血～ *leukemia* /结肠～ *colon cancer* /直肠～ *carcinoma of the rectum* /喉～ *cancer of the throat* /胰岛细胞～ *islet-cell carcinoma*

【癌变】【医】canceration; cancerization

【癌病】【医】carcinomatosis

【癌扩散】【医】metastasis (of cancer); spread of cancer

【癌魔】【医】demon of cancer

【癌切除术】【医】carcinectomy

【癌细胞】【医】cancer cell

【癌症】【医】cancer; carcinoma: ～研究基金会 *Cancer Research Foundation* /他最终战胜了～。*He finally overcame the cancer.* /医生断定汤姆患的是～。*The doctor concluded that Tom's disease was cancer.*

【癌转移】【医】metastasis of cancer

ǎi

嗳 show dissent or displeasure

矮 ① short: 她不像她妈妈;她很高,而她妈妈很～。*She is unlike her mother; she is tall and her mother is very short.* ② low: 他建造的房子～而宽敞。*He built the house low and wide.* ③ be lower than; be inferior to

【矮凳】low stool

【矮墩墩】pudgy; dumpy; stocky

【矮个儿】person of short stature; short person

【矮林】bosquet; spinney; low woods

【矮胖】bosquet; dumpy; short and stout: 一个～的女人 *a dumpy woman*

【矮人】① dwarf ② pigmy or pygmy: 他们的儿子是个～。*Their son is a dwarf.*

【矮小】short and small; undersized; little; undersized: 他的孩子们因营养不良而身材～。*His children were dwarfed by insufficient food.* /他被关在一间～的屋子里。*He was shut up in a small room.*

【矮子】short person; dwarf

蔼[1] [书] friendly; amiable; affable: 和～ *amiable* /我总觉得他是一位和～可亲的人。*I've always found him a most amiable fellow.*

蔼[2] [书] lush; luxuriant

【蔼蔼】① lush; luxuriant ② dim; dark; hazy ③ numerous

【蔼然】kind-hearted; amiable; genial; gentle

【蔼然可亲】kindly; amiable; affable

霭 [书] mist; haze: 晨～ *morning haze* /暮～ *evening haze*

ài

艾[1] ① Chinese mugwort (Artemisia argyi); moxa ② (Ài) a surname

艾[2] [书] ① old; aged ② the aged; the elderly

艾[3] [书] end; halt; stop: 方兴未～ *be fast unfolding; be in the ascendant*

艾[4] [书] pretty; beautiful; handsome

【艾滋病】AIDS (Acquired Immune Deficiency Syndrome): ～委员会 *Aids Committee* /～研究中心 *Aids Research Centre* /～研究基金会 *Aids Research Foundation*

唉 express sadness or regret

see also āi

爱 ① love; have profound affection: 那个小伙子～上了这个姑娘。*The boy fell in love with the girl.* /他对他妻子的～现在已经幻灭了。*His love for his wife is now dead.* /没有孩子的人不知道什么叫～。*He knows not what love is that has no children.* /他把他的～写在诗歌里。*His love was written into his poem.* ②be fond of; like: 这个商店是我最～去的地方。*This shopping is my favourite resort.* /他～用夸大的词句。*He is fond of using high-sounding phrases.* ③ cherish; hold dear; treasure: 拥军～民 *support the army and cherish the people* /他宣扬的教义要旨是～天下所有的人。*The essence of his religious teaching is love for all men.* ④ be apt to; be in the habit of

【爱不释手】be fond of sth that one can hardly put it down

【爱才如命】cherish talent as much as one cherishes

【爱财如命】skin a flea for its hide; love money as much as life itself

【爱巢】love nest

【爱称】diminutive; pet name

【爱戴】adore; love and esteem; beloved: 他是人民～的领袖。*He is the beloved leader of the people.*

【爱迪生】Thomas Alva Edison (1847-1931), American inventor

【爱尔兰】Ireland; Eire: ～人 *Irish; Irishman* /～语

A

Irish /联合王国包括北～和威尔士。*The United Kingdom includes Northern Ireland and Wales.*

【爱尔兰共和国】Republic of Ireland; Eire

【爱尔兰共和军】Irish Republican Army

【爱抚】show tender; care for; have tender affection for:谁来～这些穷人呢? *Who cares for the poor?*

【爱国】be patriotic; love one's country: ～统一战线 *patriotic united front* / ～卫生运动 *patriotic sanitation campaign* / ～主义 *patriotism* /没有人相信他是一个～者。*Nobody believed he was a patriot.*

【爱好】① be fond of; be keen on; take on; take great pleasure in:我～轻音乐。*I'm very fond of light music.* ② interest; hobby:舞蹈是她一生的～。*Dancing was the love of her life.* /他是一个音乐～者。*He is a music-lover.* /不要根据人们的穿着～来评价他们。*Don't judge people according to their taste in clothes.*

【爱护】cherish; treasure; take good care of:要～身体。*Good care should be given to your health.*

【爱见】[方] like; be fond of:邻居们都很～那个孩子。*The neighbours are fond of the child.*

【爱克斯光】【物】X-ray; Roentgen ray:照～ *have an X-ray taken* / ～透视 *fluoroscopy*; *X-ray examination* / ～诊断 *X-ray diagnosis*; *Roentgen diagnosis*

【爱克斯射线】【物】X-ray

【爱怜】tender affection; compassion

【爱恋】be in love with; feel deeply attached to

【爱侣】sweethearts; lover

【爱美】set great store by one's appearance; like to look smart; be fond of fine clothes

【爱面子】save face; be keen on face-saving; be sensitive about one's reputation

【爱莫能助】willing and yet unable to help; be willing to lend a hand but unable to do so; be willing to help, but one's hands are tired

【爱慕】adore; admire; envy; long for

【爱琴海】Aegean Sea (part of the Mediterranean between Greece and Anatolia)

【爱情】love (between man and woman); affection:柏拉图式的～ *platonic love* / ～歌曲 *love song* / ～小说 *romance novel*; *live story* / ～是不能买卖的。*Love can neither be bought nor sold.* /有～必有妒忌。*Love is never without jealousy.* / ～不分贫贱与高贵。*Love lives in cottage as well as in courts.*

【爱人】husband or wife; spouse; sweetheart; lover

【爱沙尼亚】Estonia: ～共和国 *Republic of Estonia* / ～人 *Estonian* / ～语 *Estonian*

【爱上】lose one's heart to; be gone on; be sweet on; fall in love with

【爱神】God of Love; Amor; Cupid; Eros

【爱斯基摩人】Eskimo

【爱屋及乌】love me, love my dog; love for a person extends even to the crows on his roof; love for a person extends to everything associated with her or him

【爱惜】value; cherish; treasure; use sparingly: ～人才 *treasure men of talent* / ～人力和物力 *treasure manpower and material resources* /老人～那女孩,就好像她是自己的女儿一样。*The old man cherished the girl as if she were his daughter.*

【爱心】compassion; love; sympathy:让世界充满～。*Fill the world with love.*

【爱新觉罗】Aisin Gioro, family name of Manchu royalty, e. g. Aisin Gioro Puyi (1906-1967), the last emperor (1909-1911) of the Qing Dynasty

【爱因斯坦】Albert Einstein (1879-1955), noted scientist of theoretical physics: ～相对论 *Einstein's principle of relativity* / ～是一个天才。*Einstein was a genius.*

【爱憎】love and hate: ～分明 *understand what to love and what to hate*; *know whom to love and whom to hate*

隘 ① narrow ② pass:险～ *strategic pass*

【隘谷】ravine

【隘口】pass

【隘路】defile; narrow passage

碍 hinder; obstruct; be in the way of:旅行者们一路上被暴风雨所阻～。*The travelers were hindered by storms throughout their journey.* /不要妨～他的工作。*Don't hinder him in his work.* /帮帮忙,不要～事。*Help out; don't hinder.* /嘈杂声妨～了我的写作。*The noise hindered me in my writing.* /横在大路上一棵倒下的树是障～。*The fallen tree lying across the road is an obstacle.* /他的身体不好,这是他完成计划的一个障～。*His poor health is an obstacle to the fulfillment of his plan.*

【碍口】be too embarrassing to mention

【碍面子】afraid to wound sb's sensibilities; for fear of hurting sb's feelings

【碍事】① be in the way ② matter; be of consequence

【碍手碍脚】be in the way; be in a hindrance

【碍眼】① be unpleasant to look at; be offensive to the eye ② be out place

暧 [书] dim

【暧暧】[书] dark; dusk: ～远人村。*The distant village is shrouded in the deepening shadows of dusk.*

【暧昧】① (of attitude, intention etc.) ambiguous; equivocal:他的答复非常～。*His reply was full of ambiguities.* ② (of behaviour) shady; dubious; questionable

ān

安[1] ① peaceful; at ease; quiet; calm; undisturbed:国泰民～。*The country is prosperous and the people live in happiness.* ② stabilize:使某人～心 *calm sb down*; *set sb's mind at ease* ③ be content; be satisfied ④ safe; secure; in good health ⑤ place in a suitable position; find a place for ⑥ fit; fix; install: ~空调 *install air-conditioners* ⑦ bring a charge against; claim credit for sth ⑧ be up to; harbour ⑨ (Ān) a surname

安[2] [书] ① where ② (used in a rhetorical sentence) how

安[3] 【电】ampere

【安邦定国】bring peace and stability to the country; make the state stable and safe from disturbances

【安步当车】walk over leisurely instead of riding in a carriage; walk rather than ride; go on foot rather than by car

【安插】get a position for sb; place in a certain position; assign to a job

【安达曼海】Andaman Sea (northeastern part of the Indian Ocean)

【安道尔】Andorra: ~人 *Andorran*

【安的列斯群岛】Antilles Islands

【安第斯山脉】the Andes Mountains

【安定】① (of life, political situation, etc.) stable; quiet; settled ② stabilize; maintain: ~的生活 *a stable life*; *a settled life* / ~社会秩序 *maintain social order* / ~人心 *reassure the public* / ~团结的政治局面 *political stability and unity* ③ diazepam; valium: ~药 *tranquilizer*; *sedative*

【安顿】① arrange for; settle down; find a place for: 她把孩子~在托儿所便走了。*She left her child to the care of the nursery and went away.* ② tranquil; peaceful: 她是一个好母亲,没费多少事就把孩子~睡了。*She was a great mother that she bedded the children down without much trouble.*

【安放】place; lay; put in a certain position: 他在灯后~了一面大镜子。*He placed a big mirror behind the lamps.*

【安分】be law abiding; know one's place; keep one's place; not go beyond one's bounds: 你还是~一点儿吧。*You should know your place.*

【安分守己】law-abiding and well-behaved; know and keep one's place: 一家人~地过日子。*The whole family lived quietly and contentedly.*

【安抚】appeased; pacify; placate: 我建议用一辆新车取代这辆车,以~他们。*I tried to appease them by offering to replace the car with a new one.*

【安哥拉】Angola: ~人 *Angolan*

【安圭拉】Anguilla, an island in the West Indies

【安好】safe and sound; well; in good health

【安家】① settle down; settle: 他们已经在农村~落户了。*They have settled in the countryside.* ② set up a home; get married: 她收入不高,还没有条件在城里~。*She isn't earning enough to get married and start a family in the city.*

【安家费】allowance for setting up a new home; family allowance

【安家立业】settle down and embark on a career

【安检】security check: 乘客必须通过~才能登机。*Passengers are requested to go through a security check before boarding the plane.*

【安静】① quiet; noiseless: 老师要我们~下来。*The teacher told us to be quiet.* ② peaceful; calm: ~! *Keep calm!*

【安居】settle down (in a place): ~工程 *housing project for low-income urban residents*; *low-cost housing project*; *affordable housing project* / ~乐业 *live and work in peace and contentment*

【安卡拉】Ankara, capital of Turkey

【安康】good health: 祝您~。*Wish you the best of health.*

【安澜】[书] ① (of a river, etc.) flow calmly in its natural course ② peaceful; tranquil

【安乐】easy; comfortable; peaceful and happy; free from worry: 他过着一种很~的生活。*He leads a very easy life.*

【安乐死】mercy killing; painless death; euthanasia

【安乐窝】cosy nest: 经营~ *feather one's cosy nest*

【安乐椅】arm chair; easy chair

【安理会】Security Council: ~常任代表 *Permanent Representative to the Security Council*

【安曼】Amman, capital of Jordan

【安谧】[书] peaceful; tranquil

【安眠】sleep peacefully: ~药 *sleeping pill or tablet*; *soporific*

【安秒】【电】ampere-second

【安民】reassure the public; pacify the public or people

【安民告示】notice to reassure the public

【安民恤众】improve the conditions of people and maintain order

【安宁】peaceful; free from disturbance; calm; tranquil: 那个小镇上一片~气氛。*An atmosphere of peace pervaded the small town.*

【安排】arrange; manage; settle; fix up; make arrangements for: 该由我来~这次旅行。*It is up to me to arrange the trip.* /今天晚上你有什么~? *What do you have on for tonight?* /他~了自己的财产处理问题。*He arranged for the disposal of his property.* /那个编辑终于把广告~在报纸上了。*The editor inserted an advertisement in a newspaper at last.* /我曾希望能去度假,但~却不是这样。*I had hoped to be on holiday but things were ordered otherwise.*

【安培】【电】ampere: ~计 *ammeter*; *amperemeter* / ~数 *amperage*

【安贫】content with poverty

【安贫乐道】be willing to suffer poverty and unwilling to leave the right track; find contentment in poverty and joy in one's principle; happy to lead a simple and virtuous life

【安琪儿】angel

【安寝】be asleep; go to bed

【安全】safe; secure: 他~地回到了家。*He came home in safety.* / ~别针在尖端有一个金属套。*A safety pin has a metal covering over the pointed* end. /不要站在那里，那里不～。*Don't stand there; it's not safe.*

【安全岛】safety island; pedestrian island

【安全灯】safety lamp

【安全阀】【电】safety valve; overload valve; protection valve

【安全工作区】area of safe operation (ASO)

【安全局】safety bureau

【安全帽】safety helmet

【安全门】emergency exit

【安全期】【医】safe period

【安全系数】safety coefficient or factor; something to fall back on

【安全装置】safety gear; safety apparatus

【安然】safe; secure; peacefully; at rest

【安然无恙】get off with a whole skin; keep a whole skin; escape unscathed; be safe and sound

【安如磐石】as solid as a rock

【安如泰山】as secure as Mount Tai; as firm as a rock

【安设】set up; install; fix

【安身】make one's home; take shelter; have a roof over one's head

【安身立命】head settle down to a quiet life and get on with one's work; settle down in one's life and career

【安神】calm the nerves; soothe the nerves

【安生】① peaceful; restful ② quiet; still：这孩子一会儿也不～。*The child simply won't keep quiet.*

【安适】quiet and comfortable; contented

【安舒】at ease and relaxed; in peace and comfort

【安睡】sleep soundly

【安徒生】Hans Christian Andersen (1805-1875), Danish author celebrated for his fairy tales

【安危】safety; safety and danger：关心国家的～ *be concerned about the safety of the country*

【安慰】① be comforted; feel happy：～那个孩子 *say a few words to comfort the child; give the child a few words of comfort the child; give the child a few words of comfort* /她的话给了我极大的～。*What she said comforted me greatly.* /自从她母亲死后，宗教成了她唯一的～。*After her mother died, the religion is her only resource.* ② console：～奖 *consolation prize* /～赛 *consolation event or match*

【安稳】① smooth and steady：～着地 *land smoothly* ② (one's behaviour) quiet and calm

【安息】① rest; go to sleep ② rest in peace; at rest：愿她在天之灵～吧！*May her soul rest in heaven.*

【安息日】【宗】Sabbath：守～ *keep the Sabbath* /不守～ *break the Sabbath*

【安闲】carefree; leisurely：～自得 *carefree and content* /上个月，她在乡下～地度过了假期。*Last month, she had a free and easy holiday in the country.*

【安详】composed; serene; unruffled; unhurried：～的神情 *a serene look* /～的微笑 *a serene smile* /举止～ *behaviour with composure*

【安享】enjoy in peace：～清福 *enjoy blessing of quiet, peaceful life* /～天年 *comfortable all rest of one's life*

【安歇】① go to bed; retire for the night ② take a rest

【安心】set one's mind to; at east; rest：在没有获得真相之前，他是不会～的。*He will not rest until he knows the truth.* /母亲听到他平安到达的消息就～了。*His mother was relieved at the news of his safe arrival.*

【安逸】easy; comfortable; leisure：贪图～ *be bent on seeking comfort and ease* /她喜欢～地坐着。*She likes to sit in comfort.*

【安营】set up a camp; camp out：～扎寨 *pitch a camp; encamp* /战士们在树林中～扎寨。*The soldiers camped out in the woods.*

【安于】be satisfied with; be accustomed to：～现状 *be satisfied with things as they are* /～职守 *stay at one's post* /你不要～现状，要继续更努力工作。*You must not be satisfied with things as they are; you'd better work harder than before.*

【安葬】bury：成千上万的人死了，被～在他们自己修建的城墙下面。*Thousands of men died and were buried under the wall they built.*

【安置】assemble; fix; fit; install; arrange for：～费 *settlement allowance; placement allowance* /灯被～在墙上。*The lamp is fixed to the wall.*

【安装】set up; install; erect; fix; mount：～工 *installer; mounter* /～图 *installation diagram or drawing* /～电话不费多少时间。*The installment of the phone will not take along.* /办公室的电话已经～好了。*The telephone has been installed in the office.*

桉

【植】eucalyptus

【桉树】【植】eucalyptus

【桉油】eucalyptus oil

氨

【化】hydrogen nitride; ammonia：合成～ *synthetic ammonia*

【氨苯磺胺】sulfanilamide

【氨化】【化】ammoniate

【氨基】【化】amino; amino-group：～醇 *amino-alcohol* /～酸 *amino acid* /～酮 *aminoketone*

【氨气】【化】ammonia

【氨水】【化】ammonia water; ammonia solution

庵

①［书］hut ② nunnery; Buddhist convent：尼姑～ *nunnery*

【庵堂】［方］nunnery; Buddhist convent

谙

［书］know well; be well-versed

【谙达】be conversant; be familiar

【谙练】skilled; conversant

【谙事】be sensible; have sense

【谙熟】be conversant with; be proficient in：～语言 *be well versed in language* /～艺术 *be well-versed in art*

鹌

【鹌鹑】quail：～蛋 *quail's egg* /他非常喜欢吃～蛋。*He likes to eat quail's eggs very much.*

鞍 saddle：给马备～ *put a saddle on a horse* /人靠衣装，马靠～。*Feathers make fine birds.* /她把马～放在马背上。*She put the saddle on the horse's back.*

【鞍鼻】saddle nose

【鞍架】saddle-tree

【鞍马】①【体】pommelled horse; side horse ②［书］saddle and horse; life on horseback

【鞍前马后】run before or behind the master's horse; act as a faithful attendant

【鞍子】saddle

ǎn

俺 ［方］① we; our (excluding those addressed)：～们都是北方人。*We all are from northern.* ② my; I：～爹 *my father; my dad* /～娘 *my mother; my mum* /～兄弟 *my brother* /～村 *our village*

埯 ① dibble ② hole for planting seeds ③ a cluster of：一～面粉 *a cluster of powder*

铵 【化】ammonium：硫酸～ *ammonium sulphate* /～离子 *ammonium ion* /～盐 *ammonium salt*

揞 apply medicinal powder to a wound：你最好～一些消炎粉。*You'd better apply some medicinal powder.*

àn

岸[1] bank; coast; shore：湖～ *lakeside* /江～边 *on the bank of a river* /海～边 *on the coast* /她家在河的南～。*Her home is on the south bank of the river.* /河～上那棵大树也许可供我们避雨。*That big tree on the bank of the river might afford us shelter from the rain.* /我每天早晨在～上散步。*I take a walk along the bank every morning.* /她知道她离海～不远了。*She knew she was near the shore.* /我们沿湖～走着。*We walked along the shore of the lake.* /她将在早上八点钟从法国海～出发。*She is going to set out from the French coast at eight o'clock in the morning.* /～上的一些人对着船上的人大声叫喊她，但是她没有听见。*Some people on the bank called out to the lady in the boat, but she did not hear them.* /他把球抛回到～上。*He threw the ball back to the bank.*

岸[2] ［书］① tall; high ② arrogant：道貌～然 *be sanctimonious*

【岸边】shore side; side：船向～划去。*The boat pulled for the shore.* /海侵蚀了～。*The sea has eaten into the shore.*

【岸标】shore beacon

按[1] ① press; push down：她画画时你来～住纸。*You will hold the paper steady while she draws.* /那个淘气的孩子～了门铃。*The naughty boy pressed the doorbell.* /只要～一下这个按钮就可以启动这台发动机了。*Press this button, and you will start the engine.* ② restrain; control ③ keep one's hand on ④ leave aside ⑤ according to：～比例协调发展 *proportionate and coordinated growth* /～件计工 *piece work pay* /～性质分类费用账户 *natural expense account* /政府各部门都必须始终～宪法办事。*All the departments of the government must always act constitutionally.* /宇航员们～计划成功地从月球返回到地球。*The astronauts succeeded in returning from the moon to the earth according to the plan.*

按[2] ①［书］refer to; check ② comment; note (by the editor, author, etc.)

【按比例】in proportion; at the ratio; by a ratio of

【按兵不动】hold one's troops where they are; take no action：大家都动起来了，你怎么还～呢？*Everybody else has started work; why do you sit there doing nothing.*

【按部就班】follow the prescribed order

【按键】key; press key：～式电话 *push-button telephone*

【按揭】［方］mortgage：～贷款 *mortgage loan* /～利率 *mortgage rate* /～购房 *take out a mortgage to buy a house*

【按劳分配】distribution according to work

【按理】according to reason; normally：～说你该早点来这儿。*Normally, you should come here earlier.*

【按脉】feel the pulse：过来，让张大夫～。*Come here; let doctor Zhang feel your pulse.*

【按摩】【医】massage：～器 *massager* /～师 *massager; masseur* /女～员 *masseuse* /这个院里有很多～师。*There are many massagers in this yard.* /～可以放松疲劳的肌肉。*A massage relaxes tired muscles.*

【按捺】hold back; control; restrain：～不住内心的激动 *be unable to hold back one's excitement*

【按钮】push button; depressed button：～开关 *press-button switch; button switch* /那盏灯的～在哪里？*Where is the press-button of the lamp?*

【按期】on time; on schedule：会议将～举行。*The meeting will begin on schedule.* /他～完成了任务。*He finished his task on schedule.*

【按时】on time; on schedule：你一定要～上学，不要迟到。*You must go to school on time; don't be late.* /幸运的是飞机～到达。*Fortunately the plane was on time.*

【按说】in the ordinary course of events; normally; ordinarily：～节目早就该结束了。*Normally the programme should be finished earlier.*

【按图索骥】look for a fine horse with the aid of its picture — try to locate sth by following up a clue or do sth mechanically

【按需分配】distribution according to need

A

【按语】note; comment:编者~ *editor's note*
【按照】according to; in accordance with:一切完全~规则做 *do everything in exact accordance with rules* / ~礼节 *according to protocol* / ~惯例 *according to the custom* /李经理~实际情况制定了下一步的工作。*Manager Li made out the next work in the light of actual conditions.*
【按钟点】by the hour:那家工厂~付给工人工资。*The factory paid workers by the hour.*
【按住】hold

胺 【化】amine

【胺酸】【化】amino acid
【胺盐】【化】amine salt

案[1] old-fashioned long narrow table

案[2] case; law case:破~ *crack a criminal case* / 他是这个谋杀~的帮凶。*He is an accessory to the murder.*

【案板】kneading board; chopping board
【案秤】counter scale; platform balance
【案底】record of previous offences:他是一个有~的罪犯了。*He was a criminal with a record of previous offences.*
【案牍】[书] office documents and correspondence
【案犯】the accused; offender; suspect
【案件】case; law case; legal case:民事~ *civil case* /刑事~ *criminal case* /行凶抢劫~ *a case of robbery with violence* /律师已受理了这个~。*The advocate has undertaken the case.* /这个~在庭外解决。*The case was settled out of court.*
【案卷】file folder; records; archives
【案例】case
【案情】case; details of a case
【案头】on one's desk; on one's table: ~日历 *desk calendar*
【案由】brief; summary
【案子】old-fashioned long, narrow table; long board serving as a table or counter; case:乒乓球~ *pingpong table* /一个很难办的~ *a difficult case to prove* /谁将审理下个~? *Who will judge the next case?* /法官将于明天对~进行判决。*The judge will decide the case tomorrow.*

暗 ① dark; dim; dull:这幅画色彩太~。*There is too much dark in this painting.* /云层使天空灰~。*Clouds are greying the sky.* ② hidden; secret:沉默有时~指同意。*Silence sometimes implies consent.*

【暗暗】secretly; inwardly; to oneself: ~跟踪 *follow sb secretly* /看了弟弟的来信,我不禁~高兴。*After reading my brother's letter, I could not help laughing in my heart.* /我在心里~起誓,必须通过这次考试。*I swear to myself; I must pass the exam.*
【暗堡】bunker:当他的朋友追赶他时,他偷偷地藏到了~的后面。*When his friends ran after him, he hid behind a hunker secretly.*
【暗藏】hide; conceal: ~金银珠宝 *conceal treasures*
【暗娼】illicit prostitution; unregistered prostitute
【暗处】dark place; obscure corner; secret place:那个罪犯白天躲在~,希望没有人能认出他来。*The criminal hid himself in a dark place during the day hoping no one would recognize him.*
【暗淡】dim; dismal; dull; faint:前途~ *bleak prospect* /心情~ *dismal mood* /这灯的光线极其~。*The lamp gave very little light.* /他最近非常劳累,脸色~。*He is very tied recently and looks very gloomy.* /如果这个月底她还不能设计出新型产品,那她将面临着失去这份工作,她的前途也将十分~。*If she can't devise new models of products until the end of this month, she will lose this job and her future will be very bleak indeed.*
【暗道】secret path or tunnel:这个院子里有多处~。*There are several tunnels in this yard.*
【暗地里】secretly; inwardly; on the sly; on the quiet:我们~送到他家一些食物。*We inwardly sent some food to his home.* /别让王经理知道我们~告发了他。*Don't let manager Wang know we sang on him.*
【暗斗】secret struggle; underplay:明争~ *both open strife and veiled struggle*
【暗渡陈仓】engage in sth covertly while making a feint in the open, esp. carry on an illicit love affair
【暗访】investigate in secret; make secret inquiries: ~民情 *make secret inquires into the condition of the people*
【暗沟】covered sewerage; underground drain:教室的旁边有许多~。*There are many underground drains near the classroom.*
【暗害】kill secretly; stab in the back; murder:背后~某人 *stab sb in the back; give sb a stab in the back*
【暗含】imply; be implicit
【暗号】secret signal; countersign:以~为准开始行动 *go into action on a secret signal*
【暗箭】stab in the back; arrow shot from hiding; attack by a hidden enemy: ~伤人 *injure sb by underhand means* / ~难防 *hidden arrows are difficult to guard*
【暗礁】① concealed obstacle ② submerged rock
【暗枪】sniper's shot
【暗杀】assassinate: ~者 *assassin* /在一次聚会中,他的小弟弟被~了。*His younger brother was assassinated in a big party.*
【暗伤】① internal injury; invisible injury ② internal damage
【暗示】drop a hint; suggest; imply; implicit; intimate: ~的恐吓 *an implicit threat* /在合同中~的 *implicit in the contract* /他的老板~他要更努力工作。*His boss hinted that he ought to work harder.* /她~希望他离开。*She gave him a hint that she would like him to leave.*
【暗送秋波】make eyes at sb; make secret overtures to sb
【暗算】plot against; entrap

【暗锁】built-in lock
【暗滩】hidden shoal
【暗探】spy; detective; secret agent: ~敌方行动 *spy on the enemy's movements*
【暗无天日】complete darkness; total absence of justice
【暗喜】be pleased secretly
【暗笑】laugh in one's sleeve; snigger
【暗语】code word
【暗指】insinuation; hint at; infer
【暗喻】metaphor
【暗中】① in the dark: ~摸索 *grope in the dark* ② in secret; on the sly: ~勾结 *make secret deals with sb; collude with* /她~流泪。*Tears stole down her check.*
【暗自】inwardly; secretly; to oneself: ~高兴 *secret rejoicing* / ~盘算 *secretly calculate* / ~思量 *turn sth over in one's mind secretly; say sth to oneself* / ~庆幸 *secretly congratulate oneself; consider oneself lucky*

黯 gloomy; dim
【黯淡】gloomy; dim
【黯然】① dim; faint; be eclipsed ② low-spirited; dejected: ~泪下 *shed tears sadly* / ~失色 *be cast into the shade; be eclipsed; pale into insignificance* / ~神伤 *feel depressed* / ~销魂 *extremely sad and depressed*

āng

肮 dirty: ~话 *dirty words*
【肮脏】①dirty; filthy: ~的条件 *dirty condition* / ~和疾病形影相随。*Dirt and disease go hand in hand.* ② mean; foul; dirty: ~的勾当 *dirty work; a foul deed*

áng

昂 ① hold (one's head) high; raise ② high; soaring:群情激~。*Popular feeling ran high.*
【昂贵】expensive; costly; exorbitant:她支付不起那件~的衣服。*She can't pay the expensive clothes.*
【昂首】hold one's head high: ~阔步 *stride along with one's chin up; stride proudly ahead*
【昂扬】high-spirited; excited: 斗志~ *have high morale; be full of fight; be militant*

àng

盎[1] ancient vessel with a big belly and a small mouth
盎[2] [书] brimming; abundant; vigorous; full of life
【盎然】abundant; full; overflowing:趣味~ *full of interest* /生机~ *overflowing with vigour* /春意~。*Spring leads a sweet atmosphere to everything on earth.*
【盎司】ounce

āo

凹 concave; hollow; sunken; dented: ~凸不平 *uneven; full of bumps and holes* /那个老奶奶的眼睛~下去了。*The old granny's eyes have sunk in.*
【凹痕】pit; dent; indenture:桌子下面有个~。*There was a depression under the table.*
【凹面】concave surface; camber concave: ~镜 *concave mirror*
【凹凸】concave-convex: ~镜 *concave-convex lens* / ~不平 *uneven; rough* / ~印刷 *embossing; die stamping*
【凹纹】design in intaglio
【凹陷】hollow; sunken; depressed; pit:她的眼睛~,像个外国小孩。*She has sunken eyes, like a foreign child.*

熬 cook in water; boil; stew: ~蔬菜 *stewed vegetable*
see also áo
【熬心】extremely worried; filled with anxiety:孩子太小,真让人~。*It is worrisome that the baby is too small.*

áo

敖 (Áo) a surname
【敖包】*aobao*, heap of sand, stone or earth laid out as a road marker or boundary sign by Mongolians, formerly also worshipped as habitation of spirits

遨 [书] stroll; saunter
【遨游】travel; stroll:汤姆最近没在家,去~四海了。*Recently Tom was not at home and roamed about the various parts of the world.*

嗷
【嗷嗷】indicate cries of pain: ~待哺 *cry piteously for food*

熬 ① cook into gruel; boil: ~鸡汤 *cook chicken stew* ② decoct: ~药 *decoct medical herbs* ③ endure; bear; stand:为了孩子他都~白了头发。*He suffered so much that his hair had turned grey prematurely for his children.*
see also āo
【熬煎】torture; suffer
【熬头儿】hope for a better life:那个大学生觉的日子没有~,就离开了公司。*The college student left his*

company, as he had nothing to look forward to in life.

【熬夜】stay up late; work all night; burn the midnight oil

翱 soar; take wing

【翱翔】soar; hover; take wing: 鸟儿在树林中展翅~。*Birds spread their wings and begin to soar.* / 雄鹰在空中~。*Eagles hover in the sky.*

鳌 huge legendary sea-turtle

【鳌头】head of a carried legendary turtle on the stone steps leading to the main hall of the Imperial Palace, steps which the best successful scholar at the palace examination was permitted to ascend: ~独占 *take possession of the sea monster's head; the champion; win first prize*

鏖 engage in fierce battle

【鏖战】fight hard

ǎo

拗 [方] bend so as to break; twist and break: 他气得把铅笔~了。*He was so angry as to break a piece of pencil in two.*

see also ào; niù

【拗陷】【地】depression

袄 a short Chinese-style coat or jacket: 夹~ *lined jacket* / 棉~ *cotton-padded jacket* / 皮~ *fur to coat; fur garment*

媪 [书] old woman

ào

坳 col; depression in a mountain range: 山~ *hollow in the hill*

拗 disobedient; refractory

see also ǎo; niù

【拗口】hard to pronounce; twist the tongue: ~令 *tongue twister*

傲 proud; unyielding; arrogant; haughty; refuse to yield to; defy

【傲骨】lofty and unyielding character; innate pride; self-esteem

【傲慢】arrogant; overbearing; impudent; haughty: ~无礼 *be insolent and rude* / ~的态度 *an arrogant attitude*

【傲气】haughtiness air of arrogance: 讨厌某人的~ *dislike sb for his arrogance* / 我们公司的总经理~十足。*Our general manager is full of arrogance.*

【傲然】proudly; unyieldingly: ~屹立 *stand to proudly*

【傲视】show distain for; look down upon; turn up one's nose: ~权势 *hold power and authority in disdain*

奥[1] ① difficult to comprehend: 深~ *unfathomable; profound; abstruse* ② southwest corner of a house

奥[2] 【物】oersted (Oe)

【奥德赛】*Odyssey*, Greek hexameter epic poem in 24 books attributed to *Homer*

【奥地利】Austria: ~人 *Austrian*

【奥林匹克】Olympics: ~村 *Olympics Village* / ~精神 *Olympic spirit* / ~运动会 *Olympic Games; Olympiad* / ~委员会 *Olympic Committee* / ~体育中心 *Olympic Sports Centre*

【奥秘】profound mystery; secret: 根据这一线索，他解答了这个~。*In this way, he was able to solve the mystery.*

【奥妙】profound; secret; subtle: 这个孩子很聪明，竟然看出了其中的~。*The child was too clever to have got at the secret behind it.* / 其中并无~。*There is nothing secret about it.*

【奥斯卡】Oscar: ~金像奖 *Oscar-popular term for the Academy Award*

【奥斯陆】Oslo, capital Norway

【奥斯曼帝国】Ottoman Empire (1290—1922)

【奥委会】Olympic Committee: 国际~ *International Olympic Committee (IOC)*

【奥匈帝国】Austro-Hungarian Empire (1867-1918)

【奥运会】Olympiad; Olympic Games

澳[1] inlet of the sea; bay ② Macao: 港~同胞 *compatriots in Hong Kong and Macao* / ~门特别行政区 *Macao Special Administrative Region*

澳[2] Australia: ~大利亚人 *Australian* / ~大利亚联邦 *Commonwealth of Australia* / 苏格兰队负于~大利亚队。*Scotland lost to Australia.* / 他是我在~大利亚期间的唯一的中国伙伴。*He was my only Chinese companion during my stay in Australia.*

懊 annoyed; regretful; vexed; remorseful

【懊悔】regret; repent of: ~莫及 *be too late to repent* / ~不已 *no end of regret* / 我非常~自己不礼貌地对待了客人。*I was sorry that I had been unfriendly to the guests.*

【懊恼】annoyed; upset; remorseful: 不要为失败而~。*Don't be upset for the failure of the experiment.*

B

bā

八 eight：~百年 *eight hundred years*; *long time*; *long period* / ~个人在值班。*Eight people are on duty.* /现在~点钟了。*It is eight now.* /她的表是~点十分。*Her watch says ten past eight.* /以前大多数人干的是~小时工作日。*Most people worked an eight-hour day before.* / ~加六等于十四。*Eight plus six equals fourteen.*

【八宝】eight treasures (choice ingredients of certain special dishes)：~饭 *eight-treasure rice pudding*

【八边形】octagon

【八成】① eighty percent：~新 *eight percent new*; *mostly new* / ~熟 *not quite ripe* ② most likely; probably：~他不来了。*Most likely he won't come at all.*

【八方】all directions; eight points of the compass：~呼应 *responses from every direction*; *cooperation all sides* /四面~ *all directions*; *all around* /一方有难，~支援。*When trouble occurs at one spot, help comes from all quarters.*

【八哥】【动】mynah; crested

【八股】eight-part essay; stereotyped writing

【八卦】the Eight Diagrams; be meddlesome; superstitious：~在她们村里特别盛行。*The Eight Diagrams are very popular in their village.*

【八国联军】the Eight-Power Allied Force, aggressive troops sent by Britain, America, Germany, France, tsarist Russia, Japan, Italy, and Austria in 1900, to suppress the anti-imperialist Yihetuan Movement of the Chinese people

【八进制】【数】octonary number system; octal：~计数器 *octal counter* / ~译码器 *octal decoder* / ~调试程序 *octal debugger*

【八九不离十】very near; about right：她猜个~。*She has made a very close guess.*

【八路军】the Eighth Route Army

【八面玲珑】be smooth and slick; be able to get along well with everybody：他非常讨厌~的人。*He dislikes slick people very much.*

【八旗】eight Banners (Manchu military-administrative system established in the early 1600's and kept throughout the Qing Dynasty)：~制度 *Banner system* / ~子弟 *profligate children of privileged families*

【八仙】① the Eight Immortals ②【植】hydrangea：~过海，各显神通 *like the Eight Immortals going across the sea*; *each in his own way* / ~桌 *Eight Immortals table*

【八月】① August：我是~中旬回南京的。*I returned to Nanjing in the middle of August.* ② the eight moon; the eighth month of the lunar year：去年~节，我们全家一起在院子里赏月。*Last Mid-Autumn Festival, our family enjoyed the moon in the yard.*

【八折】twenty percent discount：按~出售 *sell at a discount twenty percent* /我们按商品目录上的价格打~。*We make a discount of twenty percent off the prices in the catalogue.*

【八字】character：~形 *splayed* / ~还没见一撇儿。*Nothing tangible is in sight yet.*

巴[1] ① hope earnestly：~不得天下雨。*Hope it raining earnestly.* ② cling to; stick to ③ get stuck to ④ crust ⑤［方］be next to; be close to：他的工厂~着一条河。*His factory is close to a river.*

巴[2] ① name of principality of the Zhou Dynasty ② eastern part of Sichuan Province ③ (Bā) a surname

巴[3] 【物】bar：微~ *microbar* /毫~ *microbar*

巴[4] bus：大~ *bus* /小巴 *minibus*

【巴比伦】Babylon (ancient city on the Euphrates, capital of the Babylonian kingdoms)

【巴不得】be eager to：我~早点离开这儿。*I am eager to leave here earlier.* /他~有这么一个出国的机会。*He jumped at the chance to go abroad.*

【巴尔干】the Balkans：~半岛 *the Balkan Peninsula* / ~国家 *Balkan states* / ~山脉 *Balkan Mountains*

【巴尔扎克】Honore de Balzac (1799—1850), French novelist

【巴伐利亚】Bavaria：~人 *Bavarian*

【巴格达】Baghdad, capital of Iraq

【巴基斯坦】Pakistan：~人 *Pakistani*

【巴结】fawn on; flatter; make up to; curry favour with; try to please sb：~权势人物 *curry favour with influential people* / ~老师 *try to win teacher's favour*

【巴库】Baku, port city on the Caspian Sea and capital of Azerbaijan

【巴拉圭】Paraguay：~人 *Paraguayan*

【巴勒斯坦】Palestine：~人 *Palestinian* / ~解放组织 *Palestine Liberation Organization (PLO)*

B

【巴厘】Bali, mountainous island of Indonesia: ~人 *Balinese*

【巴黎】Paris, capital of France: ~圣母院 *Notre-Dame de Paris* / ~人 *Parisian* / ~是个古老而繁华的城市。*Paris is an old and busy city.*

【巴马科】Bamako, capital of Mali

【巴拿马】Panama: ~人 *Panamanian* / ~运河 *the Panama (canal)*

【巴塞罗那】Barcelona, city and province of Catalonia in NE Spain

【巴士底狱】the Bastille

【巴望】① hope; look forward to: 那群孩子~早日见到他们的新老师。*The Children hope they will be able to see their new teacher earlier.* ②hope for: 别灰心,有~。*Don't give up; now there is something to look forward to.*

【巴西】Brazil: ~人 *Brazilian* /在~举行国际足球比赛的主意,将对其的未来产生巨大的影响。*The idea to hole an international football match will have a great effect on the future of Brazil.*

【巴西利亚】Brasilia, capital of Brazil

【巴眨】wink; blink: ~眼睛 *blink the eyes*

【巴掌】palm; hand: 打他一~ *slap him on the cheek*

扒 ① hold on to; cling to: ~车 *jump into a bus or train* / ~墙头儿 *hold on to the top of the wall* ② dig up; pull down: ~一幢楼 *pull down a building* / ~泥 *rake mud* ③ push aside; take off: 那个小孩子把鞋袜一~就上床了。*Taking off his shoes and socks, the child went to bed.*
see also pá

【扒钉】cramp

【扒开】push aside

【扒拉】touch lightly; remove; push lightly: ~算盘子儿 *move the beads of an abacus up and down; click away at an abacus*

芭 【植】fragrant grass; plant; flower

【芭蕉】【植】plantain; banana: ~扇 *palm-leaf fan*

【芭蕾舞】ballet: ~演员 *ballet dancer* /很遗憾,我们错过了昨天精彩的~演出。*It's a pity that we missed the wonderful ballet performance last night.*

吧 ①[象] crackling: ~的一声,椅子断了。*The chair broke off with a snapping sound.* ②[方] draw on one's pipe; smoke: 请~一口。*Please have a drag.* ③ bar: 酒~侍者 *bartender*
see also ba

【吧嗒】[象] patter; click: 雨点~~地打在房顶上。*Big raindrops pattered on the roof.*

疤 ① scar: 横过他脸上的长~ *a long scar across his face* /她头上的刀伤已结~了。*The cut on her head scared over.* ② a scar-like mark: 玻璃杯上的~ *mark on the glass*

【疤痕】scar; cicatrix; sore; spot

捌 (used for the numeral 八 on cheques, receipts, etc. to avoid mistakes or alternations) eight

笆 basket

【笆篱】[方] fence

bá

拔 pull out; pull up; draw: ~出手枪 *draw one's pistol* / ~出刀 *draw a sword* / ~钉 *draw a nail* / ~出瓶塞 *draw a cork from a bottle* /这些树根很好~。*These roots pull easily.* /这位老人的牙很容易~。*The old man's teeth draw easily.* ② suck out ③ select; promote; choose; pick: 她是从几百人的候选人中选~出来的。*She was selected from hundreds of candidates.* ④ lift; raise ⑤ surpass: 出类~萃 *be distinguished from one's kind; stand out among one's fellows* ⑥ capture; seize ⑦ cool ⑧ drawing

【拔草】pull up weeds: 过去他常常放学后去~。*He used to pull up weeds after school.*

【拔出】pluck out: ~刺进手指的刺 *pluck out a thorn in one's finger*

【拔除】uproot; pull out; remove; eradicate: ~杂草 *weed out the rank grass*

【拔刀相助】unsheathe one's sword and go to the rescue of another; take up the cudgels against an injustice

【拔地而起】rise straight from the ground: 万丈高楼~。*High buildings rose abruptly out of the ground.*

【拔掉】tear up; pull out: 你的那颗坏牙应该~。*Your bad tooth should be pulled out.*

【拔河】【体】tug-of-war: 昨天他们学校举行了~比赛。*Yesterday, a tug-of-war match was held in their school.*

【拔尖】① tiptop; outstanding: 李平的英语成绩~。*Li Ping is at the top of English.* ② push oneself to the front; push oneself forward; feel one is superior to others

【拔苗助长】try to help the saplings grow by pulling them upward; spoil things by excessive enthusiasm

【拔起】pull up

【拔腿】① make a step; take to one's heels: 没有回答我的问题,他~就走了。*Before answering my questions, he swung abruptly around on his heels and stalked off.* ② get away; extricate oneself: 还有其他事情要做,我不能~就走。*For having other things to do, I can't get away.*

【拔牙】pull out a tooth; extract a tooth: ~钳 *dental forceps* /牙医用~钳子顺利地为我拔掉一颗牙。*The dentist pulled out a tooth for me easily by dental forceps.*

跋[1] cross mountains: 长途~涉 *make a long and arduous journey* / ~山涉水 *scale mountains and ford streams; travel over land and water* / 红军战士~山涉水。*The soldiers of Red Army travelled across mountains and rivers amid diffi-*

culties.

跛[2] postscript; colophon:序～ *preface and postscript*

【跛扈】domineering; bossy:那个小孩为什么那么～? *Why does the little child get to be so domineering?*

【跛涉】trudge; trend:在雪中～ *trudge through the snow* /他沿着荒芜的路～了数小时。*He trudged the deserted road for hours.*

【跛文】postscript; epilogue

bǎ

把[1] ① hold; grasp:～住停车手柄 *hold abort handle* /战士们～着枪。*The soldiers held guns in their hands.* ② hold (a baby for it to relieve itself):给婴儿～尿 *hold a baby out to piss* ③ control; dominate:～好舵 *be firm at the helm* ④ guard; watch; keep:～守大门 *guard a gate* /妈妈～贵重的东西藏在保险箱里。*My mother kept her valuables in a safe.* ⑤ close to:～着门口 *close to the door* ⑥ hold together ⑦ give; offer:那个孩子太不懂事了,她差点要～旧照片扔掉了。*The child was too impolite to throw out the old photo.* ⑧ handlebar:三轮车～ *handlebar of a tricycle* ⑨ bunch; bundle:草～ *a bundle of straw*

把[2] ① be used when the object is the receiver of the action of the ensuing verb:小孩～作业做了。*The kid finished his homework.* /她～花浇了。*She watered the flowers.* /别～她当客人。*Don't treat her like a guest.* ② indicate the receiver of the action when it is busy, tired, worry, angry etc., followed by a complement:那个孩子现在还没回来,～她妈妈吓坏了。*Her mother was scared stiff that she didn't come back until now.* ③ show that sth undesirable has happened

把[3] indicate the approximate number:个～月前他回来过。*He returned his home a month or so ago.*

把[4] refer to a relationship of sworn brotherhood:他们是拜～子兄弟。*They became sworn brothers.*

see also bà

【把柄】handle; excuse:操作～ *operating handle* /活动～ *free handle* /固定～ *fixed handle* /留给人们说闲话的～ *give people a handle for gossip*

【把持】① control; check ② dominate; monopolize:～整个公司 *control whole company*

【把舵】have the helm; take the helm; have the rudder

【把关】① guard a pass:重兵～。*The pass was heavily guarded.* ② check on; make the final check:把好质量关 *guarantee the quality of products*

【把酒】raise one's wine cup; hold wineglass; drink:～言欢 *converse cheerfully over a glass of wine* /明月几时有,～问青天。*When can we enjoy a bright moon? Raising the wine up to my lips, I ask heaven.*

【把揽】monopolize; control; take sole possession of:他独自～大权。*He keeps all power in his own hands by himself.*

【把门】guard a gate; keep guard at the door:～的人不让任何人进来。*The entrance guard didn't allow anybody inside.*

【把守】guard:～大门 *guard the gate* /～关口 *guard the pass*

【把手】handle; grip; handlebar:装上～ *fit a handle on* /制动～ *binding handle* /手制动～ *hand brake handle* /门～ *door handle* /杠杆～ *lever handle* /开关～ *switch handle* /手动换向～ *manual reversing handle*

【把握】① keep; hold ② seize; grasp:我～住了这篇讲话的要点。*I grasped the main points of the speech.* ③ assurance; certainty:那群孩子们有～取得比赛的胜利。*The children have full confidence in the game's victory.*

【把戏】① acrobatics; jugglery ② trick; game

靶 target; reins; bridle:打～ *target practice; shooting practice* /环～ *round target* /中～ *hit the target*

【靶标】target

【靶场】range; firing ground:打～ *target range*

【靶心】bull's eye:射手的那支箭正中～。*The archer's shot was a perfect bull's eye.*

【靶子】target; aim

bà

坝 ① dam:三峡大～ *Three Gorges Dam* /拦河～ *checking dam* /分水～ *diverting dam* /土～ *fill dam* /防洪～ *flood dam* /闸～ *gate dam* /主～ *key dam* /河谷里正建一座新水～。*A new dam is now being built at the valley.* /战士们筑起土～,防止洪水泛滥。*The soldiers built banks of earth to hold back the floodwaters.* /河水被水～截住了。*The river has been dammed up.* ② dike; embankment ③ sandbar; shoal ④ plain; flatland

【坝顶】dam crest

【坝基】foundations of a dam; the base of a dam

【坝田】strath

【坝址】damsite

【坝子】① dam ②[方] flatland

把 ① grip:刀～儿 *handle of a knife* ② stem:苹果～ *petiole of an apple*

see also bǎ

爸 pa; dad; father:上个月,我～出差去上海了。*Last month, my father went Shanghai for business.*

罢 ① stop; cease:～诉 *abandon a prosecution; withdraw a lawsuit* /～业 *shopkeepers' strike* /决不～休 *will not give up; will not let the matter drop* /在小河前面建立一个大花园的计划因缺少资金而作～。*The project of building a big park was* abandoned for want of funds. ② dismiss; terminate; relieve; remove: ~职 *remove from office*; *dismiss* ③ finish: 说~, 他便离开了办公室。*With these words he left his office.*

【罢笔】stop writing: 他决定就此~, 再也不做了。*He decided to stop writing and never did it again.*

【罢黜】① dismiss from office ② ban; reject

【罢工】strike; go on strike; walk off the job: ~者 *striker* / 工人们在~, 因为他们要求增加工资。*The workers were striking because they wanted more salary.* / ~预定星期五开始。*The strike is due to begin on Friday.* / 政府不得不出动军队镇压工人~。*The government has to call out the army to suppress the workers' strike.*

【罢官】dismiss from office; remove from office: 他的哥哥因受贿而被~。*His elder brother was dismissed from office for taking bribes.*

【罢课】strike of students; boycott classes: 那时, 学生们正在~。*The students were striking on that time.*

【罢了】(bàle) just, merely; only: 不要再骗我了, 你只是想出去玩~。*Don't cheat me again; you just want to go out to play.*

【罢了】(bàliǎo) let it pass: 这没什么, 我不过做了我应该做的事~。*I have only done what I ought to; that's all.*

【罢免】recall; dismiss from office; remove sb from his job: ~权 *right of recall* / 通过投票表决, 李经理被~了职务。*Manager Li was recalled by voting.*

【罢赛】go on strike; refuse to participate in a competition: 昨天部分运动员在比赛中~。*Yesterday, parts of sportsmen were on strike in the games.*

【罢市】shopkeeper's strike; cease trade; suspend business as a protest

【罢手】give up; let the matter drop: 他不干完此事决不~。*He will not lay it down until it is finished.*

【罢演】go on strike; refuse to participate in a performance

【罢战】end hostilities; stop fighting; cease fire

【罢职】dismiss; remove

霸 ① chief of feudal princes ② tyrant; bully; despot: 恶~ *local despot* ③ hegemony ④ dominate; lord it over; rule by force ⑤ (Bà) a surname

【霸道】(bàdào) ① strong; willful; rule by force of dictators ② domineering; overbearing; violent in action: 横行~ *play the bully*

【霸道】(bàdao) strong; potent: 这种酒太~了, 你最好不要喝太多。*The liquor is quite strong; you'd better not drink too much.*

【霸气】arbitrary; domineering

【霸权】hegemony; supremacy: ~主义 *hegemonism* / ~者 *hegemonist* / 企图取得世界~地位 *attempt to attain world domination* / 美国的~更强大了。*America's supremacy is stronger.*

【霸王】① conqueror ② despot; overlord

【霸业】achievements of a leader of feudal lords; conquest

【霸占】seize by force; forcibly occupy; seize: ~别国领土 *forcibly occupy the territory of another country*

【霸主】overlord; hegemony; powerful chief

ba

吧 ① show consultation, suggestion, request or command: 别哭了~! *Don't cry, please.* / 别说了~? *Stop, please.* ② show agreement or approval: 好~, 我出席这个会。*Ok, I will attend the meeting.* ③ indicate doubt or surprise: 他不熟悉这里的情况~? *He is unfamiliar with the situation here, isn't it?* ④ indicate probability: 我们会在晚饭时见到她~。*Perhaps we'll meet her at dinner time.* ⑤ indicate a pause after suppositions, concessions, or conditions: 比如他~, 他喜欢帮助别人。*For example, he likes helping other people.*

see also bā

bāi

掰 ① break off with hands: ~苹果 *break off an apple* ② fall apart ③ analyze; examine

【掰腕子】hand wrestling; wrist wrestling: 你们两个人来~。*You two have a wrist-wrestling contest with each other.*

bái

白[1] ① white: 像雪一样~ *as white as snow* / ~水泥 *white cement* / ~砂糖 *refined white sugar* / ~皑皑的雪 *pure white snow* / ~头发 *white hair* / ~葡萄酒 *white wine* / 黑和~形成明显的对比。*Black and white shows a striking contrast.* / 有~必有黑, 事物各有缺陷。*Every white has its black, and every sweet its sour.* ② bright; light: 东方发~。*It dawns in the east.* ③ clear: 真相大~。*Everything is clear now.* / 那个老板决定调查那件事直至真相大~。*The boss chooses to look into the matter till the truth is out.* / 听说她从事的是不明不~的职业。*I heard that she has engaged in rather shady occupation.* ④ pure; blank ⑤ in vain: 你不要~辛苦了。*You may save your pains.* / 她所做得尝试~费心机。*What she had attempted was made without result.* ⑥ free of charge; gratis ⑦ white (symbol of reaction): ~区 *the White Area* ⑧ funeral ⑨ unfriendly look: ~某人一眼 *give sb a cold stare* ⑩ (Bái) a surname

白[2] wrongly written; mispronounced: 念~字 *mispronounce a word*

白[3] ① explain ② spoken part ③ dialect ④ vernacular

【白白】for nothing; in vain：我～浪费了时间。*I wasted my time in vain.*

【白班】day shift：这个星期我上～。*I'm on day shift this week.*

【白斑】hickie; vitiligo

【白报纸】newsprint

【白璧微瑕】a spot in white jade a slight blemish or small failing of a person's character; a minor defect of anything that would otherwise be perfect

【白璧无瑕】flawless jade

【白布】plain white cloth

【白菜】cabbage; Chinese cabbage：中国人爱吃～。*Chinese like eating Chinese cabbage.*

【白痴】① idiocy ② idiot：她曾经被认为是个～。*She used to be considered to be an idiot.*

【白炽】white heat; incandescence：～灯 *incandescent lamp*

【白唇鹿】white-lipped deer

【白醋】light coloured vinegar

【白搭】no use; no good; no purpose; in vain：把这事告诉他也是～。*It's no use to tell him.*

【白大褂】light gown：她是穿～的。*She is a doctor or nurse.*

【白带】【生理】whites; leucorrhea

【白蛋白】【生化】albumin

【白道】①【天】moon's path ② normal society; law-abiding citizenry

【白瞪眼】anxious but unable to do anything

【白发】white hair; grey hair：～苍苍 *gray-haired; hoary-haired*

【白饭】plain cooked rice; rice with nothing to go with it：他去年吃了一年～。*Last year he ate meals without paying it.*

【白费】waste; in vain; be of no avail：～心机 *scheme in vain; make futile efforts* / ～蜡 *for nothing; in vain; useless* /他们的好心没有～。*Their kindness has not been wasted.*

【白粉】① face powder ②［方］chalk; white wash ③ heroin：～病 *powdery mildew*

【白宫】the White House, official residence of the US president in Washington, DC

【白骨】bones of the dead; white bones

【白骨精】① white Bone Demon (in the novel Pilgrimage to the west) ② sinister and ruthless woman

【白果】ginkgo; gingko

【白鹤】white crane

【白喉】【医】diphtheria

【白糊糊】whitish; milky：她的衣服上有～的面粉。*Her clothes were covered with whitish powder.*

【白狐】【动】arctic fox

【白花】【纺】lap waste

【白花花】shining white：看到～的银子，她非常惊讶。*It's very surprise for her to see the gleaming silver coins.*

【白化】【医】albinism：～病 *albinism* / ～病人 *albino* / ～体 *albino*

【白话】① unrealizable statement; empty promise ② gossip; chitchat ③ vernacular; the written form of modern Chinese：～诗 *free verse written in the vernacular* / ～文 *writing in vernacular Chinese; vernacular Chinese* / ～文开始流行。*The writing in the vernacular became popular.*

【白桦】【植】white birth

【白晃晃】gleaming; white and bright：～的匕首 *shining dagger*

【白灰】① lime ②［方］white-wash

【白金】platinum; silver

【白金汉宫】① British royal family ② Buckingham Palace

【白晶晶】sparkling white

【白鲸】【动】beluga; white whale

【白净】fair and clear

【白酒】alcohol; white spirit

【白卷】unanswered examination paper; blank examination paper：那个小孩子这次考试又交了～。*The child handed in a blank paper in this examination.*

【白开水】plain boiled water

【白口铁】white (pig) iron

【白蜡】white wax; insect wax

【白蜡树】Chinese ash

【白兰】【植】gardenia：～地 *brandy* / ～瓜 *honeydew melon; Wallace melon*

【白脸】① white face, face painting in Beijing opera, etc., traditionally for the villain：他在京剧中唱～。*He plays the villain in Beijing opera.* ② fair complexion

【白磷】【化】white phosphorus

【白领】white-collar：～阶层 *white-collared workers, white-collar employees*

【白令海】Bering Sea：～峡 *Bering Strait*

【白鹭】egret

【白马王子】prince riding a white horse-Prince Charming

【白茫茫】(of cloud, mist, snow, floodwater, etc.) vast expanse of whiteness：在辽阔的田野上，～的一眼望不到头。*The fields covered with snow became a vast expanse of whiteness stretching to infinity.*

【白蒙蒙】(of smoke, vapour, mist, etc.) whitish and indistinct：屋里充满了～的烟雾。*The room was full of whitish smoke.*

【白米】polished rice：～饭 *cooked rice*

【白面】flour; fine flour：～书生 *a young handsome scholar* / ～儿 *heroin*

【白沫】frothy saliva; foam

【白嫩】fair and delicate

【白内障】【医】cataract

【白皮书】white paper; white book

【白旗】white flag (indicate surrender or cross the fronts)

【白鳍豚】【动】white-flag dolphin

【白求恩】Henry Norman Bethune (1890-1939), Canadian surgeon who came to Yan'an in 1938 to assist the Chinese struggle against Japanese aggression

【白热化】turn white-hot; reach a crisis or climax; white-hot:他俩的争论达到了～的程度。*The debate between them became white-hot.*
【白人】white person; Caucasian
【白刃】naked sword; naked blade; a sharp knife: ～战 *hand-to-hand fighting; bayonet charge*
【白日】① sun ② day: ～做梦 *indulge in wishful thinking; a walking dream; daydream; a pure fancy; build castles in the air*
【白色】① white; whiteness ② White (as a symbol of reaction): ～区 *a White area* / ～军 *the White army* / ～政权 *White regime*
【白手】empty handed; with bare hands: ～起家 *start from scratch; be self-made*
【白薯】sweet potato:烤～ *baked sweet potato*
【白水】① plain boiled water ② clear water
【白糖】white sugar
【白体】【印】lean type
【白天】daytime; day:大～我不喜欢学习。*I don't like studying in broad daylight.*
【白条】① unofficial receipt ② slaughtered poultry or animal, stripped of hairs or feathers, or with head, feet and entrails removed: ～猪 *pig carcass*
【白铁】tin plate
【白头】① hoary-headed; white-haired; old age:祝你们～偕老。*We hope that you two will live together till you are old and grey.* ② unsigned; anonymous
【白兔】white rabbit
【白皙】[书] white skinned; blond:她的皮肤～,像她妈妈。*She has a fair complexion, like her mother.*
【白细胞】white blood cell; white blood corpuscle
【白锈病】【植】white rust
【白血病】【医】leukaemia
【白血球】【医】white blood cell
【白雪公主】Snow White:《～和七个矮人》*Snow White and the Seven Dwarfs*
【白眼】supercilious look; scornful look
【白眼珠】white of the eye
【白眼狼】ungrateful, heatless villain
【白杨】white poplar
【白夜】white night
【白衣】① white frock; nurse: ～天使 *angels in white-hospital nurses* ② man without a degree or official post; commoner
【白蚁】【动】termite; white ant
【白银】silver
【白纸黑字】written in black and white; commit sth to paper
【白昼】daytime; daylight
【白字】wrongly written character; mispronounced character: ～连篇 *reams of wrong characters; full of mispronounced or wrong words*
【白族】Bai nationality:他的父亲是～。*His father is a Bai.*

bǎi

百 ① hundred:九～天 *nine hundred days* /好几～人出席了这位著名指挥家的告别音乐会。*Hundreds of people attended the famous director's farewell concert.* /我～分之～同意。*I am 100 percent in agreement.* ② numerous; all kinds of:千方～计 *by all manners or methods* / ～忙之中 *in the midst of pressing affairs*
【百般】① in a hundred and one ways; in every possible way; by every means: ～劝慰某人 *try every means to soothe sb* / ～刁难 *create obstructions of every description; raise all manner of difficulties*
【百宝箱】treasure box
【百倍】a hundred-fold; a hundred times
【百病】all kinds of diseases and ailments
【百尺竿头,更进一步】reach at a higher point; make still further progress; make still more efforts; win still further achievement; continue to do better
【百川归海】all rivers empty into the sea; all trends tend in one direction; everyone turns to sb for guidance; all roads lead to Rome
【百读不厌】be worth reading a hundred times:这本书～。*You never get tired of reading this book.*
【百端】① various ② undertaking of all kinds
【百发百中】a hundred shots, a hundred bull's eyes; be a crack shot
【百废待举】a thousand and one things wait to be done
【百分】per cent; percent:旷课的学生占～之几? *What percentage of the students was absent?* /听说明星的代理人的佣金是～之二十。*Hearing that the cut of stars' agent is 10 percent.*
【百分比】percentage:按～计算 *in terms of percentage*
【百分表】dial gauge
【百分点】percentage point
【百分号】percentage symbol (%); percent sign
【百分率】percent; percentage
【百分数】percentage
【百分之百】absolutely; entirely; hundred percent: 我有～的把握能赢这场比赛。*I have a hundred percent sure to win this game.* /她～同意她儿子所做的事情。*She is 100 percent in agreement what her son had done.*
【百分制】hundred-mark system; percentage system
【百感交集】mixed feelings; a multitude of feeling surge up
【百合】【植】lily; lily bulb
【百花齐放,百家争鸣】let a hundred flowers blossom and a hundred schools of thought contend
【百花盛开】a hundred flowers are in full blossom
【百花争艳】a hundred flowers contend in beauty; the flowers are a riot of colour
【百货】general merchandise: ～商店 *department*

store

【百家】① hundred schools of thought ② many families：～姓 *Book of Family Names*

【百家争鸣】contention of numerous schools of thought in the period of the spring and Autumn Annals, and the Warring States

【百洁布】scouring pad

【百科全书】encyclopedia：老师告诉我们～的新版本有许多改进之处。*The teacher told us the new edition of the encyclopedia embodies many improvements.* /一部好的～就是知识宝库。*A good encyclopedia is a mine of information.*

【百孔千疮】riddled with gaping wounds; afflicted with all ills

【百口难辩】difficult to get at the truth

【百老汇】Broadway

【百里挑一】pick; one in a hundred

【百忙】while fully engaged：感谢您在～之中抽空见我。*Appreciate the time you spared away from your work for our meeting.*

【百年】a hundred years; century：～纪念 *centenary*

【百年树人】It takes a hundred years to make education bear fruit.

【百年大计】a project of vital and lasting importance

【百年好合】have a harmonious married life

【百思不解】incomprehensible; not to understand through deep in thought; remain perplexed despites much thought

【百岁】a hundred years：人生～古来稀。*It is seldom that a man lives to be a hundred years old.*

【百听不厌】worth hearing a hundred times：这个故事～。*You never get tired of hearing this story.*

【百万】million：～富翁 *millionaire*

【百闻不如一见】seeing is believing; it is better to see once than hear a hundred times; seeing for oneself is a hundred times better than hearing from others

【百无聊赖】bored to death; languish in boredom; overcome with boredom; no know what to do with oneself：她～地躺在床上看书。*Having nothing better to do, he laid on bed to read a book.*

【百无一失】no risk at all; surefire; perfectly safe

【百姓】common people; civilians; people：～生活富足。*The people are well off.*

【百业】various trade; all business：～萧条 *all business languishes*

【百叶】louver：～窗 *shutter*; *blind* / ～箱 *thermometer screen*

【百依百顺】all obedience; obedient in everything; docile and obedient

【百战百胜】keep the field; ever triumphant

【百战不殆】fight a hundred battles with no danger of defeat

【百折不挠】persistent efforts; stubborn; unbending; pull through; keep on fighting in spite of all setback

柏

① cypress; cedar ② (Bǎi) a surname *see also* bó

【柏树】cypress; cedar

【柏油】pitch; tar; asphalt; mineral pitch：～路 *asphalt road*; *tarmac road*

摆

① place; lay; put：把书～在桌子上 *put books on the table* ② put off; show off：～架子 *put on airs* ③ sway; swing ④ pendulum：单～ *simple pendulum* /复～ *compound pendulum* ⑤ set forth; state

【摆布】① arrange; decorate; furnish; put sth in order：她是一个受环境～的人。*She is a fool of circumstances.* ② order about

【摆出】put; put on：他～傲慢的态度。*He put on an air of assumption.* /新英汉辞典下个月就会在书店里～来。*The new English-Chinese dictionary will appear in the bookstores next month.*

【摆地摊】set up a temporary stall to sell on the street

【摆动】sway; swing; wave：墙上的指示针来回～。*The pointer on the wall flickered.*

【摆渡】ferry; ferry across

【摆放】put; place; arrange; lay：～在我们面前的任务 *the task confronting us* /把工具～整齐 *tools in order*

【摆好】set sth in order; commend：请把工具～。*Please set the tools in order.* / ～你的电脑开始工作吧。*Please lay the computer and begin to work.*

【摆架子】assume great airs; put on airs; go about with one's head high in the air：他不能容忍～的人。*He can't stand for those who put on airs.*

【摆阔】parade one's wealth; show a desire for pomp and extravagance; be ostentatious and extravagant

【摆擂台】set up a stage for contest and invite challengers

【摆列】play; display

【摆门面】keep up appearances

【摆弄】① move back and forth; fiddle with：老师不应该让孩子们～危险的化学品。*Teachers shouldn't have let the children fool about with dangerous chemicals.* ② order about; manipulate ③ do; handle

【摆平】treat fairly; punish

【摆谱儿】show off; try to appear rich and elegant; try to impress

【摆设】furnish and decorate：～得很雅致 *be tastefully furnished*

【摆事实，讲道理】present the facts and reason things out

【摆手】① wave one's hands ② shake one's hand in disapproval

【摆摊儿】spread out goods for sale in booth; set up a stall; maintain a large staff or organization

【摆脱】get rid of; throw off; break away from：那个教会想～国家的束缚。*The church wanted to get rid of the control of the state.* /现代的很多规章制度～了旧的传统规则。*Modern rules have broken away from the old traditional rules.*

【摆宴】feast; host a banquet
【摆样子】do sth for show:她们做朋友只是～。*They are friends only in show.*
【摆针】pointer
【摆钟】pendulum clock
【摆桌】give a feast:明天他们要结婚,在北京宾馆～。*They will marry tomorrow and invite some people to dinner in Beijing Hotel.*

bài

败 ① be defeated; beat; lose:残～*be crushingly defeated* /在德国他们竟然将主队击～。*They smeared the home team actually in German.* ② beat; defeat:她们5:0击～对手。*They beat their opponents 5 to 0.* ③ fail:～军之将 *general of a defeated army* ④ spoil; ruin: ～胃口 *spoil one's appetite* ⑤ counteract ⑥ decay; wither:腐～的食物 *putrid food* ⑦ ruin
【败北】suffer defeat; be defeated in a war
【败笔】a faulty stroke in calligraphy or painting; a faulty expression in writing; a faulty part in a piece of painting; a faulty expression in writing
【败兵】defeated army; routed troops
【败坏】① ruin; undermine; corrupt: ～名誉 *blacken sb's good name; damage sb's reputation* /你的行为会～你的名望的。*Your behaviours will ruin your reputation.*
【败火】【中医】relieve inflammation or internal heat
【败家子】spendthrift; wastrel; prodigal; black sheep: ～不会守业。*A prodigal does not safeguard his heritage.* / ～回头了。*The prodigal has returned.* /那个吝啬的父亲竟然有一个～的儿子。*The miserly father has a prodigal son actually.*
【败将】loser; defeated general
【败局】lose game; losing battle
【败类】scum of community; degenerate:民族～ *national traitors; scum of a nation*
【败露】fall through and stand exposed; be brought to light; be uncovered:阴谋终于～了。*In the end the conspiracy was brought to light.*
【败落】decline (in wealth and position); wane:昔日的繁荣正在～。*The past prosperity is on the wane.* /他们家族的势力～了。*The reputation of his family is waning.*
【败诉】lose a lawsuit: ～方 *the party losing a lawsuit* /昨天他的一个朋友～了. *One of his friends lost a lawsuit yesterday.* /昨天判决宣告他～了,他非常难过。*The judgement passed against him yesterday, so he was very unhappy.*
【败退】retreat in defeat
【败兴】① dampen sb's enthusiasm; disappoint:感到～ *be disappointed* /使某人～ *spoil the pleasure of sb* /我们发现他不在家,不得不～而归。*We found he was not at home, so we had to come back disappointed.* ②[方] unlucky; unfortunate
【败仗】defeat; lost battle:打～ *be defeated in battle*
【败阵】defeat; be beaten; be defeated: ～而逃 *lose the field and take to flight*
【败走】flee in defeat: ～麦城 *suffer a major defeat; have one's Waterloo*

拜 ① do obeisance: 烧香～佛 *burn incense and pray to Buddha* / ～神 *worship a deity* ② congratulate:春节团～ *gather together to exchange greetings during the Spring Festival* ③ visit; make a courtesy: ～亲访友 *visit relatives and friends* ④ appoint; entitle sb with ceremony:诸葛亮被刘备～为丞相。*Zhu Geliang was made prime minister by Liu Bei* ⑤ formally establish a relationship:我准备～你为师。*I'm ready to formally acknowledge you as my teacher.* ⑥ be used before verbs:你的文章我们早已～读了。*We have read your article earlier.* ⑦ (Bài) a surname
【拜把子】become sworn brothers: ～弟兄 *sworn brothers*
【拜拜】bye-bye; see you:她给我们说了声～就走了。*She said bye-bye to us and went away.*
【拜辞】bid farewell to; take leave of sb
【拜倒】prostrate oneself; bow before sb; fall on one's knees:那个年轻人～在那个漂亮的姑娘脚下。*The young man groveled himself at the feet of the pretty girl.*
【拜读】have the honour to read:希望有一天我能～您的大作。*I wish I had pleasure of pursuing your work one day.*
【拜访】pay a visit; call on; drop in:下个月我去～你。*I'll pay you a visit next month.* /你顺路～时喝杯茶,好吗? *Would you like to drop in and have a cup of tea?* /他们明天要去～过去的老师。*They will call on their former teacher tomorrow.*
【拜会】pay an official call; visit, call on; pay a call
【拜见】pay a formal visit; call to pay respects; meet one's senior; meet one's superior
【拜金】worship of money: ～主义 *money worship*
【拜客】pay visits; call on:外出～ *go round to make social calls*
【拜年】pay a New Year call; wish sb a Happy New Year; send New Year greetings
【拜认】acknowledge sb
【拜师】formally acknowledge sb as one's master or teacher:他独身一人来到这个大城市～求学。*He went to this big city by himself to pay respect to a teacher and seek for knowledge.*
【拜寿】congratulate an elderly person on one's birthday; offer birthday felicitations:明天我和父母去给奶奶～。*Tomorrow, my parents and I will congratulate granny on her birthday.*
【拜堂】be wed; perform the formal wedding ceremony; make formal bows to the groom's parents at the traditional wedding ceremony
【拜天地】(bride and groom) bow to heaven and earth as part of the traditional wedding ceremony
【拜托】request sb to do sth; entrust:可以～您帮我

捎个信给父母吗？*Would you kindly take a message to my parents?*

【拜谒】① pay a formal visit; call to pay respects: ~二老 *call to pay respects to two old persons* ② pay homage: ~人民英雄纪念碑 *pay homage at the Monument to the People's Heroes*

稗 ① barnyard grass ② unofficial

【稗草】【植】barnyard grass; barnyard millet

【稗官野史】book of anecdotes; unofficial history: 你看到出自~的书吗？*Have you read books from unofficial history?*

【稗史】private record of events

bān

扳 ① pull; turn ② win back what has been lost: 他们终于~成了平局。*At last they managed to draw a match.*

see also pān

【扳动】move; pull: ~按钮 *operate the button*

【扳机】trigger: 双~ *double-set trigger* /前~ *fore trigger* /机械式~ *mechanical trigger* /他无意中扣发了步枪的~。*He accidentally triggered his rifle.* /要开枪就扣动~。*To fire the gun, pull the trigger.*

【扳手】① spanner; wrench ② lever

【扳子】spanner; wrench

【扳钻】twist-drill

班 ① class; team; grade: 辅导~ *tutorial class* /短期培训~ *short-term training course* /长期培训~ *long-term training course* /我们~上有三名外国学生。*There are three foreign students in our class.* /王刚比~上任何人学习都好。*Wang Gang studies better than anyone else in the class.* ② shift; duty: 今天她值~。*It's on her duty today.* /公共汽车每5分钟一~。*The buses run every five minutes.* ③ squad: ~长 *a squad leader* ④ troupe: 戏~ *theatrical troupe* ⑤ a bunch of; a group of: 这~小孩很早就回家了。*The bunch of the children went home very early.* ⑥ regularly-run; scheduled ⑦ withdraw; deploy; move: ~兵 *call back troops; deploy forces*

【班禅喇嘛】Panchen Lama

【班车】regular bus service; scheduled bus; shuttle service: 每天有~。*There is regular bus service everyday.*

【班次】① order of classes; grades at school; classes: 她~比我高。*She was in a higher class than me.* ② number of runs or flights

【班底】① ordinary members of a theatrical troupe ② cast

【班房】jail; prison: 他年轻时曾经坐了几天~。*He had been detained for a few days when he was young.*

【班干部】class cadre

【班会】class meeting: 下周五开~。*The class meeting will be holding on next Friday.*

【班机】airliner; flight

【班级】class; grade: 李梅认识这个~的每一个学生。*Li Mei knows each students of the class.* /王芳拒绝把自己的女儿编入自己的~。*Wang Fang refused to have her daughter in her class.*

【班门弄斧】show off one's skill with the axe before Lu Ban (the ancient master carpenter); show off one's scanty knowledge in the presence of an expert; teach one's grandma to suck eggs; teach a fish to swim: 在老师面前你用不着~。*You don't have to teach a fish to swim.*

【班期】timetable; schedule

【班师】order the troops to withdraw from the front

【班头】chieftain; head of a gung

【班图斯坦】Bantustan, in south Africa

【班长】monitor; team leader: 她是我们的~。*She is our monitor.* /我们~在考试中成绩优异，因而显得非常高兴。*The monitor looks very happy for his performance in the examination.*

【班主任】grade or class adviser; head-teacher: 我的~向我要一份关于我生病的证明。*My head teacher asked me to give him a reference about my illness.*

【班子】① theatrical troupe ② organized group; task group: 领导~ *a leading body; leader group*

【班组】teams and groups; working teams

般[1] sort; kind; way: 十八~武艺 18 *types of martial arts-every kind of skill*

般[2] kind; way; like; sort

【般配】match; suit

see also bō; pán

颁 promulgate; issue; distribute; confer; publish

【颁布】① issue; promulgate: ~法令 *promulgate a decree* /~命令 *issue an order*

【颁发】① issue; promulgate ② award: ~奖金 *award a bonus* /由于他的勇敢，他被~了一枚奖章。*He was awarded a medal for his braveness.*

【颁奖】award prizes; give out an award: 给优胜者~ *distribute prizes to the victors*

【颁行】promulgate

斑 ① spot; speck; speckle; stain: 泪~ *tear stain* ② spotted: ~驴 *zebras* /~鹿 *spotted deer* /~马 *zebra*

【斑白】grizzled; greying: 两鬓~ *greying at the temples; with greying temples*

【斑斑】full of stains; full of spots: 他回来时浑身血迹~。*He returned with blood-stained.*

【斑驳】mottled; motley

【斑点】spot; speck; stain; dot; fleck: 当她长大后脸上有一些~。*She has spots on her face after she grows up.* /得了这种病，脚上会出现~。*In this disease spots appear on the legs.* /这只小狗灰色带白~。*This dog is grey with white speckles.*

【斑痕】stain; mark

【斑羚】goral

【斑马线】zebra crossing
【斑鸠】turtledove
【斑斓】multicoloured; gorgeous; bright-coloured: 五彩~ *a blaze of multifarious colours*
【斑纹】stripe; streak; scaling: ~布 *marble cloth*
【斑岩】【地】porphyry
【斑疹】【医】macula: ~热 *spotted fever*
【斑竹】【植】mottled bamboo

B

搬 ① move; remove; take away: ~上银幕 *be presented on film* / 请给我~张椅子和桌子。*Get me a chair and a table, please.* ② move; migrate ③ copy: 生~硬套 *copy mechanically and apply indiscriminately*
【搬兵】ask for help; call in reinforcements: 他没有别的办法了,只得去~了。*He had no other ideas and had to ask for help.*
【搬动】① move: 王小姐个子太小,不能~桌子。*Miss Wang is too short to move the table.* ② send out; dispatch; deploy
【搬家】move house; migrate: ~公司 *house-moving company* / 玛丽早就~了。*Mary moved away long ago.* / 听说我们公司下个月就要~了。*I hear that our company will move next month.*
【搬弄】① fiddle with: 别~那堆书。*Don't fiddle with the book.* ② show off: ~自己 *show off oneself* ③ stir up trouble: ~是非 *tell tales; sow dissension*
【搬迁】move; relocate: ~户 *relocated households* / 爸爸向我提供大笔款项让我~,所以我决定离开这里。*My father has offered a large sum of money for me to go away, so I am determined to leave here.*
【搬移】move; remove
【搬用】copy; apply indiscriminately
【搬运】carry; transport: ~费 *shifting charge; removal expense; portage* / ~工 *porter; docker* / ~设备 *handling equipment; handling facility*

bǎn

坂 [书] slope

板 ① board; plate: 黑~ *blackboard* / 让他们用~把边门钉上。*Let's board the side door up.* ② shutter; door plank ③ blackboard: 制图~ *drawing board* / 布告~ *notice board* / 钻~ *dread board* ④ clappers: 我有一副竹~。*I have a pair of bamboo clappers.* ⑤ accented beat ⑥ unnatural ⑦ hard like a plate ⑧ look stern or grave; look serious
【板报】blackboard newspaper
【板擦】black board eraser
【板凳】wooden bench; stool
【板斧】broad axe
【板块】【地】plate: ~学说 *plate tectonics*
【板栗】Chinese chestnut
【板书】① writing on the blackboard ② words written on the blackboard
【板刷】scrubbing brush; brush eraser
【板条】【建】lath; batten: ~箱 *crate*
【板牙】① [方] front tooth; incisor ② molar ③【机】screw die; threading die
【板眼】①【音】measure; metre ② orderliness; method ③ [方] idea
【板直】① old-fashioned and tactless ② look serious
【板纸】paperboard; board
【板滞】stiff; dull
【板子】① board; plank ② birch or bamboo for corporal punishment; ferule

版 ① printing plate: 胶~ *offset plate* / 铅~ *stereotype* / 排~ *compose type* ② edition: 初~ *first edition* / 再~ *republish; reprint* / 修订~ *revised edition* / 标准~ *standard edition* ③ page: 头~ *front page* ④ board frames
【版本】edition: ~学 *bibliology* / 这是该词典的第二~。*This is the second edition of the dictionary.*
【版次】order of the edition
【版画】engraving; etching; print
【版刻】carving; engraving
【版面】① space of a whole page ② typeface: ~设计 *layout*
【版权】copyright: ~局 *Copyright Bureau* / ~研究会 *Copyright Research Society* / ~所有 *all rights reserved; copyright reserved* / ~法 *copyright law* / ~页 *copyright page* / ~保护 *copyright protection* / ~保护期 *copyright duration*
【版式】format
【版税】royalty; copyright royalty
【版图】domain; territory: 他拥有一些著名作家珍贵的~作品。*He owns some valuable territory work of well-known authors.*
【版型】matrix

钣 metal plate: 钢~ *steel plate*

bàn

办 ① handle; do; manage: 代~进口 *importing on customer's behalf* / 代~所 *agency* / 老板要去北京~事了。*Our boss will get a few errands to do in Beijing.* ② carry out; run: 那个漂亮的小姑娘到这里来是代替她妈妈~几件小事的。*The pretty girl came here to execute a few small commissions for her mother.* ③ purchase ④ punish by law: 惩~罪犯 *punish a criminal*
【办案】handle a case; take charge of a case
【办报】run a newspaper
【办差】perform missions; do errands for the government
【办到】get sth done; accomplish: 原来认为办不到的事,现在~了。*What was thought impossible has now been done.*
【办法】way; means; measure: 有些老人喜欢处理事务的老~。*Some old men like the older ways of*

doing things.

【办公】handle official business：～时间 *office hours* /～厅 *administrative department* /我们公司不需要增添任何～人员。*There's no call for any office workers now.*

【办公室】office：他带着他的作品，来到教授的～。*He came to professor's office, taking along his works.* /～的工作人员凑钱给老板买了一件生日礼物。*The workers in the office clubbed together to buy their boss a present for her birthday.*

【办理】handle；deal with；conduct；do：～手续 *go through the formalities* /我现在习惯～这类的事情。*I'm used to dealing with matters of this sort.* /我来～这件事。*I will take up this matter.*

【办事】handle affairs；work：～处 *agency* /～机构 *administrative office or body* /～认真 *work conscientiously* /无论办什么事都要凭良心～。*Whatever you have done should act according to your conscience.*

【办学】conduct a school；run a school：按学术自由的～方针 *run a school on the principle of academic freedom*

半 ① half；semi：～公里路程 *half a kilometer of distance* /～波放大器 *half-wave amplifier* /我们每人有～。*We had half each.* /她们有～数的来了。*Half of them are here.* /那个孩子～睡着。*He was half asleep.* /现在是七点～了。*It's half past seven.* /良好的开端等于成功的一～。*Well begun is half done.* ② in the middle；halfway：～夜 *midnight* ③ little；the least bit：一星～点 *just a little*；*tiny bit* ④ partly：～信～疑 *half-believing, half doubting*

【半百】fifty years of age：那个老人已年过～了。*The old man is over fifty.*

【半辈子】half a lifetime：他花了～时间来研究历史。*It cost him half a lifetime to research the history.*

【半壁江山】half of the country

【半边】half of sth；one side of sth：～天 *half the sky*

【半波】【电】half wave；semiwave：～输电 *half-wave electric transmission* /～区 *half-wave zone* /～整流器 *half-wave rectifier*

【半场】half a game；half court

【半成品】semi-finished product；semi-manufactures

【半岛】peninsula：山东～*Shandong Peninsula*

【半导性】semiconductivity

【半导体】semi-conduction：化合物～ *compound semiconductor* /元素～ *element semiconductor* /集成～ *integrated semiconductor* /金属氧化物～ *metal-oxide semiconductor* /～晶体 *semi-conduction crystal* /～收音机 *transistor radio* /～材料 *semiconductor material*；*semiconducting material*

【半道儿】halfway；midway；on the way：那个孩子在去学校的～迷路了。*The child lost his way halfway to the school.*

【半地下室】semi-basement

【半吊子】① person who is not sensible ② dabbler smatterer ③ trifler；dawdler

【半独立】semi-independent

【半对称】hemihedral

【半封建】semi-feudal；semi-feudalism：旧中国是一个～半殖民地国家。*Old China was a semi-feudal and semi-colonial country.*

【半干旱】semi-arid

【半工半读】part work, part study：他～念完了大学。*He worked his way through college.*

【半公开】semi-overt；semi-open

【半固体】【物】semisolid

【半官方】semi-official

【半价】half price；fifty percent discount：该家商店里的所有衣服～出售。*All the clothes of this shop sell at half price.*

【半截】half：～铅笔 *half of a pencil*

【半斤八两】much of muchness；six of one and half a dozen of the other

【半金属】【物】semimetal

【半晶体】【物】semi-crystal

【半径】radius；semi-diameter

【半决赛】【体】semifinals

【半绝缘体】【物】semi-insulator

【半空】①in mid-air；in the air ② half-empty；not full

【半路】① halfway；midway；on the way；in progress ② halfway through：～出家 *switch to new profession or a hew field of study late in life* /～夫妻 *couple married halfway through life*

【半票】half-price ticket

【半旗】half-mast

【半球】hemisphere

【半晌】quite a while；for a long time：～午 *about noon*；*almost noon* /他想了～才想起来。*It was quite some time before he recalled it.*

【半身】half of one's body：～像 *half-length photo*

【半数】half；half the number：有～的学生都来了。*Half of the students come here.*

【半天】half a day；a long time：他～说不出话来。*He remained tongue-tied for a long time.*

【半透明】translucent；semitransparent：～体 *translucent body*

【半途】halfway；midway：做事决不能～而废 *never do anything by halves*

【半推半就】yield with seeming reluctance

【半脱产】partly excused from work；partly released from productive labour

【半文盲】semiliterate

【半信半疑】half-believing；doubtful

【半夜】half of a night；midnight；late at night：～三更 *in the depth of night*；*in the middle of night* /她经常工作到～。*She often works till midnight.* /昨天～她家的邻居猛烈地敲她家的门。*There was a furious knocking at the door at midnight yesterday by her neighbour.*

【半元音】semivowel

【半圆】semicircle

【半月】half-moon：～潮 *fortnightly tide* /～刊 *semimonthly*

【半自动】semi-automatic：实现～化 *realize semi-automation* / ～步枪 *semi-automatic rifle*
【半自治】semi-autonomous
扮 ① make up；play the part of；disguise oneself as：装～成羊的狼 *a wolf disguises itself as a sheep* ② put on（an expression）③［方］thresh；beat
【扮鬼脸】make faces：那个可爱的孩子向他奶奶～。*The lovely child made faces at his granny.*
【扮相】stage appearance：她的～如何？*How about her stage appearance?*
【扮演】have a role；play the part；act：导演让那个著名的演员～一位科学家。*The director cast the famous actor as a scientist.* /他～一个残疾青年。*He was cast as a handicapped youth.*
【扮装】make-up
伴 ① companion；partner：伙～ *companion；partner* /他是你的～吗？*Is he your partner?* ② accompany：闪电通常～有雷声。*Lightning usually accompanies thunder.*
【伴唱】vocal accompaniment；accompany：玛丽由钢琴～。*Mary sang to the accompaniment of the piano.*
【伴君如伴虎】Accompany the emperor is to be in the company of the tiger.
【伴郎】best man at a wedding
【伴侣】companion；partner；mate：他一直是她的忠实～。*He was been a faithful mate to her.*
【伴娘】bridesmaid
【伴随】company；follow
【伴同】accompany；go together
【伴舞】be a dancing partner；accompany a singer with dance
【伴星】【天】companion(star)
【伴音】audio；sound accompaniment；aural
【伴奏】accompaniment：在音乐的～下跳舞 *perform dances to the accompaniment of music* /我的妻子唱歌，我弹琴给她～。*My wife sang and I accompanied her on the piano.*
拌 ① mix ② quarrel
【拌和】mix；blend：～机 *mixing machine*
【拌浆机】grout mixer
【拌嘴】［方］quarrel；squabble；bicker
绊 stumble；trip：～了一跤 *trip over sth*
【绊倒】trip；stumble：我被一把椅子～在地上。*I stumbled against a chair.* /那个淘气的孩子在路上～了。*The naughty boy stumbled along the road.*
【绊脚】trip；tie up person's movements：～石 *stumbling block；obstacle*
【绊住】entangle；successfully hinder movement
【绊子】trip；restraining rope；hobble
瓣 ① petal：花～ *petal* ② segment；clove ③ fragment；piece ④ valve；lamella ⑤［量］a petal；a leaf：切成六～儿 *cut into six*
【瓣膜】【生】valve
【瓣片】【植】limb

bāng

邦 nation；state；country：礼仪之～ *land of ceremony and propriety* /联～ *federation；union* /友～ *friendly nation* /邻～ *neighbouring country；neighbour state*
【邦国】［书］nation；country
【邦交】rations between two countries；diplomatic relations
帮[1] ① assist；help；aid：让他来～你拿这些包吧！*Let him assist you with these bags.* /你能～我修理自行车吗？*Can you help me repair the bike?* /妈妈总是～我收拾房间。*My mother always helps me get the room tidy.* ② be hired；work：你在～短工吗？*Do you work as seasonal help?*
帮[2] ① side；upper：鞋～ *upper of a shoe* ② outer leaf：他喜欢吃白菜～。*He likes eating outer leaf of cabbage.*
帮[3] ① gang；band；clique：匪～ *bandit gang* ②［量］a group of；a band of；a gang of a group of children ③secret society
【帮办】① assist in management：～军务 *assist in handling military affairs* ② deputy；assistant
【帮厨】help in the mess kitchen
【帮倒忙】do sb a disservice；be more of a hindrance than a help
【帮工】① help with farm work ② helper；farm hand；work assistant；seasonal labour
【帮会】secret society；underworld gang
【帮伙】gang；band
【帮教】help and educate
【帮忙】help；give a hand；lend a hand；do a favour，do a good turn：这是我第一次请你～。*This is the first favour that I have been asked of you.*
【帮派】faction：～活动 *factionalism；gang activities*
【帮腔】① vocal accompaniment；join in singing behind the stage ② speak in support（of sb）；echo sb；back sb up；give vocal support：李阿姨老给她女儿～。*Aunt Li always keeps chiming in with her daughter.*
【帮手】helper；assistant：她配得上做你的～。*He is worthy of your assistant.* /王秘书是老板的得力～。*Secretary Wang is a good help to his boss.*
【帮闲】① serve as a hireling or hack ② hack writer；literary hack
【帮凶】① serve as an accomplice or hack；assist in a crime or evil；be an accomplice ② accomplice；accessory
【帮佣】maid；servant
【帮助】assist；help：我希望你能～我照顾一会孩子。*I hope you can help me look after my baby for a while.* /当刘芳英语学习遇到困难时，总是她的哥哥～她克服了。*When Liu Fang had difficulty with her English，her elder brother pulled her through.* /你的建议对我的～很大。*Your advice*

was a great help to me.

bǎng

绑 bind; tie up:捆~*tie up*; *bind* /请~紧囚犯的双臂。*Please bind the prisoner arms together.* /匪徒用绳子把他~在座位上以免那个孩子逃跑。*The gangsters bind the child to the seat with rope lest he should escape.*

【绑带】bandage

【绑匪】kidnapper

【绑架】① kidnap; abduct:上周那个著名的女演员遭到了~。*Last week the famous actress was kidnapped.* /那个孩子的家长认为他们的孩子已被~了。*The parents thought their child has been abducted.* ②【农】stake

【绑票】kidnap sb and hold him to ransom

【绑线】binding wire

【绑扎】tie up; bind up; wrap up:他不得不自己~伤口。*He had to bind up the wound by himself.*

榜 ① list of names posted up; published list of names:光荣~*honour roll*; *roster of honour* ② announcement; notice

【榜首】the top candidate of an examination:这首歌曲流行后,它的录音带销量跃登畅销带的~。*After the song was a hit and its recording tape rose to No. 1 on the bestseller list.*

【榜眼】second place of the first grade in China's highest imperial examinations during the Ming and Qing dynasties

【榜样】example; role model; pattern:雷锋为我们大家树立了好~。*Lei Feng set a good example to us all.* /王丽的勇敢是大家的~。*The courage of Wang Li is an example to us all.*

膀 ① arm; shoulder:人的肩~*shoulders of a person* /他是一个肩~宽的男人。*He is a man with broad shoulders.* ② wing:翅~*wing of a bird*

【膀臂】① reliable assistant ② upper arm

【膀阔腰圆】broad shouldered and solidly-built; of a powerful build; husky

【膀子】upper arm; sing

bàng

蚌 freshwater mussel; clam

see also bèng

棒 ① stick; club; cudgel: ~叶病毒 *club-leaf virus* /工人们用~在废料堆里乱捣。*The workers poke among the waste materials with a stick.* ② terrific; good; strong; excellent

【棒冰】[方] ice-sucker; frozen sucker; ice-sucker

【棒槌】① wooden club ②[方] clumsy; awkward

【棒料】【冶】bar stock

【棒球】baseball: ~场 *baseball field* /~队 *a baseball team* / ~投手 *pitcher* /那个孩子非常喜欢打~。*The child likes playing baseball very much.* /那个国家以~而闻名。*That country is prominent in baseball.*

【棒糖】lollipop; sucker

【棒针】thick knitting needle

【棒子】① stick; club; cudgel ②[方] maize; corn: ~面 *corn-meal*; *corn flour*

傍 ① draw near; be close to ② towards; nearly ③ follow; lean on

【傍边儿】near

【傍大款】lean on a moneybags; find a sugar daddy; rely on someone with a lot of money; accompany a rich man; attach to money bags

【傍晚】toward evening; at nightfall; at dusk

【傍午】toward noon

【傍依】be close to; near

谤 [书] slander; defame; vilify; smear:那个老人宣称在会上他受人诽~。*The old man claimed he was slandered at the meeting.*

【谤毁】[书] slander; calumniate

磅[1] ① pound ② scales ③ weigh: ~体重 *weigh oneself*

磅[2] 【印】point

【磅秤】platform scale; platform balance: ~车 *scale car*

镑 pound:他花了二十~买了这本书。*It cost* 20 *pounds for the book.*

bāo

包 ① wrap:把书~起来 *wrap things up* /那个小姑娘用一张纸把花~起来。*The little girl folds a piece of paper round the flowers.* ② bundle; parcel pack; package ③ bag ④ a packet of: 一~旧衣服 *a bundle of old clothes* /她去商店给她的丈夫买了~香烟。*She went supermarket to buy a packet of cigarettes for her husband.* ⑤ swelling ⑥ yurt:蒙古~ *Mongolian yurt* ⑦ surround; encircle ⑧ include; contain ⑨ undertake to fulfill an assignment ⑩ guarantee; assure ⑪ hire; charter: ~辆汽车 *hire* (*or charter*) *a car* ⑫ (Bāo) a surname

【包办】① take sole charge of ② monopolize: ~婚姻 *arranged marriage or match*

【包庇】shield; cover up: ~某人的过失 *cover up sb's faults*

【包藏】contain; harbour; conceal: ~恶意 *harbour evil designs*

【包产】make a production contract; take full responsibility for output quotas: ~到户 *fix farm output quotas for each household*

【包场】make a block booking; book all or most of the seats in the theatre or cinema; book all or part of the tickets for a film show or play

【包车】① vehicle hired by an individual for a certain period of time; chartered car or bus ② bus or trolley ③ hire a car for a period of time; charter

【包饭】① meals thus arranged; meals thus supplied ② supply or get meals at a fixed rate; board

【包房】① compartment; chartered room ② rent a room for a period of time

【包袱】① cloth wrapper ② a bundle wrapped in cloth ③ load; burden ④ joke or laughing stock

【包干】be responsible for a task until it is completed; undertake to do a job until it is completed: ~制 *overall rationing system*; *scheme of payment partly in kind and partly in cash*

【包工】① undertake to perform work within a time limit and according to specifications; contract for a job ② contractor; head of contracted labour: ~队 *contracting team* / ~头 *labour contractor* / ~制 *labour contract system*

【包管】assure; guarantee

【包裹】① wrap up; bind up ② package; bundle; parcel: 邮政~ *postal parcel*; *postal packet* / ~单 *parcel form* / ~收据 *parcel receipt* /邮递员把你的~放在了办公室里。*The postman left your packages in your office.*

【包含】contain; embody; include: 海水中~盐。*Seawater contains salt.*

【包涵】excuse; forgive; bear with: 我英文讲得不好,请多多~。*Excuse me for my poor English.*

【包换】guarantee to accept the return or exchange

【包机】① charter a plane ② chartered plane; chartered flight

【包括】include; cover; consist of; incorporate; embrace: 他的发言~了他所有的论点。*His statement embraces all his arguments.* /这个文章~了一些有趣的例子。*The article contained some interesting examples.*

【包揽】monopolize all work to serve private ends; undertake the whole thing; take on everything: ~词讼 *engage in pettifoggery*

【包罗】embrace; cover; include

【包罗万象】all-embracing; all-inclusive; cover and contain everything; embrace everything under the sun: 制定一个~的计划 *draw out an all-inclusive plan*

【包络】【数】envelope: ~曲线 *envelope curve* / ~函数 *envelope function*

【包赔】guarantee to pay compensations

【包皮】① wrapping; wrapper ②【生理】prepuce; foreskin

【包容】tolerant; magnanimous ② contain; hold

【包身工】indentured labourer

【包退】money back guarantee: ~包换 *guarantee change of article or refund if unsatisfactory*; *refund or change for a better one*

【包围】surround; close round; encircle; besiege; encompass: ~圈 *ring of encirclement* /以农村~城市。*Encircle the cities from the rural areas.*

【包厢】box; opera house

【包圆儿】① buy the whole or the remaining lot ② finish up or off

【包扎】wrap up; bind up; pack: 医生把他受伤的头部~起来。*The doctors bandaged up his injured head.*

【包治】guarantee a cure; not receive fees until the patient is cured: ~百病 *guarantee to cure all diseases*

【包装】① pack; package ② encase: ~材料 *packaging*; *wrapping* / ~设备 *packaging equipment*; *packing facility* / ~纸 *wrapping paper* /此货用帆布~。*The goods are packed in canvas.* /我们明天动身,但我的行李还没有进行~呢。*We leave tomorrow, but I haven't begun to pack yet.*

【包子】① steamed stuffed bun ②【冶】ladle

【包租】① rent for subletting ②［旧］fixed rent for farmland irrespective of the harvest ③ hire for a period of time: ~合同 *charter contract*

苞[1] bud: 含~欲放 *flower in bud*

苞[2] ［书］profuse; luxuriant

【苞米】［方］corn; maize

【苞片】【植】bract

【苞叶】【植】bracteal leaf

孢 spore

【孢子】spore: ~植物 *cryptogam*

胞 ① afterbirth; placenta ② born of the same parents ③ fellow countryman; compatriot: 侨~ *countrymen residing abroad*; *overseas compatriots*

【胞弟】full brother

【胞芽】【植】gemma

【胞衣】【医】afterbirth; secundines

剥 strip; peel; shell; skin

see also bō

【剥皮】peel; skin: 这些树被~了。*The trees are stripped of their bark.*

【剥皮工】stripper

龅

【龅牙】bucktooth

煲 ［方］① cooking pot; boiler: 电饭~ *electric cooker*

褒 ① praise; honour with praise; decoration or gift; commend: ~贬人物 *pass judgement on persons* ② loose; large

【褒贬】pass judgement on; comment; appraise: 不加~ *make no comment*; *complimentary or otherwise*

【褒奖】commend and award; praise and honour: 应该受到~ *deserve praise and award*

【褒扬】praise; commend: ~爱国精神 *commend the patriotic spirit*
【褒义】commendatory sense; laudatory meaning: ~词 *commendatory term*

báo

雹 hail; hailstone
【雹子】hail; hailstone: ~猛落下来把玻璃砸破了。*Hail fell with such violence that it broke windows.*
薄 ① thin; flimsy: 稀~ *thin; rare* /这冰太~,载不起你的重量。*The ice is too thin to bear your weight.* ② coldly; shabbily ③ weak; light ④ infertile; poor
see also bó; bò
【薄板】【冶】sheet metal; sheet
【薄饼】pancake; wafer; thin pancake
【薄脆】crisp fritter: ~饼 *wafer; waffle; snap*
【薄片】flake
【薄田】infertile land

bǎo

饱 ① be full; be replete; have eaten one's fill: 酒足饭~ *have drunk and eaten to one's heart's content* ② full; plump ③ fully ④ satisfy ⑤ embezzle
【饱尝】experience; feast one's eyes on: 她小时候~了辛酸的生活。*She had met with many trials of life.*
【饱嗝儿】belch; burp
【饱和】saturation: 旧汽车市场已经~。*The market for the used car is saturated.*
【饱经沧桑】have been through the vicissitudes of life; have witnessed or experienced many changes in life
【饱经风霜】having had one's fill of hardships and difficulties; weather-beaten
【饱满】full of; plump; rounded
【饱暖】be well fed and clad; more than enough to eat and wear
【饱受】have a full measure of; suffer (insult, grievances, etc.) to the fullest extent
【饱学】learned; erudite; scholarly: ~之士 *a learned scholar; a man of great erudition*
【饱足】be satisfied; be content
宝 ① treasure; riches; valuables: 珠光~气 *bedecked with jewels; resplendent with jewels* /珠~ *pearls and jewels* ② precious; treasured ③ a kind of gambling device ④ your: ~号 *your shop*
【宝宝】darling; baby; darling child; dear: ~装 *infant clothes*
【宝贝】① treasure ② darling; dear; baby ③ cherish; love ④ crank; good-for-nothing
【宝刀】a treasured sword; especially valued or antique knife: ~不老。*A good sword remains always sharp.*
【宝地】① well-situated place ② your place
【宝典】treasured book
【宝顶】top of an emperor's mausoleum
【宝盖】canopy of an imperial carriage
【宝贵】① valuable; precious: ~的经验 *valuable experience* / ~的文物 *precious cultural relic* ② valuc; treasure: 幽默是一个人的~资产。*A sense of humour is a great asset for a person.*
【宝剑】a double edged sword
【宝眷】your wife and children; your family
【宝盒】box of treasures; jewel box
【宝库】treasure house; treasury; any valuable collection: 图书馆是知识的~。*The library is a storehouse of knowledge.*
【宝蓝】bright blue
【宝器】valuable article
【宝气】be with jewelry: 那个老板的夫人穿得浑身珠光~。*The boss's wife stinks with jewelry.*
【宝山】treasure mountain
【宝石】precious stone; gem; jewel: 那条金项链在她的~箱里。*The gold necklace is in her jewel case.* /上个月她看到了嵌有~的王冠。*Last month she saw a crown embedded with jewels.* /金刚钻是一种~。*Diamond is a precious stone.*
【宝书】treasured book
【宝塔】pagoda; dagoba: 从~上层可以眺望周围。*The pagoda's upper stories may be used to view the surrounding area.*
【宝物】treasure
【宝藏】treasure; hidden treasure; precious deposit: 发掘地下~ *unearth buried treasure; tap mineral resources*
【宝座】throne
保 ① defend; protect; safeguard: 劳~ *labour protection; labour insurance* / ~养汽车 *maintain a car* ② keep; maintain in good condition; preserver ③ guarantee; ensure: 担~ *assures; guarantee* /投~ *insure; take out an insurance policy* ④ bail ⑤ guarantor; guarantee ⑥ division ⑦ (Bǎo) a surname
【保安】ensure public security; maintain law and order ensure safety: ~队 *peace preservation corps*
【保本】break even; protect any investment; keep the capital intact
【保镖】① act as a bodyguard; escort ② bodyguard; armed escort
【保不住】① most likely ② impossible to maintain
【保藏】preserve; keep in store: 在低温下~得很好 *store well at low temperature*
【保持】keep; hold; preserve; maintain: ~独立的见解 *keep independent views* /那个经理通常在会上~沉默。*The manager generally keeps silent at a meeting.*
【保存】preserve; keep; conserve: 古埃及人懂得~尸体使之不腐烂的方法。*The ancient Egyptians knew ways to preserve dead bodies from decay.*

【保单】warranty; guarantee slip
【保底】① protect an investment ② guarantee a minimum sum
【保兑】confirm: ~银行 *confirming bank*
【保费】insurance fee
【保付】guaranteed of payment
【保管】① take care of; manage; maintain ② storekeeper ③ certainly; surely
【保函】letter of guarantee; letter of credit
【保护】protect; safeguard; take care of; defend: ~贸易政策 *policy for the protection of trade; protectionist policy* / ~主义 *protectionism* /我们应该~益鸟。*We should protect helpful birds.*
【保皇】defend the emperor or king: ~派 *royalist* / ~党 *royalists; monarchist party*
【保加利亚】Bulgaria: ~人 *Bulgarian* / ~语 *Bulgarian language*
【保家卫国】protect our homes and defend our country; safeguard our homeland
【保价】value insured: ~包裹 *insured parcel*
【保驾】protect; escort the Emperor; protect an important person
【保荐】recommend
【保健】health care; health protection: 妇幼~ *health care for women and children; mother and child care* / ~操 *setting-up exercises; fitness exercise* / ~食品 *health food* / ~站 *health centre; community clinic*
【保洁】keep the environment clean; do sanitation work
【保举】recommend for promotion
【保龄球】bowling; bowling ball
【保留】① retain; keep; maintain ② hold back ③ have reservations: 对这一事实的看法得有所~。*This fact must be taken with some reservation* ④ save
【保密】maintain secrecy; keep sth secret; keep confidential: ~局 *National Security Agency; National Security Bureau* /这些资料一定要~。*The information will be treated as strictly confidential.*
【保姆】① domestic child care nurse; baby sitter ② housemaid ③［旧］nursery or kindergarten worker
【保暖】keep warm
【保票】warranty; certificate of guarantee; written guarantee
【保全】① save from damage; assure the safe of; guard; deep intact; preserve ② maintain; repair
【保释】release on bail; bail: ~人 *bailsman* /把某人~出狱 *bail sb out of prison*
【保守】① guard; keep safe; secure ② conservative: ~思想 *conservative ideas; conservative thinking* / ~党 *Conservative Party; Tory Party*
【保送】recommend sb for admission to school; send sb on recommend action
【保胎】prevent miscarriage; help retain the fetus
【保卫】defend; guard; safeguard: ~祖国 *defend one's country*
【保温】keep warm; preserve heat: ~瓶 *thermos; vacuum flask*
【保鲜】retain freshness: ~期 *length for preservation; best before* / ~剂 *anti-staling agent* / ~膜 *plastic wrap*
【保险】① insurance: 人寿~ *life insurance* / ~公司 *insurance company* /学校里所有的学生和老师都参加了人身~。*All the pupils and teachers in the school are covered against accidents.* ② maintain; repair; keep in good condition
【保修】guarantee; maintenance; guarantee to keep sth in good repair: ~单 *warranty* /这块表~两个月。*This watch is guaranteed for two months.*
【保养】① take good care of one's health; keep fit; preserve ② keep in good repair; service; maintenance; upkeep: 他的新汽车一直~得很好。*His new car has always been properly maintained.*
【保佑】bless and protect: 愿上帝~你。*God bless you!*
【保育】child care; child welfare: ~员 *child care worker; nurse*
【保障】ensure; guarantee; safeguard
【保证】ensure; pledge; guarantee: ~人 *guarantor; sponsor* / ~金 *earnest money; margin; bail* / ~书 *guarantee; written pledge; letter of guarantee* /制造厂商对这种手表~用三年。*The manufactures guarantee the watch for three years.* /如果你~下课以前回来,你可以出去。*You can go out as long as you promise to be back before class.*
【保值】hedge appreciation
【保质】ensure or guarantee the quality of a product: ~期 *date stamping* / ~保量 *ensure both quality and quantity*
【保重】take care of oneself; look after oneself: 请多多~! *Please be careful of your health!*

鸨 ①【动】bustard ② procuress; madam: 老~ *procuress; brothel keeper*
【鸨母】procuress; keeper; bawd

葆[1] ①［书］nurture; preserve ②（Bǎo）a surname

葆[2] ［书］luxuriant growth

堡 fort; fortress
see also bǔ
【堡礁】barrier reef
【堡垒】fort; bastion; stronghold; blockhouse
【堡寨】walled village; walled village

bào

报 ① tell; report; announce: 喜~ *bulletin of glad tidings* /她向老师~告了昨天所发生的事情。*She told her teacher what had happened yesterday.* ② respond; reply ③ recompense: 以怨~德 *recompense good with evil* ④ retaliate; revenge ⑤ retribution ⑥ newspaper: 他喜欢饭后读~。*He likes reading newspaper after dinner.* ⑦ journal; periodical

【报案】report a case; report to the police an act violating the law or endangering social security

【报表】tables for reporting statistics; report forms; forms for reporting to the higher organizations:财务~ *balance sheet* /损益~ *profit-and-loss report*

【报偿】repay; reward; remuneration; recompense: 读这些书能得到~。*These books repay the labour of reading.*

【报仇】revenge; avenge:我赢了他一盘棋之后给了他一个~的机会。*After I had beaten him at chess I gave him a chance to get his revenge.*

【报酬】reward; remuneration; pay

【报春】be a harbinger of spring; herald spring: ~花 *primrose; fairy primrose*

【报答】repay; requite:我总有一天会~你的。*I will repay you some day.*

【报单】entry; tax declaration

【报到】check in; register; report for duty; report one's arrival

【报道】report; cover; information; story

【报恩】pay a debt of gratitude; requite favours; pay sb's kindness

【报废】scrap; discard as useless; be declared worthless:这台计算机太慢,不得不~了。*The computer is so old that it has to be scrapped.*

【报复】avenge; make reprisals; retaliate; pay sb in one's own coin

【报告】① report; inform; make known; announce ② speech; talk; lecture; advisory: ~文学 *reportage* /总结~ *summing-up report; summary report*

【报关】declare sth at the customs; apply to the customs; make a customs declaration; entry: ~表 *customs debenture; declaration form* / ~证书 *customs clearance certificate*

【报官】report to the authorities

【报馆】newspaper office

【报国】serve the country worthily; dedicate oneself to the service of one's country

【报户口】apply for permanent residence; register one's domicile; apply for a residence permit

【报话】① radio communication: ~员 *radio operator* / ~机 *transmitter-receiver set; handle-talkie*

【报价】【经】quoted price; offer; quotation: ~单 *quotation of prices*

【报架】newspaper holder; newspaper rack

【报界】the press; the news circle; the media; press circles:她的贫困家庭引起了~的关注。*Her poor family attract much attention in the media.*

【报警】report to the police; give an alarm: ~器 *alarm; warning device*

【报刊】the press; newspapers and periodicals: ~杂志 *newspaper and magazines* / ~发行 *distribution of newspapers and periodicals*

【报考】enter oneself for an examination; register for examination

【报密】inform against sb

【报名】sign up; sign; enroll; enlist; enter one's name

【报幕】announce items of a programme; screen and stage announcement: ~员 *announcer*

【报盘】【经】offer

【报批】submit to a higher authority for approval

【报社】newspaper office

【报时】give the correct time: ~器 *chronopher*

【报税】make a statement of dutiable goods; declare dutiable: ~单 *taxation form*

【报摊】news-stand; news stall

【报亭】news-stand; kiosk selling newspaper and periodicals

【报童】newspaper delivery boy; street newsboy; newsboy

【报务】work of sending and receiving messages: ~员 *radio operator; radioman*

【报喜】report success; announce good news; announce glad tidings: ~不报忧 *report the good news but not the bad; hold back unpleasant information; report only what is good while withholding what is unpleasant*

【报销】① apply for reimbursement; submit an expense account; claim payment or refund:他一到办公室,便向财务部要求~他的差旅费。*As soon as he came to his off office, he asked for reimbursement of his travelling expenses from the financial division.* ② hand in a list of expended articles ③ [口] write off; wipe out; discard

【报晓】herald the break of day:晨鸡~。*The crowing of roosters at dawn heralded the break of day.*

【报效】repay sb's kindness by working hard for him; render service to repay sb's kindness

【报信】inform; give information; notify; deliver a message

【报修】report for repair

【报应】retribution; judgement

【报忧】report unpleasant; notify disappointing news

【报怨】avenge a grievance; respond to a grievance: 不要以德~。*Don't return good for evil.*

【报账】apply for reimbursement; render an account; submit an expense account for refunding

【报纸】① newspaper; journal:不要给他今天的~了,他已经看过了。*Don't give him today's newspaper for he had read them.* ② newsprint

刨 ① plane; planing machine; planer:槽~ *grooving plane* ② plan sth down; plane smooth; shave: ~桌子 *plane a table*
see also páo

【刨冰】water ice; powdered ice; shavings of ice: ~机 *ice shaver*

【刨床】planer; planing machine

【刨工】wood shavings

【刨子】plane

抱[1] ① clasp in the arms; hug; embrace; cherish; hold in the arms:两国总统热烈地拥~在

一起。*The Presidents of the two countries warmly embraced each other.* /她把她的小孩~起来。*She took her child in her arms.* ② have one's first child or grandchild:恭喜你快~孙子了。*Congratulation you will soon be a grandmother.* ③ adopt (a child):她家没有孩子,只得从医院~了一个孩子。*She adopted a baby from a hospital for she had no children.* ④[方] hang together ⑤[方] fit well ⑥ harbour; cherish ⑦[量] armful

抱[2] hatch(eggs); brood: ~窝 *sit* (*on eggs*); *brook*; *hatch* / 我家的一只母鸡~窝了。*A hen in my home is sitting.*

【抱病】be ill; be in bad health

【抱不平】be outraged by an injustice:打~ *champion the cause of a person who has suffered wrong*

【抱残守缺】be conservative; cherish the old and preserve the outworn

【抱成一团】hang together; gang together; gang up

【抱佛脚】clasp Buddha's feet-profess devotion only when in trouble; make a last minute effort

【抱负】ideal; ambition; aspiration:他是个有~的年轻人。*He is a young man with high ideals and aspirations.*

【抱恨】have a gnawing regret; be overwhelmed with remorse

【抱歉】regret; be sorry; feel apologetic: ~,今天他来不了。*I'm sorry that he can't come her today.*

【抱头鼠窜】cover the head with one's hands and run away like a rat; clasp one's head and scurry away in a panic

【抱养】adopt (a child)

【抱怨】complain; grumble; grouse:她老~自己个子矮。*She always complains she is too short.*

趵 spring forth; bounce

豹 leopard; panther:海~ *seal* /猎~ *cheetah* / 金钱~ *leopard*

【豹猫】leopard cat

【豹子】leopard, panther:昨天孩子们去动物园看~去了。*Yesterday the children went to the zoo to see leopards.*

鲍 ① abalone; salted fish ② (Bào) a surname

【鲍鱼】① abalone ②[书] salted fish

暴[1] ① sudden and fierce:残~ *brutal*; *savage* ② savage; harsh and tyrannical; fierce:狂风~雨 *violent storms* ③ irritable; hot-tempered ④ (Bào) a surname

暴[2] ① bulge; stand out; stick out; bulge ② expose; broadcast; reveal

暴[3] ruin; spoil; soil; waste:自~自弃 *give oneself up as hopeless*

【暴病】a sudden illness; fall ill; sudden attack of disease:昨天,他突然得了~,被送进了一家医院。*Yesterday, he was suddenly seized with a severe illness and was sent to a hospital.*

【暴跌】drop; slump; steep fall; break

【暴动】riot; insurrection; rebellion; uprising

【暴发】① have suddenly become rich; get rich quickly: ~户 *upstart*; *riche*; *nouveau* ② break out; eruption

【暴风】① violent storm; tempest; windstorm: ~雪 *blizzard wind*; *snowstorm*; *blizzard* / ~雨 *storm*; *rainstorm* ② storm(force 11 wind); hurricane

【暴君】despot; tyrant

【暴力】① force; violence: ~革命 *violent revolution* ② force as exercised by the state

【暴利】extravagant profits; windfall:不要以不正当手段牟取~。*Don't reap colossal profits by illegitimate means.*

【暴戾】ruthless and tyrannical; savage

【暴敛】forcible collection of (taxes):在旧社会里,政府经常横征~。*In old society, the government often extorted excessive taxes and levies.*

【暴露】bare; expose; reveal; bring to light

【暴乱】rebellion; revolt; riot: ~者 *rioter*; *rebel*

【暴民】mob; rioters; mobster

【暴怒】fury; violent rage

【暴晒】be under the blazing sun; be exposed to the sun

【暴殄天物】be recklessly wasteful of nature's bounties

【暴跳】move violently; stamp with fury: ~如雷 *be in a towering rage*; *fly into a violent temper*

【暴徒】mobster; ruffian; rioter; thug; bully

【暴行】outrage; savage act; ferocity

【暴刑】savage act; cruel punishment; torture; unruly conduct

【暴雨】rainstorm; hard rain; downpour:在一个~的天气里,她独自离开了家。*In a rainstorm day, she left her home.*

【暴躁】hot tempered; irritable

【暴涨】boom; rise suddenly and sharply

【暴政】tyranny; tyrannical rule; despotic rule

曝

see also pù

【曝光】exposure; bar: ~表 *exposure meter*

爆 ① explode; burst:引~装置 *igniter*; *detonator* ② crop up ③ pop; quick-fry

【爆发】① erupt ② break out:战争很快~了。*The war broke out soon.* ③ (of feeling, incident, etc.) burst out

【爆冷门】surprise; unexpected turn of events

【爆裂】burst; crack

【爆米花】popcorn; pop rice

【爆破】blow up; blast; explode: ~作业 *blasting operation*

【爆炸】explode; blast; detonate: ~装置 *explosive device* /这次~造成了很多人员伤亡。*The blast caused many loss of human life.*

【爆竹】firecracker; maroon

bēi

杯 ① cup：举～ *raise one's glass* /茶～ *tea cup* /来一～啤酒怎么样？*How about a cup of beer?* ②（prize）trophy；cup：金～ *gold cup* /世界～ *world cup* /优胜～决赛 *cup-final* ③［量］used usu. of liquids：两～水 *two glasses of water* /～弓蛇影 *mistake the reflection of a bow in the cup for a snake—extremely suspicious*

【杯酒】cup of wine：～释兵权 *relieve the generals of their commands at a feast*

【杯水车薪】drop in the bucket；trying to put out a burning cartload of faggots with a cup of water — an utterly inadequate measure

【杯子】glass；cup

卑 ① low；low-lying ② low rank ③ low character；inferior in quality ④［书］modest；humble：～辞厚礼 *humble words and handsome gifts*

【卑鄙】① mean；despicable：～手段 *contemptible means；dirty tricks* ②［书］inferior and ignorant；worthless

【卑恭】humble and respectful

【卑躬屈膝】cringe；bow and scrape；act servility

【卑贱】① lowly；humble origin：她总是说自己出身～。*She always said that she was of lowly origin.* ② menial；lowly

【卑劣】base；mean；despicable

【卑陋】① mean；lowly ② degrading

【卑怯】base and cowardly

【卑屈】cringing；obedient and docile

【卑微】petty and low

【卑下】① lowly；base ② humble

【卑职】［书］① lowly post；humble position ②（used by a subordinate official in addressing superiors）your humble subordinate；I

背 ① carry on the back：她～着孩子不得不离开了家乡。*She had to leave her hometown carrying her child on her back.* ② bear；shoulder：我～不起这样的恶名。*I can't should a bad name.* ③［量］indicate what can be borne by one person on the back：那个孩子～着一捆柴火下山了。*The little child left the mountain with a bundle of firewood.*
see also bèi

【背包】backpack；rucksack；knapsack；infantry pack；field pack ②【军】blanket roll：战士们打了～，准备离开那个村庄。*The soldiers tied up blanket rolls and were ready to leave the village.*

【背包袱】take on a mental burden；have a weight or load on one's mind

【背带】① braces；suspenders ② sling；straps（for a knapsack）

【背负】① carry on the back ② bear；have on one's shoulder：那个学生～着父母的希望离开了家乡。*The student carried in his heart the expectations of his parents and left his hometown.*

【背黑锅】［口］be unjustly blamed；be made a scapegoat；take the blame for others：我们没有必要为他～。*We have no use for taking the blame for him.*

【背债】be in debt；be saddled with debts

悲 ① melancholy；sad；sorrowful：少壮不努力，老大徒伤～。*If a person does not work hard when young, it will be of no use for him to regret when old.* /我永远不会忘记是你使我们处于可～的境地。*I will never forget it is you that make us be in a deplorable state.* ② compassion：慈～ *compassionate；merciful* /大慈大～ *be immensely compassionate and merciful*

【悲哀】grieved；sad：她是那么的～，以至于一句话也说不上来。*She was so sad that can't say anything.*

【悲惨】bitter；miserable；tragic：～的生活 *miserable life*

【悲愤】grief and indignation：～填膺 *be filled with grief and indignation*

【悲歌】① sing with solemn fervour ② sad song

【悲哽】choke with grief

【悲观】pessimistic：～主义 *pessimism* /～厌世 *be pessimistic and world-weary*

【悲欢离合】joys and sorrows：人有～，月有阴晴圆缺。*Men have joys and sorrows, they part or meet again；the moon may be bright or dim, she may wax or wane.*

【悲剧】tragedy；misfortune

【悲伤】sad；mournful；sorrowful：她因失去了儿子而过分～。*She was grief ridden for losing her dear son.*

【悲叹】lament

【悲恸】be extremely grieved

【悲痛】grieved；sorrowful：化～为力量 *turn grief into strength*

【悲喜交集】joy tempered with sorrow；grief mingled with joy

【悲壮】moving and tragic；solemn and stirring：他很欣赏～的歌曲。*He enjoys solemn and heroic songs.*

碑 stele；stone tablet：人民英雄纪念～ *monument to the People's Heroes*

【碑额】top part of a tablet

【碑记】record of events inscribed on a table

【碑碣】［书］upright stone tablet

【碑刻】engraving on a tablet；inscription on a tablet

【碑林】forest of steles

【碑铭】inscription on a tablet

【碑帖】rubbings from a stone inscription

【碑文】inscription on a tablet

【碑志】record of events inscribed on a tablet

běi

北[1] ① north：华～ *north China* /～屋 *a room with a southern exposure* ② North standing for the developed countries：南～对话 *North-South dialogue*

北[2] ［书］be defeated：败～ *suffer defeat* /敌军连战皆～。*The everywhere defeated in one battle after another.*

【北爱尔兰】northern Ireland; Ulster
【北半球】northern Hemisphere
【北冰洋】the Arctic(Ocean)
【北大荒】Great Northern Wilderness (in northeast China)
【北斗星】the Big Dipper; Plough
【北方】① north ② northern part of the country, esp. the area north of the Yellow River：～人 *northerner*
【北国】northern part of the country
【北海】North Sea
【北寒带】the north frigid zone
【北回归线】【地】the Tropic of Cancer
【北极】① North Pole; Arctic Pole ② north magnetic pole
【北美洲】north America
【北美自由贸易区】north America Free Trade Area (NAFTA, including Canada, the USA and Mexico, established in 1994)
【北面】① north; northern side ② face north
【北纬】north latitude：～20 度 *20th parallel of north latitude*
【北温带】north temperate zone

bèi

贝 ① mollusk; shellfish：～类 *shellfish*; *molluscs* ② cowrie ③ (Bèi) a surname
【贝雕】shell carving
【贝多芬】ludwig van Beethoven (1770-1827), great German composer
【贝尔】①【物】bel(B) ② Alexander Graham Bell (1847-1922), Scottish American scientist and inventor：～实验室 *Bell Telephone Laboratory*
【贝尔法斯特】Belfast, capital of Northern Ireland
【贝尔格莱德】Belgrade, capital of Yugoslavia
【贝壳】shell
【贝雷帽】beret
【贝鲁特】Beirut, capital of Lebanon
【贝丘】【考】shell mound

备 ① be equipped with; have; possess：德才兼～ *have both ability and moral integrity* ② get ready; prepare：万事俱～，只欠东风。*Everything is ready, but the opportune moment has not come.* ③ provide against; prepare against take precautions against ④ equipment ⑤ fully; in every possible way
【备案】put on record; enter(a case) in the records
【备查】for future reference：所有公司文件都要存档～。*All company's documents should be kept on file for reference.*
【备份】①［方］serve as a figurehead; fill a nominal post ② spare ③【电】back-up
【备货】stock; get in a supply of goods
【备件】spare parts：你那里还有～吗? *Have you some spare parts?*
【备考】(an appendix, note, etc) for reference
【备课】(of a teacher or student) prepare one's lessons：昨天，李老师～到深夜。*Teacher Li prepared his lessons until late at last night.*
【备料】① get the material ready ② prepare feed
【备品】machine parts; tools kept in reserve; spare parts or tools
【备忘录】① memorandum ② memorandum; Filofax
【备用】alternate; spare; reserve：请为我准备一些～款项。*Please prepare some reserve founds for me.*
【备战】prepare for war：扩军～ *arms expansion and war preparations*
【备注】remarks：请把～写在纸上。*Please put the remarks on the paper.*

背[1] ① back of the body; dorsum：揩～ *scrub one's back with a towel* ② back of an object

背[2] ① with the back towards：他～对着学生们站着。*He stood with his back to the students* ② turn away ③ leave; go away ④ do sth behind sb's back ⑤ recite from memory ⑥ violate; break ⑦ out-of-the-way ⑧ unlucky：最近他很～。*Recently he is very unlucky.* ⑨ hard of hearing *see also* bēi

【背部】back of the body
【背后】① behind; at the back ② behind sb's back
【背井离乡】leave one's native place
【背景】① backdrop; scenery; stage setting ② background
【背离】① leave：小时候他就～了故乡。*When he was a child, he had to leave his homeland.* ② depart from
【背面】back; reverse side：请阅～。*Please turn over(PTO).*
【背叛】betray; forsake
【背弃】abandon; desert; go back on
【背人】① concealed from the public ② out of the way
【背时】① out-of-date; behind the times ② unlucky
【背书】① recite a lesson from memory; repeat a lesson ②【经】endorsement (on a cheque)
【背水一战】fight with one's back to the river or wall-fight to win or die; fight a last-ditch battle
【背诵】recite：小时候，他能够～好多诗歌。*He can recite many poems when he was a little child.*
【背心】vest; waistcoat
【背影】figure viewed from behind
【背运】unlucky; unfortunate
【背着手】with one's hands clasped behind one's back：他太着急了，不得不～来回踱步。*He was so worried to walk to and fro with his hands behind his back.*

倍 ① times; -fold：六～ *six times* ② double; redoubles; twice as much
【倍加】all the more; redouble：我们必须～努力学

习。*We must redouble our efforts to study.*
【倍率】magnifying power
【倍数】①【数】multiple：十二是三和四的～。*Twelve is a multiple of three or four.* ② times; quotient of one number divided by another
【倍增】redouble; multiply：～器 *multiplier*
悖 ① be contrary to; go against ② perverse; erroneous ③ confused; puzzled
【悖理】contrary to reason
【悖论】paradox
【悖谬】absurd; preposterous
被[1] quilt：鸭绒～ *eiderdown quilt*; *down quilt*
被[2] ① cover ② meet with; encounter
被[3] ① used in a passive sentence to introduce the agent or doer：他～选为总统。*He was elected the President of the country.* ② used to form a passive verbal phrase
【被保护国】protectorate
【被保护人】ward
【被保险人】insurant; the insured; insured person
【被剥削阶级】exploited class
【被剥削者】the exploited
【被乘数】【数】multiplicand
【被除数】【数】dividend
【被单】①(bed) sheet ② quilt cover
【被担保人】guaranteed person
【被动】passive：～语态 *passive voice*
【被俘】be captured; be taken prisoner：在战争中她的儿子～了。*Her son was captured in the war.*
【被告】【律】defendant; the accused：～席 *defendant's seat*; *dock*
【被害人】【律】victim; injured party
【被加数】【数】summand
【被监护人】a person under guardianship; ward
【被减数】【数】minuend
【被劫持者】hijack victim; hijackee
【被拘留者】【律】internee; detainee
【被里】underneath side of a quilt
【被面】the facing of a quilt; outside cover of a quilt
【被迫】be forced; be compelled：她～离开学校到上海打工去了。*She was forced to leave school and went Shanghai to work.*
【被褥】bedclothes; bedding
【被套】① bedding bag ② quilt case ③ cotton wedding for a quilt
【被提名人】nominee
【被统治者】the ruled
【被窝儿】quilt folded to form sth like a sleeping bag
【被选举权】right to be elected
【被选举人】the elected
【被压迫民族】oppressed nation
【被罩】quilt slip; quilt case
【被子】quilt：早上起来一定要叠～。*You must make the bed when you get up in the morning.*

辈 ① generation; rank：小～ *member of a lower (or younger, or junior) generation in the family hierarchy* / 同～ *of the same generation* / 先～ *elder generation*; *ancestors*; *forebears* ② the like; people of a certain kind ③ lifetime：她后半～子过得很幸福。*She led happy life in the latter party of her life.*
【辈出】come forth in large numbers：人才～。*A large number of talented people are coming to the fore.*
【辈分】position in the family hierarchy; seniority
【辈子】all one's life; lifetime
惫 fatigued; exhausted
【惫倦】tired
焙 bake over a slow fire
【焙粉】baking-powder
蓓
【蓓蕾】bud：～初放。*The flowers are in bud.*

bei

呗 ① used to show that sth is self-evident ② used to express reluctant agreement or concession

bēn

奔 ① dash; run quickly; (of a horse) gallop：万马～腾 *ten thousand horses galloping ahead* ② rush; hurry; hasten：战争爆发了，战士们～赴前线。*The war broke out and soldiers hurried to the front.* ③ run away; flee
see also bèn
【奔波】be busy running about; dash about; hurry back and forth; rush about
【奔驰】run quickly; dash; speed; run fast
【奔窜】flee; stampede; run away
【奔放】uninhibited; bold and unrestrained：那个小姑娘具有豪爽～的性格。*The little girl is of bold and dynamic personality.*
【奔赴】rush to; hurry to (a plane)
【奔流】① pour; flow at great speed ② flowing stream
【奔忙】bustle or dash about
【奔跑】race; run away
【奔丧】hasten home for the funeral of a parent or grandparent
【奔驶】speed; move with great speed
【奔逃】run away; flee
【奔腾】① gallop：万马～。*A thousand horses were galloping ahead.* ② surge forward; roll on in waves：～不息 *roll on ceaselessly*
【奔腾处理器】【电】Pentium CPU (central process-

ing unit)
【奔腾芯片】【电】Pentium chip
【奔向】march on towards
【奔走】go around; rush about; run around: ~相告 *run around spreading the news; lose no time in telling each other the news*

B

běn

本[1] ① root or stem of a plant:无~之木 *tree without roots* ② foundation; basis; origin:勤奋是成功之~。*Diligence is the foundation of success.* ③ capital; principal ④ central; chief; main ⑤ original; initial ⑥ one's own; native ⑦ this; present ⑧ based on; according to ⑨[量] used of flowering plants

本[2] ① book:户口~ *residence book* /账~ *account book; ledger* ② edition; copy; version:精装~ *deluxe edition* ③ script ④ memorial presented to the emperor: 奏~ *memorial to the throne* ⑤[量] used of books of various kinds:他送我了六~书。*He gave me six books.*

【本本主义】book worship; bookishness; dogmatism
【本币】basic unit of a national currency
【本部】headquarter; main part
【本埠】this town or city; local: ~邮件 *local mail*
【本初子午线】first meridian; prime meridian
【本地】local:那个商人把~的特产卖到北京。*The businessman sold his local specialty to Beijing.*
【本分】① one's duty; one's job ② honest; contented and law-abiding; decent:她是个~的孩子。*She is a decent guy.*
【本国】one's own country: ~产品 *domestic product* / ~语 *native language; mother tongue*
【本行】① one's line; field of study; one's own profession:教育不是她的~。*Education is not her line.* ② one's current profession:三句话不离~ *can never say three sentences without talking shop; can hardly open one's mouth without talking ship*
【本家】member of the same family; relative with the same surname
【本届】current; this year's: ~联合国大会 *the current session of the U. N. General Assembly*
【本金】① capital ② principal
【本科】undergraduate course: ~生 *college student; undergraduate*
【本来】① original:你知道他~的意思吗? *Do you know his original meaning?* ② at first; originally ③ of course; naturally; as a matter of course; it goes without saying: ~嘛,你就得离开这儿。*It goes without saying that you have to leave here.*
【本来面目】truth; true features; objective reality; true colours:我早就看清这帮人的~。*I have seen these people in their true colours.*
【本垒】【体】(of baseball) home base; home plate
【本利】principal and interest
【本领】skill; ability; capability
【本命年】every 12th year after the year of one's birth
【本末】ins and outs; whole course of an event from beginning to end:每件事情都有~。*Everything has a beginning and an end.* ② the fundamental and the incidental
【本末倒置】take the branch for the root; put the non-essentials before the fundamentals; put the incidental before the fundamental; put the cart before the horse:强调方法而忽视内容是~。*To put emphasis on method at the expense of content is to put the cart before the horse.*
【本能】instinct: ~行为 *instinctive behaviour*
【本年度】this year; the current year: ~国家预算 *the national budget for this fiscal year*
【本票】cashier's cheque; promissory note
【本钱】① capital; principal ② ability, etc. that one can rely on; asset; what is capitalized on; sth used to one's own advantage
【本人】① I; me; myself ② oneself; in person
【本色】(Běnsè) true qualities; distinctive character:劳动人民的~ *the true qualities of the labouring people*
【本色】(Běnshǎi) natural colour: ~布 *gray cloth; unbleached and undyed cloth*
【本身】oneself; in oneself
【本事】skill; ability; capability
【本题】subject under discussion; point at issue
【本体】①【哲】noumenon; thing-in-itself ② main part of a project: ~论 *ontology*
【本土】① one's native country or land ② metropolitan territory ③【农】native soil
【本位】①【经】standard:金~ *gold standard* / ~货币 *standard or basic unit of a national currency* ② department or unit one works in: ~主义 *selfish departmentalism; departmental selfishness; working solely in the interests of one's own department or unit*
【本文】① this text; this article: ~谈的是我国教育方面的一些问题。*The article deals with certain problems in our national economy.* ② original text:那本小说的~只有两千多字。*The original text of the novel is only a little over 2,000 characters long.*
【本息】principal and interest
【本小利微】small capital and little profit — a small business; small investment bringing scanty profit
【本性】nature; inherent quality:江山易改,~难移。*The rivers and mountains may be changed, but it is hard to alter a man's character.*
【本意】original intention; original idea
【本源】origin; source:探索事物的~ *explore the origin of things*
【本着】in line with; in the light of; in accordance with; in conformity with: ~真诚合作的精神,经理出差去了上海。*In the spirit of sincere cooperation, our manager went on business to Shanghai.*
【本职】one's duty or job:他根本就不安心~工作。*He didn't content with his job at all.*
【本质】essence; nature; innate character; intrinsic

quality:透过现象看～ *see through the appearance to the essence*
【本子】① book; notebook ② edition ③ diploma; certificate
【本族语】native language; mother tongue
【本罪】【宗】actual sin
苯 【化】benzene; benzol
【苯胺】【化】aniline
【苯酚】【化】phenol
【苯甲酸】【化】benzoic acid
【苯乙烯】【化】styrene
畚 ① bamboo scoop; wicker scoop; dustpan ② scoop with a dustpan
【畚箕】bamboo or wicker scoop; dustpan

bèn

奔 ① go straight towards; make straight for:全国人民～小康。*The people throughout the country are heading for comfortable-off society.* / 嫦娥～月。*Chang E flies towards the moon.* ② towards:出租车～火车站驶去。*The taxi sped by towards the train station.* ③ (of one's age) approach; get close to; get on for:我妈妈是～七十的人了。*My mother is getting on for seventy.* ④ be after; go about:我是～着这份工作来山东的。*I'm after the job to come Shandong.*
see also bēn
【奔命】be in a desperate hurry
【奔头】sth to strive for; prospect; advantage
笨 ① stupid; foolish; dull:脑子～ *slow-witted; stupid; dull-witted* ② clumsy; awkward ③ cumbersome; unwieldy; awkward: ～重的机器 *heavy (or cumbersome) machine* /这张桌子太～。*This table is too cumbersome.*
【笨蛋】idiot; fool; dunce:你真是一个～。*What a fool you are.*
【笨活儿】heavy unskilled work; heavy manual labour:他年轻时干了不少～。*When he was young, he did a lot of heavy work.*
【笨口拙舌】slow of speech; inarticulate; clumsy in speech; not particularly articulate
【笨鸟先飞】clumsy birds have to start flying early — the slow need to start early
【笨手笨脚】clumsy (with one's hands and feet); all gauche; all one's fingers are thumbs; awkward
【笨头笨脑】① slow; slow-witted; stupid ② clumsy; cumbersome
【笨重】① heavy; cumbersome; unwieldy:她年纪大了,手脚～,行动迟缓。*She was so old that she was slow and clumsy in movement.* ② hard and strenuous
【笨拙】clumsy; awkward; stupid

bēng

崩 ① collapse:山～地裂。*Mountains collapse and the ground cracks.* ② crack; burst; split; broke ③ (of sth bursting) hit sb or sth; hit and smash:爆竹～了那个孩子的眼睛。*The firecracker went off in his eye.* ④［口］shoot; execute by shooting ⑤ (of an emperor) die:皇帝驾～了。*The emperor passed away.*
【崩坏】crumble; crack and fall
【崩溃】collapse; crash; crumble; fall apart
【崩裂】burst apart; crack
【崩落】collapse and roll down:山石～。*Mountain rocks were rolling down.*
【崩塌】collapse; crumble
【崩陷】fall in; cave in
绷[1] ① stretch tight; draw tight; strain:别把绳子～的太紧了。*Don't overstrain the rope.* ② tight; taut ③ spring; bounce ④ baste; tack; pin:她妈妈擅长～被子。*Her mother is good at sewing a cover on to the head of a quilt.* ⑤ be barely able to subsist; manage with difficulty ⑥ frame matting ⑦ embroidery frame
绷[2] ［方］swindle; cheat
see also běng; bèng
【绷带】bandage
【绷子】① embroidery frame; hoop; tambour ② frame matting
嘣 ［象］sound of palpitations or explosions:看到他进来,我心里～～直跳。*My heart was thumping when I saw him coming.*
【嘣豆儿】roasted broad beans

béng

甭 ［方］don't need to:你～管了,把它交给我吧! *Don't bother; leave it to me.*

běng

绷 ① pull (a long face):那个老师～着脸给我们说话。*The teacher pulled a long face to talk with us.* ② strain oneself
see also bēng; bèng
【绷劲】strain oneself; strain one's muscles with bated breath
【绷脸】look displeased; pull a long face; be sullen

bèng

泵 pump:离心～ *centrifugal pump* /轴流～ *axial-flow pump; axial pump*

【泵房】pump house
【泵排量】pumpage; pump delivery
【泵推力】thrust of pump
【泵压】pumping pressure

迸 ① spout; spurt; blurt out; burst forth: 那个孩子太紧张了，半天才～出几个字来。*The child was too nervous to blurt out a few words.* ② break to pieces suddenly

【迸发】burst forth; burst out: 教室里～出一阵笑声。*There was an outburst of laughter in the classroom.*
【迸溅】burst forth; slash: 火花～ *sparks flying about*
【迸裂】split; burst(open)
【迸散】dash out in all directions
【迸射】spew; spout; squirt: 子弹从那个著名的教堂里～出来。*Bullets were spewing out from the famous church.*

蚌
see also bàng

【蚌埠】Bengbu, major city in Anhui Province

绷 ① split open; crack: 桌子～了一道缝。*The table has a crack in it.* ②［口］(used before certain adjectives) very: ～脆 *very crisp* / ～直 *exceptionally straight* / ～亮 *shining bright*
see also bèng; běng

【绷瓷】crackleware

镚 small coin

【镚子儿】［方］least bit of money; penny: 他是个吝啬鬼，一个～也不给他儿子。*He was a miser and didn't give his son a penny.*
【镚子】small coin: 我一个钢～也没有了。*I have no small coins with me.*

蹦 leap; jump; spring: 欢～乱跳 *alive and kicking*

【蹦蹦车】noisy motorized tricycle; small motorized three-wheel transport vehicles
【蹦蹦跳跳】lively; bouncing and vivacious
【蹦跶】bounce or jump about at last gasp: 那个罪犯就像秋后的蚂蚱，～不了几天了。*Like grasshoppers after autumn, the criminal was on their last legs.*
【蹦迪】disco dancing
【蹦豆儿】① roasted broad beans ② little child
【蹦高儿】leap; jump
【蹦极跳】【体】bungee-jumping
【蹦子】［方］leap; jump: 那个孩子一个～跳上了窗台。*The child landed on the window at one leap.*

bī

逼 ① force; press; drive; compel: 官～民反。*It was the rulers who drove the people into rebellion.* ② press for; extort: 学校～她交学费。*The school pressed her for payment of tuition.* ③ press on towards; advance on; close in on: 战士们直～城下。*The soldiers pressed up to the city wall.* ④［书］narrow

【逼供】try to force sb to confess; extort a confession: 严刑～ *extort a confession by atrocious torture*
【逼婚】force a girl or woman to marry
【逼近】approach; press on towards; close in on
【逼迫】force; compel; coerce
【逼人】pressing; threatening: 寒气～。*There is a nip in the air.* /情势～。*The situation is pressing.*
【逼上梁山】hound sb to death; be compelled to act desperately; have no alternative but to join the Liangshan Marsh rebels — be driven to rebel
【逼视】gaze fixedly at; look at from close-up; stare intently at
【逼死】hound sb to death: 那个孩子是被她妈妈～的。*The child was driven to commit suicide by her mother.*
【逼问】force sb to answer; interrogate; question closely
【逼债】press for debt repayment; dun
【逼真】① lifelike; true to life: 这幅画画得真～。*The picture is really true to life.* ② distinctly; clearly

bí

荸

【荸荠】water chestnut (Eleocharis tuberosa), the plant or its tuber

鼻 ① nose: 鹰钩～ *aquiline (or Roman) nose* / 酒精～ *brandy nose; acne rosacea* ②［书］start; pioneer; originate

【鼻癌】【医】rhino-carcinoma
【鼻孔】nostril
【鼻梁】bridge of the nose
【鼻腔】【生理】nasal cavity
【鼻青脸肿】bloody nose and swollen face: 被打得～ *be badly battered; be beaten black and blue*
【鼻涕】nasal mucus; snivel: 流～ *have a running rose*
【鼻咽】【生理】nasopharynx; rhinopharynx: ～炎 *nasopharyngitis; rhinopharyngitis* / ～癌 *nasopharyngeal; carcinoma*
【鼻炎】【医】rhinitis
【鼻翼】wing of nose
【鼻音】【语】nasal sound: 那个小孩说话带～。*The little child speaks with a twang.*
【鼻子】nose
【鼻祖】earliest; ancestor; originator (of a tradition, school of thought, etc.); founder

bǐ

匕 ① an ancient type of spoon ② dagger：图穷~见 *when the map as unrolled, the dagger was revealed*

【匕首】dagger

比[1] ① compare；contrast；emulate；compete：无与伦~ *incomparable*；*unparalleled* / 你~不上他。*You can't compare with him.* ② be like；match；be similar to：寿~南山 *live as long as the hills-wish sb longevity* ③ gesture；gesticulate ④ do according to；copy ⑤ compare to ⑥ ratio；proportion ⑦ to（in a score）⑧ than

比[2] ① close together；next to ② depend on；gang up with ③ recently ④ by the time；by then

【比比皆是】can be seen everywhere；such is the case everywhere：这种桌子市场上~。*This kind of table can be found everywhere in the market.*

【比方】① analogy；compare to ② take for instance；take for example ③ if；suppose

【比分】【体】score：~领先 *score in one's favour* / ~落后 *score against one*

【比划】① gesture；gesticulate：那个丢失的孩子~着说了好多。*The losing child talked a lot with the help of gestures.*

【比价】① rate of exchange；price ratio；price comparison：人民币与美元的~ *rate of exchange between the RMB and the US Dollar*

【比较】① compare；contrast ② than ③ rather；fairly；comparatively：~成本 *comparative cost*

【比利时】Belgium：~人 *Belgian*

【比例】① proportion；scale：成正~ *direct proportion* / 成反~ *inverse proportion* ② ratio

【比例尺】① scale：这幅图片的~是十万分之一。*The scale of the picture is* 1:100,000. ② architect's scale；engineer's scale

【比邻】① neighbour；next-door neighbour：海内存知己，天涯若~。*A bosom friend afar brings a distant land near.*

【比率】ratio；rate

【比目鱼】flatfish；flounder

【比如】such as；for example；for instance：他喜欢吃水果，~苹果，桔子等等。*He likes eating fruits, such as apples, oranges etc.*

【比赛】contest；match；competition：昨天你看那场足球~了吗？*Did you watch the football match yesterday?*

【比上不足，比下有余】better than some，though not as good as other；fair to middling；can pass muster；not up to those above，but above those below — middling；tolerable

【比试】① have a contest；take a competition ② make gestures；measure with one's hand or arm

【比武】take part in Wushu contest；martial arts competition；competition in military skills：~招亲 *marry whoever can defeat one in a martial arts contest*

【比翼】fly wing to wing：~齐飞 *pair off wing to wing*；*fly side by side*；*keep each other company all the time*；*help each other to make progress* / 在天愿作~鸟，在地愿为连理枝。*On high, we'd be two love-birds flying wing to wing; on earth, two trees with branches twined from spring to spring.*

【比喻】metaphor；analogy；figure of speech；simile：这只是一个~的说法。*This is just a figure of speech.*

【比照】① according to；in the light of ② contrast

【比值】specific value；ratio；rate

【比重】①【物】specific gravity ② proportion：农业在整个国民经济中占的~比以前大多了。*The proportion of industry in the national economy as a whole is more than before.*

妣［书］deceased mother：先~ *my deceased mother*

彼 ① that；those；the other；another：不分~此 *make no distinction between one's own and sb else's*；*be on very intimate terms* ② other party；one's opponent

【彼岸】other bank；other side：我的老家在太平洋的~。*My hometown is on the other side of Pacific.* ② ideal state of mind that one yearns for

【彼此】① each other；one another：她的态度很友好，因此我们~相处得很融洽。*She is very friendly to me, so we live in peace and amity together.* ② used in reduplication to indicate that all concerned are about the same：你说我态度不好，咱俩~~。*You said I was not kind to you; maybe, we are on the same plane.*

【彼一时，此一时】that was one situation，and this is another；the situation is different now；times have changed

秕（of grain）not plump；blighted

【秕谷】blighted grains

【秕糠】① chaff ② worthless stuff

笔 ① pen；pencil；writing brush：奋~疾书 *wield one's brush furiously* ② technique of writing，calligraphy or drawing：文~ *style of writing* / 败~ *flaw in a good piece of writing* ③ write；pen：亲~ *in one's own hand-writing*；*in one's own hand* ④ handwriting ⑤［量］used to indicate sums of money or business：那个商人做了一~好生意。*The businessman did a good deal in business.* ⑥［量］stroke in Chinese painting or calligraphy：我真不敢相信这个孩子竟然写得一~好字。*I can't believe that the little child writes a good hand.*

【笔答】give a written answer；answer in writing

【笔刀】carving knife；graver；burin：把你的~借我用一下。*Please lend your knife tome.*

【笔调】（of writing）tone；style

【笔法】technique of writing，calligraphy or drawing：~细腻 *exquisite piece of writing*

【笔锋】① tip of a writing brush ② vigour of style in writing or painting; stroke; touch: ~犀利 *wield a pointed pen*; *write in a pungent style*
【笔杆子】① shaft of a pen or writing brush; penholder ② ability to write; ability to wield the pen ③ effective writer
【笔供】written confession
【笔画】① strokes of a Chinese character; number of strokes ② stroke
【笔记】① take down ② note-taking; notes ③ pen jottings — a type of literature consisting mainly of short sketches; sketch
【笔迹】a person's handwriting; hand; chirography
【笔尖】① nib; pen point ② tip of a writing brush or pencil
【笔力】vigour of strokes in calligraphy or drawing; vigour of style in literary composition
【笔录】① put down ② notes; records
【笔名】pen name; pseudonym
【笔墨】pen and ink; words; writing: 难以用~形容 *words cannot describe sth*; *sth is beyond words*
【笔顺】order of strokes observed in calligraphy
【笔体】handwriting; writing style
【笔挺】①(standing) very straight; straight as a ramrod; bolt upright: 学校门口~地站着六名战士。*At the gate of the school six soldiers were standing bolt upright.* ② well-ironed; trim; stiff: 他穿着~的西装来到了学校。*He came to the school dressed in an immaculate western-style suit.*
【笔筒】pen container; brush pot
【笔误】① make a slip of the pen ② words written wrong due to carelessness
【笔芯】① pencil lead ② refill (for a ball-point pen)
【笔形】(of Chinese characters) forms of strokes and their combinations
【笔译】written translation
【笔直】perfectly straight; straight as a ramrod; bolt upright

鄙 ① low; mean; vulgar: 卑~ *mean*; *base*; *despicable* ② my ③[书] despise; disdain; scorn ④[书] out-of-the-way place
【鄙陋】shallow; superficial; ignorant
【鄙人】① I; your humble servant ② uneducated or ignorant person
【鄙视】despise; look down upon; belittle; disdain: 我~那些说谎的人。*I despise those who always say a lie.*
【鄙俗】vulgar; philistine
【鄙屑】scorn; despise
【鄙夷】disdain; despise

bì

币 money; currency: 金~ *gold coin* / 银~ *silver coin* / 硬~ *coin* / 纸~ *paper currency*; *note* / 人民~ *RMB* / 外~ *foreign currency* / 本~ *standard money*
【币值】currency value
【币制】currency system; monetary system

必 ① certainly; surely; necessarily: 有求~应 *respond to every plea*; *grant whatever is requested* / 这种情况下我~帮助你。*I surely help you in this situation.* ② must; have to; ought to: 有法~依,执法~严。*Laws must be observed and strictly enforced.*
【必不可少】absolutely necessary; indispensable; essential
【必定】① must; have to; be bound to; be sure to ② be resolved to; be certain to
【必然】① inevitable; certain: 不要伤心了,这是事物发展的~趋势。*Don't be so sad, you know it was the inexorable trend of the development of events.* ②【哲】necessity: ~性 *necessity*; *inevitability*; *certainty* / ~规律 *inexorable law*
【必修】required; obligatory; mandatory: ~课 *required course*
【必须】must; have to; necessary: 你~谦虚谨慎,否则你将失去这场比赛。*You must be imperative to remain modest and prudent, or you will lose the match.*
【必需】essential; indispensable; necessary: ~品 *daily necessities*; *articles for daily consumption*
【必要】necessary; essential; indispensable: ~性 *necessity* / ~劳动 *necessary labour*
【必由之路】only way; road or route must follow or take

毕 ① finish; complete; conclude: 礼~后在学校门口集合。*You will get together at the gate of the school after the completion of the ceremony.* ②[书] fully; altogether; completely: 真相~露 *reveal one's true features*; *show one's true colours* ③ nineteenth of the twenty-eight constellations into which the celestial sphere was divided in ancient Chinese astronomy ④(Bì) a surname
【毕恭毕敬】reverent and respectful; extremely deferential: 那群学生~地听着教授的报告。*The group of the students listened to the report of the professor with extreme deference.*
【毕竟】after all; all in all; in the final analysis; when all is said and done
【毕露】reveal completely; be completed exposed
【毕生】all one's life; lifetime
【毕业】graduate; finish school: ~班 *graduating class* / ~分配 *job assignment on graduation* / ~论文 *graduation thesis or dissertation* / ~设计 *graduation project* / ~实习 *graduation field work* / ~证书 *diploma*; *graduation certificate*

闭 ① shut; close: 请~上眼睛跟我来。*Please follow me while you close your eyes.* ② stop up; obstruct ③ stop; end ④(Bì) a surname
【闭关】① close a city gate; block a pass; close the country to the outside world ②【宗】(of a monk) stay secluded meditating and studying

scriptures for a fixed period; be in seclusion
【闭关锁国】cut off one's country from the outside world; shut one's door to the international community; close the country to the rest of the world
【闭关自守】adopt a closed-door policy; close the country to the outside world; follow a policy of national isolation
【闭会】close a meeting; end a meeting
【闭经】【医】amenorrhoea
【闭卷】closed-book: 昨天我们通过了~考试。*We have passed the closed-book examination yesterday.*
【闭口】not speak up; keep one's mouth shut: ~不谈 *refuse to say anything about*; *avoid mentioning*
【闭门羹】be belied entrance; be denied entrance
【闭门思过】do re-thinking behind closed doors; ponder over one's mistakes in seclusion
【闭门谢客】close one's door to visitors; stop receiving visitors; refuse to receive any guest
【闭门造车】act blindly; shut oneself off from reality; make a cart behind closed doors
【闭幕】①lower the curtain; the curtain falls: 报告在观众热烈的掌声中~。*The curtain of the report fell to the loud applause of the audience.* ② conclude; close: ~式 *closing ceremony*
【闭塞】① stop up; block: 管道~ *blocked pipe* ② out-of-the-way; backward ③ unenlightened ④【医】occlusion
【闭音节】【语】closed syllable
【闭月羞花】[书] (of a woman) one's beauty outshines the moon and puts the flowers to shame; be exceedingly beautiful

庇 shelter; screen; protect; shield
【庇护】shield; shelter; put under one's protection; take under one's wing: ~所 *sanctuary*; *asylum*

毖 [书] caution: 惩前~后 *punish past wrongdoing to caution those to come*; *learn from past errors to avoid future mistakes*

陛 [书] flight of steps leading to a palace
【陛下】your Majesty; His or Her Majesty: 国王~ *his Majesty the King* /女王~ *her Majesty the Queen* /天皇~ (*Japan*) *His Imperial Majesty*

毙 ① die; get killed: 击~ *shoot dead* ② execute; shoot ③ fall down; collapse
【毙命】meet a violent death; get killed

秘
see also mì
【秘鲁】Peru: ~人 *Peruvian*

敝 ① [书] shabby; worn-out; ragged ② my; our; this: ~人的家乡在山东。*My hometown is Shangdong Province.* ③ decline; worsen
【敝帚自珍】value one's own old broom — cherish sth of little value simply because it is one's own

婢 slave girl; servant girl
【婢女】slave girl; servant girl

愎 wilful; self-willed: 刚~ *obdurate*; *recalcitrant*

蓖
【蓖麻】【植】castor-oil plant; ricinus
【蓖麻油】ricinus oil; castor oil

痹 【中医】pain or numbness caused by cold, dampness, etc; rheumatism
【痹症】illness caused by wind, cold or dampness, characterized by aching and numbness in the limbs or all over the body

裨 [书] benefit; advantage: 于事无~。*It won't do any good.*
see also pí
【裨益】benefit; advantage; profit

辟[1] [书] monarch; sovereign: 复~ *restore a monarchy*; *restoration*

辟[2] [书] ward off; keep away

辟[3] [书] (of a sovereign) summon sb and confer on him an official post
see also pì
【辟邪】exorcise evil spirits; ward off baneful influences

碧 ① [书] green jad ② bluish green; blue
【碧波】blue waves
【碧空】pale blue sky; azure sky: ~万里 *vast clear skies*
【碧蓝】bluish green; blue; turquoise
【碧绿】dark green: 我们看不到~的田野的尽头。*We can't see the end of the expanse of green fields.*
【碧螺春】green tea originally produced in the Taihu Lake area
【碧玉】jasper — a kind of greenish jade: 她是一个小家~的女孩。*She is a pretty girl of a humble family.*

蔽 cover; shelter; hide: 那个可怜的孩子衣不~体。*The poor child had nothing but rags on his back.*

弊 ① fraud; abuse; malpractice: 舞~ *practise fraud*; *engage in corrupt practices* /作~ *cheat* (*as in an examination*) ② harm; disadvantage
【弊病】① ill; evil; malady; malpractice: 在我们的生活中存在着许多社会~。*There are a lot of social ills in our life.* ② drawback; disadvantage
【弊端】abuse; corrupt practice; malpractice

壁 ① wall ② sth resembling a wall: 铜墙铁~ *a bastion of iron — an impregnable fortress* ③ cliff ④ rampart; breastwork
【壁报】wall newspaper
【壁橱】built-in wardrobe; cupboard; closet
【壁灯】wall lamp; bracket light
【壁虎】【动】gecko; house lizard
【壁画】mural(painting); fresco: 敦煌~ *Dunhuang frescoes*
【壁垒】rampart; barrier: 关税~ *tariff wall* /贸易~

trade barrier ② line of demarcation or division
【壁炉】fireplace
【壁球】squash rackets; squash
【壁纸】wallpaper

避 ① avoid; evade; shun: ～而不见 *avoid meeting sb* ② prevent; keep away; repel
【避风】① take shelter from the wind ② lie low; stay away from trouble
【避讳】(bìhuì) avoid a taboo
【避讳】(bìhui) ① taboo; word or phrase to be avoided as taboo ② evade; dodge
【避雷针】lightning rod
【避免】avoid; refrain from; avert
【避难】take refuge; seek asylum: ～所 *refuge; sanctuary; asylum*
【避实击虚】stay clear of the enemy's main force and strike at his weak points
【避暑】① be away for the summer holidays; spend a holiday at a summer resort ② prevent sunstroke
【避税】tax avoidance
【避嫌】avoid suspicion; avoid doing anything that may arouse suspicion
【避邪】ward off evil spirits
【避孕】contraception: ～套 *condom*
【避重就轻】avoid the impartment and dwell on the trivial; evade major responsibility and take minor

臂 ① arm ② upper arm
【臂章】① armband; armlet ②【军】shoulder emblem

璧 round flat piece of jade with a hole in the middle (used for ceremonial purposes in ancient China)

biān

边 ① side (of a geometrical figure) ② brim; side; edge; margin: 无～无际的大海 *a boundless ocean* ③ border; hem: ～卡 *border checkpoint; border checkpost* ④ frontier; boundary: ～防部队 *frontier guards* ⑤ limit; bound ⑥ close by ⑦ part; side ⑧ near; next to; close to ⑨ (Biān) a surname
【边岸】bank; shore
【边陲】[书] border area; frontier: 他的家乡在一个～小镇。*His hometown is a frontier town.*
【边防】frontier defence; border defence: ～哨 *border sentry* / ～战士 *frontier guard*
【边幅】one's dress; one's appearance: 她是一个不修～的女孩子。*She is careless about her dress.*
【边关】frontier pass; strategic pass at the border
【边际】limit; bound; boundary; margin: ～投资 *marginal investment* / ～成本 *marginal cost* / ～需求 *marginal demand* / ～效益 *marginal benefit*
【边疆】border area; borderland; frontier; frontier region: 她爸爸去～支援建设去了。*Her father went to the border area for supporting the construction of the border areas.*
【边界】boundary; border: ～线 *boundary line*
【边境】frontier; border; border area: ～贸易 *frontier trade*
【边框】frame; rim
【边门】side door; wicket gate
【边区】border area; border region
【边塞】frontier fortress
【边沿】edge; fringe
【边缘】① brink; verge; edge; fringe; periphery ② marginal; borderline: ～海 *marginal sea* / ～学科 *borderline discipline*
【边远】remote; far from the centre; outlying
【边寨】borderland village; stockaded village stronghold on the border area

砭 ① stone needle (used in ancient time) ② use stone needles in acupuncture in ancient time; pierce; castigate: 针～时弊 *castigate the social abuses of the time*

编 ① weave; plait: ～辫子 *plait one's hair* ② organize; group; arrange ③ edit; compile ④ write; compose ⑤ invent; make up ⑥ copy; book ⑦ volume ⑧ authorized or stipulated strength or size; establishment
【编程】【电】program
【编导】write and direct: 这部电影是他叔叔～的。*The film were all written and directed by his uncle.* ② playwright-director
【编队】form into columns; organize into teams ②【军】formation
【编发】edit and release (manuscript, news, etc.): 新华社～了伊拉克战争爆发了消息。*The Xinhua News Agency released the broken of Iraq War.*
【编号】① number ② serial number
【编辑】① edit; compile ② editor; compiler: 毕业后,她成了一位～。*After graduation, she became an editor.*
【编剧】① write a play, scenario, etc. ② playwright; screenwriter; scenarist
【编码】【电】code; encode: ～程序 *code program*
【编目】① make a catalogue; catalogue ② list
【编年】annalistic; chronological: ～史 *annals; chronicle* / ～体 *annalistic style; chronological style*
【编排】arrange; lay out; work out: 那个校长～了下个学期的课程表。*The headmaster worked out a sheet for the next term.* ② write and rehearse
【编审】① edit and finalize; read and edit ② senior editor
【编外】not on the regular payroll; not on the permanent staff: ～人员 *irregulars; temporary staff*
【编舞】① choreography ② choreographer
【编修】① compile; edit; revise ② imperial compiler
【编选】select and edit; compile
【编演】write and produce; create and perform: 他们正在为新年～节目。*They are creating and putting on a show for New Year.*

【编译】① edit and translate ② editor-translator
【编印】edit and print; publish
【编造】① compile; draw up; work out ② create out of imagination ③ make up; invent; fabricate
【编者】editor; compiler
【编织】weave; knit; plait; braid
【编制】① weave; plait; braid ② work out; draw up ③ authorized strength or size; establishment: 战时～ *wartime establishment*
【编钟】chime bells; serial bells
【编著】write; compile
【编撰】write; compile
【编纂】compile

蝙

【蝙蝠】【动】bat: 你见过～吗? *Have you seen bats?*
【蝙蝠衫】upper outer garment with batwing sleeves

鞭 ① whip; lash: 马～ *horsewhip* ② iron nodular staff used as a weapon in ancient China ③ sth resembling a whip: 你上课时用教～吗? *Do you use your pointer when you have a class?* ④ penis of certain male animals used as medicine or cooked as food ⑤ string of small firecrackers ⑥ ［书］flog; whip; lash
【鞭策】spur on; urge on; encourage
【鞭长莫及】beyond the reach of one's power; too far away to be helped
【鞭笞】flog; lash; castigate
【鞭打】whip; lash; flog; thrash
【鞭挞】lash; castigate
【鞭子】whip

biǎn

贬 ① demote; relegate: ～为庶民 *be degraded to the status of a commoner* ② reduce; depreciate; devalue: 褒～ *praise and censure*
【贬斥】①［书］demote ② denounce; belittle and exclude; discriminate against
【贬词】derogatory term; expression of censure
【贬低】belittle; play down; deliberately underestimate; depreciate
【贬义】derogatory sense; pejorative meaning
【贬值】① devalue; devaluate ②【经】devalue ③ diminish in value; depreciate
【贬职】［书］demote

扁 flat
see also piān
【扁担】carrying pole; shoulder pole
【扁豆】① hyacinth bean ②［方］kidney bean
【扁平】flat: ～胸 *flat chest* / ～足 *flatfoot*
【扁桃体】【生理】tonsil: ～肥大 *hypertrophy of tonsils* / ～切除术 *tonsillectomy* / ～炎 *tonsillitis*
【扁圆】oval; oblate: 请你在黑板上画一个～形。*Please draw oral shape in the blackboard.*

匾 ① horizontal inscribed board: 他们的校门口挂着一块～。*An inscribed board hung above the gate of their school.* ② silk banner embroidered with words of praise ③ big round shallow basket
【匾文】inscription on a horizontal board

褊 ［书］narrow; cramped
【褊狭】narrow; cramped: 气量～ *small-minded; narrow-minded*

biàn

卞 ①［书］impetuous ②（Biàn）a surname

苄 【化】benzyl: ～醇 *benzyl alcohol*
【苄基】【化】benzyl

变 ① change; become different: 你～了。*You became different.* ② change into; turn into; become: 你已经～成另一个人了。*You have changed into another people.* ③ transform ④ changeable ⑤ sell off cone's property ⑥ flexible ⑦ unexpected turn of events
【变把戏】juggle; conjure; perform conjuring: 我听说那个陌生人是个～的。*I heard that the newcomer was a conjurer.*
【变本加厉】worsen; become aggravated; be further intensified
【变成】change into; turn into; transform into; become: 几年过去了，那个小姑娘～成一位漂亮的女士。*Several years passed, the little girl became a beautiful lady.*
【变电站】transformer substation
【变动】① change: 人事～ *personnel changes* ② alter; modify
【变法】【史】introduce institutional reforms; political reform: 维新～ *constitutional reform and modernization*
【变革】① change; transform: 在过去的十年里，中国发生了很大的社会～。*In the passed ten years, it happened great social changes in China.* ②【地】revolution
【变更】change; alter; modify: 下周我们要放假了，所以我们的学习计划要～了。*Next week we will have a holiday, so we have to change our plans of study.*
【变故】accident; misfortune; unforeseen event; catastrophe
【变卦】go back on one's word; change one's mind; break one's promise
【变化】change; vary: ～无常 *constantly changing; changeable*
【变幻】change irregularly; fluctuate
【变换】① vary; alternate ②【数】transform: ～系数 *transformation coefficient*
【变价】appraise at the current rate: 这批书将～出

售。*The books will be sold at the current price.*
【变节】make a political recantation; turn one's coat; betray one's country; recant one's faith
【变脸】① suddenly turn hostile ② change facial expression rapidly (to show extreme anger, fear, etc)
【变量】【数】variable: ~函数 *variable function*
【变卖】sell off one's property: 他被迫~了产业来还债。*He was forced to sell off his estate for paying for his debts.*
【变频】【电】frequency conversion: ~器 *frequency converter* / ~管 *converter tube*
【变迁】change; vicissitude: 时代~ *changes of the times*
【变色】① change colour; discolour: 脸不~心不跳 *one's face does not change colour, nor does one's heart beat faster-without a trace of fear* ② change countenance; become angry; show signs of displeasure
【变数】①【数】variable: 常数与~ *constants and variables* ② variable factor; variable
【变速】【机】speed change; gearshift: ~器 *change gear* / ~运动 *variable motion*
【变态】① metamorphosis ② deformation ③ abnormal; aberrant
【变通】be flexible; stretch a point; accommodate sth to circumstances: 你最好根据不同情况作一些适当的~。*You'd better make appropriate adaptations in the light of specific conditions.*
【变为】change into; turn into; become; change into
【变现】【经】realization
【变相】in disguised form; covert: ~涨价 *disguised price increases*
【变心】cease to be faithful; transfer one's affection to another person; break faith
【变形】① be out of shape; become deformed: 她太胖了,身材都~了。*She is so fat that she has lost her shape.* ②【物】deformation; distortion ③ metamorphosis; change from human into nonhuman shape and vice versa
【变型】change category; change type; change into a different type
【变性】① denaturation ② change sex by surgical means: ~手术 *transsexual operation*
【变压】【电】voltage transformation: ~器 *transformer*
【变样】become different; change in shape or appearance
【变质】① go bad; deteriorate: 这盘菜已经~了。*The plate has gone bad.* ②【地】metamorphism: ~岩 *metamorphic rock*
【变种】mutation; variety ② variant; variety: 机会主义的~ *variety of opportunism*

便[1] ① convenient; handy: ~于运输 *easy to transport* ② when an opportunity arises; when it is convenient: 悉听尊~ *suit your own convenience; act at your own discretion; do as your please* ③ informal; plain; ordinary ④ piss; urine or stool: 粪~ *excrement; night soil* ⑤ excrete; relieve oneself: 大~ *shit; defecate; evacuate bowels* /小~ *piss; urinate*

便[2] ① used in the same way as 就 but more formal: 我们五点钟~起床了。*We have got up on five o'clock in the morning.* ② indicating a hypothetical concession
see also pián
【便池】toilet bowl; urinal
【便当】① convenient; handy ② fast food in box
【便道】① pavement: 行人走~。*Pedestrians walk on the pavement.* ② shortcut: 抄~走 *take a shortcut* ③ makeshift road
【便饭】① ordinary meal; simple meal; potluck ② have informal dinner: 明天李教授请学生们吃~。*Tomorrow professor Li will invite the students having potluck with us tomorrow.*
【便服】① everyday clothes; informal dress ② civilian clothes; civvies; mufti
【便笺】① note ② memo; memo pad; notepaper
【便捷】① convenient; easy ② nimble; quick; agile
【便览】brief guide: 出去玩时,买本旅游~来指导自己。*When you visit some places, please buy a guidebook to guide yourself.*
【便利】① convenient; easy: 现在山东的交通很~。*Now there are good transport facilities in Shandong Province.* ② facilitate: 拖拉机使耕作~ *tractors facilitate farming*
【便门】side door; wicket door
【便秘】constipation
【便民】for the convenience or benefit of the people: ~商店 *convenience shop*
【便盆】bedpan
【便士】penny
【便条】note
【便携式】portable: ~计算机 *portable computer*
【便衣】① civilian clothes; plainclothes: ~警察 *plain clothes detective* ② plainclothesman
【便于】easy to; convenient for

遍 ① all over; everywhere: 朋友~天下 *have friends all over the world* ②[量](denoting an action from beginning to end) time: 这部电影我看过三~了。*I have seen the film three times.*
【遍布】be located everywhere; spread all over
【遍地】all over the place; all around; everywhere
【遍及】extend all over; reach everywhere
【遍体鳞伤】be beaten black and blue; be a mass of bruises; be covered all over with cuts and bruises

辨 differentiate; distinguish; discriminate: 明~真伪 *discriminate between truth and falsehood*
【辨别】tell apart; differentiate; distinguish; discriminate: ~力 *ability to see things in their true light; discerning power*
【辨明】clearly distinguish; strictly discriminate: 在

这里我们几乎～不了方向。*We can't take our bearings in this place.*

【辨认】identify; recognize:我从来没有见过他,所以也不能～。*I have never seen him, so I can't recognize him.*

【辨析】differentiate and analyse; discriminate:词义～ *semantic discrimination and analysis*

【辨证】textual research and discrimination

辩 argue; debate; dispute:能言善～ *have the gift of the gab; be eloquent and persuasive*

【辩白】try to justify oneself

【辩驳】rebut; refute; dispute:无可～ *beyond all dispute; irrefutable*

【辩才】[书] eloquence; oratory

【辩护】① argue in favour of; speak in defence of; defend ②【律】plead; defend: ～人 *defender; counsel* / ～权 *right to defence* / 出庭～ *defend a case in court*

【辩解】give an explanation; try to defend oneself; explain away; make excuses:不要为自己～了。*Don't try to defend for yourself.*

【辩论】argue; debate: ～会 *a debate*

【辩证】① investigate; authenticate; textual research and discrimination: ～地看问题 *look at things dialectically* ② dialectical: ～唯物主义 *dialectical materialism*

辫 ① plait; braid; pigtail:那个小姑娘喜欢梳小～儿。*The little girl likes wearing his hair in braids.* ② mistake or shortcoming that may be exploited by an opponent; handle ③ sth resembling a braid

【辫子】① plait; braid; pigtail ② sth resembling a plait ③ handle

biāo

标 ① tip of a tree; treetop 树～ *treetop* ② outward sign; superficiality; symptom: ～本兼治 *treat a disease by looking into both its root cause and symptoms* ③ mark; sign:路～ *road sign* ④ label; put a mark on:用红墨水～上记号 *put a mark with red ink* / ～上～签 *put a label on* / ～价 *put a price tag on* ⑤ standard; quota; requirement:达～ *reach the standard; meet the requirement; fulfil the quota* ⑥ tender; bid:中～ *win a contract through bidding* / 开～ *open sealed tenders* ⑦ prize; award:夺～ *compete for first prize; win the championship* / 锦～赛 *championship* ⑧【军】regiment in the Qing Dynasty ⑨ [量] used only with the numeral-:一～人马来到了我们村庄。*A group of soldiers came to our village.*

【标榜】① brag about; flaunt; parade:西方国家一直～他们的自由平等。*The western countries always flaunt their banner of liberty and equality.* ② boost; excessively praise:不要再～自己了,我们都知道你是个什么样的人。*Don't sing your own praises; we have know what you are.*

【标本】① specimen; sample:动物～ *animal specimen* ② root cause and symptoms

【标兵】① parade guard ② example; role model; pacesetter

【标尺】① staff; surveyor's rod ② staff gauge ③ rear sight

【标点】① punctuation: ～符号 *punctuation mark* / 我写了一篇带～的小诗。*I wrote a poem with punctuation.* ② punctuate

【标杆】① surveyor's pole ② model; example for others to follow

【标号】grade; marks and symbols

【标记】sign; mark; symbol

【标价】mark a price; price; marked price:商店里的所有商品必须明码～。*All the goods in the store must be at a marked price.*

【标明】mark; indicate

【标签】label; tag:那个售货员正在图书上贴上～。*The salesman is sticking a label on the books.*

【标示】mark; indicate: ～牌 *sign post; marker*

【标售】sell by tender; put a price-tag on sth for sale

【标题】title; caption; heading; headline

【标新立异】create sth new and original; put forward novel ideas to show one is different from the ordinary run; start sth new in order to be different; do sth unconventional

【标语】slogan; poster: ～牌 *placard* / 张贴～ *put up slogans*

【标志】① sign; mark; symbol; hallmark ② indicate; symbolize

【标致】(usu. of women) beautiful; pretty:那个小姑娘长得很～。*The little girl is very pretty.*

【标准】① standard; criterion:国际～ *international standard* ② standardized; conforming to a standard: ～产品 *standardized product*

彪 ① [书] young tiger; stripes of a tiger ② [量] used only with the numeral-:一～人马闯入了我们的学校。*A detachment of troops rushed into our school.* ③ (Biāo) a surname

【彪悍】intrepid; doughty; valiant

【彪形大汉】burly chap; tall and strong man; hefty fellow; husky fellow:她雇了一个～做她的保镖。*She hired a tall and strong man as her safeguard.*

膘 fact of an animal:长～ *put on flesh; flesh out*

飙 [书] very strong wind; violent wind; hurricane; whirlwind

【飙车】drive a car at top speed

【飙风】strong wind; gale

【飙升】rise quickly; rocket:汽车的价格一路～。*The price of the cars is rocketing.*

镖 dartlike weapon:保～ *bodyguard* / 飞～ *flying dart*

【镖局】commercial firm for providing armed bodyguards; a professional establishment which provided armed escorts

【镖客】armed escort
【镖头】head of escort; chief bodyguard: 他曾当过~。*He has been a head of escort.*

biǎo

表 ① outward appearance; outside; surface; external: ~里不一 *think in one way and behave in another*; *by hypocritical* / 由~及里 *proceed from the outside to the inside*; *penetrate the surface to get at the essence* ② relationship between the children or grand-children of a brother and a sister or of sisters ③ show; demonstrate; express: 送你一份礼物以~我们的心意。*Give you this gift to express our appreciation.* ④ administer medicine to bring out the cold ⑤ model; example ⑥ memorial to an emperor usually on an important event ⑦ table; form; list: 价目~ *price list* / 时间~ *timetable*; *schedule* / 履历~ *curriculum vitae*; *resume* / 工资~ *payroll* ⑧ pole used as a sun dial ⑨ meter; gauge: 电度~ *electric meter*; *watt-hour meter*; *kilowatt-hour meter* / 水~ *water meter* ⑩ watch; clock: 我家有一块老怀~。*Our families have an old pocket watch.*
【表白】express or state clearly; profess; vindicate; explain oneself
【表层】surface layer
【表达】show; express; convey; voice: ~力 *power of expression* / ~方式 *way of expression* / 我不知道如何对我的妻子~我的爱意。*I don't know how to express my love to my wife.*
【表带】watchband; watch strap: 既然你的表都丢了, 那你的~也就没用了。*You have lost your watch, so it is no use of your watchband.*
【表弟】cousin; younger male cousin
【表哥】cousin; older male cousin
【表格】form; table: 我要填写这个~吗? *Shall I fill in this form?*
【表功】① claim merit for oneself; brag about one's deeds ② [书] commend; cite; honour
【表姐】cousin; older female cousin
【表决】vote; decide by note: ~权 *right to vote*
【表里】① outside and inside; one's outward show and inner thoughts: ~如一 *think and act in one and the same way* ②【中医】exterior and interior
【表露】show; reveal: 她是那样的悲伤, 但脸上一点也没~出来。*She was so sad, but there is nothing to show in her face.*
【表妹】cousin; younger family cousin
【表面】① surface; face; outside ② appearance; superficiality: ~现象 *superficial phenomenon* ③ dial plate
【表明】indicate; make known; make clear
【表皮】【生】epidermis; cuticle
【表亲】cousin; cousinship
【表情】① express one's feelings ② look; expression; countenance: 面部~ *facial expression*
【表示】① express; show ② indication; manifestation
【表述】present; convey; explain; state: 在大会上, 他~了自己的愿望。*He stated his wishes in the meeting.*
【表率】example; model
【表态】make known one's position; commit oneself; declare where one stands: 在大会上他明确~支持我。*He took a clear-cut stand to support me.*
【表现】① show; display; manifest ② behaviour; performance ③ show off: 这是第一次来这儿工作, 你最好~一下自己。*It's the first time to work here, you'd better show off yourself.*
【表演】① perform; act; play; exhibition: ~赛 *exhibition match* ② demonstrate
【表扬】praise; commend: ~信 *commendatory letter*
【表语】【语】predicative
【表彰】commend; cite (in dispatches)
【表侄】nephew; son of a male cousin on the distaff side
【表侄女】niece; daughter of a female cousin on the distaff side

婊
【婊子】bastard; whore; prostitute; son of a bitch

裱 ① mount (a picture, etc.) ② paste paper on (a wall, ceiling, etc.); paper
【裱糊】paper (a wall, ceiling, etc.)
【裱装】mount: ~字画 *mount calligraphic works and paintings*

biào

摽 ① be arm in arm; tie fast; fasten together ② cling to one another: 那两小孩子老~在一起玩。*The two of the little children hang together to play all the time.*

biē

瘪
see also biě
【瘪三】[方] bum; wretched-looking tramp who lives by begging or stealing

憋 ① bottle up; hold back; suppress: ~足劲 *burst with energy* ② feel oppressed; suffocate; stifle ③ [方] force; keep watch on ④ snap; break
【憋闷】be dejected; feel oppressed; be depressed
【憋屈】feel depressed; be down-hearted

鳖 soft-shelled turtle
【鳖甲】【药】turtle shell

bié

别[1] ① leave; part: 离乡～亲 (*often forced to*) *leave one's native place*; *go away from home* / 久～重逢 *meet again after a long separation* / 临～赠言 *parting advice* ② other; another: ～处 *another place*; *elsewhere* / ～无选择 *be left with no choice*; *have no alternative* / ～无出路。*There's no other way out.* ③ change; around ④ (Bié) a surname

别[2] ① differentiate; distinguish ② distinction; difference: 差～ *difference*; *disparity* / 千差万～ *differ in thousands of ways* ③ category; classification

别[3] ① fasten with a pin or clip ② stick in ③ trip up: ～腿 *stick one's leg out to trip sb up* ④ deliberately hinder the advance of a bike or car with one's own

别[4] ① don't: ～离开我。*Don't leave me alone.* ② usu. followed by 是, indicating conjecture of sth against one's own wish

see also biè

【别称】another name; alternative name: 请说出山东的～。*Please tell us another name of Shandong.*

【别出心裁】try to be different; start sth unique or original; adopt an original approach

【别处】other places; elsewhere: 我们不知道～是否有卖这本书的。*We don't know whether other places sell the book.*

【别动队】special detachment; commando; fifth column: ～员 *ranger*; *commando*

【别管】① no matter (who, what, etc.) ② leave alone; never mind

【别具匠心】show ingenuity; have originality

【别具一格】have a distinctive style; have a style of one's own

【别开生面】develop a new style; break a new path; break fresh ground; start sth new; be out of the common run

【别来无恙】[书] I trust all has been well with you since we last saw each other; I believe you've been in good health since we parted

【别论】another matter; different story

【别人】other people; others

【别树一帜】set up a new banner; found a new school of thought; have a style of one's own

【别墅】villa: 听说他们在家乡买了一套～。*I heard that they had bought a villa in their hometown.*

【别说】not to mention; let alone; say nothing of

【别提】no need to mention; you can well imagine

【别无他图】have no other intentions: 她嫁给我, 真是～。*She married with me and had no other intentions.*

【别样】① other ② different style

【别有用心】have ulterior motives

【别针】① safety pin; pin ② brooch: 这个～很漂亮。*The brooch is very beautiful.*

【别致】unique; original; novel; exquisite; unconventional

【别字】incorrectly written or mispronounced character; malapropism: ～连篇 *be riddled with wrongly written characters*

蹩 [方] sprain (one's ankle or wrist)

【蹩脚】[方] shoddy; poor; inferior: ～货 *inferior goods*; *poor stuff*; *shoddy work*

biě

瘪 ① shrivelled; shrunken; deflated: ～花生 *blighted peanuts* ② be on a spot

see also biē

【瘪陷】shrivelled; sunken

biè

别 [方] sway; bring round; persuade sb to change one's idea

see also bié

【别扭】① awkward; uncomfortable; difficult to deal with ② not see eye to eye; not get on well: 闹～ *be at odds*; *fall out*

bīn

玢 [书] a kind of jade

宾 ① guest: 国～ *state guest* / 相敬如～ (*of a married couple*) *treat each other with respect and courtesy* (*as if they were host and guest*) / 喧～夺主 *presumptuous guest usurping the host's role*; *minor issue taking precedence over a major one* / ～客盈门。*One's horse was filled with guests.* ② (Bīn) a surname

【宾格】[语] objective case

【宾馆】guesthouse

【宾客】guests; visitors

【宾朋】friends and guests: ～满座。*The house is packed with friends and guests.*

【宾语】[语] object: 间接～ *indirect object* / 直接～ *direct object*

【宾至如归】where guests feel as comfortable as if they were at home; home from home

【宾主】host and guest

彬

【彬彬有礼】affable and courteous; polite; urbane

傧

【傧相】① attendant of the bride or bridegroom at a wedding: 女～ *bridesmaid* / 男～ *best man* ② [古]

master of ceremony

滨 ① bank; shore; brink; water's edge ② be close to; border on

缤

【缤纷】in riotous profusion:五彩~ *riot of colours*; *multi-coloured*

濒 ① be close to; border on ② on the brink of; on the point of

【濒临】be close to; on the verge of; border on

【濒危】① be in imminent danger: ~ *endangered species* ② be critically: ~病人 *critically ill person*; *dying patient*

bìn

摈 [书] discard; get rid of; reject

【摈斥】reject; keep out; dismiss; exclude: ~异己 *dismiss those who hold different opinions*

【摈除】discard; get rid of; dispense with

【摈弃】abandon; discard; cast away

殡 ① lay a coffin in a memorial hall ② carry a coffin to the burial place

【殡车】hearse

【殡殓】corpse and carry it to the grave

【殡仪馆】the undertaker's; funeral parlour or home

【殡葬】funeral and interment

鬓 temples; hair over the temples:干~ *dry ice*

【鬓发】hair over the temples

bīng

冰 ① ice:干~*dry ice* ② feel cold:这水太凉,有点~手。*The hands feel very cold in the icy water.* ③ put in a place packed with ice ④ sth resembling ice

【冰雹】hail; hailstone

【冰川】glacier: ~湖 *glacial lake* / ~平原 *glacier plain*

【冰岛】Iceland: ~人 *Icelander*

【冰灯】coloured ice of various shapes with lights inside; ice lantern

【冰雕】ice sculpture; ice carving

【冰冻】① freeze: ~地区 *frost zone* / ~疗法 *ice therapy* / ~三尺,非一日之寒。*It takes more than one cold day to freeze three feet of ice; the trouble is deep-rooted or Rome was not built in a day.* ② [方] ice

【冰糕】ice cream; ice-lolly; popsicle

【冰柜】freezer; refrigerator

【冰花】① ice-flower ② iced object of art ③ frost flower; frost; rime

【冰冷】ice-cold

【冰凉】ice-cold:天太冷了,你的手冻得~。*It's too cold, your hands are ice-cold.*

【冰淇淋】ice cream

【冰清玉洁】pure as ice and spotless as jade; noble or impeccable in character

【冰球】①【体】ice hockey: ~场 *rink* / ~棍 *ice stick* ② puck

【冰山】① ice-covered mountain ② iceberg: ~一角 *tip of the iceberg* ③ supporter one cannot long rely on

【冰霜】austere manner; stern countenance:冷若~ *look frosty and stern*

【冰糖】crystal sugar; rock candy: ~葫芦 *candied haws on a stick*

【冰天雪地】world of ice an snow

【冰箱】① icebox ② refrigerator; fridge

【冰鞋】skating boots; skates:小时候我有一双漂亮的旱~。*When I was a child, I had a beautiful roller skates.*

【冰心】moral purity; loyal heart; pure and innocent soul

【冰雪聪明】brilliant; extremely intelligent; extraordinarily bright

【冰柱】icicle

兵 ① weapons; arm: ~戎相见 *appeal to arms*; *open hostilities*; *meet on the battleground* / ~不血刃 *no swords are stained with blood — win victory without shedding a drop of blood* /短~相接 *fight at close quarters* ② soldier:征~ *conscription* /新~ *recruit* /老~ *veteran* ③ army; troops: 骑~ *cavalry* / 炮兵 *artillery* ④ private ⑤ about war or military affairs:纸上谈~ *theorize abstractly without referring to reality* ⑥ (in chess) pawn

【兵败如山倒】a completely routed; an army in flight is like a landslide; a routed army collapses like a landside

【兵变】mutiny

【兵不厌诈】there can never be too much deception in war; nothing is too deceitful in war; all's fair in war

【兵部】【史】ministry of war

【兵多将广】have vast military forces; have numerous troops and many generals; very large army with many able generals — very powerful military warship

【兵法】art of war; military strategy and tactics

【兵工厂】arsenal; ordnance; munitions factory

【兵荒马乱】turmoil and chaos of war; troops on the rampage

【兵家】① military strategist in ancient China ② soldier; military commander:胜败乃~常事。*For a military commander, winning or losing a battle is a common occurrence.*

【兵谏】exhortations backed up by force of arms; coerce the ruler by force of arms into acceptation one's exhortations

【兵精粮足】well-trained troops and abundant supplies or provisions

【兵来将挡,水来土掩】counter measure for measure;

stop soldiers with generals and on-rushing water with earth-counter move for move

【兵力】military strength; armed forces: ~不足 *be short of armed forces*

【兵临城下】the city is under siege; enemy troops are at the city gate

【兵马】troops and horses; military forces

【兵马俑】【考】terra cotta warriors and horses:秦朝~ *Qin Dynasty terra cotta warriors and horses*

【兵器】weaponry; weapons; arms:在这些~中挑选一件你喜欢的。*Please choose one you like among these weapons.*

【兵强马壮】well-trained soldiers and sturdy horses-well-trained and powerful army

【兵权】control of the armed forces; military leadership; military power

【兵团】army group; armed force

【兵种】branch of one of the arms:装甲兵是陆军~的其中一支。*The armoured force is one of the arms of the army.*

【兵卒】[旧] soldier

屏

see also bǐng; píng

【屏营】in fear and trepidation; trembling with fear

bǐng

丙 ① third of the ten Heavenly Stems ② third: ~等 *third grade*; *grade*

秉 ① hold; grasp; control: ~笔 *wield a brush* ②[古] capacity unit ③(Bǐng) a surname

【秉报】report to one's superior or senior

【秉赋】natural endowment; gift ②inherit; be endowed with

【秉公】justly; impartially: ~执法 *be level-handed in dispensing justice*; *handle cases according to law*

【秉性】nature; temperament; disposition

【秉直】[书] upright; just; integrity:他为人~。*He is a person of integrity.*

柄 ① handle:铁锹~ *handle of a shovel* /勺~ *handle of a spoon* ② stem (of a flower, leaf or fruit):叶~ *leafstalk* ③ opportunity that may serve as evidence against sb; anything affording an advantage or pretext to an opponent:把~ *evidence against sb*; *handle* /话~ *subject for ridicule* /笑~ *laughing stock* ④[书] power; be in control ⑤[量] used of things with a handle

【柄权】hold a position of power and influence

饼 ① round flat cake:月~ *moon cake* /烙~ *unleavened pancake* ② sth shaped like a cake:柿~ *dried persimmon*

【饼干】biscuit; cracker: ~烤炉 *biscuit oven*

屏 ① hold one's breath:他~住气,眼睁睁地看着小偷溜走了。*He held his breath by staring the thief going away.* ② get rid of; reject *see also* bīng; píng

【屏除】get rid of; remove; dismiss; overcome:你们要~成见,更多的去关心对方。*You'd better overcome your prejudices and care about each other more.*

【屏息】hold one's breath: ~不动 *holding one's breath*

禀 ①[书] report; petition:回~ *report back* ② written report to one's superior ③ receive; be endowed with

【禀报】[书] report (to one's superior)

【禀呈】[书] respectfully submit

【禀赋】gift; natural endowment:汤姆~聪明。*Tom is gifted with keen intelligence.*

【禀告】report:那个孩子已经把发生的事情~老师了。*The child had reported the happened events to his teacher.*

【禀性】nature; disposition:他是个来自农村的孩子,~淳朴。*He comes from countryside and is simple and honest by nature.*

【禀奏】present a proposal; submit a memorial to the throne

bìng

并[1] ① simultaneously; side by side: ~发症 *complication* / ~肩 *shoulder to shoulder* ② used before a negative for emphasis, usu. as a retort ③ and; besides

并[2] combine; merge; incorporate:去年几个小医院~成一个综合性的医院。*Several small hospitals merged into a comprehensive one.*

【并存】coexist; exist side by side

【并发】be complicated by; erupt simultaneously: ~感染 *accompanying infection*

【并驾齐驱】run neck and neck; keep abreast of sb; be on a par with

【并肩】shoulder to shoulder; side by side; abreast: ~而行 *walk abreast* / ~作战 *fight side by side*

【并举】develop simultaneously; carry on (two things) at the same time

【并列】stand side by side; be juxtaposed:王丽和张刚两人~榜首。*Wang Li and Zhang Gang appeared side by side at the top of the list of successful candidates.*

【并排】side by side; abreast

【并且】① and; also; as well as ② furthermore; moreover; in addition

【并入】merge into; incorporate in

【并吞】swallow; annex; merge

【并行】① walk side by side ② carry two on more things at the same time ③【电】parallel: ~存储 *parallel storage* / ~处理机 *parallel processor*

【并用】use two things simultaneously; apply methods simultaneously

【并重】lay equal stress on; pay equal attention to

病 ① illness; disease; sickness:血液~ *blood diseases* /传染~ *infectious disease; contagious disease* /职业~ *occupational disease* /心脏~ *heart trouble; heart disease* /皮肤~ *skin disease; dermatosis* /结核~ *tuberculosis(TB)*/艾滋~ *acquired immune deficiency syndrome(AIDS)* ② be ill; be sick:因为工作太操劳他~倒了。*He was ill for he worked so much.* ③ secret passion; syndrome ④ fault; defect:这是社会的一个通~。*This is one of common problems of society.* ⑤ do harm to ⑥ blame

【病变】pathology; pathological change

【病床】sickbed; hospital bed

【病毒】virus

【病房】ward (of a hospital); sickroom:她被转移到了隔离~。*She was moved to the isolation ward.*

【病根】① incompletely cured illness; old complaint ② root cause of trouble

【病故】die of illness

【病号】sick personnel; patient; invalid:老~ *valetudinarian; chronic invalid*

【病假】sick leave: ~条 *doctor's note or certificate for sick leave*

【病句】faulty sentence:他的文章里有很多~。*There are many faulty sentences in his article.*

【病理】pathology: ~诊断 *pathological diagnosis* / ~学 *pathology*

【病历】medical record; case history

【病例】case of illness

【病魔】evil spirit of illness: ~缠身 *be afflicted with a lingering illness*

【病情】state of one's illness; patient's condition

【病人】patient; sick person; invalid

【病容】sickly look:那个小姑娘面带~。*The little girl looks unwell.*

【病史】medical history; clinical notes; case history

【病逝】die of illness; pass away:他妈妈去年~了。*His mother passed away last year.*

【病态】① sickly appearance:那个小孩装作~的样子,想不去上学。*The little child pretended to be ill in order not to go school.* ② morbid state; pathosis: ~心理 *morbid psychology* ③【数】ill condition

【病痛】slight illness; disorder; indisposition; ailment

【病危】be critically ill; be dangerously ill; be terminally ill:看到妈妈的~通知他哭了。*He cried at the critical condition notice of his mother.*

【病休】sick leave

【病秧子】[口] chronic invalid; valetudinarian; person who is chronically ill

【病因】cause of illness; pathogeny:没有人知道他的~。*Nobody knows his pathogeny.*

【病友】ward mate; inmate; friend made while one is in hospital:他和几个~成了好朋友。*He and several ward mates became good friends.*

【病愈】recover (from an illness); get over (one's illness)

【病源】cause of a disease; root trouble

【病院】specialized hospital:精神~ *mental hospital*

【病症】disease; illness:疑难~ *difficult and complicated cases*

【病重】seriously ill

【病状】symptom (of a disease)

摒 get rid of; dismiss

【摒除】get rid of; renounce

【摒弃】discard; abandon: ~前嫌 *dispense with all previous ill will* / ~坏习惯 *discard bad habits*

bō

拨 ① move with hand; turn; stir; dial:他正在~动算盘子儿。*He is moving the beads on the abacus.* ② assign; allocate: ~200斤大米给村民 *assign 200 jin rice to the villagers* ③ turn round ④[量] group; batch:轮~ *by turns*

【拨付】make payments as earmarked; appropriate cash of money

【拨号】dial a number; dial: ~电话 *dial telephone*

【拨开】push aside:她~人群看到了丢失了的儿子。*She pushed through the crowd and saw her losing son.*

【拨款】① allocate funds:教育~ *allocate funds for education*

【拨乱反正】set things right; restore things to order; set things to rights; bring order out of chaos

【拨弄】① move to and fro with the hand ② order about; manipulate ③ stir up; incite: ~是非 *stir up trouble by gossip*

【拨云见日】dispel the clouds and see the sun shining through — restore justice; enlighten

【拨正】set right; correct

波 ① wave:秋~ *autumn ripples — the bright and clear eyes of a beautiful woman* /微~ *ripples* ②【物】wave:声~ *sound wave* /光~ *light wave* /电磁~ *electromagnetic wave* /短~ *short wave* /中~ *medium wave* /长~ *long wave* ③ unexpected turn of events ④[方] run; rush:东奔西~ *run hither and thither; rush about*

【波长】wavelength

【波导】【物】wave guide

【波动】① undulate; fluctuate; rise and fall:近来那个学生的情绪有些~。*Recently the student is in an unsettled state of mind.* ②【物】wave: ~学 *wave theory*

【波段】wave band:听说八~以上的收音机才可以收听到美国之音。*I hear that radios with more than eight wave bands can receive the Voice of America.*

【波恩】Bonn, formerly capital of West Germany

【波峰】【物】wave crest

【波哥大】Bogota, capital of Colombia

【波谷】【物】trough

【波及】spread to; involve; affect:这次反战大罢工~到全世界。*The strike of anti-war affected the*

whole world.
【波兰】Poland：~人 *Pole* / ~语 *Polish*
【波澜】great waves; big waves; billows：~起伏 *waves rise and fall*; *unfolds one climax after another* / ~壮阔 *surging forward with great momentum*; *enormous expanse of roaring waves*
【波浪】wave：~起伏 *waves rising and falling*
【波利尼西亚】Polynesia：~人 *Polynesian* / ~语 *Polynesian*
【波罗的海】Baltic Sea
【波斯】Persia：~人 *Persian* / ~语 *Persian* / ~湾 *Persian Gulf* / ~猫 *Persian cat* / ~帝国 *Persian Empire*
【波速】wave velocity
【波涛】great waves; billows：我终于见到了~汹涌的大海。*Finally I saw the roaring sea.*
【波纹】① ripple ② corrugation：~管 *corrugated pipe*
【波音】①【音】mordent ② Boeing：~747 飞机 *Boeing 747*
【波折】twists and turns：他求学的故事比较~。*The story of his study took an unexpected turn.*

玻

【玻利维亚】Bolivia：~人 *Bolivian*
【玻璃】① glass：那个盘子是由~制成的。*The plate is made of glass.* ② transparent plastic; things that look like glass：有机~ *organic glass*

钵 ① earthen bowl：饭~ *rice bowl* ② alms bowl (of a Buddhist monk)
【钵盂】Buddhist monk's alms bowl

般

see also bān; pán
【般若】【宗】highest wisdom

饽 bun; cake
【饽饽】① pastry ② steamed bun; cake

剥 used only in compounds

see also bāo
【剥夺】① strip (be force); expropriate ② deprive (by law)：~自由 *deprivation of freedom* / ~政治权利终身 *deprive sb of one's political rights for life*
【剥落】① peel off ②【地】exfoliation
【剥削】exploit：~阶级 *exploiting class* / ~制度 *exploitation system* / ~者 *exploiter* /被~者 *the exploited*

菠

【菠菜】spinach
【菠萝】pineapple：~是我最喜欢吃的水果了。*Pineapples are my favourite fruits.*
【菠萝蜜】jackfruit

播 ① sow：夏~ *summer sowing* /秋~ *autumn sowing* ② broadcast; spread：新闻联~ *national news on TV*
【播出】broadcast; transmit; be on the air：他们制作的节目正在~。*The programme they made is on the air.*
【播发】broadcast on the air：电视台选择了一些新闻~。*The TV station chose some news to broadcast.*
【播放】① transmit by radio; go on the air; broadcast
【播弄】① order sb about; manipulate ② stir up; incite; instigate; discord：~是非 *stir things up*; *sow dissension*; *foments discord*
【播撒】scatter; broadcast：春天，农民经常在农田里~一些种子。*In spring, farmers often broadcast some seeds in the field.*
【播送】broadcast; transmit
【播音】transmit; broadcast
【播映】televise; show on television; transmit by television
【播种】(bōzhǒng) sow seeds; sow; seed：~机 *seeder*; *grain drill*
【播种】(bōzhòng) grow by sowing seeds：~季节到了。*The sowing season is coming.*

bó

伯[1] ① father's elder brother; uncle ② eldest (of brothers)
伯[2] earl; count
【伯父】father's elder brother; uncle
【伯爵】earl; count：~夫人 *countess*
【伯乐】a good judge of talent
【伯母】aunt; wife of father's elder brother

驳[1] [书] (of different sorts or colours) mixed
驳[2] ① barge; lighter ② transport by lighter ③ extend
驳[3] refute; reject; gainsay
【驳斥】rebut; refute; denounce
【驳倒】outargue; demolish one's argument
【驳回】turn down; overrule; reject
【驳面子】not show due respect for sb's feelings; offend sb's sensibilities; make sb lose face

帛 [书] silks：玉~ *jade and silks*
【帛画】painting on silk

泊 ① be at anchor; moor; berth：停~ *cast anchor* ② stop; stay for a time：最近他漂~不定。*Recently he wandered from place to place.* ③ park：~车 *park a car*
see also pō
【泊位】【交】berth：~费 *berthage*

柏

see also bǎi
【柏拉图】Plato (c. 428—348BC), Greek philosopher

B

【柏林】Berlin

勃 ［书］prosperous; rigorous; thriving: 蓬～ *vigorous; thriving*

【勃勃】thriving; vigorous; exuberant: 生机～ *full of life*

【勃发】① thrive; prosper ② break out; erupt

【勃郎宁】Browning (a type of automatic pistol)

【勃起】【生理】erection; erect

【勃然】① vigorously ② suddenly; excitedly: ～大怒 *fly into a rage*

脖 ① neck: 他的～子很长。*He has a long neck.* ② sth shaped like a neck

【脖子】neck

博[1] ① rich; abundant; plentiful: 中国地大物～。*There are vast in territory and rich in natural resources in China.* ② big; wide: 宽衣～带 *in loose garments* ③ knowledgeable and well informed: 旁征～引 *be well documented; quote copiously to support one's viewpoints* /那位老教授知识渊～，可以通今～古。*The old professor is conversant with things past and present.*

博[2] ① win; gain ② gamble

【博爱】universal fraternity; universal love; universal brotherhood

【博大】extensive rich: 中国的文化～精深。*The culture of China has extensive knowledge and profound scholarship.*

【博得】win; gain

【博而不精】have wide but not expert knowledge; know sth of everything but not a lot about anything

【博古通今】be learned and well-informed; possess a wide knowledge of things ancient and modern — erudite

【博览】read widely or extensively: 他从小就～群书了。*When he was a child, he had read widely.*

【博览会】fair; exposition

【博取】try to gain; court

【博士】① doctor: ～学位 *doctor's degree; doctorate* ②［古］person specialized in a skill ③［古］official title of a specialist in charge of the dissemination of learning

【博士后】① post-doctoral research; post-doctoral studies ② one who is engaged in such research or studies

【博闻强记】have wide learning and a powerful memory; have encyclopedic knowledge

【博物馆】museum

【博学】learned; erudite: 那个英语老师是个～多才的人。*The English teacher is learned and versatile.*

【博引】quote extensively: 旁征～ *well-provided with a wide range of authoritative quotations; well-documented*

渤

【渤海】Bohai Sea

搏 ① wrestle; fight; struggle ② pounce on ③ beat; throb

【搏动】beat rhythmically; throb

【搏斗】wrestle; fight; struggle: 生死～ *life-and-death struggle*

【搏击】strike; fight with

【搏战】wrestle; struggle

膊 arm: 赤～ *bare to the waist*

薄[1] ① small; slight; meagre: ～弱环节 *vulnerable spot; weak link* /我们厂技术力量相当～弱。*There are quite fewer qualified technical personnel in our factory.* /自从他俩吵了架后，感情就淡～了。*Since they quarrelled with each other, they remained indifferent.* ② frail; weak: 单～ *thin and weak* ③ unkind; ungenerous; mean ④ despise; belittle ⑤ (Bó) a surname

薄[2] ［书］approach; hear: 日～西山。*The sun is setting behind the western hills.*

see also báo; bò

【薄产】small property

【薄礼】modest gift; small present: 上周日他送老师了一些～。*He gave some small presents to his teacher last Sunday.*

【薄利】small profits: ～多销 *small profits and good sales*

【薄命】(usu. of women) born under an unlucky star; ill-fated

【薄膜】① membrane ② film

【薄片】thin slice; thin section: 请把那个苹果切成～。*Please cut the apple into think slices.*

【薄情】fickle; inconstant in love

【薄弱】weak; frail

bǒ

跛 lame; limping

【跛脚】lame; crippled

【跛行】limp along

【跛子】lame person; cripple

簸 ① winnow with a fan; ② toss up and down

see also bò

【簸荡】rock; roll: 风越来越大，小船开始～起来。*The wind was stronger and stronger, and the boat began to rock.*

【簸动】① jolt; bump; toss

【簸箩】winnowing basket; wicker basket

bò

see also báo; bó

【薄荷】【植】mint; peppermint: ～糖 *peppermint*

candy

簸

see also bǒ

【簸箕】① winnowing pan ② loop (of fingerprint pattern) ③ dustpan

bo

卜 carrot

see also bǔ

啵 ［方］used to indicate consultation, suggestion, request, command, etc.

bū

逋 ［书］①flee; disappear ② owe; delay; evade; default; be behind in payment

【逋逃】flee; fugitive

【逋亡】flee; escape; abscond

bǔ

卜 ① divination; fortune-telling: 他是一个～卦先生。*He is a fortune-teller.* ②［书］foretell; predict: 吉凶未～ *cannot predict the good or bad outcome*

see also bo

【卜辞】oracle inscriptions of the Shang Dynasty on tortoiseshells or animal bones

【卜骨】oracle bone

【卜卦】divine by the Eight Diagrams

【卜问】pray and consult the oracle

补 ① mend; repair: ～胎 *mend a puncture* / ～裤子 *mend trousers* ② fill up; add supplement; make up for: ～偿费 *compensation; compensatory payment* / ～偿差额 *make up a deficiency* /请把漏了的字～上。*Please supply the missing words.* ③ nourish: 多喝点鸡汤，～～身子。*Drink more chicken soup to build up your health.* ④ benefit; help; use

【补白】filler; additional explanation

【补办】do sth after the time it should have been done; repay a kindness or favour

【补报】① make a supplementary report; make a report after the event ② repay a kindness; repay a favour; repay favours granted

【补偿】① compensate; make up ② compensation: ～贸易 *compensation trade*

【补充】① replenish; supplement; make-up; add: 她晚上教课以～正常收入。*She supplements her regular income by doing a bit of teaching in the evening.* ② additional; supplementary: ～读物 *supplementary reading material* / ～条款 *subsidiary; supplementary provisions*

【补丁】patch: 那个可怜的孩子的裤子上满是～。*The poor child's trousers are full of patches.*

【补发】pay retroactively; reissue; supply again: ～增加的工资 *pay increased wages retroactively*

【补过】make up for a fault; make amends for mistakes: 将功～ *make amends for one's mistake by meritorious deeds*

【补给】provision; supply; replenishment; feed: ～品 *supplies*

【补济】supply

【补角】【数】supplementary angle

【补救】remedy; rectify: 这类罪过不可～。*Such evils are beyond remedy.*

【补考】make up; make-up examination; supplementary examination

【补课】① make up missed lessons; remedial teaching: 放学后老师给那个生病的孩子～去了。*After class, the teacher helped the sick child make up the lessons he had missed.* ② make up for; remedy the weak areas in one's work

【补漏】repair; stop leaks; make up deficiencies

【补苗】【农】fill the gaps with seedlings

【补票】buy a ticket which one failed to get at the booking office

【补品】supplies; tonic; cordial

【补其所短】make up for one's shortcomings and defects

【补缺】fill up a vacancy; supply a deficiency

【补税】pay an overdue tax; pay the dodged duty

【补台】boost sb; help sb strengthen one's position

【补贴】① subsidize ② subsidy; allowance: 给学生伙食～ *give a food subsidy to students*

【补习】take lessons after school; attend make-up lessons

【补修】repeat a course one has failed

【补选】by-election

【补血】enrich the blood

【补牙】【医】fill a tooth; tooth filling

【补养】take a tonic food to build up one's health

【补药】tonic; supplies; invigorator

【补衣服】patch clothes

【补语】complement

【补助】subsidy; supply needs; allowance: 接受政府～ *receive subsidy from the government*

【补足】make up for; make complete; fill reinforcement

【补足语】complement

捕 catch; seize; arrest

【捕风捉影】speak or act on hearsay evidence

【捕俘】capture

【捕获】catch; capture; seize; succeed in catching; acquire: 那些小偷在作案时被当场～。*The thieves were caught red-handed.*

【捕捞】fish for; catch: ～季节 *catching season* / ～量 *amount of fishing* / ～业 *fishery* /河里的鱼～得过多。*The river was fished too much.*

【捕猎】catch (wile animals); hunt
【捕虏】capture; take prisoner
【捕拿】arrest; capture; catch:政府已经下令～那个罪犯。*The government has issued a warrant to capture the criminal.*
【捕杀】catch and kill
【捕食】prey on; catch and feed on; prey on
【捕头】head constable; sheriff
【捕鱼】① catch fish; fish; ② fishing:他们整天都在河里～。*They fished all day in the river.*
【捕捉】catch; seize

哺 ① feed (a baby); nurse:嗷嗷待～ *cry piteously for food* ② food of chewing; food in one's mouth
【哺乳】suckle; nurse; breast-feed:～动物 *mammal* /～室 *nursing room* /～瓶 *feeding bottle*
【哺养】feed; rear:为了工作,她不得不把孩子交给她的姐姐～。*For her work, she has to leave her child under her elder sister's feeding.*
【哺育】①[书] feed:在充满爱的环境下～成长 *be reared in an atmosphere of love* ② develop; foster; nurture

堡 bourg; village
see also bǎo
【堡子】[方] village; walled-in bourg; walled-in bourg hamlet

bù

不 ① not; no:他～爱说话。*He dose not like talking.* /他的女儿长得～漂亮。*His daughter is not pretty.* ② (used before certain nouns to form an adjective) un-; in-; dis-:～法行为 *illegal act* ③ used as a negative reply to a question:他～喝酒吗?——不,他喝。*Doesn't he drink wines? Yes, he does.* ④ used at the end of a sentence to indicate that it is a question:你走～? *will you go?* ⑤ used between a verb and its complement to indicate negation:门被锁上了,那个女孩子出～来了。*The door was docked and the little child cannot get out.* ⑥ no matter (how, where, etc):什么好～好的,你都得离开那儿。*No matter what is good or bad, you have to leave here.* ⑦ either... or ⑧ (used in certain ceremonial expressions) needn't; don't:～客气。*Don't mention it.*
【不安】① intranquil; not peaceful; unrest; unstable:坐立～ *be restless; be on pins and needles* ② disturbed; restless; uneasy:她神色有点～,好像发生什么事了? *It seemed something happened for she looked troubled.* ③ sorry
【不卑不亢】neither haughty nor bumble; neither supercilious nor obsequious
【不备】① unprepared; not ready; off guard:乘其～ *catch sb off guard* ② (used at the end of a letter) that's all for now; there's more than I can tell you in this time
【不比】unlike; no match for; inferior to
【不必】need not; not have to; not be necessary:～太认真,只是个玩笑而已。*Don't take it seriously; it's just a joke.*
【不变】unchanged; constant:～资本 *constant capital*
【不便】① inappropriate; inconvenient; unsuitable:那位老人行动有点～。*The old man has a little difficulty in moving about.* ② short of cash; hard up:能借给我一些钱吗,我最近手头有点～。*Can you lend some money to me for I have no money at hand recently?*
【不测】mishap; accident; contingency:～风云 *unforeseen storms* /他随着带着一把刀以防～。*He always carries a knife preparing for any contingency.*
【不耻下问】not feel ashamed to seek advice from one's people below
【不辞】① without saying good-bye ② not refuse or shirk
【不错】① correct; right:你说的一点也～。*What you said is quite right.* ②[口] not bad; pretty good
【不打自招】give oneself away; make a confession without duress; disclose unintentionally
【不单】① not the only:参加会议的～有李老师班的人。*There are not the only class of teach Li.* ② not only; not merely
【不但】not only
【不当】unsuitable; improper; inappropriate:那封措辞～的信令他很生气。*He was very angry at the letter with inappropriate wording.*
【不道德】immoral; unethical
【不得】(bùdé) must not; may not; should not; not be allowed
【不得】(bude) can't; mustn't
【不等】very; differ:大小～ *differ in size*
【不定】① hard to say; not for certain; hard to predict:说～他考不过这次考试呢。*It's hard to say that he couldn't pass the examination.* ② indefinite; indeterminate:～积分 *indefinite integral* /～期航班 *nonregular service* /～根 *adventitious root* /～芽 *adventitious bud* /～冠词 *indefinite article* /～方程 *indeterminate equation*
【不动声色】stay calm and collected; maintain one's composure; not bat an eyelid
【不端】improper; dishonourable:品行～ *having bad conduct; ill-behaved*
【不断】constant; continuous; unceasing; uninterrupted
【不对】① incorrect; wrong:昨天你所做的都是～的。*What you had done yesterday was incorrect.* ② (used by itself to express disagreement) no ③ amiss; abnormal; queer ④ be in disagreement; not in harmony; not on good terms; be at odds
【不乏】no lack of; not rare:他所说的倒是～其事。*What he said is such things are not rare.*

【不法】illegal; lawless; unlawful: ~行为 *illegal acts*; *unlawful practice* / ~小贩 *lawbreaking pedlar* /昨天警察抓到了那些~之徒。*The policemen seized the lawless persons yesterday.*

【不凡】unconventional; extraordinary; out of the common run:那个小姑娘太骄傲,总是自命~。*The little girl is always so pride that she considers herself out of the ordinary.*

【不防】taken by surprise; not ready; caught unawares

【不妨】might as well; there is no harm in

【不菲】considerable; great:她丈夫送她一个价值~的项链作为生日礼物。*Her husband sent her invaluable necklace as her birthday gift.*

【不服】remain unconvinced; refuse to obey; not give in to

【不符】not conform to; be inconsistent with:她所说的与事实~。*What she said is inconsistent with the facts.*

【不复】no longer:那旧楼房已经~存在了。*The old building is no longer in existence.*

【不干不净】unclean; filthy:俗话说~,吃了没病。*The saying says unclean food don't cause disease.*

【不干涉】nonintervention; noninterference:互不~内政 *noninterference in each other's internal affairs*

【不甘心】not reconciled to; not resigned to

【不敢】dare not; not dare:李苹~去学校了,因为她没有完成作业。*Li Ping dare not go to school, because she didn't finish her homework.*

【不更事】have not seen the world; have not experience life; inexperienced in life:他少~,你就原谅他吧! *Please forgive him for he is too young to know the world.*

【不共戴天】swear not to live under the same sky (with one's enemy) — be absolutely irreconcilable

【不苟】not casual; careful; conscientious: ~言笑 *reserved*; *reticent* /一丝~ *be meticulous*

【不够】not enough; insufficient; lacking; inadequate

【不顾】① never think of; never care ② in spite of; regardless of:她~一切去寻找丢失的儿子。*She is looking for her losing son at any cost.*

【不关】not get involved; have nothing to do: ~你的事,请走开。*Please go away it has nothing to do with you.*

【不管】in spite of; no matter; regardless of: ~上不上课,我都得去学校。*No matter whether there is any classes or not, I will get to school.*

【不光】① not the only one; not the only thing ② not only

【不规则】irregular: ~动词 *irregular verb*

【不轨】against the law or discipline

【不过】① (used as an intensifier after an adjective):再好~ *can't be better* ② no more than; only; merely: ~一个小孩子 *a little child only* ③ but; however; yet:我不同意你的意见,~我们还可以商量。*I disagree with you, but we can continue our discussion.*

【不过如此】just so-so; passable; barely acceptable

【不含糊】① unambiguous; unequivocal; explicit ② really good; not ordinary ③ show no fear; not be afraid of

【不寒而栗】shiver all over through not cold; tremble with fear

【不好意思】① fell embarrassed; shy; be ill at ease; bashful ② find it embarrassing to do sth

【不合】① be unsuited to; not conform to; be out of keeping with ②[书] should not; ought not ③ at odds; not get along well; be on bad terms

【不和】① not get along well; be on bad terms; be at odds:因房子问题他和哥哥闹得~。*His elder brother and he are on bad terms for house.* ② discord:他尽力制造我们之间的~。*He tries his best to sow discord between us.*

【不怀好意】not with the best of intentions; cherish malicious intentions; harbour evil designs

【不欢而散】part in a foul mood; break up in discord

【不慌不忙】calm; leisurely; unhurriedly:他~地走了。*He went away unhurriedly.*

【不会】① be unlikely; will not ② have not learnt to; be unable to ③ used to express reproach for the non-performance of an action

【不讳】① without concealing anything:直言~ *be frank and outspoken* /供认~ *candidly confess*; *make a clean breast of everything*

【不惑】not to be perplexed; be free from doubts:四十而~。*At forty I came to be free from doubts.*

【不及】① not as good as; inferior to ② fall short of; not be afraid of ③ find it too late

【不计其数】countless; innumerable

【不假思索】readily; without thinking

【不结盟】nonalignment: ~国家 *nonaligned countries*

【不解】① not understand; fail to comprehend ② indissoluble

【不禁】can't help; can't refrain from

【不仅】① not the only one ② not only

【不进则退】Not to forge ahead is to slip backward; Move forward, or you'll fall behind.

【不景气】【经】① depression; recession; slump ② depressed state

【不胫而走】run apace; get round fast; spread like wildfire:他们离婚的消息~。*The news that they had divorced ran apace.*

【不久】soon; before long; soon after; not long after:他走后~他母亲就去世了。*His mother died soon after he had left.*

【不拘小节】not bother about trifles; not be punctilious; not be fettered by petty conventions; not niggling

【不堪】① cannot bear or stand ② unbearably; impossibly: ~入目 *not fit to be seen* ③ (used after words of bad meaning) utterly; extremely

【不堪回首】cannot recall the past; find it unbearable to recall cannot bear to look back on
【不堪入耳】revolting; offensive to the ear; disgusting
【不堪一击】collapse at the first blow; cannot withstand a single blow
【不可】① cannot; should not; must not: 什么事都~一概而论。*Anything should not make sweeping statements.* ② used together with to indicate what one is set to do: 我真有其他事情要做,今天非走~。*I have really other thing to do; I just have to go.*
【不可估量】inestimable; incalculable; beyond measure
【不可救药】① incurable; beyond cure; past praying for ② hopeless
【不可收拾】hopeless; irremediable; unmanageable; out of hand: 不要着急,事情还没到~的地步。*Don't worry; things are not getting out of hand.*
【不可思议】inconceivable; unthinkable; unimaginable: ~的是他竟然通过了考试。*It was unimaginable that he had passed the examination.*
【不可同日而语】cannot be put on a par; there's no comparison between them; cannot be mentioned in the same breath
【不可一世】flaunting one's superiority; consider oneself unexcelled in the world; extremely arrogant: 我讨厌他~的样子。*I dislike his air of extreme arrogance.*
【不客气】① impolite; rude: 李阿姨说了几句~的话后就走了。*Aunt Li made some rude remarks and then left.*
【不快】① be unhappy; be displease; be in low spirits ② be indisposed; feel under the weather; be out of sorts
【不愧】be worthy of; prove oneself to be; deserve the title of: 李医生~为人民的好医生。*Doctor Li is worthy of the people's good doctor.*
【不赖】[方] not bad; good; fine: 他的衣服~。*His clothes are not bad.*
【不劳而获】reap without sowing
【不理】ignore; refuse to acknowledge; pay no attention to
【不力】not exert oneself; be ineffective; incompetent
【不利】① unfavourable; harmful; disadvantageous ② unsuccessful: 出师~ *lose the first battle*
【不良】bad; harmful; unhealthy: 他有~的工作习惯。*He has undesirable work habit.*
【不料】unexpectedly; to one's surprise
【不留余地】leave no room; make no allowance
【不露声色】not show one's feelings, intentions, etc.
【不伦不类】neither fish nor fowl; nondescript: 他看起来像一个~的人。*He seems like a nondescripts.*
【不论】no matter (what, who, how, etc.); whether... or... ; regardless of
【不满】resentful; discontented; dissatisfied; unhappy
【不妙】not too encouraging; far from good; anything but reassuring: 他知道事情看起来~。*He knew things were none too encouraging.*
【不明】① unknown; not clear: 自从去年他离开以后就下落~了。*Since he left last year, his whereabouts was unknown.* ② fail to understand: ~事理 *lack common sense; be unreasonable*
【不明不白】obscure; doubtful; dubious; unclear: 我必须解释清楚,不能这样~地离开。*I must explain it to you; I can't leave unclearly.*
【不谋而合】agree without prior consultation; happen to hold the same view
【不能】cannot; must not; should not: 我们~把钥匙给你。*We can't give the keys to you.*
【不怕】not fear; not be afraid of: 不要对着我们大喊,我们~你。*Don't shout at us; we are not afraid of you.*
【不配】① be unworthy of; be unqualified for; not deserve: 你~当一名教师。*You are unqualified for a teacher.* ② not match: 你们俩彼此~。*You are not a well-matched pair with each other.*
【不偏不倚】even-handed; impartial; unbiased
【不平】① uneven; wrong; not smooth: 一群孩子们经过了崎岖~的山路来到了一个小村庄。*The group of children passed rugged mountain path and came to a small village.* ② injustice; unfairness ③ indignant; resentful
【不平衡】disequilibrium; imbalance: 在中国农业和工业发展~。*There is the disequilibrium between the development of industry and agriculture in China.*
【不期而遇】meet unexpectedly; meet by chance; have a chance encounter
【不起眼】negligible; unimportant; ordinary; not be noticeable; not be attractive: 我们不能相信那个~的老人是一位将军。*We can't believe that the ordinary old man is a capital.*
【不巧】unfortunately; as luck would have it
【不切实际】unrealistic; unpractical; impracticable: 他总是有一些~的想法。*He always has some impracticable ideas.*
【不求甚解】not seek to understand things thoroughly; be content with a superficial understanding
【不屈】unyielding; unbending: 英勇~ *valiant and unyielding*
【不然】① not so: 他看起来很诚实,其实~。*He looks very honest, but actually this is not so.* ② (used at the beginning of a sentence to express disagreement) no ③ or else; otherwise; if not
【不仁】① heartless; no benevolent: ~不义 *show no benevolence* ② numb; benumbed: 麻木~ *apathetic*
【不忍】cannot bear
【不容】not tolerate; not allow; not brook: 其中一名罪犯说出了~否定的事实。*One of the criminals said out the undeniable fact.*
【不容置疑】beyond doubt; allow of no doubt

【不如】not equal to; would be better; not as good as; inferior

【不善】① bad; evil; ill:来者~。*Those who came might not be motivated by friendship.* ② not good at; quite impressive

【不声不响】secretly; quietly:她~地走开了。*She went away quietly.*

【不胜】① cannot stand; cannot bear; be unequal to:他太累了,感觉体力有点~。*He was too tired and physically unequal to the task.* ② used between two identical verbs to indicate difficulty:防~防 *cannot avoid (danger, mistake, etc.) in all cases* ③ very; extremely; deeply ④ less than; worse than

【不失时机】lose no time; seize the opportune moment; not let the opportunity slip:那个小伙子~地和那位漂亮的姑娘说上几句话。*The young fellow seized the opportune moment to talk with the pretty lady.*

【不时】① frequently; from time to time; often ② at any time; at an unexpected moment

【不是】fault; blame:你不要抱怨我,这是你的~。*You don't complain about me; it's your fault.*

【不适】out of sorts; indisposed; not well

【不爽】① not well; out of sorts; in bad mood:她的话令我感到很~。*Her words made me in bad mood.* ② accurate; without discrepancy

【不速之客】gatecrasher; uninvited guest; unexpected visitor

【不同】distinct; different; not alike

【不同凡响】outstanding; out of the ordinary; out of the common run:他的父亲是一位~的将军。*His father is an outstanding capital.*

【不痛不痒】superficial; perfunctory; scratching the surface

【不妥】not proper; inappropriate:不去上学,恐怕有些~。*I'm afraid it isn't the proper way to not go to school.*

【不畏】be unafraid; defy

【不闻不问】take no notice of; not bother to ask; show no interest in sth; be indifferent to sth

【不问】① pay no attention to; disregard; ignore:~事情的是非曲直,她就对我大嚷。*She shouted at me without looking into the rights and wrongs of the case.*

【不务正业】① not do decent work; not live by honest labour ② ignore one's proper occupation; not attend to one's proper duties.

【不惜】not stint; not spare; not scruple:要~一切代价寻找那群丢失的孩子们。*We will look for the losing children at all costs.*

【不限】without limit; unrestricted

【不相称】unsuited; unmatched

【不详】not quite clear:那个孩子的身世~。*Little is known about the little child.*

【不像话】① absurd; unreasonable ② outrageous; scandalous; shocking

【不像样】① in no shape to be seen; not fit to to be seen; unpresentable ② (used as a complement after) beyond recognition:他的书包破得~。*His bag worn to shreds.*

【不孝】be unfilial; act contrary to filial piety

【不屑】think sth not worth doing; disdain to do sth; feel it beneath one's dignity to do sth

【不谢】don't mention it; not at all; you are welcome

【不懈】untiring; unremitting; indefatigable:坚持~ *persevere unremittingly*

【不兴】① outdated; outmoded; out of fashioning ② not allowed ③ (used only in rhetorical questions) can't

【不行】① be out of the question; be out allowed; be not permissible ② not be equal to; not work ③ dying ④ be no good ⑤ used as a complement after 得 awfully; extremely; terribly:我累得~了。*I'm terribly tired.*

【不幸】① unfortunate; ill-fated; sad ② unfortunately ③ misfortune; bad luck; adversity

【不修边幅】be slovenly; be untidy; not care about one's appearance

【不朽】eternal; immortal:革命先烈们创建了~的功绩。*The heroes of the revolution created enduring achievements.*

【不许】① not allow; not permit; must not ② can't; couldn't

【不言而喻】it goes without saying; it is self-evident

【不厌其烦】take great pains; be very patient; not mind taking all the trouble

【不要】don't: ~离开我。*Don't leave me alone.*

【不要紧】① it doesn't matter; not be serious; be of no importance: ~,我会陪你一块走。*It doesn't matter for I will go with you.* ② it looks all right... but...; it does not seen serious... but...

【不要脸】shameless; brazen; have no sense of shame

【不一样】of different kinds

【不宜】inadvisable; inappropriate; not suitable:少儿~ (*of movies, books, etc.*) *not fit for children; X-class*

【不遗余力】do one's utmost; spare no effort; do sth to the best of one's ability

【不义之财】dishonest gains; undeserved wealth

【不亦乐乎】① (used as a complement after 得) extremely; awfully ② isn't it a great pleasure:有朋自远方来,~? *Is it not a great pleasure to have friends coming from afar?*

【不翼而飞】① spread fast; spread like wildfire ② disappear unexpectedly

【不由自主】involuntarily; can't help; can hardly prevent

【不育症】【医】barrenness; sterility

【不远千里】might light of travel in a thousand Li; go to the trouble of travelling long distances; make light of travelling from afar

【不约而同】think the same without prior consultation; take identical action or share identical views without previous consultation

【不在】① not be in; be absent:他~家。*He is not at home.* ② die; be dead:李老师~了,留下了妻子和孩子。*Teacher Li died and left his wife and children.*

【不在意】① pay no attention to; take no notice of; ② not mind

【不择手段】unscrupulously; by fair means or foul; by hook or by crook:我是他唯一的姐姐,他却~地骗我。*I am his only sister, but he cheats me by unscrupulous.*

【不争气】disappoint one's hopes; fail to live up to expectations; by disappointing

【不正之风】evil social practices; unhealthy tendency; malpractice

【不知不觉】unconsciously; unwittingly; without one's being aware of it

【不知所措】not know what to do; be at a loss; be at one's wits' end:看到这么多钱,她~了。*Looking at so much money, she didn't know what to do.*

【不知所云】not understand what sb is driving it; not know what sb is talking about

【不值】not worth:我所做的~的一提。*What I have done is not worth mentioning.*

【不止】more than; not limited to; without end

【不至于】cannot go so far; be unlikely

【不置可否】hedge; be noncommittal; not express an opinion; decline to comment:我问你的意见呢,你不能~。*I am asking your opinion; you can't evade the issue.*

【不中用】useless; no good; unfit for anything

【不周】thoughtless; not attentive and satisfactory:招待~ *not be attentive enough to guests*

【不准】not allow; forbid; prohibit: ~吸烟。*No smoking!*

【不自量力】overrate one's own abilities; overreach oneself; not have a proper measure of oneself

【不足】① insufficient; inadequate; not enough ② should not

【不足轻重】worthless; negligible

【不足为奇】nothing to be surprised at

【不足与谋】not worth consulting with

【不做声】keep silent; not say a word:面对那个问题,他就是~。*The teacher asked him for a while; he didn't say a word at the questions.*

布 ① cotton cloth ② cloth

【布帛】cloth and silk; cotton and silk textiles

【布达拉宫】the Potala (the former palace of the Dalai Lamas, in Lhasa, Xizang)

【布达佩斯】Budapest, capital of Hungary

【布道】preach the Gospel; evangelize

【布丁】pudding

【布告】① notice; bulletin:同学们帮助他贴了很多~。*The students helped him put up lots of notice.* ② proclaim; announce in a bulletin

【布景】scenery; setting

【布局】① layout; distribution:城市~ *the layout of a city* ② composition (of a picture, piece of writing, etc.) ③ position; opening moves

【布施】【宗】alms giving; charities

【布娃娃】cloth doll; doll made of cloth:女儿生日时我送她一个~。*I gave my daughter a cloth doll for her birthday.*

【布鞋】cloth shoe

【布衣】① cotton clothes ②[古] commoner

【布置】① fix up; tidy up; arrange:房间由她来~。*She will arrange the room.* ② assign; give instructions about

步 ① step; pace:这里离教室只有几~路。*There are only a few steps away from the classroom.* ② stage; step:工作要一~一~地做。*The work should be done step by step.* ③ condition; situation; state:事情发展到这一~不容易。*It was gotten into such a state.* ④ walk; go on foot: ~入车站 *walk into the bus station*

【步兵】① infantry; foot ② infantryman; foot soldier

【步步】step by step; at every step :敌人~~逼进。*The enemies pressed forward steadily.*

【步步退让】incessant retreats

【步步登高】ascend step by step; rise steadily in one's career

【步步高升】gradually rise to eminence

【步步为营】advance gradually and dig in at every step; consolidate at every step; act cautiously

【步测】measure by paces; pace out

【步调】pace; step: ~一致 *march in step; keep in step; act in union*

【步伐】step; pace: ~整齐 *keep perfect formation; (march) in steps*

【步法】footwork (in dancing, sports, etc.)

【步犁】walking plough

【步履蹒跚】walk haltingly; hobble along

【步履维艰】have difficulty walking; walk with difficulty

【步枪】rifle

【步人后尘】follow in sb's footsteps

【步哨】sentry; sentinel

【步行】go on foot; walk

【步韵】use the rhyme sequence of a poem (when replying to it)

【步骤】step; measure; move

【步子】step; pace

部 ① part; section; division; region:中~ *central part* /内~ *inside* /外~ *outside* ② unit; department; ministry; board:农业~ *the ministry of agriculture* /收购~ *purchasing department* ③ headquarters:海军司令~ *headquarters of the navy* ④ troops:战斗~队 *fighting force* ⑤ command ⑥[量] of movies, books, etc. ⑦[量] of machines or vehicles ⑧ (Bù) a surname

【部队】① army; armed forces ② troop; unit: ~番号 *code designation*

【部分】part; section; portion:这本书分成三个~。

The book is divided into three parts.

【部件】part; unit; subsystem; component

【部落】tribe: ~首长 *chieftain of a tribe* / ~首领 *tribal chief* / 古代印第安~的习俗非常奇特。*The customs of ancient Indian tribes are very strange.*

【部门】department; branch; class; section

【部属】① subordinate; troops under one's command ② affiliated to ministry

【部署】deploy; arrange; map out; lay out: 完成军队的巧妙~ *perfect a clever disposition of troops*

【部委】ministries and commissions: 国务院各~ *ministries and commissions under the State Council*

【部位】position; location; region; place

【部下】① troops under one's command ② subordinate

【部优】ministry-recognized quality product: ~产品 *high-quality products by ministry*; *ministry-graded quality product*

【部长】minister; head of a department: 财政~ *minister of finance* / 对外联络部~ *head of the International Liaison Department* / 司法~ *minister of justice* / 他是新任教育~。*He is the new minister of Education.*

埠 ① city; metropolis: 本~ *this city* / 外~ *other city* ② wharf; town or city with a port ③ [旧] trading port; port city

簿 book: 把公司的账~给我看一下。*Please give me the account book.*

【簿册】notebook

【簿记】① bookkeeping: ~员 *bookkeeper* / 复式~ *double-entry bookkeeping* ② check and register

【簿子】notebook; book

B

C

cā

擦 ① scratch; rub: ~胳膊 *scratch one's arm* / ~火柴 *strike a match* / ~眼镜 *rub one's glasses* /摩~起电或起热。*Friction generates heat or electricity.* ② wipe; towel: ~汗 *wipe the sweat* / ~地板 *mop the floor* / ~皮鞋 *shine shoes* ③ apply: ~药膏 *apply ointment* / ~唇膏 *apply lipstick* / ~粉 *powder one's face* ④ brush past; shake; touch lightly:燕子~着海面飞翔。*The swallow is shaving the sea level.* /他与她~肩而过。*He brushed past her.* ⑤ shred: ~土豆丝 *shred potatoes*

【擦边】near; close to:他六十~。*He is on the right side of sixty.*

【擦边球】【体】edge ball; touch ball (in table tennis)

【擦除】erase; scratch

【擦亮】scour; shine: ~铜像 *shine the bronze statue*

【擦亮眼睛】remove the scales from one's eyes; alert oneself; be vigilant:我们要~以防对手的花招。*We should sharpen our vigilance to guard against our opponent's tricks.*

【擦伤】scrape; abrasion; chafe; scratch

【擦洗】wipe dean; wash; dean (with water or alcohol, etc.): ~自行车 *clean one's bike*

cāi

猜 ① guess; conjecture; speculate: ~谜语是她的爱好。*Guessing riddles is her hobby.* ② suspect; doubt: 不要乱~疑。*Don't suspect groundless.*

【猜测】guess; conjecture; surmise:这只是~。*This is pure surmise.*

【猜度】surmise; conjecture:他在~事情的真相。*He is wondering the truth of the incident.*

【猜忌】be suspicious and jealous: ~使它们无法友好相处。*Suspicion and jealousy make them can't get along well.*

【猜谜儿】① guess a riddle ② guess:有话直说,我不想~。*Please come to the point straightly; I don't want to guess.*

【猜拳】play the finger-guessing game:喝酒~很有趣。*It is fun playing more while drinking.*

【猜透】guess correctly; see through; figure out:想~他的意图是很难的。*It's difficult to figure out his intention.*

【猜想】guess; suppose; suspect:他反复~她的暗示。*He keeps guessing her indication.*

【猜疑】be suspicious; be distrustful; have misgivings: ~破坏了他们的友谊。*Distrust undermined their friendship.*

【猜中】solve a riddle; guess right:只有他~了这个谜语。*He is the only one who sowed the riddle.*

cái

才[1] ① ability; capability; talent; gift:人~济济 *an abundance of capable people*; *a galaxy of talent* /德~兼备 *have both talent and political integrity* ② talent; a capable person:天~ *genius* ③ people of a certain type:奴~ *slave* /庸~ *mediocrity* ④ (Cái) a surname

才[2] ① a moment ago; just: ~上课。*The class has just begun.* ② indicate sth happens later than is expected:会议快结束了他~来。*He didn't appear until the meeting was ending.* ③ indicate sth happens only under certain conditions:只有好好学习,~能取得好成绩。*Good performance can only be achieved after hard work.* ④ indicate sth new has happened after an expression of reason or condition:经他解释之后,老师~明白争执的原因。*The teacher learned the reason of argument only after his explanation.* ⑤ used for emphatic assertion or contradiction (of ten followed by 呢 at the end of the sentence):我~不等呢。*I definitely won't wait.* /你以为他很善良? ~不是呢? *You think he is a kind guy? Not him!* ⑥ indicate that after comparison sth is small in amount or low in frequency:这条裙子~20 元。*The skirt costs only twenty yuan.* /我的外甥~3 岁,已经认识不少字了。*My nephew is merely three, and he has already learned quite a few words.*

【才分】inherent ability; talent: ~超群 *of outstanding talent*

【才赋】talent

【才干】ability; competence; talent:增长~ *enhance one's abilities* /老板很欣赏他的~。*The boss appreciates his capability very much.*

【才高八斗】be gifted with rare literary talents

【才华】literary or artistic talent; brilliance:她很有~。*She is highly gifted.*

【才华横溢】have superb talent; brim with talent
【才略】talent for scheming; ability and sagacity
【才貌】talent and beauty; talent and appearance: ~双全 *both talented and beautiful* / ~出众 *of outstanding talent and distinguished looks*
【才能】capability; endowment; talent; ability: 她有非凡的演说~。*She has remarkable talent of speech.*
【才女】gifted female; woman with a literary talent
【才气】literary talent
【才情】literary and artistic talent; imaginative power: 展示~ *demonstrate one's talent*
【才识】ability and insight: ~过人 *be endowed with remarkable talent and insight* / 弗兰克是一个有~的工程师。*Frank is an engineer with talent and insight.*
【才疏学浅】have little talent and learning
【才思】imaginative power; creativeness (in writing): ~敏捷 *have a facile imagination* / 他在写作上有~。*He is creative in writing.*
【才学】scholarship; erudition; talent and learning: 毛主席读书万卷~出众。*Chairman Mao had read volumes and was a remarkable scholar.* / 史密思先生在物理方面很有~。*Mr. Smith is very erudite in physics.*
【才艺】talent and skill
【才智】brilliance; ability and intelligence; ability and wisdom
【才子】gifted scholar: ~佳人 *genius and beauty* / 风流~ *a gallant young scholar*

材 ① timber: 钢~ *steel products; rolled steel* ② material: 教~ *teaching material* ③ coffin: 水晶棺~ *crystal coffin* ④ ability; tank; aptitude: 人~ *talents* ⑤ capable person: 长大成~ *grow into a talented person*
【材料】① material: 建筑~ *construction material* ② data; material: 档案~ *archival material* / 收集~ *gather material; collect detail* / 原始~ *original data* ③ makings; stall; ingredients: ~力学 *mechanics of materials* / ~科学 *material science* / 她是当教师的好~。*She has the makings of a teacher.*
【材质】texture; quality of material: 这台仪器要求特殊~。*The instrument requires special material quality.*

财 wealth; money: 爱~如命 *skin a flea for its hide; be crazy for money* / 守~奴 *miser*
【财宝】money and valuables
【财帛】wealth; money; money and silk (often used as gifts)
【财产】property: 保护生命~ *protect the life and property* / 国家~ *state property* / 公共~ *public property* / 私有~ *private property* / ~关系 *property relation* / ~估价 *property assessment* / ~继承 *inheritance of property* / ~清理 *property inspection* / ~损失 *property damage* / ~债券 *property bond* / ~转让 *transfer of property*
【财大气粗】he who own money speaks louder than others; wealth breeds arrogance
【财阀】magnate; tycoon; plutocrat
【财富】wealth; riches: 物质~ *material wealth* / 精神~ *intellectual wealth* / 文化~ *cultural wealth* / 劳动创造~。*Labour creates wealth.*
【财经】finance and economy: ~学校 *colleges of finance and economics* / 完善~体制 *consummate the financial and economic system* / ~纪律 *financial and economic discipline* / ~报道 *a report on finance and economics*
【财会】finance and accounting: ~专业 *the major of finance and accounting*
【财力】financial resources (or power): ~雄厚 *have abundant financial resources* / 由于~不足，工厂暂停。*Without sufficient financial resources, the factory stopped running temporarily.*
【财粮】money and grain: ~供应 *the supply of money and grain*
【财路】approaches to acquire wealth: 广开~ *open all possible avenues for wealth*
【财贸】finance and trade: ~部门 *the department of finance and trade* / ~专业 *the major of finance and trade*
【财迷】moneygrubber; miser: 出了名的~ *notorious miser* / ~心窍 *money-grubbing; mad about making money*
【财权】① right of property; ownership of property ② control over wealth; economic right; financial power: 掌管~ *control over financial matters*
【财神】God of Wealth; extremely rich person; person or institution in charge of financial matters: 在庙里敬~ *salute the God of Wealth in the temple*
【财势】wealth and power: 追求~ *pursue wealth and power* / 这个老板有~。*He is a boss with wealth and power.*
【财税】finance and taxation: ~制度 *financial and taxation system* / 整顿~秩序 *rectify the orders of finance and taxation*
【财团】financial group; consortium: 金融~ *financial consortium*
【财务】financial affairs: ~报表 *financial reporting; financial (statement)* / ~管理 *financial administration* / ~往来 *financial transaction* / ~监督 *financial supervision* / ~科 *financial section* / ~自主 *financial autonomy* / ~制度 *financial system* / ~总监 *Chief Financial Officer (CFO)*
【财物】property; belonging: 爱护公共~ *protect public property* / 个人~ *personal property; personal effects*
【财源】financial resources; source of revenue: ~滚滚 *be abundant in financial resources*
【财运】luck in money matters: ~亨通 *run of good luck in making money* / ~不佳 *be unlucky in making money*
【财政】public finance: ~部 *ministry of finance* / ~收支平衡 *balance of revenue and expenditure* / ~赤字 *financial deficits* / ~拨款 *budgetary appropriations* / ~补贴 *financial subsidy* / ~机关 *fi-*

nancial institution / ~年度 *financial year*

【财主】[旧] rich man; moneybags

裁 ① cut (paper, cloth, etc.) into parts:量体~衣 *cut the garment according to the figure; act according to actual situation* / ~纸条儿 *cut paper into strips* / ~开包裹 *cut the package open* ② cut; reduce; dismiss: ~减经费 *reduce the budget* /这家企业最近~了几人。*The enterprise dismissed several people recently.* ③ judge; decide; determine: 仲~ *arbitrate* ④ control; check; sanction: 制~ *sanction* ⑤ type of writing: 小说体~ *style of the novel* ⑥ mental planning; selection: 别出心~ *try a different idea*

【裁并】cut down and merge: ~机构 *abolish or merge organizations*

【裁撤】dissolve; disband: 公司~了两个科室。*The company has disowned two offices.*

【裁处】judge and decide; consider and handle; decide and deal with: 短时间内这事很难~。*This matter is difficult to settle in short time.*

【裁定】rule; adjudicate: 法官~该发言人证词无效。*The judge ruled the speaker's testimony was invalid.*

【裁断】consider and decide: 慎作~ *consider it over before deciding*

【裁夺】consider and decide: 由经理~此事该如何处理。*It is up to the manager to determine how to handle the problem.*

【裁度】[书] surmise; guess; judge: 他的话很模糊,不好~。*What he said is too ambiguous to catch the point.*

【裁缝】tailor; dressmaker

【裁减】reduce; trim; cut down; lay off: ~线条 *trim the lone* / ~军备 *reduce armaments* / ~人类 *lay off the staff* / ~支出 *cut down the expenditure*

【裁剪】cut out

【裁决】adjudicate; rule: 依法~ *adjudicate according to law*

【裁军】disarmament; reduce armament: ~会议 *disarmament conference*

【裁判】①【律】judge ②【体】referee; umpire: 足球赛~员 *the referee of the football match*

【裁员】reduce staff; cut down: 为减少开支,公司决定~。*To cut down the expenditure, the company decided to reduce the staff.*

【裁纸机】trimmer; paper cutter

【裁制】① sanction; punish ② restrain; check ③ cut and sew; make a dress

cǎi

采[1] ① pick; gather; pluck: ~药 *pick medicinal herbs* / ~蘑菇 *gather mushrooms* ② mine; extract: 开~石油 *extract petroleum* ③ select; choose; adopt: ~取行动 *adopt actions*

采[2] spirit; complexion: 神~飞扬 *be in high spirits* /无精打~ *be depressed; be dispirited* /半~ *elegant manner*

【采办】purchase; stock up: ~学习用品 *purchase article for study* / ~年货 *purchase goods for the Spring Festival*

【采编】gather and edit: 新闻~ *news coverage and editing* /报社~人员 *staff writers of the newspaper office*

【采场】【矿】stope: 露天~ *opencast stope; outdoors stope*

【采伐】out down; fell; cut timber; log

【采访】cover; interview; gather news; hunt for materials: ~知名教授 *interview a famous professor* / ~开会情况 *cover a conference*

【采风】collect folk songs

【采购】choose and purchase: ~仪器 *purchase instruments* / ~团 *purchasing mission* / ~员 *payer; purchasing agent* / ~站 *purchasing station*

【采光】【建】get light; daylighting: ~系数 *light coefficient* / ~井 *light well*

【采集】collect; gather: ~标本 *collect specimens* / ~数据 *collect data*

【采掘】dig up; excavate: ~设备 *equipment for excavation*

【采矿】mining: ~工业 *mining industry* / ~工人 *mining worker*

【采录】collect and record: ~民歌 *collect and record folksongs* / ~地方戏曲 *collect and record local operas*

【采买】① buy; purchase: ~日常用品 *purchase articles for daily use* ② purchaser buyer

【采煤】coal mining; coal extraction; coal cutting: ~机 *coal mining machine* / ~工作面 *coal face*

【采纳】accept; adopt: ~合理建议 *accept rationalization recommendations*

【采暖】heating: ~设备 *heating facilities* / ~和通风 *heating and ventilation*

【采取】take; adopt; carry out; assume: ~防守措施 *carry out defensive measures* / ~具体行动 *take concrete action*

【采石】【建】quarry: ~场 *quarry; stone-pit*

【采收】pick; gather

【采撷】[书] ① pick; pluck: ~奇花异草 *pluck exotic flowers and grass* ② gather; collect

【采血】【医】blood-taking; blood collection: ~检验 *take some blood for examination*

【采样】①【建】sampling ② sample; spot-check: 我们要学统计学,就必须知道如何~。*We have to know how to spot-check when we learn statistics.*

【采用】employ; adopt; use: ~科学方法 *adopt scientific methods* / ~新工艺 *adopt new technology*

【采择】select and choose; select and adopt: ~最佳方案 *select and adopt the optimum plan*

【采摘】pick; pluck: ~茶叶 *pick tea leaves*

【采种】【农】seed collecting

彩 ① colour: 五~缤纷 *blazing rich colour* ② variety; brilliance; splendor: 精~的表演 *a brilliant performance* / 丰富多~ *rich and colourful* ③ applaud; cheer: 喝倒~ *make catcalls* ④ prize：中～ *win a prize* ⑤ blood from wound：挂～ *be wounded* ⑥ colored silk；variegated silk：张灯结～ *decorate with lanterns and streamers*

【彩笔】colour pencil；crayon

【彩车】float（in a parade）；ornamented car

【彩绸】coloured silk

【彩带】coloured ribbon

【彩蛋】① painted eggshells ② preserved gee

【彩灯】colourful lantern；colourful lights；lampion

【彩电】colour television；colourcast；colour TV sat

【彩虹】rainbow

【彩绘】coloured drawing or pattern：人体～ *coloured drawing on body* / ～陶瓷 *ceramics decorated with coloured drawings*

【彩卷】colour film

【彩礼】betrothal gifts：送～ *present betrothal gifts* / 拒收～ *refuse betrothal gifts*

【彩练】coloured ribbon

【彩排】dress rehearsal：开幕式～ *the dress rehearsal of the opening ceremony* / 演出～ *the dress rehearsal of the performance*

【彩棚】decorated tent；colourful tent

【彩票】lottery ticket

【彩旗】coloured flag；bunting；coloured banner

【彩球】① colour balloon ② coloured silk ball

【彩色】multicolour；variegation；colour：～玻璃 *stained glass*

【彩云】rosy clouds；pink clouds

【彩照】colour photo

【彩纸】① coloured paper ② colour photographic paper

睬 pay attention to；take notice of：不要理～他的甜言蜜语。*Don't pay attention to his honeyed words.*

踩 ① step on；trample：～高跷 *walk on stilts* / 不要～踏庄稼。*Don't tread on the crops.* / 不要～草坪。*Don't step on lawn.* ② belittle；disdain；trample on：他喜欢吹捧自己而～低别人。*He likes flattering himself while disdaining other's.*

【踩灭】tread out：～引爆装置 *tread out the ignitor* /请～烟头。*Please tread out the end of cigarette.*

【踩线】step on line；foot-fault

【踩油】step on the gas

【踩闸】step on the brake

cài

菜 ① vegetable；greens：～汤 *vegetable soup* / 泡～ *pickled vegetables*；*pickles* ② food；rape ③ dish；course：荤～ *meat dishes* / 素～ *vegetable dishes* ④ wild herbs：靠糠～度日 *live on chaff and wild herbs*

【菜板】chopping board

【菜帮子】outer leaves

【菜单】menu；bill of fare

【菜刀】kitchen knife；chopper

【菜地】vegetable plot

【菜墩子】chopping block

【菜瓜】snake melon

【菜花】① cauliflower ② rape flower

【菜窖】vegetable cellar；clamp

【菜篮子】①vegetable basket ②non-staple-food supply

【菜农】vegetable grower；truck farmer

【菜圃】vegetable plot；vegetable garden

【菜谱】① menu；bill of fare：请把～递给我。*Please give me the menu.* ② cookery-book；cookbook ③ recipe

【菜畦】vegetable bed；small sections of a vegetable plot

【菜青】dark greyish green：脸色～ *dull greenish complexion*

【菜色】look famished；be pallid for the sake of hunger：脸呈～ *look famished* / 那家人因缺乏足够食物而脸色～。*The family looked famished for lack of enough food.*

【菜市】food market

【菜摊】vegetable stall

【菜系】style of cooking

【菜心】heart（of a cabbage, etc.）

【菜肴】cooked dishes：美味～ *delicious cooked food* / 这些～都是胡萝卜做的。*All of the cooked dishes were made of carrots.*

【菜油】rape oil；rapeseed oil

【菜园】vegetable garden：他正在～里看书。*He is reading books in the vegetable garden.*

【菜籽】① vegetable seeds ② rapeseed：～饼 *rapeseed cake* / ～油 *colza oil*；*rape oil*

cān

参[1] ① join；take part in；enter；participate：～军 *join the army* ② refer；consult：相互～照 *cross reference*

参[2] call to pay one's respects；pay warship to

参[3] impeach sb before the emperor：在皇帝面前～丞相一本 *impeach the prime minister before the emperor*

see also cēn；shēn

【参拜】pay homage to；pay respect to：～国王 *pay respect to the king* / ～黄帝陵 *pay homage to Mausoleum of the Yellow Emperor*

【参半】half；half-and-half；fifty-fifty：喜忧～ *half delighted, half worried*

【参变量】【数】parameter

【参禅】（Buddhist）sit in deep meditation for penetration of truth：～悟道 *sit there attentively meditating in order to arrive at the realm of truth*

【参股】purchase shares；become a shareholder in enterprises

【参观】visit；tour；have a look around：～名胜古迹 *have tours to interesting places and historical spots*

/ ~团 *visiting group*; *tour group* / ~日程 *schedule of a visit* /欢迎~。*Visitors are welcome.*
【参劾】[书] impeach
【参加】① join; attend; take part in; participate in: ~会议 *attend a meeting* / ~考试 *take an examination* / ~社交活动 *take part in social activities* / ~文学协会 *join the literary association* ② give (advice, suggestion, etc.):这项技术如何推广,请你~意见。*Please give your view about how to popularize the technology.*
【参见】① see also; refer also to; cf.: ~第三章 *see chapter Three* ② pay one's respects to (a superior, etc.): ~公主 *pay respects to the princess*
【参军】join the army; enlist:他感觉~很光荣。*He feels that it's very honourable to join the army.*
【参看】① see also ② consult; read sth for reference:为写这篇论文,他~很多书籍。*To write the paper, he consulted many books.*
【参考】① consult; refer to: ~相关资料 *consult relevant data* ② reference; information: ~手册 *reference manual* / ~书 *reference book* / ~书目 *bibliography*; *list of reference book* / ~资料 *reference material* / ~文献 *reference literature* /仅供~。*For reference only.*
【参量】【数】parameter: ~变化 *parametric variation*
【参谋】① staff officer: ~长 *chief of staff* ② give advice; advise; serve as an adviser:这件事你给我~~如何做好。*Please give me your advice about how to do this thing.*
【参评】be sent in for public appraisal or competitive selection: ~作品 *works nominated for appraisal and selection* / 这部小说是~作品之一。*The novel is one of the works sent in for public appraisal.*
【参赛】take part in a match; enter competition: ~选手 *contestant*; *athletes for a match*
【参试】① take part in an experiment: ~科研人员 *scientific research personnel who take part in the experiment* ② take or sit for an exam:报名~ *sign up for the exam*
【参数】【数】parameter:分布~ *parameter of distribution* / ~方程 *a parametric equation*
【参天】reaching to sky; tower; very tall
【参谒】[书] ① pay homage to sb (before his tomb) ② a superior
【参选】① enter into an election contest; run in an election: ~的政界头面人物 *prominent political figures running in the election* ② enter a contest for public appraisal: ~作品 *works entered for appraisal and selection (in a contest)*
【参议】①[书] participate in policy making discussion: ~国事 *take part in the deliberation of state affairs* ② advise; counsel: ~员 *senator* / ~院 *senate*
【参与】participate in; have a hand in; involve oneself in: ~某事 *have a hand in the matter* / ~制订方案 *participate in the establishment of a blue print*
【参阅】consult; see also; refer to
【参赞】① counsellor:商务~ *commercial counsellor* / 农业~ *agricultural counsellor* ②[书] act as an adviser
【参展】participate in an exhibition; supply exhibits for an exhibition: ~作品 *works on display (at an exhibition)* / ~单位 *units participating in the exhibition*
【参战】enter a war; take part in a battle; participate a warfare: ~国 *belligerent state* / 这场战争有六个国家~。*Six countries were involved in the war.*
【参照】consult; refer to: ~经验 *refer to experience* / ~物 *object of reference*
【参政】participate in politics: ~议政 *participate in the deliberation and administration of state affairs* / ~党 *participating party* / 每个公民都有~的权利。*Every citizen has the right participating in politics.*
【参酌】consider (a matter) according to the actual conditions; deliberate:再三~,他们才决定执行计划。*They decided to carry out the plan after much deliberation.*

餐 ① eat:聚~ *dine together*; *have a dinner party* ② food; meal:中~ *Chinese food* /西~ *western food* /快~ *snack* ③[量](for meals):一日三~ *three meals a day*
【餐布】table linen
【餐车】dining car; diner; restaurant car:公园里有~。*There are dining cars in the park.*
【餐馆】eatery; restaurant; cookshop: ~文化 *restaurant culture* / ~老板 *restaurateur*
【餐巾】dinner cloth; table napkin: ~纸 *napkin paper*; *serviette*
【餐具】tableware; dinner service; mess kit: ~柜 *buffet*; *cupboard*; *sideboard*
【餐盘】① meal tray ② dinner plate
【餐券】meal ticket; meal coupon
【餐室】dining room; cenacle
【餐位】seats in a restaurant
【餐饮】food and drink:免费~ *free food and drinks* / ~业 *catering (trade)*
【餐桌】dining table

cán

残 ① incomplete; deficient; disabled:老弱病~ *the old, weak, sick and disabled* / ~缺的课本 *incomplete textbooks* ② remaining; remnant:风卷~云 *strong wind scattering wisps of clouds*; *make a clean sweep of sth* ③ savage; ferocious; cruel; barbarous:凶~成性 *be cruel by nature* ④ injure; damage:摧~ *beat cruelly* /身~志坚 *deformed health but adamant will*
【残败】incomplete; dilapidated; decrepit: ~不堪 *thoroughly defaced*; *be damaged beyond recognition*

【残暴】ruthless; brutal; cruel and ferocious; savage: ~统治 *ruthless rule* / 他是一个~的人。*He is a brutal person.*

【残杯冷炙】remains of a meal; leftovers: 做人要有气节,不能靠别人施舍的~生活。*A man should have a sense of dignity; he should not live on others leftovers.*

【残兵败将】remnants of a defeated army: 收拾~ *regroup the remnants of the army*

【残喘】dying breath; last gasps (of dying person): 苟延~ *be at one's last gasp* / 敌人只能~一时。*The enemies were at their last gasps.*

【残次】imperfect; defective; substandard: ~品 *defective product; wastrel* / 这台洗衣机有~。*The washing machine is a defective product.*

【残存】remain; remain; survive: ~物 *survivor*

【残废】① crippled; disabled; hand; capped; invalid: 他身体~了。*He has been disabled.* ② cripple; disabled person: 一场车祸使他成了~。*A traffic accident made him a disabled man.*

【残骸】remains; wreckage; wreck; debris: 失事飞机~ *the wreck of a crashed plane* / 敌舰的~ *the wrecks of the enemy warships*

【残害】cruelly injure or kill; slaughter: ~无辜百姓 *slaughter innocent civilians* / ~忠良 *mercilessly persecute loyal and upright persons*

【残花败柳】faded flowers and withered willows — fallen female

【残货】shopworn goods; damaged or substandard goods: 甩卖~ *dump substandard goods*

【残迹】indistinct vestige; remaining trace: ~犹存。*Faint traces are still visible.*

【残疾】deformity; handicap: ~人 *the handicapped*

【残旧】broken and shabby; dilapidated

【残局】① the final phase of a game of chess ② the situation after a failure: 收拾~ *clear up the mess; pick up the pieces*

【残酷】cruel; brutal; ruthless: ~折磨 *excruciate atrociously* / 勇敢面对~的现实 *bravely confront the harsh reality*

【残留】remain; be left over

【残年】① evening of life; declining years: 这位老人已是风烛~。*The old man is like a candle in the wind.* ② last days of the year

【残品】damaged article; defective goods

【残破】broken; dilapidated; shabby: ~的家具 *dilapidated furniture* / ~的书 *a broken book*

【残缺】incomplete; fragmentary; with parts missing: ~的字典 *incomplete dictionary*

【残忍】cruel; ruthless: ~的天性 *cruel nature*

【残杀】murder; massacre; slaughter: 自相~ *mutual slaughter*

【残生】① one's remaining years: 了结~ *put one's remaining life to an end* ② one's miserable life

【残损】be damaged; broken: 减少运输途中~商品 *reduce damaging goods in transit*

【残阳】the setting sun

【残余】remnants; remains; vestiges; survivals; stub; rump: 封建~ *feudal vestiges* / ~的雪茄烟蒂 *the stub of a cigar*

【残月】① waning moon; crescent moon ② setting moon: 晓风~ *breezes at dawn and the fading moon*

【残渣】residue; dregs; garbage

【残照】setting sun; evening glow: 天边一抹~给大山披上了神奇的色彩。*The trace of evening glow on the horizon wrapped around the mountain with a fantastic colour.*

蚕 silkworm: 养~ *raise silkworms*

【蚕豆】broad bean; horsebean

【蚕茧】silkworm cocoon; pod

【蚕农】silkworm raiser

【蚕桑】growing mulberry and breeding silkworms (as an industry)

【蚕食】nibble: ~政策 *nibbling policy*

【蚕丝】natural silk; silk: ~蛋白 *fibroin*

【蚕叶】mulberry leaves

【蚕蛹】silkworm chrysalis

【蚕子】silkworm seed; silkworm egg

惭 feel ashamed: 自~形秽 *feel unworthy; have a sense of inferiority* / 大言不~ *be shamelessly boastful*

【惭愧】be ashamed of: 对你照顾不够,我深感~。*I feel ashamed very much for not caring you enough.*

【惭色】[书] ashamed countenance; guilty expression: 面带~ *look ashamed*

cǎn

惨 ① miserable; pitiful; tragic: 悲~遭遇 *a miserable experience* / 悲~的事故 *a sorrowful accident* / ~不忍睹 *be too horrifying to look at* ② savage; merciless: ~遭杀害 *be murdered brutally* ③ to a serious degree; disastrously; terribly: 累~了 *terribly tired*

【惨案】① massacre: 流血~ *bloody massacre* ② disaster; tragedy

【惨白】deathly pale; ghastly: 面容~ *deathly pale countenance*

【惨败】suffer crushing defeat; smashup: 险遭~ *narrowly elude a disastrous defeat*

【惨变】① horrible change; disastrous turn of events ② (complexion) change greatly due to fear, sorrow, etc.: 听到这一消息,他脸色~。*Hearing the news, his face turned horribly pale.*

【惨不忍睹】too horrified to look at

【惨淡】① gloomy; dismal; bleak: ~灯光 *dim lamp light* ② dreary; desolate; depressed: 神情~ *depressed look* / 生意~ *dull business; slack trade* ③ take great pains; laborious

【惨毒】vicious; brutal; merciless: 心肠~ *cold-blooded heart*

【惨祸】horrible disaster; frightful calamity: 轮船失

事,造成重大~。*The shipwreck caused a horrible disaster.*

【惨叫】heart-rending shriek

【惨境】dire straits; miserable condition; wretched plight:接连不断的灾祸使他陷入了~。*The disasters came one after another, which made him in hopeless light.*

【惨剧】tragedy; calamity; a dreadful; fatal event

【惨绝人寰】extremely tragic; catastrophic; exceedingly brutal:~的大屠杀 *catastrophic massacre* / ~暴行 *most atrocious brutalities*

【惨厉】miserable; desolate; sorrowful:~哭声 *heart-breaking cry* / ~的嘶鸣 *sorrowful neighing*

【惨烈】① miserable; tragic:~的场面 *miserable scene* ② heroic:~牺牲 *sacrifice heroically* ③violent; fierce; horrible:~的战斗 *a fierce battle*

【惨然】saddened; grieved:她的~一笑让他心碎。*Her grieved smile made his heart break.*

【惨杀】murder; massacre; slaughter

【惨死】die tragically:他~在敌人的刀下。*He died tragically under the enemy's whittle.*

【惨痛】deeply grieved; painful; bitter:~的教训 *a bitter lesson*

【惨无人道】very cruel and inhuman; brutal barbarous:~迫害 *inhuman persecution*

【惨遭不测】die an unexpected death; meet a miserable end:他在飞机失事中~。*He died tragically in the plane wreck.*

【惨重】grievous; disastrous; heavy:~的代价 *a grievous cost* /损失~ *suffer heavy losses* /伤之~ *suffer disastrous casualties*

【惨状】miserable condition; pitiful sight:空难现场的~使人目不忍睹。*The scene of the air crash was too dreadful to look at.*

càn

灿 bright; splendid; dazzling:金~~的油菜花 *bright-golden rape flowers*

【灿烂】magnificent; splendid; resplendent; brilliant; refulgent:星光~ *brightly shining stars light* /光辉~的成就 *magnificent achievements* / ~的前程 *brilliant future* / ~民族文化 *refulgent national culture*

【灿然】bright; brilliant; beaming:~微笑 *smile brilliantly* / ~的阳光使人心情舒畅。*The bright sun makes us happy.*

cāng

仓 storehouse; warehouse:粮食满~。*The granary is full of grain.*

【仓储】keep in storehouse

【仓促】hastily; hurriedly; suddenly:~应战 *accept battle in haste* /不要~下结论。*Don't jump to conclusions.* /时间~,我准备的不够充分。*I didn't prepare sufficiently due to the pressing time.*

【仓皇】in a flurry; in panic:~逃窜 *flee in a flurry; flee in confusion* / ~退却 *retreat in panic*

【仓皇失措】be scared out of one's wits; get into a panic:面对危急情况,最重要的是不要~。*Don't panic when faced with emergent danger — that's the big thing.*

【仓库】warehouse; storehouse; storage; depositary; depot:~保管员 *warehouseman* /清理~ *check warehouse stocks*

苍 ① blue; green:白发~~ *hoary-haired; greyhaired* / ~松翠柏 *verdant pines and cypresses* ②gray; ashy ③[书] heaven; sky:上~ *heaven overhead* ④(Cāng) a surname

【苍白】① pale; pallid; wan② feeble; weak; insufficient:她的论据~无力。*Her argument is feeble.*

【苍苍】① gray; ashen:白发~ *hoary-haired* ② deep blue:天~,野茫茫。*The shy is dark blue and the prairie is boundless.* ③ luxuriant; vast and hazy; boundless

【苍翠】dark green; verdant:~的山峦 *verdant mountains*

【苍劲】① old and strong; old and hardy:~的古柏 *the old and hardy pines* ② vigorous; bold:他的书法~有力。*His hand writing is vigorous and forceful.*

【苍老】① old; aged:这场灾难使他一夜之间~了许多。*The disaster made him aged overnight.* ② vigorous; forceful

【苍凉】desolate; bleak:月色~ *melancholy moonlight*

【苍茫】① vast; boundless:~的大海 *vast ocean* / ~大地 *boundless land* ② indistinct:夜色~。*Gathering dusk extends far into the distance.*

【苍生】the common people:天下~ *the common people all over the world*

【苍天】① the blue sky ② Heaven:~保佑我们。*May Heaven bless us.* / ~不容! *Heaven forbid!*

【苍鹰】【动】goshawk

【苍蝇】fly:~不叮无缝的蛋。*Flies go for cracked eggs — evil people corrupt only those who have weakness.*

【苍郁】verdant and luxuriant

沧 (of the sea) dark blue

【沧海】the sea; the deep blue sea

【沧海一粟】a drop in the ocean:在浩荡的革命队伍中,个人不过是~。*An individual in the midst of the vast and mighty revolutionary troops is nothing but a drop in the ocean.*

【沧桑】seas change into mulberry fields — time brings great changes to the world:饱经~ *have experienced many vicissitudes of life*

舱 ① cabin:客~ *passenger cabin* /密封~ *sealed cabin* ② module:指挥~ *command module*

【舱壁】bulkhead

【舱底】bilge
【舱口】hatchway; hatch: ~盖 *hatch; hatch cover*
【舱门】port; hatch door; cabin door
【舱面】deck: ~货 *deck cargo* / ~舱室 *deckhouse*
【舱室】cabin: ~小孔 *scuttle*
【舱外】【航】outside the cabin; extra-vehicular: ~操作 *extravehicular operation* / ~环境 *extravehicular circumstance*
【舱位】① cabin seat or berth ② shipping space

cáng

藏 ① hide; conceal: 东躲西~ *flee hither and thither; hide here and there* /把钱~在枕头下。*Hide the money under the pillow.* /她喜欢把话~在心里。*She likes hiding her feedings.* ② store; lay by: 阁楼上有大量~书。*Many books are stored in the attic.*
see also zàng
【藏藏掖掖】conceal
【藏躲】hide: 无处~ *have no place to hide*
【藏奸】① harbour evil intentions; bear ill will: 笑里~ *evil intentions are hidden behind smiles* ② unwilling to do one's best to help others
【藏经阁】depository of Buddhist scriptures
【藏猫儿】hide-and-seek: 小孩喜欢~玩。*Children like playing hide-and-seek.*
【藏匿】conceal; hide; go into hiding: 罪犯~在一个破庙里。*The criminal hid in a shabby temple.*
【藏身】hide oneself; go into hiding: ~之处 *hiding place; hideout*
【藏书】① collect books: 他爱好~。*He has the hobby of collecting books.* ② collection of books: 宝贵的~ *precious books*
【藏头露尾】give a partial account of; tell part of the truth; but not all of it: 他说话~的。*He spoke evasively.*
【藏掖】① try to cover up: ~躲闪 *dodge and hide* ② covered things: 他做事光明正大,从来不~着。*He always acts above board, without hiding anything.*
【藏拙】hide one's in adequacy by keeping quiet: 在这么多知名画家面前,我就~吧。*I had better not reveal my poor skill before so many well-known painter.*
【藏踪】conceal one's tracks; hide: 他多年~于深山。*He hid in the remote mountains for years.*

cāo

操 ① grasp; hold: 稳~胜券 *be sure of success* ② act; do; operate: 重~旧业 *resume one's old profession; restart one's old trade* ③ speak (a language or dialect): ~外地口音 *speak with accent* ④ drill; exercise: 健美~ *aerobics; callisthenics* ⑤ conduct; behaviour: 节~ *moral integrity* ⑥ (Cāo) a surname
see also cào
【操办】conduct; make arrangements; take care of: ~婚事 *make arrangements for a wedding*
【操场】playground; sports ground; drill ground
【操持】① handle; manage: ~家务 *manage housework* ② plan and make preparations for; arrange: ~政事 *handle the government affairs* /他负责~一切准备工作。*He is in charge of making all preparations.*
【操刀】be in command hold a knife
【操典】【军】drill book; drill manual; drill regulations
【操劳】① work hard: ~过度 *overwork oneself* /妈妈终年~。*Mom manages housework drudgingly all the year around.* ② take care; look after: 您介意多~这事吗? *Would you mind taking care of this?*
【操练】drill; practise; train: ~士兵 *drill the soldiers* / 实际~ *practical drill*
【操切】rash; hasty; over hasty; head-over-heels: 不要~采取行动。*Don't rush into taking actions.*
【操神】look after; take care; tax one's mind; bother: 她整天为孩子~。*She taxes her mind on children all day.*
【操守】moral character; personal integrity
【操心】worry about; take pains; wrack one's brains: 孩子已经长大了,不要太~了。*Children have grown up; don't worry about them so much.* /为了工程的按时完工,他可没有少~。*He took a lot of trouble to ensure the completion of the project on time.*
【操行】behaviour or conduct: ~评语 *remarks on a student's behaviour* / ~端正 *well-behaved; having good conduct*
【操演】drill; demonstration: 同学们在为运动会开幕式~。*Students are drilling for the opening ceremony of the sports meet.*
【操之过急】act too hastily; act with undue haste; carry sth too hastily: 慢慢来,不要~。*Take it easy; Don't act too hastily.*
【操纵】① operate; control; command: 远距离~ *remote control* /无线电~ *radio control* ② rig; manipulate: ~国家政策 *manipulate national policy* /幕后~ *pull the strings; manipulate from behind the scenes*
【操作】operate; manipulate; handle; manage: ~说明书 *operating manual* /独立~ *operate on one's own* / ~程序 *operate sequence* / ~程序图 *flow diagram; flow chart* / ~代码 *operate code*

糙 rough; coarse: ~纸 *rough paper* /粗~ *coarse; crude*
【糙粮】[方] coarse food grain (e.g. maize, sorghum, etc.)
【糙米】brown rice; unpolished rice

cáo

曹 ① [书] used to indicate plural number: 尔~ *all of you* ② (Cáo) a surname
【曹白鱼】Chinese herring

漕 water transport

【漕船】ships for carrying grain

【漕河】canal for transporting tribute rice

【漕粮】grain transported by water

【漕运】(in feudal times) transporting grain to the capital by water

槽 ① trough：水～ *water trough* /马～ *manger* ② groove；slot：挖～ *dig a groove* ③［量］(of doors，windows，etc.)：一～门 a door ④［方］raise piglets enough until they are big enough for sale：一～猪 a litter of piglets

【槽车】tank track

【槽口】【机】notch

【槽头】trough (in a livestock shed)：～兴旺 *stable full of sturdy livestock*

【槽牙】molar

cǎo

草[1] ① grass：青～ *green grass* /枯～ *withered grass* /疾风劲～ *hardy grass in the strong wind* ② straw：～绳 *straw rope* ③ female (of animals)：～鸡 *hen*

草[2] ① careless；hasty；rough；sloppy：～～收场 *come to a hasty end*；*hastily wind up* (*the performance*) /～～了事 *rush through the work* /他的字很～。*His handwriting is very sloppy.* ② draft：起～文件 *draft a file*

【草案】draft (of a plan，law，etc.)：计划～ *draft plan* /协议～ *draft agreement* /宪法～ *draft constitution*

【草包】① straw bag；straw sack ② idiot；wind bag；block head；good-for-nothing：他是个地道的～。*He is really a good-for-nothing.*

【草本】① herbaceous：～植物 *herbs* ② original draft (of a manuscript)

【草编】straw weaving；straw knitting

【草草】carelessly；hastily：～过目 *read through carelessly* /这篇文章我只～看了一遍。*I have just skimmed through the article.*

【草场】meadow；pasture；grassland；grazing land；do sth slovenly

【草丛】thick growth of grass：～里有许多虫子。*There are many insects in the thick growth of grass.*

【草底儿】［口］draft；manuscript

【草地】① grassland；meadow；pasture：～上有成群的牛羊。*There are herds of cattle and sheep on the grassland.* ② lawn；grassplot：～网球 *lawn tennis*

【草垫子】straw mattress；pallet：她跪在～上祈祷。*She is kneeling on the pallet praying.*

【草稿】rough draft；manuscript；preliminary draft：打～ *make a rough draft*

【草根】grass root：小时候我喜欢吃一种很甜的～。*I liked eating a kind of sweet grass roots in childhood.*

【草灰】① plant ash；barilla ② greyish yellow：～色的封面 *greyish yellow cover* /听到这个消息，她吓得面色～。*On hearing the news*，*her face turned to greyish yellow with scare.*

【草绿】grass green

【草莽】① a thick growth of grass ② wildness；uncultivated land：～英雄 *green wood hero*；*hero of the bush* /我是一个～之人。*I rose from the common people.*

【草帽】straw hat：～辫 *plaited straw*

【草莓】strawberry：～口味 *straw berry flavour*

【草民】① common people；commoner ②［旧］I；me

【草木】vegetation；plants and trees；grass and trees

【草木皆兵】every bush and tree looks like an enemy — a state of extreme nervous ness as if surrounded by enemies；imaginary pears：风声鹤唳，～。*The moan of the wind*，*the cry of the cranes and the rustle of the grass all sounded like the lurking enemy army.*

【草拟】draft；draw up：～文件 *draft a document* /～方案 *draft a plan*

【草棚】thatched shack；straw shed

【草皮】sod；turf

【草坪】lawn：修剪～ *now the lawn*

【草签】initial：～协议 *initial an agreement*

【草书】grass characters；calligraphy executed with strokes flowing together；Chinese characters written in the cursive hand

【草率】carelessly；perfunctorily；sloppily：～从事 *act rashly*；*do a sloppy job* /不要～下结论。*Don't draw a conclusion perfunctorily.*

【草体】running hand of a phonetic alphabet

【草图】sketch map；draft

【草屋】hut；thatched hut

【草席】straw mat

【草鞋】straw sandals：他穿一双～过了冬。*He lived through the winter with one pair of straw sandals.*

【草药】medicinal herbs；herbal medicine

【草野】① common people；ordinary people：～之人 *untitled commoner* ② coarse and rude

【草鱼】grass carp

【草原】grasslands；prairie：辽阔的～上马儿跑。*Horses run in the grasslands.*

【草约】draft treaty；protocol；draft agreement

【草泽】①grassy marshland；swamp；morass：一望无际的～ *boundless swamp* ② among commonalty

【草纸】① rough straw paper ② toilet paper

cè

册 ① volume; book: 工作人员名～ *personnel roll* / 学生～ *student's register*; *student's roll* / 相～ *photo album* / 纪念～ *autograph album* / 装订成～ *be bound into book form* ② grant on a imperial edict ③ [量] copy; volume: 这本书已印刷二万～。*Twenty thousand copies of the book have been printed.* / 这部小说一共有三～。*This novel is on three volumes.*

【册封】confer titles of nobility on: 他被～为太子。*He was made the crown prince.*

【册立】make a crown prince or empress

【册子】book; volume: 小～ *booklet*; *brochure*; *fly-sheet*

厕 lavatory; toilet; washroom; restroom: 公～ *public toilet* / 女～ *women's (room or toilet)*

【厕所】lavatory; toilet; W. C

侧 ① side; lateral: 左(右)～ *the left (right) side* / 河的两～都种着垂柳。*Weeping willows are planted on both sides of the river.* ② lean; incline: 他正～着身子睡觉。*He is sleeping on one side.*

【侧耳】incline the head and listen; strain one's ears: ～倾听 *listen attentively*; *be all ears*; *prick up one's ears*

【侧根】lateral roots

【侧击】① make a flank attack on ② attack sb by talks or letters: 旁敲～击 *beat about the bush*

【侧力】side force; lateral fore

【侧廊】side porch; aisle

【侧门】side door; side entrance

【侧面】side; aspect; flank: 从～了解情况 *find out about the situation from indirect sources* / 他的遭遇只是旧社会穷人生活的一个～。*His miserable experience was only one side of the life of the poor in the old society.*

【侧图】side view

【侧面像】profile

【侧目】sidelong glance (with fear or indignation): 他在村里横行霸道,令人～相看。*His tyrannizing in the village was feared by the villager.*

【侧身】① on one's side; sideways: 公共汽车上很拥挤,他不得不～站着。*It is very crowded in the bus; he has to stand sideways.* ② participate in: ～教育界 *be one member of teaching profession*

【侧视】look askance at; look sideways at; shoot a sideline at: ～图 *side view*; *profile*

【侧室】[旧] ① side roam ② concubine

【侧卧】lie on one's side

【侧线】① siding ② lateral line (of fishes, amphibians, etc.)

【侧向】side direction: ～分力 *cross component force* / ～加速 *side acceleration*

【侧翼】【军】flank

【侧影】silhouette; profile: 飞船的～ *the profile of the airship* / 通过这篇小说可以看到当时土地改革的一个～。*The novel presents a reflection of the land reform of the time.*

【侧泳】【体】sidestroke

【侧枝】arm; twig; branch; offshoot

【侧重】lay particular emphasis on; stress: 这篇文章～谈了农业污染问题。*The keynote of the article is the problems of agricultural pollution.*

测 ① survey; fathom; measure: ～体温 *take one's temperature* / ～风向 *determine the wind direction* / ～土深 *measure the depth of soil* ② infer; conjecture: 变幻莫～ *unpredictable*; *capricious*; *fickle* / 居心叵～ *with hidden intention*; *have ulterior motives*

【测报】observe and predict: 气象～ *weather forecasting* / ～汛情 *flood survey and forecast*

【测程仪】【交】log; mileage meter

【测点】landmark; measuring point

【测定】determine by measuring or surveying; gape; measure; fathom

【测度】① measure ② conjecture; estimate; infer: 市场行情难以～。*It is difficult to conjecture the market quotations.*

【测杆】measuring staff; surveying rod; station pole

【测谎器】lie detector; polygraph

【测绘】survey-cartography and drawing; map: ～员 *surveyor*; *cartographer* / ～飞机 *air-mapping plane* / ～卫星 *cartographic satellite*

【测角】goniometry: ～器 *goniometer*; *angle meter*

【测井】well logging

【测距】measure distance: ～仪 *range finder*; *diastimeter*

【测控】observe and control: 卫星～中心 satellite observation and control centre

【测力计】dynamometer

【测量】measure; survey; gape; determine: ～温度 *measure the temperature* / ～速度 *measure the speed* / ～仪器 *surveying instrument* / ～学 *surveying* / ～员 *surveyor*

【测流计】current meter

【测漏】leak hunting; track down a leak

【测评】determine and review

【测深仪】depth-sounder; echo sounder

【测试】survey; measure; test: ～仪器 *test an apparatus* / ～设备 *checkout gear* / ～数据 *test data* / ～技术 *testing technique* / 英语～ *English test*

【测算】measure and calculate: ～地震震级 *measure the earthquake magnitude*

【测探】① find out; ferret out; fathom: 她内心的奥秘很难～出来。*The interpersonal secrets in her heart are hard to ferreted out.* ② measure and survey

【测向仪】direction finder; goniometer

【测验】test; quiz: 几何～ *a geometry test*

策[1] ① bamboo or wooden slips used for writing on in ancient China ② type of essay which candidates should write at the imperial examinations ③ plan; scheme; strategy: 良～ *sound strat-*

egy; *good plan* /失 ~ *wrong decision*; *take a false step*

策[2] ① whip:鞭 ~ *spur on*; *urge on* /扬鞭 ~ 马 *whip a horse on with a riding crop* ② plan; plot

【策动】instigate; stir up; machinate; whip and drive: ~叛乱 *instigate a rebellion*

【策划】plan; design; plot; scheme; hatch; mastermind: ~企业改革方案 *make an enterprise reform plan* / ~阴谋 *hatch a plot* /幕后 ~ *plot behind the scenes*

【策励】encourage; spur on:你的教诲将时刻 ~ 着我努力学习。*Your encourage will constantly spur me on hard work.*

【策略】① tactics; strategy:作战 ~ *battle tactics* / ~上的失误 *tactical error* ② tactful:下次和他谈判要更 ~ 一些。*Be more tactful when negotiating with him next time.*

【策源地】source; place of origin; cradle; hotbed: 战争 ~ *a hotbed of war* /革命 ~ *cradle of revolution*

cēn

参

see also cān; shēn

【参差】uneven; irregular: ~错落 *uneven and irregular*

【参差不齐】uneven; irregular; varying; not uniform:同学们的阅读理解水平 ~。*The students have different levels of reading comprehension.*

cén

岑 ① small but high hill ② (Cén) a surname

【岑岑】[书] causing pain in the head:我的头 ~。*I have a splitting headache.*

【岑寂】silent; solitary; quiet: ~的山谷 *silent valley*

涔 [书] ① profusion of water ② excessive rain

【涔涔】① dripping; streaming (of sweat, tears or rain):热汗 ~ *sweating all over* /泪 ~ *tears streaming down* ② gloomy; overcast; dark:雪意 ~。*It threatens to snow.* ③ suffer from swelling pain; depressed; swollen:心绪 ~ *emotionally upset*; *in a flutter*

céng

层 ① overlapping: ~层叠出 *appear repeatedly*; *occur frequently* ② [量] layer; tier; stratum: 一 ~ 灰尘 *a layer of dust* /一 ~ 奶油 *a layer of cream* /湖面上结了一 ~ 薄冰。*A thin sheet of ice formed on the lake.* ③ [量] story; floor:高 ~ 建筑 *high building*; *tower block* /她家在一 ~。*She lives on the ground floor.* ④ component part in a sequence:她的话还有另外一 ~ 意思。*What she said has another implication.* /他的评语中有两 ~ 含义。*His remark has two shades of meaning.*

【层报】submit or report a matter to higher authorities through proper channel step by step:这件事经过 ~,终于反映到中央政府。*The matter was finally brought before the central government after it had been reported from one level to another.*

【层层】layer upon layer; tier upon tier; ring upon ring; at each level: ~把关 *check at each level* / ~包围 *surround ring upon ring* / ~梯田 *tier upon tier of terraces* / ~排列 *tier up*

【层出不穷】emerge in an endless stream; be too numerous to be counted:新事物 ~。*New things are emerging in quick succession.* /他的闪光点子 ~。*His glittery ideas are coming out one after another.*

【层次】① arrangement of ideas (in writing or speech):这篇文章 ~ 不清。*The article lacks unity and coherence.* ② administrative levels:为提高工作效率,我们必须减少机构 ~。*To improve work efficiency, we must simplify the administrative structure.* /他和我 ~ 不同,没有共同语言。*He and I are in different levels, and we have no common language.* ③ gradation:色彩的 ~ *colour gradations*

【层叠】one on top of another; tier upon tier; over lapping:山峦 ~ *tier upon tier of mountains*

【层积云】【气】stratocumulus

【层理】【地】bedding; stratification

【层流】【物】laminar flow

【层峦】range upon range of mountains; peaks rising one higher than another: ~起伏 *range upon range of undulating mountains* / ~叠嶂 *range upon range of mountains*

【层面】①【地】bedding: ~构造 *bedding structure* ② scope or aspect of sth on a certain level or of a cross section:

【层压】【化】lamination: ~玻璃 *laminated glass*

曾 once; ever; before:我 ~ 问过他这个问题。*I once asked him about the question.* /她 ~ 去过美国。*She has been to America.*

see also zēng

【曾经】once; ever:我 ~ 做过导游。*I was once a tourist guide.*

【曾经沧海】have sailed the seven seas; have experienced great things: ~难为水。*One who has crossed the deep blue seas thinks nothing of mere rivers — to a sophisticated person there is nothing new under the sun.*

cèng

蹭 ① rub; scrape; scratch; grind:小猪在墙上~痒痒。*The pig is scratching its back against the wall.* /他用袖子把课桌上的灰~掉了。*He wept the dust away from the desk with his sleeve.* /我的手~破了皮。*I grazed my hand.* ② be smeared with:小心别~身上机油。*Be careful that you don't stain your clothes with engine oil.* /他~了一身灰。*His clothes are smeared with dust.* ③ dawdle; dillydally:一步步往前~ *drag oneself along inch by inch* /快点,别磨~了。*Hurry up! Don't dawdle.* ④[方] cadge; scrounge; freeload for sth:~吃~喝 *scrounge meals and drinks* /看~戏 *go to the theatre free of charge*

【蹭吃】freeload for food; freeload for meals

【蹭抹】rub:把地上的血迹~掉。*Scrub off the bloodstain on the ground.*

chā

叉 ① fork:刀~ *knife and fork* /木~ *wooden fork* /钢~ *steel fork* /鱼~ *fish spear* ② X-sign; cross:在错误的答案上打上~。*Put a cross on the wrong answer.* ③ work with a fork; fork:~秸秆 *fork stalk* / ~鱼 *spear fish*
see also chá; chǎ; chà

【叉车】forklift; forklift truck

【叉接】【机】forked joint

【叉烧】barbecued pork; grill (marinated pork):~肉 *grilled pork*

【叉手】cup one hand in the other before the chest:~施礼 *raise one's folded hands to one's chin to salute sb*

【叉腰】akimbo:她双手~地站在那里。*She stood there with arms akimbo.*

【叉子】fork:用~吃饭 *eat with a fork*

杈 wooden fork; hayfork; pitchfork
see also chà

差 ① difference; discrepancy; dissimilarity:补足~额 *make up the difference* (*or the balance*) /时~ *time difference* /丝毫不~ *perfectly correct; in total agreement* ②【数】mathematics difference ③[书] somewhat; slightly; barely:~强人意 *be barely satisfactory*
see also chà; chāi; cī

【差别】difference; disparity:城乡~ *the gap between the city and the countryside* /年龄~ *disparity in age* / ~关税 *differential rates of duty; differential duties* / ~汇率 *differential exchange rates* / ~对待 *discriminate*

【差错】① error; mistake; slip:计算上的~ *calculating errors* /她工作上很少出~。*She seldom makes mistakes in her work.* ② mishap; accident; unforeseen:血浆的运输不能出任何~。*Whatever unexpected mustn't happen to the transit of blood plasma.*

【差额】difference; balance; margin:进出口贸易~ *imbalance between imports and exports* /补足~ *make up the balance* / ~税 *variable levies*

【差额选举】multi-candidate election; competitive election

【差价】price difference:地区~ *regional price differences* /季节~ *seasonal price differences* /批零~ *the price difference between wholesale and retail*

【差距】gap; disparity; spatial difference:缩小~ *reduce* (*or narrow*) *the gap*

【差强人意】be barely satisfactory; be satisfactory in a manner:她的成绩~。*Her performance is barely satisfactory.*

【差误】mistake; error; slip

【差异】difference; divergence; diversity; discrepancy:气候~ *difference on climate* /文化~ *difference in culture*

【差值】D-value; differential value

插 ① insert; stick in:把笔帽~上 *insert the pen in its cap* /把插头~上 *insert the plug in a socket* / ~门 *bolt the door* /山峰直~云霄。*The peaks penetrate into the clouds.* /他把手~在口袋里取暖。*He put his hands in pockets for warm.* ② interpose; insert; cut in:在文字中~入一些图片。*Insert some pictures in the words.* /不好意思,让我~句话。*Excuse me; let me get a word in.*

【插班】join a class in the middle of the course; enroll late in class: ~生 *late enrollee; mid-course student*

【插播】insert (an item) in a radio or TV programme:在电视剧中~广告 *insert advertisement in the TV play*

【插翅难飞】be difficult to fly away even with the aid of wings; be unable to escape even if furnished with wings

【插队】① jump the queue; cut in a line ② (in 1960s and 1970s) go to live and work in a production team of a rural commune: ~落户 *go and settle as a member of a production team* / ~知青 *school graduate living and working as a member of a rural production team*

【插杠子】poke one's nose into sb's business; meddle; butt in:别到处~! *Don't poke your nose in everybody's business.* /他在我们中间~,真卑鄙! *He is really contemptible to drive a wedge between us.*

【插管】【医】intubate

【插花】① insert or arrange flowers in a vase, basket, etc. ② mingle; inter mingle; mix:我们在棉花地里~种着豇豆。*We grow cowpeas in between the cotton crops.*

【插话】① interpose remarks:别~! 让他继续讲解下去。*Don't interrupt; let him go on explaining.* ② interruption; interposed words:他的~有很深的含义。*His remark has deep meanings.* ③ digression; episode:这一段～使他的文章更加精彩。*This digression makes his article much more wonderful.*

【插脚】① gain a foothold; find a place to stand:大厅里人很多,无法～。*There are so many people in the hall that I can't squeeze in.* ② be engaged in; be involved in:事情很复杂,我们最好别～。*The matter is so complicated that we'd better not intervene.*

【插科打诨】① (of an actor) make impromptu comic gestures and remarks ② jesting, buffoonery:他喜欢～。*He is fond of making gags.*

【插孔】plughole; socket; jack; spigot

【插口】① socket jack; spigot:电脑～ *socket for the computer* ② interrupt; chip in; cut in:他～阐明自己的观点。*He chipped in, clarified his own viewpoint.*

【插屏】table plaque; table screen

【插曲】① songs in a film or play; interlude ② episode; interlude:这只是整个故事的一个～。*This is merely an episode in the whole story.*

【插入】① insert:文章中～了几幅图片。*Several pictures have been inserted in the article.* ②【电】plug in: ～部件 *plug-in unit*

【插身】① squeeze in; edge in:难以～ *difficult to squeeze in* ② get involved in; take part in:不要～在这事里头。*Don't get involved in the matter.*

【插手】① get involved in, take part in; lend a hard:我很想帮你一把,可不知道该如何～。*I really want to help you, but I don't know how to.* ② meddle in intervene; have a hand in; poke one's nose into:不管你的事,不要你～。*It is none of your business; Don't poke your nose into the affair.* /他的老婆也想～企业管理。*His wife also wants to intervene in the management of the enterprise.*

【插头】【电】plug 三脚～ *three-pin plug*

【插图】① bolt; latch; thumb lock ② plug

【插叙】narration interspersed with flashbacks

【插秧】transplant rice seedings or shoots; set out rice-plants: ～季节 *time for rice-transplanting*

【插页】insert; inset

【插足】① gain a foothold; put one's foot in ② get involved in:第三者～ *involvement of a third party* /他们之间的事,你又何必～? *This is their matter; why do you get involved in?*

【插嘴】interrupt; chip in:她说个没完没了,别人无法～。*She kept on speaking without pause, leaving no chance for others to chip in.*

【插座】【电】socket; outlet; receptacle:弹簧～ *cushion socket* /多用～ *multi-purpose socket*

chá

叉 [方] block; jam
see also chā; chǎ; chà

茬 ① stubble:麦～儿 *wheat stubble* /豆～ *bean stubble* ② crop:二～花生 *second crop of peanuts* /这块地一年种两～。*This plot can produce two crops a year.* ③ batch:又一～毕业生 *a new group of graduates*

【茬口】① crops for rotation ② soil on which a crop has been parted and harvested:红薯～ *land on which sweet potato has been grown and harvested* ③ opportunity; chance; juncture:趁着这个～,我们考托福吧。*Let's seize the opportunity to take the exam of TOEFL.*

【茬子】stubble; stalks and roots of a harvested crop: ～地 *stubble land* /胡～子 *moustache stubble*

茶 ① tea; tea leaves: ～场 *tea farm; tea plantation* /采～ *pick tea leaves* ② tea (the drink):绿～ *green tea* /红～ *black tea* /花～ *jasmine tea* /砖～ *brick tea* /清～ *tea without refreshments* /浓～ *strong tea* /沏～ *make tea* ③ certain kinds of drink or liquid food:奶～ *cream tea* /菊花～ *chrysanthemum tea* /杏仁～ *almond paste* /油～ *paste made of flour, beef fat and other ingredients* ④ dark brown: ～色玻璃 *dark brown glass*

【茶杯】teacup

【茶匙】tea spoon

【茶道】tea ceremony

【茶点】tea and pastries; tea and cookies; refreshments

【茶碟儿】sauce (for holding a teacup)

【茶饭】food and drinks; meal:他为期末考试深深担心,几乎不思～。*So deeply worried about the final exams, he almost lost his appetite for meals.*

【茶缸子】mug

【茶馆】teahouse:开～ *run a teahouse*

【茶褐色】dark brown

【茶壶】teapot; tea kettle

【茶花】camellia

【茶话会】tea party

【茶几】tea table; teapoy; side table: coffee table

【茶鸡蛋】egg boiled in water blended with tea, spices, soy sauce, etc.

【茶具】tea set; tea service

【茶客】① customer in a teahouse ②[旧] tea dealer; tea merchant

【茶楼】teahouse (with two or more storeys)

【茶农】tea grower; tea farmer

【茶盘】tea tray

【茶色】dark brown; tawny: ～眼镜 *dark brown glasses*

【茶树】tea shrub; tea tree; tea plant

【茶水】tea or boiled water: ～站 *tea-stall*

【茶摊】roadside tea-stall

【茶亭】tea-booth; tea-stall; tea-kiosk

【茶托】saucer

【茶碗】tea bowl; large teacup

【茶叶】tea leaves; tea: ～蛋 *tea eggs*

【茶油】tea-seed oil; tea oil

【茶余饭后】over a cup of tea or after a meal — at one's leisure: ～,他常看一些小说。*He often reads some novels at his leisure.*

【茶盅】handless tea cup
【茶砖】tea brick
【茶座】① teahouse (usu. outdoor); tea stall ② seats in a teahouse or tea garden

查 ① check; examine; inspect: ~产品质量 *check the quality of a product* / ~血 *have a blood test* / ~卫生 *make a sanitation inspection* / ~电表 *read the electricity meter* ② look into; investigate: ~清事实真相 *find out the truth about sth* / ~个水落石出 *get to the bottom of a matter; investigate sth thoroughly* ③ look up; consult: ~字典 *look up a word in the dictionary; consult a dictionary* / ~档案 *look into the archives* / ~资料 *consult reference materials (on a special subject)*

【查办】investigate and deal with accordingly: 撤职~ *dismiss sb from his post and prosecute him* / ~案件 *investigate into a case*
【查抄】make an inventory of a criminal's possessions and confiscate them
【查处】investigate and deal with accordingly
【查档】look into the files; rummage through the archives
【查点】check the number or amount of; make an inventory of: ~出席人数 *check the attendance; check the number of people present* / ~货物 *make an inventory of the goods*
【查对】check; verify: ~账目 *check the account* / ~原文 *check against the original (text, manuscript, etc.)* / ~数字 *verify the figures* / ~无误 *examined and found correct; verified*
【查房】make the rounds of the wards in a hospital; (in some hostels) make a routine check of the rooms: 值班护士每夜多次~。*Nurses on duty make several rounds of the wards during the night.*
【查访】go around and make inquiries; investigate: ~被盗珠宝的下落 *track down the stolen jewelry* / 多方~案情 *make extensive inquiries about the crime*
【查封】seal up; close down: ~房屋 *seal up the house* / ~违法经营的公司 *close down the companies that conduct business activities forbidden by the law*
【查号台】directory inquiries; information desk
【查核】check; examine: ~账目 *check accounts* / 经过反复~,确认计算无误。*We have verified the calculation by repeated checks.*
【查户口】check residence cards; check on household occupants
【查获】hunt down and seize; ferret out; track down: ~大量走私品 *ferret out a good number of smuggled goods* / ~逃犯 *track down an escaped criminal*
【查禁】prohibit; ban; suppress: ~黄色书刊 *ban pornographic publications* / ~走私活动 *suppress smuggling*
【查究】investigate and ascertain; follow up a case; look into and find out: ~责任 *find out who should hold responsibility*
【查勘】survey; prospect: ~地形 *survey the terrain* / ~矿产资源 *prospect for mineral deposits* / ~水文 *survey hydrology*
【查看】look over; inspect; examine: ~驾驶执照 *check one's driving licence* / ~水情 *look into the water level* / ~地图 *look up a map*
【查考】try to ascertain; examine; do research on: ~这批文物的年代 *try to ascertain the date of this lot of cultural treasures* /无处~。*There is no source for verification.*
【查扣】check and detain: ~违禁录像带 *check and detain contraband video-tapes*
【查明】ascertain through investigation; find out; ascertain: ~起因 *find out the cause* / ~事实真相 *find out the truth*
【查票】examine or check tickets
【查铺】make a bed check; go the rounds of bed at night: 特殊时期,值班老师每晚都要到学生宿舍~。*In special time, teachers on duty will make a bed check in the students' dormitories.*
【查讫】checked: 这笔账目已~。*The account has been checked.*
【查清】investigate thoroughly; check up on: ~他的来历 *check up on him; find out his background* /你负责~这件事情的来龙去脉。*It is up to you to find out how the matter started and developed.*
【查哨】go the rounds of guard posts; inspect the sentries
【查实】verify: 案情已经~。*The case has been verified.*
【查收】check and accept (mail /goods): 寄上两本书,请~。*Please find two books enclosed herewith.*
【查税】make a tax inspection
【查问】① question; inquire; interrogate: ~口令 *challenge for a password* ② inquire about: ~是否收到此信 *check to see if the letter is received*
【查无实据】investigation reveals no evidence; give the benefit of doubt: 事出有因,~。*The charge may not be without cause, but investigation furnishes no real evidence.*
【查寻】search for; inquire about: ~失散多年的兄弟 *look for a long-missing brother*
【查询】inquire about; inquire into: ~电话号码 *inquire about a telephone number* / ~地址 *inquire about one's address* / ~台 *information desk*
【查验】check; examine: ~护照 *examine a passport* / ~行李 *inspect the luggage*
【查阅】look up; consult: ~科技文献 *consult technical literature* / ~参考书 *look up references*
【查账】accounts; audit accounts; examine accounts: ~报告 *audit report*
【查找】look for: ~失主 *look for the owner of a lost property* / ~资料 *gather data* / ~病毒 *look for virus*
【查证】investigate and verify; check: ~属实 *be checked and found to be true; be verified* /他的话,

句句可以～。*What he said can bear strict scrutiny.*

搽 apply; put on:～粉 *powder one's face* /～豆花膏 *put on vanishing cream* /～油 *put on lotion; apply ointment* /～药水 *apply liquid medicine*

【搽脂抹粉】apply powder and paint; prettify; whitewash

楂 short, bristly hair or beard; stubble:胡子～ *stubbly beard*

碴 [方] be cut (by broken glass, chinaware, etc.):她的手被玻璃～破了。*She cut her fingers on the broken glass.*

【碴儿】① broken pieces; fragments:冰～ *small pieces of ice* /玻璃～ *fragments of glass* /骨头～ *crushed bones* ② sharp edge of broken glass, china, etc.:他不小心碰到碗～,把手指头拉破了。*Unguardedly, he happened to touch the sharp edge of the broken bowl and cut his fingers.* ③ the cause of quarrel:没事找～ *find fault with sb; pick a quarrel with sb* ④ sth just said or mentioned:接～ *take the cue* ⑤ impetus; tendency:这不是好～。*This is not a good tendency.*

察 examine; look into; scrutinize; observe:～勘 *make a field survey* /～其言,观其行 *examine his words and watch his deeds; check what he says against what he does* /体～民情 *acquaint oneself with the condition of the people; watch the public mood*

【察访】investigate through visit and observation; look into; go about to find out:实地～ *make an on-the-spot investigation* /暗中～ *make a secret investigation trop*

【察觉】be conscious of; become aware of; perceive; detect:我已～出他情绪不好。*I have been aware that he was in bad mood.* /我没有～到任何危险。*I didn't sense any danger.*

【察看】inspect; observe; watch; look carefully:～地形 *survey the terrain* /～现场 *inspect the scene*

【察探】investigate; detect; scout:～敌情 *scout an area to obtain information about the enemy; gather intelligence about the enemy*

【察言观色】try to read a person's thoughts from his words and facial expression; observe the words and gestures of sb:她很讨人喜欢,因为她很善于～。*She is very popular because she is very good at watching other's every mood.* /～,相机行事。*Watch one's mood and act accordingly.*

【察验】examine; check; test:～项链的成色 *examine the percentage of gold in a necklace*

檫 【植】sassafras

chǎ

叉 part so as to form a fork; fork:～着腿站着 *stand with one's legs apart*

see also chā; chá; chà

chà

叉 fork:劈～ *with both legs apart*

see also chā; chá; chǎ

杈 branch (of a tree):树～ *tree branch* /打棉花～ *trim cotton plants*

see also chā

岔 ① branch off:从主路～开 *branch off from the main road* ② diverge; turn off:为走捷径,他～上了小道。*To find a crosscut, he turned off into a side road.* ③ change the topic (of conversation); interrupt:老师有意把话～开了。*The teacher changed the topic deliberately.* ④ accident; mistake:你放心吧,路上不会出～的。*Don't worry; nothing will go wrong on the way.* ⑤ stagger:把办公时间～开。*Stagger office hours.*

【岔口】fork (in road); road junction:

【岔流】branch stream; (of a river) tributary outlet into the sea:这条河有两条～。*This river has two tributary outlets into the sea.*

【岔路】branch road; byroad; side road

【岔子】accident; trouble; setback; mistake:他是个很有经验的司机,几十年来从没有出过～。*He is an experienced driver, and has never had an accident during the decades.*

刹 Buddhist temple; Buddhist monastery:古～ *an ancient Buddhist temple* /宝～ *Buddhist dagoba*

see also shā

【刹那】instant; split second:一～ *in an instant; in a flash* /～间 *in a split second; in the twinkling of an eye*

衩 slit or vent in the side of a garment:这条裙子两侧面开～了。*The skirt has slits on both sides.*

诧 be surprised:惊～ *be surprised; be amazed*

【诧异】be surprised; be astonished; be amazed:～神色 *a surprised look* /他反常的举动,使我们非常～。*His strange behaviour made us very astonished.*

差 ① differ from; fall short of:相～甚远 *extremely different* /这个分数离老师的期望还～得远。*The mark still falls far short of what the teacher expected.* ② wrong; mistaken:这你可说～了。*You are wrong here.* ③ be wanting; be less than; be short of:～十分九点 *ten (minutes) to nine* /一个月～两天 *two days less than a month* /～一个人 *one person short* /我还～你二十元。*I still owe you twenty yuan.* ④ not up to standard; poor; inferior:成绩～ *poor performance* /～等生 *poor student* /他太～劲了,你离他远点。*You had better stay away from him, since he is such a mean guy.*

see also chā; chāi; cī

【差不多】① almost; nearly:他~十岁了。*He is almost ten years old.* /他的话~是毫无意义。*What he said almost means nothing.* ② about the same; similar:兄弟俩长得~。*The two brothers look very much alike.* /两家的经济状况~。*The economic conditions of the two families are similar.* ③ just about right; just about enough; not far off; not bad; just so-so:他的生意还~。*His business is not bad.* /水稻熟得~了。*The rice is just about ripe.*

【差不多的】ordinary people; the average person:这种常识,~都知道。*This common sense is known by everyman.*

【差等】(of students level) below the average: ~生 *poor student*

【差点儿】① not quite up to the mark; not good enough:这道菜味道~。*The dish doesn't taste very nice.* /他的技术还~。*His technique is not quite up to the mark.* ② almost; nearly; on the verge of:我~没赶上飞机。*I almost missed the plane.* /他~赢了这场比赛。*He almost won the contest.* /看到成绩单,她~哭出来。*On the sight of the school report card, she hold back her tears with difficulty.*

【差劲】be too bad; disappointing:今晚的舞会太~了。*The ball tonight is no good at all.*

【差生】slow student; poor student: ~不应该受到歧视。*Slow students should not be discriminated.*

chāi

拆 ① tear open; tear apart; undo: ~信 *open a letter* / ~机器 *disassemble a machine; strip a machine; take a machine apart* /把这个组~了。*Break up the group.* ② pull down; dismantle; demolish: ~大楼 *pull down a building* / ~桥 *dismantle a bridge*

【拆除】pull down; demolish; remove; dismantle: ~临时建筑物 *pull down temporary buildings*

【拆穿】expose; unmask; give the lie to; debunk: ~骗局 *expose a fraud* / ~阴谋 *uncover a conspiracy* / ~西洋镜 *strip off the camouflage; expose a trick*

【拆毁】demolish; pull down; tear down: ~祭坛 *pull down the sacrificial altar*

【拆伙】disband; dissolve a partnership; part company:这个公司已经~了。*The company has been dissolved already.*

【拆借】daily interest rates on short-term private loans

【拆开】take apart; open; separate; disassemble: ~包裹 *open the parcel* /没有东西可以将我们~。*Nothing can separate us.*

【拆迁】remove as a result of the pulling down the original houses: ~工程 *resettlement project*

【拆墙脚】undermine; cut the ground; pull the rug from under sb's feet:你的所作所为是拆市场经济体制的墙脚。*What you do undermines the market economic system.*

【拆散】(chāi sǎn) break (a set):小男孩把玩具~了。*The little boy broke the toy.*

【拆散】(chāi sàn) break up (marriage, family, etc.):战争~了许多幸福的家庭。*The war broke up many happy families.*

【拆台】pull away a prop; undermine; cut the ground from under sb's feet:工作中,互相~,没有任何好处。*It is no good counteracting each other's efforts in our work.*

【拆洗】unpick and wash; wash after removing the lining of a padded coat, quit, etc. strip and clean: ~被褥 *unpick and wash beddings*

【拆线】【医】take out stitches: ~刀 *seam ripper*

【拆卸】disassemble; dismantle; dismount

钗 hairpin (formerly worn by women for adornment):银~ *a silver hairpin*

差 ① assign; dispatch; send on an errand: ~去请大夫 *send for a doctor* / ~他去签订合同 *dispatch him to sign the contract* ②[旧] messenger; errand-boy:听~ *errand-boy; servant* ③ job; official post; errand:肥~ *cushy job; lucrative job* /因公出~ *be away on business* / ~人 *policeman*
see also chā; chà; cī

【差旅费】allowances for a business trip

【差遣】send on an errand or mission; dispatch; assign:听候~ *be at sb's disposal*

【差使】(chāishǐ) send; dispatch; assign; appoint

【差使】(chāishi) billet; commission; job:找份~ *look for a job*

【差事】assignment; errand:看门是他的临时~。*Guarding the entrance is his temporary job.*

chái

柴 ① firewood:砍~ *cut firewood* ②[方] bony into fleshy:骨瘦如~ *be scrawny; be all skin and bones*

【柴草】firewood; faggot; fuel:烧~ *burn firewood*

【柴火】firewood; faggot

【柴鸡】small-bodied chicken

【柴米】rice and fuel — daily necessaries: ~夫妻 *impoverished couple who married for convenience*

【柴米油盐】fuel, rice, oil and salt — chief daily necessities

【柴油】diesel oil

【柴油机】diesel engine:船用~ *marine diesel engine* /陆用~ *stationary diesel engine*

豺 jackal

【豺狼】jackals and wolves — cruel and evil people

chān

搀[1] ① help by the arm; support with hand: ~老爷爷过街 *help the old grandpa across the street*

搀[2] mix; adulterate; mingle: 酒里~了水。*This wine has been adulterated with water.* /油和水~不到一块儿。*Oil and water do not mix.*

【搀兑】mix different substances together: 牛奶里~点水 *mix some water with the milk*

【搀扶】support sb with one's hand; help by the arm: 她~奶奶进屋。*She helped grandma into the room.*

【搀和】① mix; mingle; blend: 粗粮细粮~着吃 *have a mixed diet of fine and coarse grain* ② meddle; interfere: 不是你的事就最好别~。*You'd better not meddle with what is not your business.*

【搀假】adulterate

【搀水】dilute

【搀杂】mix; blend; mingle; dope: 不要把不同颜色的衣服~在一起洗。*When you do washing, Don't mix up clothes of different colours.*

chán

谗 slander or abuse (sb behind his back); backbite

【谗害】slander or calumniate sb in order to harm him; frame sb up; persecute: ~忠良 *vilify and harm loyal courtiers* / ~老百姓 *persecute the common people*

【谗言】slanderous talk; calumny: 不要轻信~。*Don't swallow false charges.*

婵

【婵娟】① (of a women) lovely; beautiful; graceful ~女孩 *a lovely girl* ② the moon: 但愿人长久，千里共~。*May we live a long life, and share the moonlight together though thousands of miles apart.*

馋 greedy; gluttonous: ~猫 *greedy-guts* / ~鬼 *greedy-guts* /看见人家打羽毛球，他就~得慌。*At the sight of others playing badminton, his hands will itch.*

【馋涎欲滴】mouth drooping with greed; have eyes bigger than the belly

【馋嘴】① greedy; gluttonous ② glutton; a greedy eater

潺

【潺潺】murmur; babble; gurgle: ~溪流 *babbling brook; murmuring stream*

禅【宗】① prolonged and intense contemplation; deep meditation: 参~悟道 *try to reach into the realm of truth by meditation* /坐~ *sit in meditation* ② Buddhist; Buddhism
see also shàn

【禅房】monastic room; Buddhist temple

【禅林】Buddhist temple

【禅堂】meditation room; Buddhist shrine hall

【禅心】mind totally at peace

【禅院】Buddhist temple or monastery; Buddha Hall

【禅杖】Buddhist monk's staff; Buddhist cane

【禅宗】the *Chan* sect of Buddhism in China; Dhyana

孱 weak; frail

【孱弱】① (of physique) weak; frail; delicate; feeble: 体质~ *have fragile health* ② weak; impotent; powerless ③ insubstantial; thin

【孱微】[书] insignificant; small: 出身~ *come from a humble family*

缠 ① twine; wind: ~钢丝 *wind steel wire* / ~毛线团 *wind the wool into a ball* /他腿上~着绷带。*His leg was bandaged.* /绳子~在了树干上。*The rope twined around the tree.* ② tangle; tie up; pester: ~着不放 *fasten onto (sb or sth) like a leech* /胡搅蛮~ *plague sb with unreasonable demands; argue vexatiously and tediously* /两股线~在了一起。*The two threads got tangled up.* ③ [方] deal with: 这家伙很难~。*This fellow is very difficult to deal with.*

【缠绵】① (of an illness or emotion) lingering; abiding: 情愿~ *abiding affection* /乡思~ *be tormented by homesickness* /疾病~ *have a lingering illness* ② touching; moving; sentimental: 笛声非常~。*The tune of the flute is exceedingly melodious and sentimental.*

【缠绵悱恻】exceedingly sentimental; mushy; full of pathos

【缠磨】[口] bother; pester; nag: 许多事情~着他，使他不得安宁。*Many things are bothering him, which makes him uneasy.*

【缠绕】① twine; bind; wind: 他的手腕上~着一条蛇。*There is a snake twining around his wrist.* ② worry; harass; bother; pester: 她被孩子~着，无法走开。*She was pestered by the children and couldn't go away.*

【缠身】twine round one; bog one down; be tied down: 家务~ *be bogged down with housework* /债务~ *be debt-ridden* /病魔~ *be pestered by serious illness*

【缠手】troublesome; thorny; sticky; be hard to deal with: 这事情变得更~了。*The matter becomes much more knotty.*

【缠足】foot-binding

蝉 cicada

【蝉联】continue to hold a post or title: ~世界冠军 *retain a world championship*

【蝉蜕】① cicada slough (used as a Chinese medicine) ② [书] free or extricate oneself

【蝉翼】cicada's wings: 薄如~ *be as thin as a*

cicada's wings

【蝉翼纱】【纺】organdie

chǎn

产 ① give birth to; be delivered of; bear: ~卵器 *ovipositor* / ~卵期 *egg-spawning* (*or laying*) *season* / 难~ *difficult delivery* / 顺~ *easy or normal delivery* ② produce; yield: 高~ *high yield* / ~煤 *produce coal* ③ product; produce: 特~ *special local product* ④ property; estate: 家~ *family property* / 房地~ *real estate*

【产出】output: ~系数 *output coefficient*

【产床】【医】obstetric table

【产地】place of origin; provenance: 原料~ *source of raw materials*

【产儿】① newborn baby ② outcome; result; product: 科技革命的~ *product of the scientific technological revolution*

【产房】【医】delivery room

【产妇】lying-in woman; puerpera

【产后】postpartum; postnatal: ~护理 *postnatal care*; *puerperal care*

【产假】maternity leave

【产科】obstetrical department; obstetrics; maternity department: ~医生 *obstetrician* / ~病房 *obstetrical or maternity ward*

【产量】production; output; yield: 粮食~ *grain output* / 单位面积~ *yield per unit area*

【产卵】(of birds and poultry) lay eggs; (of fish; frogs, etc.) spawn: ~洄游 *spawning migration*

【产品】product; produce: ~质量 *the quality of products* / ~专利 *product patent* / 农~ *farm product* / 副~ *sideline* / 知识密集型~ *knowledge-intensive product* / 合格~ *qualified product* / ~包装 *the packaging of product* / ~保证书 *product warranty* / ~结构 *product structure*

【产前】prenatal; antenatal: ~护理 *antenatal or prenatal care*

【产钳】【医】obstetric forceps

【产权】property right: ~管理 *property rights administration* / ~拍卖 *equity auctioning* / ~转让 *transfer of property right*

【产生】① produce; engender; cause: ~效果 *come into effect* / ~误解 *cause misunderstanding* / ~很大的影响 *exert a great influence* / ~连锁反应 *produce a chain reaction* ② emerge; arise; come into being: 新政党的~ *emergence of a new political party*

【产物】outcome; product; result; offspring: 时代的~ *outcome of the times* / 必然的~ *inevitable result*

【产销】production and marketing: ~平衡 *coordination of production and marketing* / ~旺。*Both production and marketing are thriving.*

【产需】production and demand: ~平衡 *production-demand balance*

【产业】① estate; property ② industry: ~革命 *the Industrial Revolution* / ~结构 *industrial structure* / ~界 *industrial circles* / ~军 *the army of industrial workers* / ~税 *industrial tax* / ~资本 *industrial capital*

【产值】output value; value of output: 国民经济总~ *gross national product* (*GNP*)

【产仔】give birth to young animals; farrow: 猪每胎可~多只。*A sow can bear several piglets per litter.*

谄 flatter; fawn on; toady to; adulate

【谄媚】flatter; fawn on; adulate; toady

【谄上欺下】be servile to one's superiors and tyrannical to one's subordinates; fawn on those above and bully those below

【谄笑】ingratiating smile: 胁肩~ *cringe and smile obsequiously*

【谄谀】sweet talk; toady; flatter

铲 ① shovel; spade: 铁~ *iron shovel* / 锅~ *slice* ② work with a shovel or spade: ~煤 *shovel coal* / 把地~平 *scrape the ground even*; *level the ground with a spade*

【铲车】forklift truck

【铲除】root out; uproot; eradicate; abolish; eliminate: ~杂草 *root out weeds* / ~封建思想 *eradicate old feudal ideas*

【铲子】shovel; spade; trowel

阐 explain; expatiate; expound

【阐发】elucidate: 这篇文章详尽地~了革命的历史意义。*This article dedicates the historical significance of the revolution in great detail.*

【阐明】expound; clarify; expose: ~观点 *clarify one's viewpoint*

【阐释】explain; expound; interpret; elucidate; give a profound: 她对交通规则作了详细的~。*She gave a detailed explanation of the traffic regulations.*

【阐述】expound; elaborate; set forth: 这篇文章系统地~了社会的发展规律。*This article systematically expounds the laws of social development.*

【阐扬】expound and propagate; expound and advocate: ~真理 *expound and propagate truth* / ~爱国主义 *expound and advocate patriotism*

chàn

忏 repent; confess

【忏悔】① repent; be penitent: 他深深~自己虚度了黄金时代。*He deeply regretted that he had wasted his golden ages.* ②【宗】confess: 向神父~自己的过错 *confess one's sins to a priest*

【忏悔节】【宗】Shrovetide; Shrove Tuesday

颤 quiver; tremble; vibrate: 她笑得浑身发~。*She was shaking with laughter.* / 爬到山顶时，我累得两腿打~。*When I climbed the mountain-*

top, my legs were shaking with tiredness.

【颤动】quiver; vibrate; tremble: 声带～ *vibration of the vocal words* /树叶在秋风中～。*The leaves quivered in the autumn wind.*

【颤抖】shake; tremble; quiver; shiver: 吓得两腿～ *shake in one's shoes* /她激动得声音都在～。*Her voice quivered with excitement.*

【颤栗】shudder: 一想到那恐怖的情景,她的心就会～。*She will shudder at the thought of that horrible scene.*

【颤巍巍】unsteady; tottering; faltering: 老太太～地朝门口走去。*The old lady hobbled towards the door.*

【颤音】trill; shake

【颤悠】shake; quiver; flicker: ～的烛光,映照着她安详的脸。*The flickering candlelight shined upon her serene face.* /垂柳在风中轻轻地～着。*The weeping willows are swaying in the wind.*

chāng

昌 prosperous; flourishing

【昌盛】thriving; prosperous; flourishing: 建设一个繁荣～的国家 *build a prosperous country*

【昌言】[书] ① correct statement; proper remarks; worthy advice ② speak frankly; make a straightforward statement

猖 ferocious; fierce; savage

【猖獗】rampant; unbridled violence: ～一时 *be rampant for a while; run wild for a time* /最近,在中国,传染病"SARS"十分～。*Recently, the contagion of SARS (Severe Acute Respiratory Syndrome) is very rampant in China.*

【猖狂】savage; furious; outrageous: ～的反攻 *furious counterattack* / ～的挑衅 *reckless provocation*

娼 prostitute: 逼良为～ *compel a woman to prostitution* /男盗女～ *behave like thieves and whores*

【娼妇】bitch; whore

【娼妓】prostitute; harlot; streetwalker

鲳 silvery pomfret; butterfish

【鲳鱼】silvery pomfret; butterfish

cháng

长 ①long: ～路 *a long road* /很～的海岸线 *a very long coastline* /昼～夜短 *long days and short nights* /悠～的历史 *a long history* ② length: 这栋温室全～六十米。*The length of the greenhouse is sixty metres.* ③ strong point; forte: 取～补短 *learn from others strong points to offset one's weakness* ④ be good at; be proficient in: 她～于绘画。*She is good at drawing.*
see also zhǎng

【长臂猿】【动】gibbon

【长波】long wave: ～通讯 *long-wave communication* / ～辐射 *long-wave radiation*

【长城】① the Great Wall: 不到～非好汉。*He who does not reach the Great Wall is not a true man.* ② impregnable bulwark

【长处】strong point; merit; virtue; forte; good quality: 充分发挥每个人的～ *bring everyone's strengths into full play* /每个人都有自己的～。*Everybody has his own strong points.*

【长传】【体】throw a long pass

【长此以往】if things go on like this; if things continue this way; if things remain what they are: 他每天除了赌博什么都不干,～如何得了? *He does nothing but gambling everyday; if he goes on like this, what will become of him?*

【长存】live forever; be everlasting

【长凳】backless bench

【长笛】flute

【长度】length: ～测量 *linear measurement* /两条绳子的～一样。*The two ropes are about the same length.*

【长短】① length: 这条裤子～正合适。*The trousers are just the right length.* ② mishap; accident: 万一孩子有个～,怎么办? *What of anything should happen to the child?* ③ right and wrong; good and bad; strong and weak points: 她讨厌背后议论别人的～。*She dislikes gossiping about people behind their backs.* ④ [方] anyway; whatever: 这条裙子的～她不喜欢。*She likes this skirt no matter what you say.*

【长方形】rectangle; oblong

【长工】long-term labourer; farm labourer hired by the year

【长跪】kneel on one's stomach; kneel down with a straight back

【长号】【音】trombone

【长河】① long river; large river ② Milky Way ③ endless flow: 历史的～ *the long process of history* /在真理的～中,认识是无止境的。*In the endless flow of truth, cognition has no end.*

【长话短说】make a long story short

【长假】① long leave of absence; extended leave: 请～ *ask for a long leave of absence* ② resignation

【长江】Changjiang River; Yangtze River: ～三角洲 the Yangtze Delta / ～三峡工程 the Tree Gorges Project / ～后浪推前浪。*As in the Yangtze River the waves behind drive on those before — the new would always push on the old.*

【长颈鹿】【动】giraffe

【长久】for long; for a long time; permanently: ～打算 *long-term plans* /他们的友谊无法持续～。*Their friendship has no means to keep for long.*

【长久之计】long-term plan; permanent solution: 这不是～。*This is not a permanent solution.*

【长距离】long distance: ～赛跑 *a long-distance race*

【长空】sky: 飞机在万里～翱翔。*The airplanes are soaring in the vast sky.*

【长裤】trousers; slacks; pants
【长龙】long queue:买火车票的人排成~。*People stood in a long queue to buy train tickets.*
【长矛】long spear; lance; pike
【长眠】eternal sleep; death: ~地下 *lie buried* /无数先烈~在这片土地上。*Countless martyrs are buried in the area.*
【长年】① all the year round; for a long time:战士们~驻守在祖国的边关。*The soldiers garrison on the frontier juncture of our country all the year round.* ②[书] long life; longevity; long-lived
【长年累月】year in year out; over the years; all the year round
【长袍儿】long gown (worn by men)
【长跑】long-distance running; long-distance race: ~健将 master long-distance runner
【长篇大论】lengthy article or speech; be prosy and diffuse:新闻稿忌讳~。*Press releases taboo long-windedness.*
【长期】prolonged; long-term; long-lasting; age-long: ~存在的问题 *long-standing problem* / ~合作 *long-term cooperation* / ~政策 *long-term policy* / ~天气预报 *long-range weather fore cast* / ~贷款 *long-term loan* / ~亏损 *run at a loss for years* / ~信贷 *long-term credit* / ~债券 *long-term bond*
【长期共存】long-term coexistence: ~,互相监督,肝胆相照,荣辱与共 *long-term coexistence and mutual supervision of various parties, treating each other with all sincerity and sharing weal and woe*
【长驱直入】drive straight in; push deeply into:我军~,势如破竹。*Our army drove straight in, carrying everything on the way.*
【长衫】long gown (worn by men)
【长舌】long-tongued-fond of gossip; gossipy: ~妇 *gossipy woman; loquacious woman*
【长生不老】live forever and never grow old; perpetual rejuvenation: ~药 *elixir of life*
【长生果】[方] peanut; groundnut; pinder
【长石】【矿】feldspar
【长逝】pass away; be gone forever:溘然~ *pass away quite unexpectedly*
【长寿】long life; longevity; long-lived:祝您健康~! *I wish you good health and a long life.*
【长丝】【纺】filament
【长叹】deep sign: ~一声 *have a deep sign*
【长统靴】high boots
【长统袜】stockings
【长痛】long dull pain: ~不如短痛 *be better to have short, sharp pains than long, dull pains; be better to have a quick, though painful solution*
【长途】① long-distance: ~运输 *long-distance transport* / ~旅行 *long trip* ② long-distance call or bus:坐~汽车 *take a long-distance bus* / ~电话 *long distance or trunk call; toll call* / ~电话局 *long-distance exchange; toll office; toll centre* / ~电信局 *long-distance telecommunications bureau*
【长线】overproduction; oversupply: ~产品 *product in excessive supply; oversupplied product*
【长项】sth one is good at; one's strong point
【长吁短叹】moan and groan; utter sighs and groans; whine:她走来走去,不时地~。*She walked to-and-fro, moaning and groaning from time to time.*
【长须鲸】【动】finback (a whale)
【长夜】① long night; eternal night:漫漫~ *endless night* ② period resembling dark night: ~难明。*There seemed to be no end to the dark days.* ③ all night
【长于】be good at; be adept in; specialize:她~唱歌。*She is adept in singing.*
【长元音】【语】long vowel
【长圆】oval; egg-shaped: ~脸 *oval face*
【长远】long-term; long-range: ~的利益 *long-term interests* / ~目标 *long-range objective* / ~规划 *long-term plan*
【长征】① expedition; long march:万里~,始于足下。*A long journey of ten thousand li begins with a single step.* ② the Long March (of the Chinese Worker's and Peasants' Red Army in 1934 — 1935)
【长治久安】lasting stability and durable peace; prolonged political stability
【长住】live in a place for a long time; reside permanently; settle
【长足】[书] legs and bounds; rapid:取得~的进步 *make great strides; make rapid progress* /有了~的发展 *have scored considerable achievements*

场 ① level open space; threshing ground:晒~ *sun the harvested crops on the threshing ground* /打~ *threshing* ②[方] country fair; market:赶~ *go to the country fair* ③[量] spell; period:一~大雨 *a heavy rain* /一~硬仗 *a hard battle* /大干~ *go all out; exert one's utmost* /他生了一~气。*He was very angry.*
see also chǎng
【场院】threshing ground; sunning ground

肠 ① intestines:大~ *large intestine* /小~ *small intestine* ② sausage:鸡肉~ *chicken sausage* / ~衣 *casting for sausages*
【肠癌】【医】intestinal cancer
【肠胃】intestines and stomach; stomach; belly: ~不好 *suffer from indigestion*
【肠炎】enteritis
【肠子】intestines

尝[1] ① taste; try the flavour of:卧薪~胆 *sleep on brush-wood and taste gall; under go self-imposed hardships* / ~~咸淡 *try a bit to see if it tastes just right* / ~菜肴 *savor the dishes* ② experience; be aware of; come to know:备~艰辛 *experience all the hardships* / ~到甜头 *become aware of the benefits of; come to know the good of*

尝[2] ever; once:我们在网上聊了很久,但还未~见面。*We have chatted on net for a long time, however, we have never meet yet.* /我何~拒绝过你。*I have never said "no" to you.*
【尝试】attempt; try; venture; have a shot:为何不

C

~一下? *Why not have a try?* /为了振兴企业,他们~了各种方案。*In order to develop the enterprise vigorously, they have tried various plans.*

【尝受】experience; taste (the bitterness of life, etc.); go through (hardships, sufferings)

常 ① ordinary; common; normal: 人之~情 *normal human feelings* /习以为~ *be accustomed to* ② constant; invariable: 冬夏~青 *remain green throughout the year*; *evergreen* ③ frequently; usually; often: ~来~往 *exchange frequent visits*; *pay frequent calls on each other* /她~来这里。*She often comes here.*

C

【常备】be always prepared; be constantly standing: ~药品 *household medicine*; *common medicine*

【常备不懈】be always on the alert; be ever prepared: 军人要~。*Soldiers should be ever prepared against any eventuality.*

【常备军】standing army; permanent force

【常常】often; frequently; usually; many a time: 她周末~加班。*She often works overtime on weekends.* /她~坐在那里发呆。*She often sits there staring blankly.*

【常规】① convention; rule; routine; common practice: 按照~办事 *follow the routine* /打破~ *break with conventions* ②【医】routine: 血~ *routine blood test*

【常轨】normal practice (or course): 我们可以遵循~来解决这类事情。*We can follow the normal practice to settle such sort of matters.*

【常会】regular session (or meeting): 公司领导每季度举行一次~。*The leaders in the company hold regular meetings once every quarter.*

【常见】be common; be usual: ~病 *common disease*; *common ailment* /这类现象十分~。*Such phenomena are very common.*

【常客】a frequenter (of a restaurant, theatre); a frequent guest or customer

【常理】general consent; commonsense; customary practice

【常量】【物】constant: ~和变量 *constants and variables*

【常绿】evergreen: ~植物 *evergreen plants*; *evergreens* / ~灌木林 *evergreen shrubbery*

【常年】① throughout the year; all the year round; year in year out; long-term: 他~坚持体育锻炼。*He persists in physical training all the year round.* ② average year: 在这个地区,大豆~亩产四百公斤左右。*In this area, per mu yield of soybean for an average year is about 400 kilograms.*

【常青】evergreen: 四季~ *have green leaves throughout the year*

【常情】reason; common sense; human nature: 不合~ *contrary to reason*; *against common sense*

【常人】ordinary people

【常任】standing; permanent: 安理会~理事国 *permanent member of the Security Council* / ~代表 *permanent representative* / ~理事 *standing member of a council*

【常设】standing; permanent: ~机构 *standing body*; *permanent organization* / ~委员会 *permanent committee*

【常识】① elementary knowledge; general knowledge: 卫生~ *elementary knowledge of hygiene and sanitation* / ~课 *general knowledge course* ② common sense: 出国要申请签证是~。*It's common sense to apply a visa when you want to go abroad.*

【常事】common occurrence; commonplace happening: 备课至深夜对他来说是~。*It's common occurrence for him to sit up preparing for lessons far into the night.*

【常数】【数】constant: ~项 *constant term*

【常态】normal behaviour; normality; normalcy: 一反~ *contrary to one's normal behaviour* /恢复~ *return to normal*

【常谈】trite remark; platitude

【常温】① normal atmospheric temperature (between 15℃ and 20℃) ② homoiothermy: ~动物 *homoiothermal animal*; *warm blood animal*

【常务】① standing; permanent: ~秘书长 *permanent secretary-general* / ~委员 *member of the standing committee* / ~理事 *executive council member* / ~董事 *managing director* ② routine; day-to-day business: 主持~ *be in charge of day-to-day business*

【常言】common saying; proverb: ~道:熟能生巧。*As the saying goes, practice makes perfect.*

【常用】in common use; often used or quoted: ~药材 *medicinal herbs most in use* / ~词语 *everyday expression* / ~字 *basic word*

【常住】① reside permanently: ~之地 *permanent residence*; *somewhere one has resided* / ~居民 *inhabitant*; *permanent resident* / ~人口 *permanent population* ②【宗】changeless; permanent

【常驻】resident; permanent: ~大使 *resident ambassador* / ~代表 *permanent representative* / ~联合国代表团 *permanent mission to the United Nations* / ~外交使节 *permanent diplomatic envoy* / ~记者 *resident correspondent*

偿 ① repay; compensate for: 补~ *compensate*; *make up* / ~债 *pay a debt*; *discharge a debt* ② meet; fulfill; satisfy: 得~夙愿 *have fulfilled one's long-cherished wish* /如愿以~ *achieve what one wishes*

【偿付】pay back; pay; reimburse: 延期~ *deferred payment*; *delay the payment of a debt*

【偿还】repay; payback; return for; redeem: 分期~债务 *pay a debt in instalments* /如数~ *pay back the exact amount*

【偿命】pay with one's life (for a murder); a life for a life

【偿清】settle; clear off; pack back in full: ~债务 *clear off one's debts*

徜

【徜徉】[书] wander about; roam; stroll; saunter: ~于浩瀚的知识海洋中 *sail in the immensity ocean knowledge*

嫦

【嫦娥】Goddess in the Moon

chǎng

厂 ① factory; mill; plant; works: 玩具 ~ *toy factory* /面粉 ~ *flour mill* /钢铁 ~ *iron and steel works* /飞机制造 ~ *airplane plant* /造船 ~ *ship yard* /电影制片 ~ *studio*; *film studio* /糖 ~ *sugar refinery* /纺织 ~ *textile mill*; *spinning mill* ② yard; depot: 煤 ~ *coal yard*

【厂房】① factory building ② workshop

【厂规】factory rules and regulations

【厂家】① factory; manufacture: 有些 ~ 因生产伪劣产品受到起诉。*Many factories were prosecuted for making false and inferior products.* ② factory owner; factory management

【厂矿】factories and mines: ~协作 *cooperation between factories and mines*

【厂区】production area of a factory

【厂商】① factory owner: 承包 ~ *contractor* ② factories and shops.

【厂长】factory director; factory manager: ~负责制 *system of overall responsibility by the factory director*

【厂址】the site or location of a factory

场 ① gathering place used for a particular purpose: 战 ~ *battlefield* /篮球 ~ *basketball court* /运动 ~ *sports ground* /广 ~ *square* /剧 ~ *theatre* /赌 ~ *gambling house* ② stage: 上 ~ *enter stage* /下 ~ *exit stage* ③ scene: 第二幕 第二 ~ *act* Ⅱ, *scene* Ⅱ ④【物】field: 电 ~ *electric field* /磁 ~ *magnetic field* ⑤[量]: 一 ~ 演出 *a performance* /一 ~ 噩梦 *a nightmare* /一 ~ 足球赛 *a football match*

see also cháng

【场磁铁】【电】field magnet

【场次】number of showings of a film, play, etc.

【场地】space; place; site; lot: 比赛 ~ *competition arena*; *competition ground* /活动 ~ *playground*; *space for activities* /施工 ~ *construction site*

【场合】situation; occasion; context: 外交 ~ *diplomatic occasion* /正式 ~ *formal occasions* /公开 ~ *in public*; *openly* /说话要分 ~。*Think of the social context whenever you speak.*

【场记】① log (for film shooting, theatrical performance, etc.) ② log keeper; script holder

【场界灯】【航】boundary lights

【场景】①【戏】scene: 富有特色的 ~ *scene with special features of its own*; *scene with a distinctive flavour* /逼真的 ~ *life like scene* ② sight; scene; picture: 热火朝天的劳动 ~ *picture of overflowing labour enthusiasm* /依依惜别的 ~ *sentimental parting scene*

【场面】① scene; spectacle (in drama, fiction, etc.): 这部电影有不少动人的 ~。*There are many moving scenes in the film.* ② spectacle; occasion; scene: 盛大的 ~ *a grand occasion* /壮观的 ~ *sublime spectacle* ③ appearance; front; facade: ~活 *polite platitude for the occasion*; *civil banalities* / ~人 *very sociable person*; *person of prestige*; *celebrity* / ~上 *on social occasions*; *in social life*

【场所】place; arena; venue: 公共 ~ *public place* /娱乐 ~ *place of recreation*; *place of entertainment* /热闹 ~ *place busting with noise and activity* /蚊蝇孳生的 ~ *breeding ground of flies and mosquitoes*

【场子】large place (for an activity)

敞 ① (of houses, yards, etc.) spacious; roomy: 这间书房太宽 ~ 了。*This study is too big.* ② open; uncovered: ~着门 *leave the door open* / ~衣露胸 *with one's coat unbuttoned*

【敞车】① open wagon; open freight car ② flatcar

【敞怀】① with one's shirt unbuttoned; bare one's chest ② unrestrainedly; open mindedly: ~痛饮 *drink to one's heart's content*

【敞开】① open wide: ~窗户 *keep the window wide open* / ~心扉 *open one's mind to* / ~思想 *say what's in one's mind*; *get things off one's chest* ② unstinted; unlimited: ~供应 *supply without limit*

【敞亮】① bright and spacious: ~的教室 *bright and spacious classroom* ② clear-minded: 她虽然不能说话,但心里很 ~。*Her mind is very clear, though she can't speak out.*

【敞篷车】open car

【敞胸露怀】bare one's chest

氅 cloak: 大 ~ *cloak*

chàng

怅 disappointed; sorry

【怅然】disappointed; upset: ~不语 *be speechless with disappointment* / ~离去 *walk away disappointedly* / ~若失 *feel depressed and perplexed*

【怅惋】sigh with regret; deeply regret: ~不已 *can hardly repress a feeling of deep regret*

【怅惘】distracted; listless: 无限 ~ *be overcome with a feeling of infinite anxiety* /神色 ~ *look anxious and depressed* /飞机在天边消失了,她仍然 ~ 地站在机场。*Even after the airplane had flied out of sight, she still stood solicitously in the airport.*

畅 ① smooth; unimpeded: 流 ~ *easy and smooth*; *fluent* ② free; uninhibited: ~饮 *drink one's fill*

【畅达】①smooth; fluent: 译文 ~。*The translation reads smoothly.* ② pass unimpeded: 交通 ~ *have a good transport and communications net work*

【畅怀】to one's heart's content; as much as one likes: ~大笑 *laugh to one's heart's content*

【畅快】free from inhibitions; carefree; happy:心情~ *have easy of mind; be carefree and happy; be in a happy mood* /玩得~ *have a good time; have a wonderful time*

【畅所欲言】speak out freely; speak without any reservation; your out what one wishes to say; get sth off one's chest; express with zest and gust:这次会议很呆板,我们没能~。*The meeting was very formalistic, and we couldn't pour out what we wishes to say.*

【畅谈】talk freely and to one's heart's content; chat or speak glowingly of: ~人生的理想 *talk freely and glowingly about one's ambition of life* / ~国内外大好形式 *speak glowingly of the excellent situation at home and abroad* / ~美好的前程 *speak frankly and eagerly about one's brilliant future*

【畅通】unblocked; unimpeded: ~无阻 *pass unimpeded; go unhindered* /信息~。*The flow of information is unimpeded.*

【畅想】think freely; set no bounds to imagination; give free rein to one's imagination: ~灿烂的明天 *freely image a gorgeous picture of the future*

【畅销】be in great demand; sell briskly and easily; sell well; have a ready market:中国茶叶~国外。*Chinese tea sells well on foreign market.* /他们公司的产品很~。*Products made in their company are in great demand.*

【畅行无阻】pass unimpeded; proceed without hindrance

【畅叙】chat cheerfully (usually about old times): ~友情 *relive an old friendship*

【畅游】① enjoy a good swim: ~长江 *enjoy a good swim in the Changjiang River* ② enjoy a sighting tour: ~名胜古迹 *enjoy a delightful trip to interesting places and historic spots*

倡 initiate; advocate

【倡导】initiate; propose; promote; advocate: ~和平共处五项原则 *initiate the Five Principles of peaceful coexistence*

【倡议】propose; proposal; initiate: ~书 *written proposal; proposal* / ~者 *initiator* / ~权 *diplomacy initiative* / ~保护环境 *propose protecting environment* / ~植树造林 *propose forest plantation* / ~组织学术讨论会 *propose holding seminars*

唱 ① sing: ~国歌 *sing the National Anthem* /独~ *solo* /合~ *chorus* /二重~ *duet* /三重~ *trio* /四重~ *quartet* /五重~ *quintet* ② call; cry: 雄鸡~晓 *cock crowing at dawn* ③ a song or singing part of a Chinese opera

【唱本】the libretto or scrip of a ballad-singer

【唱词】libretto; words of a ballad

【唱段】aria:京剧中精彩的~ *a wonderful aria from a Beijing opera*

【唱对台戏】put on a rival show; enter into rivalry with sb; set oneself against sb:他总是故意和我~。*He always puts on rival shows against me on purpose.*

【唱反调】sing a different tune; strike a discordant tune; speak or act contrary to

【唱高调】make high-sounding statements; say fine-sounding things; use high-flown words; affect a high moral tone: ~无济于事。*Fine-sounding words won't help matters.*

【唱歌】sing:她喜欢~。*She likes singing.*

【唱和】① one sing a song and the others join in the chorus:彼此~ *when one starts singing, another joins in* ② when one writes a poem, the other comes up with, another in reply, usually using the same rhyme sequence

【唱红脸】wear the red makeup of the stage hero; play the hero; appear generous and kind

【唱机】phonograph; gramophone; record player

【唱空城计】① perform the empty-city stratagem — present a bold front to conceal a weak defence ② have all or most of the staff vacated:大家都出去搞推销了,只留下经理一人~。*With everyone else promoting sales outside, merely the manager is left.*

【唱老调】sing the hackneyed tune; harp on the same old theme:文章要有创新,不要总是~。*You should have innovative ideas when you write; Don't always harp on the same old theme.*

【唱片】phonograph or gramophone record; disc; platter:放~ *play a gramophone record* /灌~ *cut a disc; make a record*

【唱票】call out the names of candidates while counting ballots: ~人 *teller*

【唱戏】sing and act in an opera; put on a theatrical performance

【唱主角】play the leading role:这次的音乐晚会由她来~。*She will play the leading role in the music evening.*

chāo

抄[1] ① copy; transcribe: ~资料 *copy data* / ~家庭作业 *copy sb's homework* /照~原文 *make a verbatim transcription of the original* ② copy; lift; plagiarize: ~别人的文章 *plagiarize (from) somebody else's writing*

抄[2] ① search and confiscate; make a raid upon: ~赃物 *search for and confiscate the booty* / ~了土匪的老窝 *make a raid upon the bandits' den* ② take a shortcut; outflank: ~敌人侧翼 *outflank the enemy* ③ fold in the sleeves: ~着手站在一边 *stand by with folded arms*

抄[3] grab: ~起铁锹就干活 *grab a shovel and plunge into the job*

【抄本】hand-copied book; transcript; copy:《红楼梦》~ *a handwritten copy of A Dream of Red*

Mansions

【抄道】take a shortcut：～迫击 *chase by taking a shortcut*

【抄后路】outflank and attack (the enemy) in the rear; turn the enemy's rear

【抄获】search and confiscate; search out; ferret out：～财宝 *search for and confiscate treasure*

【抄家】search the house and confiscate the property

【抄件】duplicate; copy：现将报告的～转发给你。*A copy of the report is forwarded to you herewith.*

【抄近路】take a shortcut

【抄录】make a copy of; copy; quote：这段文字是从报上～的。*This paragraph is quoted from a newspaper article.*

【抄没】ransack and confiscate：～家产 *ransack sb's house; search sb's house and confiscate his property*

【抄身】search sb; make a body search; frisk sb

【抄手】① fold (one's arms) ② dumpling soup; wonton

【抄送】make a copy for; send a duplicate to：～有关单位 *send duplicates to the relevant units*

【抄袭】① plagiarize; copy; lift ②borrow indiscriminately from other's experience：不要盲目～别人的经验。*Never copy other's experience blindly.* ③ launch a surprise attack on the enemy by making a detour

【抄写】copy; transcribe：～文件 *transcribe the document* /～员 *copyist*

【抄斩】(in feudal times) confiscate sb's property and have him executed

吵

【吵吵】[方] be noisy; make a row; kick up a racket：安静点儿，不要～。*Be quiet; Don't make such a row.*

see also chǎo

钞

paper money; banknote：现～ *cash*

【钞票】banknote; paper money; bill：印刷～ *print notes* /大额～ *notes of large denominations* /这张～是假的。*This is a counterfeit banknote.*

超

① exceed; surpass; overtake：赶～世界先进水平 *catch up with and surpass the advanced world level* /捐款～万元。*The donation exceeded ten thousand yuan.* ② transcend; go beyond：～现实 *go beyond reality; transcend realism; be unrealistic* ③ ultra-; super-; extra-：～水平发挥 *exert oneself and gain a result better than expected one*

【超薄】ultra-thin：～镜片 *ultra-thin glasses* /～切片 *ultra-thin section*

【超编】overstaff; exceed the personnel quota：～人员 *excess personnel; redundant staff*

【超标】surpass the set standard; exceed a quota：因～排放污水而被罚款 *be fined for excessive discharge of waste water*

【超产】overfull a production target or quota：～百分之十 *exceed the production quota by 10%*

【超常】supernormal; hypernormal; extraordinary：～儿童 *supernormal child* /智力～ *be a person of extraordinary intelligence*

【超车】overtake other vehicles：不准～ *no overtaking*

【超出】overstep; go beyond; exceed：～定额 *exceed the quota* /～意料 *exceed one's expectations* /～范围 *go beyond the scope* /～法律权限 *go beyond the law; overstep one's jurisdiction; be extralegal*

【超导】【物】superconduction：～材料 *superconducting material; superconductor* /～电性 *superconductivity* /～技术 *superconducting technology* /～体 *superconductor* /～元素 *superconducting element*

【超度】【宗】expiate the sins of the dead; release souls from the purgatory：～众生 *save the living souls from the sea of misery*

【超短波】ultrashort wave

【超短裙】miniskirt

【超额】exceed norm; above quota; overfulfil or exceed the quota：～完成生产指标 *overfulfil the production quota; surpass the production target*

【超凡】① transcend the worldly; overcome the worldly desire and attain sainthood ② out of the common run; extraordinary; outstanding; super mundane; uncommon：技艺～ *extraordinarily skilful*

【超负荷】overload; excess load：～运转 *run with excess load; overloading operation*

【超高速】ultrahigh-speed; hypervelocity：～巨型计算机 *giant ultra-high speed computer*

【超高压】①【物】superhigh pressure ②【电】ultra-high voltage (UHV); extra-high tension (EHT)：～输电系统 *ultrahigh-voltage transmission system*

【超过】overtake; outstrip; surpass; exceed：～历史最高记录 *top all previous records* /～规定的速度 *exceed the speed limit*

【超级】super：～明星 *superstar* /～市场 *supermarket* /～油轮 *supertanker* /～大国 *superpower* /～公路 *super high way; free way*

【超假】overstay one's leave：无故～是不允许的。*Overstaying your leave without special reason is not permitted.*

【超龄】overage：～队员 *overage member of a team*

【超媒体】hypermedia

【超期】beyond the fixed term of service：这台机器的使用年限～了。*The machine has been running beyond its guaranteed life.*

【超期服役】extended service in the army; extended active duty：～的队员 *overage team member*

【超前】① ahead of times; aiming at the future; transcending the present：～教育 *future-oriented education* ② surpassing past generations：～绝后 *unrivalled in the past and not likely to be matched in the future* ③【电】lead

【超群】head and shoulders above all others; preeminent：才学～ *be outstanding both in knowledge and talent*

【超然】aloof; detached：他对她的事情持～的态度。*He took a detached attitude toward her matters.*

【超人】① out of the common run; superhuman; exceptional：～的毅力 *superhuman fortitude* / ～的记忆力 *exceptionally good memory* ② superman

【超生】①【宗】be reincarnated ② be lenient; be merciful; spare sb ③ have more children than the plan allows; give unplanned births

【超声波】ultrasonic wave; supersonic wave：～疗法 *ultrasonic therapy*

C

【超俗】be free from vulgarities; be unconventional

【超速】① exceed the speed limit ② hypervelocity：～粒子 *hypervelocity particle*

【超脱】① be free from conventions; be unconventional; be original：他的字体很～。*His calligraphy has an unconventional grace.* ② be detached; stand or keep aloof; keep distance from：～感情的困扰 *keep aloof from emotional difficulties* / 任何人都不可能～现实。*No one can possibly detach himself from reality*

【超音速】supersonic speed：～喷气机 *superjet* / ～战斗机 *supersonic fighter-plane*

【超员】exceed the designated number：这艘船大大～。*This ship is far overloaded with passengers.*

【超越】surpass; transcend; overstep; exceed; surmount：～自我 *outdo oneself; transcend oneself* / ～障碍 *surmount an obstacle* / ～射击 *overhead fire*

【超载】【交】overload; surcharge：～能力 *overload capacity*

【超支】overspend; live beyond one's income：她很会计划，从不～。*She is such a good planner that she never lives beyond her income.*

【超重】① overload ② overweight：～信件 *overweight letter* / ～行李 *excess luggage* ③【物】superheavy：～元素 *superheavy element*

【超自然】supernatural：～的力量 *supernatural force*

cháo

巢 nest：归～ *bird return nest* / 鸟～ *bird's nest* / 蚁～ *ant's nest* / 蜂～ *honeycomb; beehive*

【巢居】dwell in trees

【巢窟】den; lair; nest; hideout

【巢穴】lair; den; nest; hideout：匪徒的～ *a bandits' den*

朝 ① court; government：在～ *be in power* ② dynasty：唐～ *the Tang Dynasty* / 改～换代 *dynastic changes* ③ emperor's reign ④ have an audience with (a king, emperor, etc.); make a pilgrimage to：百鸟～凤 *all birds pay homage to the phoenix* / ～见皇帝 *have an audience with the emperor* ⑤ facing; towards：～北走 *go northward* / 四脚～天 *lie or fall down flat on one's back* / 他～我微笑。*He smiled at me.*

see also zhāo

【朝拜】① pay respects to (a sovereign) ② worship

【朝臣】courtier; government official

【朝代】dynasty; reign

【朝服】court dress in feudal China

【朝纲】the laws of an imperial court：领先～ *promulgate court disciplines*

【朝贡】present tribute to an emperor; pay tribute to an imperial court

【朝贺】pay one's respects to (the sovereign)：新君登基，百官～。*When the new emperor ascended the throne, all the courtiers came to pay their respects.*

【朝见】have an audience with; be received by (the emperor)：～天子 *have an audience with the emperor*

【朝觐】①［书］have an audience with an emperor ② make a pilgrimage：～圣地 *make a pilgrimage to a sacred place*

【朝圣】【宗】pilgrimage; hadj：到麦加～ *make a pilgrimage to Mecca*

【朝廷】① royal court ② imperial government

【朝鲜】Korea：～人 *Korean* / ～语 *Korean* / ～半岛 *Korean peninsula*

【朝鲜族】① Korean nationality in China ② Korea people

【朝向】① turn towards; face：向日葵总是～太阳。*Sunflowers always turn towards the sun.* ② exposure：两座房子的～不同。*The two houses different exposures.*

【朝阳】be exposed to the sun; sunny：～的房间 *rooms which can get bright sunlight*

【朝野】① the court and the commonalty：～上下，井然有序。*The whole nation is in good order.* ② the government and the public

【朝政】court affairs; affairs of state; court administration：处理～ *handle court affairs*

嘲 ridicule; deride; sneer：冷～热讽 *taunt and jeer; scathing sarcasm* / 解～ *try to ward off a taunt with a lame excuse; try to explain things away when been laugh at*

【嘲讽】sneer at; taunt; mock; ridicule：他被她～的微笑激怒了。*He was irritated by her ironical smile.* / 不要～别人的过失。*Never cast ridicule upon one's fault.*

【嘲弄】mock; poke fun at; ridicule：成了别人～的对象 *become a butt for ridicule* / ～历史的人必将被历史所～。*Those who mock history are doomed to be mocked by history.*

【嘲笑】laugh at; ridicule; deride; jeer at; sneer at：忍受别人的～ *endure the ridicule of others* / 被人～，他感到非常尴尬。*Being a target for derision, he felt very embarrassed.*

潮 ① tide：学～ *student strike; campus upheaval* / 浪～ *tide* / 心血来～ *be seized by a whim; have a sudden impulse; act on the spur of the moment* ② social upsurge; current; tide：学～ *student movement; student unrest; campus up-*

heaval /思～ *trend of thought* /新～ *new current*; *new fashion* ③ damp; moist:饼干返～了。*The cookies have got damp.* /这被子很～。*The quit is very damp.*

【潮红】(of face or skin) flush:两颊～ *be flushed in both cheeks*

【潮乎乎】damp; dank; clammy; moist:这房间～的。*The room is pretty dank.*

【潮流】① tide; tidal current ② trend; current:顺应历史～ *go along with the historical trend* /跟上时代的～ *follow the current of the times*

【潮气】moisture in the air; humidity; damp:若仓库里～太大,粮食就容易发霉。*The grain is liable to mildew if the humidity in the barn is too high.*

【潮热】【中医】hectic fever

【潮润】① damp humid ②teary:想到伤心的往事,她双目～。*At the thought of the heartrending bygones, her eyes blurred with tears.*

【潮湿】damp; clammy; moist:地下室太～,不能住人。*The basement is too damp to serve as living rooms.*

【潮水】tidewater; tide; tidal water:欢乐的人群如～般涌向海滩。*Hordes of joyous people streamed into the sea beach.*

【潮位】tide mark:～曲线 *tide curve*

【潮汐】morning and evening tides; ocean tide:～表 *tide table* /～测站 *tide station* /～预报 *tide prediction* /～能 *tidal energy* /～发电站 *tidal power station*

【潮汛】spring tide

【潮涌】surge forward like a tide; roll like a tide:心事如～。*All feelings welled up in one's heart like tidal waters.*

chǎo

吵 ① make a noise; disturb:别～他。*Don't disturb him.* /他们～得我没法睡。*So much noise did they make that I couldn't get a wink* /不要把婴儿～醒了。*Don't wake the baby up!* ② quarrel; squabble; wrangle:～～闹闹 *wrangle*; *kick up a row* /不要因为一点小事就～起来。*Don't quarrel over a mere trifle.*
see also chāo

【吵架】quarrel; squabble; wrangle; have words with sb:他们夫妻俩老为孩子的事～。*The couples are always quarrelling over their child.* /他存心要和我～。*He intended to quarrel with me.*

【吵闹】① wrangle; kick up a row; bicker:他们为了钱的事～不休。*They quarrelled on and on over money matters.* ② harass; disturb:他讨厌正在思考时被人～。*He dislikes being disturbed when he is thinking.* ③din; hubbub:大厅里一片～声。*A hubbub was heard in the hall.*

【吵嚷】shout in confusion; make a racket; clamour:你们在～什么? *What are you clamouring for?*

【吵嘴】quarrel; bicker; squabble; have a row:她从不跟别人～。*She has never quarrelled with anybody.*

炒 ① stir-fry; fry:～饭 *fried rice* /～鸡蛋 *scrambled eggs* /～肉丝 *stir-fried shredded pork* /～花生 *roasted peanuts* ② speculate; promote:～股票 *speculate in stocks* /～地皮 *speculate in real estate*; *speculate in building land* /～得很热 *promote sth so that it becomes a hot item*; *be raised artificially high in price* ③[方] sack; fire

【炒菜】① stir-fry; make dishes:她喜欢～。*She likes making dishes.* ② a stir-fried dish:我要了两个～和一碗米饭。*I ordered two stir-fried dishes and one bowl of rice.* ③ promote; speculate

【炒股】profiteer with stocks; speculate in stocks

【炒锅】frying pan

【炒汇】speculate in foreign currency; buying and selling foreign currency

【炒冷饭】stir-fry leftover rice — say or do the same old thing; dish up the same old stuff; rehash:她的话尽是～。*There's nothing new in her speech.*

【炒面】① fried noodles with shredded meat and vegetables ② parched flour:开水冲～ *mix parched flour with boiling water*

【炒勺】round-bottomed frying pan with a handle

【炒鱿鱼】[方] stir-fry squid — give sb the sack; dismiss sb; fire sb:他被老板炒了鱿鱼。*He was fired by his boss.*

【炒作】profiteering activities

chē

车 ① vehicle:公共汽～ *bus* /叉～ *forklift* /汽～ *motor car*; *motor vehicle*; *automobile* /火～ *train* /无轨电～ *trolley bus* /自行～ *bicycle*; *bike* /救护～ *ambulance* /货～ *freight truck*; *goods wagon* /灵～ *hearse* /餐～ *dining car* /开车 *drive (a car)* ② wheeled instrument; wheeled machine:纺～ *spinning wheel* /吊～ *crane*; *hoist* /水～ *water wheel* ③ machine:开～ *start a machine* /停～ *stop the machine* ④ lathe; turn:～光 *smooth sth on a lathe* ⑤ lift water by waterwheel ⑥[方] turn (one's body or limb)
see also jū

【车把】hand bar; shaft

【车把式】car-driver; carter

【车帮】side or sideboard of a cart or truck

【车床】lathe; turning machine:万能～ *universal lathe*

【车次】① train number ② motorcoach number

【车道】traffic lane:快～ *speed lane* /慢～ *normal lane*

【车灯】light or lamp on a vehicle (e. g. headlights, bicycle lamp, etc.)

【车队】convoy; motorcade

【车费】fair

【车夫】[旧] cart-driver; carter

【车工】① lathe work ② turner; lathe operator: ~车间 *turning shop*
【车钩】coupler; coupling
【车轱辘】[口] wheel (of a vehicle)
【车号】licence number (of a vehicle)
【车祸】traffic accident; road accident
【车技】trick-cycling
【车间】workshop; shop: 装配~ *assembly shop; fitting shop* / ~主任 *workshop director*
【车库】garage
【车筐】bicycle basket
【车辆】vehicles: 来往~ *traffic vehicles* /前面施工,~绕行。*Road construction ahead; please make a detour.*
【车裂】tear sb asunder by five carts (a cruel punishment in ancient China)
【车流】traffic flow: ~不息 *an incessant stream of vehicles — heavy traffic*
【车轮】wheel(of a vehicle)
【车牌】licence plate; number plate
【车篷】awning for a vehicle
【车票】ticket for a vehicle
【车身】① body of a vehicle ② [方] turn away; turn round
【车手】motorist
【车水马龙】endless stream of horses and carriages — heavy traffic: 门前~。*The courtyard was thronged with visitors.* / 大街上~。*The street looks very busy with an incessant stream of buses and car.*
【车速】① speed of a vehicle ② speed of a lathe
【车胎】tyre
【车头】① the front part of a vehicle ② engine (of a train)
【车帷】curtain in a carriage
【车尾】rear of a vehicle
【车位】parking place: 这个停车站有六十个~。*The parking lot has sixty parking places.*
【车厢】railway carriage; railway compartment
【车削】【机】turning
【车辕】shaft (of a cart, etc.)
【车载斗量】be enough to fill carts and be measured by the bushel — common and numerous: 像他这样的人在这里~。*People like him come by the bushel here.*
【车闸】brake(of a vehicle): ~失灵。*The brake doesn't work.*
【车站】station; stop; depot: ~候车室 *station hall; waiting room*
【车照】driving licence
【车辙】rut
【车轴】axletree; axle
【车主】owner of a vehicle
【车子】① a small vehicle (such as a car, pushcart, etc.) ② [方] bicycle

chě

扯 ① pull; drag: 东拉西~ *drag in all sorts of irrelevant matters; ramble* / ~着她的袖子 *pull her by the sleeve* / ~着嗓子喊 *shout at the top of one's voice* /她把两件不相干的事~在了一起。*She lumped the two irrelevant things together.* ② tear: 她把信~得粉碎。*She tore the letter to pieces.* ③ [口] buy(cloth, thread, etc.): ~二尺布 *buy two chi of cloth* ④ chat; gossip: ~闲活 *gossip* / 别把话~远了。*Don't wander from the topic.*
【扯白】[方] lie; tell a lie
【扯淡】[方] talk nonsense: 别瞎~! *Don't talk nonsense.*
【扯后腿】hold sb back from action; be a drag on sb; be a hindrance to sb: 农业搞不好,就会扯工业的后腿。*A backward agriculture would be a hindrance to industry.*
【扯谎】tell a lie; lie: 他在~。*He is telling a lie.*
【扯家常】talk about everyday matters; chit-chat
【扯皮】dispute over trifles; argue back and forth; wrangle: 双方互相~,推卸责任。*They argued back and force, each trying to shift the blame onto the other.*
【扯平】break even; even up: 你再给我20元,咱俩就~了。*Give me another twenty yuan, and we will be quits.*

chè

彻 thorough; penetrating; complete: 透~的理解 *perfect understanding* /响~云霄 *resound through the skies; soaring; echo to the skies*
【彻底】thorough; thoroughgoing; full: ~改变 *radical change* / ~调查 *full investigation* / ~否定 *totally reject; reject categorically* / ~完蛋 *be finished for good* / ~放弃 *abandon thoroughly* /这房间需要~的打扫。*The room needs a thorough cleaning.*
【彻骨】to the bone: 寒风~。*The cold wind chills one the bone.*
【彻头彻尾】out and out; through and through; downright; sheer; head over heals: ~的骗局 *downright fraud; sheer fraud; deception from beginning to end*
【彻夜】all night; all through the night; from dusk to dawn: ~苦读 *study all night; burn the midnight oil* /实验室里的灯火~通明。*The lights were ablaze in the laboratory all through the night.*

坼 [书] split open; crack: 天旱地~。*The ground cracked after a long drought.*
【坼裂】[书] split open; crack

掣 ① pull; tug; drag ② draw: 他赶紧~回手去。*He rapidly drew back his hand.* ③ flash past: 电~雷鸣。*Lightning flashed and thunder rolled.*
【掣电】(of lighting) flash
【掣肘】hold sb back by the elbow; impede; handi-

cap; make things difficult for sb:这件事办得很顺利,没有人~。*With no one making difficulties, the matter was settled very smoothly.* /他们没法继续旅行,因为风雪在~。*Due to obstruction by the deep snow, they can't go on travelling.*

撤 ① remove; take away: ~除障碍 *remove obstacles* / ~火 *put out the fire; stop heating* / ~一道菜 *take a dish away* / ~去餐具 *take away the dishwares* ② dismiss: 他的职务被~了。*He was dismissed from his post.* ③ withdraw; evacuate; retreat: 立即后~ *withdraw immediately* ④ [方] (of smell, weight, etc.) reduce; take off: ~味儿 *reduce the smell* /向农村~ *retreat to the countryside*

【撤兵】withdraw troops: 停火~ *cease hostilities and withdraw troops*

【撤除】remove; dismantle: ~军事设施 *dismantle military installations* / ~渎职领导的职务 *dismiss the malfeasant leaders from their offices*

【撤防】withdraw a garrison; withdraw from a defended position

【撤岗】withdraw the sentries; withdraw the guard

【撤换】dismiss and replace; recall; replace: ~人选 *recall candidates*

【撤回】① recall; withdraw: ~军队 *withdraw troops* ② retract; revoke; withdraw: ~声明 *retract a declaration* / ~起诉 *withdraw a charge; revoke a court action*

【撤军】withdraw troops

【撤离】withdraw from; evacuate; leave: ~阵地 *abandon a position* / ~危险地带 *withdraw from the danger area*

【撤诉】(of the plaintiff) drop a lawsuit; withdraw an accusation: 经调解,她同意~了。*She agreed to drop the lawsuit after intermediation.*

【撤退】withdraw; retreat; evacuate; pull out: 全部~ *full pull out* /安全~ *make good one's retreat* / 密集的轰炸迫使敌人~了。*The saturation bombing forced the enemy to retreat.*

【撤席】clear the table (after a feast): ~后,端上了一些甜点。*Desserts were sewed after the table was cleared.*

【撤销】cancel; revoke; rescind; abolish: ~职务 *dismiss sb from his post* / ~处分 *rescind a penalty* / ~禁令 *lift a ban* / ~决议 *annul a decision* / ~合同 *abandon a contract* / ~定货单 *retreat an order*

【撤职】remove sb from office; dismiss or discharge sb from his post; eliminate: ~查办 *discharge sb from his post and prosecute him*

【撤走】withdraw; leave; evacuate: ~军队 *withdraw the army*

澈 (of water) clear; limpid: 清~见底 *crystal clear; crystalline*

chēn

抻 pull out; stretch: 把衣服~平。*Stretch and smooth out the clothes.*

【抻面】① hand-pulled noodles ② make noodles by drawing out the dough by hand

嗔 [书] ① be angry; be displeased ② be annoyed (with sb); blame

【嗔怪】blame; rebuke; upbraid

【嗔怒】become angry; get angry: ~而言 *speak angrily*

【嗔色】angry expression; sullen look: 她面带~,瞪了她丈夫一眼。*She looked displeased and glared at his husband.*

chén

臣 ① official under a feudal ruler; subject; minister: 忠~ *loyal court official* ② (used by court officials when addressing the emperor) your vassal; I

【臣服】[书] submit oneself to the rule of; acknowledge allegiance to

【臣民】subjects of a feudal ruler

【臣子】an official in feudal times

尘 ① dust; dirt: 轻~ *light dust* /除~装置 *dust removing device* /吸~器 *dust remover; vacuum cleaner* /一~不染 *spotless; very clean* ② this world; worldly affairs: 红~ *world of mortals; vanity fair* ③ [书] *traces*: 步人后~ *follow the trail of sb; follow in sb's footsteps*

【尘埃】dust; dirt: ~传染 *dust infection* /放射性~ *radioactive dust*

【尘暴】dust storm; dust devil

【尘封】dust-laden; covered with dust

【尘垢】dirt and dust; dust and filth: 他带着满脸的~回来了。*He came back with dust and dirt all over his face.*

【尘海】human world: 茫茫~ *immense human world*

【尘世】this world; this mortal life

【尘事】worldly affairs: 纷繁的~ *numerous and complicated worldly affairs*

【尘俗】① this world; vulgar world; mortal life ② worldly; earthly

【尘土】dust; dirt; soil: 满身~ *be covered all over with dust* /风一来,吹得~飞扬。*The wind was blowing, flying a cloud of dust.*

【尘烟】① cloud of dust: ~滚滚 *clouds of dust churning* ② smoke and dust: ~弥漫 *be heavy with smoke and dust*

【尘缘】predestined bonds of this world; human bondage; carnal thoughts: ~未断。*One has not broken free the bonds of this world.*

辰 ① celestial bodies: 日月星~ *the hosts of heaven* ② any of the traditional twelve two-hour periods of the day：一个时～ *one of the two-hour periods*; *two hours* ③ time; day; occasion：诞～ *birthday* /良～美景 *beautiful sceneries in a good day*

【辰时】the period of the day from 7a. m to 9a. m

【辰星】Mercury

沉 ① sink：石～大海 *like a stone dropped into the sea* /月落星～。*The moon is down and the stars have set.* ②［喻］keep down; lower; sink：好长一段时间没有他的消息，我的心都～下去了。*My heart sank, for I haven't got any news from him for a long time.* ③ subside：地基下～ *subsidence of foundations* ④（of degree）deep; profound ⑤ heavy：这只箱子很～。*This box is very heavy.* ⑥ feel heavy or uncomfortable：我的头有点～。*My head feels a bit heavy.* /我的两条腿很～。*My legs are very heavy.*

【沉沉】① heavy：麦穗～地垂下来。*The ears of wheat hang heavy on the stalks.* ② deep; profound：心事～ *have a heavy heart*; *be laden with anxiety* /暮霭～。*Dusk is falling.*

【沉甸甸】heavy：～的钱包 *heavy wallet* / ～的谷穗 *heavy ears of millet* /想到作业还没有写完，我心里就～的。*The thought of the unfinished homework weighs heavily on my mind.*

【沉淀】① precipitate; form a sediment：～池 *precipitating tank* / ～剂 *precipitating agent* / ～物 *sediment*; *precipitate* /药水～了。*There is some sediment in the liquid medicine.* ② accumulation; accretion：文化～ *accretion of culture*

【沉浮】① sink and rise; drift ② ups and downs in one's life; vicissitude

【沉积】① deposit; sediment：～作用 *deposition*; *sedimentation* /桌面上～了厚厚一层灰。*There is a thick layer of dust sediment on the desk.* ② sedimentation; settlement ③ accumulation; accretion

【沉寂】① quiet; still; silent：一声尖叫声划破了深夜的～。*A screech broke the silence of the night.* ② no news

【沉降】subside：～缝 *settlement joint*

【沉浸】be immersed in; be steeped in; be permeated with：～在美丽的回忆中 *be immersed in beautiful memories* / ～在极大的喜悦之中 *be immersed in great joyance*

【沉静】① quiet; calm：放假了，学校里～下来。*All was quiet in the campus during the vacation.* ② calm; serene; placid; be gentle and quiet：～的神色 *a serene look* /他的性格很～。*She is a very placid girl.*

【沉沦】sink into：不甘心～ *refuse to submit to degradation* / ～于罪恶的深渊里 *sink deep into the iniquity of sin*

【沉闷】① dull; oppressive; depressing; dreary; gloomy：实验室的气氛太～了，让人无法忍受。*The atmosphere in the laboratory is unbearably oppressive.* ② depressed; in low spirits; retiring：性格～ *have a retiring nature* ③ not outgoing; withdrawn; tedious：他这个人很～。*He is rather withdrawn.*

【沉迷】indulge in; wallow：～于酒色之中 *be excessively fond of wine and woman*; *be addicted to drinking and womanizing*; *be extremely indulged in sensual pleasures and dissipation*

【沉湎】［书］indulgent; wallow in; be given to：～于儿女之情 *indulge in romantic sentiments*

【沉没】sink; founder; submerge：打捞～已久的轮船 *salve a long-sunken ship*

【沉默】① reticent; taciturn; uncommunicative：他的妻子去世后，他变得更加～了。*He has become even more reticent since his wife died.* ② silent; wordless; speechless：上课了，我们要保持～。*The class began, so we had to keep quiet.*

【沉溺】be addicted to; wallow; indulge; be given to：～于醉生梦死的生活里 *indulge in dissipation*

【沉睡】be fast asleep; be sound asleep; be sunk in sleep

【沉思】think deeply; ponder; meditate; contemplate; be lost in：陷入～之中 *be lost in thought*; *be deep in meditation*

【沉痛】① with a deep feeling of grief or remorse; be deep in sorrow：～的哀悼 *profound condolences* ② deeply felt; bitter

【沉稳】① steady; prudent; discreet：他处事很～。*He is very prudent in handling matters.* ② sound; steady; untroubled：小宝贝睡得很～。*The baby is in sound asleep.*

【沉陷】① sink; cave in; subside; settlement：洪水后路基～了。*The flood made the roadbed cave in.* ② get bogged down; be lost in a muse; contemplate：老奶奶终日～于往事的回忆中。*The old grandma was lost in memories of the bygones all the time.*

【沉毅】steady and strong; determined; steadfast; resolute：这位经理～果断。*The manager is steadfast and resolute.*

【沉吟】① recite or read（poetry）in a low voice ② mutter to oneself; ponder; be unable to make up one's mind：她～了良久才去打电话。*She pondered for a long time before she made the phone call.*

【沉勇】brave and composed

【沉鱼落雁】（of a woman）be lovely enough to make fish sink and birds settle; be extremely beautiful; be breath-taking beautiful

【沉郁】depressed; gloomy; downcast：她的心情很～。*She feels very depressed.*

【沉冤】gross injustice; grievous wrong that remains unrighted; an unredressed grievance of long standing：他十年～，终得昭雪。*He was finally rehabilitated after suffering a gross injustice for ten long years.*

【沉渣】① sediment, dregs; dross ② dregs of society

【沉重】① heavy：～的脚步 *heavy steps* / ～的打击 *a severe blow* /怀着～的心情 *with a heavy heart* /你

将为你所做的事情付出～的代价。*You are to pay a high cost for what you did.* /他感到肩上的担子很～。*He felt that he was shouldering a heavy responsibility.* ② serious; critical:我听说他奶奶的病情～。*I heard that his granny was critically ill.*

【沉住气】keep calm; keep cool; be steady: ～,不要打草惊蛇。*Keep cool! Don't act rashly and alert the enemy.*

【沉着】① cool-headed; composed; steady; calm: ② sediment; clog

【沉醉】be heavily drunk; become into excited; immerse oneself in: ～于节目的欢乐中 *be into excited with the happy atmosphere of the festival*

陈[1] ① lay out; put on display: ～兵百万 *deploy a million troops* ② state; explain:此事当另函～述。*The matter will be explained in detail in a separate letter.*

陈[2] ① old; stale ② (Chén) a surname

【陈兵】mass troops; deploy troops

【陈醋】mature vinegar

【陈放】display; lay out:展厅里～着各种飞机模型。*Various plane models are displayed in the exhibition hall.*

【陈腐】old and decayed; stale; trite; outworn; obsolete: ～的观念 *outworn ideas*

【陈规】outmoded conventions:墨守～ *stick to old customs and habits* / ～陋习 *outmoded customs and habits; outmoded conventions and irrational practices*

【陈货】old stock; shopworn goods:甩卖～ *markdown sale of old stock*

【陈迹】old traces; relic; things of the past

【陈酒】old wine; mellow wine

【陈旧】outmoded; obsolete; old-fashioned; out-of-date; shabby:你们厂的设备太～了。*The equipments of your factory were out-of-date.*

【陈粮】surplus grains of the preceding year(s); stale grain

【陈列】display; exhibit; set out:展览柜里～着各种蝴蝶标本。*Butterfly specimens are on display in showcases.*

【陈年】of many years' standing; preserved for a long time dried orange peel

【陈皮】【药】dried tangerine;dried orange peel

【陈设】① display; exhibit; set out:客厅里～着几件古董。*Several antiques are displayed in the parlour.* ② furnishings:豪华的～ *luxurious furnishings* /客厅里的～朴素大方。*The drawing room was furnished in simple and good taste.*

【陈述】state; explain: ～自己的观点 *state one's viewpoint* / ～句 *declarative sentence*

【陈说】state; explain

【陈诉】state; recount; recite; make a plea

晨 morning

【晨操】morning exercises

【晨光】light of the early morning sun; dawn

【晨练】morning exercise; morning practice

【晨夕】morning and evening:他们～相处了半年多。*They were together from morning till evening more than half of a year.*

【晨曦】first rays of the morning sun; light at dawn

【晨星】①【天】morning star ② stars at dawn:寥若～ *as few as stars at dawn*

chèn

衬 ① line; place sth underneath:映～ *set off* /里面～一件马甲 *wear a vest underneath* ② serve as a foil to; provide a background for; set off ③ lining; liner:领～儿 *collar lining*

【衬布】lining cloth

【衬垫】①【机】liner:接合～ *joint liner* ② pad

【衬裤】underpants; pants

【衬里】lining

【衬裙】underskirt; slip; petticoat

【衬衫】shirt; blouse

【衬托】set off; serve as a foil to:这个金色镜框把你的油画～得更加美丽。*This gold frame sets off your oil painting very well and makes it much more beautiful.*

【衬衣】① shirt ② undergarments; underclothes

【衬字】word inserted in a line of verse for balance or euphony

称 fit; match; suit:匀～ *symmetrical; well-proportioned*

see also chēng; chèng

【称身】fit:这条裙子你穿着很～。*This skirt fits you perfectly.*

【称心】find sth completely satisfactory; be gratified:日子过得很～ *live a very contented life* /找一个～的郎君 *find a husband after one's heart*

【称心如意】after one's own heart; to one's heart's content; very gratifying and satisfactory: ～的工作 *a most satisfying job*

【称愿】feel gratified (especially at the misfortune of a much-hated person)

【称职】be competent; be qualified; fill a post with credit: ～的教练 *qualified coach* /不管怎样,他是一个～的老师。*He is a competent teacher at any rate.*

趁 ① take advantage of (time, opportunity, etc.) avail oneself of:我想～此机会讲一下我的学习情况。*I'd like to take this opportunity to tell you something about my study.* ② while:他～别人不注意的时候,偷偷溜走了。*He sneaked away while nobody took any notice of him.* ③［方］own; possess; have: ～几个钱 *have several money*

【趁便】when it is convenient; when it is no extra trouble; at one's convenience:他出差到北京要～看望一下几位老同学。*When he is on a business trip to Beijing, he will call on several old classmates.*

【趁火打劫】loot a burning house — take advantage of sb's misfortune to make trouble for him; fish in troubled waters

【趁机】take advantage of the occasion; seize chance; seize the opportunity: ～逃跑 *seize the opportunity to escape* / ～彻底打扫房间 *make use of the chance to give the room a thorough cleaning*

【趁空】avail oneself of leisure time; when one has time to spare: 我～洗了头发。*I washed my hair when I happened to have some time to spare.*

【趁钱】[方] *have lots of money*; *be rich*: 这位商人很～。*This merchant is rolling in money.*

【趁热打铁】strike while the iron is hot; make hay while the sun shines

【趁势】take advantage of favourable situation: ～创办一个新企业 *seize the favourable chance to launch a new enterprise* / ～发起进攻 *seize the opportunity to launch an attack promptly*

【趁早】as early as possible; at the first opportunity; before too late; better sooner than later: 你有一点低热，～去看大夫吧。*You are running a slight fever*; *you'd better go and see a doctor right away.* /时不待人，你～决定自己的研究方向吧。*Time waits for no man*; *you'd better decide your own research direction as early as possible.*

chēng

称[1] ① call; style: 人们～他为国王。*People called him king.* ② say; state: 据外交部发言人～ *according to the Foreign Ministry spokesman* ③[书] praise; commend: ～叹不已 *praise profusely* /杭州以风景优美著～。*Hangzhou is famous for its beautiful scenery.* ④ name: 俗～ *popular name*

称[2] weigh: ～～苹果有多重。*See how much the apples weigh.*
see also chèn; chèng

【称霸】play the bully; seek hegemony; dominate: ～世界 *dominate the world*

【称便】find sth a great convenience: 饭店服务周到，顾客无不～。*The restaurant provides excellent service to the satisfaction of all guest.*

【称病】plead illness; claim to be ill; offer illness as am excuse: 他～辞职。*He resigned on the excuse of illness.* /他～不肯出席会议。*Pleading illness, he declined to attend the meeting.*

【称道】commend; praise; speak approvingly of; acclaim: 连声～ *praise again and again*

【称得起】deserve to be called; be worthy of the name: 他～是一位伟大的发明家。*He deserves to be called a great inventor.*

【称帝】proclaim oneself emperor

【称号】title; name; designation: 优秀教师的光荣～，她受之无愧。*She is worthy of the glorious title of best teacher.*

【称呼】① call; address: 我该怎么～他呢? *What should I call him*? ② a form of address

【称快】express one's satisfaction; express joy and jubilation

【称量】weigh; measure sth's weight

【称奇】speak admiringly of; regard as amazing

【称颂】praise; extol; eulogize; pay tribute to: 备受～ *be extolled profusely*; *be highly praised* /每个人都～周总理的丰功伟绩。*Everybody extol Premier Zhou's great achievements.*

【称王称霸】*act like an overlord*; *lord it over*; *domineer*: 他在这一带～，到处为非作歹。*He acts like an overlord in this region and commits crimes here and there.*

【称为】be called; be known as

【称谓】appellation; title; form of address

【称羡】express one's admiration or envy; praise and admire: 他的高超技艺令人～。*His outstanding skill is admired boundlessly.*

【称谢】thank; express one's gratefulness: ～不止 *thank sb again and again*

【称兄道弟】call each other brothers; be on intimate terms

【称誉】sing the praise of; praise; acclaim: 他被～为"人民的好公仆"。*He was acclaimed as a good "people's servant."*

【称赞】praise; acclaim; commend: 她的论文受到了导师的～。*Her lecture was praised by her tutor.* /他没有陶醉于大家的～声中。*He didn't indulge in popular commendation.*

撑 ① prop up; support: 他坐在大树下，双手～着下巴沉思。*He was sitting under a big tree in deep thought, with his chin held in both hands.* ② push or move with a pole ③ maintain; keep up: 他累得实在～不住了。*He is so tired that he can't hold out any longer.* /她～不住，笑了。*She could not help laughing.* ④ open; unfurl: ～开口袋 *hold open the bag* ⑤ fill to the point of bursting: 吃～了 *be full up*; *be bursting at the seams* ⑥【机】brace; stay

【撑臂】【机】brace; supporting arm

【撑场面】keep up appearances; maintain the front: 他常常借钱来～。*He often borrows money to keep up appearances.*

【撑持】prop up; shore up; sustain: ～动荡不安的局面 *shore up a unsteady situation*

【撑杆】① vaulting pole; flexible long pole: ～跳高 *pole vault*; *pole jump* ②【机】stay bar; stay-pole

【撑死】[方] at the outside limit; at most: 这件衬衣～也就值50美金。*This shirt is worth $50 at most.*

【撑条】【机】stay

【撑腰】support; back up; bolster up: 有我们给你～，你还怕什么呢? *We are all behind you, so what's there to fear*?

瞠 [书] stare

【瞠目】stare (in embarrassment, fear, confusion, etc.): ～不知所答 *stare blankly*, *at a loss for a appropriate reply*

【瞠目结舌】stare tongue-tied; stare dumb-founded; be amazed and speechless

chéng

成[1] ① accomplish; succeed: 马到~功 *win instant success; achieve immediate victory* /功到自然~。*Constant effort yields sure success.* ② become; turn into: 水结~冰了。*The water froze into ice.* /绿树~荫。*The trees give welcome shade.* /请把苹果切~两半。*Please cut the apple into halves.* ③ help sth to materialize; help sb to achieve sth ④ achievement; result: 坐享其~ *reap where one has not sown* /一事无~ *accomplish nothing* ⑤ fully developed; fully grown ⑥ established; ready-made: 既~事实 *accomplished fact* ⑦ in considerable numbers or amounts: ~箱的书籍 *boxes of books* /产量~倍增长。*Output has doubled and redoubled.* ⑧ OK; all right: 什么时候都~。*Any time will do.* / ~! 就这样定了。*OK. That's settled.* /你不出席这个会议可不~。*No. You must attend the meeting.* ⑨ able; capable: 你可真~。竟然能在这么短的时间内想出答案。*It was really smart of you to come up with the answer in such short time.*

成[2] one tenth; ten percent: 九~新 *ninety per cent new* /增产两~ *twenty per cent increase in output; output increased by twenty per cent*

【成败】success or failure: ~得失 *success or failure* / ~机会均等 *even chance; even odds*

【成本】cost: 降低~ *reduce the cost* /生产~ *production cost* /固定~ *fixed cost* /总~ *aggregate cost* /边际~ *marginal cost* / ~分析 *cost analysis* / ~核算 *cost accounting* / ~价格 *cost price* / ~结构 *cost structure* /会计 *cost accounting* / ~效益 *cost benefit*

【成材】① grow into useful timber; grow to full size ② become a useful person: 父母希望他能早日~。*His parents hope that he can soon become a useful person.*

【成仇】become enemies; turn hostile (to each other)

【成堆】form a pile; be in heaps: ~的蔬菜 *heaps of vegetables* / ~的问题都必须在近期内解决。*We must settle heaps of problems in the near future.*

【成分】① composition; component part; ingredient: 营养液的~ *the composition of the nutrient fluid* ② one's class status; original or current; one's profession or economic status: 定~ *determine sb's class status*

【成个儿】① grow to a good size: 橘子已经~了。*The oranges have grown to a good size.* ② be well formed; be in the proper shape: 他的字写得不~。*His handwriting is shapeless.*

【成功】succeed; achieve success: 良好的开端是~的一半。*Well begun is half done.* /祝你~! *Wish you success.* /大会开得圆满~。*The congress was a consummation.*

【成规】established practice; set rule; groove; rut

【成果】achievement; fruit; gain; positive result: 劳动~ *fruits of one's labour* /科研~ *achievements in scientific research* / ~累累 *an abundance of achievements*

【成婚】get married

【成活】survive: 新栽的树苗全都~了。*The new saplings have all survived.*

【成绩】result; achievement; success: 取得骄人的~ *achieve excellent successes* /他的学习~很好。*He does very well in his studies.*

【成家】① (of a man) got married: 他还没有~。*He hasn't got married yet.* ② become an expert

【成见】preconceived idea; prejudice; bias

【成交】strike a bargain; conclude a transaction; clinch a deal: ~额 *volume of business*

【成就】① achievement; success; attainment; accomplishment: 取得了突出的艺术~ *score outstanding artistic merits* /他是个卓越~的科学家。*He is a scientist of great attainments.* ② achieve; accomplish

【成立】① found; establish; setup: ~一家子公司 *set up a subsidiary company* /举行~大会 *hold an inaugural meeting* ② be tenable; hole water: 这个论点因为论据不足,不能~。*This argument is untenable for lack of grounds.*

【成例】precedent; existing model: 这件事有~可循。*There are precedents to follow in this case.*

【成眠】fall asleep; go to sleep

【成名】become famous; make a name for oneself; establish one's reputation: 她以写言情小说~。*She made a name for herself by writing romance fictions.*

【成命】order already issued; decision already announced: ~难违。*One shouldn't defy the issued order.*

【成年】① grow up; come of age: ~人 *grown-ups; adults* ② [口] all year; year in and year out; year after year: ~在外 *be away from home all year* / ~累月 *year in year out; for years and years*

【成批】group by group; in batches: ~的工人 *groups of workers* / ~生产 *mass production; serial production* / ~处理 *batch processing* / ~的货物 *batches of goods*

【成品】end product; finished product

【成气候】be hopeful; be promising (often used in the negative): 这么点小事如果办不好,也就不能~了。*You can't get anywhere if you can't do such trifles well.*

【成器】grow up to be a useful person: 玉不琢,不~。*A piece of jade can't be made into anything valuable unless it is carved.*

【成亲】get married: 她最终与她心爱的男人~了。*She got married with her beloved man finally.*

【成全】help sb to achieve his aim; help sb to succeed

【成群】in groups; in crowds; in large numbers: ~的牛羊 *herds of cattle and sheep*

【成人】① grow up; become full-grown: 长大~ *be grown to manhood* ② adult; grown-up: ~电影 *adult film*

【成仁】[书] die for a righteous cause

【成事】① succeed; accomplish sth: 谋事在人, ~在天。*The planning lies with man, the outcome with Heaven or Man proposes, God disposes.* ② [书] sth that is finished or past; bygones

【成事不足,败事有余】unable to accomplish anything but can very well serve as a mischief-maker; never able to achieve anything but quite capable of ruining it; never make but always mar: 这个人~,不足以承担重任。*This guy can never make buy always mar; he cannot assume important tasks.*

【成熟】ripe; mature: ~期 *mature period; maturity* / ~林 *mature forest* / ~产业 *mature industry* /小麦~了。*The wheat is ripe already.* /条件~。*The conditions are ripe.*

【成双】form a pair

【成俗】become social custom or convention

【成算】preconceived idea or plan: 别指望他,他心里没有什么~。*Don't count on him; he has no preconceived ideas in his mind.*

【成套】form a complete set: ~设备 *complete sets of equipment*

【成天】[口] all day long; all the time: ~忙忙碌碌 *be kept busy all day long* /她~上网聊天。*She chats on net all the time.*

【成为】become; turn into: 把我国建设~繁荣昌盛的社会主义国家 *turn our country into a prosperous socialist country*

【成文】① existing writing ② written: ~法 *written law; statute law; statutory law*

【成问题】be a problem; be open to question

【成像】【物】formation of image; imagery

【成效】effect; result: 初见~ *win initial success*

【成心】intentionally; on purpose; deliberately: 你~让我难堪。*You intentionally embarrassed me.* /他不是~跟你过不去。*He didn't deliberately make difficulties for you.*

【成形】①take shape: 他的人生观已经~。*His philosophy has begun to take shape.* ②【医】repair damaged tissues or organs: 骨~术 *osteoplasty* ③【医】have a normal shape: 大便~。*The stool is in normal shape.*

【成型】shaping; forming: ~铸件 *mould casting*

【成性】by nature; become sb's second nature: 暴戾~ *be ruthless and cruel by nature*

【成药】patent medicine; pharmacist-prepared medicine; ready-made medicine

【成也萧何,败也萧何】the same person can contribute to both your success and downfall; success or failure are both due to the same person or factor

【成衣】①[旧] tailoring ② ready-made clothes; ready to-wear

【成衣店】tailor's shop; tailor's; dress-maker's

【成议】an agreement already reached: 在这个问题上双方已有~。*The two sides have already reached an agreement on this issue.*

【成因】cause of formation; contributing factor; origin

【成语】set phrase; idiom

【成员】member: 俱乐部~ *members of a club* /调查小组的正式~ *full members of the investigation group* / ~国 *member state*

【成灾】cause disaster; plague: 害虫~ *disaster caused by pests*

【成章】① constitute a good piece of writing; come out as a article: 出口~ *have an outstanding eloquence* ② logical; systematic: 顺理~ *follow a rational line to do some work well*

【成长】grow up; grow to maturity: 健康~ *healthy growth; sound growth* /小树苗正茁壮~。*The seedlings are growing vigorously.*

丞 [旧] assistant; assistant officer; auxiliary official

【丞相】prime minister (in ancient China); chief minister

呈 ① assume (form, colour, etc.); manifest: 龙凤~祥 *prosperity brought by dragon and the phoenix; extremely good fortune* /叶子~椭圆形。*The leaf is oval in shape.* /她脸上~不悦之色。*Her face took on a grouchy expression.* ② submit; present ③ petition; memorial

【呈报】submit a report; report a matter (to a superior) in writing: 这件事需要向上级~。*This matter should be reported to the higher authorities.*

【呈递】present; submit

【呈览】submit sth to a higher authority for perusal

【呈请】apply: ~上级批准 *apply to the higher level for approval*

【呈文】a document submitted to a superior; an official petition

【呈现】present; appear; emerge; take on: ~出新面貌 *take on a new look*

【呈献】respectfully present: 他把礼物~给国王。*He presented the gifts with formality to the king.*

诚 ① sincere; honest ② [书] really; actually; indeed

【诚笃】[书] extremely sincere and earnest

【诚服】be completely convinced; have genuine admiration; submit oneself willingly

【诚惶诚恐】with reverence and awe; in fear and trepidation: 老板竟把如此重要的工作交给他,真让他~。*It filled him with fear that he had been entrusted with such an important task by his boss.*

【诚恳】sincere; earnest; true-hearted: 态度~ *be sincere in what one does and say* / ~问候 *cordial greetings*

【诚朴】sincere and simply; honest: ~的乡亲 *honest folk*

【诚然】① truly; really; indeed: 这~是个不错的主

意。*This is indeed a great idea.* ② no doubt; to be swore; admittedly:勇敢～可贵,但智慧也绝不可少。*Trustiest braveness is very important, however brightens is indispensable as well.*

【诚实】honest: ～可靠 *honest and dependable*

【诚心】① sincere desire; wholeheartedness; sincerity ② sincere and earnest; devout

【诚信】faith; honesty

【诚意】good faith; sincerity:缺乏～ *lack sincerity* / 以实际行动来表明自己的～。*Show one's good faith by actual deeds.*

【诚挚】sincere; cordial:在～友好的气氛中 *in a cordial and friendly atmosphere*

承 ① hold; bear:支～点 *bearing point* ② undertake; contract ③ be indebted; be granted a favour: ～您过奖。*You flatter me.* ④ convince; carry on:继～ *inherit; carry on* /子～父业。*The son carries on his father's business.* ⑤ accept

【承办】undertake: ～土木工程 *undertake civil engineering projects* /这事该由广告公司一手～。*It was up to the advertising agency to take the whole task.*

【承包】contract: ～果园 *contract to the orchard* / ～饭店 *contract to a restaurant* /把工程～给一家建筑公司 *contract a project out to a building company* / ～合同 *contract* / ～商 *contractor* / ～责任制 *system of contracted responsibility; contract system* / ～制 *contract system; contracting out system*

【承保】undertake insurance; accept insurance: ～单 *open cover* / ～通知书 *cover note*

【承担】undertake; bear; assume: ～一切费用 *bear all the costs* / ～义务 *undertake the obligation* /对一切后果～全部责任 *shoulder full responsibility for all the consequences*

【承当】① bear; take on; assume: ～责任 *bear the responsibility* ②[方] agree; promise

【承兑】【经】honour; accept: ～票据 *acceptance bill* / ～人 *acceptor*

【承继】① be adopted as heir to one's uncle ② adopt one's brother's son as his heir ③ inherit; carry forward: ～祖业 *inherit ancestral property*

【承建】(of a project) contract to construct:新宿舍楼由一家建筑公司～。*A construction company has contracted to build the new dormitory building.*

【承接】① hold out a vessel to have a liquid poured into it ② continue; carryon: ～上文 *continued from the preceding paragraph* ③ undertake; bear; accept; take in

【承揽】contract to do a whole job; undertake an entire project: ～文物修复业务 *contract to restore artifacts to their original shapes*

【承蒙】be granted a favour; be accorded a kindness; be indebted (to sb for a kindness): ～热情招待,不胜感激。*I'm deeply grateful for the cordial.*

【承诺】promise to undertake; undertake to do sth; commit oneself to do sth:口头～ *orally promise to do sth* /既然我已经～尽全力帮你,就不会反悔。*Since I have promised to do my best to help you, I will not go back on my word.*

【承情】be much obliged; own a debt of gratitude: 你对我的帮助,我～不尽。*I will always remain indebted to you for your help.*

【承认】① admit; acknowledge; recognize; concede; confess: ～错误 *admit one's mistake; acknowledge one's fault* / ～他的重要贡献 *acknowledge his important contribution* ② give diplomatic recognition; recognize: ～世界上只有一个中国 *recognize that there is only one "China" in the world*

【承上启下】form a connecting link between the preceding and the following (as in a piece of writing, etc.):这句话起到～的作用。*This sentence serves as a link between what goes before and what comes after.*

【承受】① bear; support; endure; sustain: ～住种种考验 *be able to endure every kind of trial* ② inherit:她～了父亲的全部遗产。*She inherited all her father's property.*

【承袭】① adopt; follow: ～旧制 *follow the old system* ② inherit

【承先启后】inherit the past and usher in the future; serve as a link between past and future

【承运】① undertake the transportation of (goods) ②[书] (of a ruler) be ordained by Heaven:奉天～ *be ordained by Heaven*

【承载】bear the weight of: ～能力 *bearing capacity; load-bearing capacity; carrying capacity*

【承重】load-bearing; bearing: ～墙 *bearing (or load-bearing) wall*

【承转】transmit; forward a document to the next level above or below

城 ① city wall; wall: ～郭 *inner and outer city wall; city wall* ② city:东～ *the eastern part of the city* ③ town:县～ *country town*

【城邦】city-state

【城堡】castle; citadel

【城池】[书] city wall and moat; city

【城防】city defence

【城府】[书] shrewdness; sophistication:老板～很深。*The boss is an astute person.*

【城根】sections of a city close to the city wall

【城关】the area just outside a city gate

【城壕】moat

【城隍】①[书] moat ② town god; city god: ～庙 *town god's temple*

【城际】inter-city: ～快车 *inter-city express*

【城建】urban construction: ～规划 *urban (or city) planning*

【城郊】outskirts of a town; suburb:我们的大学位于～。*Our university is located on the outskirts of the town.*

【城里】inside the city; in town: ～人 *city dwellers; townspeople* / ～生活 *city life; urban life*

C

【城楼】gate tower; city gate tower:天安门~上红旗飘飘。*Red flags are flaunting on the rostrum of Tian An Men.*
【城门】city gate
【城墙】city wall
【城区】city proper
【城市】town; city:工业~ *industrial city* / ~规划 *city planning; urban planning* / ~建设 *urban construction* / ~环境 *urban environment* / ~污染 *municipal pollution* / ~经济学 *urban economics* / ~贫民 *urban poor; city poor* / ~居民 *city dwellers; urban population* / ~生态学 *urban ecology* / ~化 *urbanization*
【城乡】urban and rural; town and country: ~差别 *difference between town and country* / ~结合 *integration of town and country* / ~贸易 *urban and rural trade* / ~交流 *exchange between town and country*
【城镇】cities and towns: ~户口 *urban residence registration*

乘[1] ① ride: ~飞机 *by plane* / ~公共汽车去动物园 *go to the zoo by bus* / ~马 *ride a horse* / ~船 *go by boat* ② take advantage of; avail oneself of: ~敌不备 *take the enemy by surprise* / ~胜追击 *chase in the flush of victory* / ~夜出击 *attack under cover of night*

乘[2] 【数】multiply:二~三等于六。*Two times three is six.*

【乘便】when it is convenient; when there is a trouble; at one's convenience:请~帮我买点东西。*Please help me buy some goods at your convenience.*
【乘法】【数】multiplication: ~表 *multiplication table*
【乘方】【数】① involution ② power
【乘风破浪】ride the wind and cleave the waves; brave the wind and waves; have a high ambition as riding the waves
【乘号】【数】multiplication sign; times sign
【乘机】seize the opportunity
【乘积】【数】product
【乘客】passenger
【乘凉】enjoy the cool; relax in a cool place
【乘龙快婿】an excellent or idea son-in-law
【乘幂】【数】power
【乘人之危】take advantage of sb's precarious position:真正的君子决不会~。*A genuine honourable man will never pounce upon anybody in trouble.*
【乘胜】exploit or follow up a victory: ~追击 *pursue enemy troops in retreat; follow up a victory with hot pursuit; chase enemy troops on the crest of a victory*
【乘数】【数】multiplier
【乘务员】attendant on a train; steward or stewardess; conductor or conductress
【乘隙】take advantage of a loophole; seize the opportunity; exploit sb's mistake as one's own account: ~猛攻 *exploit the enemy's blunder to make a violent attack*
【乘兴】while one is in high spirits; come on a impulse: ~而来,兴尽而返 *arrive in ebullient good spirits and depart well content*
【乘虚】take advantage of a weak point; act when sb is off guard: ~偷袭 *make a sneak attack when there is an opening in the enemy's defence*
【乘虚而入】break through at a weak point; act when one's opponent is off guard; exploit the weakness of one's opponent:疾病在人们身体虚弱的时候就会~。*Diseases are liable to attack a person when he becomes weak physically.*

盛 ① fill; ladle: ~饭 *fill a bowl with rice* ② hold; contain:这个阶梯教室可以~三百人。*This theater can hold three hundred people.* /这个箱子里~了很多书。*This box contains many books.*
see also shèng
【盛殓】encoffin
see also shèng

程 ① rule; regulation:② order; procedure:历~ *course* ③ journey; stage of a journey:全~ *entire journey* ④ distance:远~ *long-distance; long-range* /射~ *field of fire* ⑤ [书] measure; estimate
【程度】① level; degree:文化~ *level of education; degree of literacy* /政治觉悟~不同 *various degrees of political consciousness* ② extent; degree:在一定~上 *to a certain extent*
【程式】form; pattern; formula: ~化 *stylization*
【程序】① order; procedure; course; sequence:生产~ *production procedure* /法律~ *legal procedure* ② programme: ~存储器 *program memory* / ~处理机 *programme processor* / ~寄存器 *programme register* / ~编制器 *programme compiler* / ~计算器 *programme counter* / ~库 *programme library* / ~卡 *programme card* / ~分析 *programme analysis* / ~分配 *programme allocation* / ~设计 *automation programming* / ~管理 *programme management* / ~语言 *programme language*

惩 ① punish; penalize: ~恶劝善 *punish evildoers and encourage people to do good* /依法~处罪犯 *punish a criminal in accordance with the law* ② guard against; warn; be on the alert against
【惩办】punish; penalize:依法~ *punish according to law mete out severe punishment*
【惩处】punish; penalize; discipline:严厉~贪污犯 *severely punish embezzlers* /严加~ *mete out severe punishment*
【惩罚】punish; penalize:免受~ *exempt from punishment* /因扰乱社会治安受到~ *be punished for disturbance of the social peace* / ~权 *power of punishment; punitive power*
【惩戒】punish sb to teach him a lesson; discipline as a warning:他因为偷税被吊销了执照以示~。*His licence was revoked as a punishment for tax dodging.*

【惩前毖后】learn from past mistakes to avoid future ones：～治病救人 *learn from past mistakes to avoid future ones, and cure the sickness to save the patient*

【惩一警百】punish one to warn a hundred; make an example of sb：严厉打击首犯，以达到～的效果。*Severely punishing the prime criminal aims at warning others.*

【惩治】punish; mete out punishment to：～腐败分子 *punish corrupt officials*

澄 ① limpid; clear; transparent ② clear up; clarify; precipitate
see also dèng

【澄清】① clear; bright; transparent：湖水碧绿～。*The lake is green and clear.* ② clear up; clarify; settle：～事实 *clarify facts* / ～误会 *clear up misunderstanding*

橙 ① orange：～树 *orange tree* ② orange colour

【橙红】salmon pink; orange red

【橙黄】orange：这件上衣是～色的。*This coat is orange in colour.*

【橙子】orange

chěng

逞 ① show off; flaunt ② carry out (an evil design); succeed (in a scheme)：阴谋得～ *succeed in a plot* ③ indulge; give free rein to

【逞脸】[方] be wilful and arrogant because one is in sb's graces：别～，好好做作业。*Stop acting like a spoilt child and do your homework attentively.*

【逞能】show off one's skill; parade one's ability：这家伙喜欢～。*This fellow is fond of showing off.* / 没有本事就别瞎～。*If you are not the stuff, you'd better be quiet.*

【逞强】flaunt one's superiority; exhibit one's power：～好胜 *parade one's superiority and strive to outshine others*

【逞性子】act recklessly; be wayward; act on impulse：遇事要冷静，而不要～。*You should keep cool in all circumstances and never act on impulse.*

【逞凶】act violently; go berserk; act with murderous intent

骋 [书] ① gallop ②give free rein to

【骋怀】give free rein to ones thoughts and feelings; enjoy oneself to one's heart's content

【骋目】look into the distance; look as far as one's eyes can see：～远眺 *scan distant horizons*

chèng

秤 balance; weigh; steelyard：用～称一称 *weigh sth in a balance (or on the scales)* /杆～ *steelyard; level scales* /弹簧～ *spring scales*
see also chèn; chēng

【秤锤】the sliding weight of a steelyard

【秤杆】the arm of a steelyard

【秤钩】steelyard hook

【秤盘子】the pan of a steelyard

【秤砣】[口] the sliding weight of a steelyard

chī

吃 ① eat; take：～水果 *eat fruits* / ～苹果 *eat an apple* / ～药 *take medicine* / ～饱 *eat one's fill; be full* / 请随便～些橘子吧。*Help yourself to some oranges, please.* ② have one's meals; eat somewhere; dine ③ live off; live on; scrounge off ④ absorb; soak up ⑤ annihilate; wipe out; take (in a chess game)：～掉敌人一个团 *annihilate an enemy regiment* / ～一个子儿 *take a piece (in chess)* ⑥ suffer; bear; incur：肩膀上～了一枪 *get wounded by a shot in the shoulder* ⑦ understand; grasp：他来这儿的目的，我～不准。*I'm not sure why he comes here.* ⑧ endure; withstand; take：我才不～这一套。*I won't take all this lying down.*

【吃白饭】① eat without paying; not earn a honest living; live off others：他这个人不务正业，一直～。*He doesn't do any honest work and lives off other all along.* ② sponge on sb：～的 *parasite; good-for-nothing* ③ eat rice alone

【吃饱了撑的】be restless from overeating (said of sb doing sth silly or senseless)

【吃不饱】① not have enough to eat ② (of factories, etc) cannot operate at full capacity; operate under capacity：由于原料不足，我们厂一直处于～状态。*Owing to the shortage fo raw materials, our factory has not been running at full capacity.*

【吃不开】be unpopular; won't work：他这个人很倔，在公司～。*As a very fractions man, he is unpopular in our company.*

【吃不来】not be fond of certain food; find that the food doesn't suit one's taste：我～辣的。*I'm not fond of hot food.*

【吃不了】cannot finish (all the food)：我～这么一大碗米饭。*I can't finish such a bowlful of rice.*

【吃不了兜着走】get more than one bargained for; land oneself in serious trouble：谁若进了这个屋，我让他～。*Who enters the room, I will make him sorry for it.*

【吃不上】① have nothing to eat; cannot afford to eat; cannot get sth to eat：穷得一天～一顿饱饭 *be too poor to afford one square meal a day* ② miss a meal

【吃不下】have no appetite for; be unable to eat more：我饱了，实在～了。*I'm full; really, I can't eat any more.* /他不太舒服，～饭。*He is not very comfortable and has no appetite for food.*

【吃不消】cannot bear; cannot endure or stand (exertion, fatigue, etc.):天气热得真让人～。*It is unbearably hot.* /这任务太重,我～了。*This task is too heavy for me; I can't bear it any more.*

【吃不住】be unable to bear; can not support:书太多,这个书架～。*This bookshelf is not strong enough to hold so many books.*

【吃穿】food and clothing

【吃醋】be jealous (of a rival in love)

【吃大户】mass seizure and eating of food in the homes of landlords during famines (as in pre-liberation China)

C

【吃得开】be popular; be much sought after; be a favourite of:只有本事,到哪儿都～。*One who has ability is welcome anywhere.*

【吃得苦中苦,方为人上人】only by enduring the hardest of hardships can a person hope to rise in society

【吃得来】be able to eat; not mind eating:牛肉我～,但不特别喜欢。*I can eat beef; however, I'm not overfond of it.*

【吃得上】① be available on the market:现在冬天也能～黄瓜。*Nowadays cucumbers are available even in winter.* ② can afford to eat:农民现在～白面了。*Farmers can afford wheat flour now.* ③ be in time for a meal; be able to get a meal:六点之前赶回到学校,我们还能～晚饭。*If we get back to our school before 6pm, we won't be too late for supper.*

【吃得下】have an appetite for; be able to eat:他的胃口很好,能～好多东西。*He has got such an enormous appetite that he can have much food.*

【吃得消】be able to endure or stand:再熬一个通宵,我也～。*I can stand working throughout another night.*

【吃得住】be able to bear; be strong enough to support:这座桥虽然破,但过大卡车还能～。*Though the bridge is shabby, it still can bear the weight of a heave-duty lorry.*

【吃豆腐】[方] ① flirt with a woman; take liberties with a woman:休想吃我的豆腐! *Don't try to flirt with me.* ② crack a joke; tease; make fun of sb ③ visit the bereaved to offer one's condolences

【吃耳光】get a slap in the face; get a box on the ear

【吃饭】① eat; have a meal:～了! *Dinner is ready!* /你今晚在哪儿～? *Where will you have your supper?* ② keep alive; make a living:靠唱歌～ *make a living by singing*

【吃官司】be prosecuted; be involved in a legal action; serve a jail term

【吃馆子】[口] eat in a restaurant; dine out:我很少～。*I seldom dine out.*

【吃喝风】unhealthy practice of feasting on public funds

【吃喝玩乐】eat, drink an be merry:人生并不全是～。*One should have higher goal in life than mere pleasure-seeking.*

【吃花酒】[旧] carouse in the company of prostitutes

【吃回扣】receive rebate; get commission

【吃荤】eat meat:喜欢～ *be fond of meat; prefer meat*

【吃紧】① be critical; be hard pressed:这种商品在市场上很～。*These kinds of commodities are in short supply in the market.* ② essential:这个地方最～,要特别注意。*This part is most essential, please pay special attention to it.*

【吃惊】be surprised; be amazed; be shocked; be startled; be taken back:大吃一惊 *be flabbergasted*

【吃苦】bear hardships; suffer:～在前,享受在后 *be the first to bear hardships and the last to enjoy comforts* /怕～就干不了大事。*Those who fear hardships will not accomplish anything great.*

【吃亏】① suffer losses; come to grief:他～的原因就在于他的自私。*The reason that he suffers losses consists in his own selfishness.* ② at disadvantage:他个子不高,打篮球～。*He is short and that puts him a disadvantage in playing basketball.* /他口吃,学语言有点～。*As a language learner, he is at disadvantage for his stammer.*

【吃老本】live off one's past gains; rest on one's laurels

【吃里爬外】live off one person while cater to his enemy; live on one person while secretly serving another; secretly work for the opponent of one's benefactor

【吃力】requiring effort; labourious; strenuous; be a strain:～不讨好 *do a thankless job; work hard (for sb) but get little thanks; spare no pains but get no gains* /单独完成这个任务对于他来说是相当～的。*It is fairly strenuous for him to accomplish this task on his own.*

【吃奶】(of a baby) suck the breast:～的孩子 *a sucking child; suckling*

【吃偏饭】eat better-than-average meals in the mess; enjoy special privilege; be specially treated:临近考试,老师给他～。*The teacher taught him specially as the examination drew near.*

【吃请】accept an invitation to dinner:～是腐败的一种表现。*Accepting invitations to dinner is one of the signs of corruption.*

【吃软不吃硬】be susceptible to persuasion; but not to coercion:你应该和他好好商量,而不是大吵大嚷,因为他是那种～的人。*You should consult with him, not shout at him because he is the sort of person who yields to soft rather than hard tactics.*

【吃食】(of bird or animal) eat; feed:那些鸟正在～。*The geese were feeding.*

【吃水】①[方] drinking water:这个地方～很困难。*It is difficult to get drinking water in this place.* ② absorb water; be absorbent:这种纸特别～。*This type of paper is very absorbent.* ③【航】draught; draft:～线 *water line*

【吃素】① be a vegetarian; be on a vegetarian diet;

abstain from eating meat ② not killing; not effective:小心点,他的拳头可不是~的。*Be careful; his fists are not for decorative purposes.*
【吃透】understand thoroughly; have a thorough grasp of sth:他的话我吃不透。*I can't thoroughly understand his words.* / 重在~文件精神,而不能拘泥于字面的理解。*It is more important to grasp the essence of the document than to define the phraseology.*
【吃闲饭】be a loafer or sponger; lend an idle life
【吃现成饭】eat what is already prepared by sb else — enjoy the fruits of others' work; benefit from other people's labour
【吃香】[口] be very popular; be in great demand; be much sought-after
【吃一堑,长一智】a fall into the pit, a gain in your wit
【吃硬不吃软】be open to coercion rather than persuasion
【吃斋】practise abstinence from meat and fish for religious reasons; be a vegetarian for religious reasons
【吃着碗里看着锅里】keep looking at the pot while eating from one's bowl — be covetous of what one does not have yet; be insatiably greedy
【吃重】① arduous; strenuous; heavy:翻译这篇文章很~。*It is arduous to translate this article.* ② loading capacity:这辆车~两吨。*This truck has a loading capacity of two tons.*
【吃罪】take the blame:父亲让他离开这儿,怕他~不起。*His father let him leave here and worried that he couldn't afford to take the blame.*

笞 [书] beat with a whip, cane, stick, etc:鞭~ *whip; flog*
【笞刑】flogging as a punishment

嗤 [书] sneer
【嗤笑】laugh at; sneer at; jeer at:为人~ *be made a laughing-stock; be sneered at*
【嗤之以鼻】give a snort of contempt; lookdown one's nose at; despise:人们都对他庸俗的行为~。*People looked down their noses at his vulgar behaviour.*

痴 ① silly; idiotic; stupid; foolish ② be infatuated; be crazy:~心女子负心汉 *an innocent girl infatuated with a heartless man* / 书~ *bookworm* ③ [方] insane; mad; crazy
【痴爱】dote on; experience unrequited love; carry the torch:他~自己的孙子。*He doted on his grandson.*
【痴呆】① silly; stupid; idiotic; dull-witted ② [医] dementia:先天性~ *congenital dementia*
【痴愣】be dazed; be in a trance; stare blankly:他~地看着妈,半天说不出话来。*He stared at his mother blankly, tongue-tied.*
【痴迷】infatuated; obsessed; crazy
【痴情】① deep passionate love; sentimental longing; infatuation ② be infatuated; be sentimentally attached:她对音乐特别~。*She is obsessed with music.*
【痴人说梦】idiotic nonsense; idiot's day-dream:他的话只不过是~罢了。*His words are nothing but idiotic nonsense.*
【痴想】① be lost in thought; be lost in reverie ② wishful thinking; daydreaming; illusion
【痴心】obsession; infatuation; deep passionate love:无论如何,你都不要辜负了她的一片~。*Don't disappoint her deep love for you at all events.*
【痴心妄想】illusion; wishful thinking; daydreaming; fond dream:不肯努力就想取得突出的成就,简直是~。*It is really sheer illusion if you want to achieve outstanding achievements without hard work.*

chí

池 ① pool; pond:浴~ *bathing pool* / 鱼~ *fish pond* ② an enclosed space with raised sides ③ stalls (in a theatre) ④ [书] moat:城~ *city* ⑤ (Chí) a surname
【池塘】pond; pool
【池浴】take a bath in a common bathing pool
【池沼】a large pond; pool
【池子】[口] ① pond; pool ② common pond in a bathhouse ③ dance floor ④ stalls (in a theatre); orchestra

弛 [书] relax; loosen; slacken:文武之道,一张一~。*The cardinal principal of governance is to alternate tension with relaxation.*
【弛缓】ease; calm down:紧张的气氛渐渐~下来。*The torsion eased gradually.* /他的心情~下来。*He calmed down.*
【弛懈】relax; slack; slacken:刻苦攻读,不可一日~。*We must work hard at our studies without relaxing for a day.*

驰 ① (of vehicle, horse, etc.) speed; race; gallop:一匹马飞~而过。*A horse sped past.* ② promulgate; spread ③ [书] aspire; crave; desire:心~神往(*make*) *one's thoughts go to (sb or sth)*
【驰骋】[书] gallop
【驰名】famous; well known:中外~ *renowned at home and abroad* / ~商标 *well known trademark; famous trademark*
【驰驱】① gallop ② do one's utmost in sb's service

迟 ① tardy; slow:动作~笨 *move clumsily* ② delayed; late:姗姗来~ *be slow in coming* ③ (Chí) a surname
【迟迟】slow; tardy: ~决定 *come to a decision after so much delay*
【迟到】be late (to come or arrive): ~半小时 *be half an hour late* / ~是个坏习惯。*Being late is a bad habit.*
【迟钝】slow; obtuse; slow-witted
【迟缓】slow; tardy; sluggish:这件事进展~。*This matter isn't making a good progress.*
【迟留】delay; stay on; stop over: ~数月 *stay for a*

C

few more months

【迟效肥料】slow-release fertilizer; slow-acting fertilizer

【迟延】delay; retard:毫不~的执行 *carry out without delay*

【迟疑】hesitate; be indecisive

【迟疑不决】hesitate to make a decision; be irresolute; be undecided: ~等于失去时机。*Remaining undecided equals to let the chance slip.*

【迟早】sooner or later:她~会走的。*She will go sooner or later.* /幸福~会属于你的。*Happiness will belong to you sooner or later.*

【迟滞】① sluggish; stagnant ② dull; slow ③【军】delaying (action)

【迟重】slow and heavy:脚步~ *slow and heavy steps*

持 ① hold; grasp: ~相同观点 *hold a same opinion* / ~友好态度 *take a friendly attitude* ② support; maintain ③ manage; run; handle:操~家务 *manage household affairs* ④ control; hold under duress ⑤ oppose; confront

【持法】enforce the law

【持家】run one's home; keep house: ~有方 *be good at running one's home* /勤俭~ *be industrious and thrifty in running one's home*

【持久】lasting; enduring; protracted: ~力 *staying power; endurance* / ~和平 *lasting peace* / ~战 *protracted warfare* /我希望你对学习的兴趣~。*I wish your interest in study would last.*

【持论】present an argument; put a case; express a view

【持平】unbiased; fair; impartial

【持球】【体】(as in volleyball) holding

【持续】continue; sustain:使国民经济~稳定增长 *bring about a sustained, stable growth in the national economy* / ~努力 *sustained effort* / ~电流 *sustained current* / ~增长 *sustained growth*

【持有】hold: ~护照 *hold a passport*

【持正】[书] ① uphold justice; be just ② be impartial

【持之以恒】persevere; persist; pursue a matter with determination:做学问要~。*Perseverance is essential for intellectual pursuit.*

【持重】prudent; cautious; discreet

匙 spoon:汤~ *soup spoon* /茶~ *teaspoon*

see also shi

踟

【踟蹰】hesitate; waver: ~不前 *hesitate to move forward*

chǐ

尺 ① *chi*, a traditional unit of length ② rule; ruler:卷~ *band tape; tape measure* ③ instrument in the shape of a ruler:戒~ *ruler used by a teacher in old days to beat the palm of a student as a punishment*

【尺寸】① size; measurement; dimensions:土地的~ *measurement of a land* ② [口] proper limits for speech or action; suitability; propriety:说话有~ *speak properly on social occasions*

【尺牍】correspondence; epistolary writing

【尺度】criterion; standard; scale; yardstick:货币是价值的~。*Money is the measure of value.*

【尺短寸长】sometimes a *chi* may prove short while a *cun* may prove long — everyone has his strong and weak points

【尺骨】【生理】ulna

【尺码】size; measures:你穿多大~的衬衫? *What size shirt do you wear?*

【尺子】ruler

齿 ① tooth:咬牙切~ *gnash or clench one's teeth* /牙~ *tooth* /恒~ *permanent tooth* /乳~ *milk tooth* /臼~ *mortar* /门~ *front tooth; incisor* /犬~ *canine tooth* /义~ *false tooth* /蛀~ *decayed tooth* ② tooth-like part of an object; tooth: ~轮箱 *gear box* / ~轮传动 *gear drive* / ~轮泵 *gear pump* /梳~儿 *teeth of a comb* /轮~ *teeth of a cogwheel* ③ toothed: ~轮 *toothed wheel; gear* ④ stand side by side; regard as of one's own:不~于人类 *not he regarded as one of humanity; be not worthy of the name of a human* ⑤ [书] age:稚~ *very young* ⑥ [书] mention; speak of

【齿鲸】toothed whale

【齿轮】gear; toothed or cog wheel:伞~ *bevel gear* / ~组 *gear cluster*

【齿冷】[书] arouse one's infinite scorn

【齿条】【机】rack

【齿龈】【生理】gums

侈 [书] ① wasteful; extravagant ② exaggerate

【侈靡】[书] extravagant; wasteful:过着~的生活 *lead a life of dissipation and debauchery*

【侈谈】[书] ① talk glibly about; prate about; prattle about: ~永久和平 *prate about eternal peace* ② high-sounding words

耻 ① shame below ② humiliation; ignominy; infamy:引以为~ *regard as a disgrace*

【耻辱】shame; disgrace; humiliation

【耻笑】hold sb to ridicule; sneer at; mock; ridicule:不要~他人。*Never sneer at others.*

chì

叱 [书] denounce or rebuke loudly; shout at

【叱呵】shout at; bawl at

【叱骂】scold roundly; curse; abuse

【叱责】scold; upbraid; rebuke

【叱咤风云】commanding wind and storm; shaking heaven and earth; thundering; enormously powerful: ~的英雄 *all-conquering hero*

斥[1] scold; upbraid; denounce; reprimand

斥[2] repel; dismiss; exclude:同性相~。*Two like electric charges repel each other.*

斥[3] [书] pay; spend ④ expand; open up

【斥骂】reproach; scold; berate

【斥退】① dismiss sb from his post ②[旧] expel from a school ③ shout at sb to go away

【斥责】reprimand; rebuke; denounce:厉声~ *severely reprimand*

【斥逐】expel; oust; drive away

【斥资】[书] pay the expenses: ~建校 *donate money to found a school*

赤 ① a kind of red slightly lighter than vermilion ② red: ~颜色 *red colour* ③ revolutionary; communist: ~色政权 *revolutionary government* ④ loyal; devoted; faithful; single-hearted: ~心 devotion ⑤ bare ⑥ empty ⑦ pure (gold):金无足~。*There is no such thing as a hundred percent pure gold.*

【赤背】naked to the waist; bareback

【赤膊】barebacked:打~ *be stripped to the waist*

【赤诚】absolutely sincerity: ~相待 *be absolutely sincere*

【赤胆忠心】utter devotion; absolute loyalty; complete dedication:对人民事业~ *be absolutely loyal to the cause of the people*

【赤道】① the equator ②【天】the celestial equator ~仪 *the equatorial telescope*

【赤豆】red bean

【赤褐色】russet

【赤红】crimson; flushed

【赤金】pure gold; solid gold

【赤露】bare: ~着手臂 *with bared arms*

【赤裸】① naked: 全身 ~ *stark-naked* ② undisguised; totally unsheltered: ~原野 *open country*

【赤裸裸】① without a stitch of clothing; stark naked ② undisguised; naked; open

【赤身】without a stitch of clothing; naked

【赤手空拳】barehanded; unarmed; with bare fists: 他~,勇敢地和歹徒搏斗。*He fought against gangsters barehanded bravely.*

【赤条条】have not a stitch on; be stark-naked

【赤心】sincere heart; genuine sincerity; wholehearted devotion:

【赤子】① a newborn baby ②[书] the people:海外~ *overseas compatriots* / ~之心(*with*) *complete innocence*

【赤字】deficit; red ink:财政~ *financial deficit* /弥补~ *make up a deficit*

【赤足】barefooted; barefoot

饬 [书] ①put in order; rectify; readjust ② order: ~其照办无误 *order sb to act inconformity with the demand* ③ prudent

【饬令】(usu. used in official documents) order

炽 flaming; ablaze

【炽烈】burning atmosphere:炉火~。*The stove is burning vigorously.*

【炽情】ardent emotion; passion

【炽热】① white-hot; fervent: ~的太阳 *a blazing sun* ② passionate

【炽盛】flaming; ablaze; flourishing:他有着~的探索欲。*He has a burning desire for exploration.*

翅 ① wing ② shark's fin ③ wing-like part of an object

【翅膀】① wing ② part of which looks or functions like a wing

【翅果】【植】samara

【翅脉】【动】rein of the wing of an insect

眙 [书] ① stare; gaze ② stare in surprise

敕 imperial order; edict

【敕令】(of an emperor) issue an edict; imperial edict

chōng

冲[1] ① thoroughfare; important place ② charge; rush; break; dash:横~直撞 *dash around like mad; barge or charge about* / ~出重围 *break loose from heavy enemy encirclement* ③ clash; collide ④【天】opposition

冲[2] ① pour boiling water on:她给我~了一杯绿茶。*She made a cup of green tea for me.* ② rinse; flush:把鞋子~一~ *rinse the shoes* ③【摄】develop: ~胶卷 *develop a roll of film* ④ cancel out; offset

冲[3] [方] a stretch of flatland in a hilly area

see also chòng

【冲程】【机】stroke

【冲刺】【体】spurt; sprint:向终点~ *make a dash towards the tape*

【冲动】impulse; get excited; be impetuous:凭一时~ *act on impulse*

【冲断层】【地】thrust fault

【冲锋陷阵】① charge against the enemy line; charge ahead in battle; fight barely:他在战场上~,立下许多战功。*He won distinction on the battlefield for his extraordinary valour.* ② fight valiantly for a just cause:他是抗洪中~的英雄。*His image is that of a here charging ahead bravely on fighting against the flood.*

【冲昏头脑】turn sb's head; be or get carried away: 被胜利~ *be dizzy with success*

【冲击】① lash; beat against; break on:狂涛~着岩石。*Furious wares lashed the rock.* ② charge; assault ③ challenge; affect:新思想~旧思想。*Traditional concepts have been challenged by new ideas.*

【冲量】【物】impulse

【冲突】conflict; clash; contradict:武装~ *armed conflict*

【冲撞】① hit; bump; strike; ram ② offend; give offence to

充 ① full; sufficient ② fill; stuff ③ serve as; act as ④ pretend to be; pose as ⑤ (Chōng) a surname

【充斥】flood; congest; be full of:外国商品～市场。*The markets were flooded with foreign goods.*

【充当】serve as; act as; play the part of: ～领导 *act as a leader* / ～好人 *serve as a good man*

【充电】charge (a battery, etc.): ～器 *charger*

【充耳不闻】refuse to hear; turn a deaf ear to:他～别人的意见。*He turned a deaf ear to other people's opinion.*

【充分】① full; abundant; sufficient:人民享有～的人权。*The people enjoy fall human right.* ② to the best of one's ability; as far as possible: ～发挥 *give full play to one's ability*

【充公】confiscate:受贿财物必须～。*The bribes and gifts must be all confiscated.*

【充饥】appease one's hunger; allay one's hunger: 靠水果～ *allay one's hunger with fruits*

【充军】be transported to a distant place for penal servitude; banish

【充满】① fill:会场里～了温暖的气氛。*The assembly hall was filled with warmth.* ② be filled with; be full of; brim with; be permeated with: 屋里～阳光。*The room is fall of sunshine.*

【充沛】plentiful; abundant; full:精力～ *be energetic*

【充其量】at most; at best:歌唱比赛他～能得个第二名。*He can at best win a second prize in the singing contest.*

【充气】air charging; air inflation

【充任】fill the post of; hold the position of:他～班长。*He held the position of monitor.*

【充塞】fill up; cram:她心里～着悲伤。*Her heart is filled with sadness.*

【充实】① substantial; rich:内容～ *rich is content* ② substantiate; enrich; replenish: ～数据库 *substantiate the date base*

【充数】make up the number; serve as a stopgap; pass muster:大多数人是～的。*The most of people were there to make up the number.*

【充血】【医】hyperaemia; congestion of blood

【充溢】be full to the brim; be exuberant; be overflowing:学生们的脸上～着喜悦。*The students' faces beamed with pleasure.*

【充裕】plentiful; abundant; ample; sufficient:时间～ *have plenty if time*

【充足】adequate; sufficient; abundant; ample:水分～ *full of water*

舂 pound; pestle: ～米 *husk rice with mortar and pestle*

憧

【憧憬】long for; look forward to

chóng

虫 ① insect; worm ② certain sort of people:懒～ *lazybones; idler*

【虫害】insect pest

【虫牙】carious or decayed tooth

【虫灾】a plague of insects

【虫子】insect or worm

重 ① repeat; duplicate:书买～了 *duplicate the purchase of a book by mistake* ② again; once more: ～写 *rewrite* ③ layer:远渡～洋 *travel across the oceans* / 多～关卡 *numerous checkpoints*

see also zhòng

【重播】rebroadcast a programme

【重操旧业】resume one's old trade; work at one's old job

【重唱】【音】ensemble of two or more singers, each singing one part:二～ *duet* / 三～ *trio* / 四～ *quarter*

【重重】layer upon layer; ring upon ring:陷入～困难 *be encircled with numerous difficulties*

【重蹈覆辙】follow the track of the overturned cart — follow the same old road to ruin; follow the same old disastrous road

【重叠】overlapping; one on top of another:山峦～ *range upon range of mountains*

【重发球】【体】let service; let

【重返】return; go back: ～前线 *return to the front*

【重犯】repeat (an error or offence)

【重逢】meet again; have a reunion:久别～ *meet again after a long separation*

【重复】① reappear; repeat:这篇文章多处～。*This article is repetitive many times.* ② repeat; duplicate: ～劳动 *duplication of labour*

【重归于好】be reconciled; be reunited

【重合】【数】coincide

【重见天日】see the light of day again; be delivered from oppression or persecution

【重建】rebuild; reconstruct; reestablish

【重起炉灶】set up a new store or kitchen — start afresh; begin all over again

【重审】try again after the original court verdict has been nullified by the higher court; retrial

【重生】① be revived or resurrected ② regrow

【重孙】[口] great-grandson

【重提】bring up again:旧事～ *recall past events*

【重围】tight encirclement:敌军深陷～。*The enemy found themselves trapped in a tight encirclement seriously.*

【重温】review; revive: ～旧梦 *revive and old dream; revive an old experience*

【重现】reap pear

【重新】again; once more: ～做人 *start one's life afresh*

【重修旧好】renew cordial relation; become reconciled; bury the hatchet

【重演】① restage ② recur; reenact; repeat:悲剧～ *tragedy repeated* / 历史的～ *history repeating itself*

【重阳】Double Ninth Festival (9th day of the 9th lunar month)

【重洋】seas and oceans

【重印】reprint

【重整旗鼓】rally one's force after a defeat

【重奏】ensemble of two or more instrumentalists, each playing one part
【重组】① reorganize; reshuffle ② re-engineering
崇 ① high; lofty; sublime: ~山 *high mountain* ② esteem; worship; respect: 推~ *hold in esteem; praise highly* ③ (Chóng) a surname
【崇拜】worship; adore; admire: ~英雄 *hero worship*
【崇奉】believe in: ~真理 *believe in the truth*
【崇高】lofty; sublime; high; noble: ~的品德 *virtuous character*
【崇敬】esteem; respect; revere
【崇山峻岭】high mountains and lofty ridges
【崇尚】uphold; advocate
【崇洋媚外】worship things foreign and fawn on foreigner or foreign powers

chǒng

宠 dote on; bestow favour on; indulge: ~妃 *favourite imperial concubine* / ~爱孩子 *dote on a child*
【宠爱】made a pet of; dote on
【宠儿】pet; favourite; darling: 命运的~ *the darling of fortune* / 时代~ *the idol of the day*
【宠惯】spoil or pamper a child; indulge
【宠姬】favourite concubine
【宠辱不惊】remain indifferent whether favoured or humiliated
【宠物】pet
【宠幸】favour bestowed by one's superior; bestowing favour on a person of inferior rank

chòng

冲[1] ① vigorously; with plenty of dash bluntly: 鲍伯说话很~。*Bob speaks bluntly.* ② (of smell) strong: 这酒很~。*The wine is quite strong.* ③ [方] scold; tell off
冲[2] ① facing; towards: 窗户~北开。*The windows face north.* / 我是~他来的。*My coming was aimed at him.* ② on the basis of; one the strength of; because: ~你这句话,我相信你。*Because of your words, I believe you.*
冲[3] 【机】punching

see also chōng
【冲床】【机】punch (press); punching machine
【冲模】【机】die
【冲压】【机】stamping; punching: ~机 *punching machine*

chōu

抽[1] ① take out from in between; draw: 病来如山倒,病去如~丝 *disease comes on horseback and go away on foot; illness comes like an avalanche, but goes like reeling silk* / 从文件夹里~出报表 *take a reporting out of the file* ② take a part from a whole: ~出点时间作运动 *try to find time to practice* ③ (of certain plants) put forth (buds, etc.): 小麦~穗了。*The wheat is in the ear.* ④ obtain by drawing: ~水 *draw water*
抽[2] ① shrink: 这种材料一下水就~。*This material shrinks in water.* ② lash; whip; thrash: 向奴隶狠~鞭子 *give the slave a furious whip*
【抽测】spot check: 机器出厂前,被~。*The machine was spot checked before it went to the market.*
【抽查】selective examination; spot-check; spot test; sample: ~产品 *spot-check the product*
【抽搐】【医】twitch; tic: 肌肉~ *twitch of the muscle*
【抽打】lash; whip; slash
【抽搭】sob
【抽调】transfer; second: ~物资 *transfer materials*
【抽动】twitch; have a spasm; jerk spasmodically
【抽风】①【医】convulsion ②[口] crazy; lose one's sense: 别~了! *Don't be crazy!* ③ pump in air: ~机 *air pump*
【抽检】spot check
【抽奖】draw lots (to give out prizes); draw a winning number (for lottery) sweepstake; etc.: ~仪式 *ceremony for drawing lots to choose winners*
【抽筋】① pull out a tendon ② cramp: 他的腿~了。*He is having a cramp in the leg.*
【抽空】manage to find time
【抽气机】exhaust fan; air extractor; air pump
【抽泣】sob
【抽签】draw or cast lots
【抽取】take out a part
【抽穗】head; ear
【抽缩】shrink; contract
【抽屉】drawer
【抽头】① take a percentage of (the winnings in gambling, etc.) ②【电】tap: ~电路 *tap circuit*
【抽象】abstract; general; vague: 从~到具体 *proceed from the abstract to the concrete* / ~代数 *abstract algebra* / ~思维 *conceptualization*
【抽选】select; close
【抽烟】smoke: 禁止~ *no smoking*
【抽验】sample testing; spot check
【抽样】sample; sampling: 随机~ *random sampling* / ~分布 *sampling distribution* / ~分析 *sampling analysis* / ~误差 *sampling error*
【抽噎】sob
【抽油泵】【油】oil-well pump

chóu

仇 ① enemy; foe: ~人 *enemy; personal enemy* ② hatred; enmity; grudge: ~外心理 *anti-foreign sentiment; xenophobia* / ~冤 *rancour; hatred; enmity*
【仇敌】[书] enemy; foe

【仇恨】① enmity; hatred; hostility: 满腔～ *be burning with hatred* ② hate
【仇家】personal enemy; foe
【仇杀】murder committed in revenge
【仇深似海】entertain a hatred as great as the ocean
【仇视】regard as an enemy; look upon with hostility; be hostile to
【仇怨】grudge; grievance; hatred

惆 [书] disappointed; aggrieved

【惆怅】disconsolate; sad: 辞别父母后,他产生一种～失落之感。*After bidding farewell to his parents; he was seized with a feeling of ennui and melancholy.*

绸 silk; silk fabric: ～布 *silk fabric*

【绸缎】silks and satins
【绸缪】sentimentally attached
【绸子】silk fabric

畴 [书] ① farmland: 平～千里 *a vast expanse of cultivated land* ② kind; division: 范～ *category* ③【物】domain: 场～ *field domain*

酬 ①[书] propose a toast; toast ② social intercourse; friendly exchange: ～对 *reply; respond; retort* /我最近应～多。*I have hand many social engagements recently.* ③ fulfill; realize: 壮志未～ *without fulfilling one's noble aspirations* ④ reward; payment

【酬报】reward; requite; repay; recompense
【酬宾】bargain sales: 周末大～ *special season sale during weekend*
【酬答】① reward sb for his kindness ② respond with a poem or speech
【酬金】payment for one's service; monetary reward; remuneration
【酬劳】① reward (sb) for his service ② recompense; reward
【酬谢】reward sb for his kindness
【酬应】① socializing: 不善～ *socially inept* ②[书] respond; reply; retort: ～如流 *quick at response*

稠 ① thick: ～糊 *thick and sticky* /粥很～。*The porridge is very thick.* ② dense

【稠密】dense; thick: 小草～ *thick grass*
【稠人广众】a large crowd; a big gathering: 在～前表演,她已经不是第一次了。*It was not the first time she had ever acted before such a big audience.*

愁 ① be worried; be anxious: 他～得直哭。*He is so worried that he cannot refrain from tears.* ② sadness; sorrow: 乡～ *homesickness*

【愁苦】anxiety; distress
【愁眉】knitted brows; worried look: ～不展 *with a worried frown*
【愁眉苦脸】have a worried look; look miserable; pull a long face: 看这几天你～的,有什么麻烦吗? *I've noticed these casts few days that you've been looking rather unhappy; what's the matter?*
【愁闷】feel gloomy; be in low spirits
【愁思】gloomy thoughts; melancholy reveries: ～如麻 *be distressed by a skein of gloomy thoughts*
【愁绪】[书] gloomy moon: ～全消 *one's gloomy had totally disappeared* / ～满怀 *be filled with gloomy moon*

筹 ① chip: 酒～ *chips used to keep count in a drinking game* ② prepare; plan; raise: ～款 *raise money* ③ resource; way; means: 一～莫展 *at the end of one's resources*

【筹办】make preparations; make arrangements: ～运动会 *plan to hold a sports meeting*
【筹备】prepare; arrange: ～委员会 *preparatory committee* / ～组 *planning group*
【筹措】raise (money): ～学费 *raise tuition*
【筹划】plan and prepare: ～有方 *be good at planning*
【筹集】raise (money): ～基金 *raise funds*
【筹建】prepare to construct or establish sth: ～学校 *make preparations for setting up a school*
【筹款】raise funds; raise money
【筹码】chip; counter
【筹募】collect (funds): ～捐款 *collect donations*
【筹资】fund raising

踌

【踌躇】① hesitate; shilly-shally: ～不决 *hesitating and irresolute* / ～不前 *hesitate to move forward* ②[书] be satisfied; be filled with pride
【踌躇满志】enormously proud of one's success

chǒu

丑 ① second of the twelve Earthly Branches ② ugly; unsightly; hideous: 长得～ *bad-looking* ③ disgraceful; shameful; scandalous: 家～ *shameful things of a family* /家～不可外扬。*Domestic shame should not be made public.* ④ clown; comedian ⑤ (Chǒu) a surname

【丑八怪】[口] very ugly person
【丑旦】female clown
【丑恶】ugly; repulsive; hideous: ～灵魂 *ugly soul*
【丑化】discredit; smear; vilify: ～现实 *paint a distorted picture of the real life*
【丑话】① vulgar or coarse language ② blunt words: ～说在前头。*I must tell you bluntly.*
【丑剧】farce
【丑角】① comic role ② (in real life) down; comedian; buffoon
【丑陋】ugly
【丑事】a disgraceful affair; scandal
【丑态】ugly performance; buffoonery: ～百出 *cut a despicable figure* / ～毕露 *reveal all one's hideous feature*
【丑闻】scandal
【丑行】scandalous conduct; misconduct

瞅 [方] look at: 让他～～ *let him have a look*

【瞅见】[方] see; have or catch a glimpse (of sth or sb)

chòu

臭 ① smelly; foul; stinking: ~豆腐 *strong-smelling preserved bean curd* / ~鸡蛋 *rotten egg* ② disgusting; disgraceful: 名声~ *have a bad reputation* ③ inferior; poor; bad ④ harsh; severe; relentless ⑤ [方] (of a bullet) dud
【臭虫】bedbug
【臭豆腐】strong-smelling presented bean card
【臭烘烘】stinking; foal-smelling; smelly
【臭美】[口] show off shamelessly; be disgustingly smug
【臭名】bad reputation; notoriety: ~远扬 *be notorious far and wide* / ~昭著 *of ill repute; notorious*
【臭气】bad (or offensive) smell; stink: ~熏天 *stink to high heaven*
【臭味相投】be birds of a feather; be two of a kind
【臭氧】【化】ozone: ~层 *ozonosphere; ozone layer*
【臭鼬】【动】skunk

chū

出[1] ① go; come out: ~屋 *go out of house* ② come; arrive: ~发港 *port of departure* ③ exceed; go beyond: 排球~了端线。*The volleyball is out of bounds.* ④ issue; put up; offer; give: ~节目 *give a performance* ⑤ produce; from practice ⑥ arise; emerge; happen; occur: 近年来世界~现了很多素食者。*Quite a few vegetarians have emerged in the world in recent years.* ⑦ publish ⑧ put forth; vent: 拿某人~气 *take it out on sb* ⑨ be quoted from ⑩ emerge; appear; show: 水落石~ *when the water subsides the nocks emerge — the whole thing comes to light* /人才辈~。*People of talent are coming to the fore in large numbers.* ⑪ (of rice, etc.) rise well (with cooking) ⑫ pay out; spend: 入不敷~ *one's earrings are insufficient for one's needs*
出[2] ① dramatic piece; chapter in a romance: 一~戏 *a play* ② used after a verb to indicate direction or completion of an action: 找~缺点 *detect the shortcoming* ③ used after an adjective to indicate a higher degree: 多~了两个杯子。*We have two more cup.*
【出版】come off the press; publish; come out: ~权 *right of publication* / ~社 *publishing house* / ~物 *publican* / ~者 *publisher*
【出殡】carry a coffin to the crematory; hold a funeral procession
【出兵】dispatch troops
【出操】drill or do exercises
【出差】① be away on official business; be on a business trip ② do short term tasks in transport, construction, etc.
【出产】① produce; manufacture ② produce; products
【出厂】leave the factory: ~价 *producer price*
【出场】① come on the stage; appear on the scene ② enter the arena or sports ground: ~运动员名单 *list of players for the match*
【出车】① dispatch a vehicle ② be out driving a vehicle: 没有司机~。*No drivers are out at work.*
【出丑】make a fool of oneself; cut a poor or sorry figure; bring shame on oneself: 当众~ *make an exhibition of oneself*
【出处】source (of a quotation or allusion): 典故~ *the source of the allusion*
【出错】make mistakes; go wrong
【出道】(formerly of an apprentice) start working as a journeyman after serving one's apprenticeship; embark on one's career; become known: ~前他是个舞者。*He was a dancer before he became known.*
【出点子】offer advice; make suggestions: 他善于~。*He is good at offering advice.*
【出动】① set out; start off: 部队及时~。*The troops set off in time.* ② send out; dispatch; call out ③ turn out
【出尔反尔】go back on one's word; contradict oneself: 他是一个~的人。*He is the sort of man to go back on his word.*
【出发】① set off; set out; start (off); leave ② start from; proceed from: 从大局~ *from the overall interests* / ~信号 *starting signal*
【出发点】① the starting point of a journey ② starting point (in a discussion argument, etc.): 研究问题的~ *the starting point for a study of the problem*
【出访】go abroad on an official visit; visit (foreign countries): ~可以加强友好关系。*Tour can farther strengthen the friendly relations.*
【出份子】club together (to buy a gift for sb. etc.)
【出风头】get a lot of publicity: 喜欢~ *enjoy being the centre of attention*
【出伏】ending of the dog days or hot season
【出阁】(of a woman) leave her boudoir; get married; marry
【出格】① out of the ordinary; outstanding ② overstep the bounds: 这事做的有点~。*That's going a bit too far.*
【出工】go to work; show up for work
【出轨】① be derailed ② overstep the bounds
【出国】go abroad ~热 *crazy of going abroad*
【出海】go to sea; put out to sea: ~通道 *access to the sea* /他父母~捕鱼去了。*His parents went fishing on the sea.*
【出汗】sweat; perspire: 出一身汗 *break into a sweat*
【出航】① set out on a voyage; sail ② (of a plane) take off; set out on a flight
【出活】be efficient; yield good results in work
【出货】delivery of goods: ~单 *delivery order*

C

【出击】【军】① lunch an attack; make a sally ② hit out; attack:不要四面~。*Don't strike out in all direction.*
【出家】go to a monastery or a nunnery; become a monk or run
【出价】bid; offer a price
【出嫁】(of a woman) get married; marry
【出界】【体】out-of-bounds; outside; out
【出借】lend (things other than money)
【出境】① leave the country: ~签证 *exit visa* ② leave a region
【出口】① speak; utter:不要~伤人。*Don't speak bitingly.* ② leave the port:轮船已经~。*The ship has left the port.* ③ export ④ exit:地铁~ *subway exit*
【出来】① come out:太阳~了。*The sun has come out.* ② emerge; arise; appear:问题一~,我们就采取行动。*As the problem comes out, we will take actions at once.*
【出力】① put forth one's strength; exert oneself; make great efforts ② output power:~试验 *service test*
【出列】【军】come out of the ranks: ~! Fall out!
【出猎】go hunting
【出笼】① just off the steamer ② [贬] (sth bad) come out into the open; come forth:这谬论一~,立即受到舆论抨击。*As soon as fallacies came out; they met with withering criticism from the press.* ③ sell in large quantities; dump; inflate
【出娄子】get into trouble; be in trouble; go wrong
【出路】way out; outlet
【出乱子】go wrong; get into trouble
【出落】grow (prettier):几年不见,这姑娘~得更加漂亮了。*The girl has grown prettier than ever since I last saw her several years ago.*
【出马】go into action; take the field:亲自~ *take up the matter oneself*
【出卖】① offer for sale; sell ② sell out; betray; barter away: ~灵魂 *sell one's soul*
【出毛病】be or go out of order; go wrong; break down.
【出门】① go out ② be away from home; go on a journey ③ [方] (of a woman) get married; many
【出面】act in one's own capacity or on behalf of an organization; appear personally:以个人名义~ *act in his own name*
【出名】① famous; well-known; celebrated: ~的明星 *famous star* ② use the name of; lend one's name
【出没】appear and disappear: ~无常 *appear and disappear suddenly and unpredictably*
【出谋划策】give counsel; make designs:这件事是由他~的。*He's the brain behind this.*
【出纳】① receive or pay out money or hills ② cashier; teller ③ receive and lend books: ~员 *cashier teller*
【出其不意】take sb by surprise; catch sb unawares; catch sb on the hop:攻其不备~。*Attack where the enemy is unprepared and act where thy do not expect it.*
【出奇】unusually; extraordinarily:说话慢的~ *incredibly slow talk* / ~制胜 *win by making a surprise move*
【出气】take it out on sb; give vent to one's anger
【出勤】① turn out for work ② be out on duty; make a business trip
【出去】go out; get out
【出缺】fall vacant
【出让】sell articles of one's own: ~商店 *sell one's shop*
【出人头地】rise head and shoulders above others:不是每个人都希望~。*Not everyone hope to become outstanding someday.*
【出人意料】exceeding all expectations; beyond all expectation
【出任】[书] take up the post of
【出入】① come in and out: ~请随手关门。*Please close the door behind you when you come in or go out.* ② discrepancy; divergence; difference:这两次报告有~。*There is some discrepancy between the two reporting.*
【出入证】pass (identifying a staff member, etc.)
【出色】outstanding; remarkable; splendid: ~的青年 *an outstanding young man*
【出山】① leave a hilly region ② enter politics as a government official; take up a post or task
【出身】① family background; class origin ② one's previous experience or occupation ③ [旧] first appointment in the ladder of official promotion: 翰林~ *be first appointed as a member of the Imperial Academy.*
【出神】be spellbound:看得~ *watch spellbound*
【出生】be born: ~登记 *registration of birth* / ~日期 *date of birth* / ~地 *birthplace* / ~率 *birthrate* / ~证 *birth certificate*
【出生入死】go through fire and water; brave untold dangers:战争中~的英雄 *a hero who risk death in the war*
【出师】① finish one's apprenticeship ② [书] launch a campaign
【出使】serve as an envoy abroad; be sent on a diplomatic mission: ~美国 *be sent as an envoy to America*
【出示】① show; produce: ~护照 *show one's passport* ② [书] put up a notice
【出世】① come into the world; be born ② come into being; come into existence; be born ③ renounce human society; stand aloof from the mortal world ④ soar into the skies: 横空~(*of mountains*) *tower majestically into the heavens*
【出事】meet with a mishap; have an accident: ~地点 *site of an accident*
【出手】① get (hoarded goods etc.) off one's hands; dispose of; sell:这批自行车要尽快~。*We should try to dispose of these bikes as soon as*

possible. ②produce; offer:这点小礼物实在拿不~。*I really couldn't offer such a small gift.*
【出售】offer for sale; sell
【出书】publish books
【出数儿】[口] (of rice) rise well with cooking
【出台】① appear on the stage; enter ② come out from behind the scenes; come into the open ③ make sth public; publicize
【出逃】① set examination paper ②set a topic
【出题】set examination paper
【出庭】appear in court; enter an appearance: 昨天他~作证了。*He appeared in count as a witness yesterday.*
【出头】① extricate oneself from miserable circumstances ② (of sth) show its tip, jut out; stand out ③ appear personally; act on behalf of; take the lead:枪打~鸟。*The leading bird gets shot first — One who takes the lead usually bears the brunt of attack.* ④a little over; odd:三十~ *just a little over thirty*
【出头露面】make a public appearance; be in the limelight:她爱~。*She likes the limelight.*
【出徒】complete one's apprenticeship
【出外】leave home; be away: ~度假 be away on holiday
【出席】attend; be present
【出息】① promise; prospects; future:有~的孩子 *promising child* ②[方] progress:这孩子比去年~多了。*The boy has improved greatly since last year.* ③[方] temper; culminate; train
【出现】appear; emerge
【出血】①[方] pay up; cough up ②【医】haemorrhage; bleeding
【出行】go on a trip to other places
【出巡】royal progress; tour of inspection
【出言】speak; remark
【出演】perform; play the role of; atc as
【出洋】[旧] go abroad
【出洋相】cut a sorry figure; make an exhibition of oneself
【出迎】go or come out to meet sb:列队~ *line up to welcome sb*
【出游】go on a tour or trip
【出于】stem from; be motivated or dictated by; proceed from: ~自愿 *of one's own free will*
【出狱】come out of prison; be release from prison
【出院】leave hospital: ~证明 *hospital discharge certificate*
【出渣】tap; slag tap: ~口 *slay notch; cinder notch*
【出战】go into battle: ~告捷 *have succeed the battle*
【出账】① enter an item of expenditure in accounts ②[方] (item of) expenditure
【出诊】(of a doctor) visit a patient at home; pay a home visit; make a house call: ~费 *house visit charges*
【出阵】① go into battle ② take part (in a kind of activity)
【出证】go evidence; bear witness; testify
【出众】be out of the common run; be out of the ordinary; be outstanding:才华~ *of outstanding ability*
【出资】provide funds; put in capital: ~办校 *provide capital for setting up a school*
【出自】come from; proceed from; stem from
【出走】leave; run away; flee:仓促~ *ran away in a hurry*
【出租】let; rent out; hire out: ~游船 *rowboats for hire* / ~柜台 *rent or hire out counters* (in a store, shop, etc.)

初 ① at the beginning of; in the early part of: 上个世纪~ *the beginning of the last century* ② first (in order):最~几年 *first few years* ③ for the first time; only just begun:和好如~ *restore good relations; be on good terms again* / ~次见面 *first meeting* ④ elementary; rudimentary: ~认识 *elementary recognize* ⑤ original ⑥ (Chū) a surname
【初版】① be published for the first time ② first edition
【初步】tentative; initial; preliminary: ~告捷 *tentative success* / ~方案 *tentative programme*
【初潮】【生理】menophania
【初创】newly established; initial: ~阶段 *initial stage*
【初春】early spring; first spring month
【初次】the first time
【初等】elementary; primary: ~数学 *elementary mathematics*
【初冬】early winter; first winter month
【初犯】① first offender ② first offence
【初稿】first draft; draft:请把~给我。*Please give the first draft to me.*
【初会】first encounter; first meeting
【初婚】① first marriage ② newly married; newly wed
【初级】elementary: ~产品 *primary products* / ~阶段 *primary stage* / ~小学 *lower primary school*
【初加工】【机】preliminary working
【初见成效】achieve an initial success
【初交】new acquaintance
【初具规模】begin to take shape
【初来乍到】newly arrived; now (to a job or place)
【初恋】① first love: ~的苦涩 *bitterness of one's first love* ② just fall in love:他们看起来总是像在~。*They always seem to just fall in love with each other.*
【初露头角】begin to show ability or talent ~的新画家 *budding artist*
【初年】the first year of a historical period:清朝~ *in the first years of the Qing Dynasty*
【初期】initial stage; early days
【初秋】early autumn
【初日】rising sun
【初审】preliminary check or examination; preliminary evaluation: ~法庭 *court of first instance*
【初生牛犊】newborn calf: ~不畏虎 *newborn calves*

are not afraid of tigers — young people are fearless
【初始】initial; first; primary
【初试】① first try ② preliminary examination
【初速度】【物】initial velocity
【初夏】first month of summer; early summer
【初选】primary election
【初学】begin to learn; be a beginner:他是个～者。*He is just a beginner.*
【初夜】① wedding night: ～权 *right of first night* ② early evening
【初叶】early years of a century
【初诊】(of a patient) first visit (to a doctor or hospital)
【初值】【数】initial value
【初中】junior secondary school
【初衷】one's original intention:不改～ *not change one's original intention*

chú

除[1] ① get rid of; eliminate: ～霜 *defrost* /为民～害 *rid the people of a scourge* ② except; in addition to: ～此之外,别无他图 *have no other plan in mind except this* ③ divide ④［书］offer or confer
除[2]［书］steps to a house
【除暴安良】get rid of bullies and bring peace to the people
【除草】weeding: ～机 *seeder* / ～剂 *weed killer; herbicide*
【除法】【数】division
【除非】① only when; only if; unless:若要人不知,～己莫为。*If you don't want others to know, you'd better not do it.* ② except
【除根】dig up roots; root out; be cured once and for all; get a permanent care
【除号】【数】division sign
【除旧布新】do away with the old, usher in the new; ring out the old ring in the new
【除了】① except; except for ② in addition to; apart from
【除名】expel; dismiss
【除数】【数】divisor
【除外】except; not counting; not including
【除夕】New Year's Eve
厨 ① kitchen:下～ *serve as a cook* ② cook; chef:名～ *famous chef*
【厨房】kitchen: ～用具 *kitchen (or cooking) utensils*
【厨师】cook; chef
【厨艺】culinary art
锄 ① work with a hoe; hoe: ～草 *hoe up weeds* ② uproot; eliminate; wipe out:斩草～根 *cut the weeds and dig up the roots; stamp out the source of trouble* / ～强扶弱 *suppress the strong and aid the weak*
【锄地】weed or loosen the soil with a hoe
【锄奸】ferret out spies; eliminate traitors
【锄头】①［方］hoe ② pickaxe
雏 young (bird): ～莺乳燕 *young orioles and swallows*
【雏鸟】nestling; fledgling
【雏儿】［口］① young bird ② young inexperienced person; fledgling
【雏形】① embryonic form; embryo ② model; miniature
橱 cabinet; closet:壁～ *built in cabinet*
【橱窗】① glass-fronted billboard ② shopwindow; showcase
【橱柜】cupboard

chǔ

处 ① get along (with sb):好相～ *easy to get along with* ②be situated in; be in a certain condition ③ manage; handle; deal with ④［书］dwell:住～ *residence; dwelling place; lodging* ⑤ sentence; punish
see also chù
【处罚】punish; penalize
【处方】① write out a prescription; prescribe ② recipe; prescription: ～药 *prescription medicine (or drug)*
【处分】① take disciplinary action against:行政～ *administrative disciplinary measure* ②［书］handle; manage; deal with
【处境】unfavourable situation; light: ～危险 *be in a dangerous situation*
【处决】put to death; execute:依法～ *put to death in accordance with the law*
【处理】① handle; deal with; dispose of: ～国家大事 *conduct state affairs* ② treat by a special process:用油～ *treat with oil* ③ sell at reduced price: ～价 *bargain price*
【处理机】processor:数据～ *date processor* /中央～ *central processor*
【处理品】goods sold at reduced price
【处女】virgin; maiden: ～作 *maiden work; first effort* / ～膜 *hymen* / ～地 *virgin land* / ～峰 *virgin peak or mount* / ～航 *maiden flight or voyage*
【处身】place oneself: ～涉世 *the way one conducts oneself in society*
【处世】conduct oneself in society: ～哲学 *philosophy of life*
【处死】put to death; execute
【处心积虑】incessantly scheme; deliberately plan
【处刑】【律】condemn; sentence
【处治】punish
【处于】be (in a certain condition)
【处之泰然】take things calmly; remain unruffled
【处置】① handle; deal with; manage; dispose of

② punish

杵 ① pestle：木～ *wooden pestle* / ～臼 *mortar and pestle* ② wooden dub used to pound clothes in washing ③ poke (with sth long and slender)

础 plinth：基～ *foundation*；*base*

储 ① store up ② heir to the throne prince ③ (Chǔ) a surname

【储备】store for future use；lay in；lay up：～鸡蛋 *store up eggs*

【储存】lay in；lay up；deposit：～水果 *deposit the fruits*

【储放】store；deposit：～食品 *deposit one's food*

【储户】depositor

【储积】① store up；save ② stock；saving

【储集】collect and store up：～汽油 *stock up gasoline*

【储量】reserves

【储气】gas storage：～罐 *gas tank*

【储蓄】deposit；savings

【储油】oil storage：～罐 *oil tank*

【储运】store up and transport

楚 ①［书］suffering ② clear；neat：清～ *be clear* ③ name of a state under the Zhou Dynasty and later one of the seven hegemonic states of the period of the warring states ④ name for the region covering Hunan and Hubei，esp. Hubei ⑤ (Chǔ) a surname

【楚楚可怜】delicate and charming；attractive

chù

处 ① place：住～ *accommodation*；*lodging* ② part；point：长～ *strong point*；*forte* /心灵深～ *deep down in one's heart* ③ division；office；department：问询～ *inquiry desk* ④［量］：三～错误 *three mistakes*

see also chǔ

【处处】everywhere；in all respects：～掣肘 *hinder (sb) at step*；*make difficulties (for sb) at every turn*

【处所】place；location

【处长】head of a department or office；division or section chief

怵 ［书］fear；fright

【怵目惊心】be extremely nervous，afraid or shocked at the sigh of sth

畜 domestic animal；livestock

see also xù

【畜生】① domestic animals ② beast；dirty swine

触 ① touch；contact；hit：～电 *get an electric shock* ② more sb；stir up sb's feels：～景生情 *the scene brings back past memories*

【触动】① touch：她在黑夜中行走，忽然～了什么东西。*Going in the dark，she suddenly touched something.* ② collide (against sth)；offend；affect：～利益 *affect somebody's interest* ③ move；touch；stir up：这支歌～了我的心弦。*The song touched me to the heart.*

【触发】detonate by contact；touch off；spark off；trigger：～战争 *sparked a war* / ～地雷 *trap mine* / ～电路 *trigger circuit* / ～器 *flip-flop*

【触犯】violate；infringe：～法律 *break the law*

【触及】touch：～事件本质 *get to the essence of a matter*

【触礁】① ran (up) on rocks；strike a reef or rock ② run into difficulty；be snarled

【触觉】【生理】tactile or tactual sensation；sense of touch

【触媒】【化】catalyst；catalytic agent

【触目】① meet the eye：～皆是 *can be seen everywhere* ② attracting attention：～惊心 *startling*；*shocking*

【触怒】make angry；infuriate；enrage

【触碰】touch

【触手】【动】tentacle

【触痛】① touch a tender；touch sore spot：这句话～了她。*The words touched her* ②【医】tenderness

黜 ［书］remove or dismiss sb from office；reject

【黜免】［书］dismiss (a government official)：他被～官职。*He was removed from office.*

chuāi

揣 ① hide or carry in one's clothes；tack：～在怀里 *hide sth in the bosom* / ～着明白装糊涂 *pretend to know nothing while knowing all about it* ②［方］(of animals) be pregnant：马～上了驹子。*The horse is in foal.*

see also chuǎn

【揣手儿】tuck each hard in the opposite sleeve

chuǎi

揣 ①［书］estimate；conjecture；surmise：～情度理 *judge by reason and by the normal conduct of human affairs* ② (Chuǎi) a surname

see also chuān

【揣测】guess；suppose；conjecture

【揣度】［书］make a rough estimate of；appraise；estimate；calculate：妄加～ *make a wild conjecture*

【揣摩】try to fathom；try to figure out；elicit by careful study

【揣想】guess；conjecture

C

chuài

踹 ① kick (forward with sole and heel): ~开门 *kick the door open* ② trample; step in: ~进泥里 *trample it into the mud*

【踹腿儿】[方] kick the bucket; die

chuān

川 ① river: 冰~ *glacier* / 高山名~ *high mountains and famous rivers* ② plain: 一马平~ *vast expanse of flat land; great stretch of land*

【川贝】【药】tendril-leaved fritillary bulb

【川流不息】flow past in an endless stream: 参观者~。*Visitors come in an endless stream.*

穿 ① pierce through; penetrate: 子弹射~了他的肝。*A bullet pierced his liver.* ② go through; pass through; cross: ~过公路 *cross the highway* ③ thread: 用珠子~项链 *thread beads to make necklace* ④ wear; put on; be dressed in; have... on: ~鞋 *put on shoes* / ~得朴素 *be simply dressed*

【穿插】① alternate; arrange by turns; do or perform by turns: 音乐和诗歌~进行。*Music alternated with verse.* ② insert; weave in; interweave: 图片中~了一些对话。*The dialogues are weaved in the pictures.*

【穿戴】dress; apparel: ~整齐 *be neatly dressed*

【穿过】walk from one side to the other; cross (over)

【穿孔】①【医】perforation: 胃~ *gastric perforation* ② bore a hole; punch a hole; perforate: ~纸带 *punched tape* / ~带读器 *perforated tape reader* / ~腐蚀 *pitting corrosion* / ~卡 *punch card*

【穿山甲】①【动】pangolin ② pangolin scales

【穿梭】shuttle back and forth: 明如~ *the sun and the moon shuttle back and forth-time flies* / ~机 *space shuttle*

【穿堂风】draught

【穿透】pass through; perpetrate

【穿衣镜】full-length mirror

【穿越】pass through; cut across: 铁路~崇山峻岭。*The railway runs across high mountains*

【穿凿】give a farfetched or strained interpretation; read two much meaning into sth: ~附会 *give strained interpretations and drew farfetched analogies-distort (the evidence, the original, etc.)* / 这篇论文多处~。*The paper gives wrong interpretations in many places.*

【穿针引线】act as a go-between; try to make a match

【穿着】dress; apparel: ~高雅 *dress elegantly*

chuán

传 ① pass; convey; hand down: 一脉相~ *come down in one continuous line; be in the same strain* / 世代相~ *hand sth down from generation to generation* ② pass on (know ledge, skill, etc.); impart; teach: ~手艺 *teach the skill* ③ spread: 坏事~千里。*Bad news runs apace.* ④ transmit; conduct: ~电 *conduct electricity* ⑤ convey; express: 只可意会,不可言~ *can be apprehended but not expressed* ⑥ summon: ~审 *summon sb to court* ⑦ infect; be contagious: ~上流感 *have come down with the flu*
see also zhuàn

【传帮带】(of experienced people) pass on experience, help and guide now hands

【传播】① disseminate; spread: ~知识 *spread knowledge* ②【物】propagation: 直线~ *rectilinear propagation*

【传布】disseminate; propagate; spread

【传抄】make private copies of (a manuscript, document, etc. which is being circulated)

【传达】① pass on (information. etc.) transmit; relay; communicate: ~命令 *transmit an order* ② reception and registration of callers at a public establishment ③ janitor: ~室 *reception office; janitor's room*

【传代】pass on from generation to generation

【传单】leaflet; handbill

【传导】①【物】conduct (heat, electricity, etc.): 金属都有~作用。*All metals are conductor.* ②【生理】transmission: 神经纤维他外界的刺激~给大脑。*Nerve fibres transmit to the brain.*

【传道】deliver a sermon; preach

【传递】transmit; deliver; transfer

【传粉】【植】pollination: ~媒介 *pollination medium*

【传感器】【电】sensor; transducer: 激光~ *laser sensor*

【传呼】pass on a telephone message or call sb to answer the phone: ~机 *beeper*

【传话】pass on a message

【传家宝】① family heirloom ② a cherished tradition or heritage: 艰苦朴素是我们的~。*Hard work and plain living are a cherished heritage of us.*

【传教】do missionary work

【传令】transmit (or dispatch) orders: ~惩罚 *punish sb in a dispatch*

【传媒】① media; vehicle ② mass media; the media

【传票】①【律】(court) summons; subpoena: 发出~ *issue a summons* ② accounting voucher

【传奇】① tales of the marvellous ② a form of drama of the Ming-Qing period, immensely long with an verge of forty or more scenes ③ legend; romance: 他爷爷是一个~式的人物。*His grandpa was a legendary figure.*

【传情】express amorous feelings
【传球】pass the ball to a teammate
【传染】infect; be contagious: ~病 *infectious disease* / ~病院 *hospital for infectious diseases; isolated hospital* / ~性 *infectiousness; contagion*
【传神】vivid; lifelike: ~之笔 *a vivid touch (in writing or touching)*
【传声器】micro phone
【传世】be handed down from ancient times: ~珍宝 *a treasure handed down from ancient times*
【传授】pass on (knowledge, skill, etc.); impart; teach: ~知识 *impart knowledge to*
【传输】【电】transmission: ~损耗 *transmission loss*
【传说】① pass from mouth; it is said; they say ② legend; tradition: 民间~ *popular legend*
【传诵】be widely read; be on everybody's lips
【传送】convey; deliver: ~信息 *convey information*
【传颂】be on everybody's lips
【传统】tradition: ~观念 *traditional ideas* / ~艺术 *traditional art* / 革命~ *revolutionary tradition*
【传闻】① it is said; they say: ~不如亲见。*To see it is better than hear about it.* ② hearsay; rumour; talk: ~失实。*The rumour proved unfounded.*
【传销】pyramid selling
【传信】①［书］pass on to others what one believes in ② pass on a message
【传讯】【律】summon for interrogation or trial; subpoena
【传言】① hearsay; rumour ② pass on a message ③ make a speech
【传扬】spread (from mouth to mouth): 美名~天下。*One's good name spreads far and wide.*
【传谕】［旧］relay instructions from a superior or an elder
【传阅】circulate for perusal
【传真】① portraiture ② facsimile; fax: 收到~ *receive a fax* / ~机 *fax machine; fax*
【传旨】pronounce an imperial edict
【传宗接代】have a son to carry on one's family name

船 ship; boat

【船板】deck a boat
【船帮】① side of a ship; shipboard ② merchant fleet
【船舶】ships; shipping: ~证书 *ship's papers*
【船埠】wharf; quay
【船舱】① ship's hold ② cabin
【船厂】shipyard; dockyard
【船底】bottom
【船队】fleet; flotilla
【船夫】boatman
【船工】boatman; junkman; sailor
【船户】① one who owns a boat and makes a living as a boatman; boatman ②［方］boat dweller
【船货】freight; cargo
【船级】ship's class
【船籍】registry; nationality of a ship
【船壳】hull
【船老大】［方］① chief crewman of a wooden ② boatman
【船票】boat ticket; ship ticket; steamer ticket: 你能帮我买一张~吗? *Would you like help me buy a ship ticket?*
【船期】sailing date
【船艄】stern
【船身】hull
【船手】boatman; junkman
【船台】(building) berth; shipway; slipway; slip
【船体】body of a ship; hull
【船桅】mast
【船尾】stern: ~部 *quarter* / ~楼 *poop* / ~轴 *stern shaft*
【船坞】dock; shipyard
【船舷】side (of a ship or boat); gunwale
【船运】ship; transport by water
【船闸】(ship) lock
【船长】captain; skipper
【船只】vessels; shipping
【船主】① captain (of a ship); skipper ② shipowner

chuǎn

喘 ① breathe heavily; gasp for breath; pant: 气~吁吁 *huffing and puffing* ②【医】asthma: 他有~病。*He is a victim of asthma.*

【喘气】① breathe (deeply); pant; gasp ② take a breather
【喘息】① pant; gasp for breath ② breather; breathing spell; respite
【喘吁吁】puff and blow

chuàn

串 ① string together: 贯~ *run through; penetrate; permeate* ②［量］string; bunch; cluster: 羊肉~ *mutton cubes roasted on a skewer; shashlik* / 一~香蕉 *a cluster of banana* ③ conspire; gang up: ~骗 *gang up to swindle (sb)* ④ get things mixed up: 电话~线 *get the (telephone) lines crossed* ⑤ go from place to pace; go about; rove: ~亲访友 *go visiting one's relatives and friends* ⑥ play a part (in a play); act: 反~ *play a role one is not trained for* ⑦ string

【串行】① (in reading or typing) skip a line; confuse two lines ② series: ~计算机 *series machine*
【串讲】① (of a teacher) explain text sentence by sentence ② give a summing-up of a text after going over it paragraph by paragraph
【串门子】［口］call on sb; drop in
【串气】gang up; collude with: 暗中~ *be in secret collusion*
【串通】① gang up; collaborate; collude: 法官与证

人暗中~。*The judge acted in collusion with the witness.* ② establish contact with; get in touch with

【串通一气】work hand in glove; act in close collaboration:两人~,互相包庇。*Acting in collaboration, the two of them shield each other.*

【串味】(of food or drinks) absorb the smell of sth with a peculiar odour:这两种食品不应该放在一起,以免~。*The two kind of food should not be put together, or they might get a peculiar odour.*

【串演】play the role of; act the role of

C

chuāng

创 wound; trauma:战争的~伤 *war scar; wounds of war* /重~敌军 *inflict heavy casualties on the enemy*

see also chuàng

【创痕】scar

【创口】surface of a wound

【创伤】wound; trauma:精神~ *emotional trauma*

【创痛】pain from an injury

疮 ① sore; skin ulcer:冻~ *chilblain* ② wound:刀~ *sword wound*

【疮疤】scar

【疮口】open part of a sore

【疮痍满目】a scene of devastation meets the eye everywhere; one sees suffering and destruction everywhere

窗 window:纱~ *screen window* /气~ *transom* /百叶~ *shutters*

【窗扉】casement (of a window)

【窗格子】window lattice

【窗户】window; casement: ~的旁边有一颗大树。*There is a big tree near the window.*

【窗花】paper-cut for window decoration

【窗口】① window:坐在~ *sit by the window* ② wicket; window:在这个~买票 *buy tickets at this window* ③ window on people's life — serving the people directly: ~工业 *industry bearing directly on people's life* ④ channel; medium:发挥~作用 *serve as a medium* ⑤ reflection; showcase:眼睛是心灵的~。*Eyes are the window of the soul.*

【窗框】window frame

【窗帘】curtain; draper

【窗幔】large window curtain

【窗明几净】with bright windows and clean tables; bright and clean

【窗台】windowsill

chuáng

床 ① bed:单人~ *single bed* /折叠~ *folding bed* ② implement or appliance shaped like a bed:车~ *lathe* ③[量] used of sth that corers a bed:一~被子 *one quilt*

【床单】sheet:昨天我买了两条新~。*Yesterday I bought two new sheets.*

【床垫】mattress

【床架】bedstead

【床铺】bed

【床身】【机】lathe bed

【床头】the head of a bed; bedside: ~柜 *bedside cupboard*

【床位】berth; bunk; bed

【床沿】the edge of a bed

【床罩】bedspread; counterpane

【床第】[书] bed mat — the bed as a place of conjugal intimacies: ~之言 *pirate talk between husband and wife; pillow talk*

chuǎng

闯 ① rush; dash; charge:江湖~荡 *make a living wandering from place to place* /横冲直~ *charge about furious; run amuck* ② temper oneself (by battling through difficulties and dangers): ~出一条新路 *break a new path; blaze a trail* ③ go around; by busy running about:走南~北 *journey north and south; travel widely* ④ get into or bring on (sth undesirable)

【闯荡】make a living away from home; venture out into the world

【闯关】fight one's way through a fortresses; break through barriers

【闯红灯】① go against a red light; jump a red light ② violate law and discipline; break down a barrier or limit

【闯祸】bring disaster; get into trouble

【闯将】pathbreaker; a daring general

【闯劲】pioneering; spirit of a pathbreaker

【闯牌子】work hard to establish a name for oneself

chuàng

创 start (doing sth); achieve (sth for the first time); create: ~新貌 *found a new view*

see also chuāng

【创办】establish; set up: ~学校 *set up a school*

【创编】write; create

【创高产】achieve a high yield

【创汇】earn net foreign exchange profit from exports: ~产品 *foreign-exchange-earning products*

【创纪录】break a record; register a new record

【创见】original idea; creative thinking

【创建】found; establish: ~新学派 *found a new school of thought*

【创举】pioneering work or undertaking:伟大的~ *great undertaking*

【创刊】publication: ~号 *first issue or number*

【创立】found; originate:那所学校是他父亲~的。*The school was found by his father.*

【创利】make or earn a profit
【创牌子】(of enterprises) produce and establish a brand name
【创设】① found; create; set up ② create (conditions, etc.)
【创始】originate; initiate:马克思和恩格斯是科学社会主义的～人。*Marx and Engels were the founders of the theory of scientific socialism.*
【创世主】【宗】creator
【创税】pay taxes: ～大户 *big taxpayer*
【创新】bring forth new ideas; blaze new trails:不断～ *constantly bring forth new ideas*
【创业】start an undertaking; do pioneering work: ～精神 *pioneering spirit*
【创意】break fresh ground in imaginative cut
【创优】① achieve success ② make bland-name or high quality products
【创造】create; produce; bring about: ～本能 *the ability of creation* / ～力 *creative power or ability* / ～性 *creativeness*; *creativity*
【创作】① write; produce; create: ～思想 *ideas guiding artistic (or literary) creation* ② creative work; creation:文艺～ *literary and artistic creation* / ～方法 *mode of writing*

chuī

吹 ① blow; puff: ～灰之力 *just a small effort*; *effort needed to blow away a speck of dust* /睡觉前一定把灯～灭。*You must blow out the lamp before you have a sleep.* ② play (wind instruments): ～箫 *play the vertical flute* / ～口琴 *play the mouth organ* / ～口哨 *whistle* ③ (of wind) blow:风～雨打 *be weather-beaten* ④ [口] *boast*; *brag*: ～喇叭 *given to unctuous praise* /自～自擂 *blow one's own trumpet* ⑤ flatter; compliment:又～又拍 *do one's utmost to flatter* ⑥ [口] break off; break up; fall through:他们俩～了。*The couples have broken up.*
【吹玻璃】【化】glass blowing: ～机 *glass blower*
【吹吹打打】beating drums and blowing trumpets; piping and drumming; making an ostentatious show
【吹打】① play wind and percussion instruments ② be hit:经受风雨的～ *withstand the onslaught of storms* ③ blow off (dust, etc.) ④ [方] hurt sb my offer sire remarks:说话～人 *speak sarcastically* ⑤ [方] *blow one's horn*; *brag*
【吹打乐】【音】ensemble of Chinese wind and percussion instruments
【吹荡】stir (by wind)
【吹灯拔蜡】[方] kick the bucket; fall from power
【吹动】(of wind) blow; sway
【吹风】① be in draught; catch a chill:小心～着凉。*Be careful not to get in draught and catch cold.* ② dry (hair, etc.) with a blower ③let sb in on sth in advance; give a cue; brief
【吹风机】blower (for drying hair); hair drier
【吹拂】① (of a breeze) sway; stir ② [书] praise and recommend sb
【吹管】【机】blowpipe
【吹胡子瞪眼】forth at the mouth and glare with rage; foam with rage:他总是对儿子～。*He was always foaming with rage at his son.*
【吹拉弹唱】blow, pull, pellet and sing-perform various kinds of instrumental as well as vocal music:他多才多艺,～,无所不能。*He is quite a versatile artist, good at all kinds of instrumental as well as vocal music.*
【吹冷风】blow a cold wind over; throw cold water on:不要给人家～。*Don't pour cold water on others.*
【吹毛求疵】find fault; pick holes; nitpick; cavil at
【吹牛】boast; brag; talk big: ～大王 *boaster*; *braggart*
【吹弹】play musical instruments: ～之声,不绝于耳。*The sound of the musical instruments lingers in one's ears.*
【吹嘘】lavish praise on (sb); boast:自我～ *self-praise*

炊 cook a meal
【炊饼】steamed round flat cake
【炊具】cooking utensils
【炊事员】cook (or kitchen) staff
【炊烟】smoke from kitchen chimneys: ～袅袅 *smoke spiraling from kitchens*

chuí

垂 ① hang down; droop:柳丝在空中悬～着。*Willow branches are hanging down to the midair.* ② [书] used to kind action of other people, (usu. one's seniors) to wards one: ～询 *condescend to inquire* ③ [书] spread; hard down; go down in history; bequeath to posterity:名～千古 *one's reputation will resound throughout the ages*; *one's good name will be recorded in history* / ～示后世 *set a shining example for posterity* ④ [书] approach; hear; be close to; verge on
【垂成】[书] on the verge of success:功败～ *suffer defeat when success is in sight*
【垂钓】fish with a hook and line; go angling
【垂范后世】pass on to posterity as a shining example
【垂挂】hang down
【垂泪】shed tears; weep
【垂怜】show sympathy (as for one's subordinates who have met with misfortune)
【垂帘听政】(of an empress or mother queen) attend to court affairs from behind a screen
【垂柳】weeping willow
【垂落】droop; fall

【垂暮】[书] ① old age: ~之年 *in the evening of one's life* ② near sunset; just before sundown
【垂盼】solicitude from a senior man
【垂泣】weep; shed tears
【垂青】[书] look upon sb with favour
【垂手】① with hands down; easily ② with the hands at one's side; respectfully: ~可得 *be extremely easy to obtain*
【垂死】moribund; dying: ~的命运 *approaching doom*
【垂头丧气】crestfallen; dejected
【垂危】① be critically ill; be at one's last gasp ② (of a nation) be in great peril
【垂涎】drool; slaver; covet: ~欲滴 *one's mouth waters; one's mouth drools with greed; be greedy* / ~三尺 *have sb's saliva three feet long; drool with envy*
【垂杨柳】weeping willow
【垂直】perpendicular; vertical

陲 [书] frontier; border: 边~ *frontier or border area*

捶 beat (with a stick or fist); thump; pound: ~背 *pound sb's back*
【捶打】strike; beat; thump
【捶胸顿足】thump one's chest and stamp one's feet

槌 mallet; beetle: 棒~ *wooden club (used to beat clothes in washing)* / 鼓~儿 *drumstick*

锤 ① metal ball with a chin or long handle (used as a weapon in ancient times); hammer: 铁~ *iron hammer* ② sth shaped like a hammer: 纺~ *spindle* ③ hammer: 钉~ *nail hammer* / 汽~ *steam hammer* ④ hammer into shape; knock with a hammer
【锤锻】[机] hammer forging
【锤炼】① temper ② polish; refine: ~语言 *refine one's diction*
【锤子】hammer

chūn

春 ① spring: ~风化雨 *life-giving spring breeze and rain; salutary influence of education* / ~去秋来 *with the change of seasons; with the passage of time* / ~暖花开。*Spring has come and the flowers are in bloom* ② a year's time; year ③ love, lust: 有女怀~ *girl longing for love; girl in love* ④ vital energy; life: 妙手回~ *bring the dying back to life* ⑤ (Chūn) a surname
【春播】spring sowing
【春风】① spring breeze ② [书] favour; kindness ③ kind and pleasant countenance
【春风得意】be flushed with success; ride on the crest of success
【春风满面】beaming with satisfaction; radiant with happiness
【春光】sights and sounds of spring; spring scenery: ~融融。*Spring fills the air with warmth.*
【春季】spring; springtime; spring season: ~作物 *spring crops*
【春假】spring vacation; spring holiday
【春节】Spring Festival; Chinese's New Year's Day
【春卷】spring roll (a thin sheet of dough, rolled, stuffed and fried)
【春兰】orchid; cymbidium
【春令】① spring ② spring weather: 冬行~。*The winter is mild like spring.*
【春梦】spring dream; pipe dream
【春日】① spring ② [书] spring sun
【春色】① spring scenery: ~满神州。*Spring reign all its gorgeous beauty in this sacred lard.* ② flushed look under the influence of alcohol; joyful look: 满面~ *be flushed with joy*
【春色满园】signs of spring are visible everywhere in the garden
【春笋】spring bamboo shoots
【春天】spring; springtime
【春心】ardent desire for love; ardent love; lust
【春汛】① spring flood; spring freshet ② spring (fishing) season
【春意】breath of spring; hint of spring: ~盎然。*Spring is very much in the air.*
【春游】spring outing
【春雨】spring shower; spring rain: ~贵如油。*Rain dropping spring time is as precious as oil.*
【春运】transport during the Spring Festival period
【春种】spring sowing: ~秋收 *spring sowing and autumn harvest*
【春装】spring clothing; spring dress

chún

纯 ① pure; unmixed: ~毛 *pure wool* ② pure and simple: ~系无稽之谈。*It's nonsense, pure and simple.* ③ accomplished: 工夫不~。*The shill is far from accomplished.*
【纯度】degree of purity
【纯化】purification
【纯洁】pure; unselfish and honest: 她是一位心地~的姑娘。*She is pure in thought.*
【纯净】pure; clean
【纯利】net profit
【纯朴】simple; unsophisticated: ~敦厚 *simple and honest*
【纯收入】net income
【纯熟】skillful; well versed: 技术~ *highly skilled*
【纯损】net loss
【纯真】pure; sincere: ~无暇 *pure and innocent*
【纯正】pure; unadulterated: 动机~ *have no selfish motives* / 酒味~。*The wine has a pure taste.*
【纯种】purebred: ~牛 *purebred cattle*

唇 lip: 上(下)~ *upper (lower) lip*
【唇齿音】[语] labiodental
【唇膏】lipstick

【唇枪舌剑】cross verbal sword; argue heatedly
【唇舌】argument：费一番～ *take a lot of explaining or arguing* /白费～ *a waste of breath*
【唇亡齿寒】if the lips are gone, the teeth will be cold; if one (of two interdependent things) falls, the other is in danger; share a common lot
【唇音】【语】labial

淳 pure; honest: ～朴 *simple-hearted and honest*

鹑 quail

醇 ① mellow wine; good wine ② pure; mellow; rich：酒味～。*The wine is mellow.*
【醇和】(of quality, taste, etc) mellow; pure
【醇厚】mellow; rich

chǔn

蠢 ① wriggle ② stupid; foolish; dull; clumsy: 愚～ *stupid; clumsy; foolish*
【蠢笨】clumsy; awkward; stupid
【蠢材】idiot; fool
【蠢蠢欲动】ready to start wriggling; ready to make trouble
【蠢动】① wriggle ② create disturbances; carry on disruptive activities
【蠢货】blockhead; dune; idiot
【蠢驴】idiot; donkey; ass
【蠢人】fool; blockhead
【蠢事】a stupid thing：别做那～。*Don't do that stupid thing.*
【蠢头蠢脑】stupid-looking
【蠢猪】idiot; stupid swine; ass

chuō

戳 ① jade; poke; thrust: 在纸上～一个洞。*Poke a hole in the paper.* ② sprain; blunt：钢笔尖儿～了。*The nib is blunted.*
【戳穿】① puncture ② by bare; expose: ～谎言 *give the lie to sth*
【戳记】stamp; seal
【戳子】stamp; sea：在文件上盖个～。*Put a seal on a document.*

chuò

啜 sip; suck: ～茶 sip tea

绰 ample; spacious
【绰绰有余】more than sufficient; enough and to spare
【绰号】nickname：他的～叫小猪。*He has got the nickname of "young pig".*

辍 stop; cease: ～学 *discontinue one's study* / ～工 *stop work*
【辍笔】stop in the middle of writing or painting

cī

刺 sound of hearing, friction

see also cì
【刺啦】the sound of ripping, tearing, or scratching: ～的一声，他划着了火柴。*Scratch; she struck a match.*
【刺溜】the sound of slipping

差 grade; class; grading

see also chā; chà; chāi

疵 flaw; defect: ～点 *flaw; fault*

cí

词 ① word; term：遣～造句 *choice of words and construction of sentences* /同义～ *synonym* /反义～ *antonym* /技术～ *technical term* ② speech; statement：开幕～ *opening speech* /台～ *lines (of an opera or play)* ③ classical poetry conforming to a definite pattern：宋～ *such poems of the Song Dynasty*
【词典】dictionary
【词法】【语】morphology
【词干】【语】stem
【词根】【语】root
【词汇】vocabulary; words and phrases：常用～ *common words* / ～表 *word list; vocabulary; glossary*
【词句】words and phrases; expressions：空洞的～ *empty phrases*
【词类】【语】parts of speech
【词库】【语】lexicon; word bank
【词素】【语】morpheme
【词条】entry：请把这些～拼在一起。*Please put the entries together.*
【词头】【语】prefix
【词形】【语】morphology
【词性】【语】syntactical functions and morphological features that help to determine a part of speech
【词序】【语】word order
【词义】【语】the meaning of a word
【词语】words and expressions; terms
【词源】【语】the origin of a word; etymology
【词组】【语】word group; phrase

茨 ① thatch (a roof) ②【植】puncture

祠 ancestral temple: ～堂 *ancestral hall; memorial temple*

C

瓷 porcelain; china: ~碗 *china bowl* / 细~ *fine china*
【瓷漆】enamel paint; enamel
【瓷器】porcelain; chinaware
【瓷实】solid; firm; substantial: 他的身体很~。*He is solidly built.*
【瓷土】porcelain clay; china clay
【瓷砖】ceramic tile; glazed tile

辞 ① diction; phraseology: 修~ *rhetoric* ② a form of classical Chinese ③ take leave: ~别家乡 *leave one's hometown* ④ decline: 申请~职 *ask to be relieved of one's duties* ⑤ dismiss; resign ⑥ shirk: 不~劳苦 *spare no effort*
【辞别】bid farewell to; say good-bye to: ~妻子 *bid farewell to one's wife*
【辞呈】(written) resignation: 提出~ *submit* (*or hand in*) *one's resignation*
【辞典】dictionary; lexicon
【辞工】① dismiss (a labourer or employee); discharge: 老板辞了他的工。*The boss dismissed him.* ② quit one's job; resign: 他~不干了。*He's quit his job.*
【辞旧迎新】ring out the old year and ring in the new
【辞令】language appropriate to the occasion: 外交~ *diplomatic language* / 善于~ *good at speech*; *eloquent*
【辞让】politely decline
【辞世】depart his life; pass away
【辞书】dictionary; lexicographical work
【辞岁】bid farewell to the outgoing year; see the old year out; celebrate the lunar New Year's Eve
【辞退】dismiss; discharge
【辞谢】decline with thanks
【辞行】say goodbye to friends or relatives before setting out on a journey
【辞藻】flowery language; rhetoric
【辞章】① poetry and prose; prose and verse ② art of writing; rhetoric
【辞职】resign; quit; hand in one's resignation

慈 ① kind; loving ② mother
【慈爱】kindly affection
【慈悲】mercy; benevolence; pity: 发~ *have pity*; *be merciful*
【慈和】kindly and amiable
【慈眉善目】a benign countenance
【慈母】loving mother
【慈善】charitable; benevolent; philanthropic: ~事业 *charities* / ~机关 *charitable institution*; *philanthropic institution*
【慈祥】kind: ~的面容 *a kind face*

磁 ① magnetism: ~铁 *magnet* / ~场 *magnetic field* ② porcelain; china
【磁场】【物】magnetic field
【磁带】(magnetic) tape: ~录音机 *tape recorder*
【磁道】track
【磁感应】【物】magnetic induction
【磁钢】magnet steel
【磁化】【物】magnetization: ~水 *magnetized water*
【磁极】【物】magnetic pole
【磁卡】magnetic card: ~电话 *card phone* / ~锁 *magnetic card lock*
【磁力】【物】magnetic force
【磁疗】magnet therapy
【磁盘】magnetic disk: ~操作系统 *disc operation system*
【磁石】① magnetic ②【电】magnet: ~发电机 *magneto*
【磁体】【物】magnetic body; magnet
【磁铁】【物】magnet: 永久~ *permanent magnet*
【磁通量】【物】magnetic flux
【磁头】magnetic head (of a recorder)
【磁性】【物】magnetism; magnetic: ~炸弹 *magnetic bomb*
【磁针】magnetic needle

雌 female
【雌花】female flower
【雌黄】orpiment
【雌蕊】pistil
【雌性】female
【雌雄】male and female: 决一~ *have a showdown* (*to see which side will emerge victorious*)

cǐ

此 ① this: ~话 *this word* / ~处 *this place*; *here* / ~人 *this man* / ~类 *this kind* / ~辈 *such people* ② here and now
【此岸】【宗】this shore; temporality
【此地】this place; here: ~人 *local people* / ~无银三百两 *no 300 taels of silver burial here* (*the sign put up by the man in the folk tale over the place where he had hidden some money*) — *a clumsy denial resulting in self-exposure*
【此后】after this; hereafter
【此呼彼应】as one calls out, another responds; echo and echoes: 口号声~。*Sounds of slogans resounded back and forth.*
【此间】around here; here: ~已有传闻。*It has been so rumored here.*
【此刻】at this moment; now
【此起彼伏】rise and fall alternately; recur
【此时】right now: ~此刻 *at this very moment* / ~此地 *here and now*
【此外】besides; moreover; in addition
【此致】greeting written at the end of a letter addressed to somebody by name

cì

次 ① order; sequence: 依~ *one by one in due order* / 车~ *train number* ② second; next: ~

日 *next day* ③ second-rate; inferior: ~品 *goods of poor quality*; *defective goods* ④ time; occasion: 三~ *tree times* / 首~ *first time* ⑤ (Cì) a surname
【次大陆】subcontinent
【次等】second-class; inferior
【次品】substandard products; defective goods
【次数】number of times; frequency: ~不多 *not very often*
【次序】order; sequence
【次要】less important; secondary minor
【次音速】subsonic
【次之】take second place
【次中音号】【音】tenor horn

伺 *see also* sì
【伺候】wait on; serve: 难~ *hard to please*; *fastidious*

刺 ① thorn; splinter: 鱼~ *small bone of a fish* / 手上扎了个~。*Get a horn in one's hand.* / 她说话带~。*There was a ring of sarcasm in one's words.* ② pick; stab ③ assassinate: 被~ *be assassinate* ④ irritate; criticize: 讽~ *satirize*
see also cī
【刺柏】Chinese juniper; Taiwan juniper
【刺刀】bayonet
【刺耳】ear piercing; unpleasant to the ear: ~的话 *harsh words*
【刺骨】piercing to the bones
【刺槐】locust
【刺激】① stimulate: 物质~ *material incentive* ② upset; irritate: 这一不幸的消息给了她很大~。*She was upset by the bad news.*
【刺客】assassin
【刺杀】① assassinate ② bayonet charge
【刺探】make secret inquires; pry; spy: ~军情 *gather military intelligence*
【刺猬】hedgehog
【刺绣】embroidery
【刺字】① tattoo ② (in former times) brand a criminal by tattooing

赐 bestow; confer: 天~ *bestowed by heaven* / ~恩 *bestow favours* / 请~复。*Please favour me with a early reply.*
【赐福】blessing
【赐教】condescend to teach; grant instruction: 不吝~ *please favour (or enlighten) me with your instructions*; *be so kind as to give me a reply*
【赐予】grant; bestow

cōng

匆 hurriedly; hastily: ~促应战 *give battle in a hurry* / 来去~~ *pay sb a flying visit*; *make hurried visits*
【匆匆】in a rush; in haste: 行色~ *be in a rush getting ready for a trip or journey* / ~做了报告 *make a hurried speech*
【匆促】hastily; in a hurry: 时间~ *be pressed by time*
【匆忙】hastily; in a hurry: 走的很~ *leave in a hurry*

葱 onion; scallion: 大~ *green Chinese onion* / 小~ *spring onion*
【葱白】very light blue: ~儿 *scallion stalk*
【葱翠】fresh green
【葱花】chopped spring onion
【葱茏】verdant; luxuriantly green: 草木~ *luxuriant vegetation*
【葱绿】pale yellowish green
【葱头】onion
【葱郁】verdant; luxuriantly green

聪 ① faculty of hearing ② acute hearing
【聪慧】bright; intelligent
【聪明】bright; intelligent; clever: ~能干 *bright and capable* / ~反被~误。*Clever people may be victims of their own cleverness.*; *cleverness may overreach itself.*
【聪明一世,糊涂一时】clever all one's life but stupid this once; smart as a rule but this time a fool
【聪颖】bright; intelligent: ~过人 *surpass others in intelligence*; *be exceptionally bright*

cóng

从 ① follow: 孩子们跟~母亲进了房间。*The children followed their mother into the room.* ② comply with; conform with; follow; obey: 言听计~ *listen to sb's words and follow his counsels*; *have implicit faith in sb* / 士兵们必须服~军官的命令。*The soldiers must follow the officer's orders.* ③ join; be engaged in: 他~事烤面包行业。*He follows the trade of baker.* ④ secondary; accessary ⑤ relationship between cousins, etc. of the same paternal grandfather or great-grandfather ⑥ follower; attendant ⑦ in a certain manner or according to a certain principle ⑧ (follow by negative) ever
【从长计议】give the matter further thought and discussion; take one's time in reaching a decision
【从此】from now on; since then; henceforth
【从而】thus; thereby
【从犯】accessory criminal; accessory
【从简】conform to the principle of simplicity: 一切~ *dispense with all unnecessary formalities*
【从教】be engaged in the teaching profession; be a teacher: 给~三十年的教师颁奖。*Awards are conferred for those who have been engaged in the teaching profession for thirty years.*
【从句】subordinate clause
【从军】join the army; enlist
【从来】always; all along: 她~没去过非洲。*She has never been to Africa.*
【从略】be omitted: 此处引文~。*The quotation is o-*

mitted here.
【从命】comply with sb's with; obey an order:欣然～ *gladly comply with sb's wish*
【从前】before; in the past; formerly:她～不爱学习。*She didn't like study before.*
【从戎】join the army; enlist
【从容】① clam; unhurried: ～不迫 *remain cool-headed and steady* ② plentiful:时间很～。*There is still plenty of time.*
【从事】① go in for; be engaged in: ～科研工作 *be engaged in scientific research* / ～文学创作 *take up writing as a profession* ② deal with:慎重～ *act cautiously; steer a cautious course* /军法～ *dealing with according to military law*
【从属】be subordinate to
【从速】as soon as possible; without delay: ～处理 *attend to the matter as soon as possible*
【从天而降】descend from heaven:灾祸～ *a disaster descended from heaven*
【从头】from the beginning
【从小】from childhood:他～就喜欢音乐。*He's loved music ever since he was a child.*
【从刑】【律】accessory punishment
【从业】obtain employment: ～人员 *the employed*
【从一而终】be faithful to one's husband to the end
【从中】out of; from among: ～渔利 *profit from* / ～吸取教训 *draw a lesson from it*
【从众】follow the public opinion: ～行事 *act in conformity with the majority*

丛 ① crowd together ② clump; thicket; grove ③ a group people or things
【丛集】① crowd together; pile up:债务～ *debts piling up* ② collected writing
【丛刊】a series of books; collection
【丛林】jungle; forest
【丛生】① grow thickly:荆棘～ *be overgrown with brambles* ② break out:百病～ *all kinds of diseases and aliments breaking out*
【丛书】a series of books; collection:自学～ *self-study series*
【丛杂】motley

còu

凑 ① put (or gather) together; pool: ～在一起 *crowd together* ② take advance of; happen by chance:正～上是个星期六。*It happened to be Saturday.* ③ moves close to; press near: ～近点儿。*Move closer, please.*
【凑份子】club together (to present a gift to sb)
【凑合】① gather together; collect; assemble:昨天我们～在一起打牌。*Yesterday we gathered together to play card.* ② improvise:请大家在会议前做好准备不要临时～。*Please prepare before the meeting; don't speak offhand.* ③ passable:他的英语还～。*His English is not too bad.*
【凑钱】pool money
【凑巧】luckily; by coincidence:真不～! 他出去了。*What a bad luck! He is not in.*
【凑趣儿】① show a similar interest (just to please sb):他也说了几句玩笑话,～。*He also cracked a few jokes to make everybody happy.* ② make a joke about; make fun of:别拿我～。*Don't make fun of me.*
【凑热闹】① join in the fun ② add trouble to:他们够忙的了,别去～了。*They are busy enough as it is; leave them alone.*
【凑手】at hand; within easy reach:一时不～,我拿不出那么多钱来。*It happens I haven't got so much money on me at the moment.*
【凑数】make up the number or amount

cū

粗 ① wide; thick: ～铁链 *a thick iron chain* / ～绳 *a thick rope* ② coarse; crude; rough: ～砂纸 *coarse sandpaper* /活干得很～。*The work is crudely done.* ③ husky; hoarse (of sb's voice): ～声～气 *with a gruff voice* ④ careless; negligent: ～疏 *be careless* / ～心大意 *be negligent* ⑤ rude; coarse; unrefined: ～里～气 *rough* ⑥ roughly
【粗暴】rude; rough; brutal
【粗笨】clumsy; unwisely
【粗鄙】coarse
【粗布】① coarse cloth ② homespun cloth
【粗糙】rough; coarse; crude:皮肤～ *rough skin* /做工～ *crudely made; of poor workmanship*
【粗茶淡饭】homely meal
【粗大】① thick; bulky: ～的手 *big strong hands* ② loud: ～的嗓门 *a loud voice*
【粗放】① free and easy ② extensive: ～型发展 *extensive growth*
【粗犷】① rugged; straightforward and uninhibited ② rough; boorish
【粗豪】① forthright; straightforward: ～坦率 *forthright and candid* ② raucous; gruff
【粗花呢】【纺】tweed
【粗话】coarse language
【粗活】heavy manual labour; unskilled work
【粗加工】rough machining; roughing: ～制成品 *roughly process product*
【粗粮】coarse food grain (e. g. maize, sorghum, millet, etc. as distinct from wheat and rice)
【粗劣】of poor quality
【粗陋】coarse and crude
【粗鲁】rude; boorish
【粗略】rough; sketchy: ～的了解 *some rough ideas about sth*
【粗眉大眼】bushy eyebrows and big eyes; heavy features
【粗浅】superficial; shallow
【粗人】① a rough fellow; a rash person ② an unrefined person; boor:我是个～,说话直来直去,你别

见怪。*I am a bit of a boor, so I hope you won't mind if I speak bluntly.*
【粗纱】【纺】roving: ~机 *fly frame*
【粗俗】coarse; unrefined
【粗算】rough estimate or calculation
【粗通】have a rough idea; know a little: ~文墨 *be just able to read and write*
【粗细】① (degree of) thickness:这样~的沙子最合适。*Sand this fine will be just right.* ② crudeness or fineness; degree of finish; quality of work:庄稼长的好坏,也要看活的~。*Whether the crops grow well or not depends also on how the work is done.*
【粗线条】① thick lines; rough outline: ~的描写 *a rough sketch* ② rough-and-ready:我不喜欢他~的工作方法。*I don't like his slapdash way of doing things.*
【粗心】careless; thoughtless
【粗心大意】negligent; careless; inadvertent
【粗野】rude; boorish
【粗轧】roughing (down): ~机 *roughing mill*
【粗枝大叶】crude and careless; sloppy slapdash
【粗制滥造】manufacture in a crude and slipshod way
【粗中有细】there's finesse in sb's roughness; usually careless, but sometimes sharp; crude in most matters, but subtle in some
【粗重】① (of voice, etc.) loud and jarring ② big and heavy; bulky: ~的钢管 *big and heavy steel tubes* ③ thick and heavy:眉毛浓黑~ *bushy black eyebrows* ④ heavy: ~的活计 *heavy work*
【粗壮】① sturdy; brawny; strong:身材~ *be sturdily built* ② (of voice) deep and resonant

cù

促 ① promote; urge:催~ *urge; hasten* ② hurried; urgent:呼吸短~ *pant be short of breath* / 匆~启程 *set out hastily*
【促成】help to bring about; facilitate: ~那对情人的婚事 *hope to bring about a happy union of the lovers*
【促进】promote; accelerate: ~贸易 *promote trade*
【促销】promote the sale (of goods); sales promotion
【促使】impel; spur; encourage: ~他人做出更大努力 *impel others to greater efforts*

猝 sudden; abrupt; unexpected
【猝然】suddenly; abruptly; unexpectedly: ~决定 *make a sudden decision*
【猝死】【医】sudden death

醋 ① vinegar ② jealousy (as in love affairs)
【醋罐子】a jealous person
【醋酸】【化】acetic acid: ~纤维 *acetic fiber*

簇 ① cluster; bunch:一~鲜花 *a bunch of flowers* ② from a cluster; pile up:花团锦~ *rich multicolored decorations*
【簇居】live in a community
【簇生】(of plants, flowers etc.) grow in clusters
【簇新】brand new
【簇拥】cluster round (sb)

蹙 ① pressed; cramped:穷~ *in dire straits* ② knit (one's brows): ~额 *knit one's brows; frown*

蹴 ① kick ② tread

cuān

蹿 ① leap up:猫~到树上去了。*The cat leaped up into the tree.* ② spray; spurt:我鼻子~血了。*Blood spurted from my nose.*
【蹿房越脊】(of swordsmen, robbers, etc. in old Chinese novels) leap from roof to roof

cuán

攒 collect together; assemble:自己~一台计算机 *assemble a computer oneself*
see also zǎn
【攒聚】gather closely together
【攒三聚五】(of people) gather in knots; gather in threes and fours

cuàn

窜 flee; scurry:东逃西~ *flee in all directions* / 鼠~ *scurry like rats* / 敌人狼狈~逃。*The enemy fled in utter confusion.*
【窜犯】raid; make an inroad into: ~边境的匪徒 *the bandits that invaded the border area*
【窜改】distort; misrepresent; tamper with; falsify: ~历史 *distort history* / ~记录 *tamper with the minutes* / ~账目 *falsify accounts*
【窜扰】harass: ~活动 *harassment*
【窜逃】flee in disorder: scurry off

篡 usurp: ~权 *usurp power* / ~位 *usurp the throne*
【篡夺】usurp; seize
【篡改】tamper with; falsify; distort: ~历史 *distort history*
【篡国】usurp state power
【篡位】usurp the throne

cuī

催 ① hurry; urge; press: ~促她早回家 *urge her to return home as soon as possible* ② has-

ten; expedite; speed up
【催逼】press (for payment of debt, etc.)
【催促】urge; press; hasten
【催肥】fatten
【催化】【化】catalysis: ~剂 *catalytic promoter* / ~反应 *catalytic reaction*
【催款单】【经】prompt; prompt-node
【催泪弹】tear bomb; tear-gas grenade
【催眠】lull (to sleep); hypnotize; mesmerize
【催奶】stimulate the secretion of milk; promote lactation
【催生】(of an expectant mother's family) send gifts over to convey best wishes
【催熟】【农】accelerate the ripening (of fruit)
【催吐剂】【药】emetic
【催醒剂】【药】analeptic
【催租】press a tenant to pay rent; press for payment of rent

摧 break; destroy
【摧残】wreck; destroy; devastate: ~身体 *ruin one's health*
【摧毁】destroy; smash; wreck
【摧枯拉朽】(as easy as) crushing dry weeds and smashing rotten wood
【摧眉折腰】bowing and scraping
【摧折】break; snap setback

cuì

脆 ① fragile; brittle: 这纸太~。*This kind of paper is too fragile.* ② crisp: ~梨 *crisp pear* ③ (of voice) clear: 嗓音~ *a crisp voice*
【脆骨】gristle (as food)
【脆弱】(of health or feeling) fragile; frail; weak: 感情~ *emotionally fragile*
【脆性】【冶】brittleness

萃 come together; assemble
【萃集】gather; assemble: 船舶~ *ships gathering*
【萃聚】gather; assemble: 群英~ *heroes of our time getting together*
【萃取】【化】extraction

啐 spit: ~他一口 *spit at him*

淬 temper by dipping in water oil, etc.; quench
【淬火】quench: ~剂 *hardening agent*; *quenching liquid* / ~硬化 *quench hardening*

瘁 overworked; tired: 心力交~ *be physically and mentally tired from overwork*

粹 ① pure: ~白 *pure white* ② essence; the best: 精~ *the best*
【粹美】perfect; flawless: 品学~ *a man of flawless character and eminent scholarship*

翠 ① emerald green; green ② kingfisher ③ jadeite
【翠蓝】bright blue; azure
【翠绿】emerald green; jade green
【翠鸟】kingfisher

cūn

村 ① village; hamlet ② rustic; boorish
【村口】entrance to a village
【村落】village; hamlet
【村民】villager; village people
【村舍】cottage
【村寨】stocked village; village: ~相望 *neighbouring village within sight of each other*
【村长】village head
【村镇】villages and small towns
【村庄】village; hamlet
【村子】village; hamlet

皴 (of skin) chapped (from the cold); crashed: 孩子的手~了。*The child's hands were chapped from the cold.*
【皴裂】(of skin) chapped (from the cold)

cún

存 ① exist; live; survive: 他在灾难中幸~。*He survived from the disaster.* ② store; keep: ~粮 *store up grain* ③ accumulate; collect ④ deposit: 钱~在银行里 *deposit money in a bank* ⑤ leave with; check: ~车处 *parking lot* ⑥ reserve; retain: 他从不~东西。*He never reserves anything.* ⑦ remain on balance; be in stock: 他每月有两千元~款。*He has a surplus of* 2000 *yuan every month.* ⑧ cherish; harbour: 不~幻想 *harbour no illusions*
【存案】register with the proper authorities
【存查】file for reference
【存车处】parking lot (for bicycles)
【存储】storage; memory: ~容量 *memory capacity* / ~器 *memory (of a computer)*
【存单】deposit receipt: 定期~ *time certificate*
【存档】keep in the archives; file
【存底儿】keep the original draft; keep a file copy
【存放】① leave in sb's care ② deposit
【存根】counterfoil; stub: 支票~ *check stub*
【存户】depositor
【存货】goods in stock: 减价出售~ *a clearance sale*
【存款】deposit; bank savings: 活期~ *current account* / 死期~ *deposit or saving accounts*
【存身】take shelter; make one's home
【存亡】live or die; survive or perish: 生死~的战斗 *a life-and-death struggle*
【存项】credit balance; balance
【存心】intentionally; deliberately; on purpose: 我不是~这么做的。*I didn't do it on purpose.*
【存疑】leave a question open
【存在】exit: ~这种可能性。*There is the possibility.*

【存折】deposit book; bankbook
【存执】counterfoil; stub

cǔn

忖 turn sth over in one's mind: 思～ *ponder; mull over*
【忖度】speculate; conjecture
【忖量】① think over; turn over in one's mind: 在做决定前,他～了很长时间。*He thought it over for a long time until he made the decision.* ② guess: 我在～他那番话的意思。*I kept wondering what he really meant.*

cùn

寸 ① a traditional unit of length(=1/30 meter) ② small; very little; very short: 肝肠～断 *be heart-broken; be deeply grieved* ③ (Cùn) a surname
【寸步】a tiny step; a single step
【寸步不离】follow sb closely; keep close to sb; be always at sb's elbow
【寸步不让】refuse to yield an inch; not budge an inch
【寸步难行】be unable to move even a single step; unable to do anything
【寸草不留】leave not even a blade of grass; be devastated
【寸金难买寸光阴】money can't buy time; time is more precious than gold
【寸进】a little progress; a small advance: 略有～ *have made just a little progress*
【寸土必争】fight for (or contest) every inch of land
【寸心】① feelings: 聊表～ *as a small token of my feelings* ② heart; mind: ～不忘 *bear it in mind*

cuō

搓 ① rub with the hands: ～手取暖 *rub one's hands together to warm them* ② (in tennis, table tennis, cricket, etc.) shop: 一板一板的把球～过去 *return every shot with a chop*
【搓板】washboard
【搓球】【体】chopping
【搓揉】rub; knead; twist: 他把信～成一团。*He crumpled the letter into a ball.*
【搓澡】give or get a rubdown with a damp towel
磋 consult
【磋商】consult: 我们将与有关部门～后决定。*We will make a decision after consultation with the departments concerned.*
撮 ① gather; bring together ② pick up; scoop up with a dustpan or shovel; hold: ～一锹土 *scoop up a shovel of dirt* ③ extract; summarize ④ pinch; handful (of bad people): 一～盐 *a pinch of salt* / 一小～匪徒 *a handful of bandits*
【撮合】make a match; act as good-between
【撮弄】① make fun of; play a trick on ② tease abet; instigate; incite
【撮要】make an abstract; outline essential points: 把工作情况～上报 *submit an outline report on one's work* / 论文～ *an abstract of a thesis*
蹉
【蹉跌】trip and fall-make a slip
【蹉跎】waste time: ～岁月 *idle away one's time*

cuó

痤
【痤疮】acne (a skin disease)

cuò

厝 ① lay; place ② place a coffin in a temporary shelter pending burial
【厝火积薪】a fire beneath a pile of faggots — a hidden danger
挫 ① frustrate; defeat ② subdue; lower: ～敌人的锐气 *deflate the enemy's arrogance*
【挫败】frustrate; foil; defeat: 遭到严重的～ *suffer a serious defeat*
【挫伤】①【医】contusion; bruise ② dampen; blunt; discourage: 不要～群众的积极性。*Don't dampen the enthusiasm of the masses.*
【挫折】setback; reverse: 遭受～ *suffer setback*
措 ① arrange; manage; handle: ～置得当 *be handled properly* / 惊慌失～ *be seized with panic* / 不知所～ *be at loss what to do; be at one's wit's end* ② make plans
【措辞】word: ～不当 *inappropriate wording* / ～强硬 *strongly worded*
【措施】measure; step: 采取重大～ *adopt an important measure*
【措手不及】be caught unprepared: 打他个～ *make a surprise attack on them*
【措置】handle; manage; arrange: ～得当 *be handled properly*
锉 ① file ② make smooth with a file; file
【锉屑】filing
错 ① interlocked and jagged; intricate; complex: 盘根～节 *with twisted roots and gnarled branches-complicated and difficult to deal with* ② wrong; mistaken; erroneous: 从头～到底 *completely wrong* / 你弄～了。*You're got it wrong.* ③ (used in the negative) bad; poor: 他的成绩～不了。*His grade is sure to be good.* ④ grind; rub:

~牙 *grind one's teeth* ⑤ make way; move out of the way:劳驾往那边~一~。*Would you mind making a room for me?* ⑥ alternate; stagger:这两个会不能同时开,得~一下。*We can't hold the two meetings at the same time; we must stagger them.* ⑦ be out of alignment:这行没排齐,中间~进去了一点。*This line is not straight; it's a little crooked in the middle.* ⑧ fault; demerit:这不是他的~,不怨你。*You are not to blame; it's his fault.*

【错爱】undeserved kindness or favour

【错案】misjudged case

【错别字】wrongly written or mispronounced characters

【错处】fault; demerit

【错怪】blame sb; wrongly

【错过】miss; let slip: ~机会 *miss an opportunity*

【错角】【数】alternate angle

【错觉】illusion; misconception:这样会给人造成~。*This will give people a false impression.*

【错开】stagger:把日子~ *stagger the days off*

【错乱】in disorder in confusion:精神~ *insane*

【错落】in disorderly profusion; deranged

【错位】【医】dislocation:肘关节~ *dislocation of the elbow*

【错误】① mistake; error:犯~ *make a mistake; commit an error* / ~百出 *full of mistakes* ② wrong; mistaken; error; blunder: ~的结论 *wrong conclusion*

【错字】wrongly written character

【错综】crisscross; intricate

【错综复杂】intricate; complex:这条通往城里的路~。*The road to the city is intricate.*

D

dā

奆 ①［书］big-eared ② droop; hang down

【奆拉】droop; draggle; loll; hang down: ~着脑袋 *hang one's head* /她眼皮~着,一定是困了。*Her eyelids drooped and she was sure to be sleepy.*

搭 ① put up; build; erect: ~个简易戏台 *put up a makeshift stage* / ~帐篷 *pitch a tent* / ~一个简陋的木屋 *put up a tousy wooden house* ② hang over; put over:将毛巾~在椅背上吧。*Hang the towel over the back of the chair.* ③ throw in more; add (time, money, people, etc.) ④ touch; join together; come into contact:将两根电线~在一起 *touch the two wires together* /这件事跟你不~边。*You didn't have something to do with this matter.* ⑤ lift sth together; give ab a hand: 你能~把手帮我把衣柜挪走吗? *Can you give me a hand to remove this wardrobe?* ⑥ travel by or take (a conveyance):开车中途~上某人 *pick sb up* /安德森昨晚~飞机走了。*Anderson went by plane last right.*

【搭伴】travel together; join sb on a trip; in company with sb:下班后你愿意跟我~走吗? *Would you like to go with me after going off work?*

【搭车】lift; hitchhike:被雨淋湿了的一对夫妇招手要求~。*A couple soaked by the rain waved hands to ask for a g lift.*

【搭乘】travel by:她每天~班车回家。*She went home by regular bus every day.*

【搭档】① team up; work together; cooperate:同一位老朋友~。*Team up with one's old friend.* ② partner:我们是老~了。*We're old partners.*

【搭话】① talk to each other; converse with:宴会上没人乐意跟他~。*No one was ready to talk to him in the banquet.* ② send word; pass on (or deliver) a message:他让我~给你说可能会晚点回家。*He asked me to tell you that he might go home late.*

【搭伙】① join as partner; form partnership:我想跟他们~一块儿去看电影。*I want to join them to see a film.* ② eat regularly in (a mess, eatery, etc.):他中午在单位食堂~。*He ate in the eatery of his unit at room.*

【搭架子】① make an outline: get sth roughly into shape; build a framework:这项任务我们基本上已搭好了架子。*We have gout the task roughly into shape.* ②［方］put on airs

【搭肩】① help sb lift sth onto the shoulder ② step on other's shoulder to reach a certain height:他们~爬上悬崖。*They climbed on the cliff by stepping on each other's shoulders.*

【搭救】rescue; save; rescue sb in distress: ~伤员 *rescue the wounded*

【搭客】① passengers ②［方］lift; take on passengers

【搭理】(usu. used in the negative) respond; answer; take notice of; acknowledge

【搭卖】sale with aged goods; tied sale

【搭配】① pair; arrange in pairs or groups; be in close coordination:劳动时男女要合理~。*We should make a proper proportion of boys and girls at the time of labour.* ② agree with; collocation: 宾语与谓语不~。*The object didn't agree with the predicate.*

【搭腔】① answer; respond; continue sb's saying:我问了半天她也不~。*I asked her for times, but she didn't answer at all.* ②［方］converse; talk to each other:他们俩几年没~了。*The two of them haven't spoken a word to each other for years.*

【搭桥】① build a bridge ② act as a go-between; integrate ③【医】bypass

【搭讪】strike up a conversation with sb; say sth to smooth over an awkward situation:那边的小伙儿正跟漂亮女孩~。*The young fellow was trying to strike up a conversation with a pretty girl.*

【搭售】sale with aged goods; tided sale

答

see also dá

【答理】(usu. used in the negative) respond; answer; take notice of:我问了他两遍,他都没~我。*I repeated my question, but he didn't answer me.* /她很高傲,不爱~人。*She is supercilious and standoffish.*

【答声】answer aloud; reply; response:这么多人,居然没人~。*There ware so many people, but nobody answered.*

【答应】① answer; reply; respond:我喊你,你怎么不~? *Why don't you answer my call?* ② promise; agree; pledge; comply with:我~你的事一定会做到。*I'm sure to do what I complied with you.* /你~过我会来参加晚会的。*You'd promised me that you would come to the party.*

褡

【褡包】a long, broad girdle outside jacket
【褡裢】① a long, rectangular bag (sewn up at both ends with an opening in the middle) worn round at the girdle or across the shoulder ② the wrestlers jacket, made of several layers of cloth

dá

打 [量] dozen:一~笔记本 *a dozen notebooks* /两~钢笔 *two dozen pens* /论~出售 *sell by the dozen*
see also dǎ

达 ① extend; go through to:这儿的交通四通八~,从而带来了很大的经济效益。*The transportation here extends in all directions, which brings great economic profits.* ② reach; arrive at; amount to; get to:他们将于明天下午抵~北京。*They will arrive at Beijing tomorrow afternoon.* /教授们的讨论长~三个小时。*They discussion among professors lasted for three hours.* ③ be understanding; understand thoroughly:她通情~理,赢得了别人的尊重。*She understands which gains the respect of others.* ④ communicate; express; transmit:请把老师的建议相互转~一下。*Please pass on the suggestion of teachers to others.* ⑤ eminent; distinguished; notable: ~官贵人 *high officials and notables*
【达标】reach a required standard:废水必须~排放。*Wastewater must reach the required standard before drainage.*
【达成】reach(agreement): ~交易 *strike a bargain* / ~谅解 *reach an understanding* /双方就合作问题~一致。*The two parties reached agreement on cooperation.*
【达旦】until the night
【达到】achieve; reach; attain: ~先进水平 *reach advanced levels* / ~高潮 *reach a high tide* / ~要求 *achieve the requirement* /这张演出海报~了预期效果。*The playbill attained the anticipated effect.* /到目前为止,销售量已~了三千台。*The sales volume has amounted to 3000 till now.*
【达观】be philosophical; take things philosophically:他处事~,无忧无虑。*He always takes things philosophically without worries.*
【达官】high officials:他总喜欢与~贵人打交道。*He always likes contacting with high officials and dignitary.*
【达赖喇嘛】Dalai Lama
【达意】express (or convey) one's ideas or feelings:他在批阅过程中发现几篇词不~的文章。*He found several compositions which words couldn't convey the ideas during perusing.*

沓 [量] pile (of paper, etc.); pad:一~报纸 *a pile of newspaper* /一~钞票 *a pad af bank notes* /一~卡片 *a pile of cards*
see also tà
【沓子】[量] pile (of paper, etc.); pad:一~圣诞卡片 *a pile of Christmas cards*

答 ① answer; reply; respond: 回~问题 *answer the question* /他被通知下周五~辩。*He is informed to defend the dissertation next Friday.* ② reciprocate; reward; repay; return (a visit, etc.): ~谢 *express one's appreciation*
see also dā
【答案】answer; solution; key:问题的~ *solution to the problem* /这就是你正寻找的~。*This is the answer you are looking for.*
【答拜】return a visit
【答辩】reply (to a charge, argument); defend a thesis (or dissertation):他们给他的~以高度评价。*They sang high praise for the deface of her thesis.*
【答词】thank-you speech; answering speech; reply:向观众致~ *give the thank-you speech to the audience*
【答对】reply; answer; respond: 无言~ *say nothing to reply (or answer)*
【答非所问】give an irrelevant answer to a question:请正视问题,不要~。*Please face the question and don't give the irrelevant answer.*
【答复】answer; reply:对这个问题的~ *answer to this question*
【答话】answer; reply:她很害羞,在陌生人面前不爱~。*She is very shy and doesn't like replying in full of strangers.*
【答卷】① answer the questions of the test paper:认真~,不要左顾右盼。*Answer the paper carefully and don't look around.* ② an examination or test paper which has been answered:标准~ *a test paper with standard answers*
【答数】【数】answer (to an arithmetic problem)
【答问】① answer one's questions ② a question-and-answer form
【答谢】express appreciation (for sb's kindness or hospitality); acknowledge: ~宴会 *return banquet* /如此感情,我们无以~。*We couldn't find way to repay your great kindness.*
【答疑】answer questions by a teacher: 需要~的同学可以留下来。*Students who have questions may stay now.*

鞑
【鞑靼】tartar: ~语 *Tartar Language* / ~人 *Tartar*

dǎ

打 ① strike; hit; knock: ~钟 *strike a bell* / ~门 *knock at the door* /有人在~稻子。*Someone is threshing rice there.* ② break; smash:是他~了杯子。*It's he who broke the cup.* ③ beat; hit; fight; attack:不要在公共场所~架。*Don't fight in public.* /解放军~了一场胜仗。*The PLA fought a victorious battle.* ④ deal with; make contact with:鲍里斯是一个很难~交道的人。*It's*

hard to make contact with Boris. ⑤ construct; build: ~地基 *lay the foundation* ⑥ make; forge: ~家具 *make furniture* / ~刀 *forge a knife* ⑦ mix; stir; beat: ~浆糊 *mix paste* / ~鸡蛋 *beat eggs* ⑧ tie up; pack; bale: 将行李~包 *pack one's luggage* ⑨ knit; weave: ~毛衣 *knit a sweater* / ~草鞋 *weave straw sandals* ⑩ draw; mark; paint: ~手印 *put one's fingerprint* (*on document*) / ~邮戳 *make a stamp or an envelop* ⑪ spray: 给作物~农药 *spray insecticide to crops* ⑫ open; dig; drill: ~井 *dig* (*or sink*) *a well* / ~洞 *drill a hole* ⑬ raise; hoist: ~伞 *hold an umbrella* / ~起精神 *exert oneself* ⑭ send; dispatch; transmit: ~电话 *make a phone call* / ~信号 *send a signal* ⑮ issue; receive: ~借条 *write a receipt for loan* / ~介绍信 *write a letter of introduction* ⑯ remove; get rid of: ~蛔虫 *take medicine to remove the roundworm* ⑰ ladle; draw: ~井水 *draw water from a well* ⑱ buy: ~票 *buy a ticket* /去食堂~饭 *go to the dining room to buy meal* ⑲ catch; hunt: ~鱼 *catch fish* / ~野兔 *hunt have* ⑳ gather in; collect; reap: ~柴 *gather firewood* / ~小麦 *reap wheat* ㉑ calculate; include: ~上路费,他们损失了上万元。*Including the cost on road, they lost almost* 10,000 *yuan.* ㉒ hire (a taxi): ~车回家 *go home taking a taxi* ㉓ draw up: ~草稿 *make* (*or draw up*) *a draft* ㉔ do; engage in: ~夜班 *be on night shift* /明天我去城里~工。*Tomorrow I will go to city to do temporary job.* ㉕ play: ~秋千 *get on* (*or have*) *a swing* / ~排球 *play volleyball* ㉖ make some body actions: ~手势 *gesticulate*; *make a gesture* / ~哈欠 *make a yawn* ㉗ adopt; use: 来~比喻 *draw an analogy* ㉘ guess (a riddle)
see also dá

【打把势】① practice martial arts: 他每天早上都练习~。*He practices martial arts every morning.* ② dance for joy: 听到这个消息,孩子们在草地上~。*Hearing the news, children danced on the grass to express their joy.*

【把靶】target (or shooting) practice: ~场 *target* (*or shooting*) *range* /他~很准。*He shoots at a target practically.*

【打白条】write IOUs (instead of paying cash): 请付现金,这里不准~。*Please pay the cash because it is forbidden to write IOUs here.*

【打摆子】[方] suffer from malaria

【打败】① defeat; vanquish; conquer; subdue: 他有信心~对手。*He is full of confidence to defeat his opponent.* ② suffer a defeat; be defeated: 她在选举中被~了。*She was defeated in the election.*

【打扮】① dress (or make) up; deck out: 她喜欢把自己~得漂漂亮亮。*She likes decking out well.* ② appearance of dressing: 他看上去就是学生~。*He is dressed like a student at the first sight.*

【打包】① bale; pack: ~费 *packing charges* ② take the residuary meal away after eating in a restaurant: 请将这个菜~。*Please put this dish in a lunch-box.* ③ unpack

【打包票】vouch for; guarantee: 我敢~他是诚实的。*I can vouch for him that he is honest.*

【打苞】(of wheat, sorghum, etc.) from ears; ear up

【打抱不平】come out in defense of the weak (or justice): 他总是爱~。*He always likes taking up the cudgels for the injured party.*

【打边鼓】say sth from the sidelines: 你在边上~,这件事肯定能成。*It will be successful as long as you put in a word or two from the sidelines.*

【打草惊蛇】beat at the grass to alert snakes — act rashly and alert the enemy

【打岔】interrupt; break in: 别人谈话时不要~。*Don't break in when others are talking.*

【打场】thresh grain (on a threshing ground)

【打成一片】become one with: identify oneself with; integrate: 与群众~ *identify oneself with the masses*

【打冲锋】① charge (in a battle): 带领士兵~ *lead the soldiers to charge the enemy's position* ② take the lead; be in the vanguard

【打虫子】take medicine to get rid of intestinal parasites or worms

【打蛋器】egg-whisk

【打倒】topple; fall; overthrow: ~帝国主义! *Down with imperialism!*

【打得火热】be as thick as thieves; be close with others: 这两人最近~。*The two persons are on intimate term recently.*

【打的】[方] take a taxi

【打底】① eat sth before having a drink: 你可以先吃点东西~。*You may eat something now before drinking.* ② feel definite: 这件事是否能做好,我心里总有点不~。*I feel indefinite whether I can do it well.*

【打底子】① sketch (a plan, picture, etc.): 他习惯写文章前~。*He is used to making a sketch before writing.* ② lay a foundation: 学习任何东西要从小打好底子,这非常重要。*It is important to lay a good foundation from childhood to learn everything well.*

【打地铺】sleep on the floor; have a shakedown on the floor or on the ground: 今天晚上我可以~。*I can make a shakedown on the floor tonight.*

【打点】① get (luggage, etc.) ready: 旅行之前~好行李。*Pack your luggage before journey.* ② bribe

【打点滴】(in nursing) put on a drip: 他感冒了,正在医院~。*He is putting on a drip in hospital for his cold.*

【打掉】destroy; knock out; wipe out: ~敌人的碉堡 *wipe out the blockhouse of enemy* / ~一盏灯 *knock a light out*

【打动】move; touch: 这番话一定会~他。*It is sure to move him emotionally by these words.*

【打赌】bet; wager; make a bet: 我敢~是你错了。*I bet that you are wrong.*

【打断】① break:阿默斯特的腿是在战争中被~的。*It was in a battle that Amherst had his leg broken.* ② interrupt, cut short:我的演讲被他的闯入~了。*My speech was interrupted for his rushing.* /当别人写作时,不要~其思路。*Don't interrupt their train of thoughts when others are writing.*

【打盹儿】doze; take a nap:中午时~有利于下午的工作。*It is advantageous to the work afternoon after taking a nap at noon.*

【打哆嗦】shiver; shudder; tremble:冻得~ *shiver with cold* /吓得~ *shudder with fear*

【打耳光】slap sb in the face; box sb's ears:不要总是打孩子耳光。*Don't always slap the boy in his face.*

【打发】① send (on errand); dispatch:妈妈~弟弟去买了一瓶醋。*Mum sent my younger brother to buy a bottle of vinegar.* ② dismiss; get rid of sb:他干得不好,被老板~走了。*He was dismissed by the boss for his bad work.* ③ kill time; while away (one's time)

【打翻】overturn; invert; strike down:小船被风浪~了。*The boat was overturned by stormy waves.* /他起身时把杯子~了。*He knocked the cup over when standing up.*

【打分】mark; grade (student's exams, etc.):这位评委~很低。*This evaluation committee gave very low marks.*

【打稿】draw up a draft

【打嗝儿】[口] belch; burp

【打更】① sound the night watches ② go on night patrol

【打埂】【农】ridging

【打工】hire out for job; work part-time; go out to do a temporary job: ~妹 *employed female worker* /现在许多农民都去城里~。*Nowadays quantities of peasants go to the city to do a temporary job.* /他边上学边~。*He does a part-time job as he studies.*

【打谷场】threshing ground (or floor)

【打鼓】① beat a drum ② feel uncertain:对于能否通过考试,他心里直~。*He felt worried and nervous whether he can pass the exam.*

【打官腔】talk like a bureaucrat; speak in an official tone:他官不大,说话却喜欢~。*He ranks low but speaks in a bureaucratic tone.*

【打官司】go to court or law; engage in a lawsuit

【打光棍】stay single; remain a bachelor; live alone:他都快四十了,还在~。*He still lives alone although he is almost forty years old.*

【打滚】① roll about:她肚子疼得在地上~。*She rolled on the ground for her stomachache.* ② live under certain circumstances for a long time:他从小在泥里~长大的。*He grew up in the mud since childhood.*

【打哈哈】make a joke; tease; make fun:你净~,不要逃避问题。*You are drays making fun; Don't escape the problem.*

【打哈欠】yawn

【打鼾】snore

【打夯】ramming; tamping: ~机 *ramming machine*

【打滑】① skid (of vehicle wheels) on the ground without mooring forward:车轮在雪地上直~。*The wheels skidded on the ground full of snow.* ② slip slide

【打诨】make a joke

【打火】strike sparks from a flint; strike a light

【打火机】lighter

【打击】strike; knock; hit; attack: ~报复 *retaliate; take revenge* / ~犯罪 *crackdown criminal activities* /他受到了沉重~。*He was heavily stricken.*

【打家劫舍】loot; plunder:最近有一犯罪团伙到处~。*A mass of criminal is plundering everywhere recently.*

【打假】check and accept counterfeit products

【打架】come to blows; scuffle; fistfight

【打尖】① stop for refreshment when traveling ② 【农】topping

【打江山】fight to win dominative position (or to be a ruler)

【打浆】beat (in paper making): ~机 *beating engine; beater*

【打交道】deal with; make contact with:他是一个很难~的人。*It is hard to get along with him.* /我们曾跟那家公司打过交道。*We've even made contact with that company.*

【打搅】disturb; trouble:他在睡觉。不要~他了。*Don't disturb him for he is sleeping.* /可以~您一下吗? *May I trouble you a minute?*

【打劫】rob; plunder; loot:她在路上被~了。*She was robbed on the road.*

【打结】① tie a knot ② be tongue-tied:感到舌头~ *fell tongue-tied*

【打卡】punch card: ~机 *punch-card machine; punched-card machine* /每天上班前他们都要~。*They punch card everyday before working.*

【打开】① open; unfold: ~钱包 *open the wallet* / ~包裹 *untie the package* ② turn on; switch on: ~收音机 *turn on the radio* ③ widen; open up: ~眼界 *widen one's field of vision* / ~僵局 *open up the deadlock*

【打开天窗说亮话】speak frankly; put one's cards on the table: ~吧,不要吞吞吐吐了。*Let's talk rankly and don't mince matters.*

【打瞌睡】doze off; snooze; nod:他一直在~,因为昨晚熬夜了。*He is always dozing for he stayed up late last night.*

【打孔】punch; drill a hole: ~机 *punching machine*

【打垮】defeat; rout; strike down:将敌人~ *defeat the enemy completely*

【打捞】① salvage; get out of the water: ~沉船 *salvage a sunken ship* / ~海藻 *salvage the algae* ② fishing ③ rescue

【打擂】join in an open contest

【打冷噤】shiver; tremble; shudder:冻得~ *shiver with cold*

【打冷枪】snipe; attack in the back:在背后~是不光彩的事。*It's contemptible to snipe on the sly.*

【打量】① measure with the eye; look sb up and down; estimate:他上下~着我,好像我们好久没见似的。*He looked at me up and down as if we've not seen for a long time.* ② think; suppose; reckon:我~她完不成任务。*I think she can't finish the task.*

【打乱】disturb; upset; disarrange; throw into confusion: ~次序 *disturb the order* / ~安排 *upset the arrangement* /她的不期而至~了我的全部计划。*Her unexpected arrival disturbed all my plan.*

【打马虎眼】[方] act dumb to feign ignorance of something; try to fool sb by acting dumb

【打埋伏】① lie in ambush; trap ② hold sth back for one's own use

【打闷棍】① beat sb. with a club without knowing ② give sb. a blow by surprise

【打磨】polish; burnish; shine

【打牌】① play cards or mahjong:我喜欢在业余时间~。*I am fond of playing cards in my spare time.* ② (in international or domestic politics) exploit for one's own end

【打喷嚏】sneeze

【打破】break; smash: ~僵局 *break a deadlock (or stalemate)* / ~记录 *break a record* / ~常规 *break the common rule* / ~旧框框 *break the old set pattern* / ~铁饭碗 *break the iron rice bowl*

【打破砂锅问到底】ask questions till bottom of the matter; look for details of one thing:研究要有~的精神。*When searching we should learn to get to the bottom of everything.*

【打气】① inflate; pump up; blow up:给轮胎~ *blow up the tyre* ② bolster the morale; cheer up

【打钎】drill a blasting bole in rock with a hammer and a drill rod

【打前站】act as an advance party:不用着急,有人~了。*Don't be worried for someone has set out in advance.*

【打情骂俏】flirt with the opposite sex; tease one's lover by pretending to the displeased

【打秋千】get on a swing; have a swing

【打趣】banter; chaff; tease; make fun of:弗格斯没事总爱拿小孩~。*Fergus always made fun of little children.*

【打圈子】① circle:羽毛在空中~,慢慢飘了下来。*A feather made a circle in the sky and floated down slowly.* ② get bogged down:在琐事上~是毫无意义的。*It's none of sense to get bogged down in minor issues.*

【打拳】make shadowbox; practice boxing

【打群架】engage in a gang fight

【打搅】disturb; trouble

【打散】break up; scatter; disperse:将原有顺序~ *break up the formal orders*

【打扫】sweep; clean: ~卫生 *do some cleaning* / ~房间 *clean a room* / ~残局 *clean up the final situation of a failure*

【打闪】lightning; flash

【打食】① (of birds and beasts) hunt for food ② take medicine to remedy indigestion

【打手】hatchet man; hired roughneck or thing:他以充当~为生。*He made a living by serving as a latchet man.*

【打水漂儿】play ducks and drakes; squander:我小时候经常在河边~。*I'm used to playing ducks and drakes by the river in my childhood.* /拿着钱~。*Play loose with money.*

【打算】plan; intend: 做长远~ *be prepared for the long-term plan* /我~明年去上海旅游。*I'm planning to have a tour to shanghai next year.*

【打算盘】① calculate(on abacus) ② be calculating; scheme; plan:他是一个善于打小算盘的人。*He is a man who is good at be calculating.*

【打碎】smash; break into pieces:是谁~了玻璃? *Who broke the glass into pieces?*

【打胎】have an (induced) abortion; induce abortion

【打探】fish for; make inquires: ~消息 *fish for information*

【打铁】forge iron; work as a blacksmith:趁热~ *strike while the iron is hot*

【打听】ask (or inquire) about; make inquire: ~消息 *make inquire about information* /能向您~一下路吗? *Excuse me; may I ask the way?*

【打通】get through (phone call, etc.); open up: ~电话 *be able to get through (on the telephone)* / ~院墙 *make an opening in the courtyard wall* / ~关系 *bribe official in charge*

【打头】① take the lead:这事儿得有人~。*Someone should take the lead to do it.* ②[方] from the beginning: ~儿起她就没搞明白这件事。*She didn't understand this thing from the very beginning.*

【打头风】contrary wind; against the wind

【打头炮】fire the first shot; be the first to speak or act:如果有人~,这件事就容易多了。*It will be much easier if someone acted first.*

【打头阵】fight in the ran; take the lead; spearhead

【打退】repulse; beat back:将敌人~ *repulse the enemy*

【打退堂鼓】retreat; back out; fall back:关键时刻我们不能~。*We can't back out at the key time.*

【打围】encircle and hunt down (animals)

【打下】① overcome (or capture) a city ② lay(a foundation); set a basis: ~扎实的基础 *lay a sturdy foundation*

【打先锋】be a pioneer; fight in the van; take the lead

【打响】① start shooting; begin to exchange fire:前线的战斗~了。*The war began in the front.* ② win initial success; win first round:我们成功地~了第一炮。*We've succeeded at the first step.*

【打消】give up; dispel: ~顾虑 *dispel mismanages* / ~计划 *give up the plan* /她临时~了去看电影的念头。*She gave up the idea to go to see a film*

D

temporarily.
【打小报告】rat(or inform) secretly on sb
【打雪仗】have a snowball fight; throw snowballs
【打眼】① drill ②［方］catch the eye; attract attention
【打样】① draw a design ②【印】make a proof：～机 *proof press*
【打烊】(of stores, shops, etc.) close for night
【打印】① put a seal on; affix stamp on ② cut a stencil and mimeograph; mimeograph ③ print：～格式 *print format* /草稿要～出来。*The draft needn't be printed out.*
【打印机】printer：激光～ *laser printer* /～终端 *typewriter terminal*
【打油诗】doggerel; ragged verse
【打游击】① fight as a guerrilla; join the guerrillas：同敌人～ *fight as a guerrilla with the enemy* ② no fixed place to work, sleep, etc.
【打预防针】have a preventive injection; take precautions against sth：提前给你们～了，这个任务很难完成。*Warn you in advance that this task is difficult to finish.*
【打圆场】mediate a disputer (or quarrel); smooth things over
【打杂儿】do odd jobs：他只不过是个～的。*He is only an odd-jobber.*
【打造】forge：～一把斧子 *forge an axe*
【打仗】fight; wage war
【打招呼】① say hello; greet sb：你刚才跟谁～？*Who did you greet just now?* ② notify; let sb know; warn：走之前请跟我～。*Let me know before you go.* /这不怪我，我已经跟他们～了。*It's none of my business for I've waved them.*
【打折扣】① sell at a discount; allow a discount：这件衬衣不～。*This shirt doesn't sell at a discount.* ② detract：说到做到，不～ *carry out one's pledge to the letter*
【打针】give (or have) an injection; inject
【打制】forge; make：～斧头 *forge an axe*
【打肿脸充胖子】act as a fat person by slapping one's face until it is swollen — try to maintain one's self-respect to do sth strained
【打中】hit the mark (or target)：～靶心 *hit the bull's-eye* /～要害 *hit the vital point*
【打主意】① think of an idea; devise a plan：要报考哪所大学你要早～。*You should make up your mind earlier about which university to choose.* ② scheme; try to obtain：你要小心，他们在打你的主意。*Be careful for they're thinking of scheming you.*
【打住】stop; hold; come to a half (in speech or writing)：看到领导进来，他立马～了。*He stopped quickly when he saw the leader coming.*
【打转】spin; rotate; revolve：车轮在泥里～。*The car's wheels kept spinning in the mud.* /孩子们在围着她～。*The children were revolving around her.*
【打桩】piling：～机 *pile driver*
【打字】type; typewrite：～机 *typewriter* /～员 *typist*
【打嘴巴】slap sb on face：你说错话了，真该～。*You should deserve a slap on you face because you've said the wrong words.*
【打坐】(of a Buddhist or Taoist monk) sit in meditation

dà

大[1] ① big; large; great：～桌子 *a big desk* /～头衔 *big rank* /一～片土地 *a large area* ② strong; heavy：雨太～了，不要出去了。*Don't go outside for it is rains heavily.* /团结起来力量～。*Unity is strength.* ③ loud; high：噪音太～，我听不清楚。*The noise is so loud and I can't hear your words clearly.* ④ main; general; important：～任务 *an important task* /～路 *main road* /～问题 *major issue; big problem* ⑤ size：你家房子有多～？*How large is your house?* /你穿多～号鞋子？*What size shoes do you wear?* ⑥ age：您今年多～岁数了？*How old are you?* /我姐比我～两岁。*My elder sister is two years older than me.* ⑦ eldest：他是我们家老～。*He is my elder child.* /～哥 *one's eldest brother* ⑧ your：～作 *your writing* /～名 *your name* ⑨ used before a phrase of time to stress on it：～热天穿这么多？*Why do you wear so much daring such a hot day?*

大[2] ① greatly; to a great degree：～吃一惊 *surprise sb greatly* /～为改观后的城市，我几乎认不出来了。*I can hardly recognize the city after unexpected change.* ② used after 不 to indicate a low degree or few times：不～出门 *go outside infrequently* /不～爱说话 *tend to speak little*

大[3]［方］① father ② uncle

see also dài
【大巴】［方］bus
【大白】①［方］whiting：～浆 *whitewash* ② come out; make known to public; be fully exposed：真相～了。*The truth has been made known to all.*
【大白菜】Chinese cabbage
【大白话】colloquial words
【大白天】daytime; broad daylight：这是～，你不用担心。*You needn't be worried for it is in broad daylight.*
【大白天说梦话】daydream; say sth that can't be done
【大败】① defeat (or vanquish) completely; put to rout：解放军在战斗中～敌军。*The PLA men defeated the enemy utterly in one battle.* ② suffer a crushing defeat：在选举中～ *suffer a crushing defeat in the election*
【大班】① top class in a kindergarten ② boss of a foreign firm in old china ③ a large class (of students)
【大阪】Osaka (of Japan)
【大板车】large handcart

【大办】do sth in a big way; arrange (a wedding, feast, etc.) exaggeratedly

【大半】① more than half; most; great part: ~年 *more than half a year* /霍尔等了~辈子。*Hall has waited in most of his lifetime.* ② most probably (or likely):这工作弗朗西斯~是完不成了。*Frances probably isn't able to finish the work.*

【大本营】① the supreme headquarters (or base) of an army ② base camp (of an activity):这是我们军训的~。*This is the base camp of our military training.*

【大便】① defecate; shit; have a bowel movement: ~不通(*suffer from*) *constipation* ② stool; human excrement; shit:化验~ *have one's stool examined*

【大兵】① solider ② great force; big battle

【大兵团】large troop formation

【大饼】a kind of big flatbread

【大不列颠】Great Britain (comprising England, Wales and Scotland)

【大不了】① at the worst: ~今晚熬夜。*If the worst comes to the worst, we'll stay up all night.* ② (used in the negative) alarming; serious:不要哭,这没什么~的。*There is nothing serious; don't cry.*

【大步流星】at a stride; with vigorous strides:他~地走向广场。*He walked toward the public square.*

【大部分】great part; for the most part:来听报告的~是学生。*The majority coming to listen to the report are students.*

【大部头】voluminous work: ~的书 *book in voluminous volumes*

【大材小用】waste one's talent on a petty job:你在这家公司工作,简直是~。*It's a waste of your talent to work in this company.*

【大菜】① the major or last course of a feast ② Western food; European food

【大操大办】arrange (a wedding, funeral, feast, etc.) in an exaggerated way

【大肠】【生理】large intestines: ~杆菌 *colon bacillus*

【大潮】surging tide

【大吵大闹】kick up a row; make a din (or scene):不要在公共场合~。*Don't kick up a row in public.*

【大车】① cart ② a call of engine driver

【大臣】minister (of a monarchy); high officials

【大吃大喝】eat and drink indulgently:反对~ *oppose eating and drinking extravagantly*

【大吃一惊】be greatly surprised (or shocked); be quite taken aback

【大虫】[方] tiger

【大酬宾】crazy sale; give a large discount

【大出血】①【医】massive hemorrhage ② bargain sale; colossal spending: ~价格 *bargain price* /昨天的酒席是你~办的吗? *Did you dig deep into your pocket to arrange the feast yesterday?*

【大锤】sledgehammer

【大慈大悲】【宗】great mercy; be infinitely compassionate (or merciful)

【大葱】green Chinese onion

【大错特错】completely wrong; seriously mistaken:你们先前的计划是~。*The former plans you've made are absolutely wrong.*

【大大】greatly; enormously; tremendously:出口量~增加。*The exports have risen greatly.*

【大大咧咧】[方] careless; casual:他表面~,但实际上很认真。*He seems careless in appearance, but he is careful in fact.*

【大胆】audacious; bold; daring: ~的设想 *a bold imagine* /的提议 *a bold proposal* / 你真~! *How dare you!*

【大道理】major (or general) principle; great truth:他只会讲~,不会实干。*He only knows talking in generalities and don't know doing work.*

【大灯】headlight (of a car)

【大堤】dike; dam; embankment

【大敌】formidable; archenemy:如临~ *like confronting a mortal enemy*; *be an one's guard for all possible dangers*

【大抵】generally speaking; more or less; on the whole: ~相同 *more or less the same*

【大地】earth; mother earth; land:祖国~ *land all over the country* /春回~。*Spring returns to the earth.*

【大典】① great (or grand) ceremony:开国~ *founding ceremony* (*of a state*) ② a body of classical writings; canon

【大调】【音】major: C~奏鸣曲 *sonata in C major*

【大动干戈】go to war; make a big fuss over:为这点事儿~不值得。*It didn't worth making a big fuss over such a trivial matter.*

【大动脉】①【医】main artery: aorta ② main artery of communication

【大豆】soybean

【大度】[书] magnanimous; open minded:为人~ *be a magnanimous man* / ~包容 *be magnanimous and tolerant*

【大队】① a military unit or group ② production brigade (of a rural commune) ③ a large body (of); a large number: ~人马 *a large contingent of troops*; *a large body of marchers, parades, etc.*

【大多】mostly; for the most part:今天的水果~已卖完了。*Most of the fruits today have been sold out.*

【大多数】great (or vast) majority; most; bulk:他的做法得到了~人的认可。*His action won recognitions of the vast majority.*

【大发雷霆】be furious; fly into a rage:看到窗户玻璃被孩子们打破了,他~。*He flew into a rage seeing that the glass of the window was broken into pieces by children.*

【大法】fundamental law and constitution of a nation

【大凡】generally speaking; in most cases: ~好好复习的都不用担心考试。*Generally speaking, those who have gone over the lessons carefully needn't worry about the exam.*

【大方】①［书］experts ② generous; openhanded ③ natural and poised; unaffected; elegant:举止～ *have dignified air*; *have an easy manner* ④ be in good taste; tasteful:她的衣着很～。*The style of her dress is in good taste.*

【大方向】general orientation

【大放厥词】talk a lot of nonsense; boast or brag wildly; spout a stream of empty rhetoric

【大放异彩】shine with unusually brilliant results

【大粪】① human excrement ② night soil

【大风】① fresh gale ② strong wind:据天气预报,明天有～。*There will be a strong wind through weather forecast.*

【大风大浪】① wind and waves; great storms ② great upheaval:他是经历过～的人。*He is a man who has gone through great social upheavals.*

【大幅度】substantially; by a big margin; to a great extent:～提高 *increase by a wide margin* /他的学习态度有了～改善。*His attitude to study has improved by a big margin.*

【大副】first mate; chief officer

【大腹便便】potbellied; paunchy

【大概】① general idea; broad outline:这件事你知道个～就可以了。*It is enough for you to know the general idea of this matter.* ② general; approximate:～的估计 *a rough estimate* /的印象 *general impression* / ～的想法 *general idea* ③ probably; presumably; most likely:明天～要下雨。*It will probably rain tomorrow.*

【大纲】outline; synopsis:教学～ *syllabus*

【大哥】① eldest brother ②［口］elder brother (a polite form of address for a man about one's own age)

【大哥大】① mobile phone; cellular phone ② super boss; a powerful person

【大革命】① great revolution:法国～ *the French Revolution* ② the Great Revolution in china (1927-1927)

【大公无私】① unselfish; selfless ② perfectly impartial

【大功】great achievement; extraordinary service

【大姑子】［口］husband's elder sister; sister-in-law

【大鼓】bass drum

【大褂】Chinese unlined long gown; rob

【大观】magnificent spectacle; grand sight:洋洋～ *magnificent view*

【大规模】large-scale; massive:～生产 *large-scale production*

【大锅饭】big pot rice — everyone in the same situation; extreme equalitarian

【大过】serious offence; big mistake:记～ *record a serious mistake*

【大海捞针】fish for a needle in ocean; look for a needle in haystack

【大喊大叫】① scream; shout at the top of one's voice ② conduct vigorous propaganda

【大好】① be very good; excellent:～风光 *excellent view* / ～形势 *excellent situation* ② fully recover

【大号】① large size:～鞋 *large-size shoes* ② your (given) name ③ tuba; bass horn

【大合唱】chorus; cantata

【大亨】big shot; tycoon; magnate

【大红】bright red; crimson

【大后方】① vast rear area ② areas under KMT rule during the War of Resistance Against Japan in China

【大后年】three years from now

【大后天】three days from now

【大户】① wealthy and influential family ② large family ③ individual unit that is celebrated in a certain field

【大话】big words; boast; bragging:讲～ *talk big*

【大黄蜂】hornet

【大黄鱼】large yellow croaker

【大茴香】【植】anise; star anise

【大会】① plenary meeting; general membership meeting; conference:全国人民代表～ *National People's Congress* ② mass meeting; mass rally:纪念～ *a commemorative meeting*

【大伙儿】［口］we all; everybody; mate

【大祸临头】disaster is forthcoming; a calamity is about to happen

【大惑不解】be extremely puzzled; be completely confused

【大吉大利】be extremely lucky; greatly auspicious:祝你～！*Wish you very good luck!*

【大集体】big collective

【大计】a major issue of lasting importance; a matter of fundamental importance:共商～ *discuss matters of vital importance*

【大家】① all of us; everybody:～都要来开会吗？*Will everybody be here to attend the meeting?* ② authority; master:书法～ *a great master of calligraphy* /语言～ *leading expert on philology* ③ rich and influential ancient family:～闺秀 *a girl from a good family*

【大家庭】extended family; big family; community:社会～ *community of society*

【大驾】you:恭候～ *wait respectfully for your gracious presence* /有劳～ *have to rely on your efforts*; *have to ask you the take the trouble*

【大奖】grand prize; top prize; big award or prize:～赛 *prize-giving competition* /她在演讲比赛中获得了～。*She was awarded the grand prize in the lecture competition.*

【大将】①【军】senior general ② high-ranking officer; chief general

【大教堂】cathedral

【大街】main street:逛～ *go window-shopping* / ～小巷 *streets and lanes*; *in every street and alley*

【大捷】great victory

【大姐】① eldest sister ② elder sister (a polite form of address for a woman about one's own age)

【大姐大】［口］woman with power

【大襟】the front of a Chinese garment with buttons on the right

【大惊失色】turn pale with fright：听到这个消息，她～。*She turned pale with fright when she heard the news.*

【大惊小怪】be alarmed at sth ordinary; make an unwarranted fuss：你不值得为这点儿小事～。*You didn't worth making a fuss about such a trifle.*

【大静脉】【生理】vena cava

【大舅子】［口］wife's elder brother; brother-in-law

【大局】situation in general; overall public interest：顾全～ *take the overall situation into account* /事关～，你要小心。*You should be careful for it's an issue that concerns the whole situation.*

【大举】carry out (a military operation) on a large scale：～进攻 *mount an offensive on a large scale*

【大军】① army; main forces：援助～ *main forces for support* ② large contingent：医疗～ *large contingent of medical treatment*

【大开眼界】open one's eyes; broaden one's horizon

【大课】enlarged class; lecture given to a large number of students

【大快人心】affording general satisfaction; give a lift of the heart

【大块头】［方］a person who is tall or bulkily

【大款】［口］magnate; moneybag; upstart

【大括弧】brace

【大牢】［口］prison; jail：关进～ *cast into prison*

【大老粗】uncouth fellow; uneducated person; rough and ready fellow

【大老婆】primary or first wife in polygamy

【大礼拜】two-day weekend (in contrast with one day off)

【大礼堂】auditorium; big assembly hall

【大理石】marble

【大力】energetic; vigorous：～提倡 *devote major efforts to advocate*

【大力士】muscleman; a man of extraordinary strength

【大梁】①【建】large roof beam ② the main prop

【大量】① large quantity：～信息 *large quantities of information* / ～事实 *a host of facts* / ～证据 *a vast amount of evidence* ② generous; magnanimous：宽宏～ *magnanimous; broad-minded; generous*

【大料】［方］aniseed

【大溜】main current; main trend; great number (of persons); majority (of the people)：随～ *follow the crowd; conform to the majority; follow the tread*

【大楼】multi-storeyed building：摩天～ *skyscraper* / 办公～ *office building*

【大陆】① continent; mainland：～架 *continental shelf* / ～漂移 *continental drift* ② China's mainland; mainland of China

【大路】main road; big street

【大略】① general idea; broad outline：了解事情的～ *get a general idea of the matter* ② roughly：你可以～讲一下他的情况。*You may speak about him briefly.* ③ great vision

【大妈】① aunt; father's elder brother's wife ② aunt (an affectionate or respectful from of address for an elderly woman)

【大麻】① hemp ② marijuana; hashish

【大麦】barley

【大忙】very busy：～季节 *busy season*

【大猫熊】giant panda

【大帽子】a big hat — an exaggerated categorize of a person's status; political label：～压人 *intimidate people by pinning political labels on them*

【大门】main entrance; front door; gate

【大米】(husked) rice

【大面儿】［方］general appearance; surface：～上过得去就可以了。*It is enough that it's basically all right.*

【大民族主义】big-nationality chauvinism

【大名】① one's formal personal name ② your (given) name

【大名鼎鼎】famous; well-known; big-name; celebrated：～的人物 *a well-known person*

【大漠】great desert

【大模大样】with a swagger; in a ostentatious manner：～地走进办公室 *step into the office with a swagger*

【大拇指】thumb：竖起～叫好 *hold up one's thumb in approval*

【大拿】［口］① person with power; boss：我们这里厂长说了算，他是～。*The director has the final say here; he is the boss.* ② expert; authority：在力学方面，他是我们这里的～。*In mechanics, he is the expert here.*

【大男子主义】male chauvinism

【大难】catastrophe; disaster：～临头 *be faced with imminent catastrophe* / ～不死，必有后福。*One who survives a catastrophe is bound to have good fortune in the future.*

【大脑】【生理】cerebrum

【大逆不道】treason and heresy; worst offence; sedition

【大年】① good year; year of bumper harvest ② lunar year in which the last month has 30 days ③ Spring Festival

【大年初一】［口］first day of the lunar year; lunar New Year's Day

【大年夜】［方］lunar New Year's Eve

【大娘】［口］① aunt; father's elder brother's wife ② aunt

【大排档】side walk snack eatery

【大炮】① artillery; big gun; cannon ②［口］one who talks big or speaks boastfully

【大篷车】① (covered) wagon ② covered truck or lorry (for carrying goods); caravan：组织～送货下乡 *send goods into the country in caravans*

【大批】large quantities of; a good deal of：～食物 *large quantities of food* / ～供应 *supply in a large quantity*

【大气】① atmosphere; air：～层 *atmospheric layer* / ～污 *air pollution* / ～折射 *atmospheric refrac-*

D

tion ② heavy breathing：吓得连～也不敢出 *catch one's breath in fear* ③ carry oneself with ease and confidence；generous：他在朋友面前很～。*He is generous in front of friends.* ④ great momentum：～磅礴 *be of great momentum*

【大气候】general political climate；major situation or tendency

【大器】① treasure ② great talent：这孩子将来必成～。*The child is bound to become a celebrated person in the future.*

【大器晚成】great vessels take years to produce — great minds mature slowly；a great talent takes time to mature

【大千世界】the boundless universe

【大前年】three yeas ago

【大前提】major premise

【大前天】three days ago

【大权】power or authority to decide on major issues：～在握 *hold power in one's hands*；*wield the scepter*

【大人】① adult；grown-up ②［旧］Your Excellency ③ used in a letter to be a respectful address for one's parents or seniors：母亲～ *dear mother*

【大人物】important person；big shot；VIP

【大扫除】general cleaning；give a thorough cleaning to

【大嫂】① eldest brother's wife；sister-in-law ② elder sister（a respectful address for a woman about one's own age）

【大厦】large building；mansions：公共～ *public mansions*

【大少爷】① eldest son（of a rich family）② a spoilt or dandy son of a rich family；spendthrift；playboy：～作风 *behaviour of a spoilt boy of a rich family*；*style of life of pampered youngsters*

【大舌头】［口］a thick-tongued person；lisper

【大婶儿】① aunt；father's younger brother's wife ② aunt（a respectful from of address for a woman about one's mother's age）

【大声疾呼】cry as loud as possible；loudly appeal to the public

【大牲畜】draught animal

【大失所望】greatly disappointed；to one's great disappointment

【大师】great master；master：国画～ *master of traditional Chinese painting* / 象棋～ *great master of Chinese chess*

【大师傅】（dàshīfu）Great Master，courtesy title used to address a Buddhist monk

【大师傅】（dàshifu）cook；chef

【大使】ambassador：特命全权～ *ambassador extraordinary and plenipotentiary* / 驻外～ *ambassador to a foreign country* / ～馆 *embassy* / ～级会谈 *talks at ambassadorial level*

【大事】① great event；major issue；gigantic task：国家～ *affairs of state* / 人生～ *most important event in one's life* ② overall situation ③ in a big way：～渲染 *play up greatly*；*immensely exaggerate* / ～夸张 *distend grossly*

【大事记】chronicle of events；record of important events

【大势】general trend of events：～所趋，人心所向 *trend of the times and will of the people*；*the general trend and popular feeling* / ～已去 *the end of one's force*；*be all up with sb*

【大是大非】cardinal questions of right and wrong：事关～的问题。*It's related with major matters of principle.*

【大手笔】① work of an authority or writing of a great calligrapher ② a well-known writer

【大手大脚】extravagant；wasteful；lavish：花钱～ *spend extravagantly*

【大叔】① uncle；younger brother of one's father ② uncle（a respectful form of address for a man about one's father's age）

【大暑】Great Heat-the 12th of the 24 solar terms

【大树底下好乘凉】［谚］a big tree affords good shade；an influential friend，relative or mentor provides protection and help

【大水】flood

【大肆】without restraint；wantonly：～掠夺 *plunder wantonly* / ～宣扬 *propagate viciously*

【大堂】①［旧］courtroom of magistrate ② hall ③ lobby（of a hotel）：～经理 *manager on duly*

【大提琴】violoncello；cello

【大题小作】（or be little）a major issue

【大体】① main principle；general interest：识～ *keep the general interest in mind* ② generally；by and large；more or less；approximately：～相同 *more or less the same* / 他～上同意了我的想法。*He agreed with me by and large.*

【大田】land for growing field crops：～作物 *field crop*

【大厅】hall

【大庭广众】（before）a big crowd；in public；（on）a pubic occasion：～之下丢丑 *lose one's face in public*

【大同】① Great Harmony（an ideal or perfect society）② be essentially the same

【大同小异】much the same（or large identical）but with minor differences；be almost alike

【大头】① a mask of big head ② the bigger end of sth；main part：抓～儿 *grasp the major issue* ③ a person deceived on account of his generosity：拿～ *sponge a person who is generous*

【大头菜】【植】rutabaga

【大头钉】pin

【大团圆】① happy reunion（of a family，etc.）② happy ending：以～结束 *end with a happy ending*

【大腿】thigh

【大腕】distinguished personage（or star）in literature，art，etc.

【大无畏】dauntless；utterly fearless；indomitable：～的英雄气概 *dauntless heroism*

【大西洋】the Atlantic（Ocean）：～公约 *Atlantic Pact*

【大喜】①［口］overjoyed; great rejoicing：您～啦！*Congratulations*！② wedding; marriage：今天是他们～的日子。*Today is their wedding day.*
【大虾】prawn
【大显身手】display one's skill fully; be at one's best; distinguish oneself; cut a brilliant figure：到你～的时候了。*It's time for you to display your skill to the full.*
【大显神通】display one's prowess; give full play to one's remarkable ability
【大相径庭】be widely divergent, be entirely different; be strikingly at variance
【大小】① big or small：国家不论～，应该一律平等。*All countries, big or small, should be equal.* ② size：箱子的～ *the size of the case* / 这双鞋我穿～正合适。*These shoes are just my size.* ③ degree of seniority：说话没个～ *speak to elderly people impolitely* ④ adults and children：他们家～五口。*There are five people in their family altogether.*
【大校】【军】senior colonel
【大写】① capital form of a Chinese numeral：～金额 *amount in words* ② capitalization; upper case：～字母 *capital letters*
【大兴】go in for sth in a big way：～土木 *go in for large-scale construction* / ～调查研究之风 *energetically encourage the practice of conducting investigations and studios* / ～问罪之师 *point an accusing finger at*
【大猩猩】gorilla
【大型】large-scale：～企业 *large enterprise* / ～音乐会 *full-length concert* / ～轧钢厂 *heavy steel rolling plant* / ～客机 *giant airliner*
【大行星】【天】major planet
【大熊猫】giant panda
【大修】【机】overhaul; repair thoroughly
【大选】general election
【大学】university; college
【大学生】university student; college student; undergraduate
【大循环】【生理】systemic circulation
【大雅】［书］elegance; refinement; good taste
【大烟】opium：～鬼 *opium addict*
【大言不惭】brag unblushingly
【大雁】wild goose
【大洋】① ocean ② silver dollar
【大洋洲】Oceania; Oceanica
【大样】①【印】full-page roof ②【建】detail drawing
【大摇大摆】strutting; swaggering; walk haughtily：旁若无人似的，他～地闯进了门。*Superciliously, he walked into the door as bold as brass.*
【大要】main points; gist：内容～ *gist of the content*
【大爷】① a lazy, arrogant and self willed man：～作风 *arrogant manner* ②［口］father's elder brother; uncle ③［口］uncle (a respectful form of address for an elderly man)
【大业】great cause; great undertaking：国家统一～ *great cause of national reunification*
【大衣】overcoat; topcoat
【大姨】［口］mother's elder sister; aunt
【大姨子】［口］wife's elder sister; sister-in-law
【大义】righteous cause; cardinal principles of righteous ness：深明～ *be deeply conscious of what is righteous*
【大义凛然】inspiring awe by upholding justice; uphold the cause of righteousness
【大意】① general idea; main points; gist：文章～ *gist of an article* ② careless; negligent; inattentive：他总是～，书包丢了也难怪。*It's no wonder that he lost his bag for he was always careless.*
【大音阶】【音】major scale
【大印】great seal; seal of power
【大有】① plenty of; a great deal of：～益处 *be for great benefit* ②［书］good (or bumper) harvest：～之秋 *autumn of good harvest*
【大有可为】have bright prospects; be well worth doing：设施栽培～。*There are bright prospects for facility culture.*
【大有人在】there are plenty of such people; such people are by no means rare：支持他的人～。*Such people as advocate him are by no means rare.*
【大有文章】there is more to it than meets the eye; there is something behind all this
【大有作为】there is full scope for one's talents; be able to develop one's ability to the full：这是可以让你～的地方。*This is a place for you to develop your ability to the full.*
【大雨】heavy rain
【大元帅】generalissimo
【大员】［旧］high-ranking official
【大院】courtyard; compound：海军～ *the compound of nary*
【大约】① approximately; about; around：～有二十人到会。*About 20 people attended the meeting.* ② probably; likely：他～不会来了。*He will probably not come here.*
【大跃进】the Great Leap Forward (1958—1959)
【大运河】the Grand Canal
【大杂烩】hodgepodge; hotchpotch
【大杂院儿】compound occupied by many households
【大张旗鼓】on a grand scale; in a big way; with a big display of flags and drums：～地宣传 *propagate in a big way*
【大丈夫】true man; real man; man courage
【大志】high aim; lofty aim; exalted ambition; high aspirations：胸怀～ *cherish lofty aim*
【大治】great order：～之年 *the year of great order*
【大致】roughly; by and large; more or less
【大智若愚】the wise appears dumb; a man of great wisdom often seems slow-witted
【大中型】large and medium-sized
【大众】the people; the masses; the crowd of people：～歌曲 *popular songs* / ～电影 *popular films*

/ ~媒体 *mass media*

【大众化】popularize: ~品味 *taste of the ordinary people*

【大洲】continent

【大主教】【宗】archbishop

【大专院校】universities and colleges; institutions of higher education

dāi

呆 ① dull; slow-witted: 目睹了那场惨剧后,他变~了。*After witnessing the tragedy, he became slow-witted.* ② wooden; be in a daze; blankly: ~~地站着 *stand blankly* / ~~地看 *stare at sth in a daze* ③ stay: 她总喜欢~在家里。*She always likes staying at home.*

【呆板】inflexible; rigid; still: 色调~ *a rigid tone* / 表情~ *a stiff expression* / 你的做事方法太~了。*You are so inflexible in the way of doing something.*

【呆若木鸡】dumb as a wooden chicken; dumbstruck; transfixed (with fear or amazement): 这个消息使他~。*The news made him dumb as a wooden chicken.*

【呆头呆脑】stupid; dull-looking

【呆账】bad debt

【呆滞】① dull: 目光~ *with a dull look in one's eyes* ② sluggish; idle: ~的市面 *idle business conditions* / 资金~ *idle capital*

【呆子】blockhead; simpleton; idiot

dǎi

歹 bad; evil; vicious: 为非作~ *do evil*

【歹毒】sinister and vicious; be malicious and ruthless

【歹人】bandit; burglar; gangster

【歹徒】scoundrel; ruffian

【歹心】evil or vicious intent: 可别把人家的好心当了~。*Don't take the goodwill for evil intent.*

逮 capture; catch: 将小偷~住 *catch the thief* / 猫~老鼠。*Cats catch mice.*
see also dài

dài

大 used in the following phrases
see also dà

【大夫】[口] doctor; physician

【大黄】【植】chinese rhubarb

【大王】king (usu. used in traditional operas or novels)

代[1] ① take the place of: 请~我向他问好。*Please give him my regards.* ② acting: ~市长 *acting mayor*

代[2] ① historical period; dynasty: 现~ *modern times* / 唐~ *Tang Dynasty* ② generation: ~新人 *a new generation* ③ generation

【代办】① do sth for sb; manage on behalf of another: 这件事你必须自己完成,不能~。*You must finish it by yourself and it couldn't be acted on your behalf.* ② charge d affaires: 临时~ *charge d affaires ad interim* / ~处 *Office of the Charged Affaires*

【代笔】ghostwrite; write (a letter, etc.) on one's behalf: 这封信是由我~替他写的。*This letter is written by me on his behalf.*

【代表】① delegate; representative; deputy; exponent: 全国人大~ *deputy to the National People's Congress* ② represent; stand for: 他的作品~了那个时代的风尚。*His work represented the fashion of that time.* ③ in the name of; on behalf of: 他~教育界发了言。*He spoke on behalf of the educational circles.*

【代词】【语】pronoun

【代沟】generation gap

【代购】buy on one's behalf; act as a purchasing agent: ~代销点 *purchasing and marketing agency* / 这个商店可以为你办理~。*The shop can act as a purchasing agent for you.*

【代号】code name

【代价】cost; price: 医生们接到命令要不惜任何~救活那位英雄。*The doctors received the order to save that hero at any cost.*

【代课】teach for an absent teacher; take over a class for an absent teacher

【代劳】do sth for sb; take trouble on sb's behalf: 我姐姐病了,这件事由我~可以吗? *My elder sister is ill; may I do it for her?*

【代理】① act for sb in a responsible position: 他的律师将~他处理这个事件。*His lawyer will act for him to deal with this matter.* ② act as agent

【代码】code: ~文件 *code file*

【代庖】[书] do in sb's place; do what is sb else's job

【代培】train sb for (an organization)

【代乳粉】milk powder substitute

【代售】be commissioned to sell; sell goods on a commission basis: ~车票 *be commissioned to sell tickets*

【代数】algebra: ~方程 *algebraic equation* / ~和 *algebraic*

【代替】replace; substitute for; take the place of: 现在电话在很大程度上~了书信。*Nowadays, communication by telephone has taken the place of writing letters to great degree.*

【代为】replace; for (sb): ~保管 *take care of sth for sb*

【代销】be commissioned to sell sth usu. as a sideline: ~店 *shop commissioned to sell certain goods*

【代谢】①【生】metabolize：新陈～ *metabolism* ② supersession

【代序】on article used in lieu of a preface (or by way of introduction)

【代言人】spokesman; mouthpiece

【代用】substitute：～材料 *substitute material* / ～品 *substitute; ersatz*

【代职】act on sb's behalf; function in an acting capacity

迨 [书] ① by the time; wait till：～后再议 *discuss it later* ② before sth happens

带[1] ① belt; ribbon; tape：丝～ *silk ribbon* / 皮～ *leather belt* ② tyre：车～ *car tyre* ③ zone; area; belt：热～雨林 *tropical rain forest*

带[2] ① take; bring：我可以～相机进去吗? *May I go in with the camera?* / 你～来了什么好消息吗? *Do you take us good news?* ② do sth incidentally：请随手～门。*Please close the door conveniently.* ③ have; bear; show：面～笑容 *have a smile on one's face* / ～有时代特色 *have the characteristic of the time* ④ having sth attached; with：～花园的房子 *house with a garden* / 他连跑～跳地走了。*He went away running and jumping.* ⑤ head：～领军队 *lead an army* / ～研究生 *be a tutor of postgraduates* ⑥ look after; bring up; raise：她是由姑姑～大的。*She was brought up by her aunt.* ⑦ drive; bring along; give impetus to：大家的热情都被他～动起来了。*The enthusiasm of all was brought along by him.*

【带病】in spite of illness：～值班 *be on duty in spite of illness*

【带操】【体】gymnastics with ribbons

【带刺儿】be sarcastic：说话～ *speak sarcastically*

【带电】electrified; charged; live：～作业 *live-wire work* / ～粒子 *charged particle*

【带动】drive; bring along; give impetus to：以点～全面 *use the experience of pilot units to promote progress in on entire area* / ～经济发展 *give impetus to the development of the economy*

【带劲】① energetic; forceful：他们干活儿很～。*They worked like horses.* ② interesting; exciting; wonderful

【带锯】【机】band saw

【带菌者】【医】carrier

【带累】implicate; involve：让我自己去吧，不能再～你了。*Let me go there on my own; I shouldn't trouble you any more.*

【带领】lead; guide; take sb to a place：在厂长的～下，全厂获得了很好的经济效益。*Under the leadership the manager, the factory won notable economic profits.*

【带路】show or lead the way; act as a guide：谁要为我们～上山? *Who will lead us the way to the mountain?*

【带路人】guide; leader

【带头】take the lead; be a pioneer; be the first; take the initiative：～作用 *a leading role* / ～在会上发言 *be a pioneer to speak at the meeting* / ～人 *leader; foregoer*

【带头羊】bellwether

【带徒弟】train or take on an apprentice

【带信儿】take or bring a message

【带鱼】hairtail; ribbonfish

【带职】be absent from duty without relieving one's post：～学习 *go on a study course without being relieved of one's post* / ～培训 *in-service training*

【带子】belt; band; tape; ribbon

殆 [书] ① danger; defeat：危～ *be great dangerous* / 百战不～ *fight a hundred battles without danger of defeat* ② almost; nearly：～尽 *be almost wiped out*

贷 ① loan; credit：农～ *agricultural loan* / 信～ *credit* ② borrow or lend：他们从银行～款买的房子。*They bought the house by borrowing money from the bank.* ③ shirk; shift (responsibility) ④ forgive; mercy：严惩不～ *punish mercilessly*

【贷方】credit; credit side

【贷款】① provide a loan; grant a loan; extend credit：从银行～ *get a bank loan* ② loan; credit：低息～ *low-interest loan* / ～利率 *loan interest rate* / ～期限 *term of a loan*

待[1] ① treat; deal with：以礼相～ *treat with courtesy* / 真诚～人 *be sincere with people* ② entertain：～客 *entertain a guest*

待[2] ① wait for; await：～机行事 *wait for an opportunity to take actions* ② need：自不～言 *this goes without saying* ③ about to; going to：我正～上车，看到了她跑过来。*I was about to get on the train when I saw her running towards me.*

【待到】await; by the time; when：～山花烂漫时，她在丛中笑。*When the mountain flowers are in full bloom, she will smile in them.*

【待机】await the opportune moment; bide one's time：～而动 *wait for an opportunity to take actions*

【待价而沽】wait for the highest bid; watch the market to wait for the most favourable price

【待考】need checking：他所说的是否属实～。*Whether what he said is true or not need being checked.*

【待命】await orders：原地～ *stay at the former place to await orders*

【待人】the way one gets along with people：～处世 *the way one treats people and conducts oneself in society*

【待时而动】bide one's time; wait for the right moment to act

【待续】to be continued

【待业】wait for a job; wait for employment; unemployed：～青年 *youth waiting for a job* / ～人口 *unemployed population* / ～人员的增多是一个很大的社会问题。*The increasing of job-waiting people is a big social problem.*

【待遇】① treatment：政治～ *political treatment* / 第一流的～ *first-class treatment* ② pay; wages; salary; remuneration：这家公司的优厚～是他留下来

的主要原因。*The attractive salary of this company is the main reason of his stay.*
【待字】[书] not betrothed yet
怠 idle; slack; indolent: 倦 ~ *be tired*; *worn out* / 懈 ~ *be lax* (*or sluggish*)
【怠惰】idle; lazy; remiss; indolent
【怠工】slow down: go show
【怠慢】① cold-shoulder; slight; ignore deliberately: 是你太不礼貌了,不怪别人~你。*Don't blame others for their old shouldering; it's you who were so impolite.* ② used by a host to show his modesty: 太~了。*I'm afraid that I've been a poor host.*
袋 ① bag; pocket; pouch; sack: 布 ~ *cotton bay* / 衣 ~ *pocket* / 旅行 ~ *travelling bag* ② [量] 一~面粉 *a sack of flour* / 抽一~烟 *smoke a pipe*
【袋鼠】kangaroo
【袋装】in bags: ~咖啡 *coffee in bags*
【袋子】bag; packet; sack
逮 ① [书] reach: 力所不 ~ *beyond one's reach or power* / ~夜 *till night* ② arrest
see also dǎi
【逮捕】arrest; take into custody; commit to prison: 协约国要~并惩罚战犯。*Entente countries will arrest and punish the war criminals.*
戴 ① wear; put on: ~上围巾 *put on one's muffler* ② respect; esteem: 爱 ~ *love and respect* (*or esteem*) ③ (Dài) a surname
【戴高帽子】① wear a dunce's cap ② flatter; make compliment: 他的提升依赖于给领导~。*His promotion depended on flattering the leaders.*
【戴绿帽】be a cuckold; the husband whose wife has another or lover outside marriage
【戴帽子】be branded as; stigmatize
【戴罪立功】atone for one's crime by doing good deeds; make amends for one's wrong doing
黛 a dark pigment used by women in ancient times to paint their eyebrows
【黛蓝】dark blue
【黛绿】[书] dark green

dān

丹 ① red: ~砂 *cinnabar* ② pallet; powder
【丹顶鹤】red-crowned crane
【丹毒】【医】erysipelas
【丹凤眼】slanting eyes: 那个可爱的小姑娘长着一双~,两道柳叶眉。*The lovely girl is with slanting eyes and arched brows.*
【丹桂】【植】orange osmanthus
【丹麦】Denmark: ~人 *Dane* / ~语 *Danish*
【丹皮】root bark of the tree peony
【丹青】[书] red and green colours-painting: ~妙笔 *superb of a great master*
【丹田】pubic region: 气运~ *inhale a deep breath*
【丹心】loyal heart; loyalty

担 ① carry on a shoulder pole: ~水 *carry water with shoulder pole* ② take on: undertake: ~责任 *take on responsibility* / ~风险 *run risks*
see also dàn
【担保】guarantee; assure; vouch for: 出口信贷~ *export credit guarantee* / ~金 *bail*; *bond* / ~期 *period of guarantee* / ~人 *guarantor*; *guarantee* / ~信贷 *secured credit* / 我敢~玻璃是那群踢球的孩子打破的。*I assure you that the glass was broken by the children who played football just now.*
【担不是】take the blame; take on responsibility: 大家都有责任,不能让她一个人~。*All of us should be blamed and we won't put all the blame on her.*
【担待】① forgive; excuse ② take on responsibility: 你们不要管了,这事儿由他~。*Leave it alone and let him bear the responsibility.*
【担当】take on; undertake; assume: ~重任 *take on heavy responsibilities* / 这项工作你干不合适,应该由男孩子~。*You don't fit in with this work and it shouldn't do by boys.*
【担负】bear; shoulder; take on; be charged with: ~责任 *shoulder responsibility* / 手术费用将由他~。*He will pay for the operation.*
【担架】stretcher; litter: ~队 *stretcher team* / ~员 *stretcher bearer* / 他被护士用~从战场上抬了下来。*He was carried by nurses from battlefield on a stretcher.*
【担惊受怕】feel alarmed; remain in state of anxiety
【担任】assume office of; take charge of; hold the post of: ~会议主席 *be chairman of the meeting* / 谁~你们的班长? *Who is your monitor?*
【担心】worry; feel anxious: 不要为我~,我会照顾好自己的。*Don't worry about me; I will take good care of myself.*
【担忧】worry; be apprehensive; feel anxious: 国家的危难需要每个人来~。*The danger of the whole country need apprehensiveness of everybody.*
单[1] ① one; single ② odd: ~只鞋 *an odd shoe* ③ singly; solitary: 把药~独放着,以防误服。*Put the medicine in a certain place singly in case of drinking it carelessly.* ④ simple: 简~ *simple*; *uncomplicated* ⑤ thin; weak: 势~力薄 *weak in power* ⑥ unlined
单[2] only; alone: ~这点就可以给他定罪。*Only this point can declare him guilty.*
单[3] ① sheet: 床 ~ *bed sheet* ② list; bill: 菜 ~ *menu* / 名 ~ *name list* / 节目 ~ *playbill*
【单摆】【物】simple pendulum
【单板】veneer
【单帮】traveling trader working on one's own: 跑~ *travel around trading on one's own*
【单倍体】【生】monoploid; haploid
【单边】【经】unilateral: ~进口 *unilateral import* / ~贸易 *unilateral trade*
【单薄】① thin (of clothing) ② weak; frail; feeble: 你身体太~了。*You have such a poor physique.* ③ insubstantial; flimsy; thin: 论据~ *feeble argument* / 内容~ *insubstantial content*

【单产】yield of per unit area
【单车】[方] bicycle
【单程】one way: ~车票 *one-way ticket* / ~公车 *one-way bus*
【单纯】① pure; simple:思想~ *pure in mind*; *unsophisticated* /不要把事情想的那么~。*Don't think the matters so simply.* ② alone; purely; merely: ~追求个人利益 *pursue individual interests done*
【单纯词】【语】single-morpheme word
【单词】① individual word; word:背~ *memorize words* ② single-morpheme word
【单打】【体】singles:男子~ *men's singles* /他在羽毛球~中夺冠。*He won championship in men's singles of badminton.*
【单打一】① concentrate on one thing only ② have a one-track mind
【单单】only; alone:大家都同意了,~他有异议。*Everybody agreed except him.*
【单刀】① short-hilted broadsword ② single-broadsword ③ event
【单刀直入】speak out without beating about the right to the point; straight for ward:他们一坐下就~地进入了话题。*They came straight to the point as soon as they sat down*
【单调】monotonous; dull; drab; boring:生活~ *dull life* /色彩~ *dull colour*
【单独】alone; by oneself; independent; exclusive:我想和他~呆一会儿。*I want to stay with him alone.* /外出旅游时要听从导游的安排,不要~行动。*Submit yourselves to the tourist guide and don't take independent actions when travelling outside.*
【单发】【军】single shot: ~射击 *single shot*
【单方面】one-sided; unilateral: ~毁约 *break the promise unilaterally*
【单飞】【航】solo flight
【单峰驼】【动】one-humped camel; dromedary; Arabian camel
【单幅】【纺】single width
【单干】① work by oneself; work on one's own; do sth single-handed:这项工作靠你自己~是完不成的。*The work can't be finished on your own.* ② individual farming; farming: ~户 *a peasant family still farming on its own after agricultural cooperation*
【单杠】【体】① horizontal bar ② horizontal bar gymnastics
【单个儿】① alone; individually:天太晚了,不要~回去了。*It's too late and don't go back individually.* ② odd one:这球拍~卖吗? *Are rackets sold by the piece?*
【单轨】single track
【单号】odd numbers (of tickets, seats, etc.)
【单簧管】【音】clarinet
【单机】① single engine ② single computer unconnected with another
【单季稻】single harvest rice
【单价】【经】unit price ②【生】univalent
【单间儿】separate room or single room (in a hotel, restaurant, etc.)
【单脚跳】【体】hop
【单句】【语】simple sentence
【单据】receipt; bill; voucher; documents attesting to the giving or receiving of money, goods, etc.:货运~ *shipping documents* /核对~ *check the bill*
【单卡】single cassette deck
【单口相声】cross talk performed by one actor only
【单跨】【建】single span
【单利】【经】simple interest
【单恋】unrequited love; one-sided love
【单片机】single or one chip computer
【单枪匹马】single-handed; alone; by oneself:他~地闯入虎穴。*He rushed to the hazardous spot single-handed.*
【单亲】single parent:她在~家庭中长大,性格孤僻。*She grows up in one-parent family, which lead to her unsociable character.*
【单人床】single bed
【单人房】single room
【单人舞】solo dance:跳~ *dance a solo*
【单日】odd-number days (of the month)
【单弱】frail; feeble; weak and thin:她身体~,完不成这项任务。*She isn't able to finish the task for her fragile constitution.*
【单色】monochromatic: ~电视 *monochromatic television* / ~胶印机 *single-colour offset press*
【单身】① unmarried person; single person:你打算一辈子~吗? *Do you want to be single the whole life?* ② live alone; unaccompanied; not be with one's family: ~在外,一定要多加小心。*Living alone away from home, you must be careful.*
【单身汉】bachelor; single
【单生花】【植】solitary flower
【单声道】【物】single track
【单数】① odd number ②【语】singular number
【单线】【纺】monofilament
【单体】【化】monomer
【单位】① unit (as a standard of measurement):长度~ *unit of length* /重量~ *unit of weight* /货币~ *monetary unit* /以毫米为~计算 *measure by the millimeter* ② unit (as an organization, department, division, section, etc.):事业~ *institution* /企业~ *enterprise* /行政~ *administrative unit* /基层~ *basic unit*
【单位圆】【数】unit circle
【单位制】system of unit
【单细胞】single cell; unicellular: ~动物 *unicellular animal*
【单线】① single line ② one-way (contact); single-line (link):大部分地下工作人员都~联系。*Most of the people doing underground work had single-line contact with each other.* ③【交】single track: ~铁路 *single-track railway*
【单相思】unrequited love; one-sided love
【单向】one-way; unidirectional: ~电路 *one-way*

D

circuit / ~收费 *charge unidirectional*

【单项】【体】individual event: ~比赛 *individual competition*

【单行本】① separate volume (or edition) ② off-print

【单行道】one-way street:大都市里~很多。*There are many one-way streets in metropolis.*

【单性花】【植】unisexual flower

【单眼】simple eye

【单眼皮】single-fold eyelid

【单叶】【植】simple leaf

【单一】single; unitary; one-track:样式~ *unitary style* / ~汇率 *unitary exchange rate* / ~经济 *single-product economy* / ~税 *single tax*

【单衣】unlined garment

【单翼机】monoplane

【单音词】【语】monosyllabic word; monosyllable

【单元】① unit of teaching materials:今天讲第2~。*Today we will learn Unit 2.* ② residential unit: ~楼 *apartment building*; *block of flats* /他们家住三号楼五~四号。*They live in No 4, Entrance 5, Building 3.*

【单子】① list; bill; form:填~ *fill in a form* ② bed sheet:床~ *bed sheet*

【单字】① individual Chinese character ② separate word (of a foreign language)

耽[1] [书] abandon oneself to

耽[2] indulge in: ~于游乐 *indulge in pleasure*

【耽搁】① stop over; stay:赶快出发吧,不要在这儿~太久。*Set out as soon as possible and don't stop over here so long.* ② delay; detain; postpone:他昨天早上起太晚了,把考试~了。*He got up so late yesterday morning as to miss the examination.*

【耽误】delay; hold up:他的话毫无意义,简直是在~时间。*His words had no sense at all; simply he was wasting time.*

殚 [书] exhaust; use up; wear out: ~心 *demote oneself heart and soul to*

【殚精竭虑】make one's brains; meditate deeply on sth

dǎn

胆 ① gallbladder ② courage; bravery; boldness:壮~ *boost sb's courage*; *embolden* ③ a bladder-like container: ~胆 *glass loner of a thermos*

【胆大】bold; audacious: ~包天 *audacious in the extreme* / ~妄为 *act in foolhardy manner*; *reckless* / ~心细 *bold but cautious*; *be daring and scrupulous*

【胆敢】dare to; have the audacity to

【胆固醇】【生化】cholesterol

【胆寒】terrify; lose one's nerve; be struck with terror

【胆量】courage; guts; boldness; bravery; pluck: ~很大 *hare plenty of guts*

【胆略】courage and resourcefulness; mettle: ~过人 *have unusual courage and resourcefulness*

【胆囊】【生理】gallbladder: ~炎 *cholecystitis*

【胆怯】timid; cowardly; be afraid of one's own shadow:她生性~,不敢跟陌生人说话。*She was born with timidity and never dared to speak with strangers.*

【胆石】【医】cholelith; gallstone

【胆识】courage and insight; audacity: ~过人 *be with unusual courage and insight*

【胆酸】【生化】cholic acid

【胆小】timid; cowardly: ~怕事 *be timid and fear getting into trouble* / ~鬼 *coward*; *yellowbelly*

【胆小如鼠】as timid as a mouse; chicken-hearted

【胆战心惊】tremble with fear; horribly frightened; be panic-stricken:他做了亏心事,整天~。*He did unconscionable things and was terror-stricken all day long.*

【胆汁】【生理】bile

【胆子】courage; nerve; boldness:好大的~! *What a nerve!* /你~可真大,连领导都敢顶撞。*You have such a big nerve as to contradict the leader.*

掸 brush lightly; whisk dust: ~衣服 *bush the dust off one's clothes* /墙上的灰尘用鸡毛掸子才能~干净。*The wall can be dusted clean only by feather duster.*

【掸子】whisk or duster (usu. made of chicken feathers or strips of cloth):鸡毛~子 *feather duster*

dàn

石 [量] a unit of dry measure for grain

see also shí

旦[1] ①[书] dawn; daybreak:通宵达~ *all right till dawn*; *all through the night* ② day:元~ *New Year's Day*

旦[2] 【戏】a actress or female character type in opera

旦[3] 【纺】denier

【旦角儿】female character type in Chinese operas; role of female actress

【旦夕】[书] this morning or evening; in a short while; in a day's time:危在~ *in deadly peril*

【旦夕之间】between morning and evening; in a day's time

但 ① but; yet; still; nevertheless:虽然获得了很多荣誉,~他从不骄傲。*Although he has achieved so many honors, he is never arrogant.* ② merely; only: ~求无愧于心 *merely wish to have clear conscience*

【但凡】without exception; so long as; in every case: ~跟他熟悉的人,都欣赏他的性格。*Whoever acquaints himself with him admires his nature.*

【但是】but; yet; still; nevertheless:他虽然赢了,~很不光彩。*He won but he was unhonoured.*

【但愿】wish; hopefully; if only: ~明天别下雨。*If only it would not rain tomorrow.*

担 ① a unit of weight (=50 kilograms) ② shoulder-pole load:一~水 *two buckets of water (carried on a shoulder pole)* ③ carrying people and the loads on it; burden; load:重~ *heavy burden*

see also dān

【担担面】[方] a hot spicy noodle with peppery sauce as eaten in Sichuan

【担子】① a pole and the loads on it ② burden; load:日常工作的沉重~ *the heavy burden of daily work*

诞[1] ① birth ② birthday:华~ *glorious birthday*

诞[2] absurd; fantastic:荒~ *fantastic; incredible; absurd*

【诞辰】[书] birthday

【诞生】be born; come into being: ~地 *birthplace* / 新中国~于1949年10月。*New China was born in October, 1949.*

啖 [书] ① eat ② feed ③ entice; bait ④ (Dàn) a surname

淡 ① think; light:天高云~。*The sky is height and the clouds are pale.* ② tasteless; weak: ~酒 *weak wine* / ~菜 *food with very little salt* ③ (of colour) light; pale: ~黄色 *light yellow* / ~红 *pink* ④ indifferent; cool; unconcerned: ~然 *indifferently; coldly* ⑤ slack; dull: ~季 *slack season* ⑥ [方] meaningless; nonsense:扯~ *talk nonsense*

【淡泊】[书] living tranquilly without seeking fame and wealth:他一生~名利。*He was indifferent to fame and wealth through his life.*

【淡泊明志】live a simple life showing one's cool in life; live simply to express one's ambition

【淡薄】① thin; light:雾逐渐~了。*The mist thinned gradually.* ② become faint; dim; hazy: 随着时间的流逝,我对他的印象已渐渐~了。*My impression on him has become dim gradually as time goes on.* ③ tasteless; weak:酒味~。*The wine tastes weak.* ④ cold; indifferent:感情~ *be with distant relationship*

【淡出】fade out

【淡淡】① thin; light; slight; pale: ~的浮云 *thin floating clouds* / ~的远山 *distant mountains with haziness* ② cool; indifferent; unconcerned ③ [书] (of wares or ripples) undulating

【淡化】① desalination:海水~ *desalination of sea water* ② weaken: ~宗派思想 *weaken the idea of faction*

【淡季】off season; slack season:旅游~ *slack season for tourism* /争取做到蔬菜~不淡,旺季不烂。*Strike for an ample supply of vegetables in the off seasons and aroid waste in the peak periods.*

【淡漠】① indifferent; apathetic; aloof:他不关心集体,对什么事都很~。*He is not concerned about the collective and is indifferent to everything.* ② faint; dim:印象~ *hare a hazy impression*

【淡墨】light ink

【淡青】light greenish blue

【淡然】indifferent; coldly; unconcerned: ~处之 *treat sth indifferently*

【淡水】fresh water: ~鱼 *freshwater fish* / ~养殖 *freshwater aquaculture* / ~湖 *freshwater lake*

【淡忘】fade from one's memory:难过是没有用的,你要学着去~。*You should learn to fade it from your memory for sadness is of nonsense.*

【淡雅】simple but elegant; light; no strong:颜色~ *elegant colour* / ~的香气 *light fragrance*

【淡妆】be in light make-up

弹 ① ball; pellet:玻璃~儿 *little glass ball* ② bullet; bomb:手榴~ *grenade*

see also tán

【弹道】trajectory; path of projectile: ~弧线 *ballistic curve* / ~火箭 *ballistic rocket* / ~设计 *ballistic design* / ~学 *ballistic*

【弹弓】catapult; slingshot

【弹痕】bullet (or shot) mark: ~累累 *be covered with bullet marks*

【弹夹】charger; cartridge dip

【弹尽粮绝】run out of ammunition and provisions; exhaust one's supplies of food and ammunition

【弹壳】shell case; cartridge case

【弹坑】(shell) crater

【弹片】shell fragment; splinter; shrapnel

【弹膛】chamber (of a gun)

【弹头】bullet; warhead; projectile nose

【弹丸】① pellet; ball ② bullet; shot ③ [书] (of a place) very small or tiny: ~之地 *a tiny area; very small bit of land*

【弹药】ammunition: ~库 *ammunition depot; ammunition storehouse* / ~手 *ammunition man (or beaver)* / ~所 *ammunition supply point*

【弹子】① pallet shot from a slingshot ② marble:弹~ *play marbles* ③ [方] billiards: ~房 *billiards room*

蛋 ① egg ② an egg-shaped thing:泥~儿 *mud ball*

【蛋白石】【地】opal

【蛋白质】protein: ~工程 *protein engineering* / ~塑料 *protein plastics*

【蛋粉】egg powder; powdered egg

【蛋糕】cake

【蛋羹】egg custard

【蛋黄】yolk

【蛋鸡】layer; laying hen

【蛋壳】eggshell

【蛋清】egg white

【蛋用鸡】layer

氮 【化】nitrogen (N)

【氮肥】nitrogenous fertilizer

dāng

当[1] ① equal; match：门～户对 *be well-matched in social and economic status for marriage* ② ought to; should; must：他～负主要责任。*He should take the main responsibility.* ③ work as; serve as; be：民主选举后，他～了厂长。*He served as the factory after the democratic election.* ④ bear; deserve：你一定能～此重任。*You are sure to take on this heavy task.* ⑤ manage; be in charge of; direct：～家 *run the household* ⑥ face; in sb's presence：～着他面谈 *talk in his presence*

当[2] just at (a time or place)：～我进门时，她正在大扫除。*When I came in, she was doing some clearing.*

当[3] clang; sound of striking a bell：～的钟声 *the tolling of a bell*
see also dàng

【当班】be on duty; be on a shift; on turn：他每天～三个小时。*He is on duty for three hours everyday.*

【当兵】be a soldier; serve in the army

【当场】on the spot; then and there; in the act：～抓住 *be caught red-handed (or in the act)* / ～达成协议 *reach an agreement on the spot*

【当场出彩】make a spectacle of oneself; give the show away on the spot

【当初】originally; at that time; at beginning：经过认真考虑后，他改变了～的设计。*He changed the original design after deliberate consideration.* / 早知今日，何必～？*If you had know that it would come to this, you would not have acted the way you did.*

【当代】the present age; the contemporary era; in an epoch：～意识 *consciousness of the contemporary era* / 金庸是～著名作家。*Jin Youg is a famous contemporary writer.*

【当道】① block one's way：别～站着。*Don't stand in the way.* ②［贬］be in power; hold reins (or sway)：坏人～好人受害。*When scoundrels are in power, good people suffer.*

【当地】local; in the locality：～政府 *government of a locality* / ～时间 *local time* / ～的居民 *local inhabitants* / 这是～特产。*It's the special local product.*

【当断不断】fail to make a decision when one should; demur or be hesitant

【当机立断】decide quickly (or on the spot); make a decision promptly and opportunely：面对紧急情况，机长～地做了决定。*Facing the crisis, the aircraft commander made a prompt.*

【当即】immediately; at once; right away：～签订协约 *sign a treaty at once*

【当家】manage household affairs; manager：她～有道。*She has a right way to be a good housekeeper.* / 她是我们厂里的好～。*She is a good manager of our factory.*

【当家作主】be master in one's own house; be master of one's own affairs：社会主义社会人民～。*The people are the masters of their own country in socialism.*

【当街】① facing the street：～正建着一座高楼。*A tall building is constructed facing the street.* ②［方］in the street

【当今】nowadays; at present; now：和平与发展是～世界的两大主题。*Peace and development are the two major themes of the whole world now.*

【当局】① the authorities：政府～ *the government authorities* ② those involved：～者迷，旁观者清。*The spectators see the chess game better than the players — blundering are those concerned.*

【当空】high above in the sky：明月～。*A bright moon hangs in the sky.*

【当口儿】this or that very moment; just at this time：战斗紧张激烈的～援兵来了。*The reinforcements came at the very moment that the war was intense.*

【当啷】clang; clank

【当量】【化】equivalent (weight)：克～ *gram equivalent* / ～浓度 *equivalent concentration*

【当令】in season：现在穿这身衣服正～。*This clothing is just in season to be worn.*

【当面】to sb's face; in sb's presence; face to face：～说好话，背后下毒手。*Say nice things in sb's presence and stab him behind his back.*

【当年】① in those days：～他身强力壮。*In those years, he was very strong.* ② the prime of life：他正～。*He is in his prime.*

【当前】① at present; current：～的首要任务 *the prime task at present* ② the current international situation ③ before one; facing one：大敌～ *faced with formidable foe*

【当权】hold power, hold sway; be in power

【当然】① of course; certainly; without doubt：经理～应该为自己的员工负责。*The manager certainly should be responsible for his staff.* ② natural：～之事 *natural thing* / ～同盟 *natural ally* ③ natural; *ex officio*：～成员 *ex officio member*

【当仁不让】not decline to shoulder a responsibility; in good cause do not lag behind; take sth as one's obligation：该～的时候就不要谦让。*Don't modestly decline when you should take the responsibility as your obligation.*

【当时】then; at that time; for the moment：～我不在场。*I was not on the spot at that time.*

【当事】① be in charge; exercise control：坏人～好人倒霉。*When bad people exercise control, good people suffer.* ② concerned ③ agent; authorities or parties concerned

【当事国】the country (or state) directly involved

【当事人】①【律】party (to a lawsuit); litigant ② agent concerned; person (or party) involved; interested party：～应该出来解决问题。*The per-*

son concerned should come out to solve the problem.

【当头】① head on; right overhead: ~一棒 *a head-on blow* /烈日~。*The hot sun is right overhead.* ② imminent; facing or confronting one: 国难~。*The country was faced with an imminent disaster.*

【当头棒喝】a blow and a shout — give a sharp warning to sb

【当头炮】direct attack or criticism

【当务之急】pressing demand of the moment; argent matter: ~是把局面控制住。*To control the whole situation is the top priority at present.*

【当下】at owe; instantly; immediately: 他一见这场面,~就愣住了。*He stared blankly instantly seeing the scene.*

【当下手】be assistant or subordinate of sb; serve sb by doing unimportant things: 今天我掌勺,你给我~。*Today I will cook and you serve as my assistant.*

【当先】be in vanguard; at the head; in the front ranks: 奋勇~ *fight bravely in the van*

【当心】be careful; be ware of: 路上~点。*Be careful on the road.* /~别踩着小麦。*Take care not to step on the wheat.*

【当选】be elected: 市长以多数票~。*The mayor was elected by a majority vote.*

【当一天和尚撞一天钟】toll the bell as long as one is a monk — take a passive attitude towards one's work; do as little as possible

【当政】be in power; hold sway; be in office

【当之无愧】be worthy of; fully deserve (a title, an honour, etc.); deserve the reward: 受到表扬,他~。*He fully deserved the praise.*

【当中】① in the middle; in the centre: 这座城市~是一条河。*Arriver flows in the middle of the city.* ② among: 校长站在同学们~讲的话。*The president made a speech among the students.*

【当众】in public; in open court; in everyone's presence: ~表态 *take a public stance* / ~宣布判决 *declare the court decision in public*

【当众出丑】make an exhibition of oneself

裆 ① crotch (of trousers); rise ②【生理】crotch

dǎng

挡[1] ① get in the way of; block; keep off: 一辆大卡车~住了我们的去路。*A big truck blocked our way.* ② shelter: 遮风~雨 *shelter sb from wind and rain* /谁站在窗口~着亮了? *Who stood in front of the window and block the light?*

挡[2] ① fender; blind: 炉~儿 *fire screen* /窗~子 *window blind (or shade)* ② gear: 前进~ *forward gear* /高速~ *top gear* /挂~ *put into gear*

【挡车】【纺】operate a number of textile machines and check the quantity and quality of products: ~工 *loom tender*

【挡驾】turn away a visitor with some excuse

【挡箭牌】shield; pretext; excuse; pretense: 他以腿疼为~不参加劳动。*He didn't go to labour on the pretext that his leg ached.*

【挡泥板】mudguard; fender

【挡土墙】【建】retaining wall

党 ① party; political party: 执政~ *ruling party* ② the Party (the communist party of China): 向~靠拢 *draw close to the Party* ③ clique; faction; gang ④[书] be partial to; take sides with ⑤[书] kinsfolk; relatives: 父~ *father's kinsfolk* ⑥ (Dǎng) a surname

【党报】party newspaper (or organ)

【党费】party membership dues

【党风】style of party work; conduct of Party members: 加强~建设 *strengthen the construction of Party's work style*

【党纲】party programme

【党籍】party membership: 开除~ *expel from the Party*

【党纪】party discipline: ~国法 *party discipline and state laws*

【党课】party lecture; party class: 上~ *attend a party lecture*

【党魁】[贬] party boss (or chieftain)

【党龄】party standing: ~要从预备期算起。*Party standing should count from the probationary period.*

【党派】party; political parties and groups; party groupings: ~关系 *party affiliation* / ~政治 *party politics*

【党旗】party flag

【党人】members of a political party; partisan

【党徒】① follower; member of a clique or reactionary political party ② henchman

【党委】Party committee

【党务】party work; party activities; party affairs

【党小组】Party group

【党校】Party school

【党性】Party spirit; Party character: ~纯正 *have a pure Party spirit*

【党羽】[贬] adherents; henchmen; members of a clique

【党员】party member: ~要起带头作用。*The party member should take the leading role in everything.*

【党章】party constitution

【党证】party card; membership card

【党政分工】separation of Party work and government work

【党支部】Party branch

【党中央】Central Committee of the Party; Party Centre: 紧密团结在~周围 *unite closely around Central Committee of the Party*

【党总支】general Party branch

dàng

当[1] appropriate; prop; right:只要措施得~就没问题。*There are no problems if you take the right measure.*

当[2] ① match; be equal to:以一~十 *pat one against ten* ② regard as; treat as; take for ③ think:你做的那些事不要~我不知道。*Don't think that I haven't known what you did.* ④ pawn:把房子~了 *pawn one's house*

当[3] ① sth pawned; pawn; pledge:赎~ *redeem sth pawned* ② that very (day, year, etc.)
see also dāng

【当成】regard as; consider as; treat as; take for:他把谬论~了真理。*He considered the fallacy as truth.*

【当年】the same year; that very year:这个新建的厂子~就收回了投资。*This newly built factory regained the investment that very year.*

【当票】pawn ticket

【当铺】pawnshop: ~老板 *pawnbroker*

【当日】the same day; that very day:你可以~来回。*You may take a one-day round trip.*

【当时】right away; at once; immediately:那个公司~就签约雇佣了她。*The company signed the contract with her right away.*

【当天】the same day; that very day:他~就走了。*He went back that very day.*

【当真】① take seriously; accept as true:他只是开个玩笑而已,不用~。*Don't take it seriously; he was only making a joke.* ② really; really true:几天后,他~给我送来了一盆水仙花。*Several days later, he really brought me a basin of narcissus.*

【当作】treat as ;regard as; look upon as:他被~有能力的律师。*He is regarded as a capable lawyer.*

宕 [书] delay:延~ *procrastinate; postpone*

荡[1] ① swing; sway; move; wave: ~秋千 *play on a swing* /一片叶子在水中飘~。*A leaf was drifting on water surface.* ② loaf:游~ *loaf about* ③ rinse; wash; wash away:涤~ *wash away* ④ clear away: sweep off:倾家~产 *lose family fortune*

荡[2] loose in morals; licentious in conduct:淫~ *licentious; lewd; lascivious*

荡[3] shallow lake; marsh:芦苇~ *a reed marsh*

【荡涤】[书] cleanse; clean up; wash away:他的一番话~了人们心灵上的污秽。*What he said cleansed the human mind of all its spiritual filth.*

【荡妇】[书] ① vamp; woman of licentious in conduct ② prostitute

【荡气回肠】heartrending; soul-stirring

【荡然无存】all gone; with nothing left; be fully dissipated

【荡漾】ripple; undulate:一叶扁舟在湖面~。*A small boat was rippling on the lake.* /春天来了,柳枝随风~。*Spring comes and willow branches ripple in the breeze.*

档 ① shelves (for files); pigeonholes:归~ *file a document; place on file* ② files; archives:查~ *consult the files* ③ crosspiece (of a table, etc.) ④ grade; order:低~产品 *low-grade products*

【档案】files; record; dossier; archives: ~室 *archives room* / ~馆 *archives* / ~柜 *filing cabinet*

【档次】grade grading:在企业内部,要扩大工资差额,拉开~。*An enterprise should expand the difference of income among workers.*

dāo

刀 ① knife; sword:菜~ *kitchen knife* /军~ *saber* ②【机】culling tool:车~ *lathe tool* ③ sth shaped like a knife:冰~ *ice skates* ④ [量] one hundred sheets of paper ⑤ (Dāo) a surname

【刀把子】① handle (or hilt) of a knife ② things that may be used against sb; handle ③ military power; power: ~攥在他手里,穷人上哪里说理去。*He controlled the power and the poor had no place to be judged between right and wrong.*

【刀背】back of a knife blade

【刀兵】① weapons; arms:动~ *resort to arms* ② fighting; war: ~之战 *disaster of war*

【刀叉】knife and fork

【刀锋】knife point or edge: ~锐利。*The edge of the knife is sharp.*

【刀耕火种】slash-and-burn cultivation: ~的年代没有文明。*No civilization existed during the period of slash-and-burn cultivation.*

【刀光剑影】the glint and flash of cold steel — heated combat

【刀痕】mark or scar left by a knife-cut

【刀架】【机】tool carrier; tool past

【刀口】① edge of a knife ② crucial point; where it is needed most; right place where a thing can be put to best use; right spot:把劲儿使在~上。*Do efforts on the crucial point.* /钱要花在~上。*Spend your money where it is needed most.* ③ cut; incision: ~化脓了。*The cut festered.*

【刀片】① razor blade ②【机】bit blade

【刀枪】sword and spear; weapon: ~入库 *put the weapons back in the arsenal*

【刀枪不入】neither swords nor spears can penetrate; (of a human body) invincible

【刀鞘】sheath; scabbard

【刀刃】① edge of a knife ② crucial point; where it is needed most

【刀山火海】mountain of swords and sea of fire — an extremely dangerous place which is difficult to get through:那是~,你也敢闯? *It's a most dangerous place; dare you go?*

【刀伤】knife wound; stab; gash

【刀子嘴,豆腐心】[口] (have) a sharp tongue but a soft hear

叨

see also tāo

【叨叨】talk on and on; chatter like a magpie:她也不嫌累,整天一个人~不停。*She is not worried about tiredness and talks on and on all day long.*

【叨唠】[口] talk on and on; chatter away; babble: 你在~些什么? *what are you babbling?*

dǎo

导 ① lead; guide:领~ *lead; leader* / ~入正途 *lead sb to the right direction* ② teach; instruct; direct:教~ *instruct; teach* /辅~ *coach; tutor* ③ transmit; conduct: ~电 *conduct electricity* / ~热 *conduct heat*

【导播】a special person who instructs performance and supervises the whole programme in TV station

【导弹】guided missile:防空~ *antiaircraft missile* / 远程~ *long-range missile* /地对空~ *ground-to-air missile* / ~防御系统 *Missile Defense System* / ~部队 *missile force* / ~跟踪船 *missile-tracking vessel* / ~核潜艇 *nuclear submarine armed with guided missiles* / ~基地 *missile base* / ~系统 *guided missile system*

【导电】conduct electricity; electric conduction: ~性能 *electric conductivity* / ~率 *conductivity*

【导读】give guidance to reading

【导风板】【航】baffle

【导购】provide guidance for purchase: ~小姐 *sales girl; shopping guide*

【导管】①【机】conduit; pipe; duct:冷却~ *cooling duct* /金属~ *metal conduit* ②【生】vessel; duct

【导轨】【机】slideway; guide; guide way: ~磨床 *slideway grinder*

【导航】navigation; path finding: 天文~ *celestial navigation* / ~灯 *range lights* / ~台 *navigation station; no direction radio beacon (NDB)*

【导火线】① (blasting) fuse ② direct cause; a small indent that touches a big one:战争的~ *an incident that touches off the war* /整个事件的~ *direct cause of the whole event*

【导轮】【机】guide pulley; pilot wheel

【导论】introduction; introductory remarks

【导尿】【医】catheterization

【导热】【物】conduct heat; heat conduction: ~性能 *capacity of heat conduction* / ~系数 *thermal conductivity*

【导师】① tutor; teacher; supervisor:研究生~ *supervisor of postgraduate* ② leader of a cause; mentor teacher:革命~ *mentor of a revolution*

【导数】【数】derivative

【导体】【物】conductor

【导线】【电】conducting wire; lead: ~管 *conduit*

【导向】① lead to:这次会谈~两个地区的经济合作。*The talks led to the cooperation of the two areas.* ② direction of guiding; orientation:舆论~ *orientation of public opinion*

【导言】introduction; introductory remarks; preface

【导演】① direct (a film, play etc.):他~过许多故事片。*He directed many feature films.* ② director

【导游】① conduct a sightseeing tour:谁将为我们~? *Who will guide us in the tour?* ② tour guide: ~证书 *tourist guide certificate*

【导源】① river rises in; have a source in (of a river):黄河~于青海。*The Yellow River rises in Qinghai Province.* ② originate; derive:成功~于勤奋。*Success derives from diligence.*

【导致】lead to; bring about; result in; cause:小过失~了大悲剧。*A small fault led to a large tragedy.* /什么~了二战发生? *what resulted in world war* Ⅱ?

岛 island

【岛国】island nation; country consisting of one or more islands

【岛屿】islands; islands and islets

捣 ① beat with a pestle etc.; pound: ~米 *husk rice with a pestle and mortar* / ~蒜 *pound garlic into pulp* /用胳膊肘~某人 *nudge sb with elbow* ② cause trouble; create a disturbance

【捣蛋】make trouble:这孩子从小就调皮~。*The child was always making trouble when he was very young.*

【捣动】① turn over ②[方] incite; instigate; stir up

【捣鼓】[方] fiddle with; move back and forth; meddle with:手表被他~坏了。*My watch didn't work because of his meddling.*

【捣鬼】play tricks; sow discord; do mischief:这件事情办不成,肯定是有人在里面~。*There must be someone doing mischief which can explain the failure of the work.*

【捣毁】destroy; break down; smash up

【捣乱】make trouble; disturb; stir up a row: ~现状的提问 *question disturbing present conditions* / 你别跟我~了,我现在正忙着呢。*I'm busy now; Don't disturb me.*

【捣碎】pound to pieces

倒[1] ① fall; topple:摔~ *fall down* /我的自行车被撞~了。*My bicycle was run down.* ② fail; collapse; be on the decline; bankrupt:那家公司~了。*This company went bankrupt.* ③ (of voice) become hoarse:嗓子~了 *lose one's voice*

倒[2] ① change; exchange: ~座位 *swap (or charge) seats* / 你在哪儿~车? *Where did you change the bus?* ② sell out:把铺子~给别人 *sell the shop out to others* ③ move around:你该换个大房子了,这屋子连身儿都~不开。*It's time for you to buy a bigger house; there is no place to move around in this room.*

see also dào

D

【倒把】engage in speculation and profiteering; speculate:投机~ *speculate and profiteer*
【倒班】change shifts; work in shifts; work by turns:昼夜~ *work in shifts round the clock* /他和我~,以便能参加儿子的毕业典礼。*He changed shifts with me so as to attend the commencement of his son.*
【倒闭】go bankrupt; close down:这家银行~了。*This bank wont bankrupt.*
【倒毙】fall down and die; drop dead: ~街头 *drop deal in the street*
【倒戈】change sides in the war; transfer one's allegiance; defect: ~卸甲 *lay down arms to switch sides in a war*
【倒换】① take turns; rotate: ~着照顾病人 *take turns to look after the patient* ② rearrange (sequence, order, etc.); replace: ~位置 *exchange seats*
【倒汇】deal illegally in foreign currency
【倒卖】scalp; resell at a profit; speculate: ~文物 *scalp historical objects*
【倒霉】have bad luck; unlucky; be out of luck:是你自己不努力,不要怨自己~。*You didn't have bad luck, just because you didn't pay out enough efforts.*
【倒手】① change hands (of merchandise, etc.): 他把房子~给了朋友。*This house changed hands from him to his friend.* ② shift from one hand to the other:皮箱太重,我在路上倒了把手。*The leather suitcase was so heavy that I shifted it from one hand to the other on the way.*
【倒塌】collapse; fall down; topple
【倒台】fall from power; collapse
【倒腾】[口] ① rummage; move; shift:要下雨了,赶紧把粮食~到屋里。*It is to rain carry the grain into the house quickly.* ② replace; exchange; rearrange:人手少,事情多,~不开。*It is hard to cope, with so few hands and so much to do.* ③ rend; buy in and sell out; trade in:他~古董。*He trades in antique.*
【倒头】touch the pillow; lie down: ~便睡 *tumble into bed; fall asleep quickly as soon as one touches the pillow*
【倒胃口】lose one's appetite; spoil appetite:这顿饭真让我~。*The dinner spoiled my appetite.* /她的打扮让人看了~。*What she dressed disgusted people infinitely.*
【倒休】take a work day off in exchange of a holiday
【倒爷】profiteer; wheeler-dealer
【倒运】①[方] have bad luck; unlucky; be out of luck ② transport goods for trade by buying cheap and selling dear
【倒账】bad debt

祷 ① pray:祈~ *pray; say one's prayers* ②[旧] ask earnestly
【祷告】pray; say one's prayers
【祷文】prayer

蹈 ①[书] tread; step:赴汤~火 *jump into the water and walk through fire — be ready to risk one's own life* /循规~矩 *follow the usual rules and regulations* ② skip; trip:手舞足~ *dance for joy*
【蹈袭】follow slavishly; imitate; copy: ~前人 *follow predecessors slavishly*

dào

到[1] ① arrive; reach:飞机半夜~北京。*The airplane will arrive in Beijing at midnight.* ② go to; leave for:你要~哪去? *Where are you going?* ③ used as the complement of a verb to show the result of an action:说~做~ *put words into deeds* /我一定能做到。*I'm sure to do it.*

到[2] up till; up to:截止~现在 *up to now; so far* /学~老 *study up to the old age* /从小~大排列 *put in order from small one to big one*

到[3] thoughtful; considerate:他想得很周~。*What he thought was attentive and satisfactory.*

【到岸价格】【经】cost, insurance and freight(CIF)
【到场】be present; turn up; show up:上尉~后,士兵们肃静了。*The soldiers came to silence when the captain showed up.*
【到处】at all places; everywhere; about: ~找人帮忙 *look for persons for help everywhere* /厂长陪客人~参观。*The factory director showed the guests up everywhere.*
【到达】arrive; reach; get to: ~目的地 *arrive at the destination* /客人~后,跟我打声招呼。*Warn me when the guest reaches here*
【到底】① through; to the end:贯彻~ *carry out (or implement) to the end* ② at last; finally; in the end:事情~成功了。*It succeeded in the end.* ③ on earth:你~是怎样算出那道题的? *How did you work the question out on earth?* ④ after all: ~还是女人心细。*The woman was scrupulous after all.*
【到顶】reach the summit; reach peak performance; can't be improved
【到会】attend a meeting; be present at a meeting: 数一下~人员。*Count the person present at the meeting.*
【到家】① get home; arrive home:他傍晚时才~。*He arrived home at dusk.* ② reach a very high level; be perfect:她的表演还不~。*Her performance is far from perfect.*
【到来】arrival; advent:新世纪的~ *arrival of the new century* /暴风雨即将~。*The rainstorm will arrive soon.*
【到期】become due; terminate; expire; mature: ~协议 *mature agreement* /合同已经~了。*The contract has expired now.*
【到任】take office; assume a post; arrive at one's post

【到手】in one's hands; come into one's possession: ~的肥肉 *fatty meat in possession*
【到头】to the end; at an end:顺着这条路走~,就是他家。*His home is situated at the end of this street.*
【到头来】finally; in the end; ultimately:他很懒惰,~导致了期末考试的不及格。*He was very lazy which led to his failure in the final exam.*
【到位】reach the designated place; be in position
【到职】take office; assume a post; assume a post; arrive at one's post
倒[1] ① put upside down; be inverted; inverse: 把照片拿~了 *hold the photograph upside down* /这两个数字的次序~了。*The order of the two numbers is reversed.* ② reverse; move backward: ~椅子 *back a chair* ③ pour out; tip; empty: ~杯水 *pour a glass of water* / ~垃圾 *dump rubbish*
倒[2] ① on the contrary; instead:妹妹~比姐姐高。*On the contrary, the younger sister is taller than her elder sister.* ② indicating unexpectedness:我~要听听他的意见。*I'd like to hear his opinion.* ③ indicating concession:质量~挺好,就是价钱贵点。*The quality is fine, but it's a little expensive.* ④ indicating the notion that the matter is not as one thinks:你说得~简单,你试试看。*It's easy to say; you may try to do it.* ⑤ indicating an urging or questioning:你~说说看。*We'll hear what you are to say.*
see also dǎo
【倒背如流】recite a passage backward fluently — know sth thoroughly by heart
【倒背手】with one's hands behind one's hand:校长~走进了教室。*The headmaster entered the classroom with his hands behind his back.*
【倒不如】it would be better to
【倒彩】booing; hooting; catcall:喝~ *make catcalls*
【倒插门】(of a man) marry into and live with one's bride's family
【倒车】back a car:这地方太窄了不好~。*This place is too narrow to back the car.*
【倒春寒】abnormal coldness after spring comes
【倒打一耙】recriminate; put the blame on the victim; make false countercharges:我帮了她她反而~陷害我。*I helped her but she recriminated to frame me.*
【倒挡】reverse gear
【倒飞】【航】inverted or upside down flight
【倒灌】flow backward; reverse flow; (of sea water or flood) flow from a lower to a higher level:海水~ *reverse flow of sea water*
【倒立】① stand upside down:树的影子~在水中。*The tree is reflected upside down in the water.* ②【体】handstand
【倒流】flow backwards; flow up stream: 河水~ *flowing backwards of the river water* /污水~进入房屋。*They drain water flew back into the house.*
【倒赔】lose money instead of making money; sustain losses in business
【倒数】(dàoshǔ) count backwards; count in reverse order: ~第一行能看清吗? *Can you see the first line from the bottom clearly?* /期末考试他考了~第一。*He ranked the last one in the final exam.*
【倒数】(dàoshù)【数】reciprocal
【倒锁】be locked in by sb from the outside:他被敌人~在屋子里。*He was locked in by the enemies.*
【倒贴】① pay instead of making a profit:不但没赚,反而~了两千元。*I lost 2,000 yuan instead of making any profit.* ② (of a woman) keep a gigolo; pay for the up keep for her paramour
【倒退】go backwards; fall back; retrogression: ~到上个世纪的一个事件 *an event back to the last century* /在许多问题上公开~ *retrogress in many problems publicly* /他哆嗦着从门口~了出去。*He went backwards out the door with tremble.*
【倒行逆施】try to turn the wheel of history back; attempt to go against the trend of history; do sth in a perverse way:法西斯的~最终受到了历史的惩罚。*The perverse acts of the Fascists was finally punished by history.*
【倒许】perhaps; maybe:你要的鞋子这家商店没有,另一家~会有。*This store sells the shoes you want; maybe another store will do.*
【倒叙】flashback; cutback
【倒悬】[书] be in sore straits as hanging by the feet
【倒因为果】reverse cause and effect; take cause for effect
【倒影】inverted image; inverted reflection in water
【倒置】place sth upside down; invert:本末~ *put the cart before the horse* / ~发动机 *inverted engine*
【倒转】reverse; on the contrary; turn the other way round: ~来说,他的话也有一定道理。*What he said was some reasonable the other way round.*
【倒装】【语】inversion: ~词序 *inverted word order*
盗 ① steal; rob; filch, burgle:那家超市昨晚被~。*The supermarket was stolen last night.* ② thief; robber; bandit:强~ *robber*; *bandit*
【盗版】illegal copy; pirate copy; piracy: ~书籍 *pirate copy of a book* / ~影碟 *pirated video disc* /严厉打击~行为。*Strike the action of piracy severely.*
【盗伐】fell trees illegally; stealthily cut down trees: ~森林 *fell trees of a forest unlawfully*; *illicit logging*
【盗匪】robber; bandit; mobster
【盗汗】【医】night sweat
【盗卖】steal and sell to gain ill-gotten property: ~文物 *steal and sell historical objects*
【盗墓】rob a tomb: ~人 *grave robber*
【盗窃】steal: ~企业机密文件 *steal the secret files of an enterprise* / ~犯 *thief* / ~罪 *larceny*; *robbery*; *theft*
【盗用】embezzle; usurp: ~公款 *defalcate*; *embez-*

zle public funds / ～他人名义 *usurp the name of others*

【盗贼】robber; bandit; thief; embezzler

悼 mourn; grieve: 哀～ *lament*; *mourn*

【悼词】memorial speech

【悼念】mourn for; grieve over: ～死者 *mourn for the deceased*; *grieve over sb's death*

道[1] ① way; road; path: 能告诉我去火车站的～儿怎么走吗? *Can you tell me the way to the railway station*? ② course; channel: 河～ *course of a river* ③ way; orientation; method: 养生之～ *way to keep fit* ④ doctrine; principle ⑤ Taoism; Taoist: ～教 *Taoism* / ～士 *Taoist priest* ⑥ superstitious sect ⑦ line: 画一条～儿当界限。*Draw a line to be the boundary*

道[2] ① for long and narrow objects: 一～小溪 *a small stream* / ～线 *line* / 一～彩虹 *a rainbow* ② used for obstacles such as doors, walls, etc.: 过两～门 *pass through two doors* / 落二～幕 *ring down the second curtain* ③ for orders, questions, etc.: 一～命令 *an order* / 一～公文 *an official document* / 两～算术题 *two art arithmetic questions* ④ used for stages in a procedure, etc.: 一～手续 *one procedure* / 还有一～菜 *have one more course*

道[3] ① say talk; speak: 能说会～ *have the gift of gab*; *be good at good at expressing oneself* / 说三～四 *make thoughtless comments* ② say (usu. used in the words quoted): 她说～: "跟我们一起走吧。" *She said.* "*Let's go together.*" ③ express: ～谢 *thanks* ④ think; suppose: 我～是谁呢, 原来是你。*Oh it's you*; *I thought it was somebody else.*

【道白】spoken parts or lines in an opera

【道别】① say goodbye and leave; bid farewell: 依依不舍地～ *say goodbye reluctantly* ② say goodbye before setting out on a journey: 一清早他来跟我～。*Early in the morning he came to say goodbye to me.*

【道岔】switch; points

【道场】① Taoist or Buddhist rites (performed to save the souls of the dead) ② place where the Taoist or Buddhist rites are performed

【道道儿】[方] way; idea; method: 发财的～ *a way to get rich* / 他说不出个～来。*He can't give a convincing explanation.*

【道德】morals; ethics; morality: ～败坏 *morally degenerate* / ～标准 *moral standards* / 职业～ *professional ethics* / 商业～ *business ethics* / 作为校长, 他要求在学校里保持高的～标准和礼貌规矩。*As a president*, *he asked for high moral standards and polite rules in school yard.*

【道高一尺, 魔高一丈】as virtue rises one foot, vice vises ten; the good is strong, but the evil is ten times stronger; the more illumination, the more temptation

【道姑】Taoist num

【道观】Taoist temple

【道号】Taoist name

【道贺】congratulate; offer congratulations: ～他儿子毕业。*Congratulate him on his son's graduation.*

【道家】Taoist school (a school of thought in the spring and Autumn and Warring States periods); Taoists

【道教】【宗】Taoism (as a religion)

【道具】stage property; pro

【道理】① truth; principle; hows and whys: 跟他讲解物理学的～ *explain the principle of physics to him* ② reason; argument: 他的话似乎很有～。*What he said seems quite reasonable.* / 跟这种人没有～可讲。*It's impossible to reason with such a person.*

【道路】road; way; path: 修一条平坦的～ *repair a level road* / 铺平～ *pave the way for* / 为企业发展肃清～ *clear the way for the development of enterprise* / 小心点, 前面的～崎岖不平。*Be careful*; *the road in front is rugged.*

【道貌岸然】be sanctimonious; appearance of man of dignity and integrity; pose as a person of high morals: 他看上去～, 实际上是个伪君子。*He, who posed as a person of high morals, was a sanctimonious hypocrite in fact.*

【道袍】Taoist robe

【道破】point out frankly; lay sth bare; reveal sb's secret: 一语～天机 *lay the secret bare with one mark*

【道歉】apologize to; make an apology: 他因为迟到而向女主人～。*He apologized to the hostess for his lateness*

【道士】Taoist priest

【道听途说】hearsay; pick up what has been heard on the way; rumour: 那是他～来的, 不可信。*That is only his hearsay, and is not to be taken seriously.*

【道谢】express one's thanks; thank

【道义】morality and justice: ～上的支持 *moral support*

稻 rice; paddy: 水～ *paddy* / 旱～ *upland rice*

【稻苞虫】rice plant skipper

【稻草】rice straw: ～人 *scarecrow*

【稻谷】paddy; rice

【稻糠】rice chaff

【稻烂秧】seedling blight of rice

【稻螟虫】rice borer

【稻穗】rice ear

【稻田】paddy; rice field: ～养鱼 *fish culture in rice fields*

【稻秧】rice seedlings; rice shoots

【稻种】rice seeds

【稻子】rice; paddy

dé

得[1] ① get; obtain; gain: ～奖 *win a prize* /这次比赛谁～了冠军? *Who won championship in the competition?* ② (of a calculation) result in; be equal to:三三～九。*Three multiplied by three is nine.* ③ fit; proper; suit:这种钢笔很～用。*This kind of pen is suitable for use.* ④[书] satisfied; complacent ⑤[口] be finished; be ready: 饭～了。*Dinner is ready.*

得[2] [口] ① used to express one's approved or prohibition: ～了,说定了。*OK! That's settled then.* / ～了,我知道了。*That's enough; I know it.* ② (used to express one's helplessness) look: ～,又算错了。*Look! I've calculate it wrong again!*

see also de; děi

【得便】when it's convenient; when somebody is free: ～请到我办公室来一下。*Come to my office when you're free.*

【得病】become (or fall) ill; contract a disease:他得了传染病,被隔离了。*He was isolated for his contagious disease.*

【得不偿失】gain can't make up for losses:他开垦了一块～的荒地。*He reclaimed a wasteland in which he lost more than he gained.*

【得逞】[贬] succeed; have one's way; accomplish in an evil purpose:他们扰乱社会治安的阴谋未～。*Their plot to throw the society into disorder fell through.*

【得宠】[贬] be in sb's good graces:她在老师面前很～。*She is in her teacher's good graces.*

【得出】reach (a conclusion); obtain; arrive; confirm (a calculation):你最后～的结论是错误的。*The final conclusion you came to was wrong.* / ～计算结果了吗? *Have you confirmed the answer after calculation?*

【得寸进尺】give sb an inch and he wants a yard; be insatiable

【得当】befitting; proper; suitable: ～的措施 *proper measures* /措辞～ *properly worded*

【得到】get; obtain; attain; receive: ～允许 *get permission* /病人在医院里～了很好的照料。*The patients were taken good care of in hospital.*

【得道多助,失道寡助】a just cause enjoys abundant support while an unjust cause finds little

【得法】in the proper way; be properly done; get the knack:他用这把锯很～。*He had a proper way to use this saw.*

【得分】score:连得三分 *win three points in a row* /他在发球时～。*He scored in serving the ball.*

【得过且过】muddle along; let things drift:你该结束～的生活了。*It's time for you to stop the life of muddling along.*

【得计】succeed in one's scheme:他们夺取对政治控制权的阴谋未～。*They failed in their scheme to seize the control of the state.*

【得奖】win a prize; be awarded a prize: ～者 *prizewinner* /她在演讲比赛中～。*She won a prize in the lecture competition.*

【得劲】① feel well:近来腿脚～。*I haven't been feeling well in legs and feet recently.* ② fit for use; handy:改进后的工具用起来很～。*The tools improved fit for very use.*

【得救】be saved; be rescued:被洪水围困的村民～了。*The villagers besieged by flood were rescued.*

【得空】be at leisure; be free: ～我一定去拜访您。*I am sure to call on you when I'm free.*

【得了】① used to express a suggestion:你走～,不用管我。*You just go and don't worry about me.* ② that's enough; hold it: ～,我知道你又在吹牛。*Well! I know you are boasting again.*

【得力】① benefit from; get help from: ～于日常积累 *benefit from daily accumulation* ② capable; competent: ～助手 *capable assistant*

【得人心】popular; be supported or beloved by the people:经理的讲话很～。*What the manager said was very popular among staff.*

【得胜】succeed; triumph; win a victory:旗开～ *win first engagement; win speedy success*

【得失】① gain and loss; success and failure; acquire and lose:不计较个人～ *care little about personal gains and losses* ② advantages and disadvantages; merits and demerits:两种措施各有～。*Each of the two measures has its advantages and disadvantages.*

【得势】[贬] be in power; get the upper hard

【得手】succeed in; go smoothly; come off:做买卖～ *go smoothing in the business*

【得体】appropriate; proper; befitting one's position:话讲得很～ *speak properly*

【得天独厚】be rich in natural resources; abound in gifts of nature; be richly endowed by nature:这里是～的葡萄种植区。*This area enjoys the special favour of nature to plant grapes.*

【得悉】hear of; learn about: ～你平安抵达后,我才会放心。*I will feel relieved if I hear of your safe arrival.*

【得闲】be free; be at leisure

【得心应手】① masterly; with facility; with high proficiently:他对英语的学习～。*He is in his element in English study.* ② 毕竟还是自己的笔用得～。*After all a pen of one's own writes very well.*

【得宜】appropriate; proper; suitable:处理～ *deal with a problem properly*

【得以】so that... can (may)...:充分发扬民主,使每个人的意见～发表出来。*Carry democracy on fully, thus everyone can express his (or her) opinion.*

【得益】benefit from; profit:老师的教导,使学生们～匪浅。*These students benefited a lot from the teacher's instruction.*

【得意】proud of oneself; complacent:这点成就,不值得～。*Such inconspicuous achievements were not worth your complacence.*

【得意忘形】feel dizzy with success; be intoxicated by one's success:受到表扬,她有点～了。*She got dizzy with praise.*

【得意洋洋】look triumphant; be proud immensely

【得志】enjoy success; achieve one's ambition; have a successful career:少年～ *have a successful career when young*

【得罪】off end; displease; affront:他很耿直为此～了不少人。*He offended many people for his honesty and frankness.*

德 ① virtue; moral character:高尚的品～ *noble moral character* ② heart; mind:同心同～ *be of one heart and mind* ③ kindness; favour:感恩戴～ *be deeply grateful for*

【德才兼备】have both ability and political integrity

【德高望重】(of an old person) enjoy noble character and high prestige; with great virtue and universal reputation

【德国】Germany: ～人 *German*

【德行】① moral integrity; moral caliber (or conduct) ②［方］disgusting; hideous; repugnant:看他那臭～。*Look, how repugnant the fellow is!*

【德语】German (language)

【德育】moral education; ethical training

【德治】rule of virtue

de

地 used after an adverbial modifier and before a verb to form an adverbial adjunct:深思熟虑～思考 *consider sth deliberately* /他大大～扫了我的兴。*He stroke deep damp over me.*
see also dì

的 ① used after an attribute:鲜红～旗帜 *a scarlet flay* /沉重～桌子 *a heavy table* ② used after a phrase or word to indicate people or things:做生意～人 *business man* /她爱穿红～。*She is always dressed in red clothes.* ③ used after a predicate to stress implementer, time way etc.:谁开～门? *Who opened the door?* /他是昨天来～。*He came here yesterday.* ④ used at the end of a declarative sentence to indicate certainty:你干得可真够漂亮～。*You really did a remarkable job.*
see also dí; dì

得 ① used after an adverbial modifier to express possibility or capability:我们可粗心不～。*We must be careful.* /这凳子太凉坐不～。*The stool is too cool to sit.* ② used between a verb and complement to express possibility:我搬～动。*I can remove it.* /你能请～动他参加晚会吗? *Can you invite him to the evening party?* ③ used after a verb or an adjective to link a implement of degree or result:起～早 *get up early* /冷～打哆嗦 *shiver with cold* /跳～欢 *dance to one's heart's content*
see also dé; děi

děi

得 ① need:明天你～带上弟弟去上学。*You should take your younger brother to go to school tomorrow.* /这间房子我～用一个小时打扫。*It will take me an hour to clean this room.* ② must; have to:作业没完成就～挨批。*You had to be criticized because you didn't finish your homework.* ③ will be sure to; certainly will:快走,呆会儿天～要黑了。*Hurry up; it will be dark soon.*
see also dé; de

dēng

灯 ① lamp; light; lantern:油～ *oil lamp* /电～ *electric lamp* /信号～ *signal lamp* /探照～ *searchlight* ② burner:酒精～ *alcohol burner* ③ value; tube:五～收音机 *five-value radio set*

【灯标】beacon; beacon light

【灯彩】① colored lantern making; festoon lighting ② festival decorative coloured lanterns

【灯船】light ship; light vessel

【灯光】① lamplight: ～变亮了。*The light became bright.* ② (stage) lighting:舞台～ *stage lights; lighting* / ～师 *juicer*

【灯红酒绿】red lanterns and green wine — scene of debauchery

【灯花】snuff (of a candlewick)

【灯火】lights; candlelight's: ～辉煌 *ablaze with lights* / ～管制 *blackout*

【灯节】the Lantern Festival (the 15th of the first lunar month)

【灯具】lamps and lanterns

【灯笼】lantern:打～ *carry (or hold) a lighted lantern*

【灯笼裤】knickerbockers; knee-length or ankle-length trousers worn during sports or informal occasions

【灯谜】riddles written on lanterns; lantern riddles:他从小就喜欢猜～。*He liked guessing lantern riddles when he was a child.*

【灯泡】light bulb; bulb: 40 瓦～ *40 watt bulb* /螺口～ *screw socket bulb*

【灯丝】filament (in light bulb or value)

【灯塔】lighthouse; beacon

【灯头】① lamp holder; electric light socket:螺丝口～ *screw socket* ② holder for the wick and chimney of a kerosene lamp

【灯芯】lampwick; wick

【灯油】lamp-oil; kerosene; paraffin oil

【灯语】lamp signal

【灯座】lamp stand

登 ① ascend; mount; scale: ～上宝座 *ascend the throne* / ～上顶峰 *reach the summit* ② publish; record; register; enter:在报纸上～条广

告 *advertise in a newspaper* / 他的文章刊～在杂志上了。*His article was published in the magazine.* ③ ripen (of grain): 五谷丰～ *have a bumper harvest of cereals* ④ step on; tread; stand: ～在桌子上挂灯笼 *stand on the table to hang the lantern* ⑤ pedal; treadle; ride; press down with the foot: ～自行车 *ride a bicycle* ⑥ put on (shoes or trousers): 听到这个消息,他～上鞋就去了学校。*Hearing the news, he put his shoes on quickly and went to the school.*

【登岸】go ashore; disembark

【登报】publish in the newspaper; report in the newspaper: 这条公告～了。*The announcement appeared in the newspaper.*

【登场】① be carried to the threshing ground: 小麦已经～。*The wheat has been carried to the threshing ground.* ② come on stage: 粉墨～ *ascend the stage with powder and rough make-up; do one's costume and appear on he stage* / ～人物 *characters in a play*

【登峰造极】reach acme; reach the limit; (of calligraphy, drawing, etc.) reach a very high level: 他的字写得到了～的地步。*He has reached the peak in calligraphy.*

【登高】① ascend a light: ～望远 *ascend a height to view distantly* ② climb mountains on the Double Ninth Festival

【登革热】【医】dengue fever

【登广告】advertise

【登机牌】boarding card

【登基】ascend the throne; crown; be enthroned

【登记】register; check in; enter one's name: 住宿～ *check in (at a hotel)* / ～结婚 *marriage registration* / ～簿 *register; registry* / ～处 *registry*

【登临】climb a hill to enjoy a broad and distant view; visit famous mountains, places of interest, etc.

【登录】① enroll; register ② entry

【登陆】land; disembark: ～部队 *landing force* / ～艇 *landing boat (or craft)* / ～母舰 *landing-craft carrier*

【登门】call at sb's house: ～拜访 *pay sb a visit* / ～谢罪 *call at sb's house to apologize for offense*

【登山】climb; mountain-climbing; mountaineering: ～队 *mountaineering expedition (or party)* / ～服 *mountaineering apparel* / ～鞋 *mountaineering boots* / ～临水 *scale the summit and face the water* / ～越岭 *up hill and down dale*

【登时】at one; immediately; right away; then and there: 她～脸就红了。*She blushed with shame the and there.*

【登台】mount the platform; go on the stage and perform: ～表演 *perform on the stage*

【登堂入室】pass through the hall into the inner chamber — reach a higher level in one's study; become more proficient in one's profession

【登月飞船】lunar excursion vehicle

【登载】publish (in newspapers or magazines): 那起交通事故被～在了各种报纸上。*All the newspapers reported the accident.*

噔 thump; thud; dump: 箱子～地摔在了地上。*The case fell thudding on the floor.*

蹬 pedal; treadle; ride; press down with the foot; step on

【蹬技】juggling with the feet

【蹬腿】① stretch out one's legs; kick one's legs ② [口] kick the bucket; die; pass away

děng

等[1] ① class; grade: 优～生 *top students* / 分为两个～级 *classify into two grades* ② kind; sort

等[2] ① equal: 相对～ *be equal* ② wait; await: ～人 *wait for a person* / ～公车 *wait for a bus* / 我们正～候领导视察。*We are awaiting the inspection of leaders.* ④ when; till; by the time: ～天黑了再开灯吧。*Turn on the light till dark.*

等[3] ① [书] used after a personal pronoun or a noun referring to people to express plurality: 一干人～ *a group of people* ② and so on; and so forth; etc.: 我去超市买来了鸡蛋、油等。*I bought rice, eggs, oil and so on from the supermarket.* ③ used to end after an enumeration: 硬盘、显示器、调制解调器～硬件 *hardware such as hard disk, display and modem*

【等边三角形】equilateral triangle

【等差】[书] gradation of difference; equal difference

【等次】grade; place in series; hierarchy: 按大小将苹果划分～。*The apple is graded according to size.*

【等待】wait for; await: ～最佳时机 *await an optimum opportunity*

【等到】when; till; by the time: ～那时候,我该毕业了。*I will graduate by that time.*

【等而下之】from that grade down; loner down: 最好的尚且如此,～的就不必看了。*Even the best is not worth much; we needn't look at those lower down.*

【等份】equal portion; an equally divided part of sth

【等高线】【地】contour(line): ～地图 *contour map*

【等号】【数】equal-sign; equals mark

【等候】wait for; await; expect: ～客人到来 *expect the coming of the guests* / ～英雄凯旋归来 *expect the hero to return triumphant*

【等级】① grade; rank: 商品的～ *grades of goods* ② order and degree; social status; social estate: ～制度 *hierarchy; social estate system* / 古代社会～森严。*The society was rigidly stratified in antiquity.*

【等价】be of equal value; equivalence: ～交换 *exchange at equal value* / ～物 *equivalent* / ～原理 *equivalence principle*

【等距离】equidistance: 我和他到学校是～的。*He and I are equidistant to school.*

【等离子体】【物】plasma: ～激光器 *plasma laser* / ～物理学 *plasma physics*

D

【等式】【数】equality
【等同】equate; be equal:这两件事有本质区别,你不能将它们～起来。*The two matters are quite different in essence; you can't equate them.*
【等温线】【气】isotherm
【等闲】① ordinary; unimportant; lightly: ～视之 *regard as ordinary (or unimportant)* ② careless; random; casually:不要～度过你的黄金岁月。*Don't fritter away your golden years.* ③ for no reason
【等效】【电】equivalent: ～电路 *equivalent circuit* / ～电源 *equivalent source*
【等压面】【气】isobaric surface; constant pressure surface
【等压线】【气】isobaric line; isobar
【等腰三角形】【数】isosceles triangle
【等音】【音】enharmonic
【等于】① be equal to; be equivalent to:二乘四～八。*Two multiplied by four is eight.* ② amount to; be tantamount to; have no difference:不要再推辞了,你就～帮我个忙吧。*Don't decline me again; you may take it for a help to me.*

dèng

凳 stool; bench:石～ *stone bench*
【凳子】stool
澄 (of liquid) settle; clarify; precipitate
see also chéng
【澄清】(of liquid) settle; become clear; clarify:等水～了,你再洗衣服。*Wait till the water has settled before you wash your clothes.*
磴 ① stone steps on a hill path ② used for steps or stairs:这楼梯有多少～? *How many steps does this flight of stairs have?*
瞪 open one's eyes wide; glare; stare:我又没做错事干吗～我? *I didn't do something wrong and why are you glaring at me?*
【瞪眼】① open one's eyes wide; glare; stare:看到海市蜃楼的景象,我瞪大了眼。*Seeing the scene of mirage I opened my eyes wide.* ② get angry with sb; glare at sb:他冲我直～。*He glared at me all the time.*

dī

低 ① low:薪水～ *have a low salary* /气压～ *low atmospheric pressure* / ～水位 *low water level* ② hang down; let drop: ～头 *hang one's head*
【低产】law yield: ～作物 *low-yielding crop* / ～油井 *stripper well; stripped well*
【低潮】low tied (or ebb): ～线 *low-water line (or mark)* /今天他的情绪处于～。*He emotion is at low tide today.*
【低沉】① overcast; somber; cloudy:天气很～,一定是要下雨了。*It is sure to rain for the sky is overcast.* ② (of voice) low and deep: ～的语调 *a low and deep tone* ③ low-spirited; dismal; downcast:消极～ *negative and low-spirited*
【低成本】low cost
【低垂】droop; hang low: ～着头 *hang one's head low* /柳枝～。*The sallow hangs low.*
【低档】low grade; be of low quality: ～产品 *low-grade products*
【低等动物】lower animal
【低地】lowland
【低调】low key: ～演说 *a low-key speech* /他说话很～。*He speaks in a low-key way.*
【低估】underestimate; underrate:反动派总是～人民的力量。*The reactionary always underestimates the power of people.*
【低谷】valley — all-time low; bottom:走出～ *get out of the bottom*
【低耗】low cost; low consume
【低级】① elementary; primary; rudimentary: ～动物 *lower animal* ② vulgar; filthy; low: ～趣味 *bad taste; vulgar interests*
【低贱】humble; low and degrading:出身～的人 *a person of humble birth*
【低空】low altitude; low level: ～飞行 *low-altitude flying* / ～导弹 *low-level (or low-altitude) missile* / ～轰炸 *low-level bombing*
【低栏】【体】low hurdles
【低廉】cheap; low-priced:价格～。*Prices are low.*
【低劣】inferior; low-grade; mean; bad:质量～ *be of inferior quality* /态度～ *have a bad attitude*
【低龄化】become younger in age
【低落】downcast; dismal; depressed:情绪～ *be in low spirits*
【低眉顺眼】obedient; be submissive and servile
【低能】mental deficiency; feeble-minded; moronism: ～儿 *imbecile; changeling; retarded child*
【低频】【物】low frequency: ～段 *low-frequency range* / ～输出 *low-frequency output* / ～变压器 *low-frequency transformer*
【低气压】【气】low pressure; depression
【低人一等】inferior to others; be lower-ranking: ～的职位 *inferior position*
【低三下四】① lowly; humble; mean: ～的人家 *a degrading family* ② servile; obsequious; cringing: ～的拍马屁行为 *an obsequious action* / ～地跪下求饶 *kneel down to beg abjectly for mercy*
【低烧】【医】low fever; slight fever
【低声】in a low voice; under one's breath; undertone:他们在一个角落～谈话。*They were talking in a low voice at a corner.*
【低声波】【物】infrasonic wave
【低声下气】soft-spoken and submissive; humble; be obsequious:他在领导面前总是～。*He was always soft-spoken and submissive in front of leaders.*
【低碳钢】【冶】low-carbon steel

【低头】① bow (or hang) one's head: ~认错 *bow one's head and admit one's mistake* ② yield; submit: 他面对挫折从不~。*He never yielded the frustration.*
【低洼】low-lying: ~地 *low-lying land*
【低微】① (of voice, sound, income, etc.) low: 用~的声音讲话 *speak in a low voice* / ~的收入 *low income* ② lowly; humble; degrading: 出身~的人 *a person of humble origin*
【低温】① low temperature ②【气】microthermal: ~气候 *microthermal climate* ③【医】hypothermia: ~疗法 *cryotherapy; crymotherapy*
【低下】(of status or living standards) low: 社会地位~ *be of low social status*
【低消耗】low consumption (of raw materials, fuel, etc.): 以高产~为目标 *aim at high production and low consumption*
【低血糖】【医】hypoglycemia
【低血压】【医】hypotension
【低压】①【物】low pressure: ~计 *low-pressure gauge* ②【电】low tension; low voltage: ~输送 *low-voltage transmission* ③【气】low pressure; depression: ~气流 *low-pressure air current* ④【医】minimum pressure
【低音】【音】bass: ~提琴 *double mass; contrabass*
【低音控制】bass control
【低云】【气】low clouds

堤 dike; dyke; embankment: 河~ *river embankment; levee*
【堤岸】embankment
【堤坝】dykes and dams
【堤防】dike; embankment: 修固~ *repair and strengthen the dyke* / ~工程 *dyke building; embankment project*

提
see also tí
【提防】be on guard against; be wary of; watch out for; beware of: 为了~传染病扩散，我们采用了有效措施。*We have take efficient measures against the spread of contagious disease.*
【提溜】[方] carry; bring along: 他~着两条鱼进了厂长家。*He went to the home of the factory manager with two fishes in hands.*

滴 ① drip: ~眼药 *put drops in one's eyes* / 水龙头在不停~水。*Water kept dripping from the faucet.* ② drop: 几~眼泪 *some drops of tears* / ~血 *a drop of blood*
【滴鼻剂】nose drops; collunarium
【滴答】① ticktack; tick: 雨打在玻璃上，~~地响。*Striking on the glass, the rain kept pattering.* ② drip: 屋顶上~着水。*Water is dripping down from the roof.*
【滴管】dropper
【滴灌】【农】drip irrigation; trickle irrigation
【滴漏】water clock; clepsydra; hourglass
【滴水不漏】① watertight; flawless; allow of no lap holes; leave nothing for others to nit-pick: 这件事她做得~。*She left nothing for people to nit-pick in doing this thing.* ② closely endorsed
【滴水成冰】freezing cold; water freezes when it drips: 严寒的北方~。*Water freezes as soon as it drops in freezing north.*
【滴水穿石】dripping water can wear through a stone: 不懈的努力会迈向成功，这就是~的道理。*Constant efforts bring success; this is the principle that drops of water wear holes in stone.*
【滴水石】dripstone
【滴水瓦】drip-tile (placed at either end of an eaves)
【滴眼剂】eye drops

镝 【化】dysprosium (Dy)
see also dí

dí

迪 [书] enlighten; guide: 启~ *enlighten; stimulate*
【迪斯尼乐园】Disneyland

的 true; really; indeed: ~确 *indeed; certainly; really*
see also de; dì
【的确】indeed; really: 他昨天~回家了。*He really went home yesterday.*
【的士】[方] taxi

敌[2] ① fight; resist; oppose; withstand: 寡不~众 *be hopelessly outnumbered* ② match; be equal to: 匹~ *be well-matched* / 势均力~ *balance of forces* ③ enemy; foe; adversary: 天~ *natual enemy*
【敌对】hostile; opposed; antagonistic: ~分子 *hostile; a hostile element* / ~情绪 *feelings of enmity*
【敌国】enemy state
【敌后】enemy's rear area: 深入~ *go deep into the enemy's rear area* / ~根据地 *base areas behind enemy lines*
【敌军】enemy; enemy troops; enemy forces
【敌忾】[书] hatred against the enemy: 同仇~ *share a common feeling of a bitter hatred against the enemy*
【敌情】enemy's situation
【敌人】enemy; foe: 同~斗争到底 *fight against the enemy to the end*
【敌视】stand against; be hostile or antagonistic to; regard with hostility: 我们的政策从不~任何国家。*Our policies are never hostile to any countries.*
【敌手】① match; adversary; opponent; rival: 同~竞争 *compete with one's opponent* ② enemy hands: 落入~ *fall into enemy hands*
【敌探】enemy spy
【敌伪】the enemy and the puppet regime (during the War of Resistance Against Japan): ~人员 *enemy and puppet personnel*
【敌我矛盾】contradictions between ourselves and

the enemy
【敌意】hostility; enmity; animosity

涤 ［书］wash; cleanse: 洗～ *wash*; *wash up*

【涤除】was away; discard; do away with; eliminate: ～社会旧习 *do away with social outdated customs*

【涤纶】【纺】polyester fibre: ～长丝 *polyester filament*

笛 ① bamboo flute: ～声 *fluting* / ～手 *flautist* ② whistle: 汽～ *hooter* / 警～ *hooter*; *alarm whistle*

【笛子】bamboo flute

嘀

【嘀咕】① murmur; whisper; talk in whispers: 你在～些什么? *What are you murmuring*? ② guess; have misgivings; have sth one's mind; ponder: 我～这件事好长时间了。*It's been on my mind for a long time.*

嫡 ① of or by the wife: ～长子 *the wife's eldest son* ② of lineal descent closely related; orthodox

【嫡传】be handed down from the master directly

【嫡亲】blood relations; own; close paternal relations: ～姐妹(弟兄) *blood sisters* (*brothers*)

【嫡堂】(cousins) of the same paternal grandfather by the direct line: 他们是～兄弟。*They are cousins of the same paternal grandfather.*

【嫡系】① direct line of descent: ～重孙 *great-grandson of direct line of descent* ② one's own clique; under one's direct control: ～部队 *troops under one's direct control*

镝 ［书］arrowhead: 鸣～ *whistling arrow*

see also dī

dǐ

邸 residence of a high official

【邸宅】mansion

诋 ［书］slander; defame

【诋毁】slander; defame; vilify; calumniate: 他的名誉受到～。*His reputation was slandered.*

抵[1] ① support; prop; sustain; brace: 用手～着下巴 *prop one's chin in one's hand* / 这棵花由两根棍儿～着。*The flower was supported by two sticks.* ② resist; withstand: ～住诱惑 *resist the temptation* ③ compensate; make up for: 你要拿什么来～债? *What will you take to pay off your debts*? ④ mortgage: 以房做～ *mortgage a house* ⑤ balance; set off: 付出与收获相～。*Paying and gains are exactly equal.* ⑥ be equal to; match; be equivalent: 我干活～不上他。*I can't match with him in doing work.*

抵[2] ［书］reach; get to; arrive at: ～京 *arrive in Beijing*

【抵偿】compensate; make up for; atone for; make good: 谁来～我的损失? *Who will compensate my lost*?

【抵触】conflict; clash; contradict: 有～情绪 *have resentful feelings* / 当个人利益与集团利益相～时，应服从集体利益。*When individual interests clash with collective interests, we should obey the latter one.*

【抵达】reach; get to; arrive: 你什么时候～北京? *When will you arrive in Beijing*?

【抵挡】resist; ward off; keep out; check; withstand: ～风寒 *keep out the wind and the cold* / ～敌人的进攻 *resist the attack of the enemy*

【抵换】substitute for; take the place of; replace

【抵抗】resist; stand up to; withstand: ～侵略 *resist aggression* / 对疾病的～力 *one's resistance to disease*

【抵赖】refuse to admit; deny; repudiate; disavow: 不容～ *brook no denial* / 在事实面前你是无法～的。*You can't attempt to deny something before facts.*

【抵命】pay with one's life: 杀人～。*He who kills must give his life.*

【抵消】offset; cancel out; neutralize; counteract: ～药物的作用 *counteract the effect of a medicine* / 他的真诚道歉～了她的愤怒情绪。*His sincere apology mitigated her anger.*

【抵押】mortgage: 以人格作～ *raise a mortgage on one's personality* / ～贷款 *mortgage loan* / ～贷款 *mortgage financing* / ～合同 *mortgage contract* / ～信贷 *mortgage credit* / ～市场 *mortgage market* / ～银行 *mortgage bank*

【抵御】resist; withstand: ～严寒 *resist the severe cold* / ～外敌入侵 *resist foreign invasion* / ～自然灾害 *withstand natural calamities*

【抵债】pay a debt in kind or by labour

【抵制】resist; boycott; reject: ～不良思想的影响 *resist the influence of harmful ideas*

【抵罪】be punished by law for a crime

底[1] ① bottom; base; sole: 海～ *seabed*; *seafloor* / 鞋～ *tread*; *sole of shoe* ② ins and outs of a matter: 亮～ *pull all one's cards on the table*; *state one's views* ③ rough draft: 打个～儿 *make a draft* ④ record: 查查～儿 *look up the record* ⑤ end of a year or month: 年～ *end of a year* ⑥ background: 白黄～花 *yellow flowers on a white background* ⑦ (Dǐ) a surname

底[2] what

底[3] here; this

【底版】negative; photographic

【底册】bound copy of documents kept on file

【底层】① ground floor; first floor ② bottom; the lowest rung: 在奴隶社会中奴隶们处于社会最～。*Slaves lived at the lowest rung in slave society.*

【底稿】draft; manuscript
【底火】① fire in a stove before fuel is added ②【军】primer; ignition cartridge
【底价】base price; floor
【底架】【机】chassis
【底牌】cards in one's hand; hand:亮~ *show one's hand*
【底盘】bed or chassis of a motor vehicle
【底片】negative; photographic plate: ~模糊不清了。*The photographic plate was blurry.*
【底漆】undercoat; priming paint; primer
【底气】① physical strength give out by thoracic or abdominal resonance:他唱起歌来~十足。*He has good resonance in singing.* ② vigour; basic strength and confidence:以我的能力和水平来干这件事,我感到~不足。*I feel little confident to do this thing with my ability and level.*
【底色】【纺】bottom
【底视图】【机】bottom view
【底数】①【数】base number ② the truth or root of a matter:看到他没来,我心里就有了~。*Seeing that he didn't come, I knew how the matter stood.*
【底图】【地】base map
【底细】ins and outs; detailed information; inside story:你了解这人的~吗? *Do you know the ins and outs of this man?*
【底下】① under; below; beneath:他在大树~乘凉。*He was enjoying the cool in the shade of a big tree.* /汗透过他的夹克渗到~的衬衣。*Sweat penetrated into his shirt through the jacket.* ② next; later; afterwards:你们~要做的事是到操场集合。*What you will do next is to gather on the playground.*
【底线】① baseline (of football court, etc.) ② spy; planted agent
【底子】① bottom; base:鞋~ *sole of a shoe* ② foundation; base: ~薄 *have a weak foundation* /他数学~好。*He has a good grounding in mathematics.* ③ rough draft; sketch:正式写之前先打个~。*Make a draft before you write formally.* ④ copy kept as record:你留~了吗? *Do you keep a copy as a record?* ⑤ remnant; leftover:只剩货~了。*There are only remnants of stock loft.*
【底座】base; pedestal; foundation

骶

【骶骨】【生理】sacrum

dì

地

① the earth:天~ *heave and earth* ② land; soil; ground:山~ *hilly land* /平~ *flat ground* ③ land; fields:湿~ *everglade* /下~干活儿 *work in the fields* /这块儿~很肥沃。*This land is fertile.* ④ floor; ground:水~磨石 *terrazzo* /水泥~ *cement floor* ⑤ place; locality; area:产~ *producing area* /站在原~ *stand in the former place* ⑥ position; situation:不败之~ *invincible position* ⑦ background; ground:一块白~黄花的布料 *a cloth with yellow flowers on a white background* ⑧ distance:还有一站~就到了,我们走过去吧。*It's only one bus stop from here and let's go on foot.*
see also de
【地板】floor board; floor:木~ *wood floor* /马赛克~ *mosaic floor* /水泥~ *cement floor* / ~蜡 *floor wax*
【地堡】【军】bunker; blockhouse; pillbox; fort
【地表】surface of the earth: ~径流 *runoff of the earth's surface*
【地步】① condition; situation; state; plight:既然你弄到这样的~,我也无话可说了。*Since you got into such a mess, I had nothing to say now.* ② extent; degree:他工作到废寝忘食的~。*He worked so hard that he forgot food and sleep.* ③ room for action; elbowroom:我得给自己留~。*I should give myself elbowroom.*
【地蚕】[方] cutworm
【地槽】【地】geosyncline: ~学说 *theory of geosyncline*
【地产】landed estate (or property); real estate: ~经纪人 *land agent* / ~投机商人 *land-jobber* / ~银行 *land bank* / ~税 *real estate tax*
【地秤】weighbridge
【地磁】【物】geomagnetism; terrestrial magnetism: ~场 *geomagnetic field* / ~赤道 *magnetic equator* / ~仪 *magnetometer* / ~学 *geomagnetism*
【地大物博】(a country) vast in territory and abundant in natural resources
【地带】zone; district; terrain; region; belt:森林~ *forest region* /严寒~ *zone of bitter cold*
【地道】(dìdào) tunnel: ~战 *tunnel warfare*
【地道】(dìdao) ① genuine; from a well known place for a certain product; one hundred percent: ~的药材 *genuine medicinal herbs* ② pure; typical: ~的美国口语 *pure American spoken English* ③ work be up certain standard; well-done:他干得一手~的木工活儿。*He did excellent carpentry.*
【地点】place; site; locale; location:施工~ *site of construction* /你们的劳动~是主楼后面的树林。*Your working place is the woods behind the main building.*
【地电】terrestrial electricity
【地动】[口] quake; earthquake: ~山摇。*The earth trembled and the mountains swayed.*
【地洞】hole in the ground; burrow
【地段】area sector (or section):这是个做生产的好~。*This section is a good area for doing business.*
【地方】(dìfāng) ① locality (as distinct from the central administration):中央与~ *central and local authorities* / ~组织 *organization of local authorities* ② local: ~武装 *local armed forces* / ~保护主义 *regional protectionism* / ~病 *endemic*

disease / ～志 *local chronicles* / ～色彩 *local colour* / ～戏 *local drama* / ～自治 *local self-government*

【地方】(dìfang) ① place; space; room: 他到什么～去了? *Where did he go?* /这～太小了放不下一张床。*This space is too small to place a bed.* ② part; respect: 剧中最动人的～ *the most touching part of an opera*

【地瓜】[方] ① yam bean ② sweet potato

【地广人稀】an area with much land and few people; small population for a large area

【地核】【地】the earth's core

【地基】① ground ② foundation

【地极】【地】terrestrial pole

【地级市】prefecture-level city

【地价】price of land

【地脚】lower margin (of a page)

【地窖】cellar; storage pit; basement

【地界】① abuttal; the boundary of a piece of land ② jurisdiction

【地久天长】everlasting; as long as the heaven and earth endure

【地块】【地】massif

【地牢】dungeon

【地雷】(land) mine: ～战(*land*) *mine warfare* / 埋～ *plant mines*

【地理】① geographical features of a place: ～环境 *geographical surroundings* / ～位置 *geographical position* / ～坐标 *geographical coordinates* / ～民情 *the place and its people* ② geography: 世界～ *world geography* /自然～ *physical geography* /经济～ *economic geography* / ～学 *geography*

【地力】soil fertility; productivity of the land

【地利】① favourable geographical position; topographical advantages: 天时～ *favourable climatic condition and geographical position* ② land productivity

【地沥青】asphalt; bitumen

【地裂】(of the ground) cleave; fissure; rift: 山崩～ *landslide and ground rifting*

【地龙】earthworm

【地龙墙】【建】sleeper wall

【地漏】【建】floor drain

【地貌】landforms; the general configuration of the earth's surface; physical contours: ～学 *geomorphology*

【地面】① ground; the earth's surface: ～以上 *above ground* / ～沉降 *surface subsidence* / ～导航 *area navigation* / ～卫星站 *ground satellite station* / ～子午线 *terrestrial meridian* ②【建】ground; floor: 水泥～ *cement floor* / 水磨石～ *terrazzo floor* / ～砖 *floor tiles* ③ region; district; area; territory: 先头部队已经进入江苏～。*The advance forces have been in Jiangsu Province.* ④ local; in the locality: 他在～儿上很有名望。*He enjoys good fame and prestige among the local people.*

【地名】place name

【地膜】plastic films used for covering plants: ～覆盖 *covering the ground with plastic films*

【地盘】domain; territory under one's control; sphere of influence: 争夺～ *compete for share of influence* / 抢占～ *race to seize (or control) domains*

【地皮】① surface of ground: 阴雨天～潮湿。*The ground is moist during overcast and raining days.* ② land for building

【地痞】local ruffian; local riffraff; bad eggs

【地平线】horizon

【地铺】shakedown; improvised bed: 打～ *make an improvised bed on the floor*

【地契】owning contract

【地堑】【地】graben

【地壳】【地】the earth's crust: ～变形 *diastrophism* / ～均衡说 *isostasy*

【地勤】【航】ground service; ground duty: ～人员 *ground crew*

【地球】the earth; the global: ～保持日 *Earth Day* / ～村 *global village* / ～动力学 *geodynamics* / ～反照 *earthlight*; *earthshine* / ～化学 *geochemistry* / ～年代学 *geochronology* / ～日 *Earth Day* (*April 22*) / ～外天文学 *extraterrestrial astronomy* / ～物理学 *geophysics* / ～仪 *terrestrial globe*

【地区】① area; district; region: 亚太～ *Asia and Pacific region* /热带～ *the tropical area* /多山～ *a mountainous region* / ～冲突 *regional conflict* / ～合作 *regional cooperation* / ～封锁 *barriers between regions* / ～经济 *regional economies* ② prefecture: ～代码 *area code* / ～法院 *regional court*

【地权】land ownership: 平均～ *equalization of land ownership*

【地热】【地】the heat of the earth's interior; subterranean heat; terrestrial heat: ～资源 *geothermal resources* / ～发电 *geothermal power generation* / ～电站 *geothermal power plant*

【地史学】historical geology

【地势】terrain; relief; topography; physical features of a place: ～图 *hypsometric map*

【地税】land tax

【地摊】roadside stall; articles displayed on side walk floor: 摆～ *set up a stall on the street*

【地毯】carpet; rug

【地铁】subway; underground railway; tube: ～站 *subway station*

【地头】① edge of a field: 那个小伙子坐在～上。*The young fellow sat at the edge of a field.* ② [方] this place; the area: 他初来乍到, ～儿生。*He has just arrived and doesn't know this place well.* ③ lower margin (of a page)

【地图】map: 世界～ *world map* / ～学 *cartography* / ～投影 *map projection*

【地位】① position; status; place; standing: ～平等 *be equal in status* /政治～ *political position* /社会～ *social position* /经济～ *economic status* ② place (as occupied by a person or a thing)

【地温】【气】earth temperature; ground temperature: ～计 *geothermometer* / ～梯度 *geothermal* gradient

【地物】surface features; man-made surface features of a region

【地峡】isthmus:巴拿马~ *the Isthmus of Panama*

【地下】① underground; subterranean: ~迷宫 *underground labyrinth* / ~通道 *underpass* / ~水位 *water table* / ~铁道 *subway* / ~停车场 *subterranean parking* ② underground; secret activity: ~党 *underground party organization* / ~工作 *underground work* ③ on the ground:从~拣起 *pick up sth from the ground*

【地线】【电】earth wire; ground wire:接~ *connect the earth wire*

【地心】【地】the earth's core: ~引力 *terrestrial gravity*

【地形】topography; terrain; general configuration of the earth's surface: ~图 *relief map* / ~学 *topography; geomorphology* / ~走向 *lay of the land*

【地衣】【植】lichen

【地狱】hell; nether world inferno:她过着~一般的生活。*She lived an infernal life.*

【地域】district; region:中国~广阔。*China is vast in territory.*

【地震】earthquake; seism:里氏6.8级~ *6.8 magnitude on the Richter scale* / ~波 *seismic wave* / ~带 *seismic belt* / ~观测 *seismological observation* / ~检波器 *geophone* / ~烈度 *earthquake intensity* / ~学 *seismology*

【地址】address: ~常数 *address constant* / ~类型 *address style* / ~存储器 *addressed memory* /能把你的通信~给我吗? *May I get your mailing address?*

【地志学】topology

【地质】geology: ~概况 *general situation of geology* / ~调查 *geological survey* / ~学 *geology; geognosy* / ~报告 *a geological report* / ~年代 *geological time* / ~图 *geologic map*

【地中海】the Mediterranean (sea)

【地轴】the earth's axis

【地主】① landlord; landowner: ~阶段 *the landlord class; landocracy* ② host:尽~之谊 *exercise the duties of the host*

【地租】land rent; ground rent: ~剥削 *exploitation through land rent* /实物~ *rent in kind*

弟 younger brother

【弟弟】brother; younger brother

【弟妹】① younger brother and sister ② younger brother's wife; sister-in-law

【弟兄】brothers:亲~ *blood brothers* / ~二人 *the two brothers*

【弟子】disciple; follower; pupil

的 target; bull's eye:无~放矢 *shoot at random — aimless and vainly*

see also de; dí

帝 ① the supreme Being; god:上~ *God* ② monarch; emperor:称~ *come to the throne* ③ abbreviation of imperialism:反~反封建斗争 *struggle against imperialism and feudalism*

【帝国】empire:罗马~ *Roman Empire*

【帝国主义】imperialism: ~侵略 *imperialist aggression* / ~者 *imperialist*

【帝王】emperor; monarch

【帝制】autocratic monarchy; monarchy

递 ① pass; hand over; transmit; deliver: ~口信 *take a message to sb* /把书~给我。*Hand me the book, please.* ② in the proper order; successively

【递补】fill vacancies in the proper order

【递加】increase by degrees; progressively increase: 他的债务逐日~。*His debts have increased successively every day.*

【递减】decrease by degrees; progressively decrease

【递交】present; submit; hand over: ~国书 *present the credential* / ~辞职报告 *send in one's resignation*

【递解】escort (usu. a criminal) from one place to another: ~回籍 *send (usu. a prisoner) back to one's native place under escort*

【递进】go forward one by one; move forward in order of sequence

【递送】send; deliver (letters, files, etc.): ~信件 *deliver letters* /这封密函是经过千辛万苦~过来的。*This secret letter was delivered through innumerable hardships.*

【递眼色】give sb message by a wink; wink at sb:他向我递了个眼色,让我忍耐一下。*He gave me a wink to restrain myself.*

【递增】progressively increase; increase by degrees: 节假日出国旅游的人逐年~。*People who go abroad for a trip on festival and holidays have increased progressively every year.*

第[1] used before numeral to indicate ordinal numbers: ~条 *the first item*

第[2] ①[书] grades in which successful candidates in the imperial examinations were placed:及~ *pass grades in the imperial examinations* ② residence of a high official:门~ *family status; pedigree*

【第三者】① the third person (or party) to a dispute:既然决定不了,让我们听听~的意见吧。*Since we can't make a decision, let's listen the opinion of the third party.* ② third party; paramour; person having an affair with either the husband or the wife: ~插足 *the involvement of a third party in one's family life*

【第五纵队】fifth column

【第一】first; at the head; in the first place; primary; most important:这次选举中他得票~。*He ranked the first in the election.* /把安全放在~位。*Safety first.*

【第一夫人】the First Lady (wife of president of a country)

【第一家庭】the First Family (family of head of state)

【第一手】firsthand：～资料 *firsthand material*；*primary sources*

【第一线】forefront；first（or front）line：教学～ *the first line of teaching*；*classroom lecturing*

谛 ①［书］attentively；careful：～听 *listen attentively* /～思 *think over*；*consider carefully* ② meaning；significance：真～ *true essence*；*truth*

蒂 the base of a fruit，flower，etc.：并～莲 *twin lotus flowers on one stack*（*symbol of a loyal couple*）

缔 form；combine；conclude

【缔交】① establish diplomatic relations ② form friendship：～数年 *form a friendship for many years*

【缔结】concluded；establish；wrap up：～盟约 *conclude a treaty*（*or convention*）/～邦交 *establish diplomatic relations* /～停战协定 *wrap up an armistice*

【缔盟】ally；form an alliance

【缔约】conclude（or sign）a treaty：～国 *signatory*（*state*）*to a treaty*

【缔造】found；create：～共和国 *found the republic*

diān

掂 weigh in the hand：用手～～，你就知道有多重了。*Weigh this in your hand；you will know its weight.*

【掂量】① weigh in the hand：～一下这石块有多重。*Weigh the stone in your hand.* ② think over；weigh up：让他们～着办吧。*Let them do as they think fit.*

【掂算】estimate；calculate；figure：我～着，我们十二点才能到。*I estimate that we will reach there at* 12:00.

颠[1] ① crown（of the head）② top；peak：山～ *mountain top* /塔～ *the top of a pagoda*

颠[2] ① jolt；bump：汽车～得厉害。*The bus bumped badly.* ② fall；turn over；topple down ③［方］rum；jump and run；go away：整天跑跑～～ *be on the go all day long* /对不起，他早～儿了。*Sorry，he has already gone away.*

【颠簸】jolt；bump；toss：拖拉机在山路上～着前进。*The tractor bumped along the mountain road.* /海浪很大，船～得厉害。*The boat was tossed violently because of the hard sea wave.*

【颠倒】① put or turn upside down；reverse；invert；transpose：箱子里有贵重东西，不要放～了。*Because there is precious thing in the box，don't put it upside down.* /把这两个字～一下，读起来更上口。*Transpose there two words and the sentence are easy to read aloud.* ② confused；disordered：神魂～ *be infatuated*；*one*；*mind is confused*；*be crazy with losing of loved ones be out of mind*

【颠倒黑白】confound black and white；stand the facts on their heads：事实不是这样的，你不要～。*Don't turn black into white for the fact is not like this.*

【颠倒是非】confound right and wrong；confuse truth and falsehood；turn things upside down

【颠覆】overturn；subvert；topple：～政权 *subvert the state power* /～活动 *subversive activities*；*subversion* /任何～活动都将以失败告终。*Any subversion will end in failure.* /汽车～在路边。*The car fell to the roadside and overturned.*

【颠来倒去】over and over：不要～，说个没完。*Do not keep harping on the the same thing.*

【颠沛流离】drift from place to place，homeless and miserable；wander about in a desperate plight：战争使人民～。*The war made people drift away from home and had a vagrant life.*

【颠扑不破】indestructible；irrefutable；indisputable：～的真理 *irrefutable truth*

【颠三倒四】disorderly；confused；incoherent；disconnected：你说话不要～。*Do not talk incoherently.*

巅 mountain top；peak；summit

【巅峰】summit；mountain peak

癫 mentally deranged；insane：疯～ *insane*

【癫狂】① demented；insane ② frivolous

【癫痫】【医】epilepsy

diǎn

典[1] ① standard；law；canon ② standard work of scholarship ③ allusion；literary quotation：用～ *use allusions* ④ ceremony：庆～ *celebrations*

典[2] ①［书］be in charge of ② mortgage；pawn

【典当】mortgage；pawn：～东西 *pawn sth* /～行 *pawn shop*

【典范】model；example；paragon

【典故】allusion；literary quotation

【典礼】ceremony；celebration

【典卖】mortgage

【典契】mortgage contract

【典型】① typical case（or example）；model；type：抓～ *grasp typical cases* ② typical；representative：～案例 *a typical case*

【典押】mortgage；pawn

【典雅】cultured；refined；elegant

【典狱】prison warden

【典质】mortgage；pawn

【典制】laws and institutions

点[1] ① drop（of liquid）：雨～儿 *raindrops* ② stain；spot；dot：斑～儿 *stain*；*spot* /墨～儿 *ink spot* ③ dot stroke（in Chinese characters）④【数】point：两～之间直线最短。*The line between two points is the shortest.* ⑤ place；point ⑥ aspect；feature：疑～ *dubious point* /要～ *main points* /特～ *tea and cookies*；*tea bread* ⑦ appointed time ⑧ refreshments

点[2] ① decimal point ② a little, a bit; some:小～儿 *a little smaller* /喝～儿水 *drink some water* /你好～了吗? *Are you feeling a little better?* ③ used in counting items:几～意见 *some suggestions* /此次大会有三～主要内容。*The conference contains three main points.* ④ o'clock:上午十～ *ten o'clock in the morning* /几点了? *What time is it?*

点[3] ① put a dot: ～个点作个记号 *put a dot to make a mark* ② touch on briefly; skim:船夫用篙一～,船就走了。*The boatman pushed the boat off with a shove of the pole.* /他讲话时～了这件事。*He touched on the matter in the speech.* ③ drip: ～眼药 *put drops in the eyes* ④ plant in holes; dibble: ～种 *dibble seeds* ⑤ count one by one: ～货 *check over goods; take stock* ⑥ select; choose: ～歌 *request a song* ⑦ hint; point out:他一～就透。*He took a hint quickly.* ⑧ light; burn; kindle: ～烟 *light a cigarette* /性子火爆,一～就着。*He's got a fiery temper and flares up at the slightest provocation.* ⑩ embellish; adorn; ornament:装～居室 *decorate the sitting room*

【点播】request a programme from a radio station:听众～的歌曲 *songs requested by the audience*

【点拨】teach; show how to do sth:他曾受过名师～。*He was instructed by a master before.*

【点菜】choose dishes from a menu; order food

【点唱】(of an audience) request a song (an aria from a traditional opera)

【点钞机】money counting machine (for bills only)

【点穿】lay bare; expose; bring sth out into the open

【点滴】① a bit; a little: ～经验 *limited experience* /～积累 *accumulate little by little* ②【医】intravenous drip:打葡萄糖～ *have an intravenous glucose drip*

【点定】[书] make corrections or revisions:这篇文章无所～。*The article needed no polishing.*

【点对点传输】【电】point to point transmission

【点焊】spot (or pointing) welding

【点火】① catch a fire; ignite: ～试验 *firing run* ② stir up trouble:煽风～ *fan the flames*

【点货】check over goods; tally the cargo

【点击】click

【点将】① [旧] muster one's officers and assign them tasks ② name a person for a particular job

【点交】hand over item by item

【点名】① call the roll: ～册 *roll book* /今天上课老师～了。*The teacher called the roll in class today.* ② mention sb by name:他～要我去办这件事。*He named me as the one he wanted to do this.*

【点明】point out; put one's finger on: ～问题所在 *point out the cause of the trouble*

【点破】point out bluntly; bring something out into open; lay bare:他的真实意图马上被我～了。*I pointed out what he was really after at once.*

【点燃】light; kindle; ignite: ～火炬 *light a torch* /～生命之光 *ignite the light of one's life*

【点染】① add details to painting ② touch up a piece of writing

【点射】① firing in bursts ② fixed fire

【点石成金】turn a stone into gold with a tough; turn a crude essay into a literary gem

【点收】check and accept:按清单～货物 *check the goods against a list before acknowledging receipt*

【点数】check the number; count:这是我还你的钱,请～。*Here is the money I returned to you; please count it.*

【点题】bring out the theme

【点头】nod one's head; nod: ～同意 *nod assent* /～承认 *recognize sth by nodding* /她还没～。*She hasn't given the go-ahead yet.*

【点心】light refreshment; pastry; dim sum; dessert

【点穴】hit a vital point; touch vital points on the adversary's body to cause internal injury

【点验】examine item by item

【点阵】【物】lattice: ～打印机 *dot matrix printer*

【点种】dibble in the seeds

【点缀】① embellish; ornament; decorate; adorn ② use sth merely for show:房间里摆束花作为～。*Put a bundle of flowers in the room for show.*

【点子】① drop(of liquid):雨～ *raindrops* ② spot; dot; speck:泥～ *speck of dirt or mud* ③ beat (of percussion instruments):鼓～ *drumbeat* ④ key point:这话说到～上了。*This remark hit the nail on the head.* ⑤ idea; pointer:出～ *make suggestions* /他鬼～多。*He is full of clever ideas.*

碘 【化】iodine (I)

【碘仿】【化】iodoform

【碘化银】sliver iodide

踮 stand on tiptoe:看见他在睡觉,她～着脚走了出去。*Seeing that he was sleeping, she walked out of the room on tiptoe.*

diàn

电 ① electricity: ～波 *electric wave* ② telegram; cable:加急～报 *urgent telegram* ③ give or get an electric shock: ～了我一下。*I got a shock.*

【电霸】electricity tyrants

【电棒】[方] (electric) torch; flashlight

【电报】telegram; cable:无线～ *wireless telegraph* /有线～ *wire telegram* /～等级 *telegram message precedence* /～挂号 *cable address; telegraphic address* /～机 *telegraph* /～局 *telegraph office*

【电表】① meter for measuring electricity ② kilowatt-hour

【电冰箱】(electric) refrigerator; fridge

【电铲】electric shovel

【电场】electric field: ～强度 *electric field intensity*

【电唱机】electric gramophone; phonograph, record player

D

【电车】① tram; tramcar; streetcar ② trolleybus; trolley

【电池】cell; battery:太阳能~ *solar cell* /干~ *dry cell* / ~充电器 *battery charger*

【电磁】electromagnetism: ~波 *electromagnetic wave* / ~感应 *electromagnetic induction* / ~铁 *electromagnet*

【电导】conductance: ~仪 *conductivity gauge*

【电灯】electric Lamp; electric light: ~泡 *electric (light) bulb* /我们村子里终于有了~。*Electric light has finally come to our village.*

【电动】power with electricity; electric: ~泵 *motor driven pump*; *electric pump* / ~车 *electrically operated motor car* / ~发电机 *motor generator* / ~割草机 *power-operated mower* / ~机 *motor* / ~计分器 *electric scoring apparatus* / ~力学 *electro dynamics* / ~势 *electro-motive force* (*EMF*) / ~剃刀 *electric shaver* / ~玩具 *battery operated toy*

【电度表】kilowatt-hour meter; watt-hour meter; electric meter

【电镀】electroplate:无氰~ *electroplating without using cyanide*

【电饭煲】electric cooker

【电风扇】electric fan

【电工】① electrical engineering: ~技术 *electrotechnics* / ~器材 *electrical appliances* / ~学 *electrical engineering*; *electrotechnics* ② electrician

【电功率】electric power

【电灌站】electric pumping station

【电光】light produced by electricity; lightning

【电棍】electric prod

【电焊】electric welding: ~机 *electric welding machine*; *electric welder* / ~条 *welding electrode*; *welding rod*

【电荷】electric charge; charge:正~ *positive charge* /负~ *negative charge*

【电弧】electric arc: ~炉 *arc furnace* / ~切割机 *arc cutting machine*

【电化学】electrochemistry

【电话】① telephone; phone:无线~ *wireless telephone* / ~薄 *telephone dictionary* /长途~ *long distance call* /热线~ *hot line* / ~号码 *telephone number* / ~会议 *telephone conference*; *teleconference* / ~机 *telephone* / ~增音机 *telephone repeater* / ~卡 *telephone card* / ~亭 *telephone booth* /请别把~挂了。*Please hold the line a minute.* ② phone call:打~ *make a phone call*; *phone sb*; *call sb up*; *give sb a ring*; *ring sb* /我正在接~。*I am on the telephone now.*

【电汇】telegraphic money order; remittance by telegram; telegraphic transfer:请将货款~给我。*Please send the remittance for goods to my office.*

【电机】electric machinery: ~厂 *electrical machinery plant* / ~工程 *electrical engineering*

【电机车】electric locomotive

【电吉他】electric guitar

【电极】electrode

【电键】telegraph key; key; button

【电解】electrolysis: ~分离 *electrolytic dissociation* / ~质 *electrolyte* / ~液 *electrolyte*

【电介质】dielectric

【电锯】electric saw

【电抗】reactance: ~器 *reactor*

【电缆】electric cable; cable

【电老虎】electricity tiger

【电烙铁】① electric iron ② electric soldering iron

【电离】ionization: ~层 *ionosphere* / ~化 *ionize*

【电力】electric power; power: ~工程 *electric power project* / ~供应 *supply of electricity*; *power supply* / ~工业 *power industry* / ~机械 *electrical power equipment* / ~消耗 *power consumption* / ~机车 *electric locomotive* / ~网 *power network* / ~线 *power line*; *electric line of force* / ~系统 *power system*

【电疗】【医】electrotherapy:短波~ *short-wave therapy*

【电料】electrical materials and appliances

【电铃】electric bell

【电流】electric current:载波~ *carrier current* /反向~ *reverse current* / ~强度 *current intensity*

【电炉】① electric stove; electric furnace ② hot plate: ~钢 *electric steel* / ~炼钢法 *electric furnace process* /工业~ *electric furnace*

【电路】(electric) circuit

【电路图】circuit diagram

【电码】(telegraphic) code: ~本 *code book*

【电门】electric switch

【电脑】electronic brain; computer: ~病毒 *computer virus* / ~犯罪 *computer crime* / ~空间 *cyberspace* /微~ *micro-computer* / ~顾问 *computer adviser* / ~记事本 *personal digital assistant* / ~中心 *electronic computer centre*

【电钮】push button; button:按~ *press* (*or push*) *a button*

【电瓶】storage battery; accumulator: ~本 *storage battery car*

【电气】electric: ~工程 *electrical engineering* / ~设备 *electrical equipment* / ~机车 *electric locomotive*

【电气化】electrification; electrify:农业~ *electrification of agriculture* / ~铁路 *electric railway*

【电器】electrical equipment (or appliance):家用~ *household electrical appliances*

【电热】electric heat; electrothermal: ~丝 *heating wire* / ~毯 *electric blanket* / ~杯 *electric heating jug* / ~器 *electric heater*

【电容】electric capacity; capacitance

【电扇】electric fan

【电视】television; TV:看~ *watch television* (*or TV*) /彩色~ *colour television* /黑白~ *black-and-white television* /闭路~ *closed-circuit television* / ~屏幕 *television screen* / ~广告 *television advertising* / ~剧 *TV play or drama* / ~台 *television station* / ~信号 *television signal* / ~新闻 *television news* / ~转播 *telecast*; *replay a TV programme* / ~实况转播 *live television coverage*; *live telecast* / ~网 *television network* / ~机 *television*

receiver; *television set* / ~系列片 *TV series* / ~连续剧 *TV series*; *television serial*
【电枢】armature: ~线圈 *armature coil* / ~绕组 *armature winding*
【电刷】【机】brush: ~触点 *brush contact*
【电台】① transmitter-receiver; transceiver ② broadcasting (or radio) station
【电烫】permanent hair styling or waving; permanent wave; perm
【电梯】lift; elevator: 乘~上去 *go up by lift*
【电筒】torch; flashlight
【电网】electrified wire netting; live wire entanglement
【电位】【电】potential: ~差 *potential difference*
【电线】wire: ~杆 *(wire) pole*
【电信】telecommunications: ~业务 *telecommunication service* / ~局 *telecommunication bureau*
【电刑】electric instruments of torture; electrocute
【电学】electricity (as a science)
【电讯】① (telegraphic) dispatch: ~从四面八方发来 *dispatches from far and near* ② telecommunications: ~联系中断。*Telecommunications connection is cut off.*
【电压】voltage: ~表 *voltmeter* / ~不稳 *unstable voltage*
【电眼】electric eye; magic eye
【电唁】send a telegram or message of condolence
【电冶金】electrometallurgy
【电椅】electric chair
【电影】film; movie; motion picture: 有声~ *sound film* / 无声~ *silent film* / 彩色~ *colour film* / 黑白~ *black and white film* / ~发行公司 *film distribution company* ~导演 *film director* / ~演员 *film actor (or actress)* / ~剧本 *scenario* / ~明星 *film or movie star* / ~节 *film festival* / ~院 *cinema; movie (house)* / ~周 *film week* / ~字幕 *film caption* / ~说明书 *film synopsis* / ~译制厂 *film dubbing studio*
【电源】power supply; power source; mains: 接上~ *connect with the mains* / ~插座 *power socket* / ~开关 *power switch*
【电灶】electric cooking stove
【电闸】master switch; electric switch
【电钟】electric clock
【电子】electron: 热~ *thermal electron* / 正~ *positive electron* / 负~ *negative electron*; *negatron* / ~器件 *electronic device* / ~图书 *electronic books* / ~报刊 *electronic press* / ~层 *electronic shell* / ~出版物 *E-journal* / ~伏特 *electron volt* / ~工程学 *electronic engineering* / ~公告牌 *electronic bulletin board* / ~管 *radio tube*; *vacuum tube* / ~计算机 *electronic computer*; *computer* / ~枪 *electron gun* / ~琴 *electronic organ* / ~邮件 *email* / ~邮箱 *email box* / ~束 *electron beam* / ~表格 *spreadsheet* / ~数据处理 *EDP*; *electronic data processing* / ~透镜 *electron bens* / ~显微镜 *electron microscope* / ~学 *electronics* / ~游戏 *video game*; *TV game* / ~云 *electron cloud*
【电阻】【电】resistance: ~率 *resistivity*; *specific resistance*
【电钻】electric drill

佃 rent land (from a landlord)
【佃户】tenant (farmer); renter
【佃农】tenant peasant; tenant farmer
【佃租】land rent

店 ① shop; store: 理发~ *barber's shop* / 书~ *book store* ② inn: 住~ *stop at an inn* / 开~ *keep an inn*
【店铺】shop; store
【店堂】shop (or store) room
【店员】shop assistant; salesclerk; clerk; salesman or saleswoman

玷 ① flaw in a piece of jade ② blemish
【玷辱】be a disgrace to; bring disgrace on
【玷污】sully; stain; tarnish

垫 ① put sth under sth else to raise it or make it level; fill up; pad: ~路 *repair a road by filling the holes* / 把桌子~平 *put sth under the leg of a desk to make it level* ② pay for sb and expect to be paid back later: 我带的钱不够,你先替我~上吧。*I haven't enough money on me; will you please pay for me now?* ③ pad; cushion; mat: 杯~ *cup cushion*
【垫背】[方] take the blame for others; be made a scapegoat
【垫付】pay for sb and expect to be repaid later
【垫肩】shoulder pad
【垫脚石】stepping-stone
【垫款】money paid for sb to be paid back later
【垫密片】【机】gasket: 气缸~ *insulation spacer*
【垫球】under pass; under toss
【垫片】【机】① spacer: 绝缘~ *insulation spacer* ② shim: 轴承~ *bearing shim*
【垫平】level up: 把路~ *level a road*
【垫子】mat; mattress; pad; cushion: 蹭鞋~ *door mat* / 体操~ *gym mat* / 椅~ *chair cushion* / 弹簧~ *spring mattress*

淀 ① form sediment; settle; precipitate ② shallow lake
【淀粉】starch; amylum
【淀粉酶】【生化】amylase

惦 remember with concern; be concerned about; keep thinking about: ~着某事 *keep think about sth*
【惦记】remember with concern; worry about; keep thinking about: 他总是~着那件没有完成的工作。*He's always thinking about the unfinished work.*
【惦念】keep thinking about; be concerned about; worry about: 离家多年,我非常~我的父母。*Having been away from home for many years, I think about my parents very much.*

奠 ① establish; settle ② make offerings to the spirits of the dead
【奠定】establish; settle: ~基础 *lay a foundation*
【奠都】establish or found a capital: ~北京。*Bei-*

jing has made the capital.

【奠基】lay a foundation: ~石 *foundation stone; cornerstone*

【奠仪】a gift of money made on the occasion of a funeral

殿 ① hall; palace; temple: 宫~ *palace* /太和~ *the Hall of Supreme Harmony* ② march at the rear ③ at the rear

【殿后】bring up the rear: 你先走,我~。*You go first while I'll bring up the rear.*

【殿堂】① palace ② temple hall: 艺术~ *palace of art*

【殿下】your Highness; His (or her) highness

靛 indigo

【靛蓝】indigo: ~色 *indigo-blue*

【靛青】① indigo-blue ② [方] indigo

癜 purplish or white patches on the skin: 白~疯 *vitiligo*

diāo

刁 ① tricky; sly ② artful: 这话实在是~。*The words are really crafty.*

【刁悍】cunning and fierce

【刁滑】cunning; crafty; artful

【刁民】[旧] unruly people

【刁难】create difficulties; make things difficult; deliberate harassment; obstruct: 百般~ *create obstructions of every description*

【刁钻】tricky; sly; cunning; artful: 发球~ *tricky service*

【刁钻古怪】sly and capricious; be cunning and peculiar: ~的脾气 *a strange cranky temper*

叼 hold in the mouth: ~着烟卷 *with a cigarette dangling from one's lips* /猫~着一只老鼠。*A cat ran with a mouse in its mouth.*

凋 wither: 松柏长绿不~。*The pine and cypress remain green and will not wither all the year round.*

【凋敝】① (of life) hard ② (of business) depress; ragged

【凋零】① withered; fallen and scattered about: 草木~。*Grass and trees have withered.* ② decline; be on the wane ③ pass away; die: 老辈~。*The older generation is dying off.*

【凋落】wither and fall

【凋谢】① wither and fall ② die of old age

貂 marten; ermine; mink

【貂皮】marten; fur of marten; pelt of marten

【貂裘】marten coat

碉 pillbox; blockhouse

【碉堡】pillbox; blockhouse

【碉楼】military watchtower

雕 carve; engrave; sculpt

【雕虫小技】insignificant skill; literary skill of no order

【雕花】① carve patterns of designs on woodwork ② carrying: ~玻璃 *engraved glass; cut glass*

【雕刻】carve; engrave: ~刀 *carving tool; burin* / ~工艺 *artistic carving* /玉石~ *jade carving* / ~师 *carver; engraver*

【雕漆】carved lacquerware

【雕塑】sculpture

【雕像】stature; carved figure: 石膏~ *gesso statue* / 半身~ *bust* /小~ *statuette*

【雕琢】① cut and polish (jade, etc.) ② write in an ornate style

diào

吊 ① hang; suspend; dangle: 树上~着秋千儿。*There is a swing hanging in the tree.* ② lift up or let down with a rope, etc.; haul: 把木料~上顶层。*Lift up the timber to the top floor.* ③ put in a fur lining, line: ~皮袄 *line a coat with fur* ④ revoke; withdraw ⑤ crane

【吊膀子】[方] flirt; try to get fresh with a woman

【吊车】crane; hoist: ~轨道 *crane runway*

【吊床】hammock

【吊打】hang up and beat sb

【吊灯】pendent lamp

【吊斗】cableway bucket

【吊儿郎当】be careless and casual; fool around: 他整天~,不努力学习。*He fools around all day long not studying hard.*

【吊杆】【机】boom; jib: 起重机~ *crane boom* / ~托架 *boom crutch well-sweep*

【吊杠】【体】trapeze

【吊钩】【机】(lift) hook; hanger

【吊古】reminisce about the past on visiting a historical site

【吊环】【体】rings: 摆荡~ *swinging rings* /静止~ *still rings*

【吊货盘】platform (or tray) sling

【吊架】【机】hanger: 平衡~ *balance hanger*

【吊景】【戏】drop scene

【吊链】chain sling; sling chain

【吊铺】hanging bed; hammock

【吊桥】① drawbridge ② suspension bridge

【吊表】pay condolence call; visit the bereaved to offer one's condolences

【吊嗓子】train one's voice; exercise one's voice

【吊扇】ceiling fan

【吊死】hang by the neck; hang oneself

【吊索】sling: 钢丝~ *wire sling* /绳~ *rope sling*

【吊桶】well-bucket; bucket

【吊袜带】(stocking) suspenders; garters

【吊胃口】tease; flirt; tantalize

【吊线】plumb line

【吊销】revoke; withdraw: ~驾照 *revoke a driving licence* / ~营业执照 *revoke a business licence* / ~护照 *withdraw a passport* / ~签证 *cancel a visa already issued*
【吊孝】[口] pay a condolence call
【吊唁】condole; offer condolences: ~函电 *messages of condolence*
【吊装】【建】hoisting
钓 ① fish with a hook and line; angle: ~鱼 *angle; go fishing* ② pursue (personal fame); hunt for; seek: 沽名~誉 *fish (or angle) for fame and compliments*
【钓饵】bait
【钓竿】fishing rod
【钓钩】fishhook
【钓具】fishing tackle
【钓鱼】go fishing; angle
调[1] ① transfer; shift; move: 他已经~到我们单位了。*He has been transferred to our unit.* ② investigate: ~查 *look into; research; survey*
调[2] ① accent; tone: 他说话有很重的河南~儿。*He speaks with a heavy Henan accent.* ②【音】key: B~ *key of B* ③ air; tune; melody: 定~ *call the turn; set the keynote* ④【语】tone; tune: 升~ *rising tone (or tune)* / 降~ *falling tone (or tune)*
see also tiáo
【调兵遣将】① move troops; deploy forces; dispatch officers and men ② mobilize and organize manpower
【调拨】① allocate and transfer; allocation and delivery of consumer goods: ~物资 *allocate materials* ② abet; instigate
【调查】investigate; inquire into; survey; ascertain; check: 现场~ *on-the-spot investigation* / 社会~ *a social investigation* / ~报告 *findings report* / ~团 *fact-finding mission* / ~者 *inquirer; investigator*
【调车场】switchyard
【调档】ask for the applicant's dossier
【调动】① transfer; shift: ~人员 *transfer personnel* / ~工作 *transfer sb to another post* ② manoeuvre; muster; more troops: ~大批的部队 *move troops by the thousands* ③ bring into play; mobilize; arouse: ~一切积极因素 *bring every positive factor into play*
【调度】① dispatch (trains, buses, etc.): ~货车 *dispatch trucks* ② manage; control: 生产~ *production management* ③ dispatcher: ~员 *dispatcher* / 他是电车公司的~。*He is the dispatcher of trolley company.*
【调防】【军】relieve a garrison
【调号】①【语】tone make ②【音】key signature
【调虎离山】lure the tiger out of the mountains; (fig) lure the enemy away from his base
【调回】recall (troops; etc.): ~原公司 *recall sb to the original company*
【调集】assemble; muster; mass: ~人马 *assemble forces* / ~人员 *assemble persons*
【调离】be transferred from one place of job (to another):
【调令】transfer order: 蒂娜的~已经发出了。*The order for Tina's transfer has been sent out.*
【调门儿】① pitch: ~太高了,我唱不上去。*The tune is pitched too high for my voice.* ② point of view; tone (of one's words); argument: 这篇文章的~太高了。*This article utters high-sounding words.*
【调派】send; assign
【调配】allocate; deploy: ~饲料 *allocate feedstuff* / 合理~劳动力 *rational deployment of manpower*
【调遣】dispatch; assign: ~军队 *dispatch troops* / 服从~ *obey an assignment*
【调任】be transferred to another post: 他已经~市长。*He has been transferred to be the mayor.*
【调式】【音】mode
【调用】transfer (under a unified plan); transfer to a specific job: ~干部 *transfer cadres* / ~程序 *calling program* / ~人手 *transfer the hands*
【调运】allocate and transport: ~大批蔬菜到北京 *allocate large quantities of greenstuff to Beijing*
【调职】be transferred to another post
【调子】①【音】tune; melody: 定~ *call the tune; set the keynote* ② tone (of speech); view
掉[1] ① fall; drop; shed; come off: ~眼泪 *shed tears* ② fall behind; drop: ~队 *drop out; fall behind* ③ lose; be missing: 我把钱包~了。*I've lost my wallet.* / 这本字典~了几页。*Several pages are missing from this dictionary.* ④ decrease; lower: 由于工作辛苦,他最近~了五公斤肉。*For the heavy work, he lost five kg recently.*
掉[2] ① wag; shake; sway: ~尾巴 *wag the tail* ② turn; turn back: ~过脸去 *avert one's face; turn one's face* ③ exchange; swap: ~座儿 *change seats*
掉[3] used after certain verbs to indicate removal: 擦~ *wipe off* / 洗~ *wash out* / 吃~ *eat up* / 卸~玻璃 *remove glass*
【掉包】stealthily substitute one thing for another
【掉队】drop out; fall behind: 快点,千万别~。*Hurry up; Don't fall behind by all means.*
【掉换】shift; swop; exchange; change: 这双鞋不合适,~一下好吗? *These shoes are not of the right size; could I change them for others?*
【掉魂】be frightened out of one's wits
【掉价】① fall in price go down in price: 电视机~了。*The price of TV set has come down.* ② lower one's status: 我干这事并不~。*What I did was not beneath the dignity of mine.*
【掉色】lose colour; fade: 这件上衣~。*The coat faded.*
【掉书袋】fill one's writing with quotations to parade learning
【掉以轻心】treat sth lightly; let down one's guard; adopt a casual attitude; lower one's guard: 情势危急,千万不能~。*How critical the state of affairs*

is! Don't treat thing highly.
【掉转】turn round：~身子 *turn round* (*one's body*)

diē

爹 father; dad; pa：~娘 *father and mother*
跌 ① fall; tumble：~进水坑 *tumble into a pond* /他不小心~倒在地。*He fell over carelessly.* ② drop; fall
【跌打损伤】injuries from falls, fractures, contusions and strains
【跌倒】fall; tumble down：他被石头绊了一下，~了。*He stumped over a stone and fell.*
【跌跌撞撞】stagger along：他醉了，走路~。*He staggered along as he was drunk.*
【跌幅】amount or size of decrease
【跌价】go down in price; devalue; sell off：手机开始~。*The price of mobile phone has dropped.*
【跌跤】① fall; trip and fall：② make a mistake ③ meet with a setback
【跌落】① fall; decent ② (of value) drop; sag

dié

迭 ① alternate; replace; substitute：政府更~ *reshuffle of government* ② repeatedly; time and time again：人才~出 *talents emerged one after another* ③ in time
【迭次】repeatedly; time and time again：~造访 *call on sb repeatedly*
【迭代】iterate
【迭连】continually; in succession：最近她~出差错。*She made mistakes several times recently.*
【迭起】happen repeatedly; occur frequently：新春晚会上，高潮~。*One climax followed another in the New Year party.*
谍 ① espionage ② spy; intelligence agent
【谍报】secret information obtained through espionage; intelligence：~员 *secret agent*; *spy*
喋
【喋喋不休】chatter away; talk endlessly; rattle on：我再也忍受不了他的~了。*I can't put up with his endless talking any more.*
【喋血】bloodshed; bloodbath
牒 official document or note; certificate
叠 ① pile up; repeat ② fold：折~椅 *folding chair* / ~被子 *make the bed*
【叠句】【语】reiterative sentence
【叠影】ghosting
【叠韵】【语】characters with similar vowel formation
碟 small dish; saucer
【碟子】small dish; small plate
蝶 butterfly
【蝶骨】【生理】sphenoid bone
【蝶泳】butterfly stroke

dīng

丁 ① man; male; adult：雷切尔家有三个男~。*There are three men in Rachel's family.* ② members of a family; population：添~ *have another baby born into the family* ③ a person engaged in a certain type of occupation：园~ *gardener* ④ small cubes of vegetable or meat：土豆~ *diced potato* ⑤ the fourth of the ten Heavenly Stems (天干) ⑥ fourth ⑦ (Dīng) a surname
【丁当】ding-dong; jingle; clatter：远处传来一声~响。*There is jingle somewhere.*
【丁点儿】[方] a little bit：你说得~没错。*You are absolutely right.* /我只剩这一~钱了。*I have only this poor money left.*
【丁零当啷】cling-clang; jingle-jangle
【丁烷】【化】butane：~气 *butagas*
【丁香】【植】① lilac ② clove：~园 *clove plantation* / ~油 *clove oil*
【丁字】T-shaped：~尺 *T-square* / ~街 *T-shaped road junction* / ~梁 *T-girder*; *T-beam*
叮 ① sting; bite：蚊子~了他的脸。*A mosquito bit him on the face.* ② say again to sb：我又~了她一句，确信她明天会来。*I asked her again to make sure she will come tomorrow.*
【叮嘱】urge again and again; exhort again and again：母亲再三~我多穿衣服别着凉。*Mother urged me again and again to wear more clothes against the cold.*
盯 fix one's eyes on; gaze at; stare at：萨宾一动不动地~着显示器。*Sabin looked at the monitor fixedly without any movement.* / ~住这个坏蛋。*Keep a close watch on the bad egg.*
【盯梢】shadow sb; tail sb：他们被警察~了。*They were tailed by the police.*
钉[1] nail; tack：图~ *drawing pin*; *thumb tack*
钉[2] ① follow closely; tail; stick with：侦探正~着一个嫌疑分子。*A detective is tailing a suspicious character.* ② keep asking or reminding：你要~着他做作业。*You must remind him to do his homework.*
【钉齿耙】spike-tooth harrow
【钉锤】nail hammer; claw hammer
【钉帽】head of a nail
【钉耙】(iron-toothed) rake
【钉人】【体】watch an opponent in a game：~防守 *man-to-man defence*
【钉鞋】spiked shoes; spikes; brush shoes
【钉子】① nail; tack; pin ② planted agent; saboteur：~户 *tarter*

dǐng

顶 ① top; crown of the head:秃～ *be bald* /房～ *roof* ② carry on the head:头上～着一罐酒 *carry a pitcher of wine on one's head* ③ gore; butt:这只羊老～东西。*The goat often butts something.* ④ push from below or behind; push up:用千斤顶～汽车 *jack up a car* /嫩芽～开了土。*The sprouts have pushed up the earth.* ⑤ go against:战士们～着暴风雪前进。*The soldiers marched ahead in the snowstorm.* ⑥ retort; answer back:他～回了我的抗议。*He rejected my protest.* ⑦ cope with; under take:任务虽重,我们还是～了下来。*Hard as the task was, we managed to get it done.* ⑧ substitute; take the place of; replace: ～别人的名字 *assume sb else's name* ⑨ equal; be equivalent to ⑩ [量] used of sth that has a top:一～帽子 *a cap; a hat* ⑪ most; very; extremely: ～有用 *very useful* / ～漂亮 *very beautiful* /我～喜欢英文歌曲。*I like English songs very much.*

【顶班】① take over other's shift while he is absent ② work full time; work on regular shifts

【顶板】【矿】roof; ejector plate:直接～ *immediate roof*

【顶吹】【冶】top blown: ～转炉 *top-blown converter*

【顶灯】overhead light; dome light (of a car)

【顶点】①【数】vertex apex ② top; peak; zenith

【顶端】summit; top end

【顶多】at (the) most; at best:托马斯～是个工程师。*Thomas is at best an engineer.*

【顶风】upwind; against the wind; head wind

【顶峰】peak; summit:生意～ *the zenith of one's business*

【顶骨】【生理】parietal bone

【顶呱呱】tip-top; first-rate

【顶好】① best; very good ② had better; it would be best:你～留在这里。*You'd better stay here.*

【顶尖】top; best; topmost: ～高手 *topmost figure* / ～建筑师 *top level architect* / ～人物 *topmost figure*

【顶梁柱】pillar; backbone

【顶门儿】the front top of the head

【顶棚】ceiling joist; paper ceiling

【顶球】【体】head (a ball)

【顶少】at least

【顶事】be useful; serve the purpose:这药可～了! *The medicine is a great help!*

【顶替】take sb's place; substitute; replace:他不在时谁来～? *Who's going to take his place when he is absent?* ② get a job at one's parent's place of work when the parent dies

【顶天立地】of indomitable; of gigantic stature: ～的男人 *dauntless man*

【顶头】① against; come directly: ～风 *against wind* ② top; end:这条街～有个书店。*There is a bookstore at the end of this street.*

【顶碗】balancing a stack of bowls on the head

【顶芽】【植】terminal bud

【顶用】be of use or help; be effective; be serviceable:来年他就～了。*He'll be of help next year.* /我觉得电话留言机一点也不～。*I think answer machine is no use.*

【顶针】thimble

【顶住】hold out against; with stand; stand up to: ～一切压力 *withstand all pressure* / ～诱惑 *resist temptation* / ～风浪 *weather a storm*

【顶撞】contradict (one's elder or superior); talk back: ～父母 *contradict one's parents*

【顶嘴】[口] answer back; talk back; reply defiantly:孩子不应该跟父母～。*Children shouldn't talk back to their parents.*

鼎 ① an ancient cooking vessel with two loop handles and three (or four) legs:三足～ *tripod* ② [书] the throne; state power ③ [方] pot; pan ④ great; grand

【鼎沸】[书] like a boiling cauldron; noisy and confused:人声～ *seething mass of people; bawling crowd*

【鼎力】[书] your kind effort; your great help: ～支持 *support sb with all one's effort* /我们真的很感激你的～相助。*We really appreciate your great help.*

【鼎立】stand like the legs of a tripod; tripartite con formation

【鼎盛】in a period of great prosperity; at the height of power and splendour:国力～ *in the heyday of a nation*

【鼎新】[书] innovate; reform:革故～ *introduce reforms*

【鼎足】three legs of a tripod-three powers

dìng

订 ① conclude; draw up; agree on: ～单 *order list* / ～合同 *enter into (or make) a con tract* / ～计划 *formulate (or work out) a plan* / ～日期 *agree on a date* / ～条约 *conclude a treaty* ② subscribe to (a newspaper, magazine, etc.):增～ *place a new order* /续～ *renew one's subscription* ③ revise; make corrections:修～ *revise* ④ staple together:她把散页～了起来。*She stapled the loose leaves together.*

【订单】order for goods; order form

【订费】subscription rate

【订购】order goods; place an order for sth

【订户】① subscriber (to a newspaper or periodical) ② a person or household with a standing order for milk, purified water, etc.

【订婚】be engaged (to be married); be betrothed

【订货】order goods; place an order for goods: ～代理人 *indent agent* / ～付款 *cash with order (CWO)* / ～量 *quantity (or size) of order*

【订交】make friends (with sb)

【订金】an initial payment; earnest money

【订立】conclude (a treaty, agreement, etc.); make (a contract etc.): ~贸易协定 *conclude a trade agreement*
【订书机】① stapling machine; stapler ② book binding machine
【订约】conclude a treaty; make a contract
【订阅】subscribe to (a newspaper, periodical, etc.)
【订正】make corrections; emend: ~了原稿中的错误。*Corrections have been made to the manual scripts.*

钉 ① nail: ~马掌 *nail on horse shoes* / ~钉子 *drive in a nail* ② sew on: ~扣子 *sew a button on*

定 ① calm; stable; quiet: 心神不~ *be distracted*; *be uneasy* ② fixed; determined; settled; established ③ fix; set; make certain: ~计划 *make a schedule* / 截止日期~于明天。*The deadline is set for tomorrow.* ④ subscribe to (a news paper, magazine, etc.): ~去北京的机票 *book a plane ticket to Beijing* ⑤ [书] surely; certainly; absolutely; definitely: ~可完成 *be sure to finish*
【定案】① decide on a verdict; reach a conclusion ② judgement; final decision; verdict
【定都】choose a site for the capital; establish a capital: ~北京 *make Beijing the capital*
【定夺】make a final decision: 这事儿让老板~吧! *Let the boss make a final decision on this matter!*
【定额】quota; norm; standard: 生产~ *production quota* / ~补贴 *quota subsidy* / ~制 *quota system*
【定岗】fix responsibility; set work requirements for a position
【定稿】① finalize a manuscript, text etc. ② final version or text
【定格】① freeze frame ② fixed paler or model
【定冠词】【语】definite article in English grammar
【定规】① established rule or practice ② [方] insist on; be determined
【定价】① bid; fix a price: 给商品~ *fix the prices of goods* ② charge; fixed price; list price: 这本书~十元。*The marked price of the book is 10 yuan.*
【定见】definite opinion; set view
【定金】earnest; deposit; down payment
【定居】settle down; settle; live in: 他们决定在广东~。*They've decided to settle down in Guangdong.*
【定局】① unchangeable conclusion; final settlement; inevitable out come ② settle; finally: 这事还没有~, 改天再议。*The matter isn't settling yet; we can take is up again someday.*
【定礼】bride-price; betrothal gift
【定理】theorem: 基本~ *fundamental theorem*
【定例】routine; usual practice; set pattern: 周日开会已成~。*It is a usual practice that we have a meeting every Sunday.*
【定量】① determine the amounts of the components of a substance: ~分析 *quantitative analysis* ② fix the amount or quantity: ~供应 *rationing* ③ fixed quantity; ration
【定律】law: 万有引力~ *the law of universal gravitation*
【定论】final conclusion: 对于这部影片的评价, 目前尚无~。*There is no final conclusion about this film.*
【定苗】【农】final singling (of seedlings)
【定名】name; denominate
【定期】① fix a date; set a date ② regular; periodical: ~体检 *regular physical checkup* / 不~刊物 *non periodic publication* / ~存款 *fixed deposit*; *time deposit* / ~贷款 *term loan*; *time loan*; *fixed loan* / ~抵押 *term mortgage* / ~抵押贷款 *time mortgage loan* / ~付款 *scheduled payment* / ~信用证 *time letter of credit*
【定钱】deposit; earnest (money)
【定亲】engagement (usually arranged by parents); betrothal
【定情】pledge love
【定然】certainly; definitely: 她~会喜欢这首诗。*She definitely will like this poem.*
【定神】① concentrate one's attention: 我~细看, 她眼里含着泪。*Looking hard, I found tear in her eyes.* ② collect oneself; pull oneself together: 先~下来再走。*Calm down before you go.*
【定时】① at fixed time; at regular intervals: ~服药 *take medicine at regular intervals* ② fix the time; time: ~引爆 *time an explosion*
【定时器】timer; timing controller
【定势】fixed pattern: 思维~ *fixed pattern of thinking*
【定位】① orientate; position ② orientation; fixed position; location
【定息】fixed interest
【定弦】① tune a stringed instrument ② [方] make up one's mind; have a fixed idea
【定向】① fix the orientation of ② directional: ~爆破 *directional blasting* / ~分配 *predetermined assignment of job for a student, etc.*
【定心】① feel relieved; feel at ease: 孩子找到了, 这下他们可~了。*Now that the child was found, they could feel relieved.* ②【机】centring: ~装置 *centring device*
【定形】① setting; boarding: 热~ *heat setting* ② take form; take shape
【定型】finalize the design; fall into a pattern; take form; take shape
【定性】① determine the nature (of an offence or a case) ② determine the chemical composition of a substance: ~分析 *qualitative analysis*
【定义】definition: 下~ *define*; *give a definition*
【定语】【语】attribute: ~从句 *a attributive clause*
【定员】fixed number of staff or passengers: 这辆公汽~96人。*The bus has a seating capacity of 96 people.*
【定则】【物】rule: 右手~ *right-hand rule* / 左手~ *left-hand rule*
【定制】① established rule or practice ② have sth

custom-made：～家具 *have furniture made to order*

【定罪】declare guilty；convict sb（of a crime）

【定做】have sth made to order

锭 ①【纺】spindle ② ingot-shaped tablet（of medicine，metal，etc.）③［量］used of sth like an ingot：一～银子 *a silver ingot*

【锭模】【冶】ingot mould

【锭速】rotational speed of a spindle

【锭子】【纺】spindle

dīu

丢 ① lose；mislay：他～了个手机。*He lost a mobile phone.* /我把钢笔～哪儿了？*Where did I leave my pen?* ② throw；cast；toss：不要随地～垃圾。*Don't litter，please.* ③ put aside；lay aside：他早把学习～在脑后。*He has forgotten all about his study.* /我的英语～了好几年了。*I haven't used my English for years.*

【丢丑】be disgraced；lost face：真～！*What a pity!* /你这样做太～了。*It was really disgraceful of you to act like that.*

【丢掉】① lose：我把信用卡～了。*I lost my credit card.* ② throw away；cast away；discard：～幻想 *cast away illusions* /～压力 *discard stresses*

【丢饭碗】［口］lose one's job

【丢盔弃甲】throw away one's shield and armour；be badly defeated and run away

【丢脸】lose face；be disgraced：不要怕～。*Don't be afraid of losing face.*

【丢面子】lose face；feel humiliated：这不是～的事。*There's nothing to be ashamed of.*

【丢弃】abandon；get rid of；discard

【丢人现眼】make a fool of oneself

【丢三落四】forget this and that；be careless and sloppy

【丢失】wash one's hand of；give up：她～不管了。*She washed her hands of the business.*

【丢眼色】wink at sb；signal with a wink：我几次向他～，但他都没注意到。*I winked at him several times；but he didn't take my cue.*

【丢卒保车】（as in playing Chinese chess）give up a pawn to save a castle — sacrifice minor things to save major ones

dōng

东 ① east：城～三十里 *thirty li east of the city* /～城 *eastern part of the city* ② master owner：房～ *landlord* /股～ *stockholder* ③ host：今天我做～。*It's my treat today.*

【东半球】eastern Hemisphere

【东北】① northeast ② northeast china；the Northeast

【东奔西跑】run around here and there；rush around；bustle about：他为事业～。*He was rushed off his feet for his business.*

【东窗事发】the plot hatched in secret is exposed；the secret is out

【东倒西歪】stumble；unsteady；tottering；lying in disorder：～的椅子 *rickety chairs* /三个醉鬼～地在街上走。*Three drunken men staggered along the street.*

【东道主】one who treats sb to a meal；host：做～ *play host；be the host* /～国 *host country*

【东方】east：日出～。*The sun rises in the east.*

【东风】① east wind；spring wind ② driving force of revolution：万事俱备，只欠～。*Everything is ready except one key element.*

【东海】the East China Sea

【东家】master；boss；landlord：少～ *young master*

【东拉西扯】drag in irrelevant matters；talk at random；ramble：他的报告～，没有主题。*He talked randomly in his lecture without any subject.*

【东盟】association of southeast Asian Nations（ASEAN）

【东南】① southeast ② southeast China；the Southeast

【东南亚】Southeast Asia

【东挪西借】borrow from everybody

【东欧】eastern Europe

【东跑西颠】rush here and hurry there；run busily around

【东拼西凑】scrape together；knock together：他的文章是～来的。*His article is just scissors-and-paste work.*

【东山再起】stage a comeback；resume one's business

【东西】① east and west ② from east to west：这个小镇～五百米。*The small town is 500 metres from east to west.* ③ thing；stuff：收拾好～再离开。*Put your things in order before you leave.* /没有一成不变的～。*Nothing is immutable.* ④（used to express affection or hatred for person or animal）thing；creature：真不是～！*What a mean creature!*

【东亚】East Asia

【东张西望】gaze or peer around；glance around；look about in all directions：她站在那儿～。*She stood there glancing around.*

【东正教】the Orthodox Eastern Church

冬 ① winter：隆～ *deep winter* ② the sound of beating a drum，knocking at a door，etc.；dub-a-dub；rat-a-tat

【冬储】store sth in winter or for winter use

【冬耕】winter ploughing

【冬菇】dried mushrooms picked in winter

【冬瓜】wax gourd；white gourd

【冬灌】winter irrigation

【冬寒】winter cold

【冬候鸟】winter bird

【冬季】winter：～施工 *winter construction* /～体育运动 *winter sports* /～作物 *winter crop*

【冬眠】winter sleep; hibernation
【冬青】【植】Chinese ilex
【冬笋】winter bamboo shoots
【冬天】winter: 去年～，他去了上海出差，到现在还没有回来。*He didn't come back until now since he went business last winter.*
【冬小麦】winter wheat
【冬训】winter training
【冬汛】winter fishing season
【冬衣】winter clothes
【冬泳】winter outdoor swimming; swimming freezing water in winter
【冬运会】winter sports meet
【冬至】the Winter Solstice-the 22nd of the 24 solar terms, marking the sun's position at 270° on the ecliptic
【冬装】winter dress or clothes

氡 【化】radon (Ru)

dǒng

董 ①［书］direct; superintend; supervise ② director; trustee
【董事】director; trustee: 常务～ *executive director*
【董事会】board of directors (in an enterprise); board of trustees
【董事长】chairman or president of the board of directors

懂 understand; know: ～日语 *know Japanese* / 那孩子一点也不～礼貌。*The little child has no good manners.* / 不要不～装～。*Never pretends to know when you don't.*
【懂得】understand; know; grasp: 没人～他在干什么。*No one knew what he was doing.* / 他～读书的重要性。*He knows the importance of reading.*
【懂行】［方］know the business; know the tricks
【懂事】sensible; intelligent: 他怎么这么不～? *How can he be so thoughtless?*

dòng

动 ① more; stir: 风吹～水面。*A breeze stirred the river.* / 我没～过你的单放机。*I haven't touched your walkman.* ② act; get moving: 轻举妄～ *act rashly* / 经过动员，所有学生都～起来了。*After the mobilization meetings, all the students got moving.* ③ change; alter: 他把设计作了些改～。*He has made some alterations on the design.* ④ use: ～脑筋 *use one's head* / ～嘴皮子 *pay lip service* ⑤ touch (one's heart); arouse: ～感情 *be carried away by emotion; get worked up* / 晓之以理，～之以情 *appeal to reason as well as human compassion* / 他的故事很～人。*His story is very touching.* ⑥［方］eat; drink: 不～荤腥 *never eat meat or fish*
【动笔】take up the pen or brush; start writing or painting: 她最近很少～作画。*She hasn't done much painting recently.* / 想清楚后再～。*Think it over before you start writing.*
【动不动】easily; frequently; at every turn: ～就发火 *flare up easily* / ～就哭 *often break down and weep; be apt to cry*
【动产】movable property; personal property; movables: ～税 *movable property tax* / 不～ *immovable property*
【动词】【语】verb: ～不定式 *infinitive* / ～短语 *verbal phrase*
【动粗】［方］resort to violence
【动荡】turbulence; upheaval; unrest: ～的局势 *a turbulent situation*
【动荡不安】turbulent; in turmoil: 世界局势～。*The world is in turmoil.*
【动肝火】get angry; flare up
【动感】dynamic; graphic
【动工】① being construction; start building: 新公路已～了。*The construction of the new highway has started.* ② under construction: 前方正在～，车辆请绕行。*Construction site ahead; please choose another way.*
【动滑轮】movable pulley
【动画片】animated cartoon; cartoon
【动火】get angry; flare up
【动机】motive; intention: ～不纯 *have impure (or mixed) motives* / 你这样做的～是什么? *Why did you do so?*
【动静】① the sound of sth astir: 教室里一点～也没有。*Nothing was stirring in the classroom.* ② movement; activity: 监视敌方～ *keep a close watch on the enemy's activities*
【动力】① motive power; power ② motive or driving force; impetus: 发展的～ *motive force of development* / ～反应堆 *power reactor* / ～机 *motor; engine* / ～系统 *power system* / ～学 *dynamics; kinetics* / ～装置 *power set* / 他工作的～很大。*He is strongly motivated in his working.*
【动量】【物】momentum: 广义～ *generalized momentum* / ～矩 *moment of momentum* / ～守恒定律 *the law of conservation of momentum*
【动令】【军】command of execution
【动乱】turmoil; disturbance; upheaval; turbulence: ～时期 *time of turmoil* / 社会～ *social unrest* / ～年代 *years of upheaval*
【动脉】【生理】artery: ～脉搏 *arterial pulse* / ～血 *arterial blood* / ～血压 *arterial pressure* / ～弓 *arch of aorta*
【动名词】【语】gerund
【动摩擦】【物】dynamical friction
【动能】【物】kinetic energy
【动怒】lose one's temper; flare up
【动平衡】【物】dynamic balance
【动气】［口］take offence; get angry
【动情】① be moved or touched; become excited ② become enamoured
【动人】moving; touching: ～的场面 *moving scene* /

～的事迹 *stirring deeds* /楚楚～（*of women*）*beautiful*; *attractive*

【动人心弦】tug at one's heartstrings; be deeply touching

【动身】go on a journey; leave (for a distant place):他决定明天～。*He made up his mind to leave tomorrow.*

【动手】① start work; get to work:亲自～ *do it oneself* ② touch; handle:爱护展品,请勿～。*Please don't touch the exhibits.* ③ raise a hand to strike; hit out:～打人 *raise one's hand to hit sb* / ～动脚 *get fresh with sb*

【动手术】① operate on sb; perform an operation ② have an operation; be operated on ③ effect a big change or reform

【动态】① trends; developments:科技新～ *recent developments in science and technology* ② dynamic state: ～变量 *dynamic variable* / ～分析 *dynamic analysis* / ～经济学 *dynamic economics* / ～平衡 *dynamic balance* / ～数据交换 *dynamic date exchange* (*DDE*) ③ motion and expression; behaviour

【动弹】move; stir:这只狗不能～了。*The dog could not move a little.*

【动听】interesting or pleasant to listen to:他的故事很～。*His story is very interesting.*

【动土】break ground; start building

【动窝儿】[方] start moving; make a move:不管你怎么说,他就是不～。*Whatever you say, he just won't stir.*

【动武】use force; start a fight; come to blows

【动物】animal: ～界 *the animal kingdom* / ～蛋白 *animal protein* / ～淀粉 *animal starch* / ～胶 *animal glue* / ～群落 *animal community*

【动向】trend; tendency:新～ *new trend*

【动心】have one's enthusiasm or interest aroused; be attracted

【动型】subject to torture; torture

【动摇】shake; waver:信仰～ *waver in one's belief* / 什么也～不了他的信心。*Nothing can shake his confidence.*

【动议】motion:紧急～ *urgent motion* /通过～ *adopt a motion*

【动用】put to use; employ: ～武力 *use force* / ～大量人力 *employ a huge a mount of manpower*

【动员】mobilize; arouse: ～报告 *mobilization speech* / ～大会 *mobilization meeting* /学生都被～起来植树。*All the students were mobilized to plant trees.*

【动植物】animals and plants: ～检疫 *quarantine of animals and plants*

【动真格】do sth for real; take sth seriously

【动作】① movement; motion; action: ～敏捷 *quick in one's movements* /优美的体操～ *graceful gymnastic movements* ② act; start moving:分析一下他下一步的～。*Let's examine what he do next.*

冻 ① freeze:河水～上了。*The river has frozen.* ② jelly ③ feel very cold; freeze: ～死我了! *I'm freezing!* /小心别～着。*Take care so you won't catch cold.*

【冻冰】freeze:湖面～了。*The lake is frozen on the surface.*

【冻疮】chilblain:生～ *have chilblains*

【冻害】【农】freeze injury

【冻僵】frozen stiff; numb with cold

【冻结】① freeze; congeal ② (of wages, prices, etc.) freeze:工资～ *wage free* / ～的资产 *frozen assets* / ～资金 *frozen fund*; *blocked fund*

【冻凝】congeal: ～点 *congealing point*

【冻伤】frostbite

【冻死】freeze to death; freeze and perish; die of cold

【冻土】frozen earth, ground, or soil

【冻雨】【气】sleet

栋 ①[书] ridgepole ②[量] used of housing: 一～楼房 *a building*

【栋梁】ridgepole and beam; pillar:社会～ *pillar of the state* / ～之材 *one with the makings of a states man*

洞 ① hole; cavity:窑～（*mountain*）*cave* /漏～ *loophole* /城门～儿 *archway of city gate* ② [书] penetrate; pierce ③ [书] penetratingly; thoroughly

【洞察】see clearly; have an insight into: ～力 *insight*; *discernment* / ～是非 *distinguish unequivocally between right and wrong* / ～一切 *see everything clearly* / ～下情 *be well-acquainted with the situation at the grass-roots level*

【洞彻】understand thoroughly; see clearly: ～事理 *be sensible and wise*

【洞穿】① pierce; penetrate ② have an insight into; under stand fully

【洞达】understand thoroughly

【洞房】bridal or nuptial chamber

【洞房花烛】wedding; wedding festivities

【洞若观火】see sth as clearly as a blazing fire

【洞识】know clearly

【洞天】cave heaven — fairyland:别有～ *a place of unique, charming beauty*

【洞悉】know clearly; understand thoroughly: 我们已经～你来的目的了。*We have known clearly why you come.*

【洞晓】have a clear knowledge of

【洞穴】cave; cavern

【洞烛】see through; discern clearly

恫 [书] fear

【恫吓】threaten; intimidate

胴 ① trunk; body ② [书] large intestine

【胴体】① trunk; carcass ② body

dōu

都 ① all:他们～上学去了。*All of them have gone to school.* /兄妹俩～病了。*Both brother*

and sister were taken ill. ② used together with 是 to show the cause: ~是你的错。*It's your entire fault.* ③ even: 他只顾抽烟,一声~不吭。*He kept on smoking, without a single word.* /连他自己~不知道怎么了。*Nobody, not even himself, knew what's going on.* ④ already: ~七点半了,还不去上课! *Why don't you go to school? It's already seven thirty.*
see also dū

兜[1] ① pocket; bag: 裤~儿 *trouser pocket* /上衣~儿 *coat pocket* /双手插~ *with hands in one's pockets*

兜[2] ① wrap up in a piece a towel ② more round; go in a circle: 公汽在车站附近~圈儿。*The bus went around the bus stop again and again.* ③ canvass; solicit: ~生意 *canvass business* ④ take upon oneself; take responsibility for sth: 一切后果他~着。*He will take full responsibility.* ⑤ disposes all the details of the matter

【兜底】reveal all the details (of sth disreputable or sb's disreputable past); uncover the whole inside story: 兜一个人的老底 *drag up the seamy side of sb's life*

【兜风】① catch the wind; shield against the wind: 帆破了,~不住。*The sails are torn; they won't shield against the wind.* ② go for a drive, ride or sail; go for a spin: ~去! *Let's go for a spin.*

【兜揽】① canvass; tout: ~生意 *tout for business* ② take upon oneself (sb else's work): 这些麻烦事都是他~来的,应该他自己处理。*These troubles are all of his own making, and should be solved by himself.*

【兜圈子】① go round in circles; circle ② beat about the bush: 别再~了,直说吧! *No more beating about the bush; speak straight to the point.*

【兜售】peddle; hawk: ~假冒伪劣商品 *peddle fake or shoddy goods*

【兜子】pocket; bag

dǒu

斗 ①[量] dou, unit of dry measure for grain (=1 decaliter) ② a dou measure ③ an object shaped like a cup or dipper: 漏~ *funnel* /车~ *sidecar* /烟~ *pike* ④ ancient wine vessel
see also dòu

【斗胆】make bold; venture: 恕我~,这件事不应该这么做。*May I make bold to suggest that you should not do it like that.*

【斗笠】wide-rimmed bamboo hat

【斗篷】① cloke; mantle ②[方] bamboo hat

抖 ① tremble; shiver; quiver: 浑身直~ *tremble all over* ② shake; jerk; flick: ~掉雨衣上的水 *shake the water off the rain coat* /一~缰绳 *jerk the reins* ③ uncover the inside story; expose ④ rouse; stir up; cheer up: ~起精神 *pluck up one's spirits* ⑤ (used sarcastically) preen oneself

【抖动】shake; tremble; vibrate; quiver

【抖搂】[方] ① shake off; shake out of sth: 把包里的东西全部~出来。*Shake a bag to empty it.* ② expose; bring to light: 他们干的那些事全被~出来了。*Everything they did has been brought to light.*

【抖擞】enliven; rouse; in vigour at: ~精神 *brace or cheer up; pull one self together*

【抖威风】throw one's weight about

陡 ① steep; precipitous: 这个山坡很~。*The mountain slope is very steep.* ② suddenly; unexpectedly: 天气~变。*The weather changed all of a sudden.*

【陡槽】【水】chute

【陡度】【物】gradient: 压力~ *pressure gradient*

【陡峻】precipitous and perilous

【陡立】rise steeply

【陡坡】steep slope for declivity

【陡峭】precipitous; sheer: ~有深谷 *sheer ravine*

【陡然】suddenly; abruptly: ~上升 *up suddenly*

【陡直】very steep; sheer

dòu

斗 ① fight; tussle: 拳~ *fist fight; fisticuffs* ② struggle against; denounce: 与天~ *fight against nature* ③ contest with; compete with: 狐狸再狡猾也~不过好猎手。*The fox can't escape a seasoned hunter.* ④ make animals fight: ~蛐蛐 *cricket fight* ⑤ fit together; put together: 大家把收集的信息~起来。*Let's piece together the information we have gathered.*
see also dǒu

【斗法】① fight (each other) with magic power ② contend by artifice or trickery; use stratagems

【斗鸡】① game cock ② cockfight ③ game in which all players hop round on one leg and each tries to strike the other with the other led

【斗牛】bullfight: ~士 *matador; bullfighter*

【斗殴】fight

【斗气】take things personally and nurse a grudge

【斗士】fighter

【斗争】① struggle; fight; combat: 阶级~ *class struggle* /思想~ *ideological struggle* ② expose; denounce; accuse ③ strive for; fight for: 为自由而~ *fight for freedom* /为真理而~ *fight for truth*

【斗志】will to fight; fighting will; morale: ~昂扬 *have high morale; be full of fight*

【斗智】fight a battle of wits

【斗嘴】① quarrel; have an angry exchange; bicker ② banter

豆 ① pod-bearing plant or its seeds; peas ② sth like a bean: 花生~ *peanut* /土~ *potato*

【豆瓣儿酱】thick brood-bean sauce

【豆包】steamed bun with sweetened bean paste filling

【豆饼】soya-bean cake; bean cake

【豆豉】fermented soya beans; salted or otherwise
【豆腐】bean curd: ~干 *dried bean curd* / ~脑儿 *jellied bean curd* / ~皮 *skin of soya-bean milk*
【豆类】pod
【豆浆】soya-bean milk
【豆角儿】[口] fresh beans in pod; fresh kidney beans
【豆科】【植】the pulse family; bean or pea family
【豆蔻年华】(of a girl) thirteen or fourteen years of age
【豆面】bean flour
【豆萁】[方] bean stalk
【豆沙】sweetened bean paste: ~糕 *cake with sweetened bean paste filling*
【豆芽儿】bean sprouts
【豆油】soya-bean oil
【豆渣】bean dregs
【豆汁】① fermented drink made from ground beans ② [方] soya-bean milk
【豆制品】bean product
【豆子】① pod-bearing plant or its seeds ② bean-shaped thing

逗[1] ① tease; play with: ~你玩儿 *tease you* / 她拿玩具~小孩玩。*She is tantalizing a child with a toy.* ② provoke; amuse; attract: 小婴儿真~人喜欢。*The baby is really a joy.* ③ [方] amusing; funny: 这人真~! *What a funny man!*

逗[2] stay; stop
【逗号】comma (,)
【逗乐儿】[方] provoke laughter; amuse
【逗留】stay; stop: 假期他在家~了几天。*He stayed at home for several days in the school vacation.*
【逗弄】play with; make fun of: 她~你呢! *She is kidding you!*
【逗趣儿】[方] set people laughing (by funny jokes)
【逗人】arouse interest; amuse
【逗笑儿】[方] amusing
【逗引】play with; tease: ~小狗玩 *play with a puppy*

痘 ① smallpox; variola ② smallpox pustule ③ vaccine (lymph): 种~ *vaccinate*
【痘苗】(bovine vaccine)
【痘疱】【医】pock pustule

dū

都 ① capital: 建~ *establish a capital* ② big city; metropolis
see also dōu
【都城】capital (of a country)
【都会】big city; metropolis
【都市】city; metropolis: ~化 *urbanization* / ~生活 *urban life*

督 superintend and direct: 监~ *supervise*
【督察】① superintend; supervise ② supervisor; superintendent
【督促】supervise and urge: ~学生努力学习 *urge the students to study hard*
【督导】supervise and direct: ~员 *supervisor*
【督军】military governor in the early gears of the Republic of China
【督励】[书] urge and encourage
【督师】supervise military operation

嘟 ① toot; honk: 车喇叭~~响。*The car tooted.* ② [方] pout: 小孩气得~着嘴。*The child pouted peevishly.*
【嘟噜】① [量] bunch; cluster: 一~葡萄 *a bunch of grapes* ② hang down in a bunch; sag ③ trill: 打~儿 pronounce with a trill; trill
【嘟囔】mutter to oneself; mumble: 你在~些什么呀? *What are you mumbling about?*

dú

毒 ① poison; toxin: 食物中~ *food poisoning* ② narcotics; drugs: 吸~ *take drugs* ③ poisonous; noxious; poisoned: 有~气体 *poisonous gas* ④ vicious; malicious; cruel; fierce: 用心狠~ *with vicious intent* / ~打 *beat up; beat relentlessly* ⑤ kill with poison; poison: ~老鼠 *poison rats* ⑥ poison
【毒草】① poisonous weeds ② harmful speech or writing
【毒刺】poisonous sting
【毒饵】poisoned bait
【毒谷】【农】poison grains (planted with seeds to kill harmful insects)
【毒害】① defile; poison (sb's mind); harm (sb's health) with narcotics: 暴力电影~青少年心理。*Violent fills poison the minds of young people.* ② murder by poisoning ③ pernicious influence; poisonous stuff
【毒化】poison; spoil: ~社会风气 *debase social morality*
【毒剂】toxic; toxicant
【毒辣】sinister; diabolic; malignant: 手段~ *ruthless means*
【毒理学】【医】toxicology
【毒品】narcotics; drugs: ~走私 *drug traffic*
【毒气】poison gas: ~弹 *gas bomb*
【毒杀】kill with poison
【毒蛇】poisonous snake; viper
【毒手】violent treachery; wicked trap
【毒死】poison; kill with poison: 没有人知道她是被儿子~的。*No one knows she was poisoned by her son.*
【毒素】① toxin; poison ② poison; pernicious influence
【毒物】poisonous substance; poison
【毒腺】【动】poison gland
【毒刑】cruel corporal punishment; torture

【毒性】toxicity; poisonousness
【毒牙】venom fang
【毒药】poison; toxicant
【毒液】liquid poison; venom
【毒瘾】drug addiction
【毒汁】liquid poison; venom

独 ① only; single: ~生子 *only son* ② alone; by oneself; on one's own: ~居 *live in solitude* ③ old people without offspring; the old and childless ④ only; solely; alone: 大家都鼓掌,唯~他没有。*Everybody applauds except him.*

【独霸】dominate exclusively; monopolize: ~市场 *corner the market*
【独白】soliloquy; monologue
【独步】be unequalled; be unmatched; be unrivalled: ~天下 *be unmatched in the world*
【独裁】dictatorship; autocratic rule: ~者 *dictator* / ~统治 *autocratic rule* / ~政治 *autocracy*
【独唱】solo: ~歌曲 *solo song*
【独处】live alone; live on one's own
【独创】specialty; original creation: ~精神 *creative spirit* / ~性 *originality*
【独当一面】cope with one sector or field on one's own; take charge of a department or locality: 他在单位~。*He copes with his job in the company all on his own.*
【独到】original: ~见解 *original view* / ~之外 *specific characteristics*; *distinctive qualities*; *unique style*
【独断】arbitrary; dictatorial
【独断专行】make arbitrary decisions and take peremptory actions; act willfully on one's own
【独家】sole; the only one; exclusive: ~经营 *sole agent* / ~代理 *sole agency* / ~新闻 *exclusive report* / ~采访 *exclusive interview*
【独角兽】unicorn
【独角戏】monodrama; one-man show
【独具匠心】show unusual ingenuity; have originality
【独来独往】come and go all alone; be a loner
【独揽】arrogate to oneself; monopolize: ~大权 *arrogate all power to oneself*
【独立】① stand alone ② independence: 宣告~ *proclaim independence* / ~战争 *war of independence* ③【军】independent: ~营 *independent battalion* ④ be come independent or separate ⑤ independently; on one's own: ~思考 *think for oneself*
【独联体】Commonwealth of Independent States (CIS)
【独轮车】wheelbarrow
【独苗】only son of a family
【独木桥】single-plank or single; log bridge; difficult path
【独木舟】dugout canoe
【独幕剧】one-act play
【独辟蹊径】open a new road for oneself; develop a brand new style or a method of one's own
【独身】① live alone ② unmarried; single: ~主义 *celibacy*
【独生女】only daughter
【独生子】only son
【独生子女】only child
【独树一帜】fly one's own colours; be unique
【独特】unique; distinctive: ~的表现手法 *novel way of expression* / ~的风格 *unique style*
【独体字】【语】single-element character
【独吞】take exclusive possession of sth
【独舞】solo dance
【独行其是】do what one thinks is right regardless of other's opinions
【独眼龙】person blind in one eye; one-eyed person
【独一无二】unique; unparalleled; unmatched
【独占】have all to oneself; monopolize
【独占鳌头】come out first; be the champion
【独资】exclusive investment / ~经营 *single proprietorship*; *exclusive ownership*
【独资企业】exclusive investment enterprises: 外商~ *enterprise with exclusive foreign capital and management*
【独自】alone; by oneself: 尤里~在街上徘徊。*Urey is wandering on the street.*
【独奏】(instrumental) solo: 钢琴~ *piano solo* / ~会 *recital (of an instrumentalist)*

读 ① read out; read aloud: ~课文 *read a text aloud* ② read: 这首诗值得一~。*The poet is worth reading.* ③ attend school: ~小学 *attend primary school*

【读本】reader; textbook
【读卡机】card reader
【读入】【电】read-in
【读书】① read; study: 她~很用功。*She is very diligent in her studies.* ② attend school: 我~时她在学校当老师。*She's a teacher when I was at school.*
【读数】reading: 温度计~ *thermometer reading* / ~误差 *reading error*
【读图】interpret drawings
【读物】reading material: 儿童~ *reading matter for children*; *children's books* / 通俗~ *popular literature*
【读音】pronunciation
【读者】reader: ~来信 *letters form readers* / ~文摘 *Reader's Digest*

渎[1] [书] show disrespect or contempt: 亵~ *blaspheme*; *profane*

渎[2] ditch; drain

【渎职】malfeasance; dereliction of duty: ~者 *malfeasant* / ~罪 *crime of misconduct in office*

椟 [书] casket; case; box

犊 calf: 初生牛~不怕虎。*Young people are fearless.*

牍 ① wooden tablets or slips for writing (in ancient tines) ② documents; archives; correspondence: 文~ *official documents and corre-*

spondence

黩 ① blacken; defile; sully ② act wantonly; act rashly

【黩武】[书] militaristic; warlike; bellicose: 穷兵~ *use all one's military might in a war of conquest*

dǔ

肚 tripe

【肚子】tripe

see also dù

笃 ① sincere; faithful; earnest: ~爱 *love deeply*; *be devoted to* ② be seriously ill; be in a critical condition: 危~ *be terminally ill*

【笃诚】sincere and faithful

【笃厚】honest and kind-hearted; sincere and magnanimous

【笃实】① honest and loyal ② solid; sound: 学问~ *sound scholarship*

【笃守】abide by faithfully

【笃信】faithfully believe in; be a devout believer in

【笃学】be diligent in study; studious; devoted to study

堵 ① stop up, block; plug up: ~住出口 *plug up on exit* /回家的路上~车了。*There's a traffic jam at my way home.* ② stifled; suffocated; oppressed: 胸口~得慌 *feel suffocated*; *feel a constriction of the chest* /心里~得难受 *have a load on one's mind* ③ [书] wall: 观者如~。*There was a crowd watching.* ④ [量] used of walls: 一~墙 *a wall*

【堵车】traffic jam; traffic congestion

【堵击】intercept and attack: ~逃敌 *cut off the enemy's retreat route*

【堵截】intercept: ~敌机 *intercept enemy airplanes*

【堵塞】stop up; block up: 交通~ *traffic hold-up*; *traffic jam* /下水道又~了。*The sewer has been blocked again.*

【堵嘴】gag sb; silence sb: 她用鸡蛋堵住他的嘴。*She stopped him from speaking out with an egg.*

赌 ① gamble: 聚~ *set up a gambling party* ② bet: 打~ *make a bet*

【赌本】① money to gamble with; gambling money ② resources for risky ventures

【赌博】gambling

【赌场】gambling house; gambling den

【赌风】vice of gambling; the common and unhealthy practice of gambling

【赌鬼】gambler

【赌棍】hardened or professional gambler

【赌局】gambling party; gambling joint

【赌具】gambling paraphernalia; gambling device

【赌窟】gambling den

【赌气】feel wronged and act rashly; act willfully in a pique: 她~不跟他说话。*She kept from talking with him in a fit of pique.*

【赌钱】gamble

【赌徒】gambler

【赌债】a gambling debt

【赌咒】take an oath; swear

【赌注】stake: 下~ *put down a stake*

【赌资】gambling money

睹

【睹物思人】think of the person at the sight of the thing — the thing reminds one of its owner

dù

杜 ① birch-leaf pear ② block; prevent; stop: 以~流言 *so as to forestall gossip*

【杜鹃】①【动】cuckoo ②【植】azalea

【杜绝】stop; put an end to: ~腐败 *put an end to corruption* / ~浪费 *put an end to waste*

【杜梨】birch-leaf pear

【杜撰】fabricate; make up: 这故事可不是~的。*This story is not made up.*

肚 belly; abdomen; stomach

see also dǔ

【肚肠】① stomach and intestines ② heart; intention: 热心~ *enthusiastic and warm-hearted*

【肚带】bellyband; girth

【肚量】appetite; capacity or need for food

【肚皮】[方] belly: 填饱~ *fill the stomach*

【肚脐】navel; belly button

【肚子】① belly; stomach: ~疼 *have a stomachache* /一~气 *full of pent-up anger* ② a belly-shaped thing: 腿~ *calf of one's leg*

妒 be jealous of; envy; be envious of

【妒恨】hate out of jealousy; be jealous of

【妒火】agony of jealousy: ~中烧 *burn with jealousy*

【妒忌】be jealous of; envy: ~心 *jealousy*

【妒贤嫉能】be jealous of capable and virtuous people

【妒意】feeling of jealousy; jealousy: 满脸~ *very image (or picture) of jealousy*

度 ① linear measure ② degree of a quality: 硬~ *hardness* /湿~ *humidity* /浓~ *density* ③ limit; extent; degree: 兴奋过~ *be overexcited* ④ tolerance; magnanimity: 气~ *tolerance* ⑤ consideration: 把个人安危置之~外 *give no thought to personal safety* ⑥ a unit of measurement for angles, temperature, etc.; degree: 90~角 *an go degrees angle* /北纬33~ *latitude 33°N* /三~电 *kilowatt-hours* /五十~的温水 50 *degrees centigrade water* ⑦ occasion; time: 一年一~ *once a year* ⑧ spend; pass: 欢~春节 *joyously celebrate the Spring Festival*

see also duó

【度荒】tide over a famine; tide over a lean year

【度假】spend one's holidays; go vacationing: ~村

vocational village / ~胜地 holiday resort

【度量】tolerance; magnanimity: ~大 broad-minded; magnanimous / ~小 narrow-minded

【度量衡】length, capacity and weight; weights and measures: ~学 metrology

【度日】eke out a living or an existence; subsist (in hardship):艰难~ make a miserable living

【度日如年】one day seems like a year; time hangs heavy; days drag on like years

【度数】number of degrees; reading:你的眼镜多少~? What's the strength of the lenses of your glasses?

渡 ① cross; go across: ~河 cross a river /飞~重洋 fly (across) many oceans ② tide over; pull through: ~过难关 tide over a difficulty; pull through ③ ferry (people, goods, etc.) across ④ ferry crossing

【渡槽】aqueduct

【渡场】【军】crossing site; ferry crossing

【渡船】ferryboat; ferry

【渡河点】point of crossing

【渡口】ferry crossing; ferry

【渡轮】ferryboat

【渡桥】temporary bridge; makeshift bridge

【渡鸦】【动】raven

【渡越】cross; negotiate: ~天险 cross a natural barrier

镀 plating:电~ electroplating galvanizing

【镀槽】coating bath

【镀层】coating: ~金属 coated metal

【镀金】① gold-plating; gilding ② become gilded (said of students who went abroad to study in order to enhance their social status)

【镀银】silver-plating; silvering

duān

端[1] ① end; tip; extremity:两~ both ends /笔~ tip of a pen ② beginning; start ③ point; aspect:仅举数~ just to mention a few points ④ reason; cause:无~ without any reason

端[2] ① upright; proper: ~坐 sit bolt upright /品行不~ of improper behaviour ② hold sth level with both hand; carry: ~上饭菜 serve a meal / ~两杯茶 carry two cups of tea

【端点】【数】end point

【端点用户】an end user

【端口】port

【端量】look up and down; size up

【端倪】① clue; indication; inkling:毫无~ have no due whatever ② conjecture; predict:事态复杂,实难~。Prediction is hardly possible as things are so complicated.

【端平】① just; fair; impartial ② make fair and just ③ hold level

【端午节】the Dragon Boat Festival (the 5th day of the sth lunar month)

【端详】① details:细说~ give a full and detailed account ② dignified and serene:举止~ be have with serene dignity ③ look sb up and down:她久久地~这个小伙子。She looked the young kid over for a long time.

【端绪】inkling; clue; thread of thought:他对这件事怎么也理不出~。He could not sort the matters out.

【端正】① upright; regular:五官~ have regular features ② proper; correct:品行~ having good conduct; well-behaved ③ rectify; correct: ~思想 correct one's thinking / ~动机 straighten out one's intentions / ~学习态度 take a correct attitude toward study

【端庄】dignified; sedate; stately

duǎn

短 ① short; brief: ~发 short hair /泰勒给我们做了一个简~的讲座。Taylor gives us a brief lecture. ② lack; owe: ~你两块钱。I owe you two yuan. ③ short coming; weakness; fault:护~ shield a fault

【短兵相接】fight at close quarters; engage in hand-to-hand fighting

【短波】shortwave

【短不了】① cannot do with out:生命~水。Water is indispensable to life. ② cannot avoid; have to:今后~还要请你帮忙。Most likely I'll have to ask you for help again.

【短程】short distance; short range: ~飞机 short-haul airplane

【短处】shortcoming; fault; weakness

【短粗】short and thick; stocky

【短促】very short; very brief:呼吸~ be short of breath; gasp; pant /时间~,我们必须加速。We must speed up for the limited time.

【短大衣】short overcoat; car coat

【短刀】dagger; short sword

【短笛】[音] piccolo

【短工】casual labourer; seasonal labourer

【短号】cornet

【短见】① shortsighted view ② suicide:自寻~ commit suicide

【短距离】short distance

【短裤】short pants; shorts

【短路】【电】short circuit; short: ~保护装置 short-circuit protection device

【短命】die youg; be short-lived

【短跑】dash; sprint: ~运动员 dash man; sprinter

【短片】short film; short

【短评】short commentary, brief comments

【短期】short-term: ~计划 short-term plan / ~培训 short-term training / ~贷款 short-term loan / ~分析 short-run analysis / ~国库券 short-term government bond / ~行为 short-sighted action / ~预

测 *short-term forecasting*
【短浅】narrow and shallow:目光～ *be short-sighted* /见识～ *be inexperienced*
【短枪】short arm; handgun
【短缺】shortage; short; lacking:资金～ *be short of funds* / ～产品 *products in short supply*
【短裙】short skirt
【短少】deficient; short; missing
【短视】① near-sightedness; myopia ② lack foresight; be short-sighted
【短寿】of short life; short-lived
【短统靴】ankle boots
【短途】short distance
【短袜】socks; anklets
【短尾猴】【动】stump-tailed monkey; macaque
【短小】short and small:篇幅～ *limited in length*
【短小精悍】①(of a person) short but strong and capable ②(of writing) short and pithy; terse and forceful
【短讯】news in brief
【短训】short-term training: 短期～ *short-term training course*
【短语】【语】phrase
【短元音】【语】short vowel
【短暂】of short duration; transient; brief: ～的休息带来更高的工作效率。*A short rest can lead to higher work efficiency.*
【短装】be dressed in a Chinese jacket and trousers

duàn

段 ①[量] section; segment; part:一～时间 *a period of time* ② rank ③ paragraph; passage: 名家名～ *famous arias by famous artist*
【段落】① paragraph: ～大意 *main idea of a paragraph* ② phase; stage:我们的节日告一～了。*Out programme has been completed.*
【段子】【戏】aria; piece:传统～ *traditional arias*
断[1] ① break; snap:一刀两～ *sever at one cut-make a complete break* ② break off; cut off; stop: ～电 *cut off the supply of electrical power*; *cut power* / ～了联系 *be out of contact* ③ quit; give up: ～烟 *give up smoking*; *quit smoking*
断[2] ① judge; decide:诊～ *diagnosis* /当机立～ *make a prompt decision* ②[书] absolutely; utterly; decidedly: ～不可信 *absolutely incredible* / ～无可能 *absolutely impossible*
【断案】① try or hear a case; settle a lawsuit ② conclusion (of a syllogism)
【断壁】① broken walls:残垣～ *dilapidated walls* ② cliff; steep
【断层】fault: ～带 *fault zone* / ～面 *fault-plane* / ～线 *fault-line* / ～作用 *faulting* / ～地震 *fault earthquake* / ～湖 *fault lake* / ～山 *fault mountain* /文化～ *break in cultural continuity*
【断肠】heartbroken
【断代】division of history into periods: ～史 *periodic history*
【断档】out of stock; sold out
【断电】power failure; power cut
【断点】breakpoint; breaking point
【断定】form a judgement; conclude; determine:我～我们下午没课。*I'm sure we have no class this afternoon.*
【断断】absolutely: ～骄傲不得。*One should never get conceited.*
【断断续续】on and off; intermittently: ～地说 *speak haltingly*
【断根】① have no offspring; be childless ② be completely cured
【断后】① have no progeny ② cover a retreat; bring up the rear
【断乎】(often used in the negative) absolutely: ～不同 *absolutely impermissible*
【断交】① break off a relationship ② sever diplomatic relations
【断句】① make pauses in reading unpunctuated ancient writings ② punctuate
【断绝】break off; cut off; sever: ～邦交 *break off diplomatic relations*
【断粮】run out of grain (or food)
【断裂】① split; break ② crack; fracture: ～带 *fracture zone*
【断路】①【电】open circuit; broken circuit: ～器 *circuit breaker* ② waylay; hold up; block the road to rob: ～劫财 *commit highway robbery*
【断面】section:横～ *cross-section* / ～图 *sectional drawing*; *section*
【断奶】wean:给孩子～ *wean a child*
【断片】part; extract; fragment; passage
【断气】① breath one's last; die ② cut off or stop the gas (supply)
【断然】① resolute; drastic:采取～措施 *take drastic measures* ② flatly; absolutely; categorically: ～拒绝 *flatly refuse*
【断送】forfeit or lose (one's life, future, etc.); ruin:这个错误～了他升迁的机会。*The mistake ruined his promotion.*
【断头】① broken end ② cut off sb's bead; behead: ～台 *guillotine*
【断弦】snap the lute string-lose one's wife
【断线】①(of string or thread) break:风筝～了。*The flying kite has broken away from its string.* ② discontinue; be interrupted:面临～危险 *face the danger of being discontinued*
【断续】[书] intermittently; off and on
【断言】say (or state) with certainty; assert (or affirm) categorically
【断语】conclusion; judgement:妄下～ *draw unwarranted conclusions*; *jump to conclusions*
【断章取义】quote out of context; garble a statement, etc.
【断肢】severed limb: ～再植 *replantation of a severed limb*
【断子绝孙】may you die sonless; may you be the

last of your line

椴 【植】(Chinese) linden

煅 ① forge: ~铁 *forge iron* ② calcine

【煅烧】calcine

【煅石膏】calcined gypsum; plaster

锻 forge: ~铁 *forge iron*

【锻打】① beat with a forging hammer; forge ② temper; steel; toughen

【锻工】① forging: ~车间 *forging shop*; forge ② forger; blacksmith

【锻件】forging

【锻接】forge welding

【锻炼】① do exercises; have physical training: 每天~1小时 *take an hour's exercise every day* ② temper; steel; toughen: ~坚强的意志 *build up a strong will* / 劳动~ *temper oneself through manual labour*

【锻压】forging and pressing: ~机 *forging press*

duī

堆 ① pile up; heap up; stack: 桌子~满了各种书。*The desk is piled with all kinds of books.* ② heap; pile; stack: 柴火~ *pile of firewood* / 草~ *haystack* / 土~ *mound* ③[量] heap; pack; crowd: 一~灰烬 *a heap of ashes* / 一~人 *a crowd of people* / 一~废话 *a pack of nonsense*

【堆场】freight yard; stacking ground

【堆存】store up; keep in store

【堆放】pile up; stack: 库房里~了许多旧电脑。*A lot of old computers are piled in the storehouse.*

【堆肥】【农】compost

【堆焊】【机】built-up welding

【堆积】① pile up; heap up: ~如山 (*of things*) *heap in a mound*; (*of work, etc.*) *pile up like a mountain* ②【地】accumulation

【堆砌】① pile up ② load one's writing with fancy phrases: ~辞藻 *string together ornate phrases*

【堆石坝】rock-fill dam

【堆笑】put on a smile; wear a grin from ear to ear: 满脸~ *be all smiles*; *one's face is wreathed in smiles*

duì

队 ① row of people; line; queue: 站~ *line up* ② team; group; band: 足球~ *football team* ③ Chinese Young Pioneers ④[量]: 一~士兵 *a column of soldiers*

【队部】the office or headquarters of a team, etc.: 消防队~ *headquarters of the fire brigade*

【队列】formation: ~训练 *drill*; *formation drill*

【队伍】① troops; armed force: ~就要出发了。*The troops are about to set out.* ② ranks; contingent: 革命~ revolutionary ranks

【队形】formation: 成战斗~ *in battle formation*

【队友】fellow player; fellow member of a grouper team

【队员】team member; team player

【队长】①【体】captain: 篮球队~ *the captain of an basketball team* ② team leader: 生产队~ *production team leader*

对 ① answer; reply: ~答如流 *respond fluently* / 无以为~ *not know how to answer* ② treat; cope with; counter: 面~困难 *be faced with difficult* ③ be trained on: ~着镜子修面 *shave one's face looking into the mirror* ④ bring into coordination or contact; fit; match: ~暗号 *exchange code words* ⑤ suit; agree; get along: 文不~题 *content of an essay at variance with its title* / ~胃口 *suit one's taste* ⑥ compare; check; identify: ~笔迹 *identify the handwriting* ⑦ set; adjust: ~表 *set one's watch*; *synchronize watches* / ~焦 *adjust the focus* ⑧ mix; add: 给我~点热水,太凉了。*Add some hot water to me*; *it's too cold.* ⑨ mutual; face to face: ~骂 *call each other names* / ~饭 *have a drink together* ⑩ divide into halves ⑪ opposite; opposing: ~岸 *the opposite bank* ⑫ right; correct: 猜~了 *guess right* / 你~了。*You are right.* ⑬ antithetical couplet; couplet: 喜~ *wedding couplet* ⑭[量] pair; couple: 一~花瓶 *a pair of vases* / 一~石狮 *a pair of stone lions* ⑮ with regard to; concerning: ~学生负责 *responsible for students*

【对案】diplomacy counterproposal

【对白】dialogue

【对半】① half-and-half; fifty-fifty: ~儿分 *go halves* ② double: ~的利 *a double profit*

【对比】① compare; contrast: 新老~ *compare the new with the old* / 今昔~ *contrast the present with the past* / 鲜明的~ *sharp contrast* ② ratio: ~度 *contrast ratio* / ~剂 *contrast medium* / ~色 *contrast colour* / 双方人数~是一对二。*The radio between the two sides is one to two.*

【对簿】[书] be tried(in court): ~公堂 *be interrogated in court*

【对不起】① I am sorry; excuse me; pardon me; I beg your pardon: ~,你刚才说什么? *Excuse me, what was that again?* ② let sb down; do a disservice to; be unfair to: ~父母 *be unworthy heirs of one's parents*

【对策】the way to deal with a situation; countermeasure; solution; countermove: 上有政策,下有~。*Whatever policy the higher-ups may adopt, people down below know how to circumvent it.* / 我们还没找到~来应对当前形势。*We have not found ways and means to cope with the present situation.*

【对唱】musical dialogue in antiphonal style; antiphonal singing

【对称】symmetry: ~变换 *symmetry transformation*

/ ~轴 *axis of symmetry*

【对答】answer; reply

【对待】treat; approach; handle:认真~问题 *adopt a serious attitude towards the problems*

【对得起】treat fairly; not let sb down; be worthy of:为你做这么多事,我觉得总算~你了。*I didn't think I let you down for so many things I've done for you.*

【对等】reciprocity; equity:在~的基础上 *on the basis of reciprocity* / ~待遇 *reciprocal treatment* / ~贸易 *counter-trade*

【对调】exchange; swap: ~工作 *exchange jobs*

【对顶角】【数】vertical angles; vertically opposite angles

【对方】other party; opposite side: ~付费电话 *collect call*

【对付】① deal with; cope with; counter; tackle:我能~。*I can manage.* ② make do:这台旧电脑你先~着用吧。*Try to make do with this old computer for now.*

【对歌】singing in antiphonal style

【对光】set a camera; focus a camera, microscope, etc.:自动~ *automatic focusing*

【对过】opposite; across:我家~就是书店。*The bookstore is just opposite my house.* / ~的房间就是她的办公室。*Her office is just opposite mine.*

【对号】① check the number: ~入座 *take one's seat according to the number on the ticket; sit in the right seat* ② fit; tally:我听说过这个人,但一直没和他本人对上号。*I know of the man but haven't been able to identify him.* /他说的和做的不~号。*What he did doesn't match what he said.* ③ check mark; tick

【对话】dialogue; conversation:夫妻~ *dialogue between couples*

【对换】exchange; swap

【对讲机】intercom

【对角】【数】opposite angle

【对角线】【数】diagonal line

【对接】①【航】dock; connect ②【机】butt joint; abutting joint: ~焊 *butt welding*

【对襟】Chinese-style jacket with buttons down the front

【对劲】① be to one's liking; suit one:这笔写起字来很~。*The pen writes very well.* ② normal:这事儿看起来有点不~儿。*There seems to be something fishy about it.* ③ get along(well); be on good terms with:他们几个一向很~。*They have always got along very well.*

【对酒当歌】one should sing merrily over one's wine

【对局】play a game of chess, etc.:我每天都跟父亲~。*I played a game of chess with father everyday.*

【对抗】① antagonism; confrontation:两国间的~ *confrontation between two states* ② resist; oppose:武力~ *resist by force*

【对口】①(of two performers) speak (or sing) alternately: ~词 *rhymed dialogue* / ~快板儿 *rhymed clapper talk* / ~相声 *cross talk; comic dialogue* ② be geared to the needs of the job; fit in with one's vocational training:专业~ *a job suited to one's special training* ③ to one's taste; palatable: ~味 *suit one's taste*

【对垒】stand facing each other; fight each other; be pitted against each other:两军~ *two armies pitted against each other*

【对立】oppose; contradict; be antagonistic to; against: ~情绪 *antagonism* /自由与纪律并不~。*Freedom and discipline are not contradictory to each other.*

【对立面】opposite; antithesis:矛盾的~ *opposites in a contradiction*

【对立统一】unity of opposites: ~规律 *law of the unity of opposites*

【对联】antithetical couplet (written on scrolls, etc.)

【对流】convection; convection current: ~换热 *convective heat transfer*

【对路】① meet the requirement; satisfy the need; be just right:商品~ *marketable goods; good that sell well* ② be to one's liking; suit one:这些措施绝对是~的。*These are welcome measures.*

【对门】①(of two houses) face each other ② the building or room opposite:照相馆~是一所邮电局。*There is a post office opposite the photo studio.*

【对面】① opposite; across:街~有家影院。*There is a cinema on the opposite side of the road.* ② right ahead; right in front: ~来了一辆车。*A car came towards us.* ③ face to face:老师要和你~谈。*The teacher will talk about it with you personally.*

【对内】internal; domestic; home: ~政策 *domestic policy* / ~销售 *sell at home(or in the home market)*

【对事不对人】concern one self with facts and not with individuals

【对手】① opponent; adversary; rival ② match; equal:棋逢~ *find one's match* /打游戏你不是他的~。*You are no match for him in computer games.*

【对数】【数】logarithm: ~表 *logarithmic table* / ~函数 *logarithmic function*

【对台戏】rival show:演~ *stage a rival show* /他不该跟我们唱~。*He should not challenge us.*

【对头】① correct; on the right track:他这样看问题就~了。*Now he is thinking along the right line.* ② normal; right:你的脸色不~。*You are not looking well.* ③ get on well; hit it off:过去他俩不大~,现在却十分合得来。*The two didn't get along very well but now they hit it off well.* ④ enemy:死~ *sworn enemy* ⑤ opponent; adversary; rival

【对外】external; foreign: ~工作 *external work* / ~关系 *foreign relations* / ~扩张 *external expansion* / ~援助 *aid to foreign courtiers* / ~政策 *foreign policy*

【对外开放】(the policy of) opening to the outside

world; the open policy: ~,对内搞活 *opening to the outside world and invigorating the domestic economy*

【对外贸易】foreign trade: ~指数 *foreign trade index number*

【对味儿】① suit one's palate; be tasty: 今天的饭菜很~。*Today's meet is very nice.* ② seem all right: 你的话似乎不太~。*What you said doesn't sound quite right.*

【对虾】prawn

【对象】① target; object: 调查~ *object for investigation* / 研究~ *object of study* ② boy or girl friend: 找~ *look for a partner in marriage*

【对眼】cross-eye

【对弈】[书] play chess

【对应】homologous; corresponding: ~物 *homologue* / ~原理 *correspondence principle* / ~措施 *countermeasure*

【对于】about; concerning; with regard to

【对照】contrast; compare: 英汉~读本 *an English-Chinese bilingual textbook* / 形成鲜明~ *make a sharp contrast*

【对折】① 50% discount ② fold in half

【对着干】① adopt a confrontational approach; set oneself against ② compete with sb in work

【对证】verify; check; establish evidence through personal confrontation: 死无~。*Dead men bear no witness.*

【对症下药】suit the medicine to the illness; suit the remedy to the case; prescribe the right remedy for an illness

【对质】confrontation in a law court between two parties: ~权 *right of confrontation*

【对峙】stand facing each other, neither side willing to give in; confront each other: 两军~。*The two armies are locked in a face-off.*

【对准】① aim at; point at: ~靶子 *aim at the target* ②【机】alignment: 轴~ *shaft alignment*

【对子】a pair of antithetical phrase, etc.

兑 ① exchange; convert ② honour (a bill, etc.); cash (a money order, check, etc.): 汇~ *remittance* ③ add (water, etc.); mix; mingle: 往锅里~水 *pour some water into the pot*

【兑付】cash (a check, etc.)

【兑换】exchange; convert: 把外币~成人民币 *convert foreign currency into RMB* / ~率 *rate of change; exchange rate* / ~券 *bank draft; money order*

【兑奖】cash in a lottery ticket (that has won a prize)

【兑现】① cash (a check, etc.) ② honour (a commitment, etc.); fulfill; make good: ~诺言 *live up to one's word; fulfill one's promise*

dūn

吨 ①[量] ton ② register ton ③ shipping ton; tonnage

【吨公里】ton kilometer

【吨位】tonnage

敦 honest; sincere

【敦促】urge; press: ~他尽快答复 *request him to make an early reply*

【敦厚】honest and sincere: 质朴~ *simple and sincere*

【敦请】sincerely request; cordially invite; earnestly request

【敦实】stocky; thickset: 他长得很~。*He is of stocky build.*

墩 ① mound: 土~ *mound* ② a block of stone or wood: 树~ *stump* ③[量] cluster: 一~稻秧 *a cluster of rice seedlings*

【墩布】mop; swab

【墩子】a block of stone or wood: 菜~ *chopping block*

蹲 ① squat on the heels: 两人~在树下下棋。*They are squatting under a tree, playing chess.* ② stay: 她整天~在家。*She stays all day at home.*

【蹲班房】[口] be in jail; be imprisoned

【蹲苗】【农】restrain the growth of seedlings for the roots to develop better

dǔn

盹 doze; take a nap: 他上课时常打~儿。*He often dozes off at class.*

趸 ① whole sale ② buy whole sale: ~货 *buy goods wholesale*

【趸船】landing stage; pontoon

【趸卖】sell wholesale

【趸批】wholesale: ~买进 *buy wholesale*

dùn

囤 a grain bin

see also tún

炖 ① stew: ~牛肉 *stewed beef* ② warm sth by putting it in a container in boiling water: ~酒 *warm (up) wine*

砘 ram loose soil with a stone-roller after sowing

钝 ① blunt; dull: 刀~了。*The knife is blunt.* ② stupid; dull-witted

【钝化】inactivation: ~剂 *passivator* / ~金属 *passive metal*

【钝角】【数】obtuse angle：～三角形 *obtuse triangle*
【钝拙】clumsy；awkward

盾 shield

【盾牌】① shield；buckler ② pretext；excuse

顿[1] ① pause：看到她，他～了一下。*He paused when he saw her.* ②（in Chinese calligraphy）pause in writing in order to reinforce the beginning or ending of a stroke ③ arrange；handle；settle ④ kowtow；stamp ⑤ suddenly；immediately：～悟 *suddenly realize the truth* ⑥［量］used to indicate frequency：一天三～饭 *three meals a day*

顿[2] tired：困～ *dog-tired*；*fatigued*

【顿挫】pause and transition（in rhythm or melody）
【顿号】a slight-pause mark（、），used to set off items in a series
【顿河】the Don（River in European Russia）
【顿时】at once；instantly；all of a sudden：喜讯传来，我们～欢呼起来。*We broke into cheers as soon as we heard the good news.*
【顿悟】realize in a flash；be suddenly enlightened
【顿足不前】come to a standstill

遁 ① escape；flee；fly：远～他乡 *flee far away from home* ② hide；lie low；disappear

【遁词】subterfuge；quibble
【遁入空门】with draw from secular life and become a monk or nun
【遁形】lie low；hide one's identity

duō

多[1] ① many；much；more；a lot of：很～苹果 *many apples* /很～外国朋友 *many foreign friends* /请～～提问。*Please feel free to ask questions.* /要学的知识还很～。*There is a lot more to learn.* ② excessive；over：～疑 *oversensitive*；*over suspicious* ③ exceed the original；have more or too much：这儿～了三棵树。*There are three more trees.* ④ have sth in a abundance：这里春天～风，夏天～雨。*Here we have a lot of wind in spring and a lot of rain in summer.* ⑤ over a specified amount more than：一周～ *more than one week* / 五十～岁 *over fifty years old* /一百～人 *more than one hundred people* ⑥（Duō）a surname

多[2] ①（used in questions）to what extent：他～大了？*How old is he?* /这扇门有～高？*How high is the door?* ②（used in exclamations）to what an extant：这儿～热呀！*How hot it is!* /～好的人呀！*What a fine person!* ③ to an unspecified extent：～复杂的问题他都能解决。*He could handle even the most complex problem.*

【多半】① the greater part；majority；most：这班学生中男生占～。*Most of the students are boys in this class.* ② most probably；very likely：他～不在家。*He probably isn't at home.*
【多倍体】【生】polyploid：～植物 *polyploid plant*
【多边】multilateral：～会谈 *multilateral talks* /～公约 *multilateral pact or convention* /～贸易 *multilateral trade* /～条约 *multilateral treaty* /～外交 *multilateral diplomacy*
【多边形】【数】polygon
【多变】changeable；varied：天气～ *changeable weather* /形势～ *volatile situation*
【多波段】multiple-band
【多才多艺】versatile；gifted in many aspects：她是个～的女孩。*She is a versatile girl.*
【多层次】multilevel：～推销 *multilevel marketing*
【多产】prolific：～作家 *a prolific writer*
【多吃多占】take more than is due to one；grab more than one's share
【多愁善感】sentimental and susceptible
【多此一举】make an unnecessary move：何必～？*Why go to all this bother?*
【多次】many times；repeatedly；on many occasions：他曾～访问我们学校。*He's visited our school many times.*
【多弹头】multiple warhead：～导弹 *multiple warhead missile*
【多党制】multiparty system；multi-party system
【多动症】hyperactivity
【多多益善】the more，the better
【多发病】frequently occurring disease
【多方】in many ways；in every way
【多方面】in many ways；many-sided
【多功能】multifunction；multi-purpose：～厅 *multipurpose hall*
【多会儿】［口］① when；what time：你～回来？*When will you come back?* ② ever；at any time：～我有空，就给你回电话。*I'll call you back when I'm free.*
【多极】【电】multipolar：～发电机 *multipolar generator*
【多极化】multi-polarization
【多孔】porous：～板 *perforated plate* /～砖 *porous brick*；*perforated brick*
【多口相声】cross talk or conic dialogue performed by more than two persons
【多快好省】achieve greater，faster，better and more economical results
【多亏】thanks to；luckily：～你的到来 *thanks to your coming* /～你给我们的建议。*We were lucky to have your advices.*
【多劳多得，少劳少得】more pay for more work and less pay for less work
【多虑】be overanxious，be full of misgivings
【多伦多】Toronto，largest city in Canada
【多么】① used in exclamations to what all extent：～好的天气啊！*How sunny it is!* /～好玩！*What fun!* ② to an unspecified extent：不管～忙，他总能抽出时间来画画。*How ever bury he was，he always manage to find spare time for painting.*
【多媒体】multimedia：～电脑 *multi-media computer* /～光盘 *multimedia CD*

D

【多米诺骨牌】dominoes：～理论 *domino theory*
【多米诺效应】domino effect
【多面手】a many-sided person；a versatile person；an all－rounder
【多面体】【数】polyhedron
【多民族国家】multinational country；country with many ethnic groups
【多谋善断】resourceful and decisive；sagacious and resolute
【多幕剧】a play of many acts；a full-length drama
【多瑙河】Danube（River）：～文化 *Danubian culture*
【多年】many years；for years
【多年生】【植】perennial：～植物 *perennial plant*
【多尿症】【医】polyuria
【多情】tender and affectionate（to a person of the opposite sex）：～自古伤离别。*Lovers always suffer the sorrows of parting.*
【多日】many days；long time
【多如牛毛】as many as the hairs on an ox；countless；innumerable：计算机类图书～。*There are innumerable books about computer.*
【多色】polychrome：～染料 *polygenetic dyes* /～印刷 *polychrome printing*
【多少】① number；amount：～不等 *vary in amount* ② somewhat；more or less；to some extent：～有点遗憾 *feel sorry to some extent* /～有点沾沾自喜 *feel somewhat conceited* ③ how many；how much：你有～钱？*How much money do you have?* /这西红柿～钱一公斤？*How much are those tomatoes per kilo?* ④ expressing an unspecified amount or number：我不知道他在家呆～天。*I don't know how long he will stay at home.*
【多时】a long time：等候～ *wait a long time*
【多事】① meddlesome；do what is unnecessary or superfluous：你何必～？*Why should you bother?* ② troubled；eventful：～之秋 *eventful period of time*；*troubled times*
【多数】majority；most：绝大～ *overwhelming majority* /绝对～ *absolute majority* /相对～ *relative majority* /～表决 *decision by majority* /～票 *majority vote* /决议以～微弱通过。*The resolution was carried by a small majority.*
【多糖】【化】polysaccharide；polysaccharide
【多头】①（on the stock exchange）bull；long：～市场 *long market*；*bull market* ② many chiefs or bosses：领导～ *with too many leaders*
【多退少补】refund for any overpayment or supplementary payment for any deficiency（after a round sum is paid in advance for a batch of goods）
【多谢】many thanks；thanks a lot
【多心】over sensitive；suspicious：他对我的话～了。*He is over sensitive what I said.* /放松点，别～。*Take it easy and don't take it to heart.*
【多学科】multidisciplinary；interdisciplinary
【多样】diversified：款式～ *many diverse styles*
【多样化】diversify；vary：～的艺术风格 *a variety of artistic styles* /～经营 *diversification*
【多一事不如少一事】avoid trouble wherever possible；the less trouble，the better；let sleeping dogs die
【多余】unnecessary；surplus；superfluous；redundant：删掉～的词 *delete redundant words* /～农产品 *surplus farm produce*
【多元论】【哲】pluralism：～者 *pluralist*
【多云】【气】cloudy：～转阴 *from cloudy to overcast*
【多灾多难】be dogged by bad luck；be plagued by frequent disasters
【多中心】polycentric：～主义 *polycentrism*
【多种多样】varied；manifold：艺术的形式是～的。*The forms of art are many and varied.*
【多种经营】diversified economy；diversification：～方式 *various methods of business operation*
【多姿】very charming：～多彩 *very charming and colourful*
【多嘴】have a big mouth；shoot off one's mouth：～多舌 *gossipy and meddlesome*；*long-tongued* /初来乍到，别～！*Being a stranger here，you'd better keep your mouth shut!*

咄 ① used to show amazement or to berate ② berate；be shocked
【咄咄逼人】arrogant；overbearing；aggressive：他那～的态度，令我非常讨厌。*His overweening manner annoyed me very much.*
【咄咄怪事】height of absurdity

掇 pick up
【掇弄】［方］① repair；fix：电脑经他一～就好了。*The computer worked again after he fixed it up.* ② stir up；incite；manipulate

duó

夺[1] ① take by force；seize；wrest：强词～理 *resort to sophistry* ② force one's way：～门而出 *force open the door and rush out*；*force one's way out* /眼泪～眶而出 *be unable to hold back the tears* ③ contend for；compete for；strive for：～得冠军 *carry off the first prize* ④ deprive
夺[2] make a decision
【夺标】① win the trophy；win a championship：～呼声最高 *be a likely champion* ② have one's tender accepted；win bid
【夺冠】win the championship；come first；take first place
【夺回】recapture；retake；seize back：～阵地 *recapture a position* /～一局 *win a game*（*after losing one or more*）；*pull up by a game* /～发球权 *win back service*
【夺目】dazzle the eyes
【夺取】① capture；seize；take by force；wrest：～主动权 *seize the initiative* ② strive for：～更大的胜利 *strive for even greater victories*

【夺权】seize power; take over power
【夺占】capture; seize; carry

度 ［书］surmise; estimate: 审时～势 *judge the timing and size up the situation*
see also dù

踱 pace; stroll: ～来～去 *pace to and fro; pace up and down* /他独自一人在屋里～着方步。*He strolled in the room with measured steps.*

duǒ

朵 ［量］: 一～花 *a flower* /一～白云 *a whitish cloud*
【朵儿】flower; blossom

垛 ① crenel; battlements ② ［量］used of a window, wall, etc.
see also duò
【垛堞】battlement; crenel: 有～的城堡 *crenellated castle*
【垛口】crenel
【垛子】battlement; crenel: 城～ *battlements on a city wall*

躲 ① hide(oneself): ～在角落里 *hide in a corner* / ～在柜子里 *hide in a closet* /你快～起来! *Quick, hide yourself!* ② avoid; dodge: 你怎么老～着她? *Why do you keep avoiding her?*
【躲避】① hide(oneself) ② avoid; elude; dodge: ～困难 *shy away from difficulties*
【躲藏】hide or conceal oneself; go into hiding: 他被迫～起来。*He was forced to go into hiding.*
【躲躲闪闪】be evasive; hedge; equivocate
【躲风头】go into hiding or lie low until sth blows over
【躲懒】shy away from work; shirk
【躲难】take refuge; seek asylum
【躲闪】dodge; evade: 老大爷～不及，被自行车撞着了。*It was too late for the old man to get out of the way and he was be knocked down by the bicycle.*
【躲债】avoid a creditor

duò

驮
see also tuó
【驮子】① a load carried by a pack-animal; pack ② ［量］used of caravan goods: 三～货 *three packs of goods*

剁 chop; cut: ～为肉泥 *hack to pieces*

垛 ① pile up neatly; stack: 把干草打好捆，～起来。*Bale the hay and pile it up* ② pile; stack: 柴火～ *a pile of faggots*
see also duǒ

舵 rudder; helm: 掌～ *be at the helm*
【舵柄】tiller
【舵轮】steering wheel; helm
【舵手】steersman; helmsman
【舵位】quartermaster's grating; helmsman's post

堕 fall; sink: ～地 *fall on the ground*
【堕落】degenerate; sink low: ～成为罪犯 *degenerate into a criminal* /腐化～ *corruption and degeneration* /自甘～ *resign oneself to degeneration; give oneself up to a life of degeneration*
【堕入】sink into; lapse into; land oneself in: ～陷阱 *fall into a trap* / ～情网 *fall in love; be hit by Cupid's arrow*
【堕胎】have an (induced) abortion

惰 lazy; idle; indolent
【惰性】①［化］inertia: ～气体 *inert gas* / ～元素 *inert element* ② passive attitude; passivity

跺 stamp (one's foot)
【跺脚】stamp one's foot: 气得直～ *stamp one's foot with fury*

E

ē

阿 play up to; pander to; cater to: 刚正不～ *standing on principles and not yielding to pressure; upright and above flattery*
see also ā

【阿胶】donkey-hide gelatin

【阿弥陀佛】【宗】① *Amitabha Buddha* (who presides over the Western Paradise and whose name is used as an incantation repeated by the faithful) ② (used as an exclamation) may Buddha preserve us; Buddha be praised

【阿谀奉承】flatter; toady to; curry favour with

婀

【婀娜】(of a woman's carriage) lithe and graceful; supple and graceful: 体态～ *be of lithe and graceful figure*

é

讹 ① erroneous; wrong; mistaken: ～字 *wrong words (in a text)* / 以～传～ *circulate erroneous reports; spread a wrong message* ② extort under false pretences; blackmail; bluff: ～人 *blackmail sb; bluff sb*

【讹传】false or unfounded rumour

【讹谬】error; mistake

【讹索】blackmail; extort under false pretences

【讹误】error

【讹诈】extort under false pretences; blackmail: ～钱财 *extort money under false pretences*

俄 very soon; presently; suddenly

【俄罗斯】Russia: ～人 *Russian* / ～语 *Russian language*

【俄罗斯帝国】the Russian Empire (1721-1917)

【俄罗斯联邦】the Russian Federation

【俄罗斯族】① the Russian nationality (or the Russians) ② the Russians (or Russia)

娥 pretty young woman: 宫～ *palace maid; maid of honour* / 嫦～ *goddess of the moon*

鹅 goose: 天～ *swan*

【鹅蛋脸】egg-shaped face; oval face

【鹅黄】light yellow

【鹅卵石】cobblestone; cobble

【鹅毛】goose feather: ～扇 *goose feathers fan* / ～大雪 *snow flakes as big as goose feathers — heavy snow*

【鹅绒】goose down

蛾 moth: 蚕～ *silk moth*

额[1] ① forehead ② a horizontal tablet; a horizontal zonal inscribed board

额[2] a specified number or amount: 定～ *quota*

【额定】specified (number or amount); rated: ～功率 *rated power* / ～马力 *rated horse power* / ～输出 *nominal output*

【额度】quota; specified amount

【额骨】【生理】frontal bone

【额角】frontal eminence

【额数】a specified amount, figure or number

【额头】forehead

【额外】extra; additional; added: ～开支 *extra expenses* / ～收入 *additional in come*

ě

恶
see also è; wù

【恶心】① feel like vomiting; feel queasy; feel sick: 小时候我一坐车就感到～。*I always felt sick on a vehicle when I was young.* ② disgusting; repugnant: 那人做的事真叫人～。*His behaviour is repugnant.* ③［方］rotten; lousy ④［方］show up; embarrass; humiliate

è

厄 ［书］① strategic point: 险～ *strategic pass; strategic point* ② disaster; adversity; hardship: 遭～ *meet with disaster* ③ be in distress; be stranded: 登山队～于风暴，未能如期登上顶峰。*The mountaineers were stranded in a storm and failed to reach the peak on schedule.*

【厄尔诺现象】【气】*El Nino* phenomenon

【厄瓜多尔】Ecuador: ～人 *Ecuadorian*

【厄境】miserable plight; difficult situation; predicament: 在～中保持乐观 *remain cheerful in adversity* / 遭～ *land oneself in one predicament after an-*

other

【厄运】adversity; misfortune: ~难逃 *hard to escape the misfortune*

扼 [书] ① clutch; grip: ~其手腕 *clutch at his wrist* / ~住他的咽喉 *clutch at his throat* ② guard; control

【扼杀】strangle; smother; throttle: ~新事物 *smother new emerging things* / ~在摇篮里 *strangle in the cradle* /企图把新思想~在萌芽状态中 *try to nip new ideas in the bud*

【扼守】hold (a strategic point); guard: ~阵地 *hold a position* / ~出口 *hold the mountain pass*

【扼要】concise; to the point: 简明~ *brief and to the point*

【扼制】control; restrain; check: ~心中怒火 *restrain (or control) one's anger*

呃 used to express an exclamation, a reminder, etc.

垩 ① chalk (a soft, white, powdery limestone) ② whiten with chalk

恶 ① evil; guilt; wickedness: 无~不作 *stop at nothing in doing evil* /十~不赦 *guilty of unpardonable evil* ② fierce; vicious; ferocious: 一场~战 *a fierce battle* /穷凶极~ *extremely cruel and vicious* ③ bad; evil; wicked: ~势力 *evil forces* see also ě; wù

【恶霸】local tyrant or despot; local bully: ~地方 *despotic landlord*

【恶报】retribution for evildoing; judgement: 恶有~报。*Evil is rewarded with evil.*

【恶臭】a foul smell; stench: 厕所充满了~。*The W. C. was filled with a foul odour*

【恶斗】fierce fight; ferocious fist fight

【恶毒】vicious; malicious; venomous: ~的诽谤 *venomous slander* / ~攻击 *viciously attack* /手段~ *vicious means*

【恶感】ill feeling; ill will: 对某人有~ *have a grudge against sb*

【恶鬼】① evil spirit ② wicked person; devil

【恶棍】ruffian; scoundrel; bully

【恶果】evil consequence; bad result; disastrous effect: 自食~ *suffer the consequences of one's evildoings*

【恶狠狠】venomous; fierce; ferocious: 她~地给了他一巴掌。*She gave him a ferocious slap.*

【恶化】worsen; deteriorate; take a turn for the worse: 病人的病情~了。*The patient's condition is deteriorating.* /形势越来越~了。*The situation is getting worse and worse.*

【恶疾】a foul or nasty disease

【恶劣】bad; odious; disgusting: 天气~ *inclement weather* / ~行径 *disgusting conduct* /手段~ *mean (or dirty) tricks*

【恶骂】shout vicious abuse

【恶眉恶眼】fierce look; a very fierce expression

【恶名】a bad name; a bad reputation; in fanny

【恶魔】① demon; devil; evil spirit ② monster; vicious thug

【恶气】① a bad odor; a foul smell ② insult; outrage ③ grievance; resentment: 出口~ *vent one's grievance* ④ anger; fury

【恶人】an evil person; a vile creature; villain: ~当道。*Evil people were in power.*

【恶少】wicked young man from a wealthy or influential family; young ruffian

【恶声恶气】angry voices and hard words

【恶事传千里】bad news spreads for and wide

【恶习】bad or pernicious habit: 染上~ *contract a bad habit; fall into evil ways*

【恶性】malignant; pernicious; vicious: ~刑事案件 *case of vicious crime* / ~通货膨胀 *galloping (or runaway) inflation*

【恶言】rude language; coarse language: 口出~ *use abusive language; wag one's vicious tongue* / ~相向 *exchange hot words*

【恶意】evil or ill intentions; ill will; malice: ~攻击 *spiteful attack* / ~中伤 *slander*

【恶兆】ill omen; bad omen

【恶浊】foul; filthy: 空气~ *foul air*

【恶作剧】a practical joke; a mischievous prank; mischief: 闹~ *be up to mischief; play a practical joke*

饿 ① hungry: 挨~ *go hungry; starve* /我~极了。*I'm starving.* / ~了吃什么都甜如蜜。*Any food is tasty when one is hungry.* ② starve: 别~着小狗。*Don't starve the dog.*

【饿饭】[方] go hungry; go without food

【饿虎扑食】like a hungry tiger pouncing on its prey: 那人~地扭住了我。*He pounced on me like a hungry tiger.*

萼 【植】calyx

【萼片】【植】sepal

遏 check; restrain; prohibit: 沮~ *stop; prevent*

【遏抑】suppress; contain; keep down: 不可~的怒火 *uncontrollable fury*

【遏止】check; hold back; restrain: ~侵略 *check aggression*

【遏制】keep within limits; contain; restrain: ~革命 *contain a revolution* / ~愤怒的情绪 *check one's anger* / ~政策 *policy of containment*

愕 astounded; stunned; dazed: 惊~ *be shocked*

【愕然】stunned; astounded: ~四顾 *look around is astonishment*

【愕视】look in astonishment; stare wide-eyed

腭 【生理】palate: 硬~ *hard palate* /软~ *soft palate*

【腭裂】【医】cleft palate

【腭音】【语】palatal

鹗 osprey; fish hawk

颚 ① mandible (of an arthropod); jaw: 上~ *upper jaw* ② palate

【颚骨】jawbone

E

噩 shocking; frightening; upsetting

【噩耗】sad news of the death of a beloved person: ~传来,犹如晴天霹雳。*The grievous news came like a bolt from the blue.*

【噩梦】nightmare; frightening or horrible dream: 那些日子的生活真是一场~。*Life in those days was a real nightmare.*

鳄 crocodile; alligator

【鳄蜥】crocodile lizard

【鳄鱼】crocodile; alligator

ēn

恩 ① kindness; favour; grace: 施~ *bestow favours* / 忘~ *be ungrateful*; *be devoid of gratitude* ② (Ēn) a surname

【恩爱】conjugal love; be deeply in love with each other: ~夫妻 *an affectionate couple*

【恩赐】bestow (favours, charity, etc.); patronize

【恩德】kindness; favour; grace: ~无量 *infinite kindness*

【恩典】① favour; grace; benevolence: 皇上的~ *royal favour* ② bestow a favour or kindness on sb; be clement to sb: 求老爷~~! *I beg your excellency's grace.*

【恩断义绝】all love and kindly feeling are dead; a marriage or friendship breaks down completely

【恩格斯】Friedrich Engels (1820—1895), one of the founders of scientific socialism or Marxism

【恩惠】favour; kindness; grace; bounty

【恩将仇报】return evil for good; requite kindness with enmity; bite the hand that feeds one

【恩情】loving kindness; favour: 我永远也忘不了老师对我的~。*I shall never forget my teacher's loving-kindness to me.*

【恩人】benefactor

【恩深义重】a great debt of gratitude

【恩威并用】make a combined use of favour and disfavour (as in controlling one's subordinates); use both the mailed fist and the velvet glove

【恩怨】gratitude and resentment; resentment; grievance: ~分明 *know dearly to whom to show gratitude and against whom to feel resentment* / 不计较个人~ *not allow oneself to be swayed by personal feelings*

【恩重如山】kindness as heavy as a mountain; great favour

【恩准】gracious approval of the monarch

èn

摁 press (with the hand or finger): ~按钮 *press (or push) a button* / ~电铃 *ring an electric bell* / ~手印 *register one's fingerprint*

【摁钉儿】drawing pin; thumbtack

【摁扣儿】snap fastener

ér

儿[1] ① child ② youngster; youth; young man: 英雄~女 *young heroes and heroines* ③ son: 他有五~二女。*He has five sons and two daughters.* ④ male

儿[2] used as a suffix and transcribed as r in pinyin

【儿茶】①【植】acacia catechu ② catechu

【儿歌】children's song; nursery rhymes

【儿皇帝】puppet emperor

【儿科】(department of) paediatrics: ~医生 *paediatrician*

【儿女】① sons and daughters; children: ~都已长大成人。*The children have all grown up.* ② young man and woman (in love)

【儿女情长】love between man and woman is long; cherish deep affection for each other: 英雄气短,~。*The aspirations of a hero are over whelmed by the love between man and woman.*

【儿时】childhood

【儿孙】children and grandchildren; descendants; posterity: ~满堂 *many children and grandchildren in the family*

【儿童】children: ~节 (*International*) *Children's Day* / ~读物 *children's book* / ~节目 *children's program* / ~文学 *children literature* / ~心理学 *child psychology* / ~医院 *children's hospital*

【儿媳妇儿】daughter-in-law

【儿戏】trifling matter: 视同~ *regard as a mere trifle* / 这可不是~。*It's no trifling matter.*

【儿子】son

而 ① and; as well as: 伟大~艰巨的任务 *a great and arduous task* / 这篇文章长~空。*This article is long-winded and lacks substance.* ② and yet; but; while on the other hard: 朴素~大方 *simple but with good taste* / 有其名~无其实 *in name but not in reality* ③ so that; in order to: 因病~辞职 *resign on health grounds* ④ (used with 由,从,自,etc.) to: 由上~下 *from top to bottom* / 由远~近 *approach from afar* ⑤ connecting an adverbial element to a verb: 顺流~下 *go down stream* / 不欢~散 *part in discord*

【而后】after that; then: 三思~行。*Think twice before you act.*

【而今】now; at the present time

【而立】[书] thirty years of age: 三十~ *at thirty on should be well established in one's life*

【而且】and; and also; but also; moreover

【而已】nothing more; that is all; only: 说说~,别当真。*Don't take it too seriously; it was only a casual remark.* / 我只是个学生~。*I'm just a student; that's all.*

ěr

尔 [书] ① your; you: ~等 *you*; *all of you* ② so; like that: 果~ *if so* ③ that: ~时 *at that time* ④ only; just: 无他,但手熟~。*It is just that I am familiar to it.*

【尔后】[书] thereafter; subsequently; hence-forth: ~的事情我就不清楚了。*I have no idea what happened afterwards.*

【尔虞我诈】mutual deception; each trying to cheat or outwit the other

耳[1] ① ear: 内~ *inner ear* /中~ *middle ear* ② any ear-like thing: 木~ *edible fungus* ③ on both sides; flanking; side

耳[2] [书] only; just

【耳背】hard of hearing; deaf

【耳边风】sth that goes in one ear and out the other; a puff of wind passing the ear — unheeded advice: 他把父母的劝告当作~。*He turned a deaf ear to his parents' advice.*

【耳鬓厮磨】[书] (of a boy and girl) play together ear to ear and temple to temple — have close childhood friendship

【耳垂】【生理】earlobe

【耳聪目明】have good ears and eyes — have a dear understanding (of the situation)

【耳朵】ear: ~尖 *have sharp ears* /穿~ *have one's earlobe's pierced* (*for wearing earrings*)/ ~软 *credulous*; *easily influenced*; *susceptible to flattery*

【耳房】smaller rooms on both sides of the main room or of the wings

【耳福】the good for tune of heaving sth rare or beautiful: 大饱~ *enjoy to the full listening to music*, *singing*, *etc.*

【耳根清净】have peace for one's ears (free from nagging, quarrel, etc.); have a quiet and peaceful environment

【耳垢】earwax

【耳光】slap on the face; box on the ear: 打~ *slap sb's face*

【耳环】earrings

【耳机】earphone; earpiece: 戴上~ *put on the earphones*

【耳聋】be deaf

【耳鸣】【医】tinnitus; ringing in the ear: 我~。*My ears are ringing.*

【耳膜】tympanic membrane

【耳目】① what one sees and hears; knowledge; in formation: ~不广 *not well-informed* ② one who spies for sb else: 他~众多。*His men are everywhere.* ③ ears and eyes: 掩人~ *prevent sb from seeing or hearing of sth*

【耳目一新】find everything fresh and new: 我们一到这个小山村,顿时觉得~。*We found everything fresh and new the moment we entered the small mountain village.*

【耳濡目染】be imperceptibly influenced by what one sees and hears: 他父母都是画家,平日~,所以他也爱好美术。*His parents are both painters, and under their daily influence, he is passionately fond of arts.*

【耳塞】① mini-earphone ② earplug

【耳生】be unfamiliar to the ear; sound rather strange: 这个人的话音听起来~。*This man's voice sounds unfamiliar to me.*

【耳屎】[口] earwax

【耳熟】familiar to the ear: 这名字听起来好~,好像在哪儿听过。*The name sounds so familiar, I seem to have heard it somewhere.*

【耳听八方】have keen ears; be very alert

【耳听为虚,眼见为实】what you hear maybe false, what you see is true.

【耳闻】hear of or about: 此事早有~。*I heard about it long ago.*

【耳闻不如目见】seeing for oneself is better than hearing from others

【耳闻目睹】what one sees and hears: 其间我~了不少有趣事儿。*During the time I saw and heard many funny things.*

【耳蜗】【生理】cochlea

【耳咽管】【生理】Eustachian tube; auditory tube

【耳语】whisper in sb's ear; whisper: 他们俩在大树下低声~。*They are whispering under a tall tree.*

【耳坠】earring; eardrop

迩 [书] near; close: 遐~驰名 *know far and wide*

饵 ① cakes; pastry: 果~ *candies and cakes*; *confectionery* ② bait: 鱼~ *fishing bait* ③ [书] entice; tempt: ~以生利 *use great wealth as a bait*; *tempt sb by offering pots of money*

【饵料】① fishing bait ② insect killer; insecticide

【饵子】(fishing) bait

èr

二 ① two: ~十 *twenty* / ~楼 (*UK*) *first floor*; (*US*) *second floor* / ~公斤 *two kilograms* ② different: 不~价 *fixed price*; *no bargaining* /三心~意 *of two minds*; *shilly-shally*

【二八】sixteen: 年方~ *be only sixteen years of age*

【二把刀】[方] ① have a smattering of a subject ② smatter

【二把手】the second top leader of a unit; second-in-command

【二百五】① [口] a stupid person: 你别~了! *Don't be silly*! ② [方] dabbler; smatterer

【二重唱】【音】(vocal) duet

【二重性】dual character (or nature); duality

【二重奏】【音】(instrumental) duet

【二等】second-class; second-rate: ~舱 *second-class cabin* / ~公民 *second-class citizen* / ~功 *merit citation class*

E

【二副】【航】second mate; second officer

【二锅头】a strong, colourless liquor distilled from sorghum (so called because it is distilled twice), popular in northern China

【二话】(often used in the negative) demur; objection: ~不说 *without demur* / 你尽管吩咐,我决无~。*If you have any instructions, please let me know and I will not hesitate to carry them out.*

【二婚】remarry

【二级风】【气】force 2 wind; light breeze

【二极管】【电】diode: ~整流器 *diode rectifier*

【二进宫】① traditional play in Beijing opera ② detained or sentenced for a second time; in and out of prison twice ③ do sth for a second time

【二进制】【电】binary system; binary mode: ~编码器 *binary coder* / ~计算机 *binary computer* / ~数 *binary number* / ~数字 *binary digit*

【二郎腿】[方] cross-legged: 跷起~ *sit cross-legged*

【二愣子】a rash fellow

【二流子】idler; bum

【二硫化物】【化】bisulphide

【二十四节气】the twenty-four solar terms

【二手】① assistant; helper: 我给你当~。*I'll act as your assistant.* ② second-hand: ~货 *second-hand goods* / ~资料 *second-hand information*

【二踢脚】double-bang fire cracker

【二氧化碳】【化】carbon dioxide: ~灭火器 *carbon-dioxide bottle*

【二氧化物】【化】dioxide

【二月】① February ② the second month of the lunar year; the second moon

【二战】world War Two

【二者必居其一】either one or the other; one way or the other

贰 ① two ② transfer one's allegiance; turn one's coat

【贰臣】court official who transferred his allegiance to a new ruler; turncoat official

F

fā

发 ① issue; send (out); deliver; give out; distribute: ~短信息 *send a short message* / ~信号 *give a signal* / ~通知 *hand out a notice* / ~传单 *distribute leaflets* ② discharge; shoot; emit; launch: ~射人造卫星 *launch a manmade satellite* ③ speak; express: ~出呻吟 *utter a groan* / ~表意见 *express an opinion* ④ generate; come or bring into existence: ~芽 *germinate* / ~电 *generate electricity* /种子~芽了。*The seeds have sprouted.* ⑤ expand; develop: ~展市场经济 *expand the market economy* /雨水和阳光促使植物生长~育。*Rains and summer suns develop the plants.* ⑥ (of foodstuffs) rise or expand when soaked or fermented: ~酵 *ferment* ⑦ discover; expose; open up: ~现新油田 *discover new oil field* /要揭~以前的错误。*The mistakes of the past should be exposed.* ⑧ diffuse; disperse; evaporate; volatilize: 挥~油 *volatile oil* /树木散~着清香。*The trees sent forth a delicate fragrance.* ⑨ become; get into a certain state: 她脸色~白。*Her face looks pale.* /树木开始~绿。*The trees are beginning to turn green.* ⑩ show one's feeling; elicit: 饿得~慌 *feel faint with hunger* / ~怒 *get angry* / ~慈悲 *show mercy* ⑪ feel: 胳膊~麻 *have pins and needles in one's arms* /她腿有点~酸。*She felt weak and sore in the legs.* ⑫ set out; start; depart; begin an undertaking: 夕~朝至 *set off in the evening and arrive in the next morning* /整装待~ *fully equipped for a journey; ready and waiting* ⑬ [量]: 五~炮弹 *five shells* /十~子弹 10 *rounds of ammunition*; 50 *cartridges*
see also fà

【发案】(of a case) occur: ~地点 *the scene of the occurrence of a case* /过去那个地方的犯罪案件~率很高。*Before there was a high incidence of criminal cases in that district.*

【发榜】publish a list of successful applicants or candidates

【发包】contract out: 把这项工程~给一家外国公司 *contract a project out to a foreign company*

【发报】transmit a message by radio, telegraphy, etc.: ~机 *transmitter* / ~台 *transmitting station*

【发背】① become hard of hearing ②【中医】*carbuncle on the back*

【发标】*issue bidding documents*

【发表】publish, issue; announce: ~演说 *deliver or make a speech* / ~文章 *publish an article* / ~社论 *publish an editorial* / ~声明 *make or issue a statement*

【发病】(of a person) fall ill; (of a disease) come on: ~率 *incidence (of a disease)*

【发布】issue; release: ~命令 *give an order; issue an order* / ~消息 *give out information* / ~新闻 *release news*

【发财】get rich; make a fortune: 我肯定这笔买卖他们一定~了。*I bet they were making a pile out of the deal.*

【发颤】quiver; tremble: 她的声音有些~。*There was a tremble in her voice.*

【发潮】fell damp; become damp: 睡觉时不要盖~的被子。*Don't sleep between damp quilts.*

【发车场】departure yard or track

【发愁】worry; become sad; be anxious: 我非常~女儿的健康。*I am very anxious about my daughter's health.*

【发出】issue (orders, etc.); send (letter, message, etc); send out; give out: ~邀请 *send out an invitation* / ~警告 *send out a warning; sound a warning*

【发喘】be short of breath; pant

【发达】① developed; flourishing: ~国家 *developed country* /经济~ *have well-developed economy* /四肢~ *have well-developed arms and legs; have powerful arms and legs* ② develop; promote: ~交通 *develop transport system*

【发呆】look blank; stare blankly; be in a daze; be in a trance: 他整天~。*He has been in a trance all day.* /他盯着我的脸~。*He looks blankly at my face.*

【发电】generate electricity (or power): ~量 *generated energy; electric power production*

【发电厂】power plant; power station; generating plant: 火力~ *thermal power plant* / ~容量 *station (or power plant) capacity* /风力~ *wind power plant*

【发电机】generator; dynamo: 永磁~ *magneto generator* / ~容量 *generator capacity* / ~机 *generating set (or unit)* / ~出了故障。*The generator has broken down.*

【发电站】power station: 水力~ *hydro-power station*

【发动】① start; launch: ~汽车 *start a car; set a car going* / ~内战 *launch (or unleash) a civil war* / ~进攻 *launch an attack* ② arouse; call into action; mobilize: ~群众 *mobilize (or arouse) the masses*

【发动机】engine; motor: 汽油~ *gasoline engine* / 内燃~ *inner-combustion engine* / ~输出功率 *engine output*

【发抖】shiver; shake; tremble; quiver: 冻得~ *shake (or shiver) with cold* /气得~ *tremble with anger; shake all over with anger*

【发放】provide; grand; extend; distribute; ~货款 *grant a credit; extend a credit; grant a loan* / ~物资 *distribution of materials*

【发奋】① work energetically; exert oneself: ~读书 *work hard at one's studies* ② make a firm resolution

【发疯】go mad; go crazy; be out of one's mind; become insane; lose one's senses: 为了能挣更多的钱,他~似地工作。*In order to make more money, he worked like crazy.*

【发福】put on weight; grow stout

【发糕】steamed sponge cake

【发稿】① distribute news dispatches: 截至~时,我们都没有见到她。*We didn't see her at press time.* ② send manuscripts to the press

【发给】grant; distribute; issue

【发光】① be glow; be luminous; give off light ②【物】luminescent: ~材料 *luminescent material*

【发汗】induce perspiration; sweat

【发号施令】issue orders; order people about: 不要对别人~。*Don't order other people about.*

【发慌】feel nervous; get flustered or flurried

【发挥】① bring into play; give scope to; give free rein to: ~想象力 *give free rein to one's imagination* ② elaborate; develop (idea, theme, etc.)

【发昏】① feel dizzy; feel giddy ② lose one's head; become confused; be out of one's mind: 你一定是~了,竟然放弃这么好的机会。*You must be out of mind for you gave up so good chance.*

【发火】① catch fire; fire ② go off; detonate ③ be on fire; break out ④ get angry; lose temper

【发货】send out goods; dispatch goods; deliver goods: ~单 *dispatch list* /按期~ *dispatch the goods on schedule*

【发家】build up a family fortune

【发奖】award prizes; present prizes: ~仪式 *prize giving ceremony* /昨天他参加了那个~大会。*He attended the prize-giving meeting yesterday.*

【发酵】ferment; leaven: ~粉 *yeast powder* / ~剂 *leavening agent*

【发觉】find; detect; discover; realize

【发掘】explore; excavate; unearth

【发狂】go mad; go crazy; go berserk

【发困】[口] feel sleepy; feel drowsy: 刚起床不久,我又有点~了。*I felt a little sleepy after I got up for a while.*

【发落】deal with (an offender)

【发霉】go mouldy; become mildewed

【发明】① invent ②[书] *expound*

【发难】① rise in revolt; launch an attack ② raise a difficult question for discussion

【发怒】get angry; flare up; fly into a rage; lose one's temper: 最近他总是无端~。*Recently he always flares up for no reason at all.*

【发胖】put on weight; gain weight; get fat

【发配】banish; exile; be transported to a distant place for penal servitude: 他爷爷被~到边疆多年。*His grandpa was exiled to a border area for many years.*

【发脾气】lose one's temper; get angry; fly into a rage; throw a tantrum

【发票】invoice; receipt; bill: ~存根 *invoice stub* / 凭~报销 *reimburse one's expenses with the receipts* /开~ *make an invoice*

【发起】① initiate; sponsor: ~革命运动 *initiate a revolutionary campaign* / ~人 *initiator; sponsor* / ~国 *sponsor nation* ② start; launch

【发情】【动】oestrus; oestrum; heat; rut: ~周期 *oestrous cycle*

【发球】【体】serve a ball: ~失误 *miss a service* /换~ *change service*

【发热】① have a fever; have a temperature ② generate heat; give out heat ③ be hotheaded

【发散】① (of rays, etc.) diverge; diffuse: 气体~ *diffusion of gases* / ~思维 *divergent thinking* ②【中医】*let out the internal heat; disperse the internal heat with sudorifics*

【发丧】① announce a death; send out an obituary ② hold a funeral; arrange a funeral; carry a coffin to the graveyard

【发烧】① have a fever; have a temperature ② give oneself to; be infatuated

【发烧友】[方] enthusiastic fan; fancier; zealot; fan; audiophile

【发射】① launch; discharge; fire; project: ~导弹 *launch a guided missile* / ~塔 *launching tower* ②【物】*transmit; emit*: ~电波 *transmit radio waves* / ~天线 *transmitting antenna*

【发生】happen; occur; take place: 咱们看看那边究竟~了什么事情。*Let's see what happened on earth.*

【发誓】swear; pledge; take an oath; vow

【发售】sell; put on sale

【发送】① transmit by radio: 他去~电报去了。*He went out for transmitting by radio.* ② send; dispatch: ~货物 *dispatch goods*

【发酸】① turn sour; taste sour ② feel weak and sore; ache slightly ③ (of one's nose, eyes, etc.) tingle with sorrow

【发现】① find; discover: 他在院子里~了那个丢失的盒子。*He found the missing box in the yard.* ② notice detect; become award of

【发祥地】place of origin; birthplace

【发泄】let off; give vent to

【发薪】pay wages; pay salaries: 又到了~的日子了。*It's time for paying wages again.*

【发信】post a letter; mail a letter; send a letter

【发行】issue; publish; release; put on sale: ~公

债 *issue of government bonds* / ～银行 *bank of issue*

【发虚】① feel apprehensive; feel diffident; lack in self-confidence ② feel feeble and weak

【发芽】germinate; sprout: ～率 *germination percentage*

【发言】make a statement; take the floor; deliver a speech: ～稿 *text of a statement or speech* / ～权 *right to speak* / ～人 *spokesman*

【发炎】inflammation

【发扬】① develop; promote; foster; carry on: ～民主 *promote democracy* / ～优良传统 *carry on a fine tradition* ② make full use of; make the most of

【发痒】itch; tickle

【发音】pronounce; articulate; enunciate; vocalize: ～器官 *vocal organs*

【发育】growth; development: ～期 *period of growth* / ～健全 *physically well developed* / ～不全 *underdevelopment*

【发源】rise; originate: ～地 *place of origin*

【发晕】feel dizzy; feel giddy

【发展】① develop; grow; expand; promote: ～权 *right of development* ② development: ～模式 *mode of development*

【发胀】① swell: 他忽然感觉肚子有点～。*Suddenly he felt a little bloated.* ② feel distended

【发作】① break out; show effect: 她的毒瘾开始～。*She is craving the drug.* /酒性开始～。*The alcohol began to take its effect.* ② flare up; have a fit of anger

fá

乏 ① lack; be short of: 缺～经验 *be inexperienced; have little experienced; have little experience* /缺～了解 *lack understanding* ② tired; weary: 一天工作下来,他感觉浑身～力。*After one day's work, he felt weary all over.* ③ exhausted; worn-out

【乏顿】[书] weary; fatigued

【乏货】good-for-nothing

【乏倦】fatigued; tired

【乏困】tired; run-down

【乏累】tired; run-down

【乏力】① incapable; short of strength ② weary

【乏煤】used coal

【乏汽】dead steam; steam exhaust

【乏人】useless person; good-for-nothing

【乏味】tasteless; dull; insipid

伐 ① fell; cut down: ～倒 *felling* / ～倒的大树 *felling area* /在林中～木 *log in the woods* ② attack; strike; send an expedition against: 征～ *send a punitive expedition* /讨～叛逆 *send armed forces to put down a rebellion* ③ boast about oneself; sing sb's own praises: ～善 *sing one's own praise*

【伐木】lumbering; logging; cutting; felling: ～业 *lumbering* / ～工人 *lumberman* / ～场 *lumber-mill*

罚 punish; penalize; fine; forfeit: ～不当罪 *be unduly punished; suffer inappropriate punishment*

【罚出场】【体】foul out

【罚金】fine; forfeit

【罚酒】make sb drink wine

【罚款】① impose a fine ② forfeit; penalty: 违约～ *fine for breaching a contract*

【罚球】(in soccer) penalty kick; (in basketball) penalty shot: ～线 *penalty line*

阀[1] powerful person or family: 财～ *financial magnate*

阀[2] valve: 安全～ *safety valve*

【阀门】【机】valve: 他把～关了。*He turned off the valve.*

筏 raft: 木～ *wooden raft* /竹～ *bamboo raft*

【筏道】log chute; logway

【筏子】raft

fǎ

法[1] ① law; statute: 遵纪守～ *observe law and discipline; abide by the law and observe discipline* /刑～ *criminal law* /民～ *civil law* /想～ *idea; view; opinion* /想方设～ *use all means; do everything possible* /婚姻～ *marriage law* ② way; mode; method ③ standard; model ④ follow; emulate: 效～先贤 *follow the example of the sages of the past* ⑤ magic; trick

法[2] 【物】farad (F)

【法案】proposed law; bill

【法宝】①【宗】*sutras* ② magic weapon or formula

【法场】execution ground

【法典】code; statute book

【法定】legal; statutory: ～货币 *legal tender* / ～期限 *legal time limit; prescription* / ～监护人 *legal guardian* / ～休假日 *legal holiday* / ～继承人 *legal heir* / ～代理人 *legal representative; statutory agent* / ～股本 *authorized share capital* / ～年龄 *legal age; lawful age*

【法官】judge; justice: 那个～尽放空炮。*The judge was all talk.*

【法规】laws and regulations; statutes

【法国】France: ～人 *French; Frenchman* / ～梧桐 *plane tree*

【法纪】law and discipline: 遵守～ *observe law and discipline* /目无～ *act in utter disregard of law and discipline*

【法拉第】Michael Faraday (1791-1897), English chemist and physicist: ～定律 *Faraday's law*

【法郎】franc

【法力】①【宗】power of the Buddhist doctrine;

F

dharma power ② magic power; supernatural power

【法令】decree; order; laws and decrees:最近政府颁布了很多~。*Recently the government promulgated many decrees.*

【法律】law; statute: ~规定 *legal provisions* / ~程序 *legal procedure*

【法盲】person ignorant of the law; one who lacks legal knowledge

【法人】【律】legal person; juridical person; artificial person; corporation: ~代表 *legal representative* / ~股 *shares held by legal persons*; *corporate shares* / ~团体 *body corporate*

【法师】master of the Law (title of respect for a Buddhist or Taoist priest)

【法术】magic arts; witchcraft

【法庭】court; tribunal:国际~ *international court* / 军事~ *military tribunal*

【法网】net of justice; arm of the law: ~恢恢,疏而不漏。*Large though its meshes may be, the wide net of justice lets no criminal through.*

【法西斯】fascist: ~主义 *fascism* / ~组织 *fascist organization* / ~统治 *fascist rule*

【法学】law; science of law; jurisprudence

【法医】legal medical expert

【法语】French (language)

【法院】law court; court; court of justice:地方~ *local court* /最高人民~ *supreme People's Court*

【法则】① law; rule ②[书] *laws and regulations*

【法治】rule of law; government by law: ~国家 *country under the rule of law*

【法制】legal system; legal institutions; legality

【法子】method; way:她想了一个好~来对付他。*She thought a good idea to deal with him.*

fà

发 hair:黑~ *black hair* /乌黑的头~ *jet-black hair* /金~ *golden hair*; *blonde hair* / 秀~ *beautiful hair* /满头白~ *grey headed*; *hoary-headed*; *silver-haired* / ~短心长 *short in the hair but long in wisdom* / ~际 *hairline* / ~蜡 *pomade* /我们不敢相信她染~了。*We can't believe that she had her haired dyed*
see also fā

【发辫】plait; braid; pigtail

【发夹】hairclip; barrette; bobby in

【发胶】hair spray; hair jelly; gel-mousse:抹~ *apply hair jelly to one's hair*

【发廊】hairdresser's; beauty parlor or salon

【发妻】[旧] first wife

【发卡】hairclip; hairpin; bobby pin:妈妈送给我~。*My mother gave hairclips to me.*

【发乳】hair cream

【发屋】① hairdresser's; barber's ② beauty salon

【发型】hairstyle; hair fashion; hairdo

【发油】hair tonic; brilliantine; hair oil

【发指】be filled with indignation

【发指眦裂】become so angry that one's hair stands on end and one's eye sockets burst; boil with anger

fān

帆 ① sail:扬起风~ *hoist the sails*; *set sail* /一~风顺 *plain or smooth sailing* ②[书] *sailing boat* / ~板运动 *sailboarding*; *windsurfing* / ~板运动员 *windsurfer*

【帆板】【体】sailboard; windsurfer

【帆布】canvas; sailcloth: ~包 *canvas bag* / ~鞋 *canvas shoes* ~船 *canvas boat* / ~床 *cot*; *camp bed* / ~带 *canvas belt*

【帆船】sailing boat; sailing ship; sailing vessel

【帆篷】sail; canvas

【帆樯】mast

番 ① aborigines; barbarian; foreign:生~ *aboriginal savage* ② used in names for certain plants originally introduced from abroad: ~瓜 *pumpkin* / ~石榴 *guava* (*psidium guajava*)

【番号】designation of a military unit

【番茄】tomato: ~酱 *tomato sauce*:她喜欢喝~汁。*She likes drinking tomato juice.*

藩 ① fence; hedge ② screen; barrier ③ feudatory; vassal state: ~国 *vassal state* / ~镇割据 *separatist rule by military governors*

【藩篱】fence; barrier

【藩属】vassal state; feudatory

翻 ① turn:他~了我的衣服。*He turned my clothes over.* ② look through; search; rummage:她~了所有的盒子都没有找到。*She rummaged all over the box, but she found nothing in them.* ③ overturn; reverse: ~供 *withdraw a confession* ④ cross; get over: ~过河 *cross a river* ⑤ double; multiply ⑥ translate; interpret ⑦[口] *quarrel fall out*; *break up*

【翻案】overturn a verdict; reverse a verdict

【翻版】reprint; refurbished version; copy

【翻车】① overturn ② run into difficulties; be defeated

【翻船】① capsize ② be defeated; suffer a setback

【翻动】shift (sth from one position to another); move:汽车每次转弯,行李箱里的工具就会来回~。*The tools shift around in the car boot every time when it turns a corner.*

【翻斗】tipping (or skip) bucket: ~车 *tipcart*; *end tipper*; *skip car* / ~卡车 *tipping lorry*; *tip lorry*; *tipper truck*; *tipper*

【翻番】double; increase by a specified number of times

【翻覆】① overturn; turn over; turn upside down:天地~ *world-shaking change*; *cataclysmic change*; *great and thorough change* / 江中的一条渔船~了。*A fishing boat on the river overturned.* /火车~。*A train turned over* ② toss from side to side:她整夜在床上~,不能入眠。*She couldn't sleep, but kept tossing and turning in bed all night.*

【翻改】remake (old clothes); turn: ~裙子 *have an skirt turned*

【翻盖】renovate or rebuild (a house): 那座大楼关闭进行~。*The building was closed for renovation.*

【翻杠子】【体】do gymnastics on parallel bars or horizontal bar

【翻个儿】[口] turn over: 那辆汽车在路上翻了个儿。*The car turned over on the road.*

【翻跟头】turn a somersault; loop the loop; (of an aircraft) fly in a completely circle vertically: 那些体操运动员正在垫子上~。*The gymnasts on the gym mats were turning somersault.* /飞机不断地在空中~。*The aircraft was looping the loop continuously.*

【翻耕】plough

【翻供】withdraw a confession; revoke a confession; retract one's testimony

【翻滚】① seethe; roll; churn: 稻浪~ *rolling of rice* /小孩儿跌进了~的激流中。*The child fell into the seething waters of the rapids* ② roll about; toss about; tumble about; writhe: 病人痛得在地上~。*The patient was writhing on the ground in agony.* /孩子在地板上~嬉戏。*The child was tumbling about on the floor.*

【翻悔】back out (of a commitment, promise, etc.); renege; fail to keep (a promise, one's word, etc.)

【翻江倒海】holding back rivers and overturning seas — overwhelming; tremendous

【翻旧账】rake up old scores; bring up old scores again

【翻来覆去】① toss and turn; toss from side to side ② again and again; repeatedly

【翻脸】suddenly turn hostile; fall out; turn against sb: ~不认人 *turn against a friend; turn one's back on an old associate*

【翻山越岭】go uphill and down dale; cross over mountain after mountain; tramp over hill and dale

【翻身】① turn over: 那个孩子~从床上爬了起来。*The little child rolled off the bed.* ② stand up; free oneself: ~做主人 *stand up and be master of one's own fate*

【翻腾】(fānténg) tuck dive: 向内~三周半 *backward tuck dive with three-and-a-half somersaults*

【翻腾】(fānteng) ① surge; seethe ② turn sth over and over

【翻天覆地】earth-shaking; world-shaking

【翻箱倒柜】rummage through chests and cupboards; ransack boxes and chests

【翻新】renovate; revamp; recondition; make over: 花样~ *present the same old thing in a new guise*

【翻修】rebuild; renovate; restore to good condition: ~汽车 *repair a car* /去年我们家的老房子~了。*Our old house was renovated last year.*

【翻译】① translate; interpret: ~机 *translation machine* ② translator; interpreter: 他哥哥在这次会议中担当了~。*His elder brother acted as an interpreter in the meeting.*

【翻印】reprint; reproduce

【翻阅】leaf through; look over; glance over: 今天下午我要去图书馆~一些报刊杂志。*I'm going to the library to look over newspapers and magazines.*

【翻越】get over; climb over; surmount

【翻云覆雨】produce clouds with one turn of the hand and rain with another — be given to playing tricks; be tricky and deceitful; keep shifting one's ground; be shifty and capricious

【翻造】rebuild; renovate

fán

凡[1] ① commonplace; ordinary: 不同~响 *quite extraordinary* /~庸之辈 *common herd* /超~脱俗 *rise above the general run of people* ② the earth; this mortal world: 仙女下~ *fair maiden descending to the world; celestial beauty coming down to earth*

凡[2] ① all; any; every: ~这个班的学生必须参加这次活动。*All the students in the class must attend this activity.* ② in all; altogether

【凡尘】this world; this mortal life

【凡尔赛】versailles: ~宫 *Palace of Versailles* /~和约 *Treaty of Versailles*

【凡夫俗子】①【宗】*layman* ② common run of people; ordinary people

【凡间】mortal world

【凡例】guide to the use of a book, etc.; notes on the use of a reference book, etc.

【凡人】①[书] ordinary person; common people ② mortal

【凡士林】Vaseline; petrolatum

【凡事】everything: ~小心 *be careful in whatever one do*

【凡是】every; any; all: ~听过弗里曼讲演的人都很敬佩他。*All who listened to Freeman's speech admired him very much.*

【凡俗】ordinary; common

【凡响】common music; ordinary music: 她所做的非同~。*What she had done was quite extraordinary.*

【凡心】mortal desires; worldly desires

【凡庸】ordinary; commonplace

矾 【化】vitriol: 明~ *alum*

【矾土】alumina: ~水泥 *alumina cement*

钒 【化】vanadium

【钒铝合金】vanalium

烦 ① vexed; annoyed; upset: ~人 *vexing; annoying* /~絮 *miscellaneous and disorderly* /不知道为什么他最近有点心~意乱的。*We don't know why he was terribly upset recently.* ② be tired of：～厌 *tired of*；*fed up with* /～言碎语 *tiresome loquacities*；*over elaborate and tedious remarks* ③ superfluous and confusing：～请 *ask*；*request* ④ trouble：～难 *knotty*；*troublesome*

【烦愁】worried and depressed

【烦乱】depressed and perturbed

【烦闷】depressed；unhappy；moody

【烦恼】worried；upset；vexed

【烦扰】① bother；disturb：这么晚来～你，非常抱歉。*I'm sorry to have disturbed you so late.* ② feel disturbed

【烦琐】loaded down with trivial details

【烦心】annoying；vexatious；worrisome：让人～的孩子 *a vexatious kid*

【烦躁】agitated；fidgety；irritable and restless

樊 ①［书］fence ②（fán）a surname

【樊篱】① fence；hedge ② barriers；trammels

【樊笼】bird cage — place or condition of confinement：她终于冲破了旧传统的～。*At last she shake off the shackles of the old tradition.*

繁 ① in great numbers；numerous；manifold：～花似锦 *flourishing scene of prosperity*；*a multitude of blossoming flowers* ② procreate；multiply：～殖场 *breeding ground*

【繁多】various；numerous

【繁分数】【数】complex fraction

【繁复】heavy and complicated

【繁华】thriving；flourishing；busy；prosperous：他家在城里～的地区附近。*His house is near the downtown district.*

【繁忙】busy；bustling：他总是说他公务～。*He always says he is busy with official duties.*

【繁茂】lush；luxuriant：枝叶～ *with luxuriant foliage*

【繁荣】① thriving；booming；flourishing；prosperous：市场～ *flourishing market* /中国是一个～富强的国家。*China is a rich, strong and prosperous country.* ② promote；make prosper

【繁荣昌盛】thriving prosperous

【繁荣富强】powerful, rich and prosperous

【繁体字】original complex form of the simplified Chinese characters；full-form characters

【繁文缛节】over elaborate formalities；red tape

【繁星】array of stars

【繁衍】［书］multiply；procreate；increase gradually in number

【繁育】breed；raise：～优良品种 *breed good strains*

【繁杂】many and diverse；various；miscellaneous：他妻子去世后，他不得不做～的家务活。*He had to do miscellaneous household chores after his wife died.*

【繁殖】breed；procreate；propagate；reproduce：～力 *reproductive capacity* /～率 *rate of reproduction reproductive capacity*

【繁重】heavy；strenuous；onerous；toilsome：他在工厂里干一些～的体力劳动。*He does some strenuous manual labour in the factory.*

fǎn

反 ① inside out；inverse；in an opposite direction：你把衣服穿～了。*You have put your clothes on inside out.* ② turn；turn over；reverse ③ return；counter：违～政策 *run counter to the policy* /违～交通规则 *violate traffic regulations* /～诘 *counter with a question*；*ask in retort* /适得其～ *be just to opposite to what one wished*；*run counter to one's desire* ④ be against；oppose：～法西斯 *fight against fascism* /～腐败 *combat corruption* ⑤ revolt；rebel：起～ *revolt*；*rebel* /造～ *rebel*；*rise in rebellion* /谋～ *conspire against the state*；*plot a rebellion* ⑥ analogize；reason by analogy：举一～三 *draw inferences about other cases from one instance* ⑦ instead；on the contrary

【反败为胜】turn the tables（on sb）；turn defeat into victory；turn the tide

【反比】inverse relation；inverse ratio：～例 *inverse proportion*

【反驳】refute；retort；rebut

【反差】contrast

【反常】unusual；abnormal；strange；perverse：最近，他经常做一些～的行为。*Recently he often does some abnormal behaviour.*

【反潮流】go against the tide；swim against the stream

【反衬】set off by contrast；serve as a foil to

【反冲】【物】recoil；kick：～效应 *recoil nucleus*

【反串】（of Chinese opera actors or actresses）not pay one's customary role；play a reversed role；act a role other than one's own

【反唇相讥】answer back sarcastically；reply with a sarcastic rebuttal

【反动】① reactionary：～统治 *reactionary rule* /～势力 *forces of reaction*；*reactionary forces* ② reaction

【反对】oppose；be against；fight；combat：～种族歧视 *oppose racial discrimination*

【反而】on the contrary；instead

【反复】① again and again；over and over again；repeatedly：经过～的思考，她决定留下来。*She decided to stay after turning it over in her mind again and again.* ② go back on one's word；back out；chop and change ③ relapse；reversal；setback

【反复无常】behave capriciously；blow hot and cold；be changeable：她是个～的人。*She is a capricious person.*

【反感】dislike；turn unkindly to；be disgusted with；be averse to

【反革命】① counterrevolutionary：～组织 *counterrevolutionary organization* /～罪行 *counterrevolutionary crime* ② counterrevolutionaries：政府镇压

了这次～行动。*The government cracked down on the counterrevolutionaries.*

【反攻】counteroffensive; counterattack

【反光】① reflect light: ～灯 *reflector lamp* ② reflection of light

【反函数】【数】inverse function

【反话】irony; ironic remark: 她老爱说～。*She always speaks ironic remarks.*

【反悔】go back on one's promise; go back on one's word

【反击】beat back; counterattack; hit back

【反抗】revolt; resist; rebel: 消极～ *passive resistance* /有压迫就有～。*Where there is oppression, there is resistance.*

【反科学】anti-science

【反客为主】turn from guest into host — gain the initiative; turn the tables

【反恐怖主义】anti-terrorism

【反馈】feedback

【反例】counterexample

【反面】① reverse side; wrong side; back ② contrary; negative side: ～教材 *negative example which may serve as a lesson* ③ reverse side of a state of affairs, a problem, etc.

【反目】have a falling-out; fall out (esp. between husband and wife)

【反扒】crack down on pickpockets: 她爸爸是一个～能手。*Her father is a good hand at catching pickpockets.*

【反派】villain (in drama, etc.); negative character: 那个著名的演员在剧中演了一个～人物。*The famous actor acted the part of the villain in the play.*

【反叛】rebel; revolt

【反扑】pounce on sb again after being beaten off

【反其道而行之】act in a diametrically opposite way; do exactly the opposite

【反倾销】anti-dumping

【反三角函数】【数】inverse trigonometric function

【反射】①【物】*reflection*: 声音～ *reflection of sound* ②【生理】*reflex*: 条件～ *conditioned reflex*

【反身代词】【语】reflexive pronoun

【反思】reflect; introspect; self-examination

【反诉】【律】counterchange; counterclaim

【反锁】be locked in or out: 他出不来了,门被～了。*He can't come out for the door was locked from outside.*

【反胃】【医】feel nauseated; feel queasy; regurgitation; gastric disorder causing nausea

【反问】① ask a question in reply; ask in retort ②【语】*rhetorical question*

【反响】echo; repercussion; reverberation: 他的演讲引起了不同的～。*His speech evoked conflicting responses.*

【反向】reverse; opposite direction: ～电流 *reverse current*

【反省】self-examination; self-questioning; engage in introspection

【反义词】【语】antonym

【反应】react; respond: 化学～ *chemical reaction*

【反映】① reflect; mirror; show: 这篇文章～了广大市民的看法和意见。*This article reflects the wishes of the city residents.* ② report; make known: 向领导～情况 *report to the leader*

【反正】(fǎnzhèng) restore things to order; put things on the right track: 拨乱～ *bring order out of chaos*

【反正】(fǎnzheng) ① used to indicate the same result despite different circumstances: 不管怎么样,～我不想走。*In any case I don't want to go.* ② used to convey certainty or resolution

【反证】disproof; counterevidence

【反之】otherwise; whereas; conversely; on the other had

【反作用】reaction; counteraction: ～力 *reacting force*

返 return; come back; go back: ～聘 *be reposted or employed after one's retirement* / ～程 *return journey; on one's return back* / ～工 *redo one's job; do poorly done work over again* /流连忘～ *enjoy oneself so much as to forget go home; cannot tear oneself away; linger on with on thought of leaving*

【返潮】get damp; get moist: 在雨季,屋里容易～。*Things in houses get damp easily in the rainy season.*

【返归】return; go back

【返航】return to base or port; be on the homeward journey

【返还】return; restore; send back; give back: 公司决定把钱～给员工。*The company decided to give back the money to their employees.*

【返回】return; come back; go back: ～回卫星 *recoverable satellite* / ～故土 *return to one's homeland*

【返老还童】regain one's youthful vigour; feel rejuvenated in one's old age

【返璞归真】return to one's original nature; recover one's original purity and simplicity; go back to nature

【返青】【农】(of transplanted seedlings or winter crops) turn green

【返销】(of state-purchased grain) be sold back to a grain-producing area (in cases of natural disaster, etc.)

【返校】(of students) return to school: 周末过去了,我们不得不～了。*Weekend past, we had to return to school.*

【返修】refix; repair again

【返祖现象】【生】reversion; atavism

fàn

犯 ① violate; go against; offend: 违～纪律 *violation of discipline* /违～校规 *violate school*

regulations ② attack; assail; invade; work against: 互不侵～条约 *nonaggression treaty* ③ criminal; offender; culprit: 刑事～ *criminal offender* ④ have a recurrence of (an old illness); revert to (a bad habit): 他的老毛病又～了。*He reverted to his bad habit.* ⑤ commit (a crime, mistake, etc.): ～重罪 *commit a serious crime*

【犯案】(of a criminal) be found out and brought to justice

【犯病】fall ill again; have a relapse; have an attack of one's old illness

【犯愁】be anxious; worry; fell uneasy

【犯法】break the law; violate the law: 这是～的事情,你最好不要去做。*You'd better not to do it for it is an offence against the law.*

【犯规】① break the rules; break the regulations ②【体】*foul*: 发球～ *foul service* /技术～ *technical foul*

【犯浑】act unreasonably; be perversely tactless in one's behaviour: 他又～了,别理他。*Don't talk with him; he ran wild again.*

【犯急】get restless; become impatient

【犯忌】violate a taboo

【犯贱】behave badly; conduct oneself below one's dignity

【犯科】violate laws and decrees: 作奸～ *commit crimes in violation of the law; commit offences against the law*

【犯困】feel sleepy; feel drowsy: 我～了,先回去了。*I feel sleepy and go first.*

【犯难】feel uneasy; feel embarrassed

【犯上】go against the king or emperor; defy one's superiors, elders, etc.: ～作乱 *defy one's superiors and start a rebellion*

【犯罪】commit a crime; commit an offense: ～集团 *criminal gang* / ～分子 *criminal; offender* / ～率 *crime rate* / ～现场 *scene of a crime*

饭 ① cooked rice or other cereals: 炒～ *fried rice* ② meal: 早～ *breakfast* /午～ *lunch* /晚～ *supper* /剩～ *leftover dishes*

【饭菜】① meal; repast; food ② dishes to go with rice, steamed buns, etc.

【饭店】① hotel: 他住在一家四星级的～里。*He lived in a four-star hotel.* ②[方] *eatery; restaurant*

【饭馆】eatery; restaurant

【饭锅】① pot for cooking rice; rice cooker ② job; means of livelihood: 昨天他被砸～了。*He lost his job yesterday.*

【饭盒】mess tin; dinner pail; lunch-box

【饭局】banquet; feast; dinner party: 自从他当了公司的经理后,天天都有～。*He attends dinner parties every day since he became the manager of the company.*

【饭来张口,衣来伸手】have only to open one's mouth to be fed and hold out one's arms to be dressed — lead an easy life, with everything provided; live the life of a parasite; be waited on hand and foot

【饭量】appetite: 她很瘦弱,但是～却很大。*She is very slim and weak, but she has an enormous appetite.*

【饭票】meal ticket; mess card

【饭厅】dining hall; dining room; mess hall

【饭桶】① rice bucket ② big eater; piggish eater ③ good-for-nothing; fathead

【饭碗】① rice bowl ② job; means of livelihood

【饭庄】(big) restaurant

【饭桌】dining table

泛 ①[书] float ② emerge; turn: 苹果～红了。*The apples are turning red.* ③ flood; inundate: 洪水～滥 *be seriously inundated with flood* ④ general; extensive: ～～而谈 *talk in generalities; speak in vague terms* / ～～之交 *casual or nodding acquaintance*

【泛称】general term

【泛读】extensive reading

【泛泛】① common; ordinary: ～之辈 *mediocre person* ② general; not deep-going

【泛滥】① be in flood; overflow; overspill; inundate ② spread unchecked

【泛滥成灾】disaster caused by flooding water; run wild

【泛论】have a general discussion

【泛水】【建】flashing

【泛指】be used in a general sense; make a general reference

范 ①[书] *matrix; mould; pattern* ② model; example: 示～ *set an example; demonstrate* ③ limits; range ④ [书] *restriction*: 防～ *be on guard; remain vigilant* ⑤(Fàn) a surname

【范本】model for calligraphy or painting

【范畴】① category: 基本～ *basic category; primary category* ② range; domain; realm

【范例】example; model

【范围】limits; range; scope: 他参加了全省～内的考试。*He attended the examination with in the whole province.*

【范文】model essay

贩 ①(of traders) buy to resell: ～商品 *buy goods for resale* ② vendor; trader; pedlar: 摊～ *street pedlar*

【贩毒】drug trafficking; traffic in narcotics: 我们不能相信他是一个～者。*We can't believe that he is a drug trafficker.*

【贩卖】sell; trade; peddle: ～人口 *traffic in human beings*

【贩运】traffic; transport goods for sale

【贩子】trader; monger: 战争～*warmonger*

梵 ① of ancient India ② Buddhist

【梵蒂冈】Vatican

【梵宫】Buddhist temple

【梵文】Sanskrit

fāng

方[1] ① square: ~凳 *square stool* ②【数】power; involution: 立~ *cube* / 平~ *square* / Y 的七次方 *seven power of Y* ③［量］*used for square things*: 两~玉玺 *two imperial jade seal* / 三~石头 *three cube meter of* ④ direction: 四面八~ *in all directions* ⑤ prescription: 开处~ *make out a prescription* ⑥ *method; way; mean*: 想~设法 *try every means; do everything possible* / 指导~ *give proper guidance* ⑦ honest; upright

方[2] ① then; just then; just at the time: ~今盛世 *in this age of prosperity* ② only; just: 年~18 *be just eighteen years old*

【方案】work scheme or plan; work programme: 养老金~ *a pension scheme* / 有创意的~ *an imaginative scheme* / 提出一项改建厂区的~ *launch a programme to redevelop production area of the factory*

【方便】① convenient; handy ② proper; suitable; appropriate: 要是不~的话, 我们就不去你们家了。*If it is not appropriate, we can't visit you.* ③ have money to spare ④［口］go to the lavatory

【方步】measure steps: 迈~ *walk with a measured tread*

【方才】just now; just; not until: ~他来过这儿。*Just now he came here.*

【方程】equation: 二次~ *quadratic equation* / 高次~ *equation of higher degree* / 线性~ *linear equation* / 解~ *solve an equation* / ~组 *group of equations*

【方寸】① square cun (=1/9 square decimetre) ②［书］heart: ~已乱 *with one's mind in a turmoil; greatly upset*

【方队】square array; phalanx

【方法】way; method; means; approach

【方格】check; pattern of squares

【方根】【数】root: 二次~ *square root*

【方框】square case; square frame

【方括号】square brackets

【方面】side; field; aspect; respect: 在这一~, 我做的比你好。*In this respect, I do it better than you have done.*

【方式】way; mode; fashion; pattern: 生活~ *way of life; mode of life*

【方糖】sugar cube; lump sugar

【方位】① direction and position; bearing: 确定~ *find one's bearings* ② point of the compass

【方向】orientation; geographical direction

【方兴未艾】be in the ascendant; be just unfolding

【方言】【语】dialect; local dialect: ~学 *dialectology*

【方圆】① neighbourhood; surrounding area ② squares and circles: 不以规矩, 不成~。*You cannot draw squares and circles without the compass and square — nothing can be accomplished without norms or standards.* ③ circumference

【方丈】(fāngzhàng) square zhang

【方丈】(fāngzhang) ① abbot's room in a Buddhist temple ② abbot

【方针】policy; guiding; principle: ~政策 *general and specific policies* / 基本~ *fundamental policy*

【方正】① foursquare and upright ② upright; righteous; straightforward: 他为人~。*He is an upright person.*

【方桌】square table.

坊 ① lane (use, as part of a street or lane name); alley: 街~ *neighbourhood* ② memorial archway: 牌~ *memorial archway (or gateway)*

芳 ① fragrant; sweet-smelling: ~馥的花朵 *a sweet smelling flower* ②［书］your: 请问~名? *Could you tell me your name?* ③ flowers and plants: ~草连天。*The grassland seems to merge with the sky.* ④ virtuous; good (name or reputation): 流~百世 *leave a good name through the age* ⑤ (Fāng) a surname

【芳草】fragrant grass: ~如茵 *carpet of green grass*

【芳龄】age of a girl; age of a young woman

【芳名】① name of a girl or young woman ② good name or reputation

【芳容】good looks

【芳香】(of flowers or plants) fragrant; aromatic

【芳心】heart of a young lady: 他很爱她, 但无奈她~已许。*He loves her very much; but she has loved other man in her heart.*

fáng

防 ① prevent; guard against: 在公共汽车上一定要谨~扒手。*Beware of pickpockets in a bus.* ② defend; protect: 边~ *frontier defence* ③ dyke; embankment: 堤~工程 *dyke building; embankment project* ④ (Fáng) a surname

【防暴】anti-riot; riot protection: ~车 *anti-riot vehicle* / ~警察接到任务后就出发了。*The riot policemen set out as soon as they received the task.*

【防不胜防】hard to guard against; impossible to defend effectively

【防潮】dampproof; moistureproof: ~砖 *moistureproof brick*

【防尘】dustproof

【防弹】bulletproof; shellproof: ~玻璃 *bulletproof glass* / ~背心 *bulletproof vest*

【防盗】guard against theft; take precautions against burglars: ~门 *anti-theft door* / ~锁 *burglarproof lock*

【防冻】frostbite prevention; freeze-proof; antifreeze

【防毒】protect against toxins; protect against poison gas: ~面具 *gas mask*

【防范】be on guard; keep a lookout: ~非典 *guard against SARS* / ~火灾 *take precautions against fire* / ~小偷 *look out for pickpockets*

【防风】protect against the wind; provide shelter from the wind: ~灯 *hurricane lamp* / ~带 *wind-*

break belt / ~林 *windbreak forest* / ~风衣 *windcheater* / ~罩 *windshield*

【防辐射】radiation protection; protect against radiation

【防腐剂】antiseptic; preservative

【防寒】protect against cold weather: ~服 *winter outerwear*

【防旱】take precautions against drought; control drought

【防洪】control flood; prevent flood:他们已经采取了~措施。*They have taken flood control measures.*

【防护】protect; shelter: ~林 *shelter-forest*

【防患未然】provide against possible trouble; take preventive measures

【防火】① prevent fires ② fireproof: ~墙 *fire wall*

【防空】air defence; antiaircraft defence: ~洞 *air-raid shelter* / ~部队 *air defence forces* / ~导弹 *air defence missile* / ~警报 *air-raid warning* / ~演习 *air-defence exercise; air-raid drill*

【防涝】prevent waterlogging

【防沙堤】sand-control dyke

【防身】defend oneself against violence; act in self-defence

【防守】defend; guard:他儿子被派去~要塞了。*His son was sent to garrison a fort.*

【防暑】heatstroke prevention:夏天采取一些~措施是必需的。*It's necessary to take measures to prevent heatstroke.*

【防水】waterproof: ~层 *waterproof Layer*

【防微杜渐】nip in the bud; check at the outset

【防线】line of defence

【防锈】rust-resistant; rustproof: ~层 *antirust coating* / ~剂 *rust inhibitor*

【防汛】flood control; flood prevention: ~指挥中心 *flood-control headquarters*

【防疫】epidemic control; epidemic prevention: ~站 *epidemic prevention station*

【防御】defend; guard:他们部队的~力量非常强大。*The defence capabilities of their army are very strong.*

【防灾】take precautions against natural calamities

【防震】shockproof; quakeproof; antiseismic

【防止】avoid; guard against; prevent:为了~传播非典型肺炎,我们采取了很多措施。*All of us took many measures to keep off the infection of SARS.*

【防治】prevention and cure; prophylaxis and treatment: ~病虫害 *prevention and control of plant diseases and elimination of pests*

妨 harm; hamper; hinder; impair; impede: ~害公共安全 *threaten public security* / ~碍经济发展 *hamper the growth of the economy*

【妨碍】hamper; hinder; impede; obstruct:由于发生了交通事故,~了交通。*An accident took place and caused block traffic.*

【妨害】harm; damage; impair

房 ① house; building:他家住楼~。*He lives in storeyed building.* ② chamber; bedroom; room: 产~ *delivery room; lying-in room* / 新~ *bridal chamber* ③ shop; store: 药~ *drug store* ④ house like structure: 蜂~ *beehive* /子~ *ovary* ⑤ branch of an extended family: 长~ *eldest branch* ⑥ [量] used for branches of an extended family ⑦ (Fáng) a surname

【房产】real estate; house property: ~主 *owner of a house* / ~税 *house property tax*

【房地产】real estate; real property

【房顶】roof; housetop

【房东】landlord or landlady; owner and lessor of a house

【房间】room:他和女朋友在学校附近租了一套~住。*He and his girlfriend rent a room.*

【房客】lodger; tenant (of a flat, house, room, etc.)

【房契】title deed (for a house)

【房屋】building; house

【房主】house-owner

【房子】building; house

【房租】rent (for a house, flat, etc.); rental:这套房子的~太贵了。*The monthly rent for this flat is very expensive.*

fǎng

仿 ① copy; imitate; model on; be like; resemble: ~制的古玩 *replica of an antique; imitation curio* / ~古家具 *pseudo-classic furniture* / ~造珍珠 *imitation pearl; olivet* ② characters written after a calligraphy model

【仿佛】① as if; seemingly ② be similar

【仿古】modelled after an antique; in the style of the ancients: ~建筑 *pseudo-classic architecture*

【仿建】copy the style of another building

【仿冒】forge; counterfeit: ~签名 *forge a signature*

【仿生学】bionics

【仿宋】【印】imitation Song-Dynasty-style typeface

【仿效】follow the example of; model on; imitate: ~榜样 *imitate; model on follow the example of* / 他是一个真正的英雄,值得我们~。*He is a real hero, who is worth being followed.*

【仿造】copy; model on

【仿照】follow; imitate

【仿真】【电】emulate; simulate: ~技术 *simulation technology*

【仿制】copy; imitate; model on: ~品 *imitation; copy*

访 ① call on; visit; pay a visit:昨天晚上李老师又去家~了。*Yesterday evening, Mr. Li visited the parents of his schoolchildren again.* ② seek by inquiry or search

【访查】inquire; investigate; go about making inquires

【访谈】interview and discuss:你看到关于他的~节目吗? *Have you watched the programme of an interview discussion about him.*

【访问】call on; interview; visit:国事~ *state visit*

纺 ① spin ② thin silk cloth

【纺车】spinning wheel

【纺纱】spinning:~厂 *cotton spinning mill*

【纺织】spinning and weaving; textile:工厂 *textile mill* /她妈妈是一名~工人。*Her mother is one of textile workers.*

fàng

放 ① release; let go; set free: ~他走吧,我不想再见到他。*Let him go; I don't want to see him again.* ② set off; let off; give out:上周末,我们全家去公园~风筝了。*Our family went to the park to fly a kite last week.* ③ stop; knock off; have a holiday:现在工人们~工了。*The workers knock off now.* ④ show; play; turn on: ~电影 *play a film* ⑤ let oneself go; give way to; act with abandon ⑥ kindle; light; fire: ~火 *set fire* ⑦ lend money at interest; loan: ~贷 *grant or extend credits* ⑧ expand; make larger; let out:我想知道能否再把照片~大一些。*I wonder if you can have those photographs larger.* ⑨ put; lay; place ⑩ add ⑪ moderate (one's attitude, behaviour, etc.) ⑫ lay aside; store away; keep long ⑬ (of flowers) blossom; open

【放暗箭】shoot an arrow from behind — stab sb in the back; injure people by treacherous means

【放长线,钓大鱼】throw a long line to catch a big fish — adopt a long-term plan to secure sth big

【放出】emit; give out; let out

【放大】enlarge; blow up; magnify: ~镜 *magnifying glass*

【放荡】① debauched; dissolute; dissipated:她曾经是一个~的女人。*She had been a loose woman.* ② unconventional: ~不羁 *unconventional and unrestrained*

【放电】discharge

【放毒】① harm with poison; put poison in food, water, etc. ② spread poisonous ideas; poison minds with evil ideas; make vicious remarks

【放飞】let go; release; allow to take off

【放风】① let in fresh air; ventilate ② let prisoners out for exercise ③ leak certain information; circulate news; spread rumours ④ [方] be on the lookout; act as a lookout

【放歌】sing heartily and loudly

【放过】let off; let slip by:他爸爸最终~了他。*His father let him off at last.*

【放火】① set fire to; commit arson:杀人~ *commit murder and arson* ② create disturbances

【放假】have a holiday; have a vacation; have a day off:再有一星期他们就要~了。*They will have a vacation after one week.*

【放开】have a free hand in doing sth; relax control: ~价格 *relax control over prices*

【放宽】relax restrictions; liberalize:银行~利率已经两周了。*Banks have liberalized interest rates for two weeks.*

【放浪形骸】refuse to be bound by convention; fly in the face of convention; be unconventional and unrestrained; be defiant of convention

【放亮】begin to shine; give out light:天刚刚~,她就起床学习了。*She got up for studying when the day was just breaking.*

【放牧】put out to pasture; herd; graze

【放炮】① fire a gun ② set off firecrackers ③ blasting; shot fire:这儿正在~,请离开这儿。*Blasting here; please go away.* ④ blow out ⑤ shoot off one's mouth

【放屁】① break wind; fart ② talk nonsense

【放弃】abandon; give up; forfeit:为了儿子,她~了这次出国机会。*She gave up the opportunity of going abroad for her son.*

【放青】graze; put out to pasture

【放晴】(of sky) clear up:天一~,我们就出去玩。*We will go out to play as soon as it clears up.*

【放权】delegate powers to lower levels; transfer power to a lower level

【放热】exothermic; exothermal; emitting: ~反应 *exothermic reaction*

【放任】let alone; indulge; not interfere:他太忙了,不得不对自己的孩子~不管。*He is too busy to leave his children to themselves.*

【放哨】be on sentry or on patrol; stand sentry:那位哨兵正在门口站岗~。*The sentry is being posted at the gate.*

【放射】radiate: ~线 *radioactive rays*

【放射性】【物】radioactivity; activity: ~元素 *radioactive element*

【放生】free captive animals

【放手】① have a free hand; go all out:相信他们,让他们自己~工作吧! *Please believe them and give them a free hand in their work.* ② let go; let go one's hold ③ release one's control; hand over to sb else

【放肆】wanton; unbridled:他的~行为令我们很生气。*His unbridled behaviour made us very angrily.*

【放松】loosen; relax; slacken:考试结束后,他~了自己。*He relaxed himself after the examination.*

【放下】lay down; put down:听到那个消息,他~工作回家了。*He put down his work and went home on hearing the news.*

【放下屠刀,立地成佛】drop one's cleaver and become a Buddha — achieve salvation as soon as one's gives up evil

【放心】trust sb; have confidence; rest assured; set one's mind at rest: ~吧,我一定会通过这次考试的。*You can rest assured that I can pass the examination.*

【放行】let sb or sth pass; get clearance: ~单 *release permit; clearance paper*

【放学】① school lets out; classes are over; dismiss

class ② school holidays

【放眼】scan widely; take a broad view: ~世界 *have the whole world in view*

【放羊】① look after sheep pasture sheep; graze sheep:他过去常常放学后去~。*He used to pasture sheep after school.* ② throw the reins off; drift along; be reinless

【放养】breed (fish, silkworm, etc.) in a suitable environment

【放映】project; show: ~室 *projection room* / ~机 *projector* / ~员 *projectionist*

【放债】lend money for interest

【放之四海而皆准】universally applicable; valid everywhere

【放置】place; put; lay up; lay a side:他把桌子~好就出去了。*He put the tables in their proper place and went out.*

【放逐】send into exile; banish

【放纵】① indulge; let sb have one's own way; connive at:作为一名老师来说你太~学生了。*You indulged your students as a teacher.* ② boorish; unrestrained; uncultured; undisciplined

fēi

飞 ① (of birds, etc.) fly; flit:蝴蝶从窗台上~走了。*The butterfly flew away from the window.* ② (of an aircraft or its occupants) fly:盖恩斯明天要从欧洲~往美国。*Gaines will fly from Europe to the United States tomorrow.* ③ hover in the air; flutter in the air:大雪纷~。*It's snowing thick and fast.* ④ rapidly; speedily; swiftly: ~车赶往学校 *speed to the school* ⑤ disappear through volatilization or vaporization:灰~烟灭 *vanish like so much smoke; become ashes and smoke* ⑥ very extremely ⑦ unexpected; unfounded; accidental: ~祸 *unexpected disaster*

【飞奔】speed off; tear along; dash

【飞镖】① ancient spear like weapon ② darts (a game):他喜欢玩~。*He likes playing darts.*

【飞车】drive a car or ride a bicycle with great speed

【飞驰】speed along

【飞虫】winged insect

【飞船】① airship; dirigible ② spaceship; spacecraft

【飞弹】① rocket; missile ② stray bullet

【飞碟】①【体】frisbee:投~ *flip a frisbee* ② flying saucer; unidentified flying object (UFO)

【飞短流长】spread embroidered stories and malicious gossip

【飞蛾扑火】a moth darting into a flame — bring destruction upon oneself; courting one's own doom; seek one's own doom

【飞黄腾达】make rapid advances in one's career; get rapid promotion; have a meteoric rise

【飞机】plane; aircraft; airplane; airplane:无人驾驶~ *robot plane; pilotless aircraft* / 喷气式~ *jet plane* / 超音速~ *supersonic aeroplane*

【飞溅】splash; spatter

【飞快】① very past; with great rapidity; at lighting speed ② extremely sharp; razor-sharp; keen-edged

【飞毛腿】① fleet-footed; swift of foot ② fleet-footed runner

【飞沫】splatter drops; flying particles of liquid: ~传染 *infection through breathing in flying particles of the saliva*

【飞禽走兽】birds and beasts; fauna

【飞人】① trapeze:空中~ *flying trapeze* ② fastest runner; best sprinter; best athlete:世界~ *best man sprinter in world*

【飞沙走石】sand flying about and stones hurtling through the air

【飞速】at full speed

【飞腾】fly swiftly upward; climb rapidly; soar

【飞吻】blow a kiss

【飞舞】dance in the air; flutter; whirl:落叶~。*The fallen leaves are dancing in the air.*

【飞翔】fly; hover; circle in the air:展翅~ *spread wings and fly*

【飞行】flying; make a flight: ~半径 *flying radius* / ~表演 *exhibition flight* / ~人员 *aircrew* / ~行速度 *flying speed* / ~员 *pilot*; *flyer*; *aviator*

【飞檐走壁】leap onto roofs and vault over walls

【飞眼】make eyes; ogle

【飞扬】① float; rise; fly upward ② in high spirits

【飞跃】leap: ~地发展 *develop by leaps and bounds*

【飞贼】① burglar who makes one's way into a house over walls and roofs ② intruding enemy airman; air marauder

【飞涨】(of prices, water level, etc) soar; shoot up; skyrocket

【飞针走线】ply one's needle nimbly; do skilful needlework

【飞转】turn swiftly; revolve swiftly

妃 ① imperial concubine:贵~ *highest ranking imperial concubine* ② wife of a prince; etc.: 王~ *princess consort*

【妃嫔】imperial concubine

【妃子】imperial concubine

非 ① error; evil; wrong; wrongdoing:文过饰~ *cover up one's errors* ② not conform to; go against; run counter to: ~法行为 *illegitimate action* / ~法手段 *illegal means* ③ censure; oppose; find fault with:口是心~ *say yes and mean no; say one thing and mean another* ④ not; not-; un-; in- ⑤ simply must; have go to ⑥ deteriorate ⑦ used to indicate wilfulness or determination

【非比寻常】out of the ordinary; unusual; extraordinary

【非常】① extraordinary; special; uncommon; unusual:昨天他们公司召开了~会议。*Their company held the extraordinary session yesterday.* ② highly; extremely; very: ~感谢你的帮助。*Thank you very much for your help.*

【非常规】non-conventional: ~战争 *non-conventional warfare*

【非但】not only

【非法】illegal; illicit; illegitimate; unlawful: ~移民 *illegal immigration* / ~收入 *illicit income* / ~同居 *illicit cohabitation* / ~侵入 *trespass* / ~政府 *outlaw government* / ~结社 *illegal association* / ~行医 *practise medicine without a license*

【非凡】extraordinary; uncommon; outstanding: 她具有~的能力。*She is of extraordinary talent.*

【非分】overstepping one's bounds; assuming; presumptuous: 他对她有~之想。*He has presumptuous desires to her.*

【非公莫入】no admittance except on business

【非官方】unofficial: ~消息 *news from unofficial sources*

【非会员】nonmember: ~国家 *nonmember country*

【非婚生子女】children born out of wedlock; illegitimate children

【非金属】nonmetal: ~材料 *nonmetallic material*

【非晶体】amorphous body

【非军事】non-military: ~用途 *non-military use* / ~目标 *non-military objective* / ~化 *demilitarize* / ~区 *demilitarized zone* / ~人员 *civilian personnel*

【非礼】rude; impolite; improper; assault: 来而不往，~也。*It is impolite not to reciprocate.*

【非卖品】article not for sale: 这些书是~。*The books are not for sale.*

【非贸易】nontrade; noncommercial: ~合同 *noncommercial contract*

【非盟国】non-allied country

【非命】① violent death; unnatural death: 她的哥哥死于~。*Her elder brother died a violent death.* ②【哲】*refute fatalism*

【非难】blame; censure; condemn; reproach

【非亲非故】neither relative nor friend; neither kith nor kin; not in any way related: 我们~，他却给了我这么多钱。*We are neither relative nor friend; he gave me so much money.*

【非人】①［书］*not the right person* ② inhuman: 他在国外曾受到过~的待遇。*He had received inhuman treatment in abroad.*

【非同儿戏】not child's play

【非同小可】not small or trivial matter

【非我莫属】I, and I alone, deserve it; it is definitely mine

【非线性】nonlinear: ~经济学 *nonlinear economics*

【非议】blame; condemn; reproach: 她所做的无可~。*What she had done is beyond reproach.*

【非正式】informal; unofficial: ~会议 *informal meeting*

【非政府】nongovernment; nongovernmental

【非洲】Africa

【非专业】non-professional

菲 (of flowers and grass) luxuriant and rich with fragrance: 芳~ *fragrance of flowers and plants*

see also fěi

【菲菲】① luxuriant and beautiful ② richly fragrant

【菲律宾】the Philippines: ~人 *Filipino*

扉 door leaf

【扉页】【印】title page

蜚

【蜚短流长】spread malicious gossip

【蜚声】［书］make a name; make one's mark; become famous; establish one's reputation: 她~歌坛十年。*She has been a woman of great renown in singing circles for ten years.*

【蜚语】gossip; rumours

霏 ① fall thick and fast: 细雨~~ *incessant drizzle* ② flutter; disperse

【霏霏】(of rain, snow, mist, cloud, etc.) think and fast

【霏微】heavy with mist or drizzle

绯 red

【绯红】bright red; scarlet

鲱 Pacific herring

féi

肥 ① fat: ~羊 *fat sheep* / ~差 *fat job; lucrative post* ② fertile; rich: ~沃的土地 *fertile land* ③ fertilizer; manure: 施~ *spread manure* ④ feather one's nest: 损公~私 *feather one's nest at public expense; seek private gain at public expense* ⑤ benefit; profit: 年底分~ *divide up the spoils at the end of year* ⑥ loose-fitting: 这鞋太~了。*The shoes too large.*

【肥肠】pig's large intestines

【肥大】① large; loose: 他喜欢穿~的衣服。*He likes wearing loose clothes.* ② fat; plump ③【医】*hypertrophy*

【肥厚】① plump; fleshy ② fertile and deep ③【医】(of human organs) hypertrophy: ~性鼻炎 *hypertrophy rhinitis*

【肥力】【农】fertility (of soil)

【肥料】fertilizer; manure: 有机~ *organic fertilizer* / 无机~ *inorganic fertilizer*

【肥美】① rich; fertile: ~的土地 *rich soil* ② plump; fat; luxuriant ③ fleshy and delicious

【肥胖】fat; corpulent: 他变得越来越~。*He became fatter and fatter.*

【肥缺】lucrative job; lucrative post

【肥肉】fat meat

【肥实】① fat; stout; rich in fat ② affluent

【肥水不流外人田】no rich water should be let out of one's own fields.

【肥硕】big and fleshy; large and firm-fleshed

【肥田】① fertilize the soil; enrich the soil ② fertile land; rich soil

【肥沃】fertile; rich: 他们家的田地很～。*The fields of his home are fertile.*
【肥皂】soap: ～盒 *soap box* / ～泡 *soap bubble* / ～粉 *soap powder* / ～剧 *soap opera* / ～水 *soapsuds*
【肥壮】stout and strong
腓 calf (of the leg)
【腓骨】【生理】fibula

fěi

匪 ① bandit; brigand; gangster; robber: 绑～ *kidnapper* / 劫～ *robber; highwayman* ② not; no: 获益～浅 *reap no little benefit*
【匪帮】bandit gang
【匪巢】bandit's lair
【匪军】bandit troops
【匪徒】bandit; gangster: 一帮～冲进了学校。*A gang of bandits rushed into the school.*
【匪夷所思】(of ideas) unimaginably queer; out of the ordinary; bizarre; fantastic
诽 calumniate; slander
【诽谤】slander; calumniate; libel: ～罪 *crime of defamation*
菲 ①［古］*radish or red turnip* ②［书］*poor; humble; unworthy*
see also fēi
【菲薄】① humble; poor: 她用～的工资支助弟弟上学。*She supported her younger brother's study with her poor salary.* ② belittle; despise
悱 ［书］laden with sorrow sad at heart
斐 ［书］rich with literary grace; (of literary talent) striking; brilliant
【斐济】Fiji: ～人 *Fijian* / ～语 *Fijian*
【斐然】① of striking literary talent ② splendid; brilliant: 成绩～ *splendid results*
【斐然成章】show striking literary merit or talent
翡 ［古］halcyon
【翡翠】① halcyon ② jadeite

fèi

吠 bark; yap; yelp
【吠叫】bark
【吠影吠声】when one dog barks at a shadow all the others join in — slavishly echo others
肺 lung
【肺癌】cancer in the lung; lung cancer; carcinoma of the lung
【肺病】pulmonary tuberculosis (TB); lung disease
【肺动脉】pulmonary artery
【肺腑】bottom of one's heart: ～之言 *words from the bottom of one's heart*
【肺活量】(of lungs) vital capacity
【肺结核】pulmonary tuberculosis (TB)
【肺静脉】pulmonary vein
【肺囊肿】pulmonary cyst
【肺脓肿】pulmonary abscess
【肺泡】pulmonary alveolus
【肺气】【中医】vital energy
【肺气肿】pulmonary emphysema
【肺循环】【生理】pulmonary circulation
【肺炎】pneumonia
【肺叶】【生理】lobe of the lung
【肺硬变】【医】cirrhosis of lung; pulmonary cirrhosis
【肺脏】lungs
废 ① give up; abandon; abolish; abrogate; reject: ～矿 *abandoned mine* / 半途而～ *give up halfway* ② useless; disused; waste: ～钢 *scrap steel* / ～金属 *metal scrap* / ～热 *waste heat* ③ disabled; maimed ④［书］*depose; dethrone*: 那个皇帝把太子给～了。*The emperor deposed the crown prince.*
【废除】abolish; abrogate; repeal: ～令 *abatement order* / ～农权制 *abolish serfdom*: 政府～了过时的法律。*The government repealed the obsolete laws.*
【废黜】① banish; dismiss from office ② dethrone; depose
【废帝】dethroned emperor; depose an emperor
【废话】nonsense; rubbish; superfluous words: 少～,赶紧学习。*Not more rubbish; study in a hurry.*
【废料】waste; waste material; scrap
【废票】① invalidated ticket: 她收集了很多～。*She collects many invalidated tickets.* ② spoilt vote
【废品】① waster product; reject: ～收购站 *salvage station* / ～回收 *waste recovery* ② scrap; junk
【废气】waste gas; waste steam; exhaust steam: ～处理 *waste gas treatment*
【废弃】abandon; discard; cast aside; fall into disuse
【废寝忘食】forget all about food and sleep; (work day and night) without eating or sleeping
【废人】① disabled person ② good-for-nothing
【废水】waste water; liquid waste: ～处理池 *purification tank for liquid waste* / ～处理场 *waste water processing station* / ～氧化池 *waste oxidation basin*
【废铁】scrap iron
【废物】(fèiwù) waste material; trash: ～处理 *waste treatment; waste disposal* / ～利用 *make use of waste material; recycling of wastes*
【废物】(fèiwu) dimwit; good-for-nothing
【废墟】debris; ruins
【废液】liquid waste; used or waste water
【废渣】waste residue; slag; dross
【废止】annul; abolish; put to an end
【废纸】waste paper: ～篓 *wastebasket; scrap basket*

【废置】put aside as useless

沸 boil：～水 *boiling water*

【沸点】【物】boiling point
【沸沸扬扬】bubbling and gurgling；in a hubbub
【沸滚】boiling
【沸泉】【地】near-boiling spring（a spring with a temperature of over 80℃）
【沸腾】①【物】boil；bubble；ebullition ② boil over；seethe with excitement：热血～ *one's blood boils*
【沸涌】boil over；surge：听到那个消息，她的心情～。*She felt an upsurge of emotion on hearing the news.*

费 ① fee；charge；expenses；fare：生活～ *living expenses* /他已经交纳了半年的水电～。*He has paid charges for water and electricity of half a year.* ② cost；expend；spend：母亲在佩里的教育上花～了不少心血。*Mother took great pains with Perry's education.* ③ be wasteful；expend too quickly：枉～精力 *waste one's spirit* ④（Fèi）a surname

【费唇舌】take a lot of talking or explaining
【费工】take a lot of work；require a lot of labour
【费工夫】take time and energy；be time-consuming
【费解】puzzling；unintelligible；hard to understand：她所做的令人～。*What she had done was hard to understand.*
【费尽心机】tax one's ingenuity；lack one's brains（in scheming）
【费劲】need great effort；go to great pains；be strenuous
【费力】exert great effort
【费力不讨好】work hard but to no avail；do a hard but thankless job
【费钱】cost a lot；be costly
【费神】① would you mind；may I trouble you ② tax one's energy；be exhausting
【费时】take time；be time-consuming：写作即～又费力。*Writing takes time and energy.*
【费事】give a lot of trouble；take a lot of trouble；be troublesome：不要～了，我们出去吃饭吧。*Don't bother to cook；we'll get out to eat.*
【费心】① give great care；take much trouble ②［口］may I trouble you；would you mind
【费用】cost；expenses：生活～ *cost of living*
【费嘴皮子】waste one's breath；talk nonsense：你不必～了，我已经决定放弃了。*Don't waste your breath any more；I have decided to give up.*

痱

【痱子】med. prickly heat
【痱子粉】prickly-heat powder

fēn

分 ① divide；part；separate：这篇文章可以～四段。*This article can be divided to four paragraph.* ② assign；allot；differentiate：～派工作 *assign jobs* ③ distinguish；distribute；tell：你是个好人，不能是非不～。*You are a kind man and can't make no distinction between right and wrong.* ④ branch（of organization）：公安～局 *sub-bureau of public security* /～理处 *subbranch of a bank*；*suboffice* /国内～行 *home*（*or domestic*）*branch* /国外～行 *oversea branch* ⑤ fraction：通～ *reduce fractions to a common denominator* ⑥ used in spoken forms of fractions：十～之一 *one-tenth* ⑦［量］fen，a unit of length（$=\frac{1}{3}$ centimetre）⑧［量］fen，a unit of area cone tenth of a mu＝66.666 square metres ⑨［量］fen，a unit of weight（one tenth of a qian＝$\frac{1}{2}$ gram）⑩ minute ⑪ of interest rate ⑫ point；mark ⑬ fen，a fractional unit of money in China
see also fèn

【分包合同】subcontract
【分包商】sub-contract
【分贝】【物】decibel（db）
【分崩离析】come apart；disintegrate
【分辨】① distinguish；distinguish；tell：～是非 *distinguish between right and wrong* ②【物】resolution：～误差 *resolution error*
【分辩】defend oneself；offer an explanation
【分别】① part；leave each other；say goodbye to each other ② distinguish；difference ③ in different way；differently ④ respectively；individually；separately
【分兵】divide forces：～两路同敌人战斗。*The troops separated and fought against enemies by two different routes.*
【分布】be distributed（over an area）；be dispersed
【分部】branch；subsection
【分餐】meal served individually
【分册】separately published part of a book
【分权】share：他们约定挣钱以后～。*They make an agreement to share the money they have made.*
【分词】【语】participle：过去～ *past participle* /现在～ *present participle*
【分寸】proper limits for speech or action；sense of propriety or proportion：她妈妈说话很有～。*Her mother talks appropriately.*
【分担】share responsibility for：～费用 *share the expenses*
【分道】【体】lane
【分道扬镳】go different ways；each going one's own way；part company
【分等】classify；grade
【分店】branch：他爸爸是那个超市～的经理。His

father is a manager of the branch of the supermarket.
【分段】in sections; sector by sector
【分队】troop unit corresponding to the platoon or squad; detachment; element
【分而治之】divide and rule
【分发】① distribute; hand out ;issue:老师给同学们~了试卷。*The teachers handed out examination papers to the students.* ② assign to a post; appoint to a job
【分封】enfeoff: ~制 *system of destinations*
【分赴】leave for different destinations
【分割】divide; break up; carve up; cut apart; separate
【分隔】divide; isolate; partition; separate: ~变压器 *isolating transformer*
【分工】division of labour: ~合作 *share out the work and help one another; have division of labour as well as cooperation*
【分管】be in charge of; assume personal responsibility for
【分号】① semicolon ② branch
【分红】draw dividends; share profits; share out bonus:按股~ *dividends on shares*
【分洪】flood diversion: ~区 *flood-diversion area* / ~闸 *flood-diversion sluice*
【分化】① break up; become divided; split up:贫富~越来越大。*The polarization of rich and poor becomes larger and larger.* ②【生】(of cells, etc.) differentiate
【分化瓦解】split; divide and demoralize: ~犯罪分子 *disintegrate the criminals*
【分会】branch (of a society, committee, association, etc.); sub-committee; chapter
【分机】(telephone) extension:告诉我你的~号码。*Please tell me your extension number.*
【分级】classify; grade
【分家】① divide up family property and live apart ② break up; split up
【分解】① separate into parts; break up; dismantle ②【化】decompose; resolve: ~热 *decomposition heat* ③ make peace; mediate ④ disintegrate:很多事情的变化都是从内部开始~的。*Many changes disintegrate from within.* ⑤ disclose; recount dividing line; line of demarcation
【分居】① (of a married couple) live separately ② (of family members) live apart
【分句】【语】clause
【分开】① come apart; separate; be away from each other:他俩总是吵架,不得不~。*They always quarrelled with each other and had to come apart.* ② cause to separate or part
【分类】classify:接价值进行~ *classify according to values*
【分离】① separate; sever ② part; leave
【分裂】① division; fission:细胞~ *cell division* ② divide; break up; split: ~主义 *splittism*
【分流】① distributaries; split-flow ② split-flow of human resources ③ repositioning of redundant personnel
【分路】① go along separate routes; go from several directions:我们要~了,就在这里说再见吧! *Will say good-bye to you; we will be go along separate routes.* ② shunt: ~电流 *branch current*
【分泌】【生理】excrete; secrete: ~基因 *secretory gene*
【分娩】① childbirth; parturition ② give birth to the young
【分秒】minute and second; instant:在学习方面他~必争。*He seizes every minute and second on study.*
【分明】① clear; distinct; unmistakable ② clearly; evidently; plainly: ~是你做错。*It's very clear that you have done wrongly.*
【分母】【数】denominator
【分派】apportion; share; assign
【分配】① allot; allocate; distribute:按劳~ *to each according to one's work* ② assign; dispose:今年大部分毕业生服从了~。*Most of university graduates accepted the jobs assigned to them this year.* ③ distribution: ~制度 *distribution system*
【分批】① in batches; in turn; group by group:大家可以~出去玩。*We can go out group by group.* ②【经】instalment; job lot: ~生产 *job production*
【分期】by stages: ~付款 *payment by instalments*
【分歧】dispute; difference; divergence:在孩子教育问题上,他们又有很大的~。*They have a deep difference on children's education.*
【分清】tell from; distinguish; draw a clear distinction between:他太小了,不能~好坏。*He is too young to draw a distinction between good and evil.*
【分权】division of a power or authority
【分散】① diffuse; scatter; decentralize:上课时他总是~注意力。*He always distracts his attention in class.* ② hand out; distribute
【分身】spare time (from one's main work to attend to sth else);find time: ~术 *magic of replicating oneself*
【分神】give some attention to; divert sb attention
【分式】【数】fraction: ~方程 *fractional equation*
【分手】part; part company; say god-bye
【分数】① core; mark; grade; point:在这次测试中她考了高~。*she got high marks in this test.* ②【数】fraction; functional number:真~ *proper fraction* /假~ *improper fraction*
【分水岭】①【地】watershed; divide ② dividing line; line of demarcation
【分送】send; distribute
【分摊】contribute; apportion; share: ~费用 *share the expenses*
【分头】① parted hair:他留了个~。*He has a part in his hair.* ② separately; severally
【分文】single cent; single penny: ~不取 *not take a single cent*

【分析】analyse：~员 *analyst*
【分享】share；partake of
【分销】distribution：~渠道 *distributional channel* / ~店 *retail shop*
【分晓】① outcome；result；solution ② see or understand clearly
【分校】branch school；branch campus
【分心】① divert sb's attention；distract sb's attention；我不能为你~。*I can't divert my attention on you.* ② may I trouble you.
【分秧】【农】separate seedlings for planting
【分页】paging
【分忧】share sb's cares and burdens；share sb's worries；help sb to get over difficult problems
【分赃】share the booty；share the loot；divide the spoil：他们~时被警察抓住了。*They were caught while they divided the spoils.*
【分针】minute hand (of a clock or watch)
【分支】branch；affiliate；subdivision
【分值】value of a workpoint，etc. (as in the production team)
【分钟】minute
【分子】①【数】numerator(in a fraction) ② molecule：~论 *molecular theory*
【分组】divide into groups：今天我们~讨论这个问题。*Today we will discuss the problem in groups.*

芬 fragrance；sweet smell

【芬芳】fragrant；sweet-smelling
【芬兰】Finland：~人 *Finn*；*Finlander* / ~语 *Finnish*
【芬香】fragrance；sweet smell

吩

【吩咐】tell；order；instruct：请您~。*Please tell me what we should do.*

纷 ① many and various；profuse；diverse；numerous：落英缤~*fallen petals lie in tumultuous abundance*；*petals fall in riotous profusion* ② confused；chaotic；disorderly：众说~纭 *opinions vary*；*opinions are widely divided*；*opinions differ widely*

【纷繁】numerous：每天她不得不应付~的工作。*Everyday she has to deal with the complexities of work.*
【纷飞】fly about disorderly；swirl in the air
【纷纷】① numerous and confused；profuse ② one after another；all at once；in succession：大家~离开了学校。*People left the school one after another.*
【纷乱】chaotic；helter-skelter；numerous and disorderly
【纷忙】in a rush and a muddle；extremely busy
【纷扰】tumult；confusion；turmoil
【纷杂】numerous and disorderly；diverse and confused
【纷争】dispute；quarrel；wrangle
【纷至沓来】come in a continuous stream；come thick and fast；come as thick ad hail

氛 atmosphere

【氛围】atmosphere

酚 phenol

【酚醛】phenolic aldehyde
【酚酞】phenol phthalein

fén

坟 grave；tomb

【坟场】graveyard；tomb
【坟墓】grave；tomb
【坟头】grave mound
【坟茔】① grave；tomb ② graveyard；cemetery
【坟冢】grave；tomb

焚 burn

【焚化】cremate；incinerate
【焚毁】destroy by fire；burn down
【焚烧】burn；consume with flames；set on fire
【焚书坑儒】burning books and burying Confucian scholars alive(by the first emperor of the Qin Dynasty)

fěn

粉 ① powder：漂白~ *bleaching powder* / 骨~ *bone meal*；*bone dust* / 每顿饭后吃一服药~ *take a powder after each meal* / 面~ *flour* ② cosmetics in powder form：爽身~ *talcum powder* / 牙~ *tooth powder* / 咖喱~ *curry powder* ③ turn to powder；become powder：石头被砸得~碎。*The stones are smashed to smithereens.* ④ noodles or vermicelli made from flour，bean，sweet potato starch，etc.：通心~ *macaroni* ⑤ pink

【粉笔】chalk
【粉刺】【医】chalk
【粉红】pink；rosy：她身着~的服装。*She dressed in pink.*
【粉墨登场】make oneself up and go on stage-embark
【粉皮】sheet jelly made from bean or sweet potato starch
【粉身碎骨】have one's body smashed to pieces and one's bones be crushed to pulp；die the most cruel death
【粉刷】① whitewash：~房间 *whitewash rooms* ②［方］plaster；layer of protective plaster
【粉丝】vermicelli made from bean starch，etc.
【粉碎】① broken into pieces ② crush；smash；shatter：他们又一次~了敌人的进攻。*They crushed another enemies.*
【粉条】starch noodles

【粉线】tailor's chalk line
【粉蒸肉】pork steamed with ground rice flour

fèn

分[1] ① component; element: 灰~ *ash content* / 水~ *moisture content* ② what is within one's right or obligation: 他做的太过~了。*What he had done was going too far.* ③ affection; friendly feeling: 看在老同学的~上 *for old classmate's sake*

分[2] [书] expect; know; think

see also fēn

【分量】weight: 在世界上中国是一个非常有~的国家之一。*China is one of the countries that carries weight in the world.*
【分内】one's job; one's duty
【分外】① beyond one's duty; beyond one's due; beyond one's job: 对她,你不能有~之想。*You can't have inordinate wish to her.* ② especially; particularly
【分子】element; member: 先进~ *advanced element* /骨干~ *core member*; *key member* /积极~ *active member*; *activist*

份 ① share; part; port; portion ② [量] a set; a copy: 给我一~报纸。*Please give me a copy of newspaper.* ③ used after 年,月,省,县 to form a unit
【份额】portion; share
【份礼】gift in the form of cash
【份儿菜】set-portion dish
【份儿饭】set meal
【份子】① one's share of expenses for a joint undertaking, as in buying a gift for a mutual friend: 她结婚的时候,我们凑~了。*We gave our share of expanses for her marriage.* ② gift of money; gift in the form of cash

奋 ① act vigorously; brace up; exert oneself: ~起直追 *exert all one's strength to catch up* ② raise; lift; take up: ~笔疾书 *take up a pen and write swiftly*
【奋不顾身】dash ahead regardless of personal safety
【奋斗】fight; struggle; strive; work hard: 他为考上大学而努力~。*He strives for entering universities to study hard.*
【奋发】brace oneself up; exert oneself; rouse oneself: ~图强 *go all out to achieve success*
【奋进】advance bravely; forge ahead courageously
【奋力】do all one can; spare no effort; exert oneself to the utmost
【奋起】① brace up; exert oneself; rise with force and spirit ② lift with force; raise with force
【奋勇】be dauntless; summon up all one's courage and energy
【奋战】fight bravely; work strenuously: 我们要为自己~到底。*We will struggle to the bitter end for freedom.*
【奋争】struggle with might and main

粪 ① dung; droppings; faeces; excrement: 大~ *human excrement*; *night soil* ② [书] apply manure
【粪便】night soil; excrement and urine
【粪车】dung-cart; night-soil cart
【粪池】manure pit; cesspool
【粪肥】manure; dung
【粪筐】manure basket; manure collector's bin
【粪土】dung and dirt; muck

愤 anger; fury; indignation resentment
【愤愤不平】feel aggrieved; be indignant
【愤恨】furiously detest; indignantly resent: 他的所作所为激起了我们的~。*What he had done aroused our resentment.*
【愤慨】indignation
【愤懑】[书] disgruntled; resentful
【愤怒】anger; fury; indignation; wrath
【愤世嫉俗】detest the world and its ways; be cynical; loathe the ways of the world

fēng

丰 ① abundant; plentiful; rich: 收入~厚 *handsome income* ② great ③ graceful; fine; good: 朱丽叶长得很~满。*Juliet has a quite plump figure.* ④ (Fēng) a surname
【丰碑】monument; monumental work
【丰登】bumper harvest: 五谷~ *abundant harvest of all crops*; *bumper grain harvest*
【丰富】① abundant; plentiful; rich: 资源~ *rich in natural resources* / ~多彩 *rich and varied* ② enrich
【丰功伟绩】great achievements; signal contributions; magnificent exploits and great feats
【丰厚】rich and thick; rich and generous: 奖金~ *handsome bonus* /植被~ *rich vegetation*
【丰满】① full; plentiful: ~的稻子 *full rice* ② full and round; well-grown
【丰年】bumper harvest year; good year; year of abundance: 瑞雪兆~。*A timely snow foretells a bumper harvest.*
【丰饶】rich and fertile
【丰盛】abundant; lavish; rich; sumptuous
【丰收】bumper harvest; big harvest
【丰硕】abundant; rich; plentiful and enormous: 近几年她爸爸在科学领域取得了~的成果。*In recent years, her father has scored great successes in science fields.*
【丰衣足食】have ample food and clothing; be well-fed and well-clad
【丰盈】① (of one's figure) full and round; well-developed: 体态~ *have a full figure* ② rich; plentiful: 食物~ *have plenty to eat*
【丰腴】① plump; well-rounded ② fertile; abun-

dant; plentiful
【丰裕】in plenty; well provided for
【丰足】abundant; plentiful:她过着衣食～的生活。*She has plenty of food and clothing.*

风 ① wind; breeze:春～ *spring breeze* /二级～ *light breeze* ② as swift as wind; speedily:巴顿走路像一阵～。*Barton walks as swift as wind.* ③ custom; atmosphere; practiced: 班～ *class spirit* /党～ *conduct of Party member; work style of a political party* /世～日下。*Public morals are deteriorating day by day.* ④ style; attitude:他的文～相当好。*His style of writing is quite good.* ⑤ information; news: 闻～而动 *act without delay on hearing the news; answer a call with immediate action* ⑥ rumour; hearsay:每个人都不要听见～就是雨。*Everyone should not speak merely upon hearsay.* ⑦【中医】used innermost certain disease:破伤～ *tetanus* ⑧ view; scene: ～景 *landscape; scenery* ⑨ (Fēng) a surname
【风暴】storm; tempest; windstorm
【风标】weathercock; weather vane
【风波】disturbance; storm; trouble; rumpus:她在他们之间挑起了一场～。*She made a rumpus between them.*
【风采】① graceful bearing; elegant demeanour ② literary grace or talent
【风车】① wind mill ② winnower ③ pinwheel (a toy)
【风尘】① wind and dust-travel fatigue:他看起来满脸～。*He looks travel-stained.* ② hardships or uncertainties of an unstable society or wandering life
【风尘仆仆】have endured the hardships of a long journey; worn out by a long journey
【风驰电掣】swift as the wind and quick as lightning
【风吹草动】rustle of grass in the wind — a sign of disturbance or trouble; sign of anything untoward brewing
【风吹雨打】① the wind blows and the rain beats; be buffeted by wind and rain; be exposed to the weather ② rough conditions
【风度】bearing; demeanour; manner: ～翩翩 *have a graceful manner or bearing*
【风帆】① sail ② sailing boat; junk
【风范】bearing; demeanour; manner
【风风火火】① in a hurry; hastily and rashly ② active; dynamic
【风风雨雨】① repeated difficulties and hardships:那两位老人～走过了五十年了。*The two old have spent the countless hardships of the last fifty years.* ② gossip; groundless talk
【风格】① style; spirit ② character; integrity
【风骨】① strength of character: ～高洁 *be of noble and stainless character* ② vigour of style
【风光】(fēngguāng) scene; sight; view:我非常欣赏田园～。*I enjoy idyllic scene very much.*
【风光】(fēngguang)［方］in style; ostentatious and extravagant
【风寒】cold; chill:至从去年她染～后一直躺在床上。*She always lies in bed since she caught a bad cold last year.*
【风和日丽】bright sun and gentle breeze; sunny and genial weather.
【风花雪月】① wind, flowers, snow and moon — referring originally to certain types of literary works and later to effete and sentimental writings in general ② lead a dissipated life ③ love affair
【风华正茂】at life's full flowering; in one's prime; in the flower of youth
【风化】① decency; morals ②【地】weathering: ～壳 *crust of weathering*
【风火墙】fire wall
【风景】landscape; scenery: ～区 *scenic spot*
【风镜】goggles
【风卷残云】a strong wind scatters wisps of clouds — make a clean sweep of sth
【风口】① place where there is a draught:不要站在～上。*Don't stand in the draught.* ②【地】wind gap ③【冶】(blast) tuyere:渣～ *slag tuyere*
【风浪】① stormy waves; storm ② stormy experience; hardship:在他的一生中他遇到过很多～。*In his whole life he met all kinds of hardship.*
【风力】force of wind; power of wind: ～发电站 *wind power station*
【风凉话】irresponsible and sarcastic remarks
【风铃】wind-bells or aeolian bell hung on the eaves of pagodas or temple buildings
【风流】① distinguished and accomplished; refined and tasteful; outstanding ② talented in letters and unconventional in life style; unrestrained in spirit and behaviour: ～才子 *free-mannered gifted scholar* ③ dissolute; loose; romantic:不要谈论人的～韵事。*Don't talk about other's romantic affair.*
【风马牛不相及】have nothing at all to do with each other; be totally irrelevant
【风貌】① style and features; ethos:精神～ *mental outlook* ② appearance and manner; looks and bearing ③ appearance; view
【风靡】fashionable; in vogue: ～一时 *become fashionable for a time*
【风平浪静】the wind has dropped and the waves have subsided; calm and tranquil:生活不可能永远～。*The life can't be calm for ever.*
【风起云涌】① rising wind and rolling clouds ② rolling on with full force; surging and fast-changing
【风气】 atmosphere; common practice; general mood:在社会上～正变得越来越不好。*The general mood of society becomes worse and worse.*
【风琴】organ:他五岁时开始弹～了。*He began to play the organ when he was only five years old.*
【风情】① information about wind-force and wind direction ② bearing; demeanour ③ thoughts and feelings ④ flirtatious expression; amorous feeling ⑤ lifestyle; local conditions and customs:民族～

cultures and customs of the ethnic minorities

【风趣】humour; wit: 大家都喜欢～的人。*All the people like a man of charm and wit.*

【风骚】① [书] literary excellence; literature in general ② coquettish; flirtatious: 不要在这里卖弄～。*Don't play the coquette here.*

【风沙】dust storm; sand blown by the wind

【风扇】electric fan; fan

【风尚】prevailing custom; practice: 尊师重教已成为一种社会～。*Honouring the teacher and revering his teachings has become a common practice to stress decorum and manners.*

【风声】① the sigh or sough of the wind ② news; rumour; word: 你听到什么～了吗? *Have you heard any news?*

【风声鹤唳】moaning of the wind and cry of cranes — fleeing army's suspicion of danger at the slightest sound

【风湿】【医】rheumatism: ～性关节炎 *rheumatism*; *rheumatic disease* / ～性心脏病 *rheumatism of heart*

【风蚀】【地】wind erosion

【风霜】wind and frost — hardships experienced in life

【风水】location of a house or tomb, suppose to have an influence on the fortune of a family; geomancy; geomantic omen: 这是一块～宝地。*This is a place of good geomantic omen.*

【风俗】social custom' custom: ～习惯 *customs and habits*

【风速】wind speed; wind velocity

【风调雨顺】good weather for the crops; propitious winds and rains, favourable weather

【风头】① trend of things; trend of events: 老师让他回家避避～. *The teacher lets him go home to lie low until the dust has settled.* ② publicity one receives; public attention; the limelight: 在这次节目中她出尽了～。*In this program, she was very much in the limelight.* ③ the way the wind blows

【风土人情】local conditions and customs

【风味】distinctive flavour; local colour; special flavour: ～小吃 *typical local delicacy*

【风险】danger; risk: ～赔偿 *indemnity for risk* / ～资本 *risk capita*; *venture capital*

【风箱】bellows; wind chest

【风向】wind direction; how the wind blows: ～标 *wind vane*

【风行】① be in fashion; be popular; be come prevalent: ～一时 *be all the rage for a time* ② fast; rapidly: 雷厉～ *do sth vigorously and speedily*

【风雪】wind and snow; snow storm

【风雅】① literary pursuits ② elegant; polite; refined: 她妈妈是一个举止～的人。*His mother has refined manners.*

【风言风语】canard; groundless talk; slanderous gossip

【风衣】wind breaker

【风油精】【医】essential balm

【风雨】① wind and rain ② stress and hardships

【风雨交加】the wind howls and the rain pour down; it's wet and windy; it's raining and blowing hard

【风雨同舟】in the same storm-tossed boat — stand together through thick and thin

【风云】wind and cloud-stormy or unstable situation

【风疹】【医】nettle rash; urticaria

【风筝】kite: 上周末我们家一块去颐和园放～了。*Our family went to Summer Palace for flying a kite last weekend.*

【风烛残年】old and ailing like a candle guttering in the wind

【风姿】graceful bearing; charm

枫 ① maple ② Chinese sweet gum

【枫树】leaves of gum

【枫叶】leaves of Chinese sweet gum, maple, etc. which turn red in autumn

封[1] ① confer (a title, territory, etc.) upon: 加～ *confer a title upon sb* ② (Fēng) a surname

封[2] ① close; seal: 他家的商店被查～了。*His store was closed down.* ② envelope wrapper ③ [量] for sth enveloped: 昨天她收到了三～请帖。*She received three invitations yesterday.*

【封闭】① seal; cap: 我们进行了为期一周的～式训练。*We have conducted closed door training for one week.* ② seal off; close: ～系统 *closed system*。

【封舱】hatch sealing

【封存】seal up for safekeeping

【封地】feudal estate

【封顶】① (of a plant) cease growing any taller ② put a ceiling on; set the maximum rate

【封冻】freeze over: ～期 *period of freezing weather*

【封火】bank a fire

【封建】① system of enfeoffment ② feudalism: ～王朝 *feudal monarchy* / ～剥削 *feudal exploitation* ③ pertaining to feudal

【封镜】finish making a film

【封口】① seal; heal; close ② shut up; speak with a tone of finality

【封门】seal up a door (so that people are forbidden to enter the room or house)

【封面】① title page of a thread-bound book ② front and back cover of a book ③ front cover

【封皮】① envelope ② paper wrapping; wrapper

【封妻荫子】confer titles of honour on the wife of a deserving official and hereditary ranks on his descendants

【封杀】strangle; smother

【封山】seal or close a mountain pass

【封锁】blockade; lock: 实行经济～ *enforce an economic blockade* / ～线 *blockade line*

【封条】strip of paper used for sealing; paper strip seal

【封装】seal up and pack

【封嘴】① seal sb's lips ② speak with a tone of finality

疯 ① crazy; mad; deranged; insane: ~话 *incoherent utterance; rot* /戈尔登爱撒酒~。*Golden usually acts crazy when he is drunk.* ② without restraint: 这个假期里他玩~了。*He enjoyed himself with abandon during this vacation.* ③ (of a plant, grain crop, etc.) spindled

【疯疯癫癫】mentally deranged; act like a lunatic

【疯狗】mad dog; rabid dog: 昨天她被~咬了。*She was bit by the mad dog.*

【疯狂】crazy; unbridled; wild

【疯牛病】mad cow disease; bovine spongiform encephalopathy (BSE)

【疯人】madman; deranged person; lunatic: ~院 *lunatic asylum; madhouse; mental hospital*

【疯长】overgrow; spindle

【疯子】lunatic; madman; nut

峰 ① crest; peak; summit: 主~ *highest peak in a mountain range* ② hump; peak-like thing: ~驼 *three camels hump* ③ [量] *used of camels*: 三~骆驼 *three camels*

【峰巅】peak; summit

【峰回路转】amidst surrounding elevations and winding roads; be full of twists and turns; make an abrupt transition

【峰会】summit (meeting)

【峰峦】ridges and peaks: ~起伏 *mountain ranges rise and fall*

【峰年】peak year

【峰态】[数] kurtosis

【峰值】peak value; crest value: ~点 *peak point*

烽 beacon

【烽火】① beacon-fire (for giving border alarm in ancient china); beacon: ~台 *beacon tower* ② flames of war: ~连三月, 家书抵万金。*With turmoil of battle three months on end, a letter from home is worth a fortune in gold.*

【烽烟】beacon fire; beacon; flames of war

锋 ① sharp point or cutting edge of a sword, knife, etc. ② forefront; leading edge ③ [气] front: 冷~ *cold front*

【锋芒】① cutting edge; spearhead ② talent displayed; outward show of one's talent: ~毕露 *make a full display of one's talent; show off one's ability*

【锋面】[气] frontal surface

【锋刃】sharp point or cutting edge of a knife, word, etc.

【锋锐】① keen; sharp ② dashing spirit: 这次会议上她大出~。*She caught a lot of attention in the meeting.*

蜂 ① bee: 养~场 *bee yard* ② wasp ③ in swarms

【蜂巢】honeycomb; beehive

【蜂刺】sting of a bee or wasp

【蜂毒】bee venom

【蜂蜜】honey

【蜂鸣器】buzzer

【蜂农】bee-keeper; apiarist

【蜂王】queen bee; queen wasp

【蜂窝】① bechive; honeycomb ② honeycomb-like thing: ~炉 *honeycomb briquet stove*

【蜂箱】beehive; hive

【蜂拥】swarm; flock: ~而至 *come swarming* /上课铃一响, 同学们~而入。*As soon as the bell rang, the students swarmed into the classroom.*

féng

逢 ① encounter; come across; meet: 你我萍水相~, 我凭什么帮助你? *We met by chance like patches of drifting duckweed; why shall I help you?* ② (Féng) a surname

【逢凶化吉】turn ill luck into good; turn misfortune into fortune

【逢迎】make up to; curry favour with; fawn on: 他老爱~别人。*He always likes currying favour with others.*

缝 sew; stitch: ~扣子 *sew on a button* /我不相信她会~衣服。*I can't believe that she can sew clothes.*

see also fèng

【缝边】stitch-hem; hem: ~器 *hem-stitcher; hemmer*

【缝补】sew and mend

【缝合】suture; sew up: 医生帮他~了腿上的伤口。*The doctor helped him stature a cut on his leg.*

【缝纫】sewing; tailoring: ~车间 *tailoring workshop* / ~机 *sewing-machine*

【缝线】[医] suture

【缝制】sew

fěng

讽 ① mock; satirize; allude euphemistically: ~刺小说 *satirical novel* /~谏 *remonstrate with the sovereign by euphemism* ② [书] chant; intone

【讽嘲】mock; satirize; sneer

【讽刺】mock; ridicule; satirize: ~诗 *satirical poem* / ~文学 *satirical literature; ironical literature; satire*

【讽喻】parable; allegory: 他写了好多文章~时政。*He writes a lot of articles to allude to current politics in parables.*

唪 chant in a loud voice

【唪经】(of Buddhists or Taoists) recite or chant

fèng

凤 phoenix

【凤蝶】swallowtail butterfly; swallowtail

【凤冠】phoenix coronet (worn by an empress or imperial concubine and also used formerly as a bride's headdress)

【凤凰】phoenix (凤 being the male and 凰 being the female)

【凤凰木】royal poinciana (Delonix regia); flamboyant (tree)

【凤凰竹】hedge bamboo (Bambusa multiplex)

【凤梨】pineapple (the plant and its fruit)

【凤毛麟角】(precious and rare as) phoenix feathers and unicorn horns; rarity of rarities

【凤仙花】garden balsam; balsam

奉 ① offer; submit; give or present with respect ② receive (orders, etc.): ~领导命令,我们明天就离开上海。*We will leave Shanghai on the orders from the leader.* ③ regard with respect; look upon... as ④ wait upon; attend to ⑤ used to refer to sth one does for the other party

【奉承】flatter; fawn upon; toady; bow and scrape

【奉公】act for public interests: ~守法 *law-abiding* /克己~ *be selfless and work devotedly for public interests*

【奉还】return with thanks

【奉命】act under orders; receive orders: ~唯谨 *obey orders scrupulously*

【奉陪】keep sb company: ~到底 *have the honour of keeping sb company until the end* /我不得不离开了。恕不~。*As I have to go now, I'm afraid I won't be able to keep you company.*

【奉劝】offer a piece of advice

【奉送】give away free; offer as a gift: 作为礼物,~你几句话。*Offer some words to you as a gift.*

【奉天承运】by the Grace of God

【奉献】devote; offer as a tribute; present with respect: ~精神 *spirit of utter devotion* /把青春~给社会 *devote one's youth to society*

【奉行】pursue (a policy, etc.): 中国~独立自主的外交政策。*China pursues an independent foreign policy.*

【奉养】support and wait upon (one's parents, etc.): ~你老母亲是你的义务。*It's your duty to support and wait upon your old mother.*

【奉迎】flatter; fawn on; curry favour with

【奉召】receive a summons

【奉旨】by order of the emperor; by decree of the emperor; by imperial edict

俸 pay; salary; stipend

【俸给】salary; stipend

【俸禄】[旧] official's salary or stipend

缝 ① seam: 焊~ *welding seam* ② crack; chink

see also féng

【缝隙】crack; chink; crevice: 那两把椅子之间有~。*There's crack in the two chairs.*

fó

佛 ① Buddha: 活~ *living Buddha* ② Buddhism ③ image of Buddha; statue of Buddha

【佛法】① Buddha's teachings; Buddhist doctrine; Buddha dharma: 传布~ *spread Buddha's teachings* ② power of Buddha

【佛家】Buddhist; Buddhism; Buddhist

【佛教】Buddhism

【佛经】Buddhist scripture; Buddhist sutra

【佛龛】niche for a statue of Buddha

【佛罗里达】Florida, a state in the southeastern United States

【佛门】Buddhism: ~弟子 *follower of Buddha*

【佛事】Buddhist ceremony; Buddhist service

【佛手】【植】buddha's hand; fingered citron

【佛手瓜】【植】chayote

【佛堂】family hall for worshipping Buddha

【佛像】image of Buddha; statue of Buddha

【佛学】Buddhist learning; Buddhist philosophy: 她对~很感兴趣。*She is very interested in Buddhist philosophy.*

【佛要金装,人要衣装】as Buddha needs a gilt statue, man needs fine clothes; fine feathers make fine birds

【佛争一炷香,人争一口气】as Buddha needs incense, so man needs self-respect

【佛珠】beads; rosary

【佛祖】Buddha; Buddhist patriarch; founder of a Buddhist sect

fǒu

否 ① deny; negate ②[书] no; not: 你是学生吗? ~。*Are you a student? No.* ③ used at the end of a question ④ used after 是,能,可, etc. to indicate a choice or question

see also pǐ

【否定】① deny; negate ② negative

【否决】vote down; reject; veto: ~权 *veto power*

【否认】deny; disavow; repudiate

【否则】if not; or else; otherwise: 请你立刻走开,~我叫警察了。*Please go away; otherwise I call the police.*

fū

夫 ① husband: 前~ *ex-husband* ② man: 匹~ *ordinary man* ③ manual worker; person engaged in manual labour ④ [旧] *conscripted labourer*

【夫唱妇随】the husband sings and the wife follows — domestic harmony; wife being her husband's echo; conjugal felicity

【夫妇】husband and wife; married couple: 那对新婚～出去旅行了。*The newly married couple went out for travelling.*

【夫妻】husband or man and wife

【夫权】authority of the husband

【夫人】lady; madam

【夫婿】[书] husband

【夫子】① [旧] term of address for a scholar ② [旧] my husband ③ pedant: 你真是一个老～。*You are really an old pedant.*

孵 hatch; brood; incubate

【孵化】hatch; incubate

【孵卵】brood; hatch; incubate

【孵卵器】incubator

【孵育】hatch; incubate

敷 ① apply (powder, ointment; etc.): 医生在为患者背部～药。*The doctor is applying ointment to the back of the patient.* ② spread; lay out: ～设轨枕 *lay a sleeper* ③ be sufficient for: 入不～出 *income falling short of expenditure*; *unable to make ends meet*; *living beyond one's means*

【敷料】[医] dressing

【敷设】① lay (pipes, etc.) ② lay (mines); place: ～地雷 *lay land mines*

【敷贴】apply ointment or plaster (to an affected part of the body)

【敷衍】① act in a perfunctory manner; go through the motions; do just enough to satisfy sb; muddle through: 他对这次事故采取了～的态度。*He acted in a perfunctory manner to the accident.* ② barely get by; just manage

【敷衍塞责】perform one's duty in a perfunctory manner muddle through one's work

【敷衍了事】do sth perfunctorily; muddle through sth

【敷衍搪塞】go through the motions; explain away

fú

伏[1] ① lean over; bend over: 她～在床上睡着了。*She lied prostrate on the bed and slept.* ② fall; go down: 波浪起～ *roaring waves rise and fall* / 群山～ *meandering mountains ranges* ③ hide: 敌人中了我们的埋～。*The enemy fell into our ambush.* ④ any of the three nine-day periods constituting the hottest season of the year: 今年天气已经入～。*It is beginning the hottest season this year.* ⑤ yield; admit: 罪犯已经～法。*The prisoner was executed.* ⑥ subdue; overcome: 降～野马 *break in wild horse*

伏[2] volt

【伏安】volt-ampere

【伏案】bend over one's desk; lean over a table

【伏笔】hint foreshadowing later developments in a story, essay, etc.; foreshadowing

【伏兵】troops in ambush; ambush: 在路上他们遇上了～。*They met troops in ambush on their way.*

【伏尔加河】Volga River (major river in western Russia)

【伏法】be executed; be put to death

【伏击】ambush: 他们决定在半道上～敌人。*They decided to ambush the enemies in their half way.*

【伏暑】hot season; height of summer

【伏特】[电] volt

【伏帖】① at ease; comfortable ② docile; obedient; submissive

【伏卧】lie on one's stomach; drop to the ground

【伏汛】summer flood

【伏诛】[书] be executed

【伏罪】plead guilty

芙

【芙蕖】[书] liter. lotus

【芙蓉】[植] ① cottonrose hibiscus ② lotus

扶 ① support with the hand; place a hand on sb or sth for support: 老人～着桌子站起来。*The old man got on his feet by leaning on a table.* ② hold up; straighten up; help sb up: 把铁棒～起来 *straighten up an iron bar* ③ lead a hand; assist: 搀～某人下马 *assist sb from the saddle* / ～某人站起 *assist sb to his feet* ④ (Fú) a surname

【扶病】(do sth) in spite of illness: 他～坚持学习。*In spite of illness, he goes on study.*

【扶不起的阿斗】weakling whom nobody can help to succeed

【扶持】① support sb with one's hand; help sb to stand and walk ② give aid to; foster; help sustain

【扶老携幼】holding the old by the arm and the young by the hand; bring along the old and the young

【扶贫】aid-the-poor; aid a poverty-stricken area; help the poor: ～计划 *aid the poor programme*

【扶手】① handrail; banister ② armrest

【扶梯】① staircase with banisters ② [方] *ladder*

【扶危济困】help those in danger and relieve those in need; help those in distress and aid those in peril

【扶养】bring up; foster: ～费 *support payment* / 他每月交给老人一些～费。*He gives some support pant to told man.*

【扶正】① [旧] make a concubine one's official wife ② set upright or straight

【扶植】cultivate; foster; prop up; promote: ～新政府 *prop up a new government*

【扶助】assist; help; support

F

拂 ① caress; stroke: 春风~面 *a spring breeze sweep one's face* ② flick; whisk: ~去头发上的尘土 *whisk the dust off the hair* ③ go against (sb's wishes)

【拂尘】horsetail whisk

【拂动】brush slightly against; stroke; sway gently

【拂拭】wipe off; whisk off: 她轻轻~掉衣服上的灰尘。*She wiped the dust off her clothes.*

【拂晓】before dawn: 明天我们~就要起床。*We will get up before dawn tomorrow.*

【拂袖而去】leave with a flick of one's sleeve — go off in a huff

【拂煦】(of wind) bring warmth: 和风~。*A gentle breeze is warm and pleasant.*

服 ① clothes; dress; attire: 中山~ *Chinese tunic suit* /西~ *Western-style clothes* ② wear or put on (clothes): 他为他母亲~孝。*He wore mourning clothes for his mother.* ③ serve: ~兵役 *serve in the army* ④ obey; submit: 这个孩子一点也不~管教。*This child did not submit himself to others' management at all.* ⑤ take (medicine) ⑥ convince: 心~口~ *be thoroughly convinced* ⑦ be used to; be accustomed to ⑧ (Fú) a surname

see also fù

【服从】obey; submit (oneself) to; be subordinated to

【服毒】take poison

【服法】(fúfɑ) directions on how to take a medicine: 你知道这种药的~吗? *Do you know how to take the pill?*

【服法】(fúfǎ) obey or abide by the law

【服气】be convinced; be won over

【服软】① be amenable to persuasion ② admit or acknowledge defeat; give in: 在我们面前他从来不~。*He is not be cowed by us.*

【服丧】be in mourning (for the death of a kinsman, etc.)

【服饰】dress; attire; dress and personal adornment: 她带了很多~给我们。*She brought many dresses to us.*

【服侍】wait upon; attend to; nurse

【服输】admit defeat; acknowledge defeat

【服帖】① appropriate; fitting; neat; well-arranged ② compliant; docile; obedient; submissive

【服务】be in the service of; give service to; service: 那个酒店向我们提供了良好的~。*The hotel supplied good service for us.*

【服刑】serve a sentence (in prison)

【服药】take medicine: 医生要求我们按时~。*The doctor demands we take medicine on time.*

【服役】be on active service; enlist in the army; serve in the army: 超期~ *be on an extended term of service*

【服用】① take (medicine): 由于~了药物,他感觉有点困。*He felt a little sleepy for taking medicines.* ②[书] clothing and articles for daily use

【服装】clothing; costume; dress; garment: 民族~ *national costume*

氟 【化】fluorine

【氟化氢】【化】hydrogen fluoride

【氟化物】【化】fluoride

俘 ① capture; take prisoner; seize: 昨天他在家里被~了。*Yesterday he was seized at home.* ② captive; prisoner of war: 战~ *prisoner of war (POW)*

【俘获】① capture ②【物】*capture*: 裂变~ *fission capture*

【俘虏】① capture; take prisoner: 昨天他们共~了50名敌人。*Yesterday they captured fifty enemies.* ② captured personnel; prisoner of war (POW)

浮 ① float ②[方] *swim*: 他能~一百米远。*He can swim* 100 *metres.* ③ flighty; superficial: 学习很~ *superficial study* ④ temporary; provisional ⑤ movable; portable ⑥ empty; hollow ⑦ exceed; surplus; redundant

【浮标】buoy

【浮尘】floating dust; surface dust: 屋里满是~。*The house was filled with floating dust.*

【浮沉】go up and down; drift along; now sink, now emerge

【浮荡】float in the air

【浮雕】relief: ~塑像 *relief sculpture*

【浮动】① drift; float ② fluctuate; rise and fall ③【经】*float*: ~汇率 *floating exchange* /~价格 *floating price*

【浮光掠影】hasty and casual; skimming over the surface; superficial

【浮华】flashy; ostentatious; showy: 他哥哥在城里过着~的生活。*His elder brother leads a showy and luxurious life.*

【浮夸】boastful; exaggerate

【浮力】【物】buoyancy

【浮面】surface

【浮名】bubble reputation; empty name; vain glory

【浮萍】【植】duckweed

【浮浅】shallow; superficial

【浮桥】floating bridge; pontoon bridge

【浮现】appear before one's eyes; reveal; show: 她的脸上~出幸福的笑容。*An expression of happy smile showed on her face.*

【浮想联翩】thoughts thronging one's mind

【浮选】【矿】flotation

【浮游】① swim ② roam about; go on a pleasure trip

【浮员】redundant personnel: 公司决定削减~。*The company decided to cut down the redundant personnel.*

【浮云】floating cloud: ~蔽日 *like a floating cloud obscuring the sun — in reference to treacherous court officials deluding the monarch*

【浮躁】impetuous; impulsive: 他办事太~。*He acts on impulse.*

【浮肿】【医】dropsy; edema; oedema

符 ① tally issued by a ruler to a general or envoy as credentials in ancient China：虎～ *tiger tally* ② symbol，mark；sign：音～ *musical note* ③ accord with；match；tally with：她说的和事实不～。*What she said was not tally with the facts.* ④ magic figures drawn by Taoist priests to invoke or expel spirits and bring good or ill fortune ⑤（Fú）a surname

【符号】① mark；sign；symbol：标点～ *punctuation mark* ② insignia

【符合】① accord with；be in line with；be in keeping with；tally with：他所做的正～父母的心愿。*What he had done was in keeping with his parents' wish.* ②【物】coincidence：～传感器 *coincidence sensor*

【符咒】taoist magic figures and incantations

幅 ① width of cloth：宽～布 *broad or wide cloth* ② breadth；size：巨～广告牌 *billboard of gigantic size* ③［量］used for cloth，pictures，scrolls，etc.：他送给我了一～画。*He gave me a picture.*

【幅度】extent；margin；range；scope

【幅面】width of cloth

【幅员辽阔】vast territory

辐 spoke（of a wheel）

【辐射】① radiate ②【物】radiation：～强度 *radiation intensity*

【辐照】【物】irradiation

福 ① luck；blessing；good fortune；happiness：造～后代 *benefit posterity or future generations* ②【旧】（of a woman）make a curtsy：道万～（*of a woman*）*make a greeting while curtsying* ③（Fú）a surname

【福尔马林】【化】formalin

【福分】［口］good luck；good fortune；happy lot

【福利】① material benefits；welfare；well-being：～设施 *welfare facilities*

【福气】good fortune；happy lot

【福如东海，寿比南山】happiness as boundless as the sea and longevity comparable to that of the hills；may you live a long and happy life

【福无双至，祸不单行】blessings never come in pair and misfortunes never come singly

【福相】face showing good fortune；features or countenance of good fortune：那个孩子长得很～。*The child has features suggestive of good fortune.*

【福星】lucky star；mascot：～高照 *be under the smiles of fortune；the lucky star shines high above；have one's star in the ascendant*

【福音】①【宗】gospel ② happy news；glad tidings

【福荫】protection of one's elders or ancestors

【福佑】bless and protect

蝠 bat

fǔ

抚 ① comfort；console：安～ *aid and comfort* ② foster；nurture；protect：优～ *give special care and preferential treatment* ③ press lightly；stroke

【抚爱】caress；fondle；take care of

【抚摸】caress；stroke

【抚摩】caress；stroke

【抚弄】caress；fondle；stroke：她轻轻地～着女儿的头发。*She was gently stroking her daughter's hair.*

【抚慰】comfort；console；soothe

【抚恤】comfort and compensate a bereaved family：～金 *pension for the disabled or for the family of the deceased*

【抚养】bring up；foster；raise；rear：～费 *child support payment；payment for the upbringing of one's children* / 他叔叔决定把他～成人。*His uncle decided to bring up him.*

【抚育】foster；look after；tend；nurture

【抚掌】clap one's hands

拊 ［书］clap

【拊手】clap hands：～大笑。*Clap hands and laugh heartily.*

【拊掌】［书］clap hands

斧 axe；hatchet

【斧头】axe；hatchet

【斧子】axe；hatchet

府 ① seat of government；government office ②［旧］government repository，archive or treasury of（local）government ③ mansion；official residence ④ your home；your house ⑤（Fǔ）a surname

【府邸】mansion；mansion house；residence

【府上】① your home；your house：最近～怎么样？*How about your home recently？* ② your native place

俯 ① bow（one's head）；bend forward or down：史蒂夫～身拾起地上的书。*Steve bent down to pick up the books on the floor.* ②［旧］（used in official documents or letters）deign to；condescend to

【俯冲】【航】dive：～角 *dive angle* / ～飞行 *diving flight*

【俯角】angle of depression

【俯瞰】look down at；overlook：从这里你可以～整个村庄。*You can overlook the whole country from there.*

【俯身】bend down；stoop

【俯拾即是】be easily available；be found everywhere；be extremely common

【俯视】look down at；overlook

【俯首】bow one's head；obey submissively：～甘为

孺子牛 *humbly serve the people with one's heart and soul*

【俯首帖耳】be docile and obedient; be servile; take lying down; be all obedience

【俯首听命】bow down and obey submissively; be at sb's beck and call

【俯卧】lie prostrate; lie on one's stomach: ~撑 *press-up; push up*

【俯仰】bend or lift one's head; act; move: ~运动 *pitching movement*

【俯泳】【体】breaststroke

釜 kind of cauldron used in ancient China

【釜底抽薪】take away the firewood from under the cauldron — take drastic measures to deal with an emergency

【釜底游鱼】fish swimming in the bottom of a cauldron — person whose fate is sealed

【釜山】Pusan, second largest city and seaport on the southeastern coast of the Republic of Korea

辅 ① assist; complement; supplement: ~助授粉 *supplementary pollination* / ~课 *subsidiary course* / ~币 *fractional money or currency* /相~相成 *complement each other* ② [书] areas round a national capital

【辅导】tutor; guide; give guidance in study or training: 课外~ *after-school tutoring* / ~材料 *guidance material*

【辅导员】assistant; counsellor; instructor

【辅料】subsidiary materials; supplementary materials

【辅音】【语】consonant

【辅助】① aid; assist: 他叔叔~他完成了学业。*His uncle helped him to finish his study.* ② auxiliary; subsidiary; supplementary: ~作用 *auxiliary function* / ~设备 *auxiliary equipment* / ~机构 *auxiliary organization or body* / ~车间 *auxiliary shop* / ~人员 *auxiliary personnel*

【辅佐】assist a ruler in governing a country

脯 ① dried meat: 我喜欢肉~。*I like to eat dried meat.* ② sundried candied fruit; preserved fruit: 苹果~ *preserved apple*
see also pú

腐 ① corroded; putrid; rotten; stale: ~米 *rotten rice* ② bean-curd; tofu

【腐败】① decayed; foul; rotten ② decadent; corrupt; musty; dark: ~分子 *corrupt elements* / ~的社会 *decadent society* /他们过着~的生活。*They lead a decadent life.*

【腐臭】emitting a smell of decay; decaying and stinking: ~分子 *corrupt elements* / ~堕落 *become corrupt*

【腐烂】decompose; rot; go putrid: 那些苹果已经~了,不能再吃了。*The apples have rotted and were not eaten any more.*

【腐乳】fermented bean — curd or tofu

【腐生】【生理】saprophytic: ~植物 *saprophyte* / ~链 *saprophyte chain*

【腐蚀】corrode; etch; deprave: ~剂 *corrosive; corrodent*

【腐朽】① decay; rot ② decadent; depraved; rotten: ~的作风 *rotten way of thinking*

【腐殖酸】humic acid: ~盐 *humate*

【腐殖土】【农】humus soil

【腐竹】dried rolls of bean milk cream

fù

父 ① father: 雷蒙娜的~亲去年去世了。*Ramona's father died last year.* ② male relative of a senior generation: 岳~ *father-in-law*

【父辈】elder generation; people of father's generation

【父老】elders (of a country or district): ~乡亲 *fellow countrymen*

【父母】parents; father and mother: ~把他送到一个很远的地方去读书了。*His parents sent him to a faraway place for study.*

【父母之命,媒妁之言】command of parents and the good offices of a matchmaker — the proper way of contracting a marriage

【父亲】father

【父系】① paternal: ~亲属 *relatives on the paternal side; paternal relative* ② paternal line

【父子】father and son

讣 ① announce sb's death ② obituary

【讣告】① announce sb's death ② obituary: ~栏 *obituary column*

【讣闻】obituary notice

付 ① hand or turn over; commit; give: 我们的办公室已经交~使用了。*Our office has been turned over for use.* ② pay: ~钱 *pay the money* ③ (Fù) a surname

【付出】expend; pay

【付款】pay a sum of money; make payment: ~人 *payer* / ~凭证 *payment voucher; payment certificate*

【付讫】(of a bill) paid: 现金~ *paid cash*

【付清】pay off; pay in full; pay up; clear: 所有货物的款项需一次~。*Payment for goods should be paid off in one lump sum.*

【付托】entrust; put sth in sb's charge; put in trust

【付息】pay interest

【付现】pay in cash; make cash payment

【付印】① send to the press ② turn over to the printing shop (after proofreading)

【付账】pay a bill; foot a bill

【付之一炬】burn; commit to the flames; set on fire

【付之一笑】dismiss with a laugh; laugh away

【付之东流】thrown into the eastward flowing stream — all one's efforts wasted; come to naught

【付梓】[书] turn over a manuscript for printing; send to press

负 ① carry on the back or shoulder：背～炸药包 *carry a explosive package on one's back* /肩～皮箱 *shoulder a leather suitcase* ② bear；take up：肩～重任 *shoulder an important back* ③ enjoy ④ have at one's back；rely on ⑤ suffer；sustain：他在战争中身～重任。*He suffered serious injuries in the war.* ⑥ owe；be indebted ⑦ lose；be defeated ⑧ betray；fail ⑨【数】minus；negative：～分数 *negative fraction* ⑩【电】negative：～极 *negative pole*

【负担】① bear (a burden)；carry shoulder：我～不起教育费用。*I cannot afford my educational expenses.* ② burden；load；weight；strain：精神～ *mental strain*

【负电】negative electricity

【负号】【数】negative sign

【负荷】① load；work load；performance capacity：超～ *overload*；*above capacity*

【负极】【电】negative pole

【负荆请罪】proffer a birch and ask for a flogging — offer a humble apology

【负疚】[书] fell guilty；feel conscience-stricken；be apologetic

【负离子】【物】anion

【负利率】negative interest rate

【负面】negative：～影响 *unfavourable influence* / ～效应 *negative effects*

【负气】do sth in a fit of pique：那个孩子～离开了学校。*The child left school in a fit of pique.*

【负伤】be wounded；sustain an injury

【负数】【数】negative number

【负心】untrue；ungrateful；heartless

【负隅顽抗】(of an enemy or a robber) fight stubbornly with one's back to the wall；put up a desperate struggle

【负约】break a promise；go back on one's word；fail to keep an appointment

【负载】【电】load：工作～ *operating load*

【负责】① be in charge of；be responsible for：在公司里，她～管理工作。*She is in charge of management in the company.* ② conscientious：工作～ *be conscientious in one's work*

【负债】① be in debt；incur debts ② liabilities：～管理 *liability management* /资产与～ *assets and liabilities*

【负值】【数】negative value

【负指数】【数】negative exponent

【负重】carry a heavy load；bear a heavy weight；shoulder an important task

【负罪】[书] bear the blame；plead guilty to the charge

妇 ① woman ② married woman ③ wife：夫唱～随 *harmony between husband and wife*

【妇产科】department of gynaecology and obstetrics

【妇产医院】hospital for gynaecology and obstetrics

【妇道人家】[旧] women；womenfolk

【妇科】department of gynaecology

【妇女】woman

【妇孺】[书] women and children

【妇婴】women and infants；mothers and babies

【妇幼】women and children：～保健中心 *health centre for women and children*

附 ① add；attach；append；enclose：～从 *comply with*；*agree to* /随信～发票两张。*With the letter I enclose two invoices.* ② be near；be close by；get close to：小孩把头～在桌子上。*The little kid got close to the table with his head.* ③ attach oneself to；comply with；depend on

【附龙攀凤】curry favour with people of power and position

【附笔】additional note；additional remarks；postscript

【附带】① attach；append ② incidentally；in passing；by the way ③ additional；subsidiary：～任务 *subsidiary task*

【附耳】move close to sb's ear

【附睾】【生理】epididymis ～炎 *epididymitis*

【附和】echo；chime in with：她一点主意没有，总是～别人。*She has no ideas and always chimes in with others.*

【附会】draw wrong conclusions by false analogy；strain one's interpretation

【附加】① add；attach ② additional；attached；appended：～费 *additional charge*；*surcharge* / ～条款 *additional clause* / ～险 *additional risk* / ～工资 *extra wage*；*supplementary wage* / ～税 *supertax*；*surtax*；*additional tax* / ～刑 *accessory punishment* / ～资本 *additional paid-in capital*

【附件】① annex；appendix ② enclosure ③【机】*accessories*；*attachment*

【附近】① adjacent；nearby；neighbouring：～的城市 *neighbouring city* ② close to；in the vicinity of：他在商店～工作。*He works close to the shopping.*

【附录】appendix

【附上】enclosed herewith

【附生】(of a plant) grow on another plant but not be parasitic on it：～植物 *epiphyte*

【附属】auxiliary；attached；affiliated：～中学 *attached secondary school* / ～小学 *attached primary school*

【附体】(of ghost, demon, evil spirit, etc.) bedevil a human body；be possessed

【附图】attached map；attached drawing；figure

【附言】postscript (PS)

【附议】second a motion；support a proposal

【附庸风雅】(of landlords, merchants, etc.) mingle with men of letters and pose as a lover of culture

【附着】adhere to；cling to；stick to：～力 *adhesion*；*adhesive force*

服 (for Chinese medicine) dose：他在医院买了六～药。*He bought six doses of Chinese medicine in hospital.*

see also fú

驸 horse hitched up by the side of the shaft horse；horse harnessed by the side of a team

F

【驸马】 emperor's son-in-law; husband of an emperor's daughter or sister

赴 attend; be bound for; go to: 去年他姐姐~英国学习去了。*His elder sister went to study in the England last year.*

【赴会】 attend a meeting; keep an appointment; meet sb by appointment

【赴任】 be on the way to one's post; go to one's post: 爸爸去北京~了。*My father went to his post to Beijing.*

【赴汤蹈火】 go through fire and water; defy all difficulties and dangers; be ready to risk one's life

【赴宴】 go to a banquet; go to a feast; attend a banquet

【赴约】 keep an appointment; meet sb by appointment ~

复[1] ① complex; compound; complicated: ~名数 *compound number* /纷繁~杂 *numerous and complicated* ② duplicate; repeat: 反~琢磨 *turn sth over in one's mind again and again*

复[2] ① turn over; turn round ② answer; reply: 请回~。*Please answer me.*

复[3] recover; resume; revenge

复[4] again; repeatedly

【复本】 duplicate

【复本位制】【经】 bimetallism

【复辟】 restore a dethroned monarch; restore the old order

【复查】 check again; reexamine: 她妈妈去医院~了。*Her mother went to hospital for reexamination.*

【复仇】 avenge; revenge: ~者 *revanchist* / ~主义 *revanchism*

【复出】 resume one's official post after rehabilitation; make a comeback

【复读】 repeat the last year of schooling due to the next level

【复发】 recur; have a relapse: ~率 *recurrence rate* / 旧病~ *have an attack of an old illness*; *have a relapse*

【复返】 come back; return: 时间一去不~。*Time comes but once.*

【复方】 ①【中医】 prescription composed of two or more recipes of herbal medicines ②【医】 medicine made of two or more ingredients; compound: ~阿司匹林 *aspirin compound* (*APC*)

【复分解】【化】 double decomposition: ~反应 *double decomposition reaction*

【复工】 return to work after a strike or layoff

【复古】 restore ancient ways; return to the ancients: ~主义 *doctrine of back to the ancients*

【复合】 compound; complex; composite: ~词 *compound word*

【复核】 ① check: 你认真~一下这些数字。*Please check the figures carefully.* ②【律】 (of the Supreme People's Court) review a case in which a death sentence has been passed by a lower court

【复婚】 remarry each other; restoration of a marriage; resumption of matrimonial relations; reunion of a couple after divorce

【复活】 ① come back to life; bring back to life; revive: 防止军国主义~ *guard against the revival of militarism* ②【宗】resurrection: ~节 *Easter*

【复旧】 restore old ways; return to the past

【复句】【语】 sentence of two or more clauses; complex or compound sentence

【复刊】 (of newspaper or magazine) resume publication

【复课】 resume classes

【复利】【经】 compound interest

【复明】 recover lost eyesight; regain one's eyesight: 听说他妈妈的眼睛~了。*It's heard that his mother regained her eyesight.*

【复命】 report back after carrying out an order; report on completion of a task

【复赛】【体】 intermediary heat; semi-finals

【复审】 ① re-check; reexamine ②【律】 review a case

【复生】 come back to life; bring back to life; revive

【复式】 double entry

【复试】 reexamination; final examination; second round of examinations

【复述】 repeat; retell: 请你~一遍课文。*Please repeat the text.*

【复数】 ①【语】 plural (number) ②【数】 complex number

【复丝】【纺】 multifilament

【复苏】 ① come back to life; resuscitate ②【经】 recovery

【复透镜】 compound lens

【复位】 ①【医】 reset; reduce: ~术 *reduction* /关节~ *reset a joint* ② be restored to the throne; resume power

【复习】 review; revise: 老师要同学们下课后要~课文。*The teacher wants his students to review the text after class.*

【复线】【交】 double track; multiple track

【复写】 make carbon copies; duplicate: ~纸 *carbon paper*

【复信】 reply; write a letter in reply

【复兴】 revive; reinvigorate; rejuvenate: 文艺~ *renaissance*

【复姓】 compound surname; two-character surname

【复学】 go back to school; resume one's interrupted studies

【复眼】【动】 compound eye (of insects)

【复业】 ① take up one's old occupation; reestablish one's business ② reopen; restart; resume business after a close-down: 昨天学校里的那家超市~了。*The supermarket of the school reopens business yesterday.*

【复叶】【植】 compound leaf

【复议】 reconsider (a decision)

【复音】【物】 complex tone

【复印】【印】copy; duplicate; photocopy: ~机 *duplicator*; *copier* / ~件 *duplicate copy* / ~纸 *duplicating paper*; *copy paper*
【复员】① return to peacetime condition ② demobilize; demob: ~军人 *demobilized soldier*
【复原】① recover from an illness; be restored to health ② restore; rehabilitate
【复杂】complex; complicated; intricate:这件事情太~了,没有人能说清楚。*The matter was so complicated that nobody can say it clearly.*
【复诊】further consultation (with a doctor); subsequent visit
【复职】be reinstated; resume one's post:他希望今年能够~。*He wishes he can get himself reinstated this year.*
【复制】duplicate; make a copy of; reproduce; reconstruct: ~品 *replica*; *reproduction*
【复种】【农】multiple cropping: ~面积 *multiple cropping area*
副[1] ① assistant; deputy; vice: ~主任 *deputy director* ② assistant post; assistant position: 团~ *subsidiary regimental commander* ③ auxiliary; complementary; secondary: ~题 *subtitle*; *subheading* / ~油箱 *auxiliary fuel tank*; *auxiliary tank* ④ correspond to; fit:名~其实 *title corresponding with reality*
副[2] ①[量] set; pair:昨天我买了一~眼镜。*I bought a pair of glasses yesterday.* ② used to indicate facial expression
【副本】copy; duplicate; transcript
【副标题】subheading; subtitle
【副词】【语】adverb
【副官】adjutant; aide-de-camp
【副驾驶员】copilot; second pilot
【副教授】associate professor; adjunct professor
【副刊】supplement:文学~ *literary supplement*
【副科】minor subject; secondary course:他不喜欢学习~。*He dislikes the minor courses.*
【副品】seconds; substandard goods
【副食】non-staple food: ~品 *non-staple food or foodstuffs*
【副手】assistant; helper
【副业】sideline; side occupation
【副职】position of a deputy
【副作用】① side effect; by-effect:你不能再吃了,这种药有~。*You can't eat any more; the medicines have a harmful side effect.* ②【机】secondary action
赋[1] bestow on; endow with; vest with:天~ *natural endowments*
赋[2] ①[旧] agricultural tax: ~课 *land and other taxes* /田~ *land tax* / ~敛 *levy taxes* ②[书] levy; impose
赋[3] ① compose; write ② rhyme prose; poetic prose: ~诗 *compose a poem*
【赋税】taxes
【赋闲】be out of office; be unemployed; be out of employment:他最近~在家。*He is out of employment and stays at home recently.*
【赋有】possess; be endowed with; be gifted with
【赋予】bestow; entrust; give
【赋值】【电】bind
傅 ① teacher; instructor ② apply; lay on
富 ① abundant; rich; wealthy:他并不~,但总是给别人钱。*He is not rich, but he always gives money to others.* ② resource; wealth ③ enrich ④(Fù) a surname
【富贵】riches and honour; wealth and rank:她出生在~人家。*She was born in a rich and powerful family.*
【富国】① rich country ② make one's country rich: ~强兵 *make one's country rich and build up its military might*
【富豪】rich and powerful people
【富丽堂皇】grand; gorgeous; splendid; magnificent
【富农】rich peasant
【富强】prosperous and strong; rich and powerful
【富饶】abundant; fertile: ~的土地 *fertile land*
【富商】rich merchant
【富士山】mount Fuji or Fujiyama, a dormant volcano which is Japan's highest peak
【富庶】rich and populous
【富态】plump; stout:他长得很~。*He is inclined to plumpness.*
【富翁】rich man; man of wealth:他做梦自己成了一个大~。*He dreamed that he became a man of wealth.*
【富有】① affluent; rich; wealthy ② rich in; full in; replete with:她~自己的个性。*She is of her strong personality.*
【富于】full of; rich in:他哥哥是一个~正义感的人。*His elder brother is a man with a strong sense of justice.*
【富裕】① prosperous; well-to-do; well-off:共同~ *common prosperity* ② enrich; make rich; make prosperous
【富余】have more than needed; have enough and to spare:他把~的钱都交给了妻子。*He gave the spare money to his wife.*
【富源】natural resources
【富足】affluent; abundant; rich; plentiful:她和妈妈过得很~。*She and her mother lead an affluent life.*
腹 ① belly; abdomen; stomach: 小~ *underbelly*; *lower abdomen* ② feelings; heart; innermost ③ empty and protruding part in the middle of a vessel or a vase
【腹背受敌】be attacked front and rear
【腹地】hinterland
【腹稿】draft worked out in one's mind; mental notes:打~ *make mental notes*; *work out a draft in one's mind*
【腹肌】【生理】abdominal muscle
【腹疾】diarrhoea

【腹膜】【生理】peritoneum
【腹腔】【生理】abdominal cavity: ~镜 *peritoneoscope*
【腹水】【医】ascites
【腹痛】abdominal pain
【腹泻】diarrhoea
【腹胀】abdominal distension
【腹足】【动】abdominal foot or leg: ~类 *gastropod*

缚 bind fast; tie up

覆 ① cover; envelop: 床上~盖着一层被子。*The bed is covered with a quilt.* ②［书］overturn; capsize; upset: 翻来~去 *toss and turn*
【覆被】cover; overspread; screen
【覆盖】① cover: 绿草~着地面。*The earth is covered with grass.* ② plant cover; vegetation
【覆灭】destruction; ruin; collapse
【覆没】①［书］(of ship) capsize and sink ② be destroyed; be overwhelmed
【覆水难收】spilt water can't be gathered up — what is done can't be undone
【覆土】cover up with soil
【覆亡】fall; downfall; collapse
【覆辙】track of an overturned cart: 重蹈~ *take the track of the overturned cart; repeat the same mistakes*

馥 ［书］fragrance
【馥馥】［书］strongly scented; richly fragrant
【馥郁】［书］sweet-scented; sweet-smelling; strong fragrance; heavy perfume: 在这里你可以闻到~的花香。*You can smell the sweet scent of flowers.*

F

G

gā

夹
see also jiā; jiá
【夹肢窝】armpit

旮
【旮旯儿】［方］① nook; corner:墙～ *corner of a wall*; *corner* ② out-of-the-way place:背～ *inaccessible recess* /山～ *a mountain recess*

伽
see also jiā
【伽利略】galileo Galilei (1564-1642), Italian astronomer, mathematician and physicist: ～望远镜 *Galilean telescope*
【伽马射线】【物】gamma ray

咖
see also kā
【咖喱】curry: ～鸡 *curried chicken* / ～牛肉 *beef curry* / ～粉 *curry powder*

嘎 ［象］screech; a loud, high-pitched sound: 公共汽车～的一声刹住了。*The bus screeched to a halt.*
【嘎巴】①［象］crack; snap:手杖～一声断成两截了。*Crack! The stick broke in two.* ②［方］form into a crust; crust:饭粒都～在锅底上了。*The bottom of the pot is all covered with rice crust.* ③ crust:粥～儿 *porridge crust*
【嘎嘎】［象］sound made by ducks or wild geese; quacking sound made by a duck; honk; quack
【嘎吱】［象］creak; the creaking sound of objects that are under great stress:三轮车在山路上～～地走着。*The tricycle was creaking along the road.*

gá

钆 【化】gadolinium(Gd)

gāi

该[1] ① ought to; should:我们本～买把新锁安在前门上。*We should have bought a new lock for the front door.* /你这么大了,～懂事一些。*At your age you ought to know better.* ② be sb's turn, duty or lot; fall to sb:下次～着经理值班。*The manager will be on duty next time.* ③ deserve; merit; serve sb right:活～！谁叫他不守纪律。*It serves him right; he shouldn't have broken the rules.* ④ probably; most likely; it is expected:再过三天,我就～放假了。*I'm due to have a holiday in three days.*

该[2] ① owe:我～你多少钱? *How much do I owe you?* /这钱是～你的。*I owe you this money.*

该[3] ① used in exclamatory sentences for emphasis:等到下雪的时候,风景～多美! *How beautiful scenery will be when it is snowing.* ②［书］this; that; said; above mentioned: ～厂 *this factory* / ～校 *the above-mentioned school* / ～项工作 *the job*
【该当】① ought to; should: ～这样。*That's as it should be.* ② deserve:你们～何罪? *What punishment do you think you deserve?*
【该死】［口］used to show one's resentment or anger: ～的暴雨! *What wretched storm!*
【该账】be in debt; owe

赅 complete; full; comprehensive:言简意～ *brief but sufficient; concise; succinct*

gǎi

改 ① change; transform; convert: ～洼地为鱼塘 *transform waterlogged land into fish pond* / 作息时间～了。*The work schedule has changed.* ② alter; revise; polish:把这件夹克～瘦点儿。*Make this jacket a bit tighter.* ③ correct; put right; remedy; mend: ～作业 *correct students' homework or papers* /痛～前非 *sincerely mend one's ways; thoroughly rectify one's errors* ④ (followed by a verb) switch over to:由汽车～乘轮船 *change from a bus to a steamboat*
【改版】【印】① change the layout of a printed sheet ② correcting
【改编】① adapt; revise; rearrange:这小说已～成电影。*The novel has been adapted for film.* ② reorganize; redesignate: ～军队 *reorganize an army*
【改变】change; alter; transform: ～主意 *change one's mind* / ～工作作风 *change the style of work* / ～航线 *alter the course*
【改朝换代】change dynasties; substitute a new re-

G

gime for the old

【改道】① change one's route:我们决定~上海。*We decided to change our route and head Shanghai.* ②(of a river) change its course:历史上,黄河曾多次~。*The Huanghe River has changed its course many times over the centuries.*

【改掉】give up; drop; discard: ~坏习惯 *give up bad habits* / ~官僚主义作风 *shake off one's bureaucratic style of work*

【改订】reformulate; revise; redraft: ~计划 *redraft a plan*

【改动】change; polish; modify:文字上做少许~ *make a few changes in wording* /规定没有任何~。*The rules remain unchanged.*

【改恶从善】change from bad to good; remove the evil and follow the good

【改革】reform: ~不合理的工资结构 *reform an unfair salary structure* /土地~ *land reform* / ~开放 *reform and open* / ~学制 *reform school system* / ~派 *reformers; reformists*

【改观】change the appearance; take on a new look; get a new look:有了新的规章制度,局面就会~。*With the new rules and regulations come into existence, things are sure to improve.* /这一胜利使战争形势大为~。*This victory changed the complexion of the war.*

【改过】mend one's ways; correct one's errors; overcome one's mistakes:勇于~ *be ready to correct one's mistakes; have the courage to correct one's mistakes* / ~自新 *correct one's errors and make a fresh start; mend one's ways*

【改行】change one's profession, occupation or trade:他由农民~经商。*He quitted his job as a farmer and went into a business.*

【改换】change over to; change; replace: ~名称 *rename* / ~地点 *change the place; move away*

【改悔】repent:死不~的罪犯 *die-hard criminal* /毫无~之意 *show not the least sign of repentance; absolutely unrepentant*

【改嫁】(of a woman) remarry:她离婚十年后又~了。*She got remarried ten years after her divorce.*

【改建】reconstruct; rebuild: ~扩建工程 *projects for renovation and expansion* / ~校舍 *reconstruction a school building* / ~医院 *reconstruction a hospital building*

【改进】improve; become better:经~的新型洗衣粉 *a new improved washing-powder* /他的工作在慢慢~。*His work is improving slowly.*

【改口】① correct oneself(in conversation); change one's tone; withdraw or modify one's previous remark:教授发现自己说错了,连忙~。*The professor corrected himself as soon as he realized he'd made a mistake.* ② address a different way

【改良】① improve; ameliorate: ~土壤 *improve the soil* / ~农机具 *improve farm implements* ② reform:改良主义 *reformism* ③【冶】modify: ~合金 *modified alloy*

【改判】【律】change the original sentence; commute; amend a judgement:由死刑~十八年有期徒刑 *commute the death sentence to eighteen years imprisonment*

【改期】reschedule; change the date; postpone; put off:会议~举行。*The meeting has been put off.* /交易会~了。*The date set for the trade fair has changed.*

【改任】change to another post; have a new appointment

【改日】another day; some other day:咱们~再商量吧! *Let's talk it over another day.*

【改善】improve; ameliorate; make better:道路~计划 *a road improvement scheme* /邮局锐意~服务质量。*The post office aims to improve its quality of service.*

【改天换地】change heaven and earth; remake nature; change the world:以~的气概 *in a spirit of changing heaven and earth*

【改头换面】[贬] make only superficial changes; change one's looks and one's face; disguise:这班人~以农民的身份出现。*These people have camouflaged themselves as farmers.*

【改弦更张】refix a bowstring-change policy; make a fresh start; change one's course; turn over a new leaf; mend one's way

【改弦易辙】make a new start; change one's direction; strike out (on) a new path

【改邪归正】forsake heresy and return to the truth; stop doing evil and reform oneself; break away from evil ways and return to a virtuous way

【改写】rewrite; adapt: ~本 *adaptation; adapted version* /这篇文章必须~才行。*This essay will have to be written.*

【改选】reelect; hold a new election: ~班长 *elect a new monitor* /教代会每年~一次。*A new representative assembly of the teachers is elected every year.*

【改元】change the designation of an imperial reign; change the title of a reign

【改造】transform; remake; remold: ~自然 *remake nature* / ~旧企业 *refurbish old plants*

【改正】correct; put right; make right; remove the mistakes from: ~拼写错误 *correct spelling mistakes* / ~液 *correction fluid*

【改装】① change one's costume or dress ② repackage; repack: ~费用 *repackaging charge; reconditioning expense* ③ reequip; refit: ~一辆汽车 *refit a car*

【改锥】screwdriver

【改组】reorganize; restructure; reshuffle: ~内阁 *reshuffle the cabinet* / ~行政机构 *restructure the administration*

G

gài

丐 ［书］① beg ② beggar：乞～ *beggar*

芥 *see also* jiè

【芥菜】【植】leaf mustard

【芥蓝】【植】cabbage mustard

钙 【化】calcium(Ca)

【钙化】【医】calcify：～作用 *calcification*

【钙镁磷肥】calcium magnesium phosphate

【钙片】calcium tablet

【钙缺乏】calcium deficiency

盖[1] ① lid；cover；cap：锅～ *the lid of a cooking pot* /茶壶～ *teapot lid* /瓶～ *cap of a bottle* /膝～ *knee-cap* /引擎～ *bonnet of an engine* ② shell (of a tortoise，crab，etc.)：乌龟～ *shell of a tortoise* ③ canopy ④ cover；place sth over：他把毯子～在膝盖上。*He covered his knee with a blanket.* /箱子没～严。*The box isn't closed properly.* /积雪覆～了大地。*Snow covered the ground.* ⑤ affix (a seal)：～公章 *put the official seal (on sth)* ⑥ overwhelm；surpass；excel：他的跳远成绩～过了所有的选手。*He excelled all the other contestants in the long jump.* ⑦ build；construct；put up(housing)：～新房 *build new houses* / ～礼堂 *build an auditorium* ⑧［方］excellent；terrific；tops：这个小说真叫～。*The novel is tops.* ⑨ (Gài) a surname

盖[2] ① about；around；approximately：与会者～几十人。*About several tens people attended the meeting.* ②［书］*for*；*because*；*in fact*：有所不知，～未学也。*If there are things we don't know，it is because we haven't learnt them.*

【盖板】blind flange；butt plate；spear plate：～接合 *concealed joint* /接头 *strap joint*

【盖菜】【植】leaf mustard

【盖戳】affix a seal；stamp；seal

【盖棺论定】when one's coffin is covered all discussion about him can be settled；final judgement can be passed on a person only when the lid is laid on his coffin

【盖帽儿】① block a shot(in basketball) ②［口］extremely good；fantastic；tops

【盖世】unsurpassed；matchless；unrivalled；unparalleled：～无双 *stand without peer in one's generation*；*be unrivaled in the world* / ～英雄 *the greatest hero in the world*；*peerless hero*；*a matchless hero*

【盖世太保】Gestapo，German secret police under Nazi rule

【盖章】seal；affix one's seal；put a stamp on：在合同上签字～ *affix one's signature and seal to a contract*

【盖盅儿】tea cup with a cover

【盖子】① lid；cover；cap；top：瓶～ *bottle top* /揭～ *lift up the lid*；*uncover* ② shell (of a tortoise，etc.)

溉 ［书］water；irrigate：灌～ *irrigate*

概[1] ① general；main；approximate：大～ *main idea*；*general outline* /梗～ *broad outline*；*gist* ② without exception；absolutely：一～而论 *treat all alike*；*be lumped together* / ～不追究。*No action will be taken (against sb for his past offences).* ③ generally；approximately：～而论之 *generally speaking*

概[2] the manner of carrying oneself；deportment：气～ *mettle*；*spirit* /慷～激昂 *impassioned*；*vehement*

【概况】general situation；brief account；survey：《各省～》*A Brief Survey of the Provinces of China*

【概括】① summarize；sum up；give a brief summary；generalize：～起来说 *to sum up* /现在把你的观点用几句话来～一下。*Now sum up your views in a few words.* ② briefly；generally；in broad outline：～地说 *put it briefly*；*put it in a nutshell*

【概括性】generality；ability to generalize or summarize

【概率】【数】probability：～论 *probability*；*probability theory* / ～分析 *probability analysis* / ～流量 *probability current*

【概略】① summary；outline：这只是小说的～。*This is only an outline of the novel.* ② brief；succinct：～说明 *brief account*

【概略图】skeleton diagram

【概论】(usu. used in books titles) outline；introduction；survey：《物理学～》*An Introduction to Physics* /《美国文学～》*A Survey of America Literature*

【概貌】general picture；overall outline：反映人民生活的～ *give a general picture of the life of the people*

【概莫能外】admit of no exception whatsoever；be without exception

【概念】concept；conception；general notion；idea：基本～ *basic concept*；*fundamental conception* /自由的～ *the concept of freedom* /看来他不大熟悉机会均等这个～。*He seemed unfamiliar with the concept that everyone should have an equal opportunity.*

【概念化】deal in generalities；conceptualize；write or speak in abstract terms：公式化、～的作品 *literary works which tend to formularize and generalize*

【概述】outline；summary；give a brief account

【概数】approximate number；round number

【概算】【经】budgetary estimate

【概要】(usu. used in book titles) essentials；outline：《英语语法～》*Essentials of English Grammar*

G

gān

干 ① dry：～燥的气候 *a dry climate* /清新可口的～白葡萄酒 *a crisp dry white wine* /井都～了。*The wells ran dry.* /我嗓子发～。*My throat feels dry.* ② empty；hollow；dry：～号 *cry aloud but shed no tears；affected wailing* /外强中～ *outwardly strong but inwardly weak* /钱都花～了。*All the money has been spent.* ③ take into nominal kinship：～妈 *nominally adoptive mother；godmother* ④［书］offend：～犯 *offend；encroach upon* ⑤ have to do with；be concerned with；be implicated in：这事与小孩无～。*It has nothing to do with the kid.* /与你何～？*What has this to do with you?* ⑥ dried food：萝卜～儿 *dried radish* /豆腐～ *dried bean curd* /葡萄～ *raisin* ⑦ in vain；to no purpose；for nothing：老师们今天不来，咱们别～等了。*The teachers are not coming today; let's not waste time waiting for them.* ⑧［方］rude；blunt；impolite：你说话别那么～。*Don't be so blunt when you speak.*
see also gàn

【干巴巴】① dried up；wizened；parched：～的土地 *parched land* ② dull and dry；insipid；vapid：文章写得～。*The article is dull.*

【干巴】dried up；shrivelled；wizened

【干杯】drink a toast：为朋友们的健康～！*Here's the health of our friends-to your health!* / ～！*Cheers! Or Bottoms up!*

【干贝】dried scallop（adductor）：～鱼翅 *shark's fin cooked with scallops*

【干瘪】① shriveled；wizened：～的老太婆 *a wizened old woman* /水果～了。*The fruit shriveled up.* ② dull and dry；drab；uninteresting：这部电影内容太～了。*The film is very flat.* ③ dry：树上挂的辣椒都已经给风吹～了。*The peppers hanging on the wall have been dried out by the wind.*

【干冰】【化】dry ice

【干菜】dried vegetable

【干草】hay：晒～ *make hay* /～垛 *haystack*

【干柴烈火】① like a blazing fire and dry wood；like a dry faggot on a blazing fire ②（of a man and a woman）caught in a burning passion

【干醋】jealously about something that is none of one's business；vicarious jealously；uncalled — for jealously：吃～ *experience vicarious jealously*

【干脆】① clear-cut；straightforward；not mince one's words；frank：～一点嘛！*Make it snappy!* /新领导为人爽快，办事～。*The new leader is straightforward and acts with decision.* ② simply；just；altogether：孩子们～一言不发。*The children simply refused to talk.*

【干打雷，不下雨】all thunder but no rain；much noise but no action；much cry but little wool

【干瞪眼】［口］watch anxiously but be unable to help；stand by helplessly；look on in despair

【干电池】dry cell：～组 *dry battery*

【干爹】（nominally）adoptive father；godfather

【干儿子】（nominally）adoptive son；godson

【干饭】cooked rice

【干纺】dry spinning：～纱 *dry-spun yarn*

【干戈】weapons of war；arms；war：动～ *take up arms；go to war* / ～四起 *civil war breaks out in the country；fighting broke out all over the country.*

【干果】① dry fruit；nuts ② dried fruit

【干旱】dry；arid：～地区 *arid area* / 战胜～ *conquer drought*

【干涸】dry up；run up：河道～。*The river dried up.*

【干货】dried food and nuts（as merchandise）；dry cargo：～船 *dry cargo ship*

【干季】dry season

【干结】dry and hard

【干净】① clean；clean and fresh；neat and tidy：把院子打扫～ *sweep the yard clean* ② completely；totally；entirely：经理把这事忘了个～。*The manager entirely forgot about this.*

【干净利落】smooth and clean；very efficient；neatly and smoothly done

【干咳】dry cough

【干枯】dried-up；withered；shriveled；wizened：～的树木 *withered trees* / ～的皮肤 *wizened skin* /村里的井～了。*The well in the village dried up.*

【干酪】cheese

【干酪素】casein

【干冷】dry and cold：天气～。*The weather is dry and cold.*

【干粮】solid food for a journey；field rations；rations for a journey：～袋 *haversack；ration bag*

【干裂】①（of parched earth，skin，lips，etc.）crack；chap；be dry and cracked：嘴唇～ *parched lips* ② season check and weather-shack

【干馏】【化】dry distillation

【干妈】（nominally）adoptive mother；godmother

【干女儿】（nominally）adopted daughter

【干呕】【医】retch

【干亲】nominal kinship：认～ *enter into an adoptive relationship*

【干扰】① disturb；break（the rest，calm，concentration of sb）；interfere；distract：～某人的工作 *interfere with sb's work* ②【物】interference；jam：～台 *jamming station* / ～波 *interference wave* / ～场 *interference field* / ～区 *range or zone interference* / ～素 *interferon*

【干涉】① interfere；intervene；meddle：～别家私事 *meddle in other family's private affairs* /武装～ *armed intervention* /互不～内政 *noninterference in each other's internal affairs* ② be related；be connected；have anything to do with：他们了无～。*There is no relation whatsoever between among them.* ③【物】interference：相互～ *constructive interference* / ～仪 *interferometer*

【干湿表】【气】psychrometer

【干瘦】skinny and wizened；bony；emaciated：～

G

的男人 *a bony man*

【干洗】dry-clean; dry cleaning: ~店 *dry-cleaner's (shop)*

【干系】responsibility; implication:汤姆同这桩案子有~。*Tom is implicated in the case.*

【干鲜水果】composite term for dried and fresh fruit

【干笑】hollow laugh; forcing smile:他~了一声。*He forced smile.*

【干薪】① salary drawn for a sinecure:领~ *hold a sinecure* ② *net salary*

【干预】interfere; intervene; interpose; meddle:这是她家内部的事情,我们不便~。*This is her family's internal affair; it is not for us to interfere.*

【干燥】① dry; arid:气候~ *arid climate* /口腔~ *xerostomia* ② dull; uninteresting; dryasdust: ~无味 *dry as dust; dull as ditchwater* ③ seasoning (of a timber): ~裂纹 *seasoning crack*

【干燥剂】drier; drying agent; desiccating agent

【干燥器】desiccator; water extractor

【干着急】be anxious but unable to do anything; be helplessly worried; stand by helplessly

甘

① sweet; honeyed; pleasant:同~共苦 *share weal and woe* / ~泉 *sweet spring water* ② willingly; readily; of one's free will:不~落后 *unwilling to lag behind* /心~情愿 *of one's own accord; willingly* / ~守清贫 *be ready to lead a poor but honest life*

【甘拜下风】show the white feather; confess oneself vanquished; willingly admit defeat; bow to sb's superiority

【甘草】【药】licorice root

【甘居中游】be content with the second best; resign oneself to a state of mediocrity; be content with the middling state

【甘苦】① sweetness and bitterness; joys and sorrows; weal and woe:同~,共患难 *share weal and woe; go through thick and thin together* ② hardships and difficulties experienced in work: ~自知。*One knows best what one has gone through.*

【甘蓝】【植】wild cabbage

【甘霖】good rain after a long drought; timely rain; seasonable rain:全国~普降。*A timely rain fell all over the country.*

【甘露】① sweet dew ②【医】manna

【甘美】sweet and refreshing:泉水~。*The spring water is sweet and refreshing.*

【甘薯】sweet potato: ~软腐病 *sweet potato soft rot* / ~黑斑病 *sweet potato black rot*

【甘甜】sweet; honeyed; joyful: ~可口 *sweet and delicious*

【甘心】① do sth willingly; be glad to do sth; be ready: ~情愿 *willingly and gladly* ② be reconciled to; resign oneself to; be content with:反动派决不~自己的失败。*The reactionaries will never take their defeat lying down.*

【甘休】willingly give up; take it lying down; be willing to stop:我们不达目的,不会~。*We will never give up until our purpose is achieved.*

【甘油】【化】glycerine: ~炸药 *dynamite*

【甘于】be willing to; be glad to; be happy to

【甘愿】willingly; readily; gladly: ~效劳 *be glad to offer one's services* / ~冒风险 *be willing to take the risk*

【甘蔗】sugarcane: ~渣 *bagasse* / ~压榨机 *cane crusher; cane press* / ~板 *cane fiber board*

【甘之如饴】enjoy sth bitter as if it were malt sugar; gladly endure hardships; be quite content even in adversity

杆

pole; staff:旗~ *flagstaff; flagpole* /标~ *surveyor's pole* /桅~ *mast*

see also gǎn

【杆子】pole; staff:电线~ *wire pole; telephone pole*

肝

liver

【肝癌】【医】cancer of the liver

【肝肠寸断】liver and intestines are cut into inches; be deep affliction; be heartbroken

【肝胆】① liver and gall: ~俱裂 *feel as if one's liver and gall both seemed torn from within; be heartbroken; be overwhelmed by grief or terror* ② true heart; open-heartedness; sincerity ③ heroic spirit; courage: ~过人 *be unsurpassed in valour*

【肝胆相照】open one's heart to sb; be in perfect sympathy with each other; show utter devotion to sb; treat each other with an open heart

【肝功能】liver function: ~试验 *liver function test* / ~正常。*The liver is functioning normally.*

【肝火】irascibility; spleen: ~旺 *hot-tempered; irascible* /动~ *get worked up; fly into a rage*

【肝脑涂地】be ready to die the cruelest death for principles; be willing to repay a favour with extreme sacrifice

【肝气】①【中医】diseases with such symptoms as costal pain, vomiting, diarrhea, etc. ② irritability

【肝素】heparin

【肝吸虫】【动】liver fluke

【肝炎】【医】hepatitis

【肝脏】liver

【肝蛭】liver fluke

【肝肿大】【医】hepatomegaly

坩

【坩埚】【化】crucible:石墨~ *graphite crucible* / ~炉 *crucible furnace*

【坩埚钢】pot steel

泔

【泔水】swill; slops; hogwash; pigwash; wash

柑

mandarin orange

【柑橘】oranges and tangerines; citrus: ~酱 *marmalade*

【柑子】mandarin orange

G

竿 pole; staff; rod: 钓鱼～ *fishing rod* /竹～ *bamboo rod* /爬～ *climbing pole; pole-climbing*
【竿子】bamboo or wooden pole
尴
【尴尬】① be awkward; be hard to deal with; be in a dilemma; be cornered: 处境～ *in an awkward position; in a dilemma* ②［方］uneasy; embarrassed: 他看起来十分～。*He looks very much embarrassed.*

gǎn

杆 ① shaft or arm of sth; rod; bar: 电线～ *wire pole; telephone pole* /秤～ *arm of a steel-yard* /箭～ *arrow shaft* /钢笔～ *pen-holder* /保险～ *bumper bar* /杠～ *lever* ②［量］used for implements with a shaft: 一～秤 *a steelyard* /一～枪 *a rifle* /一～红旗 *a red flag*
see also gān
【杆秤】steelyard
【杆菌】［生］bacillus: 结核～ *tubercle bacillus*
秆 stalk; stem: 高粱～ *sorghum stalk* /麦～ *wheat stalk*
【秆子】stalk
赶 ① catch up; chase; run after; overtake: 追～世界先进水平 *measure up to advanced world level* /你追我～ *emulate one another; each trying to outstrip the other* /～先进 *catch up with the advanced* /追～ *run after; chase after* ② try to catch; rush for; hurry; dash for: ～末班车 *try to catch the last bus* ③ hurry through; rush through; dash off: ～任务 *rush through one's job* ④ drive: ～大车 *drive a cart* ⑤ drive away; drive off; expel: 把敌人～出中国 *drive the enemy out of China* /～下台 *drive sb off the stage* ⑥ happen to; run into; encounter; avail oneself of: ～上一场雪 *run into a snow* ⑦ go to a place: ～集 *go to a local market* ⑧ till; by; until: ～黑我就走。*I'll be leaving at dusk.*
【赶不及】there is not enough time to do sth; be too late for sth: 公共汽车 8:00 开，再不动身就～了。*The bus sails at 8:00; I'm afraid we won't be able to make it if we do not start off right now.*
【赶不上】① be unable to catch up with; lag behind: 孩子们已经走远了，～了。*The children are pretty far away by now and we won't be able to catch up with them.* ② there is not enough time to do sth; be too late for sth ③ fail to have; miss: 好事我总～。*Opportunity never knocks at my door.*
【赶场】①［方］go to a local market or village fair ② (of a performer) rush from one performance to another performance in other place
【赶超】catch up and overtake; catch up with and surpass: 在科学上～世界先进水平 *catch up with and surpass the advanced world level in the field of science*
【赶得及】there is still time; be able to do sth; can still to make it
【赶得上】① can catch up; be able to keep up with: 同学们先走，我～你们。*Classmates go first; I'll be able to catch up with you.* ② have time to do sth; be able to do sth; be able to make it; be in time for ③ be able to meet with; have: ～好天气，我们就去公园吧。*If the weather is fine, we'll go to the park.*
【赶集】go to a local market; go to a country fair
【赶紧】lose no time; hasten; be quick; hurry: ～解释 *hasten to explain* /～刹车 *quickly put on the brakes* /～回家 *hurry home*
【赶尽杀绝】drive away and exterminate everyone; spare no one; kill all; wipe out the whole lot
【赶考】go and take the imperial examination: 进京～ *go to the capital to sit for the imperial examinations*
【赶快】at once; quickly; hurriedly: ～回家 *go home at once* /～跟我走。*Come along with me at once.*
【赶路】push on with one's journey; rush; hurry
【赶忙】hurry; hasten; rush: 他～道歉。*He hastened to apologize.* /听到儿子的脚步声，母亲～去开门。*The mother hurried to open the door when he heard the footsteps of her son.*
【赶前不赶后】be better to hurry at the beginning than to rush at the last moment; rather be early than too late
【赶巧】happen to; it so happens that; as luck would have it; do sth by chance: 我～在一家旧书店里买到这本书。*I got this book by chance at a second-hand bookstore.*
【赶上】① overtake; catch up with; keep up with; keep pace with: ～末班车 *catch the last bus* /～时代的步伐 *keep abreast of the times* ② run into; happen to; encounter; be in time for: 没～公共汽车 *miss the bus* /～午饭 *be in time for lunch* ③ have time do sth; be able to make it: 恐怖分子还没～还手，就被消灭了。*The terrorists were shot down before they had time to fight back.* ④ force; drive; compel: 把猪～卡车。*Drive the pigs on a truck.*
【赶时髦】follow the fashion; try to be in the swim; try to be in the trend
【赶鸭子上架】drive a duck onto a perch; make sb do sth entirely beyond his capacity
【赶走】drive out; drive away: ～侵略者 *drive out the invaders* /～羊群 *drive away the flock of sheep*
敢 ① brave; courageous; bold; having no fear: 勇～些！*Be brave!* ② dare; brave; have sufficient courage to do sth; endure or face without showing fear: ～于面对批评 *brave one's critics* /我再也不～回去看一眼了。*I 've never dared go back to look.* /我不～要求他加薪。*I daren't ask him for a rise.* ③ be sure; be certain; have the confi-

dence to：我不～说老板究竟什么时候来。*I am not sure just when the boss will come.* ④［书］make bold；venture；take the liberty：～问 *I venture to ask*；*may I ask*

敢[2]［方］can it be that

【敢怒而不敢言】feel indignant but not dare to speak out；choke with silent fury；hold back one's anger and not dare to speak out；suppress one's rage

【敢说敢为】dare to speak and act；have the courage to expressing one's opinion

【敢死队】dare-to-die corps；suicide squad

【敢想敢干】have the courage to think and act

【敢于】dare to；be bold in；have the courage to；be brave：～承担责任 *dare to shoulder a responsibility* /～面对现实 *have the courage to face the reality*

【敢在太岁头上动土】dare to leap on an earth god's head to make trouble；provoke sb far superior in power

【敢作敢当】be bold enough to do sth and accept responsibility for it；have the courage to accept the consequence of one's doing

【敢作敢为】dare to do everything；be decisive and bold in action；be afraid of no difficulties

感 ① feel；sense；have the sensation of；be aware of：他～到自己错了。*He sensed that he himself was wrong.* /她～到冷。*She felt cold.* ② move；touch；affect：～人 *touching*；*moving* /深有所～ *be deeply touched* ③ be thankful；be grateful；be obliged：～激不尽 *be extremely thankful* ④【中医】be affected；catch (cold)：外～风寒 *catch a cold* ⑤ sense；feeling；impression：快～ *pleasant sensation*；*delight* /优越～ *sense of superiority*；*superiority complex* /民族自豪～ *a sense of national pride* /幽默～ *sense of humor* /反～ *disgust*；*aversion* /好～ *good opinion*；*liking* /随～ *informal essay*；*jottings* /读后～ *impressions of a book or an article* /新鲜～ *a feeling of freshness* ⑥【摄】sensitize

【感触】thoughts and feelings；feeling；sensation：深有～地说 *say with deep feeling*

【感到】feel；sense；be aware of：～冷 *feel cold* /～悲哀 *feel sad* /她虽然什么也没说，但我已～她不喜欢这个主意。*Although she didn't say anything, I sensed that she didn't like the idea.*

【感动】move；touch；affect：～的流下眼泪 *be moved to tears* /深为某人的精神所～ *be deeply touched by one's spirit* /格兰特的演讲～了所有的听众。*Grant's lecture struck a deep chord in the entire audience.*

【感恩】feel grateful；be thankful；be obliged：～不尽 *be everlastingly grateful* /～图报 *be grateful to sb and seek ways to return his kindness*

【感恩戴德】feel deeply grateful；bear a debt of gratitude for past kindness；be thankful for sb's goodness

【感恩节】Thanksgiving Day

【感奋】be moved and inspired；be enthused；be fired with enthusiasm：演讲令人～。*The speech fired everyone with great enthusiasm.*

【感官】sense organ；sensory organ：～的印象 *sense perception*

【感光】【摄】sensitize：～度(*light*) *sensitivity* /～纸 *sensitive paper* /～性 *photo nasty*；*photoelectric sensitivity* /～计 *sensitometer* /～树脂版 *photopolymer plate*

【感化】reform a misguided person through persuasion, etc.；help sb to change (by education and persuasion)：～教育 *reformatory education* /～院 *reformatory*

【感怀】① recall with emotion；bring back to mind with emotion：～往事 *recall past events with deep feeling* ② reflections；thoughts；recollections：新春～ *thoughts on the Spring Festival*

【感激】feel thankful；be grateful；be obliged；feel indebted：不胜～ *be deeply grateful* /～不尽 *feel indebted forever* /～涕零 *shed grateful tears* /～之至 *be extremely grateful* /很～你给我的帮助。*I'm very grateful for your help.*

【感觉】① feeling；sensation；sense perception；impression：温暖的～ *sensation of warmth* /这只是我个人的～。*That's only my own feeling.* ② sense；feel；become aware of；perceive：～到某人的忧愁 *sense sb's sorrow* /～论 *sensualism* /～神经 *sensory nerve* /～过程 *sense process* /～特性 *sense quality* /～区 *sensory area* /～中枢 *sensorium* /你～怎么样？*How do you feel now?*

【感慨】sigh with emotion：～万千 *be full of myriad emotions* /～流涕 *be moved to tears* /～万端 *all sorts of feelings well up in one's mind* /～系之 *sigh with deep emotion* /提起过去那段经历，他～万千。*When he spoke of those hard times, he sighed a great sorrow.*

【感抗】【电】inductive reactance；positive reactance

【感冒】① cold；flu：流行性～ *flu*(*influenza*) /患～ *catch a cold*；*have a cold* ② catch cold；have a touch of flu：小心别～。*Take care not to catch cold.* ③ be interested in；enthusiastic about：他对物理不～。*He is not interested in physics.*

【感念】remember with gratitude；recall with deep emotion：～不忘 *always recall sb with deep emotion* /我将永远～母亲的好处。*I shall always remember my mother's kindness to me.*

【感情】① feeling；emotion；sentiment：动～ *be carried away by one's emotions* /伤～ *hurt sb's feelings* /～流露 *betray one's emotion* ② affection；attachment；love：他对姐姐的～很深。*He has a deep love for his older sister.*

【感情冲动】emotional impulse；act on a momentary impulse；be carried away by one's emotions

【感情洋溢】an exuberance of feeling；overflowing with emotion

【感情用事】give oneself over to blind emotions；

G

give way to one's feelings; abandon oneself to emotion; act according to one' sentiment:要冷静,不要~。*Keep a cool head; Don't act impetuously.*

【感染】① infect; taint:细菌~ *bacterial infection* /防止再~ *avoid reinfection* /手术后~ *postoperative infection* /因~伤口发炎。*The wound was inflamed by infection.* ② inspire; infect; affect; influence:艺术~力 *artistic appeal* /他的乐观情绪~了周围的人。*He infected everyone with his optimism.*

【感人肺腑】touch one deeply in the heart; touch the chords of one's heart; touch one to the heart; touch one to the depth of one's soul

【感伤】sad; sentimental; sorrowful; maudlin:令人~的音乐 *sentimental music* /一部~的爱情小说 *a sentimental love story* /~自己不幸的身世 *feel sad about one's bad lot*

【感受】① be affected by; catch: ~风寒 *be affected by the cold; catch a chill* ② feel; experience; be impressed:父母去世以后,他~到了生活的艰辛。*He experienced the hardships of life after his parents' death.*

【感叹】sigh with feeling: ~词 *interjection; exclamation* / ~号 *exclamation mark; exclamation point* / ~句 *exclamation sentence* /她发出了无可奈何的~。*She sighed helplessly.*

【感物伤怀】be deeply affected at seeing sth; touched to one's soul

【感悟】come to realize; become aware (of sth)

【感想】thoughts; reflections; impressions; feelings:你对此事有何~? *What are your feelings about this matter?* /请你谈谈看了这部影片后的~。*Please tell us your impressions of the film.*

【感谢】thank; be grateful; be thankful:表示衷心的~ *express heartfelt thanks* / ~信 *letter of thanks* /真是太~你了。*Thank you very much indeed.* /我们~他们鼎力相助。*We thanked them for all their help.*

【感性】perception; perceptiveness:认识的~阶段 *the perceptual stage of cognition* / ~认识 *perceptual knowledge* / ~运动 *nastic move* / ~知觉 *sense impressions*

【感应】① response; reaction; interaction ②【生理】irritability ③【电】induction:电磁~ *electromagnetic induction* /静电~ *electrostatic induction* / ~干扰 *inductive interference* / ~式话筒 *inductor microphone* / ~场 *induction field* / ~电动机 *induction motor* / ~电压调节器 *induction-voltage regulator* / ~率 *inductivity* / ~线圈 *induction coil; inductor* / ~计 *induction meter* / ~热 *induction heat*

【感召】move and inspire; impel; influence:在党的政策的~下 *under the influence of the Party's policy*

【感知】①【哲】perception ② feel; sense; become aware of:他对自己问题的严重性有所~。*He seems to be aware of his serious problem.*

橄

【橄榄】【植】① Chinese olive (Canarium album); the fruit of the canary tree ② (oil) olive: ~绿 *olive green* / ~油 *olive oil* / ~枝 *olive branch-a symbol of peace* / ~石 *olivine*

【橄榄球】【体】rugby; American football

擀 roll (dough, etc.): ~饺子皮 *roll out dumpling wrappers* / ~面条 *make noodles*

【擀面杖】rolling pin

gàn

干 ① do; work: ~得很好! *Well done!* /巧~ *work skillfully; do sth in a clever way* /埋头苦~ *immerse oneself in hard work* /肯~ *ready to work; willing to do sth* /咱们开始~吧! *Let's get started!* ② trunk; stem; main part; mainstay:树~ *tree-trunk; trunk* /骨~ *backbone; hardcore* ③ cadre: ~群关系 *relations between cadres and the masses* ④ competent; capable; able: ~将 *capable person* / ~员 *a capable official* /这位经理精明强~。*The manager is a man of great ability.* ⑤ fight; strike: ~到底 *fight to the bitter end* ⑥ work as; go in for; hold the post of; assume the office of:他~过会计。*He was once an accountant.*

see also gān

【干部】cadre; public functionary or servant:各级领导~ *leading cadres at all levels* / ~政策 *policy to the cadres* / ~带头 *cadres stand in the van to* /大学里有许多学生~可供挑选。*The university has a large selection of student cadres.*

【干才】① capability; ability; competence:这个人颇有点~。*He is a man of considerable ability.* ② capable or able person

【干掉】[口] kill; get rid of; put out of the way; bump off:他给黑社会的歹徒~了。*He was killed off by an underworld thug.*

【干活】work; do a job; work on a job:他们到工厂~了。*They all went to work in the factory.* / ~去吧。*Let's go to work.*

【干架】① quarrel squabble:那两口老~。*The couple often quarrels.* ② come to blows; fight

【干将】capable or able person; go-getter

【干劲】drive; vim; vigor:鼓~ *rouse one's enthusiasm* /冲天~ *boundless energy*

【干警】police officers; constables; cadres and police

【干练】capable and experienced; capable; able:他的确是精明~的人才。*He is really capable and bright man.*

【干流】trunk stream; mainstream; master stream

【干吗】[口] ① why on earth; whatever for; why: ~这么认真? *Why take it so seriously?* ② what to do:你想~? *What are you up to?*

【干渠】【水】trunk canal; main canal
【干事】secretary or clerical worker in charge of sth: 宣传~ *person in charge of publicity work*
【干线】main line; trunk line; main; artery: 公路~ *main highway* / 交通~ *main lines of communication (or transportation)*
【干休所】cadres' sanatorium; sanatorium for retired cadres

gāng

冈 ridge (of a hill): 山~ *low hill; hillock*
【冈比亚】the Gambia: ~人 *Gambian*
【冈比亚河】Gambia River
扛 ① lift with both hands: 力能~鼎 *powerful enough to lift a ding* ②[方] (of two or more people) carry together
see also káng
刚 ① firm; strong; hard; indomitable: ~柔 *hard and soft; firm and flexible* / 以柔克~ *overcome hardness by softness* / 他的性情太~。*He has a very strong character.* ② just; exactly; precisely: 不大不小,~合适 *neither too big nor too small, just fit* / 这件背心我穿上~好。*This vest fits me perfectly.* ③ barely; only; just; no more than: 这块棉布~够做一件衬衣。*This piece of cotton is just enough for a shirt.* ④ just; only a short while ago: 会议~开始。*The meeting has just begun.* / 他~走。*He just left.*
【刚愎自用】be set in one's way; be perverse in temper; self willed and conceited; headstrong
【刚才】just; a moment ago; just now; a short time ago: 她比~好一点了。*She is a little better than she was a moment ago.* / 他~还在这儿呢。*He was around a short time ago.*
【刚刚】① just; exactly; only; barely: 他考试~及格。*He barely passed the examination.* ② a short time ago; just now: 报纸~到。*The newspaper came just now.* / 不要打扰他,他~躺下。*Don't disturb him; he went to bed only a moment ago.*
【刚果】the Congo: ~河 *the Congo (River)* / ~人 *Congolese* / ~语 *Congolese (language)* / ~红 *Congo red*
【刚好】① just; exactly; precisely: 人数~够。*There is just enough people.* / 你们来得~。*You've come in the nick of time.* ② happen to; it so happens that; as luck would have it: ~总经理在这儿,你就跟他谈谈吧。*The general manager happens to be here; you'd better talked over with him.*
【刚架】【建】rigid frame; stiff frame: ~结构 *rigid-framed structure*
【刚健】vigorous; energetic; forceful; robust: 迈着~的步伐前进 *march forward with firm and vigorous steps*
【刚劲】bold; vigorous; sturdy: 笔力~ *write in a bold hand*
【刚劲有力】powerful and vigorous; vigorous and forcible
【刚…就…】as soon as; no sooner than: 刚过立春,天气就异乎寻常地热。*It got unusually hot just after the beginning of spring.*
【刚烈】fiery and forthright; upright and unyielding; strong character and moral integrity: ~女子 *woman of strong character and integrity*
【刚强】firm; staunch; unyielding; steadfast: 意志~ *strong-willed; iron-willed* / 性格~ *be of firm character* / ~铁汉 *a man of steel*
【刚柔相济】exercise a combination of inflexibility and yielding; temper force with mercy; couple hardness and softness
【刚体】【物】rigid body
【刚性】【物】rigidity: ~结构 *rigid structure* / ~支架 *rigid support*
【刚毅】resolute and steadfast: ~果断 *resolute and decisive*
【刚硬】① firm; unbending; unyielding: 性格~ *strong character* ② strong; tough: ~的口气 *uncompromising tone* ③ hard; solid: ~的工具 *hard tools*
【刚正】staunch and upright; honorable; principled
【刚正不阿】upright and never stooping to flattery; standing on principles and not yielding to pressure
【刚直】upright and outspoken; frank and straightforward
肛 anus: 脱~ *prolapse of the anus (or rectum)*
【肛裂】【医】anal fissure
【肛瘘】【医】anal fistula
【肛门】【生理】anus
纲 ① outline of fishing net: 网~ *warp; heap rope (of a fishing net)* ② key link; outline; guiding principle: 大~ *outline* / 政~ *political principle* / 总~ *general outline* / 规划~要 *the outline of a plan* ③【生】class: 亚~ *subclass*
【纲纪】[书] law and order; discipline: ~国法 *discipline, morale; law and order* / 整顿~ *restore order and strength discipline*
【纲举目张】once the outline of a fishing net is pulled out, all its meshes open; once the key link is grasp, everything falls into place; when the general plan is laid out, the details are easy to arrange
【纲领】programme; guiding principle; guidelines: 最高~ *maximum programme (of a government, political party, etc.)* / ~性文件 *programmatic document*
【纲目】(usu. used in book titles) detailed outline (of a subject); outline; compendium
【纲要】① outline; sketch; general thoughts: 先写~,再写全文。*Make an outline before you write the article.* ② (usu. used in book titles) essentials; compendium: 《英语语法~》*Essentials of English Grammar*

钢 steel: ～铁长城 *great wall of steel* / ～刀 *steel knives* / 炼～工业 *industry that produces steel* / 废弃的炼～厂 *deserted steel mills* / 槽～ *channel steel* / 扁～ *flat steel* / 不锈～ *stainless steel* / 超高强度～ *super-high strength steel* / 工具～ *tool steel* / 弹簧～ *spring steel* / 低碳～ *low carbon steel* / 铸～ *cast steel* / 轧～ *steel rolling* / 冷轧～ *cold-rolled steel* / 优质 *high quality steel* / 硅～ *silicon steel* / 软～ *soft steel*; *mild steel* / ～是铁炼成的。*Steel is made from iron.*

【钢板】① steel plate; plate: 薄～ *steel sheet*; *sheet steel* / 厚～ *steel plate* / 成型～ *shaped steel plate* / 锅炉～ *boiler plate* / 网眼～ *perforated plate* / 造船～ *ship plate* ② spring (of a motorcar, etc.) ③ stencil steel board

【钢笔】pen; fountain pen: ～尖 *pen nib* / ～水 *ink* / ～画 *pen drawing*

【钢材】steel products; steels; rolled steel

【钢尺】steel rule

【钢带】steel band; steel belt; steel strip

【钢锭】steel ingot

【钢构件】steel member; steel part

【钢鼓】steel drum

【钢箍】steel hoop

【钢骨水泥】reinforced concrete

【钢管】steel tube; steel pipe: 焊接～ *welded steel pipe* / 无缝～ *seamless steel tube* / 异形～ *chapped pipe*

【钢轨】rail (for trains, etc.); tracks: ～探伤仪 *rail flaw detector* / ～连接板 *joint fastening*

【钢号】【冶】steel grade

【钢花】spray or sparks of molten steel: ～飞舞 *sparks of molten steel flying*

【钢筋】steel bar

【钢筋混凝土】reinforced concrete

【钢筋铁胆】have an iron resolve and steel sinews

【钢筋铁骨】a body strong as iron; muscles of iron; muscles of steel

【钢锯】hacksaw: ～架 *hacksaw frame* / ～条 *hacksaw blade*

【钢盔】(steel) helmet

【钢坯】【冶】billet; steel feed; steel billet: 大～ *bloom*

【钢片琴】【音】celesta

【钢钎】drill rod; drill steel

【钢琴】piano: 大～ *grand piano* / ～家 *pianist* / 弹～ *play the piano*

【钢水】【冶】molten steel: ～包 *steel ladle*

【钢丝】(steel) wire: ～垫子 *spring mattress* / ～床 *spring bed* / ～钳 *combination pliers*; *cutting pliers* / 走～ *walk the wire*; *walk a tightrope* / ～绳 *steel cable*; *wire rope*; *wire cable* / ～网 *steel wire gauze*

【钢索】cable wire; steel rope; wire rope

【钢铁】① iron and steel; steel: ～厂 *steelworks* / ～公司 *iron and steel company* / ～工业 *iron and steel industry* ② strong; firm; staunch: ～意志 *iron will* / ～汉子 *man of steel*; *strong guy*

【钢印】① steel seal; embossing seal ② embossed stamp: 上面盖了公司的～ *bear the embossed stamp of the firm*

【钢珠】steel ball (in the ball bearing); ball bearing; ball

缸 ① vat; jar; bowl; crock: 水～ *water vat* / 酒～ *wine jar* / 金鱼～ *goldfish bowl* / 一口大～ *a big vat* ② compound of sand, clay, etc. for making earthenware ③ a jar-shaped or vat-shaped vessel: 汽～ *cylinder* / 烟灰～ *ashtray*

【缸管】earthen pipe

【缸盆】glazed earthen basin

【缸瓦】compound of sand, clay, etc. for making earthenware

【缸砖】clinker (tile); quarry tile

【缸子】mug; bowl: 茶～(*tea*) *mug* / 搪瓷～ *enamel mug*

gǎng

岗 ① hillock; mound: ～地 *farm land on low hills* / ～台 *sentry stand*; *police stand* / 山～ *low hill*; *hillock* / 乱坟～ *unmarked common graves* / ～峦起伏 *undulating hills* ② sentry; guard; post: 布～ *post sentries* / 站～ *stand sentry*; *keep guard* / 下～ *come off sentry duty*; (*of workers*) *be made redundant*; *be laid off* / 交通～ *traffic police post* ③ ridge; welt; wale

【岗警】policeman on point duty

【岗楼】watchtower

【岗哨】① lookout post; sentry post ② sentry; sentinel: 设置～ *post sentries* / 流动～ *soldier on patrol duties*; *patrol*

【岗亭】sentry box; police box

【岗位】post; job; station: 坚守～ *stand fast at one's post*; *stick to one's guns* / ～津贴 *job subsidy* / ～培训 *on-the-job training* / 离开～ *quit a post* / 走上新的～ *take up a new post*; *take on a new job*

【岗位责任制】system of post responsibility (for the work done by each individual at his post)

【岗子】① hillock; mound: 土～ *earth hillock* ② ridge; wale; welt: 他背上肿起一道～。*There is a welt on his back.*

港 ① port; harbor: 良～ *a good harbour* / 天然～ *natural harbor* / 海～ *seaport*; *harbor* / 军～ *naval port* / 鱼～ *fishing port* / 自由～ *free port* / 出发～ *port of departure* / 停靠～ *port of call* / 目的～ *port of destination* / 深水～ *deep-water port* ② airport: 飞机离～。*The plane has taken off.* ③ short for Hong Kong; HK

【港澳同胞】compatriots in Hong Kong and Macao

【港币】Hong Kong dollar; Hong Kong currency

【港督】(before 1 July, 1997) governor of Hong Kong

【港府】(before 1 July, 1997) Hong Kong government

【港客】visitors and guests from Hong Kong region

【港口】port; harbor:沿海～ *coastal port* / ～吞吐量 *traffic (of a port)* / ～费用 *port charge* / ～惯例 *custom(s) of the port* / ～税 *port dues* / ～河段 *harbor reach* / ～建筑线 *pierhead line*
【港人】Hong Kong residents
【港商】Hong Kong businessman
【港式】Hong Kong style; Hong Kong fashion
【港湾】harbor
【港务】harbor administration: ～代表 *representative of port authorities*
【港务费】harbor dues; port rate
【港务监督】harbor superintendency administration
【港务局】port office

gàng

杠 ① thick stick or club; thick staff; stout carrying pole:撬～ *pinch bar; crowbar; pry* /顶门～ *thick staff used to prop up the door leaf from inside* ②【体】bar:单～ *horizontal bar* /双～ *parallel bars* /高低～ *uneven (parallel) bars; asymmetric bars* ③ rod-like spare parts used for machine tools:丝～ *guide screw; leading screw* /保险～ *bumper* ④ thick line (drawn beside or under words in reading, correcting papers, etc.) ⑤ cross out; delete:他把草稿中不必要的词句都～掉了。*He crossed out all the superfluous words and phrases in the draft.*
【杠棒】stout carrying pole
【杠杆】lever; heaver; pry bar: ～臂 *lever arm* / ～原理 *lever principle* / ～率 *leverage* /经济～ *economic levers* / ～定律 *lever law* / ～作用 *leverage; lever action*
【杠杠】① rules; regulations:退休要有个年龄～。*There should age limits for retirement.* ② criterion; standard:划出几道政策～ *define certain policy criterion*
【杠铃】【体】barbell: ～片 *disc (of a barbell)*
【杠子】① thick pole; stout carrying pole ②【体】bar ③ thick line marks errors ④ rules; regulations; standard

gāo

高 ① tall; high: ～大的树 *a tall tree* / ～山大川 *high mountains and great rivers* /她比我～。*She is taller than me.* ② advanced; superior; top: ～质量 *top quality; high quality* / ～水平 *advanced level* / ～速度 *high speed* ③ loud: ～喊 *shout loudly; raise a cry* ④ height; altitude: 飞行～度 *flying altitude* /塔的～度 *height of a tower* ⑤ of a high or higher rank: ～年级 *higher (or senior) grades* ⑥ your; his; their:你的～见 *your opinion* ⑦ high-priced; dear; expensive:要价太～ *ask too high a price*
【高矮】height: ～不一 *some tall and some short* / 姐妹俩～差不多。*The two sisters are about the same height.*
【高昂】① hold high (one's head, etc.):战士们～着头通过主席台。*The soldiers passed the rostrum with their heads held high.* ② high; elated; jubilant:斗志～ *have high moral* /情绪～ *be in high spirits* ③ high-priced; expensive; dear; costly:为此我们付出了～的代价。*It cost us dearly.*
【高傲】supercilious; arrogant; haughty; self-respecting; high-minded
【高标号】high grade: ～水泥 *high-grade cement*
【高不成,低不就】be unfit for a higher post but unwilling to take a lower one; too choosy to succeed; can't have one's heart's desire but won't stoop to less; be unable to achieve one's heart's desire but unwilling to accept less
【高不可攀】too high to be reached; difficult to reach; so tall that it was out of reach; unattainable
【高才生】brilliant student; whiz kid; outstanding student
【高层云】【气】altostratus
【高产】high yield; high production: ～田 *high-yield field* / ～作物 *high-yield crop* / ～稳产 *achieve high and stable yield* /创～ *achieve high yield*
【高唱】① sing loudly; sing with spirit: ～赞歌 *sing the praises (of sb or sth)* / ～战歌 *sing battle songs* ② talk glibly about; call out loudly for; prate:他们一面～反腐败,一面疯狂受贿。*They are prating about "against corruption" but frenziedly taking bribes.*
【高超】superb; outstanding; excellent:技艺～ *superb skill* /见解～ *excellent idea*
【高超音速】【物】hypersonic speed: ～火箭 *hypersonic rocket* / ～飞机 *hypersonic aircraft*
【高潮】① high tide; high water: ～线 *high-water mark or line* / ～面 *high-water level* ② upsurge; high tide:经济建设的新～ *new upsurge in economic construction* ③ climax:全剧的～ *the climax of the play*
【高大】① tall and big; tall:身材～ *be of tall and sturdy stature* / ～的建筑物 *tall building* ② lofty; noble:雷锋的～形象 *the lofty image of Lei Feng*
【高蛋白】high protein: ～食品 *high protein food*
【高档】top grade; high class; top quality; superior quality: ～商品 *high-grade goods* / ～服装 *superior quality clothing*
【高等】higher; senior; advanced: ～哺乳动物 *higher mammal* / ～数学 *higher mathematics* / ～法院 *high court* / ～教育 *high education* / ～植物 *higher plant* / ～化学 *advanced chemistry*
【高低】① height; pitch:山崖的～ *the height of a cliff* ② relative superiority or inferiority; difference in degree:难分～ *hard to tell which is better* ③ sense of propriety; appropriateness:他说话不知～。*He had no sense of discretion when he star-*

G

ted to talk. ④［方］on any account; just:嘴都说破了,他～不参加我们的聚会。*I talked myself hoarse, but he just wouldn't take part in our party.* ⑤［方］at long last

【高低杠】【体】uneven (parallel) bars; asymmetric bars

【高低角】【军】angle of site

【高地】① highland; upland; elevation; high place: ～田 *highland field* ②【军】height:无名～ *nameless height*

【高调】① lofty tone; high-sounding words:唱～ *say fine-sounding things* ②【摄】high tone

【高度】① height; altitude; elevation:树的～ *the height of a tree* /在海拔6000米的～上飞 *fly at a height of 6000 meters above sea-level* ② highly; to a high degree: ～赞扬 *speak highly of* / ～概括 *succinct generalization* / ～评价 *hold in high regard* / ～发展的工业国 *highly developed industrial country* / ～表 *altimeter* / ～规 *height gage*

【高额】huge amount; great number: ～利润 *high profit* / ～租金 *rack-rent*

【高尔夫球】① golf: ～棒 *golf club* / ～场 *golf course*; *golf links* / ～俱乐部 *golf club* / ～袋 *golf bag* ② golf ball

【高分低能】high scores and low ability; good at taking exams but poor in practice

【高分子】【化】high polymer; macromolecule: ～化学(*high*) *polymer chemistry* / ～化合物 *macromolecular compound*; *high-molecular compound* / ～聚合物 *high polymer*

【高风亮节】exemplary conduct and nobility of character; have a sharp sense of integrity; noble character and sterling integrity

【高峰】peak; summit; height:世界第一～ *the highest peak in the world* /人口出生～期 *a baby boom* / ～会议 *summit meeting* / ～期 *peak period*

【高峰时间】rush hour; peak-hour

【高干】high-ranking official; senior cadres: ～子弟 *children of senior cadres* / ～病房 *wards for senior cadres*

【高高在上】sit up high in a leading position; hold oneself aloft; stand high above the masses; keep aloof from the masses

【高个儿】tall person

【高跟鞋】high-heeled shoes

【高工】senior engineer

【高官厚禄】high position and handsome salary; high position and a large income; high official with a high salary; high official with high pay

【高贵】① noble; exalted; high; morally elevated: ～品质 *noble quality* ② highly privileged; elitist: ～的家族 *exalted family*

【高积云】【气】altocumulus

【高级】① senior; high-ranking; high-level; advanced: ～将领 *high-ranking general officers* / ～干部 *senior cadre* / ～研究 *advanced studies* ② high-grade; high-quality; advanced: ～墨水 *high-quality ink* / ～读本 *advanced reader* / ～会晤 *summit talk* / ～经理 *senior manager* / ～人民法院 *Higher People's Court* / ～研究员 *senior research fellow* / ～职称 *senior academic or professional rank* / ～神经活动 *higher nervous activity* / ～中学 *senior high school* / ～语言 *high-level language*

【高技术】high-technology; high-tech: ～产品 *high-tech products* / ～产业 *high-tech industry* / ～领域 *fields of high-technology* / ～园 *high-tech park* / ～开发区 *high-technology development zone*

【高加索山脉】the Caucasus Mountains

【高价】high price; excessive price: ～出售 *sell at a fancy price* / ～收购 *buy at a high price* / ～货物 *expensive goods* / ～出让 *go off at high price* / ～勒索 *demand extortionate prices* / ～待沽 *wait for the opportunity to sell at high price*

【高架公路】flyover

【高架桥】viaduct

【高架铁道】overhead railway; elevated railway

【高见】brilliant idea; your, his or their view:实在是～。*It is really a brilliant idea.*

【高洁】noble and unsullied: ～的品德 *noble and unsullied character*

【高精尖】high-grade, precision and advanced (industrial products):我们研究所拥有一百多台～设备。*Our institute boasts over 100 pieces of sophisticated equipment of high grade and precision.*

【高就】(find a) better job; (move up) a higher position:另有～ *have landed a better job* /另请～。*You may leave and have a better job elsewhere.*

【高举】hold high; hold aloft: ～着奖杯 *hold the cup high* / ～革命的红旗 *hold high the revolutionary red banner*

【高聚物】【化】high polymer

【高踞】stand above; set oneself above; lord it over

【高峻】high and steep:山势～。*The mountains are high and steep.*

【高亢】① loud and sonorous; resounding: ～的歌声 *sonorous singing* ② (of terrain) high:平整～地六十亩 *level out 60 mu of high land* ③［书］supercilious; arrogant; haughty:生性～ *arrogant by nature*

【高考】college or university entrance examination: 参加～ *take part in college entrance examination*

【高科技】high technology; high-level science and technology: ～企业 *high-tech enterprises*

【高空】upper air; high altitude: ～飞行 *high-altitude flight* / ～病 *altitude sickness* / ～作业 *work high above the ground* / ～气象学 *aerology* / ～缺氧 *high-altitude anoxia* / ～爆炸 *high air burst* / ～槽 *high-level trough* / ～飞行服 *pressure suit*; *pressurized suit* / ～风 *upper wind*; *wind-aloft*

【高跨比】【建】rise-span ratio; rise-to-span ratio

【高栏】【体】high hurdles

【高利贷】usury; usurious loan:放～ *practise usury* / ～者 *usurer*; *loan shark*; *vampire*

【高粱】kaoliang, Chinese sorghum: ～米 *husked kaoliang* / ～饴 *sorghum candy*; *sweets or candy made of sorghum syrup*

【高龄】①［套］advanced age；venerable age：八十～ *the advanced age of 80* /～社会 *aged society* ② older than usual：～学员 *students above the average age*

【高楼大厦】high buildings and large mansions；many-storied buildings；tall buildings；high-rise：如今的中国，～随处可见。*There are skyscrapers and high-rises everywhere in China nowadays.*

【高炉】【冶】blast furnace：～煤气 *blast furnace gas* /～寿命 *life of a blast furnace*

【高氯酸】【化】perchloric acid

【高论】enlightening remarks；brilliant opinion

【高帽子】① tall paper hat（worn as a sign of humiliation）；dance's cap ② flattery；empty title or honor：她喜欢戴～。*She likes to flattery.*

【高门】tall gate-a rich and powerful family：～望族 *rich and distinguished family*

【高锰酸钾】【化】potassium permanganate

【高密度】high density：～存储（器）*high density storage*

【高妙】ingenious；masterly；skilful：笔法～ *masterly writing skills*

【高名】① brilliant；clever；wise；smart：医术～ *have superb medical skill* /他的所作所为一点也不～。*What he had done is not at all clever.* ② wise or brilliant person：另请～。*Find someone better qualified（than myself for the job）.*

【高难】highly difficult；superior and difficult：～动作 *difficult movements that require superior skills* /～技巧 *a superior and difficult technique*

【高能】high-energy：～燃料 *high-energy fuel* /～物理学 *high-energy physics* /～电子 *high-energy electron*

【高攀】make friends or claim ties of kinship with someone of a higher social position：～不上 *be beyond one* /不敢～。*I dare not aspire to such an honor.*

【高朋满座】guests and friends filled up the room；many guests of exalted rank were present；a great gathering of distinguished guests

【高频】high frequency：超～ *ultrahigh frequency* /～扬声器 *tweeter* /～干扰 *high-frequency interference* /～电流 *high-frequency current* /～手表 *high-frequency watch*

【高品位】high-grade；high-rank

【高聘】be appointed to a high position

【高气压】high atmospheric pressure；high barometric pressure：～区 *high-pressure area*；*region of high barometric pressure*

【高强】excel in；be master of：武艺～ *excel in martial arts*

【高强度】high strength；high tension；high intensity：～钢 *high strength steel*；*high-duty steel* /～部件 *high-strength part* /～电流 *high-intensity current* /～铸铁 *high-strength cast iron*

【高跷】stilts：踩～ *walk on stilts*

【高球】【体】high ball；lob：放～ *send a ball in a lob*；*lob*

【高热】high fever

【高人】①［书］holy hermits；hermits and recluses ② great scholar；master hand；distinguished personage

【高人一等】be superior to ordinary people；be a cut above others；be a head taller than others：你不要老以为自己～。*Please don't always think your are a cut above others.*

【高僧】eminent monk：有道～ *eminent and learned monk*

【高山病】mountain sickness

【高山大川】high mountains and great rivers

【高山反应】altitude reaction；altitude sickness

【高山流水】lofty mountains and flowing waters-referring to a person who appreciates one's talents，a bosom friend，or elegant music

【高尚】① noble；lofty：～的品质 *noble character* /～的人 *noble-minded person* /～的理想 *lofty ideas* ② meaningful；refined；elegant：谈吐～ *refined speech* /～的娱乐 *tasteful entertainment*

【高烧】high fever：发～ *have a high fever*；*run a high fever*

【高射机关枪】antiaircraft machine gun

【高射炮】antiaircraft gun or artillery

【高深】advanced；profound；recondite；abstruse：～的造诣 *of great attainment* /～的学问 *erudite scholarship* /～莫测 *too profound to understand*；*too high and deep to be measured*

【高升】be promoted；move up to a higher position：他最近得到了～。*He got a promotion recently.*

【高视阔步】walk with one's head held high；swagger about；carry oneself proudly；prance

【高手】past master；master-hand；ace；expert：网球～ *tennis ace* /国际象棋～ *master chess player* /他在计算机方面是有名的～。*He's a well-known master-hand in computer.*

【高寿】① longevity；long life：祝您～！*Wish you a long life!* ② your venerable age：老大爷，您今年～？*May I ask how old you are，Grandpa?*

【高斯】Karl Friedrich Gauss（1777-1855），German mathematician，astronomer and physicist：～定律 *Gauss' theorem* /～函数 *Gauss' function*

【高耸】tall and erect；towering：～入云 *reach to the clouds* /国际大饭店～在广场上。*The International Hotel towers over on the square.*

【高速】high speed；top speed：～发展 *develop at high speed* /～前进 *advance at top speed* /～车 *speed car* /～档 *top gear*；*high gear* /～公路 *expressway* /～摄影 *high-speed handling* /～打印机 *high-speed printer* /～存储器 *high-speed memory* /～缓冲存储器 *cache memory*；*cache* /～钢 *high-speed steel*；*rapid steel* /～阅读器 *high speed*

【高抬贵手】be generous；be lenient；be magnanimous；not be too hard on sb

【高谈阔论】talk with eloquence；talk volubly；indulge in loud and empty talk；talk in a lofty

strain
【高碳钢】【冶】high-carbon steel
【高汤】①（meat or chicken）soup-stock ② thin soup
【高堂】① great hall; large hall ②［书］one's parents: ~老母 *aged mother*
【高头大马】① big strong horse ②（of people）tall and big; tall and strong: ~的小伙子 *tall and strong young man*
【高徒】outstanding disciple: 严师出~。*A strict teacher produces outstanding students.*
【高危】① high and dangerous ② extremely dangerous
【高纬度】high latitude; circumpolar latitude
【高温】high temperature: ~计 *pyrometer* / ~天气 *megathermal weather* / ~车间 *high-temperature workshop* / ~作业 *high-temperature operation* / ~消毒 *high temperature sterilization* / ~淬火 *quench hot* / ~切削 *high temperature machining* / ~场 *high temperature field*
【高屋建瓴】pour water off a steep roof; sweep down irresistibly from a commanding height; operate from a strategically advantageous position; be strategically situated
【高下】relative superiority or inferiority
【高消费】high level consumption; excessive consumption
【高效】highly effective; highly efficient: ~节能 *energy-efficient* / ~肥料 *concentrated fertilizer* / ~政府 *highly-efficient government*
【高校】institution of higher learning; universities and colleges
【高新技术】advanced technology; high technology; hi-tech
【高薪】high salary; high pay; good income: ~聘请 *engage sb at a high pay*
【高兴】① glad; happy; cheerful; pleased: 见到老师很~。*I'm glad to meet my teacher.* / 她听了这个好消息非常~。*She was very happy to hear the good news.* ② be willing to; be glad to; be happy to: 你不~去看戏，就去上网好了。*If you don't like going to the theatre, you can connect to the Internet instead.*
【高性能】high performance: ~飞机 *high performance aircraft*
【高血压】【医】high blood pressure; hypertension
【高压】①【气】high pressure: ~锅炉 *high-pressure boiler* / ~风 *high-pressure blast* / ~锅 *pressure cooker* / ~水龙 *water cannon* ②【电】high tension; high voltage: ~电缆 *high-tension cable* / ~电流 *high-tension current* / ~线 *high-tension line or wire* ③【医】maximum pressure ④ high-handed: ~手段 *high-handed measures* / ~政策 *high-handed policy*
【高雅】elegant; graceful; refined: 格调~ *elegant and graceful style*
【高研】senior research fellow; high-level researcher
【高音】【音】high pitch; high-pitched voice: 男~ *tenor* / 女~ *soprano*
【高原】plateau; highland; tableland: 青藏~ *Qinghai-Tibet plateau* / ~湖 *plateau lake*
【高瞻远瞩】look far ahead from a high place; take a broad and long view; stand high and gaze far; have great foresight
【高涨】① rise; upsurge; run high: 群众热情~。*The enthusiasm of the masses ran high.* / 物价日益~。*Commodity prices are running high with each passing day.* ②【经】boom
【高招】［口］good idea; clever move; smart trick: 你的~真多。*You have so many good ideas.*
【高枕无忧】sleep with any anxiety; rest easy; sleep peacefully without cares; sleep with an easy mind
【高知】intellectuals with senior professional titles
【高中】senior middle school; senior secondary school
【高指标】high targets in production
【高姿态】lofty stance; generous attitude: 你要~，不要和同学们计较。*Be generous and tolerant; let your classmates off.*
【高祖】（paternal）great-great-grandfather
【高祖母】（paternal）great-great-grandmother

羔 lamb; kid; fawn: 小羊~ *lamb*; *kid* / 鹿~儿 *fawn*
【羔皮】lambskin; kidskin; kid: ~手套 *kid gloves*; *kids*
【羔羊】① lamb; kid ② innocent and helpless person; scapegoat: 替罪的~ *scapegoat*
【羔子】lamb; kid; fawn: 小猪~ *piglet*

睾
【睾丸】testis; testicle: ~炎 *orchitis*

膏 ① fat; grease; oil: 春雨如~。*Rain in spring is as precious as oil.* ② paste; cream; plaster; ointment: 牙~ *toothpaste* / 软~ *ointment* / 药~ *ointment*; *salve*
see also gào
【膏粱】fat meat and fine grain; rich food: ~子弟 *children of wealthy family*; *good-for-nothing sons of the idle rich*
【膏药】【药】medicated plaster; plaster: 贴~ *apply a plaster to* / 狗皮~ *dog-skin plaster*; *shoddy goods*
【膏腴】［书］fertile: ~之地 *fertile land*

篙 punt-pole: 竹~ *bamboo punt-pole*
【篙竿】［方］punt-pole

糕 cake; pudding: 蛋~ *cake* / 发~ *steamed sponge cake* / 年~ *New Year cake*（*made of glutinous rice*）
【糕饼】［方］cake; pastry
【糕点】cake; pastry
【糕干】sweetened rice floor（as a substitute for powdered milk）

gǎo

搞 ① do; go in for; carry on; be engaged in: ～阴谋诡计 *go in for intrigue and conspiracy* / ～改革 *carry on reforms* / 他是～法律的。*He is in the law.* ② make; achieve produce; work out: ～几个菜 *prepare a few dishes* / ～计划 *draw up a plan* / 这个车间在～新产品。*The workshop is trying to produce a new product.* ③ get; get hold of; wangle: ～钱 *raise money*; *make money* / 我去～点水来。*I will go and fetch some water.* ④ set up; start; organize: 这个工厂是由一个工程师～起来的。*This factory was started by an engineer.* ⑤ make sb suffer; fix sb: 全班合起来～我。*The whole class joined hands in making things difficult for me.* ⑥ produce a certain effect or result; cause to become: 把某人～臭 *make sb's name stink*; *discredit sb*

【搞臭】discredit; put to shame; humiliate: 他一心要把女孩～。*He is bent on discrediting the girl.*

【搞出】make; work out; produce; achieve: ～成果 *achieve results*

【搞错】make mistakes; mistake: 我把他们俩～了。*I mistook the one for the other.*

【搞掉】get rid of; do away with: 把这堆垃圾～ *get rid of this rubbish dump* / 把某人～ *put someone out of the way*

【搞对象】go steady; date; keep steady company

【搞鬼】play tricks; scheme in secret; be up to mischief; play foul

【搞好】make a good job of; do well: ～邻里关系 *foster good relations with one's neighbours* / ～团结 *strengthen unity*

【搞坏】damage; spoil; impair: ～身体 *impair one's health*

【搞活】vitalize; enliven; invigorate: ～企业 *rejuvenate an enterprise* / ～市场 *enliven the market* / ～经济 *enliven the economy*

【搞垮】disrupt; undermine

【搞乱】confuse; muddle; mess up: 把秩序～了 *get the order confused*

【搞特殊化】use one's position to pursue personal perquisites and privileges

【搞头】have a point (in doing sth); be worth doing: 这事没～。*There is no point in doing that.*

【搞糟】mess up; make a mess

缟 thin white silk used in ancient China

【缟素】white mourning apparel or dress: 一身～ *be dressed in deep mourning*

槁 withered

【槁枯】withered; haggard

【槁木】withered tree; dead tree: 形如～ *look like a withered tree*; *look haggard*

镐 pick; pickaxe: 电～ *electric pick*

【镐头】pick; pickaxe

稿[1] [书] stalk of grain; straw

稿[2] draft; sketch; manuscript: 初～ *first draft* / 修改～ *revised draft* / 拟～ *make a draft* / 先打个～再画 *make a sketch before painting*

【稿本】manuscript: ～目录 *written catalogue*

【稿费】payment for an article or book written; contribution fee; author's remuneration: 这家出版社的～标准较高。*This publisher offers a better rate of remuneration.*

【稿件】contribution; manuscript

【稿约】notice to contributors

【稿纸】squared or lined paper for making drafts or copying manuscripts

【稿子】① draft; sketch: 起草～ *make a draft* ② manuscript; contribution: 这个～是史密斯写的。*Mr. Smith wrote this article.* ③ idea; plan: 同学们心里还没个准～。*The students haven't got any definite plan yet.*

gào

告 ① tell; inform; notify; make sth known: 通～周知 *make a public announcement* / 电～ *inform by telegraph* / 无可奉～。*No comment.* / 把你的住处～诉我。*Tell me where you live.* ② sue; make a legal claim; accuse; take sb to court: 上～ *appeal to a higher court* / 到法院去～他。*Go to court and sue him.* ③ ask for; request; solicit: ～假 *ask for leave* ④ declare; announce; notify: 不～而别 *leave without saying goodbye* / 自～奋勇 *volunteer for the job* ⑤ announce or declare the completion of sth: ～一段落 *come to the end of a stage*

【告白】① public notice or announcement ② profess; express: ～内心的忧虑 *express one's worries* ③【经】bill

【告别】① leave; part from; go away from: 向亲友～ *take leave of one's relatives and friends* ② say goodbye to; bid farewell to: 挥手～ *wave farewell* / 向遗体～ *pay one's last respects to the deceased* / ～词 *farewell speech*; *valediction* / ～演出 *farewell performance* / ～宴会 *farewell banquet* / 我明天向老师～去。*I will go to say goodbye to my teacher tomorrow.*

【告病】ask for sick leave: 他～还乡。*He returned to his home-town on account of illness.*

【告成】complete; finish; accomplish: 大功～。*The great task is accomplished.* / 这部小说历时十年方始～。*This novel took ten years to complete.*

【告吹】fizzle out; fall through; fail: 这个计划最终～了。*Eventually the plan fell through.*

【告辞】take leave (of one's host)

【告贷】ask for a loan; turn for loans; borrow money:四处~ *try to borrow money right and left* / ~无门 *have nowhere to turn for loans* / ~很难。*It is very difficult to borrow money.*

【告发】inform against (sb to the police); report (an offender); accuse sb (of an offence); denounce: ~同案犯 *split on an accomplice*

【告急】① be in an emergency; be critical:前方~。*The situation at the front is critical.* ② report an emergency; ask for emergency help: ~的电报 *cable asking for emergency help* /前线频频~。*The front-line units repeatedly signaled for help.*

【告假】ask for leave: ~一周 *ask for a one-week leave*

【告捷】① win victory; be victorious: 全线~ *be victorious on all fronts* ② report a victory; notify a victory:立即发短信向家里~ *send home a short message*

【告诫】warn; caution; admonish; exhort

【告警】report an emergency; sound an alarm; give a warning: ~系统 *warning system* / ~阀 *alarm valve* / ~灯 *lamp making stand*

【告老】retire because of age: ~还乡 *retire on account of old age and return to one's native place*

【告密】inform against; report against: ~者 *informer*

【告罄】run out; use up; be exhausted:弹药~。*Ammunition has run out.* /市面上的纯棉内衣~。*Pure cotton underwear has been sold out in the market.*

【告饶】beg for mercy; ask pardon; throw oneself on sb's mercy:求情~ *plead for mercy*

【告示】① notify; inform; announce:我们按照海报上~的时间,按时进入电影院。*We went to the cinema at the time as announced in the poster.* ② bulletin; official notice; placard:安民~ *notice to reassure the people* ③[旧] slogan; poster

【告诉】tell; inform; notify; let know:他把那消息~了全家的人。*He told the news to everybody in the his family.* /她~你姓名了吗? *Did she tell you her name?* /有用着我的地方,请~一声。*In case you need my help, do let me know.*

【告退】① ask for leave from a meeting to withdraw from a meeting, etc.:随着演出结束,观众全都~。*As the show came to a close, all the audiences departed.* ② withdraw (from an organization)

【告知】inform; notify; tell

【告终】come to an end; end up:以失败~ *end in failure; come to grief in the end*

【告状】① go to court against sb; bring a case; bring a lawsuit against sb; sue:向法院~ *bring an action against sb in the court* ② complain about sb to his superior; report to the superior:他在我妈妈面前告了我一状。*He lodged a complaint against me with my mother.*

诰 ①[书] order; enjoin; admonish ②[古] written admonition ③ imperial mandate

【诰封】conferment of honorary titles by imperial mandate

【诰命】① imperial mandate ② women on whom titles were conferred by imperial mandate; a titled lady

膏 ① lubricate; oil; grease: ~车 *lubricate the axle of a cart* /在轴上~点儿油 *put some lubricant on the axle* ② dip a brush in ink and smooth it on an inkstone before writing

see also gāo

gē

戈 dagger-axe (an ancient weapon)

【戈壁】①【地】gobi ② the Gobi Desert

【戈兰高地】Golan Heights (Syrian territory occupied by Israel)

疙

【疙瘩】① swelling on the skin; wart; lump:墙上尽是~。*The wall is dotted with pimples.* ② lump; knot:面~ *small round lumps of dough* ③ knot in one's heart; hang-up:老师帮我解开了心头的~。*The teacher helped me rid myself of my hang-up.*

【疙疙瘩瘩】[口] rough; knotty; bumpy

咯

see also kǎ

【咯噔】click; clump: ~~的皮靴声 *clump of boots (on the floor)* /心~~地跳个不停 *heart keeps thumping in the chest*

【咯咯】①[象] cluck; chuckle; cackle ② chuckle; titter giggle:她~地笑着,开心极了。*She was chuckling, extremely delighted.*

【咯吱】creak; groan:地板被他踩得~~响。*The floor creaked under his heavy steps.*

哥 ① (elder) brother:大~ *eldest brother* /四~ *forth elder brother* ② form of address for the elder male relative of one's generation:表~ *elder cousin* ③ friendly way of addressing males of older acquaintances

【哥哥】(elder) brother

【哥伦比亚】① Colombia (The Colombia Republic): ~人 *Colombian* ② Columbia: ~特区 *District of Columbia* / ~大学 *Columbia university* / ~河 *Columbia River* / ~广播公司(*US*) *columbia broadcasting system (CBS)* / ~号航天飞机 *Space Shuttle Columbia*

【哥伦布】Christopher Columbus (1451-1506), Italian navigator

【哥儿们】[口] ① brothers ② buddies; cronies; pals: ~义气 *brotherhood loyalty; gang spirit*

【哥斯达黎加】Costa Rica: ~人 *Costa Rican*

【哥特式】【建】gothic: ~建筑 *Gothic architecture* / ~式家具 *Gothic Chippendale* / ~式教堂 *Gothic cathedral* / ~艺术 *Gothic art*

【哥特体】【印】gothic print; black letter

胳

【胳臂】arm:粗壮的~ *brawny arms*

【胳膊】arm:~腕子 *wrist* /~肘儿 *elbow*

【胳膊拧不过大腿】the arm is no match for the thigh; the weak can not contend with the strong; the wagon must go whither the horses draw it

【胳膊肘儿往外拐】one's elbow turns to the wrong side; side with outsiders instead of one's own people

鸽 pigeon; dove:哨~ *pigeon whistle* /~派 *dovish* /白~ *white pigeon* /信~ *homing pigeon; carrier pigeon* /和平~ *peace pigeon*

【鸽子】pigeon; dove: ~笼 *dovecote; pigeon house; loft*

搁 ① put; place; lay: 把箱子~在房里 *put the trunk in the room* /你把东西~下。*Put down your things.* ② put aside; leave over; shelve: 耽~ *delay; hold up* /这些问题她总是~不下。*She is unable to put the problems out of her mind.* ③ add; put in:多~点儿糖。*Put in more sugar.* *see also* gé

【搁笔】put aside the pen or brush; lay down the pen; stop writing or painting: ~沉思 lay down the pen lost in thought

【搁浅】① run aground; get stranded:小船~了。*The boat was stranded on the river bank.* ② held up; reach a deadlock; come to a deadlock

【搁置】shelve; lay aside; put aside; pigeonhole: ~一项动议 *shelve a motion* /~争议 *put aside a dispute* /事件重大,不能~。*The event is too important to be delayed.*

割 ① cut; sever; mow: ~麦子 *cut or reap wheat* /~草 *cut grass; mow* /~开 *cut open; rip open* /~掉 *cut off; get rid of* ② divide; give up:切~ *sever; divide*

【割爱】give up what one treasures; part with some cherished possession:忍痛~ *part reluctantly with what one treasures*

【割草机】mower

【割除】cut off; cut out; remove; exercise: ~扁桃体 *cut off the tonsil; remove the tonsil* /~肿瘤 *remove a tumor*

【割断】sever; cut off; break off: ~电话线 *cut telephone wires* / ~手指 *cut off one's fingers* / ~联系 *sever relations break off ties*

【割胶】tap rubber

【割炬】【机】cutting torch

【割据】set up a separatist regime by force of arms; carve out a vast track of land and establish an independent regime:封建~ *feudal separatist rule* /军阀~ *nation carved up into a number of separate regimes by rival warlords*

【割捆机】【农】self-binder; binder; reaper-binder

【割礼】【宗】circumcision

【割裂】cut apart; sever; separate:把问题~开来看 *look at the problem in isolation.*

【割让】cede: ~领土 *cession of territory* / ~国 *cessionary state; ceding state*

【割舍】give up; part with; give away:难以~ *find it hard to part with* /她~不下自己的儿子。*She found it hard to part with her son.*

【割线】【数】secant; secant line

歌 ① song:恋~ *love song* /国~ *national anthem* /唱支~儿 *sing a song* /儿~ *children's song* /民~ *folk song* ② sing; chant:纵情高~ *sing loudly and without constraint* /高~一曲 *chant a melody* /讴~ *sing the praise of; celebrate in song*

【歌本】songbook:她喜欢收集~。*She is fond of collecting songbooks.*

【歌唱】① sing:纵情~ *sing heartily* / ~家 *singer; vocalist* ② sing the praise of; praise (through songs, poems, etc.); extol: ~伟大的祖国 *extol our great motherland* / ~友谊 *laud friendship*

【歌词】words of a song

【歌功颂德】sing merits and praise virtues; eulogize sb's virtues and achievements; glorify a ruler's character and accomplishments

【歌喉】(singer's) voice; singing voice: ~婉转 *have a beautiful voice* /嘹亮的~ *resonant singing voice*

【歌后】most accomplished female singer; singing queen

【歌剧】opera: ~剧本 *libretto* / ~演员 *opera performer* / ~院 *opera house* / ~团 *opera troupe or company*

【歌诀】formulas or directions put into verse

【歌迷】song fan or devotee

【歌片儿】song sheet

【歌谱】music score of a song; music of a song:填写~ *set a song to music*

【歌曲】song:流行~ *popular song* /校园~ *campus song*

【歌手】singer; vocalist:青年~ *young singer* /女~ *female singer*

【歌颂】sing the praises of; eulogize; laud:齐声~ *extol in unison*

【歌坛】song circles: ~新秀 *new stars in song circles*

【歌舞】song and dance: ~剧 *song and dance drama* / ~片 *musical* / ~团 *song and dance troupe* / ~厅 *song and dance hall*

【歌舞升平】sing and dance to extol the good times; sing and dance in celebration of peace

【歌星】singing star; star singer

【歌谣】ballad; folk song; nursery rhyme:民间~ *folk songs*

【歌咏】singing: ~比赛 *singing contest* / ~会 *singsong meeting; singsong* / ~队 *singing team; singing group*

gé

革[1] ① leather; hide: ~制品 *leather goods* /面~ *upper leather* /皮~ *leather; hide* /人造~ *im-*

G

itation leather; *artificial leather* /制～ *process hides*; *tan* ② (Gé) a surname

革[2] ① change; reform; alter; transform: 改～ *reform* /变～ *transform*; *change* ② remove sb from office; expel; get rid of: 斥～ *dismiss sb from office*

see also jí

【革除】① abolish; get rid of; eliminate; do away with: ～弊端 *do away with malpractices* ② expel; dismiss; discharge; remove sb from office: ～公职 *dismiss from public service*

【革故鼎新】discard the old ways of life in favor of the new; reform the set rules to create sth new; destroy the old and establish the new

【革履】leather shoes: 西装～ *in Western dress and leather shoes*

【革命】① revolution: 资产阶级～ *bourgeois revolution* /参加～ *join the revolution* /将～进行到底 *carry the revolution through to the end* /～意志 *revolutionary will* /～精神 *revolutionary spirit* ② radical change; transformation; revolution: 技术～ *technical revolution* /产业～ *industrial revolution* /～化 *revolutionize* /～家 *revolutionary*; *revolutionist* /～性 *revolutionary character* /～英雄主义 *revolutionary heroism*

【革新】innovate; renovate; improve: 技术～ *technological innovation* /～思想 *innovative ideas* /～派 *reform party*; *reformers*

【革职】dismiss; remove sb from office; expel: ～查办 *discharge sb from his post and prosecute him* /他受到了～的处分。*He was punished with dismissal.*

阁 ① pavilion (usu. two-storied): 楼台亭～ *pavilions, terraces, and towers* ② cabinet: 改组内～ *reshuffle a cabinet* /倒～ *bring down a cabinet* /～僚 *member of a cabinet* ③ [旧] woman's chamber; boudoir: 出～ *get married*; *marry* ④ rack; shelf: 束之高～ *tie sth up and place it on the top shelf*

【阁楼】attic; garret; loft: 我租了一间～。*I rented a garret.*

【阁下】your Excellency or His or Her Excellency: 敬请～光临。*Your Excellency's presence is cordially requested.*

【阁员】member of a cabinet: 内阁～ *cabinet member*

格[1] ① square (formed by crossed lines); check: 在黑板上打方～儿 *square off the blackboard* /表～ *form*; *table* /把字写在～里。*Write the characters in the squares.* ② division (horizontal or otherwise): 横～纸 *ruled paper* /三～儿的书架 *a bookcase with three shelves* ③ standard; rule; pattern; style: 规～ *standard*; *specification* /合～ *up to standard* /破～ *make an exception*; *break a rule* ④ character; personality; style; manner: 人～ *character*; *personality* /风～ *style*; *manner*

格[2] 【语】case: 主～ *the nominative case* /宾～ *the objective case*

【格但斯克】Gdansk, industrial port and shipping building centre in northern Poland

【格调】① (literary or artistic) style: ～优雅 *elegant style* /伤感的～ *sentimental ethos* ② [书] one's style of work; one's moral quality: ～高尚的人 *person of integrity and lofty ideas*

【格斗】grapple; wrestle; fistfight: 勇敢地与歹徒～ *bravely grapple with a ruffian*

【格格不入】be misfits; be out of tune with sb; be incongruous; feel out of one's element: 与时代～ *be out of tune with times*

【格局】pattern; layout; structure: 这个医院的～与别处不同。*This hospital has a different setup from others.* /在这场足球比赛中，我队始终保持"四四二"的～。*Throughout the football match our team kept to the 4-4-2 patterns.*

【格林尼治时间】greenwich mean time (GMT)

【格鲁吉亚】Georgia: ～人 *Georgian* / ～语 *Georgian*

【格律】rules and forms of classical poetic composition (with respect to tonal pattern, rhyme scheme, etc.): 诗词～ *poetical meter*; *metrical pattern of poetry*

【格杀勿论】kill with lawful authority; kill anybody who puts up resistance; kill on the spot with the authority of the law

【格式】form; pattern; standardized style: 公文～ *the form of an official document* /按规定的～写 *write in the set form* /书信～ *form of a letter*

【格外】① especially; all the more; extraordinarily: 雪地上开车要～小心。*You've got to be especially careful when you drive on snow.* /今天天气～冷。*It is exceptionally cold today.* ② extra; additional; added

【格言】maxim; motto; aphorism

【格子】squares; check; chequer: 用尺打～ *square (the page) off with a ruler* / ～纸 *squared paper* / ～布 *checked fabric*; *check*

葛 ①【植】kudzu vine ② poplin

【葛根】【药】root of kudzu vine

搁 bear; stand; endure; sustain: 丝巾～不住搓揉。*Silk scarves won't stand rubbing.*

see also gē

蛤 clam

see also há

【蛤蜊】clam

隔 ① separate; cut off; partition; stand between: 远～重洋 *be separated by vast oceans* /分～ *separate*; *divide* /两国～海相望。*Our two countries are on the opposite sides of the sea.* ② at a distance; at a interval: 间～ *setting apart*; *intermission* /相～很远 *at a great distance from each other*

【隔岸观火】watch a fire from the other side of the river; look on at sb's trouble with indifference; show utter unconcern

【隔壁】next door：～第二间 *next door but one* /～邻居 *next-door neighbor* /住在一家医院的～ *live next-door to a hospital*

【隔断】① separate；cut off；lie between；obstruct ②【建】partition（wall，board，etc.）

【隔行如隔山】difference in trade makes one feel worlds apart；different professions are separated as by mountains

【隔阂】① estrangement；misunderstanding：制造～ *foment feelings of estrangement* /消除～ *remove understanding* /产生～ *cause estrangement* ② barrier：语言上的～ *language barrier*

【隔绝】cut off；separate；isolate；insulate：与世～ *be cut off from the outside world* /～噪音 *insulate against noise*

【隔离】keep apart；isolate；separate；segregate：种族～ *racial segregation*；*apartheid* /～审查 *be taken into custody and under investigation* /～病房 *isolation ward* /～带 *dividing strip* /～栅 *isolation fencing* /非典病人已经～了一周。*The SARS patient has been in isolation for a week.*

【隔膜】① lack of mutual understanding；estrangement：孩子们之间有些～。*The kids are rather estrangement from each other.* ② unfamiliar；strange；not versed

【隔片】【机】spacer

【隔墙】【建】partition（wall）

【隔墙有耳】walls have ears；walls have cracks and partitions have ears；be aware of eavesdroppers

【隔热】【建】insulate against heat：～材料 *thermal insulation material*；*heat-barrier material* /～性能 *heat-proof quality*

【隔日】day after the next；every other day

【隔扇】partition board

【隔声】【建】insulate against sound：～板 *sound insulating board* /～材料 *sound insulator*

【隔靴搔痒】scratch an itch through one's boot；make a useless attempt；fail to strike home；talk way off the mark

【隔夜】of the previous night；last night

【隔音】soundproof；sound insulating：～室 *soundproof room* /～装置 *deafening*；*sound arrester* /这教室～不错。*The classroom is impervious to sound.*

嗝 ① belch；burp：饱～ *belch*；*burp* /一连打了几个～儿 *keep belching* ② hiccup；hiccough

膈 diaphragm

【膈膜】diaphragm：横～ *diaphragm*

镉 【化】cadmium（Cd）：～灯 *cadmium lamp*

gè

个[1] ① height；size ② individual

个[2] ①［量］usually used before a noun having no particular classifier：一～西红柿 *a tomato* /三～字 *three characters* ② used before an approximate figure：每年都来～三四次 *come three or four times every year* ③ used after a verb which is followed by an object：讨～吉利 *invite luck* /睡～好觉 *have a good sleep used between a verb and a complement*：忙～不停 *be as busy as a bee* /看～仔细 *have a careful look* ④ as suffix to the classifier：那些～花草 *all those flowers and grass*

【个案】（individual or special）case：～研究 *case study*

【个把】about one；one or two；a couple of：增加～人 *add a person or two* /～月 *a couple of months*

【个别】① individual；specific；particular：～辅导 *individual coaching* /～谈话 *private talk* ② very few；one or two；exceptional：～差异 *individual differences* /～教学法 *individualized introduction* /～许可证 *individual license* /～合约 *specific contract* /～项目 *end item*

【个儿】① size；height；stature：～高 *tall* ② persons or things taken singly；each：卖苹果论斤不论～。*Apples are sold by the jin, not by item.*

【个个】each；everyone；all：教室里的人～束手无策。*No one in the classroom had any plan or suggestion to offer.* /这些同志～都是好样的。*Each and every one of these comrades has proved his mettle.*

【个股】individual share

【个人】① individual（person）；personal：～利益 *personal interests* /～电脑 *personal computer* /～得失 *personal gains and losses* /～隐私 *privacy* /以～的名义 *in one's own name* /～崇拜 *individual superstition*；*deify and worship an individual* /～存款 *individual deposits* /～技术 *personal skill* /～冠军 *individual championship* /～所得税 *personal income tax* /～投资 *individual investment* /～信用 *personal credit* /～主义 *individualism* ② I：～认为 *in my opinion*

【个体】① individual：～农业经营 *individual farming* /～生产者 *individual producer* /～商业 *business run by individuals* /～经营执照 *individual license* /～劳动者 *person who works on his own* /～所有制 *individual ownership* /～企业 *private enterprise* ② individual or household engaged in small-scale businesses：～户 *small-scale privately owned business* /～分析 *owned business* /～繁殖 *individual economy* /～经济 *individual economy* /～商贩 *pedlar*；*small retailer*

【个头儿】［方］height；size：这萝卜～大。*The carrot is huge.*

【个性】individual character；individuality；personality：～特征 *individual characteristics* /～解放 *liberation of the self*；*liberation of individual personality*

【个中】［书］therein：～奥妙 *the inside story* /～老手 *an expert in a given field*；*a big pot* /～三昧 *secret known only to experts* /～原因 *the whys and*

G

wherefores of

【个子】height; stature; build: 高～*a tall person* / 小～*a small fellow; a short person*

各 ① each; every; all; various: 全国～地 *all parts of the country* / ～兵种 *all arms of the services* / ～不相同 *differ from each other* / ～怀鬼胎 *each with his or her own axe to grind* / ～方面代表 *representatives of different fields* ② variously; respectively: 两侧～有一洞。*There is a hole on either side.*

【各按其职】stay at their posts; each minds his own business

【各半】half and half; fifty-fifty: ～对分 *divide it up fifty-fifty; divide it up on a fifty-fifty basis* / 去留的可能性～。*The chances of departure are fifty-fifty.*

【各奔前程】each pursues his onward journey; each pursues his own course; each goes his own way; everyone is anxious to get ahead

【各别】① distinct; different: ～对待 *treat differently; treat each on its (or his, etc.) own merits* ② [方] out of the ordinary; unusual; novel; peculiar: 这件夹克的样式很～。*The style of this jacket is quite unusual.* ③ odd; funny; freakish

【各不相让】each refused to give in to the other; neither is willing to give ground; each is trying to excel the other

【各持己见】each holds his own opinion; each sticks to his own version; each holds to his own statement

【各打五十大板】blame both sides without discrimination; punish the innocent and the guilty alike

【各得其所】play their proper role; have a place for everyone; everyone has fallen into his right place; each gets his due

【各个】① each; every; various: ～单位 *each unit* / ～朝代 *every dynasty* / ～方面 *all the various aspect* ② one by one; separately: ～解决 *piecemeal solution; resolve problems one at a time*

【各行各业】the various walks of life; all trades and professions; every profession and trade

【各级】all or different levels: ～政府 *governments at all levels* / ～党组织 *party organizations of all levels*

【各界】all walks of life; all circles: ～人士 *personages of various circles* / ～代表 *representatives from all walks of life*

【各尽其用】each answers the purpose intended

【各尽其责】everyone does his duty

【各尽所能】work according to one's ability; each do his best

【各尽所能,按劳分配】from each according to his ability, to each according to his work

【各尽所能,按需分配】from each according to his ability, to each according to his needs

【各就位】【体】on your marks

【各取所需】each takes what he needs

【各人】each one; everyone

【各色】of all kinds; of every description; assorted: ～人等 *people of all descriptions* / 冰箱里～的食物,一应俱全。*Our refrigerator is well stocked with food of all kinds.*

【各式各样】of all kinds; of all sorts; of all styles: ～的服装 *dresses of all styles*

【各抒己见】each airs his own views; each says his say; each one expresses his own views

【各司其职】each does his or her duty; each performs his or her own functions

【各位】① everybody: ～请注意! *Attention pleases, everybody.* / ～请入座。*Be seated please, everybody.* ② every: ～女士、～先生 *ladies and gentlemen*

【各显神通】each shows his or her special prowess; each tries for all one is worth

【各行其是】act as one pleases; act willfully; each acts in his own way

【各有千秋】each has its own merits; each has its advantages; each has his or her strong points

【各有所长】each one has his good points; everybody has his strong points; each one has sth in which he excels

【各有所好】each has his likes or dislikes; everyone has his hobby; everyone has his own particular tastes

【各执一词】each holds to his own statement; each sticks to his own version

【各自】each; respective; individual

【各自为政】act of one's free will; work each for himself; everyone goes his own way

硌 (of sth hard or bulging) press or rub against: 饭里有沙子,～牙。*There's some grit in the rice, and it hurts my teeth.*

铬 【化】chromium(Cr)

【铬钢】【冶】chromium steel; chrome steel

【铬镍钢】chrome-nickel steel

【铬铁】ferrochrome: ～矿 *chromites*

gěi

给 ① give; present; grant: ～出路 *give sb a way out* / ～他一个星期的假 *grant him a week's leave* / 我～男孩每人一个苹果。*I gave each of the boys an apple.* / 这本书是～你的。*This book is for you.* ② let; allow; make: 家里寄钱～他买书。*His family sent money to him for buying books.* / 这种小说不能～小孩看。*Children are not allowed to read such novel.* / 裙子～雨淋湿了。*The skirt got wet in the rain.* ③ for the benefit of; for the sake of; for: 我～你当向导。*I'll act as a guide for you.* ④ (used to introduce the recipient of an action) for; to: 我～老师行了礼。*I saluted my teacher.* ⑤ used directly before the verb of a passive sentence, etc. to show emphasis: 你快把桌子～收拾一下。*Please tidy up the table quickly.* / 把报纸收

起来,别叫风～刮散了。*Put away all the newspaper; don't let it get blown about.* ⑥(used after a verb to indicate the handling over of sth.) to; with:交～他一封信 *hand him a letter* /请把盐递～我。*Pass me the salt, please.* /我把收音机留～你。*I will leave the radio with you.*
see also jǐ

【给脸】save sb's face; try not to embarrass; do sb a favor:她不知好歹,～不要脸。*She doesn't know what is good for her and is fool enough to reject a face-saving offer.*

【给小鞋穿】give sb a pair of tight shoes to wear; make sb feel the pinch

【给颜色看】make it hot for sb:你如果不守时,他就要给你颜色看。*If you don't come on time, he will show you a thing or two.*

【给以】give; grant allow: ～重视 *pay attention to* / ～好评 *give good opinions; accord commendation* / ～补偿 *recompense*

gēn

根 ① root: 草～ *grass roots* /树～ *roots of a tree* /直～ *tap root* /连～拔 *pull up by the tree* ②【数】root; solution of an algebraic equation:平方～ *square root* /立方～ *cube root* ③ root; foot; base:城墙～ *the foot of a city wall* /舌～ *the root of a tongue* ④ offspring; descendant progeny:单～独苗 *sole male offspring* ⑤ cause; origin; source; root:病～ *cause of illness* /祸～ *root-cause of trouble or disaster* ⑥【化】radical:酸～ *acid radical* ⑦ thoroughly; completely; entirely ⑧[量] long thing piece:几～头发 *several strands of hair* /一～木柴 *a piece of fire wood*

【根本】① base; foundation; root:我们一定要从～上解决问题。*We should tackle the problem at the root.* ② basic; essential; cardinal; fundamental: ～原因 *basic reason; root cause* / ～变化 *fundamental change; radical transformation* / ～出发点 *basic point of departure* / ～原则 *cardinal principle* ③ at all; simply; ever:我们所有人～就不赞成你的主张。*All of us don't agree with you at all.* /我～没有说过这种话。*I have made such remarks.* ④ radically; thoroughly; completely:问题已经得到～解决。*The problem has been settled completely.* /这～行不通。*This is wholly impractical.*

【根本法】fundamental law(i. e. a constitution); a body of basic laws

【根除】thoroughly do away with; eradicate; root out; uproot: ～水患 *eliminate the scourge of floods* / ～弊端 *stamp out (or eradicate) malpractice*

【根底】① foundation; groundwork:他的中文～不错。*He has a solid foundation in Chinese.* ② cause; root; origin:追问～ *inquire into the cause of the matter?* /事故的～我不太清楚。*I'm not quite clear about the background of this accident.*

【根雕】tree-root carving (a handicraft); tree-root sculpture

【根腐病】【农】root rot

【根冠】【植】root cap

【根号】【数】radical sign

【根基】① foundation; groundwork; basis:打好～ *build up a solid foundation* / ～稳固 *have a firm foundation* ② property accumulated over a long time; resources:底子薄,～差 *poor in foundation and scanty in resources*

【根茎】【植】rhizome

【根究】make a thorough investigation of; probe into; get to the bottom of; inquire into: ～缘由 *probe into the cause* /案件真相,必须～。*A thorough investigation of the case must be made.*

【根据】① on the basis of; according to; in conformity with; in line with: ～群众的利益和愿望 *in accordance with the interests and desires of the masses* / ～具体的情况 *in the light of specific conditions; on the merit of each case* / ～天气预报 *according to the weather forecast* ② basis; grounds; foundation:毫无～ *utterly groundless* /缺乏科学～ *want of scientific basis*

【根据地】base area; base: ～军民 *army and people of a base area*

【根绝】stamp out; root out; eradicate; uproot; do away with: ～事故 *eliminate accidents* / ～腐败 *stamp out corruption* / ～非典 *root out SARS* / ～弊端 *do away with bad practice*

【根瘤】【植】root nodule: ～菌 *nodule bacteria*

【根毛】【植】root hair

【根苗】① root and shoot:长出了～ *put out shoots* ② source; root:铲除腐败的～ *eliminate the root of corruption* ③[旧](male) offspring; posterity:他不是刘家惟一的～。*He is not the only offspring of the Lius.*

【根深蒂固】deeply rooted and firmly planted; well-founded; have a firm foundation; deep-seated: ～的偏见 *deep-seated prejudice; Ingrained bias* /结束了～的官僚作风 *put an end to the deeply entrenched bureaucratic way of doing things*

【根深叶茂】be deeply rooted and thickly covered with foliage; well-established; (trees) thick with leaves and deep-rooted

【根式】【数】radical (expression)

【根由】cause; origin:追查～ *find out the whys and wherefores*

【根源】① source; origin; root:找出事故的～ *find out why the accident was made* ② originate; stem from; come from:这些现象～于无知。*These phenomena stem from ignorance.*

【根植】take root; strike root

【根治】effect a radical cure; cure once and for all; bring under permanent control: ～肺结核 *effect a radical cure of tuberculosis* / ～手术 *radical operation* / ～黄河 *permanently harness the Huanghe River*

【根子】[口] ① root (of a plant):这棵松树的～扎

得很深。*The pine is deep-rooted.* ② cause; origin; source; root:要找出犯错误的思想~。*The ideological roots of the mistake must be found out.*

跟 ① heel:右脚~ *right heel*; *heel of the right foot* /靴后~ *heel of a boot* ② follow: ~我来。*Follow me or come along with me.* /步步紧~。*Follow closely step by step.* ③ (used as a preposition to introduce the recipient of an action) with; and; to; from: ~工人农民交朋友 *make friends with workers and peasants* /我有一句话~你讲。*There is only a sentence I want to talk to you about.* ④ (used to indicate accompaniment, relationship, involvement, etc.) with: ~父母住一块儿 *live with one's parents* ⑤ (used as a preposition to show comparison) as; from:他~你一样高。*He is as tall as you.* /今天的活儿~往常一样。*Our job today is the same as before.* ⑥ and: 一楼~四楼的水管都坏了。*Water pipes on the first and forth floor are all out of order.* ⑦ (of a woman) marry sb:因为丑,她只好~了他。*She was ugly and had to marry him.*

【跟班】① join a regular shift or class; work with a team, group or class: ~听课 *audit a class* / ~劳动 *go to work in a workshop for a specified period of time* ② [旧] footman; attendant

【跟脚】① (of shoes) fit well:这双袜子大小正好,很~。*This pair of socks is exactly my size and fits well.* ② (of children) follow elders and be unwilling to leave. ③ close upon sb's heels:你刚出去,你哥哥~儿就来找你了。*Your elder brother came to see you the moment you left.* ④ [旧] wait upon the master when out on a journey: ~的 *footman*

【跟屁虫】[方] persistent follower; shadow; pest

【跟前】① in front of; near; close to:小朋友挤到了首长的~。*The kid pressed forward to be near the commanding officer.* ② just before:新年~ *shortly before New Year's Day* ③ (of one's children) living with one:同学们都不在她~。*None of the students stay with her.*

【跟上】keep pace with; catch up with; keep abreast of: ~时代的步伐 *keep pace with the times* /跟不上形势的需要 *fall short of the demands of the times* / ~形势 *keep abreast of the current situation*

【跟随】① follow; go after: ~左右 *follow one wherever one goes* /我们~着先辈的足迹前进。*We followed in the steps of forerunners and marched onward.* ② retinue; entourage

【跟头】① tumble; fall:小孩摔了个~,腿受了伤。*The child fell and injured his leg.* ② somersault: 杂技演员一口气翻了八个~。*The acrobat did eight somersaults at a stretch.*

【跟头虫】wiggler; wriggler

【跟踪】follow the tracks of; trail:雪地~ *follow sb's tracks in the snow* / ~追击 *go in hot pursuit of* / ~程序 *tracing routine* / ~信号 *tracking signal* / ~装置 *follow-up device*; *tracking apparatus*; *tracker*

gén

哏 [方] ① amusing; comical; funny; farcical: 老人笑的样子有点~。*The way of the old man laughs is quite funny.* /小孩说话的样子真~。*The way the kid speaks is really amusing.* ② clownish speech or behavior; clowning; antics: 逗~ *play the fool* /他说话带~。*There is humor in his words.*

gěn

艮[1] [方] brusque; blunt; straightforward; sharp:这女士说的话太~。*The lady put it too sharply.* /这小家伙真~。*The kid is really blunt.*

艮[2] (of food) tough; hard; leathery:发~ *turn tough* / ~苹果不好吃。*Leathery apples taste bad.*

gèn

亘 extend; stretch:横~ *lie across*; *span* / ~古及今 *from time immemorial down to the present day* /绵~数百里(*of a mountain range*) *extend for hundreds of li*

【亘古未有】no such thing from days of old; never from time immemorial down to the present day; unprecedented; unheard-of: ~奇迹 *unprecedented wonder*

gēng

更[1] ① change; alter; replace: ~换位置 change place / ~时间 *alter the time* /除旧~新 *replace the old with the new* /改弦~张 *change over to new ways*; *make a fresh start* ② [书] experience:少不~事 *young and green*; *inexperienced*

更[2] one of the five two-hour periods into which the night was formerly divided; watch:三~半夜 *in the dead of night* /巡~ *keep (night) watch*

see also gèng

【更杯易箸】bring clean cups and chopsticks; renew the feast

【更迭】change; alternate:政府~ *reshuffle of government* /内阁~ *a change of cabinet*

【更动】alter; change; modify:人事~ *personnel changes* / ~计划 *modify the plan*

【更番】by turns; alternately: ~值勤 *be on duty by turns*

【更夫】[旧] night watchman

【更改】change; alter: ~路线 *change a route* /不可~的决定 *an unalterable decision*

【更换】change; replace; alter; renew: ~衬衣 *change one's shirt* / ~零件 *renewal part*

【更年期】climacteric; menopause; change of life

【更深人静】deep in the night and all is quiet; all is quiet in the dead of night; the night is late and people are quiet:在～的时候 *at dead of night*; *in the quiet of the night*

【更生】① regenerate; revive; revitalize:自力～ *regeneration through one's own efforts* ② renew; recycle; reclaim: ～产品 *reclaimed products*

【更替】interchange; replace; alternate; change:季节～ *change of season*; *alternation of seasons* / 生产方式的～ *the replacement of one mode of production by another*

【更新】① renew; replace; update:设备～ *renewal of equipment* / 设备在不断地～。*New ones are continually replacing old equipments.* ② (of forest, plants, etc.) renew; rejuvenate; restore; renovate:品种～ *renovation of variety* / ～观念 *renew idea*; *change one's concepts* / ～投资 *replacement investment*

【更新改造】make replacements and technical innovations: ～项目 *projects of equipment renewal and technological transformation*

【更新换代】replace the old with the new; upgrade: 采用先进技术,促进产品的～ *use advanced technique to update older products*

【更新率】turnover rate

【更衣】change one's cloth:上楼～ *go upstairs to have a change* / ～室 *changing room*; *locker room*

【更正】make corrections; correct; emend:做必要的～ *make necessary corrections* / ～通知 *advice to correction* / ～凭单 *correction voucher*

庚 ① the seventh of the ten Heavenly Stems ② age:贵～ *your age* / 年～ *date of birth* / 同～ *of the same age*

耕 ① plough; till; cultivate: 秋～ *autumn ploughing* / 深～细作 *deep ploughing and intensive cultivation* ② work (for a living); do:笔～ *making a living by writing*; *take up writing*:刀～火种 *slash-and-burn cultivation*

【耕层】【地】topsoil

【耕畜】farm animal; draught animal:饲养～ *raise farm animals*

【耕地】① plough; till; cultivate:帮邻居～ *do farm work for one's neighbour* ② cultivated land:可～ *arable land* / ～面积 *area under cultivation*; *cultivated land* / 未～ *uncultivated land*

【耕具】tillage implements; farm-tool

【耕牛】farm cattle; ox used in farming

【耕耘】plough and weed; cultivate:勤于～ *work hard at cultivation*

【耕种】till; cultivate

【耕作】tillage; cultivation; farming: ～方法 *methods of cultivation*; *farming methods* / ～技术 *farming technique* / ～制度 *cropping system* / ～机械 *tillage machinery*; *farming equipment*

羹 thick soup; jelly-like food (such as custard):鸡蛋～ *egg custard* / 莲子～ *custard of lotus seeds*

【羹匙】soup spoon; tablespoon

gěng

埂 ① a low bank of earth between fields:田～ ridge / 土～ *footpath in the fields*; *earth dike* ② long, narrow mould:山～ *a hill mould* ③ earth dike or embankment:堤～ *earth dike or embankment*

耿 ①［书］bright; brilliant: ～光 *bright light* ② honest and just; upright:忠心～～为教育 *dedicated heart and soul to education work* ③ (Gěng) a surname

【耿耿】①［书］bright; brilliant: ～星河 *the bright Milky Way* ② devoted; dedicated; staunch:忠心～ *loyal and faithful* ③ have on one's mind; be troubled; worried: ～不寐 *lose sleep over sth* / ～在心 *have sth on one's mind*

【耿耿于怀】take sth to heart; deeply concerned at heart; constantly remembering in one's heart; nurse a grudge

【耿直】honest and just; honest and frank; upright; candid and outspoken:性情～ *be of honest disposition*; *be candid and outspoken* / 秉性～ *be upright by nature*

哽 ① choke: 吃饭～着了 *choke over food*; *choked by food* ② choke (with emotion); feel a lump in one's throat

【哽咽】choke with sobs:女孩～难言。*The girl was choked with sobs and words failed him.*

梗 ① stalk; stem:芹菜～ *celery stalk* / 菠菜～ *spinach stalk* / 花～ *stem of a flower* / 荷～ *lotus stem* ② a slender piece of wood or metal:火柴～ *matchstick* ③ straighten; stiffen; hold stiff:老头～着脖子一句话也不说。*The old man stiffened his neck without saying a word.* ④ obstruct; block; hinder:从中做～ *place obstacles in the way* ⑤［书］obstinate; stubborn:顽～ *obstinate* / 强～ *firm and stubborn*

【梗概】broad outline; main idea; summary; gist: 这篇小说的～ *gist of the novel* / ～表示 *skeletal representation*

【梗塞】① block; obstruct; choke:交通～ *traffic jam* / 道路～ *with the road blocked up* ②【医】infarction:心肌～ *myocardial infarction*

【梗死】【医】infarct: ～形成 *infarction*

【梗阻】① block; obstruct; hamper:山川～ *be separated by mountains and rivers*; *be far away from each other be far away and out of touch* ②【医】obstruction:肠～ *intestinal obstruction* / 不完全～ *partial obstruction*

鲠 ①［书］fishbone:如～在喉 *like a fishbone stuck in the throat* ② (of a fishbone) get caught in one's throat:小孩吃得太快,被鱼刺～住了。*The kid ate so fast that a fishbone got stuck in his throat.*

gèng

更 ① more; still more; even more: ~少 *less; fewer* / ~坏 *worse* /刮了一夜北风,天~冷了。*The weather has got even colder since the north wind blew all night.* ② [书] further; furthermore; what is more: ~进一步 *go a step further* / ~有甚者 *what is more* / ~上一层楼 *climb one story higher*
see also gēng

【更加】more; still more; even more:情况~复杂了。*The matter became even more complicated.* /我们的措施比他的~容易,~好。*Our measure is easier and better than his.*

gōng

工 ① worker; workman; laborer; working class:女~ *woman worker* /童~ *child laborer* /技~ *skilled worker; technician* /钳~ *bench work; fitter* /司炉~ *fireman* ② work; labour:上~ *go to work* /收~ *stop work; knock off* /省料省~ *save both material and labor* ③ (construction) project:动~ *begin a project* /竣~ *complete a project* /道路正在施~中。*The road is under construction.* ④ industry:化~ *chemical industry* /军~ *war industry* ⑤ man-day:这活需要十个~。*This job needs ten man-days.* ⑥ skill; craftsmanship; workmanship:唱~ (*art of*) *singing* /做~ *acting* /基本~ *basic skills* ⑦ be good at; be versed in; be expert at:~诗善书 *be well versed in writing and poetry* ⑧ exquisite; excellent; delicate; fine:这幅画用笔~巧。*The painting shows fine and skilful brushwork.* ⑨ engineer:高~ *senior engineer*

【工本】cost (of production); expense:不惜~ *spare no expense; do sth whatever the cost*

【工笔】【美】fine brushwork; traditional Chinese realistic painting characterized by fine brushwork and close attention to detail: ~画 *meticulous painting; drawing made with fine, delicate strokes*

【工兵】(army) engineer:坑道~ *sapper* /轻~ *pioneer* / ~连 *engineering company*

【工部】the Ministry of works in feudal China; the Broad of Works

【工厂】factory; mill; plant; works:钢铁~ *iron and steel works* /化~ *chemical works* / ~区 *factory district* / ~自动化 *factory automation*

【工场】workshop; shop:手工业~ *handicrafts workshop* / ~手工业 *workshop handicraft*

【工潮】worker's demonstration; worker's protest movement; strike movement:闹~ *go on strike*

【工尺】a traditional Chinese musical scale: ~谱 *a traditional Chinese musical notation*

【工程】① engineering:土木~ *civil engineering* /采矿~ *mining engineering* /电机~ *electrical engineering* /机械~ *mechanical engineering* / ~地质学 *engineering geology* / ~管理 *engineering management* / ~经济学 *value engineering; engineering economics* / ~师 *engineer* / ~造价 *cost of construction* / ~学院 *college of engineering* / ~标准 *engineering standard* / ~技术人员 *engineers and technicians* ② project; program:水利~ *water conservancy project* / ~浩大 *a gigantic project; a tremendous amount of work* /建筑~ *construction project* /安居~ *housing project* / ~进度和质量 *progress and quality of a project* /按~进度分阶段付款 *progress payment*

【工党】the Labour Party:英国~ *British Labour Party*

【工地】building site; construction site: ~负责人 *person in charge of a construction site* / ~上冷冷清清。*The construction site was a scene of desolation.*

【工段】① section a construction project ② workshop section

【工段长】section chief

【工蜂】worker (bee)

【工夫】① time:白费~ *waste one's time and energy* /老师去了没多大会~就回来了。*The teacher didn't take long to get there and come back.* ② workmanship; skill; art:苦练硬~ *practice hard to master the skill* /这位芭蕾演员可真有~。*The ballet dancer's skill is really superb!* ③ effort; work:花了好大的~ *put in a lot of work* ④ [方] at that time; when; as:正在说话的~,领导就来了。*The leader came as I was talking.* ⑤ free time; spare time; leisure:明天有~再来吧。*Come again tomorrow if you have time.*

【工会】trade union; labor union: ~会费 *union membership dues* / ~主义 *unionism; syndicalism*

【工价】labor cost

【工件】workpiece; work: ~架 *work rest* / ~夹具 *workpiece holder; (work) fixture*

【工匠】craftsman; artisan: ~师傅 *master artisan*

【工具】tool; means; instrument; implement:爱护~ *take good care of the tools* /木工~ *carpenter's tools* /运输~ *means of transport* / ~改革 *improvement of tools* / ~袋 *kit bag; workbag* / ~房 *tool house; tool storeroom* /参考~ (*in a library*) *reference tools; finding aids* /测量~ *measuring instrument* / ~箱 *toolbox; toolkit; workbox* / ~车床 *toolmaker lathe* / ~书 *reference book*

【工科】engineering course: ~学生 *student of engineering* / ~大学 *engineering university*

【工况】operating mode

【工力】① skill; expertise; craftsmanship: ~深厚 *remarkable craftsmanship* / ~不够 *lacking in skill* ② manpower; labour: ~短缺 *be short of manpower*

【工料】labor and materials (for a building project): ~成本 *flat cost*

【工龄】length of service; standing; seniority:一个

有五年～的工人 *a worker of five years standing* / ～工资 *pay based on years of service; seniority pay* / ～津贴 *seniority allowance*

【工贸】industry and trade: ～结合 *combination of industry and foreign trade*

【工农】workers and peasants: ～差别 *the difference between industry and agriculture* / ～联盟 *alliance of workers and peasants; worker-peasant alliance* / ～大众 *broad masses of workers and peasants* / ～子弟 *children of workers and peasants*

【工棚】builders' temporary shed; work shed: 搭～ *put up a work shed*

【工期】time limit for a project; schedule or deadline for a project: 延误～ *behind schedule* / 提高效率,缩短～。*Increase efficiency and shorten the time limit for the project.*

【工钱】① money paid for odd jobs; charge for a service: 做这套设备要多少～? *How much should I pay for having the equipment made?* ②［口］wages; pay: 克扣～ *dock part of the worker's pay*

【工巧】exquisite; superb; fine: ～的玉雕 *exquisite jade sculpture*

【工区】work area(a grass-roots unit of an industrial enterprise)

【工人】worker; workman; workingman: 产业～ *industrial worker* / ～阶级 *working class* / ～技术员 *technician of worker origin* /技术～ *technical worker* / ～领袖 *worker's leader* / ～运动 *labor movement* /农业～ *farm work* / ～俱乐部 *worker's club*

【工日】man-day

【工伤】injury suffered on the job; industrial injury: ～事故 *industrial accident* /因～致残 *become disabled because of Industrial injury*

【工商管理】business administration; business management: ～学院 *business school* /主修～ *major in business administration* / ～学硕士 *Master of Business Administration(MBA)*

【工商界】industrial and business circles; business circles: ～著名人士 *well-known figure in business circles*

【工商联】association of industry and commerce

【工商税】industry and commercial income tax

【工商银行】the Industrial and Commercial Bank

【工商业】industry and commerce: 私营～ *privately owned industrial and commercial enterprises*

【工时】man-hour; labor

【工事】fortifications; defense works: 构筑～ *build fortifications*

【工头】foreman; overseer

【工薪阶层】salaried worker; wage-earners

【工薪族】wage-earners

【工休日】day off; holiday: 今天是这个公司的～。*Today is a holiday in the firm.*

【工序】working procedure; process: 产品从生产到完工共需要十道～。*The product goes through a ten-step process from start to finish.*

【工业】industry: 煤炭～ *coal industry* /重～ *heavy industry* /国有化～ *nationalized industry* /基础～ *basic industry* /轻～ *light industry* /飞机制造～ *aircraft industry* /手～ *handicraft* /电力～ *power industry* /加工～ *processing industry* /机械制造～ *machine building industry* / ～成本制度 *industrial cost system* / ～大气压 *technical atmosphere* / ～电视 *industrial television* / ～基地 *industrial base* / ～品 *industrial products; manufactured goods* / ～体系 *industrial system* / ～噪声 *man-made noise* / ～总产值 *gross value of industrial output* / ～革命 *the Industrial Revolution* / ～化 *industrialize* / ～粉尘 *industrial dust*

【工艺】technology; craft; handicraft: ～流程 *technological process* / ～美术 *industrial art; arts and crafts* /手～ *handicraft* / ～品 *handicraft article; handiwork* / ～水平 *technological level* / ～要求 *technological requirements* /民间～ *folk craft*

【工友】① fellow worker; worker ② manual worker (such as janitor, cleaner, etc.); blue-collar worker

【工于心计】adept at scheming; very calculating; machiavellian

【工欲善其事,必先利其器】a workman must first sharpen his tools if he is to do his work well; success in a job presupposes ready tools

【工贼】scab; blackleg

【工长】section chief (in a workshop, or on a building site); foreman

【工整】orderly; careful and neat: 字迹～ *neatly lettered*

【工致】exquisite; delicate; fine; neat and refined

【工种】type of work in production: 我们工厂有车工、铣工、铸工、钳工等不同～。*Turning, milling foundry and benchwork are among the various jobs in our factory.*

【工转干】change of one's status from worker to cadre

【工装裤】overalls

【工资】wages; salary; pay: 基本～ *basic wages* /附加～ *supplementary wages* /货币～ *money wages* /计件～ *payment by the piece* / ～表 *payroll; pay sheet* / ～率 *wage rate* / ～制 *wage system* /实际～ *real wage* /领～ *draw one's salary; get one's pay* / 浮动～ *floating wages* /从～中扣除 *deduct from one's salary* / ～理论 *wage theory* / ～级别 *wage scale*

【工字形】I-shaped: 这座大楼呈～。*This building is I-shaped.*

【工作】① work; operate: 努力～ *work hard* / ～速度 *operating rate* / ～单位 *an organization in which one works; place of work* / ～服 *work clothes; boiler suit* / ～日 *workday* / ～语言 *working language* / ～作风 *style of work* / ～阻力 *working resistance* / ～量 *amount of work; work load* / ～台 *working table; bench* / ～样片 *film rushes* ② job; work; career: 找～ *look for a job* / 分配～ *assign jobs* /调动～ *transfer sb to another post* / ～证 *employee's card; I. D. card* ③ task;

G

work：经济～ *economic work* /社会～ *community work* /科研～ *research work* /～会议 *working conference* /～人员 *working personnel*; *working staff*/他是做消防～的。*He works in the fire brigade.* /人人都应做好本职～。*Everyone should do his own job well.*

【工作面】① face：采煤～ *coal face* /～运输机 *face conveyor* ②【机】working surface

【工作者】worker：电影～ *film worker* /教育～ *educational worker* /文艺～ *literary and art workers*; *writers and artists* /新闻～ *journalist* /音乐～ *musician*

弓 ① bow：弹～ *catapult* /弩～ *crossbow* /强～ *heavy bow* /～箭 *bow and arrow* ② bend; arch; bow：～着腰走路 *walk with one's back bent forward* /～着背 *arch one's back*; *bend low* ③ anything bow-shaped：大提琴的～ *bow of a cello* ④ wooden land-measuring dividers

【弓背】① back of a bow ② arch one's back; bend down：老人弓着背走出来。*The aged man came out bending low.* ③ hunchbacked; stooping

【弓箭】bow and arrow

【弓弦】bowstring：～乐器 *bowed instrument*; *string instrument*

【弓形】【数】① arc; segment of a circle ② bow-shaped; arched; curved

【弓腰】bend over; bend down; arch one's body; stoop

【弓子】① bow (of a stringed instrument) ② anything bow-shaped

公[1] ① public; state-owned; collective：假～济私 *jobbery*; *use public office for private gain* /交～ *hand over to the government* /归～ *make sth a public possession* /出以～心 *act in a public spirit* /充～ *confiscate* /克己奉～ *work selflessly for the public interest* ② common; general：～分母 *common denominator* ③ of the world; universal; international; metric：～海 *high seas* /～里 *kilometer* ④ make public; public：～之于众 *make known to the world*; *reveal to the public* ⑤ equitable; impartial; fair; just：秉～办理 *handle affairs equitably or impartially* /不～ *unfair*; *unjust* /大～无私 *unselfish*; *selfless* ⑥ male (animal)：这只兔子是～的。*This is a male rabbit.* ⑦ public affairs; official business：办～时间 *office time* /因～外出 *be away on official business* ⑧ duke：大～ *grand duke* /王～ *princes and dukes*

公[2] ① husband's father; father-in-law ② respectful term of address for an aged or elderly man：师～ *master's master*; *teacher's teacher*

【公安】public security：～机关 *public security organs* /～人员 *public security officers* /～局 *public security bureau* /～厅 *public security department* /～干警 *public security police* /～部 *the Ministry of Public Security*

【公案】①［旧］court desk used by a judge; court table：大堂摆着一张～。*Only one desk is placed in the courtroom.* ② complicated legal case：无头～ *intricate case without a clue* ③ controversial issue; sensational affair

【公办】government administered; state-run：～企业 *government run enterprise* /～学校 *state school*

【公报】communiqué; bulletin：新闻～ *press communiqué* /政府～ *government bulletin*

【公报私仇】use one's position to get even with another person for a private grudge; avenge a personal wrong I the name of public interests

【公倍数】【数】common multiple：最小～ *least (lowest) common multiple*

【公布】announce; publish; make public; issue; promulgate：～名单 *publish a name list* /～方案 *unfold a plan*; *lay one's plan before the public* /～法令 *promulgate a decree*

【公厕】public toilets; restroom; public lavatory

【公差】(gōngchā) ①【数】common difference ②【机】tolerance; allowable error：安装～ *(location) tolerance*

【公差】(gōng chāi) ① public errand; official business; noncombatant duty：出～ *go on a public errand*; *go on official business* ② person on a public errand

【公产】public property：私吞～ *embezzle public property* /保护～ *protect public property*

【公车】public (as opposed to private) vehicles

【公称】【机】nominal：～尺寸 *nominal dimension*

【公尺】meter; metre (m.)

【公出】be away on official business

【公畜】male animal (kept for breeding); stud

【公道】① justice：主持～ *uphold justice* /讨一个～ *ask for justice* ② fair; just; reasonable; impartial; evenhanded：说句～话 *to be fair*; *in fairness to sb* /办事～ *be evenhanded*; *be impartial* /待人～ *treat people with fairness* /买卖～ *be fair in business transaction*

【公德】public morality; social ethics：～心 *public spirit* /讲～ *have a strong sense of public morality*

【公敌】public enemy：头号～ *public enemy number one* /人民～ *an enemy of the people*

【公牍】［书］official document

【公断】① arbitrate：听候众人～ *await the verdict of the public* /～人 *umpire*; *arbitrator* ② make an impartial judgement

【公吨】metric ton (MT)

【公而忘私】forget selfishness in the interest of the public; be so devoted to public service as to forget one's own interests; be selfless

【公法】【律】① public law ② international law; law of nations：国际～ *public international law*

【公方】state ownership (in a joint state-private enterprise)：～代表 *representatives of state ownership (in a joint state-private enterprise)*

【公费】at public or state expense：～留学 *study abroad on state scholarship* /～旅游 *travel at public expense* /～医疗 *free medical service*; *public health service* /～吃喝 *wining and dining at public expense*; *junketing*

【公分】① centimeter（cm.）② gram（g.）
【公愤】public indignation；popular anger；public wrath：引起～ *arouse public indignation*
【公干】official business：你们有何～？*What important business brings you here?* /总经理将于近日来沪～。*The general manager is soon coming to Shanghai on business.*
【公告】① public notice；announcement；bulletin；proclamation：张贴～ *put up an announcement* / ～栏 *bulletin board* ② inform；announce
【公共】public；common；communal：～财产 *public property* / ～建筑 *public buildings* / ～道德 *public morality* / ～关系 *public relations* / ～卫生 *public health* / ～汽车 *bus* / ～责任保险 *public liability insurance* / ～秩序 *public order* / ～积累 *common accumulation* 。～食堂 *canteen* / ～事务 *public affairs* / ～投资 *public investment* / ～电话 *pay phone*；*public telephone* / ～基金 *public fund* / ～课 *common required course*
【公公】① husband's father；father-in-law：～婆婆待李梅如同亲生女儿一般。*Li Mei's parents-in-law treat their as her own daughter.* ②［方］（paternal）grandfather or（maternal）grandfather ③ grandpa；granddad：老～，请问到书店怎么走？*Grandpa, could you tell me how to get to the bookstore?* ④［旧］form of address for a eunuch
【公股】government share（in a joint state-private enterprise）
【公关】public relations；PR：～业务 *public relations business* / ～手法 *public relations ploy* / ～部门 *public relations department* / ～人员 *public relations officer* / ～小姐 *public relations miss* / ～部主任 *public relations manager* / ～先生 *public relations sir*
【公馆】residence（of a rich or important person）；mansion
【公国】duchy；dukedom；principality：卢森堡大～ *grand Duchy of Luxembourg*
【公海】high seas：～自由 *freedom of the open sea*
【公害】① social effect pollution；public hazard：塑料垃圾成了一大～。*Plastic rubbish has become a serious public hazard.* ② public plague；public scourge：贪污腐败已成～。*Corruption has become a public plague.*
【公函】official letter；official correspondence：来往～ *official correspondence*
【公鸡】cock；rooster：铁～ *out-and-out miser*
【公积金】accumulation fund；public reserve fund
【公祭】public memorial ceremony：各界人士为牺牲的烈士举行了～。*People from all walks of life held a memorial ceremony for the martyrs.*
【公家】［口］the state；the public；the organization：爱护～的财产 *take good care of public property* /损害～的利益 *harm public interests*
【公交】public transport：～路线 *bus line*；*public transport route*
【公斤】kilogram（kg.）；kilo
【公决】decide by the majority：全民～ *public or general referendum*
【公爵】duke：～夫人 *duchess*
【公开】① open；overt；public：～的秘密 *an open secret* / ～发表 *publish* / ～论战 *open polemics* / ～审判 *public trial* / ～报价 *public offer* / ～拍卖 *public auction* / ～赛 *open tournament* / ～投标 *open bidding*；*public bidding* / ～招标 *competitive bidding*；*competitive tender* / ～信 *open letter* /他们之间的矛盾已经～了。*Their disagreement is already in the open.* ② make public；make known to the public：～账目 *make the account known to the public* /把事情～出去 *make the matter known to the public*
【公开化】come out into the open；be brought into the open；make public；make known to the public
【公筷】serving chopsticks；chopsticks for serving food
【公款】public money；public fund：挪用～ *misappropriate public funds*
【公里】kilometre（km.）
【公理】①【数】axiom ② generally acknowledged truth；self-evidence truth；justice
【公历】the Gregorian calendar
【公立】established and maintained by the government；public：～学校 *public schools* / ～医院 *public hospital*
【公粮】agricultural tax paid in grain；grain delivered to the state；public grain：交～ *hand in grain tax*
【公量】【纺】conditioned weight
【公路】highway；road：高速～ *express highway*；*expressway* /信息高速～ *information superhighway* / ～交通 *highway communication* / ～运输 *highway transportation* / ～桥 *highway bridge* / ～容量 *highway capacity* / ～工程 *highway engineering* / ～路面板 *slab* / ～自行车赛 *road race* / ～支线 *feeder road*
【公论】public opinion；verdict of the masses：是非自有～。*Public opinion will decide which is right and which is wrong.*
【公民】citizen：中国～ *Chinese citizen* / ～身份 *citizenship* / ～投票 *referendum*；*plebiscite* / ～自由 *civil liberties* / ～权 *civil rights*；*citizenship*；*citizen's rights* / ～基本义务 *fundamental duties of citizens*
【公亩】arc（a.）
【公墓】cemetery
【公平】fair；just；impartial；equitable：～合理 *fair and reasonable* / ～的判决 *just judgement* / ～贸易 *fair trade* / ～竞争 *fair play*；*fair competition* / ～原则 *equitable principles*
【公婆】husband's father and mother；parents-in-law：伺候～ *wait upon one's parents-in-law*
【公仆】public servant：人民～ *servant of the people*
【公切线】【数】common tangent
【公勤人员】service personnel in an office；office attendants；members of the service staff

G

【公顷】hectare(ha.)

【公然】[贬] openly; undisguisedly; flagrantly; brazenly: ~背叛 *openly betray* / ~撕毁协议 *brazenly tear up an agreement* / ~破坏停战协议 *make a barefaced breach of the armistice agreement*

【公认】generally acknowledge; universally recognize; establish: ~的国际关系原则 *generally recognized principles governing international relations* / ~的领袖 *acknowledged leader* / ~的会计原则 *generally accepted accounting standard (GAAP)*

【公社】① primitive commune ② commune: 人民~ *people's commune* / 巴黎~ *the Paris Commune*

【公审】【律】① open trial; public trial ② trial openly

【公升】litre

【公使】envoy; minister: ~馆 *legation* / 特命全权~ *envoy Extraordinary and Minister Plenipotentiary*

【公式】formula: 数学~ *mathematical formula* / ~主义 *formulism*

【公式化】formulism (in art and literature); formulistic; stereotyped: ~的写作手法 *stereotyped writing*

【公事】public affairs; official business; official duties: 处理~ *attend to official duties* / 我还有很多~要办。*I still have a lot of official duties to attend to.*

【公事公办】public business should be strictly managed; public affairs should be conducted in an orthodox way; business is business

【公署】government office

【公说公有理,婆说婆有理】each of two quarreling parties insists that he is right; both parties claim to be in the right

【公司】company; corporation; firm: 钢铁~ *iron and steel company* / 保险~ *insurance company* / 进出口~ *import and export corporation* / 经营皮货的~ *firm dealing in furs* / ~所得税 *corporation income tax* / ~法 *corporation act* / ~律师 *corporation lawyer* / ~章程 *corporation by-laws*

【公私】public and private: ~兼顾 *give concurrent consideration to public and private interests* / ~分明 *be scrupulous in separating public from private interests* / ~两便 *be beneficial to both public and private interests* / ~合营 *joint state-private ownership*

【公诉】【律】public prosecution: 提起~ *institute prosecution; bring a public charge* / ~人 *public prosecutor; the prosecution* / ~权 *right of prosecution* / ~书 *bill of indictment; public indictment*

【公堂】①[旧] law court; tribunal: 私设~ *set up a clandestine tribunal* ② ancestral hall; memorial temple

【公推】recommend by general acclaim: 村长由群众~。*The village head is to be elected by all the members in it.*

【公文】official document: 传送~ *deliver official documents* / ~包 *briefcase; portfolio* / ~袋 *official envelop* / ~纸 *paper for copying official documents*

【公务】public affairs; official business: 执行~ *perform official duties* / ~车 *service car* / ~人员 *government functionary* / ~员 *government office worker; civil servant* / ~繁冗 *be overburdened with official duties*

【公物】public property: 爱护~ *take good care of public property*

【公休】general holiday; official holiday; public holiday

【公演】perform in public; give a performance: 那部电影下个月~。*The film will be put on stage next month.*

【公羊】ram; male sheep

【公议】have a public or mass discussion: 交由群众~ *pass on to the rank and file for discussion*

【公益】public good; public welfare: 热心~ *be public-spirited* / ~广告 *public-interest ads* / ~劳动 *volunteer labor* / ~事业 *public service; public welfare undertaking*

【公意】will of the public; public will: 不能违背~ *must not go against the will of the public*

【公因子】【数】common factor: 最大~ *greatest common factor*

【公营】manage by the public; be publicly-owned; be publicly-operated; public: ~经济 *the public sector of the economy; public economy* / ~企业 *public enterprise*

【公用】for public use; public; communal: ~电话 *public telephone; pay phone* / ~事业 *public utilities; public service* / ~网 *public network* / ~语言 *common language* / ~权 *commonage*

【公有】publicly-owned; public: ~财产 *public property* / ~化 *transfer to public ownership; socialize* / ~土地 *public land* / ~制 *public ownership (of means of production)*

【公寓】①[旧] lodging house; room or suite in a hotel rented by the month ② block of flats; apartment house; apartment: ~大楼 *apartment building*

【公元】the Christian era: ~2000年 A.D. 2000 / ~前200年 200 B.C.

【公园】park: 国家~ *national park*

【公约】① convention; pact; treaty: 签订~ *sign a convention* / 缔结~ *conclude a pact* / 日内瓦~ *Geneva Convention* ② joint pledge: 服务~ *service pledge (given by workers in the service trades)* / 治安~ *public security pledge*

【公约数】【数】common divisor: 最大~ *greatest common divisor*

【公允】just and sound; fair and equitable; impartial; evenhanded: 执法~ *enforce law evenhandedly* / 貌似~ *pretend to treat all sides alike*

【公债】(government) bonds; public debt: 经济建设~ *economic construction bonds* / ~发行 *public subscription* / ~券 *government securities debentures; government bond* / 购买~ *buy bonds* / 发行

G

～ *issue bonds*

【公章】official seal：在收据上加盖～ *affix an official seal to a receipt*

【公正】just; fair; impartial; fair-minded：～的裁决 *true verdict* / ～的审判 *impartial trial* / ～的仲裁人 *impartial arbitrator* / ～的舆论 *fair-minded public opinion* / ～待人 *be just to a person* / 有个裁判不～。*One of the judges was partial.*

【公证】notarize; attest：～事务 *notarial affairs* / ～处 *notary office* / ～人 *notary; notary public* / ～手续 *notarial acts* / ～委托书 *letter of commitment*

【公之于世】make known to the world; make public; reveal to the public; make public to the world

【公职】government office; official post; public employment：担任～ *hold public office* / 开除～ *discharge sb from public employment; take sb's name off the books* / ～人员 *civil servant*

【公制】the metric system：～尺寸 *metric size* / 折成～ *convert to the metric system* / ～螺纹 *metric thread*

【公众】the public：～舆论 *public opinion* / ～集会 *public rally; public gathering* / ～人物 *public figure* / ～领袖 *leader of the public*

【公主】princess

【公转】【天】revolution

【公子】son of a feudal prince or high official; sb's son：富家～ *son of a rich family*

【公子哥儿】pampered son of a wealthy or influential family; dandy; beau：张华是个典型的～。*Zhang Hua is a typical playboy.*

功 ① meritorious service or deed; achievement; merit; exploit：三等～ *merit citation class* Ⅲ / 军～ *military exploits* / 立大～ *render outstanding service* / 领导的～大于过。*The leader's achievements outweighed his errors.* ② achievement; result; effect; success：好大喜～ *crave greatness and success* / 徒劳无～ *make a futile effort* / 大～告成 *be crowned with success* / 教育之～ *the fruits of education* ③ skill; technique：基本～ *basic skill* / 练～ *practice one's skill; do exercises in gymnastics, acrobatics, etc.* / 张小姐唱～好，做～亦佳。*Miss Zhang sings well and acts gracefully.* ④ work：机械～ *mechanical work*

【功败垂成】fail in a great undertaking on the verge of success; suffer defeat when victory is within one's grasp; fall through when success in sight

【功臣】person who has rendered outstanding service; hero：开国～ *founders of a state* / 以～自居 *give oneself the airs of a hero*

【功成不居】disclaim all achievements one has made; claim no credit for one's service

【功成身退】retire after winning merit; retire from public life after a great work has done; retire after having made one's mark

【功成业就】be crowned with success

【功到自然成】constant effort yields sure success

【功德】① merits and virtues：不可忘记先辈们造这个大坝的～。*We should not forget our ancestors for the great pains they took in building the dam for us.* ②【宗】merit; benefaction; charitable and pious deeds; good deeds or works：积～ *accumulate virtue; do good deeds*

【功德无量】kindness knows no bounds; boundless beneficence; great service to mankind

【功德圆满】come to a successful end; round it off; achieve perfect virtues and merits

【功底】basic training; grounding in basic skills; foundation：～扎实 *have a good grounding in basic skills* / 天赋好，～差 *be talented but lacking in basic training*

【功夫片】martial arts movie; action movie

【功过】merits and demerits; contributions and blunders：～是非 *merits and demerits, right and wrong* / ～相抵。*Merits neutralize demerits.* / ～不分。*No distinction is made between merits and demerits.*

【功绩】merits and achievements; contribution; service; meritorious deeds：他为革命事业建立了不可磨灭的～。*He has made indelible contributions to the revolutionary cause.*

【功课】① course; lesson; subject：复习～ *review one's lessons* / 她每门～都是良。*She gets straight Bs for all the courses.* ② schoolwork; homework：做～ *do homework*

【功亏一篑】lack a basketful; fail to succeed for lack of a final effort; fall short of success at the last stage

【功劳】contribution; merit; meritorious deeds; service; credit：躺在～薄上 *rest on one's laurels* / ～属于大家。*The credit should go to every one.*

【功劳簿】record of merits

【功利】utility; material gain：热衷于～ *be keen on fame and wealth* / ～主义 *utilitarianism* / ～主义者 *utilitarian*

【功率】【物】power：～计 *dynamometer* / 额定～ *rated power* / 输出～ *output rating* / ～表 *power meter; wattmeter*

【功名】scholarly honor or official rank (in feudal times)：博取～ *seek official position* / ～富贵 *fame and fortune* / ～利禄 *position and wealth; rank, fame and fortune*

【功能】function：～锻炼 *functional training* / ～键 *function key* / ～主义 *functionalism* / ～性障碍 *functional disorder* / ～各异 *different in function* / ～失调 *functional disturbance* / ～元件 *functional element* / ～性疾病 *functional disease*

【功效】effect; efficiency; efficacy：～比原来提高了两倍。*The efficiency has increased twofold.* / 此药～非常显著。*This medicine is most efficacious.*

【功勋】exploits; feat; meritorious service：～卓著 *notable exploits*

【功业】achievements; exploits; feat; credit

【功用】function; use

攻 ① attack; take the offensive; assault; fight：远交近～ *befriend distant states while attac-*

king those nearby /火～ *fire attack* / ～城 *attack a city* / ～入敌阵 *storm into the enemy position* /围～ *besiege*; *lay siege to* /佯～ *feign attack*; *make a feint* /总～ *general offensive* /反守为～ *turn defensive into offensive* ② accuse; charge; refute:群起而～之。*Everyone points an accusing finger at him.* ③ study; specialize in; major in:专～数学 *major in math*

【攻城略地】capture territory; attack cities and seize territories

【攻打】attack; assault; assail: ～敌人的弹药库 *attack the enemy's ammunition depot*

【攻读】① study assiduously; work diligently; diligently study:刻苦～ *study hard* ② specialize in; major in; read: ～英语 *study English*

【攻关】① storm a strategic pass:突击队～没有成功。*The shock brigade failed to seize the pass.* ② tackle or overcome a key problem: ～小组 *task team* /攻下这一关,其他问题就好办了。*Once this problem is settled, others will be easy to solve.*

【攻击】① attack; assault; assail; take the offensive:发起总～ *launch a general offensive* / ～敌军阵地 *assail the enemy's position* / ～点 *a point chosen for attack*; *point of attack* ② vilify; accuse; charge; let fly at; attack:人身～ *personal attack* /蓄意～ *deliberately attack* /无端的～ *groundless charges*

【攻击机】attack plane; attacker

【攻坚】① storm fortifications; assault fortified positions: ～部队 *assault troops* / ～战 *storming of heavily fortified positions* ② tackle a thorny problem

【攻克】① capture; take; conquer; seize: ～城市 *capture a city* / ～敌人据点 *capture an enemy stronghold* ② overcome a difficult problem; surmount a thorny difficulty: ～难关 *resolve a serious difficulty*; *solve a difficult problem*

【攻破】make a breakthrough; break through; penetrate; breach: ～敌军防线 *break through the enemy defense line*

【攻其不备】attack when the enemy is unprepared; take a person unawares; strike before the enemy is prepared; catch sb by surprise

【攻取】attack and catch; storm and capture; strike and occupy: ～据点 *capture a stronghold* / ～城池 *storm and capture a city* / ～要塞 *attack and catch a stronghold*

【攻势】offensive; offence:采取～ *take the offensive* /政治～ *political offensive* / ～防御 *offensive defense* / ～作战 *offensive operation* /心理～ *psychological offensive*

【攻守同盟】an agreement between partners (in crime) not to give each other away; alliance for offense and defense; offensive and defensive alliance; pact to shied each other

【攻丝】【机】tapping: ～机 *tapping machine* / ～装置 *chasing bar*

【攻无不克】carry everything before one; be all-conquering; be ever-victorious:战无不胜,～ *take every objective one attacks and win every battle one fights*

【攻陷】capture; take; seize; storm:解放军势如破竹,一连～了好几座城池。*The PLA smashed all resistance and captured a number of cities in succession.*

【攻心】① attack the mind; try to persuade an offender to confess; mount a psychological attack; try to win over sb's heart:政策～ *try to win over or obtain a confession from a person by explaining the Party's policy* / ～战 *war of nerves*; *psychological warfare* ②【中医】be in a coma or remain in a stupor (because of sorrow or hatred); be attacked by internal heat:怒气～ *be burnt by pent-up anger*

【攻心为上】psychological offense is the best of tactics; the best way is to win over people's heart

【攻占】attack and occupy; storm and seize; strike and capture: ～敌人城池 *attack and capture an enemy city*

供 ① supply; feed; furnish; provide: ～气 *gas supply* / ～电系统 *system of power supply* / ～水 *water supply* / ～不起 *unable to meet the demand*; *unable to afford the cost* / ～油泵 *fuel feed pump* / ～油箱 *oil feeding reservoirs* ② for (the use or convenience of):仅～参考 *for your reference only* /这个饭厅可～五百人同时用饭。*This dining hall can accommodate five hundred people at a time.*

see also gòng

【供不应求】supply is unable to meet the demand; supply falls short of demand; demand outstrips supply; demand exceeds supply

【供电】supply power; supply electricity: ～调度员 *load dispatcher* / ～干线 *supply main* / ～局 *power supply bureau* / ～中心 *centre of supply*

【供过于求】supply exceeds demand; supply outstrips demand; drug on the market

【供给】supply; provide; furnish: ～生活必需品 *provide daily necessities* / ～制 *the supply system* /原料由国家～。*Raw materials are provided by the state.*

【供暖】【建】heating:热水～ *hot water heating* /蒸汽～ *steam heating* / ～、通风和空气调节 *heating, ventilating, and air conditioning* / ～设施 *heating facilities* /中央～系统 *central heating system*

【供气】【机】air feed: ～管 *air supply pipe*

【供求】supply and demand: ～关系 *the relation between supply and demand* / ～平衡 *balance between supply and demand* / ～价格 *price based on supply and demand* / ～率 *supply-demand ratio* / ～律 *law of supply and demand*

【供销】supply and marketing: ～合作社 *supply and marketing cooperative*

【供需】supply and demand: ～矛盾 *imbalance between supply and demand* /避免～脱节 *avoid the divorce of supply from demand*

【供养】provide for (one's parents and elders); support: ~老人 *support the elders* / ~孩子 *support the children*
【供应】supply; provide: 食品~ *food supply* / 计划~ *planned supply* / 免费~ *supply free of charge (or gratis)* / ~充足 *be in liberal supply* / 市场~ *supply of commodities; market supplies* / ~点 *supply centre* / ~船 *tender* / ~线 *supply line*
肱 [书] the upper arm; arm: 曲~而枕 *sleep with one's head resting on one's bent arm* / ~动脉 *brachial artery*
【肱骨】【生】humerus
宫 ① palace: 行~ *imperial palace for stays away from the capital* / 皇~ *imperial palace* ② (celestial) palace; residence of immortals: 天~ *heavenly palace* / 月~ *palace on the moon; moon* ③ temple (used in a name): 雍和~ *the Lama Temple of Peace and Harmony (in Beijing)* ④ place for cultural activities and recreation: 劳动人民文化~ *working People's Cultural Palace* ⑤【生理】womb; uterus: 子~ *uterus; womb* ⑥ (Gōng) a surname
【宫灯】palace lantern
【宫殿】palace: ~式建筑 *palatial architecture*
【宫调】【音】modes of ancient Chinese music
【宫内节育器】intrauterine device(IUD)
【宫女】maid in an imperial palace; maid of honor
【宫廷】① imperial palace; palace: ~侍卫 *imperial bodyguard* / ~政变 *palace coup* ② royal or imperial court; court
【宫外孕】【医】ectopic pregnancy; extrauterine pregnancy
【宫闱】[书] palace chambers: ~秘事 *palace secrets*
【宫刑】castration (a punishment in ancient China)
恭 respectful; courteous; reverent: ~~敬敬 *with great respect; respectfully* / 洗耳~听 *listen with respectful attention* / 不~ *disrespectful; irreverent* / ~而有礼 *be polite and respectful*
【恭贺】congratulate: ~新禧! *Happy New Year!*
【恭候】await respectfully: ~多时 *await sb for quite a while* / ~光临。*We request the pleasure of your company.*
【恭谨】respectful and cautious: 态度~ *show respect and caution* / 在领导面前你应该~从事。*You should show respect and caution before your superior.*
【恭敬】respectfully; with great respect: 学生们~地向老师行了个礼。*The students bowed respectfully to their teacher.*
【恭敬不如从命】obedience is a better way of showing respect than outward reverence
【恭请】invite respectfully; invite sincerely: ~光临。*We request the honour of your presence.*
【恭顺】respectful and submissive; respectful and compliant
【恭维】flatter; compliment: ~话 *flattery; compliments* / 他~我英语说得好。*He complimented me on my English.*
【恭喜】*congratulate*: ~发财! *Congratulations and may you be prosperous!* / ~你们大功告成。*We congratulate you on the success of your work.*
躬 ① oneself; in person; personally: ~行实践 *practice what one preaches* / 反~自问 *examine oneself; introspect* ② bend forward; bow; stoop: 鞠~致谢 *bow one's thanks* / ~身下拜 *bow down and worship* / ~身 *bend at the waist*
【躬逢其盛】be present on the grand occasion; be personally present at the gala occasion; live in times of prosperity
【躬亲】attend to personally: 事必~ *attend to everything personally; see to everything oneself*
觥 an ancient bronze wine vessel
【觥筹交错】toast each other; wine flows freely at a dinner party; wine cups and gaming chips lie about in disarray

gǒng

巩 consolidate; strengthen; solidify
【巩固】① consolidate; strengthen; solidify: ~阵地 *consolidate a position* / ~地位 *strengthen one's position* ② consolidated; strong; solid; stable: 建立~政权 *build strong political power* / ~的国防 *strong national defence*
【巩膜】【生理】sclera
汞 【化】mercury; hydrargyrum(Hg)
【汞弧】【电】mercury arc: ~灯 *mercury-arc lamp*
【汞化】【化】mercurate; mercerize: ~物 *mercuride*
【汞化合物】mercury compound
拱[1] ① cup one hand in the other before the chest (as a form of salutation) ② encompass; encircle; surround: 众星~月。*A myriad of stars surround the moon.* ③ hunch up; hump up; arch: 腰~ *arch one's back* ④【建】arch: ~道 *archway* / ~式桥梁 *arch bridge* ⑤ push without using one's hands: 用身子把门~开 *push the door open with one's body*
拱[2] ① (of pigs, etc.) dig earth with the snout; (of earthworms, etc.) wriggle through the earth: 猪~土找食。*Pigs root in the ground for food.* ② sprout up through the earth: 芽儿~出枝头了。*The buds spring up from the branches.*
【拱坝】【水】arch dam
【拱抱】surround; encircle; embrace
【拱点】【天】apsis; apse
【拱顶】【建】dome; vault
【拱梁】arched girder
【拱门】【建】arched door
【拱棚】arched shed
【拱桥】【建】arch bridge: 双曲~ *double-curvature arch bridge*
【拱手】fold one's hands in a bow; make an obei-

sance by cupping one hand in the other before one's chest：～告别 *bid farewell in a respectful manner* / ～旁观 *look on with folded arm* / ～致礼 *salute with joined hands; salute with the hands folded* / ～称谢 *join one's hands together in salute and thanks*

【拱手让人】hand over on a platter; hand over with a bow; give up sth to others without putting up a fight

【拱卫】surround and protect; defend; guard

【拱券】【建】arch

gòng

共 ① common; general; universal：公～ *public; common* / ～享 *enjoy in common* ② share：～命运 *share a common fate* / ～患难 *share hardships* ③ doing the same thing; in company; together：～存亡 *live or die together* / ～进午餐 *have lunch together* ④ altogether; in all; all told：～三万字 *a total of thirty thousand words; thirty thousand words altogether* ⑤（short for 共产党）communist Party：中～ *the CPC (the Communist Party of China)*

【共产党】the Communist Party：～人 *Communist* / ～员 *member of the Communist Party; Party member; Communist*

【共产主义】communism：～道德 *communist morality* / ～风格 *communist style* / ～精神 *communist spirit* / ～战士 *fighter for communism* / ～觉悟 *communist consciousness* / ～理想 *communist ideal* / ～运动 *communist movement*

【共处】coexist：和睦～ *live in harmony*

【共存】coexist; survive together; exist side by side

【共电】【电】common battery：～制 *common-battery system; CB system* / ～电话机 *common battery telephone set*

【共度】spend (an occasion) together; pass the time together：～佳节 *celebrate a festival together*

【共轭】【物】conjugate：～点 *conjugate point* / ～根 *conjugate rots* / ～角 *conjugate angles* / ～像 *conjugate image* / ～轴 *conjugate axis*

【共犯】【律】accomplice

【共管】condominium

【共和】republicanism; republic：～制 *republicanism*

【共和党】(US) republican Party

【共和国】republic：中华人民～ *the People's Republic of China*

【共计】add up to; amount to; total：全班～十五人。*Altogether there are fifteen people in the class.*

【共聚】【化】copolymerization：～物 *copolymer*

【共聚一堂】gather together; gather in the same hall; come together：大家～，庆祝公司成立一百周年。*Gathering together in the hall we were celebrating the centenary of the founding of our corporation.*

【共勉】encourage each other; make joint effort：愿～之。*Let us encourage each other in our endeavors.*

【共鸣】①【物】resonance：～器 *resonator* / 发生～现象。*Acoustic resonance occurs.* ② sympathetic; response：引起～ *arouse sympathy; strike a sympathetic chord*

【共栖】【生】commensalism

【共青团】communist Youth League：～员 *member of the Communist Youth League; League member* / ～支部 *branch of the Communist Youth League; League branch*

【共生】①【地】intergrowth; paragenesis：～矿 *mineral intergrowth* / ～次序 *paragenesis* ②【生】symbiosis：～细菌 *symbiotic bacteria* / ～星 *symbiotic object*

【共识】common understanding; consensus; agreement：达成～ *reach agreement* / 寻求～ *seek common understanding*

【共事】work together (at the same organization); be fellow workers：～多年 *have been colleagues for many years* / 他俩在一个公司～。*They two work in the same firm.*

【共通】① universal; applicable to both or all：～的原则 *universally applicable principles* ② shared; common：热心是老师们～的优点。*Warmth is the common merit of the teachers.*

【共同】① common; shared; joint：～边界 *common boundary* / ～账户 *joint account* / ～关心的问题 *matters of common concern* / ～语言 *common language* / ～敌人 *common enemy* / 毫无～之处 *have nothing in common at all* ② together; jointly; in conjunction：～战斗 *fight side by side* / ～努力 *make joint effort* / ～负责 *share the responsibility* / ～行动 *act in concert* / ～点 *common ground* / ～保险 *co — insurance* / ～市场 *the Common Market* / ～富裕 *common prosperity*

【共同体】community：欧洲经济～ *the European Economic Community (EEC)* / 加勒比～ *the Caribbean Community (CARICOM)*

【共享】enjoy together; share：～天伦之乐 *enjoy family happiness together* / ～胜利的喜悦 *share the joys of victory* / ～软件 *shareware* / ～原则 *mutuality principle*

【共性】general character; generality：～存在于个性之中。*Generality resides in particularity.*

【共振】【物】resonance：～器 *resonator* / ～腔 *resonant cavity* / ～灯 *resonance lamp*

【共轴】coaxial：～圆柱 *coaxial cylinders* / ～圆锥 *coaxial cone*

贡 tribute：进～ *pay tribute (to an imperial court)*

【贡品】articles of tribute; tribute

【贡税】tribute and taxes：交纳～ *pay tribute and taxes*

【贡献】① contribute; dedicate; devote：～自己的一份力量 *contribute one's share; do one's bit (for)* / 为革命事业～出自己的一生 *dedicate one's life to revolution* ② contribution; dedication; devotion; service: ～卓著 *make outstanding contributions* / 科学应该对人类有更大的～。*Science ought to make a greater contribution to humanity.*

供[1] ① lay or present (offerings) ② offerings: 上～ *lay offerings on the altar*

供[2] ① confession; deposition: 招～ *make a confession of one's crime; confess* / 口～ *statement made by the accused under examination* / 翻～ *withdraw a confession; take back one's testimony* ② confess; admit; own up: 据该犯～称 *as was confessed by the culprit*

see also gōng

【供词】a statement made under examination; confession: 在～记录上按手印 *put one's thumbprint on the recorded confession*

【供奉】① enshrine and worship; consecrate ② attendants, actors, etc., in the imperial palace

【供具】sacrificial vessel

【供品】offerings: 地上摆满了～。*The floor is loaded with offerings.*

【供认】make a confession; confess: ～不讳 *confess without hiding anything; confess everything* / 彻底～ *make a clean breast of one's crime*

【供职】hold office: 在学校～ *work in the school*

【供状】written confession; deposition

【供桌】altar table

gōu

勾[1] ① tick off; check; cross out; cancel; strike out: ～除 *tick off; write off* ② delineate; draw; sketch: 用铅笔～出轮廓图 *sketch a outline with a pencil* ③ fill up the joints of brickwork with mortar or cement; point: ～墙缝 *point a brick wall* ④ thicken: 汤里～了点芡 *add some corn starch to thicken the soup* ⑤ induce; evoke; arouse; call to mind: ～对往事的回忆 *evoke memories of the past* / ～起一腔热情 *arouse great enthusiasm* ⑥ collude with; gang up with; entice; inveigle: 他又～上了一个女人。*He has seduced yet another woman.*

勾[2] 【数】shorter leg of a right triangle

see also gòu

【勾搭】① gang up with; collude with: 他们臭味相投,很快就～在一起了。*Birds of a feather, they soon flocked together.* ② seduce; carry on (an affair) with: 她丈夫和一个女演员～上了。*Her husband has been carrying on with an actress.*

【勾股定理】【数】the Pythagorean theorem; the Pythagorean proposition

【勾画】draw the outline of; delineate; sketch; trace; draft: 他～了一幅城市发展的蓝图。*He drafted a blueprint for the development of the city.*

【勾魂】captive sb's soul; bewitch; enchant; fascinate: 他被勾掉了魂儿。*He was bewitched.*

【勾结】collude with; gang up with; collaborate with; act in collusion with: 与不法商人相～ *collude with the lawbreaking businessman*

【勾勒】① draw the outline of; sketch the contours of; delineate; draft: ～出猪的轮廓。*Sketched the outline of a pig.* ② give a brief account of; outline; sketch out: ～出游子思归的情怀 *succinctly depict the homesickness of those traveling abroad*

【勾通】collude with; work hand in glove with

【勾销】liquidate; write off; strike out; cancel: 一笔～ *write off at one stroke* / ～债务 *liquidate a debt* / ～宿怨 *sink a feud*

【勾心斗角】intrigue against each other; jockey for position; intrigue against each other

【勾引】① seduce; tempt; entice; lure: ～少女 *seduce young girls* ② induce; arouse; evoke: 他的话～起妈妈的伤心事。*What he said evoked memories of the mother's past miseries.*

佝

【佝偻】[口] with arched shoulder and back: ～着背 *hunch-backed* / ～病 *rickets*

沟 ① ditch; channel; trench; drain: 排水～ *drainage ditch; drain* / 阴～ *sewerage* / 水～ *ditch; drain* / 明～ *ditch; open sewer* ② groove; rut; gutter; furrow: 开～播种 *make furrows for sowing* / 垫～ *filed ditch* ③ waterway; gullet; gully; ravine: 乱石～ *boulder-strewn gully* / 小溪～ *brook* / 山～ *gully; ravine; (mountain) valley*

【沟槽】【军】cannelure; furrow; plow groove: ～刨 *dado plane; trenching plane*

【沟灌】【农】furrow irrigation

【沟壑】gully; ravine: ～纵横 *crisscross gullies*

【沟渠】irrigation canals and ditches

【沟通】link up; connect; join: ～思想 *get to know each other's viewpoints better; exchange ideas* / ～感情 *cultivate friendship* / ～情报 *exchange intelligence or information*

【沟沿儿】banks of a ditch or canal

钩 ① hook: 铁～ *iron hook* / ～链 *hook chain* 鱼～ *fishhook* / 挂衣～ *clothes-hook* / 称～儿 *steelyard hook* / 窗～ *window catch* ② hook stroke (in Chinese characters) ③ check mark; tick: 给正确答案打上～儿 *check the correct answer* / 在表格的方块处打～ *tick the box on the form* ④ secure with a hook; hook: ～心斗角 *intrigue against each other* ⑤ crochet: ～花边 *crochet lace* ⑥ sew with large stitches: ～贴边 *sew on an edging*

【钩针】crochet hook: ～编织品 *crochet*

【钩子】① hook ② hook-like

篝 [书] cage

【篝火】bonfire; campfire: 我们明晚举行～晚会。*We'll give a campfire party tomorrow evening.*

G

gǒu

苟 ① careless; negligent; indifferent; casual: 不~言笑 *be not indiscreet in speech and manner* ②[书] provided; if: ~富贵勿相忘。*If sb become rich, he should share weal with his friends.*

【苟安】seek a moment's peace; be content with temporary ease and comfort; live in a fool's paradise: ~一时 *seek security for a time*

【苟合】illicit sexual relations

【苟活】drag out an ignoble existence; live on degradation

【苟且】① drift along; muddle on; be resigned to circumstances: ~度日 *muddle along* ② perfunctory; careless; casual: ~了事 *dispose of sth perfunctorily.* ③ illicit (sexual relations); improper

【苟且偷安】live in a fool's paradise; seek temporary peace; be content with temporary ease and comfort

【苟且偷生】drag out an ignoble life; live (on) just for the sake of remaining alive; keep alive without serious ambition

【苟全】aimlessly preserve (one's own life); preserve (one's own life) without any sense of purpose

【苟全性命】just manage to survive: ~于乱世 *barely secure personal safety in a troubled age*

【苟同】[书] (often used in the negative) agree without giving serious thought; readily to subscribe to (sb's view): 不敢~ *beg to differ; cannot agree* /你的观点我不敢~。*I could't agree to your view.*

【苟延残喘】linger on with one's last breath of life; drag out one's feeble existence; eke out a living; try to prolong one's exhausted panting

狗 ① dog: 猎~ *hunting dog; hound* /狼~ *wolfhound* /走~ *running dog* /疯~ *mad dog*/恶~ *a ferocious (or vicious) dog* ② damned; cursed: ~东西 *that son of a bitch* /~地主 *the cursed landlord*

【狗吃屎】fall flat on the face; fall down heavily: 跌了个~ *stumble and fall flat on one's face*

【狗胆包天】monstrously audacious

【狗苟蝇营】ingratiate oneself with someone to gain one's ends; shamelessly to seek personal gain

【狗獾】badger

【狗急跳墙】a desperate dog tries to jump over the wall; a corned beast will do sth desperate; desperation drives a dog to jump over a wall

【狗拿耗子,多管闲事】a dog trying to catch mice; too meddlesome; poke one's nose into other people's business

【狗皮膏药】①【药】dogskin plaster (a plaster for rheumatism, strains, contusions, etc., formerly spread on dogskin, but now usu. on cloth) ② quake medicine; fake stuff: 卖~ *fob things off on people; practice quackery; sell quick remedies; palm things off on people*

【狗屁】boloney; bullshit; rubbish; nonsense; horseshit: ~不通 *unreadable rubbish; mere trash* / ~文章 *stodgy and worthless article* /放你的~! *Stop that nonsense!*

【狗屎】dog's droppings-worthless stuff: ~不如 *utterly worthless* /一堆臭~ *a pack of disgusting people*/堆 *pile of dog's dung*

【狗腿子】[口] hired thug; lackey; flunkey; henchman

【狗尾草】【植】green bristlegrass

【狗尾续貂】dog's tail joined to a marten; wretched sequel to a fine literary work; make an unworthy continuation of a great work

【狗窝】kennel; doghouse; one's humble home: 家里乱得像~。*The home is such a mess that it resembles a doghouse.*

【狗血喷头】pour out a torrent of abuse; curse at full blast; let loose a stream of abuse (against sb): 骂得~ *heap curses on sb*

【狗熊】① black bear ② coward; good-for-nothing; good-for-naught: 你真~。*What a coward you are!*

【狗眼看人低】be a bloody snob; act like a snob; be damned snobbish: 你别~。*Don't be snobbish.*

【狗咬狗】dog-eat-dog; dog-fight: 帝国主义~的战争 *an imperialist dog-eat-dog type of war*

【狗杂种】bastard

【狗崽子】① pup; puppy ② son of a bitch

【狗仗人势】a dog bites on the strength of his master's position; an underling gets haughty on the strength of an influential relative; bully others because of one's master's power and position

枸

see also jǔ

【枸骨】【植】Chinese holly

【枸杞子】【药】fruit of Chinese wolfberry

gòu

勾

see also gōu

【勾当】[贬] business; transaction; deal: 罪恶~ *criminal activities* /卑鄙~ *shameful trick* /不可告人的~ *business under the counter; unseemly dealings* /肮脏的~ *a dirty deal*

构 ① construct; form; build; compose: ~词 *form a word* /结~ *structure; construction*/ ~件 *structural member; component part*/ ~建 *set-up; establish* ② fabricate; make up; invent: 虚~ *fabrication* ③ literary composition: 佳~ *good piece of writing* ④【植】paper mulberry

【构成】constitute; form; compose; make up;

pose：～威胁 *pose a threat* / ～多数 *make up a majority* / ～部分 *component part* / ～犯罪的要件 *requisites to constitute a crime*

【构词法】【语】word-building; word-formation

【构架】boom; staging; structural frame; frame; framework; skeleton：钢～ *framework of steel*

【构思】work out the plot of a literary work or the composition of a painting; conceive; construct; concept：～新颖 *original in conception* /导演正在～一部电影。*The director is working out the plot of a film.*

【构图】【美】composition (of a picture)：～完美 *perfect composition*

【构想】① work out the plot of a literary work or the composition of a painting; conceive; construct ② idea; concept; plan; scheme：提出经济改革的～ *put forward a plan for economic reforms*

【构造】① structure; construction：人体～ *the structure of the human body* ②【地】tectonic; structural：～体系 *structural system* / ～板块 *tectonic plate* / ～学 *tectonics* /地质～ *geological structural* / ～序次 *structural generation* / ～地震 *tectonic earthquake* / ～运动 *tectonic movement*

【构筑】construct; build：～碉堡 *build a fort* / ～工事 *construct field works; build defenses* / ～物 *structures*

购 purchase; buy：赊～ *buy on credit* / ～粮 *purchase grain* /采～ *make purchases for an organization or enterprise; purchase* /函～ *purchase by mail* /订～ *place an order* /这部小说～于西安新华书店。*The novel was bought in Xi'an Xinhua bookstore.*

【购货单】order form; order

【购货券】purchase coupon

【购买】buy; purchase：～书籍 *buy books* / ～文具 *buy stationery* / ～大量设备 *buy a lot of equipment* / ～动机 *buying motive* / ～力 *purchasing power*

【购销】purchase and sale; buying and selling：～两旺 *brisk buying and selling* / ～持平 *balanced purchase and sale*

【购置】purchase (durables); buy：～家电 *purchase electrical household appliances* / ～实验设备 *buy lab equipment*

诟 [书] ① shame; disgrace; humiliation：～辱 *insult; humiliation* ② rebuke; revile; talk abusively; reprimand：世人～之 *be reviled by the public*

【诟病】[书] censure; denounce; condemn

【诟骂】revile; abuse; vilify; bawl out：当众～ *vilify sb in public* /竟敢～上司 *even dare to abuse one's superior*

垢 ①[书] dirty; filthy; soiled：蓬头～面 *with disheveled hair and dirty face* ② dirt; filth; stain：污～ *dirt; filth*/尘～ *dust and dirt* /牙～ *dental calculus* /油～ *grease stain* ③[书] disgrace; humiliation; insult：含～忍辱 *endure humiliation and insult; swallow insults*

够 ① enough; sufficient; adequate：这些钱～他买书的。*The money is adequate to buy the books he wanted* /我的钱～付计程车费的。*I have got enough money to pay for a taxi.* /你复制的份数～吗? *Have you made enough copies?* ② enough; sufficiently：在这条河里游泳水～深吗? *Is the river deep enough for swimming?* /你钢琴弹奏练习得不～。*You don't practice enough at the piano.* ③ quite; fairly; rather; enough：房间～大的。*The room is quite spacious.* ④ reach (sth by stretching)：你～得着那些苹果吗? *Can you reach those apples?* /我站在桌子上才能～着灯泡。*I can't reach the lamp unless I stand on the desk.* ⑤ reach (a standard or level); be up to：～标准 *be up to standard* / ～资格 *be qualified* /他当总经理～条件。*He is qualified to the general manager.*

【够本】① make enough money to cover the cost; break even; get one's money worth：这辆自行车我可骑～了。*I've got my money worth out of this bicycle.* ② the gains balancing the losses

【够格】be qualified; be up to standard：我当老师不～。*I am not qualified to be a teacher.*

【够劲儿】[口] ① (of an onerous task, etc.) almost too much to cope with; almost unbearable ② strong enough (in taste, strength, etc.)：这辣椒真～。*This pepper is really hot.* /这白酒真～。*The spirit is certainly powerful stuff.*

【够朋友】[口] be worthy of the name of a true friend; be a friend indeed

【够呛】[方] unbearable; terrible; quite the limit：累得～ *dog tired* /喝的东西真～ *appalling drink*

【够瞧的】really awful; too much：天冷得真～。*The weather is terribly cold.*

【够受的】quite an ordeal; hardly endurable：累得～ *be dog-tired*

【够数】① adequate in quantity; enough; sufficient：你领的书～。*You did get enough books to go round.* ②[方] be up to a certain standard

【够味儿】[口] just the right flavor; just the thing; quite satisfactory; really good

【够意思】① really something; terrific; wonderful; quite good：今晚的饭菜～! *Tonight's food is terrific!* ② generous; really kind; friendly：不～ *unfriendly; ungrateful*

媾 [书] ① wed：婚～ *marriage* ② reach an agreement; make peace; become reconciled ③ coition：交～ *copulate*

【媾和】make peace; become reconciled

gū

估 estimate; assess; appraise; reckon：评～ *judge and assess* /低～同学们的能力 *underestimate the ability of the students* /布什～计这项工作需要三个月。*Bush estimated that this work would take three month.*

G

【估产】① estimate the yield：这块地～八百斤。*The estimated yield of this plot of land is 800 jin.* ② appraise the assets; assess

【估计】estimate; assess; appraise; reckon; take into account; calculate：～错误 *miscalculate* / 过高～ *overestimate* / ～成本 *estimated cost* / ～风险 *calculated risk* / ～误差 *evaluated error* / 你能～它有多长吗？*Can you estimate how long it is?*

【估价】① appraise; evaluate; estimate：买汽车不事先～是不明智的。*It would be unwise to buy the car before having it appraised.* ② appraisal; valuation; estimate; estimated price：～表 *schedule of prices* / ～单 *list of cost estimates* / ～惯例 *valuation convention* / 这是最高的～。*This is an outside estimate of the price.*

【估量】appraise; assess; estimate; reckon：～双方的力量对比 *assess the balance of strength between the two sides* / 不可～的损失 *an immeasurable loss*

【估摸】[口] reckon; guess; suppose：我～着他这几天就能回来。*I reckon he will be back in a few days.*

【估税】tax assessment：～人 *assessor*

【估算】estimate; calculate; consider; impute; appraise：～产量 *estimate the yield* / ～利息 *imputed interest* / ～收入 *imputed income* / ～数据 *estimated data*

咕 [象] (of hens, etc.) cluck; (of turtledoves, etc.) coo

【咕咚】[象] thud; plump; splash：水桶～一声掉进井里去了。*The barrel fell into the well with a splash.*

【咕嘟】① [象] bubble; gurgle; gulp：汤泉～～地往外冒。*The hot spring kept bubbling up.* ② boil or stew for a long time：肉早就～烂了。*The meat is overcooked.* ③ purse (one's lips); pout：她不说话，～着嘴。*She pursed her lips with no word.*

【咕咕】[象] (of hens, etc.) cluck; (of turtledoves, etc.) coo：斑鸠～地叫。*The turtledove was cooing.*

【咕叽】① [象] squelch：他～～地走在泥泞的路上。*He was squelching down the muddy road.* ② whisper; murmur; mumble (to oneself)：她俩～了半小时。*They whispered to each other for half an hour.*

【咕隆】[象] rumble; rattle; roll：远处炮声～～地响。*Cannons rumbled in the distance.*

【咕噜】[象] ① rumble; roll：肚子～～直响。*One's stomach keeps rumbling.* ② murmur; whisper; grumble

【咕哝】murmur; mutter; grumble; whisper：老人在～些什么？*What is the old person muttering about?*

呱

see also guā

【呱呱】[书] cry of a baby：～而泣 *mewl*

【呱呱坠地】be born crying; come into this world with a cry; be brought to bed

沽 [书] ① buy; purchase：～酒待客 *buy wine to entertain a guest* ② sell：待价而～ *wait to sell at a good price; wait for the highest bid* / ～酒为生 *sell wine for a living*

【沽名钓誉】fish for fame and credit; fish for fame and social recognition; buy reputation and fish for praise; angle for compliments

姑[1] ① father's sister; aunt：小～ *youngest aunt* ② husband's sister; sister-in-law：大～子 *husband's elder sister* ③ [书] husband's mother; mother-in-law：翁～ *husband's parents* ④ nun; priestess：尼～ *Buddhist nun* / 道～ *Taoist priestess; Taoist nun*

姑[2] [书] just; for the time being; for the moment; tentatively：～置勿论 *leave sth aside for the moment*

【姑表】the relationship between the children of a brother and a sister; cousinship：～兄弟 *male cousins* / ～亲戚 *cousinship*

【姑父】the husband of one's father's sister; uncle

【姑姑】[口] father's sister; aunt

【姑老爷】a form of address for a man used by members of his wife's family

【姑妈】[口] father's (married) sister; aunt

【姑母】father's (married) sister; aunt

【姑奶奶】[口] ① sister of one's paternal grandfather; great-aunt ② married daughter ③ I, your great-aunt (used by a woman in a row)

【姑娘】① girl：乡下～ *country girl* ② daughter

【姑且】tentatively; for the moment; for the time being：～不谈 *leave sth aside for the moment* / ～不论 *let us not go into the question now* / ～试一试。*Have a try, anyhow.*

【姑嫂】a woman and her brother's wife; sisters-in-law

【姑妄听之】just to listen to sth without taking it seriously; take a story for what it is worth; see no harm in hearing what sb has to say

【姑息】appease; indulge; tolerate; placate：～养奸 *over-indulgence nurtures evil; to tolerate evil is to abet it* / ～疗法 *palliative treatment*

【姑爷】[口] a form of address for a man used by the senior members of his wife's family

孤 ① (of a child) fatherless; orphaned：遗～ *orphan* / 托～ *entrust an orphan to sb's care* ② lone; solitary; isolated; alone：～雁 *a solitary wild goose* / ～身一人 *all alone; all by oneself*

【孤傲】proud and aloof; standoffish and arrogant：去掉～的习气 *rid oneself of aloofness and arrogance* / ～不群 *too haughty to get along with others*

【孤残】the orphaned and disabled：～儿童 *orphaned and disabled children*

【孤单】① alone; lonely; solitary; friendless：～的生活 *solitary life* / 感到～ *feel lonely* / 老人很～。*The old man feels very lonely.* ② weak; inadequate：力量～ weak and helpless

【孤胆】(fight the enemy) single-handed; all alone：

~英雄 *a lone fighter; hero who fights all on his own*

【孤岛】isolated island

【孤独】lonely; solitary; alone; isolated: ~无援 *alone and with no help* /过着~的生活 *live in solitude* / ~无偶 *all alone without a mate*

【孤儿】① a fatherless child ② orphan: ~寡母 *a widow and her child* / ~院 *orphanage*

【孤芳自赏】indulge in self-admiration; remain aloof from the world; a lone soul admiring his own purity

【孤寡】① orphans and widows ② solitary; lonely; lone: ~老婆儿 *lone old woman* /老头儿 *lone old man*

【孤寂】lonely; solitary

【孤家寡人】a person in solitary splendor; a man who is completely isolated; a man without followers; a loner

【孤军】an isolated force: ~作战 *fight in isolation* / ~深入 *isolated force penetrating deep into enemy territory*

【孤苦伶仃】be alone and friendless; be alone and uncared for; be isolated and wretched; be utterly forlorn and alone

【孤老院】old folks' home; home for the aged

【孤立】① isolated; on one's own; helpless: 处境~ *find oneself in an isolated position* / ~无援 *isolated and cut off from help* ② isolate: ~敌人 *isolate the enemy*

【孤零零】solitary; all alone; lone; lonely: ~地坐在路边 *sit by the road-side all alone*

【孤陋寡闻】live in a backwater; poorly read and ignorant; rude and with no experience; out of touch the outside world

【孤僻】unsociable and eccentric: 性情~ *of an uncommunicative and eccentric disposition* /生性~ *of an odd and unsociable temperament*

【孤身】alone; all alone; all on one's own

【孤掌难鸣】cannot clap with one hand; single-handed and helpless; alone and helpless

【孤注一掷】vie money on the turn of a card; risk everything on a single throw; risk everything on one big effort; make a last desperate effort

轱

【轱辘】①[口] wheel: 自行车坏了一个~。*One of the bicycle's wheels is out of order.* ② turn; roll: ~鞋 *roller skates* /把球踢一下就~过来了。*Give the ball a kick and it will roll over here.*

骨

see also gǔ

【骨朵儿】[口] flower bud

【骨碌碌】roll round and round; move rapidly: 小孩子的眼睛~地到处看。*The little kid's eyes moved about.*

【骨碌】roll: 石块沿山坡~下来。*Stones rolled down the hillside.* /孩子们在地板上~。*The kids rolled about on the floor.*

菇 mushroom: 香~ *straw mushroom* /冬~ *dried mushroom* /春~ *spring mushroom*

辜 guilt; crime: 滥杀无~ *indiscriminately kill innocent people* /无~ *innocent*

【辜负】let down; fail to live up to; be unworthy of; disappoint: 不~父母的期望 *live up to the expectations of the people*

箍 ① fasten round; bind fast; bind round; hoop: 他用围巾把头~得紧紧的。*He fastened round the head.* ② hoop; band: 铁~ *iron hoop* /胳膊上戴着红袖~儿 *have a red band round one's arm*

【箍钢】hoop iron: ~带 *hoop steel*

【箍桶匠】cooper; hooper

gǔ

古 ① ancient; age-old: ~语 *archaism* / ~时候 *in ancient times* / ~画 *ancient paintings* / ~庙 *ancient temple* / ~书 *ancient books* ② of ancient style: ~朴 *simple and unaffected* ③[书] *simple and sincere*: 人心不~。*People nowadays are no longer simple and honest.*

【古巴】Cuba: ~人 Cuban

【古板】old-fashioned and inflexible; outmoded and rigid: 思想~ *have an outmoded and rigid way of thinking*

【古代】(referring to the period in Chinese history before the mid-19th century, and sometimes, esp. to the age of slave society) ancient times; antiquity: ~史 *ancient history* / ~文明 *ancient civilization* / ~社会 *ancient society*

【古典】① classical allusion: 引用~ *quote a classical allusion* ② classical: ~学派 *classical school* / ~芭蕾 *classical ballet* / ~建筑 *classical architecture; classical building* / ~艺术 *classical art* / ~文学 *classical literature* / ~作品 *classic*

【古董】① antique; curio; curiosity: 收集~ *collect antiques* / ~店 *antique shop* / ~商 *antiquary antiquarian* ② old fogey; outdated stuff; anachronism

【古都】ancient capital: 六朝~ *capital of six dynasties*

【古风】① ancient customs; antiquities ② form of classical poetry originated before the Tang Dynasty

【古怪】eccentric; old; strange; bizarre: 稀奇~ *rare and queer* / ~的名字 *strange name* /样子~ *odd-looking* / ~脾气 *eccentric character*

【古画】old painting

【古话】old saying; old saw: ~说,天无绝人之路。*As the old saying goes, every cloud has a silver lining.*

【古籍】ancient books: ~字画 *ancient books, calligraphy and paintings*

【古迹】historic site; place of historic interest: 名胜

~ *places of historic interest and scenic beauty*

【古今中外】at all times and in all countries; both ancient and modern, Chinese and foreign; in China or elsewhere, in modern or ancient times

【古老】ancient; age-old: ~的文明 *old civilization* / ~的传说 *legend* / ~的习俗 *ancient custom* / ~的文化 *ancient culture* / ~的学校 *age-old school*

【古朴】simple and unaffected; of primitive simplicity

【古人】the ancients; our forefathers:前不见~,后不见来者。*Behind me, I don't see the ancient men; before me, I don't see the ones to come.*

【古色古香】having an antique flavor; classic beauty; antique:他家布置得~的。*His home has an air of antiquity.*

【古生代】【地】the Palaeozoic Era

【古生界】【地】Palaeozoic Erathem

【古生物】ancient extinct life: ~学 *palaeontology* / ~化石 *fossils of ancient extinct life*

【古诗】ancient poetry: ~赏析 *appreciation of ancient poetry*

【古书】ancient books

【古铜色】bronze-colored; bronze: ~的皮肤 *bronze-coloured skin*

【古玩】antique; curio: ~商店 *antique shop*

【古往今来】from ancient to modern times; through the ages; since time immemorial

【古为今用】adapt ancient forms for present-day use; make the past serve our present-day needs; make ancient things serve the present

【古文】① prose written in the classical literary style; classical prose: ~运动 *Classical Prose Movement* ② Chinese script before the Qin Dynasty(221-206B. C.)

【古文字】ancient writing; ancient script

【古物】ancient objects; antiquities: ~陈列馆 *museum of antiquities* / ~收藏家 *collector of antiquities*

【古稀】seventy years of age:年近~ *getting on for seventy; almost seventy*

【古雅】in graceful classical style; of classic beauty and in elegant taste; of classical elegance:陈设~的书房 *reading-room laid out in a graceful classical style*

【古植物学】palaeobotany

【古装】ancient costume: ~戏 *costume play; costume piece*

谷[1] volley; gorge; ravine; gully:山~ *mountain valley* /峡~ *gorge; canyon* /河~ *river valley* /万丈深~ *fathomless ravine*

谷[1] ① cereal; grain:打~ *thresh grain* / ~类作物 *cereal crops* ② millet: ~穗儿 *ears of millet* ③［方］*unhusked rice*:稻~ *unhusked rice; paddy*

【谷仓】granary; barn

【谷草】① millet straw: ~垛 *stack of millet straw* ②［方］*rice straw*

【谷底】bottom of a valley

【谷壳】husk (of rice)

【谷物】cereal; grain; cereal crop: ~播种机 *grain drill* / ~取样机 *grain sampler* / ~干燥机 *grain dryer* / ~市场 *grain market*

【谷雨】grain rain (6th solar term)

【谷种】seed-grain; seed-corn

【谷子】① millet ②［方］unhusked rice: ~白发病 *downy mildew of millet*

汩 ［书］(of running water) gurgle

【汩汩】gurgle:河水~流过。*The gurgling river flows by.*

股 ① thigh ② section (of an office, enterprise, etc.):人事~ *personnel section* /财务~ *accounting section* ③ strand; ply:四~的电线 *electronic wire of four strands* ④ share in a company or one of several equal parts of property:入~ *buy a share; become a shareholder* /普通~ *common share* /分~ *divide into equal parts* /优先~ *preference shares; preferred stock* ⑤［量］used to indicate sth long and narrow:一~泉水(*a*) *stream of clear spring water* /一~线 *a skein of thread* (*b*) *used for gas, smell, strength, etc.*:一~劲 *a burst of energy* /一~香味 *a whiff of fragrance* ⑥［贬］used to indicate a group of people:一~土匪 *a band of bandits* /一~敌军 *a horde of enemy soldiers*

【股本】capital stock; equity: ~折价 *discount on capital stock* / ~短缺 *short of capital*

【股东】shareholder; stockholder: ~大会 *stockholder's meeting* / ~产权 *stockholder's equity* / ~基金 *shareholder's fund*

【股份】share; stock: ~转让 *share transfer* / ~红利 *stock bonus* / ~公司 *stock company* / ~银行 *joint-stock bank* / ~保险 *joint-stock insurance* / ~制 *shareholding system* / ~期权 *share option* / ~有限公司 *limited-liability company; limited company* (*Ltd.*)

【股肱】［书］right-hand man: ~之臣 *most trustworthy minister* (*of a ruler*)

【股骨】【生理】thighbone; femur

【股金】money paid for shares (in a partnership or cooperative); capital:交~ *pay for one's share* /缺少~ *short of share capital*

【股民】person who buys and sells stocks

【股票】share; stock; share certificate: ~持有人 *shareholder* / ~发行 *bond issue; stock issue; issuance* /购买~ *buy stocks* (*or shares*) / ~价格 *share price* / ~过户 *stock transfer* /炒~ *buy and sell stocks* / ~交易 *buying and selling of stocks* / ~经纪人 *stockbroker; stockjobber* / ~交易所 *stock exchange* / ~证券 *stock certificate* / ~指数 *stock index* / ~期权 *stock option* / ~行市 *current prices of stocks; quotations on the stock exchange* / ~市场 *stock market* / ~投资信托 *stock investment trust* / ~票面价值 *face value of share* / ~分割 *stock split*

【股权】stock ownership; stockholder's right

【股市】stock market: ~暴跌。*The stock market fell*

abruptly. / ～崩溃。*The stock market crushed.* / ～暴涨。*The stock market rose suddenly and sharply.*

【股息】dividend：～收益 *dividend yield* / ～限度 *dividend limitation*

【股长】section chief; head of a section

【股指】stock market index：～快速下探。*The stock market index is falling rapidly.*

骨 ① bone：恨之入～ *hate with every fibre of one's marrow; hate like poison* /胸～ *breastbone* /寒风刺～。*The cold wind chilled one to the bone.* ② skeleton; framework; structure：钢～水泥 *reinforced concrete* /伞～ *umbrella frame* ③ character; quality; spirit：傲～ *unyielding character* /风～ *strength of character*
see also gū

【骨癌】cancer in the bones

【骨刺】【医】spur

【骨干】①【生理】diaphysis ② backbone; mainstay; core：～分子 *core member* / ～作用 *act as the mainstay; play a major role* / ～项目 *key project* / ～企业 *key enterprises*

【骨骼】【生理】skeleton：～肌 *skeletal muscle* / ～系统 *skeletal system*

【骨骺】【生理】epiphysis

【骨化】【生理】ossify

【骨灰】① bone ash ② ashes of the dead：～盒 *cinerary casket* / ～坛 *cinerary urn*

【骨架】skeleton; framework：房屋的～ *the framework of a house* / ～图 *skeleton drawing* / ～结构 *skeleton structure*

【骨节】【生理】joint

【骨结核】bone tuberculosis; TB bone

【骨科】【医】(department of) orthopaedics：～专家 *specialist in orthopaedics*

【骨料】【建】aggregate：合成～ *combine aggregate* / 粗～ *thick aggregate* / 轻～ *light aggregate*

【骨瘤】【医】osteoma

【骨膜】【生理】periosteum：～炎 *periostitis*

【骨牌】dominoes：多米诺～效应 *domino effect*

【骨盆】【生理】pelvis

【骨气】strength of character; moral integrity; probity; backbone：穷人有～。*The poor people have backbone.*

【骨器】bone object; bone implement

【骨肉】flesh and blood; kindred：情同～ *as close to each other* / ～之亲 *blood relations* / ～离散 *separation of parents and children; family separation* / ～团聚 *family reunion* / ～兄弟 *blood brothers* / ～相残 *fratricidal fighting*

【骨软化】【医】osteomalacia

【骨瘦如柴】as thin as a thread-paper; be all skin and bone; emaciated like a stick; worn to a shadow

【骨髓】【生理】marrow：～炎 *osteomyelitis*

【骨炭】bone black; animal charcoal

【骨头】① bone ② character：懒～ *lazybones* /软～ *spineless creature*

【骨头架子】［口］① skeleton：她瘦得只剩下～了。*She is all skins and bones.* ② very thin person

【骨学】【医】osteology

【骨折】【医】fracture：大腿～ *fracture in the thigh* / 粉碎性～ *comminuted fracture* /开放性～ *open fracture*

【骨质疏松】【医】osteoporosis

【骨子里】［贬］in one's bones; in one's innermost nature; in reality; at bottom; in substance：从～仇恨某人 *hate sb to the marrow of one's bones*

牯 bull：水～ *buffalo*

【牯牛】bull

贾 ［书］① merchant：书～ *book seller* /商～ *merchant* ② trade; do business; engage in trade ③ buy; purchase：～马 *purchase a horse* ④ sell; afford：余勇可～ *with plenty of fight left in one*

钴 【化】cobalt(Co)

【钴弹】【军】cobalt bomb

【钴合金】cobalt alloy

【钴60】【医】cobalt-60：～放射疗法 *gammatherapy*

【钴同位素】cobalt isotope

【钴土】asbolite

蛊 a legendary venomous insect

【蛊惑】poison and bewitch; poison; harm

【蛊惑人心】befog the minds of the people; seduce the people; confuse and poison people's minds：～的讲演 *demagogic speech*

鼓 ① drum：锣～ *gong and drum* /铜～ *kettledrum* /腰～ *waist drum* /在乐队中打～ *play the drum(s) in a band* / ～声 *drumbeats* /大～ *base drum* ② drum-shaped object：石～ *drum-shaped stone block* /耳～ *eardrum* ③ beat; strike; drum; sound：～琴 *play the zither* / ～翼 *(of a bird) flap its wings; wing its way* /一～作气 *(get sth done) in sustained effort; at one stroke* ④ blow with bellows, etc.; fan：～风 *work a bellows* ⑤ rouse; summon; agitate; stir up; pluck up：～起勇气 *pluck up one's courage* / ～起精神 *summon one's spirit* ⑥ bulge; swell：钱包很～。*The purse is bulging.*

【鼓板】【音】clappers

【鼓吹】① advocate; promote; espouse：～和平 *espouse peace* / ～男女平等 *advocate the equality of men and women* / ～革命 *advocate revolution* ② ［贬］*preach; advertise; play up; trumpet*：大肆～ *a flourish of trumpets*

【鼓槌】drumstick

【鼓捣】［方］① tinker with; fiddle with：小孩正在专心致志地～闹钟。*The kid was absorbed in fiddling with a clock.* ② egg on; stir up; incite：～别人去干坏事 *incite people to do evil*

【鼓点子】① drumbeats ② clapper beats which set the tempo and lead the orchestra in traditional Chinese operas

【鼓动】① agitate; arouse; stir up; incite; instigate: ~群众 *arouse the masses* /作宣传~工作 *conduct propaganda and agitation* / ~工人罢工 *agitate the workers for a strike* ② flap: 蜜蜂~翅膀。*The bee is flapping its wings.*

【鼓风】【冶】(air) blast: 富氧~ *oxygen-enriched (air) blast* / ~机 *air-blower; blower* / ~炉 *blast furnace*

【鼓鼓囊囊】bulging: 背包里装满了书, ~的。*The backpack is bulging with books.*

【鼓劲】boost the morale; pluck up one's courage; stir up sb's enthusiasm or spirit

【鼓励】encourage; urge; spur (on): ~的话 *encouraging words* /老师~大家学习物理。*Our teacher encouraged us to learn physics.*

【鼓楼】drum-tower

【鼓膜】【生理】tympanic membrane; eardrum

【鼓弄】[口] fiddle with; play with; tinker with

【鼓起】call up; muster up; pluck up; stir up: ~精神 *stir up one's spirit* / ~勇气 *pluck up one's courage*

【鼓手】drummer; drumbeater

【鼓舞】inspire; encourage; hearten; boost: ~斗志 *inspire the fighting spirit* / ~人心 *set the hearts of the people's aflame* / ~人心的消息 *heartening news* /深受~ *feel very much encouraged*

【鼓乐】strains of music accompanied by drumbeats: ~喧天。*There is a great din of drums and pipes.*

【鼓噪】make an uproar; raise a hubbub; clamor; kick up a din: ~一时 *make a great to-do about sth for a time* / ~四起 *rise up with a great clamor; rise in a hubbub*

【鼓掌】clap one's hands; applaud: ~欢迎 *clap one's hands to welcome* /热烈~ *warmly applaud*

毂 hub of a wheel: 肩摩~击 *with jamming vehicles and jostling pedestrians*

臌

【臌胀】【中医】distension of the abdomen caused by accumulation of gas or fluid due to dysfunction of the liver and spleen; tympanites; meteorism

gù

固[1] ① firm strong; solid; stable: ~体废弃物 *solid waste* /坚~ *firm; solid* /稳~ *firm; stable; steadfast* /加~ *make sth more solid; strengthen* ② solidity; consolidate; strengthen: ~堤 *strengthen the dike* / ~防 *consolidate defense* ③ firmly; resolutely; persistently: ~请 *request sb resolutely* / ~辞 *firmly decline* ④ (Gù) a surname

固[2] ① originally; in the first place; as a matter of course ② admittedly; no doubt

【固步自封】be content with staying where one is; stand still and refuse to make progress; hold fast to one's established ideas

【固定】① fixed; static; regular; permanent: 电视台的~节目 *a regular TV programme* / ~保释金 *fixed bail* / ~工资 *fixed wage* / ~汇率 *fixed fund* / ~价格 *fixed price* / ~收入 *fixed income; regular income* / ~职业 *permanent occupation* / ~资本 *fixed capital* / ~资产 *fixed assets* ② fix; regularize: 把扣钮~一下 *fix a button*

【固化】【化】solidify: ~酒精 *solidified alcohol*

【固然】no doubt; it is true; true; of course; admittedly

【固若金汤】be as strong as iron; be secure against assault; strongly fortified; impregnable

【固沙林】sand-fixation forest; dune-fixing forest

【固守】① defend tenaciously; be firmly entrenched in: ~阵地 *tenaciously defend one's position* ② stick to; cling to; adhere to

【固态】【物】solid state: ~物理学 *solid-state physics*

【固体】solid body; solid: ~酱油 *solidified soy sauce* / ~燃料 *solid fuel* / ~水库 *solid reservoir* / ~理论 *theory of solids*

【固有】intrinsic; inherent; innate: ~属性 *intrinsic attributes* / ~性格 *intrinsic traits*

【固执】① obstinate; stubborn: 戴维很~,不会改变主意的。*David is very obstinate and won't change her mind.* ② persist in; cling to; stick to: ~己见 *stubbornly adhere to one's opinions*

故[1] ① incident; accident; happening: 意外交通事~ *a traffic accident* ② reason; cause: 借~缺席 *find an excuse to be absent* /不知何~他不回信。*I wonder why he didn't answer my letter.* ③ on purpose; intentionally; deliberately: ~作镇静 *pretend to be calm* /明知~犯 *willfully violate (a law or rule)* ④ hence; therefore; consequently; so: 无私~能无畏。*Fearlessness stems from selflessness.*

故[2] ① of the past; old; former: 黄河~道 *the old course of the Yellow River* ② die: 她父母早~。*Her parents died when she was very young.*

【故地】old haunt; former home: ~重游 *revisit old haunt*

【故都】former capital; onetime capital

【故而】therefore; hence; so; consequently

【故宫】the Imperial Palace (in Beijing): ~博物院 *the Palace Museum*

【故国】native land; native soil; motherland; native place

【故伎】stock trick; old dodge; old tactics: ~重演 *repeat the stock tricks; play the same trick again; be up to one's old trick again*

【故旧】old friends and acquaintances

【故居】former residence

【故里】native place; hometown: 他永远忘不了他荣归~的那一刻。*He can never forget the time when he returned home with honours.*

【故弄玄虚】make things look unnecessarily; cast a mist before sb's eyes; deliberately make things look mysterious

【故去】die; pass away:彼得的父亲早就~了。*Peter's father passed away a long time ago.*
【故人】old friend: ~情深 *deep affection of an old friend*
【故事】① story; tale:民间~ *folktale; folk story* /讲~ *tell a story* / ~员 *storyteller* /编~ *make up a story; spin a yarn* / ~会 *a gathering at which stories are told* / ~片 *feature film* ② plot:这部小说~性很强。*The novel has an interesting story.*
【故土】native place; native soil; native land; hometown; birthplace: 怀念~ *long for one's hometown* / ~难离。*It is hard to leave one's native land.*
【故乡】hometown; birthplace; native land
【故意】intentionally; on purpose; willfully; deliberately; knowingly: ~刁难 *place obstacles in sb's way* / ~杀人 *intentional homicide* / ~犯规 *intentional foul* / ~撒谎 *tell a deliberate lie* / ~捣乱 *make trouble on purpose* / ~犯罪 *calculated crime; intentional offence*
【故障】hitch; breakdown; stoppage; trouble; failure; fault 谁也不知道出了什么~。*No one knows what's gone wrong.*
【故作高深】pretend to be erudite and profound
【故作镇静】keep a stiff upper lip; put on a show of calmness; try to hide one's dismay
【故作姿态】make a deliberate gesture; strike an attitude on purpose; put on airs

顾[1] ① turn round and look at; look at:环~四周 *look around* 相~一笑 *smile at each other knowingly* /左~右盼 *look to the left and to the right* ② take care of; attend to; take into account:兼~ *give consideration to both* /你别只~自己。*Don't just think of yourself.* ③ pay a visit; visit; call on:三~茅庐 *call on sb repeatedly* ④ customer:主~ *customer; patron; client* ⑤ (Gù) a surname

顾[2] ① but; however; nevertheless ② on the contrary; instead

【顾此失彼】care for this and lose that; attend to one thing and lose sight another; unable to attend to everything at once
【顾大局,识大体】bear the overall situation in mind and put the general interest above all else
【顾及】take into account; attend to; give consideration to:无暇~ *have no time to attend to the matter* /大多数人的利益你~了吗? *Have you taken the interests of the vast majority of people into account?*
【顾忌】scruple; qualm; misgiving:无所~地发表意见 *air one's views without misgivings* /毫无~ *without scruple; have no scruples* /对自己的行为无所~ *feel no qualm about one's actions*
【顾家】look after one's family; attend to the family; care for one's own family:她从来不~。*She never looks after her family at all times.*
【顾客】customer; shopper; client; patron: ~服务台 *custom service* ~心理学 *consume psychology* / ~至上。*Customers First.*
【顾虑】misgiving; apprehension; anxiety; worry: 家庭~ *family cares; considerations of one's family* /玛丽~妈妈的健康。*Mary was anxious about her mother's healthy.*
【顾虑重重】be full of worries; have no end of misgivings; have scruples
【顾名思义】think what a title should imply; as the term connotes; as the name implies
【顾盼】[书] look around:左右~ *look right and left* / ~生姿 *look around charmingly* / ~自如 *gaze round free and easy*
【顾前不顾后】drive ahead without considering the consequences; act rashly
【顾全】show consideration for and take care to preserve; keep in mind: ~各方利益 *concern oneself with the interests of all sides* / ~大局 *take the interests of the whole into account; bear the overall or general interest in mind* / ~面子 *have full consideration for sb's feelings*
【顾问】adviser; consultant; counsellor:高级~ *senior adviser* /法律~ *legal adviser* / ~委员会 *consultative committee* / ~班子 *council* / ~工程师 *consulting engineer* / ~团 *advisory group*
【顾惜】take good care of; care for; value; treasure; cherish: ~自己的健康 *take care of one's health* / ~名节 *treasure one's name and integrity*
【顾影自怜】① look at one's image in the mirror and pity oneself; look at one's reflection and admire oneself; admire oneself in the mirror ② look at one's shadow and lament one's lot; feel self-pity, when looking at one's own shadow
【顾主】customer; client; patron

梏 [书] wooden handcuffs: 桎~ *fetters and handcuffs; shackles*

雇 hi re; employ; engage: ~保姆 *hire a maid* / ~长工 *employ a long-term farm hand* /解~ *discharge; dismiss; sack* / ~车 *hire a car* / ~家教 *engage a private a tutor* /我们大家~了一辆汽车。*We hired a bus between us.*

【雇工】① hire labor; hire hands ② hired laborer; hired hand:虐待~ *maltreat hired labourers* /他在经理家当~。*He works as hired hands for the boss.*
【雇农】farm hand; farm laborer:贫~ *poor peasants and farm laborers*
【雇佣】employ; hire: ~者 *employer* /被~者 *employee* / ~合同 *employment contract* / ~关系 *employer-employee relationship*
【雇佣兵】mercenary (soldier): ~役制 *mercenary system*
【雇佣军】mercenary army or troops; mercenary
【雇员】employee:高级~ *senior employee* / ~考核 *employee rating*
【雇主】employer:农民工们正在找~。*The peasants are hunting for a job.*

锢 ① plug with molten metal; run metal into cracks ② [书] hold in custody; imprison;

jail：禁～ *keep in custody*; *hold prisoner*; *imprison*

痼 chronic; enduring; inveterate：沉～ *serious and protracted illness*; *deep-rooted bad habit*

【痼疾】chronic disease; obstinate disease; incurable disease

【痼癖】addiction; inveterate weakness; deep-rooted liking for：罗伯特把吸毒的～戒了。*Albert gave up his addiction to drug.*

【痼习】inveterate habit; confirmed habit：～难改。*Confirmed habits are difficult to break.*

guā

瓜 melon; gourd：冬～ white gourd /西～ *watermelon* /苦～ *bitter gourd* /丝～ *towel gourd* /黄～ *cucumber* /香～ *muskmelon* / ～棚 *melon hut* /南～ *pumpkin*/哈密～*Hami melon*

【瓜分】carve up; divide up; partition; dismember：战利品被他们～了。*The captured equipment was divided up among them.*

【瓜葛】connection; implication; association：她和老板有些～。*She is somewhat associated with her boss.*

【瓜熟蒂落】when the melon is ripe, the calyx falls; when the melon is ripe it falls from the stalk; fruits fall off when ripe

【瓜田李下】in a melon patch or under a plum tree; liable to lay oneself open to suspicious; be found in a suspicious position

【瓜子】melon seeds：嗑～ *crack and eat melon seeds*

【瓜子脸】oval face：她那～上经常带着迷人的笑容。*There was always a charming smile on her oval face.*

呱

see also gū

【呱嗒】① [象] clip-clop; clack: ～～的马蹄声 *clatter of horse-hoofs* ② [方] mock; satirize: ～着脸 *pull along face*

【呱呱】the quacking of a duck; the croaking of a frog; the cawing of a crow: ～～叫喊的老鸹*flocks of quacking crows*

【呱呱叫】[口] tiptop; top-notch; terrific; superb; wonderful：简是个～的歌手。*Jane is a terrific singer.*

【呱唧】the sound of hands being clapped

刮[1] ① scrape; scratch; shave; scale: ～鞋上的泥 *scrape the mud off sb's shoes*/ ～铁锈 *scrape off rust* / ～胡子 *shave oneself*; *shave the beard* / ～鱼鳞 *scale a fish* /就～破一点皮。*It's only a scratch.* ② smear with (paste, etc.): ～糨子 *stiffen (cloth) by spreading paste over it*; *size* ③ plunder; fleece; rob; extort：搜～民财 *plunder people*; *extort money* ④ scold; give a dressing down：狠狠～了学生一顿 *give the student a good telling-off*

刮[2] (of wind) blow: ～大风了。*It's blowing hard.*

【刮板】【机】scraper plate; scraper; drawing template: ～运输机 *scraper chain conveyer*

【刮刀】scraping cutter; scraper; scraping knife：三角～ *triangular scraper*

【刮地皮】batten on extortions; scrape off the earth; grow rich by extortion

【刮宫】【医】dilatation and curettage (D. and C.)

【刮脸】shave (the face): ～刀 *razor* / ～膏 *shaving cream (soap)*

【刮目相看】have a completely new appraisal of sb; regard a person with special esteem; treat sb with increased respect

【刮痧】【中医】(as treatment for sunstroke) scraping the patient's neck, chest or back

【刮削】① scrape: ～器 *scraper* ② exploit; embezzle: ～得来的收入 *income from exploitation*

guǎ

剐 ① cut to pieces; dismember：千刀万～ *be cut to pieces* /是杀是～，随你便。*Behead me, or cut me to pieces, as you please.* ② cut; slit：手上～了个口子 *cut one's hand*

寡 ① few; scarce; scant: ～情薄义 *lacking in friendship and affection*; *heartless* /曲高和～ *highbrow songs find few listeners* ② tasteless; bland; thin：清汤～水 *watery soup*; *sth insipid*/ ～瘦 *boney*; *very thin* ③ widowed：鳏～ *widowers and widows* /守～ *live in widowhood*/ ～母 *widowed mother*

【寡不敌众】a few are no match for the many; a few cannot resist many; the few cannot fight the many

【寡妇】widow

【寡廉鲜耻】have no sense of shame; be lost to all sense of shame; shameless; unscrupulous and shameless

【寡人】I; your unworthy king; royal we

【寡头】oligarch：金融～ *financial oligarch*; *financial magnate* / ～垄断 *oligopoly* / ～政治 *oligarchy*

【寡言】of few words; taciturn; sparing of words：沉默～*keep silent*; *be of few words*

【寡欲清心】have few desires and cleanse the heart

【寡助】enjoy little support

guà

卦 divinatory symbols：算～ *tell fortunes* /卜～ *practice divination*; *cast a horoscope* /变～ *go back on one's words*; *break an agreement*

【卦摊儿】fortune teller's stall

挂 ① hang; put up; suspend：天上～着繁星。*Array of stars hung in the sky.* /学生把标语～在墙上。*The student put the slogan on the wall.*

G

② leave sth outstanding; be pending:好多问题一直～着呢。*Many problems have remained unsettled.* ③ ring off; hang up:电话已经～断。*The phone was hung up.* ④[方] call up; ring up; put sb through to:有空给我～个电话。*Ring me up when you are free.* ⑤ hitch ⑥ be anxious; care for; be concerned about:我会把这件事～在心上的。*I shall keep the matter in mind.* ⑦[方] be covered with; be coated with ⑧ register (at a hospital):我要～外科。*I want to register for surgery.* ⑨[量] a set or string of:一～鞭炮 *a string of firecrackers* /一～珠子 *a string of pearls* /一～辣椒 *a string of cayenne peppers*

【挂包】[方] satchel

【挂表】[方] pocket watch

【挂不住】[方] be unable to conceal one's embarrassment or agitation; give oneself away

【挂彩】① decorate with colored silk festoons; decorate for festival occasions ② be wounded in action

【挂车】trailer

【挂齿】mention

【挂挡】put into gear

【挂钩】①【交】couple (two railway coaches); hook:车后面有拖曳～。*The car has drag hook at the rear.* ② hook:衣服～ *clothes hooks* /口袋～ *bag hook* ③ link up with; get in touch with; establish contact with:工资与工作表现～ *link up salary with performance*

【挂冠】[书] resign from office; give up office and leave the place

【挂号】① register (at a hospital):～处 *registration office* /～费 *registration fee* /请排队～。*Please queue up to register.* ② send by registered mail:～信 *registered mail or letter* /～邮资 *registration charge*

【挂花】① (of trees) bloom:苹果树～季节 *time when apples are in blossom* ② be wounded in action:他腿上～两次了。*He was twice wounded in the leg.*

【挂记】miss; worry about; be anxious about; show concern for:～海外的儿子 *miss one's son who is in oversea*

【挂历】monthly calendar hung up on the wall; wall calendar

【挂零】odd:七十～ *seventy-odd*

【挂虑】be anxious about; worry about; feel uneasy:不要～你的儿子。*Please don't worry about your son.*

【挂面】fine dried noodles; vermicelli:西红柿～ *vermicelli with tomato flavoring* /鸡蛋～ *noodles with egg flavoring*

【挂名】titular; nominal; in name only; ostensible:～夫妻 *husband and wife in name only* /～委员 *titular committee member* /～合伙人 *nominal partner; ostensible partner*

【挂念】show concern for; be worried about; miss:十分～ *miss sb very much*

【挂牌】① hang out one's shingle; put up one's brass plate ② put up a tag or label; list:～股票 *listed stock* /～上市公司 *listed company; quoted company* /～证券 *quoted securities; listed securities* /～汇价 *posted rate* /～股票总值 *total value of listed shares*

【挂屏】hanging panel; vertically-hung mounted scroll; scroll:立体～ *relief panel* /一对金漆～ *a pair of scrolls in gold-lacquered frames*

【挂失】report or declare the loss of sth:到银行～ *report the loss of a cheque* /遗失汽车,必须立即向警察局～。*You must report to the police station immediately if you lose your car.*

【挂帅】be in command; take command; take charge of; assume leadership:亲自～ *take command in person* /～人物 *person in command* /该工程由经理亲自～。*The manager will assume personal command of the project.*

【挂锁】padlock

【挂毯】tapestry:劣质～ *low quality tapestry*

【挂图】① wall map ② hanging chart; wall chart

【挂心】be on one's mind; concern oneself with; be anxious for; worry about

【挂靴】(of a football player, skater, etc.) hang up shoes

【挂衣钩】clothes-hook

【挂账】buy or sell on credit

【挂职】take up a temporary post (in order to temper oneself); serve in a lower level unit for a period while retaining one's position in the previous unit

【挂钟】wall clock

褂 Chinese-style garment or jacket; gown:短～儿 *short gown* /长～儿 *long gown* /马～儿 *sleeveless mandarin jacket (worn over a gown)*

【褂子】Chinese-style upper garment; short gown; jacket:白布～ *white jacket*

guāi

乖 ① well-behaved; good; obedient:他不是一个～孩子。*He isn't a good child.* ② clever; smart; wise; alert; shrewd:嘴很～ *honey-tongued; honey-lipped* ③ contradict; contrary to reason:有～常理 *run counter to reason* ④ (of one's behavior, etc.) perverse; abnormal; headstrong

【乖乖】① well-behaved; compliant; obedient:孩子们都～地坐在地板上。*The children all sat quietly on the floor.* ② little dear; little darling:起来吧,妈妈的好～! *Stand up, mummy's little dear!* ③ good gracious; gosh; my; boy:～,这幅字写得真好! *Boy, this writing is real fine!*

【乖觉】alert; quick; smart:老鼠～得很,感觉到人就窜了。*The rat is very stand up, and will run away as soon as it feels the existence of a man.*

【乖戾】perverse; recalcitrant; unreasonable; cantankerous：生性～ *perverse by nature* /举止～ *cantankerous in behaviours*

【乖谬】absurd；abnormal；fallacious：言辞～ *absurd in speech*

【乖僻】eccentric；odd；unnatural；bizarre：行为～ *eccentric behavior*；*eccentric in one's conduct*

【乖巧】① cute；lovely ② clever；smart；wise

【乖张】① eccentric and unreasonable；odd；perverse；recalcitrant：性情～ *be of an eccentric and unreasonable character*；*be perverse by nature* /行为～ *odd in behaviours* ②［书］not smooth：命运～ *vicissitudes of life*

掴 slap；smack：～耳光 *box sb's ears*；*slap sb on the face*

guǎi

拐[1] ① change direction；turn：～过墙角 *turn the corner of a house* /公路的～角处有一个商店。*There is a store is a store at the road corner.* /见岗哨往右～。*Turn right at the police stand.* ② limp：一～一～地走 *limp along*；*walk with a limp* ③ crutch：走路架着～ *walk on crutches* /拄着～练习走路 *practice walking with crutches* ④ swindle；make away with：～宝潜逃 *abscond with treasure* ⑤［方］corner；turning：墙～ *corner of a wall*；*corner of a house*

拐[2] kidnap；abduct：～卖儿童 *abduct and sell children*

【拐脖儿】elbow（of a stove pipe）

【拐带】kidnap；abduct

【拐棍】① walking stick；crutch：拄着～ *leaning on a stick* ② sb or sth that can be depended on for help or support：妻子成了丈夫走路缺不了的～。*The wife has become indispensable to the husband whenever he wants to walk.*

【拐角】corner；turning

【拐卖】kidnap and sell；abduct and sell：～妇女 *abduct and traffic in women*；*engage in white slavery* /～人口 *kidnap and sell people*

【拐骗】abduct；kidnap；swindle：～钱财 *swindle money*（*out of sb*）/～妇女 *abduct women* /～犯 *kidnapper* /～罪 *kidnapping* /～小孩 *abduct children*

【拐弯】① turn；make a turn；turn a corner：～要慢行。*Slow down when turning a corner.* /船～的时候，请大家坐稳了。*Please hold on to sth when the boat turns.* ② turn round（in thinking or speech）；pursue a new course；reorient：他心里一时还拐不过弯来。*He hasn't straightened out his heart yet.* ③ corner；turning

【拐弯抹角】① turn a corner here and there；go beating about the bush ② speak indirectly；talk in a roundabout way；talk about things without giving a clear answer：每个人发言都不要～。*Every one should speak directly.*

【拐杖】walking stick；crutch

【拐子】①［口］cripple ② I-shaped spool or reel ③ crutch：一副～ *a pair of crutches* /拄着～行动 *go on crutches* ④ abductor；swindler

guài

怪[1] ① strange；odd；queer；bewildering；eccentric：奇形～状 *fantastic in shape or appearance* /一点儿也不～ *not at all strange* /～病 *strange disease*；*rare disease* /～念头 *fantastic idea*；*whim* /这件事～得出奇。*It's most unusual.* ② find sth strange；wonder at；be surprised：那有什么可～的？*Is that anything to be surprised at?* /真是少见多～！*What ignorance!* ③［口］rather；quite；very：那地方～冷的。*It is quite cold.* /他～不好意思的。*He felt rather embarrassed.* ④ monster；demon；evil being；fiend：妖～ *monster* /妖魔鬼～ *demons and ghosts*；*monsters of every description*

怪[2] blame；reproach：不能～史密斯。*Smith is not to blame.* /～我没照顾好孩子。*I'm to blame for not having taken care of the child.*

【怪不得】① no wonder；so that's why；that explain why：～她这么高兴，原来买了一套新房。*So that's why she is so happy*；*she bought a new flat.* ② not to blame：这事～他。*He is not to blame for this.*

【怪诞】weird；absurd；strange；fantastic；uncanny：～的想法 *weird idea* /～不经 *weird and uncanny*；*fantastic* /～的故事 *strange story*

【怪话】cynical remark；grumble；complaint：说～ *make cynical remarks* /爱说～的人 *a grumbler*

【怪里怪气】have a screw loose；eccentric；strange；queer：打扮得～的 *be peculiarly dressed up* /～的人 *an eccentric fellow*

【怪模怪样】queer in appearance and manners；queer-looking；grotesque：你穿着这衬衣显得～的。*You look grotesque in those shirts.* /小猫长得～的。*The little cat is queer-looking.*

【怪僻】eccentric；odd；peculiar；cranky：性情～的人 *an eccentric person*；*crank*

【怪腔怪调】speak in a queer way；a queer tune

【怪圈】strange phenomenon which is hard to explain；vicious circle

【怪人】eccentric；a peculiar person；a strange person；crank

【怪事】peculiar thing；absurdity；rum go：咄咄～！*What a monstrous absurdity!* /真是～，钢笔怎么不见了？*How strange! Where did my pen disappear?*

【怪胎】monster；teratism；genetic freak

【怪石嶙峋】jagged rocks of grotesque shapes

【怪物】① monster；monstrosity；freak ② eccentric person；crank；weirdie；a queer bird；oddball

【怪异】① monstrous；strange；unusual；grotesque：感到～ *find sth unusual* ② unusual phenomenon；strange phenomenon；portent；prodigy

【怪罪】blame；reproach；reprove

guān

关 ① shut；close：～窗 *close the window* / ～抽屉 *shove in the drawer* / 把门～上。*Shut the door.* / 这扇门～不上。*This door won't shut.* ② turn off；switch off：出门时随手～灯 *turn the light off as you go out* / ～电视 *switch off the TV set* ③ lock up；shut in：～进监狱 *lock up（in prison）*；*put behind bars* / 笼子里～着一只猴子。*A monkey is shut in the cage.* / 别把老人整天～在屋里。*Don't keep the old man inside all day.* ④ close down；shut down：市里～了好几家厂子。*Quite a few factories in the town closed down.* ⑤ mountain pass；a guarded passage：雄～ *impregnable pass* / 边～ *frontier pass* ⑥ customs house；customs：过～ *go through customs* ⑦ barrier；a critical juncture：闯～ *fight one's way through a fortress*；*break through barriers* ⑧ gear；joint；key：～键人物 *key figure* ⑨ involve；implicate；concern：无～紧要 *of no consequence* / 有～部门 *department concerned*

【关爱】love and care；concern and care：同学们的深切～，使她深受感动。*The concern and care shown by the students moved her greatly.*

【关隘】［书］（mountain）pass：扼守～ *guard a pass*

【关闭】① close；shut：～城门 *close the city gate* / ～门窗 *close the doors and windows* ② close down；shut down：工厂～ *the closing down of factories* / ～效应 *blackout effect* / ～指令 *out code*

【关岛】Guam，an island administered as an unincorporated territory of the United States

【关防】① measures against divulgence of secrets；security measures：～严密 *tight security measures* ②［旧］government or army seal ③［书］military position at a strategic point；fort；fortress

【关怀】show loving care for；concern for；show solicitude for：～备至 *show the utmost solicitude* / 领导～每个员工。*The leaders pays great attention to every employee.*

【关键】① door bolt；door bar ② key；hinge；crux；crucial：问题的～ *the key to the question*；*the crux of the matter* / ～时刻 *the crucial moment* / ～证人 *key witness* / ～代码 *key code* / ～字 *key word*

【关节】①【生理】joint：膝～ *knee joint* / 全身～疼痛。*I ache all over at every joint.* / ～炎 *arthritis* / ～痛 *arthralgia*；*arthrodynia* / ～脱位 *abarticulation*；*dislocation of joint* ② key link；crucial point：应该注意那些涉及犯罪的重要～。*Attention should be centred on the links that have a vital bearing on criminal offence.*

【关口】① strategic pass；checkpoint：把住各个～ *guard every checkpoint* ② juncture

【关联】be related；be connected；be linked：密切～ *closely connected* / 数学和物理学是互相～的科学。*Mathematics and physics are connected sciences.*

【关贸总协定】general Agreement on Tariffs and Trade（GATT）：～缔约国 *a contracting party to GATT, replaced now by the WTO（World Trade Organization）*

【关门】①（of a shop，etc.）close：学校下午五点～。*The school closes at 5 p. m.* ② close；shut；stop operation：工厂因为管理不善，最后只好～。*The factory had no choice but to close down in the end due to mismanagement.* ③ refuse discussion or consideration；slam the door on sth：采取～态度 *adopt a closed-door attitude* ④ be behind closed doors：我们不能～办学。*We must not run a school behind closed doors.* ⑤ last：～弟子 *last disciple（of a master）*

【关卡】an outpost of a tax office；checkpoint：～林立。*There are checkpoints everywhere.*

【关切】① kind；thoughtful；considerate：～备至 *very thoughtful* ② be deeply concerned；show concern over；care for：表示严重～ *show grave concern over* / ～地注意到 *note with concern*

【关税】customs duty；customs；tariff：保护～ *protective tariff* / 特惠～ *preferential tariff* / 免征～ *exempt sb from customs duties*；*be duty-free* / 报复性～ *retaliatory tariff* / ～壁垒 *tariff wall*；*customs barrier* / ～地区 *tariff area* / ～豁免 *exemption from customs duties* / ～法 *tariff act* / ～负担 *incidence of duty* / ～减让 *concession of tariff* / ～配额 *customs quota*；*tariff quota* / ～升级 *tariff escalation* / ～税则 *customs tariff*；*tariff schedule* / ～同盟 *customs union* / ～政策 *tariff policy*；*customs policy* / ～制度 *tariff system* / ～自主 *tariff autonomy* / ～率 *tariff rate* / ～限额 *tariff ceiling* / ～战 *tariff war* / ～普惠制 *General Preferential Duties*

【关头】moment；juncture：生死～ *moment of life and death* / 紧要～ *critical moment*

【关系】① relations；connections；ties：保持友好～ *maintain friendly ties* / 社会～ *social connections* / 国际～ *international relations* / 公共～ *public relations* / 家庭～ *family connections* / 夫妻～ *relations between husband and wife* ② relationship：要正确处理人和人之间的～。*We should correctly handle the relationship between person to person.* ③ personal connections or network：老～ *old-comrade network* ④ usu. used with 由于 or 因为 to indicate cause or reason：由于天晚的～，就谈到这里吧。*Since it is late, I will have to stop here.* ⑤ concern；affect；have a bearing on；have to do with ⑥ bearing；relevance；impact；significance：她与那个案子毫无～。*She has nothing to do with that case.* / 你回答的话跟他所问的我看不出有什么～。*I don't see any connection between your answer and his question.* ⑦ credentials showing membership in or connection with an organization；personal credentials：党、团～ *one's Party or League membership credentials*

【关系户】parties of connections；special connections; connections

【关系人】【律】party

【关系网】network of friends; connections

【关系学】art or skill of cultivating good relations with people

【关心】concern with; show solicitude for; be interested in; care for: ~群众 *care for the masses* / ~国家大事 *concern oneself with state affairs*

【关押】lock up; put in prison; put behind bars; jail; put under detention: ~犯人 *put a criminal in prison* /他因贪污而遭~。*He was locked up for corruption.*

【关于】about; on; with regard to; concerning; as regards: ~保护森林的若干规定 *regulations concerning the protection of forests* /最近,我读了几本~数学方面的书。*Recently I have read a few books about mathematics.*

【关张】[方] (of a business, etc.) close down; shut down; go out of businesses

【关照】① look after; care for; take care of; keep an eye on: 感谢你的~。*Thank you for the trouble you have taken on my behalf.* ② notify by word of mouth; tell: 如果你要离开学校,请~一声。*Please let me know if you have to leave the school.*

【关注】show concern for; pay close attention to; show solicitude for; follow with interest

观 ① look at; see; observe; watch: 察其言, ~其行 *examine one's words and watch one's deeds; check what one says against what one does* /以~后效 *see how the offender behaves in future* /察言~色 *weigh up sb's words and watch his expression carefully; watch sb's every mood* ② sight; view; spectacle: 景~ *scene; landscape* /奇~ *wonderful sight* /外~ *outward appearance* /壮~ *impressive sight* ③ outlook; view; concept; conception: 世界~ *world outlook* /乐~ *optimism* /悲~ *pessimism* /正确的人生~ *a correct outlook on life*
see also guàn

【观测】① observe and survey: ~气象 *make weather observations* / ~读数 *observed reading* / ~值 *observed value* / ~洪水的涨势 *observe and measure the flood tide* / ~机 *observation airplane* / ~误差 *error in observation* / ~员 *observer; surveyor* / ~站 *observation station; observation post* ② observe; watch; size up: ~敌情 *watch enemy movements* / ~形势 *analyze the situation*

【观察】observe; watch; survey; size up: ~地形 *survey the terrain* / ~动静 *watch what is going on* / ~病情 *keep a patient under observation* / ~国际形势 *take stock of the international situation* / ~病房 *observation or probationary ward* / ~机 *observation plane* / ~哨 *observation post* /~员 *observer*

【观点】point of view; viewpoint; standpoint: 阶级~ *class viewpoint* / ~一致 *identity of views* /对立~ *opposing view* /用发展的~看问题 *look at things from a developmental perspective*

【观风】be on the lookout; serve as a lookout; watch

【观感】impressions; observations: 谈几点~ *make a few observations* /对美国的~ *impressions of United States*

【观光】go sightseeing; see the sights; visit; tour: ~者 *sightseer; tourist* / ~旅行 *make a sightseeing tour* / ~团 *sight-seeing party; visiting group* / ~市容 *tour the city*

【观看】watch; view; look at: ~足球比赛 *watch a football match* / ~电影 *see a film*

【观礼】attend a celebration or ceremony: ~台 *reviewing stand; visitor's stand*

【观摩】inspect and learn from each other's work; view and emulate: ~教学 *demonstration lecture* / ~演出 *performance before fellow artists for the purpose of discussion and emulation*

【观念】sense; idea; concept; mentality: 加强组织~ *strengthen one's sense of organization* /私有~ *private ownership mentality*

【观赏】view and admire; enjoy the sight of: ~文艺表演 *watch theatrical performances* / ~植物 *ornamental plant* / ~鱼 *fishes for display* / ~艺术 *visual arts*

【观望】① wait and see; look on (from the sidelines): ~不前 *hesitating and stalling* /采取~态度 *take a wait-and-see attitude* ② look about; look around: 四下~ *look around*

【观象台】【天】observatory

【观瞻】① the appearance of a place and the impressions it leaves; sight; view: 有碍~ *be unsightly; offend the eye* /以此~ *assume an imposing* ② look; see; watch

【观战】watch a war; watch a battle; watch a match or contest

【观众】viewer; audience; spectator: 电视~ *TV viewer* / ~席 *auditorium (of a theatre); grandstand (of a stadium)*

纶
see also lún

【纶巾】blue-ribboned silk kerchief

官[1] ① government official; military officer; officer; officeholder: 封~许愿 *promise high posts and other favours* /大~ *a high official* /外交~ *diplomat; diplomatic officer* / ~兵 *officer and soldiers* /清~ *honest and upright official* /贪~ *corrupt official; venal official* /升~ *promotion; rise in promotion* ② official; governmental; state-owned: ~办 *run by the government; operated by official bodies* ③ public: ~厕 *public toilet; public lavatory*

官[2] organ: 感~ *sense organ* /五~ *five sense organ*

【官本位】official rank or status taken as the only criterion for judging one's social worth; official rank standard: ~意识 *rank consciousness* / ~制 *system of ranking of officials*

【官逼民反】being oppressed by officials the masses revolt against them; misgovernment drives the people to revolt; misgovernment makes the people rebel
【官兵】① officers and soldiers; officers and men: ~一致 *unity between officers and men* ②［旧］*government troops*
【官场】［贬］officialdom; official circles: ~得意 *rapid rise up the official ladder*; *successful in one's official career* / ~积习 *tradition of official circles*
【官邸】official residence; official mansion: 大使~ *ambassador's residence*
【官方】of the government; official: ~消息 *news from government sources*; *official sources* / ~机密 *official secrecy*; *official secrets* / ~没收 *official confiscation* / ~人士 *official quarters* / 以~身份 *in an official capacity* / ~文件 *official document*; *patent* / ~统计 *official statistics* / ~外汇市场 *official exchange market* / ~发言人 *official spokesman* / ~报纸 *official newspaper*; *government newspaper* / ~汇率 *official exchange rate*; *official rate* / ~牌价 *official market quotation*
【官府】［旧］① local authorities; government ② officials; feudal official
【官宦】［旧］government official: ~之家 *family of an government official* / ~世家 *an aristocratic family of official*
【官价】official price; official rate: ~汇率 *official rate of exchange* / ~美元 *official rate of US dollar*
【官架子】the airs of an official; bureaucratic airs: 别摆~! *Don't put on bureaucratic airs!*
【官阶】official rank
【官吏】［旧］government officials
【官僚】bureaucrat; bureaucracy: 封建~ *feudal bureaucrat* / ~资本 *bureaucrat capital* / ~机构 *bureaucratic apparatus* / ~买办 *bureaucrat-comprador* / ~主义 *bureaucratism* / ~主义作风 *bureaucratic style of work* / 你这人太~! *What a bureaucrat you are!*
【官了】settle according to law; settle in court
【官迷】one who is obsessed by the pursuit of government office; office-hankerer; office-seeker; careerist
【官气】bureaucratic airs; bureaucratism: ~十足 *bursting with bureaucratic airs*
【官腔】official jargon; bureaucratic tone: 打~ *speak in a bureavcratic tone*; *stall with official jargon*
【官商】① government commerce; state-operated commerce; state-run business ② government merchant; bureaucrat-like personnel in a government enterprise: ~作风 *bureaucratic ways of doing business* ③ government and private citizens
【官司】［口］lawsuit: 打~ *go to law against sb*
【官衔】official title
【官样文章】official formality; dead letter; red tape; an unpractical routine document
【官瘾】［贬］craving after office; obsession for official post; loving for public office: 格拉布的~极大。*Grub is an addicted office-seeker.*
【官员】official; officer: 政府~ *governmental official* / 外交~ *diplomatic official* / 项目~ *programme officer*
【官运】official career; political career; fortunes of officialdom: ~亨通 *have a successful official career*; *advance smoothly in officialdom*
【官职】government post; official position; office

冠 ① cap; hat: 免~照片 *bare-headed photo* / 衣~整齐 *be neatly dressed* ② corona; crown: 花~ *corolla* / 树~ *the crown of a tree* / 王~ *crown* / 牙~ *the crown of a tooth* ③ crest; comb: 鸡~ *cock's comb*; *crest*
see also guàn
【冠冕】① royal crown; official hat ② high-sounding; pompous; stately; ceremonious
【冠冕堂皇】① have a bold, noble bearing; have a bold and dignified bearing; impressive looking; ② high-toned; highfalutin; high-sounding: ~的理由 *high-sounding excuses*
【冠心病】【医】coronary heart disease: ~患者 *coronary heart patient*
【冠状动脉】coronary artery: ~硬化 *coronary arteriosclerosis*
【冠子】crest; comb: 鸡~ *cockscomb*

倌 ① stockman; herdsman; livestock keeper; keeper of domestic animals: 羊~儿 *shepherd* / 牛~儿 *cowherd* / 马~儿 *groom* ②［旧］*hired hand in certain trades*: 堂~儿 *waiter*

棺 coffin: 盖~论定 *the final Verdict can not be passed on a person until the lid is placed on his coffin*
【棺材】coffin: ~铺 *coffin shop*
【棺床】【考】coffin platform
【棺椁】【考】inner and outer coffins
【棺架】bier
【棺木】coffin

鳏 wifeless; widowered: ~居 *live as a widower*
【鳏夫】［书］an old wifeless man; bachelor; widower
【鳏寡孤独】the widower, the widow, the orphan and the childless; widows, orphans and other people without a provider

guǎn

馆 ① accommodation for guest: 小旅~ *inn* / 宾~ *guest house* / 驿~ *posthouse* / 旅~ *hotel* ② embassy; legation or consulate: 大使~ *embassy* / 总领~ *consulate general* ③ (of service trades) shop: 茶~ *tea house* / 饭~ *restaurant* / 咖啡~ *coffee house* / 照相~ *photo studio* ④ place for cultural activities: 美术~ *art gallery* / 图书~ *library* / 展览~ *exhibition hall* / 纪念~ *memorial hall* / 文化~ *culture centre*

【馆子】restaurant; eating house: 下 ~ *eat at a restaurant*

管[1] ① pipe; tube; conduit; duct: 水泥 ~ *pipe cement* / 水 ~ *water pipe* / 钢 ~ *steel pipe* / 试 ~ *test tube* / 输油 ~ *oil pipeline* ② wind instrument: 单簧 ~ *clarinet* / 铜 ~ 乐 *brass wind* ③ valve; tube: 电子 ~ *electron tube* / 晶体 ~ *transistor* / 显像 ~ *picture tube* ④ (Guǎn) a surname

管[2] ① manage; control; run; take care of; be in charge of: ~ 设备 *be in charge of equipment* / ~ 生产 *manage production* / ~ 孩子 *take care of children* / 这事我 ~ 不了。*I'm not in a position to take care of this business.* ② have jurisdiction over; administer ③ subject sb to discipline; discipline ④ concern oneself with; bother about; care about; care for; mind: 这个孩子太自私了，只 ~ 自己，不 ~ 别人。*She is so selfish and is only concerned about herself, not about others.* ⑤ provide; ensure; guarantee: 我们公司 ~ 我们吃住。*Our company provides food and accommodation.* ⑥ call: 大家 ~ 这间屋子叫家。*People call this room "the home".* ⑦ [方] from towards; to: ~ 我借钱 *borrow money from me* ⑧ [方] no matter (who, what, how, etc.); despite: ~ 它冷不冷，今天都得出发。*Cold or warm, we must set out today.*

【管保】guarantee; assure; sure

【管不住】be unable to control; cannot manage: 我哥哥非常淘气，连他老师都 ~ 他。*My elder brother is very naughty and even his teacher cannot manage him.*

【管不着】have no right to interfere; (it's) none of your concern: 这是我们自己事，你 ~。*This is our own matter; and you have no right to interfere.*

【管道】pipeline; piping; conduit; tubing: ~ 系统 *piping system* / ~ 工 *plumber; gas fitter* / ~ 敷设 *pipe laying* / ~ 安装 *piping erection* / ~ 工程 *plumbing*

【管风琴】【音】pipe organ; organ: ~ 手 *organist*

【管家】① manage a household; run a house ② [旧] steward; butler: 忠实可靠的 ~ *honest, loyal, and reliable steward* ③ manager; housekeeper

【管教】subject sb to discipline; discipline; correct

【管界】① area or land under control; sphere of jurisdiction; jurisdiction zone: 事件发生在这个省的 ~ 内。*It took place in an area under the jurisdiction of this province.* ② border of a jurisdiction zone

【管井】【水】tube well

【管窥】look at sth through a bamboo tube; have a restricted view: ~ 所及 *in my humble opinion*

【管理】① manage; run; administer; supervise: ~ 生产 *manage production* / ~ 财务 *be in charge of financial affairs* / ~ 图书 *take care of the library books* / 城市 ~ *city government* / ~ 企业 *run an enterprise* / 市场 ~ *supervise a market* / 经济 ~ *economic administration* / 商业 ~ *business management* / ~ 部门 *administrative department* / ~ 费 *management fee* / ~ 风格 *manage style* / ~ 经济学 *managerial economics* / ~ 会计 *management accounting* / ~ 买进 *management buy-in* (*MBI*) / ~ 卖出 *management buy-out* (*MBO*) / ~ 权 *administrative power; right of supervision* / ~ 人员 *administrative personnel; managerial staff; administrator* / ~ 水平 *level of administration or management* / ~ 制度 *administrative regulations* / ~ 科学 *management science* / ~ 职能 *management function* / ~ 模式 *management model; management pattern* / ~ 方法 *office procedure* / ~ 处 *administrative office* ② tend; look after; control; watch over: ~ 犯人 *watch over prisoners* / ~ 牲口 *tend drought animals* ③ take care of; look after: ~ 宿舍 *look after the dorm* / ~ 仓库 *take care of the warehouse*

【管路】【机】pipeline: 铺设 ~ *lay pipelines*

【管事】① run affairs; be in charge; be responsible ② [口] effective; of use; useful ③ [旧] steward; butler; manager; person in charge

【管束】supervise; control; restrain; check: ~ 不严 *lax in supervise* / 严加 ~ *keep sb under strict control*

【管辖】have jurisdiction over; exercise control over; administer: ~ 区 *district under the jurisdiction or administration of a large geopolitical unit* / ~ 区域 *compass of competency; jurisdictional area* / 在 ~ 范围内 *come within the jurisdiction of* / ~ 权 *jurisdiction*

【管闲事】be meddlesome; be a busybody; poke one's nose into others' business: 你别 ~。*Keep your nose out of it.*

【管弦乐】orchestral music: ~ 队 *orchestra; symphony orchestra*

【管押】take sb into custody; keep s bin custody; detain: 你不能见到他，他现在还是一个受 ~ 的罪犯。*You can't see him; he is a criminal held in custody.*

【管乐队】wind band; band

【管乐器】wind instrument

【管制】① control: 外汇 ~ *foreign exchange control* / 交通 ~ *traffic control* / 军事 ~ *military control* / ~ 灯火 *enforce a blackout* / ~ 物价 *control prices* ② put (a criminal, etc.) under surveillance: ~ 劳动 *labor under surveillance*

【管中窥豹】look at a leopard through a tube; see only one spot; have a limited knowledge of sth: ~，可见一斑 *conjure the whole thing through seeing a part of it; look at one spot on a leopard and you can visualize the whole animal*

【管状花】【植】tubular flower

【管子】tube; pipe: ~ 工 *plumber; pipe fitter* / 煤气 ~ *gas pipe*

guàn

观 Taoist temple：白云～ *white Cloud Temple*
see also guān

贯 ① pass through；penetrate；pierce：横～全国的英特网 *the internet runs cross the whole country* /学～古今 *well versed in both ancient and modern learning* ② proceed in succession；be linked together；follow in a continuous line；be connected：鱼～而入 *file in*；*enter in single file* ③ native place；birthplace：籍～ *the place of one's birth or origin*

【贯彻】carry out；implement；execute；put into effect：～党的路线 *implement the Party line* /～政策 *carry out a policy* /～群众路线 *follow the mass line* /～决议 *put into effect a resolution*

【贯穿】① run through；penetrate：铁路～南北。*The railway runs through north and south.* ② fill；permeate

【贯串】penetrate；run through；permeate；spread through

【贯通】① have a thorough knowledge of；be well versed in；master：融会～ *achieve mastery through a comprehensive study of the subject* ② link up；thread together；join up

【贯注】① concentrate on；give full attention to；be absorbed in：全神～ *be wholly absorbed* ② be connected in meaning or feeling；consistent

冠 ①［书］wear or put on a hat ② precede；crown with ③ first place；the best；champion：这里的糖产量为全国之～。*This area ranks first in the whole country for sugar output.*
see also guān

【冠词】【语】article：定～ *definite article* /不定～ *indefinite article*

【冠军】champion；first-prize winner：世界～ *world champion* /在这次比赛中汤姆又获得了～。*Tom won the first prize again in this match.*

掼 ［方］① throw；fling；hurl；cast；toss：她把手机～在地上。*She flung her mobile phone on the floor.* ② fall；throw down；tumble：他～了一个跟头。*He had a fall.* ③ thresh：～稻 *thresh rice*

【掼纱帽】［方］cast away one's official hat in anger；resign in resentment；quit office

惯 ① be used to；be accustomed to；be inured to；be in the habit of：～盗 *hardened bandit*；*professional brigand* /这是他～用的字眼。*These are his customary words and expressions.* ② indulge；spoil；pamper；coddle：孩子要管不要～。*Children should be disciplined and not indulged.*

【惯常】① habitual ② often；frequently ③ usual；normal

【惯犯】habitual offender；hardened criminal；recidivist；repeater：听说昨天警察在～的家里逮住了他。*I heard the habitual offender was caught in his home.*

【惯匪】hardened bandit；professional brigand

【惯技】［贬］customary tactic；old trick

【惯例】① convention；usual practice：按～行事 *go by convention* /国际～ *international practice* /打破～ *break with conventions* ②【律】precedent：援引～ *cite a precedent* /～法 *code of practice*；*conventional law*

【惯量】【物】inertia；inertness

【惯偷】habitual thief；hardened thief；professional thief

【惯性】【物】inertia：～定律 *the law of inertia* /～飞行 *coasting flight* /～飞行导弹 *coasting missile*；*coaster* /～领航 *inertial navigation* /～系数 *inertia coefficient* /～中心 *centre of inertia* /～导航 *inertial guidance* /～导航仪 *inertial navigator* /～力 *inertial force*；*mass force*

【惯用】① habitually practice；consistently use：～法 *customary usage* /～两面派的手法 *consistently use double-faced tactics* ② habitual；customary：～称呼 *customary title* /～手法 *habitual practice* /～伎俩 *customary tactics*

【惯于】① be used to；be accustomed to

盥 ［书］wash（the hands or face）

【盥漱】wash one's face and rinse one's mouth

【盥洗】wash one's hands and face；wash up：～用具 *toilet articles* /～室 *washroom* /～台 *washstand*

灌 ① irrigate：浇～ *watering* /漫～ *flood irrigation* /喷～ *sprinkler irrigation* ② fill；pour；cram：～药 *pour medicine down the throat* /～醉 *get sb drunk* ③ record（sound，music，etc. on a tape or disc）：～唱片 *make a gramophone record*；*cut a disc*

【灌肠】①【医】give an enema（or clyster）；clyster ② sausage

【灌溉】irrigate；water：机器～ *irrigation by pumping* /人力～ *irrigation by human power* /～面积 *irrigated area* /～渠 *irrigation canal* /～网 *irrigation network* /～系统 *irrigation system* /～站 *irrigation station*

【灌浆】①【建】grouting：～泵 *grouting pump* ②【农】(of grain) be in the milk：那对农民夫妇在小麦～时节回到了家乡。*The farmer couple returned their hometown at the time when the wheat was in the milk.* ③【医】from a vesicle（during smallpox or after vaccination）④ injection

【灌录】make a recording

【灌迷汤】bewitch with honeyed words；butter up；lay it on thick；soft-soup

【灌木】bush；shrub：～丛 *brush*；*brush-wood*；*shrubbery*

【灌区】irrigated district；irrigated area

【灌输】① channel water to another place；divert running water for use elsewhere. ② instill into；inculcate；imbue with：～科学知识 *instill scientif-*

ic knowledge into sb /给学生～爱国思想 *instill patriotism into the students*
【灌音】have one's voice recorded; have one's voice canned
【灌制】tape-record; record: ～唱片 *cut a disc* /把歌曲～在磁带上 *record the songs on tape*
【灌注】pour

鹳 【动】stork: 白～ *white stork*

罐 ① jar; pot; tin; tank; pitcher: 煤气～ *gas tank* /茶叶～ *tea caddy* /水～ *water pitcher* /酒～ *wine jar* /一～苹果酱 *a jar of apple jam* ② coal tub
【罐车】tank car; tank truck; tanker
【罐笼】cage; cage conductor: ～间隙 *cage clearance* /～格 *cage way*
【罐头】①［方］jar; pot; pitcher; tin ② tinned food; canned food: ～食品 *canned goods* /水果～ *canned fruit* /～厂 *cannery*
【罐装】canning
【罐子】pot; jar; pitcher; tin; jug: 空～ *empty tin* /两～水 *two jugs of water*

guāng

光 ① light; ray: 曙～ *first light of morning* ② landscape; scenery; sight ③ credit; glory; honour: 他决定好好学习，为父母争～。*He decided to study hard and won honour for his parents.* ④ benefit; advantage; good ⑤ bright; shiny ⑥ glorify; bring honour to ⑦ used of what the other party does for one ⑧ finish; use up: 打印纸用～了。*The print paper is used up.* ⑨ glossy; smooth ⑩bare; naked: 他～脚丫子就跑出来了。*He rushed out of the house with bare-footed.* ⑪ alone; only; merely; solely: 不要～说不做。*Don't only speak, but there's no action.* ⑫(Guāng) a surname
【光膀子】stripped to the waist
【光笔】light pen; electronic pen
【光标】cursor
【光波】【物】light wave; optical wave
【光彩】① brilliance; lustre; radiance; splendour ② honour; glory
【光尺】laser range finder; laser ranging device
【光大】① carry forward; develop; enhance; promote ② extensive; far and wide; vast
【光点】light spot
【光电】【物】photoelectricity: ～材料 *photoelectric measuring instrument* / ～计数器 *photocurrent counter* / ～晶体管 *phototransistor* / ～显像管 *photoelectric viewing tube* / ～显微镜 *photoelectric microscope*
【光度】【物】luminosity
【光杆儿】① bare trunk or stalk ② man who has lost his family
【光景】① landscape; scenery; scene; conditions; state of affairs ② probably; likely ③ around
【光控】light-operated; photo-controlled: ～开关 *photoswitch*; *light-operated switch*
【光缆】optical cable
【光临】presence
【光溜溜】bare; naked; smooth; slippery
【光芒】brilliant rays; radiance; rays of light: ～四射 *rays in all directions*
【光面】noodles served without meat or vegetables
【光敏】【物】light-sensitive; photosensitive: ～玻璃 *light-sensitive glass*; *photosensitive glass*
【光明】① light: 她仿佛看到了黑暗中的一丝～。*She seems to see a streak of light in the darkness.* ② bright; promising: 你的前途一片～。*Your future is very bright.* ③ aboveboard; guileless; openhearted: ～磊落 *open and aboveboard*
【光年】【天】light-year
【光盘】optical disk: ～驱动器 *CD－ROM driver*; *disc drive*
【光频】light frequency; optical frequency
【光谱】【物】spectrum: ～图 *spectrum chart* / ～仪 *spectrograph*/太阳～*solar spectrum* /原子～*atomic spectrum*
【光圈】【摄】aperture; diaphragm
【光荣】credit; honour; glory; distinction: ～榜 *honour roll*
【光束】【物】light beam: ～半径 *beam radius*
【光速】【物】speed of light; velocity of light
【光天化日】in broad daylight; in the light of day: ～下你做了什么? *What have you done in the light of day?*
【光头】① bareheaded; hatless; shaven head ② bald head
【光秃秃】bare; bald: ～的山岭 *bare hills and mountains/* ～的树枝 bare branches
【光纤】optical fibre; fibre optic: ～电缆 *fibre optic cable* / ～技术 *fibre optics/* ～通信 *fibre-optical communication*
【光线】light; ray: 屋子里的～不太好。*The room is not well lighted.*
【光学】optics: ～介质 *optical medium* / ～传感器 *optical sensor* / ～仪器 *optical instrument*
【光耀】① brilliant; glittering; splendid; glory; honour ② bring glory to; win honour for ③ shine brilliantly
【光阴】① time: ～似箭 *time flies* ②［方］life; livelihood
【光源】【物】light source; luminous source
【光泽】gloss; lustre; sheen
【光照】【植】illumination; shine: ～期 *light period* / ～量 *quantity of illumination* / ～度 *intensity of illumination*
【光质子】【物】photoproton
【光中子】【物】photoneutron
【光子】【物】photon: ～束 *photon beam*
【光宗耀祖】bring honour to one's ancestors

咣 ［象］ang; crash

【咣当】[象] bang; crash

guǎng

广[1] ① extensive; vast; wide ② many; numerous: 玛丽是个性格开朗的女孩,她交友很~。*Mary is active and has many friends.* ③ expand; extend; spread

广[2] ① short for Guangdong (Province) or Guangzhou (City) ② (Guǎng) a surname

【广播】① broadcast; be on the air ② radio programme; broadcast news broadcast ③ [书] widely spread; known far and wide: ~电台 *radiostation; broadcasting station* / ~稿 *broadcast script*/ ~节目 *broadcast or radio programme* / ~剧 *radio play or drama* / ~体操 *calisthenics with radio music; radio exercises* /员 *broadcaster* / ~站 *broadcaster station*

【广博】extensive; wide: 他爸爸是一个知识~的教授。*His father is a professor with extensive knowledge.*

【广场】public square; square

【广大】① extensive; vast; wide ② broad; large scale; widespread ③ many; numerous: 国家的发展依靠~人民群众。*The country's development depends on broad masses of the people.*

【广度】breadth; range; scope

【广而告之】give extensive publicity; spread far and wide

【广而言之】speaking generally; in a general sense; in general terms

【广泛】broad; extensive; wide-ranging; widespread

【广告】advertisement: ~公司 *advertising firm* / ~费 *rate of advertisement; advertising fee*

【广阔】broad; extensive; vast; wide

【广漠】vast and bare

【广义】① broad sense ②【物】generalized; general: ~方程 *generalized equation*

【广域网】wide area network (WAN)

【广征博引】quote copiously and prove extensively

犷 boorish; rustic; uncouth

【犷悍】rough and ferocious; tough and intrepid

guàng

逛 roam; ramble; stroll: 今天上午我和妈妈~街去了。*My mother and I strolled around the streets this morning.*

【逛荡】loaf about; loiter

【逛街】roam the streets; take a stroll in the streets

【逛窑子】visit a brothel; go whoring

【逛游】saunter; stroll

guī

归 ① come back; go back; return ② give back; return sth to sb: 你什么时候把钱~还我? *When will you return the money to me?* ③ be in sb's charge; put under sb's care ④ come together; converge ⑤ belong to: 这些桌子都~我所有。*All the tables belong to me.* ⑥【数】divide (on the abacus) with a one-digit divisor ⑦ used between identical verbs to indicate uselessness or irrelevance of the action ⑧ (Guī) a surname

【归案】bring to justice

【归档】file; file away; place on file

【归队】① rejoin one's unit: 他病好就~了。*He returned to his army after recovery.* ② return to the profession one was trained for

【归根结底】in the final analysis; put it in a nutshell; fundamentally

【归功】attribute the success to; give the credit to

【归国】return to one's country: ~华侨 *returned overseas Chinese* / ~观光 *return to one's homeland on a sightseeing tour*

【归航】【航】homing: ~台 *homing station*

【归还】give back; revert; return: 请帮我把书~图书馆。*Please help me return the books to the library.*

【归咎】attribute a fault to; impute the blame to

【归类】categorize; classify; sort out: 请把我给你的信件~。*Please sort out these letters I gave you.*

【归谬法】reduction to absurdity

【归纳】conclude; induce; sum up: ~法 *inductive method*

【归期】date of return

【归属】belong to; come under the jurisdiction of: ~权 *right of attribution*

【归宿】home to return to; destination; final settling place: 谁知道她的~? *Who knows her final settling place?*

【归天】pass away; go to one's glory; die

【归途】way back; way home; homeward journey

【归降】capitulate; surrender

【归向】inclination; turning towards

【归心似箭】with one's heart set on speeding home; impatient to get back; anxious to return

【归省】[书] by on family leave; return and visit one's family

【归于】① attributed to; belong to: 成功~老师。*Success is attributed to our teachers.* ② end in; tend to; result in

【归整】arrange; put in order; sort out; tidy up: 我们去她家拜访时,她正在~房间。*She is tidying up her room when we visit her.*

【归置】arrange; put in order; tidy up

【归罪】impute a fault to; put the blame on: 他总是~别人。*He always puts the blame on others.*

龟 tortoise; turtle
see also jùn
【龟背】curvature of the spinal column
【龟甲】tortoise-shell
【龟头】【生理】glans penis
规 ① compasses; dividers:他送我了一副圆~。*He gave me a pair of compasses.* ② rule; regulation ③ plan; map out ④【机】gauge ⑤ advise; admonish; counsel
【规程】rules; regulations
【规定】① provide; prescribe; specify ② rules and regulations; provisions; stipulations:他违反~了。*He went against the regulations.*
【规范】① standard; model; normal; norm:行为~ *norms of behaviour* ② regulate; standardize
【规格】condition; norms; requirement; standards; specifications
【规划】① plan; programme:城市~ *city planning* ② draw up a plan; map out a programme
【规矩】① custom; rules of a community or organization; established practice:尊敬老人是我们的老~。*To respect the olders is our established rules.* ② honest; well-behaved; well-disciplined
【规律】law; regular; pattern
【规模】large-scale; scope; scale; extent: ~经济 *economy of scale*
【规劝】advise; admonish; counsel:她根本不听我们的~。*She refused to take our advice.*
【规则】① rule; regulation; law:我们要遵守交通~。*We need to abide by traffic regulations.* ② regular: ~名词 *regular noun*
【规章】rules; regulations: ~制度 *rules and regulations*
【规整】① neat; tidy; regular:那个孩子写一手~的好字。*The child can write a neat hand.* ② put in order; tidy up
皈
【皈依】① ceremony of proclaiming sb a Buddhist ② be converted to Buddhism or some other religion
闺 ①［古］small door ② lady's chamber; boudoir
【闺房】［旧］lady's chamber; boudoir
【闺女】①［口］daughter:您的~真漂亮! *How beautiful your daughter is!* ② girl; maiden
硅 【化】silicon (Si)
【硅钢】【冶】silicon steel
【硅胶】【化】silica gel
【硅石】silica
【硅酸】【化】silicic acid: ~钠 *sodium silicate*
【硅铁】ferrosilicon
【硅砖】silica brick
瑰 marvellous; rare
【瑰宝】gem; rarity; treasure:国家的~ *national treasure*
【瑰丽】magnificent; splendid; surpassingly beautiful: ~的夜晚 *splendid night*
【瑰异】fantastic; magnificent

guǐ

轨 ① rail ② track:双~ *double track* /单~ *double track* /无~ *trackless* ③ rule; course; order:她的生活正慢慢步入正~。*His life is taking the regular course step by step.*
【轨道】① track ② orbit:进入~ *put into orbit* ③ path; trajectory ④ course; path:他不想加入他们的~。*He didn't want to follow their path.*
【轨迹】【数】locus: ~函数 *locus function*
【轨辙】beaten track; rut
【轨枕】sleeper; tie: ~板 *concrete slab sleeper*
诡 ① cunning; deceitful; tricky: ~称 *falsely allege* ②［书］eerie; uncanny; weird
【诡辩】① indulge in sophistry; quibble:他所说的完全是~。*What he said is nothing but quibbling.* ② sophistry; sophism: ~术 *sophistry* / ~家 *sophist*
【诡计】crafty plot; cunning scheme; trick: ~多端 *have a whole bag of tricks; be very crafty; have a lot of tricks up one's sleeve*
【诡谲】① strange and changeable ② eccentric; mysterious
【诡秘】furtive; secretive; surreptitious:最近他们班的几个同学行动有点~。*Some students of their class are surreptitious in their movement recently.*
【诡异】odd; abnormal; queer; strange
【诡诈】crafty; cunning; treacherous; sly
鬼 ① ghost; spirit; apparition:我不喜欢听~故事。*I dislike listening ghost stories.* ② derogatory term for a person with a certain vice or problem:你真是一个胆小~。*You are really a coward.* ③ dirty trick; sinister plot ④ damnable; terrible; wretched ⑤ stealthy; surreptitious ⑥［口］clever; smart; quick
【鬼把戏】sinister plot; treacherous scheme; monkey trick; mischievous trick
【鬼才】special talent; person having special talent:在语言方面她是个~。*She is a special talent in languages.*
【鬼点子】［方］trick; wicked idea
【鬼怪】forces of evil; ghosts and monsters
【鬼鬼祟祟】on the sly; sneaky; furtive; stealthy; in a hole and corner
【鬼话】lie; fake story; falsehood: ~连篇 *pack of lies*
【鬼魂】ghost; spirit; apparition
【鬼混】hang around; fool around
【鬼机灵】［口］clever; intelligent; smart
【鬼哭狼嚎】wail like ghosts and howl like wolves; let loose wild shrieks and howls
【鬼脸】① mask:那个孩子做着~从屋子里冲出来。

The little child rushed out the house with a mask. ② funny face; wry face
【鬼门关】danger spot; gate of hell
【鬼迷心窍】be obsessed; be possessed
【鬼使神差】doings of ghosts and gods-unexpected happenings; curious coincidence; unexpected happening
【鬼胎】dark scheme; evil plot; sinister design
【鬼头鬼脑】furtive; stealthy; on the sly
【鬼主意】evil plan; wicked idea: 不要听她的～。*Don't listen her wicked idea.*
【鬼子】devil

guì

柜 ① cabinet; cupboard ② cashier's desk; cashier's office
【柜橱】cabinet; cupboard
【柜房】cashier's office; shop cashier
【柜台】bar; counter: 她姐姐是站～的。*Her elder sister serves behind the counter.*
刽 cut off; chop off
【刽子手】① headsman; executioner ② slaughterer; butcher
贵 ① costly; dear; expensive: 这些衣服太～了。*These clothes are too expensive.* ② highly valued; valuable; precious ③ of high rank; noble ④ your: 请问您～姓? *Would you like to tell us your name?* ⑤ (Guì) a surname
【贵宾】honoured guest; distinguished guest: ～休息室 *VIP lounge or room*
【贵妃】highest-ranking imperial concubine
【贵干】your business; noble errand
【贵庚】your age
【贵贱】① cheap or expensive ② high or low social status ③ anyway; at any case; at any rate
【贵金属】noble metal; precious metal
【贵客】honoured guest
【贵人】man of eminence: ～多忘事。*Men of eminence have short memories or great men easily forget.*
【贵重】costly; precious; valuable
【贵族】aristocrat; noble; peer: 封建～ *feudal nobility*
桂[1] ① cassia; cinnamon ② sweet-scented osmanthus ③ bay tree; laurel
桂[2] ① Guijiang River in Guangxi ② another name for Guang xi ③ (Guì) a surname
【桂冠】laurel: ～诗人 *poet laureate*
【桂花】【植】sweet-scented osmanthus
【桂皮】Chinese cinnamon tree; cassia-bark tree
【桂鱼】mandarin fish
【桂圆】longan
跪 kneel: 为了让父亲原谅,他都给父亲下～了。*He dropped on his knees in order to be forgave by his father.*
【跪拜】worship on bended knees; kowtow
【跪倒】throw oneself on one's knees; prostrate oneself
【跪叩】kowtow
【跪姿】kneeling position

gǔn

滚 ① roll; trundle; tumble: ～淌 (*of tears, sweat, etc.*) *roll; stream* / 在地上打～ *roll back and forth on the floor* ② get away; bear it: 他冲我大喊"～出去"。*He shouted at me "get out of here".* ③ boil; seethe: ～水 *boiling water* / ～汤 *boiling soup* ④ bind; trim ⑤ (Gǔn) a surname
【滚蛋】get out; bear it; scram
【滚刀】【机】hobbing cutter; hob
【滚动】roll; trundle
【滚瓜烂熟】know sth by heart; be extremely fluent; have at one's fingertips; master thoroughly
【滚滚】billow; roll; surge: 波涛～ *waves surge*
【滚开】(gǔnkāi) boiling hot
【滚开】(gǔnkai) beat it; clear out; scram
【滚热】burning hot; boiling hot; piping hot
【滚烫】boiling hot; burning hot: 他递给我一杯～的咖啡。*He gave me a cup of boiling hot coffee.*
【滚筒】cylinder; roll
【滚雪球】roll a snowball; get bigger and bigger as it proceeds
【滚圆】round as a ball
【滚珠】【机】roll: ～轴承 *ball bearing*
【滚子】roller; running pulley
磙 ① roller ② level (ground, etc.) with a roller
【磙子】① stone roller ② any round-shaped rolling

gùn

棍[1] rod; stick; cane: 那个孩子带着一根木～冲进了教室。*The child rushed into the classroom with a wooden stick.*
棍[2] rascal; ruffian; scoundrel: 赌～ *gambler*
【棍棒】① club; bludgeon; cudgel ② stick or staff used in gymnastics
【棍子】club; stick; staff

guō

郭 ① outer wall of a city: 城～ *inner and outer city walls* ② (Guō) a surname
聒 noisy
【聒耳】grate on one's ears
【聒噪】[方] noisy; clamorous

锅 ① pan; pot:煎~ *frying pan* ② bowl (of a pipe, etc.)
【锅巴】rice crust; crust of cooked rice
【锅铲】slice; spatula
【锅盖】the lid of a cooking pot
【锅炉】boiler: ~房 *boiler room*
【锅台】top of a kitchen range
【锅贴儿】lightly fried dumpling
【锅烟子】soot on the bottom of a pan
【锅灶】pot and stove

蝈

【蝈蝈儿】【动】katydid; long-horned grasshopper

guó

国 ① country; nation; state:邻~ *neighbouring country* ② of the state; national: ~宾馆 *state guesthouse* / ~旗 *national flag* ③ of China; Chinese ④ (Guó) a surname
【国宝】national treasure
【国宾】state guest:他们在等~的到来。*They are waiting for the state guests' coming.*
【国策】state policy; basic policy of a state
【国耻】national humiliation
【国粹】the quintessence of Chinese culture
【国道】national road; national highway
【国都】national capital; capital
【国度】country; nation; state
【国法】law; national law; law of the land: ~难容 *not to be tolerated by law*
【国防】national defence: ~部 *the Ministry of National Defence* / ~现代化 *modernization of national defence*
【国歌】national anthem
【国格】national prestige; nation's dignity
【国号】title of a reigning dynasty
【国花】national flower:你知道日本的~是什么吗? *Do you know what's the national flower of Japan?*
【国画】traditional Chinese painting
【国徽】national emblem
【国会】parliament (UK); Congress (UK); Diet (Japan); Reichstag (Germany)
【国货】Chinese goods; China-made goods
【国籍】nationality; citizenship:双重~ *dual nationality* /去年他加入了英国~。*Last year he was naturalized as the citizen of England.*
【国计民生】national economy and people's livelihood
【国际】international; foreign; world: ~影响 *international repercussions* / ~劳动节 *International Labour Day* / ~联盟 *League of Nations*
【国家】country; nation; state:发达~ *developed country* /发展中~ *developing country* / ~大事 *state (or national) affairs* / ~队 *national team* / ~主席(*Chinese*) *president* / ~领导人 *state leader* / ~元首 *head of state* / ~机关 *state organs*; *government offices* / ~机器 *state apparatus*; *state machinery* / ~政权 *state power* / ~法 *law of the state* ; *state law* / ~机密 *state secret* / ~决算 *final accounts of state revenue and expenditure*; *final state account* / ~权力 *state power* / ~主权 *national or state sovereignty* / ~兴亡,匹夫有责。*Every man has a share of responsibility for the fate of his country.*
【国界】national boundaries
【国境】national territory: ~线 *boundary of a country* /现在出入中国~不是太难的事情了。*Now it is not difficult to leave and enter China.*
【国库】state treasury; exchequer: ~券 *treasury bill*; *state treasury bond*
【国力】national power; national strength:中国拥有雄厚的~。*China has solid national strength.*
【国立】state-maintained; state-run: ~学校 *national school*
【国门】gateway of a country
【国民】member of a nation; people of a nation: ~收入 *national income* / ~经济 *national economy*
【国难】national crisis; national calamity
【国内】internal; domestic; home:他父亲喜欢看~新闻。*His father likes reading home news.*
【国旗】national flag: ~迎风飘扬。*The national flag is fluttering in the breeze.*
【国企】state enterprise
【国情】national conditions; condition of a country
【国庆】national Day:欢度~ *celebrate National Day*
【国色天香】of ravishing beauty and heavenly fragrance; ethereal colour and celestial fragrance
【国事】national affairs; state affairs
【国势】① state of affairs in the country ② national power
【国是】[书] matter of vital importance to the state; state policy:莫谈~。*No talking about state affairs.*
【国手】national champion; topnotch person in the country; grand master; member of the national team
【国书】credentials; letter of credence; letter of commission:递交~ *present credentials*
【国税】national tax: ~局 *National Tax Bureau*
【国泰民安】the country enjoys prosperity and the people live in peace
【国体】① state system ② national prestige
【国土】land; territory: ~资源部 *Ministry of Land and Resources*
【国外】abroad; external; overseas: ~事务 *external affairs* / ~投资 *investment in foreign countries*
【国王】king; monarch
【国文】① national language ② [旧] Mandarin
【国务】state affairs: ~会议 *state conference*
【国玺】① imperial or royal seal ② national seal; seal of the state
【国宴】state banquet
【国营】state-run; state-operated
【国有】state-owned: ~企业 *state-owned enterprise*

G

【国语】national language of a country
【国葬】state funeral
【国债】national debt; treasury bond; government bond

guǒ

果[1] ① fruit; nut: 干 ~ *dried fruit* ② result; effect; consequence: 前因后 ~ *cause and effect* ③ (Guǒ) a surname
果[2] ① determined; resolute; strong-willed ② really; as expected; sure enough
果[3] really expected; sure enough
【果冻】jelly; jello
【果断】decisive; determined; resolute: 他办事精明 ~。*He handles affairs in an intelligent and decisive manner.*
【果脯】candied fruit; preserved fruit
【果酱】jam
【果林】fruit-bearing forest
【果木】fruit tree
【果农】orchardman; orchard worker; fruit grower
【果皮】skin of fruit; peel; rind
【果然】really; as expected; sure enough: 她 ~ 没有通过考试。*She did not pass the examination just as expected.*
【果肉】flesh of fruit; pulp
【果实】① fruit ② gains; fruits: 胜利的 ~ *fruits of victory*
【果树】fruit tree
【果酸】tartaric acid
【果糖】【化】fruit sugar; fructose; levulose
【果园】orchard; fruitery
【果真】① really; indeed; as expected; sure enough ② if indeed; if really
【果汁】fruit juice
【果枝】① fruit-bearing shoot; fruit branch ② boll-bearing branch
【果子】fruit; pastry
【果子狸】【动】masked or gem-faced civet
裹 ① bind; tie up; wrap ② package; bundle
【裹脚】bandages used in binding women's feet in feudal China; foot-binding — a vile feudal practice which crippled woman physically

guò

过[1] ① cross; pass; go through: 我们终于穿 ~ 了那片森林。*We went through the forests finally.* ② pass(time); spend(time): 那群孩子们度 ~ 了愉快的假期。*The children spent happy holidays.* ③ undergo; go over ④ adopt; transfer ⑤ go beyond; be over; exceed ⑥ fault; mistake: 他知道如何改 ~ 了。*He knew how to correct his mistakes.* ⑦ too; unduly ⑧ per; super; over ~ 氧化物 *peroxide*
过[2] ① used after a verb to indicate the completion of an action: 吃 ~ 饭他爸爸匆匆地走了。*His father went out in a hurry after lunch.* ② used after a verb or an adjective to indicate a past action or state
【过半】more than half
【过磅】weigh (on the scales)
【过不去】① be imposable; be unable to get by; cannot get through ② be hard on; make it difficult for ③ feel sorry
【过程】course; process
【过错】fault; mistake
【过道】corridor; doorway; passageway
【过得去】① be able to get by; can get through ② not too bad; passable; tolerable
【过度】inordinate; excessive; over: 劳累 ~ *be overworked*
【过渡】interim; stopgap; transition: ~ 时期 *period of transition*
【过分】excessive; going too far; over: 你做得太 ~。*What you have done was going too far.*
【过关】① go through an ordeal; cross a mountain pass ② pass a test; come through well; reach a standard
【过火】go too far; overdo; go to extremes; go beyond the proper limit
【过激】exceedingly drastic; extremist; radical: ~ 分子 *extremist* / ~ 行为 *excessive action*
【过继】adopt a young relative; have one's child adopted by a relative
【过奖】flatter; overprize; undeserved compliment: 你 ~ 了。*I feel flattered!*
【过节】① celebrate a festival ② festival; festive occasion
【过境】cross the frontier; be in transit; pass through the territory of a country
【过客】passing traveller; transient guest
【过来】(guòlai) come over; come up: 赶快 ~ 吧,要上课了。*It is going to have class; please come over, quick.*
【过来】(guolai) ① towards; over; up; in: 老师正朝我们走 ~。*Our teacher was going towards us.* ② come round; come to ③ go round; turn round
【过来人】old hand; person who has had the experience
【过量】excessive; immoderate; over: 昨天她服用了 ~ 的安眠药。*She took an overdose of sleeping pills yesterday.*
【过路】pass by one's way: ~ 人 *passer-by*
【过虑】be over-anxious; worry unnecessarily; worry overmuch: 你不要太 ~,孩子已经长大了。*You don't worry too much; your child has grown up already.*
【过滤】filter; filtrate: ~ 器 *filter* / ~ 嘴 *filter tip*
【过门】(of a woman) go over to a man's house-get married

【过敏】①【医】allergy:~休克 *anaphylactic shock* ② over-sensitive

【过目】look over (papers, draft documents, etc.) so as to approve; glance through or over

【过年】celebrate the New Year; spend the New Year or the Spring Festival

【过期】exceed the time limit; be overdue; pass the deadline:~作废 *become invalid after the specified date*

【过谦】too modest:您~了。*You are too modest.*

【过去】(guòqu) ① go over; pass by:她~把钱包捡起来了。*She walked over to pick the wallet up.* ② pass away; die

【过去】(guoqu) ① used after a verb to indicate motion away from the speaker:把鲜花给他拿~。*Please take the flowers over to him.* ② used after a verb to indicate turning the other side to the speaker ③ used after a verb to indicate a departure from the normal state ④ go over; pass by

【过热】① overheated ②【物】superheat; overheat; over-temperature

【过人】① outstanding; excellent:那个孩子有~的记忆。*The little child is of remarkable memory.* ② get past; get round

【过日子】get along; live:他妻子挺会~的。*His wife can manage to get along quiet well.*

【过剩】① excess:这孩子有点精力~。*The little child has excessively energetic.* ② surplus:商品~ *glut of goods* /资本~ *surplus of capital*

【过失】error; blunder; fault; negligence

【过时】① out-of-date; outdated; out of fashion ② past the appointed time

【过世】die; pass away

【过堂风】wind coming through a passageway; draught

【过头】exceed; overdo; go beyond the limit

【过往】① come and go; pass ② have friendly contact with; associate with

【过问】bother about; concern oneself with; take an interest in:老爸总是~我的私事。*My father always bothers about my private affairs.*

【过眼云烟】like a puff of smoke; as transient as a fleeting cloud

【过夜】① pass the night; stay overnight ② of the previous night

【过意不去】feel sorry; feel apologetic

【过瘾】enjoy oneself to the full; satisfy an urge; have a good time

【过硬】be really up to the mark; be able to pass the stiffest test; have a perfect mastery of sth

【过犹不及】going too far is as bad as not going far enough; going beyond is as wrong as falling short; too much is as bad as too little

【过于】excessively; too; unduly:他爸爸~劳累而被送进了医院。*His father was sent to hospital for overtired.*

【过账】transfer items (as from a daybook to a ledger); post

【过重】(of luggage, letters, etc.) overweight:行李~ *overweight luggage*

H

hā

哈 ① breathe out (with the mouth open); exhale ② (usu. reduplicated) the sound of laughing: ~~大笑 *laugh heartily*; *roar with laughter* ③ usu. reduplicated, expressing self-pride or satisfaction: ~~,我猜着了。*Aha, I've got it.*
see also hǎ; hà

【哈佛大学】Harvard University

【哈哈镜】distorting mirror

【哈哈儿】[方] a ridiculous thing; a laughing matter: 瞧~ *enjoy watching other people make fools of themselves*

【哈喇】①[口] rancid; (of oil-bearing food) having a rank smell or taste after a long period of time: 这块猪肉已经~了。*This piece of pork has gone bad.* ②[旧] kill; put sb to death: 把他~了 *kill him*

【哈喇子】[方] dribble; drivel; drool: 流~ *slobber* /他一见到肉就流~。*His mouth will water at the sight of meat.*

【哈雷彗星】【天】Halley's Comet; the Halley Comet

【哈密瓜】Hami melon (a variety of muskmelon)

【哈气】① breathe out; gasp ② breath (through the open mouth) ③ steam that forms on a window, etc.

【哈欠】yawn: 伸懒腰打~ *stretch oneself with a yawn* /你每天是不是以一个~开始工作,而不是满面笑容? *Do you start the day with a yawn instead of a smile?* /这部电影只能令人~连天。*The movie was nothing more than one big yawn.*

【哈萨克斯坦】Kazakhstan: ~人 *Kazakh* / ~语 *Kazakh (language)*

【哈瓦那】Havana, capital of Cuba, which is famous for its cigar: ~雪茄 *Havana (cigar)*

【哈腰】①[口] bend one's back; stoop: 这个老女人~捡起了支票。*The old lady stooped to pick up the cheque.* ② bow slightly to show courtesy: 不能整天对人点头~的。*One shall not always bow to show his courtesy.*

铪【化】hafnium (Hf): ~板 *hafnium plate*

há

蛤
see also gé

【蛤蟆】① frog ② toad

【蛤蟆夯】a kind of ramming machine; load rammer

【蛤蟆镜】frog sun glasses; goggles

hǎ

哈 ①[方] scold: 妈妈~了他一顿。*Mother gave him a good scolding.* ②(Hǎ) a surname
see also hā; hà

【哈巴狗】① Pekinese (a breed of dog) ② toady; sycophant: 像~一样下跪求饶不是好办法。*It is not a good idea to kneel down like a toady and beg for mercy.*

【哈达】*hada*, a piece of long thin silk, used as a sign of respect or congratulation among the Tibetans and some Mongolians nationalities: 献~ *present a hada*

hà

哈
see also hā; hǎ

【哈巴】bend one's knees outward when walking

hāi

咳 dammit; hey (expressing sadness, regret or surprise): ~,我怎么这么糊涂? *Damn it! How stupid I was!* / ~,到这儿来! *Hey! Come here!*
see also ké

【咳声叹气】heave deep sighs; sigh in despair: 他望着窗外,~。*He sighed deeply and stared out of the window.*

嗨

【嗨哟】heave ho; yo-heave-ho; yo-ho

hái

还 ① still; yet: 你~是那样。*You're still like that.* / ~有许多事情要做。*Much remains yet* to be done. /他虽然老了,可~是挺活跃。*He is old, yet active.* ② even more; still more: 今天比昨天~冷。*It's even colder than yesterday.* ③ also; too; as well as; in addition: 另外~有一件事要做。*Besides, there is something else to do.* /我喜欢香蕉,~喜欢柑橘。*I like bananas, but I like oranges, too.* ④ passably; fairly: 身体~好 *feel fairly well; be in a fairly good condition* ⑤ expressing realization or discovery of sth unexpected: 他~真有办法。*He is really smart after all.* ⑥ even: 他那么大年纪~那么干,咱们更应该加油干了。*He is still working so hard despite his old age; we should work even harder.*

see also huán

【还好】① not bad; passable; not much: "最近忙吗?" "~"。"*Are you very busy recently?*" "*So so.*" /不想~,一想就生气。*It's all right if I don't think about it; but whenever I do, I always get angry.* /"怎么样?" "~"。"*What's up?*" "*Not much.*" ② fortunately: ~,我终于找到了这本书。*I was fortunate enough to find the book.*

【还是】① still; yet: 到目前为止~没有结果。*The end has not yet come.* /她说她会迟到,但她~准时到达了。*She said she would be late, yet she arrived on time.* /他~我们的老师。*He is still our teacher.* ② expressing realization or discovery: 这个人~真了不起。*This guy is really great.* ③ expressing a preference for an alternative: 咱们~出去吧。*We'd better go out.* ④ no matter what, how etc.; whether... or...; regardless of: 她不知道是该哭~是该笑。*She didn't know whether to laugh or cry.*

孩 child; infant

【孩儿】[旧] ① (parents addressing their children) my child; my son: 我那~近日好像有点反常。*I have found something a little bit strange in my son.* ② self reference when talking to one's parents: ~想念父母大人。*I miss you, my dearest parents.*

【孩提】[书] early childhood; infancy: 我的~时代充满了辛酸的故事。*My early childhood is a book full of miserable stories.*

【孩子】① child: 男~ *boy* /女~ *girl* ② son or daughter: 他有三个~。*He has three children.*

【孩子话】silly childish talk; prattle

【孩子气】childish; puerile; immature; juvenile: 她一脸的~。*She still looks childish.* /十几岁的男孩子比女孩子更显得~。*During their teens, boys tend to be much more immature than girls.*

【孩子头】① a person who is very popular with children: 他是这附近的~。*He is rather popular with children in the neighbourhood.* ② leader of a group of children

骸 ① bones of the body; skeleton ② body: 病~ *a sick body* /残~ *remains of the body*

【骸骨】bones of the dead: 美貌不能千年,大家终究都是~。*Beauty cannot last, and we all will be skeletons under the grave stone.*

hǎi

浬 nautical mile

海 ① sea; waters close to the continents and smaller than oceans: 黄~ *the Huanghai Sea; the Yellow Sea* ② a great number of people or things: 人~ *a sea of faces; a huge crowd of people* /文山会~ *mountains of papers and seas of meetings* ③ largest; of great capacity: ~碗 *a very big bowl* / ~量 *great capacity; magnanimity* /夸下~口 *boast about what one can do; talk big* ④ [旧] (used to indicate the origin of certain plants, etc.) from overseas ⑤ [方] (usu. followed by 了 or 啦): 广场上的人可~啦! *There were countless people in the square.* ⑥ [方] randomly or aimlessly: ~找 *look high and low (for sth)* ⑦ [方] with no limit or restraint: ~吃~喝 *eat and drink to one's heart's content* ⑧ (Hǎi) a surname

【海岸】seacoast; seabeach; seashore; coast: 沿~航行 *sail along the coast* /多岩石的~ *a rocky coast*

【海岸线】coastline; beachline; shoreline: ~效应 *coastline effect* /崎岖的~ *a rugged coastline*

【海拔】height above sea level; elevation: ~3000米 *3000 metres above sea level; with an elevation of 3000 metres*

【海白菜】sea lettuce

【海报】bill; poster; playbill: 张贴~ *put up a playbill; put up a poster*

【海豹】[动] seal

【海标】seamark

【海滨】seashore; seaside; beach: 去~度假 *go to the seaside for one's holiday* / ~浴场 *seaside resort* /他在~有自己的房子。*He owns a house at the seaside.*

【海波】① wave ② hyposulfite; hypo

【海菜】edible seaweed

【海产】marine products

【海潮】sea tide

【海程】distance travelled by sea; voyage

【海船】sea boat; ship; seagoing vessel

【海床】seabed

【海带】sea-tangle; sea-tent; kelp: 我爱吃~。*I like eating kelp.*

【海岛】island (in the sea): ~居民 *islander* / ~民兵 *island militia*

【海盗】pirate; sea rover: 最早登陆中国东海岸的人应该是~。*Those who firstly landed on east coast of China should be pirates.*

【海盗船】pirate (ship); sea rover

【海堤】coastal levee; sea embankment; sea wall

【海底】the bottom of the sea; seabed; sea floor: 在~,你可以看到另一个世界。*On the sea floor, you will find quite another world.*

【海底捞月】try to fish out the moon from the bottom of the sea — strive for the impossible or illusory; a fruitless attempt; a useless effort; cry for the moon：你这样做恐怕不过是～。*I'm afraid you're attempting the impossible.*
【海底捞针】dredge for a needle in the sea; fish for a needle in the ocean; look for a needle in a haystack — impossible task：现在想要找到他无异于～。*Trying to locate him now is like searching for a needle in a haystack!*
【海底资源】seabed resources; submarine resources
【海底钻探】offshore drilling
【海地】Haiti：～人 *Haitian*
【海雕】sea eagle
【海防】coast defence：～部队 *coastal defence force* / ～前哨 *output of coastal defense* / ～艇 *coastal defense boat* / ～演习 *coastal defense exercise*
【海风】sea breeze; sea wind
【海港】seaport; dock; harbour
【海沟】oceanic trench; submarine trench
【海狗】fur seal; ursine seal
【海关】customhouse; customs：通过～ *go through customs; clear customs* / ～登记 *customs entry* / ～人员 *customs officer* / ～申报单 *customs declaration* / ～通行证 *customs pass* / ～总署 *customs head office*;（*China*）*General Administration for Customs*
【海关检查】customs inspection（or examination）：～站 *customs inspection post*
【海关检疫】customs quarantine control
【海关手续】customs formalities：办理～ *attend to the customs formalities*
【海关税收】customs revenue
【海关退税】customs drawback; rebate：～凭证 *debenture*
【海关总署】customs head office
【海光】sea light
【海龟】green turtle; sea turtle; marine turtle
【海涵】be magnanimous enough to forgive or tolerate（sb's errors or shortcomings）：此事处理欠妥，万望～。*May I crave your forgiveness for inadequacy in dealing with the matter?* / 招待不周，还望～。*Please forgive us if we have not looked after you well.*
【海话】[方] talk big; boast; bragging：他喜欢当众说～。*He likes to talk big in public.*
【海货】marine products; seafood：很多人去餐馆的时候都钟情于～。*Many people will be in favour of seafood when eating out at a restaurant.*
【海脊】sea ridge; submarine ridge
【海鲫】Japanese seaperch; surfperch
【海岬】coastal cape
【海疆】coastal areas and territorial seas
【海角】cape; promontory
【海角天涯】the corners of the sea and the end of the sky — far-off regions; the corners of the world; the ultimate ends of the world; the remotest corners of the earth：即使你在～，我的心也会陪伴你的。*My heart will be by your side even if you are in the remotest corner of the earth.*
【海进】【地】transgression of sea; advance of the sea：～沉积物 *transgressive deposit*
【海禁】band on maritime trade or intercourse with foreign countries（as during the Ming and Qing dynasties）：开～ *open country to foreign trade*
【海景】waterscape; seascape：～画 *seascape* / ～画家 *seascape artist*
【海军】navy; naval forces：～部（*US*）*Department of the Navy* / ～军官 *naval officer* / ～飞机 *naval aircraft* / ～演习 *naval manoeuvre*（*or exercise*）
【海军基地】naval base
【海军蓝】navy blue：～在六十年代的中国很流行。*The colour navy blue was once very popular in China during 1960's.*
【海军呢】navy cloth
【海军学校】naval academy
【海军战术】naval tactics
【海口】① mouth of a river where it flows into the sea ② seaport ③ brag; boast about what one can do; talk big：夸～ *boast about what one can do* / 他夸下～说要走到沙漠的另一端。*He boasted to walk to the other end of this desert.*
【海枯石烂】（usu. in an oath expressing firm will or unchanging fidelity）even if the seas may run dry and the rocks turn to dust：即使～，决心绝不动摇。*Even if the seas go dry and the rocks crumble, my will will remain firm.*
【海况】【航】sea state; sea conditions：～级 *scale of state of sea*
【海阔天空】① as boundless as the sea and sky（heavens）; as broad as the sea and sky; unrestrained and far-ranging; endless vast：到～的大世界去闯荡 *temper oneself in the wide world; brave the world* ② discursive; without restriction or limit; talk at random：～地聊个没完 *have a rambling chat about everything under the sun*
【海浪】sea wave：～发电 *sea wave power generation* /隐约传来～的声音。*The sound of sea waves could be vaguely heard.*
【海狸】【动】castor; beaver
【海里】nautical mile; sea mile：每小时航行30～的船 *vessel of 30 knots*
【海量】① magnanimity：怠慢之处，望您～包涵。*I hope you will be magnanimous enough to forgive any lack of attention on my part.* ②enormous capacity for alcoholic drinks：您是～，再来一杯！*Have another one; you can hold your liquor!*
【海岭】ocean ridge
【海流】ocean current：～动力学 *dynamics of ocean current* / ～发电 *current power generation*
【海龙】①［口］sea otter ② pipefish
【海路】sea route; sea-lane; seaway：走～ *travel by sea; go by sea*
【海轮】seagoing vessel; ocean liner
【海螺】【动】conch; sea snail; whelk
【海洛因】heroin：～瘾 *heroinism; heroin-addiction*

H

【海马】① sea horse (Hippocampus) ② walrus (*Odobenus rosmarus*)
【海鳗】【动】long-jawed conger eels; conger pike
【海米】dried shrimps
【海绵】① sponge ② foam rubber or plastic; sponge: ~包 *sponge-rubber pad* / ~冰 *sludge*
【海绵垫】foam rubber cushion
【海绵田】mellow-soil field; spongy soil
【海面】sea level; sea surface: ~反射 *sea surface reflection* / ~群落 *pelagium* / ~水平面 *geoidal horizon* / 繁星密布的夜空下是平静的~。*Below the starry night lies that quiet and peaceful sea.*
【海面升降】eustacy; eustasy: ~运动 *eustatic movement*
【海鸣】sea noise
【海南】Hainan Province
【海南岛】Hainan Island
【海难】marine perils; perils of the sea: ~例外条款 *perils of the sea exception* / ~条款 *perils clause* / ~救助 *salvage at sea*
【海内】within the four seas; throughout the land
【海内存知己,天涯若比邻】as long as one has a true friend, he is close even when far way; if in this world an understanding friend survives, then the ends of the earth seem like next door — a bosom friend afar brings a distant land near
【海泥】sea mud
【海鲇】【动】sea catfish
【海鸟】seabird; seafowl: ~粪 *guano*
【海涅】Heinrich Heine (1797—1856), German poet
【海牛】【动】manatee; sea cow; sea slug
【海鸥】【动】sea mew; sea gull
【海派】① the Shanghai school of Beijing opera ② Shanghai style: ~时装 *Shanghai fashion*
【海盘车】【动】starfish
【海螃蟹】sea crab
【海盆】【地】sea basin; ocean basin
【海蓬子】glasswort; froggrass
【海螵蛸】【药】cuttlebone; sepium
【海平面】sea level: ~气压 *sea-level pressure*
【海旗】maritime flag
【海丘】【地】oceanic rise
【海区】【军】sea area
【海渠】faro; furrow
【海雀】【动】puffin; auk; guillemot
【海商法】maritime law: ~外交会议 *Diplomatic Conference on Maritime Laws*
【海上】at sea; on the sea; offshore; maritime; marine: ~风暴 *a storm at sea* / ~事故 *accident at sea* / ~搜查 *search at sea* / ~霸权 *maritime hegemony* / 在~度过一个月 *spend a month at sea*
【海上保险】maritime or marine insurance: ~诉讼 *marine insurance action*
【海上封锁】sea blockade; naval blockade: ~不能封锁我们通向外部世界的道路。*Sea blockade shall not block our way to the outside world.*
【海上交通】maritime traffic: ~线 *sea-lane*; *seaway*
【海上贸易】maritime trade or commerce: ~一度为中国带来了丰厚的利润。*Maritime trade once brought great profits into China.*
【海上丝绸之路】silk road of the sea
【海上运输】marine transportation
【海上钻井】offshore drilling: ~平台 *offshore drilling platform*
【海上作业】offshore operation; operation on the sea: ~平台 *offshore work platform*
【海蛇】sea serpent; sea snake
【海参】sea cucumber; sea slug; trepang
【海狮】sea lion; sea dog
【海蚀】marine or sea erosion; marine abrasion; be washed and eroded by sea water: / ~海岸 *abrasion coast* / ~阶地 *marine-cut terrace* / ~平原 *marine plain*; *plain of marine denudation*
【海蚀洞】sea cave
【海市蜃楼】①【气】mirage ② castle in the air; illusions or hopes that cannot be realized: 你的理想只是~。*Your ambition may prove to be a castle in the air.*
【海事】maritime affairs: ~保险 *maritime insurance* / ~处理 *settlement of maritime case* / ~纠纷 *marine dispute* / ~仲裁委员会 *maritime arbitration commission*
【海事法】admiralty law; maritime law; marine law
【海事法庭】admiralty court; maritime court
【海誓山盟】lover's pledge of eternal loyalty; (make) a solemn pledge of love; swear inviolable oaths of mutual love and fidelity; swear by the sea and by the hills: 他们在众人面前~。*They made the solemn pledge of love before crowds of people.*
【海水】seawater; brine; the sea: ~采样 *seawater sampling* / ~淡化 *desalination of sea water* / ~工业 *marine industry* / ~老化 *marine aging* / ~入侵 *seawater invasion* / ~压力 *seawater pressure* / ~植物 *sea weed* / ~资源 *seawater resources* / ~综合利用 *seawater comprehensive utilization*
【海水不可斗量】the sea cannot be measured with a bushel — great minds cannot be fathomed: 人不可貌相,~。*People should not be judged by their appearance and the sea not measured with a bushel.*
【海水面】level of seawater; sea level
【海水养殖】marine culture; seawater aquaculture; marine cultivation: ~场 *marine aquaculture park* / ~面积 *marine aquaculture area*
【海水浴】seawater bath; sea bathing
【海损】average; sea damage; marine loss: 单独~ *particular average* / 共同~ *general average* / ~协议书 *average agreement* / ~货物 *goods damaged by sea* / ~费用 *average* / ~条款 *average clause* / ~保险 *marine insurance* / ~理算 *average adjustment* / ~理算人 *average adjuster*
【海獭】【动】sea otter
【海滩】seabeach; beach: ~砾石 *beach gravel* / ~生物 *beach organism* / ~侵蚀 *beach erosion* / ~

岩 *beach rock*

【海棠】【植】Chinese flowering crabapple; cherry-apple tree

【海塘】seawall

【海天一色】the sea melts into the sky; the sea and the sky merge into one

【海图】sea (or marine, nautical) chart; blueback: ~室 *chart room*; *chart house* / ~集 *naval atlas*

【海涂】tidal land; tidal flat; shallows

【海兔】【动】sea hare

【海豚】【动】dolphin; delphis: ~馆 *dolphinarium* / ~泳 *dolphin swimming*; *dolphin butterfly*; *dolphin fishtail* / ~油 *dolphin oil* / ~星座 *Delphinus*

【海外】overseas; abroad: 居住~ *reside (or live) abroad* / ~华人 *overseas Chinese* / ~华侨 *overseas Chinese nationals (or citizens)* / ~同胞 *compatriots overseas*/ ~投资 *overseas investment* / ~贸易 *overseas trade* / ~农业 *overseas agriculture* / ~企业 *overseas business* / ~倾销 *dumping abroad* / ~市场 *overseas market* / ~资金 *offshore fund* /大陆和~的青少年思维方式相差不大。*Teenagers home and abroad enjoy almost the same way of thinking.*

【海外版】overseas edition

【海外关系】relatives abroad: 利用~打开销路 *utilize one's overseas connections to find a market for a product*

【海外奇谈】a strange story from over the seas; a traveller's tale; a fantastic tale; a curious tale; strange stories of other countries:这只不过是~。*It is nothing but a traveller's tale.*

【海湾】bay; gulf; loch: 墨西哥~ *the Gulf of Mexico* / ~地区 *Gulf areas* / ~国家 *Gulf States* / ~战争 *the Gulf War* / ~原油 *Gulf coastal oil*

【海碗】a very big bowl; huge bowl: 喝了一~酒 *drink up a huge bowl of wine*

【海王星】【天】Neptune

【海味】seafood; choice seafood; marine food products: 山珍~ *all sorts of delicacies* / ~餐厅 *seafood restaurant* / ~什锦 *seafood cocktail*

【海峡】strait; channel:台湾~ *the Taiwan Straits* / 英吉利~ *the English Channel* /马六甲~ *Strait of Malacca*

【海峡群岛】the Channel Islands

【海鲜】seafood:如今经营~的工厂发了大财。*Nowadays factories specializing in sea food have made a fortune.*

【海相】【地】marine (or sea) facies: ~沉积 *marine deposit (or sediment)*

【海象】【动】walrus; morse

【海啸】bore; tsunami; seismic sea wave; seaquake

【海星】【动】starfish; sea star;asteroid

【海熊】【动】fur seal; ursine seal

【海寻】nautical fathom

【海牙】The Hague: ~公约 *Hague Conventions* (1899, 1907) / ~规则 *Hague Rules* / ~议定书 *Hague Protocol* / ~仲裁常设委员会 *Permanent Court of Arbitration (The Hague)*

【海牙国际法庭】International Court at the Hague

【海盐】sea salt; bay salt

【海蜒】【动】dried anchovy

【海燕】(storm) petrel; sea swallow

【海洋】seas and oceans; ocean: ~霸权 *maritime hegemony* / ~国家 *maritime state* / ~环境污染 *maritime environmental pollution damage* / ~健康 *ocean health* / ~牧场 *aquafarm*; *pasture of sea* / ~能源 *marine energy* / ~权 *maritime rights* / ~食物链 *marine food chain* / ~石油资源 *offshore petroleum resources* / ~鱼类 *marine fishes* / ~渔业 *marine fishery* / ~主权 *marine sovereignty* /地球表面大部分是~。*Most of the earth's surface is covered by sea.*

【海洋保护区】marine preserve

【海洋动物】marine animal

【海洋法】law of the sea: ~公约 *Convention of the Law of the Sea*

【海洋公约】maritime convention

【海洋环境】marine environment

【海洋生物】marine organisms: ~学 *marine biology*

【海洋石油】offshore oil: ~平台 *offshore oil extraction platform*

【海洋性气候】maritime (or marine) climate

【海洋学】oceanography; oceanology; thalassography

【海洋资源】marine resources

【海鱼】sea fish; marine fish

【海隅】[书] coastal areas; coastland

【海域】sea area; maritime space: 南海~ *Nanhai Sea waters*

【海员】seaman; sailor; mariner: ~船 *crewboat* / ~俱乐部 *seamen's club* / ~留置权 *seaman's lien* / ~营生 *sailoring* / ~用语 *nautical expression*

【海运】sea transportation; ocean shipping; ocean carriage; transport by sea: ~保险商 *underwriter* / ~代理人 *shipping agent* / ~法 *shipping law* / ~费 *ocean freight* / ~合同 *contract of ocean carriage* / ~留置权 *maritime lien* / ~贸易 *seaborne trade* / ~提单 *ocean bill of lading*; *marine bill of lading* / ~协定 *maritime agreement* / ~运单 *ocean waybill* / ~债务 *maritime loan* / ~政策 *maritime policy*

【海葬】sea-burial

【海枣】【植】date palm; date

【海藻】marine alga; seaweed; kelp; sea wrack: ~产品 *seaweed products* / ~工业 *seaweed industry* / ~加工 *seaweed processing*

【海战】sea warfare; naval battle: ~法规 *rules on naval warfare* / ~区 *area of sea operation*

【海蜇】【动】jellyfish

【海震】【地】seaquake; submarine earthquake; sea shock

醢 [书] ① minced fish or meat paste ② cut to small pieces; cut up

hài

亥 last of the twelve Earthly Branches

【亥时】[旧] period of the day from 9 pm to 11 pm

骇 be astonished; be shocked: 惊~ *frightened; panic-stricken*

【骇怪】be shocked; be astonished

【骇惧】be frightened; be terrified

【骇然】gasping with astonishment; stuck dumb with amazement: ~失色 *turn pale with astonishment; be flabbergasted* /他~道:"难道不是那么回事?" *"Isn't it the case?" He gasped.*

【骇人听闻】shocking; appalling: ~的暴行 *appalling violence* / ~的屠杀 *a horrifying killing*

【骇异】be shocked; be astonished: 不胜~ *be greatly shocked; be greatly astounded; be greatly surprised*

氦 【化】helium (He): 液态~ *liquid helium*

【氦层】heliosphere

【氦灯】helium lamp

害 ① evil; harm; calamity; injury: 为民除~ *eliminate the evil for people's sake* /早起对你没有~。*Getting up early won't do you harm!* ② harmful; destructive; injurious: ~虫 *destructive insect; pest; vermin* /吸烟对身体有~。*Smoking can be harmful to your health.* ③ do harm to; impair; cause trouble to: ~人 *do people great harm* /你弄错了地址,~得我白跑了一趟。*You gave me the wrong address and mad me go all that way for nothing.* ④ kill; murder: 谋财~命: *murder for money* ⑤ contract (an illness); suffer from: ~病 *fall ill* /这小孩~了病。*The child suffers from illness.* ⑥ feel (ashamed, afraid, etc.): ~怕 *feel afraid* /我真是为你感到~臊。*I am totally ashamed of you.*

【害病】fall ill; be sick; be ill with

【害虫】injurious or destructive insect; pest: 花园中的~ *garden pests*

【害处】harm: 多吃蔬菜不会对你的身体有~。*Eating more vegetables will not do harm to your body.*

【害口】[方] (pregnant woman) show appetite for certain foods

【害命】murder; take sb's life

【害鸟】harmful (or destructive) bird: 麻雀曾经被认为是~。*Sparrows once were considered destructive birds.*

【害怕】be afraid; be scared; fear; show the white feather; have a dread of; dreadful; have cold feet; get cold feet: ~得要命 *be scared to death; be mortally afraid* /这个小姑娘特别~打雷。*The little girl is intensely afraid of thunder.* /她们~得浑身发抖。*They are scared with trembling.*

【害群之马】an evil member of the herd; one who brings disgrace on his group; a black sheep; bad egg of the community: 到处都有~。*There is a black sheep in every flock.*

【害人不浅】no small harm is done; do people great harm

【害人虫】an evil creature; pest; vermin: 扫除一切~。*Away with all pests.*

【害人反害己】bite off one's own head; curses come home to roost; harm set, harm get; injure both others and self

【害臊】[口] feel ashamed; be bashful; be shy: 你撒了谎感到~吗? *Are you ashamed for having lied?* /他感到~,因为妻子挣钱比他多。*He felt humiliated because his wife earned more than he did.*

【害喜】suffer from morning sickness; be pregnant

【害羞】be bashful; be shy: 她干什么事都~。*She is bashful in doing anything.* /他是一个~的人。*He is a man with a shy manner.*

【害眼】have eye trouble

嗐 used to express sorrow or regret: ~! 想不到她病得这样重! *Oh, I had no ideas he was so seriously ill.* / ~,你怎么不早点告诉我呢? *Oh, why didn't you tell me earlier?*

hān

蚶 【动】blood clam: [方]毛~ *blood clam*

【蚶线】limacon

酣 ① (drink, etc.) to one's heart's content; be given to heavy drinking: 酒~耳热 *heated with wine* ② heartily; to one's satisfaction: ~歌 *sing to one's heart's content*

【酣畅】① merry and lively (with drinking) ② sound (sleep): 他们的睡袋既暖和又舒适,所以他们都睡得很~。*Their sleeping-bags were warm and comfortable, so they all slept soundly.* ③ with ease and verve; fully

【酣畅淋漓】heartily; to one's heart's content: 这首诗~地抒发了作者的感情。*This poem fully expresses the author's feelings.*

【酣梦】a sweet dream

【酣眠】sleep soundly; be fast asleep

【酣然】① merrily (drunk) ② sound (asleep): ~入梦 *fall into a sound sleep* /轮船剧烈摇摆,其余的人都在晕船,他却~入睡。*The ship was swaying violently but he slept like a log while others were being sick.*

【酣睡】sleep soundly; be fast asleep; sleep like a log: 他一直~到天明。*He slept soundly till the morning.*

【酣甜】(of sleep or dream) sweet: 进入~的梦乡 *fall into a sound and sweet sleep*

【酣饮】drink to the full; carouse

【酣战】hard-fought battle; locked in fierce battle; fight bitterly; be in the thick of battle

【酣醉】be dead drunk

H

憨 ① foolish; silly ② straightforward; naive; ingenuous; simple: 那个小伙子显得比较~。*That guy seems more ingenuous.* ③ (Hān) a surname

【憨痴】idiotic; stupid: ~的话 *stupid remark*

【憨厚】straightforward and good-natured; simple and honest: ~善良的女人 *a woman of simple goodness*

【憨态】a silly appearance; air of charming naivety: 大熊猫站在竹林中,一副~可掬的样子。*The giant panda stood in the bamboo forest, showing a simple and naive look.*

【憨笑】smile foolishly; simper: ~着说了一个拙劣的借口 *simpered a lame excuse*

【憨直】honest and simple; candid; frank; tell sb straight: 她是一个~的朋友,能够说出对我们的想法。*As a friend, she is very candid, always saying what she thinks about us.*

【憨子】[方] fool; blockhead; simpleton; idiot; ninny; dimwit

鼾 snore; sound emitted from the nose during sleep: 希望你不要仰着睡觉,这样容易打~。*I wish you wouldn't sleep on your back — it makes you snore.*

【鼾孔】snore-hole

【鼾声】sound of snoring; thunderous snores: 隔壁传来的~使我久久不能入睡。*The snoring that came from the next room kept me awake for a long time.*

【鼾声如雷】snore thunderously: 昨天夜里我听到他~。*Last night I heard him driving his pigs to market.*

【鼾睡】sound, snoring sleep; heavy sleep; snore away soundly

hán

邯

【邯郸学步】try to learn the Handan Walk — imitate others and thus lose one's own individuality; take a leaf out of another person's book: 学习外国经验切忌~。*We must avoid blind imitation when we learn from the experience of other countries.*

含 ① keep in the mouth, neither spitting nor swallowing; keep in the eyes: 嘴里~着块糖 *with a candy in the mouth* / ~着眼泪 *eyes filled with tears; eyes grown moist* ② contain inside: ~水分 *containing water or moisture* / ~养分 *containing nutrients* ③ nurse or cherish some intentions or feelings; without exposing them completely: 她的表情里~着一丝怒气。*Her face held a suggestion of anger.*

【含苞】[书] in bud: 花朵~待放。*The flowers are now in bud.*

【含苞待放】a bud just ready to burst; just budding, not yet opened

【含悲】be filled with deep sorrow

【含愤】be in resentment: ~而死 *die in resentment*

【含钙土】calcareous soil

【含垢忍辱】endure contempt and insults; be patient under obloquy; bear shame and humiliation; eat dirt: 有时候~是我们应该具有的品质。*Sometimes to endure contempt and insults should be one of our virtues.*

【含恨】nurse a grievance or hatred

【含恨在心】cherish resentment in the heart; harbour hatred against sb; nurse a hatred: 她对她的前夫一直~。*She has been harbouring hatred against her ex-husband.*

【含糊】① ambiguous; vague; imprecise; muddled: 一点也不~ *clear-cut; definite; not at all vague* /这份文件~的措辞让人很难理解。*The document's ambiguous wording makes it very difficult to follow.* ② careless; perfunctory: 这事可不能~。*We'll have to handle the matter with great care.* ③ timid and overcautious; shrinking, often combined with "not": 绝不~ *not a bit equivocal; not afraid at all*

【含糊其辞】talk ambiguously; boggle; equivocate; in vague terms; mention vaguely; mince matters; uncertain: 不要~,有话就直说吧。*Don't mince matters, but speak plainly.*/我不知道如何翻译她的话,我认为她是故意~。*I don't know how to interpret her remark. I think it was deliberately ambiguous.*

【含混】unclear; indistinct; ambiguous; vague; imprecise: 如果指示~不清,就不能怪别人犯错误。*If the instructions are not clear, you cannot blame people for making mistakes.*

【含金量】① gold content: 矿石的~ *gold content of ore* ② real worth or value: 同样是金牌,足球冠军比其他球类冠军的~要大得多。*As first prize, the championship for soccer is worth much more than those for some other ball games.*

【含泪】with tears in one's eyes: ~感谢 *thank sb with tears in one's eyes* / ~乞求 *beg with tears in one's eyes* / ~微笑 *smile through one's tears*

【含量】content: 净~ *net contents* /一吨矿砂中银的~ *the content of silver in a ton of ore*

【含怒】be in anger; be filled with anger: ~不言 *hold one's tongue angrily*

【含片】lozenge: 止咳~ *cough lozenge*

【含情脉脉】(soft eyes) exuding tenderness and love; cherish a deep feeling, but be unable to express it; cast sheep's eyes at sb; with loving eyes: 那儿来了一个富有的证券经纪人,他~地看着这位漂亮的姑娘。*There came a wealthy stockbroker who cast sheep's eyes at the beautiful girl.*

【含沙射影】hold sand in the mouth and shoot it at a shadow — injury to men inflicted by evil persons; innuendo; insinuations: ~,恶语中伤 *defame with vicious, insinuating remarks* /那个长舌妇~地散布流言。*The gossipy woman spread much scandal by innuendoes.*

H

【含漱剂】【药】gargle; collutorium

【含水】containing water or moisture: ~百分率 *percentage of moisture* / ~饱和度 *water saturation*/ ~性 *property of water-bearing*

【含水层】【地】water-bearing stratum; aquifer; aquiclude

【含水量】moisture content; water content

【含水率】moisture content

【含笑】have a smile on one's face; wearing a smile; with a smile; smilingly; grin: ~地下 *smile in the underworld*; *die with satisfaction* / ~点头 *nod smiling*; *nod with a smile* / ~谢绝 *decline politely with a smile* / ~作答 *laugh in reply*

【含笑九泉】smile in the underworld — one has nothing to regret in life; die with satisfaction: 如果你们能回来看我一眼,我也会~了。*Should you come back and have a last look at me, I would die with satisfaction.*

【含辛茹苦】suffer untold hardships; endure suffering; bear bitter hardship; put up with hardships: 妈妈~抚养我们兄弟姐妹五人长大。*Mother put up with all kinds of hardships to bring up the five sisters and brothers of us.*

【含羞】with a shy look; shyly; bashfully: ~不语 *be silent with shame*; *feel too shy to speak* / ~忍辱 *suffer humiliations* / ~自尽 *commit suicide through shame*

【含羞草】【植】sensitive plant; mimosa pudica

【含蓄】① contain; embody ② implicit; veiled: ~往往比直言更为重要。*An implication is often more important than the direct statement.* ③ reserved; withdrawn; introverted: 英国人以~著称。*English people have a reputation for being reserved.*

【含血喷人】make slanderous accusations against others; make trumped-up charges; make vicious attacks; cast malicious words to injure sb; do sb wrong; put sb in the wrong: 别理他,他只是在~对付我罢了。*Let him alone, for he is just making vicious attacks against me.*

【含饴弄孙】play with grandchildren with candy in mouth — enjoy happy old age; a life of leisure in old age

【含义】meaning; implication; import; signification; sense: 这个词有几个~。*The word carries several senses.* /这句话~深刻。*This remark has profound implications.* /科学家们一直无法确定大部分伊特鲁里亚人的刻印文字的~。*Scientists have been unable to determine the signification of most Etruscan inscriptions.*

【含有】contain; have; import: 这条河~放射性污染物质。*Water of this river contains contaminants.* / 啤酒~酒精。*Beer contains alcohol.*

【含冤】suffer a wrong; suffer an injustice; be the victim of a false or unjust charge; do sb an injustice: ~而死 *die uncleared of a false charge* /你不应使他~。*You shouldn't do him an injustice.*

【含冤莫白】suffer a wrong with no hope of being cleared; bear an injustice one cannot clear up

【含怨】bear a grudge; nurse a grievance: 老人~而死。*The old man died nursing a grievance.*

函 ①[书] case; envelope: 镜~ *case for a mirror* ② letter: 便~ *informal letter* /公~ *official letter* /贺~ *letter of congratulation* /唁~ *letter (or message) of condolence* /致~ *send a letter*; *write to sb*

【函词】【数】function

【函电】letters and cables; correspondence

【函调】investigation conducted through correspondence

【函牍】[书] letters; correspondence

【函复】reply by letter; write a letter in reply: 如能尽快~不胜感激。*Your prompt reply by letter will be very much appreciated.*

【函告】inform by letter: 请~行期。*Please inform us by letter about the date of your departure.*

【函购】purchase by mail; mail order

【函件】letters; mails; correspondence

【函聘】engage or employ by letter

【函授】teach by correspondence; give a correspondence course: ~学校 *correspondence school* / ~大学 *correspondence university* / ~教育 *education by correspondence*

【函数】【数】function: ~变换 *functional transformation* / ~常数 *function constant* / ~代数 *function algebra* / ~方程 *functional equation* / ~关系 *functional relation* / ~极限 *functional limit* / 生产~ *production function* / ~微分 *differential of function* /消费~ *consumption function* / ~运算 *functional operation*/正弦~ *sine function* /余弦~ *cosine function* /周期~ *periodic function*

【函数表】function table

【函数值】functional value

【函索】request by letter: ~即寄 *be sent on application*; *be available on request*

【函约】make an appointment by letter

琀 [书] piece of jade put in the mouth of the dead upon burial

晗 [书] dawn is on the point of breaking

涵 ① contain; embody: 海~ *magnanimity of mind (in forgiving one's error)*; *generous forgiveness* ② culvert: 桥~ *bridges and culverts*

【涵洞】culvert; ponceau

【涵盖】contain; cover; embody: 法律并没有~所有罪行。*The law does not cover all crimes.* / 这次复习~上学期我们所学的全部课程。*The review covered everything we learned last term.*

【涵管】① pipes for making culverts ② pipe-shaped culvert

【涵容】[书][套] excuse; forgive; bear with

【涵养】① ability to control oneself; self-restraint: 很有~ *know how to exercise self-control* ② conserve: 利用植树造林~水源 *conserve water through forestation*

【涵养万物】nourish and cherish all things

【涵义】meaning; implication：这个词有许多不同的～。*This word has several different meanings.* / 这个决定带有深刻的政治～。*This decision has very serious political implications.*

【涵闸】culverts and water gates

寒 ① cold：饥～交迫 *suffer hunger and cold* / 天～地冻。*The weather is cold and the ground is frozen.* ② tremble (with fear); afraid：胆～ *be terrified* / 心～ *be bitterly disappointed* ③ poor; needy：贫～ *poverty-stricken* ④［谦］humble：～舍 *my humble home*

【寒不择衣】a cold man is not choosy about clothing; all is fish that comes into his net

【寒蝉】a cicada in cold weather (which can no longer make any noise or can only make a very low noise)

【寒潮】【气】cold-air outbreak; cold wave

【寒碜】［口］① ugly; unsightly：～的形态 *an ugly shape* / ～的广告牌 *an unsightly billboard* / 他把自己所有的东西都放在一只～的手提箱里。*He put everything he owned in a battered suitcase.* ② shabby; disgraceful：你工作的高效率使我们其他人感到～。*Your productivity has put the rest of us to shame.* ③ ridicule; make fun of：这个孩子的同班同学们因为他的胆小而～他。*The child's classmates ridiculed him for his timidity.*

【寒窗】a cold window — the difficulties of a poor student; persevere in one's studies in spite of hardships：十年～苦，今日我终于得到了回报。*Ten years of hard work and today I am fully rewarded.*

【寒带】frigid zone：～环境 *cold belt environment* / ～林带 *cold forest zone*

【寒冬】severe winter

【寒冬腊月】severe winter; dead of winter; in the teeth of winter：～的，不要出去跑。*You shall not run about in such a severe winter day.*

【寒风】cold wind：迎着刺骨的～ *face a biting wind*

【寒风凛冽】a piercing cold wind — bitterly cold

【寒光】① pallid light (of the moon) ② dazzling gleam (of a sword)：～乍现 *the flash of dazzling gleam*

【寒极】【气】cold pole

【寒季】dead season

【寒悸】［方］shiver (with cold or fear)：他被他们从水中捞出来后，冷得直打～。*When they pulled him out of the water, he was shivering with cold.*

【寒假】winter vacation; winter holiday

【寒噤】shiver (with cold or fear)：当他在夜晚听见这奇怪的声音时，吓得直打～。*He shivered as he heard the strange noise at night.*

【寒苦】poverty-stricken; in financial straits

【寒来暑往】as summer goes and winter comes — as time passes; with the passage of time; change of seasons; year in and year out：～，他们的生活没有变化。*As time goes by, their life remains the same.*

【寒冷】① cold; frigid：～的气候 *a cold climate* / ～的房间 *a frigid room* ② chill; frigidity; rigour：今天早晨的空气颇有些～。*There is quite a chill in the air this morning.*

【寒冽】［书］cold; frigid

【寒流】【气】cold current; cold wave

【寒毛】fine hair on the human body：这是一个令人～倒竖的故事。*This is really an appalling story.*

【寒门】［书］① a poor and humble family ②［谦］my family

【寒漠】cold desert：～土 *cold desert oil*

【寒气】cold air; cold draught; cold：今天早上我出门时有点～袭人。*There was a chill in the air when I got out the house this morning.* / ～已不那么逼人。*The cold has decreased in severity.*

【寒峭】［书］chilly; piercingly cold

【寒秋】late autumn

【寒热】【中医】chills and fever; high temperature：～症状 *symptoms of chill and fever*

【寒色】cool colour

【寒舍】［谦］my humble home (or abode)

【寒士】［书］a poor scholar; a scholar of little means

【寒暑】① cold and heat ② winter and summer — a year

【寒暑表】thermometer：摄氏～ *centigrade thermometer* / 华氏～ *Fahrenheit thermometer*

【寒素】［书］① impoverished; poor ② poor people ③ simple; plain; crude

【寒酸】(usu. of a poor scholar) shabby and miserable; sorry; scrubby：～的家庭 *a poor family* / 他是一个工资很低的～小职员。*He is a sorry underpaid official.*

【寒腿】［口］rheumatism in the legs

【寒微】of low station; of humble origin

【寒心】① be bitterly disappointed：对某人(某事)～ *be bitterly disappointed at a person (or thing)* ② be afraid; fear：直到现在，那件事仍然让我～。*Until now I am still scared to recall that thing.*

【寒暄】exchange of conventional greetings; exchange of amenities (or compliments)：她同客人～了几句。*She exchanged a few words of greeting with the guests.*

【寒鸦】jackdaw

【寒夜】cold night; chilly night

【寒衣】winter clothes; warm clothes

【寒意】a nip (or chill) in the air：他的话让我感到了～。*His words brought me a chill in the air.*

【寒战】shiver (with cold or fear)：它使我打了一个～。*It gives me the shiver.* / 她突然全身打了一个～。*A sudden shiver came upon her.*

【寒症】【中医】symptoms caused by cold factors (e.g. chill, slow pulse, etc.)

hǎn

罕 ① rarely; seldom; unusual：一种希～的动物 *a rarely-seen animal* ② (Hǎn) a surname

【罕觏】［书］rarely seen

【罕见】seldom seen; rare：那种鸟在这个国家很～。*That bird is very rare in this country.*

【罕事】rare thing or event：铁树开花，真乃～。*It is a rare chance that flowers might grow on an iron tree.*

【罕闻】rarely or seldom heard of：世所～ *rarely heard of in this world*

【罕物】a curiosity; a rare thing：他们保留那块雕刻过的骨头并把它作为～展出。*They kept the carved bone and displayed it as a curiosity.*

【罕有】rare; unusual; exceptional：～的记忆力 *an exceptional memory* / ～的气候 *exceptional weather* / ～的机会 *a rare opportunity*

喊 ① shout; cry out; yell：老太太对那男孩大声～。*The old lady shouted at the boy.* ② call (a person)：他从街对面～我的名字。*He called my name from across the street.* ③［方］call; address：你～我老张就行了。*Just call me Lao Zhang.*

【喊话】① propaganda directed to the enemy at the front line ② communicate by tele-equipment

【喊叫】shout; cry out; scream：听众们高声～，不让演讲者讲下去。*The audience shouted the speaker down.* / 他们～表示反对。*They shouted their disapproval.*

【喊嗓子】① shout ② train (or exercise) one's voice (esp. opera singers do in an open space early in the morning)

【喊声】shout; yell; hubbub; scream; roar：疼痛时的～ *a yell of pain* / 我一路跟随着厨房传出的～。*I followed the sound of the shouts coming from the kitchen.*

【喊冤】cry out about one's grievances; complain loudly about an alleged injustice; cry out for justice：光～是没有用的。*It is no use just crying out for justice.*

hàn

汉¹ ① the Han nationality, the majority nationality of People's Republic of China ② man：老～ *old man* / 好～ *brave man*; *true man* / 不到长城非好～。*He who does not reach the Great Wall is not a true man.*

汉² the Milky Way：银～ *the Milky Way*

【汉白玉】white marble

【汉堡】Hamburg, major city and port in the north western Germany

【汉堡包】hamburger：～餐馆 *hamburger restaurants*

【汉城】Seoul, capital of the Republic of Korea

【汉奸】traitor (to China)

【汉民】［口］the Han nationality

【汉人】① the Hans; the Han people ② people of the Han Dynasty

【汉文】① Chinese language (usu. written) ② Chinese character

【汉姓】① Han surname ② Han surname adopted by people of other nationalities

【汉学】① the Han school of classical philology ② Sinology

【汉语】Chinese (language)

【汉子】① man; fellow：他是一条～。*He is a real man.* ②［方］husband

【汉字】Chinese character：～改革 *reform of Chinese characters* / ～简化方案 *the Scheme of Simplifying Chinese Characters* / ～显示 *Chinese character display* / ～注音 *phonetic transcription of Chinese characters* / ～数据库 *Chinese character database*

【汉族】the Han nationality, China's main nationality, or the Hans, distributed all over the country

汗 sweat; perspiration, the fluid excreted from the pores of the body：出～ *sweat; perspire* / 虚～ *abnormal sweating due to general debility* / 你正在出～。*You are sweating.* / 他开始出～。*He started to perspire.*

【汗斑】① sweat stain ② tinea versicolour

【汗背心】sleeveless undershirt; vest; singlet

【汗臭】bad smell of perspiration; stink of sweat

【汗褂儿】［口］undershirt

【汗碱】sweat stain

【汗脚】feet that sweat easily; sweaty feet; athletic feet

【汗津津】［口］sweaty; moist with sweat：～的头发 *sweaty hair* / 他脱下了～的衣服。*He stripped off his sweaty clothes.*

【汗孔】【生理】pore

【汗淋淋】dripping with perspiration; soaked with sweat：他跑得浑身～的。*He got soaked with sweat after running.*

【汗流浃背】sweat streaming down and drenching one's back; soaked with sweat; sweat like a pig; sweat buckets; be pouring with sweat：这可不是个简单活儿，我们一会儿就累得～了。*It was tough work; within minutes we were all sweating buckets.*

【汗马功劳】① distinction won in battle; war exploits ② one's contributions in work; render great services：他为革命立下了～。*He made great contribution to our revolution.*

【汗漫】［书］① wide-ranging but irrelevant; wide of the mark ② (of waters) vast and mighty

【汗毛】fine hair on the human body

【汗牛充栋】enough books to make the ox sweat or to fill a house to the rafters — an immense collection of books：他的藏书可以说是～。*He has an immense collection of books.*

【汗青】［书］① sweating green bamboo strips — completion of a literary undertaking ② historical records：留取丹心照～ *to show one's loyalty to the country in historical records*

【汗如雨下】break out in a sweat; be pouring with sweat; be dripping with sweat; sweat like a pig; sweat buckets：我很害怕，～。*I was extremely ter-*

H

rified and broke out in a sweat. /他~，头发粘在脸上。*He was pouring with sweat, and his hair was glued to his face.*
【汗衫】① undershirt; T-shirt ②［方］shirt
【汗水】sweat; perspiration：男人要在田地里挥洒~。*Man shall sweat in the field.* /他停下来擦去头上的~。*He stopped for a while to wipe the sweat off his face.*
【汗味】stink with perspiration
【汗腺】【生理】sweat gland
【汗颜】［书］blush with shame; feel deeply ashamed：他的成绩让我~。*His achievements made me feel deeply ashamed.*
【汗液】sweat; perspiration
【汗疹】heat rash; prickly heat
【汗珠】beads of sweat; drops of sweat：他头上布满了~。*Beads of sweat appeared on his forehead.*
【汗渍】sweat stain

旱 ① dry spell; drought：防~*take precautions against drought* /抗~ *combat (or fight) drought* /庄稼都~了。*All the crops dried up.* ② in contrast with water：~伞 *parasol* ③ dryland; land ④ on land; by land：起~ *take an overland route*
【旱冰】【体】roller-skating
【旱冰场】roller rink
【旱冰鞋】roller skates
【旱船】①［方］boat-shaped waterside house in a garden ② land boat, a model boat used as a stage prop in some folk dances
【旱道】［方］overland route
【旱稻】upland rice; dry rice
【旱地】nonirrigated farmland; dry land：~作物 *dry crop* / ~农业 *dryland farming*
【旱季】dry season：~攻势 *dry-season offensive*
【旱井】① water-retention well ② dry well (used to store vegetables in winter)
【旱涝保收】ensure stable yields despite drought or excessive rain; make gains no matter what happens; ensure a safe income：~、高产稳产 *give high and stable yields irrespective of drought or excessive rain*
【旱柳】dryland willow
【旱路】overland route：走~ *travel by land*
【旱年】year of drought
【旱情】damage to crops by drought; ravages of a drought：~严重 *be afflicted with a severe drought*
【旱獭】【动】marmot
【旱田】① dry farmland; ② dry land
【旱鸭子】① ducks raised on dry land as opposed to ducks raised by rivers and ponds ② non-swimmer：我是个~。*I am a non-swimmer.*
【旱烟】tobacco (smoked in a long-stemmed Chinese pipe)
【旱烟袋】long-stemmed Chinese pipe
【旱灾】drought
【旱作】dry farming

捍 defend; guard
【捍蔽】［书］protect; guard：~东南 *guard the southeast*
【捍拒】［书］resist; fight back
【捍卫】defend; guard; protect：~民族利益 *protect national interests* / ~祖国尊严 *defend national dignity; vindicate national honour*
【捍御】［书］defend; guard; protect：~祖国边疆 *defend the frontiers of one's country*

悍 ① brave; bold：短小精~ *not of imposing stature but strong and capable; (of essay) terse and forceful* ② fierce; ferocious：刁~ *cunning and fierce; wicked and ferocious*
【悍匪】ferocious bandit
【悍妇】termagant woman; shrew
【悍然】outrageously; brazenly; flagrantly：~镇压人民起义 *flagrantly suppress the people's uprising* / ~宣布 *brazenly declare*
【悍然不顾】in flagrant disregard of; in outrageous defiance of：~国际关系准则 *in defiance of norms of international relations*
【悍勇】［书］intrepid; dauntless：~好斗 *intrepid and bellicose*

菡
【菡萏】［书］lotus

焊 weld; solder：电~ *electric welding* / 点~ *spot welding* /冷~ *cold welding* /气~ *gas welding* /铜~ *copper welding* /电渣~ *electroslag welding*
【焊点】welding spot; soldered dot
【焊缝】welding seam; weld line：~加厚 *reinforcement of weld* / ~量规 *weld gauge*
【焊膏】soldering paste
【焊工】① welding; soldering ② welder
【焊弧】【冶】welding arc：~电压 *welding arc voltage*
【焊机】welding machine; welder
【焊接】weld; solder：电弧~ *electric arc welding* / ~操作 *welding operation* / ~变形 *welding deformation* / ~车间 *welding shop* / ~钢管 *welded steel pipe*
【焊料】welding or soldering flux; solder
【焊钳】electrode-holder or pliers
【焊枪】welding torch; welding blowpipe; welding gun
【焊丝】solder wire; welding stick
【焊条】welding rod

颔 ［书］①chin ②nod
【颔首】［书］nod：~示意 *beckon with a nod* / ~赞许 *give an approving nod; nod approvingly*

翰 ［书］① writing brush：挥~ *wield one's writing brush; write with a brush* /染~ *dye brush* ② poetry; letters; writing：文~ *official correspondence* /华~ *your esteemed letter* /书~ *calligraphy; letter*

【翰林】member of the Imperial Academy (from the Tang Dynasty onward):前清～ *member of the Imperial Academy of the former Qing Dynasty*
【翰林院】[旧] Imperial Academy
【翰墨】[书] brush and ink — writing, painting or calligraphy:名家～ *painting or calligraphy of a famous master*

撼 shake:摇～ *shake violently*
【撼动】shake; vibrate:这一重大发现～了整个世界。*This great discovery shocked the whole world.*
【撼天动地】shake heaven and earth:～的大事 *earthshaking events*

憾 regret; not feel satisfied:遗～ *regret; pity* /死而无～ *die without regret; die contented*
【憾然】disappointed:～而返 *return in disappointment*
【憾事】matter for regret:引为～ *regard sth as a matter for regret* /他昨天没来,真是件～。*What a pity he couldn't come here yesterday!*

瀚 [书] vast; immense; numerous:浩～ *vast; immense*
【瀚海】[书] vast desert:～无垠 *endless as the vast desert is*

hāng

夯 ① rammer, a tool used to ram the ground:石～ *stone rammer* (*or tamper*) ② pound with a rammer:～地 *ram the earth* ③ [方] pound; buffet; thrash:用拳头～人 *pound* (*or buffet*) *sb with fists* ④ [方] carry on one's shoulder with effort
【夯板】tamping plate
【夯锤】tamper; rammer
【夯镐】tamping pick
【夯具】rammer; tamper
【夯路机】roadpacker; steam roller
【夯土】【建】rammed earth:～坝 *rammed earth dam*
【夯土机】ramming or tamping machine; power rammer or tamper
【夯砣】heavy end of a rammer (usu. made of stone or metal)

háng

行 ① line; row:单～ *single lines* /双～ *double lines* ② occupation; profession:咱们是同～。*We are of the same trade.* ③ certain business firms or setups:银～ *bank* /车～*vehicle company* /～市 *quotations or average prices on the market* ④ seniority among brothers and sisters:排～ *ranks of seniority among brothers and sisters* /您～几? *What's your rank of seniority among your sisters and brothers?* /我～三。*I'm the third.* ⑤ measures (for things in line) line:几～字 *a few lines of words* /两～树 *two rows of trees*
see also xíng
【行帮】[旧] trade association; guild
【行辈】seniority in the family (or clan); position in the family hierarchy
【行播】【农】row planting
【行播机】row planter
【行车】[方] overhead travelling crane; shop traveller
【行当】① trade; profession; line of business ② 【戏】type of role
【行道】[方] trade; profession
【行东】[旧] owner of a trading company, workshop, mill, etc.
【行贩】pedlar
【行规】guild regulations
【行话】jargon; cant:黑道～ *cant of the underworld* /外交～ *diplomat-speak*
【行会】guild:～制度 *guild system* /～工人 *journeyman*
【行货】crudely-made goods; common stock
【行家】① expert; connoisseur; specialist:老～ *old hand* /～里手 *experts and master hands* ② be expert (at sth)
【行间】① [书] ranks of the army:出身～ *rise from the ranks* ② between lines or rows
【行距】space between rows; spacing; row spacing:栽种这种庄稼～一定要宽。*Be sure to leave a wide space between rows when planting this crop.*
【行款】format of lines in writing or typesetting
【行列】ranks:队伍～整齐 *be drawn up in orderly ranks*
【行频】line frequency
【行情】quotations (on the market); prices; market conditions:～分析 *market analysis*
【行情表】quotations list; tabulated quotations
【行市】quotations (on the market); price:～看好。*The market is picking up.*
【行伍】the ranks:～出身 *be from the ranks; rise from the ranks*
【行业】trade; profession; industry:服务～ *service trades; service industry* /建筑～ *building* (*or construction*) *industry* /广告～ *advertising profession*
【行业工会】craft union
【行业公会】craft guild; trade association (of businessmen in the same trade or industry)
【行业亏损】loss incurred by an industry; industry loss
【行业语】professional jargon; cant
【行院】[旧] ① (in the Jin and Yuan dynasties) house of prostitutes; house of actresses ② prostitute; actress
【行栈】broker's storehouse
【行长】president (of a bank); governor (usu. of an official bank):中国人民银行～ *governor of the People's Bank of China*
【行子】[方] sb or sth one doesn't like

H

吭 throat：引～高歌 *sing lustily*
see also kēng

杭 ①short for Hangzhou ②（Háng）a surname
【杭纺】soft plain-weave silk fabric made in Hangzhou
【杭剧】Hangzhou opera

航 ① boat；ship ② navigate；sail by water；fly：出～ *set out on a voyage；set sail；take off* /远～ *go on a long voyage；sail or fly to a faraway place* /通～ *be open to navigation（or air traffic）*
【航班】scheduled flight；flight（number）：～号 *flight number*
【航标】navigation mark；buoy
【航测】aerial survey
【航程】voyage；flight；distance travelled
【航船】①（in Jiangsu and Zhejiang）wooden boat that plies regularly between inland towns ② steamboat or ship（that sails in a river or on the sea）
【航次】① sequence of voyages or flights；voyage or flight number ② number of voyages or flights made
【航道】channel；sea-lane；fairway；course：国际～ *international sea-lane* /主～ *main channel* /～标 *navigable channel mark* /～水深 *fairway depth*
【航海】navigation：～家 *navigator；voyager*
【航迹】（of an airplane，ship，rocket，torpedo，etc.）flight path；track；wake：～角 *flight-path angle* /～轴 *flight-path axis*
【航空】aviation：民用～ *civil aviation* /～安全 *aviation safety* /～货运 *airfreight* /～器材 *air material* /～燃料 *aviation（or aircraft）fuel*
【航空公司】airline company；airlines；airways：中国国际～ *Air China* /联合～ *China United Airlines；（US）United Airlines*
【航天工业】space industry；astronautical industry：～部 *ministry of space industry*
【航线】air or shipping line；route；course
【航向】course（of a ship or plane）：改变～ *change course* /～误差 *course error* /指引～ *point out the way forward；provide guidance* /拨正～ *correct the course* /～指示器 *direction indicator*
【航行】① navigate by water；sail ② navigate by air；fly：飞机正向南京方向～。*The flight is flying in the direction of Nanjing.*
【航运】shipping：～业 *shipping industry* /～市场 *shipping market*
【航运保险】shipping insurance
【航运法】law of navigation

hàng

沆 ［书］vast expanse of water
【沆瀣】［书］evening mist
【沆瀣一气】［贬］like attracts like；birds of a feather flock together；act in collusion；wallow in the mire together；in league with；in cahoots with：军队被怀疑与恐怖分子～。*The army is suspected in collusion with the terrorists.*

巷 tunnel
see also xiàng
【巷道】［矿］tunnel：～掘进机 *tunnelling machine*

hāo

蒿 【植】wormwood；artemisia
【蒿草】wormwood
【蒿莱】［书］overgrown weeds
【蒿子】wormwood；artemisia
【蒿子秆儿】tender leaves and stem of crown daisy chrysanthemum（eaten as a vegetable）

薅 ① pull up（weeds，etc.）；weed by hand ②［方］pull；tug；grab
【薅草】weeding
【薅锄】weeding hoe

háo

号 ① howl；yell；bawl：北风怒～。*A north wind is howling.* ② wail
see also hào
【号呼】cry out；yell
【号叫】yell；scream；howl；bawl；roar：她一面哭，一面～着。*She yelled as she wept.* /蛇咬着了他，他痛苦地～起来。*As the snake bit him，he roared with pain.* /风穿过树林发出似～的声音。*The wind wailed through the trees.*
【号哭】wail；bawl：～不止 *keep on wailing* /一场～可能会使她好过些。*A good bawl may make her feel better.*
【号丧】（háosāng）howl or scream at a funeral
【号丧】（háosɑng）［贬］howl as if at a funeral；cry；wail
【号啕】cry loudly；wail：她～了好一阵子。*She had a good long cry.* /他突然像一个小孩一样～大哭起来。*He blubbered like a child suddenly.*

蚝 【动】oyster
【蚝豉】dried oyster meat
【蚝蘑】oyster mushroom
【蚝油】oyster sauce

毫 ① fine tapering hair ② writing brush ③ loop for balancing a steelyard（from the user's hand）④（used in the negative only）least bit；slightest degree：你们已经取得了进步，对此我～不怀疑。*There has been no doubt in my mind of the progress which you have achieved.* ⑤ a thou-

H

sand of certain units of measurement ⑥ hao, a unit of measure 1/10 of li(厘), (a) in weight, equivalent to 0.005 grams (b) in length, equivalent to 1/3 of a decimillimetre ⑦ [方] *jiao*, 1/10 of yuan

【毫安】【电】milliampere (mA or ma)

【毫不利己,专门利人】utter devotion to others without any thought of oneself

【毫法】【电】millifarad

【毫发】[书] (mostly used in the negative) hair; least bit; slightest: ~不差 *not deviating a hair's breath; without the least difference* / ~无损 *be safe and sound*

【毫发不爽】not deviate a hair's breadth; be perfectly accurate: 本次测试的结果可以说~。*Results from this test can be said perfectly accurate.*

【毫分】least; minute; slightest

【毫伏】【电】millivolt

【毫克】milligramme (mg)

【毫厘】least bit; iota: ~不差 *without the slightest error*

【毫毛】soft hair on the body; down: 他的威胁无损于我一根~。*His threats can't harm a single hair of my head.*

【毫米】millimetre (mm)

【毫米波】millimetre wave

【毫秒】millisecond (ms)

【毫末】[书] tip of a fine hair — minutest quantity or detail

【毫升】milliliter (ml)

【毫瓦】【电】milliwatt

【毫无二致】without a fraction of difference; as like as two peas; identical: 里根上台时在做法上跟执政初期的卡特~。*Early Reagan was a mirror image of early Carter.*

【毫无疑问】no doubt; without doubt: ~,氧是大气中最活泼的元素。*It goes without saying that oxygen is the most active elements in the atmosphere.*

【毫针】filiform needle in acupuncture; acupuncture needle

嗥 (of a jackal or wolf) howl

【嗥叫】(usu. of jackals and wolves) howl: 半夜里听到狼的~,感觉很害怕。*It is a dreadful experience to hear wolves howling at midnight.*

貉

see also hé

【貉绒】fine raccoon dog fur (with all the bristles pulled)

【貉子】racoon dog

豪 ① person of extraordinary powers or endowments: 文~ *literary giant* /富~ *rich and powerful person*; *tycoon* ② bold and unconstrained; magnanimous and forthright; unrestrained ③ rich and powerful ④ despotic; bullying; coercive: 土~ *local despot*

【豪侈】excessively luxurious; bold and unconstrained

【豪宕】[书] uninhibited; bold and unconstrained

【豪夺】take by force: 巧取~ *take by force or trickery; seize by hook or by crook*

【豪放】uninhibited; bold and unconstrained: 性格~ *be unbridled in character*

【豪放不羁】unconventional and uninhibited; vigorous and unrestrained: 这位诗人以~的行为而闻名。*The poet is famous for his unconventional behaviour.*

【豪富】① powerful and wealthy ② the rich and powerful; plutocrat

【豪横】(háohèng) despotic; bullying

【豪横】[方] (háoheng) of uncompromising integrity; staunch; unyielding

【豪华】① (of living) extravagant; luxurious: 你的钱不够你过这么~的生活。*Your purse will not allow you such luxury.* ② (of buildings, furniture, ornaments, etc.) sumptuous; splendid; lavish

【豪杰】person of exceptional ability; hero: 女中~ *heroine* /英雄~ *hero*

【豪举】bold move; munificent or magnificent act; extravagance

【豪迈】bold and generous; heroic: 以~的步伐踏入新的一年 *stride into the new year with pride and confidence*

【豪门】rich and powerful family; wealthy and influential clan

【豪气】heroic spirit; heroism

【豪强】① arrogant; despotic; tyrannical ② despot; bully: 江南地区的~是皇帝的主要支持者。*The landlords and despots in the south of Yangtze River are main supporters of the Emperor.*

【豪情】lofty sentiments; heroic feelings; pride

【豪情满怀】full of pride and enthusiasm; full of spirit: 站在广场上,我们~。*Standing in the square, we feel that we are filled with pride and enthusiasm.*

【豪情壮志】lofty sentiments and high aspirations

【豪绅】despotic gentry

【豪士】person of outstanding talent

【豪爽】frank; bold and unconstrained; uninhibited and straightforward; forthright: 山东的汉子多为~之士。*Men from Shandong Province are mostly bold and unconstrained.*

【豪侠】① courageous and chivalrous; gallant ②gallant man; man of courage and chivalry

【豪兴】ebullient high spirits; exhilaration; keen interest

【豪言壮语】brave or proud words; heroic remarks or words

【豪饮】drink to the limit of one's capacity; drink lustily; drink heavily; drink with abandon

【豪雨】torrential rain; heavy rain

【豪语】heroic words; brave words; bold promise; bombast

【豪猪】【动】porcupine

【豪壮】grand and heroic

【豪族】wealthy and influential clan

壕 ① moat ② trench

【壕沟】①【军】trench ② ditch

【壕堑】trench; entrenchment

嚎 ① howl; yell; bawl ② wail; cry loudly

【嚎春】howl for mating; be in heat

濠 moat：城～ *city moat*

hǎo

好 ① good; fine; nice ② be in good health; be or get well 我今天～多了。*I feel much better today.* ③ friendly; kind 这两个孩子又～了。*The two children are friendly to each other again.* ④ be easy to do; be convenient：这种衣物～洗。*This kind of clothes washes well.* ⑤ used before a verb to indicate an aspect that gives satisfaction：～，就这么办。*Ok, it's settled.* ⑥ used after a verb to indicate the completion of an action：坐～吧，要开会了。*Take your seats, please. The meeting is going to begin.* ⑦ used to express approval, agreement, conclusion, etc.：～，就照你的意思办吧。*Ok, let's do it according to your suggestion.* ⑧ used ironically to express dissatisfaction：～，这下可麻烦了。*Well, we are in trouble now.* ⑨ used as a polite formula：你～！*How do you do?*; *Hello* ⑩ for the purpose of; in order to; so that：告诉我地址，我～给她打电话。*Tell me the address so that I can call her.* ⑪［方］may; can; should; ought to：我明天～去你家吗？*May I come to your home tomorrow?* ⑫ used before certain time or numeral indicators to suggest a large number or a long time：他去过～几个国家呢。*He has been to several countries.* ⑬ used before adjectives or verbs for emphasis and with exclamatory：今天～冷！*How cold it is today!* ⑭（used before adjectives）to what extent; how：北京离上海～远？*How far is Beijing from Shanghai?*
see also hào

【好办】easy to handle or cope with：这件事很～。*That is a piece of cake.*

【好比】can be compared to; may be likened to; be just like：军民关系～鱼水关系。*The relationship between the army and the people is like that between fish and water.*

【好不】（used with exclamatory force）very; quite; so：我～容易才找到他。*It was rather hard for me to find him.* /市场～热闹。*The bazaar is quite noisy and crowded.*

【好吃】good to eat; pleasant to the taste; tasty：一道～的菜 *a tasty dish*

【好处】① good; benefit; advantage：对人民有～ *be of benefit to the people* /空谈有什么～？*What's the good of empty talk?* /每天锻炼身体对你很有～。*It is to your advantage to exercise every day.* ② gain; profit：做这种生意是有～的。*It's profitable to run such kind of business.*

【好处费】pickings; favour fee

【好歹】① good and bad; what's good and what's bad：别跟他生气，他根本就分不清～。*Don't be so angry with him, for he cannot tell what is good and what is bad.* ② mishap; disaster：万一她的母亲有个～，我们怎么交代？*What should we do if her mother were trapped in some mishap?* ③ in any case; at any rate; anyhow：～你得写完作业。*You'd better finish your homework in any case.* ④ no matter in what way; anyhow：～吃点就得了。*We will have whatever there is.*

【好端端】in perfectly good condition; when everything is all right：～的，怎么就突然病了？*How can you fall ill when in perfectly good condition?*

【好多】① plenty of; many; good deal; lots of：她读了～小说。*She read a great many novels.* ②［方］how many; how much

【好感】favourable impression; good opinion：博得～ *win (or earn) the good opinion of others* /他对左邻右舍概无～。*He's very ill-disposed towards her neighbours.*

【好钢用在刀刃上】use the best steel to make the knife's edge — use material where it is needed most; use the best material at the key point

【好过】① have an easy time; be in easy circumstances：前些年我们家的日子很不～。*In the past few years we have been in a very hard time.* ② feel well：我～多了。*I feel much better.*

【好汉】brave man; true man; hero：不到长城非～。*He who doesn't reach the Great Wall is not a true man.*

【好汉不吃眼前亏】a wise man will not fight when the odds are obviously against him; a wise man knows when to retreat：他们不是什么好人，别跟他们吵架，～。*They are no good men, better not quarrel with them, for only a fool goes looking for trouble.*

【好汉不提当年勇】a true hero is silent about his past glories

【好好儿】① in perfectly good condition; when everything is all right：～的一本书，他却给弄坏了。*He has broken a perfectly good book.* ② all out; to one's heart's content; try one's best：得～谢谢他，人家帮了那么大的忙。*We have really got to thank him for the great help offered.*

【好好先生】one who tries not to offend anybody; one who never says no; yesman; Mr. Goody-goody; creep：他是公认的～。*He is publicly considered Mr. Goody-goody.* /和他在一起工作没什么好的，除非你想做一个～。*It's no good working with him unless you are happy being a yes-man.*

【好好学习，天天向上】study hard and make progress every day

【好话】① good words; well-meant advice; useful words：领导们应该是～坏话一起听。*The leaders should listen to unpleasant words as well as pleasant words.* ② words of praise; pleasant words: 不要听了几句～就沾沾自喜。*Don't become complacent when you hear a few words of praise.*

【好坏不分】do not distinguish the good from the bad; not distinguish between those who do a good job and those who shoddy work: 你不能～。*You should be able to distinguish the evil from the good.*

【好几】① used after a round number to indicate that the fractional amount is considerable: 他今年已经三十～了。*He's well over thirty this year.* ② (before a measure word, a time word, and the numerals 百, 千, 万, etc.) quite a few; a good few: 我～年都没有看电影了。*I have not seen a film for a good few years.*

【好家伙】good god; good lord; good heavens: ～, 这小孩能吃下两大碗米饭。*Good heavens! This child can eat two big bowls of rice.*

【好价】a good (selling) price: 连草都能在市场上卖个～, 真是荒年。*An off-year it really is that even grass can be sold at a good price.*

【好景不长】good times don't last long: ～, 他很快就破产了。*Golden times are easily gone; he soon went broke.*

【好久】① a long time: 我～没有看到他了。*I haven't seen him for a long time.* ②［方］how long

【好看】① good-looking; nice: 穿红衣服的那个小姑娘很～。*The girl in red is rather good-looking.* ② interesting: 这个电影很～。*This film is interesting.* ③ honoured; proud: 他有出息了, 我脸上也～。*I will share the honour in that he becomes somebody.* ④ in an embarrassing situation; on the spot: 等着吧, 有他的～。*You can be sure he'll soon find himself on the spot.*

【好莱坞】Hollywood, centre of US movie industry located close to Los Angeles

【好了疮疤忘了疼】forget the pain once the wound is healed — forget the bitter past when released from one's suffering

【好力宝】a kind of folk singing, sometimes combined with recitation, popular in Inner Mongolia

【好脸】［口］a smiling face: 他一听我要借钱, 马上就没～了。*He pulled a long face as soon as he knew I wanted to borrow money from him.*

【好男不跟女斗】a gentleman doesn't fight women

【好歹】［口］① good and bad; what's good and what's bad ② in any case; whatever happens; at all events: ～我也不会让你走的。*I will not let you go at any events.*

【好评】favourable comment; high opinion: 报界对他的发言予以～。*The press made favourable comments on his address.*

【好气儿】［口］good humour; good temper: 那个女人一见到老公抽烟就没～。*The woman will lose temper at the scene of his husband's smoking.*

【好人】① a good (or fine) person: 他是个～。*He is a good man.* ② a healthy person: 我这个孩子不是～, 干不了重活。*My son cannot bear the heavy work for he is not a healthy person.* ③ a soft person who tries to get along with everyone (often at the expense of principle); yes-man: 他只想做个～。*He wants to be a person out of whom come no offensive words or actions.*

【好人好事】good people and good deeds; fine people and fine deeds

【好人家】① a decent family; a respectable family: 他一看就知道是～出来的人。*At first sight we can see that he is from a decent family.* ② a woman from a respectable family; a respectable woman ③［方］a wealthy family; a well-to-do family: 她真幸运嫁到了一个～。*She is lucky enough to marry a man from a wealthy family.*

【好人主义】seeking good relations with all and sundry at the expense of principle

【好日子】① auspicious day ② wedding day: 今天是他们的～。*Today is their wedding day.* ③ good days; happy life: ～不远了。*Good days are on their way.*

【好容易】to find sth very hard to handle: 他～才咽下那个饺子。*He tried his best to ingest that dumpling.*

【好商量】can be settled through discussion: 这件事～。*It's easy for us to make an agreement about the matter.*

【好生】① quite; exceedingly: 她说她～难过。*She said she was quite sad.* ②［口］carefully; properly: ～拿着这个玻璃杯子。*Handle this glass with great care.*

【好声好气】［口］in a kindly manner; gently

【好使】be convenient to use; work well: 这个圆珠笔不太～。*This ballpoint pen does not write well.*

【好事】① good deed; good turn: 为群众做～ *do people good turns* ② an act of charity ③［书］happy event; joyous occasion

【好事多磨】① the road to happiness is strewn with setbacks; good things are a long time in coming ② the course of true love never runs smooth: 真可谓～, 他们在婚前历经了种种磨难。*As is said that the course of true love never runs smooth, they suffered a lot before their marriage.*

【好手】good hand; expert; past master: 做针线活儿, 她可是把～。*She is adept at needlework.*

【好受】feel better; feel more comfortable: 听了你的话, 我～多了。*I feel more comfortable at your words.*

【好说】① used in answer to praises or thanks: ～, ～! 您过奖了! *It's very kind of you to say so, but I really don't deserve your compliment.* ② no problem: ～, 我明天早晨就会把钱送到的。*No problem. I will show you the money tomorrow morning.*

【好说歹说】try every possible way to persuade sb: 我～, 他总算答应了。*He agreed, but only after I had pleased him in every way I could.*

【好说话儿】good-natured; open to persuasion：他觉得她的父母很～。*He found her parents very affable.*
【好死】natural death：不得～ *to die a worst (horrible) death*
【好死不如赖活】even a good death is not better than a wretched existence
【好似】seem; be like：她就～我生命中的蜡烛。*She is like a candle in my life.*
【好天儿】fine day; lovely weather：今天是个～。*It's a fine day today.*
【好听】pleasant to hear：甜言蜜语更～。*Sweet talks are more pleasant to hear.*
【好玩儿】amusing; interesting：这个游戏一点都不～。*This game is not interesting at all.*
【好闻】smell good; smell sweet; fragrant：他带给我一束～的玫瑰花。*He brought me a bunch of sweet-smelling roses.* /真～！你在做什么菜？*Something smells good; what are you cooking?*
【好戏】① good play：她写了些～。*She wrote some good plays.* ② great fun (used sarcastically)：～还在后头呢。*The worst is still on its way.*
【好像】seem; be like：善行～是黑夜中的蜡烛。*Good is like a candle in the darkness.*
【好笑】laughable; funny; ridiculous; absurd; stupid：你这样做真是太～了。*It is really ridiculous for you to do so.*
【好些】quite a lot; a good deal of; a lot of
【好心】good intention：我可是～来帮助你。*I am helping you with the best intention.* /她的～却得到了恶报。*Her good intentions were repaid by evil results.*
【好心当作驴肝肺】take an honest man's heart for a donkey's liver and lungs — take sb's goodwill for ill intention：你真是～，我不管这件事了。*You have truly mistaken my good intention; thus I am determined to let this matter be.*
【好样儿的】[口] (of a man or woman) fine example; great fellow：干了这么多活，真是～。*Great fellow are you for all the heavy work you have done.*
【好一个】what a：～正人君子，连骗七家！*What an honourable man! To take seven families in successively!*
【好意】good intention; kindness：多谢您的～，可是我还是要走。*Thank you very much for your kindness, but I must be off now.*
【好意思】how can one have the face (or nerve) to do sth：你怎么～说出这种话来？*How can you have the face to talk something like this?*
【好在】fortunately; luckily：～他在这儿，要不我们真不知道怎么对付这种两难的境地。*Fortunately, he has been here, or else we wouldn't have known how to deal with such a dilemma.*
【好转】change for the better; take a turn for the better; take a favourable turn; improve：经过一个月的治疗，他的病情开始～。*After a month's treatment, he began to show the sign of turning for the better.*
【好自为之】look out for yourself：有这个机会不容易，希望你～。*An opportunity like this is not easy to come by, so I hope you'll make best use of it.*
【好走】[口] goodbye

hào

号[1] ① name：绰～ *nickname* ② assumed name; alternative name; literary name; sobriquet：吴镇(元画家)，字仲圭，～梅花道人。*Wu Zhen (a Yuan painter), whose courtesy name was Zhonggui, and the sobriquet "Taoist of the Plum Blossom".* ③ business house：银～ *bank* ④ mark; sign; signal：问～ *question mark* ⑤ order; sequence：编～ *serial number* ⑥ size：大～ *large size* /中～ *medium size* /小～ *small size* ⑦ kind; sort：这～人不好相处。*This kind of men are hard to get on with.* ⑧ person of a given type：病～ *sick personnel* ⑨ ordinal number：门牌～ *street number; house number* /今天是几～？*What's the date today?* ⑩ [量] used to indicate numbers：今天来了一百多～人。*Today more than 100 people came to work.* /已经做了几～买卖。*Several deals have been done.* ⑪ make a mark on：～一～这几样货品。*Have these items marked.* ⑫ examine

号[2] ① order ② anything used as a horn：螺～ *conch; shell trumpet* ③ any brass-wind instrument：军～ *bugle* /小～ *clarino; trumpet* ④ bugle call; any call made on a bugle：起床～ *reveille*

see also háo

【号兵】bugler; trumpeter
【号称】① be known as：昆明～春城。*Kunming is known as the City of Spring.* ② claim to be：据说他～有百万大军。*He is said to have an army claimed to be a million strong.*
【号灯】signal lamp
【号房】[旧] ① janitor's room; reception office ② janitor ③ dormitory for candidates of the imperial examination
【号角】① bugle; horn ② bugle call：吹响冲锋的～ *sound a bugle call for charge*
【号坎儿】[旧] numbered singlet worn by coolies
【号令】verbal command; order：任何不听从他～的人都会受到惩罚。*Anyone who disobeys his order will be punished.* /将军发出开火的～。*The general gave the command to open fire.*
【号码】number：电话～ *telephone number* /房间～ *apartment number* /现代人被形形色色的～包围。*Modern people are being surrounded by all sorts of numbers.*
【号码机】numbering machine
【号脉】[中医] feel the pulse
【号牌】numberplate
【号炮】signal gun

【号手】bugler; trumpeter
【号头】[口] number
【号外】extra (of a newspaper)
【号衣】[旧] livery or army uniform
【号召】call; appeal: 响应党的~ *respond to the Party's call*
【号子】① [口] mark; sing; signal ② a work song sung to synchronize movements, with one person leading

好 ① like; love; be fond of: ~表现 *like to show off* ② be liable to: ~冷 *be subject to colds*
see also hǎo

【好吃】enjoy eating good food
【好吃懒做】be fond of eating and averse to work; be gluttonous and lazy: ~可不是什么美德。*Laziness can never be a virtue.*
【好大喜功】crave for greatness and success; be ambitious for great achievements; have a fondness for the grandiose: 领导人是绝对不能~的,否则就会有灾难性的后果。*Leaders shall be modest and never crave for greatness, or all will end up with a tragedy.*
【好读书】love to read books; be fond of reading books; be addicted to study
【好高骛远】reach for what is beyond one's grasp; aim too high; bite off more than one can chew
【好客】be hospitable; keep open house; neighbourly; welcoming: ~的主人 *a hospitable host* /我去拜访他们的时候,他们总是热情~。*They are always so welcoming when I visit them.*
【好奇】be curious; be full of curiosity: 有的单身汉对婚姻很~。*Some bachelors are curious about marriage.* /不要那么~! 这不关你的事! *Don't be so nosy! It's none of your business.* /当我提到他的名字,这个女孩儿开始~起来。*When I mentioned his name, the girl became inquisitive.*
【好奇心】curiosity: 我告诉了他全部我知道的事情,但是仍然不能满足他的~。*I told him all I knew about the affair but I could still not satisfy his curiosity.*
【好强】eager to do well in everything
【好色】lust for women; love woman's beauty; be fond of women
【好色之徒】lecher; libertine
【好施乐善】be happy in doing good; enjoy helping those in need; be generous in one's charity
【好尚】one's likes or preferences; what is valued or held in esteem
【好胜】love to outshine others; seek to do others down
【好事】meddlesome; officious: 我被一个~的前台拦住了,除非我回答了他所有的问题才能进去。*I got held up by an officious receptionist who wouldn't let me in until I'd answered all her questions.*
【好事者】busybody; do-gooder; interfering man; meddling man: 这是某个~杜撰的。*This is fabricated by some busybody.* /这个老太太真是个~! 她为什么不能让我安静一会儿呢? *She's really a meddling old lady! Why can't she just leave me alone?*
【好事之徒】busybody; interfering man; meddling man: 他是个~。*He is an interfering busybody.*
【好为人师】be fond of teaching others; like to lecture people; be given to laying down the law: 人之患,在~。*The trouble with people is that they are too eager to assume the role of teacher.*
【好恶】likes and dislikes; taste: 人各有~。*Everyone has his likes and dislikes.*
【好学】studious; assiduous; diligent; be fond of learning; be eager to learn: 聪明~ *be intelligent and eager to learn*
【好逸恶劳】love leisure and hate labour; love ease and hate work
【好战】bellicose; warlike: ~分子 *bellicose elements; warlike elements* /希腊城邦激进而~。*The Greek city-states were aggressive and warlike.*

昊 [书] ① vast and boundless ② sky; heaven

【昊天】the sky; the heaven

耗[1] ① consume; cost: 这锅水快~干了。*This pot of water is boiling dry.* ② [方] waste time; dawdle: 他看书只是为了~时间。*His reading books is only for killing time.*

耗[2] bad news: 噩~ *sad news of the death of one's beloved*

【耗电量】power consumption
【耗电率】consumption rate
【耗费】consume; expend: 这个计划~了我大部分时间和精力。*This project consumed most of my time and energy.*
【耗竭】exhaust; use up: 资源~ *resources used up*
【耗尽】exhaust; use up: ~心血 *exhaust all one's energies* /有一天人类可能~地球上储备的所有有用能源。*Maybe in time, the human race will exhaust the world's store of useful energy.* /这些麻烦和困难~了他的耐心。*The trouble and difficulties have worn out his patience.*
【耗能】consume energy
【耗神】drain one's mind
【耗水量】【水】water consumption
【耗损】consume; waste; lose: ~精力 *wear sb down*
【耗资】cost (a large sum of money)
【耗子】[方] mouse; rat
【耗子药】ratsbane

浩 ① great; vast; grand ② many; much

【浩博】extensive; wide-embracing
【浩大】huge; gigantic; heavy; very great; huge; vast: ~的工程 *a huge project*
【浩荡】vast and mighty: 东风~。*The east wind blows with mighty power.*
【浩繁】heavy; large; vast and numerous: ~的开支 *heavy expenditure*
【浩瀚】[书] vast: ~的大海 *boundless sea*

【浩浩荡荡】vast and mighty：～的革命大军 *an enormous and powerful revolutionary army*

【浩劫】great calamity；catastrophe：十年～ *a ten-year calamity* /人类的～ *catastrophe for mankind* /空前～ *an unheard-of calamity*

【浩茫】［书］vast；extensive；boundless

【浩渺】（of water） extending into the distance；vast：～的水域 *a vast of water*

【浩气】noble spirit：～长存 *the noble spirit that will never perish* / ～凌云 *fully display one's noble spirit*

【浩然之气】noble spirit；moral force

【浩如烟海】vast as the open sea — a tremendous amount（of literature，data，etc.）

【浩叹】heave a deep sigh；sigh deeply

皓 ① white ② bright；luminous

【皓白】white；pure white

【皓齿】white teeth

【皓矾】【化】zinc sulphate

【皓首】［书］hoary head

【皓月】bright and luminous moon

【皓月当空】a bright moon hung shining in the sky

颢 ［书］white and shining

hē

呵[1] breathe out（with the mouth open）：一气～成 *accomplish sth at one go；carry sth through without stopping or interruption*

呵[2] scold；reprove

【呵斥】scold severely；berate；excoriate：不要～孩子，这不是他的过失。*Don't scold the child. It's not his fault.*

【呵冻】breathe out hot air to warm up frozen fingers in winter

【呵呵】［象］the sound of laughing：笑～ *laugh a bit loudly*

【呵喝】［书］shout（as a warning or reprimand）

【呵护】［书］① bless：上帝～你。*Bless you!* ② cherish；take good care of：老师对孩子们～备至。*The teacher takes great care of the little children.*

【呵禁】berate and forbid

【呵气】give a puff：她～来暖手。*She gave a puff to warm her hands.*

【呵欠】［方］yawn：她感到很困，止不住地打～。*She felt so sleepy that she couldn't stop yawning.*

【呵责】scold；give sb a dressing-down；excoriate：我的靴子上要是有泥，一进屋爸爸就～我。*If I walk in with muddy boots，dad always scolds me.*

喝 ① drink：～水 *drink water* ② drink alcoholic liquor：他不～酒。*He doesn't drink.*
see also hè

【喝叱】berate；excoriate：酒店经理总是因为礼貌问题～他的员工。*The hotel manager was always berating his staff about their bad manners.*

【喝闷酒】drink alone in low spirit

【喝墨水】drink ink — go to school：他们家就他喝过点墨水。*He is the only person who once went to school in the family.* /他喝过洋墨水呢。*He once studied abroad.*

【喝西北风】drink the northwest wind — live on air；go hungry；have nothing to eat；starve：如果你不好好学习，将来就只有～了。*Provided you do not study hard，you are sure to be starved to death some day.*

嗬 ah；oh，expressing surprise：～，真不得了！*Oh，how terrible!*

hé

禾 ①a general term for cereal crops ②［古］millet

【禾场】［方］threshing floor

【禾苗】seedlings of cereal crops

合[1] ① close；shut：～眼 *close the eyes；sleep* /缝～伤口 *sew up（or suture）a wound* /笑得～不上嘴 *grin from ear to ear* ② join；combine：～为一体 *combine（or merge）into one* ③ whole；total；entire：～家大小 *whole family* ④ not contrary to，fitting or corresponding（between one thing and another）：正～我意。*It suits me fine.* ⑤ be equal to；add up to：这件衣服做成了～多少钱？*How much does this coat cost when it is finished?* /一米～多少市尺？*How many chi is one meter equal to?* ⑥［书］proper；appropriate；necessary：理～声明。*It is deemed necessary to make a statement.* ⑦［古］（of passage at arms）round；bout：大战三十余～ *fight thirty-odd rounds* ⑧【天】conjunction ⑨（Hé）a surname

合[2] 【音】a note of the music score in ancient times，corresponding to the low tone "5" in numbered musical notation

【合办】operate or run jointly：～企业 *joint venture*

【合抱】get one's arms around（a tree，etc.）：三人～的大树 *tree so big that it makes three people to embrace it with outstretched arms* / ～之木生于毫末。*A tree that can fill the span of a man's arms grows from a downy tip.*

【合璧】combine harmoniously；match well：中西～ *harmonious combination of Chinese and Western elements*

【合编】① compile in collaboration；co-edit：我们～了这本字典。*We jointly compiled the dictionary.* ② merge and reorganize：军队～ *the merger of the two armies*

【合并】① merge；amalgamate；combine：两个组～为一个组。*Two groups merge into one.* /两家银行宣布了明年～的计划。*The two banks have announced plans to merge next year.* /女队和男队已经～。*The women's group has amalgamated with the men's.* ②（of an illness）be complicated by

another illness
【合不来】not get along well; be incompatible: 我从来没有见过这么～的一对。*I've never seen such an incompatible couple.*
【合唱】chorus: 混声～ *mixed chorus* /无伴奏～ *unaccompanied chorus* /女声～ *female chorus* /男声～ *male chorus* /童声～ *children chorus* /他先独唱,然后我们大家一起～。*He sang the verses and everyone joined in the chorus.*
【合唱曲】chorus
【合唱团】chorus; choir
【合成】① compose; compound: 录音～ *dubbing* /～镜头 *process shots* ②【化】synthesize: ～材料 *synthetic material* /～醇 *synthol* /～钢 *synthetic steel* /～燃料 *synthol*; *synfuel*; *synthetic fuel* /～汽油 *synthetic gasoline*
【合成词】【语】compound word
【合得来】get along well; be compatible
【合订本】one-volume edition; file; bound volume: 报纸的～*a file of newspapers*
【合度】right; proper; appropriate
【合而为一】【哲】two combine into one: 资本主义和社会主义最终不会～。*Capitalism and socialism will not eventually converge.*
【合法】legal; lawful; legitimate; above board; within the law: ～地位 *legal status* /～行为 *legal action* /～婚姻 *lawful marriage* /～收入 *lawfully earned income* /～身份 *legal status* /抗议者必须使用～的方式反对政府。*Protesters must only use lawful methods of opposing the government.* /他向我们保证这个合同是～的。*He assured us that the contract was honest and above board.*
【合法化】legalize; legitimize: 政府永远不会让可卡因这样的毒品～。*The government will never legalize drugs like cocaine.*
【合该】should; ought to: 那日也是～出事,他早早就下班了。*He left for home early that day, not to expect something unusual should happen to him.*
【合格】qualified; up to standard: ～的医生 *a qualified doctor*
【合格率】acceptance rate
【合格证】certificate of inspection; certificate of quality
【合共】altogether; in all: ～三万元收入 *income of 30,000 yuan in all*
【合股】① pool capital; form a partnership ②【纺】plying
【合乎】conform with (or to); correspond to; be in keeping with; accord with: ～实情 *accord with the actual situation* /～自然规律 *be in conformity with the law of nature* /～情理 *stand to reason*; *be reasonable*
【合欢】① enjoy (sexual) bliss together; make love ②【植】silk tree
【合伙】partnership; form a partnership: ～经营 *run a business in partnership* /他和弟弟～做生意。*He entered into partnership with his brother.* /年龄大的男孩～欺侮年龄小的男孩。*Older boys ganged up on younger ones.*
【合伙公司】partnership: 我最初在一家小的～工作。*My first job was with a small partnership.*
【合伙企业】partnership
【合伙人】partner
【合击】make a concerted or joint attack: 分进～ *concerted attack by converging columns*
【合计】amount to; total; add up to: 这两项开支～一千元。*The cost of the two items amounts to 1,000 yuan.*
【合计】① think over; figure out : 让我再～一下这事。*I should like to think over the matter a little.* /他们在～买彩电的可能性。*They are looking into the possibility of buying a colour TV set.* ② consult: 大家～～该怎么办。*Let's put our heads together and see what's to be done.*
【合剂】【药】mixture
【合家】the whole family: ～团圆 *a reunion of the whole family*
【合家欢】[方] a family group photo
【合脚】(of shoes or socks) fit: 我穿这双鞋非常～。*These shoes fit me perfectly.*
【合金】alloy: 二元～ *binary alloy* /三元～ *ternary alloy*
【合金钢】alloy steel
【合刊】combined issue (of a periodical)
【合口】① (of a wound) heal up ② (of a dish) be to one's taste: 你做的菜很～。*The dishes you make are very much to my taste.*
【合理】justified; reasonable; equitable: 收费～ *reasonable charges* /时间安排～ *a well worked out timetable* /～分工 *rational division of labour* /他们的回答不～。*Their answer is not reasonable.*
【合理化】rationalize: ～建议 *rationalization proposal*
【合力】① join forces; pool efforts: ～修建水库 *pool efforts to build a reservoir* ②【物】resultant (of forces)
【合流】① flowing together; confluence: 永定河和大清河在天津附近～。*The Yongding and Daqing rivers meet near Tianjin.* ② collaborate; work hand in glove with sb; in collusion with sb: 政客和军队～。*The politicians are hand in glove with the military.* ③ different schools (of thought, art, etc.) merge into one
【合龙】【建】start building a dam or bridge from the two ends, and finally join the two sections in the middle: 大坝～ *closing of a dam*
【合拢】come together; join together; gather
【合谋】conspire; plot together: ～推翻政府 *conspire to overthrow the government* /我确信他们在～对付我。*I am sure they are all conspiring against me.*
【合拍】① in time; in step; in harmony: 与音乐～ *be in time with the music* /与时代潮流～ *in step with the trend of the times* ② collaborate (on a film, etc.); shoot a film in collaboration: 这是一部中、日～的影片。*This film was jointly produced by Chinese and Japanese studios.* ③ take a

group photo or picture
【合情合理】fair and reasonable; fair and square: ～的要求 *reasonable demand* /这个建议～。*The proposal is fair and reasonable.*
【合群】① get on well with others; be sociable; be gregarious: 如果她不爱和你说话你可别生气,她只是不太～。*If she seems not to want to talk to you, don't be offended — she is just not very sociable.* ② form a group or society for mutual aid; gang up
【合扇】[口] hinge
【合身】(of clothing) fit: 你穿这件上衣很～。*The coat fits you quite well.*
【合十】put or hold the palms together before one (as a Buddhist greeting)
【合时】fashionable; trendy; in vogue; in fashion: 穿戴～ *dress fashionably* /真奇怪,喇叭裤居然又变得～了。*It's surprising that flared trousers are in vogue again.*
【合式】up to standard; in agreement with the forms and formulas
【合适】suitable; appropriate; right: 这个词用在这里不～。*This isn't the right word to use here.* /我在等一个～的时候告诉他我要辞职。*I've been waiting for a suitable moment to tell him that I will resign.*
【合手】①[方] be congenial; cooperate (with each other) ②[书] put the palms together before one in salutation
【合署】related offices handle official business together in the same building
【合算】① worthwhile; paying: 这件事还挺～的。*This is worthwhile.* /买这块手表不～。*It doesn't pay to buy such a watch.* ② reckon; calculate
【合体】① (of clothing) fit ②【语】composite character (i. e. composed of two or more elements, such as 明 composed of 日 and 月)
【合同】contract; agreement: 产销～ *production and marketing agreement* /代理～ *agency contract* /抵押～ *mortgage contract* /订立～ *conclude (or make) a contract* /雇佣～ *contract of employment* / ～纠纷 *contract dispute* /履行～ *carry out a contract* /撕毁～ *tear up a contract* / ～期限 *contract period* / ～条款 *contract terms* /销售～ *sales contract*
【合同法】【律】contract law
【合同工】contract worker
【合同医院】assigned hospital under medical insurance or public medicine system, to which people from a given organization or area go for treatment
【合同制】contract system
【合围】(in battle or hunting) surround; encircle
【合心】suit; be to one's liking; be to one's taste; appeal to; be fond of: 这条裙子你～吗? *Is the dress to your liking?* /最合我心的一点是我有机会学习外语。*What really appealed to me was the opportunity of learning a foreign language.*
【合眼】① close one's eyes; sleep: 他昨晚一夜没～。*He didn't get a wink of sleep last night.* ② die; pass away
【合演】appear in the same play or performance; perform together; co-star
【合叶】hinge
【合议庭】【律】collegiate bench (of judges, or of a judge and people's assessors); collegial panel
【合意】suit; be to one's liking (or taste); appeal to sb: 这个你～吗? *Does this suit you?* /这里的宁静氛围正合我意。*The peaceful surroundings here are very much to my liking.*
【合营】jointly operate; jointly owned: 中外～公司 *jointly-run Chinese-foreign company*
【合营企业】joint venture or enterprise
【合影】① take a group photo (or picture): ～留念 *have a group photo taken to mark the occasion* ② group photo (or picture): 毕业班～ *group picture of the graduating class*
【合用】① share: 他们在宿舍～一台电脑。*They share a computer in the dormitory.* ② serve (the purpose); of use: 这根绳子太短,不～。*The rope is too short to be of any use.*
【合于】accord with; tally with; conform to: ～国情 *accord with the conditions of a country*
【合约】contract: 签订～ *sign (or conclude) a contract*
【合葬】(of husband and wife) be buried in the same grave
【合闸】switch on; switch in
【合掌】put the palms together before one (a Buddhist greeting)
【合账】[口] make up accounts; figure out accounts
【合辙】① in rhyme: 快板很～。*Clapper talk is rhythmical.* ② in agreement: 咱们的意见一说就～。*The moment we started talking we found ourselves in complete agreement.*
【合着】[方] (expressing surprised discovery) so: ～你的病是假装的。*So you are pretending to be sick.*
【合著】write in collaboration with; co-author: 我和我的一个朋友～了这本书。*I wrote the book in collaboration with a friend of mine.*
【合资】invest or own jointly; pool capital; enter into partnership
【合资经营】joint venture: ～各方 *parties to a venture*
【合子】(hézǐ)【生】zygote
【合子】(hézi) a kind of fried pie with meat or vegetable filling
【合奏】instrumental ensemble
【合作】cooperate; work together: 分工～ *share out the work and cooperate with each other* /我事先向你保证我非常乐于～。*I pledge you in advance my willing of cooperation.*
【合作化】(a movement to) organize cooperatives: 农业～ *cooperative transformation of agriculture*
【合作经营】jointly operated; manage in cooperation
【合作社】cooperative; co-op: 农村信用～ *rural*

H

credit cooperatives

【合作医疗】cooperative medical service

【合作者】coworker; collaborator; partner: 他是我们在这个项目上的~。*He is our partner in this project.*

何 ① used in specific questions: ~人 *who?* / ~事? *What?* / 为~? *Why (or For what?)* / 有~困难? *Is there any difficulty?* / 欲~往? *Where to?* / ~不? *Why not?* / ~必如此? *Why act this way?* ② (used in rhetorical questions) how: 他学习了好久,~至于一点进步也没有? *He has been studying for a long time; how can he make no progress at all?* ③ (Hé) a surname

【何必】there is no need; why: ~去那么早? *There is no need to go so early.* / ~当真? *Why take it so seriously?*

【何不】why not: ~再试一下? *Why not try again?*

【何曾】(used in rhetorical questions) did ever: 我~说过此话? *When did I ever say that?*

【何尝】(used in rhetorical questions) ever so: 我~没警告过他,只是他听不进去。*Not that I had not warned him, but he just wouldn't listen.*

【何啻】[书] (used in rhetorical questions) can it be any less than...: ~天壤之别 *no less than the difference between heaven and earth*

【何等】① what kind: 你知道他是~人物? *Do you know what kind of person he is?* ② (used in exclamations) what; how: 这是~高超的技术! *What consummate skill!*

【何妨】why not; might as well: 说说~? *Why not speak up?* /你~试试。*You might as well have a try.*

【何故】why; what for; what is the reason for: 我不知道会议~延期。*I don't know why the meeting was postponed.*

【何苦】why bother; why: 你~在这些小事上伤脑筋? *Why bother your head about such trifles?*

【何况】① much less; let alone ② moreover; besides; in addition: 现在去看足球比赛已经太晚了,~,又开始下雪了。*It's too late to go to the football match now; besides, it's beginning to snow.*

【何乐而不为】why not do it; one would be only too glad to do it: 这是一本万利的事,你~呢? *The project cannot fail to bring enormous profit returns; why not go ahead with it?*

【何其】(used in exclamations to express disapproval) what; how: ~荒唐! *How absurd!*

【何去何从】what course to follow: ~,请速定夺! *Please decide quickly what course to follow!*

【何如】[书] ① how about; what about: ~再饮一杯茶? *How about another cup of tea?* ② wouldn't be better: 与其恨,~爱她。*It would be better to love her than to hate her.*

【何首乌】【药】the tuber of multiflower knotweed (*polygonum multiflorum*).

【何谓】[书] what is meant by; what is the meaning of: ~竞争? *What is the meaning of competition?*

【何消】what is the need: ~说,我一定会参加这个会的。*It goes without saying that I'll take part in the meeting.*

【何须】what is the need: ~如此焦虑? *What's the need for all these worries?*

【何许】[书] what place; what kind of: ~人? *What sort of person?*

【何以】[书] ① with what; how: ~见得? *What makes you think so?* ② for what reason; why: 你~要改变主意? *Why do you change your mind?*

【何用】What's the use of...? ~着急? *What's the use of hurrying?*

【何在】[书] where: 原因~? *What is the reason for it?*

【何止】far more than: 老李~是我们的老师。*Lao Li is far more than our teacher.*

【何足挂齿】be not worth mentioning; don't mention it: 区区小事,~。*Such a trifle is not worth mentioning.*

和[1] ① gentle; mild; not strong: 风~日丽 *gentle breeze and bright sun; warm and sunny weather* /心平气~ *even-tempered and good humoured; calm* ② harmonious; on good terms: ~为贵。*Harmony is what matters.* ③ settle a dispute; achieve peace: 讲~ *make peace; settle a dispute* / ~解 *become reconciled* ④【体】draw; tie: 那盘棋~了。*That game of chess ended in a draw.* /中国足球队胜了一局,~了一局,输了五局。*Chinese National Football Team won one match, drew one and lost five.* ⑤ (Hé) a surname

和[2] ① together with: ~衣而卧 *sleep all dressed* ② toward; to; indicating relationship, comparison, etc.: 她~我一样高。*She's the same height as I.* / 你~孩子讲话要通俗些。*When you speak to the child you should use a somewhat popular language.* ③ and: 我~她意见相同。*My opinion and hers are the same.* ④【数】the sum of two or more numbers: 2跟3的~是5。*The sum of 2 and 3 is 5.*

和[3] Japan; Japanese: ~文 *the Japanese language*

see also hè; hú; huó; huò

【和蔼】genial; kindly; affable; amiable: ~的笑容 *an affable smile* /态度~ *be affable in manner*

【和蔼可亲】affable; amiable; genial: 当她不忙于公事的时候是~的。*She is affable enough when she is not preoccupied with business problems.* /她~,我们相处愉快。*She was a most genial person and our stay was a very pleasant one.*

【和畅】(of a wind) gentle and pleasant: 惠风~ *a gentle and pleasant breeze*

【和风】① soft or gentle breeze ②【气】moderate breeze

【和风细雨】like a gentle breeze and light rain — in a gentle and mild way; in a genial or amiable manner: 周总理总是强调要~地对待同志。*Premier Zhou always paid enough attention to treating comrades in a genial manner.*

【和服】kimono

【和好】make one's peace with sb; be at peace with sb; become reconciled; be (become) reconciled with sb: ~如初 *be on good terms again; restore good relations* /翻脸的那对夫妻一年以后又~了。*The estranged couple reconciled after a year.*

【和合】[书] harmonious: ~文化 *culture of harmony*

【和缓】① gentle; mild: ~的风 *a gentle wind* /态度~ *adopt a mild attitude* ② ease up; alleviate; relax; relieve: ~一下气氛 *relieve the tension a little*

【和会】peace conference: 巴黎~ *Paris Peace Conference*

【和解】become reconciled; make compromise with; conciliate: 采取~态度 *adopt a conciliatory attitude* /工会和公司~了。*The labour union closed with the company.*

【和局】drawn game; draw; tie: 这场比赛打成~。*The game ended in a tie.*

【和美】harmonious: ~的家庭 *a harmonious family*

【和睦】harmony; concord; amity: 我的猫和狗相处得十分~。*My cat and dog live in perfect harmony.* /两个部落~相处。*The two tribes lived in concord.*

【和盘托出】reveal everything; hold nothing back: 他很高兴她把自己的秘密向他~。*He was glad it was to him she had revealed her secret.* /愤怒使她~。*Anger moved her to speak out.*

【和平】① peace: 世界~ *world peace* /~仪式 *peace offering* /维护~ *maintain peace* /人人都想生活在一个~的世界。*Everyone wants to live in a world at peace.* ② mild: 药性~。*The medicine is mild.* ③ peaceful; tranquil: 心境~ *peaceful mind; ease of mind*

【和平鸽】dove of peace

【和平攻势】peace offensive

【和平共处】peaceful coexistence

【和平共处五项原则】the Five Principles of Peaceful Coexistence (mutual respect for territorial integrity and sovereignty, mutual non-aggression, non-interference in each other's internal affairs, equality and mutual benefit, and peaceful coexistence)

【和平过渡】peaceful transition

【和平谈判】peace negotiation

【和平统一,一国两制】peaceful reunification and one country, two systems (a policy of the Chinese government on the Taiwan question)

【和平演变】peaceful evolution (from socialism back to capitalism)

【和平主义】pacifism: ~者 *pacifist*

【和棋】a draw in chess or other board games

【和气】① harmonious; gentle; amiable; friendly: 他们彼此很~。*They are very friendly with each other.* ② harmony; friendship: 别因为这点儿小事伤了~。*Don't let this unpleasantness hurt our friendship.*

【和气生财】amiability begets riches (a motto for businessmen): 买卖买卖,~。*Do business with a smile, and you will make a pile.*

【和善】kind and gentle; friendly; genial: 心地~ *kind-hearted*

【和尚】(in Buddhism) a general term for Buddhist monks

【和声】① soft voice; mild tone: 说话~细语 *speak in a soft voice* ②【音】harmony

【和事佬】peacemaker (esp. one who is more concerned with stopping the bickering than settling the issue)

【和谈】peace talks; peace negotiation

【和头】both ends of a coffin; front end of a coffin

【和婉】(of speech) mild and roundabout; tactful

【和谐】harmonious: ~的气氛 *harmonious atmosphere* /颜色搭配得很~。*The colours match quite well.*

【和煦】sunny; pleasantly warm; genial: 春风~。*The spring breeze is warm and pleasant.*

【和颜悦色】complaisantly; amiably; have a kind face; be kindly and affable: 她总是面带微笑,~且懂礼貌。*She is always smiling, affable and polite.*

【和衣】(sleep) with one's clothes on: ~而卧 *to sleep with one's clothes on*

【和议】peace talks; peace negotiation

【和易】unassuming; amiable; approachable: ~近人 *amiable and easy of approach*

【和约】peace treaty: 缔结~ *conclude a peace treaty*

【和悦】kindly; amiable

【和衷共济】pull together for a common cause; cooperate harmoniously; work together with one accord (in time of difficulty): 双方应该~,共度难关。*Both parties shall work together with one accord to get through the hard times.*

劾

[书] expose one's misdeeds or crimes: 弹~ *impeach*

河

① a general term for water routes: 运~ *cannel* /淮~ *the Huaihe River* /密西西比~ *the Mississippi River* /泰晤士~ *the River Thames* /~附近有一所房子。*There is a house near the river.* ② Milky Way system: ~外星系 *extragalactic nebula*

【河岸】river bank

【河北梆子】Hebei clapper opera

【河蚌】freshwater mussel; clam

【河边】bank; riverside: 沿~散步 *go for a walk along the riverside*

【河滨】riverside

【河槽】riverbed

【河川】rivers and creeks

【河床】riverbed: 很久没下雨,~已经干涸。*It's so long since it rained that the riverbed is dry.*

【河道】river course

【河堤】river embankment

【河段】section of a river; reach

【河防】① flood prevention work done on rivers, especially the Huanghe River ② military defence on the Huanghe River: ~部队 *defending troops on the Huanghe River*
【河肥】river silt used as manure
【河粉】rice noodles
【河港】river port
【河工】① river conservancy works (esp. for the Huanghe River) ② river conservancy workers
【河沟】brook; stream
【河谷】river valley
【河口】river month; stream outlet
【河口湾】firth; estuary
【河流】rivers: 多国~ *multinational river*
【河马】hippopotamus; river horse
【河内】Hanoi, capital of Vietnam
【河泥】river silt; river mud
【河曲】bend (of a river); meander
【河渠】rivers and canals; waterways
【河山】rivers and mountains; land; territory: 大好~ *beautiful rivers and mountains*; *great territory* /锦绣~ *land of enchanting beauty*
【河水】river water
【河滩】river beach
【河滩地】flood land
【河塘】river embankment
【河套】① the bend of a river ② the Great Bend of the Huanghe River
【河豚】blowfish; globefish; puffer: ~中毒 *fuguism*
【河湾】ancon; cove; river band
【河网】a network of waterways: ~平原 *river plain*
【河系】river system
【河蟹】freshwater crab
【河沿】river bank; riverside
【河鱼】river fish; freshwater fish
【河运】river transport

饸
【饸饹】a kind of noodles, usually made from buckwheat or sorghum flour

阂 cut off from; not in communication with: 隔~ *estrangement*; *misunderstanding*

盍 [书] why not: ~往观之? *Why not go and have a look at it?*

荷[1] 【植】lotus

荷[2] the Netherlands; Holland
see also hè
【荷包】① small bag; pouch ② pocket (in a garment)
【荷包蛋】poached or fried eggs
【荷尔蒙】【生理】hormone
【荷花】【植】lotus
【荷兰】Holland; the Netherlands
【荷兰人】Dutchman; the Dutch
【荷兰水】[方] aerated water; soda water
【荷兰语】Dutch (language)
【荷兰猪】guinea pig; cavy
【荷马】Homer (9th century BC), ancient Greek poet, and author of the epics *Iliad* and *Odyssey*
【荷塘】lotus pond
【荷叶】lotus leaf: ~饼 *thin pancake*
【荷叶边】(of woman's dress, etc.) flounce; furbelow; falbala

核[1] ① pit; stone; kernel: 枣~ *stone of a date* ② nucleus, sth that resembles a pit: 菌~ *sclerotium* /细胞~ *cell nucleus* ③ referring to atomic nucleus, nuclear energy, nuclear weapons, etc.: ~试验 *nuclear test* / ~战争 *nuclear war*

核[2] ① check or examine closely: ~算 *examine and calculate*; *assess* ② [书] faithful; true; real: 其文直, 其事~。*His writings are straightforward and true to the facts.*
see also hú
【核安全】nuclear security, nuclear safety: ~标准 *nuclear safety standard*
【核按钮】nuclear button (for nuclear war)
【核保护伞】nuclear umbrella
【核爆炸】nuclear explosion
【核裁军】nuclear disarmament
【核查】examine and verify; check: 我翻字典~了这个词的拼写。*I checked the spelling in the dictionary.*
【核尘】nuclear dust
【核磁共振】nuclear magnetic resonance
【核大国】nuclear power
【核蛋白】【生化】nucleoprotein
【核弹】nuclear bomb
【核弹头】nuclear warhead
【核当量】nuclear equivalent
【核电厂】nuclear power plant
【核电站】nuclear power station; nuclear plant
【核定】check; ratify; appraise and decide: ~资本 *approved capital*
【核动力】nuclear power: ~工业 *nuclear power industry*
【核对】check; verify: ~账目 *check the accounts* / ~笔迹 *identify sb's handwriting* /我们早已~过了。*We've already had a check.*
【核反应】nuclear reaction
【核反应堆】nuclear reactor
【核废料】nuclear waste
【核风险】nuclear risk
【核辐射】nuclear radiation
【核感应】nuclear induction
【核工程】nuclear engineering
【核工业】nuclear industry
【核共振】nuclear resonance
【核火箭】nuclear rocket
【核计】assess; calculate: ~成本 *assess the cost*
【核减】trim (a budget, etc.) and make cuts
【核聚变】nuclear fusion
【核军备竞赛】nuclear arms race
【核扩散】nuclear proliferation
【核理论】nuclear theory

【核力】nuclear force
【核裂变】nuclear fission
【核垄断】nuclear monopoly
【核能】nuclear energy
【核能源】nuclear power source
【核潜艇】nuclear-powered submarine
【核燃料】nuclear fuel
【核审】examine and verify
【核实】confirm; verify; check: ~数字 *verify the figures* /请他帮我们~一下这条消息。*Ask him to check the information out for us.*
【核试验】nuclear test: 地下~ *underground nuclear test*
【核衰变】nuclear decay
【核酸】【生化】nuclein; nucleic acid
【核算】calculate; adjust accounts: 成本~ *cost accounting*
【核算单位】accounting unit: 独立~ *independent accounting unit*
【核糖】【生化】ribose
【核桃】walnut: ~仁 *walnut meat* / ~油 *walnut oil*
【核威慑】nuclear deterrent: ~力量 *nuclear deterrent power*
【核威胁】nuclear threat
【核武器】nuclear weapon: ~试验 *nuclear weapons test*
【核销】cancel after verification
【核心】nucleus; core; kernel; heart: 起~作用 *play key roles* /家庭是社会的~。*The family is the nucleus of the community.* /现在我们进入问题的~部分。*Now we are getting to the heart of the matter.*
【核心人物】key person; key figure: 他是这支队的~。*He is a key person of the team.*
【核医学】nuclear medicine
【核战争】nuclear war
【核准】examine and approve
【核子】nucleon: 成对~ *paired nucleon* /裸~ *bare nucleon* / ~能 *atomic energy*
【核子学】nucleonics

龁 [书] bite

盒 ① box; case; packet: 一~薄荷 *a packet of mint* / 铅笔~ *pencil case*; *pencil-box* ② box-shaped fireworks
【盒带】cassette tape
【盒饭】box lunch
【盒式磁带】cartridge tape; cassette
【盒式胶卷】cassette film
【盒子】① box; case: 桌子上有些~。*There are some boxes on the table.* ② box-shaped fireworks
【盒子枪】[方] Mauser pistol

涸 [书] dry; dry up
【涸泽而渔】drain the pond to get all the fish; kill the goose that lays the golden eggs

颌 [书] jaw: 上下~ *the upper and lower jaw*

貉 【动】raccoon dog
see also háo

阖 [书] ① entire; whole: ~家 *the whole family* ② shut; close: ~户 *close the door*
【阖府】your whole family
【阖家】whole family: ~团圆 *reunion of all family members*
【阖眼】sleep; close one's eyes

翮 ① shaft of a feather; quill ② [书] wing (of a bird): 振~高飞 *flap the wings and soar high into the sky*

hè

吓 ① threaten: 威~ *threaten* ② to show one's disapproval: ~,怎么能够这样? *Tut-tut, how could it be like this?*
see also xià

和 ① join in the singing: 一唱百~。*When one starts singing, all the others join in.* ② compose a poem in reply: ~诗 *write a poem in reply (to one sent by a friend, etc., using the same rhyme sequence)*
see also hé; hú; huó; huò

贺 ① congratulate; celebrate: 电~ *cable a message of congratulations* ② (Hè) a surname
【贺匾】congratulatory plaque
【贺词】speech (or message) of congratulation; greetings: 新年~ *New Year message*; *New Year greetings*
【贺电】message of congratulation; congratulatory telegram
【贺卡】greeting card: 圣诞~ *Christmas card*
【贺礼】gift; present; congratulatory gift: 他给我寄了一件生日~。*He sent a birthday gift to me.*
【贺联】congratulatory couplet (written on scrolls, etc.)
【贺年】extend New Year greetings; pay a New Year call
【贺年片】greeting card; New Year card
【贺喜】offer congratulations; congratulate sb on a happy occasion: 请代我向他~。*Please convey my congratulations to him.*
【贺信】letter of congratulation
【贺仪】[书] congratulatory gift
【贺幛】congratulatory silk scroll

荷 [书] ① carry on one's shoulder or back: ~枪实弹 *carry a loaded rifle* / ~锄而归 *return home carrying a hoe on one's shoulder* ② [书] bear; take on: 身~重任 *bear heavy responsibilities* ③ burden; responsibility: 肩负重~ *shoulder heavy responsibilities* ④ [书] (usu. used in letter writing) grateful; obliged: 早复为~。*An early reply will be very much appreciated.*
see also hé

【荷载】① carry a load ② load：～分布 *load distribution*

【荷重】weight a building can bear; weight load：～系数 *load factor*

喝 shout loudly：大声～问 *shout a question to sb*

see also hē

【喝彩】acclaim; cheer：我希望你能够来比赛现场为我～。*I hope you are going to come and cheer me on in the competition.*

【喝倒彩】make catcalls; hoot：他的讲话被喝了倒彩，嘘声四起。*His speech was greeted with jeers and catcalls.* / 演员被～轰下了台。*The actors were booed off the stage.*

【喝道】[旧] (of yamen runners, etc.) shout out to pedestrians to make way for an approaching official

【喝令】shout an order

【喝向】shout out a question

赫[1] ① conspicuous; grand：显～ *distinguished and influential*; *illustrious* ② (Hè) a surname

赫[2] 【电】hertz：千～ *kilohertz* / 兆～ *megahertz*

【赫尔辛基】Helsinki, capital of Finland

【赫赫】illustrious; very impressive：～～战功 *illustrious military exploits*; *brilliant military success*/ ～～有名的人物 *an illustrious personage*

【赫然】① impressively：一只猛虎～出现在山坡上。*To our consternation, a fierce tiger suddenly appeared on the mountain slope.* ② terribly (angry)：～震怒 *get into a terrible temper*; *fly into a violent rage*

【赫兹】hertz(Hz); Hertz：～波 *Hertz wave*

褐 [书] ① coarse cloth or clothing ② brown; dark yellow：～色书包 *brown bag*

【褐煤】brown coal; lignite

【褐色】(dark) brown：这头发披散在她身上，好像～的小瀑布，波纹起伏，光彩照人。*The hair fell about her, rippling and shining like a brown waterfall.*

【褐色产品】brown goods (referring to electrical appliances such as TV sets, radios, etc., which used to be painted brown on the outside)

【褐色土】drab soil

鹤 crane：～发童颜 *white hair and ruddy complexion* / ～立鸡群 *like a crane standing among chickens — stand head and shoulders above others*; *be the flower of the flock*

【鹤嘴锄】pick; pickaxe; mattock

壑 gully; big pool：千山万～ *innumerable mountains and valleys*

hēi

黑 ① black：～发 *black hair* ② dark; (of light) dim：天～了。*It's dark.* / 那间屋子太～。*That room is too dim.* ③ secret; shady：～会 *a clandestine meeting* / ～交易 *shady deal* ④ wicked; sinister; malicious：～后台 *sinister backstage boss* ⑤ reactionary ⑥ (Hēi) short for Heilongjiang Province ⑦ (Hēi) a surname

【黑癌病】【植】black knot

【黑矮星】【天】black dwarf

【黑暗】① dark; dim; midnight：～的角落 *a dark corner* / 那是一个～无月的夜。*It was a dark, moonless night.* / 小屋子里又～又冷。*Inside the small room it was dim and cold.* / 彩色胶卷必须在彻底的～中冲洗。*Colour films must be developed in complete darkness.* ② reactionary; dark; seamy：教育史上的～时代 *a dark age in the history of education* / ～面 *the seamy side*; *a dark aspect*

【黑白】① black and white：一幅～画 *a drawing in black and white* ② right and wrong：颠倒～ *confuse right and wrong*; *call black white*; *prove that black is white and white black*

【黑白电视】black-and-white television; monochromatic television：～系统 *black-and-white system*

【黑白显像管】black and white kinescope; monochrome picture tube; black and white television picture tube

【黑白片儿】[方] black-and-white film

【黑白片】black-and-white film：多数旧电影都是～。*Most old films were made in black and white.*

【黑斑】blackspot

【黑板】blackboard：～报 *blackboard newspaper* / ～擦 *eraser*

【黑版】black print

【黑帮】reactionary gang; sinister gang

【黑不溜秋】[方] very black in appearance; swarthy

【黑尘暴】black blizzard

【黑沉沉】very dark：在这个～的夜里，我真担心自己会迷路。*It was a dark night and I was afraid I might get lost.*

【黑稻】black rice

【黑道】① dark road：拿着手电筒，省得走～。*Take a torch, or you will be groping your way in the dark.* ② dark deeds (as of robbers)

【黑灯瞎火】[口] dark; obscure; unlighted：这条路～的，我需要一个手电来照明。*The path is unlit. I need a torch to find my way.*

【黑地】unregistered land

【黑底】black matrix; black base

【黑店】[旧] an inn run by brigands

【黑鲷】black sea bream; black porgy

【黑洞洞】pitch-dark：地下室里～的。*Inside the cellar it was pitch black.*

【黑洞】【天】black hole：～热力学 *black-hole thermodynamics* / ～物理学 *black-hole physics* / ～学说 *theory of a "black hole"*

【黑豆】black soya bean

【黑度】blackness; density

【黑方】black (chess games)

【黑非洲】Black Africa

【黑更半夜】［口］in the dead of night
【黑咕隆咚】very dark; pitch-dark: 这里~的,我什么也看不见。*It's pitch dark here. I can't see a thing.*
【黑管】【音】clarinet
【黑光】black light: ~灯 *black light lamp*
【黑海】the Black Sea
【黑锅】whipping boy; scapegoat: 他们分享了利润,我却来背~。*They enjoy the profits while I have to enjoy my ruined reputation of a scapegoat.*
【黑糊糊】① black; blackened: 他满手油泥,~的。*His hands are dirty with grease.* ② rather dark; dusky: 屋子里~的。*It is rather dark in the room.* ③ indistinctly observable in the distance
【黑户】① unregistered household; unregistered resident ② a shop without a license; an illegal shop
【黑话】bandits' argot; thieves' cant; double-talk; malicious words
【黑货】① smuggled goods; contraband ② sinister stuff; trash
【黑金刚石】carbonado
【黑枯病】bacterial blight
【黑马】a dark horse; dark horse — those who have won a game unexpectedly
【黑麦】rye
【黑面包】black bread; brown bread; rye bread
【黑名单】blacklist: 警方拟定了一份通缉恐怖分子的~。*The police drew up a blacklist of wanted terrorists.*
【黑墨汁】Chinese ink; Indian ink
【黑幕】dark deeds behind the scenes; inside story of a plot; shady deal: 揭穿~ *expose a sinister project; tell the inside story of a plot* / ~重重 *curtains after a black curtain*
【黑木耳】black fungus
【黑漆漆】pitch-dark; dark; dim: 厚厚的窗帘遮住了窗户,屋子里~的。*Thick curtains covered the window — the room was quite dark.*
【黑钱】black money, usually from illegal transactions or tax-evading deals such as gambling: 洗~ *laundry black money*
【黑枪】① illegal guns ② a shot from the back
【黑人】Black people; Black; Negro: ~教育 *Negro education* / ~学科 *black studies* /南非的~人口 *the Black population of South Africa* /歧视~仍是普遍现象。*Discrimination against Blacks is still common.*
【黑色】black (colour)
【黑纱】black crape; black armband: 佩带~ *wear a mourning-band*
【黑舌症】【医】black tongue
【黑社会】criminal syndicate
【黑市】black market: ~汇兑 *black market exchange* / ~价格 *black rate* / ~交易 *off-the-books deal*
【黑手】a vicious person manipulating sb or sth from behind the scenes; evil backstage manipulator
【黑手党】Mafia; Maffia
【黑体】①【物】blackbody: ~辐射 *black-body radiation* / ~轨迹 *blackbody locus* / ~温度 *blackbody temperature* ②【印】boldface: ~字 *boldface type*
【黑铜】【冶】black copper
【黑头】black-face role — the painted-face role in traditional opera
【黑土】black earth; black soil
【黑窝】nest of illegal activities; den: 警察端了他们的~。*The police raided their den.*
【黑瞎子】［方］black bear
【黑匣子】【航】black box
【黑箱】black box
【黑心】black heart; evil mind; diabolical
【黑信】［口］anonymous letter from a hostile pen; poison-pen letter
【黑信号】【电】black signal
【黑猩猩】【动】chimpanzee
【黑熊】black bear
【黑魆魆】pitch dark
【黑压压】a dense or dark mass off: ~的人群 *a dense crowd* /天上~的乌云 *masses of dark clouds in the sky*
【黑眼珠】apple (of one's eyes)
【黑药】black powder
【黑夜】dark night: 在~里不要抄近路。*At dark night avoid shortcuts.*
【黑油油】jet-black; shiny black: ~的头发 *shiny black hair*
【黑黝黝】① shiny black ② dim; dark: 四周~的。*It is dark all around.*
【黑鱼】【动】snakeheaded fish; snakehead
【黑玉】jet
【黑云密布】dark clouds spread over the sky — the coming of a storm
【黑晕】black halo
【黑痣】pigmented naevus; mole
【黑种】the black race
【黑子】①［书］black mole ②【天】sunspot; spot: ~群 *spot group* / ~数 *sunspot number* / ~相对数 *sunspot number* / ~耀斑 *sunspot flare* / ~周 *sunspot cycle*

嘿 ① greeting or to call attention: ~,看电影去吧。*Hey, let's go to the cinema.* ② used to express satisfaction or self-congratulation: ~,咱们的房子真漂亮啊! *Hey! Our apartment is really nice!* ③ used to express surprise: ~,她哭了! *Why, she cried!*
【嘿嘿】［象］(of laughter) ha ha

hén

痕 mark; trace; stain: 水~ *water stains* /泪~ *tear stains* /伤~ *scar; bruise*
【痕迹】mark; trace; track; trail: 墨水~ *an ink mark* /雪地上的~ *tracks in the snow* /有很古老的~ *bear marks of great antiquity* /沙地上响尾蛇爬过的~ *a rattlesnake trail in the sand* /岁月在她脸上留下了~。*Age has left its traces on her face.*

【痕量】【化】trace：～分析 *trace analysis* / ～元素 *trace elements*

hěn

很 very；quite；much：～大 *very large* (*or big*) / ～多 *very much* / ～好 *very good* / ～冷的一天 *a very cold day* / 这块表～新。*The watch is quite new.* / 他这个人好得～。*He's a very good man.* / 她是一个～不错的球员。*She's quite a good player.*

狠 ① ruthless；relentless：凶～ *ferocious and ruthless* ② suppress(one's feelings)；harden (the heart)：他～下心来不被孩子的哭声烦扰。*He hardened the heart not to be disturbed by the cries of his children.* ③ firm；resolute：～抓革命，猛促生产。*Vigorously promote revolution and production.*

【狠毒】vicious；venomous；cruel；malicious；vindictive；spiteful：用心～ *with vicious mind* / 我想喜欢他，可是我无法忘记他过去对我是多么～。*I tried to like him but I couldn't forget how spiteful he'd been to me in the past.*

【狠狠】severely；roundly；relentlessly：～打击 *hit hard*；*deal heavy blows to*

【狠命】[方] use all one's strength；go all out；spare no efforts

【狠心】① harden one's heart；make up one's mind：替她着想，你要下～。*For her own good, you must harden your heart.* ② cruel-hearted；heartless：你真够～的。*You are being so callous.*

hèn

恨 ① hate；resent：怀～在心 *nurse a hatred*；*bear a grudge* / 老板们～乔·希尔。*The bosses hated Joe Hill.* ② regret：遗～ *eternal regret*

【恨不得】have a strong desire to；itch to；be dying；can't wait：她～立刻就去。*She wishes she could go immediately.* / 她～马上就知道发生了什么事。*She is dying to find out what happened!*

【恨人】[方] irritating；being a nuisance：蚊子是～的东西。*The mosquitoes are a nuisance.*

【恨事】a matter for regret；something regrettable

【恨铁不成钢】wish iron could turn into steel at once — set a high demand on somebody in the hope that he will improve：我父亲对我很失望，他是～。*My father is disappointed with me, because I failed to live up to his expectations.*

【恨入骨髓】hate to the marrow (of one's bones)；harbour a bitter hatred for sb：他对法西斯主义～。*He has a profound hatred of fascism.*

【恨之入骨】hate sb to the marrow of one's bones；bitterly hate：这次经历使他对他的老板～。*This experience left him with a deep hatred of his boss.* / 她对他～。*She hates his guts.*

hēng

亨[1] ① go smoothly ② (Hēng) a surname

亨[2] 【电】henry(H)，an inductance unit

【亨利】【电】henry：微～ *microhenry*

【亨通】go smoothly；be prosperous：万事～。*Everything is going smoothly.*

哼 ① snort；groan：他病得很重，却从不～一声。*He is seriously ill, but he never groans.* ② hum；sing casually in a low voice：他一面走一面～着歌。*He was humming a song while walking.*

【哼唱】hum；sing in a low voice：她在～一首流行歌曲。*She was humming a popular song.*

【哼哈二将】a pair of fierce men serving one master or acting in collusion with each other

【哼哼唧唧】mumble：他～说了几句话就走了。*He mumbled a few words and went off.*

【哼唧】murmur；hum；croon：你能不能大点儿声？我不知道你在～什么。*Can you raise your voice? I don't know what you are murmuring about.*

【哼气】[方] utter a sound or word：没有人～。*Not a sound was uttered among those people.*

【哼儿哈儿】[象] hum and haw；hum and ha：你别老是～的，我可是认真的。*Don't just hum and haw. I am serious about it.*

【哼唷】heave ho；yo-heave-ho；yo-ho

héng

恒 ① permanent；lasting：永～ *eternal*；*everlasting* ② perseverance；constancy：持之以～ *persevere in* (*doing*) *sth* ③ constant；common：～言 *common sayings* ④ (Héng) a surname

【恒比】constant proportion

【恒产】immovable property — real estate

【恒磁材料】permanent magnetic material

【恒等】【数】identically equal；identical：～变换 *identical transformation* / ～代换 *identical substitution* / ～定理 *identical theorem* / ～方程 *identical equation* / ～公式 *identical formula* / ～函数 *identity function* / ～式 *identical equation* / ～元素 *identical element* / ～运算 *identity operation* / ～周期 *identity period*

【恒定】constant：～波 *constant wave* / ～场 *constant field* / ～电流 *constant current* / ～电源 *stabilized power source* / ～速度 *constant speed* (*or velocity*) / ～温度 *steady temperature* / ～压力 *constant pressure* / ～振幅 *uniform amplitude* / ～周期 *constant cycle*

【恒定电压】constant voltage：～系统 *constant-voltage system*

【恒风】permanent wind

【恒负载】constant load

【恒河】the Ganges River(in South Asia):~鳄 *gavial* / ~猴 *rhesus monkey* / ~平原 *Gangetic Plain; plain of the Gangs River* / ~三角洲 *Ganges Delta*
【恒劲】persistent strength or power; staying power; stamina
【恒久】constant; enduring; lasting; lifelong; longstanding:他童年时期的经历对他的生活产生了~的影响。*His childhood experiences had an enduring influence on his life.* /她对律师有一种~的厌恶。*She had a lifelong hatred of all lawyers.*
【恒量】【物】constant
【恒流】【电】constant current:~变压器 *constant-current transformer* / ~电动机 *constant-current motor* / ~电路 *constant-current circuit* / ~调节器 *constant-current regulator*
【恒湿】constant humidity
【恒速】constant speed (or velocity):~传动 *constant-speed drive* / ~电动机 *constant-speed motor* / ~控制 *constant-speed control*
【恒温】constant temperature:~车间 *constant temperature workshop* / ~动物 *homeothermal animal* / ~法 *constant temperature method* / ~环境 *isoperibol* / ~设备 *thermostatic equipment*
【恒心】perseverance; constancy of purpose:有~的人 *a person of perseverance* /这跛童靠~学会了游泳。*By perseverance the lame boy learned to swim.*
【恒星】【天】fixed star; star:~导航 *star navigation; stellar guidance* / ~动力学 *stellar dynamics* / ~飞船 *starship* / ~光谱 *stellar spectrum* / ~际 *interstellar* / ~年 *sidereal year* / ~日 *sidereal day* / ~天文学 *stellar astronomy* / ~物理学 *stellar physics* / ~系 *stellar system* / ~小时 *sidereal hour* / ~月 *sidereal month* / ~云 *star cloud*
【恒压】【电】constant voltage:~变压器 *constant-voltage transformer* / ~电源 *constant-voltage source* / ~发电机 *constant-voltage generator* / ~器 *barostat; manostat* / ~调节 *constant potential regulation* / ~装置 *constant-voltage equipment*

姮

【姮娥】[书] goddess in the moon

珩

top gem of a girdle-pendant

【珩床】【机】honing machine
【珩磨】【机】honing:~轮 *honing wheel*

桁

【建】purlin

【桁架】truss:~跨度 *truss span*
【桁梁】longeron; braced girder
【桁条】【建】purlin; stringer

横

① horizontal; transverse:划一~道 *draw a horizontal line* ② (in geography) east-westward or vice versa:~渡太平洋 *cross the Pacific east-westwardly (or vice versa)* ③ from left to right or from right to left ④ at a right angle to the longer side of sth:~剖面 *cross (or transverse) section* /人行~道 *pedestrian crossing; zebra crossing* ⑤ place sth crosswise or horizontally:把扁担~过来 *put the carrying pole in a horizontal position* ⑥ unrestrained; turbulent:蔓草~生 *overgrown with creepers* ⑦ forcibly; without reason:~加阻拦 *willfully obstruct* ⑧horizontal stroke in a Chinese character (一):"王"字是三~一竖。*The character"王" has three horizontal strokes and a vertical one.* ⑨ in any case; anyhow; anyway:~竖我也要去。*I'll go there any way.* ⑩[方] probably; most likely:天都黑了,他~不来了。*It's already dark; he is probably not coming.* *see also* hèng

【横匾】inscribed horizontal board (over the entrance of a public building, institution, historical structure, etc.)
【横标】streamer; banner
【横滨】Yokohama, second largest city and seaport on Honshu Island, Japan
【横陈】lie across:战场上尸体~。*The battlefield was strewn with dead bodies.*
【横冲直撞】dash around madly; barge about; charge about; rampage; push one's way by shoving or bumping; jostle and elbow one's way:我们正谈话时,他~地进来了。*He barged in while we were talking.* /她~地穿过人群。*She elbowed her way through the crowd.* /他跨进屋子,~地来到我面前。*He strode into the room and barged right into me.*
【横穿】cross:~马路 *cross a road*
【横挡】crosspiece (of a table, etc.)
【横倒竖歪】in disorder:房间里的书~。*The books are in disorder in the room.*
【横笛】bamboo flute
【横渡】cross (a river); across:我们~大海过来时风浪很大。*The sea was rough when we came across.*
【横断层】【地】cross fault; transverse fault
【横断面】cross section
【横队】rank; row:排成三列~ *line up three deep*
【横幅】banner; streamer; horizontal scroll of painting or calligraphy
【横杆】【体】crossbar; overarm
【横亘】lie across; span:一座雄伟的大桥~在江上。*A magnificent bridge spans the river.*
【横贯】cross over; traverse:这条铁路~全国。*The railway traverses the country.*
【横过】cross; across:那位老人小心地~马路。*The old man walked across the road carefully.*
【横加】willfully; flagrantly; forcibly:对事实~歪曲 *distort the facts willfully* / ~指责 *make unfounded charges; hurl abuses; blame unscrupulously*
【横截面】cross-section; transverse section
【横空】across the sky:~出世 *sudden emergence of a great man* /彩虹~。*A rainbow arched across the sky.*
【横跨】stretch over or across; span:~亚欧大陆 *stretch over the Eurasian land mass*

【横梁】①【建】crossbeam; cross girder ② cross member

【横流】①(of tears) gush; stream: 他涕泪~。*Tears bathed his cheeks.* ②(of water) flow in all directions

【横眉】frown in anger; scowl

【横眉怒目】with frowning brows and angry eyes; darting fierce looks of hate: 他对敌人~。*He dared fierce looks at the enemies.* / 这位老先生只是站在那里对那个扒手~,一句话也没有说。*The old gentleman just stood there glaring at the pickpocket and did not say a word.*

【横眉竖眼】glare in anger; look daggers at; give sb a black look; scowl: 他生气地坐在那里,对我~。*He sat there angrily, looking daggers at me.* /我不知道我怎么惹着她了,我走进屋子的时候她对我~。*I don't know what I've done to upset her, but she gave me a dirty look when I walked into the room.*

【横楣】crossbeam (of a door or window frame)

【横批】a horizontal wall inscription; a horizontal hanging scroll (usually hung over a door and flanked by two vertical scrolls forming a couplet)

【横剖面】cross (or transverse) section

【横七竖八】at sixes and sevens; in utter disorder; in disorder; in a mess; in a clutter: 桌子上~地堆满了书和报纸。*The desk is cluttered up with books and papers.*

【横切】crosscut

【横肉】ugly, ferocious facial muscles: 一脸~ *look ugly and ferocious*

【横扫】① sweep across or over; sweep way: ~前进路上的一切障碍 *sweep all obstacles from one's path* ② glance quickly: 他~一眼,就看穿了他的阴谋。*He saw through his tricks at a glance.*

【横生】① grow wildly: 杂草~ *be overgrown with creepers and weeds* ② happen unexpectedly: ~是非。*A dispute unexpectedly broke out.* ③ be overflowing with; be full of: 妙趣~ *be full of wit*

【横生枝节】raise unexpected difficulties; deliberately complicate a problem: 对方在合作过程中~。*The other side deliberately complicated the issue in the cooperation.*

【横是】[方] probably; most likely: 他~不会来了。*He's not likely to come.* /他~还不到 20 岁。*I suppose him to be not yet twenty.*

【横竖】[口] in any case; anyway: ~我今天必须完成这项工作。*Anyway I must finish this work today.*

【横顺】[方] in any case; anyway: 虽然没人邀请,他~要去参加那个聚会。*Though there is no invitation, he's going to take part in that party anyway.*

【横说竖说】say again and again (in persuasion or explanation): 我~,他却置若罔闻。*My repeated talking to him just fell on deaf ears.*

【横躺竖卧】(of a number of people) lie here and there; lie in disorder: 他们在宽大的屋子里~。*They were lying in disorder in the spacious room.*

【横挑鼻子竖挑眼】[口] find fault in a petty manner; nit-pick; pick holes in; knock: 他总是对他的新女朋友~。*He is always finding fault with her new girlfriend.*

【横向】① crosswise; lateral; horizontal: ~交流 *lateral exchange* / ~协作 *cross cooperation* / ~联合 *lateral integration* /发展沿海开放城市和内地的~经济联合是很必要的。*It's necessary to expand the horizontal economic collaboration of the open coastal cities with the interior areas.* ② from east to west or vice versa: 这条河是~的。*The river goes from east to west.*

【横心】steel one's heart; resolve; be determined: 横下一条心 *resolve to do sth in desperation*

【横行】run amok; be on a rampage: ~一时 *run wild for a time* /暴徒在街道上~。*The rioters were running amok in the streets.*

【横行霸道】act like a tyrant; play the bully; ride roughshod (over); trample on; domineer: 这个地主在乡里~,为所欲为。*The landlord played the despot and did whatever he wished.*

【横行一时】run wild for a time

【横许】[方] probably; most likely: 我~能赶上那趟火车。*Probably I may catch that train.*

【横溢】①(of a river) overflow; be in flood: 河水~,淹没了两岸。*The river overflowed the banks.* ②(of talent, enthusiasm, etc.) brimming; overflowing; abundant: 才气~ *brimming with talent* /她心中喜悦~。*She was full to the brim with joy.*

【横越】fly across (from east to west or vice versa)

【横征暴敛】extort excessive taxes and levies; levy exorbitant taxes

【横直】[方] in any case; anyway

【横坐标】【数】abscissa

衡 ① the graduated arm of a steelyard ② weighing apparatus ③ weigh; measure; judge ④ [书] levelled; balanced: 平~ *balance* ⑤ (Héng) a surname

【衡量】① measure; judge: ~事非 *measure right and wrong* ② weigh; consider: ~自己的话 *weigh one's words* /他~了两种选择而决定留下来。*He weighed the alternatives and decided to stay.*

【衡量得失】weigh up the gains and losses: 我已经衡量了接受这个工作的得失。*I've been weighing up all the gains and losses of accepting the job.*

【衡平】weigh and consider in order to uphold justice

【衡平权】【律】equitable interest

【衡器】weigher; weighing apparatus

【衡情度理】consider the circumstances and judge by common sense — all things considered

【衡视】look horizontally

【衡算】accounting

【衡消】balance out: ~法 *null method*; *zero method*

【衡重杆】balanced weight lever

hèng

横 ①harsh and unreasonable; perverse: 强～ *brutal and unreasonable* ②unexpected: ～遭此难 *suffer an unexpected misfortune*
see also héng

【横暴】despotic; tyrannical; high-handed; perverse and violent

【横财】ill-gotten wealth or gains: 发～ *get rich by foul means; get a windfall*

【横祸】unexpected disaster

【横蛮】arbitrary; brute; rude and unreasonable: 这个小女孩～不讲理。*This little girl is rather rude and unreasonable.*

【横逆】a perverse and unreasonable manner; an outrageous manner: 待我以～ *treat me in an outrageous manner*

【横事】an untoward accident

【横死】die a violent death; be killed in an accident

【横恣】perverse and wanton

hōng

轰 ①[象] bang; boom: ～的一声就起火了。*The fire broke out with a bang.* ② attack with artillery or bombs; roar; rumble; explode: 抽水站～～响着开始工作了。*The pumping station roared into action.* /载货列车～～驶过。*The freight train rumbled past.* ③ drive; shoo away; hoot out: 把猫～出去。*Drive away the cat.*

【轰倒】knock down by bombardment

【轰动】stir; cause a sensation: ～文坛的作品 *a literary sensation* /这本书引起相当一阵～。*The book caused quite a stir.*

【轰动一时】create a furore; make a great stir; cause a great sensation: 该剧在纽约曾～。*The play was quite a hit in New York.* /他的垮台是当时～的大事件。*His downfall was a great sensation of the day.*

【轰赶】shoo away; drive off; hoot away: ～苍蝇 *whisk the flies off* /司机按喇叭～路上的羊。*The driver hooted at the sheep in the rood.*

【轰轰】[象] rumble; bomb; buzz: 火车～地响。*The train thundered along.*

【轰轰烈烈】on a grand and spectacular scale; vigorous; dynamic: ～的场面 *vigorous situation* /工人们展开了～的劳动竞赛。*The workers have started a vigorous labour emulation campaign.*

【轰击】① shell; bombard: ～敌人据点 *shell the enemy's stronghold* ②【物】bombard: 中子～ *neutron bombardment*

【轰隆】[象] rumble; roll: 鼓声～震天。*The drums rolled.*

【轰鸣】roar; thunder: 火车～着驶过。*The train roared past.* /我们驶出了市中心,但人来车往的声音仍在耳边～。*We drove away from the city centre, the roar of the traffic still dinning in my ears.*

【轰然】with a loud crash or bang; with big noise: 墙～倒塌。*A wall crashed to the ground.*

【轰响】thunder; roar: 大炮～。*The cannons roared.*

【轰炸】attack with bombs; bomb: 定点～ *pinpoint bombing* /远程～ *a long-range bombardment* /空军～了两个城镇。*The airforce bombed two towns.* /我们的飞机执行了一次～敌方目标的任务。*Our planes carried out a bombing raid on enemy targets.*

【轰炸机】【航】bombardment aircraft; bomber: 战斗～ *fighter-bomber* /喷气式～ *jet bomber* /无人驾驶～ *unmanned bomber; robot bomber* /重型～ *large bomber; heavy bomber*

哄 ①[象] roars of laughter; (of many people) utter sounds simultaneously ② hubbub; din
see also hǒng; hòng

【哄传】(of rumours) circulate widely: 这个消息不久就～开了。*It was not long before the news was widely circulated.*

【哄闹】(of a crowd of people) make a lot of noise; hubbub: 一群孩子在操场上～。*A crowd of children were making a hubbub on the playground.*

【哄抢】①(of a crowd of people) make a mad rush for; panic-buying: ② scramble for (public property, goods, etc.): ～国家物质 *open looting of state-owned goods and materials*

【哄然】boisterous; uproarious: ～大笑 *burst into uproarious laughter*

【哄抬】force up; bid up; drive up(prices): ～物价 *force up prices*

【哄堂大笑】set the room in a roar; set the whole table laughing; the whole room rocking with laughter: 观众～。*The audience exploded in laughter.*

【哄笑】(of a crowd of people) burst into laugher; roar into laughter

訇 loud noise: ～然 *with a loud crash*

烘 ① dry or warm by the fire: 衣服湿了,～一～。*The coat is wet; dry it over the fire.* ② use one colour in contrast with another colour, or use one thing in contrast with another, to make the latter stand out

【烘焙】cure (tea or tobacco leaves)

【烘干】① dry over fire or heat: 她在火边～手。*She dried her hands at the fire.* ②【化】stoving

【烘干机】drying apparatus; drying machine

【烘缸】dryer

【烘烤】toast; bake: 把面包～得焦黄 *toast the bread very dark* /在壁炉边把脚～暖和 *toast one's feet at the fireplace*

【烘篮】a bamboo basketwork brazier for keeping warm

【烘笼】① a basketwork frame propped over an oven or a brazier for drying clothes ②[方] a hand-held basketwork brazier

【烘托】①(in Chinese painting) add shading around an object to make it stand out ② set off by contrast; throw into sharp relief: 绿叶~红花。*The green leaves set off the red flowers.*

【烘箱】oven

【烘云托月】paint clouds to set off the moon; provide a foil for a character or incident in a literary work: ~的艺术效果 *the artistic effect of prominence through contrast*

薨 die; pass away (of feudal lords or high officials)

hóng

弘 ① great; grand; magnificent ② enlarge; expand: 恢~ *broad; magnanimous* ③ (Hóng) a surname

【弘大】grand

【弘扬】carry forward; develop; enhance: ~五四精神 *carry forward the spirit of the May 4th Movement*

红 ① red: ~气球 *red balloon* / 脸~ *red in the face* ② red cloth, etc. used on a happy event or occasion: 挂~ *hang up red festoons (or bunting)* ③ symbol of success or smoothness: 他在国内是个很走~的歌星。*He is a very popular singer in the country.* ④ revolutionary; possessing sharp consciousness: ~军 *the Red Army* / ~色政权 *the red political power* / 又~又专 *both socialist-minded and professionally proficient* ⑤ bonus; dividend: 分~ *draw (or receive) dividends; share profits*

【红案】red (chopping) board — cooking that deals with dishes, both meat and vegetable

【红白喜事】weddings and funerals

【红榜】honour roll (or board)

【红包】red envelope or paper bag containing money as a gift, tip or bonus: 送~ *hand sb a red envelope containing money*

【红宝石】ruby: ~戒指 *ruby ring*

【红宝石婚】ruby wedding anniversary — 40th wedding anniversary

【红茶】black tea

【红场】Red Square (in Moscow)

【红潮】① blush; flush: 人家一夸他,他就脸泛~。*He always blushes when praised.* ② menses; menstruation ③ red tide; red water

【红尘】human society; the world of mortals; vanity fair

【红丹】red lead; minium

【红丹漆】red lead paint

【红蛋】eggs dyed red on the happy occasion of the birth of a child and distributed as gifts to friends and relatives

【红得发紫】(of a person) extremely popular; (of an official) be at the height of one's power and influence: 那个女演员二十多岁时~,如今却默默无闻。*The actress reached the height of her popularity in the twenties, but has now been all but forgotten.*

【红灯】red light: ~亮时不可过马路。*Don't cross the street when the red light is on.*

【红灯区】red-light district

【红定】betrothal gifts to the bride's family by the bridegroom

【红豆】① red bean shrub (*Abrus precatorius*); Indian licorice; paternoster pea ② lovesickness seeds; love tokens

【红粉】rouge and powder used by women; cosmetics: ~佳人 *beautiful young woman* / ~知己 *a woman bosom friend*

【红汞】【药】mercurochrome

【红光满面】glowing with health; in the pink: 他度假归来看起来~。*He looked in the pink after his holiday.*

【红果】[方] the fruit of large Chinese hawthorn; haw

【红海】Red Sea

【红鹤】【动】ibis

【红红绿绿】in gay colours; colourful: 过年时孩子们都穿得~的。*The children were dressed in gay colours on New Year's day.*

【红狐】【动】red fox

【红花】①【药】false saffron; safflower (*Carthamus tinctorius*): 藏~ *saffron (Crocus sativus)* / ~油 *safflower oil* ②red flower

【红花草】【药】Chinese milk vetch (*Astragalus sinicus*)

【红火】flourishing; prosperous: 他很忙,生意~。*He is busy and prosperous.* /石榴花越开越~。*The pomegranate flowers are more and more flourishing.*

【红极一时】enjoy great popularity (or well-known) for a period of time

【红角】an extreme popular actor or actress

【红军】① the Red Army; the Chinese workers' and Peasants' Red Army (1928—1937) ② Soviet Union army before 1946

【红口白舌】①[方] talk rubbish; gossip randomly ② misunderstanding or dispute arising from conversation

【红利】bonus; extra dividend

【红脸】① blush: 我和陌生人说话时会~。*I will blush when speaking to strangers.* ② flush with anger; get angry: 他俩从来没有~过。*There has never been a cross word between the two of them.* ③ red face, face painting in Beijing Opera, etc., traditionally for the heroic or the honest

【红领巾】① red scarf (worn by the young pioneers): 这所学校要求低年级的学生都佩戴~。*It is required that the students in low grades wear red scarves in this preliminary school.* ② Young Pioneer: 一群~正在帮助老人打扫卫生。*A group of young pioneers are helping the old man clean his house.*

【红领章】red collar tab（as formerly on PLA uniforms）

【红柳】【植】Chinese tamarisk；rose willow

【红楼梦】*A Dream of Red Mansions*（*or The Story of the Stone*），novel published in the early Qing Dynasty by Cao Xueqin（曹雪芹）

【红绿灯】traffic lights；traffic signals

【红玛瑙】red agate；sardonyx

【红帽子】① red cap（anyone branded a Communist or a Communist sympathizer was said to be wearing a red cap before Liberation）② railway porter；redcap

【红媒】matchmaker；go-between

【红煤】［方］anthracite

【红霉素】【药】erythromycin

【红焖】stew in soy sauce：～鸡块 *stewed chicken*

【红米】red rice

【红棉】silk cotton

【红木】rosewood；mahogany：～家具 *rosewood*（*or mahogany*）*furniture*

【红男绿女】gaily dressed young men and women

【红娘】① the maid in the play *the Western Chamber*，who helps bring about the union of the lovers ② go-between；warm-hearted matchmaker

【红牌】【体】red card：出示～ *show the red card*

【红扑扑】ruddy；flushed

【红旗】red flag（or banner）（often as a symbol of revolution or of an advanced unit）：五星～ *Five-Star Red Flag*

【红旗单位】red-banner unit；advanced unit

【红旗手】red banner bearer；model worker

【红青】dark purple

【红壤】red soil（or earth）

【红人】popular figure；people being favoured by others；white-headed；fair-haired boy

【红润】ruddy；rosy：～的脸颊 *ruddy cheeks*

【红色】① red：枫叶在秋天变成～。*Maple leaves turn red in the autumn.* ② revolutionary；red

【红杉】① Chinese larch ② redwood

【红伤】gun or knife wound

【红烧】braise in soy sauce：～肉 *pork braised in brown sauce*；*red-cooked pork*

【红苕】［方］sweet potato

【红参】red ginseng

【红十字会】the Red Cross

【红事】red affair-marriage；wedding

【红薯】sweet potato

【红树】【林】mangrove

【红松】Korean pine

【红糖】brown sugar

【红桃】heart（in cards）

【红彤彤】bright red；glowing：～的火苗 *flames glowing red*

【红头文件】official document：这是刚发布的～。*This is the newly issued official document.*

【红外】infrared ray；infrared：～报警装置 *infrared-warning device* / ～成像 *infrared imaging* / ～系统 *infrared imaging system* / ～导航 *infrared navigation* / ～电视 *infrared television* / ～发射 *infrared emission* / ～辐射 *infrared radiation* / ～跟踪 *infrared tracking* / ～光谱 *infrared spectrum* / ～激光 *infrared laser* / ～胶卷 *infrared photograph film* / ～雷达 *infrared radar* / ～瞄准镜 *sniperscope* / ～目标 *infrared target* / ～扫描 *infrared scanning* / ～色散 *infrared dispersion* / ～摄影 *infrared photography* / ～天文学 *infrared astronomy* / ～天线 *infrared antenna* / ～通信 *infrared communication* / ～相片 *infrared photo* / ～遥感 *infrared remote sensing* / ～预警系统 *infrared early-warning system* / ～照相 *infrared photography* / ～制导 *infrared guidance*

【红外线】【物】infrared；infrared ray：～辐射 *infrared radiation* / ～扫描装置 *infrared scanner* / ～探测器 *infrared detector* / ～照相 *infrared photography* / ～电子学 *infranics*

【红细胞】red blood cell；red corpuscle；erythrocyte

【红线】main thread；main line

【红小豆】red bean

【红心】red heart — a heart loyal to the cause of revolution

【红星】red star（a symbol of the proletarian revolution）

【红学】studies of the Hongloumeng（《红楼梦》）；Hongloumeng scholarship

【红颜】beautiful woman；pretty appearance

【红颜薄命】beautiful women are ill-fated：自古～。*It seems a rule that beautiful women have usually suffered ill fates since ancient time.*

【红眼】① be infuriated or furious ②［方］be jealous；be envious：一见别人比她过得好，她就～。*She is always jealous of those who are better off than she is.*

【红眼病】① acute conjunctivitis ② jealousy；envy

【红艳艳】bright red

【红样】corrected proofs

【红药水】mercurochrome

【红叶】red autumnal leaves（of the maple，etc.）

【红衣主教】cardinal

【红缨枪】red-tasselled spear

【红鱼】red snapper

【红云】① red cloud ② blush；flush：两朵～飞上她的脸颊。*Two spots of colour brightened her cheeks.*

【红运】good luck

【红晕】blush；flush

【红糟】red wine dregs（used as seasoning）

【红枣】red date

【红藻】red alga

【红涨】（of one's face）be swelled with blood

【红痣】port-wine stain

【红肿】red and swollen：～的手指 *swollen finger*

【红装】［书］① gay feminine attire ② young woman

宏 ① huge；great；grand：气量宽～ *broadminded*；*magnanimous* /规模～大 *grand in scale* ②（Hóng）a surname

H

【宏博】extensive; wide: ~的知识 *extensive knowledge*

【宏才大略】a great talent and a big plan; be capable of doing great things

【宏大】spacious; vast; great; grand; grandiose: 规模~的建筑物 *buildings on a grand scale* /那的确是我所见到的最~的客厅。*It is indeed the most magnificent living-room I have ever seen.*

【宏观】①【物】macroscopic: ~概念 *macroscopic concept* / ~观察 *macroscopic observation* ② macro-: 政府的~协调功能 *the government's function of macro-coordination* / ~管理 *macro-control* / ~结构 *macrostructure* / ~决策 *overall policy decision* / ~控制 *macro control* / ~世界 *macrocosm* / ~语言学 *macrolinguistics* / ~预测 *macro-forecast* / ~指导 *macro-direction* / ~组织 *macrostructure*

【宏观经济】macro-economy: ~调节 *macroeconomic control* / ~效益 *macroeconomic results* (*or efficiency*) / ~学 *macro-economics*; *macroeconomics* / ~政策 *macro economic policy*

【宏阔】vast; broad

【宏朗】loud and clear; sonorous

【宏论】informed opinion; intelligent view: 大发~ *argue at great length*

【宏图】great plan; grand prospect: 立大志,展~ *make a great plan with noble ambition*

【宏伟】grand; magnificent: ~的宫殿 *a magnificent palace* /瀑布的~景象真是好看极了。*The magnificent scene of the waterfall is a perfect delight to the eye.*

【宏伟目标】ambitious goal; magnificent aim: 他立下了提前完成项目的~。*He set an ambitious goal to complete the project ahead of schedule.*

【宏伟事业】magnificent cause

【宏业】a great achievement

【宏愿】great aspirations; noble ambition: 他有从政的~。*He has great aspirations to a career in politics.*

【宏旨】main theme; main idea of an article: 无关~ *be irrelevant to the main idea* /时间花在无关~的小事情上 *waste time on insignificant points*

【宏壮】magnificent; great and solid

泓 [书]① (of water) deep ② [量]used in literature as a measure word: 一~清泉 *a clear spring* /一~秋水 *an expanse of limpid water in autumn*

荭

【荭草】prince's feather (*Polygonum orientale*); prince's plume

虹 rainbow

【虹彩】【气】iridescence: ~云 *iridescent cloud*

【虹膜】【生理】iris

【虹膜炎】【医】iritis

【虹吸管】siphon

【虹吸现象】siphonage

【虹鳟】【动】rainbow trout

洪 ① big; vast ② flood: 山~ *mountain torrents* /溢~道 (*water conservancy*) *spillway* ③ (Hóng) a surname

【洪波】big waves

【洪大】loud: ~的回声 *resounding echoes*

【洪都拉斯】Honduras: ~人 *Honduran*

【洪恩】great kindness; great favour

【洪泛区】floodplain; flooded area

【洪峰】flood peak: ~流量 *peak flood*; *peak discharge*

【洪福】great blessing: ~齐天 *limitless blessing*

【洪荒】chaotic state — primeval times: ~时代 *primeval ages*; *remote antiquity*

【洪亮】loud and clear; sonorous: 嗓音~ *a sonorous voice*

【洪量】① magnanimity; generosity ② great capacity for liquor

【洪流】mighty torrent; powerful current: 时代的~ *the powerful current of the times* /救生艇顺着~而下。*The mighty torrent carried the lifeboat far downstream.*

【洪炉】great furnace: 在革命的~里锻炼成长 *be tempered in the mighty furnace of revolution*

【洪脉】【中医】pulse beating like waves; full pulse

【洪水】flood; flood water: ~季节 *flood season* / ~位 *flood stage* / ~总量 *flood volume*

【洪水猛兽】fierce floods and savage beasts — great scourges

【洪灾】a big flood; inundation

【洪钟】large bell: 声若~ *have a stentorian voice*; *have a sonorous voice*

鸿 ① swan; wild goose ② [书] letters ③ grand; great ④ (Hóng) a surname

【鸿博】erudite; learned: ~之士 *a man of learning*; *an erudite person*

【鸿沟】wild gap; chasm; gulf: 不可逾越的~ *unbridgeable gulf* /期望和现实之间的~ *a gap between expectation and realities*

【鸿鹄】① swan ② a person of noble aspirations; a person with lofty ideals

【鸿鹄之志】lofty ambition; high aspirations

【鸿基】foundation for a great undertaking

【鸿毛】a goose feather — something very light or insignificant: 轻如~ *as light as a goose feather*

【鸿门宴】Hongmen feast — a meeting contrived as a trap

【鸿儒】an erudite person; a learned scholar

【鸿雁】① swan goose ② [书] letter

【鸿运】good luck

hǒng

哄 ① cheat or fool by telling lies; humbug; kid: 你不要~我。*Don't kid me.* ② keep sb in good humour through words or performance: 她很会~小孩儿。*She knows how to keep children in good humour*; *she has a way with children.*

see also hōng; hòng
【哄逗】keep (especially a child) in good humour; coax
【哄弄】[方] cheat; humbug; hoodwink
【哄骗】cheat humbug; hoodwink: 她有一套假话～人。*She has a string of words to hoodwink people.*
【哄劝】coax
【哄人】humor; make a fool of sb

hòng

讧 [书] quarrel; combats: 内～ *internal strife*

哄 uproar; horseplay: 起～ *jointly create a disturbance*
see also hōng; hǒng
【哄场】(of an audience) make catcalls; hoot
【哄闹】uproar; hubbub: 拥挤的大厅里一片～。*There was a hubbub in the crowded hall.*

hōu

齁[1] snore

齁[2] ① sickeningly sweet or salty: 这个菜咸得～人。*This dish is much too salty.* ② [方] very; awfully (usually implying disapproval): 天气～热。*It's awfully hot.*
【齁齁】[象] the sound of snoring: ～熟睡 *snore in deep slumber*
【齁声】the sound of snoring; snore

hóu

侯 ① marquis, the second of the five nobility ranks in ancient China: 封～ *offer the title of marquis to sb* ② noblemen or high officials ③ (Hóu) a surname
【侯爵】marquis
【侯爵夫人】marquise
【侯门似海】the gate of a noble house is like the sea — impassable to the common man

喉 【生理】larynx; throat: 咽～ *pharynx and larynx*
【喉癌】throat cancer
【喉管】windpipe; trachea
【喉结】【生理】Adam's apple; larynx
【喉科学】laryngology
【喉咙】throat: ～痛 *have a sore throat* / 小男孩渴得～里冒烟儿。*The boy feels parched.*
【喉痧】scarlet fever
【喉舌】mouthpiece; voice: 党的～ *the mouthpiece of the Party* / 人民的～ *voice of the people*
【喉神经】laryngeal nerve
【喉头】larynx; throat

猴 ① monkey: 金丝～ *golden monkey* ② [方] (of children) naughty ③ squat on the heels like a monkey
【猴急】feel anxious; feel worried
【猴年马月】impossible date; day that will never come
【猴皮筋儿】rubber band: 跳～ *rubber-band rope skipping*
【猴儿精】[方] ① astute; shrewd: 这家伙～的。*That fellow is very shrewd.* ② clever and mischievous person
【猴手猴脚】be careless; not be steady; act rashly
【猴头】【植】hedgehog hydnum (*Hydnum erinaceus*)
【猴戏】a show by a performing monkey; monkey show: 耍～ *give a monkey show*
【猴子】monkey: 动物园里有许多小～。*There are a lot of little monkeys in the zoo.*

hǒu

吼 ① (of animals) roar; howl: 狮～ *the roar of a lion* ② (of human or weapons) shout out of anger: 怒～ *angry shouts* / 远方传来大炮的～声。*Guns rumbled in the distance.* ③ (of wind, siren, etc.) howl; boom: 北风怒～。*The north wind was howling.*
【吼叫】roar; howl; roar; yell: 洪水～着穿过山谷。*The flood howled through the valley.*
【吼鸣】roar; rumble; thunder: 雷声～。*Thunder rumbled.*
【吼声】roar; boom; loud shouts

hòu

后[1] ① (of space) in the back; at the back; behind: ～门 *back door (or gate)* / 村～ *behind the village* ② (of time) later; not yet: ～天 *the day after tomorrow* / 日～ *in the future* / 先来～到 *in the order of arrival; first come, first served* ③ (of order) last: ～排 *back row* / ～十名 *the last ten persons* ④ offspring: 子孙～代 *descendents*

后[2] ① empress; queen ② sovereign; king (in ancient times): 商之先～ *previous sovereign of the Shang Dynasty* ③ (Hòu) a surname
【后半场】latter half; second half: ～比赛 *second half of a game (or match)*
【后半晌】[方] afternoon
【后半生】the latter half of one's life
【后半天】afternoon
【后半叶】latter half of a century: 20世纪～ *latter half of the 20th century*
【后半夜】the second half the night; after midnight: 我在～听到了奇怪的声音。*I heard a strange sound after midnight.*
【后备】reserve: ～力量 *reserve forces* / ～基金 *re-*

H

serve fund / ~物资 *reserve materials* / ~部队 *reserve units*

【后备军】① reserves ② reserve force：产业~ *industrial reserve army*; *industrial reserve*

【后背】① back (of the body)：马~ *the back of a horse* ②［方］at the back; in the rear; from behind：在某人~伺机袭击 *hang on the rear of sb*

【后辈】① posterity; descendents：传至~ *go down to posterity* ② younger generation; juniors：~需要向前辈学习很多东西。*There is a lot for younger generations to learn from the elders.*

【后边】back; rear; behind：工厂~的托儿所 *a child-care centre at the back of the factory* / 大厅在建筑物的~。*The hall is in the rear of the building.*

【后部】back; rear：屋子~的花园 *the garden at the rear of the house*

【后步】room for maneuver; leeway：留有一定的~ *retain a certain leeway*

【后尘】［书］sb's footsteps; dust raised by sb walking in front：步人~ *follow in sb's footstep*; *follow suit*

【后沉】(of a cart load, etc.) back-heavy

【后代】① later periods in history：这些都是~人的想象。*All of those are imaginations of people in later ages.* ② later generations; descendants; posterity：为~着想 *for the sake of future generations*; *in the interest of future generations*

【后殿】back chamber (of a palace); rear chamber

【后灯】taillight; tail lamp

【后爹】［口］stepfather

【后蝶】【动】queen butterfly

【后端】rear end; back end

【后盾】backing; support; supporter：这项计划有政府做~。*The plan has the backing of the government.*

【后发制人】gain mastery by attacking only after the enemy has struck

【后方】① rear：~医院 *rear (or base) hospital* /他在~工作。*He works in the rear.* ② behind; at the back; in the rear

【后防】rear defence：巩固~ *strengthen rear defence*

【后妃】empress and imperial concubines; queen and royal concubines

【后福】blessings (or good days) in the future or in one's old age

【后父】stepfather

【后跟】heel

【后宫】① living quarters for imperial concubines ② imperial concubines

【后顾】① turn back：无暇~*have no time to care for things left behind* ② look back

【后顾之忧】family worries; fear of attack from the rear; trouble back at home

【后果】result; consequence; aftermath：你要准备承担自己行动的~。*You should be ready to bear the consequences of your actions.*

【后滚翻】【体】backward roll

【后花园】back garden

【后话】part of a story to be recounted later; part of a story that is to come：这是~，暂且不提。*That is what happened later, so no more of it now.*

【后患】future trouble：根除~ *dig up the root of future trouble*; *remove the cause of future trouble*

【后患无穷】no end of trouble for the future

【后悔】regret; repent; sorry：不要在徒然的~中浪费时间。*Do not lose time in vain regret.* /我~不该对他如此宽宏大量。*I repent having been so generous to him.*

【后悔莫及】too late to repent

【后悔药】medicine for remorse; sth or sb that is supposed to relieve the pain of regret：没有卖~的地方。*What is done cannot be undone.*

【后会有期】we'll meet again some day

【后婚儿】［旧］remarried woman

【后脊梁】［方］back; backbone; spine

【后记】postscript (added to a finished book, etc.)

【后继】succeed; carry on

【后继无人】leave no successor (to carry on a tradition, transmit an art or craft, etc.)

【后继有人】there is no lack of successors; there is another generation to carry on

【后脚】① the rear foot (in walking)：前脚一滑，~也站不稳。*As the front foot slipped, the rear foot became unsteady.* ② close behind：我前脚刚走，他~到了。*Immediately after I had left he got there.*

【后襟】the back of a Chinese robe or jacket

【后进】① juniors in service ② lagging behind; less advanced; backward：~赶先进 *the less advanced striving to catch up with the more advanced* ③ person or unit lagging behind

【后劲】① aftereffect ② stamina; reserve strength

【后景】background (of a picture)

【后空翻】【体】backward somersault

【后来】① later; afterwards; by and by：~，我知道了真相。*I learned the truth later.* ② newly come; newly arrived：~的各位请坐好。*All latecomers please be seated.*

【后来居上】the latecomers surpass the old timers; the new generation will surpass the old

【后来人】successors：自有~。*There is no lack of successors.*

【后浪推前浪】the waves behind drive on those before：~，一代更比一代强。*As the waves behind drive on those before, so each new generation excels the last one.*

【后脸儿】［方］the back; the reverse side

【后路】① communication lines to the rear; route of retreat：切断敌人的~ *cut off the enemy's route of retreat* ② room for manoeuvre; a way of escape：给你自己留点~吧。*Leave yourself a way of escape.*

【后妈】［方］stepmother

【后门】① back door ② backdoor (or backstairs) influence

【后面】① back; rear; hind; behind; at the back; in the rear: 房子~有些羊。*There are some sheep behind the house.* ② later: 这个问题~我还要讲。*I will come back to this question later.*
【后母】[方] stepmother
【后脑勺儿】[方] the back of the head
【后年】[方] the year after next
【后娘】[方] stepmother
【后怕】fear after the event
【后排】back row
【后期】later stage; later period
【后起】(of people of talent) of new arrivals; of the younger generation: ~的青年作家 *budding young writers*
【后起之秀】an up and coming youngster; a promising young person
【后勤】rear services; logistics: ~部 *rear-service department*; *logistics department*; *logistics command* / ~机关 *rear-service establishments* / ~人员 *rear-service personnel*
【后儿】[口] day after tomorrow
【后人】① later generations ② posterity; descendants
【后任】successor (to a post)
【后晌】(hòushǎng) [方] afternoon; evening
【后晌】(hòushɑng) [方] evening
【后身】① the back of a person: 我只看见她的~。*I only saw her back.* ② the back of a garment: 这件衬衫的~太长了。*The back of this shirt is too long.* ③ the back of a building ④ reincarnation: 我相信那朵花就是她去世的她姐姐的~。*I believe that flower is a reincarnation of her dead sister.* ⑤ sth deriving from an earlier form; descendant: 国民党是同盟会的~。*The Kuomintang is the descendant of the Tongmenghui.*
【后生】[方] ① young man; lad ② having a youthful appearance
【后生可畏】a youth is to be regarded with respect; hold the young in awe
【后生女】[方] a young woman
【后生子】[方] a young man
【后世】① later ages:《诗经》对~的文学很有影响。*The book of Songs had great influence on the literature of later ages.* ② offspring; descendant ③【宗】next life
【后事】① (often used in traditional novels) what happened afterwards: 欲知~如何,且听下回分解。*If you want to know what happened afterwards, read the next chapter.* ② funeral affairs; arrangements after one's death
【后视镜】rear-view mirror; rear-vision mirror
【后视图】back view; rearview
【后手】①[旧] successor ②[旧] recipient (of a receipt, bill, etc.) ③ defensive position (in chess): 把某人逼成~ *drive sb into the defensive* ④ room for manoeuvre; a way of escape
【后首】[方] ① afterwards; later ② behind
【后嗣】descendants
【后台】① backstage: 他被带到~去看演员。*He was taken backstage to meet the actors.* ② backstage supporter; behind-the-scenes backer: ~很硬 *have very strong backing*
【后台老板】backstage boss; backstage supporter; behind-the-scenes backer
【后天】① the day after tomorrow ② postnatal; acquired: 知识是~获得的,不是先天就有的。*Knowledge is acquired, not innate.*
【后头】① at the back; in the rear; behind ② [方] later; future: 吃苦还在~呢。*The worst is yet to come.*
【后土】Earth; All-producing Earth
【后腿】hind legs
【后退】draw back; fall back; retreat: 遇到困难决不~ *never shrink from difficulties*
【后卫】①【军】rear guard ② (in soccer) full back; guard
【后现代主义】postmodernism
【后效】aftereffect
【后心】upper back; centre of one's back
【后行】carry out as a second step; carry out later
【后序】epilogue
【后续】① follow-up: ~部队 *follow-up troops* ② [方] remarry after the death of one's wife
【后悬】rear overhang (of a car)
【后学】a young junior scholar or student
【后腰】the small of the back
【后遗症】①【医】sequela ②aftereffect; aftermath
【后裔】descendant; offspring: 维多利亚女王的~ *the descendants of Queen Victoria*
【后影】the shape of a person or thing as seen from the back: 看~好像是个小姑娘。*From the back view it must be a little girl.*
【后援】reinforcements; backup force; backing
【后院】① backyard ② home
【后者】the latter: 很多人赞成前一种方法,但我赞成~。*Many support the former alternative, but I favour the latter.*
【后账】① accounts kept secret ② account to be settled later
【后肢】hind legs (of an animal)
【后轴】rear axle
【后缀】【语】suffix
【后坐】【军】recoil: ~指标 *recoil indicator*
【后坐力】recoil

厚 ① thick: ~纸 *thick paper* / ~棉袄 *heavy padded coat* ② (of a flat article) the extent from one surface to the opposite; thickness: 长宽~ *length, width, and thickness* /三厘米~的木板 *a 3-cm-thick plank* ③ deep; profound: 深~的友谊 *profound friendship* ④ kind; magnanimous: 忠~ *honest and tolerant* ⑤ large; generous; handsome: 优~的待遇 *handsome reward* ⑥ rich or strong in flavour: 酒味醇~。*The wine tastes mellow and strong.* ⑦ well-off; wealthy; rich: 家底儿~ *a well-off family* ⑧ favour; stress: 不负某人~望 *meet (or come up to) sb's expectations* ⑨

(Hòu) a surname
【厚爱】great kindness; treat very kindly and generously: 感谢你的~。*Thank you for all your great kindness.*
【厚玻璃】heavy sheet glass
【厚薄】① thickness: ~适中 *moderate thickness* ② show favour or disfavour
【厚布帘】drape
【厚层】thick-layer; deep-bed: ~粘土 *lean clay* / ~土壤 *deep soil*
【厚酬】handsome reward or remuneration
【厚此薄彼】favour one more than another; be biased; be liberal to one and stingy to another; say turkey to one and buzzard to another; treat with partiality
【厚待】treat kindly and generously; kind-heartedly treat
【厚道】kind-hearted; clement; tolerant; honest and kind; straight and sincere: ~的乡亲 *honest folk*
【厚地】heavy back
【厚度】thickness; land: 每层地板的~仅为一层混凝土。*Each floor is a single thickness of concrete.*
【厚墩墩】very thick: ~的棉衣 *a heavy padded overcoat*
【厚恩】kind favours; great indebtedness
【厚非】criticize; justify: 未可~ *not be altogether unjustifiable; give little cause for criticism*
【厚古薄今】esteem the past over the present; pay more attention to the past than to the present; value the past and slight the present
【厚积薄发】be well-prepared; be well-grounded
【厚今薄古】lay more stress on the present than on the past; emphasize the new and deemphasize the old
【厚金】handsome reward; liberal remuneration
【厚礼】lavish gifts; liberal presents; largesse; munificent: 一份~ *a munificent gift*
【厚利】substantial (or large; big) profit: 这项新发明会像一座金矿一样给你们带来~。*This new invention will bring you great profits like a goldmine.*
【厚脸皮】thick-skinned; brazen; shameless; impertinently bold; cheeky: ~的冒充者 *a brazen impostor* / ~的说谎者 *a shameless liar*
【厚禄】high government pay: 高官~ *a high position and a good pay*
【厚貌深情】kindly in appearance but unfathomable at heart
【厚呢】box cloth; dreadnaught
【厚片】sheet: ~云母 *sheet mica*
【厚漆】paste paint
【厚情难却】kind feelings are hard to refuse
【厚人薄己】treat others well but be frugal with oneself
【厚实】① thick and solid ② thick and sturdy: ~的肩膀 *broad and sturdy shoulders* ③ deep ard solid: 基础~ *a solid foundation* ④ [方] honest and sincere ⑤ rich; well-off: 家底~ *well-off family*
【厚死薄生】praise for the dead and contempt for the living
【厚望】great hope; high expectation: 不负~ *live up to one's expectation; not to let sb down*
【厚味】savoury; rich or greasy food
【厚谢】give sb a rich reward: 事成之后,必当~。*When the thing is done, there will be a rich reward for you.*
【厚颜无耻】impudent; shameless; brazen; cheeky; bold as brass: ~的荡妇 *a brazen hussy* / 他~地要求老板给他增加50%的工资。*He had the brass to ask his boss for a 50% pay rise.* / 不要~! *That's enough of your cheek!*
【厚谊】deep friendship or hospitality: ~比金钱更有价值。*Deep friendship is worth more than money.*
【厚意】kindness; favour; great cordiality; good will; kind thought: 多谢你的~。*Thank you for your kindness.*
【厚翼】thick wing
【厚油层】thick oil pay
【厚遇】excellent pay and conditions; high wages and good benefits
【厚葬】① an elaborate funeral; a lavish funeral ② bury with full honours
【厚重】① thick and heavy ② decorous; stately; rich and generous: ~的礼物 *generous gifts* ③ [书] honest and serious

候[1] ① wait; await: 你先在这儿~着,他一会儿就来。*Please wait a moment here; he is coming soon.* ② send one's regard to; say hello to; inquire after

候[2] ① time; season: 时~ (*the duration of*) *time; moment* ②【气】period of five days; pentad ③ condition or state (of sth changing): 症~ *disease; symptom* / 火~ *duration and degree of heating, cooking, smelting, etc.*
【候补】be a candidate; be a substitute: 中共中央~委员 *alternate member of the Central Committee of the CPC*
【候场】(of an actor or actress) wait one's turn to enter the stage
【候车】wait for a bus (or train)
【候车室】waiting room
【候虫】seasonal insect
【候机室】airport waiting room; airport lounge
【候鸟】migratory bird; migrant; visitant
【候审】【律】await trial
【候选人】candidate: 提名~ *nominate a candidate*
【候诊】wait to see the doctor
【候诊室】waiting room (in a hospital)

hū

乎[1] [书] ① a particle used in ancient Chinese to express doubt：王侯将相，宁有种～？*How should we conclude those nobles have been given blue blood on birth?* ② used in a selective question：然～，否～？*Is it right or not?* ③ used to express supposition：其是之谓～？*Is this what it is about, more or less?*

乎[2] ① suffix of a verb, an adjective, or an adverb：超～寻常 *be out of the ordinary* ② used after an adjective or adverb for rhythm's sake：迥～不同 *completely different*

乎[3] [书] oh; alas

帐[1] [方] cover：幼苗让草给～住了。*The shoots are covered by the weeds.*

帐[2] [书] ① large; spacious ② be supercilious; cold-shoulder：～而无礼 *arrogant and rude*

呼[1] ① breathe out; exhale：～出二氧化碳 *exhale carbon dioxide* ② shout; cry out ③ call：直～其名 *address sb disrespectfully by his name* ④ bleep; page：有人～我。*Somebody is paging me.* ⑤ (Hū) a surname

呼[2] [象] the sound of wind, heavy breath, or a fast-moving object：汽车～地从我身边驶过。*The car went fast past me.*

【呼哧】[象] the sound of panting; puff

【呼叱】berate; excoriate; shout at sb; scold sb

【呼风唤雨】summon wind and rain — exercise magic powers; stir up trouble; worsen the situation

【呼喊】call out; shout

【呼号】(hūháo) wail; cry out in distress：奔走～ *go round crying for help*

【呼号】(hūhào) ① call sign; call letters：～分配 *assignment of call signs* ② motto; slogan

【呼吼】whistle; roar; howl

【呼唤】① call ② shout to：妻子在～我。*My wife is calling me.*

【呼叫】① telecommunications call：～灯 *calling lamp* /～信号 *calling signal* ② shout; call out

【呼救】call for help; send out SOS signals

【呼拉圈】hula hoop

【呼啦】the sound of flapping：一面大旗在风中～作响，上写：举世无双。*A large flag flapping in the wind says; be second to none.*

【呼噜】[象] (hūlū) wheezy：我的感冒好多了，就是呼吸时还有点～声。*My cold is much better but I'm still a bit wheezy.*

【呼噜】(hūlu) [口] snore：打～ *snore*

【呼朋引类】gang up; gangsters getting together

【呼扇】① shake; tremble ② fan：小猪～着耳朵。*The small pig is fanning himself with his ears.*

【呼哨】whistle

【呼声】① cry; voice：群众的～ *the voice of the masses* /他们中布什的～最高。*Bush is the most likely of them.* ② voice of the people

【呼天抢地】lament to heaven and knock one's head on earth — utter cries of anguish

【呼吸】① breathe; respire：～困难 *lose one's breath* ② single breath — an instant：成败就在～之间。*Success or failure hinges on a single moment.*

【呼吸道】respiratory tract

【呼吸器】respirator

【呼吸器官】respiratory apparatus

【呼吸系统】respiratory system

【呼啸】scream; whizz; roar：寒风～。*The cold wind is roaring.* /风～着穿过树林。*The wind howled through the trees.*

【呼幺喝六】① shout for numbers in throwing dice; noisy shouting in gambling ② shouting right and left — arrogant

【呼应】echo; chime in with; work in accordance with：她的工作与我的正好～。*Her job works in very accordance with mine.* /你们的计划和我们的正相～，太好了！*It's great that your plans chime in with ours.*

【呼吁】appeal; call on：～援助 *appeal for aid*

【呼吁书】letter of appeal; appeal

【呼噪】noisy shouting

【呼之即来，挥之即去】have sb at one's beck and call

【呼之欲出】ready to come out at one's call; be vividly portrayed

忽[1] neglect; overlook; ignore：疏～ *overlook*

忽[2] suddenly; all of a sudden：～明～暗 *now bright, now dim*

忽[3] ① one hundred thousandth of a unit ② unit of length (= 0.00001 metre) ③ unit of weight (= 0.00001 gram)

【忽搭】the sound of flapping：船帆在微风中～作响。*The sails were flapping gently in the wind.*

【忽地】suddenly; all of a sudden：她～消失了。*She disappeared suddenly.*

【忽而】sometimes... sometimes...; now... now...：小男孩～哭～笑。*The little boy cried and laughed by turns.* /雨～下，～停。*It rains off and on.*

【忽忽】① fast; quickly (used to describe the passing of time) ② confused

【忽…忽…】sometimes... sometimes...; now... now...：～左～右 *suddenly left, suddenly right; now in one extreme, now the other* /我这是受不了这～冷～热的天气。*It is really hard for me to bear the sudden changes of the weather.*

【忽略】neglect; overlook; lose sight of; slur over：我们绝不能～那些仍然存在的错误。*Never shall we overlook those still-existing errors.*

【忽然】suddenly; all of a sudden：她～插话道："就是那样了。" *"That is it." She suddenly put in.*

【忽闪】(hūshǎn) (of a light) flash; sparkle：她的钻石在烛光中～。*Her diamonds sparkled in the candle-light.*

【忽闪】(hūshan)(of the lights or eyes, etc.) sparkle; flash: ~的大眼睛 *big flashing eyes*
【忽视】neglect; overlook; ignore; disregard: ~健康 *neglect one's health* /不可~的一股力量 *a force not to be ignored* /你可不能~安全问题。*You can't just disregard the security problem.*
【忽悠】[方] flicker: ~的烛光 *flickering lights of the candle*

烀 stew in shallow water: ~白薯 *stew sweet potatoes*

糊 plaster: 我的脸被~上了一层泥。*My face was spread a layer of mud.*
see also hú; hù

hú

囫

【囫囵】whole: ~而食 *swallow whole*
【囫囵个儿】[方] ① whole: 这孩子把一只梨~吞下去了。*The boy swallow that pear whole.* ② sleep with one's clothes on: 我总是~睡觉。*I always sleep with my clothes on.*
【囫囵觉】a sound and non-stop sleep; uninterrupted sleep; a good night's sleep: 主席太忙, 连个~也睡不成。*Our Chairman has been too busy to have a good night's sleep.*
【囫囵吞枣】swallow a date whole — lap up information without digesting it; read without doing any thinking: 读书不能够~。*You should read with understanding.*

和 complete a set in mah-jong or cards
see also hé; hè; huó; huò

狐 ①fox: 北极~ *arctic fox* /沙~ *corsac fox* /银~ *silver fox* ②(Hú) a surname
【狐步】foxtrot (a kind of ballroom dance)
【狐臭】body odour; bromhidrosis
【狐假虎威】bully people by flaunting one's powerful connections; swagger about in borrowed plumes; browbeat others by virtue of sb else's position
【狐狸】【动】fox
【狐狸精】fox spirit — a seductive woman
【狐狸尾巴】fox's tail — cloven hoof; sth that gives away the evil intention of sb like a fox tail: ~终究是藏不住的。*The devil cannot hide his cloven hoof.*
【狐媚】bewitch by cajolery; entice by flattery
【狐朋狗友】evil associates; pack of rogues
【狐裘】fox-fur robe
【狐群狗党】a pack of rogues; a gang of scoundrels
【狐死首丘】a fox dies with its face towards its den — people longing for home or mindful of his origin
【狐仙】fairy fox
【狐疑】doubt; suspicion: 满腹~ *full of suspicion*

弧 ①【数】arc ②(in ancient times) bow
【弧度】grade of arc; radian; radian measure
【弧光】arc light: ~灯 *arc lamp*
【弧面】cambered surface
【弧圈球】【体】loop drive
【弧线】pitch arc; curve: ~运动 *movement in a curve*
【弧形】arc-shaped; curve: 虹的~ *the arc of a rainbow*

胡[1] ① Hu, general term for non-Han nationalities living in the north and west of China in ancient times ② introduced objects from northern or western nationalities or from abroad: ~服 *hu dress* ③ (Hú) a surname

胡[2] recklessly; wantonly; outrageously: ~编 *coin recklessly; concoct; cook up*

胡[3] [书] why (used usually in ancient literature works): ~不归? *Why not come back?*

胡[4] moustache; beard; whiskers; sideburns

【胡扯】talk nonsense; chatter idly: 这纯粹是~。*This is sheer nonsense.*
【胡吹】boast outrageously; talk big
【胡豆】broad bean
【胡匪】[方]bandit
【胡蜂】【动】wasp; hornet
【胡搞】① meddle with sth; mess things up ② be promiscuous; carry on an affair with sb
【胡瓜】cucumber
【胡话】wild talk; ravings: 病人对护士说起~来。*The patient began to rave incoherently at the nurses.*
【胡笳】【音】Tartar reed flute, a kind of musical instruments
【胡椒】pepper: 白~ *white pepper* /~粉 *beater (or ground) pepper*
【胡搅】① pester sb; be mischievous ② argue tediously and vexatiously; wrangle
【胡搅蛮缠】argue tediously and vexatiously; plague sb with unreasonable demands
【胡来】① mess things up; fool with sth: 不知道怎么放家具就不要~。*If you don't know how to place the furniture, never make it a mess instead.* ② run wild; act irresponsibly or recklessly: 他唾他的父亲, 真是~。*It is foolhardy enough of him to spit at his father.*
【胡噜】[方] ① rub: 他不好意思地~~脑袋。*He shamefully rubbed his head.* ② sweep; scrape together: 把粉笔都~到一起去。*Scrape together all the chalks, please.* ③ manage; deal with
【胡乱】① carelessly; casually: ~吃了点东西 *have a hasty meal; grab a quick bite* /~做梦 *have wild dreams* ② at random
【胡萝卜】carrot
【胡萝卜素】【生化】carotene
【胡闹】be mischievous; run wild; make trouble: 正经点, 别~。*Be serious. Don't run wild.*
【胡琴】【音】two-stringed Chinese fiddle: 拉~ *play*

the Chinese fiddle

【胡说】talk nonsense; talk through one's hat; blather; drivel; nonsense: 别再～了。*No more nonsense, please.*

【胡说八道】nonsense; rubbish; sheer nonsense: 所有的传言都是～。*All rumours are nonsense.*

【胡思乱想】go off into flights of fancy; give way to foolish fancies; let one's imagination run freely: 有的时候我们有必要～。*Sometimes it is necessary for us to give free play to our imagination.*

【胡桃】walnut: ～肉 *walnut meat*

【胡同】lane; alley

【胡须】moustache; beard; whiskers; sideburns

【胡言乱语】talk nonsense; rave; babble about sth

【胡杨】【植】diversiform-leaved poplar (*Poplar diversifolia*)

【胡志明市】Ho Chi Minh City, major city in southern Viet Nam, formerly named Saigon

【胡诌】cook up; fabricate wild tales; drivel

【胡子】① moustache; beard; whiskers; sideburns: 一星期未刮的～*a week's growth of beard* ②［方］bandit

【胡子拉碴】a stubbly beard; a bristly unshaven chin

【胡作非为】act wildly in defiance of the law or public opinion; commit all kinds of outrages; run amuck

壶 ① kettle; pot; bottle; flask: 水～ *kettle* ②（Hú）a surname

核

see also hé

【核儿】［口］① stone; pit; core: 杏～ *apricot stone* ② sth resembling a fruit stone: 煤～ partly-burnt coals; cinders

斛 ［旧］a dry measure used in former times

葫

【葫芦】bottle gourd; calabash: 油～ *oil gourd* / 他～里卖的是什么药? *What has he got up his sleeve?*

【葫芦瓢】gourd ladle

鹄

【鹄候】await respectfully; expect: ～佳音。*I am expecting good news from you.*

【鹄发】white or grey hair: ～童颜 *hoary hair and a child's appearance — aged but healthy*

【鹄立】［书］stand erect

【鹄望】［书］eagerly look forward to

猢

【猢狲】macaque; monkey

㗅 porridge

【㗅口】keep body and soul together; eke out one's livelihood

湖 ① lake ② Huzhou, now Wuxing, Zhejiang Province ③（Hú）Hunan or Hubei: 两～ *Hunan and Hubei*

【湖笔】writing brush produced in Huzhou, Zhejiang Province

【湖滨】lakeside

【湖光山色】a beautiful scenery of lakes and mountains: 坐在家中您就可以看～。*You can enjoy a marvelous view of lakes and mountains at home.*

【湖蓝】bright blue; light blue

【湖绿】light green

【湖泊】lakes

【湖区】lake district (or region)

【湖色】light green

【湖田】land reclaimed from a lake; shoaly land

【湖心亭】a pavilion in the middle of a lake; mid lake pavilion

【湖泽】lakes and marshes

【湖沼】lakes and marshes

【湖绉】【纺】crepe silk produced in Huzhou, Zhejiang Province

煳 burnt: 肉～了。*The meat got burnt.*

【煳锅】get burnt in a pot

槲 【植】Mongolian oak (*Quercus dentata*)

【槲寄生】【植】mistletoe (*Viscum coloratum*)

【槲栎】【植】oriental white oak (*Quercus aliena*)

蝴

【蝴蝶】【动】butterfly

【蝴蝶花】①【植】fringed iris ② butterfly loop

【蝴蝶结】bowknot; bow

【蝴蝶瓦】small green tile

【蝴蝶鱼】butterfly fish

【蝴蝶装】butterfly binding, a Chinese form of bookbinding.

糊 stick; paste: 在墙上～张画 *paste a picture onto the wall*

see also hū; hù

【糊糊】［方］gruel made of ground maize, flour, etc.: 棒子～ *cornmeal gruel*

【糊里糊涂】muddle-headed; mixed up: 他老是～的。*He is always muddle-headed.*

【糊涂】① muddled; confused; bewildered: 你说的话让我有点～。*What you said made me confused.* ② confusion: 一塌～ *utter confusion* ③［方］blurred; indistinct

【糊涂虫】blunderer; bungler; idiot

【糊涂账】chaotic accounts; a mess

【糊嘴】keep body and soul together; eke out one's livelihood

hǔ

虎 ① tiger：猛~ *a fierce tiger* / 幼~ *a tiger cub* ② brave；vigorous ③［方］put on a fierce or angry look：他一看到他的儿子，就~起脸来。*He put on a solemn face at the sight of his son.* ④（Hǔ）a surname

【虎背熊腰】thick，powerful back and shoulders；tough and stocky；muscular and sturdy：一个~的拳击手 *a muscular and powerful boxer*

【虎贲】knight；warrior；brave and strong man

【虎彪彪】powerful and sturdy；robust and imposing：~的年轻人 *a robust young man*

【虎步】① vigorous steps（or strides）：他迈了两大~穿过了房间。*With two vigorous strides he crossed the room.* ②［书］exercise rule or governance（over a region）

【虎伥】helper of an evil scheme；accomplice

【虎胆】① tiger's gallbladder ② as brave as a tiger：~英雄 *hero as brave as a lion*

【虎毒不食子】even a vicious tiger will not eat its cubs — no one is willing to hurt his own children

【虎伏】【体】gyro wheel

【虎符】a tiger-shaped tally issued to generals as imperial authorization for troop government in ancient China

【虎父无犬子】eagles do not breed doves

【虎虎】mighty；imposing；vigorous

【虎将】a brave general

【虎劲】dash；dauntless drive：有一股子~ *have plenty of dash*；*be full of drive and daring*

【虎鲸】killer whale（*Orcinus orca*）

【虎踞龙盘】like a tiger crouching，a dragon curling — be located in a strategic place

【虎克定律】【物】Hooke's law

【虎口】① tiger's mouth — a dangerous situation ② the part of the hand between the thumb and the index finger

【虎口拔牙】pull a tooth from the tiger's mouth — dare the greatest danger；gear the lion in his den

【虎口夺食】snatch food from the jaws of a tiger

【虎口脱险】have a narrow（or near；hairbreadth）escape；escape from a dangerous situation

【虎口余生】be saved from the tiger's mouth；return from the tiger's lair — have a narrow escape from death；barely escape with one's life

【虎狼】tiger and wolf — cruel and ferocious；ruthless and savage：~之辈 *a ruthless and cruel person* / ~之性 *voracious nature*；*wolfish disposition* / ~之国 *a nation of savages*

【虎里虎气】strong and strapping；robust and mighty：~的大汉 *a great strapping fellow*

【虎皮】tiger skin：拉大旗作~ *use a great banner as a tiger-skin*；*dress oneself in a tiger-skin to intimidate people*

【虎气】of imposing manner

【虎钳】nip；vice：万能~ *universal vice* / ~口 *vice jaw*

【虎鲨】【动】horned shark（*Heterodontus*）

【虎蛇】tiger snake（*Notechis scutatus*）

【虎生生】mighty and vigorous；vigorous and forceful

【虎视】① glare with avarice and malice ② awe-inspiring gaze

【虎士】brave warrior

【虎视眈眈】cast greedy eyes on；look at fiercely as a tiger does；glare like a tiger eyeing its prey；eye menacingly and greedily：贪心的儿子对父亲的财产~。*The greedy son casts covetous eyes on his father's wealth.*

【虎头虎脑】（usu. of a child）looking strong and healthy：你儿子~的，真招人喜欢。*Your son looks healthy and robust*；*he is really lovely.*

【虎头拍蝇】beat a fly on the head of a tiger — unwise provocation

【虎头蛇尾】a tiger's head and a snake's tail — a fine start and a poor finish；a brave beginning and weak ending；anticlimax：在一个星期戏剧性的谈判之后，结果却是~的。*After a week of dramatic negotiations*，*all that followed was anticlimax.*

【虎威】valiant and powerful；prowess

【虎尾春冰】tread on the tiger's tail or walk on spring ice — in a precarious position；very cautious

【虎啸风生】tigers howl with the rise of winds — great men appear in response to the call of the times.

【虎啸龙吟】cries of dragons and tigers

【虎须】tiger's whiskers

【虎穴】tiger's den — a dangerous place：~追踪 *track the tiger to its lair* / 不入~，焉得虎子？*How can you catch tiger cubs without entering the tiger's lair？— Nothing venture*，*nothing have.*

【虎牙】［口］protruding canine teeth

【虎眼石】tiger's-eye

浒 waterside

唬 intimidate；bluff：你别~人了。我才不相信呢！*Quit bluffing. I don't believe it at all.* / 她没被他耸人听闻的话~住。*She wasn't intimidated by his sensational words.*

琥

【琥珀】amber：~冰 *amber ice* / ~玻璃 *amber glass* / ~树 *amber tree* / ~油 *amber oil*；*lake oil* / ~种子 *amber seed*

hù

互 mutually；each other：~济会 *mutual association* / ~通情报 *exchange information* / ~为条件 *inter-dependent*；*mutually conditional*

【互帮互学】help and learn from each other

【互比定律】law of reciprocal proportions

【互变】interconversion：～性 *enantiotropy* / ～现象 *tautomerism*

【互补】①【电】complementary；complementation；relatively complemented：～分配 *complementary distribution* / ～基因 *complementary genes* / ～理论 *complementary theory* ②【数】complementarity law；law of complementation：～群 *complementation group* / ～事件 *complementary event* / ～图 *complementation map* / ～性 *complementarity* / ～职业 *complementary occupation*

【互补色】complementary colours：～地图 *anaglyphic map* / ～观察法 *anaglyphic method*

【互不干涉】mutual noninterference

【互不侵犯】mutual nonaggression：～条约 *nonaggression treaty*

【互斥】mutual exclusion；mutex：～电路 *selecting chain* / ～现象 *mutual exclusion* / ～作用 *mutual repulsion effect*

【互导】transconductance；mutual conductance

【互等定律】equivalent law

【互反】reciprocal：～公式 *reciprocity formula* / ～函数 *reciprocal function* / ～定律 *law of reciprocity*

【互访】exchange visits：两国代表团的～ *exchange of delegations between two countries*

【互换】exchange；interchange；interconvert；reciprocate；crossing-over：～礼物 *interchange gifts* / ～功率 *interchange power* / ～码 *permutation code* / ～现象 *interconversion*

【互惠】mutually beneficial；reciprocal：～关税 *mutual preferential duties* / ～贸易 *reciprocal trade* / ～条约 *reciprocal treaty* / ～政策 *give-and-take policy*

【互惠共生】mutualistic symbiosis；reciprocal symbiosis

【互惠合作】mutual benefit and collaboration

【互见】①（of writings）mutually explanatory and supplementary ② both have；exist at the same time：瑕瑜～ *have both strength and weakness*

【互交】【生理】intercross

【互敬互爱】mutually respect and love

【互赖】interdependence

【互利】mutual benefit：在平等～的基础上 *on the basis of equality and mutual benefit*

【互利互惠】offer mutual benefit and achieve common progress

【互联】interconnection；interconnect：～技术 *interconnection technique* / ～控制 *interconnected control*

【互联网】internet；internetwork：～协议 *Internet Protocol*（*IP*）

【互连】interlinkage；interconnection：～技术 *interconnection technique*

【互免】mutual exemption：～签证协议 *agreement on mutual exemption of visas*

【互逆】reciprocal：～电容 *mutual stiffness* / ～矩阵 *reciprocal matrix*

【互让】mutual accommodation；give-and-take

【互溶】be intersoluble：酒精和水～。*Alcohol and water are intersoluble.*

【互生】【生理】alternate phyllotaxy：～现象 *mutualism* / ～叶 *alternate leaf*

【互素】【数】coprime；relatively prime：～数 *coprime numbers*

【互调】intermodulation：多信号～ *multiple-signal intermodulation* / ～失真 *intermodulation distortion*

【互通】interflow：～消息 *communicate news*

【互通有无】mutual help to make up what the other lacks；meet each other's wants；supply each other's needs

【互为因果】reciprocal causation；interact as both cause and effect

【互相】mutual；each other；one another：～爱慕 *mutual love and admiration* / ～拆台 *undermine each other's work* / ～掣肘 *hold each other back* / ～仇视 *regard each other as an enemy* / ～吹捧 *logroll* / ～抵触 *contradict each other* / ～攻击 *attack each other* / ～勾结 *collude with each other*/ ～贯通 *interpenetrate* / ～监督 *mutual supervision* / ～交换 *intercourse*/ ～联系 *interconnected* / ～配合 *coordinate* / ～牵连 *involve each other* / ～渗透 *interpenetrate* / ～信赖 *mutual trust* / ～印证 *corroborate each other* / ～制约 *mutual condition* / ～转化 *mutual transformation*

【互训】（of writings）mutually explanatory

【互应】mutual induction

【互助】mutual help；help each other；mutual aid：～合作 *mutual aid and cooperation*

【互助会】mutual help club（or society）

【互助组】① mutual aid group：学习～ *mutual help study group* ② mutual aid team（an elementary form of organization in China's agricultural cooperation）：临时～ *temporary mutual aid team*

【互阻】mutual resistance

【互作用】mutual effect；interaction：～隙 *interaction gap*

户 ① a door：夜不闭～。*Doors are not bolted at night — when law and order prevail with peoples' morality high* ② household；family：千家万～ *innumerable households or families*；*every family* ③ family status：门当～对 *be well-matched in social and economic status*（*esp. for marriage*）④ bank account：开～ *open an account* ⑤（Hù）a surname

【户部】Ministry of Revenue

【户次】household time — one household counted once

【户籍】① census register；household register：～科 *household registration section* ② registered permanent residence

【户籍法】law of population registration

【户籍警】policeman in charge of household registration

【户均】per family；per household：～收入 *per household income*；*average family income*

【户口】① number of households and population：这

个镇子有很多～。*There are many households in the town.* ② registered permanent residence and total population：报～*apply for a residence permit* /～簿 *permanent residence booklet* /长期～*permanent residence* /临时～*temporary residence* /迁～*change one's residence* /销～*cancel one's residence*

【户口管制】domicile control

【户口普查】census

【户内】indoor；indoors：～活动 *indoor activity* /～设备 *indoor equipment* /～体操 *indoor gymnastics*

【户枢】door hinge (or axis)

【户枢不蠹】a door-hinge never becomes worm eaten — constant activity staves off decay

【户庭】[书] door and courtyard

【户头】(bank) account：开～*open an account*

【户外】outdoor；in the open：～活动 *outdoors*；*in the open air* /～劳动 *outdoor labour* /～运动 *outdoor sports*

【户限】[书] threshold：跨过～*cross the threshold*

【户限为穿】a threshold worn low by visitors — an endless flow of visitors

【户养】(usu. livestock) be raised by private households

【户牖】[书] door；door and windows：他在家时整天～敞开。*The door and windows of his house are open all the day when he's at home.*

【户主】head of a household

【户子】[方] household；family

护 ① protect；guard；shield：保～*protect* /爱～*cherish*；*take good care of* ② be partial to；shield from censure；indulge：不要一味～着他。*Don't be partial to him all the time.*

【护岸】[水] bank revetment

【护岸林】protective belt (of trees) along an embankment

【护板】backplate；guard board

【护臂】bracer

【护庇】[口] shelter；shield；cover：当小孩子犯错误时，不要～他们。*Don't shield the children when they make mistakes.*

【护兵】military guard；escort

【护城河】city moat

【护持】① shield and sustain ② look after；take care of：她正在～病人。*She is looking after the patient.*

【护从】① follow as bodyguard；escort ② guard；bodyguard

【护犊子】[口] be partial to one's own child；shield the faults of one's child

【护短】shield a shortcoming or fault：他想给她～。*He wants to cover up for her.*

【护耳】earflap

【护发】capilliculture；hair care：～素 *hair conditioner*

【护封】book jacket

【护肤霜】face cream；body lotion

【护盖】protective cover

【护航】escort；convoy：～飞机 *escort aircraft* /～舰 *convoy ship* /～任务 *escort mission*

【护驾】escort the emperor；defend the king

【护肩】[方] shoulder pad (or padding)

【护栏】guardrail；rail fence

【护理】① tend；nurse：～病人 *nurse the sick* ② protect；take care of：～小麦越冬 *take good care of the wheat through the winter*

【护理人员】nursing staff

【护林】protect the forest：～防火 *protect the forest and guard against fire*

【护林员】forest ranger

【护领】detachable collar

【护路】patrol and guard a road or railway；road maintenance

【护路林】shelter belt (along a road)

【护目镜】goggles；eye protector

【护坡】[水] slope protection

【护秋】keep watch over the ripe crops (or the autumn harvest)

【护身符】① amulet；protective talisman ② a person or thing that protects one from punishment or censure

【护士】nurse：实习～*student nurse* /夜班～*night nurse* /～学校 *nurses' school*

【护士长】head nurse

【护守】guard；defend：～自己的财产 *guard one's own property*

【护送】escort；convoy：～救灾物资 *convoy vehicles bringing relief to a disaster-stricken area* /我会～你回家。*I'll escort you home.*

【护腿】[体] shin-guard；shin-pad

【护腕】[体] bracer

【护卫】① protect；guard ② bodyguard

【护卫舰】escort vessel

【护卫艇】gunboat

【护膝】[体] kneepad

【护校】nurses' school

【护养】① cultivate；nurse；rear：～秧苗 *cultivate seedlings*；*nurse young plants* ② maintain：～铁路 *maintain a railway line*

【护佑】protect；bless and protect

【护照】① passport：普通～*ordinary passport* /公务～*service passport* /外交～*diplomatic passport* ② [旧] certificate issued by the authorities to any person when he travels or takes goods through the country

【护罩】shield；mask；hood

沪 (Hù) another name for "上海"：～杭铁路 *the Shanghai-Hangzhou Railway line*

【沪剧】Shanghai opera

怙 [书] rely on (an advantage)

【怙恶不悛】be steeped in evil and refuse to repent；incorrigible；remain impenitent

【怙恃】① [书] rely on；depend on ② father and mother (used in the third person)：少失～*lose parents in childhood*

戽 ① bailing bucket, old farm tool for bailing water to irrigate fields ② bail

【戽车】noria

【戽斗】【农】bailing bucket; bailer

笏 a tablet held (before the breast) by officials when received in audience by the emperor in ancient times

瓠 gourd, a kind of annual climbing plant

【瓠果】pepo

【瓠子】a kind of edible gourd

扈 ①[书] retinue ②(Hù) a surname

【扈从】[书] ① retinue; retainer ② accompany; attend

糊 paste; gruel-like food: 辣椒~ *chili paste* /玉米~(*cornmeal*) *mush*

see also hū; hú

【糊弄】[方] ① deceive or mislead people; swindle: 你不要~人。*You should not swindle people.* ② go through the motions; be slipshod in work: 做事不应该~。*One shouldn't do his work in a careless way.*

huā

化 spend; expend: ~时间 *spend time*

see also huà

【化子】beggar

花[1] ① flower; blossom: 开~ *come into bloom* /雌~*female flower* /雄~ *male flower* ② ornamentary plant: 种~ *plant* (*or grow*) *flowers* /多漂亮的~儿呀! *How beautiful the flower is!* ③ like or shaped as a flower: 雪~儿 *snowflake* /浪~ *the foam of breaking waves* /火~儿 *spark* /印~ *printing*; *stamp duty* ④ fireworks: 放~ *let off fireworks* ⑤ pattern; design: 白地蓝~ *blue patterns on a white surface* /窗帘上的~很漂亮。*The design on the curtain is beautiful.* ⑥ decorated with flowers: 雕~家具 *furniture with carvings* ⑦ multicoloured; multipatterned: ~布 *cotton print*; *print* /头发~白 *grey-haired* / ~边 *decorative border*; *lace* /那是只~猫。*The cat looks variegated.* ⑧ blurred; dim: 我眼~了。*My eyes are blurred.* ⑨ threadbare: 衣服袖子都磨~了。*The coat is threadbare at the sleeves.* ⑩ hypocritical; tricky: 耍~招 *play tricks* ⑪ flower; cream; essence: 文艺之~ *flower of literature an art* ⑫[喻] young and beautiful woman: 校~ *campus belle* ⑬ prostitute; courtesan: 寻~问柳 *spend time with prostitutes*; *go whoring* ⑭ cotton: 轧~ *gin cotton* ⑮ particles; drops: 泪~儿 *tears* /葱~ *chopped spring onion* ⑯ young of certain animals: 鱼~ *fish fry* ⑰ smallpox: 出~儿 *get smallpox* /种~儿 *vaccinate* ⑱ wound: 挂~ *get wounded in a battle* ⑲ (Huā) a surname

花[2] spend; expend: ~一年工夫 *spend one year* /很~时间 *time-consuming* /他~了很大的劲儿去搬那块大石头。*He made a big effort to move the rock.*

【花白】(of hair or beard) gray; grizzled: 头发~ *with gray hair*; *grey-haired*

【花斑】piebald: ~马 *a piebald horse*

【花瓣】petal; petalage: 玫瑰~ *rose petals*

【花苞】bud: 长满~的枝条 *branches in full bud*

【花绷子】embroidery fame; hoop

【花边】① decorative border; lace: 带~的衣领 *a lace collar* ②【纺】cording; fancy lace; purl: 带~的裙子 *dress with lace trimmings* ③【印】fancy borders in printing ④[方] silver dollar

【花边新闻】titbits (of news); news in box; interesting sidelights: 一则关于总统的~ *a juicy titbit of gossip about the President*

【花边纸】lace paper

【花柄】flower stalk

【花布】print; cotton print

【花不棱登】[口] variegated; loud; flashy; gaudy: 这件衣服~的，不适合老师在课堂上穿着。*This coat is too fancy for a teacher to wear at class.*

【花彩】festoon: ~装饰 *festoonery*

【花草】flowers and plants

【花插】① flower pad ② container for cut flowers

【花插着】interspersed; mixed: 草地上~点缀着星形花坛。*The lawn is interspersed with flowerbeds in the shape of stars.*

【花茶】scented tea: 茉莉~ *scented jasmine tea*

【花铲】trowel; scoop

【花厂】[旧] flower shop

【花车】festooned vehicle; float

【花痴】anthomaniac

【花池子】flower bed

【花丛】flowering shrubs; flowers in clusters

【花簇】flowers in clusters; inflorescence

【花大姐】【动】potato ladybird; bug

【花大钱】pay a lot of money; pay through the nose: 如果你想买那座别墅可要~。*You'll have to pay through nose if you want that villa.*

【花旦】【戏】female role in Chinese opera

【花道】ikebana, art of Japanese flower way

【花灯】festive lantern (as displayed on the Lantern Festival)

【花点子】① trick; deceit; artifice: 他用~骗走了我的钱。*He got the money from me by a trick.* ② fancy but impractical idea

【花店】flower shop; florist's

【花雕】high-grade Shaoxing wine

【花缎】brocade; figured satin; damask: ~刺绣 *brocade embroidery*

【花朵】flower; blossom: 儿童是祖国的~。*Children are the flower of our motherland.*

【花萼】calyx: ~喷雾 *calyx spray*

【花儿】a folk song popular in Gansu, Qinghai and Ningxia

【花房】greenhouse; garden house

H

【花肥】① fertilizers or manure applied at the time of florescence for more flowers and fruits ② fertilizers or manure for flowers in pots
【花费】(huāfèi) spend; expend; cost; use up:他生活讲究，～很大。*He lived high and expended largely.*
【花费】(huāfei) expense; money spent; expenditure:铺张的～ *an extravagant expenditure* /重新装饰房屋将是一项很大的～。*Redecorating the house will be a considerable expense.*
【花粉】①【植】pollen: ～壁 *pollen wall* / ～孢子 *pollen spore* / ～病 *pollen allergy*; *hay fever* / ～抗原 *pollen-antigen* / ～粒 *microspore* / ～食品 *pollen food*; *beebread food* / ～植株 *pollen plant* ②【药】powder made of Chinese trichosanthes' root
【花秆】sighting rod; rank
【花岗岩】① granite: ～冲击物 *granite wash* / ～质层 *granitic layer* / ～状 *eugranitic* ② granite-like; stubborn
【花岗岩脑袋】granite-like skull; ossified thinking; obstinate:多年来轻易的成功把他变成了～。*Years of easy success had ossified his thinking.*
【花格】lattice: ～墙 *lattice wall* / ～装饰 *bratticing*
【花梗】stalk; scape; peduncle; flower stalk
【花骨朵】flower bud
【花鼓】flower-drum, a folk dance popular in the Changjiang valley: ～戏 *flower-drum opera, popular in Hunan, Hubei, Jiangxi and Anhui provinces*
【花冠】① corolla; chaplet:合瓣～ *gamopetalous corolla* /离瓣～*choripetalous corolla* / ～期 *garland stage* ② wreath; sumptuous hat worn by a woman on her wedding day
【花好月圆】blooming flowers and full moon — perfect conjugal bliss
【花和尚】unconventional monk (who drinks wine, eats meat, etc.)
【花盒】fireworks
【花红柳绿】① bright red blossoms and green willows ② gorgeously dressed; colourful:春节那天，孩子们打扮得～。*On Spring Festival, the children were gorgeously dressed.*
【花喉】gorge
【花候】flowering season
【花花肠子】[方] scheme; trick; craft: 他的～可多了。*He is a man full of craft.*
【花花公子】clubman; dandy; dude; coxcomb; fop; spark; toff; playboy: ～的外表 *a dandified appearance*
【花花绿绿】brightly coloured; multicoloured:穿得～的 *be colourfully dressed*
【花花世界】merry and material world; the mortal world; vanity fair: ～使这些小女孩们眼花缭乱。*The girls were dazzled by the gaiety and splendour of the metropolis.*
【花花太岁】lascivious despot or bully; king of lechers
【花环】① garland; floral hoop ② wreath:戴着～的美丽新娘 *the beautiful bride with wreath*
【花卉】① flowers and plants ②【美】painting of flowers and plants in traditional Chinese style: ～画 *flower-and-plant painting*
【花会】① flower fair ② flower display
【花甲】sixty years of age
【花架】pergola
【花架子】① showy but useless martial arts movements ② good outside but impractical in fact; show piece
【花剑】【体】foil; fleuret
【花键】【机】spline: ～轴 *spline shaft* / ～座 *splined hub*
【花匠】gardener; florist
【花椒】①【植】Chinese prickly ash ② seeds of such plant: ～粉 *seed powder of Chinese prickly ash*
【花轿】bridal sedan chair
【花秸】chopped straw
【花街柳巷】red-light district; streets of ill repute
【花镜】presbyopic glasses
【花酒】drink and make accompanied by singsong girls
【花卷】steamed twisted (or plaited) roll
【花葵】【植】tree mallow
【花魁】① queen of flowers — an epithet for the plum blossom or a famous courtesan ② celebrated prostitute
【花篮】① flower basket ② beautifully decorated basket
【花蕾】flower bud
【花里胡哨】① gaudy; garish; loud; tawdry: ～的时装 *a gaudy costume* ② showy; not reliable; florid: ～的广告战 *a splashy advertising campaign* / ～的学术版本 *a pretentious scholarly edition*
【花脸】male character in traditional Chinese opera with a darkish painted face
【花翎】peacock feather on an official's hat
【花露水】perfumed toilet water
【花面狸】masked civet; gem-faced civet
【花苗】① flower seedling: 育～ *grow seedling* ② [方] seedlings of cotton
【花名册】register; membership roster; muster roll; rota
【花木】flowers and trees (in parks and gardens): 禁止攀折～! *Don't pick flowers!*
【花农】flower grower
【花牌】face cards; court cards
【花盘】①【植】flower disc ②【机】disc chuck; faceplate
【花炮】firework and firecrackers
【花盆】flowerpot
【花瓶】① vase; flower vase; jardiniere ② a woman who gets her position by good-looking appearance instead of ability
【花圃】flower nursery; flower garden
【花谱】florilegium

【花期】florescence of plants; flowering season
【花旗】Stars and Stripes; star-spangled banner — the United States
【花旗参】American ginseng
【花旗银行】(US) First National City Bank of New York
【花扦儿】fresh flower with twig; paper flower
【花前月下】amidst flowers and in the midnight — an ideal place for lovers
【花枪】① short spear used by ancient people ② trickery; deceit: 耍～ *play tricks*
【花腔】① florid ornamentation in opera singing; coloratura ② guileful talk: 靠耍～达到目的 *achieve one's ends guilefully*
【花墙】tracery wall; lattice wall
【花俏】(of clothes) bright-coloured and fashionable
【花青】【化】cyanine: ～燃料 *cyanine dyes*
【花圈】wreath; garland: 献～ *lay a wreath (at the tomb of sb)*
【花拳绣腿】showy or fancy but not practical martial arts
【花雀】bramble finch
【花儿匠】① gardener ② artificial flower maker
【花儿针】embroidery needle
【花容月貌】as beautiful as a flower and charming as a moon — extreme beauty
【花蕊】【植】stamen; pistil
【花色】① design and colour ② variety of designs, sizes, colours, etc.: ～齐备 *a great variety of goods*
【花衫】a female role in traditional opera, stressing both acting and singing
【花哨】bright-coloured; flowery: ～的广告 *flaring advertisements*
【花生】【植】peanut; groundnut: ～饼 *peanut cake* / ～蛋白酶 *arachain* / ～豆 *shelled peanut; peanut kernel* / ～酱 *peanut butter* / ～米 *peanut; shelled peanut; pignut* / ～仁儿 *groundnut; peanut; shelled peanut* / ～糖 *peanut brittle* / ～油 *arachis oil; earthnut oil*
【花式】fancy: ～玻璃纱 *fancy glass yarn* / ～糕点 *fancy cakes* / ～跳伞 *style jumping* / ～跳水 *fancy diving* / ～游泳 *fancy swimming*
【花市】flower fair (or market)
【花饰】ornamental design; floriation; curlicue: ～窗格 *tracery* / ～图案 *fillet*
【花束】bouquet; a bunch of flowers: ～期 *bouquet stage* / ～月季 *floribunda*
【花丝】①【植】filament ② filigree: ～绸 *grisaille* / ～绒 *velvet-figured; brocaded velvet* / ～镶嵌 *filigree inlaying*
【花坛】flower bed; flower terrace; border; parterre
【花体】curlicue; curlycue; squiggle
【花天酒地】indulge in dissipation; lead a gay life; be on the tiles; have one's fling; lead a decadent and dissolute life: 他过着～的生活。*He indulged in a gay life.*
【花厅】drawing room; parlour
【花筒】cylindrical fireworks
【花头】①[方] decorative pattern; decorative figure: 印有漂亮葵花～的布 *cloth with beautiful figures of sunflower* ② trick; artifice; ruse: 他靠耍～得到了那笔钱。*He acquired that sum of money by artifice.* ③ fresh ideas; new ideas: 他的～真多。*He is full of fresh ideas.* ④ knack: 这里面有点～。*There is a knack in it.*
【花团锦簇】bouquets of flowers and piles of brocades — rich multicolored decorations; ornamental: 她走出了屋子来见我们，帽子弄得～的。*With rich multicoloured decorations on her hat, she went out of her room to meet us.*
【花纹】decorative pattern; figure; arabesquitic: 这块布上有红白方格的～。*The cloth has a pattern of red and white squares.*
【花线】①【电】flexible cord; flex ② coloured thread
【花香】potpourri; fragrance of the flowers: ～扑鼻 *the scent of flowers assails the nostrils*
【花项】[方] item to spend money on: 你一独立生活～就多了，所以应该开始攒钱了。*You should begin saving money as you'll lead an independent life and need money on many aspects.*
【花销】① spend; expend: 他在房子上～了一大笔钱。*He expended a large sum on his apartment.* ② cost; expense: 她报销了旅费～。*She was reimbursed for her travel expenses.* ③[旧] commission; taxes and levies
【花鞋】[方] embroidered shoes
【花谢】blossom fall: ～结子 *go to seed*
【花信】florescence
【花形的】floriated; floral: 以～图案装饰 *decorate with floral designs*
【花序】【植】anthotaxy; inflorescence: ～枯萎 *destruction of inflorescence* / ～轴 *rachis*
【花絮】interesting sidelights; titbits (of news): 大会～ *interesting sidelights on the convention*
【花学】anthology
【花薰】a jade vessel for perfuming; jade perfumer
【花压板】presser cut
【花芽】【植】(flower) bud; blossom bud: ～形成 *flower bud formation* / ～孕育 *flower bud initiation*
【花言巧语】blandishments; double talk; with sweet words on one's lips; smooth-tongued; slickness; fair-spoken; fine rhetoric; coax: 不为～所动 *be proof against sweet words* / ～是不中用的。*Fine words butter no parsnips.*
【花眼】presbyopia
【花秧】flower sapling
【花样】①(floral) design; pattern; variety; model: ～翻新 *innovations in pattern or design* / ～滑冰 *figure skating* / ～滑水 *acrobatic water skiing* / ～跳伞 *skydiving* / ～游泳 *synchronized swimming; water ballet* ②embroidery patterns ③ trick
【花样刀】ice skates (for figure skating)

【花艺】floriculture
【花音】grace note; grace notes
【花园】garden; flower garden: ~城市 *flower city* / ~公寓 *garden apartment*
【花展】flower show
【花账】padded accounts for bills: 开~ *pad accounts*
【花招】① showy but impractical movement in martial art ② trick; stratagem; scheme; chicanery: 别耍~! *Don't try any tricks!*
【花枝】【植】spray
【花枝招展】(of women) be gorgeously dressed; be seductively dressed; as pretty as flowers
【花种】seeds of flowering plant
【花轴】【植】floral axis; rachides; rachis
【花烛】[旧] candles with dragon and phoenix pattern used in the bridal chamber
【花子】beggar
【花子儿】①flower seed ②[方] cotton seed: ~油 *cotton-seed oil*

哗 [象]: 他的眼泪~地流了下来。*He burst into tears.*
see also huá

huá

划[1] paddle; row: ~船 *paddle a boat*

划[2] be to one's profit: ~得着。*It pays.*

划[3] scratch; cut the surface of: 把手~伤了 *have one's hand cut*
see also huà

【划不来】being not worth it; do not pay: 你过分注意那件事,有点~。*It does not deserve too much of your attention.*
【划得来】being worth it; pay; to be of profit: 做这事~。*It proves profitable.*
【划拉】[方] ① brush away: 把桌子上的东西都~掉了 *brush away the things on the desk* ② scrawl; scribble: 不要以为~几个字就可以上著名的大学。*It is not likely that you will enter a famous university only by scribbling a few words on your papers.*
【划拳】finger-guessing game — a drinking game at feasts
【划水】【体】strike water
【划算】① calculate; weigh; figure out: 我得~一下这笔生意能带来多少钱。*I shall calculate how much this business can bring in for me.* ② to one's profit: 这笔生意对我们大家都~。*The deal is profitable to all of us.*
【划艇】【体】canoe
【划子】small rowboat

华[1] ① brilliant; magnificent; splendid: 光~ *brilliance; splendour* ② corona: 月~ *diffused moonlight* ③ prosperous; flourishing: 繁~ *flourishing* / 奢~ *extravagant* ④ best part; cream: 精~ *cream; essence; elite* / 英~ *cream; the best or most outstanding persons or things; elite* ⑤ luxurious; flashy: 豪~ *luxurious; splendid* ⑥ time; years; course of time, esp. prime of youth: 韶~ *glorious youth* / 似水年~ *Time passes like flowing water.* ⑦ grizzled; grayish: ~发 *gray hair* ⑧ [书] (a term of respect) your: ~宗 *your namesake*

华[2] matter formed by sediment of mineral in spring water: 钙~ *travertine*

华[3] ① China: ~北 *north China* / ~东 *east China* / ~南 *south China* / 驻~大使 *ambassador to China* ② Chinese: 英~词典 *an English-Chinese dictionary* ③ (Huá) a surname
see also huà

【华表】ornamental columns erected (in front of palaces, tombs, etc.)
【华达呢】gabardine: ~服装 *gabardine; gabardine*
【华诞】[书] your birthday
【华灯】colourfully decorated lantern; light
【华灯初上】the time when the lights are lit in the evening
【华而不实】showy; pompous; gimcrack; slick; tinsel; flashy and without substance; superficially clever; have all one's goods in the window speciosity: ~的晚会和促销活动 *the tinsel of parties and promotional events* / 一个~的公告 *a pompous proclamation*
【华尔街】Wall Street — a street in Manhattan, New York: ~老板 *Wall Streeters*
【华尔兹】waltz: 跳~ *dance a waltz* / 他同她在屋里跳~。*He waltzed her round the room.*
【华发】[书] grey hair
【华夫饼干】waffle, a light, crisp battercake baked in a waffle iron
【华服】panoply: 身着~的将军的肖像 *portrait of the general in full panoply*
【华盖】① canopy (as over an imperial carriage); baldachin; marquee ②【天】aureole
【华工】[旧] Chinese labourers abroad
【华贵】① magnificent; luxurious; showy; costly; gorgeous; sumptuous: ~的珠宝 *magnificent jewels* ② luxurious and wealthy: ~之家 *a wealthy family*
【华里】*li*, a Chinese unit of length (=1/2 kilometre)
【华丽】magnificent; flamboyant; luxurious; pompous: 那部影片中的服装非常~。*The costumes in the film are very magnificent.* / 穿着一件维多利亚时期的~的长袍 *wear a gorgeous Victorian gown*
【华美】magnificent; resplendent; gorgeous; gayer: 挂着~挂毯的墙壁 *walls hung with gorgeous tapestries*
【华侨】overseas Chinese: ~投资公司 *Overseas Chinese Investment Company* / 归国~ *returned overseas Chinese*
【华人】① Chinese ② foreign citizens of Chinese origin or descent
【华沙】Warsaw, the capital of Poland

H

【华沙条约】the Warsaw Treaty (1955): ~组织 *the Warsaw Treaty Organization*

【华盛顿】① George Washington (1732—1799), American military leader and the first President of the United States (1789—1797). ② Washington State, a state of the northwest United States on the Pacific Ocean ③ Washington, D. C. — the capital of the United States

【华氏】Fahrenheit: ~温度 *degree Fahrenheit; Fahrenheit*

【华饰】braveness; flourish: 一段充满~的讲话 *a long speech with many rhetorical flourishes*

【华夏】an ancient name for China: ~古陆 *Cathysia* / ~子孙 *the descendants of the Chinese Nation*

【华裔】①[书] China and the neighbouring countries ② foreign citizen of Chinese origin

【华语】the Chinese language; Chinese

【华约】the Warsaw Treaty Organization

哗 noise; clamour: 喧~ *confused noise; hubbub*

see also huā

【哗变】mutiny: 船员因反抗船长而~。*The crew mutinies against its captain.*

【哗然】in a tumult in an uproar; in commotion: 听到这个消息,举国~。*The whole nation was in an uproar at the news.* /舆论~。*There was a public outcry or public Public opinion was seething with indignation.*

【哗笑】uproarious laughter; roar with laughter

【哗众取宠】talk big to impress others; try to please the public with claptrap

骅

【骅骝】[书] very swift red horse

猾 cunning; sly: 奸~ *sly*

滑 ① slippery; smooth: 下雪后地很~。*The ground is very slippery after the snow.* ② slip; slide: ~了一跤 *slip and fall* /船~入水中。*The ship slid into the water.* /剃刀一~把我的脸割破了。*The razor slipped and cut my cheek.* ③ cunning; dishonest: 狡~ *sly; tricky* /这个人很~。*This guy is very crafty.* ④ (Huá) a surname

【滑板】①【机】operating slide ②【体】skateboard ③【体】(of table tennis) feint play

【滑冰】①【体】skating; ice-skating: 花样~ *figure skating* /双人花样~ *pair skating* /速度~ *speed skating* / ~场 *skating rink* ② skate on ice

【滑不唧溜】[方] slippery: 路上结了冰,走起来~。*Ice made the path slippery underfoot.*

【滑车】①【机】block; wheel; pulley ②【生理】trochlea

【滑道】skidway; slideway; runway; slide

【滑动】slide; glide: ~闸门 *slide gate* /轴承 *sliding bearing*

【滑动摩擦】【物】sliding friction: ~系数 *coefficient of sliding friction*

【滑竿】jampan, a kind of litter

【滑轨】sliding rail; slideway

【滑旱冰】roller skate

【滑稽】① amusing; funny; humourous: 他说话很~。*He's got a funny way of talking.* ②【戏】comic talk

【滑稽戏】【戏】a kind of farce, popular in Shanghai, Jiangsu and Zhejiang Provinces

【滑溜】(huáliū) stir-fried with thick gravy

【滑溜】(huáliu) [口] smooth; silky; slippery: 这布摸起来很~。*The cloth feels smooth.*

【滑轮】【机】pulley; block: 定~ *fixed pulley* /动~ *movable pulley* / ~杆 *roller arm* / ~组 *pulley block; block and falls*

【滑腻】(of the skin) satiny; velvety; creamy: 她~的皮肤 *her satiny skin*

【滑坡】①【地】hill-creep; land slide; landslip ② go steadily downhill; slump; decline: 这个厂的生产在~。*The production in this factory is on the decrease.*

【滑橇】skidding; runner: ~式起落架 *skid landing gear*

【滑润】smooth: 大理石摸起来很~。*Marble is smooth to the touch.*

【滑水】【体】water ski: ~板 *hydro-ski* / ~运动 *water skiing*

【滑速】slip velocity

【滑梯】slide; children's slide

【滑天下之大稽】be the biggest joke in the world; absurd to the extreme

【滑铁卢】Waterloo, a place in Belgium: ~战役 *Battle of Waterloo*

【滑头】① slippery person; slicker; fox; old file ② slick; slippery; cunning; artful: 他非常~。*He is as slippery as an eel.*

【滑头滑脑】sly; cunning; crafty; slick; foxy: 他在我们面前~。*He showed a great deal of cunning before us.*

【滑翔】glide: ~飞行 *sailflying; glide* / ~运动 *gliding; sailplaning* /那个芭蕾舞女演员舞姿优美,宛如~。*So graceful was the ballerina that she just seemed to glide.*

【滑翔机】【航】glider; sailplane; air sailer: ~机场 *gliderport*

【滑行】① slide; coast: 冰上~ *slide on the ice* ② taxi: 飞机降落,在跑道上~。*The plane came in and taxied along the runway.*

【滑行道】【航】taxi strip; taxi track; taxi way

【滑雪】【体】ski; skiing: 高山~ *alpine skiing*

【滑雪板】skis

【滑雪场】ski run

【滑雪服】ski suit

【滑雪衫】ski shirt

【滑雪鞋】ski boots

【滑雪杖】ski pole; ski stick

【滑音】①【语】glide ②【音】portamento

【滑座】slide carriage; slide rest

H

huà

化[1] ① change; turn: 变～ *change; alter* /～暗为明 *change dark into light* /～悲为喜 *turn one's sadness into joy; turn one's sorrow into happiness* /～敌为友 *convert enemies into friends* /～悲痛为力量 *turn sorrow into strength* ② convert; influence: 教～ *educate and influence* ③ melt; dissolve ④ digest; dispel; remove: ～食 *help digestion* ⑤ burn up: 焚～ *burn up; incinerate* ⑥ (of monks and priests) pass away; die: 坐～ *pass away in a sitting posture* ⑦ chemistry: 生～ *biochemistry* ⑧ used as a suffix to indicate sth or sb is becoming or made to have that attribute: 丑～ *discredit* /绿～ *make (a place) green by planting trees, flowers, etc.*

化[2] 【宗】(of Buddhist monks or Taoist priests) beg alms: 募～ *collect alms*
see also huā

【化虫丸】【药】traditional Chinese pills used to kill the tiny worms living inside of one's body

【化除】eliminate; dispel; remove; clear up: ～疑虑(恐惧,烦恼) *dispel sb's doubts (fears, worries)*

【化冻】thaw; melt; defrost: 趁着没～去溜冰 *go skating before the thaw* /冻鸡应彻底～后再烹调。*A frozen chicken should be allowed to defrost completely before cooking.*

【化肥】chemical fertilizer: ～厂 *fertilizer plant* /～撒肥机 *fertilizer distributor* /～添加剂 *fertilizer additive*

【化废为宝】turn waste materials into valuable (or useful) things; make a silk purse out of a sow's ear

【化风】wind transmission

【化粪池】septic tank

【化腐朽为神奇】turn the foul and rotten into the rare and ethereal; make the useless useful; transform the corruptible into mysterious life

【化干戈为玉帛】turn hostility into friendship — put an end to war and have peace; cease hostilities and make peace; bury the hatchet

【化工】chemistry industry; chemical engineering: ～产品 *chemistry products* /～厂 *chemistry plant; laboratory* /～过程 *chemical process* /～机械厂 *chemical machine works* /～商品 *chemical goods* /～原料 *industrial chemicals*

【化公为私】turn public property into private things; embezzle (or appropriate) public property: 银行分行行长在他工作的银行里把一万美元～。*The head of the branch bank embezzled ten thousand dollars from the bank where he worked.*

【化合】【化】chemical combination: ～比例 *combining proportion* /～反应 *combination reaction* /～光 *chemiluminescence* /～价 *valence; atomicity* /～力 *combining power* /～量 *combining weight* /～热 *combining heat* /～水 *combined water; water of hydration* /～体积 *combining volume* /～作用 *combination*

【化合物】【化】chemical compound; compound: 大分子～ *macromolecular compound* /高分子～ *high polymer; highly polymerized compound* /共价～ *covalent compound* /光敏～ *light-sensitive compound* /挥发性～ *volatile compound* /加成～ *addition compound* /离子～ *ionic compound* /两性～ *amphiprotic compound* /弹性～ *elastomeric compound* /碳环～ *carbocyclic compound* /天然～ *native compound* /无机～ *inorganic compound* /吸附～ *adsorption compound* /吸收～ *absorption compound* /水是氢和氧的～。*Water is a compound of hydrogen and oxygen.*

【化祸为福】turn bad luck into a blessing; turn disaster into good luck

【化剑为犁】beat swords into ploughshares; disarm and make peace

【化解】resolve; eliminate

【化疗】chemotherapy: ～专家 *chemotherapist*

【化零为整】gather parts into a whole; assemble the parts into a whole

【化民成俗】influence the people and form moral customs

【化名】① use an assumed name: 他的真名是约翰逊,但是他常常用～史密斯。*His real name was Johnson, but he often went by the alias of Smith.* ② assumed name; alias: 诈骗犯用不同的～行骗。*The swindler worked under various aliases.*

【化募】(of Buddhist monks or Taoist priests) collect alms

【化脓】fester; suppurate; maturate; purulence; pyogenesis: 一旦弄脏了伤口,可能会～。*A dirty wound will probably fester.*

【化热】heat-transmission

【化身】① incarnation: 魔鬼的～ *devil incarnate* ② embodiment: 那位主要舞蹈演员简直是美的～。*The leading dancer is the embodiment of grace.*

【化生】①【生理】metaplasia ②[书] give birth and foster growth: 天地～万物。*Heaven and earth foster all things in universe.*

【化湿】resolving dampness

【化石】【考】fossil: 标准～ *index fossil; guide fossil; key fossil; type fossil; leading fossil* /化学～ *chemical fossils* /活～ *living fossil* /转生～ *derived fossils* /指带～ *zone fossil* /指相～ *facies fossil* /踪迹～ *trace fossil* /～带 *fossil zone* /～动物 *zoolite* /～动物学 *zoogeology* /～块 *steinkern* /～矿石 *fossil ore* /～昆虫 *fossil insect* /～马 *anchithere* /～燃料 *fossil fuel* /～人类 *fossil man* /～珊瑚 *corallite* /(古象的)～象牙 *fossil ivory* /(动物的)～遗体 *fossil remains* /～学 *fossilology* /～学家 *fossilist* /～足迹 *ichnite* /～足迹学 *ichnology* /～组合 *fossil assemblage* /～作用 *fossilization*

【化痰】【中医】reduce phlegm: 清热～ *alleviate fever and reduce phlegm* /～平喘 *resolving sputum and relieving asthma* /～散结 *reducing phlegm and resolving masses* /～生津 *act as expectorant* /～通

络 eliminating phlegm and freeing channels / ~止咳 preventing phlegm from forming and stopping coughing

【化为灰烬】turn dust and ashes; crumble to dust; be consumed by fire：大火过后，她的书全部~。*Ashes were all that remained of her books after the fire.* /整座房子不到一小时就~。*The whole house went up in smoke in less than an hour.*

【化为泡影】disappear like soap bubbles; come to naught; fail to come true：我成功的希望~。*My hopes of success have vanished.*

【化为乌有】pass into nothingness; vanish; melt into thin air; dwindle away into nothing; vanish into nothingness; go up in smoke

【化纤】chemical fibre

【化险为夷】turn danger into safety; head off a disaster; come safely out of danger; save the situation：我已濒于破产，是你借给我的钱使我~。*I was nearly bankrupt, but your loan saved my bacon.*

【化形】(of demons and ghosts) change of appearance

【化学】① chemistry：理论~*theoretical chemistry* / 有机~*organic chemistry* / ~爆炸 *chemical explosion* / ~变化 *chemical change*/ ~玻璃 *chemical glass* / ~成分 *chemical composition*; *chemical constitution* / ~沉积 *chemical deposition*; *chemical plating* / ~除草剂 *chemical herbicide* / ~除莠 *chemical weed control* / ~处理 *chemical treatment* / ~传递 *chemical transmission* / ~瓷器 *chemical porcelain* / ~地雷 *chemical mine* / ~电源 *electrochemical power source* / ~动力学 *chemical kinetics* / ~镀 *chemical plating* / ~发光 *chemiluminescence* / ~反应 *chemical reaction* / ~反应剂 *chemical reactor* / ~反应式 *chemical reaction formula* / ~方程式 *chemical equation* / ~仿生学 *chemical bionics* / ~肥料 *chemical fertilizer* / ~肥料污染 *chemical fertilizer pollution* / ~废物 *chemical waste* / ~分解 *chemolysis*; *analysis* / ~分析 *chemical analysis* / ~符号 *chemical symbol* / ~干燥 *chemical seasoning* / ~感应 *chemoreception*; *chemoreceptivity* / ~工厂 *chemical plant* / ~工程 *chemical engineering* / ~工业 *chemical industry* / ~工艺 *chemical technology* / ~海洋学 *chemical oceanography* / ~合成 *chemosynthesis* / ~合成品 *synthetic* / ~化石 *chemical fossil* / ~环境 *chemical environment* / ~火箭 *chemical rocket* / ~家 *chemist* / ~计算 *stoichiometric calculation* / ~加工 *chemical machining*; *chemical milling* / ~监测 *chemical monitoring* / ~键 *chemical bond* / ~鉴定 *chemical analysis* / ~结构 *chemical construction* / ~扩散 *chemical diffusion* / ~疗法 *chemotherapeutics*; *chemotherapy iatrochemistry* / ~蚀刻 *chemical etching* / ~试剂 *chemical reagent* / ~污染 *chemical pollution* /无机~*inorganic chemistry* / ~武器 *chemical weapon* / ~纤维 *chemical fiber* / ~性质 *chemical property* / ~岩 *chemical rock* / ~药品 *chemical*; *chemical medicine* / ~原理 *principles of chemistry* ②[口] *celluloid*：这把梳子是~的。*This comb is made of celluloid.*

【化验】laboratory test; chemical examination; assay：~报告 *analysis report* / ~单 *laboratory test report* /血常规~*ordinary blood test* / ~员 *laboratorian*; *analyst* /这矿石经~证明含金量很高。*The ore assays high in gold.*

【化缘】(of Buddhist monks or Taoist priests) beg alms; mendicant：~钵 *begging bowl* / ~和尚 *a mendicant Buddhist monk*

【化斋】(of Buddhist monks or Taoist priests) beg a vegetarian meal

【化整为零】break up the whole into parts

【化妆】make up; apply cosmetics; dressing; face-painting; prink; titivate; toilet; toilette：~膏 *pomade* / ~盒 *dressing case*; *powder box* / ~墨 *kohl*/ ~师 *dresser*; *makeup girl* / ~水 *astringent* / ~台 *dressing-table*; *dresser* / ~舞会 *costume ball* / ~香水 *beauty water* / ~椅 *dressing stool* / ~纸 *facial tissue* /她~以便看上去漂亮些。*She made up her face to look prettier.*

【化妆品】cosmetics; make up; toiletry：~工业 *cosmetics industry* / ~广告 *cosmetic urge*

【化妆室】① dressing room; powder room ②[方] toilet; lavatory

【化装】①(of actors) dress up：他~扮演一个老人。*He made up for the part of an old man.* ② disguise：~师 *makeup man* / ~室 *dressing room* / ~舞会 *costume ball*; *fancy dress ball*; *masquerade* /他~成士兵。*He disguises himself as a soldier.*

划

① divide a region into certain areas; delimit：~成分 *determine class status* / ~分区域 *divide a region into several areas* / ~清界限 *draw a clear line of demarcation* ② transfer; assign：银行已经将那笔款项~到了他的账户上。*The bank has transferred the sum to his account.* ③ plan：筹~ *plan and prepare* /你去筹~一下这件事。*Please work out a plan for this.*
see also huá

【划拨】① appropriate; transfer：政府~出一大笔钱修建学校。*The government appropriated a large sum of money for building schools.* ② assign; allot; allocate：这块地皮已经~用作建一座新医院。*That space has been allocated for a new hospital.*

【划策】scheme; plan; give counsel; offer advice

【划等号】equate one thing with another：你不能把年轻和缺乏经验~。*You shouldn't equate inexperience with youth.*

【划定】delimit; designate：~边界 *delimit a frontier*; *designate boundaries*

【划分】① divide; partition：~势力范围 *carve out spheres of influence* /地球上最大的一块陆地是沿着乌拉尔山脉~为两个大洲的。*The largest landmass is divided into two continents along the Ural Mountains.* ② differentiate; distinguish：~善恶 *distinguish good from evil*

H

【划粉】tailor's chalk
【划归】put under (sb's administration, etc.); incorporate into: 这个企业～地方管理。*The enterprise has been put under local administration.*
【划痕】scratch; score: ～规 *scratch gauge* / ～器 *scratcher* / ～硬度 *scratch hardness*
【划价】have a prescription priced (in a hospital dispensary); calculate the medical expenses: 病人交款之前需要～。*Before paying, patients have to have their prescription priced.*
【划句号】put in a period or full stop — finish doing sth; bring sth to a conclusion: 他已经给这件事迅速地～了。*He brought the matter to a speedy conclusion.*
【划框框】set limits; place restrictions
【划清】draw a clear line of demarcation; make a clear distinction: ～界限 *draw a clear demarcation line (between)* / ～是非 *make a clear distinction between right and wrong*
【划时代】epoch-making; (of an important event) beginning a new period in history: 五四运动具有～的历史意义。*The May Fourth Movement has an epoch-making historical significance.*
【划线】lineation; marking off; marking out; score; ruling: ～刀 *race knife* / ～工 *router*; *liner-off* / ～规 *marking-gauge* / ～技术 *ruling* / ～台 *marking-off table* / ～针 *marking-off pin*; *scriber* / ～支票 *crossed cheque*
【划一】① uniform; standardized: 形状尺寸～ *of uniform size and shape* ② standardize: ～制度 *standardize rules and regulations*; *make the system uniform*
【划一不二】① fixed; unalterable: ～的价格 *fixed price (no bargaining)* ② 写文章可长可短，没有～的公式。*The articles could be long or short, without rigid rules to follow.*

华 ① Mount Hua, in Shaanxi Province ② (Huà) a surname
see also huá

画[1] ① draw; paint; write: ～个圈 *draw a circle* / ～素描 *sketch*; *draw a sketch* ② picture; drawing; painting: 版～ *engraving* /壁～ *mural painting* /年～儿 *New Year picture* /人物～ *figure painting* /水彩～ *watercolour painting* /油～ *oil painting* ③ be decorated with paintings or pictures

画[2] ① draw; mark; sign: ～线 *draw a line* ② (of a Chinese character) stroke: "广"字有三画。*The character "广" is made up of three strokes.* ③ [方] horizontal stroke (in Chinese character)

【画板】【美】drawing board; palette
【画报】illustrated magazine or newspaper; pictorial
【画笔】【美】brush; painting brush; brush-pencil; hair pencil: ～图片 *paintbrush picture*
【画饼】a painted cake; pie in the sky
【画饼充饥】draw cakes to satisfy one's hunger — feed on illusions; comfort oneself with imaginations
【画布】canvas (for painting): ～绷架 *chassis*
【画草图】roughdraw; sketch; block out
【画册】album of paintings; picture album
【画船】gaily-painted pleasure boat
【画到】sign in; check in; register one's attendance: 上午的会议要求8点～。*You're required to sign in at 8 o'clock for the meeting in the morning.*
【画地为牢】draw a circle on the ground to serve as a prison — restrict one's activities to a designated area or sphere; confine sb in a small circle
【画法】【美】technique of painting or drawing; brush work; brushwork: ～几何 *descriptive geometry* /这个画家～独到。*The artist's technique of painting is unique.*
【画舫】gaily (or gorgeously) painted pleasure boat
【画符】(of a Taoist priest) draw a magic figure or incantations to exorcise spirits and bring good or ill fortune: ～念咒 *draw magic characters and sing incantations*
【画幅】① picture; painting: 美丽的田野是天然的～。*The beautiful field is a natural painting.* ② size of a picture: ～虽然不大，所表现的天地却十分广阔。*Though the size of the picture is small, the content and vista showed is boundless.*
【画稿】① (of a person responsible) endorse an official draft to indicate approval ② rough sketch (of a painting)
【画格】【影】frame
【画工】① professional artisan-painter; commercial painter ② technique of painting or drawing
【画供】【律】sign on a written confession to a crime by the accused
【画夹】painting folder
【画家】painter; artist; drawer; penman: 名～ *a famous painter*
【画架】easel
【画匠】① artisan-painter; limner ② [贬] inferior painter
【画角】[古] painted military bugle
【画境】picturesque scene: 如入～ *feel as though one were in a landscape painting*
【画镜线】picture string
【画具】【美】painter's paraphernalia
【画卷】① picture scroll ② magnificent scenery (or spectacle): 雄伟的泰山宛如一幅壮观的天然～。*The great Mount Tai is like magnificent scenery of nature.*
【画绢】silk for drawing on; drawing silk
【画刊】① pictorial section of a newspaper ② pictorial
【画框】frame (of a picture)
【画廊】① painted corridor ② (picture) gallery; salon: ～里现正展出毕加索的作品。*Picasso's works are now on display in the gallery.*
【画龙点睛】bring a painted dragon to life by putting in the pupils of its eyes — add the touch that

brings a work of art to life; add (or make) the finishing touch: 文章的结尾出人意料,乃是～之笔。*The ending of the article is out of the readers' expectation and clinches the point.*

【画论】theory of painting

【画眉】①【动】*Garrulax canorus*, a kind of thrush ② draw or blacken eyebrows

【画谜】picture puzzle; rebus

【画面】① general appearance of a picture; tableau ②【影】frame: 影片开头的几个～为高潮部分作了铺垫。*Several frames at the beginning of the film foreshadows the climax.*

【画皮】disguise or mask of an evildoer: 他用智慧剥去了这个骗子的～。*He stripped the disguise off the imposter by his wisdom.*

【画片儿】[口] a miniature reproduction of a painting

【画片】miniature; reproduction of a painting; printed pictures; picture postcard: 明星～*picture of a star*

【画屏】painted screen

【画谱】① picture copybook ② a book on the art of drawing or painting

【画圈】draw a circle with a pen; draw a circle round one's name on a document submitted for approval to show that one has read it: 办公室里的人都～后,文件将提交会议讨论。*After people in the office have drawn circles round their names, the document will be submitted for discussion on the meeting.*

【画蛇添足】draw a snake with feet to it — ruin the effect by adding sth superfluous; carry coals to Newcastle; fan the breezes; gild the lily: 这个故事的结尾实在是～。*The last part of the story is entirely unnecessary.*

【画师】① master in painting; painter; artist ②artisan-painter; professional painter

【画十字】① draw a cross on a document in place of a signature by an illiterate ②【宗】make the sign of the cross; cross oneself

【画室】studio; atelier

【画刷】paintbrush; brush

【画坛】painting or drawing world; painting or drawing circles

【画帖】a book of model paintings or drawings

【画图】① draw designs, maps, etc. ② picture: ～纸板 *drawing board* / ～员 *designer*

【画外音】【影】voice-over; offscreen voice

【画像】① draw a portrait; portray: 请人～*sit for one's portrait* ② finished portrait; portrayal: 巨幅～ *huge portrait* / ～石 *stone relief* (*on ancient Chinese tombs, shrines, etc.*)

【画押】make one's cross mark; sign: 他被逼在契约上～。*He was forced to make his cross on a contract.*

【画页】page with illustrations (in a book or magazine); plate

【画苑】place where artists or painters gather; painting world

【画院】① imperial art academy ② art academy: 江苏～ *Art Academy of Jiangsu*

【画展】art exhibition; exhibition of paintings; art show: 他举办了一次个人～,展出了他10年中的作品。*He held a one-man exhibition of his paintings covering a period of ten years.*

【画纸】drawing paper

【画轴】painted scroll; scroll painting: 山水～*scroll painting of landscape*

【画字】[方] make one's cross or mark; sign: 这个穷苦的农民在契约上画了字。*The poor and miserable peasant signed the contract.*

话 ① word; talk; saying: 谈了几句～ *have a chat; say a few words* / 收回自己的～ *take back one's words* ② speak out; talk about: 茶～ *chat or talk at a tea party*

【话把儿】subject for ridicule; handle; proverb: 你要更谨慎些 — 否则你就会成为人们的～。*Be more discreet or you'll get yourself talked about.*

【话白】①【戏】monologue; dialogue ② monologue (by a storyteller); prologue

【话本】printed versions of the prompt-books used by popular story-tellers in Song and Yuan dynasties

【话别】say a few parting words; say good-bye; take one's farewell of: 他们在车站～。*They bid farewell at the station.*

【话柄】subject for ridicule; handle; proverb: 传为～*become the joke of the town* / 他不谨慎的行为留下了～。*His careless behaviours left behind a subject for ridicule.*

【话不离宗】talk shop; speak exclusively of one's own business

【话不投机】can't see eye to eye with sb; have a disagreeable conversation; have nothing in common: ～半句多。*Without agreement between too speakers, even a single word is a waste of breath.*

【话茬儿】①[方] thread of discourse or conversation: 在会上,他接着主任的～说了下去。*He took up the thread of the director's words and went on talking on the meeting.* ② tone of one's speech: 听他的～,我们估计他下个月就要出国了。*We guess from his tone of speech that he will go abroad next month.*

【话到舌边留半句】[俗] hold some words back when one is about to say it all — one should not be too straight and pour out all one's thoughts

【话到嘴边】swallow back the words on the tip of one's tongue; have sth at the tip of one's tongue: ～又被他咽了回去。*It' on the tip of his tongue, but he swallowed it back.*

【话锋】thread of discourse; topic of conversation: 我正想深入地问一些情况,他却～一转,开始了别的话题。*I wanted to get some further information when taking with him, but he switched the topic to other subjects.*

【话家常】chitchat; exchange small talk: 这两个家

庭主妇一有时间就坐在一起～。*Whenever they are free, the two housewives will sit together and chitchat.*

【话旧】talk over old times; reminisce: 他们一边喝茶,一边～。*They talked about past events over tea.*

【话剧】modern drama; stage play: ～团 *modern drama troupe; theatrical company*

【话口儿】[方] tone of speech; note: 听这姑娘的～,好像对小伙子不太中意。*From what the girl said, she seems not satisfied with the young man.*

【话里有话】have one's tongue in one's cheek; words mean more than they say; there is more to it than meets the ear: 他～,我听了很不痛快。*His words carried some implications and made me uncomfortable.*

【话篓子】[方] chatterbox; talkative person

【话路】speech channel; speech path; telephone channel: ～系统 *speech path system*

【话梅】preserved plum; plum candy

【话频】voice frequency (VF): ～载波 *voice carrier*

【话说】① it's told that...: ～明朝时期,城郊有一个穷苦的读书人。*It is told that in the Ming Dynasty, there was a poor scholar in the outskirts of the city.* ② talk; account; narration:《～长江》*Talk About the Changjiang River*

【话题】topic of a conversation; subject of a talk: 有趣的～*an interesting subject of conversation* /学生们总爱谈论社会上的热门～。*The students tend to talk about popular topics in the society.*

【话亭】telephone box or booth; kiosk

【话筒】① telephone transmitter ② microphone: ～怯 *mike fright* / ～调制 *microphone modulation*/ ～噪声 *microphone noise* ③ megaphone

【话头】thread of discourse: 打断～ *interrupt sb; cut sb short*

【话务量】telephone traffic; traffic volume; traffic load: ～单位 *traffic unit*

【话务员】(telephone) operator

【话匣子】[方] ① gramophone ② radio: 老太太一天到晚守着个～。*The old woman kept listening to the radio all the day.* ③ chatterbox; talkative person

【话绪】mood for or interest in talking: 酒引出了他的～。*Liquor aroused his mood for talking.*

【话音】① one's voice in speech: ～电流 *speaking current* / ～识别 *speech recognition* / ～特性 *characteristics of speech sounds* ② tone; implication

【话语】speech; remark; utterance: ～分析 *discourse analysis* /他用粗鲁的～批评我。*He passed rude remarks about me.*

【话中有话】overtones in conversation; with the tongue in the cheek: 他最近和我说话时总是～。*He talks with the tongue in the cheek when meeting me recently.*

【话嘴】mouthpiece

桦 【植】birch: 白～ *white birch* /黑～ *black birch* / ～木 *birch wood*

huái

怀 ① chest; bosom: 母亲把小孩抱在～里。*The mother held the little child in her arms.* ② mind; wish: 襟～坦白 *frank and open-minded* / 无介于～ *do not mind at all* /正中下～ *be just what one wishes* ③ keep in mind; cherish; think of: ～友 *think of a friend* ④ conceive (a child): ～了双胞胎 *be expecting twins* ⑤ harbour; conceive; nurse: 满～激情 *be filled with ardour* /胸～壮志 *harbour great ambitions; have lofty aspirations* ⑥ (Huái) a surname

【怀抱】① hold or carry in the arms; embrace: ～着婴儿 *with a baby in one's arms* ② bosom: 我又回到了祖国的～。*I have returned to the embrace of my motherland.* ③ cherish; keep in mind: ～真情厚意 *with sincere and deep feelings* / ～大志者 *aspirant* ④ [书] ambition; ideal: 他～高远。*His ideals are lofty and ambitious.* ⑤ [方] babyhood: ～儿 *one's babyhood*

【怀表】pocket watch

【怀才不露】refrain from showing one's abilities; be modest about one's learning

【怀才不遇】be frustrated for all one's talent; have unrecognized talents; have talent but no opportunity to use it: 他这一生穷困潦倒且～。*He lived in poverty all his life and had no opportunity to show his talent.*

【怀春】[书] (of a young girl) harbour the amorous thoughts of love; be lovesick; be in love: 有女～。*There is a girl in love.*

【怀二心】ambidexter; janus-faced; be not faithful; double-minded

【怀古】meditate on the past; reflect on an ancient event: ～诗 *poems reflecting on ancient events*

【怀鬼胎】[喻] have evil intentions; have a bad conscience; have sinister motives; with evil in one's heart: 我总觉得这小子怀着鬼胎。*I feel the fellow has some evil intentions in his mind.*

【怀恨】bear (or have; nurse; owe; harbour) a grudge against sb or sth.; nurse hatred; bear ill will; be resentful; spiteful; have resentment rankling in one's mind: 我总觉得她对我～在心。*I always feel she has a grudge against me.*

【怀旧】recall past events or old friends (with kindly thoughts); be nostalgic; reminiscences: ～者 *nostalgist* /他上了年纪以后总是～。*He always remembered past times and old acquaintances when he became old.* / 这景象勾起我对年轻时代的～之情。*The scene awakens reminiscences of my youth.*

【怀恋】think fondly of (past time, old friends, etc.); miss

【怀念】miss; think of; cherish the memory of: ～故人 *think fondly of one's old friend* / ～当年风花雪月的美好情景 *think of that old time of the wine and roses* /我相信每个人都会～他。*I'm sure that everybody will miss him very much.*

【怀柔】make a show of conciliation in order to bring other nationalities or states under control：～政策 *policy conciliation*；*policy of placation*

【怀胎】be pregnant；conceive a baby

【怀想】think about with affection；cherish the memory of：他～他那一去不复返的青春年华。*He cherished the memory of his departed youth.*

【怀疑】① doubt；suspect；question：表示～ *cast* (*or throw*；*raise*) *doubts on sb* (*or sth*) /消除～ *dispel doubts*；*clear up suspicions* /我们并不～他能把这事干得很好。*We don't doubt that he can do a good job of it.* ② guess；suspect：我～他生病了。*I suspect him to be ill.*

【怀疑论】【哲】skepticism；skepticism：～者 *skeptic*

【怀有】cherish；harbour；owe：我们不应对所谓的裁军谈判～任何不切实际的想法。*We shouldn't harbour any unrealistic notions about the talks on the so-called disarmament.*

【怀孕】be pregnant；be with child；conceive；be in the family way；be with young；be expecting；be knocked up：～期 *pregnancy*；*gestation period* /她～6个月了。*She is six months pregnant.*

槐 ①【植】Chinese scholartree；Sophora japonica (pagoda tree) ②(Huái) a surname

【槐蚕】inchworm；geometer；looper (living on a Chinese scholartree)

【槐豆】Chinese scholartree seeds；sophora beans

【槐花】【药】Flos Sophorae；sophora flower；pagoda tree flower：～散 *Sophora Powder*

踝 【生理】ankle

【踝骨】anklebone；malleolus

【踝关节】ankle joint

【踝子骨】[口] ankle；anklebone

huài

坏 ① bad；poor；defective：～脾气 *a bad temper* / ～天气 *foul weather* / ～习惯 *bad habit* / 给人～印象 *a bad impression* /一条～新闻 *a bad piece of news* ② evil；wicked：～人～事 *evildoers and evil deeds* ③ (of things) be damaged；be ruined；broken：自行车～了。*The bicycle is broken.* /玩具摔～了。*The toy crashed and broke.* / 不加防腐剂，肉会～得快。*Meat spoils more quickly without preservatives.* ④ spoil；ruin：暴雨毁～了庄稼。*The storm ruined the crop.* / 客人们无休止的争吵当然～了他们的胃口。*The never-ending quarrel among the visitors certainly spoiled their appetite for the banquet.* ⑤ badly；awfully：气～了 *be beside oneself with rage* /累～了 *be dog-tired* /疼～了 *feel a great deal of pain*；*hurt badly* / 真把我忙～了。*I was extremely occupied.* ⑥ evil idea；dirty trick：使～ *play a dirty trick*

【坏包儿】[口] bad person；rascal；rogue：别看他小，可是出了名的～。*Though young, he is a notorious rascal.*

【坏病】deteriorated case

【坏处】harm；disadvantage

【坏蛋】bad egg；rascal；bastard：大～ *rogue* (*or knave*) *in grain*

【坏东西】rascal；bastard；scoundrel

【坏分子】bad element；evildoer

【坏话】①unpleasant words：好话～都要听。*You should listen to both praises and criticisms.* ② malicious remarks；vicious talk：讲～*talk scandal* /在背后讲别人～是不道德的。*It's immoral to speak ill of others behind their backs.* /她爱说别人～。*She has an evil tongue.*

【坏良心】heartless；a depraved conscience：一个～的人 *a person of a depraved conscience*

【坏人】bad person；evildoer；scoundrel；malefactor；villain：～内讧，好人得利。*When rogues fall out, honest* (*or true*) *men come by their own.*

【坏事】① ruin；spoil；make things worse：鲁莽只能～。*Overboldness will only make things worse.* ② bad things；evil deeds；misdoing；villainy：在一定条件下，～可以变为好事。*In given conditions a bad thing can be turned into a good one.*

【坏事传千里】ill news runs space；bad news has wings

【坏事做绝】commit terrible crimes without end；commit every evil

【坏水儿】[口] wicked idea；evil trick：满肚子～的家伙 *a wicked man*

【坏死】【医】necrosis；putrescence：～激素 *necrohormone* /局部～ *local necrosis* /骨～ *necrosis of bone* / ～组织 *slough*

【坏透】downright bad；rotten to the core；execrable；vile：～了的脾气 *a vile temper*

【坏心眼儿】[口] evil intention；ill will；dirty trick；ill-conditioned；ill-disposed；malevolent：～的女人 *a malevolent woman* / ～的老头 *an evil-minded old man*

【坏血病】【医】scurvy；vitamin C deficiency；scorbutus

【坏运气】misfortune；bad luck：他业务上的失败不是由于遇到了～，而是由于他自己的过错。*He failed in business not because of misfortune, but because of his own error.*

【坏账】bad debt of loan

【坏字】【印】batter

huān

欢 ① joyous；merry；glad；jubilant：寻～作乐 *seek pleasure*；*make merry*；*enjoy oneself* ② liking；lover：喜～ *like*；*love* /新～ *new sweetheart* /求～ *seek sexual pleasure*；*ask for sex* ③ [方] active；vigorous；with great drive；in full swing：机器转得很～。*The machine is running in full swing.* /炉火烧得很～。*The fire in the furnace is roaring.*

H

【欢蹦乱跳】healthy-looking and vivacious; dancing and jumping with joy: 小姑娘~地朝街那头走过去。*The little girl skipped down the street with joy.*

【欢畅】elated; joyous

【欢唱】sing merrily; carol: ~到深夜 *sing to one's heart's content until midnight*

【欢度】spend joyfully: ~晚年 *spend one's remaining years in happiness* /春节是合家~的佳节。*The Spring Festival is a family celebration.*

【欢歌】sing merrily: 她过去经常每天早上~。*She used to carol cheerfully every morning.*

【欢好】happy and harmonious: 两情~。*The two love each other dearly.*

【欢呼】cheer; hail; applaud; acclaim: 男孩子们为他们的足球队~。*The boys cheered their football team.*

【欢呼雀跃】shout and jump for joy; be elated

【欢聚】happy get-together; happy reunion

【欢聚一堂】get together happily; be together on a joyful occasion; enjoy a nice meeting together

【欢快】merry; cheerful and light-hearted: 她脸上的~表情 *a merry expression on her face*

【欢乐】merry; cheerful; happy; joyous: 一个~的夜晚 *a merry evening* /丰收以后到处可以看到一片~景象。*Signs of merry life could be seen everywhere after the bumper harvest.*

【欢眉喜眼】[方] be all smiles: 她听到自己获胜的消息~。*She was all smiles at the news of her win.*

【欢闹】① play joyfully; gambol; caper; frolic; romp: 小羊羔在草地上~。*Lambs gamboled in the meadow.* /孩子们睡觉前正在~。*The children are having a frolic before bedtime.* ② noise and excitement; bustle: 大都市的~ *the bustle of the big city*

【欢洽】friendly; congenial; agreeable; pleasing: 在这个小村子里他发现很少有人能与他相处~。*In this small village he found few persons congenial to him.*

【欢庆】celebrate joyously: ~节日 *celebrate a festival* / ~胜利 *celebrate the victory*

【欢声】cheers; applause: 我听到观众阵阵的~,就知道主队要赢了。*I heard the cheers of the crowd, and I knew that the host team was winning.*

【欢声雷动】give a thundering ovation; cheers resound like peals of thunder; cry out for joy

【欢声笑语】cheers and laughter

【欢实】[方] lively; full of vigour; cheerful; energetic: 这些年青学生们越干越~。*The more the young students worked, the more energetic they became.*

【欢送】see off; send off; bid farewell: ~仪式 *farewell ceremony* / ~会 *farewell party (or meeting)*

【欢腾】great rejoicing; jubilant: 举国一片~。*The whole nation is jubilant.* /万众~。*All the people were transported with joy.*

【欢天喜地】wild with joy; overjoyed; be filled with great joy; in an ecstasy of joy; in high glee; rapture; in the seventh heaven; in heaven: 听到这个好消息后我~。*I was in heaven when I heard the good news.*

【欢慰】be gratified; happy and content: 老夫妇俩似乎整夜坐在电视机前就很~了。*The old couple seems happy and content to sit in front of the television all night.*

【欢喜】① delighted; pleased; happy: 听到这个好消息,他满心~。*He was filled with joy on hearing the good news.* /女儿出生时她十分~。*She was filled with elation when her daughter was born.* ② like; love; be fond of; be keen on: 他~这个小女孩儿。*He likes the little girl very much.* /我~唱歌。*I am fond of singing.*

【欢喜冤家】quarrelsome and loving couple; quarrelsome lovers

【欢笑】laugh heartily: 他的~表达了他胜利的喜悦。*He laughed his delight at the victory.* /青松迎风~。*Green pines laugh in the breeze.*

【欢心】favour; liking; love: 赢得某人的~ *win sb's favour*

【欢欣】joy; be elated: 他们唯一的孩子是他们的骄傲和~。*Their only child is their pride and joy.*

【欢欣鼓舞】be exulting; be filled with exultation; jubilant; be elated and inspired by: ~地迈入新年 *stride into the new year in high spirits* /全国人民为成功地发射了一颗新的人造卫星而~。*The people all over the country exulted in the success in launching a new satellite.*

【欢颜】[书] joyous expression; smiles: 她看见我时露出~。*She smiled when she saw me.*

【欢宴】fete; festivity; entertain sb to dinner in happy times: 结婚~很热闹。*The wedding festivities were very gay.*

【欢迎】① welcome; greet; meet: ~会 *welcome meeting* /夹道~ *line the streets to give sb a welcome* / ~到中国来! *Welcome to China* ② be popular; receive favourably; be well received: 我们~你的热心帮助。*We welcome your kind help.*

【欢迎词】address of welcome; welcoming speech

【欢迎会】reception; party for meeting or welcoming sb

【欢迎惠顾】welcome to enjoy sb's service

【欢娱】[书] happy; joyous; gay: 过着~的生活 *lead a gay life*

【欢愉】happy; joyous; joyful; merry: ~的心情 *a joyful heart* /一阵~的笑声 *a peal of merry laughter*

【欢悦】joyous; merry; pleasure: 放鞭炮能增添节日的气氛,给人们充分表达~兴奋之情的机会。*Setting off firecrackers can add to the festive atmosphere and offer an outlet for people's pleasure and excitement.*

【欢跃】exultant; jubilation; joy; very pleased; leap for joy: 人们因胜利而~。*The people were exultant at the victory.*

獾

【动】badger

huán

还 ① go (or come) back; return: 生～ *come back alive*; *survive* ② give back; repay: ～清债务 *pay off one's debt* ③ give back; return: 以眼～眼,以牙～牙 *an eye for an eye and a tooth for a tooth*; *tit for tat* ④ (Huán) a surname
see also hái

【还报】repay; requite; reciprocate: 他以恶语～我的善意。*He requited my kindness with cruel words.*

【还本】repayment of principal or capital: ～付息 *repay capital with interest*

【还魂】①［迷］revive after death; return from the grave ②［方］reclaim; recycle; reprocess: ～纸 *recycled paper* / ～橡胶 *reclaimed rubber* / ～植物 *resurrection plant*

【还击】① fight back; strike back; counterattack: 向敌人～ *retaliate upon one's enemy* /对诽谤者的～ *a counterattack on one's detractors* ②【体】riposte (in fencing)

【还籍】return to one's native place

【还价】counter offer; counter-bid; beat a bargain; abate a price; huckster: 讨价～ *bargain over prices*; *bargain* /在黑市上讨价～ *huckster over prices on the black market*

【还口】answer back; talk back; retort: "你管不着!"他～道。"*It's none of your business!" he retorted.*

【还礼】① return a salute: 她还了礼。*She acknowledged the salute.* ② present a gift in return

【还清】pay off; wipe off: ～债务 *pay off one's debt*

【还情】repay a favour: 他们曾经帮助过我们,现在我们该～了。*It's time we repaid them a favour for the help they once offered.*

【还手】strike (or hit) back: 他先打我,我才～打他。*He hit me first, so I struck him back.*

【还俗】(of Buddhist monks and nuns or Taoist priests) resume secular life; secularization

【还席】give a return banquet or dinner

【还乡】return to one's native place

【还醒】come to; regain consciousness; revive: 新鲜空气很快就使他～过来了。*The fresh air soon revived him.*

【还言】reply; answer; retort: 我～说我不能帮助他们。*I replied that I was unable to help them.*

【还阳】【迷】come back to life after death

【还原】① restore to the original state or shape: 出门前,他把所有的书都～到原来的位置。*Before leaving, he put every book back in place.* ②【化】reduction; recondition; regeneration; revivification: ～色 *reduced colour* / ～酸 *reductic acid* / ～糖 *reducing sugar* / ～性 *reducibility* / ～氧化 *reduction-oxidation* / ～焰 *reducing flame* / ～作用 *reduction*; *reducing action*

【还愿】①【迷】redeem a vow to a god: ～供奉 *a votive offering* ②［喻］fulfill one's promise: 你许了愿就要～。*If you make a promise, you should carry it on; promise is debt.*

【还债】repay a debt: 欠债容易～难。*It's easy to get into debt than to get out of it again.*

【还账】pay one's debt; settle accounts; repay a loan

【还政于民】hand power back to the people; return the power of the government to the hands of people

【还嘴】［口］answer (or talk) back; retort: 善于～ *quick at retort* /他～说我的错误并不比他的错误小。*He retorted that it was my fault as much as he is.*

环 ① ring; hoop: 耳～ *earring* /连～ *a chain of rings* /铁～ *iron ring* ② ring, points scored in shooting or archery: 射中 10～ *hit the centre of the target* ③ link: 关键的一～ *key link*; *essential link* ④ surround; encircle: ～城马路 *ring road*; *belt highway* ⑤ (Huán) a surname

【环保】environmental protection: ～人士 *environmentalist*

【环抱】embrace; surround; encircle; hem in: 被郊区～着的城市 *a city surrounded by suburbs* /四面被山～的村庄 *a valley hemmed in by mountains*

【环衬】【印】lining paper

【环城】around the city: ～路线 *round-the-city route* / ～工事 *ceinture*

【环程旅行】circular tour

【环程票】circular ticket

【环带】① ring of light; halo ②【动】clitellum

【环刀】cutting ring

【环岛】traffic circle; roundabout; rotary

【环道】circuit; rotary road

【环封】ring seal

【环顾】［书］look round: ～左右 *look to the right and left*

【环冠】garlands

【环规】ring gauge

【环海】be surrounded by sea

【环焊】boxing

【环航】【航】circumnavigate: ～地球 *circumnavigate the earth*

【环节】①【动】segment ② link; sector: 最薄弱的～ *the weakest link* /生产～ *the manufacturing sector*

【环境】① environment: 标准大气～ *normal atmospheric environment* /沉积～ *depositional environment* /大陆～ *continental environment* /淡水～ *freshwater environment* /地质～ *geohydrologic environment* /呼吸～ *respiratory environment* /湖泊～ *lacustrine environment* /近海～ *paralic environment* /空间～ *space environment* /陆地～ *terrestrial environment* /热带～ *torrid environment* /人类～ *human environment* /深海～ *abyssal environment* /水生～ *aquatic environment* /生物～ *biological environment* /土壤～ *soil environment* /原生～ *primary environment* /远洋～ *pelagic environment* /噪声～ *noise environment* /致癌～ *carci-*

H

nogenic environment ② surroundings; circumstances; conditions; situation; state: 他做这件事是为～所迫。*He was forced by circumstances to do this.* / ～非常复杂。*The situation was complicated.*

【环流】【气】circulation; circulating current; circumfluence; circular current: ～方式 *circulating current system* / ～气体 *recycle stream* / ～指数 *circulation index*

【环论】【数】ring theory; theory of rings

【环佩】(jade) pendant

【环骑】【体】volt

【环球】① round the world: ～航行 *a voyage around the world* ② Earth; whole world: ～导弹 *global missile* / ～轰炸机 *global bomber*

【环球法】ring and ball method

【环球网】World Wide Web (www)

【环球卫星通讯】global satellite communication

【环球邮报】The Global and Mail, Canadian newspaper since 1844

【环绕】surround; circle; revolve around: 篱笆～着学校。*The fence surrounds the school.* /许多国家发射了～地球的人造卫星。*Many countries have sent up man-made satellites to circle the earth.*

【环绕速度】【天】circular or orbital velocity; first cosmic velocity

【环山】① round a mountain: ～公路 *road round a mountain* ② surrounded by mountains or hills: 三面～*surrounded by hills on three sides*

【环山带水】surrounded by hills and girdled by water

【环蛇】krait; rock snake

【环生】happen one after another; occur frequently: 险象～ *dangerous situations appear one after another*

【环食】【天】annular eclipse (of the sun or the moon): ～带 *path of annular eclipse*

【环视】look around: 他们～四周,但玛丽已经不在了。*They look around but Mary is already gone.*

【环式】ring type: ～空间 *ringed space* / ～炉 *circular furnace* / ～线圈 *toroidal coil*

【环数】cylinder number

【环丝】circumfili

【环伺】watch closely from all round

【环算子】【数】ring operator

【环太平洋】circum-Pacific: ～地区 *circum-Pacific region* / ～地震带 *circum-Pacific seismic belt* / ～构造带 *tectonic belt*

【环眺】look (far) around

【环网】looped network

【环卫】environmental sanitation

【环系】【化】ring system

【环细胞】choanocyte

【环线】ring route; circular route: ～地铁 *belt subway*; *circular subway route*

【环向漂移】toroidal drift

【环行】going in a circle; make a circuit

【环形】annular; ring-like: ～安装 *looping-in* / ～波导 *disc waveguide* / ～齿轮 *ring gear* / ～电枢 *ring armature* / ～防御 *all-round defence*; *perimeter defence* / ～供电 *annular electric supply*; *loop feeding* / ～交叉 *traffic circus*; *rotary* / ～晶体管 *annular transistor* / ～开关 *ring switch* / ～脉冲 *loop pulse*; *loop impulse* / ～系统 *loop system* / ～线圈 *loop coil*

【环游】travel or tour round: ～世界 *travel round the world*; *go on a tour round the world*

【环状】cyclic; annular; ring-like: ～扩散 *encircling diffusion* / ～领 *ruff* / ～软膏 *cricoid* / ～软骨 *cricoid* / ～物 *annulation* / ～效应 *annular effect* / ～腺 *ring glands* / ～线 *loop-line* / ～星系 *ring galaxy* / ～星云 *ring nebula*

【环子】ring; link: 铁～ *iron hoop*

寰 extensive region

【寰球】the earth; the whole world

【寰宇】[书]the earth; the whole world

缳 [书] ① noose: 投～ *to hang oneself* ② strangle

huǎn

缓 ① slow; unhurried; sluggish: 迟～ *slow*; *tardy* / ～步而行 *walk unhurriedly* ② delay; postpone: ～两天再办 *postpone sth for one or two days*; *do sth after a short time* /刻不容～ *be of great urgency* ③ relaxed; not tense: 紧张局势已经迟～。*The tense situation has eased off.* ④ come to; revive: ～口气再往前走 *walk on after a short break* /病人昏过去又～过来。*The patient fainted and then came to.*

【缓办】delay action; put off a project: 今日可做的事不要到明天～。*Don't put off until tomorrow what can be done today.*

【缓兵之计】stratagem to gain a respite; stalling tactics; measures to stave off an attack; delay under a pretext; trick to gain time

【缓步】walk slowly; stroll; saunter: 我们～穿过了这个公园。*We strolled through the park.*

【缓步代车】stroll or walk in a leisurely way instead of going by car: 路途不远,我们可以～。*It's not far away, so we can have a slow walk instead of riding in a carriage.*

【缓冲】buffer; cushion; buff; dampen; amortize; separate the two sides in a conflict so as to lessen tensions: 他的帽子帮助～了打击。*His hat helped to cushion the blow.* / 药物～了他的病痛。*The drug buffered his pain.*

【缓冲剂】【化】buffer

【缓冲气袋】air bag

【缓冲器】【机】buffer; bumper cushion: 存储～ *memory buffer* /地址～ *address buffer* /反相～ *inverter buffer* /载波～ *subcarrier buffer* /矩阵～ *matrix buffer* /输出～ *output buffer* /弹簧～ *spring buffer* /通信～ *communication buffer* /视频～ *vid-*

eo buffer /数据～ *data buffer* /载频～ *carrier buffer* /中心～ *central buffer* /字符～ *character buffer*

【缓冲作用】cushioning effect; buffer action; buffering

【缓动】slow-action; slow-motion: ～环 *slug* / ～控制 *inching control*

【缓发】【物】delay: ～粒子 *delayed particle* / ～衰变 *delayed decay* / ～质子 *delayed proton* / ～中子 *delayed neutron*

【缓和】① relax; ease up (tensions): 国际紧张局势有所～。*The international tension relaxed.* /自从开始边界争端的谈判以来,两国关系已趋～。*The relationship between the two countries has eased since the beginning of the talks on the border conflicts.* ② alleviate; mitigate; defuse: ～矛盾 *mitigate contradictions*

【缓化剂】【化】negative catalyst; moderator

【缓缓】slowly; gradually; step by step: 他们～演奏那首序曲。*They played the overture at a fairly slow tempo.*

【缓急】① pressing or otherwise; of greater or lesser urgency: 轻重～ *relative importance or urgency; order of priority* ② emergency; urgent affairs; difficulty: ～相助 *help each other in time of emergency*

【缓颊】[书] intercede for sb; put in a good word for sb

【缓建】postpone construction

【缓缰】slacken (or loosen) the reins

【缓解】relieve; alleviate; ease: ～紧张局面 *relieve the tension* /一种～感冒症状的药品 *a drug that alleviates cold symptoms* /从未～的疼痛 *pain that never eased*

【缓慢】slow; sluggish; laggard: ～的心跳 *a slow heartbeat* / ～的生长 *sluggish growth* /行动～ *slow in action*

【缓凝剂】retarder

【缓辔】give (a horse) the reins; slacken the reins

【缓坡】gentle slope; glacis; low pitch

【缓期】suspend; postpone a deadline; delayed schedule: ～付款 *delay payment* /判处强度劳动两年,～执行一年。*The sentence was two years' hard labour suspended for a year.*

【缓气】get a breathing space; have a respite: 让我缓口气。*Let me get my breath back.*

【缓图】plan slowly and carefully

【缓限】delay; put off; postpone the deadline; suspend; extend the time limit: ～三个多月的贷款 *extend a loan for three more months*

【缓行】① move; walk or drive slowly; amble: 他开车～去超级市场。*He drove slowly to the supermarket.* /这匹马正在溜蹄～。*The horse is walking at an amble.* ② delay; postpone implementation

【缓刑】【律】reprieve; probation; temporary suspension of the execution of a sentence; suspend a jail sentence: 对犯人～ *place an offender on (or under) probation* /给囚犯～ *to reprieve the prisoner* /对判刑的人宣布～ *grand a respite to a condemned man*

【缓刑犯】【律】probationer

【缓刑制度】system of probationary suspension

【缓性】phlegmatic temper; slow effect: ～药 *medicine that produces slow effects*

【缓醒】[方] come to; come round; regain consciousness: 往他脸上泼些水,他很快就能～过来。*Pour some water on his face — he'll soon come round.*

【缓役】【军】deferment (of military service)

【缓议】shelve; defer the discussion: ～一项计划 *to shelve a plan*

【缓征】postpone the imposition of a tax or levy

huàn

幻 ① imaginary; unreal; illusory: 梦～ *illusions; dream* ② change magically: 变～ *change irregularly*

【幻灯】① slide show: 放～ *show slides* /看～ *watch a slide show* ② slide projector; magic lantern: ～放映员 *lanternist; projectionist* / ～盒 *slide magazine* / ～片 *filmstrip* / ～扫描器 *slide scanner*

【幻灯机】slide projector; optical lantern; epidiascope

【幻化】change magically: 舞台上的幕布～成一片片雪花。*The curtain on the stage changed magically into flakes of snow.*

【幻景】illusion; mirage; blaze: 在～中,沙漠有时会现出湖泊的形象。*In a mirage the desert will mimic a lake.*

【幻境】dreamland; fairyland: 这真是个～。*This is a veritable fairyland.*

【幻觉】illusion; hallucination; pink elephants; stardust: 产生成功唾手可得的～ *under the delusion that success is at hand* /光学～ *optical illusion*

【幻梦】dream; fantasy; illusion; daydream: 一场～ *be an idle dream*

【幻灭】(of illusions or sth unreal) vanish into thin air; illusions shattered by reality; disillusion: 许多老百姓对现政府的希望完全～了。*Many common people are very disillusioned with the present government.*

【幻视】【医】photism; visual hallucination: ～术 *pseudoscopy* / ～效应 *pseudoscopic effect*

【幻术】magic; conjuring; sorcery: 这人用～从他的帽子里变出六只兔子。*The man used magic to produce six rabbits from his hat.*

【幻数】【数】magic numbers

【幻听】【医】phonism; acousma

【幻想】① fancy; imagine; dream: 让我在可以～的时候尽情地～吧。*Let me fancy while I may.* /她～自己成了一个真正的艺术家。*She imagines herself to be a true artist.* ② illusion; fantasy; dream: 充满～ *be full of fancies* /这个年轻人生活

H

在～的世界里。*The young man lives in a world of fantasy.*
【幻想曲】【音】fantasia
【幻象】phantom; phantasm; vision; mirage: 梦中的～ *phantom of a dream*
【幻象性错觉】idolum
【幻影】unreal image; phantom; rainbow; ghost: 往事的～ *the phantom of things past*

奂 [书] ① abundant; plentiful; numerous ② (of writing) brilliant

宦 ① official: 官～ *government official* ② be an official: 仕～ *have an official career* ③ eunuch ④ (Huàn) a surname
【宦场】officialdom; official circles
【宦官】eunuch
【宦海】[喻] (sea of) officialdom; official circles: ～浮沉 *the vicissitudes of official life; floating and sinking in the official seas*
【宦门】[书] family of officials: ～公子 *young man from an official family*
【宦囊】[书] savings saved during one's official career
【宦情】[书] desire or aspiration for an official career: 少无～。*A young man hasn't aspiration for an official career.*
【宦途】[书] official career
【宦游】[书] go from one place to another hunting an official position; leave home and take up government employments: ～人 *office-seeker*

换 ① exchange; trade: 互～ *exchange* / 交～条件 *conditions of exchange* ② change: ～衣服 *change one's clothes* ③ exchange (coupon for money or one currency for another); convert: 把美元～成人民币 *convert US dollars into RMB*
【换班】change shifts; take over the duty or work; relieve a person on duty: ～工作 *work in shifts* / 五点钟有人来和我～。*I'm to be relieved at five.*
【换币机】money exchange machine
【换茬】【农】change of crops
【换车】change trains or buses; transfer: 我从家到学校要换两趟车。*I have to change buses twice to get to school from my home.* / 他不得不在上海匆忙～。*He had to make a quick change at Shanghai.*
【换乘】change; transfer: ～另一辆公共汽车 *transfer to another bus*
【换船】transfer; change ships
【换代】① (of a dynasty or regime) change: 改朝～ *dynastic changes* ② replace; regenerate
【换挡】【机】shift gears: ～分离叉 *declutch shift fork* / 自动～ *shift gears automatically* / 上山时要换第二挡。*Change into second gear when you go up the hill.*
【换档键】shift key
【换发球】【体】change of service
【换防】【军】relieve a garrison
【换房】exchange housing: ～大会 *housing exchange fair*
【换俘】【军】exchange of prisoners
【换俘协定】agreement for exchange of prisoners; cartel
【换岗】relieve a sentry; change the guard: 哨兵的～ *relief of a sentry*
【换个儿】[口] exchange position; change places: 我和你～好吗? *May I exchange seats with you?*
【换工】exchange labour
【换骨脱胎】be born again; fundamental change: 她简直是～。*She thoroughly remoulded herself.*
【换购】purchase by way of barter
【换辊】roll change: ～装置 *changing rig; roll-changing gear*
【换行】line feed: ～字符 *line feed character; new-line character*
【换汇】earn foreign exchange
【换货】exchange goods; barter: ～协定 *barter agreement*
【换季】change garments according to the season; put on different clothes for a new season
【换脚】change of feet
【换接】changing-over; change: ～开关 *reversing switch* / ～频率 *commutating frequency*
【换届】replace or re-elect when a term of office expires: 他的总统任期明年将届满,政府面临～。*His term of office as president will expire next year and new members of the government will be elected.*
【换景】【戏】scene shifting
【换句话说】in other words; namely; that is to say: 你未经同意就拿了那本书,～,你偷了它。*You took the book without permission; in other words, you stole it.*
【换料】reloading; change material: ～工具 *refuelling tool*
【换马】change horses (half way); have sb replaced (before his term ends): 不要中途～。*Don't have him replaced before his term is over.*
【换码】escape: ～符号 *escape character*
【换毛】moult: 小燕子在～。*The young swallows are moulting.*
【换脑筋】[喻] change one's way of thinking: 形势发展这么快,你也该～了。*The situation is changing and developing so rapidly, and you should change the way of thinking accordingly.*
【换气】take a breath (in swimming); aeration
【换气扇】ventilation fan
【换气孔】loophole
【换气装置】air interchanger
【换钱】① change money; break a bill or note: 我在哪儿可以～,把英镑兑换成美钞? *Where can I change my English money for dollars?* ② sell: 这些废品可以～。*The waste can sell for money.*
【换亲】(of two families) exchange daughters in marriage to each other's sons
【换取】exchange or barter for; get in return: 我们用烟草和橡胶～毛皮。*We bartered for furs with tobacco and rubber.*
【换热】heat transfer: ～系数 *coefficient of heat*

transfer
【换热器】heat exchanger; heat-exchanging unit
【换人】【体】substitution (of players)
【换算】【数】matrixing; scaler; conversion: ～表 *conversion table* / ～电路 *scale unit* / ～公式 *reduction formula* / ～机构 *change-over mechanism* / ～速度 *corrected speed* / ～周转量 *conversion of freight mileage*
【换汤不换药】[喻] the same medicine with a different name — a change in form but not in content; make a superficial change; old stuff with a new label
【换帖】become sworn brothers by exchange of papers bearing each other's name, age, origin and other personal and family information: ～兄弟 *sworn brothers*
【换位】【数】conversion: ～法 *conversion method* / ～矩阵 *commutator matrix*
【换位思考】put oneself in another's shoes and think in his or her terms
【换文】exchange of notes or letters: 通过～达成谅解 *reach understanding through an exchange of letters*
【换席更酌】food and wine are served afresh; wine is again served
【换洗】change and wash (clothing, sheets, etc.)
【换相】【电】commutation
【换向】changing-over; change: ～齿轮 *tumbler gear* / ～电流 *current of commutation* / ～机构 *changement; reversing mechanism* / ～开关 *change-over switch; reversing switch*/ ～控制 *reverse control; commutation control* / ～区域 *commutating zone* /试验 *commutation test* / ～系统 *exchange system* / ～周期 *commutation cycle*
【换血】blood transfusion — reorganization by introducing fresh personnel; recast
【换心】[方] intimate; understanding: ～朋友 *bosom friend; intimate friend*
【换性】transsexual
【换牙】(of a child) grow permanent teeth
【换言之】[书] in other ways; that is to say; namely: 他被法庭判为无罪，～，法庭依法律不能定他的罪。*He was found innocent in the court, that is to say, the court could not convict him legally.*
【换样】change in pattern; vary
【换药】redress (a wound, etc.); change bandage; change dressings; change a medical prescription
【换页】form feed
【换油】oil change; replacement of oil: ～周期 *drain period*
【换羽】(of birds) moult; moulting
【换约】exchange of notes or letters; exchange treaties
【换置】hyperphoric: ～作用 *hyperphoric alteration*
【换置法】hypallage obversion

唤 call out; summon: 呼～ *call; shout* / ～鸡 *call back the chicken* / ～狗 *call back the dog*
【唤起】① arouse: ～热情 *arouse sb's fervour* / ～责任感 *recall sb to a sense of his duties* ② call; draw; recall; evoke: ～往日回忆的歌曲 *songs that evoke old memories* /那封信～了她对往事的回忆。*Old memories awoke in her when she read the letter.*
【唤审】subpoena
【唤头】percussion tool (used by itinerant grinders, barbers, etc.) to attract customers
【唤醒】awaken; wake up: 杜鹃花的味道～了我对许多年前那个下午的记忆。*The scent of the azaleas awakened my memory of that afternoon years ago.*

涣 melt; vanish; dissolve
【涣涣】[书] (of water or flood) overflowing: 水～ *vast expenses of water*
【涣然冰释】(of ice) melt away; disappear; thaw out: 我们之间的误会～。*The misunderstanding between us has been cleared up.*
【涣散】lax; slack; demoralized: 士气～。*The troops are demoralized.* / 对于学校～的纪律她感到震惊。*She was shocked at the slack discipline in the school.*

浣 ① wash; rinse ② [旧] any of the three ten-day divisions of a month
【浣衣】wash clothes
【浣纱】wash yarn
【浣熊】【动】racoon

患 ① trouble; disaster: 灾～ *suffering; disaster* /祸～ *disaster* /有备无～。*Where there is a precaution, there is no danger.* ② anxiety; worry: 忧～意识 *sense of concern for the fate of one's country; sense of crisis* ③ contract; suffer from an illness: ～感冒 *catch a cold* / ～脚气 *have beriberi*
【患病】fall ill; suffer from a disease; be ill: 她母亲在医院里，～很重。*Her mother's seriously ill in hospital.*
【患处】affected part (of a patient's body); wounded part: 包扎～ *dress a wound*
【患得患失】be mindful of personal gains or losses; be swayed by selfish considerations of gains and losses
【患难】trials and tribulations; adversity; trouble: 他们的友谊是由于共～而结成的。*Their friendship was forged by shared adversity.*
【患难弟兄】brothers in affliction
【患难夫妻】husband and wife who have been through difficult times together
【患难见知己】a friend in need is a friend indeed; prosperity makes friends and adversity tries them
【患难与共】share hardships and difficulties; go through thick and thin together
【患难相依】share one's hardships through thick and thin; share weal and woe
【患难之交】tested friends; friend in need: 我们是～。*We are companions in adversity.*
【患者】patient; sufferer: 医生在医院里看视他的～。

The doctor visited his patients in hospital.

焕 shining; glowing

【焕发】① shine; glow; irradiate: 精神～ *be full of vigour* / ～喜气的脸 *a face irradiated with joy* ② display vigour; cheer up: 吃完午饭后他很快～了兴致。*He had lunch and soon cheered up.* / 新的希望又使他～了活力。*He was rejuvenated by new hope.*

【焕发青春】(of old people, etc.) radiate the vigour of youth; rejuvenate: ～革命青春 *fresh with revolutionary vigour*

【焕然】bright; splendid; brilliant; glowing

【焕然一新】take on an entirely new look; look brand new; have a bright and new look: 整修后的学校～。*The school took on a new look after refitting.*

豢 feed or keep (animals)

【豢养】feed; keep: ～家禽 *feed poultry*

擐 [书] wear; put on: ～甲执兵 *put on one's armour and take up arms*

huāng

荒 ① waste; uncultivated: 地～了。*The land lies waste.* ② desolate; out of the way; wild; barren: ～村 *deserted village* ③ famine; crop failure: 备～ *prepare against natural disasters* ④ wasteland; uncultivated land: 垦～ *open up virgin soil* / 开～ *open up wasteland* / 生～ *virgin soil* / 沙～ *sandy wasteland* ⑤ out of practice; rusty; neglect: 他把英文～了。*His English is rusty.* ⑥ serious shortage; scarcity: 煤～ *shortage of coal* / 房～ *housing shortage* ⑦ unreasonable; absurd; ridiculous ⑧ [方] uncertain ⑨ [书] loose; dissipated; indulged; self-indulgent

【荒草】weeds: ～丛生 *overgrown with weeds*

【荒村】isolated (or deserted) village; hamlet

【荒诞】absurd; fantastic; incredible: ～的想法 *fantastic idea* / ～故事 *old wives' tales*

【荒诞不经】unbelievable; fantastic; absurd; preposterous: ～的计划 *fantastic schemes* / 用茶匙铲煤是～的。*It would be preposterous to shovel coal with a teaspoon.* / 我从来没有听过如此～的话! *I've never heard anything so ridiculous!*

【荒诞派】the absurd: ～戏剧 *theatre of the absurd* / ～作家 *absurdist*

【荒诞无稽】be a wild legend; absurd; irrational; incredible; groundless; be beyond belief: 他讲的关于如何在雪崩中逃生的故事简直～! *His story about how he escaped an avalanche is totally beyond belief.*

【荒诞主义】absurdism

【荒诞主义者】absurdist

【荒岛】a deserted island; an uninhabited island

【荒地】badlands; waste; wasteland; wild; wilderness: 北方大草原的～ *the wilds of the northern steppes* / 这个园子逐渐变成了～。*The garden is turning into a wilderness.*

【荒废】① leave uncultivated; lie waste: ～的土地 *uncultivated ground* ② neglect; be out of practice: 对历史有点～了 *a bit rusty on history* / ～学业 *neglect one's studies* ③ fall into disuse; leave completely unattended to: 这条街道～了。*This street has fallen into disuse.*

【荒古】remote antiquity

【荒寒】desolate and cold

【荒旱】drought

【荒秽】[书] lie waste; go out of cultivation

【荒火】bush fire; prairie fire

【荒货】[方] junk; waste; scrap

【荒瘠】bleak and barren; wild and infertile: ～的土地 *wild and infertile land* / 沙漠是～的土地。*The desert is barren land.*

【荒寂】desolate and still

【荒郊】desolate outskirts; outside a town; wilderness

【荒凉】desolate; brumal; deserted; lonely; lorn; stark: 满目～ *a scene of desolation* / 月球多石的、～的表面 *the rocky, desolate surface of the moon* / 他住在一个～的山村里。*He lives in a lonely mountain village.*

【荒乱】in great disorder; in turmoil: 处于工人罢工造成的～中的国家 *a country in turmoil over labour strikes*

【荒谬】absurd; paradoxical; ridiculous; preposterous: 他们的要求是～的。*Their request is absurd.* / 他对事故发生的原因作了～的解释。*He gave an incredible explanation of the cause of the accident.*

【荒谬绝伦】extremely absurd; absolutely preposterous; an absurdity carried to its ultimate point: ～的想法 *nonsensical ideas* / 你怎么会想到要带毒品到那个国家去,这简直～! *How could you even think of bringing drugs into the country — it's completely idiotic.*

【荒漠】① desolate and vast; wild: ～的土地 *vast and wild land* ② desert; wilderness: 文化～ *a cultural wasteland* / 一望无际的～ *a vast expanse of desert* / 北极～ *arctic desert*

【荒年】famine year; lean year

【荒僻】desolate and out of the way; wild and remote; deserted: 过去的～土地变成了富饶的谷仓。*That remote barren land has blossomed into rich granaries.*

【荒歉】crop failure; famine; deficiency: 每年有很多人死于～。*Many people die of famine every year.*

【荒沙】barren sand

【荒山】barren mountain: 绿化～ *clothe barren mountains with greenery* / ～造田 *open up land on barren hills*

【荒山野岭】barren hills and wild mountains

【荒疏】out of practice; rusty: 学业尚未～。*The*

subjects learned are still fresh in mind. /你的英语要继续学下去,否则会~的。*Keep up your English or it will get rusty.*
【荒数】[方] rough figure; approximate number
【荒率】[书] careless; rash
【荒滩】barren (or uncultivated) beach
【荒唐】① absurd; fantastic; cockeyed; flimflam; ludicrous: 这话真~。*The words are ridiculous.* / 他穿着那种制服看起来很~。*That uniform makes him look absurd.* ② dissolute; loose; wanton: ~的生活 *dissipated life* / ~的小说 *a wanton novels*
【荒颓】desolate and rundown
【荒无人烟】desolate and uninhabited; no human habitation
【荒芜】arid; lie waste; be overgrown with weeds; go out of cultivation
【荒墟】waste open land; debris; ruins
【荒野】wilderness; the wilds; bush; boondocks; moor
【荒淫】dissolute; debauched: ~的生活 *a life of debauchery*
【荒淫无耻】dissipated and shameless; lead a life of luxury and debauchery
【荒原】wasteland; wilderness; wild country: 北极的~*the Arctic wilderness*
【荒政】[书] neglect public duties or state affairs
【荒置】leave unused; discard; abandon: ~家园 *abandon one's home*
【荒冢】abandoned grave; desolate and uncared-for grave; nameless grave: ~埋骨 *bury someone's decaying bones in the burying-ground*
【荒子】semifinished product
慌 flurried; flustered; confused: 别~,一切都会好的。*Take is easy, and all will be fine.*
慌 awfully; unbearably: 累得~ *be tired out; be worn out; be dog-tired; be played out* / 我心里急得~。*I am rather worrying about it.*
【慌促】*be in a hurry and unprepared*: ~之中得出的结论不一定有道理。*It is not necessarily reasonable to rush to a conclusion.*
【慌慌张张】in a flurry; in a hurry; in haste; hurriedly: 我们~做了决定,没顾上考虑细节。*We made the decision in a hurry without thinking about the details.*
【慌乱】get confused; fall into a flutter; flurried; alarmed and bewildered: 不能~,我们能够找到出路的。*Keep your nerve, and we will find the way out of here.*
【慌忙】in a great rush; helter-skelter; in a flurry; hurriedly; hastily: ~跳起来 *hurriedly jump to one's feet*
【慌神儿】be scared out of one's wits
【慌手慌脚】in a rush; not careful enough: 年轻人不能老是这么~。*As young men, you should not be always in a rush.*
【慌张】flurried; flustered: 神色~ *look flustered*

huáng

皇 ① great; grand: 堂~ *grand; magnificent* ② emperor; sovereign: 女~ *empress* / 玉~大帝 *Jade Emperor* ③ (Huáng) a surname
【皇朝】dynasty
【皇城】imperial city
【皇储】crown prince
【皇帝】emperor: 从前,有一位~热衷于漂亮的新衣服胜过其他一切。*Many years ago there lived an Emperor, who cared more for fine new clothes than for anything else.*
【皇恩】imperial beneficence; imperial favour: ~浩荡 *vast and mighty shall be the imperial favour*
【皇宫】imperial palace
【皇冠】imperial crown
【皇后】empress; queen
【皇皇】magnificent; splendid: ~巨著 *a monumental works*
【皇家】royal; imperial: ~空军 *the Royal Air Force* / ~海军陆战队 *the Royal Marines*
【皇历】[口] lunar almanac
【皇粮】① [旧] public grain: 交~ *pay grain tax* ② funds, goods, etc. provided by the government: 他是吃~的,所以工作很稳定。*He works in government, so he leads a stable life.*
【皇陵】imperial mausoleum
【皇亲】relative of the emperor
【皇亲国戚】kinsman or relative of the emperor
【皇权】imperial power or authority
【皇上】emperor; His Majesty; Your Majesty
【皇室】① imperial family ② royal court; imperial government
【皇太后】empress dowager
【皇太子】crown prince
【皇天】Heaven; Great Heaven
【皇天不负苦心人】heaven helps those who help themselves
【皇天后土】Heaven and Earth: 放弃~ *relinquish the crown* /她拒不接受~。*She refused the crown.*
【皇位】throne
【皇庄】imperial estate
【皇子】emperor's son; prince
【皇族】royal or imperial clan
黄[1] ① yellow: 麦田一片金~。*The fields were yellow with wheat.* ② gold ③ yolk: 双~蛋 *egg with two yolks* ④ decadent; obscene; pornography: 扫~ *wipe out pornography and prostitution* ⑤ the Huanghe River: 引~工程 *project of diverting the water of the Huanghe River* ⑥ Huang Di, a legendary emperor in the remote ages of China: 炎~子孙 *descendents of Yan Di and Huang Di — the Chinese people* ⑦ (Huáng) a surname
黄[2] fail; come to nothing; be off: 这件事~不了。*This business will not fail.*

H

【黄包车】［方］rickshaw；rickshaw；ricksha
【黄宝石】oriental topaz
【黄骠马】white-spotted yellow horse
【黄菠萝】【药】bark of the cork tree
【黄檗】【植】amur cork；cork tree
【黄菜】［方］scrambled eggs：摊～ *scrambled eggs*
【黄灿灿】bright yellow；golden：～的头发 *golden hair*
【黄丹】yellow lead
【黄疸】【医】jaundice；icterus
【黄道】【天】ecliptic：～坐标 *ecliptic coordinate*
【黄道带】zodiac
【黄道吉日】propitious or auspicious date；lucky day：这是开张的～。*This is a propitious day to start a new business.*
【黄澄澄】glistening yellow；golden：～的麦穗 *golden ears of wheat*
【黄帝】Huangdi or Yellow Emperor
【黄豆】soybean：～芽 *soybean sprouts*
【黄泛区】area formerly flooded by the Yellow River
【黄蜂】wasp
【黄瓜】cucumber
【黄瓜香】garden burnet
【黄冠】① yellow hat（of a Taoist priest）② Taoist priest
【黄海】the Huanghai Sea；the Yellow Sea
【黄河】the Huanghe River；the Yellow River：～流域 *the Huanghe Valley* / ～三角洲 *the Huanghe Delta*
【黄褐色】yellow-brown；tawny；tan：～的皮手套 *tan leather gloves* /狮子～的鬃毛 *the lion's tawny mane*
【黄花】① chrysanthemum ② day lily ③ without sexual experience
【黄花菜】day lily
【黄花女儿】【口】virgin girl
【黄花鱼】yellow croaker
【黄化】【植】yellowing；etiolation：～病 *yellows*
【黄桦】yellow birch；silver birch
【黄昏】dusk；twilight：近～时下雨了。*It rained late in the afternoon.* / ～是司机容易出事的时间。*Twilight is a dangerous time for drivers.*
【黄昏恋】old people's love
【黄酱】salted and fermented soya paste
【黄教】the Yellow Sect（a sect of Lamaism in Tibet）
【黄金】gold：～价格 *price of gold*；*gold rate* / ～市场 *gold market*
【黄金分割】【数】golden section；extreme and mean ratio
【黄金时代】① the golden age：伊丽莎白时期是英国戏剧的～。*The Elizabethan period was the golden age of English drama.* ② prime of one's life：他的～已经过去。*He is past his prime.*
【黄金时间】prime time；peak viewing time：～广告 *prime-time advertising*
【黄酒】yellow rice wine
【黄口小儿】immature young man；callow young fellow；an ignorant youth：～的话也常有道理 *out of the mouths of babes and sucklings*
【黄葵】musk mallow（*Hibiscus moschatus*）
【黄蜡蜡】wax yellow；sallow；colourless：～的脸色 *a waxen complexion*
【黄蜡】beeswax；cera flava
【黄鹂】oriole
【黄连】【药】the rhizome of Chinese goldthread（*Coptis chinensis*）
【黄连木】【植】Chinese pistache
【黄连素】【药】berberine
【黄粱梦】Golden Millet Dream — daydream；pipe dream：我总希望能够环游世界，不过这似乎只是～。*I'd always wanted to travel around the world, but it seemed nothing more than a pipe-dream.*
【黄麻】jute：～袋 *gunnysack*；*gunny bag*
【黄毛丫头】［贬］a silly little girl；chit of a girl
【黄梅季】rainy season
【黄梅戏】Huangmei opera，a form of regional opera popular in central Anhui Province
【黄米】glutinous millet
【黄牛】① ox；cattle ②［方］tout；scalper：～票 *scalper's ticket* ③ unreliable person；person who breaks his or her promises
【黄牌】【体】yellow card：这个运动员在足球比赛中吃了一张～。*This athlete got a yellow card in the football match.*
【黄袍加身】be draped with the imperial yellow robe by one's supporters — be made emperor
【黄皮书】yellow book — International Certificate of Vaccination
【黄泉】netherworld：命归～ *go to the netherworld*；*die* / ～之下 *the netherworld*；*dwelling place of the dead*
【黄雀】siskin
【黄壤】yellow earth；yellow soil
【黄色】① yellow：～的帽子 *a yellow cat* ② decadent；vulgar；pornographic：～歌曲 *lewd song* / ～书刊 *obscene publication*（*or books*）/ ～电影 *pornographic movie*；*sex film*；*blue film*
【黄色人种】yellow race
【黄鳝】rice-field eel；finless eel
【黄熟】【农】yellow maturity；yellow ripeness：～期 *stage of yellow maturity*（*or ripeness*）
【黄鼠】ground squirrel；suslik
【黄鼠狼】yellow weasel
【黄鼠狼单咬病鸭子】a yellow weasel will take an ill duck as his victim — only the weak will be bullied
【黄鼠狼给鸡拜年】a weasel makes a courtesy call to a chicken — harbour evil intentions；have evil motives：我看那家伙是～，没安什么好心。*I can see that guy through, and he can hardly has any good intention.*
【黄汤】［贬］rice wine；liquor：他灌了几口～就开始吹牛。*He began boasting after drinking a little.*

【黄糖】［方］brown sugar
【黄体酮】【生理】progesterone
【黄铁矿】pyrite
【黄铜】brass
【黄铜矿】chalcopyrite
【黄土】【地】loess
【黄土高原】loess plateau
【黄烟】［方］tobacco
【黄羊】Mongolian gazelle
【黄杨】【植】Chinese littleleaf box
【黄杨木】boxwood
【黄莺】【动】oriole
【黄油】① grease：～枪 *grease gun* ② butter：～面包 *bread and butter*
【黄鱼】① yellow croaker ②［旧］stowaway passenger who pays the driver or sailor ③［方］gold bar：大～ *big gold bar* (*ten taels*)
【黄种人】yellow man；Mongoloid

惶 fear；anxiety；trepidation
【惶惶】in a state of anxiety；on tenterhooks；alarmed
【惶惶不可终日】be in a constant state of anxiety
【惶惑】perplexed and alarmed；apprehensive
【惶遽】［书］frightened；scared
【惶恐】terrified：～万状 *be seized with fear*；*be frightened out of one's senses*
【惶恐不安】in a state of trepidation
【惶悚】［书］terrified

煌 bright；brilliant
【煌煌】bright；brilliant

锽 a kind of weapon in ancient times
【锽锽】sound of bells and drums

潢[1] ［书］pool；pond

潢[2] dye or colour paper：装～ *decoration*

璜 semi-annular jade pendant

蝗 【动】locust
【蝗虫】locust
【蝗灾】plague of locust

磺 sulphur：硝～ *nitre and sulphur*

簧 ① reed ② spring：表～ *the spring of watch*
【簧风琴】reed organ；harmonium
【簧片】reed
【簧乐器】reed instrument

huǎng

恍 ① all of a sudden；suddenly ② seem；as if：～若身临其境 *as if one is placed in the atmosphere*
【恍惚】① in a trance；absentminded：精神～ *be in a trance* ② (of seeing，hearing，and memory) dimly；seemingly：我～看见他了。*I was faintly aware of his sight.*
【恍然】suddenly；all of a sudden：～醒悟 *wake up to the truth in an instant*
【恍然大悟】suddenly see the light；suddenly realize what has happened：他～。*A light broke in upon him.*
【恍如隔世】as if being cut off from the outside world for ages；as if had been in the remote past
【恍悟】wake up to reality suddenly；suddenly come to realize the truth

晃 ① dazzle ② flash past：有个人影儿一～。*A figure flashed past.*
see also huàng
【晃眼】① dazzle：很～ *be dazzlingly bright* ② twinkling：一～二十多年过去了。*Twenty-odd years have passed in a twinkling.*

谎 ① lie；falsehood：撒～ *tell a lie*；*lie* / 要～ *exorbitant price asked by a seller* ② tell lies；lie
【谎报】lie about sth；make a false report about sth：～成绩 *give a false account of one's achievements* / ～军情 *make a false report about the military situation*
【谎称】falsely claim to be；pretend to be：当敌人盘问的时候，他～是小商贩。*When inquired by enemies, he pretended to be a peddler.*
【谎话】lie；falsehood：～连篇 *tell a pack of lies*
【谎价】excessive price；exorbitant price
【谎骗】deceive：他那热情的样子没有能够～我们很久。*His friendly manner did not deceive us for long.*
【谎信】［方］unproved information；rumour
【谎言】lie；falsehood：～掩盖不了事实。*Lies cannot cover up facts.*

幌 ［书］heavy curtain
【幌子】① shop sign；sign board ② pretence；cover；front：打着……～ *in the guise of*；*under the pretence of* ③［喻］ade；a front

huàng

晃 shake；sway：摇～ *rock*；*sway* / 树枝来回～。*The branches are swaying to and fro.*
see also huǎng
【晃荡】① rock；sway；swing；② saunter；loaf
【晃动】shake；rock；sway：他坐在椅子上～。*He sat rocking in his chair.*
【晃梯】balancing on an upright ladder
【晃摇】rock；shake；sway
【晃悠】shake from side to side；wobble：他拿着绳子的一端～呢。*He is now swaying with one end of the rope in hand.*

huī

灰 ① ash：炉～ *stove ashes* /烟～ *tobacco* (*or cigarette*) *ash* /他的骨～将安葬在坦桑尼亚。*His ashes will be buried in Tanzania.* ② dust；powder：青～ *graphite powder* ③ lime；(lime) mortar：抹～ *apply mortar* ④ grey：银～ *silver-grey* ⑤ depressed；disheartened：心～意懒 *be disheartened*

【灰暗】murky grey；gloomy

【灰白】pale；ashen；greyish white：她脸色～。*She looks pale.*

【灰败】dingy；dreary

【灰不溜丢】[贬][方] grey and dull

【灰菜】lamb's-quarters；goosefoot

【灰尘】dust；dirt：请把汽车上的～洗掉。*Please wash the dirt off the car.*

【灰沉沉】(usu. of the sky) dull grey；dull：

【灰顶】mortared or plastered roof

【灰斗】ash bucket；hod

【灰飞烟灭】become ashes and smoke；vanish like smoke：问题仍在，不会～的。*The problem won't just disappear.*

【灰膏】slaked lime；plaster

【灰姑娘】Cinderella，heroine of a famous folk tale

【灰浆】mortar；plaster

【灰烬】ashes：化为～ *be reduced to ashes*

【灰鲸】grey whale (*Eschrichtius robustus*)

【灰领工人】grey collar worker

【灰溜溜】① dull grey；dingy：② depressed；crestfallen：他～地溜出了房间。*He slipped shamefacedly out of the room.*

【灰霉】grey mold：～病 *grey mold* /～酸 *grisic acid*

【灰蒙蒙】dusky；overcast

【灰泥】plaster

【灰棚】[方] ① straw ash shed ② mortar-roofed hut

【灰雀】bullfinch

【灰色】① grey ②[喻] pessimistic；gloomy ③[喻] obscure；ambiguous：

【灰色收入】grey income — extra income earned by part-time job

【灰沙】dust and sand

【灰鼠】squirrel

【灰铁】grey (or pig) iron

【灰头土脸儿】[方] ① (of head or face) covered with dust：打扫完卫生，他～的。*He was dirty all over after cleaning and sweeping.* ② gloomy；downhearted

【灰土】dust

【灰心】lose heart；discouraged：不要～。*Don't be discouraged.*

【灰心丧气】extremely dishearten；very much dejected：我们永远不能～。*We shall never abandon our hope.* /不管遇到什么困难，我们绝不能～。*No matter what difficulties may come, we must never lose heart.*

【灰熊】【动】grizzly bear

诙 [书] ① tease good-humouredly ② mock；ridicule

【诙谐】humorous；jocular；witty；jocose；scherzando：一句～妙语 *a witty saying* /～地说 *speak in jest*

【诙谐曲】humoresque；humouresque

挥 ① wave；move；shake；wield：大笔一～ *with one stroke of the writing brush* ② wipe off：～汗 *wipe off one's sweat* ③ command (an army) ④ scatter；disperse

【挥斥】[书] ① criticize；scold ② bold and unrestrained；uninhibited

【挥动】wave；shake；brandish

【挥发】volatilize；(of a liquid and some solids) change into gas or vapor in normal atmospheric temperature

【挥发性】volatility；volatileness：～化合物 *volatile compound*

【挥发油】volatile oil

【挥戈】brandish one's weapon；advance boldly

【挥翰】[书] wield one's writing brush；write (with a brush)

【挥汗如雨】dripping with sweat

【挥毫】[书] wield one's brush；write or paint (with a brush)

【挥霍】① squander；spend freely：他已～掉父母留下的钱。*He has been prodigal of the money left by his parents.* /他因为酗酒～掉了自己的积蓄。*He threw away his savings by drinking too much.* ② [书] lively；free and easy

【挥金如土】spend money like dirt；spend money like water；be lavish with one's money

【挥泪】wipe off one's tears；shed tears

【挥洒】① sprinkle or spray (water)；shed (tears) ② paint or write with ease ③ [书] free and unrestrained

【挥师】command an army

【挥手】wave (one's hand)；wave：～作别 *wave sb good-bye* /～致意 *wave greetings to sb*

【挥舞】wave；brandish；shake：他～着手帕表示欢迎。*He waved the handkerchief in welcome.*

咴

【咴儿咴儿】[象] (of a horse) neigh

恢 extensive；vast

【恢诞】exaggerated；fantastic；absurd

【恢复】recover；restore；resume：～健康 *recover one's health*；*recuperate* /～名誉 *rehabilitate one's reputation*/ ～外交关系 *resume diplomatic relations with (a country)* /他动手术后仍在～中。*He is still recuperating from his operation.*

【恢弘】[书] ① broad；extensive；magnanimous：气度～ *broad-minded* ② develop；carry on

【恢恢】[书] extensive；vast：天网～。*The net of heaven has large meshes.*

【恢廓】[书] ① large-minded ② expand；spread

袆 [古] sacrificial robe for the queen or empress (in ancient times)

晖 sunshine; sunlight: 春~ *spring sunshine*

辉 ① brightness; splendour: 光~ *radiance; glory* /落日余~ *sunset glow; the last of sunset brilliance* ② shine

【辉煌】glorious; splendid; brilliant: ~的成就 *brilliant achievements*

【辉煤】glossy coal; glance coal

【辉映】shine; reflect: 交相~ *reflect radiance to each other*/ 大海~着灿烂的阳光。*The sea reflected back the bright sunlight.*

麾 ① standard of a commander, usually used in ancient time ② [书] command

【麾下】[书] ① under one's command ② a respectful address to a general or commander

徽[1] ① emblem; badge: 国~ *national emblem* / 校~ *school badge* ② fine; glorious

徽[2] (Huī) Huizhou of Anhui Province

【徽标】emblem; insignia; logo: 爱的~ *an emblem of love* /在飞机的不同部分有五个~。*There are five insignia on various parts of the plane.*

【徽带】cummerbund; kummerbund

【徽调】① the Anhui musical style ② [旧] Anhui opera

【徽号】glorious title; title of honour

【徽记】mark; sign; logo; insignia: 翼梢上的~清晰可见。*The insignia was visible on the wingtip.*

【徽墨】Huizhou inkstick, the best of its kind

【徽章】badge; insignia: 空军的~ *the emblem of the air force* / ~设计者 *emblematist*

【徽帜】[书] flag (or banner) as a symbol

huí

回[1] ① wind; circle: 巡~ *go the rounds; tour* ② return; go back: ~原单位工作 *go back to work in one's original unit* ③ turn around: 他~身看到了我。*He turned around and saw me.* ④ answer; reply: 我刚给他~了电话。*I just called him back a minute ago.* ⑤ report (to higher authorities, etc.): 校长提的问题我已经~答了。*I have reported back to the principal about the question he asked.* ⑥ decline; refuse; cancel: 她~了他聚会的邀请。*She declined his invitation to that party.* ⑦ [量] time; occasion: 他来过两~。*He has been here twice.* ⑧ [量] (in Chinese novels) chapter:《红楼梦》共一百二十~。*Dreams of the Red Chamber has 120 chapters.*

回[2] ① Hui nationality ② (Huí) a surname

【回拜】pay a return visit or call: 她翌日~了这位教授。*She paid a return visit to the professor the next day.*

【回报】① report back ② repay; requite: 我怎样才能~您的厚爱? *How can I do something in return for your kindness?* ③ retaliate; get one's own back: 美德即是美德的~。*Virtue is its own reward.*

【回避】① avoid; evade; dodge; shun: ~矛盾 *dodge contradictions* /生病期间他~了一切社交。*During his illness, he shunned all society.* ② (as of a judge or witness) avoidance; challenge; recuse: 与本案被嫌疑人有亲友关系的人应自行~。*A person who has an intimate relationship with the suspect of this case should withdraw of his own accord.*

【回避制度】avoidance system; challenge system

【回禀】[旧] report back (to one's superior)

【回驳】refute

【回茬】second crop: ~小麦 *wheat as second crop in the year*

【回肠】①【生理】ileum ② [书] worried; agitated; anxious

【回肠荡气】(of music, poems, etc.) soul-stirring; thrilling; inspiring

【回肠九转】one's mind occupied with anxiety and worries

【回潮】① get damp or wet again: 在雨季东西很容易~。*Things easily get damp in rainy season.* ② [喻] resurgence; reversion: 思想~ *an ideological relapse*

【回程】return trip: 在~的路上,他病倒了。*He fell ill on the return trip.*

【回春】① return of spring: 大地~。*Spring returns to the world again.* ② [喻] bring back to life: 妙手~ *bring the dying back to life*

【回答】answer; reply; respond; in answer to: 那个男孩立即做出了~。*The boy gave a quick answer.*

【回单】short note acknowledging receipt of sth

【回荡】resound; reverberate: 牧羊人的歌声在山间~。*The shepherd's songs reverberated in the valleys.*

【回电】① wire back: 请即~。*Wire back soon.* ② a telegram in reply

【回跌】(of prices) drop or fall after a rise

【回返】come or go back; return

【回访】pay a return visit

【回奉】return

【回复】① reply (to a letter) ② restore; return to original state or condition: 让我们用想象把北京~到三十年代的样子。*Let's just imagine and restore Beijing to what it was in the 1930's.*

【回购】buy back; counter-purchase: ~交易 *buy-back deal*

【回顾】review; look back

【回顾展】retrospective exhibition

【回光返照】last glow of the setting sun — momentary recovery of consciousness just before death

【回光镜】reflector

【回归】① return: 香港~祖国 *Hong Kong return to the motherland* ②【统】regression

【回归带】tropical zone

【回归年】【天】tropical year; solar year
【回归线】【地】tropic：南～ *Tropic of Capricorn* /北～ *Tropic of Cancer*
【回锅】cook again; heat up：这碗菜要～才能吃。*Heat up the dish before eating.*
【回锅肉】twice-cooked pork; stir-fried boiled pork slices
【回国】return to one's country or motherland：她学成～。*She returned to her country after finishing studies.*
【回航】【航】return to base; return to port
【回合】round; bout：这个拳手在第一个～中取得了胜利。*The boxer got a first-round victory.*
【回护】defend; shield; be partial to a party
【回话】① answer; reply：这个农民回了官老爷的话。*The peasant answered the question by the local official.* ② reply; answer：明天给你～。*I'll give you an answer tomorrow.*
【回还】return：他再也没有～。*He didn't return forever.*
【回环】winding; zigzagging
【回击】fight back; return fire; counterattack
【回家】go home; return home
【回见】[口] see you later; see you soon
【回教】Islam; Mohammedanism
【回敬】return a compliment; do or give sth in return：～你一杯酒。*I'll drink a toast in return.*
【回绝】decline; refuse; reject
【回空】(of vehicles and ships) make the return trip empty
【回口】[方] answer back; talk back; retort：不要～，那不礼貌。*Don't answer back. It's rude.*
【回扣】rebate; sales commission：拿～会影响我们的声誉。*Taking kick-back will ruin our reputation.*
【回来】① return; come (or get) back：她马上就～。*She'll come back soon.* ② back (here)：跑～ *run back* /把借出去的钱要～。*Recall the money on loan.*
【回廊】winding corridor
【回老家】[口] die; be no more：送他～。*Kill him!*
【回礼】① return a salute ② give a gift in return：他很快找了个理由给我回了礼。*He soon found an excuse and gave me a gift in return.* ③ return gift：这份～让他很意外。*The return gift surprised him a lot.*
【回历】Islamic calendar
【回流】backflow; return：河水～ *backflow of a river* /人才～ *return of talents*
【回笼】① steam again ② withdraw (currency) from circulation
【回笼觉】sleep again after waking up in the morning
【回炉】① melt down：废铁～ *melt down scrap iron* ② bake again：～烧饼 *bake again the cakes*
【回路】① way back ②【电】return circuit; return loop
【回銮】(of an emperor) return from outside
【回落】(of water levels, prices, etc.) fall or drop after a rise
【回门】the bride visits her parents with her newly-wed husband a few days after their wedding
【回民】Hui people：他是～。*He is a Hui.*
【回眸】(usu. of a woman) look back; glance back：～一笑 *glance back and smile*
【回娘家】(of a newly-wed woman) visit her parents
【回暖】get warm again after cold weather
【回聘】re-engage for work; re-employ
【回迁】move back; return：工程竣工后，居民又～了。*The inhabitants moved back when the project was completed.*
【回青】[方] turn green
【回请】give a return banquet; return hospitality
【回去】① return; go back：你来晚了一步，他刚～。*You are a little late; he has just gone back.* ② back：拿～ *take it back*
【回绕】winding; zigzagging
【回身】turn around
【回神】[口] recover from shock (or absent-mindedness)
【回升】rise again; pick up：气温开始～。*The temperature is going up again.*
【回生】① return to life ② be out of practice; get rusty
【回声】echo：这个峡谷以～闻名。*The canyon is famous for producing echoes.*
【回声学】catacoustics
【回师】bring back the troops; (of troops) move back
【回收】① retrieve; recover; reclaim：～废物 *recycle waste* ② take back; retrieve; recover
【回收站】collection depot
【回收装置】retrieving device
【回手】① turn round and stretch out one's hand：他出了屋子，又～带上了门。*He went out and turned round to close the door.* ② hit back; return a blow
【回首】① turn one's head; turn round ②[书] look back; recollect：不堪～ *can't bear to think of the past* /～童年的艰苦岁月，他深有感触。*When recalling his childhood of hardship, he lost himself in thought.*
【回书】[书] reply; letter in reply
【回赎】redeem
【回思】recall; bring back to the mind
【回溯】recall; look back upon：～战争年代 *recall the war years*
【回天】reverse a hopeless situation
【回天乏术】unable to save a situation
【回天之力】ability to reverse a hopeless situation; extraordinary power
【回条】a short note acknowledging receipt of sth; receipt
【回帖】[旧] receipt (for postal remittance)

【回头】① turn round; turn one's head: ~观望 *turn round and look back* ② return; go back: 一去不~ *never return after one's departure* ③ repent: 现在~还不算晚。*It's still not late to repent now.* ④ later: ~再说。*Let's discuss it later.*
【回头见】see you later; cheerio
【回头客】regular customer; frequenter: 这个商店有很多~。*Many people shopping here are regular customers.*
【回头路】[喻] the road back to where one started: 千万不能走~。*Never take the road of retrogression.*
【回头人】[方] widow
【回头是岸】[喻] repent and be saved: 苦海无边, ~。*The sea of bitterness is boundless; repent and the shore is at hand.*
【回味】① aftertaste ② call sth to mind and ponder over it: 小女孩仔细~着老人的话。*The little girl pondered over words of that old man.*
【回味无穷】leave prolonged aftertaste
【回席】invite sb to dinner in return for his or her hospitality; give a return banquet
【回戏】cancel a performance (of a traditional opera)
【回翔】circle round; wheel
【回响】reverberate; echo; resound
【回想】recall; think back; recollect: 这些照片使我~起我的学生时代。*The photographs reminded me of my schooldays.*
【回销】(of the state) resell (to the place of production)
【回心转意】change one's mind; come round
【回信】① write back; reply: 我正在给父亲~。*I am now writing back to my father.* ② letter in reply: 他正在焦急地等待丈夫的~。*She is waiting anxiously for her husband's letter in reply.*
【回形针】(paper) clip
【回修】return sth for repairs
【回叙】① flashback ② recount; recall
【回旋】① circle round; wheel: 风卷着树叶在院子中~。*The wind whirled the leaves around the yard.* ② manoeuvre
【回旋曲】【音】rondo
【回忆】recall; memories: ~对比 *recall the past and contrast it with the present* /这张相片勾起了他幸福的~。*The photograph evoked his happy memories.*
【回忆录】memoirs; reminiscences
【回音】① echo; resound ② reply; respond
【回音壁】Echo Wall (in the Temple of Heaven, Beijing)
【回应】reply; answer; response
【回映】(of light, etc.) reflect
【回佣】[方] sales commission; kickback
【回援】(of an army) turn round to reinforce or rescue
【回赠】give sb a present in return: 他收了我的礼物, 但一点儿东西也没有~我。*He accepted my presents and didn't give me any in turn.*
【回涨】(of water level, etc.) rise again
【回执】a short not acknowledging receipt of sth receipt
【回转】① go back; return: ~家乡 *return to one's hometown* ② turn round
【回族】the Hui Nationality, national minority in China
【回嘴】[口] answer or talk back; retort: 受到父母的斥责时不能~。*We cannot try to retort when scolded by our parents.* /他再批评你,不要~。不理他就是了。*If he criticizes you again, don't retaliate; just ignore him.*

茴

【茴香】【植】① fennel ② [方] aniseed: ~豆 *beans flavoured with aniseed*

洄 [书] (of water) whirl

【洄游】migration: 产卵~ *spawning migration*

蛔 roundworm

【蛔虫】roundworm, ascarid: 我又不是你肚子里的~,怎么能知道你要什么。*I am not to probe into your mind; how should I know what you truly want?*
【蛔虫病】roundworm disease; ascariasis

huǐ

悔 regret; repent: 亡羊补牢, ~之未晚。*It shall never be too late to mend.*

【悔不当初】regret a previous mistake; regret having done sth: 早知今日, ~。*If I'd known then what was going to happen, I wouldn't have done as I did.*
【悔改】regret and reform; repent and mend one's way: 他对他的所作所为毫无~之意。*He shows no repentance for what he has done.*
【悔过】repent one's error; be repentant: 他为过激的举止~。*He repented of his intemperate behaviour.*
【悔过书】written statement of repentance; written confession
【悔过自新】repent and turn over a new leaf; repent and make a fresh start; repent and start anew
【悔恨】deplore; regret; be filled with remorse; the worm of conscience: ~失误 *deplore one's faults* / 他非常~自己轻率的举动。*He lamented his thoughtless acts.* / ~使他内心非常痛苦。*Remorse preyed upon his mind.*
【悔恨交加】mixed feelings of remorse and shame; be stung by remorse: 他因为没有帮助她而~。*He was filled with remorse and shame for his failure to help her.*
【悔婚】break an engagement for marriage
【悔棋】retract a false move in a chess game

【悔悟】awake from sin; realize one's error and show repentance: 毫无~之意 *show no sign of repentance*

【悔之晚矣】be too late to repent; too late for remorse; cry over split milk: 她曾经想过好好工作,如今~。*She had been thinking of working hard, but now it is too late.*

【悔罪】show penitence (or repentance); contrite: ~的罪人 *a penitent sinner* /怀着谦恭并~的心情 *with a humble and contrite heart*

毁 ① destroy; ruin: 谁~了这个收音机? *Who broke this radio?* ② burn up: 烧~ *destroy by fire* ③ defame; slander: 诋~ *slander* ④ [方] make over (finished old clothes, etc.): 这两个凳子是一张旧桌子~的。*The two stools were made out of an old table.*

【毁谤】defame; slur; slander; calumniate; calumniate; smear: ~他的政治对手 *slandered his political opponent* / 他在我的朋友面前~我。*He slandered me in front of my friend.*

【毁掉】damage; destroy; break down; finish; ruin; consume; go to sticks and staves: ~某人的一生 *make a wreck of sb's life* /不要~那个盒子——它也许有用。*Don't destroy that box — it may be useful.*

【毁害】destroy; damage; ruin; demolish: 人们经常~许多野生植物。*People often destroy many wild plants.*

【毁坏】demolish; depredate; destroy; devastate; dilapidate; ratten; ruin; scuttle: 大火~了图书馆的书。*The fire ruined the books in the library.*

【毁林】deforest; disafforest

【毁灭】destroy; exterminate; ballyhack; consume; wrack and ruin: 面临~的威胁。*Ruin now stares in the face.*

【毁圮】[书] ruin; collapse: 在1976年,无数的房屋因唐山地震而~。*Numerous houses collapsed as a result of the Tangshan Earthquake in* 1976.

【毁弃】ruin; scrap; annul; cassation

【毁容】disfigure: 被一道深深的伤疤~的脸 *a face disfeatured by a deep scar*

【毁伤】injure; damage; hurt: ~半径 *radius of damage; radius of rupture*

【毁尸灭迹】chop up a corpse and obliterate all traces; bury the corpse in order to destroy all traces of one's crime

【毁损】damage; derogation; derogation; impair; mutilation: 因使用而~ *be impaired by use*

【毁于一旦】be destroyed in a day (or moment)

【毁誉】praise or blame; praise or condemnation: 不计~ *be indifferent to people's praise or blame*

【毁誉参半】get both praise and censure; have a mixed reception

【毁誉失当】inappropriate in giving praise

【毁约】break one's promise; annul a contract or treaty: 他在最后时刻~。*He reneged on the contract at the last minute.*

huì

卉 a general term for grass: 花~ *flowers and plants*

汇[1] ① converge: 小溪~入湖泊。*The brooks converge into a lake.* ② gather together ③ things collected; assemblage; collection: 词~ *vocabulary; lexicology*

汇[2] ① remit: 给家里~点钱 *send money to one's family; remit money home* ② foreign exchange: 创~ *earn foreign exchange*

【汇报】report: 我将向校长~你的情况。*I will report your situation to the headmaster.*

【汇报演出】a report-back performance

【汇编】① compile; collect ② collection; compilation; corpus: 旁征博引的~ *an erudite compilation* ③【电】assembly

【汇单】money order; remittance slip

【汇兑】① remittance: 国内~ *domestic remittance* ② exchange: ~管制 *exchange control* / ~率 *rate of exchange* / ~银行 *exchange bank*

【汇费】remittance fee

【汇丰银行】Hong Kong and Shanghai Banking Corporation

【汇合】converge; join

【汇集】collect; compile; converge: 学生在礼堂~。*The pupils assembled in the school hall.*

【汇寄】remit

【汇款】① remit money ② remittance: 即速~不胜感激。*A prompt remittance would be appreciated.*

【汇款单】money order; remittance slip

【汇款人】remitter

【汇流】converge; flow together

【汇流平原】confluence plain

【汇拢】gather together; converge; assemble

【汇票】draft; bill of exchange: 邮政~ *postal order; (postal) money order*

【汇融】converge; mix together

【汇算】settle accounts; wind up accounts

【汇展】joint exhibition

【汇总】gather; collect: 把材料~上报 *collect data for the higher level; present an itemized report to the higher level*

会[1] ① get together; assemble: 咱们就在这里~齐吧。*Let's assemble here.* ② meet; see: 你~过他没有? *Have you ever met him?* ③ gathering: 群众大~ *mass rally* /开~ *hold a meeting* ④ certain unions or associations: 工~ *trade (or labour) union* /学生~ *student union (or association)* ⑤ temple fair: 赶庙~ *go to the fair* ⑥ pilgrimage; religious festival; village thanksgiving festival ⑦ a small-scaled association for mutual help composed of people who contribute regularly to a common fund and draw from it by turns ⑧ city or capital (usu. administrative centre): 都~ *capital* /省~ *provincial capital* ⑨ opportunity;

occasion：适逢其～ *happen to be present at the right moment* ⑩［书］happen to ⑪［书］surely；certainly：长风破浪～有时。*There will be a day when we will succeed.*

会[2] ① understand；grasp：误～ *misunderstand*；*mistake* /领～ *understand*；*comprehend* ② be acquainted with；have knowledge of：他～英文。*He knows English.* ③ can；be able to：她～滑冰。*She can skate.* ④ be good at；be skilful in：能说～道 *have a gift of the gab*；*a talkative person* ⑤ be likely to；may：我想他不～不懂。*I don't think he may not understand it.*

会[3] pay；foot：我～过饭费了。*I've paid for the meal.*

see also kuài

【会标】symbol of an event or a meeting

【会餐】dine together；have a dinner together：很多公司都有周末～。*Many companies offer their staff weekend dinner party.*

【会操】a joint drilling（or exercises）

【会场】meeting place；site of a conference

【会钞】pay（or foot）the bill

【会车】（of vehicles）cross；pass by each other

【会费】membership dues

【会馆】［旧］guild hall；provincial or country guild

【会海】sea of meetings — numerous meetings

【会合】join；meet；converge；assemble

【会合点】【军】meeting point；rendezvous

【会合周期】【天】synodic period

【会话】conversation

【会徽】emblem of an organization；logo

【会籍】membership of a society（or an association，etc.）

【会见】meet；meet with；have a meeting with

【会聚】assemble；meet；flock together

【会考】general standard examination（for graduating students in a particular area）

【会客】receive visitors（or guests）

【会客室】reception room

【会门】superstitious sects and secret societies

【会盟】meet to form alliances（in ancient China）

【会面】meet

【会期】① date of a conference or meeting ② duration of a meeting

【会齐】gather；assemble

【会旗】flag of a conference

【会签】countersign；countersignature；jointly sign a document

【会亲】［旧］mutual visit between a newly-wedded couple's relatives

【会儿】［口］moment：等一～。*Wait a moment.* /用不了多大～。*It will not take a long time.*

【会商】hold a conference or consultation

【会审】① joint hearing（or trial）：举行～ *conduct a joint trial* ② make a joint checkup（of some bill，etc.）

【会师】（of forces marching from different places）join at a certain place

【会首】leader or chief of a society，association，etc.

【会水】be able to swim：我不～。*I can't swim.*

【会所】headquarters or office building of a nongovernmental organization

【会谈】talks；negotiation：举行～ *carry out talks*

【会堂】meeting hall；assembly hall；conference hall

【会通】［书］achieve mastery through a comprehensive study of the subject

【会同】together with

【会务】routine affairs of a conference

【会悟】［书］realize；come to understand

【会晤】meet：两国外长定期～。*The foreign ministers of the two countries meet regularly.*

【会衔】jointly sign a document

【会心】understanding；knowing：～的微笑 *an understanding smile*

【会演】joint performance；festival：戏曲～ *opera festival*

【会要】book of economic and political institutions and regulations of a dynasty

【会议】① meeting；conference；convention：明天我们将举行～来讨论这件事。*We will hold a meeting tomorrow to discuss the matter.* ② council；conference

【会议室】meeting-room

【会意】①【语】combined meaning；associative compounds ② understanding；knowing；sly：～的表情 *a knowing expression* /她向桥牌搭档使了个～的眼色。*She cast a sly glance at her bridge partner.*

【会阴】【生理】perineum

【会饮】drink together

【会友】① fellow members of a society，club，organization，etc. ②［书］make friends

【会员】member

【会员国】member state or nation；member

【会员证】membership card

【会员资格】status of a member；membership

【会战】①【军】meet for a decisive battle ②［喻］join in a battle；launch a mass campaign

【会长】the president（of an association or society，etc.）

【会账】pay a bill

【会诊】consultation of doctors；group consultation：中西医～ *hold group consultations of doctors practicing Chinese and Western medicine*

【会址】① the site of an association ② the site of a conference or meeting

【会众】① audience（at a meeting）②［旧］members（of a secret society）

【会子】period of time；a moment：说～话儿 *chat for a moment*

讳 ① avoid as taboo：忌～ *taboo*；*avoid as taboo* /直言不～ *speak without reservation*；*mince no words* ② taboo；forbidden word ③（in feudal society）the name，regarded as taboo，of

a deceased emperor or head of a family
【讳疾忌医】hide one's sickness for fear of treatment; conceal one's fault for fear of criticism
【讳忌】taboo
【讳莫如深】carefully avoid mentioning sth; not utter a single word about sth
【讳饰】avoid and cover up
【讳言】dare not or would not speak up; keep sth secret; hush up: 毋庸～。*There is no need to keep it secret.*

荟 [书] luxuriant growth of plants
【荟萃】gather together or assembling of distinguished people or exquisite objects: 京剧～ *selection of Beijing Opera*

诲 teach; instruct: 教～ *teaching; instruction*
【诲人不倦】be tireless in teaching
【诲淫诲盗】propagate sex and violence

绘 paint; draw: 描～ *depict; describe*
【绘画】painting; drawing: 我从没见过这么美的～。*I've never seen such beautiful drawings.*
【绘声绘色】vivid; lively: ～的描述 *a vivid description*
【绘事】[书] matters concerning painting; painting business
【绘图】mapping; sketch: ～员 *draftsman*
【绘像】draw portraits
【绘制】draw: ～图表 *draw a diagram*

贿 ① [书] money; wealth; property ② bribe; offer sth to sb in order to get him to do sth: 受～ *accept (or take) bribes* / 行～ *practise bribery; give bribes; bribe*
【贿赂】bribe: 政府采取强治措施惩治～。*The government took strong measures again bribery.*
【贿赂公行】people give and accept bribes openly; corruption is rife
【贿通】bribe; buy over
【贿选】practice bribery at an election; get elected by bribery

烩 ① braise: ～豆腐 *braise bean curd* ② cook various food mixed together: ～饭 *rice or shredded pancakes cooked with meat, vegetables and water*

彗 [书] broom
【彗尾】【天】tail of a comet
【彗星】【天】comet

晦 ① the last day of a lunar month ② dark; obscure: 隐～ *obscure; veiled* ③ night: 风雨如～ *wind and rain sweeping across a gloomy sky — a grim situation* ④ [书] hide; cover up: 韬光养～ *hide one's capacities*
【晦暗】dark and gloomy: 心情～ *feel gloomy*
【晦迹】[书] live in seclusion
【晦明】[书] ① day and night ② bright or dark
【晦暝】[书] dark; dim: 风雨～。*It was dark with wind and rain.*
【晦气】① unlucky; whammy: 真～! *What bad luck!* ② dark or gloomy complexion when one meets adversity or is ill: 一脸～ *with a gloomy complexion*
【晦涩】obscure; unclear; hard to understand: 他喜欢用～的句子表达思想。*He tended to use those words that can hardly be understood to convey himself.*

秽 ① dirty: 污～ *filthy* ② ugly; abominable: 淫～ *obscene; bawdy*
【秽德】[书] filthy behaviour; evil conduct
【秽迹】[书] dirty record
【秽乱】licentious; debauched
【秽气】bad smell; stink: 这儿～冲天。*It smells rather bad here.*
【秽土】rubbish; dirt
【秽闻】[书] ill repute
【秽亵】[书] ① filth; dirt ② obscene; salacious: ～言语 *coprolalia*
【秽行】[书] abominable behaviour
【秽语】dirty words; obscene language
【秽浊】dirty; filthy

惠 ① favour; kindness; benefit: 恩～ *favour; benefit* ② do others a favour: 根据互～原则进行贸易 *establish trade relations according to the principle of mutual benefits* ③ kind; gracious ④ (Huì) a surname
【惠风】[书] gentle breeze
【惠顾】your patronage: 顾客的～ *the kind patronage of our customers*
【惠临】your gracious presence
【惠灵顿】Wellington, capital of New Zealand
【惠然】friendly; kind
【惠予】kindly; be kind enough to
【惠允】your generous permission or consent
【惠泽】[书] favour; benefit
【惠赠】your kind presents

慧 intelligent; bright: 智～ *wisdom; intelligence* / 明～ *bright; clever*
【慧根】【宗】talent to thoroughly understand Buddhist teachings
【慧黠】[书] clever and sly
【慧心】enlightened mind; wisdom
【慧眼】insight; mental discernment

蕙 【植】a species of orchid
【蕙心】[书] (of a woman) pure heart

hūn

昏 ① dusk: 晨～ *at dawn and dusk* ② dark; dim: 天～地暗 *murky heavens over a dark earth; dark all around* ③ dizzy; dazed: 发～ *feel giddy (or dizzy)* ④ faint; lose consciousness: 她～过去了。*She has fainted.*
【昏暗】dim; dusky

H

【昏沉】① murky; dark: 夜色～ *murky twilight* ② dazed; befuddled: 他躺在地上, 头脑～, 浑身无力。*He lay on the ground, dazed and weak.* /病人整天～沉的。*The patient was in a daze all day long.*
【昏倒】faint; lose consciousness: 听到这个悲惨的消息, 她立刻～了。*She passed out immediately at the bad news.*
【昏黑】dusky; dark
【昏花】dim-sighted; blurred
【昏话】absurd remark; nonsense
【昏黄】pale yellow; faint
【昏昏欲睡】drowsy; sleepy
【昏厥】faint; swoon
【昏君】a fatuous and self-indulgent ruler
【昏聩】decrepit and muddle-headed
【昏乱】① dazed and confused ② [书] confusion and disorder
【昏迷】stupor; coma; shock: ～不醒 *remain unconscious*
【昏睡】lethargic sleep
【昏死】faint; swoon; coma
【昏天黑地】① dark; dim: 这样一个雨夜, ～, 泥泞的路越发难走了。*On such a dark night with the heavy rain, we found it was increasingly difficult to walk along the muddy road.* ② dizzy; lose conscious ③ perverted; decadent ④ complete chaos ⑤ dark rule and social disorder
【昏头昏脑】with one's mind numb; muddleheaded
【昏眩】dizzy; giddy
【昏庸】fatuous; muddle-headed; foolish
【昏晕】faint; dizzy

荤 ① chicken, duck, meat, fish, etc.: 不吃～ *do not eat meat*; *be a vegetarian* ② strong-smelling vegetables such as onions, garlic, etc.: 五～ *the five strong-smelling vegetables* ③ vulgar; dirty: ～笑话 *dirty jokes*
【荤菜】meat dish
【荤话】vulgar remarks; dirty words
【荤口】coarse language (in performance)
【荤腥】meat or fish
【荤油】lard

婚 ① marry: 已～ *married* /未～ *single*; *unmarried* ② marriage
【婚变】divorce
【婚假】wedding leave
【婚嫁】marriage
【婚检】physical check-up before marriage
【婚礼】wedding ceremony; wedding
【婚恋】fall in love and get married
【婚龄】① years of marriage ② (legally) marriageable age
【婚配】married
【婚期】wedding day
【婚纱】wedding garment
【婚事】marriage; wedding
【婚书】[旧] marriage certificate
【婚俗】customs of marriage
【婚外恋】extramarital love; affair
【婚姻】marriage; matrimony: ～自主 *marry on one's own*; *marriage decided by oneself*
【婚姻法】marriage law
【婚姻介绍所】matrimonial agency
【婚姻状况】marital status
【婚约】marriage contract; engagement

hún

浑 ① (of water) muddy; turbid: ～水坑 *a muddy water pool* ② (in cursing) foolish; stupid ③ simple and natural ④ whole; all over: ～身是汗 *sweat all over* ⑤ (Hún) a surname
【浑蛋】skunk; bastard; son of a bitch
【浑噩】ignorant; simple-minded
【浑厚】① simple and honest ② simple and vigorous: 笔力～ *bold and vigorous strokes* ③ (of voice) deep and resonant bass
【浑话】impudent remark
【浑浑噩噩】ignorant; simple minded; muddle headed
【浑家】wife
【浑括】all in all; in a word; generally speaking
【浑朴】simple and honest
【浑球儿】[方] rascal; wretch; son of a bitch
【浑然】① integrated; unified: ～天成 *like nature itself*; *integral whole* ② completely; fully: ～不觉 *be fully unaware*
【浑然一体】a unified entity; an integral whole
【浑如】exactly like
【浑身】from head to foot; all over: ～是胆 *be brave at every pore*; *be filled with guts*
【浑水摸鱼】fish in troubled waters — make a profit in troubled situation
【浑说】talk rubbish
【浑似】exactly like
【浑天仪】[古] ① armillary sphere ② celestial globe
【浑圆】perfectly round

珲 [书] a kind of jade

馄
【馄饨】ravioli; wonton, dumpling soup

魂 ① soul ② mood; spirit: 教师被誉为人类灵～的工程师。*A teacher is praised as an architect of man's soul.* ③ lofty spirit of a nation, army, etc.
【魂不附体】be scared out of wits; feel as if one's soul had left one's body
【魂不守舍】① in a trance; absent-minded ②be terrified
【魂飞魄散】be frightened out of one's wits; almost swooning with fright
【魂灵】soul
【魂魄】soul

【魂牵梦萦】miss very much; pine for

hùn

诨 joke; jest: 打~ *make comic remarks*

【诨名】nickname

混 ① mix; confuse: 在羊毛中~棉花 *mix cotton into wool* / 为了避免弄~,底部也贴上了标签。*To avoid confusion, the bottom is labeled too.* ② pass for; pass off as: 蒙~过关 *have passed off* / 鱼目~珠 *pass off fish eyes as pearls* ③ muddle on; drift along: ~日子 *drift along aimlessly* / 鬼~*fool around* ④ get along with: 新来的英语老师和学生们~得很熟。*The new English teacher gets along well with the students.* ⑤ thoughtlessly; irresponsibly: ~出主意 *put forward irresponsible suggestions*

【混编】mixed grouping

【混充】pass oneself off as: ~内行 *pass oneself off as an expert*

【混沌】① chaos, the primeval state of fear and the universe according to folklore ② simple-minded: ~无知 *simple-minded and ignorant*

【混饭】make a living as best as one can: 这儿的工作很没意思,我不过是~而已。*The job is very boring; I stay here just for making a living.*

【混纺】①[方] blending: ~织物 *blend fabric; union* ② blend fabric

【混合】mix; blend; mingle: 教授把三种东西~在一起。*The professor mixed the three together.* / 蓝色和黄色~产生绿色。*Green results from blending blue and yellow.*

【混合物】mixture: 那~很难尝。*The mixture tasted horrible.*

【混混儿】[方] scoundrel; idler

【混迹】unworthily mix with

【混交】【林】trees of two or more species growing together

【混交林】mixed forest

【混乱】confused; chaotic; confusion; chaos: ~不堪 *be in utter disorder*

【混凝剂】【化】coagulant

【混凝土】【建】concrete

【混日子】muddle along; drift along; loaf: 他整天就是~。*He just idles away his days.*

【混世魔王】devil incarnate

【混事】muddle along

【混同】confuse; mix up: 把价值和价格~了 *confuse value with price*

【混为一谈】confuse sth with sth else

【混淆】confuse; mix; confound

【混淆黑白】mix up black and white

【混淆视听】mislead the public

【混淆是非】confound right and wrong

【混血儿】a person of mixed blood; half-breed; mongrel

【混杂】mix up; intermix; interweave; jam; motley

【混战】battle royal; dogfight; melee; scuffle

【混账】scoundrel; rascal; son of a bitch

【混浊】muddy; turbid: ~的河 *a muddy stream*

【混子】person unworthy of his title; imposter

【混作】【农】mixed cropping (or cultivation)

huō

豁[1] split; break; crack: ~了一个口。*There was a breach.*

豁[2] give up; sacrifice: ~出几天时间 *spend several days regardless of anything*

see also huò

【豁出去】go ahead at any price; sacrifice anything for a purpose: ~性命 *risk one's life; go all out regardless of danger to ones'life*

【豁口】split; breach; crack: 打开~ *open a breach*

【豁子】[方] ① opening; break: 盘子上有个~。*There is an opening in the plate.* ② harelipped person

【豁嘴】①[口] harelip ②a harelipped person

攉 shovel (sth piled up) from one place to another: ~土 *shovel the soil* / ~煤机 *coal shoveller*

huó

和 mix (powder) with water in a paste: ~面 *knead dough* / ~泥 *knead wet clay*

see also hé; hè; hú; huò

活[1] ① live; grow: 人必须呼吸才能~。*Human beings can only live by breathing.* / ~到老,学到老。*One is never too old to learn; live and learn.* ② alive; living: 她还~着! *She is still alive!* ③ save; feed: ~人无数 *save countless lives* ④ movable; moving: 灵~ *flexible* ⑤ vivid; lively: 把这个角色演~可不容易。*It is rather hard to give life to this character.* ⑥ exactly; simply: ~像一只老虎 *be like a tiger very much*

活[2] ① work: 木工~儿 *woodwork* ② product: 这~儿做得真好。*This product is well made.*

【活靶】【军】moving target

【活扳子】spanner

【活版】【印】letterpress; typography

【活宝】[贬] funny fellow

【活蹦乱跳】alive and kicking

【活便】[方] ① flexible; agile ② convenient; handy

【活地图】walking map

【活地狱】hell on earth; living hell

【活底】false bottom

【活动】① move about; exercise: 冬眠的动物把~减少到大大低于一般的水平。*The hibernating animals move far below the ordinary level.* ② act for some purpose ③ shaky; unsteady ④ flexible; movable ⑤ activity for some purpose; campaign: 一项阻止人们吸烟的~ *a campaign to stop people*

H

smoking /课外～太多,占去了我们很多宝贵的学习时间。*Too many extracurricular activities take up too much of our precious time for study.* ⑥ wangle; maneuver

【活动家】activist; public figure

【活泛】① nimble; flexible ② have spare money; in good economic condition

【活佛】①【宗】Living Buddha ② Buddhist monk who helps people in difficulty and saves people from danger

【活该】① serve one right: ～如此 *get what one deserves* ②［方］should; be destined: 我～有救,碰上了这样的好医生。*With such a good doctor, I should be saved.*

【活化】activation

【活化石】living fossil

【活话】non-committal words; indefinite remarks

【活活】① while still alive: ～饿死 *starve to death* ② completely; almost: 她～是个疯子! *She looked like a complete maniac.*

【活火山】active volcano

【活计】① handicraft work; handiwork; manual labor ② handiwork; work

【活件】【电】liveware

【活见鬼】it's sheer fantasy

【活校】proof-reading that checks the original and the proofs

【活局子】［方］trap; trick

【活口】① living witness (or survivor) to a crime ② prisoner or criminal who can provide information ③ support oneself or one's family: 我靠写作～。*I support myself by writing.*

【活力】energy; juice; livingness; marrow; snap; spark; vigour; vim; vires: 充满青春～ *be brimming with youthful vigour* /大城市中充满～的街道 *the vibrant streets of a big city*

【活灵活现】lifelike; vivid: 他把梦境讲得～的。*He gave us a vivid picture of his dream.*

【活领】detachable collar

【活路】(huólù) ① thorough path ② workable (or feasible) method ③ means of subsistence

【活路】(huólu) manual or physical labour

【活络】［方］① loose; shaky; unstable ② flexible

【活埋】bury alive

【活门】【机】valve

【活命】① scrape along; eke out an existence; earn a living ②［书］save one's life ③ life

【活泼】① lively; vivacious; vivid; alive: 明快～的曲调 *a bright vivacious strain* /一个～的人,总是充满活力并且总在做事。*A lively person is full of life and is always doing things.* ②【化】reactive

【活菩萨】saviour; Buddha incarnate

【活期】current: ～储蓄 *current deposit* / ～贷款利率 *call rate* / ～借款 *call money demand loan*

【活气】lively atmosphere

【活契】conditional sales contract

【活钱儿】① cash; handy money ② extra income

【活塞】【机】piston plunger stopcock

【活色生香】［口］lifelike; vividly: 报道写得～,我也仿佛身临其境。*The report was so descriptive; I felt as if I were there.*

【活生生】① real; in real life: ～的例子 *actual example* ② while still alive

【活食】live earthworms, insects fish, etc. served as bigger animals' food

【活受罪】living death

【活栓】bibcock stopcock tap ventil

【活水】flowing water; running water

【活体】living body

【活脱儿】look exactly like

【活现】appear vividly; come alive

【活像】as like as two peas; have a close resemblance to

【活性】【化】active; activated

【活血】【中医】invigorate blood circulation

【活阎王】［喻］devil incarnate; demon king

【活页】leaflet: ～笔记本 *loose-leaf notebook* / ～乐谱 *sheet music* / ～纸 *filler*; *loose leaves*

【活跃】① activity; be up and doing; fizz; flourish; in full; swing; vibrancy: ～的人 *a stirring person* / ～于外交界 *move in diplomatic circles* /商业十分～。*There is much activity in trade.* ② animate; stimulate; enliven: ～市场 *enliven the market*

【活跃分子】activist

【活捉】hold captive; take alive

【活着】alive; aboveground; on one's pins; on the hoof; see the sun: 我们所捕的鱼还～。*The fish we caught is still alive.*

【活字】【印】movable type or letter

【活字版】movable type; original font

【活字典】a walking dictionary; walking dictionary

huǒ

火 ① fire: 炉～ *fire in the stove* ② firearms; ammunition: 军～ *munitions* /开～ *open fire* ③【中医】internal heat, a disease cause that leads to inflammation, red and swollenness, fidgets, etc.: 上～ *suffer from excessive internal heat* /败～ *relieve inflammation or internal heat* ④ red ⑤ urgent; pressing' anger; temper: 他发～儿了。*He flared up.* ⑥ prosperous; brisk: 这里生意很～。*Business here is very brisk.* ⑦ (Huǒ) a surname

【火把】torch

【火棒】lighted torch in the performance of acrobatics

【火爆】① fiery; impetuous ② vigorous; prosperous

【火并】open fight between factions

【火柴】match: 一盒～ *a box of matches*

【火场】scene of a fire

【火车】train

【火车头】① railway engine; locomotive ② leader of a group or sth which plays a leading role

【火车站】railway station

【火炽】vigorous; flourishing

【火刀】［方］steel (for flint)
【火电】thermal power
【火电厂】thermal power plant
【火电站】thermal power station
【火夫】［旧］① fireman; stroker ② mess cook
【火攻】attack with fire
【火钩子】fire hook
【火罐儿】【中医】cupping jar or glass
【火光】flame; blaze: ~冲天。*The flames lit up the sky.*
【火锅】chafing dish; hotpot
【火海】sea of fire
【火红】① red as fire; fiery; flaming ② prosperous; thriving
【火候】① duration and degree of heating, cooking, etc. ② level of attainment ③ crucial (or important) moment
【火狐】red fox
【火花】① spark ② matchbox picture
【火花塞】【机】sparking plug
【火化】cremate
【火鸡】turkey
【火鸡舞】turkeytrot
【火急】urgent; pressing
【火急火燎】be very anxious (or worried)
【火剪】① fire-tongs ② curling tongs; curling irons
【火碱】caustic soda
【火箭】rocket: 发射~*fire a rocket*
【火箭炮】rocket gun
【火箭筒】rocket launcher
【火井】gas well
【火警】fire alarm
【火镜】convex lens
【火具】ignition apparatus or equipment
【火炬】torch: ~点亮了。*Torches are lighted.*
【火炕】heated brick bed
【火坑】pit of hell; abyss of suffering
【火口】【地】crater
【火口湖】crater lake
【火筷子】fire-tongs
【火辣辣】① burning; scorching② hurt; burn ③ anxious; flushed ④ (of person) bold and resolute; (of language) acerbic; sharp
【火力】① thermal power: ~发电站 *thermal power station* ②【军】firepower; fire ③ cold-resistant capacity of the human body
【火力点】firing point
【火力电】thermo-power generation
【火力圈】field of fire
【火力群】concentration of firing position
【火镰】steel (for flint)
【火亮】①［方］spark ② bright
【火龙】① fiery dragon — a procession of lanterns or torches ②［方］air channel
【火笼】［方］bamboo basket brazier
【火炉】(heating) stove: 生~*light a stove*
【火冒三丈】flare up; be furious
【火帽】【军】percussion cap
【火煤】kindling
【火苗】flame
【火磨】power driven mill; electric mill
【火泥】fire clay
【火捻】① firelighter ② fuse
【火炮】gun; cannon
【火漆】sealing wax
【火气】① anger; temper: 他~大了些,大家别拿他的话太当回事儿。*He has got hot temper; we shall not take his words too seriously.* ② heat in human body ③【中医】internal heat
【火器】【军】firearm
【火钳】fire-tongs; fire-poker
【火枪】firelock
【火墙】① hot wall ② fire net
【火情】state (or condition) of a fire
【火球】fireball
【火雀】fire finch
【火热】① burning hot ② fervent; fiery ③ intimate; fall in love: 她俩打得~。*They two are enamored.* ④ intense
【火山】volcano: ~爆发 *volcanic eruption*
【火上浇油】add fuel to the flames; pour oil on the flames — aggravate the situation: 我的话如同~,他们吵得更激烈了。*My words simply worsened the situation and they got into an even more furious quarrel.*
【火烧火燎】① feel extremely hot ② be fidgeted with anxiety
【火烧眉毛】the most urgent situation
【火烧云】morning glow; evening glow
【火舌】tongues of fire; licking flame
【火绳】kindling rope
【火石】① flint ② artificial flint
【火势】state of the fire
【火树银花】fiery trees and silver flowers — display of fireworks and a sea of lanterns
【火速】at top speed; at once: ~完成工作 *finish the work at once*
【火损】fire damage
【火炭】live charcoal; burning wood
【火塘】［方］fire pit
【火烫】① burning hot; fiery ② have one's hair permed with hot curling tongs
【火头】① fire; flame ② degree and duration of heating; smelting, etc. ③ place where a fire started ④ anger; fare-up
【火头上】at the time of one's anger
【火腿】ham; gammon
【火腿蛋】ham and egg
【火网】cross fire
【火匣子】［方］coffin of inferior quality
【火险】① fire insurance: 给房子保~ *insure one's house against fire* ② fire danger
【火线】① battle (or firing, front) line: 轻伤不下~ *refuse to leave the front though having minor wounds* ②【电】live wire
【火星】①【天】Mars ② spark: 工厂的烟囱白天黑糊

糊的好像不动，但一到晚上就冒～。*The dark chimneys of the factory seem still in the day, but at night, they all spark.*
【火刑】execution by fire
【火性】hot temper
【火眼】【医】pinkeye
【火眼金睛】piercing (or discerning) eyes
【火焰】flame
【火药】gunpowder
【火药桶】powder key — a dangerous place：形势越来越紧张，该地区已经成为～，任何小事均能激起一场动乱。*Rising tensions have turned the area into a powder-keg and any incident could set off a riot.*
【火药味】smell of gunpowder
【火引子】material for starting a fire
【火印】mark made by burning
【火油】［方］kerosene
【火源】source of combustion; fire starter
【火灾】conflagration
【火葬】cremation
【火葬场】crematorium
【火躁】［方］impetuous
【火针】【中医】hot-needle acupuncture
【火种】kindling material
【火烛】things that may cause a fire
【火柱】column of fire
【火箸】［方］fire-tongs
【火砖】firebrick

伙[1] mess; food; meals

伙[2] ① partner; mate：同～儿 *partner; companion; pal* ②partnership; company：合～ *form a partnership* /入～ *join in a partnership* ③ (for people) group; crowd：一～歹徒 *a band of scoundrels* ④ combine; join：他们合～开了一家饭馆。*They clubbed together to run a restaurant.*
【伙伴】partner; companion：与某人结成～关系 *enter into partnership with sb*
【伙犯】accomplice
【伙房】kitchen (in a school, factory, etc.)
【伙夫】［旧］mess cook
【伙耕】club to cultivate
【伙计】① partner; mate ②［旧］salesman; shop assistant
【伙食】food; mess; meals
【伙食科】catering office
【伙同】in league with; in collusion with; gang up with sb
【伙友】partners and friends
【伙子】group; gang; band

huò

或 ① maybe; perhaps：他已经出发，明日上午～可到达。*He has set off, and perhaps will arrive tomorrow morning.* ② or; either... or：～多～少 *more or less* /同意～反对 *for or against* ③［书］somebody; someone ④［书］a little bit; slightly：不可～缓 *cannot wait any longer*
【或…或…】or; either... or...：～胖～瘦 *fat or thin* / ～早～晚 *whether early or late* / ～迟～早 *sooner or later*
【或是】or; either：她不知道该哭～该笑。*She didn't know whether to laugh or cry.*
【或许】may; maybe; perhaps：～我还会在那儿碰见你呢。*Maybe I'll see you there.*
【或则】or; either... or：你要么自己来，～就托人办理这件事。*Either you come in person, or you entrust somebody with the matter.*
【或者】① perhaps; maybe：～那封信今天能到。*Perhaps the letter will come today.* ② or; either... or...：汤姆～杰克要来。*Tom or Jack is coming.* /要么我们现在走，～永远在这呆下去。*Either we go now or we remain here forever.*

和[1] mix or blend powder or grain-like substances, or mix with water：～药 *mix the medicine (with some water)*

和[2]［量］time of rinsing; adding water when decocting medical herbs：二～药 *second decoction* /衣服已经洗了两～。*The clothes have been rinsed twice.*
see also hé; hè; hú; huó
【和弄】［方］① mix; blend ② sow discord
【和稀泥】［喻］mediate differences at the sacrifice of principle; paper over differences

货 ① money：通～ *currency; current money* ② goods; commodity：进～ *stock with goods* /订～ *order goods* ③ referring to the one being cursed：笨～ *fool; idiot* /蠢～ *blockhead; dunce* ④［书］sell
【货比三家】compare different offers before buying：买东西要～，挑最合适的。*You should compare prices offered by different suppliers and take the most reasonable one.*
【货币】money; currency
【货舱】cargo hold
【货仓】warehouse; freight house
【货差】cargo loss or damage
【货场】goods (or freight) yard
【货车】freight car (or train)
【货船】freighter; cargo ship (or vessel)
【货单】manifest; waybill; shipping list
【货到付款】cash on delivery(COD)
【货到即提】delivery on arrival
【货店】［方］store; shop
【货柜】① goods counter ②［方］container
【货机】【航】air freighter
【货价】commodity price; price of goods
【货架子】① goods shelves ② luggage-carrier of a bicycle
【货款】payment for goods
【货郎】itinerant pedlar; street vendor
【货郎担】itinerant pedlar's load
【货郎鼓】rattle-drum

H

【货流】flow of goods or freight
【货轮】freighter; cargo ship (or vessel)
【货棚】goods shed
【货票】invoice; delivery order
【货品】kinds or types of goods
【货色】① goods: ~齐全。*Goods of every description are available.* ②[贬] stuff; trash; rubbish:你知道他是什么~吗? *Do you know what stuff he is made of?*
【货损】freight (or cargo) damage
【货摊】stall; stand
【货梯】freight elevator
【货位】① car load ② storage space
【货物】goods; freight; commodity; merchandise: 载有大量~的飞机 *an aeroplane carrying a heavy freight* / ~整齐到达。*The goods arrived in good order.*
【货物税】excise tax
【货箱】packing box; container
【货样】sample goods; pattern
【货源】source of goods; supply of goods
【货运】freight transport: 通过~发送货物 *send the goods freight*
【货运单】waybill
【货运费】shipping cost
【货运量】volume of freight
【货运列车】goods (or freight) train
【货运周转量】rotation volume of goods (or freight) transport
【货栈】warehouse; storehouse
【货真价实】genuine goods at a fair price
【货主】owner of cargo

获 ① capture; catch:俘~ *capture*; *take prisoner* ② get; obtain:不劳而~ *reap where one has not sown* ③ reap; harvest: 收~ *gather in ripe crops*
【获得】gain; obtain; get; pick up; acquire; win; achieve; attain: ~广泛支持 *win a wide support* / ~全场喝彩 *bring down the gallery* / ~有关敌人的重要情报 *gain important information about the enemy's plans* /这个机灵的小伙子设法~那个标致女孩的欢心。*The cute lad did all he could to win the pretty girl's favour.*
【获得性】【生理】acquired character: ~免疫 *acquired immunity* / ~免疫缺损综合症 *acquired immune deficiency syndrome (AIDS)*
【获奖】win a prize; be rewarded: ~作品 *prize-winning works*
【获救】be rescued or saved from (death, disaster, etc.):他因医生而~。*His life was saved by the doctor.*
【获利】make a profit; clean up; accrual; reap profits: 每卖一只橘子~一便士 *make a penny profit on each orange*
【获取】acquire; gain; get: 那位新闻记者立即着手~这些重要的资料。*The journalist immediately set out to obtain these important facts.*
【获赦】be pardoned:他被~释放。*He was pardoned and released.*
【获胜】win; carry it; prevail; rack up; win: 偶然~*win by chance* /以绝对优势~ *prevail against great odds*
【获释】be released; be set free; get off: ~出狱 *be released from the prison*
【获悉】[书] learn (of an event); be informed of: ~火车事故的详情 *to learn the details of the train wreck*
【获益】benefit; profit: 学生们真心希望从老师对他们的作文的评语中~。*The students do hope to profit from the teacher's comments on their compositions.*
【获知】learn: 我是从他那里~的。*I learn it from him.*
【获准】obtain permission: 如果你想早走的话,必须得到~。*You must ask permission if you want to leave early.*

祸 ① misfortune; disaster: 车~ *traffic accident* /大~临头 *disaster is imminent* /闯~ *get into trouble*; *bring disaster* ② ruin; bring disaster upon
【祸不单行】misfortune never comes singly; it never rains but it pours; an evil chance seldom comes alone
【祸从口出】out of the mouth comes evil; trouble comes out of the words uttered
【祸从天降】a disaster descends from heaven
【祸端】[书] the source of the disaster
【祸福】weal and woe: ~与共 *share weal and woe*
【祸根】the root of evils; the cause of ruin; bane
【祸国殃民】bring calamity to the country and the people; cause great harm to the state and the people
【祸害】① disaster; ruin ② scourge: ③ damage; destroy
【祸患】disaster; calamity
【祸乱】disastrous disorder; turmoil
【祸起萧墙】trouble arises behind the walls of one's own family — trouble arises within the home
【祸事】disaster; calamity; mishap
【祸首】chief culprit; arch-criminal
【祸水】[喻] a person who is the source of trouble; bane
【祸胎】the root of the trouble
【祸心】evil intent
【祸殃】disaster; calamity; curse: 遭受~ *suffer disaster*; *undergo calamity*
【祸种】the root (or source) of the trouble

惑 ① be puzzled; be wildered; cannot tell right or wrong: 大~不解 *be extremely puzzled* ② delude; mislead: 迷~ *puzzle*; *confuse* /谣言~众 *spread rumors to mislead people*
【惑乱】confuse; befuddle
【惑众】delude or confuse people

霍 ① fast; quickly ② (Huò) a surname
【霍地】suddenly

【霍霍】①［象］磨刀～ *sharpening one's sword; sabre-rattling* ② flash：电光～。*The lightning flashed.*
【霍乱】① cholera ②【中医】acute gastroenteritis
【霍然】① suddenly; quickly：他～起身。*He stood up suddenly.* ②［书］(of an illness) be cured quickly：～病愈。*The illness was cured quickly.*
【霍闪】［方］lightning

豁 ①open; open-minded ②exempt; remit

see also huō
【豁达】be generous and open-minded; be frank：～大度 *open-minded and generous*
【豁朗】sanguine; optimistic
【豁亮】① roomy and bright：一间～的房子让人心情愉快。*A bright room makes people happy and cheerful.* ② (of one's voice) loud and clear; sonorous
【豁免】exempt; remit：～某人纳税 *exempt sb from taxation* /享有不受起诉的～权 *be granted immunity from prosecution*
【豁然】suddenly; all of a sudden
【豁然开朗】suddenly see the whole thing clearly; be enlightened all of a sudden see the light clearly

藿 ［书］leaves of pulse plants

【藿香】【药】wrinkled giant hyssop

J

jī

几1 a small low table：茶～儿 *tea table* /窗明～净 *bright and clean*

几2 ［书］ almost, nearly：～近于零 *virtually nothing* / ～可乱真 *good enough to pass for genuine*
see also jǐ

【几案】table

【几乎】① close to; nearly; practically：～人人都喜欢音乐。*Almost everyone likes music.* /这个月～没有好天气。*We've had practically no fine weather this month.* ②almost; hardly：我～忘了。*I almost forgot it.* /我～给吓死了。*I was near dead with fright.*

【几乎不】hardly; barely：我～理解你的意思。*I can hardly understand you.*

【几近】be close to; almost：～疯狂 *be almost crazy*

【几率】【数】probability：～单位 *probit* / ～密度 *probability density* / ～守恒 *conservation of probability*

讥 ridicule; satirize; mock：冷～热讽 *with freezing satire and burning irony; with biting sarcasm*

【讥嘲】ridicule; satirize; mock; sneer; taunt; poke fun at：他们～这个主意。*They mocked at the idea.* /这出戏～了政府。*The play ridicules the government.*

【讥刺】［书］ ridicule; satirize

【讥讽】ridicule; satirize; throw out innuendoes against; a flea in one's ear; poke fun of; taunt：你为什么～我的建议? *Why do you ridicule my proposal?* /他们～那个男孩儿的胆小。*They mocked at that boy's timidity.* /我不想打架,他就反复地～我。*I didn't want to fight and he taunted me repeatedly.*

【讥诮】［书］ ridicule; sneer at; deride; taunt：～某人无知 *deride sb's ignorance* /那群人～落选的政客。*The crowd jeered at the politicians who had failed in the election.*

【讥笑】ridicule; taunt; sneer at; gibe; deride; jeer：这个孩子的同班同学们因为他的胆小而～他。*The child's classmates gibed at him for his timidity.* / 观众将演说者～下台。*The audience jeered the speaker off the stage.* /他们～他穷。*They taunted him with being poor.*

击 ① bit; hit; strike：海浪拍～着海岸。*Waves beat the shore.* /他被子弹～穿腿部。*He was struck in the leg by a bullet.* ② attack; assault：声东～西 *look one way and row another* /游～ *guerrilla warfare* /迎头痛～ *deal a head-on blow* ③ bump into; come in contact with：撞～ *ram; dash against; strike* /目～ *see with one's own eyes; witness*

【击败】defeat; beat; vanquish; outplay：有的国家可能被～,但决不能被征服。*Some countries may be defeated but can never be conquered.* /她在竞争中～了对手。*She defeated her opponents in the competition.*

【击毙】shoot dead; kill：罪犯被～了。*The criminal was shot to death.*

【击沉】bombard and sink：～敌舰 *sink the enemy warships*

【击打】hammer; beat：～草坪上的球 *hit the ball onto the green* /他用拳头～对手。*He hammered the opponent with his fists.*

【击倒】bowl over; clobber; knock down; lay; strike down：他一拳～了对手。*He knocked down his opponent with one blow.*

【击发】pull the trigger (of a gun); percussion：～机 *percussion lock* / ～装置 *arming mechanism; firing gear*

【击鼓】beat a drum; drum

【击鼓传花】one is drumming while the others pass round a spray of blossom — a drinking game

【击鼓鸣冤】beat the drum outside the court to lodge a complaint against some injustice

【击毁】smash; wreck; shatter; destroy

【击剑】【体】fencing：～场 *fencing strip* / ～服 *fencing clothes* / ～运动员 *fencer*

【击溃】defeat; overwhelm; conquer; annihilate; bring sb to their knees; rout; put to flight; smash; crash：～敌人 *put the enemy to rout* /军队训练有素,武器精良,轻易～了叛军。*The army was well-trained and well-armed, and had little difficulty in defeating the rebels.*

【击落】shoot down; bring down; down：～一辆敌机 *shoot down an enemy plane*

【击破】break up; destroy; rout：各个～ *destroy one by one*

【击球】【体】batting：～率 *batting average* / ～手 *batsman; batter* / ～位置 *batter's box*

【击水】strike waters in swimming

【击退】beat back; repel; repulse; fight off：～敌人的进攻 *repulse the enemies' attacks*

【击掌】① clap one's hands ② strike one's own palms：～为定 *swear it to sb palm against palm*

【击中】hit; roquet; hit the mark：～要害 *hit the*

needle; hit the right nail on the head; strike home /枪~了警官的肩膀。*The bullet hit the police officer in the shoulder.*

叽 [象] the sound of a bird chirping or talking in a low voice: 鸟儿~~地叫。*The birds were chirping.*

【叽咕】talk in a low voice; whisper; mutter: 他向邻座的人~。*He is whispering to his neighbour.*

【叽叽嘎嘎】[象] the sound of cackling: 房门老是~响。*The door always creaks.*

【叽叽喳喳】[象] chirp; twitter: ~地说办公室闲话 *twitter over office gossip*

【叽里旮旯儿】[方] every nook and cranny: 她找遍了每一个~。*She has searched every nook and cranny.*

【叽里咕噜】[方] the sound of sb talking indistinctly or of sth rolling around: 她们~说个没完没了。*They gabbled away twenty to the dozen.*

【叽里呱啦】[象] the sound of loud talk or chatter

饥[1] hungry; starved; famished: 又~又渴 *be hungry and thirsty* /那孩子看来很~饿。*The child looked half famished.*

饥[2] famine; crop failure: 大~之年 *a year of great famine*

【饥不择食】be too hungry to be picky and choosy; one hungry is not choosy about his food; beggars cannot be choosers; hunger is the best sauce

【饥肠】[书] empty stomach

【饥肠辘辘】be so hungry that the stomach is beginning to gurgle

【饥饿】hungry; starved: ~的样子 *a hungry look* /中午他又累又~。*At noon he was tired and hungry.*

【饥寒】hunger and cold

【饥寒交迫】live in hunger and cold; be poverty-stricken; be miserable with cold and hungry

【饥荒】① famine; crop failure: 每年有很多人死于~。*Many people die of famine every year.* /庄稼遭受水灾毁坏的地方都在闹~。*There is hunger in all the places where the crop was spoilt by the flood.* ② [口] be hard up; be short of money ③ [口] debt: 拉~ *run into debt*

【饥馑】[书] famine; crop failure: 由于战争和~,非洲成百万的人死去。*Millions of people in Africa continue to die because of war and famine.*

【饥民】famine victim; famine refugee: 他看上去很瘦,好像一个~。*He looks terribly thin, like a famine victim.*

【饥色】malnourished look (on one's face): 面有~ *look pallid because of hunger*

玑 ① [书] a pearl that is not quite round: 珠~ *pearl; gem* ② an ancient astronomical instrument

机 ① machine; engine: 电唱~ *record player; electric phonograph* /电话~ *telephone* /电视~ *television; TV* /发动~ *engine; motor* /缝纫~ *sewing machine* /录像~ *videotape recorder* /录音~ *recorder; tape recorder* /复印~ *duplicating machine* /收音~ *radio* /自动售货~ *automatic vending machine* ② aircraft; aeroplane; plane: 班~ *airliner* /轰炸~ *bomber* /客~ *passenger plane* /战斗~ *fighter plane* /直升~ *helicopter* ③ (of the beginning or changing of things) crucial point: 生~ *lease of life* /危~ *crisis* /转~ *a favorable turn; a turn for the better* ④ chance; occasion; opportunity: 随~应变 *play to the score; do as the changing circumstances demand* /坐失良~ *miss the boat* ⑤ organic: 有~体 *organism* ⑥ key link or central link for a success or failure; sth secret: 军~ *military plan; military secret* /日理万~ *attend to numerous affairs everyday* ⑦ motive; intention: 动~ *motive* ⑧ flexible; quick-witted: 神~妙算 *wonderful foresight*

【机变】[书] adapt oneself to circumstances

【机不可失,时不再来】don't let slip an opportunity as it may never come again; opportunity knocks but once

【机舱】① engine room (of a ship) ② passenger compartment (of an aircraft)

【机场】airport; airfield; aerodrome: 国际~ *international airport* /军用~ *military airfield* /民用~ *civil airport*

【机车】locomotive; engine: 电池~ *accumulator locomotive* /电力~ *electric locomotive* /发动机~ *motor locomotive* /辅助~ *booster locomotive* /内燃~ *diesel locomotive* /汽油~ *gasoline locomotive* /双~ *double locomotive* /蓄电池~ *battery locomotive* /蒸汽~ *steam locomotive*

【机船】motor vessel

【机床】machine tool: 重型~ *heavy machine tool* /精密~ *precision machine tool*

【机电】mechanical and electrical: ~产品 *mechanical and electrical products*

【机动】① power-driven; motorized: ~车辆 *motor driven vehicle* ② flexible; expedient; mobile: ~灵活处置 *deal with flexibly* /~作战 *fight with some flexibility* ③ in reserve; for emergency use: ~力量 *reserve force* /~粮 *grain reserve for emergency use* /~时间 *time kept in reserve* /~资金 *fund kept in reserve; reserve fund*

【机动性】mobility; maneuverability; flexibility

【机房】① generator or motor room ② engine room (of a ship)

【机耕】【农】tractor-ploughing: ~面积 *cultivated land plowed by machinery*

【机耕船】boat tractor; wet-field tractor

【机工】mechanic; machinist; ~车间 *machineshop; mechanical department*

【机构】①【机】mechanism: 传动~ *transmission-mechanism* ② organization; setup: 教育~ *educational institution* /金融~ *financial setup* /军事~ *military establishment* /科研~ *scientific research institute* /权力~ *organ for power* /政府~ *government organization* ③ the internal structure of an organization: ~改革 *structural reform* /调整~ *adjust the organizational structure*

【机关】①【机】mechanism; gear that serves as the

J

essential part in a machine：启动～ *starting gear* ② machine-operated：～布景 *machine-operated stage scenery* ③ institutions; office; organ; body：军事～ *military organization* /领导～ *leading bodies* /行政～ *administrative organization* ④ stratagem; intrigue：～算尽 *use up all one's tricks*; *for all one's calculations and scheming* /识破～ *see through a trick*

【机关报】the official newspaper of a political party, a government, etc.; organ

【机关干部】government functionary; office worker

【机关工作】office work

【机关刊物】the official publication of a party, government, etc.

【机关炮】cannon

【机关枪】machine gun

【机关算尽】use up all one's tricks; for all one's calculations and scheming

【机会】opportunity; chance：错过～ *lose a chance*; *miss the bus* /～难得。*Opportunities are few and far between*; *now or never*! /我想要给他一次～。*I want to give him a chance.*

【机会成本】opportunity cost

【机会均等】equal opportunities

【机会主义】opportunism

【机降】airland：～部队 *airlanded forces*

【机井】motor-pumped well

【机警】alert; sharp-witted; vigilant; watchful; keep one's eyes open：～的战士 *a vigilant soldier* /她～地监视敌人。*She kept watch alertly on the enemy.*

【机具】machines and tools

【机理】mechanism：腐蚀～ *corrosion mechanism*

【机灵】clever; smart; sharp; quick; intelligent; alert; shrewd：她相当～。*She knows a trick or two.* /班里的一些孩子比另一些～。*Some children in the class are quicker than others.* /他非常～，如果你的论证中有任何纰漏，他都会发现。*He is razor sharp — if there's any weakness in your argument, he will spot it.*

【机灵鬼】a clever person

【机密】① secret; confidential; classified：～文件 *confidential documents*; *classified papers* ② sth secret; secret：泄露～ *let out a secret* /这种技术被视为～。*The technology is considered confidential.*

【机敏】alert and resourceful：～的才智 *nimble wits* /～的年轻女子 *a wide wake young man*

【机谋】［书］stratagem; artifice; scheme：为了得到晋升，他用尽了～。*He used every stratagem in order to be promoted.*

【机能】【生理】function; enginery：～错乱 *parafunction* /～低下 *underactivity* /～亢进 *hyperfunction* /～紊乱 *disorder* /～障碍 *a functional obstruction* /～转换 *change of functions*

【机器】machine; machinery; apparatus：国家～ *state apparatus*; *state machine* /战争～ *war machine*

【机器人】robot：电动～ *electromotive robot* /工业～ *industrial robot* /家用～ *domestic robot* /人形～ *anthropomorphic robot* /智能～ *intelligent robot*

【机器油】lubricating oil; lubricant

【机枪】machine-gun：轻～ *light machine-gun* /重～ *heavy machine-gun*

【机枪手】machine gunner

【机巧】adroit; ingenious：一个～的计划 *an ingenious scheme*

【机体】①【生】organism ②【航】airframe

【机头】nose (of an aircraft)

【机尾】tail (of an aircraft)

【机务】machine operation and maintenance：～段 *maintenance section*

【机务人员】① maintenance personnel ② ground crew

【机械】① machinery; machine; mechanism：大型～ *big machinery* /工业～ *industrial machinery* /杠杆和滑轮是简单～。*Levers and pulleys are simple machines.* ② mechanical; inflexible; rigid; fixed：～地工作 *work rigidly*

【机心】①［书］diabolical scheme; cunning idea ② movement (of a watch or clock)

【机型】① type (of an aircraft) ②model (of a machine)

【机要】confidential; departments in charge of confidential or important work：～秘书 *confidential secretary*

【机宜】general principles of action; guidelines：面授～ *brief sb on how to behave* /请示～ *ask for guidelines* (*from one's superior*)

【机翼】【航】wing (of an aircraft)

【机油】engine oil; machine oil：～加入口 *oil filling hole* /～冷却器 *oil cooler*

【机遇】［书］favourable circumstances; opportunity; good fortune：千载难逢的～ *the opportunity of a lifetime*; *a golden opportunity*

【机缘】good luck; lucky chance

【机运】① opportunity; chance：他所需要的是一个能展示他的能力的～。*All he needs is an opportunity to show his ability.* /得到这个工作是千载难逢的～，如果你拒绝就是一个傻瓜。*This job is the chance of a lifetime*; *you'd be a fool not to take it.* ② fate：他相信这一切都是～决定的。*He believes that everything is decided by fate.*

【机载】airborne：～导弹 *air-launched missile* /～电视 *airborne television* /～火箭 *aircraft rocket* /～雷达 *airborne radar*

【机长】aircraft (or crew) commander

【机罩】bonnet (of an aircraft); hood

【机制】① machine-processed; machine-made：～纸 *machine-made paper* ② mechanism：发育～ *developmental mechanism* /激发～ *excitation mechanism* /金融～ *financial mechanism* /会计～ *accounting mechanism* /免税～ *exemption mechanism*

【机智】quick-witted; resourceful; be nobody's fool; astute：～地处理某事 *be resourceful in settling a matter* /他是个～的政客，很快就升到了该党领导的位置。*He was an astute politician who*

quickly rose to the top of the party.
【机杼】[书] ① loom conception (of a piece of writing)
【机子】[口] ① loom ② a small machine (e.g. a sewing machine, a telephone) ③ trigger
【机组】①【机】unit; set; assembling unit: 动力~ *power unit* /发电~ *generating unit*; *generating set* ② aircrew; flight crew

肌 muscle; flesh: 背~ *dorsal muscles* /骨骼~ *skeletal muscle* /横~ *transverse muscle* /横纹~ *striated muscle* /环~ *circular muscle* /睫状~ *ciliary muscle* /颈~ *cervical muscle* /平滑~ *smooth muscle*; *involuntary muscle* /三角~ *deltoid muscle* /心~ *cardiac muscle* /腋~ *axillary muscle* /纵~ *longitudinal muscle*
【肌病】【医】myopathy
【肌肤】[书] (human) skin
【肌腱】【生】tendon
【肌浆】carcoplasm; sarcoplasm: ~蛋白 myogen
【肌紧张】muscular tension
【肌理】[书] skin texture
【肌力】myotome
【肌群】muscle group
【肌肉】muscle; flesh: 腹~ *abdominal muscle* /~抽搐 *jerk* /~抽筋 *crick*; *kink* /~拉伤 *pulled muscle* /~收缩 *contraction of muscle* /~弹性 *tonicity* /当你走路时, 你在运动腿上的~。*When you walk you exercise your leg muscles.*
【肌肉学】mycology
【肌糖】【生化】inositol: ~原 *muscle glycogen*
【肌体】human body; organism
【肌细胞】muscle cell; myocyte
【肌纤维】【生理】muscle fibre: ~瘤 *myofibroma*
【肌炎】【医】myitis; myositis
【肌硬化】myosclerosis

鸡 fowl; hen; cock: 公~ *cock* /母~ *hen* /小~ *chicken*
【鸡巴】[口] cock; penis
【鸡雏】chink; chicken
【鸡蛋】egg: 炒~ *scrambled eggs* /煮~ *boiled eggs*
【鸡蛋糕】sponge cake
【鸡蛋羹】steamed egg custard
【鸡蛋里挑骨头】look for a bone in an egg — find fault; nitpick: 请你不要对我所作的每件事~。*I wish you'd stop trying to pick holes in everything I did.*
【鸡蛋碰石头】an egg strikes a stone — attack sb far stronger than oneself
【鸡飞蛋打】the hen flies away and the eggs break - all is lost
【鸡飞狗跳】hens flying and dogs running — a total disorder: 当土匪们听说军队走近了就立刻~地逃跑了。*The bandits fled in disorder at once when they heard that the army was marching near.*
【鸡冠】cockscomb
【鸡冠花】【植】coxcomb; cockscomb
【鸡奸】sodomy; buggery: ~者 *sodomite*
【鸡叫】crow
【鸡肋】[书] chicken ribs — things of little value
【鸡零狗碎】fragmentary: ~的回忆 *fragmentary memories*
【鸡毛掸子】feather duster
【鸡毛蒜皮】chicken feathers and garlic skins — trifles; trivia: 报纸上充满了~的小事和闲言碎语。*The newspaper was full of trivia and gossip.*
【鸡鸣狗盗】crow like a cock and snatch like a dog — small tricks: 我鄙视这些~之徒。*I look down upon those men who can only play small tricks.*
【鸡皮疙瘩】goose pimples; goose bumps: 我被吓得起了一身~。*I was so terrified that my flesh creeps.*
【鸡皮鹤发】wrinkle skin and white hair — an old age
【鸡犬不留】even fowls and dogs are not spared — a mass slaughter; massacre; total extermination: 新来的殖民者把部落村民杀得~。*All of the tribesmen were being exterminated by the new settlers.*
【鸡犬不宁】even fowls and dogs are not left in peace — a great turmoil; utter commotion; clamour: 我听到楼下闹得~, 就跑下去看个究竟。*I heard a commotion downstairs and ran down to see what was happening.*
【鸡犬升天】even fowls and dogs ascend to heaven with sb — one's relatives are promoted easily or begin to live a wealthy life due to one's great success
【鸡肉】chicken (as food)
【鸡舍】chicken coop
【鸡虱】chicken louse
【鸡食】chicken feed
【鸡松】fried chicken floss
【鸡汤】chicken broth
【鸡尾酒】cocktail: ~会 *cocktail party*; *cocktail reception*
【鸡瘟】chicken pest
【鸡窝】chicken coop; roost
【鸡窝里飞出金凤凰】a phoenix flies out of a chicken coop — a miracle; an unbelievable event: 他考上了大学, 对于这个贫寒的家庭来说, 这可真是~。*He will start college, which is really a miracle to such a poor family.*
【鸡心】① heart-shaped: ~领 *V-neck* ② heart-shaped pendant
【鸡鸭鱼肉】chicken, duck, fish and meat — variety of food; rich food
【鸡眼】【医】corn; clavus
【鸡杂】chicken giblets
【鸡子】[方] chicken
【鸡子儿】[方] (hen's) egg

奇 ① (of number) odd: 一、三、五、七是~数。*One, three, five and seven are odd numbers.* ② [书] fractional amount; odd lots: 六十有~ *sixty odd*
see also qí
【奇函数】【数】odd function
【奇数】【数】odd number; uneven number

唧 spurt; squirt: ~他一身水。*Water spurted all over him.*

【唧咕】whisper; murmur; talk in a low voice：她整个晚上都在男朋友耳边～。*She kept whispering something in her boyfriend's ear the whole evening.*

【唧唧】[象] (of insects) chirp

【唧唧嘎嘎】[象] creak; giggle：这辆车走动时～地响。*The cart creaked as it moved along.* /她～笑了一阵。*She had a fit of the giggles.*

【唧唧喳喳】[象] chirp; twitter：麻雀～的叫声 *the chirp of a sparrow*

【唧哝】whisper; talk in a low voice：她～着说她觉得很害怕。*She whispered that she felt very afraid.*

积 ① amass; store up：堆～ *accumulate; pile* /日～月累 *accumulate over the years* ② long-standing; age-old：郁～ *pent-up* ③【中医】indigestion：食～ *dyspepsia; indigestion* ④ product by multiplication：乘～ *product*

【积案】a long-pending case

【积弊】age-old abuses

【积储】keep; store up, lay up; stockpile：食物被～在地下室里。*Food is stored in the basement.*

【积存】store up; lay up; stockpile：我们总是～足够的纸张，以防不够用。*We always keep plenty of spare paper, in case we run out.*

【积德】accumulate merit by good works; accumulate virtue：～行好 *do good deeds and dispense charities*

【积淀】sediments accumulated over the years

【积肥】collect (farmyard); store compost

【积分】①【数】integral：不变～ *invariant integral* /不定～ *indefinite integral* /初～ *first integral* /代数～ *algebraic integral* /定～ *definite integral* /共轭～ *conjugate integral* /角～ *angular integral* /完全～ *complete integral* /无穷～ *infinite integral* /线～ *curvilinear integral* ② accumulated points (in sports)

【积愤】pent-up indignation：倾吐～ *pour out one's pent-up grievances*

【积垢】accumulated filth

【积毁销骨】repeated calumny can bring about one's ruin

【积极】① positive：做出～贡献 *make positive contribution* / ～的援助 *positive help* ②active; enthusiastic; vigorous：采取～措施 *adopt vigorous measures* /他～地为人们做好事。*He is active in doing good to others.* /他对体育运动很～。*He is enthusiastic for sports.*

【积极分子】activist; enthusiast：工会～ *union actives*

【积极性】enthusiasm; zeal; initiative; ardour：革命的～ *revolutionary zeal* /劳动～ *enthusiasm for labour*

【积渐】gradually：我～明白了他的意图。*Gradually, I began to understand his purpose.*

【积聚】accumulate; amass; gather; build up; collect：～力量 *build up strength* /她用手指触摸架子的顶部，看看是否有灰尘～。*She ran her finger along the top of the shelf to see if any dust had gathered.*

【积劳】[书] be overworked for a very long period

【积劳成疾】[书] fall ill from constant overwork

【积累】① accumulate; gather：他在工作中～了丰富的经验。*He has accumulated a wealth of experience in his work.* /大部分员工都去休假了，所以工作～起来了。*Most of the employees have gone on vacation and the work is piling up.* ②【经】accumulation (for expanded reproduction)：逐年增加公共～和个人收入 *increase public accumulation and personal income year by year* / ～与消费 *accumulation and consumption* / ～率 *rate of accumulation*

【积木】building blocks; toy bricks

【积年累月】for years on end; year after year：他～地在这片土地上劳作。*He works hard on this land year after year.*

【积欠】① have one's debts piling up：我要尽快还清～的各种债务。*I will clear up all my outstanding debts as soon as possible.* /我本不想卖掉汽车，但是迅速～的债务让我不知如何是好。*I don't want to sell the car, but my debts are piling up so quickly that I am at a loss what to do.* ② outstanding debts; arrears：穷苦的老人无力偿还～。*The old miserable man was unable to clear up all outstanding debts.*

【积善】performance of one good deed after another

【积少成多】amass gradually; many a pickle makes a mickle

【积食】[方] (of children) have indigestion：这个小男孩～了，没有胃口吃东西。*The child has indigestion and has lost his appetite.*

【积温】sum of the difference between average temperature and given temperature over a given period of time

【积习】inveterate (or ingrained) habit; long-standing practice; deep-rooted habit：～难改。*Ingrained habits cannot be cast off overnight; it is difficult to get rid of deep-rooted habits.*

【积蓄】① save; store; put aside; accumulate：～力量 *accumulate strength* /他们～煤以备过冬。*They lay in stores of coal for winter.* ② savings：他把～拿出来买房子。*He took out his savings to purchase a house.*

【积雪】accumulated snow：路上～很深。*The roads are deep in snow.* / ～盈天。*Accumulated snow is over an inch.*

【积压】overstock; pile up：物资～ overstocking of materials /资金～ let funds lie idle /不要让货物～。*Don't keep materials too long in stock.*

【积雨云】【气】cumulonimbus

【积郁】【医】smouldering; pent-up：～成疾 *fall ill from stasis*

【积怨】accumulated rancour; piled-up grievances; complaints

【积云】【气】cumulonimbus：层～ *stratocumulus* /卷～ *cirrocumulus*

【积攒】[口] save (or collect) bit by bit：～钱币 *collect coins* /他省吃俭用，～学费。*He economized* on food and clothing to save for his tuition. /他把零花钱～下来,想买件礼物。*He saved up his pocket money in order to buy a present.*

【积重难返】bad old practices die hard; ingrained habits are hard to change

【积铢累寸】save every tiny bit; accumulate bit by bit: 他们～攒下了这些钱供儿子上大学。*They saved the money bit by bit for their son's college education.*

【积贮】store up; lay in: 战斗前,他～了足够的力量。*He stored up enough energy before the fight.*

屐 ① clogs; wood slippers ② shoes in general

姬 ①(in ancient China) a complimentary term for women ② concubines in ancient times: 宠～ *a concubine in high favour* ③[旧] a professional female singer: 歌～ *singing girl*; *female entertainer* ④(Jī) a surname

基 ①(of a building) base: 地～ *groundsill*; *groundwork*; *toft* /路～ *roadbed* ② basic; fundamental; primary: ～调 *fundamental key* ③【化】(of chemistry) radical; base, a unit of atoms in a molecule of a chemical compound: 氨～ *amina*; *amina-group* /氢～ *hydrogen radical*

【基本】① foundation:人民是国家的～。*The people are the foundation of a nation.* ② basic; fundamental; elementary; essential; prime: ～原则 *basic principles* /～观点 *basic concept* /～知识 *elementary knowledge* /他们之间存在着～分歧。*Fundamental differences exist between them.* ③ main; essential: ～条件 *main condition* /人猿的～不同是智慧。*The essential difference between apes and man is intelligence.* ④ basically; in the main; on the whole; by and large: 情况～属实。*It has been found to be basically true.*

【基本词汇】【语】basic vocabulary; basic word-stock

【基本单位】basic unit

【基本电荷】【物】elementary charge

【基本工资】basic wage (or salary)

【基本法】basic law

【基本功】basic training; basic skill; essential technique: 练好～ *have a thorough training in basic skills*; *master the basic skills*

【基本国策】basic policy of the state; basic state policy

【基本建设】capital construction

【基本粒子】【物】elementary particle

【基本路线】basic line

【基本矛盾】【哲】fundamental contradiction

【基本上】① fundamentally; on the whole: 她～不适合教师这一工作。*She is fundamentally unsuited to the job as a teacher.* ② on the whole; in the main: 工程～完成了。*The project has been finished on the whole.*

【基波】【物】fundamental wave; fundamental harmonic

【基层】basic level; primary level; grass-roots unit: ～单位 *basic unit*; *grass-roots unit*; *unit at the grass-roots level* /～干部 *cadre at the basic (or grass-roots) level* /～选举 *elections at the basic level* /领导深入～了解情况。*The leading cadre went down to the grass-roots level to gain an understanding of the situation.* /镇人民代表大会是我国～政权组织。*The people's congress of a town is an organization of political power at the grass-roots level in our country.*

【基础】① foundation: 这个建筑的～很牢固。*This building has a solid foundation.* ② foundation; base; basis: 物质～ *material base* /理论～ *theoretical basis* /农业是国民经济的～。*Agriculture is the foundation of the national economy.* ③ economic base

【基地】base: 原料～ *source of raw material* /1849年,马克思到了英国,并把伦敦作为他从事革命工作的～。*In 1849, Marx went to England and made London the base for his revolutionary work.*

【基点】① centre; focus: 研究工作的～ *the focus of research efforts* ② basic point; starting point: 分析问题是解决问题的～。*The analysis of a problem is the starting point for its solution.* ③【测】base point (BP)

【基调】①【音】fundamental key; main key ② keynote: 定下会议的～ *set the keynote for the conference* /讲话的～ *basic idea of the speech*

【基督】【宗】Christ, title given to Jesus, meaning the Saviour

【基督教】① Christianity; Christian religion ② Protestantism

【基督徒】Christian

【基尔特】guild: ～社会主义 *guild socialism*

【基肥】【农】base manure; base fertilizer

【基干】① backbone; hard core: ～民兵 *primary militia*; *core members of the militia* ② cadres at the basic level

【基极】【电】base: ～电流 *base current*

【基价】base price

【基建】capital construction: ～工程 *capital construction project*

【基金】fund: 积累(消费)～ *accumulation (consumption) fund* /福利～ *welfare fund* /救济～ *fund for relief* /专用～ *fund for special use*

【基金会】foundation

【基色】primary colours

【基生】sprout from the bottom part of a stem: ～叶 *basal leaf*; *bathyphyll*

【基石】foundation stone; cornerstone: 剩余价值学说是马克思经济理论的～。*The doctrine of surplus value is the cornerstone of Marx's economic theory.*

【基数】①【数】cardinal number ②【统】base

【基态】【物】ground state: 原子的～ *atomic ground state*

【基体】substance constituting the major part of a compound

【基线】①【数】base ②【测】datum line

【基岩】【矿】bedrock

【基业】property, inheritance, family estate, etc., considered as a foundation on which to build

【基因】【生】gene：等位～ *allele* /断裂～ *split gene* /互补～ *complementary gene* /恢复～ *restoring gene* /稀释～ *dilution gene* /显性～ *dominant gene* /抑制～ *inhibiting gene* /隐性～ *recessive gene*

【基音】【音】fundamental tone

【基于】base on; because of; found on; ground on：～上述理由 *for the above-mentioned reasons*

【基质】【生】stroma; substrate; matrix：～细胞 *stroma cell*

【基准】①【测】datum：～点 *datum point* / ～边 *reference edge* / ～面 *datum plane* / ～线 *datum line* ② standard; criterion：教育～ *educational criteria*

期 ［书］an exact year, or a complete month：～年 *anniversary* / ～月 *a month*
see also qī

赍 ［书］①hold (in mind); harbour：～志而殁 *die without fulfilling one's ambitions* ② give; present

【赍发】［书］give sb money; help sb：～盘缠 *give sb traveling expenses*

【赍恨】［书］feel regretful

【赍赏】grant a reward

犄

【犄角】(jījiǎo)［方］edge and corner; cutting line where two sides meet：墙～儿 *the corner of a wall* /桌子～儿 *the corner of a table*

【犄角】(jījiao)［方］horn：牛～ *ox horns*

缉 seize; arrest：通～逃犯 *order the arrest of a criminal at large*

【缉捕】seize; arrest：～人员 *hounds of law*

【缉查】① search; check; inspect ② inspector：海关～ *customs officer*

【缉毒】① crack down on drug trafficking ② arrest drug traffickers

【缉获】capture; arrest：罪犯在企图逃离时被～。*The criminal was captured when trying to flee.*

【缉拿】seize; arrest; apprehend：～凶手 *apprehend the murderer* /罪犯昨天被～了。*The criminal was arrested yesterday.*

【缉私】seize smugglers; suppress smuggling; search for smuggler：～船 *anti-smuggling patrol boat*

畸 ① lopsided; unbalanced ② irregular; abnormal ③［书］a fractional amount (over that mentioned in a round number)

【畸变】① abnormal change ②【物】distortion

【畸形】① deformity; malformation：先天～ *congenital malformation* ② lopsided; unbalanced：纠正经济～发展的现象 *check the occurrence of lopsided economic development*

跻 ［书］ascend; mount：～于世界强国之列 *rank among the powerful nations of the world*

【跻身】mount; ascend; rank among：他在比赛中～前三名。*He ranked the first three in the competition.*

箕 ① dustpan or winnowing pan made of bamboo strips or iron sheets ② (of a fingerprint) crescent loop ③ a star constellation, one of the twenty-eight constellations ④ (Jī) a surname

稽[1] ① check; exam：无～之谈 *a tale of a tub; fantastic talk; traveler's tale* ② argue; answer back：反唇相～ *back talk; recriminate* ③ (Jī) a surname

稽[2] ［书］stay; delay：不得～延时日。*There must not be any delay of time.*

【稽查】① check, inspect; investigate ② inspector：铁路～ *a railway inspector*

【稽核】check; examine; audit：～账目 *audit accounts*

【稽留】［书］hold up; delay：因事～ *be detained by business*

【稽延】［书］put off; postpone：～时日 *stall*

激 ① (of water, etc.) swash; surge：～起浪花 (*of waves*) *break up into a spray* ② fall ill from getting wet; catch a cold：他被雨～病了。*He got a chill from getting wet in the rain.* ③［方］chill (by putting in ice water, etc.)：她把西瓜放在冷水里～。*She chilled the melon in the ice water.* ④ arouse; excite; incite; provoke; stir up：刺～ *provoke; stimulate* /我希望你不要～起麻烦。*I hope you're not trying to stir up trouble.* ⑤ (of motion; tone; etc.) excited and indignant：慷慨～昂 *impassioned* ⑥ violent; radical：偏～ *extreme*

【激昂】excited; roused：群情～。*Public feeling was aroused; popular feeling ran high.*

【激昂慷慨】rousing; passionate; emotional：当谈到战争时，这个老兵变得～。*The veteran got very emotional when he talked about the war.* /他～地描写了贫苦农民的生活。*He wrote with great feeling about the life of the miserable poor peasants.*

【激变】violent change; cataclysm：形势发生了～。*The situation has taken a radical turn.*

【激荡】① surge; rage：心潮～ *thoughts surging in one's mind* ② agitate：～人心的歌声 *songs that agitate people's hearts*

【激动】① excited; roused; exhilarated：孩子看到他的礼物时非常～。*The child became very excited when seeing his gift.* /他整夜未睡，为选举的胜利～万分。*He stayed awake all night, exhilarated by his election victory.* /再过几分钟就要宣布获胜者，观众的心情十分～。*There were only a few minutes to go before the winner was announced and the excitement of the audience was intense.* ② stir; heat; inspire; excite：我们深为这个消息所～。*We were deeply stirred by the news.*

【激发】① arouse; stimulate; set off; stir up; activate：他奇怪的表情～了我的好奇心。*His strange expression aroused my curiosity.* ②【物】excite：～热 *thermal excitation* / ～能 *excitation energy*

【激奋】excited; exhilarated：他的话使我精神～。*His words exhilarated my spirits.* /他知道这个问题可能引起群情～ *He realized the intensity of people's feelings on this issue.*

【激愤】wrathful; indignant; enraged: 心情～ *be filled with indignation*
【激光】laser; laser light: ～唱机 *laser disc player; compact disc player* / ～唱片 *laser disc; compact disc (CD)* / ～测量 *laser gauge* / ～打印机 *laser printer* / ～导航 *laser navigation* / ～光纤 *laser fibre* / ～化学 *laser chemistry* / ～枪 *laser gun* / ～通信 *laser communication* / ～束 *laser beam* / ～育种 *breeding with laser*
【激光器】laser; laser device
【激化】sharpen; intensify; become acute: 进一步～矛盾 *make the contradictions more acute*.
【激活】【物】activate: ～剂 *activator*
【激将】prodding sb into action; goading sb into action: ～法(*method of*) *prodding sb into action*
【激进】radical; militant: ～分子 *radical* / ～派 *radicals; militants* / ～主义 *radicalism*
【激剧】① intense; acute; sharp; strong: ～的思想斗争 *intense conflicts of thought* ② rapid: ～的发展 *a rapid development*
【激浪】torrential waters
【激冷】【治】shock chilling
【激励】urge; inspire; stimulate: 老师～我做出更大的努力。*The teacher inspired me to make greater effort.*
【激烈】① intense; sharp; fierce; violent; acute: ～的冲突 *sharp conflict* / ～的争论 *heated argument* /他用～的语言羞辱我。*He used a violent language to insult me.* ② (of feeling, etc.) uplifting: 壮怀～ *with lofty aspiration*
【激灵】[方] shock; startle; give a start: 我拍了拍他的肩膀,他吓得一～。*He gave a start when I tapped him on the shoulder.*
【激流】turbulent current; rapids
【激怒】provoke; enrage; exasperate; wind sb up; needle; nettle: 我相信他不会无缘无故地打人,你一定～了他。*I'm sure he wouldn't just hit someone for no reason; you must have provoked him.* /他装作满不在乎来～我。*He pretended to be free of care to wind me up.* /我的话显然～了他。*My words clearly nettled her.*
【激切】[书] vehement; strong; intense; fervent; full of passion: 言辞～ *words full of passion*
【激情】strong emotion; enthusiasm: 满怀～ *be filled with enthusiasm*
【激素】【生】hormone: 垂体～ *hypophyseal hormone; pituitary hormone* /雌性～ *estrogen hormone* /催产～ *oxytocic hormone* /催乳～ *lactogenic hormone* /睾丸～ *testicular hormone* /花粉～ *pollen hormone* /黄体～ *luteal hormone* /甲状腺～ *thyroid hormone* /抗生长～ *antigrowth hormone* /昆虫～ *insect hormone* /脑～ *brain hormones* /肾上腺～ *suprarenal gland hormone* /生长～ *growth hormone* /雄性～ *male hormone; sex hormone* /孕～ *progestational hormone* /植物～ *plant hormone* /组织～ *tissue hormone*
【激扬】① drive out evil and usher in good ② excited and high-spirited ③ encourage; urge: ～士气 *boost the morale*
【激增】increase sharply; rise steeply: 产量～ *steep rise in output* /二战以后,世界人口～。*The world population shot up after World War II.*
【激战】fierce fighting; fierce battle
【激涨】sharp rise in prices; jump in prices: 物价～。*There was a sharp rise in prices.*
【激浊扬清】drain away the mud and bring in fresh water

羁 [书] ① bridle; headstall ② restrain; control: 放荡不～ *bold and unconstrained* ③ stay; delay
【羁绊】[书] fetters; yoke: 摆脱传统习惯的～ *shake off the yoke of traditional custom*
【羁愁】nostalgia; homesickness
【羁缚】tie; fetter: 他为责任所～。*He is fettered by responsibility.*
【羁勒】[书] control; restraint; yoke: 摆脱～ *throw off the yoke*
【羁留】① stop over; stay: 他会在此处～一段时间。*He will stay here for a period of time.* ② detain: 警察～了许多疑犯进行审问。*The police detained several suspects for questioning.*
【羁押】[书] detain; take into custody; confine: 他因涉嫌谋杀,仍在～当中。*He is still being detained now, on suspicion of murder.* /开庭审判之前你将被～。*You will be kept in custody until your trial.*

jí

及[1] ① reach; up to: 波～ *spread to* /由表～里 *from the outside to the inside* /力所能～ *within one's power* ② in time for: ～时 *in season; in time* /～早 *as soon as possible; in good season* /望尘莫～ *too far behind to catch up with* ③ match; be as good as; can compare with: 我不～他。*I cannot compare with him.* ④ [书] think of by analogy; take into account: 推己～人 *put oneself in the place of another* ⑤ (Jí) a surname
及[2] and; as well as: 一把刀～一把汤匙 *a knife and a spoon* /编辑～校对者都在加班工作。*The editors as well as the proofreaders are working overtime.*
【及第】pass an imperial examination
【及锋而试】try while the point is sharp; attack when the army is in up high morale
【及格】pass a test, examination, etc.; pass: ～分数 *pass mark* /老师让所有报考者都～了。*The instructor passed all the candidates.* /他考试不～。*He failed the examination.*
【及冠】(of a young man) come of age (usu. at 20); attain full age
【及龄】reach a required age: ～儿童 *children who have reached school age*
【及门】[书] be directly taught by a master: ～弟子 *disciples directly taught by a master*
【及时】① timely; in time; without delay: 这场雨很～。*The rain has come at the right time.* ② at

once; promptly: ~采取有效措施 *take effective measures without delay* /我~打断了她。*I interrupted her at once.*

【及时行乐】carpe diem; grasp every opportunity to eat, drink and be happy; enjoy pleasure in good time

【及时雨】① timely rain; auspicious rain ②timely help; a friend in need

【及物动词】【语】transitive verb

【及早】at an early date; as soon as possible: 我会~把这本书还给你。*I will return the book to you as soon as possible.*

【及至】until; up to; by: 我一直在说,~声音嘶哑。*I talked until I was hoarse.* /~今天上午十点,他完成了这项工作。*He had finished the work by ten o'clock this morning.*

吉 ① lucky; auspicious: 凶多~少 *bode ill rather than well* /逢凶化~ *turn ill luck into good* ② (Jí) a surname

【吉卜赛人】Gipsy; Gypsy

【吉卜赛语】gypsy

【吉利】lucky; fortunate; auspicious: 他希望抽到一个~数字。*He hoped to draw a lucky number.*

【吉隆坡】Kuala Lumpur, capital of Malaysia

【吉尼斯】Guinness (Book of Records)

【吉普车】jeep; bantam

【吉期】wedding day

【吉庆】happy occasion; auspicious occasion: 在这~之时,让我们举杯为幸福的新人祝福。*On this most auspicious occasion may I take the opportunity of proposing a toast to the happy couple.*

【吉庆有余】auspicious happiness in superabundance

【吉人天相】all is well that ends well; heaven helps a good man; heaven rewards the good

【吉日】auspicious day; lucky day: 今天一定是我的~,每一件事都那么顺心。*This must be my lucky day; every thing seems to be going right.*

【吉时】good time; auspicious occasion

【吉他】【音】guitar: ~弹奏者 *guitarist*

【吉祥】lucky; auspicious

【吉祥如意】be as lucky as desired; good fortune as one wishes: 祝来年~ *wish sb good luck in the coming year*

【吉祥物】mascot: 我们把熊猫作为~。*We had a panda as our mascot.*

【吉星】lucky star

【吉星高照】one's star is rising or in the ascendant; bring sb good luck and success in life

【吉凶】good or ill luck: 人生充满~。*Our life is full of various good or ill luck.*

【吉凶未卜】no one knows how it will turn out; cannot predict the outcome, good or bad; fate unknown

【吉言】auspicious words; blessing: 我很感激他的~。*I appreciate his auspicious words very much.*

【吉兆】good omen (or sign): 冒险行动已显示出~。*Auspices for the venture seemed favorable.* /看到今天的好天气,他说:"也许这是一个~。" *Seeing the fine weather today, he said, "Maybe this is a good omen."*

岌 [书] (of a mountain) lofty; towering

【岌岌】① (of a mountain) high; lofty; towering ② dangerous; precarious: ~可危 *in imminent danger; be placed in jeopardy; in a tottering position*

汲 ① draw water from a well: ~水 *draw water* ② (Jí) a surname

【汲汲】[书] be anxious; hunger for: ~于富贵 *be anxious for wealth*

【汲取】draw; derive; scoop: 从实践中~知识 *derive knowledge from practice*

级 ① level; rank: 高~ *high level* /低~ *low level* /上~ *higher level; superior* /下~ *lower level; subordinate* ② grade; class name of the school establishment; division of the school year: 四年~ *grade four* /高年~ *senior grade* /升~ *promote to a higher grade* ③ step: 石~ *stone steps* ④ [量] step; tier: 十几~台阶 *a flight of a dozen steps*

【级别】rank; level; distinction: 工资~ *wage scale* /这种~的羊毛可以以相当低的价格卖出。*This grade of wool can be sold at a fairly low price.*

【级数】【数】progression; series: 等比~ *geometric progression* /等差~ *arithmetic progression* /~求和 *summation of series* /~展开 *series expansion*

极 ① the utmost point; extremity: 登峰造~ *reach the limit; reach the peak of perfection* ② (of the earth, magnet, or electric circuit) pole: 南~ *the Antarctic Pole; the South Pole* /北~ *the Arctic pole; the North Pole* /阳~ *anode; anticathode* /阴~ *cathode; kathode* ③do one's utmost: 物~必反。*Things will develop in the opposite direction when they become extreme.* ④ last; highest: 罪大恶~ *flagrance; be guilty of the most heinous crimes* ⑤ of the highest degree; extremely: ~困难的问题 *exceedingly difficult problem* /~艰难 *with the greatest difficulties* /~冷 *freezing cold*

【极大】maximum: ~原理 *principle of the maximum*

【极大值】【数】maximum; maximum value: ~问题 *maximum problem*

【极地】polar region: ~冰川 *polar glacier* /~高压 *polar high atmospheric pressure* /~轨道 *polar orbit trajectory* /~航空 *polar aviation* /~土壤 *arctic soil*

【极点】the limit; the utmost: 感动到了~ *be extremely moved* /兴奋到~。*The excitement was at its maximum.* /他不负责任到了~。*He is the limit of irresponsibility.*

【极顶】① peak; top of a mountain: 山的~终年积雪。*The mountain peaks are covered with snow all the year.* ② extreme: ~讨厌 *annoying in the extreme* ③ extremely; utterly: 她对他~憎恶。*She utterly detests him.*

【极度】① extremely: ~高兴 *extremely pleased* ② extreme; limit; utmost: ~黑暗的一夜 *a night of exceeding darkness*

J

【极端】① extreme：走～ *go to extremes* /爱和恨是两个～。*Love and hate are extremes.* ② extreme; utter; exceeding; all or nothing：～的热爱 *immoderate enthusiasm* / ～危险 *extreme danger* /我无法同意他关于婚姻问题的～看法。*I cannot agree with his extreme views on marriage.*
【极端分子】wild man; extremist; radical; fanatic; zealot; diehard; lunatic fringe：政府谴责所有那些像～一样要求社会公正的人。*The government condemns all people who want some form of social justice as extremists.*
【极端主义】ultraism; extremism
【极恶】enormity：罪行～ *the enormity of the crime*
【极风】polar wind
【极光】【天】aurora; polar lights：～暴 *auroral storm* /～反射 *auroral reflection* /～弧 *auroral arc* /～极 *auroral poles* /～亮度 *auroral brightness* /～温度 *auroral temperature* /～吸收 *auroral absorption*
【极好】splendid; excellent; perfect; wonderful：这套新衣服真是～！*The new clothes are perfectly wonderful!*
【极尽能事】do everything possible to do sth：在会上，他对校长极尽吹捧之能事。*He spared no effort to flatter the principal at the meeting.*
【极口称赞】praise highly (or lavishly)：观众对这部电影～。*The audience praised the film highly after seeing it.*
【极乐鸟】bird of paradise
【极乐世界】【宗】Pure Land; Western Paradise
【极力】exert oneself to the utmost; spare no effort：她为她的迟到～辩解。*She tried her best to excuse herself for being late.* /教师～称赞她功课好。*The teacher was extolling her work to the skies.*
【极量】①【药】maximum dose ② maximum：这种卡车最大的载重～是一吨。*The maximum load for this lorry is one ton.*
【极面】【数】polar face
【极目】look as far as one can：～远眺 *gaze into the distance*
【极年】polar year
【极品】[书] ① highest grade; best quality; masterwork; nonesuch：～手表 *a watch of best quality* ② highest ranking (official)
【极其】most; extremely; profoundly：～精美的艺术品 *the most elegant work* /～美丽的少女 *a girl of exceeding beauty* /他见到我～高兴。*He was so glad to meet me.*
【极区】【地】polar regions：～航行 *polar navigation*
【极圈】【地】polar circle：北～ *the Arctic Circle* /南～ *the Antarctic Circle*
【极权】totalitarian
【极少量】minute quantity; thimbleful
【极射线】polar rays
【极盛】heyday; zenith; acme：～时期 *golden age; prime* /写于这位作家事业的～时期的小说 *a novel written at the peak of the writer's career* / 他正处在财富的～时期。*He was at the zenith of his fortunes.*
【极为】extremely; most：～伤心 *extremely sad* /晚会～精彩！*That party was the most!*
【极细】minuteness：～粉末 *superfine powder*
【极限】the limit; the maximum; the ultimate：确立～ *establish a maximum* /那是我所能做到的～。*That is the utmost I can do.*
【极小】【数】minimum：～方程 *minimal equation* /～函数 *minimal function* /～极限 *minimum limit* /～向量 *minimal vector*
【极刑】capital punishment; death penalty：处以～ *give sb the death penalty; put sb to death*
【极值】【数】extreme value; limit value：～场 *extremal field* /～点 *extreme point* /～分布 *extremal distribution* /～调节 *extreme regulation*
【极致】of highest attainments
【极轴】【数】polar axis; polaxis
【极昼】polar day
【极左】ultra-left：～思潮 *ultra-left trend of thought*
【极坐标】polar coordinate：～导航 *polar coordinate navigation* /～定位系统 *polar-coordinate model* /～方程 *polar equation* /～纸 *polar-coordinate paper*

即[1] ① be near; approach; be close to：若～若离 *keep sb at an arm's length* ② attain; assume; undertake ③ at once, promptly：成功～在眼前。*Success is in the immediate future.* ④ at present; prompted by the occasion

即[2] [书] ① be; mean：荷花～莲花 *lotus, namely lotus flower* /假如一个人失踪七年，～作已经死亡论。*If a person is missing for 7 years, he is presumed dead.* ② at once; immediately; in no time：一触～发 *on the verge of breaking out* ③ even; even if; even though：～无他人支援，也能按期完成任务。*Even though others cannot offer support, we can finish the task on time.*
【即便】even; even if; even though：～价格上涨，他也会买那辆汽车。*He's going to buy the car even if the price is raised.* /你应该经常锻炼，～每天10分钟。*You should often exercise — even if it's only 10 minutes a day.*
【即或】even; even if; even though; though：～是最轻微的声音也会使他失眠。*Even the slightest sound would prevent him from falling asleep.*
【即将】be about to; soon; be on the point; before long：国庆～来临。*National Day is drawing near.* /他～离开中国。*He is about to leave China.* /他～结婚。*He will get married soon.*
【即景】[书] (of a literary or artistic work) the scene rouses one's creative impulse; be inspired by what one sees
【即景生情】be inspired by what one sees; the scene brings back memories
【即刻】at once; instantly; immediately; right away; lose no time：他～就回来。*He will be back soon.* /我们最好～开始工作。*We'd better start work right away.* /我认为你应该～回家。*I think you ought to get back home without delay.*
【即令】even; even if; even though：～天气好，我也不会出去。*Even if it's fine, I will not go out.*

【即日】① this or that very day：这项法律～生效。*The law is effective this day.* ② within the next few days；soon：这本书～出版。*The book will be published recently.*

【即如】as；like：～他所说，就要下雨了。*As he said, it was going to rain.*

【即若】［书］even；even if；although：～可能不会成功，但他们仍努力尝试。*Though they may not succeed, they will still try.*

【即时】immediately；at once；instantly：～投产 *put into production at once*

【即食】（of food）instant：～面 *instant noodles*

【即使】even；even if；even though：～我不去，他也会去的。*He will go even if I don't.* /～破产我也要试一下。*I'll do it if I go bankrupt in the attempt.*

【即世】［书］pass away；die

【即事】write out of inspiration

【即位】① take one's seat ②（of feudal rulers）ascend the throne or take office；enthronement

【即席】［书］① impromptu；offhand：～赋诗 *compose a poem impromptu* /～发表谈话 *make an impromptu speech* ② take one's seat：宾主～ *hosts and guests taking their seats*

【即行】carry out right away（or immediately）：～枪决 *carry out the execution right away*

【即兴】impromptu；extemporaneous：～之作 *improvisation*

亟 ［书］earnestly；urgently：～待解决 *demanding prompt solution*

笈 ［书］① book case ② books；books and record：古～ *ancient books*

急 ① worried；impatient；hurried；hasty：焦～ *worried；anxious* /～着完成任务 *be anxious to fulfill a task* ② worry；make anxious：我的孩子学习跟不上，真～人！*I am so worried about my child because he cannot catch up with his classmates at school.* ③ irritated；annoyed：他～了。*He got angry.* ④ fast；rapid and violent：水流很～。*The current is swift.* ⑤ urgent；pressing：不～之务 *business that is not urgent* ⑥ emergent；critical：告～ *be in an emergency；report an emergency* /当务之～ *urgent affairs* ⑦ be eager to extend help to public affairs or other people's difficulty：～人之难 *be eager to help those in need*

【急案】urgent case

【急巴巴】hasty；in a hurry

【急奔】dash：我们赶在关门之前向银行～。*We dashed to get to the bank before it closed.*

【急变】abrupt change；unexpected crisis

【急病】acute disease

【急不可待】be extremely anxious；can scarcely wait：他～要知道比赛结果。*He is extremely anxious to know the results of the contest.*

【急茬儿】［方］urgent matter；emergency case：这是～，可不能耽误了。*It is an urgent matter which cannot be delayed.*

【急赤白脸】［方］face turning red，or pale due to anger or anxiety

【急匆匆】hurriedly；in a hurry；in haste：他～地做了决定，没顾上考虑细节。*He made the decision in a hurry without thinking about the details.*

【急促】① hurried；rapid：远处枪声～。*The gunfire in the distance was rapid.* /他听到一阵越来越近的～的脚步声。*He heard rapid footsteps approaching.* ②（of time）short；pressing：时间很～。*Time is pressing；time is running short.*

【急电】urgent telegram；urgent cable

【急方】【中医】emergency prescription

【急功近利】eager for quick success and instant benefit

【急火】① quick fire；high heat：～煮不好饭。*Quick fire cooks no good rice.* ② pent-up fury

【急急巴巴】in a hurry；hurriedly；in haste：他们～地离开，忘记锁上门。*They left in a hurry and forgot to lock the door.*

【急件】urgent document

【急进】① radical：～派 *radical party* ② quick or rapid movement

【急救】first aid；emergency treatment：采取～措施 *take first-aid measures*

【急救包】first-aid dressing

【急救车】ambulance；emergency vehicle

【急救站】dressing station；first-aid station

【急救中心】first-aid centre

【急剧】rapid；sharp；sudden：～上升 *rise sharply* /销售额～减少。*There was a sharp decrease in gross sales.*

【急遽】rapid；sharp；swift：一辆～行驶的卡车撞倒了一个穿过马路的女孩儿。*A truck traveling at high speed struck a girl crossing the street.*

【急流】torrent；rapid stream；rapids：他在～中小心地驾船。*He steered the ship carefully through the swift currents.*

【急流勇进】press on in the teeth of difficulties

【急流勇退】resolutely retire at the height of one's career；make a quick retreat before a crisis

【急忙】in a hurry；in a rush；in haste

【急难】①［书］be anxious to help people in trouble ② misfortune；grave danger：他现在正处于～之中。*He is now in dire straits.*

【急迫】critical；pressing；urgent：～时刻 *a critical moment* /～的需要 *a pressing demand* /～的口信 *an urgent message*

【急起直追】rouse oneself to catch up；make haste to catch up with sb

【急切】① eager；urgent；imperative：女儿～地把她写的诗念给我听。*My daughter was eager to read me the poem that she had written.* ② in haste；in a hurry：她～地把好消息告诉我。*She made haste to tell me the good news.*

【急人所急】be anxious to help those in grave danger；be eager to meet the needs of others

【急如星火】in a frantic hurry；extremely urgent：这件事～。*This is a matter of great urgency.*

【急事】urgent matter；urgent case；pressing business：他有～，先走了。*He has left for he has something urgent to do.*

J

【急速】very fast; at high speed：火车～驰过村庄。*The train sped through the village.*
【急湍】① swift current; rushing water ② swift; rapid：溪流～ *swift stream*
【急弯】a sharp turn
【急务】pressing work; urgent task：有～在身 *have some urgent task on hand*
【急行军】rapid march
【急性】① acute：～传染病 *acute infectious disease* /～阑尾炎 *acute appendicitis* /～呼吸道疾病 *acute respiratory disease* ② impatient; impetuous; rash：她太～了，不愿听我解释。*She is too impatient to listen to my explanation.*
【急性病】①【医】acute disease ② impetuosity
【急性子】① impatient; impetuous ② impetuous person：～不适合这项工作。*An impetuous person is not fit for the job.*
【急需】① be badly in need of; need urgently：我们～资金。*We are badly in need of funds.* ② urgent need; crying need：以应～ *meet a crying need*
【急眼】[方] ① get angry; furious：我说的话把他惹～了。*My words made him furious.* ② be anxious; be worried about sth：她一～，连话都说不出来。*She cannot even utter a word when she is extremely anxious.*
【急用】urgent need：这些钱你留着～。*You can keep the money for a rainy day.*
【急于】be anxious to; wildly; anxious; be impatient to do sth：我～想知道结果。*I'm anxious to know the result.* /不要～下结论。*Don't jump at conclusion.*
【急于求成】overanxious for quick results; impatient for success
【急躁】① irritable; hot-tempered：她不高兴时，容易～。*She was irritable when she was unhappy.* ② impatient; rash：对孩子们不要～。*Don't be impatient with your children.* /要防止～情绪。*Guard against rashness.*
【急诊】emergency case; emergency treatment：～室 *emergency ward*
【急症】sudden attack or onset of an illness
【急智】quick wittedness
【急中生智】show resourcefulness in an emergency; hit upon an idea in peril; think up a device in an emergency
【急骤】rapid; hasty：～的脚步声 *hurried footsteps*
【急转弯】take a sudden turn; make a radical change：向左～ *a sharp turn to the left*
【急转直下】(of a situation, etc.) take a sudden turn and then develop rapidly; develop rapidly after a sudden change

疾[1] ① disease; sickness：积劳成～ *break down from constant overwork* ② suffering; difficulty ③ hate; abhor：痛心～首 *with bitter hatred*

疾[2] fast; quick：手～眼快 *with quick hands and keen eyes — nimble*

【疾病】disease; illness; sickness; ailment：战胜～ *triumph over illness*
【疾步】at full speed; with quick steps
【疾驰】gallop away; whirl off：～的车辆 *a car running at full speed*
【疾恶如仇】hate evil like an enemy
【疾风】①【气】moderate gale ② gale; strong wind
【疾风知劲草】sturdy grass outstands strong winds
【疾患】[书] disease; illness
【疾苦】hardships; difficulties：关心群众的～ *be concerned about the weal and woe of the people*
【疾驶】speed past
【疾首蹙额】with aching head and knitted brows — express great disgust
【疾书】write swiftly：奋笔～ *write swiftly*
【疾言厉色】harsh words and sturdy looks
【疾疫】[书] disease; illness
【疾走】walk quickly：我看见他在街上～。*I see him walk quickly on the street.*

棘 ① sour jujube ② thorny bushes; brambles：披荆斩～ *break through brambles and thorns* ③ prick; puncture

【棘刺】① bristle (on a porcupine's back, etc.) ② prickle or thorn
【棘轮】【机】ratchet (wheel)
【棘手】thorny; sticky; knotty; ticklish：～的问题 *thorny problem; a hard nut to crack*
【棘爪】【机】detent; pallet; pawl

集 ① gather; collect ② country fair; market：赶～ *go to fair; go to market* ③ collection; anthology：全～ *complete works* /诗～ *a collection of poems* /文～ *collected works* /选～ *selected works; selections* ④ volume; part：十～电视剧 *a ten-part teleplay* ⑤ set; assemblage ⑥ (Jí) a surname

【集部】literary works; one of the major categories in ancient Chinese book collections
【集成】① collection ②【电】integration：计算机～制造 *CIM (computer integrated manufacturing)*
【集成电路】integrated circuit
【集股】raise capital; form a stock company
【集合】① gather; assemble; rally; mass; congregate：我们～在他周围。*We gathered around him.* /老师把学生～在操场上。*The teacher assembled the students on the playground.* /人群～在广场上听总统讲话。*The crowds congregated in the square to hear the President.* /士兵已经～起来进行检阅。*The soldiers have mustered for inspection.* ② gather together; collect：～材料 *collect materials* ③【数】set; assemblage; collection
【集合号】bugle call for fall-in
【集合论】【数】set theory
【集合名词】【语】collective noun
【集会】assembly; meeting; congregation; convocation：毕业生～ *convocation of graduates* /群众～ *a mass rally* /友好～ *a "good-will" gathering* /政治～ *a political rally*
【集结】build up; concentrate; mass; rendezvous：～军队 *concentrate troops* /～力量 *build up strength*
【集锦】a collection of selected specimens：图片～ *collection of choice pictures*

J

【集聚】gather; collect; centralize: ～一堂 *assemble together in one place*
【集刊】collected papers of an academic organization
【集拢】gather together: 一大群人～过来看看发生了什么事。*A large crowd of people gathered to see what was happening.*
【集录】collect and compile
【集贸市场】fair; local market
【集权】centralization of state power: ～政治 *centralized politics*
【集日】market day
【集散】(of goods, etc.) collect and scatter
【集散地】collecting and distributing centre: 毗邻著名学府,这个地方是个大规模的图书～。*Near several famous universities, it's a large-scaled collecting and distributing centre of books.*
【集市】country fair; market: ～贸易 *country fair trade* / 我们学校附近有个很大的～。*There's a big market near our school.*
【集思广益】draw on collective wisdom and absorb all useful ideas; pool the wisdom of the masses
【集体】(of an organization, group or society of people as a whole) collective: ～防卫 *collective defence* / ～经济 *collective economy* / ～利益 *collective benefit* / ～领导 *collective leadership* / ～农庄 *collective farm* / ～所有制 *collective ownership* / ～舞 *group dancing* / ～主义 *collectivism*
【集体化】collectivization: 农业～ *collectivization of agriculture*
【集团】group; circle; clique; bloc: 军事～ *military bloc* / 统治～ *ruling clique*; *ruling circle* / 社会～ *social group* / 盗窃～ *gang of robbers*
【集训】assemble for training: ～班 *class for training athletes*
【集邮】philately; stamp collecting: ～册 *stamp album* / ～家 *philatelist*
【集约】intensive: ～经营 *intensive farming*
【集约化】intensification
【集运】(usu. of goods) transport by group
【集镇】town; market town
【集中】centralize; collect; concentrate; focus; muster; pool: ～火力 *concentrate fire* / ～优势兵力 *muster superior forces* / ～精神工作。*Concentrate on your work or focus your mind on work.*
【集中供暖】【建】central heating
【集中营】concentration camp
【集注】① concentrate; focus; pay attention to sth: 大家的目光都～在我身上。*All eyes were focused on me.* ② variorum
【集装箱】container: ～船 *container ship*
【集资】collect money; raise funds: ～办学校 *raise funds for opening up schools*
【集子】anthology; collection

楫 oar

辑 ① collect; compile (esp. information and material to be arranged in a book, report, etc.): 纂～ *compile*; *edit* ② parts divided according to the contents or order of publication of a collection of books or materials
【辑录】compile; collect: ～成册 *be compiled into books*
【辑要】summary; abstract: 会议事项～ *abstract of the proceedings at the meeting*
【辑佚】① compile scattered writings ② book thus compiled: 《唐诗～》*A Collection of Scattered Poems of the Tang Dynasty*

嵴 ridge of a mountain or hill

嫉 ① be envious; be jealous ② hate; detest: 愤世～俗 *hate the world and vulgar affairs*
【嫉妒】envy; be jealous of: 宁可让人～,不要让人怜悯 *better be envied than pitied* / 他～我的成就。*He is jealous of my success.* / 他～他的同学,认为他才应该受到表扬。*He is jealous of his classmate because he thinks he should be praised.*
【嫉恨】envy and hate
【嫉贤妒能】envy the good and the capable

瘠 [书] ① lean; thin and weak ② (of soil) barren; poor: 贫～ *barren*
【瘠薄】barren; unproductive: ～的土壤 *poor soil*
【瘠瘦】① lean and thin ② barren
【瘠田】barren land

鹡
【鹡鸰】【动】wagtail

藉 ①[书] tread on; insult: 狼～ *in disorder*; *scattered about in a mess* ② (Jí) a surname
see also jiè

籍 ① book; record: 古～ *ancient books* / 史～ *historical records* ② place of origin; native place: 原～ *ancestral home*; *original home* ③ registry; roll: 党～ *party membership* / 户～ *census register*; *registered permanent residence* ④ (Jí) a surname
【籍贯】the place of one's birth or origin; native place: 我的～是辽宁。*Liaoning Province is my hometown.*
【籍没】[书] register and confiscate sb's property

jǐ

几 ① how many: ～个人? *How many people?* / 你来～天了? *How many days have you been here?* / 你妹妹～岁了? *How old is your younger sister?* ② a few; some: ～千 *thousands of* / ～十 *scores (or dozens) of* / ～亿 *hundreds of millions of* / 所剩无～。*Only very few were left.*
see also jī
【几曾】at what time in the past; when: 虽然他很淘气,可是我～说过他? *Though he is very naughty, when did I scold him for that?*
【几次三番】time and again; repeatedly; often and often: 她～向我强调诚实的意义。*She repeatedly impressed on me the value of honesty.*
【几多】[方] how; how many; how much: 这筐苹果～重? *How much does this basket of apples weigh?* / 他不知道为这个工程度过了～不眠之夜。*He thought about the project in many sleepless*

nights.
【几分】a bit; a little; somewhat; rather: 这件上衣我穿着有～大。*The coat looks a bit large on me.* / 我有～惊讶。*I was somewhat surprised.* / 他有～疲倦了。*He was rather tired.*
【几何】①［书］how much; how many: 不知尚有～ *uncertain how much is left or how many are left* ②【数】geometry: 不变～ *invariant geometry* / 初等～ *elementary geometry* / 代数～ *algebraic geometry* / 高等～ *higher geometry* / 积分～ *integral geometry* / 解析～ *analytic(al) geometry* / 绝对～ *absolute geometry* / 立体～ *solid geometry*
【几何体】solid
【几何投影】geometric projection
【几何图形】geometric figure
【几何学】geometry: 解析～ *analytic geometry*
【几何元素】geometric element
【几经】experience several times: ～沧桑 *go through the mill; marked by vicissitudes*
【几内亚】Guinea: ～人 *Guinean*
【几内亚湾】Gulf of Guinea, a large inlet of the Atlantic Ocean bordering on the coast of Guinea
【几儿】［方］what date: 你～来的? *When did you come here?*
【几时】what time; when: 你～见他哭过? *When did you ever find him crying?*
【几许】［书］how much; how many: 不知～。*No one can tell how much.*

己 ① oneself; one's own: 各抒～见 *each airs his own views* / 舍～为人 *sacrifice one's own interests for the sake of others* ② the sixth of the ten Heavenly Stems; the sixth
【己方】one's own side
【己见】one's own opinion
【己任】one's own duty or responsibility: 引为～ *regard as one's own duty*
【己所不欲,勿施于人】do as you would be done by others; don't do to others what you don't want others to do to you

挤 ① crowd; pack: ～作一团 *huddle together* ② jostle; push against: 人多～不过去 *cannot push one's way through because it is too crowded* / ～到队伍的前面 *push to the front of the line* / 他～进了拥挤的公共汽车。*He squeezed into a crowded bus.* ③ press; squeeze: ～掉水分 *squeeze water out of sth* / 把牙膏从管里～出来 *extrude toothpaste from the tube* / 鞋子太～脚。*Shoes are pressing on my toes.* ④ exclude; push aside: 排～ *elbow out; push aside; squeeze out*
【挤出】squeeze out; force out; extrude: ～人群 *squeeze one's way out of the crowd; push one's way through the crowd*
【挤兑】a run on a bank
【挤对】［方］force sb to submit or yield: 他不愿意,就别～他了。*If he is not willing to do that, just let him be.*
【挤咕】［方］wink: 他向我～眼,示意我小点儿声。*He winked at me to speak lower.*
【挤满】crowd; pack; packed; crowded: 车已经～了。*The car is filled to capacity.* / 房间里～了客人。*The room was crowded with guests.*
【挤眉弄眼】make eyes; wink one's eyes at; wink: 我不知道他～的是什么意思。*I didn't know what he meant by winking.*
【挤奶】milk (a cow, etc.)
【挤压】extrude; press: 塑料从细孔～出来形成纤维。*Plastic material is extruded through very small holes to form fibres.*
【挤牙膏】squeeze toothpaste out of a tube — be forced to tell sth bit by bit: 快点说,不要～! 我已经不耐烦了。*Make a clean breast of it. Don't talk bit by bit. I am getting impatient.*
【挤轧】engage in internal strife or infighting
【挤眼】wink at sb
【挤占】squat; commandeer: 士兵～民房用作办公室。*The soldiers commandeered the house to use as offices.*

济
see also jì
【济济】(of people) many; numerous: 人才～ *an abundance of capable people*
【济济一堂】a galaxy of talents gather together

给 ① supply; provide: 自～自足 *autarky* / 补～ *supply; replenishment* ② ample; wealthy: 家～人足。*All live in plenty.*
see also gěi
【给付】pay money; pay
【给水】water supply: ～工程 *water supply engineering*
【给养】provisions; victuals; rations: ～不足 *be short of provisions* / ～充足 *be abundantly provisioned*
【给予】［书］give; render; offer: ～补助 *give subsidies to sb* / ～协助 *render assistance to sb*

脊 ① (of man or animal) spine; backbone: ～椎骨 *vertebra* ② ridge: 屋～ *ridge of a house* / 山～ *chine; ridge of a mountain*
【脊背】back (of a human being or any other vertebrate)
【脊梁】［方］back (of the human body): 国家的～ *the backbone of a country*
【脊梁骨】backbone; spine: 他从马上跌下摔断了～。*He broke his spine in a fall from a horse.*
【脊神经】spinal nerve
【脊髓】spinal cord
【脊索】【动】notochord
【脊索动物】vertebrate
【脊柱】spinal or vertebral column; rachis
【脊椎】① vertebra; back ② spine; back-bone
【脊椎动物】vertebrate
【脊椎骨】vertebra; spine

掎 ［书］① pin down; tie up ② tow; pull; draw
【掎角之势】tactic of dividing one's forces to pin down the enemy

麂 【动】muntjac

【麂皮】chamois (leather)
【麂子】[口] muntjac

jì

计 ① count; calculate: 共~ *count up to*; *sum to* / 不~其数 *countless*; *numerable* ② meter; gauze: 体温~ *clinical thermometer*; *thermometer* / 血压~ *blood-pressure meter*; *sphygmomanometer* ③ idea; stratagem: 缓兵之~ *stalling tactics* / 妙~ *wrinkle* / 百年大~ *a project of vital and lasting importance* ④ plan: 为工作方便~ *for the purpose of convenience in work* ⑤ consider; concern oneself; care: 不~成败 *not care whether one succeeds or not* ⑥ (Jì) a surname
【计策】stratagem; plan; device; ploy; tactic: 小心别中了他的~。*Be careful not to fall into his trap.*
【计程表】taximeter
【计程车】taxi
【计程仪】【航】log: 电~ *electric log*
【计酬】calculate the sum of payment; pay: 这项工作按劳~。*You will be paid according to your labour.*
【计工】assessment of work done
【计划】① plan; idea; scheme; policy: 她想出了一个~惩罚他。*She thought of a plan to punish him.* /一切按~进行。*Everything went according to plan.* /政府的救济~很快陷入了困难。*The government's relief scheme soon ran into difficulties.* ② plan; map out; work out; formulate: 我们~下周开会讨论。*We plan to hold a meeting to discuss it next week.* /他已经~好了自己的职业生涯。*He has his career all mapped out.*
【计划经济】planned economy
【计划生产】planned production
【计划生育】family planning; birth control: ~政策是中国的一项基本国策。*Family planning is one of China's basic policies.*
【计价】valuation: ~过低 *undervaluation* / ~过高 *over valuation*
【计件】reckon by the piece: ~付酬 *pay by the piece* / ~工人 *piece-worker*; *rate worker* / ~工资 *piece rate wage* / ~制 *piece system*
【计较】① care; bother about: 我不~他所说的话。*I don't care what he says.* /我从不~这些。*I never bother about such things.* ②argue: 我不愿与你~。*I don't want to argue with you.* ③ consider; think over: 此事暂且不论, 到时再作~。*Don't discuss it at present. Let's just play it by ear.*
【计量】measure; calculate; estimate
【计量经济学】econometrics
【计量心理学】psychometrics
【计量学】metrology
【计略】[书] scheme; stratagem
【计谋】trick; scheme; trap; conspiracy; intrigue: 他精心设计了一个~。*He devised a stratagem carefully.*
【计上心来】come up with a good idea suddenly: 他突然~。*All of a sudden, an idea came across his mind.*
【计生委】family planning commision
【计时】reckon by time: ~工 *time work* / ~工资 *payment by the hour*; *time wage*
【计时器】hourmeter; hour counter
【计时赛】【体】timetrial
【计时员】【体】timekeeper
【计数】(jìshǔ) count; calculate: 不可~ *countless*
【计数】(jìshù) count: ~器 *counter* /以十为单位来~ *count by tens*
【计算】① calculate; figure; compute; count: ~开支 *figure expenses* / 生产成本应当~精确。*The cost of production should be precisely calculated.* / 据~损失有200元。*The losses are computed at* 200 *yuan.* ②consideration; planning: 你做事该有个~。*You should plan well the things you will do.* ③ scheme; trap: 我上回被他~了。*I was tricked by him last time.*
【计算机】computer: 普及~的应用 *popularize the computer application*
【计议】consider; consult: 他们~着比赛的组织办法。*They are discussing how to organize the match.*

记 ① remember; bear in mind: 永~不忘 *treasure up in one's memory* / ~住这件事! *Remember it!* / 我一时~不起来他的名字。*His name escaped my memory.* ② write down; record: ~在本子上。*Write down the words in the notebook.* ③ notes; record (written account): 日~ *diary*; *journal* /笔~ *note* /游~ *travel notes* ④ mark; sign: 标~ *earmark*; *marker*; *sign* ⑤ birthmark: 他后背上有块黑~。*He has a black birthmark on the back.* ⑥[量][方] usu. used of certain actions: 一~耳光 *a slap in the face*
【记仇】bear grudges; harbour bitter resentment: 你是我的哥哥, 不管你说过什么我都不会和你~。*You are my elder brother and I will not bear you grudges no matter what you've said.*
【记得】remember; bear in mind: 你还~我吗? *Do you still remember me?*
【记分】keep the score; record the points; register a student's marks: ~册 *markbook* / ~员 *scorekeeper*; *scorer*
【记功】cite sb for meritorious service; record a merit
【记工】record workpoints: ~员 *workpoint recorder*
【记挂】[方] be concerned about; keep thinking about; miss: 母亲十分~远方的儿子。*Mother missed his son far away very much.*
【记过】record a demerit
【记号】mark; sign; symbol: 在上面作个~。*Put a mark on it.*
【记恨】bear grudges: 我知道他为那个事故~我。*I know he has a grudge against me for that accident.*
【记录】① take notes; record: 他对校长的发言作了~。*He put down the content of the headmaster's*

speech. /她总是把花的钱～下来。*She always keeps a record of how much money she spends.* ② notes; record:会议～ *minutes of a meeting* /课堂～ *classroom record* /学业～ *academic record* /原始～ *original record* /有～以来最热的夏天 *the hottest summer on record* ③ recorder ④ record: 保持～ *hold a record* /打破～ *break a record*; *cut a record*

【记录片】documentary film:大型～ *full length documentary film*

【记录员】notetaker

【记名】put down one's name; sign: 无～投票 *vote without signing one's name*

【记念】miss; think of: 他时刻～国外的丈夫。*She keeps thinking of her husband abroad.*

【记取】remember; bear in mind: ～教训 *remember the lessons*

【记认】① identify; distinguish: 你能～这书上的笔记吗? *Can you identify the handwriting on this book?* ②［方］sign; mark: 他在自家的每件东西上都做了～以防别人误拿。*He marked all the things in his house to prevent them being taken by mistake.*

【记事】① keep a record of events: 撰史书～ *keep a record of events by writing history* ② account; annal; chronicle

【记事儿】(of a child) begin to remember things: 我那时已经能～了。*I could remember things at that time.*

【记述】record and narrate; give an account of: 这篇作文～了我的大学生活。*This composition gives an account of my college life.*

【记诵】commit to memory and be able to recite; learn by heart

【记协】journalist's association

【记下】note; put down: 我～了他的新电话号码。*I made a note of his new telephone number.* /我～了飞机起飞的时间。*I noted the time of the plane's taking off.*

【记性】memory: ～好 *have a good memory* /～坏 *have a poor memory*

【记叙】narrate: 生动的～ *a vivid narration*

【记叙文】narration; narrative

【记忆】① remember; recall; recollect: 我认出了他,却～不起太多关于他的事。*I recognized him but I couldn't recollect much about him.* /这是一个值得～的事件。*It is an event worth remembering.* ② memory; recollection: 她因年迈而～模糊。*Age has clouded her memory.* /我对这件事的～与他不同。*My recollection of the incident differs from his.*

【记忆力】memory: 他～好。*He has a good memory.* /我对数字的～很差。*I have a bad memory for figures.* /奶奶的～极差。*Grandmother has a memory like a sieve.*

【记忆犹新】remain fresh memory; remember vividly; distinctly remember: 那一幕我至今～。*That scene remained fresh in my memory.* /那件事我～。*I remember it as if it were yesterday.*

【记载】① put down in writing; keep a record; put on record: 对这一地区的气温变化有详细的～。*Temperature variations in this area are recorded in detail.* ② record; account: 历史～ *historical records*

【记账】keep accounts; keep books: ～买卖 *transaction for account* /请记我的账。*Please charge to my account.*

【记者】reporter; newsman; journalist; correspondent: 随军～ *a war correspondent* /特派～ *special correspondent* /体育～ *sports journalist*

【记者证】press card

【记住】remember; learn by heart; bear in mind; commit to memory: 我会～你说的话。*I will bear in mind what you've said.*

伎 a professional female singer or dancer in ancient China

【伎俩】trick; intrigue: 这是他惯用的～。*It's his favourite trick.* /他对我玩弄了卑鄙的～。*He played a dirty trick on me.*

纪[1] discipline: 军～ *military discipline* /违法乱～ *break the law and violate discipline* /遵～守法 *abide by the law and discipline*

纪[2] ① record; write down ②［古］epoch (1 epoch equals twelve years in ancient time): 世～ *century* ③【地】period: 侏罗～ *Jurassic Period*

【纪纲】［书］① law ② moral standard

【纪检】inspect discipline: ～部门 *discipline inspection department*

【纪律】discipline: 财经～ *finance and economic discipline* /财务～ *financial discipline* /财政～ *fiscal discipline* /劳动～ *labour discipline* /遵守～ *observe discipline* /违反～ *breach of discipline* /军队～严明。*The army is strict in discipline.*

【纪年】① a way of numbering the years: 公元～ *Christian era* ② chronological record of events: ～体 *chronological order*

【纪念】① commemorate; mark; in memory of: 金婚～ *gold wedding anniversary* /这座纪念碑是为了～所有在战争中牺牲的战士。*The monument was built in memory of all the soldiers who died in the war.* ② keepsake; memento: 他在回国前送我一张照片作为～。*He gave me his picture as a keepsake before returning to his country.*

【纪念碑】monument; memorial: 人民英雄～ *Monument to the People's Heroes*

【纪念币】commemorative coin

【纪念册】commemorative book (or album)

【纪念馆】memorial hall: 曹雪芹～ *Cao Xueqin Memorial Hall*

【纪念品】souvenir; memento

【纪念日】commemoration day

【纪念塔】memorial tower

【纪念堂】memorial (or commemoration) hall

【纪念邮票】commemorative stamp

【纪念章】souvenir badge; medal

【纪实】record of actual events

【纪实文学】documentary writing

【纪事】① narrate; record facts: ～诗 *narrative po-*

em ② record of facts or historical events
【纪委】commission for inspecting discipline
【纪行】travel notes
【纪要】summary; minutes: 会议～ *summary of the meeting*
【纪元】① beginning of an era ② epoch; era: 开辟科学上的新～ *mark an epoch in science*
【纪传体】history presented in a series of biographies

技 ability; skill: 一～之长 *professional skill*; *specialty* /口～ *gastriloquy* /黔驴～穷。*All tricks have been exhausted.*
【技法】skill; technique: 他的绘画～很独特。*His technique in painting is unique.*
【技工】① skilled worker ② mechanic; technician
【技击】art of attack and defence
【技能】technique; mastery of a technique: 基本～ *basic skill* /听说～ *audiolingual skills* /阅读～ *reading skill*
【技巧】① skill; craftsmanship: 美发～ *skill in hairdressing* /写作～ *writing technique* /这门课将传授你成为一个成功的代理人的～。*This course will give you the skills you need to become a successful deputy.* ②sports acrobatics
【技穷】at one's wit's end
【技师】engineer; technician: 汽车～ *an automotive technician*
【技士】junior technician
【技术】① technology; technique; skill: 超声波～ *ultrasonic technology* /国防～ *defense technology* /模拟～ *analogue technique* /农业～ *agricultural technique* /科学～是第一生产力。*Science and technology are the first productive force.* /由于外科手术～的发展，心脏移植手术的成功率已经有了很大提高。*Thanks to new surgical techniques, heart replacement operations have become much more successful.* ②technical plant or equipment
【技校】technical school
【技痒】itch to display one's skill: 他看见别人打篮球，不觉～。*When he saw others playing basketball, he was itching to show his skill.*
【技艺】artistry; skill: 他做饭的～很高明。*He is very skillful in cooking.*

系 tie; fasten: ～安全带 *fasten one's seatbelt* / ～衣服扣子 *button up a jacket* / ～鞋带 *tie the shoe laces* / ～领带 *wear ties*
see also xì
【系泊】moor (a boat)
【系留】moor (a balloon or airship)

忌 ① be jealous of; envy: 猜～ *be jealous and suspicious* ②fear; dread: 顾～ *scruple* /肆无～惮 *run riot*; *unbridled*; *stopping at nothing* ③ abstain from; avoid; shun: ～食生冷 *avoid cold and uncooked food* ④ quit; give up: ～烟 *give up alcohol* / ～酒 *give up alcohol*; *abstain from drinking*
【忌辰】anniversary of the death of an ancestor, parent, etc.
【忌惮】[书] dread; be afraid; fear; for fear of: 出于对竞选失败的～，政府官员不敢增加税收。*Government officials fear that if they increase taxes they will lose the election.*
【忌妒】be jealous of: 他～任何人的成就。*He is jealous of everybody's achievement.* /她的～和猜疑毁掉了她的婚姻。*Her jealousy and suspicion ruined her marriage.*
【忌恨】detest; hate; loathe: 他～所有的外国人。*He hates all foreigners.*
【忌讳】① taboo: 和伊斯兰教谈论吃猪肉是犯～的。*It violates the taboo to talk about eating pork with Moslems.* ② avoid as harmful; abstain from: 做学问最～浅尝辄止。*You should avoid being satisfied with a smattering of knowledge when you learn something.* ③ [方] vinegar
【忌口】avoid certain food; be on a diet: 他为减肥而～。*He is on a diet to lose weight.*
【忌日】[迷] date on which certain things should be avoided
【忌食】① avoid certain food for the benefit of one's health or medical treatment: ～冷食 *avoid cold food* ② avoid certain food out of religion: 印度教徒～牛肉。*Hindus avoid beef.*

际 ① border; edge: 边～ *bound*; *limit* /天～ *horizon* /一望无～ *stretch to the horizon* ② in; inside: 脑～ *in one's head* ③ between; among: 国～ *international* ④ occasion; time: 危难之～ *at a critical moment* ⑤on the occasion of; when: ～此盛会 *on the occasion of this grand gathering* ⑥ circumstances; one's experiences or lot
【际会】come across; run into
【际涯】[书] boundary: 渺无～ *boundless*
【际遇】[书] opportunity; spell of good fortune

妓 prostitute; whore
【妓女】prostitute; whore
【妓院】brothel: 逛～ *visit a brothel*

季 ① season (consisting of three months): 一年分四～。*A year is divided into four seasons.* ② a period of time: 淡～ *slow season*; *dull season*; *dead season* /雨～ *rainy season*; *monsoon* /旺～ *midseason*; *high season*; *rush season* ③ last: ～世 *the declining years of a dynasty* ④ last month of a season ⑤ the fourth or youngest among brothers: ～弟 *the fourth or youngest brother* ⑥ (Jì) a surname
【季报】quarterly bulletin (or report)
【季春】last month of spring
【季冬】last month of winter
【季度】quarter (of a year): 第一～ *the first quarter (of a year)* /～报告 *a quarterly report*
【季风】【气】monsoon: 冬～ *dry monsoon* /夏～ *wet monsoon*
【季风气候】monsoon climate
【季风雨】monsoon rain
【季父】[书] uncle; youngest uncle
【季候】[方] season
【季节】season: 交配～ *a mating season* /农忙～ *a busy farming season* /农闲～ *a slack farming sea-*

son

【季节性】seasonal:~性变化 *seasonal variation* / ~行业 *seasonal trade*

【季军】third place in a contest

【季刊】quarterly publication

剂 ① a pharmaceutical or other chemical preparation:药~ *medicament* /麻醉~ *anaesthetic; anesthetic* ②【化】agent:杀虫~ *insecticide; pesticide* /冷冻~ *coolant; cryogen; refrigerant* ③ a small piece of dough ④[量] used of concoctions of herbal medicine:一~药 *a dose of medicine (or drug)*

【剂量】【药】dosage; dose

【剂量计】【化】dosimeter

【剂量学】【化】dosimetry

【剂型】【药】form of a drug

荠

【荠菜】【植】shepherd's purse

迹 ① mark; trace:足~ *footmark; footprint* /血~ *bloodstain* /笔~ *a person's handwriting* /踪~ *tail; trace; trail* ② remains; vestige:古~ *historic site* /陈~ *vestige of the past* ③ outward sign; indication

【迹象】indication; sign

济 ① cross a river:同舟共~ *in the same boat* ② aid; help (the poor):救~金 *relief fund* /接~ *give financial help to sb* ③ be of help; benefit:无~于事 *of no help; of no use*
see also jǐ

【济急】meet the emergency; relieve sb in need

【济困扶危】help the distressed and those in peril

【济贫】relieve the poor:劫富~ *rob the rich to relieve the poor*

【济世】be of help to the people and society:行医~ *practise medicine to help people*

【济事】be of help; helpful:这么做根本不~。*It didn't help at all.*

【济助】give material help

既 ①(of action) finished; done with:保持~有的成绩 *keep the acquired achievement* ② since; now that:~要提高英语水平,就要每天练习。*Since you want to improve your English, you should practise every day.* ③[书] finished; done:食~ *the second contact of a total eclipse* ④ both... and; as well as:~高且大 *tall and massive* /~快又好 *both quick and well done*

【既成事实】accomplished fact:承认~ *accept a fait accompli* /造成~ *present a fait accompli; make sth an accomplished fact*

【既得利益】vested interest

【既定】set; fixed; established:~目标 *set objective (or goal)* /~方针 *established policy*

【既而】[书] later; subsequently:~雨霁,欣然登山。*After the rain stopped, we began to climb the mountain happily.*

【既来之,则安之】since you are here, you may as well stay and make the best of it

【既然】since; as; now that; seeing that:~如此,我们不用再谈了。*Since it is so, we don't have to talk about it any more.*

【既是】since; as; now that:~如此,再没什么可说的了。*Since that is so, there is no more to be said.*

【既遂】【律】accomplished offence:~罪 *accomplished (or completed) offence*

【既往】① past:一如~ *as in the past* ② past affairs

【既往不咎】forgive sb's past misdeeds; let sb off from his past misdeeds; let bygones be bygones

【既约分数】【数】fraction in the lowest terms; reduced fraction

觊 [书] hope; covet

【觊觎】[书] covet; cast greedy eyes on:他~邻居的财富。*He coveted his neighbour's wealth.*

继 ① continue; follow:前赴后~ *advance wave upon wave* /日以~夜 *day and night* ② then; afterwards:她初感头晕,~又呕吐。*She felt dizzy at first and then threw up.*

【继承】① inherit; succeed:~王位 *succeed to the throne* /他~了大笔遗产。*He succeeded to a fortune.* ② advance; carry on:~传统 *carry on the tradition* /过去流传下来的优良传统应该加以~。*The valuable traditions handed down to us from the past should be followed.* ③ continue the work left by the deceased

【继承法】law of succession

【继承权】right of succession; right of inheritance

【继承人】heir; inheritor:法定~ *heir at law* /合法~ *the right heir* /假定~ *heir presumptive* /旁系~ *heir collateral* /直系~ *heir in tail* /他已经把他的事业移交给他的~了。*He's turned over his business to his successors.*

【继承税】inheritance tax

【继电器】【电】relay

【继而】then; afterwards:我们先是一惊,~哄堂大笑。*We were surprised at first and then burst into laughter.*

【继父】stepfather

【继后】then; afterwards:他开始接受,~又拒绝了。*He accepted it at first, and then refused to do so.*

【继进】continue to advance

【继母】stepmother

【继女】stepdaughter

【继任】succeed sb in a post:~首相 *succeed sb as Prime Minister*

【继室】one's second wife

【继嗣】[书] ① be adopted ② adopted son

【继往开来】carry forward the cause of our predecessors and forge ahead into the future; carry on the past and open a way for future

【继位】succeed to the throne

【继续】① remain; continue; go on; keep up (on); resume; go back to; start again:~前进 *march on* /~跑 *race on* /~做 *keep doing; go on doing* /~向前行进一公里 *continue on for another one kilometer* /休息之后谈判~进行。*The negotiations continued after a break.* /他伤得很严重,不

能～篮球生涯了。*He was so seriously injured that he was unable to resume his basketball career.* ② continuation：中国革命是伟大的十月革命的～。*Chinese revolution is the continuation of the great October Revolution.*

【继子】① adopted son ② son of one's spouse by previous marriage

祭 ① offer sacrifices to ② hold a memorial ceremony for the dead：公～烈士 *hold a public memorial ceremony for the martyrs* ③ wield sth magic：～起法宝 *wield a magic wand*

【祭典】ceremony to offer sacrifices

【祭奠】hold a memorial ceremony for sb

【祭礼】① sacrificial ceremony ② sacrificial offerings

【祭灵】hold a memorial ceremony in a mourning hall or in front one's coffin

【祭品】sacrificial offerings；oblation

【祭器】sacrificial utensil or vessel

【祭扫】sweep a grave and pay respects to the dead

【祭神】offer a sacrifice to one's gods

【祭祀】offer sacrifices to Gods or ancestors

【祭坛】sacrificial altar；altar

【祭天】offer a sacrifice to Heaven；worship Heaven

【祭文】funeral oration；elegiac address

【祭享】offer sacrifices to a god

【祭仪】［书］① sacrificial offerings；oblations ② ceremony of offering sacrifices

【祭幛】large sheet of silk with inscription showed at a funeral

悸 ［书］（of the heart）throb with terror；palpitate：心有余～ *one's heart still fluttering with fear*

【悸动】（of heart）throb with terror

【悸栗】tremble with fear：我一想到这件事就浑身～。*I tremble with fear at the very thought of it.*

寄 ① send；post：～包裹 *send a parcel by post* /～钱 *remit money* ② entrust；place：～希望于未来 *place hopes on the future* /他把孩子～在父母家。*He parked his child at his parents.* ③ depend on；attach oneself to ④ adopted：～父母 *foster parents*

【寄殡】lay a coffin in a place temporarily

【寄存】deposit；leave with；check：～费 *deposit charge* / 把包～在寄存处 *leave one's bag in the checkroom*

【寄递】deliver a letter

【寄放】leave with；leave in the care of：他把他的宠物～在我家。*He left his pets with me.*

【寄费】postage：免～ *postage free* /欠～ *postage due* /航空～ *airmail postage* /普通～ *ordinary postage*

【寄怀】［书］express one's feelings

【寄籍】stay away from home for quite a long time：～北京 *stay in Beijing for a long time*

【寄件人】sender

【寄居】live away from home：我上中学期间～在姑姑家里。*I stayed with my aunt during my middle school life.*

【寄卖】consign for sale on commission；put up for sale in a secondhand shop：～商店 *commission shop*

【寄卖品】consignment merchandise

【寄卖商店】secondhand shop；commission store

【寄情】express one's feelings：～山水 *write about mountains and rivers to vent one's feelings*

【寄人篱下】live under sb's roof — depend on sb for a living

【寄身】［书］stay in a place for a short time

【寄生】①【生】parasitism ② parasitic：～生活 *parasitic life*

【寄生虫】① parasite：～病 *parasitic disease* ② a person who leads a parasitic life

【寄生动物】parasitic animal

【寄生植物】parasitic plant

【寄食】live with a relative

【寄售】consign（for sale on commission）：～商店 *commission shop*

【寄宿】① lodge；put up ②（of students）board

【寄宿生】resident student；boarder

【寄宿学校】boarding school

【寄托】① entrust（to the care of sb）：年轻夫妇把孩子～在邻居家里。*The young couple entrusted the child to the care of their neighbour.* ② place hope on；repose in：人们的希望～在他身上。*The hope of the people rested on him.*

【寄销】consignment

【寄信】send（or post）a letter

【寄信人】addresser；sender

【寄秧】raise rice seedlings temporarily in a field

【寄养】entrust one's child to the care of sb；ask sb to bring up one's child：他自幼～在舅舅家。*He was brought up by his uncle.*

【寄意】send one's regards

【寄予】① place（hope，etc.）on：父母对他～了很大希望。*His parents place much hope on him.* ② show；express：我对这可怜的孩子～无限同情。*I felt much sympathy for that poor boy.*

【寄语】［书］send word

【寄寓】①［书］lodge；stay away from home：～他乡 *stay away from home* ②place（hope，etc.）：这篇文章～了他对祖国的热爱。*The article conveys his love for his motherland.*

【寄主】【生】host（of a parasite）

寂 ① silent；quiet ② quiet；lonely；solitary：孤～ *lonesome*

【寂寂】quiet；still

【寂静】quiet；still；silent：～的夜晚 *a still evening* /大厅里～得能听得到一根针掉在地上。*It was so quiet in the hall that you could hear a pin drop.*

【寂苦】lonely and distressed

【寂寥】［书］quiet；still：～的小村庄 *a quiet small village*

【寂灭】① die out；perish ②【宗】nirvana

【寂寞】① lonely；lonesome：当作家是一种很～的生活。*Working as a writer can be a very lonely existence.* / 他走后，我们都觉得万分～。*We all felt absolutely desolate when he left.* ② still；quiet：～的原野 *still field*

【寂寞】quiet; silent: 屋子里一片~。*Everything was very still inside the room.*
【寂然】[书] still; silent; quiet
绩 ① make hemp fibres into thread or rope: 纺~ *twist flax fibres and weave* ② achievement; gain: 成~ *result; success; achievement* /战~ *military successes*
【绩效】performance; achievement: ~显著 *prominent achievement*
霁 [书] ① cease raining or snowing; clear up after rain or snow: 雪初~。*It has just stopped snowing and is clearing up.* ② cool down: 色~ *calm down after a fit of anger*
【霁红】bright red colour used in glazing pottery
【霁色】blue colour similar to that of the sky after rain
【霁威】[书] cease to be angry
【霁月光风】bright moon and gentle breeze — open and aboveboard
暨 ① [书] and; as well as ② [书] to; up to: 从古~今 *from ancient times to the present* ③ (Jì) a surname
稷 ① millet, an ancient cereal crop ② the god of grains as worshipped by ancient emperors as the number one cereal crop: 社~ *country*
鲫 【动】crucian carp
【鲫鱼】【动】crucian carp; crucian
冀[1] [书] hope; long for: 希~ *look forward to; hope for*
冀[2] (Jì) ① another name for Hebei Province ② a surname
【冀求】hope to get sth: 他~那个职位已久。*He has been coveting that position for a long time.*
【冀图】hope; desire; long for: 他~东山再起。*He hoped to resume his former position.*
【冀望】[书] hope; look forward to: 他给我看他失踪的女儿的照片~我能认出她。*He showed me a picture of his missing daughter in the hope that I might recognize her.*
骥 [书] ① a thoroughbred horse: 按图索~ *try to locate something by following up a clue* ② virtuous and competent person

jiā

加 ① add; plus: 增~ *increase; add; augment* /火上~油 *add fuel to the fire* /二~二等于四。*Two plus two is four.* ② increase; rise; raise: 添砖~瓦 *contribute one's bit* /增~工资 *increase one's wages* ③ put in; append: ~引号 *put in the quotation marks* / ~注解 *append notes to* ④ carry out a certain action: 横~阻挠 *willfully obstruct* / 不~考虑 *not consider at all* ⑤ (Jiā) a surname
【加班】work overtime; work extra hours: 老板强迫我们~。*The boss forced us to work overtime.*
【加班费】overtime pay; overtime wages
【加班加点】be on overtime; put in extra hours
【加倍】① double; be twice as much: 债务不久就~了。*The debt soon doubled.* /他工作得很好,他们给了他~的工资。*He worked so well that they doubled his wages.* ② redouble; double: ~努力 *redouble one's efforts* / ~注意 *be doubly careful*
【加标点】punctuate: 加上标点,意思就清楚了。*When it is punctuated, the meaning becomes clear.*
【加餐】add a snack; have an extra meal
【加长】lengthen: ~衣服 *to lengthen a dress*
【加车】(put on) extra buses or trains
【加衬】lining; planking: 这件夹克衫有一层图案的~。*The jacket had a patterned lining.*
【加成】【化】addition: ~反应 *addition reaction; addictive reaction* / ~晶体 *addition crystal* / ~率 *markup percentage* / ~物 *addition product*
【加大】increase; augment: 持续的雨水~了洪水水量。*Continuing rains augmented the floodwaters.*
【加碘盐】iodized salt
【加尔各答】Calcutta, a city of eastern India
【加法】【数】addition; process of adding: ~表 *addition table* / ~定理 *sum rule* / ~公式 *addition formula* / ~机 *adding machine* / ~速度 *addition speed* / ~元件 *adding element* / ~运算 *add operation*
【加封】① paste a paper strip seal on sth ② confer another title on sb
【加工】① process: ~奶酪 *process cheese* /工业~ *industrial processing* /食品~ *food processing* /影片~ *film process* ② polish, treat raw material or non-finished product so that it is polished; refine: 文字~ *polish the words in the article*
【加固】consolidate; reinforce: ~堤坝 *reinforce dikes and dams* /她在任职的第一年内~了自己的权力。*She consolidated her power during her first year in office.*
【加官晋爵】be promoted to a higher rank; advance in one's position; rise in the official world
【加害】do harm to sb; injure: ~于人 *do sb harm; do sb an injury*
【加号】【数】plus sign (+)
【加厚】intensification; thickening
【加急】① be rapid and intense ② urgent: ~电报 *urgent telegram (or cable)* / ~电话 *express telephone service*
【加减】add and subtract: ~运算符 *adding operator*
【加减乘除】add, subtract, multiply and divide
【加减法】addition and subtraction
【加紧】step up; speed up; intensify: ~筹备 *speed up preparation* / ~生产 *step up production* / ~训练 *intensify the training*
【加劲】put more effort into sth: 再加把劲儿! *Put more effort into it!*
【加剧】intensify; aggravate: 痛苦~了她的病情。*Grief aggravated her illness.*
【加快】① speed up; quicken; accelerate: ~步子 *quicken one's step* / ~改革 *accelerate the reform* ② procedure for the passenger of a slow train ticket to take a fast train: 我的火车票要~。*I want to exchange this train ticket for a faster one.*

【加宽】broaden; widen: 这条路需要～。*This road needs to be widened.*
【加勒比海】Caribbean Sea
【加勒比人】Carib; Galibi
【加利福尼亚】California, a state on the Pacific coast of the United States: ～州人 *Californian*
【加料】① feed in raw material: 自动～ *automatic feeding* ② reinforced: ～药酒 *reinforced tonic wine*
【加料机】charger
【加料孔】charging aperture; feed opening
【加料口】charge door
【加榴炮】gun-howitzer
【加仑】gallon: 标准～ *proof gallon*
【加码】①［旧］raise the price of commodities; overcharge ② raise the stakes in gambling ③ raise the quota: 层层～ *raise the quota at each level*
【加盟】join an alliance or union
【加密】【电】encrypt: ～技术 *encryption techniques* / ～软件 *encryption software*
【加密狗】【电】softdog
【加冕】coronation; crowing: ～典礼 *coronation ceremony* / ～日 *coronation day*
【加拿大】Canada: ～人 *Canadian* / ～广播公司 *Canadian Broadcasting Corporation* / ～航空公司 *Air Canada* / ～骑警 *Mountie* / ～银行 *Bank of Canada* / ～萬苣 *horseweed*
【加纳】Ghana: ～人 *Ghanaian*
【加捻】【纺】twisting: ～机构 *twisting mechanism*
【加蓬】Gabon: ～人 *Gabonese*
【加强】① intensify; strengthen; reinforce; augment: ～控制 *tighten the screws* /黄昏将至,搜索～了。*The search intensified as dusk approached.* / 和谈期间,敌人力量已大为～。*The enemy has greatly strengthened during the truce talks.* ②【军】reinforced: ～排 *reinforced platoon* / ～连 *reinforced company*
【加权】【数】weighting; weighted
【加热】heat; warm; heating; warming: 放在火上～ *heat it over the fire* / ～表面 *area of heating surface* / ～处理 *furnace run* / ～电流 *heating current* / ～分裂 *thermal cracking*
【加热炉】furnace; mill furnace; stove
【加热器】heat booster; heater; heating appliance
【加入】① add; mix; put in: 多～点热水 *to add more hot water* ② join; accede to: ～搜索 *join in the search* /我国政府～了该条约。*Our government acceded to the treaty.*
【加入国】acceding state
【加塞儿】［口］push into a queue out of turn; queue-jump
【加赛】【体】additional tie-breaking match
【加上】① add; give: ～10%服务费 *add on a 10% service charge* ② moreover; in addition; furthermore
【加深】deepen; aggravate: ～理解 *get a deeper understanding* /他的皱纹由于操劳过度而日益～。*His wrinkles deepen day by day through overwork.*
【加湿器】humidifier
【加时赛】【体】play-off
【加试】add another exam: 据我所知,这次考试要～口语。*As far as I know, oral part has been added to this exam.*
【加数】【数】addend
【加速】speed up; quicken; expedite: ～社会主义建设 *accelerate socialist construction* /建筑商答应～修理。*The builders promised to expedite the repairs.*
【加速度】【物】acceleration: 重力～ *acceleration of gravity*
【加速器】【物】accelerator: 粒子～ *particle accelerator* /直线～ *linear accelerator*
【加速室】accelerating chamber
【加速运动】【物】accelerated motion
【加速折旧】accelerated depreciation
【加温】raise the temperature; heat up: ～设备 *warming-up device* / ～时间 *warm-up time*
【加线】【音】ledger line; leger line
【加薪】raise the salary (or pay)
【加以】① used before a disyllabic verb to indicate how to deal with sb or sth mentioned earlier: 有了问题要及时～解决。*Problems should be resolved in good time.* ② in addition; moreover: 我不喜欢滑冰,～冰又太薄。*I don't like skating; moreover, the ice is too thin.*
【加意】with attention to sth, with special care: ～保护 *protect with special care*
【加油】① oil; lubricate: 在车的齿轮上～ *lubricate the gears of a car* ② refuel: 那架飞机在北京～后继续飞行。*The plane refueled at Beijing and flew on.* ③ make more effort: 请你在功课上再加点油。*Please put more effort into your school work.*
【加载】loading; straining; stressing: ～电压 *onload voltage* / ～天线 *loaded antenna*
【加重】① make or become heavier; increase the weight: ～任务 *add to one's tasks* ② become more serious; aggravate: ～危机 *aggravate the crisis* / 她的病情～了。*Her illness has become more serious.* /寒冷的天气使他的病情～了。*The cold weather aggravated his illness.*
【加罪于人】cast the blame on sb; shift a blame to others

夹 ① press from both sides; place in between: 书里～着一张卡片。*The book has a card inserted in between its leaves.* / 鞋～脚。*The shoe pinches.* ② carry sth under one's arm: ～着书包 *carry a schoolbag under one's arm* ③ place or stay in between: 把这张纸～在相册里 *put the piece of paper in the photo album* ④ mix; mingle: ～在人群里 *mingle with the crowd* ⑤ clip; folder: 发～ *hair clip* / 文件～ *folder; binder* /皮～ *wallet; pocketbook* /衣～ *clothes peg*
see also gā; jiá
【夹板】① boards for pressing sth or holding things together; clamping strap ②【医】splint: 石膏～ *plaster splint* / ～接合 *fish joint*
【夹板气】between two fires; receive pressure from two opposite sides: 受～ *get blamed by both*

sides; caught between two fires
【夹层】【建】mezzanine; double layer
【夹层玻璃】sandwich glass
【夹带】① smuggle; carry in a secret way: ~一封信进/出监狱 smuggle a letter into/out of a prison ② notes taken into an examination
【夹道】① narrow lane; passageway ② line both sides of a street: ~欢迎 line the street to welcome; welcoming crowds lining the streets
【夹缝】a narrow space between two adjacent things; crevice
【夹攻】attack from both sides; converging attack: 内外~attack from within and outside/左右~ under the crossfire from left and right
【夹击】pincer attack; converging attack
【夹角】【数】included angle
【夹紧】fastening motion; gripping; pinch; vise; clamp: 像老虎钳一样~某物 get a vice-like grip on sth
【夹具】【机】clamping apparatus; jig; fixture; holing device
【夹锯】saw pinching
【夹克】jacket
【夹七夹八】incoherent; confused; at random: 他喝得这样醉,说起话来~。He was so drunk that he was quite incoherent.
【夹钳】【机】clam; clamp
【夹枪带棒】with a sting in one's words; lashing out in all directions
【夹生】half-cooked
【夹生饭】① half-cooked rice ② a job (or tsk) still not finished
【夹馅】stuffed (pastry, etc.)
【夹心】with filing: ~饼干 sandwich biscuits /~蛋糕 layer cake / ~糖 bonbon /~涂层 sandwich coat
【夹叙夹议】narration interspersed with comments
【夹杂】be mingled with; be mixed up: 她说话~着南方口音。She speaks with a slight southern accent.
【夹竹桃】【植】(sweet-scented) oleander
【夹注】interlinear notes
【夹子】clip; tongs; clamp; folder; hook: 点心~ cake tongs /晒衣~ clothes peg; clothes pin

伽 see also gā
【伽利略】Galileo, Italian astronomer and physicist: ~望远镜 Galilean glass; Galilean telescope

佳 good; beautiful: 才子~人 gifted scholars and beautiful ladies /风景绝~ extremely beautiful scenery
【佳话】an anecdote or a good deed; a much-told story: 传为~ become an interesting story on everybody's lips
【佳节】happy festival time; joyous festival: 欢度~ celebrate the joyous festival /每逢~倍思亲。On every festive occasion we miss all the more our dear ones far away.
【佳境】① beautiful place ② the most enjoyable or pleasant stage: 渐入~ become more and more pleasant and interesting
【佳句】beautiful line; well-turned phrase
【佳丽】① (of looks, scenery, etc.) beautiful ② [书] beauty; woman with extreme beauty
【佳酿】[书] vintage wine
【佳偶】[书] ① happy married couple: ~天成 a good match as if made in Heaven ② ideal spouse
【佳品】excellent product
【佳期】① wedding (or nuptial) day ② dating time for lovers
【佳趣】good taste and charm
【佳人】[书] beautiful woman; beauty
【佳肴】delicacies; delicious food
【佳音】welcome news; favourable reply: 静候~。I am waiting for the news of your success.
【佳作】a fine piece of writing; an excellent work; masterpieces: 欣赏他的~ appreciate a masterwork of his

珈 (in ancient times) an ornament use by women

枷 cangue, an implement of punishment that is tied around the neck in old times
【枷锁】yoke; shackles; chains; fetters: 打碎封建~ smash the feudal shackles /摆脱奴隶制的~ throw off the chains of slavery

浃 [书] soaked; drenched: 汗流~背 sweat streaming down and drenching one's back; soaked with sweat

痂 scab, dry crust: 结~ form a scab
【痂皮】crust; crusta

家[1] ① family; household: 勤俭持~ be industrious and thrifty in running a family /我们~共有4口人。There are four people in my family. /全~都起得很早。The whole household was up early. ② home: 回~ go home /他~在北京。His home is at Beijing. ③ place where one belongs: 校长出去开会了,不在~。The principal is not in his office — he has just left for a meeting. ④ a person or family engaged in a certain trade or having a certain status: 农~ peasant family /酒~ wine shop /渔~ boatman ⑤ a specialist in a certain field: 艺术~ artist /政治~ politician /作曲~ composer; musician ⑥ school of thought: 儒~ Confucian school /百~争鸣。A hundred schools of thought contend. ⑦ (in card games, etc.) player or contestant: 上~ the player whose turn comes just before /下~ the player whose turn comes next ⑧ my: ~父 my father /~母 my mother ⑨ domestic animal; livestock ⑩ [方] tamed; domesticated: 这兔子已经养~了,不会跑的。This rabbit has been tamed, so it will not run away. ⑪ [量] used of families or enterprises: 两~饭馆 two restaurants /三~商店 three shops ⑫ (Jiā) a surname

家[2] ① used as a suffix to indicate a specified kind of people: 姑娘~ the girls ② [方] used

J

after a man's name, referring to his wife: 老三~ *third son's wife*
【家财】family property; penates
【家产】family property or fortune
【家长里短】[方] domestic chitchat; gossip
【家常】the daily life of a family; domestic trivia: 叙~ *chitchat*; *engage in small talk*
【家常便饭】① homely food; simple meal ② common occurrence; routine; all in the day's work; usual practice
【家常菜】home cooking
【家常话】small talk; chitchat
【家丑】a skeleton in the cupboard (or closet); family scandal; domestic shame
【家丑不可外扬】domestic shame should not be made public; don't wash your dirty linen in public
【家畜】domestic animal; livestock: ~传染病 *murrain* / ~繁殖 *livestock reproduction* / ~流行病 *epizootic* / ~饲料 *feed stripper* / ~医院 *veterinary hospital* / ~用车箱 *stockcar* / ~展览会 *cattle show*
【家传】① handed down from older generation of the family ② spread from one family to another
【家传户诵】become a household word; be sung in every family and chanted in every house
【家传秘方】a secret recipe handed down in the family
【家祠】clan hall; ancestral temple
【家慈】[书][谦] my mother
【家当】[口] family property; family belongings: ~中落。*The means of the family is declining*; *one's family fortunes declined.*
【家底】family property accumulated over a long time: ~薄 *without substantial resources*; *not financially solid* /我的~就这么多。*All my resources are here.*
【家电】household appliance
【家丁】[旧] private retainer in a big family
【家法】① theories and research methods handed down from master to pupil ② domestic discipline in a feudal household ③ a rod or stick for punishing children or servants in a feudal household: ~伺候 *inflict a punishment on a servant or sb*
【家访】a visit to the parents of children at school or young workers
【家风】family custom and tradition
【家父】[谦] my father
【家鸽】pigeon; homing pigeon
【家馆】[旧] family school run for children in rich families
【家规】family rules
【家户】[方] family; household
【家伙】[口] ① tool; utensil; weapon: 这~挺好使。*This is a very handy tool.* ② fellow; guy: 坏~ *villain*; *scoundrel* ③ domestic animal
【家计】[书] family livelihood
【家祭】family ceremony held in memory of the dead
【家家】every family
【家家户户】every family (or household)
【家家有本难念的经】each family has its own problems
【家教】① family education: ~甚严 *be strict with one's children* ② private tutor
【家境】the financial situation (or condition) of a family: ~贫寒 *with one's family in straitened circumstances*
【家具】furniture: 一件~ *a piece of furniture* / ~商 *furnisher* / ~师 *cabinetmaker*
【家眷】① wife and children; one's family ②one's wife
【家君】[书][谦] my father
【家口】member of a family; the number of people in a family
【家累】family burden (or cares)
【家里】① at home; in the family: 他现在在~。*He is at home now.* ②[口] one's wife: 我~不让多喝酒。*My wife always prevents me from drinking much.*
【家门】① the gate of one's house ② [书] family ③ [方] member of the one's own clan or family ④ family background
【家庙】ancestral temple or shrine
【家母】[谦] my mother
【家奴】bond servant (or slave)
【家破人亡】with one's family ruined and its members killed; the members of one's family are partly dispersed and partly dead
【家仆】servant; myrmidon: 忠实的~ *one's obedient servant*
【家谱】family tree; genealogy; pedigree: ~鉴定 *family judging*
【家雀儿】[方] sparrow
【家禽】domestic fowl; poultry: ~霍乱病 *chicken cholera* / ~饲养场 *poultry farm*
【家人】① family member: 我的~都很关心我。*All my family members care about me much.* ② [旧] servant
【家史】family history: 这位老贫农有一本用血泪写成的~。*The old poor peasant has a family history written in blood and tears.*
【家世】[书] family background: ~贫寒 *be of plebeian origin* / ~小说 *saga novel*
【家事】① household affair: 过多的~占用了很多时间,让我无暇从事创作。*Mountains of household affairs occupied so much of my time that I could hardly write.* ② [方] family's financial situation
【家室】① family ② wife ③ [书] house
【家什】[口] utensils, tools, furniture, etc.
【家书】letter to or from home
【家书抵万金】a letter from home is worth ten thousand pieces of gold
【家塾】[旧] family school
【家属】family member: 每人允许带一名~。*One family member is allowed to go along.*
【家鼠】home mouse
【家私】[口] family property or fortune
【家庭】family; household
【家童】[旧] boy servant

【家徒四壁】have nothing but the bare walls in one's house — be extremely destitute; a house empty of all furniture
【家屋】residential house
【家无二主】a house can't have two masters
【家务】household duties：～劳动 *housework*; *household chores* /承担所有的～ *take on all the household duties*
【家乡】hometown; native place
【家乡话】native dialect
【家小】① wife and children ② wife
【家信】letter to or from one's family
【家兄】［谦］my elder brother
【家训】［书］parental instruction
【家宴】family dinner (or reception)
【家养】tame; domesticate
【家业】① family property ②［书］knowledge or skill handed down from one's ancestor
【家用】① family expense ② for household use; domestic：～冰箱 *domestic refrigerator* /～计算机 *home computer* /～录音机 *home recorder*
【家用电器】household appliance
【家喻户晓】known to every family; widely known; known to all
【家园】① home; homeland：重建～ *rebuild one's homeland* /印度是大象的～。*India is the home of elephants.* ②［方］grown in a home garden
【家贼】thief in the family：～难防。*A thief within a house is hard to guard against.*
【家宅】home; homestead
【家长】① head of a family ② parent or guardian of a child：～会 *a parents' meeting*
【家长式】patriarchal
【家长统治】patriarchy
【家长制】patriarchal system
【家长作风】highhanded way of dealing with people
【家珍】family heirloom
【家政】household management
【家种】① cultivated ② grown in one's own garden
【家主】head of a family
【家传】household biography
【家资】family property
【家子】［口］family：这一～就靠他呢！*He supports the whole family.*
【家族】clan; family：我们～在这个村子里住了一百多年了。*Our family has lived in this village for over a hundred years.*

袈

【袈裟】a patchwork outer vestment worn by a Buddhist monk

笑 (in ancient times) chopsticks

嘉 ① good; fine ② praise; commend：精神可～。*The spirit is worthy of praise.* ③ (Jiā) a surname
【嘉宾】honoured guest; welcome guest
【嘉奖】bestow praise, honour or reward：传令～ *cite sb for meritorious service* /给予某人～ *award commendation on sb*
【嘉奖令】citation
【嘉礼】wedding; marriage ceremony
【嘉勉】［书］praise and encourage; urge sb to greater efforts with words of encouragement
【嘉许】［书］praise; approve：值得～的努力 *a pious effort*

jiá

夹 double-layered：～裤 *lined trousers* /～被 *lined quilt*
see also gā; jiā

荚 pod, long seed vessel of peas and beans：豆～ *pod* /皂～ *Chinese honey locust* /槐树～ *the pod of Chinese scholar tree*
【荚果】【植】pod; legume
【荚膜】【植】capsule

戛 ［书］knock gently; tap
【戛戛】［书］① difficult：～乎难哉！*How impossible the job is!* ② new; original; novel：～独创 *have great novelty*
【戛然】［书］① loud and clear twitter：～长鸣 *long and loud cries* ② ～而止 *cease abruptly*; *come to an abrupt end*

铗 ［书］① pincers; tongs ② sword; sabre：长～ *a long sword* ③ the hilt (or handle) of a sword

颊 cheek：两～绯红 *with rosy cheeks* /她奔上楼梯到了六楼，两～涨得通红。*Her cheeks became red after she ran up the stairs to the six floor.*
【颊骨】cheekbone
【颊囊】【动】cheek pouch

蛱

【蛱蝶】a kind of butterfly with wings of various bright-coloured speckles; vanessa

跲 ［书］trip and fall

jiǎ

甲[1] ① the first of the ten Heavenly Stems ② ranking first; surpassing the others：桂林山水～天下。*The mountains and rivers in Guilin are the finest in the world.* ③ (Jiǎ) a surname

甲[2] ① shell; carapace：龟～ *tortoise shell* ② nail：指～ *nail* ③ armour：盔～ *a unit of armour* /装～车 *armoured car* (*or vehicle*)

甲[3] ［旧］a unit of civil administration
【甲板】deck, any of the floors of a ship：前～ *foredeck* /后～ *after deck*; *quarter deck* /上～ *upper deck* /下～ *lower deck* /主～ *main deck* /我们去～上散步吧。*Let's have a walk round the deck.*

【甲板间】between decks
【甲兵】［书］① armour and weaponry; military equipment ② soldier in armour
【甲虫】beetle: ~类 *coleoptera*
【甲醇】【化】carbinol; methanol; methyl alcohol; wood alcohol: ~分解 *methanolysis*
【甲肝】hepatitis A
【甲沟炎】【医】paronychia
【甲骨文】inscriptions on bones or tortoise shells of the Shang Dynasty (c. 16th -11th centuries BC)
【甲级】first rate; Class A
【甲壳】shell; crust
【甲壳动物】crustacean
【甲醛】【化】formaldehyde: ~尿素 *urea formaldehyde* / ~溶液 *formalin; formaldehyde solution* / ~水 *formalin*
【甲烷】【化】firedamp; methane: ~细菌 *methane bacteria* / ~指示计 *metanometer*
【甲午战争】Sino-Japanese War of 1894-1895
【甲鱼】soft-shelled turtle
【甲羽】vane
【甲晕】half moon
【甲胄】［书］armour
【甲状腺】【生】thyroid gland

岬 ① promontory; cape ② a narrow passage between two mountains
【岬角】cape; promontory; bill; nook

胛 either of the parts behind the shoulders
【胛骨】shoulder blade, either of the flat triangular bones of the upper back
【胛子】［方］shoulder

钾 【化】potassium (K): 苯基~ *phenyl potassium* / 乙基~ *ethyl potassium*
【钾肥】potash fertilizer

假 ① false; fake; bogus; counterfeit: ~和平 *phoney peace* / 弄虚作~ *fiddler; falsification* / 以~乱真 *mix the false with the genuine* ② suppose; presume ③ if; supposing ④ borrow; avail oneself of: 狐~虎威 *bully people by borrowing one's powerful connections*
see also jià
【假扮】disguise oneself as; dress up as: 他~成一女子。*He disguised himself as a woman.*
【假币】false coin; faked (or forged) money
【假臂】arm-prosthesis
【假钞】forged note; counterfeit note
【假充】pretend to be; pose as: ~内行 *pretend to be an expert* / ~英雄 *pose as a hero*
【假传圣旨】deliver a false imperial edict — give a fake order
【假窗】blank window
【假慈悲】crocodile tears; insincere sorrow: 当他知道她被解雇了时, ~了一阵。*He shed crocodile tears when he knew she was fired.*
【假道】via; by way of: ~伦敦的旅行 *travel via London*
【假定】① suppose; grant; assume: ~这是真的 *assume this to be true* / ~我们赢了彩票。*Suppose we win the lottery.* / 我们~他通过了考试。*We grant that he has passed the exam.* ② hypothesis
【假动作】【体】deceptive movement; feint
【假发】wig; hairpiece; toupee: 戴~ *wear a wig*
【假分数】【数】improper fraction
【假峰】apparent front
【假负载】false load; dummy load
【假根】【植】rhizoid
【假公济私】job; jobbery; gain private ends in a public cause; seek one's own profit in public affairs
【假拱】【建】false arch; blind arch
【假果】【植】pseudocarp; false fruit
【假花】artificial flower
【假话】lie; falsehood: 你的~给自己带来麻烦。*You have lied yourself into trouble.* / 你怎能说出这种~? *How can you utter such falsehoods?*
【假借】① make use of outside forces; use false pretences: ~他人名义 *under the guise of other's name* ②【语】phonetic loan characters ③［书］be tolerant towards; bear with: 对于坏人坏事,他从不~。*He never tolerates any evildoers and evil deeds.*
【假近视】pseudomyopia
【假科学】pseudoscience
【假哭】crocodile tears; snivel; weep Irish
【假令】［书］in case
【假冒】pass oneself off as; palm off (a fake as genuine): ~他人专利 *pass off the patent* / ~酒 *fake spirits*
【假寐】［书］catnap; doze: 他~了大约一小时。*He dozed (off) for about an hour.*
【假面】mask; false front
【假面具】① mask; false front ② hypocrisy; pretence: 摘下~ *throw off one's mask*
【假面舞会】masked ball; masquerade
【假名】① pseudonym; false name ② kana; a Japanese syllabary: 片~ *katakana* / 平~ *hiragana*
【假命题】false statement; false proposition
【假模假式】put on an act; pretend to be serious
【假年轮】false annual ring
【假皮】imitation leather
【假仁假义】hypocrisy; sham kindness and goodness
【假妊娠】false pregnancy; pseudo-pregnancy
【假如】if; in case; on condition that: ~有人来电话,就说我不在家。*If anyone calls tell them I'm not at home.*
【假若】if; suppose; in case: ~你学过打字,就容易找工作了。*If you learned to type you would easily find a job.*
【假嗓子】falsetto
【假山】rockery: ~花园 *rock garden*
【假设】① suppose; assume; grant: 我们大家可以一起走 —— ~其他人不耽搁的话。*We can all leave together — assuming that the others aren't late.* / ~有个公司想出售一种新的早餐麦片粥。*Suppose a company has a new breakfast cereal to sell.* ② fiction ③ hypothesis: 科学~ *a scientific hypothesis*
【假声】【音】falsetto

【假声带】false vocal cord
【假使】if; in case: ~那是真的,我们该怎么办呢? *If that is true, what should we do?*
【假释】【律】parole; release on probation: ~犯 *parolee*
【假手】① do sth through sb else ② artificial hand; hand prosthesis
【假手于人】through the instrumentality of sb else; make sb else to do the job; transfer
【假数】【数】mantissa
【假说】hypothesis; premise; presumption
【假死】①【医】suspended animation; asphyxia ②【动】play possum (or dead); feign death: ~状态 *torpor; thanatosis*
【假托】① on the pretext of; on the presence of: 他~身体不佳先走了。*He left before the others on the pretext of ill health.* ② pass oneself off as ③ by means of; through the medium of: 职位空缺可~报纸公之于众。*Vacant positions can be made known through the medium of the press.*
【假戏真做】a false thing becomes true
【假想】imagination; hypothesis; supposition
【假想敌】【军】imaginary enemy; hypothetical foe
【假想作业】dummy activity
【假响应】spurious response
【假象】① false appearance: 识破~ *see through a false appearance* /给人以~ *give a false impression* ②【地】pseudomorph
【假小子】tomboy
【假惺惺】hypocritically; unctuously: ~的夸奖 *hypocritical praise* /他们的友好完全是~的。*Their friendliness was only pretence.*
【假眼】ocular prosthesis; artificial eye
【假药】imitation (of fake) medicine
【假以辞色】speak to someone kindly and encouragingly
【假意】① unction; insincerity; hypocrisy: 虚情~ *put up a phoney show; be pure hypocrisy* ② pretend: ~奉承 *cheap flattery*
【假孕】【医】pseudocyesis
【假造】① forge; counterfeit: ~证件 *forge a certificate* ② invent; fabricate: 他们~证据并威胁目击者。*They fabricated evidence and threatened witnesses.* /他为缺席~了一个巧妙的借口。*He invented an ingenious excuse for his absence.*
【假账】false account
【假正经】hypocrisy; prudery
【假肢】artificial limb
【假装】pretend; make believe; make as if; put on; fake sth: 老板进来时他~在看一份重要的文件。*He pretended to be reading an important paper when the boss entered.*

檟 (in ancient books) Chinese catalpa or tea tree

jià

价 ① price: 减~ *reduce the prices; mark down* /廉~ *sale price; cheapness* /无~之宝 *invaluable asset* ② worth; value: 等~交换 *exchange of equal values* /估~ *evaluate; appraise* ③【化】valence: 共~ *covalence* /原子~ *atomic valence* /氧是二~元素。*Oxygen is a two-valence element.*
see also jiè; jie
【价格】price: 浮动~ *floating price* /优惠~ *favoured price* /调整~ *readjust a price* /每种型号的~显示在荧光屏上。*The price of each model is shown on the screen.*
【价款】cost; money for sth sold
【价码】[口] price: 你认为这个~合理吗? *Do you think the price is reasonable?*
【价目】market price: ~表 *price list*
【价内税】taxes included in the calculated prices
【价签】price tag
【价钱】price: ~公道 *a fair price* /那幢房子因~太高而卖不出去。*The house didn't sell because the price was too high.*
【价态】valence state
【价外税】taxes not included in the calculated prices
【价位】price level; price
【价值】① value: 变现~ *cash realizable value* /垫付~ *advanced value* /估计~ *assessed value* /核定~ *authorized value* /交换~ *exchange value* /偶然~ *accidental value* /清算~ *abandonment value* /商业~ *commercial value* /调整~ *adjust value* ② worth; cost; value: 毫无~ *worthless; count for nothing; not worth a continental* /你的建议很有~。*Your advice has been of great value.*
【价值连城】invaluable; priceless: ~的绘画作品 *invaluable paintings* /~的珠宝 *priceless jewels*
【价值量】magnitude of value

驾 ① harness; draw (a cart, etc.): 并~齐驱 *run neck and neck* ② drive; operate: ~飞机 *pilot a plane* /腾云~雾 *speed across the sky; ride the clouds* ③a general term for vehicles in ancient times: 劳~。*Excuse me.* /大~光临。*You honour us with your presence.* ④ the emperor's cart, referring to the emperor: 保~ *escort the emperor* /候~ *wait for your arrival*
【驾崩】(of an emperor) pass away; die
【驾到】arrive
【驾临】your arrival; your esteemed presence: 恭候~。*Your presence is requested.*
【驾轻就熟】do a familiar job with ease; handle a job with ease because of previous experience
【驾驶】drive; sail; pilot: ~轮船 *pilot a ship* /~飞机 *pilot a plane* /小心~。*Drive with caution!*
【驾驶舱】【航】control cabin; cockpit
【驾驶员】driver; pilot: 作为一个~,你千万不能酒后开车。*As a driver, you mustn't drive after drinking wine.*
【驾驶执照】driving licence; driver's licence

【驾驭】① drive ② control; master; dominate: ~自己的命运 *master one's destiny*

【驾辕】pull a cart or carriage from between the shafts; be hitched up

【驾云】① fly in the air by magic; levitate ② walking on air; treading on air

架 ① frame; shelf; etc.: 窗~ *window frame* / 脸盘~ *washstand* / 行李~ *luggage rack* / 衣~ *clothes hanger* / 书~ *bookcase*; *bookshelf*; *bookstack*; *bookstand* ② erect; put up: ~电话线 *set up telephone lines* / ~桥 *put up (or build) a bridge* ③ fend off; ward off: 难以招~ *be hard to ward off one's blows* ④ kidnap; abduct: 强行~走 *carry sb away by force* ⑤ support; help: 他受伤了,咱们~着他走吧。*He is wounded; let's help him to walk.* ⑥ fight; quarrel: 劝~ *try to part quarrelling*; *mediate* ⑦ [量] usu. for things with machinery or on a tripod or a stand: 一~飞机 *a plane*

【架不住】[方] ① cannot sustain (the weight); cannot stand (the pressure): 这椅子~这么重的东西。*The chair cannot sustain such heavy weight.* ② be no match for; fail to compete with: 情况再复杂,也~我们准确的判断。*However complicated the situation is, it is no match for our exact judgement.*

【架次】sortie: 出动飞机30~ *fly thirty sorties*

【架得住】[方] can bear (or stand): 这点压力,我~。*I can bear the pressure definitely.*

【架构】① build; construct: ~一座桥 *to construct a bridge* ② framework; scaffold: 这座跨江大桥是钢骨~。*This bridge over the river has a steel framework.* ③ structure; pattern; configuration: 理论~ *framework of the theory* / 语法~ *grammar structure*

【架空】① built on stilts; aerial; overhead: ~管道 *overhead pipe* / ~铁路 *overhead railway* ② impractical; unpractical: 这个理论实际上是~的。*In fact, the theory is impractical.* ③ kick upstairs; make sb a puppet (or tool); render unfeasible

【架设】erect; put up: 在两条河之间~起一座桥。*A new bridge has been set up between the two rivers.*

【架势】① posture; stance; manner: 摆出一副盛气凌人的~ *assume a domineering posture* ② [方] judge by the appearances of things

【架线】stringing: ~工 *lineman*; *overhead line worker*

【架秧子】[方] kick up a row: 他没有什么主意,只会起哄~。*He is not resourceful at all; all he can do is creating a disturbance.*

【架子】① shelf; rack; frame: 洗衣房的晾衣~ *drying rack for laundry* / 他把书从~上拿走。*He took the book off the shelf.* ② outline; framework: 他先把所画物体的~画在纸上。*He drew the outline of the objects on the paper at first.* ③ airs; arrogant manner: 他因为知识丰富而喜欢摆~。*He always puts on high airs with his learning.* ④ stance; posture: 一看他做饭的~,就知道他是内行。*I know he must be a dab hand at the sight of his cooking posture.*

假 holiday; vacation: 病~ *sick leave* / 放~ *have a holiday or vacation* / 事~ *leave of absence* / 请一天~ *have a day off* / 目前史密斯先生正在度~。*Mr. Smith is on holiday at present.* see also jiǎ

【假期】① vacation; holidays: 我一年有四个星期的~。*I can get four weeks holiday a year.* ② period of leave

【假日】holidays; day off: 法定~ *official holidays* / 最近持续的坏天气总是破坏我的~。*The continuous bad weather in these days always spoiled my vacations.*

【假条】① application for leave ② leave permit: 病~ *doctor's certificate for sick leave*

嫁 ① (of a woman) marry; get married: 她母亲要把她~给一个诚实的小伙子。*Her mother will marry her to an honest man.* ② shift; transfer (disaster or hatred): ~怨 *shift the hatred to sb else*

【嫁祸于人】shift the misfortune onto sb else; put the blame on sb else

【嫁鸡随鸡,嫁狗随狗】[旧] once a girl has married, she must be faithful to his husband forever

【嫁接】【植】graft: 将一个品种~到另一个品种上 *graft one variety on (or in) another* / 同类~ *congenial graft* / 自然~ *natural graft* / 异种~ *heteroplastic graft*; *xenoplastic graft*

【嫁娶】marriage

【嫁人】[口] (of a woman) get married; marry: 她两年前就已经~了。*She got married two years ago.*

【嫁妆】dowry; trousseau: 老两口为女儿置办了一份丰厚的~。*The old couple dowered their daughter lavishly.*

稼 ① sow: 耕~ *ploughing and sowing* ② grain; cereals; crops: 庄~ *crops*

【稼穑】[书] sowing and reaping, a general term for farm work

jiān

尖 ① pointed; tapering: 把铅笔削~了。*Have the pencil sharpened.* ② (of voice) shrill; piercing: ~声~气 *in a shrill voice* ③ (of senses) keen; sharp: 眼~ *have sharp eyes*; *have a keen sight* / 耳朵~ *have sharp ears* ④ make (one's voice, etc.) shrill or sharp: ~着嗓子 *in a shrill voice* ⑤ point; tip (small or sharp end): 笔~儿 *nib*; *pen-point* / 针~儿 *the point of a needle* / 指~ *fingertip* ⑥ (of people or things) the best of the same kind; the cream: ~儿货 *goods of the best quality* ⑦ [方] stingy; miserly: 这人太~,一点都不吃亏。*He is a meanie, always trying to profit at others' expense.* ⑧ sharp-tongued; caustic

【尖兵】①【军】point; vanguard: ~连 *point (or*

vanguard) *company* ② trailblazer; pathbreaker; pioneer:科学种田的～*pioneers in scientific farming*

【尖刀】sharp knife; dagger

【尖点】【数】cusp; cuspidal point:～轨迹 *cuspidal locus* /～指数 *cusped index*

【尖顶】pinnacle; acme; tip:～部 *ogival*; *ogive*

【尖顶帽】peaked cap; cap with a visor

【尖顶饰】【建】finial

【尖端】① tip; point; pointed end; external point; nib; acme:天线的～*the point of the antenna* ② advanced; sophisticated:～技术 *sophisticated technique*

【尖峰】【物】spike; peak:～电压 *spike voltage* /～现象 *spike phenomenon* /～性能 *spiking behaviour*

【尖拱】【建】pointed arch

【尖叫】scream; yell:痛得～*yell with pain* /她害怕地～起来。*She screamed with fear.*

【尖刻】acrimonious; caustic; biting; barbed:～的言论 *caustic remarks* /引起～的批评 *excite scathing comment* /他的话并不～。*His words had no bite.*

【尖口钳】clipper

【尖括号】angle brackets (< >)

【尖冷】biting cold; piercing cold

【尖厉】(of voice or sound) piercing; high-pitched:～的叫声 *a shrill cry*

【尖利】① sharp; keen; cutting; edgy:～的刀 *a sharp knife* /针头～的针 *a needle with a sharp point* ② shrill; piercing:～的笛声 *a shrill whistle*

【尖溜溜】[方] very sharp:～的嗓子 *a sharp voice*

【尖嫩】(of voice) thin and delicate

【尖劈】wedge

【尖锐】① keen; sharp-pointed:像刺刀一样～*as keen as razors* ② sharp; keen; biting; penetrating:～的批评 *incisive criticism* /～的观察 *a penetrating observation* /他的评语非常～。*His remark has a biting edge to it.* ③ shrill; piercing:～的声音 *a shrill sound* (*or voice*) ④ intense; sharp; acute:～的思想斗争 *sharp mental conflicts*

【尖酸】pungent; acrimonious; tart:～的讥讽 *pungent satire* /～的讽刺作品 *mordant satire* /他的反驳带着强烈的～口气。*His retort was delivered with a strong note of vinegar.*

【尖酸刻薄】tart and mean; bitterly sarcastic:她总是用～的语言挖苦人。*She always uses bitter sarcasm.*

【尖头】sharp point; tip

【尖头棒】gad

【尖子】① point; tip ② top; the best of its kind; the cream of the crop:～学生 *outstanding student*; *top student* ③ sudden rise in pitch (in opera singing)

【尖子班】class of top students

【尖钻】pointed drill; awl

【尖嘴薄舌】have a caustic and flippant tongue

【尖嘴猴腮】pointed mouth and ape's cheek — have a wretched appearance

【尖嘴钳】long flat nose pliers

【尖嘴鱼】pipefish

奸[1] ① wicked; evil ② betray one's country or monarch ③ traitor:汉～*traitor* (*to China*) /内～*a secret enemy agent within one's ranks*; *hidden traitor* ④ crafty:藏～耍滑 *hide the evil intention by acting in a slick way*

奸[2] illicit sexual relations:通～*commit adultery*

【奸臣】treacherous court official; traitor minister:～当道。*The treacherous court officials govern the state.*

【奸党】cabal; clique or person disloyal to the country or certain monarch

【奸恶】[书] sly and evil

【奸夫】adulterer; intrigant

【奸妇】adulteress; paramour

【奸猾】treacherous; crafty; deceitful

【奸计】trickery; an evil plot:他们设～陷害皇后。*They plotted against the queen.* /他所有的～注定要失败。*All his intrigues are doomed to failure.*

【奸佞】[书] ① crafty and flattering ② crafty sycophant

【奸情】adulterous affair; amour

【奸人】evildoer; malefactor

【奸商】profiteer; sharp-shooter

【奸徒】perfidious person

【奸污】rape; seduce:～妇女 *rape a woman*

【奸细】spy; enemy agent:狡猾的阴谋家可以成为最好的～。*Crafty plotters make the best intelligence agents.*

【奸险】wicked and crafty; malicious; treacherous

【奸笑】sinister smile; villainous smile

【奸邪】[书] ① crafty and evil; treacherous ② crafty and evil person

【奸雄】a person who achieves high position by unscrupulous scheming; arch-careerist

【奸淫】① illicit sexual relations ② rape; seduce:～罪 *carnal intercourse*

【奸贼】traitor; conspirator

【奸诈】fraudulent; crafty treacherous:～的人 *a man of deceit* /他用～的手段取得了那个职位。*He got the position by fraudulent means.*

歼 annihilate; exterminate; wipe out; destroy:全～灭入侵敌人 *destroy all the intruding enemy*

【歼轰机】【军】strike fighter

【歼击】attack and destroy

【歼击机】fighter plane; fighter

【歼灭】annihilate; wipe out; destroy:在这次袭击中敌军被彻底～了。*The enemy force was annihilated completely during the attack.*

【歼灭射击】annihilation fire

【歼灭战】war of annihilation

坚 ① strong; solid; hard:其～无比 *as hard as a brick*; *adamant* ② a heavily fortified point; strong-hold:攻～战 *storming of heavily fortified positions* /无～不摧 *all-conquering*; *overrun all*

J

fortifications ③ firmly; resolutely: 意志~定 *be resolute* ④ (Jiān) a surname

【坚壁】place in a cache; cache: 把粮食~起来 *hide grain from the enemy*

【坚壁清野】strengthen defences and clear the fields; leave no provisions for the enemy

【坚不可摧】indestructible; invincible; resistant; unconquerable; unbeatable: ~的信念 *indestructible faith* / ~的堡垒 *an impregnable fortress*

【坚持】insist (on); stick (or hold) to; keep up; persist in; uphold; adhere to: 我们~自力更生。*We insist on (or upon) self-reliance.* / 他一直~学习英语。*He persists in the study of English.* / 我们将~按计划行事。*We will adhere to our plan.*

【坚持不懈】hold on consistently; unremitting: 通过~的努力,他终于通过了考试。*He finally passed the examination by unremitting efforts.*

【坚持不渝】persevering; persistent: 我们~地支持你们的正义斗争。*We perseveringly support the just struggles of yours.*

【坚持己见】stubbornly and arbitrarily cling to one's own course: 在这个问题上,他~。*He held on to his own views on this issue.*

【坚定】① firm; resolute; steady; staunch: 有~的生活目的 *have a firm purpose in life* / ~的革命者 *a staunch revolutionary* ② strengthen; fortify: ~信念 *fortify one's conviction*

【坚定不移】constant; keep a stiff upper lip; unswerving; hold the line; unrelenting: ~的信仰 *an unshakable faith* / ~的奉献 *unswerving devotion*

【坚固】solid; strong; firm; sturdy: ~的联盟 *a firm ally* / 新建的大桥非常~。*The new bridge is a very solid construction.*

【坚固性】sturdiness; ruggedness

【坚果】【植】nut; nut fruit: 我喜欢吃~。*I like to eat nuts.*

【坚决】adamant; determined; firm; resolute: ~反对 *resolutely oppose* / 他下了决心,~惩治那些贪官污吏。*He was adamant in his determination to punish the corrupt officials.*

【坚苦】arduous; difficult; tough

【坚苦卓绝】tireless and indomitable; showing the utmost fortitude: ~的战争 *an extremely hard and bitter war*

【坚牢】solid; strong: ~的基础 *a solid base*

【坚强】① strong; firm: 表明自己~的决心 *declare one's strong determination* ② strengthen: ~国防 *strengthen national defence*

【坚强不屈】firm and unyielding

【坚忍】steadfast and persevering

【坚韧】tough and tensile; firm and tenacious: 这种新型材料很~。*This new kind of material is very tenacious.*

【坚忍不拔】firm and indomitable; unyielding; invincible: ~的勇气 *indomitable courage*

【坚如磐石】solid as a rock; as steady as a rock: 我们的决心~。*Our determination is as solid as rocks.*

【坚实】① solid; substantial: 只有打下~的基础,才能进行下一步的学习。*You cannot further your study unless a solid foundation is laid.* ② strong; sturdy: 他的体格~。*He is a man of substantial build.*

【坚守】stick to; hold fast to; stand fast: 节日期间我们~岗位。*We stuck to one's post in holidays.*

【坚挺】① strong and powerful ②【经】strong: 市场上美元~。*The US Dollar is strong in the market.*

【坚信】firmly believe; be firmly convinced; be fully confident of: 他~这一理论。*He has infinite faith in this theory.* / 我们~他会打败对手。*We firmly believe that he will beat his opponent.*

【坚信不疑】firmly believe: 大家对他的诚实~。*All have profound faith in his honesty.*

【坚毅】firm and persistent: ~的面容 *a firm countenance*

【坚硬】hard; solid: 这种木头十分~。*This kind of wood is very hard.*

【坚贞】faithful; constant; loyal: 她是个~的妻子。*She is a faithful wife.*

【坚贞不屈】remain faithful and unyielding; stand firm and unbending: 面对酷刑,革命者~。*Facing cruel torture, the revolutionary remained firm and faithful.*

间 ① between; among: 彼此~ *between each other* / 劳资之~ *between labour and capital* ② within a definite place, time, or crowd of people: 田~ *field; farm* / 晚~ *in the evening; at night* ③ room: 车~ *workshop* / 衣帽~ *cloakroom* ④[量] used for room: 一~房 *a room* / 一~卧室 *a bedroom*

see also jiàn

【间不容发】not a hair's breadth in between — the situation is extremely critical

【间架】① framework or structure of a house ② structure of a Chinese character ③ structure of an essay

【间距】interval; separation; spacing; space between: 一英里的~ *the space of a mile*

【间量】[方] area of a room; floor space

【间奏曲】【音】intermezzo

浅

see also qiǎn

【浅浅】[书][象] the sound of flowing water

肩 ① shoulder: ~并~ *side by side* ② take on; shoulder; undertake: 身~重任 *shoulder great responsibilities* ③[方] carry on the shoulder: ~起扁担 *carry the pole on one's shoulder*

【肩膀】shoulder: 耸~ *shrug one's shoulders* / 他~宽阔。*He is a man with broad shoulders.*

【肩带】aiguillette; baldric; sash

【肩负】take on; undertake; bear; shoulder: ~光荣任务 *undertake a glorious task*

【肩关节】shoulder joint

【肩胛】[书] shoulder

【肩痛】【医】omalgia

【肩头】① on the shoulder：我们～的担子不轻。*The responsibilities on our shoulders are very heavy.* ②［方］shoulder：他两个～不一样高。*He has one shoulder a little higher than the other.*
【肩窝】hollow part of the shoulder
【肩炎】【医】omitis
【肩章】shoulder-strap; shoulder loop; shoulder ornament
【肩周炎】【医】periarthritis
【肩注】【印】shoulder notes

艰 difficult; hard：步履维～ *walk with great difficulty*
【艰巨】arduous; formidable; onerous：～的任务 *an arduous task*
【艰苦】arduous; difficult; hard：～创业 *pioneer an enterprise with painstaking efforts* /一次长期、～而疲惫不堪的战争 *a long, arduous, and exhausting war.*
【艰苦奋斗】work hard; struggle hard amid difficulties
【艰苦朴素】hard work and plain living; be plain in one's style of living
【艰苦卓绝】the utmost fortitude; extremely hard and bitter
【艰难】difficult; hard：在～的岁月里成长 *be brought up in difficult days*
【艰难困苦】difficulties and hardships：这位老人尝遍了～。*The old man has endured all kinds of difficulties and hardships.* /～，玉汝于成。*Difficulty is the nurse of greatness.*
【艰难曲折】difficulties and setbacks：成功的路上总会有～。*Difficulties and hardships can be always found on the way to success.*
【艰难险阻】difficulties and obstacles; hardships and dangers
【艰涩】intricate and obscure：文字～ *involved and abstruse writing*
【艰深】difficult to understand; abstruse：这篇文章对小学生来说过于～。*This article is too abstruse for pupils.*
【艰危】difficulties and dangers
【艰险】hardships and dangers：不避～ *in spite of all difficulties and perils*
【艰辛】hardships：历尽～ *experience all kinds of hardships; go through all kinds of tribulations*

监 ① supervise; inspect ② prison：收～ *take into custody; put in prison* /女～ *women's prison*
see also jiàn
【监测】monitor; observe and measure：环境～ *monitoring the environment* /我们会在夜间～病人的状况看情况是否有好转。*We will be monitoring the patient's progress during the night to see if there is any improvement in his condition.*
【监测器】monitor：电动～ *electric monitor* /定位～ *fixed site monitor* /空气微粒～ *air particle monitor* /通道～ *doorway monitor* /污染～ *contamination monitor*
【监察】supervise; control; inspect
【监场】invigilate or monitor in an examination
【监督】① supervise; control; monitor; oversee：～部门 *supervisory department* /～调查组 *supervise a team of investigators* /接受人民～ *subject oneself to supervision by the masses* /项目经理在～一个项目小组的工作。*The project manager oversees a group of programming staff.* ② supervisor; foreman：安全～ *safety supervisor*
【监犯】prisoner; convict; inmate：～每天锻炼一个小时。*The prisoners get an hour of exercise each day.*
【监房】prison; jail：很多～已经人满为患。*Many prisons are now seriously overcrowded.*
【监工】① supervise work; oversee ②supervisor; overseer; overlooker; foreman：这个～非常严格但很公平。*The supervisor was a strict but very fair man.*
【监管】keep watch on; supervise and control
【监规】prison regulations
【监护】①【律】guardianship; tutelage ② observe, tend and nurse：这个病人必须二十四小时～。*The patient needs nursing round the clock.*
【监护权】【律】guardianship：被授予孩子～的成年人 *an adult who is given custody of the child*
【监护人】guardian; guarder：她是这个孤儿的～。*She acts as a guardian for the orphan.*
【监禁】take into custody; imprison; put in jail; put in prison; imprisonment; incarcerate; intern; detention：他被～了两年。*He was imprisoned for two years.*
【监考】① invigilate; monitor examinations：～历史 *invigilate (at) a history exam* ② monitor; invigilator：他是这个考场的～。*He is the invigilator of the examination hall.*
【监考人】invigilator
【监控】① monitor and control：～程序 *monitor routine* ② supervise and control
【监牢】prison; jail：他因盗窃在～中度过了一年。*He spent a year in jail on a charge of theft.*
【监理】inspect and handle; supervise
【监票】scrutinize balloting
【监票人】scrutineer; ballot examiner
【监舍】prison house; cell：这就是囚禁他多年的～。*Here is the cell where he was incarcerated for many years.*
【监事】supervise; member of a supervisory committee：～会 *board of supervisors*
【监视】watch; keep watch on; scout; keep sb under surveillance; keep sb under observation：～敌人的行动 *keep watch on the movements of the enemy*
【监视器】monitor：闭路～ *closed-circuit monitor* /电视波形～ *a television wave form monitor* /晶体～ *crystal monitor* /视频～ *video monitor* /误差～ *error monitor* /序列～ *sequence monitor*
【监视人】guard; sentinel
【监视哨】【军】supervisor
【监视卫星】surveillance satellite
【监视信号】supervisory signal

【监视站】monitoring station
【监守】take care of; guard
【监守自盗】embezzle; defalcate; misappropriate; custodian turned thief; inside job: 他~了大量的钱用于赌博。*He embezzled large amounts of money to finance his gambling.*
【监听】monitoring: 我们一直在~敌方的电台广播,设法查探他们的秘密计划。*We have been monitoring the enemy's radio broadcasts to try to find out their secret plans.*
【监外就医】undergo medical treatment outside the prison under surveillance
【监外执行】executing a sentence outside of jail; serving sentence outside the prison under surveillance
【监押】① imprison; put in jail: 在他~期间,我不能去看他。*I was never able to visit him during his periods of detention.* ② send away under escort
【监狱】prison; jail: 关进~ *throw into prison; put in prison* /他蹲~已5年了。*He has been in prison for five years.*
【监证】check and affirm
【监制】① supervise the manufacture of sth ② supervise the shooting of (films, etc.)

兼 ① double; twice ② simultaneously; concurrently (involving or having more than one): 德才~备 *have both ability and moral integrity* /身~数职 *hold several posts simultaneously*
【兼爱】universal love
【兼备】have both... and...; combine... with...: 德才~ *have both political integrity and ability* /文武~ *be well versed in civilian as well as military affairs*
【兼并】annex; acquire; merger: 土地~ *annexation of land*
【兼程】travel at double speed: ~前进 *advance at the double* /日夜~ *travel day and night*
【兼而有之】have both at the same time
【兼顾】give consideration to (or take account of) two or more things: 公私~ *give consideration to both public and private interests*
【兼毫】Chinese writing brush made of a mixture of weasel's and goat's hair
【兼课】① do some teaching in addition to one's main occupation ② hold two or more teaching jobs concurrently
【兼人】[书] one person who is equal to two
【兼任】① hold a concurrent post ② do part-time job
【兼容】① embrace all; be tolerant: ~并包 *include in one and monopolize it; all embracing* ②【物】compatible: ~计算机 *compatible computer* /~硬件 *compatible hardware*
【兼容并包】absorb anything and everything
【兼容性】compatibility: ~检验 *compatibility test*
【兼善天下】benefit all the people in the world: 达则~。*If a person is successful in his career, he should try his best to benefit all the people.*
【兼施】apply various methods simultaneously: 软硬~ *resort to both soft and hard methods*
【兼听则明,偏信则暗】heed only one side and you will be benighted
【兼优】be good in more than one field
【兼之】[书] furthermore; besides: 这房子太贵,~离上班地点也太远。*The house is too expensive, and furthermore, it's too far from the office.*
【兼职】① hold two or more posts at the same time ② part-time job: ~教师 *part-time teacher (or faculty)*

笺 ① annotation; commentary ② writing paper; small piece of paper: 便~ *notepaper* /信~ *letter paper* ③ letter: 华~ *your esteemed letter*
【笺札】[书] letter; correspondence
【笺纸】writing paper; letter paper
【笺注】[书] notes and commentary on ancient texts

渐 [书] ① soak; be saturated with ② flow into: 东~于海 *flow east and empty into the sea*
see also jiàn
【渐染】[书] be imperceptibly influenced

犍 bullock; castrated bull: 老~ *bullock*
【犍牛】bullock
【犍子】[方] bullock

缄 seal; close: 上海刘~ (*as written on an envelope*) *from Liu in Shanghai*
【缄封】seal a letter
【缄口】[书] keep one's mouth shut; hold one's tongue: ~不言 *keep silent; hold one's tongue* /~结舌 *bite the lip or tongue* /对自己的希望~不谈 *be reticent about one's hope*
【缄密】firmly sealed; shut tight
【缄默】keep silent; be reticent: 保持~ *remain silent* /他对个人生活保持~。*He was close about his personal life.*
【缄札】[书] letter; correspondence

煎 ① fry (in shallow fat): ~鱼 *fried fish* /~豆腐 *fried bean curd* ② simmer in water; decoct: ~药 *decoct medical herbs* ③ [量] (used for herb medicine) decoction: 头~药 *first decoction* /二~药 *second decoction*
【煎熬】suffering; torture: 受尽~ *suffer all kinds of torments* /在不知结果中等待的~ *the torture of waiting in suspense*
【煎逼】force; compel; coerce: ~下的供认 *a confession obtained by force*
【煎饼】thin pancake; battercake
【煎膏】condensed decoction
【煎锅】frying pan
【煎剂】decocta; decoction
【煎饺】fried dumpling
【煎心】be overwhelmed with worry and anxiety: 我父亲有许多~的事。*My father has a lot of worries.*
【煎药】boil medicine; tisane
【煎灼】deeply worried: 他的生意亏本了,内心~。*His business is losing money and he is extremely worried.*

jiǎn

囝 [方] ① son ② son and daughter

拣 select; choose: 挑肥~瘦 *choose whatever is to one's personal advantage* /~好的给我拿几个 *choose the best ones for me* /她就会~好听的说。*She is good at flattering.*

【拣了芝麻丢了西瓜】pick up the sesame seeds but overlook the watermelons — be mindful of minor matters to the neglect of major ones

【拣便宜】buy on the cheap; get the better of a bargain

【拣选】choose; select: ~优质药材 *select the high grade medicine*

【拣择】choose; select: ~吉日成婚 *choose an auspicious day for marriage*

茧 cocoon: 蚕~ *silkworm cocoon* /作~自缚 *become entangled in one's own contradictions* /冬天多数虫子作~。*Most worms cocoon in winter.*

【茧子】①[方] silkworm cocoon ② callus: 手掌上的~ *calluses on one's palms*

柬 general term for letter, visiting card, invitation, etc.: 请~ *invitation card*

【柬埔寨】Cambodia; Kampuchea: ~人 *Cambodia*; *Kampuchean* / ~语 *Cambodia*; *Kampuchean language*

【柬帖】short letter; note

俭 frugal; thrifty: 勤~ *industrious*; *frugal* /省吃~用 *pinch and scrape*; *pinch and screw*

【俭朴】thrifty and simple; economical: 生活~ *lead a thrifty and simple life*

【俭省】frugal; economical: ~的饮食 *a frugal diet* /对能源最~的利用 *the most economical use of energy* /我努力在购物时做到~,只买自己需要的东西。*I'm trying to be more economical when I go shopping, and only buy what I really need.*

【俭以养廉】thrift nourished modesty

【俭约】[书] thrifty; frugal; economical; careful: 他生活~,从不浪费任何东西。*He was a very thrifty man who never wasted anything.*

捡 collect; pick up: ~柴火 *pick up firewood* /~了芝麻,丢了西瓜 *pick up the sesame seeds but overlook the watermelons*; *strain at a gnat and swallow a camel*

【捡漏】【建】repair the leaky part of a roof; plug a leak in the roof

【捡漏儿】[方] find fault (with sb)

【捡破烂儿】pick odds and ends from refuse heaps

【捡拾】collect; pick up: 他~了一些柴火。*He gathered some firewood.*

检 ① examine; check: 体~ *physical check-up* ② restrain oneself ③ (Jiǎn) a surname

【检测】test and determine: 对酸含量进行~ *test for acid content* /对抗体的存在进行~ *test for the presence of an antibody* /老师要~学生的英语水平。*The teacher will examine the students in English.*

【检测器】detector: ~法则 *detector law*

【检查】① examine; inspect; check up (on); go through; go over; look over: ~工作 *check up on work* /~身体 *have a physical examination* /新闻~ *press censorship* /列车员走下火车,~了轨道。*The conductor got off and checked the rails.* /医生给她作了仔细的~。*The doctor examined her carefully.* /他买这辆车之前仔细~了一番。*He inspected the car before he bought it.* ② review; reference; check: 这本词典留着~用。*Keep this dictionary for reference.* ③self-criticism: 他因为多次迟到而写~。*He wrote a self-criticism for being late frequently.*

【检查团】inspection party

【检查员】inspector

【检查站】checkpost; inspection station

【检察】[书] procuratorial work

【检察官】public procurator; public prosecutor; prosecuting attorney

【检察机关】procuratorial organ

【检察院】procuratorate: 军事~ *military procuratorate*

【检察长】chief procurator

【检场】[旧] ① arrange or collect stage property with the curtain up ② person responsible for arranging or collecting stage property when the curtain is up

【检点】① examine; check: ~行李 *check the luggage* ② be cautious or careful: 言行有失~ *be careless about one's words and acts*

【检校】examine and check

【检举】report to the authorities; inform against; impeach: ~盗窃行为 *inform against theft* /他们~他受贿。*They accused him of taking bribes.*

【检举人】accuser; offence-reporter: 我不怕面对我的~,我已经做好准备要证明我的清白。*I am not afraid to meet my accusers and I am prepared to prove my innocence.*

【检举箱】a box for accusation letters

【检举信】letter of accusation

【检漏】【电】leak hunting; leakage detecting: ~器 *leak detector*

【检录】【体】call the roll and guide sportsmen into the arena

【检票】have tickets checked

【检视】check; examine: ~现场 *check the scene*

【检索】look up sth (in books, reference, etc.) retrieve; search: 确定~ *deterministic retrieval* /随机~ *stochastic retrieval* /资料~ *data retrieval*

【检讨】① self-criticism: 作~ *make a self-criticism* ②[书] review; study: ~形势 *to review the situation*

【检修】examine and repair; overhaul: ~机器 *overhaul a machine* /全面~ *a complete overhaul*

【检修周期】overhaul period

【检寻】check and look for

【检验】test; examination; exam; inspect: 运动员的耐力~ *a test of an athlete's endurance* /~商品

质量 *examine the quality of the products* /防火官员定期～大楼。*The building is regularly inspected by a fire-safety officer.*
【检疫】quarantine：实施～ *perform quarantine* /出口～ *export quarantine* /国际～ *international quarantine* /国内～ *internal quarantine* /海港～ *quarantine of a sea-port* /进口～ *import quarantine* /植物～ *plant quarantine*
【检疫员】quarantine officer
【检疫站】quarantine station
【检疫证明书】quarantine certificate; yellow book
【检阅】① review; inspect：～仪仗队 *review a guard of honour* /司令～了部队。*The commander inspected the troops.* ② browse; glance over：～报纸 *browse through the newspaper*
【检阅台】reviewing stand
【检字表】word index
【检字法】【语】indexing system for Chinese characters：部首～ *indexing system by radicals*

减 ① subtract：五～三就得二。*If you subtract 3 from 5, you get 2.* ② decrease; minus：失败使信心渐～。*Lack of success decreases confidence.*
【减编】staff reduction
【减产】reduction of output; drop in production
【减除】wipe out; get rid of
【减低】lower; slow down; reduce：～房租 *lower the rent of a house* /～运费 *freight cutting*
【减法】【数】subtraction：串行～ *subtraction with serial operation* /～电路 *subtraction circuit* /～输出 *subtract output*
【减肥】reduce; lose one's weight：～疗法 *bantingism* /～药丸 *diet pill* /要想～就得多喝水。*To lose weight you need to drink lots of water.*
【减幅】damp; amplitude reduction：～常数 *damping constant* /～电流 *decaying current* /～运动 *weight reducing exercise* /～振荡 *damped oscillation*
【减号】【数】minus sign (-)
【减缓】retard; slow down：～进程 *slow down the pace*
【减价】reduce the price; mark down：～出售 *sell at a reduce price* /～五元 *reduce five yuan from the price*
【减免】① mitigate (a punishment) ② reduce; remit：～某人的学费 *reduce sb's tuition* /～债务 *abate a debt*
【减轻】lighten; ease; alleviate; mitigate; abate：这药～了他的痛苦。*The medicine abated his pain.* /我能～你的负担吗? *Can I ease you of your burden?*
【减却】go down; drop
【减去】minus：30～10是20。*30 minus ten leaves 20.*
【减热】abstraction of heat
【减弱】weaken; bate; lower; slack; trail off：暴风雨正在～。*The storm is weakening.* /随着黄昏的来临,光线逐渐～。*Light lessens as evening comes on.* /他的声音～成耳语。*His voice sank to a whisper.*
【减色】impair the excellence of; lose luster：盗窃行为使他的形象大为～。*Theft spoiled his image greatly.*
【减杀】weaken; lessen; reduce
【减少】reduce; lessen; decrease：～编制 *reduce the staff* /～风险 *reduce risks* /据说这位经验丰富的老编辑能把印刷错误几乎～到零。*This experienced editor is said to be able to reduce the misprints to almost nil.* /节假日行人车辆～了。*Traffic decreases on holidays.*
【减湿】dehumidify：～器 *dehumidifier*
【减数】【数】subtrahend
【减税】abatement of tax; tax abatement; tax reduction：～让利 *reduce tax on enterprises and allow them to retain more profits*
【减速】slow down; decelerate; retard：汽车～过桥。*The motorcar slowed up over the bridge.*
【减速度】deceleration
【减速阀】deceleration valve
【减损】decrease; reduce; cut down：增益～ *increase profit and reduce loss*
【减缩】reduce; cut down：必须～用煤量。*It is necessary to decrease the amount of coal used.*
【减退】go down; drop; subside：那支球队的胜利所激起的狂热之情没有～。*The wild enthusiasm the team's victory aroused did not subside.*
【减薪】reduce salary
【减刑】【律】reduce a penalty; commute a sentence; mitigate a sentence; abatement from penalty
【减削】cut down; reduce：～经费 *cut down the outlay*
【减压】reduce pressure; decompress：～变压器 *negative boosting transformer* /～舱 *deck decompression chamber* /～装置 *decompressor; reliever*
【减员】① depletion of numbers; personnel reduction：战斗～ *depletion of combat strength* ② cut down the number of personnel
【减灾】reduction of natural disasters
【减震】shock absorption; damping：～板 *vibration damper plate* /～材料 *vibration-absorptive material* /～架 *dynamic mount* /～力 *damping force* /～筒 *damper cylinder* /～作用 *cushioning effect*

剪 ① scissors; clippers; shears：电～ *electric scissors* ② anything like scissors：火～ *firetongs* ③ cut with scissors; clip; trim：～树篱 *shear a hedge* /～羊毛 *shear a sheep* /从杂志上～下一篇文章 *clip an article from a magazine* ④ wipe out; exterminate
【剪报】① cut out (useful information) from newspaper ② press clipping
【剪裁】① cut out (a garment)：这条裙子～得很好。*The dress was well cut.* ② prune; cut out unwanted material：这篇文章还需要～。*You still have to do a lot of pruning on this article.*
【剪彩】cut the ribbon at an opening ceremony：～仪式 *ribbon-cutting ceremony* /各有关部门的领导同志出席了～仪式。*Leading comrades of various departments concerned were present at the ribbon-*

cutting ceremony.

【剪草机】grass (or lawn) mower

【剪除】wipe out; annihilate; exterminate: 我们～消灭了敌人的力量。*We annihilated the enemy.*

【剪刀】scissors; shears: 一把～ *a pair of scissors*

【剪刀差】scissors movement of prices; scissors difference: 价格～ *price scissors* /缩小～ *narrow the price scissors*

【剪断】cut through; nip off; shear off: 有人在夜里～了绳子,现在船已经跑了。*Somebody had cut the rope during the night and now the boat was gone.*

【剪辑】①【影】montage; film editing: ～导演 *montage director* /～车间 *film-editing department* ② recut; re-edit: 电影录音～ *highlights of a live recording of a film*

【剪接】montage; film editing

【剪力】shearing force: 冲击～ *impact shear* /纯～ *pure shear* /负～ *negative shear* /惯性～ *inertia shear* /有效～ *effective shear* /正～ *positive shear* /组合～ *combined shear* /～波 *shear wave* /～墙 *shear wall* /～曲线 *curve of shearing force*

【剪毛】shearing; clipping

【剪灭】wipe out; exterminate: ～异己 *wipe out the dissident*

【剪票】punch a ticket: 不久列车员走过来～了。*Soon the guard on the train came and clipped our tickets.*

【剪切】【机】shearing: ～层 *shear layer* /～冲头 *cutting punch* /～面积 *section of shear* /～阻力 *shearing resistance*

【剪切力】【物】shearing force

【剪贴】① clip and paste (in a scrapbook or on cards) ② cut out

【剪压力】shearing pressure

【剪影】① paper-cut silhouette ② outline; sketch

【剪枝】【林】lopping; pruning; trimming

【剪纸】paper-cut; scissor-cut

【剪纸艺术】kirigami

【剪子】scissors; shears; clippers: ～剪不断铁丝。*Scissors won't cut through wire.*

睑 [书] eyelid

简[1] ① brief; simple; simplified: 言～意赅 *concise and comprehensive* ② simplify: 精兵～政 *better troops and simplify administration* ③ (Jiǎn) a surname

简[2] ① bamboo slips used for writing on in ancient times ② letters; correspondence: 书～ *letters*

简[3] [书] select; choose

【简板】【音】a kind of percussion instrument with two flat wood or bamboo pieces

【简报】bulletin; brief report: 会议～ *conference bulletin*; *brief reports on conference proceedings*

【简本】abridged edition

【简笔画】sketch

【简编】short course; abridged edition: 《中国文学史》*A Brief History of Chinese Literature*

【简便】simple and convenient; handy: ～的方法 *a simple and convenient method* /做事要周到,不能只图～。*One should do everything up brown instead of thinking only of one's own convenience.*

【简称】① acronym; abbreviation; short form: 业务～ *service abbreviation* ②be called sth for short: Ben 通常为 Benjamin 的～。"*Ben*" *is usually short for* "*Benjamin*".

【简单】① simple; brief: 一项～的任务 *a straightforward task* /人们赞赏它那～直率的风格。*People appreciate its simple and direct style.* /对他来说开张支票是个十分～的手续。*Writing a cheque is quite a simple procedure to him.* ② ordinary; commonplace: 他能写出这么好的文章,真不～。*He's marvel to be able to write such a good article.* ③ oversimplified; cursory; offhand: ～地处理 *deal with things in a casual way*

【简牍】[书] ① bamboo slip ② letter; correspondence

【简短】brief; terse; short: 对事件～的陈述 *a brief account of the incident* /冷淡而～的欢迎 *a cold and brief welcome* /因为下雨,仪式举行得很～。*The ceremony was abbreviated by rain.*

【简而言之】make a long story short; briefly speaking; sum up; in short; in brief; to put it in a nutshell: ～,结婚是件麻烦事。*In short, marriage is a carriage of trouble.* /我可以说很多,但是～,这个项目是个彻底的失败。*I could say a lot more, but to put it in a nutshell, the project was a complete failure.* /～,你被解雇了。*Briefly, you're fired!*

【简分数】【数】common fraction; simple fraction

【简古】[书] brief and archaic: 文笔～ *archaic and terse style of writing*

【简化】simplify; streamline: ～方程 *reduced equation* /～工序 *simplify working progress* /这个合同包含的内容太多,我正在想办法～它。*The contract contains too much content and I am trying to find ways of simplifying it.*

【简化汉字】① simplify Chinese characters ② simplified Chinese characters

【简洁】succinct; terse; pithy; concise: ～有力的文体 *a terse and vigorous style*

【简捷】① simple and direct; forthright: 她提出的问题很～。*The question she raised is quite straightforward.* ② simple and quick

【简截】simple and direct

【简介】① introduce briefly ② synopsis; brief introduction: 人物～ *the synopsis of the characters*

【简况】brief account (or introduction)

【简括】brief but comprehensive; compendious: ～的说明 *a brief explanation*

【简历】biography note; curriculum vitae (CV); resume

【简练】terse; succinct; pithy: 她的文章文字～。*Her essay is succinct in style.*

【简陋】simple and crude; shabby: 设备～ *simple e-*

quipment /～的家具 *shabby furniture*
【简略】simple; compact; brief; sketchy; thin: 一个过于～的介绍 *a too sketchy introduction*
【简慢】negligent; short: 他是要人,招待上不能～。*He is a VIP, so we cannot be negligent to him.*
【简明】concise; succinct: ～英汉字典 *a concise English-Chinese dictionary*
【简明扼要】terse and clear; concise: 你的发言～。*Your presentation is concise and to the point.*
【简朴】simple and unadorned; plain: 生活～ *plain living; a simple and frugal life*
【简谱】【音】numbered musical notation
【简切】simple and to the point
【简缩】simplify; cut; reduce: 我～了开支。*I reduced my expenditure.*
【简体】① simplified ② simplified Chinese character
【简体字】simplified Chinese character
【简帖】[旧] letters; correspondence
【简图】sketch; diagram; abbreviated drawing: 画～ *make a sketch*
【简写】① write a Chinese character in its simplified form ② simplify a book for beginners
【简写本】simplified edition
【简讯】news in brief
【简言之】briefly; in short; in a word; in sum; in a nutshell; sum up: ～他不想干了。*In a word, he wants to quit the job.*
【简要】brief; concise: ～的描述 *a brief description*
【简易】① simple and easy: 引进一种～的方法 *introduce a simple and easy method* ② simply constructed or equipped: ～病房 *simply equipped ward*
【简约】① brief; concise; sketchy: 一定要确保你的答案～而清晰。*Make sure that your answers are as clear and concise as possible.* ② thrifty and simple
【简则】brief rules
【简札】[书] letters; correspondence
【简章】general regulations: 招生～ *general regulation for enrolling students*
【简政】streamline administration
【简直】① simply; just: ～是浪费时间。*It's a sheer waste of time.* / 我～热死了。*I am simply melting with heat.* ② [方] may just as well
【简装】plainly-packed: ～书 *plainly-packed books*

碱 ① soda: 纯～ *soda (ash)* ② alkali: 有效～ *available alkali* ③ be corroded by alkali: 这间房子的墙都～了。*The wall in the room is corroded by alkali all over.*
【碱地】alkaline land
【碱电池】alkaline cell
【碱化】【化】alkalize; alkalify; basify
【碱金属】【化】alkali metals: ～化合物 *alkali metals compound* / ～盐 *alkali metals salt*
【碱溶液】aqueous alkali
【碱色】alkaline colour
【碱石灰】soda lime
【碱水】water containing soda
【碱土】【农】alkaline earth
【碱土金属】alkaline-earth metals
【碱性】【化】alkalescence
【碱液】lye: ～清洗 *caustic dip*
【碱渣】caustic sludge
【碱值】base number
【碱中毒】alkalosis

蹇 ① [书] lame; crippled: ～滞 *poor and unlucky* /命运多～ *suffer many a hardship during one's life* ② [书] unlucky; difficult ③ [书] inferior horse; donkey ④ (Jiǎn) a surname

jiàn

见[1] ① see; catch sight of: 罕～ *infrequence; infrequency* /喜闻乐～ *love to see and hear* /视而不～ *turn a blind eye to sth* ② meet with; be exposed to: 胶卷不能～光。*Films are not to be exposed to light.* ③show evidence of; appear to be: 病～好 *seem to be recovering from an illness* ④ (of literature) refer to; see: ～上 *see above* / ～下 *see below* ⑤ meet; call on: 接～ *see; interview* ⑥ view; opinion: 固执己～ *stick to one's guns; sit tight* /主～ *definite idea; one's own view* /成～ *prejudice* ⑦ (Jiàn) a surname

见[2] [书] ① used before a verb to indicate the passive ② used before a verb in polite requests
【见爱】be liked or loved: 承蒙～。*I am greatly honoured by your high opinion of me.*
【见报】appear in the newspaper: 这条消息已经～了。*This piece of news has been published in the newspaper.*
【见不得】① not to be exposed to: 这种材料～光。*This kind of material is not to be exposed to light.* ② not fit to be seen or revealed: ～人的勾当 *shameless deed* ③ [方] unable to put up with: 我～人撒谎。*I cannot put up with lying.*
【见长】be good at; be skillful in: 他以诗歌写作～。*He is good at writing poems.*
【见称】[书] be known; be praised: ～于世 *be well-known by everyone*
【见得】seem; appear: 他说的不～准确。*What he said might not be correct.* /何以～? *How so?*
【见地】insight; judgement: 颇有～ *have keen insight*
【见多识广】experienced and knowledgeable; have great experience; have been around; have seen a great deal; be a man of the world; sophisticated; worldly: 他是个～的人。*He is a man of the world.*
【见方】[口] square: 一米～ *one metre square*
【见访】[书] your call; your visit: 承蒙～,不胜荣幸。*I'm greatly honoured by your visit.*
【见分晓】be clear; be sorted out: 比赛结果还未～。*The result of the contest is still not clear.*
【见风是雨】take wind as sure sign of rain — jump to conclusion

【见缝插针】stick in pin wherever there is a room — make use of every bit of one's time; utilize every bit of space
【见告】[书] keep me informed
【见怪】mind; take offence: 我说的话您别~。*I hope you will not take any offense at my words.*
【见怪不怪】not be surprised by anything unusual; be used to something uncommon: ~,其怪自败。*Fear not the fearful, and its fearfulness disappears.*
【见鬼】① ridiculous; fantastic: 真~,刚放在这里的书就不见了! *It is fantastic that the book I placed here a minute ago disappeared.* ② go to hell; go to the devil: 让他~去吧! *To hell with him!*
【见好】get better; mend: 父亲的病~。*Father is getting better.*
【见好就收】leave well enough alone; stop before going too far away
【见后】see below
【见机】as the opportunity arises; according to the conditions
【见机行事】act according to circumstances; use one's discretion
【见教】[套] favour me with your advice; instruct me: 有何~? *Is there something you want to instruct me?*
【见解】view; opinion; idea: 阐述自己的~ *set forth one's opinion*
【见礼】salute; greet
【见利忘义】forget what is right at the sight of money; sacrifice principle for profit
【见谅】[书] excuse me; forgive me
【见面】meet; see: 昨天是我们第一次~。*We met for the first time yesterday.*
【见面礼】present given to sb at first meeting
【见面熟】[口] hail-fellow-well-met
【见票】demand: ~即付 *payable at sight*
【见弃】be discarded or rejected
【见钱眼开】open one's eyes wide at the sight of money; be moved at the sight of money
【见轻】(of illness) get better
【见仁见智】different people have different views; opinions differ from each other: 大家对这个问题~,看法不一。*Different people held different views about the issue.*
【见世面】see the world; widen one's horizon
【见识】① enrich one's experience; get more information ② knowledge; experience: 长~ *widen one's knowledge* / ~短浅 *lacking knowledge and experience*
【见死不救】stand calmly by while another is drowning — see someone in great danger indifferently: 医生是不能~的。*A doctor cannot turn away a dying man.*
【见外】regard sb as an outsider: 在我家里一定别~。*Just make yourself at home.*
【见闻】what one see and hears; information: 增长~ *broaden one's knowledge*
【见习】learn on the job; probation; internship: 一年~期 *one-year probation*
【见习生】intern; probationer
【见习医生】intern
【见下】see below; vide infra
【见效】become effective; take effect: 药物~很快。*The medicine became effective soon.*
【见笑】① [谦] incur ridicule by one's poor performance ② laugh at me (or us): 唱得不好,请别~! *Please don't laugh at me if I can't sing well.*
【见义勇为】be ready to act for a just cause; have the courage to do what is right
【见异思迁】change one's mind the moment one sees something new; be inconstant or irresolute
【见长】grow perceptibly: 他的脾气~。*He became more and more irritable.*
【见证】① be a witness to ② witness; testimony: 历史~ *the testimony of history* / 一个证人提供的~说被告当时喝醉酒了。*A witness gave testimony that the accused was drunk at that time.*
【见证人】eyewitness; witness; observer: 事故的~ *a witness to the accident*
【见罪】[书] take offence; be blamed

件 ① [量]: 一~事 *a matter; a thing* / 两~衣服 *two articles of clothing* ② things that can be counted: 部~ *units* / 零~ *parts* ③ letter; paper; document: 来~ *letter; correspondence* / 文~ *document* / 信~ *letters; mail*

间 ① space in between; opening: 当~儿 *in the middle* ② estrangement; grudge: 亲密无~ *as thick as thieves; be on intimate terms* ③ separate; disconnect: 黑白相~ *black alternating with white* / 晴~多云 *fine, occasionally cloudy* ④ sow discord: 离~ *alienate; cast in a bone between; come between; estrange* / 反~计 *a stratagem of sowing distrust among enemies* ⑤ thin out (seedlings) *see also* jiān

【间壁】next door; next-door neighbour
【间谍】spy: 军事~ *military spy*
【间谍飞机】spy plane
【间谍活动】espionage
【间谍网】espionage network; spy ring
【间谍卫星】spy satellite
【间断】be disconnected (or interrupted): 他~大学学业到军队去服役。*He interrupted college to serve in the army.*
【间伐】【林】intermediate cutting — cutting down some trees to speed up the growth of a forest: ~强度 *intensity of intermediate cutting*
【间隔】① interval; intermission: 以10英尺的~排列 *arranged at intervals of ten feet* / ~了好久他才回了电话。*There was a long interval before he answered the telephone.* ② separate: 围栏把奶牛和猪~开。*A fence separated the cows from the pigs.* / 树与树之间~5米 *space out the trees five metres apart*
【间隔号】【语】separation dot-punctuation mark separating the day form the month
【间或】occasionally; now and then; sometimes: 我们~去田野里散步。*We go for walks in the fields*

occasionally.

【间接】indirect; secondhand：那场火灾造成了巨大的～损失。*The fire caused terrible indirect losses.*

【间苗】【农】thin out seedlings or young shoots：～机 *plant thinning machine*

【间隙】① interval; gap; space：利用工作～学习 *study in the intervals of one's work* /在谈话的～你能听到钟的滴答声。*You could hear the clock ticking every time there was a lull in the conversation.* ②【机】clearance：～结构 *interstitial structure* / ～宽度 *gap width* / ～配合 *clearance fit* / ～损耗 *clearance loss* / ～修正 *gap correction* / ～运动 *intermittent motion*

【间歇】intermission; intermittence; pause：短暂的～后，听众突然爆发出欢呼声。*After a pause the audience broke into cheers.* /现在有一个短暂的～。听到铃声后立刻回到你们的座位上。*There will now be a short intermission; please return to your seats at once when you hear the bell.*

【间杂】be mixed：～其间 *get mixed up in it*

饯[1] give a fare well dinner

饯[2] candy; preserve：蜜～ *candied fruit*

【饯别】give a farewell dinner：～友人 *give a friend a farewell dinner*

【饯行】give a farewell dinner：我们为他～。*We gave a fare well dinner for him.*

建[1] ① build; construct; erect：新～ *be built newly* / ～桥 *construct a bridge* ② establish; found; set up：～校 *found a school* ③ propose; advocate

建[2] ① the Jianjiang River, in Fujian Province ② refer to Fujian Province

【建材】building materials

【建党】① found a political party ② Party-building：～路线 *line for Party-building*

【建档】place sth on file; set up a new file

【建都】found a capital：明代～北京。*The Ming Dynasty made Beijing its capital.*

【建盖】build; construct

【建功】do a deed of merit：～立业 *render meritorious service and make a distinguished career*

【建国】① found (or establish) a state ②build up a country：勤俭～ *build up our country through diligence and frugality*

【建交】establish diplomatic relations：～国 *country having diplomatic relations* / ～谈判 *negotiation for establishing diplomatic relations*

【建军】① found an army ② army building：～路线 *line for army building*

【建军节】Army Day (1 August)

【建立】① start; build; found：～家庭 *set up a family* / ～政权 *start a regime* ②establish; build up：以事实为依据～论点 *build an argument on fact* /这个发现～了他的声望。*The discovery established his reputation.* /这所学校～于1980年。*The school was founded in 1980.*

【建设】build; construct：国防～ *building of national defense* /经济～ *economic development* /加快社会主义～ *speed up the socialist construction*

【建设部】Ministry of Construction

【建设性】constructive; positive：～意见 *constructive suggestions*

【建树】① make a contribution; contribute; score an achievement：他在文学上很有～。*He made a great contribution to literature.* ② contribution; achievement：颇有～的人 *a man of high attainments*

【建议】① propose; suggest：～修改法律 *propose a change in the law* /我～马上动身。*I propose to set off immediately.* / 他～出去走走。*He suggested going out for a walk.* ② suggestion; advice; proposition：合理的～ *a piece of reasonable advice*

【建造】build; construct：～房屋 *build a house*

【建政】build up political power

【建制】organizational system：部队～ *the organizational system of the army*

【建筑】① build; erect; put up ② structure; building：这古堡～奇妙。*The castle is curious in structure.*

【建筑师】architect：总～ *chief architect*

【建筑物】building; structure：这所新医院是一座大～。*The new hospital is a big building.*

荐[1] ① recommend; introduce：毛遂自～ *volunteer one's services* /推～ *recommend* ②［书］offer; present

荐[2] ①［书］grass; straw ② grass cushion

【荐拔】［书］recommend sb for promotion

【荐举】propose sb for an office; recommend：～他做那项工作 *recommended him for the job*

【荐贤】recommend persons of virtue and ability

【荐引】［书］recommend：她获大力～担任这个职务。*She was strongly recommended for the post.* /在上次会议上，好几个成员～了他。*At the last meeting, he was proposed by several members.*

【荐擢】［书］recommend sb for promotion：我们～他来填补这一空位。*We put his name forward for the vacant seat.*

贱 ① low-priced; inexpensive; cheap：～买～卖 *buy and sell at low price* /这东西真～。*The goods are really cheap.* ② lowly; humble：贫～ *poor and lowly* /卑～ *humble* ③ abject; base：下～ *shameless*; *base* ④ (humble word) my：～姓 *my surname* / ～恙 *my ailment*; *my illness*

【贱骨头】①［粗］miserable wretch ②［谑］self-imposed sufferer

【贱货】① cheap or shoddy goods ②［粗］miserable wretch; good-for-nothing

【贱民】①［旧］person of a lower social status ② Pariah, the lowest status in India

【贱人】(usu. used in old novels) contemptible woman; slut

【贱视】look down upon; despise

剑 sword; sabre：短～ *stiletto* /花～ *foil* /击～ *fence* /刀光～影 *glint and flash of cold steel*

【剑拔弩张】with swords drawn and bows bent; at

daggers drawn; saber rattling; at sword's point: 世界在冷战中～。*The world lives at daggers drawn in a cold war.*
【剑柄】handle of a sword; hilt
【剑道】(Japan) kendo
【剑客】swordsman
【剑麻】【植】sisal hemp
【剑眉】straight eyebrows slanting upwards and outwards
【剑桥】Cambridge, city in Cambridgeshire, England
【剑桥大学】Cambridge University
【剑鞘】scabbard; sheath
【剑伤】sword cut
【剑术】art of fencing; swordsmanship: ～教练 *fencing master* /～师 *fencer*
【剑舞】sword dance
【剑侠】knight-errant or swordsman who champions the cause of the downtrodden
【剑杖】sword cane

涧 ravine; gully: 山～ *mountain stream*

监 ① an imperial office or officer: 国子～ *the Imperial College (the highest educational administration in feudal China)* /钦天～ *Board of Astronomy* ② (Jiàn) a surname
see also jiān
【监本】books printed by successive Imperial Colleges

健 ① strong; healthy: 强～ *strong and healthy* /保～ *health care; health protection* ② strengthen; toughen; invigorate: ～脾 *invigorate the function of the spleen* ③ be good at; be strong in
【健步】walk with vigorous strides: 他～走过来握住了我的手。*He strode towards me and shook my hand.* /他～走进办公室请求道歉。*He marched straight into the office to demand an apology.*
【健步如飞】walk as if on wings; walk quickly and vigorously
【健存】(of elderly people) be still living and healthy
【健斗】be good at fighting
【健儿】① valiant fighter ② good athlete: 体育～为祖国赢得了荣誉。*Good athletes have won honour for the motherland.*
【健将】① master; expert ② master of a sport; top notch player: 足球～ *top notch football player*
【健康】① health; physique: 恢复～ *bring back to health* /恢复～ *recover one's health* /心理～ *mental health* /对大多数人来说～比金钱更重要。*Health is more important to most people than money.* /祝你～。*I wish you good health.* ② healthy; fit; sound: 孩子们看来很～。*The children look very healthy.*
【健康证明书】health certificate
【健朗】strong and hearty
【健美】strong and handsome; vigorous and graceful
【健美操】callisthenics; body-building exercise
【健美运动】body building
【健苗】healthy seedling
【健全】① sound; sane; healthy: 身心～ *sound in mind and body* ② perfect: 一套～的设施 *a set of perfect equipment* ③ strengthen; improve: ～民主集中制 *strengthen democratic centralism*
【健身】keeping fit; body-building
【健身操】setting-up exercise
【健身房】gymnasium; gym
【健身器】【体】fitness or body-building equipment
【健谈】be a good talker: 她可真～! *What a talker she is!*
【健忘】forgetful; having a bad memory: 这个老人很～。*The old man had a bad memory.* /他有时～。*He is sometimes forgetful.*
【健忘症】【医】amnesia
【健旺】healthy and vigorous
【健在】[书] (of aging people) be still living and healthy
【健壮】healthy and strong: 我体格～。*I am strong in body.*

舰 warship; naval vessel: 航空母～ *aircraft carrier* /旗～ *flagship* /战～ *warship* /主力～ *capital ship*
【舰船】ships and warships
【舰队】fleet; naval force: 南海～ *the Nanhai Sea Fleet* /海军～ *naval fleet* /～正在和航空部队进行联合演习。*The fleet is manoeuvring in combination with the air unit.*
【舰桥】commanding bridge on a warship
【舰日】day a warship spends at sea
【舰首】bow: ～炮 *bow chaser*
【舰艇】naval ships and boats; naval vessels: 作战～ *combat ship*
【舰尾】stern
【舰尾炮】stern chaser
【舰位】berth (in a harbour); (of a warship) location (on high seas)
【舰载】carrier-borne; ship-based
【舰长】captain (of a warship)
【舰只】warship; naval force
【舰嘴】rostrum

渐 gradually; by degrees: 循序～进 *in proper sequence; progress in an orderly way step by step* /生意日～兴隆。*Business in on the up grade.*
see also jiān
【渐变】① gradual change; wear ②【生】anamorphism; anamorphosis
【渐次】[书] gradually; one after another
【渐渐】gradually; by degrees; little by little: ～从店员上升到经理 *rise by degrees from clerk to manager of the store* /他激动的心情～平息了。*His excitement gradually died down.* /陆地～向海边倾斜。*The land slopes to the sea by a gradual descent.*
【渐进】advance gradually; progress step by step: 循序～ *advance step by step in due order*
【渐入佳境】gradually entering enjoyable circumstances; be getting better

【渐愈】convalesce：患者～。*The patient convalesced nicely.*
【渐晕】vignetting：～效应 *vignetting effect*

谏 ［书］（in former times）persuade one's sovereign or superior to correct his mistakes：直言劝～ *use blunt words to remonstrate*
【谏官】official whose duty is to remonstrate with the emperor
【谏劝】admonish；advise
【谏诤】［书］criticize sb's faults frankly

践 ① trample；tread ② keep one's promise：实～ *practise*；*put into practice*
【践履】［书］① trample；tread ② carry out；act on
【践诺】［书］keep one's promise；keep one's words：他不是那种可以～的人。*He is not a person whose promise you can build on.*
【践踏】① tread：不要～庄稼。*Don't tread on the crops.* ② trample；ride roughshod over：肆意～他国主权 *wantonly trample on the sovereignty of other countries*
see also jiǎn

毽
【毽子】shuttlecock，a Chinese toy kicked in a game：踢～ *kick the shuttlecock*

腱 【生理】tendon，tough，thick and white cord that joins muscle to bone
【腱损伤】tendon injury
【腱子】（beef or mutton）shank

溅 splash；spatter：～了一身泥 *be spattered with mud all over* /被搅拌的冰淇淋～到柜台上。*Whipped cream splashed onto the counter.* /热油向四面八方～开。*Hot grease spattered in all directions.*
【溅落】splash down：精确～ *a precision splashdown*
【溅落区】water landing area；splash area
【溅落点】splash point
【溅射】sputtering；spurting；spotter

鉴 ① mirror ② reflect；mirror：光可～人。*The surface is so finished that it can reflect a man's image.* ③ inspect；examine ④ sth that can serve as warning or lesson：前车之覆，后车之～。*The overturned cart ahead is a warning to the ones behind.* ⑤ used in letters：张先生台～ *Dear Mr. Zhang, may I draw your attention to the following.*
【鉴别】discern；distinguish；discriminate：～能力 *ability to differentiate* /～真伪 *discriminate the true from the false* /无法～颜色 *unable to discriminate colors*
【鉴察】［书］scrutinize；examine；inspect
【鉴定】① appraisal；evaluation：学业成绩～ *accomplishment evaluation* /设备～ *appraisal of equipment* /通过国家～ *pass state appraisal* ② judge；appraise；identify；determine：～产品质量 *appraise the quality of a product*
【鉴定人】identifier；surveyor
【鉴定书】testimonial；written appraisal
【鉴定委员会】certifying commission
【鉴定会】appraising meeting
【鉴戒】warning；object lesson：把这次事故引为～ *take warning from an accident*
【鉴谅】［书］used to ask for understanding or forgiveness：有失远迎，务乞～。*We sincerely hope you'll excuse us for any negligence in meeting you in time.*
【鉴貌辨色】try to read sb's mind by observing the expression on his face
【鉴频】frequency discrimination
【鉴赏】appreciate：～艺术品 *appreciate works of art* /培养～力 *cultivate the appreciation*
【鉴赏家】connoisseur
【鉴于】since；as；considering；in view of：～他只学了一年英语，他说得是很好的。*Considering he's only been learning English a year, he speaks it very well.* /～她的表现，大家选她为班长。*In view of her performance, she was elected as monitor.*
【鉴证】① distinguish and confirm ② confirm the authenticity, legality of a contract

键 ① linchpin, a piece of iron passed through an axle ②［书］bolt（of a door）③ key（of some musical instruments；typewriter, etc.）：琴～ *a piano key* ④【化】bond：共价～ *covalent bond*
【键半径】【化】bond radius
【键长】【化】bond length
【键电子】bonding electrons
【键角】bond angle
【键盘】keyboard；fingerboard
【键式】key-type：～开关 *key switch*
【键条】key bar
【键组】keyboard

踺
【踺子】【体】（in gymnastics）round-off；somersault：～后空翻 *backward somersault in the air*

箭 ① arrow；weapon with a metal point at one end and shot to the distance with a bow：射～ *shoot an arrow* /他像～一般飞快地逃走了。*He ran away like an arrow.* ② the distance an arrow flies
【箭靶】target for archery
【箭步】sudden big stride forward：他一个～出了房间。*In a big stride he came out of the room.*
【箭垛子】① battlements；parapet ② target for archery
【箭杆】arrow shaft
【箭头】① arrowhead；arrow tip ② arrow（as a sign）
【箭托】arrow rest
【箭在弦上】there can be no turning back；a point of no return
【箭在弦上，不得不发】an arrow fitted on the bow — string can't avoid being discharged

jiāng

江 ① a general name for big rivers: 松花~ *the Songhuajiang River* ② the Yangtze River, the biggest river in China ③ (Jiāng) a surname

【江岸】river bank

【江北】① areas north of the lower reaches of the Yangtze River ② north of the Yangtze River

【江潮】tidal bore; tide at a river mouth

【江东】① the lower reaches of the Yangtze River ② an area on the south of the Yangtze River

【江防】① preventive project or works against flood along a river, esp. along the Yangtze River ② defense works along the Yangtze River

【江河】rivers: ~水雷 *river mine*

【江河日下】go form bad to worse; be on the decline; fall away: ~的帝国 *an empire on the decline*

【江湖】① rivers and lakes — all corners of the country; the wide world: 流落~ *drift about homeless* ② *itinerant entertainers, quacks, etc.*

【江郎才尽】a Jianglang depleted of his talents; the inspiration has dried up

【江流】river; waters

【江轮】river steamer

【江米】polished glutinous rice

【江米酒】fermented glutinous rice

【江米纸】paper made of glutinous rice

【江南】① regions south of the Yangtze River ② south of the Yangtze River

【江山】① rivers and mountains; land; landscape: ~如此多娇。*Beautiful and glorious is the land.* ② country; state power; territory: 打~ *fight to win state power*

【江山易改,本性难移】a leopard never changes his sports; the child is father of the man

【江水】river water

【江天】the sky over the river

【江心】the middle of a river

【江洋大盗】an infamous robber; a notorious bandit leader

将 ①[书] support; take: 扶~ *support* ② take care of one's health ③[方] (of animals) drop: ~驹 *drop a pigling* ④[书] do sth: 慎重~事 *handle a matter with care* ⑤ (in Chinese chess) check, move one's pieces so as to treat or attack the opponent's jiang or shuai under direct attack ⑥ prod; incite; challenge: ~他去反对她 *challenge him to contradict her* ⑦ with; by means of: 恩~仇报 *bite the hand that feeds one; repay kindness with ingratitude* ⑧ used to introduce the object before the verb: ~门关上。*Close the door.* ⑨ will; be going to: 飞机~起飞。*The plane will take off.* ⑩ partly... partly... ⑪[方] used between a verb and its complement of direction: 走~进去 *walk in* ⑫ (Jiāng) a surname

see also jiàng

【将才】just now; a moment ago

【将次】[书] be going to; will; shall

【将错就错】over shoes over boots; leave a mistake uncorrected and make the best of it; make the best of a bad bargain

【将功补过】make amends for one's fault by good deeds; atone for a crime by meritorious actions

【将功赎罪】make amends for one's crimes by good deeds

【将计就计】countermine; turn sb's trick against himself; counterplot; meet one's scheme for another

【将将】[方] just; only; exactly: 他~及格。*He got exactly the passing score.*

【将近】close to; nearly; almost: ~黄昏。*It was close upon dusk.* /他~50了。*He is getting on for fifty.*

【将就】make do passable; not too bad; make do with make the best of; put up with: ~着用 *make do with it* /晚餐我们只好~吃面条了。*We'll have to make do with the noodles for supper.*

【将军】① (in Chinese chess) check ② embarrass; challenge: 你是想将我的军吗? *Are you trying to embarrass me?* ③ general: 他是名伟大的~。*He is a great general.* ④ high-ranking military officer

【将军肚】pot-belly; big belly

【将来】future: 我们~会尽力做得更好些。*We will try to do better in the future.* /谁能知道~会发生些什么? *Who can tell what will happen in the future?*

【将息】rest; recuperate

【将心比心】put oneself in sb's shoes; think of others; be empathic

【将信将疑】half believing, half doubting; be half in doubt; shilly-shally

【将养】rest; recuperate: 好好~。*Take a good rest.*

【将息】rest; recuperate

【将要】be going to; will; shall: 我明年~毕业。*I will graduate next year*

姜[1] ① ginger ② the stalk of ginger

姜[2] (Jiāng) a surname

【姜花】garland-flower

【姜黄】①【植】turmeric: ~根 *turmeric root* ② sallow; the ginger's colour: ~的脸 *a sallow face* /他的头发带一点~色。*His hair was a bright shade of ginger.*

【姜太公钓鱼,愿者上钩】[俗] a willing victim letting himself be caught

【姜汤】ginger decoction

豇

【豇豆】① cowpea ② the pods and the seeds of cowpea

浆 ① thick liquid：纸～ *paper pulp* /豆～ *soybean milk* /糖～ *syrup* ② stiffen cloth or clothes with starch or millet gruel：～衣服 starch clothes

【浆果】【植】berry

【浆纱】【纺】sizing；slashing

【浆纱机】slasher；dresser；tape frame

【浆洗】wash and starch

【浆细胞】plasma cell

【浆液】serous fluid：～膜 *serosa* /～细胞 *serous cell*

【浆纸机】coating machine

僵 ① numb；stiff；not flexible：我的手冻～了。*My hands are numb with cold.* ② deadlock：千万别闹～了！*Don't bring things to a deadlock* ③［方］be grave；be serious：他～着脸。*He looks serious.*

【僵板】［方］① stiff；rigid：～的面孔 *straight face* ② harden：～田 *hardened field*

【僵蚕】inactive silkworm（before it sheds its skin）

【僵持】refuse to budge（or give in）

【僵化】petrify；become rigid；ossify；stereotyped：思想～ *a rigid way of thinking* /脑筋是易于～的。*It is easy for the mind to ossify.*

【僵局】deadlock；impasse；logjam；stalemate：打破～ *break a deadlock* /会议因工资问题而陷入～。*The meeting deadlocked over the wage issue.* /双方在谈判过程中陷入了～。*The two parties reached an impasse in the negotiations.*

【僵冷】numb with cold

【僵尸】corpse

【僵石】loess doll

【僵死】be dead as mutton；be stone dead

【僵硬】① stiff；hard-shelled：～的脖子 *a stiff neck* /他的舌头变得有点～。*His tongue became a bit stiff.* ② rigid；inflexible：～的官僚主义让我恼火。*I get very annoyed with rigid bureaucracies.* /缺少变革应归罪于～的社会习俗。*The lack of change may be ascribed to the inflexibility of social customs.*

【僵直】rigidity；spasticity：～的纪律 *rigid discipline*

【僵滞】dull and rigid；inflexible：～的眼光 *glassy stare*

缰 rein；halter；trace：脱～ *bolt* /信马由～ *ride a horse without holding the reins — run about without aims*

【缰绳】reins；halter：牵着马的～走 *take a horse by the halter* /骑马的人拉紧～，马停住了。*The rider pulled on the reins, and the horse stopped.*

疆 ① border；boundary：边～ *border area*；*frontier*；*border land* /～域 *territory*；*domain* ②（Jiāng）refer to Xinjiang

【疆场】battlefield：～捐躯 *lay down one's life on the battlefield* /驰骋～ *gallop across the battlefield* /他们在～上牺牲。*They died in battle.*

【疆界】boundary；border；frontiers

【疆土】territory

【疆埸】［书］① field borders ② national borders：这条河是两国的～。*The river is the boundary between the two countries.*

【疆域】territory；domain

jiǎng

讲 ① say；speak；tell：～德语 *speak German* /～故事 *tell a story* /～出真相 *speak the truth* /很难～这件事谁对谁错。*It's hard to say who is right in this matter.* ②explain；make clear；interpret：把道理～清楚 *state the reasons clearly* /这个字有两个～法。*The word has two meanings.* ③ talk over；consult：～价 *bargain* /～条件 *negotiate the terms* ④ as far as sth is concerned；when it comes to：～技术，他显然不如你。*When it comes to technique, he is not your match evidently.* ⑤ pay attention to；emphasize：～道德 *stress on moral* /～速度 *pay attention to the speed* /～文明 *stress on decorum*

【讲道】preach；sermonize

【讲法】① the way of saying a thing；wording；formulation ② statement；version；argument：这是此事的另一种～。*This is another version of the issue.*

【讲稿】the draft or text of a speech；lecture notes

【讲古】tell former stories or legends

【讲和】make peace；settle a dispute；become reconciled：我的解释使这对夫妻～了。*My explanation reconciles the husband with the wife.*

【讲话】① speak；talk；address：她从来不居高临下地对听众～。*She never spoke down to her audience.* /足球队长向队员～。*The football captain addressed his team.* ② censure；condemn；reproach：你对待老师礼貌不周，难怪别人要～了。*You treated your teacher with bad manners; no wonder others reproached you.* ③ speech；talk：他的～吸引了很多人。*His speech draws large audiences.* ④ talks：语法～ *An Introduction to Grammar*

【讲价】bargain：如果你～，他们可能会把降低。*If you bargain with them, they might reduce the price.*

【讲价钱】① haggle over the price；bargain：她和卖书的人～，直到他把书便宜地卖给了她。*She bargained with the bookseller till he sold her the books cheaply.* ② negotiate the terms；insist on the fulfillment of certain conditions：不要和我～，我已经下定决心了。*There is no room for negotiation, as I have made up my mind.*

【讲解】explain；interpret：～课文 *explain the texts*

【讲解员】guide；interpreter

【讲究】① be particular about；pay attention to；stress；strive for：～卫生 *pay attention to hygiene* /～衣着 *be particular about what one wears* ② careful study：为老人选择礼品大有～。*Choosing gifts for elderly people need careful study.* ③ exquisite；tasteful：～的服装 *elegant dress* /房间布置很～。*The room is decorated exquisitely.*

【讲课】teach；lecture

【讲理】① reason with sb；argue：我要和他～。*I*

J

will argue with him. / 你最好心平气和地同他～。*You'd better reason things out with him calmly.* ② listen to reason; be reasonable; be sensible: 蛮不～ *be extremely unreasonable* / 一个～的人 *a reasonable person*

【讲论】① talk about; discuss: 他从不～政治。*He never talks about politics.* ② be about; explain; expound: 这是一本～诗歌的书。*This book is about poetry.*

【讲明】explain; make clear; state explicitly: 我向他～了道理。*I explained the reasons to him.* / 我已经～2点钟出发。*I have made it clear to set out at two o'clock.*

【讲排场】go in for pomp; hanker after vainglory

【讲评】comment on and appraise: ～我们的作业 *comment on our homework*

【讲情】intercede; plead for sb: 替女儿向父亲～ *intercede with the father for the daughter*

【讲求】be particular about; pay attention to; stress: ～实效 *stress on practical results* / ～效率 *strive for efficiency*

【讲师】lecturer

【讲授】lecture; instruct; teach: ～英语 *lecture on English* / 十年前他在大学～语文。*He taught Chinese at a college ten years ago.*

【讲述】tell about; give an account of; narrate; relate: ～一个实验的过程 *narrate the process of an experiment*

【讲台】platform; dais; rostrum: 登上～ *mount the rostrum*

【讲坛】①（speaker's）platform; rostrum: 你的问题将由～上的人作答。*Your questions will be answered from the platform.* ② forum（for public discussion）: 这个公园是人们发表政治见解的～。*The park is a forum for political ideas.*

【讲堂】lecture room; classroom

【讲题】① explain the exercise problems ② subject of a lecture; topic of a speech

【讲习】lecture and study: ～所 *institute for instruction*

【讲学】give lecture; discourse on an academic subject: 应邀出国～ *be invited to give lectures abroad*

【讲演】① give a speech or lecture: 他将就世界和平问题发表～。*He will lecture on the world peace.* ② speech; lecture

【讲义】teaching materials; lecture notes

【讲桌】lecture desk

【讲座】a course of lectures; series of lectures

奖 ① encourage; reward: 努力工作者～ *reward those who work hard* ② award; prize: 得～ *win a prize* / 安慰～ *consolation prize* / 荣誉～ *prize of honour* / 诺贝尔～ *the Nobel Prize*

【奖杯】cup（as a prize）; trophy; plate: 温布尔登网球赛～ *the Wimbledon tennis trophy* / 他曾多次荣获歌唱比赛的～。*He has won several cups for singing.*

【奖惩】rewards and punishments; rewards and penalties: ～条例 *regulations concerning rewards and penalties*

【奖金】money award; bonus; premium: 和平～ *peace prize* / 加班～ *attendance bonus* / 年终～ *December bonus; year-end bonus* / 团体～ *group bonus*

【奖励】encourage and reward; award; reward: ～制度 *system of reward* / 学校因为她表现好～了她。*The school awarded her a prize for her good performance.*

【奖牌】medal: 他赢得了射击～。*He won a medal for shooting.*

【奖品】prize; award; trophy: 给优胜者授予～ *award prizes to the winners*

【奖旗】（silk）banner（as an award）

【奖券】lottery ticket; gift coupon

【奖赏】award; reward: 那是对美德的～。*It's a reward for virtue.*

【奖售】① sales incentive; reward sale ② sell as a reward

【奖学金】scholarship: 一等～ *major award* / 二等～ *minor award*

【奖章】medal; decoration: 授予某人～ *award sb with a medal* / 金质～ *gold medal* / 银质～ *silver medal* / 铜质～ *bronze medal*

【奖状】certificate of merit; certificate of an award: 发此～，以资鼓励。*Issue this certificate as an encouragement.*

桨 oar

【桨板】paddle board

【桨耳】thole; tholepin

【桨轮】paddle wheel

【桨手】boatman

jiàng

匠 ① craftsman; person with special skill: 木～ *carpenter; squareman* / 铁～ *blacksmith* / 能工巧～ *skillful craftsman* ②［书］person of great achievement in a certain field: 文学巨～ *a great master in literature*

【匠气】（of sculpture or painting）mediocre with no originality

【匠人】artisan; craftsman

【匠心】［书］craftsmanship; ingenuity: ～独具 *have great originality; show distinctive ingenuity*

降 ① drop; fall: 气温下～。*The temperature drops.* / 起伏的山丘逐渐向海岸缓～。*The rolling hills fall gently toward the coast.* ② lower; reduce: ～低价格 *lower the price* ③（Jiàng）a surname

see also xiáng

【降班】send（a student）to a lower grade

【降半旗】flag flown at half-mast: ～致哀 *fly a flag at half-staff as a sign of mourning*

【降半音】【音】flat

【降等】degradation

【降低】reduce; cut down; drop; lower: ～成本 *cut the cost* / ～房租 *lower the rent of a house* / ～废品

率 *reduction in the number of rejects* / ~功率 *reduce power* / ~生活水准 *lower the living standard* /气压在~。*The air pressure is falling.* /价格~了。*Prices dropped.* /我不愿~自己的身份去跟这样一种粗鲁的人讲话。*I wouldn't lower myself to speak to such a rude person.*

【降调】【语】falling tone

【降幅】(of prices, income; etc.) the range of falling: 今年油的价格~很大。*The prices of oils have fallen by a big margin this year.*

【降格】[书] lower one's standard or status

【降格以求】set one's aim lower than usual; settle for a second best

【降号】【音】flat

【降级】① reduce to a lower rank; demote ② send (a student) to a lower grade

【降价】reduce (or lower) the prices: 这种裙子过时了,我们只好~。*This kind of skirt is out of date, and has to bring down the price.*

【降解】degradation: ~代谢 *katabolism*/ ~作用 *degradation*

【降临】befall; arrive; come: 黑夜迅速~。*Night fell quickly.*

【降落】descend; land: 安全~ *land safely* /强迫~ *forced landing* /由于大雾,飞机无法~。*The plane cannot land because of the bad fog.*

【降落区】dropping zone

【降落伞】parachute

【降幂】【数】descending power

【降旗】lower a flag: 船长命令~休假一周。*Captain gave the order to lower the flags for a week holiday.*

【降生】[书] be born

【降水】【气】precipitation: 人工~ *artificial precipitation*

【降水概率】【气】precipitation probability

【降水带】precipitation zone

【降水量】precipitation; amount of precipitation

【降水量学】hyetology

【降温】① lower the temperature (as in a workshop): 采取~措施 *take measures to lower the temperature* ② drop in temperature ③ cool down; decrease: 出国热已经~。*The craze of going abroad has already waned.*

【降雪】snowfall

【降雪量】snowfall

【降压】①【电】step-down: ~变压器 *step down transformer* / ~电阻器 *voltage dropping resistor* / ~调节器 *set down voltage regulator* ② bring high blood pressure down ③ depressurization; pumpdown

【降压片】【药】hypertension pill

【降雨】moisture; rainfall: 人工~ *artificial rainfall* /对流性~ *convective rainfall* / ~强度 *rainfall intensity* / ~指数 *pluvial index*

【降雨量】rainfall: 年~ *annual rainfall*

【降职】demote: 他由中士~到下士。*He was demoted from sergeant to corporal.*

【降旨】issue an imperial edict

将 ① general: 少~ *major general* ② lead; command
see also jiāng

【将兵】command troops

【将才】① talent as a field commander ② man with military talent; born general

【将官】(jiàngguān) general

【将官】(jiàngguan) high-ranking military officer

【将领】high-ranking military officer; general

【将令】military orders: 传~ *issue the commanding general's order*

【将门】the family of a general

【将门虎子】a capable young man from a a distinguished family

【将士】[书] officers and men

【将帅】commander-in-chief

【将校】generals and field officers; high-ranking officers

【将指】① middle finger ② big toe

洚 [书] be in flood; overflow: ~水 *floodwater*

绛 crimson; deep red

【绛紫】dark reddish purple

强 stubborn; unbending: 倔~ *obstinate*; *unyielding*
see also qiáng; qiǎng

【强嘴】talk back; reply defiantly; answer back

酱 ① a thick sauce made from fermented beans, wheat, etc.: 甜面~ *a sweet sauce made of fermented flour* ② cooked or pickled in soy sauce: ~黄瓜 *pickled cucumber* ③ pickle in soya sauce ④ paste; jam: 芝麻~ *sesame paste* / 辣椒~ *chilli sauce*

【酱菜】vegetables pickled in soy sauce; pickles

【酱豆腐】fermented bean curd

【酱坊】shop making and selling sauce, pickles, etc.

【酱缸】jar for making or keeping thick soya bean sauce

【酱肉】pork cooked in soy sauce

【酱色】caramel; dark reddish brown

【酱油】soy sauce; soy

【酱园】a shop making and selling sauce, pickles, etc.; sauce and pickle shop

【酱紫】dark reddish purple

犟 stubborn; obstinate; unyielding

【犟劲】obstinacy; stubbornness; doggedness: 他的~使他拒绝道歉。*Sheer obstinacy prevented him from apologizing.*

【犟嘴】reply defiantly; answer back; talk back

糨 thick: 粥熬得太~了。*The porridge is too thick.*

【糨糊】paste, mixture of flour, water, etc. for sticking things together: 打~ *make paste*

【糨子】paste

jiāo

交 ① deliver; pass on; hand over: 移～ *hand over*; *make over*/ ～作业 *hand in one's homework* /这事就～给我吧。*You can just leave it to me.* ② reach; come: 快～夏至了。*The Summer Solstice is coming near.* ③ (of time; place, etc.) joining part: 夏秋之～ *when summer is changing into autumn* ④ intersect; cross: 两条直线～于A点。*One line intersects the other at A.* ⑤ associate with: ～朋友 *make friends* ⑥ friendship; acquaintance: 邦～ *relations between two countries* /绝～ *split chums*; *break off relations* / 一面之～ *have met for only once* ⑦ mate; breed: 杂～ *cross-fertilize*; *crossbreed*; *intercross* ⑧ exchange; communicate: 打～道 *contact with sb or sth*; *deal with* /水乳～融 *as well mixed as milk and water — in complete harmony* ⑨together; at the same time: 饥寒～迫 *suffer hunger and cold* / 内外～困 *be put into difficulties inside and outside*

【交白卷】① hand in a blank examination paper ② completely fail to accomplish a task: 他什么也没做,回去只好～。*He didn't do anything at all and he had nothing to report back.*

【交班】hand over to the next shift; turn over one's duty

【交办】entrust (sth to one's subordinates); send (sb) on an errand

【交杯酒】drink the nuptial cup; drink "cross-cupped wine"

【交兵】[书] be at war; wage war: 两国～,不斩来使。*Two countries at war would not kill each other's envoys.*

【交叉】① intersect; cross; crisscross: 马路通常以直角～。*Streets usually intersect at right angles.* / 沿着这条路走,然后在第二个～口向右拐。*Go down this street, then turn right at the second crossing.* ② overlapping: ～的意见 *the overlapping ideas* ③ alternate; stagger: ～进行 *do alternately*

【交差】report to the superior after accomplishing a task: 我正在发愁如何～。*I am worrying about my account for my mission.*

【交错】① interlock; crisscross: 道路纵横～。*The roads crisscross.* ②【机】staggered: ～比例 *alternate proportion* / ～层 *cross-bedding* / ～抽样 *zigzag sampling* / ～函数 *alternate function* / ～矩阵 *alternate matrix* / ～纹理 *cross lamination* / ～周期 *stagger cycle*

【交代】① hand over: ～工作 *hand over one's job* ② tell; leave words: ～得清清楚楚 *give a clear-cut order* ③ explain; make clear; brief: ～任务 *assign and explain a task oneself* ④ confess: ～罪行 *confess a crime*

【交待】finish; end sadly: 要是飞机出了事,这条命也就～了。*If the plane had an accident, my life would be over.*

【交道】contact; dealings: 打～ *have dealings with sb*

【交底】tell sb what one's real intentions are; put all one's cards on the table: 相互～ *tell each other the bottom line*

【交点】①【数】point of intersection; crossover point ②【天】node

【交叠】crossover; overlapping; blend

【交锋】cross swords; engage in a battle or contest: 与敌人～ *fight a battle with the enemy*; *engage the enemy in battle*

【交付】① pay: ～定金 *pay down payment* ② hand over; deliver; consign: ～表决 *put to the vote* / ～日期 *due date* / ～运营 *be open to traffic*

【交割】① complete a business transaction ② delivery: ～日期 *date of delivery* /工作正在～。*The goods are just being turned over.*

【交工】hand over a complete project

【交公】hand over to the collective or the state

【交媾】sexual intercourse; copulation

【交好】be on friendly terms: 两国～。*The two countries befriend each other.*

【交合】① link together ② sexual intercourse

【交互】① each other; mutual ② alternately; in turn: 两种方法可以～使用。*The two methods can be used in turn.*

【交欢】[书] make friends with sb

【交还】give back; return

【交换】① exchange; swap: ～战俘 *exchange of prisoners of war* / ～礼物 *exchange gifts* / ～意见 *exchange ideas* / ～资料 *swap data* /比赛结束时,运动员像往常一样～了服装。*At the end of the game, players traditionally exchange shirts with each other.* ② business exchange: 商品～ *exchange of commodities*

【交汇】(of current; etc.) converge

【交会】rendezvous; intersection: ～点 *point of intersection* / ～面 *encounter plane*

【交火】fight; exchange fire

【交货】delivery; consignment: 分批～ *partial delivery* /即期～ *prompt delivery* /远期～ *forward delivery*

【交货单】delivery order

【交货港】port of delivery

【交货期】date of delivery

【交集】(of different feelings) be mixed; occur simultaneously: 悲喜～ *mixed feelings of grief and joy*

【交际】social intercourse; communication: 善于～ *be a good mixer* /语言是人们的～工具。*Languages are means of making communication.*

【交际花】[贬] social butterfly; society woman

【交际舞】ballroom dancing; social dancing

【交加】[书] (of two things) accompany each other; occur simultaneously: 风雪～ *a raging snowstorm* /贫病～ *be plagued by both poverty and illness*

【交角】①【航】inclination ②【数】angle of intersection

【交接】① join; connect ② hand over and take over: ~班 *relief of a shift* ③ associate with: 他善于~朋友。*He is good at making friends.*
【交结】① associate with ② [书] connect with each other: ~盘错 *interconnect and crisscross*
【交界】(of two or more places) have a common boundary
【交卷】① hand in an examination paper ② fulfill one's task; carry out an assignment
【交警】traffic police; traffic policeman
【交口】① with one voice: ~称赞 *be praised by one and all* ② [方] converse; talk: 我们久未~。*We have not been talking to each other for a long time.*
【交困】beset by troubles: 内外~ *be beset with difficulties both at home and abroad*
【交流】① flow simultaneously: 涕泪~ *shed tears and have a runny nose* ② exchange; interflow; interchange: ~经验 *exchange experience* /文化~ *cultural exchange*
【交流电】alternating current generator; alternator: ~磁铁 *alternating electromagnet*
【交纳】pay (to the state or an organization); hand in: ~所得税 *pay income tax*
【交配】mating; copulation: ~期 *mating season*
【交迫】hard pressed on both sides
【交情】friendship; friendly relations: 老~ *longstanding friendship* / ~甚笃 *have sincere and deep friendship* /我们是老~了。*We have longstanding friendship.* /我和那个经理~很好。*I'm on familiar terms with that manager.*
【交融】blend; mingle: 水乳~ *blend as well as milk and water — in complete harmony*
【交涉】negotiate; make representations: 虽然经过多次~,事情仍然没有解决。*The problem has not been solved though repeated negotiations have been made.*
【交手】fight hand to hand; be engaged in a hand-to-hand fight; come to grips
【交售】sell (to the state): 向国家~更多棉花 *sell more cotton to the state*
【交泰】union; harmony: 日月~ *union of the sun and the moon*
【交谈】talk with each other; converse; chat: 亲切~ *have a heart-to-heart talk*
【交替】① supersede; replace: 新老~ *the new replace the old* ② alternately; in turn: 昼夜~。*Night and day alternate.*
【交通】① be connected; be linked: 阡陌~ *crisscross of paths in fields* ② traffic; communications: ~堵塞 *traffic jam* /城市~ *municipal traffic* / ~事故 *traffic accident* /洪水使~陷入瘫痪。*Traffic was paralyzed by the flood.* ③ liaison: 跑~ *do liaison work* ④ liaison man; underground messenger: 地下~ *underground liaison man* ⑤ [书] associate with; collude with
【交头接耳】speak in each other's ears; whisper to each other; bill and coo; head to head: 你难道不知道~是不礼貌的吗? *Don't you know it's rude to whisper?*
【交往】association; contact: 和正当的人~ *in contact with the right people*
【交尾】mating; pairing; coupling
【交恶】fall foul of each other; become enemies
【交相辉映】enhance each other's beauty
【交响曲】【音】symphony
【交响诗】【音】symphonic poem
【交响乐】【音】symphony; symphonic music
【交响乐队】symphony orchestra; philharmonic orchestra
【交卸】hand over office to a successor
【交心】lay one's heart bare; open one's heart to sb
【交椅】① an ancient folding chair ② armchair ③ post; position: 他在单位里坐第一把~。*He is the leader in his unit; he occupies the highest post in his unit.*
【交易】business; deal; trade; transaction: 黑市~ *black market bargain* /做成一笔~ *make a deal* /禁止非法~ *ban illegal transactions* /劳务~ *service transaction* /买卖~ *bargaining transaction* /配额~ *rationing transaction* /期货~ *forward (or futures) transaction* /双边~ *bilateral transaction* /委托~ *agency transaction* /现金~ *cash transaction* /虚市~ *bogus transaction*
【交易会】trade fair
【交易所】exchange: 证券~ *stock exchange; security exchange* / ~价格 *exchange price*
【交谊】[书] friendship; friendly relations
【交谊舞】"friendship dance" — social dance; ballroom dance
【交游】[书] make friends; keep company: ~广阔 *have a wide acquaintance; have a wide circle of friends*
【交战】be at war; fight; wage war: ~地带 *war zone* / ~状态 *state of war*
【交战国】belligerent countries (or states, nations)
【交账】① hand over the accounts ② account for: 我们该怎么向他~? *What are we going to say to him?*
【交织】interweave; intertwine; mingle: 惊异和喜悦~在一起。*Joy mingled with surprise.*

郊 suburbs; outskirts: 西~ *the western suburbs* /远~ *the outer suburbs; the remoter outskirts of a city*
【郊区】suburban district; suburbs; out-skirts: 他住在~,而在城里工作。*He lives in the suburb and works in the city.* /他住在巴黎~。*He lives on the outskirts of Paris.*
【郊外】the countryside around a city; outskirts
【郊游】outing; excursion: 海滨~ *an outing at the beach*

浇[1] ① sprinkle water on; pour water on: 大雨把他全身都~透了。*The downfall made him drenched.* ② water; irrigate: ~地 *irrigate the fields* ③ cast: ~铅字 *cast lead into type; make type*

浇[2] [书] cold; harsh; mean

【浇版】【印】casting：~机 *casting machine*
【浇薄】[书]（of customs, manners, etc.）mean; unkind：人情~ *indifferent to the feeling of others* / ~之世 *the age of demoralization*
【浇补】casting-on; cast-on
【浇灌】① pour; mould：~混凝土 *pour concrete* ② water; irrigate：~荒地 *irrigate the desert*
【浇冷水】throw a damp over; throw a wet blanket on; throw cold water on：他给女儿的热情~。*He dampened down his daughter's ardour.*
【浇漓】[书]（of customs; morals; etc.）degenerate
【浇勺】pony ladle
【浇水】watering：请给草地~。*Please water the lawn.*
【浇头】[方] gravy with meat or vegetables poured over rice or noodles：~面 *noodles with sauce*
【浇注】①【冶】pour（melted metal, cement mixed with water, etc.）into a mould：~槽 *pouring basin* / ~点 *pour point* / ~温度 *pouring temperature* ② devote; give：他把全部心血~在学生身上。*He devoted himself heart and soul to his students.*
【浇铸】【冶】casting; pouring：金属~ *metal founding* / ~点 *pour point* / ~间 *casting bay*

娇 ①（of women, children, flowers, etc.）pretty; tender; charming：嫩红~绿 *tender blossoms and delicate leaves* ② finicky; fragile; frail：才干了一小时的活就说累，她未免太~了。*She began complaining about tiredness after working for just one hour; she's too frail.* ③ pamper; spoil：小孩不能太~！*Don't pamper your child!*
【娇嗔】（young woman）be coquettishly to be angry
【娇宠】pamper; spoil：~孩子 *spoil one's child* / 谁都喜欢偶尔让人~一下。*Everybody enjoys being spoiled from time to time.*
【娇滴滴】delicately pretty; affectedly sweet：一个经常生病的~的孩子 *a delicate child who is often ill*
【娇儿】a darling son
【娇惯】pamper; coddle; spoil：他是有钱人家~的孩子。*He is a pampered child of the rich.*
【娇贵】① spoiled; coddled ② delicate and fragile：这些~的箱子完整无损地运到了。*The fragile boxes arrived intact.*
【娇憨】young and ignorant
【娇客】① son-in-law ② a pampered person
【娇媚】① coquettish：~的女子 *a coquettish woman* ② sweet and charming
【娇嫩】① tender and lovely：~的花瓣 *a tender petal* ② fragile; delicate：~的幼苗 *delicate seedlings*
【娇娘】beautiful young lady
【娇女】beloved daughter
【娇妻】young and pretty wife
【娇气】① fragile; delicate：~的植物必须妥为保护以避免风霜的侵袭。*Delicate plants must be protected from cold wind and frost.* ② squeamish; finicky：去掉~ *get rid of squeamishness* / ~十足 *be full of finicality*
【娇娆】enchantingly beautiful
【娇柔】gentle and demure
【娇弱】tender and delicate
【娇生惯养】have been delicately brought up; be pampered and spoiled; be accustomed to delicate living：这个孩子从小~。*The child was brought up in clover.*
【娇声娇气】speak in a seductive tone
【娇态】sweet and charming manner
【娇娃】a pretty girl
【娇小】petite; delicate：~的身材 *a petite figure*
【娇小玲珑】delicate and exquisite; petite and dainty
【娇羞】coy：~的女郎 *a coying maiden*
【娇艳】delicate and charming; tender and beautiful
【娇养】pamper（a child）; spoil：这个小女孩被~得不像话 —— 父母对她是有求必应。*The little girl is terribly spoilt — her parents give her everything she asks for.*
【娇纵】indulge（a child）; pamper; spoil：他对他的孩子太~了。*He indulges his children too much.*

姣 [书] beautiful; pretty; handsome

骄 ① conceited; arrogant; haughty; proud：戒~戒躁 *guard against arrogance* ②[书] intense; fierce; violent：~兵必败 *an arrogant army is bound to lose*
【骄傲】① arrogant; conceited; be cocky：~自大的人 *an arrogant person* / 他在小有成就之后变得~起来。*He became conceited after only modest success.* ② be proud of; take pride in：为能报效国家而~ *be proud to serve one's country* / 我们的足球队对今年战无不胜甚感~。*Our football team feels proud that it has won every match this year.* ③ pride：万里长城是民族的~。*The Great Wall is the pride of our nation.*
【骄横】arrogant and imperious; overbearing：~的态度 *an overbearing manner*
【骄横跋扈】throw one's weight around; lordly and imperious
【骄矜】[书] self-important; proud：~自负 *be proud and conceited*
【骄慢】arrogant; haughty：~的女孩子在学校常常不受人欢迎。*A haughty girl is always unpopular at school.*
【骄气】overbearing airs; arrogance
【骄人】① villain holding sway ②treat others overbearingly
【骄奢淫逸】extravagant and dissipated; a luxurious and dissipated life; wallowing in luxury and pleasure
【骄阳】[书] the scorching sun; blazing sun：~似火 *the sun blazing like a ball of fire*
【骄躁】be arrogant and flippant
【骄子】① the son in favour ② a person in favour：天之~ *an unusually lucky person*
【骄纵】arrogant and willful

胶 ① glue; gum: 乳~ *emulsion* /鱼~ *fish glue* /皮~ *hide glue* /万能~ *all-purpose adhesive* ② glue; stick: 相框坏了,请尽快把它~上。*The picture frame is broken, so please glue it soon.* ③ sticky; gluey ④ rubber
【胶版】offset plate
【胶布】① rubberized fabric; blanket cloth ② adhesive plaster
【胶草】gum-plant
【胶层】substratum; bond line
【胶带】rubberized tape; adhesive tape
【胶合】agglutinate; veneer
【胶合板】plywood; veneer board: ~工业 *plywood industry* /~内层 *backing of veneer*
【胶接】cementing; glue joint
【胶卷】film; roll film: 彩色~ *colour film* /黑白~ *black and white film*
【胶囊】capsule; cachet
【胶泥】clay; cement
【胶粘】gum; glue off: ~水泥 *mastic* /~涂料 *bonded coating*
【胶皮】①【化】(vulcanized) rubber: ~带 *rubber belt* ②[方] rickshaw
【胶片】film: 电影~ *cinefilm* /缩微~ *microfiche*
【胶片厂】photographic film plant
【胶圈】rubber ring
【胶水】glue; mucilage
【胶鞋】rubber shoes; rubbers; tennis shoes
【胶靴】high rubber overshoes; galoshes
【胶衣】glaze; gel coat
【胶印】【印】offset printing; offset lithography
【胶原】collagen: ~蛋白 *collagen*
【胶纸】gummed paper: ~带 *masking tape*
【胶着】deadlocked; stalemated: ~状态 *deadlock; stalemate*

教 teach; instruct: 我来~你怎么学英语。*I'll teach you how to learn English.* /陈老师~语文。*Mr. Chen teaches Chinese; Mr. Chen instructs us in Chinese.*
see also jiào
【教书】teach school; teach: 他在大学~。*He teaches in the college.*
【教书育人】impart knowledge and educate people
【教书匠】pedagogue
【教学】teach school; teach

椒 any of several hot spice plants: 花~ *Chinese prickly ash* /辣~ *chilly; red pepper* /胡~ *pepper*
【椒房】imperial concubine's residence
【椒盐】a condiment made of roast prickly ash and salt; spiced salt: ~排骨 *spareribs with spiced salt*

蛟
【蛟龙】flood dragon, a mythical creature capable of invoking storm

焦[1] ① burnt; charred: 舌敝唇~ *one's tongue and lips are parched — wear oneself out in pleading* /饭烧~了。*The rice is burnt.* ② coke: 炼~ *coking* ③ anxious; worried: 心~ *extremely worried* ④ (in traditional Chinese medicine) certain parts of the body: 上~ *part of the body cavity above the diaphragm housing the heart and lungs* /下~ *part of the body cavity below the umbilicus housing the bladder, kidneys and bowels* ⑤ (Jiāo) a surname

焦[2] joule, a measure of energy or work
【焦愁】be worried; be anxious: 母亲为他的病而~。*Mother was anxious for his illness.*
【焦点】①【数】【物】focal point; focus: 虚~ *virtual focus* /实~ *real focus* ② focus: 透镜的~ *the focus of a lens* ③ central issue: 成为世人瞩目的~ *be the focus of world attention*
【焦度】focal power
【焦耳】【物】joule: ~定律 *Joule's law* /~积分 *joule integral* /~热 *joule heat*
【焦烦】irritable; agitated
【焦黑】burned black
【焦化】【化】coking: ~产品 *coke chemicals* /~气体 *coking gas*
【焦黄】sallow; brown: 面色~ *a sallow face*
【焦急】anxious; worried: 他~地等待考试结果。*He was worried about the result of the exams.*
【焦距】【物】focal distance; focal length: 这张照片看上去有些滑稽,我想你是忘了给照相机调~了。*This photograph looks funny; I think you forgot to focus the camera.*
【焦渴】terribly thirsty; parched
【焦枯】dried up; withered
【焦劳】[书] worry and trouble about: 为国~ *be deeply concerned about the country's affairs*
【焦雷】a clap of thunder
【焦裂】split apart or crack because of a serious shortage of water: ~的土地 *cracked ground*
【焦炉】coke oven
【焦虑】worried; feel anxious: 把你的~讲出来 *speak out your worries* /我们都为他的安全而~。*We are all anxious about his safety.*
【焦煤】coking coal
【焦墨】thick ink
【焦热】extremely hot
【焦思】rack one's brains; feel anxious
【焦炭】coke: ~塔 *coking drum* /~砖 *coalite*
【焦糖】caramel
【焦头烂额】in a sorry plight; in a terrible fix; utterly exhausted from overwork: 他真是~,钱丢了,又没赶上回家的末班车。*He was in a sorry plight — he had lost his money and missed the last bus home.*
【焦土】scorched earth — ravages of war, fire, etc.: 大火以后一片~。*After the fire everything lay in ruins.*
【焦心】[方] feel terribly worried
【焦油】【化】tar; pez; coke tar: ~沥青 *tar asphalt* /~酸 *tar acid*
【焦枣】fire-dried stoned dates
【焦躁】restless with anxiety; impatient: 别这么~。*Don't be so restless.*

【焦躁不安】restless and ill tempered
【焦轴】focal axis
【焦炙】terribly worried; burning with anxiety; on pins and needles
【焦灼】[书] deeply worried; very anxious: 儿子的失踪让她~万分。*She was worried about her missing son.*

跤 fall: 摔了一~ *stumble and fall*

鲛 【动】shark

蕉 any of several broadleaf plants: 香~ *banana* /美人~ *canna*; *Indian shot*
see also qiáo
【蕉麻】【植】abaca; Manila hemp
【蕉农】banana producer

礁 ① reef; rock: 暗~ *submerged reef* ② coral reef
【礁壁】reef wall
【礁岛】reef island
【礁鹿】key deer
【礁石】reef; rock; riff
【礁岩】【地】reef rock

jiáo

矫
see also jiǎo
【矫情】[方] argumentative; unreasonable; quarrelsome: 犯~ *argue unreasonably*

嚼 masticate; chew; munch: 咬文~字 *play with words*; *word-splitting* /细~慢咽 *chew carefully and swallow slowly*
see also jué
【嚼裹儿】[方] expenses for living
【嚼舌】① wag one's tongue; chatter; gossip: 你不应该听~的话。*You shouldn't listen to gossip.* ② argue meaninglessly; squabble: 我没功夫和你~。*I have no time to squabble with you.*
【嚼烟】chewing tobacco
【嚼用】[口] expenses for living
【嚼子】bit (of a bridle); snaffle

jiǎo

角[1] ① horn: 牛~ *oxhorn* /羊~ *sheep horn* ② (in ancient times) musical wind-instrument used in the army: 号~ *bugle* ③ objects in the form of a horn: 皂~ *Chinese honey locust* /菱~ *water caltrop*; *water chestnut* ④ cape, usu. used in place names: 镇海~ *Zhenhai Cape*, *in Fujian Province* ⑤ corner: 桌子~ *the corner of a table* /墙~ *corner of wall* /天涯海~ *the ends of the earth* /英语~ *English corner* /他把名字写在卷子的左下~。*He wrote his name on the left hand corner of the paper.* ⑥【数】angle: 直~ *a right angle* /锐~ *a sharp angle* /钝~ *an obtuse angle* /反射~ *reflex angle* ⑦ quarter; an angled part of a whole: 一~饼 *a quarter of a pancake* ⑧ a star constellation, one of the twenty-eight constellations

角[2] a fractional unit of money in China, which equals 1/10 of *a yuan* or 10 *fen*
see also jué
【角半径】angular radius
【角边】arm of angle; leg of angle
【角变换】angular transformation
【角材】angle section
【角尺】angle square
【角蛋白】【生化】keratin
【角点】angular point
【角动量】angular momentum; moment of momentum
【角度】①【数】angle: 把照相机转个~ *to angle a camera* /从任何~看都很漂亮的建筑物 *a handsome building looked at from any angle* ② point of view; angle: 他改变写报告的~,以取悦听众。*He angles his reports to please his listeners.*
【角缝】angle seam
【角钢】angle iron; angle steel: ~截面 *angle cross section* /~支柱 *angle post*
【角间距】angular separation
【角距】angle pitch; angular distance
【角楼】a watchtower at a corner of a city wall; corner tower; turret
【角落】corner; nook: 我独自坐在~里。*I sat by myself in the corner.*
【角膜】【生理】cornea: ~白斑 *walleye*
【角球】【体】corner kick
【角速度】angular velocity
【角体积】angular volume
【角运动】angular motion
【角质】【生理】cutin; keratin

侥
【侥幸】luck; by a fluke; accidentally obtaining profit or avoiding bad luck: 他怀着~心理作弊。*He cheated in the exam nursing the idea of leaving things to chance.* /他~得救。*He was snatched from the jaws of death.*

佼 [书] beautiful; pretty; handsome
【佼佼】[书] above average; outstanding

狡 cunning; crafty; sly
【狡辩】quibble; indulge in sophistry: 无理~ *sheer sophistry*
【狡猾】sly; crafty; cunning; tricky: ~的政客 *a tricky politician* /她父亲是一个~的老执法官。*Her father was a wily old attorney.*
【狡计】crafty trick; ruse: 和那个人做生意可要小心,他~多端。*Be careful when you do business with that man: he is full of craft.*
【狡狯】[书] deceitful; crafty: ~的人 *a man of deceit*

J

【狡兔三窟】a wily hare has three burrows — a foxy person has more than one hideout
【狡黠】[书] sly; crafty; cunning
【狡诈】deceitful; crafty; cunning: 为人～ *of deceitful temperament* /他用光明正大的方法得不到的东西,就采取～的手段。*When he couldn't get what he wanted openly and honestly, he resorted to low cunning.*

饺 a kind of dumpling (made by stuffing meat and vegetables in a wheaten wrapper): 水～ *boiled dumpling* /蒸～ *steamed dumpling*
【饺子】dumpling, wheaten food with finely chopped meat and vegetable as stuffing

绞 ① twist; entangle: 铁索是用许多铁丝～成的。*Many iron wires twist into an iron chain.* /好多问题～在一起,把我都闹糊涂了。*With so many problems mixed up with each other, I am quite confused.* ② twist; wring: 把毛巾～干 *wring out a wet towel* ③【机】reaming: ～孔 *ream a hole* ④ kill sb by hanging from a rope around the neck: 明天一早他将作为间谍被～死。*He will be hanged as a spy early tomorrow morning.* ⑤ wind: ～着辘轳打水 *raise the water by winding the windlass* ⑥ skein: 一～纱 *a skein of yarn*
【绞车】winch; windlass; hoister; cable winch: ～架 *turntable*
【绞刀】【机】reamer; drift
【绞合】twisting; strand: ～天线 *stranded antenna wire*
【绞架】gallows
【绞接】【机】splice; wringing
【绞尽脑汁】rack one's brains; task one's mind: 他～地想他把钱放在哪儿了。*He racked his brains trying to remember where he had put the money.*
【绞轮】reel
【绞盘】capstan; winch: 推杆～ *bar capstan*
【绞肉机】meat grinder
【绞杀】① hang sb ② strangle; throttle: 她觉得她的创造力被～了。*She felt her creativity was being strangled.*
【绞纱】【纺】skein: ～染色 *skein dyeing*
【绞索】(the hangman's) noose; hemp death cord
【绞痛】【医】angina; colic pain: 心～ *angina pectoris*
【绞线】stranded conductor
【绞刑】death by hanging; hanging; sentence to be hanged; sentence to the gallows: ～架 *gallows (tree)* /将某人处以～ *send sb to the gallows*

铰 ① cut with scissors: 把布～开 *cut the cloth* ②【机】reaming hinge
【铰床】【机】reamer
【铰刀】①【机】broach; fraise; reamer ②[方] scissors
【铰接】【机】join with a hinge; articulate: ～框架 *hinged frame*
【铰具】reamer
【铰孔】【机】reaming; scan: ～车床 *reaming lathe*
【铰链】hinge; butt hinge: ～接合 *hinge joint*

矫[1] ① straighten out; rectify; remedy ② (Jiǎo) a surname

矫[2] brave; strong

矫[3] feign; pretend

see also jiáo

【矫健】strong and vigorous; robust; full of vim and vigour: ～的运动员 *a vigorous player* /～的步伐 *vigorous strides*
【矫捷】vigorous and nimble; brisk: ～的一跃 *a nimble leap*
【矫命】[书] counterfeit an order; issue false orders
【矫情】[书] be affectedly unconventional
【矫揉造作】affected; artificial; extremely unnatural: 他的态度～。*His manners are affected.* /他～地笑了一笑。*He smiled in an unnatural manner.*
【矫饰】feign in order to conceal sth; dissemble
【矫形】【医】orthopaedics: ～外科 *orthopedic surgery*
【矫正】correct; put right; rectify: ～发音 *correct sb's pronunciation mistakes* /～视力 *correct defects of vision*
【矫正术】diorthosis
【矫治】correct and cure: ～口吃 *correct and cure stammer*

皎 ①[书] clear and bright: ～月当空。*A luminous moon is shining in the sky.* ② (Jiǎo) a surname
【皎皎】very clear and bright; glistening white
【皎洁】(of moonlight) bright and clear

脚 ① foot: 赤～ *barefoot* /手忙～乱 *hurry-scurry* /他～上受了伤。*He got hurt in the foot.* ② base; foot: 墙～ *the foot of a wall* /山～ *the foot of a mountain* ③[方] refer to things relevant to carrying and transporting manually
【脚板】[方] sole (of the foot)
【脚背】instep
【脚本】script; scenario: 电影～ *film script* /～作者 *scenarist; scriptwriter*
【脚脖子】[方] ankle: 扭了～ *sprain one's ankle*
【脚步】① step; pace: 迈着蹒跚的～ *walk with tottering steps* /～轻快 *be light of foot* ② footstep; pace: 放慢～ *slow down one's pace*
【脚踩两只船】straddle two boats — have a foot in either camp
【脚灯】① footlights ② night light
【脚蹬子】pedal; treadle
【脚凳】footrest; footstool
【脚底】[方] sole (of the foot)
【脚垫】callus on the sole of the foot
【脚夫】[旧] ① porter ② one who hires out his donkey or horse to riders and leads or follows it on foot
【脚跟】heel; footing: 站稳～ *stand firm*
【脚光】footlight
【脚行】[旧] ① a business concern operating a porters' service ② porter
【脚后跟】heel

【脚户】[方] porter
【脚踝】【生理】malleolus; ankle
【脚架】foot stool
【脚迹】footprint; footmark; track
【脚尖】the tip of a toe: 踮着～ *walk on tiptoe* /～舞 *toe dancing*
【脚劲】[方] strength of one's legs
【脚扣】foot clasp (for climbing posts)
【脚力】① strength of one's legs ② porter ③ payment to a porter
【脚镣】fetters; shackles: 囚犯戴上了～。*Shackles were placed on the prisoner's feet.*
【脚炉】foot warmer; foot stove
【脚马】straw of rope, etc. worn over ordinary shoes to prevent sliding
【脚盆】a basin for washing feet
【脚蹼】flippers; fin
【脚气】【医】① beriberi; barbiers ② athlete's foot
【脚钱】[旧] payment to a porter
【脚刹车】service brake
【脚手架】scaffold; scaffolding
【脚踏】pedal: ～板 *foot-plate*; *foot rest*
【脚踏车】bicycle
【脚踏船】pedalo
【脚踏实地】have one's feet planted on solid ground — earnest and down-to-earth: 你必须始终～。*You must always build on firm ground.*
【脚腕子】ankle
【脚下】① underfoot ② [方] the present moment; at present ③ [方] near at hand; close: 大年～ *close to the Spring Festival*
【脚心】arch (of the foot); arch
【脚癣】【医】ringworm of the foot; athlete's foot
【脚丫子】[方] foot
【脚印】footprint; footmark; track: 他把～留在了身后的沙滩上。*He left footprints behind him on the sand.*
【脚闸】coaster brake
【脚掌】sole (of the foot)
【脚爪】[方] claw; paw; talon
【脚指头】[口] toe
【脚趾】toe
【脚柱】socle; stilt
【脚注】footnote
【脚镯】anklet; bangle

搅 ① stir; mix: 把粥～匀了。*Stir the porridge thoroughly.* ② annoy; disturb: 胡～ *be annoying* /隔壁的音乐声太大，～得我难以入睡。*The music in the neighbourhood produced a too big noise to make me fall asleep.*
【搅拌】stir; agitate; mix; beat; whisk: ～油漆 *stir the paint* /在喝汤之前先～一下。*Stir the soup before tasting it.* /～这些鸡蛋直到它们蓬松。*Carry on beating the eggs until they're light and fluffy.*
【搅拌机】mixer; puddle mixer
【搅拌器】treater; plunger
【搅棒】splash bar
【搅缠】pester; disturb
【搅动】① mix; stir; whip: 把汤放在锅里加热并不时地～。*Heat the soup in a pan and stir it regularly.* ② disturb; mess up
【搅街】[方] (of prostitutes) walk in the street to solicit patrons
【搅浑】stir and make muddy; deliberately create confusion
【搅混】[方] mix; blend; mingle
【搅和】[方] ① mix; blend; mingle: 把糖和面粉～在一起。*Blend the sugar and flour.* /他熟练地把面粉和鸡蛋～在一起。*He expertly whisked the eggs and flour together.* ② mess up; spoil: 别～他人之事。*Don't mess in the affairs of others.*
【搅局】upset a scheme or plan
【搅乱】confuse; throw into disorder: 繁杂的情节把我～了。*The complex plot fuddles my comprehension.* /他们问了我许许多多的问题，把我～了。*They asked me so many questions that I got confused.*
【搅扰】disturb; annoy; bother: 我小睡的时候不要～我。*Don't disturb me while I am taking my nap.*

剿 suppress; put down: 围～敌人 *encircle and annihilate the enemies*
【剿除】exterminate; wipe out
【剿匪】suppress bandits
【剿灭】exterminate; wipe out: ～残余土匪 *exterminate the remnants of the bandits*

缴 ① hand over; pay: ～学费 *pay the tuition fee* ② force sb to hand over; capture: ～了敌人的武器！*Disarm the enemies!*
【缴裹儿】[方] living expenses
【缴获】capture; seize: ～许多战利品 *seize a lot of booty*
【缴纳】pay: ～罚款 *pay the penalty*
【缴枪不杀】Lay down your arms and we'll spare your lives!
【缴税】pay taxes
【缴销】hand in for cancellation: ～营业执照 *hand in business license for cancellation*
【缴械】① disarm ② surrender one's weapons; lay down one's arms

jiào

叫[1] ① cry; shout: 狗～ *bark* /鸡～ *crow* /男孩大～救命。*The boy cried for help.* /她高兴得大声～了起来。*She shouted for joy.* ② call; greet: 你的电话～通了。*Your call has been put through.* /我把他～来了。*I called him over.* ③ order; hire: 他替她～了一辆出租车。*He called her a taxi.* /请替我～菜。*Please order for me.* ④ name; call: 你～什么名字? *What's your name?* /这种材料～不锈钢。*The material is named stainless steel.* ⑤ [方] male (animal): ～驴 *jackass*

叫[2] ① let; order: 这件事应该～他知道。*We should let him know about the matter.* ② ask; order: 大夫～他注意休息。*The doctor ordered him to rest often.* ③ by (to introduce the doer of an action): 他～雨淋了。*He got wet.*
【叫板】(in traditional opera) call for music

【叫春】(of cats) mating call
【叫喊】shout; yell; howl: 牙科大夫把牙拔出时，她痛得大声～起来。*She cried with pain when the dentist pulled the tooth out.* /她对淘气的孩子们～。*She yelled at the mischievous children.*
【叫好】applaud: 她讲完后，听众～。*When she finished her speech, the audience applauded.*
【叫号】① call out the numbers (of waiting patients, etc.) ②[方] sing a work song to synchronize movements ③[方] provoke by words; challenge
【叫花子】[口] beggar
【叫花子鸡】beggar's chicken (whole chicken baked in a mud coating)
【叫唤】① cry out; call out: 疼得～ *cry out with pain* ② (of animals, birds, insects, etc.) cry; call
【叫绝】shout "bravo!"; applaud: 拍案～ *applaud by thumping the table*
【叫苦】complain of hardship or suffering; moan and groan: 暗暗～ *groan inwardly*
【叫苦连天】complain to high heaven; complain bitterly
【叫驴】jackass
【叫骂】shout curses
【叫卖】cry one's wares; peddle; hawk: 在市场大声～货物 *cry one's wares in the marketplace* /沿街～ *hawk one's wares in the streets*
【叫门】call at the door to be let in
【叫名】① name ②[方] nominal; titular
【叫屈】complain of being wronged; protest against an injustice: 喊冤～ *cry out about one's grievances*
【叫嚷】shout; howl; clamour
【叫嚣】clamour; raise a hue and cry: 拼命～ *raise a terrific hue and cry*
【叫醒】wake up: 请在八点钟～我。*Please wake me up at 8 o'clock.*
【叫阵】challenge an opponent to a fight when two armies meet
【叫座】draw a large audience; draw well; appeal to the audience; be a box-office success: 这部电影很～。*This film is quite a box-office success.*
【叫做】be called; be known as: 这种饮料～鸡尾酒。*This kind of liquor is called cocktail.* / 他～迈克。*He is called Mike.*

觉 sleep: 午～ *midday nap* /睡个好～! *Have a good sleep!*
see also jué

校 ① check; proof read: ～稿子 *proofread the draft* ② compare; contrast
see also xiào
【校本】collated edition (of a book)
【校测】calibrate and test: ～功率 *calibrate and test power*
【校场】[旧] drill ground for practicing martial arts
【校点】check against the authoritative text and punctuate
【校订】check against the authoritative text
【校读】proofreading
【校对】① check against a standard; calibrate ② proofread; proof: 按原稿～一下文章 *proofread an article against the original manuscript* ③ proofreader
【校对员】corrector; proof-reader
【校改】read and correct proofs
【校勘】collate
【校色】【印】colour correction
【校图】check of drawing
【校验】verification; check; proof: ～点 *checkpoint* /～方位 *check bearing* /～仪表 *check meter*
【校样】【印】proof sheet; proof: 付印～ *final proof* /同意把～付印 *pass the proofs for press*
【校阅】① read and revise ②[书] review
【校正】proofread and correct; rectify: ～仪器 *rectify an instrument*
【校正信号】correction signal
【校注】check against the authoritative text and annotate
【校准】calibration
【校准表】calibration scale

轿 sedan (chair): 上～ *enter a sedan chair*
【轿车】①[旧](horse-drawn) carriage ② bus; closed car: 这种小～是上海产的。*This kind of car is made in Shanghai.*
【轿夫】sedan carrier; one who lives by carrying sedans
【轿子】sedan (chair)

较[1] ① compare: ～差 *relatively poor* /两物相比～ *compare one thing with another* /他今天～昨天好多了。*He is much better today than yesterday.* ②[书] dispute: 斤斤计～ *haggle over every ounce; be calculating* /锱铢必～ *quibble over every penny*

较[2] [书] obvious; clear: 彰明～著 *very obvious*
【较比】[方] comparatively; relatively; fairly; quite
【较劲】① match strength: 暗中～ *have a tacit contest with sb* ② set oneself against ③ require special effort: 眼下正是～的时候。*Now we must put special efforts on it.*
【较量】① measure one's strength with; have a contest: 势均力敌的～ *close contest* ②[方] haggle; argue; dispute
【较为】comparatively; relatively; fairly: 人类是地球上出现得～晚的一种生物。*Man is a comparatively new creature on the surface of the earth.*
【较真】[方] serious; earnest: 他真的～了。*He really took it seriously.*
【较著】[书] obvious

教 ① teach; instruct: 请～ *consult* /因材施～ *teach students in accordance of their aptitude* ② religion: 佛～ *Buddhism* /伊斯兰～ *Islam* /政～分离 *the separation of church and state* ③ (Jiào) a surname
see also jiāo

【教案】① teaching plan; lesson plan ②【历】Missionary case (an incident involving foreign missionaries)
【教本】textbook
【教鞭】(teacher's) pointer
【教材】teaching material
【教程】course of study: 语法～ *A Course in Grammar*
【教导】instruct; teach; give guidance: ～有方 *skillful in teaching and able to provide guidance* / 牢记某人的～ *remember sb's instruction by heart*
【教导员】political instructor
【教父】god-father
【教父教母】godparents
【教改】educational reform
【教工】teaching and administrative staff (of a school)
【教官】drillmaster; instructor
【教规】rules of a religion; canon
【教化】[书] enlighten by education
【教皇】【宗】pope; pontiff: 罗马～ *the Supreme Pontiff*
【教会】(the Christian) church: ～学校 *missionary school*
【教诲】[书] teaching; instruction: 谆谆～ *earnest teachings* / 他们未能通过谆谆～使学生们热爱知识。*They failed to inculcate students with love of knowledge.*
【教具】teaching aid
【教科书】textbook
【教练】① train; drill; coach: 我正在为赛跑进行～。*I am training for the race.* ② coach; instructor; trainer: 足球～ *football coach*
【教龄】length of service as a teacher
【教母】god-mother
【教女】god-daughter
【教派】religious sect; denomination
【教区】parish; diocese
【教师】teacher; schoolteacher: 代课～ *supply teacher* / 高级～ *senior teacher* / 兼课～ *part-time teacher* / 科任～ *departmental teacher* / 理科～ *science teacher* / 模范～ *model teacher* / 女～ *woman teacher* / 实习～ *apprentice teacher* / 小学～ *elementary teacher* / 新～ *beginning teacher* / 正式～ *certificated teacher* / 专职～ *full-time teacher*
【教师节】Teacher's Day
【教士】priest; clergyman; Christian missionary
【教室】classroom; schoolroom
【教授】① instruct; teach: 他在学校～历史。*He teaches history at school.* ② professor: 访问～ *visiting professor* / 副～ *an associate professor* / 交换～ *exchange professor* / 名誉～ *honorary professor* / 这个～的课生动有趣。*This professor's classes are lively and interesting.*
【教唆】instigate; abet; put sb up to sth: ～盗贼抢劫银行 *abet the thief in robbing the bank* / ～犯罪 *abet the commission of a crime* / ～叛乱 *instigate a rebellion*
【教唆犯】abettor; instigator
【教唆罪】instigation to a crime; solicitation
【教堂】church; cathedral; chapel: 他们在～中做礼拜。*They are in church, attending a service.*
【教条】dogma; doctrine; creed; tenet: 政治～ *a political dogma*
【教条主义】dogmatism; doctrinairism
【教廷】the Vatican; the Holy See
【教头】① chief military instructor (in Song Dynasty) ②[口] coach; instructor; trainer
【教徒】believer (or follower) of a religion: 基督～ *Christian* / 天主～ *(Roman) Catholic*
【教委】Commission of Education (now Ministry of Education)
【教务】educational administration: ～处 *Dean's office; office of teaching affairs*
【教习】①[旧] teacher; instructor ②[书] teach; train: ～绘画 *teach sb painting*
【教学】the process of teaching; education
【教学法】pedagogy
【教训】① chide; teach sb a lesson: 父亲教训了儿子一顿。*Father taught the son a lesson.* ② lesson; moral: 历史的～ *lessons of history*
【教研室】teaching and research section
【教养】① bring up; train; educate: ～子女 *bring one's children up* / 把她～成护士 *train her as a nurse* ② breeding; upbringing; education; culture: 有良好～的人 *a person of fine breeding* ③【律】correction; reeducation: 劳动～ *reeducation through labour*
【教养员】kindergarten teacher
【教养院】indoctrination centre; house of correction
【教义】religious doctrine; creed
【教益】[书] benefit gained from sb's wisdom; enlightenment
【教友】【宗】fellow; brother; sister
【教友会】Society of Friends; Quakers
【教育】① education: 大学～ *college education* / 高等～ *advanced education* / 贵族～ *aristocratic education* / 函授～ *correspondence education* / 免费义务～ *free and compulsory education* / 启蒙～ *formative education* / 青少年～ *adolescent education* / 全面～ *all-round education* / 他所接受的全部学校～加起来不过一年。*His whole school education added up to no more than one year.* ② teach; educate; inculcate: 应该～儿童讲老实话。*Children should be taught to speak the truth.*
【教员】teacher; instructor
【教正】[书] give comments and criticisms: 送上拙著一部，敬希～。*Please give your comments and criticisms on my presented work.*
【教职员】teaching and administrative staff
【教主】the founder of a religion
【教子】god-son
【教子有方】bring up one's children in a proper way

窖 ① cellar (or pit) for storing things: 白菜～ *cellar for storing Chinese cabbage* ② store sth in a cellar or pit: 把白薯～起来 *store the sweet potatoes in a pit*
【窖藏】store sth in a cellar or pit; hoard

【窖穴】cellar or pit for storing things
【窖子】［口］cellar or pit for storing things
酵 ferment; leaven
【酵母】yeast：活～ *viable yeast* /酒精～ *alcohol yeast* /饲料～ *nutrient yeast* /原～ *false yeasts* /种～ *dona yeast*
【酵素】ferment; enzyme：活性～ *active ferment*
【酵子】［方］leavening dough

jiē

节 see also jié
【节骨眼】［方］critical juncture; vital link; crisis：在这个～，你可不能走。*You shouldn't leave at this critical moment.* /你来的正是～。*You've come in the nick of time.*
【节子】knot (in wood)
阶 ① steps; stairs：台～ *step*; *sidestep* ②rank：军～ *military rank*
【阶层】①(social) stratum：低收入～ *the lower-income classes* ② class：劳动者～ *labouring class*; *working people*
【阶乘】【数】factorial：四的～ *the factorial of 4* /～函数 *factorial function* /广义～ *generalized factorial* /向量～ *factorial of a vector*
【阶地】【地】terrace：低潮～ *low-tide terrace* /断层～ *fault terrace* /海岸～ *coastal terrace* /海成～ *marine terrace* /宽谷～ *strath terrace* /潜伏～ *plunging terrace*
【阶段】stage; phase：过渡～ *a passing phase* /学步～ *the toddler stage* /经历三个～ *pass through three phases*
【阶级】①［书］steps; stairs ②［旧］rank ③(social) class：中产～ *middle class* /工人～ *working class* /有产～ *proprietary class* /～差异会造成国家的分裂。*Class differences can divide a nation.*
【阶梯】a flight of stairs; ladder
【阶梯教室】theater; amphitheatre; amphitheater
【阶调】contrast：～系数 *contrast factor*
【阶下囚】prisoner; captive
疖
【疖子】【医】furuncle; boil
皆 all; every：比比～是 *can be found everywhere* /尽人～知 *upon the table*; *everybody knows* /一着不慎，满盘～输。*One careless move loses the whole game.*
【皆大欢喜】everybody is happy; to everyone's satisfaction
【皆伐】【林】clear felling
结 bear (fruit)：开花～果 *blossom and bear fruit* /什么样的树～什么样的果。*Different trees bear different fruits.* see also jié
【结巴】① stammer; stutter：他一紧张就～。*He stammered when he was nervous.* /他～地道歉。*He stuttered (out) an apology.* /发言者丢掉了讲稿就开始～了。*The speaker faltered after dropping his notes.* ② stammerer; stutterer：那些～经常接受语言治疗。*Those stutterers often receive speech therapy.*
【结巴颏子】［方］stammerer; stutterer
【结果】bear fruit：桃树每年夏天～。*Peach trees bear fruit every summer.*
【结实】① solid; sturdy; durable：～的布 *durable cloth* ② strong; sturdy; tough：小伙子很～。*The young man is very strong.* /这个孩子有～的双腿。*The child had sturdy legs.*
接 ① come close to：短兵相～ *fighting at close quarters* /交头～耳 *whisper to each other* ② connect; join：～电线 *connect wires* ③ catch; take hold of：把球～住 *catch the ball* ④ receive：～电话 *receive a phone call* ⑤ meet; welcome：到机场～朋友 *meet one's friends on the airport* ⑥ take over; replace：～好革命班 *be worthy successors to the revolution* ⑦ (Jiē) a surname
【接班】① take one's turn on duty：我们下午2点～。*We'll take our turn on duty at 2 p. m.* ② take over from; succeed; carry on：老人要由年轻人来～。*The old men will be succeeded by the young people.*
【接班人】successor：社会主义～ *successors to the socialist cause*
【接茬儿】［方］① pick up the thread of a conversation ② after that; and then：随后他们～商量晚上开会的事。*After that, they began to discuss the meeting, which would be held in the evening.*
【接触】① come into contact with; get in touch with：我在旅途中～到许多新鲜事物。*I came into contacting with many new things in the trip.* /我们应加强与外部世界的积极～。*We should strengthen our active contact with the outside world.* ② engage：与敌人～ *engage the enemy* ③【电】contact：～不良 *loose contact*
【接二连三】one after another; in quick succession; repeatedly：他们～地站起来离开了办公室。*They got up and left the office one after another.* /～的疾病差一点要了他的命。*Diseases in rapid sequence nearly brought an end to his life.*
【接发球】【体】receive; return of service
【接防】relieve a garrison; relieve
【接风】give a dinner for a visitor：～洗尘 *give a dinner of welcome*
【接骨】【医】set a broken bone：～法 *synthetism*
【接骨术】【医】osteopathy; coaptation; bonesetting
【接管】take over control; take over：～生意 *take over the business*
【接轨】① connect the rails ② integrate; get onto the track：与国际惯例～ *follow international practice*
【接合】【机】joint：气密～ *airtight joint*
【接合处】junction; joint
【接合点】【军】junction point
【接合体】conjugant

【接火】[口] ① start to exchange fire ②【电】energize

【接济】give material assistance to; give financial help to; offer pecuniary aid to: 他急需～。*He is in urgent need of financial help.*

【接驾】greet an emperor; welcome an emperor

【接见】receive sb; grant an interview to: ～外国记者 *give an interview to foreign journalists*

【接近】be close to; near; approach: 性能～完美。*The performance approaches perfection.* / 这里是禁区不许～。*It is not allowed to approach the forbidden area.* / 虽然比赛赢了，但比分非常～。*Although the game was won, it was a very near thing.* / 她说的情况非常～事实。*What she said was very close to home.*

【接境】border on; share a common border

【接客】① (of a hotel, etc.) receive lodgers or guests ② (of a prostitute) receive or sleep with a patron

【接口】① continue the conversation; cut in ② join ③ opening that is cut when grafting ④ interface

【接力】work by relays: 火炬～ *torch relay*

【接力棒】relay baton

【接力赛跑】relay race; relay

【接力站】relay stations

【接连】on end; in a row; in succession: 四季的～ *the succession of the seasons* / ～获丰收 *reap several bumper harvests running* / 会议～开了两个小时。*The meeting lasted 2 hours on end.*

【接轮】cock wheel; third wheel

【接纳】① admit (into an organization): 他被律师协会～。*He was admitted to the bar association.* ② adopt; accept: 他～了我的意见。*He took out my advice.*

【接片】【影】splicing

【接气】coherent; consistent: 这个说法与你昨天会上的发言不～。*This statement is not consistent with what you said at yesterday's meeting.*

【接洽】take up a matter with; arrange (business, etc.) with; consult with: 与有关单位～ *take up the matter with departments concerned; consult with departments concerned*

【接腔】pick up the thread of a conversation: 他说完话，大家谁也没有～。*After his speaking, no one went on the topic.*

【接亲】[口] (of the bridegroom) go to the bride's home to escort her to the wedding

【接壤】border on; be contiguous to; be bounded by: ～地区 *contiguous areas* / 英格兰与威尔士～。*England is contiguous with Wales.*

【接任】take over a job; replace: 他～我当队长。*He replaced me as captain.*

【接入】insert; join up; switch on: ～电路 *place in circuit*

【接生】deliver a child; practice midwifery: ～婆 *midwife*

【接事】take over a job

【接收】① receive; accept: ～无线电信号 *receive radio signals* ② take over (property, etc.); expropriate: ～一个企业 *take over an enterprise* ③ admit: ～新成员 *recruit new members*

【接收端】receiving terminal (or end)

【接收机】receiver; radio set: ～干扰 *receiver interference* / ～灵敏度 *receiver sensitivity*

【接手】① take over (duties, etc.): 经理要求你～这个项目。*The manager asked you to take over the project.* ②【体】baseball, softball catcher

【接受】accept: ～礼物 *accept a gift* / ～邀请 *accept an invitation* / ～歉意 *accept apologies* / ～劝告 *take sb's advice*

【接谈】receive sb to discuss things

【接替】take over; replace: ～他作俱乐部主席 *succeed him as chairman of the club*

【接头】① connect; join; joint: 把两根线～ *connect two threads* ② contact; get in touch with; meet: ～地点 *contact point* ③ be familiar with; know about: 我刚来，这件事我还不～。*I am a stranger here and I don't know anything about it.* ④【纺】piecing; tying-in

【接头儿】connection; joint; junction: 万向～ *universal joint*

【接吻】kiss

【接线】【电】wiring: ～板 *terminal block; patch board* / ～布局 *wiring topology* / ～点 *wiring point* / ～图 *connection diagram; wiring diagram*

【接线员】switch board operator

【接续】continue; follow

【接应】① come to sb's aid; coordinate with; reinforce ② supply: 村子里水～不上。*Water was in short supply in the village.*

【接援】reinforce and aid

【接站】meet sb at the station

【接着】① catch: 她扔出了球，～！*She threw the ball. Catch!* ② follow; carry on: ～读书吧！*Carry on with your reading!* / 我们～唱歌吧！*Let's go on singing.*

【接枝】stem grafting

【接旨】receive (and accept) an imperial edict

【接踵】[书] following on sb's heels: 摩肩～ *jostle each other in a crowd*

【接种】【医】vaccinate; inoculate: 这小孩已经～了牛痘疫苗。*The child has been vaccinated against smallpox.*

秸 straw; stalks left after threshing: 麦～ *wheat straw*

【秸秆】straw

【秸子】[方] crop stalks after threshing: 苞米～ *corn stem; maize stalk*

揭 ①tear off: ～下这张膏药 *tear off the plaster* / 把包装纸从礼物上～下来 *tear the wrappings off the present* ②lift: ～开锅盖 *lift the lid of a cooking pot* ③expose; show up ④[书] raise; hoist ⑤ (Jiē) a surname

【揭榜】① announce the results of an examination ② tear off a notice inviting applications for jobs, etc. from a wall to show accepting of the invitation

【揭不开锅】[口] have nothing in the pot — have

nothing to eat; go hungry: 他失业以后,家里就~了。*Since he lost his job, the whole family has been in hunger.*

【揭穿】expose; disclose; lay bare; show up: 我们~了他的阴谋。*We exposed his plot.*

【揭疮疤】pull the scab right off sb's sore; touch sb on the raw

【揭底】reveal the inside story

【揭短】rake up sb's faults, shortcomings or weaknesses

【揭发】expose; unmask; bring to light: ~隐私 *reveal sb's secrets* / 对贪官污吏的罪行一定要毫无保留地予以~。*The crime of the corrupt officials must be exposed without any reserve.*

【揭盖子】take the lid off sth; bring sth into the open

【揭竿而起】start an uprising; rise in rebellion

【揭露】expose; unmask; ferret out; lay bare: ~非法活动 *lay bare illegal activities* / ~真相 *uncover the truth; make a disclosure of the truth*

【揭秘】unveil a mystery; break a secret

【揭幕】① unveil (a monument, etc.); inaugurate: 为塑像~ *unveil a statue* / 为展览会~ *inaugurate an exhibition* / 举行一个社区中心的~仪式 *inaugurate a community centre* ② raise the curtain; begin

【揭幕式】unveiling ceremony

【揭破】expose; lay bare; reveal; disclose; divulge: 他的犯罪活动最终被一个记者~。*His criminal activities were finally exposed by a journalist.*

【揭示】① announce; promulgate ② reveal; bring to light: ~身份 *reveal one's identity* / 进一步的调查~了事情的真相。*Further investigation revealed the true facts.*

【揭晓】announce; make known; publish: 比赛结果已经~。*The result of the contest has made known.*

喈

【喈喈】[书] ① (of sounds) harmonious: 鼓钟~。*Bells and drums resounded.* ② the sounds of birds: 鸡鸣~。*A cock is crowing.*

嗟

[书] sigh

【嗟悔】[书] be regretful

【嗟来之食】food handed out in contempt; handouts

【嗟叹】[书] sigh: ~不已 *sigh without ceasing*

街

① street: 大~ *avenue; main street* / 我在~上碰见他。*I met him in the street.* ② [方] fair; market

【街道】① street: 打扫~ *clean a street* / 美化城市~ *beautify the city streets* ② residential district; neighbourhood: ~办事处 *subdistrict office* / ~工厂 *neighbourhood factory* / ~派出所 *neighbourhood police substation* / ~食堂 *neighbourhood or community canteen* / ~医院 *neighbourhood hospital*

【街灯】streetlight; streetlamp

【街坊】[口] neighbour: 隔壁~ *a next-door neighbour*

【街垒】street barricade

【街门】a gate or door facing the street

【街面儿】[方] ① (activities, etc.) in the street ② neighbourhood

【街市】downtown streets

【街谈巷议】town talk

【街头】street; street corner: ~音乐家 *street musicians* / ~小丑 *a street juggler* / ~服装 *street clothes*

楷

[方] Chinese pistache

see also kǎi

jié

孑

[书] alone; lonely

【孑然】[书] solitary; lonely; alone: ~一身 *all alone in the world*

【孑遗】[书] the few survivors (of a disaster, massacre etc.)

节[1]

① joint; knob: 骨~ *joint of bones* / 关~ *joint; arthrosis* ② part; division: 音~ *syllable* ③ [量] section; length: 两~课 *two periods classes* ④ festival; holiday: 妇女~ *Women's Day* / 国庆~ *National Day* / 劳动~ *Labour Day* / 青年~ *Youth Day* ⑤ abridge ⑥ economize; save: 精简~约 *simplify administration and practise economy* ⑦ item: 情~ *plot* / 细~ *details* ⑧ moral integrity: 保持晚~ *maintain one's moral integrity in one's later years* ⑨ (Jié) a surname

节[2]

【航】Kn knot, a measure of the speed of a ship (1 knot equals 1 nautical mile per hour)

see also jiē

【节哀】[书] restrain one's grief (used in offering one's condolences): ~顺变 *restrain one's grief and accord with inevitable changes*

【节疤】bulging part of the bamboo and reed; joint

【节本】abridged edition; abbreviated version: 《红楼梦》*abridged edition of A Dream of Red Mansions*

【节表】section table

【节操】[书] high moral principle; moral integrity

【节点】【电】panel point; hybrid; node: ~电压 *node voltage* / ~方程 *nodal equation* / ~位移 *nodal displacement*

【节妇】[旧] woman who maintain unmarried after the death of her husband or after her engagement

【节概】[书] high moral principle; moral integrity

【节候】season and climate

【节货】goods supplied at festival time

【节假日】festivals and holidays

【节俭】thrifty; frugal: 一个~的主妇 *a thrifty housewife* / ~是一种美德。*It is a virtue to practice thrift.*

【节减】save and economize: ~开支 *reduce expenses*

【节节】successively：～胜利 *win many victories in succession*
【节孔】knothole
【节礼】gifts (or presents) sent in holidays
【节理】jointing; fissure：～面 *joint plane*
【节令】climate and other natural phenomena of a season：～不正 *not in the right season*
【节流】① reduce expenditure：开源～ *opening up the source and regulating the flow* ②【机】orificing; choke：～管 *throttle pipe* /～门 *gate throttle* /～嘴 *flow nipple*
【节录】extract; excerpt
【节律】the rhythm and pace of moving things：代谢～ *metabolic rhythm* /发育～ *developmental rhythm* /心动～ *rhythm of heart*
【节略】① capsule; except：演讲稿的～ *excerpt of a speech* ② reduce and save; omit ③ memorandum; aide-memoire
【节目】① programme; item (on a programme)：钢琴演奏～ *a programme of piano pieces* /我看了一个有关儿童的～。*I watched a programme about children.* ② item; list
【节目单】programme; playbill：一出剧的～包括演员表和与该剧有关的其他情况。*A programme for a play contains a list of the actors' names and other information about the play.*
【节能】save energy：～灯 *energy-saving lamp* /～灶 *energy-saving stove*
【节拍】【音】metre; beat：～频率 *beat frequency*; *clock frequency*
【节气】a day marking one of the 24 divisions of the solar year in the traditional Chinese calendar; solar terms
【节日】festival; red-letter day; holiday：整个镇上充满了欢乐的～气氛。*A happy festival atmosphere pervaded the whole town.*
【节省】economize; save; use sparingly; cut down on：～时间 *save one's time* /～精力 *save one's energy* /～经费 *retrench funds*
【节食】be moderate in eating and drinking; be (or go) on a diet
【节外生枝】① side issues or new problems crop up unexpectedly ② create side issues; cause complications
【节选】excerpts; extracts
【节要】main points of an extract; abstract：论文～ *gist of the extract from an essay*
【节衣缩食】economize on food and clothing; live frugally
【节油器】economizer; fuel-economizing device
【节余】① save ② surplus (as a result of economizing)
【节育】birth control：～环 *intrauterine device (IUD)* /～手术 *birth control surgery*
【节欲】continence; check one's selfish desire
【节约】practise thrift; economize; save：～用水 *economize on water* /～能源 *energy saving* /我们应该～用油，否则世界上就不会有油留下了。*We should save oil, or else there won't be any left in the world.* /他提出一个～人力物力的计划。*He came up with a plan that would economize on manpower and material resources.*
【节肢动物】arthropod
【节制】① direct; demand：这支队伍归你～。*The troop is under your command.* ② control; check; be moderate in：～饮食 *be moderate in eating and drinking*
【节奏】① rhythm：～明快 *lively rhythm* ② tempo：快～ *quick tempo* /慢～ *slow tempo*

讦 ［书］expose sb's past misdeeds：攻～ *rake up sb's past and attack him*

劫[1] ① rob; plunder; loot：趁火打～ *loot a burning house* ② compel; coerce

劫[2] disaster; misfortune：浩～ *great calamity*

【劫持】kidnap; hold under duress; hijack：～飞机 *hijack an airplane*
【劫夺】seize (a person or his property) by force
【劫匪】highwayman; robber
【劫富济贫】rob the rich and assist the poor
【劫后余生】be a survivor of a disaster：他～，因为他落到一个雪堆上。*He escaped death only because he landed in a snowdrift.* /如果我们能在这场危机中～，公司的前景还是光明的。*If we can come through this crisis the company's future looks bright.*
【劫机】air piracy; hijacking of aircraft：～者 *hijacker*; *skyjacker*
【劫难】disaster; calamity：他们祈求上帝保佑他们躲过～。*They prayed to God to protect them from further calamity.*
【劫掠】plunder; loot：～城里所有贵重的东西 *plunder all the valuable things in the city*
【劫数】【宗】inexorable doom; predestined fate：～难逃。*There is no escape from fate.*
【劫洗】loot; sack
【劫狱】break into a jail and rescue a prisoner
【劫运】adversity; misfortune

杰 ① outstanding person; hero：豪～ *gallant man* /英～ *hero* ② outstanding; prominent：人～地灵 *remarkable place turning out outstanding men*

【杰出】outstanding; remarkable; prominent：～的政治家 *conspicuous statesman* /～的作家 *distinguished writer*
【杰作】masterpiece; masterwork：毕加索的画都是～。*Picasso's paintings are all masterpieces.*

诘 ［书］interrogate：反～ *ask in retort* /盘～ *cross-examine*; *interrogate*

【诘难】［书］censure; rebuke; denounce
【诘问】［书］cross-examine; interrogate
【诘责】［书］censure; rebuke

拮

【拮据】in low water; short of money：我最近手头～。*I am hard up recently.*

洁 clean：整～ *tidy*; *neat* /纯～ *chaste*; *holy*; *immaculate*

【洁白】pure white; spotlessly white: ~的衣服 *spotless white dress*
【洁白无瑕】spotless white
【洁净】clean: ~的衣服 *clean clothes* / ~的手套 *spotless gloves* / ~的心 *a clean heart*
【洁具】sanitary equipment
【洁癖】cleanliness; mysophobia
【洁身自好】preserve one's moral integrity: ~的生活 *a clean life*

结 ① tie; weave: ~网 *weave a net* /张灯~彩 *decorate with lanterns and streamers* ② knot: 死~ *dead knot* /在一根绳子上打~ *tie a knot in a piece of string* /解开一个~ *untie* (*or undo*) *a knot* ③ join; assemble: 集会~社 *assembly and association* ④ settle; conclude: 归根~底 *in the final analysis* ⑤ [旧] written guarantee: 具~ *sign an undertaking*
see also jiē
【结案】wind up a case; close a case
【结拜】[旧] become sworn brothers or sisters
【结伴】go with: ~而行 *go* (*or travel*) *in a group*
【结冰】freeze; ice over: 地下室里的水管~了。*The pipes froze in the basement.*
【结彩】adorn (or decorate) with festoons
【结肠】【生理】colon: ~炎 *colonitis*
【结成】form; establish: ~同盟 *form an alliance*
【结仇】start a feud; become enemies: 他们之间曾经~。*There once existed animosity between them.*
【结存】① cash on hand; balance: 现款~已经不多了。*There isn't much cash on hand.* ② goods on hand; inventory
【结单】statement of account
【结党营私】form a clique to pursue selfish interests; band together for selfish purposes
【结发夫妻】husband and wife by the first marriage
【结构】① structure; composition; construction: 人体~ *structure of the human body* /组织~ *framework of organization* ②【建】structure; construction: 钢~ *steel structure* ③【地】texture
【结关】customs clearance: ~费用 *clearance fee* / ~港口 *port of clearance*
【结果】① result; outcome: 他的努力得到好~。*His hard work brings about good results.* ② kill; finish off: 他被~了。*He is killed.*
【结合】① combine; unite; integrate; link: 使理论与实践相~ *combine theory with practice* ② marry; be united in wedlock
【结核】①【医】tubercle; tuberculosis: 骨~ *bone tuberculosis* ②【矿】nodule: 锰~ *manganese nodule*
【结核病】tuberculosis: 假~ *spurious tuberculosis* / 牛~ *bovine tuberculosis* /禽~ *avian tuberculosis* / 吸入性~ *aerogenic tuberculosis*
【结汇】settlement of exchange
【结婚】marry; get married; be married: ~登记 *marriage registration* / ~仪式 *wedding ceremony* / ~证书 *marriage certificate* /他很高兴他和一个活泼的姑娘结了婚。*He is glad that he married a girl of spirit.* / 草率~后悔多。*Marry in haste and repent at leisure.*
【结伙】gang: ~斗殴 *gang fighting*
【结集】① collect articles, etc. into a volume ② concentrate; mass: ~军队 *concentrate troops*
【结交】make friends with; associate with: 不要和不诚实的孩子~。*Don't associate with dishonest boys.*
【结焦】coking; coke
【结晶】① crystallize: 糖在什么温度下~? *At what temperature does sugar crystallize?* ② crystal: 盐~ *salt crystals* ③ crystallization; product: 智慧的~ *a crystallization of wisdom*
【结局】final result; outcome; ending: ~并不像他天真地希望的那样。*The outcome was not what he fondly expected.* /战争的~是日本无条件地投降了。*The war ended with Japan's unconditional surrender.*
【结论】① conclusion (of a syllogism): 假~ *false conclusion* /不要过早下~。*Don't leap to a conclusion.* ② conclusion; verdict: 历史的~ *the verdict of history*
【结盟】form an alliance; ally; align: 不~政策 *nonalignment policy*
【结膜】【医】conjunctiva
【结膜炎】【医】conjunctivitis
【结囊】【生理】sacculation
【结幕】① last act; final act ② ending; final result; grand finale
【结欠】balance due: 去年~五百元。*The balance due of last year is 500 yuan.*
【结亲】①[口] marry; get married ②(of two families) become related by marriage
【结清】settle; square up: ~债务 *settle a debt* / ~账目 *square accounts* (*with sb*)
【结舌】tongue-tied; unable to say anything
【结社】form an association: ~自由 *freedom of association*
【结石】【医】stone; calculus: 胆~ *gall stone* /肾~ *kidney stone*
【结识】get acquainted with sb; get to know sb: 我在火车上~了她。*I got to know her on train.*
【结束】end; finish; conclude; wind up: 大会以国歌作为~ *conclude the rally with the national anthem* /晚会到半夜才~。*The party did not end until midnight.*
【结束语】concluding remarks
【结算】settle accounts; close (or wind up) an account: ~单据 *document of settlement* / ~贷款 *loan for the settlement of accounts* / ~日 *account day*
【结尾】① ending; winding-up stage: 皆大欢喜的~ *a happy ending* ②【音】coda
【结业】complete a course; wind up one's studies
【结义】[旧] become sworn brothers or sisters
【结余】cash surplus; surplus; balance: 银行~ *a balance at the bank*
【结语】epilogue; concluding remarks
【结缘】form ties (of affection, friendship, etc.)
【结怨】contract enmity; incur hatred: 他们分手后并

不。No hatred was incurred after their parting.
【结扎】【医】ligation; ligature: 输卵管～ *tubal ligation*
【结账】settle (or square) accounts; balance the books
【结转】carry-over; carry down: ～库存量 *carry-over stock*
【结子】knot

桔
【桔梗】the root of balloonflower

桀 the last ruler in the Xia Dynasty, said to be a tyrant
【桀骜不驯】[书] wild and intractable; obstinate and unruly

捷[1] quick; swift: 敏～ *prompt*; *quick*

捷[2] victory; triumph: 大～ *a major victory*
【捷报】news of victory; report of a success
【捷报频传】a steady flow of news of victories; reports of victory come in quick succession; news of successes keeps pouring in
【捷径】shortcut; bee line: 我们可以走～节省时间。*We can save time by taking a shortcut.*
【捷克】Czech: ～共和国 *Czech Republic* / ～语 *Czech language*
【捷足先登】the swift-footed arrive first; the early bird catches the worm — those who are quick in action will achieve the goals first

婕
【婕妤】female official in the palace of the Han Dynasty

睫 eyelash: 目不交～ *not sleep a wink*
【睫毛】eyelash; lash: ～膏 *eye black*
【睫腺】ciliary glands

截 ① cut; sever: 把木头～成两端 *cut the log in two* ② [量] section; chunk: 一～儿木头 *a log* ③ stop; check: 把马～住! *Stop the horse!* ④ end; close (by a due date or time): ～至三月 *by the end of March*
【截长补短】take from the long to add to the short; make up a deficiency by the surplus
【截断】① cut off; block; truncature: ～河流 *dam a river* / 这个港口与世界各地的通航被～了。*The harbour was blocked from the rest of the world.* / 敌人的退路已经被～。*The enemy's line of retreat was cut off.* ② cut short; interrupt: ～电流 *interrupt an electric current* / 别～我。*Don't interrupt me.*
【截夺】piracy
【截稿】deadline for receiving articles
【截获】intercept and capture: ～情报 *intercept information* / 这些成包的毒品在运到前被海关～了。*The parcels of drugs were intercepted by the Customs House before they were delivered.*
【截击】intercept (enemies)
【截击导弹】interceptor missile
【截击机】interceptor
【截距】nodal increment; intercept: ～式 *intercept form*
【截流】dam a river: ～工程 *project of damming a river*
【截留】intercept and hold on to; withhold: 把钱～ *withhold the money* / ～上缴利润 *retention of profits which out to be turned over to the state*
【截门】pipe valve
【截面】【数】section: 横～ *cross section* / 正～ *normal section*
【截取】cut off a section of sth: ～一段铁丝 *cut out a section of wire*
【截然】sharply; completely: ～不同 *completely different*; *different as black and white* / 这和他以前提的建议～相反。*This is the inverse of his earlier proposal.*
【截瘫】【医】paraplegia
【截枝】lopping: ～林 *stem-shoot forest*
【截肢】【医】amputation
【截止】① end; close: ～到本月底 *be closed by the end at this month* / 报名就要～了。*The registration is coming to an end.* ②【电】cut-off; blockage: ～电流 *cut-off current* / ～电压 *cut-off voltage*
【截至】by (a specified time); up to: ～目前 *up to now*
【截锥】frustum of a cone; truncated cone: ～体 *frustum of a cone*
【截子】[量] section; length; chuck: 我的英语水平和他差一大～呢! *His command of English is much better than mine.*

碣 stone tablet with a round top: 残碑断～ *remains and broken parts of tablets*

竭 ①use up; exhaust: 声嘶力～ *shout oneself hoarse* ②[书] dry up: 枯～ *dry up*
【竭诚】wholeheartedly; with all one's heart: ～为您服务 *serve you whole heartedly*
【竭尽】use up; exhaust: ～全力 *spare no effort*
【竭力】do one's utmost; use every ounce of one's energy; try by every possible means: ～反对 *strongly oppose* / ～宣传 *assiduously propagate* / ～支持 *give all-out support*
【竭泽而渔】drain the pond to get all the fish — sacrifice future profit to present gains

jiě

姐 ① elder sister, an elder female relative with the same parents ②elder sister, an elder female relative of the same generation in the clan: 表～ *elder female cousin* ③ a general term for young women
【姐夫】elder sister's husband; brother-in-law
【姐姐】elder sister; sister
【姐妹】① sisters: 同胞～ *sister of the whole blood* ② brothers and sisters

【姐儿们】sisters
【姐丈】elder sister's husband; brother-in-law

解 ① separate; divide: 瓦～ *collapse*; *go to pieces* ②untie; undo: ～衣服 *undress* ③dispel; allay ④ interpret; explain: 注～ *annotation*; *note* ⑤ understand; comprehend: 令人不～ *puzzling*; *hard to understand* ⑥ relieve oneself: 大～ *make stools* /小～ *urinate* ⑦ solution, the value of an unknown number in an algebraic equation ⑧ solve; calculate: ～方程 *solve an equation*
see also jiè; xiè

【解饱】[方] (of food) satisfy hunger: 她认为面条比米饭～。*She thinks that noodles are better than rice in satisfying one's hunger.*
【解馋】satisfy a craving for good food
【解嘲】try to explain things away when ridiculed: 自我～ *find excuses to console oneself*
【解愁】put an end to one's worry
【解除】remove; relieve; get rid of; release: ～某人的职务 *remove a man from office* / ～心中偏见 *liberate the mind from prejudice* / ～某人的痛苦 *release sb from his suffering* / ～婚约 *renounce an engagement* / ～武装 *disarm troops*
【解答】answer; explain: 他～了我的问题。*He answered my question.*
【解冻】①thaw; unfreeze: ～季节 *thawing season* / 把冻肉放在外面，直到～。*Leave the frozen meat out until it thawed* ② unfreeze (funds, assets, etc.): ～资产 *unblocked assets*
【解毒】① detoxify; detoxicate ②【中医】relieve internal heat or fever
【解饿】satisfy one's hunger: 吃点儿东西～。*Eat something to satisfy your hunger.*
【解乏】recover from fatigue: 好好睡一觉，解解乏。*Have a good rest to get over your fatigue.*
【解法】【数】solution: 这道题有三种～。*There are three solutions to this problem.*
【解放】① liberate; emancipate: ～区 *liberated area* / ～生产力 *liberate the productive forces* / ～思想 *free oneself from old ideas* /我的家乡是在1949年～的。*My hometown was liberated in* 1949. ② Liberation (signifying the termination of Kuomintang rule in mainland China in 1949)
【解放军】the Chinese People's Liberation Army
【解放战争】① war of liberation ②China's War of Liberation (1945-1949)
【解雇】discharge; dismiss; fire; sack: 他因为泄露机密而被～。*He was sacked for revealing a confidential source.*
【解恨】vent one's hatred; have one's hatred slaked: 我要为他～。*I will slake his hatred.*
【解甲归田】take off one's armour and return to the land; be demobilized
【解禁】lift a ban: ～之后，涌入了大批的申请者。*When the ban was lifted there was a sudden rush of applicants.*
【解酒】relieve the effect of alcohol
【解救】save; rescue; deliver: ～工作受到恶劣天气的妨碍。*The rescue attempt was impeded by bad weather.* /我们来～他，把他从火海里拉了出来。*We came to his rescue and pulled him out of the fire.*
【解决】① solve; resolve; settle: ～问题 *resolve a conflict* / ～冲突 *resolve a problem* /现在你该跟他把争端～了。*It's time you settled your dispute with him.* ② dispose of; finish off
【解开】untie; undo; unfasten: ～纽扣 *undo a button* /我必须把这个结剪掉，因为我解不开它。*I had to cut the knot because I couldn't untie it.*
【解渴】quench one's thirst: 我发现这种饮料非常～。*I find these drinks very thirst-quenching.* /我们在一个小村子停下来～，顺便给车加油。*We stopped in a small village to quench our thirst and refuel the car.*
【解铃系铃】let him who tied the bell on the tiger take it off — whoever started the trouble should end it; in order to untie the bell, the person who tied it is required
【解螺旋】uncoiling: ～作用 *despiralization*
【解码】decipher; decode: ～器 *demoder*; *decoder*
【解闷】divert oneself (from boredom): 我们下棋～。*We diverted ourselves by playing chess.*
【解密】declassify: 这些文件已经～。*These documents have now been declassified.*
【解难】(jiěnán) solve a difficult problem; relieve sb of difficulties: 释疑～ *remove doubts and solve puzzles*
【解难】(jiěnàn) rescue sb from danger or disaster: 消灾～ *get rid of calamities and remove dangers*
【解囊】[书] open one's purse (to help sb with money): ～相助 *help sb generously with money*
【解聘】dismiss an employee (usu. at the expiration of a contract): 他因不诚实而被公司～。*He was dismissed by the company for his dishonesty.*
【解剖】① dissect: 尸体～ *autopsy* ② analyze; examine: ～一篇文章 *analyze an article*
【解剖刀】scalpel; scalper
【解剖学】anatomy: 人体～ *human anatomy*
【解气】vent one's spleen; work off one's anger: 他用咒骂来～。*His anger vented itself in curses.*
【解劝】soothe; mollify; comfort; console: 我因他的不幸遭遇而～他。*I comforted him for his misfortunes.* /我尽了最大努力～女儿，许诺给她买一个新玩具。*I did my best to console my daughter by promising to buy her another doll.*
【解热】【中医】relieve internal heat or fever
【解任】[书] be relieved of one's office
【解散】① dismiss: ～集会 *dismiss a congregation* ② dissolve; disband: 网球俱乐部已经～了。*The tennis club has disbanded.*
【解释】explain; expound; interpret: ～问题的复杂性 *expound the intricacies of the issue* /你能～一下你为什么迟到吗? *Can you explain why you were late?* /你对这些作何～? *What interpretation would you place on them?*
【解释权】power of interpretation; right of interpretation

【解手】① relieve oneself; go to the toilet (or lavatory) ②[书] part company
【解说】explain orally; comment: 教授正在对一个术语加以~。*The professor was explaining orally on a term.*
【解说词】commentary; caption
【解说员】commentator; announcer
【解体】disintegrate: 信仰的~ *the disintegration of belief* /封建制度的~ *the disintegration of the feudal system*
【解脱】①【宗】moksa; moksha ② free (or extricate) oneself: 我终于从繁重的家务事中~出来了。*I finally extricated myself from heavy housework.* ③ absolve; exonerate: 你不该为他~,我知道是他的错。*You should not absolve him from responsibility; I know it's his fault.*
【解围】① force an enemy to raise a siege; rescue sb from a siege ② help sb out of a fix; save sb from embarrassment
【解悟】come to understand
【解析几何】【数】analytic geometry
【解疑】① dispel doubts and misgivings ② explain a difficult point
【解忧】allay sorrow; assuage grief
【解约】terminate an agreement; cancel a contract: ~金 *cancellation money* /~书 *letter of cancellation*
【解职】dismiss from office; discharge; relieve sb of his post: 他因贪污而被~。*He was discharged for corruption.*

jiè

介[1] ①put (or come) between: 媒~ *intermedium; medium* /在那儿你无法看到海,因为有房子~于其间。*You can't see the sea from there because the house intervenes.* ②introduction: 内容简~ *a brief introduction of the content* ③mind: 不必~意! *Don't take it seriously!* ④ (Jiè) a surname
介[2] armour; shell: ~虫 *beetle; dung beetle* /~胄之士 *men in armour*
介[3] [书] upright: 耿~ *honest and frank*
介[4] [古] (in old drama scripts) a word indicating motion or action: 打~ *the action of fight*
【介词】【语】preposition
【介夫】[书] soldier in armour; warrior
【介怀】mind; take offence: 毫不~ *not mind at all*
【介木】cap-sill
【介壳】shell (of oysters, snails, etc.)
【介壳虫】scale insect
【介然】[书] ① firm and steadfast ②have sth on one's mind: ~于怀 *take sth seriously* ③ extraordinary; unusual
【介入】intervene; interpose; get involved: ~行为 *intervening act* /别让别人~进你的麻烦中去。*Don't involve other people in your trouble.*
【介绍】① introduce; present: 主席把讲演者~给听众。*The chairman introduced the speaker to the audience.* ② recommend; suggest: ~新方法 *introduce sb to a new method* ③ let know; brief: ~情况 *brief sb on the situation*
【介绍人】① introducer; sponsor ② matchmaker
【介绍信】① letter of introduction ② letter of recommendation
【介意】take offence; mind: 对此我毫不~。*I don't care at all.* /一定不要~你姑姑严格要求你。*You must not mind if your aunt is strict with you.*
【介值定理】intermediate value theorem
【介质】【物】medium; agent; media
【介子】【物】meson; mesotron: ~场 *meson field* /~动力学 *mesodynamics* /~云 *meson cloud*

价 [书] (in early times) a dispatched person on an errand; messenger
see also jià; jie

戒 ① take precautions: 力~骄傲 *strictly avoid arrogance* ② drop; give up: ~烟 *give up smoking* ③ things forbidden to do: 开~ *do things which are forbidden to do* ④ Buddhist monastic discipline: 清规~律 *regulations, taboos and commandments for Buddhists or Taoists* ⑤ ring: 钻~ *diamond ring*
【戒备】guard; take precautions; be on the alert: ~森严 *be heavily guarded*
【戒尺】[旧] teacher's ruler for beating pupils
【戒除】give up; drop; stop: ~恶习 *give up a bad habit*
【戒刀】Buddhist monk's knife
【戒忌】① taboos: 一度被视为~的许多问题现在可以公开谈论了。*Questions and problems that were once taboo are now discussed openly.* ② be wary of violating a taboo
【戒骄戒躁】guard against arrogance
【戒惧】be frightened and watchful
【戒绝】give up; stop
【戒律】【宗】religious discipline; commandment: 清规~ *regulations and taboos*
【戒条】【宗】religious discipline
【戒心】vigilance; wariness: 我对他怀有~。*I am on my guard against him.*
【戒严】enforce martial law; impose a curfew; cordon off an area: ~地区 *district under martial law* /宣布~ *declare martial law*
【戒严法】martial law
【戒严令】order of martial law
【戒严状态】state of siege
【戒指】(finger) ring: 结婚~ *wedding ring* /他送给她一枚订婚~。*He gave her an engagement ring.*

芥 ① mustard ② grass: 尘~ *thin and slender*
see also gài
【芥菜】leaf mustard
【芥蒂】[书] ill feeling; unpleasantness; grudge: 我总觉得她对我心怀~。*I always feel she has a*

J

grudge against me.

【芥末】mustard：～鸭掌 *duck webs with mustard*

【芥子】mustard seed：～碱 *sinapine* /～素 *myroxin* /～油 *mustard oil*

【芥子气】【化】mustard gas：～中毒 *mustard gas poisoning*

【芥子油】mustard oil

届 ① fall due ②［量］time；session：应～ *graduating students or pupils*

【届满】at the expiration of one's term of office：在任期～时 *at the expiration of one's term of office*

【届期】when the day comes；at the appointed date：～未归 *fail to return on the appointed date*

【届时】when the time comes；at the appointed time；on the occasion：～请出席。*Your presence is requested for the occasion.*

界 ① boundary：边～ *boundary*；*border* /我们的花园有一边以小河为～。*Our garden is bordered on the side by a stream.* ②range；scope：眼～ *outlook*；*horizon* ③circles；fields：教育～ *educational circles* /经济～ *financial circles* /军～ *military circles* /文化～ *cultural circles* /学术～ *academic circles* /政～ *political circles* ④ primary division；kingdom：动物～ *the animal kingdom* /植物～ *the vegetable kingdom* ⑤【地】group：古生～ *the Paleozoic group*

【界碑】boundary tablet；boundary marker

【界标】boundary mark

【界层】interlayer

【界定】specify the limits；delimit：你应该给他的权限做一个～。*You should make his power specified.*

【界河】boundary river：这条河是两国的～。*The river is the boundary between the two countries.*

【界面】boundary；interface

【界外球】【体】out-of-bounds；out

【界限】① demarcation line；dividing line；limits；bounds：划清～ *make a clear distinction* ② limit；end：凡事都有～。*There is a limit to everything.* /你的要求必须在合理的～之内。*Your desires must be within reasonable bounds.*

【界线】① boundary line：石墙是两个农场的～。*A stonewall marked the boundary between the two farms.* ② dividing line；limits：不要混淆是非～。*Don't confuse the right and wrong.* ③ edge；verge

【界约】border agreement（between two neighbouring countries）

【界址】location of a dividing line：清查～ *find out where the dividing line lies*

【界桩】boundary marker；boundary stone

疥 【医】scabies

【疥疮】【医】scabies

【疥蛤蟆】toad

【疥癣】mange；scab：羊～ *sheep scab*

诫 warn；admonish：告～ *warn*；*give warning* /上次惨痛的教训我们一定要永远记住，引以为～。*No one must ever forget last bitter lesson and we must all take warning from it.*

借[1] ① borrow：向他～钱 *borrow money from him* /她昨天从图书馆～了一些书。*She borrowed some books from the library yesterday.* ② lend：～钱给他 *lend him money*

借[2] ① use as a pretext ② take advantage of；make use of：我～此机会向大家表示感谢！*I'd like to take this opportunity to show my gratitude to you all.*

【借差】debit balance

【借词】【语】loanword；loan

【借代】rhetorical devices such as metonymy

【借贷】① borrow or lend money：～利息 *loan interest* /～资本 *loan capital* ②debit and credit sides

【借刀杀人】kill sb by another's hand；harm sb through a third party

【借调】temporarily transfer；be on loan：他～到农业部工作了。*He is on loan to the Agriculture Ministry.*

【借读】study at a school on a temporary basis

【借端】[书] use as a pretext；find a pretext：～挑衅 *make use of anything as a pretext for seeking a quarrel*

【借方】debit side；debit：银行在我账户的～透支金额。*The bank debited my account for the overdrawn check.*

【借风使船】sail the boat with the help of the wind — achieve one's purpose through the agency of sb else

【借古讽今】use the past to disparage the present；make use of the ancient to satirize the present

【借故】find an excuse：他～未去。*He didn't go on some pretext.*

【借光】① benefit from association with sb or sth：他能出国全是借了姐姐的光。*Thanks to his sister's help, he went abroad.* ② excuse me：～让我过去！*Please make a way for us!*

【借花献佛】present Buddha with flowers given by another — make a gift of sth given by another；borrow sth to make a gift of it

【借火】ask for a light：劳驾，借个火。*Excuse me；would you mind giving me a light?*

【借鉴】use for reference；draw lessons from；draw on the experience of：～外国经验 *use the experience of other countries for reference* /他的作品～了其他作曲家的乐曲。*He borrowed music from other composers.*

【借景】borrow the scenery outside a garden to harmonize with that within

【借镜】use for reference；draw on the experience of

【借酒浇愁】drown one's sorrows in wine；drown care in the wine cup；get drunk in order to forget one's troubles

【借据】receipt for a loan；IOU

【借口】① use as an excuse（or pretext）：他～牙痛不去学校。*He used his toothache as a pretext for not going to school.* ② excuse；pretext：工作太忙不能成为不学习的～。*Too much work is no excuse for not studying.*

【借款】① borrow or lend money; ask for or offer a loan: ~企业 *borrowing enterprise* ② loan

【借尸还魂】revive in a new guise; use a corpse to resurrect a dead soul

【借宿】stay overnight at sb else's place; put up for the night: 他昨晚在朋友家~。*He found a lodging in a friend's house yesterday.*

【借题发挥】make use of the subject to elaborate one's own ideas; give vent to one's pent-up feelings on some extraneous pretext

【借条】receipt for a loan (IOU)

【借问】may I ask: ~去动物园怎么走? *Could you tell me the way to the zoo?*

【借以】so as to; for the purpose of; by way of: 我给您献花~表达敬意。*I show my respect to you by way of presenting these flowers.*

【借用】① borrow; have the loan of: 英语~了许多语言的词。*English has borrowed from many languages.* /我能~您的字典吗? *May I borrow your dictionary?* ②use sth for another purpose: ~一句谚语 *quote a proverb*

【借喻】borrowed analogy; metonymy

【借约】loan agreement; loan contract

【借阅】borrow (books, magazines, etc.) for reading: ~报纸 *borrow newspapers for reading*

【借债】borrow money; raise (or contract) a loan: ~是不幸的开始。*He that goes a borrowing goes a sorrowing.*

【借账】borrow money; contract a loan

【借支】ask for an advance on one's pay

【借重】rely on for support; enlist sb's help

【借住】stay at sb else's place temporarily: 我今晚能否~在你家? *May I stay in your home tonight?*

【借助】have the aid of; draw support from: 他~词典学习外语。*He learned the foreign language with the help of a dictionary.*

解 send under guard: 把犯人~到县里 *send the criminal to the county under guard*
see also jiě; xiè

【解差】guards escorting prisoners

【解送】send under guard

藉 ①[书] mat; mattress ② place sth underneath: 枕~ *lying close together*
see also jí

jie

价 ①[方] used for emphasis after a negative adverb: 不~! *No!* ② suffix (added to certain adverbs): 成天~吵 *make noises all day long*
see also jià; jiè

jīn

巾 a piece of cloth: 餐~ *table napkin* /毛~ *towel* /头~ *scarf* /围~ *scarf* /浴~ *bath towel*

【巾帼】① ancient woman's headdress ②woman

【巾帼英雄】heroine

【巾帼须眉】women who act and talk like a man

斤[1] ① a traditional unit of weight (1 jin equals 10 liang or 0.5 kilograms) ② added to the name of sth measured by weight to form a general term: 煤~ *coal*

斤[2] (in ancient times) a tool used for felling trees

【斤斗】[方] somersault

【斤斤】be particular (about small matters)

【斤斤计较】haggle over every ounce; be calculating; be excessively mean in one's dealings: 多年来,他的经历把他变成了一个~的人。*Over the years his experiences have turned him into someone calculating.*

【斤两】weight: 发言者话语的~ *the weight of the speaker's words*

今 ① now; the present: 从~往后 *from now on* ② this; of this year: ~春 *this spring* ③[书] this: ~次 *this time*

【今不如昔】be worse than before

【今草】a type of cursive hand

【今非昔比】today we are no longer as we have been; times change

【今后】from now on; in the days to come; henceforth; hereafter; in future: 我发誓~再也不说谎话。*I promise never to lie henceforth.*

【今年】this year

【今儿】[方] today: ~是星期天。*Today is Sunday.*

【今人】moderns; contemporaries; people of our era

【今日】① this day; today ②present; now: ~人们似乎不像过去那么有礼貌了。*People don't seem as polite now as they used to be.*

【今生】this life

【今世】① this life ② this age; the contemporary age

【今天】① this day; today: ~是星期一。*Today is Monday.* /一个~抵得上两个明天。*One today is worth two tomorrows.* ② the present time; nowadays: ~的问题 *today issues* / ~的一代人 *the today generation*

【今文】modern script (used in the Han Dynasty)

【今昔】the present and the past; today and yesterday: ~对比 *contrast the present with the past* /北京的~ *Beijing's yesterday and today*

【今译】modern translation; modern-language version: 古诗~ *ancient poems rendered into modern Chinese*

【今音】modern (as distinct from classical) pronunciation of Chinese characters

【今朝】①[方] today ② the present; now

金 ① metal: 五~ *the five metals (gold, silver, copper, iron and tin)* ② money: 基~ *funds* /现~ *cash* ③ ancient metal percussion instrument: 鸣~收兵 *beat the gongs and withdraw the army* ④ gold (Au): 镀~ *gild* /赤~ *deep coloured gold* /她戴了一枚~戒指。*She wore a gold*

J

ring. ⑤ valuable; honourable ⑥ golden: ～发 *golden hair* ⑦ (Jīn) a surname
【金榜】[旧] a list of successful candidates in the imperial examinations
【金榜题名】have passed the examination; succeed in the government examination
【金本位】gold standard: ～制 *gold standard*
【金笔】(quality) fountain pen
【金币】gold coin
【金碧辉煌】(of a building, etc.) looking splendid in green and gold; resplendent and magnificent
【金边】Phnom Penh, capital of Cambodia
【金箔】goldleaf; gold foil
【金不换】not to be exchanged even for gold; invaluable; priceless: 浪子回头～。*A prodigal's return to normal life is more valuable than gold.*
【金灿灿】glittering
【金蝉脱壳】slip out of a predicament like a cicada sloughing its skin — escape by crafty scheme
【金唱片】best seller
【金雕】golden eagle
【金额】[书] amount (or sum) of money
【金饭碗】a golden bowl — a well-paid occupation
【金粉】① lead powder ② pollen ③ gold bits
【金风】[书] autumn wind: ～送爽 *cooling autumn wind*
【金刚】Buddha's warrior attendant: 四大～ *four guardian warriors*
【金刚经】【宗】diamond sutra
【金刚砂】emery; corundum; carborundum
【金刚石】diamond: ～矿区 *diamond field*
【金刚石婚】60th or 75th anniversary of a marriage
【金刚钻】diamond: 没有～,别揽瓷器活。*Don't try to mend porcelain wares unless you have a diamond cutter. — Don't undertake a hard job if you don't have the ability to do it.*
【金戈铁马】a symbol of war; military hardware
【金工】metalworking; metal processing: ～机械 *metalworking machinery*
【金瓜】a kind of pumpkin
【金光】golden light: ～大道 *golden road; bright road*
【金龟】tortoise
【金龟婿】rich son-in-law
【金龟子】【动】chafer; cockchafer; dor; dorbeetle; tumble bug; tumblebug
【金贵】[口] precious; valuable: 在这个地区水是很～的。*Water is very precious in this area.*
【金黄】golden yellow; golden
【金婚】golden wedding, 50th wedding anniversary
【金货币】gold money
【金鸡独立】standing on one leg like a cock (a posture in Chinese martial arts)
【金甲虫】goldbug
【金奖】gold award
【金匠】goldsmith
【金菊】golden aster
【金橘】【植】kumquat
【金具】armour clamp
【金科玉律】the golden rule
【金口玉言】a golden mouth and pearly words — precious words; utterances that carry great weight
【金库】national (or state) treasury; exchequer; burse; cashbox: 银行～ *the coffers of a bank*
【金块】gold bullion
【金矿】gold ore
【金矿床】gold deposit
【金矿区】gold field; goldfield
【金矿物】gold mineral
【金兰之交】close and intimate friendship
【金銮殿】the Hall of Golden Chimes (a popular name for the emperor's audience hall)
【金缕玉衣】【考】jade clothes sewn with god wire
【金泥】gold mud
【金牛座】【天】Taurus
【金瓯】[书] golden goblet — national territory: ～无缺 *golden bowl remaining intact — unimpaired territorial integrity*
【金牌】gold medal
【金器】gold plate
【金钱】money: ～至上 *value money above everything else* / 他拍卖财产来换取～。*He made money on the sale of his properties.* / ～并不一定总带来幸福。*Money doesn't always bring happiness.*
【金枪鱼】【动】tuna
【金秋】autumn
【金融】finance; banking: 国际～ *international finance* / 贸易～ *trade finance* / 农业～ *agricultural finance* / 市场～ *market finance*
【金嗓子】golden voice — beautiful voice
【金色】golden; gold: ～的太阳 *golden sun*
【金闪闪】golden bright and dazzling: ～的阳光 *dazzling sunlight*
【金石】① [书] metal and stone — a symbol of hardness and strength ② inscriptions on ancient bronzes and stone tablets
【金属】metal: 纯～ *simple metal* / 脆性～ *brittle metal* / 惰性～ *inert metal* / 复合～ *composition metal* / 痕量～ *trace metal* / 碱性～ *basic metal* / 浇灌～ *capping metal* / 晶体～ *crystalline metal* / 稀有～ *less-common metal* / 液态～ *fluent metal* / 有机～ *organic metal* / 杂质～ *contaminating metal* / 中性～ *neutral metal* / 重～ *heavy metal*
【金丝猴】【动】golden monkey; snub-nosed monkey
【金丝雀】【动】canary; canary bird
【金丝绒】pleuche
【金丝燕】【动】esculent swift
【金丝枣】a variety of Chinese date
【金条】gold bar
【金屋藏娇】settle one's young wife in a golden house — keep a mistress in a splendid house
【金无足赤,人无完人】gold cannot be pure and man cannot be perfect
【金星】①【天】Venus ② golden star
【金言】precious words; valuable words
【金钥匙】a golden key — a good method to solve a difficult problem
【金叶】【冶】gold leaf

【金银】gold and silver
【金银合金】electrum
【金银本位制】gold and silver bimetallism
【金银财宝】money and treasure
【金银花】【植】honeysuckle
【金银块】bullion
【金银丝】purl
【金鱼】goldfish：～缸 *goldfish bowl*
【金鱼草】【植】snapdragon
【金鱼虫】【动】water flea
【金玉】［书］gold and jade — valuable；precious
【金玉良言】golden saying — invaluable advice
【金玉其外，败絮其中】a person with good looks but empty-minded
【金盏草】【植】calendula；marigold
【金盏花】【植】marigold
【金针】①［书］needle used in sewing and embroidery ②【中医】acupuncture needle ③ dried day lily flower
【金针菜】【植】① day lily ② day lily flower
【金枝玉叶】golden branches and jade leaves — be born in the purple
【金字塔】pyramid
【金字招牌】a gold-lettered signboard — a vainglorious title
【金子】gold：闪光的未必都是～。*All is not gold that glitters.*

津[1] ① saliva：生～止渴 *help produce saliva and slake thirst* ② sweat：遍体生～ *perspire all over* ③ moist；damp

津[2] ferry crossing；ford：问～ *make inquiries*

【津巴布韦】Zimbabwe：～人 *Zimbabwean*
【津渡】［书］ferry crossing
【津津】① tasty；interesting：甜～ *pleasantly sweet* ②（of water or sweat）flow：汗～ *sweaty*
【津津乐道】take delight in talking about；enjoy elaborating on：对自己的成就～ *relish talking about one's achievement*
【津津有味】eat with appetite；be very fond of；do sth with interest：他听得～。*He listened with great interest.*
【津梁】bridge and ford — help；aid
【津贴】① financial aid；subsidy；allowance；subvention：出差～ *travelling allowance* /工资性～ *wage-equivalent subsidy* /膳宿～ *accommodation allowance* /物价～ *dearness allowance* /月～ *monthly allowance* /职务～ *duty allowance* ②give financial aid；subsidize

衿 ①［书］girdle；belt

矜 ① pity；sympathize with ② conceited；arrogant：自～其功 *sing high praise for one's own achievements* ③ reserved；restrained

【矜持】restrained；reserved；withdrawn；introverted；inhibited：这个曾经活泼的女孩儿现在变得很～。*The young girl, once so lively, became introverted now.* /他现在已经不再～。*He has come out of his shell.*
【矜夸】conceited and boastful

筋 ① muscle ② tendon；sinew：牛蹄～ *tendons of beef* ③ veins that stand out under the skin ④ anything that resembles a tendon or vein：钢～ *steel bar* /橡皮～ *rubber band*

【筋道】［方］①（of food）tough and chewy：这面条挺～。*The noodles are very chewy.* ② sturdy old man
【筋斗】①［方］somersault：翻～ *turn a somersault* ② fall；tumble（over）：摔了个～ *fall*；*have a fall*；*have a tumble*；*tumble over*
【筋骨】bones and muscles — physique：锻炼～ *take exercise*；*build one's body*
【筋节】muscles and joints — vital links in a speech or essay
【筋疲力尽】exhausted；played out；worn out；tired out；all in；dead-beat；dog-tired：这次旅行后我们都～了。*We are all exhausted after the journey.* /因为游逛得～，他们都睡着了。*Weary with wandering, they fell asleep.*
【筋肉】muscles
【筋条】fillet

禁 ① bear；endure：弱不～风 *too weak to stand a gust of wind — extremely delicate* ② restrain oneself：不～笑起来 *cannot help laughing* /他怂恿我接受一只香烟时，我就～不住了。*When he urged me to accept a cigarette, it was more than I could bear.*
see also jìn

【禁不起】① be unable to stand（tests，trials，etc.）：～考验 *fail to stand a test* ②can't help（doing sth）；can't refrain from
【禁不住】① can't stand ② can't help；can't refrain from：他～流下了眼泪。*He couldn't refrain from shedding tears.*
【禁得起】be able to stand（tests，trials，etc.）
【禁得住】be able to bear or endure：你认为这些管子能～多少压力吗？*How much pressure do you think the pipes will stand?* /孩子穿的鞋应该～磨损。*Children's shoes need to be able to withstand constant wear and tear.*
【禁受】bear；stand；endure：～时间考验 *stand the test of time*

襟 ① front of a garment：对～ *a kind of Chinese style jacket with buttons down the front* ② brothers-in-law whose wives are sisters：～兄 *husband of one's wife's elder sister* ③ mind；bosom：胸～ *mind*；*breadth of mind*

【襟度】［书］breadth of mind；tolerance
【襟怀】bosom；（breadth of）mind：～坦白 *frank*；*sincere*

jǐn

仅 only；merely：～是皮肉之伤 *merely a flesh wound* /他～一个月就完成了这个项目。*He finished the project within only one month.*
see also jìn

【仅见】rarely seen：世所～ *have no parallel anywhere*
【仅仅】only；merely；alone：这～是个开头。*This is merely the beginning.*
【仅只】only；merely：我们不～满足于填饱肚子。*We are not merely content to fill the stomach.*
尽[1] ① to the greatest extent：～着力气做 *do sth to the best of one's ability*；*do one's best* ② within the limits of：～着我给你的这些钱花。*Don't spend more than the sum I gave you.* ③ give priority to：先～着旧衣服穿 *wear the old clothes first* ④ extreme；furthest：～里头 *at the extreme inside*
尽[2] ［方］keep on doing sth：这些日子～下雨。*We're having a lot of rain these days.*
see also jìn
【尽管】① feel free to；not hesitate to：有问题～提。*Don't hesitate to ask questions.* ②［方］always；all the time：有病早些治，～耽搁着也不好。*You'd better see a doctor early；your always delaying it does you no good.* ③ though；even though；in spite of；despite：～他很穷却很快乐。*Though he was poor he was happy.* /～我可能失败，我也要试一下。*I will try it，though I may fail.* /～天气不好，我还是去上学了。*I went to school as usual in spite of the bad weather.*
【尽快】as quickly（or soon，early）as possible：～制定新的计划 *make a new plan as soon as possible*
【尽量】to the best of one's ability；as far as possible：我会～照顾好她的。*I will try my best to look after her.* /我们将～努力地执行这个计划。*We will carry out the plan to the best of our ability.*
【尽让】［方］let others take precedence
【尽先】give first priority to：～照顾老年人 *give priority to the old*
【尽早】as early as possible；as soon as possible：我们还是～告诉他这件事吧。*Let's tell him about it as soon as possible.*
【尽自】［方］always；all the time：要想办法解决问题，别～诉苦。*You should find a way to solve the problem instead of complaining all the time.*
紧 ① tight；taut：绑～ *tie it tightly* ② fast；firm：把门关～ *make the door fast* ③tighten：拧～螺丝 *tighten this screw* ④ tight；close：绷得很～的鼓膜 *a tight drumhead* /这双鞋太～了。*This pair of shoes is too tight.* ⑤ urgent；pressing：抓～时间 *make the best use of time* /任务很～。*The task is pressing.* ⑥ short of money：我现在手头～。*I am short of money at present.*
【紧巴巴】① tight：这双鞋我穿着～的。*The shoes are tight for me.* ② hard up；short of money：她现在的日子～的，我们应该帮帮她。*She was in low water now and we should give her a hand.*
【紧绷绷】① tightly drawn ②（of one's facial expression）taut；sullen：～的面容 *a sullen face*
【紧逼】press hard：步步～ *press on at every stage*
【紧凑】compact；terse；well-knit：情节～ *a well-knit plot*
【紧跟】follow closely：～形势 *keep in step with the situation*
【紧箍咒】the Incantation of the Golden Hoop（in the novel *Pilgrimage to the West*）— inhibition；sth used to keep sb under control
【紧急】urgent；pressing；critical：～的口信 *an urgent message* /～关头 *critical moment* /～抢救 *emergency rescue* /～支援 *emergency aid* /他似乎没有意识到情况的～。*He didn't seem to realize how grave it was.*
【紧邻】close neighbour；next-door neighbour
【紧锣密鼓】a wild beating of gongs and drums — intense public campaign in preparation for some evil scheme：他竞选总统的各项准备正在～地进行着。*An intense publicity campaign is going on in preparation for his bid for the presidency.*
【紧密】① close together；inseparable：他被～监视。*He was kept under close custody.* /让我们团结得更～些。*Let's unite still more closely.* ②rapid and intense：～的雨点 *a heavy rain*
【紧迫】pressing；urgent；imminent：时间～ *be pressed for time* /据说形势很～。*The situation is said to be rather critical.*
【紧俏】（of goods）in great demand but short supply：～物品 *badly needed goods*
【紧缺】in short supply；badly needed：用水～。*Water is in short supply now.*
【紧身】close-fitting undergarment
【紧缩】reduce；retrench；tighten：～开支 *cut down expenses* /～生产 *curtail production*
【紧要】critical；crucial；vital；major；central；pivotal：无关～ *of no importance* /所有的信息都必须准确，这一点十分～。*All the information must be accurate — that's absolutely central.*
【紧张】① nervous；keyed up：因焦虑而神经～。*Nerves taut with anxiety.* /演说的人～得咳嗽了一声。*The speaker gave a nervous cough.* ② tense；intense；strained：～的生活 *a intense life* /它们之间的关系相当～。*The relations between them are rather strained.* ③in short supply；tight：用水～。*Water is in short supply.*
【紧着】［口］speed up；press on with；hurry：时间不多了，咱们～干吧！*Little time is left. Let's hurry.*
锦 ① brocade：蜀～ *Sichuan brocade* ② bright and beautiful：～霞 *rose tinted clouds*
【锦标】prize；trophy；title
【锦标赛】championship contest；championships：世界～ *world championship*
【锦缎】brocade；damask
【锦鸡】【动】golden pheasant
【锦纶】polyamide fibre
【锦囊妙计】wise counsel；a secret master plan
【锦旗】silk banner（as an award or a gift）
【锦上添花】add flowers to the brocade — make what is good still better
【锦心绣口】elegant thoughts and flowery speech
【锦绣】as beautiful as brocade；beautiful；splendid
【锦绣河山】beautiful landscape
【锦绣前程】bright prospect；be promising

【锦衣玉食】beautiful dresses and delicious food — live an extravagant life

谨 ① careful; cautious: ~记在心 *bear in mind* ② sincerely; solemnly: ~向您表示祝贺。*I wish to extend to you my sincere congratulations.*

【谨饬】[书] prudent; careful; cautious; circumspect

【谨防】guard against; beware of: ~假冒 *beware of imitations* / ~有误 *caution oneself against error* / ~扒手。*Beware of pickpockets*

【谨慎】prudent; careful; cautious; circumspect: ~的回答 *a careful answer* / 谦虚~ *be modest and prudent* / 他非常~,把每一个细节都核对过了。*He was careful enough to check up every detail.*

【谨小慎微】overcautious in small matters; overcautious: 她一向~。*She is always cautious in the extreme.*

【谨严】careful and precise

【谨言慎行】speak and act cautiously; be careful with one's words and actions

瑾 [书] a beautiful jade

jìn

仅 [书] nearly; approximately: 士卒~万人。*The soldiers numbered nearly ten thousand.*
see also jǐn

尽 ① finished; exhausted: 取之不~ *inexhaustible* / 弹~粮绝 *exhaust one's supplies of food and ammunition* ② [书] die; perish: 同归于~ *perish together* ③ to the limit: 山穷水~ *at the end of one's tether; at one's wit's end* ④ use up; exhaust: 仁至义~ *do what by humanity and duty; show extremely forbearance* / 筋疲力~ *be used up; exhausted* ⑤ try one's best: ~责任 *do one's duty* ⑥ all: 人~皆知 *known to everybody*
see also jǐn

【尽处】terminal point; end: 巷子~,又是一番风景。*At the end of the lane was still attractive scenery.*

【尽付东流】all is thrown into the eastward flowing stream — all one's efforts wasted

【尽欢】enjoy oneself very much

【尽力】do all one can; try one's best: 我会~完成你交给我的任务。*I will do all I can to finish the task you assigned me to do.*

【尽力而为】do one's best; exert every effort

【尽量】(drink or eat) to the full

【尽情】to one's heart's content; as much as one likes: ~歌唱 *sing to one's heart's content* / 晚会上,大家~欢乐。*Everyone enjoyed himself very much at the party.*

【尽然】entirely satisfactory: 我看他说的不~是真的。*In my opinion, what he said could not be considered as truth.*

【尽人皆知】be known to all; be common knowledge: ~,金字塔是埃及的象征。*It is well known that the pyramid is the sign of Egypt.*

【尽人事】do what one can (to save a dying person, etc.); do all that is humanly possible (though with little hope of success): ~,听天命 *do all that is humanly possible and leave the rest to God*

【尽如人意】just as one wishes; be satisfactory: 文章的结构还不~。*The structure of the article is still not up to everyone's expectation.*

【尽善尽美】the acme of perfection; perfect: 他的译文可说是~。*His translation can be said perfect.*

【尽释前嫌】forget all former grudges: 在我的调解下,他们两人~。*I mediated between the two, and they finally forgot all former grudges.*

【尽收眼底】have a panoramic view: 站在高山之巅,美景~。*Standing on the top of the mountain, the entire beautiful scenery came into view.*

【尽数】total number; whole amount: 三天内你必须把所有欠款~归还。*You must return all the borrowed money within three days.*

【尽头】end: 铁道的~ *the end of the railway*

【尽夕】[书] whole night: ~不寐 *lie awake all night*

【尽孝】be filial to one's parents

【尽心】with all one's heart: 他~照顾生病的母亲。*He took care of his sick mother with all his heart.*

【尽心竭力】(do sth) with all one's heart and might

【尽兴】to one's heart's content; enjoy oneself to the full: ~而归 *return after thoroughly enjoying oneself*

【尽言】[书] ① say all one has to say; express oneself fully in words ② plain exhortation

【尽意】① express fully one's feelings or intentions: 他在诗作中~地抒发了对她的爱恋。*He expressed fully his love to her in his poem.* ② to one's heart's content: 我~地度过了一个假期。*I enjoyed myself fully this holiday.*

【尽义务】do one's duty; fulfill one's obligation; be a volunteer; work for no reward: 不要忘记对父母~。*Do not forget your duty to your parents.*

【尽责】do one's duty; discharge one's responsibility

【尽职】fulfill one's duty: 你应该~教导你的学生。*You are duty bound to educate your students.*

【尽忠】① be utterly loyal: ~报国 *be loyal and patriotic* ② sacrifice one's life; lay down one's life: 为国~ *sacrifice one's life for the country*

进 ① advance; move forward: 前~ *move forward* / 不~则退。*Move forward, or you'll fall behind.* ② enter; come into; get into: ~大门 *enter the gate* / ~屋 *come into the room* ③ take; receive: ~款 *income* / 他今年~了不少钱。*He earned much this year.* ④ submit; present: ~一言 *give a word of advice* ⑤ into; in: 把衣服放~箱子里 *pack clothes into a trunk* ⑥ any of the several rows of houses within an old-style residential compound: 这房子是两~院子。*This house has two courtyards.*

【进逼】close in on; advance on; press on towards: 步步~ *steadily close in*

【进兵】dispatch troops to attack (a place); forge ahead: 向南部~ *march towards the south*

【进补】take tonic; take extra nourishment: 冬令 ~ *take tonic in winter*

【进步】① advance; progress; improve: 在老师的帮助下,他 ~ 很快。*He progressed rapidly with the help of his teacher.* /他的英文 ~ 很大。*His English improved a lot.* ② (politically) progressive: ~ 青年 *progressive youth* / ~ 书刊 *progressive publications* / ~ 力量 *progressive forces*

【进餐】have a meal: 他邀我一同 ~。*He invited me to have supper together.*

【进谗】[书] speak ill (of sb before elders or superiors)

【进程】course; process; progress: 工作 ~ *the progress of work* /战争影响历史的 ~。*Wars have influenced the course of history.*

【进城】① go into town ② enter the big cities

【进出】① pass in and out: 车辆一律由西门 ~。*Vehicles go in and out through the western gate.* ② (business) turnover: 这个店每天有几千块钱的 ~。*This shop has a daily turnover of several thousand yuan.*

【进出口】① exits and entrances: 剧院 ~ *exit and entrance of a theatre* ② imports and exports: ~ 公司 *import and export corporation* / ~ 贸易 *import and export trade* / ~ 贸易总额 *total volume of import and export trade* / ~ 业务 *imports and exports* / ~ 申报 *import and export declaration* / ~ 总额 *total export-import volume*

【进抵】(of troops) reach (a place)

【进度】① rate of progress (or advance): 加快 ~ *quicken the tempo* ② planned speed; schedule: 制定合理的 ~ *make a reasonable schedule* / ~ 控制 *progress control*

【进度表】progress chart; progress schedule

【进而】and then; after that: 先巩固知识, ~ 提高。*Solidify your knowledge first and then learn more.*

【进发】set out; start: 向香山 ~ *head for the Fragrant Mountain*

【进犯】intrude into; invade: 敌军准备 ~。*The enemy troops are ready to invade.*

【进风口】air intake

【进奉】submit; present: ~ 珍宝 *present treasures*

【进攻】attack; assault; offensive: 敌人向左翼 ~。*The enemy attacked on the left flank.*

【进贡】① pay tribute (to a suzerain or emperor) ② grease (or oil) sb's palm

【进化】evolution: 飞跃 ~ *drastic evolution* /趋同 ~ *convergent evolution* /人为 ~ *artificial evolution* /适应 ~ *adaptive evolution* /研究人类的 ~ *study the evolution of man*

【进化论】the theory of evolution; evolutionism

【进货】stock (a shop) with goods; lay in a stock of merchandise: ~ 成本 *purchase cost* / ~ 价格 *prime cost*

【进击】advance on (the enemy)

【进见】call on (sb holding high office); have an audience with

【进酒】[书] urge sb to drink (at a banquet)

【进军】march; advance: 向敌人 ~ *march against the enemy*

【进口】① enter port; sail into a port ② import ③ entrance: 剧场 ~ *entrance of a theater* ④【机】inlet: 鼓风 ~ *blast inlet*

【进款】[口] income; receipts

【进来】come (or get) in; enter: 请 ~ 吧! *Come in, please!*

【进来】(jìnlái) come in; enter: 请 ~ 吧! *Please come in!*

【进来】(jìnlai) in (here): 她从街上跑 ~。*She ran into the room from the street.*

【进料】【机】feedstock; charge-in; feed: ~ 板 *feed board* / ~ 端 *feed end* / ~ 加工 *processing with imported materials* / ~ 盘 *entry table* / ~ 室 *feed space*

【进门】① go in ② learn the rudiments of sth ③ (of a woman) get married and move into the bridegroom's family

【进取】keep forging ahead; be eager to make progress; be enterprising: ~ 心 *initiative*; *enterprising spirit* / ~ 精神 *enterprising spirit*; *push* /他是一个有 ~ 心的年轻人。*He is an enterprising young man.*

【进去】(jìnqù) go in; get in; enter: 一个人站在门口阻止大家 ~。*There was a man at the door trying to stop people from going in.*

【进去】(jìnqu) in; into: 闯 ~ *break in*; *barge in*

【进入】enter; get into: ~ 角色 *enter into the spirit of a character* /她 ~ 了梦乡。*She sank into a deep sleep.* /她要 ~ 名牌大学学习的梦想实现了。*Her dream to enter the famous university came true.*

【进深】the depth or length of a house, yard or room

【进食】take food; have one's meal

【进士】a successful candidate in the highest imperial examinations

【进水管】water inlet

【进水口】blast-hole; water inlet

【进水塔】intake tower

【进退】① advance and retreat ② sense of propriety: 不知 ~ *have no sense of propriety*

【进退两难】find it difficult to advance or to retreat — be in a dilemma; be in a nice; between the devil and the deep sea; catch-22; no-win situation: 这真是 ~: 如果投资,就要冒破产的危险;如果不投资,就要冒失去市场份额的危险。*This is a dilemma: invest, and risk going bankrupt, or not invest and risk losing your share of the market.*

【进退维谷】in a dilemma; between the devil and the deep blue sea; be up a tree; a catch-22; no-win situation: 我现在真是 ~: 如果我告诉他,他会生气;如果我不告诉他,他会为此冲我发火。*It's a no-win situation — if I tell him, he'll be upset, but if I don't he'll be mad at me for not telling him.*

【进位】【数】carry (a number, as in adding)

【进贤】[书] recommend or recruit an able and virtuous person

【进香】offer incense in a temple; worship in a temple: ~ 客 *Buddhist pilgrim*

【进项】income; receipts

【进行】① be in progress; be underway; go on: ~调查 *make an investigation* ② carry on; carry out; conduct: ~侦察 *conduct a survey* ③ be on the march; march; advance
【进行曲】【音】march: 义勇军~ *March of the Volunteers*
【进行时】【语】progressive tense
【进修】make advance studies; receive advanced training; take a refresher course: ~班 *class for advanced studies* / ~学校 *in-service training school* / ~出国 *go abroad for further studies*
【进言】offer a piece of advice or an opinion
【进一步】go a step further; further: ~的调查 *further investigation* /他~指出他不愿与她合作。*He stated further that he would not cooperate with her.*
【进益】①［书］progress (in study, etc.) ② income; earning
【进展】make progress; make headway: 取得很大~ *make a mighty advance* /工作没有~。*The work is not advancing.*
【进占】march on and take (a place)
【进站】get in; pull in: 准时~ *pull in the station on time*
【进账】income; receipts
【进针】【中医】inserting needle
【进驻】enter and be stationed in; enter and garrison

近 ① near; close: 舍~求远 *seek far and neglect what lies close at hand* / 路程很~。*It's very near.* ② approaching; nearly: 年~五十 *getting on for fifty* /他的年收入~万美元。*His income approximated ten thousand dollars a year.* ③ intimate; closely related: 亲~ *be close to*; *be on intimate terms with* ④［书］simple; easy to understand: 言~旨远 *simple words but deep meaning*
【近岸】alongshore; in shore: ~航行 *hug*; *coastal navigation*
【近便】close and convenient: 咱们找个~的旅馆休息吧。*Let's have a rest at the nearest hotel.*
【近臣】［旧］minister close to an emperor
【近场】near field: ~距离 *distance of near field*
【近程】short range: ~回波 *near echo* / ~雷达 *short range radar*
【近刺】【军】short thrust; short lunge
【近代】① modern times: ~史 *modern history* ② capitalist era
【近道】shortcut: 走~ *follow a shortcut*; *cut corners*
【近地点】【天】perigee: ~潮 *perigean tide*
【近地轨道】near-earth orbit
【近点】【天】near-point: ~角 *true anomaly* / ~年 *anomalistic year* / ~月 *anomalistic month* / ~周 *anomalistic revolution*
【近东】the Near East
【近端】near-end: ~串话 *near-end crosstalk*
【近古】the age of recent antiquity (in Chinese history, the period from the 9th to the mid-19th century)
【近海】coastal waters; inshore; offshore: ~测量 *offshore survey* / ~构造 *offshore structure* / ~水域 *offshore waters*
【近红外】【物】near infra-red: ~光谱 *near infra-red spectrum* / ~线 *near infra-red ray*
【近乎】① close to; little short of: ~不可能 *almost impossible* ②［方］intimate; friendly: 和那女孩套~ *try to be friendly with the girl*
【近郊】outskirts of a city; suburbs; environs: ~居住区 *bedroom community*
【近景】【摄】close shot
【近距】low coverage
【近距离】close range; close quarter
【近况】recent developments; how things stand: 你~如何? *How are you getting along?*
【近来】recently; of late; lately: 我~未见过他。*I haven't seen him lately.* / ~情况变得如此糟糕,以致他决定卖掉房子。*Things got so bad recently that he decided to sell his apartment.*
【近邻】near neighbour: 远亲不如~。*A good neighbour is better than a relative far away.*
【近路】shortcut: 咱们抄~从田里穿过去吧。*Let's take a shortcut across the field.*
【近旁】nearby; near: 她来自~的一个村庄。*She came from a nearby village.*
【近期】in the near future; short term: ~目标 *immediate term objective* /我~没有出国的打算。*I have no intention of going abroad in the near future.*
【近前】［方］nearby; near
【近亲】close relative; near relation: ~繁殖 *inbreeding*; *close breeding* / ~结婚 *intermarriage*
【近情】reasonable; sensible
【近人】① a person of modern times or alive at present ②［书］one's close associate or friend: 我把他看作~。*I regard him as my friend.*
【近日点】【天】perihelion
【近日距】【天】perihelion distance
【近世】modern times; modern age
【近视】① myopia; nearsightedness: 我开车不得不戴眼镜,因为我~。*I have to wear glasses for driving because I am short-sighted.* ② shortsightedness: 这种做法很~。*This move is shortsighted.*
【近视眼】① myopia; nearsightedness ② myopic or nearsighted person: 她是个~,可是外出仍然不愿意戴眼镜。*She is as blind as a bat but still refuses to wear her glasses when she goes out.*
【近视矫正】myoporthosis
【近世】modern times: ~代数学 *modern algebra*
【近水楼台】waterside pavilion — a favourable position
【近水楼台先得月】a waterfront pavilion gets the moonlight first — the advantage of being in a favoured position
【近似】approximate; similar: 勾画出嫌疑者的~肖像 *sketch an approximate likeness of the suspect* / 她对这个问题的看法和我的很~。*Her views on this matter are similar to mine.*
【近似值】approximate value

【近体字】【语】proxemics
【近卫军】① armed escort of monarch ②（esp. in Europe）crack troops；Guards
【近义词】【语】near-synonym
【近因】immediate cause
【近影】picture taken recently；recent photo
【近于】little short of；border on：～疯狂 *little short of crazy* / ～奇迹 *be little short of miraculous*
【近在咫尺】be close at hand；a very short distance away
【近战】① fighting at close quarters；close combat ② close combat：～武器 *close-in weapons*
【近朱者赤，近墨者黑】one takes on the colour of one's company；he who plays with pitch must defile his fingers；he that lives with cripples learns to limp

妗
【妗母】［方］wife of one's mother's brother；aunt
【妗子】［方］① wife of one's mother's brother；aunt ② wife of one's wife's brother

劲 ① energy；strength：用～ *put forth strength* ② spirit；vigour：干活起～儿 *be vigorous in working* ③ air；manner；look：瞧他那骄傲～！*How arrogant he looks!* ④ interest；relish：老看电视真没～儿。*It's no fun watching TV all the time.*
see also jìng
【劲道】［方］strength；energy；effort
【劲头】① strength；energy ② vigour；spirit；drive；zeal：有～ *have a high spirit* / 这些年轻人～十足，但还不够仔细。*These young people are full of vigour, but fail in carefulness.*

晋[1] ① enter；promote：～京 *go to the capital* ② promote：加官～爵 *set promotion*
晋[2]（Jìn）① another name for Shanxi Province ②（Jìn）a surname
【晋级】［书］rise in rank；be promoted：～考试 *an examination for promotion*
【晋见】call on（sb holding high office）；have an audience with
【晋升】［书］promote to a higher office：那个年轻的陆军军官已被～为上尉。*The young army officer was promoted to the rank of captain.*
【晋谒】［书］call on（sb holding high office）；have an audience with
【晋职】［书］be promoted to a higher post

烬 cinder：烛～ *candle ashes* / 灰～ *ash*；*cinder*

浸 ① soak；steep：把种子放在水里～一～ *have the seeds soaked in water* ② be soaked；be steeped：衣服让汗～湿了。*The clothes were soaked with sweat.* ③［书］gradually；increasingly：交往～密 *gradually get into closer contact*
【浸沉】soak；immerse
【浸出】infusion；leach；lixiviate：～率 *leaching rate*
【浸焊】dip soldering
【浸剂】【药】infusion
【浸礼】【宗】baptism；immersion
【浸礼会】【宗】Baptist church
【浸没】① submerge；flood：～深度 *submergence* ② be immersed in；be permeated with：我们～在悲痛的气氛中。*We were immersed in grief.*
【浸泡】soak；immerse；steep：把水果～在盐水里 *steep fruits in brine* / 她把脏衣服～在水里。*She soaked the dirty clothes in water.*
【浸取】leaching：～率 *extraction rate*
【浸染】① be contaminated；be gradually influenced：这些年他～了一些不良习气。*He has been contaminated with some bad habits these years.* ② soak；infiltrate ③【纺】dip-dye
【浸润】① soak；infiltrate：雨水～土壤。*Rainwater soaks through the earth.* ②［书］gradually influence ③【物】adhesion ④【医】infiltration：～麻醉 *infiltration anesthesia*
【浸透】soak；saturate；steep；infuse：被雨水～ *be saturated by the rain*
【浸种】【农】seed soaking（in water）：～催芽 *soaking seeds to hasten germination*
【浸渍】soak；ret；macerate：～处理 *dipping treatment* / ～法 *infusion process*；*immersion method* / ～试验 *immersion test*

禁 ① forbid；ban：严～用火！*No fire!* ② imprison；detain：监～ *take into custody*；*imprison* ③ what is forbidden by law and custom：犯～ *violate a prohibition* ④（in former times）a place where the emperor lives：紫～城 *the Forbidden City*
see also jīn
【禁闭】place in confinement（as a punishment）；keeping custody：关～ *be placed in confinement* / ～室 *guardhouse*
【禁兵】imperial guard
【禁带】forbidden band；forbidden zone
【禁地】forbidden area；restricted area；out-of-bounds area
【禁锢】①［旧］debar from holding office ② keep in custody；imprison：他被～在一个小屋子里。*He was kept in a small room.* ③ confine：打破习惯的～ *break through the shackles of habit*
【禁果】【宗】forbidden fruit
【禁忌】① taboo：在这个部落酒是～。*Alcohol is a taboo in this tribe.* / 这种行为属～之列。*This behaviour is under taboo.* ② avoid；abstain from：～生冷 *abstain from cold or uncooked food* / ～油腻 *abstain from peppery or greasy food*
【禁忌症】【医】contraindication
【禁绝】totally prohibit；completely ban：这家商店已经～了假货。*This shop has got rid of all fake goods.*
【禁军】imperial guards
【禁猎】game refuge；preserve
【禁猎期】closed season
【禁猎区】suspended hunting area
【禁例】prohibitory regulations；prohibitions：触犯～ *violate the prohibitions*

【禁令】prohibition; ban: 解除～ *lift a ban*
【禁脔】a chunk of meat for one's exclusive consumption; one's exclusive domain
【禁区】① forbidden zone; restricted zone: 军事～ *military restricted zone* ② (wildlife or plant) preserve; reserve; natural park ③【医】forbidden band ④【体】(of football) penalty area; (of basketball) restricted area
【禁食】jejunitas; fasting
【禁书】banned book
【禁卫军】troops that protect the capital city or imperial palace
【禁物】banned goods and materials
【禁线】forbidden line
【禁夜】curfew
【禁欲】be ascetic: ～修行 *mortify the flesh*
【禁欲主义】asceticism
【禁运】embargo: 石油～ *oil embargo* /解除～ *lift (or raise) an embargo* /政府已对参与国际恐怖主义的国家实施武器～。*The government has imposed an arms embargo on countries involved in international terrorism.*
【禁止】prohibit; ban; forbid; outlaw: ～入内 *No entrance*! ; *No admittance*! /～停车 ! *Parking forbidden*! / ～拍照! *Cameras are forbidden*! /在大多数戏剧院里～吸烟。*Smoking is prohibited in most theaters.* /新的校规～在教室里吃东西。*The new school rule bans eating in classrooms.*
【禁制品】banned products or goods
【禁阻】prohibit; ban; forbid; prevent; stop: ～作用 *inhibitory action*

觐 present oneself before a monarch, or go on a pilgrimage
【觐见】[书] present oneself before (a monarch); go to court; have an audience with

噤 ①[书] keep silent ② shiver: 寒～ *shiver with cold*
【噤若寒蝉】as silent as a cicada in cold weather — keep quiet out of fear

jīng

茎 ① stem; stalk: 根～ *rhizome* /鳞～ *bulb* /球～ *corm* /攀援～ *climbing stem* /匍匐～ *creeping stem* /空心～ *cane stalk*/垂体～ *hypophyseal stalk* ② anything like a stem or stalk: 剑～ *sword handle* ③ [量]: 数～小草 *a few small blades of grass*

京[1] ① capital city; the capital of a country: 进～ *go to the capital* ② (Jīng) Beijing ③ (Jīng) a surname

京[2] [古] (a national numeral) ten million
【京白】【戏】parts in Beijing opera spoken in Beijing dialect
【京城】the capital of a country
【京都】① the capital of a country ② Kyoto, a city in Japan
【京官】[旧] officials with posts in the capital
【京胡】jinghu, a two-stringed bowed instrument with a high register; Beijing opera fiddle
【京华】[书] the capital of a country
【京剧】Beijing opera: ～唱腔 *music for voices in Beijing opera*
【京派】the Beijing school of Beijing opera
【京腔】Beijing accent
【京师】[书] the capital of a country
【京味】of special Beijing flavour; with Beijing characteristics: ～小吃 *snacks of Beijing flavour*
【京戏】[口] Beijing opera
【京油子】[旧] Beijing sharper
【京韵大鼓】【戏】story-telling in Beijing dialect with drum accompaniment

泾 ①[方] brook; stream ② (Jīng) Jing River
【泾渭分明】as different as the waters of the Jinghe and the Weihe — entirely different; have nothing in common: 我们的政治观点～。*We are just worlds apart in our political views.*

经[1] ①【纺】warp, threads running along the length of cloth ②【中医】arteries and veins inside the human body ③【地】longitude: 东～ *east longitude* ④ administer; manage: ～国之才 *ability to manage a country* ⑤[书] put to death by hanging: 自～ *hang oneself* ⑥ constant; normal: 荒诞不～ *fantastic*; *ridiculous* ⑦ canon; classic: 佛～ *Buddhist scripture* /圣～ *the Holy Bible* /古兰～ *the Koran* ⑧ menses: 停～ *amenorrhoea* ⑨ (Jīng) a surname

经[2] ① through; pass through: 饱～风霜 *weather-beaten* /途～北京 *pass through Beijing* /～他一说我才明白。*I got to know it through him.* ② experience; undergo: ～风雨 *face the world and brave the storm*
see also jìng
【经常】① day-to-day; everyday; daily: ～工作 *day-to-day work* ② frequently; constantly; regularly; often: 我～去拜访他。*I often visit him.* /我认识他,但不～往来。*I know him, but I don't frequently visit him.*
【经幢】【宗】stone pillar inscribed with Buddha's name or Buddhist scripture
【经典】① classics: ～作家 *writer of classics* ② scriptures: 佛教～ *Buddhist scriptures* ③ classical: 马克思主义～著作 *Marxist classics*
【经典力学】【物】classical mechanics
【经度】【地】longitude: 天文～ *astronomical longitude* /地理～ *geographic longitude* /真～ *true longitude*
【经度测量】longitude determination
【经度线】meridian
【经断】【医】menopause
【经费】funds; outlay: 这个计划因为缺少～而作罢。*The project was abandoned for want of funds.*
【经管】be in charge of: ～人事 *be in charge of personnel*
【经过】① process; course: 事情的全部～ *the whole*

course of the incident ② pass; go through: 火车～时发出了很大的响声。*The train made a big noise when passing.* /事非～不知难。*A man can hardly appreciate the difficulty of a job unless he tries his hand at it.* ③ go on; continue: 这次谈判～了一年的时间。*The negotiation has taken one year.* ④ as a result of; after; through: ～翻修的房子 *a house that is undergoing renovations*

【经籍】[书] ① Confucian classics ② books generally (with special reference to ancient texts)

【经纪】① manage (a business) ② manager; broker ③ [书] handle; look after

【经纪人】broke; middleman; agent: 房地产～ *estate agent*

【经济】① economy: 单一～ *single product economy* /封建～ *feudal economy* /个体～ *individual economy* /工业～ *industrial economy* /国民～ *national economy* /国营～ *state-owned economy* /规模～ *economy of scale* /货币～ *money economy; monetary economy* /集体～ *collective economy* /集约～ *intensive economy* /计划～ *planned economy* /民用～ *civilian economy* /农村～ *rural economy* /商品～ *commodity economy; commercial economy* /社会主义～ *socialist economy* /市场～ *market economy* /小农～ *small peasant economy; small-scale peasant economy* /信用～ *credit economy* /自然～ *natural economy* ② of industrial or economic value; economic ③ financial condition; income: ～宽裕 *well off; well-to-do* ④ economical; thrifty ⑤ [书] manage the country

【经济效益】economic performance; economic results; economic effectiveness; economic benefit

【经济学】economics: 部门～ *departmental economics* /动态～ *dynamic economics* /公共～ *public economics* /工业～ *industrial economics* /古典～ *classical economics* /管理～ *managerial economics* /规范～ *normative economics* /国际～ *international economics* /货币～ *monetary economics* /静态～ *static economics* /均衡～ *equilibrium economics* /开发～ *development economics* /劳动～ *labor economics* /垄断～ *monopoly economics* /农业～ *agricultural economics; agrarian economics* /平衡～ *balance economics* /企业～ *business economics* /森林～ *forest economics* /实用～ *applied economics* /实证～ *positive economics* /数量～ *quantitative economics* /司法～ *judicial economics* /统计～ *statistical economics* /新古典～ *neoclassical economics* /新凯恩斯派～ *Neo-Keynesian economics* /信息～ *information economics* /应用～ *practical economics* /政治～ *political economics* /总量～ *aggregate economics*

【经久】① prolonged: ～不息的掌声 *prolonged applause* ② durable: 颜色～不退。*The colour is fast and will not fade.*

【经理】① handle; manage ② manager; director: 部门～ *divisional manager* /财务～ *financial manager* /地区～ *area manager* /副～ *deputy manager* /公关～ *public relations manager* /区域～ *regional manager* /业务～ *office manager; operation manager* /总～ *general manager*

【经历】① go through; undergo; experience: 这个国家正在～一场可怕的战争。*The country is in the throes of a dreadful war.* /他们是～了经济危机和世界大战的一代人。*They were of the generation that had lived through the Depression and a world war.* ② experience: 这本书是以她的～写的。*The book is based on her experiences.*

【经略】[书] manage and manoeuvre: ～之才 *talent in military and administrative affairs*

【经纶】[书] statecraft; statesmanship: 满腹～ *talent for managing state affairs*

【经络】【中医】Main and collateral channels, regarded as a network of passages, through which vital energy circulates and along which the acupuncture points are distributed

【经脉】【中医】passages through which vital energy circulates, regulating bodily functions

【经贸】economy and trade

【经贸委】State Economic and Trade Commission

【经年累月】for years and years; year in year out

【经期】(menstrual) period: ～错后 *delayed menstrual cycle* / ～延长 *menostaxis*

【经商】engage in trade; be in business: 他很有～的天分。*He is born for a businessman.*

【经手】handle; deal with: ～人 *person handling a job, etc.* /这件事是我～的。*It's I who dealt with the matter.*

【经受】undergo; experience; withstand; stand; go through: 这个国家正在～人口迅速增长所带来的压力。*The country is undergoing the strains of rapid population growth.*

【经售】sell on commission; deal in; distribute; sell: 本店～电子产品。*Our shop sells electronic products.*

【经书】Confucian classics

【经天纬地】have heaven and earth under one's control — have great ability

【经纬】① meridian and parallel lines ② main threads; reason: ～万端 *have too many things to attend to* ③ [书] plan and administer ④ [旧] Confucian classics, etc.

【经纬度】【地】latitude and longitude

【经纬仪】theodolite; transit

【经文】passages from the Confucian classics or religious scriptures

【经线】①【纺】warp ②【地】meridian (line)

【经销】sell; distribute: ～商 *distributor*

【经心】careful; mindful; conscientious: 漫不～ *be careless to do sth*

【经学】study of Confucian classics

【经血】【中医】menses; menstruation

【经验】① experience: 交流～ *exchange experience* /直接～ *direct experience* /总结～ *sum up experience* ② go through; experience

【经验论】empiricism: ～者 *empiricist*

【经验之谈】wise counsel of an experienced person; remarks of an experienced person

【经意】careful; mindful: 我不～泄漏了秘密。*I let*

out the secret unconsciously.

【经营】① manage; operate; run; engage in: ~范围 *business scope* /~副业 *engage in sideline production* /我的丈夫~一家小餐馆。*My husband manages a small restaurant.* /他在~一家大农场。*He is now running a large farm.* ② plan and organize: 苦心~ *take great pains to build up* (*an enterprise, etc.*)

【经营成本】operating cost

【经营权】power of management

【经由】via; by way of: ~北京去天津 *go to Tianjin via Beijing*

【经传】① Confucian classics and commentaries on them; Confucian canon ② classical works; classics: 他名不见~。*He is not well known.*

荆 ① chaste tree; bramble: 披~斩棘 *break through brambles and thorns* /负~请罪 *proffer a birch and ask for a flogging — offer a humble apology* ② (Jīng) a surname

【荆棘】thistles and thorns; brambles; thorny undergrowth

【荆条】twigs of the chaste tree (used for weaving baskets, etc.)

菁

【菁华】the best; essence; cream; quintessence; the pick of the bunch: 这个公司的~员工被国外的高薪职位吸引走了。*The cream of this company's employees are attracted abroad by highly paid jobs.*

【菁菁】[书] lush; luxuriant

旌 ① (in ancient times) banner hoisted on a feather-decked mast ② [书] praise; commend; extol: 以~其美 *use it to praise his virtue*

【旌表】(of an emperor) confer a memorial archway or horizontal inscribed board on sb for loyalty or filial piety

【旌旗】banners and flags: ~招展。*The banners and flags are fluttering in the wind.*

惊 ① start; surprise: 大~小怪 *a storm in a teacup; fuss; like a hen with one chicken* /心~肉跳 *have the jitters* ② shock; alarm: 打草~蛇 *act rashly and alert the enemy* ③ (of horses, mules, etc.) shy; stampede: 马~了。*The horse shied.*

【惊诧】surprised; amazed; astonished; can't believe: 她盯着那张照片,脸上露出~的表情。*She stared at the picture with an amazed expression on her face.*

【惊颤】tremble with fear: 一想到要发生的事她就浑身~。*She trembles with fear to think what will happen.* /那奇怪的声音让我~。*That strange noise sent shivers down my spine.*

【惊动】alarm; alert; disturb; startle; trouble: 不要~病人。*Don't disturb the patient.*

【惊愕】[书] stunned; stupefied; staggered: 他~地发现他并不能合法地拥有他所购买的房子。*He was staggered to find that he did not legally own the house he had bought.*

【惊弓之鸟】a bird startled by the mere twang of a bow-string — a badly frightened person

【惊骇】[书] frightened; panic-stricken; scared; terrified; petrified: 不要如此~!那只不过是雷声。*Don't be frightened; it's only thunder.*

【惊鸿】startled swan — elegance of a beauty: ~艳影 (glimpse of) lithe and graceful figure of a beauty

【惊呼】cry out in alarm; utter a cry of alarm; shriek

【惊慌】alarmed; scared; panic-stricken: ~失措 *be all in a fluster; be terrified out of one's wits; be panic-stricken* /这个人~失措。*The man was seized with panic.*

【惊魂】the state of being frightened: ~甫定 *have just got over the state of terror* / ~未定 *not yet recovered from a fright*

【惊悸】[书] palpitate with fear

【惊叫】cry in fear; scream with terror; shriek: 突然一声可怕的~吓得过路人愣住了。*A sudden terrible shriek froze the passenger to the spot.*

【惊惧】alarmed and frightened

【惊遽】[书] startle; panic

【惊觉】wake up with a start

【惊厥】① faint from fear: 他的死讯让母亲~。*His death made his mother faint.* ②【医】convulsions

【惊恐】alarmed and panicky; terrified; panic-stricken; seized with terror: 老师把~万状的学生们带到安全处。*The teacher led the frightened students to safety.*

【惊雷】a sudden clap of thunder; frightening thunder: 于无声处听~。*You could hear thunderous warning in that dead silence.*

【惊乱】alarmed and disordered

【惊梦】wake up from a dream with a start

【惊奇】wonder; be surprised; be amazed: 我~地看着他,没想到又见到他了。*I looked at him in surprise — I didn't expect to see him again.*

【惊扰】alarm; agitate: 我们自己解决这件事吧。不要~他了。*Let's deal with it by ourselves. Don't bother him.*

【惊人】astonishing; amazing; alarming; astounding: ~的成就 *amazing success* /潜水艇以~的速度从水中驶过。*The submarine moved through the water at an astonishing speed.* /这些小孩儿钢琴弹得这么好,太~了! *It's amazing to see those little children playing the piano so beautifully.*

【惊世骇俗】astound the world with an extraordinary idea, action, etc.

【惊悚】alarmed and frightened

【惊叹】exclaim with admiration; marvel: 我为他所取得的成绩~。*I marvel at the achievements of his.*

【惊叹号】exclamation mark

【惊涛骇浪】terrifying waves; a stormy sea — a situation full of danger: 他曾经历过很多~。*He has gone through many hardships in his life.*

【惊天动地】shaking heaven and earth; earth-shaking; world-shaking

【惊悉】［书］be shocked or distressed to learn：～张老师不幸逝世 *be distressed to learn of the passing way of Mr. Zhang*
【惊喜】pleasantly surprised：～万分 *be extremely happy*
【惊吓】frighten；scare；terrify；give sb a fright；startle：摘掉那个面具，你会让孩子们受到～。*Take that mask off — you're frightening the children.* /巨大的噪音使他受了～，他手中的杯子摔到地上。*The big noise startled him and he dropped his glass on the floor.*
【惊险】alarmingly dangerous；breathtaking；thrilling：～的演出 *breathtaking performance*
【惊险片】thriller
【惊险小说】thriller（fiction）
【惊羡】wonder；marvel：他们的技艺令人～。*We marveled at their skill.*
【惊心动魄】soul-stirring；profoundly affecting：～的场面 *soul-stirring scene*
【惊醒】（jīngxǐng）① wake up with a start：他半夜里被～，发现天花板正在滴水。*She'd woken up in the middle of the night to find water dripping through the ceiling.* ② rouse suddenly from sleep；awaken：噪音～了我。*The noise awoke me.*
【惊醒】（jīngxing）sleep lightly；be a light sleeper：她睡觉很～，容易被很小的声音吵醒。*She was always a light sleeper，likely to be woken by the slightest sound.*
【惊讶】surprised；amazed；astonished；astounded：医生对于病人的迅速康复感到很～。*The doctor was amazed at the patient's rapid recovery.* /我非常～公司居然不付我薪水。*I was staggered that the company simply refused to pay me.*
【惊疑】surprised and bewildered
【惊异】surprised；amazed；astonished；astounded：人们都很～，他放弃了成功的演艺生涯成为了一个政治家。*People were astounded that he gave up a successful acting career to become a statesman.*

晶 ① glittering；brilliant：亮～～ *glittering；sparking* ② quartz；crystal：斑～ *porphyritic crystal* /水～ *quartz* /茶～ *yellow quartz* /砂～ *sand crystal* /烟～ *smoked crystal* ③ any crystalline substance：结～ *crystallization*
【晶晶】［书］bright；glittering
【晶粒】【物】grain
【晶亮】bright；glittering
【晶态】【物】crystalline state
【晶体】crystal：单～ *single crystal；unit crystal* /单质～ *elemental crystal* /发光～ *luminescent crystal* /发射～ *transmitting crystal* /分子～ *molecular crystal* /共价～ *covalent crystal* /介质～ *dielectric crystal* /离子～ *ionic crystal* /天然～ *natural crystal* /微～ *fine crystal* /无色～ *clear crystal* /镶嵌～ *mosaic crystal* /有机～ *organic crystal* /正～ *positive crystal*
【晶体管】transistor：～音机 *transistor radio*
【晶体学】crystallography
【晶莹】sparkling and crystal-clear；glittering and translucent：泪光～ *glistening teardrops*
【晶状体】【生理】crystalline lens

腈 【化】nitrile
【腈纶】acrylic fibres

睛 eyeball：目不转～ *fix eyes on sth* /画龙点～ *bring the painted dragon to life by putting in the pupils of its eyes — make the finishing point*

粳 a round-grained rice that is glutinous or non-glutinous
【粳米】polished round-grained non-glutinous rice

兢
【兢兢】careful；cautious：战战～ *tread on eggs；with fear and anxiety*
【兢兢业业】cautious and conscientious：她一生～地工作。*She works conscientiously all her life.*

精 ① fine；refined；polished：～金 *fine gold* ② spirit；essence；extract：酒～ *alcohol；spirits of wine；ethanol* /味～ *monosodium glutamate* /糖～ *saccharin；saccharine* ③ perfect；essential：去粗取～ *discard the dross and select the essence* ④ fine；delicate：体大思～ *broad in conception and meticulous in details* ⑤ smart；clever；shrewd：这孩子可～了。*That's really a smart child.* ⑥ proficient；skilled：博而不～ *have wide but not expert knowledge* /他～于绘画。*He is skilled in painting.* ⑦ spirit；attention；vigour：聚～会神 *gather oneself together；be all attention* ⑧ sperm；semen：受～ *fecundation；impregnation* ⑨ spirit；demon：妖～ *evil spirit* /狐狸～ *fox spirit — a seductive woman* ⑩［方］very；extremely：～瘦 *very lean* /～光 *with nothing left*
【精白】pure white：～米 *polished white rice*
【精本】de luxe edition
【精兵】picked troops；crack troops：宫殿由忠于国王的～守卫。*The palace is guarded by elite troops loyal to the emperor.*
【精兵简政】streamline the administrative structure；do away with redundancies in organization
【精彩】① brilliant；splendid；wonderful；superb；marvellous：～的发言 *excellent speech* /演员的表演很～。*The actor gave a superb performance.* ②［书］expression；spirit
【精巢】【生理】spermary；testis；testicle
【精诚】［书］absolute sincerity；good faith：～团结 *unite as one*
【精诚所至，金石为开】extreme sincerity can affect even metal and stone — complete sincerity can conquer all
【精赤】① naked；nude ②［方］be naked from the waist down
【精虫】【生】spermatozoon
【精萃】cream；pick；choice
【精粹】succinct；pithy；terse
【精打细算】count every cent and make every cent count；pinch pennies；careful calculation and strict budgeting：我们的收入很少，必须～。*With so little income，we must make every cent count.* /

在制定家庭预算时，你要学会～。*You should learn to practice economy in making out the household budget.*
【精当】precise and appropriate：用词～ *precise and appropriate wording*
【精到】precise and penetrating
【精雕细镂】work at sth with the care and precision of a sculptor — work at sth with great care
【精读】① read carefully and thoroughly：我～了这本书。*I read this book carefully.* ② intensive reading
【精度】precision；accuracy：～指数 *index of precision*
【精纺】spinning：～机 *spinning-frame*
【精干】①（of a body of troops，etc.）small in number but highly trained；crack ② keen-witted and capable；smart and efficient；capable；able-minded
【精耕细作】intensive and meticulous farming；intensive cultivation
【精工】refined；delicate
【精怪】goblins；spirits；demons
【精光】① with nothing left：他的儿子把钱花得～。*His son spent all money.* /我已经把英语忘得～。*I have clean forgotten English.* ② bright and clean；shiny：他穿着时尚，头发梳得～。*He wore in fashion，with his hair combed smooth.*
【精悍】① capable and energetic；smart and efficient ② pithy and poignant：文笔～ *pithy and pungent writing*
【精华】① cream；essence；quintessence：取其～ *get（or skim）the cream of* ②［书］brilliance；radiance：日月之～ *radiance of the sun and moon*
【精简】retrench；simplify；cut；reduce：～课程 *cut down the curriculum* /～机构 *simplify administrative structure* /～节约 *simplify administration and practise economy；retrench and economize*
【精力】energy；vigour；vim：～充沛 *full of energy* /他把～全都放在工作上。*He devoted all his energies to his job.*
【精练】concise；succinct；terse：语言～ *refined language* /～的风格 *a succinct style* /他用～且有逻辑的方式阐述了他的观点。*He expressed his arguments in a concise and logical way.*
【精炼】【冶】refine；purify：糖，油和金属在使用前须先～。*Sugar，oil and metals are refined before use.*
【精良】excellent；superior；of the best quality：装备～ *well-equipped*
【精灵】① spirit；demon ②［方］（of a child）clever；bright；intelligent
【精馏】【化】rectification：～酒精 *rectified alcohol*
【精美】fine；nice；exquisite；elegant：～的食品 *delicacies* /～绝伦 *exquisite beyond compare* /她戴着一条～的珍珠项链。*She was wearing an exquisite pearl necklace.* /展现给我们的房子非常～。*The apartment we were shown was extremely elegant.* /多么～的衣服啊！*What a gorgeous dress!*
【精密】precise；accurate：～机床 *precision machine tool* /～仪器 *a precise instrument* /～铸造 *precision casting*
【精妙】exquisite
【精明】astute；shrewd；intelligent；sagacious：～的老人 *a sagacious old man* /他是个～的律师，什么花招都懂。*He is a shrewd lawyer who knows all the tricks.*
【精明强干】intelligent and capable；able and efficient
【精磨】【机】finish grinding；precision grinding
【精囊】【生理】seminal vesicle
【精疲力竭】exhausted；worn out；tired out；spent：这天的事情使我～。*The day's events completely drained me of all strength.*
【精辟】penetrating；incisive；pithy：～的分析 *incisive analysis*
【精品】fine works（of art）；quality goods；articles of fine quality：～皮鞋 *top-quality leather shoes* /艺术～ *artistic work of excellent quality*
【精气神儿】［口］vigour；energy
【精巧】exquisite；ingenious；subtle：～的机器 *ingenious machine*
【精确】accurate；exact；precise：～的天平 *an accurate scale* /～的测量 *a precise measurement*
【精确度】measure of precision
【精肉】［方］lean meat
【精锐】crack；picked：～部队 *picked troops*
【精深】profound；deep：这是个～的理论。*The theory is abstruse.*
【精神】（jīngshén）① spirit；mind；consciousness：共产主义～ *communist spirit* /时代～ *the spirit of the age* /你要做好～准备。*You have to be mentally prepared.* ② essence；gist；spirit：领会文件的～ *try to understand the gist of the document*
【精神】（jīngshen）① vigour；vitality；drive：～好 *in good spirits* /打起～ *keep up one's spirits* /恢复～ *recover one's spirits* /他很没～。*He is rather listless.* ② lively；spirited；vigorous；smart：这小伙子真～。*The young man is in fine fig.*
【精神病】mental disease；mental disorder；psychosis
【精神失常】have lost one's marbles；be deranged：这个可怜的女人～很多年了。*The poor woman's mind has been deranged for many years.*
【精神食粮】spiritual food；nourishment for the mind
【精神文明】spiritual civilization；cultural and ideological progress：物质文明和～ *spiritual and material civilization*
【精神支柱】ideological prop
【精神状态】state of mind：他的～很差。*He is in low spirits.*
【精审】［书］（of writings，plans，opinions，etc.）carefully thought-out
【精瘦】skinny：～的孩子 *a skinny child*
【精饲料】concentrated feed
【精髓】marrow；pith；quintessence：道德的～ *the essence of morality*
【精通】be proficient in；have a good command of；

J

master：他～法语。*He is proficient in French; he has a good command of French.* /他对当地语言如此～让我吃惊。*His familiarity with the local language surprised me.*

【精微】profound and subtle

【精卫填海】Jingwei, the mythical bird trying to fill up the sea with pebbles — dogged determination to achieve one's purpose

【精铣】【机】finish milling

【精细】① meticulous; fine; careful：这件事母亲考虑得十分～。*Mother carefully thought out the matter.* ② shrewd; astute

【精心】meticulously; painstakingly; elaborately; with great care：我们正在为总统的来访做～的准备。*Elaborate preparations were being made for the president's visit.* /他公布了所有他～收集的数据。*He published all the data that has been painstakingly collected.*

【精选】①【矿】concentration ② selected; carefully chosen：～农作物 *the cream of the crop* /～商品 *choice goods*

【精研】study hard：～外文 *study foreign languages diligently*

【精盐】refined salt; table salt

【精要】pithy; essence

【精液】【生理】seminal fluid; semen

【精益求精】constantly improve sth; keep improving; strive for perfection; refine on sth：他努力使自己的教学法～。*He refined on his methods of teaching.*

【精英】essence; cream; flower; elite; the best：足球队的～ *the football team's elite* /本届的～毕业生将获得高薪职位。*The cream of this year's graduates will get high-paid jobs.*

【精于】be skilful in; be expert at：他～绘画。*He is expert in painting.*

【精湛】consummate; exquisite; superb：钢琴家的～技艺使全场观众惊诧不已。*The pianist's virtuosity has amazed all the audience present.*

【精制】make with extra care; refine：这些家具都是～而成。*The furniture was made with extra care.*

【精致】fine; exquisite; delicate; superb：屋子的中间是一张～的橡木桌子。*In the centre of the room was a splendid oak table.*

【精忠】utterly (or unreservedly) loyal：～报国 *serve one's country with selfless loyalty*

【精装】①(of books) clothbound; hardback; hardcover：～书 *hardcover books* ②(of goods) elaborately packed：～糖果 *elegantly-packed candies*

【精壮】able-bodied; strong

【精子】【生理】sperm; spermatozoon：副～ *accessory sperm* /巨～ *giant spermatozoon* /无核～ *apyrene sperm*

鲸 whale：雌～ *cow whale* /雄～ *bull whale* /蓝～ *blue whale* /捕～ *whale fishing*

【鲸鲨】whale shark

【鲸吞】swallow like a whale; annex (a large tract of territory)：蚕食～ *nibble away like a silkworm or swallow like a whale — occupy territory in many ways*

【鲸须】baleen; whale fin

【鲸油】sperm; sperm oil; spermaceti; train oil; whale oil

【鲸鱼】whale

【鲸脂】blubber

jǐng

井[1] ①well：打～ *sink a well* /枯～ *dry well* /落～下石 *drop a stone on sb who has fallen into a well — hit sb when he is in trouble* ② a well-shaped space：天～ *small yard* /矿～ *mine shaft (or pit)* ③ village; settlement：背～离乡 *leave one's native place* ④ a star constellation, one of the twenty-eight constellations ⑤(Jǐng) a surname

井[2] neat; orderly：秩序～然 *in good order*

【井壁】wall of a well：～取样 *side-wall sampling*

【井底】① bottom of a well ②【矿】shaft bottom; pit bottom

【井底之蛙】a frog in a well — a person with a very limited outlook

【井灌】【水】well irrigation

【井架】① petroleum derrick ②【矿】headframe; headgear

【井井有条】in perfect order; shipshape; methodical; systematic：她慢慢地、～地把所有纸张都放回卷宗。*She worked slowly, methodically putting all the pages back into their files.* /你应该更加～地安排你的文章，使要点更加清晰。*You need to organize your article in a more systematic way so that the main points are shown more clearly.*

【井口】① mouth of a well ②【矿】pithead ③ wellhead：～气 *wellhead gas*

【井喷】petroleum blowout

【井然】[书] orderly; neat and tidy; shipshape; methodical; in good order：乘客们上车秩序～。*The passengers boarded the bus in good order.*

【井然有序】apple-pie order; eutaxy; neat：我的母亲做事总是～。*My mother was always neat in everything she did.*

【井水不犯河水】well water does not intrude into river water — I'll mind my own business; you mind yours; one should care his own business：我们俩从此～。*Since then we didn't interfere with each other.*

【井台】a raised platform around a well

【井位】well location; well-site

【井下】in the pit; in the shaft：～作业 *operation in a pit*

【井盐】well salt

【井邑】[书] city; town

颈 neck：长～鹿 *giraffe*

【颈动脉】【生理】carotid; carotid artery

【颈静脉】【生理】jugular vein

【颈联】third antithetical couplet in a lüshi poem (the fifth and sixth lines)
【颈项】neck
【颈椎】【生理】cervical vertebra
【颈子】[方] neck

景[1] ① view; scenery: 良辰美~ *beautiful scene in a good day* ② condition; situation: 盛~ *a grand occasion* /远~ *perspective; prospects* ③ setting; scenery (of a film): 外~ *outdoor scene* /实~ *scene shot on location* ④ scene (of a play): 第一幕第二~ *Act I, Scene II* ⑤ (Jǐng) a surname

景[2] admire; respect

【景点】scenic spots
【景观】① landscape: 自然~ *natural landscape* ② sights worth seeing: 人文~ *sights of human interest*
【景况】situation; circumstances: 他们的~逐渐恶化。*Their situation is getting worse.*
【景慕】[书] esteem; revere; admire: 他是一个受人~的诗人。*He is a respectable poet.*
【景片】a piece of (stage) scenery; flat
【景气】prosperity; boom: 不~ *in depression; slump*
【景区】scenic spot
【景色】scenery; view; scene; landscape; sight: 这里~宜人。*The scenery is pleasing here.* /我往窗外看,除了几座高楼,什么~也没有。*There's no view from my window except of some tall buildings.*
【景物】scenery; scene: 他停下来欣赏~。*He stopped to admire the scenery.*
【景象】scene; sight; picture: 孩子在街上跑的常见~ *the familiar sight of the children running along the street* /港湾中的船只构成了美丽的~。*The boats in the harbour make a beautiful scene.*
【景仰】respect and admire; hold in deep respect: 他受到大家的爱戴和~。*He was greatly loved and esteemed.*
【景遇】[书] circumstances; one's lot: 他这些年~很好。*He is getting on very well in recent years.*
【景致】view; scenery; scene

儆 warn; admonish: 杀一~百 *execute one as a warning to others*

憬 [书] awake; come to understand

【憬悟】wake up to reality; come to see the truth, one's error, etc.

警 ① alert; vigilant ② keen; sharp; acute: 机~ *alert and resourceful* ③ warn; alarm: 惩一~百 *punish one as a warning to others* ④ emergency; alarm: 报~ *give an alarm* ⑤ police; policeman: 民~ *people's police* /武~ *armed police*

【警报】alarm; warning; alert: 拉~ *sound the alarm* /解除~ *all clear* /我一看到黑烟,马上就发出~。*I raised the alarm as soon as I saw the black smoke.*
【警报器】siren; alarm
【警备】guard; garrison: ~部队 *garrison troops* /~司令部 *garrison headquarters*
【警察】police; policeman: 交通~ *traffic police* /治安~ *security police* /~在跟踪他。*The police are on his track.*
【警察局】police station (or office)
【警车】police car; police van
【警笛】① police whistle ② siren
【警督】police supervisor
【警服】police uniform
【警告】① remind; alert: 医生~我要注意睡眠不足的危险。*The doctor alerted me to the danger of not getting enough sleep.* ② warn; caution; admonish: 他~我不要单独去那里。*He warned me not to go there alone.* /父亲~他不要忘记锁上自行车。*His father cautioned him not to leave his bicycle unlocked.* /我向他发出最后的~,告诉他如果再迟到就要被开除。*I gave him a final warning and told him that if he was late again he would be fired.* ③ warning (as a disciplinary measure): 撤销~处分 *withdraw a disciplinary warning*
【警官】police officer: ~,我做错什么事了吗? *Have I done something wrong, officer?*
【警棍】① policeman's baton; truncheon ②【旧】policeman who abused his power
【警号】① warning signal ② number-badge a policeman wears on his uniform
【警徽】police emblem
【警戒】① warn; admonish ② be on the alert against; guard against; keep a close watch on: 战斗~ *combat security*
【警戒部队】outpost troops; security force
【警戒色】【动】warning (or aposematic) coloration
【警戒水位】warning water level; warning stage
【警戒线】cordon
【警句】aphorism; epigram: ~名言 *famous sayings and pithy remarks*
【警觉】① vigilance; alertness: 他的话引起了我的~。*What he said aroused my vigilance.* /照顾小孩儿需要一直保持~,你不知道他们接下来要做什么。*Looking after young children requires constant vigilance — you never know what they'll get up to next.* ② sound an alarm; warn against
【警力】police force; police power
【警犬】police dog; patrol dog
【警世】warn the world; admonish the world: ~良言 *wise counsel that admonishes the world*
【警惕】be on guard against; watch out for; be vigilant; keep one's eyes open (or peeled): 我们必须要~恐怖主义活动。*We must be on guard against terrorist activities.*
【警惕性】vigilance: 保持~ *on one's guard* /丧失~ *off one's guard* /我们要提高~。*We should heighten our vigilance.*
【警卫】(security) guard: ~连 *the guard company* /门口有~站岗,防止有人出入。*There are guards at the gate to prevent anyone getting in or out.* /犯人由武装~押了进来。*The prisoner was brought in under armed guard.*
【警务】police affairs; police service

J

【警衔】police rank
【警械】police apparatus or instruments
【警醒】① be a light sleeper：奶奶睡觉很～。*My grandma is a very light sleeper.* ② warn；caution；alert
【警语】aphorism；epigram
【警员】① general term for police ② police constable：一级～ *Police Constable，Class I*
【警钟】alarm bell；tocsin：敲～ *sound the alarm* / 这些可怕的数字为社会敲响了～。*These appalling statistics have set the alarm bells ringing in the society.*
【警种】police services

jìng

劲 strong；powerful：刚～ *sturdy*；*vigorous* / 疾风知～草。*Sturdy grass understands high winds — strength of character is tested in a crisis.* *see also* jìn
【劲拔】［书］powerful
【劲吹】（of the wind）blow fiercely：北风～。*The northern wind is blowing hard.*
【劲敌】formidable adversary；strong opponent（or contender）
【劲风】strong wind
【劲急】strong and swift
【劲健】strong and forceful：笔力～ *vigorous calligraphy*
【劲旅】［书］strong contingent；crack force
【劲射】（in football，etc.）forceful or powerful shot
【劲升】①（of rocket，etc.）rise with a powerful thrust ② quick rise in one's position
【劲直】［书］staunch and honest
【劲卒】［书］valiant soldiers：良将～ *good commanders and valiant soldiers*

径 ① track；foot-path：山～ *mountain path* ② way；road；means：捷～ *a short cut*；*crosscut* / 独辟蹊～ *develop a new style or a new method of one's own* ③directly；straight：～向有关人士联系 *directly contact with the people concerned* ④ diameter：半～ *radius* / 口～ *bore*；*caliber*
【径道】［书］footpath；track
【径流】［书］runoff：地表～ *surface runoff* / 地下～ *groundwater runoff* / ～调节 *runoff regulation*
【径赛】【体】track：～项目 *track event* / ～选手 *track sportsman*
【径庭】［书］very unlike：大相～ *entirely different*
【径行】do sth on one's own
【径直】straight；directly；straightaway：道路～通向北方。*The road runs directly north.*
【径自】without leave；without consulting anyone：你可～处理这件事。*You could deal with it on your own.* / 她～走了。*She turned away without leave.*

净[1] ① clean：把手洗干～。*Wash your hands clean.* ② wash；make clean：～脸 *wash one's face* ③ with nothing left：吃～ *eat up* / 钱用～了。*The money is used up.* ④ net；pure：～收入 *net income* ⑤ nothing but；only：地上～是纸屑。*There were nothing but wastepaper all over the ground.* / 他～爱胡扯。*He likes to waffle all the time.*

净[2]（in the traditional opera）painted-face role
【净白】pure white
【净产值】net output value
【净出口国】net exporting country
【净额】net amount
【净高】clear height
【净化】purify；cleanse；clean：～污水 *purify sewage water* / ～语言 *purify the language*
【净化剂】clarifier；purificant
【净价】net price
【净洁】pure and clean
【净尽】completely used up；with nothing left
【净口】purify the language in folk art performance
【净跨】【建】clear span
【净宽】clear width
【净亏】net loss
【净利】net profit（after taxes）
【净面】wash one's face
【净身】（of a man）be castrated
【净室】clean and tidy house or room（usu. a nun's or monk's）
【净手】①［方］wash one's hands ②［婉］relieve oneself
【净桶】nightstool；closestool；commode
【净土】①【宗】Pure Land；Paradise of the West ② any clean，unpolluted place
【净心】① free from care ② have a peaceful and quiet mind
【净意】［方］① on purpose；by design：他～踩我的脚。*He stepped on my foot on purpose.* ② purposely；specially
【净余】net balance；remainder；surplus
【净增】net increase
【净值】net worth；net value
【净重】net weight：这盒食品～1000克。*This box of food has a net weight of one thousand grams.*

经 【纺】warping
see also jīng
【经纱】warp yarn

胫 shin：不～而走 *get round fast*；*spread fast*
【胫骨】【生理】shin bone；tibia
【胫节】（of insects）tibia；tibiae

痉
【痉挛】fit；convulsion；cramps；spasm：肌肉～ *muscle spasm*；*a convulsive movement of the muscles* / 面部～ *facial spasm* / 强直性～ *tonic spasm* / 胃～ *spasm of the stomach* / 习惯性～ *habit spasm*

竞 ① compete；contend ②［书］strong；powerful：南风不～。*The southerly wind is gentle.*

J

【竞渡】① boat race ② swimming race
【竞技】sports; athletics: ~状态良好 *be in top form*
【竞赛】contest; competition; emulation; race: 军备~ *arms race*; *armament race* /劳动~ *labour emulation* /~运动 *emulation drive*
【竞相】compete; vie: ~购买 *vie in buying sth*
【竞选】enter into an election contest; campaign for (office); run for: ~运动 *an election campaign* / ~总统 *run for president*
【竞争】compete; rival; vie; contest: ~产品 *rival products* /~公司 *rival companies* /~机制 *mechanism of competition* /~价格 *competitive price* /~力 *competitiveness* /~学校 *rival schools* /在这方面没有人能同他~。*No one could rival him in this respect.* /小书店显然不能同连锁书店~。*The small bookstores simply can't compete with the big chains.* /他说要和我~工会的领导职务。*He said he would fight me for the leadership of the labour union.*
【竞争机制】competitive mechanism
【竞争价格】competitive price
【竞争性】competitiveness
【竞逐】compete and pursue
【竞走】【体】heel-and-toe walking race: 公路~ *highway walking race*

竟[1] ① finish; complete: 读~ *finish one's reading* /未~之业 *the unfulfilled cause* ② whole; throughout: ~日读书 *reading the whole day* ③ [书] in the end; finally: 有志者事~成。*Where there is a will, there is a way.*

竟[2] to one's surprise; unexpectedly: 他~在两年之内学会了三门外语。*It is amazing that he grasped three foreign languages within only two years.*
【竟敢】have the audacity to do sth; dare: 他~在我的家里如此放肆! *He dares to behave like that in my house!*
【竟然】① unexpectedly; to one's surprise; actually: 他~通过了考试。*To our surprise, he passed the examination.* ② have the cheek to do sth: 他~当众说谎。*He has the cheek to tell lies before the public.*
【竟日】the whole day; all day long
【竟至】actually go so far as to: 他脚疼, ~不能行走。*The pain in his foot was such as to stop his walking.*

靓 [书] make up; dress up
see also liàng
【靓妆】[书] (of a woman) gorgeously dressed

敬 ① respect: 尊~ *respect*; *esteem*; *worship* ② respectfully; reverently: ~请光临 *request the honour of your presence* ③ offer politely: ~茶 *serve tea (to a guest)* /~酒 *propose a toast* ④ (Jìng) a surname
【敬爱】respect and love: 令人~的老师 *a respectable teacher*
【敬辞】term of respect; polite expression
【敬而远之】stay at a respectful distance form sb; keep at a respectful distance
【敬奉】① piously worship ② offer respectfully; present politely
【敬服】respect and admire: 我~他的人品。*I esteem and admire his character.*
【敬告】beg to inform
【敬贺】congratulate with respect; send respectful greetings to
【敬候】① await respectfully: ~回复 *wait to hear from sb* ② greet sb respectfully: ~起居 *inquire after sb's health with respect*
【敬酒】propose a toast; toast: 相互~ *exchange toasts*
【敬酒不吃吃罚酒】refuse a toast only to drink a forfeit — submit to sb's pressure after first turning down his request; submit to compulsion rather than persuasion
【敬老院】home of respect for the aged; old folk's home
【敬礼】① salute; give a salute: 立正~ *stand at (the) salute* ② used at the end of a letter: 此致~ *with best regards*
【敬慕】respect and admire; think highly of; look up to: 我很~他,因为他非常勇敢。*I've always looked up to him because he has so much courage.*
【敬佩】esteem; admire; respect: 我~他事业有成。*I admire him for his success in business.*
【敬若神明】worship sb as deity; worship: 他把她~。*He worships the very ground she walks on.*
【敬上】yours truly
【敬挽】with deep condolences from sb
【敬畏】hold in awe and veneration; revere
【敬献】present politely: ~礼品 *present gifts*
【敬仰】revere; venerate: 当受贿的事实被揭露后,他们开始反对曾经~的领袖。*When the fact of taking bribes was revealed they turned against the leader they had once revered.*
【敬业】dedicate oneself to work or study: ~精神 *professional dedication*
【敬意】respect; admiration; tribute: 他果断而坚决地处理了这件事,使我们对他满怀~。*With his firm and decisive handling of the dispute, he had earned the respect of ours.* /我对你所做的善事充满了~。*I am full of admiration for the charity work you have done.*
【敬赠】respectfully presented by sb
【敬重】deeply respect; revere; honour; hold sb in high esteem: 所有认识他的人都很~他。*He was held in high esteem by all who knew him.* /他为人正直,我对他十分~。*I respect him for his honesty.*
【敬祝】sincerely wish

靖 ① quiet; peaceful: 安~ *peace and tranquility* ②make tranquil; pacify: ~边 *pacify the border regions* ③ (Jìng) a surname
【靖国】stabilize the country
【靖国神社】(Japan) Yasukuni Shrine; Japanese shrine for the war-dead built in Tokyo in 1869: 参拜~ *pay homage to Yasukuni Shrine*

【靖乱】put down a rebellion

静 ① still; calm: 安～ *quiet; peaceful* /风平浪～ *calm and tranquil* ② quiet; silent: 你该～下来好好想一想了。*You should calm down and think it over.* ③calm; quieten: 请～一～! *Please be quiet.* ④ (Jìng) a surname

【静磁场】【物】magnetostatic field

【静电】【物】static electricity: ～纺纱 *electrostatic spinning* /～喷漆 *electrostatic paint spraying* /～扫描 *electrostatic scanning* /～印刷 *electrostatic copying or printing* /她的头发～很强。*Her hair was full of static.*

【静电场】electrostatic field

【静电感应】electrostatic induction

【静电荷】electrostatic charge

【静电计】【物】electrometer

【静电学】electrostatics

【静观】watch quietly; observe calmly: ～其变 *watch the changes calmly*

【静候】quietly wait for: ～佳音 *quietly waiting for the good news*

【静寂】quiet; silent: ～的街道 *a quiet street*

【静力学】【物】statics

【静脉】【生理】vein: 大～ *systemic veins*

【静脉曲张】【医】varix; varicosity

【静脉炎】【医】phlebitis

【静脉注射】【医】intravenous injection

【静谧】[书] quiet; still; tranquil

【静摩擦】static friction

【静摩擦力】【物】static friction force

【静默】① become silent ② mourn in silence; observe silence: ～致哀 *mourn in silence; observe a moment's silence in mourning*

【静穆】solemn and quiet

【静悄悄】very quiet

【静态】① static state: ～平衡 *static equilibrium* /～特性 *static characteristic* /～控制 *static control* ② (observe and study) from the static point of view: ～分析 *static analysis* /～研究 *study of static state*

【静物】still life: ～画 *still-life drawing* /～摄影 *still-life photography*

【静心】peace of mind: ～继续工作吧。*Quieten down and get on with your work.*

【静养】rest quietly to recuperate; convalesce; have a rest-cure; convalesce

【静园】stilling the park

【静止】static; motionless; still; immobile; not move a muscle; at a standstill: ～的水 *static water* /他站在门口,～不动。*He stood motionless in the doorway.* /好长一段时间她都～不动,好像在发呆。*For a time she remained immobile, seemingly in a trance.*

【静坐】① sit quietly ② sit still as a form of therapy ③ sit-down; sit-in: ～罢工 *sit-down (strike)*

境 ① border; boundary: 边～ *border; frontier* /国～ *national territory* ② place; area: 如入无人之～ *like entering an unpeopled land — smashing all resistance* ③ situation; circumstances: 事过～迁。*The events have passed and the times have changed.*

【境地】condition; circumstances: 处于贫困的～ *be in reduced circumstances*

【境界】① boundary ② extent reached; state; realm

【境况】(financial) condition; circumstances: ～不好 *be badly off* /～好 *be well off*

【境域】① condition; circumstances; situation ② area; realm; domain

【境遇】circumstances; one's lot: 个人～不同。*Everybody has his own lot.*

镜 ① looking glass; mirror: 哈哈～ *distorting mirror* /三棱～ *bevelled mirror* ② lens; glass: 放大～ *magnifier* /花～ *presbyopic lenses* /显微～ *microscope* /望远～ *telescope*

【镜花水月】flowers in a mirror or the moon in the water — an illusion

【镜框】① picture frame ②spectacles frame

【镜面】mirror face; mirror plane: ～抛光 *mirror polish*

【镜片】lens

【镜台】dressing table

【镜头】① camera lens: 变焦距～ *variable-focus lens* /标准～ *standard lens* /广角～ *wide-angle lens* /远摄～ *telephoto lens* ② shot; scene: 特写～ *close-up*

【镜匣】a wooden case with a looking glass and other toilet articles; dressing case

【镜箱】① (of a camera) dark room or chamber ② bathroom medicine cabinet whose door is faced with a mirror

【镜子】① mirror; looking glass: 照～ *look into the mirror* ② [口] glasses; spectacles

jiōng

驷 [书] ① (of horses) stout and strong ② fine steed

jiǒng

炅 [书] ① sunlight ② bright

迥 [书] ① far apart; remote: 山高路～ *high mountains and long road* ② widely different: ～若两人 *look like a different person*

【迥乎】widely different

【迥然】far apart; widely different; widely different: ～不同 *utterly different; not in the least alike* /不同国家的习俗～相异。*Customs differ much in different countries.*

【迥异】widely different: 我们俩性情～。*We are poles apart in temperament.*

炯 [书] bright; shining

【炯炯】[书] (of eyes) bright; shining: 目光～ *sparkling eyes* /他目光～有神。*He has a pair of*

bright pioneering spirit

窘 ① in straitened circumstances; hard up：生活很～ *live a hard life* ② awkward; embarrassed：我遇到他时觉得很～。*I felt rather embarrassed when I met him.* ③ embarrass：他用尖刻的话～我。*He embarrassed me with bitter remarks.*

【窘促】［书］① poverty-stricken ② hard pressed; embarrassed; in a predicament：当我要在很多人面前发言的时候就会很～。*I always get really embarrassed when I have to give a talk in front of a lot of people.*

【窘境】awkward situation; predicament; plight：我突然发现自己处于一种最为尴尬的～。*I found myself suddenly in a most awkward predicament.*

【窘况】awkward situation; predicament; plight：他缓解了我的～。*He eased my embarrassment.*

【窘困】awkward; in a difficult position：显然他感到非常～。*It was obvious that he was very embarrassed.*

【窘迫】① poverty-stricken; very poor ② hard pressed; embarrassed; in a predicament：poverty-stricken; very poor; be embarrassed：她的双颊发红，显得十分～。*Blushes showed her embarrassment.*

【窘态】embarrassed look：露出一副～ *show embarrassment*; *look embarrassed*

jiū

纠[1] entangle

纠[2] assemble; band together

纠[3] ①［书］inform against; supervise ② correct; rectify：有错必～。*Mistakes once found must be corrected.*

【纠察】① maintain order at a public gathering ② picket：担任～ *act as a picket*

【纠察队】pickets

【纠缠】① get entangled; be in a tangle：与警方的～ *entanglements with the police* /～不清的事情 *entangled affairs* ② nag; worry; pester; harass：他还有事，别～他。*He is busy; stop nagging at him.* /女儿～我，让我为她买那本书。*My daughter badgered me to buy her that book.* /房东不断～拖欠房租的房客。*The landlord harassed tenants who were behind in their rent.*

【纠缠不清】too tangled up to unravel; get terribly entangled：在这个公司里人与人之间～。*The inter-person relationship has been too complex in this company.*

【纠错】error correction：～程序 *error correcting routine* /～系统 *error correction system*

【纠纷】dispute; issue; trouble; complication：边界～ *boundary dispute* /家庭～ *household quarrel* /无原则～ *unprincipled dispute* /这个问题会引起～。*The problem will give rise to troubles.* /这场旷日持久的～似乎没有尽头。*There seems to be no end in sight to this long dispute.*

【纠风】get rid of professional malpractices

【纠葛】entanglement; dispute; complication：感情～ *emotional entanglement*

【纠合】［贬］gather together：～众人 *call* (*or round up*) *a group of people*

【纠集】［贬］get together; muster; gang up; collect：那些小伙子～起来反对政府。*Those young guys ganged up against the government.*

【纠结】be entangled with; be intertwined with：她的长发和玫瑰丛～在一起。*Her long hair entangled itself in the rose bush.*

【纠偏】rectify a deviation; correct an error：～救弊 *rectify a deviation*; *correct an error*

【纠正】correct; put right; put sb straight; set sb straight; redress; cure：～错误 *remedy a fault* /～拼写错误 *correct spelling mistakes* /他认为饮料和食品是免费的，我们必须～他的想法。*He thought the food and drink were free, so we had to set him straight.*

鸠［书］turtledove：斑～ *turtledove* /绿～ *green pigeon*

【鸠形鹄面】gaunt and emaciated; haggard; skin and bones

【鸠占鹊巢】the turtle-dove occupies the magpie's nest — seize another person's home, etc. for one's own use

究 ① study carefully; investigate：研～ *study*; *research* /推～ *examine*; *study* /追～ *look into*; *find out* ②［书］after all; actually：～非长久之计。*After all, this is not a permanent solution.*

【究办】investigate and deal with：依法～ *be investigated and dealt with according to law*

【究诘】［书］interrogate; cross-examine：我向她～这件事，她拒不回答。*She refused to be interrogated about this matter.*

【究竟】① outcome; what actually happened; consequence：我们都想知道个～。*All of us want to know what actually happened.* ② actually; exactly：这～是怎么一回事？*What on earth is the matter?* ③ after all; anyway; in the end：我们～是一家人。*After all, we are in the same family.*

【究问】probe into; interrogate

【究真儿】［方］study seriously：每件事都～，早晚得累死。*If you try to take everything seriously enough, you will very soon be worn out.*

赳

【赳赳】valiant; gallant：雄～ *gallant*; *valiant*

阄 lot, a folded piece of paper used in drawing lots：抓～儿 *draw lots*

揪 tight; seize (with the hand)：～头发 *grab one's hair* /～断了绳子 *snap a rope with a pull*

【揪辫子】seize sb's pigtail — seize upon sb's mistakes or shortcomings; capitalize on sb's vulnerable point：他揪住了我的辫子。*He capitalized on the mistakes made by me.*

【揪揪】［方］① creased; crumpled; not smooth：这

料子容易～在一起。*The material crumples easily.* ② have a heavy heart; in gloom; be upset: 他心里一直～着,因为他的女友离他而去了。*He was very upset because his girlfriend had gone away.*

【揪痧】【中医】a popular treatment for sunstroke or other febrile diseases by repeatedly pinching the patient's neck, etc. to achieve congestion

【揪心】[方] anxious; worried; agonizing; gnawing: 令人～的痛苦 *an agonizing pain*

啾

【啾唧】[象] the chirping of birds or insects

【啾啾】[象] ① the chirping of birds: 小鸟在树林中快乐地～叫个不停。*The birds are chirping merrily in the trees.* ② a piteous cry

jiǔ

九 ① nine: ～本书 *nine books* / 这个小女孩明天将庆祝她的～岁生日。*The little girl will celebrate her ninth birthday tomorrow.* / 传说猫有～条命。*The legend said that cats have nine lives.* ② the eighty-one days beginning from the day of the Winter Solstice, each of the following nine nine-day periods is called a "nine" ③ many; numerous: 三六～等 *various grades and ranks*

【九边形】【数】enneagon; nonagon

【九重霄】highest of heavens

【九鼎】① legendary nine tripods ② sth of heavy weight or great importance: 一言～ *a word that carries much weight*

【九龙】Kowloon, in Hong Kong

【九龙壁】Nine-Dragon Screen (an imperial decoration)

【九牛二虎之力】the strength of nine bulls and two tigers — tremendous effort; an immense amount of energy: 我们费了～才完成了任务。*We made great effort to accomplish the mission.*

【九牛一毛】a single hair out of nine ox hides — a drop in the ocean; negligible; next to nothing: 我急需经济援助,他所给我的钱不过是～。*I am in urgent need of financial help; the money he has given is just a drop in the ocean.*

【九品】① nine grades of official rank in dynastic China ② ninth grade

【九秋】ninety days of the autumn season

【九曲回肠】knot in one's stomach — melancholy

【九泉】[书] the Nine Springs — the nether world; grave: 含笑～ *smile in the underworld* / ～之下 *after death; in the nether world*

【九死一生】a narrow escape from death; survival after many hazards; a hairbreadth escape; a slim chance of surviving; be at death's door: 真是～。*It's a near touch.*

【九天】[书] the highest heavens; heaven: ～揽月 *clasp the moon in the Ninth Heaven*

【九头鸟】① legendary bird with nine heads ② cunning man

【九五】imperial throne: ～之尊 *the imperial throne*

【九霄】highest heavens

【九霄云外】beyond the highest heavens — far; far away; throw to the winds: 她把我们的忠告抛到了～。*Our advice to her fell onto deaf ears.*

【九渊】[书] abyss

【九州】① the nine divisions of China in remote antiquity ② a poetic name for China ③ Kyushu, a city in Japan

【九族】[旧] nine degrees or forms of kinship: 祸灭～ *bring death penalties upon all of one's relatives*

久 ① for a long time; long: 年深日～ *as the years go by* / 一小时之～ *an hour long* / 那是很～以前的事情了,我不想提它。*It all happened a long time ago. I'd rather not talk about it.* / 我能呆多～就呆多～。*I'll stay as long as I can.* ② of a specified duration: 你来了多～了? *How long have you been here?*

【久别】long separation: ～重逢 *meet again after a long separation*

【久病成医】[俗] prolonged illness makes a doctor of a patient

【久而久之】in the course of time; with the lapse of time; as time passes: ～,我们成了好朋友。*Gradually, we became good friends.*

【久负盛名】have long enjoyed a good reputation

【久旱逢甘雨】a good rain after a long drought — to have a long-felt need satisfied

【久假不归】put off indefinitely returning sth one has borrowed; appropriate sth borrowed

【久经】① experience for a long time: ～锻炼 *well-steeled* / ～考验 *long-tested; seasoned* / ～世故 *well-experienced in the ways of the world* ② happen long ago

【久久】for a long, long time: 我～地盯着那尊铜像。*I stared at the bronze statue for a long time.*

【久炼成钢】steel is made through prolonged tempering — practice makes perfect

【久留】stay long: 抱歉,我不能～。*I am sorry. I can't stay long.*

【久违】[套] how long it is since we last met; I haven't seen you for ages: ～了。*I haven't seen you for a long time.*

【久闻大名】I have long heard of your name

【久悬不决】long unsettled: ～的问题 *unsettled issue of long standing*

【久仰】[套] I've heard about you for a long time; I've long been looking forward to meeting you

【久已】for a long time; long since: 我～未回家乡了。*I have not been back to my hometown for some time.* / 这种机器～不用了。*This kind of machines has long since been out of use.*

【久远】far back; ages ago; remote: ～的过去 *the remote past*

玖¹ nine (used for the numeral "九" on cheques, etc.)

玖² [书] a jade-like light-black stone

灸【中医】moxibustion, a medical treatment

韭

【韭菜】fragrant-flowered garlic; (Chinese) chives

【韭黄】hotbed chives

酒 ① wine; drinks; liquor; spirits: 白 ~ *liquor* / 陈 ~ *old wine* / 烈 ~ *strong wine; spirit* / 葡萄 ~ *wine* / 啤 ~ *beer* / 鸡尾 ~ *cocktail* / 香槟 ~ *champagne* / 我父亲经常喝 ~。*My father often drinks beer.* ② (Jiǔ) a surname

【酒吧】bar

【酒吧老板】barkeeper

【酒吧调酒员】mixologist

【酒保】[旧] barkeeper; barman; bartender

【酒杯】wine glass

【酒不沾唇】never touch wine

【酒菜】① food and drink: 供应 ~ *serve food and drink* ② food to go with wine or liquor

【酒厂】brewery; winery; distillery

【酒橱】cellaret

【酒单】winelist

【酒德】good drinking habit

【酒店】① wineshop; public house ② hotel

【酒逢知己千杯少】among bosom friends, a thousand cups of wine are too few: ~, 话不投机半句多。*If you drink with a bosom friend, a thousand cups are too few. If you argue with a man, half a sentence is too much.*

【酒馆】public house; pub; tavern

【酒鬼】[贬] drunkard; sot; alcoholic; drunk; winebibber; toper: 跟他谈话毫无意义。他是个不可救药的 ~。*There's no point talking to him; he is a hopeless drunk.* / 他的父亲是一个 ~, 经常喝的烂醉如泥。*His father was an alcoholic who often drank himself to death.*

【酒过三巡】when the wine has been round three times

【酒酣耳热】warmed with wine; mellow with drink: 几杯酒下肚后, 我们感到 ~。*After a couple of bottles of wine we were all beginning to feel mellow.*

【酒后失态】forget oneself in one's cups

【酒后失言】make indiscreet remarks under the influence of alcohol

【酒后吐真言】wine in, truth out

【酒壶】wine pot; flagon; stoup

【酒会】cocktail party

【酒家】① wineshop; tavern; restaurant ②【旧】waiter in a wineshop

【酒浆】[书] wine

【酒窖】wine cellar

【酒酵母】distiller's yeast

【酒精】ethyl alcohol; alcohol; spirits of wine: 纯 ~ *absolute alcohol* / 发酵 ~ *fermentation alcohol* / 饮料 ~ *beverage alcohol*

【酒精灯】alcohol burner; spirit lamp

【酒精含量】alcoholicity

【酒精炉】spirit stove

【酒具】drinking utensils

【酒力】① capacity for liquor ②influence of alcohol

【酒帘】(in former times) a wineshop sign in the form of a streamer

【酒量】capacity for liquor; one's drinking capacity: 他 ~ 很大, 没有丝毫醉意。*He carries his liquor like a gentleman.*

【酒令】drinkers' wager game

【酒囊饭袋】wine skin and rice bag — a good-for-nothing; a useless person good only for drinking

【酒酿】fermented glutinous rice; sweet fermented rice

【酒钱】tips

【酒肉朋友】wine-and-meat friends; fair-weather friends; mercenary acquaintance

【酒色】① wine and women — sensual pursuits; debauchery: ~ 之徒 *voluptuary* ② the colour of wine

【酒食】food and drink

【酒水】① drinks ② [方] feast; banquet

【酒徒】winebibber; toper

【酒文化】spirits culture

【酒窝】dimple: 她一笑, 脸上露出了 ~。*Her cheeks dimpled as she smiled.*

【酒席】feast; banquet: 结婚 ~ *wedding feast; marriage feast*

【酒兴】elation caused by intoxicants; rapture with wine

【酒宴】feast; banquet

【酒药】yeast for brewing rice wine or fermenting glutinous rice

【酒意】a tipsy feeling: 他已有几分 ~。*He was slightly tipsy.*

【酒糟】distillers' grains

【酒糟鼻】acne rosacea; brandy nose

【酒质】vinosity

【酒足饭饱】have drunk and eaten to one's heart's content

【酒醉】drunkenness: 你应该感到羞耻, ~ 成这个样子。*You should be ashamed of yourself — getting drunk like that.*

jiù

旧 ① past; outdated; old: ~ 社会 *the old society* / 因循守 ~ *lockstep* ② old; used; worn: ~ 书 *old book* / ~ 车 *used car* / ~ 衣服 *worn clothes* ③ former ④ old friend; old friendship: 故 ~ *old friends and acquaintances*

【旧案】① a court case of long standing ② old regulation; former practice: 一切按照 ~ 办理。*Handle all cases according to former regulations.*

【旧病】old (or chronic) complaint: ~ 复发 *recurrence of an old illness; have a relapse*

【旧部】former subordinates

【旧地】a once visited place: ~ 重游 *revisit a once familiar place*

【旧调重弹】harp on the same string; sing the same old tunes: 他 ~。*He is telling the same old story.*

【旧都】former capital
【旧恶】old grievance; old wrong: 不念~ *forgive an old wrong*
【旧故】old friend
【旧观】former appearance; former state: 恢复~ *be restored to original form* / 新建了几座教学楼之后,我们的学校已经一改~。*Our school has taken on a completely new look with several new teaching buildings built.*
【旧好】[书] ① old friendship: 重修~ *reestablish an old friendship* ② old friend
【旧话重提】repeat an old tale
【旧货】① old things; old stuff ② second-hand goods: ~店 *junk shop; secondhand shop; commission shop*
【旧家】[书] old and well-known family
【旧交】old acquaintance; old friend
【旧教】Catholicism
【旧金山】(US) San Francisco
【旧居】former residence; old home
【旧历】the old Chinese calendar; the lunar calendar
【旧例】old practise
【旧貌换新颜】new scenes replace the old
【旧梦】past experience: ~重温 *renew a sweet experience of bygone days*
【旧民主主义革命】democratic revolution of the old type; old-democratic revolution
【旧脑筋】an old way of thinking
【旧年】① [方] last year ② the lunar New Year
【旧瓶装新酒】new wine in an old bottle — new content in old form
【旧情】old or former friendship; former affection: ~不忘 *remember a former friendship*
【旧日】former days; old days: 他依然是~的模样。*He looks just like what he used to be.*
【旧社会】old society (usu. referring to China before 1949)
【旧诗】old-style poetry; classical poetry
【旧石器】【考】paleolith
【旧石器时代】【考】the Old Stone Age; the Paleolithic Period: ~文化 *Paleolithic culture*
【旧时】old times; old days: 我~的同学昨天来看我。*My old classmates came to visit me yesterday.*
【旧式】old type; old style: ~服装 *old-style clothes* / ~家庭 *old-fashioned family* / ~婚姻 *traditional marriage* / ~自行车 *bone shaker*
【旧事】an old matter (or affair); a past event: 希望你不要~重提。*I hope you will not rake up those matters of the past.*
【旧书】① secondhand book ② ancient book; ancient text
【旧俗】old customs
【旧套】outmoded style; former style: 摆脱~ *get rid of the outmoded style*
【旧闻】old lore; old news; past events
【旧物】① past heritage ② lost territory
【旧习】old habit and custom: ~难改。*It's difficult to change old habits and customs.*
【旧学】old Chinese learning (as distinct from the new or Western learning)
【旧业】① old trade or profession ② ancestral estate; family fortune
【旧友】old acquaintance; old friend
【旧怨】old grudge; old scores: 由于两家的~,他已多年不与岳父母说话。*Because of an old feud, he never spoke to his wife's parents for years.*
【旧约】【宗】The Old Testament
【旧章】old rules
【旧账】old debt; old feud
【旧知】old friend
【旧址】site (of a former organization, building, etc.)
【旧制】① old system ② the old system of weights and measures

臼 ① mortar: 石~ *stone mortar* ② mortar-shaped things
【臼齿】molar
【臼齿动物】gnawer

咎 ① blame; fault: 引~自责 *blame oneself for a misdeed* ② punish; blame: 既往不~ *forgive sb's past misdeeds; let bygones be bygones* ② [书] bad fortune: 休~ *good and bad fortune; weal and woe*
【咎由自取】have only oneself to blame
【咎有应得】get what one deserves

疚 [书] remorse: 负~ *feel guilty* / 内~ *guilty conscience*

柩 a coffin with a corpse in it: 灵~ *a coffin containing a corpse*

厩 stable; cattle-shed
【厩肥】barnyard manure

救 ① rescue; save: 呼~ *call out for help* ② help; relieve: ~人济世 *help others and remake the world*
【救兵】relief troops; reinforcements: 他去搬~了。*He has gone to ask for reinforcements.*
【救场】save the show (or performance): ~如救火。*To save a show is as urgent as to put out a fire.*
【救国】save the nation
【救护】relieve a sick or injured person; give first-aid; rescue
【救护车】ambulance
【救护队】ambulance corps
【救护站】aid post
【救荒】send relief to a famine area; help to tide over a crop failure
【救活】bring sb back to life; revive
【救火】fight a fire; try to put out a fire: 抱薪~ *add fuel to the fire — use a wrong method to stem off a disaster* / ~扬沸 *put out a fire and shake the boiling*
【救火车】fire truck; fire engine
【救火帽】smoke helmet
【救火梯】pompier
【救急】help sb to cope with an emergency; help meet an urgent need

J

【救济】extend relief to; relieve the distress of: ~金 *relief fund* / ~粮 *relief grain; relief food* / ~物资 *relief supplies* / ~地震灾民 *go to the relief of earthquake victims*

【救驾】save the emperor from danger — save sb from a hard situation

【救苦救难】help the needy and relieve the distressed

【救命】save sb's life: ~恩人 *benefactor who has saved sb's life*

【救命稻草】straw to clutch at

【救人一命,胜造七级浮屠】to rescue one person from death is better than to build a seven — storied pagoda for the god

【救生】save life (esp. through the prevention of drowning)

【救生筏】life raft

【救生圈】life buoy

【救生索】life line; lifeline

【救生艇】lifeboat

【救生演习】boat drill

【救生衣】life jacket; air jacket; life buoy; life vest

【救生员】life guard; lifeguard

【救世军】salvation army

【救世主】【宗】the Saviour; the Redeemer

【救死扶伤】heal the wounded and rescue the dying

【救亡】save the nation from extinction: ~图存 *fight for the survival and salvation of the nation*

【救星】liberator; emancipator; saviour

【救应】aid and support; reinforce

【救援】rescue; come to sb's help: 一次~行动 *an attempt at a rescue*

【救援车】wrecking car

【救灾】provide disaster relief; send relief to a disaster area; help the people tide over a natural disaster

【救治】bring a patient out of danger; treat and cure: ~伤病员 *give treatment to the sick and wounded*

【救助】help sb in danger or difficulty: 海难~ *salvage at sea* / 自愿~ *salvage by voluntary action* / ~条款 *salvage clause*

就[1] ① come near: ~着昏暗的灯光写字 *write by dim lamplight* / 迁~ *indulge* / 避重~轻 *avoid the important and dwell on the trivial* ② undertake; engage in: 按部~班 *follow the prescribed order* ③ used in a passive sentence to introduce an action ④ accomplish; make: 功成名~ *render outstanding service and be famous* / 造~人才 *bring up qualified personnel* ⑤ with regard to; taking advantage of: ~近上学 *go to a nearby school* ⑥ (of food, etc.) go with: ~咸菜吃饭 *have rice to go with pickles* ⑦ the range of an action: 他们~这个问题进行了讨论。*They had a discussion aiming at the problem.*

就[2] ① at once; right away: 我~走。*I' m leaving.* / 这个小孩~要上学了。*The child is going to go to school.* ② as early as; already: 风一早~停了。*The wind subsided in the morning.* ③ as soon as; no sooner... than: 我刚进门,电话铃~响了。*No sooner had I entered the room, than the phone rang.* / 他一到达~给我写信。*He wrote to me as soon as he arrived.* ④ used to indicate that sth comes naturally under certain conditions: 只要努力,~能进步。*You can make a progress so long as you work hard.* / 谁愿意去,谁~去。*Anybody who wishes to go can just go.* ⑤ as much as; as many as: 他三天来一次,你一天~来两次。*He came here only once in three days, but you came twice in one day.* ⑥ used between two identical words to express tolerance: 大点儿~大点儿吧,买了算了。*It doesn't matter that it is a little larger; just take it!* ⑦ used to indicate that sth has been like this all the time: 房间本来就小,来了这么多人~更拥挤了。*The room is small as it is, and it gets more crowded with so many people.* ⑧ only; merely: 他~爱看书。*He only likes reading.* / 为什么我~不能去? *Why is it I that cannot go there?* ⑨used to express resolve: 别说了,我~不去! *Shut up. I won't go there definitely.* ⑩ exactly; very; right: 邮局~在那边。*The post office is just over there.* / 这~是我想要的书。*This is exactly the book that I look for.*

就[3] even if: 你~送来,我也不要。*I will not take it even if you send it here.* / 天~是再冷,我也得去。*I shall go there even if it gets colder.*

【就伴】keep sb company; accompany sb: 咱们一起~上学吧。*Please accompany me on the way to school.*

【就便】at sb's convenience; while you're at it: 你~帮我买一支笔。*Please buy me a pen on your way.*

【就餐】have a meal; eat; dine: 在外~ *dine out*

【就此】at this point; here and now; thus: 这项工作~告一段落。*The work has thus come to a close.*

【就道】set out on a journey; start off (or out)

【就地】on the spot: ~审判 *on-the-spot trial* / ~调解 *on-the-spot mediation*

【就地取材】draw on local resources; draw on local talents; gather material on the spot

【就地正法】execute summarily

【就读】[书] attend school: 他的儿子~于清华大学。*His son studies at Tsinghua University.*

【就范】submit; give in: 他终于使我~。*He finally made me yield.*

【就合】[方] ① accommodate oneself to; make do with; yield to: 我就吃碗面~了。*I will make do with a bowl of noodles.* ② curl up; twist

【就教】go to sb for advice or instructions

【就近】(do or get sth) nearby; in the neighbourhood; without having to go far: 我们~找个旅馆吧。*Let's find a hotel in the neighbourhood.* / 他感到很疲惫,天气也变得越来越热,他~找了个阴凉处坐下。*His weariness and the increasing heat determined him to sit down in the first convenient shade.*

【就里】inside information; inside story: 不知~ *have no inside information*

【就木】［书］be laid in a coffin — die：行将～ *about to die*
【就擒】be seized；be captured：束手～ *allow oneself to be captured without putting up a fight*
【就寝】retire for the night；go to bed
【就任】take up one's post；take office：～总统 *assume the office of the President*
【就势】making use of momentum
【就使】［书］even if；even through
【就势】make use of momentum
【就是】① used usu. with 了，at the end of a sentence to give force to the statement：我一定办到，你放心～了。*You can rest assured that I can make it.* ② yes，that's right；exactly；precisely：～，～，你说得很对。*Exactly；what you said is quite right.* ③ even if；even：～小孩子也知道这个。*Even a child knows it.*
【就是说】that is；that is to say：三天之后，～星期三。*Three days from now，that's to say Wednesday.* /她是个好学生，～，她在学校里得高分。*She is a good student；that is，she gets good grades in school.*
【就事】［旧］take up one's post
【就事论事】deal with a matter on its merits：我是～。*I just confine myself to facts as they are.*
【就手】while you're at it；at one's convenience：～把窗户打开。*Open the window beside you.*
【就算】［口］even if；granted that：～我得一路走着去，我也要走到那里。*Even if I have to walk all the way I'll get there.*
【就位】take one's place
【就席】take one's seat at a banquet
【就刑】be executed
【就绪】be in order；be ready；be arranged：一切准备～。*Everything is arranged well.*
【就学】go to school；attend school
【就要】near；about to；going to：晚会～开始了。*The evening is about to begin.*
【就业】obtain employment；take up an occupation；get a job：公平～ *fair employment* /～范围 *number of jobs available* /～机会 *job openings；employment opportunities* /～指数 *employment index*
【就医】seek medical advice；go to a doctor；go to hospital for treatment
【就义】be executed for championing a just cause；die a martyr
【就诊】seek medical advice；go to a doctor
【就正】solicit comments（on one's writing）：～于读者 *request the readers to offer their criticisms*
【就职】assume office：～典礼 *inaugural ceremony* /～演说 *inaugural speech*
【就中】① between them ② among them
【就座】take one's seat；be seated

舅 ① mother's brother；uncle ② wife's brother；brother-in-law：妻～ *wife's brother；brother-in-law* ③［书］husband's father：～姑 *husband's parents*
【舅父】mother's brother；uncle
【舅妈】［口］wife of mother's brother；aunt
【舅嫂】［口］wife of wife's brother；sister-in-law
【舅子】［口］wife's brother；brother-in-law

jū

车 chariot，one of the pieces in Chinese chess
see also chē

且 ①［书］（in classical Chinese）equal to "啊"：狂童之狂也～。*How conceited the child is!* ② a character used in people's names
see also qiě

苴
【苴麻】female plant of hemp

拘 ① arrest；detain ② constrained；restrained：无～无束 *unconstraint* ③ inflexible ④ limit；restrict：不～一格 *not stick to one pattern*
【拘板】［方］stiff；formal：他对任何人都很～。*He's very formal with everybody.*
【拘捕】① arrest；take into custody：非法～ *false arrest* ② detention；provisional apprehension：他被处以一个月～。*He received a punishment of a month detention.*
【拘传】【律】summon sb for detention
【拘管】keep in custody
【拘谨】overcautious；reserved：他态度～。*He is stiff in manner.* /她太～了，不主动和别人交朋友。*She is too reserved to take the initiative in making acquaintances.*
【拘禁】take into custody；detain：法官命令把他～一个月。*The magistrate remanded him in custody for a month.*
【拘礼】be punctilious；stand in ceremony：我们是好朋友，不必～。*We are good friends，aren't we? Don't stand in ceremony.*
【拘留】detain；hold in custody；intern：警察～了许多疑犯进行审问。*The police detained several suspects for questioning.*
【拘留所】house of detention
【拘留证】detention warrant
【拘挛】① cramps；spasms ②［书］rigidly adhere to：～章句 *rigidly adhere to the wording*
【拘泥】① rigidly adhere to（formalities，etc.）；stick to sb；be nice about sth：～小节 *stand on trifles* /不要过分～于形式。*Don't be too nice about form.* ② uneasy；restrained：举止～ *be ill at ease*
【拘票】arrest warrant；warrant
【拘牵】［书］restrain；confine
【拘束】① restrain；restrict：他的行动受到～。*He is restricted in his movements.* ② constrained；awkward；ill at ease：我在他家里感到～。*I felt ill at ease at his home.* /我们告诉他不要～，想讲什么就讲什么。*We told him to let loose and say whatever he wants to.*
【拘押】take into custody；detain
【拘役】【律】criminal detention

【拘囿】rigidly adhere to; be confined to：他的论文明显～于成说。*His thesis is obviously confined to the accepted theory.*
【拘执】rigid; inflexible：他做事～。*He is rather inflexible in handling things.*
【拘滞】inflexible; rigid

狙 ①（in ancient times）a kind of monkey ②［书］spy
【狙击】snipe：～战 *sniping action*

居 ① reside; dwell：分～（*of husband and wife*）*live separately* ② house; residence：新～ *new house* ③ in a certain position：～中 *be placed in the middle* / 材料的昂贵费用使价格～高不下。*The high cost of materials keeps up prices.* ④ assert; hold a position：以专家自～ *pride oneself on one's expertise* ⑤ store up; lay by：奇货可～ *hoard as a rare commodity* / 囤积～奇 *forestall; hoard for a higher price* ⑥［书］be at a standstill：岁月不～。*Time and tide wait for no man.* ⑦ used in the names of some restaurants ⑧（Jū）a surname
【居安思危】think of danger in times of safety; be vigilant in peace time; be prepared for danger in times of safety
【居多】be in the majority：这个公司以男性职员～。*Man employees in this company are in the majority.*
【居高临下】occupy a commanding position（or height）：这座塔～可望全城。*The pagoda offers a commanding view of the whole city.* / 老板习惯于用～的调子和我说话。*The boss is used to speaking to me in a commanding tone.*
【居功】claim credit for oneself：～自傲 *parade one's own merit*
【居积】［书］accumulate（wealth）
【居家】live at home; run a household：～勤俭 *manage a family economically*
【居间】（mediate）between two parties：～人 *mediator* / 他在劳资双方间～调停达成和解。*He mediated a settlement between labour and management.*
【居留】reside：长期～ *permanent residence*
【居留地】habitat
【居留权】right of residence
【居民】resident; inhabitant：当地～ *local residents* / 固定～ *permanent residents* / 非固定～ *non-permanent residents* / 一个村的～ *the inhabitants of a village*
【居民点】residential area
【居奇】hoard and speculate：囤积～ *hoard and profiteer*
【居然】① unexpectedly; actually; to one's surprise; go so far as to：他这次考试～没通过。*To my surprise, he didn't pass the exam.* / 他们～撕毁了全部合同。*They went so far as to tear up all the contracts.* / 他～能做出这种事。*He has the cheek to do such a thing.* ②［书］obvious; evident
【居丧】［书］be in mourning; observe mourning for one's dead parent
【居士】① lay Buddhist ② retired scholar
【居室】room：三～的房间 *a three-room apartment*
【居所】residence; dwelling place
【居停】① stop and stay（at a place when traveling）②［书］landlord; host
【居首】to lead; rank first：他的考试成绩～。*He came out the first in the exam.*
【居委会】neighbourhood committee; residents' committee
【居心】harbour（evil）intentions：～不良 *harbour evil intentions* / 他～何在？*What is he up to?*
【居心叵测】with hidden intent; with ulterior motives
【居于】occupy（a certain position）：他在公司～重要地位。*He occupies an important position in the company.*
【居中】①（mediate）between two parties：～调停 *mediate between two parties* ② be placed in the middle
【居住】live; reside; dwell：我的祖父～在乡下。*My grandfather dwells in the countryside.*
【居住国】country of residence
【居住面积】living space
【居住证】residence permit

驹 ① colt：千里～ *winged steed* ② foal：马～子 *colt; filly*
【驹子】foal

疽 【中医】subcutaneous ulcer

掬 hold with both hands：以手～水 *scoop up water with one's hands*

椐 （in ancient books）a kind of tree with swelling joints, used for walking stick

雎
【雎鸠】a waterfowl mentioned in ancient texts

鞠[1] ①［书］rear; bring up：～育 *rear; bring up* ②［书］bend ③（Jū）a surname

鞠[2] a ball used in play in ancient times
【鞠躬】① bow：～致谢 *bow one's thanks* ②［书］in a discreet and scrupulous manner
【鞠躬尽瘁】bend oneself to a task and exert oneself to the utmost; spare no effort in the performance of one's duty：～，死而后已 *bend one's back to a task until one's dying day* / 他是个苛刻的老板，要求他的手下～。*As a demanding boss, he expected total loyalty and dedication from his employees.*
【鞠养】［书］rear; bring up

jú

局[1] ① chessboard：棋～ *chessboard; chess game* ② a game of chess or of other contests; set：第二～（*of table tennis, etc.*）*second game; second set* ③ situation; position：大～ *overall situation* / 时～ *the current political situation* ④ tolerance; magnanimity：器～ *magnanimity* ⑤ party; gathering：饭～ *dinner party* ⑥ trap; trick：骗～

fraud; swindle ⑦ restrain; constrain

局[2] ① part ② bureau; department: 教育~ *bureau of education* /劳动~ *labour bureau* /旅游~ *travel bureau* /税务~ *customs bureau* /统计~ *statistic bureau* /专卖~ *monopoly bureau* ③ functional office: 邮~ *post office* ④ shop: 书~ *bookshop*

【局部】part; locality: ~地区 *parts of an area*

【局促】① narrow; cramped ②［方］(of time) short ③ feel or show constraint; feel ill at ease: 下周就要交论文了,现在才开始做调查,时间显得很~。*You have to hand in the paper next week, and time is too short to finish it since you just began to make the research.*

【局度】［书］tolerance; forbearance

【局量】［书］tolerance

【局面】① aspect; phase; situation: 打开~ *open up a new prospect* ②［方］scope; scale

【局内】take part in

【局内人】a person in the know; insider

【局骗】swindle; cheat: 他的钱财被~了。*He was cheated out of his money.*

【局势】situation: ~非常复杂。*The situation was complicated.* /我们开始认清~的严重性。*We woke up to the situation.*

【局外】have nothing to do with; be an outsider: 置身~ *keep oneself away from sth*

【局外人】a person not in the know; outsider

【局限】limit; confine: 请你把话题~在当前的问题上。*Please confine your remarks to the current issues.* /美并不~于外表。*Beauty is more than skin-deep.*

【局限性】limitations; restrictions

【局域网】local area network (LAN)

【局长】bureau head; director

【局子】［口］police station

菊 ① chrysanthemum: 雏~ *daisy* /翠~ *China aster* /赏~ *visit a chrysanthemum show* ② (Jú) a surname

【菊花】chrysanthemum: ~酒 *chrysanthemum wine*

【菊科】【植】composite family

【菊坛】theatrical circles; Beijing opera circles

【菊展】chrysanthemum show

焗 【方】① steam food in a sealed container: 盐~鸡 *steamed chicken in dense-salty water* ② feel suffocated; be stifled

【焗油】① treat hair with cream to make it soft and shiny ② hair treatment cream

橘 ① tangerine tree ② tangerine; orange: 柑~ *oranges and tangerines* /金~ *kumquat*

【橘柑】［方］tangerine

【橘红】① tangerine (colour); reddish orange ②【药】dried tangerine peel

【橘黄】orange (colour)

【橘汁】orange juice

【橘子】tangerine

jǔ

咀 chew: 含英~华 *relish the joys of literature*

【咀嚼】① masticate; chew: 食物在吞咽前要仔细~。*Chew your food well before you swallow it.* ② mull over; ruminate; chew the cud: 我反复~这件事的含义。*I chew over the meaning of the matter.*

沮 ①［书］stop; prevent ② feel dejected; in gloom

see also jù

【沮遏】［书］prevent

【沮丧】① dejected; depressed; dispirited; disheartened; despondent; crestfallen: 他神情~。*He looks dejected.* ② depress; dispirit; dishearten: 阴天总是使我~。*The cloudy days always depress me.* /坏消息使他很~。*The bad news disheartened him.*

矩 ① square; carpenter's square ② regulations; rules: 循规蹈~ *follow rules and orders; conform to convention*

【矩臂】【物】moment arm

【矩尺】carpenter's square

【矩心】【数】centre of moment

【矩形】rectangle: ~点阵 *rectangular lattice* /~电压 *rectangular voltage* /~分布 *rectangular distribution* /~矩阵 *rectangular matrix* /~系数 *squareness factor*

【矩阵】【数】matrix; array: ~存储器 *matrix storage; matrix memory* /~代数 *matrix algebra* /~电路 *matrix circuit* /~定理 *matrix theorem* /~法 *matrix method* /~方程 *matrix equation* /~分数 *matrix fraction* /~分析 *matrix analysis* /~力学 *matrix mechanics* /~列 *rectangular array* /~模式 *matrix pattern* /~群 *matrix group* /~组 *set of matrixes*

举 ①lift; raise: 高~红旗 *hold high the red banner* /回答问题前请先~手。*Please hold up your hands before answering questions.* ② deed; act; move: 壮~ *feat* /多此一~ *bring owls to Athens; hold a candle to the sun* /一~一动 *every act and every move* ③ start ④［书］give birth to: ~一男 *give birth to a boy* ⑤ elect; choose: 推~他为班长 *elect him as monitor* ⑥ successful candidate in the imperial examinations at the provincial level in the Ming and Qing dynasties ⑦ cite; enumerate: 列~ *enumerate; particularize; specialize* ⑧［书］all; whole: ~家南迁。*The whole family moved to the south.*

【举哀】go into mourning: 全国~ *observe a national mourning* /~三天 *go into mourning for three days*

【举案齐眉】a wife lifts the tray to a level with her eyebrows to show great respect for her husband — the couple love and respect each other

【举办】conduct; hold; run: ~辩论会 *hold a debate* /~展览会 *put on an exhibition; hold an exhibi-*

tion

【举报】report; tip; tip off; report on: 收到大量~ *receive a lot of tips* /他向领导~我。*He reported me to the head.*

【举报制度】the offence reporting system

【举杯】raise one's glass: 让我们~祝他健康。*Let's drink to his health.*

【举步】[书] take a step: ~维艰 *have difficulty in taking a step*

【举出】enumerate; itemize; cite as example: ~一个典型的例子 *show a typical example*

【举措】behave; move; act: 预期的~ *an expectant move* /~失当 *make an ill-advised move; make a false move*

【举动】act; movement; behaviour: ~缓慢 *be slow in action* /~规矩 *be on one's good behaviour* /这个~旨在给妇女带来更多的自由。*The act aims at greater freedom for women.* /你要密切注意他的~。*You should keep a close eye on his movements.*

【举发】report an offender; inform against sth

【举凡】[书] ranging from... to...; all... such as: ~来过这里的人都要赞叹这美景。*All people coming here ranging from young to old highly praise the beautiful scenery.*

【举国】the whole nation; entire nation: ~悲痛。*The whole nation was heart-broken with grief.* /~欢腾。*The whole country is in jubilation.*

【举火】[书] ① light a fire: ~为号 *make a fire for a signal* ② light a kitchen fire (or stove)

【举架】[方] the height of a house: 这房子~矮。*This house is quite low.*

【举荐】recommend: ~他做那项工作 *recommend him for the job*

【举例】for example (or instance); give an example; illustrate; citing: 演讲人说他将设法~说明。*The speaker said he would endeavor to illustrate.* /请~。*Please give an example.*

【举目】[书] raise the eyes; look: ~远眺 *look into the distance*

【举目无亲】be a stranger in a strange land; find no kin to turn to; have no one to turn to (for help)

【举棋不定】be unable to make up one's mind; hesitate; uncertain what to do next; be in two minds about sth: 面对这两件礼物,他~究竟挑哪一件给她母亲。*He hesitated over the choice between the two gifts for his mother.* /我在买房这件事上~。*I wavered over buying a house.* /你要还是~,我们就来不及了。*If you keep shilly-shallying like this we'll be late.*

【举起】lift; raise; put up: 他~手臂过头顶。*He raised his arms above his head.*

【举人】a successful candidate in the imperial examinations at the provincial level in the Ming and Qing dynasties

【举世】all over the world

【举世闻名】be known to all the world

【举世无双】unrivaled; matchless: 这个花瓶是~的工艺品。*The vase is of matchless workmanship.* /贝利是~的足球健将。*Pele was in a class of his own as a footballer*

【举世瞩目】attract worldwide attention; become the focus of world attention: ~的成就 *achievements of world interest*

【举事】[书] rise in insurrection

【举手】rise one's hand: 赞成者请~。*Those in favour, please raise your hands.*

【举手之劳】lift a finger — a very easy job: 不必谢我,这不过是~。*No need to thank me; it's nothing for me to do that.*

【举行】hold (a meeting, ceremony, etc.): ~罢工 *stage a strike* /~会议 *hold a meeting* /~仪式 *have services; perform a ceremony; solemnization*

【举一反三】draw inferences about other cases from one instance; infer other things from one fact; learn by analogy

【举义】rise in revolt

【举债】borrow; float a loan

【举证】quote; put to the proof

【举止】bearing manner; mien: ~大方 *be decent in manner; bear oneself well* /~要与你年龄相称。*Act your age.* /她的~像个天生的领导。*She acts like a born leader.* /她~文雅。*She always conducts herself like a lady.*

【举止言谈】one's behaviour and conversation

【举重】weight lifting: ~运动员 *weight lifter*

【举足轻重】hold the balance; play a decisive role; carry weight: ~的地位 *decisive position*

龃

【龃龉】[书] the lower and upper teeth not meeting properly — disagreement; discord

踽

【踽踽】[书] walk alone: ~独行 *walk alone; walk in solitude*

jù

巨 ① enormous; gigantic; huge: ~幅标语 *a huge poster* ② (Jù) a surname

【巨变】great (or radical) change: 山乡~ *tremendous changes in a mountain village*

【巨擘】[书] ① thumb ② authority in a certain field: 诗坛~ *prince of poets*

【巨齿鲸】[动] bottlenose whale

【巨齿龙】[考] megalosaur

【巨大】great; huge; immense; massive: ~的改进 *an immense improvement* /~的成功 *a huge success* /~的跨国公司 *a mammoth multinational corporation* /燃放鞭炮会产生~的噪声,严重污染大气。*Setting off firecrackers makes a tremendous noise and causes serious air pollution.*

【巨额】huge sum or amount; enormous: ~财富 *immense amount of treasure* /~费用 *enormous expenses* /他有~的金钱。*He has a mint of money.*

【巨富】① great wealth ② magnate: 工业~ *an in-*

J

dustrial magnate /那位上校是当时的～之一。*The colonel was one of the richest nabobs of his day.*
【巨构】① tall building ② great work
【巨猾】[书] very cunning person：老奸～ *crafty old scoundrel*
【巨祸】huge disaster (or calamity)
【巨奸】[书] treacherous person
【巨匠】[书] great master; giant：莎士比亚是一位文坛～。*Shakespeare is a giant among writers.*
【巨款】vast sums：一笔～ *a colossal sum of money*
【巨浪】billow; surge; very rough sea：大火像～一般滚过原野。*The flames billowed over the prairie.*
【巨量】large number of; great deal of
【巨流】a mighty current：汇成一股～ *converge into a mighty current*
【巨鲈】black sea bass
【巨轮】① large wheel：历史的～ *the wheel of history* ② large ship：远洋～ *large oceangoing shop*
【巨鸟】roc; a big bird
【巨人】① giant; colossus; Titan; bouncer：泥足～ *colossus with clay feet* ② a person who has made a great contribution：物理学界的～ *a giant in the field of physics*
【巨人症】【医】gigantism
【巨商】big businessman; business tycoon
【巨石】【考】megalith
【巨室】① big house ② old and well-known family
【巨胎】giant embryo
【巨头】magnate; tycoon：钢铁～ *steel magnate* /石油～ *oil magnate* /美国工业～ *titan of American industry*
【巨万】[书] millions：这项工程耗资～。*The project cost a large amount of money.*
【巨细】big and small：事无～ *all matters, big and small*
【巨细胞】【生理】giant cell：～瘤 *giant-cell pneumonia*
【巨纤维】giant fibres
【巨星】【天】giant star：～系 *giant galaxy* ② outstanding person：歌坛～ *super singing star*
【巨型】giant; heavy; colossal：～纪念碑 *a colossal monument* /这架新飞机看起来像一只～的鸟。*The new airplane looked like a gigantic bird.*
【巨眼】[书] mental discernment; insight：～识人 *have an insight to judge a person*
【巨著】monumental work; magnum opus：历史～ *a magnum opus of historic significance*
【巨子】[书] authority; tycoon：文坛～ *an tycoon in literature*

句 ① sentence：陈述～ *assertive sentence* /否定～ *negative sentence* /复合～ *composite sentence* /感叹～ *exclamatory sentence* /简单～ *simple sentence* /省略～ *elliptical sentence* /条件～ *conditional sentence* /造～ *make sentences* /主～ *main sentence* ② [量] used of language：一～口号 *a slogan*
【句点】period; full stop
【句读】pause at the end of a sentence or of a phrase
【句法】① sentence structure ②【语】syntax：～分析 *syntactic analysis*
【句号】period; full stop
【句型】sentence pattern：～练习 *pattern drills*
【句子】sentence：～成分 *sentence element; part of a sentence* /这是一个难懂的～。*This is a dark sentence.*

讵 [书] used to introduce a rhetorical question：～料 *Who could have expected that...?*

拒 ① resist; repel：抗～ *resist* ② refuse：来者不～ *accept everything*
【拒捕】resist arrest
【拒付】【经】refuse payment
【拒绝】refuse; reject; turndown; decline：病人～治疗。*The patient refused treatment.* /他们～了我的提案。*They rejected my proposal.* /她～了我提出的帮助。*She declined my offer of help.* /她断然～了他的邀请。*She rebuffed the invitation from him.*
【拒聘】decline an appointment
【拒人于千里之外】keep people at a distance of one thousand li — be arrogant and unapproachable：对于失意落魄的朋友，不要～。*Don't turn your back on friends who are down and out.*
【拒收】reject; refuse to accept：他～这笔巨款。*He refused to accept the large amount of money.*
【拒载】(of a taxi driver) refuse to take passengers

具[1] ① tool; utensil：餐～ *farm implements* ② [书] ability; talent：才～ *capability* ③ [书] [量]：一～石磨 *a stone mill*

具[2] ① have; possess：初～规模 *have begun to take shape* ② [书] provide; furnish：物品毕～。*All the things were ready.* ③ [书] state; write out：条～时弊 *list current malpractices*
【具保】sign a guarantee：联名～ *jointly sign a guarantee for sb*
【具备】possess; have; be provided with：我～了申请条件。*I have qualifications for application.* /这个孩子～入学条件。*The child is qualified to be admitted to a school.*
【具领】draw; receive：～失物 *receive lost property*
【具名】put one's name to a document; affix one's signature：～盖章 *sign and seal*
【具体】① exact; concrete; detailed：～的时间 *the exact time* /你能解释得再～一些吗？*Can you explain it more specifically?* /我们谈得很～。*We talked about it in concrete terms.* ② particular; specific：～的人 *the specific person* ③ apply theory to a certain person or thing：这项政策～到这个单位，应该采取下列有效措施。*When the policy is applied to this specific unit, the following effective measures should be taken.*
【具体而微】small but complete; similar in shape but smaller in proportions; miniature
【具文】dead letter; mere formality
【具有】have; possess：～中国特色的社会主义 *socialism with Chinese characteristics* /这个年轻人～非凡的智谋。*The young man possessed great tact.* /新发明～极好的前景。*The new invention contains wonderful possibilities.* /这件事对我来说

重大意义。This matter is of great significance to me.

炬 torch：火～ torch

沮 see also jǔ

【沮洳】mire caused by rotten plants

俱 ［书］all；altogether：面面～到 attend to each and every aspect of a matter

【俱乐部】club：她属于作家～。She belongs to the Author's club.

【俱全】complete in all varieties：一应～ be available in all varieties

倨 ［书］haughty；arrogant：前～后恭 first supercilious and then deferential；change from arrogance to humility

【倨傲】haughty；arrogant：他因～而不受欢迎。He is unpopular for being haughty.

剧[1] ① drama；play；show：电视～ television drama /独幕～ one-act play /歌～ lyric drama /广播～ radio drama /历史～ historical play /话～ drama ②（Jù）a surname

剧[2] acute；severe：病～ be critically ill

【剧本】play；drama；script；libretto：～已经送交导演了。The script has been delivered to the director.

【剧变】violent or drastic change

【剧场】theatre：露天～ open air theatre /～里在演什么戏？What's playing at the theatre?

【剧跌】drop violently；plummet：此地房价～。House prices have plummeted in this area.

【剧毒】deadly poisonous

【剧烈】violent；tense；acute；severe；fierce：～的疼痛 an acute pain /～的社会运动 radical social changes /胃痛再次～发作了。A severe attack of stomachache began again.

【剧目】a list of plays or operas：保留～ repertoire

【剧评】a review of a play or opera；dramatic criticism

【剧情】plot of a play or opera：～复杂 intricate plot /～简介 synopsis

【剧痛】acute or severe pain：生孩子的～ the pangs of childbirth /他无法忍受这～。He couldn't stand the acute pain any more.

【剧团】theatrical company；opera troupe：芭蕾舞～ ballet troupe

【剧务】① stage management ② stage manager

【剧院】① theatre ② theatrical company；opera troupe

【剧增】increase sharply：他今年的收入～。His income of this year increased sharply.

【剧涨】rise rapidly：价格又在～。Prices are soaring again.

【剧照】stage photo

【剧中人】characters in a play or opera

【剧终】the end of（a drama，play，etc.）；curtain

【剧种】① type of traditional opera ② type（or genre）of drama art

【剧组】play staff

【剧作】drama；play

【剧作家】playwright；dramatist

据 ① occupy；seize：～为己有 take forcible possession of sth ② rely on；depend on：～山险 take advantage of a mountain defile ③ according to；on the basis of：～我看 in my opinion /～调查 on the basis of investigation /引经～典 chapter and verse ④ evidence；certificate：证～ evidence；proof /字～ written pledge /真凭实～ conclusive evidence；hard evidence /无凭无～ having no evidence

【据称】it is said；it is alleged：～，那个小偷已经被捕了。It is alleged that the thief has been arrested.

【据传】people are saying that：～物价要上涨。Rumour has it that prices are going to rise.

【据此】on these grounds；in view of the above；accordingly：～可知，他说的是谎话。From this we know he was lying.

【据点】strongpoint；stronghold

【据理】according to reason

【据理力争】argue strongly on just grounds

【据情】according to facts：～上报 report the facts to one's superior

【据实】according to reality

【据守】defend；guard；be entrenched in：～要塞 hold a fort

【据说】it is said；allegedly：～他们要结婚了。It is said that they are going to marry. /我没去过那个地方，～那地方很好。I've never been there but it is，by all accounts，a lovely place.

【据为己有】seize by force：她把那些没人认领的物品～。She possessed herself of the unclaimed goods.

【据闻】it is said；allegedly

【据悉】it is reported：～这项研究已经取得了很大进展。It is reported that the research is progressing rapidly.

【据险】rely on mountainous terrain

【据有】have；hold；occupy；take possession of

距[1] distance：差～ gap；difference；disparity /相～深远 far from each other

距[2] spur，a sharp growth on the back of cock's shin

【距角】【天】elongation

【距离】① be apart or away from；be at a distance from：～这里约 20 公里 be about 20 kilometres away from here /上海到北京～多远？What is the distance between Shanghai and Beijing? ② distance：远～ long distance；remote /保持～ keep distance /直线是两点之间的最短～。A straight line is the shortest distance between two points.

惧 fear；dread：临危不～ face the music；face danger fearlessly

【惧内】［书］henpecked

【惧怕】fear；dread：在任何时候，我们都不应该～困

J

难。*In no conditions should we dread difficulties.*
【惧色】a look of fear：面无～ *look undaunted*

惧 ［量］for animal power（enough to pull a plough，cart，etc.）

飓

【飓风】【气】hurricane

锯 ① saw：手～ *handsaw* /电～ *electric saw* ② cut with a saw；saw：～树 *cut a tree with a saw* /他把木头～成三块。*He sawed the wood into three pieces.*
【锯齿】sawtooth
【锯床】【机】sawing machine
【锯末】sawdust
【锯木厂】sawmill
【锯条】saw blade
【锯屑】sawdust
【锯子】［方］saw

聚 gather；assemble：欢～ *happy union*；*happy get-together*
【聚宝盆】treasure bowl — place rich in natural resources；cornucopia
【聚变】【物】fusion
【聚变反应】fusion reaction
【聚餐】dine together；have a dinner party
【聚赌】gambling group or party；group gambling
【聚光灯】spotlight；focus lamp
【聚光镜】condensing lens
【聚合】① assemble；get together ②【化】polymerization
【聚合物】【化】polymer
【聚汇】flow together；converge
【聚会】① gather；get together ② get-together；party：我们在她的～上玩得很开心。*We had a good time at her party.*
【聚伙】gang up
【聚积】accumulate；amass；collect；build up：～力量 *build up strength*；*gather forces* /房屋不经常打扫，尘土就会～起来。*Dust and dirt soon accumulate if a house is not cleaned regularly.*
【聚集】gather；assemble；crowd：云在～，要下雨了。*The clouds are gathering*；*it's going to rain.* /一群人不久就～在他的周围。*A crowd soon gathered round him.*
【聚歼】round up and annihilate
【聚焦】【物】focusing
【聚精会神】concentrate one's attention；be all eyes and ears：他～看书的时候，门铃响了起来。*He was engrossed in the book when the doorbell rang.*
【聚居】inhabit a region
【聚居点】settlement region：维吾尔族～ *regions where the Uygur nationality lives in compact communities*
【聚敛】amass wealth by heavy taxation：～钱财 *amass wealth and property by heavy taxation*
【聚拢】gather together：人们～过来，想知道发生了什么事情。*People gathered round*，*curious to know what was happening.*
【聚落】village or hamlet；settlement
【聚齐】assemble：学生们在校门口～了。*The students have assembled at the school gate.*
【聚散】meet and separate
【聚生】grow together
【聚首】［书］gather；meet：我们何时才能再～？*When shall we meet again?*
【聚讼】hold different opinions and fail to agree：～纷纭。*Opinions differ widely.*
【聚谈】meet to talk
【聚糖】【生化】polysaccharid；polysaccharide
【聚头】［书］gather；meet
【聚星】【天】multiple star
【聚蓄】accumulate；build up：他由于投资精明而～了一笔财产。*By investing wisely she accumulated a fortune.*
【聚议】meet for discussing sth
【聚饮】drink together；have a drinking party
【聚众】gather a crowd：～斗殴 *crowd to engage in an affray*

踞 ① crouch or sit：龙蟠虎～ *a coiling dragon and a crouching tiger — a forbidding strategic point* ② occupy：盘～ *be entrenched*
【踞傲】arrogant；haughty
【踞守】guard；be entrenched in

遽 ① hastily；hurriedly：～下断言 *make hasty judgements*；*jump to conclusions* ② frightened；alarmed
【遽然】［书］suddenly：～离去 *leave suddenly*

juān

捐 ① relinquish；abandon：为国～躯 *sacrifice one's life for the country* ② contribute；donate：募～ *solicit contributions*；*appeal for donations* /他～给医院很多钱。*He donated a lot of money to the hospital.* ③ a kind of tax：房～ *a tax on housing* /车～ *a tax on a vehicle*
【捐款】contribute money；contribution：这些钱是世界各地向饥民提供的～。*This money came from world wide contributions on behalf of the sufferers by the famine.*
【捐弃】［书］abandon；relinquish：～前嫌 *cast away past grievances*
【捐钱】donate money
【捐躯】go to one's death：为国～ *sacrifice one's life for one's country*
【捐生】sacrifice one's life
【捐税】taxes and levies
【捐献】contribute；donate：请惠予～。*Contributions are requested.*
【捐赠】contribute（as a gift）；present；donate
【捐助】offer（financial or material assistance）：校长号召大家提供食品和衣物～灾民。*We are called for by the principal to contribute food and clothing for the relief of the victims.*
【捐资】give financial assistance：～办学 *donate money to set up a school*

J

涓 ［书］a tiny stream

【涓埃】［书］insignificant; negligible: ~之功 *insignificant contribution*

【涓滴】a tiny drop; a very small amount of water: ~归公。*Every bit goes to the public treasury.*

【涓涓】trickling sluggishly: 小河~流过峡谷。*The brook trickled through the valley.*

娟 ［书］beautiful; graceful

【娟秀】beautiful; graceful: 字迹~ *beautiful handwriting*

圈 ① shut in a pen; pen in: 把猪~起来 *pen in the pigs* ②［口］lock up: 别老把孩子~在家里！*Don't shut the child up at home all the time.*
see also juàn; quān

镌 ［书］engrave: ~碑 *engrave a tablet*

【镌刻】engrave

juǎn

卷 ① roll up; curl; furl: ~头发 *curl one's hair* / ~纸 *roll up the paper* ② sweep off; carry along: 风~残云 *a clean sweep of sth* ③ roll; reel: 胶~ *roll of film* / 烟~儿 *cigarette* / 纸~儿 *a roll of paper* ④ steamed roll: 春~儿 *spring rolls* ⑤［量］: roll; reel: 一~布 *a roll of cloth* / 一~磁带 *a roll of tape* / 一~烟草 *a roll of tobacco.*
see also juàn

【卷笔刀】pencil sharpener

【卷层云】【气】cirrostratus

【卷尺】tape (measure)

【卷发】curly hair; wavy hair; crimped hair

【卷积云】【气】cirrocumulus

【卷帘门】folding door

【卷铺盖】get fired; get the sack: 经理叫他~。*The boss gave him the boot.*

【卷曲】curl; curly: 她的头发自然~。*Her hair waves naturally.*

【卷起】roll (or turn) up: 他把这张画~以使它不被损坏。*He rolled up the picture so that it does not get damaged.* /他~袖子想要和我打架。*He rolled up his sleeves ready to fight with me.*

【卷入】involve: 我~了一场纠纷。*I was involved in a dispute.* /她~了邻居间的争端。*She was enmeshed in the neighbours' dispute.*

【卷舌音】【语】retroflex

【卷逃】escape with valuables; make off with valuables

【卷筒】reel

【卷土重来】stage a comeback

【卷烟】① cigarette: ~厂 *cigarette factory* / ~纸 *cigarette paper* /薄荷~ *mentholated cigarette* /烤烟型~ *Virginian-type cigarette* ② cigar

【卷云】【气】cirrus

【卷轴】reel: 天线~ *aerial reel*

【卷子】steamed roll

帣 ［书］turn up one's sleeves
see also juàn

锩 (of the edge of a knife, sword, etc.) be rolled up

juàn

卷 ① book; volume; file; paper: 长~ *a long volume* ② (of a book) section; fascicle: 第一~ *the first fascicle* ③ examination paper: 交~ *hand in an examination paper* ④ file; dossier: 查底~ *look through the original files*
see also juǎn

【卷次】volume serial number

【卷头语】foreword; preface

【卷轴】［书］scroll

【卷子】① examination paper: 出~ *set a test paper* /看~ *mark examination papers* ② ancient hand-copied book that could be rolled up

【卷宗】① file: 机密~ *confidential file* ② folder

帣 ［书］bag
see also juǎn

隽 ①［书］meaningful ② (Juàn) a surname

【隽永】［书］(of speech or article) meaningful

【隽语】pithy remark

倦 ① weary; tired: 疲~ *tired; worn out* ② be weary; be bored: 孜孜不~ *tirelessly; diligently* /诲人不~ *be tireless in teaching*

【倦怠】tired and sleepy

【倦容】tired appearance

【倦色】tired expression

【倦意】tiredness; weariness; sleepiness

【倦游】［书］be weary of wandering and sightseeing

狷 ［书］① impetuous; rash ② upright; incorruptible

【狷傲】［书］detached and haughty

【狷急】［书］irritable in temper

【狷介】［书］upright; honest: ~之士 *upright person*

【狷狭】［书］be narrow-minded

绢 thin, tough silk: 手~儿 *handkerchief*

【绢本】silk scroll

【绢纺】silk spinning

【绢花】silk flower

【绢画】classical Chinese painting on silk

【绢丝】spun silk: ~织物 *spun silk fabric*

【绢子】［方］handkerchief

圈 ① pen; fold; sty: 羊~ *sheepfold* /猪~ *pigsty* ② (Juàn) a surname
see also juān; quān

【圈舍】livestock's pen

【圈养】rear livestock in pens

【圈猪】pigs that raised in sites

眷 ① relatives; family dependant: 家~ *wife and children; one's family* ②［书］have ten-

der feeling for
【眷爱】love deeply; have deep affection for
【眷顾】[书] take care of
【眷怀】remember fondly; miss very much
【眷眷】[书] yearn for; think of frequently
【眷口】[书] family dependants
【眷恋】[书] be sentimentally attached to (a person or place): ~过去 *feel nostalgic about one's past*
【眷念】[书] think fondly of; feel nostalgic about
【眷属】① family dependants ② married couple: 愿天下有情人终成~。*May all lovers in the world become couples.*
【眷佑】[书] show loving care for and bless
【眷注】[书] show solicitude for: 深承~ *be deeply grateful to sb for his loving care*

juē

屩 [书] straw sandals

撅[1] ① stick up: ~嘴 *pout (one's lips)* ② contradict; make sb embarrassed: 他~了我一顿。*He embarrassed me to my face.*

撅[2] break; snap: 把筷子~断了 *have the chopsticks snapped*

jué

决[1] ① decide; determine: 犹豫不~ *be in two minds; yea and nay; hesitate* ② definitely; certainly: ~无此事。*No such things ever happened.* ③ decide the outcome ④ execute a person: 枪~ *execute by shooting*

决[2] be breached; burst: 堵塞~口 *stop up a breach*

【决不】never; by no means: ~食言 *never go back on one's word* /我~向他妥协。*I will never make compromise with him.*
【决策】make policy; make a decision
【决策机构】policy-making body
【决策人】policy maker
【决堤】breach or burst a dyke
【决定】① decide: 她~先把钱包上交。*She decided to turn the wallet in first.* /他最终~出国。*He made up his mind to go abroad finally.* ② decision; resolution: 我们好不容易才做出离开的~。*We took the difficult decision to leave.* ③ determine: 考试成绩可能会~你的前途。*The exam results could determine your future.* ④ decisive: ~因素 *decisive factor*
【决定论】【哲】determinism
【决定权】power to make decision: 有最后~ *have the final say*
【决定性】decisiveness
【决斗】① duel ② decisive struggle
【决断】① make a decision ② resolution; decisiveness; determination: 她是个有~的人。*She is a woman of determination.*
【决计】① have decided; have made up one's mind: 我~明天就走。*I've decided to go tomorrow.* ② certainly; surely: 我说的~不会错。*What I've said definitely can't be wrong.*
【决绝】① sever; cut off ② firm; determined: 他态度~。*He is rather determined.*
【决口】breach; break: 堵住~ *close up a breach*
【决裂】break; break with: 与过去~ *break with the past*
【决然】① firmly; resolutely ② definitely; undoubtedly
【决赛】finals: 半~ *semifinals* /参加~ *run in the finals; play in the finals* /网球~ *the tennis finals*
【决胜】determine the victory
【决胜局】【体】deciding game (or set)
【决死】life-and-death
【决算】final accounts
【决心】will; determination: ~书 *a written statement of determination* /他是一个~获胜的候选人。*He is a candidate with the will to win.*
【决一雌雄】fight it out
【决一死战】do or die; fight to the death
【决疑】solve difficult problems
【决议】resolution: 撤销~ *revoke a resolution* /通过~ *adopt a resolution*
【决意】set one's mind; determine: 我~证明他的无辜。*I determine to prove his innocence.*
【决狱】[书] try a court case
【决战】a decisive battle: ~决胜 *determine to fight and win*

诀[1] ① rhymed formula: 口~ *mnemonic rhyme* /歌~ *formula put into rhyme* ② knack; secret of success: 秘~ *a special skill* /妙~ *a clever way*

诀[2] bid farewell; part: 永~ *part for ever*

【诀别】bid farewell; part: 这是一次痛苦的~。*It's a painful farewell.*
【诀窍】secret of success; key to success; knack: 成功的~ *secret of success* /掌握了~就容易了。*It's easy once you've got the knack of it.*
【诀要】[书] secret of success

抉 [书] pick out; single out

【抉剔】pick and choose: ~精华 *pick out the essence*
【抉瑕掩瑜】pick out flaws to cover up the radiance of the jade — comment harshly so as to write off the good points
【抉择】[书] choose; select: 作出~ *make one's choice*
【抉摘】[书] ① choose ② expose and condemn: ~弊端 *expose and castigate malpractices*

角[1] ① role; part: 主~ *leading role* ② role in traditional Chinese opera: 旦~ *a female role* ③ actor or actress: 丑~ *clown* /名~ *a famous actor or actress*

角[2] contend; wrestle: 口~ *quarrel; bicker*

J

角[3] an ancient wine vessel

角[4] a note of the ancient Chinese five-tone scale

角[5] (Jué) a surname

see also jiǎo

【角抵】ancient wrestling

【角斗】wrestle

【角斗场】wrestling ring

【角力】wrestle

【角色】① type of role：派～ *choose the cast* ② part; role; character; player：反面～ *negative character* /正面～ *positive character* /这是剧中最难扮演的～。*This is the most difficult part in the play.*

【角逐】contend; contest; compete

珏 ［书］two pieces of jade stuck together

觉 ①(of human or animal organs) sense; feel：不知不～ *unconsciously* /视～(听～，嗅～，味～，触～) *a sense of sight* (*hearing*, *smell*, *taste*, *touch*) /最近我一直～着不太舒服。*I have been feeling not well recently.* ② wake up：如梦初～ *as if waking from a dream* ③ become aware (or awakened)：自～自愿 *of one's own free will*

see also jiào

【觉察】sense; read; find; detect; perceive; become aware of：他～到大家并不欢迎他。*He sensed that he was unwelcome.* /你～到他的敌意了吗？*Are you aware of his hostility?* /我～到了他态度的转变。*I perceive a change in his attitude.*

【觉得】① feel：我～今天很冷。*I feel it's very cold today.* ② think：我～他不是一个诚实的人。*I don't think he is an honest man.*

【觉悟】① consciousness; awareness：政治～ *political consciousness*; *political understanding* ② begin to understand：他终于～到自己错了。*He finally realized he was wrong.* ③【宗】awakening; illumination

【觉醒】awaken：第三世界的～ *the awakening of the Third World*

绝 ① cut off; sever：掌声不～ *prolonged applause* /络绎不～ *in an endless stream* ② used up; exhausted：斩尽杀～ *kill all* ③ hopeless; desperate ④ die; pass away：悲痛欲～ *be sorrowful to death* ⑤ unique; superb：拍案叫～ *strike the table and shout bravo* ⑥ extremely; most：～大多数 *most*; *the overwhelming majority* /～早 *extremely early* ⑦ absolutely; in the least：～无此意 *have absolutely no such intentions* ⑧ a type of poem, consisting of four lines, five or seven characters each

【绝版】out of print：他想要的那本书已经～。*The book he wanted has been out of print.*

【绝笔】① last words written before death ②［书］best works, painting, etc.

【绝壁】precipice; cliff：多悬崖的～ *a precipitous bluff.*

【绝不】① never; on no account; not at all; by no means; in no circumstances：我～吃西餐。*I will never eat western style food.* ② be anything but：他～自私。*He is anything but selfish.*

【绝产】① crop failure ② heirless property or an inheritance the heir wishes to give up

【绝唱】① acme of perfection ② last singing or song before one's death

【绝处逢生】be unexpectedly rescued from a desperate situation：我～。*I saved my neck by mere chance.* /他让我～。*He gave me new hope of life.*

【绝代】［书］peerless：～佳人 *incomparable beauty*; *unrivalled beauty*

【绝倒】［书］roar with laughter：他的幽默让我们～。*His humour split our sides.*

【绝地】① extremely dangerous place ② hopeless situation：他已身陷～，无人能救。*He fell into a hopeless situation and nobody could save him.*

【绝顶】① extremely; utterly：他是个～聪明的孩子。*He is an extremely clever boy.* ②［书］highest peak：泰山～ *the top of Mount Tai*

【绝对】① absolute：～安静 *absolute silence* /～信任 *absolute trust* /～优势 *absolute advantage*; *absolute superiority* /～真理 *absolute truth* ② based on the condition without considering all the others：～零度 *absolute zero* /～误差 *absolute error* ③ absolutely; completely; utterly; fully：这～不可能。*It's absolutely impossible.* /他～适合这个工作。*He is suitable for the job in every way.* /没有他的帮助，我们～不可能按时完成任务。*Without his help it would have been utterly impossible for us to complete the task on time.* ④ most; extreme：这些孩子～大多数都是少先队员。*Most of the children are Young Pioneers.*

【绝根】without offspring (or descendants)

【绝非】① never; by no means; in no case：～偶然 *by no means fortuitous* ② by anything but：他～一个负责的人。*He is anything but responsible.*

【绝后】① without descendants ② never to be seen again：空前～ *unique*

【绝户】① without offspring or issue ② childless person (or family)

【绝活】one's best skill

【绝技】consummate skill

【绝迹】disappear; vanish; be extinct：地球上的许多动物已经～。*Many kinds of animals have been extinct on the earth.*

【绝交】break off relations (as between friends or countries); sever relations with：他们俩因为意见不同而～。*They two parted company because they hold different opinions.* /她那样对待我，所以我和她～了。*I've finished with her after the way she's treated me.*

【绝经】【生理】menopause

【绝景】extremely beautiful scenery

【绝境】①［书］remote place ② hopeless situation; impasse; blind all

【绝句】a poem of four lines, each containing five or seven characters

J

【绝口】① cease talking：他对我的发型赞不～。*He gave unstinted praised about my hairstyle.* ② keep one's mouth shut：从那以后，他对改建房子的许诺～不提。*Since then he has never mentioned his promise to rebuilt the house.*
【绝粒】[书] run out of food
【绝路】① cut off the way out ② road to ruin；blind alley；impasse；disaster：走上～ *head for one's doom*
【绝伦】[书] unsurpassed；peerless：荒谬～ *height of absurdity*
【绝门】① family without offspring：～绝户 *family without child* ② job no one takes up：这一行快要～了。*This trade is going to die out.* ③ unique skill ④ unexpected：他说的话太～了。*What he's said is too much.*
【绝密】top-secret；most confidential；classified：他终于设法得到了大使馆里的～文件。*He finally managed to obtain top-secret documents in the embassy.*
【绝妙】extremely clever；wonderful；perfect；splendid；superb：～的好诗 *an excellent poem* /～的景观 *superb scenery*
【绝灭】be extinct
【绝命书】① suicide note ② note written on the eve of one's execution
【绝品】peerless work of art
【绝棋】"dead game" of chess
【绝情】break off relations；be heartless；unthankful；ungrateful
【绝群】unsurpassed；superb
【绝然】completely；entirely：这双胞胎姐妹俩的性格～不同。*The twin sisters have totally different characters.*
【绝热】【物】heat insulation：～变化 *adiabatic change* /～方程 *adiabatic equation* /～过程 *adiabatic process* /～冷却 *adiabatic cooling* /～系数 *adiabatic coefficient* /～指数 *adiabatic exponent*；*adiabatic index*
【绝塞】[书] remote frontier fortress
【绝色】[书] (of a woman) extremely beautiful
【绝食】fast；go on a hunger strike
【绝世】[书] ① peerless：～珍品 *peerless treasure* ② die；pass away
【绝收】no harvest at all
【绝嗣】[书] without offspring (or descendents)
【绝望】despair；hopeless；in despair：他～地向他的伙伴挥了挥手。*He waved desperately to his companion.* /他被一种～的感觉包围着。*He was overwhelmed by a feeling of despair.* /他用一种～的姿势扔掉了手中的钱并哭了起来。*In a despairing gesture he threw away the money in his hands and cried.*
【绝无仅有】unique；only one of this kind：一个人的每一个基因组都是～的。*Each set of genes in unique to the individual.*
【绝响】[书] lost music
【绝续】dying out or surviving；life or death
【绝学】[书] ① lost learning ② profound learning
【绝艺】unique art (or skill)
【绝育】【医】sterilization：～手术 *sterilization operation*
【绝缘】① be cut off from；be isolated from：他几乎完全与外界～了。*He was almost completely cut off from the outside world.* ②【电】insulation：～导线 *insulated wire* /～涂层 *insulation coating* /～性能 *insulating property*
【绝缘体】insulator：电～ *electrical insulator* /电池～ *battery insulator* /耐火～ *refractory insulator* /气体～ *gaseous insulator* /双～ *double insulator* /无机～ *inorganic insulator* /有机～ *organic insulator*
【绝缘子】insulator：玻璃～ *glass insulator* /高压～ *high tension insulator* /天线～ *aerial insulator* /橡皮～ *rubber insulator* /蓄电池～ *accumulator insulator*
【绝早】very early；extremely early：他～就动身了。*He set off extremely early.*
【绝招】① unique art or skill ② unexpected tricky move
【绝症】incurable disease
【绝种】become extinct；die out

倔

see also juè
【倔强】obstinate；stubborn；pig-headed；willful；won't listen to reason：他很～，不肯承认自己错了。*He was very obstinate and didn't admit he was wrong.* /我竭尽全力劝说他不要辞职，但是他～得像头骡子。*I tried everything to persuade him not to resign, but he was as stubborn as a mule.*

掘

dig：临渴～井 *not dig a well until one is thirsty — start acting too late*
【掘进】【矿】driving；drifting tunneling：快速～ *quick tunnelling*
【掘土机】excavator

崛

[书] rise abruptly
【崛起】[书] ① (of a mountain, etc.) rise abruptly ② rise (as a political force)：抗日游击队～于广大农村。*The anti-Japanese guerrillas rose in the vast rural areas.*

厥[1]

faint；lose consciousness：晕～ *dizzy*；*faint*

厥[2]

[书] ① his；her；its；their：～父 *his or her father* ② only then：左丘失明，～有《国语》。*Only when Zuoqiu Ming lost his sight did he compile Remarks of Monarchs.*

谲

[书] ① cheat；swindle：正而不～ *honest and never cheat* ② strange：诡～ *crafty*；*cunning*
【谲诈】cunning；double-dealing；sneaky；crafty；canny；tricky：他是个～的商人。*He was a foxy trader.*

蕨

【植】brake (fern)
【蕨类植物】pteridophyte

橛

a short wooden stake
【橛子】a short wooden stake；wooden pin

噱 ［书］ loud laughter：可发一～ *make one laugh out loud*
see also xué

爵[1] the rank of nobility；peerage：公～ *duke* /侯～ *marquis* /伯～ *earl*；*count* /子～ *viscount* /男～ *baron*

爵[2] an ancient wine vessel

【爵禄】［书］ rank of nobility and the emoluments that go with it
【爵士】① knight ② sir
【爵士舞】jazz dance
【爵士乐】jazz；jazz music：～队 *jazz band* /～迷 *jitterbug*
【爵位】rank of nobility；title of nobility

蹶 fall；suffer a setback；stumble：一～不振 *be unable to recover from a setback*
see also juě

矍 ［书］ stare in surprise

【矍铄】［书］（of old people）hale and hearty：精神～的老人 *hale and energetic old man*

嚼 masticate；chew：咀～ *masticate*；*chew*
see also jiáo

攫 grab（with the claw）：～为己有 *possess oneself of sth*

【攫取】seize；grab：～暴利 *rake in exorbitant profits*

juě

蹶
see also jué

【蹶子】（of mules，horses，etc.）give a backward kick

juè

倔 gruff；surly：这人真～。*The guy is rather surely.*
see also jué

【倔巴】［方］ surly；gruff；sulky：这个小孩儿很～，总是由着自己的性子来。*He was a sulky little boy who always got his own way.*
【倔头倔脑】blunt of manner and gruff of speech

jūn

军 ① army；armed forces：参～ *take up arms* /常备～ *standing army* /海～ *the navy* /解放～ *liberation army* /空～ *air force*；*air service* /陆～ *land army*；*land forces* /野战～ *a field army* /劳动者大～ *an army of workers* ② army，a unit of the armed forces consisting of two or more divisions

【军备】armament；arms：扩充～ *engage in arms expansion* /裁～ *reduce armament*
【军备竞赛】armament race
【军兵种】arms and services of the armed forces
【军博】Military Museum of the Chinese People's Revolution
【军部】army headquarters
【军操】military drill
【军车】military vehicle
【军船】naval ship
【军刀】sabre；soldier's sword
【军队】armed forces；troops；army：召集～ *muster in troops*
【军队标号】military symbol
【军队番号】designation of a military unit
【军阀】warlord；military strongman
【军阀割据】separatist warlord regime
【军法】military criminal code；military law
【军法审判】court-martial
【军方】the military
【军费】military expenditure：～开支 *military spending*
【军风】military style（or spirit）
【军风纪】soldier's bearing and discipline
【军服】military uniform；uniform
【军服呢】army coating
【军港】naval port
【军鸽】pigeon for military use
【军歌】army song
【军工】① war industry ② military project
【军功】military exploit
【军功章】medal for military merit
【军官】officer：高级～ *high-ranking officers* /见习～ *officer on probation* /～学校 *military school*
【军管】military control
【军管会】military control commission
【军规】military discipline
【军棍】［旧］ cane for corporal punishment in the army
【军国主义】militarism
【军号】bugle
【军徽】army emblem
【军婚】marriage of serviceman or servicewoman
【军火】arms and ammunition：～交易 *deal in arms* /～走私 *munitions smuggling*
【军火库】arsenal
【军火商】munitions merchant；arms dealer
【军机】① military plan：贻误～ *delay the fulfillment of a military plan* ② military secret：他因泄漏～而被关进监狱。*He was put into prison for leaking a military secret.*
【军机处】office in the Qing Dynasty that helped the emperor to handle confidential military and political affairs
【军籍】military status；one's name on the army roll：开除～ *discharge sb from the army*
【军纪】military discipline
【军舰】warship；naval vessel
【军阶】military rank

J

【军界】military circles
【军垦】reclamation of wasteland by an army unit
【军控】arms control
【军礼】military salute
【军力】military strength
【军粮】army provisions：~库 *military grain depot*
【军烈属】family members of active servicemen or of martyrs
【军龄】length of military service
【军令】military orders：执行~ *carry on a military order* / ~如山。*Military orders cannot be disobeyed.*
【军令状】written pledge that makes oneself punished by military law in case one fails to execute an order or fulfill a mission
【军旅】[书] army；armed forces
【军绿】army green
【军马】① army horse ② troops；soldiers
【军帽】army cap
【军民】army and people：~关系 *army-people relations* / ~团结 *the unity between the army and the people*
【军民共建】joint efforts by the army and the people
【军命】military mission (or order)
【军品】products for military use
【军棋】military chess
【军旗】army flag；ensign
【军器】[旧] ordnance；armament
【军情】military situation：他是敌方派来刺探~的。*He is dispatched by the enemy to spy on our military movements.*
【军区】military region (or area)：北京~ *Beijing Military Command* / 省~ *provincial military command*
【军权】military power (or leadership)
【军犬】military dog
【军人】soldier；armyman：复员~ *a demobilized soldier* / 这是一个由~政府统治的国家。*This is a country ruled by the military.*
【军容】soldier's discipline, appearance and bearing：~整肃 *keep up military bearing*
【军师】[旧] military counselor (or adviser)
【军史】history of an army
【军士】noncommissioned officer (NCO)
【军事】military affairs：~部署 *military deployment* / ~路线 *military line* / ~训练 *military training*
【军售】arms sale
【军书】[书] military documents and registers
【军属】soldier's dependents (or family)
【军帖】[旧] military proclamation
【军团】army group
【军屯】troops engaged in farming and garrison duties
【军威】military prestige (or reputation)
【军委】Military Commission of the Central Committee of the Communist Party of China
【军伍】[旧] troops；army
【军务】military affair
【军衔】military rank：~制度 *system of military ranks*
【军饷】soldier's pay and provision：克扣~ *embezzle soldier's pay and provisions*
【军校】military school
【军械】ordnance；armament：~库 *ordnance depot*
【军械处】ordnance department
【军械库】ordnance depot
【军心】soldier's morale：~振奋 *the high morale of the troops*
【军需】① military supplies：~工厂 *military supplies factory* / ~品 *military supplies；artillery* ② [旧] quartermaster
【军需库】military supply depot
【军需品】military supplies
【军训】military training：学生们在这个学期要参加~。*The students will take part in military training this term.*
【军衣】military uniform
【军医】medical officer
【军营】military camp
【军用】for military use：~地图 *military map* / ~飞机 *military aircraft* / ~物资 *military supplies*
【军邮】army post (or mail)
【军乐】martial music；military music：~队 *military band*
【军运】military transport
【军长】army commander
【军政】① military and political ② military administrative work：~人员 *military administrative personnel* ③ army and government：~关系 *relations between the army and the government*
【军政府】military government
【军职】official post in the army
【军制】military system
【军种】(armed) services
【军转民】(of a factory) convert from manufacturing military products to civilian products
【军装】military uniform
【军资】military supplies

均 ① equal；even：平~ *average* / 势~力敌 *all square；nip and tuck* ② all；without exception：各项准备工作~已就绪。*All the preparation has been completed.*
【均等】equal；fair：机会~ *equal opportunities*
【均分】divide equally：我们将~这些钱。*The money will be divided equally among us.*
【均衡】balanced；harmonious：东西方国家之间的权力~ *equilibrium of power between Western and Eastern countries* / 有时有一点儿损失，有时有一点儿盈余，但总的来说是~的。*Sometimes there is a slight loss and sometimes a slight surplus, but in general they balance out.*
【均衡论】【哲】theory of equilibrium
【均势】equilibrium of power (forces)：新政党的壮大打破了力量的~。*The growth of the new political party upset the balance of power.*
【均摊】share equally
【均温】average temperature
【均一】even；uniform

【均夷】【地】grade：~平原 *graded plain*
【均匀】even；well-distributed：涂得~的清漆 *an even application of varnish*
【均沾】share equally：利益~ *share the profits equally*
【均值法】averaging method

龟 *see also* guī
【龟裂】① (of skin) chap：许多人的皮肤在冬天容易~。*Many people's skin chaps easily in winter.* ② (of parched earth) be full of cracks：天久不雨，田地~。*Owing to lack of rain for a long time, the field is full of cracks.*

君 ① monarch；sovereign：国~ *monarch* ② gentleman：诸~ *gentlemen*
【君临】① monarch's rule：~天下 *rule the country* ② approaching；drawing near
【君权】monarchical power
【君上】[书] monarch；sovereign
【君王】monarch；emperor
【君主】monarch；sovereign：立宪制~ *a constitutional monarch*
【君主国】monarchical state — the imaginary land of the virtuous
【君主立宪】constitutional monarchy
【君主制】monarchy
【君主专制】autocratic monarchy
【君子】man of noble character；superior man：伪~ *hypocrite*
【君子报仇，十年不晚】even ten years isn't a long time for a gentleman to seek vengeance
【君子成人之美】a gentleman is always ready to help others attain their aims
【君子坦荡荡】a gentleman is open and magnanimous
【君子协定】gentlemen's agreement
【君子一言，驷马难追】a word spoken is past recalling
【君子之交淡如水】the friendship between gentlemen is as pure as crystal

钧 ① an ancient unit of weight：千~一发 *hang by a thread — in imminent peril* ② a kind of wheel used in making pottery：陶~ *potter's wheel* ③ (term of respect for one's senior or superiors) you；your
【钧安】[书] wish you good health
【钧鉴】[书] your attention
【钧命】[书] your order
【钧启】[书] yours sincerely
【钧谕】[书] your written advice
【钧座】[书] Your Excellency

菌 fungus
*see also*jùn
【菌肥】bacterial manure
【菌核】【植】sclerotium
【菌苗】【医】vaccine

皲 (of skin) chap
【皲裂】[书] (of skin) chap：他的嘴唇在大风中~了。*His lips chapped in the strong wind.*

jùn

俊 ① pretty；handsome：这姑娘长得真~。*The girl is very pretty.* ② of outstanding talent
【俊杰】a person of outstanding talent；hero：识时务者为~。*One who understands the times is a hero；those who suit their actions to the times are wise.*
【俊丽】beautiful and elegant
【俊髦】[书] person of outstanding talent
【俊美】pretty；beautiful；handsome：~的少年 *a handsome young man*
【俊气】pretty；delicate
【俊俏】[口] pretty and charming
【俊伟】[书] be gifted with eminent talent and insight
【俊秀】pretty；good-looking：容貌~的小姑娘 *a pretty girl*
【俊雅】[书] pretty and tasteful
【俊逸】[书] handsome, free and easy

郡 prefecture, an ancient area of administration that was smaller than a country before the Qin Dynasty and bigger than a county since the Qin Dynasty

峻 ① (of mountains) high and steep：高山~岭 *high mountains and lofty ranges* ② harsh；stern：严刑~法 *harsh laws and severe punishments*
【峻拔】(of mountains) high
【峻急】[书] ① (of water currents) rapid：~的河流 *a rapid river* ② stern；impetuous
【峻厉】severe；stern；grim
【峻峭】high and steep：~的山 *a steep hill*；*precipitous hills* / ~的峡谷 *an abrupt canyon*
【峻险】dangerously steep
【峻泻】empty the bowels with drastic purgatives
【峻直】high and straight

骏 steed
【骏马】fine horse；steed
【骏足】[书] fine horse；steed

菌 mushroom
see also jūn
【菌柄】(of fungus) stem
【菌伞】(of fungus) cap
【菌子】[方] gill fungus

竣 complete；finish：大事告~。*The project has been completed.*
【竣工】complete (or finish) a project：该项目已~。*The project has been completed.*

K

kā

咔 ［象］click; clack:他进屋后,门～地关上了。*The door clicked shut behind him.*

咖 see also gā

【咖啡】coffee:牛奶～ *white coffee; coffee with milk* /速溶～ *instant coffee* /煮～ *make some coffee* /我要一杯～。*I want a cup of coffee.*

【咖啡伴侣】coffee mate

【咖啡杯】coffee cup

【咖啡豆】coffee bean

【咖啡壶】coffee pot

【咖啡色】coffee colour; dark brown

【咖啡厅】coffee bar; café

喀 ［象］the sound of coughing or vomiting

【喀吧】［象］snap; crack:他～一声关上了箱盖。*He snapped down the lid of the box.*

【喀布尔】Kabul, capital of Afghanistan

【喀嚓】［象］crack; snap: ～一声树枝断了。*The branch broke with a crack.* /士兵～一声立正。*The soldiers snapped to attention.*

【喀哒】［象］click: 门锁的～声 *the click of a door latch* /她故意使鞋跟发出～声。*She clicked her heels on purpose.*

【喀麦隆】Cameroon: ～人 *Cameroonian*

【喀秋莎】① Katyusha, a girl's name ② multi-barrel rocket launcher

【喀斯特】【地】karst: ～地区 *karst* / ～地形 *karst topography* / ～水 *karst water*

【喀土穆】Khartoum, capital of the Sudan

kǎ

卡 ① calorie: 大～ *kilocalorie*; *kcal* ② card: 成绩～ *report card* /登记～ *register card* /考勤～ *clock card* /赊账～ *charge card* /调试～ *debug card* /信用～ *credit card* /资料～ *data card* ③ cassette: 双～录音机 *double-cassette recorder* ④ truck; lorry:十轮～ *ten-wheeled truck*
see also qiǎ

【卡宾枪】carabin; carbine; escopeta; machine carbine: ～手 *carbineer*

【卡车】truck; lorry:翻斗～ *tip truck*; *skip lorry* /搅拌机～ *agitator truck* /军用～ *army lorry* /冷藏～ *reefer truck* /履带～ *crawler truck* /平板～ *flat bed lorry* /轻型～ *pickup truck* /油罐～ *tanker truck* /重型～ *heavy-duty truck*

【卡车起重机】truck crane

【卡尺】【机】caliber gauge or rule; slide calliper rule: 游标～ *vernier callipers*

【卡带】cassette tape

【卡丁车】【体】Carting car, a mini Formula-One-styled racing car

【卡规】measuring tool used to measure axles and convex workpieces

【卡介苗】【药】BCG (Bacille Calmette-Guérin) vaccine; TB vaccine

【卡拉OK】karaoke, a form of entertainment in which one sings against a pre-recorded backing

【卡片】card; fiche:穿孔～ *aperture card* /工资～ *pay card* /索引～ *an index card* /食谱～ *a recipe card* /文摘～ *abstracts card* / ～穿孔 *card punching* / ～盒 *card box* / ～目录 *card catalogue* / ～索引 *card index* /我用～学英语单词。*I learn English by cards.*

【卡钳】【机】calipers:内～ *inside calipers* /外～ *outside calipers*

【卡萨布兰卡】Casablanca, seaport and largest city of Morocco

【卡塔尔】Qatar: ～人 *Qatari*

【卡特尔】【经】cartel:反萧条～ *anti-depression cartel* /钢铁～ *steel cartel* /稳定价格～ *price stabilization cartel*

【卡通】① animated cartoon: ～片 *animated cartoon film* ② cartoon; strip cartoon

咯 cough up:把鱼刺～出来 *cough up the fishbone*
see also gē

【咯痰】cough up phlegm

【咯血】【医】spit blood; haemoptysis

kāi

开[1] ① open; turn on: ～抽屉 *open a drawer* / ～门 *open the door* / ～锁 *open a lock*; *unlock* / ～灯 *turn on the light* ② exploit; make an opening; open up: ～路 *cut out a path*; *clear a path* / ～矿 *open up a mine*; *exploit a mine* ③ come lose; open out:衣服扣儿～了。*The button has come untied.* /公园里的花都～了。*The flowers in the park come into bloom.* ④ thaw out:我家门前的河～了。*The frozen river in front of my home has thawed out.* ⑤ lift a ban ⑥ start; operate:

~车 drive a car / ~船 sail; set sail / ~机器 operate a machine; run a machine ⑦ (of troops, etc.) set out: 听说两团人马就要~进城里。*It's heard that two regiments will move into the city.* ⑧ run; set up: ~工厂 *run a factory* / ~医院 *set up a hospital* ⑨ start; begin: ~先例 *create a precedent* ⑩ hold (a meeting, exhibition, etc.): ~会 *hold a meeting* / ~欢送会 *hold a farewell party* ⑪ make out; write out: ~发票 *make an invoice* / ~药方 *write out a prescription* ⑫ pay (wages, fares, etc.) ⑬ [方] fire; sack: 他昨天被老板~了。*He was fired by the boss yesterday.* ⑭ boil: 水~了。*The water is boiling.* ⑮ serve (a meal, etc.): ~席 *serve dinner; serve a meal* ⑯ [方] eat up: 他把一盘饺子都~了。*He ate up the whole plate of dumplings.* ⑰ used after a verb or an adjective: 这话都传~了。*The word has got about.* / 她一见了我,就聊~了。*She began to chat with me as soon as she saw me.* / 下了两天雨,天就冷~了。*It's getting cold after two days' raining.* ⑱ percentage; proportion: 我们把收入按四六~分成。*We divided the earning in the proportion of four to six.* ⑲【印】(of standard size of printing paper) division of a whole: 十六~ *sixteenmo; 16mo* / 三十二~ *thirty-twomo; 32 mo.* ⑳ (Kāi) a surname

开² carat: 十四~金 *14 carat gold*

开 used after a verb: 躲~ *stand aside; ward* / 睁~眼 *open one's eyes* / 这房间太小,坐不~这么多人。*The room is too small for so many people to be seated.*

【开拔】(of troops) move

【开办】open; set up; establish; start; found: ~工厂 *start a factory* / ~一所学校 *set up a school*

【开本】【印】format; book size: 四~ *quarto* / 八~ *octavo* / 十六~ *16mo*

【开笔】① [旧] begin learning to write poems and essays: ~学书 *begin to practise calligraphy* ② [旧] time for taking up the writing brush in a year: 新年~ *start writing in the new year* ③ start writing a book or an article

【开编】start compiling or editing: 这本书已经~。*Somebody has begun to edit the book.*

【开标】open sealed tenders: ~日期 *tenders opening date*

【开播】① (of a radio or TV station) begin broadcasting: 这个地方电台已经~。*The local radio station has begun broadcasting.* ② begin broadcasting a programme: 这个电视剧是昨天~的。*This teleplay began to be broadcast yesterday.* ③ begin sowing

【开采】mine; extract; exploit: 单翼~ *one-way mining* / 地上~矿物 *open pit mining* / 二次~ *second mining* / 干法~ *dry mining* / 自动化~ *automated mining* / ~石油 *exploit oil*

【开舱】break bulk; break out a cargo

【开槽】open a slot; make a notch: ~机 *groover; notching machine* / ~脉冲 *slotted impulse* / ~线 *slotted line* / ~砖 *notched brick*

【开衩】(of a coat) vent: 中间~ *centre vent*

【开场】begin; open: 戏已经~。*The play has already started.*

【开场白】① prologue of a play ② opening speech: 她用一个重大事件做了~。*She opened with an important event.*

【开车】① drive or start a car, train, etc. ② set a machine going

【开诚布公】open-hearted; in all sincerity and frankness; above-board: 我们进行了~的交谈。*We had a frank and straight talk.*

【开秤】begin business

【开初】at the beginning; at first: ~我不知道她是这样一个虚伪的人。*At first, I didn't know she was such a hypocritical person.*

【开除】expel; discharge; fire; sack: ~学籍 *expel from school* / ~公职 *discharge sb from public employment* / 你被~了! *You are fired!* / 她因盗窃被~。*She was sacked for stealing.*

【开船】set sail; sail

【开创】open; initiate; found; set up: ~新纪元 *open a new epoch* / ~新局面 *create a new situation*

【开春】beginning of spring; early spring

【开打】【戏】acrobatic fighting

【开裆裤】open-seat pants; split pants

【开刀】① behead: ~问斩 *execute by beheading* ② [喻] make the first target of attack; punish: 她准备拿我~。*She intended to punish me first as a warning to others.* ③ operate: 病人明天~。*The patient will be operated on tomorrow.*

【开导】give guidance to sb; enlighten: 让我来~~她吧。*Let me straighten her out.* / 她耐心地~女儿。*She explained and made her daughter understood patiently.*

【开倒车】turn back the wheel of history; turn the clock back; return to the past

【开道】① clear the way: 鸣锣~ *beat gongs to clear the way (for officials in feudal times)* ② [方] make way

【开灯】switch (turn) on the light: 天黑了,请~! *It's dark now; please turn on the light.*

【开动】① start; set in motion; bring into operation: ~机车 *set the engine in motion* ② move; march

【开冻】thaw: 地面~了。*The ground has thawed out.*

【开端】beginning; start: 好的~ *flying start; running start* / 文明的~ *the dawn of civilization* / 我们已经有了一个良好的~。*We have already made a good beginning.*

【开恩】show mercy; bestow favours

【开尔文】【物】degree Kelvin; Kelvin: ~方程 *Kelvin equation* / ~效应 *Kelvin effect*

【开发】(kāifā) ① develop; exploit: ~矿藏 *exploit mineral resources* / ~新产品 *develop new products* / ~自然资源 *tap natural resources* / 国土~ *land development in the country* / 水力~ *water power development* ② bring into play; develop: ~智力 *tap intellectual resources*

【开发】(kāifa) pay; distribute: ~车钱 *pay traveling expenses*

【开发区】Open Economic Zone (OEZ); coastal open regions

【开发银行】development bank

【开饭】① serve a meal ② be in service: ~时间 *dining hours; service hours*

【开方】① write out a prescription ②【数】extraction of a root; evolution: 开平方 *extraction of the square root* /开立方 *extraction of the cube root*

【开房间】[方] rent a room in a hotel

【开放】① blossom; come into blossom: 玫瑰花~了。*The roses have come into bloom.* ② be open to the public: 这家诊所不对外~。*The clinic isn't open to outsiders.* /这个国家的博物馆对公众免费~。*The museums in this country are open to the public free of charge.* ③ outgoing; open-minded: ~的性格 *an outgoing personality*

【开赴】march to; be bound for: ~战场 *march to the front*

【开工】① (of a factory, etc.) go into operation: ~不足 *be operating under capacity* ② (of a construction project, etc.) start work: 大桥的建设已经~。*The construction of the bridge has begun.*

【开工率】utilization of capacity; operating rate

【开沟】ditching; guttering: ~机 *ditching machine; trench digger* / ~平地 *dig ditches and level land*

【开关】①【电】switch; switchgear: 场~ *field switch* /触发~ *trigger switch* /单向~ *unidirectional switch* /电~ *electric switch* /断点~ *breakpoint switch* /多路~ *multiway switch* /负荷~ *load switch* /光敏~ *light activated switch* /数字~ *digital switch* /双极~ *bipolar switch* /双向~ *a two-way switch; bilateral switch* /显示~ *display switch* /小型闸刀~ *baby knife switch* /应急~ *emergency switch; intervention switch* /闸刀~ *chopper switch; knife switch* /制动~ *brake switch* /终端~ *dead end switch* /主~ *main switch; master switch* /组~ *group switch* / ~盒 *switch box* ② button; knob: ~按钮 *switch knob; shift knob*

【开光】①【宗】enshrine a Buddha statue ②[谑] have one's hair cut; shave

【开锅】boil: 牛奶已经~十分钟了。*The milk has been boiling away for 10 minutes.*

【开国】found a state: ~大典 *founding ceremony of a state* / ~元老 *the founder of the state*

【开焊】(of welded joint) snap

【开航】① become open for navigation ② set sail: ~日期 *sailing day* /请问这船什么时候~? *Could you please tell me when the ship will sail?*

【开河】① (of a river) thaw ② construct a canal

【开后门】open the back door — offer advantages to one's friends or relations by underhand means: 他经常滥用权力,为亲戚~。*He always abuses his powers to secure advantages for his relatives.*

【开户】open an account: 我在银行以你的名义~。*I opened an account at a bank in your name.*

【开花】① blossom; bloom: ~结果 *blossom and yield fruit* /花园里的树正在~。*Those trees in the garden are blossoming.* ② explode: 炸弹在敌人中间~。*The bomb exploded among the enemies.* ③ burst with joy: 他表面镇静,其实心里乐开了花。*He kept calm in appearance but burst with joy inside.* ④ (of experience, etc.) spread; known to all: 这种先进经验已经遍地~。*The advanced experience has spread to everyone.*

【开花弹】fragmentation bullet; high explosive shell

【开化】① become civilized ② thaw: 冰在~。*The ice is thawing.*

【开怀】to one's heart's content; heartily: ~畅饮 *drink to one's heart's content; drink heartily*

【开怀儿】[口] give birth to the first child

【开荒】open up (or reclaim) wasteland

【开会】hold a meeting; attend a meeting: 我们明天上午要~。*We will hold a meeting tomorrow morning.*

【开荤】① begin a meat diet ② have a novel experience

【开火】① fire; open fire: 向敌人~ *fire at the enemy* ② attack (in speech or writing): 报界因总统未遵守竞选时的诺言而向其~。*The president was attacked by the press for failing to keep a campaign promise.*

【开伙】① run a mess or cafeteria ② provide food

【开豁】① open and clear: 房子看起来十分~。*The room looks open and clear.* ② become broadened or enlightened: 听了他的话,我心里很~。*His words widened my view.*

【开机】① start a machine ② start shooting a film, TV play, etc.

【开集】【数】opener; open set

【开霁】[书] clear up (after rain or snow)

【开价】① charge or ask a price ② opening price; initial price

【开架】① (of a library, etc.) open-stack: ~阅览室 *open-stack reading room* ② (of a store, etc.) open-shelf

【开间】①[方] about 1/3 metres, the standards width of a room in an old-style house: 单~ *narrow one-room house* ② width of a room: 这间房子~不大。*The room is a little narrow.*

【开缄】[书] unseal (a letter, etc.)

【开疆】[书] open up territory

【开讲】begin lecturing: 教授刚~,他就睡着了。*He fell asleep the moment the professor began lecturing.*

【开奖】draw and announce the winning ticket in a public lottery

【开胶】become unglued

【开解】console; soothe: 说什么也不能~他。*No words availed to straighten him out.*

【开戒】break an abstinence; break one's resolution

【开金】(of gold) carat; gold alloy: 12~ *12-karat gold*

【开禁】lift a ban; rescind a prohibition

【开镜】start shooting a film, TV play, etc.

【开局】①（of a game）start; begin ② beginning

【开具】prepare or write out（a list, certificate, etc.）：请为我～清单。*Please write out a clear statement for me.*

【开卷】①［书］open a scroll or book：～有益。*Reading is always profitable.* ② open-book examination

【开掘】① dig：～水井 *dig a well* ② deeply explore and fully express（subject matter, character, etc.）：我们应该向真实生活进行～。*We should explore and portray real life.*

【开课】① begin school; begin classes ②（in college）offer a course; teach a subject：张老师这学期为我们～。*Mr. Zhang will give lectures to us this term.*

【开垦】open up（or reclaim）wasteland：～荒地 *reclaim; land reclamation*

【开口】① open one's mouth; begin to speak：～说话 *loose sb's tongue* /他就是不～。*He held his tongue firmly.* /你有什么办法能让他～吗？*Could you find a way to make him speak?* ② put the first edge on a knife; sharpen

【开口闭口】say the same thing again and again; repeat many times：他～地炫耀他在考试中的高分。*He cannot open his mouth without talking about his high grades in the exam.*

【开口钳】open mouth tongs

【开口子】①（of a dyke）break; burst ② stretch a rule or regulations（in favour of sb or sth）：挪用公款的口子可不能开。*No one should ever give the green light to embezzlement.*

【开快车】① step on the gas; speed：酒后～ *drunk driving and speeding* ② hurry through one's work; speed up the works：时间够用，不必～。*There is enough time left, so you can do it with ease.*

【开旷】wide and spacious

【开矿】open up a mine; exploit a mine

【开阔】① open; wide; vast：～的广场 *an open square* ② tolerant; liberal：他是一个心胸～的人。*He is a broad-minded man.* ③ widen：～眼界 *broaden one's outlook* / ～思路 *expand one's mind*

【开阔地】【军】open terrain; open ground

【开朗】① open and clear：豁然～ *suddenly see the light* ② cheerful; sanguine; optimistic：她是一个性格～的姑娘。*She is a girl with a bright and pleasant disposition.*

【开犁】① start the year's ploughing ② plough the first furrow as a guideline

【开例】create or set a precedent：没有人敢～。*No one dared to create a precedent.*

【开脸】①［旧］a girl changes her hair style when getting married ②（in sculpture, etc.）carve the face of a figure

【开列】list; make a list：～名单 *make a list of names*

【开裂】crack; burst open：镜子～了。*The mirror cracked.*

【开路】① open a way; open a new road; pioneer ② take the lead; lead the way ③【电】open circuit：～电压 *open-circuit voltage* /～控制 *open circuit control* / ～试验 *open-circuit test* / ～线圈 *open coil*

【开绿灯】give the green light; tolerate：这件事我们不可对他们～。*We must not give them the green light to do it.*

【开罗】Cairo, capital of Egypt：～会议 *Cairo Conference* / ～宣言 *Cairo Declaration*

【开锣】①【戏】strike the gong to start a performance ②（of a game）begin; start：校际排球比赛即将～。*The inter-college volleyball matches will start soon.*

【开门】① open the door — do sth in public：～办学 *carry out open-door education* / ～整风 *public rectification* ②（public organizations, units, etc.）open; begin business：这家饭馆十点～。*The restaurant opens at 10 am.*

【开门红】make a good beginning：新年第一笔生意就赚了，真是～。*We made great profits from the first business of the year; it is really a flying start.* /你新学期～使我很高兴。*I'm pleased that you've made such an auspicious start to the new term.*

【开门见山】the door opens on a view of mountains — come straight to the point; speak bluntly; put it bluntly：会上，他～地说出了自己的想法。*He came straight to what he thought at the meeting.*

【开门揖盗】open the door to the robbers; invite disaster by letting in evil-doers：你这样做无异于～。*Your behaviours are just like putting the cat near the goldfish bowl.*

【开蒙】［旧］teach children to learn to read and write;（of children）begin to learn to read and write

【开明】enlightened; liberal：～人士 *enlightened personage* /开明～ *enlightened gentry* / ～的思想 *liberal ideas*（*or views*）

【开幕】① curtain rises; begin a performance：晚会～了，观众报以热烈的掌声。*The curtain rose, and the audience applauded ardently.* ② open; inaugurate：展览会下周～。*The exhibition will open next week.*

【开幕词】opening speech or address

【开幕式】opening ceremony; inauguration

【开年】① beginning of a year ②［方］next year

【开拍】start shooting（a film, TV programme, etc.）

【开盘】【经】opening quotation（on the exchange）：～价格 *opening price*

【开炮】① open fire with artillery; bombard ② fire or level criticism at：向错误～ *severely criticize mistakes and errors*

【开辟】① open; start：～航线 *open an air*（*or sea*）*route* / ～专栏 *start a special column* ② develop; promote：～新局面 *make a breakthrough* ③ creation of the world

【开篇】① introductory song in some local operas in China ② beginning of a literary work

K

【开瓢儿】［方］（used humorously）break one's head：他让人给～了。*His head was broken in a fight.*

【开票】① open the ballot box and count the ballots ② make out an invoice or bill：发货时别忘了给顾客～！*Don't forget to make out an invoice when you deliver goods.*

【开屏】（of a peacock）spread its tail：孔雀～ *peacock spreading its tail*

【开普敦】Capetown，port city of South Africa

【开普勒】Johannes，Kepler（1571-1603），German astronomer and physical scientist：～定律 *Kepler's law* /～轨道 *Keplerian orbit*；*Keplerian ellipse* /～望远镜 *Kepler telescope*

【开启】① open：自动～ *open automatically* ② start；begin：～新局面 *start a new phase*

【开腔】begin to speak；open one's mouth：他都半天没～了。*He kept silent for a long time.*

【开枪】fire；shoot；fire a round：他向目标瞄准并～。*He aimed and fired at the target.* /他一路～，逃出监狱。*He shot his way out of prison.*

【开窍】① have one's ideas straightened out；begin to know the truth：他逐渐～了，知道自己可能无意中得罪了她。*He gradually came to know that he must have offended her unconsciously.* ② children begin to gain knowledge or understand things：这个男孩儿～很晚。*The boy began to understand things very late.* ③［方］（used sarcastically）see（the ways of）the world：他一直住在乡下，根本不～。*He lived in the countryside since he was born and has never seen the outside world.*

【开球】【体】（in soccer）kick off；（in basketball）start the game；（in volleyball）serve：～开得好 *serve well*

【开区间】【数】open interval

【开区域】【数】open region

【开缺】［旧］（of a position）become vacant：～候补（*of a position*）*fall vacant*

【开刃儿】put the first edge on a knife

【开赛】begin a match，game，etc.

【开山】① cut into a mountain（for quarrying，etc.）：～筑路 *cut mountains to construct roads* ② open the mountains for grazing ③【宗】build the first temple on a famous mountain

【开山祖师】founder of a religious sect or a school of thought；founding father

【开衫】cardigan：男～ *cardigan for men* /女～ *cardigan for women*

【开烧】［方］sleep in the open wilderness by a campfire

【开设】① open（a shop，factory，etc.）：～医院 *establish a hospital* ② offer（a course in college，etc.）：这所大学～了传播学课程。*The university offers courses in communications.*

【开审】start the trial：～日期 *hearing time*

【开始】① start；begin；initiate；commence：～改革 *initiate a reform* /认识从实践～。*Knowledge begins with practice.* /他从18岁就～了他的教师生涯。*He commenced his career as a teacher when he was 18.* ② start doing：～写作业 *start doing one's homework* ③ initial stage；beginning；outset；initiation；commencement：旅途的～是枯燥无味的。*The beginning of the trip was dull.* /刚刚～，就遇到了困难。*Problems arose at the very outset.*

【开市】①（of a shop）reopen after a cessation of business ② first transaction of a day's business：～价 *opening quotation*

【开释】release（a prisoner）；set free

【开首】［方］at the start；at first

【开涮】［方］tease；make fun of：少拿我～！*Don't make fun of me!*

【开水】① boiling water：用～沏茶 *make tea with boiling water* ② boiled water：白～ *plain boiled water*

【开榫】【机】mortise and tenon：～机 *mortising machine*；*tenoning machine*

【开锁】unlock

【开台】begin a theatrical performance：～锣鼓 *gongs and drums introducing a theatrical performance*

【开膛】gut；disembowel（poultry，livestock，etc.）

【开天窗】①（of a syphilitic）have a rotten nose ②［旧］put in a skylight- leave a blank in a publication（to show that sth has been censored）

【开天辟地】when heaven was separated from earth — creation of the world；since the dawn of history：～头一遭 *the first time in human history*

【开庭】【律】open or hold a court session：～审理（*the court*）*hold hearing* /本案本周～。*The court will hear the case this week.*

【开通】（kāitōng）① inspire；cultivate：～民智 *cultivate public intellect* ②（of communication lines or routes）be put into use：～高速公路 *put the highway into use*

【开通】（kāitong）① open-minded；liberal：一个思想～的人 *an open-minded person* ② liberate；enlighten：你最好～～他的思想。*You'd better enlighten him.*

【开头】① start；begin："你看完那本书了吗？""我刚开了个头。""*Have you finished the book yet?*" "*No，I've just started it.*" ② start sth；make a start：警方的调查已经开了头。*The police had started their investigation.* ③ beginning：万事～难。*Things are always difficult at the beginning.*

【开脱】absolve；vindicate：～责任 *free sb from responsibility* /关于此事他的过失已被～。*He was absolved of blame in the matter.*

【开拓】① open up；pioneer：～进取 *forge ahead* /～精神 *the pioneer spirit* /～市场 *develop markets* /～型人才 *talent of pioneering type* ②【矿】developing；opening

【开拓者】pioneer：航空业的～ *a pioneer in aviation*

【开外】over；above；beyond：他看上去有五十～了。*He looks over fifty.*

【开玩笑】① play a joke；joke：不要和那位老人～。*Don't joke with that old man.* ② regard as a trifling matter；treat casually：这种事可不能～，这关

K

看一个人的名誉。*This is no joke; it's related to one's reputation.*

【开胃】① whet the appetite; stimulate the appetite; get up one's appetite: ~酒 *aperitif* / ~品 *appetizer* / ~食品 *appetizer* ②［方］amuse oneself; make fun of

【开销】① pay expenses ② expense: 日常~ *daily expenses*

【开小差】①（of a soldier）desert; sneak off; go AWOL: 集体~ *be deserted in a body* /战争期间~的士兵要受到严惩。*A soldier who deserts his post in time of war is punished severely.* / ② be absent-minded: 他因为上课时~受到了批评。*He was criticized for being absent-minded at class.*

【开小灶】prepare special food for sb; give special favour to sb: 老师经常给后进生~。*The teacher often gave the students who lag behind special instruction.*

【开心】① feel happy; be delighted: 他取得了进步，父母很~。*His parents are rejoiced at his progress.* /孩子们玩积木玩得很~。*The children have a fun with the building blocks.* ② amuse oneself; make fun of sb: 你不要拿我~！*Stop teasing me!*

【开心果】【植】pistachio

【开心丸】words of comfort

【开行】start a car, train, ship, etc.: 快点！船就要~了！*Hurry up! The ship is to sail at once.*

【开学】school opens; term begins: 学生们九月~。*The students will begin a new term at September.*

【开学典礼】school's opening ceremony

【开颜】smile; beam

【开眼】open sb's eyes; broaden one's vision: 他到北京来了一趟，算是~了。*He really broadened his horizon after travelling in Beijing.*

【开演】（of a play, movie, etc.）begin: 电影六点半~。*The film will begin at half past six.*

【开洋】［方］dried, shelled shrimps

【开业】①（of a shop, etc.）start business ②（of a lawyer, doctor, etc.）open a private practice: ~行医 *practise medicine*

【开夜车】work late into the night; sit up late at work: 我今晚只有~才能按时完成任务。*I have to burn the midnight oil in order to finish the job on time.*

【开音节】【语】open syllable

【开印】start printing: 本报今日四点~。*The newspapers will be printed at four today.*

【开映】（film）start showing

【开元音】【语】open vowel

【开园】picking starts at an orchard or melon field

【开源节流】open up the source and regulate the flow — increase income and reduce expenditure; tap new resources and cut dow expenses

【开云见日】disperse the clouds and see the sun — remove misunderstanding

【开凿】cut; dig: ~隧道 *dig a tunnel*

【开斋】①（of one on a vegetarian diet）resume a meat diet ②【宗】come to the end of Ramadan

【开斋节】【宗】Lesser Bairam; Festival of Fastbreaking

【开展】① develop; launch; promote: ~技术革新 *carry out technical innovation* /妇女组织决定~一项全国性的"同工同酬"运动。*Women's organizations have decided to launch a nationwide campaign for "equal work, equal pay".* /警方已经针对这个老人的失踪~了调查。*Police have opened an investigation into the old man's disappearance.* ②（of an exhibition）open ③ open-minded; enlightened: 思想~ *be open-minded*

【开战】① make war; open hostilities: 他认为人类频繁~是因为其侵略的本性。*He believes that men make war frequently because they are by nature aggressive.* ② battle against sth: 向封建主义~ *combat feudalism*

【开张】① start a business: 这家超市明天~。*The supermarket will open a business tomorrow.* ② make the first transaction for the day: 我今天还没~呢。*I haven't made the first transaction today.* ③ beginning; start ④［书］open-minded; receptive ⑤［书］vast and magnificent: 气势~ *with great momentum*

【开仗】① make war ②［方］fight: 你看，他们俩又~了。*Look! Those two are fighting again!*

【开账】① make out a bill ② pay or take the bill: 我已经~了。*I have paid the bill.*

【开征】levy（taxes）; tax: ~所得税 *collect income tax*

【开支】① pay; spend: 他的学费由父母~。*His tuition is paid by his parents.* ② expenses; expenditure: 节省~ *reduce expense* ③［方］pay wages or salaries: 我明天~。*I'll get my pay tomorrow.*

【开罪】offend; displease: 他经常~那些本可以帮助他的人。*He often offended those who might have been helpful to him.*

揩 wipe; rub: 把脸~干净 *wipe one's face clean*

【揩布】rag; dishcloth: 用~擦桌子 *clean a table with a rag*

【揩拭】clean; cleanse: ~桌面 *clean the table*

【揩油】get petty advantage; scrounge: 他揩了公家的油，拿了一些公款。*He pocketed a portion of public funds.*

kǎi

凯 ① triumphant strains; triumphant; victorious: 奏~而归 *return in triumph* ②（Kǎi）a surname

【凯恩斯】John Maynard Keynes（1883-1946）British economist: ~经济学 *Keynesian Economics* / ~主义 *Keynesianism*

【凯风】［书］south wind

【凯歌】paean; triumphant songs: ~归来 *return with songs of triumph*

【凯旋】triumph: ~柱 *triumphal column* / ~而归 *return in triumph*

【凯旋门】① triumphal arch ② Arch of Triumph; Arc de Triomphe (in Paris)

恺 [书] happy and harmonious

铠 armour: 铁~ *armour; mail*

【铠甲】(suit of) armour

【铠装】【电】armour; shield; sheath: ~玻璃 *armoured glass*

慨 ① indignant: 愤~ *indignation; soreness* ② sigh with emotion ③ generous: 慷~ *unstinting; generous*

【慨然】① with deep feeling: ~长叹 *heave a sigh of regret* ② generously; without stint: ~相赠 *give sth as a gift generously* /她~允诺借钱给我。*She generously promised to lend me money.*

【慨叹】sigh with regret: "我希望当时告诉了他真相," 她~到。"*I wish I had told him the truth," she sighed with regret.*

【慨允】consent readily: ~捐助 *kindly promise to contribute*

楷 ① model; pattern ② regular script, a type of popular Chinese calligraphy: 小~ *the regular script in small characters* /正~ *regular script*
see also jiē

【楷模】model; example: 他是诚实的~。*He is a model of honesty.* /老师的守时为学生们树立了一个~。*The teacher set a good example for the students by being punctual.*

【楷书】regular script

【楷体】① (of Chinese calligraphy) regular script ② block letter (of phonetic alphabet)

kài

忾 [书] hatred: 同仇敌~ *share a bitter hatred of the enemy*

kān

刊 ① engrave: ~石 *engrave on a stone* /停~ (*of a newspaper, magazine, etc.*) *stop publication* ② publication: 月~ *a monthly publication; monthly* /周~ *a weekly publication; weekly* /纪念~ *memorial volume* /特~ *special issue* ③ delete; correct: 不~之论 *perfectly sound proposition*

【刊本】edition of a book: 原~ *original block-printed edition*

【刊播】publish and broadcast (an item of news)

【刊布】[书] print and publish

【刊登】publish; carry: ~消息 *publish the news* /所有的报纸都~了这则消息。*All the newspapers carried the news.*

【刊定】revise and finalize

【刊发】publish; carry

【刊后语】postface

【刊刻】cut blocks; block-print

【刊落】[书] delete; strike out

【刊授】teach through publications; give courses through periodicals

【刊头】masthead of a newspaper or magazine: 设计~ *design a newspaper masthead*

【刊物】publication: 内部~ *restricted publication* /非法~ *illegal publication*

【刊误】correct errors in printing

【刊误表】errata; corrigenda

【刊行】print and publish

【刊印】set up and print; block-print

【刊载】publish; carry: 分期~ *serially published* /晚报~了这个故事。*The evening papers carried the story.*

【刊正】proofread and correct; rectify

看 ① guard; look after: ~门 *guard the entrance* / ~家 *look after the house* ② keep under surveillance: ~住他 *detain him*
see also kàn

【看财奴】miser; skinflint; tightwad; cheapskate: 他抱怨说丈夫是个~,从来不给她钱花。*She complains that her husband is a miser who never lets her have any money.*

【看管】① guard; watch: ~犯人 *guard the prisoner* ② look after; attend to: 他们在我们不在时~事务。*They attended our affairs during our absence.*

【看护】① nurse; look after: ~病人 *look after the patient* / ~婴儿 *watch a baby* /她~孩子。*She nursed the children.* ② [旧] hospital nurse

【看家】① look after the house; house-sit ② outstanding ability; special skill

【看家本领】one's stock-in-trade; one's special ability

【看家狗】watchdog

【看家戏】play or opera one is particularly good at

【看门】① look after the house ② door-keeper; janitor

【看门人】gate keeper; watchman

【看青】keep watch over ripening crops

【看守】① look after; take care of ② watch; guard: ~一群羊 *watch a flock of sheep* /狗~着房子。*The dog guarded the house.* ③ jailer; turnkey: 女~ *wardress; matron*

【看守所】lockup; detention house

【看押】take into custody; detain: 罪犯被警方~。*The police took the criminal into custody.*

【看养】① raise; rear: ~牲口 *raise livestock* ② look after; bring up: ~孩子 *look after a child*

勘 ① read and correct the text of: 校~ *collate* ② investigate; survey: 踏~ *make a field survey*

【勘测】survey: 地质~ *geological survey* /地形~ *topographical survey* / ~队 *survey party*

【勘察】① reconnoiter: ~地形 *terrain reconnaissance* ②【地】prospect; survey: 实地~ *on-the-spot survey*

【勘定】① survey and determine ② [书] check and ratify; appraise and decide

K

【勘校】collate; proofread
【勘界】boundary settlement
【勘探】exploration; prospecting: 磁性～ *magnetic prospecting* /地质～ *geological exploration* /地震～ *seismic prospecting* /电磁～ *electromagnetic prospecting* /电法～ *electrical prospecting* /海床的～和开发 *exploration and exploitation of seabed* /无线电～ *radio prospecting* /重力～ *gravity prospecting*
【勘问】[书] question; interrogate
【勘误】correct errors in printing
【勘误表】errata; corrigenda
【勘验】inspect; examine
【勘正】proofread and correct
龛 niche; shrine: 佛～ *Buddha's niche; Buddhist altar*
【龛影】【医】niche (the location or image of an ulcer as observed in an X-ray)
堪 ① may; can: 不～设想 *cannot be imagined; be dreadful to contemplate* ② bear; endure: 不～回首 *can't bear to look back* /不～一击 *can't withstand a single blow*
【堪布】【宗】① lama in charge of the commandments ② head or abbot of a lamasery ③ title of a monk official in the former Tibetan local government
【堪察加半岛】Kamchatka Peninsula (in northeast Russia)
【堪达罕】[方] elk; moose
【堪当重任】be capable of holding an important position; be capable of shouldering important tasks
【堪培拉】Canberra, capital of Australia
【堪萨斯】Kansas, state in central United States
戡 suppress; put down; quell
【戡乱】[旧] suppress (or put down) a rebellion
【戡平】succeed in suppressing a rebellion

kǎn

坎[1] ① one of the Eight Diagrams, representing water ② ridge: 田～ *a raised path through fields* ③ [书] pit; hole
坎[2] 【物】candela
【坎肩儿】sleeveless jacket; vest: 皮～ *leather waistcoat* /棉～ *padded sleeveless jacket*
【坎井】① pit; trap; pitfall ② abandoned well
【坎坷】① bumpy; rough: 山路～ *rugged mountain path* ② [书] full of frustrations: 她一生～。*Her life was full of frustrations.*
【坎儿】critical moment; important juncture
【坎子】raised ground: 土～ *mound*
侃[1] [书] ① upright and honest ② cheerful; happy
侃[2] [方] chat idly: 这个人可能～了。*The guy is a real talker.*
【侃大山】[方] chat idly; gossip: 老板一走，他们就继续～。*The boss walked away and they returned to their gossip.* /不要～了，我们是来谈公事的。*Stop chatting, we are here to talk business*
【侃侃】[书] ① joyful ② upright and straightforward ③ with ease and composure
【侃侃而谈】speak with ease and assurance; speak unhurriedly and assuredly
【侃爷】[方] big talker; gossip: 不要告诉他任何私事，他可真是个～。*Don't tell him anything private — he is a terrible gossip.*
砍 ① chop; cut: ～树 *chop at a tree; hew a tree* /把树枝～下来 *cut off a branch* /渔夫在冰上～出一个洞来。*The fisherman chopped a hole in the ice.* ② cut; reduce: 从计划中～去一些项目 *cut some projects from the plan* ③ [方] throw at sth or sb: 拿砖头～狗 *throw bricks at the dog*
【砍刀】chopper; broadsword
【砍伐】fell (a tree); cut down: ～木材 *fell timber* /他们在荒野中～出一条路。*They cleaved a path through the wilderness.*

kàn

看 ① see; look at; watch: ～书 *read* / ～电影 *see a film; go to the cinema* /～电视 *watch TV* / ～我的新衣服！*Look at my new dress!* ② view; consider; judge: 全面～事物 *view things in their totality* /我～他能胜任。*I think he is competent.* /我～他是个内行。*I consider him as an expert.* /我～形势很危险。*I judge the situation very dangerous.* ③ visit; go to see: 我昨天去～了一个朋友。*I visited a friend of mine yesterday.* ④ regard; treat: 另眼相～ *treat sb with special respect* /我把他当哥哥～。*I regard him as my elder brother.* ⑤ treat (a patient or an illness): 我的病恐怕～不好了。*I'm afraid my illness won't get cured.* ⑥ take care of; look after: 照～病人 *attend to the sick* /你不在家时，我将照～你的孩子。*I'll take care of your baby when you are away.* ⑦ used to show sth is going to happen: 别跑！～摔着！*No running! Mind you don't get stumbled!* ⑧ try and see: 试试～ *have a try* /等等～ *wait and see*
see also kān
【看病】① (of a doctor) see a patient: 大夫正在～。*The doctor is treating a patient now.* ② (of a patient) see a doctor; consult a doctor: 我感冒了，下午要去～。*I've caught a cold and I will see the doctor this afternoon.*
【看不出】unable to detect or judge: ～真假 *cannot tell whether sth is genuine or fake*
【看不惯】can't bear the sight of; hate to see sb or sth: 我～这些拍马屁的人。*I hate to see those flatterers.*
【看不起】look down upon; belittle; scorn; despise; turn up one's nose at; make light of: 她～穷人。*She belittles the poor.* /你没有任何理由～他。*You've no reason to think scorn of him.*
【看成】look upon as; regard as: 他们被～最有希望

K

的运动员。*They are regarded as the most promising players.*

【看承】[书] look after; take care of

【看出】see; make out: ~苗头 *see a sign of sth* /我一眼就~他心情不好。*At first sight I knew he was in low spirit.*

【看穿】see through: 我一眼就~了你那套把戏。*I saw through your little game at a glance.* /没有人~他的伪装。*Nobody saw through his disguise.* /我~了他的阴谋。*I was wise to his schemes.*

【看错】mistake sb or sth for; be mistaken: 我~人了,还以为您是我的邻居。*I mistook you for my neighbour.*

【看待】regard; consider; treat: 我们把他当自家人~。*We treat him as a member of our own family.*

【看得起】think highly of; think much of: 他似乎很~那个作家。*It seems that he thinks highly of that writer.*

【看低】underestimate; understate; belittle; trivialize: 我认为你~了年轻人在社会中的重要性。*I think you are understating the importance of young people in the society.* /千万不要~沟通的价值。*Never underestimate the value of communicating.*

【看跌】(of market prices) be expected to fall: 最近股市~。*The stock market tends to be bearish recently.*

【看法】① view; point of view; opinion: 你的~如何? *What's your opinion?* /我能知道你对这个问题的~吗? *May I know your views on the question?* ③ [口] unfavourable opinion or judgement

【看风色】see or find out which way the wind blows: 别担心他。他很会~并照顾好自己。*Don't worry about him; he can see which way the wind is blowing and will look after himself.*

【看风使舵】trim one's sails to the wind; serve the time; see how the wind blows: ~者 *time-server*

【看好】① look up; get better: 旅游市场~。*The tourism market is getting better.* ② expect sb or sth to win: 这场比赛我~北京队。*I expect Beijing Team to win the match.*

【看见】catch sight of; see: 你刚才~校长了吗? *Did you see the headmaster just now?* /我看了,但是什么也没~。*I looked but saw nothing.* /我~了一张奇怪的脸。*I caught sight of a strange face.*

【看开】accept an unpleasant fact with equanimity; resign oneself (to a hard situation)

【看看】① look carefully; examine: 你~,这是赝品。*Examine carefully and you'll find it is a counterfeit.* ② soon; in a moment: ~时间不早了,我便向他们告辞。*Soon it is late, and I said good-bye to them.*

【看客】[方] spectators; viewers; onlooker

【看破】① see through: ~骗局 *see through a trick* ② become disillusioned; take nothing to heart: ~红尘 *see through human vanity* /你要学会~名利,自在地生活。*You should learn to regard fame and gain as noting and then live a happy life.*

【看齐】① dress: 向右~! *Dress right, dress!* ② keep up with; emulate: 在学习上你要向先进者~。*You should keep up with the more advanced ones in studying.*

【看起来】it looks as though; appear; seem: ~我们必须走了。*It appears that we must go.* /~他很满意这个计划。*He seems to be satisfied with the plan.*

【看轻】underestimate; look down upon; belittle; disguise; scorn: 不是我~他的成果,他确实从同事那里获得了很多帮助。*I don't mean to belittle his achievement, but he did have a lot of help from his colleagues.*

【看清】① see clearly: 你能~黑板吗? *Can you see clearly the blackboard?* ② realize: 他终于~了形势的严重性。*He finally realized the gravity of the situation.*

【看热闹】watch the scene of bustle; look on: 他站在一旁~。*He looked on passively.*

【看人下菜】[喻] treat people according to their social status; be snobbish: 我的邻居真会~。我被解雇后,他就不和我说话了。*My neighbour was so snobbish; just because I was fired, he didn't even talk to me.*

【看上】fall in love with sb; settle on: 你是不是~了隔壁的姑娘? *Have you fallen in love with the girl in neighbourhood?* /他~了这块表。*He likes this watch.*

【看手相】tell someone's future by examining the lines on the palm of one's hand

【看台】【体】stands; bleachers

【看透】① understand completely: 我彻底~了他的用意。*I understand fully his meaning.* ② see through: 看不透那件事 *be unable to see through that matter* /他~了我的心思。*He had an insight into my mind.*

【看望】visit; see: 我明天要去医院~病人。*I will visit the sick in the hospital tomorrow.*

【看相】tell sb's fortune by reading one's face: 他最近想请人~。*He wants to visit a fortune-teller recently.*

【看笑话】watch sb make a fool of himself or herself; make a mockery: 如果那个人被释放了,我们的法律体系就被人~了。*If that man gets released, it will make a mockery of our legal system.*

【看涨】(of market prices) be expected to rise; be on the rise: 行情~。*Market will be strong.*

【看中】settle on; be satisfied with sb or sth: 他~了那件白衬衫。*He is quite satisfied with that white shirt.*

【看重】regard as important; value; think a lot of: 我很~你的劝告。*I value your advice much.*

【看作】regard; look upon; consider; think of; take the view that: 她总是穿着怪异,被大家~怪人。*He always wore strange clothes and was widely regarded as eccentric.* /大部分人把达·芬奇~是个伟大的艺术家,事实上他还是个伟大的科学家。*Most people think of Leonardo da Vinci as a great artist, but in fact he was also a great scientist.*

瞰 ① overlook：鸟～ *get a bird's-eye view* ②［书］peep；look

kāng

康 ① healthy：安～ *safe and sound* ②［书］well-being；affluence：～年 *good year* ③（Kāng）a surname
【康复】recover；recuperate：祝您早日～。*Hope you'll soon be well again.*
【康复中心】health recovery centre
【康健】healthy
【康乐】peace and happiness
【康乃馨】【植】carnation；clove pink（*Dianthus caryophullus*）
【康宁】［书］healthy and sound
【康平】［书］peace and stability
【康泰】［书］healthy；peaceful：身体～ *healthy；in good health*
【康庄大道】broad road；main road

慷
【慷慨】① vehement；fervent ② generous；liberal：～援助 *generous assistance*
【慷慨陈词】speak with fervour；present one's views vehemently
【慷慨激昂】impassioned；vehement
【慷慨解囊】help sb generously with money；give money freely：他为朋友～。*He lavished money on his friends.*
【慷慨就义】go to one's death like a hero；die a hero
【慷他人之慨】be generous at the expense of others；be liberal with other people's money；make free with other's money

糠 ① chaff；bran；husk：稻～ *paddy chaff* / 米～ *rice bran* ② spongy：萝卜～了。*The radish has gone spongy.*
【糠秕】① chaff；bran ② worthless stuff
【糠麸】chaff；bran；husk
【糠虾】opossum shrimp；mysis
【糠油】oil abstracted from bran
【糠疹】【医】pityriasis

káng

扛 carry on the shoulder；shoulder：～枪 *shoulder a gun* / 他肩上～了一只箱子。*He was carrying a box on his shoulder.*
see also gāng
【扛长工】work as a farmhand on a yearly basis
【扛大个儿】［方］work as a stevedore or porter
【扛活】work as a farm labourer

kàng

亢 ① high：高～ *loud and sonorous* ② haughty：不卑不～ *behave modestly but without undue self-effacement* ③ excessive ④ a star constellation, one of the twenty-eight constellations ⑤（Kàng）a surname
【亢奋】excessively excited；in high spirits：～的运动员很快就平静下来了。*The excessively excited athlete soon calmed down.*
【亢旱】sever drought
【亢进】【医】hyperfunction；sthenia：甲状腺机能～ *hyperthyroidism*
【亢礼】［书］salute each other as equals

伉 ①［书］equal；（of spouse）fit for each other ②［书］lofty；tall ③（Kàng）a surname
【伉俪】married couple；husband and wife：结为～ *be married；get married*
【伉直】［书］honest；upright

抗 ① resist；combat：对～ *confront；withstand；antagonize* / 抵～ *counteract；fight back；resist* ② defy；refuse：～粮 *resist the grain levy* / ～租 *stop paying rent* ③ contend with；be match for：分庭～礼 *stand up to sb as an equal；act independently and defiantly*
【抗暴】fight against violent repression
【抗辩】① contradict；refute：彬彬有礼地～是很难做到的。*It's difficult to contradict someone politely.* ②【律】counterplea；demurrer：进行～ *put in a demurrer* / 他们是来应诉，不是～的。*They didn't came to raise defences，but to challenge the court jurisdiction.*
【抗病】【农】disease-resistant.
【抗病毒】antiviral：～性 *antiviral property*
【抗虫害】【农】pest-resistant
【抗磁】【物】diamagnetism：～材料 *diamagnetic material*
【抗倒伏】【农】lodging-resistant；resistant to lodging
【抗丁】fight against press-ganging：～抗粮 *resist press-ganging and the grain levy*
【抗冻剂】anti-freezing agent
【抗辐射】radio resistance；radiation hardening
【抗腐蚀】resistant to corrosion
【抗干扰】anti-interference：～素 *anti-interferon*
【抗旱】fight a drought；combat a drought：～性 *drought resistance* / ～作物 *drought-resistant crops*
【抗衡】rival；compete；match；act as a counterweight to：处于激烈的～中 *be in a fierce rivalry*
【抗洪】fight a flood：～排涝 *fight the flood and drain waterlogged areas*
【抗婚】refuse to marry the person chosen by one's family
【抗击】resist；fight back：～侵略者 *resist the aggressors*
【抗静电】antistatic electricity：～剂 *antistat*
【抗拒】resist；defy；refuse：～从严 *severe punish-*

ment to those who refuse to confess their crimes / ~心理 *negativism* / 自然规律是不可~的。*One can never resist the laws of nature.*

【抗捐】refuse to pay levies

【抗涝】prevent water-logging

【抗粮】refuse to hand in grain

【抗命】① defy orders; disobey ② defy one's destiny

【抗日战争】War of Resistance against Japanese Aggression (1937—1945)

【抗生素】【药】antibiotic: 广谱~ *broad spectrum antibiotic*

【抗税】refuse to pay taxes

【抗诉】【律】appeal against a judgement; protest

【抗体】【医】antibody

【抗氧化】antioxidant: ~剂 *antioxidant*

【抗药性】【医】resistance to drugs

【抗胰岛素】【生化】anti-insulin

【抗议】protest; object: ~书 *protest letter* / 提出~ *lodge a protest* / 激起多方面的强烈~ *excite bitter protests from many sources* / 他挥舞拳头，用强烈的语言表示~。*Waving fists, he objected in strong language.* / 成千上万的工人和学生~美国参战。*Thousands of workers and students demonstrated against US involvement in the war.*

【抗抑郁剂】【医】antidepressant

【抗御】resist and defend against

【抗原】【医】antigen

【抗灾】fight or combat natural disasters

【抗战】① war of resistance against aggression ② War of Resistance Against Japanese Aggression (1937-1945)

【抗震】① anti-seismic: ~设计 *aseismatic design* ② take preventive measures to reduce the loss as caused by an earthquake: 防震~ *prevent and reduce the loss from an earthquake* / ~救灾 *combat the earthquake and do relief work*

【抗争】oppose; resist; fight for; work for; campaign: 世界上每个国家的妇女都要为平等~。*In every country of the world women have had to fight for equality.* / 他一直为变更有关同性恋的法律而~。*He kept campaigning to change the law on homosexuality.*

炕 ① *kang*, a brick bed ② [方] bake or dry by the heat of a fire

【炕梢】further end of a *kang*; cooler end of a *kang*

【炕头】① warmer end of *a kang* ② edge of a *kang*

【炕席】kang mat

【炕桌儿】table used on *kang*

kǎo

考[1] ① test; quiz; question: 他居然把老师给~住了。*It's amazing that his question has baffled his teacher.* ② take (or give) an examination, test, etc.: 补~ *make-up exam* / ~大学 *take college entrance examination* / 期中~ *mid-term examination* ③ check; inspect ④ investigate; study: 参~ *consult; refer to*

考[2] [书] one's father; one's deceased father: 先~ *my late father* / 如丧~妣 *look as if one has lost one's parents — look utterly wretched*

【考妣】[书] deceased parents

【考查】check; examine: ~学生成绩 *check students' work*

【考察】① inspect; investigate on the spot: 出国~ *go abroad on a tour of investigation* / 俄、美小组有权互相~对方的导弹基地。*Russian and American teams have the right to inspect each other's missile sites.* ② observe and study

【考场】examination room

【考点】examination place

【考订】examine and correct

【考分】result of an examination

【考古】① engage in archaeological studies: ~发现 *archaeological discovery* ② archaeology

【考古学】archaeology: ~家 *archaeologist*

【考官】[旧] examiner: 主~ *chief examiner*

【考核】check; assess: 工作~ *assessment of work* / ~标准 *assessment criteria*

【考绩】assess or appraise staff performance

【考究】① observe and study; investigate ② fastidious; choosy: 他对吃的东西很~。*He is very nice in his food.* ③ exquisite; fine: ~的缝纫 *fine sewing* / ~的酒杯 *an exquisite chalice*

【考据】textual criticism (or research)

【考卷】examination paper

【考量】consider; ponder; mull over; brood; muse; contemplate; meditate: 你应该给他时间仔细~。*You should give him time to consider.* / 他说每一句话都要仔细~。*He pondered his every word thoroughly.*

【考虑】consider; think over: 他~到法国去度假。*He is thinking of going to France for his holiday.* / 我们必须~他的意愿。*We must consider his desire.* / 他在回答我的问题之前仔细~了一下。*He reflected before answering my question.*

【考评】assess and evaluate

【考期】date of examination

【考勤】check on work attendance

【考区】area or regional examination centre

【考取】pass an entrance examination

【考生】candidate for an entrance examination

【考试】examination; test: 驾驶~ *driving test* / 他通过了英语~。*He passed English examination.*

【考释】do textual research and make explanations

【考题】examination question

【考问】examine orally

【考验】test; trial; ordeal: 他们的友谊经受了时间的~。*Their friendship stood the test of time.*

【考证】① textual criticism; textual research ② engage in textual research and criticism

拷 flog; beat

【拷贝】copy: ~机 *copying press* / ~纸 *copying paper*

【拷打】flog; beat

【拷问】torture during interrogation：严刑～ *subject sb to severe torture during interrogation*

栲 【植】evergreen chinquapin

【栲栳】 wicker basket

烤 ① bake or dry by the fire；roast；toast：～白薯 *baked sweet potatoes* ② warm oneself by the fire：～手 *warm one's hands by a fire*

【烤电】【医】diathermy

【烤火】 warm oneself by a fire

【烤架】 gridiron

【烤炉】 oven：搁架式～ *shelf oven；rack oven* / 固定底～ *fixed sole oven*

【烤面包】 toasted bread

【烤漆】 stove varnish

【烤肉】 barbecue；roast meat

【烤箱】 oven；toaster

【烤鸭】 roast duck

【烤烟】 flue-cured tobacco

【烤羊肉串】 mutton shish kebab

kào

铐 ① handcuffs：手～ *cuff；handcuffs；shackle* ② put handcuffs on sb：把犯人～起来 *handcuff the criminal*

【铐子】［方］ handcuffs

犒 reward with food and drink

【犒劳】① reward with food and drink ② rewarded food and drink

【犒赏】reward a victorious army, etc.：～三军 *feast and offer bounties to the army*

靠[1] ① lean against；lean on：～着桌子 *lean against the table* / 她们背～背坐着。*They sat back to back.* ②（of sth）lean or stand against：竹竿～在门上。*The bamboo stood against the back of the door.* ③ get near；come up to：船～岸了。*The ship has pulled in to shore.* ④ depend on；rely on：要想致富，只能～我们自己。*We can only depend on ourselves to become rich.* ⑤ trust：可～ *reliable；trustworthy* / 他办事很可～。*He is most dependable in whatever he does.*

靠[2] 【戏】military officer's armour

【靠岸】pull in to shore：～条款 *shore clause*

【靠把】【戏】stage armour

【靠背】back（of a chair）

【靠背椅】chair

【靠边】① keep to the side：～儿站 *stand aside；out of the way, please!* ②［方］ reasonable；sensible：这话说得还～儿。*That sounds reasonable.*

【靠边儿站】stand aside；get out of the way：～，让我过去。*Stand aside for me to pass.*

【靠不住】unreliable；untrustworthy：他说的话～。*What he said is unreliable.*

【靠得住】reliable；trustworthy：他是个～的人。*He is a man to be relied upon.*

【靠垫】cushion

【靠接】【植】grafting by approach；inarching：割裂～ *inarching by cleaving*

【靠近】① near；close to：那条船～海岸航行。*The ship kept close to the coast.* ② draw near；approach：禁区不许～。*It is not allowed to approach the forbidden area.*

【靠拢】draw close；close up：向左～！*Left close!*

【靠谱】reasonable；sound

【靠山】backer；patron：他是这个组织的主要经济～。*He is the organization's chief financial backer.* / 他急于在公司里找到一个～。*He is eager to get a backing in the company.*

【靠山吃山，靠水吃水】those living on a mountain get their living from the mountain；those living near the water get their living from the water — live on what the locality provides

【靠手】（of a chair）armrest

【靠枕】back cushion

【靠准】［方］ reliable；dependable；trustworthy：这消息～吗？*Is the information reliable?*

kē

坷

【坷垃】［方］ clod：打土～ *break clods*

苛 ① exacting；severe；harsh ② tedious；overelaborate：～礼 *overelaborate ritual*

【苛暴】［书］ harsh and cruel；tyrannical

【苛察】［书］ exacting；overcritical

【苛待】treat harshly；be hard upon：不要～这个年轻人，他还缺少经验。*Don't be too hard on the young man；he is still inexperienced.*

【苛捐杂税】exorbitant taxes and levies；multifarious taxes

【苛刻】harsh；relentless：待人～ *be hard on others* / 我不能接受他提出的～条件。*I cannot accept the harsh terms put forward by him.*

【苛求】be exacting；be overcritical；judge too harshly：最受宠爱的孩子往往最容易被～。*Sometimes it is the most loved child who is treated the most harshly.*

【苛性】【化】causticity：～钾 *caustic potash；kali* / ～碱 *caustic alkali* / ～钠 *caustic soda；sodium hydroxide*

【苛杂】［书］ exorbitant taxes and levies

【苛责】criticize；excoriate：～缺点 *make harsh criticism of one's shortcomings*

【苛政】tyrannical or oppressive government；tyranny：～猛于虎。*Tyranny is even more to be dreaded than tigers.*

珂 ［书］① a jade-like stone ② an ornament on a bridle：玉～ *a jade ornament*

【珂罗版】collotype：～印刷 *collotype printing*

柯 ①［书］ stalk or branch：交～错叶 *with branches intertwined and leaves touching each other* ②［书］ *axe-handle；helve* ③（Kē）a surname

科[1] ① a term of division; discipline; department: 学～ *branch of study* / 文～ *liberal arts*; *humanities* / 理～ *science*; *natural sciences* / 本～ *undergraduate programme* / 专～ *vocational study* / 内～ *medical department* / 外～ *surgery department* ② administrative section: 财务～ *finance section* / 总务～ *general affairs section* ③ imperial examination during the period from the Sui and Tang dynasties to the Qing Dynasty: 登～ *pass the imperial civil examinations* ④ old-type Chinese opera schools: 坐～ *undergo professional training at an old-type Chinese opera school* ⑤【生】family: 狮子属于肉食类的猫～。*The lion belongs to the carnivorous cat family.* / 槐树是豆～植物。*The pagoda tree is a leguminous plant.*

科[2]［书］① legal articles or clauses: 犯～ *violate the law* / 金～玉律 *golden rule and precious precept*; *laws and regulations* ② impose a punishment: ～以罚金 *impose a fine on sb*

科[3] actor's or actress' actions and expressions in classical Chinese drama: 笑～ *laughs*

【科白】【戏】actions and spoken parts in classical Chinese drama

【科班】① old-type traditional opera school ② regular professional training: ～出身 *be a professional by training*

【科场】place where an imperial civil examination was held

【科处】impose a punishment: ～徒刑 *sentence sb to imprisonment*

【科第】grading of successful candidates in the imperial civil examination

【科幻】science fiction: ～小说 *science fiction*

【科技】science and technology: ～创造 *scientific and technological creation* / ～成果 *scientific and technological achievements* / ～大学 *university of science and technology* / ～进步 *advance of science and technology* / ～人才 *scientific research and technological personnel*

【科教】science and education: ～兴国 *make the country strong through science and education*

【科教片】science and educational film

【科举】imperial civil examination

【科盲】person who is ignorant of science

【科目】① subject; course: 必修～ *obligatory course* / 考试～ *an examination subject* ② grades of successful candidates in imperial civil examinations

【科普】popular science

【科室】administrative or technical offices; units at section level: ～人员 *office personnel*

【科威特】Koweit; Kuwait: ～人 *Kuwaiti*

【科学】① science: 保健～ *health science* / 边缘～ *borderline (or boundary) science* / 尖端～ *advanced science* / 精密～ *exact science* / 精神～ *mental science* / 人文～ *humanities* / 社会～ *social sciences* / 生命～ *life science* / 自然～ *natural science* / ～是老老实实的学问。*Science means honest, solid knowledge.* ② scientific: ～知识 *scientific knowledge* / ～种田 *scientific farming* / ～文献 *scientific literature*

【科学院】academy of sciences: 中国～ *Chinese Academy of Sciences*

【科研】scientific research: ～成果 *findings of scientific research* / ～机构 *scientific research institute* / ～经费 *cost of scientific research* / ～人员 *scientific research personnel*

【科员】a member of an administrative section

【科长】section chief; section manager

砢

【砢碜】［方］ugly; shabby or disgraceful

棵［量］used of plants: 一～树 *a tree* / 一～大白菜 *a (head of) Chinese cabbage*

【棵儿】size (of plants): 这棵树～很大。*This tree is very big.*

【棵子】［方］stem or stalk (of crops)

颏 chin, the lowest part of the face

嗑［方］words; talk: 唠～ *have a chat*

see also kè

稞

【稞麦】highland barley, raw material of the chief food of the Tibetans

窠 nest; burrow: 蜂～ *beehive*

【窠臼】［书］set pattern (usu. of writing or artistic creation): 不落～ *not be bound by conventions*

颗［量］used of round articles or granules: 一～牙齿 *a tooth* / 一～珠子 *a pearl*

【颗粒】① anything small and roundish ② (of cereals) each grain: ～归仓 *get every grain to the granary*; *harvest every single grain*

磕 ① knock (against sth hard): ～破头 *bump and break one's head* ② knock (sth out of a container): ～烟斗 *knock out one's pipe*

【磕巴】① stutter; stammer; lisp: 她～着向我道歉。*She stuttered out an apology to me.* / 他一紧张往往～。*He stammered when he was nervous.* ② one who stammers: ～需要经常接受语言治疗。*Those who stutter need regular speech therapy.*

【磕打】knock; knock out: 请把书上的泥巴～下去。*Please knock the dry mud off the book.*

【磕磕绊绊】① stumble; stagger; limp: 喝了一瓶酒后，他～地走上楼梯上了床。*Having drunk a bottle of wine, he stumbled upstairs and into bed.* ② hindrance; difficulty; trouble; snag: 两口子过日子免不了～。*Difficulties are only to be expected in a couple's life.*

【磕磕撞撞】stagger along; stumble: 我被击中了头部，～地走出了房间。*I was hit on the head and managed to stagger out of the room.*

【磕碰】① knock against; bump against: 他走路时，沉重的摄影机～着他的臀部。*The heavy video camera knocked against his hip as he walked.* / 虽然她眼瞎了，却能在附近活动并且不～到其他东西。*Although she is blind she can move around here without banging into things.* ② clash; squabble; rumpus; quarrel:他们之间总是发生~,但过后不久他们就忘了。*Squabbles frequently break out between them but they're soon forgotten.*

【磕碰儿】①[方] chip in a utensil ② setback; difficulty:尽管有许多~,我还是决心要出国。*In spite of all the setbacks I am still determined to go abroad.* /婚姻中难免有~。*Marriage has its ups and downs.*

【磕头】kowtow

【磕头碰脑】① bump against things on every side:淘气的小男孩整天~的。*The naughty boy bumps himself all the day.* ② rub elbows with each other; meet often:我们在同一所学校,整天~的。*We are in the same school and meet frequently.* ③ clash or quarrel between people:他们俩总是~的。*They are always in conflicts.*

【磕膝盖】[方] knee

【磕牙】[方] chat; banter:闲~ *engage in chitchat*

瞌

【瞌睆】[方] sleep; doze

【瞌睡】sleepy; drowsy:打~ *have a nap*

【瞌睡虫】①(in traditional stories) sleep-inducing insect ② sleepyhead:他是个不可救药的~! *He is an incurable sleepyhead!*

蝌

【蝌蚪】tadpole

【蝌子】[方] tadpole

髁 【生理】condyle

ké

壳 shell, a hard outer covering:鸡蛋~ *egg shell* /核桃~ *walnut shell*
see also qiào

咳 cough:干~ *dry cough*
see also hāi

【咳喘】asthmatic cough

【咳嗽】cough:~糖浆 *cough syrup* /感冒使我~。*My cold made me cough.*

揢 [方] ① get stuck; wedge:抽屉~住了。*The drawer is stuck.* ② make things difficult; create difficulties:他总是~我。*He is always trying to make things difficult for me.*

kě

可[1] ① approve; agree:许~ *permit; allow* /认~ *approve* /不加~否 *neither approve nor deny* ② can; may:~大~小 *may be big or small* /牢不~破 *unbreakable; indestructible* ③ need doing; be worth doing:这个电影~看。*The film is worth seeing.* ④[书] about:年~四十 *at the age of about forty* /重~百斤 *weigh about* 100 *jin* ⑤[方] go as far as is possible:他疼得~地打滚。*He rolled all over the place in pain.* ⑥ be fully recovered ⑦(Kě) a surname

可[2] ① but; yet:我很喜欢那块表,~它太贵了。*I like the watch very much, but it's too expensive.* /她虽然很累~很高兴。*She was very tired and yet very glad.* ② used for emphasis:她唱歌~好听了! *She sings very well.* /他跑得~快了,谁都赶不上他。*He ran so fast that nobody could catch up with him.* ③ used to ask a rhetoric question:~不是吗? *Isn't it so?* ④ used in a question to express doubt:这话~是真的? *Is that true?* /你~曾跟他说过这件事? *Did you ever mention it to him?*

可[3] fit; suit:~人意 *agreeable to one; just what one wants* /这条裙子你~心吗? *Does the dress suit you?*
see also kè

【可爱】lovely; likeable; charming; delightful:~的祖国 *my beloved country* /这花儿真~。*What a lovely flower!*

【可保】insurable:~财产 *insurable property* / ~价值 *insurable value*

【可悲】sad; deplorable; miserable; lamentable:~的失败 *a miserable failure* / ~的是,我弄丢了那张票。*Sad to say, I lost that ticket.*

【可比】comparable:我们的汽车和你们的是不~的。*Our car is not comparable with yours.*

【可比性】comparability:国际~ *international comparability*

【可鄙】contemptible; mean:~的动机 *a mean motive* / ~的屈服 *abject submission* /那是对朋友玩弄的一出~的把戏。*That was a contemptible trick to play on a friend.* /你抛弃你的妻子是~的。*It is despicable to desert your wife.*

【可不】right; exactly:"我看您老七十上下。""~,今年五月就整七十了。""*I guess you are around seventy.*""*Exactly, I will reach seventy this May.*" /"听说您的儿子个子很高。""~,足有1米8呢!""*I heard that your son is very tall.*""*You said it! He is 180 cm high.*"

【可怖】horrible; terrible:~的事故 *a horrible accident*

【可拆】removable; detachable:~部分 *free section; removable section*

【可乘之机】opportunity that can be exploited to sb's advantage; an opportunity given by:我们不会给他任何~! *We will not give him any opportunity that can be made use of by him.* /他的不慎重给了敌人反对他的~。*His indiscretions gave his enemies a handle to use against him.*

【可持续发展】sustainable development

【可持续增长】sustainable growth

【可耻】shameful; disgraceful:~的行为 *a disgraceful conduct* /作弊是~的行为。*Cheating is shameful behaviour.*

【可丁可卯】① to the exact number; exactly:设计工作中必须~,因为一点小的失误也会造成很大差异。*You have to be very exact in the design, because a small mistake can make a big difference.* ② meticulous; inflexible; adamant:他是个~的人,绝不会收下你的礼物。*She was inflexible; she would have none of your gifts.* /他~,拒绝改变主意。*He was so adamant that he refused to change his mind.*

【可歌可泣】heroic and moving; epic; capable of evoking praises and tears

【可耕】【农】arable; cultivable: ~层 *arable layer*

【可耕地】arable land; cultivable land

【可观】① be worth seeing:我认为这部电影是~的。*I think the film is worth seeing.* ② considerable; sizable: ~的收入 *a respectable income* /损失相当~。*The losses are considerable.*

【可贵】valuable; commendable; admirable:精神~ *praiseworthy spirit*

【可好】just at the moment:我正要给他打电话,~他就给我打过来了。*I was about to give him a call when he phoned me.*

【可恨】hateful; detestable; abominable: ~的罪行 *detestable crimes; hateful crimes*

【可回收】recoverable; retrievable: ~卫星 *retrievable satellite* / ~运载火箭 *recoverable launching vehicle*

【可嘉】laudable:校长感谢孩子们~的勇气。*The headmaster thanked the children for their courage, which he said was most commendable.* /为使双方重归于好,他做出了~的努力。*He has made a praiseworthy attempt to bring the two sides together.* /他在这篇作文上所作的努力是~的。*He made a creditable effort on the composition.*

【可见】① it is evident that:由此~,他欺骗了大家。*It is clear that he cheated all of us.* ② visible: ~极光 *visual aurora*

【可见度】visibility

【可见光】【物】visible light

【可见光谱】visible spectrum

【可敬】worthy of respect; respectable:一位~的老人 *a respectable old man*

【可卡因】cocaine: ~瘾 *cocaine addiction*

【可靠】reliable; dependable: ~的消息来源 *a reliable source of information* /这很~吗? *Is it quite certain?* /~的人是可以信任的。*A trust worthy person is the one that you can trust.*

【可靠性】reliability; probability of reliability:安全~ *safe reliability* /高~ *high reliability* /使用~ *use reliability; work reliability* /线路~ *circuit reliability* /最大~ *maximum reliability* / ~保证 *reliability assurance* / ~函数 *reliability function* / ~系数 *reliability coefficient* / ~指数 *reliability index*

【可可】cocoa: ~奶 *cocoa milk* / ~粉 *cocoa powder* / ~豆 *cocoa beans* / ~香精 *cocoa essence; cocoa flavour* / ~油脂 *cocoa butter*

【可可儿的】[方] just at the moment:我正想出去晾衣服,~就下起雨来。*I was about to dry the clothes in the sun when it began to rain.*

【可垦地】reclaimable land

【可控】controllable; steerable: ~成本 *controllable costs* / ~费用 *controllable expenses*

【可口】agreeable to the taste; palatable; tasty; delicious: ~的菜肴 *tasty dishes* /是胡椒让菜肴如此~。*It is the pepper which gives the dish its delicious flavour.*

【可口可乐】Coca-Cola

【可怜】① pitiful; poor; miserable: ~的家伙 *a poor fellow* /那些乞丐的生活多~呀! *What a wretched life those beggars lead!* ② pity; have pity on:我~你。*I pity you.* /我们一点也不~那个倒霉的骗子。*We had little sympathy to spare for the unfortunate swindler.* /她~那些饥饿的孩子们。*Her heart yearned for the starving children.* ③ meager; miserable; wretched:少得~ *pathetically meager* /他们给犯人少得~的定量。*They fed the prisoners miserable rations.* /他的学术水平低得~。*His academic standards were pathetic.*

【可怜巴巴】pitiable; pitiful:他看上去~的,身体因饥饿而格外虚弱。*He looked pitiful, his body very weak with hunger.*

【可怜虫】pitiful creature; poor fellow; pilgarlic:这个~立刻就后悔自己所犯的罪行了。*The pathetic creature regretted his crime immediately.*

【可能】① possible; probable; likely: ~范围内 *in so far as it is possible* /科学家现在正在努力去探索这是否有~。*Scientists are now trying to discover if this is possible.* /今天~会有暴风雨。*A storm is probable today.* ② possibility; probability:你有~去国外工作吗? *Is it a possibility that you will work abroad?* ③ probably; perhaps:把鞋从火炉边拿走,不然就~烧着的。*Take away the shoes from the heat of the fire, or they might get burnt.* /他明天~来。*Perhaps he will come tomorrow.*

【可能误差】possible error

【可能性】possibility; probability:极小的~ *remote possibility* /有几种~。*There are several possibilities.* /看来他通过考试的~不大。*There seems to be little probability of his passing the exam.*

【可逆】reversible: ~变化 *reversible change* / ~定理 *law of reciprocity* / ~反应 *reversible reaction* / ~函数 *invertible function* / ~矩阵 *invertible matrix*

【可怕】frightening; fearful; dreadful; terrible; scary; terrifying: ~的贫穷 *fearful poverty* / ~的热 *the dreadful heat* /这有什么~的? *What is there to be afraid of?* /核战争的料想是~的。*Nuclear war is a frightening prospect.* /他向我们讲述了发生过的~的事情。*He gave us a spine-chilling account of what have happened.*

【可欺】① easily teased or bullied:不要把我的沉默视为~。*Don't take my silence for a sign of weakness.* ② easily duped; gullible:老实~ *be simple-minded and gullible*

【可气】annoying; troublesome; bothersome; exasperating: ~的苍蝇一直在屋子里飞。*The annoying flies kept flying in the room.*

【可巧】as luck would have it:我正想从图书馆借这本书,~他就有一本。*I was going to borrow the*

K

book from the library when I found that he just got one.

【可亲】genial; amiable:当她对孩子说话的时候,显得十分~。*She looks amiable enough when she speaks to children.*

【可取】desirable; advisable:一无~ *nothing to recommend* /这个方法是~的。*This course of action is advisable.* /这几个学生各有~之处。*Each of the students has his special advantages.*

【可燃】combustible; inflammable

【可燃物】combustible matter

【可人】[书]① one who has apparent merits or desirable qualities ② person one loves; sweetheart ③ satisfying; pleasant: ~的小女孩儿 *a beautiful and attractive girl*

【可溶】【化】soluble: ~于水 *be soluble in water*

【可溶物质】soluble substance

【可溶性】【化】solubility: ~淀粉 *soluble starch* / ~物质 *soluble matter* / ~盐 *soluble salt*

【可熔】【化】fusible; meltable: ~保险丝 *electric fuse*

【可身】[方](of clothing) be a good fit:她穿这套衣服很~。*The suit fits her nicely.*

【可食】edible: ~菌 *edible fungus*

【可是】① but; yet; however:我本来要写信的,~把你的地址弄丢了。*I was going to write, but I lost your address.* /这本书很贵,~很值。*The book is expensive; however, it's worth it.* ② used for emphasis

【可视电话】picture-phone; videophone

【可视数据】【电】videotex; viewdata

【可视图文】【电】videotex

【可数名词】【语】countable noun

【可体】(of clothing) fit nicely:他穿这件衬衫很~。*The shirt fits him nicely.*

【可贴现票据】bankable bill

【可望而不可即】within sight but beyond reach; unattainable:那对我来说是一个~的目标。*That is an unattainable goal to me.*

【可谓】[书] it may be said; it may be called:这个机会~千载难逢。*This may be the chance of a life-time.* /他~全心全意为人民服务。*You can say that he serves the people heart and soul.*

【可恶】abhorrent; loathsome; hateful; detestable: ~之极 *utterly detestable*

【可惜】unfortunately; regrettable; it's a pity: ~他昨天没来。*It is a pity that he didn't come yesterday.* /她是个漂亮的姑娘,~有抽烟的毛病。*She is a pretty girl who has an unfortunate habit of smoking.*

【可惜了的】[方] it's too bad; what a pity; what a shame; unfortunately:"她因为大雪错过了音乐会。""~,她早就盼着了。"*"She missed the concert because of the heavy snow." "What a shame! She was really looking forward to it."*

【可喜】gratifying; heartening; satisfying:取得~的成绩 *achieve gratifying achievements*

【可想而知】one can imagine; be imaginable:他有三个小孩,~负担有多重。*He has three children to foster, and you can imagine how heavy the burden is.*

【可笑】① ridiculous; ludicrous; idiotic: ~的建议 *a ridiculous suggestion* / ~之至 *be ridiculous in the extreme* /我认为那个建议非常~,我不能相信任何一个有头脑的人会同意它。*I find that suggestion absolutely ludicrous and can't believe that any intelligent person would agree with it.* ② funny; amusing:他与人谈话时有一种~的眨眼睛的习惯。*He has a funny habit of blinking when talking with others.*

【可心】after one's heart; satisfying:她终于买了一顶~的帽子。*She finally bought a hat that she really liked.*

【可信】authentic; believable; credible; creditable: ~性 *credibility* / ~的证人 *credible witness*/ ~的故事 *a creditable story*

【可信度】reliability

【可行】feasible; workable: ~的计划 *a feasible plan*

【可行性】feasibility; practicability: ~报告 *feasibility report*

【可压缩】compressible: ~气体 *coercible gas*

【可疑】suspicious; dubious: ~行为 *suspicious behavior* /我认为这很~。一个没有工作的人怎么可能有这么多的钱? *It seems very suspicious to me; how can a man with no job have so much money?* /他卷入一些~的活动中。*He has been involved in some dubious activities.*

【可以】① can; may:我~进来吗? *May I come in?* /他~用你的字典吗? *Can he use your dictionary?* ② very good; passable:她说英文还~。*She speaks English very well.* ③ terrible; awful:她那张嘴真~! *What a sharp tongue she has got!*

【可意】gratifying; satisfactory:你的答案在他来看一定不会是~的。*Your answer will be anything but satisfactory to him.*

【可遇而不可求】may come by something with luck, but not by searching for it

【可用资产】available capital

【可造之材】a person suitable for training

【可憎】hateful; detestable; disgusting: ~的行为 *disgusting behaviours*

【可着】make the best use of sth:你就~这张纸画吧。*You can just make do with this paper.*

【可知论】【哲】theory of the knowability of the universe

【可知性】【哲】knowability

渴 ① thirsty:我很~。*I'm very thirsty.* /天热时我常感到~。*I often feel thirsty when it's very hot.* ② yearningly

【渴待】expect eagerly or yearningly; hanker after:人们~战争结束。*All the people yearn for an end to the war.*

【渴慕】admire greatly; dream of; yearn for:他拥有每个人都~的大产业。*He owns the biggest business anyone dreams of.*

【渴念】dream of; yearn for; long for:他~成为一名著名作家。*He dreamt of becoming a famous writer.*

【渴盼】look forward to; expect eagerly; crave:犯人最～自由。*Above all the prisoners yearned for freedom.*

【渴求】hope eagerly; strive for; crave:我一直～爱情和友谊。*I've always craved love and friendship.* /他的评论给了我一种～已久的认同感。*His comments gave me the feeling of recognition I craved for a long time.*

【渴望】long for; thirst for; crave:他～掌权。*He is thirsty for power.* /他～看到她。*He yearned to see her.* /我～出国旅行。*I am eager to travel abroad.*

【渴想】long for; want to know eagerly:我～知道考试结果。*I am anxious to know the result of the exam.*

kè

可

see also kě

【可汗】Khan, a title of rulers of ancient nationalities

克[1] ① can; be able to:不～分身 *unable to attend to anything else; be fully occupied* ② overcome:以柔～刚 *subdue toughness with softness* ③ win victory; conquer; capture:攻无不～ *all conquering; ever-victorious* /连～数城 *capture several cities one after another* ④ digest

克[2] set a strict limit: ～日完成 *set a time limit for the fulfillment of sth*

克[3] gram, a unit of weight (1 gram = 1/1000 kilogram)

【克敌制胜】defeat an enemy and win a victory

【克服】① overcome; conquer: ～困难 *surmount difficulties* / ～缺点 *rectify one's shortcoming; overcome one's shortcomings* /我终于～了恐高症。*I finally conquered my fear of heights.* ② put up with; make do:膳宿条件不是很好,咱们就～一下吧。*The accommodation here is not so satisfactory, but we can make do with it.*

【克复】recover; recapture: ～失地 *recover lost territory*

【克格勃】KGB (Russian acronym for the former Soviet State Security Committee); member of KGB

【克己】① be strict with oneself; be unselfish; self-control; self-command; self-master ② (of shops) reasonable; at low prices:价钱～ *reasonable price* ③ frugal:生活～ *live a frugal life*

【克己奉公】deny oneself and work wholeheartedly for the public interest; work selflessly for the public interest

【克己复礼】(as a Confucian ethical idea) exercise self-restraint and return to propriety

【克扣】embezzle part of what should be issued; deprive secretly: ～工资 *pocket part of the other person's wages*

【克拉】carat (about 0.2 gram)

【克里米亚】Crimea: ～会议 *the Crimea Conference* / ～战争 *the Crimean War*

【克里姆林宫】Kremlin: ～学 *Kremlinology*

【克利特岛】Crete, an island of southeast Greece in the eastern Mediterranean Sea

【克隆】clone: ～羊 *cloned sheep*

【克罗地亚】Croatia: ～共和国 *Republic of Croatia* / ～人 *Croat; Croatian*

【克期】set a time limit; set a date

【克勤克俭】be industrious and frugal; practise economy and diligence

【克日】set a date: ～完成 *set a time limit for the fulfillment of sth*

【克什米尔】Kashmir: ～人 *Kashmiri; Kashmirian* / ～羊毛料 *kerseymere*

【克食】help the digestion

【克星】jinx; natural enemy

【克抑】[书] control; restrain; suppress:她努力～住自己的怨恨。*She tried with all her might to bridle her resentment.* /他极大地冒犯了我,但是我～住自己的情绪并保持礼貌。*He offended me intensely, but I managed to control myself and remain polite.*

【克制】restrain; control:他能极好地～自己的脾气。*He controls his temper admirably.* /他难以～好奇心。*He had difficulty restraining his curiosity.*

刻 ① carve; engrave: 雕～ *carve and paint* ② unit of time when the water clock was used to measure time ③ quarter (of an hour):三点一～ *quarter past three* ④ moment: 即～ *at once; right now* /顷～ *in a moment* ⑤ in the highest degree: 深～ *penetrating; profound* ⑥ harsh; mean; biting:苛～ *harsh; biting*

【刻板】① cut wood at metal blocks (for printing) ② inflexible; stiff:他的表演很～。*His acting is mechanical.*

【刻薄】acerb; mean; unkind; cynical; caustic; tart; nasty: ～话 *caustic remarks* /待人～ *be harsh towards others* /言语～的演说 *an acrid speech* /你对她太～了。*You are too mean to her.* /我无法忍受他～的批评。*I cannot bear his biting criticism.* /他经常～地评论他的同事。*He often makes nasty comments about his colleagues.*

【刻薄鬼】meanie

【刻不容缓】no time to delay; be extremely urgent; cannot be delayed even a moment:这件事～。*It brooks no delay; it is of great emergency* /抑制通货膨胀是～的。*Getting inflation down is at the top of the agenda.*

【刻刀】nicking tool; burin

【刻毒】venomous; spiteful; malicious; malice; vindictive: ～的言论 *a venomous remark* /我受够了这村子里～的流言。*I've had enough of the malicious gossip that goes on in this town.* /离婚后,她的前夫变得越来越～。*After the divorce, her ex-husband became increasingly vindictive.*

【刻度】graduation (on a vessel or instrument):收音机～ *graduation of receiver* /线性～ *linear*

graduation
【刻度盘】division circle; dial scale: ~指针 *dial needle*
【刻度线】scale; scale mark
【刻工】① carving skill ② carver; engraver
【刻骨】engraved on one's bones; deeply ingrained: ~仇恨 *nurse an inveterate hatred for; harbour a bitter hatred for*
【刻骨铭心】remember to the end of one's life:他们的爱情让他~。*He will remember the love between them forever.*
【刻画】① engrave or draw ② depict; portray: ~入微 *portray to the life* / ~战争的恐怖 *depict the horrors of war*
【刻苦】① hardworking; painstaking; industrious: ~钻研 *study assiduously* / ~的研究者 *an unwearied researcher* /他学习~。*He is diligent in his studies.* ② thrifty; frugal:生活~ *lead a simple and frugal life*
【刻漏】water clock
【刻镂】carve; engrave
【刻露】[书] profound but lucid
【刻面】facet
【刻深】[书] ① deep; profound ② severe; harsh
【刻石】① carve or engrave a stone ② severe; harsh
【刻蚀】【地】sculpture; corrosion; mechanical erosion
【刻图】needle drawing; engraving: ~法 *scribing* / ~工具 *scribing tool*
【刻下】at present; right now: ~很忙 *be very busy right now*
【刻写】① cut stencils ② [书] carve; engrave
【刻意】strive sedulously: ~求精 *perfect one's skill assiduously*
【刻针】cutting stylus
【刻舟求剑】carve on gunwale of a moving boat — take measures without attention to the changes in circumstances
【刻字】carve or engrave characters on a seal, tablet, etc.

恪 [书] respectful and scrupulous
【恪守】scrupulously abide by (a treaty, promise, etc.): ~本分 *scrupulously abide by one's duty* / ~不渝 *adhere faithfully to sth; strictly abide by sth* / ~诺言 *honour one's promise* / ~法律 *reverently observing the law* /在这场辩论中她~中立,因为她对这个问题不感兴趣。*She kept neutral in this argument, as she wasn't interested in the subject.*
【恪遵】obey orders

客 ① visitor; guest: 宾~ *guest; visitor* /稀~ *rare visitor* /不速之~ *uninvited guest* /来~了。*We have a guest.* ② passenger; traveller:乘~ *passenger* ③ live or settle in a strange place: ~死他乡 *die abroad* ④ traveling merchant:珠宝~ *travelling jeweller* ⑤ customer; patron:顾~ *customer; client* ⑥ a person engaged in a particular purpose:说~ *persuader* /侠~ *a person adept in martial arts and ready to chivalrous conduct* /政~ *politician* ⑦ independent of human consciousness; objective ⑧ [量] used for food or drinks:三~布丁 *two helpings of pudding*
【客边】[方] alien land; strange land
【客边人】[方] person who lives in an alien land
【客舱】passenger cabin (on a ship, plane, etc.): 头等~ *first-class cabin*
【客场】【体】other team's home court (or ground)
【客车】① passenger train; passenger car ② coach; bus
【客船】passenger ship
【客串】(usu. of an amateur) play a part in a show as a guest performer: ~一电视系列剧 *guest on a television series*
【客店】inn; tavern:住~ *put up at an inn*
【客队】【体】visiting team
【客饭】① ordinary meal arranged for a visitor ② set meal
【客贩】trader from outside the area
【客房】① guest room ② room (in a hotel): ~经理 *resident manager* / ~服务员 *room-service waiter*
【客观】① objective, existing outside the mind:人类意识属于主观,物质世界属于~。*Human consciousness belongs to the subjective, while the material world belongs to the objective.* ② objective, not influenced by personal feelings:她看问题很~。*She looks at problems quite objectively.*
【客官】[旧] patron
【客馆】[旧] guest house
【客户】① [旧] tenant (farmer) ② [旧] immigrant; non-native resident ③ customer; client:大~ *major customer (or client)* / ~借款 *a charge to a customer's account*
【客机】passenger plane; airliner
【客籍】① province into which a settler has moved ② a settler from another place
【客家】Hakka: ~人 *Hakka (people)*
【客家话】Hakka dialect
【客居】live abroad; live away from home
【客流】volume of passenger traffic; passenger flow
【客流量】passenger flow
【客轮】passenger ship
【客满】be booked up:旅店已经~。*The hotel was well-filled; the hotel is filled to capacity.*
【客票】passenger ticket
【客气】① polite; courteous: ~话 *polite words* ② speak or behave politely:别~! *Please don't stand on ceremony.; Please don't bother.*
【客人】① guess; visitor: ~们三五成群地离去。*The guests departed in small groups.* ② patron; customer:小店里都是~。*The little shop is full of customers.*
【客商】traveling merchant (or trader)
【客死】die in a strange land
【客随主便】the guest must suit the convenience of the host
【客堂】[方] drawing room

【客套】① polite formulas; civilities ② make polite remarks; exchange courtesies：不讲～ *do away with formalities* /他们谈论正题前～了几句。*They exchanged greetings before coming to the subject.*
【客套话】polite formulas
【客体】object
【客厅】parlour; drawing room
【客位】seats reserved for guests or passengers
【客姓】surname of a non-native person
【客运】passenger transport：～量 *volume of passenger transport* / ～列车 *passenger train* / ～站 *passenger depot station*
【客栈】inn：～老板 *innholder*
【客座】① seat or place for a guest ② professional person invited to work temporarily in a institution：～教授 *guest or visiting professor* / ～指挥 *a guest conductor*

课[1] ① class; lecture：讲～ *give a lecture* /上～ *have class*; *attend a class* ② subject; course：必修～ *required course*; *compulsory course* /选修～ *elective course* ③ class; period：我们上午有四节～。*We have four classes in the morning.* ④ lesson：第五～ *Lesson Five* ⑤ section, division or subdivision of certain administrative units：会计～ *accounting section* /教务～ *educational administration section*

课[2] ① a kind of tax in ancient times ② levy; collect：～以重税 *impose a heavy tax on sb*

课[3] a session at divination fortune-telling：起～ *start session in divination by tossing coins, etc.*

【课本】textbook：语文～ *textbook in Chinese*; *Chinese textbook*
【课表】school or class schedule
【课程】course; curriculum：～编排 *construction of curriculum* / ～计划 *syllabus* / ～模式 *curriculum model* / ～设计 *curriculum design*
【课间】break (between classes)
【课间操】setting-up exercises during a break (between classes)
【课件】courseware
【课卷】students' written work
【课目】① subject; course ②【军】course
【课时】class hour; period：每周授课4～ *teach 4 periods a week*
【课室】classroom：宽敞的～ *a spacious classroom*
【课税】impose tax; levy：～过重 *overtax* / ～过低 *undertax* / ～基础 *tax base*
【课堂】classroom：～教学 *classroom instruction* / ～讨论 *classroom discussion*
【课题】① topic for class discussion ② question or topic for study; task：提出新的～ *pose a new problem*; *set a new task*
【课题组】research group
【课外】after school; extra-curricular：～读物 *out-of-class reading material* / ～活动 *extra-curricular activities* / ～阅读 *outside reading*
【课文】text
【课业】lessons; classwork; schoolwork：荒废～ *neglect one's studies* /我认为学生们的～负担太重。*I think the students suffer much from the schoolwork.*
【课余】after school; after class：你通常～都做些什么？*What do you usually do after school?*
【课桌】school desk

骒 female (mule or horse)

【骒马】mare

嗑 crack sth (shelled or hard) between the teeth：～瓜子 *crack melon seeds*
see also kē

锞

【锞子】a small ingot of gold or silver

溘 ［书］suddenly：～逝 *pass away suddenly*; *die surprisingly*

【溘然】［书］suddenly：～长逝 *pass away suddenly*

kěn

肯[1] flesh attached to the bone：中～ *draw blood*; *be to the point*

肯[2] ① agree; consent：他不～来。*He wouldn't come over.* ② be willing to do sth：～学习 *be eager to learn* ③［方］be liable to; often happen：这几天～下雨。*It often rains recently.*

【肯定】① affirm; confirm; approve：～成绩，指出缺点 *affirm the achievements and point our the shortcomings* /我要用实验来～我的想法。*I will make experiments to confirm my ideas.* /总经理～了这个计划。*The general manager approved the plan.* ② affirmative; positive：～的回答 *affirmative answer* / ～的评论 *positive criticism* ③ doubtless; sure：我们～能提前完成任务。*We can surely fulfill the task before the time limit.* /他八点以前～会到的。*He will doubtlessly arrive by 8 o'clock.* ④ definite; clear：请给我一个～的答复。*Please give me a definite answer.*
【肯尼迪】John Fitzgerald Kennedy (1917-1963), 35th President of the United States (1961-1963)
【肯尼亚】Kenya：～人 *Kenyan*
【肯塔基】Kentucky, state in central southeastern United States

垦 cultivate (land); reclaim (wasteland)：～田 *cultivate farmland*

【垦覆】make furrows between rows of trees, plant manure crops and plough them under to enrich the soil for the trees
【垦荒】open up wasteland; reclaim virgin soil
【垦区】reclamation area
【垦殖】cultivate wasteland
【垦种】reclaim and plant; open up and cultivate

恳 ① sincerely; earnestly：～谢 *thank sincerely* ② request; entreat; beg：敬～ *respectfully request*

【恳辞】decline in all sincerity; beg off earnestly
【恳切】sincere; earnest：他～地想帮助她，但是被拒地了。He was sincere in his wish to help her but was refused. /她～地向教授请教这个问题。She consulted the professor about this question earnestly.

【恳请】cordially invite; earnestly request: ～您的帮助。*Your assistance is earnestly requested.* /我要～她帮我一个忙。*I'd like to ask her a favour.*

【恳求】beg sincerely; implore; beseech: 她～我让她出去。*She implored me to let her go out.* /"原谅我吧。"她～道。"*Please forgive me*," *she pleaded.* /她～律师尽一切努力证明她的清白。*She begged her lawyer to do everything possible to prove her innocence.*

【恳谈】have a heart-to-heart talk: 我和父亲～了整个下午。*I talked with my father sincerely the whole afternoon.*

【恳托】make a sincere request

【恳挚】[书] earnest; sincere: 请接受我～的感谢。*Please accept my hearty thanks.*

啃 gnaw; nibble: 老鼠把抽屉～坏了。*The rats have damaged the drawer by gnawing it.*

【啃骨头】pick a bone; gnaw at a bone: 那只狗在～。*The dog is gnawing at the bone.*

【啃啮】gnaw; nibble: 鱼在～鱼饵。*The fish were nibbling at the bait.* /焦虑和恐惧不断～着他,让他睡不着觉。*Anxiety and fear gnawed constantly at his heart, preventing him from falling asleep.*

【啃青】[方] ① (of people) reap green or unripe crops for food ② (of sheep, draught animals, etc.) nibble green crops

【啃书本】study hard; bury oneself in books: 不要光～,要把理论应用于实践。*Don't just read books; you should put the theories in the books into practice.*

kèn

掯 【方】① push down hard ② oppress; force: 勒～ *force sb to do sth* ③ (of eyes) contain; hold: 她眼里～着泪。*Her eyes welled with tears.*

kēng

坑 ① pit; hole; hollow: 粪～ *manure pit* /泥～ *mud puddle* /水～ *puddle* ② tunnel; gallery: 矿～ *pit* /煤～ *coal pit* ③ [古] bury alive: ～杀 *bury alive (in a pit)* ④ entrap; cheat: 他把我～了。*He cheated me.* ⑤ (Kēng) a surname

【坑道】①【矿】pit; gallery ②【矿】tunnel: ～工事 *tunnel defences; tunnel fortifications*

【坑害】entrap; ensnare: 你怎么能～朋友,让他买假货? *How can you entrap your friend into buying a fake?*

【坑井】gallery and pit

【坑坑洼洼】bumpy; full of pits and holes: 我们走在一条～的乡村小路上。*We are walking on a bumpy country road.*

【坑蒙】swindle; cheat; double-cross: 这些推销员非常狡猾,不要让他们～你。*These salesmen are very sly; don't let them cheat you.* /他说的是真话,他没有～我。*What he said is truth; he didn't swindle me.* /我坚信那个推销员～了我100元钱。*I am convinced the salesman did me out of 100 yuan.*

【坑骗】cheat; defraud; fiddle: 如果我发现你在～我,你可就有苦头吃了。*If I find out you've been fiddling me you're in big trouble.* /他们通过使用假名字和假证件～了税务部门。*They defrauded the Tax Department using false names and forged certificates.*

【坑人】cheat; deceive; trick: 他专门用花言巧语～。*He always deceives people with sweet words.*

【坑子】[口] pit; hole

吭 utter a sound or a word: 一声不～ *without saying a word* /有什么需要帮忙的,你就～一声。*If you need my help, just tell me.*
see also háng

【吭哧】① puff; puff and blow: 老爷爷上了楼以后直～。*The grandpa was puffing after going upstairs.* ② work hard: 他～了好几天才写出这篇作文。*He has been working on this composition for several days and finally finished it.* ③ hem and haw; prunes and prism: 他～了半天我也没有听明白。*He hemmed and hawed for quite a while, but I still couldn't understand him.*

【吭气】utter a sound or word: 他只是看着墙,不～。*He just looked at the wall without uttering a word.*

【吭声】utter a sound; breathe a word: 任凭他说什么你也别～。*Don't utter a single word no matter what he says.*

硁 [书] the sound of striking stones

【硁硁】[书] shallow and bigoted: ～之见 [谦] *my humble and shallow view*

铿 [象] clang; clatter

【铿锵】(of sound) sonorous and rhythmic: ～悦耳 *sonorous and pleasant* /这首诗读起来音调～。*This poem reads sonorous.*

【铿然】[书] sonorous and forceful

kōng

空 ① empty; hollow; unreal: ～碗 *an empty bowl* / ～话 *empty talk* / ～想 *unrealistic thought* ② air; sky: 真～ *vacuum* /今晚夜～明亮。*The stars overhead are very bright tonight.* ③ for nothing; in vain; fruitless: ～忙一阵 *make fruitless efforts* /落～ *come to nothing; fail through* /～欢喜 *rejoice too soon*
see also kòng

【空瘪】empty and shrunken: ～的麦穗 *withered ears of wheat*

【空舱费】dead freight

【空肠】【生理】jejunum
【空敞】open and vast; spacious: ~的操场 *a spacious playground*
【空城计】presenting a bold front to conceal a weak defence
【空挡】【机】neutral gear:挂 ~ *put* (*a car*, *etc.*) *in neutral gear*
【空荡荡】empty; deserted; bare: ~的教室里只有他一个人。*He was the only person in the empty classroom.* /他的脚步声回荡在~的通道里。*His footsteps echoed in the empty passage.* /屋子~的,只有一张床。*The room was completely bare except for a bed.*
【空洞】① empty; hollow:内容~的文章 *article empty of matter* /他的讲话很~。*His speech is devoid of content.* ② cavity:肺~ *pulmonary cavity*
【空洞洞】empty; deserted:我回来后发现房子漆黑一片且~的。*I came back to find the house dark and deserted.*
【空洞无物】empty; devoid of content: ~的文章 *an article empty of matter*
【空乏】① poverty-stricken; poor ② empty and dull: ~的生活 *a dull life*
【空翻】【体】somersault; flip:前~ *forward somersault* /后~ *backward somersault*
【空泛】vague and general:你说得太~了,请具体一点儿。*What you've said is too general; please put it in a specific way.*
【空防】【军】air defence
【空房】① empty room:旅馆的一间~ *a vacant room in a hotel* /为什么你要去看那间~呢? *Why do you want to look at that empty room?* ② house in which a wife lives while her husband is away:丈夫出国后,她独守~已经两年了。*She has lived a lonely life for two years since his husband went abroad.*
【空腹】① on an empty stomach:明天体检要求~。*The physical examination tomorrow requires an empty stomach.* ②[书] ignorant; without learning
【空喊】speak loudly without taking action: ~是没有用的。*It's no use clamouring without taking action.*
【空耗】waste:不要~时间! *Don't waste your time!*
【空话】empty talk; hollow words:这篇文章~连篇。*This article is full of pages of empty verbiage.* /这个年轻人爱说~。*The young man indulges in idle talk.*
【空怀】(of animals) non-pregnant; barren
【空幻】visionary; illusory:她以为他爱她,但这是~的。*She thought he loved her but it was illusory.*
【空际】in the sky; in the air
【空寂】open and silent; deserted and quiet:湖边~无人。*It's deserted and silent by the lake.*
【空架子】mere skeleton; bare outline:我的计划还只是个~。*My plan is just a skeleton now.*
【空间】space; room:外层~ *outer space*
【空间站】space station
【空降】airborne: ~部队 *airborne force*
【空姐】[口] air hostess
【空军】air force: ~部队 *air force*; *air component* / ~基地 *AFB*; *air base* / ~力量 *air power* / ~司令部 *air command*
【空空如也】completely empty:他坐在那儿,面前是个~的盘子。*He was sitting there with a completely empty plate in front of him.*
【空口】① eat dishes without rice or wine ② only give a verbal statement; pay lip service: ~约定有什么用? *What's the use of a verbal contract?*
【空口说白话】pay lip service:我根本不相信他,他总爱~。*I don't trust him at all; he always pays lip service.*
【空口无凭】a mere verbal statement is no guarantee
【空旷】open and spacious: ~的原野 *open and spacious field*
【空阔】open and vast
【空雷】aerial mine
【空灵】indescribably free; free and natural
【空论】idle talk; empty talk:发~是没有用的。*Giving empty talk is of no use.* /他的话只不过是吓人的~,你不必太认真了。*His words were just idle threats; you don't have to take them seriously.*
【空落落】empty; deserted:送走了孩子,他觉得~的。*After seeing off his child, he felt lonely.*
【空门】①【宗】Buddhism ② (of football) unguarded gate
【空濛】[书] misty:烟雾~ *vast expanse of drifting mist*
【空名】① empty title:"董事长"只是他的~。"*Chairman of the board*" *is just his empty title.* ② undeserved reputation
【空难】air disaster; air crash
【空气】① air:新鲜~ *fresh air* /~污染 *air pollution* /月球上没有~和水。*There is no air or water on the moon.* ② atmosphere: ~紧张。*The atmosphere was tense.*
【空前】unparalleled; unprecedented: ~繁荣 *be thriving as never before* / ~高涨 *soar to unprecedented heights* / ~盛况 *extraordinarily grand occasion*
【空前绝后】unprecedented and unrepeatable: ~的成功 *an unprecedented success*
【空腔】【物】cavity: ~电路 *cavity circuit*
【空勤】air duty: ~人员 *aircrew*
【空身】carry no luggage; carry nothing:他~去了北京。*He went to Beijing without taking anything with him.*
【空驶】travel empty
【空手】① empty-handed ② without a model or a sample (in a painting or embroidery)
【空手道】【体】karate
【空速】【航】air speed
【空谈】① prattle; idle talk:停止如此可笑的~! *Stop such ridiculous idle talk!* ② indulge in empty talk:他只会~。*He is all talk.*
【空调】① air-conditioning: ~设备 *air-conditioning unit* ② air-conditioner
【空头】①【经】(of the stock exchange) bear;

short-seller ② nominal；empty

【空头支票】① rubber or dud cheque；bad cheque：开～ *write a bad cheque* ② empty promise：我已经习惯了他给我开～。*I have been used to his lip service.*

【空投】air drop；paratroop：～伞 *aerial delivery parachute* /～鱼雷 *aerial torpedo；hydrobomb* /救援物资已经～到地震区。*Supplies were parachuted into the earthquake zone.*

【空文】① *empty writing；verbiage* ② ineffective plan，rule，etc.：这些规章制度被看作是一纸～。*Those rules and regulations are regarded as ineffective ones.*

【空袭】air raid；air attack：～警报 *air-raid alarm；air alert*

【空想】① indulge in daydreaming；daydream about：他开始～他有了钱以后会是什么样子。*He began to daydream about what he would be like if he had a lot of money.* ② daydream；idle dream；pipe-dream：我知道这些念头不过是一个女孩儿浪漫的～。*I know that these ideas are nothing more than a girl's romantic daydreams.*

【空心】①（of trees，etc.）become hollow inside ② hollow；air core：～导线 *hollow conductor*

【空心菜】【植】water spinach（Ipomaea aquatica）

【空心萝卜】hollow-turnip — person without genuine ability

【空虚】hollow；void：他心中有悲痛的～感。*There was an aching void in his heart.*

【空穴来风】an empty hole invites wind — weakness lends wings to rumours；no smoke without fire：他否认偷了钱，但自是～。*He's denied stealing the money but of course there's no smoke without fire.*

【空言】impractical words；empty talk：他用～欺骗那个单纯的小女孩儿。*He cheated that naive girl by sheer empty talk.*

【空邮】send mail by air

【空域】airspace

【空运】air transport：～救灾物资 *airlift relief supplies*

【空运单】airway bill

【空运费】air freight

【空运能力】lift capacity

【空载】（of machinery，equipment，etc.）operate without load：～卡车 *empty truck*

【空战】air battle

【空中】① in the air；in the sky：～传来的花香 *the scent of the flowers wafted through the air* ② by radio

【空重】empty weight

【空转】① operate without a load：～速度 *idling speed；idle speed* ②（of wheels）turn without moving forward；spin

【空转轮】idler pulley

kǒng

孔 ① hole；opening；cavity；hollow；aperture：鼻～ *nostril* /弹～ *bullet hole* /检查～ *access hole* /箭～ *arrow hole* /卡片～ *card hole* /毛～ *pore* /膜～ *iris opening* /排气～ *air exit hole* /钥匙～ *keyhole* /针～ *the eye of a needle；pinprick* /轴～ *axle hole* /无～不入 *be all-pervasive；seize any opportunity* /装料～ *receiving opening* /你要在纸盒子上留出足够大的～，这样里面的昆虫才能呼吸。*Make sure you leave a big enough opening in the top of the paper box so that the insects in it can breathe.* ②［量］used for caves：一～土窑 *an earthen cave-dwelling* ③（Kǒng）a surname

【孔道】narrow passage

【孔洞】hole；opening；hollow：这些～是蛀虫弄的。*These little holes are made by woodworms.* /一只鸟在一棵倒地的树木的～中栖息。*A bird was sitting in the hollow of a fallen tree.*

【孔方兄】money；cash：我最近急缺～。*I am hard pressed for money recently.*

【孔教】Confucianism

【孔径】diameter of aperture：～规 *calliper gauge* /～角 *aperture angle* /～天线 *aperture antenna*

【孔孟之道】doctrines of Confucius and Mencius

【孔庙】Confucian temple

【孔雀】a bird of Juno；peacock；peafowl：～开屏 *peacock fanning out its tail in a splash of colours* /她像～般高傲。*She was as proud as a peacock.*

【孔隙】small hole or opening：瓶子底部有一道～。*There's a hole in the bottom of this bottle.* /雨水通过屋顶的～渗入屋子。*Rain was dripping into the room from a leak in the roof.*

【孔穴】cavity；hole：一束光线从屋顶的～中照射进来。*A shaft of light came in through a hole in the roof.*

【孔眼】small hole or opening：她堵住了蚊帐上的～，以防蚊子飞进来。*She sewed the curtain to stop the mosquitoes getting in from the opening.*

【孔子】Confucius（551—479BC），Chinese philosopher，educator and founder of Confucianism in late Spring and Autumn Period

恐 ① fear；dread：惶～ *terrified；fear* /有恃无～ *secure in the belief that one has strong backing* /诚惶诚～ *with reverence and awe* ② terrify；frighten ③ I'm afraid：～不可信 *probably not trustworthy*

【恐怖】scare；fright；terror；horror：～感 *a feeling of terror* /白色～ *the White Terror* /当他谈到一个乞丐在街上被杀害的～情形时，不禁哭了起来。*He couldn't help crying as he told of the horror of seeing a beggar killed in the street.* /走在黑暗里使他想起了被抢劫的～经历。*Walking in the dark reminded him of the terror of being robbed.*

【恐怖分子】terrorist：在袭击中，～杀害了许多无辜的人。*The terrorists killed many innocent in the attack.*

【恐怖统治】a reign of terror; reign of terror; terrorism
【恐怖小说】horror fiction
【恐怖主义】terrorism
【恐吓】frighten; terrify; scare; threaten: ～信 *letter of intimidation* /他总是～那个小女孩儿,以至于她讨厌见到他。*He terrified her so much that she hated seeing him.* /我们不会有任何麻烦,他只是在～我们。*We're not really going to get into any trouble — he is just trying to scare us.* /如果我不服从,他～说要打我。*I was threatened with a beating if I didn't obey.*
【恐慌】panic:金融～ *financial panic* /经济～ *economic panic*/同性恋～ *homosexual panic* /银行～ *banking panic* / ～万状 *be all panic* /剧院失火时,引起一阵～。*When the theater caught fire, there was a panic.*
【恐惧】fear; terror:无所～ *fear nothing* /他突然感到一阵～。*A sudden fear came over him.*
【恐龙】【考】dinosaur
【恐怕】① indicating doubt or anxiety about consequences: ～我们是迟到了。*I'm afraid we're late.* /他小声和我说话,～吵醒了母亲。*He whispered to me for fear of waking up her mother.* ② indicating an estimation: ～要下雪了。*It looks like snow.*

倥

【倥偬】[书] ① pressing; urgent:戎马～ *burdened with the pressing duties of a soldier* ② poverty-stricken

kòng

空 ① leave empty or blank: ～出一间房 *leave a room empty* / ～出一些时间 *leave some time unoccupied* ② unoccupied; vacant: ～房 *a vacant house* / ～地 *vacant lot; open ground* / ～椅子 *a vacant chair* ③ free time; vacant place:屋子里都是东西,一点～儿也没有。*The room was full of objects and there was no vacant space at all.* /你明天有～儿吗? *Will you be free tomorrow?*
see also kōng
【空白】margin; blank; empty: ～磁带 *a blank tape* / ～支票 *a blank cheque* /请在这一页顶端的～处写上你的姓名。*Write your name in the blank spaces at the top of the page.* /那时我的脑中一片～。*My mind was a complete blank at that time.*
【空白点】blank spot; blank
【空当】① gap; empty space ② break; interval:两餐饭之间的～ *an interval between meals* /插播广告的～ *a break for the commercial*
【空地】① unused land; open space:屋前有一块～可以种菜。*In front of the house there is an unused land, which can be used to plant vegetables.* ② extra room; space available:屋角还有点儿～,正好放一个书架。*There is extra space in a corner of the room just for a bookshelf.*
【空额】vacancy:他调走后公司里出现一个～。*His transfer caused a vacancy in the firm.*
【空格】blank; blank space (as on a form)
【空格键】space key
【空缺】① vacant position; vacancy:你认为公司里谁能顶替这个～? *Who do you think can fill the vacant position in this company?* ② gap; vacancy:填补～ *fill a gap; fill a vacancy*
【空日】undesignated date in certain calendars
【空隙】① gap; interval; hole; aperture:我透过墙上的～看到了发生的事情。*I watched what had happened through a gap in the wall.* ② opportunity:他很好地抓住了这个～。*He took good advantage of the opportunity.*
【空暇】free time; spare time:他一有～就读书。*He reads whenever he is free.*
【空闲】① free; leisurely:等老师～下来,你再问问题。*You can consult the teacher when he becomes free.* ② leisure; free time:你～时间做些什么? *What do you do in your leisure time?* /我～了就会来拜访你。*I'll visit you at my leisure.* ③ unused; idle:我们应该充分利用～设备。*We should make a full use of the unused equipment.*
【空心】on an empty stomach:这药得～吃。*You have to take the medicine on an empty stomach.*
【空余】free; square; vacant: ～时间 *free time* / ～房间 *a vacant room*
【空子】① unoccupied space; free time:抽个～给我打个电话。*Call me up when you have free time.* ② opening; chance; loophole:小心点,他很会钻～。*Be careful! He is good at availing himself of loopholes to realize his aims.*

控[1] accuse; charge:指～ *accuse; charge*

控[2] control; dominate:失～ *out of control* /遥～ *remote control; telecontrol*

控[3] ① keep unsupported:我的腿都～麻了。*My legs went numb from hanging in midair.* ② turn (a bottle, jar, etc.) upside down to let the liquid inside trickle out:把瓶子～干 *turn the bottle upside down to empty it completely*
【控方】【律】prosecuting party: ～证人 *prosecuting witness*
【控告】charge; accuse:他被～偷了一个钱包。*He was charged with stealing a wallet.* /这项～可能要判五年徒刑。*The charge carries a possible sentence of five years.* /警方～他谋杀。*The police accused him of murder.*
【控购】【经】control institutional purchases: ～指标 *quota for controlled institutional purchases*
【控股】【经】holding: ～公司 *holding company*
【控诉】accuse; denounce: ～旧社会 *denounce the society before liberation*
【控御】① control and drive (a horse, etc.) ② dominate; control; check; curb: ～愤怒 *place a curb on one's anger* /她无法～自己,勃然大怒。*She couldn't control herself and became furious.* /我努力～自己的脾气。*I try my best to keep my temper in check.*
【控制】control; dominate; command; curb; check;

rule; restrain: ~自己 *command oneself* /这台机器是自动~的。*The machine is automatically controlled.* /不要总是想~别人! *Don't always want to dominate others!* /他~住了想要哭的冲动。*He checked an impulse to cry.* /他难以~住强烈的好奇心。*He had difficulty restraining his strong curiosity.*

kōu

抠 ① dig with a finger or sth pointed: ~了个洞 *dig a small hole* / ~鼻孔 *pick one's nose* ② carve; cut decorative patterns: 在书架上~花纹 *carve a pattern on a bookshelf* ③ delve into; study punctiliously: 死~书本 *pay too much attention to book knowledge; be inflexible in studying* ④ mean; stingy; miserly: 她这个人很~。*He is a stingy person.*

【抠门儿】[方] stingy; miserly; mean; tight-fisted: 他真的很~,一生中从来没有借过钱给别人。*He is really mean; he's never lent anyone money in his life.* /他们很富有,却很~。*They are rich, but they are terribly stingy.*

【抠搜】① dig out with one's finger or something pointed ② stingy; mean: 这个老板是我为之工作过的最~的人。*The boss is the meanest man I had ever worked for.* ③ dawdle; loiter: 干工作不要抠抠搜搜的。*Don't loiter over your job.*

【抠字眼儿】find fault with the choice of words; split hairs in choice of words

眍 (of eyes) become sunken

【眍瞜】(of eyes) sink in; be sunken: 他病了一场,眼睛都~了。*He became sunken — eyed after the illness.*

kǒu

口 ① mouth: 开~ *open one's mouth to speak* /信~开河 *run off at the mouth; shoot off one's mouth* /异~同声 *all with one voice; with one mouth* /住~! *Shut your mouth.* /真难相信这话出自你的~。*It's unbelievable that these sounds are in your mouth.* ② one's taste: ~重 *a salty taste* ③ people: 家~ *family members* ④ sth like a mouth: 袋~ *bag mouth* /火山~ *the mouth of a volcano* /瓶子~ *mouth of a bottle* ⑤ entrance; gateway: 河~ *river mouth* /海~ *seaport* /关~ *gateway; strategic pass* ⑥ gateways in the Great Wall: ~北 *area north of Zhangjiakou, Hebei Province* ⑦ cut; hole: 伤~ *wound* /决~ (*of a dyke*) *be breached; burst* ⑧ general category or division grouping organs, institutions, etc.: 教育~ *department of education* ⑨ edge of a knife, etc.: 刀还没开~。*The knife hasn't the first edge yet.* ⑩ the age of a mule, horse, etc.: 两岁~的母马 *two-year-old mare* ⑪ [量]: 一~刀 *a knife* /三~之家 *family of three* /一~猪 *a pig* /一~锅 *a pot*

【口岸】port: 通商~ *trading port* /入境~ *port of entry*

【口碑】public praise: 他在这一带~很好。*He enjoyed a good reputation in this area.*

【口才】eloquence; speechcraft; talent for speaking: 她~很好,所以被派去参加谈判。*She is eloquent and so is assigned to take part in the negotiation.*

【口彩】auspicious remark

【口沉】[方] ① salty ② be fond of salty food

【口称】say; allege: 他~支持我,实际上却在拆我的台。*He said he would support me, but he acted against me in fact.*

【口吃】stutter: 你注意到了吗,那孩子说话有些~? *Do you notice that the child speaks with a slight stammer?*

【口齿】① enunciation: ~清楚 *have clear enunciation* / ~不清 *a twist in one's tongue; inarticulacy* / ~伶俐 *glib; saponaceous* ② age of horses, donkeys, mules, etc.

【口臭】【医】bad breath; halitosis

【口出狂言】talk boastfully or wildly: 这个小孩儿居然在大庭广众之下~。*Surprisingly, the little child talked wildly at a public occasion.*

【口传】pass on by word of mouth

【口传心授】oral instruction and rote memory

【口疮】aphtha; canker; mouth ulcer

【口袋】① bag; sack: 面~ *flour sack* ② pocket: 他在~里装满了食物。*He filled his pockets with food.*

【口淡】[方] not too salty; lightly-seasoned

【口德】restraint in one's speech: 说话留点~。*Use proper restraint when you speak.*

【口风】one's intention revealed in saying: 漏~ *betray one's intention in advance; give oneself away; let the cat out of the bag*

【口风琴】mouth organ; harmonica

【口服】① profess to convinced: ~心服 *be utterly convinced* / ~心不服 *be convinced in appearance; saying one is convinced but not really so at heart* ② take orally (medicine): ~药 *medicine to be taken orally; oral medicine* /不可~。*Not To Be Taken Orally.*

【口服避孕药】oral contraceptive

【口服液】oral liquid

【口服疫苗】oral vaccine

【口福】the luck to eat sth delicious; gourmet's luck: 我真有~。*I am lucky enough to have such a delicious meal.*

【口腹】food and drink

【口干舌燥】have one's mouth parched and one's tongue scorched — be extremely thirsty: 在大热天里走了一会儿,我就感到~。*I felt extremely thirsty after walking a while in that scorching day.*

【口感】texture of food

【口供】statement made by the accused under examination; testimony

【口号】① slogan; watchword:喊~ *shout slogans* ② [旧] countersign; password

【口红】lipstick

【口技】gastriloquy; art of imitating sounds; ventriloquism; vocal mimicry: ~表演者 *gastriloquist*; *ventriloquist*

【口碱】[方] alkali produced in northwestern China

【口角】quarrel; fray; brawl:昨天我和她发生了~。*I have a quarrel with her yesterday.* /他们的~毫无意义。*The fray between them is meaningless.*

【口角炎】【医】perleche

【口紧】closemouthed:他是一个~的人,值得信任。*He is really a clam and worth trusting.*

【口径】① caliber; diameter: ~测量器 *calibrater*; *calibrator* ② requirements; specifications: ~吻合 *meet the requirements exactly* ③ approach; version:对~ *arrange to give the same account* /统一~ *agree on a uniform version* (*or account*) /他们对这件事的叙述~不同。*Each of them has a version of the accident respectively.*

【口镜】【医】mouth mirror

【口诀】a pithy formula; mnemonic rhyme:乘法~ *rhyming multiplication table*

【口角】quarrel; brawl; bicker; fray:他们就儿子的教育问题~起来。*They had a quarrel about their son's education.*

【口渴】thirsty:我~了。请给我一杯水。*I am thirsty; please give me a glass of water.*

【口口声声】say again and again; repeatedly declare: 他~说爱我,我却认为行为比语言更重要。*He says he loves me again and again, but I think actions speak louder than words.*

【口溃疡】【医】canker sore

【口粮】grain ration; provisions:目前我们的~充足。*Our provisions are plentiful at present.*

【口令】① word of command ② password; watchword:主~ *master password* / ~应至少包含5个字母。*The password should contain at least five letters.*

【口沫】saliva; spittle

【口气】① manners of speaking; the way one speaks: ~强硬 *in strong terms* / ~太大 *open one's mouth* (*too*) *wide* /听到这些,他立刻改变了~。*On hearing this, he changed his manners of speaking at once.* ② what is actually meant; implication: 听他对我说话的~,好像对这件事很感兴趣。*He talked to me with the implication that he was interested in it.* ③ tone; note: 她的话中有一种自满的~。*There was a tone of self-satisfaction in her speech.*

【口器】mouthparts (of an arthropod)

【口腔】【生理】oral cavity

【口腔病】【医】oral disorder

【口腔镜】mouth mirror

【口腔科】stomatology: ~医生 *stomatologist*

【口腔外科】oral surgery

【口腔学】stomatology

【口琴】mouth organ; harmonica; harmonicon:吹~ *play on the mouth organ*

【口轻】① not too salty; lightly-seasoned ② be fond of food that is lightly-seasoned ③ (of livestock) young

【口若悬河】eloquent; speak with a flow of eloquence; well-spoken: ~的演讲者 *an eloquent speaker*; *a fluent speaker*

【口哨儿】whistle (with one's lips):吹~ *whistle* /他对马吹~。*He whistled to the horse.*

【口舌】① quarrel caused by what one says: ~是非 *quarrel caused by gossip* ② talking round; talk in persuasion, arguing, etc.: ~费尽 *have a great deal of talking* /我费尽~才说服他休息。*I talked a lot to persuade him to have a rest.*

【口实】[书] ① cause for gossip; handle:你这样做无异于授人~。*Your doing this way is just to provide your critics with a handle.* ② excuse; pretext:她以生病为~不来开会。*She didn't attend the meeting on the pretence of her illness.*

【口试】oral examination; oral test:参加~ *take an oral examination*

【口是心非】duplicity; say yes and mean no; play a double game:选民对他的~逐渐生厌。*The electorate is growing tired of his posturings.*

【口授】① teach by oral instruction:这首歌是由民间艺人世代~流传下来的。*This song has been passed down from generation to generation by the folk artists' oral instruction.* ② dictate: ~遗嘱 *dictate a will*

【口述】oral account:他~,我记录。*He gave an oral account and I put down what he said.*

【口水】saliva:淌~ *run saliva*; *slobber*; *run at the mouth*

【口说无凭】words alone are no proof; words of mouth alone don't carry conviction

【口诵】read out loud; read aloud

【口诉】accuse orally

【口算】① chant out the result while doing mental calculation ② poll tax

【口谈】talk; speak: ~和平 *talk about peace*

【口条】pig's or ox's tongue

【口头】(kǒutóu) ① in words:他只是~上答应了。*He only promised in words.* ② verbal; oral: ~表决 *voice vote*; *acclamation* / ~汇报 *oral report* / ~抗议 *verbal protest* / ~描述 *word picture* / ~练习 *oral practice*

【口头】(kǒutou) [方] taste (of fruit or melons):这个西瓜的~很好。*The watermelon tastes good.*

【口头禅】tag; pet phrase

【口头文学】unwritten literature; oral literature

【口头协议】verbal agreement

【口头语】pet phrase:他的~是:"我的上帝!" *His pet phrase is "My god".*

【口味】① flavour or taste of food:本地~ *local flavour* ② one's taste or liking:这道菜很合我的~。*The dish is to my taste.*

【口吻】① muzzle; snout ② tone; note:听她的~,似乎是在开玩笑。*It seems that there is a note of fun in her voice.*

K

【口误】a slip of the tongue:刚才他说上午的时候实际上是想说下午,这是一个~。*When he said in the morning he meant "in the afternoon" — a slip of the tongue.*
【口香糖】cachou; chewing gum; chutty
【口信】oral message:请你带个~给他好吗? *Would you mind giving him a message?*
【口形】【语】degree of lip-rounding
【口型】shape of the mouth when one speaks:别人唱歌时他只是做~,但是没有人注意到这些。*He only mouthed the words as the others sang, but nobody noticed that.*
【口血未干】the moment it is made; before the ink is dry
【口译】oral interpretation: ~者 *interpreter*
【口音】(kǒuyīn)【语】oral speech sounds
【口音】(kǒuyin) voice:听他的~,我看他是北方人。*Judging from his voice, I think he is from the north.* ② accent:浓重的南方~ *a broad Southern accent* /她说话带沈阳~。*She speaks with a Shenyang accent.*
【口语】① spoken language:英语~ *spoken English; oral English* ②[书] slander; calumniation
【口谕】[旧] oral instruction or directive by higher authorities
【口占】[书] ① dictate: ~书信 *dictate a letter* ② improvise poetry:他立即~了一首新词。*He improvised a new verse at once.*
【口罩】gauze mask; surgical mask
【口重】① salty; heavily seasoned ② be fond of salty flavour
【口诛笔伐】condemn both in speeches and in writing
【口子】①[量] used of people:你们家有几~? *How many are there in your family?* ②[口] my husband or wife:我们那~到上海出差去了。*My husband (or wife) has gone on business in Shanghai.* ③ opening; breach; gap; rift:炮弹片在墙上炸的大~ *a large gap in the wall where the artillery shell had exploded* ④ cut; crack; hole:他腿上的~正在流血。*The cut on his leg is bleeding.*

kòu

叩 ① knock: ~门 *knock at a door* ② kowtow, a sign of courtesy in the old days ③[书] inquire; ask:略~生平 *ask generally about one's life*
【叩拜】(an old form of formality) show one's respect by kowtowing
【叩齿】teeth-clicking (a method of dental care)
【叩打】knock; tap:他用手指轻轻~着房门。*He knocked at the door gently with his finger.*
【叩关】①[书] seek an audience with the monarch of a foreign state ②[书] knock at the door ③【书】launch an attack upon a fortress ④ (of football; etc.) attack the goal
【叩见】[书] call on (one's superior)
【叩首】kowtow
【叩头】kowtow: ~求饶 *kowtow to ask to be spared (from punishment, etc.)* /他认为给这个女人~是奴颜婢膝的行为。*He thought it an obsequious act to kowtow before that woman.*
【叩问】[书] make inquiries: ~缘由 *inquire into the reasons*
【叩喜】[旧] offer congratulations by kowtowing
【叩谢】express thanks by kowtowing; express earnest thanks
【叩询】[书] make inquires

扣 ① buckle; button up:把门~上 *latch the door* ② place a bowl, cup, etc. upside down:用盘子把菜~上 *cover the dish with a plate* ③ accuse unjustly; frame up:他被~上了小偷的帽子。*He was framed as a thief.* ④ take into custody; detain; arrest:那个间谍被~了起来。*The spy has been detained.* ⑤ deduct; give a discount:打七~ *give a seventy percent discount* /不折不~ *one hundred percent; without discount or deduction* ⑥ knot; loop:活~ *a slip knot* ⑦ button; buckle:大衣~ *coat button* ⑧【体】smash; spike: ~球 *spike a ball* ⑨【纺】reed ⑩ circle of thread (of a screw):螺丝拧了三~ *give the screw three twists*
【扣除】deduct; take away:公司将从你的薪水中~收入所得税。*The company will deduct income tax from your salary.*
【扣发】withhold; hold: ~奖金 *withhold the bonus*
【扣减】deduct; subtract:通过从B栏中~A栏中的数字,你可以算出你的整体收入。*You can calculate the overall income of yours by subtracting the amount in column A from the amount in column B.* /考试中字迹不清楚将被~分数。*Marks may be deducted for illegible handwriting in the examination.*
【扣篮】【体】dunk shot; over-the-rim shot
【扣留】detain; arrest: ~走私犯 *detain the smuggler* /警方~了一个嫌疑犯。*The police has arrested a criminal suspect.*
【扣帽子】put a political label on sb:给人胡乱~ *put labels on others indiscriminately*
【扣人心弦】soul-stirring; exciting; thrilling:这真是一场~的比赛,可惜最后我们输了。*It was really an exciting match, but we lost it at last.*
【扣杀】【体】smash or spike (the ball):大力~ *(in volleyball) spike the ball powerfully*
【扣审】【律】detain and interrogate
【扣题】keep to the point; be relevant to the subject:这句话很~。*This sentence is in keeping with the theme.*
【扣头】discount; rebate
【扣压】withhold; shelve: ~书面材料 *withhold the written material*
【扣押】① detain; hold in custody:他的汽车被警察~。*His car was held in the custody of the police.* /他被当作嫌疑犯~。*He is detained as a suspect.* ②【律】seize
【扣子】① knot ② button:看,你把大衣的~扣错了。

K

Look, you have buttoned up your coat the wrong way. /这条裙子用~,那条用拉链。*This dress buttons, but that one zips.* ③(in traditional literature or story-telling) abrupt break in a story to create suspense

寇 ①invader; bandit: 敌~ *the invading enemy* /外~ *aggressor; invader* ② invade: 入~ *make an incursion* ③(Kòu) a surname

【寇边】[书] invade the frontier

【寇仇】mortal enemy; foe

【寇盗】bandit; robber

蔻

【蔻丹】nail polish

【蔻蔻】cocoa

kū

枯 ①(of a plant, etc.) withered; dried up; die: ~草 *withered grass* / ~木 *dead tree* ②(of a well, river, etc.) dried up ③ thin and haggard ④ dull; boring; dry ⑤[方] dregs; residue: 麻~ *sesame residue*

【枯病】【植】rot

【枯草热】【医】hay fever

【枯肠】[书] impoverished mind

【枯瘁】withered; haggard; drawn; washed-out; deathlike: 她眼睛深陷,面容~。*She was haggard with cavernous eyes.*

【枯干】dried-up; withered: 花瓶里都是~的花。*The vase was full of withered flowers.*

【枯槁】①(of plants) withered; shriveled ② haggard; drawn; washed-out: 他面容~,看上去又老又虚弱。*His face was drawn, and he looked old and weak.* /面容~的外科医生说,他已经两天没有睡觉了。*The surgeon who looked extremely haggard said that he had not slept for the past two nights.*

【枯骨】dry bones; skeleton

【枯耗】deplete; exhaust

【枯涸】dry up; exhaust: 我家门前的小河已经~了。*The river in front of our house has dried up.*

【枯黄】withered and yellow: ~的庄稼 *withered yellow crops*

【枯瘠】barren; infertile: 他们想在~的土地上种树。*They wanted to plant on the barren land.*

【枯寂】dull and lonely: ~的生活 *dull and lonely life*

【枯焦】dried-up; withered: 很久没有下雨,禾苗都~了。*The crops all withered for it hasn't rained for a long time.*

【枯竭】① dried up; exhausted: 水源~。*The water source has dried up.* ②(of energy, money, etc.) exhaust; deplete: 旅行过后我们的体力都~了。*We were all exhausted after the journey.*

【枯井】dry well

【枯窘】[书] dried up

【枯木逢春】come to life again like a withered tree in spring — get a new lease of life; good fortune that comes after a long spell of bad luck

【枯荣】(of grasses and trees) luxuriate and wither; rise and fall

【枯涩】dry and puckery

【枯瘦】haggard; emaciated; skinny: ~的老人 *a skinny old man*

【枯熟】【农】dead ripeness

【枯水】low water: ~河 *wadi*

【枯水期】dry season; low-water season

【枯索】[书] ① devoid of vitality; wizened ② dull and dry

【枯萎】wither: 花在寒冷的天气里~了。*The flowers withered in the cold.*

【枯萎病】【植】blight; wilt

【枯朽】dry and decayed: 院子里的老树~了。*The old tree in the yard became dry and decayed.*

【枯哑】(of voice) low and hoarse

【枯燥】insipid; dry; boring: ~的谈话 *insipid conversation* / ~的演讲 *a dry lecture* /这本书~无味。*The book is dry as dust.* /她过着~的生活——只有学习,没有玩乐。*She led a humdrum existence — all study and no play.*

【枯枝】dry stick: 一枝~落在他的头上。*A dry stick fell on his head.*

【枯坐】sit idly: 他~在窗前,想了一个下午。*He thought for the whole afternoon by the window, sitting idly.*

哭 cry; weep; sob; wail: 痛~流涕 *cry one's eyes out; wail* /当她知道自己考试未通过时忍不住~了。*She couldn't help weeping when she knew that she failed the exam.* /小孩儿~着睡着了。*The little child sobbed himself to sleep.*

【哭包子】[口] child liable to crying; crybaby

【哭鼻子】[口] cry; weep: 他的儿子动不动就~。*His son weeps often.*

【哭哭啼啼】keep crying or sobbing; weep and wail: 小女孩~地要新衣服。*The little girl is wailing for new clothes.*

【哭脸】[方] cry; weep

【哭灵】wail bitterly before a bier, tomb or memorial tablet

【哭闹】cry and make noises; weep: 婴儿醒了开始~起来。*The baby woke up and began to cry.*

【哭泣】weep; cry: 这个女人为丈夫的死大声~。*The woman sobbed loudly at his husband's death.*

【哭腔】①(in traditional opera) sobbing tune ② speak with sobs: 他带着~向我讲述了事情的经过。*He told me what had happened with sobs.*

【哭穷】go about saying how hard up one is; complain of poverty

【哭丧】lament sb's death by loud wailing

【哭丧棒】staff used by the son of the deceased in a funeral procession

【哭丧着脸】wear a long face; look displeased (or unhappy): 不要一整天都~! *Don't wear a long face the whole day!*

【哭声】cry; tearful voice: ~载道。*Cries of misery were heard the whole length of the way.*

K

【哭诉】accuse in tears; complain tearfully; sob out:他在～他的遭遇。*He is sobbing out his grievances.*
【哭天抹泪】[贬] wail and whine:她在我们面前～。*She sobbed her heart out before us.*
【哭笑不得】not know whether to laugh or to cry; find sth both funny and annoying:他们的错误的称赞让我～。*I was embarrassed by their mistaken compliment.*

堀 [书] dig a hole
【堀穴】cave; cavern

窟 ① cave; hole; burrow:石～ *stone cave* /狡兔三～ *a foxy person has more than one hideout* ② den; lair:赌～ *a gambling den* /匪～ *a robbers' den* /魔～ *den of monsters*; *den of evil* /贫民～ *slum*
【窟窿】① hole; cavity:冰～ *ice-hole* /香烟掉在地板上,把地毯烧出了～。*A cigarette dropped on the floor and burnt holes in the carpet.* ② debt; deficit:拉～ *get into debt* ③ loophole
【窟窿眼儿】small hole:我不能穿这双袜子了,那上面有～。*I cannot wear that pair of socks, as it's got a hole in it.*
【窟穴】lair; den
【窟宅】den or lair (usu. of bandits, etc.)

骷
【骷髅】human skeleton; human skull

kǔ

苦 ① bitter:这药很～。*This medicine tastes bitter.* ② pain; suffering; hardship:愁眉～脸 *pull a long face*; *snoot* /吃～耐劳 *bear hardships and stand hard work* /同甘共～ *share weal and woe* ③ make sb suffer from sth; give sb a hard experience:这件事可～了他。*This matter gave him a hard time.* ④ suffer from; be troubled by:～雨 *too much rain* /～旱 *suffer from drought* ⑤ do sth with patience; doing one's best:～劝 *earnestly persuade* / ～学 *study sth painstakingly* ⑥ [方] too much; to excess:指甲修得太～ *trim one' snails too short*
【苦熬】endure; go through:他生病后开始～岁月。*He spent every day with pain after he fell ill.*
【苦不堪言】(of a person) suffer untold hardship:那些日子我的经历真是～。*The hardship I suffered those days is beyond description.*
【苦差】hard and unprofitable job; thankless job:我认为销售是一件～。*I think sale promotion is a hard job.*
【苦楚】suffering; misery; distress:我一肚子的～无人诉说。*I can find no one to confide my suffering.*
【苦处】suffering; hardship; difficulty:你能想象他为一个如此吝啬的老板工作的～吗? *Can you imagine his hardship in working for such a mean boss?*
【苦胆】gall bladder; gall
【苦丁茶】① evergreen tree with oval leaves ② beverage made from such leaves
【苦斗】wage an arduous struggle; fight hard:～私心 *fight hard against selfishness*
【苦厄】affliction; hardship; suffering; torture:他经历的～似乎到头了。*There seemed to be an end to his hardship.*
【苦干】work hard; make painstaking effort:他把成功归结于勤学～。*He owes his success to studying diligently and working hard.*
【苦根】root cause of impoverishment or suffering
【苦工】① hard labour; forced hard work:长年的～使他显得衰老。*Hard labour all the year round made him look old.* ② person who does hard labour:当～ *work as a coolie*; *do hard labour*
【苦功】painstaking effort; hard work:下～ *take pains*
【苦瓜】①【植】balsam pear ② bitter gourd:他长了一张～脸。*He has a miserable look.*
【苦果】bitter fruit-evil consequence; bitter pill:自食～。*As you make your bed, you must lie on it.* /这次失败是他难以下咽的～。*The defeat was a bitter pill for him to swallow.*
【苦海】sea of bitterness; abyss of misery:脱离～ *get out of the abyss of misery*
【苦寒】① bitterly cold; frigid:天气～ *extremely cold weather* ② poor; impoverished:世代～ *be poor for generations*
【苦旱】① suffer from drought ② extremely dry
【苦活儿】hard and unprofitable job:干～ *do a hard and low-paying job*
【苦尽甘来】after suffering comes happiness; no sweet without sweat; after rains comes fair weather
【苦境】hard and painful circumstances; miserable plight:他身处～,仍不改初衷。*Though he was in a pitiable plight, he still stuck to his original ideals.*
【苦酒】① wine with tart flavour ② [方] vinegar ③ awful result; evil consequences:自饮～。*Drink as you have brewed.*
【苦口】① admonish in earnest: ～相劝 *earnestly admonish* ② bitter to the taste:良药～利于病。*Good medicine tastes bitter but cures sickness.*
【苦口婆心】advise sb in earnest; persuade sb patiently; press:我不喜欢那个男人,但是母亲～劝我嫁给他。*I don't like that man, but my mother pressed me to marry him.*
【苦苦哀求】flagitate; press one's suit:他～我放他走。*He implored me miserably to let him go.* /我～哀求,但是他仍然拒绝。*I was practically on my knees but he still refused.*
【苦况】difficult position; straits; plight; predicament
【苦乐】joy and sorrow; happiness and hardship:～观 *view on hardship and happiness*
【苦力】coolie

【苦闷】depressed; dejected; downhearted:她走后我感到很～。*I felt extremely depressed after her leaving.*
【苦命】bitter or sad fate; ill-fated life: ～的孩子 *a child with a sad fate*
【苦难】tribulation; misery; suffering:被压迫人民的～ *the miseries of the oppressed people*
【苦恼】trouble; agony; distress; plague; writhe; affliction:他为失眠所～。*He was troubled with insomnia.* /他正～着呢。*He is in agony now.* /母亲为孩子的肥胖而～。*Mother was distressed by her child's fatness.*
【苦肉计】ruse of inflicting an injury on oneself to win the trust of one's enemy or critic
【苦涩】① bitter and astringent; acrid ② pained; bitter:他～地笑了笑。*He smiled bitterly.*
【苦水】① bitter water: ～井 *bitter-water well* ② gastric secretion rising to the mouth ③ suffering; grievance:吐～ *pour out one's grievances*
【苦思冥想】ponder long and hard; meditate; mull; muse; reflect:他坐在炉火前,～这个问题。*He sat down in front of the fire pondering this problem.* /作为一个年轻人,他花费了很长时间～生活的意义。*As a young man, he had spent a lot of time meditating upon the purpose of life.*
【苦痛】suffering; misery; pain: ～让他迅速成长。*Suffering made him grow quickly.*
【苦头】suffering; bitterness:吃尽～ *go through all kinds of sufferings* /他蛮横无理,我要让他尝尝～。*I'll make him pay for his insolence!*
【苦夏】loss of appetite and weight in hot summer
【苦想】think hard; contemplate; mull; reflect:他～宇宙的秘密。*He contemplated the mystery of the universe.*
【苦笑】forced smile; strained smile
【苦心】trouble taken; pains: ～研究 *hammer away* /煞费～ *rack one's brains*
【苦心孤诣】endeavour single-heartedly; do sth with great pains
【苦行】【宗】ascetic practice; asceticism
【苦行僧】ascetic monk
【苦刑】cruel torture:受～ *suffer from cruel torture*
【苦言】[书] words unpleasant to the ear; unpleasant advice
【苦役】【律】hard labour:服～ *serve ons's time in hard labour*
【苦于】① be troubled; suffer:从前他～不识字。*He suffered from illiteracy in the past.* /我～缺钱。*I feel the pinch.* ② be worse than:他的情况～我。*His situation is worse than mine.*
【苦战】① bitter fighting ② fight a hard battle; work hard:通宵～ *work hard the whole night*
【苦中作乐】enjoy life in adversity; seek joy in hardship
【苦衷】private suffering or difficulty:难言的～ *suffering that one is reluctant to mention*

K

kù

库[1] ① warehouse; storehouse:军火～ *arsenal* /水～ *reservoir* /汽车～ *garage* ② (Kù) a surname
库[2] 【电】coulomb
【库兵】① [书] weaponry in the armoury or storage ② [旧] soldier guarding a warehouse
【库藏】have in storage
【库存】stock; reserve; storage: ～股份 *treasury stock* / ～过剩 *overstock* / ～现金 *cash on hand*
【库房】storehouse; storeroom:两间～ *two-room storehouse*
【库券】treasury bond
【库容】storage capacity
裤 trousers; pants:长～ *trousers* /短～ *shorts* /牛仔～ *jeans* /石棉～ *asbestos trousers* /体操～ *gym trousers*
【裤衩】pants; underpants
【裤袋】trousers pocket; hip-pocket:后～ *hip pocket*
【裤裆】crotch (of trousers); seat of trousers
【裤管】[方] trouser leg
【裤脚】① bottom of a trouser leg ② [方] trouser leg
【裤料】panting; trousering
【裤筒】[方] trouser leg
【裤头】[方] underpants; undershorts
【裤腿】trouser leg
【裤线】creases (of trousers):熨～ *crease a pair of trousers with an iron*
【裤腰】waist of trousers
【裤腰带】waist belt; trousers belt
【裤子】trousers; pants; slacks
酷 ① cruel; extremely ruthless ② extremely; very
【酷爱】ardently love; adore; like very much:她～游泳。*She is keen on swimming.*
【酷寒】severe cold
【酷旱】harsh drought
【酷好】be extremely fond of; like very much; be keen on:他妻子～烹饪。*His wife is extremely fond of cooking.*
【酷吏】a cruel (feudal) official
【酷烈】[书] ① cruel; fierce ② (of fragrance or aroma) very strong ③ blazing; flaming: ～的阳光 *flaming sunlight*
【酷虐】cruel; ruthless
【酷热】extremely hot: ～的天气 *a boiling day*/天气～,屋子里的状况让人无法忍受。*The weather was baking hot and conditions in the room are unbearable.*
【酷暑】the intense heat of summer; high summer
【酷似】be the very image of; be the spitting image of; resemble very closely:她长得～我妹妹。*She bears a close resemblance to my younger sister.* /

那个人～你哥哥 *That guy is the spitting image of your elder brother.* /他剪短了头发以后，看上去～一个男孩儿。*With her hair cut short, she could easily have been mistaken for a boy.*

【酷肖】[书] be the very image of; be the living image of; resemble very closely：他的容貌～他父亲。*His features bore a strong resemblance to his father's.*

【酷刑】cruel (or savage) torture

kuā

夸 ① boast; exaggerate; overstate; overrate：他把自己～成了这个队伍的领导。*He is stretching the truth to say that he is the leader of the group.* ② praise：他把儿子～上了天。*He praised his son to the skies.*

【夸大】exaggerate; overstate; magnify：～事实 *stretch the facts* /他们认为危险被～了。*They thought that the dangers were overstated.* /他～了自己在这次活动中的重要性。*He inflated his own importance in the activity.*

【夸大其词】exaggerate; overstate; overemphasize; overdo; make an overstatement："我快饿死了。""不要～，你一小时以前刚吃过午饭。""*I am starving.*""*Don't exaggerate — you had your lunch just an hour ago.*"

【夸父追日】overestimate oneself and try to do sth beyond one's ability

【夸海口】boast wildly：他～说他曾和总统共进早餐。*He boasted that once he had had breakfast with the president.*

【夸奖】praise; commend：由衷的～可让一个人更快地进步。*A sincere compliment may make a person progress more quickly.*

【夸克】【物】quark

【夸口】boast; brag; crow：我是他唯一信赖的人，这不是～，是事实。*I am the only person he trusts. I'm not bragging — it's true.*

【夸夸其谈】spread oneself; windbaggary; be full of hot air; be all talk

【夸示】show off; flaunt：他向我们～他的财富，想让我们羡慕他。*He flaunted his riches to make us envy him.*

【夸饰】give an exaggerated account

【夸说】① praise; commend ② brag about; show off：他不停地～他的父母多么有钱。*He kept bragging about how rich his parents were.*

【夸脱】quart (one fourth of a gallon)

【夸耀】show off; boast of：～自己的学习成绩 *boast about one's grades in school*

【夸赞】speak highly of; praise

【夸张】① exaggerate; overstate：毫不～地说，我一年时间就能挣100万。*It is no exaggeration to say that I could earn 1 million Yuan within a year.* ② hyperbole; exaggeration, a figure of speech that uses overstatement for emphasis

【夸嘴】[口] boast; brag

kuǎ

侉 [方] ① speak with an accent (esp. a provincial accent)：他说话有点～。*He speaks with some accent.* ② big and clumsy：～大个儿 *big clumsy fellow*

【侉子】[方] one who speaks with a heavy provincial accent

垮 fall; collapse：繁重的工作把他累～了。*The onerous work broke him down.* /那个厂子要～了。*That factory is going bankrupt.*

【垮台】collapse; fall down：他因虚荣心太重而～。*His vanity was his downfall.*

kuà

挎 ① carry sth on the arm：她手臂上～着篮子。*She carries a basket on the arm.* ② carry over the shoulder：肩上～着书包 *carry a bag over the shoulder*

【挎包】satchel; haversack

【挎斗】sidecar (for a motorcycle or bicycle)

胯 hip

【胯裆】crotch (of trousers)

【胯骨】hipbone; innominate bone

【胯下之辱】crawl between another's legs — to drain the cup of humiliation; be humiliated

跨 ① stride; step：～进门去 *step into a doorway* /～过小溪 *stride a brook* ② bestride; straddle：～上战马 *mount a war-horse* /横～中心线的轿车 *a car straddling the centerline* ③ go beyond; cut across：亚洲地～寒、温、热三带。*Asia extends across the frigid, temperate and tropical zones.* ④ attach to the side of sth：～间 *small side room*

【跨步】stride; step：他充满信心地～向我走来并和我握手。*He strode confidently towards me and shook my hand.*

【跨部门】trans-department

【跨度】span; skip distance; bounce：固定～ *fixed span* /经济～ *economic span* /梁～ *beam span* /内～ *interior span*

【跨国公司】multinational corporation; transnational corporations

【跨过】step over; stride over：他小心地～了地上的白线。*He stepped over the white line on the ground carefully.*

【跨矩】moment of span

【跨距】span; spread; spacing：～中心 *centre of span*

【跨栏】【体】hurdle race; the hurdles：200米～ *200m hurdles* /～运动员 *hurdler; hurdle runner*

【跨年度】go beyond the year：～预算 *a budget which spans two years*

【跨线】overline：～桥 *flyover; overpass*

【跨项】spanned item

K

【跨学科】interdisciplinary
【跨越】stride over; stride across:铁路~高山。*Rails span mountains.*

kuǎi

㧟[1] [方] scratch: ~痒痒 *scratch an itch*
㧟[2] [方] ① carry on the arm: ~着竹篮 *with a small bamboo basket on one's arm* ② scoop; ladle:她从口袋里~出面粉。*She scooped flour out of the bag.*

kuài

会 compute
see also huì
【会计】① accounting; accountancy:财务~ *financial accounting* /成本~ *cost accounting* /分析~ *analytical accounting* /公司~ *corporate accounting* /管理~ *administrative accounting* /现值~ *current value accounting*/预算~ *budgetary accounting* /折旧~ *depreciation accounting* /资产~ *assets accounting* ② accountant; bookkeeper:助理~ *assistant accountant*
【会计师】① accountant; senior accountant:独立~ *independent accountant* /管理~ *managerial accountant* /注册~ *chartered accountant* ② [旧] private professional accountant
块 ① lump; piece; block:冰~ *ice cubes* /木~ *wood block* /这屋子用石~造成。*The house is built of blocks of stone.* ② [量]:一~面包 *a piece of bread* /一~手表 *a wrist watch* ③ yuan, the basic unit of money in China:五~钱 *five yuan*
【块儿八毛】one yuan or less: ~的我还有,多了就不一定了。*There is only one yuan or less left in my pocket. I'm not sure whether I can find more.*
【块规】block gauge; end block
【块茎】【植】tuber: ~作物 *tuber*
【块垒】[书] gloom; depression
【块儿】① size; stature:这些小伙子的~都挺大。*All of the young men are big and tall.* ② [方] place: 住这~的人我都认识。*I know everyone here.*
【块石】riprap rock: ~灰 *lump lime*
【块体】block; bulk: ~移动 *mass movement*
【块头】[方] size:别看他~大,却没什么力气。*Big as he is, he is very weak.*
【块皂】cake soap
【块状】bulk; lumpish; nubbly: ~根 *tuberous root* / ~石墨 *blocky graphite* / ~糖 *loaf sugar*
快 ① quick; fast; rapid; swift:很~找出错误 *quick to find fault* /跑得~的人 *a swift runner* /这个表~了。*The watch is fast.* ② speed:这车能跑多~? *How fast can this car go?* ③ hurry up; make haste:赶~,你就要迟到了! *Hurry up! You will be late.* /她赶~将好消息告诉了她母亲。*She made haste to tell her mother the good news.* ④ be about to; be going to; soon:我~30岁了。*I am going to be thirty.* /他~回来了。*He will be back soon.* /他从事教育工作~十年了。*It's almost ten years since he has been engaged in education.* ⑤ clever; quick-witted:这个小男孩儿脑子很~。*The little boy is quick-witted.* ⑥ sharp; keen: ~刀 *a sharp knife* ⑦ straightforward:心直口~ *frank and outspoken* ⑧ happy; glad:大~人心 *to the general satisfaction of all* ⑨ [旧] sheriff
【快板儿】rhythmic comic talk or monologue to the accompaniment of bamboo clappers
【快报】bulletin; newsflash
【快波】fast wave: ~睡眠 *fast wave sleep*
【快步】【军】half step; quickstep; trot
【快步流星】stride; walk with vigorous strides: ~地奔向目的地 *rush to the destination* /我看见他生气地~走开了。*I saw him striding angrily away.*
【快步舞】gallop; jig
【快餐】snack; fast food: ~面 *instant noodles* / ~馆 *fastfood restaurant; snack bar*
【快车】express train; express bus: ~道 *fast traffic lane*
【快当】quick; prompt:他办事~。*He is quick at work.*
【快刀斩乱麻】cut the knot with a sharp knife — make a quick decision:我们必须~,否则一切都晚了。*We have to take resolute and effective measures to solve the problem immediately, or everything is late.*
【快递】express delivery; expressage: ~服务 *fast mail service*
【快感】pleasant feeling; delight
【快攻】【体】quick attack; fast break
【快活】gay; cheerful; lively; happy: ~的日子 *happy days*
【快件】express delivery luggage, goods, etc.:寄~ *send sth by express mail*
【快捷】(of speed) quick; fast: ~的沟通方式 *fast way of communication* / ~的生活节奏 *the fast pace of life*
【快捷菜单】【电】shortcut menu
【快捷键】【电】keyboard shortcuts; shortcut key
【快镜头】snapshot
【快乐】gay; happy; joyful; cheerful: ~的样子 *a joyful look* /祝你圣诞~。*Merry Christmas to you.* /书籍是她~的主要源泉。*Books are her major source of enjoyment.*
【快马加鞭】at top speed; do fast job; spur the flying horse at high speed:要按时完成任务,我们还需要~。*In order to finish the task in time, we'll have to accelerate the speed.*
【快慢】speed:这条船的~怎么样? *What's the speed of the boat?*
【快慢针】index lever
【快门】【摄】shutter:按下~ *click the shutter*
【快门按键】tripper
【快门开关】shutter release

K

【快人】a straightforward man; an outspoken person
【快人快语】an outspoken man speaking his mind
【快事】pleasure; joy; a happy event: 她以烹饪美食为~。*She delights in cooking lovely meals.*
【快手】a quick worker: 他是我们单位有名的~。*He is a well-known quick worker in our unit.*
【快书】quick-patter, rhythmic storytelling accompanied by bamboo clappers
【快速】fast; quick: ~采取措施 *swift to take steps*
【快艇】speedboat; motorboat
【快艇车】land yacht
【快慰】pleased; glad: 母亲收到儿子的信感到十分~。*The mother was very pleased to receive her son's letter.*
【快信】express letter
【快性】[方] outright; straightforward: 她是一个~的人。*She is straightforward.*
【快婿】son-in-law after one's heart: 乘龙~ *ideal son-in-law with a high social status*
【快讯】flash; news flash: 发~ *flash the news*
【快要】be about to; be going to: ~下雨了。*It's going to rain.* / 我~出国了。*I am about to go abroad.*
【快意】pleased; satisfied; joyful; happy: 这消息让他十分~。*The news pleased him very much.*
【快运】express
【快照】snapshot; snap: 拍~ *take a snap of sb*
【快嘴】one who is quick to express his opinions

侩 [旧] middleman: 市~ *sordid merchant; market broker*

狯 [书] cunning; sly: 狡~ *crafty; foxy; cunning*

脍 [书] ① meat sliced into small pieces ② cut meat or fish into thin slices

【脍炙人口】minced meat suits everyone's taste — be on everybody's lips; enjoy great popularity; win universal praise: 他的很多作品~。*Many of his works are popular and much relished.*

筷 chopsticks: 碗~ *bowls and chopsticks*

【筷子】chopsticks: 一双~ *a pair of chopsticks* / 火~ *fire-tongs*

kuān

宽 ① wide; broad: 3米~ *3 metres wide* / ~边草帽 *broad-brimmed straw hat* / ~肩膀 *broad shoulders* ② width; breadth: 这条街有多~? *What is the width of this street?* ③ extend: 放~两个多月的贷款 *extend a loan for two more months* / 知道那个男孩脱离了危险,我们才放~了心。*We were relieved after we knew that the boy was safe.* ④ generous; lenient: 从~处理 *treat with leniency* ⑤ well-off; wealthy: 他现在手头~,你可以向他借点钱。*He is well-off now, and you can borrow money from him.* ⑥ (Kuān) a surname

【宽波段】broadband; wide range: ~天线 *broadband antenna*

【宽敞】spacious: 他儿子给他买了一套~的房子。*His son bought him a commodious apartment.*
【宽场】wide field
【宽畅】free from worry; glad; happy: 他是个胸怀~的人。*He is always cheerful in his mind.*
【宽绰】① spacious; commodious: ~的礼堂 *a commodious auditorium* ② relieved; relaxed: 听了他的话,我心里~多了。*His words made me feel greatly relieved.* ③ well-off: 村民的日子比过去~多了。*The villagers lead a much better off life than before.*
【宽大】① spacious; wide: ~的大厅 *a spacious hall* ② lenient; generous; tolerant: 心怀~ *broad-minded* / 他在这件事上表现出难得的~。*He showed uncommon generosity in this matter.* / 法官对他很~。*The judge was lenient with him.* ③ lenient; receive clemency: ~处理 *deal with leniency*
【宽大为怀】be magnanimous; lenient
【宽贷】pardon; forgive: 如果再犯,我永远不~你。*I'll never forgive you if you make the same mistake again.*
【宽带】broad band: ~测量 *wide-band width measurement* / ~发射 *broadband transmission* / ~接收机 *broadband receiver* / ~匹配 *broadband matching* / ~信号 *broadband signal*
【宽待】treat with leniency; treat sb liberally: ~战俘 *treat the POWs liberally; treat prisoners of war leniently*
【宽度】width; breadth: 半峰~ *half-peak breadth* / 半值~ *half breadth* / 角~ *angular breadth* / 谱线~ *breadth of spectrum line* / 自然~ *natural breadth* / 总~ *overall breadth* / 最大~ *extreme breadth* / 这条河的~是多少? *What's the breadth of this river?*
【宽泛】broad; covering a wide range: 这个词的意思很~。*The meanings of the word cover a wide range.*
【宽幅】(of cloth) wide in width
【宽幅犁】big base plow
【宽广】broad; extensive; vast: ~的沙漠 *a vast expanse of desert* / 你应该心胸~,不要拘泥于小事。*You should learn to be broad-minded and never stick to trivia.*
【宽和】generous and kind: ~待人 *be generous and kind to others*
【宽宏】magnanimous; broad-minded: 他~的态度深深感动了我。*His magnanimous attitude moved me deeply.*
【宽宏大量】be kind and generous; large-minded; magnanimous: 我们的领导~。*Our leader is a magnanimous person.*
【宽洪】① (of voice) broad and resonant: 他~的声音让人难忘。*His broad and resonant voice is unforgettable.* ② large-minded; magnanimous
【宽厚】① broad and thick: ~的胸膛 *broad chest* ② kind and generous; magnanimous: ~待人 *be generous to people* ③ (of voice) deep and broad: ~的嗓子 *loud and rich voice*

【宽假】[书] pardon; forgive:最近我手头紧张,能否~几日? *Could you give me a few days' grace for I'm not well-off recently.*

【宽解】ease sb's anxiety:母亲烦心的时候,姐姐总能设法~。*When mother gets annoyed, my sister can always manage to ease her of her trouble.*

【宽旷】vast; extensive: ~的草原 *extensive grassland*

【宽阔】vast; wide; broad: ~的道路 *a road of great width* /这个学校有~的操场。*The school has an extensive play ground.*

【宽屏幕】wide screen; big screen

【宽让】lenient; tolerant:他还小,你要~一些。*He is still young, and you should be tolerant to him.*

【宽饶】pardon; forgive; show mercy:我真诚地请求他的~。*I throw myself on his mercy sincerely.*

【宽容】tolerant; lenient:让我们互相~并互相谅解。*Let's be tolerant and understanding with each other.*

【宽赦】pardon; forgive: ~别人是一种美德。*Forgiving others is a kind of virtue.*

【宽舒】① happy; glad:心境~ *in a cheerful mood* ② spacious and smooth:新修的街道平整~。*The newly repaired street is smooth and spacious.*

【宽恕】pardon; excuse; forgive: ~我们吧! *Have mercy on us!* /他不是一个轻易~人的人。*He is not a man who forgives easily.* /我们应该~这个年轻人无意中犯下的过错。*We should pardon the young man his mistake made unconsciously.*

【宽松】① spacious; commodious:房子里坐上5个人还是比较~的。*The room allows five people to sit comfortably.* ② glad; relaxed: ~的环境 *relaxed environment* /得知丈夫的病情不严重,她心里~多了。*Knowing that her husband was not in serious condition, she felt much relaxed.* ③ loosen; relax: ~衣带 *loosen one's belt* ④ well-off; in good financial condition:经济~ *be well-off*; *be comfortably off* ⑤ loose and comfortable:怀孕后,她只能穿~的衣服。*She had to wear loose and comfortable clothes during her pregnancy.*

【宽慰】comfort; console:我们尽力~那悲痛的孩子。*We all tried our best to comfort the distressed child.* / 她母亲遭遇车祸时我们设法~她,但很难奏效。*We tried to console her when her mother had an traffic accident, but it was very difficult.* /听到这个消息,我甚感~。*I was greatly relieved at the news.*

【宽限】extend a time limit: ~日期 *days of grace* /我们请求老师~几天。*We asked the teacher to extend the deadline a few days.*

【宽心】feel relieved; be at ease:听说孩子们都安全到达,她才~。*Her mind was at ease knowing that the children arrived safely.*

【宽心丸】reassuring words; words of comfort:他的话对我来说是一颗~。*His remarks made me feel at ease.*

【宽延】extend:校长把我们的假期~了一周。*The headmaster extended our holiday by one week.*

【宽衣】take off one's coat:请~! *Please take off your coat.*

【宽以待人】be broad-minded to others: ~才能得到尊重。*You can win respect by treating others liberally.*

【宽余】① broad-minded and joyful ② well-off; well-to-do: ~的日子 *a well-off life*

【宽裕】well-off; well-to-do:手头~ *be quite well off*; *be in easy circumstances* /时间~。*There is enough time to spare.*

【宽窄】width; breadth:这条街的~是多少? *What's the breadth of this street?*

【宽展】[方] ① free from worry; happy; glad:听了他的解释,我的心才~了。*I felt relieved at his explanation.* /儿子一直没找到工作,他的心情难以~。*He cannot help worrying about his son as he hasn't found a job.* ② wide; broad:她家门前有一个~的庭院。*There is a broad and level courtyard in front of her house.* ③ ample; well-off:手头~ *be well-off*

【宽纵】indulge:不要~孩子! *Never indulge your child!*

髋 hip

【髋部】hip

【髋骨】【生理】hipbone; innominate bone

【髋臼】acetabulum; cotyle

kuǎn

款[1] ① sincere ② receive with hospitality; treat cordially: ~客 *entertain a guest*

款[2] ① section of an article in a legal document: 第三条第四~ *article 3, section 4* ② fund; a sum of money:贷~ *loan* /汇~ *remit money* ③ names of author or recipient at the beginning or end of a painting, calligraphy, etc.:上~ *recipient's name; addressee* /下~ *author's name; signature* /落~ *put the names of the sender and the recipient on a painting* ④ style; design; pattern:新~服装 *a new styled costume* ⑤ [量] kind; style:两~西点 *two kinds of confection*

款[3] [书] knock: ~门而入 *knock at a gate and enter — invade a frontier*

款[4] [书] slowly; leisurely:柳枝~摆。*The willow twigs sway gently.*

【款步】slow steps:她~走在乡间的小路上。*She walked with leisurely steps on the country way.*

【款待】treat cordially:非常感谢您对我们的盛情~。*Many thanks for the hospitality you showed us.*

【款额】a sum of money:所剩~有限。*The amount of money left is limited.*

【款附】[书] sincerely submit to sb's authority

【款款】[书] ① hearty; sincere:他深情~地望着那个漂亮的姑娘。*He looks at the pretty girl with deep affection.* ② slowly:风筝~飞上高空。*The kite flew slowly into the sky.*

【款留】cordially urge (a guest) to stay:我们诚恳~他多留几日,他却执意要走。*We urged him cor-*

dially to stay for another period of time, but he insisted on his leaving.

【款洽】［书］happy and harmonious：我们亲如姐妹，情意～。*We are as intimate as sisters and cherish cordial and harmonious feelings to each other.*

【款曲】［书］① treat with courtesy：不善～ *socially inept* ② heartfelt feelings：互通～ *express cordial feelings mutually*

【款式】design；style：他的服装都是流行～。*All his clothes are fashionable.* /这裙子的～已经过时了，买一条新的吧！*The design of the dress is out of date; go and buy a new one.*

【款闲】［方］chat：一群家庭主妇在院子里～。*A group of housewives are chatting in the yard.*

【款项】① sum of money；fund：救灾～ *a disaster fund* /这个工程需要大笔～。*The project requires a large sum of money.* ② section（in a legal document，etc.）；paragraph：修改合同～ *revise some sections of a contract*

【款爷】［方］rich people；moneybags；upstart

【款识】① characters inscribed on certain articles：钟鼎～ *inscription on ancient bronze objects* ② signature（of author on a painting，calligraphy，etc.）

【款子】fund；sum of money：我上周汇出的～你们收到了吗？*Have you received the sum of money I remitted last week?*

kuāng

匡 ①［书］correct；rectify：过则～之 *correct an error when it occurs* ②［书］help；save：～我不逮 *assist me to do what I cannot do* ③［方］estimate roughly：～一～ *calculate roughly；estimate* ④ out of one's expectation：不～ *didn't expect* ⑤（kuāng）a surname

【匡扶】［书］correct and assist；uphold

【匡复】［书］save（a country from perishing，etc.）

【匡计】roughly estimate：～成本 *roughly estimate the cost*

【匡济】［书］help to relieve

【匡救】help to save or remedy

【匡算】roughly calculate：～现金开支 *roughly calculate the cash expenditure*

【匡正】rectify；correct：～错误 *rectify errors*

诓 hoax；deceive：你别想～我！*You can by no means cheat me!*

【诓骗】cheat；deceive；dupe：他～我说出了秘密。*He duped me into telling the secret.*

哐 ［象］sound of a crash or bang

【哐当】［象］bang；crash：～一声关上了门 *turn and bang the door*

【哐啷】［象］bang；crash：饭盒～一声掉在了地上。*The lunch box fell to the ground with a crash.*

筐 basket：一～土 *a basket of soil*

【筐子】small basket：菜～ *vegetable basket*

kuáng

狂 ① crazy；mad：发～ *go mad；go crazy* /妒忌得发～ *be mad with jealousy* ② violent：股票价格～跌。*The stocks slumped.* ③ wild；unrestrained；unruly：欣喜若～ *jump out of one's skin；be wild with great joy* ④ wildly arrogant：你这话可说的有点～。*It seems that your remarks are a little conceited.*

【狂傲】wildly arrogant；haughty：大家普遍认为他很～，难以接近。*He was widely regarded as being haughty and difficult to make approach to.*

【狂暴】wild；violent；brutal；savage：他是一个～的人，难以控制脾气。*He was a violent man who couldn't control his temper.* /这个男孩是他父亲～毒打的受害者。*The boy was a victim of savage beatings by his father.*

【狂悖】［书］wildly arrogant

【狂奔】rush violently；run about madly：他突然开始在街上～。*All of a sudden, he began to run about madly on the street.*

【狂飙】hurricane

【狂草】an excessively free cursive style（in Chinese calligraphy）

【狂潮】［喻］turbulent tidewater

【狂放】unruly；untrammeled；undisciplined：～的年轻人 *an unruly young man*

【狂吠】howl；bark furiously：当我向那只狗扔石头时，它～起来。*The dog howled when I threw a stone at it.*

【狂风】① fierce wind：～巨浪 *wild winds and huge waves* ②【气】hole gale：～警报 *whole-gale warning*

【狂风暴雨】violent storm；furious storm — a dangerous situation

【狂轰滥炸】violent and indiscriminate bombing；bomb savagely：敌军日夜不停地～。*The enemy kept up their bombardment day and night.*

【狂欢】rapturous；carnival；triumphant

【狂澜】raging waves：力挽～ *make vigorous efforts to change the situation；save a critical situation*

【狂乱】mad；crazy；deranged：向出口处一阵～的拥挤 *a frenzied rush for the exits*

【狂怒】wildly angry；be furious；frenzied rage；towering rage：通常情况下，人们在～之下很难有理智的举动。*It's usually the case that people seldom behave in a rational way when in a furious state.*

【狂虐】savage and vicious

【狂气】arrogance：他说话时总是带着一股～。*He carries an air of arrogance whenever he speaks.*

【狂犬病】hydrophobia；rabies / ～疫苗 *rabies vaccines*

【狂热】fever；fanaticism；enthusiasm；furor；mania：～地喜爱摇滚乐 *be mad about rock-and-roll* /他～地迷恋她。*He is wild about her.* / 看比赛的人群变得～起来。*The crowd at the game went crazy.*

【狂人】① maniac; lunatic:战争~ *war maniacs* /小心!那个人开车像个~一样! *Be careful! That man is driving like a maniac!* ② extremely arrogant person

【狂态】display of wild manners

【狂涛】① roaring billows ②【气】very high sea

【狂妄】wildly arrogant; frantic; wanton: ~的野心 *a wild ambition* /他是如此~——他认为他的想法总是最好的。*He's so arrogant — he just assumes that his ideas are always the best.*

【狂喜】wild with joy; overjoyed; enrapt:母亲为这个消息而~。*Mother was overjoyed at the good news.* /整个队伍因胜利而~。*The whole team exulted at the victory.*

【狂想】① fancy; fantasy ② vain hope

【狂想曲】【音】rhapsody; fantasia

【狂笑】laugh wildly

【狂言】ravings; wild remarks; wild language:口出~ *talk wildly* /满口~的疯子 *a raving lunatic*

【狂野】violent and rough

【狂躁】rash and impatient:谈了一个小时以后,他渐渐变得~起来。*He was growing impatient and rash after an hour's talk.*

诓 ① deceive; hoax: 你别~我。*No deceiving me!* ②[方] lie; falsehood:扯了个~ *tell a lie*

【诓语】lies; falsehood

kuàng

圹 ① open grave; coffin pit:打~ *dig a coffin pit* ②[书] open country

【圹埌】[书](of an open country) boundless

旷 ① vast and spacious:空~ *open and spacious* ② happy; free from worries:心~神怡 *relaxed and happy; carefree and happy* ③ neglect; waste ④ loose; loose-fitting: 螺丝~了。*The screw has worn loose.* ⑤(Kuàng) a surname

【旷达】[书] broad-minded:胸襟~的老人 *a broad-minded old man*

【旷代】[书] matchless (unequaled) in one's times: ~文豪 *an eminent writer incomparable in one's times*

【旷荡】① open and broad ② free and open; broad-minded

【旷废】neglect; waste: ~学业 *neglect one's studies*

【旷费】waste: ~时间 *waste one's time*

【旷工】stay away from work without reasonable reason: 厂里规定~要扣奖金。*It is stipulated in the factory that staying away from one's work without reason result in a deduction in one's bonus.*

【旷古】① from time immemorial: ~未闻 *sth never heard* ② remote antiquity

【旷课】be absent from school without leave; play truant; cut classes; stay away from school:孩子因~受到父亲的惩罚。*The child was punished by his father for playing truant.*

【旷朗】spacious and bright

【旷日持久】extend over days; protracted; prolonged; long-drawn-out: ~的辩论 *a prolonged debate*

【旷世】[书] ① unequalled in one's generation: ~功勋 *remarkable exploits in one's time* ② last a long, long time

【旷野】wilderness; open field: ~荒郊 *deserted countryside*

【旷远】① open and faraway ②[书] long ago

况[1] ① condition; situation:近~ *recent condition* ② compare: 以古~今 *draw parallels from history* ③(Kuàng) a surname

况[2] [书] much less; let alone:青年尚不能为,~老人乎? *Even a young man cannot do this, let alone an elderly man.*

【况且】besides; moreover:他这么年轻,~又聪明,一定能学好外语。*He is very young; moreover, he is quite clever, so I'm sure he can grasp the foreign language.* /现在去听音乐会已经太晚了,~,又下雪了。*It's too late to go to the concert now; besides, it's beginning to snow.*

【况味】[书] ① situation; condition: ~萧条 *be desolate; be lonely* ② charm; appeal:房间装饰过后,自有一番~。*After decoration, the room holds a special appeal to us.*

矿 ① mineral deposit ② ore:含铀~ *uranium-bearing ore* /黄铜~ *yellow ore* /煤~ *coal ore* /钛铁~ *titanic iron ore* ③ mine:下~ *go to work at the mine*

【矿藏】mineral resources:开发~ *develop mineral resources* / ~丰富 *rich in mineral resources*

【矿层】ore bed; seam:可采~ *workable seam*

【矿产】mineral deposits; minerals: ~分布 *the distribution of mineral deposits* / ~综合利用 *complex utilization of valuable minerals* /中国的~丰富。*China is rich in minerals.*

【矿车】tramcar: ~轨道 *tramroad* / ~减速器 *car retarder*

【矿尘】mine dust: ~测定 *mine dust surveying* / ~浓度 *mine dust density*

【矿床】【地】mineral deposit; ore deposit:海底~ *submarine deposit* /金属~ *metalliferous deposit* / ~评价 *evaluation of deposits*

【矿带】ore belt; ore zone

【矿灯】miner's lamp

【矿点】site of a mineral deposit

【矿工】miner; pitman

【矿化】mineralize: ~水 *mineralized water*

【矿浆】ore pulp

【矿井】mine shaft; groove: ~通风 *mine ventilation* / ~安全 *mine safety* / ~事故 *mine accident*

【矿警】mine police

【矿坑】pit

【矿料】dressed ore

【矿区】mining area

【矿泉】mineral spring; spa

【矿泉水】mineral water:一瓶~ *a glass of mineral water*

【矿砂】ore in sand form

【矿山】mine：~机械 *mining machinery* /~运输 *mine haul*; *mine haulage*
【矿石】mineral; ore：一块~ *a piece of ore* /~处理 *ore-processing* /磷~ *phosphorus ore* /深成~ *hypogene ore* /原~ *crude ore*
【矿田】ore field
【矿物】mineral：饱和~ *saturated mineral* /次生~ *secondary mineral* /非晶质~ *amorphous mineral* /浮散~ *float mineral* /可燃性~ *inflammable minerals* /铝铁~ *alferric mineral* /轻~ *light mineral*/生物~ *biogenic mineral* /释放~ *released mineral* /稀有~ *rare mineral* /原生~ *primary mineral* /战略~ *strategic mineral* /指示~ *index mineral* /自生~ *authigenic mineral*
【矿物质】mineral substance
【矿盐】rock salt
【矿样】sample ore
【矿冶】mining and metallurgy
【矿业】mining industry：~经济 *mining industry economics* / ~投资 *mine industrial capital investment*
【矿源】mineral resources
【矿渣】slag：高炉~ *blast-furnace slag*
【矿柱】mine prop; post; ore pillar：~强度 *pillar strength*

框[1] frame; case：窗~ *window frame* /画~ *picture frame*

框[2] ① set pattern; restriction ② draw a frame round：用红线把标题~起来 *frame the heading in red* ③ put in a straitjacket; restrain; confine：你不能把他~得太死！*You can't restrain him too much!*

【框架】①【建】frame; framing; skeleton frame; sash：~基础 *frame foundation* / ~结构 *frame construction*; *skeleton structure* /把那幅画装进~ *frame up the picture* ② framework：~协议 *framework agreement*
【框框】① frame; circle：他用红笔在图片四周画了个~。*He drew a circle around the picture with a red pen.* ② restriction; convention：打破老~，走工业发展的新道路。*Break down the old conventions and follow the new road in developing industry.*
【框图】block diagram; flow diagram：~语言 *block-diagram language*
【框子】frame：镜~ *the frame of a mirror*

眶 the socket of the eye：热泪盈~ *one's eyes filled with tears*

kuī

亏 ① lose money; have a deficit：盈~ *profit and loss* /~了一百元 *have a deficit of* 100 *yuan* ② short; deficient：功~一篑 *fail to build a mound for want of one final basket of earth — fall short of success for lack of a final effort* /理~ *be in the wrong* ③ treat unfairly：咱们是朋友，我还能~了你？*We are friends; how can I treat you unfairly?* ④ fortunately; luckily：~的他告诉我，否则我就上当了。*Thanks to his reminding, I did not get taken in this time.* ⑤ used to show sarcasm：~你还学过英语，这么简单的单词都不会拼。*And you have learned English, how come you can't spell such a simple word?*

【亏本】lose one's capital; suffer a loss：~卖出 *sell sth at a loss*
【亏产】fail to fulfill the production target
【亏秤】① give short measure：你可别~，我是老顾客了。*Never give short measure; I am a frequenter here.* ② lose weight：这些蔬菜~了好几斤。*The vegetables lost quite a few kilograms.*
【亏待】treat unfairly：他~你了吗？*Is he short with you?* /他说我们~了他。*He said that he suffered slights from us.*
【亏得】① thanks to; luckily：~我们出发前雨停了。*Fortunately the rain stopped before we set off.* / ~他的帮助，我才顺利通过了口语考试。*Thanks to his help, I passed the oral exam without difficulties.* ② used to indicate irony：~他还是你的好朋友，你遇到困难他都不管。*Fancy an intimate friend of yours not lending you a hand when you meet difficulties.*
【亏短】deficient; lack：~分量 *deficient in weight*
【亏负】① fail; not live up to：他~了我们的期望。*He failed to live up to our expectations.* ② treat unfairly; let down：大家没有~你的地方。*We have never done anything unfair by you.*
【亏耗】loss by a natural process
【亏空】① be in debt; be in the red：出现严重的~ *sustain a huge loss*; *show a heavy deficit* ② debt; deficit; bankruptcy：如果我偿清了所有的~，我就分文不剩了。*If I pay all my debts I shall have no money left.*
【亏累】spend more than one makes; unable to make both ends meet：由于经营不善，这个商店连年~。*The shop has been in the red for many years due to poor management.*
【亏欠】have a deficit; be in red：近期~ *deficit for the current term*
【亏折】lose money in business
【亏蚀】① eclipse of the sun ② lose money in business; deficit：弥补~ *cover the deficit* ③ wear and tear; loss：设备~严重 *serious depreciation of equipment*
【亏损】① loss; deficit：~条款 *deficit clause* /~总额 *total loss* /这家公司的盈利远远超过了~。*The company's profits greatly outweighed its losses.* ② general debility
【亏心】have a guilty conscience; conscience-stricken：做~事 *do sth against one's conscience*

岿

【岿然】[书] towering; lofty：~不动 *steadfastly stand the ground*
【岿巍】[书] tower above others

盔 ① basin-like pottery container：瓦~ *earthen pot* ② helmet：钢~ *steel helmet* ③ helmet-shaped hat：头~ *cyclist's helmet*

【盔甲】suit of armour
【盔头】decorative hat worn by performers in traditional opera
【盔子】basin-like pottery container
窥 ① peep:管中~豹 *look at a leopard through a tube — a narrow view of sth* /管~蠡测 *look at the sky through a bamboo tube and measure the sea with a calabash — limited knowledge; a narrow view of sth* ② pry; spy
【窥豹一斑】see one spot on a leopard — see only part of a whole
【窥测】spy out: ~方向 *keep an eye on which direction the wind blows*
【窥察】peep; pry about:我从窗子里~她的动静。*I peeped through the window to see what she was doing.*
【窥管】look at sth through a bamboo tube — have a narrow view
【窥见】detect; get a glimpse of:我~她在人群当中。*I glimpsed her among the crowd.*
【窥器】【医】speculum
【窥视】peep at; spy on:从锁眼中~ *peep through a keyhole*
【窥视镜】peephole; spyhole
【窥伺】be on watch for: ~良机 *lie in wait for a good opportunity*
【窥探】spy upon; pry about:在幕后~ *peep behind the scenes* / ~别人的事务 *spy into other people's activities*

kuí

逵 [书] road; thoroughfare
葵 common name for certain herbaceous plants with big flowers:蒲~ *Chinese fan palm* /向日~ *sunflower*
【葵花】sunflower: ~油 *sunflower oil*
【葵花子】sunflower seeds
【葵扇】palm-leaf fan
揆 [书] ① estimate; guess; speculate: ~其本意 *guess one's original meaning* ② principle; criterion; standard ③ be in charge of:以~百事 *be in charge of a number of affairs* ④ formerly used to refer to a man in charge of government affairs:阁~ *prime minister*
【揆度】[书] estimate; surmise:不可~ *inestimable* / ~建房的费用 *estimate for the building of a house* /她~事实。*She surmised the truth.*
【揆情度理】consider and judge by common sense: ~,他一定会同意我们的想法。*Weighing the pros and cons, he will surely agree with our views.*
睽 [书] separate; part
【睽别】[书] part; leave: ~多日 *separate for many days*
【睽隔】[书] separate; be away from
【睽绝】separate; sever; cut off
【睽离】[书] part; leave: ~有年 *part for one year*
【睽违】[书] separate; part: ~数载。*It's years since we parted.*
魁 ① chief; head:罪~祸首 *chief criminal* ② big and tall; burly
【魁岸】[书] tall and burly:身材~ *a tall and strong figure*
【魁首】① number one; best and brightest:文章~ *the best article* /女中~ *the most excellent woman*
【魁伟】strong and tall:她丈夫身材~。*Her husband is tall and strong.*
【魁梧】big and tall; stalwart; full-bodied; strapping; brawny: ~大汉 *a great strapping fellow*
【魁星】① four stars in the bowl of the Big Dipper ② god that govern literature and writing
【魁元】[书] number one successful candidate
睽 [书] go against; violate
【睽睽】stare; gaze:众目~ *all eyes gazing; everybody staring; in the public eyes*
【睽异】[书] be at variance

kuǐ

傀
【傀儡】puppet; stooge: ~国 *a puppet state* / ~政府 *a puppet government* / ~政权 *puppet regime* /那个工会代表受到了指责,被说成资方的~。*The union representative was accused of being a puppet of the management.*
【傀儡戏】puppet show (or play)
跬 [书] half a step
【跬步】[书] half a step: ~难行 *difficult even to take a small step*
磈
【磈磊】[书] ① stones in a heap ② depression; gloom

kuì

匮 [书] deficient
【匮乏】[书] deficient; short of sth:资源~ *deficient in natural resources* /水源严重~ *an acute water shortage*
【匮竭】[书] in short supply; exhausted:精力~ *be completely exhausted*
【匮缺】[书] deficient; short of sth:力量~ *deficient strength* /钱财~ *short of money*
喟 [书] sigh
【喟然】[书] the manner of sighing: ~长叹 *draw a long breath and sigh; heave a deep sigh*
【喟叹】[书] sigh with deep feeling: ~不已 *cannot*

help sighing

馈 present; give as a gift: ~以鲜果 *give fresh fruits as a gift*

【馈送】present a gift

【馈遗】[书] make a present of sth

【馈线】【电】feed line

【馈献】present a gift (to one's seniors)

【馈赠】present a gift; make a present of sth: ~礼品 *present gifts*

溃 ①(of floodwater, etc.) burst: ~堤 *burst a dyke* ②[书] break through an encirclement ③disperse; fall to pieces: 敌军~散 (*of troops*) *be defeated and dispersed* ④fester; ulcerate

【溃败】be crushed; be routed; be defeated: 彻底~ *a complete rout* / 拿破仑的军队在滑铁卢全军~。*The forces of Napoleon were vanquished at Waterloo.*

【溃兵】routed troops

【溃不成军】(of an army, etc.) be utterly routed: 战斗刚开始,敌人就~了。*The enemy's troop was routed at the beginning of the war.*

【溃决】(of a dyke or dam) burst

【溃军】routed troops or army

【溃烂】【医】fester; ulcerate

【溃乱】collapse into chaos

【溃灭】crumble and fall: 旧世界必定~。*The old world is bound to crumble and ruin.*

【溃散】stampede; break: 敌人~逃跑。*The enemy broke and fled.*

【溃逃】escape in disorder; flee; run away: 敌人~了。*The enemy fled in disorder.*

【溃退】beat a disorderly retreat

【溃围】[书] break through an encirclement: ~而逃 *broke through the encirclement and fled*

【溃疡】【医】ulcer; canker: 局部~ *local ulcer* / 口腔~ *a mouth ulcer* / 热~ *heat canker* / 十二指肠~ *duodenal ulcer* / 胃~ *gastric ulcer* / 细菌性~ *bacterial canker*

愦 [书] muddled; confused

【愦乱】[书] dazed and confused; befuddled

愧 ashamed; conscience-stricken: 羞~ *ashamed; tuck one's tail* / 问心无~ *have a clear conscience* / 于心有~ *have a guilty conscience*

【愧服】[书] consider oneself inferior to sb

【愧汗】[书] sweat from a sense of shame: 我因撒谎而~不已。*I am ashamed for having lied.*

【愧恨】ashamed and remorseful: 他因作弊而深感~。*He was deeply ashamed and remorseful of his cheating in the exam.*

【愧悔】ashamed and regretful: 我说的那些让他丢了工作的话令我~不已。*My words that made him lose his job made me bitterly ashamed and regretful.*

【愧疚】[书] feel ashamed and remorseful: 我现在知道了你说的是真话,我很~当时没有相信你。*I realize now that you were telling the truth, and I'm ashamed and remorseful that I didn't believe you at that time.*

【愧领】[谦] accept humbly

【愧色】look of shame: 他面带~。*There is a look of shame on his face.*

【愧痛】pain from shame

【愧心】guilty conscience

裍 [方] ① knot: 活~儿 *slip knot* / 死~儿 *fast knot* ② tie; fasten: 把牲口~上 *tie a draught animal to a pole* (*or tree, etc.*)

聩 [书] deaf; hard of hearing: 昏~ *decrepit and muddle-headed* / 发聋振~ *rouse the deaf and awaken the unhearing*

篑 [书] (in ancient times) basket for holding earth: 功亏一~ *fail to build a mound for want of one final basket of earth — fall short of success for lack of a final effort*

kūn

坤 ① one of the Eight Diagrams representing the earth: 乾~ *heaven and earth; the universe* ② female; feminine: ~鞋 *women's shoes*

【坤包】lady's handbag; lady's purse

【坤表】women's watch

【坤角儿】[旧] actress (in traditional opera)

【坤宅】[旧] family of one's wife

昆 [书] ① elder brother: ~弟 *brother* ② offspring: 后~ *descendants; children*

【昆布】【药】kelp

【昆虫】insect: 寄生性~ *parasitic insect* / 肉食~ *carnivorous insect* / 食虫~ *entomophagous insect* / 食叶~ *defoliating insect* / 植食性~ *phytophagous insect*

【昆虫学】entomology; insectology

【昆腔】【戏】melodies which originated in Kunshan, Jiangsu Province in Yuan Dynasty

kǔn

捆 ① tie; bind: 把行李~上 *tie up one's baggage* ② bundle; bunch: 韭菜~ *bunch of leek* ③ [量]: 一~报纸 *a bundle of newspaper*

【捆绑】bind; tie up: 人质被~起来,扔在屋子的角落里。*The hostage was bound and left in a corner of the room.*

【捆缚】truss up; bind; tie: 登山者出发前把绳子~在腰间。*The climber tied a rope around his waist before setting off.*

【捆扎】tie up; fasten: 我把所有的书~起来,放在床下。*I tied up all the books and put the bundle under the bed.*

【捆子】bundle; bunch: 蔬菜被绑成~,装上卡车。*The vegetables were tied in bunches and put on the truck.*

悃 [书] sincere: ~诚 *sincere; unaffected*

【悃愊】[书] utterly sincere: ~无华 *in real earnest;*

K

honest and simple

壸 [书] a path inside the imperial palace

kùn

困 ① be stranded; be hard pressed:内外交~ *beset with difficulties both at home and abroad* /我~在那陌生的城市,既没有钱,又没有朋友。*I was stranded in the strange town without money or friends.* ② surround; hem in; encircle:被敌人围~ *be hemmed in by the enemies* ③ difficulties:急人之~ *be anxious to help those in difficulty* ④ tired; exhausted:人~马乏 *the exhausted troops* ⑤ sleepy:你~了就睡吧。*Go to bed if you feel sleepy.* ⑥ [方] sleep:他~了整整一上午的觉。*He slept away the whole morning.*

【困惫】[书] exhausted:她~之极,躺在了枕头上。*Her strength was exhausted and she fell back on the pillow.*

【困顿】① tired out; weary; worn-out:我下班后感到~。*I felt weary after work.* ② in financial straits; poverty-stricken:她一生都过着~的生活。*She has lived in poverty all her life.* /自从她丈夫去世,她一直处于~之中。*She has been in great straits since her husband died.*

【困厄】dire straits; distress:他最终在~中获得了成功。*He eventually succeeded in desperate straits.*

【困乏】tired; fatigued:病人容易~。*The patient fatigues easily.*

【困惑】puzzled; confused; bewildered; at a loss:使人~而混淆的复杂逻辑 *a complexity of logic that bewilders and confuses* /这封信使我~不解。*This letter puzzles me.*

【困觉】[方] sleep:他习惯于午饭后~。*He is used to having a nap after lunch.*

【困境】difficult position; dilemma; straits; plight:处于~中 *be in an awkward predicament* /他关心的是怎样帮助他们的公司走出~。*The ideas of how to help their company get out of dilemma occupied his mind.*

【困窘】embarrassing; in a difficult position; awkward:令人~的问题 *an embarrassing questions*

【困局】predicament; straits

【困倦】drowsy; sleepy:一个使人~的夏天下午 *a drowsy summer afternoon*

【困苦】hardship; deep distress; poverty:~的生活 *a life of hardship*

【困难】① difficulty:这个问题的~很多。*This question is full of difficulties.* ② poverty-stricken:家境~却虚摆场面 *live in genteel poverty*

【困扰】perplex; puzzle; haunt:这个问题~着我。*I was puzzled by the question.* /怕被发现的忧虑~着他。*He was haunted by fear of discovery.*

【困人】tiring; drowsy:~的天气 *drowsy weather* /~的活儿 *a very tiring job*

【困守】defend against a siege

kuò

扩 enlarge; expand; magnify:~地 *expand one's land (or territory)*

【扩版】(of a newspaper, novel, etc.) enlarge the format of the pages:本杂志将于明年~为100页。*This magazine will increase the number of its pages to 100 as from next year.*

【扩编】(of an army) enlarge the establishment; increase the troop strength:~部队 *enlarge an army*

【扩充】enlarge; expand; strengthen:把该书~为4卷 *extend the book to four volumes* /我们在~生产规模以便生产出更多更好的电视机。*We're enlarging the production scale to produce more and better TV sets.*

【扩大】enlarge; expand; broaden:~对外开放 *open wider to the outside world* / ~企业自主权 *enlargement of the powers of the enterprises to make their own decisions* / ~销路 *expand sales* / ~战果 *exploit victory* / ~会议 *enlarged session* / ~一个词的含义 *extend the sense of a word* /~知识面 *extend the range of one's knowledge; broaden one's horizon* /人类借助雷达来~自己的视野。*Man extends his eyes with radar.* /很不幸,事态的影响正在~。*Unfortunately, this affairs' influence is expanding.*

【扩大化】magnify or extend wrongly:不要使事态~ *not let the problem get out of hand*

【扩大再生产】extended reproduction

【扩建】expand; extend:~工厂 *expand a factory* / ~工程 *extension project* / ~项目 *extended construction*

【扩军】expand armaments:~备战 *arms expansion and war preparations*

【扩容】【电】expand the capacity

【扩散】spread; diffuse:核~ *nuclear proliferation* /癌~ *proliferation of cancer*

【扩销】expand sales

【扩写】expand a short article into a long one without changing the original meaning

【扩胸器】chest develop; chest expander

【扩音器】megaphone; loudspeaker

【扩印】enlarge and print a photo

【扩展】expand; extend; develop:那位作者把他的短篇小说~为长篇。*The writer expanded his short novel into a long one.* / 这个村子的地界~到河边。*This village expands to the riverside.*

【扩张】extend; expand; enlarge:~主义 *expansionism* /吸气使胸腔~ *expand the chest by inspiration* /他的权力~到别国。*His power extends to other lands.*

括 ① draw together; contract; tighten up:~发 *draw together the hair* ② include:包~ *include* /总~ *sum up* ③ bracket:把这句话~起来。*Bracket the sentence.*

【括号】brackets:方~ *square brackets* /尖~ *angle brackets*

K

【括弧】parentheses：把这两个词括在圆括弧里。*Put these two words in parentheses.*

阔 ① wide；broad：高谈～论 *spout*；*talk bombastically* ② wealthy；rich：摆～ *flaunt one's wealth* /他很～。*He is very rich.*

【阔别】be separated for a long time：～三载 *have been separated for three years* / ～多年的战友 *long separated comrades in arms* / 我们已经～多年。*We have not seen each other for years.*

【阔步】stride：～前进 *stride forward*；*advance with big strides* / ～高论 *take big strides and give a high-flown talk*

【阔绰】liberal with one's money：举止～ *be extravagant in behaviour* /生活～ *lead an extravagant life*

【阔佬】man of wealth；rich man

【阔气】luxurious；extravagant；pompous：摆～ *make a pompous show*；*display one's wealth*

【阔人】rich people

【阔少】wealthy man's son

【阔野】vast expanse of open country

【阔叶林】broad-leaved forest

【阔叶树】broadleaf tree：～材 *broad-leaved wood*

廓 ① wide；extensive：寥～ *boundless*；*vast* ② expand；enlarge：～大 *expand*；*enlarge* ③ outline：轮～ *outline*；*rough sketch*

【廓落】［书］open and still

【廓清】① clean up；clarify：～事实 *clarify matters* ② clear away；remove：～积弊 *sweep away outstanding abuses*

【廓张】［书］spread；expand：噪声～开去。*The noise spread into the air.*

K

L

lā

垃

【垃圾】rubbish; waste; garbage; refuse; junk:可燃~ *combustible rubbish* /生活~ *household garbage* /碎屑~ *detritus rubbish* /勿乱丢~。*Don't litter.* /车库里满是~。*The garage is full of junk.*

【垃圾处理】garbage disposal; refuse treatment

【垃圾堆】dump; garbage heap:那些可耻的言论早已被扔进历史的~。*Those vile remarks have already been thrown onto the rubbish heap of history.*

【垃圾发电】garbage power

【垃圾焚化】incineration of garbage: ~炉 *garbage furnace; refuse burner*

【垃圾食品】junk food

【垃圾箱】dustbin; garbage can:请把这袋垃圾丢到~去。*Take the bag of rubbish to the dustbin, please.*

【垃圾债券】junk bond

拉[1] ① pull; drag; draw: ~窗帘 *draw the curtain* /把你的椅子往桌前~一~。*Pull your chair to the table.* /一匹马~着大车沿着大路走。*A horse pulled the cart along the road.* /孩子~着我的手。*The child tugged at my hand.* ② convey by vehicles; haul:这辆小汽车只能~4个人。*The car can only carry four persons.* /他们用力把船~上岸。*They hauled the boat up onto the shore.* ③ move (troops to a place):把主力~出去 *move the main force out* ④ play (a musical instrument): ~小提琴 *play the violin* ⑤ drag out; draw out: ~下脸 *pull a long face* ⑥ [方] bring up:把他~大可真不容易。*It's quite difficult to bring him up.* ⑦ help; assist:你能~我一把吗? *Could you give me a hand?* ⑧ drag in; involve in:我被~进了他们的争吵。*I was implicated in their quarrel.* ⑨ solicit; win over: ~选票 *canvass votes* / ~订户 *solicit for subscriptions* ⑩ organize; put together: ~团伙 *form a gang* ⑪ canvass; solicit: ~广告 *solicit advertisements* ⑫ [方] chat: ~家常 *have a chat*

拉[2] have a bowel movement; empty the bowels: ~屎 *empty the bowels; shit*

see also lá; lǎ

【拉巴】[方] ① take great pains to bring up (a child):这些年都是他一个人把这几个孩子~大的。*He brought up the children by himself these years.* ② help; support; promote:我对业务还不太熟悉,我们组长经常会~我。*I have not been familiar with the business yet, and the group leader always gives me a hand.*

【拉帮结伙】recruit people to form a faction; gang up; band together; form cliques:那些人~,无恶不作。*They formed cliques and committed all sorts of crimes.*

【拉鼻儿】[口] sound a siren; blow a whistle

【拉场子】① perform in a street or in marketplaces ② make a name; put on a show to spread one's reputation:他刚来公司,想尽快拉开场子。*He is a new employee in the company and wants to be known by everyone soon.*

【拉扯】① drag; pull:小女孩~着我的袖子。*The little girl is pulling my sleeve.* ② take great pains to bring up (a child):他是由姑姑~大的。*He was brought up by his aunt.* ③ help; support; promote:多亏有他~我,我才能取得这些成绩。*With his help and support, I achieved these achievements.* ④ gang up with; rope in:他和一些不正经的人~在一起。*He gangs up with some dubious fellows.* ⑤ implicate; drag in:别把我~进去。*Don't drag me in.* ⑥ chat:他们俩在闲~。*They are chatting freely.*

【拉大旗,作虎皮】use a great banner as a tiger-skin — deck oneself out and intimidate people; deck oneself out and frighten people

【拉搭】[方] chit-chat:他俩一边排队,一边~起来。*They chatted when standing in a queue.*

【拉倒】forget about it; leave it at that; drop it:你不同意,就~。*Since you don't agree, let's forget about it.* /既然你不接受我的劝告那就~。*Since you refuse to take my advice, let's drop it.*

【拉丁】① [旧] press young men into military service ② force people into service

【拉丁美洲】Latin America: ~人 *Latin American* / ~经济委员会 *Economic Commission for Latin America* / ~自由贸易区 *Latin American Free Trade Market*

【拉丁文】Latin: ~圣经 *Vulgate*

【拉丁字母】the Latin alphabet; the Roman alphabet

【拉肚子】[口] suffer from diarrhoea; have loose bowels

【拉夫】[旧] pressgang; press people into service (for an army, etc.)

【拉杆】【机】① pull rod; drag link; draw bar: ~端 *drag link end* / ~固定点 *draught link anchorage*

/ ~[illegible]体 *drag link body* / ~支座 *drag link bearing* ② telescopic: ~三角支架 *tripod with telescopic legs*

【拉歌】challenge to sing:晚会开始前,我们两个班互相~儿。*We two classes challenged each other to sing before the evening began.*

【拉钩】①(of two people) hook up the little fingers of each other and give them a pull as a sign of keeping promise ②【机】drag hook; draw hook

【拉呱儿】[方] chat

【拉关系】[贬] try to establish a relationship with sb; cotton up to; make advances to sb without an introduction:拉同学关系 *claim old school ties*/没想到他居然和经理秘书拉上了关系。*To my surprise, he has cottoned up to the secretary of the manager.*

【拉后腿】hold sb back; be a drag on sb; be a hindrance to sb:我决定继续学习,家里应该不会有人~。*I have decided to further my study and I don't think anyone will hold me back in my family.*

【拉花儿】festoon

【拉话】[方] chat; chit-chat:他每次来这里都和那个小姑娘~。*Whenever he comes here, he will chat with that girl.*

【拉簧】【机】draw spring; drag spring

【拉饥荒】[口] be in debt; get into debt; run short of money:很幸运我今年没有~。*It's very lucky that I didn't get into debt this year.*

【拉家常】chat about daily things:两个主妇在河边~。*Two housewives are chatting by the river.*

【拉家带口】be burdened with a family:我~的,如今丢了工作,可怎么办啊? *I am burdened with a family, but now I lost my job. What shall I do?*

【拉架】try to stop people from fighting each other:他们俩刚才打起来了,是我拉的架。*They were fighting each other just now and I separated them.*

【拉交情】[贬] try to form ties with; cotton up to:说实话,我真是不愿意去他那里~。*To be frank, I am unwilling to claim friendship with him.*

【拉脚】transport persons or goods by cart

【拉近乎】[贬] cotton up to; try to form ties with sb:不知为什么,他最近总是跟我~。*He tries to get in with me recently, but I don't know why.*

【拉锯】① work a two-handed saw ② be locked in a seesaw struggle

【拉锯战】seesaw battle

【拉开】① pull open; open; draw back: ~门 *open the door* / ~窗帘 *draw back the curtain* ② increase the distance between; widen the gap: ~距离 *increase the distance; space out* /比分逐渐~。*The gap in the score was gradually widening.*

【拉客】①(of inns, small restaurants, hotels, etc.) solicit guests or diners ②(of taxi drivers, etc.) carry passengers ③(of prostitutes) solicit patrons

【拉亏空】be in debt; get into debt:他拉了很大的亏空。*He gets into a mountain of debt.*

【拉拉队】cheering team (or squad); rooters: ~员 *rooter*

【拉拉杂杂】*not well organized and without a central theme; lump together things in a confused way*:他的信写的~,让我费解。*His words in the letter are in disorder, which made me quite confused.*

【拉力】pulling force; tension

【拉力表】pull dynamometer

【拉力器】chest-developer; chest-expander

【拉力弹簧】tension spring; draught spring

【拉力赛】【体】(cross-country) rally

【拉练】camp and field training

【拉链】zip fastener; zipper; slide fastener:她拉上了裙子的~。*She zipped up her dress.*

【拉拢】draw sb over to one's side; win over; gain over; rope in:不要受坏人~。*Don't get roped in by bad people.*

【拉买卖】canvass business orders; solicit business

【拉毛】nap; gig

【拉门】sliding door

【拉面】[方] hand-pulled noodles

【拉皮条】[方] act as a procurer or pimp

【拉偏手儿】show partiality to one side when stopping a brawl

【拉平】① bring to the same level; even up; make even: ~比分 *even the score up; level the score* ②【航】flare-out

【拉纤】① tow (a boat): ~者 *tracker* ② act as go-between:保媒~ *act as go-between in arranging a marriage*

【拉萨】Lhasa, capital of the Tibetan Autonomous Region

【拉三扯四】wander from the subject; not stick to the point:他说话总爱~。*He always wanders from the subject in talking.*

【拉山头】form a faction:在我们的集体里禁止~。*Forming individual factions is forbidden in this collectivity.*

【拉伤】pull; injure by straining

【拉伸】draw; stretching; traction: ~长度 *tensile elongation* / ~试验 *tensile test* / ~弯曲 *stretch bending*

【拉生意】solicit trade; canvass trade

【拉手】handle:门~ *door handle*

【拉丝】wiredrawing

【拉斯维加斯】Las Vegas, gambling city in Nevada, USA

【拉锁】zip fastener; zipper

【拉套】①(of an extra animal) help pull a cart ② [方] help others:我心甘情愿为他~卖力。*I am most willing to slave for him.*

【拉条】【机】brace; stay

【拉脱维亚】Latvia: ~人 *Latvian*

【拉稀】[口] have loose bowels; have diarrhea

【拉下脸】① [口] not spare sb's sensibilities:我~来批评他。*I couldn't bring myself to dress him down.* ② [口] look displeased; pull a long face:他一看到我立刻~来。*He put on a stern expression at the sight of me.*

【拉下水】[喻] pull sb into the water — drag sb into the mire; make an accomplice of sb; corrupt sb:小心点,我看他想把你~。*Be careful! I think he tends to corrupt you.*

【拉线】act as go-between

【拉秧】【农】uproot plants after their edible portions have been harvested

【拉杂】rambling; promiscuous; ill-organized: ~地谈了一通 *make a rambling speech*

【拉闸】switch off power or electricity

【拉账】be in debt; get into debt

邋

【邋里邋遢】slovenly; sloppy: ~的外表 *a slovenly appearance*

【邋遢】unkempt; slovenly; seedy; dowdy; sloppy; dingy: ~的房间 *a sloppy room* /她是个~的女人。*She is a frump.*

lá

拉

slash; slit; cut: ~下一块肉 *cut off a piece of meat* /我手上~了一个口子。*I cut my hand.*

see also lā; lǎ

lǎ

拉

see also lā; lá

【拉忽】[方] careless; negligent:你可真~,居然把钱包忘在出租车上了。*You are careless enough to leave your wallet on the taxi.*

喇

【喇叭】① brass-wind instruments in general or any of these instruments: 吹 ~ *blow a trumpet* ② loudspeaker; horn (in a car):汽车~ *an automobile horn* /收音机里有个~。*There is a loudspeaker in a radio.*

【喇叭花】(white-edged) morning glory

【喇叭裤】bell-bottom trousers; bell-bottoms; flares

【喇叭裙】flared skirt

【喇叭筒】[口] ① horn; megaphone ② microphone

【喇嘛】【宗】lama

【喇嘛教】【宗】Lamaism

【喇嘛庙】【宗】lamasery

là

落

① leave out; be missing:这句话你~了一个字。*A character is missing in this sentence.* /她总是被~下,因为她老是不在。*She always misses out, because she's never there.* ② leave behind:我把雨伞~在教室里了。*I left the umbrella in the classroom.* ③ lag behind:他~在我后面。*He lagged behind me.* /我的家庭作业~下了。*I've got behind with my homework.*

see also lào; luò

腊

① the ancient practice of sacrifices to the gods in the twelfth month of the Lunar year: ~尽冬残 *the end of the lunar year* ② (of fish, meat, etc.) cured in winter, especially in the twelfth lunar month: ~鱼 *cured fish* ③ (Là) a surname

【腊八】the eighth day of the twelfth lunar month

【腊八醋】vinegar with garlic soaked in it

【腊八粥】rice porridge with nuts, beans, dried fruit, etc. eaten on the eighth day of the twelfth lunar month

【腊肠】sausage

【腊梅】【植】winter sweet

【腊日】day of winter sacrifice, usu. the eighth day of the twelfth lunar month

【腊肉】cured meat; bacon; preserved ham

【腊味】cured delicacies

【腊月】the twelfth month of the lunar year; the twelfth moon

蜡

① wax: 白 ~ *white wax* /石 ~ *paraffin wax* ② candle: 点 ~ *light a candle*

【蜡白】(of one's face) pale

【蜡板】① small wax scale ② tool for making white wax

【蜡版】mimeograph stencil (already cut)

【蜡笔】wax crayon: ~画 *crayon drawing* / ~画家 *crayonist*

【蜡布】cerecloth; patent cloth

【蜡虫】wax insect

【蜡床】tool for making white wax

【蜡刀】wax spatula

【蜡豆】wax bean

【蜡封】wax-sealed

【蜡膏】【药】cerate

【蜡光纸】flint-glazed paper; glazed paper

【蜡果】wax fruit

【蜡花】snuff (of a candlewick)

【蜡画】encaustic painting

【蜡黄】wax yellow; waxen; sallow: 面色 ~ *wear a waxen complexion; look sallow*

【蜡菊】【植】strawflower

【蜡泪】drips from a burning candle; wax guttering

【蜡疗】【医】wax therapy

【蜡模】【冶】wax matrix

【蜡皮】【药】wax coating (of a pill)

【蜡扦】candlestick

【蜡染】【纺】wax printing; batik: ~服饰 *wax-printed costumes and ornaments*

【蜡熟】【农】yellow maturity

【蜡树】wax tree

【蜡塑】wax sculpture

【蜡台】candlestick

【蜡丸】① hollow wax-ball with a pill or some secret message in it ② a wax-coated pill

【蜡像】wax figure; waxwork: ~馆 *waxworks museum*

【蜡纸】① wax paper ② stencil paper; stencil: 刻 ~ *cut a stencil*

【蜡烛】(wax) candle: ~头 *candle end* / ~心 *wick*

/洞里很黑,他就点了一些~来照明。*The cave was quite dark inside, so he made some candles to give light.*

辣 ① peppery; pungent; hot:辛~的评论 *peppery criticism* /胡椒是~的。*Pepper is hot.* ② (of taste) sting; bite; burn:~眼睛 *make the eye sting* /干辣椒使我的嘴里发~。*The chili burned my mouth.* ③ cruel; ruthless; venomous; vicious:心狠手~ *be vicious and ruthless; wicked and merciless*

【辣根】【植】horseradish

【辣乎乎】peppery; hot: ~的番茄酱 *a spicy tomato sauce*

【辣酱】thick chilli sauce

【辣椒】hot pepper; chilli:红~ *hot red pepper* /青~ *green capsicum; hot green pepper* /~粉 *paprika; chilli powder*

【辣手】① ruthless method; vicious device:他的~可多着呢! *He is full of ruthless devices.* ②[方] vicious; ruthless:一个~的妇人 *a ruthless woman* ③[口] thorny; troublesome; knotty:一个~的问题 *a thorny problem; a hot potato*

【辣丝丝】a little hot:汤的味道~的。*The soup tastes a little peppery.*

【辣酥酥】a little hot

【辣味】piquancy; pungency; peppery taste

【辣油】chilli oil

【辣子】① hot pepper; cayenne pepper; chilli ② hot-tempered woman:最好别去招惹那个~。*You'd better not get a rise out of that termagant.*

la

啦 expressing exclamation, interrogation, etc.:上课~! *Hey! It's time for class.*

lái

来[1] ① come; arrive:到我这儿~。*Come to me.* /他从日本~。*He comes from Japan.* ② take place; come up:问题~了。*Problems have cropped up.* /下午冰雹~了。*Sleet came on in the afternoon.* ③ used as a substitute for a more specific verb:让我~吧。*Let me do it.* /这样可~不得。*It won't do this way.* /我们去跳舞,你~不~? *We're dancing; will you join us?* ④ used to show possibility or capability:这件事我做不~。*I am not able to do it.* /你和他一定能处得~。*I am sure that you can get along well with him.* ⑤ used in front of a verb to indicate a intended action:要不要我~帮你? *Do you need my help?* /大家~想想办法。*Let's think of a way to solve the problem.* ⑥ used after another verb to indicate what one has come for:他看望我~了。*He came to visit me.* ⑦ used between two verbs or verbal phrases to indicate the purpose of the former action:我们要开个会~讨论一下这个问题。*We'll have a meeting to discuss the problem.* ⑧ used at the end of a sentence to indicate a past action or state:我何时这么说过~的? *When did I say so?* /刚才我们讨论~着。*We had a discussion just now.* /我昨天去游泳~。*I went swimming yesterday.* ⑨ future; next; coming:~岁 *the coming year* ⑩ indicating a period of time that lasts from the past up to the present:自古以~ *ever since the ancient times* /从~ *from the past to the present; always* /上个月~ *since last month* /这一年~他进步很快。*He has made rapid progress in the past year.* ⑪ (used to indicate an estimated number) about; around:十~个 *about ten* /三米~长 *about three metres long* /两米~深 *about two metres deep* ⑫ used after the numerals to indicate enumeration ⑬ (Lái) a surname

来[2] used as a syllable filler in folk ballads:正月里~是新春。*The first lunar month is the beginning of spring.* /你织布~我耕田。*You weave thread into cloth while I plough the field.*

来[3] ① used to indicate motion towards the speaker:进~ *come in* /出~ *come out* /拿~ *bring it here* /一只鸟飞过~。*A bird is flying hither.* ② used after a verb to indicate the result or estimation:说~话长。*It's a long story.* /看~你已经知道了。*It seems that you have known it.*

【来宾】(invited) guest; visitor: ~登记簿 *visitor's book* /~室 *guest chamber* /~席 *seats for guests*

【来不得】won't do; be impermissible:这是一个科学问题,~半点虚伪。*This is a matter of science, which permits no dishonesty.*

【来不及】there's not enough time (to do sth); it's too late (to do sth):赶火车已经~了。*It's too late to catch the train.* /我看平信~了,我们还是用特快专递吧。*I don't think an ordinary mail can catch the time; we'd better send it by EMS.*

【来朝】come to court; come to pay tribute (to the emperor)

【来潮】① (of the tide) rise; flow:他心血~要学绘画。*Prompted by a sudden impulse, he decided to learn drawing.* ②【生理】have a period; menstruate

【来到】arrive; come:好天气终于~了。*Good weather has arrived at last.* /我们今天上午~北京。*We arrived in Beijing this morning.*

【来得】[口] ① competent; equal to; be able:这些岗位她都~。*She is competent to all these posts.* ② emerge (from a comparison) as; come out as:打电话比写信~快得多。*Calling is much quicker than writing a letter.*

【来得及】have time (for sth); be able to do sth in time; be able to make it:赶快去,还~。*Go at once while there's still time.* /看样子还~。*It seems that we can still make it.*

【来得早不如来得巧】[俗] to arrive early is not so good as to arrive at the most opportune moment

【来电】① send a telegram here: ~祝贺 *send telegram of congratulations* ② power coming on again:两个小时后,终于~了。*Power was finally on two hours later.* ③ incoming telegram; your message: ~收悉。*Your message received.*

【来而不往非礼也】It is impolite not to reciprocate: ~,我们也该去回访他们。*It's improper not to pay a return visit to them.*

【来犯】come to attack us; invade our territory:没有敌人敢~。*No enemies dare to attack us.*

【来访】come to visit; come to call: ~者 *visitors* /明天美国总统~我国。*The President of USA will come to visit our country tomorrow.*

【来复枪】rifle

【来复线】【军】rifling

【来稿】incoming manuscript; your manuscript: ~截至5月31日。*The deadline for contributions is May 31.* /编辑手中本月~不足以成刊。*The editor is short of contributions for the issue of this month.*

【来归】① come over and pledge allegiance ②[古](of a woman) join a man in marriage

【来函】[书] incoming letter; your letter:请~洽谈。*Please negotiate by mail.*

【来鸿】[书] a letter from faraway

【来回】① make a round trip; make a return journey; go there and come back: ~票 *return ticket; round-trip ticket* /从我家到车站~要走20分钟。*It takes twenty minutes to walk from my home to the station and back.* ② back and forth; to and fro: ~移动 *move to and fro*

【来回来去】[方] back and forth; over and over again:他~说这几句话。*He repeated the sentences again and again.*

【来火】flare up; get angry:他为一点小事就~。*He flew into a fury for the slightest reason.*

【来件】communication or parcel received:我阅读了所有~。*I have read all the incoming documents.*

【来劲】[方] ① full of enthusiasm; in high spirits:他越说越~。*The longer he spoke, the more enthusiastic he became.* ② exhilarating; exciting; thrilling:我们打败了对手,真~! *How exciting it is that we beat our rivals.* ③ jest with; annoy; offend:他已经让步了,你就别~了。*He has conceded to you; don't offend him any more.*

【来客】guest; visitor:谢绝~参观。*Visitor is not admitted.*

【来来往往】come and go; go to and fro:这种~的交流对文化是有利的。*This kind of give and take is beneficial to our culture.*

【来历】origin; source; antecedents; background; past history:他~不明。*He is of questionable antecedents.*

【来临】arrive; come; approach:春天~了。*Spring approaches.* /新年即将~。*The new year is drawing near.*

【来龙去脉】ins and outs; whence and whither; origin and development:弄清事情的~ *find out the cause and effect of the incident; be clear about the ins and outs of a problem*

【来路】(láilù) ① incoming road; approach:他挡住了我的~。*He blocked my way.* ② source; origin:被解雇断了他的~。*Being fired cut off his source of income.*

【来路】(láilu) origin; antecedents: ~不明 *unknown source or origin; of questionable antecedents*

【来路货】[方] imported goods

【来年】the coming year; next year: ~二月他将年满20。*He will be twenty next February.*

【来去】① round trip: ~大概需要十天。*The round trip will take about ten days.* ② come and go: ~自由 *come and go freely* ③[方] contact with sb:从此他们再无~。*Hence they never contacted each other.*

【…来…去】back and forth; over and over again:翻来覆去 *toss and turn* /飞来飞去 *fly back and forth* /眉来眼去 *flirt with each other*

【来人】bearer; messenger: ~汇票 *bearer draft* /~支票 *bearer check*

【来日】the days to come; the future:时间不早了,我们~再谈吧。*It's already late; let's discuss it some other day.* /他自感~无多,已经开始写遗嘱。*He felt that there wasn't much time left and began to make his testament.*

【来日方长】there will be ample (or plenty of) time; have years ahead of sb: ~,你又何必着急呢? *Why are you so anxious? There is plenty of time.*

【来生】next life; hereafter:你相信有~吗? *Do you believe in a hereafter?*

【来使】envoy; messenger:两国交兵,不辱~。*The envoy should not be humiliated even though two countries are at war.*

【来世】next life; afterlife:他希望~灵魂得到拯救。*He hoped to win salvation hereafter.*

【来事】①[方] deal with people:这小姑娘可会~儿了,我们都很喜欢她。*The girl really has a way with people and we all like her very much.* ②[方] be all right; will do:这么做不~。*It will not do.* ③[书] future events:谁会知道~呢? *Who can tell what will happen in the future?*

【来势】gathering momentum; oncoming force: ~汹汹 *bear down menacingly; come to look for trouble*

【来书】[书] ① send a letter here ② your letter: ~已阅,备感欣慰。*I have read your letter and felt much relieved.*

【来头】① connections; backing:他~不小。*He has powerful backing.* ② the motive behind (sb's words, etc.); cause:他说话有~。*He said it with a motive.* ③ the force with which sth breaks out; gathering momentum:他一见~不妙,就立刻躲到了门后。*Seeing things turn worse, he hid behind the door at once.* ④[口] interest; fun:看电视多没~,我们出去游泳吧。*It's not at all interesting to watch TV; let's go swimming.*

【来往】(láiwǎng) come and go: ~车辆 *vehicles coming and going* /客人们~不绝。*Guests are coming and going ceaselessly.*

【来往】(láiwang) ① dealings; contact; intercourse:业务~ *business dealings* ② have contact

or dealings：我和他没有～。*I have no dealings with him.*
【来文】document received
【来向】direction of sth coming：你要根据风的～调整机器的位置。*You should set the machine by the way the wind blows.*
【来项】income；receipts：今年我的～减少了很多。*I draw a much smaller income than ever this year.*
【来信】① send a letter here：请经常给我～。*Please write to me frequently.* ② incoming letter；your letter：我今天上午收到了他的～。*I received his letter this morning.*
【来意】one's purpose in coming：～不善 *come with ill intent*
【来由】reason；cause：他没～地责备我。*He blamed me without any reason.*
【来源】① source；origin：你的报告～很完备。*Your report is thoroughly sourced.* /这条消息～可靠。*The news comes from a reliable source.* /这些词的～是不可知的。*The origins of these words are unknown.* ② originate；stem from：～于过去的习俗 *customs stemming from the past* /正确决定～于正确的判断。*Correct decisions stem from correct judgement.*
【来源国】sending country；country of origin
【来者】① the things to come or the generations to come ② any person or thing that comes or has come
【来者不拒】all are welcome；all comers are welcome；keep open doors；no comer is rejected：她对于向她献殷勤的男子都是～。*She never rejected a man who pays court to her.*
【来者不善，善者不来】he who comes is certainly well prepared to fight with us or get us into a corner
【来着】［口］used at the end of affirmative sentences or special questions，indicating a past action or state：你刚才说什么～？*What were you saying just now?* /她叫什么～？我忘记了。*What's here name? It dies away from my memory.*
【来之不易】hard to come by；be not easily won；be hard won；be not easily come by；hard-earned：这些成绩～啊。*These achievements have not been easily won.*
【来自】come from：～远方 *come from afar*

莱 ①［书］【植】lamb's-quarters ②［古］waste land outside a town
【莱比锡】Leipzig，a city in Germany
【莱塞】【物】laser
【莱茵河】Rhine，a river in central and western Europe

lài

徕 ［书］bring gifts to or send one's wishes in recognition of services provided：劳～ *send gifts to sb to win his allegiance*

赉 ［书］grant；bestow：赏～ *give a reward*

睐 ［书］① cock-eyed；squint ② look at；glance：明眸善～ *shining eyes and attractive looks*

赖[1] ① rely on；depend on：仰～ *depend on sb or sth for support* /她的学费依～于父母。*She relies on her parents for tuition.* ② brazen；rascally：耍～ *act rascally* ③ hang on in a place：他～在我家不肯走。*He continues to stay in my home and refuses to clear up.* ④ deny one's mistakes or responsibility；go back on one's words：事实俱在，想～是不可能的。*The facts are all clear and cannot be denied.* ⑤ falsely accuse；blame sb wrongly：是你做错了，不能～别人。*You shouldn't put the blame on somebody else.* ⑥ blame：这事不～他。*He's not to blame for that.* ⑦（Lài）a surname

赖[2] bad；not good：她唱得真不～。*She really sings well.*
【赖氨酸】【生化】lysine
【赖词儿】［方］lie；words meant to put the blame on sb else：她非但不自己承担起责任来，还当着我的面编～。*Instead of taking the responsibility upon herself, she threw the lie in my face.*
【赖婚】deny marriage；refuse to marry（after engagement）
【赖皮】① rascally；shameless；unreasonable：耍～ *play the rascal*；*act shamelessly* ② act rascally（or brazenly）：～是没有用的，你最好马上离开！*It's useless to act in such a shameless way*；*you'd better leave at once.*
【赖学】［方］play truant；cut class
【赖债】repudiate one's debt：我相信他不会～。*I am sure that he will not repudiate his debt.*
【赖账】① repudiate a debt ② go back on one's word：她刚刚答应要在我们厂投资，可是一转眼就～了。*She promised to invest in our factory a minute ago, but went back on her words immediately.*
【赖子】rascal；shameless people

濑 ［书］swift water；rapids

癞 ①【医】leprosy ②［方］favus of the scalp
【癞病】leprosy
【癞疮】【医】impetigo
【癞瓜】［方］bitter gourd
【癞蛤蟆】toad：～想吃天鹅肉 *crave for sth one is not worthy of*
【癞皮狗】mangy dog；loathsome creature
【癞头】favus-infected head；scabby head
【癞头疮】scabies on the head
【癞癣】favus；ringworm
【癞子】① favus of the scalp ② a person affected with favus on the head

籁 ① an ancient musical pipe ② sound coming from holes；noise：万～俱寂。*All is quiet.*

lai

唻 ［方］① used at the end of a question, equal to 呢:你们在干什么～? *What are you doing?* ② equal to 啦:她长得可漂亮～! *What a beautiful woman she is!* ③ equal to 来着:她刚才说什么～? *What did she say just now?*

lán

兰 ①【植】orchid; cymbidium ②【植】fragrant thoroughwort ③【植】lily magnolia ④（Lán）a surname

【兰草】① fragrant thoroughwort ② orchid

【兰花】① cymbidium; orchid ② sword-leaved cymbidium

【兰花学】orchidology

【兰交】［书］bosom friend; close friend

【兰谱】genealogical records exchanged by those who have sworn brotherhood

岚 ［书］mist; haze on hillside:山～ *mountain mists*

【岚烟】mountain mist

拦 ① block; hinder; bar; hold back:一个陌生人～住我问路。*A stranger stopped me and asked directions.* /他～住了我的去路。*He stood barring my way.* /他～着我不让我和她结婚。*He obstructed me from marrying her.* /大雨阻～了军队的前进。*Heavy rains were a check on the army's advance.* ② direct right at: ～腰一棍 *give sb a blow right on the waist*

【拦挡】block; obstruct:他们～我,不让我进门。*They stopped me and don't let me in.*

【拦道木】road fence; roadblock

【拦柜】shop counter

【拦河坝】a dam across a river; dam

【拦洪坝】a dam for holding back floodwater; a dam for flood control

【拦击】① intercept and attack ②【体】volley

【拦劫】waylay and rob; mug

【拦截】intercept: ～增援的敌人 *intercept enemy reinforcements*

【拦路】block the way: ～抢劫 *hold up; waylay; block the road in order to rob; block the road and rob the passers-by*

【拦路虎】a road-blocking tiger — obstacle; hindrance; bar:他的英语很差,这是他学习先进知识的～。*His poor English is a bar to his learning the advanced knowledge.*

【拦水坝】check dam

【拦网】【体】(in volleyball) block:单人～ *one-man block* /双人 *two-man block*

【拦蓄】retain (water); impound: ～山洪 *impound mountain torrents*

【拦腰】(hold) by the waist; round the middle:大坝把河水～截断。*The dam cuts the river in the middle.*

【拦阻】block; hold back; obstruct:谁也～不了他去参军。*Nobody can stop him from joining the army.*

栏 ① fence; hurdle; railing:高(低)～赛跑 *the high (low) hurdles* /木～ *a wooden fence* /铁～ *iron balustrade* /栅～ *fence; railing* ② bar; pen; shed:牛～ *cowshed* /羊～ *sheep pen* ③ column (in a newspaper or magazine):广告～ *advertising column* /新闻～ *news column* /专～ *special column* /每页分三～。*Each page has three columns.* ④ column (of a form):备注～ *remarks column* /请把这～的数字加起来。*Please add up this column of figures.* ⑤ board for attaching notices:布告～ *bulletin board; notice board*

【栏板】breast board

【栏肥】barnyard manure

【栏杆】railing; banisters; balustrade:船边～ *gunwale railing* /固定～ *fixed railing* /桥～ *bridge railing* /瞭望台～ *observation platform railing*

【栏槛】banister; railing

【栏目】the heading or title of a column (in a magazine, newspaper, etc.):很多报纸都设有读者～。*There are reader columns in many kinds of newspapers.*

【栏栅】［方］railing; barrier

阑 ［书］①（of time）late; near the end:夜～人静 *in the dead hours of the night; in the stillness of the night* ② presume; make bold to do sth: ～出 *leave without permission*

【阑干】［书］across; crisscross

【阑入】［书］① enter a place that is forbidden to one ② mix; mingle

【阑珊】［书］coming to an end; wane; decline:意兴～ *one's enthusiasm declines*

【阑尾】【生理】appendix; vermix

【阑尾炎】【医】appendicitis

蓝 ① blue:浅～ *light blue* /深～ *dark blue* /蔚～ *sky blue* ②【植】indigo plant ③（Lán）a surname

【蓝宝石】sapphire

【蓝本】① writing upon which later work is based; chief source ② original version (of a literary work)

【蓝筹股】【经】blue chip

【蓝带】【地】blue band

【蓝靛】① indigo ② indigo blue; dark blue

【蓝矾】【化】chalcanthite; vitriol; blue copperas

【蓝钢】【冶】blue steel

【蓝粉】【冶】blue powder

【蓝黑】blue-black: ～墨水 *blue-black ink*

【蓝晶】aquamarine

【蓝晶晶】bright blue: ～的海水 *blue and glittering sea water*

【蓝鲸】blue whale

【蓝栎】blue oak

【蓝领】blue-collar: ～工人 *blue-collar worker*

【蓝绿】blue-green; cyan

【蓝玛瑙】blue agate

【蓝皮书】blue book; blue paper
【蓝券】blue chip shares
【蓝色】blue; blueness: ~晶体 *blue coloured crystal* / ~星体 *blue stellar object* / ~颜料 *blue pigment*
【蓝色盲】blue blindness; trianopia; acyanoblupsia
【蓝色素】【化】cyanine
【蓝闪石】【矿】glaucophane
【蓝舌病】blue tongue disease
【蓝石英】【矿】siderite; azure quartz
【蓝田猿人】【考】Lantian Man
【蓝图】① blueprint: 绘制~ *draw a blueprint for sth* ②[喻] plan; scheme
【蓝土】【地】blue ground
【蓝星】【天】blue star
【蓝盈盈】bright blue
【蓝藻】【植】blue-green algae

谰 [书] ① slander; deny; malign ② deny

【谰言】calumny; slander: 无耻~ *shameless slander*

澜 billows; waves: 力挽狂~ *try one's best to stem a raging tide — make vigorous efforts to turn the situation* / 推波助~ *make a stormy sea stormier — add fuel to the fire*

褴

【褴褛】ragged; shabby: 衣衫~ *be dressed in rags; be shabbily dressed*

篮 ① basket: 竹~ *bamboo basket* ②【体】goal; basket: 投~ *shoot a basket* ③ basketball: 女~ *women's basketball team*

【篮板】【体】backboard
【篮板球】【体】rebound: 他抓住~投篮入网。*He grasped the rebound and sank a basket.*
【篮筐】basketry
【篮球】【体】basketball: 打~ *play basketball* / ~场 *basketball court* / ~队 *basketball team* / ~季 *basketball season*
【篮圈】【体】ring; hoop; basket
【篮坛】basketball circles
【篮子】basket: 一~桃子 *a basket of peaches*

lǎn

览 take a look at; see; view: 浏~ *skim over; glance over* / 游~ *go sightseeing; tour* / 博~群书 *read widely (or extensively)* / 一~无余 *take in everything at a glance*

【览胜】[书] visit scenic spots: 泰山~ *go sighting on Mount Tai*

揽 ① take into one's arms; hold: ~镜自照 *hold up a mirror to look at one's own reflection* / 她把女儿~在怀里。*She clasped her daughter to her bosom.* ② fasten with a rope, etc.: 她用绳子~上了柴火。*She tied a rope around the firewood.* ③ take on; canvass: 承~ *contract for* / 推功~过 *owe one's achievements to others and take the blames on oneself* ④ take hold of; grasp: ~权 *arrogate power to oneself* / 包~一切 *undertake the whole thing*

【揽承】agree (or contract) to do a job; take on (a job, etc.): 他把这个任务~下来。*He undertook the task.*
【揽工】[方] worker who has worked for a long time
【揽活】take on work: 几个出租车司机在路边~。*Several taxi-drivers were soliciting work by the roadside.*
【揽权】arrogate all powers to oneself
【揽胜】[书] have a panoramic view of the scenery
【揽总】assume overall responsibility; take on everything: 这个工程由我~。*I am in overall charge of the project.*

缆 ① cable; mooring rope ② thick rope: 电~ *power cable; wire* ③ moor (a ship)

【缆车】cable car; trolley
【缆道】track cable; cableway
【缆绳】anchor line; rope
【缆索】thick rope; cable; hawser: ~起重机 *cable crane*

榄 olive

【榄香】elemi: ~素 *elemicin*

懒 ① lazy; idle; slothful: 偷~ *loaf about* / 好吃~做 *be gluttonous and lazy* ② sluggish; languid: 伸~腰 *stretch oneself*

【懒虫】[口] lazybones
【懒怠】① indolent; lazy ② not in the mood to do sth; be too lazy to do sth: 我~写作业。*I don't feel like doing my homework.* / 她~和丈夫谈论那件事。*She was not in the mood to discuss it with her husband.*
【懒得】not feel like; not be in the mood to; be disinclined to: 我~给他写信,还是打电话吧。*I don't want to write to him; I'll just give him a call instead.*
【懒惰】lazy; idle: 一个~的学生 *a shiftless student* / 他生性~。*He has a sluggish disposition.* / 不要助长他的~。*Don't encourage him in his idle ways.*
【懒骨头】[口] lazybones
【懒汉】sluggard; idler; lazybones: 他是一个~。*He is a lazy fellow.* / 他是个优秀的工程师,但在个人习惯方面却是个~。*He is an excellent engineer, but a slob in his personal habits.*
【懒猴】【动】slender loris; loris
【懒懒散散】be slack in sth; lazy and loosened; indolent and sluggish: 他工作~。*He is negligent in his work.*
【懒散】sluggish; negligent; indolent: ~的步子 *a slack pace* / ~的员工 *slothful employees* / 不要这样~,振作起来。*Don't be so sluggish; pull yourself together.*
【懒熊】【动】sloth bear
【懒洋洋】languid; listless: 他今天~的。*He was in a languid mood today.* / 他手插在口袋里~地从我身边走了过去。*He slouched past me with his hands in his pockets.*
【懒于】too lazy to do sth; not enthusiastic about

L

sth:我~给她回信。*I am lazy to write back a letter to her.*

làn

烂 ① mashed; mushy pappy:用铁锤把竹竿砸~ *smash bamboo stems with a hammer* /稀粥~饭 *the thin gruel and the pulpy rice* /肉烧得很~。*The meat is very tender.* ② rot; decay: ~水果 *spoiled fruits* /没有人来摘这些成熟的水果,它们已经开始~了。*The ripe fruit began to rot when no one came to pick it.* ③ torn to pieces; tattered:破铜~铁 *odds and ends of copper and iron* / 破衣~衫 *worn-out clothes* / ~纸 *pieces of torn paper* ④ messy; confused; disorderly ⑤ very; thoroughly

【烂糊】(of food) mashed; pulpy:粥煮得真~。*The rice gruel is cooked quite mushy.* /这些蔬菜你烧得太久了,都~了。*You've boiled these vegetables too long; you've boiled them to a pulp.*

【烂漫】① bright-coloured; brilliant:山花~ *bright mountain flowers in full bloom* ② unaffected; natural:天真~ *naive; innocent*

【烂泥】mud; slush:汽车陷入了~。*The car got stuck in the mire.*

【烂熟】① thoroughly cooked:牛肉烧的~。*The beef is thoroughly cooked.* ② know sth thoroughly:台词背得~ *learn one's lines thoroughly* /他把课文背得~。*He learned the text by heart.*

【烂摊子】a shambles; an awful mess:他把这件事弄成了~。*He's made a mess of the job.*

【烂污】[方] ① watery faeces ② (esp. of a woman) dissolute; loose: ~货 *loose woman; whore*

【烂账】① messy accounts ② bad loan; bad debts

【烂醉】dead drunk

【烂醉如泥】be dead drunk; as drunk as a jellyfish; be as drunk as a lord:他在圣诞节聚会上~。*He got absolutely sizzled at the Christmas party.*

滥 ① overflow; flood:河水泛~。*The river was overflowing.* ② excessive; without restraint: ~交朋友 *choose friends indiscriminately* /狂轰~炸 *indiscriminate bombing* /宁缺毋~ *rather go without than have sth shoddy*

【滥调】hackneyed tune; worn-out theme; hackneyed phrase; platitude; tag:陈词~ *over used expressions; hackneyed and stereotyped expressions*

【滥伐】【林】deforestation; excessive logging: ~树木 *fell trees indiscriminately*

【滥杀无辜】indiscriminate killing of innocent people

【滥套子】hackneyed phrases

【滥用】abuse; misuse; stretch; strain; use indiscriminately: ~公款 *irregularities in use of public funds* / ~职权 *abuse one's power; misuse of authority; override one's commission; stretch one's power* /他~金钱寻欢作乐。*He lavished money upon his pleasures.*

【滥竽充数】pass oneself off as one of the players in an ensemble — to be included in a group just to fill in a vacancy; be a layman who passes himself off as an expert; make up the number

lāng

啷

【啷当】[方] ① (of age) about; around:他三十岁~。*He is about thirty years old.* ② and so on:他穿得挺讲究,帽子、夹克、皮鞋~的样样全新。*He is daintily dressed with everything on him brand-new, such as hat, jacket, leather shoes and so on.*

láng

郎 ① an ancient official title:侍~ *vice minister* ② form of address to some people:伴~ *best man* /货~ *street vendor* /新~ *bridegroom* ③ my darling:情~ *my darling* ④ son of another person:令~ *your son* ⑤ (Láng) a surname

【郎才女貌】a brilliant young scholar and a beautiful woman — a perfect match

【郎当】① (of clothes) loose-hanging; untidy; unfit ② discouraged; dejected:他看上去郎郎当当的。*He looks dejected.* ③ (of a person) useless:他有个~的儿子。*His son is good for nothing.*

【郎舅】a man and his wife's brother

【郎君】(used by a woman) husband:我何时才能找到如意~啊? *When can I find an ideal husband?*

【郎中】① [古] an official title ② [方] a physician trained in herbal medicine; doctor

狼 【动】wolf: ~群 *wolf pack* /披着羊皮的~ *a wolf in sheep's clothing; a wolf in lamb's skin*

【狼狈】in a tight corner; be in an awkward position; be flustered; lose one's presence of mind: ~逃窜 *flee in panic* /他的到来弄得她很~。*She was put in a fluster by his coming.*

【狼狈不堪】be all in a fluster; be hard-pressed; be in an awkward predicament; like a drowned mouse:我忽然发现自己处于一种~的境地。*I found myself suddenly in a most awkward predicament.*

【狼狈为奸】act in collusion (or cahoots) with each other; collude with sb in doing evil

【狼奔豕突】run like wolves and rush like boars — tear about like wild beasts; flee in panic

【狼疮】【医】lupus: ~结节 *lupoma* /红斑~ *lupus erythematosus*

【狼狗】wolfhound; wolf dog

【狼孩】wolf-child

【狼毫】a writing brush made of weasel's hair

【狼獾】【动】carcajou; wolverene; wolverine

【狼藉】[书] at sixes and sevens; in total disorder or disarray; in a messy state; scattered about:声

名 infamous; notorious /她家的厨房总是杯盘~。The cups, bowls and dishes always lie about in great disorder in her kitchen.
【狼戾不仁】be vicious and cruel; ruthlessly cruel
【狼戾无亲】without natural affection
【狼吞虎咽】eat (one's food) like wolves and tigers; avaricious; gulp; gorge; gobble up:他~地吃了一顿美餐。He wolfed down a good meal. /那饥饿的孩子~地吃饭。The hungry boy was devouring his dinner.
【狼心狗肺】① rapacious as a wolf and savage as a cur — of wolfish cruelty; cold-blooded; beastly ② heartless and ungrateful; unthankful
【狼牙】① wolf's tooth; wolf's fang ②【植】cryptotaeneous cinquefoil
【狼烟】the smoke of wolves' dung burnt at border posts in ancient China to signal alarm
【狼烟四起】smoke signals rising from all sides — war alarms raised everywhere
【狼子野心】a wolf cub with a savage heart — a wolfish nature; wolfish ambition

琅 [书] ① a kind of jade ② pure white
【琅玕】[书] a pearl-like stone
【琅琅】[象] a tinkling or jingling sound; the sound of reading aloud:书声~ the sound of reading aloud /~上口 easy to pronounce

桹
【桹桹】[象] the sound of striking wood

廊 veranda; corridor; porch:长~ a covered corridor; long corridor /画~ picture gallery /走~ passage; corridor
【廊道】gallery
【廊庙】[书] imperial court
【廊檐】the eaves of a veranda
【廊子】porch; corridor; veranda

榔
【榔槺】bulky; cumbersome: ~的包裹 a cumbersome parcel
【榔头】hammer

硠 [书] sound of water dashing on rocks

锒
【锒铛】①[书] iron chains ② clank; clang:犯人走路时脚镣~作响。The prisoner's ankle chains clanked as they walked.
【锒铛入狱】be chained and thrown into prison

稂 [古]【植】Chinese pennisetum; weeds
【稂莠】weeds; pennisetum and green bristlegrass — evil persons

lǎng

朗 ① light; bright:明~ bright and clear /晴~的天气 a fine day /豁然开~ be suddenly enlightened ② (of sound) loud and clear
【朗读】read aloud; read loudly and clearly: ~能使我们加深对诗歌的理解。Reading poetry aloud makes us understand it better.
【朗朗】①[象] the sound of reading aloud:教室里传出~书声。The sound of reading aloud came out from the classroom. ② bright; light:乾坤~ as bright as sun and moon
【朗生】[旧] Tibetan household slave
【朗声】in a clear loud voice:"是"。他~答道。"Yes." He said in a clear and loud voice.
【朗诵】read aloud with expression; recite; declaim; deliver a recitation: ~一首诗 recite a poem
【朗月明星】a bright moon and illuminating stars
【朗照】[书] ① shine; illuminate ② observe (or examine) publicly

làng

莨
【莨菪】【植】(black) henbane: ~碱 tropine

浪 ① wave; billow; breaker:乘风破~ ride the wind and cleave the waves /风平~静 calm and tranquil /后~推前~。Waves urge waves. /海~敲击岩石。Sea waves dash against the rocks. ② things undulating like waves:热~ a heat wave /麦~ rippling wheat; waves of wheat ③ unrestrained:放~ dissolute; lax /孟~ rash; rough and rude ④[方] ramble; roam: ~游 travel freely /流~ tramp; roam about; lead a vagrant lift
【浪潮】tide; wave:革命的~ the tide of revolution
【浪荡】① loiter about; loaf about: ~一辈子 loaf through life /一个~的人 an idle fellow ② dissolute; dissipated: ~子 dissipater; rakehell /~不羁 dissipated and unrestrained
【浪得虚名】have unearned reputation
【浪费】waste; squander; be extravagant:反对~ combat waste /~的人 a lavish spender /不要~水,没有多少了。Don't waste the water; there isn't much. /他们在无意义的争论中~精力。They are dissipating their energies in pointless argument. /她疯狂购物~钱财。She blew a fortune on a shopping spree.
【浪花】① the foam of breaking waves; spindrift: ~飞溅 a spray of water ② episodes in one's life
【浪迹】wander about; roam about: ~江湖 wander about (all corners of the country) /~萍踪 drift about without any trace like running water or duckweed /~天涯 wander all over the world
【浪漫】① romantic; poetic: ~的气氛 a romantic

atmosphere / ~派诗人 *the romantic poets* ② unconventional; loose; licentious; dissolute: 他是一个颇有才气而又~的作家。*He is a brilliant and dissolute writer.*

【浪漫主义】romanticism: ~者 *romanticist* / ~运动 *Romantic Movement* (*in Europe in the late* 18th *and the early* 19th *centuries*)

【浪木】swing log (used for physical exercise)

【浪人】① tramp; vagrant ② (Japanese) ronin; gangster

【浪蚀】wave cut; wave erosion: ~海岸 *wave erosion coast* / ~作用 *marine erosion*

【浪涛】great waves; billows: ~汹涌 *rolling waves*

【浪头】[口] ① wave ② trend: 赶~ *go with the tide*

【浪涌】【电】surge: ~电流 *surge current* / ~电压 *surge voltage*; *power surge*

【浪游】travel about without any definite destination; loaf; wander

【浪语】① lewd remarks ② nonsense; rubbish ③ indulge in irresponsible remarks: 他的~无凭。*His idle remarks are groundless.*

【浪子】prodigal; loafer; wastrel

【浪子回头】return of the prodigal son; a prodigal (son) becomes good; turn over a new leaf: ~金不换。*A prodigal who returns is more precious than gold.*

lāo

捞 ① drag for; scoop up; dredge out; pull out (from the water): 打~ *get out of the water*; *salvage* / ~鱼 *net fish*; *catch fish* / 大海~针 *look for a needle in a bottle of hay* ② get by improper means: ~外快 *get extra income* / ~一把 *reap some profit*; *cash in on sth*; *profiteer* / 他们趁机~了不少好处。*They took the chance of it and benefited a lot.* ③ [方] walk off with sth: 他顺手~了一支钢笔。*He walked away with a pen.*

【捞本】win back lost wagers; recover one's losses; recoup oneself: 他这次想把本捞回来。*He wants to recover his losses this time.*

【捞稻草】① clutch at a straw ② (try to) take advantage of sth; (try to) make capital of sth: 你想从中~吗? *Do you think that you can capitalize on it?*

【捞饭】rice boiled, strained and then steamed

【捞摸】[口] feel about in water — try to gain some unfair advantage; gain profits by improper ways: 谁也不知道他从中~了多少好处。*Nobody knows how many advantages he gained from it.*

【捞取】① scoop up from a liquid; drag for: 塘里的鱼可以随时~。*One can net fish in the pond any time.* ② fish for; gain; reap: ~政治资本 *fish for political capital* / 他一下子~了一万美元。*He earned $ 10,000 in one scoop.*

【捞着】get the opportunity (of doing sth): 昨天那顿饭,我没~吃。*I missed that meal yesterday.*

劳 ① work; labour: 不~无获。*No pains, no gains.* ② trouble sb with sth: ~您帮个忙。*Will you please do me a favour?* ③ labourer; labour: ~资合同 *contract between labour and capital* / ~资纠纷 *trouble between labour and management* ④ fatigue; toil: 任~任怨 *willingly bear the burden of hard works* ⑤ merit; achievement; feat: 汗马功~ *war exploits*; *one's contributions in work* ⑥ reward; bring gifts to: ~军 *bring greetings and gifts to army units* ⑦ (Láo) a surname

【劳保】① labour insurance: 享受~待遇 *enjoy the benefit of labour insurance* ② labour safety (or protection): ~医疗 *labour-protection medical care* / ~条例 *labour protection regulations* / ~用品 *appliances for labour protection*

【劳步】thanks for coming: 请勿~。*Please don't bother to come.*

【劳瘁】[书] exhausted from excessive work; worn-out: ~而卒 *die wearied and worn*

【劳动】(láodòng) ① work; labour: 体力~ *manual labour* / 脑力~ *mental labour* ② physical labour; manual labour: 参加~ *go and do manual labour* ③ do physical labour: 大家~热情很高。*Everyone worked with great enthusiasm.*

【劳动】(láodong) cause sb trouble (by asking a favour): ~你关上门。*Will you please close the door?*

【劳动成本】labour cost

【劳动锻炼】temper oneself through manual labour

【劳动保护】labour safety: ~设施 *labour safety devices*

【劳动保险】labour insurance

【劳动成果】fruit of labour

【劳动对象】subject of labour

【劳动法】labour law

【劳动服】work clothes; overalls

【劳动服务公司】labour service company

【劳动改造】reform (of criminals) through labour; reform through forced labour

【劳动观点】attitude to labour: 增强~ *improve one's attitude to labour*

【劳动合同】labour contact: ~制 *contract labour system*

【劳动和社会保障部】Ministry of Labour and Social Security

【劳动纪律】labour discipline

【劳动价值论】labour theory of value

【劳动教养】reeducation (of juvenile delinquents, etc.) through labour

【劳动节】International Labour Day (May 1st)

【劳动经济学】labour economics

【劳动力】① labour (or work) force; labour; manpower: ~不足 *short of manpower* / ~分配 *distribution of labour force* / ~过剩 *surplus labour* / ~价格 *price of labour power* / ~价值 *value of labour power* / ~结构 *structure of the labour force* / ~流动 *labour flux* / ~买卖 *buying and selling of labour power* / ~商品 *labour power as a commodity* / ~市场 *market for labour*; *market for manpower*

/ ~调配 *allocation of the labour force*; *deployment of manpower* / ~周转 *labour turnover* / ~资源 *human resources*; *pool of labour power* ② capacity for physical labour; ability to work: 丧失~ *lose one's ability to work* ③ able-bodied person: 全~和半~ *able-bodied and semi-ablebodied workers*

【劳动量】quantity of work; work output

【劳动密集】labour intensive: ~型产品 *labour-intensive product*/ ~型行业 *labour-intensive industry*

【劳动模范】model worker

【劳动强度】labour intensity; intensity of work

【劳动权】right to work

【劳动人口】labouring population

【劳动人民】working people; labouring people

【劳动人民文化宫】Working People's Cultural Palace

【劳动日】workday; working day

【劳动审查】labour audit

【劳动生产力】labour productive power

【劳动生产率】labour productivity; productivity

【劳动市场】labour market

【劳动手段】means (or instruments) of labour

【劳动条件】working conditions

【劳动者】labourer; worker: ~素质 *quality of workers*

【劳动资料】means (or instruments) of labour

【劳顿】[书] fatigued; wearied: 旅途~ *fatigued by a journey*

【劳而无功】toil with no gain; a fruitless attempt: 没想到我的努力居然~。*Little do I think that I worked fruitlessly.*

【劳而无怨】work hard without any complaint: 只要能对你有所帮助,我~。*As long as it is helpful to you, I'll work hard without repining.*

【劳乏】tired; weary; overworked: 尽管父亲很~,他还是到车站来接我。*Tired as my father was, he still met me in the station.*

【劳烦】[方] trouble: ~你再说一遍好吗? *Would you please say that again?*

【劳方】labour: ~代表 *representative of the working people*

【劳改】reform through labour: ~犯 *a prisoner serving a sentence of reform through labour* / ~农场 *reform-through-labour farm*

【劳工】① labourer; worker: ~运动 *labour movement* ② [旧] coolie

【劳绩】merits and accomplishments

【劳驾】excuse me; may I trouble you (to do); would you mind doing sth: ~,能告诉我去动物园怎么走吗? *Excuse me, could you tell me the way to the zoo?* / ~把那本书递给我好吗? *May I trouble you to pass me that book?*

【劳教】reeducation through labour: ~农场 *reeducation-through-labour farm*

【劳金】[旧] money given for work; pay

【劳倦】tired; fatigued: 工作了一天后,我很~。*I feel very tired after working the whole day.*

【劳军】take greetings and gifts to army units; comfort soldiers: ~抚民 *reward the soldiers and pacify the people*

【劳苦】toil; hard work: 他不辞~地帮助我。*He spared no pains to help me.*

【劳苦功高】have achieved great success through hard work; have performed a valuable service with high merits

【劳劳碌碌】toil; work hard

【劳累】① tired; run-down; overworked; exhausted: 他~过度。*He overworked himself.* ② trouble sb: 最近总是~您,真是不好意思。*I'm sorry to have troubled you so many times recently.*

【劳力】① labour; work ② labour; labour force: ~密集型产品 *labour-intensive product* / ~密集型产业 *labour-intensive industry* ③ [书] labour with one's strength; do manual work: ~者治于人。*Those who labour with physical strength are governed by others.*

【劳碌】work hard; toil: 母亲终日~。*My mother works hard all day long.*

【劳民伤财】exhaust the people and drain the treasury; harass the people and waste money; spend blood and money

【劳模】model worker

【劳伤】【中医】internal lesion caused by overexertion

【劳神】① be a tax on (one's mind); bother; trouble: 你现在身体不好,不要过于~。*You're in poor health, so don't overtax yourself.* ② will you please; will you mind doing sth: ~帮我照看一下行李。*Would you please keep an eye to my luggage?*

【劳神费力】tax one's mind and strength; weary mind and use strength

【劳师】[书] ① take greetings and gifts to army units ② tire troops: ~远征 *tire the troops on a long expedition*

【劳师动众】mobilize too many troops — drag in lots of people (to do sth): 你不必~叫这么多人来的。*You needn't have dragged in so many people to come here.*

【劳什子】[方] nuisance

【劳损】【医】strain: 肌腱~ *muscular strain*

【劳务】labour services: 购买~ *purchase of services* / ~报酬 *remuneration for personal services*; *reward for personal services* / ~费 *service charge* / ~出口 *the export of labour services* / ~合作 *cooperation in the field of labour service* / ~交换 *labour exchanges* / ~市场 *labour market*

【劳心】① take pains; have on one's mind ② [书] work with one's mind or brains: ~劳力 *labour and toil with mind and body* / ~者治人。*Those who labour with minds govern others.* ③ [书] be worried

【劳燕分飞】the shrike and the swallow flying in different directions — part from each other; going in different ways; the couple is forced to part

【劳役】①【律】penal servitude; forced labour ② corvee: 服~ *do corvee labour* ③ use (as a draught animal)

【劳役地租】rent in the form of service

【劳逸结合】combine exertion with rest; alternate work with rest; alternate work with rest and recreation; strike a proper balance between work and rest

【劳资】labour and capital

【劳资冲突】conflict between the employer and the employee

【劳资法庭】industrial court

【劳资关系】relations between labour and capital

【劳资合作】collaboration between labour and capital

【劳资纠纷】trouble between labour and management

【劳资两利】benefit both labour and capital

【劳资谈判】collective negotiations

【劳作】①［旧］manual work, a school subject ② do manual labour:农民们正在田里～。*The peasants are labouring in the fields.*

牢 ①［书］fold; pen; stables:亡羊补～ *mend the fold after a sheep is lost* ②［古］animals for sacrificial rites:少～ *sacrificial sheep and pigs* ③ prison; jail:蹲～ *be in jail; be put into prison* /死～ *a condemned ward* ④firm; durable; fast:记～ *bear firmly in mind* /把小船拴～。*Make the boat fast.*

【牢不可破】unbreakable; indestructible; be too strong to break:～的友谊 *unbreakable friendship; durable friendship.*

【牢房】prison cell; ward

【牢固】firm; secure; strong; solid: ～的信念 *a firm belief* /～的基础 *a solid foundation* /～的后盾 *a powerful and secure backing* /地基很～。*The foundations are very firm.* /尽管被车撞了,柱子仍然很～。*Despite being hit by the car, the post was still firm.*

【牢记】keep (or bear) firmly in mind; remember well: ～不忘 *embedded in one's memory; bear in one's mind* / ～在心 *never forget; keep firmly in mind*

【牢靠】① firm; strong; sturdy: ～的墙 *stout walls* /～的绳子 *a strong rope* /这梯子～吗? *Is this ladder secure?* ② dependable; reliable

【牢牢】firmly; safely:他们把囚犯～地关起来。*They keep the prisoner secure.* /车子～地陷在泥塘里。*The car was stuck fast in the mud.*

【牢笼】① cage; bonds:冲破～ *shake off the bonds* ② trap; snare:陷入～ *fall into a trap* ③［书］win over ④［书］bind up; tie

【牢骚】① complaint; grumble; grievance; discontent:发～ *grumble at sth; voice one's discontent* / ～满腹 *be full of complaints about sth; have a perpetual grudge against sth* ② complain; grumble:他～了半天。*He kept complaining for quite a long time.*

【牢实】firm and solid; secure and steady

【牢稳】(láowěn) safe; reliable:这种时候在家里待着是最～的。*It is good to be safe at home under such a situation.*

【牢稳】(láowen) (of objects) stable; secure; firm:把桌子放～了。*Make the table steady.*

【牢狱】prison; jail:他身陷～。*He is put into prison.*

唠

see also lào

【唠叨】chatter; be garrulous:他一见我就～个不停。*He chatters endlessly whenever he sees me.* /别～了! *Stop your gab!* /妻子～一件又一件烦心事时,他开始打哈欠。*He began to yawn while his wife rambled on about one grievance after another.*

【唠唠叨叨】babble on and on; repeating over and over again; repeat constantly:我奶奶～,没完没了。*My grandmother can talk the hind leg off a donkey.*

铹 【化】lawrencium (Lr): ～化合物 *lawrencium compound*

痨 tuberculosis; TB; consumption:肺～ *phthisis; pulmonary tuberculosis*

【痨病】【中医】tuberculosis; TB; consumption; phthisis: ～学 *phthisiology*

lǎo

老 ① old; aged: ～农 *old farmer* /白头偕～ *live to old age in conjugal bliss* ② elderly person; senior person:王～ *venerable Wang* /尊～爱幼 *respect for the old and care for the young* ③ die:他的祖父上个月～了。*His grandfather passed away last month.* ④ experienced; seasoned ⑤ old; of long standing: ～毛病 *a chronic ailment* /～同事 *old colleagues* ⑥ outdated; outmoded; old-fashioned: ～思想 *old-fashioned idea* ⑦ original; same; traditional: ～地方 *same place* /～规矩 *traditional rules* /他还是～样子,我一眼就认出他来了。*His appearance remained unchanged, and I recognized him at the first sight.* ⑧ overgrown: ～菠菜 *overgrown spinach* ⑨ tough; hardened:鸡蛋煮～了。*The eggs are overcooked.* ⑩【化】change in quality; deteriorate:防～剂 *antioxidant* ⑪ (of colour) deep; dark: ～红 *dark red* ⑫ long; for a long time: ～没见你了。*I haven't seen you for ages.* ⑬ often doing sth; frequently:他～提起这件事。*He always mentions it.* /他～是不在家。*He lives in the street.* ⑭ very: ～远 *far away* /～高 *very high* ⑮［口］the youngest:他是家里的～儿子。*He is the youngest son in the family.* ⑯ used before a person to indicate order or before some animals or plants: ～杨 *Lao Yang* /～鼠 *mouse* ⑰ (Lǎo) a surname

【老媪】［书］old woman

【老八辈子】outdated; age-old; ancient; stale; outworn:那是～的新闻了。*That news is stale.*

【老把戏】an old trick; outmoded method:你的～骗不了人了。*Your old trick cannot deceive anybody now.*

【老白干儿】［方］white spirit; strong liquor

【老百姓】［口］common people; ordinary people;

civilians; civvies:每个国家的~都渴望世界和平。*The common man in every country is anxious for world peace.*

【老板】① shopkeeper; proprietor; boss; employer:~狠狠地批评了我。*My boss dressed me down.* ②[旧] a respectful address for famous opera actors or organizers of theatrical troupes

【老板娘】shopkeeper's wife; proprietress

【老半天】[口] a long time:他~不说一句话。*He kept silent for a long time.*

【老伴儿】[口] (of an old married couple) husband or wife:我~去年去世了。*My wife passed away last year.*

【老鸨】a woman running a brothel; procuress; madam

【老辈】one's elders; old folks:我们应该尊敬~。*We should respect our elders.*

【老本】① principal; capital:他把~都输光了。*He lost his last stakes.* ② past experience, glory, etc.:我们不能吃~,而要开创新的局面。*We shouldn't live off our past glory; we have to start a new business.*

【老鼻子】[方] an awful lot; plenty of:他家的藏书~了。*There are a lot of books in his home.*

【老表】① a male cousin (on the maternal side) ②[方] a polite form of address to a male stranger:刚才有一个~来问路。*A man came to ask directions just now.*

【老兵】old soldier; veteran; campaigner

【老病】① chronic illness; old trouble:他的~时常折磨他。*He suffered from his chronic illness frequently.* ② old and sick; ageing and declining:他现在~无能。*Being old and sick, he can do nothing now.*

【老病号】be on the sick list; patron

【老伯】uncle (used in addressing a friend of father's generation)

【老伯伯】grandpa (used to address elderly people)

【老不正经】old but still licentious

【老不拘礼】the old and the sick need not observe the conventions

【老不死】a person who has outlived his usefulness; an old debauchee:他们认为我这个~是家里的累赘。*They think that I have outlived my usefulness and become a drag to the family.*

【老巢】nest; den; lair

【老成】experienced; steady; adultly:少年~ *young but steady* /~持重 *experienced and prudent*; *mature wisdom* /他是一个~的孩子。*He is a child who is old for his years.*

【老诚】honest and sincere: ~忠厚 *tolerant and honest*

【老处女】old maid; spinster

【老粗】an uneducated person; a rough and ready chap:我是个~,没什么学问。*I'm a rough man without much learning.*

【老搭档】old partner; old workmate

【老大】①[书] old (in age) ② eldest child; eldest among siblings:我是家里的~,有责任照顾好弟弟妹妹。*I'm the eldest child in our family; I should assume the responsibility of taking care of my younger brothers and sisters.* ③[方] the captain of a boat:船~ *boatman*; *captain* ④ greatly; very:他心里~的不高兴。*He felt greatly annoyed.*

【老大不小】[口] have grown up and be no longer a child:你也~的了,该结婚了。*You have grown up; It's time for you to get married.*

【老大哥】elder brother

【老大难】long-standing, big and difficult (problem):这是我们厂的一个~问题。*It's a knotty problem of long-standing in our factory.*

【老大娘】(a polite form of address to an old woman, esp. a stranger) aunty; granny:我陪这位~去看了医生。*I accompanied the granny to the doctor's.*

【老大徒伤悲】vainly regret in old age one's laziness in youth

【老大爷】(a polite form of address to an old man, esp. a stranger) uncle; grandpa:你见过那位~吗? *Have you ever seen that grandpa?*

【老旦】【戏】the role of an elderly woman in traditional opera

【老当益壮】be old in age, but young in spirit; old but vigorous; become more energetic with age; a green old age:他真是~。*He is old in age but young in spirit.*

【老道】[口] Taoist priest

【老到】[方] experienced; mature:你最好向~的顾问请教。*You'd better consult an experienced counselor.*

【老底】① sb's past; sb's unsavoury background:我揭穿了她的~,让她恼羞成怒。*I dig up her unsavory past, which made her ashamed into anger.* ② family fortune

【老弟】① young man; young fellow; my boy: ~,你能帮我一个忙吗? *My boy, could you do me a favour?* ②[方] younger brother:我~今年要上大学了。*My younger brother will go to college this year.*

【老调】① old tune; hackneyed theme; platitude:乏味的~ *milk-and-water platitudes* /满纸~ *writings full of platitudes* ② local opera popular in Baoding, Hebei Province

【老调重弹】sing the same old song; beat over the old ground; harp on the same string; harp on the old tune:现在他又开始~了。*Now he's started on his hobby horse.*

【老掉牙】very old; out of date; obsolete; antediluvian; corny: ~的笑话 *a corny joke*

【老豆腐】① processed bean curd ②[方] bean curd made in the northern style

【老坟】ancestral grave

【老夫】[书] I used by an old man to refer to himself: ~就不相信这个毛孩子能办到! *I don't believe that the little child can manage it.*

【老夫老妻】an old married couple

【老夫少妻】old man with a young wife

【老夫子】①[旧] tutor in a private school ② advisor (in the Qing Dynasty) ③ pedant; a bookish man

【老赶】[方] ① inexperienced in the ways of the world; green:他真～,连自助餐都不知道。*He has seen so little of the world that he doesn't know a self-service restaurant.* ② greenhorn; fool; blockhead:她在工作上是一个～。*She is green to her job.*

【老疙瘩】[方] one's youngest child:～在家里很受宠。*My youngest daughter is white-headed in the family.*

【老公】(lǎogōng) [方] husband:你～干什么工作? *What does your husband do?*

【老公】(lǎogong) [方] eunuch

【老公公】①[方] grandpa (used by children in addressing an old man) ②[方] husband's father; father-in-law ③[旧] eunuch

【老姑娘】① old spinster; old maid; maiden lady ② the youngest daughter:她最疼爱～了。*She is very fond of the youngest daughter.*

【老古板】fuddy-duddy; stick-in-the-mud

【老古董】① old-fashioned article; antique:他年纪虽大,脑子里却没有多少～。*Old as he is, he has few old-fashioned ideas in his mind.* ② old fogey; fuddy-duddy

【老骨头】[口] old guy:我这把～不中用了。*I am old and useless.*

【老鸹】[方] crow

【老规矩】old rules and regulations; convention; established custom or practice:我们还得按～办事。*We'll follow the convention.*

【老汉】① old man:一个～正在赶驴。*An old man is driving a donkey.* ② I (used by an old man):～我身子很硬朗。*I am quite healthy.*

【老好人】[口] a benign and uncontentious person who is indifferent to matters of principle; one who tries never to offend anybody; goody-goody; Mr. Nice Guy:他是个毫无原则的～。*He is a man who never offends anybody without regard to principles.*

【老狐狸】old fox; crafty scoundrel:这只～诡计多端。*The crafty scoundrel is up to all dodges.*

【老糊涂】dotard; doited:他是～了。*He is old and confused.*

【老虎】【动】tiger:母～ *tigress; shrew*

【老虎窗】[方] dormer; luthern; dormant window

【老虎凳】rack (an instrument of torture)

【老虎屁股摸不得】like a tiger whose backside no one dares to touch — a person who cannot tolerate differing opinions; not to be provoked

【老虎钳】① vise ② pincer pliers

【老虎灶】[方] huge kitchen range for boiling water

【老虎嘴里拔牙】pull a tooth from a tiger's mouth — dare the greatest danger

【老花镜】presbyopic glasses

【老花眼】presbyopia

【老化】①【化】ageing:加压～ *pressure ageing* /界面～ *interfacial ageing* /人工～ *artificial ageing* /氧～ *oxygen ageing* ② (of people) ageing:干部～ *the aging of cadres* /人口～ *ageing population* ③ (of knowledge, etc.) become outdated; obsolete:知识～ *the aging of knowledge*

【老话】① old saying; saying; adage:正如～说的 *as the saying goes* ② remarks about the old days:他竟然忘了自己说过的～。*He forgot what he had said about the past actually.*

【老皇历】last year's calendar — ancient history; obsolete practice:这些～应该丢掉了。*The obsolete practice should be discarded.*

【老黄牛】willing ox — a person who serves sb whole-heartedly:他是人民的～。*He serves the people whole-heartedly.*

【老几】① order of seniority among brothers or sisters:你排行～? *Where do you come in the family?* ② used in rhetorical questions to express disparagement:你算～呀,你怎么敢教训我? *Who do you think you are? How dare you teach me?*

【老骥伏枥,志在千里】an old steed in the stable still aspires to gallop a thousand li — an old hero still cherishes high aspirations

【老家】① native place; old home ② ancestral home:你～在哪儿? *Where do you come from?*

【老奸巨猾】old file; a crafty old scoundrel; a wily old fox

【老江湖】[旧] a person who has seen much of the world; a man of long experience:这点把戏骗不过他这个～的。*Such easy trick can in no way fool the man who has experienced much of the world.*

【老将】① veteran; old-timer:～出马,一个顶俩。*When a veteran goes into action, he can do the job of two.* ② commander-in-chief — king in Chinese chess

【老交情】long-standing friendship; an old friend:他不顾～,拒绝帮我的忙。*He refused to help me, not considering the long-standing friendship between us.*

【老景】life and situation in old age

【老境】① old age; the sear and yellow leaf:他渐入～,对生活十分悲观。*He is getting old and takes a pessimistic view of life.* ② life and circumstances in old age:～凄惨 *miserable life in old age*

【老旧】outmoded; obsolete; old-fashioned:～的服装 *unfashionable attire* /～的建筑物 *an outdated building* /～的思想 *old-fashioned ideas*

【老框框】old ways of doing things; outmoded conventions:只有打破～,才能有所进步。*Only by breaking away from convention can we progress.*

【老辣】① shrewd and ruthless; experienced and vicious:他是个～的商人。*He is a shrewd and vicious merchant.* ② (of style of handwriting, etc.) smooth and vigorous

【老来俏】[口] (of a woman) become prettier as one gets old; an old ewe dressed lamb fashion; play the coquette:我最看不惯～的人。*I dislike those women who are old but coquettish.*

【老老少少】old and young

【老老实实】behave oneself; (act) honestly and

unmoral; in earnest; without affectation: 我们要~地向他学习。*We should learn in earnest from him.*

【老泪纵横】the old man wept bitterly; tears flowing from aged eyes: 老母亲见到我,~。*My mother's tears coursed down her cheeks when she saw me.*

【老礼】old custom: 你们年轻人不必拘泥于~。*You young men needn't confine yourself to the old etiquette.*

【老例】old practice; precedent; old custom: 你要我做的事有~吗? *Is there a precedent for what you want me to do?*

【老脸】①[谦] old face; reputation: 我的~如今已经不值钱了。*My prestige is useless now.* ② a thick-skinned person; cheeky

【老脸皮】thick-skinned; brazen-faced: 她老着脸皮干下去。*She brazened it out.*

【老练】seasoned; experienced; tactful; seasoned; be expert in sth: 办事~ *be experienced and work with a sure hand* / 他在外交上很~。*He is old in diplomacy.*

【老林】[林] virgin forest

【老龄】old age: ~保险 *old-age insurance* / ~问题 *ageing problem*

【老路】① old road: 我们走~回家吧。*Let's follow the old path to go home.* ② beaten track; old rut: 走~ *follow the beaten track; slip back into the old rut*

【老妈子】[旧] old amah; maid servant

【老马识途】an old horse knows the way; an old hand is a good guide; know the ropes

【老迈】aged; senile: ~昏庸 *senile and fatuous; old and muddle-headed*

【老毛病】old trouble; old weakness: 嫉妒别人是我的~。*Being jealous of others is an old weakness of mine.*

【老耄之年】[书] senile age

【老帽儿】[方] dull layman: 这个~根本不懂如何与人相处。*The foolish bumpkin has no knack of getting along with others.*

【老门槛】[方] an old hand; an expert at the game

【老米】[方] old (or stale) rice

【老面】[方] leavening dough

【老面孔】① old face: 我在晚会上看到了很多~。*I saw many old faces in the evening.* ② same old thing: 我早腻烦了这些~。*I am fed up with those old things.*

【老面皮】[方] brazen; cheeky

【老谋深算】circumspect and farseeing; experienced and astute: 他办事谨慎,~。*He is scheming and calculating, making every move only after mature deliberation.*

【老衲】[书] old Buddhist monk; I (used by an old Buddhist monk to refer to himself)

【老奶奶】① paternal great grandmother: 我的~已经年过七十。*My grandmother is over seventy.* ② old granny (a respectful form of address used by children to refer to an old woman)

【老脑筋】old way of thinking; be old fashioned: 你该换换~。*You should change your old way of thinking.*

【老蔫儿】[方] taciturn person: 那个~其实是个颇有心机的人。*That reticent guy is quite a calculating person actually.*

【老年】old age

【老年斑】senile plaque

【老年大学】university for senior citizens

【老年间】former times; ancient times

【老年期】① gerontic; senescence; old age ②【地】topographic age

【老年人】old people; the aged; elderly people; senior citizens

【老娘】① old mother ② [方] (used by a married or middle-age woman to refer to herself) I, your old mother: ~我今天要教训教训你。*I'll give you a lesson today.*

【老娘们儿】[方] ① a married woman ② [方] woman: ~懂什么? *A woman knows nothing.* ③ wife: 这是我们家~。*This is my wife.*

【老牛拉破车】like an old bullock pulling a rickety cart — to creep slowly along; drag along at a snail's pace; making slow progress

【老牛舐犊】an old cow licking her calf — a parent doting on his or her child; parental love

【老农】① old farmer; experienced peasant: 那个~教会了我如何种植这种蔬菜。*That old farmer taught me how to grow this kind of vegetable.* ② farmer: 他是个富裕的~。*He is a well-to-do farmer.*

【老牌】① old brand: ~店铺 *old brand shops* ② *old-timer; veteran*: ~特务 *experienced spy*

【老派】① old-fashioned; conservative: 现在看这种电影已经很~了。*It is not the fashion to see such kind of films.* ② an old-fashioned person; conservative: 我不喜欢和一个~一起工作。*I don't like to work with an old fogey.*

【老婆】[口] wife: 我~是个医生。*My wife is a doctor.*

【老婆婆】[方] ① granny: ~,让我帮您提篮子吧。*Granny, let me carry the basket for you.* ② husband's mother; mother-in-law: 我~住院了。*My mother-in-law is in hospital now.*

【老婆子】① old biddy: 那个~可真饶舌。*That old biddy is really garrulous.* ② my old woman: 我~是个急脾气。*My wife is a quick temper.*

【老气】① mature and steady: 对于这个年龄,她可算~。*She is mature and steady for her age.* ② (of clothes) dark and old-fashioned: 快脱下这~的衣服。*Take off the old-fashioned clothes at once.*

【老气横秋】① arrogant on account of one's seniority; show off one's seniority ② lacking in youthful vigour: 邻居的小伙子显得~的。*The young man in my next-door neighbour looks decrepit.*

【老前辈】one's senior; one's elder; old-timer: 这位~在我们村子里深受尊敬。*The senior is held in great esteem in our village.*

【老腔老调】① the old tunes and melodies ② (of a child, etc.) sound like an adult: 这小孩讲起话

来～的。*The little child speaks like an adult.*
【老亲】① old relatives ② old parents
【老区】old liberated area; old revolutionary base areas
【老拳】fist：他吃了我一记～。*I stroke him hard with the fist.*
【老人】① old man or woman; the aged; the old：病人和～需要我们帮助。*The sick and the aged need our help.* ② one's aged parents or grandparents
【老人家】① a respectful form of address to an old person：这位～是离休干部。*The venerable old man is a retired cadre.* ② parent
【老人星】【天】Canopus
【老弱病残】the old, weak, sick and disabled
【老弱残兵】old, weak and wounded troops; motley troops unfit for battle
【老弱妇幼】old and weak people, women and children
【老弱无能】become so old and weak that one has lost his capacity to do any useful work
【老三届】those who graduated from junior high schools and high schools in 1966, 1967 and 1968 in China and were deprived of chances for further education due to Cultural Revolution
【老少】old and young：～良伴 *good companions for children as well as adults* / ～无欺 *cheat neither the old nor the young* / ～咸宜 *suitable for both young and old*
【老少爷们】［方］both old and young men：村里的～都去种地了。*Both old and young men in our village are plowing the land.*
【老身】I (used by an old woman)：～体弱多病。*I am weak and sick.*
【老声老气】speaking with a steady voice; the sound and look of an old person
【老生】【戏】the male role in traditional Chinese opera
【老生常谈】commonplace; platitude; truism; trite remarks; a home truth：他所说的无非是～而已。*What he has said is a mere commonplace.*
【老师】teacher：女～ *a woman teacher* /我们昨天参加了王～的婚礼。*We attended Mr. Wang's wedding yesterday.*
【老师傅】master; craftsman; experienced worker
【老实】① honest; frank：～可靠 *on the up-and-up* /做～人，说～话，办～事 *be an honest person, honest in word and honest in deed* /他的～全是装出来的。*His honesty is all put on.* ② well-behaved; good：她在学校里一向很～。*She behaves very well at school.* ③［婉］simple-minded; naive; easily taken in
【老实巴交】［方］soft-spoken and timid：他专欺负～的人。*He's always bullying those who are honest and timid.*
【老实相告】to tell the truth
【老是】always; all the time：他～在同一家餐厅用餐。*He always dines at the same restaurant.*
【老式】old style; old fashioned：一套～黑西服 *a conservative dark suit*

【老手】old hand; old stager; veteran：政治斗争的～ *a veteran of political campaigns* /这方面我是～，你骗不了我。*I'm an old hand at this game; you can't trick me.* /所有这些年轻人都是驾驶～。*All the young men are expert drivers.*
【老寿星】①（a respectful form of address to refer to old people）venerable old people ② an elder people whose birthday is being celebrated
【老鼠】mouse; rat：这里一些地方甚至白天都能看见～。*In some places here rats can be seen even in the day time.*
【老鼠过街，人人喊打】a rat running across the street, with everybody shouting, "Kill it!"; be chased by all like a rat running across the street — an extremely unpopular figure; a person or object of universal condemnation
【老鼠见到猫】(as terrified as) a mouse confronting a cat; (tremble before sb like) a mouse before a cat：他见到他老爸就好像～。*He is terrified like a mouse before a cat when he catches sight of his father.*
【老死】die a natural death
【老死不相往来】grow old and die without having had any dealings with each other — never be in contact with each other：我和他～。*We will not visit each other all our lives.*
【老太婆】old woman：我这个～只能靠儿女了。*As an old woman, I can only depend on my kids.*
【老太太】① old lady：我刚才看到一个驼背的～走过去。*I saw a bow-backed old lady pass by just now.* ② (a polite term) your mother; his or her mother; my mother, mother-in-law or grandmother：我家～每天早上都锻炼身体。*My mother takes exercise every morning.*
【老太爷】① elderly gentleman ② (a polite term) your father; his or her father; my father, father-in-law or grandfather：你家～近来身体怎么样？*How is your father recently?*
【老态龙钟】senile; doddering; old and clumsy; be stooped with age：他～的样子让我认不出来。*I could hardly recognize him from his senile and clumsy appearance.*
【老汤】① residual sauce ②［方］residual salt water from previous salting or pickling
【老套子】out-of-date practices (or convention); outmoded ways of doing things：遵循这些～会把你的思维限制在狭窄的范围内。*Following the outmoded practices will restrict your thinking within narrow limits.*
【老天爷】God; Heavens; good heavens：～，我的钱包丢了！*My God, I lost my wallet.*
【老天爷有眼】old heaven has eyes — there is divine justice after all
【老头儿】old man; old chap：这～真可怜。*The old man is really miserable.*
【老头子】① old fogey; old codger ②［口］my old man：我那个～是个烟鬼。*My old man smokes like a chimney.* ③ chief of a secret society
【老外】［口］① layman：在语言学方面我是个～，还请您多多指教。*I am a raw hand on linguistics; please kindly give me your advice.* ② foreigner: ~学中文是一件很难的事。*It's quite difficult for a foreigner to learn Chinese.*

【老顽固】old stick-in-the-mud; old diehard; old fogey:这个~不肯接受我们的建议。*The old diehard refused to accept our advice.*

【老王卖瓜,自卖自夸】Lao Wang selling melons praises his own goods — to praise one's own work; each bird loves to hear himself sing; every cook praises his own broth

【老挝】Laos: ~人 *Lao* / ~语 *Laotian (language); Lao* / ~人民民主共和国 *People's Democratic Republic of Laos*

【老窝】lair; den

【老弦】【音】the thicker inner string on the erhu, etc.

【老相识】old acquaintance:我们是~了。*We are old acquaintances.*

【老乡】① fellow-townsman; fellow-villager:你们是~吗? *Do you come from the same town?* ② a friendly form of address to a rural person: ~,这村里有多少人啊? *Buddy, could you tell me how many people are there in the village?*

【老相】looking older than one's age

【老小】① grown-ups and children; one's family:一家~ *the whole family* ② wife

【老兄】brother; man; old chap: ~,我们很久没见面了。*Brother, we haven't seen each other for a long time.*

【老羞成怒】be furious at being disgraced; get angry to cover up one's shame; fly into a rage out of shame:我的一番话惹得他~。*He lost his temper from embarrassment on hearing my words.*

【老朽】① decrepit and behind the times ②[谦](used by an old man) I; my senile self:让~送送你们吧。*Let me see you off.*

【老朽昏庸】old, worthless, dull and mean

【老眼光】old ways of looking at things; old views; out-dated opinions:千万别拿~看她,她已经变了很多了。*Don't judge her by what she used to be; she has changed a lot.*

【老眼昏花】dim-sighted from old age

【老爷】① master; bureaucrat; lord:庄园~ *the lord of the manor* ②[旧](used by a servant) a respectful address to a master: ~派人去请医生了。*Master has sent for the doctor.* ③ grandfather; grandpa ④ old; old-fashioned: ~车 *an old car*

【老爷们儿】[方] ① man:你是~,当然应该挣钱养家。*It's natural for you, a man to earn bread for the family.* ② husband:他~只知道混日子。*His husband dawdled away his time.*

【老爷爷】① great grandfather ② grandpa (used by children in addressing an old man): ~,让我扶您过马路吧。*Grandpa, let me support you to go across the road.*

【老爷子】[方] ① a respectful form of address to an old man ② my (old) father; your (old) father:你家~看上去很健康。*Your father looks very healthy.*

【老一辈】older generation: ~无产阶级革命家 *proletarian revolutionaries of the older generation*

【老一套】the same old stuff; the same old story; old rut

【老鹰】black-eared kite; hawk; eagle

【老油子】wily old bird; old campaigner; sophisticate

【老有所养】elderly will be looked after properly; provide for the elderly

【老幼咸宜】be suitable (or good) for people of all ages

【老于此道】well-experienced in this matter; consummate:要说逢迎上级,他可是~。*He is quite adept in ingratiating himself with his superior.*

【老于世故】versed in the ways of the world; worldly-wise

【老玉米】[口] maize; Indian corn; corn

【老妪】[书] old woman:昔日的美女如今已成了~。*The beauty in former days is now an old woman.*

【老妪能解】intelligible even to a common senile woman:她的文章写得~。*Her articles are easily understandable even to an ordinary old woman.*

【老丈】[书] an old gentleman

【老丈人】one's father-in-law

【老账】① old debts; long-standing debts:他还没有还清~。*He still hasn't paid off his old debts.* ② old scores:我和那家伙有些~要清算。*I have some old scores to settle with that fellow.*

【老者】old man:我爷爷是一位受人尊敬的~。*My grandfather is a respected old man.*

【老着脸皮】unabashedly; unblushingly:他~不肯承认事实。*He is unabashedly denying the facts.*

【老主顾】regular customer:他可是这个小店的~了。*He is a regular customer of the little shop.*

【老资格】old-timer; veteran; senior: ~的教师 *a senior teacher*

【老子】[口] ① father:他~对他很严厉。*His father is very strict with him.* ② I, your father (said in anger, contempt or in fun): ~天下第一。*I'm number one in the world.*

【老字号】an old name in business — an firm or shop of long standing

【老总】① [旧] an old form of address to a soldier ② general; commander (used as an affectionate form of address of the PLA)

【老祖宗】① ancestor; forefather; old ancestress; progenitor: ~的智慧 *the wisdom of our progenitors* ② grandpa: ~,您要照顾好自己,我以后会常来看您的。*Grandpa, take good care of yourself; I will visit you often.*

佬 [贬] man; guy; fellow:阔~ *a rich guy* / 美国~ *Yankee* / 外国~ *foreigner*

姥 [口]

see also mǔ

【姥姥】① [方] (maternal) grandmother; (maternal) grandma ② [方] midwife

【姥爷】(maternal) grandfather; (maternal) grandpa

铑 【化】rhodium (Rh):镍~合金 *nickel rhodium*

潦 [书] ① pouring rain ② running pools of water on the road
see also liáo

lào

络
see also luò

【络子】① string bag ② spindle

唠 [方] chat; talk about; speak:他们昨晚顺便来~了一会儿。*He dropped in for a chat last night.*
see also láo

【唠扯】[方] chit; chitchat:别~了,咱们开始工作吧。*No more chatting; let's start to work.*

【唠嗑】[方] chat; engage in chitchat:祖母每天和邻居~消磨时间。*My grandmother kills time by chatting with neighbours every day.*

烙 ① brand; iron: ~衣服 *iron clothes* ② bake in a pan: ~馅饼 *bake pies*

【烙饼】a kind of pancake; flapjack; latke

【烙花】pyrograph

【烙画】pyrograph; poker-picture

【烙铁】① flatiron; iron:电~ *electric iron* ② soldering iron

【烙印】brand; stigma:罪恶的~ *the brand of villainy* /打上阶级的~ *be stamped with the brand of a class* /这些牛身上都有我打的~。*These cattle have my brand on them.* /这件事在他心中留下了永久的~。*The accident has branded him for life.* /她的脸上有饱经苦难的~。*Her face bears the stamp of suffering.*

涝 ① waterlogging:防~ *prevent waterlogging* ② floodwater:排~ *drain off the floodwater*

【涝洼地】waterlogged lowland

【涝灾】damage or crop failure caused by waterlogging; natural calamity caused by waterlogging

落
see also là; luò

【落不是】get blamed (for an alleged fault):他替我~。*He bears the blame of me.*

【落汗】[口] stop sweating:快到屋里歇会儿,落落汗。*Come in and have a rest to dry off.*

【落价】fall (or drop) in price; go down in price; mark down:牛肉~了。*Price for beef dropped.*

【落架】[方] head on ruin; (of a family) decline:照他这么挥霍,这个家迟早要~。*If he continues to be so prodigal in his expenditures, his family will collapse sooner or later.*

【落炕】[方] stay in bed with illness; be laid up:她~两年了。*She has been sick in bed for two years.*

【落儿】[方] means of support; living:找~ *seek a living* /他生活有~。*He leads a comfortable life.*

【落忍】[方] not feel sorry or apologetic:让她为我的婚礼花费了这么多时间,我心里怪不~的。*I feel rather sorry to occupy much of her time for my wedding.*

【落色】discolour; fade:这种绸布料子不会~。*The colour in this silk material will not fade.* /阳光使我的衣服~。*Sunshine discoloured my clothes.*

【落枕】① have a stiff neck (caused by cold or an awkward sleeping posture) ② (of one's head) touch the pillow:他太疲倦了,一~就睡着了。*He was so tired that he fell asleep as soon as his head hit the pillow.*

酪 ① junket:乳~ *cheese* ② thick fruit juice; sweet paste made from crushed nuts:花生~ *peanut cream*

lè

乐 ① happy; glad; cheerful:欢~ *happy and gay* /寻欢作~ *go to town; be on the tiles* ② enjoy; be glad to do sth:喜闻~见 *be glad to see and hear* ③ laugh:他忍不住~了。*He couldn't help laughing.* ④ (Lè) a surname
see also yuè

【乐不可言】be unspeakably happy; enjoy extreme pleasure

【乐不可支】overwhelmed with joy; overjoyed; be beside oneself with joy:得知自己涨了工资,他~。*He was beside himself with happiness when he knew he had a rise in wages.*

【乐不思蜀】so happy as to forget home and duty; too happy to think of home:他~,让我们很失望。*He is indulging in pleasure and forgets his duty completely, which makes us very disappointed.*

【乐此不疲】always enjoy it; never be bored with it:对于写作,他~。*He never gets tired of writing.*

【乐道】take delight in talking about sth:津津~ *dwell upon with great relish*

【乐得】readily take the opportunity to; be only too glad to:如果他邀请我参加聚会,我~赴约。*If he invites me to the party, I am glad to go.*

【乐观】optimistic; hopeful; sanguine:~的展望 *an affirmative outlook* /事情的发展是很~的。*The prospects are very bright.* /我们会按时完成任务,对这一点,我是很~的。*I'm hopeful that we'll fulfil the task on time.* /他对于成功很~。*He is sanguine of success.*

【乐观主义】optimism: ~者 *optimist*

【乐呵呵】buoyant; happy and gay:她整天~的。*She is happy and gay all the time.*

【乐和】[方] happy; cheerful:放假的时候,一定到我家来~~。*Be sure to come to my home to get together for fun on holidays.*

【乐极生悲】extreme joy begets sorrow; after joy comes sadness; joy at its height engenders sorrow; when the cup of happiness overflows, disaster follows

【乐趣】delight; pleasure; joy:电视给亿万人带来~。*Televisions give delight to millions of people.* /园艺工作是他的~之一。*Gardening is one of his chief enjoyments.*

【乐善好施】be given to doing charitable work; always glad to give to charities; be prodigal of benefactions

【乐事】pleasure; delight：他生活中的一大～就是听音乐。*One of the greatest pleasures of his life is listening to music.* /她以烹饪美食为～。*She delights in cooking lovely meals.*

【乐陶陶】［书］cheerful; happy; joyful

【乐天】carefree; happy-go-lucky person

【乐天派】① carefree; easygoing ② sanguine person; optimist

【乐天知命】submit to the will of Heaven and be content with one's lot; rest content; be content with what one is：他是个～的人。*He is easily contented.*

【乐土】land of happiness; paradise; promised land

【乐意】① be willing to; be ready to：我不～帮助他。*I'm not willing to help him.* /我～照你的建议去做。*I am agreeable to do what you suggest.* ② pleased; happy：～的神色 *a delighted look* /一听说我们不带他去公园，他立刻就不～了。*He became unhappy immediately when he heard that we would not take him to the park.*

【乐于】be happy to; take delight in：～助人 *be ready to help others; be happy to render help to others* /我～从命。*I am most happy to obey.* /他～接受主席这个任命。*He accepted the appointment of a chairman with pleasure.*

【乐园】① paradise; fairyland; Eden：人间～ *earthly paradise* ② playground; amusement park：儿童～ *children's playground* /迪斯尼～ *Disneyland*

【乐在其中】happiness within; find pleasure in it：创作的过程是～啊。*You can always find pleasure in writing.*

【乐滋滋】［口］contented; pleased：他脸上带着～的表情。*He wears a contented expression on his face.*

【乐子】［方］① fun; pleasure：别拿我找～。*Don't make fun of me.* ② a laughable matter; sth that makes one laugh：他大白天一头撞在一棵树上，这事成了大家的～。*In the daytime he ran bump into a tree, which made all of us laugh.*

勒[1] ①［书］headstall ② rein in：悬崖～马 *rein in one's horse at the brink of the precipice — wake up to and avoid danger at the last moment* ③ coerce; force：～捐 *compel sb to make money contributions* ④［书］command

勒[2] ［书］carve; engrave：～石 *inscribe on a stone tablet*

勒[3] 【物】lux

see also lēi

【勒逼】force; coerce：他～我妥协。*He coerced me into compliance.*

【勒克斯】【物】lux; metre-candle：～计 *luxmeter*

【勒令】compel (by legal authority); order：～停业 *be closed down by order* /～退学 *rusticate (a student)*

【勒派】f[illegible] sb to pay levies or do corvee labour; impose upon：～税款 *levy a tax*

【勒索】extort; blackmail：～赎金 *hold sb to ransom* /进行敲诈～ *practice extortion* /他向我～钱财。*He extorted money from me; he squeezed money out of me.*

【勒诈】racketeer; extort

le

了 ① used to indicate the completion of an action or a change：他睡～两个小时。*He slept for two hours.* /两个男孩打～一架。*The two boys had a fight.* /他把这个消息告诉～每个人。*He told the news to everybody.* /我到～上海就会给你打电话。*I will phone you as soon as I arrive in Shanghai.* ② used to indicate a change or new circumstances：天晴～。*The sky cleared.* /你的孩子会说话～吗？*Can your child speak yet?* /等你病好～，我们一块儿去爬山。*When you recover from illness, we'll climb the hill together.* /他明白～是有人在挑拨离间。*He realized that someone sowed the seeds of discord.* /别说～！*Shut up!* /好～，我知道了。*All right. I see it.*

see also liǎo

lēi

勒 ① tie sth tight; tighten：～紧裤带 *pull in one's belt* /带子太松了，再～一～。*The strap is too loose; tighten it up a bit.* ②［方］force; compel：老板～着我们加班干活。*The boss compelled us to work overtime.*

see also lè

【勒掯】［方］force sb to do sth; make things difficult for sb; compel：他没有～我，是我自愿答应的。*He didn't force me to do anything at all; I made the promise quite voluntarily.*

【勒脚】【建】plinth

léi

累

see also lěi; lèi

【累累】①［书］haggard; gaunt; listless ② clusters of; heaps of：果实～ *fruit hanging in clusters*

【累赘】① wordy; verbose：～的文件 *a wordy document* /～的记者 *a verbose correspondence* /他是一个～且令人厌倦的演讲者。*He is a prolix, tedious speaker.* ② burdensome; cumbersome：他要照顾这些年幼的儿女，真是～。*It's really burdensome to look after his several young kids.* ③ encumbrance; burden; nuisance：不要做一个～的人。*Don't make yourself a nuisance to others.* /这么多行李真是个～。*Such a lot of luggage is really a*

L

burden.

雷 ① thunder：春～ *spring thunder* /隆隆的～声 *a long roll of thunder* ②【军】mine：布～ *lay mines* /扫～ *sweep mines* /探～ *detect mines* /鱼～ *torpedo* /手～ *antitank grenade* ③（Léi）a surname

【雷暴】【气】thunderstorm；lightning storm；thunder-gust：高空～ *high-level thunderstorm* /局部～ *isolated thunderstorm* /冷锋～ *cold-front thunderstorm* /热～ *heat thunderstorm*

【雷贝琴】【音】rebab

【雷场】minefield

【雷池】limit；confinement：～之限 *the utmost limit one can go* /不敢越～一步 *dare not go beyond the limits*

【雷达】radar：全景～ *panoramic radar*

【雷打不动】not to be shaken by thunder —（of an arrangement or plan）not to be altered under any situation；unshakable：我们的安排～。*In no circumstances will our arrangement be changed.*

【雷电】thunder and lightning：～交加 *lightning accompanied by peals of thunder*；*a thunderstorm*

【雷电计】【气】ceraunograph

【雷动】thunderous：欢声～ *thunderous cheers*

【雷锋】Lei Feng（1940 — 1962）：～精神 *Lei Feng spirit — the spirit of serving people whole heartedly*

【雷公】Thunder God

【雷汞】【化】mercury fulminate

【雷管】detonator；detonating cap；blasting cap；primer：电～ *electric detonator*

【雷击】be struck by lightning；thunderbolt；thunderstroke

【雷克雅未克】Reykjavik，capital of Iceland

【雷厉风行】with the power of a thunderbolt and the speed of lightning —（carry out orders，policies，etc.）vigorously and speedily；vigorously and resolutely；in a sweeping manner：～的工作作风 *vigorous and speedy style of work*

【雷龙】【考】brontosaurus

【雷米封】【药】rimifon

【雷鸣】① thunder：～电闪。*Thunder rumbles and lightning flashes.* ② thunderous：～般的掌声 *thunderous applause*

【雷鸟】【动】ptarmigan；white partridge

【雷声大，雨点小】loud thunder but small raindrops — full of sound and fury but with little action；much said but little done；much cry and little wool；big beginning with a small ending

【雷霆】① thunderclap；thunderbolt ② thunder-like power or rage；wrath：他对我大发～。*He thundered against me.*

【雷霆万钧】as powerful as a thunderbolt；an irresistible force；a crushing blow；devastating punch

【雷同】① duplicate；identical：他的发言与校长的发言～。*He used the headmaster's identical words.* ② echoing what others have said

【雷雨】【气】thunderstorm：～交加 *storm accompanied by peals of thunder* /～大作 *the storm bursts with a tremendous peal of thunder and a rush of rain*

【雷雨云】【气】thundercloud；thunderhead

【雷阵雨】【气】thunder shower

擂 ① pestle；pound：～药 *pestle medicine* ② beat；hit：～了一拳 *give sb a punch*
see also lèi

【擂钵】mortar

镭 【化】radium（Ra）：～同位素 *radium isotope*

【镭疗】【医】radium therapy

【镭射】laser：～影碟 *laser videodisc*；*video compact disc*（*VCD*）

【镭射气】radium emanation

【镭针】radium needle

羸 ［书］① emaciated；thin：身病体～ *a physical wreck* ② exhausted；tired

【羸老】［书］senile and thin

【羸弱】［书］thin and weak；frail：他生病后身体～。*He is frail after his illness.* /近来父亲更加～了。*Father has been getting feebler lately.*

【羸瘦】［书］thin and weak；gaunt：你应该吃多一点，你太～了。*You should eat more*；*you're too thin and weak.*

lěi

垒[1] build by piling up bricks，stones，etc.：～猪圈 *build a pigsty* /他～了一道墙。*He built a wall.*

垒[2] ①【军】wall；rampart；fort：堡～ *fort*；*fortification* ② base：全～打 *home run* /～审 *base umpire* /～外球员 *fieldsman* /～线 *base line*

【垒城】【军】garrison town

【垒球】softball：～棒 *softball bat* /打～ *play softball*

累[1] ① accumulate；pile up；amass：积～经验 *gather experience* /日积月～ *accumulate day by day and month by month* /她积～了丰富的藏书。*She accumulated a good library.* ② repeated；running：连篇～牍 *long and tedious writings* ③ build by piling up bricks，stones，etc.

累[2] involve；implicate：拖～ *drag*；*ball and chain*；*get sb into trouble*
see also léi；lèi

【累次】time and again；repeatedly：他～向我强调学习英语的重要性。*He repeatedly impressed on me the importance of learning English.*

【累代】generation after generation；for generations：两个部落～没有来往。*The two tribes haven't contacted each other for generations.*

【累犯】① recidivist ② recidivism

【累积】accumulate；gather

【累及】implicate；involve；drag in；entangle：～无辜 *make the innocent suffer*；*compromise the guiltless*；*involve the innocent* /我不想～家人。*I don't want to entail misery on my innocent family members.*

【累计】① add up:数字~起来是100。*The figures add up to* 100. ② accumulative total; grand total:他~负债十万元。*His debts totaled up to* 100,000 *yuan.*
【累加】accumulation; summation: ~误差 *add up error*
【累进】progression: ~率 *graduated rates* / ~增长率 *progressive increase rate*
【累累】① again and again; many times:盗窃案在这个地区~发生。*Theft happened repeatedly in this area.* ② innumerable; countless:罪行~ *have committed numerous crimes*
【累卵】a stack of eggs — liable to collapse at any moment; precarious:形势危如~。*The situation is extremely dangerous.*
【累年】for years in succession; year after year: ~战乱 *be at war year after year*
【累日】[书] for days; day after day: ~下雨 *rain for days on end.*
【累世】for many generations; generation after generation
【累黍不差】not an iota of difference; accurate:她的描述与事件的事实~。*She gave an accurate account of the accident.*
【累退税】【经】regressive tax
【累月】month after month
【累月经年】for months and years on end; for years; year in, year out:他~从事野外勘探工作。*He is out on field exploration year after year.*

磊

【磊磊】[书] heaps of (stones)
【磊落】① open and upright:光明~ *open and above board* ② [书] many and jumbled:山峰~ *jumbled mountain peaks*

蕾 flower bud; bud:蓓~ *bud*

【蕾铃】【植】cotton buds and bolls

lèi

肋 rib; costal region:拱~ *arch rib* / 横~ *lateral rib* / 两~ *both sides of the chest* / 片~ *laminated rib* / 曲~ *curved rib*

【肋叉子】[方] rib
【肋弓】【生理】arcus costarum; arch of rib
【肋骨】【生理】rib
【肋间】【生理】intercostal: ~肌 *intercostal muscle* / ~神经 *intercostal nerve*
【肋膜】pleura
【肋膜炎】【医】pleurisy
【肋木】【体】stall bars
【肋条】[方] ① rib ② animal ribs; spareribs:猪~ *pork ribs*
【肋窝】arm pit
【肋奏】【音】obbligati: ~声部 *obbligati*

泪 tear; teardrop:流~ *weep* / 热~ *scalding tears* / 含~微笑 *smile through one's tears* / ~干肠断 *weeping one's eyes out and heart-broken* / ~干声竭 *one's tears dry up and his voice fails him* / 催人~下 *draw tears*

【泪光】glistening teardrops
【泪痕】tear stains; traces of tears:满面~ *tear-stained face; face with traces of tears* / ~斑斑 *(one's face) bathed in tears; be wet with tears; tear-stained*
【泪花】tears in one's eyes:他~晶莹。*His eyes sparkled with tears.*
【泪流满面】one's face is covered with tears; the tears course down one's cheeks; be dissolved in tears
【泪涟涟】be all tears; in tears
【泪囊】dacryocyst; lacrimal sac; saccus lacrimalis
【泪器】lacrimal apparatus
【泪人儿】in tears; all tears:她哭得像个~。*She was bathed in tears.*
【泪如泉涌】the tears run like a bubbling spring; a stream of tears; one's tears gushed forth in floods
【泪如雨下】be in a flood of tears; burst into a flood of tears; one's eyes rain tears
【泪水】tear; teardrop:他勉强挤出一滴~。*He squeezed out a tear.* / 她眨着眼睛忍住~。*She blinked back the tears.*
【泪汪汪】(eyes) brimming with tears; tearful; (one's eyes) swimming with tears:她~地向我诉说。*She complained tearfully to me.*
【泪窝】tearpit
【泪腺】lachrymal gland
【泪眼】tearful eyes: ~晶莹 *with a brilliant sparkle in one's eyes* / ~迷濛。*One's eyes are dim with tears.*
【泪液】tear
【泪珠】teardrop: ~从她的面颊流下。*Tears rolled down her cheeks.*
【泪竹】mottled bamboo

类 ① class; category; kind:分~ *classify* / 我把这些书整理成新的和旧的两~。*I sorted the books into new ones and old ones.* ② resemble; be similar to:画虎~犬 *try to draw a tiger but end up with the likeness of a dog — attempt sth over-ambitious and end in failure*

【类比】【逻】analogy: ~论证 *analogous argumentation* / ~推理 *analogism*
【类别】classification; category; family:他们属于同一~。*They belong to the same category.*
【类蛋白】【生化】albuminoid; plastein; proteinoid
【类定义】class definition
【类风湿性关节炎】【医】atrophic arthritis; rheumatoid arthritis
【类固醇】【生化】steroid; steride: ~激素 *steroid hormone*
【类函数】class function
【类金属】【化】metalloid
【类晶体】【化】crystalloid
【类名词】【语】class noun
【类群】fauna or flora:海洋动物~ *marine fauna* / 聚居植物~ *resident flora*

【类人猿】【考】anthropoid (ape)
【类似】similar; analogous:我保证不再发生~的事情。*I guarantee against the occurrence of similar incidents.* /这个报告与上次会议上我们讨论过的那份~。*This report was analogous with the one we discussed at the last meeting.* /她处理问题的方式和她父亲~。*She resembles her father in the way she deals with things.*
【类天花】【医】alastrim
【类同】roughly the same; alike; similar
【类推】analogize; reason by analogy:照此~ *on the analogy of this*
【类新星】【天】nova-like star
【类星体】【天】quasar; quasi-stellar object (QSO)
【类星系】【天】quasi-stellar galaxy
【类型】kind; type; mold; form; category:我不喜欢那种~的表演。*I don't enjoy that type of show.*
【类脂】【生化】lipoid; lipids

累 ① tired; fatigued; weary:我下班后感到很~。*I felt weary after work.* ② wear out; tire out; strain: ~眼睛 *strain the eyes* ③ toil; work hard:你~了一天了。*You have been working all day.*
see also léi; lěi
【累乏】tired out; worn out: ~的笑容 *a weary smile*
【累死累活】work like a dog; work extremely hard:我~,还不是为了让你们过得好一点儿。*I worked like a dog to make you lead a better life.*

擂 arena; ring:打~ *take up the challenge* /~主 *one who gives an open challenge*
see also léi
【擂鼓呐喊】beat the drums and shout
【擂鼓助威】beat the drums to encourage
【擂台】a platform for martial contests; ring; arena:摆~ *give an open challenge*/ ~赛 *an arena contest (or match)*

lei

嘞 similar to 喽:何必麻烦~? *Why bother?*

lēng

唥 [象] the sound of turning wheels, etc.:纺车~~地转着。*The spinning wheel creaked round.*

léng

崚
【崚嶒】[书] (of mountain) high

棱 ① edge; corner; arris:有~有角 *angulate* ② ridge; raised angle:瓦~ *rows of tiles on a roof*
【棱角】① edges and corners ② edge; pointedness; sharp point; incisiveness:他的批评颇有~。*His criticism is rather incisive.*
【棱镜】prism; glass prism; optical prism; step lens:多面~ *multifaceted prism* /半~ *half prism* /二向~ *dichroic prism* /反射~ *reflector prism* /反像~ *a reversing prism* /光谱~ *spectroscopic prism* /三~ *triangular prism* /色散~ *dispersing prism* /双~ *double prism* /五~ *penta prism* /折射~ *refracting prisms*
【棱坎】[方] bank; ridge
【棱棱睁睁】rude; forbidding in manner:他这人办事~的,得罪了不少人。*He is always rude in manner and offends many people.*
【棱面】facet (of a cut jewel or prism)
【棱台】【数】frustum of a pyramid
【棱纹】cord weave: ~棉绒 *raglan cord*
【棱柱】【数】prism:三~ *triangular prism*
【棱柱体】【数】prism:斜~ *oblique prism* /正~ *regular prism* /直~ *right prism*
【棱锥】pyramid:多~ *polygonal pyramid* /截~ *truncated pyramid* /六~ *hexagonal pyramid* /内接~ *inscribed pyramid* /三~ *triangular pyramid* /外切~ *circumscribed pyramid* /斜~ *oblique pyramid* /正~ *regular pyramid* /~面 *pyramidal surface* /~台 *frustum of a pyramid*
【棱子】[方] edge:冰~ *edge of a piece of ice*

lěng

冷 ① cold: ~水 *cold water* /~空气 *cold air* /如果你觉得~,就把上衣穿上。*Put on your coat if you feel cold.* /我感觉~。*I'm rather chilly.* ② [方] (of food) cool:等水~一~再喝。*Let the water cool off before you take it.* ③ cold in manner; icy; frosty: ~面孔 *a frosty look* /我们~~地回绝了他。*We turned him down cold.* /他~~地看了我一眼。*He gave me an icy look.* ④ desolate; deserted; forlorn: ~清清 *cold and dreary* ⑤ strange; unusual; uncommon: ~姓 *a rare surname* ⑥ unwelcomed; neglected ⑦ done in secret; covert:放~枪 *fire sniper's shot* ⑧ discourage; dampen:心灰意~ *dejected; dispirited; crestfallen* ⑨ (Lěng) a surname
【冷板凳】cold bench — an indifferent post or a cold reception:坐~ *be given a low job without much work; get frosty reception; be kept waiting*
【冷冰冰】① cold in manner; frosty: ~的面孔 *a frosty look* /~的欢迎 *an icy welcome* ② (of objects) ice-cold; icy:我双手~的。*My hands are icy.*
【冷兵器】【军】cold steel
【冷不丁】[方] suddenly; unexpectedly
【冷不防】unawares; suddenly; unexpectedly; without warning; off base; by surprise
【冷餐】buffet: ~招待会 *buffet reception*
【冷舱】(on a ship) refrigerating chamber
【冷藏】refrigeration; cold storage: ~包装纸 *locker paper* /~仓库 *cold store* /~车 *refrigerator car* /~船 *refrigerated vessel* /~柜 *freezer* /~间 *spring-*

house/ ~库 cold store; icebox; refrigerator /~设备 refrigerating equipment / ~箱 bunker; refrigerator; chill box

【冷场】① awkward silence on the stage when an actor enters late or forgets his lines:这个年轻的演员~了。*The young actor forgot his lines.* ② awkward silence at a meeting: ~持续了很长时间,每个人都很不自在。*For quite a long time nobody broke the ice and all of us present were ill at ease.*

【冷嘲热讽】jeer and sneer at sb; pour ridicule on sb; with freezing irony and burning satire; with biting sarcasm:他对我~。*He gave me a dig.*

【冷处理】【机】cold treatment

【冷床】【农】cold bed; cold frame; skid bank: ~播种 *seeding in cold frame* / ~育苗 *propagating seeding in cold frame*

【冷脆】【冶】cold short: ~材料 *cold short material*

【冷淡】① sluggish; slack: ~的市场 *a sluggish market* /这周的买卖很~。*Trade is slack this week.* ② cold; indifferent: ~的接待 *a cold reception* / ~的表情 *a frosty look* / ~的微笑 *an icy smile* /观众对新电影反应~。*The audience showed a cold response to the new film.* /我对政治表示~。*I am indifferent about politics.* ③ treat coldly; give the cold shoulder; slight:他~我。*He slighted me.*

【冷冻】freeze; freezing: ~舱 *freezing room* / ~法 *freezing method* / ~干燥 *freeze-drying* / ~机 *freeze drier; icebox; refrigerator* / ~剂 *cryogen; refrigerant; coolant* / ~疗法 *cold therapy; cryotherapy* / ~灭菌法 *cold sterilization* / ~切片 *frozen section* / ~室 *freezer compartment* / ~手术 *cryosurgery* / ~探针 *cryoprobe* / ~温度 *cryogenic temperature*/我把几瓶水放进冰箱里~。*I put a bottle of water in the ice-box to chill.*

【冷风】① cold wind ② rumour; gossip:吹~ *spread gossip*

【冷敷】【医】cold compress: ~法 *cold application; cold compress*

【冷宫】cold palace — a place to which disfavoured queens and concubines are banished; limbo:打入~ *be consigned to limbo; be shelved*

【冷光】①【物】cold light: ~灯 *cold light lamp* / ~手术灯 *cold light operating lamp* ② cold eyes; cold expression

【冷柜】refrigerator; ice box

【冷害】【农】damage to plants caused by a sudden drop in temperature; frost damage

【冷汗】cold sweat:出了一身~ *break out into a cold sweat*

【冷荤】cold meat; cold buffet

【冷货】① goods not much in demand; dull goods ② frozen product

【冷寂】cold and still; forlorn: ~的夜晚 *a cold and silent night*

【冷加工】【机】cold working

【冷箭】an arrow shot from hiding; sniper's shot:放~ *make a sneak attack*

【冷浇注】【冶】cold cast

【冷噤】shiver; chill:打~ *have a chill* /他的话让我打了一个~。*His words gave me the shiver.*

【冷静】①［方］(of a place) quiet; still:到了晚上,街道~下来。*The street became quiet in the evening.* ② sober; calm: ~的性格 *a cold nature* / ~的谈判者 *a cool negotiator* /她需要时间~下来。*She needed time for tempers to cool.* /他非常~。*He is as cool as a cucumber.* /表演者在准备上场时沉着~。*The performer was composed as she readied herself for her entrance on stage.* /她~下来后向我道了歉。*Later she sobered down and apologized to me.*

【冷峻】grave and stern: ~的表情 *a stern expression*

【冷库】cold storage; freezer

【冷酷】harsh; unfeeling; callous; grim; cold-hearted: ~的事实 *cold facts* / ~无情 *cold-blooded; as hard as nails* /谎言掩盖不住~的现实。*Lies cannot cover up grim reality.*

【冷厉】cold and stern:他~的目光让我无地自容。*His icy look made me feel too ashamed to show my face.*

【冷脸子】［方］cold face; severe expression:他这几天都拉着~。*He puts on a frosty expression all these days.*

【冷落】① unfrequented; desolate:狭窄~的街道 *an unfrequented narrow street* ② treat coldly; cold-shoulder; leave sb out in the cold:他工作太忙,~了家人。*He was too busy to care about his family members.* /我感到受了~。*I feel slighted.*

【冷门】① (of a profession, trade or branch of learning) receives little attention; unpopular; not in great demand: ~货 *goods not much in demand* /考古学是~专业吗? *Is archaeology an unpopular major?* ② an unexpected winner; dark horse:爆~ *a surprise hit* /比赛出了~。*A dark horse emerged in the contest.*

【冷漠】cold and detached; unconcerned; indifferent; nonchalant:他受到~的欢迎。*He was given a chilly welcome.* /他对我的请求表现~。*He is indifferent to my appeals.*

【冷凝】【物】condensation:毛细~ *capillary condensation* /骤~ *quench condensation* /蒸汽~ *vapour condensation* / ~泵 *condenser pump* / ~点 *condensation point* / ~管 *cold trap; condensation tube* / ~过程 *condensation process* / ~排水 *condensed water outlet* / ~器 *condenser* / ~塔 *condensing tower* / ~液 *condensate liquid* / ~装置 *condensing unit*

【冷暖】① changes in temperature: ~自知 *know by oneself whether it is cold or warm* /你要注意~。*You should be careful about changes of temperature.* ② well-being:干部应该关心群众的~。*Cadres should be concerned with the well-being of the masses.*

【冷盘】cold dish

【冷僻】① deserted; out-of-the-way; unfrequented: ~的村子 *a deserted village* ② rare; unfamiliar: ~的字眼 *rarely used words*

L

【冷气】① cool air ② air conditioning: ~机 *air conditioner* / ~瓶 *air bottle*; *air reservoir*
【冷气团】【气】cold air mass
【冷枪】sniper's shot: 打~ *fire a sniper's shot*
【冷峭】① biting cold: ~的风 *a biting wind*; *a cutting wind* ② *scathing* (*remarks*); *caustic*: ~的批评 *a cutting criticism*
【冷清】cold and cheerless; desolate; lonely; deserted: 他在林场过着~的生活。*He leads a lonely life in the tree farm.*
【冷清清】cold and cheerless; desolate; lonely; deserted: 过去拥挤的小镇现在变得~。*The little town which was usually so thronged now became desolate.*
【冷泉】cold spring
【冷却】become or make cool; cool-off: 泡在水中~一下 *take a dip to cool off*
【冷却剂】coolant; cooling agency: ~材料 *coolant material* / ~回路 *coolant circuit*
【冷热病】①[方] malaria ② capricious changes in mood; sudden waxing and waning of enthusiasm: 他的毛病就是爱犯~。*His shortcoming is his mercurial nature.*
【冷若冰霜】as cold as ice and frost; have an icy (or chilly) manner; look severe: 他对待下级总是~。*He always adopts a chilly manner in treating his subordinates.*
【冷色】cool colour
【冷涩】① (of water, etc.) cold; chilly: ~的泉水 *very cold spring* ② (of one's voice) harsh and low ③ rare: 他的文章用了太多~的词语。*He used too many rare words and expressions in his article.*
【冷森森】chilly; chilling: ~的房间 *a chilly room*
【冷食】cold drinks and snack: ~店 *cold drink and snack bar*
【冷室】refrigerating room; refrigerating compartment (in a refrigerator)
【冷水】① cold water: 他对我泼~。*He cast a chill over me.* /不要对他们的热情泼~。*Don't chill their enthusiasm.* ② unboiled water: ~环流 *cooling water circulation* / ~养殖 *cold water culture* / ~浴 *cold bath* / ~浴室 *frigidarium*
【冷丝丝】a bit chilly
【冷飕飕】(of wind) chilling; chilly
【冷铁】【冶】chill; iron chill
【冷笑】sneer; laugh grimly; sardonic grin; grin with dissatisfaction, helplessness, bitterness, etc.: 他的~让我难堪。*He sneered me out of countenance.*
【冷星】【天】cool star
【冷血动物】① cold-blooded animal ② an unfeeling person; a cold-hearted person: 他对这个可怜的孩子毫无怜悯,真是个~。*He showed little mercy to the miserable child; what a coldhearted person!*
【冷言冷语】sarcastic comments; ironical remarks; mocking words
【冷眼】① with a cold eye; with cool detachment: 他~观看我们的窘态。*He looked at our poor situation with a cold eye.* ② cold shoulder; cold manner
【冷眼旁观】look on with a cold eye; look on coldly as a bystander; stand aloof and look on with cold indifference: 他对于别人的困境总是~。*He always stands aloof over others' sad plight.*
【冷眼相看】look coldly upon...; look at sth coldly; look with a cold eye: 我~这场所谓的改革。*I look unfavourably upon the so-called reform.*
【冷饮】cold drink: 给我来一瓶~。*Give me a bottle of cold drink.*
【冷语】cold words (or remarks)
【冷语冰人】attack sb with cold remarks: 我无法忍受他的~。*I could not bear the sting of his tongue.*
【冷遇】cold reception; cold shoulder; a cold welcome: 遭到~ *meet a cold reception*
【冷轧】【冶】cold rolling; cold reduction: ~机 *cold-rolling mill* / ~压缩 *cold-rolling reduction*
【冷战】(lěngzhàn) cold war: ~分子 *cold warrior* / ~时期 *cold war period* / ~思维 *cold-war thinking* / ~语言 *language of the cold war*
【冷战】(lěngzhan) [口] shiver: 打~ *shiver with cold*
【冷铸】【冶】chill casting
【冷字】a rarely used word; an unfamiliar

lèng

愣 ① absent-minded; stupefied; distracted: 发~ *absent-minded*; *look distracted* ② [口] rash; reckless: 他说话太~。*He speaks too bluntly.* ③ [方] stubbornly; willfully: 他~是不肯听我解释。*He refused to listen to my explanation willfully.*
【愣干】[口] do things rashly; do things recklessly; persist in going one's own way: 要遵守操作规程,不能~。*You've got to observe the working regulation; you can't do things any way you like.*
【愣神儿】[方] stare blankly; be in a daze: 他站在窗前~。*He stood by the window lost in thought.* /她似乎在~。*Her mind seemed to have blanked out.*
【愣说】[口] stubbornly assert; insist: 他~我骗他。*He insisted that I have cheated him.* /他~我偷了他的钱包,可是拿不出任何证据。*He alleged that I had stolen his money but he has given no proof.*
【愣头愣脑】rash; impetuous; reckless: ~的求爱者 *a rash wooer*
【愣头儿青】[方] rash (or brusque) fellow; hothead
【愣着】dumb; not moving: 他~不说话。*He kept dumb as an oyster.*
【愣住】be taken aback; be struck dumb: 他吓得~了。*He is struck dumb with fear.*

睖 [方] stare in dissatisfaction
【睖睁】stare blankly; be in a daze: 别~了,快去写作业。*Don't stare blankly; go to do your home-*

work.

lī

哩

see also lǐ; li

【哩哩啦啦】[口] scattered; sporadic; here and there: ~的与会者 *spotty attendance* / 农民在院子里~撒了些谷子喂鸡。*The farmer scattered the corn in the yard for the hens.*

【哩哩啰啰】[口] verbose and unclear in speech; rambling and indistinct: 妹妹~抱怨了半天,我却没弄明白她的意思。*My younger sister uttered a stream of complaints, but I was quite confused about her meaning.*

【哩溜歪斜】[方] ① crooked; twisted: 虽然他有学问,写字确是~的。*Although he is learned, his handwriting is irregular and illegible.* ② waddle; stagger: 醉汉~地走过来。*The drunkard staggered along.*

lí

厘 ① (of certain measurement) one hundredth ② *li*, (a) a unit of length (=1/3 millimetre) (b) a unit of weight (=0.05 grams) (c) a unit of area (=0.666 square metres) ③ *li*, a unit of Chinese currency (=0.001 yuan) ④ *li*, a unit of monthly interest rate (=0.1%): 月利率二~七 *a monthly interest of* 0.27% ⑤ a fraction: 分~不差 *without the slightest error* ⑥ regulate; rectify

【厘定】[书] collate and stipulate (rules and regulations, etc.): ~规章制度 *stipulate rules and regulations*

【厘革】[书] rectify and reform

【厘金】a former provincial transit duty in the Qing Dynasty

【厘克】centigram (cg)

【厘米】centimeter (cm)

【厘秒】centisecond

【厘升】centiliter (cl)

【厘正】[书] correct; revise

狸

【狸猫】leopard cat

【狸藻】【植】bladderwort

【狸子】leopard cat

离[1] ① leave; part from; separate: 别~ *be separated* / 他们被迫彼此分~。*They were forced to part from one another.* / 油和水容易分~。*Oil and water tend to separate.* / 船被吹~航道。*The ship was blown off course.* ② from; off; away: 请问~这里有多远? *Could you please tell me how far is it from here?* / 车站~这里只有几分钟的路程。*The stations are only a few minutes' walk away.* / 公园~我家很近。*The park is not far from my home.* ③ go without; be independent of: 她~不开电视。*She cannot be without a TV set.* ④ (Lí) a surname

离[2] ① *li*, one of the Eight Diagrams, representing fire

【离岸价格】【经】free on board (FOB)

【离别】part (for a long period); leave; bid farewell: ~故土 *part from one's native shore* / ~时的一瞥 *a farewell glance* / 他们在~时哭了。*They cried at parting.*

【离不开】① can't do without: 我~家人的支持。*I can't do without the support of my family members.* / 他们是~的朋友。*They are inseparable friends.* ② too busy to get away; be too busy with the job on hand: 我现在~。*I cannot afford to get away for a moment.*

【离愁】[书] the sorrow of parting; the pain of separation: ~别恨 *grief of parting; the feeling of separation; parting sorrows*

【离队】leave the ranks; leave one's post; be demobilized: 禁止擅自~! *It's forbidden to leave one's post without permission.*

【离格儿】[口] go beyond what is proper; be out of place: 说实话,你做得太~了。*To be frank, you are going too far.*

【离宫】a temporary abode for an emperor on progresses; provisional imperial palace

【离合】separation and reunion: 悲欢~ *vicissitudes of life; the sorrows and joys of partings and meetings*

【离合器】【机】clutch: ~壳 *bell housing; clutch housing* / ~盘 *clutch cushion* / ~踏板 *clutch pedal*

【离核】【植】freestone

【离婚】divorce; break a marriage: 请求~ *sue for a divorce* / ~率 *the divorce rate* / ~判决 *divorce decree* / ~申请书 *divorce petition* / ~诉讼 *divorce proceedings* / ~者 *divorcee* / 去年她和丈夫~了。*She was separated from her husband last year.* / 这对新婚夫妇~了。*The new couple divorced each other.*

【离间】alienate; sow discord (or dissension); estrange; drive a wedge between; set one party against another: ~计 *the scheme of sowing dissension* / ~主仆两人 *estrange the master and the servant* / 他企图~我们的关系。*He attempts to drive a wedge between us.* / 他散播谣言~那两个朋友但失败了,因为他们彼此完全信任。*He spread rumour to alienate the two friends but ended up with failure because they had complete faith.*

【离解】【化】dissociation: ~度 *degree of dissociation* / ~扩散 *dissociative diffusion* / ~率 *rate of dissociation* / ~平衡 *dissociation equilibrium*

【离境】leave a country or place: ~签证 *exit visa* / ~许可证 *exit permit*

【离开】eave; depart from; deviate from: 不准~房间 *not allowed to leave the room* / 他~了妻子。*He left his wife.*

【离离】[书] (of plants, etc.) luxuriant; exuberant：～原上草，一岁一枯荣。*The luxuriant grass on the plain withers and flourishes again year after year.*

【离乱】be separated by war：经历过～的人尤其珍惜这和平的日子。*Those who have been separated by war especially value peace.*

【离叛】betray

【离谱】go beyond what is proper; be out of place; far off the beam：你说得也太～了。*What you've said is unbelievable.* /他猜得都很～。*His guesses were all very wide of the mark.*

【离奇】strange; odd; fantastic; bizarre：～的行为 *odd behaviour* /～的故事 *fantastic story* /这事儿很～。*This is a very odd business.* /事实比虚构的故事还～。*Truth is even stranger than fiction.*

【离弃】abandon; desert; forsake：～家园 *abandon one's home*

【离情】sad feelings at parting：～别绪 *parting sadness*

【离去】split; leave：他不忍～。*He doesn't have the heart to leave.*

【离群索居】live in solitude; live all alone; cut oneself from the society：他过着～的生活。*He left the crowd and lived alone.*

【离任】leave one's post：～回国 *leave one's post for home*

【离散】(of relatives) be dispersed; be scattered about; be separated from one another：骨肉～。*The family were scattered in different places.*

【离世】① be free from worldly cares; isolate oneself from society ②［婉］pass away

【离索】［书］desolate and lonely; forlorn

【离题】digress from the subject; stray from the point; beside the point：～太远 *digress too far from the subject* /他乱讲一气，都是～的话。*He rambled and did not speak to the point.*

【离题万里】be remote from the subject; be too far from the subject; completely off the point

【离析】［书］① disintegrate; crumble; break up：分崩～ *fall into pieces; collapse* ② analyse

【离席】leave the table or a meeting：她不到9点就～了。*She left the meeting before 9.*

【离心】① be at odds with the community (or the leadership)：他和我已经～。*We are not of one mind now.* ② centrifugal; eccentric

【离心泵】centrifugal pump; volute pump

【离心机】【机】centrifuge; centrifugal：间歇式～ *batch centrifuge* /净化～ *clarifying centrifuge* /离子～ *ionic centrifuge* /连续～ *continuous centrifuge* /密封～ *hermetic centrifuge* /水动～ *water driven centrifuge* /台式～ *desk centrifuge* /斜角～ *angle centrifuge* /蒸发式～ *evaporative centrifuge*

【离心离德】torn by dissension and discord; disunity

【离心力】【物】centrifugal force

【离心作用】centrifugal action; centrifugal effect

【离休】(of veteran cadres) retire：我爷爷是一位～老干部。*My grandfather is a retired veteran cadre.*

【离异】［书］divorce; separate：父母～ *with one's parents divorced*

【离辙】［口］off the track; off the beam; off the point

【离职】① leave one's job temporarily; be suspended from office：～考查 *leave one's job temporarily to do a investigation* ② leave office; resign：他上个月～了。*He resigned last month.*

【离子】【物】ion：带电～ *charged ion* /二价～ *divalent ion* /复合～ *compound ion* /共轭～ *conjugate ion* /碱～ *alkali ion* /三价～ *trivalent ion* /亚铁～ *ferrous ion* /阳～ *cation* /阴～ *anion* /自由～ *free ion*

【离子计】ionometer

【离子加速器】ion accelerator

【离子键】electrovalent bond; ionic bond

【离子交换】【化】ion exchange：～材料 *ion exchange material* /～技术 *ion exchange technique* /～剂 *ion exchanger* /～容量 *ion exchange capacity* /～水 *ion exchange water*

【离子强度】ionic strength

【离子束】【物】ion beam; ionic beam：～抛光 *ion beam polishing* /～清洗 *ion beam cleaning*

骊

［书］pure black horse

【骊歌】［书］farewell song

梨

pear：鳄～ *alligator pear* /鲚～ *anchovy pear* /砂～ *Chinese pear* /无仁～ *free-stone pear* /雪～ *snow pear* /～脯 *preserved pear*

【梨膏】【药】pear syrup (for the relief of coughs)

【梨果】【植】pome

【梨子】pear

犁

plough; plow：他们用～劳动。*They work with a plough.* /种庄稼前必须～地。*You must plow the land before planting crops.*

【犁刀】【农】plough coulter

【犁耕】【农】ploughing：～阻力 *plowing resistance*

【犁沟】furrow：～底 *sole* /田间深深的～使人不易从中穿过。*The deep furrows made it difficult to walk across the field.*

【犁铧】ploughshare; share：～背 *share back* /～钢 *share steel*

【犁牛】［方］farm cattle

【犁杖】［方］plough

黎

①［书］multitude; host ②［书］black ③(Lí) a surname

【黎巴嫩】Lebanon：～人 *Lebanese*

【黎锦】a kind of brocade popular among the *Li* people

【黎民】［书］the common people; the multitude：～百姓 *the populace*

【黎明】dawn; daybreak：在～时刻 *at sunrise (or dawn)* /～即起 *get up at dawn; get out of bed at cockcrow; up with the lark* /～即起，洒扫庭除。*Rise at dawn and sweep the courtyard.*

罹

［书］meet with; be caught in; suffer from：～病 *suffer from a disease*

【罹患】［书］suffer (from illness)

【罹难】［书］die in a disaster or an accident; be

murdered

篱 fence; hedge:防雪～ *snow protection hedge*

【篱笆】(bamboo or twig fence); hurdle:电～ *electric fence* /柳条～ *wicker fence* /～匠 *fencer* /为了安全,他又扎了一道～。*He made another fence to keep safe.* /～靠桩,好汉要帮。*A fence needs the support of the stakes; an able man needs the assistance of other people.*

【篱芥】hedge mustard

【篱落】[书] (bamboo or twig) fence

【篱墙】wattled wall

蠡 [书] ① gourd ladle; dipper ② seashell

【蠡测】[书] measure the sea with a calabash shell — make a superficial estimate of sth:管窥～ *have a narrow and superficial view; have a shallow understanding of sth*

lǐ

礼 ① ceremony; rite:婚～ *wedding* /葬～ *burial rites; funeral* ② courtesy; manners; etiquette:回～ *return the courtesy* /失～ *discourtesy* /他们彼此之间彬彬有～。*They use much ceremony with each other.* ③ gift; present:贺～ *gift as token of congratulation* /送～ *give a present* ④ [书] treat with courtesy

【礼拜】① religious service:做～ *go to church* ② [口] week:上～ *last week* ③ [口] day of the week:～一 *Monday* /～六 *Saturday* ④ [口] Sunday:今儿过～。*Today is Sunday.*

【礼拜寺】【宗】mosque

【礼拜堂】church

【礼拜天】[口] Sunday

【礼宾】protocol: ～官员 *protocol officer* /～活动 *protocol activities*

【礼宾司】the Department of Protocol; the Protocol Department: ～司长 *Director of the Protocol Department*

【礼部】the Ministry of Rites in feudal China

【礼成】ceremony is over (said by the master of ceremonies)

【礼单】a list of presents

【礼多人不怪】a man's hat in his hand never does him any harm; courtesy is never to blame; one won't be blamed for being extra-polite

【礼法】rules of etiquette; the proprieties

【礼佛】【宗】pray to Buddha

【礼服】ceremonial robe or dress; full dress; formal attire:结婚～ *wedding dress or suit* /晚～ *evening dress*

【礼盒】gift box

【礼花】fireworks display:放～ *let off fireworks*

【礼教】the Confucian or feudal ethical code:吃人的～ *cannibalistic feudal ethics*

【礼节】courtesy; etiquette; protocol; ceremony; proprieties:不拘～ *without ceremony* /待客～ *the rites of hospitality* /讲究～ *stand on ceremony* /社交～ *social etiquette* /外交～ *diplomatic etiquette* /最高～ *full ceremony* /烦琐的～ *trivial formality* /介绍认识时的握手～ *the ceremony of shaking hands when introduced* /我们对新来的邻居进行了～性拜访。*We paid a courtesy visit to the new neighbours.*

【礼金】a gift of money

【礼帽】a hat that goes with formal dress

【礼貌】① courtesy; politeness; manners:他们对我们很有～。*They showed us great courtesy.* /～对于人们之间的融洽相处是很重要的。*Manners are important to happy relations among people.* ② courteous; polite; mannerly:有～的回答 *a polite reply*

【礼炮】*salvo*; (*gun*) *salute*

【礼品】gift; present: ～商店 *gift and souvenir store*

【礼聘】cordially enlist the service (of sb):登门～ *call on sb in order to enlist his or her service*

【礼券】gift coupon or card

【礼轻情意重】the gift is trifling but the feeling is profound; the thoughtfulness is worth far more than the gift itself

【礼让】give precedence to sb out of courtesy or thoughtfulness; comity

【礼尚往来】① Courtesy demands reciprocity. ② deal with a man as he deals with you; pay a man back in his own coin; give as good as one gets

【礼数】[口] courtesy; etiquette

【礼俗】etiquette and custom:不拘～ *not constrained by etiquette*

【礼堂】assembly hall; auditorium

【礼物】gift; present:圣诞～ *a Christmas gift* /我生日时收到了许多～。*I received many presents on my birthday.*

【礼贤下士】(of a ruler or a high minister) treat worthy men with courtesy; be courteous to the wise and condescending to scholars

【礼仪】ceremony and propriety:他向我表示了应有的～。*He exercised due courtesy towards me.* /结婚典礼必须符合当地的～。*The wedding ceremony had to be consistent with local protocol.*

【礼仪之邦】a state of ceremonies ; a land of propriety and righteousness:中国是～。*China is a country of ceremonies.*

【礼义廉耻】propriety, righteousness, honesty, and a sense of shame

【礼遇】courteous reception:受到～ *be accorded courteous reception*

【礼赞】① praise ②【宗】pray

【礼治】rule by rites

李 ①【植】plum ② (Lǐ) a surname

【李代桃僵】① palm off a substitute for the real thing; substitute one thing for another ② sacrifice oneself for another person

【李下瓜田】in a melon patch or under a plum tree — liable to lay oneself open to suspicion; liable to get into trouble

L

【李下之嫌】be suspected of a theft; be under suspicion of stealing
【李子】【植】plum

里¹ ① lining; liner; inside: 衣服~儿 *the lining of a coat* ② inner: ~屋 *inner room* /报纸的~页 *the inside pages of a newspaper*

里² ① neighbourhood: 邻~ *people of the neighbourhood* ②［书］native place; hometown ③［古］administrative unit of twenty-five neighbouring households ④（Lǐ）a surname

里³ Chinese unit of length（=1/2 kilometer）

里⁴ ① in; inside: 家~ *in one's home* ② used to indicate a location: 这~ *here* /那~ *there*

【里昂】Lyons, a city of east-central France
【里边】inside; in; within: 这扇门从~开。*The door opens from within.* /屋子~有三个人。*There are three people in the room.*
【里程】① mileage: 通车~ *traffic mileage* ② course of development; course: 革命~ *the course of the revolution*
【里程碑】milestone; landmark; milepost: 电灯的发明是人类历史上的一个~。*The invention of the electric light was a milestone in the history of man.*
【里程表】odometer; hodometer; velometer
【里出外进】irregular; uneven
【里带】［口］inner tube（of a tyre）
【里勾外联】in collusion with forces within and without; hand in gloves with outsiders
【里海】Capital Sea, land-locked salt lake between Europe and southwest Asia
【里脊】tenderloin: ~肉 *tenderloin*
【里间】inner room
【里拉】lira（former Italian monetary unit）
【里里外外】outside and inside; ins and outs; within and without: 家里~全靠妈妈操持。*My mother handles all affairs both inside and outside.*
【里弄】［方］① lanes and alleys; neighbourhood ② neighbourhood: ~工作 *work on a neighbourhood committee*
【里面】inside; interior: 橘子的外皮是苦的，可~是甜的。*The outside of an orange is bitter, but the inside is sweet.*
【里手】① the left-hand side（of a running vehicle or machine）②［方］expert; old hand: 行家~ *expert*
【里斯本】Lisbon, capital of Portugal
【里通外国】have（or maintain）illicit relations with a foreign country; have treasonous relations with a foreign country
【里头】inside; interior
【里外里】［方］① adding the two sums; in all: 他的工资有1000元，又拿了1500元奖金，~这个月挣了2500元。*His earns a salary of 1,000 and a bonus of 1,500; all together, he got 2,500 this month.* ② no matter how you figure it out; either way
【里外夹攻】make a front and rear attack; attack from within and without; be attacked from inside and out
【里外受气】be bullied at home and outside
【里巷】lanes and alleys
【里应外合】act from inside in coordination with forces attacking from outside; act from the inside in coordination with sb from the outside
【里约热内卢】Rio de Janeiro, the largest city of Brazil
【里子】lining: 缎~ *lining satin*

俚 vulgar; rustic

【俚歌】a rustic song; a folk song
【俚曲】popular music; pop
【俚俗】vulgar; rustic; unrefined
【俚语】slang: 军队~ *army slang* /学生~ *schoolboy slang*

哩 mile
see also lī; li

浬 ［旧］nautical mile; sea mile

理 ① texture; grain: 木~ *grain in wood* /肌~ *skin texture* ② reason; logic: 不近情~ *unreasonable* /合~ *conforming to reason; reasonable* ③ natural science, esp. physics: 数~化 *mathematics, physics and chemistry* ④ manage; run; deal with: 代~ *act for sb* /日~万机 *attend to numerous affairs everyday* ⑤ put in proper order; tidy up: ~东西 *put things in order* / ~思路 *get one's ideas into shape* ⑥ take notice of; pay attention to: 置之不~ *put sth on one side; turn one's back upon sth; wave aside* ⑦（Lǐ）a surname

【理财】manage money matters; conduct financial transactions: 他善于~。*He is good at managing financial affairs.*
【理睬】pay attention to; show interest in: 没人~这事。*Nobody pays any attention to this matter.*
【理当】ought to; should; naturally: 你~向他道歉。*You should apologize to him.*
【理当如此】it's only right and proper; that's just as it should be
【理发】①（of men）get a haircut;（of women）go to the hairdresser's ② give a haircut; do sb's hair
【理发店】barber's shop; barbershop; hairdresser's
【理发师】barber; hairdresser
【理工科】science and engineering: ~大学 *college（or university）of science and engineering* /~大学生 *science student*
【理合】［旧］（used in official documents）ought to; should
【理化】physics and chemistry
【理会】① understand; comprehend: 你~我的意思吗? *Do you understand what I mean?* ② take notice of; pay attention to: 我不~这些无聊的事情。*I'm not interested in such senseless matters at all.* /他屡屡求助均无人~。*All her appeals for help fell on deaf ears.* ③［旧］argue; debate ④［旧］take care of; deal with
【理货】tally: ~单 *tally sheet* /~公司 *tally company*
【理解】understand; comprehend; make out: 即使我

不同意你的观点但我能～。*I can understand your point of view even though I disagree with it.* /我很难～他为什么要这样对待自己的父亲。*It was difficult for me to comprehend why he treated his father this way.* /我不太～你的意思。*I can't quite seize your meaning.* /很明显,他们茫然的表情说明他们并不～我说的话。*It was obvious from their blank expressions that what I was saying was over their heads.*

【理解力】faculty of understanding; understanding; comprehension: ～强 *be quick in the uptake* /他对古诗的～很强。*His understanding of ancient poems is very good.* /这个问题超出了我的～。*The problem is beyond my comprehension.* /他的～迟钝。*He is low of comprehension; he is green in judgement.*

【理科】① science (as a field of study) ② science department in a college: ～博士 *Doctor of Science* (*D. Sc.*) /～硕士 *Master of Science* (*M. Sc.*) /～学士 *Bachelor of Science* (*B. Sc.*)

【理亏】be in the wrong: ～心虚 *have a guilty conscience; become scared, knowing justice is not on one's side; feel apprehensive because one is not on solid ground* /～语塞 *lose in the argument because one is in the wrong*

【理疗】【医】physiotherapy: ～设备 *modality; physiotherapy equipment* /～学 *physiatrics* /～科 *department of physiotherapy*

【理论】① theory; principle: ～联系实际 *integration of theory with practice* /～水平 *theoretical level* /～素养 *theoretical attainment* /～学习 *study of theory* /～上听起来是对的。*It sounds right in theory.* ② argue; debate: 我和她～了好久,但她拒绝接受我的建议。*I argued with her for a long time, but she refused to accept my advice.*

【理念】【哲】idea

【理赔】settlement of claim; settle a claim; settlement of claims; payment of claims: ～处 *claims department* /～代理人 *settling agent*

【理气】【中医】regulating the flow of vital energy and removing obstruction to it

【理屈】be in the wrong; have a weak case

【理屈词穷】fall silent on finding oneself bested in argument; be unable to advance any further arguments; be condemned out of one's own mouth: 他～就开始耍赖。*He found himself devoid of all argument and began to act shamelessly.*

【理事】① handle matters: 当家～ *rule the roost* ② member of an executive council or of a board of directors; director; manager: 常任～国 *permanent member state of a council* /～会 *council; board of directors; board of management*

【理顺】rationalize; straighten out: ～各方面的关系 *bring into better balance the relations between the various sectors*

【理算】adjustment: ～费 *adjustment fee* /～人 *adjuster*

【理所当然】of course; as a matter of course; naturally; as it should be; go without saying: 帮助别人对他来说是～的。*It comes natural to him to help others.*

【理想】① ideal; aspiration: 他的～毁于现实。*All his ideals were destroyed by reality.* ② be ideal; be perfect: 他的新工作很～。*His new job is ideal.* /这个季节的天气十分～。*The weather of this season is perfect.* /她是这个职位的～人选。*She was the perfect person for the position.*

【理想国】Utopia, an ideally perfect place, especially in its social, political, and moral aspects

【理想化】idealize; idealization: ～方法 *method of idealization*

【理想气体】【物】ideal gas; perfect gas: ～定律 *ideal gas law* /～方程 *equation for ideal gases*

【理想现实主义】ideal realism

【理想主义】idealism: ～者 *idealist*

【理性】① rational ② the rational faculty; reason: 恢复～ *come to one's sense*

【理性力学】rational mechanics

【理性论】rationalism: ～者 *rationalist*

【理性认识】【哲】rational cognition; rational knowledge

【理学】natural science: ～硕士 *Master of Science* (*MS or MSc*) /～博士 *Doctor of Science* (*DS or DSc*)

【理学士】bachelor of science

【理应】ought to; should: 你～告诉他实情。*You should tell him the truth.* /孩子～服从他们的父母。*Children should obey their parents.*

【理由】account; regard; justification; reason; ground; argument: 辞职的～ *a ground for resignation* /他有～认为我不喜欢他。*He thinks, with reason, that I don't like him.* /老板询问她迟到的～。*The boss inquired about her reason for being late.*

【理喻】reason with sb: 不可～ *would not listen to reason*

【理直气壮】be courageous with sufficient reasons; with perfect assurance

【理智】① reason; intellect: 恢复～ *be restored to reason* /你应该用～来解决问题。*You should use reason to solve problems.* ② rational

锂　【化】lithium: ～电池 *lithium cell; lithium battery* /～青铜 *lithium bronze*

鲤　【动】carp

【鲤庭之训】instructions from one's father

【鲤鱼跳龙门】like a carp leaping into the Dragon's Gate — gain literary advancement; get rapid promotion

lì

力　①【物】force; power; energy: 斥～ *expulsive force* /磁化～ *magnetizing force* /分～ *component force* /浮～ *buoyancy force; levitating force* /惯性～ *inertia force* /合～ *composite force* /拉～ *traction force; towing force* /离心～ *centrifugal force* /摩擦～ *friction force* /内～ *inner force; internal force* /守恒～ *conservative force* /外～ *ap-*

parent force /向心 ~ *centripetal force* /张 ~ *tension* /重 ~ *gravitational force* /阻尼 ~ *damping force* /作用 ~ *applied force* ② power; strength; ability; capacity:人 ~ *manpower* /财 ~ *financial power* /他的话有说服 ~。*There is force in what he said.* /基于她的管理能 ~,她被录用了。*She was hired on the strength of her management skills.* ③ physical strength:筋疲 ~ 尽 *extremely exhausted* / ~ 大如牛 *as powerful as an ox; be as robust as a bull* / ~ 大无比 *without equal in strength; without a match in physical prowess* ④ energetically; vigorously; try one's best; make every effort: ~ 求上进 *strive vigorously to improve oneself* ⑤ (Lì) a surname

【力臂】【物】arm; arm of force; tension arm

【力避】try hard to avoid or avert

【力不从心】ability falling short of one's wishes; unable to do as much as one would like to; ability not equal to one's ambition; bite off more than one can chew:我有时有 ~ 的感觉。*I sometimes feel inadequate.*

【力不能及】be beyond one's capacity; be beyond one's depth; be unequal to one's task

【力场】【物】field of force; force-field

【力持】insist on; uphold

【力畜】draught animal; beast of burden

【力促】make every effort to get sth done; try one's best to promote:他会 ~ 此事成功。*He will surely try his best to make it a success.*

【力挫】fight hard to defeat: ~ 对手 *defeat the opponent*

【力道】[方] ① strength; power ② role; effect:化肥比粪肥的 ~ 来得快。*Chemical fertilizers produce faster effects than barnyard manure.*

【力度】① force ②【音】dynamics ③ depth; power

【力攻】fight with might and main

【力荐】strongly recommend:我 ~ 他做那项工作。*I strongly recommend him for that job.*

【力戒】strictly avoid; do everything possible to avoid; guard against: ~ 浪费 *do everything possible to avoid waste*

【力矩】【物】moment of force; moment:合 ~ *resultant moment*

【力量】① physical strength:我要和他比 ~。*I will measure my strength with him.* ② power; force; strength:榜样的 ~ *force of example* /有生 ~ *the effective strength* /不可忽视的 ~ *a force to be reckoned with* /新生 ~ 是不可战胜的。*New emerging forces are invincible.* /团结就是 ~。*Union is strength.* /知识就是 ~。*Knowledge is power.* ③ potency; efficacy; strength:这种药 ~ 很大。*This kind of medicine is very effective.*

【力偶】【物】couple; couple of forces: ~ 臂 *arm of couple* / ~ 矩 *moment of couple* / ~ 系 *system of couples*

【力排众议】do one's utmost to hold one's own opinion against that of the majority; hold one's ground; override all objections

【力平衡】dynamic balance; dynamic equilibrium

【力气】physical strength; effort:我没有 ~ 搬这个箱子。*I haven't the strength to lift this box.*

【力气活】heavy work; strenuous work

【力求】make every effort to; do one's best to; strive to: ~ 完美 *make every effort to achieve perfectness*

【力三角形】triangle of forces; force triangle

【力所能及】in one's power; as one's ability allows; within one's reach:退休老工人主动为集体做些 ~ 的工作。*The retired workers volunteered to do what they could for the collective.*

【力图】try hard to; strive to

【力挽狂澜】do one's utmost to stem a raging tide or save a desperate situation; make vigorous efforts to turn the tide; save the critical situation

【力线】【物】flux line; line of flux: ~ 图 *force diagram*

【力心】【物】centre of force

【力行】be diligent in action; practise with earnestness

【力学】① mechanics:工程 ~ *engineering mechanics* /固体 ~ *solid mechanics* /轨道 ~ *orbital mechanics* /航天 ~ *spaceflight mechanics* /化学流体 ~ *chemical fluid mechanics* /机械 ~ *mechanics of machinery* /应用 ~ *applied mechanics* /原子 ~ *atom mechanics* /质点 ~ *particle mechanics* ②[书] study hard

【力争】① work hard for; do all one can to ② argue strongly; contend vigorously:据理 ~ *argue strongly on just ground*

【力争上游】aim high; strive for first place:不管你做什么工作,都要 ~。*Whatever your job, you must strive to be the best.*

【力证】strong evidence; convincing proof; conclusive proof:他坚信存在第九大行星,却并无 ~ 证明。*He firmly believed there was a ninth planet, but he had no conclusive proof of its existence.* /有 ~ 表明这种植物将在 10 年以后灭绝。*There is strong evidence to suggest that this kind of plant will have disappeared in 10 years.*

【力主】strongly advocate; be strongly in favour of:他 ~ 改革。*He is strongly in favour of reform.*

【力作】①[书] work hard; toil ② masterpiece:这部小说被看作是他的 ~。*This novel is regarded as his masterpiece.*

历[1] ① experience; go through:来 ~ *history; derivation; origin* /资 ~ *seniority* ② all previous (years, occasions, etc.) ③ all; one after another:遍 ~ 各地 *pass through different places* ④ (Lì) a surname

历[2] calendar:校 ~ *academic calendar* /阳 ~ *solar calendar* /阴 ~ *lunar calendar* /阴阳 ~ *lunisolar calendar*

【历朝】① successive dynasties; past dynasties ② the successive reigns of a dynasty

【历陈】state point by point; explain item by item: ~ 弊端 *explain all the disadvantages item by item*

【历程】① course; progress:人生的 ~ *life's journey* ②【化】mechanism

【历次】all previous (occasions, etc.):他在 ~ 考试

L

中均取得了好成绩。*He got good marks in all previous exams.*

【历代】① successive dynasties; past dynasties: ~名画 *famous paintings through the dynasties* ② all previous generations: ~务农 *engage in farming from generation to generation* ③ all ages

【历法】【天】calendric system; calendar

【历届】all previous (sessions, governments, etc.): ~毕业生 *graduates of all previous years*

【历尽】have gone through a lot of: ~磨难 *go through all kinds of hardships* / ~沧桑 *go through the mill; have experienced many vicissitudes of life* / ~艰险 *experience all kinds of hardships and perils; through hell and high water; pass through all trials*

【历尽艰辛】go through much suffering; drain the cup of bitterness to the dregs; go through many hardships: ~他始终忠实于我。*He remained loyal to me through thick and thin.*

【历经】go through; experience

【历久】for a long time; enduring: ~弥坚 *remain unshakable and become even firmer as time goes by*

【历来】always; constantly; all through the ages; all along; hitherto; from the old days; since a long time ago: ~如此。*It has always been so; this has always been the case.* /此类事情~如此。*Matters of this sort have been so from the old days.*

【历历】distinctly; clearly: ~在目 *be visible before the eyes; be still vivid in one's mind; clearly reappear before one's eyes*

【历练】① experience and training ② experienced; seasoned

【历年】① over the years ②【天】calendar year

【历任】① have successively held the posts of; have served successively as: 他~主任、校长等职。*He successively held the posts of director and headmaster.* ② successive: 这个俱乐部的~主席 *all the successive chairpersons of the club*

【历时】last (a period of time); take (a period of time): 比赛~10天。*The match took ten days.*

【历史】① history: 古代~ *ancient history* /近代~ *modern history* /~发现 *historical discoveries* /~剧 *a historical play* /~人物 *a historical character* /~小说 *a historical novel* /~学派 *historical school* /我们要用~的观点看待这些问题。*We should look at the problems from a historical point of view.* /~记载过去的重要事件。*History chronicles important events of the past.* ② past events: ~清白 *have a clean record* /那都是~了,不要再提了。*That is all history now. Don't mention it anymore.* /~往往重演。*History repeats itself.* ③ historical record ④ history (as a course of study); historiography: ~是我在学校中最喜爱的学科。*History is my favourite subject at school.*

【历世】all previous dynasties

【历书】almanac; ephemeris

【历数】count one by one; enumerate

【历险】experience dangers or adventures: 孩子们专注地听他讲他的~经历。*All the children listened to his adventures with eager attention.*

【历元】【天】epoch

【历月】【天】calendar month: 从三月一日到四月一日是一个~。*From March 1st to April 1st is one calendar month.*

【历钟】calendar clock

厉 ① strict; rigorous: ~行禁令 *carry out law strictly* ② severe; stern; grim: 声色俱~ *stern in voice and countenance* ③ (Lì) a surname

【厉鬼】an evil spirit

【厉害】① severe; sharp; cruel; fierce: 他是一个很~的人。*He is a merciless person.* ② terrible; formidable; serious: 我困得~。*I am extremely sleepy.* /那个小孩感冒得很~。*The children had a terribly bad cold.*

【厉色】a stern countenance: 正言~ *speak with stern countenance*

【厉声】in a stern voice: ~斥责 *scold with an irritating voice*

【厉行】strictly enforce; rigorously enforce; make great efforts to carry out: ~节俭 *practise economy strictly; make every penny count* /~改革 *make great efforts to carry out reforms*

立 ① stand: 倒~ *stand upside down; handstand* /站~ *remain standing* /直~ *stand straight* ② erect; set up: ~旗杆 *set up a flagpole* ③ upright; vertical: ~式冰柜 *vertical refrigerator* ④ found; set up; establish: 建~一个朝代 *erect a dynasty* /建~一个殖民地 *found a colony* /父母必须为孩子树~好榜样。*A parent must set a good example for the children.* ⑤ sign; conclude: ~字据 *sign a note* ⑥ [书] ascend the throne: 自~为王 *make oneself king* ⑦ appoint; adopt: 他被~为继承人。*He is adopted as an heir.* ⑧ exist; live: 自~ *stand on one's own feet* /势不两~ *at daggers drawn; irreconcilable* ⑨ immediately; at once: ~办此事。*The matter must be dealt with at once.* ⑩ (Lì) a surname

【立案】① register; put on record ②【律】place a case on file for investigation and prosecution: ~侦察 *place on file for investigation and prosecution*

【立标】day-mark

【立场】position; stand; standpoint: ~鲜明 *take a clear-cut stand* /你对这个问题的~是什么? *What's your position on the problem?* /看到形势的变化,他立刻改变了~。*Seeing the altered situation, he changed his stand at once.*

【立档】establish a file or archives

【立等】wait for sth to be done immediately: ~可取 *have sth ready while waiting; wait and have things ready before you get tired by standing*

【立地】① set one's feet on the ground: 顶天~ *stand on one's feet between heaven and earth — of indomitable spirit* ② location of a tree ③ on the spot; immediately: ~成佛 *become a Buddha immediately*

【立定】① halt: ~! *Halt!* ② stand firm ③ resolute-

ly determine：~主意 *make up one's mind*
【立定跳远】【体】standing long jump
【立法】make (or enact) laws; legislate：~程序 *legislative process* / ~会议 *legislative assemblies* / ~机构 *legislative assembly body*; *legislature* / ~机关 *legislative body*; *legislature* / ~委员会 *legislation committee*; *legislative council*
【立方】①【数】cube：5的~是125。*The cube of 5 is 125.* ② cube root ③［量］cubic metre; stere
【立方尺】cubic foot
【立方根】【数】cube root
【立方厘米】cubic centimeter
【立方米】cubic metre
【立方面】cubic plane
【立方体】cube：~系数 *cubicity factor*
【立竿见影】set up a pole and you see its shadow — produce instant results; get an quick effect
【立功】render meritorious service; do a deed of merit; win honour; make contributions：立大功 *render outstanding service* / ~者受奖。*Those who render meritorious service receive awards.* /这个战士立了一等功。*The soldier won a first class merit.*
【立功赎罪】do good deeds to atone for one's crimes; perform merits to atone for one's misdeeds
【立柜】clothes closet; wardrobe; hanging cupboard
【立国】found a state; build up a nation
【立国之本】foundation underlying all our efforts to build the country
【立户】① register for a household residence card; register for permanent residence ② open an account with the bank
【立即】immediately; at once; promptly：~执行 *be sentenced to death and executed immediately* /他~给了我答复。*He answered me promptly.* /我~想到了一个主意。*The idea occurred to me at once.*
【立交】【建】grade separation
【立交桥】viaduct; overpass; flyover
【立脚点】① perspective; standpoint ② footing
【立决】［书］summary execution
【立刻】immediately; at once; right away：看到我，他~站了起来。*He stood up immediately when he saw me.* /我~就去。*I'll go right away.*
【立领】straight collar
【立论】① set forth one's views; present one's arguments ② argument; position; line of reasoning
【立马】①［书］pull up a horse ②［方］immediately; at once; right away
【立米】cubic metre
【立面图】elevation; elevation drawing
【立木】body; standing tree：~度 *crop density*; *amount of growing stock* / ~蓄积 *growing stock*
【立绒】cut velvet; upright pile
【立射】【军】fire from a standing position
【立身处世】the way one conducts oneself in society
【立身扬名】gain fame and position
【立时】immediately; at once; right away
【立时三刻】［方］right away; at once
【立誓】take an oath; vow：他~要减肥。*He vowed that he would lose weight.*
【立式】【机】vertical; upright：~车床 *vertical lathe* / ~钢琴 *giraffe* / ~搅拌机 *vertical paddle mixer* / ~拉门 *vertically sliding door* / ~离心机 *vertical centrifugal machine* / ~磨床 *vertical grinder* / ~蒸汽机 *vertical steam engine*
【立嗣】［书］adopt an heir
【立陶宛】Lithuania：~人 *Lithuanian* / ~语 *Lithuanian (language)*
【立体】① three-dimensional; stereoscopic ②【数】solid：正方体和长方体都是~。*The cube and the quadratic prism are all solids.* ③ all-round; triphibious：~交叉桥 *overpass*; *flyover* ④ a three-dimensional effect：~动画 *three-dimensional cartoon*
【立宪】constitutionalism：君主~ *constitutional monarchy* / ~政体 *constitutional government*; *constitutionalism*
【立项】put a project under an authorized plan
【立言】expound one's ideas in writing; achieve glory by writing
【立业】① start one's career ② buy an estate：成家~ *get married and build up family property*
【立意】① be determined; make up one's mind：他~要当一名律师。*He is determined to be a lawyer.* ② conception; approach：~新颖 *show an interesting new approach*
【立于不败之地】be in an unassailable position; base oneself on sure ground; be invincible; establish oneself in an invulnerable position
【立约】conclude a treaty; draw up an agreement (or a contract)：~者 *promisor*
【立账】open an account
【立正】stand at attention
【立志】resolve; be determined：他~改进工作。*He resolved firmly to do better work.* /我~毕业后到农村去。/*I have determined on going to the countryside after graduation.* /她~成为作家。*She aspired to become an author*
【立轴】① vertical scroll of painting or calligraphy; wall scroll ②【机】vertical shaft; upright shaft
【立传】glorify sb by writing his biography
【立锥之地】land just enough to stick an awl into — an inch of standing room：无~ *not possess a speck of land*
【立姿】【军】standing position
【立字】sign an agreement, a contract, a receipt, etc.
【立足】① have a foothold somewhere：~社会 *establish oneself in society* /他安排儿子~商界。*He established his son in business.* ② base oneself upon
【立足点】① foothold; footing ② standpoint; stand：他在这个集体中找到了~。*He got a footing in the collective.*
【立足之地】a place to put one's feet on — a place to live in; a firm hold; an anchor point; an inch

of land to stand on; a place for living

吏 [旧] ① clerk ② official; mandarin: 官 ~ *government official*

【吏胥】[书] petty official

【吏治】[旧] administration of local officials

丽[1] beautiful; pretty: 华 ~ *magnificent*; *gorgeous* / 秀 ~ *delicate and pretty*

丽[2] [书] attach to; adhere to: 附 ~ *connected with*; *joined to*

【丽风】northwest wind

【丽人】[书] a beautiful woman; a beauty

【丽日】[书] bright sun

【丽月】second month of the lunar calendar

【丽质】beauty (of a woman): 天生 ~ *a born beauty*

励 ① encourage; exert oneself: 鼓 ~ *encourage*; *actively support* / 勉 ~ *persuade sb to greater effort* ② (Lì) a surname

【励精图治】exert oneself to make the country prosperous; arouse one's all efforts to build a strong state

【励志】[书] be determined to fulfil one's aspirations

呖

【呖呖】[象] chirping sound

利 ① sharp; keen: ~ 刃 *a sharp blade* / ~ 爪 *sharp claws* ② favourable; convenient: 吉 ~ *good fortune* ③ benefit; advantage: 无 ~ *without benefit* ④ profit; interest; gains: 薄 ~ 多销 *small profits and quick returns* / 营 ~ *seek profits* / 连本带 ~ *both principal and interest* ⑤ benefit: 自私自 ~ *selfish*; *egocentric* / 损人 ~ 己 *Roman holiday*; *harm others to benefit oneself*; *reap profits at the expense of others* ⑥ (Lì) a surname

【利比里亚】Liberia: ~ 人 *Libyan*

【利比亚】Libya: ~ 人 *Libyan*

【利弊】advantages and disadvantages; pros and cons: ~ 得失 *advantages and disadvantages, merits and demerits*; *gain and loss*; *pros and cons* / 你做出决定之前一定要权衡 ~。*You should weigh the advantages and disadvantages before making the decision.*

【利多弊少】the advantages outweigh the disadvantages: 这个计划 ~。*This plan will do more good than harm.*

【利福平】【药】rifampicin; rifampin (RFP)

【利滚利】at compound interest

【利国利民】benefit the nation and the people; bring profit to one's country and the people

【利害】advantages and disadvantages; gains and losses: ~ 昭然 *clearly point to where interests or dangers lie* / 他一向努力工作,不计 ~ 得失。*He always works very hard regardless of gains or losses.*

【利害得失】advantages and disadvantages

【利己主义】egoism: ~ 者 *egoist*

【利金】[方] interest

【利口】① a glib tongue; sharp tongue ② [方] tasty and refreshing: 这种苹果真 ~。*This kind of apple is very tasty and refreshing.*

【利令智昏】be blinded by lust for money; bend one's principles to one's interest

【利禄】[书] rank and wealth: ~ 熏心 *be enthusiastic about wealth and emolument*

【利率】【经】rate of interest; interest rate: 提高 ~ *raise profit rate* / ~ 补贴 *interest rate subsidy*

【利落】① agile; nimble; dexterous: 他做事 ~。*He is an agile worker.* ② neat; orderly: 屋子收拾得很 ~。*The room is neat and tidy.* ③ settled; finished: 这件事总算 ~ 了。*I finally finished it.*

【利马】Lima, capital of Peru

【利尿】【医】diuresis: ~ 剂 *diuretic*; *emictoria*

【利器】① a sharp weapon ② good tool; efficient instrument

【利钱】interest (on an investment)

【利权】economic rights (esp. of a country)

【利人利己】benefit other people as well as oneself

【利人主义】altruism

【利润】【经】profit: 边际 ~ *marginal (or net) profit* / 超额 ~ *abnormal profit* / 纯 ~ *net profits* / 存货 ~ *inventory profit* / 定额 ~ *quota profit* / 额外 ~ *extra profit* / 合理 ~ *reasonable profit* / 巨额 ~ *fat profit* / 可变 ~ *variable profit* / 毛 ~ *gross profits* / 免税 ~ *tax-free profit* / 平均 ~ *average profit* / 剩余 ~ *surplus profit* / 实际 ~ *actual profit* / 税前 ~ *pre-tax profit* / 虚构 ~ *fictitious profit* / 应税 ~ *assessable profit* / 预期 ~ *anticipated profit* / 账面 ~ *book profit* / ~ 被亏损抵消。*The gains are balanced by the losses.*

【利市】① [书] profits ② [方] a good market ③ [方] lucky: 讨个 ~ *just for luck* ④ [方] tip

【利税】【经】profit and tax

【利他主义】altruism: ~ 者 *altruist*

【利息】【经】interest (on an investment): 存款 ~ *interest on deposit* / 假定 ~ *hypothetical interest* / 累计 ~ *accumulated interest* / 免税 ~ *tax-exempt interest* / 派生 ~ *derivative interest* / 贴现 ~ *discount interest* / 投资 ~ *interest on investment* / 债券 ~ *bond interest* / 资本 ~ *capital interest* / 借款付七分 ~ *pay 7% interest on a loan*

【利益】interest; benefit; profit: ~ 集团 *interest group* / 公共 ~ *the public interests* / 个人 ~ 须服从集体 ~。*The interest of the individual must be subordinated to those of the collective.*

【利用】① use; utilize; make use of: 充分 ~ 自然资源 *make full use of the natural resources* / 她善于 ~ 时间。*She employs her time wisely.* ② take advantage of; exploit: ~ 职权 *presume on one's position* / 不要 ~ 他们的热情好客。*Don't presume on their hospitality.* / 投机商 ~ 石油短缺大捞一笔。*Profiteers cashed in during the gasoline shortage.*

【利用率】availability; coefficient of utilization; operating factor; output coefficient; use factor

【利诱】lure by promise of gain: 威逼 ~ *use both the carrot and the stick*

【利于】be of advantage to; benefit

【利欲熏心】be obsessed with the desire for gain; be overcome by covetousness; be blinded by greed

【利嘴】glib tongue; sharp tongue: ~ 巧舌 *have the*

gift of the gab

沥 ① drip; trickle: 披肝~胆 *be loyal and faithful* ② drop: 余~ *last drops; dregs*

【沥陈】[书] sincerely state (one's view, opinion, etc.)

【沥涝】waterlogging

【沥沥】[象] the sound of wind or of flowing waters

【沥青】pitch; asphalt; bitumen: 天然~ *natural asphalt* / ~路面 *bituminous pavement*

【沥水】waterlogging caused by excessive rainfall

枥 [书] manger

例 ① example; instance: 举~ *give an example* ② precedent: 破~ *make an exception* / 史无前~ *unprecedented* ③ case: 案~ *law case* / 病~ *case of illness* ④ rules; regulations: 条~ *regulations; rules* ⑤ regular; routine: ~套 *regular practice*

【例程】routine

【例规】① convention; usual practice ② [旧] money gift offered according to established practice ③ rules; regulations

【例会】regular meeting

【例假】① official holiday; legal holiday ② [婉] menstrual period; period

【例句】illustrative sentence; example sentence

【例如】for instance; for example (e. g.); such as: 他们出口许多水果,~橘子、柠檬等等。*They export a lot of fruit, such as oranges, lemons, etc.*

【例题】a problem designed to illustrate a principle or method; example

【例外】① be an exception ② exception: 这个城市中的大多数建筑物都不太好看,但这座教堂是个~。*Most of the buildings in this city are rather unattractive, but this church is an exception.*

【例行】routine: ~程序 *routine* / ~程序库 *routine library* / ~分析 *routine analysis* / ~检查 *routine inspection*

【例行公事】① routine; routine business ② mere formality

【例言】introductory remarks; notes on the use of a book

【例证】illustration; example; case in point: 典型~ *a typical example* / 记住要在上下文中给出这个词的~。*Remember to provide an illustration of the word in context.*

【例子】[口] example; case; instance: 这部词典有很多说明词语用法的~。*This dictionary has many examples of how words are used.* / 我可以给你举几个~。*I can quote you several instances.*

疠 [书] ① plague; pestilence ② ulcer; sore

【疠疫】[书] epidemic disease

戾 [书] ① crime; sin: 罪~ *crime; sin* ② perverse; tyrannical: 暴~ *cruel and fierce*

隶 ① be subordinate to: 附~ *be under; attach to* ② person in servitude: 仆~ *servant* ③ runner of government office in feudal China ④ one of the ancient styles of Chinese calligraphy

【隶农】[书] slave on a farm

【隶书】official script, an ancient style of calligraphy current in the Han Dynasty (206 B. C. -A. D. 220)

【隶属】be subordinate to; be under the jurisdiction or command of: ~关系 *system of administering; affiliations of* / 这支部队~市警备区。*The army is under the command of the municipal garrison.*

【隶卒】runner of government office in feudal China

荔

【荔枝】litchi; lichee

栎 【植】oak

俪 ① of a pair; parallel ② husband and wife; couple

【俪影】a husband and wife appearing in public or in a photograph

莅 [书] arrive; reach: ~席 *be present at a banquet*

【莅会】be present at a meeting

【莅临】[书] arrive; be present

【莅任】[书] (of officials) assume one's office

栗[1] ① chestnut tree ② chestnut: 火中取~ *pull sb's chestnuts out of the fire* / 甜~ *sweet chestnut* ③ (Lì) a surname

栗[2] tremble; shudder: 不寒而~ *shiver all over though not cold*

【栗暴】a knock on the head with the knuckles

【栗栗】fearful look: 战战~ *with fear and trepidation*

【栗然】[书] trembling; shuddering

【栗色】chestnut colour; maroon: ~土 *chestnut-coloured soil*

【栗鼠】[动] squirrel

【栗子】chestnut

砺 [书] ① whetstone ② sharpen; whet: 砥~ *harden oneself by self-discipline*

【砺石】[书] whetstone

砾 gravel; shingle: 瓦~ *rubble; broken tiles*

【砾层】gravel bed

【砾煤】pebble coal

【砾石】gravel; grail

【砾岩】conglomerate; conglomeration

唳 [书] cry (of a crane, etc.): 风声鹤~ *a fleeing army's suspicion of danger at the slightest sound*

笠 large bamboo or straw hat

粝 [书] coarse rice

粒 ① small particles; grain: 米~儿 *grains of rice* ② [量] used with granular objects: 一~种子 *a grain of seed*

【粒肥】granulated fertilizer

【粒径】【地】grain size; particle size; grain diameter: ~分布 *size distribution*

【粒子】(lìzǐ)【物】particle: 带电~ *charged particle*

【粒子】(lìzi) grain; granule; pellet: 豆~ *soybean*

grain

痢 【医】dysentery

【痢疾】dysentery：恶性～ *malignant dysentery*

li

哩 ［方］① used like 呢 but not in interrogative sentence：太阳已经升起来～。*The sun has risen.* ② used in enumeration, like 啦：碗～，筷子～，都已经摆好了。*Bowls, chopsticks are all set out on the table.*

see also lī；lǐ

liǎ

俩 ［口］① two：他们～ *the two of them* /他们～都是医生。*Both of them are doctors.* ② some；a few；several：就来了这么～人啊！*Only these few people!*

lián

连[1] ① link；join；connect：把它们～在一起！*Link them together!* /这条马路把两个村庄给～起来了。*This road joins the two villages.* /你能用一根线把它们～上吗？*Can you join them together with a piece of string?* ② one after another；in succession：接～的失败 *a succession of failures* /他接～给我们讲了五个笑话。*He told us five jokes one after another.* ③ including：～我在内一共十个人出席了会议。*There were ten people in the meeting including me.* ④【军】company：一～步兵 *a company of foot* ⑤（Lián）a surname

连[2] even：我做的菜他～尝也没尝一下。*He never even tasted the food I cooked.* /～小孩儿都能看懂他写的诗。*Even a child can understand his poem.*

【连本带利】both principal and interest；both capital and interest；profit as well as capital；total of capital and interest

【连比】【数】continued proportion（or ratio）（e.g. 1:3:9:27:81）

【连鬓胡子】［口］whiskers；full beard：他留着～。*He wears whiskers on his cheeks.*

【连播】chain broadcast：他正在收听长篇小说～。*He is listening to the chain broadcast of a novel.*

【连词】【语】conjunction：比较～ *conjunction of the comparative* /否定～ *negative conjunction* /假定～ *suppositive conjunction* /让步～ *concessive conjunction* /时间～ *temporal conjunction* /转折～ *adversative conjunction*

【连带】① related：人的作风和思想是有～关系的。*A person's work style is related to his ideology.* ② involve；implicate：他的仇人竭力想把他～进谋杀案中。*His enemies tried to implicate him in the murder.* ③ in passing；incidentally

【连…带…】① indicating the inclusion of two items：连工带料，一共多少钱？*How much is it with material and labour all together?* ②（indicating the simultaneous occurrence of two actions）and；while：连蹦带跳 *hopping and skipping* /连打带骂 *scold and beat sb at the same time*

【连裆裤】① child's pants with no slit in the seat ② ［方］collude；gang up

【连队】【军】company

【连发】【军】running fire：～步枪 *repeater* /～射击 *burst*（*of fire*）/～手枪 *repeater*

【连根拔】pull up by the roots；uproot：把头发～ *pull hair out by the roots* /把腐败现象～ *root out corruption*

【连亘】［书］（of mountain ranges）continue；extend

【连贯】① link up；piece together；hang together ② coherent；consistent：一篇内容～的文章 *a coherent essay*

【连贯性】sequence；coherence；continuity

【连锅端】take all the pots and pans — take or get rid of the whole lot；stock and barrel：伪军据点被敌军～了。*The puppet troop's stronghold was completely destroyed by the guerrillas.*

【连环】a chain of rings；connecting ring：～计 *a set of interlocking stratagems* /～漫画 *comic book*

【连环画】a book（usu. for children）with a story told in pictures；picture-story book

【连脚裤】infant's pants with bootees attached

【连接】join；link：新的公路将把这个岛与大陆～在一起。*The new bridge will link the island to the mainland.* /这条公路把北京和天津～起来。*The road connects Beijing and Tianjin.* /这两个部件～得不好。*The two parts do not connect properly.* /铆接是～金属元件的最简单的方法。*Riveting is the simplest way to join metal parts together.*

【连接号】【语】hyphen（-）

【连结】concatenate；joining-up copulation；structural connection；junction；anastomose

【连襟】husbands of sisters

【连裤袜】panty-hose

【连累】implicate；involve；get sb into trouble：别～她。*Don't get her into trouble.* /经理说："我不想听任何人说他不愿意被～。"*The manager said: "I don't want anybody saying they don't want to get involved."*

【连理枝】two trees with branches interlocked — a loving couple

【连连】repeatedly；again and again：他～点头。*He nodded again and again.*

【连忙】hastily；hurriedly；promptly；at once；in haste：看见妈妈回来，他～把电视关上。*Seeing his mother coming, he turned off the TV hurriedly.*

【连绵】continuous；unbroken；uninterrupted：～不断 *without stop*；*incessantly* /～不绝 *in an unbroken line*；*in succession*；*without break*；*continuous succession* /阴雨～ *a succession of wet and overcast days*

【连年】in successive years; in consecutive years; for years running; for years on end:村子里~丰收。*The village has good harvests in successive years.*

【连篇】① one article after another; a multitude of articles ② throughout a piece of writing; page after page:白字~ *pages and pages of wrongly written characters*

【连篇累牍】lengthy and tedious; at great length; one article after another; floods of ink:他这篇文章里废话~。*He keeps on repeating nonsense at great length in his article.*

【连翘】①【植】golden bell; weeping golden bell; weeping forsythia ②【药】the capsule of weeping forsythia

【连任】be reappointed or reelected consecutively; renew one's term of office:他想~。*He wanted to renew his term of office.*

【连日】for days on end; day after day:我~来一直接到匿名信。*I received anonymous letters for days on end.*

【连声】say repeatedly: ~称赞 *rain praises on (sb)* / ~认错 *hasten to acknowledge one's error* / ~叫苦。*One cried out one's bitterness without ceasing.*

【连升三级】continue to advance three steps

【连锁】linked together

【连锁店】chain store

【连锁反应】chain reaction

【连天】① for several days in a row; for days on end: ~连夜 *for days and nights running* ② continuously; incessantly ③ (of a mountain, the horizon, flames, etc.) touch the sky:炮火~。*Gunfire licked the heavens.*

【连通】feed through; connection; connected; intercommunication: ~公式 *connection formula* / ~矩阵 *connection matrix*

【连通器】communicating vessels; connecting vessels: ~定律 *law of connected vessels*

【连同】together with; along with:请把这本书~这张照片一起带给他。*Please take the book along with the picture to him.*

【连系】linkage; connection: ~动词 *copulative verb; linking verb* / ~法 *connection method*

【连写】(in Chinese phonetic transcription) write the two or more syllables of a word together

【连续】continuously; successively; in a row: ~评述 *running commentary* / ~获得丰收 *a sequence of bumper harvests; reap bumper harvests in succession* /他~三天没有给我打电话。*He didn't call me on three successive days.* /他~三年获"优秀学生"称号。*He won the title of "excellent student" for three years in a row.* /他已经~三天没有吃东西了。*He hasn't eaten anything for three days at a stretch.* /数字1、2、3是一组~数字。*The number 1, 2, 3 are consecutive.* /大脑需要~不断的供血。*The brain needs a continuous supply of blood.*

【连续剧】serial; soap opera:电视~ *TV soap opera*

【连续性】continuity; solidity; sequence; continuance:分段~ *piecewise continuity* /几何~ *geometrical continuity* /经济~ *economic continuity* /局部~ *local continuity*

【连夜】① the same night; that very night; all through the night:他~赶了回去。*He hurried back that same night.* /罪犯~潜逃。*The criminal escaped in the dark of night.* ② for nights on end; several nights running

【连衣裙】a woman's dress; dress

【连阴天】cloudy weather for several days running

【连阴雨】an unbroken spell of wet weather

【连用】use consecutively; use together:你~了两个意思相同的词。*You use together two words that share the same meaning.*

【连载】publish in instalments; serialize: ~小说 *serial story* /他的小说将以~的形式发表。*His novel will appear in serial form.*

【连长】company commander

【连着】in succession; continuously:他~唱了两首歌。*He sang two songs in succession.*

【连中三元】succeed in three successive examinations

【连轴转】work day and night; work round the clock

【连珠】like a chain of pearls or a string of beads — in rapid succession: ~妙语 *sparkling discourse; scintillate witticisms*

【连珠炮】continuous firing; drumfire:这小姑娘说话好像~。*The little girl chattered away like a machine gun.*

【连属】[书] join; link: ~成篇 *join (pieces) to form a complete whole*

【连缀】① join together; put together ②【语】cluster

【连字号】【语】hyphen (-)

【连作】【农】continuous cropping; sequential cropping

【连坐】be punished for being related to or friendly with sb who has committed an offence

怜 ① feel tender toward sb or sth; be sympathetic with; be kind toward sth:可~ *pity; have a pity on sth* ② love tenderly

【怜爱】love tenderly; have tender affection for sth:这孩子真叫人~。*What a lovely child!*

【怜悯】pity; take pity on; have compassion for:他投给我~的一瞥。*He cast a sympathetic glance to me.* /出于~,我给了他200元钱。*Out of pity, I gave him 200 yuan.* /他情不自禁地~起那个可怜的人来。*He could not help having compassion for the poor creature.*

【怜悯心】(sense of) sympathy:为什么你对他毫无~呢? *Why did you show little mercy to him?* /他博得了我的~。*He won my sympathy.*

【怜惜】take pity on; have pity for:不要~骗子! *Don't have pity for those who cheat!*

【怜香惜玉】love a fragrant jade-like maid — to have a tender heart for the fair sex; be fond of women; have a tender heart for the fair sex

【怜恤】[书] take pity on; have compassion for

L

帘 ① flag as shop sign: 酒~ *wineshop sign* ② curtain; screen: 窗~ *a window curtain* /门~儿 *door curtain*

【帘布】cord fabric (in tyres)
【帘幔】curtain
【帘幕】(heavy) curtain
【帘子】[口] (hanging) screen; curtain

莲 ①【植】lotus ② lotus seed

【莲步】[书] graceful steps of a beauty: 轻移~ *take light, graceful steps*
【莲房】[书] ① lotus pod ② monk's bedroom
【莲花】lotus flower; lotus
【莲藕】lotus rhizome; lotus root: ~同根 *joined together like lotus and its root*
【莲蓬】seedpod of the lotus
【莲蓬头】[方] shower nozzle
【莲蓬子儿】①【植】lotus seed ② lotus-seed-shaped things
【莲肉】edible part of lotus seed
【莲心】① the heart of a lotus seed ② [方] lotus seed
【莲子】lotus seed
【莲宗】【宗】Pure Land Sect
【莲座】① bottom of lotus flower (like an inverted cone) ② a Buddha's seat in the form of a lotus flower

涟 [书] ① ripples ② (of tears) continually flowing

【涟洏】[书] weeping copiously
【涟漪】[书] ripples: 池水~ *ripples on a pool*

联 ① unite; join: 关~ *be related* ② antithetical couplet: 寿~ *longevity (or birthday) couplet*

【联邦】federation; union; commonwealth: 帝国~ *imperial federation* /英~ *the British Commonwealth of Nations* /波多黎各~ *the Commonwealth of Puerto Rico*
【联播】radio hookup; broadcast over a radio network: 新闻~节目 *joint news programme* /~节目时间 *network time*
【联产承包】contract with remuneration linked to output
【联产承包责任制】【农】contract system of responsibility linked to production; output-related system of contracted responsibilities
【联产计酬】link payment to output
【联唱】a form of folk art performance; hooked up: 民歌~ *serial singing of folk songs*
【联大】United Nations General Assembly
【联单】receipt or other document in duplicate: 三~ *receipt in triplicate*
【联队】①【军】wing (of an air force) ②【体】united team ③ (of some armies) regiment
【联防】① joint defence; joint command of defence forces ②【体】joint defence
【联合】① unite; ally: 他号召自由派和保守派~起来支持社会改革的推行。*He called on the liberals and conservatives to unite to support the expansion of the social program.* /在这个问题上我们要~在一起。*We must all stand together on this issue.* /他富有煽动性的演说让工人们~起来对抗残暴的资本家。*His stirring speeches helped rally the workers to fight against the merciless capitalists* /全世界无产者，~起来! *Working men of all countries, unite!* ② joint; combined: ~对外 *concerted action towards our foreign counterparts* /我们~举办了这次展览会。*We jointly organized the fair.* ③ combination; alliance; union; coalition: ~起来就是力量。*In union there is strength.* ④【生理】symphysis
【联合大学】associated university
【联合贷款】syndicated loan
【联合抵制】boycott: 他们~那种商品。*They boycotted that commercial product.*
【联合国】the United Nations (U. N.): ~安全理事会 *United Nations Security Council* /~大会 *General Assembly* /~儿童基金会 *United Nations Children's Fund* /~教科文组织 *United Nations Educational, Scientific, and Cultural Organization (UNESCO)* /~经济及社会理事会 *United Nations Economic and Social Council (ECOSOC)* /~军 *Armed Forces for U.N.* /~开发计划处 *United Nations Development Program (UNDP)* /~秘书处 *United Nations Secretariat* /~粮农组织 *United Nations Food and Agriculture Organization* /~人口活动基金 *United Nations Fund for Population Activities* /~日 *United Nations Day* /~世界知识产权组织 *United Nations World Intellectual Property Organization* /~宪章 *Charter of the United Nations* /~宣言 *Declaration by the United Nations* (1943)
【联合会】federation; union: 学生~ *a federation of students* /农业合作社~ *Federal of Agricultural Cooperatives*
【联合企业】integrated complex: 钢铁~ *integrated iron and steel works*
【联合收割机】combine (harvester): 电动~ *electrically driven combine* /谷物~ *cereal combine* /平地~ *level land combine* /小型~ *baby combine*
【联合体】organic whole; association
【联合王国】United Kingdom (composed of England, Wales, Scotland and Northern Ireland); UK
【联欢】have a social gathering; have a get-together: 新年~ *New Year party* /~晚会 *evening party*
【联机】on-line: ~操作 *on-line operation*
【联接】① link; join ②【航】mate
【联结】join; connect; link; bind: 文化交流是~各国人民友谊的纽带。*Cultural exchange is the tie of friendship that joins the people of all countries.* /最近发生的许多事情使我们~在一起。*Many things that happened recently bind us together.*
【联军】allied forces; united army
【联络】① start or keep up personal relations; make or maintain contact or liaison ② contact (between people); liaison: 他经常与我~。*He is in constant touch with me.* /她和许多同学有~。*She*

L

comes into contact with many classmates.

【联络处】liaison office

【联络网】liaison network

【联络员】liaison man

【联络站】liaison station

【联袂】［书］go, come, etc. together：～而行 *walk hand in hand*

【联盟】alliance; coalition; league; union：工农～ *alliance of the workers and peasants* / 国际～ *the League of Nations* / 两个国家组成～反对侵略者。*The two countries formed a union against invaders.* / 两国形成了～。*The two countries made an alliance.*

【联名】jointly signed; jointly：～倡议 *jointly initiate* / ～请愿 *send a petition with joint signatures; send a letter which a group of people have signed*

【联翩】in close succession; together：～而至 *arrive in close succession; one person coming close on the heels of another* / ～思考 *brain-storming*

【联赛】［体］league matches：我们队在足球～中参加比赛。*Our team plays in the football league.*

【联手】join hands (with a person)：～调查 *joint investigation*

【联体双生】［生理］conjuncted twins

【联网】network; network access

【联席会议】joint conference; joint meeting

【联系】① contact; touch; connection; relation：我仍然在努力和那个繁忙的官员～。*I am still trying to get in touch with the busy official.* / 最近我的同事会～你，并对你进行简短的电话测试。*Recently one of our staff will contact you and ask you to complete a quick test on phone.* ② integrate; relate; link; get in touch with：这两个事件似乎有～。*The two events seem to be related.* ③ arrange; negotiate：～工作 *talk business*

【联想】connect with mentally; connect in the mind; associate with：你没有理由把这两件事～在一起。*You have no reason to connect the two events.* / 这是一个极易引起～的地方。*The place is rich in associations.*

【联谊】keep up a friendship; strengthen the bonds of friendship

【联谊会】union; sodality

【联姻】［书］(of two families) be related by marriage; form an alliance by marriage：他们两家现已～。*Their families are now connected by marriage.*

【联姻缔亲】unite in marriage：两家～ *unite two families by marriage*

【联营】joint venture：～公司 *related company* / ～商店 *chain store* / ～作业 *associated operations*

【联运】through transport; through traffic：水陆～ *land-and-water coordinated transport* / ～费率 *combination rate* / ～票 *through ticket* / ～提单 *combined transport bill of lading*

【联展】joint exhibit

廉 ① clean and honest ② cheap; inexpensive：物美价～ *good quality and low-priced* ③ (Lián) a surname

【廉察】secretly investigate

【廉耻】integrity and a sense of honour

【廉价】low-priced; cheap：～处理 *concessional disposal* / ～货币政策 *policy of easy money* / ～小说 *dime novel* / 他～买进很多物品。*He bought cheap a lot of goods.* / 我们不得不～出售了这所房子。*We had to undersell the house.*

【廉洁】honest and clean; incorruptible：这个部门中似乎没有多少～的人。*There seem to be very few incorruptible men left in this department.*

【廉洁奉公】have integrity and be public-spirited; have integrity and work always in the interest of the public：依法行事要求法官必须～。*Everything must be done according to the law, so judges must be honest in performing their official duties.*

【廉明】(of officials) upright and incorruptible

【廉正】upright and honest

【廉正爱民】be upright, honourable and have the interests of the people at heart

【廉政】honest and clean government; incorrupt government

【廉政公署】(HK) Independent Commission Against Corruption

【廉政建设】build or establish a clean government

【廉政专员】(HK) Commissioner Against Corruption

鲢 ［动］silver carp

镰 sickle

【镰刀】sickle

liǎn

琏 an ancient vessel for broomcorn millet

敛 ① hold back; keep back ② ［书］restrain：收～ *weaken or disappear; show restraint* ③ gather; collect; accumulate：聚～ *levy tax and get rich* / 横征暴～ *extort heavy taxes and levies*

【敛步】check one's steps; hold back from going

【敛财】accumulate wealth by unfair means

【敛迹】［书］① temporarily desist from one's evil ways; lie low ② restrain oneself ③ go into retirement：～山林 *live in deep mountains as a hermit*

【敛钱】［口］collect money; raise money：他正忙于为这个项目～。*He is busy raising money for the project.*

【敛容】［书］assume a serious expression

【敛声屏气】hold one's breath

【敛足】［书］check one's steps; hold back from going：～不前 *hold one's steps and refuse to go further*

脸 ① face; countenance：笑～ *a smiling face* / 板着～ *draw a long face* / 愁眉苦～ *have a face as long as a fiddle* / 她有一张漂亮的～。*She has a beautiful face.* / 她把～转向一边。*She turned her face away.* / 父亲的～搭拉下来。

Father's countenance fell. ② front：鞋～儿 *the front of a shoe* ③ feelings; face：无～见人 *fly from the face of men* ④ facial expressions：他向婴儿做鬼～逗他发笑。*He made faces at the baby to make it laugh.*

【脸薄】shy; bashful

【脸蛋儿】(usu. children's) cheeks; face：多漂亮的～呀！*What a lovely face!*

【脸憨皮厚】shameless：～的冒充者 *a brazen impostor*

【脸红】① blush (with shame or embarrassment)：他为自己的说的话感到～。*He blushed at what he'd said.* ② flush with anger; get excited：他气得～。*He reddened with anger.*

【脸红脖子粗】get red in the face from anger or excitement; turn red in the gills; flush with agitation

【脸急】hot-tempered; irritable

【脸颊】cheeks; face：红润的～ *rosy cheeks*

【脸面】① face ② face; self-respect; sb's feelings：看我的～，不要生他的气。*For my sake, don't get angry with him.* /他急于挽回～。*He is eager to save his face.* /虽然她犯了错误，但她说是别人让她这么做的，以保全～。*Though she'd made a mistake, she saved face by saying someone else had told her to do so.*

【脸盘儿】the cast of one's face

【脸盆】washbasin; washbowl：～架 *washstand*

【脸皮】① skin of the face ② feelings; sensibilities ③ face; cheek; sense of shame：他竟有～说这话？*Did he have the face to say that?*

【脸谱】【戏】types of facial makeup in operas

【脸色】① complexion; look：白皙的～ *fair complexion* ② facial expression：～沉郁 *look very sour* /～发青 *blue in the face* /～阴沉 *look sullen* /～阴郁 *have a face like a fiddle*/他立刻变了～。*He changed his countenance at once.*

【脸上无光】make sb lose face; lose face; one's face is out of countenance — losing prestige

【脸膛儿】[方] face

【脸形】the shape of one's face; facial features

【脸子】[方] ① pretty face, looks, appearance ② unpleasant facial expression ③ face; feelings：他是个要～的人。*He minds his own prestige very much.*

liàn

练 ① white silk ② [书] treat, soften and whiten silk by boiling ③ practise; drill; train：主队和客队在一起～球。*The home team and the visitors are practising together.* /老师让学生～英语语法。*The teacher drilled her students in English grammar.* /我每天～马拉松。*I trained daily for the marathon.* ④ experienced; skillful：老～ *experienced and assured* ⑤ (Liàn) a surname

【练笔】① practise writing ② practise calligraphy

【练兵】① troop training; training：～场 *drill ground; parade ground* /～房 *drill hall* /日夜～ *drill soldiers day and night* ② training

【练操】(of troops, etc.) drill

【练达】[书] experienced and worldly wise：～老成 *experienced, sincere and honest*

【练队】drill in formation; drill for a parade

【练功】do exercises in gymnastics, *wushu*, acrobatics, etc.; practise one's skill：他正在～。*He is practicing.*

【练手】try one's hand (at some skill); practise one's skill：我想成为一个美发师，所以经常在朋友头上～。*I wanted to be a hair stylist and used to practise my skill on my friends.*

【练武】① learn or practise martial arts ② learn or practise military skills

【练习】① practise; work at; work on：你～得不够。*You don't practise enough.* /如果你不～，是不会成为一名优秀运动员的。*You won't become an excellent athlete if you don't practice.* /如果你想成为一名职业舞蹈家就要勤奋～。*You'll have to really work at it if you want to be a professional dancer.* ② exercise (in a book); drill; practice：～本 *exercise book* /口头～ *oral work* /书面～ *written work* /～要适度，你要为比赛保持良好的精神状态。*Take it easy in training today; you need to be in great shape for the match.* /这是一本关于指法～的书。*This is a book of exercises to improve finger flexibility.*

【练习曲】【音】etude

炼 ① refine; smelt; work：提～ *refine; extract; abstract* ② temper with fire ③ polish

【炼丹】(try to) make pills of immortality (as a Taoist practice)

【炼钢】steelmaking; steel-smelting：～厂 *steel plant; steel-smelting plant* /～炉 *steel-smelting furnace*

【炼焦】【化】make coke; coke：～法 *coal-coking process* /～炉 *coke-oven; coking still* /～煤气 *coke-oven gas*

【炼金术】alchemy：～士 *alchemist*

【炼句】try to find the best turn of phrase; polish and repolish a sentence

【炼乳】condensed milk; evaporated milk：～工厂 *condensery*

【炼铁】iron-smelting：～厂 *ironworks* /～炉 *blast furnace; iron-smelting furnace*

【炼油】① refine oil ② extract oil by heat ③ eat edible oil

【炼油厂】rendering plant; (oil) refinery

【炼狱】①【宗】purgatory ② abyss of sufferings or misery

【炼制】【化】refine：石油～ *petroleum refining*

【炼字】cudgel one's brains for the right word; try to find the exact word

恋 ① love; be enamoured of：热～ *be madly in love* ② long for; feel attached to：～家 *reluctant to be away from home*

【恋爱】① romantic love; love affair：～关系 *love affair* /～结婚 *love match* /～小说 *love story* ② be in love; have a courtship: 热~ *fall head over heels in love* / 谈~ *be in love*; *have a love affair* / 他与玛丽正在~。*He was in love with Mary.*

【恋父情结】【心】Electra complex

【恋歌】love song

【恋家】be reluctant to leave one's home

【恋旧】① yearn for the past; long for the good old days ② yearn for old friends

【恋恋不舍】be reluctant to part from; hate to see sb go; can't bear to part with; hard to tear oneself away

【恋母情结】【心】Oedipus complex

【恋慕】have tender feelings towards; adore: 他从小就~邻家的女孩儿。*He has adored the girl in the neighbourhood since his childhood.* / 我看到他脸上闪过~的神色。*I saw an expression of tender devotion come over his face.*

【恋情】① attachment; affection ② romantic love: 他和秘书的~广为人知。*His love affair with his secretary is well publicized.*

【恋群】① be attached to one's own people ② (of animals) be gregarious: 猴子~。*The monkey is a gregarious animal.*

【恋人】sweetheart; loved one; girlfriend or boyfriend: 你应该给你的~送花。*You should send flowers to the one you love.*

【恋童癖】【心】pedophilia

【恋物癖】【心】fetishism

【恋栈】(of an official) be loath to give up his post (as a horse is loath to leave its stable)

【恋战】be over-zealous in fighting

殓 lay a body in a coffin; encoffin: 收~ *have corpse buried*

链 ① chain: 项~ *necklace* ② cable length (= 1/10 of a nautical mile, or 185.2m)

【链传动】【机】chain drive: ~装置 *chain and sprocket driving device*

【链带】chain belt

【链反应】【化】chain reaction

【链轨】chain hook; sling

【链化合物】chain compound

【链环】chain link; chain iron

【链角】chain angle

【链接】【电】interlinkage; interlinking; catenation; chaining: ~对象 *linked object* / ~检索 *chaining search* / ~类型 *link type* / ~码 *conca-tenation code* / ~命令 *chained command*

【链锯】chain saw

【链霉素】streptomycin; Futostrep; Rimocidin

【链球】【体】① hammer event ② hammer

【链式反应】chain reaction

【链锁】chain lock: ~爆炸 *chain explosion* / ~反射 *chain reflex* / ~反应 *chain reaction* / ~聚合 *chain polymerization*

【链条】① chain ②【方】roller chain (of a bicycle); chain

【链子】① chain ② roller chain (of a bicycle, etc.); chain

楝 【植】chinaberry

liáng

良 ① good; nice; fine: 善~ *good and honest* / ~马 *a fine horse* / ~药 *good medicine* ② good people: 除暴安~ *get rid of bullies and bring peace to good people* ③【书】very; very much; indeed: 用心~苦 *have really given much thought to the matter* / 这个讲座让我获益~多。*I benefit a great deal from the lecture.* ④ (Liáng) a surname

【良材】① good timber ② talented people

【良策】good plan; sound strategy: 她想出了一条~。*She came up with a fine plan.*

【良辰】① auspicious day: 择~开张 *choose an auspicious day for the opening of a shop* ② fine day

【良辰吉日】auspicious occasion; a fortunate hour and a lucky day: 她择了~为女儿完婚。*She selected a lucky day for her daughter's wedding.*

【良辰美景】a pleasant day coupled with a fine landscape; (such) a beautiful day in (such) pleasant surroundings: 我们该好好利用这~。*We should take fully advantage of the beautiful scene on the bright day.*

【良导体】【物】good conductor

【良方】① effective prescription; good recipe: 医生的~治好了我的背痛。*The doctor's effective prescription cured the pain in my back.* ② good plan; sound strategy: 你认为幸福婚姻有什么~? *What's your prescription for a happy marriage?*

【良港】fine harbour: 天然~ *fine natural harbour*

【良好】good; well: 感觉~ *feel fine*

【良机】【书】good (or golden) opportunity: 莫失~。*Don't let this good opportunity slip.*

【良家】【旧】a respectable family

【良将】fine general: 一代~ *one of the best generals of his time*

【良金美玉】good gold and a beautiful gem — one's high integrity or profound learning

【良久】【书】a good while; a long time: 她因这个问题沉思~。*She contemplated the problem for a long time.*

【良马】fine horse; fine steed

【良民】【旧】good citizen; law-abiding people

【良能】【哲】intuitive ability

【良禽择木】a fine bird chooses a tree to nestle in — to choose a master to serve

【良人】【古】① my goodman; my husband ② common people

【良师益友】good teacher and helpful friend

【良田】good farmland; fertile farmland: ~美池 *rich fields and fine pools* / ~万顷 *thousands of acres of fine land*

【良宵】【书】happy evening: 共度~ *spend a happy evening together*

【良心】conscience: ~发现 *one's better nature asserts itself*; *stung by conscience* / ~有愧 *conscience-stricken*; *guilty conscience* / ~谴责 *the stings of conscience*; *pricks of conscience*; *One's*

L

conscience pricks one. 我们应该凭[illegible]做事。*We should obey what conscience dictates.*

【良性】① good; favourable ②【医】benign

【良性循环】benign cycle between; sound cycle of economic activities; virtuous circle; favorable spiral

【良性肿瘤】benign tumour

【良言】good advice

【良药】good medicine

【良药苦口利于病,忠言逆耳利于行】[谚] good medicine is bitter in the mouth but good for the disease; honest words offend the ear but are good for the conduct

【良莠不齐】the good and the bad are intermingled; a motley crowd:市场上的书籍~。*There are good books and also bad ones in the market.*

【良友】beneficial friend

【良缘】a good match; a happy match for marriage

【良知】【哲】intuitive knowledge

【良知良能】【哲】innate knowledge and ability instinct

【良种】①【农】improved variety:水稻~ *improved varieties of rice* ② fine breed: ~繁育 *stock breeding; seed stock breeding* / ~家畜 *breeding stock*

凉 ① cool; cold: ~茶 *cold tea* /乘~ *relax in a cool place* ② disheartened; disappointed:听了这话,我的心~了半截儿。*On hearing this, my heart sank.* /他感到心里很~。他那么信任这些人。*He felt extremely let down. He had trusted these people so much.*
see also liàng

【凉白开】[口] cold boiled water

【凉拌】(of food) cold and dressed with sauce: ~菜 *cold vegetable dish in sauce*

【凉菜】cold dish

【凉窗】[方] screen window

【凉碟】cold dish (in a plate)

【凉粉】bean-starch noodles

【凉糕】cake made of glutinous rice served cold in summer

【凉快】① nice and cool; pleasantly cool:天气很~。*It is very cool.* ② cool oneself; cool off:我要出去~~。*I'm going outside to cool off.*

【凉帽】summer hat; sun hat; straw hat

【凉面】cold noodles dressed with sauce

【凉棚】① mat-awning; mat shelter ② hand or hands spread out above one's eyes (to shelter them from strong light)

【凉气】cool air:阵阵~ *waves of cool air*

【凉爽】nice and cool; pleasantly cool:她享受着清早的~时刻。*She is enjoying the cool of early morning.* /一阵~的清风拂过湖面。*A cool and refreshing breeze swept over the lake.*

【凉水】① cool water ② unboiled water

【凉丝丝】coolish; rather cool; a bit cool:山泉~的。*The mountain stream was cool and refreshing.*

【凉飕飕】(of wind) chilly; chill: ~的风 *a chill wind*

【凉台】balcony; veranda

【凉亭】wayside pavilion; summer house; kiosk

【凉席】summer sleeping mat (of woven split bamboo, etc.)

【凉鞋】sandals; foothold

【凉药】【中医】medicine of a cold nature (for reducing fever or inflammation); antipyretic

【凉意】a slight chill in the air

【凉枕】a kind of pillow used in summer

梁[1] ① roof beam:顶~ *top beam* /栋~ *beam and rafters* /横~ *cross beam* /斜~ *sloping beam* /枕~ *sleeper beam* ② purlin:正~ *ridge purlin* ③ bridge:桥~ *bridge* ④ ridge:鼻~ *nose bridge* /山~ *mountain ridge* /水平~ *horizontal beam* /尾~ *tail beam*

梁[2] (Liáng) a surname

【梁地】land on a mountain ridge; ridge land

【梁桥】beam bridge

【梁上君子】gentleman on the beam — burglar; thief

【梁柱】beam column: ~结构 *beam column construction; beam column structure*

【梁子】①[方] ridge (of a mountain or hill) ② story synopsis for an item of *quyi* or folk art performance, such as story telling, etc.

【梁座】beam seat

量 ① measure: ~体温 *take sb's temperature* /裁缝给我~尺寸做衣服。*The tailor measured me for a suit.* ② estimate; size up:打~ *measure with eye* /思~ *consider; think over*
see also liàng

【量棒】length bar

【量杯】measuring glass; graduate

【量表】scale

【量程】measurement range; measuring range; span: ~电路 *range circuit* / ~开关 *range switch* / ~扩展 *range extension* / ~迁移 *span shift* / ~误差 *range error* / ~转换 *range switching*

【量尺】graduated stick; measure gauge; measuring rule; measuring scale; scaled rule

【量度】【数】measurement

【量规】gauge; metric gauge: ~校准 *gauge calibration* / ~因数 *gauge factor*

【量角器】protractor

【量具】measuring tool (or implement): ~刃具 *measuring and cutting tool*

【量块】measuring block; gauge block

【量瓶】measuring flask

【量筒】【化】graduated (or volumetric, measuring) cylinder; graduate

【量针】measuring needle (or pin)

粮 ① grain; food; provisions:杂~ *food grains other than wheat and rice; miscellaneous cereals* ② farm tax; grain tax:公~ *agricultural tax paid in grain*

【粮仓】① granary; garner:修~ *repair a barn* ② granary; rice bowl:美国的中西部是全国的~。*The Mid-West is the granary of the US.*

L

【粮草】army provisions; rations and forage (or fodder): ~齐备。*Provisions for the troops were already prepared; there are plentiful supplies of all kinds.*
【粮道】grain route
【粮店】grain shop
【粮行】[旧] wholesale grain shop
【粮荒】grain shortage; food scarcity: 闹 ~ *have a famine*
【粮库】grain depot
【粮秣】army provisions; rations and forage; grain and fodder
【粮农】grain farmer
【粮农组织】Food and Agricultural Organization (FAO)
【粮票】food coupon; grain coupon
【粮食】grain; cereals; food: 主要 ~ *staple food* / ~充足。*Provisions are plentiful.*
【粮税】farm tax: 交纳 ~ *pay grain tax*
【粮田】grainfield
【粮饷】[旧] provisions and funds for troops
【粮油贮藏】grain and oil storage
【粮栈】wholesale grain store; grain depot
【粮站】grain distribution station; grain supply centre

粱 [书] ① a fine strain of millet: 高 ~ *common sorghum* ② good food; fine grain: 膏 ~ *fat meat and fine grain — choice food*
【粱肉】[书] fine grain and meat — choice food

liǎng

两[1] ① two: ~本书 *two books* / 她们有 ~ 个小孩儿。*They have two children.* ② both (sides); either (side): ~侧 *both sides* / 势不 ~ 立 *at daggers drawn; irreconcilable* ③ some; a few: 你就说 ~ 句吧! *Just say a few words.*

两[2] ① *liang*, a unit of weight (=50 grams) ② [旧] tael, a unit of weight for silver or gold (about 31 grams)
【两岸】① both banks; either bank: ~垂柳 *weeping willows on either bank* ② both sides of the Taiwan Strait: 海峡 ~ 同胞 *people of the same flesh and blood on both sides of the Strait*
【两岸三地】China's mainland, Taiwan and Hong Kong
【两败俱伤】both sides suffer (or lose); neither side gains; both being defeated and wounded
【两半儿】two halves; in half; in two: 把苹果切成 ~。*Cut the apple in half.* / 碟子摔成了 ~ 儿。*The dish is broken in two.*
【两倍】twofold; double; twice as much: ~的剂量 *a double dose* / 10是5的两倍。*Ten is the double of five.*
【两边】① both sides; both directions; both places: 公路 ~ 都有树。*There is a line of trees of either side of the highway.* ② both directions; both places: 敌人从 ~ 进攻。*The enemy attacked from both directions.* ③ both parties; both sides: ~讨好 *carry favour with both sides* / 在这一点上 ~ 达成了一致意见。*Both sides agreed on this count.*
【两边倒】lean now to one side, now to the other; waver; vacillate: 看来他的态度是 ~, 似乎同意这个行动, 又似乎认为这很愚蠢。*He seemed to vacillate between approving of the actions and finding them foolish.* / 他仍然没有做出决定, 对于这个建议还是 ~。*He hasn't decided yet — he's still blowing hot and cold about the suggestion.*
【两便】① be convenient to both; make things easy for both ② be beneficial to both: ~之法 *mutually beneficial solution*
【两鬓斑白】with graying temples; graying at the temples: 这是一个 ~ 的老人。*This is an old man with graying temples.*
【两不误】neglect neither... nor...: 她可真是学习工作 ~。*She neglects neither work nor study.*
【两侧】two flanks; two sides; ambo: 两头石狮位于入口处 ~。*Two stone lions flanked the entrance.*
【两重】double; dual; twofold: ~意义 *double meaning* / 对于儿子而言, 她肩负着母亲和教师的 ~ 任务。*She played a dual role of mother and teacher to her son.* / 我们的目标有 ~: 首先是增产, 然后是节支。*Our objectives are twofold — first, to increase production and second, to cut expenses.*
【两重性】【哲】dual nature; duality
【两次】twice: 缺席 ~ *be absent twice* / 分 ~ *at twice; in twice* / 那个问题你已经问过我 ~ 了。*You've asked me that question twice.*
【两次三番】again and again; over and over (again); many a time; repeatedly: 他 ~ 地向我借钱。*He came to borrow money from me again and again.*
【两党制】two-party system; bipartisan system
【两抵】balance or cancel each other: 收支 ~。*Make both ends meet; the account balance.*
【两地分居】(husband and wife) live in two places
【两点论】【哲】the doctrine that everything has two aspects
【两点透视】two-point perspective
【两耳不闻窗外事, 一心只读圣贤书】busy oneself in the classics and ignore what is going on beyond one's immediate surroundings
【两分法】【哲】dichotomy method; law of one dividing into two
【两个文明】two types of civilization, i. e. both material progress and cultural and ideological advancement; material and spiritual civilization: ~一起抓。*Efforts must be made to build a society that is advanced both materially and culturally and ideologically.*
【两虎相争】a struggle between two tigers — a fight between two big powers: ~, 必有一伤。*When two tigers fight, one is sure to lose.*
【两回事】two entirely different things; two different matters: 我喜欢她和我赞成她的意见是 ~。*To endorse her opinions is entirely different from the fact that I like her.*

【两极】① the two poles of the earth：～地区 *polar regions* ②【物】the two poles（of a magnet or an electric battery）③ two opposing extremes：～相通。*Extremes meet.*

【两极分化】polarization；division（of a group，society，etc.）into two opposing extremes

【两件套】two-piece dress

【两脚规】① compasses ② dividers

【两可】① both will do；either will do；could go either way：模棱～ *ambiguous* ② maybe，maybe not；could go either way：他能否获胜还在～。*He may or may not win.*

【两口儿】husband and wife；married couple：小～ *the young couple*

【两口子】［口］husband and wife；couple：这～总是在吵架。*The couple is always in a quarrel.*

【两肋插刀】help（one's friend）at the loss of one's life

【两立】exist side by side；coexist：势不～ *at daggers drawn；irreconcilable*

【两利】be good for both sides；benefit both

【两两】in pairs：三三～ *by twos and threes*

【两面】① two sides；both sides；two aspects；both aspects ② both directions：～夹击 *attack from both directions* /～受敌 *be between two fires；be threatened from both quarters* ③ having a dual（or double）character；dual；double：～夹攻 *make a pincer attack* /有～性格的人 *a man with a double character* /每个问题都有～。*There are two sides to every question.*

【两面光】（try to）please both parties

【两面派】① double-dealer；the vicar of Bray ② double-dealing；double-crossing：～手法 *double-faced tactics* /他对我耍～，卷走了所有的钱财。*He double-crossed me and escaped with all the money.*

【两面三刀】double-dealing；double cross；play a double game；carry fire in one hand and water in the other：我最讨厌～的人。*I disgust those who say one thing and do another.*

【两面性】dual nature；duplicity；ambivalence

【两难】face a difficult choice；be in a dilemma as to whether to go or not；be on the horns of a dilemma：我进退～，不知道是否该把实情告诉他。*I was in a dilemma as to whether to tell him the truth or not.*

【两旁】both sides；either side：河～花儿盛开。*Flowers bloom on both sides of the river.*

【两栖】①【生】【军】amphibious：～部队 *amphibious forces* /～攻击舰 *amphibious assault ship* /～作战 *amphibious warfare* /～动物 *amphibious animal；amphibian* /～动物学 *amphibiology* /～植物 *amphibious plant；amphibian* ② working or engaged in two fields：影视～明星 *star in both films and TV programmes*

【两讫】【商】the goods are delivered and the bill is cleared

【两清】square accounts between buyer and seller，or between debtor and creditor

【两全】be satisfactory to both parties；have regard for both sides：～之策 *a plan which satisfies both claims*

【两全其美】satisfy both sides；satisfy rival claims：你能不能想一个～的办法？*Could you present a method，which makes the best of both worlds?*

【两手】① skill；ability：他有～儿。*He is very clever.* ② dual tactics：～空空 *be left with nothing whatsoever；（come back）empty-handed* /～准备 *prepare oneself for both eventualities；have two string to one's bow*

【两条腿走路】walking on two legs — balance the relations between two aspects，etc.

【两头】① both ends；either end ② both parties；both sides：～落空 *fall（to the ground）between two stools；If you run after two horses，you will catch none.* /～为难 *find it hard to please either party；find it difficult to satisfy two conflicting demands* ③ two places；both places：他在自己家和父母家～住。*He lives in his own home and his parent's home in turn.*

【两下里】① both parties；both sides ② two places：一家人怎么能～住？*How can the family members live in two places?*

【两下子】① a few times；several times：他试了～，但没成功。*He tried several times but failed.* ② a few tricks of the trade：她还真有～！*She is really smart!*

【两相情愿】by mutual consent；both parties being willing：她们的婚姻是～的。*The marriage is of their own free choice.*

【两厢】① wing-rooms on either side of a one-storey house ② both sides：站立～ *stand on either side*

【两相】【电】two-phase：～电动机 *two-phase motor* /～电路 *quarter-phase circuit* /～系统 *binary system* /～制 *quarter-phase system*

【两小无猜】（of a little boy and a little girl）be innocent playmates：青梅竹马，～。*A little boy and a little girl played innocently together.*

【两性】① both sexes ②【化】amphoteric

【两袖清风】（of an official）have clean hands；remain uncorrupted；an honest official remains poor all his life：他因～而赢得了大家的尊敬。*He won respects from others，as he is free from corruption and bribery.*

【两样】different：～做法，两种结果。*Two different methods，two different results.*

【两伊战争】the Iran-Iraq war

【两翼】① both wings ②【军】both wings；both flanks

【两用】dual purpose：～炉子 *dual-purpose stove* /～人才 *dual-purpose personnel*

【两院制】two-chamber system；bicameral system；bicameralism

【两造】【律】both parties in a lawsuit；both plaintiff and defendant：～诉讼 *bilateral action*

【两者不可兼得】can't eat one's cake and have it（too）；can't have one's cake and eat it

liàng

亮 ① bright; light: 明～ *bright* /鲜～的红色 *a bright red* /房间很～。*The room is very light.* ② light; brighten; shine: 上百支蜡烛点～了舞厅。*The ballroom was lit by hundreds of candles.* /燃烧的火焰照～了炉膛上方的花瓶。*The blazing fire illuminated the vase above the hearth.* /路灯彻夜～着。*Streetlights shone throughout the night.* /等指示灯～。*Wait until the indicator lights up.* ③ loud and clear; resounding: 洪～ *loud and clear*; *sonorous* ④ make loud and clear: 他～起嗓子唱了一首歌。*He lifted his voice to sing a song.* ⑤ enlightened; open and clear: 心明眼～ *be sharp-eyed and clearheaded* ⑥ reveal; show; appear; make public: 请～出你的观点。*Please air your view.*

【亮底】① reveal the whole story; disclose one's plan, stand, views, etc.; put one's cards on the table; level with sb: 他终于～了，他计划从公司辞职自己干。*He finally put his cards on the table and explained that he was planning to resign from the company to set up his own business.* ② show the result

【亮度】【物】brightness; brilliance: 场～ *field brightness* /单位～ *unit brightness* /光学～ *optical brightness* /光电～ *photoelectric brightness* /角～ *angular brightness* /绝对～ *absolute brightness* /可见～ *visible brightness* /平均～ *average brightness* /视觉～ *visual brightness* /相对～ *relative brightness* /最大～ *maximum brightness* /最小～ *minimum brightness*

【亮度差】luminance difference: ～信号 *luminance difference signal*

【亮度对比】【摄】brightness contrast

【亮度系数】coefficient of brightness

【亮分】(of a judge or umpire) show or display the marks one has given: 请评委～。*Will the judges (or umpires) please display the marks?*

【亮光】① light: 一道～ *a shaft of light*/ ～逐渐微弱，我很担心天黑之前我们不能到达。*The light was gradually fading, and I'm afraid we couldn't arrive before it became dark.* /突然的～让我直眨眼。*The sudden glare made me blink.* ② shine; reflection: 她把酒杯擦得发～。*She polished the wine glasses until they shone.*

【亮光光】shining; gleaming; bright: ～的靴子 *shiny boots*

【亮话】blunt words: 打开天窗说～。*Let's come right to the point and call a spade.*

【亮晶晶】glittering; sparkling; glistening: 她的眼睛～的。*Her eyes are sparkling.*

【亮牌子】lay one's cards on the table; have a showdown: 先不要着急～。*Don't put your cards on the table too early.*

【亮儿】[口] ① lamp; light: 照～ *give sb a light* ② light: 黑暗中的一点儿～ *a little light in the dark*

【亮闪闪】sparkling; glittering: 一对～的耳环 *a pair of sparkling earrings*

【亮堂堂】*brightly lit*; *well lit*; *brilliant*: 剧院有一个～的排练室。*The theatre has a light rehearsal room.*

【亮堂】① light; bright: 这屋子又宽敞又～。*The room is spacious and light.* /为了避免视觉疲劳，要确保你的桌子是～的。*To avoid eyestrain make sure your desk is well lit.* ② clear; enlightened: 听了他的劝说，我心里就～了。*After his persuasion, I was clear about it.* ③ (of voice) loud and clear

【亮相】① (in Beijing opera, dancing, etc.) strike a pose on the stage ② make one's debut: 距他第一次在国际网坛～已经10年了。*It's almost ten years since he made his debut in international tennis.* ③ declare one's position; state one's views: 他迟迟不肯～。*He was reluctant to show his opinions.*

【亮眼人】the bright-eyed ones (blind people's term for those who can see)

【亮锃锃】shining; gleaming: 我甚至可以在那双～的靴子里看到自己的脸。*I can even see my face in the gleaming boots.*

【亮铮铮】shining; gleaming: 他一笑，我们就能看到他那颗～的金牙。*Whenever he smiles, we will see his gleaming gold tooth.*

凉 cool; make cool; let cool by air: 让茶泡一会，～一下再喝。*Let the tea brew and cool a little before you drink it.*
see also liáng

谅[1] excuse; forgive; understand: 体～ *understand and forgive*

谅[2] I believe; I think: ～她不敢这么说。*I don't think she dare say this.*

【谅察】[书] (used in letters) ask for your understanding and forgiveness

【谅解】understand; make allowance for: 口头～ *verbal understanding* / ～备忘录 *memorandum of understanding* /双方达成了～。*The two parties reached an understanding.*

辆 [量] used with vehicles: 一～公共汽车 *a bus* /三～卡车 *three trucks*

靓 [方] beautiful; pretty: 她长的真～。*She is really pretty.*
see also jìng

【靓女】[方] a pretty girl

【靓仔】[方] a handsome young man

量 ① [古] bulk measure: 重～ *weight* ② capacity: 容～ *capacity of container* /酒～ *capacity for liquor* ③ amount; quantity; volume: 热～ *quantity of heat* /降雨～ *rainfall* ④ estimate; weight: 不自～ *not take a proper measure of oneself*
see also liáng

【量变】【哲】quantitative change: ～到质变 *from quantitative to qualitative change*

【量才录用】hire personnel on the basis of their abilities; employ people according to their talents

【量词】【语】measure word; classifier
【量化】quantify; quantize: ~器 *quantizer*
【量力】estimate one's own strength or ability (and act accordingly)
【量力而行】act according to one's ability; do as much as one's resources, strength, etc.:我们原本想买比这个更大的房子,但是要~呀。*We wanted to buy a bigger house than this but we had to cut our coat according to our cloth.*
【量入为出】keep expenditures below income; base one's expenditure upon his income; make buckle and tongue meet; cut one's coat according to one's cloth
【量体裁衣】fit the dress to the figure — act according to actual circumstances; suit one's action to actual circumstances
【量小非君子,无毒不丈夫】[俗] no gentleman has a petty mind and no true man is without venom
【量刑】【律】measurement of penalty: ~标准 *criterion for imposing penalty*
【量子】【物】quantum:光~ *quantum of light* /虚~ *virtual quantum* /振动~ *vibration quantum*

晾 ① air; dry in the air: ~被子 *air the quilt* ② sun; dry in the sun: ~白薯干 *sun sliced sweet potatoes* ③ ignore; slight:他自己看书,把我~在一边。*He just read, totally ignoring my presence.* ④ cool; make cool
【晾干】dry by airing; dry in the air; airing; dry out:油漆大概要6个小时才能~。*The paint should take about six hours to dry.*
【晾晒】air; field:星期天我们常常把衣服拿到外面~。*We always air our clothes on Sundays.*
【晾台】① leave sb in the lurch ② sun terrace (for drying clothes)
【晾衣架】airer; clotheshorse; drier; clothes hanger

踉

【踉跄】stagger; stumble 在包裹的重压下,他~而行。*He was staggering under the weight of a huge parcel.* /他~着走向浴室。*He lurched towards the bathroom.*

liāo

撩 ① raise; lift up: ~起帘子 *raise the curtain* / ~起裙子 *hold up one's skirt* ② sprinkle with one's hand:她往地上~了一些水。*She sprinkled some water on the floor.*
see also liáo

蹽 [方] ① rush; speed; walk rapidly ② slip away; sneak off:他趁我不注意,~起腿就跑了。*He sneaked away when I was doing something else.*

liáo

辽 distant; faraway
【辽阔】vast; extensive: ~的领土 *vast territory* /青藏高原面积~。*The Qinghai Xizang plateau covers a vast area.*
【辽远】distant; faraway; remote: ~的边疆 *faraway frontier* / ~的天空 *distant sky*

疗 cure; treat; recuperate:电~ *electrotherapy* /理~ *physiotherapy* /化~ *chemotherapy*
【疗程】【医】course (or period) of treatment:她服了一个~的药。*She took a course of drugs.*
【疗法】therapeutics; therapy; treatment; therapia; therapeusis:超声波~ *ultrasonictherapy* /电子~ *electron therapy* /电震~ *electronic shock therapy* /电休克~ *electroshock therapy* /发热~ *fever therapy* /放射~ *radio therapy* /抗生素~ *antibiotic therapy* /麻醉~ *narcosis therapy* /喷雾~ *aerosol therapy* /针灸~ *acupuncture therapy* /职业~ *occupational therapy* /紫外线~ *ultraviolet therapy*
【疗效】curative effect:温泉对某些疾病有~。*Hot springs have curative effects on some diseases.*
【疗养】recuperate; convalesce; rest up:他的父母去海滨~了。*His parents have gone to the seaside to recuperate.*
【疗养院】sanatorium; convalescent hospital (or home)

聊[1] ① merely; just; rather: ~表谢意 *just a token of gratitude* / ~以塞责 *just to meet the bare requirements* / ~以自娱 *just to entertain oneself* ② a little; slightly: ~胜一筹 *just a little better* ③ (Liáo) a surname

聊[2] [书] rely on; depend:民不~生。*The masses have no means to live.*

聊[3] chat:我们~了一会儿。*We chatted for a while.*
【聊备一格】may serve as a specimen
【聊表寸心】indicate (my) feelings for you; just to show my gratitude; just a token of gratitude
【聊赖】sth to live for; sth to rely on:百无~ *extremely bored*
【聊且】tentatively; for the moment:这些书~算我的一点儿心意。*Those books are just a token of my regard.*
【聊胜于无】better than nothing; a bit in the morning is better than nothing all day
【聊天儿】[口] chat; gab; small talk; talk in an easy friendly way:通过~,我加深了对他的了解。*I understand him better through chatting.*
【聊以解嘲】manage somehow to relieve embarrassment; make a feeble attempt to explain things away when ridiculed
【聊以自慰】just to console oneself
【聊以卒岁】[书] just to tide over the year

僚 ① official:官~ *official; bureaucrat* ② an associate in office:同~ *companion; colleague*
【僚机】【军】① wing plane; wingman ② wingman
【僚舰】【军】consort (ship)
【僚属】[旧] officials under sb in authority; subordinates; staff
【僚友】[旧] colleagues (in the same government office)

【僚佐】[旧] assistants in a government office

寥 ① few; scanty ② quiet; silent: 寂~ *deserted and lonely* ③ [书] vast

【寥廓】[书] boundless; vast: ~天际 *the boundless sky* / ~星空 *vast starlit sky*

【寥寥】very few: ~数笔 *with a few strokes* / ~数语 *a few words; in a nutshell* /除了~几个行人外,街上空空如也。*The streets were empty except for a few stray passers-by.*

【寥寥可数】very few; just a sprinkling of; hardly any: 学校里的黑人学生~。*There are almost no black students at the college.*

【寥寥无几】very few left; scanty; sparse; a scanty few: 虽然是星期一的早晨,街上的行人却~。*Although it was Monday morning there were hardly any people around.*

【寥落】① few and far between; sparse; scattered: 由于吹过平原的风持续不断,这一带树木~。*Trees are sparse in this area because of the continuous wind that blows across the plains.* ② deserted

【寥若晨星】as sparse as the morning stars; few and far between

撩 tease; tantalize; stir up

see also liāo

【撩拨】① tease; banter: 他用俏皮话~那个小女孩。*He teased that little girl with jest.* ② incite; provoke

【撩动】provoke; stir up: ~心弦 *pluck one's heartstrings*

【撩动肝火】stir up anger; excite one's wrath; provoke agitation; needle: 不管你说什么,都不要提到他的前妻,那会撩动他的肝火。*Whatever you say, don't mention his ex-wife; it's like a red rag to a bull.*

【撩逗】tease; provoke: 学校的孩子们常常~他,因为他很胖。*The kids at school used to tease him because he was overweight.*

【撩惹】provoke; incite: 你~了一场争吵。*You have stirred a quarrel up.* /他装作心不在焉~我生气。*He pretended to be absent-minded in order to wind me up.*

【撩人】stir; excite: 景色~人。*The scenery provokes people's interest.*

嘹

【嘹亮】resonant; loud and clear: 歌声~。*The singing is loud and clear.*

獠

【獠牙】tush; tusk; ivory: 青面~ *be green-faced and long-toothed — have fiendish features*

潦

see also lǎo

【潦草】① (of handwriting) hasty and careless; illegible: 笔迹~ *cramped handwriting — a scrawl* ② sloppy; slovenly: ~塞责 *do one's work in a careless and neglectful way* /他干事儿很~。*He always works in a slipshod way.*

【潦倒】be frustrated; be down on one's luck: ~不堪 *have gone down in the world; in very poor circumstances* / ~而死 *die a dog's death; die like a dog* / ~困顿 *in deep water; penniless and frustrated; down and out*

寮 [方] small house; hut

【寮房】① monk's cell or hut ② [方] shed; hut

缭 ① entangle; twine ② sew with slanting stitches

【缭边】stitch a hem; hem

【缭乱】[书] confused; in a turmoil: 眼花~ *be dazzled; dazzling*

【缭绕】curl up; wind around: 歌声~。*The song lingered in the air.*

燎 (of fire) spread; burn

see also liǎo

【燎荒】burn the grass on wasteland

【燎泡】blister raised by a burn or scald

【燎原】set the prairie ablaze: ~烈火 *a blazing prairie fire* /星星之火,可以~。*A single spark can start a prairie fire.*

liǎo

了[1] ① finish; complete; fulfill; settle: ~案 *conclude a case* /不~~之 *leave it unsettled* /没完没~ *endless; non-stop; without stop* / ~此一生 *end this life* / ~此夙愿 *fulfil this predestinate love* ② can: 受不~ *cannot stand it* /做得~ *can do it* ③ [书] entirely; a bit: ~无惧色 *not show a trace of fear; look completely undaunted; not a bit of fear* / ~无生趣 *without any joy of life; lose all interest in life*

了[2] understand; know; realize: 明~ *understand*

see also le

【了不得】① extreme; terrific: 小姑娘高兴得~。*The little girl was extremely happy.* ② awfully; terribly: 没什么~的事。*There is nothing serious.*

【了不起】① amazing; terrific; extraordinary: ~的成就 *wonderful achievement* /自以为~ *think oneself terrific* /多么~的一幅画! *What an amazing picture!* ② serious; grave: 没有你说得那么~。*It's not as serious as you said.*

【了当】① frank; straightforward; forthright ② settled; in order: 安排~ *properly arranged* ③ [旧] handle; manage: 自能~得来 *can handle it by oneself*

【了得】① horrible; terrible: 那还~! *How horrible!* ② [旧] extraordinary; outstanding: 他的本事~。*He is a capable person.*

【了断】finish; settle; wind up; bring to an end: 这事迟早应有个~。*It should be got through with sooner or later.* /她想尽快~这场争吵,因为她要

去赶飞机。*She wanted to wind the quarrel up quickly because she had a plane to catch.*

【了结】finish; settle; wind up; bring to an end:我们之间的关系已经～。*Everything is finished between us.* /我要尽快把这些信件～,这样在回家的路上就可以把它们发出去。*I'd like to get all these letters finished so I can mail them on my way home.* /这个月底以前我会～我的工作。*I will have concluded my work by the end of this month.*

【了解】① understand; comprehend:看起来一些人并不～跳伞是一项危险的运动。*It seems that some people don't understand that parachuting is a dangerous sport.* ② find out; acquaint oneself with; inquire into sth: ～全部事实 *inquire into the whole matter* /我们必须设法～全部情况。*We must try to find out about the whole situation.*

【了局】① end; ending ② solution; settlement:你这样哭也不是个～。*Keeping crying is after all no solution.*

【了了】[书] know clearly:不甚～ *not too clear about sth*

【了却】settle; solve:这也算～了我的一桩心事。*It really took a load off my mind.*

【了然】understand; be clear:一目～ *be clear at a glance*

【了如指掌】know sth like the palm of one's hand — be extremely familiar with sth; be perfectly clear of sth:他对这些政策～。*He knows these policies like the back of his hand.*

【了事】dispose of a matter; finish up sth; get sth over:草草～ *get through sth in a careless way; rush through sth*

【了无】not at all; not the least: ～睡意 *not at all sleepy*

【了悟】[书] understand; realize; comprehend:我尚不能～这其中的意义。*I cannot yet comprehend the meaning in it.*

【了账】settle a debt or an account:就此～。*It's all settled.*

燎 singe; scorch: ～着了头发 *have one's hair singed*
see also liáo

liào

尥

【尥蹶子】①(of mules, horses, etc.) give a backward kick ② lose one's temper; get angry:那个顽皮的男孩儿又～了。*That naughty boy is losing his temper again.*

料[1] ① expect; predict:不出所～ *as was expected* ② take care of:照～ *look after; take care of*

料[2] ① material; stuff:木～ *timber; lumber* /燃～ *fuel* ② feed; fodder:草～ *forage; fodder* ③ [量] prescription:配一～药 *make up a prescription* ④ [量] a former measure unit for timber

【料仓】feed bin; bunker; stock bin

【料场】stock ground

【料到】foresee; expect:我没～她会撒谎。*I didn't expect her to lie.*

【料定】know for sure

【料及】[书] expect; foresee; anticipate:我未～他的到来。*I didn't expect his coming.*

【料酒】cooking wine

【料理】① arrange; manage; attend to; take care of: ～后事 *make arrangements for a funeral* / ～家务 *look after household affairs* /一切都～得很好。*Everything is well arranged.* ② cooking; cuisine:日本～ *Japanese cuisine*

【料峭】[书] chilly:春寒～。*There is a chill in the air in early spring.*

【料事如神】predict like a prophet; foretell with miraculous accuracy

【料想】expect; think; presume:结果不如～的好。*The results were below expectations.*

【料子】① material for making clothes:这衣服是用昂贵的～制成的。*The dress is made from a very expensive material.* ② [方] woolen fabric:他想买些～做件上衣。*He wanted to buy some woolen fabric to make up a jacket.* ③ wood; timber ④ [口] makings; material:跳高运动员的～ *material for a high jumper* /当我第一次看见她打网球,我就知道她是冠军的～。*When I first saw her play tennis I knew that there was a future champion in the making.*

撂 ① put down; drop: ～下担子 *put down the burden* ② knock down; throw down: ～跤 *wrestle* ③ cast aside; leave behind; discard; abandon:他～下一家人,自己当兵去了。*Leaving behind his family, he went to join the army.*

【撂地】show acrobatic skill in open spaces

【撂荒】[方] let a piece of farmland go to waste

【撂手】refuse to have anything more to do with the matter:这件事我～不管了。*I will wash my hands of this matter.*

【撂挑子】put down the load — give up one's responsibilities; wash one's hands of the matter:挨了批评后,他干脆～不干了。*He threw up his job after he was criticized.*

瞭 survey or watch from a height

【瞭哨】[方] stand sentry (or sentinel)

【瞭望】① look far into the distance (usu. from a height) ② watch from a height or a distance; keep a lookout

【瞭望哨】lookout post

【瞭望塔】sightseeing tower; lookout tower

【瞭望台】observation tower; lookout tower

镣 shackles; fetters

【镣铐】fetters and handcuffs; shackles; irons; chains:戴上～ *be shackled; be in chains*

liē

咧

see also liě; lie

【咧咧】［方］① speak carelessly; gossip; talk nonsense; blabber ② (of a child) cry; sob: 小孩儿一直在～。*The child is crying all the time.*

liě

咧 ① grin: ～着嘴笑 *on the broad grin; laugh from ear to ear* /他高兴得～开嘴笑。*He was grinning with delight.* ②［方］talk: 胡～ *talk nonsense*

see also liē; lie

【咧嘴】draw back the corners of the mouth; grin: 她疼得直～。*She grinned with pain.*

裂 ［方］open; sever; part in the middle

see also liè

【裂巴】［方］bread

liè

列 ① arrange; form a line; line up: 罗～理由 *set out one's reasons* ② list; enter in a list: 名～榜首 *be the first in the list of successful candidates* / ～出要买的东西 *list the items to buy* ③ row; rank: 后～ *the rear rank* ④［量］used of a series or row of things: 一～客车 *a passenger train* ⑤ kind; sort: 他应在候选人之～。*He should be among the candidates.* ⑥ each and every; various: ～国 *various countries* ⑦ (Liè) a surname

【列兵】【军】private

【列车】train: 高速～ *high-speed train* /工程～ *engineering train* /国际～ *international train* /混编～ *mixed unit train* /架桥～ *bridge train* /救护～ *ambulance train* /空中～ *aerial train* /临时～ *conditional train*

【列岛】*a chain of islands; archipelago*: 澎湖～ *the Penghu Islands*

【列队】line up: ～欢迎 *queue up to welcome sb*

【列国】the various countries, states, or kingdoms: 周游～ *tour various countries*

【列举】enumerate; list; reel off: 发言人～我们的要求。*The spokesperson enumerated our demands.* / 这本导游书～了1,000多家旅店和饭馆。*The guidebook listed over 1,000 hotels and restaurants.* /她能够～出这个歌星所有唱片的名称。*She could reel off the names of all the records the singer ever made.*

【列宁】Vladimir Ilyich Lenin (1870-1924), leader of the Russian Revolution (7 Nov. 1917) and founder of Leninism

【列宁格勒】Leningrad, a city of northwest Europe-an U.S.S.R.

【列宁主义】Leninism: ～者 *Leninist; Leninite*

【列强】［旧］the Great Powers

【列位】all of you; gentlemen; ladies and gentlemen: ～请坐。*Ladies and gentlemen, be seated, please.*

【列席】attend (a meeting) as an observer or a non-voting delegate; sit in on: ～旁听 *attend a meeting as an observer* / ～作陪 *sit at the same table with the guest of honour*

【列席代表】delegate without the right to vote; non-voting delegate

【列支敦士登】Liechtenstein: ～人 *Liechtensteiner*

【列祖列宗】successive generations of ancestors

劣 ① bad; inferior; of low quality: 恶～ *base; mean* ② minor

【劣等】of inferior quality; low-grade; poor: ～生 *an inferior student* / ～品 *inferior goods* / ～羊毛 *peddler's wool* /决不允许放过任何～品。*No inferior products should be allowed to pass.*

【劣根性】deep-rooted bad habits; an inherent weakness: 国民的～ *inherent weakness of a nation*

【劣弧】【数】minor arc

【劣迹】misdeed; evil doing: ～昭彰 *have a notorious record* /我们不接受有～的人。*We do not accept people with scandalous doings.*

【劣马】① inferior horse; nag ② vicious horse; fiery steed

【劣绅】evil gentry: 土豪～ *local tyrants and evil gentry*

【劣势】inferior position; unfavourable situation: 数量上的～ *numerical inferiority* /在这场比赛中我们处于绝对～。*We were reduced to absolute inferiority in the match.*

【劣质】of poor (or low) quality; inferior: ～产品 *product of inferior quality* / ～酒精 *faints* / ～煤 *dross*

【劣种】inferior strain (or breed, stock)

冽 ［书］cold; chill; icy: 凛～ *piercingly cold*

洌 ［书］(of water or wine) crystal-clear: 清～ *clear; lucid*

烈 ① strong; violent: 激～ *intense; sharp; acute* ② upright; stern: 刚～ *upright and unyielding* ③ martyr sacrificing oneself for a just cause: 革命先～ *revolutionary martyrs* ④［书］exploits; achievements: 功～ *merits and achievements*

【烈度】intensity: 地震～ *earthquake intensity*

【烈风】①【气】strong gale ② strong wind

【烈火】raging fire; raging flames: 革命斗争的～越烧越旺。*The flames of revolutionary struggles are raging more and more fiercely.*

【烈火见真金】genuine gold fears on fire — people of worth show their mettle during trials and tribulations

【烈酒】moonshine; hard drink; strong drink; spirit

【烈马】violent or untamed horse

【烈女】① (in former times) a woman who prefers to

L

die rather than remarry, or marry after the death of her betrothed ② (in former times) a woman who dies in defence of her chastity

【烈日】burning sun; scorching sun: ~当空。*The hot sun is high in the sky.* / ~当头。*The blazing sun is shining right over one's head.* / ~炎炎。*The sun is shining fiercely.*

【烈士】① martyr: 革命~ *revolutionary martyrs* / ~纪念碑 *a monument to revolutionary martyrs* / ~陵园 *cemetery of revolutionary martyrs* / ~墓 *the tomb of a revolutionary martyr* / 向~学习 *follow the example of the martyrs* ②[书] (in former times) a man of high endeavour; hero

【烈士暮年,壮心不已】a noble-hearted man retains his high aspirations even in old age

【烈属】members of a revolutionary martyr's family

【烈暑】hot summer weather

【烈性】① spirited: ~女子 *a woman of character* ② strong; violent: ~毒药 *deadly poison*

【烈性子】① fiery disposition ② spitfire; person with a violent temper

【烈焰】raging flames; a roaring blaze

捩 twist; turn: ~转 *turn round*

猎 ① hunt: 渔~ *hunting and fishing* ② hunting: ~装 *hunting dress*

【猎豹】【动】cheetah

【猎捕】hunt; go hunting

【猎场】hunting ground; hunting field

【猎刀】hunting knife

【猎狗】【动】hunting dog; hound

【猎狐】fox terrier

【猎户】① household or family specialized in hunting ② hunter; huntsman

【猎户星云】【天】Great Nebula of Orion; Orion Nebula

【猎户座】【天】Orion: ~四边形 *Trapezium*

【猎获】capture or kill in hunting; bag

【猎获物】bag; prey

【猎具】hunting equipment; hunting outfit

【猎狼犬】wolfhound

【猎鹿犬】deerhound; elkhound

【猎奇】hunt or novelty; seek novelty: ~心理 *partiality for novelty*

【猎枪】shotgun; fowling piece; hunting rifle

【猎取】① hunt: 黄鼠狼~老鼠和鸟。*Weasels pursue rats and birds.* ② pursue; seek; hunt for: ~功名 *seek scholarly honour or official rank*

【猎人】hunter; huntsman: ~们在密林深处宿营。*The hunters camped in the midst of the thick forest.*

【猎杀】hunt and kill

【猎食】[书] hunt for food: 狼是成群~的。*Wolves hunt in packs.*

【猎手】hunter

【猎头】headhunting: ~公司 *headhunting company; talent search company*

【猎物】prey; quarry; game: 猎获了许多~。*Many good bags were obtained.* / 他成为骗子的~。*He became fair game for the crook.*

【猎艳】[书] ① rack one's brains for ornate diction ② chase after pretty women

【猎鹰】【动】falcon

【猎装】hunting suit; hunting outfit

裂 ① crack; split: 分~ *split up; break up* / 四分五~ *disintegrate; fall apart* / 我头疼欲~。*My head is splitting.* ②【植】gap

see also liě

【裂变】①【物】fission: 核~ *nuclear fission* / 诱生~ *induced fission* / 原始~ *original fission* / 原子~ *atomic fission* ② split: 这群人~成数个帮派。*The crowd split (up) into several groups.*

【裂变式原子弹】fission bomb

【裂变武器】the fission type of weapon

【裂层】【地】parting

【裂齿】carnassial tooth (of certain carnivores)

【裂缝】crack; split; rift; crevice; fissure: 云层有了~。*The clouds rifted.* / 这个杯子有一条~。*There's a crack in this cup.*

【裂痕】rift; crack; fissure: 这块玻璃有一道~。*There is a crack in the glass.* / 姐妹间的~在加深。*The rift between the siblings is growing.* / 他们的婚姻开始出现~。*Their marriage is crumbling.*

【裂化】【化】cracking (in the distillation of petroleum): ~催化剂 *cracking catalyst* / ~反应器 *cracker* / ~气 *cracked gas* / ~区 *zone of cracking* / ~蒸馏 *cracking distillation*

【裂解】【化】splitting decomposition; splitting: ~产物 *pyrolysis product* / ~病毒 *lytic virus* / ~反应 *cracking reaction* / ~气 *pyrolysis gas* / ~色谱 *pyrolysis chromatography* / ~作用 *splitting action*

【裂开】crack open; split open: 旧瓷器很容易~。*Old china cracks very easily.*

【裂口】crack; breach; split

【裂纹】① crack (the sides being still together): 横~ *cross crack* / 环状~ *annular crack* / 内埋~ *buried crack* / 疲劳~ *endurance crack* / 压制~ *pressing crack* ② crackle (on pottery, porcelain, etc.)

【裂隙】crack; crevice; fracture: 杯子上有一道~。*This cup has a crack in it.*

【裂罅】[书] crack; split; rift; crevice

【裂眦】[书] stare angrily: ~痛骂 *scold with glaring eyes*

【裂足】cleft foot

趔

【趔趄】stagger; reel: 他~着站起来。*He staggered to his feet.*

躐 [书] ① pass over; overstep; go beyond ② trample upon

【躐等】[书] skip over the normal steps; not follow the proper order: 学不~ *learn step by step*

【躐进】[书] advance by skipping necessary steps

lie

咧 [方] used like 了, 啦 or 哩: 好~。*OK!* /他来~! *He's coming.*
see also liē; liě

līn

拎 [方] lift; carry: ~着一篮子菜 *carry a basket of vegetables*
【拎包】[方] handbag; shopping bag; bag

lín

邻 ① neighbour; neighbourhood: 四~ *surrounding neighbours* /远亲不如近~。*A distant relative is not as good as a near neighbour.* ② adjacent; close; neighbouring: ~室 *an adjoining room* /越南与中国相~。*Viet Nam is contiguous to China.* ③ [古] administrative unit covering five households
【邻邦】neighbouring country: 友好~ *good neighbours*
【邻比】[书] neighbour
【邻边】adjacent side
【邻点】adjacent points; neighbouring points
【邻国】neighbouring country
【邻海】adjacent sea
【邻角】【数】adjacent angles
【邻接】border on; be next to; be contiguous to; adjoin: 矩阵~ *matrix adjacency* /我们的房子~教堂。*Our house abuts on the church.* /两家餐厅~。*The two restaurants are in close vicinity.*
【邻界效应】adjacency effects
【邻近】① be near; be close to; be adjacent to ② neighbourhood; vicinity: ~没有医院。*There's no hospital in the neighbourhood.*
【邻近色】close colour; similar colour
【邻近效应】kindred effect; proximity effect
【邻近星】【天】near stars
【邻居】neighbour: 他们是隔壁~。*They are next-door neighbours.* /月亮在宇宙中是我们最近的~。*The moon is our nearest neighbour in space.*
【邻里】① neighbourhood: ~服务站 *neighbourhood service* ② people of the neighbourhood; neighbours
【邻人】neighbour
【邻舍】[方] neighbour
【邻位】【化】ortho-position: ~化合物 *ortho-compound*
【邻线】adjacent line
【邻项】successive term
【邻域】【数】neighbourhood: ~半径 *radius of neighbourhood* / ~中心 *centre of neighbourhood*

林 ① forest; woods; grove: 边缘~ *fringing forest* /次生~ *secondary forest* /多龄~ *many-aged forest* /防风~ *wind-break forest* /防护~ *prevention forest* /放牧~ *grazing forest* /风景~ *aesthetic forest* /复层~ *compound storied forest* /公有~ *community forest* /过熟~ *overmature forest* /混交~ *mingled forest* /季雨~ *monsoon forest* /经济~ *production forest* /阔叶~ *broad-leaf forest* ② circles; group: 士~ *scholarly circles* /石~ *stone forest* ③ forestry: 农~口 *farming and forestry sector* ④ (Lín) a surname
【林产】【林】forest products: ~工业 *forest product industry*
【林场】① forestry centre; forestry station ② forestry farm; tree farm
【林丛】woods; grove
【林带】forest belt; tree belt
【林道】forest-road
【林地】forest land; woodland; timberland
【林分】【林】standing forest; stand: ~测定 *inventory of stand* / ~抚育 *stand tending* / ~改造 *stand conversion* / ~价值 *cost value of stand* / ~密度 *density of crop* / ~演进 *stand development* / ~组成 *stand structure*
【林副产品】forest by-product
【林海】immense forest
【林价】cost value of forest: ~算法 *forest valuation*
【林间】woodland: ~播种 *interseeding* / ~草地 *grass plot*
【林肯】Abraham Lincoln (1809—1865), 16th President of the United States (1861—1865)
【林垦】forestry and land reclamation
【林立】(of masts, smokestacks, derricks, tall buildings, etc.) stand (in great numbers) like a forest: ~的摩天大楼 *a forest of skyscrapers* /港口桅杆~。*There is a forest of masts in the harbour.*
【林林总总】numerous; multitudinous
【林龄】【林】age of stand
【林莽】wild jungle: ~地带 *wild jungle region*
【林木】① forest; woods ②【林】forest tree; crop; sylva: 经济~ *trees of economic value* /油料~ *oil-yielding shrubs*
【林农】forest farmer; forester
【林区】forest zone; forest region; forest district; forest
【林泉】[书] forests and streams — mountain retreat; a place for a recluse: ~之士 *recluse; hermit*
【林权】ownership of a forest
【林薮】[书] ① woods and marshes ② collection
【林涛】the soughing of the wind in forest trees
【林网】crisscross forest belts; network of forest
【林下】[书] a sylvan life — retirement from official life: ~风范 *refined culture of the hermit*
【林线】timberline; forest line
【林相】① forest form ② (of a forest) quality: ~优良 *high-quality forest*
【林型】crop type; forest type: ~图 *cover type map*
【林学】forestry (as a branch of learning)

【林业】forestry：粗放～ *extensive forestry* /城市～ *city forestry* /防护～ *protection forestry* /风景～ *aesthetic forestry* /工业性～ *industrial forestry* /集约～ *intensive forestry* /商业性～ *commercial forestry*

【林阴道】boulevard; avenue

【林园】wooden land; a park of trees and vegetation

【林缘】border; forest edge：～树 *border tree*; *marginal tree*

【林苑】hunting park (for emperors)

【林政】forestry administration

【林子】［口］woods; grove; forest

临 ① face; be close to：如～大敌 *as if confronted with a formidable enemy* /居高～下 *look down from a height* ② arrive; be present：双喜～门。*A double blessing has descended upon the family.* ③ be about to; be going to：～睡 *be about to sleep* ④copy：～帖 *practise calligraphy after a model* ⑤ (Lín) a surname

【临本】copy (of a painting, etc.)

【临别】at parting; just before parting：作为～纪念 *as a parting souvenir* / ～纪念品 *parting gift* / ～赠言 *a piece of parting advice*; *parting words*

【临产】about to give birth; parturient：～阵痛 *labour pains*; *birth pangs*

【临场】① when attending an examination; when participating in a contest：这个运动员的～经验不足。*The athlete lacks field experience.* ② come personally to the site or spot：专家将～指导。*The expert will render on-the-spot guidance.*

【临池】［书］at the pond — practicing calligraphy

【临床】【医】clinical：～表现 *clinical manifestation* / ～观察 *clinical observation* / ～记录 *clinography* / ～检查 *clinical examination* / ～讲义 *clinical lectures* / ～社会学 *clinical sociology* / ～心理学 *clinical psychology* / ～药理学 *clinical pharmacology* / ～医学 *clinical medicine* / ～遗传学 *clinical genetics* / ～应用 *clinical practice* / ～诊断 *clinical diagnosis* / ～症状 *clinical symptoms*

【临到】① just before; on the point of：～我走，他才出现。*He didn't appear until I was leaving.* ② befall; happen to：没想到这种事也能～他头上。*It's surprising that it happened to him.*

【临风】［书］facing (or against) the wind：～洒泪 *sob out one's sorrow to the wind*

【临机】［书］face an emergency; as the occasion requires：～处置 *make emergency decisions* / ～应变 *suit one's actions to changing conditions*

【临街】overlook or face the street：～的窗户 *window overlooking the street*

【临界】【物】critical; crisis：～变数 *critical variable* /～参数 *critical parameters* / ～场 *critical field* / ～磁场 *critical magnetic field* / ～等温线 *critical isotherm* / ～电路 *critical circuit* / ～电势 *critical potential* / ～电压 *critical voltage* / ～电阻 *critical resistance* / ～概率 *critical probability* / ～角 *critical angle* / ～力 *critical force* / ～密度 *critical density* / ～浓度 *critical concentration* / ～强度 *critical intensity* / ～区域 *critical zone* (*or region*) / ～态 *critical state* / ～体积 *critical volume*; *critical size* / ～条件 *critical condition*) / ～外压 *critical external pressure* / ～温度 *critical temperature* / ～误差 *critical error* / ～效应 *critical effect* / ～值 *critical value*; *marginal value*

【临界点】【物】critical point; breakthrough point; point of transition：～偏移 *stagnation point shift* / ～位移 *stagnation point movement*

【临界阻尼】critical damping：～电阻 *critical damping resistance* / ～振荡 *critical damping oscillation*

【临近】close to; close on：考试～。*The examination is close at hand.*

【临渴掘井】not dig a well until one is thirsty; make one's cloak when it begins to rain — start acting too late; make an eleventh-hour attempt：她总是～。*She always makes no preparation until the last moment.*

【临了】［口］finally; in the end：～你还是得听他的。*You will have to obey him in the end.*

【临门】① come to the house; arrive at the door：近日将有贵宾～。*The distinguished guest will arrive today.* ② facing the goal; at the goal

【临摹】copy (a model of calligraphy or painting)：这幅画是直接写生的呢，还是～的？*Was this picture painted direct from nature or from a copy?*

【临盆】be giving birth to a child; be confined; be in labour

【临期】(of a date) draw close：大会已～。*The conference is drawing near.*

【临蓐】be in labour; be about to deliver a child

【临深履薄】as if on the brink of a chasm, as if treading on thin ice — with caution and care; proceed with extreme caution

【临时】① at the time when sth is needed or is expected to happen：他事先没做准备，～着急了。*He didn't make preparation at all and headed into a rush at that occasion.* ② temporarily; for the time being：～凑合 *make do for the moment*

【临时抱佛脚】embrace Buddha's feet and pray for help in time of emergency

【临死】on one's deathbed：～前的忏悔 *a deathbed confession*

【临眺】［书］ascend a height and look into the distance

【临帖】practise calligraphy after a model

【临头】befall; happen：大难～ *be faced with imminent disaster* /他口口声声说他一定帮忙，然而事到～他什么也不帮。*He always says he'll help, but when it comes to the crunch, he does nothing.*

【临危】① be dying (from illness) ② face death or deadly peril：～不惧 *not shrink in the face of danger*; *be brave in a dangerous situation* / ～不乱 *be calm in the hour of peril*; *take a tense situation calmly*

【临问】［书］go to pay one's regards or solicit opinions

【临刑】just before execution

【临行】before leaving; on departure：～告别 *say*

goodbye to sb before departure /～匆匆，不及告别。*I left in such a hurry that I didn't have time to say goodbye.*

【临渊羡鱼】stand by a pond longing for fish：～，不如退而结网。*It's better to go back and make a net than to covet the fish by merely staring into the water.*

【临月】about to give birth

【临战】just before a battle

【临阵换将】choose a new leader in the middle of an important campaign; change commanders in the middle of a battle

【临阵磨枪】sharpen one's spear just before going into battle — start to prepare at the last moment

【临阵脱逃】sneak away at a critical juncture; flee instead of fighting; turn tail

【临终】at the point of death; immediately before one's death; on one's deathbed：～遗言 *dying wish; dying words; deathbed will; deathbed words*

淋 ① pour; drench：我在暴风雨中～得湿透。*I was drenched in the storm.* ② sprinkle; splash：往地上～点儿水 *sprinkle water over the floor*

see also lìn

【淋巴】【生理】lymph：～毒素 *lymphotoxin* / ～干 *lymph truck* / ～疾病 *lymphatic disease* / ～肉瘤 *lymphosarcoma* / ～体质 *lymphatism* / ～因子 *lymphokine* / ～组织破坏 *lymphatolysis*

【淋巴系统】lymphatic system; systema lymphaticum

【淋巴细胞】lymphocyte

【淋巴腺】lymph; lymph gland：～瘤 *lymphadenoma* / ～炎 *lymphadenitis*

【淋巴组织】lymphatic tissue; lymphoid tissue：～破坏 *lymphatolysis* / ～生成 *lymphopoiesis*

【淋漓】① dripping wet：大汗～ *dripping with sweat* ②（of a piece of writing or a speech）free from inhibition：～尽致 *vividly and incisively; in great detail; describe fully* /他这番表演，真可谓～。*He put on an act, which showed him up completely.*

【淋淋】dripping wet：她浑身湿～的。*She is drenched all over.*

【淋雨】get wet in the rain; be exposed to the rain

【淋浴】shower bath; shower：洗～ *take a shower*

琳 ［书］beautiful jade

【琳琅】beautiful jade; gem

【琳琅满目】a superb collection of beautiful things; a feast for the eyes; a dazzling array of beautiful exhibits; a collection of fine and exquisite things：超市里的物品～。*A great variety of beautiful things in the supermarket dazzled my eyes.*

【粼粼】［书］（of water, stone, etc.）clear; crystalline：碧波～ *clear, blue ripples*

嶙

【嶙嶙】［书］jagged（of peaks）

【嶙峋】［书］①（of mountain rocks, cliffs, etc.）jagged; rugged; craggy：山石～ *jagged mountain rocks* ②（of a person）bony; thin：瘦骨～ *as thin as a latch; be all skin and bone* ③ upright; unyielding：气节～ *be of unyielding integrity*

遴 ［书］select; choose carefully

【遴选】［书］① select sb for a post：～委员会 *selection committee* ② select; choose：～样品 *select samples*

潾

【潾潾】（of water）clear; limpid

璘 ［书］luster of jade

霖 continuous heavy rain：秋～ *heavy rain in autumn* /甘～ *timely rain; good soaking rain*

【霖雨】continuous heavy rain

磷 【化】phosphorus（P）：白～ *white phosphorus* /红～ *red phosphorus* /黄～ *yellow phosphorus* /块状～ *pain phosphorus* /五氧化二～ *phosphorus pentoxide* /紫～ *violet phosphorus*

【磷肥】【农】phosphate fertilizer

【磷钙土】phosphate rock; phosphorite

【磷光】【物】phosphorescence：～分析 *phosphorescence analysis* / ～光谱 *phosphorescence spectrum*

【磷化物】【化】phosphide

【磷酸】【化】orthophosphoric acid; phosphoric acid：亚～ *phosphorous acid*

【磷酸钙】calcium phosphate

【磷酸盐】phosphors phosphate; phosphate：～肥料 *phosphate fertilizer*

【磷虾】【动】krill; euphausiid

【磷脂】lipoid; lipin; phospholipid; phosphatide

【磷中毒】phosphorism

鳞 ① scale：鱼有～。*Fish have scales.* ② scale-like：遍体～伤 *beaten black and blue; be covered with bruises or injuries*

【鳞斑】fish-scale; fleck scale

【鳞波】［书］ripples

【鳞翅类】【动】lepidoptera：～昆虫 *lepidopter; lepidopterid* / ～昆虫学 *lepidopterology* / ～学者 *lepidopterist*

【鳞次栉比】（of buildings）like fish scales and comb teeth; in tight rows; row upon row：城市里的高楼～。*The tall buildings in the city are arranged in close order.*

【鳞甲】scale and shell（of fish or reptile）

【鳞介】［书］aquatic animals

【鳞茎】【植】bulb：～兰 *laughing jackass*

【鳞鳞】①［书］as many as scales：强敌～ *numerous formidable enemies* ② sheets of cloud; shimmering ripples：～的白云 *sheets of white cloud*

【鳞皮病】【植】psorosis; scaly bark

【鳞片】① scale（on fish or insects' wings）②【动】squama; palea ③【植】bud scale

【鳞伤】be covered with wounds

【鳞爪】［书］scales and claws — small bits; fragments; odd scraps: 关于天文学我只知道一鳞半爪。*My knowledge about astronomy is very superficial.*

麟 [书] (Chinese) unicorn: 凤毛~角 *rarity of rarities*

【麟凤】rare treasures

【麟凤龟龙】the unicorn, the phoenix, the tortoise, and the dragon (formerly called the "four spiritually endowed beings") — worthy men; various kinds of good people

【麟角】① unicorn horns ② rarities; rare things

【麟趾呈祥】may the hoofs of the unicorn bring you much luck — may you have many good sons!

lǐn

凛 ① cold; frigid ② austere; severe; stern: ~若冰霜 *have a forbidding manner* ③ [书] afraid; fearful: ~于夜行 *dread going on a journey at night*

【凛冽】piercingly cold; biting cold: 寒风~ *biting wind*

【凛凛】① cold ② stern; awe-inspiring: 威风~的将军 *a majestic-looking general*

【凛然】stern; awe-inspiring: 正气~ *show awe-inspiring righteousness*

廪 [书] ① granary: 仓~ *public granary* ② *grain*

檩 【建】purlin: 上~ *upper purlin*

【檩条】【建】purlin

【檩子】[方] purlin

lìn

吝 ① stingy; mean; miserly: 不~赐教 *not be grudging in giving advice* ② (Lìn) a surname

【吝色】reluctant to give

【吝啬】stingy; niggardly; miserly; mean: 他是个~的老板,克扣工人们的衣食。*He was a miserly boss who grudged the workers food to eat, and clothes to wear.* /她节省但不~。*She practices economy without being stingy.*

【吝啬鬼】miser; niggard

【吝惜】grudge; stint; be stingily about; hold stingily on to; grudge: 他~仆人们的食物。*He grudged the food his servants ate.* /小孩很~那件礼物。*The baby held stingily on to the gift.*

赁 hire; rent: ~工 *hire help* /租~ *rent; lease; hire*

淋 filter; strain: 过~ *filter*

see also lín

【淋病】【医】gonorrhoea

líng

伶 [旧] actor or actress: 名~ *famous actor or actress*

【伶仃】① left alone without help; lonely: 孤苦~ *alone and uncared for* ② weak and thin: 瘦骨~ *all skin and bones*

【伶俐】clever; bright; quick-witted: 聪明~ *intelligent and clever* /口齿~ *speak sensibly and well*

【伶俜】[书] lonely; solitary

【伶人】[旧] actor or actress

【伶牙俐齿】have the gift of the gab; have a glib tongue; have a ready tongue

灵 ① clever; bright: 失~ *be out of order* ② spirit; soul; intelligence: 心~ *the soul; the mind* ③ fairy; sprite: 精~ *spirit; demon* ④ effective: 这药很~。*The drug works well.* ⑤ hearse; of the deceased: 扶~ *carry the hearse* /停~ *deposit coffin pending burial*

【灵便】① nimble; agile: 老人的耳朵不太~。*It's hard for the old man to hear.* ② easy to handle; handy: 这是一只~的小保险箱。*This is a handy little safety box.*

【灵车】hearse; dead wagon

【灵床】① bier ② a bed kept as it was when the person was alive

【灵丹妙药】a magic (or wonder) drug; a miraculous cure; panacea; sovereign remedy

【灵幡】funeral banner

【灵符】[迷] magic figures drawn by Taoist priests to invoke or exorcise spirits and bring good or ill luck

【灵府】[书] the mind; the faculties

【灵感】inspiration (for creative work); afflatus: 诗的~ *poetic afflatus* /诗人与艺术家往往由自然得到~。*Poets and artists often draw their inspiration from nature.*

【灵怪】① gods and spirits; demon ② [书] mystical; strange; unusual

【灵光】① a divine light ② halo (round the head of a god) ③ [方] excellent; effective: 你教给我的办法很~。*The method you taught me is very effective.*

【灵盒】cinerary casket

【灵慧】intelligent; clever

【灵魂】① [迷] soul: ~不死 *immortal soul* ② soul; spirit: 教师是人类~的工程师。*A teacher is an architect of man's soul.* ③ conscience; soul: 他为了金钱而出卖了自己的~。*He sold his soul for money.* ④ decisive factor; soul: 他是整个集体的~。*He is the very life and soul of the collectivity.*

【灵魂深处】in the innermost recesses of the heart; in the depth of one's soul; to the bottom of one's soul

【灵魂转世】【宗】metempsychosis

【灵活】① nimble; agile; quick: ~的脚 *nimble feet* /~的头脑 *a supple (or agile) mind* /~敏捷 *ac-*

tive and intelligent; *vivacious* ② flexible; elastic: 我可以在这周或者下周来拜访你,我的计划是相当~的。*I can visit you this week or next week*; *my plan is fairly flexible*.

【灵机】sudden inspiration; brainwave

【灵机一动】seized by a sudden impulse; with a sudden inspiration; a bright idea occurs; a flash of wit; a glimmer comes into one's eyes:~,计上心来。*One suddenly has a brain wave and finds a good solution*.

【灵境】[书] fairyland; wonderland

【灵柩】a coffin containing a corpse; bier

【灵快】nimble;quick:手脚~ *be agile in movement*

【灵猫】【动】civet (cat)

【灵媒】spirit medium

【灵妙】wonderful; clever

【灵敏】sensitive; keen; agile; acute: ~的一跃 *a nimble leap* /他头脑~。*He has a keen brain.* /狗有~的嗅觉。*A dog has an acute sense of smell.*

【灵敏度】① sensitivity:仪表~ *meter sensitivity* /有效~ *effective sensitivity* /最佳~ *optimum sensitivity* ② accuracy; precision

【灵牌】spirit tablet

【灵气】① intelligence:这个孩子很有~。*The child is of high intelligence.* ② (in legendary) miraculous power or force

【灵巧】dexterous; nimble; skillful; ingenious: ~的手 *a facile hand* / ~的手指 *nimble fingers* /小女孩儿像鹿一样~。*The little girl is as nimble as a deer.*

【灵寝】a place where a coffin containing a corpse is kept

【灵台】①[书] the mind; the heart ② a platform on which a coffin or a cinerary casket is placed

【灵堂】mourning hall

【灵通】① having quick access to information; well-informed:她是消息~人士,这件事你可以去问她。*She is always well informed*; *you can consult her about it.* ②[方] be useful:这个工具很~。*The tool is of great use.* ③[方] agile; quick:心眼儿~ *be quick-witted*

【灵童】soul boy:十世班禅转世~ *reincarnated soul boy for the 10th Panchen Lama*

【灵透】[方] clever

【灵位】temporary memorial tablet

【灵犀】magic horn — heart-beat in unison:心有~一点通 *understand each other without so many words*

【灵心慧性】intelligent and talented

【灵性】① intelligence; aptitude:他在语言方面很有~。*He has an aptitude of language.* ② intelligence(of animals)

【灵秀】(of scenery) beautiful

【灵验】① efficacious; effective:中药治这种病是~的。*Traditional Chinese medicine for this kind of disease is efficacious.* ② (of a prediction, etc.) accurate; right:这个老人说的话果然~。*What the old man said turned out to be accurate.*

【灵异】① deities and spirits ② magical; mystical

【灵芝】【药】magic fungus — glossy ganoderma

【灵知】【宗】gnosis

囹

【囹圄】[书] jail; prison:身陷~ *be thrown into prison*

泠 ①[书] clear and cool; chilly: ~风 *cold wind* ② (Líng) a surname

【泠泠】[书] ① cool ② (of sound) clear and far-reaching

【泠然】[书] clear and far-reaching

玲

【玲琅】tinkling of jade

【玲玲】[书] the tinkling of pieces of jade

【玲珑】① (of things) ingeniously and delicately wrought; exquisite:小巧~ *small and exquisite* ② (of people) clever and nimble:八面~ *able to win favour on all sides*; *sail with very wind*; *manage to please everybody*

【玲珑剔透】① exquisitely carved; beautifully wrought ② bright-minded; smart

瓴 [书] water jar; jar with ears:高屋建~ *pour water off a steep roof — operate from a strategically advantageous position*

铃 ① bell:门~ *door bell* / ~响时,她已在座位上等候。*When the bell rang*, *she was waiting in her seat.* ② bell-shaped objects:哑~ *dumbbell* ③ boll; bud:棉~ *cotton boll*

【铃钹】bell cymbals

【铃锤】bell clapper

【铃铛】small bell

【铃铎】bell hanging from the eaves

【铃鼓】【音】tambourine

【铃扣】bellpull

【铃鸟】bellbird

【铃舌】clapper

【铃声】the tinkle of bells; the ringing sound of a bell

凌¹ ① invade; insult:欺~ *bully and humiliate* ② approach; close ③ rise high; soar aloft:盛气~人 *overbearing* ④ (Líng) a surname

凌² [方] ice:冰~ *icicle*

【凌波】ride the waves; walk over ripples: ~仙子 *a fairy walking over ripples*

【凌晨】in the small hours; before dawn:次日~ *in the small hours of the next day*

【凌迟】(in imperial times) the punishment of dismemberment and the lingering death

【凌驾】place oneself above; override; rise above others; outstrip:将个人利益~于集体利益之上 *place personal interest above collective interest*

【凌空】be high up in the air; soar or tower aloft: ~射门 *make a volley shot*

【凌厉】swift and fierce; quick and forceful: ~的攻势 *a quick and powerful attack*

【凌乱】in disorder; in a mess; messy: ~无序 *confused and disordered*; *in a litter*; *in a mess*

【凌虐】[书] maltreat; tyrannize over
【凌日】【天】transit
【凌辱】insult; humiliate:甘受～*sit down under insults* /忍受～*swallow an insult*
【凌侮】insult:我评论了她的新裙子,却被她视为～。*I commented about her new skirt and she took it as an insult.*
【凌汛】spring flood caused by melting river ice; ice run
【凌夷】[书] decline; be on the wane:国势～。*The state is in decline.*
【凌云】[书] reach the clouds; soar to the skies
【凌云壮志】have a strong resolution to reach the clouds — soaring aspirations; lofty aspiration
【凌杂】in disorder; in disarray

陵 ① hill; mound:山～*hill; mound* ② imperial tomb:十三～*the tombs of 13 Ming emperors* ③ [书] bully; violate:以强～弱。*The strong bully the weak.*
【陵迟】[书] decline
【陵谷】hills and valleys
【陵居】live on the highland
【陵墓】[书] mausoleum; tomb
【陵寝】[书] emperor's or king's resting place; mausoleum
【陵替】[书] ① (of law and order) break down ② decline; decay
【陵园】funerary park; cemetery:烈士～*cemetery of revolutionary martyrs*

聆 [书] hear; listen
【聆教】hear your instruction; listen to your wise advice
【聆取】[书] listen to (advice, etc.):～意见 *listen attentively to the criticism*
【聆听】[书] listen(respectfully)

菱 [书] ling; water caltrop
【菱角】ling; waternut; water caltrop
【菱形】diamond; rhombus; lozenge

棂 window lattice; latticework

翎 feather; plume; quill:孔雀～*peacock plumes; peacock feather*
【翎毛】① plume; feather ② a type of classical Chinese painting featuring birds and animals
【翎子】① peacock feathers worn at the back of a mandarin's hat ② long pheasant tail feathers worn on warriors' helmets in traditional operas

羚 ①【动】antelope; chamois ② antelope's horn
【羚黄鼠】【动】antelope squirrel; antelope chipmunk
【羚牛】【动】takin
【羚羊】【动】antelope; gazelle:印度～*Indian antelope*

绫 damask silk
【绫罗】different kinds of silk:～绸缎 *silk and satin; silks and brocades*
【绫子】damask silk; thin satin

零[1] ① fractional; fragmentary:化～为整 *bring up the parts into a whole* /化整为～*break up the whole into parts* ② extra; fraction:全校学生一千挂～。*There are ten hundred students in the school.* ③ placed between two numbers to indicate a smaller quantity following a larger one: *a year and two days* ④ zero sign; nought:～点二 *nought decimal two* ⑤ nil; nought:三比～*three goals to nil* /他的希望是～。*His prospects were approaching zero.* ⑥ zero (on a thermometer):～上5度 *5 degrees above zero* /～下10度 *10 degrees below zero* ⑦ (Líng) a surname

零[2] ① wither and fall:飘～*fade and fall* ② [书] fall:涕～*shed tears*
【零部件】components and parts; accessories and repairs
【零差】homodyne:～检波 *homodyne detection* /～探测 *zero-difference detection*
【零代数】null algebra; zero algebra
【零蛋】duck's egg — nought; zero:他考试得了个～。*He got a zero mark in the exam.*
【零点】00:00 hour; zero hour; midnight; null point
【零丁】lonely
【零度】zero; zero degree:绝对～*absolute zero* /气温已经降到～。*The temperature has fallen to zero.*
【零度等温线】zero isotherm
【零复位】resetting of zero
【零概率】zero probability
【零工】① odd job; short-term hired labour:打～*do odd jobs* ② odd-job man; casual labourer
【零功率】zero energy; zero power:～平衡 *zero energy balance*
【零函数】null function; zero function
【零花】① spend money on minor purchases; incidental expenses:你留着这点钱在路上～吧! *Keep this money for incidental expenses on the way.* ② [口] pocket money
【零活】odd jobs; chores
【零件】spare parts; spares:组装～*spare-parts assembly*
【零料】fragmentary material; odd piece; remnant:～出售 *remnant sale*
【零零落落】scattered; by ones and twos:一些～的村子 *a few scattered villages*
【零落】① (of plants) withered; stripped of leaves ② decline; decay:～不堪 *be far gone in decay* ③ scattered; sporadic; by ones and twos:～的枪声 *sporadic shooting*
【零七八碎】① scattered and disorderly ② miscellaneous trifles; odds and ends:我买这些～的东西花了不少钱。*I spent quite a lot of money on these odds and ends.*
【零钱】① small change; spare parts; spares:请把这一百块钱换成～。*Please give me small change for this one hundred-yuan note.* ② pocket money; extra money

【零敲碎打】do sth bit by bit, off and on; adopt a piecemeal approach
【零散】scattered：～资金 *scattered funds*；*dispersed funds*
【零时】zero hour
【零食】between-meal nibbles；snacks：吃～ *eat between meals* /大部分女孩子都喜欢吃～。*Most girls like snacks.*
【零售】sell retail；retail：～店 *retail shop*（*or store*）/ ～价格 *retail price* / ～总额 *total volume of retail sales* /这种药～10 元。*The drug retails at 10 yuan.*
【零售商】shopkeeper；tradesman
【零售税】purchase tax
【零售业】retail trade
【零数】the remaining sum beyond the round figure；remainder；fractional amount
【零碎】① scrappy；fragmentary；piecemeal：～的回忆 *fragmentary memories* ② odds and ends；oddments；bits and pieces
【零头】① the remaining sum beyond the round figure；fractional amount：五块钱～ *the odd five yuan* ② remnant（of cloth）：一块儿～布 *a remnant*
【零位】zero position：～电压 *total null voltage* / ～偏角 *null angle* / ～偏移 *zero drift* / ～平衡 *null balance*
【零星】① fragmentary；odd；piecemeal：～时间 *scrappy time* ② scattered；sporadic：～小雨 *occasional drizzles*
【零线】null line；zero curve；zero line
【零讯】scraps of news（often used as a column title）
【零用】① spend money on minor purchases ② pocket money
【零增长】zero growth：人口的～ *zero population growth*
【零值】zero values
【零指数】【数】zero exponent
【零嘴】［方］between-meal nibbles；snacks

龄 ① age；years：老～ *old age* /同～ *the same age* /学～儿童 *school-age children* ② length of time；duration：工～ *length of service*；*years of service* ③instar：蛹～ *pupal instar*

鲮 【动】① dace ② pangolin

【鲮鱼】【动】dace

lǐng

令 ［量］ream：一～新闻纸 *a ream of newsprint*
see also lìng

岭 ① mountain；ridge：崇山峻～ *high mountain ridges* /翻山越～ *tramp over hill and dale*；*cross over mountain after mountain* ② mountain range：大兴安～ *the Great Xing'an Mountain* ③ the Five Ridges

领 ① neck ② collar：翻～ *turn-down collar* /软～ *soft collar* /衣～ *collar of dress* ③ collarband；neckband：圆～儿 *round collarband* ④ outline；main point；gist：提纲挈～ *bring out the essence* /纲～ *outline* ⑤［量］a piece of：一～长袍 *a gown* /一～草席 *a straw mat* ⑥ lead；head：他把我们～到他家。*He led us to his home.* /他们～我们到了办公室。*They guided us to the office.* /秘书～求职者到应到的部门。*The secretary steered the applicants to the proper departments.* ⑦ possess；own：占～ *occupy*；*capture* ⑧ get；receive；draw；claim：～奖 *receive a prize* /认～ *claim sth* /招～ *announce the finding of lost property* /你的车子出事之后，～保险金了吗？*Did you claim on the insurance after your car accident?* ⑨ accept；take：你的好意我心～了。*I appreciate very much your kindness.* ⑩ understand；grasp：心～神会 *understand tacitly*
【领班】① head a work group ② gaffer；foreman
【领兵】① lead troops ② a military officer
【领唱】① lead a chorus ② leading singer（of a chorus）
【领带】necktie；tie：～别针 *tiepin* / ～绸 *tie silk* / ～夹 *tie bar*
【领导】① lead；exercise leadership ② leadership；leader：集体～ *group leadership* / ～者与被～者 *the leadership and the led* / ～班子 *leading group*（*or body*）/ ～方法 *method of leadership* / ～干部 *leading cadre*（*or officials*）/ ～核心 *leading nucleus* / ～集团 *leading group* / ～权 *hegemony* / ～艺术 *leadership skill* / ～作风 *work style of the leadership* /他是那家工厂的～。*He is the leader of that factory.*
【领导有方】exercise good leadership
【领地】① manor（of a feudal lord）；domain ② territory：海外～ *overseas territory*；*overseas possession*
【领队】① lead a group ② the leader of a group, sports team, etc.
【领港】① pilot a ship into or out of a harbour；pilot ②（harbour）pilot
【领工】① lead people in their work ② headman；ganger；foreman
【领钩】hook and eye on the collar
【领馆】consulate：总～ *consulate-general*
【领海】territorial waters；territorial sea：～范围 *extent of territorial waters* / ～权 *maritime domain*；*command of the sea* / ～线 *boundary line of territorial waters*
【领航】① navigate；pilot ② navigator；pilot
【领花】①（bow）tie ② collar insignia
【领会】understand；comprehend；grasp：那是我无法～的问题。*That problem is beyond my grasp.* /你能～她所说的话的意图吗？*Could you comprehend the meaning of her words?*
【领舰】leader
【领江】① navigate a ship on a river ② river pilot
【领教】① receive instructions, used to express thanks for sb's advice or performance：你说得很对，～，

~！*You are quite right; thanks for your advice.* ② ask sb's advice or opinion：我有几个问题向您~。*I wish to consult you on a few questions.* ③ experience; encounter：他们的伎俩，我们早就~过了。*We've had experience of their tricks.* /他们的作风我已经~了。*I have had plenty of experience of their style of work.*

【领结】bow tie; cravat

【领巾】scarf; neckerchief：红~ *red scarf*

【领空】territorial sky (or air); territorial air space：~权 *sovereign right over territorial sky*

【领口】① collarband; neckband ② the place where the two ends of a collar meet

【领扣】collar button; collar stud

【领陆】territorial land; land domain

【领路】lead the way：~人 *guide*

【领略】have a taste of; understand; appreciate; realize：~大概 *get a general impression of things* / 我~了川菜的风味。*I relished Sichuan dishes.*

【领命】take orders or instructions：~而去 *leave with an order*

【领情】feel grateful to sb; appreciate the kindness：对于他的好意，我很~。*I'm very grateful to him for his kindness.*

【领取】receive; draw; get：~退休金 *draw a pension* / ~薪水 *draw one's salary* / ~公共救济金 *be on the rates*

【领事】consul：代理~ *acting consul* / 副~ *vice consul* / 总~ *consul-general* / 美国驻中国~ *the American consul at China*

【领受】accept (kindness, etc.); receive

【领属】possess and control; have dominion over：~关系 *relationship between a superior and a subordinate*

【领水】① island waters ② territorial waters

【领头】[口] take the lead; be the first to do sth：谁来~？*Who will take the lead?*

【领土】territory：~裁判权 *territorial jurisdiction* / ~管辖权 *jurisdiction within territory* / ~扩张 *territorial expansion; territorial aggrandizement* / ~权 *sovereign right over territory* / ~完整 *territorial integrity* / ~要求 *territorial claim* / ~野心 *territorial ambition* / ~争端 *territorial disputes* / ~主权 *territorial right*

【领舞】① lead a dancer ② leading dancer

【领悟】comprehend; grasp：点头表示~ *nod comprehension* / 她对这一课题有深刻的~。*She has a thorough grasp of this subject.*

【领洗】【宗】receive baptism; be baptized

【领先】be in the lead; lead; take the lead：遥遥~ *hold a safe lead* / 跑了一半赛程后我~了。*After the first half of the race I was leading.* / 我们队在半场时~五分。*Our team held a lead of five points at the half.* / 在国内，这家公司在汽车维修方面处于~地位。*In the country, this company is in the lead when it comes to car maintenance.*

【领衔】head the list of signers (of a document); be the first on a name list

【领袖】leader：杰出的~ *a distinguished leader* / 反对派的~已被逮捕。*The leader of the opposition has been arrested.*

【领养】adopt (a child)：当他发现自己是被~的时，开始寻找自己的亲生父母。*When he discovered he was adopted, he began to search for his biological parents.*

【领有】possess; own

【领域】① territory; domain; realm ② field; sphere; domain; realm：思想~ *ideological sphere* / 文学~ *the region of literature* / 艺术~ *the world of art* / 你研究的~是什么？*What's your field of study?*

【领章】collar badge; collar insignia

【领主】feudal lord; suzerain

【领子】collar：他抓住了我的~。*He seized me by the collar.*

【领奏】① lead an instrumental ensemble ② leading player in an instrumental ensemble

【领罪】admit one's guilt; plead guilty

lìng

另 ① another; other：~结新欢 *throw sb over for sb else — said of lovers* / ~立门户 *live in a separate house* / ~谋生路 *find another way of living* / ~有所爱 *have another sweetheart* / ~做打算 *make some other plans; seek some other ways* / ~作它图 *take another line of policy; make another plan* / 请给我~一个。*Please give me another.* ② in addition; moreover：学费是二百元，书费~收。*The tuition fee is 200 yuan and books are extra.*

【另案】a separate case

【另当别论】be looked at differently; be considered from another angle：如果他还是个孩子，那就~了。*It'll be another case if he is still a child.*

【另起炉灶】① set up another kitchen — make a fresh start; start all over again ② set up one's own kitchen — go one's own way：他们两年前就离开公司，~了。*They left the company and set up their own one two years ago.*

【另请高明】find some better person (than myself); find someone better qualified (than myself)：你们给的薪水这么低，我无法接受，你们还是~吧。*I cannot accept the job with so low salaries; please find someone more competent than myself.*

【另外】in addition; besides; another：那完全是~一回事。*That's quite another matter.* /他给了我一本书，一个计算器，~还有一些钱。*He gave me a book, a calculator and some money besides.*

【另行】(do sth) separately：具体开会时间我们会~通知你。*We will notify you the specific time of the meeting later.*

【另眼相看】① regard (or look up to) sb with special respect; give sb special treatment ② view sb in a new, more favourable light; see sb in a new light

【另议】discuss separately：此事~。*This matter will*

L

be discussed separately.

令[1] ① issue an order：通～全国 *issue a general order throughout the nation* ② order；command：军～ *military orders* /～出法随 *rigorous enforcement of the law* /～出如山。*Every order is as firm as a mountain.* ③ make；cause：这个消息～我兴奋不已。*The news made me excited very much.* ④ drinker's wager game：猜拳行～ *play a finger-guessing drinking game* ⑤ an ancient official title：县～ *county magistrate*

令[2] season：时～ *season of the year*

令[3] ［书］① good：巧言～色 *pleasing words and smooth manner* ② your：～慈 *your mother* /～兄 *your brother*

令[4] brief song-poem；short lyric

see also lǐng

【令爱】your daughter

【令箭】an arrow-shaped token of authority（used formerly in the army）：拿着鸡毛当～ *use a chicken feather as an arrow token of authority；make a mountain out of a molehill*

【令郎】your son

【令名】［书］good name；good reputation

【令亲】your relative

【令人】make one：～发指 *make one's hair stand on end；make one's blood boil* /～费解 *pass comprehension；beyond comprehension* /～寒心 *casting a chill over sb；bitterly disappointing* /～喷饭 *choke with laughter；rouse laughter* /～捧腹 *make sb hold his belly with laughing；make one burst out laughing* /～深思 *call for deep thought；make one ponder* /～神往 *cause one to crave for；cause sb to have a strong desire for* /～生厌 *make one feel disgusted* /～痛心 *cut one to the heart* /～心酸 *cause sb's heart to ache；make sb want to cry out of pity* /～心碎 *break a person's heart* /～作呕 *turn one's stomach；make one sick；make one throw up*

【令堂】your mother

【令闻】［书］good name；good reputation

【令行禁止】any order will be carried out；any prohibition will be heeded

【令仪令色】of good deportment and of good look

【令誉】［书］good reputation

【令正】your wife

【令尊】your father

liū

溜 ① slip；slide：一条蛇从草丛中～过。*A snake slithered across the grass.* ② sneak off；slip away：她悄悄～走未被人看见。*She slipped away without being seen.* /小孩儿～上了床。*The child slipped into bed.* /守卫转身时窃贼～了进去。*The thieves sneaked in when the guard had his back turned.* ③ smooth：～圆 *smooth and round* ④ ［方］take a look；glance：他～了那本书一眼，什么也没说。*He just took a look at the book and said nothing.* ⑤ along：～着路边走 *walk along the road* ⑥ ［方］very：～净 *extremely clean*

see also liù

【溜边】① keep to the edge（of a road，river，etc.）② dodge；avoid：一遇到困难，他就～。*He dodges the difficulty whenever he meets it.*

【溜冰】① skate：～板 *skateboard* /～场（*skating*）*rink* /～鞋 *skating shoes；roller skate* /学生们在～。*The students are skating on the ice.* ② ［方］roller-skate；go roller-skating

【溜达】［口］stroll；saunter；go for a walk：吃完饭出去～～吧。*Let's go for a stroll after the meal.*

【溜掉】slip；vanish：她想早点儿从岗位上～。*She wanted to sneak off from work early.*

【溜光】［方］① very smooth；sleek；glossy：他的头发梳得～。*He combed his hair very smooth.* ② totally bare；not a bit left：山上的树砍得～。*All the trees on the mountain have been felled.*

【溜号】［方］sneak away；slink off：我最近上课老～。*I am always absent-minded at class recently.*

【溜滑】① slippery；smooth：～的鹅卵石 *smooth pebbles* ② sly；cunning：～的商人 *a cunning merchant*

【溜溜儿】［方］① whole；full：我在这儿～等了你一个小时。*I wait for you here for a whole hour.* ② burst；fit ③ secretly：他～地出去了。*He went out stealthily.*

【溜溜转】turn round and round；spin continuously：我这一上午被他支使得～。*I was ordered about by him for the whole morning.*

【溜门】break into（a house）to steal：～撬锁 *burglary and lock-picking*

【溜平】［方］smooth and level

【溜须拍马】［口］smooth sb's beard and pat his horse's hindquarters — lick sb's boots；toady to；fawn on

【溜之大吉】sneak away；slip away；slope off；slink off；seek safety in flight：他今天很早就从办公室～了。*He sneaked away from work very early today.* /当大家忙于交谈的时候，我～去参加朋友的聚会。*When everyone was busy talking I slipped away to join my friend's party.*

【溜走】leave stealthily；slip away；slink；slope off：今天老板不在，他抓住这个机会早早～了。*The boss was away，and he took the opportunity to slope off home very early.*

瞄 ［方］look

蹓 saunter；stroll：～马路 *stroll around the streets*

see also liù

liú

刘 （Liú）a surname

【刘海儿】bang; fringe

浏 [书] ①(of water) clear; limpid ②(of wind) swift

【浏览】glance over; scan; skim through; browse; look through: ~报纸 *browse through the newspaper* /我认为这本书值得~一下。*I think the book is worth skimming through.*

留 ① remain; stay: 如果你愿意,你可以~下来吃晚饭。*You can stay for supper if you like.* /我们正努力说服女儿在学校里多~一年。*We are trying to persuade our daughter to stay at school for another year.* /她决定仍然~在现在的岗位上。*She has decided to remain in her present job for the time being.* ② study abroad: ~美 *study in America* ③ ask sb to stay; keep sb where he is: 我只~你一会儿。*I shall just keep you for a while.* ④ concentrate on ⑤ keep; save: ~座位 *reserve a seat for sb* ⑥ accept; take: 他~下了我送的礼物。*He accepted the gift I sent him.* ⑦ leave behind: 你要不要给他~个话? *Would you like to leave a message for him?* ⑧ (Liú) a surname

【留班】[口] (of pupils, etc.) fail to go up to the next grade (or year); repeat the year's work; stay behind

【留别】[书] give sb a parting gift or write a poem for him when taking leave of him: ~赠言 *parting words of advice*

【留步】don't bother to see me out; don't bother to come any further: 请~,不必远送。*Please don't bother to come any further.*

【留成】retain a portion (of earnings, profits, etc.): ~利润 *retained profits* / ~外汇 *retained foreign exchange earnings*

【留传】hand down (to descendants); leave sth to posterity: 这个故事一代代~下来。*The story is left to pass on to later generations.*

【留存】① preserve; keep: 请让秘书~这些文件。*Please ask the secretary to keep these documents.* ② remain; be extant

【留待】wait until later: 这件事还是~以后讨论吧。*Let's discuss it later.*

【留得青山在,不怕没柴烧】as long as the green hills last, there'll always be wood to burn — where there is life, there is hope

【留都】one-time capital; old capital after a new one has been established

【留后路】keep a way open for retreat; leave a way out: 他甚至没有给自己~。*He even didn't leave a way out for himself.*

【留后手】leave room for manoeuvre

【留级】(of pupils, etc.) fail to go up to the next grade (or year); repeat the year's work; stay in the same class; repeat the same grade: ~生 *repeater*; *holdover*

【留恋】be reluctant to leave (a place); can't bear to part (from sb or with sth); recall with nostalgia

【留门】leave a door unlocked or unbolted

【留面子】let sb keep some self-respect; let sb down gently: 他在会上给我留了面子,我很感激。*He let me down gently at the meeting and I am really thankful to him.*

【留念】accept or keep as souvenir: 合影~ *have a group picture taken as a souvenir* /我们在学校门口合影~。*We had a photo taken as a memento before the gate of the school.*

【留鸟】【动】resident (bird)

【留情】show mercy or forgiveness: 手下~ *show mercy to sb*

【留任】retain a post; remain (or continue) in office

【留神】be careful; take care; look out for: ~别碰头! *Mind your head!*

【留声机】gramophone; phonograph: ~唱片 *single*

【留守】① act for the emperor during his absence from the capital ② stay behind to take care of things; stay behind for garrison or liaison duty (after the main force has left): ~女士 *grass widow* / ~人员 *rear personnel*

【留宿】① put up a guest for the night ② stay overnight; put up for the night: 我昨晚~于一家小旅店。*I stayed at a small inn last night.*

【留尾巴】leave loose ends: 不能~。*Don't leave anything unfinished.*

【留校】be assigned to work at one's alma mater after graduation

【留心】be careful; take care: ~别写错了。*Mind you don't write it wrong.*

【留学】study abroad: ~德国 *study in Germany*

【留学生】student studying abroad; student abroad; returned student: 公费~ *government-funded student* /自费~ *self-supporting student*

【留言】leave one's comments; leave a message: ~簿 *visitors' book* /他现在不在,您要~吗? *He is not in now; would you like to leave a message?*

【留洋】[旧] study abroad

【留一手】hold back a trick or two (in teaching a trade or skill): 师傅对徒弟留了一手。*The master held back some tricks of the trade from this apprentice.*

【留意】① be careful; look out: 过马路时要~。*Look out when you are crossing the street.* ② pay attention to; notice: 你~一下报纸上有没有这篇文章。*Please pay attention and find whether this article is on the newspaper.*

【留影】① take a photo as a memento; have a picture taken as a souvenir ② a picture taken as a souvenir: 儿时~ *photo of one's childhood*

【留用】① continue to employ; keep on: 降职~ *be demoted in office* ② keep for use

【留有后路】leave oneself enough leeway for sth

【留余地】allow for unforeseen circumstances; leave some leeway

【留职】retain one's post: ~停薪 *leave without pay*; *temporary retirement from office*

【留驻】remain stationed

流[1] ① flow: ~口水 *slobber*; *slaver* /这条河~过小村中央。*The river flows through the middle of the village.* ② drift; wander: 飘~ *drift about*

③ spread; circulate ④ degenerate:放任自～ *let things drift* ⑤ send into exile;banish ⑥ stream; current:上～ *upper reaches* ⑦ sth like a stream of water:电～ *electric current* /寒～ *cold current* ⑧ class; grade; rate:三教九～ *people of all sorts*

流[2] 【物】lumen

【流弊】corrupt practices; abuses; evil of long standing

【流别】① river branch; tributary ② types or genres (of literature)

【流冰】drift ice: ～群 *ice pack*

【流播】[书] spread; circulate; hand down

【流布】[书] spread; disseminate

【流产】①【医】(of a woman) have a miscarriage; miscarry; abortion; amblosis:人工～ *induced abortion* /晚期～ *late abortion* /习惯性～ *habitual abortion* /先兆～ *threatened abortion* /自然～ *natural abortion* ② (of a plan, etc.) miscarry; fall through:她的尝试归于～。*Her attempt proved abortive.* /这个计划～了。*The plan miscarried.*

【流畅】(of writing) easy and smooth; fluent; smooth:他的文章读起来都很～。*His articles read very smoothly.* /这首诗的韵律优美～。*The cadence of the poem flowed gracefully.*

【流程】① a distance traveled by a stream of water: 生命的～ *life span* ② technological process ③【矿】circuit:破碎～ *crushing circuit*

【流程表】flow table

【流程分析】process analysis

【流程图】flow chart; flowsheet; flow diagram

【流传】spread; circulate; hand down: 广为～ *spread far and wide*

【流窜】flee hither and thither: ～作案 *flee hither and thither to commit offenses*

【流弹】stray bullet; bullet

【流荡】① flow; float ② roam about

【流动】① (of water, air, etc.) flow; circulate:缓缓～的水 *slow-moving water* ② go from place to place; be on the move; be mobile: ～的社会 *a mobile society* / ～图书馆 *a mobile library*

【流毒】① exert a pernicious (or baneful) influence: ～甚广 *exert a widespread pernicious influence* ② pernicious (or baneful) influence

【流芳】[书] leave a good name: ～百世 *hand down a good reputation to a hundred generations*; *leave a good name forever*

【流放】① banish; send into exile: ～犯 *transport* /她被～到国外。*She was banished out of the country.* /政府被推翻后,皇室被～。*When the government was overthrown, the royal family was exiled.* ② float (logs) downstream

【流风】[书] customs handed down from past generations: ～余韵 *lasting influence*; *surviving influence(of poets)*

【流感】【医】flu; influenza; grippe: ～病毒 *influenza virus* / ～性肺炎 *influenza pneumonia*

【流光】[书] ① time ② flittering light, esp. moonlight

【流火】①[方] filariasis ②【中医】erysipelas on the leg; inflammatory disease with redness of skin

【流口水】make one's mouth water; run of the mouth; drool

【流寇】① roving bandits ② roving rebel bands

【流浪】roam about; lead a vagrant life: ～江湖 *wander far and wide by the river and lake*; *be an outlaw among the rivers and lakes* / ～生活 *vagabondage*; *a vagrant life*

【流浪汉】fugitive; tramp; vagrant

【流泪】burst into tears; burst out one's eyes; tears running down one's face

【流离】[书] wander about as a refugee or vagrant: ～颠沛 *homeless and wandering from place to place* / ～迁徙 *wander about without a fixed home*

【流离失所】become destitute and homeless; wander about homeless

【流丽】(of writing or calligraphy) fluent and elegant

【流利】① fluent:他说英语很～。*He speaks fluent English.* ② smooth:这支新钢笔水不～。*This new pen doesn't write smoothly.*

【流里流气】rascally; not serious or proper:这条街上总有几个～的小青年在晃荡。*There are always some young hooligans lingering in the street.*

【流连】be reluctant to leave; linger on

【流连忘返】indulge in pleasures without stop; enjoy oneself so much as to forget to go home; on the scoop

【流量】① volume of flow; rate of flow; flow; discharge: ～表 *module*; *flowmeter* / ～测定 *hydrometry* / ～恢复 *flow recovery* / ～调节 *flow control* ② flow of traffic:交通～ *flow of traffic*

【流量计】flowmeter

【流露】show unintentionally (one's thoughts or feelings); reveal; betray: ～真情 *reveal one's true feelings* /他的许多诗篇都～出对祖国的热爱。*He shows ardent love for his country in many of his poems.*

【流落】wander about destitute:你不该让你的孩子～街头。*You shouldn't let your children roam the streets.*

【流落他乡】left behind in a strange land; be stranded in a strange land:这些年他一直～。*He wandered destitute far from home these years.*

【流氓】① rogue; hoodlum; hooligan; gangster:小～ *young rogue* ② immoral (or indecent) behaviour; hooliganism; indecency:耍～ *behave like a hoodlum* / ～习气 *ruffianism* / ～行为 *hooliganism*; *indecent behaviour*

【流氓无产者】lumpen proletariat

【流民】refugee

【流明】【物】lumen (LM): ～当量 *lumen equivalent*

【流脑】[医] epidemic cerebrospinal meningitis

【流年】①[书] fleeting time:似水～ *time passing swiftly like flowing water* ② (in fortune-telling) prediction of a person's luck in a given year: ～不

利 *an unlucky year*; *down on one's luck this year*
【流派】school; sect:文学~ *school of literature*
【流盼】[书] ① amorous glances ② cast amorous glances at; make sheep's eyes at
【流气】① rascally ② rascally behaviour; hooliganism
【流散】scatter; drift
【流沙】① shifting sands; drifting sands; quicksand ② river silt ③ mud and sand in between rock formation: ~层 *sand layer*
【流觞】(in ancient times) a kind of drinking game
【流失】① run off; be washed away: ~河 *lost river* /水土~ *soil erosion* ② loss(of resources, etc.); drain:人才~ *brain drain* ③ (of students) drop out
【流食】liquid food
【流矢】stray arrow
【流势】the force and velocity of a current
【流逝】(of time) pass; elapse:光阴~。*Time flows.* /随着时间的~,他逐渐忘了这件事。*With the passage of time, he gradually forgot it.*
【流水】① flowing water ② turnover(in business)
【流水席】feast at which guests are served as they come
【流水线】assembly line; flow line: ~操作 *pile line operation* / ~处理 *pipelining processing* / ~生产 *flow-line production* / ~作业 *flow process*; *assembly line method*; *conveyer system*
【流水账】day-to-day (bookkeeping) account; current account
【流水作业】assembly line method; flow process
【流苏】tassels; edging; fringe: ~花边 *macrame*
【流俗】[贬] prevalent custom; current fashion
【流速】①【机】velocity of flow: ~计 *kinemometer*; *tachometer* ② water conservancy; current velocity
【流淌】(of liquid) flow:他受伤很重,血顺着手臂~下来。*He had been badly wounded and the blood was flowing down his arm.*
【流体】【物】fluid: ~层 *fluid layer* / ~动力学 *fluid dynamics*; *flow mechanics* / ~静力学 *fluid statics*; *hydrostatics* /~力学 *fluid mechanics* / ~压力 *fluid-power pressure* / ~运动 *fluid motion* / ~运动学 *hydrokinematics*
【流通】(of air, money, commodities, etc.) circulate:商品~ *circulation of commodities* /货币~滞缓。*Money circulates slowly.*
【流亡】be forced to leave one's native land; go into exile: ~者 *refugee* / ~政府 *government-in-exile*
【流徙】① wander about ② send into exile
【流涎】slaver; slobber; drivel
【流线】flow line; streamline; line of flow: ~图 *motion pattern*; *streamlined diagram*
【流线型】streamlined: ~汽车 *streamlined car* / ~支柱 *streamline wire*
【流向】① the direction of a current ② the direction of the flow of personnel, commodities, etc.:我们应该重视人才的~问题。*We should pay attention to the orientation of talents.*
【流泻】(of liquid or light) pour out; gush out
【流星】①【天】meteor; shooting star: ~尘 *meteoric dust* / ~群 *meteoric stream*; *meteor stream* / ~体 *meteoric body* / ~雨 *meteor* (*or meteoric*) *shower* ② an ancient weapon, composed of two iron balls fixed on a long iron chain ③ (in acrobatics) meteors:火~ *fire-meteors* /水~ *water-meteors*
【流星赶月】like a meteor chasing the moon — at top speed:他~般往家赶。*He rushed back home.*
【流刑】(in former times) the punishment of banishment
【流行】popular; prevalent; fashionable; be in vogue; trendy; in; be all the rage: ~色 *fashionable colour* /我喜欢唱~歌曲。*I like to sing popular songs.* /当我第一次听到这张唱片时,我就知道它一定会~。*When I first heard the record, I knew it would be a hit.* /这家商店很适合那些喜欢~服饰的人。*This shop is perfect for those who want fashionable clothes.* /60年代中期,甲壳虫乐队的发型十分~。*In the mid-sixties, Beatles haircuts were really trendy.* /是街上的孩子,而不是设计师决定什么~。*It's the kids on the street who decide what's in, not the designers.*
【流行病】epidemic disease
【流行病学】epidemiology
【流行性感冒】grippe; influenza
【流血】lose blood; shed blood; draw blood; bleed: ~冲突 *sanguinary conflict* /他一只眼睛肿了,鼻子在~。*His eye was swollen and his nose was bleeding.*
【流言】rumour; gossip; false news: ~传播迅速。*Gossip tends to circulate quickly.* / ~止于智者。*A wise man does not believe in rumours.*
【流言蜚语】tattle and prate; a word of rumour; hearsay; rumours and gossip:出于嫉妒,他开始散布关于我的~。*Out of jealousy, he has started to circulate false stories about me.*
【流溢】run over; flow over the brim
【流萤】firefly; glowworm
【流域】river valley; river basin; drainage area:黄河~ *the Huanghe River valley* / ~面积 *drainage area* / ~盆地 *drainage basin* / ~综合治理 *comprehensive reclamation of river basin*
【流质】【医】liquid diet (for patients)
【流转】① wander about; roam; be on the move ② (of goods or capital) circulate:资金~ *the circulation of funds* ③ [书]

琉

【琉璃】coloured glaze: ~塔 *glazed pagoda* / ~瓦 *glazed tile*
【琉璃球】① small glazed ball ② smart; clever ③ cunning; sleek ④ miser; niggard
【琉球群岛】(Japan) Ryukyu Islands, a chain of islands in the western Pacific

硫【化】sulphur (S):化合~ *combined sulfur* / 活性~ *active sulfur* /有机~ *organic sulfur*
【硫胺】thiamin; thiamine
【硫化】【化】vulcanize: ~钙 *calcium sulfide* / ~钾

potassium sulfide / ~氢 hydrogen sulfide / ~橡胶 vulcanized rubber; vulcanizate

【硫化物】【化】sulfid; sulfide; sulfured; sulphide

【硫磺】brim stone: ~群岛 volcano islands / ~温泉 sulphur spring

【硫酸】【化】sulphuric acid; vitriol oil: ~钙 calcium sulphate / ~镁 bitter salt / ~铜 bluestone / ~锌 zinc sulfate

馏 distil

see also liù

【馏分】【化】fraction; cut: 轻~ light fraction (or cut) / 重~ heavy fraction (or cut)

骝 (in ancient books) a red horse with black mane and tail

榴 【植】pomegranate

【榴弹】【军】high explosive shell

【榴弹炮】【军】howitzer

【榴弹枪】grenade launcher

【榴火】[书] the fiery red of pomegranate blossoms

【榴莲】【植】durian

飗

【飗飗】[书] (of breeze) blow

瘤 tumour: 恶性~ malignant tumour; cancer / 良性~ benign tumour

【瘤牛】【动】zebu

【瘤胃】【动】rumen: ~细菌 rumen bacteria

【瘤子】tumour

柳[1] ①【植】willow: 白~ white willow / 垂~ a weeping willow / 脆~ brittle willow / 黑~ black willow / 匍匐~ creeping willow / 五蕊~ laurel willow ②【天】Liu, one of the twenty-eight constellations in ancient Chinese astronomy ③ (Liǔ) a surname

【柳暗花明】dark willows and blooming flowers — a new vista

【柳暗花明又一村】there is a way out (for somebody); every cloud has a silver lining

【柳编】wickerwork

【柳草】willow herb

【柳笛】willow whistle made of bark from a young willow tree

【柳罐】wicker bucket

【柳兰】willow herb

【柳眉】arched eyebrows (of a woman): ~倒竖 raise (her) eyebrows in anger / ~倒竖，杏眼圆睁 with (her) eyebrows raised and eyes distended with fury

【柳树】willow; osier

【柳丝】fine willow branches; wicker

【柳条】willow twig; osier; wicker: ~筐 wicker basket / ~帽 wicker safety helmet / ~箱 wicker suitcase; wicker trunk / ~椅 basket chair

【柳絮】willow catkins

【柳腰】small waist; soft waistline: ~袅袅 graceful willowy waistline / ~纤手 soft waistline and slender hands

【柳叶刀】lance

【柳叶眉】arch eyebrows

【柳阴】shade of willow trees

【柳枝】withy; willow branch: ~轻拂。The willows are swaying lightly in the breeze.

【柳子】clumps of willow trees

绺 ①[量] tuft; skein; lock; wisp: 一~头发 a lock of hair ②[方] steal

【绺子】① lock; tuft; skein: 一~长发 a wisp of long hair ②[方] gang of bandits

锍 sulfonium; matte: 白~ white matte / 混合~ mixed matte

【锍化物】sulfonium compound

liù

六 six: ~个人 six persons

【六重唱】(vocal) sestet; sextet; sextette

【六重奏】(instrumental) sestet; sextet

【六畜】the six domestic animals (pig, ox, goat, horse, fowl and dog): ~不安 even the six domestic animals have no peace — in great turmoil

【六和弦】six chord

【六合】[书] the six directions — north, south, east, west, up and down; the world; the universe

【六甲】[旧] pregnancy: 身怀~ be pregnant

【六角】hexagonal: ~晶体 hexagonal crystal / ~螺丝 hexagonal screw / ~头 hexagon head

【六角形】hexagon: ~结构 hexagonal structure / ~手风琴 concertinist

【六开】【印】sixmo

【六路】six directions (above, below, front, back, right, and left)

【六面体】hexahedron: ~装置 cubic apparatus

【六亲】the six relations (father, mother, elder brother, younger brother, wife, children); one's kin

【六亲不认】disown all one's relatives and friends: 自从他升了官，就~了。He has disdained to recognize his relatives and friends since he was promoted.

【六亲无靠】cannot rely on any one of the six relationships — nobody to turn to; helpless: 这个可怜的孤儿~。The miserable orphan has no relatives or friends to depend on.

【六神】spirits in charge of the six vital organs — state of mind

【六神无主】all six vital organs failing to work properly — distracted; out of one's wits; at a loss what to do; in a state of utter stupefaction: 她一遇事就~。She is out of her wits whenever she meets some urgent things.

【六弦琴】【音】guitar

【六欲】【宗】six sensory pleasures — all kinds of human desires: 七情~ various human emotions and desires

【六指】① a six-fingered hand ② one whose hand

L

has six fingers

遛 ① saunter; stroll: ~大街 *saunter along the streets* ② walk by leading a domestic animal

【遛遛】take a walk: 我们准备到公园~。*We are ready to take a stroll in the park.*

【遛马】walk a horse

【遛鸟】go for a walk in a quiet place with a bird

【遛食】[方] walk after a meal (to help digestion)

【遛弯儿】[方] take a walk; go for a stroll: 咱们出去遛个弯儿吧。*Let's take a walk.*

馏 heat up; reheat: ~包子 *heat up buns by steaming*

see also liú

溜[1] ① swift current; turbulent flow ② [方] rapid; swift: 他走得很~。*He walks very fast.* ③ rain-water from the roof ④ eaves gutter: 水~ *roof gutter for running water* ⑤ row; line: 一~新楼房 *a row of new buildings* ⑥ surroundings; nearby place ⑦ [方] exercise: ~嗓子 *train one's voice*

溜[2] [方] fill (a crevice, fissure, etc.); plaster; paste: ~窗缝 *seal with paper the cracks around a window*

see also liū

【溜子】①【矿】scraper-trough conveyer ② [方] gang of bandits ③ [方] rapid flow of water; rapids

镏

see also liú

【镏子】[方] (finger) ring: 金~ *gold ring*

蹓 saunter; stroll; ~大街 *stroll around the streets*

see also liū

鹨 [方] pipit: 田~*paddy-field pipit*

lóng

龙 ①【动】dragon ② dragon as the symbol of the emperor; imperial: ~床 *imperial bed* / ~袍 *imperial robe* ③ anything shaped like a dragon or with the pattern of a dragon on it: ~车 *dragon float* ④【考】a huge extinct reptile: 恐~ *dinosaur* ⑤ [方] (of a bicycle rim) twisted ⑥ (Lóng) a surname

【龙船】dragon boat (a dragon-shaped racing boat)

【龙的传人】descendants of the dragon — the Chinese nation

【龙灯】dragon lantern

【龙飞凤舞】like dragons flying and phoenixes dancing — lively and vigorous flourishes in calligraphy

【龙凤呈祥】prosperity brought by the dragon and the phoenix; in extremely good fortune

【龙肝凤髓】the dragon's liver and the phoenix's marrow — great delicacies

【龙宫】the palace of the Dragon King

【龙骨】① a bird's sternum ②【药】fossil fragments ③ keel: ~板 *keel plate* / ~墩 *keelblocks* / ~木 *rising wood* / ~线 *keel-line* / ~翼板 *garboard*

【龙骨车】dragon-bone water lift; square-pallet chain-pump

【龙井】Dragon Well tea (a famous green tea produced in Hangzhou, Zhejiang Province)

【龙卷风】tornado: ~带 *tornado belt*

【龙马精神】the vigour of a dragon or horse — vigorous spirit of the aged

【龙门阵】spin a yarn; shoot the bull

【龙舌兰】【植】century plant; maguey; American aloe; agave: ~酒 *pulque*

【龙生九子】the dragon has nine sons and each of them is different from the others — brothers born of the same parents differ from each other

【龙生龙,凤生凤】dragons beget dragons, phoenixes beget phoenixes — like father, like son; like begets like

【龙潭虎穴】a dragon's pool and a tiger's den — a dangerous spot

【龙套】【戏】① costume with dragon designs, worn by groups of soldiers or attendants in traditional opera ② actor playing a walk-on part in traditional opera; utility man: ~角色 *walking-on*

【龙腾虎跃】dragons rising and tigers leaping — a scene of bustling activity

【龙头】① rap; faucet; tap; cock: 开~ *turn the cock on* / 关~ *turn the cock off* / 弹簧~ *spring faucet* ② [方] handlebar (of a bicycle) ③ leader: 大企业当~,带动中小企业 *bring along medium and small enterprises with large enterprises playing the leading role* ④ [方] chieftain; boss

【龙王】the Dragon King (the God of Rain in Chinese mythology): ~庙 *Temple of the Dragon King*

【龙虾】lobster trap; lobster pot; lobster; crayfish; prawn

【龙须草】【植】Chinese alpine rush

【龙须面】dragon whiskers noodles — long, thin noodles

【龙眼】【植】longan

【龙争虎斗】fighting between a tiger and a dragon — matched forces; a fierce struggle between well-matched opponents; a contest between giants

【龙钟】[书] decrepit; senile: 老态~ *senile*; *doddering*

【龙舟】dragon boat: ~赛 *dragon-boat race*

茏

【茏葱】verdant; luxuriantly green

珑 ① jade for asking rain ② [象] rumbling ③ bright

【珑璁】① [书] [象] the tinkling sound of metal striking against metal or of jade striking against jade ② verdant and green

【珑玲】[书] ① [象] the tinkling sound of metal striking against metal or of jade striking against jade ② bright; shining

砻 ① rice huller ② hull (rice with huller)

【砻糠】rice chaff

栊 [书] ① bar: 窗～ *window with bars* ② pen; cage

聋 deaf; hard of hearing: 全～ *as deaf as an adder (post, door; door-post)* /装～作哑 *pretend to be deaf and dumb; pretend to be ignorant of sth* / 老人～了一只耳朵。*The old man is deaf of one ear.* / 不肯倾听别人意见的人是最～的人。*None is so deaf as those that won't hear.*

【聋哑】deaf and dumb; deaf-mute: ～人 *deaf-mute* / ～学校 *school for deaf-mutes*

【聋子】a deaf person; the deaf

笼 ① cage; coop: 鸡～ *chicken coop* /鸟～ *birdcage* ② [旧] wooden framework for confining prisoners: 牢～ *cage (for prisoners)* ③ steamer: 蒸～*food steamer* ④ [方] put each hand in the opposite sleeve

see also lǒng

【笼火】[方] light a coal fire with firewood; make a fire

【笼屉】food steamer; utensil for steaming food

【笼头】headstall; halter

【笼型】cage model; cage type: ～结构 *cagelike structure* / ～式 *cage type formula*

【笼形】cage type: ～阀 *cage type valve* / ～结构 *cage structure* / ～天线 *cage antenna; birdcage antenna* / ～线圈 *basket coil; basket*

【笼养】cage culture

【笼中鸟】caged bird — person deprived of freedom

【笼子】cage; coop; basket; container

【笼嘴】muzzle (put over the mouth of an animal)

隆 ① grand; solemn ② prosperous; thriving: 这个店生意兴～。*This shop's business is brisk.* ③ deep; intense; profound: ～寒 *severely cold* ④ bulge; swell up: ～起 *swell or be swollen up* ⑤ (Lóng) a surname

【隆雕】grand relief; high relief

【隆冬】midwinter; the depth of winter: ～盛暑 *in the deep winter and high summer* / ～时节 *at the time of bitter winter*

【隆隆】[象] rumble; boom: 雷声～ *the rumble of thunder* /火车～地驶过。*The train rumbled past.*

【隆起】①【地】rise; bulge; hump; lifting: ～带 *uplifted zone* / ～区 *bulge region; rise region* ② swell; bulge; protrude: 她仔细挑选衣服,来掩盖～的肚子。*She chose her clothes carefully to hide the bulging belly.* /父亲～的肚子像一个大篮球。*Farther's belly protruded like a huge basketball.*

【隆情】deep or intense feeling: ～厚谊 *profound sentiments of friendship*

【隆盛】① abundant; flourishing; prosperous ② grand; magnificent: ～的仪式 *stately ceremony*

【隆重】grand; solemn; ceremonious: ～欢迎 *roll out the red carpet* / ～集会 *hold a grand rally* / ～礼仪 *an impressive ceremony* /他们受到～的欢迎。*A ceremonious welcome was was accorded to them.*

窿 [方] gallery

lǒng

垄 ① ridge: 麦～ *ridge in a wheat field* /在～上种玉米 *sow maize on ridges* ② raised path between fields ③ ridge-like things: 瓦～ *tile ridges*

【垄播】bed planting; sowing on ridge

【垄断】monopolize: 差别～ *discriminative monopoly* /工业～ *industrial monopoly* /国家～ *state monopoly* /私人～ *private monopoly* /外贸～ *foreign trade monopoly* /完全～ *absolute monopoly* /政府～ *public monopoly* /这家公司～了鞋业。*This company has monopolized the shoe industry.*

【垄沟】【农】field ditch; furrow: 开～ *make a furrow*

【垄灌】ridge irrigation

【垄作】【农】ridge culture

拢 ① close; shut: 她笑得合不～嘴。*She grinned from ear to ear.* ② approach; draw near; reach: 快～学校了 *will reach the school soon* ③ sum up; add up ④ gather up; hold together: 母亲把孩子～在怀里。*The mother held her child in her arms.* ⑤ comb (hair): 她出门前～了～头发。*She combed her hair before she went out.*

【拢岸】(of a ship) come alongside the shore

【拢共】altogether; all told; in all: 吃饭的～有十个人。*There were altogether 10 people at the dinner.*

【拢音】carry sound well

【拢账】[方] sum up the accounts

【拢子】a fine-toothed comb

【拢总】altogether; in all; in total; all told: 恐怕这里的人～不到一百。*I am afraid there are fewer than a hundred people here, all told.*

笼 ① cover; envelope: 夜色～住了大地。*The earth is gradually shrouded in dark.* ② bamboo trunk or case

see also lóng

【笼括】encompass; seize all

【笼络】win sb over by any means; draw over; rope in; entice; tempt; ensnare: ～人心 *cultivate popularity; try to win the people's support by hook or by crook; befriend sb*

【笼统】general; sweeping; in general terms: 这么说未免太～了。*That statement is rather too sweeping.* /那是一个非常～的评论。*That's a very sweeping statement.*

【笼罩】envelop; shroud: 晨雾～在湖面上。*The lake is shrouded in morning mist.* /静寂～了小村子。*Stillness envelops the small village.*

【笼子】[方] a large box or chest; trunk

lòng

弄 [方] lane; alley: 里～ *lane; alley*

see also nòng

【弄堂】[方] lane; alley; alleyway

lōu

搂 ① gather up; rake: ~干草 *rake up hay* ② hold up; tuck up: ~起袖子 *tuck up one's sleeves* ③ squeeze; extort:他这两年~了不少钱。*He has made a fortune these years.* ④[方] pull: ~扳机 *pull a trigger* ⑤[方] check:你有空把账~一~。*Check the accounts when you are free.*

see also lǒu

【搂头】[方] head-on; directly

【搂头盖脸】hit on the head and in the face:他拿起砖头~地向那个人扔过去。*He took a brick and threw it right in that person's face.*

瞜 [方] glance; look at:让我~一眼。*Let me have a look.*

lóu

娄 ①[方] weak; debilitated:他的身体可~啦。*He is in poor health.* ②[方] get bad because of overripeness; go bad:这个西瓜~了。*The watermelon has gotten bad.* ③ one of the twenty-eight constellations ④(Lóu) a surname

【娄子】[口] trouble; blunder: 桶~ *make a blunder; get into trouble*

喽

see also lou

【喽啰】① the rank and file of a band of outlaws ② underling; lackey

楼 ① a storied building:办公~ *office building* / 教学~ *classroom building* ② storey; floor: 八层~ *a eight-storey building* ③ superstructure: 城~ *city-gate tower* ④(used of certain kinds of shops) house; mansion:酒~ *restaurant* /青~ *brothel* ⑤(Lóu) a surname

【楼板】【建】floor; floorslab

【楼层】【建】storey; floor

【楼道】corridor; passageway

【楼房】a building of two or more storeys

【楼阁】① pavilion; tower ② multi-storey house:空中~ *castle in the air*

【楼面】【建】floor: ~面积 *floor area* / ~系统 *floor system*

【楼上】【建】upstairs: ~住的是一位退休老工人。*A retired worker lives upstairs.*

【楼台】①[方] balcony; gallery ②[书] a high building; tower:近水~先得月 *a waterfront building gets the moonlight first — enjoy the benefits of a favourable position*

【楼梯】stairs; staircase; stairway:上~ *ascend stairs* /下~ *descend stairs* / ~扶手 *stair railing* / ~间 *stair half* / ~栏杆 *stair railing* /这个~通往哪里? *Where does this staircase lead to?*

【楼厅】circle; balcony

【楼下】downstairs:他到~吃早饭。*He went downstairs to breakfast.*

【楼座】balcony

耧 an animal-drawn seed plough; drill

【耧播】【农】sow with a drill

【耧车】animal-drawn seed plough; drill barrow

蝼 【动】mole cricket

【蝼蛄】mole cricket

【蝼蚁】mole crickets and ants; nobodies; nonentities

lǒu

搂 ① hug; embrace:他~住他的女儿。*He hugged his daughter.* ②[量] circular length when one's hands meet in stretching out one's arms:一~粗的树 *a tree whose trunk one can get one's arms around*

see also lōu

【搂抱】hold in one's arms; hug; embrace; cuddle; nestle:我把小狗~在怀中。*I nestled the puppy in my arms.* /那对恋人又是亲吻又是~。*The lovers kissed and cuddled.*

篓 basket:纸~ *wastepaper basket*

【篓子】deep basket

lòu

陋 ① ugly; plain:丑~ *ugly* ② rough; coarse: 粗~ *crude; coarse* ③ narrow; humble; mean: ~巷 *a narrow (or mean) alley* ④ vulgar; corrupt ⑤(of knowledge) limited; shallow:浅~ *superficial; shallow* /孤~寡闻 *ignorant and ill-informed*

【陋规】objectionable practices

【陋识】superficial idea; shallow view

【陋室】a humble room; a cramped flat

【陋俗】undesirable customs

【陋习】corrupt customs; bad habits: ~难改。*Bad habits are not easily broken.*

镂 engrave; carve

【镂骨铭心】remember to the end of one's life; remember forever with gratitude

【镂花】ornamental engraving: ~雕刻 *through-carved work*

【镂刻】① carve; engrave ② impress deeply (on the mind); engrave:这段经历~在我的记忆里。*The experience was engraved into my memory.*

【镂空】pierced work; reticulated work; openwork; fretwork; hollow out

瘘 ①【医】fistula:胆~ *biliary fistula* /肛~ *anal fistula* /尿~ *urinary fistula* /食管~ *esophage-*

al fistula ②［书］scrofula

【瘘管】fistula; syrinx: ～试验 *fistula test*

漏 ① drip; leak; seep: 屋顶～出的水滴在地面上。*Water dripped off the ceiling onto the floor.* /空气慢慢地从气球中～走。*Air is leaking slowly from the balloon.* ②（of a container）leak: 锅～了。*The pot is leaking.* ③ water clock; clepsydra: 铜～ *copper water clock* ④ disclose; divulge: 走～风声 *leak out information* /这家公司拒绝透～他们的计划。*The company refused to divulge its plan.* /警方昨天透～了人质的身份。*The victim's identity was disclosed by police yesterday.* ⑤ leave out; be missing ⑥ miss; leave out: 遗～ *miss; leave out* /疏～ *negligence; slip*

【漏报】fail to declare; omit to report or declare（sth taxable）: ～应税货品 *evade declaration of dutiable goods*

【漏电】leak electricity: ～保护 *earth leakage protection* /～流 *leakage current; stray current* /～路径 *leakage path*

【漏洞】① leak: 房顶有～，雨正往里进。*There's a leak in the roof and the rain is coming in.* ② flaw; hole; loophole; weakness: 新的税法有许多～ *The new tax law has a lot of holes in it.* /这个理论的～在于它假设所有的人都有同样的想法。*The weakness in this theory is that it assumes all people share the same idea.*

【漏洞百出】full of loopholes; with gasping holes everywhere: 他对这件事的描述～。*His account of the matter won't hold water.*

【漏斗】funnel; hopper: ～进料 *hopper feed*

【漏斗车】hopper car; hopper wagon

【漏斗口】hopper opening

【漏风】① leak air; not be airtight: 窗户～。*There are some leaks in the window.* ② speak indistinctly through having one or more front teeth missing ③（of information, secrets）leak out

【漏光】leak light

【漏锅】colander

【漏壶】water clock; clepsydra; hourglass

【漏排】omit some words or passages in printing due to carelessness

【漏气】blow-by; blowing: ～阀 *steam leak-off valve* /～率 *leak rate*

【漏勺】strainer; colander

【漏税】evade payment of a tax; evade taxation

【漏脱】omit; leave out: 无一～ *with nothing left out*

【漏网】slip through the net; escape unpunished

【漏网之鱼】（as）fish escaping from the net;（as）a fish escaped through the seine

【漏泄】①（of water, light, etc.）leak out; filter ② let out; leak; divulge; give away: ～答案 *leak the answers*

【漏泄春光】send a secret message; send news secretly; give away a secret

【漏验】omission of examination

【漏夜】in the dead of night

【漏雨】leakage of rain

【漏子】①［口］funnel: 酒～ *wine funnel* ② flaw; hole; loophole: 由于收入所得税立法上的～，他只交了很少的税金。*He pays very little tax because of some loophole in income tax legislation.*

【漏嘴】let slip a remark; make a slip of the tongue

露

see also lù

【露丑】make a fool of oneself in public: 出乖～ *make an exhibition of oneself*

【露底】let the secret out; reveal the inside story: 她一不小心～了，说出了公司新产品的名字。*She inadvertently let slip the name of the company's new product.*

【露富】show one's wealth; show one's riches

【露脸】① become known（by doing sth）; be successful; shine ②［方］make an appearance; show up: 他都好几天没～了。*He hasn't shown up for several days.*

【露马脚】give oneself away; let the cat out of the bag: 很抱歉，我想我已经露出了马脚。*I'm very sorry; I think I have let the cat out of the bag.*

【露面】show one's face; make（or put in）an appearance; appear or reappear on public occasions: 那个流行歌手已经很久没在公众场合～了。*The popular singer hasn't appeared on public occasions for quite a long time.*

【露苗】（of seedlings）emerge; sprout

【露怯】［方］display one's ignorance; make a fool of oneself

【露头】① show one's head ② appear; emerge: 太阳刚～，我们就起床了。*The sun had hardly appeared when we got up.*

【露馅儿】let the cat out of the bag; give the game away; spill the beans; let slip; blow the gaff: 你和他谈话时是不要提到他的生日，否则就～了。*Don't mention his birthday when you talk to him, or you'll give the game away.* /她让我们的全部计划～了。*She has blown the gaff on all our plans.*

【露相】［方］show one's true colours

【露一手】make an exhibition of one's abilities or skills; show off: 一有机会他总会～ *He seizes every opportunity to show off.*

lou

喽 ① used after a verb to refer to an anticipated or envisaged action: 我吃～饭就走。*I'll go as soon as I've eaten.* ② used at the end or in the middle of a sentence to attract attention: 水开～。*Look, the water is boiling.*

see also lóu

lū

撸 ①［方］strip: 她～起袖子开始干活儿。*She rolled up her sleeves and began to work.* ② discharge; dismiss: 校长～掉了他的秘书职务。*The president dismissed him from his post as secretary.* ③ blame; rebuke:她因为经常迟到被老板～了一顿。*She was blamed by her boss for being late often.*

【撸子】[方] a small pistol

噜

【噜苏】[方] long-winded; wordy

lú

卢 (Lú) a surname

【卢比】rupee (a currency used in India and some other South Asian countries)

【卢布】rouble; ruble

【卢浮宫】Louvre (museum and art gallery in Paris that used to be the chief palace of French kings)

芦 ①【植】reed ② (Lú) a surname

【芦荡】reed marshes

【芦花】reed catkins

【芦荟】【植】barbados aloe; aloes

【芦苇】【植】reed; ditch reed: ～荡 *reed marshes*

【芦席】reed mat

【芦莺】reed warbler

庐[1] hut; cottage: 茅～ *thatched cottage*

庐[2] (Lú) a surname

【庐山真面目】the true face of Mt. Lu — the real appearance of a person or thing; one's true character; one's true features

【庐舍】[书] house; farmhouse

垆[1] black earth: ～土 *black soil*

垆[2] an adobe table in an ancient wineshop; wineshop; 当～ *keep a wineshop*; *serve in a wineshop*

【垆坶】[地]loam: ～土 *loamy soil*

【垆埴】[书] black clay; dark clay

炉 ① stove; furnace: 煤气～ *gas stove* / 煤油～ *kerosene stove* ② [量] used of what is made or contained in a furnace, stove or oven: 一～钢 *a heat of steel*

【炉壁】furnace wall; oven wall

【炉灰】stove ash; breeze

【炉火】stove fire; furnace fire

【炉火纯青】the stove fire (for making pills of immortality) begins to glow a pure blue — attain high degree of perfection; high degree of technical or professional proficiency: 他的书法达到了～的地步。*He attained perfection in calligraphy.* / 这些～的摄影作品很了不起。*The technical perfection of these photographs is outstanding.*

【炉门】fire door; furnace door; opening of a stove

【炉身】stack; furnace shaft; furnace stack

【炉室】oven chamber

【炉台】stove top

【炉膛】the chamber of a stove or furnace

【炉套】boiler clothing; furnace jacket

【炉体】furnace body; furnace stack

【炉条】fire bars; grate

【炉瓦】tile

【炉灶】kitchen range; cooking range: 另起～ *make a new start*

【炉渣】slag; cinder: ～水泥 *slag cement* / ～砖 *cinder brick*

【炉子】stove; oven; furnace

鸬

【鸬鹚】cormorant

颅 【生理】cranium; skull

【颅盖】braincap

【颅骨】cranial bones; skull

【颅腔】cranial cavity

lǔ

卤 ① bittern: 点～水 *dribble bittern* ②【化】halogen ③ stew in soy sauce: ～蛋 *spiced corned egg* ④ thick gravy: 打～面 *noodles served with thick gravy* ⑤ *thick infusion*: 茶～儿 *strong tea*

【卤菜】pot-stewed meat or fowl

【卤化】【化】halogenate

【卤化物】【化】halide; haloid

【卤鸡】pot-stewed chicken

【卤水】① bittern ② brine: ～湖 *brine lake*

【卤素】【化】halogen

【卤味】pot-stewed fowl, meat, etc. served cold

【卤制】stew in soy sauce

【卤质】alkali (found in soils)

虏 ① capture; take prisoner ② captive: 俘～ *captive*; *prisoner of war* (*P. O. W.*) ③ [古] slave ④ [书] enemy

【虏获】① capture (men and arms) ② men and arms captured: 她被出卖后被敌人～ *He was betrayed and then captured by the enemy.*

掳 capture; ransack

【掳掠】pillage; loot: 房子被盗贼～一空。*The house has been ransacked by robbers.* / 在暴乱中他的商店被闯入并遭～。*His store was broken into and looted during the riot.*

鲁[1] ① stupid; dull ② rude; rough

鲁[2] (Lǔ) ① another name for Shandong Province ② a surname

【鲁钝】dull-witted; obtuse; stupid

【鲁莽】crude and rash; rash; impulsive; hotheaded; impetuous; hasty; without a second thought: 对待思想上的毛病绝不能采取～的态度。*In treating an ideological malady, one must never be crude.*

【鲁直】rash and blunt

橹[1] scull (at boat's stern)

橹[2] [书] big shield

lù

陆 ① land:大~ *continent; mainland* ② (Lù) a surname

【陆半球】【地】the continental hemisphere; the land hemisphere

【陆标】【航】landmark

【陆沉】(of land) submerged in the sea — (of territory) occupied by enemy troops

【陆地】dry land; land; terrace; earth: ~土壤 *terrestrial soil* /他们在~上旅行。*They travelled by land.*

【陆风】【气】land breeze

【陆海空三军】the army, navy and air force

【陆基】【地】continental rise

【陆架】continental shelf

【陆军】ground force; land force; army: ~飞机 *army aircraft*

【陆离】varicoloured:光怪~ *grotesque in shape and gaudy in colour*

【陆路】land route

【陆桥】land bridge

【陆禽】birds that can only fly a short distance

【陆上】land: ~车辆 *ground vehicle* / ~保险 *overland transportation cargo insurance*

【陆相】land facies; continental facies: ~沉积 *continental deposit; continental sediment*

【陆续】one after another; in succession:学生们~离开教室。*The students left the classroom one after another.*

【陆运】land transportation: ~提单 *inland bill of landing*

录 ① record; copy:抄~ *copy down* ② tape-record: ~磁带 *copy a tape* ③ use; hire:摘~ *make extracts* ④ register; record:目~ *catalogue* /语~ *a book of quotations*

【录播】recorded broadcast

【录放】record and play back

【录供】【律】take down a confession or testimony during an interrogation

【录取】enroll; recruit; admit: ~分数线 *minimum passing marks for admission* / ~名额 *number of enrollees* / ~通知书 *enrollment notification* /她被北京大学~了。*She is enrolled at Peking University.* /我们收到了你的学费支票后,~就算完成了。*Once we have received a cheque for the course fees your enrolment will be complete.*

【录像】to videotape; to video

【录像带】videotape:这个信息可以录在~上。*The information can be put on a videotape.*

【录像机】video recorder; videotape recorder; video

【录像片】video show; video film

【录音】sound-recording: ~报告 *tape-recorded speech* / ~车间 *film recording department* /机器正在~。*The machine is recording now.*

【录音带】magnetic tape; tape

【录音电话】answer machine; telegraphone; answer phone

【录音机】tape recorder; cassette recorder; recorder:我们经常在英语课上使用~。*A recorder is often used in our English class.*

【录音棚】sound-recording studio

【录音师】mixer; recordist

【录影】record a scene video

【录用】employ; take sb on the staff; hire:他们拒绝~一个从监狱出来的人。*They refused to employ a man who just came out of prison.* /这家公司因为没有~足够的女性员工而被起诉。*The company has been accused of not hiring enough women.*

【录制】record: ~唱片 *make a gramophone record*

赂 [书] ① send a gift; bribe ② (gift of) goods or money

鹿 ①【动】deer:白唇~ *white-lipped deer* /公~ *stag; buck* /梅 ~ *spotted deer* /母~ *doe* /豚~ *hog deer* /小~ *fawn* /~群 *a drove of deer* ② (Lù) a surname

【鹿皮】deerskin: ~裤 *buckskin* / ~鞋 *moccasin*

【鹿茸】【中医】pilose antler (of a young stag)

【鹿死谁手】at whose hand will the deer die — who will win the prize; who will gain supremacy:究竟~,现在还不好说。*It's hard to predict now who will win at last.*

【鹿特丹】Rotterdam, principal port of the Netherlands

【鹿砦】【军】abatis

绿

see also lǜ

【绿林】the greenwood — brigands; outlaws: ~好汉 *forest outlaws; swordsmen of the Robin Hood type; a hero of the bush; greenwood heroes*

禄 ① official's salary in feudal times:俸~ *official's salary* /高官厚~ *high position and handsome emolument* ② (Lù) a surname

【禄位】[书] official rank and salary

碌 ① mediocre:庸~ *commonplace and unambitious* ② busy:忙 ~ *busy going about one's routine*

【碌碌】① mediocre; commonplace: ~无能 *devoid of ability; a commonplace kind of man with no ability to speak of* / ~无为 *a miserable person with no accomplishment of any kind to his credit* ② busy with miscellaneous work: ~一生。*One has been bustling and hustling all his life.*

路 ① road; path:公~ *high road* /环形~ *belt road* / 条条大~通罗马。*All roads lead to Rome.* /沿着这条~走,你就会找到的。*Keep to the path and you cannot miss it.* ② distance; journey:远~ *long journey; long way* /祝你一~顺风! *A pleasant journey to you!* ③ means; way:活~ *means of subsistence; way out* ④logic; method:思~ *train of thought* ⑤ region; distance:外~货

nonlocal goods ⑥ route：八～军 *the Eighth Route Army* ⑦ sort；class；grade；两～货 *two different sorts of goods* /他们俩是一～人。*These two are the same sort.* ⑧（Lù）a surname

【路边】wayside；road side

【路标】① road sign ②【军】route marking；route sign

【路不拾遗】no one picks up and pockets anything lost on the road — a society where the moral standard is high

【路程】distance travelled；journey：漫长而艰难的～ *a long and difficult journey*

【路单】① travel permit；pass ② waybill

【路灯】street lamp；road lamp

【路堤】embankment

【路段】a section of a highway or railway：～养路工 *lengthman*

【路费】traveling expenses

【路风】work style of the railway workers；quality of the railway service

【路规】railway rules and regulations

【路轨】①（steel）rail ② track

【路过】pass by or through（a place）

【路徽】railway logo

【路基】roadbed；bed：～排水 *subgrade drainage*

【路祭】[旧] offer sacrifices by the roadside as a funeral procession passes

【路劫】highway robbery；holdup；mugging

【路警】railway police

【路径】① route；way ② method；ways and means

【路考】（of driving，etc.）road test

【路口】crossing；intersection：十字～ *crossroads*

【路况】road condition；traffic

【路面】road surface；pavement：～电车 *streetcar* / ～平整机 *smoother*

【路牌】street nameplate

【路人】passerby；stranger

【路上】① one the road ② on the way：她在回家的～遇到抢劫。*She was robbed while en route for her home.*

【路数】① way；approach ② a movement in martial arts ③ exact details；inside story

【路条】travel permit；pass

【路透社】Reuters；Reuter's News Agency

【路途】① road；way ② way；journey：到海滨～有多远？*How long is the journey to the coast?*

【路线】① route；itinerary：旅行的～ *the route of a journey* ② line

【路遥知马力】distance tests a horse's stamina — judge people after a period of time

【路遥知马力，日久见人心】a long journey proves the stamina of a horse and the passage of time tells the true from the false

【路障】roadblock；barricade

【路子】① social connections；pull：他通过～找到了工作。*He got a job through pull.* ② way；approach；means；method：据说他用不正当的～赢得了那次选举。*It's said that he used dishonest means to achieve victory in the election.*

辘

【辘轳】well-pulley；windlass；winch

【辘辘】[象] the rumbling sound of cart rumbled down the road：饥肠～ *one's stomach growling from hunger* /车轮的～声 *the rumbling of car wheels*

戮[1] kill；slay：杀～*slaughter*

戮[2] [书] join；unite

【戮力同心】make concerted efforts；join hands；work together in a coalition

璐 [书] beautiful jade

簏 ① [书] woven bamboo trunk ② [方] bamboo basket

【簏簌】[书] hanging down；drooping

鹭 【动】egret；heron

【鹭鸶】【动】egret

麓 [书] the foot of a hill or a mountain：山～ *the foot of a mountain*

露[1] ① dew：蜜～ *honey dew* /致死～ *dew of death* ② syrup；fruit juice：杏仁～ *essence of almond*

露[2] ① in the open；outdoors：风餐～宿 *eat in the wind an sleep in the dew — be exposed to inclement weather on a journey* ② reveal；betray；show：吐～ *reveal*；*confide* /揭～丑陋面目 *expose the ugly features of the enemy*

see also lòu

【露布】① [书] war proclamation ② [书] announcement of victory in an army ③ [古] an unsealed imperial edict or memorial to the throne ④ [方] notice；bulletin；playbill

【露点】dew point

【露骨】thinly veiled；undisguised；barefaced

【露酒】alcoholic drink mixed with fruit juice

【露水】[口] dew：～夫妻 *illicit lovers* /～之欢 *temporal joy*

【露宿】sleep in the open

【露台】[方] flat roof（for drying clothes，etc.）

【露天】① in the open（air）；outdoors：～放映 *outdoor film projection* / ～开采 *opencut*；*openwork* / ～游泳池 *outdoor swimming pool*；*open air swimming pool* ② open-air；open：～码放 *open-air storage*

【露头角】（of a young person）beginning to show ability or talent；budding：初～的运动员 *a budding sportsman* /参加会议的，有不少是新～的作家。*Present at the meeting were a number of new writers.*

【露营】①【军】camp（out）；encamp；bivouac ② go camping

【露珠】dewdrop：～晶莹 *sparkling dewdrops* / 叶子上的～*drops of dew on the leaves*

L

lǘ

驴【动】donkey; ass: 赶~ *drive a donkey* / 骑~ *ride a donkey* / ~车 *donkey cart*

【驴唇不对马嘴】donkeys' lips don't match horses' jaws — incongruous; irrelevant; be beside the point; have no bearing on; be neither here nor there: 她在会上提到的几个事实~。*She mentioned several impertinent facts in the meeting.* / 她提出的问题和讨论~。*She raised a question extraneous to the discussion.*

【驴打滚】①［旧］snowballing usury ② pastry made of steamed glutinous millet flour mixed with sugar

【驴肝肺】donkey's liver and lungs — ill intent: 他把我的好心当成~。*He took my goodwill for ill intent.*

【驴年马月】year of the donkey and month of the horse — a time that will never come

【驴皮影】［方］leather-silhouette show; shadow play

【驴子】［方］donkey; ass

闾 ①［书］the gate of an alley ②［书］neighbourhood: 乡~ *home village* ③ (in ancient times) a village of twenty-five families ④ (Lǘ) a surname

【闾里】［书］native village; hometown

【闾巷】［书］alley; lane; alleyway

【闾阎】［书］① a neighbourhood of commoners ② the common people

【闾左】［书］a poor neighbourhood; poor people

lǚ

吕 (Lǚ) a surname

【吕剧】【戏】Lǚ opera (of Shandong Province)

【吕宋烟】Luzon cigar; cigar

侣 associate; companion: 伴~ *partner*; *companion*

捋 smooth out with the fingers; stroke: ~胡子 *stroke one's beard*

see also luō

旅[1] stay away from home; travel: 商~ *company of traveling merchants*

旅[2] ①【军】brigade: 混成~ *a mixed brigade* ② force; troops: 劲~ *powerful army* ③［书］jointly; together

【旅伴】traveling companion; fellow traveller

【旅程】route; itinerary; journey

【旅次】［书］a stopping place on one's journey

【旅店】inn

【旅费】traveling expenses; viaticum

【旅馆】inn; hotel: ~登记簿 *hotel register* / 这家湖畔~可接待 20 多位客人。*The lakeside hotel can accommodate 20 guests.*

【旅进旅退】always follow the steps of others, forward or backward — have no views of one's own; do as others do

【旅居】live away from one's native place; sojourn

【旅客】hotel guest; traveler; passenger: 出境~ *outgoing passenger*; *outward passenger* / 单身~ *individual passenger* / 入境~ *incoming passenger*; *inward passenger* / 中转~ *transfer passenger* / ~名单 *manifest*; *passenger list* / ~席 *passenger seat* / 机场上挤满了因航班延迟而滞留的~。*The airport was jammed with passengers from delayed flights.*

【旅社】hotel

【旅舍】［书］hotel

【旅途】journey; trip: ~劳顿 *the hardships of travel*; *weariness from a tiring journey* / 明早我就要踏上~。*I am going on a trip tomorrow morning.* / 祝你~愉快。*I wish you a good journey*; *a pleasant journey to you!*

【旅行】travel; journey; tour: ~结婚 *marriage trip* / ~团 *touring party* / ~支票 *traveller's check* / ~指南 *guidebook* / 大家都说~能让人增长见识。*All said that travel broadens the mind.*

【旅行包】gripsack; travelling bag

【旅行车】beach wagon; estate car; station wagon

【旅行社】travel service; travel agency

【旅行癖】wanderlust: 他不可抑制的~让他在一年内游览了 8 个国家。*His incurable wanderlust pushed him to travel 8 countries within a year.*

【旅行社】travel agency; travel bureau

【旅游】tour; tourism: ~车 *touring car*; *tourist bus* / ~胜地 *tourist attraction* / ~事业 *tourist industries*

【旅长】【军】brigade commander

铝【化】aluminium (Al): ~箔 *aluminum foil* / ~锅 *aluminium pot* / ~矿 *aluminium ore* / ~铜 *aluminum bronze*

【铝合金】【冶】aluminium alloy: ~结构 *aluminium alloy structure*

【铝土】【化】alumina: ~矿床 *bauxite deposit*

稆 (of grains) self-grow: ~生 *naturally-grown*; *self-sown*

偻[1]［书］crooked

偻[2]［书］directly; at once: 不能~指 *unable to point out straight away*

屡 repeatedly; time and again: ~建奇功 *have repeatedly established wonderful merits* / ~劝不听 *keep one's own course in spite of repeated admonitions* / ~遭不测。*A succession of misfortunes has befallen someone.*

【屡次】time and again; repeatedly; frequently: 她~为妇女解放问题疾呼。*She has repeatedly spoken out for woman liberation.*

【屡次三番】again and again; over and over again; many times; time after time: 她~地告诉我:"那是不可能的。" *Again and again I was told by her "it's impossible".* / 我~提醒他要谨慎。*I' ve reminded him over and over again that he should be cautious.*

【屡见不鲜】common occurrence; nothing new; be

everywhere; be ten a penny; be a dime a dozen: 20年前没有听说过手机,但是现在已经～了。*No one had even heard of mobile phones twenty years ago, but now they're everywhere.* / 如今在北京,经理是～的。*These days managers are a dime a dozen in Beijing.*

【屡教不改】refuse to mend one's ways despite repeated disciplinary action

【屡屡】time and again; repeatedly; frequently: 我被～拒绝。*I've been rejected hundreds of times.* / 她总是说要和丈夫离婚,却又～回到他的身边。*She always says she's going to divorce her husband, but time and time again she goes back to him.*

【屡试不爽】put to repeated tests and proved right; time-tested; have the same result every time

缕 ① thread: 千丝万～ *countless ties* ② in fine detail: 条分～析 *analyze point by point* ③ [量] strand; lock: 一～头发 *a lock of hair*

【缕陈】[书] state in detail (esp. when reporting to a superior)

【缕缕】continuously

【缕述】state in detail; give all the details; elaborate; go into details (or particulars): 简单一点。如果你逐条～,人们会感到厌烦。*Be brief; if you go into too much detail people will get bored.*

【缕析】make a detailed analysis

履 ① shoe: 草～ *sandals* / 削足适～ *cut one's foot to fit in the shoe — accommodate oneself to existing conditions without any logic* ② walk on; step on: 如～薄冰 *on thin ice; tread as on eggs — act with extreme caution* ③ footstep: 步～轻盈 *walk with easy step* ④fulfill; carry out: ～约 *keep an appointment*

【履带】【机】caterpillar tread; track

【履历】one's personal record (of education, work experience, and attainments); antecedents

【履险如夷】go over a dangerous pass as if walking on level ground — cope with a crisis without difficulty

【履行】perform; fulfil; carry out: ～公务 *perform one's official duty* / ～合同 *comply with an agreement; fulfil a contract; performance of a contract* / ～义务 *carry out obligations; comply with one's duty*

【履约】[书] keep a promise, pledge, agreement, appointment, etc.

lǜ

律 ① law; rule; regulation: 纪～ *discipline* ② [书] restrain; discipline; keep under control ③ (Lǜ) a surname

【律己】discipline oneself; self-restraint: 严以～ *be strict with oneself* / ～正人。*He who laughs at a hunchback should walk very straight himself.*

【律例】laws, statutes and precedents

【律令】laws and decrees; laws and statutes

【律师】lawyer; barrister; solicitor; attorney: ～费 *a retaining fee* / ～事务所 *law office; law firms* / ～协会 *bar association*

【律条】① legal articles or clauses; law ② norm; standard: 做人的～ *code of conduct*

虑 ① consider; ponder: 考～ *consider; ponder* / 深谋远～ *foresight; providence; be deeply thoughtful and farseeing* / 疑～ *misgivings* ② concern; worry: 过～ *worry too much*

率 rate; ratio; proportion: 汇～ *rate of exchange* / 利～ *interest rates* / 利用～ *utility ratio; use ratio* / 人口增长～ *the rate of population growth* / 税～ *a tax rate* / 死亡～ *death rate; the mortality rate* / 通货膨胀～ *the rate of inflation*
see also shuài

绿 green: 她穿着～衣服。*She was dressed in green.*
see also lù

【绿茶】green tea

【绿灯】① green light (a traffic signal) ② green light —permission to go ahead: 你不能给欺骗行为开～。*You shouldn't give the green light to cheating.*

【绿地】greenery patches(in a town or city)

【绿豆】mung bean; green gram

【绿豆糕】a pastry made of mung bean flour

【绿豆芽】mungbean sprout

【绿矾】【化】copperas; green-vitriol

【绿肥】green manure

【绿化】make (a place) green by planting trees, flowers, etc.; afforest: ～城市 *plant trees in the city* / ～祖国 *green our motherland* / ～带 *seeded strip* / ～面积 *green space (or area)*

【绿卡】green card — permanent residence permit

【绿帽子】a green hat or turban — the state of being a cuckold

【绿茸茸】lush green

【绿色和平组织】Greenpeace, an international environmental organization

【绿色食品】green food

【绿色植物】green plants

【绿细胞】【植】green cell

【绿阴】shade (of a tree)

【绿茵】green meadow: ～场 *football field*

【绿莹莹】glittering green

【绿油油】fresh green; shiny green

【绿玉】【矿】emerald; aquamarine; beryl; greenstone

【绿藻】【植】green alga

【绿洲】oasis

氯 【化】chlorine (Cl): 电解～ *electrolytic chlorine* / 活性～ *active chlorine* / 液态～ *liquid chlorine* / 游离～ *free chlorine*

【氯仿】【化】chloroform: ～中毒 *chloroformism*

【氯化铵】【化】ammonium chloride

【氯化钾】【化】potassium chloride

【氯化钠】【化】sodium chloride

【氯霉素】【药】chloramphenicol; chloromycetin

【氯气】【化】chlorine

【氯酸】【化】chloric acid: ～钙 *calcium chlorate* /

～钾 *potassium chlorate* / ～铁 *ferric chlorate*

滤 filter; strain: 过～ *filter* / ～除杂质 *filter out impurities*

【滤杯】filter bowl

【滤饼】filter cake; residue

【滤波】filtering; filtration; smoothing: ～电路 *filter circuit* / ～技术 *filter technique* / ～效应 *filter effect*

【滤层】filtering layer

【滤光】filtering: ～玻璃 *filter glass* / ～镜 *light filter; ray filter*

【滤器】filter; colander; sifter

【滤网】sieve; strainer mesh; screen

【滤液】filtrate

【滤渣】residue; filter residue

【滤纸】【化】filter paper: ～反应 *filter paper test*

【滤嘴】filter; tip

luán

峦 ［书］mountains or hill in a range

【峦嶂】screen-shaped mountain peaks

孪 ［书］twin

【孪生】twin: ～姐妹 *twin sisters*

【孪生面】【物】twinning plane

栾 ①【植】goldenrain tree ②（Luán）a surname

挛 contraction: 痉～ *spasm; convulsions*

【挛缩】contracture

鸾 a mythical bird like the phoenix

【鸾俦】［书］husband and wife: 永结～ *forge ties of abiding matrimony*

【鸾凤】a married couple: ～和鸣 *a happily married couple; have a happy married life*

銮 ① a small tinkling bell on a horse or a carriage ② an imperial carriage

【銮驾】imperial carriage

【銮铃】tinkling bells on a carriage

【銮舆】imperial carriage

luǎn

卵 ① egg; spawn; ovum: 成熟～ *mature egg* / 端黄～ *telolecithal ovum* / 全裂～ *holoblastic ovum* / 受精～ *fertilized egg; zygote* ②【生理】zygote ③［方］testicles; penis

【卵白】white of an egg; albumen

【卵巢】【生理】ovary; ovarium: ～囊肿 *ovarian cyst* / ～切除 *oophorectomize* / ～萎缩 *ovarian atrophy* / ～炎 *oophoritis; ovaritis* / ～周期 *ovarian cycle*

【卵黄】yolk; vitellus: ～蛋白 *livetin* / ～激素 *vitellogenic hormone* / ～素 *vitellin*

【卵块】egg mass

【卵磷脂】【生化】lecithin; ovolecithin

【卵泡】egg follicle; ovarian follicle: ～细胞 *follicle cell*

【卵生】【动】oviparity: ～动物 *ovipara*

【卵石】cobble; pebble; shingle

【卵细胞】egg cell; ovum

【卵学】oology

【卵翼】［贬］cover with wings as in brooding; shield: 在帝国主义的～下 *under the aegis of imperialism; shielded by imperialism*

【卵子】（luǎnzǐ）【生理】ovum; egg

【卵子】（luǎnzi）［方］testicles; penis

luàn

乱 ① in a mess; disordered: ～混 *in confusion* / 杂～ *messy; disorderly* / ～作一团（*become*）*a scene of chaos; in great confusion* ② riot; turmoil; upheaval: 兵～ *turmoil caused by war* / 叛～ *armed rebellion* ③ confuse; mix up: 以假～真 *mix the false with the genuine* ④ unsettled; disturbed: 心烦意～ *be vexed; be perturbed* ⑤ arbitrary; random: ～吃 *feed oneself with all kinds of food* / ～跑 *run all over the place* / ～说一通 *make irresponsible remarks* ⑥ promiscuous sexual behaviour: 淫～ *pruriency; sexual promiscuous*

【乱兵】mutinous soldiers; totally undisciplined troops

【乱臣】treacherous minister; rebellious subject: ～贼子 *treacherous ministers and traitors; rebels and traitors*

【乱点鸳鸯】cause an exchange of partners by mistake between two couples engaged to marry

【乱纷纷】disorderly; confused; chaotic

【乱坟岗】unmarked common graves; unmarked burial-mounds

【乱哄哄】in noisy disorder; in a hubbub; tumultuous; in an uproar; 屋里～的，你要大点声说话。*The room is rather noisy, and you've got to raise your voice*

【乱乎】［口］in confusion; in chaos

【乱离】be separated by war; be rendered homeless by war

【乱伦】commit incest

【乱民】［旧］rebellious people; rebels

【乱蓬蓬】disheveled; tangled; jumbled; untidy; unkempt; scruffy; bedraggled: 你没有必要仔细整理这个男孩儿的衣服，五分钟内他就又会变得～的。*There's no point dressing the boy up; he looks untidy within five minutes.* / 她知道自己的外表～的。*She was conscious of her rather disheveled appearance.*

【乱七八糟】at sixes and sevens; disorder; in an awful mess; be clutter up: 整个房间～。*The room is totally out of order.* / 这些抽屉简直是～，我从来也找不到我想找的东西。*The drawers are so untidy, and I can never find what I'm looking for.* / 房间里～地堆着旧家具。*The room was cluttered*

up with old furniture.
【乱石】stone riprap
【乱世】troubled times; turbulent days: ~英雄 *heroes in a troubled time* / ~出英雄。*Heroes emerge in troubled times.*
【乱摊子】the hopeless mess:他们给我留下了这个~。*They left me the mess.*
【乱弹琴】act or talk like a fool; talk nonsense
【乱套】[方] muddle things up; turn things upside down
【乱腾腾】confused; upset
【乱腾】confused; disorderly; restless
【乱营】[方] be thrown into confusion; be in disarray
【乱葬岗子】unmarked common graves; unmarked burial-mounds
【乱糟糟】① chaotic; in a mess: 屋子里~的。*The room is in a mess.* / 他的桌子上~地堆满旧杂志。*His desk is cluttered up with old magazines.* ② confused; perturbed
【乱真】(of fakes) look genuine:他做的木头汽车可以~了。*His wooden car looks very much like genuine one.*
【乱子】disturbance; trouble; disorder

lüě

掠 [方] take up
see also lüè

lüè

掠 ① plunder; pillage; sack:士兵们劫~宫殿,找寻珠宝。*The soldiers ransacked the palace for hidden treasure.* ② brush past; skim over; pass quickly:燕子~檐而过。*The swallow swept past the eaves.* / 她的形象忽然~过我的脑海。*Suddenly her image crossed my mind.* ③ [书] lash with stick or whip
see also lüě
【掠夺】plunder; rob; pillage
【掠取】seize; grab; plunder:早期的殖民者常常~当地居民的财物。*Early colonists often took grab of local people's properties.*
【掠视】look around; sweep one's eyes over
【掠影】panorama; bird's-eye view

略[1] ① brief; simple: 粗~ *rough*; *sketchy* / ~备水酒 *have prepared some ordinary wine* / ~表寸心 *just to show one's gratitude* ② summary; outline: 要~ *outline*; *summary* ③ omit; leave out:从~ *be omitted* / ~而不谈 *omit to mention*; *skip over without reference to*

略[2] strategy; scheme:策~ *tactics* / 方~ *overall plan*

略[3] seize; capture:侵~ *invade* / ~池攻城 *seize territories and attack cities*; *capture territory*

【略称】abbreviation; shortened form
【略略】slightly; briefly
【略去】omit; leave out; miss out:我的文章中的采访部分在发表时被~了一些。*Some parts of the interview which I had included in my article were omitted from the published one.* / 他向我们做了解释,但~了一些细节。*He explained it to us but left some details out.*
【略胜一筹】be a stroke; be one upon sb; just a little better; slightly better
【略识之无】know only a few simple characters
【略图】sketch map; sketch
【略微】slightly; a little; somewhat; not much; not very; a tiny bit:这对双胞胎一模一样,只是其中一个比另一个~高一点儿。*The twins are exactly the same, except one is slightly taller than the other.* / 这座城市~有一些变化,但基本上还是我记忆中的样子。*The city had changed a little but basically it was just as I remembered it.* /我对你的健康~有些担心。*I'm a tiny bit worried about your health.*
【略为】slightly; a little; somewhat:文章~短了些,但很精彩。*The article is a little bit short but it is wonderful.*
【略语】abbreviation; shortening
【略知皮毛】have only a superficial understanding (of a subject)
【略知一二】have a smattering of; have a rough idea; know a little; just a little

lūn

抡 ① swing; brandish ② throw; fling
*see also*lún

lún

仑 [书] method; logical sequence

伦 ① ethics; human relations ② order; logical sequence: 语无~次 *incoherent* ③ match; peer: 不~不类 *nondescript* ④ (Lún) a surname
【伦巴】rumba (a dance)
【伦比】[书] rival; equal: 无与~ *unrivaled*; *peerless*
【伦常】feudal order of importance or seniority in human relationships
【伦敦】London, capital and largest city of the United Kingdom
【伦次】coherence; logical sequence
【伦理】ethics; moral principles: 经济~ *economic ethics* / 医学~ *medical ethics* / 不同阶级有不同的~。*Different classes have different ethics.*
【伦理学】ethics
【伦琴】【物】rontgen (or roentgen): ~射线 *roentgen-rays*

抡 [书] choose; select: ~材 *select suitable material*
see also lūn

沦 ① sink: 沉~ *perish; be submerged* ② fall; decline: ~为历史的罪人 *become a person condemned by history*

【沦落】① be homeless: ~街头 *be driven into the street — become a beggar* ② [书] fall low; come down in the world; be reduced to poverty ③ sink; fall; degenerate: ~风尘 *fall into professions not socially respectable*

【沦没】① sink; submerge ② (of humans) die

【沦丧】be lost; be ruined: 国土的~使我们深感痛心。*The lost of land made us deeply hurt.*

【沦亡】① (of a country) be annexed (or conquered) ② be lost; be depraved

【沦陷】① (of territory, etc.) be occupied by the enemy; fall into enemy hands: ~区 *enemy-occupied area* ② [书] submerge; inundate; flood; drown

纶 ① [书] black silk ribbon; silk tassel ② [书] fishing line ③ synthetic fibre: 涤~ *polyester fibre*
see also guān

轮 ① wheel: 备用~ *replacement wheel* / 从动~ *driven wheel; engaged wheel* / 飞~ *cog free wheel* / 风~ *wind wheel* / 负重~ *bogie wheel* / 滑~ *pulley wheel* / 棘~ *paw wheel* / 介~ *intermediate wheel* / 离合~ *castle wheel* / 链~ *sprocket wheel* / 磨~ *abrasive wheel* / 水~ *a water wheel* / 凸~ *cam wheel* / 尾~ *rear furrow wheel* / 蜗~ *worm wheel* / 叶~ *vane wheel* / 主动~ *driving wheel* ② something like a wheel: 年~ *annual ring* ③ steamboat; steamer: 江~ *river steamer* / 游~ *pleasure-boat* ④ take turns; do by turns: 下次~到我发言了。*It's my turn to give a presentation next time.* ⑤ [量]: 一~明月 *a bright moon* / 一~新的谈判 *a new round of negotiation*

【轮班】in shifts; in relays; in rotation: 几组人~工作。*Groups of men worked in relays.*

【轮埠】harbour; port

【轮尺】caliper scale

【轮船】steamer; steamship; steamboat: 远洋~ *ocean steamer*

【轮次】① in turn; by turns: ~上场 *enter the field one after another* / 她们~做不同的工作。*They took it in turns to do different jobs.* ② number of turns or rounds

【轮渡】(steam) ferry

【轮番】take turns: ~轰炸 *bomb in waves*

【轮辐】spoke; arm of wheel

【轮换】rotate; take turns: 如果你们都想使用这台电脑,就只好~了。*If you all want to use the computer, you'll have to take it in turns.*

【轮回】①【宗】Buddhism samsara; transmigration ② coming again and again

【轮机】① turbine ② motorship engine; engine

【轮奸】(of two or more men) rape a woman in turn; gang-rape

【轮空】【体】bye: 抽签~ *draw a bye*

【轮廓】① outline; contour; rough sketch: ~线 *outline; borderline; curve* / 我看到了大楼朦胧的~。*I saw the shadowy outline of the building.* ② general or rough idea: 我对这件事只知道一个大致的~。*I have got only a rough idea of the matter.*

【轮流】take turns; do sth in turn; share; alternate: 我和她~开车,这样就不会太疲倦。*She and I shared the driving so it wasn't as tiring.*

【轮牧】rotation grazing: ~场 *rotated pasture*

【轮生】【植】verticillate: ~叶序 *whorled phyllotaxy*

【轮胎】tyre: 飞机~ *aircraft tire* / 废~ *scrap tire* / 抗滑~ *adhesion-type tire* / 空气~ *air tire* / 实心~ *solid tire* / 战斗用~ *combat tire* / 重载~ *heavy duty tire* / 小心,你的~有一只快没气了。*Be careful; one of your tyres is down.*

【轮辋】rim (of a wheel); felly; wheel rim

【轮位】wheel order

【轮休】① (of land) lie fallow in rotation ② have holidays by turns; rotate days off; stagger holidays

【轮训】training in rotation

【轮养】alternate culture; rotary culture

【轮椅】wheelchair

【轮值】on duty by turns

【轮周】circumference of wheel: ~速度 *rim velocity*

【轮轴】【物】wheel and axle; wheel shaft: ~轴承 *wheel bearing*

【轮转】① rotate ② [方] take turns

【轮子】wheel

【轮作】【农】crop rotation; succession of crops: ~周期 *period of crop-rotation; rotation cycle*

lǔn

埨 [方] ridge (in a field)

lùn

论 ① discuss; comment: 辩~ *debate* / 评~ *comment; discuss* ② view; opinion; statement: 社~ *editorial* / 舆~ *public opinions* ③ theory; doctrine: 宿命~ *fatalism* / 相对~ *the theory of relativity* ④ mention; regard; 相提并~ *mention in the same breath* ⑤ weigh; decide on: 按质~价 *determine the price according to the quality* ⑥ by; in terms of: ~件 *by the pieces* / ~天 *by the day* / ~交情 *in terms of friendship* ⑦ (Lùn) a surname

【论辩】argue; debate; have a row: 这夫妻俩的所有时间似乎都在~。*The couple seems to spend all their time arguing.* / 我不想挑起~,所以我保持沉默。*I didn't want to start an argument, so I kept quiet.*

【论处】decide on sb's punishment; punish: 依法~

be punished according to law
【论敌】one's opponent in a debate
【论点】argument; thesis: 老一套的 ~ *stock argument* / 提出 ~ *put forward an argument* / 鲜明的 ~ *clear-cut argument* / 正确的 ~ *valid argument* / 我认为他的~是站不住脚的。*I don't think his argument hold water.*
【论调】[贬] view; argument; opinion; theory: 我反对这种~。*I object to such views.* / 他持一种荒谬的~。*He holds an absurd view.*
【论断】inference; judgement; thesis; conclusion: 在得出~之前,这个建议应该仔细推敲。*The proposal will need to be examined thoroughly before any conclusions can be reached.* / 她的行动总是建立在合理的~之上。*Her actions are always based on sound judgement.*
【论功行赏】award people according to their contributions
【论据】grounds of argument; argument: 纯理论性~ *academic argument* / 法律~ *legal argument* / 建设性~ *constructive argument* / 他能提供无可辩驳的~。*He can offer an indisputable argument.*
【论理】① reason (with sb): 我们想和她~,但是她根本不听。*We have tried to reason with her, but she just won't listen to us.* ② normally; as things should be: ~他该向我道歉。*He should have apologized to me.* ③ logic: 合乎~ *be logical* ③ reason things out
【论理学】[旧] logic
【论难】argue; wrangle; debate
【论述】discuss; expound
【论说】① exposition and argumentation ② [口] normally; as things should be
【论坛】forum; tribune: 读者~ *readers' forum* / 教育~ *education forum* / 人民~ *tribune of the people* / 这份报纸的读者来信栏是公众意见的~。*The letters column of this newspaper is a forum for public argument.*
【论题】【逻】proposition
【论文】thesis; dissertation; treatise; paper: 毕业~ *graduation thesis* / 学位~ *dissertation* / 答辩~ *oral defence of one's dissertation* / 他发表了一篇关于时事的~。*He published a paper on current events.*
【论战】polemic; debate: 他们之间展开了一场激烈的~。*A drastic debate was launched between them.*
【论争】argument; debate; controversy: 关于如何惩治罪犯的~ *a debate about the punishment for criminals*
【论证】① demonstration; proof ② expound and prove ③ grounds of argument: ~方式 *way of argumentation* / ~过程 *process of argumentation*
【论著】treatise; work; book: 他的~既多又很有分量。*Great and many are his works.*
【论资排辈】arrange in order of seniority; give top priority to seniority in promotion
【论罪】decide on the nature of the guilt

luō

捋 rub sth long: ~树叶 *strip a twig of its leaves*
see also lǚ
【捋虎须】stroke a tiger's whiskers — take great risks
啰
see also luo
【啰唆】① talkative; long-winded; wordy; chatty: 多年没见,她还是那个很~而又热心肠的女人。*We hadn't seen each other for years but she was still the same chatty, warm-hearted woman.* ② fussy; overelaborate; troublesome

luó

罗[1] ① a net for catching birds: 天~地网 *tight encirclement* ② catch birds with a net: 门可~雀。*It's possible to catch sparrows on the doorstep — having few visitors.* ③ collect; gather together: 网~人才 *enlist able persons* ④ spread out: 星~棋布 *spread out like stars in the sky or chessmen on the chessboard* ⑤ sieve; sifter ⑥ sift; sieve ⑦ a kind of silk gauze: ~衣 *garment of thin silk* / ~扇 *silk gauze fan* ⑧ (Luó) a surname
罗[2] [量] (translation) gross; twelve dozen
【罗布】spread out (over a large area); scatter
【罗浮宫】the Louvre Museum in Paris, France
【罗锅】(luóguō) ① humpbacked; hunchbacked ② humpback: 他是个~。*He is a humpback.* ③ arched: ~桥 *arch bridge*
【罗锅】(luóguo) bend (the back); arch
【罗汉】【宗】arhat
【罗汉豆】[方] broad bean
【罗汉果】【植】mangosteen
【罗经】【航】compass: 磁~ *magnetic compass*
【罗掘】[书] try very hard to raise money: 四处~ *run about to raise money*
【罗口】【纺】rib cuff or rib collar; rib top (of socks)
【罗列】① spread out; set out ② enumerate; cite: 光~事实还不够,必须加以分析。*It's not enough just to enumerate the facts; you've got to analyse them, too.*
【罗马】Rome, the capital and largest city of Italy: 条条大路通~。*All roads lead to Rome.*
【罗曼蒂克】romantic (a transliteration)
【罗盘】compass: 磁针~ *magnetic needle compass* / 感应~ *induction compass* / 告警~ *alarm compass* / 航空~ *aircraft compass* / 天文~ *celestial compass* / 小~ *baby compass* / 星象~ *astro compass*

L

/ 袖珍 ~ *pocket compass* / 夜光 ~ *luminous compass* / ~ 的盘面 *compass card* / ~ 上的方位 *the points of the compass*

【罗圈】the round frame of a sieve

【罗圈腿】① bowlegs; bandy legs ② bowlegged; bandy-legged

【罗宋汤】borsch; bortsch

【罗网】net; trap: 自投 ~ *step right into the trap*

【罗纹】rib; whorl (in fingerprint): ~ 被面 *rib backing* / ~ 机 *rib knitting machine*

【罗帐】curtain of thin silk

【罗织】[书] frame up: ~ 罪名 *frame a case against sb; cook up charges*

【罗致】enlist the services of; secure sb in one's employment; collect; gather together: ~ 人才 *recruit talents*

萝 【植】trailing plants: 藤 ~ *Chinese wistaria*

【萝卜】radish; turnip: 青 ~ *green turnip* / 一捆 ~ *a bunch of radishes* / ~ 泡菜 *pickled radish* / ~ 青菜,各有所爱。*It's difficult to cater for all tastes.*

逻 patrol: 巡 ~ *patrol*

【逻辑】logic: 辩证 ~ *dialectical logic* / 并行 ~ *parallel logic* / 传统 ~ *traditional logic* / 动态 ~ *dynamic logic* / 分布 ~ *distributed logic* / 符号 ~ *symbolic logic* / 负 ~ *negative logic* / 概率 ~ *probabilistic logic* / 归纳 ~ *inductive logic* / 静态 ~ *static logic*

锣 【音】gong: 鸣 ~ *strike the gong*

【锣鼓】① gong and drum: ~ 喧天 *a deafening sound of gongs and drums* ②【音】traditional percussion instruments

箩 bamboo basket

【箩筐】a large bamboo or wicker basket

骡 【动】mule

【骡子】mule

螺 ①【动】spiral shell; snail: 田 ~ *field snail* / 海 *conch* ② whorl (in fingerprint)

【螺钿】mother-of-pearl inlay

【螺钉】screw; nut bolt; mechanical bolt: 木 ~ *wood screw* / ~ 帽 *cap of screw*

【螺号】conch; shell trumpet

【螺桨】【机】propeller

【螺距】【机】(screw) pitch; thread pitch: ~ 角 angle of pitch / ~ 偏差 *screw-pitch deviation*

【螺孔】screw hole

【螺帽】blind nut

【螺母】【机】(screw) nut: ~ 车床 *nut lathe* / ~ 护圈 *nut retainer*

【螺栓】【机】(screw) bolt: ~ 头 *bolt head; gib head*

【螺丝】[口] screw

【螺丝扳手】monkey spanner

【螺丝板】jam plate

【螺丝刀】screwdriver

【螺丝钉】[口] screw

【螺丝扣】[口] thread (of a screw)

【螺丝母】[口] (screw) nut

【螺丝起子】screwdriver

【螺丝钳】clamp

【螺丝眼】screw eye

【螺丝钻】auger; tommy bar

【螺纹】① whorl (in fingerprint) ②【机】thread (of a screw): ~ 管 *screwed conduit*

【螺线】spiral; spire; helix: ~ 管 *solenoid coil* / ~ 轨道 *spiral orbit*

【螺旋】① spiral; helix ②【物】screw

【螺旋扳手】screw wrench

【螺旋桨】【机】(screw) propeller; screw: ~ 叶 *propeller blade; airscrew blade*/ ~ 轴 *airscrew shaft; propeller shaft*

【螺旋桨飞机】propeller-driven aircraft

【螺旋梯】cockle stairs

【螺旋体】【微】spirochaeta: ~ 感染 *spirochaete infection*

luǒ

裸 naked; exposed; bare: 赤 ~ *naked*

【裸奔】streaking

【裸地】bare area; bare land

【裸露】uncovered; exposed: 他们的上身都 ~ 着。*They were all bare from the waist up.*

【裸露癖】【心】exhibitionism

【裸视】①see with one's naked eyes ② naked eyesight; unaided eyesight

【裸体】naked; nude: ~ 表演 *nudie* / ~ 画 *a painting of a nude* / ~ 模特 *nude model*

【裸线】bare wire; naked wire

【裸眼】naked eye

【裸子植物】gymnosperm

luò

洛 (Luò) a surname

【洛阳纸贵】paper becomes expensive in Luoyang — a good work makes people copy them

骆 ①【动】a white horse with a black mane (in ancient books) ② (Luò) a surname

【骆驼】camel: ~ 毛 *camel hair* / ~ 绒 *camel hair cloth*

络 ① net-like thing: 丝瓜 ~ *loofah* ②【中医】subsidiary channels in the human body: 脉 ~ *a general name for arteries and veins* ③ enmesh ④ twine; wind: ~ 丝 *winding silk*
see also lào

【络腮胡子】whiskers; full beard

【络纱】【纺】doff

【络绎】[书] in an endless stream; proceed in a steady stream

【络绎不绝】in an endless stream

硌 ［书］large stone (on mountains)

落 ①fall; drop:坠~ *go down*; *pitch*; *fall* / ~太阳~山了。*The sun is set.* ② set; go down:降~ *descend*; *land* ③ lower; let down ④ decline; come down:沦~ *be reduced to poverty*; *fall low* ⑤ fall behind ⑥ stay; leave behind:不~痕迹 *leave no trace* / 小鸟在树上~着。*The small bird is resting on a tree.* ⑦ whereabouts:下~ *whereabouts* ⑧ settlement; residence:村~ *small village* ⑨ fall into; belong to:今天政权~在人民手里了。*The political power has passed into the hands of the people nowadays.* ⑩ get; gain: ~不是 *get blamed in the end* / ~埋怨 *take the blame* ⑪ write; put down
see also là;lào

【落榜】fail in an entrance examination; fail as a candidate:听到高考~的消息,她大哭起来。*She cried into tears at the news of failing the college entrance examinations.*

【落笔】put pen to paper; start to write or draw: ~之前一定要三思。*Think before you start to write.*

【落标】fail to win a bid (or election, competition, etc.):她~了。*She failed in the election.*

【落泊】［书］① be in dire straits; be down and out ② casual; unconventional: ~潦倒 *be in dire status*; *be down and out*

【落槽】① low water ②［方］family fortunes declining ③ fit a tenon into a mortise ④［方］settled; at rest

【落草】① take to the greenwood; take to the heather; become an outlaw: ~为寇 *become an outlaw*; *turn to banditry* ②［方］(of a baby) be born

【落差】①【水】drop in elevation (between) two points in a stream ② gap:心理~ *psychological gap*

【落潮】ebb tide

【落尘】dust fall

【落成】(of a building, etc.) be completed: ~典礼 *inauguration ceremony*

【落得】get; end in:搞阴谋诡计的人,必然~可耻的下场。*Plotters come to no good end.*

【落地】① fall to the ground ② (of a baby) be born

【落地窗】French window

【落地灯】floor lamp; standard lamp

【落地生根】①【植】air plant; life plant ② take root; strike root

【落地式】console mode; floor type

【落第】fail in an imperial examination

【落点】①【体】placement (of a ball) ②【军】point of fall

【落发】take the tonsure — become a Buddhist monk or nun: ~为僧 *shave one's head and become a Buddhist monk*

【落黑】［方］get dark

【落后】① be behind; fall behind; lag behind; drop behind:他故意~,想要抽根儿烟。*He deliberately lagged behind so he could have a cigarette.* ② behind schedule ③ backward; behind the times: ~就要挨打 *lag behind and be vulnerable to attacks* / 他们技术上很~。*They were backward in technique.* / 英国在这一领域日渐~于竞争对手。*Britain is increasingly dropping behind her competitors in this field.*

【落户】① settle:她终于在北京~。*She finally settled down in Beijing.* ② register for residence

【落花流水】like fallen flowers carried away by flowing water — in a sorry plight; beat sb into fits

【落花生】peanut; groundnut

【落花有意,流水无情】while the dropping flowers pine for love, the heartless brook babbles on — unrequited love

【落荒】［旧］take to the wilds — be defeated and flee the battlefield; take to flight: ~而逃 *be defeated and flee the battlefield*; *take to filght*; *turn tail and run*

【落基山】the Rocky Mountains

【落价】fall in price; drop in price

【落脚】stay (for a time); stop over; put up:天色已晚,找个地方~吧。*It's getting dark now*; *Let's take a stay somewhere for the night.*

【落井下石】drop stones on someone who has fallen into a well — hit a person when he's down

【落空】come to nothing; fail; fall through

【落款】① write the names of the sender and the recipient on a painting, gift or letter; inscribe (a gift, etc.) ② names of the sender and the recipient written on a painting, letter or gift; inscription (on a gift, etc.)

【落泪】shed tears; weep:听到他悲惨的故事,我~了。*I was in tears at his miserable story.*

【落铃】shedding of cotton bolls

【落落】① natural and graceful: ~大方 *unrestrained and at ease* ② standoffish; aloof; unsociable

【落马】① fall off a horse ②［喻］be defeated

【落寞】lonely; desolate:一个人坐在咖啡馆里,她觉得很~。*Sitting alone in the pub, she felt desolated.*

【落墨】put pen to paper; start to write or draw

【落幕】the curtain falls; lower the curtain:当戏剧~时,观众的掌声经久不息。*When the play came to an end, the audience applauded again and again.*

【落难】meet with misfortune; be in distress:他们成为~兄弟。*They became brothers in misfortune.*

【落魄】［书］① in dire straits; down and out; come down in the world ② casual; unconventional

【落日】the setting sun

【落生】［方］(of a baby) be born

【落实】① practicable; workable ② fix (or decide) in advance; ascertain; make sure ③［方］feel at ease:她心里总是不~。*She just can't set her mind at ease.*

【落市】［方］(of fruits, vegetables) be out of season ② (of market) close

【落水】fall into water — fall into evil ways

【落水狗】dog in the water — a bad person who is

down

【落汤鸡】(of a person) like a drenched chicken; like a drowned rat; soaked through; drenched and bedraggled

【落体】【物】falling body

【落网】(of a criminal) fall into the net — be caught; be captured

【落伍】① fall behind the ranks; straggle; drop behind; drop out ② outdated; outmoded; out of date; behind the times; backward; unfashionable:我想我真是有点～了,手提电脑是什么东西呢? *I'm afraid I'm a bit behind the times — what exactly is a luggable computer?* /他认为如今为了家庭而放弃工作已经～了。*He thinks that it's unfashionable these days to give up one' job for one's family.*

【落选】fail to be chosen (or elected); lose an election

【落叶归根】falling leaves settle on their roots — a person residing elsewhere finally returns to his native land

【落叶树】deciduous tree

【落英】[书] ① fallen or falling flowers: ～缤纷。*Here and there are fallen flowers.* ② new-bloomed flowers

【落账】make an entry in an account book; enter sth in an account

【落照】the glow of the setting sun

【落座】take a seat(in restaurants, theatres, etc.)

摞 ① pile up; stack up ② [量] stack; pile:一～书 *a stack of books*

luo

啰 used at the end of a sentence to indicate affirmation:你去就好～。*Ok, you go there.* *see also* luō

M

m̄

姆

【姆妈】[方] ① mum; mother ② aunt, a respectful address for an elderly married woman: 李家～ *Aunt Li*

ḿ

呒 [方] have not; nothing

【呒啥】[方] nothing; have not; it doesn't matter; that's all right: ～关系。*It doesn't matter.* /～听头。*There's nothing worth listening.*

呣 why; what: ～,真的吗? *Oh, really?* /～,你刚才说什么? *Eh? What did you say just now?*
see also m̀

m̀

呣 yes; um-hum: ～,我知道了。*Yes, I see.*
see also ḿ

mā

妈 ① ma; mum; mummy; mother: 我～是医生。*My mother is a doctor.* ② the address for a married woman of the elder generation: 舅～ *maternal aunt (wife of mother's brother)* /姑～ *paternal aunt (father's sister)* ③ [旧] a middle-aged or old maidservant: 老～子 *maid* /王～ *maid Wang*

【妈妈】① [口] ma; mum; mom; mummy; mommy; mother: "你在做什么呀,～?" "*What are you doing, mom?*" /她是这两个男孩儿的～。*She was the mother of these two boys.* /爸爸～们也被邀请参加聚会。*The mums and dads are invited to the party, too.* /亲爱的,过来坐到～膝盖上。*Dear, come and sit on mummy's knee.* ② [方] aunt, a respectful form of address for an elderly woman

【妈祖】Mazu, a goddess of the sea in Chinese legendary: ～庙 *Mazu temple*

孖 [方] couple; twin

【孖仔】[方] boy twins

抹 ① rub; wipe; mop: ～地板 *mop the floor* /吃饭前要～桌子。*Wipe the table clean before dinner.* ② slip sth off: 他把帽子～了下来。*He took off his hat.* /突然间她的脸就～下来了。*She became serious suddenly.*
see also mǒ; mò

【抹布】wiper; rag; duster: 她用一块～擦地板。*She washed the floor with a rag.*

【抹搭】[方] (of eyelids) half close; droop: 她的眼皮悲哀地～下来。*Her eyelids drooped sadly.*

【抹脸】[口] put on a stern expression; be strict with sb all of a sudden: 我对他抹不下脸来。*I cannot show anger to him.* /一看到我,她立刻抹下脸来。*She put on a stern expression at the sight of me.*

【抹澡】[方] rub oneself down with a wet towel

蚂
see also mǎ; mà

【蚂螂】[方] dragonfly

麻
see also má

【麻麻黑】[方] (it is) dusk; (it) becomes dark: 天～了,我看不太清东西。*Dusk was gathering and I couldn't see things clearly.*

【麻麻亮】[方] (it is) just dawning; at daybreak; at dawn; bright and early; at the crack of dawn: 天～的时候我就醒了。*I woke up at dawn.* /天刚～,我就起床去钓鱼。*I got up at the crack of dawn to go fishing.*

摩
see also mó

【摩挲】caress; stroke gently: 母亲～我的手。*Mother caressed my hand.* /他～婴儿的头。*He stroked the baby's head.*

má

吗 [方] what: 干～? *What for?* /～事? *What's the matter?* /你说～? *What did you say?*
see also mǎ; ma

麻[1] ①【植】a general term for hemp, flax, etc.: 蓖～ *castor-oil plant* /剑～ *sisal hemp* /

生～ *raw hemp* /亚～ *fiber flax* /洋～ *ambary hemp* ② fibre of fibrous crops：心乱如～ *with one's mind like entangled hemp — be utterly confused* /我的裙子是～的。*My dress is linen.* ③ sesame：～糖 *sesame candy*

麻[2] ① rough；coarse：墙面是～的。*The surface of the wall is rough.* ② pitted；spotted：～脸 *a pockmarked face* ③ spotted；dotted；speckled ④（Má）a surname

麻[3] numb；tingle：冻～的脚趾 *toes numb with cold* /手臂发～ *feel pins and needles in an arm* /坐的时间长了，我的腿发～。*I have a tingle in my legs after sitting for a long time.*
see also mā

【麻包】gunnybag；gunnysack；sack：这个老农把马铃薯装进了～。*The old peasant put the potatoes into sacks.*

【麻痹】①【医】paralysis；palsy：功能性～ *functional paralysis* /进行性～ *progressive paralysis* /免疫～ *immunologic paralysis* /脑性～ *cerebral palsy* /神经～ *neural paralysis* /消瘦性～ *wasting palsy* /小儿～（脊髓灰质炎）*infantile paralysis* /延髓性～ *bulbar paralysis* /中枢性～ *central paralysis* ② benumb；lull；blunt；lower one's guard；slacken one's vigilance：～人们的意志 *lull people's will* /即使没有情况发生，我们也不能～大意。*Though there is nothing unusual, we can't be off our guard.*

【麻布】① gunny（cloth）；sackcloth；burlap ② linen

【麻袋】gunnybag；gunnysack；burlap sack：西红柿被小心地装进了～。*The tomatoes were put into sacks carefully.*

【麻刀】【建】hemp；hair：～灰泥 *hemp-fibred plaster*

【麻捣】［书］hemp；hair

【麻点】mottling；pock；burn；spot：镜子上的小～ *pits on a mirror* /当她怀孕的时候，她脸上有～。*She had spots on her face when she was pregnant.* /这只母鸡灰色带白～。*This hen is gray with white speckles.*

【麻豆腐】［方］cooking-starch residue

【麻烦】① troublesome；cumbersome；inconvenient：把这些东西送回商店要求退换太～了。*It's more trouble than it is worth to take it back to the shop and ask for a replacement.* /他们发现窗子被打破后一定会有～。*There's sure to be a fuss when they find the window's broken.* /你看，有一辆车可真～，保险，税款，维修等等接踵而来。*It's really troublesome to have a car, you know — insurance, tax, repairs, etc. come one after another.* ② put sb to trouble；trouble sb；bother：找～ *look for trouble；ask for trouble；find fault with* /这点小事不要去～他了。*Don't bother him with such trifles.* /我能～你关上门吗？*Can I trouble you to shut the door?* /对不起，给你添～了。*Sorry to have troubled you so much.*

【麻纺】the spinning of jute, hemp or flax；bast fibre spinning

【麻沸散】【药】Chinese anesthesia drugs

【麻风】【医】leprosy；lepra

【麻秆】hemp stalk

【麻花】① fried dough twist ②［方］（of clothes）wearing thin；worn out；threadbare：一件～的外衣 *a threadbare coat* /看，你的衣服袖子都～了。*Look, your coat has worn thin at the sleeves.*

【麻将】mahjong：打～ *play mahjong* /～牌 *mahjong pieces；mahjong tiles*

【麻酱】sesame paste

【麻秸】stalk of skinned bast-fibre plant

【麻经儿】string of raw flax

【麻雷子】a kind of fire-crackers

【麻利】① deft；nimble；quick and neat；dexterous；一位～的技工 *a dexterous mechanic* /她手脚～。*She is keen and quick in her work.* /她能～地使用这些工具。*She is handy with the tools.* ②［方］quickly；fast：他～地跑了出来。*He ran out quickly.*

【麻脸】a pockmarked face：那个～的守门人很蛮横。*The warder with a pockmarked face is really overbearing.*

【麻面】pitted ski；pitting surface；skim：～磨损 *pitted wear*

【麻木】① numb；have no feeling；can't feel anything：我的脚冻得～了。*My feet were benumbed with cold.* /自从那次事故以后，他的腰部以下就～无知觉了。*Since that accident, he can't feel anything below the waist.* ② apathetic；blunt；insensitive；unmoved：他的孤立使他对别人的感情～不觉。*His isolation has made him blunt about the feelings of others.* /她躺在地板上痛苦地呻吟。她的女儿却～地看着她。*She was on the floor groaning in pain；her daughter looked on unmoved.* /有时候，医生对于病人的感觉是～的。*Doctors are sometimes insensitive to their patients' feelings.*

【麻木不仁】apathetic；insensitive；dead to all feeling；inert；be callous to sth；listless；torpid：他对谴责～。*He is callous to rebuke.* /我的老板是如此～，他从来不会注意到我已经精疲力竭了。*My boss is so insensitive that he never notices when I am exhausted.*

【麻钱】［方］coin；copper

【麻雀】（house）sparrow：公～ *cock sparrow*

【麻雀虽小，五脏俱全】Small as the sparrow is, it possesses all its internal organs — small but complete：这套公寓可谓～。*The apartment is small, but it possesses all necessary objects.*

【麻雀战】sparrow warfare, a form of guerrilla warfare

【麻纱】① yarn of ramie, flax, etc. ② cambric；haircords；dimity

【麻绳】rope made of hemp, flax, etc.

【麻省理工学院】（US）Massachusetts Institute of Technology（MIT）

【麻石】chiseled stone

【麻酥酥】slightly numb; tingling:他把绳子系在我的手腕上,不一会儿我就感觉~的。*He tightened the rope around my wrists and my hands felt slightly numb soon.*
【麻线】flaxen thread; linen thread
【麻药】anaesthetic
【麻衣】hemp mourning garment
【麻油】sesame oil; teel oil
【麻疹】【医】measles:出血性~ *hemorrhagic measles* /~疫苗 *measles vaccine* /~是一种传染性疾病。*Measles is a contagious disease.*
【麻织品】fabrics of flax, hemp, etc.; linen fabrics
【麻子】① pockmarks ② a person with a pockmarked face
【麻醉】①【医】anaesthesia; narcosis:局部~ *local anaesthesia* /全身~ *general anaesthesia* /药物~ *drug anaesthesia* /中药~ *herbal anaesthesia* ② corrupt (sb's mind); poison:这些书籍~了他的思想。*These books poisoned his minds.*
【麻醉剂】anaesthetic; narcotic: ~瘾 *narcomania* / ~中毒 *lit*
【麻醉精神疗法】【医】narcosynthesis
【麻醉疗法】narcosis therapy; sleep therapy
【麻醉品】narcotic; drug: ~管制 *drug control* /可卡因是一种~。*Cocaine is a rind of anaesthetic.*
【麻醉师】anaesthetist
【麻醉学】anaesthesiology; narcology
【麻醉药】narcotic; anaesthetic: ~瘾 *letheomania* / ~委员会 *Commission on Narcotic Drugs*

mǎ

马 ①【动】horse:母~ *mare* /小~ *pony* /战~ *battle steed* /~跑得很快。*Horses run very fast.* /好~无须加鞭。*A good horse should be seldom spurred.* ② horse, one of the pieces in Chinese chess ③ big: ~勺 *ladle* /~蜂 *hornet*; *wasp* ④ (Mǎ) a surname
【马鞍】saddle; bridge piece: ~形 *shape of a saddle*; *U-shape*
【马鞍革】saddle leather
【马鞍石】saddle pebble
【马帮】a train of horses carrying goods; caravan
【马宝】【药】bezoar of a horse; dust ball
【马背】horseback:这个小男孩骑在~上。*The boy is on horseback.*
【马背岭】【地】horseback
【马鞭】horsewhip
【马表】【体】stopwatch
【马不停蹄】a horse galloping — without a moment's respite; make a hurried journey without stop; nonstop:我们~地赶到目的地。*We rushed nonstop to the destination.*
【马槽】manger; horse feed:狗占~ *dog in the manger* /马被拴在~上。*The horse is tied up to the manger.*
【马车】① (horse-drawn) carriage; wagon ② cart
【马车夫】groom; cart driver
【马齿徒增】just like a horse increasing its number of teeth with the years — grow old with nothing accomplished; outgrow one's usefulness:这些年我不过是~。*These years, I just became old without anything achieved to show others.*
【马齿苋】【植】purslane
【马齿玉米】dent corn
【马刺】spur
【马褡子】saddle-bag
【马达】motor: ~效应 *motor effect* /~润滑油 *motor-oil* /车里变冷的时候,就让~开动一会儿。*When it gets cold in the bus, let the motor run a while.*
【马达加斯加】Madagascar: ~人 *Madagascan* /~语 *Malagasy (language)*
【马大哈】① careless; forgetful; negligent; slack:一个~乘客把钱包忘在了出租车上。*A forgetful passenger left his wallet on the taxi.* /你的作文里都是拼写错误。以后不要再这么~了。*Your composition is full of spelling mistakes; try not to be so careless in future.* ② a careless person; scatterbrain:这孩子是个~。*He is a careless child.*
【马刀】sabre
【马到成功】be victorious the moment the battle steeds arrive — win success immediately upon arrival; win instant success:祝你~。*I wish you a speedy success.*
【马道】parkway; bridle path
【马德堡半球】【物】Magdeburg hemispheres
【马德里】Madrid, capital of Spain: ~人 *Madrilenian*
【马灯】barn lantern; lantern
【马镫】stirrup
【马店】an inn for drivers of carts and caravans
【马丁炉】Martin furnace; open hearth furnace
【马丁·路德·金】Martin Luther King, Jr. (1929-1968), American Black Baptist minister and civil rights leader
【马豆】horsebean
【马队】① a train of horses carrying goods; caravan ② a contingent of mounted troops; cavalry
【马耳东风】in at one ear and out the other; pay no attention to what one said:我的话对他来说就是~。*He doesn't care what I've said at all.*
【马耳他】Malta: ~人 *Maltese* /~语 *Maltese language* /~热 *Malta fever*
【马尔代夫】Maldives: ~人 *Maldivian*
【马尔萨斯】Malthus (Thomas Robert, 1766-1834), British economist who wrote *An Essay on the Principle of Population* (1798): ~人口论 *Malthusian Theory of Population*
【马贩子】horse dealer
【马房】stable; livery stable
【马粪】horseshit
【马粪纸】strawboard
【马蜂】hornet; wasp
【马蜂窝】hornet's nest:捅~ *stir up a hornet's nest — cause a great trouble*

【马竿】blindman's stick; white stick
【马革裹尸】be wrapped in horsehide after death — die on the battlefield; die in the last ditch
【马褂】mandarin jacket (worn over a gown)
【马倌】groom; stableman
【马海毛】【纺】mohair
【马海绵】horse sponge
【马号】① public stable ② long-tubed bugle
【马赫】① Mach (Ernst, 1838-1916), Austrian physicist and philosopher ②【物】Mach: ~数 *Mach number*
【马赫表】Machmeter
【马赫主义】【哲】Machism
【马后炮】belated action or advice; belated effort; action that is too late: 放 ~ *make a belated effort* / 你说的这些都是~。*What you've said is definitely too late.*
【马虎】careless; perfunctory; casual; skimpy; palter with sth; slack: 工作 ~ *be careless in one's work* / ~了事 *finish the work perfunctorily* / 她把精力集中在照顾孩子上,其他的事都~了事。*She concentrated on looking after her child, skimping other matters.*
【马蟥】【动】horseleech
【马鸡】【动】eared pheasant
【马甲】① armour for a horse ②[方] a sleeveless garment; vest
【马架】① small shack ② triangular wooden rack for carrying things on one's back
【马鲛】【动】sierra
【马嚼子】bar bit
【马脚】sth that gives the game away: 露出 ~ *show the cloven hoof — give oneself away*
【马厩】stable
【马驹子】[口] foal; colt or filly
【马具】horse gear: ~革 *skirting leather*
【马可·波罗】Marco Polo (1254-1324), an Italian traveler who stayed in China from 1275 to 1292
【马可福音】【宗】The Gospel According to Mark
【马可尼】Marconi (Guglielmo, 1874-1937), Italian physicist: ~天线 *Marconi antenna*
【马克】① mark (German monetary unit) ② markka: 芬兰 ~ *Finnish markka*
【马克思】Karl Marx (1818-1883), German proletarian revolutionist, economist and philosopher
【马克思列宁主义】Marxism-Leninism: ~者 *Marxist-Leninist*
【马克思主义】Marxism: ~辩证法 *Marxist dialectic* / ~基本原理 *basic principles of Marxism* / ~哲学 *Marxist philosophy* / ~者 *Marxist* / ~政治经济学 *Marxist political economy*
【马克·吐温】Mark Twain (1835-1910), American writer
【马裤】riding breeches; overall
【马拉松】①【体】Marathon: ~赛跑 *marathon race* / ~游泳 *a swimming marathon* ② marathon; lengthy: 长达六小时的 ~ 式的讲话 *a marathon speech of 6 hours*
【马来半岛】the Malay Peninsula
【马来群岛】the Malay Archipelago
【马来西亚】Malaysia: ~人 *Malaysian*
【马来语】Malay (language)
【马兰花】【植】flagger
【马里】Mali: ~人 *Malian*
【马里兰】Maryland: ~人 *Marylander*
【马里亚纳海沟】Mariana Trench
【马里亚纳群岛】Mariana Islands
【马力】【物】horsepower (h. p.): 开足 ~ *at full speed* / 有效 ~ *effective horsepower*
【马利亚】Virgin Mary: 圣母 ~ *Holy Mary*
【马列主义】Marxism-Leninism
【马林鱼】【动】marlin
【马铃薯】potato: 烤 ~ *baked potato* / ~片 *potato chips*
【马铃薯淀粉】potato flour
【马六甲海峡】the Strait of Malacca
【马龙胆】horse gentian
【马笼头】head harness; bridle
【马鹿】【动】red deer; wapiti
【马路】road; street; avenue: 柏油 ~ *an asphalt street* / 逛 ~ *have a walk in the streets; do the block*
【马路消息】hearsay; gossip; speculation; talk; reports: 我们在席间互相交流 ~。*We exchanged gossip at dinner.* / 记者必须学会区分事实和 ~。*Journalist must learn to distinguish between fact and hearsay.*
【马路新闻】street-gossip; hearsay; rumour: 我离开镇子半年了,当我回来时急于听到最新的 ~。*I'd been out of town for half a year, and was eager to hear all the latest gossip when I came back.*
【马螺】【动】horse conch
【马骡】【动】mule
【马锣】small grass gong
【马马虎虎】① careless; casual; slack; lax; negligent; remiss: 我很惊讶她居然成了会计 — 她对待钱总是 ~。*I was surprised she got the job as an accountant — she's always been very careless with money.* / 工作中不要 ~。*Don't get slack at your work.* / 虽然她做家务 ~,却是一个关心备至的母亲。*Although rather lax in the routine of housekeeping she was a caring mother.* ② not very good; just passable; so-so: 我的英语水平也就 ~。*My English is just so-so.* / 她的历史知识 ~。*She has a passable knowledge of history.*
【马奶】mare's milk
【马尼拉】Manila, the capital and largest city of the Philippines
【马趴】fall on one's face: 摔了个大 ~ *fall flat on one's face*
【马皮】horsehide
【马匹】horses
【马屁精】[贬] adulator; bootlicker; sycophant; flatterer; ear banger: 国王被 ~ 包围得太久了。*The king has been surrounded by flatterers for too long.*

M

【马其顿】Macedonia; Macedon: ~共和国 *Republic of Macedonia*
【马其诺方程】Mathieu equation
【马其诺防线】Maginot Line
【马前卒】pawn; cat's-paw: 他是这场阴谋中的~。*He is a pawn in the scheme.*
【马枪】carbine; pistol
【马球】【体】polo: ~装 *polo coat* /~棍 *polo stick*
【马赛】Marseille, France's second largest city
【马赛进行曲】Marseillaise, national anthem of France
【马赛克】【建】mosaic: ~地板 *mosaic floor*
【马上】at once; immediately; straight away; right away: 我们~动手。*We'll start working straight away.* /他们到家后~打了电话。*They phoned immediately when they reached home.* /~停下来。*Stop it this instant.* /电话一响,她就~站了起来。*She was on her feet in a flash when the phone rang.*
【马勺】ladle
【马绍尔群岛】Marshall Islands
【马失前蹄】the horse stumbles — make a mistake by accident: 这个著名运动员在这场重大比赛的表演中~。*The famous athlete made a big mistake in his performance in such an important tournament.*
【马虱】horse louse
【马氏体】【冶】martensite: ~硬化 *martensitic hardening* /~铸铁 *martensitic cast iron*
【马首是瞻】take the head of sb's horse as guide — follow sb's lead; look up to sb for direction: 我将惟你~。*I will just follow your lead.*
【马梳】currycomb
【马术】horsemanship: ~师 *horseman* /~演员 *equestrian; rider*
【马刷】dandy brush
【马斯喀特】Muscat, capital of Oman
【马太福音】【宗】The Gospel According to Matthew
【马提尼酒】martini
【马蹄】① horse's hoof ②［方］water chestnut
【马蹄拱】mosque arch
【马蹄莲】【植】common calla
【马蹄铁】① horseshoe iron ② U-shaped magnet; horseshoe magnet
【马蹄蟹】horse crab
【马蹄星云】【天】Horse Shoe Nebula
【马蹄形】the shape of a hoof; U-shaped: ~磁铁 *horseshoe magnet*
【马蹄袖】horse-hoof-shaped cuff
【马铁】malleable cast iron
【马桶】① nightstool; stool; closestool; commode; chamber pot ② toilet: ~座圈 *toilet seat* /抽水~ *flush toilet*
【马头琴】【音】a bowed stringed instrument with a scroll carved like a horse's head, used by the Mongol nationality
【马尾矿】【地】horsetail ore
【马尾松】【植】mason pine
【马尾藻】【植】sargassum; gulfweed
【马戏】circus: 演~ *run a circus* /~篷 *big top*
【马戏团】circus troupe: 流动~ *a travelling circus* /~小丑 *a circus clown*
【马歇尔计划】the Marshall plan
【马熊】【动】brown bear
【马修方程】【数】Mathieu equation
【马靴】riding boots
【马缨花】【植】silk tree
【马贼】［旧］mounted gangsters
【马扎】campstool; folding stool
【马掌】① cutin skin of a horse's hoof ② horseshoe
【马桩】hitching post
【马鬃】horse's mane

吗

see also má; ma
【吗啡】【药】morphine; morphia
【吗啡中毒】morphinism: ~者 *morphinomaniac; morphiomaniac*

玛

【玛钢】malleable (cast) iron
【玛瑙】agate: 白~ *white agate* /带~ *band agate* /蛋白~ *opal agate* /蓝~ *blue agate* /血点~ *blood agate* /云~ *clouded agate*
【玛瑙玻璃】agate glass
【玛瑙壳】agate shell
【玛雅文化】Maya civilization (c. 1st – 16th centuries)

码[1] ① code; sign indicating number: 尺~ *size* /价~ *marked price* /密~ *cipher code* /数~ *numeral; number* ② device used to indicate number: 筹~ *counter; chip* ③［量］the same thing; thing of the same kind: 一~事 *the same thing* /两~事 *two different things*

码[2] ［口］stack; pile up: ~砖头 *pile up bricks* /孩子们正在高兴地~积木。*The children are piling up building blocks happily.*

码[3] yard, a unit of length (=3 feet or 0.9144 metres)

【码尺】yard measure; yardstick
【码钉】hitch pin
【码放】put (or place) things in good order: 他的书~得井井有条。*His books are put in perfect order.*
【码头】① wharf; dock; quay; pier: 浮~ *pierhead pontoon* /客运~ *passenger dock* /货运~ *freight dock* ②［方］port city; commercial and transportation centre: 跑~ *travel from port to port as a trader*
【码头泊位】quay berth
【码头费】wharfage; dock charge
【码头工人】docker; longshoreman; dockhand; dockworker; lumper
【码洋】(of books) total price
【码子】① numeral: 苏州~ *Suzhou numerals* ② counter; chip ③［旧］cash under one's control; ready money

【码组】code character; code block

蚂

see also mā; mǎ

【蚂蟥】【动】leech

【蚂蚁】ant:我见到树下有一大群~。*I saw a swarm of ants under the tree.*

【蚂蚁搬泰山】ants can move Mount Tai — the united efforts of the masses can accomplish mighty projects

【蚂蚁啃骨头】ants gnawing at a bone — plod away at a big job little by little

【蚂蚁缘槐】ants climb up and down the locust tree — little people inflated with pride

mà

杩

【杩头】board at both sides of a bedside or a door leaf

蚂

see also mā; mǎ

【蚂蚱】[方]【动】locust

骂 ① call names; abuse; curse:对~ *call each other names* /不要~人! *Don't swear at people.* /他~那些淘气的男孩。*He shouted insults at the naughty boys.* /他迎面对我一顿痛~。*He greeted me with a stream of abuse.* ② scold; condemn; reproach:责~ *scold; reprove* /我~了他一顿。*I gave him a good dressing down.*

【骂大街】shout abuse in the street

【骂架】quarrel; wrangle; have a row:他们俩一见面就~。*They began to quarrel at the moment they meet each other.*

【骂街】shout abuses in public; call people names in public:他对着邻居~。*He hurled abuses at his neighbour in public.*

【骂骂咧咧】intersperse one's talk with curses; be grumbling and swearing; be foul mouthed:那个孩子教养差,说话总是~。*The child is ill-bred and foul mouthed.*

【骂名】bad name; infamy:留下千古~ *earn oneself eternal infamy*

【骂娘】abuse; curse:他气愤得~。*He was so angry that he swore at his mother.* /他的头撞到了门上,然后就开始使劲~。*He hit his head on the door and cursed furiously.*

【骂人】abuse; swear at; call one names; rail at; curse; reprove; scold:他接起电话,就听到电话那端的人开始~。*He picked up the phone and received a torrent of abuse from the other end.*

【骂山门】[方] curse roundly; abuse:他~的本事着实令我们震惊。*His ability of abusing shocked us greatly.*

【骂阵】① curse roundly at the enemy in order to provoke him into accepting a battle ② [方] shout abuses in public

ma

吗 ① used at the end of a sentence to indicate doubt:您是张先生~? *Are you Mr. Zhang?* /他回来了~? *Has he been back yet?* ② used to form a pause in a sentence before a topic:这件事~,我们都有责任。*As for this matter, we are all to blame.*

see also má; mǎ

嘛 ① indicating that sth is obvious:有意见就提~。*Why don't you make your suggestions if you have any?* /你别生气,他还是个孩子~。*Don't be angry; after all, he is a child.* ② indicating an expectation:你不要走得那么快~! *Could you walk a little slowly?* ③ marking a pause to draw one's attention to the following words:其实~,这件事很好做。*As a matter of fact, it's quite easy to do.*

mái

埋 ① bury; cover:她把脸~在枕头里。*She buried her face in the pillow.* /成千上万的人死了,被~在他们自己修建的城墙下面。*Thousands of men died and were buried under the wall they built.* ② hide; conceal:隐姓~名 *conceal one's identity*

see also mán

【埋藏】① hide in the earth; bury:这一带地下~着丰富的矿产。*There are rich mineral deposits in this region.* ② hide; conceal; bury; disguise; mask:她把秘密~在心里。*She buried the secret deep within herself.*

【埋伏】① lie in ambush; lie in wait for; ambush:设置~ *lay (or set) an ambush* /中~ *fall into an ambush* /指挥员把他的部队~在树林里准备凌晨发起攻击。*The commander ambushed his troops in the woods for the morning attack.* ② hide; lie low:平静的背后~着危险。*Danger lay hidden behind the peace.*

【埋名】keep one's identity hidden

【埋没】① cover up (with earth, snow, etc.); bury:沙土~了田地。*The farmland is buried by earth and sands.* ② neglect; stifle: ~才能 *hide one's talents in a napkin* /~和浪费人才 *stifle and waste many talents*

【埋青】bury green manure in the fields as base fertilizer

【埋设】fit sth underground

【埋汰】[方] ① dirty:你的手真~! *How dirty your hands are!* ② insult; ridicule:你这不是~我吗? *You are making fun of me, aren't you?*

【埋头】bury oneself in; immerse oneself in; be engrossed in: ~苦干 *immerse oneself in hard work* /他~工作。*He buried himself in his work.* /他~看书忘记了时间。*Engrossed in his book he forgot the time.*

【埋线】sunken cord

【埋葬】① bury (a dead person):他们~了死者。*They buried the dead.* ② destroy; wipe out; ruin: ~旧世界 *smash the old world* /如果报界知道了这件事,他的婚姻、名誉和事业就被~了。*If the newspapers find out about this, it could ruin his marriage, his reputation, and his career.*

【埋针】imbedding needle：～疗法 *needle-embedding therapy*
【埋置】imbedding; embedding：～层 *buried layer* /～深度 *buried depth*
【埋钻】drill failures

霾 thick haze：北极～ *arctichaze* /干～ *dry haze* /光学～ *optical haze* /烟～ *smoke haze*
【霾层】【气】haze layer

mǎi

买 ① buy; purchase; get：～一栋房子 *purchase a house* /他～不起新车。*He was not able to afford a new car.* /我～了一件新衬衫。*I bought a new shirt.* /这件家具～得真是便宜。*The piece of furniture was a real buy.* /我们经常到这里～东西。*We often shop here.* ②（Mǎi）a surname
【买办】comprador：～阶级 *comprador class* /～资产阶级 *comprador bourgeoisie* /～资本 *comprador capital* /～资本家 *comprador capitalist* /～资本主义 *comprador capitalism*
【买单】pay for a meal (at a restaurant)：服务员，～。*Bill please, waitress.*
【买椟还珠】keep the glittering casket and give back the pearls to the seller — show lack of judgement; lack of discrimination
【买方】buying party; buyer; purchaser：～贷款 *buyer's credit* /～市场 *buyer's market*
【买关节】[旧] offer bribes to facilitate one's operations; bribe (or buy off) sb：囚犯向看守～，想得到烟和酒。*Prisoners were bribing jailers for cigarettes and alcohol.*
【买好】try to win sb's favour; play up to; curry favour with：他急于向人～。*He is anxious to please.* /他向老板～。*He curries favour with his boss.*
【买价】buying price; purchasing price
【买进】buy in; buy up：～订单 *buying order* /～现货 *spot purchase*
【买空】short purchase; bull; buy long
【买空卖空】① speculate (in stocks, etc.); speculate on the rise and fall of prices ② engage in profiteering activities
【买路钱】①[旧] paper money thrown on the road during a funeral procession ② toll money asked by highwaymen
【买卖】buying and selling
【买卖公平】buy and sell at reasonable prices; pay fairly for sth
【买卖婚姻】mercenary marriage; venal marriage
【买卖人口】deal in human beings
【买卖】① purchase and sale; transaction; deal：做～ *go into business; make a deal; do some business* /～兴旺。*The business is brisk.* /～成交。*The bargain is closed.* /这笔～使他赚了一大笔。*The transaction afforded him a good profit.* /我向你们保证，这桩～对我们大家都有利。*I can assure you that this deal is profitable to us all.* ② shop; store：他现在有自己的～了。*He has his own shop now.*
【买卖人】[口] businessman; trader; merchant
【买面子】have regard for sb's face; defer to sb
【买通】grease sb's hand; bribe; buy over; buy off：她靠行贿～了那个警察。*She bought the policeman off by bribery.*
【买账】acknowledge the superiority or seniority of; show respect for：没人买他的账，他很尴尬。*Nobody shows respect for him and he looks embarrassed.*
【买主】buyer; customer; purchaser：可能的～ *prospective buyer* /～信用 *buyer's credit* /～意图 *buyer's buying intention*
【买醉】buy liquor and drink one's full：她因过度悲伤而～酒家。*She bought liquor and became drunk in the wine house due to over sadness*

mài

迈[1] walk; step; stride：～了一大步 *take a stride* /他气愤地～出房间。*He strode angrily out of the room.* /他向门口～了一步。*He took a step towards the door.*

迈[2] old; advanced in age：年～ *aged; senile*

迈[3] mile (used in the speed of vehicles)：一小时走70～ *go seventy miles per hour*
【迈阿密】Miami, a city of southeast Florida of the United States
【迈步】take a step; make a step; step forward：向前迈一步 *take one pace forward* /迈出了重要的一步 *make an important move*
【迈方步】walk with measured steps; stride slowly and steadily
【迈进】stride forward; advance with big strides; forge ahead：我们要向更高的目标～。*We should strive to scale new heights.*

麦[1] ① general term for wheat, barley, rye, etc：大～ *barley* /荞～ *Indian wheat* ② wheat：春小～ *spring wheat* /冬小～ *winter wheat* ③（Mài）a surname

麦[2]【电】maxwell
【麦草】[方] wheat straw
【麦茬】【农】① wheat stubble ② land that has been sown to a new kind of crop after the wheat harvest：～地 *a field from which wheat has been reaped*
【麦场】thrashing floor for wheat
【麦当劳】(US) McDonald's Corporation, a fast-food restaurant chain
【麦地那】Medina, city in Saudi Arabia
【麦粉】wheat flour
【麦麸】wheat bran; millfeed
【麦秆】【农】wheat straw
【麦秆虫】skeleton shrimp
【麦管】straw
【麦季】season for wheat harvest
【麦加】Mecca, the holiest city of Islam and a pilgrimage site for all devout believers of the faith
【麦碱】ergine
【麦角】【药】ergot：～胺 *ergotamine* /～毒碱 *ergotoxine* /

~固醇 *ergosterol* / ~精 *ergotin* / ~生物碱 *ergot alkaloid* / ~酸 *ergotic acid* / ~中毒 *ergotism*

【麦秸】wheat straw：~画 *straw patchwork*

【麦精】malt extract：~鱼肝油 *cod-liver oil with malt extract*

【麦糠】wheat bran

【麦克风】microphone；mike：落地式~ *a floor microphone* / 手持式~ *a hand-held microphone* / 他使用~以便人人都能听见他的讲话。*He used a microphone so that everyone could hear him.*

【麦口】［方］ripening stage of wheat

【麦浪】rippling wheat；billowing wheat fields：田野里金色的~ *golden waves of wheat in the field*

【麦芒】awn of wheat

【麦苗】【农】wheat seedling

【麦片】oatmeal：~粥 *oatmeal porridge*

【麦淇淋】margarine

【麦清蛋白】【生化】leucosin

【麦秋】wheat harvest season

【麦收】wheat harvest

【麦乳精】extract of malt and milk；malted milk

【麦收】wheat harvest

【麦穗】wheat head

【麦莛】wheat stalk

【麦芽】malt：绿~ *green malt* / 气干~ *air dried malt* / 糖化~ *diastatic malt* / 硬粒~ *steely malt*

【麦芽醇】maltol

【麦芽酒】malt liquor

【麦芽乳】malted milk

【麦芽糖】【生化】malt sugar；maltose：~酶 *maltase*

【麦芽汁】wort；beerwort

【麦哲伦】Ferdinand Magellan（1480-1521），Portuguese navigator

【麦子】wheat：种~ *raise wheat*

卖 ① sell：变~ *sell off*（*one's property*）/ 她把她的旧自行车~给了我。*She sold her old bicycle to me.* / 在这个季节西瓜~得很贵。*Watermelons are selling high this season.* / 这些手表是要~的。*These watches are for sale.* ② betray：我被~了。*I've been sold.* / 我在任何情况下都不会出~朋友。*In no condition shall I betray my friends.* ③ do one's utmost；try one's best：~劲儿 *exert all one's strength*；*spare no effort* ④ show off：~功 *brag one's merit* / ~巧 *show off one's petty cleverness* ⑤［量］dish（used in old-time restaurants）

【卖唱】sing for a living：~为生 *make a living by singing*

【卖出汇率】selling rate

【卖出价】selling rate

【卖出现货】spot sale

【卖春】prostitution

【卖大号】（of a shop）sell retail goods as wholesale；sell retail goods in large quantity

【卖呆】［方］①（of a woman）stand idly at the gate and watch what's going on in the street ② be in a trance ③ watch the fun

【卖底】［方］deliberately let out a secret

【卖恩】do a favour with an ulterior motive

【卖方】selling party；seller：~市场 *seller's market* / ~信贷 *seller's credit*

【卖功】brag；show off one's contribution

【卖狗皮膏药】sell quack remedies — practise quackery；palm things off on people；fob sb off with

【卖乖】show off one's petty cleverness

【卖关节】take bribes from sb and do him a favour

【卖关子】stop a story at a climax to keep the listeners in suspense；keep people guessing；be deliberately mystifying：结果怎么样？快说吧，别~了。*How did it end? Come on! Don't keep us guessing.*

【卖国】betray one's country；turn traitor to one's country：~条约 *traitorous treaty* / ~贼 *traitor*（*to one's country*）/ ~通敌 *betray one's country into the hands of the enemy*

【卖好】curry favour with；ingratiate oneself with；play up to；fawn on：向老师~的学生 *students apple-polishing the teacher* / 她向上司~。*She fawned on her superior.* / 他向富有的叔叔~。*He slavered over his rich uncle.*

【卖价】selling price

【卖劲】exert all one's strength；spare no effort：他干活很~。*He works very hard.* / 他~地帮她学英语。*He spared no effort to help her learn English.*

【卖老】flaunt one's seniority；put on the airs of a senior：倚老~ *take advantage of one's seniority*

【卖力】do one's best；exert one's utmost；exert all one's strength；spare no effort；do all one can；give one's all；to to great lengths to do sth：他~地帮助我。*He did all he can to help me.* / 他们为我的生日聚会真的很~。*They really pulled out all the stops for my birthday party.*

【卖力气】① exert all one's strength；exert oneself to the utmost；do one's utmost；struggle to do sth：你在功课上应该再卖点力气。*You should put more effort into your schoolwork.* ② make a living by manual labour

【卖命】① work very hard for sb；sweat blood；work oneself to the bone for sb：你何必为这种人~？*Why should you work so hard for such a person?* ② die（unworthily）for；give one's life unworthily：没有人愿意为这个暴君的私利~。*Nobody wants to die for the tyrant's self-interest.*

【卖弄】parade；show off；make a show of；flaunt；flourish：~才华 *parade one's talent* / ~学问 *make a show of one's learning* / ~玄虚 *make a mystery of sth* / 我认为他是在女孩子们面前~。*I think he was trying to show off in front of the girls.* / 他是一个富人，但是他从不~财富或者浪费金钱。*He's a very rich man but he doesn't like to flaunt his wealth or waste his money.*

【卖俏】play the coquette；coquette；flirt

【卖人情】show favours for one's own ends；do sb a favour；do sb a good turn；oblige：我可以卖他一个人情，把他推荐到这个职位上。*I am able to do him a favour by recommending him for the posi-*

tion. /我经常向他～，他却从来都不领情。*I always oblige him, but he was never grateful.*

【卖身】① sell oneself or a member of one's family ②［口］sell one's body; sell one's soul: ～投敌 *sell out oneself to the enemy*

【卖身投靠】barter away one's honour for sb's patronage; prostitute one's honour

【卖笑】(of a prostitute or a singing girl) show a smiling face and flirt

【卖解】［旧］make a living by performing acrobatic tricks: 跑马～ *trick horse riding*

【卖艺】make a living as a performer: 街头～ *be a street-performer*

【卖淫】prostitution

【卖友】betray one's friend

【卖主】seller: ～留置权 *vendor's lien* /～市场 *seller's market*

【卖嘴】show off one's verbal skill

【卖座】(of a theatre, etc.) draw large audiences; (of a restaurant, teahouse, etc.) attract large numbers of customers: 那出戏可～了。*That play draws audiences; that play draws well.*

脉 ①【生理】arteries and veins: 动～ *artery* /肺动～ *pulmonary artery* /肝动～ *hepatic artery* /肝静～ *hepatic vein* /冠状动～ *coronary artery* /静～ *vein* /主静～ *cardinal vein* ② pulse: 病～ *abnormal pulse* /号～ *feel the pulse* ③ vein (of leaves or insects' wings): 叶～ *leaf vein* /翅～ *wing vein* ④ range; line: 山～ *mountain range* /矿～ *mineral vein*
see also mò

【脉案】【中医】diagnosis

【脉冰】vein ice

【脉波】【医】pulse wave

【脉搏】pulse: 医生搭了我的～。*The doctor felt my pulse.* /他的～每分钟八十次。*His pulse was at eighty.*

【脉搏压】pulse pressure

【脉冲】【物】pulse; impulse: ～功率 *impulse power* /～技术 *pulse technique*

【脉动】【物】【天】pulsation: ～电流 *pulsating current* /～电压 *pulsating voltage*

【脉动星】【天】pulsating star

【脉动周期】pulsation cycle

【脉管炎】【医】angitis; vasculitis

【脉候】pulse manifestation

【脉金】①【中医】consultation fee ② grain of gold in quartzite

【脉理】①［书］run; alignment: 山川～ *run of mountains and rivers* ②【中医】principles of traditional Chinese medicine

【脉络】①【中医】general name for arteries and veins; system of blood vessels ② veins (of a leaf, etc.) ③ train (or thread) of thought; sequence of ideas: ～分明 *present ideas clearly and logically*

【脉门】location on the wrist where the throbbing of the pulse is visible

【脉息】pulse: ～微弱 *weak pulse*

【脉象】【中医】pulse condition; type of pulse

【脉岩】dyke rock; vein rock

【脉诊】【中医】diagnosis by feeling the pulse

mān

嫚 ［方］girl
see also màn

mán

埋
see also mái

【埋怨】complain; blame; grumble; murmur; mutter: 工人们～工资过低。*The workers complained that the wages were too low.* /我认为她没有什么可～的。*I don't think she has anything to grumble about.* /他自己犯了错误，还～别人。*He made a mistake himself, but he put the blame on others.*

蛮 ① savage; fierce; rough; unreasoning: 野～ *savage; cruel* /～不讲理 *be impervious to reason; willful; cannot be brought to reason* /胡搅～缠 *pester unreasonably* ② rash; brute; reckless ③ ancient derogatory name for China's southern nationalities ④［方］pretty; quite: ～漂亮 *very beautiful* /这道菜～好吃。*The dish is quite delicious.*

【蛮缠】pester sb endlessly: 胡搅～ *harass sb with unreasonable demands* /我正忙着，不要～。*I'm busy; Don't bother me all the time.*

【蛮干】act rashly; act recklessly; be foolhardy: 不顾后果，危险～ *act rashly regardless of consequences and danger* /他只知道～。*He merely behaves recklessly; he is merely foolhardy.*

【蛮横】arbitrary; rude and unreasonable; peremptory: ～之极 *be insolent to the extreme* /～的要求 *unreasonable demands* /～的态度 *an overbearing manner* /他说话的态度～。*He spoke in a peremptory manner.*

【蛮荒】① barbarous and remote: ～时代 *barbarous age of remote antiquity* ②［书］remote and culturally backward place

【蛮劲】sheer animal strength: 他的～不小。*He possesses sheer animal strength.*

【蛮性】savage nature; rude behaviour

【蛮子】［旧］barbarian (used by northerners to refer to southerners in a contemptuous way): 南～ *barbarian from the south*

谩 cheat; deceive: ～天～地 *try to deceive everybody*
see also màn

see also màn; wàn

【蔓菁】turnip

馒

【馒首】[方] steamed bun

【馒头】steamed bun; steamed bread

瞒

hide; conceal; cover up; disguise; mask; bottle sth up: 隐~ *hold back; cover up* /欺~ *dupe; kid* /实不相~ *to tell the truth* /这件事不必~他。*There is no need to keep him in the dark about it.* /告诉我怎么了,想~着是没有好处的。*Tell me what's the matter — it won't do any good just bottling things up.*

【瞒哄】deceive; fool; trick; hoodwink; pull the wool over sb's eyes: 你想~我吗? *Do you want to fool me?* /老实说,我们本意并不想~你,只是让你知道这件事没有什么好处。*Honestly, our intention wasn't to deceive — it just would do no good on you to tell you about it.* /别想~我,我知道你已经结婚了。*Don't try and pull the wool over my eyes — I know that you've got married.*

【瞒骗】deceive; trick; cozen; outwit; dupe; humbug: 小偷~过警察跑掉了。*The thief outwitted the police and escaped.* /捐献者们被~说他们的钱将用于救济孤儿。*Contributors were tricked into believing their money would be used for helping the orphans.*

【瞒上欺下】perform deeds of deceiving those above and bullying those below: 他善于~。*He is inclined to hoodwink his superiors and bully his inferiors.*

【瞒天过海】cross the sea by a trick — practise deception: 很奇怪他居然~闯过了所有难关。*It's unbelievable that he managed to bluff his way through all the difficulties.*

【瞒心昧己】deceive oneself; deceive and muddle oneself: 如果你认为你的钱挣的光明正大,那么你就是~。*If you think you earned the money in a decent way, you are deceiving yourself.*

鳗

【鳗草】【植】eelgrass

【鳗毒】eel poison; eel venom

【鳗鲡】【动】eel

mǎn

满[1] ① full; filled; packed; stuffed; crammed: 客~ *full house* /她的眼里~含泪水。*Her eyes were full of tears.* ② fill; replenish; top up: 他把瓶子装~水。*He filled the bottle with water.* ③ expire; complete: 我的俱乐部会员资格已期~。*My membership in the club has expired.* /我已经年~18岁。*I have reached the age of 18.* ④ fully; completely; entirely: 他看起来~高兴的。*He looks very happy.* ⑤ satisfied; contented: 心~意足 *on top of the world; be satisfied with sth* /他对自己的工资不~。*He is discontent with his salary.* ⑥ smug; proud; conceited: 自~ *conceited; self-satisfied* /~招损 *lose by pride*

满[2] ① Man or Manchu nationality ② a surname

【满不在乎】not worry at all; not care in the least; indifferently; nonchalantly: 他对于那些恶意的评价~。*He doesn't care the ill intentioned comments in the least.* /那位老人对于寒冷的天气~。*The old man showed a casual disregard for cold weather.*

【满城风雨】(become) the talk of the town; topic of the town; (create) a sensation; (create) quite a stir raise a big uproar: 关于他的传闻已经闹得~了。*The hearsay of him has become the talk of the town.*

【满打满算】reckoning in every item (of income or expenditure); at the utmost: 这次旅行~2000元钱足够了。*Taking every item into consideration, the trip needs just 2,000 yuan.* /我~能待三天。*I can stay for three days at most.*

【满当当】full; packed; be filled with; be stuffed with: 教室里~的坐满了学生。*The classroom is packed with students.* /越来越多的宾客到达,直到屋子被装得~的。*More and more guests arrived until the house was bursting at the seams.* /他嘴里~地塞满了食物。*His mouth was crammed with food.*

【满登登】[口] full; be full to capacity; be packed out; bulging: 他从~的书包里拿出一本书。*He took a book out his bulging bag.*

【满点】reach working hours: 出满勤,干~ *guarantee full attendance and full working hours*

【满电压】full voltage

【满额】fulfil the (enrolment, etc.) quota

【满分】full marks: 他考试得了~,受到老师的表扬。*He got full marks in the exam and was praised by his teacher.*

【满服】[旧] be at the expiration of a mourning period

【满腹】be full of: 这个新来的人总是~牢骚。*The new comer is always complaining about something; the new comer is full of grumbles.*

【满腹狐疑】feel extremely suspicious: 他对这个结论~。*He has grave doubts about the conclusion.*

【满腹经纶】be possessed of learning and ability; an encyclopedic mind: 那个做讲座的学者真是~。*The scholar who is giving a lecture is full of learning and wisdom.*

【满腹珠玑】with a belly full of pearls — a mind full of valuable ideas

【满功率】full power

【满共】[方] in all; altogether: 屋子里~有10个人。*Altogether there were ten people in the room.* /学院学生~有1000人。*The students of the college totaled 1, 000.*

【满汉全席】a full, formal banquet, combining Manchurian and Chinese delicacies

【满怀】① be filled with; be imbued with; be full of: ~豪情 *be filled with boundless pride* / ~杀机 *be filled with the lust to kill* / ~希望 *be full of hope* / ~信心 *be full of confidence* ② bosom: 撞了个~ *bump right into sb* ③ (of sheep, cattle, etc.) be all pregnant; bear a full crop of young

【满刻度】full scale (FS): ~偏转 *full-scale meter deflection*

【满坑满谷】in every valley and ravine — in large numbers; in great abundance; can be seen everywhere: 谷仓里的粮食~。*The barn is heaped with grain.*

【满口】① whole of one's mouth: ~假牙 *whole set of artificial teeth* / ~余香 *leave a lingering fragrance in one's mouth* ② (of accent) standard; (of speech) completely: ~胡言乱语 *talk nonsense* / 他是~的南方口音。*He talks with a heavy southern accent.* ③ unreservedly; profusely: ~答应 *readily promise*

【满脸】all over the face: ~堆笑 *be all smiles; force a smile* / ~通红 *face reddens all over* / ~皱纹 *full of wrinkles*

【满满当当】full; bulging; be packed out; full to the brim: 她的衣柜塞得~的。*Her wardrobe is full.* /厨房的水池里~地塞满了脏盘子。*The sink of the kitchen is full to the brim with dirty plates.*

【满满登登】filled; full: 观众把礼堂挤得~。*A big audience filled the hall.* /他手里的袋子~地装满了糖果。*In his hand was a bag, bulging with candies.*

【满门】the whole family: ~抄斩 *exterminate every one of the family*

【满门桃李】a lot of pupils; many disciples

【满面】all over the face; have one's face covered with: ~愁容 *look very worried* / ~春风 *beam with joy; radiant with happiness* / ~红光 *have a fine colour in one's cheeks; glowing with health* / ~笑容 *be all smiles* /他泪流~。*Tears bathed his cheeks.*

【满目】meet the eye on every side: 琳琅~ *full of beautiful things in eyes; feast for the eyes*

【满目疮痍】see evidence of people's distress everywhere; in a state of devastation; the sight of a war-worn area

【满脑子】one's whole mind: 他~的怪念头。*His mind is filled with weird ideas.*

【满拧】[方] entirely contrary; opposite: ~的意见 *contrary opinions* /她的行为和她的语言是~的。*She engaged in practices entirely antithetical to her words.* /他所说的话与事实~。*His statement contradicts with the facts.*

【满排】【印】set solid

【满期】expire; come to an end: 我的护照再过两个月就~了。*My passport expires in a month.*

【满腔】have one's bosom filled with: ~仇恨 *filled with an inveterate hatred for sb* / ~怒火 *be filled with boiling anger (or indignation)* / ~热忱 *enthusiastically in all earnestness* / ~热血 *full of enthusiasm*

【满勤】have full attendance: 他因出~而受到表扬。*He was praised for full attendance.*

【满山遍野】all over the mountains and plains — quite a lot of; numerous: ~的花朵 *flowers all over the hills*

【满身】from head to foot; all over: ~是汗 *be all of a sweat; be sweating all over*

【满师】(of an apprentice) complete serving one's time; serve out one's apprenticeship: 他已经~。*He has been out of his apprenticeship.*

【满世界】[方] everywhere: 我们~找你。*We have looked everywhere for you.*

【满堂】① entire audience; all those present: ~欢笑 *a hall filled with joy* ② have a full house: 这个电影院天天~。*The cinema is fully packed everyday.*

【满堂彩】bring the house down: 她的舞蹈博得了~。*Her dancing won a storm of applause.*

【满堂灌】(of a teacher) cram students: 我们的语文老师只会~,实际上我并没有记住多少东西。*Our Chinese teacher is force-feeding us at class and I can remember little in fact.*

【满堂红】all-round victory; success in every field: 我们公司的管理搞得~。*The management of our company is successful in every department.*

【满天】all over the sky: ~乌云 *overcast sky* / ~繁星 *sky studded with twinkling stars*

【满天飞】[喻] go everywhere: 他这个人总是~。*He is always running about.*

【满天星】【植】baby's breath (*Gypsophila*)

【满孝】[旧] finish the prescribed period of mourning for a deceased elder

【满心】have one's heart filled with: ~欢喜 *be filled with joy; be very pleased* /我~希望能见到他。*I hope from my very heart that I will see him.*

【满眼】① have one's eyes filled with: ~泪水 *eyes filled with tears* ② meet the eye on every side: ~绿树 *green trees greeting the eye everywhere*

【满意】satisfied; pleased; content: 我的答复你~吗? *Are you satisfied with my reply?* /几句好话就足以使他~了。*Simple praise is enough to content him.* /很难使每个人~。*It's difficult to please everybody.*

【满语】Manchu (language)

【满员】① be at full strength: 应保证主力部队~。*It should be ensured that the main forces are kept at full strength.* ② (of a train, etc.) have all seats taken; fully packed up: 列车~了。*The train is fully booked up.*

【满月】① full moon ② a baby's completion of its first month of life: 他们聚会庆祝孩子~。*They held a party to celebrate the baby's full month after birth.*

【满载】① loaded to capacity; be fully loaded; be laden with: ~吃水 *load draught* / ~吃水线 *load water line* / ~排水量 *load displacement* ② full load (FL)

【满载而归】return home fully loaded; be much profited by one's trip; return from a rewarding journey
【满招损,谦受益】one loses by pride and gains by modesty
【满洲】① old name for the Manchu nationality ② [旧] Manchuria, northeastern China
【满足】① satisfied; content; contented: 我们切不可~于仅仅有一点点书本知识。*We should never content ourselves with a little book knowledge only.* ② satisfy; meet(needs, demands, etc.): ~人民的需要 *meet the needs of the people* /他们的欲望得到了~。*Their aspirations are fulfilled.* /我的回答~了他的好奇心。*My answer appeased his curiosity.* /赞美使他们的虚荣心满得到~。*The compliments tickled their vanity.*
【满族】the Manchu nationality, or the Manchus
【满嘴】one's whole mouth
【满座】have a capacity audience; be all booked up; have a full house: 场场~ *have a capacity audience for every show* /~高朋 *a remarkable gathering of friends* /~皆惊。*Everyone present is amazed.* /当足球馆~后,让更多的人进来是有危险的。*Once the football stadium was full to capacity, it would have been dangerous to let more people in.*

螨 【动】mite; acarid: 疥~ *itch mite* /羽~ *feather mite* /蛛~ *plant mite*

màn

曼 ① gently; gracefully: 轻歌~舞 *soft music and graceful dances* ② prolonged: ~声 *lengthened sounds*
【曼彻斯特】Manchester, an industrial city in northwest England
【曼谷】Bangkok, the capital and largest city of Thailand
【曼哈顿】Manhattan, a borough of New York City in southeast New York
【曼妙】[书] (of dancing) lithe and graceful
【曼荼罗】【宗】mandala
【曼声】(sing or recite in) lengthened sounds: ~而歌 *drawl out a song*
【曼延】draw out (in length); stretch

谩 disrespectful; rude
see also mán
【谩骂】hurl invectives; revile; vituperate; fling abuse; rail; revile; throw dirt at sb: 他~他的邻居。*He uttered invectives against his neighbour.* /我再也无法忍受她的~。*I couldn't bear her abusive words any more.*

墁 ① pave the floor with bricks, stones, etc.: 花砖~地 *pave the floor with ornamental bricks* ②【方】plaster a wall

蔓 tendrilled vine
see also mán; wàn
【蔓草】creeping weed
【蔓花生】runner bean; runner peanut
【蔓荆】wild pepper
【蔓生植物】trailing plant
【蔓生作物】vine crop
【蔓延】spread; extend; pervade overspread; spill over: 疾病在这个国家~很快。*The illness spread quickly in the country.* /火从工厂~到附近的房舍。*The fire spread from the factory to the houses near by.* /从这个地区开始的种族冲突正在向其他城市~。*Racial conflicts, which began in this area are beginning to spill over into other cities.*

幔 curtain; screen: 布~ *cotton curtain* /窗~ *window curtain*
【幔帐】curtain; screen; canopy
【幔子】[方] curtain; screen

漫 ① overflow; brim over; flood: 河水~过了几个农场。*The river overflowed several farms.* /碗里盛的汤~出来了。*The bowl is brimming over with soup.* ② in all places; everywhere: 雾气~天。*The mist fills the sky.* ③ broad; extensive: 岁月~~ *the long years* ④ casual; random: ~无目的 *aimless* /红旗~卷。*Red banners fluttered freely.* ⑤ no; not
【漫笔】literary notes; sketch: 灯下~ *sketches by lamplight*
【漫不经心】pay no heed to; careless; casual; negligent; heedless; absent-minded: ~的回答 *a casual reply* /你讲话不能如此~! *You shouldn't be so careless about your speech.*
【漫步】stroll; ramble; roam: 海滨~ *stroll the beach* /他们整个上午都在林中小径上~。*They spent the whole morning rambling woodland paths.* /我们~走过树林。*We rambled through the woods.*
【漫长】very long; endless: ~的康复期 *a lengthy convalescence* /我不知道如何度过~的假期。*I have no idea about how to spend the long vacation.* /革命走过了~而曲折的道路。*The revolution has followed a long and tortuous course.*
【漫反射】【物】diffuse reflection: ~镜 *diffuse reflector* /~率 *diffuse reflection factor*
【漫画】caricature; cartoon: ~家 *cartoonist*
【漫话】chat freely; talk in an informal way
【漫卷】(of banners) flutter (or wave) freely
【漫流】① rainwater flowing in small streams ② overflow; brim over
【漫骂】fling abuse; insult: 她听到男孩们在~她。*She heard the boys hurling abuse at her.*
【漫漫】very long; boundless; endless: ~黄沙 *boundless desert* /长路~。*The road is endless.* /寒冷的冬天似乎~无尽头。*The cold winter days seemed unending.*
【漫灭】wear away; blur; obliterate: 字迹~。*The words become blurred.*
【漫山遍野】all over the mountains and plains; over

hill and dale

【漫射】【物】diffusion：～带 *zone of diffuse scattering* / ～光 *diffused light* / ～角 *scattering angle*

【漫谈】an informal discussion；a random talk：～会 *informal meeting*；*informal discussion* / ～现代中国文学 *random talk on modern Chinese literature* / ～国际形势 *a casual talk about the international situation* / 我们～了一会儿。*We talked randomly for a while.*

【漫天】① filling the whole sky；all over the sky：雪花～飞舞。*The snow is drifting everywhere.* ② boundless；limitless：～大谎 *a monstrous lie*

【漫天要价】ask an exorbitant price：～，就地还钱。*The seller can ask an exorbitant price*；*the buyer can make a down-to-earth offer.*

【漫无边际】① boundless；infinite：～的沙漠 *boundless desert* / 宇宙是～的。*The universe is infinite.* ② straying far from the subject；rambling；discursive；digress；lose the thread：～的演讲 *a rambling speech* / 你解释原因的时候，请注意不要～。*When you are explaining your reasons, be careful not to stray from the point.*

【漫无止境】no bounds；without limit；boundless；infinite：人类求知的欲望是～的。*A man sets no bounds to his desires for knowledge.*

【漫延】stretch；extend：浮油一直～到地平线。*The oil slick stretched all the way to the horizon.* / 尼罗河一直～到维多利亚湖。*The River Nile extends as far as Lake Victoria.*

【漫溢】overflow；flood；brim over：河水～过河岸。*The river overflowed its banks.*

【漫游】go on a pleasure trip；roam；wander：到乡村去～ *go for a country ramble* / ～全国 *roam about the country* / ～世界 *roam about the world*

【漫语】① random remarks ② informal talk（in titles of books，articles，etc.）：《时间～》*Remarks on Time*

慢[1] ① slow；sluggish：反应～ *be slow to react* / 我的手表～了。*My watch is slow.* ② take one's time；defer；hold over；put off：且～！*Just a moment*！③ no；not

慢[2] cold；unenthusiastic：傲～ *haughty* / 怠～ *neglect*；*snub*；*slight*

【慢板】【音】lento

【慢波】slow wave：～波长 *slow wave wavelength* / ～电路 *slow wave circuit*

【慢车】slow train：乘～ *take the slow train*

【慢车道】slow lane；inside lane

【慢词】long poem of slow rhythm

【慢待】① treat coldly（or rudely）：他今天～了我。*I received bad treatment from him today.* ② treat（a guest）inadequately：今天～了，请多包涵。*Forgive us for our inadequate hospitality.*

【慢道】let alone；needn't say：专家都无法解答这个问题，更～我们普通人了。*Even an expert cannot answer the question, let alone we common people.*

【慢动作】action slow；slow motion：～摄影 *slow motion*

【慢工出细活】fine workmanship comes from slow work

【慢火】slow fire；gentle heat

【慢件】non-express delivery

【慢镜头】【影】slow motion：～电影 *slow motion film*

【慢慢腾腾】leisurely；very slow；sluggish；take one's time：他做事～的。*He does work sluggishly.* / 火车～且拥挤不堪，这个旅行糟糕透了。*The train was slow and crowded and the journey was awful.*

【慢慢悠悠】leisurely；slowly；unhurriedly：～地说 *speak slowly* / ～地走 *jog* / 如果你～地开车，你就会在汽油上省钱。*You will save money on gas if you drive your car at low speed.*

【慢跑】jogging

【慢坡】a gentle slope

【慢说】let alone；to say nothing of：～是你，就连老师都不知道答案。*Even the teacher doesn't know the answer, to say nothing of you.*

【慢速】low speed；idling：～摄影 *low-speed cinematography*

【慢腾腾】at a leisurely pace；unhurriedly；sluggishly；slowly：他在～地写信。*He is writing a letter slowly.* / 服务员这么～的，我们都快迟到了。*That waiter is so slow — we are going to be late*！/ 交通堵塞很严重，我们～地开着车。*We were driving at a snail's pace, as the traffic was so heavy.*

【慢条斯理】slowly；leisurely；unhurriedly；at a slack pace：他总是～地和别人说话。*He always speaks to others in a leisurely manner.* / 她开始做填字游戏，落笔准确且～。*She began to fill in the crossword, with precise, unhurried strokes of the pencil.*

【慢性】chronic：～病 *a chronic disease* / ～毒药 *slow poison* / ～结肠炎 *chronic colitis*

【慢性鼻炎】【医】chronic rhinitis

【慢性阑尾炎】【医】chronic appendicitis

【慢性中毒】chronic poisoning

【慢性子】① phlegmatic temperament ② slowpoke；slowcoach：他是个～。*The man is a slowpoke.*

【慢悠悠】unhurried；leisurely；dawdle：如果你这样～地看，我们今天根本买不完东西。*We'll never get all the shopping done today if you dawdle like this.* / 她周末起得很晚，然后～地吃早饭。*She gets up late on weekends and takes a leisurely breakfast.*

嫚 ［书］scorn；despise；insult

see also mān

缦 ［书］plain silk fabrics

镘 ［书］trowel

【镘板】floating rule；hand float

【镘子】trowel

māng

牤

【牤牛】［方］bull
【牤子】［方］bull

máng

芒 ①【植】Chinese silvergrass ② awn; beard: 麦～ *awn of wheat*
【芒草】Chinese silvergrass
【芒刺】prickle
【芒刺在背】feel prickles down one's back — feel extremely nervous and uneasy: 每当想起他批评我的话,我都感到～。*Whenever I recall his criticizing words, I am ill at ease.*
【芒果】【植】mango: ～罐头 *canned mango*
【芒硝】【化】mirabilite
【芒针】elongated needle: ～疗法 *long needle therapy*

忙 ① busy; fully occupied; have a lot to do: ～得不可开交 *have one's hands full* / ～得团团转 *run round in circles* / 我今天很～。*I am very busy today.* / ～中出错。*Haste makes waste.* ② hurry; rush; hasten: 他白～了。*All his haste was of no use.* / 她急～回家。*She hastened home.*
【忙不迭】hastily; hurriedly: 她～地将好消息告诉了我。*She made haste to tell me the good news.*
【忙叨】［方］busy: 你～啥呢? *What are you busy with?*
【忙乎】be busy; bustle about: 她在瞎～些什么? *What is she fussing about?*
【忙活】(mánghuó) ① be busy with sth; be busy doing: 她这几天正～。*She is busy with the work these days.* ② an urgent piece of work; a pressing job: 这是件～。*It's an urgent job.*
【忙活】(mánghuo)［方］be busy; bustle about: 我这几天～搬家呢。*I am busy with moving these days.* / 我～了一个星期,真希望有个轻松的周末。*I've been on the go all week — I'm looking forward to a relaxing weekend now.*
【忙里偷闲】snatch a little leisure from a busy life; steal a moment of leisure under pressure of a heavy job
【忙碌】be busy; bustle about; on one's toes; be engaged in doing sth: 她的心情不好,但是她的丈夫太～,根本没注意。*She was in bad mood, but her husband was too busy to notice.* / 工人们正～着建桥。*The workers were occupied in building a bridge.* / 他整天～。*He had been on the go all day.* / 明天是我儿子的婚礼,为了做好筹备我简直是～不堪。*It's my son's wedding ceremony tomorrow; I've been absolutely rushed off my feet getting ready for it.*
【忙乱】be in a bustle; bustle about; be in a rush and a muddle; tackle a job in a hasty and disorderly manner: 离婚和破产的官司使得他的生活陷入一片～当中。*With divorce and bankruptcy proceedings pending, his personal life was in a muddled rush.* / 别指望他们帮忙,他们现在也处于～之中。*Don't expect any help from them — they are snowed under at the moment.*
【忙人】busy person: 他是个大～,你很难见到他的。*He is a busy man and you can rarely see him around.*
【忙线】engaged line
【忙音】busy tone
【忙于】be busy with: 她～家务。*She is busying herself about the house.* / 他～写作。*He occupied himself with writing.*
【忙月】① busy farming season ②［方］casual labourer hired during the busy season

杧

【杧果】【植】mango

盲 ① blind: 色～ *colour blindness* / 雪～ *snow blindness* / 夜～ *night blindness* / 昼～ *day blindness* ② illiterate: 文～ *illiterate person* / 扫～ *eliminate illiteracy* ③ blindly: ～干 *go it blindly*
【盲肠】【生理】caecum; blind gut; appendix
【盲从】follow (or obey) blindly: 我不能忍受的就是他们对他的～。*What I can't stand is their blind obedience to him.*
【盲打】touch system
【盲道】blind track — grooved track for the blind
【盲点】【生】blind spot; scotoma
【盲动】act blindly; act rashly: 处理这样的大事一定不能～。*We cannot act rashly in dealing with such a critical issue.*
【盲动主义】putschism: ～者 *putschist*
【盲干】act aimlessly or rashly: 你要动脑筋,不要～。*Use your brains and never act rashly.*
【盲沟】blind drain
【盲流】① blind influx — unchecked flow of population (from the countryside or small towns to the large cities) ② person who blindly migrates to urban areas
【盲目】blind; ignorant: ～排外 *blind rejection of foreign things* / ～乐观 *unfounded optimism* / 我～地回答了这个问题。*I made a blind stab at answering the question.* / 我们对任何人都不能～崇拜。*We should not put blind faith in anybody.* / 她～地相信他的品质。*She has a blind faith in his quality.*
【盲目性】blindness (in action): 克服～ *curb blindness in one's action*
【盲棋】blind chess; blindfold chess
【盲区】【电】blind area (or zone)
【盲人】the blind; a blind person: ～地图 *map for the blind person* / ～学校 *a blind school* / ～院 *blind asylum*
【盲人摸象】several blind men trying to size up an

elephant, each mistaking the part he touches for the whole animal — take a part for the whole; draw a conclusion from incomplete information

【盲人瞎马】a blind man on a blind horse — rushing headlong to disaster; beset with danger

【盲人阅读器】optacon

【盲文】① braille: ~图书馆 *braille library* /~印刷 *braille printing* ② braille publication

【盲校】school for the blind

【盲信】undelivered letter

【盲学】typhlology

【盲眼点】blind ocellus

【盲鱼】blindfish

【盲字】braille

茫 ① boundless and indistinct; vast: 渺~ *distant and indistinct* ② ignorant; in the dark; at sea: 迷~ *confused*; *perplexed*

【茫茫】boundless and indistinct; vast: ~的沙漠 *a vast expanse of desert* /~大海 *a vast sea*; *boundless sea* /我感到前途~。*I feel my prospects are bleak.*

【茫昧】[书] ① dim; gloomy; blurred: 记忆~ *a dim memory of the past*

【茫然】① ignorant; in the dark; at a loss: ~不知所措 *be at a loss what to do*; *be at sea*; *be at one's wit's end*; *not know how to do with sth* /他表情~。*He looked blank.* /这件事使我感到~。*I feel completely in the dark on this question.* ② frustrated; disappointed: ~若失 *be lost in thought*

【茫无头绪】bemused; bewildered; completely at a loss; be in a hopeless muddle; be all at sea; not know where to begin: "发生了什么事?"~的老人问门外的警察。*"What's happening?" asked the bewildered old man as he opened the door to the policeman.*

mǎng

莽[1] rank grass; thick weeds: 草~ *wild jungle*; *wilderness* ② [书] vast; limitless ③ (Mǎng) a surname

莽[2] rash; reckless; rude: 鲁~ *reckless*; *rush one's fences*

【莽苍】① (of scenery) blurred; misty ② open country

【莽汉】a boorish fellow; boor

【莽莽】① (of plant growth) lush; rank; luxuriant: 丛林中~的植物 *rank vegetation in the jungle* /山坡上树林~。*Luxuriant forests covered the hillside.* ② (of fields, plains, etc.) vast; boundless: ~群山 *boundless mountains*

【莽原】wilderness overgrown with grass

【莽撞】saucy; imprudent; crude and impetuous; rash: ~的司机 *a reckless driver* /~的决定 *a rash decision* /年轻人常比老年人~。*Youngsters are usually more impetuous than old people.* /他还未看清楚是谁就上去打招呼,实在是太~了。*He was very foolhardy to say hello to the person without seeing clearly who he is.*

漭

【漭漭】[书] vast and boundless

蟒 【动】boa; python

【蟒蛇】【动】boa; python

māo

猫 ① cat; feline: 波斯~ *Persian cat* /灵~ *civet cat* /小~ *kitten* /~喜欢抓老鼠。*Cats like to catch mice.* /他像~盯耗子般盯着我。*He watched me as a cat watches a mouse.* ② [方] go into hide: 那个小孩儿~了起来。*The child hid himself.*

see also máo

【猫耳洞】cat's-ear-shaped cave served as a shelter for soldiers

【猫科】【动】Felidae: ~动物 *feline*; *felid* /狮子和豹子是~动物。*Lions and leopards are some of the big cats.*

【猫哭老鼠】the cat weeping over the dead mouse — shed crocodile tears; hypocrisy; weep over an onion

【猫儿腻】[口] cunning plot; trick; scheme: 我看他玩了~。*I think he played a trick on it.*

【猫儿食】[喻] small appetite

【猫儿眼】【矿】cat's eye; cymophane

【猫鼠同眠】the cat and the rat sleep together — collude with sb as partners in crime; thieves and police working together; in league with; in cahoots with; hand in glove with: 我怀疑这里的某个职员和抢劫银行的匪徒~。*I suspect that one of the clerks was in league with the gang who robbed the bank.*

【猫头鹰】【动】owl

【猫熊】【动】panda; giant panda

【猫眼】[方] peephole (fixed in a door); spyhole

máo

毛[1] ① hair; feather; fur; down: 鸡~ *chicken feather* /睫~ *eyelash*; *lash* /绒~ *fine hair*; *down* /多如牛~ *as many as the hairs on an ox — innumerable* ② wool: 美利奴羊~ *merino wool* /人造~ *imitation wool* /这套衣服是~做的。*The dress was made of wool.* ③ mildew; mould: 长~ *be covered with mildew* ④ semifinished; rough; crude: ~铁 *crude iron* ⑤ gross: ~重 5 吨 *gross weight 5tons* ⑥ little; small: ~孩子 *little child* ⑦ (of currency) devalue; depreciate: 钱~了。*The money has been devalued.* ⑧ (Máo) a surname

毛[2] ① careless; rash: ~楞楞 *rash*; *reckless* ② *scared*; *frightened*:她被吓~了。*She is panic-stricken.* ③[方] get angry:我把他惹~了。*I made him very angry.*

毛[3] [口] mao, a fractional unit of money in China; ten tents:三~钱 *three mao*; *thirty cents*

【毛白杨】【植】Chinese white poplar

【毛背心】woolen vest

【毛笔】writing brush: ~画 *brush drawing*

【毛边】(of books, etc.) selvage

【毛边纸】writing paper made from bamboo

【毛病】① trouble; breakdown; mistake: 出~ *go wrong*; *be out of order* /我的手表出了点~。*Something has gone wrong with my watch.* ② bad habit; defect; shortcoming:不守时是他最大的~。*Not being punctual is his greatest shortcoming.* /你唯一的~是粗心大意。*Your only fault is carelessness.* /每个人都有些小~。*Everyone has his little weaknesses.* ③[方] illness:老~ *inveterate disease* /他心脏有点儿~。*He suffers from heart trouble.*

【毛玻璃】frosted glass; ground glass

【毛布】coarse cotton cloth; coarse calico

【毛糙】rough; crude; coarse; careless: ~龟裂的手 *rough, chapped hands* /他手脚~而打碎了母亲最喜爱的花瓶。*He broke his mother's favourite vase through rough handling.* /这个渔夫的皮肤黑且~。*The fisherman's skin was dark and coarse.*

【毛茶】semi-made tea

【毛虫】caterpillar; bristle worm:东方天幕~ *eastern tent caterpillar* /胡桃~ *walnut caterpillar* /列队~ *processionary caterpillar*

【毛刺】【机】burr

【毛涤】polyester wool

【毛豆】young (or fresh) soya bean

【毛发】hair (on the human body and head)

【毛发倒竖】with one's hair standing on end — be terrified; frightened; scared:等一下我会向你讲述这个谋杀案,它足以让你~。*Wait until I tell you about the murder — it will make your hair stand on end.* /劫匪拿枪指着我的头,我吓得~。*The robber had the gun pointed at my head and I was absolutely petrified.*

【毛纺】wool spinning:粗梳~ *woolen spinning* /精梳~ *worsted spinning* /~厂 *woolen mill*

【毛根】hair root

【毛茛】【植】buttercup; tall crowfoot; blister flower

【毛估】roughly estimate:请帮我~一下修理楼梯的费用。*Please roughly estimate for the repairs to the stairs.*

【毛骨悚然】with one's hair standing on end; with one's blood run cold — absolutely terrified; shuddered all over; thrilling; creeping:令人~的故事 *a thrilling story* /这个恐怖电影让人~。*The terrible film made us horrified.* /我知道有一个人正在跟踪我,我吓得~。*I knew a man was following me, and I was scared to death.*

【毛孩】hairy child

【毛孩子】[口] a small child; a mere child:他还是个~,根本不知道这件事的重要性。*As a mere child, he is unaware of the importance of the matter.*

【毛蚶】【动】bloody clam

【毛烘烘】hairy; furry; woolly: ~的小猫 *furry cat*

【毛乎乎】furry; hairy

【毛活儿】[口] wool knitting

【毛尖】a kind of high-quality Chinese tea

【毛脚女婿】son-in-law to be

【毛巾】towel; facecloth: ~厂 *towel mill* /~架 *towel rail* /拧~ *wring a towel*

【毛巾被】toweling coverlet

【毛孔】【生理】pore

【毛口】【机】burr:去~ *burring*

【毛裤】long woolen underwear; woolen pants

【毛里求斯】Mauritius: ~人 *Mauritian*

【毛里塔尼亚】Mauritania: ~人 *Mauritanian*

【毛利】gross profit: ~分析 *gross profit analysis*

【毛利率】gross profit rate

【毛利人】Maori, a member of a people of New Zealand

【毛粒】【纺】woollen fabrics

【毛料】woolen cloth; woollen staff: ~衣服 *woollen clothes*; *woollens*

【毛柳】【植】almond willow

【毛驴】donkey:赶~ *drive a donkey*

【毛毛】[方] baby

【毛毛虫】caterpillar

【毛毛雨】① drizzle; fine rain:昨天下了一整天~。*It drizzled the whole day yesterday.* ② tip off; give sb some information about sth in advance:在正式通知他之前,你可以先给他下点~。*You can tip him off before he is informed of it formally.*

【毛蠓】【动】moth fly

【毛囊】hair follicle

【毛呢】woolen cloth; wool coating

【毛坯】① semifinished product ②【机】blank: ~尺寸 *blank dimension*

【毛皮】fur; pelt: ~里子 *a fur lining* /~帽子 *fur hats*

【毛片】① unprocessed film ② pornographic film

【毛票】[口] banknotes of one, two or five *jiao* denominations

【毛渠】sublateral canal; sublateral

【毛茸茸】hairy; downy: ~的羊 *woolly sheep*

【毛纱】【纺】wool yarn:粗纺~ *woolen yarn* /精纺~ *worsted yarn*

【毛手毛脚】careless (in handling things); slipshod; act recklessly; superficial; be brash and clumsy:你有足够的时间,所以根本没有理由如此~地做工作。*You have plenty of time, so there is no excuse for careless work.* /他是个~的司机,但是却从来没有出过事故,真是个奇迹! *He's always been a reckless driver — it's a miracle that he's never had an accident.*

【毛数】approximate number

【毛遂自荐】offer one's services as Mao Sui (of the

Warring States Period) did — volunteer for a job:他～当厂长。*He recommended himself to be the director of the factory.* /没有人愿意～从事这样可怕的工作。*No one would volunteer for such a horrible job.*
【毛损】gross loss
【毛笋】the shoot of mao bamboo
【毛太纸】a kind of writing paper
【毛毯】woollen blanket:他在床上铺了一条～。*He put a woolen blanket on the bed.*
【毛桃】wild peach
【毛体积】bulk volume
【毛头纸】a kind of soft white paper for wrapping or used over a window lattice in traditional Chinese architecture
【毛窝】［方］cotton padded shoes
【毛细胞】hair cell
【毛细管】① capillary: ～充血 *capillary congestion* / ～孔 *capillary bore*
【毛细渗透】capillary percolation
【毛细现象】【物】capillarity
【毛细血管】【生理】blood capillary: ～瘤 *capillary hemangioma*
【毛细作用】【物】capillary action
【毛虾】shrimp
【毛线】knitting wool; woolen yarn: ～针 *knitting needle*
【毛腺】【生理】hair gland
【毛丫头】［口］a chit of a girl; little girl
【毛芽】【生】hair bud
【毛洋槐】rose-acacia
【毛样】【印】galley proof; rough proof
【毛腰】［方］arch one's back; stoop:他～往桌下看。*He stooped to look under the table.*
【毛衣】knitted garment; pullover; cardigan; woolen sweater; sweater; woolly:织～ *knit a sweater*
【毛躁】① short-tempered; irritable:他脾气～。*He was an irascible man.* ② rash and careless:你太～了,在文章中犯了这么多错误。*You are so careless that you made so many mistakes in the article.*
【毛泽东】Mao Zedong (1893-1976), the founder of the People's Republic of China
【毛泽东思想】Mao Zedong Thought
【毛泽东著作】Works of Mao Zedong
【毛织品】① wool fabric; woolens ② woollen knitwear
【毛重】gross weight:这个包裹～10公斤,包括箱子。*The gross weight of the package is 10 kilos, including the box.*
【毛猪】【商】a live pig
【毛装】binding books without trimming
【毛子】①［旧］westerner ②［旧］［方］bandit ③［方］a tuft of fine hair or thread

矛 spear; lance; pike:长～ *lance; pike*

【矛盾】① conflicting; contradictory: ～的观点 *conflicting views* /相互～的论述 *contradictory statements* ②【哲】contradiction: ～的普遍性 *universality of contradiction* /主要～ *principal contradiction* /～的主要方面 *principal aspect of a contradiction* /～的次要方面 *secondary aspect of a contradiction* /～的统一 *unity of opposites* /～的转化 *transformation of a contradiction* ③ problem; conflict; contradiction: ～百出 *full of contradictions* /～重重 *be beset with numerous contradictions* /他今天说的与昨天说的相互～。*His statements today are in contradiction with what he said yesterday.*
【矛头】spearhead:斗争的～ *the spearhead of struggle* /批判的～指向修正主义路线。*The spearhead of the criticism is directed at the revisionist line.*

茅 ①【植】cogongrass:白～ *cogongrass* /名列前～ *come out top* ② (Máo) a surname

【茅草】【植】cogongrass: ～屋 *thatched hut*
【茅房】［口］latrine; outhouse
【茅坑】①［口］latrine pit; cesspit:占着～不拉屎 *hold on to one's post while doing nothing* ②［方］latrine; outhouse
【茅楼】［方］latrine
【茅庐】thatched cottage:初出～ *young and inexperienced; be fledgling*
【茅棚】thatched shed
【茅塞顿开】suddenly see the light; realize sth all of a sudden:经他提示,我～。*He gave me a hint and I understood it all of a sudden.* /他的话使我～。*His words are really enlightening to me.*
【茅舍】［书］thatched cottage
【茅厕】［方］latrine; outhouse
【茅台酒】Maotai, a famous Chinese spirit
【茅屋】thatched cottage; hut; straw hut

牦

【牦牛】yak

旄 ancient flag with yak's tail

猫

see also māo
【猫腰】［方］arch one's back; bend:他～亲吻小孩儿的额头。*He bent and kissed the child on the forehead.*

锚 anchor:副～ *back anchor* /电缆～ *cable anchor* /浮～ *floating anchor* /抛～ *cast anchor; drop anchor* /起～ *weigh anchor* /三爪～ *triple fluke anchor* /船抛～过夜。*The ship cast anchor for the night.*

【锚板】anchor slab
【锚臂】anchor arm
【锚标】【航】anchor buoy
【锚泊】anchorage; lie at anchor: ～泊位 *anchoring berth* /很多船只在海湾～。*Many ships came to an anchor in the bay.*
【锚地】anchorage; anchor ground
【锚定】anchorage; anchoring
【锚杆】rockbolt

【锚孔】anchor eye
【锚链】cable chain; anchor chain
【锚饰】foul anchor
【锚栓】anchor bolt
【锚位】location where a ship casts anchor; anchorage
【锚桩】anchor log

mǎo

卯[1] the fourth of the twelve Earthly Branches:点~ *call the roll in the morning*
卯[2] mortise
【卯期】[旧] deadline; time limit
【卯时】[旧] the period of the day from 5a. m. to 7a. m.
【卯榫】mortise and tenon
【卯眼】mortise
峁 small loess hills in north-west regions of China:下了一道坡,又上一道~ *go up a small hill after going down a slope*
铆 ① rivet ② riveting
【铆锤】riveting hammer
【铆钉】rivet:管形~ *tubular rivet* /开口~ *bifurcated rivet* /螺纹~ *screw rivet* /盘头~ *barrel shaped head rivet* /平头~ *flush rivet*; *flattened rivet* /实心~ *solid rivet* /圆头~ *button-head rivet*; *full head rivet* /锥头~ *bevel head rivet*
【铆缝】rivet seam
【铆工】【机】① riveting ② riveter
【铆行距】gauge of rivets
【铆合架】rivet frame
【铆合梁】riveted plate girder
【铆机】riveter:水力~ *hydraulic riveter*
【铆接】riveting; rivet joint; rivet connection: ~梁 *riveted girder* /~模 *riveting die*
【铆劲儿】①[口] make a sudden all-out effort; with a spurt of energy:我再铆铆劲儿,一定能成功。*I'll put more effort into it and I'm sure I can make it.* ②[方] have a trial of strength; compete; contest:他们俩~干呢。*They are competing in working.*
【铆枪】hitter; riveter

mào

茂 ① luxuriant; exuberant; bloom:根深叶~ *deep roots and exuberant foliage* /雨水使庭院中的植物长得繁~。*Rains made the yard bloom.* ② rich and splendid; excellent:图文并~ *excellent picture and wonderful accompanying essay*
【茂齿】[书] in the prime of life
【茂密】(of grass or trees) dense; thick: ~的丛林 *a dense jungle* /小径旁边的花儿很~。*The flowers grew thick along the path.*
【茂年】[书] vigorous years
【茂盛】①(of plants) luxuriant; exuberant; flourishing:热带~的植物 *luxuriant plants of the tropics* /花园里的植物长得~。*Those plants in the garden are flourishing.* ②(of economy, etc.) thriving; prosperous:财源~ *rich in financial resources*
冒 ① give off; emit; issue: ~泡儿 *send up bubbles* /新的问题又~出来。*A new problem arose.* /烟从烟筒~出来。*Smoke arose from the chimney.* /泉水从岩石中~出。*The spring oozes out of a rock.* /她在~汗。*She was oozing sweat.* ② risk; brave: ~着生命危险 *risk one's life* /他们~着敌人的炮火冲锋。*The charged under the enemy's gunfire.* ③ boldly; rashly; imprudently: ~入会场 *rashly enter the assembly hall* ④ falsely; pretendedly:谨防假~。*Beware of imitations!* ⑤ (Mào) a surname
【冒场】(of actors, actresses, etc.) enter stage early before one's cue
【冒充】pretend to be; pass (sb or sth) off as; impersonate; pose as: ~内行 *pretend to be an expert* /她~有经验的教师。*She passed herself off as an experienced teacher.* /他被控~警察并行窃。*He is charged with impersonating a police officer and theft.* /他~老师混进了学校。*She posed as a teacher to gain access to the school.*
【冒顶】【矿】roof fall; puking:大~ *bulk caving*
【冒渎】[书] bother or annoy a superior:你严重地~了校长。*You've annoyed the principal seriously.*
【冒犯】offend; affront: ~尊严 *violate the sanctity* /我~了他。*I gave offense to him.* /他故意~那个警察。*He offended that policeman on purpose.* /没有比提起那件事更~他的了。*Nothing displeases him more than mentioning that matter.*
【冒功】claim the credit for oneself
【冒号】【语】colon (:)
【冒火】burn with anger; get angry; flare up; blaze up:我知道了这件事心里直~。*I was burning with anger when I knew it.* /看到没人服从我的命令,我的心里直~。*I was incensed to find that my orders had been disobeyed.*
【冒尖】① be piled high above the brim:卡车上的稻草~了。*The truck is piled high with straw.* ② be a little over; be a little more than:100斤~ *a little more than 100 jin* ③ stand out; conspicuous; excellent:在这群人中他很~。*He is a conspicuous figure among those people; he stands out in particular among them.* ④ begin to crop up; appear:最近急躁情绪~了。*Impatience has cropped up recently.*
【冒金星】stars dance before one's eyes:他用拳头打得我直~。*He hammered me with his fists and I saw stars.*
【冒进】prematurely advance; advance rashly:在工作中应该避免~。*Rash advance should be avoided in our work.*

【冒领】claim what belongs to others as one's own: ~失物 *falsely claim lost articles*

【冒昧】[谦] make bold; venture; take the liberty: ~陈词 *make bold to express my views; venture an opinion* /~行事 *take liberty of doing sth; act recklessly* /你不在时我~地借用了你的钢笔。*I took the liberty of borrowing your pen while you were absent.*

【冒名】stand in sb's name; go under sb else's name; assume another's name: ~顶替 *assume the identity of another person; enter under a false name*

【冒牌】falsely use a well-known trade mark; imitation; be a fake: ~货 *imitation; fake* /~医生 *fake doctor; a pretender in medicine* /他被揭穿是个~货。*He was unmasked as a faker.*

【冒傻气】speak or act like a fool: 他冬天在海里游泳——真是~! *He swims in the sea in winter — he ought to have his head examined!*

【冒失】pert; saucy; bold-faced; rash; abrupt; thoughtless; boldfaced; impulsive; hotheaded; impetuous: ~的行为 *rash action* /他~地回答了这个严肃的问题。*He answered the serious question in a flip way.* /他~地要求和她结婚,但是现在他后悔了。*He rashly asked her to marry him and now he was regretting it.* /他~地吻了她,使她误以为他爱上了她。*He kissed her impulsively, which made her think he was in love with her.*

【冒失鬼】harum-scarum; cool hand; dare-devil

【冒天下之大不韪】risk universal condemnation; be against the world; in defiance of world opinion

【冒头】① begin to crop up; appear; emerge: 我们要防止不良倾向~。*We should try to avoid the appearance of an unhealthy trend.* ② a little over: 30岁~ *over thirty years old*

【冒险】take a risk; take chances; take the plunge: 推行~政策 *carry out an adventurist policy* /他冒着生命危险把孩子从火中救出。*He risked his life when he saved the child from the fire.* /很多人害怕~尝试新事物。*Many people are afraid to take chances and do new things.* /她决定~辞职并创业。*She has decided to take the plunge, resigning from her job and start her own business.*

【冒险主义】adventurism: ~者 *adventurist*

【冒雨】in spite of the rain: ~前往 *go in spite of the rain*

【冒支】withdraw money under an assumed name

贸 trade; commerce: 外~ *foreign trade* /财~ *finance and trade*

【贸促会】the China Council for the Promotion of International Trade (CCPIT)

【贸迁】[书] trade: ~致富 *become rich through trade*

【贸然】rashly; hastily; thoughtless; without careful consideration; without a second thought: ~得出结论 *draw a hasty conclusion* /~行事 *act rashly; go off the deep end* /我~同意接受这个工作。*Without a second thought I agreed to take the job.*

【贸易】trade: 边境~ *border trade* /补偿~ *compensation trade* /多边~ *multilateral trade* /互惠~ *reciprocal trade* /加工~ *improvement trade* /军火~ *arms trade* /农业~ *agricultural trade* /双边~ *bilateral trade* /特惠~ *preferential trade* /易货~ *goods exchanging trade* /自由~ *free trade* /主动~ *active trade* /转口~ *entrepot trade*

耄 octogenarian — very old; senile: 老~ *advanced in age*

袤 [书] length (from north to south): 广~ *vast expanse*

帽 ① cap; hat; helmet: 安全~ *safety helmet* /贝雷~ *beret* /草~ *straw hat* /礼~ *hat worn on formal occasion* /童~ *bonnet* /鸭舌~ *peaked cap* ② cover: 笔~儿 *the cap of a pen* /螺钉~ *screw cap*

【帽边】flat; brim (of a hat)

【帽翅】(in old times) the wing-like parts stretching from the back of a gauze cap for court officials

【帽灯】【矿】cap-lamp; head lamp

【帽耳】earflaps (of a cap)

【帽花】[口] insignia on a cap

【帽徽】insignia (or badge) on a cap

【帽盔儿】skullcap; helmet

【帽舌】peak (of a cap); visor

【帽檐】brim of a hat

【帽缘】marginal ridge

【帽子】① headgear; hat; cap ② label; tag; brand: 扣~ *put a label on sb* /摘~ *remove the label*

貌 ① looks; appearance; face: 面~ *face; features* /美~ *good looks* /花容月~ (*of a woman*) *fair as a flower and beautiful as the moon* /~不惊人 *an ordinary appearance; plain* /不能以~取人。*Don't judge by appearances.* ② appearance; manner; aspect: 全~ *complete picture*

【貌合神离】(of two persons or parties) be seemingly in harmony but essentially at variance; appear united outwardly but divided at heart; friendly in appearance only; double-faced

【貌似】seem to be; appear to be; seemingly: ~公正 *pretend to play fair* /~快乐 *seeming happiness* /~强大 *be seemingly strong; be strong in appearance*

【貌相】① facial features; appearance: 有的时候~似乎是求职中唯一重要的东西。*Sometimes it seems that appearance is the only thing that counts in job-hunting.* ② judge by appearance: 人不可~。*Never judge people by their appearance.*

me

么 ① suffix: 多~ *to what an extent* /那~ *then* /什~ *what* /怎~ *why; how* /这个人不那~可靠。*The person is not so reliable.* ② used in a line of verse for balance: 五月的花儿红呀~红似

火。*The flowers in May are as red as fire.*

méi

没

see also mò

【没办法】no way out; have no choice but; can't help it:这是～的事。*Nothing can be done about it.*

【没边儿】[方] ① baseless; unfounded; groundless: ～的怀疑 *unfounded suspicions* /～的控告 *a baseless accusation* /她的话证明我的怀疑绝对不是～的。*Her words confirmed that my suspicions were far from groundless.* ② without limit; excessively:他的脸皮简直厚得～。*He is extremely unashamed.* /这家餐馆饭菜很糟,但价钱贵得～。*The food was bad and the bill was excessive in this restaurant.*

【没出息】not promising; good for nothing:我看他是个～的人。*I think he is good for nothing.*

【没词儿】[口] ① can find nothing to say:他很快就～了。*He couldn't find anything to say soon.* ② be at a loss for words; get stuck; be speechless:她吓得～了。*She became speechless with fear.*

【没错儿】① to be sure; surely: ～,这就是他的书包。*I am quite sure that it is his bag.* ② be a sure success:你听我的准～。*Follow my words and you won't go wrong.*

【没得说】[方] ① be on intimate terms; keep a close relationship:咱们俩的关系～! *We are bosom friends, aren't we?* ② really good; perfect:她在学校的表现～。*Her performance at school is excellent.*

【没关系】it doesn't matter; that's all right; never mind:"对不起"。"～。" "*I am sorry*". "*It doesn't matter.*"

【没规矩】impolite; with bad manners:她很文雅,但是她的儿子很～。*She behaves very gracefully; however, her son has no manners.*

【没劲】① weak; tired:下班后,我感觉浑身～。*I felt very weak after work.* ② uninteresting; boring; dull; tedious:今天上午的课真～! *How boring the classes are in this morning.* /我们今天做的实验会很～,但是结果会很有用。*The experiment we do today won't be very interesting but the results will be useful.*

【没精打采】listless; in low spirits; out of sorts; indifferent; languid; downcast: ～的挥手 *a languid wave of the hand* /他因考试失利而～。*He was in the blues on account of his failure in exams.*

【没来由】without any cause; for no reason:他总是～地生气。*He always becomes angry for no reason.*

【没良心】without conscience; ungrateful; unthankful:你这～的孩子,你至少该说声谢谢。*You ungrateful child; you could at least say thank you.*

【没脸】feel ashamed; feel embarrassed:我～见她。*I am too ashamed to see her.*

【没…没…】① used before two synonyms to emphasize negation:没皮没脸 *shameless* ② used before two antonyms to indicate that no distinction is made:没大没小 *impolite* /没日没夜 *day and night* /没深没浅 *impudent and thoughtless*

【没门儿】[方] ① have no access to sth; have no means of doing sth:我尽了全力,可还是～。*I did my utmost but failed finally.* ② impossible:他想得一等奖,我看～。*I think it's impossible for him to win the first prize.* ③ no way; nothing doing:你想向我借钱? ～。*You want to borrow money from me? No way!*

【没命】① lose one's life; die:他在那次车祸中没了命。*He lost his life in the traffic accident.* ② recklessly; like mad; for all one's worth:他～似的追求名利。*He pursues fame and wealth desperately.* /他～地花钱。*He is reckless of expenditure.* ③ have no luck:看来我～发财。*It seems as if I haven't the luck to make a fortune.*

【没跑儿】beyond doubt; undoubtedly:他今天肯定来,～! *He will come here; that's for sure.* /她一定被提名为最佳女演员候选人,～。*It's beyond doubt that she will be nominated for the title of "best actress".*

【没谱儿】[方] be unsure; have no idea:我对于未来心里～。*I am unsure about the future.*

【没趣】feel put out; feel snubbed:自讨～ *ask for a snub*

【没商量】irretrievable; irredeemable:双方态度都很坚决,看来这事～了。*The attitudes of both parties are unshaken, and there seems no room for mediation.*

【没什么】① it doesn't matter; that's all right; never mind:我～的,你不必担心我。*I am all right; you needn't worry about me.* ② don't mention it; you're welcome:"感谢你的热情款待。""～。" "*Thank you for your hospitality.*" "*It's a pleasure.*"

【没事儿】① have nothing to do; be free; be at leisure:我明天～。咱们去看电影吧。*I will be free tomorrow; let's go to the cinema.* ② out of work:长期以来,他一直～。*He has been out of work for quite a long time.* ③ it doesn't matter; it's nothing; never mind:"对不起,我迟到了。""～。" "*I am sorry for being late.*" "*Never mind. That's all right.*" ④ nothing serious:别担心,他已经～了。*Don't worry about him; there's nothing serious.* ⑤ have no responsibility; be not implicated:你只要如实交代情况就～。*You will not be implicated in the case so long as you say everything according to the facts.*

【没事人】not care in the least; give (or take) no heed; be indifferent:她无视我的警告,像～一样。*She never heeded my warning and just behaves in her own way.*

【没事找事】① ask for trouble：你管得着他吗？真是～。*Do you have something to do with his affairs? You are asking trouble in fact.* ② find fault with; pick holes in; cavil; kick up a fuss：她对我有看法，总是～。*She is prejudiced against me and always finds fault with me.*

【没说的】① really good; perfect：他的人品真是～。*He has very good moral quality.* ② undoubtedly：～，她一定能胜任这个工作。*Undoubtedly, she is competent for the job.* ③ naturally; it goes without saying：～，这事我包了。*There's no need to say anything about it; just leave it to me.*

【没挑儿】faultless; perfect：她长的～。*She has perfectly modelled features.*

【没头苍蝇】like a headless fly — do things aimlessly：他像个～似的在外面转了一天。*He wandered aimlessly all day.*

【没头没脑】① sudden; abrupt：他说了些～的话。*He uttered several words abruptly.* ② without rhyme or reason; unprovoked：他～地就发火了。*He caught fire without apparent reasons.* ③ not consider the result：他～地把秘密说了出来。*He told the secret regardless of any result.*

【没完】have not finished with sb：我跟他～。*I won't let him off by any way.*

【没完没了】endlessly; no end; constant; incessant; nagging; unending; persistent; never-ending：孩子～地哭。*The child cried no end.* /他离开了办公室，因为受不了这里～的聒噪。*He left the office because he could no longer stand the constant gossip.*

【没戏】［方］out of the question; hopeless; without any hope

【没心没肺】unthinking：你不是小孩了，怎么办事还老是～的？*You are not a child any longer; why do you always act without thinking?*

【没心眼儿】careless; frank; simple：他是个～的人。*He is simple and frank.*

【没羞】have no shame; be unabashed：你说谎，～。*You are telling a lie, shame on you.*

【没样儿】have no manners; be ill-mannered：你是个女孩子，举止可不能～。*You are a girl, and should have good manners all the time.*

【没意思】① bored：又要出差真是～。*It's a bore having to go on business again.* ② boring; uninteresting; dull; tedious：我觉得这个音乐会很～。*I think the concert is boring.*

【没影儿】① disappear without a trace：等我赶到车站，那辆火车已经～了。*When I reached the station, the train had been out of sight.* ② groundless; unfounded; not true：谁说她要被提升？这简直是～的事。*Who said that she would be promoted? It's totally groundless.*

【没有】① not have; there is not; be without：～结果 *come to nothing* /病人一点也～好转。*The sick man is no better.* /～消息就是好消息。*No news is good news.* /这～什么不对。*There is nothing wrong about it.* ② there is not：屋子里～人。*There is nobody in the room.* /花园里～花。*There are no flowers in the garden.* ③ nobody：今天上午～谁来过这儿。*Nobody came here this morning.* ④ be not so... as：我的成绩～他好。*My grades are not as good as his.* /这项试验～我们预料的那样顺利。*The experiment didn't go as smoothly as we expected.* /他的工作～我好。*His work is inferior to mine.* ⑤ less than; not more than：～几天他就走了。*He left in several days.* ⑥ not yet：我还～毕业。*I haven't graduated yet.* ⑦ did not：我～看到那个通知。*I didn't see that notice.*

【没辙】［口］can find no way out; be at the end of one's rope：我现在是彻底～了。*I am completely helpless now.*

【没治】［方］① incurable; hopeless：医生说她的病是～了。*The doctor said that her condition was hopeless.* ② cannot do anything with sb：我拿这个固执的人是～了。*He is so obstinate that I can do nothing with him.* ③ excellent; perfect：这道菜好吃得～了。*The dish tastes perfect.*

【没准儿】maybe; perhaps：～我误会他了。*Maybe I misunderstood him.*

玫

［书］a kind of jade

【玫瑰】【植】rugosa rose; rose：白～ *cottage rose* /她非常喜欢～。*She likes roses very much.* /没有无刺的～—世上没有十全十美的幸福。*There is no rose without a thorn.*

【玫瑰红】rose colour; hermosa pink

【玫瑰花】rose：～瓣 *roseleaf* /她美如～。*She is as fair as a rose.*

【玫瑰色】rosiness：她脸上的～完全消失了。*She has quite lost her roses.*

【玫瑰紫】rosy; rose-red

枚

①［量］used for small objects：一～奖章 *a medal* /一～纪念章 *a badge* ②（Méi）a surname

【枚举】enumerate; list; number; cite one by one; reel off：不胜～ *too numerous to enumerate* /看马戏的孩子不胜～。*We found more children at the circus than we could enumerate.*

眉

① eyebrow; brow：浓～ *heavy eyebrows; thick eyebrows* /皱～ *knit one's brows* /挤～弄眼 *make eyes; wink* /迫在～睫 *be of the utmost urgency* /扬～吐气 *hold one's head high — feel proud* ② the top margin of a page：书～ *top margin*

【眉笔】eyebrow pencil

【眉端】① the space between the eye-brows ② the top of a page; top margin

【眉飞色舞】a look of exultation; enraptured; brightened up with joy; beam with joy; exultant：他因获得成功而～。*He was greatly elated by success.*

【眉峰】brows

【眉高眼低】adopt different attitudes and measures under different circumstances：他善于看人～行事。*He is good at acting according to different situations.*

【眉睫】(as close to the eye as) the eye-brows and eyelashes:迫在~ *extremely urgent*
【眉开眼笑】be radiant with smile; be all smiles; beam with joy (or delight); grin all over:她获了奖,~的。*She beamed with satisfaction as she has won the prize.* /得知国外的儿子快要结婚了,他一整天都~的。*When he heard his son abroad was going to get married, he couldn't stop grinning all day.*
【眉来眼去】make eyes at each other; exchange amorous glances; flirting glances between sexes:他们俩~,以目传情。*They exchanged amorous glances and clearly made known their passions.*
【眉棱】superciliary ridge
【眉毛】eyebrow; brow:竖起~*raise one's eyebrows*
【眉毛胡子一把抓】try to grasp the eyebrows and the beard all at once — try to attend to big and small matters all at once; all is flour that comes to his mill
【眉目】(méimù) ① one's features; looks:一个~清秀的小姑娘 *a girl with delicate features* ② logic (of writing); sequence of ideas
【眉目】(méimu) sign of a positive outcome; sign of a possible solution:这件事~不清。*It's not well organized.* /你托我办的事已经有点~了。*About that job you asked me to do, I'm beginning to get something with it.*
【眉批】notes and commentary at the top of a page; marginal notes
【眉清目秀】have delicate features; fine eyes and graceful eyebrows
【眉梢】the tip of the brow:喜上~ *look very happy*
【眉题】overline
【眉头】brows:皱~ *wrinkle one's brows*; *frown* /他~紧缩。*His brows knitted.*
【眉头一皱,计上心来】as one frowns thoughtfully, an idea strikes him; knit the brows and a stratagem comes to mind
【眉心】between the eyebrows
【眉形】camber
【眉眼】① eye and brow: ~传情 *cast amorous glances* ② appearance; looks
【眉宇】[书] forehead
【眉月】① crescent ② [书] (of women) crescent-shaped eyebrows
【眉注】headnote

莓 【植】berry:草~ *strawberry* /黑~ *blackberry*

梅 ①【植】plum:话~ *preserved plum* /酸~ *smoked plum* /乌~ *smoked plum*; *dark plum* /杨~ *red bayberry* ② plum blossom ③ plum (the fruit) ④ (Méi) a surname
【梅毒】【医】lues; syphilis: ~患者 *syphilitic* /~菌素 *luetin* /~瘤 *gumma*; *gummata*
【梅红】plum colour
【梅花】① plum blossom; plum flower ② [方] wintersweet
【梅花鹿】【动】sika (deer)
【梅树】prune tree
【梅雨】mould rains; plum rains
【梅子】【植】plum

猸

【猸子】【动】crab-eating mongoose

湄 [书] river bank

【湄公河】Mekong, a river of southeast Asia

媒 ① matchmaker; go-between:做~ *act as a matchmaker* ② intermediary:触~ *catalyst* /虫~ *insect pollination* /风~ *wind pollination*
【媒介】medium; vehicle:广告~ *advertising medium* /文化~ *cultural medium* /环境~ *environmental medium*
【媒婆】[旧] woman matchmaker
【媒人】matchmaker; go-between
【媒妁】[书] matchmaker; go-between
【媒体】medium; media: ~初始化 *media initialize* /~转换 *media conversion* /~文件 *media file*
【媒鱼】decoy-fish
【媒质】【物】medium; media:声~ *acoustic medium* /双折射~ *birefringent medium*
【媒子】decoy:鸟~ *decoy bird*

楣 lintel over a door

【楣窗】fanlight; transom

煤 coal:暗~ *dull coal* /采~ *cut coal* /粉~ *powdered coal* /腐殖~ *humic coal* /干~ *dry coal* /褐~ *brown coal* /沥青~ *asphaltite coal* /木质~ *xyloid coal* /烟~ *soft coal* /无烟~ *hard coal* /运~工 *coal haulers* /原~ *altogether coal* /藻~ *algae coal* /许多船只在大连港上~。*Many ships coal at Dalian Port.* /要不要我往火上加些~? *Shall I put some coal on the fire?*
【煤饼】briquette; coal cake
【煤仓】bunker; coal bunker
【煤藏】coal deposits
【煤层】【地】coal seam; coal bed:薄~ *thin seam* /厚~ *thick seam* / ~注水 *coal-bed flooding*
【煤车】coaler; coal car
【煤尘】braize; coal dust
【煤斗】coal bucket; coal scuttle
【煤肺】coal pneumoconiosis: ~病 *anthracosis* /~症 *soot lung*
【煤粉】buggy; braize; gum
【煤核】partly-burnt briquet; coal cinder
【煤化】carbonize
【煤精】black amber; jet
【煤矿】coal mine; coalpit: ~床 *coal deposit* /~工人 *coal miner* /~开采 *coal mining* /~事故 *coal mining accident*
【煤气】coal gas; gas:开~ *turn on the gas*
【煤气表】gasometer
【煤气灯】gas lamp; gas light
【煤气管】gas pipe
【煤气炉】gas stove; gas oven
【煤气设备】gas fittings

【煤气灶】gas burner; gas cooker; gas-oven
【煤气中毒】carbon monoxide poisoning
【煤球】(egg-shaped) briquet
【煤炭】coal: ~工业 *coal industry* /~基地 *coal base* /~资源 *coal resources*
【煤田】coalfield: ~开发 *coal field development*
【煤烟】① smoke from burning coal: ~污染 *smoke pollution* ② coal soot; soot
【煤窑】coal pit
【煤油】kerosene; paraffin: ~灯 *kerosene lamp* /~炉 *kerosene stove*
【煤渣】coal cinder: ~路 *cinder road*

酶 【生化】enzyme; ferment: 蛋白~ *protease; proteinase* /还原~ *reducing ferment; reductase* /凝固~ *coagulative ferment* /水解~ *hydrolytic ferment*

霉 ① mould; mildew: 黑~ *black mould* /青~ *blue mould* /小麦~ *wheat mildew* ② mouldy; mildewed; decayed: 发~ *become mouldy* /他兴致勃勃地研究那些发~的老照片。*She studied the mildewed old photograph with interest.*
【霉斑】mildew
【霉病】【农】mildew; mould: 黄瓜~ *cucumber mildew* /霜~ *downy mildew*
【霉菌】【微】mould; mycete: ~试验 *mould test*
【霉烂】mildew and rot
【霉气】① damp; musty ② [方] bad luck; unlucky; be out of luck: 今天在公共汽车上丢了钱包,真是~。*It's really unlucky; I lost my purse on the bus.* /真是~,所有的旅馆都客满了。*We were out of luck; all the hotels were full.*
【霉天】early summer rains
【霉头】[方] bad luck: 触~ *have a stroke of bad luck*

糜 【植】broom corn millet
see also mí
【糜子】broom corn millet

měi

每 ① every; each: ~年 *every year* /~隔两个小时 *every two hours* /~人两个 *be given two each* /~个人都知道。*Every one knows it.* /我的英语水平~天都有提高。*My English improved each day.* ② per; every time: ~战必胜 *win every battle* /~逢二十日出版 *publish every twentieth* ③ often: ~陷困境 *be always put in a sorry plight*
【每当】whenever; when; every time: ~我看到他,都毫不掩饰我的鄙夷之情。*I made no effort to hide my contempt whenever I saw him.*
【每况愈下】steadily deteriorate; go from bad to worse; go down the drain; worse and worse: 他的家境~。*His family is on decline.*
【每每】often; always; usually: ~如此。*It's usually the case.*
【每年】① every year: 我们~都去给他扫墓。*We pay our respects to him at his tomb every year.* ② [方] in the past: ~从没见过这么大的雪。*We had never seen such a heavy fall of snow in the past.*
【每时每刻】all the time; at all times: 我~都在等他的信。*I was waiting for his letter all the time.*

美[1] ① pretty; beautiful; handsome: 真善~ *the true, the good, and the beautiful* 那些玫瑰花真~。*Those roses are beautiful.* ② beautify ③ good; gratifying: 物~价廉 *of reasonable price but high quality* /他的日子过得挺~。*He leads a happy life.* ④ satisfaction: 两全其~ *make the best of both worlds* /成人之~ *help sb achieve success* ⑤ [方] self-contented; arrogant: 老师夸了他几句,他就~得了不得。*He became conceited after he got several complimentary remarks from his teacher.*

美[2] (Měi) ① America: 北~ *North America* /南~ *South America* /中~ *Central America* /拉~ *Latin America* ② United States of America; America
【美不胜收】too beautiful to be absorbed all at once; more beauty than one can take in; too many nice things for the eyes to feast on: 黄山的景色~。*The beautiful sceneries of the Huang Mountains are more than the eye can take in.*
【美餐】① tasty food; table delicacies; a dainty (or rich, luxurious) repast: 非常感谢,这真是一顿~。*Thank you very much; that was a delicious meal.* /真想不到这个小煤气炉竟能够做出如此的~。*It's hard to believe that something so tasty can be prepared on such a small gas ring.* ② eat and drink one's fill; have an excellent meal: 我在聚会上~了一顿。*I ate and drank my fill at the party.*
【美差】a cushy job; a pleasant task; junket: 到国外出差可是一件~。*It's a cushy job to go on business abroad.*
【美钞】American dollar; greenback
【美称】laudatory title; good name: 杭州有人间天堂的~。*Hangzhou enjoys the reputation of being heaven on earth.*
【美德】virtue; moral excellence: 她具有耐心的~。*She has the virtue of patience.* /他的~被逐步发现。*His merits are gradually being recognized.*
【美发】go to the hairdresser's; get a haircut
【美感】aesthetic feeling; aesthetic perception; sense of beauty: 培养~ *foster the sense of beauty* /这本书的设计给人以~。*The design of the book inspires an aesthetic feeling.*
【美工】① art designing ② art designer
【美观】pleasing to the eye; beautiful; artistic: ~大方 *simple and artistic* /食品的摆放十分~。*The food was presented in an artistic way.*
【美国】United States of America (USA); America: ~精神 *Americanism* /~梦 *the American dream* /~印第安人 *American Indian*
【美好】fine; happy; glorious: ~的一天 *a glorious day* /~的前景 *rosy prospects* /~的回忆 *happy*

memories /我们在昨天的聚会上度过了～的时光。*We had a fantastic time at the party yesterday.*

【美化】beautify; prettify; embellish: ～环境 *beautify the environment* /她竭力～自己。*She tries hard to prettify herself.* /你把一幢普通的房子～成了一座豪华公寓。*Your descriptions have glorified an average house into a mansion.*

【美景】beautiful scenery (or landscape): 西湖以～著称。*The west lake is famous for its beautiful scenery.*

【美酒】good wine: ～佳肴 *mellow wine and delicious food*

【美丽】beautiful; pretty: ～的姑娘 *a pretty girl* /这是我所见过的最～的图画。*This is the most beautiful picture I have ever seen.*

【美联社】US Associated Press (AP)

【美轮美奂】(of a new house, mansion, etc.) tall and splendid: ～的建筑 *a splendid architecture*

【美满】happy; ideal; perfectly satisfactory: ～婚姻 *happy marriage*

【美貌】① good looks; lilies and roses: 她的～吸引了他。*Her good look attracts him.* ② pretty; beautiful; fair-faced; good-looking; attractive; striking; elegant: ～的女子 *a beautiful woman* /他经常带着他～的女友出席聚会。*He always came to parties with his gorgeous girlfriend by his side.*

【美美】to one's heart's content: ～地睡了一觉 *have a sound sleep*

【美梦】fond dream: 他的想法不过是一场～。*His ideas are a fond dream.* /母亲的呼喊把他从～中拉了出来。*He was brought out of his daydream by a shout from his mother.*

【美妙】great; beautiful; splendid; wonderful; dulcet: ～的音乐 *beautiful melody* /感觉～至极。*The sensation is simply wonderful.*

【美名】good name; good reputation: 她赢得了"诗人"的～。*He won a good reputation as a poet.*

【美男子】Apollo; doll; handsome man: 她要嫁给一个年轻的～医生。*She wants to marry a handsome young doctor.*

【美尼尔氏症】Meniere's syndrome

【美女】a beautiful woman; belle

【美其名曰】call it by a good name of: ～"互相帮助" *be described euphemistically as "help mutually"*

【美人】a beautiful woman; beauty; fair: ～迟暮 *a beauty in her old age* /这姑娘是个～。*The girl is a lovely.*

【美人计】badger game; sex-trap

【美人蕉】【植】canna; Indian shot

【美人鱼】mermaid; sea-maid; sea-maiden

【美容】improve (esp. a woman's) looks; beauty treatment

【美容师】beautician

【美容院】beauty salon (or shop; parlor)

【美容专家】beauty-specialist

【美色】attractive woman; fair; beauty: 他难以抗拒～的诱惑。*He cannot resist the temptation of an attractive woman.*

【美声唱法】【音】bel canto

【美食】good food; choice food; table delicacies

【美食家】gourmet

【美食主义】epicurism; gourmandism

【美事】good luck: 真想不到能碰上这样的～。*I have never imagined that I should be blessed with such a good fortune.*

【美术】① the fine arts; art: 她极喜欢～。*She has a great taste for art.* ② painting

【美谈】anecdote; a story passed on with approval

【美味】① delicious food; delicacy: 他们为客人提供～。*They provided their guests dainties.* ② delicious; dainty; tasty; yummy; palatable: ～的馅饼 *a delicious pie* /～的巧克力糖果 *luscious chocolate bonbons*

【美西战争】Spanish-American War (1898)

【美学】aesthetics

【美言】① put in a good word for sb: 请您在校长面前为我～几句。*Please put in a good word for me before the principal.* ②［书］nice words: ～不信。*High-sounding words may not necessarily be true.*

【美艳】beautiful and glamorous

【美意】good intention; kindness: 感谢您的～。*Thank you for your kindness.*

【美育】aesthetic education; art education

【美誉】good name; good reputation: 享有～的人 *a man of good reputation* /我加入了一家享有～的公司。*I joined a firm which had a good reputation.*

【美中不足】a blemish in an otherwise perfect thing; a blemish in a thing of beauty; a fly in the ointment; some slight imperfection

【美洲】America: 北～ *North America* /南～ *South America* /拉丁～ *Latin America*

【美洲豹】【动】catamount; panther

【美洲国家组织】Organization of American States (OAS)

【美滋滋】very pleased with oneself: 他得知这个好消息时，心里～的。*He was pleased with himself when he was told the good news.*

镁 【化】magnesium (Mg)

【镁光】magnesium light

【镁光灯】flash bulb; magnesium light

mèi

妹 ① younger sister: 兄～ *brother and sister* /姐～ *sisters* ② younger female cousin: 弟～ *younger brother's wife; sister-in-law* ③［方］young girl: 外来～ *non-local girl*

【妹夫】younger sister's husband; brother-in-law

【妹妹】younger sister; sister

【妹婿】［书］younger sister's husband; brother-in-law

【妹子】［方］① younger sister; sister ② a young girl

昧 ① confused; ignorant: 愚~ *ignorant*; *benighted* / 蒙~ *ignorant*; *unlighted* / 冒~ *make bold* ② hide away; conceal; hide: 拾金不~ *not pocket the money one picks up* ③ [书] dark; dim ④ [书] offend; risk

【昧旦】[书] dawn; daybreak

【昧良心】against one's conscience; not feel guilty; have no qualms about: 他昧着良心嫁祸他人。*He shifted the misfortune onto others against his conscience.*

【昧死】[书] risk one's life: ~上言 *risk one's life to give a suggestion (to a monarch)*

【昧心】(do evil) against one's conscience: ~钱 *filthy money* / 他~地靠出卖朋友生活。*He felt no compunction about living at the expense of his friends.*

袂 [书] sleeve: 分~ *part*; *leave each other* / 联~ *hold hands*; *reunite among friends*

谜

see also mí

【谜儿】[方] riddle: 猜~ *guess a riddle*

寐 [书] sleep: 夜不能~ *cannot go to sleep at night* / 梦~以求 *long for sth day and night*

媚 ① flatter; fawn on: 献~ *make up to*; *flatter* ② attractive; lovely: 妩~ *charming*; *graceful*; *lovely* / 春光明~ *a sunlit and enchanting scene of spring*

【媚惑】seduce; bewitch: 她~他接受她的要求。*She seduced him into accepting her requirements.*

【媚上欺下】flatter the superior and bully the subordinates

【媚世】[书] try to please the public; fish for cheap popularity: ~之作 *works that please the public*

【媚态】① obsequiousness; fawning expression ② feminine charms

【媚外】fawn on foreign powers: 崇洋~ *worship foreign things and flatter foreigners*

【媚笑】coquettish smile

【媚眼】charming eyes

魅 [书] demons; monster: 鬼~ *ghosts and goblins*; *evil forces*

【魅惑】bedevil; captivate; fascinate: 他为她的美貌所~。*He was captivated by her beauty.*

【魅力】charm; glamour; enchantment; captivation; fascination; charisma: 他极有~。*He had great charm.* / 他为她的~所倾倒。*He fell victim to her glamour.* / 日落对我具有某种奇特的~。*The sunset has a certain strange fascination for me.*

【魅人】charming; attractive; enchanting; lovable; endearing; intoxicating: 她给了我们一个最~的笑容。*She gave us one of her most charming smiles.*

mēn

闷 ① stuffy; stifling; airless: 屋子里很~。*It's stifling in the room.* / 大厅又挤又~。*The hall was crowded and rather stuffy.* ② cover tightly: 把火~灭 *cover fire with ashes* / 茶刚泡上, ~一会儿再喝。*The tea has just been made; Let it draw for a while before drinking.* ③ silent; speechless: 他把话都~在心里。*He has a fit of the sulks.* ④ [方] (of sound) muffled: 他~声~气地说话。*He spoke in a muffled voice.* ⑤ shut oneself indoors: 别总是~在家里, 咱们出去走走吧。*Don't shut yourself indoors all the day; Let's have a walk outside.*

see also mèn

【闷沉沉】① stuffy; stifling: 旅馆的房间炎热且~的, 早晨我在头痛中醒来。*The hotel room was hot and stuffy, and I woke up with a headache in the morning.* / 这里~的, 我很高兴出去散步。*It is stifling here; I am glad to get out and take a walk.* ② (of voice, sound, etc.) low; muffled; hushed; subdued: 她用~的声音道了歉然后离开。*She gave a muffled apology and left.* / 他用~的声音和威胁的语气对我说: "你最好小心点儿。" *In a low, threatening whisper he said, "You'd better watch out."*

【闷锄】【农】loosen the top soil and do weeding to let the seeds germinate

【闷炉】cold stoking

【闷气】stuffy; close

【闷热】hot and suffocating; sultry; muggy: 七月~的天气 *sultry July weather* / ~的夜晚 *a muggy and airless evening*

【闷声闷气】(of voice, sound, etc.) low; muffled: "我不同意你的想法。"他~地说。"*I don't agree to your idea," he said in a low voice.*

【闷头儿】(work hard) quietly: 他不说话, 就知道~干活。*He said nothing and worked with dogged perseverance.*

mén

门 ① (of a building, vehicle, etc.) entrance: 前~ *front door*; *entrance* / 太平~ *safety door* ② door; gate: 百叶~ *blind door* / 板条~ *batten door* / 吊拉~ *overhung door* / 双扇~ *double swing door* / 隐~ *jib door* / 他开着~睡觉。*He slept with the door open.* ③ any opening: 炉~ *opening of a stove* ④ switch; valve: 电~ *switch* / 油~ *throttle* / 闸~ *throttle valve* / 水~ *sluice*; *water gate* ⑤ method; access; way: 窍~ *key*; *knack* / 入~ *know the rudiments of sth* ⑥ house; family; branch of a family: 寒~ *my humble family* / 长~长子 *the eldest son of the first branch of a family* / 喜临~。*Blessing has descended upon the house.* ⑦ sect; branch of study: 佛~ *Buddhism* / 旁~左道 *heterodoxy* ⑧ from the same master (or teacher): 同~ *taught by the same master (or teacher)* ⑨ class; category: 热~ *popular*; *in great demand* / 分~别类 *divide into different categories* ⑩ 【生】phylum: 原生动物~ *Protozoa* ⑪ position in a gambling game: 天~ *position opposite to one* ⑫

[量]:一～大炮 *a piece of artillery* /一～学问 *a branch of study* ⑬(Mén) a surname
【门把】door knob; door handle
【门板】① door plank; door sheet ② shutter:上～ *put up the shutters*
【门匾】horizontal inscribed board put above a gate (or door)
【门鼻儿】staple (of a door)
【门钹】cymbal-shaped article with a knocker on a door
【门窗】door and windows: ～布局 *fenestration* /～材料 *sash stuff* /～侧墙 *jamb wall*
【门窗框】sash: ～条 *sash bar*
【门刺】[书] visiting card
【门当户对】marry one's own kind of people; a marriage between families of equal social rank:父母希望她嫁给～的人。*Her parents expected that she will marry into a proper family.*
【门道】(méndào) gateway; doorway
【门道】(méndao) [口] ① way to do sth; knack: 技术革新的～很多。*There are all sorts of possibilities for technical innovation.* /他有一套看人的～。*He has a knack of judging people.*
【门第】[旧] family status:书香～ *an intellectual background* /他们两家～相当。*The couple's families are equal in social status.*
【门丁】[旧] doorman; gatekeeper
【门钉】round-headed decoration on the gate
【门洞儿】gateway; doorway
【门斗】small vestibule outside the door to keep off the cold, wind, etc.
【门房】① gate house; janitor's room; porter's lodge ② gatekeeper; doorman; janitor; porter
【门扉】door leaf: ～半掩。*The door is left half open.*
【门风】moral standards of a family
【门缝】a crack between a door and its frame
【门馆】① private family school in former times: ～先生 *resident private tutor* ② resident private teacher ③ living houses for hangers-on provided by aristocrats, etc.
【门户】① door: ～洞开 *with the doors wide open* /～紧闭 *with the doors tightly shut*/ ～不关紧,圣贤起贼心。*An open door may tempt a saint.* ② gateway; important passageway ③ family ④ faction; sect: ～之争 *sectarian disputes* ⑤ family status: ～相当 *equal in terms of family status*
【门户之见】sectarian bias; parochial prejudice; factional views; sectarianism:在学术问题上我们应该防止～。*We should guard against sectarian bias as far as academic issues are concerned.*
【门环】knocker
【门禁】police guard at an entrance; entrance guard: ～森严 *with the entrance carefully guarded*
【门警】police guard at an entrance
【门径】access; key; way:勤奋工作是成功的～。*Hard work is the path to success.*
【门槛】① threshold; door sill:跨过～ *cross the threshold* ② [方] way to do sth; knack; secret: ～精 *play one's card well; be shrewd* /我不知道他有什么～,但是他总是能在考试中拿高分。*I don't know what his secret is but he always gets high marks in the exams.*
【门可罗雀】you can catch birds at the door — a deserted house; visitors are few and far between
【门客】a hanger-on (or follower) of an aristocrat
【门口】entrance; doorway; door; gate:他站在学校～。*He stood in the entrance of the school.*
【门框】doorframe
【门廊】【建】porch; portico; stoop
【门类】department; class; kind; category:图书馆里有各种～的书籍。*There are different categories of books in a library.* /长篇小说、恐怖小说、科幻小说都属于小说这一～。*Novels, thrillers and science fiction all come under the heading of fiction.*
【门帘】door curtain
【门联】scrolls pasted on either side of the door forming a couplet
【门脸儿】[方] ① the vicinity of a city gate ② the facade of a shop; shop front:他们正在装饰商店的～。*They are decorating the facade of the shop.*
【门铃】doorbell; jingle bell:按～ *ring the doorbell*
【门楼】an arch over a gateway
【门路】① way to do sth; knack:有好几种～可以做成这件事。*There are several ways in which this can be done.* /他学到了做生意的～。*He acquired the knack for business.* ② social connections; pull:找～ *solicit help from potential backers; try to get sth done through pull*
【门罗主义】Monroe Doctrine (1823)
【门楣】① lintel (of a door) ② family status
【门面】① the facade of a shop; shop front:两间～ *a two-bay shop front* ② appearance; facade:装点～ *put up a facade; put on a front*
【门面话】formal and insincere remarks; lip service:她说的都是～,别当真。*What she said are routine courteous remarks; Don't take it seriously.*
【门牌】① (house) number plate ② street number; house number:你家的～是多少? *Could you tell me the number of your house?*
【门票】entrance ticket; admission ticket:不收～ *admission free* /出示～方可入场。*Entrance is permitted only on production of a ticket.*
【门球】【体】gate ball; croquet
【门儿清】[方] know everything very well:他对出版行业可是～。*He is familiar with everything about publishing.*
【门人】① pupil; disciple; follower ② a hanger-on of an aristocrat
【门扇】door leaf
【门神】door-god
【门生】① pupil; disciple; follower:得意～ *one's favourite student* ② I; your student (used by a successful candidate in an imperial examination to refer to himself before the chief examiner)
【门市】retail sales: ～价格 *retail price* /～商品

goods sold over the counter
【门闩】(door) bolt; (door) bar
【门锁】gate lock: ~开关 *door interlock switch*
【门厅】【建】hallway; entrance hall; vestibule
【门庭】① courtyard ② family status: ~衰落。*The family had declined in prosperity.*
【门庭若市】the courtyard is like a marketplace — be crowded with visitors; bustling: 他们家总是~。*His family is always swarming with visitors.*
【门徒】disciple; follower; adherent
【门外汉】layman; outsider; greenhorn: 这就是他这个~对艺术的看法。*This is just the layman's view of art.*
【门卫】entrance guard; custodian
【门下】① a hanger-on of an aristocrat ② I; your student (used by a follower or adherent to refer to himself before his master) ③ follow sb who has a special skill: 我想投在您的~学习绘画。*I wish that I could study painting under you.*
【门牙】front tooth; incisor
【门诊】outpatient service: ~病人 *outpatient; clinic patient* / ~部 *clinic; outpatient department* / ~治疗 *ambulatory treatment*
【门轴】door shaft
【门子】① gatekeeper; doorman ② social connection: 你有没有~帮我找个工作? *Could you solicit any help from your social connection to find a job for me?* ③[方]: 这~亲事老两口很称心。*The old couples are very satisfied with the marriage.*

扪 [书] stroke; touch
【扪心】[书] feel one's heart by hand — examine one's conscience: ~无愧 *feel no qualms upon self-examination; have a clear conscience* / ~自问 *feel one's chest and ask oneself — examine one's own conscience*

mèn

闷 ① feel depressed; have a tedious time: 烦~ *vexed; worried* / 沉~ *depressed in low spirits* ② sealed; tightly closed
see also mēn
【闷沉沉】depressed; gloomy: 她脸上~的表情 *a dispirited expression on her face*
【闷罐车】[方] boxcar
【闷棍】staggering blow; unexpected blow: 还没等我说话,他先给了我一~。*He greeted me with his sharp tongue before I had a chance to utter a word.*
【闷葫芦】①[喻] enigma; puzzle; riddle: 他说的话真是个~。*What he said is a riddle to me.* ② [喻] man of few words; people who always keeps silent: 他是个~,难得开口。*He is a man of reticent nature, so he seldom speaks.*
【闷酒】wine drunk in a bad mood: 别喝~了,咱们聊聊吧。*You can have a chat with me instead of drinking alone.*
【闷倦】bored and listless
【闷雷】① muffled (or dull) thunder ② unpleasant surprise; shock: 挨~ *receive a shock*
【闷闷不乐】feel bored; be in a depressed mood; in low spirits; feel blue; be down in the dumps: 他整日~。*He has been moping all day.* / 我需要一些事情来占据我的头脑。如果无事可做我就会~。*I need something to occupy my mind; I get depressed if I have nothing to do.*
【闷气】the sulks: 当我们告诉她忘了给她买礼物时,她回房间里生~去了。*When we told her we had forgotten buying her a gift, she went and sulked in her room.*
【闷郁】gloomy; depressed; despondent; morose; miserable: 我最近心情~。*I feel depressed recently.* / 当我看到他~的面孔,我知道一定发生了什么事。*When I saw his gloomy face, I knew that something mush have happened.*

焖 stew; braise: ~饭 *cook rice over a slow fire* / ~牛肉 *braised beef*
【焖锅】stew-pot; marmite

懑 [书] ① vexed; unhappy ② angry; indignant: 愤~ *feel indignant*

men

们 suffix (used after a personal pronoun or a noun to form a plural): 我~ *we* / 他~ *they* / 人~ *people* / 同志~ *comrades*

mēng

蒙[1] ① cheat; deceive; dupe: 欺~ *deceive; dupe* / 别~人。*Don't kid us.* ② make a wild guess: 这个答案是我瞎~的。*I made a guess at the answer.*

蒙[2] senseless; unconscious: 他把那个人打~过去了。*He knocked that person senseless.*
see also méng; měng
【蒙蒙亮】at the peep of day; at dawn; daybreak: 天~时,我就醒了。*I woke up at dawn.*
【蒙骗】deceive; cheat; hoodwink; delude; trick; swindle; beguile: 他用花言巧语~我。*He deceived me with fair words.* / 不坚定的消费者很容易被不道德的广告商~。*Gullible shoppers are easily duped by unscrupulous advertisers.*
【蒙事】[方] deceive; cheat: 他~呢。*He is deceiving you.*
【蒙头转向】lose one's bearings; be utterly confused; be bemused; mixed-up; be in a muddle: 复杂的情况让我~。*The complicated situation made me quite confused.*

méng

氓 (in ancient times) common people:群~ [书] *common herd*

虻 【动】horsefly; gadfly

萌 sprout; bud; germinate:故态复~ *slip back into one's old ways*

【萌动】① sprout; shoot forth; germinate; bud ② begin; start:春意~。*Spring awakens.*

【萌发】①【植】sprout; shoot forth; bud; germinate:芽在春天~。*Buds sprout in the spring; buds shoot forth in the spring.* ② emerge; appear:他~了一个坏念头。*An evil idea occurred to him.*

【萌蘖】sprout tillers: ~树 *sprouting tree* /~枝 *descendant; slip; imp*

【萌生】[书] come into being; arise:我~了强烈的好奇心。*An ardent curiosity arose in my heart.*

【萌条】young twigs

【萌芽】① sprout; shoot forth; bud; germinate: ~林 *sprout forest* /种子~。*Seeds sprout.* ② rudiment; shoot; seed; germ:一个新思想的~ *the bud of a new idea* /计划的~ *the germ of a project* /把坏事消灭在~阶段要比任其发展为严重事件效果好得多。*It's much better to nip bad problems in the bud as soon as they arise, than to let them escalate into something serious.*

【萌兆】[书] omen; foreboding; indication:他认为在去婚礼的路上遇到黑猫是一个不好的~。*He thought that his seeing a black cat on the way to his wedding was a bad omen.*

蒙 ① cover; overspread:她用一块布把桌子~上了。*She covered the table with a cloth.* ② encounter; receive; suffer:承~教导,不胜感激。*I am very grateful to your instruction.* ③ ignorance; illiteracy:发~ *teach a child to read and write* /启~ *enlighten* ④ (Méng) a surname
see also mēng; měng

【蒙版】【印】masking-out; masking

【蒙蔽】fool; hoodwink; deceive; throw dust in sb's eyes; pull the wool over sb's eyes:一时受~ *be hoodwinked for the moment* /不要被花言巧语所~。*Don't let yourself be fooled by honeyed words.* /他有意~我们。*He has deliberately deceived us.*

【蒙尘】[书] (of the emperor) be exposed to wind and dust — flee the capital due to the turmoil of war

【蒙垢】[书] be disgraced; lose face; be humiliated:整个家庭因为父亲的入狱而~。*The whole family suffered the disgrace of their father's imprisonment.*

【蒙馆】[旧] private primary school in old times

【蒙汗药】knockout drops; a kind of drug believed to have been used by highwaymen, etc. to drug their victims

【蒙哄】deceive or mislead people:他~她,使她相信他会娶她。*He deceived her into thinking he could marry her.*

【蒙混】hoodwink; deceive: ~过关 *get by under false pretences; muddle through; slip through; steal away*

【蒙眬】half asleep; drowsy; somnolent:睡眼~ *drowsy eyes*

【蒙昧】① barbaric; uncivilized; uncultured: ~社会 *uncultured society* ② ignorant; benighted; childishly ignorant: ~无知 *stupid and ignorant; unenlightened*

【蒙蒙】① drizzly; misty:窗外下着~细雨。*It is drizzling outside.* ② haze; misty:雾气~ *misty; boggy*

【蒙娜丽莎】Mona Lisa (La Gioconda), a famous painting by Leonardo da Vinci

【蒙难】be confronted by danger; suffer a catastrophe:将军昨天不幸~。*Unfortunately, the general was confronted by great danger yesterday.*

【蒙师】①[旧] old-style school teacher ② teacher who introduces one into a certain field of study

【蒙受】suffer; receive; sustain: ~不白 *be unjustly accused* /~耻辱 *suffer humiliation* /~天恩 *be in a state of grace* /~重大损失 *suffer heavy losses*

【蒙太奇】【影】montage: ~照片 *photomontage*

【蒙特利尔】Montreal, port and largest city in Canada

【蒙童】[旧] child who has just started to learn to read and write

【蒙头大睡】tuck oneself in and sleep like a log:她昨天一整天都在~。*She slept soundly the whole day yesterday.*

【蒙药】narcotic

【蒙冤】be wronged; suffer an injustice:她因~抑郁而终。*She suffered an injustice and died in gloom.*

【蒙在鼓里】live in a drum; be completely ignorant of; be kept in the dark:只有他还~。*Only he is still in the dark.*

盟[1] alliance:结~ *form an alliance* /经济同~ *economical alliance* ② sworn: ~兄弟 *sworn brothers* ③ league (an administrative division of the Inner Mongolia Autonomous Region)

盟[2] swear

【盟邦】an allied country; ally

【盟国】an allied country; ally:法国和英国在这次战争中是~。*France and England were allies in the war.*

【盟军】allied forces; allied armies: ~空军 *Allied Air Force* /~司令部 *Allied Command*

【盟誓】①[书] an oath of alliance; a treaty of alliance ② take an oath; swear; vow:当众~ *vow in public* /这个社团的每个成员都应该~永不泄露秘密。*Every member of the community has to swear an oath which says they will never reveal any of its secrets.*

【盟友】ally:我们坚定的~ *our staunch allies*

【盟员】a member of an alliance
【盟约】an oath of alliance; a treaty of alliance
【盟主】the leader (or chief) of an alliance

瞢 [书] blind; dim-sighted: 目光~然 *have a dim eyesight*

濛 [书] drizzle

【濛濛】drizzly; misty: 整日在时停时续地下着~细雨。*It drizzled off and on all day.*

曚

【曚昽】[书] dim daylight

朦

【朦胧】① dim: ~的月色 *dim moonlight* ② obscure; darkling; indistinct: ~的景色 *an obscure view*
【朦胧诗】obscure avant-garde poetry

矇 [书] blind

【矇眬】half asleep; drowsy: 睡眼~ *eyes heavy with sleep; drowsy*

měng

勐[1] [书] brave

勐[2] former administrative district in Xishuangbanna, Yunnan Province

猛 ① violent; vigorous; fierce: 凶~ *fierce; ferocious* / 火力~ *a heavy gunfire* / 突飞~进 *advance rapidly* ② suddenly; abruptly: ~一转身 *turn round abruptly* ③ with a spurt of force: ~着劲儿干活 *work with all one's efforts; try one's best to work*

【猛不防】suddenly; all of a sudden; by surprise; unexpectedly; unawares: ~后面有人推了他一下。*Suddenly someone gave him a push from the back.*
【猛冲】charge; hurl; make a break: 男孩~进屋里。*The boy charged into the room.*
【猛跌】slump; plummet; drop sharply: 股票价格~。*Stock prices plummeted.*
【猛攻】fierce attack; onslaught; attack violently: 我们向敌人右翼发起~。*We attacked fiercely on the left flank of the enemy.*
【猛击】slap; smash: 他~了我一掌。*He gave me a slap.*
【猛将】a valiant general
【猛进】proceed in rapid stride; push ahead vigorously: 突飞~ *advance by leaps and bounds*
【猛劲儿】[口] ① a spurt of energy; dash: ~将门拉开 *yank the door open* / 他一~拉断了绳子。*He jerked the rope and broke it.* ② great force: 搬重东西要用~。*You have to use concentrated force to move heavy objects.* ③ great vigour: 年轻人干活就是有股子~。*Young people always work with great energy.*
【猛力】jam on; vigorously: ~冲刺 *make a dash with all one's strength*
【猛烈】fierce; vigorous; heavy; violent: ~的风暴 *a violent storm* / 向敌人发起~进攻 *launch a fierce attack against the enemy* / 他受到野兽的~袭击。*He was savaged by wild animals.*
【猛扑】pounce on; spring on; hurl: ~向老鼠的猫 *a cat that pounced on a mouse* / 士兵向敌人~过去。*The soldier hurled himself upon the enemy.*
【猛禽】bird of prey
【猛然】suddenly; abruptly; all of a sudden: 我~想起这件事。*I recall it suddenly; in a flash I remembered.*
【猛士】a brave warrior
【猛兽】beast of prey
【猛省】suddenly realize; soon wake to
【猛醒】suddenly wake up (to the truth); be startled awake; soon wake to: 她~自己面临的危险。*She soon woke to the danger that confronted her.*
【猛药】potent drug (or medicine)
【猛增】rise greatly; skyrocket; balloon: 在这里发现了煤炭使土地价值~。*Discovery of coals here has skyrocketed land values.*
【猛涨】rise sharply; shoot up: 河水~。*The river is in spate.* / 石油价格~。*Petroleum prices skyrocketed.*
【猛鸷】hawk; eagle
【猛子】dive (into the water): 那只雄鹰一个~向兔子扑来。*The eagle dived down on the rabbit.*

蒙 (Měng) the Mongol nationality

see also mēng; méng

【蒙古】Mongolia: ~人 *Mongolian; Mongol* / ~语 *Mongol (language)*
【蒙古包】yurt; ger
【蒙古高原】Mongolian Plateau
【蒙古人种】the Mongolian stock; Mongoloid: ~性状 *mongoloid*
【蒙古族】① the Mongolian nationality, or the Mongolians (or Mongols) ② the Mongolians (or Mongols) of Mongolia
【蒙医】Mongolian medicine

锰 【化】manganese (Mn)

【锰钢】manganese steel

懵 muddled; ignorant; dull

【懵懂】muddled; ignorant: ~无知 *ignorant and dull*

蠓 【动】midge

【蠓虫儿】【动】midge; biting midge

mèng

孟 ① the first month (of a season): ~春 *the first month of spring* ② (in former times) eldest brother ③（Mèng）a surname

【孟斐斯】Memphis, an ancient city of Egypt south of Cairo

【孟加拉】Bengal：～人 *Bengali*；*Bengalese* /～语 *Bengali*（*language*）

【孟加拉湾】the Bay of Bengal

【孟浪】［书］rash；impetuous；inconsiderate：他后悔做了件～事。*He repented having done something rash.*

【孟买】Bombay, a city of west-central India

【孟秋】the first month of autumn

【孟什维克】Menshevik

【孟什维克主义】Menshevism

【孟夏】the first month of summer

【孟子】① Mencius（c. 372-289BC），Chinese famous Confucian philosopher ② Mengzi（The Book of Mencius），one of the four great texts of Confucianism

梦 ① dream：恶～ *evil dream* /从～中醒来 *awake from a dream* /黄粱美～ *a fond dream* ② dream：昨晚我～见你了。*I dreamt about you last night.* ③ illusion：幻～ *illusion*；*fancy*

【梦笔生花】dream of being a successful writer — be imaginative

【梦话】① words uttered in one's sleep；talk in one's sleep：我昨晚说～了吗？*Did I talk in my sleep last night*？② foolish talk；nonsense：满嘴～的疯子 *a raving maniac*

【梦幻】illusion；dream；reverie：～泡影 *pipe dream*；*bubbles and shadows* /她从～中清醒过来。*She wakes from her reverie.*

【梦幻曲】［音］reverie

【梦境】dreamland；dreamworld；dream

【梦寐】dream；sleep：～之事 *matters in dream and sleep*

【梦寐以求】dream of；long（or yearn）for sth day and night；crave for；hanker after：她～成为一个著名的作家。*She dreamt of becoming a famous writer.* /能够出国是他～的事。*He craves for going abroad.*

【梦乡】dreamland：进入～ *go off to dreamland*

【梦想】① vain hope；dream：上大学只是他的～而已。*Going to college is simply a fond dream for him.* ② earnest hope；dream of：我～成为全城最好的歌手。*I dream of being the best singer in the city.*

【梦魇】［医］nightmare；incubus

【梦遗】［医］nocturnal emission；wet dream

【梦呓】① sleeptalking；somniloquy ② rigmarole；foolish talk

【梦游症】［医］sleep walking；somnambulism：～者 *somnambulist*

【梦兆】［书］dream omen

mī

咪

【咪咪】［象］mew；meow（the sound made by a cat）

眯 ① narrow（one's eyes）：～着眼笑 *narrow one's eyes into a smile*；*smile with half-closed eyes* /～着眼看 *have a squint at sth* ②［方］nap；doze off：～一会儿 *take a short nap*
see also mí

【眯瞪】［方］doze off；take a short nap

【眯缝】narrow（one's eyes）：我～着眼睛想看得更清楚一些。*I narrowed my eyes to see more clearly.*

mí

弥 ① overflow；fill：～山遍野 *all over the hills and plains* ② fill：～缺 *fill a vacancy* ③ more：欲盖～彰。*The more what one tries to hide, the more it exposed.* ④（Mí）a surname

【弥补】make up；offset；compensate；remedy；make good：～赤字 *make up the deficit* /～损失 *make up for a loss*；*make good a loss* /无法～的罪过 *evils that are beyond remedy*

【弥封】fold or seal the examinee's name on an examination paper to guard against fraudulence

【弥缝】fill cracks — gloss over faults；patch up；put a good face on sth：我～了他们之间的一场无意义的争论。*I patched up a meaningless argument between them.*

【弥合】close；bridge：～裂痕 *close a rift*

【弥勒佛】Laughing Buddha

【弥留】［书］be dying：～遗言 *dying words* /父亲在～之际嘱咐儿子要还清债务。*The father urged his son to pay all the debts on his deathbed.*

【弥漫】fill the air；suffuse；pervade；be enveloped in：硝烟～ *air filled with gun smoke* /烟雾～ *heavy with smoke*

【弥蒙】（of smoke, mists, etc.）vast and vague：云雾～ *vast expanse of drifting cloud and mist* /在雾中一切东西都显得～。*In a fog everything looks vague.*

【弥撒】［宗］Mass：大～ *high mass* /小～ *low mass*

【弥散】spread or diffuse in all directions：空气中～着一股烟味。*The air is pervaded by a smell of smoking.* / 空气中～着花香。*The air was saturated with the perfume of the flowers.*

【弥散性】dispersivity：～呼吸 *diffusion respiration*

【弥天】vast；huge：～盖地 *with great momentum*

【弥天大谎】monstrous lie；outrageous lie；whopper；palpable lies；glaring falsehood：他们通过散布～和恶意的谣言毒害人们的头脑。*They poisoned people's minds by spreading glaring falsehoods and malicious rumours.*

【弥天大罪】an extraordinary crime；heinous crime；towering crime

【弥陀】［宗］Amitabha

【弥望】［书］everywhere：春色～。*It's spring everywhere.*

【弥雾】atomizing；atomization：～剂 *aerosol formu-*

lations

【弥月】［书］① a baby's completion of its first month of life：～之敬 *present for a baby just one month old* ② full month：他们新婚～。*The couple have just been married for a month.*

迷 ① lose one's way；get lost：向导领我们～了路。*The guide misled us and we got lost.* /当局者～。*The player can't see most of the game.* ② be fascinated by；indulge in；be crazy about：她的风度～住了他。*Her ways beguiled him.* /这孩子被冒险故事～住了。*The boy was enthralled by the stories of adventure.* ③ fan；enthusiast；fiend：财～ *miser* /棋～ *chess fan*；*chess enthusiast* /影～ *a movie fan* ④ confuse；enchant；fascinate：鬼～心窍 *be obsessed*；*be possessed*

【迷彩】【军】camouflage painting；pattern painting

【迷彩服】battle fatigues

【迷瞪】［方］puzzled；confused；dazed：他今天老是犯～。*He is absent-minded today.*

【迷宫】maze；labyrinth：径向～ *radial labyrinth* /声～ *acoustic labyrinth*

【迷航】（of a plane，ship，etc.）drift off course；lose one's course；get lost：那只船被风吹得～了。*The ship was blown off course.*

【迷糊】① misted；blurred；dimmed：泪水～的眼睛 *eyes blurred with tears* ② dazed；confused；muddled；perplexed：我被他的话弄～了。*I was perplexed by his words.*

【迷魂汤】① sth intended to turn sb's head；magic potion with the power to deprive a human soul ② flattery：灌～ *try to ensnare sb with honeyed words*

【迷魂阵】a scheme for confusing or bewildering sb；maze；trap：他给我摆了个～。*He set a trap for me.*

【迷惑】① puzzled；confused：我对昨天发生的事～不解。*I'm completely mystified about what happened yesterday.* ② puzzle；bewilder；confuse；perplex；baffle：～人心 *befuddle public opinion*；*confuse the masses* /不要为假象所～。*Don't be masked by false appearances.* /这个谜使我～不解。*This puzzle baffles me.*

【迷津】［书］a wild-goose chase；miss the ferry — wrong path one is often tempted to take：指点～ *show sb the right way*

【迷离】blurred；misted：～恍惚 *be in a stupor* /她泪眼～，几乎难以认出我。*She could hardly recognize me through the mist of tears that filled her eyes.*

【迷恋】be infatuated with；have a crush on；lose one's heart to：～一个女人 *be infatuated with a woman*

【迷路】① lose one's way；get lost；stray：在森林中容易～。*One easily gets lost in a forest.* ② go astray：这孩子因坏伙伴引诱而迷了路。*The boy was led astray by bad companions.* ③【医】inner ear；labyrinth

【迷乱】confused；bewildered

【迷漫】boundless and indistinct；vast and hazy

【迷茫】① vast and hazy ② confused；perplexed；dazed：他脸上是一副～的神情。*He wears a confused look.*

【迷蒙】① dim；hazy：暮色～ *enveloped in gathering dusk* ② in a trance；delirium：她陷入～状态。*She fell into a trance.*

【迷梦】pipe dream；fond illusion

【迷你】mini：～裙 *miniskirt* /～照相机 *subminiature*；*subminiature camera*

【迷人】① charming；fetching；fascinating：～的景色 *charming scenery* ② puzzle；confuse；mislead

【迷失】lose（one's way，etc.）：～方向 *lose one's bearings*；*get lost*

【迷睡】【医】sopor；catochus；eclipsis；trance

【迷途】① lose one's way：～少年 *errant youngsters* ② wrong path：～知返 *mend one's ways after realizing one's errors*；*retract from the wrong path*；*return from the lost way*

【迷惘】be perplexed；be at a loss：～的一代 *lost generation*

【迷雾】① dense fog ②［喻］anything that misleads people；miasma

【迷向】isotropic：～曲线 *isotropic curve* /～群 *group of isotropy*

【迷信】① superstition；superstitious belief；blind faith；blind worship：破除～ *do away with fetishes and superstitions* /西方一种普遍的～认为在13号房间睡觉是不吉利的。*A common superstition in western countries considered it bad luck to sleep in a room numbered 13.* ② blind faith；fetish：～书本 *book worship*

【迷醉】be fascinated by；enchant：他为这歌声所～。*He is enchanted with the singing.* /当她向我们讲述她的经历时，我们为之～。*We listened enthralled as she told us her experience.*

猕

【猕猴】【动】macaque；rhesus monkey

谜 ① riddle：灯～ *lantern riddles* /字～ *riddle about a Chinese character* ② enigma；mystery；puzzle：这件谋杀案仍然是一个～。*The murder remained a mystery.*
see also mèi

【谜底】① answer（or solution）to a riddle ② truth：揭穿～ *reveal the true story*

【谜面】clue to a riddle；conundrum

【谜团】doubts and suspicions；enigma：即使对于那些亲近的人来说，画家凡·高也是一个～。*The painter Van Gogh was an enigma，even to people who were close to him.*

【谜语】riddle；conundrum：猜～ *guess a riddle*

糜 ① gruel；porridge：肉～ *gruel with mincemeat* ② rotten；pasty：～灭 *rot away* ③ wasteful ④（Mí）a surname
see also méi

【糜烂】① rotten to the core；dissipated；debauched：～不堪 *utterly*（*or extremely*）*rotten* /我们整个假期都在抽烟、喝酒。这听起来一定很～。

M

We spent the whole holiday smoking and drinking; it must sound totally decadent. ②【医】erosion：宫颈～ *cervical erosion*

縻 ［书］harness；tie；bind：羁～ *draw over*

麋 elk

【麋羚】【动】hartebeest

【麋鹿】【动】mi-lu；David's deer

靡 waste

see also mǐ

【靡费】waste；dissipate；spend extravagantly：不要～公共财物。*Don't waste public property.*

mǐ

眯 （of dust，etc.）get into one's eyes：我～眼了。*Something has got into my eyes.*

see also mī

米[1] ① rice：白～ *cleaned rice* /红～ *red rice* /黄～ *yellow rice* /糯～ *glutinous rice* /人造～ *synthetic rice* /碎～ *broken rice* ② shelled or husked seed：花生～ *peanut seed* /小～ *husked millet* ③ anything like a grain of rice：海～ *dried shelled shrimps* ④（Mǐ）a surname

米[2] ［量］metre：立方～ *cubic metre* /平方～ *square metre* /厘～ *centimeter* /毫～ *milimetre* /那条河大约6～宽。*The river is about 6 metres wide.*

【米波】metre wave；metric wave

【米尺】meterstick；metre rule；metre scale

【米醋】rice vinegar

【米豆腐】［方］rice curd，a kind of food

【米饭】（cooked）rice：碗里有一些～。*There is some rice in the bowl.*

【米粉】① ground rice；rice flour ② rice flour noodles

【米糕】rice cake；rice pudding

【米格】MIG；Mig：～战斗机 *Mig fighter*

【米黄】cream-coloured

【米酒】rice wine

【米糠】rice bran

【米兰】Milan，a city of northern Italy northeast of Genoa：～人 *Milanese* /～银行 *Midland Bank，Ltd.*

【米老鼠】Mickey Mouse

【米粒】grain of rice

【米粮川】rich rice-producing area

【米面】① rice and wheat flour ② ground rice；rice flour ③［方］rice-flour noodles

【米色】cream-coloured：～布纹纸 *creamwove*

【米汤】① water in which rice has been cooked ② thin rice or millet gruel；rice water

【米线】［方］rice-flour noodles

【米纸】rice paper

【米制】metric system：～公约 *Metric Convention*

弭 ①［书］put down；quell；put an end to：水患消～。*The menace of floods is eliminated.* ②（Mǐ）a surname

【弭谤】［书］stop a slander

【弭兵】［书］stop a war；cease hostilities

【弭除】［书］eliminate；dispel；get rid of

【弭患】［书］remove the source of trouble；prevent troubles：～未萌 *nip trouble in the bud*

【弭乱】［书］put down a revolt；stop a civil war

靡[1] ①［书］fall with the wind：望风披～ *scatter at the sight of the oncoming force* ② excellent；fine：～曼 *charming；beautiful*

靡[2] ［书］no；not：～日不思。*Not a day passes without thinking of sth or sb*

see also mí

【靡丽】［书］magnificent；resplendent；luxurious；extravagant

【靡靡】decadent；demoralizing：～之音 *decadent music；obscene songs*

【靡然】leaning to one side：～从风 *follow the trend*

mì

觅 seek；look for；search；hunt：寻～线索 *look for clues* /～踪访迹 *follow a clue*

【觅求】search for；seek：他一生～真理。*He spent his life searching after truth.*

【觅取】search；look for；hunt for；seek：到深山老林～珍贵的木材 *search for precious timbers in the remote mountains*

【觅食】（of animal）hunt for food：狼是成群～食的。*Wolves hunt in packs.*

泌 secrete：分～消化液 *secrete digestive juices*

【泌尿器官】【生理】urinary organ

【泌尿系统】【生理】urinary system：～疾病 *urinary system disease*

秘 ① secret：奥～ *enigmatic；abstruse* ② keep sth secret：～而不露 *conceal；hide* ③ rare

see also bì

【秘宝】a rare treasure

【秘本】treasured private copy of a rare book or text

【秘藏】hide；conceal：他把偷来的钱～在山洞中。*He secreted the stolen money in the cavern.*

【秘传】hand down from generation to generation as a family secret

【秘而不宣】keep sth secret；keep quiet；not let anyone in on a secret；keep sth dark；keep sth under wraps：没有人知道他们的恋情——他们～。*No one knew about their love affair — they kept it secret.*

【秘方】secret recipe；esoteric recipe：祖传～ *esoteric recipe handed down from one's ancestors* /宽容和理解是婚姻幸福的～。*Tolerance and understanding are the recipe for a happy marriage.*

【秘府】palace repository of classics

【秘籍】rare and valuable book

【秘诀】secret; open sesame:长寿～ *a recipe for living long* /烹饪业的～ *the mysteries of cooking game* /做好这道菜的～在于烹饪时间。*The secret of this dish is in the time of cooking.*

【秘密】① secret; clandestine; confidential; underground: ～婚姻 *a secret marriage* /～会议 *meeting in camera; executive session* /～交易 *clandestine dealings* /～军事行动 *covert military operations* /～配方 *secret formula* /～情报 *confidential information* /～渠道 *back channel* /～谈判 *secret negotiations* /～途径 *back door* ② sth secret:公开的～ *open secret* /泄露～ *disclose a secret; let the cat out of the bag*

【秘史】secret history (as of a feudal dynasty); inside story:清宫～ *inside story of the Qing court*

【秘事】private affair

【秘书】secretary:机要～ *confidential secretary* /私人～ *private secretary* /行政～ *administrative secretary* /执行～ *executive secretary*

【秘书长】secretary-general

【秘书处】secretariat

【秘闻】unknown information

密 ① dense; thick; close; intensive:浓～的丛林 *a dense jungle* /紧～的花束 *compact clusters of flowers* /树木长得很～。*The trees grew thick.* ② close; intimate:亲～的朋友 *a close friend* ③ fine; delicate:精～ *precise; accurate* ④ secret; confidential:告～ *inform on sb* /绝～ *top secret* /泄～ *leak a secret* ⑤ (Mì) a surname

【密报】① secretly report; inform against sb:是谁～了这件事? *Who has reported it secretly?* ② secret report; secret message:他刚才接到一封～。*He received a confidential report just now.*

【密闭】① tightly closed:门窗～。*The doors and windows are tightly closed.* ② airtight; hermetic: ～容器 *airtight container* /～循环 *closed recirculation*

【密播】【农】dense sowing

【密不透风】① keep it secret; keep quiet:他们的计划～。*They has kept their plans under wraps.* ② airtight

【密布】be densely covered:繁星～。*Twinkling starts dotted the sky.* /乌云～。*The sky is overcast.* /这一地区地雷～。*This place is densely placed with mines.*

【密电】① cipher telegram ② secretly telegraph sb

【密度】① density; thickness:人口～ *the density of population* /居住～ *density of occupancy* /运输～ *density of freight (passenger or traffic)* ②【物】density:电流～ *ampere density* /浮力～ *buoyant density* /晶体～ *crystalline density* /摩尔～ *molar density*

【密度计】【物】densimeter; density indicator

【密封】① seal up; seal airtight; seal hermetically: ～罐头 *seal up a tin* ② sealed; hermetical; airtight; airproof: ～的文件 *sealed documents*

【密封舱】【天】capsule【航】sealed cabin; airtight cabin

【密告】secretly report; inform against sb:她向敌人～了我们的计划。*She secretly reported our plan to the enemies.*

【密会】① meet secretly:他们在花园里～。*They met secretly in the garden.* ② secret meeting; closed session

【密级】classification (of government confidential documents):请在文件上标明～。*Please mark the classification of the documents.*

【密集】concentrated; dense; serried:排列～的军队 *troops in serried ranks* /～的人群 *a dense crowd* /枪声越来越～。*The gunshots are becoming more and more intensive.*

【密件】a confidential paper (or letter); classified material

【密径】secret path

【密林】thick (or dense) wood; thicket

【密令】① give a secret order or instructions ② secret order or instructions

【密码】cipher; cipher code; secret code:用～书写 *write in cipher* /破译～ *break a code* /这封信是用～写的,我看不懂。*The letter was written in some kind of secret code which I couldn't understand.*

【密密层层】packed closed layer upon layer; dense; thick:警察把大楼～地包围起来了。*Police surrounded the building ring upon ring.*

【密密丛丛】(of grass or trees) dense; thick; luxuriant:山坡上长满～的树林。*Luxuriant forests covered the hillside.*

【密密麻麻】[口] close and numerous; thickly dotted; as thick as huckleberries:国庆节那天,天安门广场上的人～的。*The Tian'an Men Square is packed with people on the national day.*

【密密匝匝】[口] thick; dense:她脑后～梳了很多的辫子。*Dozens of braids hung thick from the back of her head.*

【密谋】conspire; plot; intrigue; scheme:歹徒～抢劫一家银行。*The criminals conspired to rob a bank.* /他们～陷害她。*They intrigue against her.* /这伙人正在～可怕的报复行动。*The gang is scheming their horrible revenge.*

【密切】① close; intimate; familiar:关系～ *be close; be on intimate terms* ② build close links; become intimate:进一步～两国关系 *forge stronger ties between the two countries* ③ carefully; closely: ～配合 *act in concert; act in close coordination* /～联系群众 *maintain close ties with the masses*

【密商】hold private counsel; hold secret talks

【密使】secret emissary; secret envoy

【密室】a room used for secret purposes

【密实】closely knit; thick; tight: ～混凝土 *dense concrete*

【密斯】(translation) miss

【密谈】secret (or confidential, private) talk; talk behind closed doors:你知道他们～的内容吗? *Do you know what they talked in their private talk?*

【密探】secret agent; spy:警方～ *a police spy*

【密纹】microgroove：～唱片 *micro-groove record*
【密西西比河】Mississippi River, the longest river of North America
【密歇根湖】Lake Michigan, one of the five Great Lakes of North America
【密信】confidential letter
【密养】dense stocking
【密友】close (or fast) friend; bosom friend; fast friend：我的心里话只对～说。*I only confide to my bosom friends.*
【密语】① code; code word ② secret talks
【密育】short intervals between births
【密约】secret agreement; secret treaty
【密钥】key secret code：～加密 *secret key encryption*
【密云不雨】dense clouds but no rain — trouble is brewing
【密召】summon secretly
【密诏】secret imperial edict
【密植】【农】close planting：合理～ *rational close planting*
【密旨】secret edict
幂 ①［书］cloth for covering sth ②［书］cover; shield ③【数】power：对称～ *symmetric power* /上～ *super power* /素数～ *powers of primes* /整数～ *power of integers*
【幂乘积】【数】power product
【幂函数】【数】power function
【幂级数】【数】power series; series of powers
【幂零】【数】nilpotent：～代数 *nilpotent algebra* /～矩阵 *nilpotent matrix*
【幂指数】【数】power exponent; potent sign
谧 ［书］quiet; peaceful：安～ *tranquil*
【谧静】serene; tranquil; calm：～的乡村生活 *a tranquil life in the country*
蜜 ① honey：巢～ *section honey* /蜂～ *honey* /酿～ *make honey* /～甜蜂蜇人。*Honey is sweet, but the bee stings.* ② honey-like thing：花～ *nectar* /苹果～ *apple honey* /糖～ *molasses* ③ sweet; luscious：甜言～语 *cajolery*; *sweet talk*
【蜜蜂】honeybee; bee：～酿蜜。*The bee makes honey.* /他被～蜇了。*He was stung by a bee.*
【蜜柑】tangerine orange; tangerine
【蜜瓜】honeydew melon
【蜜花】honey flower
【蜜饯】candied fruit; preserved fruit; sweet; paste：～草莓 *strawberry preserves* /～糖果 *sweetmeats made of fruit and sugar*
【蜜蜡】beeswax
【蜜露】honeydew
【蜜鸟】honeycreeper
【蜜色】light yellow
【蜜树】honey tree
【蜜语】sweet words：她靠对老板甜言～爬到了现在的位子。*She got where she did by honeying up to the boss.* /她用～使他相信她。*She sweet-talked him into believing her.*
【蜜源】nectar source：～植物 *nectariferous plant; bee plant*
【蜜月】honeymoon：度～ *spend a honeymoon* /他在新岗位上的～期很快过去了。*The honeymoon on his new position was soon over.*
【蜜枣】candied date or jujube
【蜜汁】honeydew

mián

眠 ① sleep：睡～ *sleep* /失眠 *suffer from insomnia* ② dormancy：冬～ *hibernate* /蚕三～了。*The silkworm has completed its third stage of dormancy.*
绵 ① silk floss ② continuous：连～ *unbroken; interminable* ③ thin; soft：软～～ *soft* ④［方］(of a person's temper) gentle：她性子很～，不爱说话。*She is of a gentle temper and seldom speaks to others.*
【绵白糖】fine white sugar; powdered sugar
【绵薄】［谦］(my) meager strength; humble effort：～之力 *one's pygmy effort*
【绵长】last a long period of time：～岁月 *a long time*
【绵绸】【纺】fabric made from waste silk
【绵惙】［书］be critically ill
【绵笃】be critically ill
【绵顿】［书］be critically ill for a long time：～在床 *be bedridden with prolonged illness*
【绵亘】(of mountains, etc.) stretch in an unbroken chain：山脉～数百里。*The mountains stretch for several hundred li.*
【绵和】［方］(of a person's temper) gentle; mild：她性情～。*She is as mild as a dove.* /他的性情太～了，即使有充分的理由，他也不会生气。*He has too mild a nature to get angry, even if he has good cause.*
【绵茧】satiny cocoon
【绵里藏针】① a needle hidden in silk floss — a firm character behind a gentle appearance; gentle but firm ② an iron hand in a velvet glove
【绵力】［谦］one's humble effort; one's limited power
【绵连】unbroken; continuous：～的雨 *continuous rain* /～不断的来访者 *a perpetual stream of visitors*
【绵毛】【植】wool; tomentum
【绵密】meticulous; detailed; well-considered：她对待工作心思～。*She was very meticulous about her work.*
【绵绵】continuous; unbroken：细雨～ *the incessant rain*
【绵软】① soft：～的手 *soft tender hand* ② weak; frail; fragile：她两腿～。*Her legs felt weak.* /他～的身体根本站不起来。*He could hardly stand up with such a frail body.*
【绵糖】fine white sugar
【绵甜】mild and sweet：～的酒 *mellow wine*

【绵土】spongy soils
【绵延】be continuous; stretch long and unbroken: ~的山脉 *mountains stretching endlessly*
【绵羊】sheep:美利奴~ *merino sheep*
【绵远】far away; distant; remote:祖父向我讲述他年轻时候曾经去过的那些~的国家。*Grandfather told me the stories of the faraway countries he had visited when he was young.*
【绵纸】tissue paper
【绵子】[方] silk floss; silk wadding
棉 ① general term for cotton and kapok:草~ *cotton* /木~ *kapok* ② cotton:纯~ *pure cotton* /皮~ *ginned cotton* /丝~ *silk cotton* /原~ *raw cotton* /籽~ *unpinned cotton* ③ cotton-like material:人造~ *artificial cotton*
【棉袄】cotton-padded jacket
【棉白杨】【植】cottonwood
【棉被】quilt with cotton wadding
【棉饼】cottonseed cake
【棉布】cotton cloth; cotton
【棉的确良】synthetic material of cotton and dacron
【棉都】Cottonopolis, the nickname for Manchester
【棉豆】butter bean
【棉纺】cotton spinning: ~厂 *cotton mill* / ~工艺 *cotton spinning* / ~业 *cotton textile industry*
【棉猴儿】hooded cotton-padded coat; (knee-length) parka; anorak
【棉花】cotton:采~ *pick cotton* / ~软而白。*Cotton is soft and white.*
【棉花包】cotton bale
【棉花胎】[方] a cotton wadding (for a quilt)
【棉花糖】cotton candy
【棉花套子】[方] a cotton wadding (for a quilt)
【棉裤】cotton-padded trousers
【棉蕾】square
【棉铃】cotton boll
【棉毛】cotton and wool
【棉毛裤】long cotton underwear; cotton-wool trousers; cotton trousers
【棉毛衫】cotton jersey; cotton-wool jersey
【棉毛毯】union blanket
【棉毛织品】linsey-woolsey
【棉农】cotton grower
【棉皮鞋】lined leather shoe
【棉签】cotton swab
【棉球】【医】tampon
【棉纱】cotton yarn
【棉石】cotton rock
【棉树】cotton plant
【棉桃】cotton boll
【棉套】a cotton-padded covering for keeping sth warm
【棉田】cotton field
【棉袜】quilted stockings
【棉纤维】cotton fibre; lint
【棉线】cotton thread; cotton
【棉鞋】cotton-padded shoes
【棉絮】① cotton fibre ② a cotton wadding (for a quilt, etc.)
【棉衣】cotton-padded clothes
【棉油】cottonseed oil: ~皂 *cotton seed oil soap*
【棉织品】cotton goods; cotton textiles; cotton fabrics

miǎn

免 ① exempt; excuse; free; immune: ~税的收入 *income exempt from taxation* /赦~罪行 *remit one's sins* / ~于刑事诉讼 *immune from criminal prosecution* /他因为身体状况不好而~服兵役。*He is exempt from military service because of his bad health.* ② avoid; evade; escape:避~灾祸 *elude a blow* /幸~于难 *escape from danger* ③ do not:闲人~进。*No admittance except on business.*
【免不得】unavoidable; inevitable; difficult to avoid:如果他继续冒险,最终~要进监狱。*If he continues to take risks, he is bound to end in prison.*
【免不了】be unavoidable; be bound to be; certainly; be sure to
【免除】① prevent; avoid: ~误会 *avoid misunderstanding* ② excuse; exempt; relieve: ~责任 *dissolution of responsibility* /外交官的日用品可以~关税。*A foreign official can be exempted from the customs duties for the basic necessities.*
【免得】so as not to; so as to avoid; lest:你最好说清楚些,~引起误会。*You'd better speak clearly so as to avoid misunderstanding.*
【免费】free of charge; free; gratis: ~搭乘公共汽车 *travel free on buses* / ~学校 *a free school*
【免冠】① take one's hat off (in salutation) ② without a hat on; bareheaded:证件上要贴~照片。*A bareheaded photo is needed for the certificate.*
【免检】exempt from inspection: ~物品 *articles exempt from examination*
【免开尊口】better shut your mouth; keep you opinion to yourself:我知道老板是不会答应的,你最好~。*I know the boss will refuse you definitely; you'd better shut your mouth.*
【免礼】be at ease; dispense with formalities
【免赔条款】franchise clause
【免票】① free pass; free ticket ② free of charge:儿童和老人可以~。*Children and elder people are free of charge.*
【免试】① be exempted from an examination ② be exempted from a test
【免税】exempt from taxation; duty-free; free of duty
【免俗】act against the common practice:不能~ *follow the common practice*; *unable to break away from convention*
【免烫】permanent press; wash and wear
【免息】free of interest

【免刑】【律】exempt from punishment
【免修】be excused from a college course：教授同意她～语文。*The professor agreed her exemption from Chinese courses.*
【免验】exempt from customs examination
【免疫】【医】immunity (from disease)：伴随～*concomitant immunity* /复合～*complex immunity* /过继性～*adoptive immunity* /获得性～*acquired immunity* /抗毒～*antitoxic immunity* /人工获得性～*artificially acquired immunity* /细胞～*cell-mediated immunity* /遗传～*genetic immunity*
【免役】exempt from military service：他因身体不好而～。*He was exempted from military service on the grounds of ill health.*
【免战牌】(in ancient times) a sign used to show refusal to fight
【免职】dismiss; remove sb from office; depose; fire; give sb the boot; relieve sb of their duties; sack：他被～了。*He was relieved of his post.* /当老板得知他因偷窃被抓住时，他立刻就被～了。*As soon as the employer heard that he had been caught stealing, she gave him his notice at once.*
【免职书】walking papers; walking ticket
【免罪】exempt from punishment

勉 ① strive; try one's best：奋～*make a great effort* ② encourage; urge：互～*encourage one another* /自～*spur oneself on sth* ③ try to do sth which is beyond one's reach

【勉力】exert oneself; strive; make great efforts; endeavour; put one's mind to sth; be at pains to do sth：～改进工作 *endeavour to improve one's work* /该公司多年来一直～提高效率。*The company constantly strove for greater efficiency in the past years.*
【勉励】encourage; urge; inspire：～上进 *incite one to make progress* /父亲～我更好地工作。*Father encouraged me to work better.*
【勉强】① manage with an effort; do with difficulty：～支持下去 *hold out with difficulty* ② reluctantly; unwillingly：他～答应了我的条件。*He accepted the terms I put forward reluctantly.* /她～说了点感谢话。*She was very grudging in her thanks.* /他～同意这个计划。*He agreed on the plan unwillingly; he acquiesced in the plan.* ③ force sb to do sth：不要～她去。*Don't force her to go.* ④ inadequate; unconvincing; farfetched：这个解释很～。*The explanation is rather unconvincing.* /让我承担这个工作实在是很～。*I am really inadequate to do the job.* /她的问候有点～。*Her greeting was a little strained.* ⑤ barely (enough); scarcely：～度日 *keep the wolf from the door; manage to make a living with efforts* /我～及格。*I barely passed the examination.* /他参加工作时～十六岁。*He was scarcely sixteen when he began to work.* /在班上他～跟得上。*He can only just rub along in class.*
【勉为其难】agree to do what one knows is beyond one's ability or power; exert oneself in spite of difficulties; make the best of a bad job

娩 childbirth; delivery

【娩出】【医】be delivered of a baby with its placenta and foetal membrane

冕 crown; coronet：加～*coronation*

【冕流】coronal streamer
【冕云】【天】coronal cloud

愐 [书] ① think; consider ② industrious; diligent

缅[1] remote

缅[2] [方] turn; roll up：～袖子 *roll up the sleeves*

【缅甸】Burma：～人 *Burman; Burmese* /～语 *Burmese (language)*
【缅怀】reminisce; cherish the memory of; recall：～往事 *recall past events with deep feelings* /～先烈 *cherish the memory of the revolutionary martyrs*
【缅邈】[书] remote; far back
【缅想】think of (past events); recall; cherish the memory of

腼

【腼腆】shy; bashful; coy：她干什么事都很～。*She is rather bashful in doing anything.* /他在陌生人面前显得很～。*He is shy in the presence of strangers.*

miàn

面[1] ① face; visage：～带笑容 *have a smile on one's face* /～露喜色。*One's face beamed with delight.* /～带病容。*One's face assumes a sickly countenance.* /他怒容满～。*He had a face like thunder.* ② face (a certain direction)：背山～水 *with hills behind and the river in front* /～南的一个窗户 *a window that faces the south* /～向党旗庄严宣誓 *stand facing the party flag and make a solemn vow* /我的房子～向一条河。*My house faces a river.* ③ surface; face：路～*road surface* /地球表～*the face of the earth* /桌～*top of a table* /玻璃～很光滑。*Glass has a smooth surface.* ④ face-to-face; directly：我会当～感谢他们。*I will thank them personally.* ⑤ cover; outside; the right side：被～儿 *top covering of a quilt* ⑥【数】surface：平～*a plane surface* /曲～*a curved surface* /球～*spherical surface* ⑦ side; aspect：正～*front; right side* /侧～*side* /他性格中勇敢的一～*the brave side of his personality* /考虑事情的各个方～*consider every aspect of the matter* /不要只看事物的黑暗～。*Don't just look on the dark side of things.* ⑧ used as a suffix to form a noun of locality：前～*in front* /后～*at the back* /外～*outside* ⑨ [量]：一～镜子 *a mirror* /一～旗 *a flag* /我见过他一～。*I saw him only once.*

面[2] ① flour; white flour: 白～ *wheat flour* /豆～ *bean flour* /小米～ *millet flour* ② powder: 把药片磨成～ *to grind the tablets into powder* ③ noodles: 挂～ *fine dried noodles*; *vermicelli* /汤～ *noodle soup* /炸酱～ *noodles served with fried soya paste* ④［方］(of food) soft and floury: 这瓜吃起来很～。*The melon tastes soft and floury.*

【面案】cook rice, make steamed bread, etc.

【面板】① board for kneading dough ② front board; front panel: ～仪表 *panel meter*

【面包】bread: 一条～ *a loaf of bread* /黑～ *black bread* /烤～ *toasted bread* /全麦～ *whole-wheat bread*

【面壁】① face the wall — not care about anything ②【宗】face the wall and mediate — be absorbed in study ③ (in former times) stand facing the wall — a kind of punishment

【面不改色】remain calm; without turning a hair; keep a straight face; keep one's head; composed; unruffled; keep a stiff upper lip: 我想做到～,但是我的手在颤抖。*I tried to stay calm but my hands were shaking.* /面对批评,他～。*He appeared unruffled by such criticism.*

【面部照片】mug shot

【面茶】seasoned millet mush

【面陈】state one's opinion personally: ～利害关系 *expound the advantages and disadvantages in person*

【面斥】criticize (or denounce) face-to-face

【面点】snacks made from wheat or flour

【面动脉】facial artery

【面对】face; confront: 军人必须勇敢而冷静地～危险和死亡。*A soldier has to confront danger and death calmly and bravely.* /警察让她～证据时她才承认偷了钱。*Only when the police confronted her with evidence did she admit that she had stolen the money.*

【面对空导弹】surface-to-air missile

【面对面】facing each other; face-to-face; front to front: ～的争论 *a face-to face argument* /我走出门,～碰上了他。*I went out of the room and found myself face-to-face with him.*

【面额】① denomination: 小～货币 *money of small denominations*

【面坊】flour mill in former times

【面肥】① leavening dough; leaven ②【农】top-dressing

【面粉】wheat flour; flour: 粗～ *middlings flour* /黑～ *grahamflour*; *brown flour* /强化～ *fortified flour* /全麦～ *whole wheat flour* /优质～ *sound flour*

【面骨】facial bone

【面馆】restaurant selling noodles, dumplings, etc.

【面和心不和】be harmonious in appearance but estranged at heart

【面红耳赤】be red in the face; be flushed; reddened; blush: 她气得～。*She flushed with anger*; *she reddened with anger.* /他的话使这姑娘～。*His remark put the girl to the blush.*

【面糊】(miànhù) ① cooked flour paste ②［方］flour paste

【面糊】(miànhu)［方］soft and floury: 土豆蒸得很～。*The steamed potatoes taste soft and floury.*

【面黄肌瘦】sallow and emaciated; lean and haggard: 长期的疾病让她～。*The prolonged illness made her lean and haggard.*

【面积】area; space: 长方形的～ *the area of a rectangle* /礼堂的坐席～ *the seating space of an auditorium* /单元～ *cell area* /临界～ *critical area* /流通～ *circulation area* /实际～ *actual area* /使用～ *usable floor space* /受压～ *compression area* /学校占地～三百亩。*The school covers an area of 300 mu.*

【面肌】facial muscle

【面颊】cheek: 她的～通红。*Her cheeks became red.*

【面角】【数】face angle

【面巾】［方］face towel

【面筋】gluten: ～蛋白 *mucedin*

【面具】mask: 防尘～ *dust mask* /防毒～ *antigas mask*; *breathing mask*; *gas mask* /消防～ *fire mask* ② mask; false facade: 一副忠诚的～ *a mask of loyalty* /他摘下了假～。*He threw off his mask.*

【面孔】face: 英俊的～ *a handsome face* /拉长了～ *pull a long face* /上课第一天我们看到许多新～。*We saw many new faces on the first day of classes.* /她的～涨得通红。*Her face blushed.* /漂亮的～就是最好的介绍信。*A good face is a letter of recommendation.*

【面宽】① width of the broad side of a room (or house) ② width of cloth

【面料】① material for making the surface (of a garment) ② veneer

【面临】be faced with; be confronted with; be up against: ～考验 *face a test* /我目前～很多困难。*I am confronted with many difficulties at present.*

【面码儿】vegetable served with noodles

【面貌】① face; features: 她的嘴唇是～最漂亮的部分。*Her lips were her best feature.* ②［喻］appearance; look; aspect: 城市～ *the appearance of a city* /政治～ *political background*

【面面观】comprehensive observation and analysis: 民俗～ *multi-dimensional view of folk-custom*

【面面俱到】pay attention to all sides; attend to each and every aspect of a matter; considerate; thoughtful: 她对我的生活照顾得～。*She is extremely considerate of my life.*

【面面相觑】look at each other in blank dismay; exchange glances in bewilderment; look at one another in embarrassment: 我们俩～,毫无办法。*We looked each other in helpless despair.*

【面膜】face pack

【面目】① face; features; visage: ～清秀 *with delicate features* /～可憎 *repulsive in countenance* /～严厉 *hard-faced*; *hard-favoured* ② appearance; look; aspect: 还其本来～ *reveal sth in its true colours* ③ self-respect; honour; sense of shame: 我

实在没有～去见他们。*I really have no face to see all of them.*

【面目全非】be changed beyond recognition; out of recognition; lose one's identity:建筑物被大火烧得～。*The building was burned beyond recognition.*

【面目一新】take on an entirely new look; assume a new aspect; put on a new face:对比十年前,我发现家乡～。*I found my hometown presenting a completely new appearance as compared with the situation ten years ago.*

【面庞】contours of the face; face:圆圆的～ *a round face*

【面盆】①［方］washbasin; washbowl ② bowl for kneading dough

【面坯儿】cooked noodles before being served with sauces and dressings

【面皮】①［方］face; cheek:你别埋怨她了,这姑娘～薄。*Stop complaining to her; the girl is very sensitive.* ②［方］wrapper (of dumpling)

【面片儿】dough strips

【面洽】discuss face to face; take up a matter with sb personally:关于合同的事情,请和她～。*You can go and see her for the contract.*

【面前】in the presence of; in (the) face of; in front of; before:在公众～讲话 *speak in the presence of a large audience* /他站在她～。*He stood before her.* /我们的～是光明的前途。*There is an infinitely bright future ahead of us.*

【面人儿】dough figurine

【面容】facial features; face; look:好心肠胜过好～。*Good looks are not as important as kindness.*

【面如土色】look ashen; look pale:吓得～ *turn pale in terror* /你～,发生了什么事? *You are as white as a sheet; what's happened?*

【面如桃花】(of a girl) rosy cheeks

【面色】complexion: ～很好 *a good complexion* /红润的～ *a sanguine complexion* /～灰白 *gray-faced*

【面纱】① veil:她出去前先用～遮住脸。*She veiled her face before she went out.* ②［喻］sth cover the truth:揭开宫廷生活神秘的～ *reveal the secrets of palace life*

【面善】① look familiar:演讲的那个人很～。*The man who is delivering a speech looks very familiar.* /我和她～不熟。*Her face looks familiar but I am not acquainted with her.* ② affable; amiable; kind: ～心狠 *be kind in appearance but evil at heart* /她是个～的人。*She is amiable to others.*

【面商】consult face to face

【面生】look unfamiliar:当着～的人,他显得十分拘谨。*He behaves restrainedly before unfamiliar people.*

【面食】cooked wheaten food:她酷爱～。*Wheaten food is her favourite.*

【面世】(of books, etc.) be published; (of goods) go into the market:他的新作品即将～。*His new work will soon be published.* /这个品牌的空调已经～了。*The air-conditioners with this brand have been put into market.*

【面试】interview; oral quiz:进行～ *go for an interview*

【面首】［书］a kept man of a noblewoman; male concubine

【面授】instruct personally: ～机宜 *personally instruct the confidential content; give confidential instruction in person*

【面熟】look familiar:我看他～。*He looks quite familiar to me.*

【面霜】cream; face cream; facial cream

【面塑】dough modeling, a kind of folk craft

【面瘫】【医】facial paralysis

【面谈】speak to sb face to face; take up a matter with sb personally:她正与一广告公司～。*She is interviewing with an advertising company.*

【面汤】(miàntāng) ①［方］hot water prepared for washing face ② water in which noodles have been boiled

【面汤】(miàntang)［方］noodles in soup

【面条】noodles:擀～ *make noodles*

【面团】dough

【面无表情】expressionless

【面无人色】look ghastly pale:吓得～ *turn ghastly pale with fright*

【面向】① face: ～南面 *face the south* ② cater to; be suited to the needs of: ～广大读者 *be suited to the needs of reading public*

【面相】［方］facial features; looks; appearance:匆忙中我没有看清他的～。*In my haste I didn't see him clearly.*

【面谢】thank sb personally

【面叙】talk face to face:就此搁笔,余容～。*I'll just stop writing and talk with you face to face about other things.*

【面议】negotiate face to face; hold personal negotiation:价格～ *negotiate the price face to face*

【面有难色】show reluctance on one's face

【面谀】［书］flatter sb to his face

【面罩】face guard; mask; visor; screen

【面值】① par value; face value; nominal value:以高于(等于、低于)～的价格出售股票 *sell shares above(at, below) par* ② denomination

【面砖】【建】face brick

【面子】① outer part; covering; outside; face:这件上衣～是红的,里面是灰的。*The coat was red outside and grey inside.* ② reputation; prestige; face:保全～ *save one's face* /他因赌博而～扫地。*He lost his reputation due to gambling.* ③ feelings; sensibilities:给～ *do sb proud* /不讲～ *show no consideration for others' sensibilities* ④［口］power:药～ *powdered medicine*

眄 ［书］look sideways at sb

【眄视】［书］give a sidelong glance; look askance at sb

miāo

喵 [象] mew; miaow (the crying sound of a cat)

miáo

苗 ① seedling; young plant; sprout: 插~ *transplant seedlings* /裸根~ *bare-rooted seedling* /烟~ *tobacco seedling* /野生~ *natural seedling* /育~ *grow seedlings* /幼~ *young sprout* ② offspring: 他是家里的独~。*He is the only son of the family.* ③ young of some animals: 鱼~ *(fish) fry* ④ vaccine: 牛痘~ *(bovine) vaccine; smallpox* ⑤ sth like a young plant: 火~儿 *flames; the tongue of flame* ⑥ Miao nationality ⑦ (Miáo) a surname

【苗床】seedbed; nursery bed: ~土壤 *nursery soil*

【苗而不秀】shoot forth but do not yield fruit — show great potentialities but fail to fulfil them

【苗肥】fertilizer applied during seedling stage

【苗木】【林】nursery stock: ~箱 *plant box*

【苗圃】nursery (of young plants)

【苗期】【农】seedling stage: ~管理 *seedling management*

【苗禽】young of poultry

【苗情】growth of seedling

【苗儿】[方] early development; sing

【苗条】(of a woman) slender; slight; slim; svelte; willowy: ~的少女 *a slender girl; a slight girl*

【苗条霜】*slimming lotion*

【苗头】symptom of a trend; suggestion of a new development; straw in the wind; indication: 要注意不良倾向的~。*Watch out for symptoms of unhealthy tendencies.* /他有在选举中获胜的~。*There are indications that he will win the election.*

【苗绣】Miao embroidery

【苗裔】[书] progeny; descendants; offspring

【苗猪】piglet; pigling

【苗子】① [方] young plant; seedling ② young successor: 她是个有前途的好~。*She is a promising young successor.* ③ [方] symptom of a trend; suggestion of a new development; straws in the wind

【苗族】the Miao nationality, or the Miaos

描 ① copy; trace: ~花 *portray a flower* ② retouch: ~底片 *retouch photographic plate*

【描红】① trace in black ink over characters printed in red (in learning to write with a brush) ② piece of paper with red characters printed on it

【描画】draw; paint; depict; describe: 孩子们正在~公园。*The children are drawing pictures of the park.*

【描绘】depict; describe; portray: ~北京风光的一组照片 *a series of pictures depicting the scenery of Beijing* /栩栩如生地~人物 *portray one's characters to life* /这个故事~了一个英雄的成长。*The story portrays the growth of a hero.*

【描记】(in monitoring) record of electrical or light curves on a screen

【描金】trace a design in gold

【描眉】pencil one's eyebrows

【描摹】① trace: ~花样 *trace a flower pattern* ② depict; portray; delineate: 那是对你的生动~。*That is a vivid description of you.*

【描述】describe; depict: 图像~ *picture description* /时域~ *time domain description* /形状~ *shape description* /~战争的恐怖 *depict the horrors of war* /~经历 *describe one's experience* /这家杂志因其对妇女的~方式不妥而遭到批评。*The magazine has been criticized for the way it portrays women.*

【描图】tracing: ~机 *tracing machine* /~员 *tracer*

【描写】describe; depict; portray: ~女主人公的内心世界 *describe the internal world of the heroine* /他不善于~。*He is not very good at description.* /这美景难以~。*The beautiful scene beggars description.*

瞄 aim; take aim at: 枪~得准 *take good aim at sth in shooting*

【瞄准】take aim; aim; train on; level at; lay; sight: 方向~ *a long course aim* /高低~ *a cross course aim* /把枪口~敌人 *train one's gun on the enemy* /她用手枪直接~强盗。*She aimed a pistol at the bandit point-blank.* /猎手~狼。*The hunter took aim at wolf.* /他在仔细~。*He is sighting carefully.*

【瞄准器】sight; sighting device

【瞄准仪】aiming sight

miǎo

杪 [书] ① top of a twig: 木~ *tree top* ② end (of a year, month, etc.): 岁~ *the end of the year*

秒 second (1/60 of a minute)

【秒摆】second pendulum

【秒表】stopwatch; chronograph

【秒针】second hand (of a clock or watch)

淼 [书] (of wide expanse of water) vast

【淼茫】(of an expanse of water) stretch as far as the eye can see; vast

渺 ① vague; distant and unclear: ~无人迹 *remote and uninhabited* /~若烟云 *as vague as mist* ② trivial; insignificant; tiny: ~不足道 *too trivial to mention*

【渺茫】① remote and indistinct; vague: 在雨中我只能看到建筑物~的轮廓。*I could just saw a vague outline of the building through the rain.* ② uncertain: 希望~ *have slim hopes; not a cat's chance; hopeless* /~的计划 *uncertain plans* /你的机会~。*Your chances are remote.*

【渺然】vague; endless:踪迹～ *disappear without a trace*
【渺无人烟】uninhabited; without a trace of human habitation:广阔的平原上～。*On these vast plains there was not a single human habitation.* /旱灾使这一地区～。*A drought brought desolation to the region.*

藐 ① small; trivial; unimportant ② look down upon; belittle; despise
【藐视】disdain; hold in contempt; despise; look down upon:公然～法律 *open disregard (or defiance) of the law* /～法庭 *contempt of court* /～困难 *scoff at difficulties* /你没有任何理由～她。*You've no right to scorn her.*
【藐小】scorn; tiny; negligible; insignificant; paltry: ～的人物 *an insignificant person* /集体的力量是伟大的,个人的力量是～的。*The power of the collective is great, while that of an individual is tiny.*

邈 ［书］far away; remote
【邈邈】［书］remote; distant
【邈远】faraway; distant; remote: ～的时代 *remote times* / ～的往事 *distant events*

miào

妙 ① good; excellent; wonderful:绝～ *most wonderful; excellent* / ～句 *excellent sentence* / ～论 *brilliant remark; sparkling discourse* / ～算 *wonderful scheme* / ～品 *fine quality goods* ② magic; clever; subtle:微～的局势 *a delicate situation* /莫名其～ *incomprehensible*
【妙笔】ingenious writing: ～生花 *write like an angel*
【妙不可言】too wonderful for words; marvelous beyond description; most amusing
【妙策】an excellent plan; a smart idea
【妙处】① an ideal place:我认为泰山是旅游的～。*I think Taishan Mountain is an ideal place for travelling.* ② advantage; merit:据说这种药的～在于可以让你长寿。*It's said that the merit of this medicine is that it helps you live longer.*
【妙计】an excellent plan; a brilliant scheme; coup; wrinkle:顿生～ *a wise idea occurs to sb suddenly*
【妙诀】a clever way; an ingenious idea; knack:她有一套学英语的～。*She has a knack of learning English.*
【妙龄】(of a girl) youthfulness; early youth; puberty
【妙龄少女】rosebud; subdeb; subdebutante
【妙趣】wit and interest
【妙趣横生】full of wit and humour; very witty; rich in wisecracks
【妙手】people with superb skills: ～丹青 *a dab at painting*
【妙手回春】(of a doctor) effect a miraculous cure and bring the dying back to life; bring a patient back to life
【妙手空空】① out of cash; moneyless ② be a pickpocket
【妙药】efficacious medicine; wonderful drug; panacea
【妙用】magical effect; magical function
【妙语】witty remark; witticism; quip: ～如珠 *endless witty remarks; sparkling sayings* / ～双关 *a clever double extender*
【妙招】clever trick; wonderful device

庙 ① temple; shrine:家～ *family shrine* ② temple or shrine where people worship their gods or a famous person in history:龙王～ *the Dragon-king Temple* /孔～ *the Confucian Temple* ③［书］imperial court:廊～ *imperial court* ④［书］late emperor ⑤ temple fair:赶～ *go to a fair*
【庙产】temple property
【庙号】temple title; posthumous title of honour given to a deceased emperor; dynastic title
【庙会】temple fair; fair:逛～ *go to the fair*
【庙堂】① the Imperial Ancestral Temple ②［书］imperial court: ～文学 *court literature*
【庙宇】temple
【庙主】abbot; Buddhist monk in charge of a temple
【庙祝】temple attendant in charge of incense and religious service; acolyte

miē

乜 ［方］squint
【乜斜】① squint ② (of eyes) half-closed: ～的睡眼 *half-closed eyes heavy with sleep*

咩 ［象］baa; bleat

miè

灭 ① (of fire, etc.) go out:灯～了。*The light has gone out.* /火～了。*The fire had died out.* ② extinguish; turn off:你走之前别忘了把灯～了。*Don't forget to turn off the light before you leave.* ③ drown; inundate ④ perish; become extinct:自生自～ *emerge of itself and perish of itself* ⑤ annihilate; destroy; erase; wipe out:消～敌人 *wipe out the enemy* /歼～全军 *wipe out a whole army* /时间磨～了她对那件事细节的记忆。*Time erased the details of the affair from her memory.*
【灭草机】weed destroyer
【灭草剂】herbicide
【灭顶】be drowned: ～之灾 *get drowned; go bankrupt; the calamity of being drowned*
【灭火】① put out a fire; extinguish a fire:进入工厂

之前请灭掉香烟的火。*Please extinguish all cigarettes before entering the factory.* ② cut out an engine

【灭火剂】fire-extinguishing agent

【灭火器】fire extinguisher; annihilator

【灭火系统】fire extinguisher system

【灭迹】destroy the evidence (of one's evildoing): 销赃～ *destroy the evidence (of one's evildoing) by disposing of the stolen goods*

【灭绝】① become extinct: 这个地区有几种鸟类已经～了。*Some of the species of birds in this area are extinct.* /一些疾病,比如说麻风病和小儿麻痹症几乎彻底～了。*Diseases such as leprosy and polio have almost completely died out.* ② completely lose: 良心～ *be totally heartless* /～人性 *inhuman; savage*

【灭菌】【医】sterilize: ～牛奶 *sterilized milk*

【灭口】do away with a witness or accomplice: 杀人～ *kill a witness to hide one's crime*

【灭门】exterminate an entire family: ～绝户 *the extinction of a whole family* /～之灾 *disaster of execution for the whole family*

【灭却】① lose: ～良知 *lose one's conscience* ② wipe out; quell

【灭鼠】deratization; rat eradication

【灭亡】be destroyed; become extinct; die out: 自取～ *invite self-destruction; draw ruin upon oneself* /走向～ *come to ruin* /种族歧视会逐渐～。*Racial prejudices will die gradually.*

【灭蚊】mosquito eradication

【灭音器】muffler

【灭种】① exterminate a race; commit genocide ② become extinct: ～的动物 *an extinct animal*

【灭族】(a punishment in ancient China) extermination of an entire family

蔑 [书] ① small; slight ② not; no; none: ～以复加 *could not be surpassed*

【蔑称】① call sb or sth in contempt ② contemptuous name

【蔑视】despise; show contempt for; scorn; disdain: ～命运 *contempt one's fortune* /她遭人～。*She was treated with disdain.* /我～撒谎的人。*I hold a liar in contempt.*

篾 ① thin bamboo strip: 苇～儿 *the rind of reed* ② husk of reed or sorghum stalks

【篾工】① bamboo craft ② bamboo craftsman

【篾货】objects made from bamboo strips

【篾匠】a craftsman who makes articles from bamboo strips

【篾片】① thin bamboo strip ② [旧] hanger-on; sycophant

【篾条】bamboo strip

【篾席】mat made of thin bamboo strips

【篾子】of thin bamboo strips

mín

民 ① the people: 公～ *citizen* /为国为～ *for the country, for the people* ② member of a nationality: 回～ *a Hui* /藏～ *a Tibetan* ③ popular; of the people ④ civilian; civil: 平～权利 *civil authorities* /平～职业 *a civilian career* /他离开军队,恢复平～生活。*He left the army and resumed civil life.*

【民办】run by the local people; privately-run: ～公助 *run by the local people and subsidized by the state* /～机构 *community-run institution* /～企业 *privately-run business* /～教师 *teacher in a community school*

【民变】mass uprising; popular revolt

【民兵】people's militia; militia: ～建设 *militia building* /～制度 *militia system*

【民不聊生】the masses live in dire poverty; the people are destitute; life is made impossible for the people; the people can hardly earn a living

【民船】ship or small boat for civilian use

【民粹派】Populists

【民粹主义】Populism

【民法】civil law: ～典 *civil code* /～通则 *civil code*

【民法学】【律】science of civil law: ～家 *civil jurist*

【民防】civil defence: ～队员 *air warder*

【民房】a house owned by a citizen; a private house

【民愤】popular indignation; the people's wrath: 激起～ *rouse the wrath of the people* /平～ *pacify public indignation*

【民风】folkways; local traits; popular customs and morals: ～淳朴。*The customs are simple and homely.*

【民夫】[旧] civilian labourer

【民负】burden (or load) on the people

【民富国强】the people are rich and the country is prosperous

【民歌】folk song

【民革】Revolutionary Committee of the Chinese Kuomintang, one of China's patriotic democratic parties

【民工】① labourer working on a public project ② peasants who works in the city

【民国】the Republic of China (1912 — 1949)

【民航】civil aviation: 中国～总局 *CAAC (Civil Aviation Department)* / ～乘客 *aviation passenger* / ～建设 *civil aviation construction* /～协定 *civil aviation agreement*

【民间】① among the people; popular; folk: ～故事 *folktale* /～文化 *folk culture* /～文学 *folk literature* /～艺术 *folk art* /～音乐 *folk music* /～药方 *folk remedy* /他是一个出身于～的领袖。*He is a leader who came from the folk.* /这个故事长久地在～流传。*For generations the story has circulated among the people.* ② nongovernmental; unofficial: ～协定 *non-governmental agreement* /～外交

people-to-people diplomacy / ~组织 *non-governmental organization* (*NGO*)

【民建】China Democratic National Construction Association

【民进】China Association for Promoting Democracy

【民警】people's police; people's policeman: 交通~ *traffic police*

【民居】civilian dwelling houses

【民力】financial resources of the people

【民盟】China Democratic League

【民命】the life of the people

【民瘼】[书] hardships of the people; the weal and woe of the people

【民女】girls from common families

【民气】public morale; popular morale

【民情】① condition of the people ② feelings of the people; public feeling: 体察~ *experience public feelings*

【民权】civil rights; civil liberties; democratic rights: ~运动 *civil rights movement*

【民权主义】the Principle of Democracy

【民生】the people's livelihood: 国计~ *national economy and the people's livelihood* / ~凋敝 *popular destitution*

【民生主义】the Principle of the People's Livelihood

【民时】(of peasants) season for farming: 不误~ *not miss the farming season*

【民事】【律】relating to civil law; civil

【民俗】folk custom; folkways: ~节 *folk customs and culture festival*

【民俗学】folklore: ~家 *folklorist*

【民委】Ethnic Affairs Commission

【民物】property of the people

【民校】① spare-time school for adults ② school run by the local people

【民心】popular feelings; common aspiration of the people: ~所向 *trend of popular feelings*; *the common aspiration of the people*

【民信】① popular trust ② civilian correspondence

【民选】elected by the people: ~政府 *democratically elected government*

【民谚】common proverb

【民谣】folk rhyme (esp. of the topical and political type)

【民以食为天】food is the first need of people; no one can survive without food

【民意】the will of the people; popular will: ~代表 *people's representative* / 顺从~ *obey the will of the people*

【民意测验】poll; public opinion poll: ~者 *pollster* / 在这次~中,只有10%的人表示他们对改革满意。*Opinion polls show that only 10% people are satisfied with the reforms.*

【民营】run by citizens: ~企业 *enterprise run by private citizens*

【民用】for civil use; civil: ~航空 *civil aviation* / ~机场 *civil airport*

【民用航空总局】Civil Aviation Administration

【民怨】resentment of people: ~沸腾 *public grievances prevail*; *seething discontent of the people*

【民乐】music, esp. folk music, for traditional instruments: ~队 *traditional instruments orchestra*

【民运】① civil transport ② privately-run transport ③ mass movement; mass campaign

【民贼】traitor to the people

【民宅】private residence

【民政】civil administration

【民政部】Ministry of Civil Affairs

【民政管理】civil administration

【民政机关】civil administration organ

【民智】educational level of the people

【民众】the masses of the people; the common people

【民主】① democracy; democratic rights: 经济~ *economic democracy* / 社会主义~ *socialist democracy* / 他的~作风使他受到人们的爱戴。*His democracy made him loved by the people.* ② democratic: ~监督 *democratic supervision* / ~联盟 *democratic union* / ~政府 *democratic government* / ~运动 *democratic movement* / ~决策 *democratic decision-making* / ~协商 *democratic consultation*

【民族】nation; nationality; ethnic group: 少数~ *ethnic group*; *minority nationality* / ~败类 *scum of a nation* / ~独立 *national independence* / ~政策 *policy towards nationalities* / 各~的团结 *the unity of various nationalities*

苠 (of crops) having a long growth period; late-maturing: ~高粱 *Chinese sorghum with a long growth period*

珉 [书] jade-like stone

mǐn

抿[1] smooth (hair, etc.) with a wet brush: 她在~头发。*She is smoothing her hair.*

抿[2] ① pucker; tuck; close lightly; furl: 她~嘴笑了。*She puckered in a smile*; *her lips curled in a smile.* / 水鸟一~翅,扎进了水里。*The water bird tucked its wings and dived into the water* ② sip: 她~了一口茶。*She sipped the tea.*

【抿子】a small hairbrush (used by a woman)

泯 vanish; die out; lose: 良心未~ *still remain some conscience*

【泯灭】die out; disappear; vanish: 他给我留下了难以~的印象。*He made an indelible impression on me.*

【泯没】vanish; sink into oblivion: ~无闻 *dead and forgotten* / 这个城市早已~无闻。*The city has passed into oblivion.*

【泯弃】give up; abandon: ~宿怨 *forget and forsake old grievances*

闽 another name for Fujian Province: ~南 *southern Fujian*

【闽菜】Fujian cuisine; Fujian cooking
【闽剧】local opera popular in northeastern Fujian Province

悯 ① pity; commiserate:悲天~人 *pity for all mankind* ②［书］sadness; sorrow
【悯惜】take pity on ; have pity for:我很~这个穷苦的老人。*I felt great pity for the poor old man.* /每个遇到不幸的人都渴望得到~。*Every man yearns for sympathy in sorrow.*
【悯恤】feel compassion for; pity:她~这些孤儿。*Her heart was filled with compassion for the orphans.* /我对他起了~之心。*I showed mercy to him.*

敏 ① agile; quick; nimble:机~的头脑 *an agile mind* /灵~的嗅觉 *an acute sense of smell* ② keen; smart:聪~ *smart*; *clever* ③ (Mǐn) a surname
【敏感】responsive; sensitive; susceptible: ~的耳朵 *a sensitive ear* / ~的心 *susceptible heart* /她很~人们对她的想法。*She is sensitive to what people think of her.*
【敏感度】sensibility; sensitivity
【敏感性】sensibility; susceptibility: ~分析 *sensitivity analysis*
【敏感元件】sense organ
【敏慧】bright; intelligent; keen
【敏捷】quick; nimble; agile; spry; adroit: ~的步伐 *a smart pace* /头脑~ *an agile mind* (*or wit*) / ~的手指 *nimble fingers* / ~的想象力 *a nimble imagination* /像蟋蟀一样~ *as spry as a cricket*
【敏锐】sharp; acute; keen: ~的观察者 *an acute observer* / ~的听觉 *sharp hearing* /她是一个思维~的女人。*She is a woman with a keen intelligent mind.* /他的演讲以~的眼光透彻地分析了国外事务。*His lecture provided penetrating insight into foreign affairs.*
【敏行】［书］work hard to cultivate one's mind

míng

名 ① name; appellation:别~ *variant name* /笔~ *pen name* /姓~ *surname and personal name* /书~ *the title of a book* /俗~ *vernacular name* /货~ *name of articles* (*or commodity*) /有~无实 *exist in name only* ② given name:这位老师姓王~志刚。*The teacher's surname is Wang and his given name, Zhigang.* ③ name; pretext:他以头痛为~不去上班。*He used his headache as a pretext for not going to work.* ④ fame; prestige; reputation:恶~ *ill fame* /享盛~ *enjoy general popularity* /声~狼藉 *make an evil reputation for oneself* /不朽之~ *undying fame* /这位作家~震全国。*The writer's fame spread all over the country.* ⑤ famous; well-known; renowned; notable:著~的小说家 *a celebrated novelist* /法国以其佳肴和美酒闻~。*France is famous for its fine food and wine.* ⑥［书］describe; express:莫以~之 *do not know what to call it* ⑦［书］have; possess:一文不~ *not have a single penny in one's pocket- be extremely poor* ⑧［量］used for persons:一~学生 *a student* ⑨ (Míng) a surname
【名不副实】the name falls short of the reality; be unworthy of the name; have an undeserved reputation; more in name than in reality:他的"三好学生"的称号总体上来说是~的。*His reputation for being an excellent student is, in general, undeserved.*
【名不虚传】be true to one's name; have a well-deserved reputation; live up to one's reputation; be equal to one's reputation
【名册】register; roll:花~ *register of names*; *muster roll* /大学~ *the College Roll* /现役军人~ *an active list* /后备役军人~ *a reserved list* /复员军人~ *a retired list*
【名产】famous product
【名称】name (of a thing or organization); definition; designation:你能叫得出这个花园里所有花草树木的~吗? *Can you name all the plants and trees in this garden?*
【名垂千古】go down in history; be on the scroll of fame:他将作为一名国际英雄~。*He will go down in history as an international hero.*
【名垂青史】go down in history; be crowned with eternal glory; figure in history; make a name in history
【名词】①【语】noun; substantive:不可数~ *noun of continuous quantity* /动作~ *action noun* /分词性~ *participial noun* /复合~ *compound noun* /个体~ *individual noun* /可数~ *noun of discontinuous quantity* /类~ *class noun* /派生~ *noun derivatives* /群体~ *noun of multitude* /谓语性~ *predicate noun* /中心~ *head noun* /专有~ *proper noun* ② term; phrase:科学~ *scientific terms* ③【逻】name
【名次】order in rank (in a name list); place (in a competition); placing:取得~ *win a place in a competition* /我们参加这次运动会不是为了争~。*We haven't come to this sports meet just to complete for places.*
【名刺】［书］visiting card; calling card
【名存实亡】cease to exist except in name; be only an empty title; have a mere nominal existence
【名单】name list; roster; rota:伤亡~ *a casualty list* /预约~ *waiting list* /他当天不能来,所以我们应把他从~上划去。*He will not come on that day so we can cross him off the list.*
【名额】the number of people assigned or allowed; quota of people:招生~ *the number of students to be enrolled* / ~已满。*The quota has been filled.*
【名分】a person's status
【名副其实】true to one's name; the name matches the reality; be worthy of the name; in name and in fact; live up to the name:这位教授~,学识渊博。*The professor really lives up to his reputation for his rich learning.*

【名古屋】Nagoya, a city of central Honshu, Japan
【名贯】[书](of a person) name and place of origin
【名贵】famous and precious; rare: ~的药材 *rare medicinal herbs*
【名号】person's (official and courtesy) name
【名讳】[旧] name of one's elders and betters or of a respected person
【名籍】[书] register; roll
【名迹】① famous historical site ② original calligraphy of a famous person ③ [书] fame and deed
【名家】a person of academic or artistic distinction; famous expert; master: 小说~ *master of novel*
【名缰利锁】the fetters of fame and wealth; the bondage of reputation and wealth
【名将】famous general; master: 网球~ *a tennis star*
【名教】the Confucian ethical code
【名节】one's reputation and integrity
【名句】a well-known phrase; a much quoted line; famous quotation
【名角儿】famous actor or actress (in traditional Chinese opera)
【名款】the name of the painter or writer inscribed on his work
【名利】fame and gain; fame and wealth: 追求~ *court fame and fortune* / ~双收 *gain both honour and money*
【名利场】vanity fair: 他已在~里混迹多年。*He has been in the pursuit of fame and wealth for many years.*
【名列前茅】head the list; come out in front; be among the best of the successful candidates: 他这次考试~。*His name stands first on the list in this exam.*
【名伶】[旧] famous actor or actress in traditional Chinese opera
【名流】distinguished personages; celebrities; somebody: 社会~ *social celebrities*
【名录】roster; roll: 会员~ *membership roster*
【名落孙山】fall behind Sun Shan (who was last on the list of successful candidates) — fail to pass the examination; be nowhere
【名门】an old and well-known family: ~望族 *notable family and great clan* / ~之后 *descendant of a notable family*
【名目】names of things; items; denomination: 巧立~ *invent various items* / ~繁多 *all sorts of items*
【名牌】① famous brand: ~服装 *clothes of famous brand* / ~大学 *prestigious university* ② nameplate; name tag
【名片】visiting card; calling card: 交换~ *exchange cards* / ~盒 *cardcase*
【名品】valuable object; treasure: 艺术~ *art treasures*
【名气】[口] reputation; fame; name: 他是个小有~的诗人。*He is a poet enjoying some reputation.*
【名人】famous person; eminent person; celebrity; personality; big name; household name: 历史~ *the great names of history* / 许多~都资助慈善事业。*Many celebrities lend their support to charity events.*
【名人录】blue book; who's who
【名山大川】famous mountains and rivers: 他对祖国的~十分熟悉。*He is quite familiar with the famous mountains and rivers of his motherland.*
【名山事业】[书] commitment to literature; an author's works destined for posterity
【名声】reputation; repute; renown: ~好 *a good repute* / 坏~ *a bad repute* / 他的~传到世界各地。*His reputation spread to all corners of the world.*
【名胜】a place famous for its scenery or historical relics; beauty spot; scenic spot; sights: 游览~古迹 *go sightseeing to places of historic interest and scenic beauty*
【名师】good teacher; master: ~出高徒。*An successful disciple owes his achievements to his master.*
【名士】[旧] ① a person with a literary reputation ② a celebrity with no official post
【名手】a famous artist, player, etc.: 象棋~ *famous chess player*
【名数】①【数】concrete number ② numeral-classifier compound
【名宿】famous scholar of the elder generation
【名堂】① variety; item: 晚会上的~真多。*There were various items in the evening.* ② result; achievement: 搞不出~ *get nowhere* / 我看他能搞出些~来。*I think he can accomplish something marvelous.* ③ what lies behind sth; reason: 他没到场,一定有什么~。*There must be some cause for his absence.* /他在搞什么~? *What is he up to?*
【名帖】visiting card; calling card
【名望】fame and prestige; good reputation; renown: 颇有~的人 *a person of some prominence* / 中国在国际上的~ *China's prestige in the world* / 北京大学享有很高的~。*Peking University has a lot of prestige.*
【名位】fame and position
【名物】the name and description of a thing
【名下】under sb's name; belonging or related to sb: 请把账记在我~。*Please charge the expenses to my account.*
【名衔】one's title: 他的~是什么? *What's his title?*
【名姓】name: 他的~很不好拼。*It's difficult to spell his name.*
【名学】logic
【名言】well-known saying; celebrated dictum; famous remark: 她说话时喜欢引用~。*She was fond of quoting the famous sayings when she speaks.*
【名义】① name: 我以他的~给你写信。*I am writing to you in his name.* /他以他父亲的~参加聚会。*He attended the party in the name of his father.* ② (usu. followed by 上) nominal; titular; in name: ~上的君主 *a titular prince* / ~主席 *nominal chairman* /他~上关心我,实际上想监视

M

我。*He cares about me in name, but keeps me under his surveillance in reality.*

【名优】① a famous actor or actress ② brand-name and high-quality

【名誉】① fame; reputation; prestige: ~扫地的政治家 *a politician of ill fame; a thoroughly discredited politician* /谦恭有礼的~ *a reputation for courtesy* /~上的污点 *a blot* (*or smirch, stain*) *on one's reputation* /她以她的~担保绝不再做这样的事。*She promised on her honour never to do such a thing again.* ② honorary: ~会员 *honorary member* /~学位 *honorary degree* /~主席 *honorary chairman*

【名媛】young lady of note: ~闺秀 *daughter of an renowned family*

【名噪一时】enjoy quite a reputation; make a noise in the world:这位作家曾~。*The writer once had a great vogue at one time.*

【名章】seal inscribed with a person's name

【名正言顺】the name is correct and what is said accords with reason — be right and proper; fitting and proper; be fully justifiable; things called by their right names:她去参加这个会议是~的。*It's fit and proper for her to take part in the conference.*

【名著】famous book; famous work; masterpiece:莎士比亚的~ *Shakespeare's famous works*

【名状】give the right name for; describe:莫可~ *beyond description*

【名字】① name or given name:教师知道全部学生的~。*The teacher knows all the pupils by their first name.* ② name (of a thing):这种花的~很特别。*This flower has a peculiar name.*

【名作】masterpiece; famous work:《蒙娜丽莎》是达·芬奇的~。*The "Mona Lisa" is Leonardo's masterpiece.*

明[1] ① bright; brilliant:鲜~的色彩 *bright, clear colours* /~月 *a full moon* /灯火通~ *be brightly lit* ② clear; distinct:表~ *make clear; state clearly* /说~ *explain; illustrate* /黑白分~ *a clear distinction between black and white* /下落不~ *whereabouts unknown* /心~眼亮 *be sharp-eyed and clear-headed* ③ open; overt; apparent:有话~说 *air one's idea openly* ④ sharp-eyed; discerning:眼~手快 *be quick of eye and deft of hand* ⑤ candid; honest:光~磊落 *on the up-and-up; open and aboveboard* /弃暗投~ *forsake darkness for light* ⑥ sight:双目失~ *go blind in both eyes* /复~ *regain one's sight* ⑦ understand; know:深~大义 *be deeply conscious of the righteousness of a cause* ⑧ [书] make clear; demonstrate:开宗~义 *make clear the purpose from the very beginning* ⑨ plainly; obviously:这些事摆~了是他干的。*This is obviously his doings.*

明[2] next; immediately following in time: ~春 *next spring* /~年 *next year*

明[3] ① the Ming Dynasty (1368-1644) ② (Míng) a surname

【明暗】light and shade: ~层次 *shade of grey* /~度 *shading value* /~扫描 *brightness scanning*

【明白】① clear; obvious; plain:这是大家都~的。*This is plain to everybody.* /他解释得很~。*He explained clearly.* ② open; unequivocal; explicit: ~的态度 *an open manner* /他~地表达了观点。*He is explicit in his views.* ③ sensible; reasonable:你是一个~人,应该知道怎么处理这件事。*You are a sensible man and you should know how to deal with it.* ④ understand; realize; know; be aware of; see: ~事理 *know what's what* /你~我的意思吗? *Do you understand what I mean?* /当那个人~是怎么回事时,禁不住笑了起来。*The man couldn't help laughing when he realized what had happened.*

【明摆着】obvious; clear:这是~的事实,你怎么能否认呢? *It's an obvious fact; how can you deny it?* /这门锁着,~他们不在家。*The door's locked, so plainly they must be out.*

【明辨是非】make a clear distinction between right and wrong; distinguish clearly between right and wrong:他很糊涂,不能~。*He is quite muddleheaded and cannot distinguish between right and wrong.*

【明察】observe clearly:所述情况,敬请~。*I respectfully await your judicious judgement about what I have said.*

【明察暗访】observe publicly and investigate privately — conduct a thorough investigation

【明察秋毫】have eyes sharp enough to perceive an animal's autumn hair — be perceptive of the minutest detail; be able to penetrate deeply into things; be able to see through a brick wall: ~的观察 *a penetrating observation*

【明畅】clear and lucid; lucid and smooth: ~的写作风格 *a lucid literary style*

【明澈】bright and limpid; transparent: ~眼睛 *clear eyes* /~如镜 *as bright and limpid as a mirror*

【明处】① where there is light:把书拿到~看,否则对视力有害。*Bring the book to the light to read, or it will do harm to your sight.* ② in the open; in public:我不想在~讨论这件事。*I do not want to discuss it in public.*

【明达】sensible; understanding: ~之人 *a man of thorough understanding*

【明德】highest virtue

【明灯】bright lamp; beacon:指路~ *beacon lighting up one's advance*

【明调】high key; tint

【明洞】open cut tunnel

【明断】[书] pass (fair) judgement

【明矾】【化】alums; white alum: ~煤 *alum coal* /~岩 *alunite rock*

【明沟】open drain; open channel: ~排水 *open ditch drainage; open drainage*

【明后天】tomorrow or the day after tomorrow:我~

会来拜访你。*I will visit you tomorrow or the day after tomorrow.*

【明晃晃】gleaming; shining: ~的刺刀 *gleaming bayonets*

【明黄】pure and bright yellow

【明慧】[书] intelligent; bright; clever

【明火】①[古] fire made by turning a bronze mirror to reflect the sun ② burning fire ③ carry torches (esp. in a robbery): ~打劫 *open robbery*

【明火执仗】carry torches and weapons (in a robbery) — do evil openly; a daring robbery; in an open way

【明鉴】① a bright mirror; a clear mirror ② your brilliant idea; your penetrating judgement

【明教】[书] your brilliant idea; your wise advice

【明洁】bright and pure

【明净】bright and clean; clear and bright: ~的窗户 *clear glass*

【明镜】a bright mirror; a clear mirror: 湖水好似一面~。*The lake is as clear as a bright mirror.*

【明镜高悬】with a bright mirror hung on high — an impartial and perspicacious judge; an fair official

【明据】clear evidence: 你可有~在手里? *Do you have any clear evidence at hand?*

【明决】sensible and resolute

【明快】① lucid and lively; sprightly: ~的节奏 *sprightly rhythm* / ~的曲调 *a lively tune* ② straightforward; forthright: 他性格~。*He is a man with a forthright character.* ③[方] bright

【明来暗往】have overt and covert contacts with sb; secret going-on: 她仍然和那些人~。*He remains contact with those people overtly or covertly.*

【明朗】① bright and clear; serene; canty: ~的天空 *serene skies* ② clear; obvious: ~化 *become clear* / 态度~ *take a clear-cut attitude* / 使责任问题~化 *clear up the question of responsibility* ③ forthright; bright and cheerful: 他是一个性格~的人。*He is always bright and cheerful.*

【明理】① sensible; reasonable: ~的父母 *understanding parents* / 任何一个~的人都知道赞扬孩子的好行为比惩罚他们的坏行为要好得多。*Any reasonable person knows that praising children for good behaviour is much better than punishing them for bad.* ② an obvious truth or fact: 这么简单的~你会不明白? *Can't you understand such an obvious fact?*

【明丽】bright and beautiful

【明亮】① well-lit; bright: 太阳很~。*The sun was very bright.* / 很快,舞台被~的灯光所覆盖。*All of a sudden the stage was flooded with brilliant light.* ② bright; shining: ~的眼睛 *clear and bright eyes* ③ become clear: 她一解释,我心里就~了。*I'm clear after she explained it.* ④ clear and loud: 歌声~ *loud and distinct singing*

【明了】① understand; be clear about: 对于事情的原因我很~。*I am clear about the cause of the matter.* ② clear; plain; manifest: 一套~的说明 *an intelligible set of directions* / 你要学会简单~地讲话。*You should learn to speak plain.*

【明令】explicit order; formal decree; public proclamation: ~嘉奖 *issue a commendation* / ~禁止 *prohibit by official order*

【明楼】① watchtower ② highest building above ground

【明码】① plain code: ~电报(*plain*) *code telegram* / ~发报 *send a telegram in plain code* ② with the price clearly marked: ~实价 *sell at marked prices*

【明媒正娶】[旧] a right and legal marriage; formal wedding

【明媚】① bright and beautiful; radiant and enchanting: 春光~ *a radiant and enchanting spring scene* ② (of eyes) bright and lovely

【明面】on the surface; obviously: 真相开始显露于~。*The truth began to surface.*

【明灭】now in view, now hidden; twinkling: ~的星空 *the twinkling of a starry sky*

【明明】obviously; plainly; undoubtedly: 那个人~是张小姐,你怎么说不是呢? *Obviously, the person is Miss Zhang, but why do you say not?*

【明明白白】plain and to the point; very clear as clear as daylight: 他~地说他不爱我。*He made it plain that he did not love me.*

【明眸】bright eyes

【明目张胆】flagrantly; brazenly; before one's very eyes; overtly; do evil things openly: ~的侵略 *flagrant aggression*

【明年】next year: 我~毕业。*I will graduate the next year.*

【明盘】[旧] negotiated price

【明器】funerary objects (used in ancient times); burial objects

【明前】a kind of green tea picked before Pure Brightness (around April 5)

【明枪暗箭】spear thrusts in the open and arrows shot from hiding — both open and covert attacks

【明枪易躲,暗箭难防】[俗] it's easy to dodge a spear in the open but hard to guard against an arrow shot from hiding.

【明抢】daylight robbery: ~暗偷 *rob both overtly and covertly*

【明渠】open canal; open channel: ~排水 *drainage by open canal*

【明确】① clear and definite; clear-cut; explicit; unequivocal; expressly: ~的指示 *explicit directions* / ~的陈述 *explicit statements* / ~的答案 *a definite answer* / ~的目的 *a specific purpose* / 我想要一个~的回答。*I want a specific answer.* / 他~拒绝了任何妥协的建议。*He unequivocally rejects any suggestions towards compromise.* ② make clear; make definite; clarify; lay it on the line; spell out: ~下一步的任务 *make clear the next task* / 她对工作还不清楚,你要~他的任务。*She doesn't understand her job so you have to spell everything out to her.*

【明儿】[口] ① tomorrow: ~见。*See you tomorrow.* ② some day: 赶~我也去报个名参加比赛。

M

I'll also enter for the competition one of these days.

【明人】① seeing person (as contrasted with the blind) ② honest man: ~不做暗事。*An honest man does not deal underhand.*

【明日】tomorrow: 我~动身。*I will set off tomorrow.*

【明日黄花】chrysanthemums after the Double Ninth Festival — things that are stale and no longer of interest; a thing of the past; topic no longer of interest: 这个话题早就成了~了。*This topic has already been stale and can interest no one.*

【明锐】① bright and keen: 目光~ *clear and keen eyes* ②［书］quick and clear: 办事~ *be quick and resolute in action*

【明睿】wise; sensible

【明若观火】as clear as day; see things very clearly

【明升暗降】kick upstairs; promote in appearance but demote in reality

【明示】explicitly instruct; clearly indicate: 考试中不能用字典, 这一点已经~。*A dictionary is not allowed to use in the test, which is clearly indicated in the regulations.*

【明誓】take an oath

【明视】photopic vision: ~距离 *distance of distinct vision*

【明说】speak frankly; speak openly: 有什么话请~。*If you want to say something, just say it plainly.*

【明堂】［方］① threshing ground ② courtyard; yard

【明天】① tomorrow: ~会下雨吗? *Will it rain tomorrow?* ② the near future: 盼望美好的~ *look forward to a bright future*

【明文】(of laws, regulations, etc.) proclaimed in writing; express provision: ~规定 *regulate in definite terms; stipulate explicitly*

【明晰】distinct; clear; lucid: ~的文体 *lucid style* / 月球上的地球阴影很~。*The earth's shadow on the moon was quite distinct.* / 安全事项应该浅显而~。*Safety guidelines need to be plain and unambiguous.*

【明细】clear and in detail: 分工~ *clear division of work* / ~表 *specification; detail list* / ~规范 *specified criteria*

【明显】clear; obvious; evident; distinct: ~的错误 *obvious errors; palpable mistakes* / ~的动机 *transpicuous motives* / ~的敌意 *evident hostility* / 一桩~的谋杀案 *a clear case of murder* / 你的学习有~进步。*There is a distinct improvement in your study.*

【明线】①【电】open-wire line; open wire: ~布线 *surface wiring; open wiring* / ~交叉 *open wire transposition* ② (in literary works) apparent sequence of events

【明晓】understand; be familiar with: 她~诗文。*She is familiar with poems and essays.*

【明信片】postcard: 美术~ *picture postcard*

【明星】①【天】Venus ② a famous performer; star: 电影~ *movie star*

【明修栈道, 暗渡陈仓】pretend to advance along one path while secretly go along another; do one thing under cover of another; feign action in one place and make the real move in another

【明秀】beautiful and bright

【明言】speak frankly: ~反对自由贸易的人 *a professed opponent of free trade*

【明眼人】a person with a discerning eye; person in the know; sensible person: ~一眼就能看出这是个骗局。*A discerning person could easily tell it's a swindle.*

【明艳】beautiful and gorgeous: 她们身着~的服装。*They were dressed in gorgeous clothes.*

【明焰】direct firing

【明喻】simile

【明早】① tomorrow morning: 我~去送他。*I will see him off tomorrow morning.* ②［方］tomorrow

【明杖】stick used by a blind person in walking

【明朝】［方］tomorrow: 切莫依赖~。*Tomorrow never comes.*

【明哲保身】be wise to protect oneself from something unfavourable; be worldly-wise and play safe; be cautious to save one's own skin

【明争暗斗】engage in overt and covert struggle; both open strife and veiled struggle; fight forth in the open and in secret

【明正典刑】carry out a death sentence according to the law

【明证】clear proof; token; evidence: 他整齐的房间就是他思维有序的~。*His neat rooms bear witness to a well-ordered mind.*

【明知】know perfectly well; be fully aware: ~故犯 *commit an error deliberately; violate knowingly* / ~故问 *ask while knowing the answer; feign ignorance and ask questions*

【明志】show one's high ideals: 淡泊~ *show high ideals by simple living*

【明智】sensible; sagacious; wise; sage: ~的领导 *a wise leader* / ~的选择 *a sensible choice* / 喝酒不过量是~的。*It is advisable not to drink too much.* / 如果你~的话, 你就应该尽早出国学习。*If you are sensible you will study abroad as soon as possible.*

【明治维新】(in Japan) Meiji Reform (1867-1912)

【明珠】bright pearl; jewel: 掌上~ *a pearl in the palm — a beloved daughter*

【明主】enlightened (or wise) ruler

【明子】pine torch; fatwood: ~木 *kindling wood*

鸣

① (of birds, insects, etc.) cry: 鸡~ *the crow of a cock* / 鸟~ *the chirp of a bird* ② sound; make a sound: 雷~ *thunder* / 汽笛~响起来。*The siren sounded.* / 爆炸的声音让我耳~。*My ears were ringing from the sound of the blast.* ③ express; voice; air: ~不平 *complain of unfairness; make complaints against injustice* / 自~得意 *show self-satisfaction; preen oneself; be ostensibly smug*

【鸣鞭】① a whip used by imperial guard of honour to keep silent ② crack a whip

M

【鸣唱】(of birds, insects, etc.) cry; chirp
【鸣笛】blow; whistle: ~致哀 *sound the siren in mourning* /警察~令汽车停下。*The policeman whistled for the motorcar to stop.*
【鸣镝】whistling (or twanging) arrow (used in ancient times)
【鸣鼓而攻之】beat the drum and launch the attack — make a scathing indictment
【鸣骨】pessulus
【鸣叫】tweet; moo; chirp; twitter: 鸟儿~的声音 *the sound of birds singing*
【鸣金收兵】beat the gongs as the signal to cease a battle; sound the retreat
【鸣锣开道】beat gongs to clear the way (for officials in feudal times) — prepare the public for a coming event; sound the gongs to clear the way
【鸣枪】fire rifles into the air; fire a shot
【鸣禽】songbird; singing bird
【鸣沙】singing sand; sounding sand
【鸣石】clapping stone
【鸣响】(of bells, guns, etc.) sound; ring: 铃声~。*The bell sounds.*
【鸣谢】express one's thanks formally: 表示衷心~ *express one's hearty thanks to sb*
【鸣冤】voice grievances; complain of unfairness: ~叫屈 *air one's discontent; call attention by shouting a grievance; call for the redress of a wrong*
【鸣钟】ring the bell; toll: 教堂~报时。*The church bell tolled the hour.*
【鸣啭】[书] (of birds) twitter; sing

茗 tea: 品~ *sample (or critically enjoy) tea*

冥 ① dark; obscure: ~夜 *dark night* ② abstruse; deep: ~思 *be deep in thought* ③ stupid; benighted; foolish ④ the underworld; the nether world: ~府 *dark hell; the nether world*
【冥暗】dim; dark: ~的角落 *an obscure corner* /我仍然记得那是一个~无月的夜。*I could still remember that it was a dark, moonless night.*
【冥钞】paper made to resemble bank money and burned for the dead
【冥府】the nether world; Hades
【冥界】ghostdom
【冥茫】[书] vast and hazy; dusky: 森林中~的光线 *the dusky light of the forest*
【冥冥】[书] ① dim; obscure: ~之中似乎有人在帮助我。*It seems that somebody is helping me in the unseen world.* ② ignorant; foolish ③ high in the sky
【冥寿】birthday anniversary of the dead
【冥思苦索】think long and hard; cudgel one's brains; muse and ponder over sth; puzzle over sth: 年轻的外科医生为一个棘手的手术~。*The young surgeon contemplated the difficult operation.* /她对着书本~着。*She was puzzling over the book.*
【冥顽】[书] impenetrably thickheaded; stupid; ignorant: ~不灵 *ignorant and stubborn*
【冥王星】【天】Pluto
【冥想】deep thought; meditation; muse; contemplate: 她一连几小时坐在那里~。*She has been sitting there musing for hours.* /我坐着~我的问题,可总是找不到解决办法。*I sat mulling over my problem without finding a solution.*
【冥衣】grave (or burial) clothes

铭 ① inscription: 墓志~ *inscription on the back of a memorial tablet* ② engrave; inscribe: 刻骨~心 *remember to the end of one's life*
【铭感】[书] be deeply grateful: ~终身 *remain deeply grateful for the rest of one's life* /~你的帮助。*I am grateful to you for helping me.*
【铭记】① bear firmly in mind; always remember: 我把他的话~于心。*His words were engraved in my heart.* /这节课我会~不忘。*I'll bear the class firmly in mind.* ② inscription; epigraph
【铭刻】① inscription: 古代~ *ancient inscriptions* /冠军的名字将被~到奖杯上。*The champion's name will be engraved on the cup.* ② be engraved on one's mind; be always remembered: 这痛苦的经历~在他记忆里。*The bitter experience was engraved on his mind.* /周总理的光辉形象永远~在人民的心中。*The shining image of Premier Zhou is indelibly engraved on the memory of the people.*
【铭牌】【机】data plate; nameplate
【铭石】stone tablet with inscription
【铭文】inscription; epigraph: 把~刻于石头上 *incise an inscription on a stone*
【铭心刻骨】be engraved on one's bones and heart — bear firmly in mind; be engraved on one's mind: 车祸的记忆对于他是~的。*The memory of the traffic accident will stay with him forever.*

溟 [书] sea; the dark ocean: 东~ *east sea*
【溟茫】[书] dusky; indistinct
【溟濛】[书] misty

暝 [书] ① (of the sky) become dark: 天已~。*Dusk has fallen.* ② evening twilight; dusk

瞑 [书] ① close the eyes: 死不~目 *die with a grievance or everlasting regret; die discontent; die with regret* ② be dim-sighted
【瞑目】close one's eyes in death — die content: 死而~ *die contented*
【瞑眩】【中医】dizziness, nausea, etc. as a side effect of drugs

螟 snout moth's larva
【螟虫】snout moth's larva
【螟蛾】snout moth
【螟害】borer pest; plague of snout moth's larva
【螟蛉】① corn earworm ② adopted son: ~之子 *a son by adoption*

mǐng

酩

【酩酊】be dead drunk：～大醉 *be completely drunken; as drunk as a lord; be dead drunk*

mìng

命[1] ① life：救～ *save one's life* /拼～ *risk one's life* /丧～ *get killed* ② life span：短～ *die young; be short-lived* ③ fate; fortune; destiny：用纸牌算～ *tell one's fortune with tarot cards* /她有一个好～。*She has a happy lot.* /他们把灾难归于～不好。*They ascribed their disaster to an unkind fate.* /她～里注定要成为一名演员。*It was her destiny to become an actress.*

命[2] ① order; command ② order; command：奉～ *receive order* /遵～ *obey order* ③ assign (a name, title, etc.)

【命案】a case involving the killing of a person; homicide case

【命笔】[书] take up one's pen; set pen to paper：欣然～ *be happy to start writing*

【命大】very lucky; be extremely fortunate：他在地震中生还，真是～。*He was extremely fortunate to survive the earthquake.*

【命定】be determined by fate; be predestined：她认为凡事都是～的。*She thought that whatever happened was predestined.*

【命妇】[旧] wife or mother of a senior official

【命根】one's very life; lifeblood; the source of life：这些书是他的～。*All these books are the lifeblood of his.*

【命官】[旧] ranking official

【命驾】[书] set off; set out

【命理学】numerology

【命令】① order; command：将军～部队向前推进。*The general has ordered an advance.* /上尉～士兵开火。*The captain commanded his men to fire.* ② order; command：下～ *give orders* /执行～ *execute a command*

【命令表】command list

【命令句】【语】imperative sentence

【命令书】mandamus; precept

【命令提示符】command prompt

【命脉】lifeblood; lifeline; vitals：经济～ *economic lifelines* /信用是消费社会的～。*Credit is the lifeblood of the consumer society.*

【命门】【中医】the gate of vitality：～之火 *fire from the gate of life*

【命名】name; nominate：这所大学以总统的名字～。*The university is named after the president.*

【命名法】nomenclature

【命数】destiny; fate; lot：掌握自己的～ *take one's fate into one's own hand*

【命题】① assign a topic; set a question：～作文 *assign a subject for a composition* ②【数】proposition：～变量 *propositional variable* /～常数 *propositional constant* /～代数 *algebra of propositions* /～演算 *propositional calculus* ③【逻】proposition

【命途】[书] one's life or experience：～多舛 *suffer a lot of setbacks in one's life*

【命相】[旧] a person's birthday in eight characters and the animal symbol of the year he was born, which could serve as the basis for a fortune-teller to predict the future of a person

【命意】① (of composition, etc.) set a theme ② meaning; implication：她写的文章总是～深刻。*She always writes articles with profound meanings.*

【命运】① fate; lot：他希望远离她，而～却偏偏另有安排。*He expected to keep away from her, but fate had decided otherwise.* /这些人在抱怨他们悲惨的～。*Those people are complaining about their miserable destiny.* ②[喻] destiny; fate：他掌握着我的～。*He has my fate in his hand.*

【命在旦夕】be at death's door; hold one's life on a precarious tenure; on one's deathbed; be dying：他意识到母亲已经～。*He realized his mother was a dying woman.* /看到她已经～，他们叫牧师来到他的床边。*When they saw that she was at death's door, they sent for the priest to come to her bedside.*

【命中】hit the target (or mark); score a hit：～目标 *hit the mark*

【命中概率】【军】hit probability

【命中率】percentage of hits; hitting accuracy

【命中偏差】deviation of impact

miù

谬 mistaken; false; wrong：荒～ *absurd; fallacious*

【谬错】falsehood; error; blunder：我已经改正了我的～。*I have amended my error.* /他造成了极大的～。*He has made a terrible blunder.*

【谬见】fallacious opinion：认为财富能带来一切是一种～。*It is a fallacy to suppose that riches could bring everything.*

【谬奖】[谦] overpraise (me); misplaced praise

【谬论】fallacy; absurd theory (or views); falsehood：常见的～ *a popular fallacy* /这～的荒诞性已被充分揭露。*The fallacy has been exposed in its naked absurdity.*

【谬说】fallacy; absurdity：这真是天大的～。*This is a fatal absurdity.*

【谬误】falsehood; error; mistake：这是极大的～。*It is grossly mistaken.*

【谬议】falsehood; fallacy

【谬种】① error; fallacy：～流传。*The fallacy has been spread.* ② scoundrel; bastard

mō

摸 ① feel; touch：～上去很光滑的表面 *a surface that is smooth to the feel* /不要～那个杯子，它很烫。*Don't touch that glass; it's very hot.*

/他轻轻地～小孩儿的头。*He stroked the child's head gently.* ② fumble; grope:她在书包里～口红。*She fumbled for a lipstick in her bag.* /她伸手去～电话。*She groped for the telephone.* ③ feel out; try to find:她早就～清了我的意图。*She has found out my intention quite early.* /我还没有～准她的脾气。*I haven't got to know her temper.* /我一点也～不透你的意思。*I haven't the faintest idea of what you mean.* ④ grope one's way in the dark:黑暗中我没～着钥匙。*I failed to feel where the key was in the dark.*

【摸彩】draw lot to determine the prize winners in a lottery

【摸底】know the real situation; try to find out the real intention or situation:他对国内的经济情况很～。*He is quite familiar with the economic situation of the country.* /我要就这个问题摸摸她的底。*I will sound her out on this question.* /我摸不清她的～。*I am rather hazy as to what her purpose is.*

【摸黑儿】[口] grope one's way in the dark: ～前进 *grope ahead through the darkness* /由于任务要求的时间紧迫,我们只好～赶路。*As the task was pressing, we had to hurry on in the dark night.*

【摸哨】attack the enemy sentinels in the dark night

【摸石头过河】[俗] travel across the river by feeling out for stones — get experience in the process of doing the job; move steadily:对于我们这是新鲜事物,所以只能～。*It's a complete new thing to all of us, and we can only gain experience while actually doing it.*

【摸索】① grope; feel about; fumble:我在黑暗中～着找电源开关。*I felt for the light switch in the dark.* /她在手提包里～护照。*She fumbled about in her handbag for her passport.* ② try to find out:经过一段时间,我～出了一些工作经验。*I found out some working experience after a period of time.*

【摸透】know (sb or sth) well; have an insight into sth; get to know clearly:她的脾气我～了。*I am familiar with her temper now.*

【摸营】steal up to an enemy's camp in the dark

mó

谟 [书] plan:宏～ *a grand plan*

馍 [方] steamed bun (or bread): 白面～ *steamed wheat flour bun*

摹 trace; copy:描～ *portray; delineate* /临～ *copy; facsimile; write from a copy*

【摹本】facsimile; copy; album of calligraphic reproduction: 文件的～ *documents reproduced in facsimile* /一幅名画的～ *a reproduction of a famous picture*

【摹古】model (or pattern) after ancient style: ～之作 *a production copied from the old style*

【摹绘】[书] draw; reproduce; describe; portray

【摹刻】① carve a reproduction of an inscription or painting ② a carved reproduction of an inscription or painting

【摹写】① copy; imitate:我要～他的文章。*I will write an article by copying his style.* ② describe; depict: ～人物情状 *depict characters in various situations*

【摹写纸】transfer paper

【摹印】① style of characters or lettering on ancient imperial seals ② copy and print (books, paintings, etc.)

【摹状】depict; portray

模 ① standard; pattern :楷～ *model; pattern* ② imitate ③ model; an exemplary person or thing:劳～ *a model worker; a labour model* /英～ *heroes and models*
see also mú

【模本】calligraphy or painting model

【模范】model; fine example: ～母亲 *a model mother* /～妻子 *a pattern wife* /～作品 *standard work* /他是诚实的～。*He is a model of honesty.* /这个孩子在关键时刻的勇敢为我们大家树立了～。*The child's courage at a critical moment sets an example to us all.*

【模仿】imitate; copy; mimic; emulate; pattern; ape; simulate:我的小女儿总是～我看书的样子。*My little daughter always copies the way I read.* /她～语文老师的一举一动来逗她的同学。*She modeled herself on her Chinese teacher to amuse her classmates.* /工人们～以前的样子建造了这座大楼。*Workers patterned this building on the previous one.*

【模糊】① blurred; indistinct; dim; hazy: ～的光线 *a dim light* /～的想法 *a vague idea* /我对那件事的记忆～不清。*My memory of the matter is only a blur; I have only a dim (or fuzzy; faint) recollection of the matter.* /我对她只有个～的印象。*I have only an indistinct memory of her.* ② blur; obscure; confuse:泪水～了我的眼睛。*Tears blur my eyes.* /浓雾～了我们的视野。*The dense fog obscured our view.* /不要～了印度和印第安那州两个地方。*Don't confuse India with Indiana.*

【模棱】vague; indistinct: ～的态度 *a vague attitude*

【模棱两可】cut both ways; on the line; yea and nay; ambiguous; equivocal:他给了我一个～的回答。*He gave me an ambiguous reply.* /法律条文是不能～的。*No ambiguous words should be used in law articles.*

【模拟】imitate; simulate; mock: ～战争 *a mimic battle* /他能惟妙惟肖地～我说话的样子。*He is able to mock the way I speak vividly.*

【模式】model; pattern:经济～ *economic model* /社会～ *social model*

【模特儿】①【美】model: 画～ *paint a model* /裸体～ *nude model* ② model:时装～ *fashion model* /她做学生时偶尔当～以赚点零用钱。*She did some modelling as a student to earn pocket-money.*

【模型】① model:轮船～ *a model of a ship* ② mould; matrix; pattern: ～板 *mould plate*

【模压】mould pressing; moulding: ~电路 *die stamp circuit* / ~机 *moulding press*; *block press*

膜 ①【生理】membrane: 鼓~ *tympanic membrane* / 呼吸~ *respiratory membrane* / 粘~ *mucous membrane* / 细胞~ *cell membrane* / 子宫粘~ *uterine mucous membrane* ② film; thin coating: 橡皮~ *rubber film* / 塑料薄~ *plastic film*

【膜拜】prostrate oneself (before an idol or person); worship: 顶礼~ *prostrate oneself in worship* / 古代民族对大自然的神秘~仪式 *the mysterious nature-worship cults of the ancient peoples*

摩[1] ① rub; scrape: 峻岭~天。*The high mountains soar into the clouds.* ② stroke; caress: 抚~ *stroke* / 按~ *massage* ③ study; mull over: 观~ *view and emulate*

摩[2] 【物】mole

see also mā

【摩擦】① rub; chafe: 衣服的高领~我的脖子。*The high collar chafed against my neck.* ②【物】friction: 滚动~ *rolling friction* / 滑动~ *sliding friction* / 火柴由~而生火。*Matches are lighted by friction.* ③ conflict; clash; friction: 内部~ *internal friction* / 大家庭的家庭成员间难免会有~。*There is inevitably some friction among the members in a big family.* / 今天边界线附近的两国军队又发生了~。*The two armies clashed near the borderline again today.*

【摩擦力】【物】frictional force; friction: ~使向下滑的箱子渐渐慢下来后停住。*Friction gradually caused the sliding box to slow down and stop.*

【摩擦面】rubbing surface; surface of friction

【摩擦阻力】frictional drag; frictional resistance

【摩登】modern; fashionable: ~服装 *modern clothes*

【摩电灯】dynamo-powered lamp (on a bicycle, etc.)

【摩尔】【化】mole: ~比热 *mole specific heat* / ~分数 *mole fraction* / ~浓度 *M*; *molarity*; *molar concentration* / ~热容 *molar heat capacity* / ~体积 *molar volume*; *mole volume*

【摩肩击毂】shoulder to shoulder and hub to hub — be crowded with people

【摩肩接踵】jostle each other on the way; be jam-packed with people: 广场上人们~。*People were jostling each other on the square.*

【摩羯】[书] male goat

【摩羯座】【天】Capricornus

【摩拉】mora

【摩洛哥】Morocco: ~人 *Moroccan*

【摩尼教】【宗】Manichean; Manicheism

【摩拳擦掌】rub one's fists and palms — be eager for a fight; roll up one's sleeves for a fight; itch for a fight: 大家~,恨不得马上投入战斗。*We all rolled up our sleeves, itching for the battle.*

【摩丝】styling mousse

【摩挲】stroke; caress: 他~小男孩的额头。*He caressed the little boy's forehead.* / 妈妈~着我的手。*Mom is fondling my hand.*

【摩天】skyscraping: ~大楼 *skyscraper*; *high-rise*

【摩托】motor: ~运动 *motorcycling*

【摩托车】motorcycle; motor bicycle; motorbike: 三轮~ *motor tricycle*

【摩托船】motor ship

【摩托艇】motorboat: ~运动 *motorboating*

【摩西】Moses, Hebrew patriarch: ~律法 *Mosaic law* / ~五书 *Pentateuch*

【摩崖】engravings on a cliff

磨 ① rub; wear: ~光的卵石 *pebbles worn smooth* / 这只鞋子~痛脚后跟。*This shoe is rubbing.* ② polish; grind; whet: ~刀 *whet the knife* / ~镜片 *grind a lens* / ~剪子 *grind scissors* / 把小麦~成面粉 *grind wheat into flour* ③ wear down; suffer: 牙痛把他~得够呛。*He suffered torments from his aching teeth.* ④ annoy; pester: 小男孩儿~他的父亲给他买玩具。*The little boy kept begging his father to buy a toy for him.* ⑤ obliterate; die out: 这种文化在几个世纪前就消~殆尽了。*This kind of culture died out centuries ago.* ⑥ waste time; idle: 她失业了,呆在家里~时间。*She is out of employment, idling away her time at home.* / 我在公园里~了许多个下午。*I whiled away many afternoons in the park.*

see also mò

【磨版】【印】grinding; plate grinding: ~工人 *grainer* / ~机 *graining machine*

【磨边】edging: ~机 *edge finishing machines*

【磨蹭】① rub lightly; stroke gently: 他一只脚在地上~,不耐烦地等着我。*He is waiting for me impatiently, with one foot rubbing lightly against the ground.* ② move slowly; dawdle: 你这样~,什么时候才完得了啊? *If you go on dawdling like this, when will you ever be able to finish?* ③ pester; nag: 她~我去看电影。*She pestered me for seeing a film.* / 她~丈夫去做她希望的事。*She nagged her husband into doing what she wanted.*

【磨齿】【机】gear grinding

【磨杵成针】rub a pestle into a needle — persistent practice makes perfect

【磨床】【机】grinding machine; grinder: 刀具~ *cutter sharpener*

【磨刀不误砍柴工】sharpening the axe won't hold up the cutting of firewood

【磨刀霍霍】sharpen one's knife to be ready for fighting

【磨刀石】grindstone; whetstone

【磨合】grinding-in; running-in: ~时间 *running-in time*

【磨砺】go through the mill; steel oneself; discipline oneself: 我要通过这次训练~我的意志和体质。*I will steel my will power and physical strength through the training.*

【磨炼】put oneself through the mill; temper oneself; steel oneself: ~人才 *cultivate talents* / 在艰苦斗争中~自己 *temper oneself in hard struggle* / 由于长时间的~,他已经适应了超负荷的劳动。*He was acclimatized by long hours to overwork.*

【磨灭】wear away; efface; obliterate:他给我留下了难以～的印象。*He gives me an indelible impression.* /许多年后战争的可怕记忆才从他头脑中～。*It takes many years for him to efface the horrible memories of a war.*

【磨难】tribulation; ordeal; suffering:他这一生备受～。*He went through all kinds of hardships all his life.*

【磨蚀】① abrasion:激流～砾石 *a swift stream abrading boulders* ② wear off; wear away; erode:我们对你的信心已经被～了。*Our confidence in you eroded.* /岁月和风雨早已～掉纪念碑上的铭文。*Time and weather had long ago effaced the inscription on the monument.*

【磨损】wear and tear; abrasion:磁头～ *head wear* /刀具～ *tool wear* /腐蚀～ *corrosive wear* /工件～ *wear of work* /均匀～ *even wear* /容许～ *allowable wear* /氧化～ *oxidative wear* /正常～ *normal wear* /这台机器基本上没有什么～。*The machine shows scarcely any sign of wear and tear.*

【磨损程度】degree of wear

【磨牙】① grind one's teeth (in sleep) ②［方］indulge in idle talk; argue pointlessly:你们怎么能把宝贵的时间浪费在～上呢? *How could you waste the precious time on endless idle talk?* ③【生理】molar; back teeth; grinding teeth

【磨洋工】dawdle over one's work; loaf on the job; potter away one's life:他因～而被开除。*He was fired when he loafed on the job.*

嬷

【嬷嬷】［方］① an elderly woman:老～ *an old granny* ② wet nurse

蘑

mushroom:鲜～ *fresh mushroom*

【蘑菇】① mushroom: ～酱 *mushroom sauce* /洋～ *meadow mushroom* /野～ *true mushroom* ② worry; pester; keep on at:他不答应我,我就和他～。*If he doesn't agree with me, I'll keep pestering him.* ③ dawdle; dillydally:别～了,该你发言了。*Don't dillydally; it's your turn to give a speech.*

【蘑菇云】mushroom cloud (esp. from nuclear explosion)

【蘑菇战术】tactics of "wear and tear"

魔

① demon; devil; fiend:病～ *serious illness* /恶～ *demon; devil* ② occult; mystic; magic:他的表演让我着～。*His performance bewitched me.*

【魔道】①【宗】domain of the devil ② witchcraft; sorcery

【魔法】sorcery; witchcraft; wizardry:看了那部电影后,他开始相信～。*He began to believe in magic after seeing the film.*

【魔方】magic square

【魔高一尺,道高一丈】Virtue dwarfs vice

【魔怪】demons and monsters; fiends

【魔鬼】devil; demon; monster: ～缠身 *be possessed by the devil* /那个凶残的地主简直是～的化身。*The cruel landlord is an incarnate fiend.*

【魔窟】den of monsters

【魔力】magical power; magic; charm:音乐的～ *the spell of music* /童话对孩子总是有巨大的～。*Children were always deeply entranced by fairy tales.*

【魔术】magic; conjuring; sleight of hand:变～ *do magic tricks* /～师 *magician; conjuror* /这人用～从空瓶子里变出一只鸽子。*The man used magic to produce a dove from an empty bottle.*

【魔头】① devil; demon ②［方］wizard

【魔王】① Prince of the Devils; erlking ② tyrant; despot; fiend

【魔影】phantom:往事的～困扰着她。*She is haunted by the phantom of things past.*

【魔掌】devil's clutches; evil hands:我们终于逃出了他的～。*We finally escaped from his evil clutches.*

【魔杖】magic wand

【魔障】obstacles or temptations set by devils; evil spirit

【魔爪】devil's talons; tentacles:他把～伸向了那个小孩儿。*He extends his tentacles to that little child.*

【魔怔】［口］obsessed; out of one's mind:他好像犯了什么～,嘴里总是念念有词。*He always mumbles something wherever as if obsessed with a demon.*

mǒ

抹

① put on; apply; smear:涂脂～粉 *apply facial make-up* /往面包上～果酱 *spread jam on a piece of bread* /有个护士正在给他的伤口～药。*A nurse is applying some medicine to his wound.* /这个孩子的脸上～得都是肥皂。*The child's face was smeared with soap.* ② clean off; wipe: ～干眼泪 *wipe one's tears away* /～把脸 *wipe one's face* ③ delete; erase; cancel:在日历上～掉已经过去的日子 *crossed the past days off the calendar* /他要求把自己的名字从光荣榜中～掉。*He required that his name be deleted from the honourable list.* /我无法～去头脑中关于那次事故的记忆。*I cannot erase all thoughts of that accident from my mind.* ④［量］used for clouds, etc:一～浮云 *a floating cloud*
see also mā; mò

【抹鼻子】［方］weep; cry:给他糖吃,不然他该～了。*Give him a candy or he will cry.*

【抹脖子】［口］cut one's own throat; commit suicide:真没想到他为了这么点小事就～了。*To our great surprise, he committed suicide for such a trivial matter.*

【抹彩】(in Beijing opera) do facial make-up

【抹黑】blacken sb's name; bring shame on; defame; discredit; spoil one's reputation:你给全家抹了黑。*You brought discredit on the whole family.* /一系列不愉快的事件给这个令人尊敬的学校

抹了黑。*A series of unpleasant incidents has tarnished the school's respectable image.*

【抹零】not count the small change (in a payment)

【抹杀】blot out; obliterate; write off: 一笔～ *write off at one stroke; deny completely* /人们一直认为他是个好妻子、好母亲,但是她最近的离婚～了这一切。*People used to think she was the perfect wife and mother but her recent divorce has spoiled all that.*

【抹稀泥】[方] try to mediate differences at the sacrifice of principle; try to gloss things over: 他说话直截了当,不想～。*He spoke in a direct way and doesn't want to gloss over anything.*

【抹一鼻子灰】suffer a snub; meet with a rebuff; be rejected: 他担心～,所以不愿意求助于她。*Fear of a rebuff has prevented him from asking for help from her.* /她不敢再谈这个话题,生怕在他那里又～。*She is scared to broach the subject with him in case he rejects her again.*

【抹子】【建】trowel

mò

末[1] ① tip; terminal; end: 刀锥之～ *point of a knife (or an awl)* ② trifles; minor details: 本～倒置 *put the cart before the horse* /舍本逐～ *attend to trifles and neglect the essentials* /细枝～节 *trivial matter of no importance* ③ end; bottom: 周～ *weekend* /月～ *end of a month* ④ dust; powder: 茶叶～儿 *tea dust* /粉～ *powder* /锯～ *sawdust* /肉～ *minced meat* /药～ *medicinal powder*

末[2] role of middle-aged man in traditional operas

【末班车】① last bus ② [口] last chance or turn: 他很幸运,赶上了分房的～。*He was very lucky to be allocated an apartment just before the policy was canceled.*

【末代】the last reign of a dynasty; last generation: ～皇帝 *last emperor of a dynasty*

【末端】end; bottom: 走廊的～ *end of the corridor*

【末伏】① the last of the three hottest periods of the year (10 days) ② the first day of the last period of the hot season

【末行】footline; terminal row

【末后】[口] last; finally; in the end; later: 你现在对他不礼貌,～还要给他道歉。*If you are impolite to him, you will have to apologize for that finally.*

【末级】final stage; last stage: ～火箭 *final-stage rocket*

【末技】petty (or insignificant) skill

【末节】minor details; nonessentials: 我们先不考虑这些～。*Let's just leave the minor details to later consideration.*

【末了】[口] last; finally; in the end: 他～还是同意了我的话。*He finally agreed with me.*

【末流】① (of a school of thought, literature, etc.) the later and decadent stage ② inferior; low-grade

【末路】dead end; impasse; blind alley: 穷途～ *go into a blind alley* /我们似乎已陷入～。*It seems that we have reached an impasse.*

【末年】last years of a dynasty or reign: 清朝～ *last years of the Qing Dynasty*

【末期】last phase (or stage); final phase: 20 世纪～ *the end of the twentieth century* /这种文学形式产生于 70 年代～。*This form of literature appeared in late seventies.*

【末日】①【宗】doomsday; Day of Judgement; Judgement Day ② end; doom: 他感到～将至。*He felt his last day was soon reached.*

【末梢】tip; end: 树枝～ *tip of a twig*

【末梢神经】【生理】nerve ending

【末世】last phase (of an age)

【末世学】eschatology

【末尾】end: 文章～的一句话非常振奋人心。*The sentence in the end of the article is very inspiring.* /到了电影～,所有主角都死了。*By the end of the movie, the main characters have all died.*

【末项】last term

【末药】【药】myrrh: ～脂 *myrrhin*

【末叶】last years (of a century or dynasty): 明朝～ *last years of the Ming Dynasty*

【末艺】insignificant skill

【末子】powder; dust

【末座】the most inferior seat of a table

没 ① sink; submerge: 船正～入水面。*The ship is sinking; the ship is submerging.* ② overflow: ～膝的雪 *knee-deep snow* /庄稼已经～人高了。*The crops have grown above the people.* ③ conceal; hide: 埋～人才 *stifle real talents* ④ seize; confiscate: 吞～ *engulf; embezzle* ⑤ to the last: ～齿 *all one's life*
see also méi

【没齿不忘】will never forget to the end of one's days; remember for the rest of one's life: 您的恩情我～。*I will not forget your kindness till death.*

【没顶】be drowned: 水深～。*The water goes above a man's head.*

【没落】decline; wane: 罗马帝国的～ *the decline of the Roman Empire* /走向～的文明 *a civilization that has begun to decay*

【没收】confiscate; expropriate: ～财产 *confiscate sb's property; expropriate sb from an estate* /海关官员～了走私物品。*The customs officials confiscated the contraband.*

茉

【茉莉】【植】jasmine

抹 ① plaster; daub: 往墙上～石灰 *daub some lime on the wall* ② turn; bypass: 拐弯～角 *talk in a roundabout way; ambages*
see also mā; mǒ

【抹灰】【建】plastering: ～涂料 *rendering*

殁 ［书］die：病～ *die of illness*

沫 ① foam；froth：啤酒～ *froth on beer* /他口吐白～。*He was foaming at the mouth.* ②［书］saliva；spittle：唾～ *saliva；spittle* /相濡以～ *help each other in an extremely difficult situation*

【沫子】foam；scum；froth：啤酒倒出来时会起～。*Beer froths when it is poured out.* /那只病狗口吐～。*That sick dog foamed at the mouth.*

陌 a path between fields：阡～ *paths in the fields* /～头杨柳 *roadside willows*

【陌路】［书］stranger：～相逢 *strangers meet on the way* /他们原来是好朋友，但是现在行同～。*They were good friends before，but now they treat each other as strangers.*

【陌生】strange；unfamiliar：他对这项工作仍很～。*He is still strange to the work.* /我对这里的路比较～。*I am unfamiliar with the roads here.*

脉

see also mài

【脉脉】lovingly；tenderly；amorously：～含情 *full of tenderness and love；full of affection*

莫 ①［书］none；no one：～不悲伤。*Everyone was sad.* ② no；not：望尘～及 *too far behind to catch up with* /一筹～展 *can find no way out* /变化～测 *so full of rapid changes as to be unpredictable* ③ do not：～提此事。*Don't mention it.* /闲人～入。*No admittance to outsiders.* ④ can it be that；is it possible that：～不是 *could it be that* ⑤（Mò）a surname

【莫不】there's no one who doesn't or isn't：～喜形于色。*Everybody is lit up with pleasure.*

【莫测高深】unfathomable；incomprehensible；enigmatic；esoteric：～的理论 *unfathomable theories* /教授的讲座～。*The professor's lecture is too profound to be understood.*

【莫大】greatest；utmost；extreme：～的耻辱 *gross insult* /～的光荣 *be greatly honoured*

【莫尔斯】Samuel Finley Breese Morse（1791-1872），American artist and inventor

【莫尔斯电码】Morse code；dot-and-dash

【莫非】can it be possible that；is it possible that：～您就是张先生？*Are you just Mr. Zhang？* /～他已经知道了那个秘密？*Is it possible that he has known the secret？*

【莫过于】nothing is more... than：我最大的爱好～绘画。*Nothing is more attractive to me than painting.*

【莫可名状】beyond description；indescribable；inexplicable；unintelligible：我现在的心情～。*What I feel now is indescribable.*

【莫可指数】beyond counting on one's fingers — countless；innumerable：新建的楼房～。*The newly built buildings are innumerable.*

【莫名其妙】① be unable to make head or tail of sth；be confused；be puzzled：这件事让我～。*I can't make head or tail of it.* /他为什么讲这番话，真叫人～。*It is quite baffling why he should have made such remarks.* ② without rhyme or reason；for no obvious reason；odd：父亲～地对我发脾气。*Father is angry with me for no apparent reason.*

【莫名一文】penniless；not have a bean — extreme poverty；poverty-stricken；badly off；impoverished：这个城市到处是～的急于卖出他们作品的艺术家。*The city is full of penniless artists desperate to sell their work.* /丈夫死后的一段时间，她～。*She was quite badly off for a while after her husband died.*

【莫逆】very friendly；intimate：～之交 *bosom friends；David and Jonathan；Damon and Pythias；sworn friend*

【莫泊桑】Guy de Maupassant（1850—1893），French short-story writer and novelist

【莫如】would be better；might as well：求人～求己。*It would be better to depend on ourselves than ask for help from others.*

【莫桑比克】Mozambique：～人 *Mozambican*

【莫斯科】Moscow，capital of the Russian Federation：～人 *Muscovite* /～宣言 *Moscow Declaration*（1957）

【莫须有】unwarranted；groundless；fabricated；fabulous：～的罪名 *trumped-up charges*

【莫扎特】Wolfgang Amadeus Mozart（1756—1791），Austrian composer

【莫衷一是】unable to agree or decide which is right；no unanimous conclusion can be drawn；unable to decide which is right as opinions vary：关于他的死因大家～。*Everyone has a version of his death and no conclusion could be drawn.*

昧 ［书］① poor eye sight ② take risks

秣 ① forage；fodder：粮～ *grain and fodder* ② feed（animals）

【秣马厉兵】feed the horses and sharpen the weapons — make preparations for war；be ready for battle

蓦 suddenly；all of a sudden

【蓦地】suddenly；unexpectedly；all of a sudden：我～想起明天有个重要的会议。*It suddenly occurred to me that I would attend an important meeting.*

【蓦然】suddenly；abruptly：～回首 *abruptly turn round* /～发怒 *a sudden outburst of temper*

漠 ① desert：大～ *vast expanse of desert* /荒～ *barren desert* ② indifferent；unconcerned：冷～ *apathetic；play it cool*

【漠不关心】indifferent；unconcerned；give short shrift；show no concern；pay no attention at all：我对于他们的行动～。*I am indifferent to their actions.* /我们平时关系很好，我身处困境时他却～。*Though he once kept on good terms with me，he is unconcerned about my current plight.*

【漠漠】① misty；foggy：～的烟雾 *a thick mist* ② vast and lonely：～荒原 *vast expanse of wasteland*

【漠然】indifferent; apathetic; unconcerned; give the cold shoulder:他对于我的愤怒表现~。*He remains indifferent to my anger.*

【漠然置之】hold loose; remain indifferent to sb or sth; show no concern for sb or sth:你怎么能对他的劝告~? *How can you turn a blind eye to his advice?* /看到电视画面上濒临饿死的儿童,谁还能够~呢? *How can anyone remain unmoved by pictures of starving children on the TV screens?*

【漠视】treat with indifference; overlook; ignore; disregard:你不能~他的存在。*You should pay attention to him.* /他~我的忠告,结果不幸出了事。*He utterly disregarded my advice and met with an accident unfortunately.*

【漠土】desert soil

寞 lonely; deserted; solitary:寂~ *lonely; desolate*

墨[1] ① ink stick; ink:研~ *rub an inkstick on an inkstone* /一锭~ *a piece of ink stick* ② ink; pigment:复写~ *copying ink* /红~ *red ink* /蓝~ *blue ink* /铝粉~ *aluminum ink* /油~ *printing ink* ③ calligraphy; painting:笔~ *writing; article* ④ literacy; knowledge:胸无点~ *be illiterate; without any learning* ⑤ rules and regulations ⑥ pitch-dark; black:近~者黑。*Touch pitch, and you will be defiled.* ⑦[书] corruption; graft:贪~ *embezzlement; graft* ⑧ tabooing the face as a kind of punishment in ancient China ⑨ (Mò) Mohist school; Mohism ⑩ (Mò) a surname

墨[2] Mexico

【墨宝】① treasured scrolls of calligraphy or painting ② your beautiful handwriting or painting

【墨笔】Chinese writing brush

【墨刀】ink knife

【墨斗】carpenter's ink marker; duct: ~轨 *ink rail*

【墨斗鱼】【动】inkfish

【墨尔本】Melbourne, a city of southeast Australia

【墨粉】powdered ink: ~鼓 *cartridge*

【墨盒】ink box; inkstone

【墨黑】pitch-dark; black as ink; inky: ~的夜晚 *a night as black as ink* /~的秀发 *jetty tresses*

【墨迹】① ink marks; ink stains: ~未干 *before the ink is dry* /~犹新 *with trace of ink still fresh* ② sb's writing or painting:这不是他的~。*It's not his calligraphy.*

【墨镜】sunglasses

【墨菊】dark chrysanthemum

【墨客】[书] literary men; men of letters

【墨吏】[书] corrupt officials

【墨绿】blackish green; dark green

【墨守成规】stick to convention; stay in a rut; stick in the mud; old methods:我们生活在一个日新月异的时代,岂能~? *We live in an era changing quickly; how could we stick to the conventions?*

【墨水】① prepared Chinese ink ② ink:红~ *red ink* /~瓶 *inkbottle* /纸上的~污迹 *a blot of ink on the paper* /我正给钢笔灌~。*I am inking a pen.*

【墨水池】inkwell

【墨西哥】Mexico: ~人 *Mexican* /~湾 *Gulf of Mexico*

【墨线】① the line in a carpenter's ink marker ② a straight line made by a carpenter's ink marker

【墨刑】tabooing the face as a punishment in ancient China

【墨鸦】①[书] scribbling ②【动】cormorant

【墨鱼】inkfish; cuttlefish; cuttle: ~骨 *cuttlebone*

【墨汁】prepared Chinese ink

【墨竹】① black bamboo ② bamboo painted in ink in a painting

镆

【镆铘】a famous double-edged sword in ancient times

默 ① quiet; silent:沉~ *keep silent* ② write from memory: ~古诗 *write the ancient poems from memory* ③ (Mò) a surname

【默哀】stand in silent tribute; pay silent tribute: ~三分钟 *observe three minutes' silence*

【默不作声】keep silence; hold one's tongue; as mute as a fish:母亲对外面发生的事情~。*Mother was silent about what happened outside.*

【默祷】pray in silence; say a silent prayer:他~能够顺利通过测验。*He prayed in silence that he could pass the test without difficulties.*

【默读】read silently

【默记】learn by heart; remember

【默剧】pantomime; mime

【默默】quiet; silent: ~对视 *gaze at each other in silence* /他~地望着我。*He looked at me quietly.*

【默默无闻】unknown to the public; without attracting public attention; in the shade:他在这个岗位上~地干了二十年。*He has worked in this position for 20 years, unknown to the public.*

【默念】① read silently:他口中~咒语。*He read the spell silently.* ② think back; meditate; recall:最近我总爱~和他在一起的日子。*I often recollect those days when I was with him recently.*

【默片】silent film

【默契】① tacitly agreed (or understood); be well coordinated:我们的队员经验丰富且配合~。*The members in our team are experienced and well coordinated.* ② secret agreement (or understanding):关于这次军事行动双方已经达成~。*The two parties have reached a secret agreement about the military action.*

【默然】silent; speechless:他坐在那里~无语,陷入沉思。*He sat there quietly absorbed in thought.*

【默认】give tacit consent to; tacitly approve; acquiesce (in):他的父母已经~了他的婚姻。*His parents have given their tacit consent to his marriage.*

【默示】【律】implied: ~承诺 *implied promise* /~承认 *implied recognition* /~担保 *implied warrant* /~放弃 *implied waiver* /~接受 *implied acceptance* /~批准 *implied ratification* /~条件 *implied term*

/～同意 *implied consent* /～信托 *implied trust* /～终止 *implied termination*

【默诵】① read silently to oneself from memory ② read (or recite) silently：学生们在～课文。*The students are reading texts silently.*

【默算】① calculate (or figure) in mind：他在～下个学期的花费。*He is figuring the cost for next semester in mind.* ② do mental arithmetic; do sums in one's heart

【默想】reflect; meditate; muse; brood; ruminate：她躺在床上～着下一步做什么。*She lay in bed musing what to do next.* /他好几天都～着受到的侮辱。*He brooded over the insult for several days.*

【默写】write from memory：你能把这首长诗～下来吗？*Could you write this long poem from memory?*

【默许】tacitly consent to; acquiesce in：我知道他的脾气，他不说话就是～了。*I am familiar with his temper; his silence can be regarded as tacit consent.* /她用微笑表示～。*She indicated tacit approval by smiling.*

【默坐】sit in silence; sit without saying a word

磨 ① mill; millstones：电～ *electric mill* /石～ *millstone* /推～ *a hand mill* ② mill; grind：～面 *mill flour* /把玉米～成粉 *grind corn into flour* ③ turn around：公共汽车上人很多，根本～不开身。*The bus is too crowded for people to turn around.*
see also mó

【磨不开】① feel embarrassed; be put out：我想当面说他两句，又怕他脸上～。*I didn't scold him in his face for fear that he would feel embarrassed.* ② cannot act impartially for fear of offending sb：我本不想接受他的邀请，可面子上又～。*I am not willing to accept his invitation, but I am afraid that it will impair our relations.* ③［方］not be convinced; not have an idea about what to do：如果你有什么～的事，尽管来找我。*If you have something uncertain, you can just turn to me.*

【磨叨】①［口］chatter away; babble：老太太从早～到晚。*The old woman babbled all day long.* ②［方］talk; gossip：你们是不是又在～新邻居？*Are you talking about our new neighbour again?*

【磨得开】① not feel embarrassed; be at ease：你当面讽刺他的文章，他能～吗？*Wouldn't he be very embarrassed if you satirize his article in his face?* ② find it embarrassing (to do sth)：他可真～，在我们家住了两周了。*He has lived in my home for two weeks without feeling embarrassed.* ③［方］be convinced; come round：这个理我～，您就放心吧。*I assure you I can see the reason well.*

【磨烦】① nag; pester：小男孩儿～我给他买糖果。*The little boy pestered me to buy him candies.* ② delay; loiter：别～了，赶快行动吧！*Let's delay no time and act quickly.*

【磨坊】mill：～工人 *millman* /～主 *millowner*

【磨盘】① nether (or lower) millstone ②［方］mill; millstones

【磨碎】attrite; bruising; squashing：～处理 *grinding treatment*

mōu

哞 ［象］moo; bellow (sound made by an ox)：牛～～叫。*The cow moos.*

móu

牟 ① obtain; seek ② (Móu) a surname

【牟利】seek private (or selfish) interests：投机商靠哄抬物价～。*Speculators seek private interests by means of driving up prices.*

【牟取】try to gain; seek; obtain：～暴利 *seek exorbitant profits*

眸 pupil (of the eye)：明～皓齿 *have bright eyes and white teeth*

【眸子】pupil (of the eye); eye

谋 ① plan; design：阴～ *plot; scheme* /足智多～ *resourceful; wise* ② strive; seek：～私利 *have an eye to the main chance* /不～私利 *not work for personal gains* /为大家～利益 *work for the interests of all the people* ③ consult; deliberate：不～而合 *happen to hold the same opinion*

【谋财害命】murder sb for one's money; murder for gain

【谋臣】emperor's counselor

【谋刺】plan an assassination

【谋反】conspire against the state; scheme for a rebellion：中央政府拒绝了这一要求后，南部各州就开始～。*When the federal government refused this request, the Southern States rebelled.*

【谋国】［书］work diligently in the interests of one's country

【谋害】① plot to murder：～亲夫 *plot against one's husband's life* ② plot a frame-up against frame：他有意～我。*He framed me deliberately.*

【谋和】sue for peace; seek reconciliation：他希望通过我的帮助和她～。*He tried to seek reconciliation with her through by my help.*

【谋划】plan; scheme：你就不能～一个办法解决这个问题吗？*Can't you find a solution to the problem?* /他～出一个弄钱的方案。*He thought of a scheme to get some money.*

【谋虑】consider carefully; ponder; contemplate; calculate：这件事事关重大，我得好好～一下。*The matter is of great importance; I'll think it over.*

【谋略】astuteness; strategy：他很善～。*He is very resourceful.*

【谋面】［书］meet each other; be acquainted with sb：我们靠书信交流，从未～过。*We communicate by correspondence and have never seen each other.*

【谋求】seek; strive for; pursue：～发迹 *carve out a career; make a career; push one's fortune* /他想方设法～改善和我的关系。*He tried every means to improve relations between us.*

【谋取】try to gain; seek: ~私利 *play one's own game; try to obtain profit for oneself*

【谋杀】murder; attempt sb's life: ~未遂 *attempted murder* / 血腥的~ *bloody murder* / 他昨晚被人~了。*He was murdered last night.*

【谋杀案】【律】case of murder

【谋杀罪】【律】offence of murder

【谋生】seek a livelihood; make a living; keep the pot boiling: ~手段 *means of subsistence* / 他靠写作~。*He earns a living by writing.*

【谋士】adviser; counsellor

【谋事】① plan matters ②［旧］look for a job; seek employment: 我要出去谋个事。*I'll go out to look for a job.*

【谋事在人,成事在天】the planning lies with man, the outcome with Heaven; man proposes, God disposes

【谋私】seek personal interests: 以权~ *seek selfish gains by abusing one's power*

【谋陷】frame; set sb up: 犯人声称他被仇人~。*The prisoner claimed that he had been framed by his enemies.* / 她并没有罪,而是被竞争对手所~。*She wasn't guilty at all; she had been set up by his rivals.*

【谋寻】seek; try to find: ~生路 *seek a livelihood*

【谋职】seek employment: 她想在广告公司~。*She wants to be employed by an advertising company.*

【谋主】mastermind

mǒu

某 ① certain; some: ~年 *in a certain year* / ~日 *at a certain date; one day; some day* / 王~ *a certain person called Wang* / 出于~种原因,他没有出席昨天的晚会。*For a certain reason, he didn't show his face at yesterday's evening.* ② (refer to oneself) yours truly: 这件事是我王~干的。*It's done by me.* ③ used instead of sb's given name to show an impolite attitude: 隔壁赵~真是太讨厌了! *That fellow Zhao in the neighbourhood is really annoying.*

【某处】somewhere; at a certain place: 他到城外~去了。*He went somewhere out of town.*

【某某】so-and-so: ~公司 *a certain company* / ~同志 *Comrade so-and-so*

【某人】a certain person; somebody; someone: ~曾给你打过电话。*Someone once phoned you.*

【某种】a certain kind: 那儿的鹿喜欢吃~野玫瑰。*The deer there like to eat a certain kind of wild rose.*

mú

模 mould; matrix; pattern: 字~ *type matrix* / 灰泥~ *stucco pattern* / 陶瓷~ *ceramic die* / 压~ *compression moulding* / 砖~ *brick die*

see also mó

【模板】①【建】shuttering; formwork ②【机】pattern plate

【模具】mould; matrix; pattern; die

【模样】① appearance; look; countenance: 她~俊俏。*She looks very pretty.* / 她的~很像她的母亲。*She takes after her mother.* / 他长得什么~? *What does he look like?* ② (of time or age) about: 过了一小时~,她终于来了。*She finally appeared after about an hour.* ③ trend; tendency: 她没有任何准备出国的~。*She doesn't show any intention of going abroad.*

【模子】mould; matrix; pattern; die: 铜~ *copper mould*

【模座】die holder

mǔ

母 ① mother: 继~ *stepmother* / 养~ *foster mother* / 有其~必有其女。*Like mother, like daughter.* ② the female elder: 舅~ *wife of mother's brother; aunt* / 祖~ *grandmother* ③ female (animal): ~狗 *bitch* / ~鸡 *hen* / ~狼 *she-wolf* / ~驴 *jennet; mare* / ~马 *mare* / ~牛 *cow* / ~羊 *ewe* / ~猪 *sow* ④ concave; nut: 螺~ *nut* ⑤ origin; mother: 酒~ *distiller's yeast* / 失败是成功之~。*Failure is the mother of success.* ⑥ (Mǔ) a surname

【母爱】mother love; maternal love: ~是世界上最神圣的感情。*The maternal love is the holiest feeling in the world.* / 缺少~对他的心理发育产生了很大的影响。*Lack of maternal love has profound effects on his psychological developments.*

【母板】mother blank; mother board

【母版】master matrix; master mask

【母分子】parent molecule

【母公司】parent company

【母国】mother country

【母机】① machine tool ②【航】mother aircraft; launching aircraft

【母舰】［旧］mother ship: 航空~ *aircraft carrier*

【母老虎】① tigress ② vixen; shrew; termagant

【母亲】mother; mater: ~节 *Mother's Day* / 我~是一位教师。*My mother is a teacher.* / ~的举止会对她的女儿产生深刻而持久的影响。*A mother's behaviours can exert a deep and lasting effect on her daughter.*

【母权社会】matriarchate

【母权制】matriarchy

【母乳】breast milk; mother's milk: ~喂养 *breast feeding*

【母树】【林】mother tree; seed tree

【母体】the mother's body; the (female) parent: ~免疫 *maternal immunity*

【母系】① maternal: ~亲属 *maternal relatives* ② matrilineal; matriarchal: ~氏族 *matrilineal clan*

【母系氏族】matriarchy: ~公社 *matrilineal com-*

mune / ~制 *matriarchy*

【母线】①【电】bus; bus bar ②【数】generatrix; generator

【母校】one's old school; Alma Mater

【母星系】parent galaxy

【母性】maternal instinct: ~本能 *maternal instinct* / 这个婴儿引发了她的~。*The baby brought out the mother in her.*

【母夜叉】① female devil ② vixen; fierce and ugly woman

【母语】① mother tongue: 用~交谈 *talk in one's mother tongue* ② parent language; linguistic parent

【母株】【植】maternal plant; mother plant

【母子】mother and child: ~之情 *love between mother and son*

牡 male: ~鹿 *buck*; *stag* / ~马 *stallion*/ ~牛 *bull* / ~竹 *male bamboo*

【牡丹】tree peony; peony: 她的脸红得像一朵~。*She blushed like a peony.*

【牡丹虽好,绿叶扶持】though the peony is beautiful, it needs the support of green leaves

【牡蛎】【动】oyster: ~床 *oyster bed* / ~筏 *oyster raft* / ~礁 *oyster bioherm* / ~苗 *spat of oyster* / ~养殖 *oyster culture* / ~养殖场 *oyster bed*; *oyster farm*

【牡竹】male bamboo

亩 a unit of area (=60 square): ~产量 *per mu yield*

【亩茬地】stubble; stubble field

拇

【拇战】finger-guessing game — a drinking game

【拇指】① thumb: ~痕 *thumbmark* / ~夹 *thumbscrew* / ~索引 *thumb index* / ~套 *thumbstall* / ~纹 *thumbprint* ② big toe

姥 [书] old lady

see also lǎo

mù

木[1] ① tree: 果~ *fruit tree* ② wood; timber: 沥青~ *bituminous wood* /松~ *pinewood* /山杨~ *axial wood* /桃花心~ *chittagonywood* /香脂~ *balsam wood* ③ wooden: ~桌 *wooden table* ④ coffin: 行将就~ *be getting nearer and nearer the coffin* ⑤ (Mù) a surname

木[2] ① plain; simple; unsophisticated; artless: 他脑袋发~。*He is a numskull.* ② numb; wooden: 呆若~鸡 *dumbstruck*; *transfixed* /我的手指被冻~了。*My fingers were numb with cold.*

【木板】plank; board: ~路 *plank road*

【木版】【印】block: ~画 *woodcut*; *wood engraving* / ~水印 *woodblock printing* / ~印刷 *block printing*

【木本】【植】xyloid; woody; ligneous: ~植物 *woody plant*; *arbor*

【木本水源】the root of wood and the source of a stream — the root of a matter; the foundation or cause of a matter

【木材】wood; timber; log; lumber: ~商 *wood-dealer*

【木柴】firewood

【木船】wooden boat

【木呆呆】stonily; be in a trance: 她~地站在门边。*She stood by the door in a trance.*

【木雕】wood carving

【木雕泥塑】like an idol carved in wood or moulded in clay — like wooden figure: 他站在墙角如~。*He stood in the corner of the room, as wooden as a dummy.*

【木钉】peg; nog; wood nail: ~鞋 *pegged shoe*

【木耳】an edible fungus (*Auricularia auricula*): 白~ *white edible fungus*; *tremella*

【木筏】raft

【木工】① woodwork; carpentry ② woodworker; carpenter

【木瓜】【植】① Chinese flowering quince ②[口] papaya

【木化】lignify: ~纤维 *lignified fibre*

【木化石】petrified wood; woodstone

【木婚】wood wedding — the 5th wedding anniversary

【木屐】clogs; wooden shoe

【木简】【考】inscribed wooden slip

【木浆】wood pulp: 化学~ *chemical wood pulp*

【木匠】carpenter

【木强】[书] upright; unyielding

【木结构】【建】timber structure; wooden structure

【木刻】woodcut; wood engraving

【木刻活字】【印】wood letters

【木刻水印】woodblock printing

【木料】timber; lumber

【木马】①【体】vaulting horse; pommelled horse; wooden horse ② (children's) hobbyhorse; rocking horse

【木马计】the stratagem of the Trojan horse; Trojan horse

【木棉】silk cotton; kapok: ~花 *common bombax flower* / ~树 *wool tree*; *tree cotton*

【木模】wooden mould

【木乃伊】① mummy ② sth rigid

【木囊】wood pocket

【木讷】[书] simple and slow (of speech): 他是一个~寡言的人。*He is a man of a plain mind and few words.*

【木偶】① wooden image; carved figure ② puppet; marionette: ~剧 *puppet show*; *puppet play* / ~片 *puppet film*; *animated doll film*

【木排】raft: ~工 *raftsman*

【木片】wood chip; spill

【木器】wooden furniture; wooden articles

【木然】stupefied: 他因酒醉而~。*He is stupefied with drink.*

【木人石心】a wooden man with a stone heart —

cruel; unfeeling; heartless; pitiless: 她抛弃了自己的女儿,真是～。*She was so heartless that she forsook her own daughter.*

【木炭】charcoal; wood charcoal: ～粉 *charcoal dust*

【木炭画】charcoal drawing

【木糖】【生化】wood sugar: ～醇 *xylitol*

【木头】[口] wood; log; timber

【木头人儿】[口] woodenhead; blockhead; slow coach: 我该如何和这个～打交道? *How could I deal with such a blockhead?*

【木纹】wood grain: ～理 *grain of wood*

【木锨】wooden spade

【木纤维】xylogen; xylon

【木屑】bits of wood; sawdust

【木星】【天】Jupiter: ～卫星 *Jovian satellite*

【木已成舟】the wood is already made into a boat — what's done is done; things past cannot be recalled

【木鱼】wooden fish (a hollow wooden block, originally used by Buddhist priests to beat rhythm when chanting scriptures)

【木枕】wood blocking; sleeper

【木制品】wood; woodwork

目 ① eye: 瞩～ *fix one's eyes upon* / 历历在～ *appear vividly before one's eyes* / 耳濡～染 *be influenced by what one constantly sees and hears* ② hole; mesh: 八十～筛 *eighty-hole sieve* ③ [书] look; see: 一～十行 *read ten lines at a glance — read rapidly* / 一～了然 *be clear at a glance* ④ item; number: 细～ *detailed items* ⑤ order: 亚～ *suborder* ⑥ catalogue; list: 剧～ *a list of plays* / 书～ *booklist* ⑦ title; name: 题～ *title*; *topic* ⑧ (in weiqi or go) eye, a unit used in counting the winnings or losses of the game

【目标】① objective; target: 军事～ *military objective* / 不要暴露～。*Don't give away your position.* / 猎人的～是一只鹿。*The hunter's target was a deer.* ② goal; aim; objective: 达到～ *achieve one's aim* / 教育～ *educational goal* / 生活～ *life goal* / 我今年夏天的～是学习游泳。*My objective this summer will be learning to swim.* / 我的～是成为一名医生。*My goal is a place in a hospital.*

【目不见睫】the eye can't see its lashes — lack self-knowledge; one doesn't know himself enough

【目不交睫】not sleep a wink; stay up; lay awake the whole night: 她～地思考下一步的策略。*She stayed up the whole night contemplating the next strategy.*

【目不窥园】not to cast one's eyes at the garden — bury oneself in one's studies; be absorbed in one's studies: 他专心写作,～。*He occupies himself in writing.*

【目不忍睹】cannot bear to look at; be too sad to look at: 车祸的惨状让人～。*One cannot bear to watch the terrible scene of the traffic accident.*

【目不识丁】not know one's ABC; be totally illiterate; not know a single word; analphabetic: 这个老农～。*The old farmer is completely illiterate.*

【目不暇接】the eye cannot take it all in; too many things for the eye to see; have no time to take in the scene as a whole; too much to watch: 超市里的物品让人～。*The goods in the supermarket are too many for one's eyes to take all in.*

【目不转睛】look with fixed gaze; regard with rapt attention; fix one's eyes on; be all eyes for sth; look at sth without winking: 孩子们～地盯着电视屏幕。*The children fix their eyes on the television screen.*

【目测】【军】visual range estimation; eye survey: ～法 *ocular estimate* / ～图 *eye draft*

【目次】table of contents; contents

【目瞪口呆】gaping; be stunned; dumbstruck; stupefied; stare in mute amazement; stand aghast: 吓得～ *strike sb dumb* / 他因惊吓而～。*He is numb with fear.* / 她～地凝视着面前的陌生男人,不相信他竟是自己的哥哥。*She gaped at the strange man before her, not believing that he was her elder brother.*

【目的】purpose; intention; goal; objective; end; motive: 教学～ *educative purpose* / 会计～ *accounting purpose* / 你做那件事的～是什么? *What is your purpose in doing that?* / 他这么做的～是想吸引你的注意。*His motive for doing so is that he wants to draw your attention.*

【目的地】destination: 直接～ *immediate destination*

【目的港】port of destination

【目的论】【哲】teleology

【目的心理学】purposive psychology

【目睹】see with one's own eyes; witness: 她～了那个事故。*She witnessed the accident.* / 如果不是亲眼～,我是不会相信的。*If I hadn't seen it with my own eyes, I would never have believed it.*

【目端】eye end

【目光】① look; gaze; eye: ～无神 *dull look* / 我的～落在报纸上一则有趣的新闻上。*My eye fell upon a piece of interesting news in the newspaper.* ② expression in one's eyes: ～炯炯 *penetrating eyes* ③ sight; vision; view: ～敏锐 *keen-eyed*; *sharp-sighted*

【目光短浅】short-sighted; improvident: ～的人 *a person of narrow vision*

【目光如豆】vision as narrow as a bean — of narrow vision; short-sighted; be myopic; see no further than what is right under one's nose

【目光如炬】① eyes blazing like torches — glare with anger ② far-sighted; have wide-vision

【目击】see with one's own eyes; witness: 我～了这件事。*I saw it with my own eyes.*

【目击者】eyewitness; witness: 事故的～ *witnesses of the accident*

【目见】see for oneself: 耳闻不如～。*Seeing is believing.*

【目今】these days; nowadays: ～,中国大部分家庭都只有一个孩子。*Nowadays, there is only one child in most Chinese families.*

【目镜】【物】eyepiece; ocular; eye lens: ～网格

eyepiece grid
【目空一切】look down upon everyone else; consider everybody and everything beneath one's notice; be supercilious; be extremely arrogant: ~的态度 *a supercilious attitude* /她~。*She was too full of herself to care about anyone else.* /我知道你做得很好,但是不要~。*I know you did well but don't let it go to your head.*
【目力】eyesight; vision: ~表 *visual chart*
【目录】① catalogue; list:图书~ *library catalogue* ② table of contents; contents: 书的前面有~,详列了书中的内容。*At the front of the book is a table of contents, giving details of what is in the book.*
【目录学】bibliography
【目论】[书] superficial view
【目偏视】squinting eyes
【目前】current; present; at the moment:到~为止,我已经攒了一万元。*I have saved ten thousand yuan so far.* /你~的工作是什么? *What is your present job?*
【目送】follow sb with one's eyes; watch sb go; gaze after:我~她远去。*I watch him going further and further away.*
【目无法纪】act in utter disregard of law and discipline; defy every law and regulation
【目无尊长】show no respect to elders and superiors
【目下】at present; at the moment: ~我正在工作。*At the moment I am working.* /~我们很忙。*At the present time, we are terribly busy.*
【目眩】dizzy; dazzled; giddy:令人~的悬崖 *a giddy precipice* /使人~的高度 *a vertiginous height; a dizzy height* /灯光令人~。*The light is too dazzling.*
【目语】communicate with the eyes
【目中无人】consider everyone beneath one's notice; have no respect for anyone; be supercilious; be overweening; with one's nose in the air:我们知道你被提升了,但是没有必要~! *We know you've been promoted but there's no need to be so smug about it!*

沐 ① wash; bathe; wash one's hair ② [书] receive ③ (Mù) a surname
【沐恩】receive a favour (or kindness)
【沐猴而冠】a monkey with a hat on — a worthless person in imposing attire
【沐雨栉风】bathed by the rain and combed by the wind — be exposed to all kinds of difficulties; toil and trouble
【沐浴】① have (or take) a bath: ~更衣 *take a bath and put on clean clothes* /~戒斋 *bathe one's body and purify oneself* ② bathe; immerse: ~阳光 *be bathed in sunlight* /整个城市都~在节日的气氛中。*The whole city was immersed in a festival atmosphere.*

苜
【苜蓿】【植】lucerne; alfalfa

牧 ① herd; tend: ~羊 *tend sheep* /游~ *move about in search of pasture* ② animal husbandry; livestock-raising
【牧草】herbage; forage grass
【牧场】① grazing land; pastureland; pasture:高产~ *rich pasture* /集约化~ *intensive pasture* /季节性~ *seasonal pasture* /天然~ *natural pasture* /永久~ *permanent pasture* /栽培~ *cultivated pasture* /这些地方有很好的~。*These lands afford good pasture.* ② livestock farm or ranch: ~管理 *livestock farm management*
【牧笛】reed pipe
【牧放】herd; tend; put out to pasture
【牧歌】① pastoral song; pastoral ②【音】madrigal
【牧工】hired herdsman
【牧马人】herdsman (of horses)
【牧民】herdsman:从前~们为了寻找新鲜的草原赶着羊群一起迁移。*Herdsmen used to migrate with their sheep in search of fresh grass.*
【牧牛工】cowhand; cowpoke; cowpuncher
【牧牛业】cowboying
【牧区】① pastureland; pasture ② pastoral area: ~供水 *water supply of pastoral area*
【牧犬】shepherd dog; sheep dog
【牧人】herdsman
【牧师】【宗】pastor; minister; clergyman: ~服 *clerical dress* /~团 *pastorate* /~职 *pastorate; pastorship*
【牧竖】[书] shepherd boy; buffalo boy
【牧童】shepherd boy; buffalo boy
【牧畜】livestock breeding
【牧羊场】sheepwalk
【牧羊女】shepherdess
【牧羊犬】collie; shepherd dog
【牧羊人】shepherd
【牧业】animal husbandry; stock raising; livestock farming:发展~ *develop stock raising*
【牧主】herd owner

钼 【化】molybdenum (Mo)
【钼合金】molybdenum alloy
【钼中毒】molybdenosis

募 collect; enlist; raise:招~ *enlist; recruit*
【募兵】recruit soldiers: ~制 *mercenary system*
【募股】raise capital by floating shares
【募化】(of Buddhist monks or Taoist priests) collect alms
【募集】raise; collect: ~资金 *raise a fund*
【募捐】solicit contributions; collect (or solicit) donations; pass (or send) round the hat:他们为新的学校~。*They passed the hat to raise funds for the new school.* /他向邻居们恳求~。*He solicited the neighbours for donations.*
【募款】raise funds (or money)

墓 tomb; grave:公~ *cemetery* /古~ *ancient tomb*
【墓碑】grave monument; tombstone; gravestone
【墓场】graveyard; cemetery
【墓道】① path leading to a grave; tomb passage ②

passage leading to the coffin chamber in an ancient tomb
【墓地】burial ground；cemetery；graveyard
【墓祭】pay respects to a deceased person at grave
【墓碣】tombstone；gravestone
【墓石】tombstone；headstone
【墓室】coffin chamber
【墓穴】coffin pit；open grave；tomb
【墓茔】grave；tomb
【墓园】cemetery；graveyard
【墓葬】【考】grave；tombs：～结构 *structure of tombs*
【墓志】inscription on the memorial tablet within a tomb
【墓志铭】inscription on the memorial tablet within a tomb；epitaph

幕 ① covering cloth；canopy：烟～ *a curtain of smoke* /夜～ *the veil of night* /谢～ *take the curtain* /在夜～的掩护下 *under screen of night* ② curtain：～启。*The curtain rises.* ③（in ancient times）governor's or general's office ④ act；scene：第一～ *the first act*；*Act 1* /这个剧分为四～，每一～有两个场景。*This play is divided into four acts，and each act has two scenes.*
【幕表】scene plot
【幕宾】［旧］① assistant to an official or general ② high official's house guest and adviser
【幕布】①（theatre）curtain ②（cinema）screen
【幕府】①［旧］office of a commanding general ② shogunate：德川～ *Tokugawa shogunate*
【幕后】behind the scenes；backstage：退居～ *retire backstage* /～策划 *manoeuvre behind the scenes* /～交易 *behind the scenes deals*；*backstage deal* /～谈判 *behind-the-scenes conference* /～指使 *direct sb behind the scenes*
【幕间区】intermezzo
【幕间时间】interlude
【幕间休息】interval（in a play，etc.）；intermission
【幕僚】［旧］assistant to a ranking official or general in old times
【幕墙】curtain wall

睦 ① harmonious；peaceful：夫妻不～。*The husband and wife don't get along well with each other.* ②（Mù）a surname
【睦邻】good-neighbourliness：～关系 *good-neighbourly relations* /～友好 *good neighbourly and friendly relations* /～政策 *good-neighbourly policy*

慕 ① admire；envy：羡～ *admire*；*envy* /仰～ *admire*；*worship* ② yearn for；long for：爱～ *love*；*adore* /思～ *think of sb with respect* ③（Mù）a surname
【慕名】out of admiration for a famous person：我是～而来。*I come to him because I admire his reputation*；*I come to see him on account of his established reputation.*
【慕尼黑】Munich，capital of Bavaria，Germany
【慕尼黑协定】the Munich Agreement（1938）
【慕尼黑阴谋】the Munich conspiracy

暮 ① evening；dusk；sunset：薄～ *dusk* ② late；declining：日～。*The day is declining.*
【暮霭】evening mist（or haze）
【暮齿】［书］old age；one's later（or remaining）years
【暮春】late spring（the third month of the lunar year）
【暮鼓晨钟】the evening drum and the morning bell（in a monastery）— the solitary life of a monk；exhorting people to lead a life of virtue
【暮景】① sunset scene；twilight ② evening of one's life；old age
【暮年】old age；declining years；evening of one's life；in the gloaming of one's age：～凄惨。*One leads a miserable life in one's old age.*
【暮气】lethargy；apathy：～十足 *lethargic* /这个年轻人看上去～沉沉。*The young man looks lifeless（or lethargic）.*
【暮秋】late autumn（the ninth month of the lunar year）
【暮色】dusk；twilight；gloaming：～苍茫 *deepening dusk*；*spreading shades of dusk* /～朦胧 *glimmering twilight* /～渐浓。*Twilight was merging into darkness.*
【暮世】modern times
【暮岁】① towards the end of the year ② old age；the gloaming of one's age；one's later（or remaining）years

穆 ① reverent；respectful：静～ *quiet and solemn* ②（Mù）a surname
【穆罕默德】Islam Mohammed（c. 570-632），founder of Islam
【穆民】believers in Islam
【穆斯林】Moslem；Muslim

N

nā

南

see also nán

【南无】【宗】Buddhism (expressing one's devotion to Buddha or Buddhism): ~阿弥陀佛! *I devote myself to Amitabha!*

ná

拿

① hold; take; bring: 不~枪的警察 *policemen without guns* /~去。*Take it.* /~来。*Bring it here.* /他手里~着一本书。*He is holding a book in his hand.* /请把这些照片~走。*Please take these photos away.* /你去~点儿水来好吗? *Will you fetch some water?* ② seize; catch; capture: 猫~老鼠。*The cat seizes a rat.* /军队~下了这个要塞。*The army seized the fort.* /罪犯在企图逃离这座城市时被~住了。*The criminal was captured when trying to escape from the city.* ③ have a firm grasp of; be able to do; be sure of: ~不准 *not be sure; feel uncertain* /家务活她样样都~得起来。*She can do every kind of housework.* /这件事你~得稳吗? *Are you sure of it?* ④ put sb in a difficult position: 他说要是不涨工资他就不干了,想~我一把。*He said he wouldn't do the job without a pay rise and tried to put me in a difficult position.* ⑤ pretend to be; put on airs: 别再~架子了。*Stop putting on such airs.* ⑥ get; gain win: 你~到工资了吗? *Have you got your salary?* /在演讲比赛中,我们班~了一等奖。*Our class won the first prize in the speech contest.* ⑦ (of a chemical agent, etc.) turn sth bad: 这块木头让药水~白了。*The chemical agent has bleached the wooden block.* ⑧ by means of; with; by: ~几句话来概括 *to sum up in a few words* /~尺量 *measure with a ruler* /~事实证明 *prove with facts* /我们不能~年轻人的穿着爱好来评价他们。*We shouldn't judge the young people by their taste in clothes.* /我们决不~原则做交易。*We will never barter away principles.* /别总是~他当小孩子。*Don't treat him as a kid.* /我简直~他没办法。*I really cannot do anything with him.* /她要是非出国不可,你又能~她怎么样? *If she insists on going abroad, what can you do about it?* /别~别人的缺点开玩笑。*Don't make fun of others' shortcomings.* ⑨ as regards; as to: ~你们的报价来说 *as to your quotation* /~质量来说,我们的产品是最好的。*So far as quality is concerned, our product is the best.*

【拿不出手】not be presentable; not good or well enough: 跟别人送你的礼物比起来,我的这个真是~。*Compared to the gifts others have given to you, mine is far from being presentable.*

【拿不起来】cannot manage: 这样的工作他~。*He cannot manage this kind of work.*

【拿不稳】not be sure of sth: 能不能干好,我也~。*I'm not sure if I can do it well.*

【拿大顶】stand on one's hands; handstand

【拿大头】① take the lion's share: 挣来的钱,他~。*He takes the lion's share of the profit.* ② take sb for a sucker; cheat sb out of his money; fleece sb: 我买这台二手电脑让人~了。*I was had over this second-hand computer I bought.*

【拿得起,放得下】can take it up or put it down — be adaptable to circumstances: ~对我来说实在不是一件容易的事。*It's difficult for me to take it up and put it down with equal ease.*

【拿得起来】can manage; can do: 他在工厂干了十年了,样样工作他都~。*He has been working in the factory for ten years and can do all kinds of work.*

【拿定主意】make up one's mind: 这事儿得你自己~。*It's up to you to make up your own mind.* /面对两种选择,她拿不定主意了。*She is wavering between two choices.*

【拿获】apprehend (a criminal); seize; catch; arrest: 银行抢劫犯被当场~。*The bank robbers were apprehended on the spot.*

【拿架子】put on airs; assume great airs; throw one's weight around; be haughty: 他以为除了他以外没人能管理好这个公司,所以整天拿着架子。*He puts on great airs thinking that the company cannot be well managed without him.*

【拿捏】[方] ① be affectedly bashful: 你有话快说,~个什么劲儿! *Speak out! Why so bashful and hesitant?* ② make things difficult for; put pressure on; threaten: 我只喝醉过一次,她就总拿这个来~我。*I only got drunk once and she is always using it against me.*

【拿破仑】Napoleon Bonaparte I (1769-1821), French Emperor (from 1804-1815): ~法典 *Napoleonic Code* /~战争 *Napoleonic Wars* (1799-1815)

【拿腔拿调】speak with an affected tone of voice: 新来的秘书说话~的,让人听了很不舒服。*The new secretary speaks with an affected tone of voice, which is really disturbing.*

【拿腔作势】be affected or pretentious; act affectedly; strike a pose:刚一升职,他就~起来了。*He turns pretentious upon promotion.*

【拿权】wield power; be in the saddle:我兄弟当上了经理,又~了。*My brother as a manager was in the saddle again.*

【拿人】[方] ① make things difficult for others; raise difficulties:他这是在故意~。*He is being difficult on purpose.* ② attract; fascinate:他们说相声很~。*Their dialogue is very fascinating.*

【拿事】have the power to do sth or to decide what to do:你已经二十岁了,也该能~了。*You are already 20 years old and should be able to make the right decisions.*

【拿手】① adept; expert; good at; skillful:~菜 *a cook's best dishes; dishes one is particularly good at making* /农活他很~。*He is good at farm work.* /尝尝这个,这可是这儿的~菜。*Try this; it is one of the best dishes served here.* ② confidence; certainty:你有~按时完成任务吗? *Are you confident you can finish the task on time?*

【拿手好戏】① the play that one does best:《罗密欧与朱丽叶》是他们的~。*Romeo and Juliet is the play that they perform best.* ② the game or trick one's good at; one's specialty; one's forte:花样滑冰是她的~。*Figure skating is her specialty.* /声东击西是他的~。*He is really good at selling the dummy.*

【拿问】[旧] detain for interrogation; be brought to trial

【拿着鸡毛当令箭】[俗] take a chicken feather for a warrant to issue orders — make a big fuss about one's superior's casual remark:经理只不过在会上开个玩笑说咖啡太甜了,他的助理就~,把采购部的人都训了一通。*The manager only joked about the coffee being too sweet at the meeting, but his assistant made a big fuss about it and reprimanded all the staff in the purchasing department.*

【拿主意】make a decision; decide; give some advice:下一步该做什么,你自己~吧。*You'd better decide for yourself what to do next.* /我们对这事儿不了解,既然你懂,就帮着拿个主意吧。*We are not familiar with this at all; since you are an expert in this field, do give us some advice.*

【拿总儿】[口] exercise overall control:爸妈不在家的时候,大姐就~。*When my parents are away, my eldest sister exercises overall control over us.*

nǎ

哪[1] ① which; what:我这里有两本字典,你要~本? *I have two dictionaries here; which one do you want?* /你是从~个国家来的? *Which country are you from?* /你喜欢~种颜色? *What colour do you like?* ② whichever; any that:不论~个队获胜,我都会高兴的。*Whichever team wins, I will be happy.* /不论你走~条路,旅途都会很艰辛。*It's a hard trip whichever road you take.* /~天有时间就过来。*Drop in any time you are free.*

哪[2] how can; how is it possible:不劳无获,~有免费的午餐? *No pains, no gains; there is no such thing as free lunch!* /~有不剥削工人的资本家? *Is there a capitalist who does not exploit workers?*

see also na

【哪个】① which:这里面~是你的? *Which of these is yours?* ② [方] who:~在用厕所? *Who is in the toilet?*

【哪会儿】① when:从~起事情成这样了? *Since when has this been going on?* /他从~起开始有了一辆汽车? *Since when has he had a car?* /要是明早八点对你来说不方便,那么~我们再碰头呢? *When else shall we meet again, if 8:00 a. m. tomorrow is not convenient for you?* ② whenever; any time:你爱~来就~来。*Come whenever you like.* /趁着经理在,抓紧把这件事定下来吧,说不准~经理又外出了。*Get this confirmed while the manager is still here, for he may leave any time.*

【哪里】① where:你到~去? *Where are you going?* /你是~人? *Where are you from?* /你~疼? *Where do you feel the pain?* ② wherever; where:~有压迫,~就有反抗。*Where there is oppression, there is resistance.* /不论你在~工作,你都必须全心全意为人民服务。*Wherever you work, you must serve the people whole-heartedly.* ③ used in rhetorical questions to express negation:我~知道他会放弃这么好的机会呢? *How could I know that he should give up such a good opportunity?* ④ [谦] not at all

【哪门子】[方] used to emphasize a rhetorical question:好好儿的,你哭~呀? *What on earth are you crying for?* /你说的是~事儿呀? *What the hell are you talking about?*

【哪能】how can; how could:都说好了的,你~出尔反尔呢? *It has already been agreed; how could you break your own words?* /"你可别骗我啊。""~呢?" *"Don't play tricks on me!" "How could I?"*

【哪怕】even; even if; even though; no matter how:~有沙尘暴我也得到工地去。*I will go to the construction site even if sandstorm comes.* /~是一滴水也不应该浪费。*We should not waste even a drop of water.* /~问题再难,他都能够答得上。*He can answer the question however hard it is.*

【哪儿】① where:电话在~? *Where is the telephone?* /你是从~弄到这个主意的? *Where did you get this idea?* ② wherever; anywhere:他好像走到~敌人就追到~。*He seems to make enemies wherever he goes.* /~需要,我就上~去。*I will go wherever I am needed.* /你喜欢~,我们就跟你到~去。*We'll follow you anywhere you like.* ③ how can; how could:我~会知道他到底在想什么? *How could I know what on earth he was thinking?* /这么多的事儿,我~能一天就处理完呢? *How could I handle so many things in one day?*

【哪儿的话】[谦] what are you saying; you shouldn't

say that:"真给您添麻烦了。""~"。"*Sorry for having caused you so much trouble.*" "*You shouldn't say that.*"

【哪些】which (ones); who; what: ~是要展出的? *Which ones are to be exhibited?* /~人反对这项提案? *Who are against this proposal?* /你这次旅行都去过~地方? *What places have you been to during this trip?*

【哪样】① what kind; what:你想把大门涂成~颜色? *What colour do you want to paint the gate?* ② whatever; whatever kind:那个超市的雨伞各式各样的,你想要~的就有~的。*They have a big variety of umbrellas in that supermarket; you can pick whatever kind you like.*

【哪知】who would have thought; who would have known

nà

那[1] that: ~本书 *that book* /~个小孩 *that child* /~时候 *at that time* /~是我的家。*That is my house.* /~是谁? *Who is that?* /~是什么? *What's that?* /~是 2001 年的事。*That was in 2001.* /我们说这道~的,不知不觉天已经亮了。*We talked about this and that without realizing that it was almost dawn.*

那[2] then; in that case:等见到了她,~你就会明白为什么我不让你去那个公司上班了。*When you see her, then you will understand why I wouldn't let you take a job in that company.*

【那达慕】Nadam Fair, a Mongolian traditional fair: ~一般是在七、八月份召开。你要是那会儿在内蒙古,千万别错过了。*Nadam Fair is usually held in July or August; Don't miss it if you are in Inner Mongolia then.*

【那当儿】at that time; in those days: ~我正在看电视。*I was watching TV at that time.*

【那个】① that (one): ~男孩 *that boy* /别担心,~一点问题也没有。*Don't worry; that's out of question.* /~你别插手。*Get yourself away from that!* ②[口] used before a verb or adjective with exclamatory force:听到这个好消息,他们~高兴劲啊,就别提了! *You cannot really imagine how happy they were at the good news.* /瞧他们聊得~起劲儿呀! *See how they are enjoying the conversation!* ③[口] used euphemistically as a predicative adjective

【那会儿】[口] at that time; then: ~我们还很小,不明白父亲那番话的意思。*At that time, we were too young to understand what father meant to say.* /希望到~我们已经写完作业了。*I hope that we will have finished our homework by then.* /快到半夜~大风才停。*It was toward midnight that the gale died down.*

【那里】there; that place:你刚从~回来,告诉我们~的气候怎么样? *You've just been there; tell us what the weather is like there.* /~的人们非常热情好客。*People there are very hospitable.* /明天到我~,我请大家吃海鲜。*Come tomorrow to my place for some seafood.*

【那么】① like that; in that way; so:你的问题有~复杂吗? *Is your problem that complicated?* /天气还没有~冷。*It isn't all that cold.* /我所做的只有~多。*I've done only that much.* /我走不了~远。*I can't walk that far.* /事情可不像你想得~简单。*It's not so simple as you have imagined.* /你~喜欢它,那我就把它送给你吧。*Since you like it so much, take it as a gift from me.* ② about; or so:估计再有~两、三天的时间就够了。*Two or three days will be probably enough.* /再有~一、两个小时,就能看到流星雨了。*We will see the meteor shower in approximately one or two hours.* ③ then; in that case; such being the case

【那么点儿】so little; so few; so trivial: ~钱,还不够我养活自己的呢。*I cannot survive with so little money.* /~事儿,你别大惊小怪的。*Don't fuss about such a trivial matter.*

【那么些】so much; so many: ~餐馆,你都试过了?! *You have dined in so many restaurants?!* /你浇~水,会把它淹死的。*With so much water you will drown it.*

【那么着】do that; do so; in that way:他~是为了咱们整个班。*He did that for the sake of the whole class.* /你再~,我就生气了。*If you do that again, I will get angry.*

【那儿】① there: ~的天气很热。*It's very hot there.* ② then; that time:打~起,她就开始研究野生动植物了。*She started studying wildlife ever since then.*

【那时】at that time; then; in those days: ~正值深秋。*It was late autumn then.* /~我正在看书。*I was reading a book at that time.*

【那些】those: ~树 *those trees* / ~房子马上就要拆了。*Those houses will soon be knocked down.* /一定不要忘记曾经帮助过你的~人。*Never forget those who have ever helped you.*

【那样】of that kind; like that; such; so:他可没你~乐观。*He is not so optimistic as you are.* /~也好,我们按你的方法试试。*That's fine too; Let's try to do it in your way.*

【那阵儿】[口] then; during that period; in those days: ~天天下雨。*There was an unbroken spell of wet weather those days.* /我们上初中~,她是我们的英语老师。*She taught us English when we were in junior high school.*

呐

【呐喊】shout loudly; cry out; whoop; battle cry: ~助威 *shout encouragement; cheer* /发出战争的~声 *set up the war whoop*

纳[1] ① admit; receive:闭门不~ *refuse to admit; shut sb out* ② accept:采~ *adopt* ③ enjoy: ~凉 *enjoy the cool* ④ put into ⑤ pay; offer:交~所得税 *pay income tax* ⑥ (Nà) a surname

纳[2] sew close stitches (over a patch, etc.): ~鞋底儿 *stitch soles (of cloth shoes)*

【纳彩】(of the bridegroom-to-be's family) present

N

gifts to the girl's family at time of betrothal

【纳粹】Nazi：他是一个顽固的～党徒。*He is a dead-end Nazi.*

【纳粹主义】Nazism

【纳贡】pay tribute (to a suzerain or emperor)

【纳罕】be surprised; marvel; wonder：我～怎么他上学总是迟到。*I wonder why he is always late for school.*

【纳贿】① accept bribes ② offer bribes

【纳谏】(of a sovereign, an elder or superior) accept an admonition; accept advice：明君通常都是乐于～的。*Wise emperors were willing to accept admonitions.*

【纳凉】enjoy the cool：夏天的时候，人们总会在晚饭后出来聊天～。*In summer, people would come out to enjoy the cool and chat after dinner.*

【纳粮】[旧] pay or hand in grain tax (to the state or to landlords)

【纳闷】[口] feel puzzled; be surprised; wonder; be perplexed：这么大的市场竟然一个人都没有，这可真叫人～。*It's really perplexing that there is no one in such a big market.* /我就～，他怎么就不给我回电话呢？*I cannot help wondering why he wouldn't return my phone calls.*

【纳米】nanometer ($nm = 10^{-9}$ metre)

【纳米比亚】Namibia, a country of southwest Africa on the Atlantic Ocean

【纳妾】take a concubine

【纳入】bring into：～正轨 *put sth on the right course* /把整个国民经济～有计划、按比例、高速度发展的轨道 *bring the country's entire economy into the orbit of planned, proportionate and high-speed development*

【纳税】pay taxes：～额 *ratal* /～年度 *tax year* /～责任 *tax liability* /～准备金 *tax reserve*

【纳税人】taxpayer：正当～ *bona fide taxpayer* /已婚～ *married taxpayer* /～抗议政府拿他们的钱去发动非正义战争。*The taxpayers are protesting against the government throwing their money into unjustified war.*

【纳头】[旧] kowtow; bow one's head (in greeting)：～便拜 *kneel down and kowtow at once*

【纳降】accept the enemy's surrender

【纳新】take in the fresh; take in a new member：他是我们的～对象。*He is a candidate for our membership.*

衲 ① patch up ② patchwork vestment worn by a Buddhist monk：老～ *I; myself (the monk)*

钠 【化】sodium (Na)：～灯 *sodium lamp*

捺 ① press down：～手印 *put one's finger-print (to a document)* ② restrain; hold back; press down：～着性子 *control one's temper* /他勉强～住心头的怒火。*He barely managed to restrain his anger.* ③ right-falling stroke (in Chinese characters)

na

哪 used after a word ending in n to tone up what is being said：谢谢您～！*Thank you!* /多好的人～！*What a nice guy!* /留点神～！*Watch out!*

see also nǎ

nǎi

乃 [书] ① be：我～一介草民。*I am nobody.* /此～两国之间生死攸关的一场战斗。*This is life-or-death battle between the two states.* /失败～成功之母。*Failure is the mother of success.* ② so; therefore：因前路难行，～在此稍事休息。*There is a hard road before us, so we take a rest for a while here.* ③ only then：今～知之。*I didn't know it until now.* /惟谦虚～能进步。*You can improve yourself only if you are modest.* ④ you; your：～兄 *your brother* /家祭无忘告～翁。*Don't forget to let your father know this on the fete-day.*

【乃是】[书] be：人民群众～真正的英雄。*The people are the true heroes.*

【乃至】[书] and even：中国革命的胜利，对全中国～全世界都具有伟大的历史意义。*The victory of the Chinese revolution had great historical significance for China and even the whole world.*

奶 ① breasts (of a female mammal) ② milk：发酵～ *fermented milk* /炼～ *condensed milk* /牛～ *(cow) milk* /羊～ *goat's milk; ewe's milk* /酸～ *sour milk* /全脂～ *whole milk* /调制～ *recombined milk* /脱脂～ *defatted milk* /无菌～ *germ-free milk* ③ suckle; breast-feed：～孩子 *breast-feed a baby* /他是奶妈～大的。*He was breast-fed by a wet nurse.*

【奶茶】tea with milk; milk tea：蒙古族喜欢喝～。*The Mongolian people enjoy milk tea.*

【奶粉】milk powder; powdered milk; dried milk：脱脂～ *defatted milk powder* /请给我冲一杯～。*Please make me a cup of milk with milk powder.*

【奶糕】a baby food made of rice-flour, sugar, etc.; brioche

【奶酪】cheese

【奶妈】wet nurse

【奶毛】foetal hair：～未退 *still with foetal hair — green; young*

【奶名】a child's pet name; infant name：他的～叫毛毛。*His infant name is Maomao.*

【奶奶】[口] ① (paternal) grandmother; grandma; granny：我～今年八十岁了。*My grandma is 80 years old this year.* ② a respectful form of address for an old woman：老～，我扶您过马路吧。*Granny, let me help you cross the road.* ③ [方] young mistress of the house

【奶牛】milch cow; milk cow; cow

【奶皮】skin formed on boiled milk; crème：不要搅

N

动牛奶好让表面结～。*Let the milk stand till it creams.*
【奶品】milk products; dairy products
【奶瓶】feeding bottle; nursing bottle; (baby's) bottle; feeder
【奶声奶气】speak in a baby or child-like voice
【奶水】[口] milk:她～不足。*She has not got enough milk to nurse her baby.*
【奶糖】toffee
【奶头】[口] ① nipple; teat ② nipple (of a feeding bottle)
【奶牙】milk tooth
【奶羊】milch goat
【奶油】cream; butter: ～分离器 *cream separator; creamer* /复鲜～ *rejuvenated cream* /～粉 *powdered cream*
【奶油小生】handsome but effeminate young man or actor
【奶罩】brassiere; bra
【奶汁】milk
【奶子】[口] ① milk ② [方] breasts ③ [方] wet nurse
【奶子酒】fermented (cow's or mare's) milk (used by Mongolians as an alcoholic drink)
【奶嘴】nipple (of a feeding bottle)

氖 【化】neon (Ne): ～灯 *neon lamp; neon light; neon* /管 *neon tube* /～气 *neon*

nài

奈 ① how; however:无～ *cannot but; be helpless* ② [书] what; how; but:将～之何? *What can you do about it?* /～援兵不至 *But the reinforcements didn't arrive.*
【奈何】① what alternative is there; what's to be done:徒唤～ *utter hopeless cries* /无可～ *have no way out; have no choice; with no alternative* /在无可～的情况下,我们只好铤而走险了。*Left with no choice, we had to take the risk.* ② [书] how; why:民不畏死,～以死惧之? *How can you threaten people with death if they have cast life aside?* ③ do sth to; cope with; deal with; handle:我～不得这群孩子。*I couldn't handle these children.*

耐 be able to bear or endure: ～得住 *can resist* /吃苦～劳 *bear hardships and stand hard work* /这种材料～得住高温。*This material can resist high temperature.* /这种布料不～洗。*This cloth doesn't wash well.* /牛仔裤比较～穿。*Jeans can stand wear and tear better.* /他再也～不住性子了。*He couldn't hold his temper any longer.*
【耐烦】be patient:显出不～的样子 *show signs of impatience*
【耐寒】cold-resistant: ～性 *cold resistance*
【耐旱】drought-enduring: ～植物 *drought-enduring plant*
【耐火】fire-resistant; refractory: ～水泥 *refractory cement* /～衬砌 *refractory lining*
【耐火砖】refractory brick; fire brick
【耐久】lasting; durable, perdurable: ～力 *durability; endurance; hardiness*
【耐看】be of lasting interest; stand scrutiny:这幅画很～。*The painting stands close examination.*
【耐苦】able to endure hardships
【耐劳】able to stand hard work; able to endure heavy labor
【耐力】endurance; staying power; stamina: ～测验 *endurance test* /那个年轻人缺乏～。*The young man lacks stamina.* /马拉松考验一个人的～。*A marathon tests one's endurance.*
【耐磨】wear-resisting; wearproof: ～性 *wearability; wear resistance*
【耐热】heat-resistant; heat-resisting; heatproof: ～性 *heat resistance*
【耐人寻味】afford for thought; provoke thinking; provide much food for thought:他的话很～。*His words are very thought-provoking.* /他的这番评论真是～啊。*His comments are not surface deep.*
【耐心】① patient:一位一向～的领导者和引路人 *an unfailingly patient leader and guide* /再～等会儿,他马上就到了。*Wait patiently for a while; he will be here soon.* ② patience:失去～ *lose one's patience; be out of patience* /她是一个很有～的人。*She is a person with great patience.*
【耐心烦】[口] patience 照顾小孩儿没～可不行。*It takes great patience to look after babies.*
【耐性】patience; endurance:我没有～了。*My patience is exhausted.*
【耐压】【物】pressure proof: ～试验 *pressure-tight test*
【耐用】durable: ～品 *durable goods; durables* /经久～ *stand wear and tear* /这种布很～。*This cloth is quite durable.* /不要把～品和易耗品放在同一个库里。*Don't stock the durables and consumables in the same storeroom.*

nān

囡 [方] ① child:男小～ *a little boy* /女小～ *a little girl* ② daughter:她有一个儿子一个～。*She has a son and a daughter.*
【囡囡】[方] little darling

nán

男[1] ① man; male: ～病房 *men's ward* /～服务生 *waiter* /～护士 *male nurse* /～学生 *boy student* /～演员 *actor* /～主人公 *hero* /～尊女卑 *concept that men are superior to women* ② son; boy:长～ *the eldest son*

男[2] baron
【男扮女装】a man disguised as a woman:他～躲过了敌人的搜捕。*He disguised himself as a woman and escaped from the enemy's manhunt.*
【男傧相】best man; groomsman

【男不男,女不女】neither fish, flesh nor fowl:他打扮得~的。*He is half dressed like a woman.*

【男厕所】① men's lavatory (or toilet, room) ② Gentlemen; Men; Gents

【男单】【体】men's singles (of tennis, table tennis, etc.)

【男盗女娼】behave like thieves and whores; be out-and-out scoundrels:他满嘴的仁义道德,却一肚子~。*All his talk is of humanity, justice and morality, while in his heart there is nothing but greed and lust.*

【男低音】【音】bass

【男儿】man:好~ *a fine man* / ~本色 *the manliness of a man*

【男方】the bridegroom's or husband's side:他是~的朋友。*He is a friend from the bridegroom's side.*

【男高音】【音】tenor: ~歌手 *tenorist*

【男耕女织】men plough the fields and women weave — an agricultural community's ideal of peace and order

【男孩儿】① boy ② son:她生了个~。*She's got a son.*

【男妓】pimp; male prostitute

【男家】the bridegroom's or husband's family

【男角】male role (in a play, film, etc.)

【男爵】baron: ~勋位 *baronage*

【男爵夫人】baroness

【男篮】men's basketball: ~队 *men's basketball team*

【男男女女】men and women:敌人将恢复轰炸的消息传来,整个社区~都骚动起来。*The whole community, men and women alike, was astir when the news came that the enemy bombing would be restored.*

【男女】① men and women:青年~ *young men and women* / ~平等 *equality of men and women; equality of the sexes* / ~应同工同酬。*Men and women should get equal pay for equal work.* ② [方] sons and daughters

【男女关系】relations between the two sexes:不正当的~ *illicit sexual relations*

【男女老少】men and women; old and young

【男排】men's volleyball: ~队 *men's volleyball team*

【男朋友】boyfriend:她的~很帅。*Her boyfriend is quite handsome.*

【男仆】footman; groom; houseboy; houseman; lackey

【男人】(nánrén) ① man ② menfolk

【男人】(nánren) [方] husband:她~在矿上上班。*Her husband works in the mine.*

【男生】man student; boy student; schoolboy

【男声】【音】male voice: ~合唱 *men's chorus; male chorus*

【男士】man; gentleman:出席这次会议的有~四名,女士五名。*Four gentlemen and five ladies attended the conference.*

【男双】【体】men's doubles (of table tennis, tennis, etc.)

【男巫】war lock; wizard

【男相】(of a female) look or behave like a man:她长得有些~。*She looks quite masculine.*

【男性】① the male sex; the sterner sex; the rougher sex ② man

【男性荷尔蒙】androgen; male hormone

【男中音】【音】baritone: ~歌手 *barytone*

【男装】menswear; men's clothing:近来女士穿~已形成一种时尚了。*It's become a fashion these days that women get dressed up in men's clothes.*

【男子】man; male: ~单打 *men's singles* / ~双打 *men's doubles* / ~团体赛 *men's team event*

【男子汉】a manly man; a real man; man:你还哪儿像个~哪? *You are far from being a real man!* / ~大丈夫,一人做事一人当。*A man should have the courage to take the responsibility for what he does.*

南 ① south:城~ *south of the city* / 向~走 *move toward south* /风从~边儿吹来。*The wind blows from the south.* ② the southern part of the country (in China, it usually refers to the area south of the Yangtze River); the south:华~ *southern China* ③ (Nán) a surname
see also nā

【南半球】the Southern Hemisphere:澳大利亚位于~。*Australia is in the Southern Hemisphere.*

【南北】① north and south: ~夹击 *make a joint attack from north and south* ② from north to south:我们这个城市~足有二十公里。*Our city extends a good twenty kilometers from north to south.*

【南北对话】North-South dialogue (i. e. dialogue between developed countries in the Northern Hemisphere and developing countries in the Southern Hemisphere)

【南北战争】American Civil War (1861—1865)

【南边】① south; the southern side:你要找的那个村子就在山~。*The village you are looking for is just south to the mountain.* ② [口] areas south of the Yangtze River

【南部】southern part; south: ~非洲 *southern Africa* /广州市位于广东省的~。*Guangzhou is in the south of Guangdong Province.*

【南方】① south ② the southern part of the country; the South:我家住在~。*I live in the South.* /他是北方人,不太习惯~风味。*As a northerner, he is not that used to the southern flavor.* /他说话带有~口音。*He speaks with a southern accent.*

【南非】South Africa

【南瓜】cushaw; pumpkin; squash: ~虫 *squash bug* / ~籽 *pumpkin seed*

【南国】[书] the southern part of the country; the South; Southland: ~风光 *southern scenery* /红豆生~,春来发几枝。*The red bean grows in the southern lands. With spring its slender tendrils twine.*

【南海】the South China Sea; the Nanhai Sea: ~舰队 *South China Sea Fleet* / ~诸岛 *South China Sea Islands*

【南寒带】the south frigid zone

【南回归线】the Tropic of Capricorn
【南货】delicacies from south China (such as dried bamboo shoots, ham, etc.)
【南极】① the South Pole; the Antarctic Pole ② the south magnetic pole (usually indicated as "S")
【南极圈】the Antarctic Circle
【南极洲】the Antarctic Continent; Antarctica
【南柯一梦】a Nanke dream — a fond dream; an illusory joy:他不遗余力地去争取总经理的位置,自以为早晚都会是他的,到头来却发现那不过是～。*He made every effort to get the General Manager's position, thinking that it would be his one day or another. But it turned out to be only a fond dream.*
【南来北往】going north and south — heavy traffic or a bustling crowd
【南美洲】South America
【南面】① face south — be a ruler (in the sense that the emperor used to sit facing south when holding court):～为王 *face south and declare himself the king* ② south; the southern side
【南南合作】South-South cooperation (i. e. cooperation among developing countries in the Southern Hemisphere)
【南欧】Southern Europe
【南腔北调】(speak with) a mixed accent:他说话～的。*He speaks with a mixture of accents.*
【南沙群岛】the Nansha Islands
【南式】(of) southern style:～糕点 *southern-style pastry*
【南水北调】divert water from the south to the north:～工程 *projects to divert water from the south to the north*
【南斯拉夫】Yugoslavia:～人 *Yugoslav*
【南纬】south (or southern latitude):船在～二十度。*The ship's latitude is 20 degrees south.*
【南温带】the south temperate zone
【南下】go down south:大军～ *large contingents of the army advancing south*
【南亚】South Asia
【南亚次大陆】the South Asian Subcontinent
【南辕北辙】try to go south by driving the chariot north — act in a way that defeats one's purpose
【南征北战】fight north and south; campaign all across the country

难 ① difficult; hard; troublesome:～的任务 *a hard task* /物理是我所学课程中最～的一门。*Physics was the hardest of my courses.* /这道题很～。*This is a difficult question.* /山路很～行。*Mountain paths are hard to travel.* ② put sb into a difficult position:这个问题可把我～住了。*The question put me on the spot.* ③ hardly possible:六个人住在一个宿舍里,～免会产生一些矛盾。*It is hardly possible for six people living in the same dormitory not to have any conflicts.* ④ bad; unpleasant:他～与同伴相处。*He's bad at getting along with his fellows.*
see also nàn
【难熬】hard to bear; hard to endure:饥饿～ *can hardly bear the hunger* /单相思是很～的。*One-sided love is really torturing.*
【难保】① there is no guarantee; cannot say for sure; it's hard to say:你要是不给我们充足的时间,那产品质量可就～了。*If you don't give us enough time, then there will be no guarantee for quality.* /今天～不下雨。*You cannot say for sure that it won't rain today.* ② difficult to preserve, protect, defend, etc.:性命～。*One's life is in danger*
【难缠】(of a person) unreasonable and hard to deal with:那个家伙很～,小心点儿! *That guy is very hard to deal with; be careful with him!*
【难产】①【医】difficult labour; dystocia ② (of a literary work, plan, etc.) be difficult of fulfillment; be slow in coming
【难吃】taste bad; be unpalatable:这顿饭可真～! *It's such an unpalatable meal!*
【难处】(nánchǔ) hard to get along with:他只是脾气暴躁些,并不～。*He is just quick-tempered, but not difficult to get along with.*
【难处】(nánchu) difficulty; trouble:这工作没有什么～。*There is nothing difficult about this work.* /有什么～尽管告诉我们。*Tell us whatever troubles you have.*
【难当】① find it hard to shoulder (a responsibility, etc.):～重任 *can hardly shoulder heavy responsibilities; can hardly undertake important tasks* ② hard to endure; unbearable; insufferable:羞愧～ *be mortally ashamed*
【难倒】daunt; baffle; beat:她被那么多还没做完的工作～了。*She was daunted by the amount of work still to be done.* /这个谜语可把我～了。*This riddle baffles me.*
【难道】used to give force to a rhetorical question:～你忘了自己说过的话了吗? *Could you have forgotten what you said before?* /这～还需要解释吗? *Isn't that self-explanatory enough?* /这样的小问题,你～就不能解决吗? *Can't you fix such a small problem?*
【难得】① not easy to get; rare; valuable:～的机会 *rare chance* /他是一个～的朋友。*He is a rare friend.* /他在一年之内两次打破世界纪录,是十分～的。*He's performed the rare feat of breaking the world record twice within one year.* /这种植物在南方很～。*It's hard to find this kind of plant in the south.* ② rarely; seldom; hardly ever:她～来我们家,让她多待会儿吧。*Seldom does she come to our home; Let her stay longer.* /这里～下一场雪。*It rarely snows here.*
【难点】a difficult point; difficulty; nodus; a hard nut to crack:这个项目～很多。*This project is full of difficulties.*
【难度】degree of difficulty; difficulty:～大 *be very difficult* /规定系汽车安全带的新法规在开始推行时是有～的。*The new law about safety belts in cars was difficult to enforce at first.*
【难分难解】① be inextricably involved (in a dispute); be locked (in a battle):两军厮杀,～。

The two opposing armies are locked in battle. ② be sentimentally attached to each other; cannot bear to part

【难怪】① no wonder: ~他今天这么高兴,原来新机器试验成功了。*No wonder he is so happy today; the test run of the new machine has succeeded.* ② understandable; pardonable:他不了解情况,搞错了也~。*You can hardly blame him for the mistake; he didn't know much about the situation.*

【难关】difficulty; crisis:度过~ *tide over a difficulty; pass a crisis* /攻克技术~ *break down a technical barrier; resolve critical technical problems*

【难过】① have a hard time:父母都下岗了,家里日子很~。*We had a very hard time when my parents were both laid off.* ② feel sad; feel bad; feel sorry; be grieved:他听到老师逝世的消息,心里非常~。*He was deeply grieved to learn that his teacher had passed away.*

【难乎为继】hard to carry on or keep up:尽管我们极为节省,生活仍~。*Though extremely frugal, we still found it hard to make both ends meet.*

【难堪】① intolerable; unbearable: ~的话 *annoying remarks* /痛苦~ *intolerable pain* /天气闷热~。*It was unbearably hot and sultry.* ② embarrassing; embarrassed; awkward: ~的沉默 *awkward silence* /他感到有点儿~。*He felt embarrassed.* /这是一个很~的问题。*This is an embarrassing question.*

【难看】① ugly; unsightly: ~的广告牌 *an unsightly billboard* /现在他把一个~的石雕头像挂在大门上。*Now he has put an ugly stone head over the gate.* ② shameful; embarrassing:小伙子干活儿要是比不上老年人,那就太~了。*It would be a shame if the young cannot do a job as well as the old.* ③ unpleasant:他听到这个消息,脸色变得很~。*When he heard the news, his face took on a very unpleasant expression.*

【难免】hard to avoid; unavoidable:没有经验,就~要走弯路。*Owing to lack of experience, we sometimes cannot avoid taking a roundabout course in our work.* /你要是走那条路,~会遇上塞车的。*If you take that road, it will be difficult to avoid traffic jams.*

【难耐】hard to bear; unbearable; intolerable:痛苦~ *intolerable agony* /一个~的不眠之夜 *a tormenting sleepless night*

【难能可贵】exceptionally commendable; be praiseworthy:那个美国人把捡到的钱包上交了,这真是~。*That American handed in the purse that he happened to pick up; it is praiseworthy.* /她有一点是~的,就是她遇事冷静。*Her one priceless asset is her unflappability.*

【难人】① difficult; delicate; ticklish:这种~的事,不好办。*It's really difficult to handle such a ticklish matter.* ② a person handling a delicate matter; a person in a difficult position:有麻烦我们帮助你,绝不叫你做~。*We will stand by you in case of trouble, and never leave you in a difficult position.*

【难色】a reluctant or embarrassed expression:当我们向他借钱时,看到他面露~。*When we asked him to lend us some money, he appeared to be reluctant.*

【难舍难分】loath to part from each other:在机场,他们俩依依惜别,~。*At the airport, the two of them could hardly tear themselves away from each other.*

【难事】a difficult matter; sth not easy to manage:世上无~,只怕有心人。*There is nothing too difficult if you put your heart into it.*

【难受】① feel ill; suffer pain:他患了流感,浑身疼得~。*He's got the flu and is aching all over.* ② feel unhappy; feel bad:朋友的离去使得她心里非常~。*She feels very unhappy over her friend's departure.* /我为他感到~。*I feel sorry for him.*

【难说】it's hard to say; hard to tell; you never can tell:战争什么时候结束还很~。*No one can tell when the war will come to an end.* /谁会在这场比赛中胜出,现在还~。*It's hard to say who will win this match.*

【难说话儿】be difficult to talk with or deal with:你这个人可真~! *You are such a difficult person!*

【难题】a difficult problem; a thorny problem; a hard nut to crack:这个关于环境保护的~把新任市长难住了。*This thorny problem on the environmental protection floored the new mayor.*

【难听】① unpleasant to the hear; unpleasant to the ear:他的嗓音可真~。*His voice is not that pleasing to the ear.* ② offensive; coarse:在女士面前,不要讲~的话。*Don't use coarse words before a lady.* /她在背后说了你很多~的话。*She has been spreading malicious gossip about you behind your back.* ③ scandalous:这种事情说出去多~! *The story will create a scandal once it gets out.*

【难忘】unforgettable; memorable: ~的一个教训 *an unforgettable lesson* /这部电影因为两位主角的精湛演技而令人~。*The film was memorable for the fine acting of the two main characters.* /这的确是我一生中最~的一天。*This was indeed the most memorable day of my life.*

【难为】① embarrass; press:她不会唱歌,就别再~她了。*Since she can't sing, don't press her to.* ② be a tough job to:一个人又要照顾老人,还得照顾孩子,真~了她。*It was quite a job for her to take care of both the old and the young.* ③ used to thank sb for doing a favour: ~你帮我们也买上了火车票。*It was really very kind of you to get the train tickets for us as well.*

【难为情】① abashed; embarrassed:我开始唱歌时,他大笑起来,使我~。*When I began to sing, he laughed and made me embarrassed.* /他们的称赞让我很是~。*I was abashed by their compliment.* ② embarrassing; disconcerting:答应吧,办不到;不答应吧,又有点~。*It is not feasible to comply, but a bit embarrassing to refuse.*

【难闻】smell unpleasant; smell bad; smell nasty: ~的气味 *bad smell; unpleasant smell* /新装修的屋子有些~。*The newly furnished room smells* bad.

【难兄难弟】two of a kind; birds of a feather

【难言之隐】sth which is awkward to disclose; sth embarrassing to mention; a painful topic; difficulties one is reluctant to mention:你有什么～？说出来,或许大家还能帮你。*What are the difficulties you are keeping to yourself? Tell us. Maybe we could help you out.*

【难以】hard to; difficult to: ～预料 *difficult to conjecture; hard to forecast* / ～启齿 *too embarrassed to say it; hard to speak out* / ～想象 *unimaginable* / ～形容 *hard to describe; indescribable; beyond description* / ～置信 *hard to believe; incredible* / 他们对事故发生的原因作了令人～置信的解释。*They gave an incredible explanation of the cause of the accident.*

【难于】hard to; difficult to:时间太短,工程～完成。*It's hard to finish the project in such a short time.*

喃

【喃喃】[象] mutter; mummer: ～自语 *mutter to oneself*

楠

【楠木】【植】nanmu (*Phoebe nanmu*)

nǎn

赧 blushing; shamefaced

【赧红】(of one's face) blush for shame; crimson from shame

【赧愧】[书] ashamed

【赧然】[书] blushing; embarrassed:她～一笑。*She blushed and smiled.*

【赧颜】[书] blush; be shamefaced

nàn

难 ① calamity; adversity; disaster; misfortune; trouble:多灾多～ *be dogged by misfortunes* /一方有～,八方支援。*When trouble occurs at one spot, help comes from all directions.* ② blame; reproach:不要～他,这不是他的过错。*Do not reproach him; it was not his fault.*
see also nán

【难胞】fellow countrymen in distress

【难船】ship in distress; sinking ship

【难民】refugee: ～营 *refugee camp* / 救济～ *provide aids to the refugees* / ～收容所 *shelter for refugees*

【难属】victim's family

【难兄难弟】fellow sufferer; people in the same boat

【难友】fellow sufferer

nāng

囊

see also náng

【囊揣】[旧] weak; cowardly; feeble

【囊膪】the flabby meat from a sow's belly

囔

【囔囔】murmur; speak in a low voice

náng

囊 ① bag; pocket; pouch:药～ *medicine bag* / 背～ *knapsack* /气～ *air bag* ② anything shaped like a bag; an object that resembles a pouch:胆～ *gall bladder* ③ [书] hold with a bag; pocket
see also nāng

【囊空如洗】be penniless; be broke to the wide; with empty pockets; broke:从赌场回来,他～。*He returned from the casino with empty pockets.*

【囊括】① include; embrace: ～四海 *bring the whole country under imperial rule* ②【体】win all: ～全部金牌 *make a clean sweep of all gold medals* / 中国队～了锦标赛上的全部四块金牌。*The Chinese team pocketed all the four gold medals at the championships.*

【囊中物】sth which is in the bag — sth certain of attainment

【囊中羞涩】[书] be short of money; be hard up

【囊肿】【医】cyst

nǎng

攮 stab:他被～了一刀。*He was stabbed.*

【攮子】dagger

nàng

齉 snuffling:受了凉,鼻子发～ *snuffle with a cold*

【齉鼻儿】① snuffle; speak through the nose:他感冒了,说话有点～。*He had a cold and spoke with a slight snuffle.* ② a person who speaks with a twang

nāo

孬 [方] ① bad ② cowardly

【孬种】[方] coward:你个～! *You coward!*

náo

呶 ［书］clamour

【呶呶】［书］talk on and on tediously

挠 ① scratch: ~痒痒 *scratch an itch* /抓耳~腮 *scratch one's head* ② hinder: 阻~ *hinder; prevent; stimy; put grit in the machine* ③ yield; flinch: 不屈不~的革命精神 *an unyielding revolutionary spirit*

【挠钩】long-handled hook

【挠头】① scratch one's head ② difficult to tackle; troublesome: 这可是件让人~的事。*This is a knotty problem.*

nǎo

恼 ① angry; annoyed; irritated: 你别~我。*Don't annoy me.* /再说我可要~了。*I will be angry if you don't stop talking like that.* ② unhappy; worried: 苦~ *miserable* /烦~ *worried; vexed*

【恼恨】resent; hate: 他是为了你好,可别~他的刻薄话。*Don't resent his harsh words, for he meant well.*

【恼火】annoyed; irritated; vexed: 长时间的等待真让人~。*It is vexing to have to wait a long time.* /孩子们的吵闹使我~。*I was annoyed by the noise of the children.*

【恼怒】① angry; indignant; furious: 如果我们迟到,老板会十分~的。*The boss will get furious if we are late.* ② annoy; infuriate: 我的话~了他,于是他再也不和我说话了。*My words infuriated him and he never spoke to me ever since.*

【恼人】irritating; annoying: 这件事真~。*This is really annoying.* /春色~ *Spring's hues are teasing.*

【恼羞成怒】get into a passion from shame; fly into a rage from shame

脑 ①【生理】brain: 大~ *cerebrum* /小~ *cerebellum* /~动脉 *cerebral artery* /用~过度 *overtax one's brain* /~是神经系统的中枢。*The brain is the centre of the nervous system.* ② head: ~袋 *head* ③ mind; brain: 动手动~ *use one's hands and brains* ④ essence: 樟~ *camphor* ⑤ remains; leftovers: 针头线~ *odds and ends*

【脑癌】【医】cancer of the brain; cerebral cancer

【脑垂体】【生理】hypophysis cerebri; pituitary body

【脑袋】［口］① head: 秃~ *bald head* ② brains; mind: 你的~真好使,十年前的事还能记得。*You've got so clever a mind that you can even remember things happened ten years ago.*

【脑电波】【生理】brain wave

【脑电图】【医】electroencephalogram (EEG)

【脑海】brain; mind: 十五年前的旧事,重又浮上他的~。*Memories of things which happened fifteen years ago flashed across his mind.* /我~里整天回荡着这个曲子,但我想不起来叫什么了。*I've had this tune on the brain all day but I can't remember what it's called.*

【脑积水】【医】hydrocephalus

【脑际】mind; memory: 祖父的形象浮现在我~。*The image of grandfather came to my mind.*

【脑浆】brains: ~迸裂 *have one's brains dashed*

【脑筋】① brains; mind; head: 动动~,你就会想出办法来的。*Use your brains and you will find the way.* ② way of thinking; ideas: 他是个旧~。*He is an old fogey.*

【脑壳】［方］head; brain case

【脑力】mental power; intelligence

【脑力劳动】mental work: ~和体力劳动的差别在不断扩大。*The distinction between mental and manual labour is increasingly expanding.*

【脑力劳动者】mental worker; brain worker

【脑瘤】【医】encephaloma

【脑颅】brainpan; cranium

【脑满肠肥】heavy-jowled and potbellied — the idle rich

【脑门儿】［口］forehead

【脑膜】【生理】meninx

【脑膜炎】【医】meningitis

【脑儿】animal brains (as food) or brain-like jellied food: 猪~ *pig's brains* /豆腐~ *jelly bean curd*

【脑疝】【医】cerebral hernia

【脑勺】［方］the back of the head

【脑神经】【生理】cranial nerve

【脑髓】brains

【脑衰竭】【医】brain fag

【脑死亡】【医】brain death

【脑细胞】brain cell

【脑下垂体】【生理】pituitary body; pituitary gland; hypophysis

【脑血管】【生理】cerebral vessel

【脑血栓】【医】cerebral thrombus

【脑炎】【医】encephalitis; cerebritis: 流行性乙型~ *epidemic encephalitis B*

【脑溢血】【医】cerebral concussion; concussion

【脑震荡】【医】cerebral haemorrhage

【脑汁】brains: 几小时来我绞尽~以期回想起她的名字。*I racked my brain for hours trying to recall her name.* /在考试中她绞尽~。*She beat her brains out during the examination.*

【脑子】① brain ② brains; mind; head: ~灵活 *quick-witted* /他~好,又用功。*He is clever and diligent.* /小伙子年轻帅气,~里却是一张白纸。*A nice enough young fellow, nothing upstairs.* /她很有~。*She has an excellent brain.*

nào

闹 ① noisy: 这里~得很,没法儿看书。*It's too noisy here for me to read.* ② make a noise; stir up trouble: 又哭又~ *make a tearful scene* ③ give vent (to one's anger, resentment, etc.): ~

脾气 *vent one's spleen; lose one's temper* /~情绪 *in low spirits* ④ suffer from; be trouble by: ~眼睛 *have eye trouble* /~肚子 *suffer from diarrhea* /~矛盾 *be at loggerheads* /你最近老是心不在焉的,怎么~的? *How come that your look so moony these days?* ⑤ go in for; do; make: ~革命 *carry out revolution* /先把问题~清楚再说。*Let's first get the thing clear.* ⑥ play for fun; tease: 打~ *horseplay*

【闹别扭】be difficult with sb; be at odds with sb: 两个人常~。*The two are always at odds with each other.* /你这不是成心跟我~吗? *You are being difficult with me on purpose.*

【闹不清】cannot tell; be unsure about: 我也~这场交通事故该怪谁。*I cannot tell who should be responsible for this traffic accident.*

【闹场】a flourish of gongs and drums introducing a theatrical performance

【闹洞房】banter or tease the newlyweds on wedding night

【闹肚子】[口] have diarrhea; suffer from loose bowels

【闹翻】fall out with sb: 他俩为了一点小事~了。*They fell out with each other over some little thing.* /因为这次争吵,邻居们~了。*As a result of the quarrel, neighbours were soon at loggerheads.*

【闹翻天】raise hell; kick up a racket: 老师不在,教室里简直~了。*The classroom was turned upside down with the teacher's absence.*

【闹鬼】① be haunted: 人们都说这房子~。*This house is said to be haunted.* ② play tricks behind sb's back; use underhand means: 我知道是他在背地里闹的鬼。*I know it's he who played tricks behind my back.*

【闹哄】[方] ① make a noise; make a fuss: 有意见你就提,~什么! *Stop making noise; if you have any objection, just say it out.* ② bustle about

【闹哄哄】clamorous; noisy: 在这个~的小镇,你很难找到一个清静的地方。*You could hardly find a quiet place in this noisy town.*

【闹饥荒】① suffer from famine ② [方] be hard up; be short of money: 快到发工资那几天他就~。*He is always hard up before payday.*

【闹剧】farce: 这次审判简直是~,因为根本没有法官出席。*The trial was a mere farce since no judge was present at all.*

【闹脾气】vent one's spleen; lose one's temper; be in a tantrum; make a scene; let off steam: 今天早上妹妹~,所以我尽早离开了家。*My younger sister was in a temper this morning so I left home as early as possible.* /每次到了睡觉的时候,这孩子就开始~。*Whenever it's time for bed the little child throws a tantrum.*

【闹气】[方] be cross with sb; be in a huff with sb; be annoyed with sb: 她正在和男朋友~,因为他忘记了她的生日。*She's annoyed with her boyfriend because he forgot her birthday.*

【闹情绪】be disgruntled; be in low spirits: 他这些天正~呢,别去惹他。*Keep yourself away from him, for he is in low spirits these days.*

【闹嚷嚷】noisy: 外面~的,发生了什么事呀? *What's all the noise about outside?* /大家在聚会上~的,我根本听不清主人在说什么。*People were making such a noise at the party that I couldn't hear what the host was saying.*

【闹市】busy streets; busy shopping centre; downtown

【闹事】make trouble; stir up trouble: 他是来寻衅~的。*He came here to stir up trouble.*

【闹腾】① make a noise; kick up a row: 孩子们整个上午都在屋子里~。*The children were making a big noise in the room the whole morning.* ② have fun; amuse oneself ③ knock together; establish: 这个商店是几个退休职工~起来的。*The shop was knocked together by several retired old workers.*

【闹天儿】[方] have bad weather: 一连好几天都~ *have an unbroken spell of bad weather*

【闹笑话】make a fool of oneself; make a stupid mistake: 不懂装懂就会~。*If you pretend to know what you don't know, you will only make a fool of yourself.*

【闹心】[方] ① be worried; be disturbed ② feel bad in the stomach: 我喝了凉水就~。*I would feel upset in my stomach if I had drunk cold water.*

【闹玄虚】purposely make a mystery of simple things; be deliberately mystifying

【闹性子】lose one's temper; become angry; throw a tantrum; make a scene: 他动不动就爱~。*She is easy to lose her temper now and then.*

【闹意见】be on bad terms because of difference in opinion; fall out with; be at odds; be at loggerheads; irreconcilable: 如果我们~的话,这个集体就不会有进步。*There could be no progress in the group while we were at odds with each other.*

【闹意气】feel resentful because something is not to one's liking; sulk: 他在家里~。*He stayed home in a sulk.*

【闹灾】be hit by a calamity

【闹着玩儿】be joking: 他是跟你~的,你别当真。*He was just joking. Don't take it seriously.* /你要是不会游泳,就别到水深的地方去,这可不是~的。*Don't go into deep water if you cannot swim; that's no joke.*

【闹钟】alarm clock: ~控制 *alarm controls*

【闹嘴】[方] quarrel; wrangle: 我和他~了。*I quarrelled with him.*

nè

讷 [书] slow (of speech): 敏于行而~于言 *quick in action but slow of speech*

【讷讷】[书] slow of speech; faltering in speech: ~不出于口 *speak under one's breath*

ne

呢 ① used at the end of a special, alternative, or rhetorical question：你学提琴～，还是学钢琴～？*Are you going to learn to play violin or piano?* /都到哪儿去了～？*What about the people? Where are they?* /我错在哪儿了～？*What have I done wrong?* /你怎么知道～？*How did you know this?* /我怎么可能不记得～？*How could I forget this?* /我是该去～，还是该留下～？*Should I go, or should I stay?* ② used at the end of a declarative sentence to reinforce the assertion：他们都要求参加比赛～。*They all want to take part in the contest.* /这药灵得很～，吃了就不疼了。*This drug is really effective. Take it and the pain will be gone.* ③ used at the end of a declarative sentence to indicate the continuation of an action or a state：他在写作业～。*He is doing his homework.* /他还在生气～。*He is still angry.* /外面下着雨～。*It's raining outside.* ④ used to mark a pause：如今～，可比往年强多了。*As for the present, things are far better than of any time before.* see also ní

něi

馁 ①［书］hungry; famished：冻～ *suffer from cold and hunger* ② disheartened; dispirited：气～ *lose heart; be disheartened* /胜不骄，败不～ *not become dizzy with success, nor discouraged by failure* ③［书］(of fish) putrid; rotten

nèi

内 ① inside; inner part or side; within：年～ *within this year* /校～ *in the school* /国～事务 *domestic affairs* /～附推荐信 *recommendation letter enclosed* /请勿入～。*No admittance.* /～有照片，请勿折。*Photos inside, please don't fold.* ② one's wife or her relatives：～人 *one's wife* /～兄 *one's wife's elder brother* ③ innermost being; bowels; internal organs：五～俱焚 *feel one's five internal organs are burning — one's heart is torn by grief or anxiety* ④［书］the imperial palace：大～ *imperial residential place*

【内包装】inner packing; internal packing

【内宾】domestic guests; home guests

【内部】① inside; interior; within：～装修 *interior decoration* /～联系 *internal relations* /在人民～ *among the people themselves* /堡垒是最容易从～攻破的。*The easiest way to capture a fortress is from within.* ② inside; restricted：～消息 *inside information* /～刊物 *restricted publication* /～参考读物 *internal reference*

【内参】internal reference：这条消息登在～上。*This piece of information is carried in the internal reference news.*

【内臣】① chamberlain ② eunuch

【内出血】【医】internal haemorrhage; internal bleeding

【内存】【电】random access memory (RAM)

【内存条】memory bank

【内地】inland; interior; hinterland：～城市 *inland city* /～人 *inlander* /我国的～ *the interior of our country*

【内弟】wife's younger brother; brother-in-law

【内定】(of an official appointment) decided at the higher level but not officially announced：听说他已被～为下一任部长。*It is said that he has been designated as the incoming minister.*

【内耳】【生理】internal ear; inner ear

【内犯】［书］enemy intrusion or invasion

【内分泌】【生理】endocrine; internal secretion：～系统 *endocrine system* /～物 *endocrine; endocritic*

【内分泌失调】【医】endocrine imbalance; endocrinopathy

【内分泌紊乱】【医】endocrine disorder

【内服】take orally：～药，每日三次，每次一片 *to be taken orally, one tablet each time, three times a day*

【内阁】cabinet：改组～ *cabinet reshuffle* /～大臣 *cabinet minister* /～会议 *cabinet council* /～危机 *ministerial crisis*

【内功】(martial art or qigong) exercises to benefit the internal organs; internal work

【内顾之忧】domestic worries; trouble at home：没有了～，工人们才能全心地投入工作。*When not distracted by the troubles at home, the workers will be devoted to their work.*

【内海】① continental sea ② inland sea：地中海是被欧洲、亚洲、小亚细亚、近东及非洲包围的一个～。*The Mediterranean Sea is an inland sea surrounded by Europe, Asia, Asia Minor, the Near East, and Africa.*

【内涵】①【逻】intension; connotation ② self-restraint：他是一个有～的人。*He is a person with self-restraint.*

【内行】① be expert at; be adept in; know the ins and outs of：对驾驶赛车很～ *be expert at driving racing cars* /他对养蜂养蚕都很～。*He knows a lot about bee and silkworm breeding.* ② an expert; a dab hand; master：向～请教 *turn to an expert for advice* /要说起幼儿教育呀，他可是～。*When it comes to teaching small children, he is an expert.*

【内耗】① energy consumed by a machine without getting any work done ② losses suffered in internal strife

【内河】inland river (or waters, waterway)：～运输 *inland water transport*

【内核】the crux of a matter; core; kernel

【内讧】internal conflict; internal strife; internal dissension; faction：～几乎使该党分裂解体。*Faction almost broke up the party.*

【内华达】Nevada, a state of the western United States
【内画】inside painting
【内画壶】glassware bottle whose interior is painted with pictures
【内踝】the medial part of the ankle
【内急】have to go to the toilet
【内奸】a secret enemy agent within one's ranks; a hidden traitor: 铲除~ *uproot the hidden traitors*
【内艰】[书] mother's funeral
【内角】【数】interior angle; internal angle
【内接多边形】【数】inscribed polygon
【内景】indoor setting; indoor scene; interior
【内径】internal diameter; inside diameter; inner diameter
【内疚】compunction; guilty conscience; conscience-stricken: ~于心 *feel compunctious* /对着自己最好的朋友说谎,我感到十分~。*I feel terribly guilty for lying to my best friend.* /奇怪的是他做了这种事却毫无~之心。*It is strange that he did such a thing without the slightest compunction.*
【内眷】female members of a family
【内科】(department of) internal medicine: ~病房 *medical ward* /~医生 *physician* /你看~还是外科? *Do you want to see a physician or a surgeon?*
【内裤】under shorts
【内涝】waterlogging
【内里】[方] the inside: 这事儿~颇有些曲折。*There are quite a few complications in this matter.*
【内力】【物】internal force
【内流河】continental river
【内陆】inland; continental: ~城市 *inland city*
【内陆国】landlocked country
【内陆湖】inland lake
【内陆盆地】inland basin
【内乱】civil strife; internal disorder: ~外患,民不聊生。*The nation was suffering from civil disorder and foreign aggression at the same time; the masses hardly had any means to live.*
【内罗毕】Nairobi, capital of Kenya
【内蒙古】Inner Mongolia: ~草原 *Inner Mongolian grasslands*
【内蒙古自治区】Inner Mongolian Autonomous Region
【内膜】【生理】inner membrane
【内幕】what goes on behind the scenes; inside story; lowdown (on): ~消息 *inside information* /这就是整个事件的~。*This is the lowdown on the whole event.*
【内难】domestic calamity; internal trouble
【内能】【物】internal energy; intrinsic energy
【内切圆】【数】inscribed circle
【内亲】relatives on one's wife's side; in-laws
【内勤】① internal or office work: ~人员 *office staff* ② office staff
【内情】inside information; inside story: 了解~ *be an insider; be in the know*
【内燃机】【机】internal-combustion engine
【内燃机车】diesel locomotive
【内热】①[书] anxiety ②【中医】internal heat — disorders due to predominance of the yang (阳)
【内人】my wife
【内容】content; substance: ~和形式的统一 *unity of content and form* /我喜欢他写作的风格,却不喜欢他写作的~。*I like the style of his writing but I don't like the content.*
【内伤】①【医】internal injury ②【中医】disorder of internal organs caused by improper diet, fatigue, emotional strains, sexual excess, etc.
【内生殖器】internal genitalia
【内室】inner room; bedroom
【内水】inland waters
【内胎】inner tube
【内廷】inner chambers in an imperial palace; imperial residence
【内外】① inside and outside; domestic and foreign: 长城~ *both sides of the Great Wall* /~反动势力 *domestic and foreign reactionary forces* ② around; about: 五十岁~ *about fifty years old*
【内外交困】beset with difficulties both at home and abroad
【内外有别】distinguish between what is for internal information and what is for external publicity
【内务】① internal affairs: ~部 *Ministry of Internal Affairs* ② daily routine tasks to keep the barracks, etc. clean and tidy: ~条令 *routine service regulations*
【内线】① planted agent ②【军】interior lines: ~作战 *fight on interior lines* ③ inside connections: ~自动电话机 *interphone* ④ inner links: ~关系 *inside network*
【内详】name and address of sender enclosed
【内向】① toward the inside: ~经济 *domestic market-oriented economy* ②【心】introversion: 性格~ *be introverted by nature* /他是~人,不轻易发表意见。*He is an introvert and seldom voices his opinion.*
【内销】sale in domestic market; for the domestic market: 出口转~ *exportable goods put on the domestic market; exportable goods sold on home market*
【内心】① heart; innermost being: 这些话发自我~深处。*These words are from the bottom of my heart.* /她向他表示~的感谢。*She gave him her heartfelt thanks.* /他~很矛盾。*He is torn by conflicting thoughts.* ②【数】incenter (of a triangle)
【内省】introspection: ~心理学 *introspective psychology*
【内兄】wife's elder brother; brother-in-law
【内秀】be intelligent without seeming so; with inward grace
【内焰】【化】inner flame
【内衣】underwear; underclothes: 棉毛~ *cotton-wool underwear*
【内因】【哲】internal cause: 唯物辩证法认为,外因通过~起作用。*Materialist dialectics holds that ex-*

ternal causes become operative through internal causes. /事物的发展基本上是由~决定的。*The development of things depends on internal causes.*
【内应】a person operating from within in coordination with outside forces; a planted agent
【内忧】① domestic trouble; domestic disorder: ~外患 *domestic disorder and foreign invasion* ②[书] anxiety
【内在】inherent; intrinsic; internal; inner: ~规律 *inherent law* /~联系 *inner link; internal relations* /~矛盾 *inherent contradictions* /~美 *inner beauty* /~因素 *internal element*
【内脏】【生理】internal organs; viscera
【内宅】inner chambers
【内债】internal debt; domestic loan
【内战】civil war: ~连年 *protracted civil war*
【内掌柜】[口] wife of a shopkeeper
【内障】cataract or glaucoma
【内争】internal strife
【内政】internal (or domestic, home) affairs: 互不干涉~ *noninterference in each other's internal affairs* /中国的~,不许任何国家干涉。*No country should be permitted to interfere in China's internal affairs.*
【内侄】son of wife's brother; nephew
【内侄女】daughter of wife's brother; niece
【内中】the inside: 你不晓得~的事。*You don't know the inside story.*
【内助】[书] wife
【内传】① anecdotal biography; life and anecdotes (of a person) ②[古] book on exegesis of classics
【内子】[书] my wife

nèn

恁 [方] ① so; such: ~大胆! *How reckless!* /要不了~些。*No need for so much.* ② that: ~时 *at that time* ③ this; this much: ~久 *so long*
【恁地】[方] ① so; like that; in that way: 不要~说。*Don't say so.* ② why; how: 这人看着面熟,~想不起来? *This person looks very familiar to me, but how come that I just cannot remember who he is?*

嫩 ① tender; delicate: ~叶 *tender leaves* /小孩儿肉皮儿~。*Children have delicate skin.* ② (of food) soft-cooked: ~豆腐 *tender bean curd* /牛排很~。*The beefsteak is very tender.* ③ light: ~绿 *light green* ④ inexperienced; unskillful: ~手 *a raw hand; a new hand* /他当工头还~了点儿。*He is not experienced enough to be the foreman.*
【嫩寒】① first days of cold weather ②[书] slightly cold
【嫩红】pink; apricot pink
【嫩黄】light yellow
【嫩绿】light green; soft green
【嫩生】[方] ① tender: 这韭菜很~。*The leek is very tender.* ② inexperienced; immature: 我侄子还~,您多照顾点儿。*My nephew is still young and immature; Please pay more attention to him.*
【嫩芽】young bud; new bud: 抽~ *bud*

néng

能 ① ability; capability; skill: 技~ *skill* /~耐 *ability; capability* ②【物】energy: 动~ *kinetic energy* /势~ *potential energy* /原子~ *atomic energy* ③ able; capable: 她可~呢,穿的衣服都是自己设计的。*She is very capable; she designs all the clothes she wears.* ④ can; be able to; be capable of: 你~爬上那棵树吗? *Are you capable of climbing that tree?* /我们~克服所有的困难。*We can overcome all the difficulties.* /他病好了,~下床了。*He has recovered and can get up now.* /有钱~使鬼推磨。*Money makes the mare go.* ⑤ (expressing possibility) can possibly: 他~原谅我吗? *Can he pardon me?* ⑥ used between 不……不 to express obligation, certainty or great probability: 这么重要的会议,你可不~不参加啊。*You must attend the meeting, for it is very important.* ⑦ may; can; be permitted to: "这儿~停车吗?" "不~。" "*Can we park here?*" "*No. Parking is not allowed here.*"
【能动】active; dynamic: 人的~作用 *man's initiative; man's dynamic role* /主观~性 *man's conscious dynamic role* /~地争取胜利 *play a dynamic role in striving for victory*
【能干】able; capable; competent: 他是一个很~的厨师。*He is a competent cook.* /这个打字员可真~。*This typist is really good at his job.*
【能歌善舞】good at singing and dancing
【能工巧匠】skillful craftsman; skilled artisan; dab hand
【能够】can; be able to; be capable of: 人类~制造工具。*Human beings can make tools.* /他~独立工作了。*He is able to work on his own now.* /下游~行驶轮船。*The lower reaches of the river are navigable for steamers.* /明天的晚会,家属也~参加。*Family members are also welcome to join tomorrow's party.*
【能耗】energy consumption
【能级】【物】energy level: 基态~ *ground state level*
【能见度】【气】visibility: 地面~ *ground visibility* /因有大雾,~降低,导致多起交通事故。*The poor visibility in the fog caused many car accidents.*
【能力】ability; capability: 支付~ *ability to pay* /他经验丰富,有~担当这项工作。*He is very experienced and has the ability to take on this responsibility.* /我们为他找到了更利于发挥他~的工作。*We found him a job more suited to his abilities.* /这项工作对学习和适应~有很高的要求。*This task has a high demand for learning and adapting capability.*
【能量】①【物】energy: ~转化 *conversion of energy* /~交换 *energy exchange* /~守恒定律 *the law of*

conversation of energy ② capabilities：别看人不多，～可不小。*Though few in number, they have enormous capacity for manoeuvre.*

【能量守恒】【物】conservation of energy; energy conservation

【能耐】［口］ability; capability：他的～真不小，一个人管这么多台机器。*He shows great skill in minding so many machines all by himself.*

【能掐会算】can foretell the future; can predict what will happen：既然你～，为什么不去买彩票呢？*Since you can foresee what will happen, why don't you buy lotteries?*

【能屈能伸】be able to stoop or to stand; submit or assert oneself as the occasion requires; be adaptable to circumstances：大丈夫～。*A man among men knows when to eat humble pie and when to hold his head high.*

【能人】able person：～背后有～。*For every able person there is always one still better.*

【能上能下】be able to work at both higher and lower levels; be ready to accept a higher or lower position

【能士】［书］talents

【能事】what one is particularly good at：极尽挑拨离间之～ *spare no effort in sowing discord*

【能手】dab; dab hand; crackerjack; expert：射击～ *a crack shot* /解决问题的～ *a trouble-shooter* /技术革新～ *an expert at technical innovation* /她是织布～。*She is a dab hand at weaving.*

【能说会道】have the gift of the gab; be a glib talker; be eloquent

【能态】【物】energy state

【能言善辩】be eloquent

【能源】energy resources; energy：可再生～ *renewable sources of energy* /～危机 *energy crisis* /～预算 *energy budget*

【能愿动词】【语】modal verb

【能者多劳】able people should do more work; an able man is always busy

ńg

嗯 used in questioning：～，你说什么？*Eh? What did you say?*

ňg

嗯 used to show surprise or disapproval：～，怎么又不见了？*Hey! It's gone again.* /～！你怎么还没去？*Why haven't you started yet?*

ǹg

嗯 used to express agreement or assent："你有空吗？"。"～。" *"Are you free?" "M-hm."* /他～了一声，就走了。*He merely said "Uh-huh" and went away.*

nī

妮

【妮子】［方］girl; lass

ní

尼 Buddhist nun

【尼泊尔】Nepal：～人 *Nepalese* /～语 *Nepali*

【尼采】Nietzsche（1844-1900）German philosopher

【尼姑】Buddhist nun

【尼古丁】nicotine：～含量 *nicotine content*

【尼加拉瓜】Nicaragua：～人 *Nicaraguan*

【尼克松】Richard Milhous Nixon（1913-1994），the 37th President of the United States（1969-1974），resigned from office because of the Watergate scandal：～主义 *Nixon Doctrine*

【尼龙】【纺】nylon：～丝 *nylon yarn* /～袜 *nylon socks*

【尼罗河】the Nile：～三角洲 *Nile delta* /～是世界上最长的河流。*The Nile is the longest river in the world.*

【尼日利亚】Nigeria：～人 *Nigerian*

【尼亚加拉瀑布】Niagara Falls

呢 (cloth made of) wool; woolen cloth; heavy woolen cloth; wool coating or suiting：厚～大衣 *heavy woolen overcoat*
see also ne

【呢喃】① swallow's twitter ②［书］whisper

【呢绒】woolen goods; wool fabric

【呢子】woolen cloth; heavy woolen cloth; wool coating or suiting

泥 ① mud; mire：黄～ *yellow mud* /火山～ *volcanic mud* /硬～ *stiff mud* ② sth like paste or pulp：土豆～ *mashed potato* /印～ *inkpad*
see also nì

【泥巴】［方］mud; mire

【泥工】［方］bricklayer; tiler; plasterer

【泥垢】dirt; grime：他满脸～。*His face is covered with dirt.*

【泥浆】mud; slurry：～泵 *slurry pump; slush pump* /焦～ *coke slurry* /粘土～ *clay slurry* /含水～ *aqueous slurry*

【泥金】coating material made of powdered gold or other metals; golden paint：～佛像 *a gilded Buddha*

【泥坑】mud pit; mire; morass：陷入～ *get stuck in the mud; be bogged down in a quagmire*

【泥流】mud flow

【泥煤】peat：带状～ *banded peat* /沥青～ *bituminous peat* /纤维～ *fibrous peat*

【泥淖】mire; bog; morass：汽车陷入了～。*The car*

got stuck in the mud.
【泥泞】① muddy; miry:雨后道路~。*The road is muddy after the rain.* ② mire; mud
【泥牛入海】like clay oxen entering the sea — never to be heard of again; gone forever:从那以后,他如~,杳无音信。*Since then, he was never heard of.*
【泥鳅】【动】loach
【泥人】clay figurine:彩塑~ *painted clay figurine*
【泥沙】silt
【泥沙俱下】mud and sand are carried along — good and bad are mixed:在革命高潮时期,各种人都来参加,未免~,鱼龙混杂。*At the high tide of the revolution, people of all descriptions flocked to join in; so inevitably the waters were muddled and the bad became mixed with the good.*
【泥石流】【地】mud-rock flow
【泥水匠】bricklayer; tiler; plasterer
【泥塑】clay sculpture
【泥胎】an unpainted clay idol
【泥胎儿】unfired pottery; virgin pottery
【泥滩】【地】(mud) flat
【泥潭】mire; morass; quagmire
【泥炭】peat:湖~ *lake peat* /盆地~ *basin peat* /山地~ *mountain peat* /原生~ *autochthonous peat*
【泥塘】mire; bog; morass
【泥土】① earth; soil ② clay
【泥瓦匠】bricklayer; tiler; plasterer
【泥雨】rain that carries a large quantity of dust
【泥浴】mud bath; bog bath: ~疗法 *mud-bath treatment*
【泥沼】mire; swamp; morass; slough
【泥足巨人】a colossus with feet of clay:列宁把帝国主义比做~。*Lenin likened imperialism to a colossus with feet of clay.*

霓 【气】secondary rainbow
【霓虹灯】neon lamp; neon light; neon

nǐ

拟 ① draw up; design; devise; draft: ~一份计划草案 *draft a proposal* /科研计划已经~出来了。*The scientific research plan has already been drawn up.* ② intend; plan: ~于明天启程 *plan to leave tomorrow* ③ imitate: ~态 *imitation* ④ assimilate; compare:把人生~作梦 *assimilate life to a dream* ⑤ suppose; guess:虚~ *suppose*
【拟订】draft: ~计划 *draft a plan*
【拟定】draw up; work out: ~城市建设规划 *map out a programme for municipal construction*
【拟稿】prepare a draft; make a draft:校长亲自~呈报上级。*The principal himself prepared this draft and submitted it to the superior.*
【拟古】model one's literary or artistic style on that of the ancients: ~之作 *a work modeled after the ancients*
【拟人】personification:使之~化 *have it personified*
【拟色】mimic colouring (of birds, insects, etc.)
【拟态】【动】mimicry; imitation:攻击~ *aggressive mimicry* /保护性~ *protective mimicry*
【拟议】① proposal; recommendation:事实证明他的~是正确的。*Facts show that his recommendations were right.* ② draw up; daft:小组一致通过了他~的学习计划。*The team unanimously adopted the study plan he drew up.*
【拟音】(produce a) sound effect
【拟作】work modeled after a certain author

你 ① you: ~是谁? *Who are you?* / ~能帮我一个忙吗? *Could you please do me a favour?* / ~要是不认得路,我叫他去接你。*If you don't know how to get here, I will ask him to pick you up at your home.* ② you (second person plural): ~方 *your side* / ~校 *your school* / ~公司 *your company* ③ (referring to any person) you; one; anyone:碰上这样一件事,~能怎么办? *What can you do in such a situation?* ④ used coordinately with 我 or 他 in parallel structures to indicate several or many people behaving the same way:三个人~看看我,我看看~,谁也不说话。*The three of them kept looking at one another without saying a word.* / ~一言,我一语,大家谈得很热闹。*A lively conversation went on with everyone joining in.*
【你们】you (second person plural): ~几个谁最大? *Who among you is the eldest?* / ~知道他是谁吗? *Do you know who he is?*
【你死我活】life-and-death; life-or-death; mortal:这是一场~的战争。*This is a life-or-death battle.*

nì

伲 [方] I; we

泥 ① cover or daub with plaster, putty, etc.; putty; plaster: ~墙 *cover the crevices in a wall with mud or plaster* ② stubborn; bigoted; obstinate:拘~ *stickle*
see also ní
【泥古】have bigoted belief in the ancients; obstinately follow ancient ways: ~不化 *stick to ancient ways*
【泥子】putty

昵 close; intimate:亲~ *very intimate*
【昵称】nickname; pet name; a term of endearment:她给他的~是"小虎"。*Her pet name for him is "little tiger".*

逆 ① contrary; counter; inverse; converse: ~反应 *inverse reaction; back reaction* /互~ *mutually inverse* ② go against; disobey; defy: ~时代潮流而动 *go against the trend of the times* ③ adverse: ~境 *adverse circumstance* ④ traitorous; rebellious: ~臣 *traitorous vassal* ⑤ [书] be ready for：～战 *prepare for the war* ⑥ beforehand；in advance

【逆差】adverse balance of trade；trade deficit：国际收支～ *an unfavourable balance of international payments* /贸易～ *unfavourable trade balance；trade deficit*

【逆产】① a traitor's property ②（of a baby）breech birth

【逆定理】【数】converse theorem

【逆耳】offend the ear；be unpleasant to the ear：～之言 *words that offend the ear* /忠言～。*Sincere advice is harsh to the ear.*

【逆反】adverse；rebellious

【逆反心理】psychology of aversion；rebellious psychology

【逆反应】【化】counter-reaction；reverse action

【逆风】① against the wind：～前行 *walk forward against the wind* ② contrary wind；head wind：我们的帆船被～耽搁了。*Our sailing boat was delayed by contrary winds.*

【逆光】【摄】backlighting

【逆弧】【物】backfire；arc-back

【逆火】backfire；flashback

【逆经】retrograde menstruation

【逆境】adverse circumstances；adversity：不管我处于～还是顺境，他一直是我的好友。*He has been a good friend to me in adversity or in prosperity.* /～是锻炼人的最好场所。*Adversity is a good schoolmaster.*

【逆来顺受】meekly submit to oppression，maltreatment，etc.；resign oneself to adversity

【逆料】see beforehand；anticipate；foresee：尚难～。*It's hard to say；there is no telling.* /事态的发展不难～。*It is not hard to foresee the course of the event.*

【逆流】① go against the current：～而上 *sail against the current* /他～游去。*He was swimming in a direction contrary to the current.* ② adverse current；countercurrent：赤道～ *equatorial countercurrent* /一股反社会主义的～ *an adverse current against socialism*

【逆旅】［书］inn；hotel：宿于～ *stay in a hotel*

【逆命题】【数】converse

【逆时针】anticlockwise；counter-clockwise：这个风车一会儿顺时针旋转，一会儿～旋转。*The windmill whirled round，clockwise，then widdershins.*

【逆水】go against the current

【逆水行舟】sailing against the current：学如～，不进则退。*Study is like sailing against the current；either you keep forging ahead or you keep falling behind.*

【逆向】against the original direction；reverse direction

【逆行】①（of vehicles）go in a direction not allowed by traffic regulations；go in the wrong direction ②【天】retrograde motion

【逆序】reverse order；backward sequence

【逆运算】reverse operation

【逆转】take a turn for the worse；reverse；deteriorate：自然规律不可～。*It is impossible to reverse the order of nature.* /形势突然～。*The situation suddenly deteriorated.*

【逆子】［旧］unfilial son

匿 hide；conceal

【匿报】withhold information

【匿藏】conceal；hide；go into hiding

【匿迹】go into hiding：销声～ *disappear from the scene*

【匿名】anonymous：我接到一个～电话警告我不要把所看到的事情报警。*I received an anonymous call warning me not to go to the police about what I'd seen.*

【匿名信】an anonymous letter

【匿影藏形】hide from public notice；conceal one's identity；lie low

睨 ［书］look askance：～视 *look sideways；cast a sidelong glance*

腻 ① greasy；oily：这个汉堡包有点～。*The hamburger is a little greasy.* ② be bored with；be tired of；be fed up with：这种日子我过～了。*I am fed up with this kind of life.* ③ meticulous：细～ *exquisite* ④ sticky；grimy：擦碗布都～了。*The dishtowel has got grimy.* ⑤ dirt；grime：尘～ *dirt*

【腻虫】【动】aphid；plant louse

【腻烦】［口］① be bored；be fed up：这些话我都听～了。*I am tired of listening to all this.* ② hate；loathe：我最～洗盘子。*I loathe washing dishes.*

【腻糊】［方］sticky；adhesive；glutinous：这张纸很～，你把果酱弄到上面了吗？*This paper feels all sticky — have you spilt jam on it?*

【腻人】① be too greasy：～的汉堡包 *a greasy hamburger* ② boring；tiring：听她教训我真～。*It's really boring to hear her lecturing at me.* ③（of a child，etc.）cling to people；pester：我儿子生病了，很～。*My son falls sick and hangs on to me all the time.*

【腻歪】［方］be bored：米饭和面条真让人～，我想换换口味。*I'm bored with rice and noodles — I want something different.*

【腻味】［方］be fed up with；be sick of；have had enough of sth；have had it：在一个地方工作那么久，你不～吗？*Aren't you fed up with working at the same place for so long?* /他问了我那么多愚蠢的问题，让我～死了。*I'm sick to death of all those stupid questions from him.*

【腻友】［书］a bosom friend；an intimate friend；a close friend

【腻子】【建】putty

溺 ① drown：～死 *be drowned* ② be addicted to：～于酒色 *be given over to wine and woman* /他沉～于酒。*He was enslaved to drinking.*

【溺爱】spoil；dote：他不爱他的妻子，却～他的孩子。*Although he doesn't love his wife，he dotes on his children.*

【溺水】drowning；sinking：～身亡 *be drowned*

【溺刑】noyade

【溺职】［书］neglect of duty; dereliction of duty:他因～而被罢官。*He was removed from office for neglect of duty.*

niān

拈 pick up (with the thumb and one or two fingers):从罐子里～出一块糖 *pick a candy out from the jar*

【拈花惹草】toy with flowers and grass — dally with women; philander

【拈阄儿】draw lots:他们通过～来决定谁请客。*They drew lots to decide who would pay the bill.*

【拈轻怕重】prefer the light to the heavy — pick easy jobs and shirk hard ones

【拈香】offer incense at a temple

蔫 ① fade; wither; shrivel up; droop:天冷了,花儿都～了。*The flowers withered in the cold.* /炎热的阳光把草晒～了。*The hot sunshine shrivelled the grass.* ② listless; spiritless; droopy:这孩子有点～,怕是病了。*The child looks a bit listless. I am afraid he's sick.* ③［方］(of temperament) slow:她做事太～。*She is slow in doing things.*

【蔫巴】［口］wither; droop:这些花儿都～了,你最好给它们浇点儿水。*These flowers are beginning to droop; you'd better water them.* /他因睡眠不足而显得很～。*He drooped from lack of sleep.*

【蔫不唧】［口］① listless; droopy; sluggish:自从收到那封信后,他老是～的。*He's been droopy ever since when he received that letter.* ② quiet; without being noticed:我还想跟他说话,没想到他～地走了。*When I was about to talk to him, he'd gone without my noticing.*

【蔫不悄儿】［方］quietly:他～往我书包里塞了一封信。*He tucked a letter in my bag quietly.*

【蔫不声】silent; quiet

【蔫耷耷】listless and droopy:她生病以后～的。*She was very listless after her illness.*

【蔫儿坏】［口］be inwardly vicious; behave in an underhand way:这人～,你加点小心。*You should be careful with him; he looks honest but is really crooked.*

【蔫头耷脑】with head hanging — dejected; listless; droopy:从大厅里走出了一群～的支持者。*Out of the hall came a crowd of dejected-looking supporters.*

nián

年 ① year:一～ *one year* /十～ *ten years* /～复一～ *year in and year out; year after year* /我到这里正好一～了。*It is just a year since I arrived here.* ② annual; yearly: ～产量 *yearly output* /～收入 *annual income* ③ age: ～过半百 *over fifty years old* ④ a period in one's life:童～ *childhood* ⑤ a period in history:明朝初～ *the beginning of the Ming Dynasty* ⑥ harvest:丰～ *an abundant year* /歉～ *a poor harvest year* ⑦ New Year:过～ *celebrate the new year* ⑧ of or for New Year ⑨［旧］friendship between those who passed the imperial examinations in the same year ⑩ (Nián) a surname

【年报】① annuals (of a learned society) ② annual report

【年辈】one's age and generation: ～相当 *of the same generation*

【年表】chronological table

【年产】annual production

【年成】the year's harvest: ～好 *good harvest* /～不好 *lean year*

【年齿】［书］age: ～尚幼 *still young in age*

【年初】the beginning of the year

【年代】① age; years; time:战争～ *the war years* /～不详 *without date* /这件古董恐怕有～了。*The history of this antique may be traced back to very early period.* ② a decade of a century:十九世纪七十～ *the 1870's* /我们出生于八十～。*We were born in the eighties.*

【年底】the end of the year

【年度】year (a twelve months period fixed for a certain purpose):财政～ *fiscal year* /～预算 *annual budget*

【年饭】family reunion dinner on the lunar New Year's Eve

【年份】① a particular year. 这两笔开支不在一个～。*These two expenditures were not incurred in the same year.* ② age; time:这件瓷器的～比那件久。*This piece of porcelain is older than that one.*

【年俸】annual salary; yearly pay

【年富力强】in the full vigour of manhood; in the prime of life; in one's prime:他在～时却遭杀害。*He was cut off in his prime.*

【年高德劭】of venerable age and eminent virtue; of advanced years and known integrity; venerable: ～的祖父被推选为主席。*My venerable grandfather was elected the Chairman.*

【年糕】New Year cake

【年根】［方］the end of the year

【年庚】the time (year, month, day and hour) of a person's birth

【年关】the end of the year (formerly time for settling accounts, thus a terrible time for the poor)

【年光】① time; years: ～易逝。*Time flies.* ② the year's harvest:今年～不好。*This year's harvest is poor.* ③［方］these days; those days:那～,不得不靠借债过日子。*In those days, we lived on debts.*

【年号】reign title

【年华】time; years:虚度～ *waste one's time; wear away one's years*

【年画】Spring Festival pictures

【年会】annual meeting:公司今年的～将在上海举行。*This year, the company's annual meeting will be held in Shanghai.*

【年货】special purchases for the Spring Festival:办

~ *Spring Festival shopping*

【年级】grade; year: 你上几~? *Which grade are you in?* /我是三~学生。*I am a student in the third grade.*

【年集】country fair at the end of the lunar year

【年纪】age: 你多大~了? *How old are you?* /他上~了。*He is an aged man.* /我觉得~大了。*I'm feeling my years.* /当你到了我的~,你就不需要那么多睡眠了。*When you reach my age, you don't need so much sleep.*

【年假】① winter holiday ② annual leave: 你有三天的带薪~。*You can enjoy a three-day paid annual leave.*

【年间】certain period of a dynasty or reign

【年检】annual inspection

【年鉴】yearbook; almanac

【年节】the lunar New Year Festival; the Spring festival

【年金】annuity

【年景】① the year's harvest ② holiday atmosphere of the Spring Festival

【年均】annual average: 这个村每户的~收入达到了一万元。*The annual average income per household in this village has reached 10,000 yuan.*

【年来】in the past year; in recent years

【年老】old; aged; advanced in years: ~多病 *be old and vulnerable to sickness* /~体弱 *be advanced in age and poor in health* /~退休 *retire on account of old age*

【年历】a calendar with the whole year printed on one sheet; single-page calendar

【年利】annual interest: ~率 *interest rate per annum*

【年龄】age: 不足~ *under age* /通过年轮,可以看出一棵树的~。*You can tell the age of a tree by its growth rings.* /~不饶人。*Age will tell.*

【年轮】【植】annual ring; growth ring

【年迈】old; aged; gerontic: ~多病 *old and sick* /他~的母亲把时间都花在了抱怨上。*His aged mother spends most of the time complaining.*

【年貌】age and appearance: ~相当 *well matched in age and appearance*

【年年】every year; year after year; year-by-year: ~丰收 *bumper harvest year after year*

【年谱】chronological life

【年青】young: 你正~,应把精力用到学习上去。*You should put more effort into studying while you are young.*

【年轻】young: ~人 *young people; the youth* /~力壮 *young and vigorous*

【年三十儿】last day of the lunar year; lunar New Year's Eve

【年少】[书] ① young: ~轻狂 *young and arrogant* ② youngster; a young man: 英俊~ *a handsome young man*

【年深日久】with the passage of time; as the years go by

【年时】(niánshí) ①[方] years; a long time ② [书] former years; the past years

【年事】[书] age (of a person): 他说自己~已高,想辞去现任职务。*He said that he wanted to resign from his current position since he was advanced in age.*

【年岁】① age: 上了~的人 *an aged person* ② years: 因为~久远,大家把这事儿都忘了。*It has been forgotten since it happened so many years ago.* ③ [方] harvest of the year: 他问了我家乡的~如何。*He asked me about this year's harvest in my hometown.*

【年头】① year: 他来北京已经有五个~了。*He has been in Beijing for five years.* ② years; a long time: 他干这行可有~了。*He has been in this field for many years.* ③ times; days: 那~,大家都提心吊胆的,怕有地震。*In those days, people were all in fear of earthquakes.* ④ harvest: 今年~好,麦子比去年多收两三成。*We have got a very good harvest this year; the wheat yield is about twenty to thirty percent more than that of last year.*

【年尾】the end of the year

【年息】annual interest

【年下】around the Spring Festival

【年限】fixed number of years: 延长工具使用~ *prolong the service life of the tool*

【年薪】annual salary; yearly pay

【年夜】the lunar New Year's Eve

【年幼】young; underage: ~无知 *young and ignorant; young and innocent*

【年月】① times: 和平~ *peaceful times* ② days; years

【年长】older in age; senior

【年终】year-end; the end of the year: ~鉴定 *year-end appraisal* /~奖 *year-end bonus*

【年资】age and years of service; seniority

【年租】annual rent

粘 ① sticky; glutinous ② (Nián) a surname

see also zhān

【粘稠】thick and sticky: ~的泥浆 *sticky mud*

【粘砂】adhering sand

鲇 【动】catfish

黏 sticky; glutinous: 胶水很~。*The paste is very sticky.*

【黏度】【化】viscosity: ~换算表 *viscosity conversion table* /~计 *viscosity meter* /~曲线 *viscosity curve* /~梯度 *viscosity gradient*

【黏附】adhere to; conglutinate: ~力 *adhesion* /这两个表面相互~在一起,我们无法把它们分开。*The two surfaces adhered to each other, and we couldn't get them apart.*

【黏合】【化】bind; bond; adhere: ~剂 *binder; adhesive; bonding agent*

【黏糊】① sticky; glutinous; tacky: 孩子们认为~的泥巴很好玩。*The kids thought the sticky clay was lovely to play with.* /骄阳让地面感觉很~。*The sun was so hot that it made the road surface tacky.* ② languid; slow-moving: 他看上去挺精神的,做起事来可~呢。*He looks smart but is really languid in doing things.*

【黏结】cohere: ~力 *cohesion*; *cohesive force* /~性 *cohesiveness*
【黏米】① glutinous rice ②［方］broomcorn millet
【黏膜】【生理】mucous membrane; mucosa
【黏土】clay:酸性~ *acid clay* /冲积~ *alluvial clay* /耐火~ *refractory clay* /砂质~ *arenaceous clay* /~岩 *clay rock*
【黏性】stickiness; viscidity
【黏液】【生理】mucus
【黏着】adhere; bond; stick together

niǎn

捻 ① twist with the fingers: ~线 *twist thread* /用几股麻~成一段绳子 *twist a length of rope from strands of hemp* ② sth made by twisting:灯~儿 *lampwick* ③［方］dredge up: ~河泥 *dredge up silt from a river*
【捻捻转儿】a wooden or plastic top set in motion by hand
【捻子】① spill; wick:药~ slender roll of medicated paper or gauze (to be inserted into wounds, etc.) ② wick:灯~ *lampwick*

辇 ① a man-drawn carriage used in ancient times ② imperial carriage

碾 ① roller and millstone; stone roller ② grind or husk with a roller: ~米 *husk rice* /~平 *level*; *roll out* ③［书］grind
【碾场】［方］thresh or husk grain on a threshing ground
【碾坊】grain mill
【碾磙子】stone roller
【碾盘】a millstone upon which a stone roller is used
【碾砣】stone roller
【碾压】(of wheel, etc.) roll over (the ground)
【碾子】roller and millstone; roller

撵 ① drive out; oust:把他~出去! *Drive him out!* /美国独立战争把英国人~了出去。*The American Revolution ousted the English.* /总统被~下了台。*The president was ousted from office.* ②［方］catch up:他跑得太快了,我~不上他。*I couldn't catch up with him since he ran so fast.*

蹍［方］step on

niàn

廿 twenty

念[1] ① think of; miss:自从他走后,我们老~着他。*We've been missing him ever since he left.* ② thought; idea:杂~ *distracting thoughts* ③ (Niàn) a surname

念[2] ① read aloud:请~一下这段儿。*Please read this passage loudly.* ② attend school:他~过中学。*He has been to middle school.*

念[3] twenty, capital form of "廿"
【念白】spoken parts of a Chinese opera
【念叨】① talk about again and again in recollection or anticipation:这就是我们常~的赵先生。*This is the Mr. Zhao we are always talking about.* ②［方］talk over; discuss:今天我有个事儿要跟大家~~。*I've got something to discuss with you today.*
【念佛】pray to Buddha:吃斋~ *be a pious Buddhist and practice vegetarianism*
【念经】recite or chant scriptures
【念旧】keep old friendships in mind; for old time's sake; remember old friends:就算是~,咱也得帮帮那些以前帮助过咱们的人哪。*Just for old time's sake, we should help those who helped us before.*
【念念不忘】bear in mind constantly; always remember; never forget:她一直~不忘的是那天桃树下的那个年轻人。*She was often reminded of the young man under that peach tree on that particular day.*
【念念有词】① mutter incantations ② mumble
【念书】① read:你打电话来的时候,我正在~呢。*I was reading when you called.* ② study:我在一中~。*I am studying in No.1 Middle School.*
【念诵】read aloud: ~经文 *chant a scripture*
【念头】thought; idea; intention:邪恶的~ *an evil thought* /你最好打消那个~。*You'd better give up that idea.*
【念物】souvenir; keepsake; memento
【念心儿】［方］souvenir; keepsake; memento:这本书送给你,做个~吧。*Keep this book as a souvenir.*
【念咒】chant incantations
【念珠】beads; rosary

niáng

娘 ① mum; ma; mother:爹~ *dad and mum* ② a form of address for an elderly married woman:婶~ *aunt*; *wife of one's father's younger brother* ③ a young woman:渔~ *a young fisherwoman*
【娘家】a married woman's parents' home
【娘舅】［方］brother of one's mother; uncle
【娘娘】① (used in speaking to or of an empress or an imperial concubine): 正宫~ *the empress* ② a name for certain goddess: ~庙 *Temple of the Goddess of Fertility*
【娘亲】mother
【娘儿】［口］woman along with her juniors, e. g. mother and child; aunt and niece or nephew: ~仨 *the mother and her two children*
【娘儿们】①［口］mother and children ②［方］the womenfolk; woman ③［方］wife
【娘胎】mother's womb:出了~ *be born*
【娘姨】［方］maidservant
【娘子】①［方］wife ②［旧］a polite form of ad-

dress for a young woman

【娘子军】a detachment of women; any contingent entirely made up of women

niàng

酿 ① make (wine); brew (wine) ② make (honey):蜜蜂~蜜。*Bees make honey.* ③ lead to; result in; give rise to: ~成大祸 *lead to disaster* ④ a way of cooking ⑤ wine: 佳~ *good wine*

【酿酒】make wine; brew beer: ~厂 *winery; brewery*

【酿造】brew; make:这酒是用大米~的。*This wine is brewed from rice.*

niǎo

鸟 bird: ~巢 *bird's nest* / ~笼 *bird cage; aviary*

【鸟巢】bird's nest

【鸟贩】poulterer

【鸟粪】① bird's droppings: ~石 *struvite* ② guano

【鸟蛤】【动】cockle

【鸟害】bird pest

【鸟尽弓藏】cast aside the bow once the birds are all killed — cast sb aside when he has served his purpose

【鸟瞰】① get a bird's-eye view; an aerial view:从山顶~全城 *get a bird's eye view of the city from the hilltop* /现场~图 *an aerial plan of the site* ② a general survey of a subject:近代史~ *a general survey of modern history*

【鸟类】birds

【鸟枪】① fowling piece ② air gun

【鸟枪换炮】replace air gun with artillery — better equipped

【鸟儿】[口] bird

【鸟兽散】scatter like birds and beasts; flee helter-skelter; stampede

【鸟语花香】birds sing and flowers give forth fragrance — a fine spring day

袅 slender and delicate

【袅袅】① curl upwards:炊烟~ *smoke curling upward from the chimneys* ② wave in the wind:垂柳~ *weeping willows dancing in the wind* ③ linger: 余音~,长久不绝。*The music lingered in the air long after the performance ended.*

【袅袅婷婷】[书] slim and supple; lissome and graceful:身材修长的模特儿们~地走过大厅。*Long-stemmed models ankled through the lobby.*

【袅娜】[书] ① (of plants) soft and slender:春风吹着~的柳枝。*The slender willow twigs were swaying gently in the spring breeze.* ② (of a female figure) delicate and graceful; willowy

【袅绕】[书] linger:歌声~。*The song lingered in the air.*

嬲 [书] ① trick; tease ② entangle

niào

尿 ① urine; piss:吓得屁滚~流 *frighten the piss out of sb* ② urinate; piss; make water:这孩子~了我一身。*The baby has wetted my clothes.* see also suī

【尿布】diaper; napkin; nappy: ~布垫 *pilch* /给孩子换~ *diaper a baby; change a baby*

【尿床】bed-wetting:一岁以后,这孩子就不再~了。*The kid never wetted the bed again after getting one year old.*

【尿道】【生理】urethra: ~炎 *urethritis* / ~造影 *urethrography*

【尿毒症】【医】uraemia

【尿管】【生理】ureter

【尿壶】chamber pot; urinal

【尿急】urgency of micturition

【尿检】【医】urinalysis

【尿炕】wet the bed

【尿素】【化】urea; carbamide

【尿酸】【化】uric acid: ~石 *uric-acid calculus*

niē

捏 ① hold or squeeze between the thumb and a finger; pinch; tweak: ~着鼻子 *squeeze the nose with the fingers* ② knead with the fingers; mould: ~泥人儿 *mould clay figurines* ③ link; bind; put together:这是两码事。不要往一块儿~。*These are two different things; Don't link them together.* ④ make up; fabricate; fudge

【捏合】① put together; bring together:爱情是要相互了解的,不能靠~。*Love needs mutual understanding, so we shall not simply put two together.* ② fabricate; fake; concoct

【捏控】falsely accuse of:他被~偷窃。*He was falsely accused of theft.*

【捏弄】① play with; fiddle with:别~那玩具熊了。*Stop fiddling with the Teddy bear.* ② manipulate; order:我再受不了让他这么~了。*I can no longer stand him ordering me about like this.* ③ discuss in private:这事他们俩一~就那么办了。*The two of them discussed the matter in private and then got it all settled.* ④ fake; fabricate

【捏一把汗】be breathless with anxiety or tension; be keyed up; be on edge:杂技演员表演走钢丝,观众都替他~。*The audience was breathless as they watched the acrobat performing ropewalking.*

【捏造】fabricate; make up; fake; concoct; trump up: ~事实 *make up a story; invent a story* / ~罪名 *trump up charges* /为了诬陷那名警察,他们~了一份报告。*To frame a case against the policeman, they faked up a report.*

niè

涅 ［书］① alunite ② dye black

【涅白】opaque white

【涅槃】【宗】nirvana — extinction of all desire and pain; death

啮 ［书］gnaw; nibble

【啮齿动物】rodent

【啮合】① clench the teeth ② (of gears) mesh; joggle; engage: ～接 *joggle joint* /这两个齿轮～在一起了。*The two cogwheels are engaged.*

【啮噬】bite; torture: 被悔恨之情～的良心 *a conscience bitten by remorse.*

嗫

【嗫嚅】［书］speaking haltingly; hem and haw; mutter and mumble; stumble over one's words: 他开会迟到了，～着他的理由。*He was late into the meeting, mumbling an excuse.*

镊 ① tweezers ② pick up sth with tweezers

【镊子】tweezers: 一把～ *a pair of tweezers*

镍 【化】nickel (Ni)

【镍币】nickel; nickel coin

【镍箔】nickel foil

【镍钢】【冶】nickel steel

【镍钴合金】【冶】alnico

蹑 ① lighten one's steps; walk on tiptoe: 他轻轻地站起来，～着脚走出去。*He stood up quietly and tiptoed out.* ② follow: ～踪 *pursue* ③ ［书］step on; tread; trample

【蹑手蹑脚】stalk; tiptoe; tread lightly; walk on tiptoe; sneak; walk gingerly: 他～地走进了卧室。*He walked gingerly into the bedroom.* /我～地走过女儿的房间，生怕惊醒她。*I tiptoed past my daughter's bedroom so as not to wake her.*

【蹑踪】［书］follow; track; pursue

【蹑足】① walk with light steps: ～潜踪 *walk stealthily* /他～走到门口。*With light steps, he walked to the door.* ② take one's position in; join a profession; follow a trade: ～行伍间 *take a position in the military force*

孽 ① evil: 妖～ *monster; evildoer* ② sin: 罪～ *sin* ③ ［书］unfaithful; disobedient: ～子 *an unfilial child*

【孽根】source of evils; root of troubles

【孽海】karmic ocean

【孽障】①【宗】sin that will lead to retribution ② ［旧］vile spawn

【孽种】① root of trouble ② vile spawn; bastard

nín

您 (showing respect) you: 老师，～早！*Good morning, sir!*

níng

宁 ① peaceful; tranquil: 康～ *peace and tranquility* ② ［书］pacify; settle: 息事～人 *make concessions to avoid trouble* ③ ［书］visit: ～亲 *visit one's parents* ④ another name for Nanjing: 沪～线 *Shanghai-Nanjing Railway*
see also nìng

【宁静】peaceful; tranquil; quiet; calm: ～的湖面 *the calm surface of the lake*/我渴望在乡村过～的生活。*I am yearning for a tranquil life in the country* /孩子们在学校上学时，家里很～。*It's peaceful at home when the children are at school.*

【宁亲】［书］visit home

【宁日】peaceful days: 国贼不除，永无～。*There will be no peaceful days unless the national traitors are rooted out.*

【宁帖】(of state of mind) tranquil; calm

【宁夏回族自治区】Ningxia Hui Autonomous Region

【宁馨儿】［书］a lovely child

拧 ① twist; screw; wrench; wring: ～毛巾 *wring out wet towel* ② pinch; tweak: ～了他一把 *give him a pinch* /他恶意地～了我一下。*He gave me a spiteful pinch.*
see also nǐng; nìng

狞 (of facial expression) ferocious; hideous

【狞笑】grin hideously; fleer

柠

【柠檬】lemon: 甜～ *sweet lemon* /野～ *wild lemon*

【柠檬茶】lemon tea

【柠檬黄】citrine; lemon-coloured

【柠檬水】lemonade

【柠檬酸】【化】citric acid

凝 ① congeal; coagulate; curdle; condense: 用鲜血～成的战斗友谊 *militant friendship cemented with blood* /牛奶～住了。*The milk has curdled.* ② with fixed attention

【凝点】【物】condensation point

【凝冻】freeze

【凝固】① solidify; curdle: 看到这一可怕情景时，我血管中的血似乎～了。*The blood in my veins curdled at the horrific sight.* /蛋白质遇热会～。*Protein becomes solid when heated.* ② inflexible; rigid: 思想～ *stereotyped in thinking*

【凝固点】【物】solidifying point

【凝合】coagulate; congeal

【凝华】【物】sublimate

【凝集】agglutinate; agglomerate

【凝胶】gel; gelatin

【凝结】congeal; coagulate; condense:湖面上~了一层薄冰。*A thin layer of ice formed over the lake.*

【凝聚】① (of vapour) condense; (of fluids) coagulate or curdle:荷叶上~着晶莹的露珠。*Glistening dewdrops have gathered on the lotus leaves.* ②【物】coacervation

【凝聚力】① cohesive force; cohesion ② cohesion:增强中华民族的~ *enhance the cohesion of the Chinese people*

【凝练】(of writing) concise; condensed; compact:~的叙述 *a compact narration*

【凝眸】[书] fix one's eyes on; look with a fixed gaze:~远望 *gaze into the distance*

【凝神】with fixed attention; attentively:~细听 *listen attentively to; be all ears* /我们都在~聆听教授的讲座。*We were listening attentively to the professor's lecture.*

【凝乳】clabber; curd

【凝视】gaze fixedly; stare; a steady look:他~着那幅油画,陷入沉思。*He gazed at the painting, lost in deep thoughts.*

【凝思】be buried in thought; be lost in thought; meditate:他坐在那儿~着往事。*He sat there meditating on his past.*

【凝望】gaze or stare at:~远山 *gaze at the distant mountains*

【凝想】be lost in thought; meditate

【凝血】cruor

【凝血剂】coagulant; coagulen

【凝脂】[书] congealed fat (to describe a woman's skin):肤如~ *smooth and glossy skin*

【凝滞】① stagnant; unmoving; sluggish:两颗~的眼珠出神地望着窗外 *look blankly out of the window with a pair of dull eyes* ② [书] condense

【凝重】① dignified; imposing:神情~ *a dignified look* ② (of sound or voice) deep and forceful:他的声音~有力。*He has a deep, powerful voice.* ③ dense; thick; heavy:~的乌云 *thick dark clouds*

【凝铸】①【冶】coagulated casting ② express; embody:这本书~了我多年的心血。*This book embodies my effort in many years.*

nǐng

拧 ① twist; screw:~开瓶盖 *screw the cap off a bottle* ② wrong; mistaken:说~了 *get the wrong way round* ③ differ; disagree; be at cross-purposes:俩人越说越~。*The more they two talked, the more they disagreed.*
see also níng; nìng

【拧劲儿】[方] disagree; be at odds; irreconcilable:他们的观点从一开始就~。*Their views have really been irreconcilable from the beginning.*

nìng

宁[1] ① would rather:我~死也不叛国。*I'd rather die than betray my country.* ② [书] could it be; could there be:山之险峻,~有逾此? *Could there be a mountain more precipitous than this?*

宁[2] (Nìng) a surname
see also níng

【宁可】would rather:他~辞职也不参加这样一种欺骗的交易。*He would rather resign than take part in such a dishonest transaction.* /~站着死,绝不跪着生。*I'd rather die on my feet than live on my knees.* /我们~租这幢房子,也不愿直接买下它。*We would rather rent the house than buy it outright.*

【宁肯】would rather:他~露宿街头,也不愿回到家去。*He would rather sleep on the street than go back home.* /与其低价把苹果卖出去,我~留给孩子们吃。*Rather than sell the apples at very low price, I would keep them for my kids.*

【宁缺毋滥】rather go without than have sth shoddy — put quality before quantity

【宁死不屈】rather die than surrender; prefer death to humiliation

【宁为玉碎,不为瓦全】rather be a shattered vessel of jade than an unbroken piece of pottery — rather die like a hero than live in dishonour

【宁愿】would rather:我~接受钱而不希望收到通常的礼物。*I would rather receive money than the usual gifts.*

佞 ① one who flatters; hypocritical:~人 *sycophant; toady* ② [书] wise; witty:不~ *me the unwise*

【佞笑】sinister smile

【佞幸】[书] ① gain favor by flattering ② a sycophantic official

拧 [方] pigheaded; stubborn:这孩子脾气真~,没人能拦得住他。*He is as stubborn as a mule; no one can stop him.*
see also níng; nǐng

泞 [书] muddy; miry

【泞泥】muddy; miry:她从雨中走进来,鞋子~,衣服湿透。*She came in from the rain, in muddy boots and wet clothes.*

niū

妞 girl:他家有两个~。*They've got two girls.*

【妞妞】[方] little girl

【妞子】[方] little girl

niú

牛[1] ① ox; cattle:公~ *bull* /母~ *cow* /奶~ *milch cow* /小~ *calf* ② stubborn; arrogant:~脾气 *obstinacy* /~气 *arrogant* ③ the ninth of the twenty-eight constellations into which the celestial sphere was divided in ancient Chinese astronomy ④ (Niú) a surname

牛² newton (used as a unit of force)

【牛鼻子】nose of an ox — the key point; the crucial element:牵牛要牵~。*We must lead an ox by the halter.* /弄清词义古今异同的情况,就牵住了学习古代汉语的~。*You will have the key to ancient Chinese studying when you understand the difference in the senses of the words.*

【牛脖子】[方] stubbornness; obstinacy; bullheadedness

【牛车】oxcart

【牛刀小试】a master hand's first small display

【牛痘】①【医】cowpox ② smallpox pustule; vaccine pustule:接种~ *give smallpox vaccination*

【牛痘苗】bovine vaccine

【牛轭】yoke

【牛犊】calf

【牛顿】① Sir Isaac Newton (1642-1727), English mathematician and physicist ②【物】newton; the SI unit of force

【牛鬼蛇神】monsters and demons — forces of evil; evil people of all descriptions; bad elements

【牛黄】【药】bezoar

【牛角】ox horn

【牛角尖】the tip of a horn — an insignificant or insoluble problem

【牛津】Oxford, a city in Britain: ~人 *Oxonian* / ~运动 *Oxford movement; Tractarianism*

【牛劲】① great strength; tremendous effort:他费了~才把大石头从马路上挪开。*He had to exert all his strength to move the big rock away from the road.* ② stubbornness; obstinacy; tenacity:这小伙子有股子~。*The lad is strong-willed.*

【牛栏】cattle pen; ox fence

【牛郎星】【天】Altair

【牛郎织女】①【天】the Altair and the Vega ② the Herd-boy and the Weaving-girl — husband and wife forced to live in different parts

【牛马】① oxen and horses — beasts of burden ② slave:过~生活 *lead a dog's life* /当~ *work as a slave*

【牛毛】ox hair — dense and thin: ~细雨 *drizzle* / 多如~ *as many as the hairs on an ox — countless*

【牛虻】【动】gadfly

【牛奶】milk:全脂~ *whole milk* /脱脂~ *defatted milk* /无菌~ *germ-free milk* /鲜~ *fresh milk* /消毒~ *pasteurized milk* / ~壶 *milk jug* / ~商 *milkman*

【牛腩】[方] sirloin; tenderloin

【牛排】beefsteak; steak:嫩~ *tenderloin steak* /生~ *raw steak*

【牛皮】① cowhide; oxhide ② tough; tensile; pliable: ~糖 *a sticky candy* ③ bragging:吹~ *brag; talk big* / ~大王 *braggart* /他老是吹~说自己足球踢得多么好。*He constantly brags about how well he plays football.*

【牛皮鞭】cowhide; cowskin

【牛皮癣】【医】psoriasis

【牛皮纸】kraft paper; kraft

【牛脾气】stubbornness; obstinacy; bullheadedness:她的~真气人。*Her obstinacy was really irritating.* /他是个~,这使得他很难相处。*He had a stubborn streak in him, which made him a very difficult person to live with.*

【牛气】[方] arrogant; overbearing:人们都说那个小伙子太~了,他自己好像还不知道。*People all think that guy is too arrogant, but he himself seems to be unaware of it.*

【牛肉】beef:带骨~ *bone-in beef* /烤~ *baked beef* / ~干 *dried beef* / ~汤 *beef broth*

【牛舍】cowhouse; cowshed

【牛虱】ox louse

【牛市】bull market — a rising market

【牛头马面】Ox Head and Horse Face, the two demon attendants of the King of Hell — vile people of all kinds

【牛蛙】【动】bullfrog

【牛尾】oxtail: ~汤 *oxtail soup*

【牛瘟】cattle plague

【牛仔裤】jeans

【牛仔帽】cowboy hat

【牛仔装】jeans wear

niǔ

扭 ① turn round; turn away:看到老师在前面,他马上~过身往回跑。*Seeing his teacher before him, he immediately turned round and ran back.* ② twist; wrench: ~断一根枯枝 *twist off a dead branch* /他用力~开了门。*He wrenched the door open.* ③ sprain; wrench: ~了手腕 *sprain one's wrist* /他跌倒时~了踝骨。*He sprained his ankle when he fell.* ④ roll; swing:她走路一~一~的。*She walks with a rolling gait.* ⑤ seize; grapple with:出纳员与抢劫银行犯~在了一起,但后来还是被摔倒在地上。*The cashier grappled with the bank robber, but was thrown to the ground.* ⑥ crooked:歪歪~~ *twisted*

【扭摆】(of one's body) sway:她~着腰慢步走来。*She walked over swaying her hips.*

【扭秤】torsion balance; torsion scale

【扭打】wrestle; grapple; tussle:他们~了起来,没人能把他们分开。*They were grappling with each other and no one could draw them asunder.*

【扭搭】[口] walk with a swing; have a rolling gait

【扭动】sway or twist from side to side; swing:一阵微风让树枝~起来。*A light wind was making the branches sway.*

【扭股儿糖】Chinese maltose candy, usually with two or three strands twisted together; twisted malt candy

【扭结】twist together; tangle up:她紧张地把手绢在手里~。*She twisted the handkerchief in her hands nervously.*

【扭矩】【物】torque; twisting moment

【扭亏为盈】make up the deficits and get surpluses

【扭捏】① walk affectedly with a swing; mincing:扭扭捏捏地走 *take mincing steps* ② be affectedly bashful:她~了大半天才说出一句话来。*She affected embarrassment for quite a while before she muttered out one sentence.*

【扭曲】① twist; contort:听到了关于他的传言,他气得脸都~了。*His face was contorted with rage when he heard the rumour about him.* ② distort:那家报纸对国际事件的刊载有时是被~的。*Those newspaper accounts of international affairs are sometimes distorted.*

【扭伤】strain; wrench:他~了腰。*He sprained his waist.*

【扭送】seize and send:把违法犯罪分子~公安部门 *seize the offender and hand him over to the public security authorities*

【扭头】① turn one's head away:她扭过头去,不再理我了。*She turned her head away and cut me dead.* ② turn round:她二话没说,~就走。*She turned and walked away without saying another word.*

【扭转】① turn round:猎人~身子,老虎扑了个空。*The hunter turned round and escaped from the tiger's catch.* ② turn back; reverse: ~乾坤 *reverse the course of events* / ~局面 *bring a radical change to the situation*

狃 be bound by; be constrained by: ~于习俗 *be bound by the custom*

忸

【忸怩】blushing; bashful:不要这么~,告诉我你怎么想的。*Don't be bashful; tell me what you think about it.*

【忸怩作态】behave coyly; be affectedly shy:我建议她使用女性的魅力,~。*I suggested that she use her feminine charm and behave coyly.*

纽 ① handle; knob:离合~ *clutch knob* / 锁~ *cage knob* ② button: ~扣 *button* ③ tie; bond ④ little fruit

【纽带】link; tie; bond:友谊的~ *ties of friendship* / 道路是城乡交流的~。*The roads are the links between the urban and rural areas.*

【纽扣】button:钉~ *sew on a button* / 扣上~ *button up one's coat*

【纽约】New York

【纽约时报】The New York Times

【纽约证券交易所】New York Stock Exchange (NYSE): ~指数 *New York Stock Exchange Index; NYSE index*

【纽子】[口] button

杻 (in ancient books) a kind of tree

niù

拗 stubborn; obstinate; difficult:他的脾气很~。*He is a stubborn fellow.*
see also ǎo; ào

【拗不过】be unable to dissuade; fail to talk sb out of doing sth:我~他,只好答应和他一起去了。*I had to agree to go with him since all my efforts to dissuade him failed.*

【拗劲】stubborn spirit; obstinacy:瞧他那~,够烦人的! *Such a stubborn man! We are all disturbed.*

nóng

农 ① agriculture; farming:他在家务~。*He is doing the farming in his hometown.* ② peasant; farmer:贫~ *poor farmer* ③ (Nóng) a surname

【农产品】agricultural products; farm products: ~的市场价格在上涨。*The market price for agricultural products is rising.*

【农场】farm:国营~ *state farm* / ~经营 *farm management*

【农村】rural area; countryside; village: ~经济 *rural economy* / ~人口 *rural population* / 我来自~。*I come from the countryside.*

【农贷】agricultural loan (or credit)

【农夫】[旧] farmer; peasant

【农妇】[旧] peasant woman

【农副产品】agricultural and side-line products

【农副业】agriculture and side-line occupations

【农耕】farming:不事~ *not conducting farming work*

【农工】① farmers and workers ② agricultural worker

【农工党】Chinese Peasants' and Workers' Democratic Party

【农行】Agricultural Bank of China

【农户】peasant household

【农活】farming work; field work

【农机】agricultural machinery; farming machinery

【农家】peasant family

【农家肥料】farm manure; farmyard manure

【农具】farm tools; farm implements

【农垦】agricultural cultivation: ~企业 *state-owned land reclamation enterprise*

【农历】the lunar calendar

【农林】farming and forestry

【农林牧副渔】agriculture, forestry, animal husbandry, sideline production and fishery (formerly regarded as the main industries of the rural areas)

【农忙】busy farming season

【农贸市场】a market of farm produce

【农民】peasant; farmer

【农民工】peasant labourer

【农民起义】peasant uprising; peasant revolt

【农民战争】peasant war

【农牧区】agricultural and pastoral areas; farming and stock breeding areas

【农奴】serf

【农奴主】serf owner

【农情】situation of agricultural production

【农人】farmer
【农桑】farming and sericulture
【农舍】farmhouse; cottage
【农时】farming season:别误了~。*Don't miss the farming season.*
【农事】farm work; farming: ~年 *crop year*; *farming year*
【农田】farmland; cropland; cultivated land; field: ~水利 *irrigation and water conservancy*
【农隙】[书] slack season (in farming)
【农闲】slack season (in farming): ~时,村里人大多数会到城里打工。*In the slack season, most of the people in the village will go to the city to find some work to do.*
【农械】farm chemical apparatus
【农学】agronomy: ~家 *agronomist*
【农谚】farmer's proverb; farmer's saying
【农药】agricultural chemical; farm chemical:喷~ *spray chemicals*
【农业】agriculture; farming:合作~ *cooperative agriculture* /集约灌溉~ *intensive irrigated agriculture* /计划性~ *planned agriculture* /世界~ *world agriculture* /自由~ *free agriculture*
【农艺】agronomy: ~师 *agronomist*
【农艺学】agronomy
【农用】agricultural; for agriculture's purpose
【农庄】farm:集体~ *collective farm*; *kolkhoz*
【农作物】crops; agronomic crop

侬 ①[方] you ②[旧] I ③(Nóng) a surname

哝

【哝哝】murmur; talk in undertones:她在姐姐耳边~了半天。*She murmured to her sister's ear for quite a while.*

浓 ① dense; thick; concentrated: ~茶 *strong tea* /~硫酸 *concentrated sulphuric acid* /~烟 *thick smoke* ②(of degree or extent) great; strong; deep: ~翠 *dark green* /~香 *heavy fragrance* /兴趣很~ *take great interest in*
【浓淡】shade; deep or light: ~相宜 *just the right shade of color*
【浓度】density; thickness; strength; consistency; concentration:当量~ *equivalent concentration* /不同~的酒精 *alcohol of different strengths*
【浓厚】① dense; thick: ~的云层 *thick clouds* ② strong; pronounced: ~的地方色彩 *pronounced local color* ③ deep; great:孩子们对足球的兴趣十分~。*These children have deep interest in playing football.*
【浓烈】strong; thick; heavy:会议充满着~的火药味。*The meeting smelt strongly of gunpowder.*
【浓眉】heavy eyebrows; beetle-browed
【浓密】dense; thick: ~的头发 *thick hair* /小径旁的玫瑰长得很~。*The rose grew thick along the path.*
【浓缩】concentrate; enrich:苹果~汁 *concentrated apple juice*; *apple juice concentrate* /~牛肉汁 *beef extract* /~溶液 *concentrated solution* /~食品 *concentrated food* /~饲料 *concentrated feed* /~铀 *enriched uranium*
【浓香】① of rich flavour; of strong aroma:茅台酒味~。*Maotai has a rich aroma.* ② strong fragrance; rich aroma:咖啡的~让我在一家小咖啡馆前停下脚步。*An aroma of coffee made me stop in front of a small café.*
【浓艳】rich and gaudy:色彩~ *in gaudy colors*
【浓郁】① strong; rich: ~的花香扑鼻而来。*The strong fragrance of the flowers assailed the nostrils.* ② dense; thick: ~的松林 *a dense pine forest* ③ strong; rich:感情~ *strong feelings* /色彩~ *rich colours* ④ great; deep: ~的兴趣 *deep interest*
【浓重】dense; thick; strong:他说话带有~的南方口音。*He speaks with a strong southern accent.* /山谷中的雾越发~了。*The fog in the valley is getting thicker still.*
【浓妆艳抹】richly attired and heavily made-up

脓 pus
【脓包】①【医】pustule ② a worthless fellow; good-for-nothing
【脓肿】【医】abscess:急性~ *acute abscess* /慢性~ *chronic abscess* /结核性~ *tuberculous abscess* /一颗病牙可使牙床~。*A bad tooth may cause an abscess on the gums.*

秾 [书] luxuriant; gorgeously blooming; resplendent: ~艳的玫瑰 *resplendent roses*

nòng

弄 ① play with; fool with:小孩儿爱~沙子。*Children like playing with sand.* /他又~鸽子去了。*He's out playing with the doves again.* ② do; manage; make; handle:这些事总得~清楚才行。*These matters should be clarified.* /他写东西,常常~到半夜才睡。*He's been diligently writing and seldom gone to bed until midnight.* /我~不好,你帮我~一~吧。*I cannot handle this properly. Please help me with it.* /~得不好,就会前功尽弃。*If things are not properly handled, our labour will be totally lost.* /别把衣服~脏了。*Don't get your coat dirty.* ③ get; fetch: ~点钱来 *make some money* /附近有家酒店,你去~点吃的来。*There is a restaurant nearby; Please go and get some food back.* ④ play: ~手段 *play tricks*
see also lòng
【弄潮】[书] paddle in the sea
【弄潮儿】① boat racer or swimmer on the tide ② a courageous person who rides on the tide
【弄臣】[书] favourite courtier of the emperor
【弄错】be mistaken; make a mistake:不会~。*There is no mistake about it.*
【弄鬼】[方] play tricks; hatch a plot:多半是他在~,否则我们早就能完成任务了。*Very possibly he was the barrier, otherwise we would have accom-*

N

plished the mission.

【弄假成真】what was said in fun is fulfilled in earnest; pretending may become truth

【弄僵】land sth in an impasse; bring to a deadlock; stalemate; come to a dead end:讨论结束了,因为很明显情况已经~了。*The discussion ended when it was clear that a stalemate had been reached.*

【弄巧成拙】go for wool and come home shorn — overreach oneself; outsmart oneself; suffer from being too smart:她本来想为班级做点好事,没想到~了。*She had got very good intention to do something for her class, but it turned out to be that she overreached herself.*

【弄权】manipulate power for personal ends; usurp power; play politics

【弄手脚】play tricks

【弄虚作假】practise fraud; employ trickery; resort to deceit:为了逃税,有的公司就~。*Some companies resort to fraud in order to evade tax.* /她靠~得以晋升。*She won her promotion by deceit.*

【弄糟】spoil; muddle; make a mess of:不要把事情~。*Don't make a mess of it; Don't spoil the whole thing.*

nú

奴 ① bondservant; slave ②[旧] I; me (self-reference of girls) ③ enslave

【奴婢】slave girl; maidservant

【奴才】① bond servant ② flunkey; lackey:一脸~相 *a servile look*

【奴化】enslave:~政策 *policy of enslavement*

【奴家】[旧] I; me (self-reference of girls)

【奴隶】slave:~贩子 *slave trader* /很久以前,许多黑人作为~被掠到美洲。*A long time ago, many black people were taken to America as slaves.*

【奴仆】servant; lackey

【奴态】servility

【奴性】servility; slavishness

【奴颜婢膝】subservient; servile; slavish:他们的~让我恶心。*Their slavish obedience disgusted me.* /他们对外~,甘心卖国求荣。*They bow and scrape like slaves to the foreigners, willing to sell the country for their own benefits.*

【奴颜媚骨】bowing and scraping; sycophancy and obsequiousness:我真看不惯他在权贵面前~的样子。*I am sick of his obsequiousness in the face of the great.*

【奴役】enslave; keep in bondage:反抗~和压迫 *resist enslavement and oppression*

驽 ①[书] an inferior horse; jade; screw: ② (of a person) dull; incompetent; stupid; incapable:~才 *a dullard*

【驽钝】[书] dull; stupid

【驽马】[书] an inferior horse; jade

nǔ

努 ① put forth (strength); exert (effort):~劲儿 *put forth all one's strength* ② protrude; bulge:~着嘴 *purse one's lips* ③[方] injure oneself through overexertion:小心点,别~着。*Be careful and don't strain yourself.*

【努力】make great efforts; work hard; try hard; exert oneself; take the trouble to:~学习 *study hard* /请放心,我们一定尽最大~把他的病治好。*Please feel assured that we will do our utmost to cure him.* /大家再努一把力。*Let's make still greater efforts.*

【努嘴】pout one's lips as a signal:她向我努努嘴,示意我先出去。*She pouted her lips at me, hinting that I go out first.*

弩 crossbow:万~齐发。*All the arrows are shot at the same time.*

【弩弓】crossbow (in ancient times)

【弩箭】arrows shot from a crossbow; crossbow arrows

nù

怒 ① anger; rage; fury:~骂 *curse furiously* /他为一点小事就发~。*He would fly into a fury for the slightest reason.* ② forceful; vigorous; dynamic

【怒不可遏】be hopping mad; boil with anger; furious; incensed; be beside oneself with rage:他~,因为他的命令没有被执行。*He was incensed to find that his orders had not been carried out.* /他为这个决定几小时~。*He raged for hours at the decision.*

【怒潮】① angry tide; raging tide ② (tidal) bore; surging tide

【怒叱】rebuke; brawl; snarl; blast; berate:他~仆人的愚蠢。*He raged at the servant's stupidity.*

【怒斥】angrily rebuke; indignantly denounce:他的老板~他的疏忽。*His boss rebuked him strongly for his negligence.* /我最好马上走。如果又回家晚了,太太一定会~我。*I'd better go right now; my wife will give me hell if I am late home again.*

【怒冲冲】in a rage; furiously

【怒发冲冠】bristle with anger; be in a towering rage

【怒放】in full bloom:~的牡丹一直都是富贵的象征。*Peony in full bloom has been the symbol of fortune.*

【怒号】howl; roar:狂风~。*The wind howled in the woods.*

【怒吼】roar; howl:雄狮~。*The lion gave a loud roar.*

【怒火】flames of fury; fury

【怒火中烧】be burning with anger (or wrath):她~。*She was in one of her uncontrollable furies.*

【怒骂】shout angry abuse; swear angrily: 她的头撞到门框上,~了一声。*She bumped her head in the doorway and swore angrily.*
【怒目】① stare with anger: ~而视 *look angrily at*; *glare at* ② glaring eyes; a fierce stare
【怒气】anger; rage; fury: 那消息使他充满~和怨恨。*That news filled him with anger and resentment.*
【怒气冲天】mad with fury; boiling with rage: 我不借给他钱,他立刻~。*He flew into a fury when I refused to lend him any money.*
【怒容】an angry look
【怒色】an angry look: 面有~ *look angry*
【怒视】glare at; glower at; scowl at: 她~着凶残的敌人。*She glared at the ruthless enemy.* /他紧握拳头,~着我。*He stared at me with his fist clenched.*
【怒涛】furious billows: ~澎湃 *billows raging with great fury*
【怒形于色】betray one's anger; look angry; be black in the face

nǚ

女 ① woman; female: ~学生 *girl student* / ~教师 *woman teacher* / ~工 *female worker*/ ~运动员 *a woman athlete* ② daughter; girl: 儿~ *son and daughter* ③ the tenth of the twenty-eight constellations
【女厕所】① women's lavatory (or toilet) ② Ladies; Women
【女儿】daughter; girl: 她有两个很漂亮的~。*She has two very beautiful daughters.*
【女扮男装】girl or woman disguised as boy or man
【女傧相】bride's maid
【女单】【体】women's singles
【女低音】【音】alto
【女儿】daughter; girl
【女儿墙】【建】parapet (of wall)
【女方】the bride's side; the wife's side
【女高音】【音】soprano
【女歌手】chanteuse
【女工】① woman worker; female worker ② woman servant ③ needlework: 她的~做得很好。*She is good at needlework.*
【女公子】your daughter; daughter of distinguished parents
【女红】[书] needlework
【女冠】[书] female Taoist priest
【女孩儿】① girl: 一个叫爱丽丝的~ *a girl named Alice* ② daughter
【女皇】empress
【女家】the bride's side; the wife's family
【女监】jail for female prisoners
【女角】female character
【女眷】the womenfolk of a family
【女篮】【体】① women's basketball team ② women's basketball game
【女郎】a young woman; maiden; girl
【女里女气】(of a man) look or act like a woman
【女伶】[旧] actress
【女流】[贬] the weaker sex; women: ~之辈 *weaker sex*
【女排】【体】① women's volleyball team ② women's volleyball game
【女朋友】girlfriend
【女气】effeminate: 她很好强,缺少~。*She is very aggressive and lacking in femininity.* /他的举止非常~。*His gestures are very effeminate.*
【女权】women's rights: ~运动 *women's movement*; *feminist movement*
【女权主义】feminism: ~者 *feminist* / ~给了许多妇女更多的工作机会。*Feminism has given many women new opportunities at work.*
【女人】(nǚrén) woman; womenfolk
【女人】(nǚren) [旧] wife
【女色】woman's beauty; feminine charms; woman as a sexual partner: 贪恋~ *be given to woman's charms*
【女神】goddess
【女生】① girl student; woman student; schoolgirl ② [方] girl; woman
【女声】【音】female voice
【女史】[旧] a woman of learning; a woman scholar
【女士】lady; madam: ~们,先生们,晚上好! *Good evening. Ladies and Gentlemen!* /请给这位~来杯啤酒。*Please bring this lady a glass of beer.*
【女式】of women's style: ~手表 *women's watch*
【女双】【体】women's doubles
【女同胞】female compatriot; woman
【女娲】a Chinese goddess who is said to create human beings and patched up the sky
【女王】queen: 英~伊丽莎白二世 *Queen Elizabeth II*
【女巫】witch; sorceress
【女相】(of a man) features of a woman
【女性】① the female sex: ~人口 *the female population* / ~比男性成熟的时间早。*Females reach maturity earlier than males.* ② woman: 新~ *modern woman*
【女婿】① son-in-law ② [方] husband
【女优】[旧] actress
【女招待】[旧] waitress
【女中音】【音】mezzo-soprano
【女主人】hostess
【女子】woman; female: 未婚~ *a single woman* / ~单打 *women's singles*
【女足】women's football

nuǎn

暖 ① warm; genial: 天气转~了。*It's getting warm.* ② warm up; warm: 烤火~手 *warm one's hands at the fire*
【暖房】① go to the bridal chamber on the eve of a wedding to offer congratulations ② call on sb who has moved into a new home to congratulate him ③ [方] greenhouse; hothouse: ~栽培 *glass cul-*

ture / ~里有好多热带植物。*There are quite a lot of tropical plants in the greenhouse.*
【暖锋】【气】warm front
【暖阁】a partitioned-off section of a large room with a heating stove
【暖烘烘】nice and warm：冬天从外面进来，觉得屋子里~的。*Coming into the house in winter, you may feel the warmth inside.*
【暖乎乎】warm; nice and warm：他的话让我们心里~的。*His words warmed our hearts.*
【暖壶】① thermos flask; thermos bottle ② a teapot or waterpot with a cosy ③ a metal or earthen hot-water bottle
【暖和】① warm; nice and warm：北京一过三月，天气就~了。*It gets warm in Beijing after March.* ② warm up; warm：热饮料使他~起来。*The hot drink warmed him.* /到火旁边来~一下。*Come near the fire and warm yourself up.*
【暖流】①【气】warm current ② warm feeling：听了她温和的言语，一股~涌上我的心头。*Her soothing words left me with a glow in my heart.*
【暖瓶】thermos flask; thermos bottle
【暖气】① steam or water heat; central heating ② central heating equipment：~管 *radiator* / ~装置 *central heating system*; *heating installation* ③ a warm gas; warm air
【暖融融】nice and warm; warm and cosy：炉火驱走了寒气，整个房间~的。*The fire has driven the cold away and made the entire room warm and cosy.*
【暖色】warm colour
【暖水瓶】thermos flask; thermos bottle
【暖袖】lengthened section of the sleeves of a padded coat to keep the hands warm in winter
【暖洋洋】warm：~的春风 *a warm spring breeze* /几句话说得我心里~的。*These words warmed my heart.*

nüè

疟 malaria; ague
【疟疾】malaria; ague：恶性~ *pernicious malaria*
【疟蚊】anopheles
虐 ① cruel; tyrannical ②［书］disaster
【虐待】maltreat; ill-treat; torture; abuse：~儿童 *maltreatment of children* / ~俘虏 *maltreat the prisoners of war* /备受~的妻子 *a much abused wife* /她不忍见动物受~。*She could not bear to see animals treated cruelly.*
【虐杀】cause sb's death by maltreatment; kill sb with maltreatment
【虐政】tyrannical government; tyranny

nuó

挪 move; shift：请把桌子~开。*Please move the table away.*
【挪动】move; shift：往前~几步。*Move a few steps forward.*
【挪借】borrow money for a short time; get a short-term loan
【挪威】Norway：~语 *Norwegian* (*language*) / ~人 *Norwegian*
【挪窝儿】［方］move to another place：天气一冷，人们都不愿意~了。*As the weather turns cold, people would rather remain at one place.*
【挪移】［方］① borrow money for a short time ② move; shift
【挪用】① divert (funds)：专款专用，不得~。*Funds should be earmarked for certain purposes and no diversion is allowed.* ② misappropriate; embezzle; peculate：~公款 *peculate the public funds* / ~抚恤金 *embezzle the pension fund* /他被判~公款罪。*He was found guilty of embezzlement.*

nuò

诺 ① promise：一~千金 *a promise that will be kept* ② "yes"：唯唯~~ *obsequious*
【诺贝尔】Noble Alfred, Swedish chemist and engineer who invented dynamite (1866) and bequeathed his fortune to institute the Nobel Prizes
【诺贝尔奖】Nobel Prize
【诺言】promise：他不遵守~，没来看我。*He broke his promise and did not come to see me.* /记住要履行~。*Remember to carry out your promise.*
喏 ［方］used to call attention to sth：~，这不就是你的那把雨伞？*There! Isn't that umbrella yours?*
懦 cowardly; faint-hearted：怯~ *timid and faint-hearted*
【懦夫】coward; craven：他说我是个~，因为我不愿去打架。*He called me a coward, because I wouldn't fight.*
【懦弱】cowardly; weak; spineless：~无能 *be weak and useless* /我们认为他很~，因为他不愿承认曾经坐过牢。*We thought it was cowardly of him no to admit he had once been to prison.*
糯 glutinous (cereal)
【糯稻】glutinous rice
【糯米】polished glutinous rice
【糯米粉】glutinous rice flour
【糯米酒】glutinous rice wine
【糯米纸】edible paper-like film made of starch, used as inner package for confectionary

O

ō

噢 expressing understanding：～，现在七点了。*Oh, it's seven o'clock now.* /～，我明白了。*Oh, I see.*

ó

哦 what; expressing doubt：～，你已经回来了？*What! Have you already come back?* /～，是这样吗？*What! Is that so?*
see also ò

ǒ

嚄 expressing surprise：～，你也跟我去呀？*What? Will you come with me?* /～，真是个了不起的母亲！*Oh, what a great mother!*

ò

哦 indicating realization or understanding：～，我忘了寄信了。*Ah, I forgot to mail the letter.*
see also ó

ōu

讴 ① sing ② folk songs
【讴歌】［书］sing the praises of; celebrate in song：他在他的新诗中～教师。*He sang high praise for the teachers in his new poem.*
【讴吟】［书］sing; chant：高声～ *sing loudly*

沤 water bubble; froth：浮～ *bubbles on water*
see also òu

瓯[1] ①［方］cup; bowl：茶～ *tea cup* /酒～ *wine cup*

瓯[2] another name for Wenzhou, Zhejiang Province
【瓯绣】Wenzhou embroidery
【瓯穴】pot hole; giant kettle
【瓯子】［方］bowl; cup

欧[1] （Ōu）a surname

欧[2] Europe：北～ *northern Europe* /南～ *southern Europe*

欧[3] 【电】ohm
【欧共体】European Community
【欧化】Europeanize; westernize
【欧美】occident：～人 *occidental*
【欧盟】European Union（EU）：～理事会 *European Union Council*
【欧姆】【电】ohm：～定律 *Ohm's law* /～表 *ohmmeter* /～线圈 *resistance winding* /比声～ *specific acoustical ohm* /标准～ *standard ohm* /倒～ *reciprocal ohm* /国际～ *international ohm*
【欧佩克】OPEC（Organization of Petroleum Exporting Countries）
【欧芹】【植】parsley
【欧亚大陆】Eurasia
【欧元】euro：～区 *euro area*
【欧洲】Europe：～电视网 *Eurovision* /～共同市场 *Euromarket* /～货币 *Eurocurrency*; *Euromoney* /～人 *European*

殴 hit; beat：斗～ *bustup*
【殴毙】beat to death
【殴打】beat; hit：互相～ *exchange blows*
【殴斗】have a fist fight
【殴杀】beat to death
【殴伤】beat and injure; contuse

鸥 gull：海～ *sea gull*

嘔 ① expressing realization, surprise or praise：～，我知道了。*Oh, I see.* /～，你比我年龄小呀！*Oh, you are younger than I am.* ②［象］*the sound of crying, etc.*：他急得～～直哭。*He was so worried that he burst into tears.*

ǒu

呕 vomit; throw up; bring up：令人作～ *make one sick; nauseating; feel like vomiting* /婴儿进食后～出一些奶是很正常的。*It is normal for a* *baby to bring up some milk after feeding.*

【呕吐】vomit; puke; retch:我吃了变质的菜后~了。*I vomited after eating the bad dish.* /味道太糟糕了,我简直要~。*It tasted so awful that I almost threw up.* /难闻的气味让我剧烈~。*The terrible smell made me retch violently.*

【呕心】exert one's utmost: ~之作 *works embodying the author's utmost exertion*

【呕心沥血】work one's heart out; strain one's heart and mind; spend one's blood:他对待工作可谓~。*He exerts his utmost effort at his work.*

【呕血】【医】spitting blood; hematemesis

偶[1] image; idol:木~ *wooden figure*; *puppet*

偶[2] ① even number:无独有~ *not come singly but in pairs* ② mate; spouse:丧~ *lose one's husband* (*or wife*)

偶[3] by chance; occasionally: ~闻 *learn by chance*

【偶对称】even symmetry

【偶尔】① occasionally; casually; sometimes; once in a while:我~10点以前睡觉。*I sometimes go to bed before ten o'clock.* /他~从书堆里抬起头来看看窗外。*He occasionally looked up from his pile of books and stared out of the window.* /要是我们能够~见面就好了。*It would be nice if we could see each other once in a while.* ② accidental; fortuitous:只有他父亲~的缺席能让他自由地谈话。*Only his father's fortuitous absence enabled him to speak freely.*

【偶发】accidental; fortuitous; by chance: ~事件 *incident*; *a chance occurrence*

【偶方】prescription with ingredients even in number

【偶函数】【数】even function

【偶合】coincidence; as it happens:你要去非洲?真是一个令人惊讶的~,我也要去! *You're going to Africa? What an amazing coincidence. So am I!*

【偶或】once in a while; occasionally; sometimes:我~去看望他。*I go to visit him once in a while.*

【偶极】【物】dipole: ~电位 *dipole potential* / ~分布 *doublet distribution* / ~流体 *dipolar fluid* / ~取向 *dipole orientation*

【偶然】① by chance; by accident; accidentally; fortuitously: ~事件 *accident* /绝非~ *by no means fortuitous* /我找这本书已经很长时间了,然后~在一家我家附近的书店里发现了它。*I'd been looking for this book for a long time and I found it quite by chance in a bookstore near my home.* /这次~的事件使他立志从政。*This fortuitous event made him decide on a career in politics.* ② sometimes; occasionally: ~情况下我不吃早饭,但通常我会吃面包、喝咖啡。*I sometimes have no breakfast at all but generally I have some bread and coffee.* /他现在搬到了另一个区,我只是~能看到他。*He has moved to another district, so I only see him very occasionally.*

【偶人】clay or wooden figure

【偶数】even number: ~行 *even number line* / ~校验 *even check* / ~页 *even page*

【偶蹄】cloot; clootie; cloven hoof: ~动物 *artiodactyl*

【偶像】idol; image: ~崇拜 *idolatry* / ~崇拜者 *idolater* /他是许多青年人崇拜的~。*He is the idol of many young people.*

【偶遇】meet by chance:我在火车上~一个老朋友。*By chance I met an old friend on the train.*

耦 [书] two people plough side by side

【耦合】【物】coupling

【耦合道】coupled channel: ~理论 *coupled channel theory*

【耦合器】coupler

【耦合线圈】coupling coil

【耦合运动】coupled motions

【耦合指数】index of coupling

藕 lotus root

【藕断丝连】Even when the lotus root breaks, the clinging fibres remain — apparently severed, but actually connected

【藕粉】lotus root starch

【藕荷】pale pinkish purple

【藕灰】pale pinkish grey

【藕节儿】joints of a lotus root

【藕色】pale pinkish grey

òu

沤 steep; soak

see also ōu

【沤肥】① make compost ② wet compost

【沤麻】【纺】ret flax or hemp

【沤田】water-logged land

怄 [方] ① be annoyed; be irritated:他还~着呢。*He is still sulky.* ② upset; annoy; irritate:他总是用话~我。*He often says something to annoy me.*

【怄气】be sulky and difficult:你们应该好好谈谈,不要总是~。*You two should have a heart-to-heart talk instead of being upset and sulky.*

P

pā

炮 ［方］① (of food) mashed; pulpy：饭煮～了。*The rice is overcooked.* ② become soft：他已经～下来了，不像原来那么强硬。*His attitude has softened, not as tough as before.*

趴 ① lie on one's stomach; lie prone：～在地上射击 *lie on one's stomach and shoot* /病人～在床上。*The patient was lying prone on the bed.* ② bend over; lean on：他～在桌子上画图。*He was bending over the desk drawing.*

【趴伏】lie on one's stomach; lie prone：他静静地～在床上。*He was lying on his stomach on the bed quiet.*

【趴架】(of house, structure, etc.) collapse; topple down

【趴窝】［方］① (of a hen) be sitting ② (of a domestic animal) lie on the ground ready to give birth ③ (of a person) be broken in health; be exhausted：他累得～了。*He is exhausted from overwork.* ④ (of a machine, vehicle, etc.) break down; be out of order：公共汽车～了，我们只好走回家。*The bus is out of order, and we have to go back home on foot.*

派

see also pài

【派司】［方］① pass：他向门卫出示了～。*He showed his pass to the guard.* ② get through; pass：他的四级考试～了。*He passed the band-4 examination.*

啪 ［象］the sound of clapping, slapping, a gunshot, etc.：～的一声把书丢在桌子上。*Slap the book down on the table.*

【啪嚓】［象］the sound of sth crashing, hitting the ground, etc.：～一声，盘子摔碎了。*The plate dropped and broke with a crash.*

【啪嗒】［象］patter：～～的脚步声 *pattering footsteps* /雨点～～地敲打着玻璃。*Rain pattered steadily against the glass.*

【啪唧】［象］patter：那孩子光着脚～～地跑。*The boy pattered along barefoot.*

【啪啦】［象］crash：沉重的箱子～一声掉到他的头上。*The heavy box landed crash on his head.*

葩 ［书］flower：奇～ *very beautiful flowers*

pá

扒 ① gather together; rake up：～草 *rake up the grass* ② ［方］scratch ③ steal; pilfer：～口袋 *pick sb's pocket* ④ stew; braise：～猪头 *braised pig-head* /～羊肉 *stewed mutton*

see also bā

【扒糕】buckwheat cake

【扒拉】［方］take a swallow of rice：他～了两口饭就跑出去和别的小孩儿玩了。*He just swallowed some rice and went out to play with other children.*

【扒犁】［方］sledge; sleigh

【扒窃】pick people's pockets; steal; pilfer：他从餐馆～了一个盘子。*He filched a plate from the restaurant.* /有人在公共汽车上～了我的钱包。*Someone lifted my wallet on the bus.*

【扒手】pickpocket

爬 ① crawl; creep：婴孩向他妈妈～去。*The baby crawled towards his mother.* /乌龟以极其缓慢的速度～着。*The tortoise crept along at an agonizingly slow speed.* ② climb; clamber：～树 *climb a tree* /～山 *climb a mountain* ③ sit up; stand up：他一早就～起来出去了。*He got up very early and went out.*

【爬虫】reptile

【爬杆】jungle gym

【爬竿】【体】① pole-climbing ② climbing pole

【爬灰】［方］scratching in the ashes — have illicit relations with one's daughter-in-law

【爬犁】［方］sledge; sleigh

【爬坡】grade climbing：～能力 *grade ability*

【爬山虎】①【植】Boston ivy ②［方］a sedan chair or litter to carry a person up a mountain

【爬升】(of an airplane, rocket, etc.) ascend; climb; gain altitude：～角 *angle of climb*

【爬绳】【体】rope climbing

【爬梯】① staircase ② vertical ladder

【爬行】① crawl; creep：虫类和蛇～。*Worms and snakes crawl.* ② work or act slowly by following the convention：～思想 mentality of trailing behind others

【爬行动物】reptile

【爬泳】【体】the crawl; crawl stroke

耙 ① rake：木～ *wooden rake* ② make smooth with a rake; rake; harrow：～地 *rake the soil level*

【耙子】rake, a kind of farming tool used to gather grains or level soil

P

筢 bamboo or iron rake

【筢子】bamboo or iron rake

pà

帕[1] handkerchief

帕[2] 【物】Pa（Pameasure），unit for intensity of pressure

【帕金森氏症】Parkinson's disease

【帕米尔高原】Pamirs

【帕斯卡】① Pascal （Blaise，1623—1662），a French mathematician and physical scientist ②【物】Pascal（Pa）：～定理 *Pascal's theorem* /～定律 *Pascal's law* /～三角 *Pascal triangle*

怕 ① fear；dread：老鼠～猫。*A mouse is afraid of a cat.* /我～去看牙医。*I dread a visit to the dentist.* /他是天不～地不～的。*Tom is a fool for danger.* ② I'm afraid；perhaps；maybe：他～不来了。*I'm afraid that he won't come.* /这个瓜～有十几斤吧。*This melon weighs more than ten jin，I suppose.*

【怕老婆】under the thumb of one's wife：他～出了名。*He is well-known as a henpecked man.*

【怕人】① dread to meet people；be shy；be timid：～的鸟 *a shy bird* /这个小女孩很～。*The little girl is shy in the presence of strangers.* ② frightening；terrifying；horrible：昨天在这里发生了一起～的事故。*There was a horrible accident here yesterday.* / 多么～的经历啊！*What a terrifying experience!*

【怕苦】be afraid of hardship：～怎么能成功呢？*How can you succeed if you are afraid of difficulties?*

【怕生】（of a child） be shy in the presence of strangers：孩子太小，～。*The child is so little that he becomes shy when he sees a stranger.*

【怕事】be afraid of getting into trouble；timid；coward：胆小～ *timid and overcautious* /她太胆小～，甚至不敢反抗他的无礼行为。*She was far too timid to protest at his unreasonable behaviour.*

【怕水】water funk

【怕死】fear death：～鬼 *coward* /革命不～，～不革命。*Revolutionaries don't fear death；cowards don't make revolution.*

【怕羞】coy；shy；bashful；sheepish：她唱歌～。*She is coy of singing.* / 这个小孩很～，躲在他妈妈后面。*The child was shy and hid behind his mother.*

pāi

拍 ① beat；tap lightly；clap；pat；slap：～球 *bounce a ball* /～手 *clap one's hands* /我轻～他的肩膀。*I patted him on the shoulder.* / 他轻轻地～了～儿子的背。*He clapped his son on the back.* ② racket；bat：苍蝇～儿 *flyswatter* /网球～儿 *tennis racket* ③ rhythm in a tune：这首歌每节有四～。*The song has four beats in a bar.* /"这首歌是几～的？""4/4 拍的。""*What time is the song in?*" "*It's s in four-four time.*" ④ take a photograph；shoot a film：～照片 *take a picture* ⑤ send（a telegraph；etc.）：～电报 *send a telegram* /～电影 *shoot a film* ⑥ flatter：能吹会～ *be good at boasting and toadying*

【拍案】strike（or bang）the table（in anger，surprise，admiration，etc.）：～大怒 *strike the table in great anger* / ～而起 *smite the table and rise to one's feet in anger* /他气得连连～。*He was enraged and struck the table for several times.*

【拍案叫绝】thump the table and shout "bravo!"；bang one's fist on the table，uttering "Superb"

【拍巴掌】［口］clap one's hands

【拍板】① beat time with clappers ② rap the gavel：～成交 *strike a bargain* ③ have the final say；make a final decision：这件事得由厂长～。*It has to be finally decided by the leader of the factory.* ④【音】clappers

【拍打】① pat；slap；clap；tap：雨水～着窗户。*Rain is slapping against the window.* /老师用尺子～课桌，直到全班学生开始听他说话。*The teacher tapped the desk with a ruler until the whole class was listening.* ② flap：～翅膀 *clap wings*

【拍档】［方］① cooperate；collaborate ② partner；cooperator：最佳～ *best partner*

【拍发】send（a telegram）：～电报 *dispatch a telegram*

【拍符号】flip symbol

【拍号】【音】time signature

【拍花】［旧］kidnap children

【拍击】lash；lap：波浪～着光滑的峭壁。*The waves lashed the smooth cliffs.*

【拍马】［口］lick one's boots；flatter；curry favour with sb；suck up to：他很反感互相～。*He dislikes complimenting with one another.*

【拍马屁】［口］lick sb's boots；flatter；soft-soap；play up to；fawn on：拍皇帝马屁的贵族们 *nobles truckling to the king* /他靠～得到晋升。*He bootlicked to get a promotion.* /他拍她马屁，她说什么他都同意。*He sucks up to her by agreeing with everything she says.*

【拍卖】① auction：把这幅画～掉 *auction the picture off；put the picture up to auction* /公开～ *public auction* /国际～ *international auction* /假～ *mock auction* /竞争性～ *competitive auctions* /零星～ *piecemeal auction* /强制～ *forced auction* /外汇～ *exchange auctions* ② selling off goods at reduced prices；sale：削价～ *a Dutch auction*

【拍卖行】auction house

【拍卖价格】auction price

【拍卖市场】auction market

【拍频】beat frequency；beat：～干扰 *beat interference* / ～率 *beat frequency* / ～振幅 *amplitude of beat*

【拍摄】take（a picture）；shoot：～全景 *shoot a*

full view / ~角度 shooting angle / 这个故事片~得挺快。This story was shot quickly.

【拍手】clap one's hands; applaud: ~称快 clap in high glee / 教师使劲地~让全班同学注意听讲。The teacher clapped hard to attract the class's attention.

【拍拖】[方] courting: 公园里有几对~的男女。There were several courting couples in the park.

【拍戏】film a play: 一群人正在我们学校~。Several people are filming in our school.

【拍胸脯】[口] vouch for; chest thumping: 我能~担保他的诚实。I vouch for his honesty.

【拍音】beat tone

【拍掌】clap one's hands: 他们随着音乐的节拍~。They clapped their hands in time to the music.

【拍照】take a picture; have a picture taken; photograph: 不准! No camera! / 请您为我~。Please take a picture for me.

【拍纸簿】writing pad; pad

【拍子】① bat; racket: 羽毛球~ badminton racket ②【音】beat; time: 二~ duple time / 三~ triple time / 四~ quadruple time / ~记号 time signature

pái

排[1] ① arrange; put in order: ~座位 arrange seats / 词典里的词是按字母顺序编~的。In a dictionary the words are arranged in alphabetical order. / 我们出发前必须把事情安~好。We must order our affairs well before we leave. ② row; line: 我坐在后~。I sit in the back row. ③【军】platoon, a military unit higher than squad in rank: ~长 a platoon leader ④[量] row; line: 一~椅子 a row of chairs / 一~石头 a line of stones / 一~书 a row of books ⑤ rehearse; practise a play: 彩~ dress rehearsal

排[2] raft; bridge: 木~ timber raft / 平~ flat raft

排[3] ① exclude; push; expel: 把水~出去 drain the water away / 力~众议 prevail over all dissenting views ② push: ~闼直入 push the door open and go straight in

排[4] pie: 苹果~ apple pie

see also pǎi

【排班】arrange an order according to class and grade

【排版】【印】composing; type setting: 打字机~ typewriter composition / 机器~ machine composition / 计算机~ computer typesetting / 计算机输出~ computer-output typesetting / 自动~ automatic typesetting

【排比】【语】parallelism; parallel construction

【排笔】broad brush made of a row of pen-shaped brushes (for painting, picture colouring, etc.)

【排便】defecate

【排摈】[书] exclude; squeeze out: 黑人投票者在选举中遭到~。Black voters are excluded from the elections.

【排布】【语】arrangement; distribution

【排叉儿】a thin and crisp deep-fried dough

【排杈儿】a kind of low and narrow partition of a room

【排场】① ostentation and extravagance; pomp and ceremony; show: 讲~已经成为了一种风气。It has become a common practice to go for ostentation and extravagance. ② ostentatious and extravagant; sumptuous; lavish: 她可真~,花掉了所有的钱来买衣服。She's really extravagant — she spends all her money on clothes. / 这个家庭举行了一次~的宴会。The family gave a sumptuous banquet. ③[方] respectable; dignified; graceful: 他有一份~的工作。He's got a graceful job.

【排斥】repel; exclude; get rid of: 静电~ electrostatic repulsion / 交换~ exchange repulsion / ~异己 discriminate against those who hold different views; exclude outsiders / 他们~十八岁以下的人加入俱乐部。They excluded people under 18 from joining the club. / 邻居们都~那一家人。The family were ostracized by the neighbourhood.

【排出】discharge; exhaust; transpire: ~蒸汽的孔 a vent discharging steam

【排除】get rid of; remove; eliminate; rule out; exclude: ~障碍 remove an obstacle / ~万难 surmount every difficulty; conquer all obstacles / 我们不能~有些人会对这些规定熟视无睹。We can't exclude the possibility that someone will turn a blind eye to the regulations.

【排挡】gear (of a car, tractor, etc.): ~间距 meros

【排档】[方] street or market stalls: 大~ a street restaurant

【排队】form a line; line up; queue up: ~上车 queue up for a bus / ~等候 wait in a line (or queue) / 在售票处~ queue up at the box office / 成批~ bulk queue / 调度~ scheduling queue / 信息~ message queue / 循环~ cyclic queues / 输出~ output queue / 优先~ priority queues

【排筏】bamboo or timber raft

【排放】① arrange in order: 桌子上~着几本书。Several books are arranged in order on the table. ② drain; discharge; let out; drain off: ~脏水 drain off the dirty water ③ (of animal) ovulate

【排废】waste discharge

【排粪】defecation; bowl movement

【排风】air exhaust

【排风扇】ventilating fan

【排骨】spareribs; pork ribs: 红烧~ pork ribs braised in soy sauce / 糖醋~ sweet and sour spareribs

【排灌】irrigation and drainage: ~船 irrigating vessel / ~网 irrigation and drainage network

【排汗】perspire

【排行】seniority among brothers and sisters: ~第二 number two in the rank

【排行榜】ranking list: 畅销书~ the best-seller list

【排号】① [口] get a number according to one's place in a line ② [方] queue; line up
【排洪】discharge floodwater
【排击】repel and attack
【排机】gang saw; frame saw
【排挤】push aside; discriminate against; crowd out; squeeze out; elbow out: 互相～ *each trying to squeeze the other out* /他感到公司里的同事总是把他～到计划之外。*He felt that his colleagues in the company were always leaving him out of their plans.*
【排检】arrange and refer to: ～法 *method of arrangement and retrieval*
【排解】① mediate; reconcile; arbitrate: ～纠纷 *mediate a dispute* /我在这对夫妻之间～。*I mediated between the wife and husband.* ② divert oneself from; dispel; assuage: 我无法～她的忧愁。*I can do nothing to assuage her grief.* /他坚定的话～了我的疑虑。*His firm words dispelled my doubts.*
【排锯】【机】gang saw; frame saw
【排涝】drain flooded (or waterlogged) fields: ～补种 *plant again after the water recedes*
【排雷】【军】removal of mines; mine clearance
【排立】stand in row
【排练】rehearse: ～节目 *have a rehearsal* /他昨晚～了他的讲演。*He rehearsed his speech last night.*
【排量】【机】displacement; output volume
【排列】① arrange; range; put in order: ～成行 *arrange in a line* /按字母顺序～ *arrange in alphabetical order* /按数字序列～数字 *arranging figures in numerical sequence* /圆形～的巨石被称为巨石阵。*The circular arrangement of megaliths is called Stonehenge.* ②【数】permutation: ～矩阵 *permutation matrix*
【排律】long poem in regulated verse
【排卵】【生理】ovulate: ～期 *period of ovulation*
【排名】sequence of names: 我在期中考试中～第一。*I came first in the mid-term examination.*
【排难解纷】mediate a dispute; iron out the differences between the disputants
【排尿】urinate; micturate; uresis: ～反射 *urinary reflex* / ～困难 *dysuria* / ～障碍 *urination disorder*
【排偶】【语】parallelism and antithesis
【排气】【机】exhaust; air-out; exit gas: ～泵 *exhaust pump* / ～风箱 *exhaust blower*
【排气管】escape-pipe; gas vent: ～道 *discharge duct*
【排遣】assuage; divert oneself (from loneliness or boredom); relieve: ～忧愁 *dispel melancholy* /没有什么能～他刻骨铭心的痛苦。*Nothing shall assuage his unforgotten pain.*
【排枪】volley of rifle fire
【排球】volleyball: 打～ *play volleyball*
【排热】heat extraction; heat rejection
【排乳】milk ejection
【排山倒海】topple the mountains and overturn the seas; overcome with an irresistible force; great in momentum and irresistible: 以～之势 *with the momentum of an avalanche; with irresistible force* /他的讲演以～的声势征服了听众。*The audience was overwhelmed by his powerful speech.*
【排射】fire a volley of guns or cannons
【排水】drain off water; drain away water: 水管～不畅。*The water pipe doesn't discharge freely.* /土地必须～以适合某些作物。*Land must be well drained for some crops.*
【排他性】exclusiveness: ～条约 *exclusive treaty*
【排闼】push: ～直入 *push the door open and go straight in*
【排头】the person at the head of a procession or formation; file leader
【排头兵】the soldier at the head of a formation — pacesetter; pacemaker: 他是学习上的～。*He takes the lead in studying.*
【排外】exclusive; antiforeign; xenophobic: 盲目～ *blind opposition to everything foreign*
【排外主义】exclusivism; exclusionism; antiforeignism
【排尾】the last person in a row or procession; the person at the end of a row, etc.
【排污】drain contamination; blow off: ～管 *drain; cesspipe*
【排戏】rehearse a play
【排险】eliminate a danger; remove a dangerous situation
【排泄】① drain (rainwater, waste water, etc.) ② excrete; let off
【排泄器官】excretory organ
【排泄物】egesta; excrement; excreta; excretion; ordure; rejection
【排泄药】【药】evacuant
【排揎】[方] scold: 你别～我,这是你的错。*Don't scold me; it's your fault.*
【排烟】exhaust fume
【排演】rehearse: 导演让我们把这几场戏反复～,直到尽善尽美。*The director made us rehearse the scenes over and over again, until they were perfect.*
【排椅】seats in a row
【排印】typesetting and printing
【排忧解难】relieve sb of worries and help solve his problems
【排运】rafting timber down the river
【排中律】【医】the law of excluded middle
【排钟】【音】chimes; tubular bells
【排字】composing; typesetting: ～工人 *typesetter; compositor* / ～机 *composing machine* / ～架 *composing frame* / ～盘 *composing stick*

徘

【徘徊】① pace up and down; walk to and fro: 他在屋子里～。*He paced up and down in the room.* ② hesitate; waver: ～歧路 *hesitate at the crossroads* ③ fluctuate; be in flux; keep changing: 他的情绪在兴奋与恐惧之间～不定。*His feelings fluctuated between excitement and fear.*

P

牌 ① board：布告～ *notice board* /招～ *shop sign*; *signboard* ② plate; tablet：车～ *number plate* /门～ *doorplate* ③ brand; trademark：名～儿产品 *goods of a well-known brand* ④ cards：打～ *play cards* /桥～ *bridge* ⑤ the tunes of *ci* or *qu*：词～ *title of a ci tune*

【牌匾】an inscribed board (fixed to a wall or the lintel of a door); tablet; plaque

【牌额】horizontal inscribed board

【牌坊】memorial archway (or gateway)

【牌号】① the name of a shop; shop sign ② trademark; brand：水泥～ *cement brand*

【牌价】① list price; posted price ② (market) quotation：股票～ *type prices* /官方～ *official market* /外汇～ *foreign exchange quotation*

【牌局】gambling game at dominoes, cards, etc.

【牌楼】① pailou, decorated archway ② temporary ceremonial gateway

【牌示】[旧] public notice; bulletin

【牌位】memorial tablet (used in ancestral worship)

【牌照】license plate; license tag; license：自行车～ *bicycle number plate*

【牌照税】licence tax

【牌子】① board：布告～ *bulletin board* ② plate; sign ③ brand; trademark：你喜欢什么～的肥皂？ *What brand of soap do you like?* ④title of a *ci* or *qu* tune

【牌子曲】a folk art form

pǎi

迫

see also pò

【迫击炮】【军】mortar

排 [方] stretch with a shoe last

see also pái

【排子车】a large handcart

pài

派 ① group; school; faction：帮～ *faction* /学～ *school of thought* /老～贵族 *aristocrats of the old school* /荷兰画～ *the Dutch school of painting* /威尼斯画～ *the Venetian school of painters* ② style; manner; air：气～ *bearing* ③[方] stylish; graceful：他长得真有～。*He is very handsome.* ④[量]：两～意见 *two different views* /形势一～大好。*The situation is excellent.* /那人讲的话纯属一～胡言。*What the man said was sheer nonsense.* ⑤[书] branch of a river ⑥ assign; send; dispatch; appoint：请求速～两个连上前线 *request the dispatch of two companies to the front* /她～人去请医生。*She sent for the doctor.* ⑦ apportion; assign：～粮～款 *levy grain and money* ⑧ censure：别～他的不是，该怪我。*Don't blame it on him, but on me.*

see also pā

【派别】group; sect; school; faction：～之争 *factional strife* /党内对立的～ *rival factions within the party* /他属于一个严格的宗教～，该派别不允许抽烟、喝酒。*He belongs to a strict religious sect that forbids smoking and drinking alcohol.*

【派兵遣将】dispatch troops and send generals

【派不是】put (or lay) the blame on sb：你不能派任何人的不是。*You can't blame anyone.*

【派差】send on a public errand：我妈妈给我～，她想让我去买点食物。*My mother asked me to go on an errand — she wanted me to buy some food.*

【派出机构】agency

【派出所】local police station; police substation：～所长 *police inspector*

【派对】[方] party：生日～ *birthday party*

【派购】(of the state) prescribe purchases (of farm produce); fix quantities for state purchase

【派活】assign sb a task (usu. manual work)：你还没给他～呢。*You still haven't assigned him any work.*

【派款】[旧] impose levies of money; levy

【派令】order of appointment

【派遣】send; dispatch：～使者 *dispatch a messenger* /～部队去中东 *send troops into the Middle East* /他们～最好的记者去报道这次事件。*They sent their best reporter to cover the event.* /地震过后，红十字～了医疗队到灾区。*After the earthquake, the Red Cross sent in medical teams to the disaster area.*

【派遣国】the sending state; the accrediting state

【派生】derive：拉丁语～出法语。*French words are derived from Latin.*

【派生词】【语】derivative

【派头】style; manner; bearing：～大 *have great style* /文雅的～ *gentle manners* /他具有挺拔的军人～。*He has the erect bearing of a soldier.* /她用优雅的～弥补了容貌上的缺陷。*What she lacked in looks she made up for with elegant style.*

【派系】groups or factions (within a political party, etc.)：学术～ *academic clique* /～纠纷几乎使该党分裂解体。*Faction almost broke up the party.*

【派性】factionalism

【派用场】put to use; turn to account：我以前学的手艺今天居然派上了用场。*It's amazing that the craft I picked up in former years is put to use today.*

【派驻】① post; station：～重兵 *station massive forces* ② accredit to：他被～里斯本任大使。*He was accredited ambassador to Lisbon.*

pān

攀 ① climb; clamber; scale：～上顶峰 *scale the peak* /～着绳子往上爬 *climb up a rope hand over hand* ② cling; grasp; hold：～住绳子 *cling to the rope* /你能不能找到手～得住的地方？*Can you find a hold for your hands?* ③ seek connections in high places：高～ *make friends or claim ties of kinship with people of a higher social position* ④ involve; implicate

【攀比】compare unrealistically; compete with the higher: ~现象 *comparing phenomenon*

【攀缠】climb and intertwine; get entangled:他的头发~在一起。*His hair is all in a tangle.*

【攀扯】implicate (sb in a crime); involve:他~进一桩抢劫案。*He is implicated in the robbery.*

【攀登】climb; clamber; scale: ~科学技术新高峰 *scale new heights of science and technology* /这是一次艰难的~。*It is a difficult climb.*

【攀登架】jungle gym (a playground apparatus for children to climb on)

【攀附】① (of a plant) climb (a support) ② seek connections with (powerful people): ~权贵 *attach oneself to persons in power*

【攀高枝儿】make friends or forge kinship with powerful or influential people; go to a better place

【攀话】[方] engage in small talk

【攀交】make friends or associate with people of a higher social position

【攀龙附凤】attach oneself to dragons and phoenixes — play up to people of power and influence; fawn upon the influential people

【攀爬】climb; shinny; speel:猴子善于~。*Monkeys climb well.*

【攀亲】① claim kinship ② [方] arrange a match; seek a match

【攀亲道故】claim ties of blood or friendship

【攀谈】engage in small talk; have a chat; chitchat:我们通过~互相了解。*We get acquainted with each other by chatting.*

【攀诬】implicate and frame: ~好人 *implicate the innocent*

【攀缘】① climb; clamber:常春藤~在墙上。*Ivy climbed up along the walls.* ② climb the social ladder through pull

【攀越】climb up and over; scale; surmount: ~一座山 *surmount a hill*

【攀折】pull down and break off (twigs, etc.):请勿~花木。*Please don't pick the flowers.*

【攀枝花】① silk cotton; kapok ② a city in southwest China

pán

爿 ① [方] thin piece of chopped bamboo or wood:柴~ *chopped firewood* ② [量] used for land:一~田 *a piece of land* ③ [量] used for shops, etc.:一~店 *a shop*

胖 [书] healthy and happy:心宽体~ *carefree and contented*
see also pàng

般 [书] joy; happiness
see also bān; bō

盘 ① [古] a kind of basin ② tray; dish; plate:一~米饭 *a dish of rice* /茶~儿 *tea tray* /一~食物 *a plate of food* /圆~ *circular tray* ③ sth shaped like a plate, tray, etc.:秤~ *the pan of a steelyard* /算~ *abacus* /棋~ *chessboard* /罗~ *compass* ④ current price; market quotation: 开~ *open quotations* /收~ *close quotations* ⑤ wind; coil: ~山公路 *winding mountain highway* /蛇~在树上。*The snake coiled round the tree.* ⑥ build with bricks: ~炕 *build a kang* ⑦ examine; check; investigate: ~账 *check accounts* ⑧ sell; transfer:招~ *put up one's shop for sale* /受~ *take over* ⑨ transfer; move; carry: 他们正在~家具。*They are moving the furniture.* ⑩ [量]:一~棋 *a game of chess* /一~磁带 *a tape* ⑪ (Pán) a surname

【盘剥】practise usury; exploit; flay:重利~ *exorbitant usury* / ~穷人 *to exploit the poor*

【盘驳】interrogate and refute

【盘查】interrogate and examine: ~可疑的人 *examine a suspicious person*

【盘缠】① coil; wind ② [口] money for the journey; travelling expenses:她把~给丢了。*She lost all her travelling funds.*

【盘车】barring; jigger; jolly: ~机 *turning engine*

【盘秤】a steelyard with a pan

【盘存】take inventory (or stock):定期~ *period inventory* /年底~ *take inventory at the end of a year*

【盘错】[书] intricate; intertwining

【盘道】winding paths; bends

【盘点】check; make an inventory of; draw up an inventory: ~存货 *take stocks; take inventory*

【盘店】transfer a business; sell one's bankrupt business:他已经把店盘给我了。*He has sold his shop to me.*

【盘费】[口] money needed for a journey; travelling expenses

【盘杠子】[口] exercise on a horizontal bar

【盘根错节】with twisted roots and gnarled branches — complicated and difficult to deal with; deep-rooted:这些人的关系~,我根本弄不明白。*The relations among those people are very complicated and I am quite confusing.*

【盘根问底】get to the heart of a matter; inquire deeply into sth:他什么事都~,很烦人! *He always tries to get to the bottom of everything, which is really irritating.*

【盘亘】[书] (of mountains) extend; interlocked with each other:森林~数百英里。*The mountains stretch for hundreds of miles.*

【盘古】Pan Gu, creator of the universe in Chinese mythology

【盘桓】① [书] pace up and down; linger; stay: ~数日 *stay for a few days in a place* /冬天~不去。*Winter lingered.* /我们在杭州~了几天,游览了各处名胜。*We spent a few days sightseeing in Hangzhou.* ② wind; coil:炊烟~直上天空。*The smoke from kitchen chimneys coiled up into the sky.* ③ wind round and round; spiral up or down:这个想法一直~脑际。*I kept thinking about it.*

【盘货】take an inventory of stock on hand; take stock

【盘获】seize; capture information by means of interrogation

【盘缴】①［方］running or operating expenditure: 他家人多，～大。*His big family requires large running expenditure.* ② travelling expenses

【盘诘】［书］cross-examine; interrogate; question: 警察仔细～我盗窃发生当日的行动。*I was interrogated at length about my activities and movements on the day of the theft.* /第一个律师～了被告达两个小时。*The first lawyer cross-examined the defendant for two hours.*

【盘结】coil around

【盘究】persistent inquiry; cross-examine and investigate: 尽管他声称自己是无罪的，但是他的罪行在～下逐渐变得明显。*Although he claimed he was innocent his guilt became clear under cross-examination and investigation.*

【盘踞】illegally or forcibly occupy; be entrenched: ～于此的敌人 *the enemy who are entrenched here*

【盘考】conduct interrogation and inquiry

【盘空】circle or whirl in the air: 当风大起来时，尘土和沙子～飞舞。*Dust and sand were whirling around in the air as the wind began to get stronger.*

【盘库】make an inventory of goods in a warehouse

【盘量】calculate; figure: 她～着造房子的费用。*She is calculating the cost of building a house.*

【盘马弯弓】ride round and round bending one's bow — assume an imposing posture but take no action

【盘弄】play with; fiddle with; fondle: 小孩儿在～一支笔。*The child is fiddling with a pen.*

【盘曲】［书］winding; curling; tortuous: 一条～的道路 *a tortuous road*

【盘绕】twine; coil; spiral; wind: 葡萄藤～在棚架上。*The vine wound about the trellis.* / 这条小路～在小山上。*The path twisted up the hill.*

【盘山】winding up a mountain: ～公路 *winding mountain road*

【盘算】calculate; consider; figure; plan: 他心中～着一件事。*He weighed a matter in his mind.* /他～算着旅行费用。*He calculated the cost of the journey.*

【盘损】adjustment debit

【盘梯】winding staircase; spiral staircase

【盘头】① a kind of woman's hair-style ②［旧］turban

【盘腿】cross one's legs

【盘陀】［书］① rocky; rugged; rough; jagged ② winding; twisting

【盘问】question; cross-examine; interrogate; carry out door-to-door inquiries: 他详细～了我。*He cross-examined me in detail.* / 警察～囚犯。*The police questioned the prisoner.*

【盘膝】［书］cross one's legs: ～而坐 *sit with one's legs crossed*

【盘香】incense coil

【盘旋】① spiral; circle; wheel; swirl; whirl: 在浪尖～的海鸥 *gulls hovering over the waves*/车队沿山路～而上。*The motorcade spiraled up the mountain.* / 鸟儿在湖面上空～。*The birds were circling around over the lake.* ② linger; stay: 在北京～数日 *stay in Beijing for a few days* ③ think over; consider: 这件事在我头脑中～很久了。*I have considered the matter for a long time.*

【盘牙】［方］molar

【盘羊】【动】argali

【盘运】carry; transport

【盘账】check (or audit, examine) accounts; audit accounts

【盘折】meandering; zigzagging; tortuous: 汽车沿着～的小路上了山。*The car climbed the winding road up into the hills.* /这座城市是一座由大门、城墙和～的小巷构成的迷宫。*The city was a maze of gates and walls and tortuous alleyways.*

【盘子】① tray; plate; dish: 桌子上有几个～。*There are some plates on the table.* ②［旧］the market quotation

磐

［书］huge rock

【磐石】huge rock; bedrock: ～之安 *as firm as a rock*

【磐石之固】as solid as a rock

蹒

【蹒跚】walk lamely; waddle; limp; stagger; totter; lurch; blunder: 那个醉汉～而行。*The drunken man lurched along.* / 老人～而行。*The old man staggered along.*

蟠

coil; curl: ～伏 *lie curled up*

【蟠结】coil; twine

【蟠龙】curled-up dragon

【蟠木】twisted tree

【蟠桃】① flat peach ② peach of immortality in Chinese mythology: ～会 *meeting of immortals at which peaches of longevity are offered*

pàn

判

① distinguish; separate ② obviously (different) ③ judge; grade: 评～ *pass judgement (on sth or sb)* ④ sentence; condemn: ～三年徒刑 *be sentenced to three years' imprisonment*

【判案】【律】decide a case; make a judgement

【判辨】distinguish; differentiate; tell sth apart; tell the difference: ～善恶 *distinguish good from evil* / 我们吃的是蛇，但是味道像鸡，我无法～这其中的不同。*We ate snake and it tasted like chicken; I couldn't tell the difference.*

【判别】differentiate; distinguish: ～是非 *distinguish between right and wrong* /这两幅画一模一样，我无法～哪个是原作，哪个是摹品。*The two paintings are so similar that I cannot distinguish between the original and the copy.*

【判处】sentence (sb) to; condemn (sb) to:他被~终身监禁。*He was sentenced to life in prison.* /杀人犯被~死刑。*The murderer was sentenced to death.*

【判词】①【律】court verdict ② conclusion; judgement

【判定】① judge; decide; determine:从一句话里很难~她的意图。*It is difficult to judge what she meant from her single sentence.* ②【机】decision: ~元件 *decision element; decision gate*

【判断】①【逻】judgement:迅速~ *be swift with one's judgement* ② judge; decide; determine:我们不应根据外表来~一个人。*We should not judge a person by his appearance.*

【判断词】【语】a defining word, such as 是, used as a link word to form a compound predicate with a noun or pronoun

【判断力】sense; the ability to judge correctly; judgement:司机对于方位有很强的~。*A driver has a good sense of locality.* /教师需要有较强的~。*Teachers need to have good judgement.*

【判罚】(in a football or basketball match) decision by a referee to penalize an offender; penalize:他们的球队因故意拖延时间而被~。*Their team was penalized for intentionally wasting time.* /他在下半场踢人犯规,被~退场。*He was ordered off in the second half for kicking another player.*

【判分】give a mark; grade:你的卷子判错分了吗? *Do you think your paper has been wrongly graded?*

【判据】① evidence ②【物】criterion

【判决】①【律】judgement; court decision: ~一个案子 *adjudicate on a case* / ~是犯人有罪。*The verdict was that the prisoner was guilty.* /法庭~他无罪。*He was adjudged to be innocent by the court.* ② decision; judgement:比赛中运动员要服从裁判的~。*An athlete should obey the umpire's judgement in a match.*

【判决令】adjudication order

【判决录】judgement book

【判决书】【律】court verdict; written judgement

【判例】【律】legal (or judicial) precedent; prejudication:国际法~ *cases in international law*

【判例案件】test case

【判例法】case law

【判明】clearly distinguish; ascertain; discover; determine; establish: ~真伪 *ascertain whether sth is genuine* /案件扑朔迷离,警方仍然无法~真相。*The case remains a mystery; the police have not been able to ascertain the true facts.* /他们还没有~事故发生的原因。*They haven't yet established the cause of the accident.*

【判然】marked (or striking) difference; obvious:两个世界~不同。*The two worlds are markedly different.*

【判若两人】have become quite a different person; judge a person to be two different persons; no longer be one's old self:她对我们的态度与从前~。*She treated us in an entirely different way.*

【判若云泥】as great a distance as between the sky and the earth; there's a world of difference between; poles apart:他们的社会地位~。*They are just worlds apart in their social positions.*

【判刑】pass a sentence on; sentence sb to; decree a punishment:判死刑 *pass a death sentence on sb*

【判罪】declare guilty; convict:因盗窃~ *convict sb of theft* /量刑~ *pass judgement and mete out punishment* /陪审团判被告犯有杀人罪。*The jury convicted the defendant of manslaughter.*

盼 ① expect; hope for; long for:期~ *yearn for; long for* ② look:左顾右~ *look right and left; look around*

【盼顾】look around; look left and right

【盼念】look forward to; long to see; be anxious to:我~知道这件事的结果。*I am eager to know the result of it.*

【盼头】hope; sth hoped for and likely to happen; good prospects:这事有~了。*The business is looking hopeful now.*

【盼望】hope for; look forward to:我~早日见到你。*I look forward to seeing you soon.* /我~今年能赚点钱。*I expect to make a small profit this year.*

叛 betray; rebel:反~ *rebel; revolt* /众~亲离 *be utterly isolated*

【叛变】betray (one's country, party, etc.); turn traitor (or renegade); collaborate:将军~,向敌人透露了重要的军事秘密。*The general betrayed his country by giving away vital military secrets to the enemies.*

【叛兵】mutinous soldiers

【叛党】betray one's party; turn traitor to one's party

【叛匪】rebel bandit

【叛国】betray one's country; commit treason: ~案 *a case of treason* / ~分子 *traitor of one's country* / ~投敌 *betray the country and go over to the enemy* / ~罪 *high treason* /他被起诉犯有~罪,其最高刑罚是死刑。*He was charged with committing treason against the country, of which the maximum penalty is death.*

【叛军】rebel army; rebel forces; insurgent troops: ~袭击了这座城市。*Rebel forces have attacked the city.*

【叛离】betray; desert; defect from: ~祖国 *betray one's country*

【叛乱】rebel; armed rebellion; revolt; mutiny:武装~ *armed rebellion* / ~爆发。*A rebellion broke out.* /农民被逼到~的边缘。*The peasants were brought to the verge of mutiny.* /经常性的~威胁着国王的统治基础。*Regular insurrections threatened the foundations of the king' rule.*

【叛卖】betray; sell out: ~祖国 *betray one's country* /当他认为他们会输掉这场战争时,他~了祖国。*When he thought they would lose the war he turned a traitor to his country.*

【叛逆】① rebel against; revolt against:当国王发现他的兄弟的~行为时,他下令处死他。*When the king found out about his brother's treachery he ordered him to be killed.* ② a person who rebel:这个~应该被判死刑。*The rebel should be sentenced to death.*

P

【叛逃】desert and flee one's country; defect:一个~到以色列的苏联公民 *a Soviet citizen who defected to Israel*

【叛徒】traitor; renegade; collaborator; turncoat:战争结束时,他作为~被执行绞刑。*At the end of the war he was hanged as a traitor.*

畔 ① bank; side:河~ *river bank*; *riverside* /湖~ *the shore of a lake* ② border (of a field)

襻 ① loop for fastening a button:纽~儿 *button loop* ② sth shaped like a button loop or used for a similar purpose:鞋~儿 *shoe strap* ③ fasten; tie:~几针 *mend with a few stitches*

pāng

乓 [象] bang:他~地一声关上门。*He banged the door shut.*

滂 [书] ① (of water) overflowing ② gushing; rushing

【滂湃】(of water) roaring and rushing

【滂沛】[书] ① (of water) surging; rushing ② (of rain) pouring; pelting:大雨~。*It rains cats and dogs.* ③ powerful; of great momentum:文辞~。*The language is forceful.*

【滂沱】torrential; pouring:大雨~ *a torrential downpour*

膀 swell:他的腿~了。*He has got swollen legs.*

see also páng

páng

彷

【彷徨】walk back and forth, not knowing which way to go; hesitate; waver:~歧途 *hesitate at the crossroads* /就在我们~不决之时,别人买下了那辆车。*While we were wavering, somebody else bought the car.*

庞[1] ① huge ② numerous and disordered ③ (Páng) a surname

庞[2] face:面~ face

【庞大】huge; colossal; gigantic; massive; be quite a size:机构~ *unwieldy organization* /~的预算 *huge budget* /一个~的团体 *a gigantic corporation* /象是~的动物。*The elephant is a huge animal.*

【庞然大物】huge monster; colossus; giant; mammoth; a leviathan

【庞杂】numerous and jumbled; unwieldy and complex:机构~ *cumbersome administrative structure* /内容~ *numerous and jumbled in content* /我每天做的工作非常~。*What I do everyday is cumbersome.*

旁 ① side:路~ *the side of the road* /站在一旁 *step aside* ② else; other:你还有~的话要说吗? *Do you want to say something else?* ③ lateral radical of a Chinese character ④ extensive

【旁白】aside (in a play)

【旁边】side; right by:他往~站,好让她过去。*He stepped aside to let her pass.*

【旁薄】boundless; majestic

【旁出】branch out from the side

【旁带】sideband:~振幅 *sideband amplitude*

【旁顾】attend to other matters:无暇~ *be too busy to care for other affairs*

【旁观】look on; be an onlooker:袖手~ *stand by with folded arms* /加入我们吧,别~了。*Join us; Don't just look on.*

【旁观者】spectator; onlooker; bystander:~者都对她的悲惨遭遇表示同情。*The bystanders sympathized with her on her miserable experience.*

【旁观者清】the spectator sees most clearly; the onlooker sees the game best

【旁轨】sidetrack; siding

【旁及】take up or be interested in other things other than the main interest:他专攻文学,~历史。*He studies literature, but also takes up history.*

【旁落】(of power, etc.) pass into others' hands:大权~,她很不甘心。*She is quite indignant about the fact that her power has slipped into others' hands.*

【旁门】side door:他拒绝从~进屋。*He refused to enter the room through the side door.*

【旁门左道】① heretical sect ② heresy; heterodoxy:陷入~ *fall into heresy*

【旁敲侧击】make oblique references; beat about the bush; fool round the stump:有话直接说,不要~。*You can go straight to the point; stop making oblique references.* /我们都不要~了,我们是来谈钱的,不是吗? *Let's not beat about the bush; we're here to talk about money, aren't we?*

【旁人】other people:一定要保密!不要让~知道。*Be sure to keep it secret; Don't make anyone else know it.*

【旁若无人】act as if there was no one else present — self-assured or arrogant; have no regard for others

【旁听】be a visitor at a meeting (in a school class, etc.); attend as a visitor or auditor

【旁听生】auditor

【旁听席】visitors' seats; public gallery

【旁骛】[书] fail to concentrate:他读书的时候能做到心无~。*He can focus all his attention on the books when he reads.*

【旁系】collateral line

【旁系亲属】collateral relatives; collaterals

【旁系血亲】collateral relative by blood

【旁征博引】quote copiously to support one's thesis; cite various authorities; well-provided with supporting material:他在文章中~。*His article is well documented.*

【旁证】circumstantial evidence; collateral evidence

【旁支】collateral branch (of a family)

【旁族】collateral family

P

【旁坐】[书] be punished for being related to sb who has committed an crime

膀

see also pāng

【膀胱】(urinary) bladder

【膀胱炎】【医】cystitis

磅

【磅礴】① boundless; majestic: 气势~ *of great momentum* /气势~的泰山 *the majestic Taishan Mountain* ② fill; permeate: 热情~ *be filled with immense zeal*

螃

【螃蟹】【动】crab

pǎng

嗙 [方] talk big; brag: 开~ *begin boasting*

耪 loosen soil with a hoe: ~地 *hoe the soil*

pàng

胖 fat; plump; stout: 发~ *put on weight* /身材~的人 *a man of stout build* /他的脸开始变~了。*His face began to fill out.* /这家商店卖~人穿的衣服。*This shop sells dresses for the fuller figure.*

see also pán

【胖大海】【药】seed of sterculia with boat-like fruit (*Sterculia scaphigera*)

【胖墩儿】[口] (esp. referring to children) roly-poly; fatty

【胖鼓鼓】fat; plump; full; bulging: ~的脸蛋儿 *chubby cheeks* /他有一张~的脸和一个可爱的笑容。*He has a plump face and a nice smile.*

【胖乎乎】plump; fleshy; chubby; pudgy; full; flabby: 婴儿~的胳膊 *the baby's plump arms* /这个小孩的脸蛋~的。*This child has plump cheeks.* /她~的嘴唇上带着迷人的微笑。*Her full lips were fixed in an attractive smile.*

【胖头鱼】【动】variegated carp; bighead

【胖娃娃】a chubby child: 一个面色健康的~ *a plump healthy-looking child*

【胖子】a fat person; fatty

pāo

抛 ① throw (down); cast (off); hurl: ~球 *throw a ball* /把钓鱼线~入水中 *cast the fishing-line into the water* /她把信件~进废纸篓。*She tossed the letter in the wastebasket.* ② abandon; cast aside: ~开礼俗 *fling propriety away* /他把自己的承诺~到了九霄云外。*He cast his promise to the winds.* /我的建议被~到了一边。*My proposal was thrown out.* ③ expose; reveal; lay bare ④ undersell; dump: ~出股票 *undersell the stock*

【抛费】[方] spoil; waste; ruin: 他习惯于~东西。*He is used to wasting things.*

【抛光】【机】polishing; buffing: 电解~ *electrolytic polishing* /干法~ *dry polishing* /化学~ *chemical polishing* /火~ *flame polishing* /金刚砂~ *diamond polishing*

【抛荒】① (of cultivated land) go out of cultivation; leave (land) uncultivated: ~地 *land that has gone to waste* ② (of study, professional work) neglect; be out of practice: ~学业 *neglect one's studies*

【抛离】abandon; leave behind: ~家乡 *leave one's hometown*

【抛锚】① drop anchor; cast anchor (of vehicles) break down; be out of order: 汽车中途~了。*The car broke down on the way.* ② [方] be suspended; discontinue: 这项工程中途~了。*The project is suspended.*

【抛媚眼】leer; ogle

【抛弃】throw away; abandon; forsake; cast aside; discard: 被~的妻子儿女 *the deserted wife and children* /他有了钱以后,就~了所有曾经给过他帮助的老朋友。*As soon as he became rich he cast aside all his old friends who once gave him some help.*

【抛却】cast aside; throw away: ~成见 *throw away prejudice*

【抛洒】throw; shed; scatter: ~热血 *shed one's blood*

【抛舍】abandon; forsake; cast aside: 他~了金钱和地位,独自去边疆创业。*He abandoned money and position, pioneering a new career in the frontier himself.*

【抛射】project; catapult; launch

【抛售】sell (goods, shares, etc.) in large quantities; undersell; dump: ~价 *closeout rate*

【抛体运动】projectile motion

【抛头颅,洒热血】shed one's blood and lay down one's life (for a just cause)

【抛头露面】[贬] show oneself up much in public; appear in public; make public appearance: 他认为女人不应该~。*He doesn't think women should appear in public.*

【抛物面】【数】paraboloid

【抛物平面】parabolic plane

【抛物曲线】parabolic curve

【抛物线】【数】parabola: 发散~ *divergent parabola* /共焦~ *confocal parabolas* /焦~ *focal parabola* /收敛~ *parabola of convergence* /双曲~ *hyperbolic parabola*

【抛掷】[书] throw; flip; cast: 垂钓者把钓线~了出去。*The angler cast the line.*

【抛砖引玉】throw away a brick in order to get a gem — offer one's (humble) opinions to elicit others' valuable ones; throw a sprat to catch a

P

whale:我先来～吧。*I'll say something so that others may come up with valuable opinions.*

泡[1] ① sth puffy and soft ②［方］spongy; soft:～枣 *spongy dates*

泡[2] ［量］used for excrement and urine:撒一～尿 *make water; urinate; piss*

see also pào

【泡货】［方］light but bulky goods

【泡桐】【植】paulownia; empress tree

【泡子】［方］a small lake

páo

刨 ① dig; excavate; burrow:～坑 *dig a pit (or hole)* /～洞 *burrow a hole* /～土豆 *dig up potatoes* /他正在花园里～地。*He is digging in his garden.* ②［口］deduct; minus; exclude; discount:9～去3等于6。*Nine minus three is six.* /～了我,我们班还有三个人参加了这个聚会。*Three persons in my class joined the party excluding me.*

see also bào

【刨除】exclude; subtract; reduce; take away:记住把这个数字从总数中～。*Remember to take this number away from the total.*

【刨分儿】deduct marks (or points) (for errors in a student's exam):这道题刨了我十分,要不然我就能及格了。*I lost ten marks on this question, or I should have passed the exam.*

【刨根儿】［口］get to the root (or bottom) of the matter:他特别爱～。*He's never satisfied until he gets to the bottom of things.*

【刨根问底】get to the root (or bottom) of things:对于什么事他都从不想当然,而是喜欢～。*He likes to get to the bottom of everything instead of taking things for granted.*

咆 ［书］(of beast) roar; howl

【咆哮】① (of beasts of prey) roar; howl:怒狮的～ *the roar of an angry lion* /狗遇到生人时,就～起来。*The dog howled when it met a stranger.* ② (of humans) roar with rage:愤怒的～ *roars of anger* /他的～声淹没了其他人的声音。*He howled down the others' voices.* ③ (of torrents) roar on; thunder:黄河～。*The Huanghe River roars on.*

狍 【动】roe deer

【狍子】【动】roe deer

庖 ①［书］kitchen ②［书］cook:名～ *famous chef*

【庖厨】［书］① kitchen ② chef; cook

【庖代】［书］do what is sb else's job

【庖丁】［书］cook; butcher

【庖丁解牛】dismember an ox as skillfully as a butcher — magical craftsmanship; do sth with great experience

【庖人】［书］cook

炮 ①【中医】prepare Chinese medicine by roasting it in a hot pan ②［书］bake; roast

see also pào

【炮格】a kind of cruel torture in ancient times

【炮姜】baked ginger

【炮炼】【药】parch and refine medicinal herbs

【炮烙】the hot pillar (an ancient instrument of torture)

【炮炙】roasting and boiling as two means of processing crude drugs

【炮制】①【中医】the process of preparing Chinese medicine, as by parching, baking, steaming, simmering, etc. ②［贬］concoct; cook up:如法～ *act after the same fashion; do what sb else has done*

袍 robe; gown:皮～ *fur gown* /睡～ *sleeping gown* /浴～ *a bath robe* /她身穿红色长～。*She robed in red.*

【袍哥】［旧］(a member of) a reactionary gang in southwest China before liberation

【袍泽】［书］fellow officers:～之谊 *friendship of fellow officers*

【袍罩儿】long gown worn over a robe; overall

【袍子】robe; gown:长～ *long gown; robe*

跑 (of a beast) dig with hoofs or paws

see also pǎo

pǎo

跑 ① run; race:短～ *short-distance running* /10英里赛～ *a 10-mile race* /参加马拉松～ *run in the marathon* /她～完了全程。*She finished the full distance.* ② escape; run away; flee:罪犯越狱逃～了。*The prisoner had escaped.* /她从房子里～到茫茫黑夜中。*She fled from the house into the night.* ③［方］walk; stroll:我们～了两公里。*We walked two kilometres.* ④ run errands; run about; go about:～买卖 *be a commercial traveller* /我要去城里～几件事。*I've got a few errands to do in town.* ⑤ leak; escape:煤气～了。*Gas was escaping.* /房顶漏了,雨～进来了。*The roof leaks; it lets the rain come in.* /报纸叫风给刮～了。*The newspaper was blown off by the wind.* ⑥ evaporate; disappear:瓶子里的汽油～了。*The gasoline in the bottle has evaporated.* ⑦ off; away:狗被吓～了。*The dog is frightened away.* /我们～题了。*We are going off the subject.*

see also páo

【跑表】【体】stopwatch

【跑步】run; march at the double; jog:～前进! *Double time!* /～对人身体有好处。*Jogging is good for people's health.*

【跑车】①【矿】(of a winch for hoisting coal in a mine) accidentally slide down ②［口］(of train conductors) be on the train ③ racing bicycle; racing bike ④【林】a kind of vehicle for conveying logs in a forest; timber carriage

P

【跑哒】[方] run about; rush about:我~了一天了,累死了。*I ran about the whole day; it's really exhausting.*
【跑单帮】make business trips on one's own account; travel around trading on one's own:他是个~的。*He is a self-employed travelling trader.*
【跑刀】【体】race skates
【跑道】①【航】runway (on an airfield) ②【体】track: ~里圈 *inside lane; inner lane* / ~外圈 *outside lane; outer lane*
【跑道儿】[口] run errands:我知道你很忙,可以让他~。*I know you are very busy, so you can ask him to run errands.*
【跑电】【电】leakage of electricity; electric leakage
【跑调】out of tune:他唱歌~。*He sings out of tone.*
【跑光】【摄】(of a film) be exposed to light accidentally
【跑旱船】a kind of folk dance
【跑江湖】wander about, making a living as a street-performer (e.g. an acrobat, fortune-teller, etc.); wander about without settling down anywhere
【跑脚】[方] lead a donkey or mule for hire
【跑街】[方] ① act as a traveling agent or salesman ② a traveling agent or salesman
【跑警报】run for shelter during an air raid
【跑空船】spout hot air
【跑了和尚跑不了庙】[俗] the monk may run away, but the temple can't run with him; the runaway monk can't run away with the temple — a fugitive must belong to some place that can provide clues
【跑龙套】【戏】play an insignificant part; play a bit role; be a utility man:我在这家公司就是~的。*I am just an insignificant member in the company.*
【跑马】① have a ride on a horse; run a horse ② horse racing: ~场 *racecourse; the turf* ③ [方] seminal emission
【跑码头】[旧] travel from port to port as a trader; be a traveling merchant
【跑买卖】be a commercial traveler; travel around doing business:他这几年~挣了不少钱。*He has earned quite a lot of money by travelling around doing business in recent years.*
【跑跑颠颠】bustle about; be on the go:他整天~的。*He is bustling about all day long.*
【跑跑跳跳】skip along; run about:院子里孩子们~的。*The children were running about in the yard.*
【跑情况】[口] run about gathering information
【跑墒】【农】loss of moisture in soil (through evaporation)
【跑堂儿的】[旧] waiter or waitress (in a wineshop, small restaurant, etc.)
【跑题】digress from the subject; stray from the point:不要~。*Don't stray from the point.* /我们已经~了。*We have digressed from the subject under discussion.* /他的评论完全~。*His remark is quite beside the mark.*
【跑腿儿】[口] run errands; do legwork; fetch and carry:我没干多少,就是~。*I didn't do much, just a bit of running around.* /妈妈叫我~去寄一封信。*My mother asked me to go on an errand — she wanted me to mail a letter.*
【跑腿子】[方] bachelor
【跑外】(of employees) travel around handling business; act as a traveling agent or salesman
【跑鞋】【体】track shoes; running shoes
【跑辙】[方] run off the track — digress from the subject; stray from the point

pào

泡 ① bubble:冒~儿 *send up bubbles; rise in bubbles* /气~ *air bubbles* ② sth like a bubble:电灯~ *electric light bulb* ③ soak; steep:用开水~茶 *steep the tea in boiling water* /她把脏衣服~在水里。*She soaked the dirty clothes in water.* ④ dawdle; dillydally:他把时间都~掉了。*He dawdled the hours away.*
see also pāo
【泡包】steam drum
【泡病号】shun work on pretence of illness; sham ill:他~在家呆着呢。*He stayed at home by malingering.*
【泡菜】pickled vegetables; pickles:朝鲜~ *kimchi* /辣~ *pungent pickle* /什锦~ *assorted pickle* /芥末~ *mustard pickle*
【泡茶】make tea
【泡饭】① soak cooked rice in soup or water ② cooked rice reheated in boiling water; gruel (from precooked rice)
【泡服】【药】be taken after being infused in hot water or decoction
【泡钢】【冶】blast steel: ~条 *blister bar*
【泡蘑菇】① temporize; use delaying tactics; stall:不要在工作上~。*Don't loiter over a job.* /她开始跟我~。*She began playing a game of stalling with me.* ② importune; pester:她经常~让我陪她去看电影。*She always pesters me to accompany her to a cinema.*
【泡沫】foam; froth; lather:肥皂~ *soap bubbles* /啤酒倒出来时会起~。*Beer froths when it is poured out.* /如果你在下巴上涂些肥皂~,你就会觉得刮脸容易多了。*If you put some lather on your chin, you'll find it much easier to shave.*
【泡沫橡胶】foam rubber; froth rubber: ~是充满了小气泡的软橡胶。*Foam rubber is soft rubber full of small air-bubbles.*
【泡沫浴】bubble bath
【泡泡纱】【纺】seersucker; taffeta; cloque
【泡泡糖】bubble gum; chewing gum
【泡汤】[方] fall flat; fall through; come to nothing; not come off; do no good; come to grief:他的生意~了,因为银行拒绝贷款给他。*His business came to grief when the bank refused to lend him money.*
【泡细胞】bladder cell

P

【泡漩】whirlpool; water current
【泡影】visionary hope, plan, scheme, etc.; bubble; zilch; in vain; get nowhere:我的希望化为了~。*My hope melted into thin air.* /我们想通过和平谈判解决争端的努力化为了~。*Our attempt to settle the dispute by peaceful negotiations proved fruitless.*
【泡澡】soak one's body in bath water
【泡子】[方] bulb; light bulb

炮 ① big gun; cannon:放~ *fire a gun* /回旋~ *flexible gun* /机关~ *machine cannon* /降旗~ *evening gun* /野战~ *field gun* ② firecrackers:花~ *fireworks and firecrackers* ③ load of explosive:点~ *set off an explosion* ④ *cannon, one of the pieces in Chinese chess*
see also páo

【炮兵】artillery; artillerymen:高射~ *anti-aircraft artillery*
【炮车】gun carriage; gun carrier
【炮床】【军】platform
【炮铳】[方] firecracker:放~ *let off firecrackers*
【炮打灯儿】[方] illuminant firecracker
【炮弹】①(artillery) shell; cannonball:空~ *blank shell* /迫击~ *mortar shell* ②[旧] cannon ball
【炮轰】(of artillery) bombard; shell:我们的城市遭到了~。*Our city was bombarded.*
【炮灰】cannon fodder
【炮火】artillery fire; gunfire:~连天。*Gunfire licks the heavens.*
【炮击】bombard; shell; mortar; gunfire:这座城市被敌人~了。*The city was bombarded by the enemy.*
【炮架】gun carriage; gun mount; bogie
【炮舰】gunboat
【炮口】gun muzzle; cannon's mouth:~焰 *muzzle flash*
【炮楼】【军】blockhouse; gun turret
【炮泥】stemming; tamping plug
【炮捻】blasting fuse
【炮身】barrel; barrel assembly
【炮声】the sound of artillery; thunder of guns:~隆隆。*Cannons boomed.*
【炮手】gunner; artilleryman
【炮塔】gun turret; turret; casemate; chin turret
【炮台】【军】a fortification with built-in cannons; battery
【炮膛】bore (of a big gun):~长度 *length of barrel; length of bore*
【炮艇】gunboat
【炮铜】【军】gunmetal; gun brass:~合金 *gunmetals*
【炮筒】barrel (of a big gun)
【炮筒子】① barrel (of a big gun) ② a person who shoots off his mouth; a hot-headed person
【炮尾】【军】gun breech
【炮位】emplacement; battery
【炮位移】【军】gun displacement
【炮眼】① porthole; embrasure ② blasthole; dynamite hole; borehole
【炮衣】gun cover
【炮战】artillery action (or engagement)
【炮仗】firecracker; cracker:放~ *fire off crackers*
【炮子儿】[口] ① small shell ② bullet
【炮座】gun platform

疱 blister; bleb

【疱锈病】blister rust
【疱疹】【医】① bleb ② herpes:带状~ *herpes zoster; zoster*
【疱疹净】【药】idoxuridine

pēi

呸 pah; bah; pooh:~!胡说八道! *Bah! That's sheer nonsense!*

胚 【生】embryo

【胚斑】germinal spot
【胚板】embryonic plate
【胚根】【植】radicle:~鞘 *coleorhiza*
【胚轨】【动】germ track
【胚孔】【生】blastopore:~痕 *blastopore rest*
【胚囊】【生理】embryo sac; blastocyst:~液 *blastochyle*
【胚培养】embryo culture
【胚球】germ ball
【胚乳】【生理】endosperm; albumen:~培养 *endosperm culture* /~细胞 *albuminous cell*
【胚胎】①【动】embryo:异位~ *adventitious embryo* ② the beginning stage
【胚胎发育】embryonic development
【胚胎培养】embryo culture
【胚胎学】embryology:~家 *embryologist*
【胚胎移植】embryo transfer; embryonic implantation
【胚体】idiosome:~腔 *embryonic coelom* /~营养 *embryotrophy*
【胚细胞】embryonic cell
【胚芽】①【植】plumule; germ; gemmule:~鞘 *coleoptile* ② bud; sprout:矛盾的~ *a contradiction in the bud*
【胚叶】【生】germinal layer
【胚子】①[俗] silkworm embryo ②[喻] breed; strain:坏~ *bad egg; bastard*

péi

陪 ① keep sb company; accompany; show:~病人 *look after a patient* /~客人 *attend a guest* /我~你一起去吧。*Let me go with you.* /她~我去看了医生。*She accompanied me to the doctor's.* ② help; assist
【陪伴】accompany; keep sb company; go along with:老太太要找个人~。*The old lady wants someone to keep her company.* /昨天他~我去看电影。*He accompanied me to the film yesterday.*

【陪绑】①［旧］(of criminals) be taken to the execution ground together with those to be executed as a form of warning ②(of an innocent person) be criticized or punished as an unwilling party：那是他自己的事，我可不想去～。*It's his business, which I don't want to be dragged into.*
【陪餐】accompany the host to entertain guests at a dinner party
【陪衬】① serve as a contrast or foil; set off; match; go with; go together; complement：在白雪的～下，红梅格外鲜艳。*The red plum blossoms stand in vivid contrast against the snow.* /她看上去很美 — 她的白丝裙极好地～了她橄榄色的皮肤。*She looked beautiful — the white silk of her dress complemented her olive skin perfectly.* ② foil; setoff：给主角做～ *play the foil to the chief actor* /她是她丈夫的～。*She is a foil to her husband.*
【陪床】act as an accompany to a hospitalized patient
【陪吊】［旧］a person employed to help with the reception of mourners at a funeral
【陪都】auxiliary or secondary capital of a country
【陪房】［旧］maids that follows the bride to her husband's family
【陪护】accompany and look after：她最近一直在医院～父亲。*She recently keeps his father company and takes care of him in the hospital.*
【陪集】coset：～码 *coset code* /～权 *coset weight*
【陪祭】a person who helps in presiding over a sacrifice or memorial ceremony
【陪嫁】［方］dowry
【陪酒】be a drinking partner
【陪客】a guest invited to a dinner party to help entertain the guest of honour
【陪奁】［方］dowry
【陪练】a training partner; ladder player：他是我的乒乓球～。*He is my training partner in table tennis.*
【陪审】【律】① act (or serve) as an assessor (in a law case) ② serve on a jury
【陪审庭】jury room
【陪审团】jury：大～ *grand jury* /小～ *trial jury; petty jury* /特别～ *special jury* /～主席 *foreman* /～意见分歧。*The jury was divided in opinion.*
【陪审席】jury box
【陪审员】juror; juryman
【陪审制】jury system; system of assessors
【陪侍】［旧］stand at the side and wait upon the seniors
【陪送】［口］① give a dowry to the bribe; dower ② dowry
【陪同】accompany：～前往参观 *accompany sb on a visit* /外宾们由经理～，观看了演出。*The foreign guests, accompanied by managers, attended a performance.*
【陪同人员】entourage：女王及其～ *the Queen and her entourage*
【陪同团】hosting team; receptionist committee
【陪夜】stay up throughout the night to look after a patient
【陪音】【音】harmonic; overtone
【陪葬】［旧］①(of a wife, concubine or slave) be buried alive with the dead ②(of figurines or objects) be buried with the dead ③(of a wife or concubine after her death) be buried by the side of her husband's grave
【陪葬品】funerary objects
【陪葬墓】subordinate tomb
【陪住】(of an inpatient's family member, etc.) stay in the ward to tend the patient

培 ① bank up (a plant, wall, bank, etc.) with earth ② train; cultivate; foster：～干 *train cadres*
【培根】Francis Bacon (1561-1626), English philosopher and essayist
【培垄】banking up
【培土】【农】earth up; bank up with earth; ridge：给玉米～ *earth up the maize*
【培土机】banking machine
【培修】repair and reinforce (earthwork)：～大堤 *repair a dyke*
【培训】train; cultivate：职业～ *train for a kind of work* /参加在职～ *take a training on the job*
【培训班】training course; training class：暑期～ *a summer vacation training course*
【培训中心】training centre
【培养】①【生】culture (microorganisms)：～细菌 *culture of bacteria* ② foster; train; develop：～艺术才能 *foster artistic talent* /～对艺术的爱好 *to cultivate a love of art* /这所大学～出很多名人。*This college has been the nurse of many famous men.*
【培育】foster; cultivate：～人才 *cultivate men of ability* /～新一代 *cultivate a new generation*
【培植】① cultivate; grow：～树苗 *grow saplings* ② foster; train：～亲信 *foster one's cohorts*

赔 ① compensate; refund; pay for：她弄丢了书，却不肯～。*She refused to pay for the book that she has lost.* ② apologize ③ lose; stand a loss：他的生意～了。*He runs a business at a loss.*
【赔本】sustain losses in business：～出售 *make a loss on goods; sell goods at a loss* /他去年在生意上接二连三地～。*He suffered loss on loss in business last year.*
【赔补】make good a loss; make up a deficit; compensate for：他们做任何事也～不了已经造成的损失。*Nothing they can do will make up for the loss they have caused.*
【赔不是】apologize：你冒犯了他，应该给他～。*You've offended him and now you should offer your apologies.*
【赔不起】be unable to make good a loss：她弄丢了同事的计算机，却～。*She was unable to compensate her colleague for the computer she had lost.*
【赔偿】① compensate; indemnify：照价～ *refund the cost* /我们现在只能～一小部分的钱。*Now we can only offer a small part of the compensation.* /我～

了他的损失。*I compensated him for loss.* ② reparations; damages：名誉～ *indemnity for defamation* /战争～ *war reparations* /精神～ *moral reparation*
【赔错】acknowledge a mistake; apologize for one's wrongdoing：我是来向您～的。*I have come to apologize to you.*
【赔垫】advance money in making payment
【赔付率】loss ration
【赔付损失】settlement of loss
【赔话】say a word in apology; apologize
【赔还】repay; pay back
【赔款】① pay money as compensation; pay reparations ② cash indemnity; reparations; amends：～选择 *settlement option* /～准备金 *claims reserve; loss reserve*
【赔了夫人又折兵】give one's enemy a wife and lose one's soldiers in the campaign — instead of making a gain, suffer a double loss; lose the bait along with the fish
【赔累】lose one's capital in business and get into debt
【赔礼】make (or offer) an apology; apologize：～道歉 *make a formal apology* /我因踩了她的脚而向她～。*I apologized to her for stepping on her foot.*
【赔钱】① sustain economic losses; lose money in business：～的买卖 *a business run at a loss* ② compensate for the loss of property
【赔情】[方] apologize
【赔小心】behave with great caution：他脾气不好，和他相处得赔着小心。*He is bad-tempered and you have to act with great caution.*
【赔笑】smile obsequiously, apologetically
【赔账】① pay for the loss of cash or goods entrusted to one ② [方] lose money in business
【赔罪】apologize; ask forgiveness for one's mistakes：你做错了事就该向人家～。*Since you've done wrong, you should make an apology.*

pèi

沛 [书] abundant; copious：精力充～ *full of energy*
【沛然】[书] copious：～雨下。*There was a heavy down-pour.*
帔 embroidered cape worn by people (esp. by women)：凤冠霞～ *phoenix coronet and colourful embroidered cape*
佩 ① wear：～徽章 *wear a badge* ② an ornament worn at the waist in ancient times：玉～ *jade pendant* ③ admire：令人钦～的老师 *an admirable teacher*
【佩带】wear; carry; bear：～徽章 *wear (or bear) a badge*
【佩戴】wear：～安全带 *wear a seat belt*
【佩刀】① wear a sword at the waist ② a sword worn at the waist
【佩服】esteem; admire; sing high praise for sb：我对她～得五体投地。*I admire her from the bottom of my heart.* /我非常～这位教授。*I have a great esteem for the professor.*
【佩剑】【体】sabre：～运动员 *sabre fencer*
【佩兰】fragrant thoroughwort (*Eupatorium fortunei*)
配 ① join in marriage：匹～ *marry; match* ② spouse (esp. wife)：原～ *one's first wife* ③ mate animals：～种 *breeding* /～猪 *breed pigs* ④ blend; mix; compound：～颜色 *mix colours* /～药 make up a prescription ⑤ apportion; assign; allot：分～ *distribution* ⑥ find sth to fit or replace sth else：～成一套 *complete the set* /～钥匙 *have a key made to fit a lock* ⑦ supporting; foil; set off; match：红花～绿叶 *red flowers set off by green leaves* /这两种颜色很相～。*The colours were a close match.* /你认为这件毛衣和这条短裙相～吗? *Do you think this sweater and this skirt go together?* ⑧ deserve; be qualified; be worthy of：他～得上三好学生的称号。*He deserves the title of an excellent student.* /你～当老师吗? *Are you qualified to teacher?* ⑨ banish; exile：发～ *send sb into exile*
【配备】① provide; equip; fit out; furnish; outfit：为新房间～家具 *furnish the new apartment* /经理给每个人～了一台电脑。*The manager allocated a computer to each employee.* /士兵们～了最新式的武器。*The soldiers were equipped with the latest weapons.* ② dispose (troops, etc.); deploy：～火力 *dispose firepower* ③ outfit; equipment：野营～ *a camping outfit*
【配比】proportion of different elements in the composition of sth
【配菜】① garnish (or trim) food ② garnishes
【配餐】① prepare mixed food according to a given standard ② assorted foods for a meal
【配餐室】pantry
【配餐员】pantryman
【配车员】car distributor
【配称】well matched; tone; set off; go together：餐巾和桌布～得很好。*The napkins were a nice match for the tablecloth.* /我们需要和地毯～的窗帘。*We need to get some curtains that will blend in with the carpet.*
【配搭】① accompany; supplement; match; blend in; complement; go together：地板与墙面不～。*The floor does not match with the wall.* /我认为红围巾与你的衣服更～。*I think the red scarf would tone in better with your coat.* ② match
【配搭儿】things that supplement or set off the principal thing
【配电】【电】(power) distribution
【配殿】side hall (in a palace or temple)
【配调】auxiliary tone; auxiliary note
【配对】① pair; make a pair; match：这两只鞋不～。*These two shoes don't match.* ② [口] (of animals) mate; pairing：鸟儿在春天～。*Birds mate in the spring.*
【配对函数】pairing function

P

【配额】quota：共同～ *common quotas* /关税～ *customs quota* /国家～ *country quotas* /进口～ *quota on imports* /绝对～ *absolute quotas* /双边～ *bilateral quota* /折旧～ *depreciation quota*

【配方】①【数】change an incomplete square form into a complete one ② fill (or make up) a prescription：医生给我开了一个治头痛的～。*The doctor wrote me a prescription for medicine for my headache.* ③ a formula for compounding a chemical or metallurgical product：肥皂～ *formula for making soap* /新药的秘密～ *the secret formula for a new medicine*

【配房】wing of a house; side house

【配购】buy rationed goods

【配股】【经】scrip issue

【配合】(pèihé) ① coordinate; concert; cooperate; concert：我们～协调。*We acted in concert.* /他们互相～并圆满地完成了工作。*They cooperated well with each other and finally successfully finished the job.* ②【机】fit：～等级 *fit quality*

【配合】(pèihe) be harmoniously combined or arranged：为什么不在篱笆旁边种些灌木，那样看上去一定很～。*Why not plant some bushes next to the fence there — they should blend in really nicely.*

【配火】tempering (of metal)

【配给】ration; rationing：石油～ *oil rationing* /信用～ *credit rationing* /资金～ *capital rationing* /当物品供应缺乏时，政府按定量～市民。*The government rationed citizens when supplies are scarce.*

【配给证】ration card

【配给制】ration system; rationing

【配件】① accessory; fitting：底盘～ *chassis fittings* /控制～ *control fitting* /连接～ *connection fittings* /自行车～ *accessory of a bicycle* ② replacement; spare part：零～ *spare parts*

【配件表】assembly parts list

【配角】① support; costar：这出戏我们俩～。*We will costar in this play.* ② supporting role; minor role; one who does secondary work

【配军】[旧] an exile

【配料】① mix ingredients in the right proportion ②【冶】burden：高炉～ *blast-furnace burden*

【配偶】[书] spouse; mate：受抚养的～ *dependent spouse* /未亡～ *surviving spouse* /你可以选择和你的～共同支付所得税或者单独支付。*You may choose to pay income tax jointly or separately from your spouse.*

【配平】①【化】balancing：～方程式 *balancing equation* ②【航】trim：～系统 *trimming system*

【配器】【音】orchestration

【配曲】set to music; compose：他为这首诗配了曲。*He sets the poem to music.*

【配色】mix colours in the right proportion：～法 *colour matching method* /～方案 *colour schemes*

【配售】ration (at state price); placing

【配水】①【水】distribution of water：～池 *service reservoir* /～闸 *water conservancy; distribution structure* ②【建】distribution：～总管 *distribution main*

【配套】form a complete set or system：～器材 *necessary accessories*

【配位】coordination

【配伍】【医】compatibility of medicines：～禁忌 *incompatibility*

【配戏】play a minor role to support a leading actor

【配药】make (or dispense) up a prescription：请去药店照这个方子配些药来。*Please go to the druggist's and have this prescription made up for me.*

【配药员】dispenser

【配页】【印】assembling (leaves of a book)

【配页机】【印】assembling machine

【配音】dub (a film, etc.)：用汉语给外国影片～ *dub a foreign film in Chinese*

【配乐】provide background music：～诗朗诵 *poetry recital with background music*

【配制】① compound; make up ② accompany; supplement

【配置】dispose (troops, etc.); deploy：～兵力 *dispose forces*

【配种】breed; breeding：～季节 *mating season* /～率 *breeding rate* /～能力 *breeding capacity*

【配子】【生理】gamete：雌～ *female gamete* /雄～ *male gamete* /兼性～ *facultative gamete*

【配子体】【生理】gametophyte：雌～ *female gametophyte*

辔 reins and bridle：鞍～ *saddle and bridle*

【辔头】bridle

霈 [书] ① heavy rain ② (of rain) heavy：雨～ *copious rainfall*

pēn

喷 spray; spurt; gush; sprinkle; shoot：从伤口～出的血 *blood shooting from the wound* /火山～火。*The volcano throws up fire.* /他把水～在花上。*He sprayed water over the flowers.*
see also pèn

【喷薄】gush; spurt：～欲出 (*of the sun*) *emerge in all its brilliant magnificence*

【喷出岩】【地】extrusive rock

【喷灯】blowtorch; blowlamp

【喷发】erupt; throw out; explode; gush：～岩 *effusive rock; volcanic; eruptive rock*

【喷发胶】hair spray

【喷饭】laugh so hard as to spew one's food; be seized with a fit of laughter that one even spews the food at dinner

【喷粉】dusting：～复印 *smoke printing*

【喷管】spray tube; jet nozzle

【喷灌】sprinkling irrigation; spray irrigation

【喷灌器】sprinkler

【喷壶】watering can; sprinkling can

【喷火车】flame-thrower

【喷火器】【军】flamethrower

【喷溅】(of a liquid when being squeezed out)

splash; spatter; jet:他把水~在我身上。*He sprayed me with water.*
【喷口】ejector; spout; lip
【喷磨】【机】abrasive blasting
【喷墨打印机】ink-jet printer
【喷墨法】【印】ink-jet method
【喷墨记录】ink jet recording
【喷漆】spray paint; spray lacquer: ~枪 *paint gun* /给家具~ *spray the furniture with paint*
【喷气发动机】jet engine
【喷气流】【航】jet wash; jet flow
【喷气燃料】jet fuel
【喷气式】jet-propelled
【喷气式飞机】jet plane; jet aircraft; jet
【喷枪】spray gun; airbrush
【喷泉】fountain: ~效应 *fountain effect* /~喷出的水束 *a jet of water sent up by a fountain*
【喷洒】spray; sprinkle:他们正在给植物~杀虫剂。*They are spraying an insecticide upon plants.*
【喷砂】sand blast; grit blast: ~处理 *blast sanding*
【喷射】spray; spurt; jet:消防队员把水流~进燃烧着的房屋。*The fireman sent jets of water into the burning house.*
【喷水】dabble; water spray: ~车 *sprayer*; *spraying car* / 喷些水,但是不要太多。*Sprinkle some water on it, but not too much.*
【喷丝头】【纺】spinning jet; spinning nozzle
【喷腾】(of water, flames, smoke, steam, etc.) spurt up; shoot up
【喷嚏】sneeze:打~时应用手帕捂住。*Use a handkerchief when you sneeze.*
【喷桶】[方] watering can; sprinkling can
【喷头】① shower nozzle ② sprinkler head
【喷涂】【化】spray coating:空气~ *air spray* /热~ *hot spray* /无空气~ *airless spray* /~设备 *spraying equipment* /~装置 *spraying plant*
【喷吐】shoot out (flames, light, gas, etc.); spurt; puff:汽艇沿河~着烟雾。*The steamboat is puffing along the river.*
【喷雾】spray; atomize:离心~ *centrifugal spray* /~法 *spray-on process* /~冷却法 *spray cooling* /~塔 *spray tower*
【喷雾器】sprayer; atomizer; inhaler
【喷涌】(of liquid) gush; spout; spurt:血从伤口中~出来。*Blood spurted out from the wound.* /水从消防龙头中~而出。*Water gushed from a hydrant.*
【喷油】oil gush
【喷油泵】【机】injection pump
【喷云吐雾】① (of a smoker) puff away:他思考问题时总爱~。*He is used to puffing away at his cigarette when thinking.* ② (of a chimney, etc.) belch forth smoke
【喷子】sprayer; spraying apparatus
【喷嘴】spray nozzle; spray head; jet:对流~ *counter-flow jet* /加速~ *accelerating jet* /冷却~ *cooling jet* /燃烧器~ *burner jet* /氧气~ *oxygen jet*

pén

盆 ① basin; port:花~ *flower pot* /脸~ *washbasin* /在零下气温里,一~水很快就会结上一层冰。*A basin of water will soon be covered with ice in freezing weather.* ② anything like a basin:骨~ *pelvis*
【盆地】【地】basin:风成~ *aeolian basin* /断层~ *fault basin* /海洋~ *ocean basin* /内陆~ *interior basin* /四川~ *the Sichuan Basin* /塔里木~ *the Tarim Basin*
【盆花】potted flower
【盆景】potted landscape; miniature trees and rockery; bonsai
【盆盆罐罐】pots and pans — household utensils:他这次搬家扔了很多~。*He threw away many household utensils when moving house.*
【盆腔】【生理】pelvic cavity
【盆腔炎】【医】pelvic infection
【盆汤】bathtub cubicle; bathhouse cubicle
【盆浴】tub bath; tub:我喜欢~胜过淋浴。*I prefer a tub to a shower.*
【盆栽】① grow (or plant) in a pot ② flowers and plants grown in flowerpots: ~植物 *potted plant*; *pot plant*
【盆子】[口] basin; pot

pèn

喷 [方] ① (of vegetables, fish, fruit, etc.) in season:西瓜~儿 *watermelon season* /螃蟹正在~儿上。*Crabs are in season now.* ② [量] crop; turn:头~棉花 *the first crop of cotton* /绿豆结二~角了。*The green beans are having the second crop of pods.*
see also pēn
【喷红】crimson; very red:听了这话,她羞得满脸~。*She blushed with embarrassment on hearing this.*
【喷香】fragrant; delicious: ~的菜肴 *delicious dishes*

pēng

抨 [书] impeach; attack in speech or writing
【抨击】attack (in speech or writing); criticize; flay; lash out at:猛烈~反对党 *lash out at the opposition party* /一部被评论家~的小说 *a novel assailed by critics* /州长因未遵守竞选时的诺言而被报界~。*The governor was attacked by the press for failing to keep a campaign promise.*
【抨弹】[书] ① attack in writing or speech; lash out at:在电视节目的采访过程中,她对她的批评者们进行了严厉的~。*She lashed out at her critics during the TV interview.* ② impeach; censure:参

议院公开～一名议员。*The Senate censured one of its members.*

怦 ［象］pound; thump：一见到她，他的心就～～跳。*His heart pounded violently at the sight of her.* /我兴奋得心～～直跳。*My heart thumped with excitement.*

砰 ［象］bang; thump：他～的一拳砸在桌子上。*He banged his fist on the table.* /烟火～地爆开了。*Bang went the fireworks.* /门～的一声关上了。*The door slammed shut.*

【砰然】a loud bang; with a thump; slam-bang：～一声，他摔了话筒。*He banged the receiver up.*

烹 ① boil; cook in water ② fry quickly in hot oil and stir in sauce：～对虾 *quick-fried prawns in brown sauce*

【烹茶】make tea

【烹饪】cooking; culinary art; cuisine：西班牙～ *Spanish cuisine* /有关园艺和～的书总是很受欢迎。*Books about gardening or cookery are always popular.* /她正在夜校上一个～班。*She is taking a cooking class at night school.*

【烹饪法】cuisine; cookery

【烹调】cook (dishes)：～书 *cookery-book* /～用具 *mess kit; mess gear* /中国式～ *Chinese cooking; Chinese cuisine* /她为丈夫～了一顿美味的饭菜。*She cooked her husband a delicious meal.* /当客人到达的时候，她仍然在～晚饭。*She was still preparing supper when her guests arrived.*

嘭 ［象］：～～的敲门声 *knocks at the door*

澎 ［方］splash; spatter：～了一身水 *be splashed all over with water*

see also péng

péng

朋 ① friends：宾～满座。*The guests and friends filled all the seats.* ②［书］form a clique ③［书］match; equal：硕大无～ *incomparably huge; huge without compare*

【朋辈】［书］friends

【朋比为奸】act in collusion; conspire; gang up to do evil; join in plotting treason

【朋党】clique; cabal：～之争 *factional strife*

【朋僚】［书］① colleagues ② friends

【朋友】① friend：交～ *make friends with sb* /知心～ *a close friend* /患难～才是真～。*A friend in need is a friend indeed.* /～之间不分彼此。*Between friends all is common.* /虚伪的～比公开的敌人更坏。*False friends are worse than open enemies.* ② boyfriend or girlfriend：这是他～。*This is his girlfriend.*

棚 ① awning of straw mats, etc. to keep off wind and rain：凉～ *mat shelter* /天～ *canopy* ② shed; shack：料～ *material shed* /牲口～ *livestock shed* /窝～ *shack; shed* /车～ *bicycle shed* /货～ *freight shed* ③ ceiling：顶～ *ceiling*

【棚户】［方］slum-dwellers; shack-dwellers：～区 *slum area*

【棚架】canopy frame; shed frame

【棚圈】covered pen (for animals); shed fold

【棚寮】［方］shack; shanty

【棚屋】hut; shack：他在一间打猎的小～里过着简单的生活。*He roughed it in a small hunting shack.*

【棚子】［口］shed; shack

蓬 ①【植】fleabane ② fluffy; disheveled：～头散发 *with disheveled hair* /乱～～的草 *fluffy and disorderly grasses* ③［量］clump; tangle：一～灌木丛 *a clump of bushes*

【蓬勃】vigorous; flourishing; full of vitality; prosperous; exuberant：朝气～的革命精神 *vigorous revolutionary spirit* /运动正在～开展。*The movement is developing vigorously.*

【蓬户】［书］a wicker door — a humble house; hut; shack

【蓬莱】Penglai Island, a fabled abode of immortals

【蓬乱】(of grasses, hair, etc.) fluffy and disorderly; rumple; rough; untidy; disheveled; unkempt：他的头发很～。*His hair is all in a tangle; his hair is rough.* /他的脏头发拢到后面梳成一个～的马尾巴。*His dirty hair was pulled back into a scruffy ponytail.*

【蓬蓬】(of grasses, trees, hair, beard, etc.) thick and disorderly; untidy; unkempt：他的头发乱～的。*His hair is unkempt.*

【蓬生麻中】a raspberry grows among the hemp — influence of good friends

【蓬松】fluffy; puffy; velvety; soft：～的枕头 *a puffy pillow* /小鸟身上的羽毛很～。*The feather of the little bird feels very fluffy.*

【蓬头垢面】with disheveled hair and a dirty face; unkempt; look a mess; scruffy; bedraggled：你干了什么？你看上去～。*What have you been doing? You look a terrible mess.* /她很清楚自己看上去～的。*She was conscious of her rather disheveled appearance.*

硼 【化】boron (B)

鹏 roc, a bird of huge size in legendary

【鹏程万里】embark on a roc's flight of 10,000 li — have an exceedingly bright future; have brilliant prospects

澎 Penghu Islands

see also pēng

【澎湖列岛】the Penghu Islands; the Penghus

【澎湃】① surge：汹涌～ *surging; turbulent* /大海中波涛～。*Waves surge in the sea.* ② great; vast and mighty：热情～ *surge of enthusiasm*

篷 ① covering or awning on sth：船～ *the mat of a boat* /敞～车 *open car* ② sail of boat：扯起～来 *hoist the sails*

【篷布】tarpaulin; awning：用～把货物盖上 *cover the goods with a tarpaulin*

P

【篷车】① box wagon; box-car ②［旧］horse-drawn carriage with a covering

【篷帐】tent; canvas:他让士兵在山顶扎～。*He tented his men on top of the hill.* /我们今晚要在～里过夜。*We will spend the night under canvas.*

【篷子】awning (or shed) (for sheltering people from the sun, rain, wind, etc.)

膨 expand; swell; extend

【膨大】expand; inflate:气球～了。*The balloon was distended.* /汽车进口增加了,但是伴随着逐步～的市场,价格仍然很高。*Car imports increased but, with an expanding market, prices stayed quite high.*

【膨化】(of rice; corn, etc.) popped; dilatation; dilation: ～食品 *dilated food; inflated food*

【膨化剂】swelling agent

【膨胀】① expand; swell; dilate:空气遇热～。*Air will expand when it is heated.* /大规模的移民使这个城市的人口迅速～。*Large scale immigration swelled the population of the city rapidly.* ② inflate:通货～ *inflation (of the currency)*

【膨胀度】dilation; dilatation

【膨胀率】expansibility; expansion ratio

pěng

捧 ① hold; carry in both hands:他手里～着一个精致的盒子。*He holds a delicate box in both hands.* ②［量］a double handful:一～大米 *a double handful of rice* ③ flatter; boost:吹～ *boost; crack up; puff; flatter* /她被～上天了。*She was exalted to the skies.*

【捧杯】(of sports competition) win the cup:这次篮球比赛广州队～。*The Guangzhou Team won the cup in the basketball match.*

【捧场】① be a member of a claque ② boost; root; sing the praises of sb; flatter:替人～ *roll logs for sb*

【捧臭脚】［贬］lick one's feet (or boots); bootlick — toady to sb:我讨厌看到他～的样子。*I hate to see his obsequious manner.*

【捧读】［书］be glad to read (your work); read with great respect:我最近～了您的大作。*I have read your works with great respect recently.*

【捧腹】split (or shake, burst) one's sides with laughter

【捧腹大笑】belly laugh; burst one's sides with laughter; be convulsed with laughter; split one's sides with laughter; roar with laughter:看到他滑稽的样子,我们大家不禁～。*At the sight of his ridiculous appearance, we laughed ourselves into convulsions.*

【捧哏】(of the supporting performer in a cross talk) play the fool to amuse the audience with words or expressions

【捧角】try to support a particular actor or actress; boost an actor or actress

pèng

碰 ① knock; bump; touch:他的膝盖～破了皮。*He broke the skin on his knee by bumping.* /碟子碗～得丁丁当当的。*The dishes and bowls slid together with a clatter.* ② meet; come across; bump into (or against):我在街上～到他。*I met him in the street; I bumped into him on the road.* /我昨天在商场～到了一位老朋友。*I run into an old buck at the department store yesterday.* ③ take one's chance; have a try:我要去～一～运气! *I'll try my luck.*

【碰杯】clink glasses (to offer congratulations)

【碰壁】run into a blank wall; run one's head against a wall; up against the wall — be rebuffed (or refused):四处～ *run into snags everywhere*/那个人很固执,我已经碰了几次壁了。*That man is really obstinate; I have been rebuffed several times.* /凭主观办事一定～。*If you do things subjectively, you'll just run into a stone wall.*

【碰钉子】meet with a rebuff; hit (or strike, run against) a snag; get the cheese:我在她面前又～了。*I run against a snag again from her.*

【碰顶】［方］at most; at best:他～今年也就能挣个一万块。*He can earn at most ten thousand yuan this year.*

【碰见】meet unexpectedly; run into; bump into; come across:真没想到,我竟然在这里～了我的老战友。*To my great surprise, I met my close comrade in arms here.* /我～他正和一个老人争吵。*I happened to see him quarrelling with an old man.*

【碰面】meet; meet with:我们约好 6 点在公园里～。*We have agreed to meet in the park at 6.*

【碰碰车】bumper car

【碰碰船】bumper boat

【碰巧】by chance; by coincidence; accidentally:那时我～在国外。*It so chanced that I was abroad at that time.* /如果～他不能来,就让他的秘书发言吧。*If, by any chance, he fails to come, we can ask his secretary to deliver the speech.*

【碰锁】spring lock

【碰头】① meet and discuss; put one's heads together:我实在想不出好办法解决这个问题,咱们～讨论一下吧。*I can hardly find a good way to solve the problem by myself; Let's put our heads together.* ②［方］kowtow: ～求饶 *kowtow for mercy*

【碰头会】brief meeting (mainly to exchange information):是该开个～的时候了。*It's high time that we held a brief meeting to exchange information.*

【碰一鼻子灰】be snubbed; meet with a rebuff; get the cold shoulder:我诚恳地请他帮忙,谁料到～。*I asked for his help sincerely, but met with an unexpected rebuff.*

【碰运气】try one's luck; take a chance:我要去～,没准儿我就考上了呢。*I'll take my chance to sit*

P

for the examination; Maybe I can pass it.
【碰撞】① collide; run into ② offend; affront; provoke: 你最好不要当众～他。*You'd better not put an affront upon him.* ③【物】collision; impact: 核～ *nuclear collision*

pī

丕 ［书］big; great: ～业 *big business* /～变 *immense change*

批[1] ①［书］slap: ～颊 *slap sb's face* ②［书］scrape ③ write instructions or comments on (a report from a subordinate, etc.): 审～ *examine and approve* ④ criticize; refute: 我挨了他一通～。*I was criticized severely by him.*

批[2] ① wholesale: 整～购进 *buy goods wholesale* ②［量］lot; group; batch: 一～货 *a batch of goods* /一～人 *a group of people* /一～新兵刚刚到达军营。*A batch of new recruits has just arrived at the camp.* /这个周末我们又要接待一～新的来访者。*We will have another lot of visitors coming this weekend.*

批[3] fibres of cotton, flax, etc.: 线～儿 *cotton fibre (for making thread or yarn)*

【批办】approve the investigation of a case
【批驳】① reject an opinion or a request from a subordinate body: ～请求 *reject a request (from a subordinate)* ② refute; criticize; rebut: 他的理论被～得体无完肤。*His theory was refuted down to the last point.*
【批处理】【电】batch processing: ～文件 *bat*
【批次】batch (of aircraft, etc.); group (of people, etc.): 生产～ *production batch* /他们是同一～到达北京的。*They arrived in Beijing in the same group.*
【批答】［书］give an official, written reply to a subordinate body
【批点】① write words and phrases for special attention or emphasis with dots or small circles: 他一边看书,一边～。*He is reading and at the same time making marginal notes.* ②［方］criticize; censure
【批斗】criticize and denounce sb (at a public meeting) during the Cultural Revolution
【批发】① wholesale; buy in bulk: ～产品 *wholesale goods* /～价格 *wholesale price* /他～货物然后在市场上出售。*He buys the goods wholesale and then sells them in the market.* /他经常～,因为这划算得多。*He always buys in bulk, because it is much more economical.* ② (of an official document) be authorized for dispatch: 这是上级～的文件。*The dispatch of the documents was authorized by the superior.*
【批复】give an official, written reply to request from a subordinate body
【批改】correct; revise: ～作业 *correct students' papers*
【批号】lot number; batch number
【批件】a report from a subordinate body with a reply by a higher-up
【批量】①（produce) in batches ② batch; lot (of products): 大～ *mass quantities* /小～ *small quantities* /～生产 *batch production*
【批零】wholesale and retail
【批判】criticize; critique: 该书对政府的政策做出了～性的分析。*The book presents a critique of the government's policies.*
【批评】① criticism: 文学～ *literary criticism*/～与自我～ *criticism and self-criticism* ② criticize; attack: ～几句是很容易的,但是你并不需要亲自处理这些问题。*It's easy to criticize, but you don't have to deal with these problems.* /他发表演讲～政府。*He delivered a speech attacking the government.*
【批示】① write instructions or comments on a report, memorandum, etc. submitted by a lower-level ② written instructions or comments on a report, memorandum, etc. submitted by a subordinate
【批条】a note with a superior's instructions or comments
【批销】wholesale: 他们～电视机。*They sell TV sets wholesale.*
【批语】remarks on a piece of writing
【批阅】annotate and comment on; annotate with comments; endorse
【批注】① annotate and comment on ② annotations and commentaries; marginalia
【批转】write instructions or comments on a report submitted by a subordinate and transmit it to units or departments concerned
【批准】ratify; approve; sanction; pass: ～建议 *give sanction to the proposals* /～宪法修正案 *ratify an amendment to a constitution* /国会～了预算。*Congress approved the budget.*
【批准书】instrument of ratification

纰 (of cloth, thread, etc.) become unwoven or untwisted; be spoilt

【纰漏】a careless mistake; a small accident; slip: 出～ *commit a mistake; make a slip*
【纰缪】［书］error; mistake

坯 ① base; blank: 铜～ *copper base* ② unburnt bricks and tiles: 打～ *make earthen bricks* ③［方］semifinished product: 面～儿 *cooked plain noodles*

【坯布】【纺】unbleached and undyed cloth; grey cloth; grey
【坯革】crust leather
【坯件】【机】blank
【坯胎】base; blank
【坯子】① base; blank ② semi-finished product ③ makings; material: 他是个当作家的～。*He is born for a writer.* /她是个演员～。*She has the makings of a good actress.*

披 ① wrap around; drape over one's shoulders; put on: ～着大衣 *have an overcoat draped over one's shoulders* /她匆忙地把围巾～在肩上。

She threw a scarf over her shoulders. /天气很冷，所以他出门前～了件衣服。*It was cold so he wrapped up before going out.* ② open; unfold; unroll: ～卷 *open a book* ③ crack; split open: 这根竹竿～了。*The bamboo pole has split.*

【披读】open a book and read; read: 尽管夜很深了，她还在专注地～文件。*Although it was late at night, she still read the documents attentively.*

【披发】①［书］with hair disheveled (or unkempt): 她急匆匆地赶了过来，～气喘。*She came in a hurry, disheveled and out of breath.* ② disheveled hair

【披风】cloak; mantle

【披拂】［书］(of a breeze) blow gently; flap

【披肝沥胆】unbosom oneself; speak without reserve; be loyal and faithful

【披挂】① put on a suit of armour ② a suit of armour

【披红】drape a band of red silk over sb's shoulders (on a festive occasion or as a mark of honour)

【披红戴花】have red silk draped over one's shoulders and flowers pinned on one's breast (as a token of honour)

【披怀】［书］treat sb sincerely

【披坚执锐】buckle on one's armour and take up weapons — go forth to battle; be ready for a combat

【披肩】① cape ② shawl

【披荆斩棘】break through brambles and thorns — blaze one's way through difficulties; hew one's way through difficulties: 经过几番～，我们终于胜利了。*We had hacked our way through various difficulties before we finally succeeded.*

【披卷】leaf through books

【披览】［书］open (a book) and read; peruse: ～群书 *read extensively*

【披沥】［书］be open and sincere

【披露】① publish; announce: 这一消息已在报上～。*The news has been published in the press.* ② reveal; show; disclose; divulge: 公司～了下一年度的生产计划。*The company has just revealed its plans of production for the coming year.* /有消息～他曾经坐牢，对此我们十分震惊。*We were greatly shocked by the disclosure that he had once been put into prison.*

【披麻戴孝】be dressed in hemp garments in mourning for one's parent

【披靡】① (of trees and grass, etc.) be swept by the wind ② be routed; flee; collapse: 所向～ (*of troops*) *carry all before one*; *sweep away all obstacles*

【披散】(of hair, mane, etc.) hang down loosely

【披沙拣金】sift out the fine gold from the sand — extract the essentials from a large mass of material

【披剃】【宗】tonsure

【披头散发】with hair disheveled; with hair in disarray; unkempt; look a mess: 现在请不要给我拍照，我看上去～的。*Please don't take my photo now; I look a mess.* /囚犯们～。*The prisoners' hair was unkempt.*

【披屋】penthouse; outhouse

【披星戴月】under the canopy of the moon and the stars — travel day and night; work from before dawn till after dark

【披阅】open and read (a book); peruse

砒

① arsenic (As) ② white arsenic

【砒霜】(white) arsenic

劈

① chop; cleave; split: ～柴 *chop wood* / ～木头 *split a log* ② cracked; broken: 钢笔尖写～了。*The pen nib is broken.* ③［方］hoarse: 他喊得嗓子都～了。*He has shouted himself hoarse.* ④ right against one's (face, head, etc.) ⑤ (of lightning) strike: 老树让雷～了。*The old tree was struck by lightning.* ⑥ a V-shaped tool

see also pǐ

【劈波斩浪】cleave through the waves — overcome all kinds of difficulties and advance

【劈刀】① chopper ②【军】sabre fighting

【劈理】【矿】cleavage

【劈里啪啦】［象］the successive sounds of crackling, etc.; pitter-patter: 我听见机枪在～不住射击。*I heard the machine guns sputtering away.* /烟火在头顶上空～爆响。*The fireworks cracked overhead.*

【劈脸】right in the face: 他～就向我提了一堆很难的问题。*He confronted me with a lot of difficult questions.*

【劈啪】［象］sputter; pit-a pat: 故障使发动机～作声。*This fault caused the engine to sputter.* /蜡烛～爆响着熄灭了。*The candle sputtered out.*

【劈山】level off hilltops; blast cliffs: ～引水 *cut through mountains to bring in water*; *split up a hill to let the water through*

【劈手】make a sudden snatch; quickly: 他～抢过我的书。*He snatched my book quickly.*

【劈头】① straight on the head; right in the face ② at the very start (or outset): 他见我进来，～就骂。*He began to heap abuse on me the moment he saw me coming.*

【劈头盖脸】right in the face: 倾盆大雨～地浇了下来。*The rain came pouring down.*

【劈胸】right against the chest

霹

【霹雷】［口］thunderbolt; thunderclap

【霹雳】thunderbolt; thunderclap: 晴天～ *a bolt from the blue*

【霹雳舞】break dance

pí

皮

① skin; cutis: 牛～ *cattle hide* /兔～ *rabbit skins* /羊～ *sheepskin* /你可以用动物的～做鞋子。*You can make shoes from the skins of animals.* ② leather; fur: ～手套 *leather gloves* /她的

大衣是～的。*Her coat is made of fur.* ③ peel; rind：橘子～ *orange peel* /香蕉～ *banana skin* /土豆～ *potato peel* /石榴～ *pomegranate rind* ④ surface：地～ *ground* /水～儿 *the surface of the water* ⑤ sheet; a broad thin piece of material：海蜇～ *jellyfish sheet* ⑥ pliable; tough：～糖 *sticky candy* ⑦ no longer crisp; soggy：饼干放～了。*The biscuits have become soggy.* ⑧ naughty：邻居家的小男孩儿真～！*The little boy in the neighbour is really naughty.* ⑨ case-hardened; apathetic; indifferent：批评他已经没有用了，他早～了。*It's no use scolding him any more; he has been used to that and doesn't care it.* ⑩ rubber：橡～ *rubber* /～筋 *rubber band* ⑪（Pí）a surname

【皮袄】fur-lined jacket

【皮包】leather handbag; briefcase; portfolio

【皮包公司】briefcase company — a fly-by-night company; a bubble company

【皮包骨头】skinny; skin and bones; bony; scraggy：一个～的孩子 *a skinny child* /他瘦得～。*He is reduced to a skeleton.* /一只～的狗在街上寻找食物。*A scraggy dog was looking for food in the street.*

【皮鞭】leather-thonged whip

【皮层】①【生】cortex：初生～ *primary cortex* /次生～ *secondary cortex* /感觉～ *sensory cortex* /海绵～ *spongy cortex* / 卵～ *egg cortex* /木栓～ *cork cortex* /听觉～ *auditory cortex* /胃～ *gastral cortex* ②【生理】cerebral cortex

【皮尺】tape measure; tape

【皮带】① leather belt：我需要一条～系裤子。*I need a leather belt to keep up my trousers.* ②【机】(driving) belt：传动～ *continuous belt*; *driving belt* /三角～ *cone belt*

【皮蛋】preserved egg

【皮垫】leather packing

【皮筏】skin raft：羊～ *goat skin raft*

【皮肤】① skin; dermis：柔嫩的～ *a soft skin* ②［书］skin-deep; shallow; superficial：这是我的～之见。*This is my superficial opinion.*

【皮肤病】skin disease; dermatosis

【皮肤科】【医】dermatological department; dermatology：～医生 *dermatologist*

【皮肤学】dermatology：～者 *dermatologist*

【皮肤炎】【医】dermatitis

【皮肤针】【中医】cutaneous acupuncture; skin needle

【皮傅】［书］give a superficial interpretation

【皮革】leather; hide：光面～ *slick-surfaced leather* /起毛～ *suede leather*

【皮革工人】leatherworker

【皮革商】fellmonger

【皮辊革】roller leather

【皮猴儿】hooded fur overcoat; fur parka; fur anorak

【皮花】ginned cotton; lint cotton

【皮划艇】【体】canoeing：～运动员 *canoeist*

【皮货】furs; peltry：～店 *fur shop* / ～商 *furrier*

【皮夹子】wallet; pocket-book：我把～弄丢了。*I lost my wallet.*

【皮匠】① cobbler; shoemaker ② tanner

【皮胶】hide glue; leather cement：～原 *collagen*

【皮筋儿】［口］rubber band

【皮开肉绽】the skin torn and the flesh gaping — badly bruised from flogging; open wound

【皮科】dermatological department

【皮脸】［口］① naughty ② shameless

【皮毛】① fur; skin and hair ② smattering; superficial knowledge：她对英语只懂得一点～。*She has only a smattering of English.* /他对所有的事都略知～，而真正的知识却一点也没有。*He knows a little amount of everything, and a knowledge of nothing.*

【皮棉】ginned cotton; lint (cotton)

【皮面】① outer skin; surface; outside ② leather cover

【皮囊】① leather bag ②［贬］the human body

【皮钱儿】leather washer

【皮球】rubber ball; ball

【皮实】① sturdy; hardy; tough：他个子矮，却很～。*He was small but sturdy.* /这种马受不了雨和寒冷的天气，一点儿也不～。*This kind of horses does not like rain and cold weather; they are not hardy animals.* ② durable：～的衣服 *durable clothing*

【皮糖】a sticky candy

【皮艇】①【体】kayaking ② kayak 单人～ *single kayak*; *one-seater kayak* /双人～ *tandem kayak*; *double kayak*

【皮桶子】fur lining (for a jacket or an overcoat)

【皮下注射】【医】subcutaneous (or hypodermic) injection

【皮线】rubber-insulated wire; rubber-covered wire

【皮屑】scurf

【皮腺】cutaneous gland

【皮箱】leather suitcase; leather trunk

【皮相】skin-deep; superficial：～之谈 *superficial talk* (*or opinion*)

【皮硝】【矿】mirabilite

【皮笑肉不笑】put on a false smile; smile hypocritically; cold smile

【皮鞋】leather shoes：擦～ *polish shoes*; *shine shoes*

【皮鞋油】shoe polish

【皮靴】leather boots

【皮炎】【医】dermatitis

【皮样瘤】dermoid tumor

【皮衣】① fur clothing：穿～ *wear furs* ② leather clothing

【皮影戏】leather-silhouette show; shadow play

【皮张】hide; pelt

【皮掌儿】outsole

【皮疹】【医】rash; quat

【皮脂腺】【生理】sebaceous glands：～肥大 *exdermoptosis*

【皮纸】tough paper made from bast fibre of the mulberry or paper mulberry, etc.

【皮质】① superficial cells (of certain internal organs) ②【生理】cortex：～素 *cortin* /～索 *cortical cord*

【皮重】tare (weight)
【皮子】① leather; hide ② fur

枇

【枇杷】loquat (the tree and its fruit)

毗

［书］① adjoin; be adjacent to ② assist

【毗连】next to; adjoin; border on; be adjacent to: 我们的农场沿河～。*Our farms join along the river.* /这座小礼堂和与它～的房子所用的砖是一样的。*The chapel is built of the same brick as the house which adjoins it.* /当地居民反对～公园建商场的计划。*Local residents are against the plan to build a shopping centre next to the park.*
【毗连国】contiguous state
【毗连区】adjacent area (or zone)
【毗邻】adjoin; border on

疲

① weary; tired; exhausted: 精～力尽 *be used up; knock up; play out; be tired out* ② slump; weaken: 乐此不～ *be extremely interested in sth; always enjoy doing sth*

【疲惫】① tired out; exhausted; weary; shattered; drained: 长途旅行之后，他已～不堪了。*After the long journey, he was extremely tired.* /农民们劳动了一天，现在十分～。*The farmers have been working all day and they are exhausted now.* /我感到浑身～无力。*All through my body I felt drained and weak.* ② tire sb out; exhaust: 持续的争吵让我们～不堪。*The constant quarrelling is tiring us out.* /这个无聊的讲座让我～。*The boring lecture exhausts me.*
【疲敝】(of manpower, resources, etc.) be running low; become inadequate
【疲病】tired and ill: ～之卒 *tired and sick soldiers*
【疲顿】［书］be tired out
【疲乏】weary; exhausted; shattered; tired out; worn out: 旅行让他十分～，他很快就睡着了。*He was tired out with travelling and slept almost at once.*
【疲竭】［书］be completely exhausted
【疲倦】tired and sleepy; weary; drained; worn out: 我刚开始工作时每天都十分～，但是现在我已经习惯了。*I was exhausted every day when I first started working, but I am used to it now.*
【疲劳】① tired; fatigued; weary; worn out; drained: 我在办公室度过了繁忙的一天，现在非常～。*I've had a busy day at the office and I am absolutely shattered now.* ② fatigue: 肌肉～ *muscular fatigue* /听觉～ *auditory fatigue* ③【机】weakening of material subjected to stress: 弹性～ *elastic fatigue* /磁性～ *magnetic fatigue*
【疲劳综合症】【医】exhaustion syndrome
【疲癃】［书］old and infirm; ageing and ailing
【疲软】① fatigued and weak ②【经】weaken; slump: 那个国家的货币在外汇市场上～。*The currency of that country is weakening on foreign exchanges.*
【疲弱】tired and weak; feeble and fatigued
【疲沓】slack; negligent: 工作～ *be slack at one's work*
【疲于奔命】be tired out by too much running around; be kept constantly on the run

啤

【啤酒】beer: 姜汁～ *ginger beer* /生～ *draught beer*
【啤酒厂】brewery
【啤酒花】【植】hops

琵

【琵琶】*pipa*, a plucked string instrument with a fretted fingerboard
【琵琶骨】［方］bladebone; scapula
【琵琶桶】barrel
【琵嘴鸭】【动】shoveler

脾

spleen

【脾寒】［方］malaria; ague
【脾气】① temper; temperament; disposition: 我和他～相投，相处得很好。*He and I got along very well, having very similar temperaments.* /她温柔而乐天的～使她赢得了学校里所有孩子的喜爱。*Her gentle and happy disposition won the hearts of all pupils of her school.* ② bad temper: 发～ *lose one's temper* /他的妻子因为他粗暴的～离开了他。*His wife left him because of his violent temper.*
【脾胃】taste; temperament: 不合～ *not suit one's taste; not be to one's liking* /两人～相投。*The two have similar likes and dislikes.*
【脾性】［方］temperament; disposition; nature: 一个～倔强的男孩 *a boy with an obstinate strong personality* /我有一种乐天的～。*I have a happy disposition.*
【脾炎】【医】lienitis; splenitis
【脾脏】【医】spleen

裨

［书］secondary; minor

see also bì

【裨将】adjutant or lower-ranking general in ancient times

貔

a kind of beast in ancient books

【貔虎】brave troops; mighty troops
【貔貅】① a mythical wild animal ② brave troops
【貔子】［方］yellow weasel

pǐ

匹[1]

① be a match for; be equal for: 难与为～ *matchless; peerless* ② alone; single: 单枪～马 *single-handed*

匹[2]

［量］① used of horses and mules: 两～马 *two horses* ② used of rolls of cloth or silk: 一～布 *a bolt of cloth* ③［方］used of hills or mountains: 一～山 *a mountain*

【匹敌】be equal to; be well matched; rival: 无可～ *matchless; peerless; without a rival* /无可～的美丽 *beauty that could never be matched* /在绘画方

P

画无人能同他～。*Nobody can rival him in painting.* /这两个摔跤选手的实力正相～。*The two wrestlers were evenly matched.*

【匹夫】① ordinary people; common people ② an ignorant person: ～之辈 *ignoramuses*

【匹夫有责】every one has the duty; every common man has his obligation: 天下兴亡，～。*Every person is responsible for the prosperity or decline of his country; every man alive has a duty to his country.*

【匹夫之勇】reckless courage; fool-hardiness; brute courage; courage without discipline

【匹练】an unrolled bolt of white silk (often used to describe a waterfall)

【匹马单枪】single-handed; alone; play a lone hand; unaided; on one's own: 我～去赴他的约。*I saw him by appointment all by myself.* /当时没有任何人，我只能～解决这个问题。*With no one else at that time I had to deal with the problem unaided.*

【匹配】①［书］mate; marry: 他们俩很～。*They are a good match.* ②【电】matching: 亮度～ *brightness matching* /阻抗～ *impedance matching*

【匹染】【纺】piece dyeing

【匹头】［方］① piece goods (or fabrics); dry goods ② bolt of cloth

仳

【仳离】［书］① (of husband and wife) be separated ② divorce one's spouse, esp. one's wife

否

① bad; wicked: ～泰 *bad and good luck* ② censure; criticize: 臧～人物 *judge and comment people*

see also fǒu

【否极泰来】out of the depth of misfortune comes bliss; the extreme of adversity is the beginning of prosperity; the darkest hour is before dawn

痞

① lump in the abdomen ② hooligan; rogue; riffraff: 地～ *local ruffian*

【痞积】mass in the abdomen; a lump in the abdomen

【痞块】【中医】a lump in the abdomen

【痞气】mass at the right hypochondrium

【痞子】［口］ruffian; riffraff

劈

① split; cut: 把木材～成两半 *cut the timber into two* /我把它～一半给你。*I'll share it out with you.* ② strip off; break off: ～掉干树叶 *break off the dry leaves* ③ open one's legs or fingers too wide

see also pī

【劈叉】【体】do the splits

【劈柴】kindling; firewood: 劈～ *chop firewood*

【劈腿】trestle; tressel

【劈账】share out proceeds; divide an amount of money

擗

① break off: ～棒子 *pick corn* ②［书］beat one's chest; pound

【擗踊】［书］beat one's breast and stamp one's feet in deep sorrow

癖

［书］addiction: 烟～ *be addicted to smoking; smoking addiction* /酒～ *drinking addiction* /洁～ *mysophobia*

【癖好】a favourite hobby; fondness; weakness (for); partiality (for): 他有下棋的～。*He has a partiality for chess.*

【癖积】hypochondriac lump; abdominal lumps of children

【癖气】innate liking

【癖习】peculiar habit: 她有很多我认为非常讨厌的～。*She has a lot of peculiar habits that I find really irritating.*

【癖性】natural inclination; proclivity; propensity: 吹毛求疵的～ *proclivity to faultfinding* /浪费的～ *a propensity to extravagance* /豪赌的～ *a propensity to extravagance for gambling*

pì

屁

① wind from bowels; fart: 放～ *break wind; fart* ② worthless or trivial matter: ～大点的事，你也放在心上? *Do you really care about such a trivial thing?* ③ what; anything: 别翻了，包里～都没有。*Stop rummaging; there is nothing in the bag.*

【屁股】①［口］buttocks; bottom; behind: 他打孩子的～。*He smacked the child's bottom.* ② (of animals) rump; haunch; hindquarters: 牛～ *rump of an ox* ③ end; butt: 烟～ *cigarette butt; cigarette end*

【屁股蛋儿】［方］buttocks; bottom; behind; backside

【屁股蹲儿】［方］buttocks; bottom: 他摔了个～。*He fell on his bottom.*

【屁滚尿流】wet one's pants (in terror); scare the shit out of sb; be frightened out of one's wits: 吓得敌人～ *get the enemies wetting their pants with fright; send the enemies fleeing helter-skelter*

【屁话】shit; nonsense; rubbish: 他说的全是～! *What he said is sheer nonsense!*

【屁事】a trifling matter; useless thing: 随便他出不出国，关我～? *Whether he will go abroad or not is totally none of my business.*

睥

【睥睨】［书］look at sb out of the corner of one's eye — look down upon sb; look scornfully at: ～一切 *look down upon everything*

辟[1]

① open up (land, territory, etc.): 开天～地 *when heaven was separated from earth — since the beginning of the history* /这一带将～为新的旅游区。*This area will be opened up as a new tourist attraction.* ② incisive; penetrating: 精～ *extractive; incisive* ③ refute; repudiate: ～邪说 *refute heresy*

辟[2]

［书］law: 大～ *capital punishment (in ancient times)*

see also bì

【辟设】open up; set up:展厅里~了一个休息室。*A resting room was set up in the exhibition hall.*
【辟谣】refute a rumour; deny a rumour:当众~ *repudiate a rumour in public* /他站出来为朋友~。*He stood up to refute the rumours about his friend.*
媲 be as good as; be equal to; be a match for; be on a par with
【媲美】be on a par with; compare favourably with; rival:在这方面没有人能与他~。*No one could rival him in this respect.* /我认为他的才能不能与你相~。*I don't think his ability is on a par with yours.* /整个亚洲没有几家体育场的设备能和这家~。*The equipment in this stadium was only matched by one or two other stadiums in Asia.*
僻 ① secluded; out-of-the-way: ~巷 *a side lane* /穷乡~壤 *a remote and backward place* /偏~的村子 *an remote and desolate village* ② eccentric; odd:孤~ *alone; isolated; solitary* /怪~ *eccentric; odd* ③ uncommon; rare:生~字 *rarely used word*
【僻典】unfamiliar allusion
【僻见】bias; prejudice
【僻径】a desolate and out-of-the-way path
【僻静】secluded; lonely: ~的地方 *a secluded place; a secluded spot* /我的童年是在一个~的小村子里度过的。*I spent most of my childhood in an isolated village.*
【僻陋】(of a place or an area) remote and backward:他们住在一个~的小山村里。*They live in a remote and backward mountain village.*
【僻壤】an out-of-the-way place:穷乡~ *a remote village*
【僻性】eccentric character; eccentricity:我无法容忍她的~。*I cannot bear her eccentric character.*
【僻远】remote; out-of-the-way
譬 example; analogy:设~ *draw an analogy*
【譬方】analogy; instance: ~说 *for example; for instance*
【譬解】[书] try to persuade; try to convince sb:我倾尽全力~他,但是没有用。*I tried my best to convince him, but it proved useless.*
【譬如】for example; for instance; such as; e. g. ; take; like:你可以挑选任何两个男生,~汤姆和约翰。*You can choose any two boys — for example, Tom and John.* /我们还有很多问题没有解决,~谁将代表我们发言? *We still haven't settled a number of problems, like who will give the speech on behalf of us.*
【譬若】[书] for example; for instance; such as:许多国家受地震的威胁,~墨西哥和日本。*Many countries are threatened by earthquakes; for example, Mexico and Japan.*
【譬语】words said by means of analogy
【譬喻】metaphor; simile; analogy:这两个~放在一起很不相配。*These two metaphors are mismatched.*

piān

片 *see also* piàn
【片儿】(of photo, picture, etc.) flat, thin piece: 相~儿 *photo* /唱~儿 *record*
【片子】① a roll of film; movie ② negative of a roentgenogram ③ gramophone record; disc
扁
【扁舟】[书] small boat; skiff:一叶~ *a small boat*
see also biǎn
偏[1] ① slanting; leaning; diverging: ~过身去 *turn sideways* /方向略~ *in a slight slanting direction* ② partial; one-sided:不~不倚 *even-handed; impartial; unbiased* ③ supplementary; supporting; auxiliary ④ different from a certain standard:工资~高。*The wage is on the high side.* ⑤ have had a meal:我~过了,您请吃吧! *I've eaten already; you just go ahead.*
偏[2] willfully; deliberately:他~不听我的话。*He simply wouldn't listen to me.* /我~不去。*I just won't go.*
【偏爱】have partiality for sth; be partial to; favour; have a preference for:对巧克力的~ *a partiality for chocolate* /他~侦探小说。*He is partial to detective novels.* /母亲不应~其任一子女。*A mother should not favour any of her children.*
【偏安】(of a feudal regime) be content to retain sovereignty over a part of the country: ~一隅 *be content to exercise sovereignty over only a part of the country*
【偏才】① cleverness in trivial matters; smartness on petty things ② talent for a particular field of human endeavour
【偏差】deviation; error; offset; variance:动态~ *dynamic deviation* /负~ *negative deviation* /航线~ *course-line deviation* /起始~ *initial deviation* /剩余~ *residual deviation* /水平~ *horizontal deviation* /随机~ *random deviation* /同步~ *synchronism deviation* /正~ *positive or plus deviation* /纵~ *longitudinal deviation* /左右~ *lateral deviation* /纠正工作上的~ *correct errors in one's work* /~减为一毫米。*The deviation is reduced to one millimeter.*
【偏宠】show particular favour to sb
【偏磁】bias magnet: ~场 *bias field* /~电流 *bias current* /~电路 *biasing circuit* /~频率 *bias frequency*
【偏待】give particularly generous treatment (to one of the parties concerned)
【偏导数】partial derivative
【偏殿】side hall in a palace or temple
【偏方】【中医】folk prescription; effective folk remedy
【偏房】① wing-room; wing of a house ② concubine

【偏废】emphasize one to the detriment of another; do one thing and neglect another:两者不可~。*Neither should be overemphasized to the detriment of the other.*

【偏锋】① oblique force of the writing brush in Chinese calligraphy ② an indirect approach to a subject in talking or writing

【偏航】going off course; off-course; yaw

【偏好】(piānhǎo)［方］it so happened that; by mere accident:我正要去找他,~就碰见他了。*I was about to call for him when I run into him.*

【偏好】(piānhào) have a special fondness for sth; have a great liking for sth:我碰巧知道他~古典音乐。*I happen to know that he's particularly fond of classical music.* /他尤其~母亲做的菜。*He was particularly partial to the dishes cooked by his mother.*

【偏护】be partial to and side with:母亲总是~弟弟。*Mother always takes sides with my younger brother.*

【偏畸】［书］unjust; unfair; biased:老师不应该对学生有所~。*A teacher should treat his students fairly.*

【偏激】extreme; radical: ~措施 *extreme measures* /意见~ *hold extreme views* /~的政治观点 *radical political views*

【偏见】prejudice; bias:种族~ *a racial bias* /经过了几个世纪依然存在的~ *prejudices that have carried through over the centuries* /法官不应存有~。*A judge must be free from prejudice.*

【偏介】［书］stubborn and aloof

【偏科】tend to go overboard on one or some courses

【偏口鱼】【动】flatfish

【偏枯】①【中医】hemiplegia ② lopsided (development, etc.)

【偏劳】used when asking for help or thanking sb for his help:谢谢你,多~了。*Thanks for all your trouble.*

【偏离】deviate; diverge; veer: ~正道 *stray from the right way* /船~了航线。*The ship drifted off its course.*

【偏门】① side door ② crooked ways or means; improper channel

【偏旁】【语】character components or basic structural parts of Chinese characters

【偏僻】remote; out-of-the-way: ~的村落 *a remote hamlet* /~的地方 *an out-of-the-way place*

【偏偏】① willfully; insistently; persistently:为什么你不叫别人去而~叫他去? *Why did you ask him to go, of all people?* /他~不肯同我们一起去上学。*He simply refused to go to school with us.* ② contrary to expectations: ~我给他打电话的时候他出门了。*Unluckily, he was not at home when I phoned him.* ③ only; alone:为什么~他不同意这个计划呢? *Of all the people here, why should he disagree with the plan?*

【偏频】offset frequency

【偏颇】［书］biased; partial; unfair:你的看法未免失之~。*You hold a prejudiced opinion.*

【偏巧】① it so happened that; as luck would have it:我刚要出门,~下起雨来。*It happened to rain when I stepped out of the door.* ② against one's expectation:他正缺钱,~邻居又来向他借钱。*He is not well-off recently; unluckily, his neighbour came to borrow money from him.*

【偏衫】Buddhist vestment draped over the left shoulder

【偏师】［书］auxiliary force

【偏食】①【天】partial eclipse:日~ *partial solar eclipse* /月~ *partial lunar eclipse* ② partiality for a limited variety of food; a one-sided diet:有些人因为~而发胖。*Some people get fat through partiality for particular kinds of food.*

【偏私】biased; partial

【偏瘫】【医】hemiplegia

【偏袒】show partiality for; be partial to one side; give unprincipled protection to; take sides with: 一项~原告的决定 *a decision that was partial to the plaintiff* /你不~任何一方是对的。*It is right for you to show no partiality to either side.*

【偏疼】［口］favour one (child, etc.) more than the others

【偏题】a catch (or tricky) question (in an examination):这次考试都是~,我肯定过不了。*The examination paper is full of tricky questions; I'm sure I'll fail it this time.*

【偏听偏信】trust only one side; be biased; be partial to:作为领导,你不能~。*As a leader, you should avoid being biased.*

【偏头痛】【医】migraine: ~患者 *migraineur*

【偏微分】【数】partial differential: ~方程 *partial differential equation*

【偏西】the sun has moved towards the west:他一觉睡到日头~。*He didn't wake up until it was late in the afternoon.*

【偏相关】partial correlation: ~系数 *partial correlation coefficient*

【偏向】① erroneous tendency; deviation:纠正~ *correct a deviation* ② favour; prefer:我~于你的建议。*I am in favour of your suggestion.* ③ shield; be partial:他~女儿。*He is partial to his daughter.* /出口政策~海外顾客。*Export policy has been biased towards overseas customers.*

【偏心】① partiality; bias:他一点都不~。*He is absolutely impartial.* ②【机】eccentric; running out

【偏心度】degree of eccentricity

【偏心角】eccentric angle

【偏心距】eccentricity; offsetting

【偏心眼儿】［口］partial; prejudiced:老师对班里的男生~。*The teacher is partial to the boys in the class.*

【偏压】【电】bias voltage; bias

【偏倚】be biased; be partial to:申请程序似乎对富裕家庭的孩子有所~。*The application procedure tends to favour children from rich families.*

【偏远】remote; faraway; out-of-the-way: ~山区 *remote districts*

【偏振】【物】polarization:光的~ *polarization of*

P

light
【偏振光】【物】polarized light
【偏执】stubbornly biased; extreme
【偏执狂】【医】paranoia: ~患者 *paranoiac*; *paranoid*
【偏重】stress one aspect at the expense of another; lay special stress on:我们不能~数量而不重质量。*We cannot unduly emphasize quantity to the neglect of quality.* /学习不应只~记忆而忽视理解。*One shouldn't only put stress on memorization while neglecting comprehension.*
【偏转】【物】deflection: ~系统 *deflection system*

犏

【犏牛】offspring of a bull and a female yak

篇 ① a piece of writing:长~小说 *novel* /诗~ *psalm*; *poem* ② printed sheet (of paper, etc.):歌~儿 *song sheet* ③[量](of article) a piece of writing; (of paper) a sheet of paper; a leaf of a book:一~论文 *a thesis* /一~文章 *a piece of writing*; *an essay*
【篇幅】① length (of an article):文章的~不必长,但要抓住要点。*The article can be short, but it should grasp the essence.* ② space (on a printed page): ~有限 *have limited space* /报纸用大~报道了这次会议。*The newspaper gave the conference considerable coverage.*
【篇目】① titles of chapters or articles in a book:我记不清这篇文章的~了。*The title of the article slipped my memory.* ② table of contents; list of articles
【篇页】leaves and pages; writing
【篇章】sections and chapters; writings: ~结构 *structure of an article*; *composition* /不朽的~ *immortal article* /改革开放为中国的发展翻开了新~。*Reform and opening up opened a new chapter in China's development.*
【篇子】[口] ① printed sheet ② essay; piece of writing

翩 [书] fly swiftly

【翩翩】① lightly (dance, flutter, etc.):蝴蝶在花丛中~起舞。*Butterflies are fluttering among the flowers.* ②[书] elegant and natural; graceful: ~少年 *an elegant young man*; *a suave young man* /风度~ *have an elegant and smart carriage*
【翩然】[书] lightly; trippingly: ~飞舞 *flutter lightly* / ~而至 *come tripping down*
【翩若惊鸿】(of a beautiful woman) walk gracefully and lightly like a startled swan
【翩跹】[书] lightly; trippingly: ~起舞 *dance with quick, light steps*; *dance trippingly*

pián

便

see also biàn

【便佞】[书] flatterer who seeks to ingratiate himself with others
【便便】bulging; swelling:毕业几年后,他变得大腹~。*He became pot-bellied several years after graduation.*
【便宜】① cheap:他买了一辆~的汽车。*He bought a cheap car.* /这条裙子这么~,真划得来。*This skirt is a real bargain at such a low price.* ② petty advantages; unearned gains:讨~ *seek advantage at the expense of others* /贪小~吃大亏。*The greed for undeserved gains may bring great losses.* ③ let sb off lightly:我们决不能~了这个骗子! *We mustn't let the cheat off lightly.*
【便宜货】a cheap article; bargain

骈 parallel; antithetical

【骈比】[书] close to each other; side by side
【骈肩】[书] shoulder to shoulder — a jostling crowd; crowded
【骈句】parallel sentences
【骈俪】art of parallelism; ornate style of writing consisting of parallel characters
【骈体】an early writing style characterized by paralleled construction of pairs of sentences and orateness
【骈阗】[书] gather; side by side; assemble
【骈文】rhythmical prose characterized by parallelism and ornateness
【骈枝】[书] ① extra toe or finger ② superfluous: ~机构 *superfluous organization*

胼

【胼手胝足】callused hands and feet; callosity forming on palms or feet due to hard labour — a life of toil; hardworking
【胼胝】callosity; callus; tyle

蹁 [书] walk with a swing or in a sidling

【蹁跹】[书] whirling about (in dancing)

piǎn

谝 [方] boast; show off: ~能 *boast one's abilities*

piàn

片 ① slice; flake; a flat, thin piece:布~ *small pieces of cloth* /雪~ *snowflakes* /纸~儿 *pieces of paper* ② TV film:制~人 *film producer* ③ section (or part) of a place:分~儿开会 *hold neighbourhood meetings* ④ cut into slices: ~肉片儿 *slice meat* / ~豆腐干 *slice bean curds* ⑤ fragmentary; partial; brief: ~言 *a few words* ⑥[量]:两~儿药 *two tablets of medicine* /一~汪洋 *a sheet of water* /一大~庄稼 *a large stretch of crops* /一~火海 *a sheet of flames* /一~新气象 *a*

P

new atmosphere /一～真心 *be all sincerity*
see also piān
【片材】sheet:～成形 *sheet forming*
【片酬】payment for making a film or TV play
【片段】part; passage; snatch; fragment:生活的～ *a slice of life* /我无意中听到他们谈话的～。*I overheard fragments of their conversation* /他太小了,只能回忆起那次事故的零碎～。*He was still too young and could recall only a fragmented account of the accident.*
【片断】fragmentary; incomplete; scrappy: ～经验 *scattered experiences* / ～的回忆 *fragmentary memories* / ～的证据 *scrappy evidence*
【片簧】【机】leaf spring
【片剂】【药】tablet; troche
【片甲不存】not a single armoured warrior remains — the army is completely wiped out:杀得敌人～ *thoroughly wipe out the enemies*
【片假名】katakana, Japanese regular script
【片金】flake gold
【片警】neighbourhood police
【片锯】blade saw
【片刻】a short while; an instant; a moment; a short space of time:稍等～ *wait a little moment* /在～功夫,她的整个人生就已经改变了。*In that brief space of time her whole life had changed.* /～之后,门关上了。*An instant later the door closed.*
【片面】① unilateral: ～之词 *one person's version of an incident* ② one-sided; single-faceted: ～地看问题 *take a one sided approach to problems* /你的观点是～的。*You hold a one-sided view.* /企业不应该～追求产值。*The enterprises should not place undue emphasis on output value.*
【片面性】one-sidedness
【片石】slabstone; flagstone; slate
【片时】a short while; a moment:请稍等～,他一会儿就到。*Please wait for a while; he will come here soon.*
【片头】titles and credits at the beginning of a film
【片瓦无存】not a single tile remains — be razed to the ground:一场大火把剧院烧得～。*The theatre was razed to the ground in the conflagration.*
【片言】a few words; a brief note: ～可决。*A single word is enough to fix the deal.*
【片言只语】(in) only a few words; a phrase or two:他的来信只有～,让我非常失望。*His letter carried only a few words, which made me very disappointed.*
【片约】contract with an actor or actress to shoot a film or TV film
【片纸只字】fragments of writing; a brief note or letter
【片状】schistose: ～保险丝 *strip fuse* / ～结构 *laminated structure* / ～侵蚀 *sheet erosion*
【片子】① a flat, thin piece; slice; flake; scrap:铁～ *small pieces of sheet iron* ② visiting card; name card

骗[1] ① deceive; cheat; fool:欺～ *deceive; dupe* /你在～我。*You are kidding me.* /你～不了她,她非常精明。*You can't fool her; she's much too clever for that.* /他竟然～他最要好的朋友以高价买了一个赝品。*He even beguiled his best friend into buying the counterfeit at a high price.* ② gain sth by cheating: ～钱 *cheat sb of his money*

骗[2]

【骗局】fraud; hoax; swindle; fiddle; trickery:和平～ *the peace hoax* /这纯粹是个～。*It's a perfect fraud.* /她因彩票～而被指控。*She has been charged with being involved in the lottery swindle.* /由于盗窃和～引起的经济损失很多。*Financial losses due to theft or fraud can be high.*
【骗马】swing (or leap) into the saddle; mount a horse
【骗取】gain sth by cheating; defraud: ～农民的土地 *cheat the peasants of their land* /他～了我的信任。*He wormed his way into my confidence.*
【骗术】deceitful trick; deception; ruse; hoax; sleight of hand; trap; put-up job:施行～ *perpetrate a fraud* /他～高明。*His art of fraud is superb.* /我很快就看穿了他的谎言和～。*I quickly saw through his lies and deceptions.*
【骗腿儿】[方] swing one's leg sideways
【骗子】cheat; swindler; impostor; trickster; bilker; con-man:政治～ *a political swindler* /她认为所有的销售人员都是～。*He thinks all sales people are cheats.* /那个律师被揭穿是个～。*The lawyer was unmasked as a faker.*
【骗子手】[方] swindler; cheat; trickster
【骗嘴】boast; talk big:他这个人只会～。*Boasting is the only thing that he is good at.*

piāo

剽 ① rob; loot ② swift; nimble: ～疾 *fierce and nimble*
【剽悍】agile and brave; quick and fierce
【剽掠】plunder; loot:昨天一群强盗～了商店。*A group of robbers looted the shop yesterday.*
【剽窃】plagiarize; lift; copy; steal: ～物 *plagiarism; plagiary* / ～者 *plagiarist* /他很生气地发现另一个作家～了他的文章。*He was furious to discover that another writer had copied one of his articles.*
【剽袭】plagiarize; lift; copy; steal:他的著作中有几篇文章是～他人的。*Several articles in his works have been lifted from other authors.* /他头脑里没有独创的想法,只是～了其他作家的想法。*He hasn't an original idea in his head; he simply plagiarizes from other writers.*
漂 ① float:一片树叶在水上～着。*A leaf is floating on the water.* ② drift:船～到海里去了。*The boat drifted out to the sea.*
see also piǎo; piào
【漂冰】flow berg; floating ice

【漂泊】① float; berth:一块木头~在水上。*A piece of wood floats on water.* ② wander from place to place; drift aimlessly; rove: ~异乡 *wander aimlessly in a strange land* /我不想继续在外国单身~了。*I want to stop gadding about unaccompanied in a foreign country.*

【漂浮】① float; stay up:玫瑰花瓣在水上~。*Rose petals float on water.* /你不会沉下去的,你肺里的空气会让你~。*You won't sink — you'll stay up because of the air in your lungs.* ② float or hover before the eyes or in the mind:他的形象在我的脑海中~。*His image hovers in my mind.* /战争的往事~在老兵的眼前。*War memories floated before the veteran's eyes.* ③ (of style of work) showy; impractical:他近期的作品风格有些~。*The style of his recent works seems a little impractical.*

【漂流】① be driven by the current; drift about: 小船在河中顺水~而下。*The boat drifted down the river.* /圆木顺流~到锯木场。*The logs were drifted down the stream to the saw-mills.* ② drift aimlessly:他在各个城市间~。*He drifted aimlessly among the cities.*

【漂萍】[书] floating about like duckweed; lead a wandering life

【漂儿】[方] float; cork on a fishing line

【漂洋过海】travel far across the ocean (or sea) — go abroad:他~去了美国。*He travelled across the ocean to the United States.*

【漂移】① drift:冰山~ *drift of an iceberg* /长期~ *long term drift* /垂直~ *vertical drift* /大陆~ *continental drift* /基线~ *baseline drift* /基准~ *datum drift* /灵敏度~ *sensitivity drift* /相位~ *phase drift* /遗传~ *genetic drift* /质点~ *particle drift* ②【电】drift:电压~ *voltage drift* /零点~ *null drift* /频率~ *frequency drift* /热~*thermal drift*

【漂游】① drift:旅行者们~而下。*The travellers drifted down the stream.* ② wander about: 四处~ *wander from place to place*

【漂悠】float slowly and gently

缥

see also piǎo

【缥缈】dimly discernible; misty:虚无~ *visionary; illusory*

飘

① float in the air; flutter; waft: ~雪花 *snow slightly* /窗帘在微风中~起。*The curtains were fluttering in the breeze.* /空气中~来一阵花香。*The scent of the flowers was wafted through the air.* ② weak; wobbly:我感觉两腿~。*My legs felt weak.* ③ frivolous; flippant:作风有点~ *behave frivolously*

【飘尘】airborne dust: ~污染 *floating dust pollution*

【飘带】streamer; ribbon

【飘荡】① drift; float; flutter:茉莉花的芳香在周围~。*The smell of jasmines floated around.* ② wander about; bum around; drift:他~街头。*He wandered the streets.* /他整个夏天都在~,现在已经身无分文。*He spent the entire summer drifting around and now he has no money left at all.*

【飘动】float (in the air or upon the waves); flutter; sway:手绢在风中~。*The handkerchief swayed in the wind.*

【飘风】[书] storm wind

【飘拂】wave; drift:白云在空中~。*White clouds were floating across the sky.*

【飘忽】① (of clouds, etc.) move swiftly; float in the air ② mobile; uncertain:他的行踪~不定。*His whereabouts are uncertain.*

【飘疾】[书] speedy; swift

【飘降】float down

【飘零】① (of flowers, etc.) withered and fallen:花在寒冷的天气里~。*The flowers withered and fell in the cold.* ② wandering; adrift; homeless: ~一身 *a solitary wanderer* /你到底在干什么? 你不能这样四处~! *What are you on earth doing? You can't wander around a country like this alone.*

【飘落】drift and fall slowly; fall down; float:一根羽毛随风~。*A feather floated down on the wind.* /雪~到各处。*The snow had drifted everywhere.*

【飘蓬】drift about; wander about

【飘飘然】① feel as if treading on air:几杯酒下肚,他感到有点~。*After drinking several cups of wine, he was tipsy.* ② be carried away with one's own importance; smug; self-satisfied; pleased with oneself; complacent:听了狐狸的奉承,乌鸦感到~了。*On hearing the flattering words from the fox, the crow became swollen-headed.* /他40出头,带有一种功成名就的~的感觉。*He was in his early forties and had the self-satisfied air of someone who has achieved fame and success.* /我考试取得了第一名,禁不住~起来。*I had come out first in the exam and was feeling inordinately pleased with myself.*

【飘飘欲仙】feel as if one were in paradise; sprightly as a fairy:置身如此美景,我感到~。*Staying in such a beautiful spot, I felt much at ease.*

【飘然】① floating in the air ② lightly:他骑上马~而去。*He rode on the horse and went away lightly.* ③ relaxed and glad: ~自在 *relaxed and free*

【飘洒】(piāosǎ) float in the air; swirl down:天空中雪花~。*Snowflakes were swirling in the air.*

【飘洒】(piāosa) free and easy; graceful; elegant:他举止~。*He behaves elegantly.*

【飘散】(of smoke, mist, etc.) drift away; float and scatter:花的香味在空气中~。*The smell of flowers floated in the air.*

【飘闪】drift and glisten

【飘逝】① drift away ② vanish; die away: ~不见 *vanish from sight*

【飘舞】wave in the wind:羽毛~落地。*The feather wavered in the wind to the floor.*

【飘扬】wave; flutter; fly (in the wind):桅杆顶端~着五星红旗。*The five-star red flag is flying at the top of the mast.*

【飘漾】float; undulate

【飘摇】① swing:烟雾~上升。*The smog rises in the wind.* ② tottering; precarious; unstable:风雨~

precarious situation; *tottering regime*

【飘曳】flicker:蜡烛~不定。*The candle flickered out.*

【飘移】drift about:船骸向海岸~。*The wreckage drifted toward shore.*

【飘逸】①［书］elegant; graceful:举止~的绅士 *an elegant gentleman* ② drift; disperse:白云~。*White clouds were dispersing.*

【飘溢】drift about; float in the air:屋子里~着咖啡的香气。*The room was permeated with the aroma of coffee.*

【飘游】roam about:在林间~ *roam about the forest*

【飘悠】drift leisurely; float in the air:气球~着升上天空。*Balloons drifted up into the sky.*

【飘展】(of flag) fly:彩旗在风中~。*Coloured flags were flapping in the wind.*

piáo

嫖 visit prostitutes; go whoring: ~妓 *go whoring*

【嫖客】whoremonger; whoremaster

【嫖宿】sleep with a prostitute

瓢 wooden dipper; gourd ladle

【瓢虫】ladybug; ladybird

【瓢泼】(of rain) very heavy: ~大雨 *heavy rain*; *torrential rain*; *raining cats and dogs*

【瓢子】［方］① wooden dipper ② spoon

piǎo

漂 ① bleach: ~布 *bleach cloth* ② wash away impurities: ~朱砂 *rinse cinnabar* /~干净衣服 *give the clothes a good rinse*
see also piāo; piào

【漂白】bleach:他把这块桌布~了。*He bleached this tablecloth.*

【漂白度】degree of bleaching

【漂白粉】bleaching powder

【漂白剂】bleacher; bleaching agent:过氧化物~ *peroxide bleaches* /含氯~ *chlorine bleaches*

【漂白土】fuller's earth

【漂染】bleaching and dyeing; bleach and dye: ~厂 *bleaching and dyeing house*

【漂洗】rinse: ~回收 *reclaim rinse*

【漂洗槽】【化】potcher

缥 ［书］① pale blue ② pale-blue silk fabrics
see also piāo

瞟 glance sideways at; askance:他~了我一眼,什么也没说。*He cast a sidelong glance at me and said nothing.*

piào

票 ① ticket; a piece of printed certificate:彩~ *a lottery ticket* /单程~ *one-way ticket*; *single ticket* /飞机~ *an airline ticket* /船~ *boat ticket* /快车~ *express ticket* /门~ *ticket for admission* /团体~ *collective ticket* /卧铺~ *berth ticket* /戏~ *a theater ticket* /站台~ *platformticket* /支~ *cheque* ② bill; note:零~儿 *small change* /一镑的~ *a pound note* ③ hostage; a person held for ransom by kidnappers: 撕~ *kill the hostage* ④［方］［量］:一~生意 *a deal*; *a transaction* ⑤ amateur performer (of Beijing opera, etc.):玩儿~ *amateur performance of Beijing Opera, etc.*; *be an amateur performer*

【票车】［方］passenger train

【票额】the sum stated on a cheque or bill; face value

【票房】① booking office (at a railway station, airport, etc.); box office (at a theatre, stadium, etc.) ②［旧］a club for amateur performers (of Beijing opera, etc.)

【票房价值】box-office value:很高的~ *be a box-office success*

【票根】counterfoil or stub (of a cheque, postal order, receipt, etc.):支票~ *a counterfoil of a check*

【票号】［旧］firm for exchange and transfer of money; exchange shop

【票汇】send a money order or bank draft

【票价】price of a ticket; admission fee; fee:开幕式的~是每张100元。*Admission to the opening ceremony is 100 yuan per person.*

【票据】① bill; note:到期未付~ *overdue bill* /应收~ *bill receivable* /流通~ *negotiable instruments* ② voucher; receipt:空白~ *blank receipt* /应付~ *bills payable* /应收~ *bills receivable* /公司在发不出工资时给职员一定的~。*A company vouchers employees when the payroll cannot be met.*

【票面】face (or par, nominal) value: ~伍圆的纸币 *bill in 5 yuan denomination*

【票面价值】face value; par (value)

【票箱】ballot box

【票选】elect by ballot; vote for sb

【票友】［旧］amateur performer (of Beijing opera, etc.)

【票证】coupons; ticket

【票庄】［旧］firm for exchange and transfer of money

【票子】bank note; paper money; bill

漂 ［方］fail to accomplish; to no avail; come to nothing:我的计划~了。*My plan came to nothing.*
see also piāo; piǎo

【漂亮】① handsome; good-looking; beautiful:我妹妹长得很~。*My sister is good-looking*; *my sister is pretty.* ② remarkable; brilliant; splendid;

smartly:他的字写得很~。*He writes a beautiful hand.* /守门员这个球救得~。*The goalkeeper made a beautiful save.*

【漂亮话】fine words; high-sounding words:光说~是没有用的,干出成绩来才算数。*Fine words butter no parsnips.*

骠 [书] ① (of horse) galloping ② brave; intrepid: ~悍 *valiant; intrepid*

piē

撇[1] neglect; discard; cast aside:先~下小事,集中精力做好这个项目。*Put aside the matters of little importance and focus your attention on the project.* /他~下一家人,独自出去谋生。*He went out to make a living, leaving behind the whole family.*

撇[2] skim: ~去汤里的沫子 *skim off the scum from the soup* /~油 *skim off the grease (or fat)*

see also piě

【撇开】leave aside; bypass: ~礼俗 *fling propriety away* /咱们把次要问题~不谈吧。*Let's leave aside questions of minor importance.*

【撇弃】discard; give up; abandon: ~处于危难中的朋友 *abandon a friend in trouble* /你应该~旧信念。*You should discard old beliefs.*

【撇清】whitewash oneself; claim to be innocent:没想到当警察来调查事故原因时,他倒先~。*To my great surprise, he whitewashed himself completely when the policeman came to investigate the cause of the accident.*

【撇脱】[方] ① simple and direct:说起来~做起来难。*It's easy to talk but hard to work.* ② frank; straightforward:他是一个~人。*He is always candid.*

瞥 glimpse:她的一~使他无言以对。*She withered him with a look.* /他一眼就~见她来了。*He saw at a glance that she was coming.* /我只是~了一眼那本书,所以没有注意作者是谁。*I just darted a look at the book and didn't notice the name of the author.*

【瞥见】get a glimpse of; catch sight of:我~她在人群当中。*I glimpsed her among the crowd.* /我在公共汽车上~他和一个妇女争吵。*On the bus, I caught sight of his quarrelling with a woman.*

【瞥视】cast a quick glance at; shoot a glance at:我们的新邻居我只~过一眼。*I caught a glimpse of our new neighbour.*

piě

撇 ① cast; throw: ~砖头 *throw a brick* /别再提了,我早把这件事~到脑后了。*No mentioning about it; I have cast the matter out of my mind completely.* ② pout one's lips in disdain:她嘴一~,把我的报告扔到了一边。*She curled her lips, throwing my report aside.* ③ the left-falling stroke in Chinese calligraphy ④ [量]:两~胡子 *two small turfs of moustache*

see also piē

【撇嘴】curl one's lips (to show contempt, disbelief or disappointment):他一~,表示怀疑。*He twitched his mouth in disbelief.*

pīn

拼[1] piece together; join together:东~西凑 *scrape together; knock together* /把两张纸~起来 *join the two pieces of paper together*

拼[2] go all out; exert one's utmost in work: ~时间 *race against time* / ~到底 *fight to the bitter end; fight to the finish*

【拼版】【印】makeup

【拼板玩具】jigsaw puzzle

【拼搏】exert oneself to the utmost; go all out in one's struggle: ~精神 *spirit of going all out to win success; combatant spirit*

【拼刺】① bayonet drill ② bayonet charge

【拼刺刀】bayonet charge

【拼凑】piece together; knock together; rig up; assemble: ~一笔钱 *scrape up a sum*

【拼攒】assemble (a car, etc.); piece together spare parts: ~一辆汽车 *assemble a car with spare parts*

【拼法】spelling:正式~ *official spelling*

【拼缝】piece:你几乎看不出那件外衣的~。*You can hardly see the join in the coat.*

【拼花地板】block floor

【拼花地面】mosaic pavement

【拼火】exchange fire

【拼接】join together; piece together:医生们只得用金属板把两块骨头~起来。*Doctors had to use a metal plate to join the two pieces of bone together.*

【拼劲儿】energy and determination; drive; resolution:小伙子们~十足。*The young men are full of energy and resolution.*

【拼力】spare no efforts to do sth; go all out; put a lot of effort into sth; be hard at:他~工作了整个上午,却仍然没有修好那辆车。*He has been hard at it all morning and he still hasn't finished mending the car.*

【拼命】① risk one's life; go all out regardless of great danger: ~抵抗 *risk the life in resistance* ② exerting one's utmost; for all one is worth; with all one's might: ~喊 *shout desperately* /为了给母亲治病,他~挣钱。*He exerted his utmost to earn money in order to cure his mother's illness.* /为了升迁,他~工作。*He is pushing himself too hard in order to get a promotion.*

【拼盘】assorted cold dishes; made dish

【拼抢】strive for the ball

【拼杀】fight desperately; grapple:与敌人~ *grapple with an enemy*

【拼死】desperately; at the risk of one's life; frantically：～挣扎 *wage a desperate struggle*

【拼死拼活】① put up a life-and-death struggle ② do one's utmost；for all one is worth；desperately：～地干 *work flat out*；*work with all one's might*

【拼图游戏】jigsaw puzzle

【拼写】spell；transliterate：～课本 *spelling book* /～错误 *spelling errors* /你的作文里满是～错误。*Your composition is full of spelling mistakes.*

【拼写法】spelling；orthography

【拼音】① combine sounds into syllables ② spell；phoneticize

【拼音文字】alphabetic language；phonetic language

【拼音字母】phonetic alphabet；phonetic letters

【拼装】assemble；fit together：～一只手表 *assemble a watch*

【拼缀】combine；stitch together

【拼字游戏】scrabble

姘 have illicit relations with sb

【姘夫】illicit male lover；paramour；adulterer

【姘妇】kept woman；mistress；paramour；adulteress

【姘居】live illicitly as husband and wife；cohabit

【姘识】[书] have illicit sexual relations after getting acquainted with each other

【姘头】paramour；mistress or lover

pín

贫[1] ① poor；impoverished：清～ *poor*；*badly off* /一～如洗 *abject poverty*；*as poor as a church*；(*as*) *poor as Job* /～不足耻，耻～乃耻。*Poverty is not a shame, but the being ashamed of it is.* ② deficient；inadequate：～油 *oil-poor* ③ [旧] used by a Buddhist monk or Taoist priest to refer to himself

贫[2] [方] loquacious；talkative：你别重复了，真～！*Stopping repeating it! You are really loquacious.*

【贫病交迫】suffer from both poverty and sickness；be poor and ill

【贫道】[谦] my humble self (used by Taoist priests)；I

【贫乏】① destitute；poor；impoverished：一个生活～的作家 *an impoverished writer* ② wretchedly lacking；meagre：常识～ *deficient in common sense* /词汇～ *meager vocabulary* /～的资源 *meager resources* /经验～ *lack experience*

【贫富不均】too much difference between the rich and the poor

【贫骨头】[方] ① a stingy (or mean) person；niggard；a person keen on petty gain：那个商人是个～。*The merchant was an avaricious fellow.* ② an idle chatterer；a garrulous person：这个～总是为一点小事唠叨个没完。*The chatterer always babbles about trifles.*

【贫雇农】poor peasants and farm labourers

【贫寒】poor；poverty-stricken；impoverished；penniless；destitute：他出身～，但是后来取得了很大的成绩。*He was born into a poor family, but achieved great achievements later.* /他家境～，家人被迫卖房以便为他治病。*His family was so impoverished that they were forced to sell the house to make him cured.*

【贫化】【矿】dilution：～燃料 *depleted fuel* /～系数 *depletion factor*

【贫瘠】barren；infertile；poor：～的土壤 *lean soil*；*poor soil* /由于干旱而变得～的地区 *a region impoverished by drought* /沙漠是～的土地。*The desert is barren land.*

【贫贱】poor and lowly；in straitened and humble circumstances：～不能移 *not to be shaken by one's poverty* /他出身～。*He is a man of poor and humble origin.*

【贫贱之交】friends in days of poverty：我们是～。*We are friends in the days when we were hard up.*

【贫苦】poor；poverty-stricken；badly off；needy；destitute；impoverished：她一生都过着～的生活。*She has lived in poverty all her life.* /他生活～，但是他的朋友比他更甚。*He was pretty poor but his friends were even worse off.* /他的摄影作品生动地表现了山区中～家庭的生活。*His photographs show vividly the lives of poverty-stricken families in the mountainous area.*

【贫矿】lean ore；low-grade ore

【贫困】poor；impoverished；in pinching poverty；destitute；penniless：～潦倒 *be on the beach*；*be penniless* /摆脱～ *shake off poverty* /他们生活在～之中。*They lived in poverty.* /丈夫死后，她的生活一度很～。*She was quite badly off for a while after her husband died.*

【贫困地区】depressed area；poverty-stricken area

【贫困化】pauperization

【贫困线】poverty line

【贫民】poor people；paupers：城市～ *urban poor*；*city pauper* /～救济税 *poor rate*

【贫民窟】slum；ghetto；rookery；bustee；shanty town：在城市～中，凶杀案的比例很高。*The murder rates are quite high in city ghettos.*

【贫民区】slum area；slum district；gutter；shanty town：她在纽约～中长大。*She grew up in a New York slum.*

【贫民学校】charity school

【贫农】poor peasant：～团 *the poor peasant league*

【贫气】① mean；miserly；stingy；niggardly：他很～，没有人愿意和他交往。*He is a miser, and nobody wants to make friends with him.* ② garrulous；loquacious：一个～的司机 *a garrulous driver*

【贫穷】poor；needy；impoverished；destitute；poverty-stricken：～人家 *a needy family* /～教会他们要谨慎花钱。*Poverty has taught them to be close with their money.*

【贫弱】(of a country) poor and weak

【贫僧】[谦] I；my humble self (a form of self-address used by Buddhist monks)

【贫相】have a mean look

P

【贫血】【医】anaemia
【贫氧层】oxygen-poor layer
【贫油】oil-poor: ~国 *oil-poor country*
【贫渣】lean slag
【贫嘴】garrulous; loquacious; talkative; chatty: 当她放松下来后，开始变得~。*As she grew more relaxed she became more and more talkative.*
【贫嘴薄舌】be garrulous and sharp-tongued; talkative

频 repeatedly; frequently: 尿~ *frequent micturition* / 这里下雨很~。*Rains are frequent here.*
【频传】(of good news, etc.) keep pouring in; come successively: 捷报~。*News of victory keeps pouring in.*
【频次】frequency
【频带】【物】frequency band
【频道】frequency channel: 一~ *Channel 1* / ~选择器 *channel selector*
【频段】frequency band; frequency range: ~分配 *frequency allocation*
【频繁】frequently; often; incessant; time after time; repeatedly: ~的地震 *the frequency of earthquakes* / 两国人民之间交往~。*There are frequent contacts between the people of the two countries.* / 我最近~地看到她。*I often see her recently.* / 她在演讲中~地提到宗教自由。*She mentioned religious freedom repeatedly in her speech.*
【频率】①【物】frequency: ~范围 *frequency range* ② frequency: 这家电台用三种不同的~广播。*This radio station broadcasts on three different frequencies.* / 这两年矿难发生的~在提高。*The frequency of mining accidents has increased these years.*
【频年】for years running; for successive years
【频频】again and again; repeatedly; frequently: ~点头 *nod again and again* / ~挥手 *wave one's hand again and again*
【频谱】【物】frequency spectrum: ~分析 *frequency analysis*
【频仍】[书] frequent; repeated: 战争~ *be torn by frequent warfare*
【频数】[书] frequent and continuous
【频移】frequency shift: ~补偿 *frequency drift compensation*

嫔 [书] ① concubine of an emperor in feudal times: 妃~ *imperial concubines* ② woman attendant at court

颦 [书] knit the brows; frown: 效~ *imitate others awkwardly*
【颦蹙】[书] knit one's brows

pǐn

品 ① article; product: 畅销~ *saleable articles* / 废弃~ *discarded article* / 免税~ *duty-free articles* / 模制~ *blocked-in article* / 日用~ *articles of daily use* / 商~ *commodity product*; *merchandise* / 食~ *articles of food* / 危险~ *hazardous article* / 赝~ *counterfeit articles* / 滞销~ *slow-moving articles* / 专利~ *patented article* ② grade; rank; class: 上~牛奶 *grade A milk*; *top grade milk* ③ official ranks in dynastic times: 七~芝麻官 *a mere grade-seven official* ④ type; kind: ~种多样 *a great variety of goods* ⑤ character; quality: 人~ *moral quality*; *moral standing* ⑥ sample; taste: ~味儿 *savour the flavour* ⑦ play (wind instrument): ~箫 *play the flageolet* ⑧ (Pǐn) a surname
【品尝】have a taste of; sample; savor: ~鸡汤 *have a taste of the chicken soup* / ~蛋糕 *sample cake* / ~生活中的酸甜苦辣 *taste joys and sorrows of life* /请~北京烤鸭。*Please try our Beijing roast duck.*
【品德】moral character; morality; quality: 她具有耐心的~。*She has the virtue of patience.* / 他已经彻底抛弃了劳动人民的优良~。*She has deserted totally the fine qualities of the working people.*
【品第】[书] ① evaluate; judge: ~高下 *assess quality* ② position; grade; rank: 这种纸张~很高。*This kind of paper is of high grade.*
【品格】① one's character and morals: 他是一个有~的人。*He is a man of character.* ② quality and style (of literary works, etc.)
【品红】① pinkish red ②【化】fuchsin; azaleine; rosein: ~碱 *rosaniline*
【品级】① official rank in feudal times ② grade; class
【品鉴】assess and judge: ~古董 *assess a piece of antique*
【品节】conduct and morals: ~高洁 *with noble character and moral integrity*
【品蓝】reddish blue
【品类】class; category: ~繁多 *different categories*
【品绿】light green; malachite green
【品貌】① looks; appearance: ~端正 *well-shaped figure and decorous appearance* ② *character and looks*; *conduct and appearance*: 这样~兼优的小伙子可不好找。*It's really difficult to find such a handsome man of good character.*
【品名】the name of an article; the name or description of a commodity
【品茗】sip tea and taste its flavour
【品目】names of things; items: ~繁多 *numerous names*
【品牌】brand: ~管理 *brand management* / ~形象 *brand image* / 好~的咖啡 *a good brand of coffee* / 消费者往往把著名~和高质量联系在一起。*Consumers always associate famous brand names with high quality.*
【品评】judge; comment on: 他善于根据人们的穿着爱好~他们。*He is good at judging people according to their taste in clothes.* / 他的作品经常为报界~。*His works are frequently commented by the press.*
【品题】[书] appraise a person
【品头论足】① make frivolous remarks about sb's appearance ② find fault with; be overcritical;

P

pick holes in：每次经理走过来，都要对我的工作～。*Whenever the manager comes around, he's always trying to find fault with my work.*

【品脱】pint：一～容量 *pint capacity* /一加仑有八～。*There are eight pints in a gallon.*

【品位】①［书］official rank ②【矿】grade ③ quality（of products, etc.）：高～的服装 *clothes of high quality*

【品味】① taste；savor：～成功的喜悦 *a taste of success* ② think over：我仔细～，才明白了他所说的话的含义。*I had thought it over before I understood the meaning of his words.* ③ quality；flavour：我喜欢这种巧克力的～。*I like the flavour of this kind of chocolate.*

【品系】strain：～杂交 *incross*；*line crossing*

【品行】conduct；behavior：～端正的人 *a moral man* /～不良 *having bad conduct*；*ill-behaved*；*be of loose morals*

【品性】moral character：就～而言，我对他十分满意。*Morally he is all that I desired.*

【品学兼优】excellent in character and learning；good both in character and scholarship

【品议】judge；appraise：经过评委会的～，这种电视被评为一等奖。*The review committee makes an appraisal that this type of TV set be awarded first prize.*

【品质】① character；quality：我们高度赞扬他的道德～。*We all think highly of his moral character.* ② quality：～低劣的货物 *goods of low quality* /～好的货物容易卖出。*High quality goods sell easily.*

【品种】①【生】breed；strain；variety：新～的羊 *a new breed of sheep* /对照～ *check variety* /选育优良～ *breeding improved variety* /杂交～ *hybrid variety* ② variety；assortment：花色～ *variety of colours and designs* /货物～齐全 *have a good assortment of goods* /你在那家专卖店可以买到至少50种不同～的蜂蜜。*You can buy at least fifty different types of honey in that specialist store.*

【品族】cattle born of the same dam

pìn

牝 female：～马 *mare* /～牛 *cow*

【牝痔】【中医】mixed hemorrhoids and perianal abscess

聘 ① engage；employ：～专家 *hire an expert* /他被～为教授。*He was engaged as a professor.* ②［书］visit a friendly country on behalf of one's government：报～ *return an official visit* ③ betroth：定～ *formally betroth* ④（of a girl）get married；be married off：出～ *get married*

【聘金】① betrothal money ② money paid when employing sb

【聘礼】① gifts given when engaging sb ② betrothal presents；bride-price：昨天男方下了～。*The man's family delivered betrothal gifts yesterday.*

【聘请】engage；hire；employ：经理决定～一个新秘书。*The manager decided to engage a new secretary.*

【聘任】engage；appoint to a position：～制 *the appointment system* /电脑公司～他担任技术顾问。*The computer company engaged him as a technical adviser.*

【聘书】letter of appointment；letter of employment；engagement contract

【聘问】［古］visit a friendly nation on behalf of one's own country

【聘用】engage；employ：～制 *system of employment under contract* /学校～了这位退休的教授。*The university employs the retired professor.*

【聘约】engagement；contract of employment

pīng

乒 ①［象］ping；bang：他～地撞在墙上。*He banged against the wall.* ② table-tennis；ping-pong：～乓赛 *table tennis game*

【乒乓】①［象］rattle：他弄得厨房里的碗盆～作响。*He rattled the dishes in the kitchen.* ② table tennis；ping-pong：打～ *play table tennis*

【乒乓球】①【体】table tennis；ping-pong ② table tennis ball；ping-pong ball：～拍 *table tennis bat* /～台 *table tennis table*

【乒坛】the table tennis circles

【乒协】table tennis association：中国～ *Table Tennis Association of the People's Republic of China*

娉

【娉婷】［书］（of a woman）have a graceful demeanour：身影～ *graceful figures*

píng

平 ① flat；even；level；smooth：一块～板子 *a flat board* /难怪桌子摇晃。地面不～。*No wonder the table wobbles；the floor isn't level.* ② make level；even；flatten：～～地 *level the ground* /～沟 *fill in a ditch* /吃完饭，她总要把桌布展～。*She smoothed the tablecloths after each meal.* ③ on the same level；on a par equal：积雪与我的膝盖相～。*The snow is even with my knees.* /比赛打～了。*The game was drawn.* /场上比分是5～。*The score is now five all.* ④ fair；just；equal：公～的交易 *an even bargain* ⑤ calm；peaceful：风～浪静 *calm* /心～气和 *even-tempered and good-humoured* ⑥ suppress；put down：～乱 *put down a rebellion* ⑦ pacify；assuage：～民愤 *assuage popular indignation* /这孩子以一个玩笑～了父母的怒气。*The child appeased her parents' anger with a joke.* ⑧ common；average：表现～～ *have average performance* ⑨【语】level tone, one of the four tones in classical Chinese ⑩（Píng）a surname

【平安】safe and sound；without mishap；well·

fine：~到达 *arrive safe and sound*；*arrive without mishap* /一路~！*Have a good trip*！

【平安无事】all is well；on good terms

【平安险】free of particular average（F. P. A）

【平白】for no reason；gratuitously；unprovoked：我~挨了一顿批评。*I was scolded for no reason at all.*

【平白无故】without any cause（or reason）；for no apparent reason；unwarranted；gratuitous：许多运动员认为随机药检是对他们的隐私的~的侵犯。*Many athletes consider random drug testing to be an unwarranted invasion of their privacy.*

【平板】① dull and stereotyped；flat；monotonous：写得~ *written in a dull style* /老师~的声音使我昏昏欲睡。*The teacher's monotonous voice almost sent me to sleep.* ② flat scraper ③ flat sheet

【平版】【印】lithographic plate：~印刷 *lithographic printing*

【平辈】of the same generation：虽然他大我20岁，但我们是~。*Although he is twenty years elder than I, we are of the same generation.*

【平布】【纺】plain cloth

【平步青云】rapidly go up in the world；have a meteoric rise；skyrocket：这个歌手~后，保镖便如影随形。*Since the singer's meteoric rise to fame, she has been accompanied by bodyguards wherever she goes.*

【平舱费】trimming charges

【平槽】The water has been on the same level with the banks.

【平产】be equal in output；have the same output：由于遇到旱灾，本地区的粮食产量和去年~。*Due to the drought, the grain yields of this area remained at the same level as last year.*

【平差】adjustment：~值 *adjusted value*

【平常】① ordinary；common：~的问题 *a common problem* /今天是很~的一天。*It was a very ordinary day today.* /他穿着~。*He is an ordinarily dressed man.* ② usually；ordinarily；as a rule：~我都是周末去看望父母。*As a rule, I visit my parents on weekends.* /我~步行去上学。*I usually go to school on foot.* ③ average；mediocre：我准备了~的晚餐。*I prepared a tolerable dinner.* /他的成绩~。*His results are the average.*

【平潮】slack water

【平车】flatcar；platform wagon（or car）

【平赤道】mean equator

【平畴】［书］level farmland；even-field

【平川】level land；flat，open country；plain：一马~ *a vast stretch of flat land*

【平喘】【中医】relieving asthma

【平旦】［书］dawn；daybreak：~即起 *get up soon after daybreak*

【平淡】flat；commonplace；insipid；prosaic；pedestrian；dull；not very interesting：~的生活 *a prosaic life* /~的谈话 *a dull conversation* /~无奇 *nothing out of the ordinary*

【平淡无奇】ordinary；prosaic；trite；nothing out of the ordinary：~的电影情节 *a pedestrian movie plot* /一个记者能把~的事件写成激动人心的新闻。*A reporter is able to write a piece of exciting news based on quite uninteresting events.*

【平等】equal；equality：~的地位 *equal standing* /~的机会 *even chances* /~的竞争 *fair competition* /男女~ *equality between the sexes* /法律面前人人~。*All men are equal before the law.*

【平等互利】equality and mutual benefit：~原则 *the principle of equality and mutual benefit*

【平底】flat-bottomed；low-heeled：~船 *flat-bottomed boat*；*flatboat*；*punt*；*junk* /~鞋 *low-heeled shoes*

【平地】① level the land；rake the ground ② level ground；flat ground；flat：我们踢足球需要一块~。*We need a level piece of ground to play football on.* /在沙砾上开了很长时间的车后，我很高兴能够来到~上。*After driving for so long on the gravel I was glad to get on an even stretch of road.*

【平地风波】a sudden wind and waves on a calm sea — a sudden，unexpected turn of events；a bolt from the blue；shock；rude awakening：这个电话无异于~，她的叔叔竟然在昨天遇害。*The telephone call contained a bolt from the blue；her uncle had been killed yesterday.*

【平地机】①【农】land leveler；grader ②【交】road grader

【平地楼台】high buildings rise from the ground — start from scratch：他的生意可是~。*He started his business from scratch.*

【平地一声雷】a sudden clap of thunder — an unexpected happy event；a bolt from the blue

【平顶】flattop：~窗 *laylight* /~锅炉 *straight boiler*

【平定】① calm down；pacify：洗个热水澡，会使你~下来的。*A warm bath will calm you.* ② quell；suppress；put down：~叛乱 *put down a rebellion* /警察~了暴动。*Police quelled the riot.*

【平凡】ordinary；common；commonplace；the person in the street：~的岗位 *ordinary post*

【平反】redress（a mishandled case）；rehabilitate：~冤案 *redress a grievance* / ~昭雪 *rehabilitate those who had been wrongfully accused* /宣布~ *announce sb's rehabilitation*

【平泛】（of writings）flat and superficial：这篇文章内容很~。*The article is superficial.*

【平方】①【数】square：25 是 5 的 ~。*25 is the square of 5.* ② square meter：20~的客厅 *a living room of twenty square metres*

【平方根】【数】square root：~法 *square-root method*

【平房】① single-story house；one-story house ②［方］house with a mortared flat roof

【平分】divide equally；share and share alike；go fifty-fifty：~线 *bisection*；*bisector* /这些钱你们~吧。*You can divide the sum of money among you.*

【平分秋色】share equally；split even；go fifty-fifty；have equal shares；leg and leg：锦标赛上这两个国家的奖牌~。*The two countries divided equally the medals in the tournament.*

【平分线】【数】bisector

【平伏】① calm down; subside; be pacified:他正发脾气呢。我们最好等他～下来再和他商量。*He is losing his temper now; we'd better discuss it with him when he calms down.* ② lie prostrate; lie flat:他～在床上。*He lay flat on the bed.*

【平幅】open width; full width

【平服】① calm down:他的心情久久难以～。*He could not calm down for a long time.* ② be convinced:对于他的能力我们都不～。*None of us were convinced of his ability.*

【平复】① calm down; subside; be pacified:母亲使哭着的孩子～下来。*Mother pacified the crying child.* ② be cured:伤口～了。*The wound is healed.*

【平光】zero diopter; plain glass: ～剂 *flatting agent* /～涂料 *flat paint*

【平巷】【矿】drift; level; entry: ～进尺 *driftage* /～运输机 *gangway conveyor*

【平和】① gentle; mild; moderate; placid:他性情～。*He is as mild as milk.* ②（of medicine）mild: ～的镇静剂 *a mild sedative* ③ calm; tranquil:经过我的反复劝说,他慢慢～下来。*After my repeated reasoning, he calmed down gradually.* ④［方］（of struggle, etc.）stop; ease:斗争日趋～。*The struggle is beginning to ease off.*

【平衡】balance; equilibrium:保持～ *maintain one's equilibrium; keep one's balance* /调整供求～ *adjust the equilibrium of supply and demand* /他失去～,跌倒了。*He lost his balance and fell over.*

【平滑】level and smooth; smooth: ～的大理石 *smooth marble* /池中的水面像镜子一样～。*The water in the pool is as even as a mirror.*

【平滑肌】【生理】smooth muscle; involuntary muscle: ～无力 *leiasthenia*

【平缓】① level; gentle:地势～ *level terrain* ② gently:水流～。*The water flows gently.* ③ mild; placid; gentle: ～的回答 *a mild answer*

【平毁】demolish; raze:那个旧工厂被～了。*The old factory was razed to ground.*

【平假名】hiragana

【平价】① stabilize prices: ～米 *low-price rice* ② reasonable price: ～交易 *fair deal* ③ par; parity:黄金～ *gold par* /假定～ *hypothetical par* /绝对～ *absolute par* /商业～ *commercial par* /暂时～ *temporary par of exchange*

【平角】【数】straight angle

【平界面】planar interface

【平靖】① pacify; tranquillize: ～内乱 *pacify the civil strife* ② tranquil; quiet:时局～ *a peaceful political situation*

【平静】calm; quiet; cool; tranquil; composed; unruffled: ～的湖面 *the calm surface of the lake* /乡村中～的生活 *a tranquil life in the country* /当我告诉他这个坏消息时,他很～。*He was calm when I told him the bad news.* /他不理会别人的嘲笑,努力保持～。*He tried hard not to lose his composure ignoring their laughter.*

【平局】draw; tie:在比赛中打成～ *square a game* /两队是～。*The teams draw.* /双方在还剩下几分钟时仍保持～。*The two parties tied the game with minutes remaining.*

【平均】① average; mean:我们每天～工作八小时。*We average 8 hours' work a day.* ② equally; share and share alike: ～分摊 *share out equally* /我来付出租车费,这样才～。*I'll pay for the taxi, to even things up.* ③【天】mean: ～太阳日 *mean solar day*

【平康】① peaceful and prosperous ②［书］brothel; red-light district

【平口钳】flat-nose pliers

【平旷】［书］（of land, fields, etc.）open and flat

【平阔】（of terrain）level and open

【平列】place side by side; put on a par with

【平流】【气】advection

【平流层】【气】stratosphere: ～顶 *stratopause*

【平炉】【冶】open-hearth furnace; open hearth

【平路机】【建】blader; bulldozer

【平乱】put down a revolt; suppress a rebellion

【平落】（of prices）drop to normal

【平脉】【中医】normal pulse

【平煤层】level coal

【平米】square metre

【平面】plane:半～ *half plane* /参数～ *parameter plane* /对称～ *symmetry plane* /校正～ *correction plane* /目标～ *objective plane* /抛物～ *parabolic plane* /扇形～ *sectorial plane* /射影～ *plane of projection* /透视～ *perspective plane* /虚设～ *fictitious plane* /振动～ *vibration plane* /正～ *horizontal frontal plane* /支撑～ *supporting plane* /主～ *principal plane* /坐标～ *coordinate plane*

【平民】common people; the populace: ～教育 *mass education* /～学校 *popular school* /政治家从不在意～。*Politicians don't care about ordinary people.* /～很少知道官方消息。*Very little official information is given to the general public.*

【平明】［书］dawn; daybreak

【平年】①【天】non-leap year; common year ②【农】average year（in crop yield, etc.）

【平平】average; mediocre; indifferent:表现～ *of average performance*

【平平当当】smoothly; without a hitch:我～办完了这件事。*I finished the job smoothly.*

【平铺直叙】tell in a simple, straightforward way; speak or write in a dull, flat style: ～的文章不吸引人。*An article with a dull and flat style can hardly attract readers.*

【平起平坐】sit as equals at the same table; be on an equal footing:我们希望在我们的学校里,教师、学生和家长能够～。*We hope that in our school, teachers, parents and students are placed on an equal footing.*

【平权】（enjoy）equal rights:男女～ *equal rights for men and women*

【平壤】Pyongyang, capital of the Democratic People's Republic of Korea（DPRK）

【平日】① on ordinary days; ordinarily; usually:我

～里都是7点起床。*I usually get up at 7 o'clock.* ② everyday; workday: 适合～里穿的衣服 *a suit for everyday wear*

【平绒】【纺】velveteen

【平射】【军】flat fire

【平射炮】【军】flat fire gun; flat trajectory gun

【平生】① all one's life; one's whole life: 他～第一次看到大海。*He saw the sea for the first time in his life.* ② usually; ever: 他～从不抽烟喝酒。*He never smoked or drank in his whole life.*

【平声】【语】level tone — the first of the four tones in classical Chinese pronunciation

【平时】① at ordinary times; in normal times; usually: ～我8点上班。*I usually go to work at 8 o'clock.* ② in peacetime: ～编制 *peacetime establishment*

【平时不烧香,急来抱佛脚】[俗] never burn incense when all is well but clasp Buddha's feet when in dire need — do nothing till the last minute; wait until the situation is desperate

【平实】[方] simple and unadorned; natural: ～的作品 *an unadorned writing*

【平世】[书] times of peace and tranquility

【平视】look straight ahead

【平手】draw: 这场比赛双方打了个～。*The match ended in a draw.*

【平水期】the period when the river water is at its normal level

【平顺】smooth-going: 计划进展～。*The plan was carried out smoothly.*

【平素】usually; habitually: 他～不爱与人交往。*Usually he hates contacting others.*

【平台】① terrace: 晚上我们坐在～上赏月。*We sat on the terrace in the evening, enjoying the beautiful full moon.* ② a house with a flat roof ③ a movable platform: ～收割机 *platform harvester*

【平坦】(of land, etc.) level; even; smooth: ～的道路易于行车。*An even road makes driving easy.* /能在～的表面上写字是最好的。*It's best to use a flat surface to write on.*

【平添】add to; give as an effect: 他的到来给家里～了许多生气。*His coming has brought much vitality to the family.* /这个收音机给老人的生活～了许多乐趣。*The radio added to the pleasure of the old man.*

【平贴】fitting and proper: 衣服熨得很～。*The clothes are ironed neatly and smoothly.*

【平头】① crew cut: 他留～。*He has a crew cut.* ② common: 我只不过是个～百姓,哪管得了这么大的事? *I am an ordinary people; how can I get involved in such an important matter?* ③ [方] (used to express round numbers) full; just; exactly: ～甲子 *exactly sixty years old*

【平头凿】butt chisel

【平头数】[方] round figure; round number

【平头正脸】have regular features

【平妥】plain, smooth and proper: 他处理事情向来很～。*He always deals with matters properly.*

【平瓦】plain roofing tile

【平尾】horizontal tail

【平温】moderate temperature

【平纹】【纺】plain weave

【平稳】① calm; steady; smooth and steady; smooth; stable: 物价～。*The prices are stable.* /他说话时声调～。*He spoke in a level tone.* /他的呼吸～。*His breathing is of even rhythm.* /卡车～地停住了。*The truck came to a smooth stop.* ② firm; steady: 请你把桌子放～。*Please make the table steady.*

【平屋】single-storey house

【平西】(of the sun) be setting: 太阳已经～,我该告辞了。*It's dusk now; I must be off.*

【平昔】in the past: 他～很孝敬父母。*He treats his parents with great filial respect in the past.*

【平息】① calm down; quiet down; subside: ～争端 *settle a dispute* /甚至一纸书面道歉都没能～这个女主人的怒气。*Even a written apology failed to placate the indignant hostess.* ② put down (a rebellion, etc.); suppress: ～暴乱 *put down a riot*

【平晓】[书] time of daybreak

【平心而论】in all fairness; objectively speaking; be frank; be honest; be fair; give sb his due: ～我也有不对的地方。*In all fairness, I am also to blame.*

【平心静气】calmly; dispassionately: 你别生气,咱们～地谈一谈。*Don't be so furious; Let's have a talk calmly.*

【平信】① ordinary mail ② surface mail

【平行】① of equal rank; on an equal footing: ～机关 *departments of equal rank* ②【数】parallel: 这些桌子和那些椅子是～的。*The tables stand in parallel with the line of chairs.* ③ simultaneous; concurrent: ～研究 *parallel study*

【平野】open country field

【平一】[书] put down rebellions and unify the land

【平移】【物】translation: ～点阵 *translational lattice* / ～对称 *translational symmetry* / ～速度 *point-to-point speed* / ～运动 *translational motion*

【平议】① judge fairly ② [书] appraise sth through discussion

【平抑】stabilize; pacify: ～物价 *stabilize the prices*

【平易】① unassuming; amiable; genial; affable; approachable: 我们的老师很～,随时愿意倾听我们的问题。*Our teacher is very approachable and always ready to listen to our problems.* ② (of a piece of writing) easy; plain

【平易近人】① easy of approach; amiable and easy of access; approachable: 他很～,而他的弟弟是个急脾气。*He is amiable and good-natured, while his younger brother was very quick-tempered.* ② (of literary works) simple; plain: 他的文章总是～,很合我的口味。*His articles are often written in a plain way, which is just to my taste.*

【平庸】mediocre; indifferent; commonplace: 才能～ *of limited ability* /该生学习刻苦,但学业～。*The student tried hard, but his work is mediocre.*

【平原】plain; flatlands: 冲积～ *fluvial plain* /堆积～ *plain of accumulation* /海底～ *submarine plain*

P

/内陆 ~ *inland plain* /盆地 ~ *basin plain* /侵蚀 ~ *plain of erosion*

【平允】[书] fair and just; equitable

【平仄】① level and oblique tones ② tonal patterns in classical Chinese poetry

【平展】① (of land, etc.) open and flat ② well smoothed out; even and smooth

【平章】[书] ① plan and prepare: ~国事 *deal with state affairs* ② comment on; pass judgement on

【平整】① level (land): ~路面 *even a road surface* /我们~了这块地以便在上面踢足球。*We leveled the piece of ground so that we could play football on it.* ② neat; even; level: 桌面是~的。*The top of the table is flat.* /我们在~的地面上做游戏。*We played games on level ground.*

【平正】① smooth and even: 这张纸很~。*This piece of paper is smooth.* ② straight; upright

【平直】① level and straight ② speak in a simple way ③ [书] upright; honest: ~的人 *an upright man*

【平治】[书] ① put in order; bring under control ② reign of peace

【平装】paperback; paper-cover; paperbound: ~本 *paperback book*; *paperback edition*

【平足】【医】flatfoot

【平作】(of farming) sowing seeds in the extensive level fields

评 ① comment; review: 短 ~ *brief comments* /书 ~ *book review* /影 ~ *film review* ② judge; assess: 他被大家 ~ 为三好学生。*He was elected excellent student by us.*

【评比】appraise through comparison; compare and evaluate: 年终 ~ *year-end appraisal of work* /通过~,大家一致认为他的作品最出色。*Through comparison and appraisal, all of us agreed that his work was the best.*

【评点】annotate; appraise and comment with words and phrases

【评定】adjudge; pass judgement on; evaluate; assess: 学业成绩 ~ *evaluation of academic performance* / ~训练成绩 *evaluate the results of training* /他写的散文被~为优秀作品。*His essays are rated as works of excellence.*

【评断】judge; arbitrate: ~是非 *judge between right and wrong*

【评分】give a mark; mark; grade; score: ~标准 *standards of grading* /老师给了我的作文好的~。*The teacher gave me a good mark for my composition.*

【评工】evaluate sb's work

【评功】appraise sb's merits (or achievements): ~摆好 *enumerate sb's merits*; *sing high praise for sb's merits*

【评估】assess; evaluate and estimate: 我们很难~结果。*It's difficult for us to estimate the possible results in advance.*

【评级】① grade (cadres, workers, etc.) according to one's performance ② grade (products) according to quality

【评价】appraise; evaluate: 动态 ~ *dynamic evaluation* /质量 ~ *quality evaluation* /正确~历史人物 *appraise historical characters correctly* /你对这本书的~如何? *How do you evaluate the book?* /现在我认识到我对她品格的~是片面的。*Now I've realized that my estimate of her character was one-sided.*

【评奖】grant awards through discussion; bonuses issued on the basis of a general voicing

【评介】review (a new book, etc.): 新书 ~ *book review*

【评剧】【戏】*pingju*, a local opera of north and northeast China

【评卷】mark examination papers

【评理】① judge between right and wrong: 谁是谁非,让大家~。*Let others judge who is right and who is wrong.* ② reason things out; have it out: 咱们找他~。*Let's go and have it out with him.*

【评论】① comment on; discuss: 不加 ~ *make no remark* /他奇怪的行为引起了很多~。*His strange behaviour caused a good deal of comment.* ② comment; commentary; review: 教育 ~ *educational review* /经济 ~ *economic review* /时事 ~ *comments on current affairs*

【评论家】critic; reviewer

【评论员】commentator

【评脉】【中医】feel the pulse

【评判】pass judgement on; decide; judge: ~胜负 *judge between contestants* /谁将~花卉展览中的蔷薇? *Who is going to judge the roses at the Flower Show?*

【评判员】judge (in sports or speech contests, etc.); adjudicator (in musical contests, etc.)

【评审】examine and appraise

【评书】storytelling (by a professional storyteller)

【评述】commentary

【评说】comment on; appraise; evaluate: 总统被要求对政治危机进行~。*The president was asked to comment on the political crisis.*

【评头论足】① make frivolous remarks about sb's looks: 对老师~是不礼貌的。*It is rude to comment on the teacher's appearance.* ② carp at; find fault with; pick holes in: 她总是对我~。*She was always carping at me.* /我认为即使是最苛刻的评论家也不能对她的表现~。*I think even the most critical reviewer could not find fault with her performance.*

【评委】member of a review committee

【评委会】review committee

【评析】comment on and analyze

【评薪】discuss and fix a person's wage grade according to his qualifications

【评选】choose through discussion: 我被~为先进工作者。*I am chosen as an advanced worker.*

【评议】appraise sth through discussion: ~委员会 *board of regents*; *appraisal committee*

【评语】comment; remarks: 品德 ~ *remarks on the conduct of a student* /他新写的小说已经获得有利的~。*His new novel has obtained favourable com-*

ments.

【评阅】read and appraise (sb's writing, etc.): ~试卷 *grade papers*

【评注】① make comments and annotation ② notes and commentary

【评传】critical biography

坪 ① level ground: 草~ *lawn*; *grass plot* /停车~ *car park*; *parking lot* ②［方］unit of area (=3.3 square metres)

【坪坝】［方］a level open space; level ground

【坪长】plateau length

【坪值】plateau value

苹

【苹果】apple: 我想吃个~。*I'd like to have an apple.* /一天一个~, 医生不上门。*An apple a day keeps the doctor away.*

凭[1] ① lean on: ~几 *lean on a small table* ② rely on; depend on: 我~自己的力量就能完成。*I can accomplish it by myself.* /公司的前途全~各位员工的努力。*The company's future is depending on everyone's efforts and contribution.* ③ proof; evidence: 文~ *diploma* /空口无~。*A mere verbal statement is no guarantee.* ④ go by; base on: ~票入场。*Admission by ticket only.* /你~什么不经允许就看我的信件? *What is the ground for your reading my letter without permission?*

凭[2] no matter (how, what, etc.): ~我怎么说, 他就是不相信。*He won't believe it no matter what I say.* / ~你跑得多快, 我也赶得上。*No matter how fast you run, I can catch up with you.* / ~我用什么方法做鸡蛋, 小孩就是不肯吃。*However I cook eggs, the child still refuses to eat them.*

【凭单】a certificate for drawing money, goods, etc.; voucher: 进货~ *purchase voucher* /原始~ *original voucher*

【凭吊】visit (a historical site, etc.) and ponder on the past: 他每年都要去李大钊墓~一番。*He pays his respects at Li Dazhao's mausoleum every year.*

【凭借】rely on; depend on; take advantage of; by means of: ~个人努力 *rely on one's own efforts* / ~我们的体力和战术, 一定能打赢这场比赛。*Relying on our physical strength and tactics, we will surely win the match.* / ~这些先进措施, 他成功地完成了这个试验。*By taking advantage of the advanced equipment, he succeeded in doing the experiment.*

【凭据】evidence; proof: 你必须提供~给警方。*You have to provide evidence to the policemen.*

【凭靠】rely on; depend on: 她的学费全~父母支付。*She relies on her parents for tuition.*

【凭空】out of thin air; without basis; without foundation; groundless; baseless: ~的怀疑 *unfounded suspicions* / ~产生的谣言 *groundless rumours* / ~捏造 *make something out of nothing*; *fabricate*; *sheer fabrication*; *make up a story* /这纯属~想象。*It's pure imagination.*

【凭栏】lean on a railing: ~细听 *lean over the railings to listen quietly* / ~远眺 *lean on a railing gazing into the distance*

【凭陵】［书］① encroach on; bully: ~邻国的领土 *encroach on the territory of a neighbouring country* / ~弱者 *bully the weak* ② rely on; depend on: ~权势 *rely on one's power and influence*

【凭恃】rely on; depend on

【凭眺】gaze from a high place into the distance: ~远方 *gaze into the distance*

【凭险】resort to natural barriers; take advantage of a strategic point

【凭信】trust; believe: 此话不足~。*These words are unreliable.*

【凭依】base oneself on; rely on: 他们~着惊人的毅力克服了重重困难。*They overcame all kinds of difficulties with amazing will power.*

【凭倚】lean on; lean against: 他~着柱子沉思。*He leant against the pillar lost in thought.*

【凭仗】rely on; depend on: ~专家的指导, 这个村的粮食获得了丰收。*Under the instruction of the expert, the villagers had a bumper harvest.*

【凭照】certificate; permit; licence

【凭证】evidence; certificate; voucher: 付款~ *evidence of payment* /记账~ *evidence for keeping account* /客观~ *objective evidence* /完税~ *tax payment receipt* /原始~ *original evidences* /自制~ *self-made evidence*

【凭准】standard

枰 chessboard

屏 ① shield; screen: 围~ *folding screen* ② a set of vertically hung scrolls: 四扇~ *four-sheet scroll* ③ screen; shield sb or sth
see also bīng; bǐng

【屏蔽】① screen; shield: 高山~着这一带地方。*The high mountain provides a protective screen for this area.* ② protective screen ③【物】screen: 电磁~ *electro-magnetic screen* /静电~ *electrostatic screen* /阴极~ *cathode screen*

【屏藩】［书］① screen and fence ② protect; shield

【屏风】screen: 竖起~ *set up a screen* /折叠~ *a folding screen*

【屏极】【电】plate: ~电路 *plate circuit* / ~电源 *plate supply* / ~回路 *plate circuit*

【屏幕】【电】screen

【屏栅】screen-grid; shield-grid: ~电压 *screen-grid voltage* / ~流 *screen current*

【屏条】a set of wall scrolls or hanging scrolls

【屏障】① protective screen: 燕山是北京的天然~。*The Yanshan Hills provide a natural defence for Beijing.* ② shield; form a protective screen

瓶 bottle; vase: 牛奶~ *a milk bottle* /花~儿 *(flower) vase* /空气~ *air flask* /量~ *graduated flask* /培养~ *culture flask* /啤酒~ *beer bottle* /汽水~ *pressurized bottle* /氧气~ *oxygen bottle* /药~ *medicine bottle* /医生给他一~药水。*The doctor gave him a bottle of liquid medicine.*

【瓶胆】glass liner (of a thermos flask)

【瓶颈】① neck of a bottle ②［喻］bottleneck: ~效

应 *bottleneck effect*
【瓶塞】bottle plug; cork: 砰地一声～飞出去了。*The cork flew off with a pop.*
【瓶装】bottled: ～饮料 *bottled drink*/～牛奶 *bottled milk*
【瓶子】bottle; vase; jar; flask

萍

duckweed
【萍泊】[书] wander about like duckweed — lead a wandering life
【萍寄】[书] live everywhere away from home
【萍蓬】[书] go adrift
【萍水相逢】(of strangers) meet by chance like patches of drifting duck-weed: 虽然我们～,我还是很愿意帮助你。*Though we have only met by chance, I am willing to help you.*
【萍踪】[书] tracks of a wanderer
【萍踪浪迹】leaving no traces like duckweed and waves; come and go without trace — persons who wander aimlessly

pō

朴

【朴刀】a sword with a long blade and a short hilt wielded with both hands
see also pò; pǔ

陂

【陂陀】[书] uneven

坡

① slope: 背风～ *lee slope* /陡～ *steep slope* /反～ *reverse slope* /缓～ *a gentle slope* /平～ *a slight slope* /山～ *hillside* /斜～ *inclined slope* /雪～ *snow slope* /仰～ *heading slope* ② sloping; slanting: 把板子～着放 *place the plank at a slant*
【坡岸】a sloping bank
【坡道】sloping path or road
【坡地】hillside fields; sloping fields: ～黄土 *slope loess*
【坡度】the degree of an incline; slope; gradient; inclination; pitch: 有五分之一～的小山 *a hill with a slope of* 1 *in* 5 /四分之一的～是指每前进四米便升高或下降一米。*A gradient of* 1 *in* 4 *is a rise or fall of one metre for every four metres forward.*
【坡积】slide rock: ～物 *slope wash*
【坡降】① slope ② gradient; slope
【坡角】slope angle
【坡口】groove: ～半径 *root radius* /～角度 *bevel angle*
【坡田】hillside fields

泊

lake: 湖～ *lake* /血～ *a flood of blood*
see also bó

泼[1]

sprinkle; splash; spill: 把坏牛奶～掉 *throw away the spoiled milk* /在地面上～水 *splash water over the floor* /一滴不～出地把杯子斟满 *fill one's cup without spilling a drop* /他把污水～在草地上。*He slopped the dirty water onto the grass.*

泼[2]

① rude and unreasonable: 撒～ *make a scene* ② [方] resolute and bold: 他做事很～。*He is decisive in behaviour.*
【泼妇】shrew; vixen; virago; callet: ～骂街。*A shrew lets loose abuse in the street.*
【泼悍】ferocious: ～的敌人 *a ferocious enemy*
【泼辣】① rude and unreasonable; shrewish: 她性格～,很难与人相处。*She is very caustic and cannot get along well with people around her.* ② pungent and forceful; bold and vigorous; daring and resolute: ～的文风 *a strong literary style* /他办事～。*He is bold and vigorous in his work.*
【泼溅】spilling; bubbling: 墨水～在书页上 *spill ink on the page* /水从水桶里～出来,落到地板上。*The water splashed out of the tub upon the floor.*
【泼赖】unreasonable: 她可真～! *She is quite unreasonable.*
【泼冷水】discourage; pour cold water on; dampen the enthusiasm (or spirits) of; throw a wet blanket on; throw cold water on: 对于他的热情,你应该鼓励,而不是～。*You should encourage him instead of dampen his enthusiasm.* /不要对他们的热情～。*Don't chill their enthusiasm.*
【泼墨】splash-ink, a technique of Chinese ink-painting: ～山水 *landscape painting done with splashes of ink*
【泼皮】ruffian; hooligan
【泼洒】splash: 别让热汤～在你身上! *Don't let the hot soup spill on your clothes.*
【泼天】extremely big; excessive: ～大祸 *catastrophe*

颇[1]

[书] partial; oblique: 偏～ *biased; partial*

颇[2]

[书] quite; rather: ～佳 *quite good* /他是一个～有野心的人。*He is a very ambitious man.* /他看上去～年轻。*He looks very young.*

pó

婆

① old woman: 老太～ *old woman* ② woman with a specific job: 媒～儿 *professional woman matchmaker* ③ husband's mother; mother-in-law: 公～ *husband's parents; parents-in-law*
【婆家】husband's family: 她结婚后住在～。*She lived in her husband's family after marriage.* /这姑娘年纪不小了,该找个～了。*The girl has reached the age for marriage.*
【婆罗门】Brahman: ～鸡 *brahma* /～参 *oyster plant*
【婆罗门教】Brahmanism; Brahminism: ～徒 *Brahmanist*
【婆母】husband's mother; mother-in-law
【婆娘】[方] ① a young married woman ② wife: 这是我～。*This is my wife.*
【婆婆】① husband's mother; mother-in-law ② [方] grandmother: 老～ *old lady; old woman*
【婆婆妈妈】① act slowly like an old woman: 动作快

点,别~的! *Hurry up! Don't dawdle any more.* ② emotionally fragile; sentimental; dodder and chat like an old woman:你这么年轻,不该~的。*You are so young and shouldn't be so sentimental.*

【婆婆嘴】① an old woman's toothless mouth ② a garrulous person; gossipy:我很讨厌这个~的女人。*I dislike very much the long-tongued woman.*

【婆娑】whirling; dancing:杨柳~。*The willows dance in the breeze.*

【婆娑起舞】start dancing; begin to trip a measure:一只蝴蝶在花丛中~。*A butterfly is fluttering among the flowers.*

【婆媳】mother-in-law and daughter-in-law:~之间容易产生矛盾。*Conflicts arise easily between mother-in-law and daughter-in-law.*

【婆姨】[方] ① a young married woman ② wife

【婆子】① [贬] woman ② wife ③ a middle-aged or elderly woman servant

皤 [书] ① white:白发~然的老人 *a white-haired man* ② big (belly):~腹瓶 *big-belly bottle*

pǒ

叵 [书] ① impossible; not ② at once; immediately

【叵测】[贬] unfathomable; unpredictable:他装作关心你,其实是居心~。*He pretended to care about you; in fact, he nursed evil intentions.*

【叵罗】a shallow wine vessel used in ancient times

【叵耐】① intolerable; cannot tolerate ② have no choice

笸

【笸篮】basket made of bamboo strips

【笸箩】a shallow basket made of wicker or thin bamboo strips

pò

朴 【植】Chinese hackberry

see also pō; pǔ

迫 ① force; compel; press; use force:他被~搬家。*He was forced to move.* /我们~使她付钱。*We compelled her to pay.* ② urgent; pressing:紧~ *urgent; pressing* /窘~ *be caught in a dilemma* /从容不~ *calm and unhurried* ③ approach; come near

see also pǎi

【迫不得已】have no alternative (but to); (do sth) against one's will:我们这样做完全是~。*We were compelled to do so.* / ~,他变卖了所有的财产。*He had no alternative but to sell all his properties.*

【迫不及待】too impatient to wait; look forward to doing sth:我~要见他。*I can't wait to see him.*

【迫促】① short; rapid:呼吸~ *be short of breath* ② urge; press:父亲~他尽快完婚。*His father urged him to hold the marriage ceremony as soon as possible.*

【迫害】persecute:残酷的~ *relentless persecution* /他受到~后,抑郁而终。*He was subjected to persecution and died in gloom.*

【迫降】【航】forced landing; distress landing:~场 *forced-landing area* /飞机起飞 20 分钟后~。*The plane made a forced landing 20 minutes after its taking off.*

【迫近】approach; get close to; draw near:大选~。*The election is drawing near.* /期末考试~,他仍然贪玩儿。*The final examination is approaching, but he still spends his time playing.*

【迫令】force; compel:他被~退学。*He was ordered to leave school.*

【迫切】urgent; pressing; imminent; imperative:~的心情 *eager desire* / ~的需要 *crying need; urgent need* / ~的愿望 *fervent wish*

【迫使】force; compel; oblige; use force; make sb do sth:警察~人群后退。*The police force the crowd back.* /坏天气~我们待在家里。*The bad weather compelled us to stay indoors.*

【迫位】peri-position:~桥 *peri-bridge*

【迫降】force the enemy to surrender

【迫胁】coerce; force:资本家~罢工者妥协。*The capitalist coerced the strikers into compliance.*

【迫在眉睫】extremely urgent; imminent; forthcoming; upcoming; be in the offing; be in sight; be around the corner:危险~。*The danger became very pressing.* /战争~。*The war is imminent.*

破 ① broken; be damaged; torn:牢不可~ *unbreakable* / ~杯子 *a broken cup* /吓~了胆 *be scared out of one's wits* ② destroy; damage:爆~ *blow up* ③ split; cleave; cut:割~手指 *cut one's fingers* /势如~竹 *irresistible force* /把一块木头~成两半 *cleave a block of wood in two* ④ change money:把1张十元钞票~成5张两元钞票 *change a ten-yuan bill into five 2-yuan bills* ⑤ break with; get rid of:~迷信,树新风 *do away with superstition and establish new customs* / ~世界纪录 *break the world record* ⑥ capture; defeat:大~敌军 *inflict a crushing defeat on the enemy* ⑦ spend; cost:~工夫 *spend one's time doing sth* ⑧ lay bare; reveal the truth of:看~ *see through* /他一语道~了我的心事。*He revealed what I am thinking in one remark.* ⑨ [讽] lousy; poor; inferior:这房子真~! *What a shabby house!* /这~天气! *What lousy weather!*

【破案】solve (or clear up) a case; crack a criminal case:迟迟没有~。*The case remains unsolved.*

【破败】① ruined; dilapidated; tumbledown; be in bad condition; be in bad repair; derelict; rundown; ramshackle:那所房子已经~不堪。*The house is dilapidated; the house is now a ruin.* /晚上我们挤在一座~的寺庙里睡觉。*At night we slept huddled together in a derelict temple.* /我们开车穿过许多~的街道。*We drove through many run-down streets.* ② deteriorate; decline; slip; get worse; go down:~的家庭 *family on the de-*

cline

【破冰船】icebreaker

【破冰雷】【军】ice mine

【破波】breaker; breaking wave: ~阻力 *wave breaking resistance*

【破布】rag:他用一块油乎乎的~擦桌子。*He used an oily rag to clean the table.*

【破擦音】【语】affricate

【破财】lose money; suffer unexpected personal financial losses: ~免灾。*An unexpected financial loss might help one avoid some potential disaster.*

【破产】① bankruptcy:过失~ *negligent bankruptcy* /假~ *fraudulent bankruptcy* ② go bankrupt; go broke; become insolvent; be ruined:那家公司因管理经营不善而~。*The company went bankrupt because of its poor management.* ③ come to naught; fall through; come to nothing; unproductive:他的阴谋彻底~了。*His plot fell through completely.*

【破产法】【律】bankruptcy law

【破钞】spend money; go to expense:今天让你~了,真不好意思。*It's so kind of you to go to expense on treating us.*

【破除】do away with; get rid of; eradicate; give up: ~社会的偏见 *break down the social prejudice* /~迷信 *banish all blind faith; do away with superstition*

【破的】hit the target; to the point:一语~ *hit the target with one remark*

【破费】spend money or time; go to some expense: 你为我买这么多礼物,真是太~了。*You really go to much expense to buy all these gifts for me.*

【破釜沉舟】break the cauldrons and sink the boats — cut off all means of retreat; be extremely resolute; cross (or pass) the Rubicon:我们只有~干到底了。*We have no alternative but to go ahead at all cost.*

【破格】make an exception; break a rule: ~提升 *break a rule to promote sb* /校长~录取了他。*The headmaster broke the rule to enroll him.*

【破瓜】(of a girl) reach 16 years of age; be 16 years old

【破关斩将】force the passes and slay enemy generals — overcome a lot of difficulties and defeat many opponents:考大学可谓~,不是件容易事啊! *To take part in the national college entrance examination is just like being involved in a war; it's by no means an easy job.*

【破罐破摔】smash a pot to pieces just because it's cracked — act recklessly when one is in a hopeless situation:出狱后,他索性~,开始混日子。*After he was released from the prison, he wrote himself off as hopeless and simply scraped by.*

【破坏】① destroy; wreck:建筑物的严重~ *wreck of the building* /敌人~了这座城市。*The enemy destroyed the city.* /这次水灾造成的~非常严重。*The destruction brought by the flood was rather serious.* ② do great damage to: ~名誉 *damage one's reputation* / ~团结 *harm unity* ③ change (a social system, custom, etc.) completely or violently: ~旧秩序 *demolish the old order* /~旧的国家机器 *smash the old state apparatus* ④ violate; break: ~纪律 *break the discipline* ⑤ destroy (the composition of a substance); decompose:维生素C受热过度就会被~。*Vitamin C is destroyed when overheated.*

【破获】① find out and arrest; uncover: ~一起盗窃案 *crack a case of theft* ② identify and capture: ~密码 *decipher a secret code*

【破击】【军】attack and destroy; wreck; sabotage: ~敌人的交通线 *wreck the enemy's communication lines*

【破击战】【军】sabotage operation

【破甲弹】【军】metal patch bullet

【破解】analyse and explain:他的~使我明白了整个事情。*His explanation helped me to understand the whole situation.*

【破戒】① break a religious precept ② break one's vow of abstinence

【破镜重圆】a broken mirror joined together — reunion of a couple after a rupture:经过多年分离,夫妻俩终于~。*The husband and wife reunited after many years' separation.*

【破旧】old and shabby; dilapidated; run-down; be in bad condition; be in bad repair: ~的家具 *old and shabby furniture* /我们一直住在一所~的旅馆里。*We have stayed in an old and dilapidated hotel.*

【破旧立新】destroy the old and build up the new

【破句】pause in reading at the wrong place; make a wrong pause:完整地理解句意才能避免~。*To avoid pause at the wrong place in reading, one has to understand thoroughly the meaning of the sentence.*

【破口】① get a cut, break, breach, tear, etc.:我手上~了。*I have got a cut on my hand.* ② hole; breach:怎么新买的衣服就有个~? *How could there be a hole in the newly bought clothes?* ③ abuse:他是个有教养的人,我不相信他会~骂人。*He is a well-bred person; I don't believe he once let loose filthy abuse.*

【破口大骂】shout abuse; let loose a torrent of abuse:他~。*He ripped out an angry oath.* /他老婆脾气很坏。稍不顺心,就对他~。*His wife is ill tempered; she is ready to shout abuse if there's anything against her.*

【破烂】① shabby; tattered; ragged; worn-out: ~的外衣 *a tattered jacket* ②[口] junk; scrap:捡~ *search worthless stuff* /母亲把我扔掉的~又都捡了回来。*Mother took back the junk, which I have thrown away.*

【破浪】cleave the waves; plough the waves:满载乘客的船正在~前进。*The ship filled with passengers is cleaving through the water.*

【破例】break a rule; make an exception; bend the rules:虽说他是校长的儿子,也不能~。*Although he is the son of the principal, we cannot break the rule for him* /在同学聚会上,他兴奋得~唱了一首

歌。*He was so excited in the reunion of the classmates that he sang a song against his own rule.* /我想我们这次还是破个例吧，毕竟这孩子只有8岁，而且他并无意要拿这些钱。*I think we should make an exception this time. The child is only 8 and he didn't mean to take the money.*

【破脸】turn against（an acquaintance or a friend）; fall out：这对好友因为利益问题破了脸。*They used to be good friends but fell out for their own interests.*

【破裂】① burst; split; rupture; crack：水管～处 *a break in the water pipe* /血管～ *rupture of blood vessel* ② break：～的家庭 *a broken home* /两国外交关系～了。*The diplomatic relations between the two countries broke down.*

【破陋】old and shabby; dilapidated; run-down; be in bad condition：我就是在这个～的房子里长大的。*It's in this dilapidated house that I grew up.*

【破落】① decline（in wealth and position）：家境～。*The family is reduced to poverty.* ② dilapidated; run-down; derelict：～的建筑 *a dilapidated building*

【破落户】a family that has gone down in the world

【破谜儿】①［口］solve a riddle ②［方］ask a riddle

【破门】① burst（or force）open the door：夜晚几个盗贼～而入。*A couple of thieves burst the door open and broke into the house.* ②（in football, handball, etc.）score a goal：临近比赛结束时我们的队伍～了。*Our team scored a goal near the end of the match.* ③【宗】（of the Christian church）excommunicate sb

【破闷】［方］kill time：我靠看电视～。*I am watching TV to kill time.*

【破灭】vanish; be shattered; fall through; melt into thin air：～的希望 *ruined hopes* /她全部希望的～ *the wreck of her hopes* /她的幻想～了。*She is disillusioned.*

【破伤风】【医】tetanus：～疫苗 *tetanus vaccine*

【破身】lose one's virginity;（of a girl）have her first sexual intercourse

【破声】speak with a loud voice

【破私立公】overcome selfishness and foster public sense

【破碎】① tattered; broken; in pieces; fall apart：～的玻璃 *pieces of broken glass* /一件稀有的瓷器支离～了。*A rare piece of porcelain is in shatters.* ② shatter; crush：这次事故～了我的梦想。*The accident shattered my dream.*

【破碎机】crusher; breaker

【破碎险】【商】risk of breakage

【破损】damaged; worn; broken：表面～ *surface damage* /减少～ *lessen breakage*

【破损险】insurance against breakage; breakage risks

【破题儿第一遭】for the first time ever：他发这么大的火真是～。*It was the first time that he was in such a temper.*

【破体字】a non-standard or form of a Chinese character

【破涕为笑】smile through tears：他拿出糖果，逗得小姑娘～。*He showed candies to the little girl, and she smiled away her tears.*

【破天荒】epoch-making; occur for the first time; be unprecedented：这种状况简直是～。*The situation is unprecedented.* /妇女有了选举权，这可是～的事。*Women are given the voting franchise for the first time in history.*

【破土】① break ground（in starting a building project, etc.）：～仪式 *ground-breaking ceremony* ② start spring ploughing ③（of a seedling）break through the soil

【破网】【体】score a goal

【破五】the fifth day of the first lunar month

【破袭战】【军】sabotage operations

【破相】（of facial features）be marred by a scar, etc.：他和别人打了一架，都～了。*He fought with others and received a scar marring his facial features.*

【破晓】dawn; daybreak：～时分，我们就出发了。*We set out at dawn.*

【破鞋】［口］slut; loose woman

【破血药】stasis-breaking drug

【破颜】break into a smile：他所做的一切只为博这漂亮姑娘～一笑。*All that he has done is just for the pretty girl's smile.*

【破衣烂衫】rags; worn-out clothes：～的流浪汉 *a tramp dressed in rags and tatters*

【破译】decode; decipher

【破约】break one's promise; break an agreement：他因为～而受到谴责。*He was condemned for breaking his promise.*

【破绽】① a burst seam：你缝补衣服上的～了吗? *Have you stitched the burst seams?* ② defect; flaw; weak point：他看出了其中的～，轻蔑地笑了。*He saw through the game and smiled scornfully.*

【破绽百出】full of flaws（or holes）：他的论证～。*His argument is full of flaws.*

【破折号】dash（—）

【破竹之势】advance like splitting a bamboo — an irresistible force

粕 ［书］dregs of rice

魄 ① soul：魂～ *soul* ② vigour; energy：气～ *boldness of vision* /体～ *physique; constitution*

【魄力】daring and resolution; boldness：工作有～ *be bold and resolute in one's work*

pōu

剖 ① cut open：解～ *dissect* /把鱼肚子～开 *cut open the belly of a fish* ② analyze; examine：～明事理 *make an in-depth analysis*

【剖白】explain oneself; vindicate oneself：～心迹 *lay one's heart bare* /他努力为旷课～。*He tried to explain himself for his truancy.*

【剖辨】analyse; distinguish

【剖断】［书］analyse and judge a case

【剖腹】paunch; cut open one's belly
【剖腹藏珠】cut one's belly to hide a pearl — die for the sake of gain; sacrifice life for money; place the trivial above the essential
【剖腹产】【医】caesarean birth
【剖腹产手术】caesarean operation
【剖解】analyse; dissect
【剖决】[书] analyse and decide
【剖露】lay bare; strip bare; reveal; expose
【剖面】section: 横～ *cross section* /纵～ *longitudinal section*
【剖明】analyse and make clear: ～利弊 *state the advantages and disadvantages in explicit terms*
【剖视】dissect and observe
【剖视图】cutaway view
【剖释】dissect and explain; analyse: 评论家～了此次选举的结果。*Commentators analysed the election results.*
【剖析】analyse; dissect: ～小说中的人物 *analyse the characters in the novel* /他们事后仔细～那项计划以便搞清它失败的原因。*They dissected the plan afterward to learn why it had failed.*
【剖心】[书] open one's heart; lay bare one's true feelings; unbosom oneself: ～以待 *unbosom oneself to sb*

póu

抔 [书] hold sth with cupped hands: 一～土 *a handful of earth — a grave*

pǒu

掊 [书] ① strike ② cut; split
【掊击】blast; lash out at; give blows

pū

仆 fall forward: 前～后继 *advance wave upon wave; one stepping into the breach as another falls*
see also pú

扑 ① dash at; throw oneself on: 小男孩儿一见到她,就～到她怀里。*The little boy threw himself on her at the sight of her.* /老虎向山羊～去。*The tiger made a spring at the goat.* /猫向麻雀猛～过去。*The cat made a pounce upon the sparrow.* ② devote oneself to; dedicate oneself: 他一心～在教育事业上。*He devoted himself to education.* ③ flap; pat: ～翅飞翔的鹰 *an eagle flapping its wings* /鱼还在岸上～～地跳动。*The fish were still flopping about on the bank.* ④ [方] bend over: 他～在桌子上看书。*He bends over the table reading.*
【扑鼻】tangy; assail the nostrils: 松叶～的香味 *the rich tangy scent of pine needles* /花香～。*A fragrant odour of the flowers assails one's nostrils.*
【扑哧】[象] the sound of snorting or fizzing, laughter, etc.: 他～一声笑了。*He tittered.*
【扑打】(pūdǎ) swat: ～苍蝇 *swat a fly*
【扑打】(pūda) pat; beat: ～地毯上的灰尘 *beat the dirt off the carpet*
【扑灯蛾子】[口] grain moth
【扑跌】① wrestling ② fall forward: 他～在地上。*He fell to the ground.*
【扑冬】[象] thump; thud; flop: 他兴奋得心头～～直跳。*His heart thumped with excitement.* /皮球～一声落了下来。*The ball fell with a thud.*
【扑尔敏】【药】chlorpheniramine
【扑粉】① face powder ② talcum powder ③ apply powder; put on powder: 出门前,她在脸上扑了厚厚的粉。*She applied much powder on her face before leaving home.*
【扑击】① pounce on; fall on; rush at: 向敌人～ *rush at the enemy* ② slap against; beat against: 波浪～岸边。*Waves beat the shore.*
【扑救】① put out a fire (to save life and property): 消防员及时赶来～了大火。*The firemen came in time and put out the fire.* ② (in volleyball, football, etc.) diving save
【扑克】① playing cards: 玩～ *play cards* ② poker: 打～ *play poker*
【扑空】fail to get or achieve what one wants; come away empty-handed; fan the air: 昨天我去找他,又～了。*Yesterday I went to see him, but again he wasn't at home.*
【扑拉】① (of birds, etc.) flap or spread (wings): 鸭子～着翅膀。*The duck flapped its wings.* ② slap; beat lightly; whisk: 他～掉身上的面包屑。*He whisks off the crumbs.* ③ (of tears, sweat, etc.) roll down; trickle down: 汗珠从他额头上～～掉下来。*The sweat trickled from his forehead.*
【扑棱】(pūlēng) [象] the sound of flapping of wings: 一只鸟～一声从灌木丛中飞出来。*A bird flew out of the bush with a flap.*
【扑棱】(pūleng) flap; flutter: 鸟～着翅膀。*The bird is fluttering its wings.*
【扑脸儿】[口] blow on one's face: 一出家门,就感到寒风～。*I felt the cold wind blowing my face the moment I got out.*
【扑亮】[方] (of day) break: 天一～,我就起床了。*I got up as soon as day broke.*
【扑落】① shake off; shake out of sth: 进门前,她～了身上的雪片。*She shook off the snowflakes before entering the house.* ② [书] scattered about; spread widely ③ plug
【扑满】earthenware money box; piggy bank
【扑面】blow on (or against) one's face; touch one's face: 春风～,十分惬意。*It is pleasing to enjoy the spring breeze caressing my face.*
【扑灭】① stamp out; put out; exterminate; extinguish: ～森林大火 *extinguish a forest fire* /～火焰 *stamp out a fire* ② exterminate; wipe out: ～

蚊蝇 *wipe out mosquitoes and flies*

【扑闪】blink; wink:小姑娘~着眼睛。*The little girl is winking.*

【扑朔迷离】complicated; puzzling; bewildering; confusing; whirling:故事的情节~。*The plot of the story is complicated.* /警方正在设法弄清一连串~的与绑架动机有关的事件。*Police are trying to make sense of a puzzling chain of events that led up to the kidnap attempt.*

【扑簌】(of tears) trickling down; roll down:她的眼泪~而下。*Her tears trickle down her cheeks.*

【扑腾】(pūtēng)[象] the sound of a heavy fall; flop; thump; thud:我们听见他~一声倒了下去。*We heard a thump as he fell.*

【扑腾】(pūteng) ① beat water with one's feet when swimming ② throb; palpitate; move up and down:他心里直~。*His heart was throbbing.* ③[方] hustle; bustle; wangle:他挺能~的。*He is quite a wheeler-dealer.* ④ spend money freely; squander; waste:父亲留下的财产他一年就给~光了。*He squandered all the properties his father left within one year.*

【扑通】[象] flop; splash; pit-a-pat:一个苹果~一声掉在水中。*An apple fell plop into the water.* /他如释重负,~一声倒在安乐椅中。*He plunked into the armchair with a sigh of relief.*

【扑翼】(of a bird) flap wings

铺 ① spread; pave; lay: ~地砖 *tile a floor* / ~开一块布 *unfold the cloth* / ~开地图 *spread out a map* /把干净的床单~在床上。*Put clean sheets on the bed* /把块布~在桌子上。*Cover the table with a cloth.* /这些砖是用来~院子的。*These bricks are to pave the courtyard.* /这条路是柏油~的。*The road is laid with asphalt.* ②[量] used for kang:一~炕 *a kang*
see also pù

【铺摆】① place goods on display; display:商贩们在街上~物品。*The peddlers are placing goods for sale on the street.* ②[方] arrange ③[方] narrate; elaborate; explain:让我给您~一下。*I'll explain it to you.*

【铺陈】①[方] spread out; arrange: ~华丽 *arrange beautifully* /屋子里~了几件新家具。*The room is furnished with several pieces of new furniture.* ② narrate in detail; elaborate:他向我们~了事情的经过。*He gave us a detailed account of the matter.* ③[方] bedclothes; bedding

【铺衬】small pieces of cloth used for patches

【铺床】make the bed; spread:他这么大了,应该让他自己~了。*He has grown up, and you should ask him to make the bed himself.*

【铺地砖】① floor tile; paving tile ② tile the floor

【铺垫】① lay; spread ② bedding ③ set off; foreshadowing:这一段为故事的高潮作了~。*This passage foreshadows the climax of the story.*

【铺盖】(pūgài) spread; over:他把毯子~到膝盖上。*He covered his knees with a blanket.*

【铺盖】(pūgai) bedding; bedclothes

【铺盖卷儿】bedding roll; bedroll; luggage roll

【铺轨】lay a railway track: ~工 *platelayer; tracklayer*

【铺轨机】track-laying machine

【铺路】① pave a road ②[喻] make necessary preparations:他的父母已经为他的将来铺好了路。*His parents have made every preparation for his future.*

【铺路玻璃】paving glass

【铺路机】paver

【铺路石】stones used to pave a road — people who sacrifice themselves for the benefit of others

【铺路砖】paving brick

【铺墁】pave the ground (with tiles, bricks, etc.)

【铺排】① plan; arrange:公司的事我已经~好了。*I have put everything in order in the company.* ②[方] extravagant; lavish:他的婚礼太~了。*His marriage ceremony is much too lavish.*

【铺平】① smooth out; spread sth out smoothly: ~纸张 *smooth out the paper* ② level; pave:这个实验为将来的研究工作~了道路。*The experiment paved the way for future research.*

【铺砌】【建】pave

【铺砂】sanding: ~层 *sand bedding*

【铺设】① lay; build (a road, railway, etc.): ~海底电缆 *lay a submarine cable* ② arrange; furnish

【铺摊】[方] spread out (paper, etc.)

【铺天盖地】blot out the sky and cover up the earth; overspread:暴风雪~而来。*The blizzard blotted out the sky and the land.*

【铺叙】narrate at length; elaborate: ~事实 *narrate the facts in detail*

【铺展】spread out; sprawl:景色好似~到无穷远。*It seems that the vista spread to infinity.*

【铺张】① extravagant; lavish; go to great expense; spare no expense: ~的皇室成员 *extravagant members of the imperial court* /他住旅馆很~,只住最好的! *When he is staying in hotels he spares no expense — only the best!* ② exaggerate; overstate:他~自己的房子的大小。*He exaggerated the size of the house he lived in.*

【铺张浪费】extravagant and wasteful:反对~ *oppose extravagance and waste*

噗 [象] puff:降落伞~地张开了。*The parachute puffed all around.*

【噗哧】[象] hiss; fizz:他~一口气吹熄了生日蜡烛。*He blew out the birthday candles with a puff.*

【噗咚】[象] thud; thump; bump:他~一声坐了下来。*He sat down with a bump.*

【噗噜噜】[象] (of tears) roll or trickle down the cheeks:眼泪像断了线的珠子~地落在她的脸上。*Tears fell like pearls from a broken string on her face.*

【噗通】[象] thud; flap:我听到卧室的屋顶有~一声响。*Overhead, in my bedroom there was a thump.*

潽 (of liquid) boil over:牛奶~了。*The milk boiled over.*

P

pú

仆 ① servant：奴～ *slave*；*lackey* / 男～ *manservant* / 女～ *maidservant* ②［旧］(referring to oneself used by man) your humble servant
see also pū

【仆从】footman；henchman；flunkey；henchman：～如云 *myriads of servants*
【仆从国】vassal country
【仆妇】［旧］older female servant
【仆仆】be travel-worn and weary；endure the hardships of travel
【仆人】(domestic) servant：雇～ *engage a servant* / ～室 *servant's room*
【仆役】(domestic) servants

匍

【匍匐】① crawl；creep；grovel：～前进 *crawl forward* / 那狗看到鞭子，便～在主人面前。*The dog grovelled before his master when he saw the whip.* ② (of plants) creep；trail
【匍匐茎】【植】stolon
【匍匐植物】【植】creeper

菩

【菩萨】① Bodhisattva ② Buddha；deity；god；Buddhist idol ③ a kindhearted person：他可真是个活～。*He is really a kind-hearted person.*
【菩萨心肠】the heart of a Bodhisattva — kindhearted；merciful：一个～的老人 *a merciful old man*
【菩提】bodhi — supreme wisdom or enlightenment
【菩提树】【植】pipal；bo tree；bodhi tree

脯 chest
see also fǔ

【脯子】breast meat (of chicken, duck, etc.)：鸡～ *chicken breast*

葡

【葡糖酸】【化】gluconic acid
【葡萄】grape：酸～ *sour grapes* / ～核 *grape stone* / ～树 *grape*；*grapevine*；*vine* / ～藤 *grape vine* / ～园 *grapery*
【葡萄虫】phylloxera
【葡萄干】raisin：～布丁 *plum duff*；*plum pudding*
【葡萄酒】grape wine；port：～酵母 *wine yeast*
【葡萄糖】glucose；grape sugar
【葡萄牙】Portugal：～人 *Portuguese* / ～语 *Portuguese (language)*
【葡萄紫】dark grayish purple

蒲¹【植】① cattail ② calamus

蒲² (Pú) a surname

【蒲包】① cattail bag；rush bag ②［旧］a gift of fruit or pastries (formerly packed in a cattail bag)
【蒲草】① stem or leaf of cattail ②［方］dwarf lily turf
【蒲垫】rush cushion
【蒲墩儿】cattail hassock used as a tool；rush cushion
【蒲公英】【植】dandelion (*Taraxacum mongolicum*)：～咖啡 *dandelion coffee* / ～素 *taraxacin*
【蒲瓜】［方］white flowered gourd
【蒲柳之姿】［谦］feel like a willow withering in autumn — be in poor health
【蒲绒】cattail wool, used for stuffing pillows
【蒲扇】cattail leaf fan
【蒲团】cattail hassock used for kneeling；rush hassock
【蒲席】cattail mat；rush mat

璞 uncut jade

【璞玉浑金】uncut jade and unrefined gold — unadorned beauty

pǔ

朴 simple；plain：俭～ *thrifty*；*frugal*
see also pō；pò

【朴厚】simple and honest；loyal and kind：一个～的村民 *a simple and honest villager*
【朴陋】crude；simple
【朴茂】［书］simple and honest；kind
【朴实】① simple；plain：～的建筑风格 *a simple style of architecture* ② sincere and honest：心地～ *simple and guileless* ③ matter-of-fact；unpretentious：他的话很～。*He spoke honestly and in a matter-of-fact way.*
【朴实无华】plain；simple and unaffected；unsophisticated：～的乡村教堂 *an unpretentious country church*
【朴素】① simple；plain：一件～的衣服 *a plain dress*；*a simple dress* / ～的发型 *a plain hair style* ② (of one's living) frugal；thrifty：养成～的生活作风 *cultivate the habit of simple and plain living* / ～大方 *plain and decent* ③ plain and unadorned：～的阶级感情 *simple class feeling* ④ undeveloped
【朴素唯物主义】naive materialism
【朴学】down-to-earth learning in the Qing Dynasty
【朴直】honest and straightforward：文笔～ *simple and straightforward writing*
【朴质】simple and unadorned；natural：～的文风 *a simple style of writing*
【朴拙】［书］sincere and unaffected

圃 garden：花～ *flower nursery* / 苗～ *seed plot*

【圃地】nursery；nursery garden

浦 ① riverside；river mouth；water's edge ② (Pǔ) a surname

【浦东开发区】Pudong Development Zone

普 ① general; universal: ~天下 *all over the world* ② (Pǔ) a surname

【普遍】universal; general; widespread; common: ~福利 *the general welfare* / ~治疗 *a universal remedy* / 一种~的误解 *a widespread misunderstanding* / 最为~使用的肥皂 *soap of the commonest sort* / 战争引起~的苦难。*War causes universal misery.* / 看电视是大家~感兴趣的事。*Watching TV is a matter of general interest.*

【普测】general survey

【普查】general investigation (or survey): 地质~ *geological survey* / 人口~ *census*

【普查员】census worker

【普度】【宗】deliver all from torment; liberate all: ~众生 *liberate all living beings from this moral world; deliver all living creatures from torment*

【普法】popularize law: ~教育 *education in the general knowledge of law*

【普及】① be universalized in; be popular; be extensively accepted: 这种教材已经~全国。*This kind of textbooks has been used all over the country.* ② popularize; disseminate; spread: 乒乓球运动的~ *the popularity of table tennis* / ~读物 *popular books* / 向广大读者~技术性刊物 *popularize technical material for a general audience*

【普及本】popular edition

【普及教育】universal education

【普及义务教育】popularization of compulsory education

【普降】(of rain or snow) fall over a large area: ~大雪 *widespread heavy snow*

【普朗克定律】Planck law

【普朗克质量】【物】Planck mass

【普利策】Joseph Pulitzer (1847-1911), American newspaper-owner and editor

【普利策奖】Pulitzer Prize

【普林斯顿】Princeton, a borough of central New Jersey north-northeast of Trenton

【普鲁士】Prussia: ~语 *Prussian* / ~主义 *Prussianism*

【普鲁士蓝】bearing blue

【普罗】proletariat

【普罗黄素】【药】proflavine

【普天同庆】the whole world (or nation) joins in the jubilation; universal rejoicing

【普天之下】everywhere under the sun; all over the world: 他很自负，认为~没有人比他更有才华。*He was so conceited that he thought there was nobody else more brilliant than he.*

【普通】plain; ordinary; common; average: ~观众 *the common spectator* / ~穿着 *everyday clothes* / 苹果在这里是很~的。*Apples are commonplace here.*

【普希金】Aleksander Pushkin (1799-1837), Russian poet

【普选】general election

【普选制】universal suffrage

【普照】illuminate all things; shine all over the world: 阳光~大地。*The sun illuminates every corner of the land.*

溥 ①[书] broad; vast ②[书] common; universal ③ (Pǔ) a surname

谱 ① table; register; record: 家~ *family tree; genealogy* / 光~ *spectrum* ② manual; guide: 棋~ *chess manual* ③ music score; music: 乐~ *music score* / 简~ *numbered musical notation* / 五线~ *staff; stave* ④ compose; set to music: 他为这首歌~了曲。*He is the composer of the song.* ⑤ a general standard; a fair amount of confidence: 他办事没~儿。*He doesn't know what he is doing.* / 我心里没~儿。*I have no definite plan yet.* ⑥ airs: 摆~ *put on airs*

【谱斑】【天】flocculus; floccule

【谱表】【音】stave; staff: 大~ *great stave*

【谱牒】[书] family tree; genealogy

【谱函数】【数】spectral function

【谱号】【音】clef: 低音~ *bass clef; F clef* / 高音~ *treble clef; G clef*

【谱级】spectrum level

【谱架】music stand

【谱曲】set (words) to music; compose music for: 他六岁时即用钢琴~。*At the age of six he was able to compose at the piano.*

【谱系】① genealogical system ② system of change of a thing ③【生理】pedigree: ~图 *pedigree chart*

【谱写】compose (music): 这支曲子是在解放战争初期~的。*The tune was composed at the beginning of the War of Liberation.*

【谱子】[口] music score; music

蹼 web

【蹼化】webbing

【蹼趾】webbed toe

【蹼足】webfoot; palmate foot

pù

铺[1] shop; store: 杂货~ *grocery*

铺[2] plank bed: 床~ *bed*

铺[3] [旧] post; courier station

see also pū

【铺板】bed board; bed plank

【铺保】[旧] guarantee for a person given by a shopkeeper; shop guarantor

【铺底】[旧] ① shop fixtures ② key money for the right to rent shop premises

【铺户】shop; store

【铺伙】[旧] shop assistant

【铺家】［方］shop; store
【铺面】① shop front: ~房 *shop building* ② sales area
【铺位】bunk; berth
【铺子】shop; store

瀑 waterfall

【瀑布】waterfall; falls; cataract: ~湖 *plunge lake*
【瀑布飞泉】waterfall and flying stream

曝 ［书］expose to the sun

see also bào
【曝光】exposure: ~表 *exposure meter* / 这两张照片的~时间不同。*These two pictures were taken with different exposures.*
【曝露】［书］expose to the open air: 他不喜欢把皮肤~在阳光下。*He hates exposing his skin to the sun.*
【曝气】aeration: ~池 *aeration tank* / ~管道 *aerated conduit* / ~塔 *aeration tower*
【曝晒】expose to the sun

P

Q

qī

七 seven:九加～等于十六。*Nine plus seven equals sixteen.* /这辆新车能载～名乘客。*The new car can carry seven passengers.*

【七…八…】used in conjunction with nouns or verbs to indicate multiplicity or disorder:七手八脚 *with many people doing sth all at once* /七疼八痒 *aches and itches of all kinds* /七老八十 *in one's seventies or eighties*

【七边形】【数】heptagon

【七彩虹】rainbow with seven colours

【七级风】【气】force 7 wind; moderate gale

【七级管】【电】heptode

【七价】【化】heptavalent; heptavalent

【七绝】a four-line poem with seven characters to a line and a strict tonal pattern and rhyme scheme

【七零八落】scattered here and there; in great disorder:侵略者被打得～,四处逃窜。*The invading army were thoroughly defeated and sent fleeing in disorder.* /～的书本散落在地上。*A few books scattered on the ground here and there.*

【七扭八歪】crooked; uneven; disorderly:这个小孩写的字～。*The child wrote a poor hand.* /他喝了酒,走路～的。*He staggered along after drinking.*

【七拼八凑】put together; knock together; piece together:用碎砖～成一道墙 *make a wall from odd pieces of brick* /用碎布～成一个枕套 *make a pillowcase from odd pieces of cloth* /这个实验室是他们自己～建起来的。*They rigged up this laboratory with their own hands.*

【七品芝麻官】lowly official, unusual referring to a county magistrate

【七七八八】off and on; various; sundry:她每天喂猪种菜,砍柴做饭,干些～的事情。*She does all the odd jobs: keeping pigs, planting vegetables, gathering firewood, preparing meals, and so on.* /他家～加起来,才有30美元的财产。*He has, off and on, 30 US dollars of property in his family.*

【七巧板】seven-piece puzzle; tangram

【七窍】the seven apertures in one's head, i. e. ears, eyes, nostrils and mouth:她～流血而死。*She was died with bleeding from every orifice.*

【七窍生烟】fume with anger; make extremely anger; infuriated; foam with rage:她被气得～,一言不发。*She was extremely anger with saying nothing.*

【七情】① seven human emotions, namely, joy, anger, sorrow, fear, love, hate and desire ②【中医】the seven emotional factors (joy, anger melancholy, brooding, sorrow, fear and shock), considered to be the internal factors of disease

【七情六欲】seven emotions and six sensual pleasures, various human emotions and desires

【七上八下】be agitated; be troubled; be in a nervous state of mind; be perturbed:我们心里～的,不知道该如何去做。*We were seriously troubled, not knowing what to do next.*

【七十二变】seventy-two metamorphoses (said of the Monkey King, in the *Pilgrimage to the West*《西游记》), who could transform himself into seventy-two forms); countless changes of tactics

【七十二行】all sorts of occupations; all sorts of professions; all sorts of trades; in every conceivable line of work

【七夕】the seventh evening of the seventh moon of the lunar calendar (when according to legend the Cowherd (牛郎) *and the Weaver* (织女) *Maid meet in Heaven*)

【七弦琴】seven-stringed musical instrument

【七星针】【中医】cutaneous acupuncture

【七言诗】a poem with seven characters to a line

【七月】① July:我们在～份有假期。*We will have our holidays in July.* ② the seventh month of the lunar year; the seventh moon

【七折八扣】various deductions; various cuts:工资本来就不多,再加上～的,剩下的连购买食品都不够。*The salary was not plentiful to start with, and after various deductions and cuts, was hardly enough to buy foodstuff.*

【七嘴八舌】lively discussion with everyone trying to get a word in; with many people talking all at once:选举结果一公布,会场上的人就～地议论开了。*Announcement of the election results touched off a lively discussion, with everybody eager to say something.*

沏 infuse; soak: ～一碗绿茶 *infuse (or make) a bowl of green tea* /用热水～中药 *soak herbs in hot water*

妻 wife

【妻弟】younger brother-in-law; the younger brother of one's wife

【妻儿老小】a married man's parents, wife and children:一家～等着他的照顾,他不得不出来打工。*He is a married man with his parents, wife and children all relying on him, so he has to go out-*

Q

side for a job.

【妻离子散】breaking up or scattering one's family：水灾使许多家庭～，家破人亡。*The flood caused countless broken families and took a heavy toll of human life.*

【妻妹】younger sister of one's wife；younger sister-in-law

【妻室】［书］wife：这个年轻人还没有～。*The young man has not get married yet.*

【妻子】（qīzǐ） wife and children

【妻子】（qīzi） wife：～为他调了一杯热饮料。*His wife mixed him a hot drink.* /他和～似乎相处得不错。*He and his wife seem to rub along all right.*

柒

① seven, used for the numeral 七 on cheques, etc. to avoid mistakes or alterations ②（Qī） a surname

栖

①（of birds） perch ② dwell；stay；live

【栖身】stay；sojourn：他们觉得世界虽大，却无处可以～。*They felt that they had no place to stay in this wide world.*

【栖息】（of birds） perch；rest：许多水鸟～在湖边的草丛中。*Many waterfowls dwell in the depths of grass on the bank of the lake.* /我们要保护好野生动物的～环境。*We should take care of the living environment of wild animals.* /鸟在电线上～。*Birds were sitting on the wires.*

【栖息地】habitat：鸟类的天然～是丛林。*Birds' natural habitat is the jungle.* /这个自然保护区是许多珍贵鸟类的～。*The nature protection zone is a habitat of many rare birds.*

桤

【桤木】【植】alder

凄

① chilly；cold；freezing：～～风雨 *cold wind and incessant rain* ② bleak and desolate：～清 *lonely and sad* ③ sad；wretched；miserable；dejected：～切 *plaintive or mournful*

【凄惨】wretched；miserable；horrible；dreadful；tragic：～的面孔 *wretched face* / ～的事故 *dreadful accident*

【凄楚】grieved；sad：她～地叹了一声。*She heaved a sigh sounded very sad.*

【凄风苦雨】wailing wind and weeping rain — foul weather；wretched circumstances

【凄寂】① desolate and still ② dreary and lonely

【凄苦】sad and miserable：十年来，老奶奶一直过着～的生活。*The grandma has led a lonely and miserable life all these ten years.*

【凄冷】desolate；chilly；cold：他感到雨中的树林异常～。*He was rather chilly in the raining forest.*

【凄厉】sad and shrill：～的哭声 *mournful, shrill cries* /寒风～。*The cold wind is wailing.*

【凄凉】dreary；desolate；dismal；miserable：晚景～ *lead a miserable and lonely life in one's old age* / 地震后到处是一派～的景象。*After the earthquake it is desolation all round.*

【凄清】chilly；bleak；gloomy：～的喊声 *a melancholy cry* / ～的月光 *chilly moonlight*

【凄然】［书］sad；mournful；sorrowful：～泪下 *shed tears in sadness* /眼神～ *wear a sorrowful expression in one's eyes*

萋

【萋萋】luxuriant：芳草～ *luxuriant green grass*

戚[1]

relative：皇亲国～ *relatives of an emperor*

戚[2]

① sorrow；grief；woe：休～与共 *share joys and sorrows* ②（Qī） a surname

【戚然】look worried；be sorrowful；be woeful；be sad：～不语 *look woeful and worried saying no word* / ～的神情 *a woeful look*

【戚友】relatives and friends

期

① appointed date；schedule time：按～完成的任务 *a programme that is on schedule* ② a period of time；phase；stage；term：假～ *vacation；holiday* /学～ *school term；semester* /长～培训 *long-term training* /短～学习 *short-term learning* ③［量］things done periodically：我是培训班的第六～学员。*I was one of the students of sixth term training class.* ④ make an appointment：不～而遇 *meet unexpectedly；meet by chance；run into* ⑤ expect；hope：我预～星期六回北京。*I expect I will return to Beijing on Saturday.*

see also jī

【期待】expect；anticipate；look forward to：我们～明天会更好。*We expect tomorrow will be better and better.* /我们～着会议的顺利召开。*All of us are looking forward to the conference hold smoothly.* /那个可怜的母亲没有～会得到那样的答复。*The poor mother did not expect that reply.*

【期汇】【经】forward exchange

【期货】【经】futures：～价格 *futures price* / ～合同 *forward contract；futures contract* / ～贸易 *futures trade* / ～交易 *futures transaction* / ～市场 *futures market*

【期间】period；time；course：圣诞节～ *in the course of Christmas Days* /在工作～ *during work time* / 会议～ *during the meeting；in the course of the conference* /演出～有一次休息。*There is a break during the performance.* /战略是指战争～一个国家整体的作战计划。*Strategy refers to the overall plans of a nation at war.* /战争～所有叛国通敌的人都可以判处枪决。*During the wartime, anyone who collaborated might be sentenced to shoot.* /这个故事发生在第二次世界大战～的日本。*The scene of this story happened in Japanese during World War II.*

【期刊】periodical：～阅览室 *periodicals reading-room* /自然科学～ *natural science periodicals* /英语～ *English periodicals* /李老师在授课前查阅了许多～。*Teacher Li looked through a number of journals before he started to teach classes.*

【期考】end-of-term examination；terminal examination

【期满】expire；come to an end；run out；end：租约

～ *the expiration of the lease* /租用～ *the expiration of tenancy* / 协议～ the expiration of the agreement /我的工作合同下月末就要～了。*My job contract will expire at the end of next month.*

【期盼】expect; look forward to: ～放假 *look forward to one's holiday* /我们非常～再次见到总经理。*We are so much looking forward to seeing our general manager.*

【期票】promissory note: ～出票人 *marker of promissory note*

【期求】hope to get; desire

【期望】hope; expect; look forward to: ～寿命 *life expectancy* /父母对孩子寄予很大的～。*Parents place high hopes on their children.* /我们不能辜负党和国家对我们的～。*We can't disappoint the expectations of our Party and our country.* /不要对我的～过高。*Don't expect too much of me.* /我们决不辜负父母对我们的～。*We will never fail to live up to what our parents expect of us.* /她是一个没有辜负父母～的好孩子。*She was a girl after the hopes and expectations of her parents.* /结果要比老师们所～的要好。*The result surpassed the teachers' hopes.*

【期望值】expected value; expectations:对孩子的～过高或过低都不利于他们的成长。*Too high or low expectations on children are not good for their growth.*

【期限】deadline; allotted time; time limit; set time:超过～ *miss a deadline* /延长合同～ *extend time limit of the contract* /停火～ *cease fire deadline* /请告诉我一个还钱的最后～。*Please tell me a deadline for paying the money.* /张老师希望我们能在最后～之前交上论文。*Teacher Zhang hopes we can submit our papers before the deadline.*

欺 ① cheat; deceive:自～～人 *cheat oneself as well as others* / ～上瞒下 *deceive one's superiors and delude one's subordinates* /不努力是不会成功的,所以你不要自～～人。*You can't succeed without working; so don't deceive yourself.* ② bully; take advantage of:以大～小 *the big bully the small* / ～软怕硬 *bully the weak and fear the strong* / ～行霸市 *bully others in a trade and monopolize the market* / ～行霸市者将会受到惩罚。*The one who bullies others for control of the market will be punished.*

【欺负】bully:富人不应该～穷人。*The rich should not bully the poor.* /大人不应该～小孩。*An adult should not treat children high-handedly.*

【欺凌】bully; humiliate; insult:任人～ *be subject to bulling and humiliation* /强大的中国再也不会受别国～。*The powerful China will never allow itself to be trodden by any other nation.* /强者不能～弱者。*The strong will never be allowed to insult the weak.*

【欺瞒】defraud; dupe; hoodwink; pull the wool over sb's eyes: ～某人(做某事) *dupe sb (into doing sth)* /孩子们再也不会受他的～了。*The children won't be her dupe any more.* / 游客受～买了假首饰。*The tourist was hoodwinked into buying fake jewels.* /一个奸诈的会计～了股东们的钱。*A dishonest accountant defrauded the stockholders of their money.*

【欺骗】cheat; dupe; deceive; hoodwink: ～视觉的幻象 *illusions that cheat the eye* / ～某人做某事 *dupe sb into doing sth* / ～公众 *befuddle the public* /他～孩子们,使他们相信他会修理那些玩具。*He deceived the children into thinking he could repair those toys.* /你这是在～你自己。*You are deceiving yourself.*

【欺人太甚】that's going too far; the humiliation is too hard to endure:这位外交官的话～,激起了其他所有国家的公愤。*The insulting words of the diplomat aroused indignation among all other counties.*

【欺辱】bully; humiliate; insult:忍受～ *swallow an insult* /二战期间,这些战俘受尽了～。*During the world war Ⅱ those POWs were insulted and humiliated in every possible way.*

【欺生】① bully or cheat strangers ② (of horses, mules, etc.) be refractory to strangers; be ungovernable by strangers

【欺世盗名】gain fame by deceiving the public or society; win popularity by dishonest means

【欺侮】bully; insult; treat sb high-handedly:这个男孩总是～其他女孩子。*The boy always bullies other girls.* /现在中国可不是好～的。*Now China is not a country to be trifled with.*

【欺压】bully and oppress; ride roughshod over:当时恶霸地主任意～那个村的穷人。*In those days the despotic landlords rode roughshod over the poor in that village.*

【欺诈】cheat; deceive; swindle:商业～ *business swindle* / ～行为 *act of swindling*

嘁

【嘁嘁喳喳】[象]chatter away; jabber away:一群孩子在操场上～的,兴高采烈。*A group of children chattered away in the playground, being in great delight.*

漆 ① lacquer; paint: ～器 *lacquer ware* / ～盒 *lacquer box* / 朱～大门 *vermilion gates* ② paint; cover with lacquer:油～笔 *painting pen* / 把窗户～成红色 *paint the window red* /把家具再～两遍。*Give furniture another two coats of paint.* /油～开始剥落。*The paint is beginning to flake off.* / 窗子上的油～已经剥落了。*The paint on the windows has flaked.* ③ (Qī) a surname

【漆包线】【电】enamel-insulated wire

【漆布】varnished cloth

【漆革】patent leather

【漆工】① lacquering; painting ② lacquerer; lacquer man; painter

【漆黑】pitch-dark; pitch-black:四周～一片 *be pitch dark all round* /那是一个～无月的夜。*It was a dark, moonless night.*

【漆黑一团】① pitch-dark: ～,他们看不到前方的路。*They could not see their way ahead in the pitch-dark.* /我们不能把将来描绘成～。*We should not paint a dark picture of the future.* ② be blind to; be entirely ignorant of; be in the dark:如何摆脱眼前的困境,他们至今心中还是～。*They are still in the dark about how to extricate the difficult position before their eyes.*

【漆画】【美】lacquer painting

【漆匠】① lacquerware worker ② lacquerer; lacquer man; painter

【漆盘】lacquer tray

【漆皮】① coat of paint ② shellac

【漆器】lacquerwork; lacquer ware: ～厂 *lacquerware plant* /脱胎～ *bodiless lacquerware*

【漆树】lacquer tree

蹊

see also xī

【蹊跷】odd; queer; mysterious; fishy:为什么他能中奖,事情有点～。*It smells fishy why he won the prize.* /那辆新车这么便宜,里面一定有～! *That new car is very cheap; there must be a catch in it somewhere!* /那个问题看起来容易,但这里面有～。*That question looks easy, but there's a catch in it.*

qí

齐 ① neat; even; uniform; in order:整～ *neat and tidy* /把杂志摆～ *arrange the magazines in order* /草坪被剪得很～。*The lawn is evenly trimmed.* /这些电线长短不～。*These wires are not even in length.* ② on a level with:院子里的花都～了窗台。*The flowers in yard have reached the windowsill.* /池水～腰深。*The pool is waist deep.* /请把～着地面的树砍断。*Please cut the tree right down to the ground.* ③ together:男女老少～上阵。*Men and women, old and young, all pitched into the work.* /球队表演精彩时,女孩子们一～跳起来为他们加油。*The girls jumped up and down together, cheering when the team has played well.* /万箭～发。*All arrows shot at the same time.* ④ all ready; all present; in order:代表都到～了。*The representatives are all present.* /现在所有的事都准备～了。*All the things are now ready.* ⑤ alike; similar; equal:人心～,泰山移。*If people work with one mind, they can even remove Mount Tai.* ⑥ (Qí) a surname

【齐备】all ready:上课所需的书都已～。*The books necessary for the class are all ready.*

【齐步走】【军】① quick march ② quick-time, march

【齐唱】【音】singing in unison; unison

【齐楚】neat and smart:衣冠～ *be well dressed*; *be smartly dressed*; *be immaculately dressed*

【齐次方程】【数】homogeneous equation

【齐集】assemble; gather; collect

【齐名】enjoy equal popularity or renown; be equally famous:在《三国演义》里关羽和张飞～。*In the novel the Romance of the Three Kingdoms Guan Yu and Zhang Fei enjoyed equal fame.* /在唐代的诗人中李白与杜甫～。*Among the Tang poets, Li Bai and Du Fu enjoyed equal fame.*

【齐全】complete; ready:这批鞋子号码～。*These batches of shoes have complete range of sizes.* /探险队员装备～。*The explorers are fully equipped.* /我们的房子设备～。*Our houses have all necessary facilities.* /商店安排了～的服务项目。*The store arranged a satisfactory series of services.*

【齐射】【军】salvo; volley

【齐声】be in chorus; be in unison: ～朗诵 *recite in unison* /人们～大哭起来。*People cried in chorus.*

【齐头并进】advance side by side; advance in parallel; do two or more things at the same time:两支队伍～。*The two teams advanced simultaneously.*

【齐心】be of one mind; share a common goal:工人们～,每天都能按时完成任务。*The workers are of one heart; they can accomplish their task on schedule everyday.* /我们只要～,事情就好办了。*When we are of one heart, everything becomes easy.*

【齐心协力】work as one; make concerted effort

【齐整】neat; well arranged; uniform:学生们总是穿得很～。*The students are always neatly dressed.*

祁 (Qí) a surname

【祁红】keemun (a kind of black tea)

其[1] ① her; his; its; their: ～家 *one's family* / ～妻 *his wife* /人尽～才,物尽～用,总之是各得～所。*Make the most suitable use of person and material, in a word, each is in one's proper place.* ② she; he; it; they:令～马上放下武器 *order him to put down his gun right away* /顺～自然 *let things take their own course* /自食～果 *reap as what one has sown* ③ that; such:生逢～时 *a person was born at that right time* /察～言,观～行 *careful weigh up a person's words and closely watch his action* /不乏～人,不乏～言。*There are not short of such people and such words.*

其[2] used as a functional word:大行～道 *sth is in popularity* /大发～威 *be furious; fly into a rage*

其[3] express conjecture or retort:舍我～谁? *Who can do it except me?*

【其次】① next; secondly; then:先讨论,～才是参观。*Let's have a discussion first and then we look around.* ② second; secondary:品质是主要的,长相还在～。*Character comes first, features second.* /内容是主要的,形式还在～。*Content comes first, form second.*

【其乐融融】happy and harmonious:老同学欢聚在一起,载歌载舞～。*When old classmates meet together, they sing and dance with great joy and delight.*

【其乐无穷】boundless happiness; infinite delight or joy:与天斗,～。*It is an immense pleasure fighting with nature.*

【其貌不扬】undistinguished features or appearance:想不到面前这位~的人竟是一位大科学家。*It was never expected that the great scientist before us was so homely in looks.*

【其实】in fact; actually; as a matter of fact: ~,这本书很容易理解。*As a matter of fact, this book is easy to understand.* / ~他是这样说的。*He actually said so.*

【其他】other; else:写完作业以前先不要考虑~的事情。*You should not consider other things before you finish your homework.* /比赛中他赶上了~的选手,最后跑了第一。*He gained on the other runners in the race and finished first.* /他一星期所完成的作业比班上~的同学都多。*He can accomplish more in a week than any other students in his class.*

【其余】the remainder; the rest; the others: ~的钱明天付。*The rest will be paid tomorrow.* / ~的人跟我来。*The others follow me.* / ~的放学后要等我们。*The rest are to wait for us after school.*

【其中】among (which, them, etc.); in (which, it etc.):我们班有60人,~男同学占70%。*There are sixty students in our class, and 70 percent of us are boys.* /我有好几个同事出席了这次会议,~有张丽和王海。*Several of my colleagues took part in this meeting; among them were Zhang Li and Wang Hai.*

奇 ① strange; queer; unusual; extraordinary: ~花异草 *exotic flowers and rare grasses* / ~谈怪论 *strange tale and absurd argument* ② surprise; unexpected; wonder; astonish:他的出现并不出~。*His appearance is not at all surprising.*
see also jī

【奇兵】troops suddenly appearing from nowhere:我们只有出~才能赢得胜利。*If we want to win this victory, it is necessary to arrange an ingenious military movement.*

【奇才】talent; genius

【奇耻大辱】extreme shame and humiliation; deep disgrace:我们必须记住这些~。*We need remember these outrageous insults and humiliations.*

【奇功】outstanding service:这支军队在抗日战争中屡建~。*This troop performed many extraordinary exploits in anti-Japanese war.*

【奇怪】strange; odd; surprising; eccentric: ~的论调 *odd views or arguments* /他出席这次会议一点也不~。*There is nothing strange about that he attended this meeting.* /当那个警察在夜晚听见~的声音时,马上从屋里跑了出来。*The policeman rushed out of the room as he heard the strange noise in the night.*

【奇观】marvelous spectacle; wonder

【奇货可居】hoard sth as rare commodity

【奇迹】wonder; miracle; marvel:工人们创造了~。*The workers performed miracles.*

【奇景】wonderful view; extraordinary sight

【奇丽】unique and beautiful: ~的海岛风光 *island scene of peculiar charm*

【奇妙】marvelous; wonderful

【奇葩】exotic and enchanting flowers:一朵科学上的~ *a wonderful work of science*

【奇巧】(of art or handicraft) of ingenious

【奇人】① odd man or woman; odd person; eccentric ② person of genius

【奇事】odd affair; strange affair; uncommon phenomenon

【奇谈】strange tale; absurd argument

【奇特】peculiar; queer; singular:科学家在海底发现了一些~的景象。*The scientists discovered some strange phenomenon in the bottom of the sea.* /她孩子的长相很~。*The appearance of her child is singular.*

【奇文】① a remarkable piece of writing ② absurd or ridiculous writing

【奇文共赏】share the pleasure of reading a remarkable piece of writing

【奇闻】sth unheard-of; a thrilling or fantastic story

【奇袭】raid; surprise attack

【奇效】(of medicine) extraordinary efficacy

【奇形怪状】sth with grotesque shape or appearance; fantastic in form: ~的面具 *grotesque mask*

【奇异】① queer; strange; bizarre; unusual: ~的孔雀 *rare peacock* / ~的花木 *exotic flowers and trees* ② surprised; curious; astounded; astonished:他们用~的眼色看着这台机器。*They all looked at this machine with curious eyes.*

【奇遇】fortuitous meeting; happy encounter; adventure:他乡~ *adventure in a distant land* /经历种种~ *go through strange adventures*

【奇缘】unexpected affair of the heart; romance

【奇珍】curio; rarity: ~异宝 *rare treasures*

【奇装异服】exotic costume; bizarre dress; grotesque or strange fashion; outlandish outfit

歧 ① branch; fork ② divergent; different:思想分~ *a difference in thought*

【歧路】branch; forked road

【歧视】discriminate against:种族~在有些国家相当严重。*Racial discrimination is a serious problem in some countries.*

【歧途】wrong road; wrong path:误入~ *be misled; go astray* /不要把年轻人引入~。*Don't lead the young astray.*

【歧义】different meanings; ambiguity; various interpretations:我们对这种解释有~。*We have another interpretations on it.*

祈 ① pray: ~风~雨 *pray for wind and rain* ② request; entreat:敬~指导。*We respectfully request your guidance or direction.*

【祈祷】pray; say one's prayers

【祈年】pray for a bumper crop

【祈请】earnestly request:我们~您的光临。*We earnestly request your coming.*

【祈求】pray for; earnestly hope; plead for: ~神灵 *pray to God* / ~幸福 *pray for happiness* / ~和平 *pray for peace* /不能~别人的恩赐,而要靠我们自己。*We must never entreat others to help us, but must rather depend ourselves.*

【祈使句】imperative sentence

Q

【祈望】wish; hope

耆 over sixty years of age

【耆年】old age

【耆老】old person

【耆绅】old gentleman

颀 ［书］tall

【颀长】tall：身材～ *a tall figure; tall in build*

【颀伟】(of human stature) tall and strong

脐 ①【生理】navel; umbilicus ② the abdomen of a crab

【脐带】【生理】umbilical cord

【脐风】【中医】umbilical tetanus

【脐炎】【医】omphalitis

萁 ［方］beanstalk：煮豆火燃豆～ *cook beans with burning beanstalks*

畦 rectangular pieces of land in a field, separated by ridges：菜～ *vegetable bed*

【畦灌】【农】border method of irrigation; plot by plot irrigation

【畦田】embanked field

崎

【崎岖】uneven; rugged：～的小路 *rugged pathway* / ～不平的山路 *rugged and uneven mountain path* / 山路～不平。*The mountain path is rugged and uneven.*

骐 ［书］black horse

骑 ① ride; sit on the back of：～骆驼 *ride a camel; be on the back of a came* / 让小孩～在肩上 *give a child a ride on one's shoulders* / 精～善射 *be exceptionally good at both horsemanship and marksmanship; excel in horsemanship and marksmanship* / 我弟弟喜欢～马。*My little brother loves to ride on a horse.* / 我的父母非常喜欢～自行车去郊游。*My parents love to bike for an excursion.* ② cavalryman; cavalry：铁～ *cavalry mounted troops; cavalry team*

【骑缝】junction of the edges of two sheets of paper：～章 *seal across the perforation*

【骑虎难下】set on the back of a tiger and find it hard to dismount; have no way to be back：虽然这件事有点～，但是我们决不能放弃。*Although we are in difficult situation in some extent, we should never discourage.*

【骑马找马】ride a horse and look for another; hold on to one's job while seeking a new one; sth one already has

【骑射】horsemanship and archery：这支部队的士兵精于～。*Soldiers in this troop excel in horsemanship and archery.*

【骑士】knight; cavalier：他是一个有～风度的人。*He is a person with knightly manner.* / ～迫使他的马在暴风雨中急速前进。*The rider forced his horse on through the storm quickly.*

【骑手】rider; horseman

【骑术】horsemanship; equestrian skill：她母亲为她的～感到自豪。*Her mother is proud of her horsemanship.*

琪 fine jade

棋 chess or any board game：～盘 *chessboard; checkerboard* / 象～ *Chinese chess* / 国际～ *(international) chess* / 下象～ *play Chinese chess* / 残～ *final phase of a chess* / 他们在下～。*They are playing at chess.* / 愿意和我下～吗？*Will you play me at chess?*

【棋逢对手】meet one's match in a chess game; be well-matched in a game

【棋谱】chess manual

【棋坛】chess fields; chess circles

【棋艺】technique of playing chess

【棋子】piece; chessman

祺 ［书］blessing; good luck

旗 ① flag; banner; standard：国～ *national flag* / 党～ *party flag* / 队～ *team pennant* / 船～国 *vessel flag nation* / 红～迎风飘扬。*The red flag is flying in the breeze.* ② of the "Eight Banners"：～人 *Manchu* ③ banner, an administrative division of county level in the Inner Mongolia Autonomous Region.

【旗杆】flag post; flagpole

【旗鼓相当】be well matched; be equal in strength or ability：这两支部队～，很难预料谁会取胜。*As the two troops are well marched, it is much difficult to predict which of them will win.*

【旗号】banner; flag：他们打着为大家服务的～牟取私利。*They pursue private interests under the banner of "serve the all"*

【旗舰】【军】flagship

【旗开得胜】win victory soon after the standard is raised; succeed from the very start; win victory in the first battle：～，马到成功。*Win speedy victory in the first battle.*

【旗袍】a close fitting woman's dress with high neck and slit skirt; cheongsam

【旗枪】flagpole with a sharp metal or wooden end

【旗手】standard bearer; colour bearer

【旗语】flag signal; semaphore

【旗帜】banner; flag; closures：高举邓小平理论伟大～ *hold high the great banner of Deng Xiaoping theory* / 大街上～招展。*The streets are decked with flags.*

【旗子】flag; banner; pennant

鳍 fin：尾～ *caudal fin*

【鳍鲸】fin whale; finback whale

【鳍足】【动】clasper：～动物 *Pinnipedia; pinniped*

麒

【麒麟】kylin; (Chinese) unicorn

【麒麟菜】【植】Chinese alpine rush (Eulaliopais binata)

【麒麟座】【天】Monoceros

qǐ

乞 ① beg (for alms, etc.); supplicate; ask (sb) humbly for sth: 行~ *go begging* ② (Qǐ) a surname

【乞丐】beggar

【乞力马扎罗山】Kilimanjaro, a volcanic massif in Tanzania

【乞怜】beg for mercy; beg for pity

【乞求】beg for; implore; supplicate; beseech; entreat: ~宽恕 *supplicate sb's forgiveness* /"救救我吧,"小女孩~道。"*Help me," the little girl implored.* /他们~她别离开。*They implored her not to leave.*

【乞食】beg for food: 沿路~ *go begging along the road*

【乞讨】beg; go begging: 向游客~ *beg money from tourists* /那个可怜的孩子被迫~。*The poor child was reduced to begging.*

【乞援】ask for assistance; beg for aid

岂 used to introduce or ask a rhetorical question: 路见不平~能不管? *How could we treat with indifference when seeing injustice on the road?* /卧榻之上,~容他人鼾睡? *How could one tolerance people snoring in one's bed?*

【岂不】wouldn't it be; isn't it: 坐飞机~更快? *Wouldn't that be much fast by air?* /这样做~更舒适? *Isn't it more comfortable to do thing this way?*

【岂但】not only: ~你进不去,恐怕总经理也不行。*Not only you are not permitted to get in, the general manager may not be permitted.*

【岂敢】① you flatter me ② how dare: 你叫我,我~不来。*I would not dare to come when you call me.*

【岂可】how could: ~出言不逊? *How could you speak insolently?*

【岂肯】how could; how would

【岂能】how could; how is it possible: ~如此无理取闹? *How could you willfully make such trouble?*

【岂有此理】outrageous; preposterous; shameless: 这样欺侮别人,真是~。*It is outrageous to bully other person just like this.* /直是~! *This is really outrageous!*

企 stand on tiptoe; look forward to; expect

【企待】look forward to; await; expect: 她非常~她男朋友情人节过来。*Her boyfriend will be expected on Valentine's Day.*

【企鹅】【动】penguin

【企及】desire strongly to achieve sth; aspire to reach; hope to attain

【企慕】admire; esteem; look up to: 我非常~她的工作。*I esteem her work highly.*

【企盼】expect; hope for; look forward to; long for

【企求】yearn for; seek for; hanker after: ~功名 *hanker after scholarly honour or official rank* / ~出国 *desire to go oversea*

【企图】[贬] attempt; seek; try: ~谋杀某人 *seek to murder sb* /阻止某人的~ *deter sb from an attempt* / ~逃避惩罚 *try to escape punishment* /那个罪犯在~逃离这座城市时被捕获。*The criminal was captured when trying to escape from the city.* /一些国家~取得世界统治地位。*Some countries attempt to attain world domination.* /那个小偷向她冲上来,并且~夺取她的手表。*The thief had rushed up to her and tried to steal her watch.*

【企望】look forward to; hope for; aspire: 我们~有一个稳定的经济环境。*We all hope for a stable economic circumstance*

【企业】enterprise; business: 大中型国有~ *large scale and medium sized state-owned enterprises* / ~法人 *legal entity* / ~管理 *business management* / ~家 *entrepreneur* / ~集团 *enterprise group; corporation* /跨国~集团 *multinational corporations* / ~文化 *enterprise culture* / ~精神 *entrepreneurship* / ~经营策略 *enterprise management tactics* / ~经营思想 *enterprise management philosophy* /有些领导极力主张改革~。*Some leaders strongly advocate the reform of government ownership of industry.*

杞 the name of an ancient kingdom during the Zhou Dynasty

【杞人忧天】like the man of Qi who fear that the sky might be fall-caught by imaginary fears

启 ① open: 开~大门 *open the gate* /张教授亲~ *to be opened by professor Zhang personally* ② start; initiate: ~行 *start on a tour* ③ enlighten; awaken; inspire ④ [书] state; inform ⑥ (Qǐ) a surname

【启禀】report (to one's superior)

【启程】set out; start on a journey: 从北京~ *set out from Beijing* / ~周游世界 *start off on a tour round the world* /旅行团已于早上~赴新加坡了。*The touring party left for Singapore this morning.*

【启齿】open one's mouth; start to talk about sth: 她把难以~的疾病告诉了大夫。*She told the doctor of her unmentionable disease.*

【启唇】open one's mouth; speak

【启迪】enlighten; inspire: 诗人受到海边美景的~而创作出他最伟大的作品。*The coast scenery inspired the poet to write his greatest works.*

【启动】start (a machine etc.); switch on; turn on: ~马达 *switch on the motor* / ~汽车 *start a car* / ~资金 *start-up fund* / ~电压 *starting voltage*

【启动期】start-up phase: 项目的~ *start-up phase of a project*

【启发】arouse; inspired; enlighten: ~他们的创造力 *arouse their creativity* /这位博士的讲话深深地~了每一个学生。*The Doctor's lecture deeply stimulated all the students.*

【启封】unseal; break or remove the seal; open a wrapper or envelop

【启航】set sail; weigh anchor: 第一艘科学考察船~远行。*The first scientific surveying ship weighed anchor for a long journey.*

【启口】open one's mouth; start to talk

【启蒙】① impart rudimentary knowledge to beginner; initiate: ~老师 *the teacher who guides his students or followers in to a specific field of study* / ~读物 *Children's primers* ② enlighten: ~教育 *enlightening education the Enlightenment* / ~时代 *the Age of Enlightenment*

【启明星】【天】Venus

【启示】enlightenment; inspiration; revelation:这一事件给了我们很多~。*This incident gave us a good deal enlightenment.* /长征的故事给了孩子们很大的~。*The story of Long March is a great inspiration to the children.*

【启事】notice; announcement: 招领~ *lost and found notice; found* /寻人~ *notice of looking for sb missing* /寻物~ *notice of looking for sth lost*

【启行】set out; set off on a journey; start on a journey: ~赴美 *set off for America*

【启用】start using:公司的新公章下周一~。*The company will start using its new seal from next Monday.*

【启运】start shipment (of goods): ~港 *port of departure* / ~地 *place of departure* / ~日期 *date of departure* /发往香港的集装箱已经~。*The containers are being shipped to Hong Kong.*

起[1] ① rise; get up; stand up:早~ *get up in the morning* /站~来 *stand up; rise to one's feet* ② move; remove; extract; pull: ~塞子 *pull the plug from sth* / ~螺钉 *draw out a screw* / ~土 *remove soil from one place to another place* / ~地雷 *clear landmines* ③ appear; raise:夏天孩子们身上容易~痱子。*It is easy to infect prickly heat on children's body in summer time.* ④ rise; grow; go up: ~风了。*The wind is rising.* / ~雾了。*The fog is rising.* ⑤ draft; work out: ~草 *make a draft* ⑥ build; set up; construct: ~一道篱笆 *build a hedge* ⑦ start; begin; initiate; launch: 发~运动 *initiate a movement* /从明天~,正式开学。*The school will formally open from tomorrow.* ⑧ obtain: ~货单 *get a manifest*

起[2] ① be used after verbs to indicate beginning: 讲到这位科学家的事迹,我们应该从头说~。*We should start from the very beginning to talk about the achievement of the scientist.* ② be used after verbs to indicate the tend of act or movement:拿~刀 *take up knife* ③ be used follow verbs and often preceded by 不 or 得 to indicate if it is within or beyond sb's ability to do sth:赔不~ *cannot afford to compensate sth*

起[3] [量] case; instance; batch; group:两~中毒事件 *two cases of toxic accidents* /今天早晨有两~人冲入了大楼。*Two groups of people rushed into the building this morning.*

【起岸】unload a ship; bring (cargo, etc. from a ship) to land

【起爆】detonate: ~装置 *detonating device*

【起笔】① the first stroke of a Chinese character ② start of each stroke in writing a Chinese character

【起兵】dispatch troops; set going an revolt

【起驳】begin shipment by barge

【起搏器】【医】pacemaker

【起步】leave; start; move:北京出租车的~价是10元。*The raising price of taxi in Beijing is* ¥10. /西部大开发处于刚刚~阶段。*The project of west exploitation is just in its start phase.*

【起草】draft; draw up: ~纲要 *draft a outline*

【起程】leave; set out; start on a journey:赴西藏的医疗队昨天~了。*The medical team left for Tibet yesterday.*

【起初】at first; originally; at the beginning; at the outset: ~我不愿意来。*I did not intend to come at the beginning.*

【起床】get up; get out of bed:孩子们已经~了。*The children are already up.* /他的妻子每天很早~。*His wife rises early every morning.*

【起床号】reveille:吹~ *blow or sound reveille*

【起道机】track jack

【起点】starting point: ~运费 *minimum freight; minimum charge per bill of lading* /把成绩作为继续前进的新~ *take achievements as starting points for further progress* /这次胜利是成功的~。*The victory is the starting point for success.*

【起点站】starting station

【起电盘】electrophorus

【起吊】lift heavy objects by crane

【起钉锤】claw hammer

【起钉钳】nail nippers

【起动】start: ~机 *starter*

【起端】origin (of an event etc.); beginning

【起飞】take off:经济~ *economic take off* /我们的航班正在~。*Our flight is taking off.* /大客机从机场~。*The huge airplane lifted from the airport.*

【起伏】rise and fall; undulate:连绵~的山冈 *rolling hillocks* /心潮~ *one's mind surge and subside alternately*

【起稿】make a draft; draft:她是讲义的~人之一。*She is one of the persons who drafted the lecture sheets.*

【起航】set sail; weigh anchor; take off

【起哄】people gathered together to create a disturbance; (of a crowd of people) jeer

【起火】① (of fire) break out; catch fire; be on fire:丛林~了。*A fire has broken out in the jungle.* ② cook meals:休息一下,~做饭。*Have a break and cook meals.*

【起货】take goods (from a warehouse or a ship etc.)

【起获】track sth down; recover stolen goods:警方~了一大批非法枪支。*The police tracked down a large numbers of illegal guns.*

【起急】[方] get anxious; be worried; get impatient:别~,慢慢说。*Don't worry; speak it slowly.*

【起家】build up; make one's fortune or fame etc.; grow and thrive:这个老板是白手~的。*This boss made his fortune from nothing.*

【起价】[方] raise prices; jack up prices

【起见】for the purpose of; in order to:为安全~ *for the purpose of security* /为方便~,请直接和她联

系。*In order to make it convenient, please connect with her directly.*

【起降】(of plane) take off and land

【起脚劲射】【体】to suddenly kick the ball towards the goal

【起劲】vigorous; energetic; zealous; enthusiastic: 讨论很～ *discuss enthusiastically* /练得很～ *train vigorously*

【起敬】express respect; inspire respect; show respect

【起居】daily life: ～室 *living room; sitting room* /住在这个小区,饮食～都很方便。*Everything about daily life in this residential district is convenient.*

【起来】① stand up; sit up; rise; rise to one's feet: ～吃点东西吧。*Sit up and eat something.* ② get up; get out of bed:快叫她～,有人等她。*Tell her to get up right away; someone is waiting for her.* ③ rise revolt; arise; arouse: ～反抗剥削 *rise against exploitation* /他的情绪好～了。*His spirits rose.* ④ upwards; up:把书从地上拿～ *pick up the books from ground* /奴隶们站～了。*The slaves have stood up.* /请把手臂抬～。*Raise your arms, please!* ⑤ used after verbs and adjectives to indicate commencement and prolongation of action or state:跳跃～ *start to jumping* /他的话引得孩子们哭了～。*His words made the children crying.* ⑥ used after verbs to indicate the end of action or the realization of goals:我记不～了。*I could not remember it.* /机器转～了。*The machine started corking.* ⑦ used after verbs to indicate impression or view:藏～ *hide out* /看～很好。*It looks wonderful.*

【起立】stand up; rise to one's feet: ～鼓掌 *standing applause* /全体～! *Stand up, everybody!*

【起落】go up and back down; rise and fall; up and down

【起落架】land gear (of an aircraft); alighting gear; undercarriage:飞机放下～顺利着陆。*The aircraft lowered its undercarriage and landed smoothly.*

【起码】① minimum; rudimentary; elementary: ～的认识 *minimum understanding* / ～的要求 *minimum demand* / ～的道德 *elementary morality* ② at least:今年参加托福考试的人～有10万。*At least* 100000 *people took TOFFEL this year.*

【起锚】set sail; weigh anchor

【起路】give a name; name

【起跑】【体】start of race: ～线 *starting line (for a race); scratch line (for a relay race)*

【起讫】the beginning and end

【起球】(of woolen etc.) pill

【起色】pick up; improvement:大夫说这个孩子的病大有～。*The doctor said that the child was beginning to pick up evidently.* /他的学习很有～。*There is a great improvement in his study.*

【起身】① get up; get out of bed:她每天五点半～做饭。*She unusual gets up at* 5: 30 *to prepare a meal.* ② go off; leave; depart:他已经～去欧洲了。*He already left for Europe.*

【起始】① at first; in the beginning: ～他不想来,最后还是改变了主意。*He didn't intend to arrive in the beginning; nevertheless, he changed his mind in the end.* ② stem from; originate from:这种建筑风格～于古希腊。*The style of architecture originated from the ancient Greeks.*

【起事】started an armed rising; rise in rebellion

【起誓】swear; take an oath:他～要攻克技术难关。*He swore that he would surmount the technical difficulty.*

【起死回生】(of a doctor's skill) bring the dying back to life; raise from the dead

【起诉】sue; prosecute; bring a suit or an action against sb: ～书 *indictment; bill of prosecution* / ～人 *suitor; prosecutor*

【起算】reckon from (a specific point); starting from:从1980年～,他已经工作了二十多年。*Reckoning from* 1980, *he has been working over twenty years.*

【起跳】【体】take off: ～板 *take off board* / ～高度 *trial height*

【起头】① start; commence; originate ② at first; in the beginning: ～他同意帮助我们。*He agreed to help us in the beginning.* ③ beginning:从～再重复一次你的话。*Please repeat your words once again from the very beginning.*

【起先】at first; in the beginning; at the outset: ～他不愿意说出心里话,后来才改变了主意。*He was not willing to talk about his innermost thoughts in the beginning, but later he changed his mind.*

【起心】[贬] cherish certain intentions; have designs on: ～不良 *cherish evil intentions*

【起薪】starting salary or wages; probationary salary

【起行】leave; set out; start on a journey; embark on a tour:登山队明天～。*The mountaineering party will set out tomorrow.*

【起眼儿】(unusual used in negative) attract attention; eye catching:她是一个不～的演员。*She is an ordinary actress.*

【起夜】get up in the night to urinate:冬天～很麻烦。*It is a trouble to get up in the night to urinate in winter.*

【起疑】cause suspicion; start to suspect; become suspicious:她的眼神令人～。*Her expression caused my suspicion.*

【起义】rise in revolt; revolt; rebel:工人～ *worker uprising* / ～部队 *insurrectionary troops* / ～爆发了。*The uprising broke out.*

【起意】[贬] harbour an evil intention; conceive a design:见钱～ *fall to evil intention at the sight of money*

【起因】cause; origin:事情的～,经过和结果 *the cause of the matter, the course of the matter and the result of the matter*

【起用】① reinstate (an official who has been removed from his post):重新～那位经理 *restore the manager to his previous position* ② promote; appoint sb to and important position: ～一批新演员 *employ a group of new actors*

【起源】originate; begin:成功～于勤奋 *success stems from diligence* /人类的～ *the origin of human being* /一切知识均～于劳动。*All knowledge originates from labour.*
【起运】start shipment: ～港 *starting harbour for shipment* /救灾物资已经～。*The relief supplies are on the way.*
【起赃】stack down and recover stolen goods; search for and recover stolen goods
【起早贪黑】work or do sth from dawn to dusk; start work early and knock off latter
【起重车】derrick car
【起重船】crane ship
【起重机】crane; derrick; hoist: ～的起吊能力 *the lifting capacity of a crane* /塔式～ *tower crane* /门式～ *portal crane*
【起皱】wrinkle; crease; crumple:老了脸上就会～。*When a person is old, his skin will wrinkle.* /他的新裤子不～。*He new trousers are crease resistant.*
【起子】① bottle opener ②［方］screwdriver:给我一把～。*Give me a screwdriver, please.* ③［方］baking powder

绮 ① figured wove silk material; damask ② beautiful; gorgeous; splendid; wonderful
【绮丽】beautiful; gorgeous: ～的风光 *a gorgeous sight*
【绮思】(of writing) beautiful thoughts
【绮霞】rosy clouds

qì

气 ① gas:沼～ *biogas; marsh gas; methane* /废～ *waste gas* /液化石油～ *liquefied petroleum gas* /煤～ *coal gas; gas* /天然～ natural gas ② air:轮胎没～了。*The tyre is flat.* ③ breath:喘～ *grasp for a breath* /断～ *stop breathing; cease to breath* /别往前走了,坐下来歇口～儿。*Don't go ahead; please sit down catch our breath.* ④ smell; odour:香～扑鼻。*A sweet smell reached one's nostril.* ⑤ weather ⑥ airs; manners:书生～ *bookishness* /傲～ *air of arrogance; haughtiness* /穷酸～ *impoverishment* ⑦ spirit; morale:鼓～ *boost the morale; cheer on* /士～ *morale* /浩～长存 *imperishable noble spirit* ⑧ get angry; be enraged; be provoked; make sb annoyed: ～得直瞪眼 *glower; glare with rage* /他～出一场大病。*He got a serious disease caused by anger.* /她这个人不爱生～,但这种话让人无法容忍。*She is not easily provoked, but these words are intolerable.* ⑨ make angry; enrage:我不是故意～老师的。*I was not purposely trying to annoy the teacher.* ⑩【中医】vital energy; energy of life ⑪ bully; insult:在办公室他受上司的～,在家里受老婆的～。*He is the target of his superior's insult in the office, and at home his wife spites him.*
【气昂昂】full of mettle; full of beans; full of dash
【气泵】air pump
【气不打一处来】full of displeasure and hostility; be filled with anger:我听到这话就～。*I was overcome with anger when I heard such words.*
【气不过】beyond endurance; can't restrain one's anger:她实在～,狠狠地掴了他一耳光。*She was beside herself with rage and gave a slap on his face.*
【气不平】make sb mad; refuse to be reconciled
【气冲冲】be furious; beside oneself with rage
【气喘】① asthma:阵发性～ *spasmodic asthma* ② be out of breath; huff and puff pant:他～吁吁地冲进教室。*He rushed into the classroom with huffing and puffing.*
【气窗】transom (window); fanlight
【气粗】① a rough temper; a fiery temper ②［贬］overbearing; domineering; overweening:有钱说话就～。*A rich man could speak in a gruff voice.*
【气促】be out of breath; breath with difficulty; be short of breath
【气垫】air cushion
【气垫船】hovercraft
【气动】pneumatic: ～开关 *pneumatic switch; air pressure switch* / ～工具 *pneumatic tool*
【气度】① tolerance; magnanimity ② bearing; appearance:他是一位～不凡的政治家。*He is an impressive looking politician.*
【气短】breathe hard; pant; be short of breath:一天的劳作使他感到～。*He felt panting after a whole day work.* ② discouraged; depressed:贫穷并没有让他～。*He was not depressed by poverty.*
【气氛】atmosphere; air; feeling in the mind that is created by a group of people or place:教室里笼罩着紧张的～。*An atmosphere of tension filled the classroom.* / ～非常阴郁沉重。*The atmosphere is so oppressive as heavy as lead.* /所有的家庭都沉浸在节日的～中。*All the family ware immersed in a festival atmosphere.*
【气愤】indignant; furious; enraged:他～极了。*He was beside himself with rage.* /她对老板的行为很～。*She was absolutely furious at the behaviour of her boss.* /那个老师～地跨进教室。*The teacher strode angrily into the classroom.*
【气腹】【医】pneumoperitoneum
【气概】noble quality; mettle; courage:英雄～ *heroic spirit* /革命浪漫主义～ *revolutionary romantic valour* /我们很钦佩红军战士大无畏的革命英雄主义～。*We strongly admire the dauntless revolutionary heroic mettle belonging to the soldiers of Red Army.*
【气缸】【机】air cylinder; cylinder
【气割】【机】gas cutting
【气功】qigong, a system of deep breathing exercises
【气鼓鼓】highly displeased; fuming with anger; furious
【气管】【生理】windpipe; trachea
【气管炎】【生理】tracheitis
【气贯长虹】inspired with a spirit as lofty as the rainbow spanning the sky; full of noble aspiration
【气焊】gas welding

【气候】① climate：海洋性～ *oceanic climate* /温和的～ *temperate climate* /严寒的～ *frigid climate* /中国南北部的～就大不相同了。*The south and north provinces of China have a very different kind of climate.* ② climate；situation：今天的国际政治～ *today's international political climate*
【气候带】climate zone
【气候图】climatic chart
【气候学】climatology
【气呼呼】in a huff；panting with rage；gasping with fury：他～地上了汽车。*He got on a bus in a huff.*
【气化】gasify
【气话】unguarded statement (or remark) made in a fit of fury：不要相信她说的～。*Don't trust what she said in a fit of temper.*
【气火】fury；wild and violent anger
【气急】panting and irritated greatly；incoherent with rage
【气急败坏】flustered and exasperated；utterly discomfited；flurried and furious：他～地从地上站起来。*He stood up from the ground in uncontrollable anger.* /他～地冲进办公室告诉老师发生的事情。*He exasperatingly rushed into the office and told the teacher what had happened.*
【气节】integrity；quality of being honest and morally upright；moral courage：共产党人坚贞不屈的～ *the unyielding integrity of a Communist*
【气井】gas well
【气绝】cease to breathe；stop breathing；die：突然～身亡 *die immediately*
【气孔】①【植】stoma ②【动】spiracle ③【冶】gas hole ④【建】air hole
【气浪】blast (of an explosion)
【气冷】【机】air cooling：～变压器 *air blast transformer* /～发动机 *air-cooled engine*
【气力】strength；energy；effort：我们要花大～提高产品的质量。*We should take a lot of effort to improve the quality of our products.* /他用尽～把石子扔进大海。*He threw a cobble into the sea with all his strength.*
【气量】tolerance；magnanimity；forbearance：他～大，不会介意这件事。*He is a broad-minded person and don't take offence this incident.* /她这个人～小，你最好别冒犯她。*She is a narrow-minded person, you'd better not offend her.*
【气量表】gas meter
【气流】① air current；airflow；air stream：～干扰 *interference in airflow* /～纺纱 *open-end spinning* /～速度 *air velocity* ② breath
【气楼】a small tower for ventilation on the of a roof
【气煤】gas coal
【气门】①【机】air drain ② (air) valve of a tyre ③【动】spiracle；stigma
【气门芯】① valve inside ② valve rubber tube of a tyre
【气闷】① upset；vexed；unhappy；worried ② stuffy；feel oppressed or suffocated
【气密】airtight；gastight；gasproof：～结合 *airtight joint* /～试验 *leakage test*；*air seal test* /～舱 *pressure cabin*
【气囊】① gasbag (of an aerostat) ② air sac (of birds)
【气恼】angry；offended；be ruffled：儿子的所作所为令人～。*What my son has done really offended me.*
【气馁】become dejected；be discouraged；lost heart：这群孩子多次失败后感到有些～。*Repeated failure had left the group of children feeling very dejected.* /失败了也决不能～。*A person should continuously keep his chin up despite failure.*
【气逆】【中医】circulation of vital energy in the wrong direction
【气派】manner；style；air：他具有艺术家的～。*He has the impressive manner of an artist.* /花园的大门很～。*The garden gate looks imposing.* /她穿警服很～。*She looks quite spirited in a police uniform.*
【气泡】air bubble；bubble
【气喷】gas blowout
【气魄】boldness of vision；breadth of spirit；adventurous courage：总工程师的设计很有～。*The plan of the general engineer demonstrates great daring.* /这支队伍登山很有～。*This team is absolutely bold and decisive in climbing a mountain.*
【气枪】air gun；pneumatic gun
【气球】balloon：热～ *hot air balloon* /我用手将～拍给儿子。*I batted the balloon over to my son with my hand.* /我不敢相信那位飞行员设法绕～飞了一阵。*I can't believe that the pilot managed to circle the balloon for some time.*
【气圈】【气】aerosphere
【气色】complexion；colour：他看起来～不错。*He looks to have a good colour.* /老奶奶～不好。*The grandma has pale complexion.* /你身体好吗？你看起来～不很好。*Are you feeling all right? You look rather pale.*
【气盛】① overbearing；arrogant ② (of writing) forceful；vigorous
【气蚀】【物】cavitation；erosion
【气室】air chamber；gas cell
【气势】momentum；imposing manner；impetus：～雄伟的人民大会堂 *the imposing Great Hall of the People* /这支部队以翻江倒海的～追击敌人。*The troop pursued and attacked the enemy with the momentum of an avalanche.*
【气势磅礴】of great momentum；powerful；full of power and grandeur (or magnificence)：中华人民共和国国歌～。*The national anthem of the People's Republic of China is full of power and grandeur.* /这是一幅～的画卷。*This is a picture scroll of great power.*
【气势汹汹】fierce；truculent；overbearing；aggressive：当时她～地同我吵起来。*She became very truculent and started arguing with me angrily.* /敌人看起来～，实际上十分虚弱。*The enemy looks fierce in appearance but feeble in reality.*
【气数】destiny；fate：柏林被攻克后，法西斯德国的～已尽了。*After Berlin was captured, the fascist*

Germany was doomed to fall.

【气态】【物】gaseous state：～废物 *gaseous waste* / ～污染 *gaseous pollution* / ～杂质 *gaseous impurity*

【气体】gas：～成分 *gas composition* / ～分离器 *gas separator* / ～采样 *gas sampling* / ～扩散 *gas diffusion* / ～浓度 *gas concentration* / ～燃料 *gas fuel*; *gaseous fuel* / ～打火机 *gas lighter* / ～是物质的一种状态。*Gas is a state of matter.*

【气体动力学】aerodynamics

【气体力学】pneumatics

【气体压缩机】【机】gas compressor

【气田】gas field

【气筒】inflator; bicycle pump

【气头上】in a fit of anger; in a temper; in a ugly mood：她在～不要和她说话。*She is in a fit of anger; Don't talk with her.*

【气团】【气】air mass

【气吞山河】filled or inspired with a spirit that can conquer mountains and rivers; full of daring

【气味】① smell; odour; flavour; scent：整个房间都是从厨房飘出的～。*The smells from the kitchen filled the room.* /那只猫闻到一只老鼠的～。*The cat nosed out a rat.* ②［贬］smack; taste：有强权单边主义的～ *smack of power unilateralism*

【气味相投】be two of a kind; be congenial to each other; be like-minded; be birds of a feather：我已向老板表示不满，并努力促使～的同事采取同样行动。*I have complained to my boss, and urged all like-minded colleagues to do the same.*

【气温】air temperature; atmospheric temperature：～停留在摄氏28度上下。*The mercury hovered around 28°C.* /昨天清晨～很低。*The temperature was very low yesterday early morning.*

【气息】① breath ② flavour; smell; scent：夏天的～ *scent of summer* /乡村～ *flavour of countryside*

【气息奄奄】be at one's last grasp; be at the point of death; breath one's last：老人病了一年多，现在已经是～了。*The old man has been ill for over a year and now is sinking fast.*

【气相】gas phase; gaseous phase：～色谱 *gas chromatography*

【气象】① meteorological phenomena：～船 *weather ship* / ～观察 *meteorological observation* / ～广播 *meteorological broadcast* / ～局 *meteorological agency* / ～雷达 *meteorological radar* / ～台(站) *meteorological station* / ～卫星 *meteorological satellite*; *weather satellite* / ～学 *meteorology* / ～灾害 *meteorological disaster*; *meteorological calamity* / ～资料 *meteorological data* / ～预报 *weather forecast* / ～服务 *weather service* / ～员 *weatherman* ② meteorology ③ atmosphere; scene：二十多年的改革开放，我们的祖国已经是～一新。*After over twenty years reform and opening to the outside world, our motherland has taken on an entirely new look.*

【气象万千】spectacular; majestic：～的烟火表演 *a spectacular display of fireworks* /从飞机上俯视绵延的雪山，～。*Looking down from an aircraft, one can see range after range of snowy mountains in all their majesty*

【气胸】【医】pneumothorax

【气虚】【中医】deficiency of vital energy

【气旋】【气】cyclone

【气血】【中医】vital energy and the state of blood in the human body

【气血两虚】【中医】deficiency of vital energy and blood

【气压】【气】atmospheric pressure; barometric pressure：高～ *high pressure* / ～表 *barometer*; *weather gauge* / ～沉箱 *pneumatic caisson.*

【气眼】①【建】air hole ②【冶】gas hole

【气焰】arrogance; bluster：不要助长敌人的～。*Don't feed the enemy's arrogance.* /我们要扑灭敌人的嚣张～。*We must put out the arrogance of the enemy.*

【气宇轩昂】have an impressive bearing; have a dignified appearance

【气郁】【中医】obstruction of the circulation of vital energy

【气韵】the spirit, character and tone of a work art or literature; flavour and tone：这部电影保留了原著的许多～。*The film retains much of the book's flavour and tone.*

【气闸】air brake; pneumatic brake

【气质】① temperament; person's nature as it effects the way he thinks, feels and behaves; disposition：她们姐妹两人的～完全不同。*The two sisters have entirely different temperaments.* ② quality; makings：他有杰出科学家的～。*He has the makings of an outstanding scientist.* /人们说她的女儿具有当明星的～。*Her daughter was being talked up as star timber.*

【气滞】【中医】stagnation of the circulation of vital energy

【气壮如牛】strong as a bull; sturdy as an ox; fierce as a bull：这个流氓表面上～，实际上胆小得像个兔子。*The hooligan looks fierce as a bull, but actually timid as a rabbit.*

【气壮山河】full of power and grandeur; imbued with sublime heroism; magnificent：～的誓言 *a magnificent pledge*

讫 ① settled; completed; paid：现金付～ *cash paid* /收～ received in full ② end

迄 ① up to; till：～今为止 *up to now*; *so far* ② so far; yet; all along：～无收效。*Up to now we have received no result.*

【迄今】up to now; to this day; so far：～为止，这件事仍记忆犹新。*This matte remains fresh in our memory to this day.* /他的病情～没有明显好转。*There has been no visible mend in his disease so far*

弃 abandon; discard; through away：鲁迅先生～医从文是为了唤醒民众。*In order to arouse the people, Mr. Lu Xun abandoned medical science and engaged in literature.*

【弃暗投明】forsake darkness for light — leave the reactionary side and cross over to the side of the people

【弃儿】abandoned child; foundling: ~院 *a foundling hospital*

【弃旧图新】turn over a new leaf: 幡然悔悟, ~。*Quickly wake up to one's error or fault and turn over a new leaf.*

【弃文从武】put down the pen and take up the sword

【弃农经商】give up agriculture production and engage in business; leave farming behind to engage in trading

【弃权】① abstain from voting: 在这次联合国表决中,中国投了~票。*China abstained from this voting of the United Nations.*

【弃婴】abandoned baby; foundling

【弃之可惜】hesitate to discard or give up sth; be unwilling to throw away

【弃置】discard; throw aside; cast away: ~的土地 *an abandoned land*

汽

gas; vapor; steam

【汽车】automobile; motor vehicle; car: 小~ *car* / 公共~ *bus* / ~用品公司 *auto products company* / ~制造厂 *motor vehicle plant* / ~司机 *driver*; *motorman*; *chauffeur*; *motorist* / ~商 *car dealer* / 出租~ *taxi*; *taxicab* / ~队 *motor transport corps*; *fleet of cars or trucks* / ~工业 *auto industry*; *car industry* / ~驾驶比赛 *gymkhana* / ~驾驶执照 *driver's license* / ~库 *garage* / ~旅馆 *motor hotel*; *motel* / ~运输 *motoring* / ~修理厂 *motor pair shop*; *auto repair garage* / ~发动机 *automobile engine* / ~废气 *automobile exhaust gases*; *automobile emission* / ~在商店的停车场上停了下来。*The car pulled up on the parking lot outside the shopping.* /我的哥哥让我搭他的~去学校。*My elder brother gave me a lift to the school in his car.*

【汽船】steamship; steamer

【汽锤】【机】steam hammer: ~打桩机 *ram steam pile driver*

【汽灯】gas lamp

【汽笛】steam whistle; siren; hooter

【汽缸】【机】cylinder: ~厂 *air cylinder factory* / ~盖 *cylinder head*

【汽锅】steam boiler; boiler

【汽化】【物】vaporization; carburation: ~调节 *vaporization adjustment* / ~效率 *vaporization efficiency* / ~器 *carburetor* / ~热 *heat of vaporization*

【汽机】steam engine; steam turbine

【汽酒】light sparkling wine

【汽轮发电机】turbo generator: ~组 *turbo-unit*

【汽轮机】steam turbine

【汽暖】steam heating (system)

【汽水】aerated water; soda water; soft drink: 柠檬~ *lemonade*

【汽艇】motorboat

【汽相】【物】vapour phase: ~反应 *vapour reaction*

【汽油】petrol; gasoline; gas: 航空~ *aviation gasoline* / 无铅~ *unleaded gasoline* / 以前他们家用~作燃料。*Before they used gasoline for the fuel.* / ~溶解油脂。*Gasoline cuts oil and grease.*

泣

① weep; sob: 饮泣 *weep in silence* ② tear

【泣不成声】choke with sob: 听到国家沦陷的消息,她~。*When she heard that her motherland fell into enemy hands, she choked with sobs.*

【泣诉】accuse while weeping; accuse amid tears; recount sth with tears: 她~了这些天所受的虐待。*She tearfully recounted the maltreatment, she'd gone through these days.*

【泣如雨下】shed tears like rain; weep copious tears

契

① contract; deed; agreement ② agree; get along well; match together: 默~ *tacit agreement or understanding*

【契合】agree with; tally with; accord with; correspond to: 与宪法精神相~ *agree with the spirit of constitution*

【契机】①【哲】moment ② turning point; juncture: 以党的十六大为~,抓住机遇,开拓创新。*With the Sixth National Party Congress a juncture, we should seize every good opportunity and be bold in blazing new trails.*

【契据】deed; contract; receipt

【契税】a tax paid by the purchaser according to a stipulation as provided in a real estate contract signed both parties

【契文】oracle bone writing

【契友】close friend; bosom friend

【契约】contract; deed; charter: 租赁~ *contract of rent* /这个~无效。*The contract is invalid.* /经理要求在~中加进一项条款。*The manager demands to add a clause in the contract.*

【契纸】title deed

砌

① build or construct sth by laying bricks or stones: ~筑砖石 *lay bricks and stones* / ~墙 *build (or make) a wall (with bricks, stones, etc.)* ② step: 雕栏玉~应犹在。*The carved balustrades and the marble steps should still exist.*

葺

①[书] cover a roof with straw; thatch ② repair; mend; fix: 修~草舍 *repair a thatched hut*

器

① implement; utensil; instrument; ware; tool: 竹~ *articles made of bamboo* /电~ *electrical equipment (or appliance)* /铜~ *bronze copper ware* ② organ: 生殖~ *reproductive organ*; *generative organ*; *genitals* /他成不了大~。*He could not accomplish any significant thing.*

【器材】equipment; material: 摄影~ *photographic equipment* /水暖~ *water supply and heating materials*

【器度】broad mindedness; tolerance

【器官】organ; apparatus: 运动~ *organ of movement* /视觉~ *organ of sight* / ~移值 *organ transplant* /眼睛是身体重要的~之一。*Eye is one of the body's vital organs.*

【器件】parts of an appliance (or apparatus) component: 半导体~ *semiconductor components*

【器具】utensil; appliance; instrument: 灭菌~ *steri-*

lizer /卫生～ *hygienic appliance* /救生～ *lifesaving appliance; life preserver* /日用～ *household utensils; articles of daily use*
【器皿】household utensils; container (esp. for use in the house):玻璃～ *glass ware*
【器物】utensils; implement; article
【器械】apparatus; appliance; instrument:医疗～ *medical appliances* /健身～ *fitness appliance*
【器械体操】gymnastics on (or with) apparatus
【器宇】[书] bearing; carriage; deportment: ～轩昂 *of dignified bearing*
【器乐】【音】instrumental music
【器乐曲】composition for an instrument
【器重】think highly of; regard highly; set great store by: ～某人 *have a very high opinion of sb* /他很聪明,教练很～他。*He is quite a clever player, and his coach thinks highly of him.*

憩 rest:小～ *take a short rest; have a short break*
【憩息】rest; relax; have a rest:战士们停止前进,到大树底下～。*The soldiers stopped go ahead and had a rest under the big tree.*

qiā

掐 ① pinch; nip; pick: ～掉嫩枝 *pinch off the young shoots* / ～一支玫瑰花 *nip off a rose flower* /他～了我的胳膊。*He pinched my arm.* /把你的烟～灭。*Put out your cigarette.* /园丁正在把玫瑰花的边芽～掉。*The gardener was nipping off the side shoots from his roses.* ② clutch; choke:他～死了一只老鼠。*He choked a mouse to death.*
【掐断】nip off; cut off: ～热水供应 *cut of the not water supply* / ～电话线 *disconnect the phone line*
【掐尖儿】① topping; pinch off young shoots, etc.: 今天地里的烟叶必须～。*The tobacco plants must be topped today.* ② dismiss; remove sb from a position; throw out:你别太出风头了,小心别人掐你的尖儿。*Don't try to enjoy yourself being the centre of attention; watch out or you might be removed from your position.*
【掐丝】wire inlay; filigree
【掐算】count or reckon on one's fingers:他～着航班起飞的时间。*He is carefully counting on his fingers what time the flight would take off.*
【掐头去尾】break off both ends:这棵甘蔗～剩下不多了。*With both ends cut off, there is not much left of this sugarcane.*

qiǎ

卡 ① wedge; get stuck:他的喉咙被鱼刺～住了。*A bone of fish sticks his throat.* /我被紧紧～在乘客中间下不了火车。*I was so tightly wedged among the other passengers, and couldn't get off the train.* ② clip; fastener:发～ *hairclip; hairpin* ③ check post:哨～ *patrol post*
see also kǎ
【卡脖子】① seize a person by the throat; have sb by the throat:那位警察卡住歹徒的脖子并制服了他。*The policeman seized the ruffian by gripping his throat.* ② have a stronghold on
【卡车】lorry:一辆～带着很多书来到了学校。*A lorry arrived at the school with many books.* /我们公司的～昨天在城外抛锚了。*The truck of our company broke down outside town yesterday.*
【卡具】【机】clamping apparatus; fixture
【卡壳】①【军】(of cartridge or shell case) jam ② get stuck; have a temporary stoppage; be unable to proceed; halt:董事会意见分歧很大,生意～了。*There had great differences of opinion in the board of directors; the business was brought to a halt.*
【卡盘】【机】chuck
【卡子】① clip; fastener:书～ *book clips* ② checkpost
【卡钻】jamming of a drilling tool; sticking of tool

qià

洽 ① be in harmony; in agreement:感情融～ *in complete harmony; in perfect harmony* /这次谈判双方意见不～。*Both sides had not seen eye to eye in this negotiations.* ② consult; discuss; arrange with: ～谈停火事宜 *hold cease-fire talks* / ～商贸易争端 *consult trade dispute*
【洽购】arrange or negotiate a purchase:打电话～钢材 *arrange the purchase of steels by phone*
【洽商】consult; talk over with:贸易～ *trade consultation* /经过几个月的艰苦～,董事会终于批准了采购合同。*After several months of hard consultation, the board of directors finally approved the purchasing contract.*
【洽谈】hold talks; negotiate; discuss together:贸易～会 *trade talks; trade symposium*

恰 ① appropriate; suitable; right and proper; fitting ② precisely; exactly; just
【恰当】proper; suitable; suitable; fitting; appropriate:使用～措施 *use proper measure* /提出～的主题 *propose a suitable theme* /这份报告里不～的地方已经被改过了。*The inappropriate words in this report have been already corrected.* /他对当前的经济形势做出了～的评估。*He made a proper evaluation about present economic situation.* /把自己的想法强加于人是极其不～的。*It's not proper to force your idea upon others.*
【恰到好处】just right (for the purpose or occasion)
【恰好】just right exactly:我们赶到汽车站时～来了一辆车。*When we arrived at the station, a bus pulled in just right.* /这些蔬菜～够做一顿3个人的饭。*These vegetables are just the right quantity for preparing a meal for three persons.* /那～是我所需要的东西。*That's exactly what I want.*
【恰恰】just; precisely; exactly:这～是他想达到的目的。*This is the exactly goal he wanted to achieve.*

【恰恰舞】cha-cha (dance)
【恰切】suitable and accurate; apt and accurate; appropriate and accurate:他的文章用词～。*The words in his article are suitable and accurate.*
【恰如其分】apt; appropriate; just right; proper: ～的赞扬 *an apt commendation* / ～的批评 *a balanced criticism*
【恰似】just like: ～你的温柔 *just like your mildness*

qiān

千 ① thousand: ～禧年 *the millennium* /这笔买卖他们赔了八～美元。*They lost $8000 on the business.* ② a great number of; a great amount of; innumerable: ～百条喜讯从四面八方传来。*Lots and lots of happy news spread from all around.*
【千安】【电】kiloampere (ka)
【千巴】【物】kilobar (kb)
【千磅】【物】kilo pounds
【千儿八百】a thousand or slightly less
【千变万化】even changing; constantly changing:股票市场错综复杂,～。*The stock market is complicated and changeable.*
【千层饼】layered pancake
【千层底】shoe sole made of many layers of cloth stitched together
【千差万别】differ in thousands of ways; vary greatly:各地的经济基础～。*Economic basic varies greatly from place to place.*
【千疮百孔】riddled with gaping wounds; afflicted with all kinds of ills
【千锤百炼】① thoroughly steeled or tempered:在复杂的国际政治斗争中经过～,他的思想方法更加成熟了。*Tempered under the complicated international political struggling, his method of thinking became even more mature.* ② be polished again and again; be revised and rewritten a lot of times; be highly finished
【千刀万剐】hack sb (enemy etc.) to a thousand pieces; punishment by dismemberment
【千吨】【物】kiloton (kt)
【千恩万谢】express a thousand thanks; extremely grateful
【千方百计】in a thousand and one ways; by every possible means; by hook or by crook: ～地招商引资 *try every possible way to attract investments from outside* / ～地提高粮食产量 *do one's best to increase the crop production*
【千分表】dial gauge; dial indicator
【千分尺】micrometer
【千分之一】one thousandth
【千伏】【电】kilovolt (kv)
【千古】① though the ages; eternal: ～笑谈 *a forever laughing stock* ② used in elegiac inscription or elegiac couplets for the deceased:某某先生～。*Eternal glory to Mr. so-and-so.*
【千古遗恨】eternal regret
【千古奇闻】a fantastic tale
【千古罪人】person of eternal guilt; villain of all time
【千赫】kilohertz
【千呼万唤】be called again and again; a thousand entreaties
【千回百转】revolve continuously; full of twists and turns:蜿蜒的小河～。*The winded stream is full of twists and turns.*
【千家万户】innumerable households or families; countless people:住房改革关系到～的大问题。*The housing system reform is of vital importance to all people.*
【千娇百媚】(of a woman) bewitchingly charming; ravishingly beautiful
【千斤】(qiānjīn) ① one thousand jin — very heavy; extremely weighty
【千斤】(qiānjin) ① hoisting jack; jack ② pawl
【千斤顶】【机】hoisting jack; jack
【千金】① a thousand pieces of gold; a large amount of money ② daughter (other than one's own)
【千军万马】thousands upon thousands of war-horses and soldiers; a mighty force
【千钧一发】hang by a hair; be in an extremely precarious situation; be in an imminent peril:在这～之际,汽车被刹住了。*In the moment of extreme crisis, the car was braked.*
【千卡】【物】kilocalorie (kcal; cal)
【千克】kilogram (kg)
【千里】a thousand *li* — long distance
【千里马】a horse that covers a thousand *li* a day; winged steed; man of great talent
【千里迢迢】from afar; thousands of *li* away:我们热烈欢迎～从南方专程前来参加签子仪式的各位领导。*We warmly welcome all those leaders who made a special tour to take part in the signing ceremony from distant south.*
【千里姻缘一线牵】a thread can draw together a fated match across a thousand *li*; persons a thousand *li* apart may be linked by marriage
【千里之堤,溃于蚁穴】one ant-hole may cause the collapse of a thousand-*li* dike; slight malignance may lead to great disaster
【千里之行,始于足下】a thousand-*li* journey is started by taking the first step; the highest eminence is to gained step by step
【千粒重】【农】thousand-grain weight
【千米】kilometre (km)
【千难万险】innumerable hazards (or dangers, risks) and hardships
【千篇一律】be stereotyped; follow the same pattern; be monotonous:他不像电影中～的商人形象,穿一身深色的套服,带一把收好的雨伞。*He did not conform to the stereotyped images of businessman in films with a dark suit and rolled umbrella.* /同学们在写作文上要有创新不能～。*Every student should constantly bring forth new ideas in his compositions, and he should not harp on the*

same old tune all the time.

【千奇百怪】all kinds of strange things; an infinite variety of fantastic phenomena; grotesque:学生们戴着～的面具参加化妆舞会。*The students wearing their grotesques masks attended the fancy dress ball.*

【千千万万】millions upon millions; innumerable; thousands upon thousands

【千秋】① a thousand years; ages; centuries ② birthday (other than one's own)

【千秋万代】generation after generation; forever; (for) thousands of years:这些精神财富将～传下去。*This spiritual wealth will be handed down from generation to generation.*

【千日红】【植】globe amaranth (*Gomphrena globosa*)

【千山万水】a thousand mountains and ten thousand river — a long and formidable journey:从瑞金到延安,红军的长征经历了～。*From Ruijin to Yan'an, the Red Army had to cross numerous mountains and rivers in their arduous journey of Long March.*

【千升】【物】kilolitre (kl)

【千丝万缕】countless ties; innumerable links; a thousand and one links:这两个组织之间有着～的联系。*There have innumerable links between the two organizations.*

【千头万绪】thousands of strands and loose ends; a multitude of things; be faced with extremely complicated situation:工作～,我们一时不知从何下手。*With a lot of tasks to perform, we simply don't know which would be the priority.*

【千瓦】【电】kilowatt (kw): ～时 *kilowatt-hour (kwh)*

【千万】① ten million; millions upon millions; countless ② be sure to; must: ～要小心呀。*Do be careful!* /～要注意交通安全。*Do take the greatest care to keep traffic safety.*

【千辛万苦】innumerable trial and tribulations; untold hardships; all kinds of hardships:历尽～,我们终于完成了任务。*After experiencing innumerable hardships, finally we completed our mission.*

【千言万语】thousands and thousands words; innumerable words (of solicitude): ～难表感激之情。*No words can express my sincere appreciation.*

【千依百顺】obedient and docile:她对她父母总是～。*She was all obedience to her parents.*

【千载难逢】not occurring once in a thousand years; very rare; once in a blue moon:你应该抓住这个～的好机会。*You should keep the chance of lifetime.*

【千兆】kilomega

【千真万确】absolutely true.

【千周】【物】kilocycle (kc)

【千姿百态】of all kinds of shapes and postures; a great variety:湖里盛开着～的莲花。*There have a great variety of lotuses blooming in the lake.*

阡 [书] a footpath between fields, running north and south

【阡陌】crisscross foot paths between fields

【阡陌纵横】foot paths crisscrossing the fields

芊

【芊芊】[书] luxuriant

扦 a short slender pointed piece (of bamboo, wood, metal etc.)

【扦插】【农】cuttage

【扦脚】[方] pedicure

【扦子】① a slender pointed stick made of bamboo, wood, metal, etc.:钢～ *steel poker* /竹～ *bamboo spike* ② a sharp-pointed metal tube used to extract samples of from sacks of grain, etc.

迁 ① move; remove: ～往北京 *move to Beijing* ② change:事过境～。*The matter is all over, and the situation is changed or a lot of water has flowed under the bridge.*

【迁都】move the capital (to another place)

【迁建】move and reconstruct the original building:由于三峡工程的原因,张飞庙被迫～。*For the reason of Three Gorges Dam Project, Zhang Fei Temple had to be moved to another place and reconstructed.*

【迁户口】change one's residence registration

【迁就】accommodate oneself to; yield to; give in to; humour:你不应～你的朋友。*You should never give in to the unreasonable demands of your friend.* /我们不能～不正之风。*We must not yield to malpractices.* /无原则的～对孩子有害。*Unprincipled accommodation will do harm to children.*

【迁居】change one's dwelling place; move (house):他已经～到上海。*He has moved to Shanghai.*

【迁离】move to another place

【迁流】[书] (of time) flow past:时光～,转眼我们老了。*Time flew past; we got old in the twinkling of an eye.*

【迁怒】vent one's anger on sb who's not to blame; take it out on sb:他自己做错了事情,却还要～别人。*He made a mistake by himself, but he took it on other persons.*

【迁徙】move; migrate; change one's abode (or residence):这些水鸟冬天～到北非。*These aquatic birds migrate to North Africa in winter.*

【迁延】delay; defer; postpone; procrastinate:由于这件事～了四十多天,访问印度的日期改在了国庆节。*This matter was delayed over forty days, so the date of visiting India was changed to National Day.*

【迁移】move; migrate; change; remove: 限制人口～ *restrict population movements* /为了躲避战争,这家工厂从城里～到了山区。*In order to escape the war, this factory was moved from urban to mountain area.* /这家商店可能要停业,要～到大城市去了。*The shopping will probably pack up and move to a big city.*

【迁移性】【动】migratory nature

钎 drill rod; drill steel; borer 钢～ *drill steel*

【钎子】rock drill; hammer drill for making hole in rock

牵 ① lead long; pull: ~骆驼 *lead a camel along* /手~手向前走 *hand in hand walk ahead* ② involve: 许多工人被~进了这次罢工。*Many workers were involved in this strike.*

【牵鼻子】lead by the nose: 我们应该牵着敌人的鼻子走。*We should lead the enemy by the nose ahead.*

【牵肠挂肚】feel deep anxiety; be very worried; be beside oneself with anxiety: 他独自乘船远行,父母对他~。*He caused his parents great anxiety by boat long distance along.*

【牵扯】involve; implicate; embroil: 他的敌人竭力想把他~进这桩丑闻。*His enemies tried to implicate him in the scandal.*

【牵掣】hold up; impede: 互相~ *hold each other up* /由于投资减少工程进度受到了严重~。*The development of the project was seriously impeded by a reduction in investment.*

【牵动】affect; worry; influence: ~全国 *affect the whole nation* / ~全身 *affect the whole body*

【牵挂】worry; care: 没有~ *free from care* /好好工作,不要~孩子们。*Do your work well and don't worry about children.*

【牵累】① tie down: 受疾病的~ *be tied down by disease* ② implicate; involve: 他不应该受这场风波的~。*He shouldn't be involved in the disturbance.*

【牵连】involve (in trouble); implicate; incriminate: 他拒绝向法庭作陈述以免受到~。*He refused to make a statement to the court in case he incriminated himself.*

【牵牛花】【植】(white-edged) morning-glory

【牵牛星】【天】Altair

【牵强】forced (interpretation, etc.); farfetched; strained: ~的比较 *a farfetched comparison*

【牵强附会】draw a forced analogy; make a irrelevant or farfetched comparison; give a strained interpretation; stretch the meaning: 你有关这次事故的推理太~了。*Your inference about this accident is too forced.*

【牵涉】involve; concern; drag in: 这是一个复杂的受贿案,很多领导干部~进了里面。*It was an absolutely complicated bribery case, which involved in many officials.*

【牵头】take the lead; lead off; take the responsibility (of arranging a meeting etc.): 最后由教育部~一百多个大学、研究所和企业参加,召开了有关大学生就业的研讨会。*Under the convening of the Ministry Education and with the participation of over a hundred units included universities, institutes and enterprises, a symposium was recently held to discuss the employment problem of graduating students.*

【牵系】link; connect; tie up

【牵线】① pull wires or strings; manipulate from behind the scenes: 这场风波显然是有人在背后~。*There must be someone manipulating from behind the disturbance.* ② act as a go-between: 这两家公司合作是我~。*I acted as a go-between for two companies to cooperate.*

【牵线搭桥】act a go-between; bring one person into contact with another

【牵一发而动全身】pull one hair and you move the whole body — a slight move in one part may affect the whole situation

【牵引】① draw; drag: 这辆机车可以~二十节火车车厢。*This locomotive can draw twenty-railway carriages.* ②【医】traction: ~器 *tractor*

【牵引车】tractor; tractor truck

【牵引飞机】towing aircraft

【牵引力】【物】traction force; pulling force; traction

【牵引能量】【交】haulage capacity

【牵引炮】towed artillery

【牵引式】【机】trail-behind; pull-type: ~播种机 *trail-behind planter* / ~滑翔机 *towed glider*

【牵制】【军】contain; pin down; tie up; check: ~敌人 *pin down the enemy* / ~行动 *containing action* / ~敌人的任务交给了十二团。*The mission of check on the enemy was assigned to the twelfth regiment.* /那个将军制订了~敌人进攻的计划。*The capital had made a plan for containing the enemy attack.*

铅 ① lead (Pb) ② lead (in a pencil); black lead:

【铅白】【化】white lead

【铅板】lead plate

【铅版】【印】stereotype

【铅笔】pencil: 红~ *red pencil* / ~芯 *lead (in a pencil); black lead* / ~画 *pencil drawing* / ~盒 *pencil case; pencil box* / ~刀 *pen-knife; pencil sharpener* /要参加考试的儿子需要一支~。*My son needs a pencil to take the exam.* /老师把~发给所有的学生。*The teacher issued pencils to all the students.*

【铅玻璃】【化】lead glass; flint glass

【铅垂线】【建】plumb line; lead line; sounding line

【铅锤】【建】plummet; plumb (bob)

【铅丹】【化】red lead (Pb_3O_4); minium

【铅弹头】lead bullet

【铅封】lead sealing

【铅球】【体】shot: 推~ *putting the shot; shot put* / ~运动员 *shot-putter*

【铅丝】① galvanized wire ② lead wire

【铅酸性蓄电池】【化】lead-acid battery

【铅蓄电池】lead storage; battery; lead accumulator

【铅印】letterpress (or relief, typographic) printing; stereotype

【铅直】vertical; plumb

【铅中毒】【医】lead poisoning

【铅字】【印】type; letter: 黑体~ *boldface* /大号~ *large type* / ~面 *type face* / ~盘 *type case; letter board* / ~合金 *type metal* /现在~印刷已经不很流行了。*Now the letter printing is not very popular.*

Q

悭

【悭吝】stingy; miserly; parsimonious

谦

modest; unassuming: ～恭 *modest and courteous*

【谦卑】humble; modest; not proud

【谦诚】modest and sincere

【谦辞】self-depreciatory expression

【谦和】modest and amiable:他是一个脾气～的人。*He is modest, pleasant and good-tempered.*

【谦谦君子】a modest, self-disciplined gentleman

【谦让】modestly decline; decline politely:你最适合承担这项工作,不要～了。*You are the right person to undertake this job; Don't decline politely.*

【谦虚】modest; self-effacing:别～了,我们知道你能胜任这项任务。*Don't be self-effacing; we know you are competent at this task.* /老张因～而赢得人们的称赞。*Lao Zhang won praises for his modesty.* /那个冠军对自己得奖非常～。*The champion is very modest about the prizes she has won.* ② make modest remarks; speak modestly:他～了几句,终于答应担任公司总经理一职。*After making several modest observations he finally agreed to hold the post of general manager in the company.*

【谦虚谨慎】modest and prudent:我们要做到～,戒骄戒躁。*We should be modest and prudent; guard against conceit and impetuosity.*

【谦逊】modest; unassuming; unpretentious:这位伟大的科学家对自己的研究成果很～。*The great scientist is modest about his research achievements.*

签[1]

① sign; autograph:请把你的姓名～到这张纸上。*Please sign your name on this paper.* ② make brief comments:请对这份报告～一个意见。*Please write a brief comment on the report.*

签[2]

① bamboo slips used for divination, gambling or casting (drawing) lots: 抽～ *cast lots; draw lots* /他抽中了上上～。*He drew one of the best lots.* ② a slender pointed piece or chip made of bamboo or wood: 牙～ *tooth pick* /竹～ *bamboo stick* /铁～子 *steel stick* ③ label; sticker: 标～ *label; sticker* /书～ *bookmarker* ④ tack (of sewing): ～裤脚 *take on the bottom of a trouser leg*

【签到】sign in; register one's attendance (at a conference or at an office etc.): 会议～处 *sign-in desk of the conference* / ～簿 *attendance book* /代表请～。*Representatives, sign in here please.*

【签订】conclude and sign (a contract etc.): ～友好合作条约 *sign a treaty of friendship and cooperation* / ～贸易合同 *sign a trade contract*

【签发】sign and issue (a document, certificate, etc.): ～一本私人护理 *issue a private passport* / ～命令 *issue an order*

【签名】autograph; sign one's name; write one's signature: ～盖章 *set one's hand and seal to; sign one's name and affix the seal* / ～活动 *signature activity* /游客请到这里～。*Tourists please sign your names here.* /请这位科学家在他的专著上～。*Please ask the scientist to autograph his monograph.*

【签收】sign after receiving sth:请～包裹。*Please receive the parcel and sign your name here.*

【签署】sign: ～协定 *sign an agreement*/ ～声明 *sign a statement* / ～人 *under signed*

【签条】① short note ② book mark

【签押】put one's name or make any other personal mark on a document

【签约】sign an agreement; sign a contract

【签证】visa: ～处 *visa section (or office)* / ～费 *visa fee* /过境～ *transit visa* /入境～ *entry visa* /出境～ *exit visa* /互免～ *mutual exemption of visas* /多次有效出入境～ *multiple entry-exit visa* /单次有效出入境～ *entry-exit visa valid for a single journey* / ～申请 *apply for a visa* / ～有效期 *the expiry of visa*

【签注】attach a slip of paper to a document with comments on it; write comments on a document (for a superior to consider):总经理在年度财务报表上作了～后把它递给了董事长。*The general manager wrote a comment on the annual financial report and then gave it to the president of the board of directors.*

【签字】sign; affix one's signature: ～仪式 *signing ceremony* / ～国 *signatory state (power); signatory* / ～后立即生效 *come into force (or effect) upon signature* /这张化验单上应该有大夫的～。*The chemical examination report should attach the signature of the doctor.*

【签子】[口] ① bamboo slip used for divination etc. ② a slender piece of bamboo or wood

qián

前

① front: ～门 *front door* ② forward; ahead: 勇往直～ *forge ahead dauntlessly; go ahead bravely; go bravely forward* ③ former; formerly: ～总理 *former premier* / ～总统 *former president (of a republic)* / ～市长 *former mayor* / ～南斯拉夫 *former Yugoslavia* ④ first; front: ～六名 *first six places* / ～两排 *first rows* / ～两轮比赛 *first two rounds of match.* ⑤ before; ago:三年～ *three years ago* /晚饭～ *before dinner* /解放～ *before liberation* ⑥ preceding: ～一阶段 *the preceding stage* / ～资本主义 *pre-capitalism* / ～身 *predecessor*

【前半场】first half (of a play, concert, game, etc.)

【前半晌】[方] morning; before noon; forenoon

【前半生】the first half of one's life or lifetime

【前半天】forenoon; morning

【前半夜】the first half of the night (form nightfall to midnight)

【前辈】senior (person); elder; the old generation; veteran:革命的老～ *revolutionaries of the older generation* /科学的老～ *scientists of the older generation* /他们中有些人是我的～。*Some of them are my seniors.*

【前臂】forearm

【前边】① in front; at the head; ahead; before:跑在队伍最～ *run ahead of the team* / ～不远有一个村庄。*There is a village ahead no far from us.* ② above; preceding: ～提到的公式 *the above-mentioned formula* / ～一段 *preceding paragraph*

【前不见古人,后不见来者】 when looking back I can't find or see the ancients; when look ahead I can't find or see the future generations either — feel extremely alone in the whole world

【前舱】forecabin; nose cabin

【前叉】front fork

【前车之覆,后车之鉴】the overturned cart ahead is warning to that of behind; we should be cautious of the mistakes of those before us

【前车之鉴】warning taken from the overturned cart ahead; lessons drawn from other's mistakes:美国的"9.11"事件对别的国家是一个～。*The September 11th Incident in the United States should be a warning to other countries.*

【前程】① prospect; future: ～似锦 *glorious future; bright prospects; rosy future* /远大～ *brilliant prospects* / ～万里 *a brilliant future; a very fine prospects* /各奔～ *everyone pursues his own cause; each goes his own way*

【前池】forebay

【前仇】old grievance; old score; old enmity: ～旧恨 *old hatred; old hostility*

【前导】① lead the way; march in front; precede: 游行队伍由工人方队～。*The square array of workers marched in front of the contingents of paraders.* ② one who leads the way; guide

【前额】forehead:她儿子的～很宽。*Her son has a broad forehead.*

【前方】① ahead; in front:奔向～ *go ahead* /正～ *right ahead* ② the front march to the front; be dispatched to the front

【前锋】vanguard:部队～已经完成任务。*The vanguard units have finished their task.* ②【体】forward:这个～很优秀。*The forward is excellent.* ③【气】front:冷空气～ *the cold front*

【前夫】former husband; ex-husband

【前赴后继】advance wave upon wave

【前功尽弃】all that has been achieved is spoiled; all one's previous efforts are wasted:我们应该继续努力,否则就会～。*We should work hard continuously, or our previous efforts will be wasted.*

【前滚翻】forward roll

【前后】around; about:2000 年～ *round 2000* /国庆节～ *about the National Day* /春节～ *round about Spring Day* ② from beginning to end; altogether:这个月～有 10 个学生访问新西兰。*There have been 10 students visiting New Zealand this month altogether.* ③ in front and behind:那座山～都有河。*There are rivers in front and behind the hill.*

【前…后…】 indicating the sequential connection between two actions or two things either in space or in time:前呼后拥 *with many retainers, attendants or adherents crowding round* /前思后想 *think over again and again* ② indicating forward or backward movements of one's body:前仰后合 *bend forwards and backwards*

【前后夹击】attack from the front and the rear at the same time:我们～敌人一定能消灭它。*If we make a simultaneous frontal and rear attack, the enemy will be wiped out.*

【前后脚儿】almost at the same time; (of two or more persons) leave or arrive almost simultaneously.

【前进】march on; go forward; forge ahead; advance:冒雨～ *advance in the rain* /急速～ *press ahead* /战士们在草地上匍匐～。*The soldiers crawled forward on the pasture.* /他策马加速～。*He whipped the horse to make it run faster.*

【前景】① foreground ② prospect; future; perspective: ～广阔 *a vast range of prospects* /无限美好的～ *boundless beautiful future (or prospects)* / ～暗淡 *bleak future; gloomy perspective* / ～辉煌 *splendid future; brilliant prospects; glorious prospects* /你们的公司～怎样? *What will become of your company?*

【前科】previous criminal record; record of previous crime:这个罪犯是有～的。*This offender has a criminal record.*

【前空翻】【体】forward somersault in the air

【前例】precedent:史无～的浩劫 *unprecedented catastrophe in history* /有～可循 *have precedent to be cited*

【前列】front rank (or row); forefront van:走在改革的～ *walk in front of the reform*

【前路】journey ahead; road ahead

【前面】in front; forward; at the head; ahead of:走在队伍～的是班长。*Walking ahead of the team is the squad leader.* /老师站在教室的～。*The teacher is standing in the front of the classroom.*

【前年】the year before last

【前怕狼,后怕虎】fear wolves ahead and tigers behind — be full of fear:如果～就永远不可能取胜。*We'll never win if we are full of fear.*

【前排】front row:我们坐～吧。*Let's seat in the front rows.*

【前仆后继】 as one falls, others step into the breach; no sooner has one fallen than other steps into the breach:无数先烈为了抗日战争的胜利,～英勇地献出了宝贵生命。*In order to win anti-Japanese war, countless martyrs, one-stepping into the breach as another fell, had fought and laid down their precious lives.*

【前妻】former wife ex-wife

【前期】earlier stage; early days

【前前后后】whole story; the ins and outs

【前情】① antecedent, cause ② old friendship; former affection

【前驱】forerunner; precursor; pioneer

【前驱期】【医】prodromal stage

【前人】forefathers; predecessors; forebears: ～的

Q

经验 *experience of predecessors*

【前人栽树,后人乘凉】earlier generations plant the trees, — in whose shade posterity will enjoy the cool — profiting by the labour of one's forefathers; toiling for the benefit of future generations

【前任】predecessor: ~市长 *former mayor* /我的~是张先生。*My predecessor was Mr. Zhang.*

【前哨】advance guard; outpost: ~战 *skirmish*

【前身】predecessor:这所大学的~是一所中学。*The predecessor of this university was a middle school.*

【前生】previous existence

【前事不忘,后事之师】past experience, if not forgotten, is a guide for the future; you will profit by bearing past experience in mind

【前视图】【机】front view

【前思后想】think over again

【前所未闻】never hear of before: ~的奇迹 *an unheard-of miracle* / ~的壮举 *a unheard-of feat*

【前所未有】never existed before; unprecedented; hitherto unknown:表现出~的诚意 *display unprecedented sincerity* /受到~的欢迎 *receive warmer welcome than ever*

【前台】① proscenium ② on stage; in public:主谋终于从幕后走到了~。*The chief instigator finally went on the stage from behind the scenes.*

【前提】① premise:大~ *major premise* /小~ *minor premise* ② prerequisite; presupposition:仔细研究市场动态是投资成功的~。*Careful study of the market trends is a prerequisite for success of investment.*

【前天】the day before yesterday: ~,他去了北京。*He went to Beijing the day before yesterday.*

【前厅】【建】antechamber; vestibule

【前庭】【生理】vestibule

【前途】prospect; future ~光明 *bright future* / ~暗淡 *gloomy future* / ~茫茫 *blurred, bleak future; unclear, gloomy prospects* /由于就业困难,很多学生都感到~渺茫。*Because of the problem of underemployment, many students felt their prospects were very bleak indeed.*

【前腿】foreleg

【前往】make for; go to; proceed to; leave for: ~工厂慰问演出 *go to the factory to make a special performance as an expression of appreciation* /旅行团已动身~加拿大。*The touring party has left for Canada.*

【前卫】①【军】vanguard; advance guard ②【体】halfback:右~ *right halfback; right half*

【前无古人】without parallel in history; unprecedented in history; have no parallel in the past

【前夕】eve:元旦~ *on the eve of New Year's Day* /圣诞节~ *Christmas Eve* /胜利~ *on the eve of victory*

【前嫌】past grievances; old grudge:尽释~ *remove all previous ill will*

【前线】frontline; front:上~杀敌 *go to the front line and fight the enemy* /离开~ *leave from the frontline*

【前项】【数】antecedent

【前言】preface; forward; introduction:画册的~ *the preface of picture album* /法典的~ *the preamble to the code*

【前言不搭后语】talk incoherently; babble disconnected phrases

【前沿】【军】forward position: ~哨所 *forward post*

【前仰后合】rock (with laughter); sway to and for:笑得~ *rock (or shake) with laughter; split one's sides laughing*

【前夜】eve:春节~ *on the eve of Spring Festival* /他的女儿是在新年~回来的。*His daughter came back on New Year's Eve.*

【前因】cause

【前因后果】entire process; cause and effect:整个案子的~已经明白了。*The whole case, its cause end effect has been fully clarified.*

【前缘】predestined relationship; foreordained affinity:我们的~已经结束。*Our predestined bond was over.*

【前院】front courtyard.

【前站】next stop on a march, tour etc. :我们为这次旅行打~。*We'll go advance to make arrangements for accommodations for this tour.*

【前兆】omen; augury; premonition; forewarning; indication:暴雨要来的~ *indications of an impending rainstorm* /地震的~ *the warning signs of an earthquake*

【前哲】ancient sages; great thinker of the past

【前者】the former

【前肢】foreleg; forelimb

【前置词】【语】preposition

【前轴】【机】forward shaft; fore axle

【前装炮】【军】muzzle-loader; muzzle-loading gun

【前缀】【语】prefix

【前奏】prelude: ~曲 *prelude* /"七七事变"是日本大举入侵中国的~。"*July 7 Incident of 1937*" *was a prelude of Japan invading China in large scale.*

虔

① pious; sincere; devout ② slaughter; plunder

【虔诚】pious; devout ~的基督徒 *a pious Christian*

【虔敬】reverent:他在他的上司面前很~。*He was all reverence before his superior.*

【虔信】devoutness; piety

钱

① coin; cash:一个铜~ *a copper (or cash)* ② money:花~ *spend money* /挣~ *make money* /零~ *small change; pocket money* /我父母每个月挣的~不多。*My parents don't make much money every month.* /愚人有~留不住。*A fool and his money are soon parted.* ③ fund; sum:我们手头缺~,明年再付给你吧。*We are short of funds so we'll pay you next year.* ④ *qian*, a unit of weight ⑤ (Qián) a surname

【钱包】wallet; purse

【钱币】coin

【钱币学】numismatics

【钱财】wealth; money 节约~ *economize on money* /浪费~ *waste of money*

【钱柜】money-locker; money-box; till

【钱粮】[旧] ① land tax ② revenue
【钱眼】hole in the centre of a copper:你别钻到~儿里去。*You should not be only a grabber.*
【钱庄】old-style private bank in China; native bank
钳 pincers; pliers; tongs:管~ *pipe gripper* /老虎~ *pincer pliers* /尖嘴~ *pointed-nose pliers* ② grip; hold with pincers; clamp ③ restrain: ~制住敌人 *stress the enemy*
【钳床】plier lathe
【钳工】① benchwork ② fitter
【钳口】① seal one's lips by force or threat ② keep silent; keep sb's mouth shut
【钳形】pincerlike:游击队对敌人形成~包围之后开始实施攻击。*After forming a pincerlike encirclement, the guerrillas began to attack the enemy.*
【钳制】clamp down on; suppress: ~性攻击 *a pinning attack*
【钳爪】【动】chela (of a crab etc.)
【钳子】① pliers; pincers; forceps
乾 ① qian, the first of the Eight Trigrams, denoting the principle of heaven, the sovereign, the male, and strength ② [旧] male
【乾坤】haven and earth; the cosmos; universe:一锤定~ *set the tune with one beat of the gong — make the final decision.*
【乾象】celestial phenomena; heavenly bodies
掮 [方] carry on the shoulder: ~一捆柴 *carry a bundle of firewood on the shoulder*
【掮客】broker 战争~ *a war broker* /政治~ *a political broker*
潜 ① latent; hidden; potential ② secretly; stealthily; on the sly: ~遁 *stealthily run away*
【潜藏】hide; be latent:他的内心~着仇恨。*A real hatred was hidden in his heart.*
【潜存】lie hidden; be latent: ~的侥幸心理是有害的。*Latent idea of leaving things to chance is harmful.*
【潜对地导弹】【军】 submarine-launched missile aimed at the objectives on land
【潜对潜导弹】underwater-under water missile
【潜伏】hide; lie low; lurk; conceal: ~的害虫 *latent pests* / ~的危险 *latent danger* / ~的疾病 *an insidious disease* /边防战士昨天在山谷里抓到一个~的特务。*The frontier guards arrested a hidden enemy agent in the ravine yesterday.*
【潜伏期】【医】incubation period; latency period: 疾病的~ *incubation period* /有些疾病~很长。*Some diseases have very long periods.*
【潜航】(of a submarine) submerged: ~深度 *submerged depth* / ~时间 *submerged time*
【潜科学】latent science; potential science
【潜力】latent capacity; potential; potentiality:在考试中你要充分发挥一切~。*You should bring all potentialities into full play in this exam.* /老师们争论如何才能充分发挥学生的最大~。*The teachers disputed how to bring into full play the potential of the students.*
【潜流】【地】undercurrent; underflow
【潜能】【物】latent energy
【潜匿】hide; keep out of sight
【潜热】【物】latent heat
【潜入】① infiltrate; sneak; slip; steal: ~白区 *slip into the White Area* / ~城内 *sneak into a town* / ~国境 *slip into the country* ② dive; submerge:那条鲸鱼慢慢~水中。*The whale slowly submerged.*
【潜水】dive; go under water: ~员 *frogman; diver* / ~打捞 *underwater salvaging* / ~器 *scuba* / ~机器人 *underwater robot* / ~服 *diving suit* / ~衣 *diving suit* / ~艇 *submarine; U boat* / ~运动 *underwater swimming* / ~钟 *diving bell* / ~泵 *sinking pump; submerged plumb* ② phreatic water
【潜台词】① unspoken words in a play left to the understanding of the audience ② implication implied sense
【潜逃】abscond:携赃款~ *abscond with illicit money* /畏罪~ *abscond to avoid punishment*
【潜艇】submarine: ~部队 *silent service*
【潜望镜】periscope
【潜心】devote oneself; with great concentration: ~攻读博士学位 *devote oneself to study for a doctorate*
【潜血】【医】occult blood
【潜移默化】exert a subtle influence on sb's character, thinking etc.; imperceptible influence:老师的言行对学生起着~的作用。*The words and deeds of a teacher exert an imperceptible influence on his students.*
【潜意识】sub-consciousness; the subconscious
【潜隐】① hide; conceal:她的笑容里~着一缕淡淡的哀愁。*Her smile contained a trace of lightly sadness.*
【潜泳】underwater swimming
【潜在】hidden; latent; potential: ~对手 *potential adversary* / ~的威胁 *hidden threat* / ~的市场 *potential market* / ~的利益 *potential profit*
【潜滋暗长】develop imperceptibly; grow and develop unconsciously
黔 1 [书] black
黔 2 another name for Guizhou Province
【黔驴技穷】 the proverbial donkey in ancient Guizhou has used up all its tricks — at the end of one's rope
【黔驴之技】tricks of the proverbial Guizhou donkey; tricks not to be feared
【黔首】[古] common people

qiǎn

浅 ① shallow: ~滩 *shoal; shallows* / ~水 *shallow water; school water* ② simple; easy: ~易 *simple and easy* / ~易读物 *easy reading* ② superficial:了解很~ *a superficial understanding* ④ not close; not intimate:交情很~ *not on familiar term* ⑤ light; pale: ~绿 *light green* / ~黄

pale yellow ⑥ not long in time：我的学历很～。*My record of formal schooling was very short.* /他俩相处的时间很～。*Both of them have not been together for a long time.*
see also jiān

【浅白】clear and plain; simple：基本原理很～。*The basic principle is simple.*

【浅薄】① shallow; superficial; scanty：学识～ *meagre knowledge*; *superficial scholarship* /文化～ *superficial culture* / ～而且糊涂的思想 *superficial and fuzzy thinking* ② frivolous; flighty; not serious：我不喜欢她～的性格。*I don't like her flighty disposition.*

【浅尝辄止】stop after obtaining a little knowledge about sth; be satisfied with a smattering of knowledge about sth：学外语不能～。*When you learn a foreign language, you should not stop striving after gaining a little knowledge about it.*

【浅成岩】【地】hypabyssal rock

【浅耕】shallow ploughing

【浅海】shallow sea; epeiric sea; epicontinental sea：～水域 *the shallow waters along the coast* / ～作业 *shallow sea operation* / ～养殖 *fish farming in shallow marine water*

【浅见】superficial view; humble opinion

【浅口鞋】shoes with low-cut uppers

【浅陋】meagre; mean：才学～ *meagre scholarship* / 内容～ *threadbare content*

【浅明】simple; plain; clear：～的真相 *an obvious truth* / ～的含义 *a simple implication*

【浅色】light colour：一件～的夹克 *a light colour jacket*

【浅水池】shallow pool; shallow end of a swimming pool

【浅说】elementary introduction：《生态～》*An Elementary Introduction of Ecology*

【浅谈】brief talk (usu. used in titles of books)：《水资源～》*A Brief Talk On Water Resources*

【浅显】plain; obvious：～的道理 *simple reason* / ～的语言 *plain language*

【浅笑】smile

【浅学】superficial knowledge; shallow learning; ill-educated

【浅易】easy; simple：～的儿童读物 *easy children's reading*

遣 ① dispatch; send：调～ *deploy*; *assign* ② dispel; expel; drive sth away; force sb to leave：消～ *divert oneself*; *while away the time*; *diversion*; *pastime*

【遣词】wording：～造句 *choice of words and building of sentences*; *wording and phrasing* / ～准确 *wording precisely* /她以用字～清新生动见长。*Her diction is noted for its freshness and vividness.*

【遣返】repatriate; send or bring sb back to his own country：～俘虏 *repatriate prisoner of war* (*P. O. W*) / ～原籍 *send one back to one's native place*

【遣散】disband; dismiss; send away; stop operating as an organization：～费 *severance pay*; *release pay* /战争结束以后，这支部队就～了。*The troop disbanded when the war was over.*

【遣送】send back; repatriate：这些非法移民被～出境。*The illegal immigrants were deported.*

谴 condemn; say that one disapproves of sb or sth

【谴责】denounce; condemn; reproach：我们一致～虐待儿童的行为。*We all condemn cruelly to children.* /有两个国家遭到国际社会的～。*Two countries were censured by the international society.*

缱

【缱绻】[书] (of lovers) deeply attached to each other

qiàn

欠[1] ① owe; be behind with; be in debt to (sb for goods etc.)：赊～ *buy sth or sell sth on credit*; *get or give credit* /拖～ *be behind with repayment of a loan*; *be in arrears* / ～情 *owe sb a debt of gratitude* /她们就～我多少钱一事进行了一番争论。*They had a dispute about how much money they owe me.* ② yawn：打呵～ *yawn*

欠[2] ① not enough; wanting; lacking, insufficient：～通顺 *not smooth enough* / ～说服力 *not be persuasive*; *not be convincing enough* ② raise slightly (a part of the body)：～身 *raise oneself slightly*; *half raise from one's seat* ③ [方] deserve to be punished：～打 *need a good hitting*

【欠安】(referring to others) feel unwell be slightly indisposed：奶奶今天身体～。*Grandma is not feeling well today or grandma is a bit under the weather today.*

【欠产】shortfall in output or production

【欠付工资】back pay; back wages

【欠佳】not good enough; not up to the mark

【欠款】money that is owing; arrears; debt：我总共～1000美元。*I owe a debt of* 1000 *US dollars in all.*

【欠缺】① be deficient in; be short of; be inadequate of：资金～ *be short of money*; *have a shortage of money* ② shortcoming; deficiency：我们的生活还有许多～。*There are still many inadequacies in our life.*

【欠条】a bill signed in acknowledgement of debt; receipt for a loan; written pledge for borrowing money or goods; IOU

【欠妥】not proper：措辞～ *not property worded* /他们处理问题～。*They didn't handle the problem properly.*

【欠息】debit interest

【欠薪】① no paying a salary on time; delay paying a salary ② back pay; overdue salaries

【欠债】be in debt; owe a debt：～人 *debtor* /我若还清所有～就一分钱不剩了。*If I pay all my debts I'll have no money left.*

【欠账】bills due; owe a debt; run into debt; outstanding account：～太多 *too much outstanding*

accounts
【欠资】postage due：～信 *postage-due letter* / ～邮包 *postage-due parcel*
【欠揍】[口] need a spanking：你太欺侮人了，真是～。*You are too rude; you need a good thrashing.*

纤 a rope for towing a boat; tow-rope; tow line
see also xiān
【纤夫】boat tracker
【纤歌】song sung by boat trackers when they are towing a boat
【纤路】towpath; towing path; track road
【纤绳】tow-rope; a rope for towing a boat

茜
【茜草】【植】madder
【茜纱】red gauze

倩[1] pretty; handsome; beautiful; attractive

倩[2] ask sb to do sth：～人发言 *ask sb to speak on one's behalf*
【倩男倩女】handsome men and pretty women
【倩影】photo or picture (of a beautiful woman)
【倩妆】attractive make-up
【倩装】handsome dress; beautiful dress

堑 moat; chasm; ditch：天～ *natural moat*
【堑壕】【军】trench; entrenchment：～工事 *entrenchment; entrenchment works*

嵌
【嵌镶】inlay; embed; set：墙上～着象牙雕的花。*The wall was inlaid with flowers carved out of ivory.*

歉 ① apology; regret：道～ *offer or make an apology; apologize* /报～ *apologize; be sorry* ② crop failure
【歉疚】be remorseful; having a guilty conscience：我因很少去看望她而感到～。*I felt guilty about visiting her so rarely.*
【歉年】lean year; poor harvest year
【歉然】regret; apologetic：～无语 *feel apologetic and say nothing* / ～微笑 *make an apologetic smile*
【歉收】poor harvest; crop failure：水稻～ *poor rice harvest* /棉花～ *bad harvest of cotton* /去年河北农作物～。*Last year the crops failed in Hebei Province.*
【歉意】regret; apology：谨表～。*Please accept my apologies or express my profound regrets; apologize sincerely.* /我没有去看望你的母亲，必须向你表示～。*I must offer you my apology for not see your mother.*

qiāng

抢 ①[书] touch：呼天～地 *cry out to heaven and knock one's head on the ground — utter cries of anguish* ② go against：～风 *walk against the wind*
see also qiǎng

呛 choke; (of smoke, etc.) make sb unable to breathe easily：烟雾几乎把小孩～着。*The fumes almost choked the child.* /什么味儿这么～鼻子？*What smell is it, which irritates the nose so much?*
see also qiàng

羌 Qiang, an ancient ethnic group in China
【羌笛】Qiang flute
【羌族】Qiang nationality living in Sichuan

枪[1] ① spear 短～ *short spear* /红缨～ *a red-tasselled spear* ② rifle; gun; firearm：机关～ *machine gun* /高射机～ *antiaircraft machine gun* /手～ *pistol; revolver* /开～ *shoot; fire a shot* ③ sth which is shaped or functions like a gun：喷～ *spray gun; airbrush*

枪[2] serve as a substitute for sb at an examination
【枪靶】target (for shooting)
【枪把】pistol grip, small of the stock
【枪崩】[口] shoot (dead)
【枪毙】execute by shooting：那个杀人犯已经被～了。*The homicide had already been executed.*
【枪刺】bayonet
【枪弹】① bullet ② cartridge
【枪法】marksmanship：他～过人。*He is an outstanding shot.*
【枪放下】(word of command) order arms
【枪杆子】rifle; gun; arm; stock of a gun：～里面出政权。*Political power grows out of the barrel of a gun.*
【枪管】barrel (of a gun)
【枪击】shoot with gun：～事件 *shooting accident*
【枪机】bolt
【枪架】arm rack; rifle rack
【枪决】execute by shooting：这些罪大恶极的犯罪分子将会被～。*These offenders with towing crimes will be executed by shooting.*
【枪口】muzzle：～要指向侵略者。*Direct the muzzle of one's gun at the aggressors.* /请把～对准靶子。*Please aim a gun at the target.* /那个孩子往后退来躲离～。*The child backed away from the gun.*
【枪林弹雨】a hail of bullets; roaring guns and flying bullets：在抗美援朝的战争中，志愿军战士在～中奋勇杀敌。*In the war to Resist US Aggression and Aid Korea, the soldiers of the Chinese People's Volunteers fought bravely with the enemies under heavy fire.*
【枪榴弹】grenade; rifle grenade
【枪炮】arms; guns

【枪杀】shoot dead
【枪伤】gunshot wound; bullet wound
【枪声】report of a gun; shot; crack: ~四起 *fusillade rise from all directions; crack break out all around* /不久他们听到了~。*Soon they heard the sound of guns.*
【枪手】(qiāngshǒu) ①[旧] spearman ② marksman; gunner: 他爸爸是一个神~。*His father was an expert marksman.*
【枪手】(qiāngshou) substitute for another person at an examination
【枪栓】rifle bolt; bolt
【枪膛】bore (of a gun)
【枪替】act as a substitute for another at examinations
【枪械】firearms; armaments; weapons
【枪眼】① embrasure; loophole ② bullet hole
【枪鱼】【动】marlin
【枪战】gun battle
【枪支】gun; firearms: ~弹药 *arms and ammunition; firearms ammunition*
【枪子儿】[口] cartridge ② bullet; shot: ~不长眼。*The bullet is no eye.*

戗 ① be in an opposite direction: ~流行舟 *sail against the flow* ② clash: 观点不同,不要说~。*If you have different views, it is not necessary to quarrel each other.*
【戗茬】be at loggerheads with: 他和妻子老是~说话。*He and his wife are always talking at loggerheads*
【戗风】against the wind: ~走路很困难。*It is very difficult to go against the wind.*

戕 [书] kill: 自~ *kill oneself; commit suicide; take one's own life*
【戕害】injure; damage: ~生命 *ruin one's life* /~健康 *ruin one's health*
【戕杀】kill ruthlessly
【戕贼】harm; undermine: ~身体 *undermine or ruin one's health*

腔 ① cavity: 口~ *the oral cavity* /鼻~ *the nasal cavity* /胸~ *thoracic cavity* /腹~ *abdominal cavity* ② tune; pitch: 低~ *low pitched tune* /高~ *high pitched tune* /唱~ *singing tunes* ③ speech; talk: 不搭~ *keep mum* /答~ *answer (a question etc.); respond (to sb or a question)* ④ accent: 北京~ *Beijing accent*
【腔调】① tune: 豫剧的~ *tunes of Henan opera* ② tone; tone of voice: 他讲话打着一副十足的官老爷~。*His speech was shot through with an arrogant tone of genuine bureaucrat.* ③ accent; intonation: 他说英语带着点威尔士~。*He speaks English with a Welsh intonation.*
【腔骨】spine of pork
【腔棘鱼】coelacanth
【腔口】[方] accent; sb's particular way of speaking: 从她说话的~知道她是上海人。*From the accent of speaking I knew she was a native of Shanghai.*

蜣
【蜣螂】【动】dung beetle

锵 [象] clang; gong ~的锣声 *clanging of gongs*

qiáng

强 ① strong; powerful; mighty: ~大的国家 *a mighty nation* /~大的军队 *a mighty army* /责任心~ *have a strong sense of responsibility* ② by force: ~占 *forcibly occupy; seize* ③ better: 我们的生活一年比一年~。*Our life is getting better and better.* /在那一点上,你比我~。*You have the advantage of me there.* ④ slightly more than; plus: 百分之六十~ *slightly more than sixty percent*
see also jiàng; qiǎng
【强暴】① violent; brutal; ferocious; savage: ~的行径 *acts of violence* ② brute force; ferocious adversary: 不畏~ *defy brute force* ③ violate (a woman, etc.); rape: 那位少女被~这件事造成了她心理上的严重创伤。*The girl's rape had a profound psychological effect on her.*
【强辩】[书] forceful argument; eloquence; expressive language, esp. to impress or persuade an audience: 他的~打动了学生。*The students were swayed by his eloquence.*
【强大】big and strong; powerful; formidable: ~的生命力 *great vitality* /~的竞争对手 *a formidable competitor* /阵容~ *have a strong line up* /听说她有~的政治背景。*It is heard that she has a strong political background.* /我们的国家和军队是~的。*Our country and army are powerful.*
【强盗】robber; bandit: ~行径 *banditry; robbery* /~逻辑 *gangster logic* /那辆经过高原的公共汽车遭到~的袭击。*Bandits have attacked buses driving through the tableland.* /~们破门而入并且偷走了很多金钱。*The robbers broke the door and stole a lot of money.*
【强敌】formidable enemies or opponents; formidable foe; strong enemy
【强的松】【医】prednisone
【强点】strong point; forte: 我们的~在于速度。*Speed is our strong point.*
【强调】stress; emphasize; underline: 总经理非常~遵守时间。*The general manager lays great stress on punctuality.* /警察~小心驾驶的重要性。*The policeman emphasized the importance of careful driving.*
【强度】intensity; strength: 劳动~ *the intensity of labour* /辐射~ *radiation intensity* /绳子的~ *the strength of a rope*
【强渡】【军】force a river; fight one's way across a river: ~长江 *force the Changjiang (Yangtze) River*
【强风】【气】strong breeze; strong wind
【强攻】storm; take by storm: 有四名士兵~进入了

那座房子。*Four soldiers stormed into the house.*

【强国】strong country; powerful nation; power:经济~ *economic power* /军事~ *military power* /世界~ *world powers* /这个王国在前几个世纪是海上~。*The kingdom was a great naval power in past centuries.*

【强悍】intrepid; doughty; valiant: ~的士兵 *a doughty soldier* /精明~ *intelligent and intrepid*

【强横】brutal and unreasonable; tyrannical; despotic: ~的态度 *despotic attitude* /他在一个~的老板手下工作。*He works for a tyrannical boss.*

【强化】strengthen; intensify; consolidate; enhance: ~训练 *an intensive training* / ~国家机器 *strengthen the state apparatus* /这种新药~了它的作用。*The new medicine has consolidated its function.*

【强记】[书] have a retentive memory:博闻~ *have encyclopedic knowledge*

【强加】impose; force; place sth unwelcome or unpleasant on sb:过去帝国主义者把殖民统治~于中国人民。*The imperialists impose their colonial rule on Chinese people in the past.*

【强加于人】impose (one's will, etc.) on others:不要把你的批评~。*Don't force your criticism on others.*

【强奸】violate (a girl); rape; defile: ~犯 *raper; rapist* / ~民意 *defile or outrage public opinion*

【强碱】【化】alkali; strong base

【强健】strong and health: ~的体格 *be physically strong; have a strong constitution; a sturdy constitution* / ~的运动员 *a sturdy player*

【强将】brilliant commander; outstanding general: ~手下无弱兵。*There are no poor soldiers under an able general.*

【强劲】powerful; forceful: ~的气流 *a strong airflow*

【强劳力】able-bodied labourer

【强力】great force: ~噪音 *forced noise* /她用~压下自己的愤怒。*She suppressed her own angers with a strong will.*

【强力霉素】【医】doxycycline

【强力起重机】【机】goliath crane

【强梁】ferocious bully; brutal force

【强烈】strong; intense; violent; powerful: ~的民族感情 *fervent national sentiments* / ~的对比 *striking or sharp contrast* / ~的愿望 *a strong aspiration; a strong desire* / ~的希望 *a strong hope* / ~的愤怒 *great indignation* / ~地震 *violent earthquake* / ~风暴 *severe storm*

【强令】arbitrary order:这栋楼已经被~拆除。*The building was demolished peremptorily.*

【强龙不压地头蛇】a mighty dragon cannot crush a snake in its old haunts — a local bully is hard to subdue

【强弩之末】an arrow at the end of its flight — a spent force

【强拍】【音】strong beat; accent beat:我的耳朵不能把~和次~区分开来。*My ears cannot differentiate a strong beat from a subsidiary strong beat.*

【强取豪夺】secure or obtain sth by force; grad and keep

【强权】power; might:不畏~ *be unafraid of might* / ~外交 *power diplomacy* / ~政治 *power politics* /正义终于战胜~。*Justice finally beat might.*

【强人】① strong man:女~ *a strong woman; a woman of exceptional ability; iron lady* ② [旧] bandit; robber

【强溶剂】【化】strong solvent

【强身】improve one's health; keep fit (by exercise or by tonics)

【强盛】(of a country) powerful and prosperous: ~的国家 *a powerful and prosperous country* / ~的民族 *a powerful and prosperous nationality*

【强手】a very capable person; person of ability or talent

【强手如林】plenty of capable persons

【强似】be better than; be superior to:今年的收成~去年。*The harvest in this year is better than that of last year.*

【强酸】【化】strong acid

【强袭】storm; take by storm

【强项】【体】strong point; forte:足球不是中国的~。*China is not strong in football.* ②[书] resolute; unyielding

【强心剂】【医】cardiac stimulant; cardiotonic

【强行】force: ~占有 *forced occupation* / ~拆除建筑 *demolishing a building without the consent of the owner* / ~突破一点 *force breakthrough at some single point* / ~通过一项法令 *force a decree through* / ~军 *forced march*

【强压】hold down; suppress; prevent (esp. one's feelings) from being expressed: ~愤怒 *suppress one's anger* / ~欢娱 *suppress one's amusement*

【强硬】tough; strong; unyielding: ~措施 *tough measure* / ~的态度 *uncompromising stand* / ~派 *hardliner; hawk* /对犯罪分子采取~方针 *take a tough line with offenders* /现在是对足球流氓采取~措施的时候了。*It's time to get tough with football hooligans.* /警察对危害公众匪徒采取~的措施。*The policemen took strong measures against dangerous mobster.*

【强有力】strong; powerful; forceful:采取~的措施 *take forceful measure* / ~的批评 *vigorous criticism*

【强于】be superior to; be better than:我们的实力略~对方。*Out actual strength is better that the opponent.*

【强占】① seize; forcibly take or occupy: ~公共财产 *forcibly take public property* / ~别国领土 *occupy the territory of another nation*

【强者】survivor; the strong and brave

【强震】【地】strong shock

【强制】force; compel; impel: ~通风 *forced ventilation* / ~劳动 *forced labour* / ~措施 *coercive measure* / ~保险 *force insurance; mandatory insurance*

【强中自有强中手】however strong a person maybe, there's always someone stronger; diamond cuts diamond

【强壮】strong; sturdy; powerful:他是个～的男子汉。*He is a strong and healthy man.* /她爷爷八十多岁了,可是还～得很。*Her grandfather is now well over eighty, but is still going strong.*

墙 ① wall:石～ *stone wall* /城～ *city wall*

【墙板】wall board

【墙报】wall newspaper

【墙壁】wall

【墙倒众人推】when a wall is about to collapse, every person gives it a push (or shove) — every person hits one who is down

【墙根】foot of a wall

【墙角】a corner formed by two walls; wall corner

【墙脚】① the foot of a wall:工人们把垃圾都堆积在～下。*The workers banked the garbage up against the wall.* ② foundation:挖～ *undermine the foundation of a wall; cut the ground from under one's feet*

【墙头】top of a wall:～草 *grass on the top of a wall sways with the wind — one who bends with the wind* / ～很低以至于人们很容易爬过去。*The walls are too low to easily climb over them.*

【墙头马上】a young woman leans over a wall and a young man comes by on the horseback — love at the first sight

【墙外汉】outsider

【墙纸】【建】wallpaper

蔷

【蔷薇】【植】rose:～科 *the rose family*

嫱 [古] lady-in-waiting

樯 [书] mast:～倾楫摧。*The mast toppled over and the oar broke.*

qiǎng

抢[1] ① seize; grab; snatch; rob; loot; scramble:～东西 *snatch a thing from one's hand* / ～银行 *rob a bank* /从她手里～走了信 *grabbed the letter from her* / ～一个最好的坐席 *scrambled for the best seats* /一帮罪犯试图合伙袭击那个女孩子子,并把她的东西～走。*A gang of criminals tried to gang the poor girl and take her things away from her.* ② vie for; compete for:～生意 *compete for business* ③ rush; hurry:～时间 *against time; lose no time*

抢[2] scrape; rub off; scratch; grind scissors and sharpen knifes

see also qiāng

【抢白】tell off; reproach; dress down; reprimand; rebuff:他的妻子～他礼貌不周。*His wife reproached him for his bad manners.*

【抢答】hurry to answer questions before others persons; vie for opportunity of replying a question

【抢渡】speedily cross:～黄河 *speedily cross the Yellow River*

【抢点】①(of a train, bus, etc.) accelerate in order to arrive on schedule; make up time ②(of a football striker, etc.) race to a favourable position

【抢夺】snatch; wrest; seize; grab:～研究成果 *seize the fruits of research* /从皇帝手里～政权 *wrested power from the emperor*/那个孩子从他妈妈手里～那本书。*The little child wrested the book out of his mother's hands.* /哪个人～了政权就成为统治者阶级。*The person who seizes the political power will be the ruler.*

【抢饭碗】fight for a job; vie for a position

【抢工】shock work

【抢购】rush to purchase:～雨伞 *a rush on umbrellas* / ～食品 *panic purchasing foodstuff* / ～风 *panic purchasing or buying*

【抢话】forestall other speakers; snatch the chance to speak right before other speakers

【抢婚】carry off a woman and marry her by force; marriage by capture

【抢建】rush to build; rush to construct:他们在冬天来临以前～了一所学校。*They did a rush job of building a school before winter.*

【抢劫】plunder; rob; loot:～案 *a case of robbery* / ～犯 *robber; pillager; plunderer* / ～罪 *pillage crime; offence of robbery* /侵略者在沿海地区～食品和女人。*The invaders plundered food and women from coast area.* /他们从那家银行～两千元人民币。*They robbed the bank of ¥ 2000.*

【抢镜头】①(of a cameraman) take a picture or a snapshot at the right moment and the vantage point ② steal the show; seek the limelight:经常～是不受欢迎的。*It is unwelcome always stealing the show.*

【抢救】rescue; save; salvage:地震中～出来的财物 *the salvage from an earthquake* /从大火中～出小孩 *rescue a child from a fire* /工作进行得很不顺利。*Rescue operations are proving not smooth.* /警察把老人从洪水中～出来。*The policemen saved the old man from the flood.* /车祸后,她的父母被迅速送到急救室～。*Her parents were rushed to casualty after the car accident.*

【抢掠】loot; plunder

【抢拍】fight for vantage point in taking news picture; seize an opportunity to take picture; rush to film

【抢亲】① traditional wedding ceremony in witch the bridegroom pretends to kidnap the bride ② take a woman for marriage by force; kidnap a woman to be one's wife

【抢收】rush in the harvest; get in the crops as soon as quickly

【抢手】shopping rush; (of goods) sell like hot cakes; (of ware) in great demand:～货 *shopping-rush commodities (or goods); sth in short supply*

【抢滩】control a ship stranded to prevent it from sinking

【抢先】forestall; to deal with or think of beforehand; anticipate:他的公司比所有的竞争者都~了一步。*His company forestalled all its competitors.* /他们赶在竞争对手之前,~把产品推向市场。*The anticipated their competitors by getting their products onto the market first.*

【抢险】rush to deal with an emergency:在解放军战士的帮助下,~工作进行得十分顺利。*Under the help of the soldiers of PLA, the emergency accident was being treated very smoothly.*

【抢修】rush to repair; rush-repair:大楼的供暖系统需要立即~。*The heating system in the building needs to be repaired right away.*

【抢眼】noticeable; attracting attention, as by being unusual or remarkable; conspicuous:由于这位歌手衣着鲜艳,发型古怪,所以总是十分~。*Because of her bright clothes and queer hairstyle, the singer is always conspicuous.* /这小伙子那长长的、女人似的睫毛很~。*The guy's long, feminine eyelashes were very noticeable.*

【抢占】① race to control; seize; race to occupy ② occupy illegally; possess sth illegally; squat:他非法~了许多公共财产。*He illegally possessed large number public properties.*

【抢种】rush-plant: ~小麦 *rush-plant the wheat*

【抢嘴】[方] ① try to beat others in being the first to talk; try to get the first word in; try to get the first chance to talk: ~是不礼貌的行为。*It is unpolite try to get the first chance to talk.* ② rush-eat; scramble for food:在宴席上~是陋习。*It is a bad habit scrambling for food in a dinner.*

强 make an effort; try hard; strive:勉~ *do sth with difficulty*

see also jiàng ; qiáng

【强逼】force; compel; coerce; liberate:他被~找第二个妻子。*He was forced to marry the second wife.* /她~自己每天练习。*She forced herself to practice daily.*

【强辩】defend oneself by sophistry; argue against all reason:

【强词夺理】argue irrationally; resort to sophistry; use lame arguments:他非但不承认错误,并且还~为自己争辩。*Not only he refused to admit his mistake, but also he defended himself by sophistry.*

【强记】memorize by rote; remember by rote; force oneself to memorize or remember:博闻~ *have wide learning (or knowledge) and a retentive memory* /通常英语考试之前同学们都~单词。*All students unusual memorize words by rote before an English examination.*

【强留】force one to stay against one's will:你可以~人,但留不住她的心。*You could force her to stay here, but you could not leave on her heart.*

【强买强卖】force sb to buy or sell sth; buy or sell under coercion unusual

【强迫】force; coerce; compel:他被~购买了那些股票。*He purchased those stocks under coercion.*

【强求】force; insist on; impose:不要~你自己和你不喜欢的人在一起。*Don't impose yourself on people whom you don't like.*

【强人所难】force sb to do sth against his will; make one to do what is beyond one's capabilities:人各有志,千万不要~。*It is unnecessary trying to make any person do what is beyond his will, for everybody has his own ideal.*

【强使】force; compel:你不要~孩子们待在家里。*You should not compel the children to stay indoors.*

【强笑】a forced smile; force a smile:以~解愁 *smile away one's vexation or grief* /我们知道她脸上是~。*We knew the smile on her face was a forced smile.*

【强征】impress; compel sb to serve in a military force; seize property by force or authority; confiscate:战时~食粮 *impress provisions in war-time* / ~兵员 *impress soldiers*

【强颜】put an air of cheerfulness; try to look cheerful

【强作解人】pretend to be in the know; feign understanding:那个骗子对这个问题煞有介事,~。*The swindler pretended to be serious about this matter and feigned knowing everything.*

襁

【襁褓】swaddle; swaddling clothes:那个可爱的婴儿被紧紧地裹在~中。*The lovely baby was tightly swaddled.*

qiàng

呛 irritate (respiratory organs):切洋葱的味道~眼。*The smell of being chopped onions irritates the eyes.*

see also qiāng

炝 ① boil sth (vegetable, etc.) in the water for a while, and then add a dressing to it ② fry sth quickly in hot oil, then cook it with sauce and water:用红辣椒~一下锅,做一碗面条。*Fry chopped red peppers in hot oil, then cook it with noodles and water.*

qiāo

悄

see also qiǎo

【悄悄】quietly; on the quiet; secretly:她~地走进大楼来。*He came into the building very quietly.*

【悄悄话】whisperings; whisper in private; a private conversation; confidential talk:这两个女孩在教室内说~。*The two girls were whispering in the classroom.*

跷 ① hold up (a finger); lift up (a leg): ~起大拇指 *hold up one's thumb* /他~起大腿坐在椅子上。*He sat in the chair with his legs crossed.* ② on tiptoe; stand on tiptoe:她~着脚从睡着的

孩子们旁边走过。*She tiptoed past the sleeping children.*

【跷蹊】fishy; suspicious:这个事件有些~。*Something is fishy about the incident.*

【跷跷板】seesaw:玩~ *play on a seesaw*

锹 shovel; spade:钢~ *shovel; spade* /用~挖 *dig with a spade*

敲 ① knock; beat; percuss; strike: ~门 *knock at the door* / ~门声 *a knock at the door* /请在墙上~出一个洞。*Knock a hole in the wall, please.* ②[口] overcharge; swindle money out of some person; blackmail; fleece: ~诈公司钱财 *swindled money from the company* /那家饭馆~了我们一笔钱。*They fleeced us at that restaurant.*

【敲边鼓】try to assist sb from the sideline; back sb up:你可以在父亲面前提出你的计划,我给你~。*You can put forward your plan in your father's face; I will back you up from the sideline.*

【敲打】① rap; tap; beat; strike:海浪~在甲板上。*The waves were beating against the deck.* /她在他的肩膀上轻轻~了几下。*She tapped him on the shoulder several times.* /她用棍子~我。*She struck me with a stick.* /他把钉子深深地~进去。*He struck the nail home.* ② say sth to irritate a person; pressurize:孩子们很懒,不~他们是不肯做任何活动的。*The children are lazy; they won't do any activity if they are not prodded into it.* /你最好~她一下。*You'd better give her memory a prod.* /不能因这件事再~他了,他已经很生气了。*We should not annoy him with sarcastic words over this matter, he is very angry.*

【敲定】determine; make the final decision:正式~ *formal decide; officially decide* /总统已经~了各部门的政策。*The president determined every departmental policy.* /法官将对这项指控的真伪做出最后~。*The judges will determine whether the charges are true or false.*

【敲骨吸髓】break one's bones and suck his marrow — cruel, bloodsucking exploitation; be a cruel bloodsucker

【敲击】beat; strike; rap; tap:他用拳头~着桌子。*He rapped the table with his fist.*

【敲警钟】sound the alarm bell — warn in advance; forewarn:艾滋病给年轻人敲了警钟。*The AIDS gives an alarm to the youth.*

【敲门砖】a brick picked up to knock on the door and thrown away after it has served its purpose — a stepping-stone to success; a mere tool to achieve sb's aim

【敲丧钟】knell; sound the funeral bell:给殖民主义~,宣告殖民统治的终结 *sound the death knell for colonialism*

【敲山震虎】a deliberate act as a warning to the opponent; make an act to give a warning to the other side

【敲诈】blackmail; extort; racketeer; shake down:这个流氓想~收款员迫使他帮他取出钱,但未能得逞。*The gangster tried to blackmail the receiver into helping him draw the money, but he failed.* /他向小孩~钱财。*He extorted money from children.*

【敲竹杠】fleece; daylight robbery; put the lug on:那家旅馆敲了我们的竹杠。*They fleeced us at that hotel.* /这是光天化日的~。*It is daylight overcharge.*

橇 sledge; sled; sleigh:乘坐雪~旅行 *travel on a sledge*

缲 hem with invisible stitches

qiáo

乔 ① tall: ~木果树 *standard fruit-tree* ② pretend to be; disguise; give sb or sth a false appearance: ~装成工人 *disguise oneself as a worker* ③(Qiáo) a surname

【乔林】high forest

【乔模乔样】insincere; in an affected manner

【乔木】【植】tree; arbor; a tree, as opposed to a shrub:

【乔迁】move to a better place; be transferred to a higher post; move; progress toward a particular state or condition; go from one residence or location to another; relocate:喜~ *congratulations on one's promotion* /我们恭贺他把家~到城外。*We felicitate that he relocated his home outside the city.*

【乔迁之喜】best wishes for one's new home

【乔装】pretend; feign; disguise: ~成教授 *disguise oneself as a professor; dress up as a professor*

【乔装打扮】smarted up; disguise oneself; masquerade:强盗~成一名司机。*The bandit masqueraded as a driver.*

侨 ① live abroad ② person living abroad; resident in foreign country:华~ *overseas Chinese*

【侨胞】countrymen residing abroad; nationals living abroad:海外~ *oversea nationals; countrymen residing abroad* /归国~ *returned overseas Chinese*

【侨汇】overseas remittance

【侨居】live abroad: ~海外 *reside in an alien nation or land*

【侨眷】dependents (or relatives) of overseas Chinese

【侨民】denizen; a national of a particular country residing abroad

【侨属】dependents (or relatives) of overseas Chinese

【侨商】overseas Chinese businessman:我们仅仅知道他是个~。*We only know he is an overseas Chinese businessman.*

【侨务】affairs concerning nationals living abroad; overseas Chinese:我们应该重视~工作。*We should pay attention to the affairs concerning nationals living abroad.*

【侨乡】an area inhabited by returned overseas Chinese and its relatives:佛山市是有名的~。*Fos-*

han city is a bigger population of returned overseas Chinese and its relatives.

【侨资】overseas Chinese capital; investment by overseas Chinese

荞

【荞麦】buckwheat

桥 bridge:铁索~ *chain bridge* /立交~ *flyover (bridge); overpass* /天~ *platform bridge* /独木~ *single-plank bridge* /架~ *build a bridge* /这座~在卡车通过时有点颤动。*The bridge quivered as the truck crossed it.*

【桥洞】bridge opening; bridge arch

【桥墩】bridge pier:筒形~ *barrel pier* /斜面式~ *batter pier* /联结式~ *braced pier* /钢筋混凝土空心~ *reinforced concrete hollow pier*

【桥涵】bridge and culvert

【桥孔】bridge opening

【桥梁】bridge:架在黄河上的~ *a bridge across the Yellow River* /两国家之间互相沟通的~ *a bridge of understanding between two nations*

【桥牌】bridge (card game):打~ *play bridge* /~要四个人玩。*It takes four persons to play bridge.*

【桥台】【建】bridge abutment

【桥头】either end of a bridge:战士们走到~就不再往前走了。*The soldiers went no farther than the bridge.*

翘 ① raise (one's head); lift up:他把他的手臂~过头顶。*He raised his arms above his head.* ② become bent or warped:木板因受潮而~曲。*The wooden board warped in the humidity.* *see also* qiào

【翘材】outstanding man

【翘棱】warp; bent

【翘盼】long eagerly; earnestly expect: ~电话 *earnestly expecting a telephone call* /我们~他的到来。*We earnestly expect his coming.* /这几个球迷~去观看足球赛。*These fans are longing to go to watch the football match.*

【翘企】eagerly look forward to; eagerly:我~着今年暑假见到你。*I'm eagerly awaiting to see you this summer vacation eagerly.*

【翘曲】turn or twist out of shape; warp

【翘首】raise one's head and look; crane one's neck

【翘望】① raise one's head and look at; turn upwards:人们都在朝上~。*The people were all looking upwards.* ② hope earnestly; expect:他们~着他们的孩子能继承家族的传统。*They earnestly hope that their children will carry on their family traditions.*

【翘足而待】wait on one's tiptoe — hope earnestly sth to happen soon:孩子们都~着圣诞晚会的开始。*The children were on tiptoe before the Christmas party.*

憔

【憔悴】wan and sallow; ill and emaciated; haggard; thin and pallid:病号~的脸 *the thin and pallid face of the invalid* /这个姑娘的眼睛深陷,十分地~。*The girl's eyes were haggard and cavernous.*

樵 ①[方] firewood ②[书] gather firewood

【樵夫】woodman; woodcutter

瞧 look; see; watch:偷~ *steal a glance* /让学生~着办吧。*Let the students do as they see fit.*

【瞧病】① (of a patient) see a doctor ② (of a doctor) see a patient

【瞧不起】despise; look down upon:这些女孩子~便宜的衣服,愿意穿最好的衣服。*These girls despise cheap clothes and will only wear the best.* /不能~乡下的孩子。*You should not look down upon the children from countryside.*

【瞧得起】think much of; think highly of sb:大家很~他。*Everybody thinks much of him.*

【瞧哈哈】[口] gloat (over other person's misfortune); have a good laugh (over people's misfortune):对于对手的厄运我们不能~。*We should not gloat over our rival's misfortune.*

【瞧见】catch sight of; notice:你~他离开房间了吗? *Did you notice him leave the house?*

qiǎo

巧 ① skillful; ingenious; clever; be good at:机~ *adroit; ingenious* /一个~妙的计划 *an ingenious scheme* /手~ *clever with sb's hands*; ~手艺 *excellent workmanship* ② cunning; deceitful; artful; clever at deceiving people:花言~语 *sweet words; blandishments* ③ opportunely; coincidentally; luckily; just right:无~不成书。*There is no story without coincidence.*

【巧辩】specious argument; argument smartly: argue skillfully

【巧夺天工】wonderful workmanship or superb craftsmanship excelling nature: so superb craftsmanship as to excel nature:这是一项~的工程。*This is a superb project.*

【巧妇难为无米之炊】even the cleverest housewife can't cook a meal without rice — a person can't make bricks without straw

【巧干】work ingeniously; do sth cleverly: ~的工人 *an ingenious worker*

【巧合】coincidence:多么~的事情啊! *What a coincidence!*

【巧计】clever device; artful scheme:他们施用~逮捕罪犯。*The arrested the criminal by resorting to a stratagem.*

【巧劲儿】① clever method; trick; knack:学习~劈柴的~ *learn the tricks of the kindling* /这里面有点~。*There is a knack in it.*

【巧匠】clever artisan; skilled workman:那些能工~建造了颐和园。*Those skillful craftsmen built the Summer Palace.*

【巧克力】chocolate: ~布丁 *chocolate pudding* /~蛋糕 *chocolate cake* /孩子拉着母亲的外衣还要~。

The child pulled at its mother's coat for more chocolate.

【巧立名目】concoct various pretexts; invent all sorts of names (or excuses): ~乱收费 *invent excuses collect fees confusedly*

【巧妙】ingenious; clever: ~的计划 *an ingenious scheme* / ~的手段 *a smart artifice* / ~的装置 *an ingenious device* /解决水果贮藏问题的~办法 *an ingenious solution to the problem of fruits storage* /这是一句~的俏皮话。*That's a clever hit.*

【巧取豪夺】work the oracle; grab and keep; secure (one's property, right etc.) by tricky or force: ~强占公共基金 *grab and keep public funds*

【巧舌如簧】talk glibly; sweet-talk; have a glib tongue like the reed of a wind instrument

【巧事】coincidence

【巧手】dexterous hands; a dab hand: 一双~ *a dab hand* /他是打高尔夫球的~。*He is a dab hand at golf.*

【巧思】a clever thought; (of art etc.) ingenious conception

【巧言令色】be hypocritical; artful talk and insinuating countenance; clever words and an ingratiating manner: 一个~的伪君子 *a hypocritical rogue*

【巧遇】chance encounter; encounter by chance; run into some person by accident: 在公园里~ *a chance encounter in the park.*

悄 ① quiet; silent; low voice: 四周静~~的。*It is quiet all round.* ②[书] grieved; sorrowful; worried; sad
see also qiāo

【寂静无声】quiet; silent: ~的学习场所 *a quiet place for studying*

【悄寂】quiet; noiseless: 当裁判员宣布竞赛的获胜者时,全场一片~。*Everyone was silent as the referee announced the winner of the competition.*

【悄然】① sorrowfully; sadly: ~泪下 *shed tears in sorrow* /老奶奶~凝视着那坍塌的房屋。*The grandma stared sadly at the ruins of her house.* ② quietly: 这个女孩~走进音乐厅。*The girl came into the concert hall very quietly.* /他昨天~离去。*He left quietly yesterday.*

【悄声】quietly; whisper: 她向邻座的人~耳语。*She is whispering to her neighbour.*

qiào

壳 shell; hard surface; crust: 胡桃~ *the shell of a walnut* /轴对称~体 *axis-symmetric shell* /地~ *lithosphere; the earth's crust* /躯~ *the body* /金蝉脱~ *escape by crafty scheme*
see also ké

【壳菜】mussel

【壳质】【生化】chitin

俏 ① pretty; smart looking; handsome; good looking; stylish ② sell well; be salable; be in great demand: 市场上这种款式夹克~的很。*This style jackets are salable in the market.*

【俏货】marketable goods; goods that sell well; highly salable goods

【俏丽】charming; attractive: ~的女孩 *a charming girl; an attractive girl*

【俏美】cute and pretty: 他的女儿真是一个~的姑娘。*His daughter really is a cute and pretty girl.*

【俏媚】attractive; handsome: 多么~的小姑娘! *What a charming girl!*

【俏皮】good-looking: smart; stylish: 她长得~得很。*She looks lively and delightful.*

【俏皮话】witty remark; quip; sarcastic remark: 不要说这么多~。*Don's say so many sarcastic remarks.*

【俏销】sell well; have a ready market

峭 ① high and steep; precipitous: 陡~的 *abrupt; cliffy; precipitous; steeper* ② stern; harsh; severe: 料~ *chilly*

【峭拔】① vigorous ② high and steep; perilous: ~的山峰 *a high and steep peak*

【峭壁】precipice: 处于失败的~边缘 *on the precipice of defeat*

【峭峻】① high and steep; perpendicular: ~的山势 *high and steep mountain* ② stern

【峭立】rise steeply: ~的悬崖 *a cliff rising steeply*

窍 ① aperture orifice 七~ *seven orifices (of the head)* ② key to sth: ~窍 *knack; know-how*

【窍门】know-how; knack; key to sth: 找~ *try to find the key to a problem; try to get the know-how*

翘 stick up; turn upwards; hold up: 他~起大拇指说:"太棒了。"*He held up his thumb and said: "It's terrific"*
see also qiáo

【翘板】seesaw

【翘辫子】kick the bucket: 他去年的溃疡差点让他~。*Last year his ulcer nearly made him pop off.*

【翘尾巴】be (or get) cocky; be haughty and snooty: 你不能因为成功而~。*You should not be cocky at your success.*

【撬杠】crowbar

【撬棍】crowbar

【撬锁】pick a lock: ~贼 *picklock*

撬 prize; pry: ~门 *pry a door open*

鞘 sheath; scabbard: 刀出~ *take the knife out of the sheath* /请把剑插进~中。*Butcher knife scabbard, please.*
see also shāo

【鞘翅】【动】elytrum

【鞘子】sheath; scabbard

qiē

切 ① cut; slice: ~下一块肉 *slice off a piece of meat* / ~蛋糕 *cut a cake* ②【数】tangency: 沿~线方向 *at a tangent*
see also qiè

【切菜】cut up vegetable

【切齿】gnash one's teeth

【切除】excision; ablation: ~一个肿瘤 *excised the tumor* / ~电影中三个场景 *excised three scenes from the film*

【切磋】learn from each other by exchanging views; compare notes: ~技艺 *learn from each other by exchanging accomplishments* / ~琢磨 *education as a gradual polishing process*

【切点】【数】point of tangency

【切断】cut off: ~电源 *cut off the power supply* / ~退路 *cut off the bridge of gold*

【切割】cut: ~机 *cutting machine* /大理石~ *cut through marble* / ~牛肉 *cut up the beef*

【切腹自杀】commit hara-kiri (or seppuku)

【切开】①【医】incision:他肚子上~了一个口子以便取出肿瘤。*An incision was made into his stomach to take out the tumor.* ② cut open: ~西瓜 *cut up a watermelon*

【切口】① notch:胶片~ *film notches* /径向~ *radial notch* ②【医】incision:二重V字形~ *double V-shaped incision*

【切面】① cut noodles ② section; plane of section: 填方~ *fill section* /纵(横)~ *vertical (cross) section* ③ tangent plane

【切片】① slice:我把面包切成片。*I sliced the bread.* ②【医】section: ~检查 *cut a section for examination under the microscope*

【切线】【数】tangent line

【切向力】【物】tangential force

【切向速度】【物】tangential velocity

【切削】【机】chipping; cutting:金属~ *metal cutting* / ~车床 *cutting machine tool*

qié

茄 eggplant; aubergine:炸~盒 *fried stuffed eggplant slices*

【茄泥】(of a dish) mashed eggplant

【茄子】eggplant; aubergine:他以前喜欢吃~。*He used to eat eggplants.*

qiě

且[1] ① just; for the time being:暂~ *just; for the time being* /你~不要着急。*You just don't worry.* /外国人也来了不少参加会议的,~不要说中国学者了。*Lots of foreigners attended the meeting, not to mention Chinese scholars.* / ~让他冷静一下。*Let him be self-possession for the time being.* ②[方] for a long time:买一块手表~使呢。*Buy a watch, it will last you quite some time.* /他~从监狱出不来了。*He will be in the prison for a long time.* ③ (Qiě) a surname

且[2] ①[书] even: ~现在也不太迟。*Even now it is not too late.* / ~连总统和总理在地震时都经受了苦难。*Even the president and the premier experienced hardship during the earthquake.* /我~更不走运。*I am even less lucky.* ② both... and:受好评的法官既有才智~聪明 *a judge well regarded for both intelligence and honesty* /这位秘书能讲~能写英语。*The secretary both speaks and writes English.* ③ almost; nearly:年~八十 *almost eighty years old*
see also jū

【且不说】let alone:他们连吃饭钱都不够,就~玩儿的钱了。*They hasn't enough money for food; let alone amusements.*

【且慢】wait a moment; not go or do so soon; hold it: ~生气 *control your angry for the moment* / ~得意。*Don's crow over too soon.*

【且…且…】while; as:且战且退 *withdraw as fighting* /且谈且走 *talk as walking*

【且说】formula for opening or continuing a story; let's begin with

qiè

切 ① correspond to; accord with; fit in:你的建议不~实际。*Your proposal does not fit in with actual circumstance.* ② be closed to:亲~接见 *a warm interview* ③ eager; keen; anxious:热~盼望春天去上海 *keen on going to Shanghai in the spring* /求胜心~ *eagerly win wish* ④ be sure to: ~记呀! *Be sure not to forget it*
see also qiē

【切齿】gnash one's teeth: ~之恨 *gnash one's teeth in hatred; cherish a bitter hatred*

【切肤之痛】keenly felt pain:他的不良行为使他的父母感到~。*His bad behaviour caused his parents a great deal of pain.*

【切骨】deep (of hatred); bitter: ~仇恨 *hatred that cuts the bone*

【切合】suit; fit in with; right and proper; appropriate: ~人民需要 *be appropriate to the people's need* /很难找到一个对每个学生都~的时间。*It is difficult to find a time that suits every student.*

【切记】be sure to keep in mind; must always remember: ~不要迟到 *be sure not to be late*

【切忌】avoid by all means; must guard against; must not do in instance:我们应该~人云亦云。*We should avoid echoing what other says by all means.*

【切近】close to; similar; near: ~实际 *close to the reality* /渔夫知道已经~海岸了,因为灯是高挂在悬崖上的。*The fisher knew he was near the shore because the light was high up on the cliffs.* /我的新车和你的那辆很~。*My new car is similar to the one you have.*

【切口】slang; secret language of a underworld gang or a certain profession; jargon; password

【切脉】【中医】pulse-feeling; feel the pulse

【切盼】expect eagerly; sincerely hope

【切迫】urgent; pressing: ~的任务 *a pressing task* /时间~。*Time is pressing.*

【切切】① earnestly; urgently: ~思念 *miss earnestly* ② (used in letter) be sure to; must do; sth must be done：～记住 *be sure to not forget* ③ used at the end of regulations or a notice, etc. to express exhortation or warning：～此令。*The order is to be regard seriously.* ④ murmuring sound：～细语 *private talk in small voice*

【切身】① of immediate concern to sb：～利益 *immediate interests* ② personal：～体验 *learn through sb's personal experience*

【切实】feasible; practical; earnest：～可行的计划 *a feasible plan* /～纠正错误 *rectify one's mistake in real earnest* /你用这笔钱继续学习绘画是我～的愿望。*It is my earnest wish that you use this money to continue you study of drawing.*

【切题】keep to the subject; keep to the point; be relevant to the topic under discussion：讲话要～。*A speech should keep to the subject.*

【切勿】(of a warning) must not：～靠近危险品 *keep off the danger* /～喧哗 *be quiet* /～倒置仪器 *keep the apparatus upright*

【切音】the system of indicating sounds by confluent consonants and syllabary

【切诊】pulse-feeling and palpation (one of the four methods of diagnosis)

【切中】hit (the mark); cut：～要害 *hit home* /～时弊 *cutting into the current evils; strike hard at the present day evils*

妾 ① concubine ② [旧] used by a woman in humble reference to herself

怯 cowardly; nervous; timid：胆～ *chicken heart; eeriness; pusillanimity* /羞～ *cannot say sth to a goose; diffidence; shyness*

【怯场】stage fright

【怯惧】timid：过于～而不敢反抗 *too timid to protest* /由于～而不敢发表意见 *timorous of venturing an opinion*

【怯懦】timid and overcautious

【怯弱】timid：需要勇敢而不是～去面对困难 *difficulties that call for bold, not timid responses*

【怯生】shy with stranger; timid and diffident in the presence of a stranger：这个小孩很～，躲在他妈妈后面。*The child was shy and hid behind his mother.*

【怯生生】shy; in a timid manner; nervous：在生人面前不要～的！*Don't be so shy in the presence of strangers.*

【怯声怯气】talk timidly; speak haltingly

【怯头怯脑】boorish; uncouth; lumpish

【怯阵】① (of a soldier etc.) feel nervous before going into battle; be battle-shy ② stage fright

窃 ① steal; pinch：偷～ *pilfer* /盗～ *brigandage; practice theft* ② secretly; furtively

【窃案】a case of pilferage; larceny; burglary

【窃夺】usurp; grab; seize by illegal means：非法～邻居的财物 *usurp a neighbour's property* /～王位 *usurp the throne*

【窃国】usurp state power

【窃据】usurp; illegally occupy：～要职 *unjustly occupy a high position*

【窃密】steal secret information; steal secrets

【窃窃私议】exchange whispered remarks

【窃窃私语】whisper; talk secretly (or privately)

【窃取】usurp; steal; seize：为某人～书 *steal sb book* /～秘密情报 *steal secret information* /～别人的劳动果实 *seize the fruit of the other's labour*

【窃听】eavesdrop; wiretap; bug ～某人家里的电话 *tap (or bug) one's home telephone*

【窃听器】bug; tapping device; tap：警察在嫌疑犯的房间安装～。*The police planted a bug in the suspect's room.*

【窃笑】laugh secretly; snicker; titter

【窃贼】thief; burglar

挈 ① lift; hoist; take up：提纲～领 *concentrate on the main points* ② take along; carry：他～作品举办展览。*He holds an exhibition taking his works with him.*

惬 be pleased or satisfied：～乎人心 *affording general satisfaction*

【惬当】apt; proper; appropriate：商业信函的～格式 *the proper form for a business letter*

【惬怀】be satisfied; be pleased：老师对学生甚为～。*The teacher felt satisfied with the students.*

【惬心】be pleased; be heartened：一个非常～的礼物 *a very satisfied gift*

【惬意】pleased; satisfied：一个非常～的约会 *a very pleased appointment*

趄 inclined; slanting：～趄 *toddle*

锲 [书] carve; engrave

【锲而不舍】keep on chipping (or chiseling) away — make unflagging effort; work with perseverance：靠～的精神这位老人终于学会了计算机。*By perseverance the old man learned to use computer.*

【挈带】take along; carry

qīn

钦 ① admire; adore; respect ② by the emperor himself：～定 *compiled and published by imperial order; (of writing) authorized by sovereign prince himself*

【钦差】imperial envoy; imperial commissioner

【钦差大臣】① imperial envoy; imperial commissioner ② a nickname for a representative of the supreme

【钦敬】admire; respect：她把老人从大火中救出来，我们都～不已。*We all admired her for the way she saved the old man from the fire.*

【钦佩】admire; adore; respect; venerate and admire：我们都～他那绝妙的幽默感。*All of us admire him for his fine sense of humour.*

【钦羡】admire and respect

侵 ① invade; intrude into; encroach on：军队～入了这个国家。*The army invaded the nation.* ② approaching：～晨 *approaching daybreak; towards daybreak; at the approach of dawn*

【侵夺】seize by force:军队~了这个要塞。*The army seized the fort.*

【侵犯】encroach on; infringe upon; violate: ~邻国 *encroach on a neighbour's land* / ~别人的权利 *infringe upon other people's right*

【侵害】encroach on; make inroads on; invade: ~他人的权益 *invade another person's rights*

【侵略】aggression; invasion: ~者 *aggressor; invader* / ~军 *aggressor troops; invading army (or troops)* / ~国 *aggressor country* /正义战争必然要战胜~战争。*Just wars are bound to triumph over wars of aggression.*

【侵权】pirate; tort; violate other's lawful rights: ~行为 *act of tort; infringement act*

【侵染】infect:他对这事毫不注意,因为他从来未受到~。*He didn't pay any attention to this matter because he never infected.*

【侵扰】invade and harass:敌人的~ *the invasion of an enemy* /疾病的~ *an invasion of disease*

【侵入】invade; intrude into: ~某人的私室 *intrude upon sb's privacy* / ~领海 *intrude into marginal sea of one country*

【侵蚀】① corrode; erode:铁锈正在~钢轨。*Rust is corroding the steel rails.* /溪流从在岩石~成一条狭窄的水道。*The stream eroded a narrow channel in the rock.* /海水~着岩石。*The sea erodes the rocks.* ② embezzle public funds bit by bit; seize (money or property) in secret bit by bit: ~公款 *misappropriate public funds bit by bit*

【侵吞】① misappropriate; embezzle:这个会计由于~由他保管的钱财而进了监狱。*The accountant was sent to prison for misappropriating money placed in his care.* ② swallow up; annex: ~别国领土 *annex another country's territory*

【侵袭】make inroads on; invade and attack; hit; assault:对别国进行突然~ *make a surprise assault on another country* /南海地区经常遭受暴雨~。*The southern coastal area is often hit by storm.*

【侵晓】dawn; before daybreak

【侵占】① invade and occupy; occupy by force:敌军准备~这座城市。*The enemy troops are ready to invade and occupy the city.* ② embezzle; seize: ~国家财产 *annex or embezzle national property* /那个会计在他工作的公司里~了一万美元。*The treasurer embezzled ten thousand dollars from the company where he worked.*

亲 ① parent:父(母)~ *father (mother)* ② blood relation; next of kin: ~儿子 *one's own son* / ~弟弟 *blood sister* / ③ kin; relative:远~ *scotch cousin* /近~ *next of kin* ④ marriage relation; match:说~ *act as a matchmaker* /姻~ *in-law* /定~ *engagement* ⑤ bride:娶~ *get married* ⑥ close; intimate: ~近的朋友 *an intimate friend* ⑦ in person: ~自 *in body; in person; oneself* / ~眼 *saw with one's own eyes* ⑧ kiss:当他告别的时候,他~了妻子。*He kissed his wife when he said good-bye.*

see also qìng

【亲爱】dear; beloved:我最~的朋友 *my dearest friend*

【亲本】parent:回交~ *backcross parent* /非回交~ *non-recurrent parent* /顶交~ *top-cross parent*

【亲笔】in sb's own handwriting: ~题词 *one's own handwriting* / ~签名 *John Hancock; autograph* / ~文件 *holograph* / ~信 *an autograph letter*

【亲代】parental generation

【亲骨肉】one's own offspring

【亲故】relatives and old acquaintances

【亲和力】【化】affinity:细胞~ *cellular affinity*

【亲近】be close to; be friendly with: ~的朋友 *a bosom friend*

【亲眷】one's relatives or one's family members

【亲口】(speak) personally:他们听他们的经理~讲的。*They heard from her manager's lips.*

【亲历】personal experience: experience personally

【亲邻】relatives and neighbours

【亲临】come in person; make personal experience: ~指导 *be present and give guidance*

【亲密】close; intimate; near and dear:他的~家庭 *his immediate family* /我是她最~的朋友。*I am one of the nearest and dearest friends.*

【亲昵】intimate; attached

【亲朋】relatives and friends; relatives and old acquaintances

【亲戚】relative:串~ *pay a call on a relatives*

【亲切】cordial; kind; warm; close: ~的问候 *a cordial greeting* / ~的话语 *a kind word*

【亲热】affectionate; intimate; loving; warmhearted:他给了她一个~的拥抱。*He gave her a warmhearted embrace.*

【亲如手足】close as brothers; dear to each other as brothers

【亲善】goodwill (between countries); friendship

【亲上加亲】marry within the clan; cement old ties by marriage

【亲身】personal; firsthand:

【亲身经历】personal experience: experience personally

【亲生】① be one's own child:孩子的~父母 *the natural parents of the child* ② one's own children or parents : ~父母 *one's own parents*

【亲事】marriage

【亲手】with one's own hands; personally

【亲疏】close and distant:无论~贵贱,一视同仁。*Treat everyone close or distant, rich or poor equally without discrimination.*

【亲属】relatives; kinsfolk:远房~ *remote relative*

【亲王】royal highness:他的哥哥死后,他被封为威尔士~。*After her elder brother died, he was created Prince of Wales.*

【亲吻】kiss:她满眼泪水~了她的孩子。*She kissed her child with tears.*

【亲狎】be improperly intimate with; be intimate and improperly familiar with

【亲信】① close and trustful ② [贬] trusted follower

【亲兄弟】blood brother

【亲眼】personally; with one's own eyes

【亲友】kith and kin; relatives and friends; one's acquaintances and relatives:来送行的～跟在开动的大客车后面叫喊。*The relatives and friends who came to say good-bye called after the departing coach.*
【亲缘】consanguinity; affinity; relationship by blood or by a common ancestor
【亲自】in body; in the flesh; myself; oneself personally; in person: ～动手 *do sth oneself* /王老师～向我母亲转达了他母亲的问候。*Mr. Wang personally conveyed his mother's message to my mother.*
【亲嘴】kiss

衾 ① quilt ② pall
【衾冷枕寒】one's quilt and pillow are cold — when one's beloved is far away he feel very lonely

qín

芹 celery
【芹菜】【植】celery

秦 ① state of Qin (897-221 BC) ② the Qin Dynasty (221-206 BC) ③ another name for modern Shanxi Province ④ (Qín) a surname
【秦川】another name for the Shanxi plain
【秦晋之好】an amity between Qin and Jin (sealed by a marriage alliance between the two royal houses) — an alliance between the two families by marriage
【秦镜高悬】nothing can escape the discerning eyes of the presiding judge
【秦岭】Qinling Mountains
【秦楼楚馆】[旧] quarters of pleasure; courtesans' quarters; brothel
【秦腔】Shanxi Opera

琴 ① Qin, one kind of seven-stringed plucked instrument in some ways similar to the zither ② musical instrument:小提～ *violin* /风～ *organ* /口～ *mouth organ; harmonica* /竖～ *harp*
【琴弓】bow
【琴键】key:钢琴～ the keys of a piano
【琴棋书画】(talent for) lute-playing, chess, calligraphy and painting-all artistic accomplishments
【琴瑟不调】conjugal disharmony; discord between husband and wife; marital disorder
【琴瑟和谐】matrimonial harmony; conjugal bliss; be on friendly terms
【琴师】stringed instrument player; stringed instrumentalist
【琴弦】string (of a musical instrument):小提琴有～。*A violin has strings.*

禽 birds; fowl:飞～ *flying birds* /家～ *fowl; poultry* /家～饲养场 *poultry farm* /珍～ *rare bird* /家～罐头 *canned poultry* /～兽之人 *impudent and wicked person*
【禽流感】bird flu
【禽龙】【考】iguanodon
【禽鸟】birds
【禽舍】artificial bird's nest
【禽兽】birds and beasts

勤 ① diligent; assiduous; toilsome; industrious: ～劳 *hardworking* /殷～ *solicitous* /他哥哥正～奋学习物理。*His brother is assiduous in the study of physics.* ② frequently often; regularly: ～理发 *have your hair cut regularly* ③ attendance:值～ *the line of duty; be on duty*
【勤奋】diligent; industrious; untiring: ～工作 *work assiduously* /学习～ *be diligent in one's studies* /这女孩比任何人都～。*The girl is more diligent than anybody else.* /她虽并不聪明,却很～,所以考试常常取得好成绩。*Though she is not clever, she is a diligent worker and has often done well in the examinations.*
【勤工俭学】work-study programme; part-work and part-study system
【勤俭】hardworking and thrifty (or frugal): ～办学 *run a school industriously and thriftily* /我们要～建国。*We should build up our country through thrifty and hard work.* /在持家方面她很～。*She is industrious and thrifty in running her household.*
【勤恳】diligent and conscientious: ～的工人 *a conscientious worker*
【勤苦】hardworking; hard work and plain living
【勤快】diligent; hardworking:这里的人民很～。*The people here are very industrious.*
【勤劳】diligent; assiduous; toilsome; industrious: ～工作 *toil at a task* /他们都是靠～致富的。*All of them get wealthy through their honest labour.*
【勤密】frequently; constantly:我认识她,但往来不～。*I know her, but I don't frequent her much.*
【勤勉】diligent; assiduous:在工作上他是一位～的人。*He is a diligent person in his work.* /这个工人是一个～的模范。*This worker is a model of diligence.*
【勤能补拙】diligence is the means by which a person makes up for his dullness
【勤朴】industrious and plain; industrious and simple: ～的人 *a industrious and plain person*
【勤勤】earnest; attentive; considerate; sincere
【勤勤恳恳】zealously and earnestly:在公司里他是一个～的人。*He is zealously and earnestly in his firm.*
【勤务】① service; duty ②【军】odd-jobman; orderly
【勤务兵】【军】orderly
【勤务员】① odd-jobman; orderly ② servant:政治官员应当是人民的～。*An officer in the government should be a servant of the people.*
【勤学苦练】study and train hard; study diligently and train hard
【勤杂】① odd jobs:在公司,她仅干一些～工作,所以她什么也不知道。*She only did odd jobs in the company, so she didn't know anything.* ② odd jobman: ～工 *odd jobman; handyman*

【勤政】a diligent government：～廉政 *be diligent and honest in one's duty*

qǐn

寝 ①sleep：废～忘食 *forget food and sleep* ② bedroom：就～ *go to bed* /寿终正～ *die in one's bed*; *pass away* ③［书］stop; end ④ coffin chamber; tomb：陵～ *mausoleum*

【寝宫】① the royal couple sleeping palace ② chamber containing the coffins of a royal couple in their mausoleum

【寝具】bedding

【寝食不安】feel uneasy even when eating and sleeping; unable to sleep and eat peacefully

【寝室】bedroom; dormitory：他和他哥哥住在同一个～。*He and his elder brother live in the same dormitory.*

qìn

沁 (of fragrance etc.) ooze; seep; exude：玫瑰的芳香～鼻。*The aroma of roses assailed my nostrils.*

【沁人心脾】seep into the heart; be refreshing; mental refreshing：我喝了一杯～的饮料。*I had a refreshing drink.* /这阵微风～。*This breeze is very refreshing.* /茉莉花香～。*The aroma of jasmine seeps into my heart.*

【沁润】(of fragrance, liquid) soak into; permeate; seep into; soak into：中国的历史神话～着我们的思想。*Our thinking is permeated by Chinese historical myths.* /雨水已～到土里去了。*The rain has soaked into the ground.*

qīng

青 ① blue; green：～山绿水 *green hill*; *blue mountain* ② black：～黛 *dark blue* ③ green grass; young crop：踏～ *walk on green lea (or meadow) — go for a walk in the country in spring* ④ young (people)：～年 *lad*; *young people*; *youth* /年～ *juvenility juvenescence* ⑤ short for Qinghai Province

【青白】pale：吓得面色～ *be pale with fright* /这几天她脸色～。*She was off colour in these days; her face looked ashen in these days.*

【青布】black cloth

【青菜】① green vegetable; greens ② pakchoi; variety of Chinese cabbage

【青苍】① dark blue (or green)：～的树木 *dark blue trees* ②［书］sky

【青草】green grass

【青出于蓝】blue comes from the indigo plant but is bluer than the plant itself — surpass one's master or teacher in learning; the student surpasses the master

【青春】youth; youthfulness：～的活力 *youthful vigour* /把壮丽的～献给党 *dedicate one's splendid youth time to serving the Party* / ～的魅力 *the fascination* / ～痘 *acne* / ～偶像 *adolescent idol* /我们不能浪费～的好时光。*We should not waste the best youthful years in our life.*

【青春饭】job for young persons only：吃～ *hold a job that lasts only as long as a person's youth*

【青春期】puberty; adolescence：国家的～ *the adolescence of a nation*

【青瓷】celadon：北方～ *northern celadon*

【青葱】verdant; fresh and green：～的树木（草地、竹林）*the verdant trees (lawns, bamboo forest)*

【青翠】verdant; fresh green：～的山冈 *the fresh green hills* /春天的大草原，满目～。*The grassland is a vast verdant expanse in spring.*

【青豆】green soya bean

【青肥】green manure

【青工】young worker

【青光眼】【医】glaucoma：急性～ *acute glaucoma* / 恶性～ *malignant glaucoma*

【青果】Chinese olive

【青海】Qinghai (a province in west China)

【青红皂白】right and wrong; black and white

【青黄不接】when the new crop is still in blade and the old one is all consumed — temporary shortage; food shortage between two harvest

【青灰】greenish lime

【青椒】green pepper：奶奶在我们家的后院里种了好多～。*In our backyard, my grandma planted a lot of green peppers.*

【青筋】blue veins：他的脸上暴起了～。*Blue veins are standing out on his face.*

【青稞】highland barley：～酒 *barley beer*

【青睐】favour; good graces：赢得某人的～ *win sb's favour* /博得某人的～ *get into sb good graces*

【青龙】① black dragon; collective name of the seven eastern constellations of the twenty-eight constellations ②【宗】the Orient God

【青楼】brothel; a house of prostitution

【青庐】black cloth tent (set up for wedding)

【青梅】green plum

【青梅竹马】green plum and bamboo house-a man and a woman who had an innocent affection for each other in childhood; both a girl and a boy playing innocently together; be innocent playmates in their childhood

【青霉素】penicillin

【青面獠牙】with green face and ferocious fangs — frightening in appearance; with green face and long teeth

【青苗】young crops; green short of grain

【青年】youth; young people：～学生 *young student*; *student youth* / ～教师 *young teacher* / ～工人 *young worker* / ～专家 *young specialist* / ～一代 *the young generation* / ～节 *Youth Day*

【青鸟】(of ancient mythology) blue bird (messenger bird for the mother goodness)

【青色】cyan
【青纱帐】the green curtain of tall crops
【青山】green hill; blue mountain:留得~在,不怕没柴烧。*As long as the Blue Mountains are there, a person need not worry about firewood.*
【青山不老,绿水长流】the green hills do not grow old, and the blue waters always remain
【青山绿水】green hills and blue waters-beautiful scenery; beautiful country scene
【青少年】young boys and girls; teen-agers; youngsters; callan; hobbledehoy: ~犯罪 *juvenile delinquency* / ~问题 *teenage problem* / ~俱乐部 *a club for teenagers*
【青史】annals of history; history:名垂~ *on the scroll of fame* / ~留名 *have one's good fame recorded in history; be crowned with eternal glory; go down in the annals of history*
【青丝】① black hair (of a woman):一缕~ *a thread of black hair* ② sliced preserved plum used as dressing on food
【青松】pine
【青蒜】garlic bolt; garlic leaves
【青苔】moss
【青天】① blue sky ② [旧] just-minded magistrate; the clear sky (a respectful sobriquet for an upright official):包~ *bao the Clear Sky; Bao, the Just-minded Magistrate* ③ as a symbol of justice
【青天白日】bright daylight
【青铜】bronze: ~时代 *the Bronze-Age* / ~像 *a statue in bronze* / ~器 *bronze ware* /铸造~ *cast bronze* /货币~ *coinage bronze* /钟~ *bell bronze*
【青蛙】frog: ~属于冷血动物。*Frogs belong to cold-blooded creatures.*
【青虾】freshwater shrimp
【青叶】leafiness
【青衣】① black cloth ② the role of an actress in Chinese Operas (the demure middle aged or young female character type)
【青蝇】greenbottle
【青油油】① dark green:麦地里是~的麦苗。*The wheat field is a stretch of dark green and lush.* ② raven: ~的头发 *raven tresses*
【青鱼】mackerel; black carp
【青云】high official position:平步~ *rapidly go up in the world; skyrocket* / ~之志 *high aspirations; lofty ideals; full of ambition* / ~直上 *rapidly advance in one's career*
【青贮】ensile; store fodder in a silo for preservation; silage

轻 ① light; of little weight:木头比铁棒~。*A wood is lighter than an iron bar.* ② small in number degree; simple; portable: ~武器 *light arm; small arm* /他的伤很~。*His wound is not at all serious.* ③ not important:任务~ *light load of task* /在这起事故中我们承担较~的责任。*We carried lighter responsibility in this accident.* ④ softly; gently: ~~地走进来 *come in very softly* / 小心~放。*Put down carefully.* ⑤ rattlebrained; rashly; impetuously: ~率从事 *act rashly* ⑥ regard sth as of not importance; belittle; make light of:重文~理 *regard liberal arts as superior to sciences* ⑦ skittish; flighty; frivolous:举止~佻 *flippant behaviour*
【轻便】① light; portable: ~铁路 *light railway* / ~机车 *light locomotive* / ~货车 *light-duty truck* / ~式 *portable type* /他只花了二百人民币就买了那台~电视机。*He only paid ¥200 for that portable television.* ② convenient and easy:这活儿干起来很~。*The work is easy to do.*
【轻薄】given to philandering; frivolous; giddy: ~的举动 *frivolous behaviour* /她是个~的女孩。*She is a giddy girl.* /他因为~妇女而受到惩罚。*He was punished for dally with a woman.*
【轻财】regard money lightly; despise wealth; belittle money: ~重义 *treasure friendship more than money; value friendship more than wealth; be big-hearted*
【轻车熟路】drive in a light carriage on a familiar road — do sth as facile as traveling along a familiar road in light carriage; do sth one knows well and can manage with easy
【轻淡】① mild; thin; dim; faint: ~的奶酪 *mild cheese* / ~的微笑 *a faint smile* ② casual; random; indifferent:对走私的~态度 *a casual attitude toward contraband*
【轻敌】underestimate the enemy; take the enemy lightly: ~意识 *consciousness to underestimate the enemy* /如果有~思想,你的损失会很惨重。*You will lose heavily if you take the opponent lightly.*
【轻度】lightly: ~污染 *lightly polluted* / ~感染 *lightly infection*
【轻而易举】sth is easy to do; easy to accomplish:她~地解决了我们的问题。*She took the easy way out of our problems.*
【轻风】light breeze
【轻拂】flick:微风~着我的脸。*The breeze is blowing on my face.* /他用毛巾~鞋上的灰尘。*He flicked the dust away from his shoes with a towel.*
【轻浮】giddy; skittish; flighty; frivolous: ~的举动 *frivolous behaviour* / ~的少女 *a flighty girl* /她的儿子生性~,什么事情都不认真对待。*Her son has a frivolous nature and won't take anything seriously.*
【轻工业】light industry
【轻轨】【交】light rail: ~铁路 *light railway* / 北京的~火车很方便。*The light rail train in Beijing is convenient.*
【轻核】【物】light nuclear
【轻缓】light and slow:他在公园~地散步。*He walks in the park with light leisurely steps.*
【轻混凝土】【建】lightweight concrete
【轻活】light work
【轻机关枪】light machine gun
【轻健】spry and light; brisk; nimble: ~的步伐 *nimble steps*
【轻捷】spry and light; springy; nimble:他的脚步很~。*His step was very springy.*
【轻金属】light metal

【轻举妄动】indiscretion; take reckless action; act impetuously; act rashly: 你不能~地对待这一问题。*You must not have the indiscretion to do this matter.*

【轻看】belittle; look down upon; underestimate

【轻口薄舌】speak impolitely; speak rudely; say nasty things about: ~的言语 *a nasty remark*

【轻快】① brisk; spry: 走路~的人 *a brisk walker* ② light; relaxed: ~的乐曲 *a lively tune*

【轻狂】extremely frivolous: ~的言辞 *extremely frivolous remark*

【轻量级】【体】lightweight: ~冠军 *the lightweight title.*

【轻慢】treat sb without proper respect; slight; treat sb rudely: 受到~ *suffer slights* / 你不应该~这位老人。*You should not treat the old man rudely.*

【轻描淡写】touch on lightly; mention casually; play down; adumbrate: 他~说出几本书的名字。*He mentioned casually a few books.*

【轻蔑】scornful; disdainful: ~的态度 *contemptuous air* / ~的脸色 *a contemptuous look* / ~的微笑 *a scornful smile* / ~的言辞 *scornful words*

【轻诺寡信】make promises easily but seldom keep them; be liberal with promises that one doesn't mean to keep them: 我们讨厌那些~的人。*We hate those persons who make promises easily but seldom keep them.*

【轻飘】① light; buoyant; fluffy: ~的羽毛 *buoyant feathers* / ~的雪花 *buoyant snowflakes* ② flighty; giddy: 她做事太~,不能照顾老人。*She is too flighty to take care of old persons.*

【轻飘飘】① light; buoyant: 雪花随风~地下落。*The snowflakes floated down on the wind.* ② nimble; agile; airy: ~的心情 *an airy mood* / ~的一跃 *a nimble leap*

【轻骑】light cavalry

【轻巧】① light and handy; light and ingenious: 这辆轿车很~。*The car is light and ingenious.* ② agile; deft: ~的手指 *dexterous fingers* / ~的脚步 *nimble feet* ③ simple; easy: 不要说得太~。*You should not talk it too easy.*

【轻轻】lightly; gently: ~地拿住它。*Hold it gently.*

【轻取】win an easy victory; win hands down; beat easily: ~对手 *beat the opponent easily*

【轻柔】soft; gentle: ~的织物 *a soft fabric* / ~的微笑 *a soft smile* / ~的一瞥 *a soft glance*

【轻软】light and soft: ~的皮大衣 *a light and soft fur coat*

【轻纱】fine gauze

【轻伤】slight wound; slight injury; minor wound

【轻生】kill oneself; commit suicide

【轻声】① in a soft voice; softly: ~说话 *whisper; speak softly* ②【语】neutral tone; light tone

【轻视】despise; look down on; belittle: 以~的眼光看某人 *look at sb with scorn* / 不要~自己。*You should not belittle yourself.*

【轻手轻脚】gently; softly: 他~地走进教室内。*He walked into the classroom gently.*

【轻率】rash; hasty; thoughtless; indiscreet: ~的决定 *a hasty decision* / 他的女儿仓促~地结了婚。*His daughter rushed headlong into marriage.*

【轻爽】relaxed; comfortable: ~的心情 *a relaxed mood*

【轻水】【化】light water

【轻松】light; relaxed: ~的家务活 *a light household task*

【轻佻】frivolous; giddy; skittish; flippant: ~无理的言语 *flippant remarks* / ~的眼神 *skittish expression in one's eyes*

【轻微】light; trifling; trifling; negligible: ~的损失 *a trifling loss* / ~的代价 *a negligible cost* / ~的感冒 *a slight cold*

【轻武器】small arm; light arm

【轻信】readily believe; be credulous: 不要~他的谎言。*Give no credence to his falsehood.*

【轻型】light: ~飞机 *light aircraft* / ~卡车 *a light truck* / ~电影摄影机 *a light video camera* / ~坦克 *light tank*

【轻言细语】gentle voice; soft-spoken

【轻扬】sway lightly; float: 树叶在风中~。*The tree leaves swayed lightly in the wind.*

【轻易】① easily; readily; simple ② lightly; rashly: 不要~答应他。*You'd better not concent him rashly.*

【轻音乐】light music

【轻盈】① slim (or slender) and graceful; lithe; nimble: ~的动作 *lithe movements* ② lighthearted; melodious: ~的笑声 *a melodious smile* / ~的歌声 *a melodious song*

【轻油】light oil

【轻于鸿毛】lighter than a feather — said of one person whose death is of no consequence

【轻载】light load

【轻重】① weight: 称称才知道~。*Only weighing it and then we know its weight.* ② degree of intensity or seriousness; relative important: 我不知道他病情的~。*I don't know how serious his illness is.* ③ propriety: ~倒置 *put a trivial thing before the important; stress trifles and overlook matters of moment* / 他说话常常不知道~。*He often speaks bluntly having no sense of propriety.*

【轻重缓急】order of importance and urgency; in order of importance and urgency; order of propriety

【轻重量级】【体】light heavyweight

【轻舟】canoe; skiff; small boat

【轻装】① light packs: ~上阵 *go into battle with light packs; join in the struggle without any burdens* / ~前进 *go head with a light pack* ② light military equipments: ~部队 *a lightly equipped troop*

【轻装简从】travel with light baggage and few attendants; travel with light packs

【轻嘴薄舌】be acerbic; speak impolitely or rudely: ~的语调 *an acerbic tone*

【轻罪】【律】misdemeanor; minor crime (or offence): 有~的经历 *have the record of petty offense*

Q

氢 【化】hydrogen:氧化～ *hydrogen oxide* /过氧化～ *hydrogen peroxide* /硫化～ *hydrogen sulphide*

【氢弹】【军】hydrogen bomb

【氢化】【化】hydrogenation: ～物 *hydride* / ～钾 *potassium hydride* / ～霉 *hydrogenase*

【氢离子】hydrogen ion

【氢气】hydrogen

【氢气球】hydrogen balloon

【氢氰酸】【化】hydrocyanic acid

【氢燃料】hydrogen fuel: ～电池 *hydrogen fuel-cell*

【氢氧】【化】oxyhydrogen: ～化物 *hydroxide* / ～焰 *oxyhydrogen flame* / ～化铵 *ammonium hydroxide* / ～化钾 *arsonium hydroxide*; *potassa hydroxide*; *potassium hydroxide* / ～化钡 *barium hydroxide* /碱性～化物 *basic hydroxide* / ～化铁 *ferric hydroxide* / ～化镓 *gallic hydroxide* / ～化锂 *lithium hydroxide* / ～化镁 *magnesium hydroxide*

【氢氧基】【化】hydroxyl group

倾 ① incline; lean; careen; bend: ～向于某事 *incline to sth* /朝东～斜 *lean to the east* /身子向后～ *bend backward*; *lean backward* ② tendency; deviation:社交～向 *communicative tendency* /电离～向 *ionization tendency* /左～ *left-leaning*; *progressive* /左～冒险主义"*Left*" *adventurism* ③ collapse:大厦将～ *a great mansion on the point of collapse* /这堆木头～倒在了地板上。*The pile of woods toppled onto the floor.* ④ overture and pour out; dump; empty: ～倒垃圾 *dump wastes* ⑤ do one's best; do all one can; use up all one's resources: ～尽全力 *exert oneself to the utmost to do sth* ⑥ overwhelm:权～天下 *one's power overbear the entire country*

【倾侧】careen:将船～修理 *careen a ship for repairing*

【倾巢】(of the enemy etc.) turn out in full force; sally forth in full force:敌人～而出。*The enemies turned out in full strength.*

【倾城】① the whole city; from all over the town: ～而出,庆贺新年。*The whole city turned out to felicitating the New Year.* ② exceedingly beautiful

【倾城倾国】(of a woman) lovely enough to cause the fall of a city or a state; extremely beautiful; devastatingly beautiful; exceedingly beautiful

【倾倒】(qīngdǎo) ① fall over; collapse; topple over:无数的房屋在暴风雨中～了。*Numerous houses collapsed during the storm.* /这船在暴风雨中～了。*The ship heeled over in the storm.* ② admire; adore:人人都为他那绝妙的幽默感而～。*Everybody admires him for his fine sense of humour.*

【倾倒】(qīngdao) empty; dump; pure out:他把箱子里的书都～在地板上。*He emptied the case of all books onto the floor.*

【倾耳】listen carefully; listen attentively; prick up one's ears: ～细听 *prick up one's ears and listen attentively*

【倾覆】upset; subvert; overturn; topple; overthrow: ～政权 *overturn a regime*

【倾家荡产】lose a family fortune; be clean broke; dissipate one's fortune; become homeless and bankrupt:吸毒使他～。*He lost all his family fortune in taking addictive drugs.* /我的家庭被那场官司搞得～。*My family was ruined by that law case.*

【倾角】①【物】dip ②【数】inclination ③【地】dip angle

【倾慕】fascinate; adore; have a strong admiration:我们～他事业有成。*We admire him for his success in business.*

【倾囊相助】empty one's purse to help sb; give generously to help sb

【倾盆大雨】waterspout; torrential rain; downpour:他们在回家的路上遇上了～。*They were caught in a torrential rain on the way going home.*

【倾洒】(of snow, tear, blood etc.) pour down; pour forth; fall down in great quantity:泪水从她眼中～出来。*Tears poured down from her eyes.*

【倾诉】pour out (one's hearts, troubles, grievances, etc.); unload:她向她的丈夫～了心里的委屈。*She poured out her chagrins to her husband.*

【倾谈】heart-to-heart talk; talk heartily

【倾听】listen attentively to: listen carefully to: ～选民的意见 *listen attentively to the views of the electorate*

【倾吐】say what is on one's mind without reservation; vent; pour: ～某人内心的想法 *poured out one's inner thoughts* / ～烦恼 *unburden oneself of one's annoyances* / ～衷肠 *breathing out one's soul*

【倾向】① tendency; trend; inclination; deviation:水质的碱性～ *the alkaline inclination of the water* /氧化～ *oxidation tendency* /政治～ *political inclination* ② be incline to; prefer :这两套衣服你～于哪一套? *Which of these two dresses do you prefer?*

【倾向性】tendentiousness; bias:对中期选举有～的报道 *a tendentious account of the medium-term elections*

【倾销】dump:向别国～商品 *dump goods into other countries* / ～价格 *dumping price*

【倾斜】① tilt; incline; slope; slant: ～的车道 *a sloping driveway* / ～的屋顶 *a roof that slopes* ② give preferential treatment; tilt in favour of: ～政策 *preferential policy*; *affirmative policy* /国家的一些政策向欠发达地区～。*The national policy inclines in favour of the undeveloped regions.*

【倾斜度】obliquity; gradient

【倾泻】come down in torrents; pour down:大雨～而下。*It's pouring down.*

【倾泄】drop down in torrents; pour down; gush out:水从消防龙头中～而出。*Water gushed out from a hydrant.*

【倾卸】tip; dump out: ～装载的石头 *dumped out the load of stones*

【倾心】① admire wholeheartedly; adore ② cordial;

sincere; do sth with all one's heart: ~支持这项计划 *wholeheartedly support the scheme* / ~交谈 *heart-to-heart talk* /一见~ *fall in love at first sight*

【倾轧】discord; engage in factional strife: 互相~ *conflict with each other* /一项结束党派~的新措施。*A new measure intended to end party strife.*

【倾注】① pour down; pour into: 山洪~到了水库里。*The flood from the mountains poured into the reservoir.* ② concentrate on; throw (energy etc.) into: 把心血~到教育事业上 *throw one's energy into education*

卿 ① minister or high official in ancient times: ~相 *high court official and chief minister* ② a emperor's form of address for a court official ③ a term of endearment used between husband and wife ④ (Qīng) a surname

【卿卿我我】(of lovers) bill and coo

清 1① unmixed; clear; pure: ~澈的水 *clear water* ② quiet; silent: ~静寂静夜晚 *the still of the night* / ~静的生活 *a quiet life* ③ distinct; clarify: 数不~ *countless*; *incomputable*; *innumerable*; *unnumbered*; *untold* /说不~ *sth hard to explain* ④ completely; thoroughly: 还~ *pay off* ⑤ settle; square; clear up; clean up: 付~债务 *to bring into balance*; *settle* /结~ *square a debt* / ~理书桌 *clean up the desk* ⑥ count: ~点一下这些橘子。*Count these oranges.*

清 2 ① Qing Dynasty (1644-1911) ② (Qīng) a surname

【清白】pure; clean; immaculate; innocent; stainless: ~的名声 *a stainless reputation* / ~无罪 *be innocent of a crime* /历史~ *have a clean curriculum vitae (or personal record)*

【清茶】① green tea ② tea served without refreshment

【清查】check: ~账目 *check accounts*

【清偿】liquidate; discharge; pay back; pay off; clear off: ~债务 *pay off one's duty* / ~贷款 *pay off a loan* / ~抵押款 *a mortgage* / ~租金 *pay off a reprise*

【清唱】sing opera arias without make up

【清澈】limpid; clear; transparent: ~的眼睛 *limpid eye* / ~的泉水 *clear conduit (or fountain)*

【清晨】morning

【清除】clear away; eliminate; get rid of; clean up; remove: ~污迹 *remove a stain* / ~路障 *remove road-block* / ~杂草 *eliminate weeds* / ~垃圾 *cleaned up the trash*

【清楚】① understand; grasp: 我不~你的话。*I don't understand you.* /我~你的意思。*I grasp your meaning.* ② clear; explicit: ~的陈述 *explicit statement* /字迹~ *a clear handwriting* /发音~ *a clear pronunciation* /月球上的地球阴影相当~。*The shadow of the earth on the moon is quite distinct.* /他在会议上讲话响亮~。*He spoke loud and clearly in the conference.* ③ be aware; know: 每个学生都~学习的重要性。*Every student is aware of the importance of study.* /我~他的历史. *I am aware of his past.*

【清纯】pretty and pure; fresh and pure

【清醇】mellow and pure (in taste or smell): ~的葡萄酒 *the sherry savour mellow and pure*

【清脆】clear and melodious: ~的歌声 *clear and melodious singing* / ~的嗓音 *a melodious voice* /百灵~的歌声 *the melodious song of a laverock*

【清单】detailed list; catalogue; inventory: 开列~ *make an inventory*

【清淡】① light; plain; delicate: ~的咖啡 *weak coffee* / ~的香气 *delicate fragrance* ② (of food) light; not greasy: ~的食物 *light food* / ~的饮料 *light drink* ③ (of business) dull; stagnant; slack: 市场上的生意十分~。*The market is extremely stagnant.*

【清党】purge within a political party; carry out a purge

【清道】① clean the street ② clean up the road (for a high official in imperil times)

【清点】check; make an inventory: ~账目 *check accounts* / ~战利品 *sort and count the booties* / ~手稿的页数 *count the page numbers of a manuscript*

【清炖】boil in clear soup with soy sauce; stew meat without seasoning: ~鸡 *stew chicken without seasoning*

【清风】cool breeze; soothing breeze: ~徐来 *A refreshing breeze is blowing slowly.*

【清福】an easy and carefree life; the happiness of a leisurely: 享~ *enjoy an easy and carefree life*

【清高】(of intellectuals) aloof from politics and material pursuits; morally lofty; morally upright: 自命~ *pretend to keep aloof from petty politics and material pursuits*

【清官】honest and upright official; respectable and morally lofty official

【清官难断家务事】even and honest and upright judge finds it difficult to settle a family quarrels

【清规】monastic rules for Buddhists

【清规戒律】① taboos and commandments; regulations, both taboos and commandments for Taoists and Buddhists ② (rigid) convention; restrictions and fetters: 打破~ *break away from rigid rules and conventions*

【清寒】① cold and clear: ~的月光 *cold and clear moon light* ② poor: ~的家庭 *a poor family*

【清寂】chilly and quiet; cold and silent

【清剿】clean up; suppress; eliminate: ~顽固分子 *clean up diehards* / ~顽匪 *suppress stubborn enemies*

【清教徒】Puritan: ~的习俗和教义 *Puritanism*

【清洁】clean: ~的空气 *clean air* / ~的饮用水 *clean drinking water* / ~的燃料 *a clean fuel* /一件~的衣服 *a clean dress* /一双~的手 *a pair of clean hands* /保持自身~ *keep oneself clean* / ~

工人 *sanitation worker*; *garbage collector*; (*street*) *cleaner* /车身~剂 *body cleaner* /每一个学生都应该注意~卫生。*Every student should pay attention to sanitation and hygiene.* /保持教室~整齐。*Keep the classroom clean and tide.* /狗是爱~的动物。*Dogs are cleanly animals.* /保持~是抵御疾病的防护措施。*Keeping clean is a safeguard against disease.*

【清结】① clear accounts; settle accounts; square accounts: ~去年的老账 *settle the old accounts of last year* ② bring to an end; wind up

【清净】① peace and quiet; clean and quiet:心境~ *keep one's heart peace and quiet* / ~的地方 *a clean and quiet place* ② clear; limpid; clean and pure: ~的湖水 *limpid lake*

【清静】quiet; serene:乡下很~。*There is quiet in the countryside.*

【清酒】①[旧] old wine as sacrificial offerings ② refresh and mellow alcoholic drink

【清口】tasty and refreshing:口香糖~。*Cachou is tasty and refreshing.*

【清朗】① resounding; loud and clear: ~的喊声 *a loud and clear shout* ② cool and bright: ~的天空 *a cool and bright sky* ③ quiet and clear: ~的夜晚 *a quiet and clear night*

【清冷】① chilly: ~的月光 *chilly moonlight* / ~的房间 *a chilly room* ② deserted; desolate; empty: ~的街道 *a deserted street* / ~的站台 *a deserted platform* / ~的会议室 *a deserted assembly room*

【清理】sort out; liquidate; put in order; clean off; clear: ~桌子 *clear the table* / ~文档 *sort out documents* / ~账目 *check up accounts* / ~债务 *clear up debts* /我们把办公室里所有的垃圾~掉吧。*Let's clear all this crap off the office.*

【清廉】free from corruption; honest and upright; fair and square:为官须~。*An official should be free from corruption.*

【清凉】cool and refreshing; cool and pleasant: ~的饮料 *cooling beverages* / ~油 *cooling ointment*; *essential balm*

【清亮】clear and resonant:那位歌手的嗓音~。*The singer has a clear and resonant voice.*

【清冽】cool; chilly: ~的秋风 *a chilly autumn wind*

【清明】① clear and bright:月光下月夜~。*The night is clear and bright under the moonlight.* ② Pure Brightness (the 5th solar term) ③ sober and calm:神志~ *be in full possession of one's faculties*; *be as cool as a cucumber* ④ (of government) clean and just; well ordered:政治~的国家 *a well ordered nation*

【清贫】(usu. of scholars in old times) be poor; be impoverished; badly off: ~的作家 *an impoverished writer* / ~的家庭 *a poor family*

【清漆】varnish:粘合~ *adhesive varnish* /气干~ *air drying varnish* /醇溶性~ *alcohol varnish*

【清泉】clear spring; limpid spring; cool spring

【清热】【中医】clearing away internal heat; remove inflammation: ~解毒 *relieve internal heat* / ~化痰 *clearing away internal heat and reduce phlegm* / ~法 *antipyretic method* / ~药 *antipyretic*

【清嗓】hawk

【清扫】broom; sweep; clean up: ~门廊 *broom the porch* / ~烟囱 *sweep a chimney* /把屋顶上的雪~除掉。*Swept snow from the roof.*

【清瘦】lean; thin; spare; slender

【清刷】clean with water; clean; scrub: ~地板 *scrub the floor*

【清爽】① fresh and cool; clean and fresh:空气~ *fresh and cool air* ② relieved; happy and relaxed:他们通过了考试,心里很~。*They felt greatly relieved when then passed the examination.* ③ [方] clean and tidy; neat: ~的衣服 *a suit of clean and tidy clothes* ④ [方] light and tasty:这碗汤很~。*The bowl of soup was light and tasty.*

【清水】clear water

【清水衙门】government office which is not very profitable; organization with inadequate funds and sandy benefits

【清算】① clear; square; settle: ~债务 *square a debt* / ~账目 *to square accounts* / ~ *clearing bank* / ~协定 *clearing argument* /请立刻~你们的欠账。*Please settle your accounts immediately.* ② expose and criticize (or condemn); liquidate: ~恶霸的罪行 *expose and punish the crimes of the bullies*

【清谈】idle talk; empty talk:别听他们无用的~。*Don't listen to their idle tales.*

【清汤】clear soup; light soup: ~寡水(*of a dish*) *watery and tasteless*

【清退】check and return: ~赃物 *check and return thievery*

【清婉】(of voice) clear and sweet: ~的歌声 *clear and sweet singing*

【清晰】distinct; clear:石头上~的纹理 *distinct grains on the stone* / ~的照片 *a clear photograph* /我的电视机图像不~。*I don't get a clear picture on my TV set.*

【清晰度】① articulation; clarity:理想传声~ *ideal articulation* /声音~ *sound clarity*

【清洗】① rinse; wash; clean:彻底~墙壁 *wash down the walls* ② purge; eliminate: ~所有的政治对手 *eliminated all political opposition*

【清闲】vacancy; quiet; at leisure:一段~时间 *a period of leisure*

【清香】delicate fragrance; faint scent:花的~ *the scent of flowers* /玫瑰的~ *the perfume of roses*

【清心】save worry: ~寡欲 *pure mind*; *be pure of heart and have few worldly desires*

【清新】① pure and fresh; fresh: ~的空气 *fresh air* ② delicate and pretty; tasteful: ~的图样 *a tasteful design*

【清醒】① sober; fresh; clear-hearted:保持~的头脑 *keep a cool heart* /这位艺术家喝酒喝得很多,但好像总是很~。*The artist drinks a lot but always seems sober.* ② regain consciousness: ~一下。*Come to your senses!*

【清秀】fine and delicate: ~的外表 *pretty and*

graceful appearance

【清雅】elegant; refined; graceful: ～的装饰 *elegant furnishings* /风格～ *a elegant style*

【清样】【印】final proof

【清一色】① (of mahjong) all of one suit ② monotone; uniform; homogeneous: 皮毛～的狗 *a dog with a monotone coat*

【清逸】new and graceful; fresh and delicate: ～笔法 a new and graceful technique of writing

【清音】① a folk art popular in Sichuan Province ②【语】unvoiced sound; voiceless sound

【清幽】(of a landscape) quiet and beautiful; quiet and deep: ～的山谷 *an enchanting and secluded hollow*

【清运】remove; clear and transport; clear: ～垃圾 *remove garbage*

【清早】early morning

【清账】① clear an account; pay off all one's debts: 我已经～了。*I have paid off all my debts.* ② cleared accounts; detailed accounts

【清真】① simple and unadorned; pure and simple ② Islamic; Muslim: ～寺 *mosque* / ～食品 *Muslim food* / ～饭店 *Muslim restaurant*

【清正】upright and just; honest and upright; clear and upright: 为官～ *be an clear and upright official*

蜻

【蜻蜓】【动】dragonfly

【蜻蜓点水】like a dragonfly skimming the surface of the water — touch on a problem lightly without going into it deeply: 学习一门技术不能～,要深入进去。*To study a technology, one should go into it deeply, not just have a superficial understanding.*

qíng

情

① feeling; affection; sentiment: 感～ *emotion; feeling* /热～ *enthusiastic* /热～欢迎 *glad hand* /热～洋溢 *ebullience* /含～脉脉 *exuding tenderness and love through eyes* /多～ *sentimental* /无～ *heartless; ruthless* ② love; passion: 爱～ *love between man and woman; personal affection; love* /恋～ *love affair* ③ intense sexual desire; sexual passion; lust: 色～ *eroticism* ④ kindness; favour: 求～ *ask for a favour* ⑤ situation; condition; circumstances: 病～ *patient's condition* /国～ *the state of a country; national conditions*

【情爱】① friendly feelings; love and care: 同学之间充满了～。*There are full of friendly feelings among the classmates.* ② (between man and woman) affection; love: ～甚笃 *in love with each other deeply*

【情报】information; intelligence: 国防～资料 *defense information* /经济～ *economic information* /飞行～ *flight information* /军事～ *military information* /业务～ *operational information* / ～员 *an intelligence agent* / ～局(处) *an information bureau; intelligence office* /电子～ *electronic intelligence* / ～系统 *intelligence channel* /搜集～ *collect intelligence* /科技～ *scientific and technological information* / ～网 *intelligence network* / ～学 *informatics; information science* /我们获得了敌方计划的秘密～。*We already had secret intelligence of the enemy's plans.*

【情不自禁】let oneself go; cannot help doing sth; be seized with a sudden impulse to: ～地大笑 *cannot refrain from laughing* / ～地哭起来 *cannot help crying*

【情操】sentiment: 高尚～ *noble sentiment* /审美～ *esthetic sentiment*

【情场】love affairs; the arena of love: ～失意 *be disappointed in love* / ～浪子 *womanizer; womanizer* / ～风波 *disturbance of love affairs*

【情痴】one infatuatedly in love; love maniac

【情敌】rival in love

【情调】sentiment; emotional appeal; taste; mood; interest: 有生活～的人 *a man of taste* /浪漫～ *romantic style* /欧洲～的建筑 *a building in European style* /他的房屋布置得非常有～。*His house is furnished in excellent taste.*

【情窦初开】(of a young girl) first awakening of love; first stirrings of love; first dawning of love

【情分】mutual affection: 朋友～ *friendship* /兄弟～ *brotherly love; fraternity*

【情夫】fancy man; lover: 他是她的～,她是他的情妇。*He is her lover; she is his mistress.*

【情妇】an illicit lover of a married man; mistress; amour

【情感】emotion; feeling: 强烈的～ *a strong feeling* /表达深厚的～ *expressed deep feeling* /宗教～ *religious feelings* /爱,恨,悲伤都是一个人的～。*Love, hatred, and grief are emotion of a person.*

【情歌】love song

【情海】deep feeling of love; deep love

【情话】① lovers' prattle; sweet nothings: 喁喁～ *whispered sweet nothings* ②［书］*intimate words; heart-to-heart talk*

【情怀】feelings; sentiments: 快乐的～ *feelings of joy* /浪漫～ *romantic feelings*

【情节】① plot; scenario: 这部小说有许多吸引人的～。*The novel had many exciting plots.* ② circumstances: ～严重 *a serious case* /还有一个重要～你没提到。*There is another important circumstance you have not mentioned.* ③ moral integrity: 高尚～ *noble moral integrity*

【情结】【心】complex; love knot; emotional ties: 自卑～ *the inferiority complex* /优越～ *the superiority complex* /阉割～ *castration complex*

【情景】scene; sight; spectacle; condition; circumstances: 一派繁荣～ *a scene of prosperity* / ～交融 *(of literary work) feeling and setting happily blended* /生日晚会的～太棒了。*The birthday party was out of sight.*

【情境】situation; circumstances

Q

【情况】① circumstances; situation; condition; case:在任何~下都不 *at no circumstances* /因为这种~ *under the circumstances* /有利的~ *advantageous circumstances* /这里的~未变。*The condition of affairs here remains unchanged.* ② military situation:摸清前线的~ *feel out the situation in front line*

【情郎】fancy man; lover; sweetheart

【情理】sense; reason:合乎~ *it stands to reason; stand to sense* /不合~ *out of all reason* /~难容 *incompatible with the accepted code of human conduct; absurd* /等三天是不合~的。*There's no sense in waiting for three days.*

【情侣】lovers; sweethearts:一对~ *a pair of lovers; two lovers*

【情面】feelings; sensibilities:不顾~ *disregard sb's feelings* /不讲~ *have no consideration for sb's feelings*

【情趣】temperament and interest: ~相投 *have similar temperaments and tastes; be temperamentally compatible* ② interest; appeal; delight: ~横生 *perfect decorum* /生活~ *life affection* /艺术~ *artistic appeal* /他的讲话~横生。*His speech is full of wit and humour.*

【情人】lover; sweetheart: ~节 *Saint Valentine's Day; Valentine's day* / ~眼里出西施。*Beauty is in the eye of beholder or in the eye of the lover, his beloved is a rare beauty.*

【情杀】murder for love

【情商】emotional intelligence quotient; emotion quotient (EQ)

【情深似海】love is as deep as the sea

【情诗】love poem

【情势】situation; circumstances: ~复杂 *The situation was complicated.*

【情书】love letter:他年轻时候写了好多~给他的妻子。*When he was young, he wrote many love letters to his wife.*

【情丝】lingering affection; tender feelings of love: ~万缕 *multitude of tender affection*

【情思】① affection; sentiment; goodwill:祖国~ *sentiments for one's mother land* ② mood; thought and feelings: ~萌动 *awakened affection*

【情死】die for love; commit suicide for love

【情态】state of affairs; spirit; mood:轻视的~ *an expression of scorn* /迷惑的~ *an embarrassed expression* /娇媚的~ *charming bearing sardonic expression*

【情态动词】【语】modal verb

【情同手足】with brotherly lover for each other

【情投意合】hit it off; be on complete agreement; find each other congenial; seeing eye to eye with each other

【情网】love net; snares of love; meshes of love:坠入~ *fall into love net*

【情文并茂】be superior in both content and language

【情形】condition; state of affairs; situation:经济~ *business situation* /实际~ *practical situation*

【情绪】① feeling; morale; mood:军队~高 *the high morale of the troops* /绝望的~ *a state of disrepair* / ~忽高忽低。*Emotion swells and subsides.* ② depression; moodiness:生日晚会将会帮助他改善抑郁的~。*A birthday party will help his depression.*

【情义】ties of friendship or comradeship; emotional attachment: ~无价 *invaluable friendship*

【情谊】friendly feelings (or sentiments):战斗~ *militant ties of friendship* /姐妹~ *sisterly affection* / ~深厚 *deep affection*

【情意】affection; friendly regards: ~绵绵 *unbroken friendly regards*

【情由】the hows and whys

【情有可原】pardonable; forgivable:这件事~。*It was excusable.*

【情欲】lust; carnal desire; sexual appetite; sexual passion

【情缘】(predestined) sentimental bond

【情愿】① aspiration; wish; be willing to:两相~。*Both are willing to.* /我~你能找到一个好职业。*I wish you would get a good job.* ② would rather; prefer: ~死也不投降。*Would rather die than surrender.*

【情韵】mood; taste; charm:她极有~,人人都喜欢她。*She had great charm, and everyone liked her.* /他为她的~所倾倒。*He fell victim to her charms.*

【情致】temperament and interest; taste; appeal

【情种】person of the sentimental type, especially the one who easily falls in love; an affectionate person

晴 fine; clear: ~朗天气 *fine weather*

【晴好】fine and beauty: ~的天气 *a fine and warm day*

【晴空】clear sky; cloudless sky: ~万里 *a clear and boundless sky; stretch of cloudless skies*

【晴朗】fine; bright; clear; sunny; shiny:一个~的日子 *a shiny day* /夜空~,星星都出来了。*The night was clear, and the stars were out.*

【晴天】fine day; sunny day

【晴天霹雳】a bolt from the blue; a lightning bolt:落榜的消息传来,犹如~。*The news of fail in civil examinations came as a bolt from the blue.*

【晴雨表】weatherglass; barometer:民意测验是市民情绪的~。*Opinion polls serve as a barometer of the citizens' mood.*

擎 hold up; lift up

【擎天柱】a man in a responsible position; pillar of state or society; mainstay

qǐng

苘

【苘麻】【植】Indian mallow

顷 1 ① unit of area equal to one hundred mu or 6.66 hectares:碧波万 ~ *a boundless expanse of blue*

顷 2 ① short while; moment; a little while:少 ~ *after a while* ② just; just now

【顷刻】in an instant; instantly:敌人的包围 ~ 被瓦解。*The encirclement of enemies collapsed instantly.*

请 ① request; ask; beg: ~ 求帮助 *a request for help* / ~ 你吃饭。*Ask you to dinner.* /她 ~ 求给点饮料。*She made a request for some drink.* /她 ~ 求我原谅她。*She begged me to forgive her.* ② invite; engage:邀 ~ 某人到我家 *invite sb to my house* / ~ 大夫 *send for a doctor* /聘 ~ 新秘书 *engage a new secretary* ③ please: ~ 来一杯水。*A cup of water, please.*

【请安】[旧] pay respects to elders; wish sb good health

【请便】do as you wish (or please); suit yourself; please yourself; please make yourself at home:你们现在坚持要走, ~ 吧。*If you insist to leave, you may do as you wish.*

【请吃】treat:下次该谁 ~ 饭? *Whose turn is it to treat next?*

【请调】ask for transferring; ask for a transfer (to a now job): ~ 申请 *application for a transfer* /他从陆军 ~ 到海军。*He has asked for a transfer from the army to the navy.*

【请功】ask the higher level to record one's meritorious deeds

【请假】ask for leave: ~ 一周 *ask for a week's leave* / ~ 一个月探亲 *ask for a month's leave going home to visit one's family* / ~ 条 *written request for leave (of absence)*

【请柬】invitation card

【请见】[书] ask to see sb; request an an audience; seek an interview with

【请教】ask for advice; ask sb's opinion; learn from; seek advice; consult:我想 ~ 您一件事。*I want to ask your opinion on this matter.*

【请君入瓮】one kindly step into the vat oneself — try what you devised against others; pay one in one's own coin

【请客】treat; play the host; entertain guests; give a dinner party; invite to dinner:这次由我 ~。*This is my treat.*

【请命】① plead on sb's behalf; beg to spare sb's life:为民 ~ *plead on people's behalf* ② [旧] ask (the higher authority) for instructions

【请求】ask; request; beg; demand; seek; entreat: ~ 一项借款 *to request a loan* /可怜的母亲 ~ 警察原谅她儿子。*The poor mother entreated the policeman to forgive her son.*

【请赏】ask (the leadership) for a reward

【请示】ask for instructions; request (or beg) instructions:向领导 ~ *ask the leadership for instructions*

【请帖】invitation:我们有六张参加这次聚会的 ~。*We had six invitations to the party.*

【请问】① please; excuse me: 你把那本字典给我好吗? *Will you please give me that wordbook?* ② should like to ask; one may ask

【请勿】please don't: ~ 吸烟! *No smoking.* / ~ 迟到。*Don't be late, please.* / ~ 随地吐痰。*No spitting.*

【请缨】[书] submit a request (or application) for a military assignment: ~ 杀敌 *volunteer for battle; submit a application for a battle assignment*

【请援】ask for aid (or support, assistance); send for reinforcement

【请愿】present a petition; petition; demand at public demonstration:为某事向某人 ~ *petition sb for sth*

【请愿书】petition:向某人提出 ~ *present a petition to sb*

【请战】ask for a battle assignment: ~ 书 *written application for a battle assignment*

【请罪】apologize; admit one's own error and ask for punishment:负荆 ~ *offer a humble apology*

qìng

庆 ① celebrate; congratulate:我们举行跳舞晚会 ~ 祝春节。*We celebrated the Spring Festival with a dance party.* ② an occasion for celebration:国 ~ *National Day* /厂 ~ *celebrations on the anniversary of the founding of a factory* ③ (Qìng) a surname

【庆典】celebration:举行开幕(闭幕) ~ *perform the opening (or closing) ceremony* /毕业 ~ *graduation ceremony* /举行 ~ *hold a celebration*

【庆贺】congratulation; celebration: ~ 胜利 *celebrate after the victory* /我向父亲 ~ 生日。*I congratulated my father on his birthday.*

【庆幸】rejoice:这孩子的痊愈使他母亲感到极为 ~。*The boy's recovery rejoiced his mother's heart.*

【庆祝】celebrate:我们 ~ 国庆节。*We celebrated our National Day.*

【庆祝会】celebration:同学们开了个 ~,最后以舞会的行式结束。*The students had a celebration, with a party to finish up with.*

亲

see also qīn

【亲家】① families related by marriage ② parent-in-law of sb's child: ~ 母 *mother-in-law of one's son or daughter* / ~ 公 *father-in-law of one's son or daughter*

磬 ① chime stone (an ancient percussion instrument made of stone or jade) ② Buddhist percussion instrument made of bronze and just like an alms bowl

罄 exhaust; use up:燃料告 ~。*The fuel is run out.* /报纸售 ~。*The newspapers were all sold out.*

【罄尽】be used up; exhausted; with nothing left

【罄竹难书】(of sins) too numerous (or many) to

record (or enumerate)

qióng

穷 ① poor; poverty-stricken; with little: 贫~的家庭 *money a poor family* ② limit; end: 无~尽的 *endless; exhaustless; inexhaustible; unending* ③ extremely; utterly: ~奢极侈 *extremely extravagant; extremely luxurious; extremely sumptuous* ④ thoroughly: ~追猛打 *vigorously (or hotly) pursue and fiercely maul*

【穷兵黩武】adopt a warlike policy; wage war frequently; use all armed might to indulge in aggressive wars; want only engage in military ventures

【穷光蛋】poor wretch; pauper

【穷极无聊】① be utterly bored; bored stiff ② absolutely senseless or absurd; disgusting: 他~的行为遭到众人的唾弃。*His behaviour disgusted everybody.*

【穷家富路】one should be thrifty at home but be amply provided while travelling

【穷尽】end; limit: 才智~ *at one's wit's end* / 财力~ *at the end of one's means*

【穷究】go into thoroughly; probe deeply into sth: ~谣言出处 *probe rumours to the bottom* / ~一件事 *probe a matter to the bottom*

【穷寇】hard-pressed enemy; tottering foe: ~勿追。*Don't press on a desperate enemy or never corner a defeated enemy.*

【穷苦】poverty-stricken; impoverished

【穷困】destitute; poor; poverty; be down and out; impoverished; miserable: ~的家庭 *a destitute family* / ~潦倒 *have no way out* / 他一生都过着~的生活。*He has lived in poverty all his life.*

【穷年累月】year after year; for years on end; for many years

【穷人】poor people; the poor; the destitute; the needy: 过~的生活 *live a life of the poor*

【穷日子】days of poverty

【穷山恶水】barren mountains and unruly (or untamed) rivers

【穷奢极欲】profuse; (live a life of) wanton extravagance; wallow in luxury: 这位艺术家过去~,结果现在穷了。*The artist was so profuse with his money that he is now needy.*

【穷酸】(of a scholar) poor and pedantic

【穷途】straitened; destitution; dead end; extreme poverty: ~潦倒 *crack up under the strain of poverty and sadness; at the end of sb's tether; desperate* / ~落魄 *no ways and means for living*

【穷途末路】at one's last gasp; be in an impasse; be (or stand) at bay; come to the end; dead end

【穷乡僻壤】remote, backward place; an area shut off from the outside world

【穷凶极恶】most barbarous; extremely violent and wicked; extremely vicious; utterly evil: 一个~的坏蛋 *a vicious rascal*

【穷则思变】poverty gives rise to a desire for change

【穷追不舍】go in hot pursuit; pursue rigorously

茕 [书] ① solitary; alone ② worried; dejected; sad

【茕茕】[书] all alone; lonely

【茕茕孑立】standing all alone

穹 [书] ① vault; dome; fornix ② sky: 苍~ *welkin; blue dome of the sky; the dome of the sky; the heavens*

【穹顶】dome; vault: 环形~ *annular vault*

【穹隆】① sky ② vault; arched roof

【穹庐】yurt; tent

【穹形】arched; vaulted; vaulted shape: 雨后彩虹在天上形成~。*A bright rainbow arched above after the rain.*

琼 ① fine jade; exquisite things ② short for Hainan Island

【琼浆】good wine; nectar: 品尝成功之~ *taste the nectar of success*

【琼楼玉宇】magnificent building; richly decorated jade palace

【琼脂】agar; agar-agar: 玉米粉~ *corn meal agar* / 卵蛋白~ *egg albumin agar* / 甘油~ *glycerin agar*

qīu

丘 ① hillock; mound: 沙~ *a sand dune* / 冰~ *ice mound* / 冻~ *frost mound* ② grave; a place of burial

【丘比特】Cupid, roman god of love

【丘陵】hills; mounds: 深海~ *abyssal hill* / 我爬上了那座~,又从另一面跑下来。*I climbed up the hill and ran down the other side.*

【丘脑】【生理】thalamus:

【丘疹】【医】papule

秋 ① autumn; fall: ~风 *autumn wind* / 晚~ *late autumn* / ~雨 *autumn rain* ② harvest time: 麦~ *wheat harvest* ③ year: 千~万代 *for thousands years; for ever; for all time* ④ a period of (troubled) time: 危难之~ *at the time of jeopardy; critical time for survival*

【秋播】autumn sowing; fall-sow

【秋波】bright and clear eyes (of a beautiful woman): 暗送~ *make eyes at somebody secretly; cast amorous glances; give the glad eye (to sb); exchange tender glances*

【秋分】the Autumnal Equinox (16th solar term)

【秋风扫落叶】like autumn wind sweeping away the fallen leaves — carry everything before one

【秋高气爽】fine autumn weather; balmy autumn day; high autumn and bracing weather; the clear and crisp autumn climate

【秋耕】【农】autumn ploughing

【秋灌】【农】autumn irrigation

【秋海棠】【植】begonia

【秋毫】newly-grown down; (of animal or bird) autumn hair: 明察~ *be perceptive of the slightest* /

之丰 tip of an autumn hair — sth so small that one can hardly see

【秋后蚂蚱】grasshopper at the end of autumn — nearing its end：日本鬼子像～，蹦跶不了几天了。*Like a grasshopper in late autumn, Japanese devils were on their last legs.*

【秋后算账】square accounts after the autumn harvest — wait until after a political movement is over to settle accounts with the leadership or the masses; bide one's time to clear the scores with sb

【秋景】① autumn scenery：欣赏不同的～ *enjoy the varied autumn scenery* ② autumn harvest：丰收的～ *abundant autumn harvests*

【秋老虎】the spell of hot weather after the Beginning of Autumn; old wives' summer

【秋凉】cool autumn days：我们～去旅游。*We'll have a journey in these cool autumn days.*

【秋粮】autumn grain crops

【秋令】① autumn ② autumn weather

【秋千】swing：这个女孩子坐在一根拴在树上的绳子上荡～。*The girl swung on the rope tied to a tree.*

【秋色】autumn scenery：她沉醉在这美丽的～中。*She indulged herself in the beautiful autumn scenery.*

【秋收】autumn harvest

【秋熟】autumn maturing; become ripe in autumn：～玉米 *autumn maturing corn*

【秋霜】① frost in autumn; autumn frost ② white hair; grey hair

【秋水】autumn waters; autumn waters-limpid eyes (of a woman)：望穿～ *looking forward to; wait with anxious*

【秋天】autumn：～树叶变黄。*Leaves turn yellow in autumn.*

【秋汛】autumn floods

【秋游】go on an outing in autumn

【秋庄稼】autumn crops

蚯

【蚯蚓】【动】earthworm

楸

【植】Chinese catalpa

qiú

囚

① imprison; jail：他被～禁了十年。*He was imprisoned for ten years.* /他被～禁了两年。*He was jailed for ten years.* ② prisoner; convict：～犯 *convict*

【囚车】prison van; prisoner's van; patrol wagon

【囚犯】jailbird; convict; prisoner：那些～曾计划逃跑。*The prisoners planned to escape.* /警察严密看守着～。*The policemen keep a close watch on the prisoners.*

【囚禁】imprison; put in jail; be sent to prison; cast sb into gaol; hold in captivity

【囚牢】prison; jail：～人数 *a jail population* / ～中的情况 *jail conditions*

【囚笼】prisoner's cage

【囚室】prison cell

【囚首垢面】with unkempt hair and dirty face：赶快整理一下你～的样子。*Please tidy your unkempt hair and dirty face in a hurry.*

【囚徒】convict; prisoner：～生产的物品 *convict goods* /过着～一样的生活 *live like convicts*

【囚衣】convict uniforms; prison garb

求

① beg; request; beseech; ask sb for sth earnestly and feelingly; entreat：应某人的请～ *at sb's request* /恳～他帮助 *begged him for help* /请～某人做某事 *beg sb to do sth* /恳～某人的恩赐 *beseech a person's favour* /有～于人 *have to look to others for help* /我～你们原谅。*I entreated your pardon.* ② strive for：力～准确 *strive for accuracy* / ～发展 *strive for further development* ③ demand：增加供给以满足需～ *supply should rise to meet demand.* ④ seek; try：～名 *seek fame* / ～助 *seek help*

【求爱】pay court to; woo; pay suit to：向漂亮的女子～ *pay court to a pretty woman*

【求成】hope for success：急于～ *be anxious for quick results; be impatient for success*

【求爹爹告奶奶】beg everywhere：你不用～，我可以帮助你。*I can help you, so you need's beg anywhere.*

【求告】entreat; supplicate; implore; beseech：苦苦～某人的怜悯 *piteously implore sb for mercy* / ～无门 *have nowhere to turn to for help*

【求根】【数】extract a root

【求购】offer to purchase; offer to buy

【求和】①【数】summation; find the sum ② sue for peace ③ (in a game) try to draw a match; try for a draw

【求婚】make an offer of marriage; propose; sue for a woman's hand：那位警察向她～，她接受了。*The policeman proposed to her, and she accepted.*

【求见】ask to see; beg for an audience; seek an audience; request an interview：他昨天去是～政府市长。*He went to the municipal government and asked to see the mayor yesterday.*

【求教】ask for advice; seek counsel：虚心～ *seek counsel with an open-mind* /昨天他到我家登门～。*Yesterday he came to my house in body to seek advice.*

【求解】(of mathematics) find the solution; solve a problem; seek solution of a question

【求借】ask for loan; ask sb to lend sth

【求救】cry for help; send (a single etc.) for help; ask sb to come to the rescue：～信号 *SOS (or GMDSS) signal; distress call (or signal)* /发出～信号 *signal an SOS; send a GMDSS*

【求偶】woo; seek a spouse; courtship

【求乞】beg：他们沿门～。*They begged from door to door.*

【求签】draw a lot before idols; draw a lot at a temple for an oracle

【求亲】seek a marriage alliance

【求情】intercede; plead; plead (or beg) for leniency; appeal to sb's mercy; ask for a favour; beg for mercy:母亲替女儿向其父亲~。*The mother interceded with the father for the daughter.* /你不要向我~告饶。*You need not beg for my leniency and mercy.*

【求全】① demand perfection ② try to round sth off:委曲~ *stoop to compromise*

【求全责备】criticize sb for falling to be perfect:我们不能对朋友~。*We shouldn't expect perfection of our friends.*

【求饶】beg for mercy; ask for pardon (or forgiveness)

【求人】ask sb for help: ~不如求自己 *better depend on oneself than ask for help from others; God helps those that help themselves; self-help is better than help from others*

【求神】pray to gods for blessing; seek God's protection

【求生】seek survival; seek for life: ~欲望 *survival wish; desire to live*

【求胜】seek victory; strive for victory: ~心切 *be too eager for success; be anxious to gain victory*

【求实】be realistic; be practical-mended: ~精神 *matter-of-fact attitude; realistic approach; down-to-earth approach*

【求索】explore; seek: ~真理 *seek a truth*

【求同存异】seek common ground while reserving differences

【求仙】① seek immortality; be in quest of immortality ② seek gods; pray to gods for blessing; seek God's protection

【求贤若渴】look for virtuous talent as if to quench one's thirst; eagerly seek after persons of worth and ability; seek talent eagerly

【求降】beg to surrender; beg to capitulate

【求学】① go to school; attend school; pursue one's studies:到海外~ *go to oversea to pursue one's studies* ② seek knowledge

【求医】see a doctor; seek medical advice; ask a doctor politely for a medical treatment

【求雨】pray for rain

【求援】request reinforcements; ask for assistance; ask for help

【求战】① seek battle ② ask to go into battle (action):士兵们~。*The soldiers were itching for the action.*

【求之不得】most welcome; more than one could wish for:对于年轻人来说这是一个~的机会。*It is a most welcome opportunity for young people.* /我真是~要到德国访问。*I'm only too glad to visit Germany.*

【求知】seek knowledge: ~欲 *an appetite for learning; thirst for knowledge*

【求值】【数】evaluation

【求职】apply for a job; look for a job:对于一个大学毕业生来说现在~很难。*Now it is very difficult for a graduate of a college to find a job.*

【求助】call for assistance; turn to sb for help; resort; seek help:她没有朋友可以~。*She has no friends to turn to.*

【求爱】pay court to

【求和】sue for peace; try to equalize the score; try for a draw

【求情】plead; ask sb for a favour:请代我向老师~。*Please plead to the teacher on my behalf.*

【求饶】beg for mercy

【求人】ask for help:她发誓说以后绝不~。*She swears that she will never ask for help later.*

【求学】study:他小的时候,不得不去外地~。*When he was a a child, he had to leave his hometown for studying.*

【求知】seek knowledge

泅 swim

【泅渡】swim across: ~黄河 *swim across the Yellow River*

【泅水】swim: ~过河 *float across the river*

酋 ① chief of a tribe ② chieftain:匪~ *bandit chief* /敌~ *enemy chieftain* /叛~必办。*The defector chief shall be punished without fail.*

【酋长】chief of a tribe; sheikh; emir: ~统辖的领地 *area of land ruled by a sheikh*

【酋长国】emirate; sheikhdom:阿拉伯联合~ *the United Arab Emirates (UAE)*

逑 [书] spouse; consort

球 ① sphere; globe:天~仪 *a celestial globe* /~面几何 *geometry of sphere* ② ball (in games):发~ *serve; take the service* /羽毛~ *badminton* /足~ *football* ③ anything shaped like a ball (or sphere):眼~ eye ball /一个钢~ *a steel ball* /一团火~ *a ball of flame* /一个毛线~ *a ball of wool* ④ the globe; the earth; world:地~人 *earthman*

【球操】【体】ball gymnastics

【球场】a ground (or court) for ball games; field:网~ *a tennis-court* /篮~ *a basketball court* /~明星 *a court star*

【球蛋白】globulin:抗体~ *antibody globulin* /血清~ *serum globulin*

【球队】team:足~ *a football team*

【球风】sportsmanship indicated in a ball game; spirit of competition as shown in ball games; (ball games) player's style: ~不正 *lack of sportsmanship*

【球技】skills in a ball game

【球菌】coccus

【球篮】basket

【球龄】ball game seniority; (of a player) length of playing a ball game:他的~超过十年。*His ball game seniority is over ten years.*

【球路】movements in a ball game; tactics in ball games

【球门】goal:守~ *keep goal*

【球迷】fan; ball game fan (or buff)

【球面】spherical surface: ~镜 *spherical mirror* /~透镜 *spherical lens* /~车床 *spherical turning lathe* / ~几何学 *spherical geometry* / ~投影 *stereographic projection* / ~应力 *spherical stress* / ~坐标 *spherical coordinate*

【球拍】racket; bat: ~拍 *tennis racket* /羽毛~ *badminton racket* /乒乓~ *table tennis bat*; *paddle* / 她用~打网球。*She played tennis with a bat.*

【球儿】① ball ② marbles: 打弹子~ *play marbles*

【球赛】match; ball game: 下周学校要举行~了。*Next week, out school will hold ball games.*

【球手】ball game player

【球台】billiard table; ping-pong table

【球坛】ball-playing circles (or world): ~新秀 *new ace player* / ~新手 *a new player*; *newcomer to the tournament* /足球~盛会 *a grand occasion for football*; *a grand gathering of football* /乒乓~的老将 *a veteran table tennis player*

【球体】sphere

【球童】caddie: 高尔夫~ *caddie*

【球网】net for ball game

【球鞋】gym shoes: 昨天她给她的儿子买了一双新~。*Yesterday, she bought a pair of gym shoes for her son.*

【球心】centre of a ball (or sphere)

【球星】ball game star; star player; ace player

【球形】spherical; globular

【球艺】ball game skills; skill in playing a ball game: ~拙劣 *maladroit skill in a ball game*

【球员】ballplayer

遒 [书] powerful; forceful; vigorous; strong and healthy

【遒劲】vigorous; powerful: ~的书法 *vigorous hand writing*

裘 [书] fur coat

【裘皮】fur: ~大衣 *a fur coat* / ~帽子 *fur hats* / ~里子 *a fur lining*

qū

区 ① area; zone; district; region: 城~ *urban district* /郊~ *suburb* /工业园~ *industrial park* /特~ *special zone* /经济特~ *special economic zone* ② distinguish; differentiate; classify ③ (as one kind administrative division) district; division: 广西壮族自治~ *the Guangxi Zhuang Autonomous Region*

【区别】① difference; distinction: 这两种解释之间存在很大~。*There is a very great difference between these two explanations.* ② differentiate; distinguish; discriminate: ~美丑 *distinguish between the beautiful and the hideous.* /我总是不能~这两种动物。*I cannot invariably make a distinction between these two kind animals.*

【区分】distinguish; differentiate: ~公鸡和母鸡 *differentiate a cock from a hen* / ~两个历史阶段 *delineate (or demarcate, mark off) two historical stages*

【区划】divide into districts: 行政~工作很重要。*The work of administrative divisions is very important*

【区徽】regional emblem: 澳门特别行政区的~ *emblem of the Macao Special Administrative Region*

【区间】part of the normal route of public transport (bus, etc.); lap; section of a route: ~车 *train or bus that travels only part of its normal route*; *suburban bus*

【区块】districts; area; block: 对渤海湾的两个~合作开发 *cooperative development of the two areas at the Bohai*

【区旗】regional flag

【区区】trifling; trivial; petty: ~小事,何足道哉。*Such a trifling thing is hardly worth mentioning.* / ~小利,不必牵挂。*Such a trifling interest is not worth considering.*

【区域】region; district; area: ~自治 *regional autonomy* / ~合作 *interregional cooperation* / ~贸易 *regional trade* / ~市场 *regional market*

【区域性】pertaining to a region; regional: ~组织 *regional organization* / ~联盟 *regional union* / ~事务 *an affair of regional significance*

曲 bent; curved; crooked: 弯~ *winding*; *curved* /弯~的道路 *a winding path* ② bend; flex; crook: ~肱而枕 *sleep with sb's head resting on one of his bent arm*; *bent sb's arm and rest his head on it* ③ wrong; unjustifiable; false; incorrect: 是非~直 *rights and wrongs* ④ leaven; yeast ⑤ (Qū) a surname

see also qǔ

【曲臂】【机】crank arm; crank radius

【曲别针】paper clip

【曲柄】【机】crank: ~销 *wrist pin*; *crank pin* / ~轴 *crank axle* / ~钻 *crank drill*

【曲尺】carpenter's square; zigzag rule

【曲拱】arched: ~石桥 *arched stone bridge*

【曲棍球】① field hockey ② hockey ball

【曲解】misinterpret (deliberately); distort; deliberately give a false meaning to (words etc.): 记者把教授的话全~了。*The reporter twisted everything the professor said.* /儿子~了妈妈的话。*The son distorted what his mother said.*

【曲径】winding path; devious trail: ~通幽 *a winding path leads to quiet seclusion*; *a winding path leading to the secluded spot*

【曲里拐弯】[口] winding; tortuous; zigzag: 公园里的小路~。*The path zigzags through.*

【曲线】①【数】curve ② sth esp. a female body, or part of it having the shape of a curve: ~板 *curve ruler* / ~图 *diagram (of curves)* / ~美 *graceful curve*

【曲意逢迎】go out of one's way to curry favour: 他常常对上司~。*He always goes out his way to ingratiate himself with his superiors.*

【曲折】① tortuous; winding; circuitous; full of twists and turns; long and indirect ② complications; intricacies; involved condition: 我们都无法理解~的情节。*All of us were unable to follow the intricacies of the plot the park.*

【曲率】【数】curvature：～计 *flexometer*

【曲面】curved surface；camber：内（外）～ *negative (positive) camber*

【曲奇饼】cookie；cooky

【曲曲弯弯】winding；meandering；full of twists and turns.

【曲射】【军】curved fire：～炮 *curved fire gun*

【曲室】secret room or chamber

【曲直】right and wrong：我们应该分清是非～。*We should make a distinction between right and wrong.*

【曲轴】【机】crankshaft；bent axle：～箱 *crankcase* / ～磨床 *crankshaft grinding machine*

【曲子】leaven；yeast

驱 ① drive (a car, horse etc.)：～车 *drive a car* / ～马 *ride on a horse* ② run quickly ③ expel；disperse；drive away；exorcise：～鬼（*of a wizard*）*exorcise spirits*

【驱策】① drive；whip on：他们的那个球进得漂亮，这极大地～了全队夺取胜利的勇气。*The magnificent goal greatly spurred the football team on to victory.* ② order people about；keep on telling sb to do things：她从小就爱～朋友。*Even as a girl she was always ordering her friends about.*

【驱车】drive；drive a car：～前往海边 *drive to the seaside*

【驱除】drive out；get rid of；repel；eliminate：～蚊子 *get rid of mosquitoes*

【驱动】【机】drive：～轮 *drive-wheel* / ～轴 *drive shaft*

【驱动器】driver：软盘～ *soft driver* /硬盘～ *hard (disc) driver* /激光～ *laser driver*

【驱赶】① drive (a car, horse etc.) ② drive away；brush away；expel：～牛群 *expel a flock of cattle*

【驱寒】dispel cold：生火～ *light a fire to keep warm*

【驱蛔灵】【药】piperazine citrate

【驱迫】drive；impel；compel；force；order about：受欲望的～，他走上了犯罪道路。*Driven by desire, he moved towards guilt.*

【驱遣】① force；compel；drive ②［书］banish；expel；deport；legally force (a foreigner, criminal, etc.) to leave a county；send sb away, especially out of the country, as a punishment：他被～，终生流放他乡。*He was banished from his motherland for life.* /他因非法入境而遭～。*He was convicted illegal entry and deported.*

【驱散】break up；scatter；disperse：警察～了抗议的人群。*The police scattered the protesting crowd.* /阳光～了浓雾。*The sun dispelled the dense fog.*

【驱使】① order about：他经常受别人～。*Other people frequently ordered him about.* ② prompt；urge：为欲望～ *be prompted by desire* /受雄心的～ *be spurred on by ambition*

【驱邪】exorcise evil spirits

【驱逐】drive out；expel；banish；oust：～出境 *deport*；*expel* /大使馆的两名随员将被～出境。*The two attaché's at the embassy will be expelled.*

【驱逐舰】【军】destroyer

【驱逐令】【律】order for ejectment；expulsion order

【驱走】drive out；get rid of；keep away

屈 ① bend；bow；crouch：～腿 *crook one's legs*；*bend one's legs* ② subdue；submit；yield：宁死不～ *rather die than submit* (*or surrender*)

【屈才】do sth unworthy of sb's talents；waste one's talents

【屈从】submit to；knuckle under to；yield

【屈打成招】confess to false charges under torture；torture someone in order to extort a confession

【屈服】subdue；submit；succumb；yield

【屈服强度】【物】yield strength

【屈光】【物】dioptric：～玻璃 *dioptric glass* / ～不正 *ametropia*

【屈驾】condescend to make the journey

【屈就】condescend to take a post offered

【屈居】be reconciled to a lower position than sb deserves；accept reluctantly a lower position than one deserves

【屈理】humiliation；dishonour

【屈死】be persecuted to death；be treated cruelly and driven to death

【屈膝】go down on one's knees；bend one's knees；submit

【屈心】have a guilty conscience；be conscience-stricken

【屈折语】【语】inflectional language

【屈指】count on one's fingers

【屈指可数】can be counted on one's fingers；very few；be rare

【屈尊】condescend；stoop；do sth that one regards as undignified or below one's level of importance

祛 dispel；remove；drive away；prevent

【祛除】dispel；get rid of；drive out；drive away：～心病 *dispel one's anxiety* / ～病魔 *drive out the demon of disease*

【祛风】【中医】dispel the wind；remove rheumatic pain or cold

【祛暑】ward off summer heat

【祛痰】facilitate expectoration；make expectoration easy：～剂 *solventia*；*expectorant*

【祛疑】［书］remove doubt；remove suspicion

蛆【动】maggot

【蛆病】myiasis

【蛆虫】① maggot ② a shameless person；scoundrel

躯 human body

【躯干】【生理】trunk；torso；body apart from the head, arms and legs

【躯壳】body (as opposed to soul)；outer form

【躯体】body；stature；soma

趋 ① hasten；rush；hurry along；move or act with speed：亦步亦～ *ape a person at every step*；*imitate one's every move* ② tend towards；head for：局势～于紧张 *The situation is tending towards tension.* /日～美好。*Get better with each passing day.* ③ (of a goose or snake) pop the

Q

head and bite people; snap at
【趋避】［书］avoid; dodge: ～道旁 *dodge to the roadside; get out of the way*
【趋奉】toady to; be obsequious: 他对老板百般～。*He was obsequious on his boss in every possible way.*
【趋附】ingratiate oneself with; pander to: ～权贵 *curry favour with powers*
【趋光性】【生】phototropism
【趋利】seek profit: 我们应该～避害，发展经济。*We should seek advantages and avoid disadvantages in developing the economy.*
【趋势】trend; tendency; inclination
【趋同】tend to converge; tend to be the same: ～论 *coherency theory*
【趋向】① lean towards; tend to ② trend; bent; direction
【趋向性】【生】taxis
【趋炎附势】curry favour with the powerful; play up to those in power
【趋之若鹜】go after sth like a flock of ducks; fall over each other to get sth

蛐
【蛐蛐儿】【动】cricket

黢 black; dark
【黢黑】pitch-black; pitch-dark

qú

渠 canal; ditch; channel; conduit
【渠道】① canal; irrigation ditch ② medium of communication; means; channel
【渠灌】canal irrigation
【渠水】canal

癯 ［书］thin; emaciated; made thin and weak

qǔ

曲 ① *qu*, a type of verse for singing originated in folk ballads, which emerged in the Southern Song and Jin Dynasties, and then became popular in the Yuan Dynasty ② song; tune or melody: 那首歌是去年风行一时的歌～。*That song was a hit last year.* ③ music (of a song): 作～ *compose music*
see also qū
【曲调】(of a song) tune; melody
【曲高和寡】highbrow songs find few singers; sth so highbrow that few persons can enjoy or understand
【曲剧】opera derived from ballad singing
【曲目】name of songs, melodies, or operas; repertoire
【曲牌】names of the tunes to which *qu*（曲）are composed
【曲谱】① the collection of tunes of *qu*（曲）② music score of Chinese operas
【曲式】【音】musical form
【曲坛】circle of *quyi*; performers
【曲线】curve: ～美 *curve of beauty*
【曲艺】folk art forms which include ballad singing, storytelling, comic dialogues, clapper talks, cross talks, etc.
【曲子】song; tune; melody

取 ① get; take; draw; fetch ② aim at; gain; seek ③ adopt; assume; select: 李梅经常把课本藏在学校里，而后来总是没能～走。*Li Mei would often hide books in the school and then failed to collect them.*
【取保】go bail for sb
【取材】draw materials
【取长补短】learn from other persons' strong points to offset one's own weaknesses; overcome one's own shortcomings by learn from other people's strong points
【取代】replace; substitute; supersede; supplant; take over; take one's place: 他对我怀恨在心，因为我～了他在办公室里的位置。*He bears a grudge against me because I took his place in the office.*
【取道】by way of; via: 她～上海去日本。*She went to Japan by way of Shanghai.*
【取得】get; gain; obtain; acquire; achieve
【取缔】outlaw; ban; prohibit
【取而代之】replace sb; supersede sb take the place of sb
【取经】① go on a pilgrimage to India for Buddhist scriptures ② learn from other persons' experience
【取景】find a view; find a scene (to pain, photograph, etc.): ～器 *viewfinder*
【取决】be decided by; be determined by; depend on: 走还是留～于你自己。*It depends on yourself whether go or stay.*
【取乐】enjoy oneself; amuse oneself; seek pleasure; find amusement: 周末她经常去酒吧～。*She often enjoys herself in bars on weekend.*
【取名】give a name; name; be named: 他们给宝贝儿子～大卫。*They'll call their baby David.*
【取闹】① kick up a row; make trouble; make a row; wrangle ② make fun of sb; amuse oneself at sb's expense; play pranks on
【取暖】warm oneself; keep warm (by fire, etc.): ～器 *heater* / ～设备 *heating facilities*
【取平】make even; make level; even up
【取齐】① make even; level ② assemble; gather; meet each other
【取巧】resort to wiles (for personal gain); resort to trickery to serve oneself (or avoid difficulties)
【取舍】decide which to accept and which not; accept or reject; make one's choice
【取胜】win victory; achieve success; score a success; triumph
【取向】orientation

【取消】cancel; call off; rescind; abolish
【取笑】ridicule; make fun of; laugh at; poke fun at
【取信】win the confidence of the others; win the trust of the others; win confidence or trust: ~于民 *gain the confidence of the people; win people's trust (or confidence)*
【取样】sampling; take a sample
【取悦】try to please; carry favour with; ingratiate oneself with sb: ~某人 *ingratiate oneself with sb*
【取证】collect evidence; gather evidence
【取之不尽,用之不竭】inexhaustible; unlimited
【取之于民,用之于民】what is taken from the people is used for the people's interests

娶 marry a woman: ~老婆 *take a wife* / ~亲 *(of a man) get married*
【娶妻】take a wife

龋
【龋齿】① tooth decay ② decayed tooth

qù

去[1] ① go; go to (a place); travel: 有~无回 *gone never to return; gone forever* /来也匆匆,~也匆匆。*Come in a hurry and go in a hurry too.* /明天三个人将会~。*Three people will go there tomorrow.* /她~飞机场接人了。*She has gone to the airport to meet somebody.* ② send there: 我已经给他~过信了。*I have sent him a letter.* /赶快给他~个电话。*Give him a call in a hurry.* ③ depart; leave: 一怒离~ *leave in anger* ④ get rid of; remove; peel; take out: 机器上的这个零件最好别~。*The part in the machine should not be removed.* /苹果~了皮再吃。*Peel the apple before you eat it.* /洗涤剂能~去衣服上的油渍。*Detergent can take out oil stains on the clothes.* ⑤ lose; forfeit: 逝~的青春 *one's lost youth* /失~同学们的尊重 *forfeit the esteem of one's classmates* /他们失~了一个好机会。*They lost a good opportunity.* ⑥ apart from (in space or time): 北京和郑州相~大约700公里。*Beijing and Zhengzhou are about 700 kilometres apart.* ⑦ pass away; die: 老奶奶昨天上午~了。*The old grandma was gone yesterday morning.*

去[2] ① used before or after a verb (to indicate an action or an intention of doing sth): 他~买东西了。*He has gone shopping.* /她到国外~了。*She has gone to oversea.* / ~叫大夫。*Go get a doctor.* /打乒乓球~。*Let's go and play ping-pong.* ② used between two verbal expressions, and a verb or a verbal structure to indicate the latter is the purpose of the former; in order to: 他回家~睡觉了。*He went home to sleep.* /她提着篮子买菜~了。*She took a basket to buy vegetables.*
【去病】cure or prevent a disease
【去臭】【化】deodorizing
【去处】① where about; place to go ② place; site; spot: 上海是购物的一个好~。*Shanghai is a good spot to go shopping.*
【去磁】deperm; demagnetize; degauss
【去垢剂】detergent
【去火】【中医】reduce internal heat; relive inflammation (or fever)
【去留】go or stay; leave or remain: 决定他们的~是一个比较困难的问题。*It is very difficult to decide whether they go or stay.*
【去路】passage; the way along which sb is going; outlet
【去年】last year: ~六月 *last June* / ~,她离开了北京去上海工作了。*She left Beijing and went to Shanghai for working last year.*
【去皮】① net weight: ~ 20吨 *twenty tons in net weight* ② remove peel or skin
【去声】【语】falling tone (the third of the four tones in classical Chinese pronunciation and the fourth tone in modern standard Chinese pronunciation)
【去世】die (of grown-up people); pass away; expire
【去势】(of animals) castrate; emasculate
【去暑】get rid of summer heat; drive away summer heat
【去岁】last year
【去伪存真】get rid of the fake and retain the genuine; discard the false and retain the true
【去污】decontamination: ~粉 *household cleanser; cleanser*
【去向】the direction in which sb (or sth) has gone; whereabouts
【去雄】【植】emasculate; castrate
【去职】no longer hold the post

趣 ① interest; amuse: 相映成~ *form a delightful contrast* ② interesting; amusing; diverting
【趣话】funny remarks
【趣事】interesting episode; amusing incident
【趣谈】interesting tale; funny remarks; amusing talk
【趣味】interest; delight; taste; liking
【趣闻】interesting hearsay; interesting news; interesting gossip; amusing anecdote

觑 [书] look; stare
【觑视】[书] look; gaze

quān

悛 [书] be penitent; repent

圈 ① ring; circle: 她生活在高级社交~里。*She lives in the highest circles of society.* /我们班把他排斥在我们的~外。*Our classmates shut him from our circle.* ② set; group ③ encircle; enclose; surround: 校长带引我们在学校里参观了一~。*The headmaster conducted us round the school.* ④ mark with a circle
see also juān; juàn

【圈点】① punctuate with periods or small (circles) ② mark words and phrases for special attention with dots (or small circles)
【圈梁】【建】girth
【圈套】snare; ploy; trap
【圈椅】round-backed armchair
【圈阅】draw a circle round one's name on a document submitted for approval to show that one has read it
【圈占】forcible occupy (land) be enclosing it; enclose and occupy; seize possession of (land, field, etc.)
【圈子】① ring; circle ② circle; group; clique

quán

权 ①[书] weigh; consider: ~其轻重 *weigh up a thing against another; weigh the relative importance (of more than one thing)* ② power; authority: 职~ *authority of office* /司法~ *judicial power* /掌~ *be in power* ③ right ④ advantageous position ⑤ flexible; expedient: 应急的~宜手段 *an expedient measure to meet an emergency* ⑥ tentatively; for the time being; provisionally
【权变】adaptability in tactics; flexibility in tactics; doing sth according to circumstances; tact
【权柄】authority; power
【权贵】influential officials; bigwigs; powers that be
【权衡轻重】weigh up one thing against another; weigh the relative importance of more than one thing
【权力】power: 应明智运用~。*Power should be used wisely.*
【权利】① authority; power; right: 他们的全部政治~必须得到保障。*Their full political rights must be safeguarded.* ② jurisdiction; extent of authority: ~斗争 *power struggle* / ~机构 *organ of power* / ~下放 *transfer (or delegate, or devolve) power to the lower levels*
【权迷心窍】obsessed with lust (intense desire) for power
【权谋】political trickery; tactics
【权能】powers and functions
【权钱交易】deal between power and money; corruption; corrupting or being corrupted
【权且】for the time being; tentatively; as a stopgap measure
【权势】power and position; power and influence: ~集团 *the establishment*
【权术】political trickery; the art of political manoeuvring; shifts in politics: 玩弄~ *play politics*
【权威】① authority; authoritativeness ② person of authority: ~人士 *authoritative sources (or person); authority*
【权位】power and position
【权限】limits of authority; jurisdiction; competence; terms of reference; power: 超过自己的~ *exceed one's powers*
【权要】influential officials
【权宜】expedient: ~之计 *expedient; makeshift device; stopgap*
【权益】rights and interests: 合法~ *legitimate rights and interests*
【权欲】the lust for power
【权责】① power and responsibility ② rights and duties
【权诈】trickery; craftiness; duplicity
【权杖】staff held as symbol of power; staff of authority as carried by political (or religious) leaders

全 ① complete ② make complete; keep intact; keep from damage (or harm) ③ whole; entire; full; all; total: 请把你在伦敦做的事情~讲给我听吧。*Please tell me about all your doings in London.* / ~城市都知道这件事。*The whole town knows of it.* ④ wholly; completely
【全部】whole; total; all; complete; entire: 她不得不说出事情的~真相。*She had to say out the full truth of the matter.* /债务必须~付清。*The debt must be paid in full.*
【全才】all-rounder; versatile mind
【全场】all those present; the whole audience; the entire house ② full-court; all-court
【全称】full name (of a thing); unabbreviated form
【全程】whole or entire journey; whole course
【全等】【数】congruent
【全等形】【数】congruent figures
【全都】every; without exception
【全额】full amount: ~保险 *full insurance*
【全反射】【物】total reflection
【全方位】comprehensive; omnidirectional; all-inclusive; all-round
【全副】full; complete; all: ~武装 *fully armed; in full battle array*
【全攻全守】【体】total play
【全国】the whole nation or country; nationwide; national; countrywide; all over the country; throughout the country: ~人民代表大会 *National People's Congress (NPC)* / ~性 *national; on a national; countrywide* / ~政协 *National Committee of the Chinese People's Political Consultative Conference (CPPCC)* /这辆卡车在~各地运送机器。*The truck conveyed machinery across the country.*
【全会】plenary meeting; plenum; plenary session: 十五届二中~ *the Second Plenary Session of the Fifteenth Central Committee of the Chinese Communist Party*
【全集】collected works; complete:《毛泽东~》*Collected Works of Mao Zedong*
【全家福】[方] ① a photograph of the whole family ② hotchpotch (an assortment of delicacies as a dish in Chinese dinner)
【全歼】annihilate; destroy completely; wipe out
【全景】panorama; complete or full view; whole scene
【全局】overall situation; general situation; the sit-

uation as a whole
【全军】① the whole or entire army ②［书］preserve military strength
【全力】with all one's strength; exert all one's strength; go all out: ~支持 *spare no effort to support; give all-out support*
【全力以赴】go all out; do one's utmost
【全麻】【医】general anaesthesia
【全貌】full view; complete picture:我们从这里可以看到大楼的~。*We can get a full view of the building from here.*
【全面】overall; general; comprehensive:总经理为改进公司的~管理做出的努力是卓有成效的。*The general manager's efforts to improve the comprehensive management in the company has been very effective.*
【全苗】【农】full-stand
【全民】whole or entire people; all the people: ~健身运动 *countrywide body-building campaign* / ~动员 *mobilization of the entire country; general mobilization* / ~党 *party of entire people* / ~公决 *referendum* / ~皆兵 *an entire nation in arms; every citizen a soldier*
【全民所有制】ownership by the whole people
【全名】full name (of a person, etc.)
【全能】【体】all-round
【全年】annual; yearly
【全盘】overall; whole; comprehensive; all
【全票】① full-price ticket ② all the votes; a unanimous vote
【全频道】all-channel
【全勤】regular or full attendance (without a single day off during a certain period): ~奖 the reward for full attendance
【全球】the whole world; the entire globe: ~定位系统 *global positioning system (GPS)* / ~通 *global system for mobile communications*
【全权】full powers, full authority; full responsibility; plenary power: ~代表 *plenipotentiary* / ~证书 *full powers*
【全然】wholly; completely; pure:这~是一次意外事故。*It was a pure accident.* /那个孩子太鲁莽了,对自己粗话可能引起的后果~不顾。*The little child is so rash that he is blind to the probable results of his rude words.*
【全日制】full time: ~学校 *a full time school*
【全色】panchromatic: ~胶片 *panchromatic film*
【全身】whole body; all over the body: ~发抖 *shiver or shake all over* / ~是汗 *sweat all over*
【全身麻醉】【医】general anaesthesia
【全神贯注】engrossed (or absorbed) in; preoccupied with; wrapped up in; with great concentration
【全胜】win all-round victory; complete victory; be completely triumphant
【全盛】flourishing; in full bloom; in the prime
【全食】【天】total eclipse:月~ *total lunar eclipse* / 日~ *total solar eclipse*
【全始全终】see sth through; stick it out to the very end; be completed
【全视图】general view; full view
【全数】total amount; whole sum
【全数字】all-digital
【全速】full speed; maximum speed; top speed; top gear: ~前进 *advance in top speed (or full speed)*
【全损】total loss
【全损险】【经】total loss only (TLO)
【全套】complete set: ~技术 *a complete set of technology*
【全体】all; total; entire: ~学生 *the whole students* / ~成员每人每周加薪100元。*A wage rises of ¥100 a week across the board.* /如果有人违反了制度,就把问题提交给~成员解决。*If someone breaks a rule, the problem goes before the whole group.*
【全天候】all-weather: ~机场 *all-weather airport* / ~飞机 *all-weather aircraft*
【全托】(put child in a) boarding nursery; total child-care
【全微分】【数】complete differential; total differential
【全文】full text: ~发表 *publish in full* /文章~如下。*The article is in full as follows.*
【全息】holographic: ~电影 *holographic film* / ~照相 *hologram* /激光~ *laser hologram*
【全线】① all fronts; the entire length; all along the line: ~反攻 *launch a counter-attack on all fronts* / ~打垮敌人 *put the enemy to rout all along the line* ② whole line:铁路~ *whole railway line* /公路~ *whole length of the road*
【全心全意】whole-heartedly; with all one's heart: ~为人民服务 *wholehearted service to the people*
【全新】entirely new; completely new; brand-new: ~的仪器 *brand-new instrument*
【全新世】【地】Recent Epoch; Holocene Epoch
【全休】a complete rest:我必须~一个月。*I must have a month's good rest.*
【全音】【音】whole tone
【全音符】【音】whole note; semibreve
【全优】excellent in all aspects
【全员】the entire staff; all members
【全责】all responsibility:我们对这起事故承担~。*We should bear all responsibility for the accident.*
【全知全能】omniscient and omnipotent
【全脂奶粉】whole milk powder
【全自动】full automation; fully automatic; fully automatic washing machine

诠［书］annotate; expound; provide a gloss
【诠释】annotate; give explanatory; glossary
【诠注】edit with notes and commentary; provide notes and commentary

荃 aromatic plant
【荃察】your esteemed approval (or understanding)

泉 ① spring:喷~ *fountain* /有一群孩子在公园的喷~中玩耍。*A group of children are playing in the fountain in the park.* ② mouth of a

spring ② ancient term for coin：～币 *ancient coin*
【泉华】【地】sinter
【泉瀑】fall formed by a flowing down spring
【泉水】spring; spring water：一股～从水管中喷出。*Spring water shot from the pipe.*
【泉眼】the mouth of a spring; spring
【泉涌】sth gush out like a fountain
【泉源】① fountainhead; wellspring; spring-head ② source：力量的～ *source of strength*

拳 ① fist ② boxing; pugilism ③ twist; curl; warp：～起胳膊 *bend one's arms*
【拳打脚踢】strike and kick; beat up
【拳击】boxing：李平在筹划这次～赛。*Li Ping is promoting this boxing match.*
【拳击手】boxer：技术熟练的～ *pugilism; a clean boxer*
【拳脚】① Chinese boxing ② fists and feet：他们～相加。*They came to blows.*
【拳曲】curl; twist; coil; bend
【拳拳】［书］sincere; earnest
【拳拳服膺】① always bear in one's mind ② have the sincere belief in; place implicit faith in
【拳师】pugilist; boxing coach
【拳术】Chinese boxing
【拳套】fixed series of both skills and tricks in Chinese boxing
【拳坛】boxing circle; boxing world
【拳头】fist：他以～回报他哥哥的好意。*He repaid his elder brother's kindness with blows.*
【拳头产品】competitive products; knockout products
【拳王】boxing champion; ace boxer; lord of the ring

痊 fully recover from an illness
【痊愈】be fully recovered; fully recover an illness：我希望她早日～。*I wish she will has a speedy recovered.*

蜷 coil; curl up
【蜷伏】curl up; huddle up
【蜷曲】coil; curl; twist
【蜷缩】curl up; roll up; huddle up
【蜷卧】lie with one's knees draw up

醛 【化】aldehyde
【醛聚合物】aldehyde polymer
【醛糖】aldose

鬈 ① curly; wavy (of hair) ② (of hair) lovely
【鬈曲】【纺】crimp; curl; crinkle

颧
【颧骨】cheek bone

quǎn

犬 dog
【犬齿】canine tooth
【犬科动物】canine
【犬马之劳】serve like the dog or horse：我一定效～。*I must offer my humble service.*
【犬儒】cynic
【犬牙】① canine tooth ② (of a dog) fang
【犬牙交错】jigsaw-like; jagged
【犬子】my son

quàn

劝 ① talk sb round by reasoning; advice; try to persuade ② encourage; urge：李老师极力～她学习再用功一些。*Teacher Li urged her to study more.*
【劝导】persuade; advice; exhort; induce
【劝告】advice, exhort; urge：他的～使我决定不再去北京学习了。*His advice determined me to go to Beijing for studying no more.*
【劝和】mediate; make peace; persuade two parties to become reconciled
【劝化】①【宗】urge persons to do good ② collect alms
【劝驾】urge sb to accept a post (or a invitation)
【劝架】try to reconcile quarrelling parties; mediate
【劝教】admonish (or advise seriously) and give guidance
【劝解】① help one to get over one's worries, etc.; mollify; allay ② mediate; make peace between
【劝诫】admonish; exhort
【劝酒】urge sb (usu. a guest) to drink (at a banquet)
【劝勉】advice (or admonish) and encourage
【劝募】solicit contributions by persuasion
【劝善】encourage persons to do good deeds
【劝说】persuade; advice; admonish：她极力～顾客买她的商品。*She pressed her clients to but her goods.*
【劝退】persuade on to quit
【劝慰】console; comfort; soothe：李平的母亲去世以后我尽力～她。*I tried to comfort Li Ping after her mother's death.*
【劝降】induce (the enemy) to capitulate
【劝学】exhort a person to study; encourage learning
【劝业场】［旧］bazaar
【劝诱】induce; bring round
【劝阻】advise one to refrain from; dissuade; advise sb not to

券 certificate; voucher; ticket

Q

quē

炔 【化】alkyne：乙～ *acetylene*

【炔烃】【化】alkyne

缺 ① be short of; be deficient in sth; lack ② absent ③ incomplete; with parts missing; imperfect ④ vacancy; unfilled position

【缺编】understaffed：这个工厂工人～。*The workers of the factory are understaffed.*

【缺档】in short supply; out of stock be understocked

【缺德】wicked; mean; vicious; rotten

【缺点】shortcoming; defect; weakness; failing; drawback：你唯一的～是不会关心别人。*Your only fault is that you can't care about others.*

【缺额】vacancy

【缺乏】be deficient in sth; be short of; be in want of; lack：这篇文章～实质性的内容。*The article is devoid of substantial matter.* /老师说他的文体～个性。*The teacher said that his style lacked distinction.*

【缺钙】【医】calcium deficiency; acalcerosis

【缺憾】imperfection; regrettable; imperfection; disappointment; regret

【缺货】be in short supply; be out of stock

【缺斤短两】give short weight (or measure)

【缺课】be absent from school (or class); miss a class：教师问起上周～的同学是否来了。*The teacher has called to know if the students who were absent for the week come here.*

【缺口】① breach; gap; shortfall：桌子边上有个～。*The table has a chipped edge.* ②【机】notch

【缺粮户】grain-deficient household

【缺漏】gaps and omissions

【缺门】gap (in a branch of learning, etc.)：这项发明填补了技术上的一个～。*This invention fills a gap in technology.*

【缺欠】① shortcoming; defect; drawback ② lack; be short of; be deficient in

【缺勤】absence from work (or duty)：因病～*be on sick leave; be absent on grounds of; illness* /～率 *absence rate*

【缺少】lack; be short of; be wanting in

【缺失】defect; flaw

【缺市】(of goods) in short supply

【缺损】① damage; worn ②【医】physiological defect; physiological deficiency

【缺铁性贫血】iron-deficiency anemia

【缺位】① (of a position) be vacant; fall vacant ② vacant position (or post); vacancy

【缺席】absent：～审判 *trial be default* /因故～ *be absent with an excuse*

【缺陷】defect drawback; flaw; shortcoming; blemish：助听器能帮助克服听力上的～。*The hearing aid helps to overcome the defects in hearing.*

【缺心眼儿】① Lack intelligence; simple-minded; be scatterbrained ② retarded; dull-witted

【缺氧】【医】oxygen deficiency; oxygen deficit

阙 ［书］fault; mistake; error：～疑 *leave a question open*
see also què

【阙如】［书］deficient; wanting

【阙文】missing parts (in a book)

qué

瘸 ［口］be lame; (walk) with a limb

【瘸腿】［口］lame

【瘸子】［口］cripple; a lame person

què

却[1] ① step back; fall back; retreat ② drive back; beat back ③ decline; reject; refuse ④ lose：忘～ *forget* /冷～ *cool off*

却[2] but; yet：当他最需要朋友的时候，他们～令他很失望。*His friends failed him when he most needed them.*

【却病】ward off or cure a disease; prevent or cure a disease：～延年 *ward off illness and prolong life*

【却步】step back (in fear or disgust); shrink：望而～ *shrink from*

【却敌】drive the enemy back; repulse the enemy

雀 sparrow

【雀斑】freckle：她的脸上有很多～。*Some freckles are on her face.*

【雀麦】【植】bromegrass; brome

【雀鹰】【动】sparrow hawk

【雀跃】jump for joy：欢呼～ *shout and jump for joy*

【雀躁】gain some kind of fame; enjoy loud fame：声名～一时 *enjoy transient or fleeting fame*

确 ① true; real; reliable; authentic 正～ *right; correct* ② rock-solid; firm; indeed

【确保】ensure; guarantee; make sure：没有什么东西能～永久的幸福。*Nothing can assure permanent happiness.*

【确定】① definite; certain ② define; determine; decide; fix; lay：～损失为200人民币 *lay the damage at ¥200*

【确乎不拔】firm and unshakable; unflinching; adamant

【确立】establish; set up

【确评】appropriate comment

【确切】① definite; appropriate; precise ② true; reliable; sure; dependable

【确认】confirm; affirm; authenticate：～书 *letter of confirmation*

【确实】① reliable; exact; sure ② really; indeed：这个学期，我们班的同学～在进步。*My classmates are really getting somewhere in this term.*

【确守】strictly abide by; faithfully abide by

【确数】exact figures; precise figure; exact number
【确信】① be certain; be convinced; firmly believe; be sure:我~今天晚上他会来。*I bet he will come here tonight.* ② reliable information
【确凿】conclusive; authentic; undeniable
【确诊】give (or make) a definite diagnosis; diagnosis
【确证】conclusively prove; prove positively

阙 ① watchtower on either side of a palace gate ② the imperial palace ③ stone carvings erected in front of a temple
see also quē

鹊 magpie:喜~ *magpie*
【鹊报】magpie's cry — good omen
【鹊巢鸠占】the magpie's nest is occupied by the turtledove — one person occupies another person's place, land, etc.
【鹊起】[书] ① act according to circumstances; seize an opportunity that rises; use one's discretion ② gain quick fame; spread
【鹊桥】Magpie Bridge — on the 7th of the 7th lunar month, the magpies spread their wings to form a bridge, thus enabling the lovers in heaven (Cowherd and weaving Girl) to meet that night: ~相会 *the reunion of lovers or long parted husband and wife*

榷 [书] discuss:商~ *discuss*

qūn

逡 [书] shrink from; yield; give in
【逡巡】[书] hesitate to move forward; not be bold enough to step ahead; hang back

qún

裙 ① skirt:短~ *short skirt* /绸~ *silk skirt* ② sth like skirt:墙~ *dado*
【裙钗】womenfolk
【裙带】① skirt belt ② connection through sb's female relatives; nepotism: ~风 *petticoat influence*; *nepotism* / ~关系 *netting through petticoat influence*
【裙礁】coral reef along the coast
【裙裤】pantskirt:她自己改变了她的~的样子。*She changed the hang of her pantskirt by herself.*
【裙子】skirt:这件~脏了,该洗一洗了。*This skirt is getting dirty; it needs washing.* /钉子钩住了她的~。*A nail caught her skirts.*

群 ① crowd group:人~ *crowd* /学校里的事故吸引了一大~学生。*The school accident drew a big crowd of students.* ② [量] group; herd; flock; swarm:一~孩子正在公园的喷泉中玩耍。*A group of children are playing in the fountain in the park.*
【群策群力】pool the wisdom and efforts of the people; make joint efforts
【群岛】archipelago; group of islands:我想知道是否日本在菲律宾~的北面。*I wonder if Japan lies to the north of Philippines.*
【群芳】beautiful and fragrant flowers; beautiful women:技压~ *outstanding skill* / ~之冠 *queen of flowers-reigning beauty*
【群峰】a chain of mountain peaks; connected mountain peaks: ~耸立 *a chain of mountain peaks towering into the sky*
【群婚】communal (marriage; group marriage)
【群集】gather; crowd together; assemble
【群居】living in groups; social; gregarious: ~动物 *social or gregarious animal* / ~昆虫 *social insect*
【群龙无首】a host of dragons without a head-a group without a leader
【群论】【数】group theory
【群落】①【生】community; colony ② building complex; group: 古建筑~ *a group of ancient buildings*
【群魔乱舞】a host of demons or monsters kinds running wild
【群殴】gang fight
【群起】all rise up (to do sth): ~而攻之 *all rise (or turn) against sb; rally together to attack sb*
【群青】【化】ultramarine
【群情】public sentiment; popular feelings; feelings of the masses: ~激奋 *every person was roused to action*
【群山】connected mountains
【群生植物】social plant
【群书】all kinds or categories of books:博览~ *be well read; be erudite*
【群体】①【生】colony ② collective; groups:科学家~ *groups of scientists* / ~取向 *group orientation* / ~行为 *group behavior*
【群威群胆】the mass heroism and spirit of daring
【群言堂】let everyone have his say; rule by the voice of the many:我们党提倡~。*Our party advocates"Letting every member have his say".*
【群英会】a gathering of heroes
【群众】① the masses; the people:由于街上~很多,车辆无法前进。*Because of the large crowd in the street the carriage was unable to pass.* ② non-Party ③ a member of the rank and file; grass roots: ~观点 *the mass viewpoint* / ~路线 *the mass line* / ~工作 *mass work* / ~运动 *mass movement; mass campaign* / ~团体 *non-governmental (or mass) organization* / ~组织 *mass (or non-government) organization*
【群众性】of a mass character: ~体育运动 *mass sports movement* / ~的技术革新运动正在该厂蓬勃开展。*The mass movement for technical innovation is vigorously forging ahead in the factory.*

Q

R

rán

然 ① accurate; correct; right: 我一再告诉他病了,他却不以为~。*I told him that he was ill, but he disagreed with me.* ② like that; so ③ [书] however; but; yet ④ used as an adjectival or adverbial suffix: 突~她大哭起来。*She cried loudly all of a sudden.*

【然而】but; yet; however: 虽然她赢了,~她并不高兴。*She won the game, but she was not glad.*

【然后】after that; afterwards; then: 你先把作业完成,~再出去玩。*You must finish your homework, and then get out to play.*

燃 ① burn; ignite; light ② set fire to; bank up: 夜间我们~起篝火做游戏。*At night we banked up the fire for fun.*

【燃点】① ignite; kindle; light ② ignition point; burning point; kindling point; kindling point

【燃料】fuel: ~电池 *fuel cell* / ~比 *fuel ratio* /这个~的问题亟待解决。*The problem of fuel presses for solution.*

【燃料库】fuel depot; fuel reservoir: 这个~的问题已经解决。*The problem of fuel depot has been solved.*

【燃眉之急】as pressing as a fire singeing one's eyebrows — one thing of great urgency; desperate need

【燃烧】① burn; kindle ② inflammation; combustion ~弹 *fire bomb; incendiary bomb* / ~点 *ignition point; burning point* / ~剂 *incendiary agent*

【燃瓶】incendiary bottle: ~热 *combustion heat* / ~烧值 *combustion value* / ~手榴弹 *incendiary grenade*

【燃油】fuel oil: ~炉 *fuel burner* / ~泵 *fuel pump*

rǎn

冉 (Rǎn) a surname

【冉冉】[书] ① (of tree branches, hair, etc.) hang down softly ② slowly; gradually: 一轮圆月~升起。*A full moon slowly rose.*

染 ① dye ② catch (a disease); acquire (a bad habit, etc.); stain; contaminate: 污~ *pollution* /感~ *infect*

【染病】contract or catch an illness; be infected with a disease

【染毒】【军】contaminate

【染发】dye the hair; tint one's hair

【染坊】dye-works; dyehouse

【染缸】dye vat; dye jigger

【染患】catch or contract an illness (or disease); be infected

【染剂】【化】dye

【染料】【化】dye; dyestuff

【染色】dyeing; colouring: ~剂 *colouring agent* / ~体 *chromosome* / ~质 *chromatin*

【染液】dye liquor

【染指】encroach upon (or on); reap a share of sth one is not entitled to

rāng

嚷

see also rǎng

【嚷嚷】① shout; make an uproar; make a noise; make a noise ② make public; make widely known: 不要再~这件事了。*Please don't breathe a word about this any more.* /这件事~出去后果不堪设想。*The consequences would be too ghastly to contemplate if the case is let out of the bag.*

ráng

瓤 ① pulp; flesh: 瓜~ *pulp of a melon* ② interior parts of sth

【瓤子】① pulp; flesh; pith ② filling

rǎng

壤 ① soil ② earth; ground ③ area; territory: 穷乡僻~ *a remote poverty-stricken place* /接~ *share a common border*

【壤地】[书] land

【壤土】①【农】loam ② territory

攘 [书] ① reject; resist; expel ② seize; snatch ③ push (or turn) up (one's sleeves) ④ trouble; disturb: 扰~ *hustle and baste; confusion*

【攘臂】[书] push (or roll) up one's sleeves and raise (or bare) one's arms (in agitation or excitement): ~高呼 *raise one's arms and shout*

【攘除】[书] get rid of; weed out; eliminate: ~邪

恶 *weed out all evils* / ～奸贼 *eliminate conspirator* / ～奸雄 *eliminate arch-careerist*
【攘夺】［书］seize; snatch: ～王权 *seize monarchical power*
【攘窃】［书］steal; pilfer: ～国宝 *steal national treasure*
【攘外】expel foreign aggression

嚷 ① shout; yell ② argue heatedly: 别～了，我们采纳你的建议。*Stop arguing; we adopt your proposal.* ③ scold; reproach
see also rāng
【嚷叫】shout; make an uproar
【嚷嚷】［方］quarrel; squabble

ràng

让 ① give way; give in; give ground; yield: 互不相～ *neither is willing to yield (or give ground)* ② offer; invite: 把同学们～进办公室。*Invite the classmates into the office.* ③ let; allow: ～我们假定这消息是真的。*Let's suppose (that) the news is true.* / ～我们携手和好吧。*Let us join hands in friendship.* ④ let sb have sth at a low price; sell: 转～ *transfer the ownership of; make over* ⑤ be used in the passive voice to introduce the doer of the action: 她的衣服～雨淋湿了。*Her clothes got wet in the rain.* /这条鱼～我给吃了。*I am the person who ate the fish.*
【让步】give in; yield; make a concession: 最后，他做出了～。*At last, he gave in.*
【让渡】transfer the ownership of; alienate
【让价】reduce the price asked
【让开】get out of the way; make way; step aside: 给我～道，不然我就开枪了。*Get out of the way, or I'll shoot you.*
【让利】cut profit for the benefit of the buyer: ～销售 *cut price sales*
【让路】make way for sb (of sth); give sb the right of way; give way
【让位】① resign sovereign authority; abdicate ② offer one's seat to sb; give up one's seat to sb ③ yield to; give way to
【让贤】yield one's to sb of virtue an talent; relinquish one's post in favour of a better qualified person
【让账】vie with each other to pay the bill (of friends eating up); insist on paying the bill
【让座】① offer (or give up) one's seat to sb ② ask (or invite) guests to be seated

ráo

饶 ① rich; abundant ② give sth extra; get sth extra; throw in: 售货员把三斤苹果称好，还～了我一个。*The salesman weighed three jin of apples for me and threw in one extra.* ③ have mercy on; let sb off; forgive: 我们不会轻～一个叛徒。*We won't let a traitor off easily.* ④［口］although; in spite of the fact that; despite
【饶命】spare sb's life: 乞求～ *beg to be spared*
【饶人】forgive sb: 得～处且～。*Forgive where you may.*
【饶舌】① loquacious; garrulous; too talkative ② say more than is proper; babble out (a secret)
【饶恕】pardon; forgive: 上周我们犯了一个不可～的错误。*We made an unforgivable mistake last week.*
【饶头】［口］give gratis; extra; throw in sth

桡 ［书］oar: ～动脉 *radial artery*
【桡骨】【生理】radius
【桡神经】【生理】radius nerve

rǎo

扰 ① harass; trouble; harry: 庸人自～ *worry about imaginary troubles* ②［书］disorder; confusion: 困～ *puzzle; perplex* ③ trespass on sb's hospitality: 我们～了他的生日宴。*We were kindly entertained at his birthday feast.*
【扰动】① turmoil; turbulence; disturbance ② disturb: ～速度 *disturbance velocity*
【扰流器】spoiler; vortex generator
【扰乱】harass; disturb; disrupt; create confusion: ～某人的思路 *interrupt sb's train of thought* / ～市场秩序 *disrupt order in the market* / ～休息 *disturb sb's rest* / ～民心 *sap public confidence*
【扰扰】［书］tumult; uproar; disturbance
【扰袭】harass and attack: ～日寇 *harass and attack Japanese aggressors*

rào

绕 ① wind; coil ② go round; circle; revolve: 火星～着太阳转。*The Mars revolves round the sun.* ③ make a detour; bypass: 你不能～过这一问题。*You cannot go round this question.* ④ confuse; baffle; befuddle; confound: 我一时被～住了，不知道该怎么办。*I got confused and didn't know what to do next.*
【绕脖子】［方］① beat about the bush; speak (or act) in a roundabout way: 你把话说清楚，别～。*Please speak clearly and don't beat about the bush.* ② involve; knotty; stiff; complicated
【绕道】make a detour; go by a roundabout route; take a devious route; by pass
【绕焊】【冶】boxing; end turning
【绕接】【电】wire-wrap connection; wrapped connection
【绕梁】(of beautiful music, etc.) reverberate; linger: ～三日 (of the sound of singing) linger and reverberate long in the air
【绕圈子】① circle; go round and round ② beat about the bush; talk or speak in a roundabout way

R

【绕弯儿】［方］go for a walk; go for a stroll; take a stroll：他正在林子里～。*He is taking a stroll in the forest.*

【绕弯子】talk (or speak) in a roundabout way; beat about the bush：我不喜欢说话爱～的人。*I don't like these persons who talk in a roundabout way.*

【绕行】① make a detour; go by a roundabout route; bypass：道路维修，车辆～。*Road is under repair and all vehicles must make a detour.* ② move or go round; circle

【绕远儿】go the long way round; be longer (of a route)：我们最好别走那条路，那样～。*We'd better not make choice of that road, or we'll go the long way round.*

【绕组】【电】winding：～线 *winding wire*

【绕嘴】(of a sentence, etc.) difficult to articulate; not smooth; tongue-twisting

rě

惹 ① invite or ask for (sth unpleasant); incur：～不快 *incur displeasure* / ～麻烦 *ask for trouble; bring trouble to oneself* ② offend; provoke; annoy：我们都～不起她。*All of us cannot afford to provoke her.* ③ attract; cause; draw：～人注意 *draw attention; attract attention* / 说话太多就会～人讨厌。*You'd better not say too more, or you'll make a nuisance of yourself.*

【惹火烧身】one who plays with fire will get one's fingers burnt — court disaster; ask for trouble

【惹祸】court disaster; invite disaster; stir up trouble; ask for trouble

【惹乱子】cause trouble; court disaster; stir up trouble

【惹怒】make sb angry; offend; annoy; provoke

【惹气】get or become angry

【惹事】stir up trouble; cause trouble; draw trouble：昨天，他又～了，都现在都不敢回家。*Yesterday he caused troubles and didn't come back home until now.*

【惹是生非】provoke a dispute; stir up trouble; kick up a fuss; create a disturbance：王明是个常常～的男孩。*Wang Ming is an ordinary boy who keeps getting into trouble.*

【惹眼】［方］conspicuous; eye-catching; attractive; showy

rè

热 ① heat：导～ *conduct heat* / 传热～ *heat transfer* ② hot：～水 *hot water* / 一杯～茶 *a cup of hot tea* / 北京的夏天一般很～。*It is generally hot in summer of Beijing.* ③ craze; fad：集邮～ *stamp collecting fad* / 足球～ *football craze* ④ fever; temperature：头疼脑～ *have a fever and a headache* / 感冒发～ *catch cold and run a fever* ⑤ ardent; chummy; warmhearted：～心 *enthusiastic* / 亲～ *affectionate; intimate; warmhearted* ⑥ popular; in great demand：～销 (*of goods*) *sell well; be in great demand* ⑦ envious; eager; full of envy：我真眼～你得到二天额外假期。*I'm so envious of you getting two extra days' holiday.* ⑧ thermal; thermo：地～能源 *geothermal energy resources*

【热爱】ardently love; deep affection; have deep love for; devotion：

【热泵】【机】heat pump

【热病】【中医】acute disease accompanied by fever; pyreticosis; febris

【热补】vulcanize (tire, etc.)

【热肠】enthusiasm; sympathetic

【热潮】mass enthusiasm; campaign, upsurge

【热忱】zeal; zest; warm-heartedness; enthusiasm

【热成形】【机】hot-forming

【热诚】cordial; warm and sincere：～待人 *be warm and sincere towards others* / ～接待 *cordially receive*

【热处理】【机】heat or thermal treatment

【热传导】heat conduction

【热脆性】【冶】hot-shortness; red-shortness

【热带】tropical zone; torrid zone; the tropics：～雨林 *selva; tropical rain forest* / ～鱼 *tropical fish* / ～草原 *savanna* / ～植物 *tropical plant* / ～风暴 *tropical storm*

【热导率】【物】thermal conductivity

【热导体】【物】heat conductor

【热得快】immersion heater

【热点】① hot spot; flash point：旅游～ *a tourist hot spot* ② attraction; centre of attention; central issue：中东是全球关注的～地区。*Middle East is the centre of global attention.* ③【物】hot-spot

【热电】【物】pyroelectricity; thermoelectricity; ～厂 *thermopile-power plant* / ～效应 *pyroelectric effect*

【热电子】thermoelectron

【热电阻】thermal resistance

【热定型】【化】heat setting; thermosetting

【热度】① degree of heat; heat：木材燃烧需要一定的～。*Wood burns only when it is heated up to a certain point.* ②［口］fever; temperature：她的～已经降下去了。*Her temperature has already come down.* ③ zeal.

【热煅】【冶】hot-forging

【热对流】【物】thermal-convection

【热风】① hot wind; hot-blast air：～干燥机 *hot air drier* / ～炉 *hot blast stove* ② (for food) hot-air oven

【热敷】【医】hot compress

【热辐射】【物】heat or thermal radiation

【热工学】【物】thermal engineering

【热狗】hotdog

【热固】【化】hot-set; heat-set：～塑料 *thermoset plastic*

【热管】heat pipe; heating pipe; radiator

【热锅上的蚂蚁】an ant on a hot pan restless; be on

pins and needles：他像～等待她答复。*He was waiting for her answer, restless as an ant on a hot pan.*

【热核】thermonuclear：～爆炸 *thermonuclear explosion* /～弹头 *nuclear warhead; thermonuclear warhead* /～反应 *thermonuclear reaction* /～反应堆 *thermonuclear reactor* /～技术 *thermonucleonics* /～武器 *thermonuclear weapon*

【热烘烘】very warm：～的风让人感觉不舒服。*I felt uncomfortable under the hot wind.*

【热乎乎】warm：～的馒头 *hot steamed bun* /屋里～的。*It was warm in the room.*

【热乎】① nice and warm; warm：～可口的饭菜 *hot and tasty food* ② warm-natured and friendly; pally; thick：他们是非常～的朋友。*They are very chummy friends.*

【热昏】［方］dizzy; giddy

【热火朝天】bustling with activity; be in full swing; buzzing with activity：～的劳动场面 *a picture of over flowing labour enthusiasm*

【热火】① in full swing; exciting：演出进行得正～。*The performance is most excitement just at the moment.*

【热货】hot commodity; popular commodities; hot cakes

【热机】【机】heat engine

【热寂】【物】heat death

【热加工】【冶】hot working, hot work

【热交换】heat exchange, heat interchange

【热交换器】heat exchanger; heat interchanger

【热聚合】【化】thermal polymerization：～物 *thermopolymer*

【热扩散】【物】thermal diffusion

【热拉伸】【冶】hot stretch

【热辣辣】burning hot; scorching：～的天 *a scorching day* /外面～的。*It's scorching outside.*

【热浪】heat wave; strong current of warm air; hot wave：～消散了。*The heat wave broke.*

【热泪】hot tears; tears

【热泪盈眶】one's eyes brimming with tears：我被他的话感动得～。*I was moved to tears by his words.*

【热力】【机】hot power：～学 *thermodynamics* /～学温标 *thermodynamic scale* /～学温度 *thermodynamic temperature*

【热恋】be passionately (or head over heels) in love; be infatuated with：他俩处在～之中。*They were passionately in love with each other.*

【热量】【物】quantity of heat：～计 *calorimeter* /～单位 *heat unit; thermal unit*

【热烈】warm; enthusiastic; animated; ardent：～欢呼 *warmly hail* /～欢迎 *warmly welcome* /～的掌声 *warm applause* /～响应党的号召 *respond to the Party's call enthusiastically* /她的优美的舞姿博得了～的喝彩。*Her graceful dancing evoked warm acclamations.*

【热裂化】【油】thermal cracking

【热流】① thermal current ② warm current：我感到一股～涌上心田。*I felt a warm current coursing in me.*

【热门】in great demand; arousing popular interest; popular：～货 *goods which are in great demand or sell well; hot item* /～专业 *a popular specialty* /～话题 *subject of great topical interest*

【热敏电阻】【电】thermal resistor

【热闹】① busy; bustling; lively：～的演出 *a lively performance* /～的超级市场 *a busy supermarket* ② have a jolly time; liven up; enjoy oneself：我们唱支歌～一下吧。*Let's sing a song to enjoy us.* ③ a scene of bustling activity; fun：我们到大街上看～吧。*Let go out to watch the fun in the street.*

【热能】【物】heat energy; thermal energy

【热喷喷】steaming hot; piping hot：一锅～的米饭 *a bowl of steaming hot rice*

【热平衡】【动】thermal equilibrium

【热气】steam; heat：锅里冒着～。*Steam is giving off from the pot.* /工人们～高，干劲大。*Every worker was full of enthusiasm and energy.*

【热气球】hot-air balloon

【热气腾腾】① steaming hot：～的米饭 *steaming hot rice* ② seething with activity; go on at a vigorous pace：麦收的景象～。*The scene of wheat harvest is in full swing.*

【热切】ardent, earnest; fervent; full of ardour

【热情】enthusiasm; zeal; ardour：爱国～ *patriotic ardour (or zeal)* /革命～ *revolutionary fervour or zeal* /～接待 *warmly receive; give one a warm reception* /那个孩子满怀～地去学习了。*The little child approached his study with enthusiasm.*

【热情奔放】overflow with emotion; bubbling with enthusiasm

【热情洋溢】brimming with warm feeling; glowing with enthusiasm：～的讲话 *heart warming speech* /～的感谢信 *a warm letter of thanks*

【热容量】【物】thermal capacity; heat capacity

【热身】warm-up：～赛 *warm-up game*

【热水袋】hot-water bag (or bottle)

【热水瓶】［口］thermos thermal flask or bottle; vacuum bottle or flask

【热塑塑料】【化】thermoplastic

【热塑性】【化】thermoplasticity

【热汤面】hot noodle soup; noodles in hot soup

【热腾腾】steaming hot：～的汤面 *steaming hot noodle soup*

【热天】hot weather; sweltering heat; hot season; hot days：那个孩子恨透了～，因为太热不能出去玩。*The child hated the hot weather for not going out to play.*

【热土】home land; native place

【热望】earnestly (or fervently) hope; ardently wish

【热污染】thermal pollution

【热物理学】thermophysics

【热线】① infrared ray ② (telephone, etc.) hot line：～电话 *hot line telephone* /服务～ *service hot-line* ③ busy route：旅游～ *busy or popular tourist route*

【热像仪】【电】thermal imaging system

R

【热销】(of goods) be in great demand; sell well: ~商品 *goods in great demand*
【热效率】heat efficiency; thermal efficiency.
【热心】enthusiastic; ardent; sincere earnest: 为乘客~服务 *warmhearted serve the passengers* / ~群众工作 *be devoted to mass work* / ~传授知识 *make earnest efforts to pass on one's knowledge* / ~公共事务 *be enthusiastic about pubic affairs*
【热心肠】[口] warm-heartedness: 他是一个~的人。*He is a person with warm-heartedness.*
【热学】【物】heat; calorifics; thermology
【热血】warm blood-righteous ardour; indignation: ~男儿 *red-blooded youth* / ~青年 *ardent youth* / 甘洒~为祖国 *be ready to lay down one's life for the mother land*
【热血动物】warm blood; warm-blooded animal
【热血沸腾】one's blood boils; burning or seethe with righteous indignation
【热压】【化】hot pressing: ~成形 *hot forming*
【热药】【中医】medicine of a hot (or warm) nature; tonics and stimulants
【热饮】hot drinks
【热源】【物】heat source
【热轧】【冶】hot-rolling
【热战】hot war; shooting war
【热障】【物】heat barrier
【热症】【中医】heat symptom-complex; febrile symptoms
【热值】【物】calorific value; thermal value
【热衷】① hanker after; hanker for; crave: 他从不~于自己的名利。*He never hankers for personal fame and gain.* ② be fond of; be keen on; be deeply interested in; be mad about: ~于足球 *be very fond of playing football*
【热中子】【物】thermal neutron
【热阻】【物】heat resistance

rén

人 ① human being; person; people; man: 黑~ *the black* / 男~ *man* / 城里~ *townspeople; city dwellers* / 她是一个地道的美国~。*She is a native of American.* ② adult; grow up: 成~ *an adult man* ③ everybody; all: ~~自危。*Everyone finds himself in danger or everyone feels insecure.* / ~手一台计算机。*Each has a computer.* ④ person considered as a worker or employee: 艺~ *actor or artist; artisan; hand; craftsman* / 工~ *worker* ⑤ personality; character: 这里的~善良朴实。*The people here are kind hearted, sincere and honest.* / 他为~慷慨。*He is generous.* ⑥ other people; people: 舍己为~ *sacrifice one's own interests for the sake of others* ⑦ state of one's health or mind: 这几天他~不高兴。*He has not been feeling happy for several days.* ⑧ hand; manpower: 我们今年不缺~手。*We are not short of hands this year.*
【人本主义】【哲】humanism
【人不犯我,我不犯人】we'll not attack unless we are attacked; if others let me alone, I will let them alone
【人不可貌相】never judge a person by his appearance
【人不为己,天诛地灭】unless a man looks out for himself, heave and Earth will destroy him; every person for himself and the devil; take the hindmost
【人不知,鬼不觉】without a soul knowing anything about it; in absolute secrecy
【人才】① person of ability; a talented person; talent; qualified personnel: 科技~ *scientists and technicians* / ~交流 *exchange of talent* / ~济济 *an abundance of talented people; a galaxy of talent* / ~市场 *employment market* / ~流动 *mobility of trained people* / ~库 *brain trust or bank; talent bank* / ~交流中心 *personnel exchange centre; talent exchange centre; job centre* / ~荟萃 *gathering of distinguished scholar; a galaxy of talent* / ~交流会 *talent fair* / ~辈出 *persons of ability emerge in succession* ② [口] hand some appearance: 一表~ *a man of striking appearance*
【人财两空】lose both people and money (as when a person's mistress absconds with his money and valuables)
【人潮】huge crowd of people; steam of people; sea of faces
【人称】【语】person: 第二~ *the second person* / 不定~ *indefinite person* / ~代词 *personal pronoun*
【人次】person-time: 参加计算机展览的总共约3000~。*Admissions to the computer exhibition totaled about three thousand.*
【人丛】crowd; crowd of people
【人道】① humanity; human sympathy: ~主义 *humanitarianism* ② human; humane ③ inhuman
【人地生疏】be unfamiliar with the place and the people; be a complete stranger; be total stranger
【人丁】population; number of people in a family: ~兴旺 *have a growing or a large family; have a flourishing population*
【人定胜天】man can conquer nature
【人堆儿】[口] crowd
【人多势众】enjoy numerical superiority and consequently great strength; overwhelm with numerical strength; dominate by sheer force of numbers
【人多智广】more people, greater wisdom
【人多嘴杂】many people, many voices (or words)
【人犯】[旧] the accused or people implicated in a crime: 所有~都被逮捕了。*All offenders were arrested.*
【人贩子】trader or trafficker in human beings
【人非草木】neither wood nor grass but man-normal human being: ~,孰能无情? *Human being is not inanimate thing; How can he be free from emotions?*
【人非圣贤,孰能无过】men are not sages, how can they be free from fault; to err is human
【人份】person-portion; portion: 麻疹疫苗2万~

twenty thousand measles vaccines

【人粪尿】【农】night soil; human waste or excrement

【人逢喜事精神爽】joy gives heart to man; joy put heart in to man

【人浮于事】have more staff (or hands) the needed; be overstaffed

【人格】① personality; moral quality; character: ~高尚 *have a noble character* /双重~ *split personality* ② human dignity:污辱~ *insult human dignity* /降低~ *stoop beneath one's dignity*; *cheapen oneself* / ~化 *personify*

【人工】① man-made; artificial: ~降雨 *artificial rainfall* / ~河 *man-made river* / ~生态系统 *artificial ecosystem* ② man-day; man power:修这座桥花了许多~。*It has taken a lot of man power to construct this bridge.* ③ manual work; manual labour; work done by hand: ~岛 *man-made island* / ~繁殖 *artificial propagation* / ~孵化 *artificial incubation* / ~更新 *artificial regeneration* / ~合成蛋白质 *synthetic protein* / ~合成胰岛素 *synthetic insulin* / ~呼吸 *artificial respiration* / ~湖 *man-made lake* / ~降水 *artificial precipitation* / ~降雨设备 *rainmaker* / ~流产 *induced abortion* / ~气候实验室 *artificial climate laboratory* / ~器官 *artificial organ* / ~授粉 *artificial pollination* / ~授精 *artificial insemination*; *artificial fertilization* / ~心肺机 *heart-lung machine* / ~选择 *artificial selection* / ~智能 *artificial intelligence*

【人海】sea of faces; huge crowd of people: ~茫茫 *blurry sea of faces*; *vast human sea* / ~战术 *human sea tactics*

【人和】harmony of people; human unity; popular support; support of the people

【人话】human speech; sensible (or reasonable) words:你这还算~。*What you say is at least reasonable words.*

【人欢马叫】people bustling and horses neighing — a busy and prosperous village scene

【人寰】[书] human world; world; man's world

【人祸】man-made calamity (or disaster)

【人际】between persons; interpersonal: ~关系 *interpersonal relationships*

【人迹】human footprints or foot marks: ~罕至 *without human trace*; *rarely visited by human being*; *uninhabited*

【人家】(rénjiā) ① household; family:富裕~ *well-off family* /村子里有 30 户~。*There are thirty households in the hamlet.* ② fiancé's family:这个 18 岁的女孩儿已经有了~。*The eighteen years old girl is engaged to be married.*

【人家】(rénjia) ① others; other other people: ~能去国外,我也能。*If others can go abroad, so I can.* ② me; I: ~想买这本书嘛。*But that book is just what I want to buy.* /你别问了,~不乐意告诉你。*I'm not willing to tell*; *you'd better not ask me.* ③ certain person or persons:把报纸给~送去。*Take the newspaper to him.*

【人间】human world; world; the earth; man's world: ~天堂 *heaven on earth* / ~奇迹 *man-made miracle* / ~悲剧 *human tragedy* / ~地狱 *hell on earth*

【人杰】[书] outstanding personality (or character)

【人杰地灵】the greatness of a person lends glory to a place; a fair place tends to produce outstanding people

【人尽其才】let every one give full play to his talent; make the best possible use of people

【人均】per capita: ~收入 *income per person*; *per capita income* / ~住宅面积 *the average living space per person* / ~国民收入 *per capita national income* / ~国民生产总值 *per capita gross national product (GNP)* / ~国内生产总值 *per capita GDP (gross domestic product)*

【人孔】【建】manhole

【人口】① population:城市~ *urban population* /农村~ *rural population* / ~减小 *population decline* /上海是一个~稠密的城市。*Shanghai is a densely populated city.* ② the number of people in a family: ~爆炸 *population explosion* / ~出生率 *birth rate*; *human fertility* / ~动态统计 *vital statistics* / ~动态学 *population dynamics* / ~分布 *population distribution* / ~负增长 *negative population growth (NPG)* / ~基数 *population base* / ~金字塔 *population pyramid* / ~老化 *aging of population* / ~密度 *population density* / ~普查 *population census* / ~死亡率 *human mortality* / ~统计 *population statistics* / ~统计学 *demography* / ~学 *demography* / ~意识 *awareness of population problem* / ~预测 *population projection* / ~质量 *population quality* / ~自然增长率 *natural growth rate of population* / ~组成 *population composition* /他们家~多。*Theirs is a large family.*

【人困马乏】both men and their steeds are worn out; exhausted

【人来疯】[方] (of children) behave like a spoiled child before visitors; show off his liveliness before guests

【人老珠黄】persons grow old like pearls turning yellow; in old age, people are like pearls whose lustre has fade

【人类】mankind; humanity: ~社会 *human society* / ~起源 *the origin in of mankind* / ~命运 *the destiny of mankind* / ~生存问题 *the problem of human existence* / ~美学 *anthropology* / ~语言学 *anthropological linguistics* / ~生态学 *human ecology* / ~遗传学 *human genetics*

【人力】manpower; labour power: ~资源 *human resources*

【人力车】① vehicle driven by man ② rickshaw

【人流】① stream of people ② induced abortion

【人龙】constant flow of people; long queue

【人伦】human relation (according to feudal ethics)

【人马】① troops; forces ② staff:原班~ *original team*

【人马座】【天】sagittarius

R

【人满为患】having too many people; overcrowded; overstaffed; overcrowded with people

【人们】the public; people; man: ~等待着伊拉克战争的结束。*The people are waiting for the end of the Iraq War.*

【人面兽心】have a human face but a wolfish heart; a beast in human form

【人面桃花】a woman's face and the peach — blossoms-the pining of lover

【人民】① the people: ~群众 *the masses* / ~代表大会 *people congress* / ~政府 *people's government* / ~战争 *people's war* / ~大会堂 *Great Hall of the People* / ~法院 *people's court* / ~公社 *people's commune* / ~检察院 *people's procuratorate* / ~警察 *people's police* / ~内部矛盾 *contradictions among the people* / ~日报 *People's Daily* / ~英雄纪念碑 *Monument to the People's Heroes* / ~武装 *people's armed forces*; *militia* / ~武装部 *people's armed forces department* / ~阵线 *popular front* ② people native to a place; natives

【人名】name of a person

【人命】human life: ~案子 *a case of homicide*; *a case of manslaughter* / ~关天,不要儿戏。*It's a matter involving someone's life there is no joking.*

【人脑】human brain

【人怕出名猪怕壮】fame portends trouble for men just as fattening does for pigs; fame is fatal to a person as fatness to a pig

【人品】① moral quality; character; moral standing; moral strength: ~好 *be of good character* ② [口] looks; bearing

【人气】popular feeling; public feeling: 市场~持续低迷。*The public's confidence in the market remains in the doldrums.*

【人弃我取】pick up what others discard have ideas of one's own

【人强马壮】both men and horses are in good fettle; have great effective strength

【人墙】【体】wall; wall of people: 筑~ *set a wall*

【人勤地不懒】where the tiller is diligent (or tireless), the land is productive

【人情】① human feelings; sensibilities; human sympathy; human nature: 不近~ *be alien to human nature*; *not amenable to reason* ② human relationship: ~练达 *be wise to the ways of world* ③ gift; present ④ favour: 顺水~ *favour done at little or no cost to oneself* / ~礼 *gift presented to strengthen interpersonal relations*; *gift presented to obtain a favour* / ~世故 *worldly wisdom* / ~冷暖 *social snobbery*

【人情味】human touch; human interest; human kindness; empathy: 这部电影充满~。*This film is full of human interest.* /他总是对穷人很有~。*He always shows human kindness to the poor.*

【人情债】the debt of gratitude

【人穷志不短】though one is poor, one has high aspiration; cherish great ambition despite sb's lowly position; poor but ambitious

【人穷志短】poverty chills or stifles ambition

【人去楼空】the person is gone and the room is empty — old sights recall to mind fond memories of the past

【人权】human right; right of human: 侵犯~ *encroach upon the rights of human* /维护~ *protect human rights*

【人群】crowd; throng

【人人】everyone; everybody: 保护文物,~有责。*It's everyone's responsibility to protect cultural relics.*

【人人自危】everyone finds himself in danger; everyone feels endangered (or insecure); nobody feels secure

【人山人海】multitude of people; huge crowds of people; sea of people

【人身】person: ~保险 *life insurance and accident insurance* / ~攻击 *personal abuse*; *personal attack* / ~事故 *accident involving casualties* / ~自由 *personal freedom* / ~安全 *personal security*; *personal safety* / ~伤害 *personal injury*

【人参】ginseng

【人生】human experience; life: ~观 *outlook on life* / ~如梦 *life is but a dream*; *life is like a dream* / ~哲学 *philosophy of life* / ~朝露 *man's life is just like the morning dew* / ~一世,草木一春。*Man has but only one life to live and grass has just one spring to prosper*; *life is short.*

【人生地不熟】be unfamiliar with the place and its people; be total stranger to the place and the people

【人生七十古来稀】men rarely live up to the age of seventy

【人声】voice

【人声鼎沸】babel of voices; hubbub of voices; terrible din

【人士】personage; public figure; person: 知名~ *well-known figures*; *celebrities* /爱国~ *patriotic personage* /官方~ *democratic personages* /各界~ *personalities of various circles* /知情~ *informed quarters* /文艺界~ *people of literary and art circles*

【人世】human world; this world; the world

【人世沧桑】man's world has witnessed many vicissitudes; tremendous changes

【人世间】human world; the world; this world

【人事】① human affair; vicissitudes in life; occurrences in human life ② personnel matter: ~调动 *transfer of personnel* / ~安排 *personnel arrangement* / ~权 *control over personnel affair* / ~更迭 *change of personnel* ③ ways of the world: 不懂~ *unaware of the ways of society*; *unaware of the ways of the world* ④ consciousness of the outside world: 不省~ *lose consciousness* ⑤ interpersonal relationship: ~纷争 *personal dispute* ⑥ sexual awareness; facts of sexual life: ~处 *personnel division* / ~档案 *personnel archives* / ~制度 *personnel system*

【人手】hand; manpower: 缺少~ *short of hands*; *shorthanded*

【人寿保险】life insurance

【人寿年丰】land yields good crops and people enjoy good heath; long life and good harvests
【人死如灯灭】a man dies the way a lamp goes out
【人梯】① human pyramid; human ladder ②［喻］a human ladder to scientific (or academic success); a man who helps another to rise to success human ladder spirit
【人体】human body: ~模型 *manikin* / ~工程学 *ergonomics* / ~节律 *biorhythm* / ~解剖学 *anthropotomy* / ~生物学 *human physiology* / ~生物钟 *biological clock* / ~特异功能 *extrasensory perception*
【人头】① human head ② the number of people: 按~分食品 *distribute food according to the number of people* ③ relations with people: ~熟 *know many people* / ~税 *poll tax*; *capitation (tax)*
【人微言轻】the worlds of the humble carry little weight
【人为】① man-made; artificial: ~错误 *artificially created errors* ② human effort: 事在~。*Human effort is the decisive factor or it all depends on human effort.*
【人为刀俎,我为鱼肉】be meat on sb's chopping block — be at sb's mercy
【人为万物之灵】human being of all creatures is the one endowed with most intelligence
【人为财死,鸟为食亡】men die for wealth, as birds die for food
【人味儿】humanity, kind-heartedness: 对待亲戚和朋友,他很有~。*He treats relatives and friends with full of humanity.*
【人文景观】a place of cultural interest
【人文科学】humanities; humane studies
【人文主义】humanism
【人无远虑,必有近忧】a man who doesn't plan for the future will find trouble at his doorstep
【人五人六】strike poses; put on an act
【人物】① personage; figure: 领导~ *a leading personage* / 英雄~ *a heroic figure* ② a person in literature; character: 典型~ *a typical character* / 反面人物 *negative character*; *villain* / ~表 *a list of characters*; *a cast of characters* / ~画 *figure painting*
【人像】portrait; figure; bust: ~靶 *silhouette target*
【人心】popular feeling; public feeling; public will; the will of the people; popularity: 得~ *have the support of the people* / 不得~ *go against the will of the people* / 振奋~ *boost popular moral* / 大快~ *most gratifying to the public* / 收买~ *buy popular support* / ~惶惶 *popular anxiety* / ~丧尽 lose or forfeit all popular sympathy / ~所向 *will of the people*; *popular sentiment* / ~向背 *whether the people are for or against* / ~如面 *the hearts of people are just as different as their faces*
【人行道】pavement; sidewalk
【人行横道】pedestrian crossing crosswalk; zebra crossing
【人性】human nature; humanity: 灭绝~ *inhuman*; *savage* / 丧失~ *utterly inhuman*; *most barbarous*
【人性】normal human feelings; attributes of human being: 不通~ *have no human conscience*; *unfeeling and unreasonable*
【人性论】the theory of human nature
【人熊】【动】brown bear
【人选】person selected; candidate
【人烟】signs of human habitation (or presence): 没有~的地方 *a uninhabited place* / ~稀少的地方 *a sparsely populated area*
【人言可畏】gossip is a fearful thing; man has to be very wary of gossip
【人仰马翻】both men and their steeds or horses are thrown off their feet locked in fierce fight; thrown in to confusion; utterly routed
【人样】① proper human appearance; human shape; proper behaviour: 脏得不像个~。*He was awfully dirty.* ② person with a future; a successful person: 我想能混出~来。*I thought that I could make the grade.*
【人影儿】① shadow of a human figure ② figure; the trace of a person's presence: 天黑路上看不见~。*It was so dark that we could see nothing on the road.*
【人有脸,树有皮】a person has a face just as a face just as a tree has bark — a person has a sense of shame
【人欲】［书］human desires; carnal pleasures
【人欲横流】unbridled indulgence of human desires or lust; moral degeneration
【人员】staff; personnel: 值勤~ *people on duty* / 外交~ *diplomatic personnel* / 行政~ *administrative personnel*; *administrative staff* / 全体~ *the whole staff* / 缺少~ *understaffed*
【人猿】anthropoid (ape)
【人缘】relations with people; relationship with people; popularity: ~好 *popular*; *enjoy popularity* / 没~ *unpopular* / 有~ *have good relations with people*
【人云亦云】echo the views of others without considering; parrot; have no views of one's own
【人造】man-made; artificial; imitation: ~冰 *artificial ice* / ~宝石 *artificial jewel*; *imitation jewel* / ~地球卫星 *man-made earth satellite*; *artificial earth satellite*; *sputnik* / ~革 *imitation leather*; *leatherette* / ~黄油 *margarine* / ~景观 *man-made scenery (or scenic spot)* / ~毛 *man-made feather*; *artificial wool* / ~纤维 *man-made (or artificial) fibre* / ~心脏 *artificial heart* / ~丝 *artificial silk*; *rayon* / ~橡胶 *artificial rubber*; *synthetic rubber*; *chloroprene* / ~棉 *staple rayon*; *artificial cotton*
【人渣】social scum (or trash); dregs
【人证】【律】testimony of an eyewitness; testimony of a witness: ~物证俱在 *availability of eye-witnesses and material evidence*
【人之常情】human nature; normal practice in human relationships
【人之将死,其言也善】sincere are the words of a dying man

R

【人治】(as distinct rule by law) rule by man
【人质】hostage:解救~ *rescue a hostage*
【人中】【中医】philtrum
【人种】ethnic group; race: ~学 *ethnology* / ~学家 *ethnologist*
【人字形】【建】herringbone
【人自为战】each man fighting only by himself

仁¹ ① kind heartiness; benevolence; humanity: ~政 *policy of benevolence*; *a benevolence government* ② (Rén) a surname

仁² kennel; stone (of a peach, etc.): 果~ *nut meat* / 桃~ *peach kernel*; *walnut meat* / 花生~ *shelled peanuts*

【仁爱】benevolence; humanity; kindheartedness
【仁慈】benevolence; kindness; mercy; merciful
【仁丹】throat lozenge
【仁德】benevolence; kindness; magnanimity; humanity
【仁弟】(be used to address one's juniors) my dear friend
【仁厚】honest and kindhearted; kind and generous
【仁人君子】benevolent gentleman; public-spirited people; kindly folk
【仁人志士】people with lofty ideals
【仁兄】(be used to address one's seniors) my dear friend
【仁义】(rényì) humanity and justice; benevolence and virtue
【仁义】(rényi)[方] gentle and sensible; amiable and reasonable
【仁义道德】benevolence and virtue; humanity, justice and virtue; virtue and morality
【仁者见仁,智者见智】the benevolent see benevolence and the wise see wisdom — opinions differ from person to person; everyone has his own views
【仁至义尽】do everything called for by one's humanity and duty; treat one person with the outmost decency and kindness; extremely tolerant

rěn

忍 ① bear; endure; stand; put up with; tolerate: ~饥挨饿 *endure the torments of hunger*; *suffer starvation* / ~住悲痛 *bear sadness* ② be hardhearted enough to; have the heart to: 惨不~睹。*It's too tragic to witness.*

【忍不住】cannot help (doing sth); unable to bear: ~哭起来 *cannot help crying* / 她痛得~了。*She was unable to bear her pain.*
【忍俊不禁】cannot help laughing
【忍耐】exercise patience (or restraint); restrain oneself
【忍气吞声】swallow a insult; swallow rude remarks; submit to humiliation; stifle one's indignation
【忍让】exercise forbearance; show forbearance; be forbearing and conciliatory
【忍辱负重】endure humiliation in order to perform important duties.
【忍辱偷生】endure humiliation in order to live or exist
【忍受】bear; endure; put up with: ~艰辛 *endure hardships* / ~折磨 *endure torments* / ~屈辱 *swallow one's humiliation*
【忍痛】suffer pain; bear pain: ~割爱 *part reluctantly with what one loves*
【忍无可忍】be pushed beyond the limit of forbearance; come to the end of one's patience; be provoked beyond endurance
【忍心】have the heart to; be hardhearted to: 她~离开她的丈夫到国外去了。*She had the heart to leave her husband and go abroad.*
【忍者】ninja
【忍住】endure; bear

荏 ①【植】common perilla ②[书] weak; cowardly; weak-kneed: 色厉内~ *ferocious in appearance but weak within*

【荏苒】[书](of time) elapse quickly; slip by: 光阴~,转眼又是二年。*Time zipped by and two years had elapsed in the twinkling of an eye.*
【荏弱】[书] weak; feeble

rèn

刃 ① edge of a knife, sword, etc.; blade: 刀~ *knife blade* ② knife; sword: 利~ *sharp sword* / 白~ *naked sword* / 白~战 *bayonet charge*; *hand to hand combat*

【刃具】【机】cutting tool; cutlery
【刃口】the edge (or blade) of a sword, scissors, etc.

认 ① recognize; identify; tell; make out; distinguish: 辨~ *identify*; *recognize* / 指~ *point out*; *identify* ② enter into a certain relationship with acknowledge: ~了个干爸 *adopt sb as one's father* / ~师傅 *apprentice oneself to sb*; *make one work as an apprentice for sb*; *acknowledge sb as one's master* ③ admit; recognize; accept: ~罪悔过 *plead guilty and repent* ④ accept as unavoidable; resign oneself to (a loss, debt, etc.)

【认不是】make an apology; acknowledge a mistake
【认出】identify; recognize; make out
【认错】admit a fault; make an apology; offer an apology; acknowledge a mistake
【认得】know; recognize
【认定】① firmly believe; hold: ~某人无罪 *maintain that one is innocent of a charge* ② confirm; affirm; decide on: ~犯罪事实 *affirmed one's crimes*
【认罚】be ready to pay the penalty; admit that one deserves punishment
【认购】offer to by; subscribe: ~股票 *subscribe for stocks*
【认捐】signal one's desire to donate a certain sum of money; offer a donation

【认可】accept; approve:点头~ *nod approval* /这个计划得到了市长的~。*This plan was approved by the mayor.*

【认领】① claim ② adopt:最后一位老奶奶~了那个可怜的孩子。*At last, one old granny adopted the poor child.*

【认命】accept fate; resign oneself to fate

【认赔】agree to pay compensation; admit an obligation to pay (for damage done, etc.)

【认亲】(in a general sense) acknowledge one's relationship with a relative; claim a family connection

【认清】recognize; see clearly; clearly recognize

【认人】(usu. said of babies) can recognize people by their looks, voices, etc.

【认生】(of children) be shy with strangers

【认识】① recognize; know; understand ② understanding; knowledge; cognition:感性~ *perceptual knowledge* /理性~ *rational knowledge* / ~过程 *process of cognition* / ~论 *theory of knowledge; epistemology* / ~能力 *cognitive ability* / ~水平 *level of understanding*

【认输】admit defeat; give in; give up; throw up (or in) the sponge

【认死理】be stubborn; be obstinate; be inflexible

【认同】① identify; regard oneself as sharing the characteristics or fortunes of sb:我对这部小说里的任何角色都难以~。*I found it hard to identify with any of the characters in the novel.* ② approve; acknowledge: ~作用 *identification* /他的观点不被大家~。*Others did not acknowledge his viewpoint.*

【认为】consider; think; believe; hold; deem

【认贼作父】take the enemy for one's father; regard the foe as kith and kin

【认账】acknowledge a debt; bear responsibility; admit what one has said or done:领导说的话也不~吗? *How can a leader go back upon what he said?*

【认真】① conscientious; earnest; serious: ~考虑 *give serious consideration to* /做~的检讨 *make an earnest self-criticism* ② take sth seriously; take to heart:他办事非常~。*He handles matters quite seriously.* /一个玩笑不要太~。*You needn't take it seriously; it was only a joke.*

【认证】【律】attestation; authentication: ~文件 *authenticated document* / ~机构 *notified bodies* / ~签字 *attest a signature*

【认知】【心】cognition: ~心理学 *cognitive psychology*

【认准】set one's mind on; firmly believe; maintain; hold

【认字】know how to read; be able to read; be literate

【认罪】plead guilt; admit that one is guilty:低头~ *hang one's head and admit one's guilt*

仞 an ancient measure of length equal to seven or eight chi:万~高山 *immeasurably high mountain*

任[1] ① appoint; engage; assign sb to a post (or position):他被~命为总经理。*He was appointed general manager.* ② assume; undertake; hold:担~ *assume the office of; hold the post of* ③ office; official post:离~ *leave one's post* /走马上~ *take office; assume a post* /调~ *be transferred to another post* ④ [量] term office:当过三~校长 *have been headmaster of the school for three terms*

任[2] ① let; allow; permit: ~任宰割 *allow oneself to be trampled upon* ② no matter (what, how, etc.): ~你怎么说,他也不接受你的建议。*No matter what you say, he won't accept your proposals.*

【任何】any; whatever; whichever:你可以告诉~人,我都觉得无所谓。*Tell whoever you like, it makes mo difference to me.* /你买~一个,都有一年的保用期。*Whichever you buy, there is one year guarantee.*

【任教】teach; be a teacher:在一所中学~ *teach at a middle school*

【任课】teach at a school

【任劳任怨】work hard regardless of others' criticism; stand the strain of labour and injustice

【任命】appoint: ~状 *letter of appointment; commission; credential*

【任凭】at one's convenience (or disposal); at one's discretion:这事不能~孩子们决定。*This matter shouldn't be left entirely to children's discretion.* ② no matter (who, how, what, etc.): ~困难多大,我们也能承担这项任务。*We can undertake the task no matter how difficult it is.*

【任凭风浪起,稳坐钓鱼船】sit tight in the fishing boat without being affected by the rising wind and waves — hold one's ground despite pressure or opposition

【任期】term of office; tenure of office: ~制 *tenure system*

【任其自然】give free rein to; let nature take its course; let things run their own course

【任人】let people do sth without restrictions; let people do what they please

【任人唯亲】appoint people by favoritism

【任人唯贤】appoint people on their merits

【任务】mission; task; assignment; job:接受~ accept or receive an assignment /执行~ *perform a mission; carry out a task*

【任性】wilful; self-willed; headstrong; wayward; capricious

【任意】① wanton; arbitrary; wilful: ~挥霍 *spend freely* / ~诬蔑 *wantonly vilify* ② unconditional; unqualified: ~四边形 *unconditional quadrilateral* / ~常数 *arbitrary constant*

【任意球】【体】free kick; free throw

【任用】appoint; assign sb to a post

【任职】be in office; hold a post: ~农业部 *hold a post in the Ministry of Agriculture*

【任重道远】the burden is heavy and the road ahead is cong — shoulder heavy responsibilities in years to come

R

纫 ① sew; stitch:缝~ *sewing*; *tailoring* /缝~机 *sewing machine* ② thread a needle

韧 pliable but strong; likely to bend but not to crack; tenacious; tough:坚~不拔 *table*; *persistent and dauntless*

【韧带】【生理】ligament

【韧度】①【纺】tenacity ②【冶】toughness

【韧劲】tenacity; stead fastness; indomitableness; dauntlessness; persevering spirit

【韧力】tenacity; stead fastness; indomitableness; daunt lessness; persevering spirit

【韧皮部】【植】bast; phloem

【韧皮纤维】bast fibre

【韧性】tenacity; toughness

轫 [书] log used to stop wheels:发~ *commence an undertaking*

妊 pregnancy

【妊娠】pregnancy; gestation: ~期 *gestation period* / ~试验 *pregnancy test*

rēng

扔 ① throw; cast; fling:把包~给她。*Throw her the bag.* ② cast aside; throw away:把这些旧衣服~了吧。*Throw the old clothes away.*

【扔掉】throw these old clothes away

【扔弃】discard; abandon; give up; cast aside

【扔下】abandon; cast aside; put aside; leave behind

réng

仍 ① remain ② frequently; often:外患频~ *be subject to repeated foreign invasion* ③ still; yet:她~没有脱离危险。*He is not yet out of danger.*

【仍旧】① remain the same:我们尽管吵过架,却~不失为最好的朋友。*In spite of their quarrel, we remained the best of friends.* ② still; yet:我回来的时候你~在这里吗? *Will you still be here when I get back?*

【仍然】still; yet:他~很忙。*He's still busy.* /我们~需要你,先别走。*We need you still; Don't go yet.*

rì

日 ① sun:赤~ *scorching sun* ② daytime; day: ~~夜夜 *day and night* ③ day:一~ *one day* /昨~ *yesterday* ④ daily; everyday:天气~凉。*It's going cooler and cooler.* ⑤ time:秋~ *autumn time*; *autumn* /往~ *the past*

【日班】day shift:我喜欢上~。*I like being on day shift.*

【日斑】【天】sunspot

【日报】daily paper; daily:人民~ *the People's Daily*

【日本】Japan: ~人 *Japanese* / ~语 *Japanese*

【日薄西山】the sun is setting beyond the western hills-be on the decline; nearing one's end; be drawing near one's doom

【日长石】【地】sunstone

【日常】day-to-day; daily; everyday: ~工作 *day-to-day work*; *routine duties* / ~事务 *day-to-day business* / ~用品 *daily necessities* / ~生活 *daily life*; *everyday life*

【日场】day show; daytime performance

【日程】schedule; programme:工作~ *work schedule*; *programme of work* /参观~ *itinerary of a visit* /比赛~ *programme of matches* / ~表 *schedule*

【日出】sunrise

【日戳】① datemark ② date stamp; dater

【日耳曼人】Germanic people

【日珥】【天】solar prominence

【日工】① day work ② day labour ③ day labourer

【日光】sunlight; daylight; sunbeam: ~灯 *fluorescent lamp*; *daylight lamp* / ~灯起动器 *fluorescent lamp starter* / ~灯镇流器 *current stabilizer* / ~浴 *sunbath* / ~效应 *sun effect*; *sunlight effect* / ~疗法 *heliotherapy* / ~皮炎 *solar dermatitis*

【日后】in the future; in the days to come: ~你一定要努力学习。*You must study hard in the future.*

【日华】【气】solar halo

【日积月累】gradually accumulate; by piecemeal accumulation; accumulate over a long period

【日记】diary; journal:写~ *keep a diary* /生产~ *production journal* / ~本 *diary* (*book*) / ~账 *daybook*; *journal*

【日间】during the day time; in the daytime

【日间不做亏心事,半夜敲门不吃惊】he who has not done sth with a bad conscience by day is not alarmed by a knock on the floor at night

【日见】day by day; with each passing day:她的病~好转。*Her illness is getting better everyday.* /这家公司~衰落。*The company is declining day by day.*

【日渐】gradually; day by day; with each passing day:他~消瘦。*He is getting thinner every day.*

【日界线】international date line; date line

【日经—道琼平均指数】【经】Nikkei-Dow Jones Average

【日景】day scene

【日久】with the passing of time; in the course of time

【日久见人心】time reveals a person's heart or character; it takes time to know a person:路遥知马力,~。*Distance is the test of a horse's strength and times a person's heart.*

【日久天长】as the years go by; after a considerable length of time; in the course of time

【日均】daily average; average per day

【日理万机】attend to numerous state affairs every day; be busy with a myriad of state affairs

【日历】calendar: ~手表 calendar watch
【日轮】sun disk; sun
【日落】sunset
【日冕】【天】(solar) corona: ~仪 coronagraph
【日暮】evening; nightfall; dusk: 我们~归来,城里已是万家灯火。*When we came back at dusk, the lamps of the town had Lighted up.*
【日暮途穷】the sun is waning and the road is ending — approaching the end of one's days; be on one's Cast Legs; head for doom, be at the end of one's rope
【日内】in a few days'; in a day or two; in a couple of days; one of these days
【日内瓦】Geneva
【日期】date
【日前】a few day age; the other day
【日趋】with the each passing day; day by day; step by step: 中东局势~紧张。*Tension is building up in the Middle East Region day and day.* / 中国经济~繁荣。*Chinese economy is becoming brisker step by step.*
【日日】every day; day after day day in; day out
【日日夜夜】night and day; day and night
【日上三竿】the sun is three poles high very late in the morning
【日射】【气】insolation: ~表 *actinometer* / ~病 *insolation; sunstroke*
【日食】【天】solar eclipse
【日坛】the Altar of the Sun (in Beijing)
【日头】[方] sun
【日托】day care: ~托儿所 *day nursery*
【日息】interest per diem; daily interest
【日心说】heliocentric theory
【日新月异】change with each passing day: 我们的国家建设~。*The Construction in our country has been undergoing great changes day by day.*
【日薪】daily way; per diem
【日夜】day and night; round the clock; night and day
【日夜商店】round-the-clock shop; day-and-night-service shop; shop open night and day
【日以继夜】night and day; round the clock
【日益】increasingly; more and more day by day
【日影】shadow cast by the sun
【日用】① of every use; of daily use: ~百货 *articles of daily use* / ~消费品 *consumer goods for daily use* / ~工业品 *manufactured goods for daily use* / ~必需品 *daily necessities; household necessities* / ~品 *articles of every use* ② daily expenses
【日语】Japanese
【日元】yen (Japanese monetary unit)
【日月】① livelihood; life: 地震期间的~真不好过。*What a hard life we had during the period of earthquake.* ② the sun and the moon
【日月重光】both the sun and the moon are shining again — back to peace and prosperity after a period of turmoil
【日月如梭】the sun and the moon shuttle back and forth — time flies
【日月星辰】the sun; the moon and the stars; heavenly bodies
【日晕】【气】solar halo
【日杂】sundry goods; daily household supplies
【日照】sunshine: ~时间 *sunshine time* / ~计 *sunshine recorder* / 长(短)~植物 *long-day (short-day) plants*
【日臻】day by day: 我们的教育制度~完善。*Our educational system is improving day by day.*
【日志】daily record; journal: 航海~ *logbook; log* / 工作~ *daily record of work* / 教学~ *daily record of teaching*
【日中】[书] ① moon ② equinox
【日子】① date; day: 定一个~ *fix a date* / 喜庆的~ *a day of jubilation* ② days; time: 他不在北京好多~了。*He has not been in Beijing for quite a long time.* ③ livelihood; life: 简朴的~ *a simple life* / 他们家的~很艰难。*The things in their family are getting very hard.* / 现在我们~好过多了。*Now our life is much easier.*

róng

戎[1] ① army; military affairs: 投笔从~ *give up academic pursuits for a military career* ② arms; weaponry

戎[2] ① ancient name for the peoples in the west of China ② (Róng) a surname

【戎马】[书] war-horse; army horse; steed: ~一生 *spend all one's life in the army* / ~生涯 *military life; army life*
【戎首】[书] warmonger; the person who starts a war
【戎装】[书] army uniform; martial attire

茸 ① (of grass, etc.) newly-grown, fine and soft; downy ② young pilose antler: 鹿~ *pilose antler (of a young stag)*

【茸长】long and untidy
【茸毛】fine hair
【茸茸】(of hair, grass, etc.) fine, soft, smooth and thick; downy: 绿~的麦苗 *a carpet of green wheat shoots* / 一头~的头发 *a head of soft, thick hair*

荣 ① grow luxuriantly; grow exuberantly; flourish: 枯~ *(of grasses and trees) luxuriate and wither; prosper and decline* ② prosper; flourishing; thriving: 欣欣向~的花园 *a flourishing garden* ③ glory; honour: 争~誉 *try to win honours* / ~立二等功 *win a second class meritorious*

【荣光】glory; honour
【荣归】return in glory (or triumph): ~故里 *return in triumph to one's native place (or hometown)*
【荣华】glory and splendour: ~富贵 *glory, splendour, wealth and rank; great wealth and high position* / 我不愿意享受~。*I am not willing to enjoy the benefits of wealth and high honour.*

R

【荣获】have the honour to obtain; get or win sth as an honour; be awarded: ~金牌 *be awarded a gold medal* / ~冠军 *win the championship* /我们认为李平在作文比赛中~一等奖是我们集体的光荣。*We call it an honour to our collective that Li Ping got the first prize in the composition contest.*

【荣枯】(of vegetation) flourishing and withering ② [喻] vicissitudes; rise and fall

【荣任】be honoured with a post; have the honour of being appointed (a position)

【荣辱】honour or disgrace; share honour or disgrace; share weal and woe

【荣升】be honoured by promotion to a higher position (or post)

【荣退】① retire from a post with honour; honourable discharge

【荣幸】be honoured (or privileged):能来你家做客,我们感到十分~。*We esteem it as a privilege to visit your family.*

【荣耀】glory; honour:他享尽了天年和~后死去。*He died full of years and honours.*

【荣膺】[书] have the honour to receive; be honoured with a decoration (or a post)

【荣誉】honour; credit; glory: ~军人 *disabled soldier* /强烈的~感 *a strong sense of honour* / ~称号 *an honourary title* /为国家赢得~ *win honour for one's country* /每个学生都应该爱护学校的~。*Every student should cherish the fine name of our school.* /一个好士兵决不会做任何会影响部队~的事情。*A good soldier does not wish to do anything, which may touch his credit.*

绒 ① fine soft hair; down:鹅~ *goose down* /羊~ *wool* /羽~ *down* ② cloth with a soft nap (or pile) on one (or either) side:丝~ *velvet* /灯芯~ *corduroy* ③ fine floss for embroidery

【绒布】lint; flannelette

【绒花】velvet flowers, birds, etc.

【绒裤】sweat pants

【绒毛】① fine hair; down; veil ②【纺】nap; pile

【绒毛膜】【生理】chorion

【绒绳】[方] knitting wool

【绒毯】flannelette blanket

【绒头绳】① wool (for tying pigtails) ② [方] knitting wool

【绒线】① floss for embroidery ② [方] knitting wool: ~编织 *chenille* / ~刺绣 *crewel work* / ~衫 *woollen sweater*

【绒绣】woollen embroidery; woollen needlepoint tapestry

【绒鸭】【动】eider

【绒衣】sweat shirt

容[1] ① contain; hold:这间教室可以~纳60名学生。*The classroom can hold sixty students.* /这座水库可~10万立方米的水。*This is a one hundred thousand cubic meters water reservoir.* ② tolerate; forgive:宽~ *tolerate* /情理不~ *incompatible with the accepted code of human conduct; contrary to reason; totally unreasonable* /不~外国干涉 *tolerate no foreign interference* ③ allow; permit:不~置疑 *allow of no doubt* /不~耽搁 *allow of no delay* / ~我再说一遍。*Let me explain once more.* ④ (Róng) a surname

容[2] ① facial expression:笑~ *smiling expression; smile* /怒~ *angry look* /满脸怒~ *wear a worried look* ② appearance; look: ~貌 *features; looks; appearance* /军~ army discipline

【容光】facial expression;

【容光焕发】one's face glowing with heath; in buoyant spirit; radiant with heath

【容华】features and bearing; features and complexion; looks: ~绝代 *of unrivalled beauty*

【容积】volume: ~吨 *measurement ton*

【容抗】【电】capacitive reactance; condensance

【容量】capacity:那只碗的~有两品脱。*That bowl has a capacity of two pints.*

【容留】give shelter to; take sb in; allow to stay; keep

【容貌】features; facial features; appearance; looks: ~较好 *beautiful and charming looks* / ~端庄 *look serene and dignified; have a pleasant appearance*

【容纳】hold; accommodate

【容器】vessel; container:那个漂亮的~是妈妈送给我的生日礼物。*My mother gave the beautiful container to me as a birthday gift.*

【容情】show mercy; put up with; tolerate

【容让】tolerant; Lenient:你不应该过于~她。*You shouldn't excessively tolerate her.*

【容忍】tolerate; put up with; condone; stand; regard (an offence) as if it were not serious or wrong:老师不能~这样的恶劣的行为。*Teachers won't have bad behaviour.*

【容色】look; appearance; farcical expression; countenance: ~泰然自若 *behave with perfect composure; look self-possessed*

【容身】take shelter; shelter oneself: 无处~ *find nowhere to shelter oneself*

【容身之地】a place to stay; shelter; refuge

【容受】① contain; hold ② endure; put up with; tolerate:他那种诡辩令人无法~。*His sophistry is intolerable.*

【容恕】tolerate and forgive; pardon: 罪不~ *one's crime can never be forgive*

【容限】【物】allowance; tolerance:光学~ *optical tolerance* / ~频率 *tolerance frequency*

【容许】① permit; allow; tolerate; let:如果资金~ *if fund permits* /如果时间~ *if time permits* /如果精力~ *if energy permits* / ~学生把话说完 *allow the student to finish what he wants to say* ② [书] possible; perhaps:他们~赞成这件事。*They may agree with this matter.*

【容颜】appearance; looks: ~憔悴 *look haggard* / ~较好 *look beautiful and charming*

【容易】① easy:说起来~做起来难。*Easier said than done.* ② easily; likely; apt:这些货物~包装。*These goods pack easily.*

【容重】unit weight

【容姿】looks; features: ~美丽 *pretty nice-looking*

蓉 ① mashed fruit; mashed seeds: 椰～ *mashed coconut kernel stuffing* ② another name for Chengdu (成都), the capital of Sichuan Province

【蓉城】another name for Chengdu

溶 dissolve; thaw

【溶洞】limestone cave: 她告诉我们她的家乡有很多～。*She told us there are lots of limestone caves in her hometown.*

【溶化】dissolve; melt

【溶汇】① dissolve and mix ② mingle; merge

【溶剂】【化】solvent; dissolvent

【溶胶】【化】sol: ～度 *solubility* / ～热 *heat of solution* / ～物 *dissolved matter*

【溶解】dissolve; thaw: ～度 *solubility* / ～热 *heat of solution* / ～物 *dissolved matter*

【溶溶】［书］broad; vast: 月色～ *flood of moonlight* / ～的湖水 *broad expanse of lake*

【溶蚀】【地】corrosion

【溶体】【化】solution

【溶性油】【化】soluble oil

【溶血】【医】haemolysis

【溶液】solution: 当量～ *normal solution*

【溶质】【化】solute

榕 【植】small-fruited fig tree; banyan

【榕城】another name for Fuzhou, the capital of Fujian Province

熔 melt; fuse; smelt

【熔池】【冶】molten bath

【熔点】【物】melting point; fusing point; fusion point

【熔度】meltability

【熔断】【电】fusing

【熔焊】【冶】burning-in; fusion welding; melting welding

【熔合】(of two or more metals) melt in to one; alloy

【熔化】melt; fuse

【熔化炉】melting furnace

【熔剂】【冶】flux

【熔接】butt fusion

【熔解】welt; fuse: ～热 *heat of fusion* / ～温度 *melting temperature*

【熔炼】① smelt: 闪速～ *flash smelting* / ～炉 *smelting furnace*

【熔炉】① smelting furnace ② crucible; furnace

【熔融】melt; fuse: ～纺丝 *melting spinning* / ～挤压法

【熔化】extrusion by melting

【熔丝】【电】fuse-element: ～断路器 *fusible circuit breaker* / ～管 *cartridge fuse*

【熔盐】【地】lava

【熔铸】casting; founding: ～工 *smelter* / ～生铁 *casting of iron*

蝾

【蝾螺】【动】turban shell

【蝾螈】【动】salamander; newt

融 ① melt; thaw: 冰雪开始～化了。*The snow and ice begin to thaw.* ② blend; merge; be in harmony: ～洽 *harmonious*; *on good or friendly term*; *getting along well* ③ circulation (of money): 金～ *finance*

【融合】merge; mix together; fuse

【融和】① pleasantly warm; genial: 天气～。*The weather was warm and genial.* ② harmonious; friendly: 她们关系～。*They were on friendly terms.*

【融化】melt; dissolve; thaw: 如果你把冰靠近火,冰就会～。*The ice will run if you put it near the fire.*

【融会】mix together; merge; fuse

【融会贯通】achieve mastery through a comprehensive study of the subject; achieve a through understanding of the subject through mastery of all relevant material

【融解】thaw; melt

【融融】① happy and chummy: 其乐～～ *happy and harmonious* ② warm: 大厅里暖～的。*It was warm in the hall.*

【融通】① circulate: ～资金 *circulate funds* ② gain a comprehensive and through understanding ③ communicate; harmonize; be or make harmonious: ～感情 *communicate feelings with each other*

【融资】finance: 贸易～ *trade financing* / ～项目 *financing project* / ～总额 *total financing* / ～方针 *credit policy* / ～租赁 *financial lease*

rǒng

冗 ① redundant; superfluous: ～词赘句 *redundant or superfluous words and expressions* ② loaded with trivial details; full of trivial details: ～杂 *miscellaneous*; *numerous and complicated* ③ busyness; busy schedule: 拨～ *find time in the midst of pressing affairs*; *put aside the various claims upon one's time (and do sth)*

【冗笔】redundancy in writing or painting; unnecessary touches or strokes

【冗长】lengthy; tediously long; long-winded, prolix; verbose

【冗词】superfluous word (in a piece of writing)

【冗繁】miscellaneous; many and diverse; full of trivial details

【冗务】multifarious routines: 他总是被～缠身。*He is always tired up with daily chores of all sorts.*

【冗员】redundant personnel: 裁减～ *reduce redundant personnel*; *cut redundant staff*

【冗赘】verbose; prolix; diffuse

róu

柔 ① soft; pliant; flexible: 儿童～软的四肢 *the supple limbs of a child* ② gentle; tender;

mild; yielding: 刚～相济 *couple hardness with softness (in dealing with people); temper toughness with gentleness* ③ soften: ～麻 *soak jute hemp, etc. to soften it*
【柔板】【音】adagio
【柔肠】soft heart; tender heart; tender feelings: ～寸断 *lovelorn; be broken-hearted* / ～百折 *deeply grieved*
【柔道】【体】judo
【柔和】mild; gentle; soft; tender
【柔滑】soft and smooth; creamy
【柔静】gentle (or tender) and quiet
【柔曼】① soft; gentle: ～的旋律 *a soft and beautiful melody; a melody of serene beauty* ② (of skin) soft and smooth; (of appearance) gentle and beautiful; good-looking; gorgeous
【柔美】gentle and lovely; soft and graceful: ～的舞姿 *graceful dance* /音色～ *soft and exquisite tone colour*
【柔媚】gentle and lovely; soft and delicate; genial: ～的微笑 *a genial smile* / ～的目光 *tender and charming eyes*
【柔嫩】tender; delicate: ～的叶子 *tender leaves* / ～的小草 *tender grass*
【柔能克刚】softness can overcome hardness; soft tactics can disarm the hardest
【柔懦】soft; timid and overcautious; weak-willed: ～的性格 *have a weak character; meek and docile by nature*
【柔情】tender feelings; tenderness: ～似水 *be passionately devoted; deep affection; boundless tender feelings* / ～蜜意 *tender affectionate love; tender affection* / ～侠骨 *tender heart and chivalrous spirit; compassionate and gallant*
【柔韧】pliable and tough; supple
【柔软】soft; lithe; supple
【柔润】soft and smooth; supple; delicate: ～的皮肤 *soft complexion; delicate skin* / ～的嗓音 *a soft and mellow voice*
【柔弱】weak; delicate: 性格～ *submissive; weak-willed; meek and mild*
【柔顺】gentle and meek; gentle and agreeable: 性格～ *have a meek disposition; meek and mild*
【柔婉】soft and mild; gentle and agreeable: ～的语调 *a soft and sweet voice; a mild tone*
【柔细】soft and fine (or thin): ～的柳条 *delicate willow twigs; soft and thin willow twigs*
【柔心弱骨】soft heart and weak bone-soft; meek; submissive; mild
【柔性】【物】flexibility: ～连接 *flexible joint* / ～塑料 *flexiplast*
【柔鱼】squid
【柔中有刚】iron fist in a velvet glove; firmness cloaked beneath gentleness; gentle but firm

揉 ① rub: ～眼 *rub one's eyes* / ～鼻子 *rub one's noses* ② knead; crumple into a ball; roll: ～面钵 *kneading trough* ③ bend; twist; reform
【揉搓】rub

糅 mix; mingle: ～杂 *mixture*
【糅合】mix; form a mixture

蹂 [书] stamp; trample:
【蹂躏】trample underfoot; trample on; ravage; ravish; devastate: ～妇女 *violate a woman; rape*

鞣 [书] tan: ～革 *tannage*
【鞣料】tanning material: ～浸膏 *tanning extract*
【鞣皮子】tan hides
【鞣酸】【化】tannic acid; tannin: ～溶液 *tan-liquor; tan-ooze; tan-pickle*

ròu

肉 ① meat; flesh: 猪～ *pork* /牛～ *beef* /肌～ *muscle* /骨～ *flesh and blood* / ～馅 *chopped meat; meat stuffing* ② pulp; flesh (of fruits): 椰子～ *coconut meat* /果～ *the flesh of fruit; pulp*
【肉包子】steamed bun with chopped meat stuffing
【肉饼】meat pie; mince pie: ～蒸蛋 *steamed minced pork with egg*
【肉搏】fight hand to-hand: ～战 *hand-to-hand combat (or fight); bayonet charge (or fighting)*
【肉畜】meat livestock; livestock raised for meat; beef cattle
【肉店】butcher's (shop)
【肉丁】diced meat: 让我再给你一些～好吗? *May I help you to some more diced meat?*
【肉冻】meat jelly; aspic: 鸭～ *duck in aspic*
【肉豆蔻】【药】nutmeg
【肉嘟嘟】plump; fat; chubby: ～的小手 *plump little hands*
【肉毒杆菌】【医】clostridium botulinum
【肉墩墩】stocky; flesh and sturdy
【肉冠】【动】comb
【肉桂】【植】Chinese cassia tree; cinnamon tree
【肉果】【植】sarcocarp
【肉红】pink; pinkish red; flesh-coloured
【肉鸡】chicken; table hen; broiler
【肉乎乎】fleshy; very fat
【肉酱】meat pulp; minced meat
【肉类】meats: ～加工厂 *meat · processing factory*
【肉瘤】【医】sarcoma
【肉麻】nauseating; fulsome; sickening; disgusting
【肉麻糜】[方] meat paste; fine minced meat
【肉末】ground meat; minced meat
【肉排】steak: 猪～ *pork chop* /牛～ *steak*
【肉皮】pork skin: 你喜欢吃～吗? *Do you like to eat pork skin?*
【肉皮儿】[方] (human) skin
【肉片】sliced meat
【肉禽】fowl; table poultry
【肉色】flesh-coloured; yellowish pick; flesh-tinted
【肉身】【宗】the mortal body; flesh
【肉食】carnivorous: ～动物 *carnivorous animal; carnivore*

【肉食】meat
【肉丝】shredded meat:一碗~面 *a bowl of noodles with shredded pork* /一盘辣椒~ *a dish of shredded meat with hot pepper*
【肉松】dried meat (esp. pork) floss; dried mince meat
【肉穗花序】【植】spadix
【肉袒】[书] strip off one's own upper garment as a token of sincere apology; make a humble apology
【肉汤】broth; meat gravy
【肉体】the flesh; human body
【肉头】[方] round and soft; soft and fleshy; chubby
【肉丸子】meatball
【肉星儿】tiny bits of meat:长时间以来我们的菜里没有见过~。*There has not been the slightest bit of meat in our dishes for a long time.*
【肉刑】corporal punishment
【肉芽】【医】granulation
【肉眼】naked eye
【肉眼凡胎】a very mundane person; common mortal; ordinary person:我们都是~。*We are all ordinary persons.*
【肉欲】sensual desire; carnal desire
【肉汁】gravy; meat juice; meat extract
【肉质】fleshy: ~果实 *fleshy fruit*
【肉制品】meat product
【肉赘】wart

rú

如[1] ① in compliance with; according; in conformity with: ~命 *in compliance with your order (or instructions)* ② like; as; as if: ~饥似渴 *as if hungering or thirsting for sth; eagerly* ③ can compare with; be as good as:在许多方面他不~我。*He is not as good as I am in many aspects.* /他哥哥的工作不~他的好。*His elder bother's work is inferior to mine.* ④ such as; for instance; for example; as:我国有许多伟大的小说家,~曹雪芹,施耐庵,蒲松龄等。*There were many great novelists, such as Cao Xueqin, Shi Naian, Pu Songling.* ⑤ be more than; surpass; exceed:质地不~样品的货物 *an inferior court goods inferior to sample* ⑥ go to; arrive at: ~厕 *go to toilet*

如[2] in case (of); if: ~若不然 *if not; otherwise*

【如常】as usual:平静~ *calm a usual* /工作~ *work as usual*
【如出一口】as if from one mouth-with one voice; in unison; unanimously
【如出一辙】be cut from the same cloth; be exactly the same; run in the same groove; follow the same pattern
【如初】as before; as always:和好~ *be on good terms against; restore good relations; be good partners again as the used to*
【如此】such; so; like that; in this way:但愿~ *wish it were so* /理应~ *rightly so* / ~伟大 *so great*
【如此等等】and so on and so forth
【如此而已】that's what it all adds up to; that's all there is to it
【如此这般】thus and thus; thus and so; in this way:他~地交代了一番。*He told me in this way.*
【如次】be as follows:原因~。*The reasons are as follow.*
【如坠烟海】as if lost on a foggy (or misty) sea; completely at a loss
【如法炮制】prepare or concoct herbal medicine by a prescribed method — follow a set pattern; follow suit
【如故】① like old friends ② as before
【如果】in case (of); if; in the event of: ~你信任我,请把你的秘密告诉我。*If you trust me, please tell me your trouble.* / ~你现在开始存钱的话,你不久就能买到你喜欢的衣服了。*If you save now, you will be able to buy the clothes soon.*
【如何】how; what:你知道~打开那扇门吗? *Do you know how to open the door?* /小偷们为~分赃而互相争吵。*The thieves quarrelled with one another about how to divide the loot.*
【如虎添翼】like a tiger that has grown wings-with might redoubled; further strengthened
【如花似锦】(of scenery, one's future, etc.) splendid; beautiful; wonderful
【如花似玉】like flowers and jade — enchantingly beautiful (woman)
【如火如荼】like a raging fire; fiery:全国掀起了~的反战运动。*Anti-war movement was under way like fire throughout the country.*
【如获至宝】as if on had found an invaluable treasure
【如箭在弦】like an arrow fitted to the bowstring-cannot but go ahead
【如胶似漆】cling or stick to each other like glue or lacquer; be deeply attached to each other
【如今】nowadays; now; today
【如旧】as before; as of old
【如狼牧羊】like a wolf shepherding sheep — trample people underfoot
【如狼似虎】a ferocious as wolves and tigers; brutal
【如雷贯耳】reverberate or resound like thunder:久闻大名,~。*Your exalted name has resounded in my ears.*
【如临大敌】as if faced with a formidable enemy — be heavily guarded
【如临深渊,如履薄冰】as though standing on the brink of an abyss or treading on thin ice — acting with extreme caution
【如芒在背】feel prickles down one's back — feel nervous and uneasy; be on pins and needles
【如梦初醒】as if awakening from a dream; wake up all of a sudden
【如期】as scheduled; on scheduled; by the scheduled time; in time: ~到达 *arrive in time*
【如其】if; in case (of)

R

【如泣如诉】(of sound, music or singing) like weeping; querulous and plaintive
【如日中天】like the sun at high noon; at the apex (or zenith) of one's power career, etc.
【如入无人之境】like entering an empty land — breaking all resistance; encountering no resistance at all; carry all before one
【如若】if; in case
【如丧考妣】as if one had cost one's parents-look utterly sad or sorrowful
【如上】as above: ~所述 *as mentioned (or stated) above*
【如实】go strictly by the facts; strictly according to the facts: ~汇报情况 *report exactly how things stand; report the situation accurately*
【如是】so; such; in this way
【如释重负】as if relieved of a heavy load: 最后他~地松了口气。*He heaved a sigh of relief at last.*
【如数家珍】as if enumerating one's family treasure-show thorough familiarity with one's subject
【如数】exactly the number or amount: ~偿还 *pay back in full* / ~缴纳罚金 *pay forfeit in full*
【如同】like; as
【如闻其声,如见其人】(so vivid description that) you seem to see and hear the person
【如下】as follow; following: 全文~。*The full text follows.*
【如心】pleased; gratified; satisfied; to one's liking
【如许】① so; such; like that ② so much; so many: 枉费~时日 *squander so much time*
【如一】identical; consistent: 表里~ *think and act in one and the same way*
【如意】① comply with one's wishes; be gratified: 万事~。*Realize all one's wishes or may all go well with you!* ② *ruyi*, an S-shaped ornamental wand or sceptre, usu. made of jade, symbolizing good fortune
【如意算盘】wishful thinking; smug calculations 他打着自己的~。*He is indulging his wishful thinking.* /他的~落空了。*His smug calculations came to nothing.*
【如影随形】like the shadow following the man — closely associated with each other; always in each other's company
【如鱼得水】feel just like fish in water; be in one's element; be in congenial company
【如愿】do as one's wishes; have one's wish fulfilled: 他去了美国,总算~了。*He went to the United States and thus had his wish fulfilled.*
【如愿以偿】have one's wish fulfilled; obtain what one wishes
【如云】cloudlike; many; abundant: 美女~ *large groups of beauties*
【如醉如痴】behave as if intoxicated and enthralled (or stupefied)
【如坐针毡】feel as if sitting on a bed of nails; be on pins and needles; be on tenterhooks; feel as if sitting on a rug full of needles

茹 ① eat: 含辛~苦 *endure suffering; endure hardships; bear hardships*
【茹毛饮血】(of primitive man) eat the raw flesh of birds and beasts; eat birds and animals raw
【茹素吃斋】go vegetarian

铷 【化】rubidium (Rb)

儒 ① Confucians; Confucianism ②[旧] scholar; learned man
【儒道】Confucianism and Taoism
【儒艮】【动】dugong; sea cow
【儒家】Confucianists: ~学说 *Confucian doctrine* / ~思想 *Confucianism*
【儒将】scholar-general
【儒教】Confucianism
【儒门】Confucian school of thought
【儒生】[旧] Confucian scholar
【儒术】Confucian teachings
【儒商】scholar-businessman
【儒雅】[书] scholarly and refined: ~风度 *scholar bearing* /风流~ *elegant in manners*
【儒医】scholar-doctor

嚅
【嚅动】(of lips) open and close
【嚅嚅】hesitate in speech; mutter and mumble

濡 ① immerse; moisten; dip in: 耳~目染 *be imperceptibly influenced by what one sees and hears* ② linger; stay
【濡笔】dip a writing brush in ink-write
【濡染】① be influenced by ② immerse; dip in imbue
【濡润】moist; wet
【濡湿】soak; become wet; make wet

孺 child: 妇~皆知 *sth known even to women and children*
【孺子】[书] child
【孺子可教】the kid is worth teaching; the young man is teachable; you could be taught, young man
【孺子牛】ox Led by the child-a servant of people

蠕 wriggle; squirm
【蠕变】① change slowly ②【物】creep; deformation
【蠕虫】worm; helminth: ~学 *helminthology*
【蠕动】① wriggle; squirm ② peristalsis
【蠕蠕】squirming; wriggling: ~而行 *crawl along; move along by wriggling*

rǔ

汝 ① you: ~辈 *you people; you* / ~等 *you people*

乳 ① breast; mamma ② milk: 牛~ *cow milk* ③ any milk-like liquid ④ newborn (animal); sucking: ~燕 *newly hatched swallow; young swallow* / ~猪 *sucking pig; suckling pig* ⑤ give birth to; reproduce. 蕃 reproduction (of animals, etc.); breed; multiply

【乳媪】wet nurse

【乳白】milky white; creamy; cream colour: ~灯泡 *opal bulb* / ~玻璃 *opal glass; opalescent glass* / ~色气球 *milky white balloon*

【乳钵】mortar (a vessel)

【乳齿】milk tooth; deciduous tooth

【乳畜】dairy cattle; milk livestock

【乳蛾】acute tonsillitis

【乳儿】nursing infant; sucking baby

【乳房】① breast; mamma ② (of an animal) udder

【乳峰】(of a woman rounded breasts)

【乳化】【化】emulsification: ~剂 *emulsifying agent; emulsifier* / ~漆 *emulsion paint* / ~油 *emulsible oil; emulsified oil* / ~液 *emulsion* /水包油~液 *oil-in-water emulsion*

【乳剂】【化】emulsion: 全色~ *panchromatic emulsion*

【乳浆】milk

【乳胶】【化】emulsion

【乳胶漆】emulsion paint; latex paint

【乳酪】cheese: ~塑料 *lactolite*

【乳糜】【生理】chyle

【乳名】infant name; child's pet name: 那个可爱的小女孩的~叫玛丽。*The lovely girl's infant name is Mary.*

【乳母】wet nurse

【乳娘】[方] wet nurse

【乳牛】dairy cattle; milch cow: ~场 *dairy farm*

【乳清蛋白】【生化】lactalbumin

【乳酸】【生化】lactic acid: ~钙 *calcium lactate* /副~ *paratactic acid* / ~酶 *lactolase*

【乳糖】milk sugar; lactose: ~尿 *lactosuria* / ~酶 *lactase*

【乳头】① nipple; teat; mammilla ② papilla: 视神经~ *optic papilla*

【乳腺】【生理】mammary gland / ~病 *mastopathy* / ~癌 *breast cancer; mastoscirrhus* / ~炎 *mastitis* / ~增生 *cyclomastopathy*

【乳香】【植】frankincense

【乳臭】smelling of milk — childish; green

【乳臭未干】still smell of one's mother's milk — greenhorn; wet behind the ears; be young and in experienced; fledgling

【乳牙】milk tooth; deciduous tooth

【乳液】emulsion

【乳罩】bra; brassiere

【乳汁】milk

【乳脂】butterfat; cream: ~奶酪 *cream cheese* / ~糖 *toffee; taffy*

【乳浊液】【化】emulsion

辱 ① disgrace; dishonour: 污~ *humiliate; insult* /那个英雄宁死不受~。*The hero would rather die than disgrace himself.* ② bring disgrace or humiliate to; be unworthy of; insult: ~没 *bring discredit to; tarnish*

【辱骂】abuse; call sb names; hurl insults upon sb

【辱命】fail to accomplish a mission; fail to accomplish an assignment

rù

入 ① enter; go in: 出~ *come in and go out* / 时已~夏。*Summer has set in.* / ~乡随俗。*When in Rome do as the Romans do.* /骑自行车出~必须下车。*Cyclists must dismount at the gate.* /海河流~渤海。*Haihe River empties into Bohai Sea.* ② join; be admitted into; become a member of: ~党 *join the party; become a party member* ③ income: 总收~ *total income* /日收~100元 *earn ¥100 a day* ④ agree with; conform to: ~理 *reasonable; sensible*

【入不敷出】income falling short · of expenditure; unable to make ends meet; living beyond one's means

【入仓】① be stored in a barn; be put in storage; store sth in a warehouse ②【经】warehousing

【入场】entrance; admission: ~券 *(admission) ticket* / ~式 *march-in ceremony*

【入超】unfavourable balance of trade; trade deficit: 近年来美国一直是贸易~国。*In recent years the United States is always a country of import surplus.*

【入肚】swallow; eat

【入耳】pleasant to the ear; pleasant or acceptable to the mind; palatable: ~的话 *pleasant words* / 不堪~ *(of language) offensive to the ear; obscene*

【入伏】beginning of the hottest days of the year; the fu days begin

【入港】①【交】enter a port; come into port ② (of conversation) find particularly congenial; in full agreement; in perfect harmony: 我们二人谈得十分~。*The two of us were deep in conversation and in full agreement with one another.*

【入股】buy a share; become a shareholder

【入骨】to the marrow: 恨之~ *hate sb to the marrow of one's bones*

【入国问禁】on entering a country, inquire about its taboos or prohibitions; ask about the prohibitions upon arrival in a foreign country

【入海口】【地】estuary

【入黑】get dark

【入户】① go to sb's home; go to sb's house ② register residence in a certain place; obtain a residence permit

【入画】be picturesque; suitable for a painting: 黄山风光处处可~。*Every bit of Huangshan scenery is worthy of a painter's brush.*

【入会】enroll as member; join a society, association, etc.

【入伙】join a gang; go into partnership; join in partnership ② join a mess; have one's meals at a canteen or mess hall:所有学生都在食堂~。*All the students eat at the mess.*

【入籍】naturalize; acquire citizenship (of a country):入日本籍 *be naturalized in Japan; become a Japanese citizen*

【入寂】(of Buddhist monks or nuns) death; pass a way; nirvana; die

【入教】be converted to a religion; embrace a religion

【入境】enter a country: ~签证 *entry visa* /办理~手续 *go through the entry formalities* / ~登记 *entrance registration* / ~证书 *entry certificate* / ~口岸 *port of entry*

【入口】① enter the mouth:不可~ *not to be taken orally!* /这种食物难于~。*This food had a nasty taste.* ② entrance:大厅~ *entrance to the hall*

【入寇】[书] invade; intrude

【入库】lay up; put in storage; be laid up: all kinds of part:所有设备都已~。*All devices have been put in storage.*

【入款】receipts; income

【入理】reasonable:他的话很~。*What he said is quite reasonable.*

【入殓】encoffin; put a corpse in a coffin

【入列】【军】join the ranks; fall in:所有士兵都已~。*All the soldiers take his place in the ranks.*

【入流】qualified:他是个不~的画家。*He is not a qualified painter.*

【入寐】fall asleep:他一夜辗转不能~。*He tossed and turned in the bed through a whole night, unable to go to sleep.*

【入门】① cross the threshold; learn the rudiments of a subject:学汉语~并不难。*Rudimentary Chinese is easy to acquire.* ② elementary course; primer:《汉语语法~》*The Elements of Chinese Grammar*

【入梦】① fall asleep; go to sleep; start dreaming ② appear in one's dream

【入迷】be enchanted; be fascinated; fill sb with great delight:这本有趣的小说使我~。*The interesting novel gets me.*

【入眠】① fall asleep ② (of silkworms) neither eat nor move (when casting of a skin)

【入魔】absolutely addicted; mad about; be infatuated; be spellbound

【入木三分】sinking deep into wood-written in a forceful hand; penetrating; piercing; incisive

【入暮】at dusk; towards evening; at nightfall; at twilight

【入侵】invade; intrude; make in roads; make an incursion:敌人再次尝试~这个国家。*The enemies made another try to invade the country.*

【入情入理】fair and reasonable; fair and just

【入射点】【物】point of incidence; incidence point

【入射线】【物】incident ray

【入神】be enthralled; be entranced; be spellbound ② superb; marvelous; wonderful

【入胜】enthralled; fascinated:引人~(*of scenery, literary works, etc.*) *fascinating; bewitching*

【入时】fashionable; modish:一件~的裙子 *a fashionable skirt*

【入世】enter society: ~不深 *lack experience of life; haven't seen much of the world*

【入室】[书] become well advanced in scholarship; attain profundity in scholastic pursuits:登堂~ *become proficient in one's profession* / ~弟子 *disciple who has inherited the mantle from his master; an initiated pupil*

【入室操戈】turn sb's words or argument against himself; refute sb with his own writings or statements

【入手】start with; begin with; take as the point of departure

【入睡】fall asleep

【入土】be buried; be interred:他快~了。*He has one foot in the grave.*

【入团】join or be admitted to the Chinese Communist Youth League

【入托】be sent to a nursery; start going to a nursery

【入微】in every possible way; in a subtle way; in every detail:体贴~ *look after sb in every possible way; attend to sb's comfort with loving care* /细腻~的画像 *an exquisite portrait*

【入闱】① [旧] enter the imperial examination hall ② be selected; be recruited out of many candidates; enter for the next round of competition

【入味】① tasty ② interesting

【入伍】join up; enlist; join the services:他最小的儿子去年应召~。*His youngest son was called up last year.*

【入席】take one's seat at a banquet, ceremony, etc.:请朋友们~。*Please be seated, every friend.*

【入乡随俗】follow local customs where you are; wherever you are, follow local customs; when in Rome do as the Romans do

【入选】be chosen; be selected

【入学】① start school: ~年龄 *school age* ② enter a school; go to school: ~考试 *examination*

【入眼】pleasing to the eye; pleasant to the eye:看得~ *look attractive* /没有一件工具他看得~的。*None of these tools were to his liking.* /他的这种行为真让人看不~。*His behaviour was most unseemly.*

【入药】be used as medicine

【入夜】at nightfall: ~后,雨越下越大。*It rained heavy and heavy after night came.*

【入狱】be put in prison; be sent to jail; be put behind bars

【入院】be hospitalized; be admitted to hospital; be put into a hospital:办理~手续 *fill out forms for admittance to a hospital; make arrangements for hospitalization*

【入账】enter an item in a account; enter into the account book

【入蛰】(of animals) go into hibernation

【入赘】marry into and live with one's bride's family

【入座】be properly seated; take one's seat

蓐 ［书］straw mat or mattress：坐～ *chair mat*

溽 ［书］damp；humid

【溽热】humid and hot；damp and close；hot and suffocating；muggy

【溽暑】sweltering summer weather

缛 elaborate；cumbersome

褥 cotton-padded mattress：被～ *bedding*；*bedclothes* / 棉～ *cotton-padded mattress*

【褥疮】【医】bedsore；decubitus ulcer

【褥单】bed sheet

【褥套】① bedding sack ② mattress cover ③ bedtick

【褥子】padded mattress；cotton-padded mattress

ruǎn

软 ① soft；flexible；supple：～椅 *soft chair* / ～底鞋 *soft-soled shoes* ② mild；gentle；soft：～媚 *gentle and soft*；*pleasant and likable* / ～饮料 *soft drinks* ③ weak；feeble；lacking strength or power：欺～怕硬 *bully the weak and fear the strong* / 他腿部发～。*His legs felt weak or he felt weak in the legs.* ④ easily moved or influenced；apt to be influenced：心～ *tender-hearted* / 他心太～。*He was too kind-hearted.* ⑤ poor in quality，ability，etc.：我们拒绝货色～的商品上市。*We refuse poor quality goods on the market.* / 面对难题他感到能力太～。*He felt quite inadequate when faced by a difficult problem.*

【软包装】soft package：～饮料 *soft packaged drinks* / 醋用～ *soft packing for vinegar*

【软币】① paper money；note ② soft money；soft currency

【软玻璃】【化】soft glass

【软磁盘】【电】diskette；floppy disk（FD）

【软蛋】① soft-shelled egg ②［方］timid and overcautious；coward

【软刀子】soft knife — one means of harming people imperceptibly

【软钉子】soft mail — a mild or tactful refusal or refutation；polite refusal；snub

【软缎】soft silk fabric in satin weave

【软腭】【生理】soft palate

【软耳朵】soft ear — a gullible person；a credulous person

【软风】① breeze ②【气】light air

【软腐病】【农】soft rot

【软钢】soft steel；mild steel

【软膏】paste；ointment

【软骨】【生理】cartilage

【软骨头】a spineless person；a coward

【软骨鱼】cartilaginous fish

【软管】flexible tube；flexible pipe；hose：～接头 *hose coupler*

【软罐头】soft package；foods packaged in carton containers

【软焊】soft soldering：～料 *soft solder*

【软乎乎】soft

【软化】① soften：～硬水 *soften hard water* / 他的态度逐渐～。*His attitude has changed from stiff to compliant.* ② win over by soft tactics；weaken：～政策 *soft tactics* ③ bate

【软和】［口］① soft：～的棉被 *a soft cotton-padded mattress* ② gentle；kind：～话 *kind words*；*soft words*

【软技术】soft technology（such as management，administration，etc.）

【软件】① software：～包 *software package* / ～库 *software library* / ～工程 *software engineering* ② quality of management，services，personnel，etc.

【软禁】place sb under house arrest；put under house confinement

【软科学】soft science

【软拷贝】soft copy

【软绵绵】① soft：～的织物 *soft fabric* / ～的音乐 *sentimental music* / ～的枕头 *soft pillow* ② weak：这些天他感到身体～的。*He felt weak in these days.*

【软磨】use soft tactics：～硬泡 *alternate use of soft and tough tactics*

【软木】cork：～塞 *cork*（*as a stopper*）

【软泥】ooze

【软盘】diskette；floppy disk：昨天因为工作需要，我们发了好多～。*We were given some floppy disks for work yesterday.*

【软片】（a roll of）film

【软弱】feeble；weak；flabby：全身～无力 *be weak in one's whole body* / 性格～ *be weak in character* / 领导～ *weak leadership*

【软弱可欺】be weak and easy to bully；be weak and easily bullied：我们不是～的人。*We are not weak persons and easy to bully.*

【软弱无能】weak and incompetent；namby-pamby；effete

【软食】soft diet；pap；soft food：李奶奶年纪大了，只能吃一些～。*Granny Li is too old to eat soft foods.*

【软水】soft water

【软酥酥】weak；limp

【软糖】jelly drops；soft candy；soft sweets

【软梯】rope ladder

【软通货】soft currency

【软卧】【交】soft berth on a sleeper：～车厢 *soft sleeper carriage*

【软席】【交】soft seat or berth；cushioned seat or berth：～卧铺 *soft-berth carriage*；*sleeping carriage with cushioned berths*

【软线】【电】flexible cord

【软性】softness；gentleness；lightness；pliability：～电影 *soft film* / ～读物 *light reading* / ～推销 *soft sell*

【软硬不吃】yield neither persuasion nor coercion
【软硬兼施】use (or employ) both hard and soft tactics; use a combination of the carrot and the stick
【软语】soft words (spoken to ask pardon, show sympathy, etc.); conciliatory remarks; gentle and kind words
【软玉】【矿】nephrite
【软玉温香】soft jade and warm fragrance — feminine charm; a woman's charm
【软炸】soft fry
【软脂】【化】palmitin: ~酸 *palmitic acid*; *palmitic acid*
【软指标】soft target
【软着陆】soft landing: ~设备 *soft-lander*
【软组织】【生理】soft tissue (such as muscles, etc.)

ruǐ

蕊 stamen; pistil: 花~ *stamen or pistil* /雄~ *stamen* /雌~ *pistil*

ruì

蚋 buffalo gnat; blackfly

锐 ① sharp; keen; acute: 目光敏~ *be sharp-eyed*; *have sharp eyes* /尖~的思想斗争 *sharp mental conflicts* ② rapid; sudden; drastic: ~减 *drop sharply*; *reduce drastically* ③ vigour; fighting spirit: 养精蓄~ *conserve one's strength and store up one's energy*
【锐不可当】be irresistible: 我军以~之势攻击敌人。*Our army attacked the enemy with overwhelming force.*
【锐角】【数】acute angle: ~三角形 *acute triangle*
【锐利】① (of a knife, etc.) sharp; keen: ~的钢牙 *a sharp knife* / ~的武器 *a sharp or powerful weapon* / ~的梭镖 *a sharp spear* ② penetrating; incisive: ~的眼光 *sharp-eyed* / ~的笔锋 *a sharp pen*; *a vigorous style*
【锐敏】keen; sharp; sensitive: keen thought: ~的思想家 *a penetrating thinker* / ~的目光 *a penetrating look* /狗的嗅觉很~。*Dogs have a keen sense of smell.*
【锐气】dash; drive: 挫敌人的~ *deflate the enemy's arrogance* / ~十足 *full of dash* /表现了运动员的~ *show the dashing spirit of players.*
【锐器】sharp tool; sharp instrument
【锐眼】sharp eyes
【锐意】strong determination: ~进取 *be determined to make progress*

瑞 auspicious; lucky
【瑞典】Sweden: ~人 *Swede*; *the Swedish* / ~语 *Swedish*
【瑞气】good omen; auspicious atmosphere
【瑞士】Switzerland
【瑞雪】timely snow; auspicious snow
【瑞雪兆丰年】timely Snow foretells a bumper harvest; a snow year, a rich year

睿 [书] be farsighted; having foresight
【睿哲】[书] wise and farsighted
【睿智】[书] wise and farsighted

rùn

闰【天】intercalation; intercalary
【闰年】leap or intercalary year
【闰日】leap or intercalary day
【闰月】leap month; intercalary month in the lunar calendar

润 ① moist; smooth; sleek: 湿~ *moist* /光~ (*of skin*) *smooth* ② moisten; lubricate: 喝点茶~~喉咙。*Drink some tea to moisten your throat.* ③ profit; remuneration; benefit: 利~ *profit* ④ embellish; touch up: ~色 *touch up*; *beautify*
【润笔】① (of a writing brush) dip in ink ② remuneration for a writer, painter or calligrapher, etc.
【润肠】【中医】lubricate the intestines; ease constipation
【润肺】【中医】moisten the lungs-make expectoration easy; facilitate expectoration
【润肤剂】emollient
【润滑】lubricate: ~油 *lubricating oil*; *lubrication oil* / ~剂 *lubricant* / ~系统 *lubricating system* / ~脂 *lubricating grease*
【润湿】① moist; damp: ~的泥土 *damp soil*; *moist soil* ② moisten; dampen; wet; soak: 露水~了她的衣服。*Her clothes were moistened with dew.*
【润饰】polish; touch up; beautify
【润养】[书] nourish: ~万物生灵 *nourish all creatures on earth*
【润燥】【中医】moisten the respiratory tract, skin, etc.
【润泽】① moist; smooth; sleek; shiny: 雨后森林显得青葱~。*After the rain, the forest looked fresh green and shiny.* ② moisten; lubricate: 细雨~着花朵。*The flowers became moist in the fine drizzle.*

ruò

若[1] as if; like; seem: 那人~有所思地吸着烟。*The man pulled thoughtfully at his pipe.*

若[2] if: ~有意见,可以提出来。*If you have differing opinion, you can put forward it.* / ~太阳晒得厉害,你就把帽子戴上。*Take a hat with you in case the sun is very hot.*

若[3] [书] you：~辈 *you people*

【若虫】【动】nymph

【若非】[书] if not; were it not for; but for

【若干】① some; certain; a certain number; a certain amount：~次 *several times* / ~名同学 *a number of students* ② how many; how much

【若何】how; what

【若即若离】be neither close nor distant; maintain a lukewarm relationship

【若明若暗】have an indistinct picture of; (of an attitude) be non-committal

【若其】[书] if; in case

【若是】if

【若无其事】as if nothing had happened; calm; casually; indifferent

【若要人不知,除非己莫为】if you don't wish people to know sth, don't do it; murder will out

【若隐若现】partly hidden and partly visible; appear indistinctly

【若有所失】feel as if something were missing; be listless 偌 so; such

【偌大】so big; of such a big size：~一个地方 *such a big place* / ~年纪 *so old; so advanced in age* / ~一座城市 *such a large city*

弱 ① weak; frail; feeble：以强凌~ *the strong bullying the weak* /体质~ *be in delicate health* /风势已~。*The wind has sunk down.* ② young; little：老~病残 *the old, weak, sick and disabled* ③ interior：我们的实力不~于对方。*Our capability is not interior to the opponent.* ④ (following a fraction or decimal) a little less than：四分之一~ *a little less than one-forth*

【弱不禁风】too weak to withstand a gust of wind; extremely delicate; frail：他参加了昨天晚上的会议以后,现在觉得身体有些~。*He is feeling a bit fragile after last night's meeting.*

【弱点】weakness; weak point：我们每个人都有~。*We all have our weakness.*

【弱冠】[旧] a young man of around twenty years old

【弱碱】【化】weak base

【弱旅】weak team

【弱脉】【中医】weak pulse

【弱拍】【音】weak beat; unaccented beat

【弱肉强食】the weak are the prey of the strong; low of the jungle

【弱视】【医】amblyopia; weak vision (or sight)

【弱手】incompetent person

【弱酸】【化】weak acid

【弱项】weak event; event in which one does poorly

【弱小】small and weak：~国家 *small and weak country*

【弱信号】weak signal

【弱音器】【音】mute; sordine

【弱智】weak-minded; mentally deficient：~儿童 *a retarded child* / ~教育 *education for the mentally retarded*

箬

【箬笠】a broad-brimmed conical bam-boo hat; bamboo hat

S

sā

仨 ［口］three：～学生 *three students* / 咱哥儿～ *we three (brothers)*

撒 ① cast；loosen；let go：～网 *cast a net* / ～手 *let go one's hold*；*let go of sth* ② throw off all restraint；let oneself go：～酒疯 *be roaring drunk*；*be drunk and disorderly*
see also sǎ

【撒旦】【宗】Satan；the Devil
【撒刁】act in a slick and shameless way；play tricks
【撒疯】① run wild；behave atrociously ② vent one's spite (or anger)
【撒哈拉沙漠】Sahara Desert：～的广阔 *the full extent of the Sahara Desert*
【撒欢儿】［方］gambol；frolic；frisk
【撒谎】［口］tell a lie；lie：昨天，在上学迟到的问题上她向她妈妈～了。*Yesterday she told a lie to her mother on late for school.*
【撒娇】behave like a spoiled child act spoiled
【撒赖】kick up a row；make a scene；act shameless；act wildly.
【撒尿】［口］piss；pee；urinate
【撒泼】be unreasonable and make a scene；make a scene and refuse to be reconciled
【撒气】(of a tyre，ball，etc.) leak；go a flat；go soft ② vent one's temper or anger
【撒手归西】go to heaven；go west；kick the bucket
【撒手锏】a sudden thrust with the mace one's trump card
【撒手人世】pass away
【撒腿】take to one's heels；scamper；beat it：～往办公室跑 *make straight for office*
【撒网】cost a net；cast one's net；pay out a net；spread a net
【撒鸭子】［方］take to one's heels
【撒野】act wildly；act rowdily；behave atrociously (or rudely)

sǎ

洒 sprinkle；spray；spill；shed：往地上～点儿水 *sprinkle some* / 往身上～香水 *spray perfume on one's clothes*

【洒泪】shed tears：～告别 *take a tearful leave*；*part in tears*
【洒落】drip：泪珠～到地下。*Drops of tear trickle down to the ground.*
【洒扫】sprinkle water and sweep the floor：～庭院 *sweep the courtyard*
【洒水车】watering car；spraying car；sprinkler
【洒脱】free and easy；unrestrained；uninhibited

撒 ① scatter；sprinkle；broadcast：～种子 *sow seeds* / ～一层盐 *spread a layer of salt* ② spill；drop：在空中～传单的飞机 *an aeroplane spilling leaflets*
see also sā

【撒播】broadcast；broadcast sowing：～机 *broadcaster*；*broadcast seeder*；*planter*
【撒肥机】fertilizer spreader or distribute；manure distributor
【撒粉】【农】dusting
【撒进】cast：渔民们一到捕鱼区就把渔网～了大海。*As soon as they reached the fishing area，the fishermen cast their nets into the sea.*
【撒施】【农】scatter fertilizer over the field；broadcast fertilizer

sà

卅 thirty

飒 ① rustle；sough：狂风～然而起。*The fierce wind rose sighing.* ② wither；wilt

【飒飒】sough；rustle：秋风～。*The autumn wind was rustling in the trees.*
【飒爽】［书］of martial bearing；valiant：英姿～ *valiant and heroic in bearing*

萨

【萨哈林岛】Sakhalin Island
【萨克管】【音】saxophone
【萨克号】【音】saxhorn
【萨摩亚】Samoa：～人 *Samoan* / ～语 *Samoan (language)*

sāi

腮 cheek

【腮帮】［口］cheek
【腮红】blush；rouge
【腮颊】cheek
【腮托】chin rest (of a viola or violin)

【腮腺】【生理】parotid gland：～炎 mumps

塞 ① fill in；squeeze in；stuff up：我一点儿也吃不下了，肚子都～满了。*I can't eat any more；my stomach's bulging.* ② stopper：瓶～ *bottle stopper* /木～ *stopper；plug*
see also sài；sè

【塞车】traffic jam
【塞尺】feeler gauge
【塞规】【机】plug gauge
【塞套】plug sleeve
【塞进】pack；whip：他妈妈把衣服～手提箱便离开了。*Her mother packed her clothes into the suitcase and left the family.* /她看了一下周围，迅速把钱～了衣袋。*She looked around and whipped it into her pocket.*
【塞牙】(of food) get stuck between the teeth
【塞子】stopper；cork

鳃 gill；branchia

【鳃瓣】gill；lamella
【鳃盖】gill cover

sài

塞 a stronghold of strategic importance：要～ *fort；fortress；fortification* /边～ *frontier fortress*
see also sāi；sè

【塞北】beyond the Great Wall
【塞尔维亚】Serbia：～人 *Serb*
【塞纳河】Seine，a river in northern France
【塞内加尔】Senegal：—～人 *Senegalese*
【塞浦路斯】Cyprus：～人 *Cypriot*
【塞外】north of the Great Wall：～风光 *scenery beyond the Great Wall*

赛[1] ① match；game；competition：volleyball game ② have a competition：比～规则 *rule of a game；rules of a contest* /参加～跑 *compete in a race* /与某人竞～以得到某物 *compete with sb for sth* ③ be comparable to；surpass：我们的生活～蜜甜。*Our life is as sweet as honey.*

赛[2] ① old practice of offering a sacrifice to gods；worshiping gods

【赛场】competition ground；arena for competition；ring；court；rink
【赛车】【体】① cycle racing；motorcycle race；automobile race ② racing bicycle；race car；racing vehicle
【赛程】【体】① distance in a event ② competition schedule
【赛次】round of competition；heat of sports：两个～ *two rounds of competition；two heats*
【赛地】venue of sports event；a place of supports contest or match
【赛段】section；leg of a long-distance race
【赛过】over take；better than；surpass
【赛会】religious procession
【赛季】competition season
【赛况】the events during a competition
【赛马】horse racing：～总会 *jockey club* /学校后面与～场为邻。*Our school backs onto the racecourse.*
【赛跑】race：长距离～ *long-distance race* /越野～ *cross-county race* /100米～ *100-metre dash* /1500米～ *1500-metre race* /和时间～ *a race against time* /十五个孩子参加～。*Fifteen children competed in the race.*
【赛区】zone (of sports and other competitions)；venue；conference (U.S.)
【赛事】sports competition；match；contest；game：他们在篮球～中输了。*They were defeated in the basketball match.*
【赛艇】【体】① rowing；yachting ② racing boat
【赛制】competition rules

sān

三 ① three：这个学校只有～学生。*There are only three students in this school.* /这个剧分为～幕，每一幕有六个场景。*This play is divided into three acts，and each act has six scenes.* ② more than two；several；many；numerous：～言两语 *in a few words；in one or two words* / ～六九等 *various grades and ranks* / ～思而后行！*Think before you act!*

【三八妇女节】international Women's Day (March 8)
【三八式步枪】38-rifle
【三百六十行】all trades and professions；all walks of life
【三胞胎】triplets
【三倍体】triploid
【三班制】three-shift working system
【三不管】come under (or within) nobody's jurisdiction；be nobody's business
【三部曲】trilogy
【三叉神经】【生理】trigeminal nerve：～痛 *trigeminal neuralgia*
【三岔路口】a junction of three roads；fort in the road
【三长两短】unexpected misfortune；sth unfortunate esp. death；unexpected calamity；mishap
【三朝元老】minister serving under three emperors；an official who stays in power under different regimes
【三重】triple；threefold：～唱 *vocal trio* /以政治家，思想家和军事家的～身份 *in the triple role of a statesman，thinker and strategist* / ～奏 (*instrumental*) *trio*
【三春】[书] the three months of spring season
【三次方程】【数】cubic equation
【三从四德】according to Confucian ethics women's three obedience and four virtues — obedience to father before marriage，to husband after marriage，and to son after husband's death；morality，proper speech，modest manner，and diligent

work

【三寸不烂之舌】a little lithe tongue; an eloquent tongue; a silver tongue; a glib tongue

【三代】three generation (father, son, and grandson)

【三等兵】(of US Army) basic private; (of US Air Force) airman third class (of US Navy) apprentice seaman

【三点式】bikini

【三碘化物】【化】triiodide

【三叠系】【地】Triassic System

【三冬】① winter; the third month of winter ② three years (or winters)

【三度存储器】【电】three-dimensional memory

【三段论法】【逻】syllogism

【三番五次】again and again; over and over again; repeatedly

【三方】tripartite: ~谈判 *tripartite negotiations*

【三废】the three waste (waste gas, water and industrial residues)

【三分球】【体】three pointer; trey

【三分像人,七分像鬼】look more like a ghost than a human

【三伏】① the three ten-day hottest periods of the year ② last of the three ten-day periods of the hot season

【三副】【航】third mate; third officer

【三纲五常】three cardinal guides (i. e. rules guides subject, father guides son, and husband guides wife) and five constant virtues (i. e. benevolence, righteousness, propriety, wisdom and fidelity) as specified in the feudal ethical code

【三个臭皮匠,赛过诸葛亮】three cobblers with their wits combined exceed Zhu Geliang the master mind — collective wisdom often proves superior; the wisdom of the masses surpass that of the wisest individual

【三个面向】the Three Orientations (education Oriented to the needs of modernization, of the world and of the future)

【三更半夜】in the depth of night; in the dead of night

【三宫六院】the three palaces and six chambers — the harem of an emperor

【三顾茅庐】make three times personal call at the thatched cottage — repeatedly re quest sb to take up a responsible post

【三光政策】policy of "burn all, kill all, loot all" once adopted by the Japanese invaders in China

【三合板】【建】three-ply board; plywood

【三合星】【天】triple star

【三合一】three-in-one

【三核苷酸】【生化】trinucleotide

【三化螟】【农】yellow rice borer

【三级风】【气】force 3 wind; gentle breeze

【三极管】triode: 晶体~ *transistor*

【三级跳远】【体】hop, step and jump; triple jump

【三季稻】triple cropping of rice

【三驾马车】① a carriage drawn by three horses ② troika; triumvirate

【三尖瓣】【生理】tricuspid stenosis: ~狭窄 *tricuspid valve*

【三缄其口】with one's lips sealed; overcautious in speech

【三讲】(a measure for Party building) three emphases (i e emphases on theoretical study, political awareness and moral rectitude): ~教育 *education on the three emphases*

【三角】① triangle ②【数】trigonometry: ~板 *set square* / ~测量 *triangulation* / ~洲 *delta* / ~债 *inter-corporate triangular debt; debt chain* / ~形 *triangle* / ~学 *trigonometry* / ~帆 *lateen sail* / ~方程 *trigonometric equation* / ~鲂 *triangular bream* / ~枫 *trident maple* / ~港 *estuary* / ~刮刀 *triangular scraper* / ~关系 *triangular relationship* / ~函数 *trigonometric function* / ~肌 *deltoid muscle* / ~巾 *sling* / ~裤 *panties; briefs* / ~恋爱 *love triangle* / ~帽 *delta wing* / ~旗 *pennant; pennon*

【三角铁】① angle iron ②【音】triangle

【三脚架】tripod; trivet; A-frame

【三教九流】① three religions (i. e. Confucianism; Taoism and Buddhism) and nine schools of thought (i. e. the Confucians, the Taoists, the *Yin-Yang*, the Legalists, the Logicians, the Mohists, the Political Strategists, the Eclectics and the Agriculturists) ② various religious sects and academic schools ③ people in various trades; people of all descriptions

【三节棍】three-section cudgel

【三九】bitter cold: ~严寒 *inclement winter weather* / ~天 *third nine-day period after the winter solstice — the coldest days of winter*

【三句话不离本行】be always talking shop; talk shop all the time

【三军】① three armed services ② the army

【三K党】Ku Klux Klan (a secret US society)

【三棱尺】three-square rule; triangular scale

【三棱镜】【物】(triangular) prism

【三连冠】win triple crown three successive championships

【三联单】triplicate form

【三令五申】repeated orders and instructions; repeatedly give injunctions

【三硫化物】【化】trisulfide

【三六九等】various grades and ranks; of all grades and ranks

【三轮儿】tricycle; pedicab

【三秒区】【体】(of basketball) 3-second area (or zone)

【三民主义】three People's Principles (Nationalism, Democracy and the People's livelihood, put forward by Dr. Sun Yatsen)

【三明治】sandwich

【三年五载】form three to five years — in several years; in a few years

【三七】【药】pseudo-ginseng

【三亲六故】relatives, friends and acquaintances;

all the kinsmen and friends
【三权分立】separation of three powers (i. e. the legislative, executive and judicial powers)
【三人行,必有我师】one of them is bound to be able to teach me something
【三三两两】in twos and threes; by twos and threes; in small groups
【三色版】【印】three-colour halftone; three-colour block: ~印刷 *trichromatic printing*
【三生】【宗】three incarnations (the present life, the previous life, and the next life)
【三生有幸】consider oneself most fortunate (to make sb's acquaintance, etc.)
【三牲】three sacrifices (pig, sheep and ox)
【三十六计,走为上计】of all the thirty-six stratagems, to quit; of all the alternatives, running away is the best
【三十年河东,三十年河西】life full ups and downs; chequered career
【三熟制】【农】triple-cropping (system)
【三思】think thrice — think carefully; ponder over: ~而后行。*Look before you leap; second thought is best.*
【三…四】① expressing confusion: 丢三落四 *be always forgetting things* ② indicating repetition: 说三道四 *make irresponsible remarks; gossip*
【三天打鱼,两天晒网】go fishing for three days and then dry the nets for two — work by fits and starts
【三天两头】every other day; from time to time
【三头肌】triceps
【三头六臂】(with) three hands and six arms — superhuman power; superman
【三围】the three vital measurements (i. e. chest, waist and hips)
【三维空间】three-dimensional space
【三位一体】①【宗】Trinity ② three forming an organic whole; trinity; three in one
【三五成群】in threes and fours; in knots
【三峡工程】three Gorges Dam Project
【三下五除二】neat and quick
【三鲜】three delicacies — delicious ingredients of dishes or fillings such as sea slug, squid, shrimp, chicken, etc: ~汤 *soup with three delicacies* / ~水饺 *boiled three delicacies dumplings*
【三相】【电】three-phase: ~电动机 *three-phase motor* / ~变压器 *three-phase transformer*
【三硝基甲苯】【化】trinitrotoluene (TNT)
【三心二意】be of two minds; waver and hesitate; shilly-shally
【三言两语】in a few words; in one or two words; casually
【三氧化物】【化】trioxide
【三叶虫】【生物】trilobite
【三月】① March ② third month of the lunar year; the third moon
【三灾八难】(children's) various illnesses and ailments; numerous adversities and calamities
【三战两胜】【体】best of three games
【三只手】[方] pickpocket
【三资企业】three kinds of foreign invested enterprises (Chinese foreign enterprise joint ventures, Chinese-foreign cooperative joint ventures, wholly foreign-owned enterprises)
【三足鼎立】stand on three legs like a tripod — triangular balance of power; tripartite confrontation

叁 three (used for the numeral 三 on cheques, etc. in order to avoid mistakes or alterations)

sǎn

伞 ① umbrella: 雨~ *umbrella* /遮阳~ *parasol; sunshade* ② sth shaped like an umbrella: 降落~ *parachute* / ~齿轮 *bevel gear*
【伞包】【军】pack
【伞兵】paratrooper; parachuter: ~部队 *parachute troops; paratroops*
【伞骨】rib
【伞降】parachuting: ~训练任务 *parachuting training programme*
【伞形科】【植】carrot family
【伞衣】【军】canopy

散 ① come loose; break up; not hold together: 柜子~架了。*The cupboard fell a part.* /纸箱~了。*Cardboard box came loose.* /谷包~了。*The sack of grain has spilled.* ② scattered: ~乱 *scattered and disorderly; in a jumble* ③ medicine in powder from; medicinal powder: ~剂 *powder* *see also* sàn
【散兵】skirmisher: ~壕 *fire trench* / ~坑 *foxhole; pit* / ~线 *skirmish line* / ~游勇 *stragglers and disbanded soldiers*
【散打】【体】a style of wrestling
【散飞子弹】【军】stray bullet; wild shot
【散工】① odd jobs; part-time jobs; short-term hired labour ② odd-job man; casual labourer; part-timer; seasonal labourer
【散光】astigmatism: ~眼镜 *astigmatic glasses*
【散户】【经】the individual investors
【散货】bulk cargo: ~船 *bulk freighter*
【散记】random notes; sketches
【散架】① collapse; fall apart; fall to pieces: 自行车~了。*The bicycle fell apart.* ② dissolve; disband
【散件】parts; components; pieces
【散居】live scattered: 这个民族~在全国各地。*People of this nationality live scattered around the country.*
【散客】walk-in
【散漫】① undisciplined; slack: 他是一个~的男孩。*He is a happy-go-lucky boy.* ② unorganized; Loose: 一篇~的文章 *a disorganized essay*
【散曲】a type of opera popular in the Yuan, ming and Qing dynasties with tonal patterns modelled on tunes drawn from folk music
【散射】【物】scattering: ~光 *scattered light* / ~波 *scattered wave* / ~通讯 *scatter communication*

【散手】free-style fistfight (or grappling)
【散碎】bits and pieces disjointed; scrappy: ~的银子 *bit and pieces of silver*
【散体】simple, direct prose style (free from parallelism)
【散文】prose: ~诗 *prose poem*
【散养】free-range raising of poultry and livestock; grazing
【散装】unpackaged; in bulk: ~白酒 *spirits in bulk* / ~货物 *bulk cargo*; *bulk freight* / ~运输 *bulk transportation* / ~饼干 *loose cookies* / ~白糖 *bulk sugar*

糁 [方] grains of cooked rice
see also shēn

sàn

散 ① break up; disperse; become separate: ~会了。*The meeting is over.* /雾~了。*The fog dispersed.* ② distribute; disseminate; scatter: ~传单 *give out handbills*; *distribute leaflets* / ~置 *scatter* ③ dispel; let out: 请打开窗户~~油烟。*Please open the windows to let me lampblack out.*
see also sǎn

S

【散播】disseminate; spread; broadcast: ~谣言 *spread rumours* / ~仇恨的种子 *sow the seeds of hatred*
【散布】spread; disseminate; distribute; scatter; diffuse: ~流言蜚语 *spread slanderous rumours*
【散步】take a walk; go for a walk (or stroll)
【散场】(of a show, etc.) be over; (of a theatre, etc.) empty after the performance
【散发】send forth; diffuse; emit; distribute
【散会】(of a meeting) be over; break up
【散伙】① (of a group, body or organization) dissolve; disband ② (of lovers, partners, etc.) break up
【散开】disperse
【散落】① fall apart; fall down; disperse ② be scattered
【散热】① dissipate heat: ~剂 *cooling agent* ② radiate heat: ~管 *cooling tube*; *radiating pipe* / ~片 *cooling fin*; *radiating fin* (*or rib*) / ~器 *radiator*; *cooler*
【散失】① scatter and disappear; vanish; be lost: 他~多年的女儿终于找到了。*His daughter who has been missing for years is found at last.* ② vaporize; dissipate; be lost
【散摊子】(of a group, organization, etc.) break up; disband; dissolve
【散席】(of a dinner party, etc.) end; come to a close
【散心】keep from worrying; drive away one's cares; relieve boredom

sāng

丧 funeral; mourning: 吊~ *pay a condolence call*
see also sàng
【丧服】mourning apparel
【丧家】family of the deceased; the family making funeral arrangements
【丧礼】funeral; obsequies
【丧乱】[书] disturbance and bloodshed; disaster
【丧门星】anyone (esp. a woman) who brings ill luck to someone
【丧事】funeral arrangements (or affairs)
【丧葬】burial; funeral: ~开支 *funeral expenses*
【丧钟】funeral bell; knell; death knell

桑 mulberry; white mulberry
【桑巴】samba (a Brazilian dance of African origin)
【桑白皮】【药】root bark of white mulberry
【桑蚕】silkworm
【桑那浴】sauna bath; sauna: 我们去洗~吧。*Let's take a sauna bath.*
【桑农】mulberry (bark) paper
【桑葚儿】[口] mulberry (the fruit)
【桑树】white mulberry; mulberry
【桑叶】mulberry leaf
【桑榆】[书] ① a place where the sun set — the west; evening ② waning day; closing y ears of one's life: ~暮景 *the evening of one's life*
【桑园】mulberry field
【桑梓】[书] one's native place

sǎng

搡 push roughly (or violently): 请不要推推~~。*Please don't push and shove.*

嗓 ① throat; larynx ② voice
【嗓门】voice: 提高~ *lift up one's voice*; *raise one's voice* /他~大。*He has a loud voice.*
【嗓音】voice: ~识别 *voice identification* /他的~悦耳。*He has a pleasant voice.*
【嗓子】① throat; larynx: 他~疼了好几天了。*He has had a sore throat for several days.* ② voice: 哑~ *hoarse voice*
【嗓子眼儿】throat

sàng

丧 lose
see also sāng
【丧胆】be terror-stricken; be terrified; be smitten with fear: 闻风~ *become terrified at the news*
【丧德】wicked; morally degenerate

【丧魂落魄】be driven to distraction; be shaken to the core

【丧家之犬】homeless dog; stray cur: 惶惶如~ *as scared as a stray cur*; *as forlorn* (*or pitiful*) *as a lost pup*

【丧尽天良】have no conscience at all; utterly devoid of conscience; conscienceless; heartless

【丧命】lose one's life; meet one's death

【丧偶】[书] be bereaved of one's spouse (esp. one's wife)

【丧气】feel disheartened; feel depressed; lose heart; become crestfallen: 不要说~话。*Stop to say demoralizing words* (*or remarks*).

【丧气】[口] be ill-starred; be unlucky; have had lucky

【丧权辱国】humiliate the nation and forfeit its sovereignty; surrender a country's sovereign rights under humiliating terms; be degrading

【丧生】lose one's life; meet one's death; get killed; die

【丧失】lose; forfeit: ~信心 *lose confidence*; *lose heart* / ~理智 *take leave of one's senses* / 不要~立场。*Please don't depart form the correct stand.* / 他已经~工作能力。*He has forfeited his ability to work.*

【丧亡】be killed; meet one's death; be subjugated

【丧心病狂】frenzied; frantic; perverse; unscrupulous: ~地进行谋杀活动 *carry on frenzied murdering activities*

【丧志】demoralized; dispirited: 玩物~ *riding a hobby saps one's will to make progress*; *demoralize oneself by indulging in material comforts*

sāo

搔 scratch: ~痒 *scratch oneself to relieve itching* / ~头皮 *scratch one's head*

【搔首】scratch one's head

【搔首弄姿】(of a woman) stroke one's hair in coquetry; posture and preen oneself; pat her own hair in a coquettish manner

【搔头】① scratch one's head: 这案子相当复杂,很~。*The case is quite complicated and perplexing.* ② [旧] hairpin; hair clasp: 玉~ *a jade hair clasp*

【搔着痒处】scratch where it itches — hit the nail on the head

骚1 disturb; upset; disrupt: ~乱 *disturbance*; *turmoil*

骚2 [书] literary writings: ~大墨客 *literary men*; *men of letters*

骚3 coquettish: ~货 *bitch*; *tart*

【骚动】disturbance; upheaval; turmoil; ferment; commotion: 引起~ *stir up a disturbance* / 观众~起来。*The viewers were in a turmoil.*

【骚话】obscene language

【骚货】woman of loose morals; tart; sexpot

【骚客】[书] poet: 文人~ *man of letters*

【骚闹】commotion; disturbance; ferment

【骚扰】harass; pester: ~社会秩序 *disrupt public order* / ~活动 *harassment*

【骚人】[书] poet

缫 reel silk from cocoons; reel

【缫丝】reeling; silk reeling: ~工人 *reeler* / ~机 *reeling machine*; *filature*

臊 smell of urine or of the fox, skunk, etc. foul smell; stench

see also sào

【臊气】foul smell; stench

sǎo

扫 ① sweep; sweep away; clear away: ~庭院 *sweep the courtyard* / ~街 *sweep the streets* ② eliminate; wipe out: ~雷 *mine clearance*; *mine sweeping* ③ pass quickly along or over; move along quickly; sweep: 他的眼睛向四周~了一圈。*His eyes swept around the audience.*

see also sào

【扫边】play a minor role in Chinese

【扫坟】sweep a grave; pay respects at sb's tomb

【扫黄】anti-pornography campaign

【扫祭】clean and offer sacrifices at sb's tomb

【扫雷艇】minesweeper

【扫雷器】mine-sweeping apparatus; minesweeper

【扫路车】street sweeper; road sweeper

【扫盲】wipe out (or eliminate) illiteracy

【扫描】【电】scanning: 行~ *line scanning* / 飞点~ *flying-spot scanning* / ~仪 *scanner* / ~周期 *scanning circle or period*

【扫灭】mop up; wipe out; exterminate: ~害虫 *exterminate pests*

【扫墓】sweep a grave — pay respects at one's tomb

【扫平】put down; crack down; crush

【扫清】sweep clean; clear away; get rid of

【扫除】① clean; clean up: 大~ *general cleaning* ② clear away; eliminate; remove; wipe out: ~障碍 *get rid of the obstacles* / ~迷信 *eliminate superstition* / ~文盲 *wipe out illiteracy*; *eliminate illiteracy*

【扫地】① sweep the floor ② (of honour, credibility, etc.) be utterly discredited; reach rock bottom; reach an all-time low; be dragged in the dust: 威信~ *lose all prestige*; *be shorn of one's prestige* / 斯文~ *bring disgrace to the intellectuals*

【扫地出门】be deprived of one's belongs and evicted; be swept out like rubbish; drive out the whole family with nothing except the clothes they have on

【扫毒】anti-drug campaign

【扫射】【军】strafe

【扫视】(of one's glance) sweep; take a sweeping glance

【扫数】all; the whole amount; the total number:

~偿清 *all paid off*
【扫榻】[书] clean the bed; sweep the bed clean: ~以待 *tidy up the guest room in anticipation of a visitor; look forward to one's visit*
【扫尾】wind up; bring to an end: ~工作 *rounding-off work*
【扫兴】dampen one's spirits; feel disappointed
嫂 ① elder brother's wife; sister-in-law: 大~ *first brother's wife* ② (the form o f address for a married woman about one's own age) sister
【嫂夫人】(form of address for a friend's wife) your wife; sister
【嫂嫂】[方] elder brother's wife; sister-in-law
【嫂子】[口] elder brother's wife; sister-in-law

sào

扫 broom
see also sǎo
【扫帚】broom
【扫帚菜】【植】summer cypress
【扫帚眉】bushy eyebrows: 两道~ *a pair of bushy eyebrows*
【扫帚星】①【天】comet ② woman who bring ill luck; jinx
瘙 scabies
【瘙痒】itch
臊 shy; diffident; bashful: 害~ *be bashful* / 替某人害~ *blush for sb* / ~得她满脸通红。*Her full face blushed scarlet.*
see also sāo
【臊脸】[方] lose face
【臊气】[方] have bad luck

sè

色 ① colour: 蓝~ *blue* / ~温 *colour temperature* / 原~ *primary colour* ② look; appearance; countenance: be visibly pleased; light up with pleasure: 面带难~ *show reluctance* ③ kind; description: 各~各样的设备 *all kinds of equipments* / 形形~~ *of all forms; of every description* ④ view; scene: 湖光山~ *beautiful view of the lake and hills* / 景~ *scenery; scene; landscape* / 深秋景~ *a late autumn scene* ⑤ quality (o f precious goods, metals, etc.): 这银子成~足。*The silver ingot is of pure quality.* ⑥ woman's beautiful looks; feminine charms: 姿~ (*of a woman*) *good looks* / ~艺双绝 *unrivalled in physical and skill* ⑦ egotism: 好~之徒 *erotic* / ~狼 *lecher; wolf; sex maniac*
see also shǎi
【色彩】① colour; hue; tint: ~鲜明 *in bright gay colours; gaudy; bright-coloured* / 地方~ *local colour* / 感情~ *emotional colouring* ② emotion; flavour; character: 文学~ *literary flavour* / 政治~ *political hue* / ~疗法 *colour therapy*
【色层谱】【物】chromatogram
【色差】①【物】chromatism; chromatic aberration ②【纺】off colour; off shade
【色带】ribbon
【色胆】boldness in erotic adventure; the lengths to which one will go for sex: ~包天 *unscrupulous in seeking carnal pleasure; be utterly reckless in sex*
【色淀】【纺】lake: 绯红~ *crimson lake* / ~染料 *lake colours*
【色调】tone; hue: 冷~ *cold tones* / 暖~ *warm tones*
【色度】①【物】chrominance: ~境 *chromoscope* ② shade of colour
【色度计】【物】colorimeter
【色鬼】sex maniac; satyr; lecher: 老~ *a lecherous old man; an old dirty man; an old lecher*
【色基】【化】colour base
【色觉】colour vision; colour sense: ~检查 *chromatoptometry* / ~检查表 *colour lest cards*
【色拉】salad: 水果蔬菜~ *fruit and vegetable salad*
【色厉内荏】fierce of mien but fain of heart ferocious in appearance but cowardly at heart
【色盲】【医】achromatopsia; colour blind: ~表 *colour test cards*
【色迷迷】cook erotic; have last in the eyes; become hazy with lust
【色谱】【物】chromatogram: ~法 *chromatography* / ~分析 *chromatographic analysis* / ~仪 *chromatograph*
【色情】pornographic; sex: ~电影 *pornographic film; porn (or blue) movie* / ~文艺 *erotology* / ~作品 *pornography; pornographic materials* / ~狂 *erotomania; sex mania* / ~文学 *erotica; pornography*
【色散】【物】chromatic dispersion
【色色】all kinds; every kind: 工具~俱全。*All sorts of tools are kept in stock.*
【色素】【生】pigment: ~斑 *pigmented spot* / ~细胞 *chromatophore* / ~痣 *mole*
【色相】colour phase ②【宗】outward appearance of thing ③ feminine charm: 出卖~ *sell her charms* / 以~事人(*of a woman*) *sell oneself*
【色艺】looks and skill; charm and skill (of a woman entertainers): ~俱佳 *remarkable or outstanding in both looks and skills*
【色釉】coloured glaze
【色欲】sexual desire; sexual urge; sexual passion; lust
【色泽】colour and lustre: ~鲜明 *bright and lustrous*
【色织厂】【纺】yarn-dyed fabric mill
【色纸】coloured paper
【色痣】【医】mole
涩 ① puckery; astringent: 苦~ *bitter and puckery*: 这些柿子很~。*These persimmons are quite puckery.* ② rough; heard-going: 地板太粗~。*The floor board is too rough.* / 理发推子~了,需要上油。*This pair of hair-clippers doesn't*

work smoothly; *it needs oiling.* ③ obscure; difficult (of writing) not smooth; hard to understand:这首诗充满了晦~的语句。*This poetry is full of obscure sentences.*

【涩脉】【中医】weak, uneven pulse

【涩滞】not smooth; rough going

啬 stingy; miserly; mean; close-fisted: 吝~ *stingy*; *niggardly*; *miserly* /吝~鬼 *miser*; *niggard*; *skinflint*

瑟 ①【音】*se*, a twenty-five-string (or sixteen-string) plucked instrument similar to the zither

【瑟瑟】① (of wind) rustle: ~的秋风 *rustling autumn wind* ② tremble: ~发抖 *be trembling or shaking all over*

【瑟缩】cower; curl up with cold:这位老妇人全身~。*The old woman was trembling all over with cold.*

塞

see also sāi; sài

【塞擦音】【语】affricate

【塞音】【语】plosive; stop

【塞责】not do one's job properly; perform one's duties perfunctorily:敷衍~ *perform one's duties in a perfunctorily manner*

sēn

森 ① tree growing thickly; full of trees: ~林 *forest* ②[书] multitudinous; in profusion ③ dark; gloomy:阴~ *gloomy and horrid*; *ghastly*; *gruesome*

【森冷】dark and cold: ~的地下室 *dark, cold cellar*

【森林】forest: ~调查 *forest survey* / ~火灾 *forest fire* / ~抚育 *tending of woods* / 原始~ *primeval forest* / ~法 *forest law* / ~覆盖率 *percentage of forest cover*; *forest acreage* / ~学 *forestry*

【森罗殿】the Hall of Darkness; Palace of the King of Hell or Hades

【森然】① (of tress) dense; thick:林木~ *thickly wooded with tall tress* ② awe-inspiring; awesome

【森森】① dense; thick; heavy:松柏~ *dense pine and cypress tress* ② gloomy; gruesome:阴~的教堂 *a ghastly-looking church*

【森严】solemn; strict; stern; forbidding:警戒~ *heavily guarded* /等级~ *rigid hierarchy* /门禁~ *the entrance is closely guarded* / ~壁垒 *strongly fortified*

sēng

僧 Buddhist monk; monk:高~ *eminent monk*

【僧道】Buddhist monks and Taoist priests; Buddhists and Taoists

【僧多粥少】many monks and meagre gruel — not enough to go round; inadequate

【僧侣】monks and priests; clergy: ~政治 *theocracy* / ~主义 *fideism*

【僧尼】Buddhist monks and

【僧人】Buddhist monk

【僧俗】clergy and laity; monks and laymen

【僧徒】Buddhist monks

【僧院】Buddhist temple; Buddhist monastery

【僧众】Buddhist monks

shā

杀 ① kill; slaughter; slay:谋~ *murder* / ~手 *killer* ② fight; battle; go into battle:这支部队最后~出了敌人的重围。*The troop fought its way out of the heavy encirclement at last.* ③ weaken; reduce; lessen abate: ~~他们的威风 *deflate their arrogance* /风势稍~。*The wind has abated.* ④[方] smart:酒精涂在伤口上让人觉得~得慌。*Alcohol smarts when it put on sb's cut.* ⑤ end:她的自传~青了。*She has just finished her autobiography.* ⑥ take off; counteract:从白菜馅里~出水。*Draw out the water from chopped cabbage.* ⑦ in the extreme; exceeding; intensely:你讲的笑~人。*What you said was absolutely ridiculous.*

【杀草强】amitrole

【杀虫剂】【农】insecticide; pesticide

【杀敌】fight the enemy; engage in battle:英勇~ *be brave in battle*; *fight heroically*

【杀害】kill; slaughter; murder

【杀回马枪】make a backward at one's enemy while pretending to retreat; give sb a backward thrust; wheel around and hit back

【杀机】murderous intentions; intent to kill:暗藏~ *harbour murderous intentions*

【杀鸡取卵】kill a hen to get the eggs; kill the goose that lays the golden eggs

【杀鸡吓猴】kill the chicken to frighten the monkey — punish someone as a warning to other persons

【杀鸡焉用牛刀】you don't use a butcher's to kill a chicken

【杀价】beat a seller down; force down the price

【杀戒】Buddhist prohibition against taking life

【杀菌】disinfect; sterilize; destroy bacteria: ~剂 *germicide*; *bactericide*

【杀戮】massacre; butcher

【杀卵剂】ovicide

【杀掠】massacre and plunder

【杀螨剂】【农】acaricide; miticide

【杀灭】kill; wipe out; eliminate

【杀气】① an aura of death; murderous look:满脸~ *with murderous expression on sb 's face* ② vent one's spleen (or ill feelings)

【杀气腾腾】ferocious; bellicose; murderous

【杀人】kill a person; homicide; murder: ~狂 *homicidal maniac* / ~灭口 *kill an eyewitness* / ~偿命 *a life for a life* / ~不见血 *kill a person with-*

S

out spilling a drop of blood — kill by subtle means / ~不眨眼 *kill without batting a eyelid; commit murder without blinking an eye*

【杀伤】inflict casualties on; kill and wound: ~力 *power of destruction* / ~武器 *anti-personnel weapon* / ~细胞 *killer cell* / ~卫星 *killer satellite*

【杀伤弹】【军】anti-personnel shell; fragmentation bomb

【杀身】lose one's life; be murdered; be killed: ~之祸 *fatal disaster*

【杀身成仁】die to achieve virtue — die for a good cause

【杀生】【宗】killing of living thing; take animal life

【杀手】assassin; killer: 职业~ *professional killer*

【杀鼠剂】rat poison; rodenticide

【杀头】behead; mete out capital punishments

【杀一儆百】execute one as a warning to others; punish one as an example to ah

杉【植】China fir
see also shān

【杉篙】【建】fir pole

【杉木】fir wood

沙[1] ① sand; grit: 黄~ *yellow sand* ② granulated; powdered: 豆~ *bean paste* ③ (Shā) a surname

沙[2] (of voice) hoarse; husky: 她嗓子发~。*She had a hoarse voice.*

沙[3] tsar

【沙坝】sandbar; sandbank

【沙包】① sand dune; sand mound ② sand bag

【沙暴】sandstorm

【沙蚕】sandworm; clam worm

【沙场】battlefield; battleground: 驰骋~ *ride on the battlefield* / 久经~ *battle*

【沙尘】dust: ~飞扬 *cloud of dust filled the air*

【沙船】large flat-bottomed junk; large junk

【沙袋】sandbag: ~鼠 *wallaby*

【沙丁鱼】sardine

【沙俄】tsarist or czarist Russia

【沙发】sofa; settee: 单人~ *upholstered armchair; sofa* / ~床 *sofa bed; studio couch* / ~椅 *couch*

【沙蜂】sand wasp

【沙岗】sand hill

【沙果】【植】Chinese pear-leaved crabapple

【沙海】expanses of desert; sea of sand

【沙害】disastrous sandstorms

【沙狐】corsac (fox)

【沙獾】sand badger

【沙荒】sandy wasteland; sandy waste: 我们国家的~必须治理。*The sandy wasteland must be cont rolled in our country.*

【沙皇】tsar; czar

【沙棘】sea buckthorn; sallow thorn

【沙金】grains of gold mixed in sand; placer gold: 这条河里~丰富。*There is abundant alluvial gold in this river.*

【沙坑】①【体】jumping pit ② sand pit

【沙梨】【植】sand pear

【沙砾】grit

【沙龙】salon: 文艺~ *the artists' salon* / 社会~ *social salon*

【沙漏】sandglass; hourglass

【沙漠】desert: ~植被 *desert vegetation* / ~化 *desertification* / ~风暴 *desert storm*

【沙鸥】【动】sandpiper

【沙盘】【军】① sand table ② sand table exercises

【沙丘】sand dune: 流动~ *shifting or moving dune*

【沙瓤】mushy watermelon pulp

【沙沙】[象] rustle: 树叶在寒风中~作响。*The leaves were rustling in the cold wind.*

【沙山】sand mountain

【沙石】sandstone; gravel

【沙司】sauce

【沙鼠】sand rat; gerbil

【沙滩】sand beach; sand: ~排球 *beach volleyball* / ~椅 *beach chair*

【沙特阿拉伯】Saudi Arabia: ~人 *Saudi Arabian*

【沙文主义】chauvinism

【沙哑】hoarse; husky: 她说话嗓音~。*She has a husky voice.*

【沙眼】trachoma

【沙浴】① sand bath (of cocks hen or turkeys) ②【医】sand bath

【沙灾】sandstorm disaster

【沙蚤】sand hopper

【沙洲】shoal; sandbar

【沙柱】dust devil; sand column

【沙锥】【动】snipe

【沙子】① sand; grit ② small grains; pellets: 铁~ *iron pellets; shot*

【沙嘴】sandspit

纱 ① yarn: ~线 *yarn* / 棉~ *cotton yarn* ② sheer; gauze: 尼龙~ *nylon sheer* / 铁~ *wire gauze*

【纱包线】cotton-covered wire

【纱布】gauze: ~绷带 gauze bandage

【纱厂】cotton mill

【纱橱】screen cupboard

【纱窗】window screen; screen

【纱灯】gauze lantern

【纱锭】【纺】spindle

【纱巾】gauze kerchief; transparent scarf

【纱笼】sarong

【纱罗】【纺】gauze

【纱染】【纺】yarn-dyed

【纱罩】① gauze covering (for food); screen covering (for food) ② (of glass lamps) mantle

刹 put on the brakes; brake; stop: ~住歪风 *check an unhealthy tendency* / 赶快~车。*Stop your car right away.*
see also chà

【刹把】【机】brake crank

【刹车】① put on the brakes; stop a vehicle by applying the brakes; step on the bakes ② stop a machine by cutting off the power turn off a machine ③ brake

砂 sand; grit: ~泵 sand pump

【砂布】emery or abrasive cloth: 刚玉~ *corundum cloth*
【砂浆】mortar: 水泥~ *cement mortar* / 石灰~ *line mortar*
【砂礓】【地】conglomerate; gravel
【沙晶】sand crystal
【砂矿】placer; placer deposit 开采~ *placer (or alluvial) mining*
【砂轮】【机】emery wheel; abrasive (or grinding) wheel
【砂轮机】grinder
【砂糖】granulated sugar
【砂土】sand soil; sand
【砂箱】【冶】sandbox; moulding box
【砂心】【冶】(sand) core
【砂型】【冶】sand mould: ~铸造 *sand casting*
【砂岩】sandstone
【砂眼】【冶】sand holes; blowholes; slag pin holes
【砂样】drilling; mud cutting
【砂纸】abrasive paper; sand paper: 金刚~ *emery paper* / ~打磨 *sand papering*
【砂质岩】arenaceous rock

铩 ① a kind of spear in the ancient ②【书】wreck; destroy; injure

【铩羽而归】return with one's wings clipped

煞 ① stop halt; check; brake; bring to close: 你的表演可以~住了。*You'd better stop performing now.* ② tighten: ~紧你的腰带 *tighten your belt*
see also shà

【煞笔】① concluding lines of an article; concluding sentences ② write the final line (of an article, letter, etc.)
【煞车】tighten up a load on a vehicle; lash down
【煞尾】① finish off; round off; wind off; complete: 我们工作时,你正在~。*You were winding up our work when we worked.* ② final stage; ending: 我不喜欢这出戏的~。*I don't like the ending of the play.*

鲨 shark

【鲨鱼】shark

shá

啥 [方] what: 这里~也没有。*There is nothing here.*

【啥子】[方] what: 那是~? *What is that?*

shǎ

傻 ① stupid; muddleheaded: ~气 *foolish; stupid* ② think or act mechanically; be bigoted: 别~干,要找窍门。*Don't just keep slogging away; you should try to get the knack of doing it.*

【傻瓜】fool; blockhead; idiot: ~照相机 *full automatic camera; foolproof camera*
【傻呵呵】simpleminded; not very clever; naive; unsophisticated: 别看他~的,心里可有数呢。*Maybe he looks very silly, but he knows what's what.*
【傻乎乎】[口] innocent; naive, simple-minded; silly; foolish: 小孩在~地笑。*The child is smiling innocently.*
【傻话】stupid talk; foolish words; silly talk; nonsense
【傻劲儿】[口] stupidity, foolishness; stupid air or manner ② sheer enthusiasm; sheer animal strength; doggedness
【傻乐】[方] laugh foolishly; giggle; laugh like an idiot
【傻里瓜唧】[方] foolish; dump
【傻脸】① [方] be dumbfounded; be stunned: 小孩在这起事故中几乎~了。*The child was stunned with fear in the accident.* ② lose face
【傻冒儿】[口] ① fool; blockhead; simpleton; idiot ② unsophisticated; naive
【傻头傻脑】look clumsy and stupid; foolish-looking
【傻小子】[口] silly lad
【傻笑】laugh foolishly; laugh like on idiot; giggle
【傻眼】be flabbergasted; be stunned; be dumbfounded
【傻样】[口] foolish look; silly look; foolish expression
【傻子】fool; nitwit; blockhead; simpleton

shà

厦 a mansion; a tall building: 高楼大~ *high-rise buildings and large mansions* / 广~ *a huge mansion*
see also xià

煞[1] evil spirit; goblin; devil; devils; fiends

煞[2] very
see also shā

【煞白】colourless; deathly pale; ghastly pale; pallid: 她脸色~。*She looks deathly pale.*
【煞费苦心】cudgel one's brains; take great pains; make a painstaking effort: 他们为了获得好成绩,可真是~。*They made a painstaking effort to obtain a good result.*
【煞后】[口] lag behind; hang back: 请您~一点儿,让老人过去。*Please step back a little and make a way for the old man.*
【煞神】demon; fiend; devil
【煞有介事】swaggering; pretensions; make a show of being in earnest

霎 moment; a very short time; instant

【霎时间】in a split second; in an instant; in a jiffy; in a twinkling

S

shāi

筛[1] ① sieve; sifter; riddle: 粗～ *coarse sieve* ② sifter; screen: ～面 *sieve flour*; *sift flour* ③ eliminating through selecting

筛[2] ① warm a pot of rice wine over a slow fire or in hot water ② pour (wine): ～酒 *pour the wine*

筛[3] strike (a gong)

【筛布】bolting cloth
【筛法】【数】sieve method
【筛分】screening; sieving; sifting: ～机 *screening machine*
【筛粉机】bolting machine
【筛管】【植】sieve tube
【筛号】screen size; screen mesh
【筛糠】[口] shiver; quiver: 吓得～ *shivered with fear*; *tremble with fear*; *shake in one's shoes*
【筛洗】dress and wash (coal, etc.) screen and wash; size and clean
【筛选】① screen; sift; sieve: 工人们在精心～矿石。*The workers are carefully screening out the ore.* ② select
【筛子】a screen; sieve; sifter: 细～ *fine sieve*

shǎi

色 [口] colour: 退～ *fade*

see also sè

【色子】dice: 掷～ *cost dice*; *throw dice*; *play dice*

shài

晒 ① (of sun) shine upon: 风吹日～ *be exposed to the wind and the sun* ② dry in the sun; bask: ～被子 *air a quilt* / ～稻 *dry rice in the sun* / ～衣服 *air clothes* ③ [方] give the cold shoulder to someone; ignore

【晒场】sunning ground (for drying grain, etc.); drying yard
【晒台】flat roof (for drying clothes, etc.); balcony
【晒图】make a blueprint; blueprint: ～纸 *blue print paper*
【晒烟】sun-cured tobacco
【晒盐】evaporate brine in the sun to make salt; make salt by evaporating brine in the sun

shān

山 ① hill; mountain: 高～ *high mountain* / ～路 *mountain path* ② anything resembling a mountain: 假～ *rockery* ③ gable: ～墙 *gable* ④ cocoons bushes of straw in which silk worms spin cocoons

【山坳】col
【山包】[方] hillock; small hill
【山崩】landslip; landslide
【山崩地裂】the mountains collapsing and the earth cracking up — cataclysm; deafening noise
【山不转水转】some change is bound to happen
【山茶】【植】camellia: ～花 *camellia*
【山产】mountain products (wild animal and plants of economic value found in the mountain which provide people with medicinal herbs, fruit, furs, etc.)
【山城】a town nestling among the mountains; mountain city: 重庆是一座～。*Chongqing is a mountain city.*
【山重水复】mountains multiply and streams double back — separated by innumerable barriers: ～疑无路，柳暗花明又一村。*Mountains multiply and the streams double back — there seems no road beyond; willows cluster darkly, blossoms shine — another village appears a heads.*
【山川】landscape; mountains and rivers — land
【山鹑】【动】partridge
【山村】mountain village
【山地】① mountainous region; hilly country; hilly country ② hillside field
【山地战】mountain warfare
【山地车】mountain bike: 昨天，妈妈给我买了一辆～。*Yesterday my mother bought a mountain bike for me.*
【山顶】the top of a mountain; the summit of a mountain; hilltop; mountaintop
【山顶洞人】【考】upper Cave Man
【山洞】cave; cavern
【山峰】mountain peak
【山旮旯儿】[方] faraway hilly area; out-of-the-way place in the mountains; remote mountain area; faraway mountain area
【山冈】low hill; hillock
【山高水长】as high as the mountains and as long as rivers — far depth of sb's kindness or friendship, or for-reaching influence of a noble character
【山高水远】① the hills (or mountains) and the rivers far away — distant, long way off ② sth unfortunate, esp., death
【山歌】folk song (sung in the fields or in mountains area)
【山根】[口] foot of a hill
【山沟】① gully; ravine; (mountain) valley ② remote mountain area
【山谷】ravine; mountain valley

【山国】① a mountainous country ② a mountainous area; a hilly region
【山河】mountains and rivers — the land of a country
【山核桃】【植】① hickory ② hickory nut
【山洪】mountain torrents: ~一泻而下。*Turbulent torrent rushed down the mountain.*
【山回路转】a winding path along the mountain ridges
【山火】mountain fire
【山货】① mountain product (such as haws, walnuts and chest nuts etc) ② household utensils made of wood, rattan, day, bamboo, etc.
【山鸡】[方] pheasant
【山脊】(mountain) ridge
【山涧】mountain stream
【山脚】foot of a mountain; foot of a hill
【山景】mountain view or scene
【山径】mountain path
【山口】mountain pass; pass
【山岚】[书] mist in mountains; haze in mountains
【山狸】【动】beaver; mountain beaver
【山梨】【植】sorb
【山里红】【植】large-fruited Chinese hawthorn
【山梁】ridge (of a hill or mountain)
【山林】wooded mountains; wooded hills; mountain forest:明天我们将进入~地区。*Tomorrow we'll enter the mountain and forest region.*
【山陵】[书] ① mountain ② royal mausoleum; tombs of emperors
【山岭】a chain of mountains; mountain ridge; mountains chain
【山路】mountain path:崎岖的~ *a rugged mountain path*
【山麓】foot of a mountain; piedmont: ~有一片白桦林。*There is a white birch grove at the foot of the mountain.*
【山峦】mountains chain; a chain of mountains: ~起伏 *an undulating chain of mountains; rolling hills*
【山萝卜】【植】scabious; scabiosa
【山脉】mountain range; mountain chain
【山门】① the gate of a monastery; the gate of a Buddhist temple ② Buddhism
【山盟海誓】(make) a solemn pledge of love; swear eternal love
【山民】mountain people (or inhabitants); Hillman; hill folk
【山姆大步】uncle Sam
【山南海北】① south of the mountains and north of the seas — remote place; far aw a y ② chat aimlessly; rambling: 他们在~地神聊。*They are shooting the breeze; they are talking everything under the sun.*
【山炮】mountain gun or artillery
【山坡】hillside; mountain slope
【山清水秀】green hills and clear waters — beautiful scenery; picturesque scenery
【山穷水尽】where the hills and the rivers end — at the end of one's pope (or tether); be in predicament
【山丘】① hillock ② tomb
【山区】mountain area
【山泉】mountain spring
【山雀】tit
【山水】① water from a mountain:用~浇灌稻田 *irrigate the rice fields with the water from the mountain* ② mountains and waters; scenery with hills and rivers:桂林~甲天下。*The scenery of Guilin is the best on earth.* ③ traditional Chinese painting of mountains and waters; landscape; landscape painting
【山水画】landscape; landscape painting
【山水相连】be linked by common mountains and waters
【山桃】mountain peach
【山头】① mountain top; hilltop; top of a mountain ② mountain stronghold; faction: ~主义 *mountain-stronghold mentality; factionalism*
【山洼】mountain valley
【山外有山】there's always a mountain beyond the mountain — there's always sth or sb better; nothing can be perfect; one should always be modest
【山窝】out-of-the-way mountain area
【山系】【地】mountain system
【山险】difficult mountain terrain; narrow mountain pass; defile
【山乡】mountain area; mountain village
【山响】thunderous; deafening: 鼓擂得~ *drums beating thunderously* /他敲得门~。*He knocked the door thunderously.*
【山魈】①【动】mandrill ② mountain elf
【山鸦】chough
【山崖】cliff
【山羊】① goat: ~胡子 *goatee* / ~绒 *cashmere* ②【体】*buck*
【山腰】halfway up the mountain
【山摇地动】hill topple and the earth quakes; earth shaking
【山药】①【植】Chinese yam ② [方] potato: ~蛋 *potato*
【山雨欲来风满楼】a wind sweeping through the tower heralds a rising storm in the mountains; a rising wind forebodes a coming storm
【山芋】[方] sweet potato
【山鹬】woodcock
【山岳】lofty mountain: ~冰川 *mountain glacier; alpine glacier*
【山楂】① (Chinese) hawthorn ② haw: ~酱 *haw jelly mountain fastness*
【山珍海味】delicacies from land and sea; delicacies of every kind
【山中无老虎,猴子称大王】the monkey proclaims himself king when there is away from the mountain; the kingdom of the blind, the one-eyed man rules
【山庄】① mountain village ② mountain villa
【山嘴】【地】spur

S

【山鳟】cutthroat trout

芟

① now (grass) ② weed out; eliminate; get rid of

【芟除】① now; cut down: ~杂草 *weeding* ② delete: 从磁盘~旧文件 *delete old files from disk drive*

【芟夷】[书] ① weed; uproot wild grass ② eliminate (certain forces)

杉

【植】china fir

see also shā

删

delete; leave out: ~除 *delete; remove; strike (or cross, cut) out* / ~除文件 *delete file; kill file*

【删繁就简】simplify sth by weeding out superfluities; simplify by cutting out t he superfluous

【删改】delete and change; revise; prune away: 略加~ *touch up* /论文已经经过了几次~。*The treatise has been revised several times.*

【删减】abridge an article; condense on article

【删节】abridge; abbreviate: ~本 *abridged edition; abbreviated version* / ~号 *ellipsis; suspension points; ellipsis dots*

【删略】delete; omit

【删削】delete; remove; cut (or strike) out

苫

straw mat: 草~子 *strow or reed mat*

see also shàn

钐

【化】samarium (Sm)

衫

unlined upper garment: 衬~ *shirt* /衣~ *clothes* /恤~ *T-shirt* /羊毛~ *wool en sweater; cardigan*

姗

【姗姗】leisurely; slowly: ~来迟 *be slow in coming; be late; arrive late*

珊

【珊瑚】coral: ~礁 *coral reef* / ~虫 *coral polyp; coral worm* / ~岛 *coral island*

栅

【栅格】【物】grid; lattice: ~结构 *lattice structure*

【栅极】【电】grid: ~电路 *grid circuit*

【栅控管】【电】grid control tube

【栅漏】【电】grid leak

see also zhà

舢

【舢板】sampan

扇

① fan: ~炉子 *fan a stove* / ~扇子 *fan oneself; use a fan* ② hit with hand; slap (sb on the face): ~她一耳光 *slap her on the face*

see also shàn

【扇动】flap: 蝴蝶~着翅膀。*The butterfly is flapping its wings.*

【扇风机】ventilating fan

煽

① fan (a fire): ~火 *fan a fire* ② incite; instigate; foment; stir up: ~诱 *incite; agitate* / ~情 *incite emotions; stir up emotions*

【煽动】incite; stir up; whip up: ~暴乱 *incite rebellion* / ~闹事 *stir up trouble; stir up unrest*

【煽风点火】inflame and agitate people; stir up trouble

【煽惑】inflame; incite; agitate

潸

[书] in tears; tearful

【潸然】[书] in tears; tearful; shed tears: 最后她已经~泪下了。*Her tears were trickling down the cheeks in the end.*

【潸潸】full of tears; in tears; tearful

膻

the smell of mutton: 腥~ *fishy; smell of fish or mutton*

shǎn

闪

① dodge; move quickly to one side; get out of the way: ~开 *step aside quickly; get out of the way; dodge; jump aside* ② sprain; twist: 昨天她~了腰。*She sprained her back yesterday.* ③ flash; sparkle: 一个念头~现在她的脑海里。*An idea flashed across her mind suddenly.* /灯泡一~就灭了。*The electric bulb flashed and it went out.* ④ lightning: ~电 *lightening* ⑤ leave behind: 我们把她~在家里了。*We left her at home.*

【闪避】dodge; sidestep; duck: 她~不及,撞上了那个人。*It was too late to dodge when she bumped into the man.*

【闪挫】【中医】sudden strain or contusion of a muscle; sprain: ~了足踝和手腕 *sprain one's ankle and wrist*

【闪点】【化】flash point

【闪电战】lighting warfare; blitzkrieg; blitz: ~术 *blitz tactics* / ~部队 *blitz units*

【闪动】flash; twinkle; move fast; scintillate flicker: 他眼中~着怒火。*His eyes flashed with anger.* /屋顶上一个人影在~。*The trace of a person's presence was flickering on the roof.*

【闪躲】dodge; evade; avoid: 他突然向右一~。*He made a sudden dodge to the right.*

【闪光】① glisten; glitter; gleam: 孩子们眼里闪着幸福的光。*The children's eyes glow with happiness.* ② flash of light: ~灯 *flashlight; flash lamp photoflash* /那个窗户在~。*Lights are flashing in those windows.*

【闪弧】【电】flashing

【闪击】(make) surprise attack: ~战 *lighting war; blitzkrieg; blitz* /这支部队~了敌人。*The troop launched a surprise attack on the enemy.*

【闪亮】glisten; glitter: 她眼里流出了两串~的泪珠。*Two chains glistening tears shed from her eyes.*

【闪露】flash: 她脸上~出喜悦的神色。*Happiness flashed across her face.*

【闪念】a sudden idea flashing across one's mind

【闪让】make way for; step aside: 给老人~道路 *step*

aside to let the old man pass 。

【闪闪】sparkling; twinkling; glistening; glittering: ~的红星 *a sparkling red star* /她的钻石在灯光中~发亮。*He diamonds sparkled in the light.*

【闪射】glitter; blaze; glisten; sparkle; shine:她的眼里~着喜悦的神情。*Her eyes sparkled with joy.*

【闪身】dodge; move or step sideways: ~进门 *move sideways through the door*

【闪失】mishap; accident:遇到一个小小的~ *meet with a slight mishap*

【闪石】amphibole

【闪烁】① twinkle; glitter; glimmer:露珠在草丛中~。*Dewdrops are glistening in the grass.* ② evasive; vague; equivocal:对我的建议他态度有点~。*He was very evasive and equivocal about my suggestion.*

【闪烁其词】dodge about; evade issues; speak hesitatingly:请回答"是"或"不是"——不要再~了。*Please answer 'yes' or 'no' — Stop hedging!*

【闪现】flash; come into view; flash before one:英雄的形象~在她的脑海中。*The image of the hero flashed across her mind.*

【闪眼】[方] dazzling: ~的灯光 *the dazzling light*

【闪耀】radiate; glitter; flash:阳光在海面上~着。*The sun is shining brightly on the sea.*

【闪熠】[书] glitter; radiate; shine; flash:星光~ *stars glittering*

【闪音】【语】flap

【闪语族】Semitic languages group (including Arabic, Hebrew, etc.)

【闪灼】shine; glitter; radiate; flicker:烛光~。*The candles are shining brightly.*

shàn

讪 ① mock; ridicule; scorn: ~谤 *malign; slander* ② embarrassed; discomfited; shamefaced:海伦娜~~地离开办公室。*Helena left the office in embarrassment.*

【讪骂】hurl abuses; rail

【讪讪】embarrassed; awkward; shamefaced; a shamed:她觉得无趣,只好~地离开办公室。*Feeling she was not wanted, she left the office in embarrassment.*

【讪笑】ridicule; mock; scoff

苫 cover with a straw mat, tarpaulin, etc.:快把货物~上。*Hurry up! Cover up the cargo.* *see also* shān

【苫布】tarpaulin

【苫席】straw mat; reed mat; mat cover

疝 hernia

【疝带】【医】truss

【疝气】【医】hernia

扇 ① fan:吊~ *pendant fan* /电~ *electric fan; ventilator* ② leaf:窗~ *window leaf* /门~ *door leaf* ③ [量] for windows; doors, etc.:一~窗 *a window* /两~门 *two doors* *see also* shān

【扇贝】【动】scallop; fan shell

【扇车】winnowing machine; winnower

【扇骨子】the ribs of a fan; the mount of a fan

【扇面儿】the covering of a fan

【扇形】① fan-shaped: ~构造 *fan structure* ②【数】sector: ~齿轮 *sector gear; segment gear*

【扇叶】【动】flabellum

【扇坠】fan pendant

【扇子】fan:两把~ *two fans*

善 ① good:心怀不~ *harbour ill intent* /从~如流 *follow what is right is a stream follows its course; readily accept good advice* ② satisfactory; good: ~策 *a wise policy; a wise move; the best policy* / ~事 *charitable deeds; good needs* ③ kind; friendly:面~心慈 *affable and Kind-hearted* /他们两个十分相~。*Both of them were quite kind and helpful to each other.* ④ make a success of; perfect:独~其身 *maintain one's own integrity* / ~始~终 *begin well and end well; stick it out; do well from start to finish* ⑤ be good at; be expert in: ~于应对 *be good at repartee* ⑥ be apt to:多愁~感 *sentimental and susceptible* / ~变 *be changeable; be apt to change* ⑦ properly:我希望你~自保重。*I hope you take good care of yourself.*

【善罢甘休】(used in the negative) leave the matter at that; let the matter rest; let it go at that:你如果不还钱,她不会~的。*If you refuse to return the money, she won't let the matter go at that.*

【善报】receive good reward; reward the good:好人将得~。*A good person will be reward with good.*

【善本】reliable text; good edition: ~书 *rare book (of a good edition)*

【善处】[书] deal properly with; conduct well

【善待】treat sb well; treat sb nicely

【善感】oversensitive

【善果】good result — the rewards of good deeds:行善事,结~。*Good deeds bear good fruits.*

【善后】properly handle the remaining problems arising roman accident, etc.:交通事故的~处理。*Deal with the aftermath of the traffic accident.*

【善举】[书] philanthropic act; charitable act

【善良】good and honest; kind; kind-hearted: ~的心愿 *good intentions; best of intention* /心地~ *kind-hearted*

【善邻】[书] be a good neighbour

【善男信女】Buddhist devotees

【善人】philanthropist; charitable person

【善始善终】start well and end well; do well from start to finish

【善事】good deeds; charitable deeds:那位老奶奶一生做了许多~。*The granny had done a lot of good deeds in her life.*

【善忘】forgetful; prone to forget

【善心】mercy; benevolence; kindness:发~ *show kindness*

【善行】kind deed; god conduct

【善意】good will; good intentions

【善有善报，恶有恶报】 good will be reward with good, and evil with evil; good an d evil will always be rewarded

【善于】be good at; be versed in: ～交际 *be good (or skilful) at socializing* / ～计算 *be adept in (or at) figures* / ～辞令 *have a ready tongue*

【善战】be good at fighting; fight like a seasoned soldier; be skilful in battle

【善终】① die a natural death; die of old age ② end well

【善自为谋】know how to look after oneself; know how to plan for oneself

禅 abdicate

see also chán

【禅让】abdicate from the throne in favour of another person

【禅位】abdicate the throne

骟 castrate (an animal); geld (a male animal); spy (a female animal): ～马 *castrate (or geld) a stud; a gelded horse*

擅 ① arrogate to oneself; act on one's own authority: ～作主张 *make a decision without authorization; act without authorization* ② be expert in; be good at: 不～辞令 *lack facility or tactful speech; not be good at speech*

【擅长】be good at; be expert in; be (well) versed in: ～歌舞 *be good at singing and dancing* / 她～书法。*She is skilled in handwriting.*

【擅断】arbitrary; dictatorial

【擅离职守】leave one's post without permission; absent oneself from his post without leave

【擅自】do sth without authorization; act without authorization

膳 meals; board: 用～ *eat one's meals*

【膳费】board expenses

【膳食】meals; food: 流质～ *liquid diet* / ～结构 *diet structure*

【膳宿】board and lodging: ～自理 *make one's own board and lodging arrangements; be responsible for one's own board and lodging*

嬗 [书] alternation; evolution

【嬗变】① evolution ②【物】transmutation: 感性～ *induced transmutation* / 自然～ *natural transmutation*

赡 ① support; provide for: ～家养口 *support a family* ② adequate; sufficient

【赡养】support; keep; maintain; provide for: ～父母 *support one's parents*

【赡养费】payment for support of one's parents; alimony

鳝 eel; finless eel

【鳝鱼】eel; finless ell

shāng

伤 ① wound; injury: 枪～ *bullet wound* / 轻～ *slight injury* / 冻～ *frostbite* / 刀～ *knife wound* ② injure; hurt; wound ③ distressed: 悲～ *sad, grieved; sorrowful* ④ get sick of sth; surfeit; overeat: 鱼吃～了。*Sick from eating too much fish.* ⑤ be harmful to; hinder: 无～大雅 *involving no major principle; not matter much*

【伤疤】scar

【伤悲】sad; depressed; sorrowful; grieved

【伤兵】wounded soldier

【伤病】injury and sickness: ～员 *the sick and wounded; sick and wounded soldiers; no effectives*

【伤残】wound and disabled: ～人 *the handicapped; the crippled; the disabled; disable person*

【伤悼】mourn for; grieve over: ～某人的辞世 *grieve over the death of sb*

【伤风】catch cold; have a cold; get a cold: ～败俗 *offend public decency; violate public decency; corrupt public morals*

【伤感】sentimental; mawkish

【伤害】injure; wound; hurt: ～身体 *be harmful to one's health* / 她～了我的感情。*She wounded my feelings.*

【伤寒】①【医】typhoid fever; typhoid ②【中医】diseases caused by harmful cold factors; cold damage; fever; febrile diseases

【伤号】wounded soldier

【伤耗】damage: 这次灾害中庄稼遭受了很大～。*The crops suffered a great damage in the calamity.*

【伤痕】scar; gash: ～文学 *trauma literature* / 她从自行车上摔下来满身～。*She was covered in bruises after falling off her bicycle.*

【伤怀】[书] sad; grieved; distressed; brokenhearted

【伤筋动骨】be injured in the tendons or bone; sustain bone injuries

【伤口】wound; gash; cut: 包扎～ *bind up a wound* / ～化脓。*The wound is festering.*

【伤面子】hurt sb's feelings or sensibilities

【伤脑筋】knotty; thorny; troublesome; bothersome: 怎样抓住那只逃跑的猴子，还真是一件～的事。*How to catch the escaped and hidden monkey is indeed a hard nut to crack.* / 食堂的卫生是一件～的事。*The sanitary condition in the dining room is a big headache.* /老刮风，真～。*It's a nuisance the way it keeps on winding.*

【伤气】①[书] feel frustrated; feel dishearten; be upset ②【中医】sap one's vitality; undermine one's constitution

【伤情】① condition of an injury or wound: 她的～越来越好转。*Her injury is getting better and better.* ② sentimental, sad, sorrowful

【伤人】① hurt sb's feeling ② injure sb; inflict injury ③ impair one's health: 贪杯～ *excessive drinking can injure your health* / 恶言～ *rude language is highly offensive*

【伤神】① overtax one's nerves; cause highly metal strain ② sad; grieved; distressed

【伤生】be harmful to life

【伤食】【中医】dyspepsia caused be excessive eating or improper diet:这几天我有些~。*I'm suffering from indigestion in these days.*

【伤势】condition of an injury or wound

【伤天害理】words or acts are in defiance of heaven and human reason — atrocious; outrageous

【伤痛】① grieved; sad; distressed ② ache; pain of a injury or wound

【伤亡】casualties; injuries or death:敌人~惨重。*The enemy suffered heavy casualties.*

【伤心】grieved; sorrowful; broken-hearted: ~落泪 *shad sad tears* / ~事 *heartbreaking affair*; *painful memory*; *agonizing affair*

【伤员】wounded personnel; wounded soldier; the wounded

汤 see also tāng

【汤汤】[书] torrentially:河水~。*The river is in spate.*

殇 [书] die young:早~ *die young*

商 ① consult; discuss:共~国是 *discuss state affairs* ② trade; business; commerce:经~ *be in business*; *engage in trade* / ~贸企业 *business and trading firm* ③ merchant; businessman; salesman; trader; dealer:客~ *consultation* /已~定的条款 *the provisions already agreed upon*

【商队】company of travelling merchants; (trade) caravan

【商法】【律】commercial or mercantile law

【商贩】small retailer; pedlar:个体~ *self-employed vendor*; *individual traders and peddlers*

【商港】commercial port

【商行】trading company; commercial firm

【商号】shop; firm; store

【商会】chamber of commerce:他爸爸是那个~的一个领导。*His father is a leader of the chamber of commerce.*

【商计】discussion; consultation

【商检】commodity inspection

【商界】business world (or circles); commercial circles

【商量】consult; discuss:我们必须找老师~一下。*We have to talk it with our teacher.*

【商标】trademark: ~名称 *brand name* / ~法 *trademark law* / ~权 *trademark right*; *trademark ownership* / ~注册 *trademark registration*

【商埠】[旧] commercial or trading port

【商场】market; bazaar; department store; mall

【商船】merchant ship; merchantman: ~队 *mercantile marine*; *merchant marine or fleet*

【商店】shop; store:百货~ *department store* /妇女用品~ *women's goods store*

【商调】transfer sb to another work post through negotiation of the two parties concerned: ~函 *letter for negotiated transfer*; *letter requesting tranfer of personnel*

【商定】decide through consultation; agree:新生录取方案已经~。*The plan for enrolling new students has been drawn up through.*

【商路】trade route

【商旅】travelling merchants; tradesmen and travellers

【商贸】commerce; business and trade; trade

【商品】commodity; goods; merchandise: ~交换 *exchange of commodities* / ~房 *commercial housing* / ~价格 *commodity price* / ~目录 *descriptive catalogue* / ~经济 *commodity economy* / ~化 *commercialization* / ~货币 *commodity money* / ~交易 *commodity transaction* / ~交易会 *trade fair*; *commodities fair* / ~结构 *commodity mix*; *commodity composition* / ~学 *merchandising* / ~检验 *commodity inspection* / ~粮 *commodity grain* / ~流通 *circulation of commodities* / ~住宅 *commercial residential building* / ~推销员 *commercial travellers*

【商洽】arrange with sb; discuss; take up (a matter) with sb

【商情】market conditions: ~晴雨表 *business barometer* / ~预测 *business forecasting* / ~研究 *market research*

【商榷】discuss; consider:我们有足够时间来认真~这个问题。*We have enough time to deliberate on the problem.* /这个结论值得~。*This conclusion is open to question.*

【商人】businessman; merchant; trader; tradesman

【商厦】department store; business plaza; emporium

【商事】commercial affairs: ~法庭 *commercial court* / ~诉讼 *commercial action* / ~仲裁 *commercial arbitration*

【商数】【数】quotient

【商谈】exchange views; confer; discuss; talk about; negotiate:~贷款规模事宜 *discuss matters relating to the volume of credit* /她先去和她的同事~,然后再做出决定。*She withdrew to confer with her colleagues before making a decision.*

【商讨】discuss; deliberate; consult

【商亭】stall; stand; kiosk

【商务】commercial affairs; business affairs: ~参赞 *commercial counsellor* / ~活动 *commercial affairs or activities* / ~旅行 *business travel* / ~代表处 *trade representative's office* / ~秘书 *commercial secretary*

【商学院】commercial college; business school

【商业】commerce; trade; business: ~部门 *business sector*; *commercial department* / ~机构 *business organization* / ~广告 *commercial advertising* / ~道德 *business ethics* / ~界 *business circles* / ~经济 *business economy* / ~经济学 *economics of commerce*; *business economics* / ~票据 *commercial bill*; *trade bill* / ~网点 *commercial net work*; *network of trading establishments* / ~信贷 *commercial credit* / ~卫星 *commercial satellite* / ~信用证 *commercial letter of credit* / ~用语 *business term* / ~中心 *commercial centre*; *business centre*

【商议】consult; confer; discuss

【商誉】goodwill; business reputation, commercial standing

【商约】commercial treaty

【商战】trade war; business competition

【商酌】consider; deliberate

墒 【农】moisture in the soil:保~ preserve the moisture of the soil /抢~ *seize the opportunity to sow while there is still sufficient soil moisture*

【墒情】soil moisture content

shǎng

晌 ① part of the day:后半~ *afternoon* ②［方］noon

【晌饭】［方］① lunch; midday meal ② extra meal in the day during the busy farming season

【晌觉】［方］afternoon nap

【晌午】midday; noon:~饭 *lunch*; *midday meal*

赏[1] ① grant a reward; bestow a reward; a word: ~金 *money reward*; *pecuniary reward* ② (Shǎng) a surname

赏[2] ① admire; enjoy; appreciate; delight in viewing: ~花 *feast one's eyes on flowers* / ~月 *feast one's eyes on the full moon*; *enjoy a beautiful full moon* ② reward; award

【赏赐】① bestow or grant a reward; award: ~他许多土地。*Give him a lot of land as a reward.* ② reward; award

【赏罚】rewards and punishments: ~分明 *be fair in meting out rewards and punishments*

【赏光】accept on initiations:请您~。*I request the pleasure of your company.*

【赏鉴】appreciate (a work of art): ~字画 *appreciate and evaluate a painting and calligraphy* / ~古董 *appreciate antiques and curios*

【赏脸】honour me with your presence; grant one the honour:你能~出席这次晚会吗? *Would you please do me the honour of taking part in the evening party?*

【赏钱】money reward; tip

【赏识】recognize the worth of; appreciate; praise; be in sb's good grace; thinks highly of:领导很~他的才能。*The superior thinks highly of his talent.*

【赏玩】admire the beauty of sth; delight in; fondle; enjoy; be fond of: ~书画 *be fond of painting and calligraphy*

【赏析】make a appreciative comment; study carefully:古曲音乐~ *appreciative comments on classical music.*

【赏心悦目】pleasing to both the eye and the mind

【赏雪】enjoy a beautiful snow scene

shàng

上[1] ① upper; up; upward: ~体 *the upper part of the body* / ~铺 *the upper berth* /他的学习成绩总是中~水平。*His school record is always above the average.* ② higher; superior; better:顶头~司 *one's immediate superior* / ~级领导 *a leading body at a higher level* ③ last; former; most recent: ~星期三 *last Wednesday* / ~个月 *last month* ④［旧］the emperor: ~谕 *imperial degree* ⑤ upward

上[2] ① go up; ascend; mount; board; get on: ~山 *go up a hill*; *climb up a mountain* / ~楼 *go upstairs*; *ascend the stairs* / ~公共汽车 *get on a bus* / ~飞机 *board a plane* / ~船 *go on board*; *go aboard a ship* ② go to; leave for: ~北京 *leave for Beijing* /我~办公室去一趟。*I'm going to the office.* ③ go ahead; forge ahead:迎着困难~ *meet difficulties head-on* ④ first (part); preceding; previous: ~册 *the first volume*; *book one* / ~半月 *first half of a year* ⑤ enter the court:这场球你们六个先~。*The six of you will play the first game.* /换人! 7号下, 11号上。*Substitution*; *player No. 11 for No. 7.* ⑥ fill; serve; supply: ~菜 *serve the dishes* / ~茶 *serve the tea* ⑦ *fix*; *place sth in position*: ~螺丝 *fix a screw* /子弹~了膛。*The gun is loaded.* ⑧ apply; pain; put on; smear:给桌子~油漆 *paint the table* /医生正在给病人脸~~药膏。*The doctor is applying ointment on the face of the sick.* ⑨ be put on record; be published; be carried (in a publication):那位战士的先进事迹~了报纸。*The soldier's model deeds have been reported on newspaper.* ⑩ wind; tighten; screw: ~发条 *wind up a watch* ⑪ begin to do sth (in work, study, etc) a t a fixed time:她今天~早班。*She is on the morning shift today.* /他~中学。*He is now in middle school.* ⑫ up to; as many as: ~百人 *no fewer than a hundred* /她已经~岁数了。*She is getting on in years.* ⑬ used after a verb expressing an up ward movement:我们十点钟爬~了山顶。*We reached the peak of the mountain at ten o'clock.* /学生成绩~去了。*The school records of students have been submitted to the higher-ups.*

上[3] ① used after a verb expressing that an aim has been achieved:当~了教师 *become a teacher* /锁~门 *lock the door* /买~汽车了 *have bought a car* ② used after a verb expressing the start and continuation of an action:她爱~了一个男孩子。*She has fallen in love with a boy.* ③ used after a verb expressing the amount or extent reached:每月读~几本书 *read several books every month* ④ on:我脸~ *on my face* /屋顶~ *on the roof* ⑤ in; within:世界~ *in the world* /书~ *in the book* /理论~ *in theory* ⑥ at (the age of):她3岁~父母都死了。*Her parents died when she was three year old.* ⑦ up; upward:向~看 *look up*

(*at sth*)
【上班】go to work; be on duty; start work hours: ~族 *office workers*
【上半场】first half (of a game, etc): ~比分是20比15。*The score in the first half was* 20 *to* 15.
【上半身】upper part of the body; above the waist
【上半夜】before midnight
【上绑】tie the arms of sb; truss sb up
【上报】① report to a higher body; report to the headship; report to the higher-ups:这件事应该立刻~市长。*This matter should be reported to the mayor.* ② appear in the newspapers
【上辈】① ancestors; forbears ② the elder generation of one's family; one's elders
【上辈子】① ancestors ② previous life; previous existence
【上臂】upper arm
【上膘】(of animals) become fat; fatten
【上表】submit a memorial to the emperor
【上宾】distinguished guest; guest of honour; honoured guest:她被总经理待为~。*The general manager treated her as honoured guest.*
【上不着天,下不着地】touch neither the sky nor the earth — be suspended in midair; be stranded halfway
【上菜】serve the dishes (of food); serve food on table
【上苍】heave; God
【上操】go out to drill; do exercise
【上策】best plan; best policy; best thing to do; best way out
【上层】upper strata; super or higher levels: ~领导 *higher leadership* / ~社会 *upper-class society* / ~路线 *the upper-level line* / ~人士 *upper circles*
【上层建筑】superstructure:国家机器属于~。*State apparatus belong to the realm of the superstructure.*
【上场】①【体】enter the court or field; participate in a contest; join in a contest ② appear on the stage; enter
【上乘】be of superior quality; first-class:一部~小说 *a finest-class novel*
【上床】go to bed; get in to bed
【上蹿下跳】① run around on sinister errands ② (of animals) running and jumping all over the place
【上达】reach the higher authorities:使民意~ *communicate the public feeling to the higher authorities*
【上代】previous generation; former generations
【上当】be taken in; be deceived; be cheated; be fooled; be duped
【上灯】light a lamp; light up; turn on the light: ~时分 *lighting-uptime*
【上等】first class; first rate; top-notch: ~皮具 *superior leather products* / ~小麦 *high-quality wheat*
【上等兵】private, first class (Chinese army); airman, first class (Chinese air force); seaman, first class (Chinese navy)
【上低音号】【音】baritone
【上帝】① God ② Lord on High that govern everything
【上调】① transfer sb to a higher post ② transfer goods, funds, etc. to higher authorities
【上冻】freeze
【上颚】① mandible (of certain arthropods) ② maxilla (of a mammal); upper jaw
【上发条】wind (a watch, etc.)
【上房】① wife (as distinguished from concubine) ② main rooms (usu. facing south, within a courtyard)
【上访】apply for an audience with the higher authorities to appeal for intervention
【上坟】visit a grave (to honour the memory of the dead)
【上风】① windward ② advantage; superior position; upper hand:占~ *get the upper hand*
【上峰】[旧] superior; higher-ups; boss:接到~的命令 *receive orders from one's superior*
【上浮】[旧] ① rise; raise; increase; go up:工资~。*The wage has raised.* /大米的价格~了。*The price of rice has gone up.* ② (of a submarine) come up; surface
【上纲】raise a minor fault to the higher plane of principle
【上岗】go to one's post; go to duty posts; take up a job
【上告】① complain to the higher authorities; appeal to a higher court ② report to a higher body
【上工】go to work; start work
【上贡】① offer up a sacrifice; lay offerings on the altar:我们通常在清明节给祖先~。*We usually offer up a sacrifice to out ancestors on Qingming.* ② oil sb's palm; give presents to the superior expecting favours in return
【上钩】rise to the bait; swallow the bait; get hooked; be enticed
【上古】ancient times; antiquity: ~史 *ancient history*
【上馆子】eat in a restaurant
【上光】① glazing; polishing ②【纺】lustring: ~版 *ferrotype plate* / ~机 glazing machine; glazer / ~蜡 *wax polish*
【上轨道】①【航】be launched into orbit ② get on the right track; begin to work smoothly
【上好】first-class; best quality; top; top-notch
【上颌】【生理】upper jaw; maxilla
【上呼吸道】【生理】upper respiratory tract: ~感染 *infection of the upper respiratory tract*
【上回】last time
【上火】①[方] get angry; flare up ②【中医】suffer from excessive internal heat (with such symptoms as constipation, conjunctivitis and inflammation of the nasal and oral cavities)
【上货】① display goods on shelves; replenish the goods shelves ② replenish stocks; replenish supplies for sale
【上级】higher level; higher authorities; one's supe-

S

rior: ~领导 *a leading body at a higher level* / ~组织 *an organization at the higher level* / ~指示 *instruction from the higher authorities*

【上计】best plan; best way out

【上佳】excellent; of superior quality; admirable

【上家】person who precedes one in play (such as in mahjong, card games, etc.)

【上浆】①【纺】dressing (of yarn, fabrics, etc.); sizing ② starching: 棉布 ~ *starching*

【上将】(Chinese Army and Air Force, US and Brit Army. US Air Force, US and Brit Marine Corps) general; (Chinese Navy, US and Brit Navy) admiral; (Brit Air Force) air chief marshal

【上交】hand in; turn over to higher authorities

【上胶】sizing: ~机 *gluing machine*

【上焦】【中医】part of the body cavity above the diaphragm housing the heart and lungs

【上缴】turn over sth (revenues, profits, etc.) to the higher authorities: ~利润 *that part of the profits turn over to the state*

【上街】① go shopping (or downtown); go to the street ② take to the street: ~游行 *demonstrate in the streets*

【上届】previous session; previous term; last: ~冠军 *defending champion* / ~毕业生 *last year's graduates*

【上界】the world above; heavenly abode

【上进】make progress; go forward: ~心 *desire for improvement*

【上劲】energetically; vigorously; with gusto: 越干越~儿 *take an increasing interest in one's work* / 他们越谈越~儿。*They get more and more excited as they talk.*

【上课】go to class; attend class; give a lesson; conduct a class: 她今天没有~。*She didn't attend class today.* /明天学校开始~。*School starts tomorrow.*

【上空】in the sky; high above

【上口】① be suitable for reading; read smoothly: 这首诗相当~。*This poem makes quite smooth reading.* ② be able to read aloud fluently: 琅琅~ *easy to read out*

【上跨交叉】【交】overpass; flyover

【上款】the name of the recipient (as inscribed on a painting or a calligraphic scroll presented as a gift)

【上蜡】waxing

【上来】① begin: 一~就吵闹 *be quarrelling from the start* ②［书］to sum up ②［书］③come up: 太阳~了。*The sun is rising.* ④ up (here): 把水桶抬~。*Bring the bucket up.* ⑤ expressing success in doing sth: 我回答不~上他的问题。*I can not give a correct answer to each of his questions.* ⑥ expressing an increase in degree: 天气热~来了。*It is getting warm.* /天色黑 ~了。*It is getting dark.*

【上联】the first line of a couplet

【上梁不正下梁歪】if the upper beam is not straight, the lower ones will go aslant; when those above behave unworthily, those below will follow suit

【上列】listed above; above

【上流】① belonging to the upper circles; high-society: ~社会 *upper class*; *high society* ② upper reaches (of a river): 黄河~ *upper reaches of the Yellow River*

【上路】① set out on a journey; start off ② on the right track: 我的工作已经~了。*I have got the knack of my job.*

【上马】① mount a horse ② start (a project, etc.): 这项工程下月~。*This project will start next month.*

【上门】① visit; drop in; go to see sb; call: 送货~ *deliver goods to the doorstep*; *door to door service* ② shut the door; lock up for the night ③ marry into and live with one's bride's family: ~女婿 *living-in son-in-law*; *son-in-law living with the bride's family*

【上面】① above; upper; over; on top of; on the surface of: 黄河~架了许多桥。*A lot of bridges have been built across the Yellow River.* ② abovementioned; aforesaid; preceding; foregoing: ~一个词 *the preceding word* / ~例子 *the above mentioned example* ③ higher level; higher ups; higher authorities: ~有命令。*There is an order from above.* ④ aspect; respect; regard: 她在英语~下了很大的工夫。*She has put a lot of effort into his study of English.* ⑤ the elder generation of one 's family; one's elders

【上年】last year

【上年纪】be getting on in year (or age)

【上盘】hanging wall

【上皮】【生理】epithelium: ~炎 *epithelitis* / ~组织 *epithelial tissue*

【上品】highest grade; highest quality; top grade

【上坡路】① uphill road; upward slope: 孩子们正在走~。*The children are walking uphill.* ② upward trend; growth; steady progress

【上漆】lacquering

【上气不接下气】pant (or gasp) for breath; short of breath; out of breath

【上去】① go up: 顺着梯子爬~ *go up along the ladder* ② used after a verb, expressing forward (or outward) direction: 向敌人冲~ *dash to the enemy* ③ up (here); rise to a place: 成绩单已经交~了。*School reports have been sent up to the higher-ups.* /把生产搞~。*We must increase our production.* ④ expressing adding or fixing: 画帖~了。*The painting has been stuck on.*

【上圈套】fall into a trap; fall into sb's trap

【上染率】【纺】dye-uptake

【上任】① take up an official post; take office: 上个月,她妈妈匆匆赶北京~了。*Last month, her mother went to Beijing in a hurry to take office.* ② predecessor

【上色】(shàngsè) best-quality; top-grade; top-notch: ~茶叶 *best-quality tea*

【上色】(shàngshǎi) colour; paint

【上山】① climb mountains ②［方］（of silkworms）go up bundles of straw（to spin co coons）

【上上】① very best; the highest: ~策 *best plan*（*or policy*）② before last: ~周 *the week before last*

【上上下下】high and low; everybody

【上身】① upper part of the body ② start weaving: 春天来了,西装该~了。*Spring is coming; we'd better start wearing our western-style clothes.* ③ upper outer garment; shirt; jacket

【上升】① rise; go up: 气温~了。*The temperature is going up.* /气球徐徐~。*A balloon is curling upwards.* ② increase; ascend: 气流~ *ascending air; up current* /今年钢产量大幅~。*The production of steel is increasing steadily this year.*

【上士】（Chinese Army, US Army）sergeant first class;（Chinese Air Force, US Air Force）technical sergeant;（Chinese Navy, US Navy）petty officer first class;（Brit Navy）chief petty officer（Brit Air Force）flight sergeant;（US Marine Corps）technical sergeant or staff sergeant;（Brit Marine Corps）colour sergeant

【上市】①（of goods）go（or appear）on the market: 苹果大量~。*There are plenty of apples on the market.* ② go to market; go shopping: ~场买米去 *go to the rice market* ③ go public; list: ~公司 *listed companies* /在深圳~ *be listed in Shenzhen* / ~规则 *listing rules* / ~股票 *listed stock or shares*

【上视图】【机】top view

【上手】① lest-hand seat; seat of honour ② get started: 那盘棋~很顺利。*Everything went smoothly from the beginning of that game of chess.*

【上书】submit a written statement to a higher authority: 向中央~ *submit a written request to the centre government*

【上述】above-mentioned; preceding

【上水】① feed water to a steam engine, radiator（of a car）, etc.: 给火车~*feed water to the train* ② upper-reaches（of a river）③ sail upstream: ~道 *water-supply line* /这是一般~水船。*The boat is sailing upstream.*

【上税】pay taxes

【上司】superior; chief: 顶头~ *one's immediate superior*（*or chief*）

【上诉】【律】appeal（to a higher court）: ~法院 *court of appeal; appellate court* /提出~ *lodge an appeal* /驳回~ *reject an appeal* / ~权 *right of appeal* /~人 *appellant; petitioner* / ~状 *petition for appeal*

【上溯】① go upstream; sail upstream; sail upstream ② trace back; date back: ~到 1850 年 *trace back to the year 1850*

【上算】profitable; paying; worthwhile: 买鱼比买肉~。*It is more economical to buy fish than meat.*

【上岁数】［口］getting on in years

【上锁】lock: 当我们赶到她家时,才发现她家已经~了。*When we got to her family, we found the door was locked.*

【上台】① ascend the platform; go up onto the platform; appear on the stage ② come to power; assume power; hold sway

【上台阶】make a new round of progress

【上堂】① go to court ②［方］（of a teacher）give a lesson

【上膛】①【军】load a gun; be loaded: 子弹已经~。*The gun is loaded.* ②【生理】palate

【上套】① hitch up a animal to a cart ② fall into a trap

【上体】［书］upper part of the body

【上天】① go up in the sky; fly sky-high（or sky wards）: 我们又一颗卫星~了。*Another satellite of ours was launched.* ② go to heaven; pass way; die ③ Heaven; God

【上天无路,入地无门】there is no road to heaven and no door into the earth; no way of escape; in deep water

【上调】（of price）raise: 肉价~了。*The price of pork has been raised.*

【上头】① higher authorities: ~有令。*There is an order from above.* ② above: 从山~往下看。*Look down from a mountain.*

【上吐下泻】throw up on top and purge down below; have loose bowels and vomit

【上味】very delicious food

【上尉】（Chinese Army, Chinese Air Force, US and Brit. Army, US Air Force, US and Brit Marine Corps）captain;（Chinese, US and Brit, Navy）lieutenant;（Brit Air Force）flight lieutenant

【上文】foregoing paragraphs; foregoing chapters; preceding paragraphs; preceding part of the text: 见~ *see above; see supra*

【上午】morning; forenoon

【上西天】go to the Western Paradise; die; pass away

【上下】① high and low: 全国~ *the whole nation* / ~一条心。*The government and the people are of one mind.* /公司~不通气。*There lacked proper channel of communication between the higher and lower level in the company.* ② from top to bottom; up and down: 她~打量着这个男孩。*She looked the boy from head to foot.* ③ relative superiority or inferiority ④（used after round numbers）about; nearly; or so; or thereabout; approximately: 他看起来 40 岁~。*He looks about forty years old.* ⑤ go up and down: 居民大楼内有电梯,~很方便。*The apartment house has lift and it easily goes up and down.*

【上下水】the water supply line and sewer

【上下文】context: 从~来看,就很容易了解作者的意图了。*From the context, we are easy to understand the author's purpose.*

【上弦】①【天】first quarter（of the moon）: ~月 *the moon at the first quarter* ② tighten to spring of; wind up a clock, toy, etc.

【上限】upper limit; the maximum permissible; ceiling

【上线】① reach the admission test scores：今年北大报名者中～的很多。*This year Beijing University have a lot of applicants who reach the admission test scores.* ② raise to the higher plane of struggle over the political line

【上香】burn incense and offer sacrifices（to gods，ancestors，etc）；burn joss sticks

【上相】come out well in a photograph；look attractive in photographs

【上校】（Chinese Army & Air Force，US and Brit Army，U. S. Air force）colonel；（Chinese Navy，US and Brit Navy）captain；（brit，Ait force）group captain

【上鞋】stitch the sole to the upper；sole a shoe

【上心】［方］in mind；set one's heart on sth be careful

【上新世】【地】the Pliocene Epoch

【上刑】torture sb to extract a confession；put to torture

【上行】①（of train）going towards the capital；upgoing；up：～列车 *upgoing train* ② upstream；upriver：～船 *an upstream boat*；*an upriver boat* ③（of document）sent to the upper levels：～公文 *a document sent to the upper levels*

【上行下效】if a leader sets a bad example，it will be followed by his subordinates；the bad example set by a person in a leading position will be followed by his subordinates

【上旋】【体】top spin：～球 *a top-spin ball*

【上选】the choicest；first-class；top grade；superior

【上学】go to school；be at school；attend school

【上旬】the first ten-day period of a month

【上演】perform；put on the stage

【上扬】increase；go up：股票价格～。*The stock price has gone up.*

【上衣】upper outer garment；jacket

【上议院】upper house；（Brit）House of Lords

【上瘾】be addicted（to sth）；get into the habit of doing sth；get hooked on sth：她吸毒～五年了。*She has been addicted to drugs for five years.*

【上映】show（a film）；screen

【上游】① upper reaches（of a river）：长江～ *the upper reaches of the Yangtze River* ② advanced position；be ahead of others：力争～ *strive for the best*

【上有天堂，下有苏杭】in heaven there is paradise，on earth there are Suzhou and Hangzhou

【上有政策，下有对策】the higher authorities have policies and the localities have their countermeasures；attempt of those below to get around the policies of their superiors

【上载】【电】upload

【上灶】do the cooking；cook

【上涨】rise；go up：米价～了2倍。*The price of rice has been gone up two times.* /湖水～。*The lake has risen.*

【上账】make an entry in an account book

【上阵】go into battle；pitch into the work；take part in a game：～杀敌 *go to the front to fight the foe*

【上肢】upper limbs

【上装】① make up（for a theatrical performance）② upper outer garment；jacket

【上座】seat of honour：～率 *box-office rate*；*occupancy*；*attendance*

尚[1] ① esteem；value；treasure；set great store by：高～ *lofty* /崇～ *uphold*；*advocate* ② prevailing custom，habits，etc. ③（Shàng）a surname

尚[2] ① still；yet：为时～早。*It is still too early.* ② even：大人～不理解，何况小孩。*Even grown-ups can't understand it，to say nothing of children.*

【尚方宝剑】the emperor's sword as a symbol of supreme authority

【尚且】even：这种事情老师～无法解释，何况学生呢？*Even the teachers cannot account for this matter；how you expect the students to know it?*

【尚书】① collection of Ancient Texts，whose compilation is generally attributed to Confucius ② a high official in ancient China ③ minister（in the Ming Dynasty an d the Qing Dynasty）

【尚武】encourage a martial or military spirit；emphasize military affairs：～精神 *a martial spirit*

shāo

捎 take along sth to or for sb；bring sth to sb：～信 *take a message for sb*
see also shào

【捎带】incidentally；in passing：你上市场的话，～一条鱼给我。*If you happen to be going to the market，please get me a fish.*

【捎话】take a message to sb；pass on a message to sb

【捎脚】pick up passengers or goods on the way：请帮忙捎一下脚。*Please give me a lift.*

烧 ① burn；set five to：～毁 *burn down* /火车～煤。*This train burns coal.* ② cook，heat：～砖瓦 *bake（or fire）bricks and tiles* / ～开水 *boil water* ③ fry after stewing or stew after frying：～茄子 *stewed eggplant* /红～鲤鱼 *carp stewed in brown source* ④ roast：～鸡 *roast chicken* ⑤ run a fever；have a temperature：赶快给孩子退～。*Hurry to bring the child's temperature down to normal.* ⑥ damage or hurt（by excessive or improper use of fertilizer；injure）：化肥施用太多，苗子全～死了。*All these seedlings were burnt by excessive use of chemical fertilizer.* ⑦ fever：他已经退～了。*His fever is gone.*

【烧包】［方］get a swollen head；be drunken with success

【烧杯】beaker

【烧饼】sesame seed cake

【烧饭】［方］do the cooking；prepare a meal

【烧高香】burn joss sticks in worship — be granted

a favour; be thankful

【烧锅】① (liquor) distillery ② vat for making liquor

【烧化】① cremate ② burn (paper, etc. as an offering to the dead)

【烧画】poker-picture

【烧荒】reclaim wasteland by burning grass and bushes

【烧毁】destroy by five; burn up; burn down; burn through

【烧火】make a fine; light a fire; build a fire; tend the kitchen fire

【烧鸡】roast chicken; baked chicken

【烧碱】【化】caustic soda

【烧结】sintering; agglomeration; agglutination: ~玻璃 *sintered glass* / ~厂 *sintering plant* / ~法 *sintering process* / ~剂 *agglutinant* / ~坩埚 *sintered crucible* / ~温度 *sintering temperature*

【烧酒】spirit (usu. distilled from sorghum or maize)

【烧烤】barbecue:韩国的~很有名。*The barbecue of South Korea is very famous.*

【烧垦】slash and burn cultivation

【烧麦】a steamed dumpling with the dough frilled at the lop

【烧毛】【纺】singeing: ~工艺 *singeing* / ~机 *singeing frame*

【烧瓶】flask (used in laboratory)

【烧伤】【医】burn:重度~ *severe burns* /三度~ *third-degree burns*

【烧香】① burn joss sticks ② bribe

【烧心】①【医】upset stomach; heartburn ②［方］(of cabbages) turn yellow at the heart

【烧纸】① burn paper money as an offering to the dead ② paper money burnt as an offering to the dead

【烧灼】burn; singe; scorch

梢 tip; the tin end of a twig, etc.:树~ *the top of a tree* /辫~ *end of a plait*

【梢条】twig; branch

【梢头】① the tip of a branch ② top log

稍 a little; a bit; a shade; a trifle; slightly: ~慢一点 *a bit slower* / ~加调整 *make slight regulation* / ~修订 *make slight revision*
see also shào

【稍稍】a little; slightly; a trifle: ~休息一下 *take a brief rest* / ~有点粗 *some what crude* /请~移动一下。*Please move a bit.*

【稍胜一筹】slightly better; a cut above

【稍逊一筹】a cut below; slightly inferior to

【稍微】a little; a bit; somewhat; a trifle; slightly: ~有点紧张 *get a bit nervous* / ~搁点糖 *put in a little sugar*

【稍许】a little; slightly; a bit

【稍纵即逝】transient; fleeting: transient; fleeting: ~的战机 *a fleeting opportunity for combat*

筲 pail (made of bamboo strips or wood) bucket

艄 ① stern ② rudder; helm;掌~ *at the helm; in control*

【艄公】① helmsman ② boatman

鞘 whiplash
see also qiào

sháo

勺 ① spoon; scoop: ~子 *ladle; scoop* /漏~ *strainer* /铁~ *iron spoon*

芍

【芍药】【植】Chinese herbaceous peony

韶 ［书］beautiful; splendid

【韶光】［书］① beautiful springtime ②［喻］glorious youth

【韶华】①［书］springtime ②［喻］glorious youth: 我们不能虚度~。*We should not idle our precious youth.*

【韶景】［书］delicate and pretty

shǎo

少 ① few; little; scanty; less:工具~ *short of tools* / ~走弯路 *avoid detours* /机会不~ *have plenty of opportunities* ② be short of; lack:缺~食物 *lack food* /我们还缺~两台电视。*We're still two TVs short.* ③ lose; be missing:墙上~了几幅画。*Some paintings are missing from the wall.* / 看~不~工具。*See if any tool is missing.* ④ stop; quit; cut out:少管闲事。*Mind your own business.* / ~来这一套。*Cut it out.* ⑤ a little; a Moment:请~候。*Wait a moment, please.*
see also shào

【少安毋躁】keep calm, don't get excited; don't get impatient, wait a while

【少不得】cannot do without; be indispensable:这里每一件事都~你。*Here we can do nothing without you.*

【少不了】① cannot do without; be bound to; cannot dispense with:这次晚会~你。*We can't do without you for this evening party.* ② plenty of; must be a lot:问题看来~。*It looks as if there are going to be quite a lot of problems.*

【少得了】(used in rhetorical question) can do without; can dispense with:明天的会议不能~她。*She must attend the meeting tomorrow; we cannot do without her.*

【少而精】smaller quantity, better quality; fewer but better; concise:用字~ *be succinct in wording* /编辑人员要~。*The editorial staffs should smaller but more efficient.*

【少见】① it's a rare pleasure to meet you ② seldom seen; infrequent; rare; unusual:这是一种~的鸟。*This is a rare bird.*

【少见多怪】the less one has seen, the more he has to wonder at; scanty experience gives rise to many surprises：用不着～。*There is nothing to be surprised.* /也许是我～。*Maybe I'm ignorant and easily surprised.*
【少量】a small amount; a few; a little; little bit
【少顷】［书］after a short while; after a few moments; soon; presently
【少生优生】have fewer but healthier babies
【少时】after a little while; a moment later; soon; presently
【少数】small number; not many; minority: ～党 *minority party* / ～民族 *minority nationality; ethnic minority* / ～民族地区 *minority nationality region* / ～服从多数。*The minority is subordinate to the majority.*
【少许】［书］a little; a few; some; modicum
【少有】rare; seldom

shào

少 young; youthful：男女老～ *men and women, old and young* / ～男 *young unmarried man; young boy* ② son of a rich family; a young master：阔～ *profligate son of the rich* ③（Shào）a surname
see also shǎo
【少白头】① young person with greying hair ② be prematurely grey
【少不更事】young and inexperienced; green
【少东家】［旧］young master; son of the master
【少儿】children; children and early teenagers: ～读物 *children's book*
【少妇】young married woman
【少管所】reformatory for juvenile delinquents; juvenile penitentiary
【少将】（U. S., Brit. and Army, Chinese and Air Force）major general;（Chinese, U. S. and Brit. Navy）rear admiral;（Brit. Air Force）air vice marshal
【少奶奶】［旧］① young mistress ② your daughter-in-law
【少男少女】unmarried young men and women
【少年】① early youth（from ten to sixteen）：她～时代一心梦想成为一个电影明星。*It was her girlhood dream to become a film star.* ② boy or girl in early teen; juvenile; teenager: ～运动员 *juvenile athletes; juvenile players* / ～读物 *juvenile reader* / ～犯 *juvenile delinquent* / ～犯罪 *juvenile delinquency* / ～宫 *children's palace* / ～先锋队 *Young Pioneers* / ～班 *juvenile college class*
【少年老成】① old head on young shoulders ② a young person lacking in vigour and drive; listless young person
【少女】young girl
【少尉】（Chinese Army and Air Force, U. S. and Brit. Army, U. S. Air Force, U. S. and Brit. Marine Corps）Second Lieutenant;（Chinese Navy, U. S. Navy）ensign;（Birt. Navy）acting sublieutenant;（Birt. Air Force）pilot officer
【少先队】young pioneers: ～员 Young Pioneer
【少相】young-looking; have a youthful appearance
【少校】（Chinese Army and Air Force, U. S. and Brit. Army, U. S. Air Force, U. S. and Brit. Marine Corps）major;（U. S. and Brit. Navy）lieutenant commander;（Birt. Air Force）squadron leader
【少爷】①［旧］young master（of the house）: ～脾气 *behaviour of a pampered*（*or spoilt*）*boy* ② your son
【少壮】young and vigorous: ～派 *powerful rising stars; the up-and-coming*
【少壮不努力,老大徒伤悲】laziness in youth spells regret in old age; and idle youth, a needy age

捎（of draught animal）draw back a step or two; shy: ～色（*of colour*）*fade*
see also shāo

哨 ① sentry post; post：观察～ *observation post* /岗～ *sentry post* / ～兵 *sentry; guard* ②（of birds）warble; chirp ③ a whistle: ～子 *whistle*
【哨岗】sentry post
【哨卡】check post; frontier sentry post
【哨所】sentry post; post：前沿～ *outpost; forward post*
【哨位】sentry post; post

稍
see also shāo
【稍息】【军】stand at ease: ～！（*a word of command*）*At ease!*

潲 ①（of rain）slant in：西～ *shant west* /北边～雨。*The rain is driving in from the north.* ②［方］sprinkle：往花上～点水。*Sprinkle the flowers with waters.*

shē

奢 ① luxurious; profligate：穷～极侈（*live a life of*）*wanton extravagance* ② excessive; extravagant; inordinate; undue: ～想 *wild wishes; extravagant hopes*
【奢侈】luxurious; extravagant; lavish; wasteful：生活～ *live in luxury* / ～品 *luxury goods; luxury items* / ～品税 *luxury tax* /宴会极其～。*The dinner was extravagant and wasteful.*
【奢华】luxurious; sumptuous: ～的生活 *an extravagant life* / ～的住宅 *a luxurious resident*
【奢靡】extravagant; lavish
【奢盼】extravagant hopes; wild expectation
【奢求】excessive demands; extravagant claims
【盼望】extravagant hopes; wild wishes

赊 buy or sell on credit
【赊购】buy on credit: ～食品 *buy food on credit*
【赊欠】buy or sell on credit
【赊销】sell on credit: ～彩电 *sell colour TV sell on credit*

【赊账】① buy or sell on credit ② outstanding bills or accounts：她有500元的～。*There was an outstanding bill of 500 yuan against her.*

猞

【猞猁】lynx

shé

舌 ① tongue ② sth shaped like a tongue：鞋～ *tongue of a shoe* /火～ *tongues of flame* ③ clapper

【舌敝唇焦】talk till one's tongue and lips are parched; talk oneself hoarse in pleading or expostulating

【舌根】root of the tongue：～音 *velar*

【舌耕】[书] teach to make a living

【舌尖】tip of the tongue：～音 *apical* /～后音 *blade-palatal* /～中音 *blade-alveolar*

【舌鳎】【动】tonguefish; tongue sole

【舌苔】coating on the tongue; tongue fur

【舌头】① tongue ② an enemy soldier captured for the purpose of extracting information

【舌下神经】lingual nerve

【舌下腺】【生理】sublingual gland

【舌咽神经】glossopharyngeal nerve

【舌炎】glossitis

【舌战】have a verbal battle with; argue heatedly：～群儒 *fight a battle of words with a group of scholars* /他们展开～。*They are engaging a verbal battle.*

【舌状花】【植】lingulate flower

折 ① break; split：绳子～了。*The rope snapped.* /桌子腿～了。*The table leg broke.* ② lose money in business
see also zhē; zhé

【折本】lose money in business：她做生意从来没有～过。*She never suffered losses in her business operations.*

【折秤】damage or loss to goods in the course of reweighing

蛇 snake：毒～ *poisonous snake*

【蛇虫】snakeworm

【蛇胆】the gallbladder of a snake; snake bile

【蛇毒】【医】snake venom; venin

【蛇管】【机】hosepipe; coiler

【蛇鳗】snake eel

【蛇皮】snakeskin

【蛇丘】【地】esker

【蛇头】① snake head ② the ring leader of illegal immigration

【蛇蜕】【中医】snake slough; exuviation

【蛇蝎】snakes and scorpions-heinous (or vicious) people; viper：～心肠 *venomous as snakes and scorpions; fiendish*

【蛇行】[书] ① move in a twisting way on the ground; crawl ② meander：小河～绕村而过。*The rivulet meandered around the village.*

【蛇形】snakelike; S-shaped

【蛇足】feet added to a snake by an ignorant artist — a superfluity

shě

舍 ① abandon; give up：难分难～ *loath to part from each other* /～弃过时的信仰 *discard outdated beliefs* ② give alms; dispense charity
see also shè

【舍本逐末】attend to trifles and neglect essentials

【舍不得】be loath to part with; hard to part with; grudge：～孩子套不住狼 *if one wishes to succeed; one has to take great risks* /我～离开孩子。*I hate to leave my children.* /他～花钱。*He is loath to spend his money.*

【舍得】be ready to part with; not grudge; be willing to give up：你～送给她这件新衣服吗？*Are you willing to send the new clothes to her?*

【舍己救人】sacrifice oneself to save sb else; save sb else life at the risk of one's own

【舍己为公】sacrifice one's own interests for the sake of public

【舍己为人】sacrifice one's own interests for the sake of public; be altruistic

【舍近求远】seek far and wide for what lies close at hand; forgo what is close at hand and seek what is far afield

【舍车保帅】(in Chinese chess) give up a chariot to save the marshal-sacrifice minor interests to major ones.

【舍脸】cast aside considerations of face：他不得～向警察求情。*He has to ask the policeman for a favour unabashedly.*

【舍命】risk one's life; (be ready to) sacrifice oneself：～陪君子 *throw in one's lot with you at the risk of my life; keep sb company at all costs*

【舍弃】give up; abandon：～享乐 *forgo pleasures* /～机会 *forgo an opportunity* /～生命 *lay down one's life*

【舍入】【数】rounding off：～误差 *rounding error; round-off error*

【舍身】lay down one's life; give one's life; sacrifice oneself：～救国 *give one's life; sacrifice oneself; give one's life for (the cause of) national salvation*

【舍生取义】sacrifice one's life for a just cause; lay down one's life for a just cause

【舍生忘死】risk one's life

【舍我其谁】if I can't do it, who can

shè

设 ① set up; from; found; establish：～立助学金 *set up a grant-in-aid* /总部～在美国。*The headquarters are established in the U. S.* ② work out; design：精心～计 *design with great care* ③

S

given; suppose:假~ *assume*; *suppose* ④[书] if; in case: ~使 *if*; *supposing that*

【设备】equipment; installation; appliances; facilities:电气~ *electrical installation* / 机器~ *machines and other equipment* / ~检修 *equipment examine and repair* / ~租赁 *equipment leasing* / ~齐全 *fully equipped* / ~精良 *well-equipped*

【设辞】[书] excuse; pretext

【设定】set: ~温度 *setting temperature*

【设法】think of a way; do what on can; try; endeavour:我们正在~解决这个问题。*We are trying to solve this problem.*

【设防】set up defences; fortify; defend with a garrison; garrison:重兵~ *heavily garrisoned* /不~的地带 *unfortified zone* /层层~ *set up defences in depth*

【设伏】[书] lay ambush

【设岗】① set up sentry posts:街上~查证件。*A number of sentries were posted in the streets to check the passes.* ② create a post (position, job, etc.)

【设计】design; plan; devise; work out a scheme: ~一种新汽车 *design a new car* / ~三峡大坝 *project the Three Gorges Dam* / ~服装 *design costume* / ~图纸 *design drawing* / ~院 *designing institute* / ~能力 *design capacity* /建设~方案 *an architectural designing scheme*

【设局】set up a trap: ~陷害 *plot a frame-up*

【设立】establish; form; set up found: ~奖学金 *set up a scholarship*

【设施】installation; facilities:市政~ *municipal installations* /防洪~ *flood control installations* /军事~ *military installations* /服务~ *service facilities*

【设使】if; supposing that

【设想】① imagine; conceive; anticipate ② have consideration for:为穷人~ *have consideration for the poor* /我们要多为青少年~。*We should give much thought to the needs of the younger generation.*

【设宴】give a banquet; provide with a feast: ~款待美国客人 *give a banquet in honour of American guests*

【设障】place obstacles; make trouble

【设营】【军】quartering; encampment

【设置】① set up; put up; establish: ~骗局 *lay a trap* /课程~ *courses offered in a college or school*; *curriculum* ② install; fix:办公室~了电话。*A telephone has been installed in the office.* / 不要给我们~这么多障碍。*Don't place so many obstacles before us.*

【设座】select a venue for a banquet; choose a place to give a banquet:明天市长~北京饭店宴请外国朋友。*Tomorrow the mayor will give a banquet at the Beijing Hotel in the honour of the foreign friends.*

社 ① an organization; agency; society:出版~ *publishing house* /信用合作~ *credit cooperative* ② a service unit:旅~ *hotel* ③ the god of the land; sacrifices to him or altars for such sacrifices

【社会】society; community:人类~ *human society* / 原始~ *primitive society* /国际~ *international community* / ~保险 *social insurance* / ~财富 *social wealth* / ~地位 *social status* / ~分工 *division of labour in society* / ~福利 *social welfare* / ~环境 *social environment* / ~实践 *social practice* / ~科学 *social science* / ~名流 *noted public figures* / ~秩序 *public order* / ~舆论 *public opinion* / ~民主党 *Social Democratic Party* / ~总供给 *total social supply* / ~科学 *social sciences* / 保障制度 *social security system* /调查 *social investigation* (*or survey*) /风气 *social morals*; *mood of society*

【社会关系】① social relation; human relations ② one's relatives and friends; one's social connections; one's relatives or relations:她的~很复杂。*She is a person with complicated social connections.*

【社会主义】socialism: ~道路 *socialist road* / ~现代化 *socialist modernization* / ~初级阶段 *primary stage of socialism* / ~法制 *socialist legal system*; *socialist legality* / ~公有制 *socialist public ownership* / ~建设 *socialist construction* / ~精神文明 *socialist spiritual civilization* / ~市场经济 *socialist market economy*

【社稷】the altars to the gods of the land and grainstate; country:江山~ *state power* / ~之臣 *bulwark of the state*; *pillar of the state*

【社交】social intercourse; social life (or contract): ~活动 *social activity*

【社论】editorial; leader; leading article: 发表~ *carry an editorial*

【社区】community: ~服务 *community service* / ~文化 *community culture*

【社团】mass organizations:文艺~ *a mass organization of art and literature*

【社戏】[旧] village theatrical performance given on religious festivals

【社员】member of a society, club, organization, etc.

【社长】chairman of the board

舍 ① house; shed; hut:牛~ *cowshed* /校~ *school buildings* /宿~ *dormitory* ②[谦] my: ~弟(妹) *my younger brother* (*sister*) ③ ancient unit of distance equal to 30 *li*:退避三~ *give way to avoid conflict*; *keep a good distance from sb* ④ (Shè) a surname

see also shě

【舍间】my humble abode; my house

【舍利】【宗】Buddhist relics; sarira: ~塔 *stupa*; *pagoda for Buddhist relics*; *Buddhist shrine*

射 ① shoot; fire:善骑~ *be excel in horsemanship and archery* /扫~ *strafe* ② discharge in a jet; spout:喷~ *spout*; *jet* /注~ *inject* ③ emit (light, heat, etc); send out:反~ *reflect* /手电筒~出一道光。*The electric torch projected a beam of light.* ④ allude to sth or sb; intimate:影~ *in-*

sinuate

【射程】range (of fire):导弹的有效～ *the effective fire range of a missile*

【射弹】projectile

【射击】fire; shoot:战士们正在向敌人～。*The soldiers were shooting at the enemy.* ②【体】shooting: ～冠军 *shooting champion* / ～场 *shooting range* / ～孔 *embrasure*; *gunport*

【射箭】① shoot an arrow ②【体】archery: ～手 *archer* / ～靶子 *rover*

【射角】elevation; angle of fire

【射界】field (or area) of fire; firing area

【射精】【生理】ejaculation

【射精管】【生理】ejaculatory duct

【射猎】hunt with bow and arrow

【射流】【物】efflux: ～技术 *fluidics* / ～喷口 *efflux nozzle*

【射门】【体】shoot (at the goal): ～手 *goal getter* / 他在球场上是一位～好手。*He is a good shooter on the football field.*

【射频】radio frequency: ～放大器 *radio frequency amplifier*

【射手】① shooter; marksman:神～ *marksman* /机枪～ *machine gunner* ②【体】goal getter

【射束】【电】beam

【射水鱼】archer fish

【射速】firing rate

【射线】【物】ray: ～病 *radiation sickness* / ～疗法 *radiotherapy*

【射影】projection

涉 ① wade; ford: ～水而过 *wade across the water* ② go through; undergo:这些孩子们～世不深。*These children have scanty experience of life.* ③ involve; implicate:牵～ *involve*

【涉笔】start writing or painting

【涉及】involve; deal with; touch upon:此案～到6位官员。*Six officers were implicated in this case.* / ～重大原则。*It is related to major matters of principle.*

【涉猎】do desultory reading; read cursorily; read at random:他读书～广泛。*He reads extensively.*

【涉禽】【动】wading bird; wader

【涉世】gain life experience; get along in the world: 青年人～不深。*Young people have seen little of the world.*

【涉讼】be entangled (or involved) in lawsuit

【涉外】concerning foreign affairs or foreign nationals; foreign-related: ～事务 *matters relating to foreign nationals, firm, etc.* / ～婚姻 *marriage between Chinese and foreigners* / ～经济法规 *laws and regulations governing business relations with foreigners*

【涉嫌】be suspected of being involved; be suspected of being implicated; be a suspect: ～杀人 *be suspected of killing a person*

【涉险】go through dangers; be engaged in an adventure

【涉足】[书] set of ot in: ～仕途 *embark on an official career*

赦 remit (a punishment); pardon

【赦令】order of pardon or amnesty; decree for pardon

【赦免】remit a punishment pardon

【赦罪】absolve sb guilt; pardon sb

摄[1] ① take in; absorb: ～取食物 *assimilate food* / ～知识 *assimilate knowledge* ② take a photo; shoot:这些照片～于公园。*These pictures were taken in the park.*

摄[2] [书] conserve (one's health)

摄[3] act for

【摄理】hold a post in an acting capacity

【摄取】① absorb; take in; assimilate: ～养料 *absorb nourishment* ② take a photo; shoot: ～一些珍贵镜头 *take some superb shots*

【摄生】[书] conserve one's health; keep fit

【摄食】(of animals) feed: 马的～习惯 *feeding habit of a horse* /母牛正在牲口棚里～干草。*The cows are feeding on hay in the barn.*

【摄氏度】Celsius; centigrade℃: ～温标 *Celsius (of centigrade) temperature scale*

【摄像】shoot pictures; make a video recording (with a video camera or TV camera)

【摄像机】video camera:电视～ *television camera* / ～取景器 *view finder*

【摄影】① take a photo (or photograph): ～留念 *take a photograph as a souvenir* / ～比赛 *photographic competition* / ～测量 *photographic surveying* /特技～ *trick photography* ② shoot film; film:内景(外景)～ interior (*exterior*) *shooting* / 全景～ *panoramic shooting* / ～迷 *shutterbug*

【摄政】act as regent: ～王 *prince regent*

【摄制】film produce: ～组 *production unit*

慑 [书] fear; dread; coerce; be awed:震～ *awe*; *frighten*

【慑服】① submit in fear; succumb ② cow sb into submission; be awed

麝 ① musk deer ② musk

【麝鹿】musk deer

【麝牛】musk ox

【麝鼠】muskrat

【麝香】musk

shéi

谁 ① who:下一个是～? *Who is the next one?* ② nobody; no one:没有～知道他的故事。*No one knows his story.* ③ somebody; someone:好像是～来过。*It seemed that somebody had come here.* ④ anybody; anyone; everybody; none

【谁个】[方] who; which person

【谁们】[方] who; what persons

【谁谁】used to refer to people whose names need not be mentioned:传着～退学了。*News about who had left school was passing around the village.*

shēn

申 ① state; express; expound; expound; explain ② another name for Shanghai

【申办】apply for the right to handle sth; apply permission to do sth; bid: ~下届奥运会 *bid the next Olympic games*

【申报】① report to a higher body or authority ② declare sth (to the customs): 入境人员必须向海关~其携带的水果。*Travellers entering the country must declare the fruits they are taking with them.*

【申辩】defend oneself; try to justify oneself; explain oneself; argue one's case; plead one's case: 你有权为自己~。*You have the right to defend yourself.*

【申斥】rebuke; reprimand: 老师~那些不到学校的学生。*The teacher reproved the students for not coming to school.* / 他玩忽职守却未受到~。*His negligence passed without reprimand.*

【申领】apply for: ~护照 *apply for a passport*

【申令】issue orders; give orders; command: ~全国 *issue orders to the whole country*

【申明】make public; declare; state: ~自己的立场 *state one's stand* / 他已经~了自己的态度。*He had already made clear his attitude.*

【申请】apply for; make an application to; present a petition to: ~退学 *ask leave school* / ~驾驶执照 *apply for a driving license* / ~入境签证 *apply for an entry visa* / ~表 *application form* / ~人 *applicant* / ~书 (*written*) *application* / 她还没有递交~书。*She had not submitted his application.*

【申述】state; explain in detail; expound: 他~了自己的来意。*He explained in detail the purpose of his visit.*

【申诉】appeal: 向上级法院提出~ *appeal to the higher law court*

【申讨】openly condemn; censure: 强烈~帝国主义的侵略罪行 *strongly condemn the crimes of imperialist aggression* / 叛徒受到了~。*The traitor was denounced.*

【申谢】express one's gratitude; extend one's thanks

【申雪】① appeal for vindication ② redress a wrong; right a wrong: 她认为对我的怀疑得到了~。*She considered that she had been completely vindicated.* / 多年的冤屈终于得到了~。*The longstanding injustice was at last redressed.*

【申冤】① redress an injustice; right a wrong ② appeal for redress of a wrong; appeal for redressing a wrong

伸 stretch; extend: ~腿 *stretch one's legs* / ~舌头 *stick out one's tongue* / ~懒腰 *stretch oneself* / 他的花园一直~展到湖边。*His garden extends as far as the cake.*

【伸开】stretch out: 把手~ *stretch out your hands*

【伸手】① stretch or hold out one's hands: 士兵~去拿枪。*The soldier reached for his gun.* ② ask for honour, money, etc. ③ meddle: 不要~管别人的事情。*Don't meddle in other's affairs.*

【伸手不见五指】so dark that you can't see your hand in front of you; pitch-dart; completely without light

【伸缩】① stretch out and draw back; lengthen and shorten; be pulled back and forth; expand and contract; ② flexible; elastic: ~性 *flexibility*; *elasticity*

【伸缩缝】【建】expansion joint

【伸头伸脑】stretch one's head to peek at; peep; spy

【伸腿】① step in (to gain an advantage) ② stretch one's legs ③ [口] kick the bucket; go west; turn up one's toes

【伸延】stretch; extend

【伸腰】straighten one's back; straighten oneself up

【伸展】spread; extend; reach; stretch

【伸张】uphold; promote; stand up for: ~正义 *uphold justice*

身 ① body: ~形 *figure*; *body* / ~怀绝技 *with unique skill* ② life: 舍~救国 *lay down one's life for national salvation* ③ oneself; personally: ~不由己 *involuntarily*; *in spite of oneself* ④ one's moral character and conduct: 修~ *cultivate one's moral character* ⑤ frame of a structure; body: 车~ *body of a car* / 树~ *trunk* ⑥ (of clothes) suit: 一~旧衣服 *an old suit* ⑦ one's lifetime

【身败名裂】lose all standing and reputation; bring disgrace and ruin upon oneself; be thoroughly discredited: 他最后落了个~。*He fell into utter disrepute at last.*

【身板】[方] body; bodily health; constitution: 老头子~一直很硬朗。*The old man still has a strong physique*

【身边】① at one's side; by one's side: 在总经理~工作 *work at the side of the general manager* ② have sth on one; (take or carry) with one: 他~总是带着很多钱。*He always has a lot of money on him.*

【身材】stature; figure: ~修长 *a tall and slender figure* / ~苗条 *a slender* (*or slim*) *figure*

【身长】① height (of a person) ② length (of a garment from shoulder to hemline)

【身段】① (dancer's) posture ② (woman's) figure

【身份】① status; capacity; identity: 暴露~ *reveal one's identity* / 以法官的~行事 *act in one's capacity as a judge* / 没有确定凶手~的线索。*There is no clue to the identity of the killer.* / 她很注意自己的重要~。*She's very aware of her status.* ② dignity: 有失~ *be beneath one's dignity* ③ [方] quality of a thing

【身份证】identity card; identification card; ID (card)

【身高】height (of a person): 她~1.55米。*She is 155 centimetres in height.*

【身故】die: 因病~ *die of disease* / 因洪水~ *die of a*

flood

【身后】after one's death

【身怀六甲】be with child; be pregnant; be in the family way:她已经～。*She is in the family way.*

【身家】oneself and one's family:他必须考虑自己的～性命。*He must take his life and the fate of the whole family into account.*

【身价】① the selling price of sb (such as a slave) ② social status

【身价百倍】① a meteoric rise in social status:一夜之间那个电影明星～。*The movie star has a sudden rise in social status.* ② rise sharply; skyrocket

【身架】[口] stature

【身教】teach other by one's own example:言传～ *teach by personal example as well as verbal instruction* / ～胜于言教。*Example is more powerful than the precept.*

【身经百战】have fought a hundred battle; have fought countless battles; be battle-hardened: ～的老兵 *a battle-tested veteran*

【身历】experience personally: ～其境 *be actually on the scene; personally go through the situation*

【身量】[口] stature; height (of a person):他～高。*He is tall.*

【身临其境】be present (or personally) on the scenes

【身强力壮】(of a person) strong; sturdy; hefty

【身躯】stature; body

【身上】① on one's body:他～穿一件夹克。*He wore a jacket.* ② carry sth with one' have sth on one:他～带着工具。*He has got tools with him.*

【身世】one's (unfortunate) lot; one's (hard) life experience

【身手】ability; talent:大显～ *fully display one's ability* /他～不凡。*He is a person of uncommon talent.*

【身受】experience personally: ～重伤 *be seriously injured or wounded*

【身体】① body:在独木桥上要保持～平衡。*Keep one's balance on the single-plank bridge.* ② health:你要注意～。*You should take care of your heath.*

【身体力行】earnestly practise what one preaches; practise what one advocates

【身条儿】[口] stature; figure:她～匀称。*She is of fine physical proportions.*

【身外之物】external things; worldly possession:金钱是～。*Money is mere worldly possession.*

【身无长物】have nothing but the necessities of life

【身先士卒】lead one's men in a charge; charge at the head of one's men; be at the forefront of struggle

【身心】body and mind: ～健康 *physically and mentally healthy* / ～交瘁 *worn out both physically and mentally*

【身形】figure:她～健美。*She has a strong and graceful figure.*

【身影】person's silhouette; from; figure

【身孕】pregnancy

【身在曹营心在汉】one lives in the Gao camp but one's heart in the Han camp; be half-hearted

【身在福中不知福】not appreciate the happy life one enjoys; you don't know when you are happy

【身正不怕影子斜】stand straight and never mind if the shadow inclines — an upright man fears no gossip

【身肢】body; trunk and limbs

【身姿】bearing; demeanour; posture:敏捷的～ *agile carriage*

【身子】[口] ① body ② pregnancy:她有了六个月的～。*She is six months pregnant.*

【身子骨儿】[方] physique; one's health:他～硬朗。*He is hale and hearty.*

呻

【呻吟】groan; moan:无病～ *moan and groan without being ill* /病人的～ *the moans of the sick*

参

ginseng:人～ *ginseng*

see also cān; cēn

绅

① sash; girdle (worn by scholars, officials etc in ancient time) ② gentry

【绅士】gentlemen; gentry: ～协定 *gentleman's agreement*

莘

【莘莘】[书] great many; numerous: ～学子 *large numbers of students*

砷

【化】arsenic (As)

【砷化物】arsenide

【砷酸铅】lead arsenate

【砷中毒】【生理】arsenic poisoning

娠

[书] pregnancy

深

① deep:根～叶茂 *have deep roots and luxuriant leaves* / ～井 *a deep well* ② hard to comprehend (or understand); difficult; profound: ～情厚谊 *profound friendship* /这个问题对中学生太～了。*This question is too difficult for middle school students.* ③ depth ④ in-depth; penetrating: ～入调查 *make a thorough investigation* ⑤ close; intimate: ～交 *intimate friendship* ⑥ (of colour) dark: ～绿 *dark green* / ～红 *deep red; crimson* /被染成～紫色的纸 *paper dyed a rich purple* ⑦ far on (in the night, season, etc.); late: ～夜 *late at night; at midnight* / ～更半夜 *in the dead night* ⑧ very; greatly; keenly; deeply: ～表同情 *have profound sympathy for sb*

【深奥】deep; abstruse; profound; recondite:一个～的问题 *a profound question*

【深不可测】unfathomable; enigmatic; of immeasurable depth:海洋中～的地方 *the ocean's unfathomable depths*

【深藏若虚】be modest about one's ability or learning; not be given to boasting or showing off

S

【深层】in-depth; depth; deep-going: ~矛盾 *deeper contradictions*

【深长】profound:意味~的笑 *a meaning smile* / 她的话意味~,值得回味。*What she said is significant and worth pondering.*

【深沉】① dark; deep:暮色~ *the dusk deepen* /他对孩子们的爱如此~。*He loves the children so deeply.* ② (of sound or voice) deep; low-pitched; dull: ~的音调 *a deep note* ③ undemonstrative; concealing one's own feelings; reserved:他只是~地一笑,没有说话。*He said nothing, but only gave a significant smile.*

【深成岩】【地】plutonic rock; plutonite

【深仇大恨】bitter and deep-seated hatred; profound hatred (or enemy)

【深处】depths; inmost part; recesses:在灵魂~ *in one's innermost soul* /在密林~ *in the recesses of the wood*; *in the depths of the forest* /我们从思想上~厌恶战争。*In our inmost hearts, we detest war.*

【深冬】severe winter

【深度】① degree of depth; depth:测量海洋的~ *sound the depth of the ocean* ② (of work understanding, etc.) profundity; depth:这篇文章缺乏~。*This article lacks depth.* ③ advanced level (or stage) of development:我们的经济建设正在向广度和~发展。*Our economic construction is developing in depth and in width.* ④ extremely; deeply: ~近视 *extremely near-sighted*

【深耕】deep culture; deep ploughing

【深谷】deep and secluded valley

【深广】deep and broad; deep and extensive:这一事件影响~。*This incident has a profound and far-reaching influence.*

【深闺】[旧] women's quarters; boudoir

【深海】deep sea: ~探测 *deep-sea exploration* / ~采矿 *deep-sea mining* / ~测量 *bathymetry* / ~带 *abyssal zone* / ~平原 *abyssal plain* / ~潜水艇 *bathyscaphe* / ~区 *abyssal region* / ~钻探 *deep-sea drilling* (DSD)/ ~资源 *deep-sea resources* / ~作业船 *deep-ocean work boat*

【深壑】deep gully

【深厚】① deep; profound: ~的感情 *profound feeling* / ~的友谊 *profound friendship* ② deep-seated; solid:这个组织有~的社会基础。*This organization has a solid foundation in the society.*

【深呼吸】deep breathing

【深化】deepen:这两个国家之间的矛盾进一步~了。*The contradictions between these two countries further intensified.*

【深加工】intensive (or down stream) processing: ~农产品 *high value added farm products*; *downstream products*

【深究】probe (or go) into a matter seriously; get into the bottom of a matter:没有必要对此事进行~。*It is no necessary to go into this matter seriously.*

【深居简出】live in the seclusion of one's own home; keep oneself apart from others

【深刻】deep; profound; deep-going; incisive: ~地领会文件的实质 *grasp the essence of a document profoundly* /这位外国朋友给我们留下~的印象。*The foreign friend made a deep impression on us.*

【深明大义】be clear as to principles; be conscious of the righteousness of a cause

【深谋远虑】think deeply and plan carefully; be thoughtful and farsighted; be circumspect and far-sighted

【深潜】deep-diving

【深浅】① depth:我们要探一下湖水的~。*We'll find out the depth of the lake.* ② shade (of colour):颜色~不同的鸟 *birds of many different hues* ③ proper limit; propriety:年轻人说话没有~。*The young man spoke thoughtlessly and often inappropriately.*

【深切】① profound; cordial; heartfelt; deep:总统~关怀他的人民。*The president was deeply concerned about his people.* /我们~怀念这位英雄。*We dearly cherish the memory of the hero.* ② penetrating; thorough:她~地感受到身体的重要。*She keenly realized the important of her health.*

【深情】profound feeling; deep affection; deep love

【深情厚谊】profound sentiments of friendship:我永远忘不了同志们的~。*I'll never forget the profound friendship that the comrades have shown for us.*

【深秋】late autumn

【深入】① go deep into; probe into: ~实际 *be in close contract with social realities*; *go deep into the realities of life* /领导干部应该~群众。*A leader should maintain close ties with the masses.* /我们的部队已经~到敌占区。*Our troops have penetrated into enemy territory.* ② through; intensive; deep-going: ~调查研究 *make a thorough investigation and study* /经过~彻底搜查未发现任何线索。*An intensive search failed to rcveal any clues.*

【深入浅出】explain profound or compiles ideas in simple terms

【深入人心】strike or take root in the hearts of the people

【深山】remote mountains: ~老林 *remote, thickly wooded mountains*

【深恶痛绝】cherish intense hatred for; hate bitterly; abhor; detest

【深信】believe strongly; firmly believe; be deeply convinced

【深夜】late at nigh; at midnight:你不能总是工作到~。*You shouldn't always work far into the night.*

【深意】profound meaning:领会他话中的~ *grasp the deep (or profound) meaning of his words*

【深幽】deep and quiet (or secluded)

【深渊】deep pool; abyss

【深远】profound; profound and lasting; far-reaching

【深造】take an advanced course of study or training; pursue advanced study:

【深深】profoundly; deeply: ~扎根 *stick deep root*

【深水】deep water: ~港 *deepwater port* / ~码头 *deepwater wharf*

【深思】think deeply about; be deep in thought; ponder deeply over

【深思熟虑】careful consideration; well-thought-out plan: ~的计划 *a well-thought out plan*

【深邃】① deep: ~的海洋 *the fathomless ocean* ② profound; abstruse: ~的哲理 *abstruse philosophical idea*

【深谈】have an in-depth conversation; discuss thoroughly; go deeply into: 这件事我已经同他进行了~。*I have gone deeply into the matter with him.*

【深透】deep and thorough: 我们必须~地理解会议精神。*We must deeply and thoroughly understand the essence of the meeting.*

【深望】sincerely hope; earnestly with

【深为】very; greatly; deeply: ~感动 *be very moved*

【深宅大院】dwelling with many rooms and spacious courtyards

【深湛】profound and thorough; superb: 技艺~ *exquisite workmanship* / ~的著作 *profound work* / ~的功夫 *consummate skill*

【深挚】deep and sincere; profound and sincere: ~的感情 *sincere and earnest feelings*

【深重】very grave; extremely serious: 罪恶~ *be guilty of all kinds of evils* / 危机~ *be in the grip of a crisis* / 我们正处在历史的~关头。*We are at a critical time in our history.*

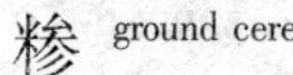

糁 ground cereal

see also sǎn

shén

什

see also shí

【什么】① what (used before a noun or by itself): 你找~? *What are you looking for?* / 你在说~? *What are you saying?* / 那是~花? *What flower is it?* ② used to refer to anything indefinite; something; anything: 我们想吃点~。*We'd like to have something to eat.* ③ (used before 都 or 也) any; every: 我~也不想吃。*I won't eat anything.* / 我~都不怕。*I'm afraid of nothing.* ④ whatever: 她演~像~。*He acts well in whatever role she plays.* / 你有~就说~。*You'll just say what's on your mind.* ⑤ indicating surprise; anger, censure or negation: ~! 没有车? *What! No car?* ⑥ indicating disapproval or disagreement: 早~! 都十点了。*Early indeed! It's ten o'clock.* ⑦ things like; such as; and so on: ~自行车呀,摩托车呀,汽车呀,他都会修。*He can repair bicycle, motor, car, anything.*

神 ① god; divine being; deity: 鬼~ *ghosts and gods* / 瘟~ *god of plague* ② expression; appearance; look: ~色慌张 *look flustered* ③ spirit; mind: ~采奕奕 *brim with energy and vitality; glowing with health and radiating vigour* ④ supernatural; magical; amazing; miraculous: ~枪手 *crack shot; sharpshooter; expert marksman* ⑤ smart; clever; incredible: 这小伙子够~的。*The guy is quite in credible!*

【神不守舍】the soul has departed from its abode; be out of one's wits; be distracted

【神不知鬼不觉】unknown to god or ghost-(do sth) without anybody knowing it; with great secrecy; in completely secrecy: 游击队~地接近敌营。*The guerrilla forces closed the enemy's camp in completely secrecy.*

【神采】demeanour; countenance; expression; look: ~飞扬 *be in fine fettle*

【神驰】one's thoughts fly to; charmed by: 对美丽的景色她心往~。*She was carried away by the beautiful scenery.*

【神道】① superstitious belief in gods, ghosts, fortune, etc ② aisle leading to the coffin chamber of an ancient grave; tomb passage ③ [口] gods; deities ④ shinto, native religion of Japan

【神甫】Father (the title of respect for a Roman Catholic priest); priest

【神怪】gods and spirits: 我喜欢~故事。*I like teratology.*

【神汉】sorcerer

【神乎】miraculous; fantastic; magical: ~其神 *causing wonder; wonderful*

【神化】deification; deify

【神话】deification; deify

【神魂】sate of mind; mind: ~不定 *be distracted; be distraught; be deeply troubled be deeply perturbed* / ~颠倒 *be infatuated* / 他被那个风骚女人弄得~颠倒。*He lose his head over the flirtatious woman.*

【神机妙算】a superb stratagem, a miracle of foresight; wonderful foresight in military operations, etc.

【神交】① friends with mutual understanding and trust (or admiration) ② friendship grown out of admiration for each other without the friends ever having met

【神经】nerve: 脑~ *cranial nerve* / 感觉~ *sensory nerve* / 交感~ *sympathetic nerve* / ~紧张 *be nervous; be jittery* / ~松弛 *be relaxed* / ~错乱 *mental disorder; be mentally deranged* / ~毒气 *nerve gas* / ~毒素 *neurotoxin* / ~官能症 *neurosis* / ~节 *ganglion* / ~解剖学 *neuroanatomy* / ~末稍 *nerve ending* / ~生理学 *neurophysiology* / ~衰弱 *neurasthenia* / ~索 *nerve cord* / ~痛 *neuralgia* / ~外科 *neurosurgery* / ~网络 *neural net* / ~神经系统 *nervous system* / ~纤维 *nerve fibre* / ~性皮炎 *neurodermatitis* / ~学 *neurology* / ~炎 *neuritis* / ~语言学 *neurolinguistics* / ~战 *war of nerves* / ~质 *nervousness* / ~中枢 *nerve centre*

【神经病】① neuropathy ② mental disorder; mental illness that causes depression or abnormal behavior; neurosis: 他为了省电把办公楼里的灯都关了,

真是～。*He's neurotic about switching lights off in the building to save electricity.*

【神经过敏】① neuroticism ② neurotic; oversensitive

【神经兮兮】[方] nervy; neurotic:她有点～。*She is a bit of a neurotic.*

【神来之笔】stroke of genius; inspired work (or writing)

【神力】superhuman strength; extraordinary power (or prowess)

【神灵】gods; divinities; deities

【神秘】mysterious; secretive; mystical: ～的大自然 *unfathomable nature* / ～的微笑 *an enigmatic smile* / ～化 *mystify*; *make mystery of* / ～莫测 *unpredictable*; *inscrutable* / ～主义 *mysticism*

【神妙】wonderful; superb; marvellous: ～的笔法 *ingenious brushwork*

【神明】gods; divinities; deities:奉若～ *worship sb or sth*; *hole sth as sacrosanct*; *make a fetish of sth*

【神女】goddess

【神炮手】crack gunner

【神品】a superb work (of art or literature); a sublime work; masterpiece

【神婆】sorceress; enchantress

【神奇】magical; mystical; wonderful; air: ～的功效 *miraculous effect*; *magical effect*

【神气】① expression; look; manner: ～十足 *putting on grand airs*; *very arrogant* ② spirited; vigorous:战士们扛着枪很～。*The soldiers look quite impressive with guns on their shoulder.* ③ putting on airs; cocky; arrogant: ～活现 *very cocky*; *self-important*

【神情】expression; look: ～沮丧 *look depressed* / ～冷漠 *look apathetic* /她看起来～愉快。*She wears a happy expression.*

【神曲】medicated leaven

【神权】① religious authority; theocracy ② divine right

【神人】① spiritual being; Taoist immortal ② person of dignified bearings

【神色】expression; look:他看起来～自若。*He is calm and collected.*

【神伤】[书] dejected; dispirited:黯然～ *feel depressed (or dejected)*

【神神道道】[口] abnormal in words and deeds; old; fantastic:这个人总是～的。*He is always strange in behaviour.*

【神圣】sacred; holy: ～的使命 *sacred mission* /保卫祖国是军队的～职责。*Defending motherland is a sacred duty of the army.*

【神思】state of mind; metal state: ～恍惚 *be distracted (or distraught)*; *be in a trance*; *beside oneself* / ～不宁 *be distracted*; *be upset*

【神似】be like in spirit or essence; be an excellent likeness:他画的猴子栩栩如生,十分～。*The monkeys he paints are most vivid and extremely lifelike.*

【神速】with lightning speed; with amazing speed: 我们的工作进展～。*Our work has made speedy progress.*

【神算】accurate prediction; miraculous foresight; marvellous prediction

【神态】expression; manner; countenance; bearing; mien:她看起来～悠闲。*She looks perfectly relaxed.*

【神通】magic powers; remarkable ability; immense capabilities:神秘武器在战场上大显～。*The magical weapon gave full play to its ability on the battlefield.*

【神通广大】be infinitely resourceful; have magic powers

【神童】child prodigy

【神投手】sharpshooter (in basketball); superb shooter (or scorer)

【神往】be carried away; be rapt; be fascinated; be charmed

【神威】martial prowess; invincible might; invincible strength; unrivalled prowess:空军的～ *the martial prowess of the air force*

【神位】spirit tablet; memorial tablet

【神仙】① supernatural being; celestial being; immortal ② a person who is free from worldly cares: ～美眷 *a happily married couple*

【神仙鱼】angelfish

【神像】picture, or statue of god or Buddha

【神效】stunning effect; amazing effectiveness; miraculous effect

【神学】【宗】theology: ～院 *theological seminary*; *school of divinity* / ～博士 *Doctor of Divinity (D. D.)*

【神医】a highly skilled doctor; a miracle working doctor

【神异】① gods and spirits ② magical; mystical; supernatural

【神鹰】【动】condor

【神勇】extraordinarily (or superhumanly) brave

【神游】[书] make a spiritual tour; range in fancy; take an imaginary trip to a place

【神韵】romantic charm (in both art and literature)

【神志】consciousness; awareness; senses: ～清醒 *be in one's right mind*; *remain fully conscious*; *be perfectly sober* /这几天她～恍惚。*She was in a trance in these days.*

【神州】the Divine Land (a poetic name for China); Sacred Land; China

shěn

审¹ ① careful; meticulous; circum: ～时度势 *judge the hour and size up the situation*; *take the stock of the situation* ② examine; check up: ～稿 *go over a manuscript*; *draft interrogate* ③ be tried for a crime: ～讯一个案件 *try a case*

审² [书] know; be aware of; be familiar:未～其详 *not know the detail*; *not be quainted with the details*

【审办】investigate and handily; try and hear (a

case); investigate and try: ~案件 *investigate and try a case*

【审查】examine; check up; go over; investigate: ~初步方案 *go over a preliminary plan* /资格~委员会 *credentials committee*

【审察】① carefully (or closely) observe; closely examine ② investigate; scrutinize

【审处】① try:这个案子已交法院~。*The case has been handed over to the court for trial.* ② deliberate and decide

【审订】examine and revise: ~讲义 *revise lecture*

【审定】examine and approve (of finalize):报上级~ *submit to higher authorities*

【审读】read and evaluate (a manuscript); check and approve:材料已经被~通过。*The material has been checked and approved.*

【审改】examine and revise; revise; edit: ~本 *draft for examination and revision (before printing)*

【审核】examine and verify; verify; check: ~预算 *verify a budget* / ~账目 *audit accounts*

【审计】audit: ~人员 *auditing personnel* / ~报告 *audit report* / ~机构 *auditing body* / ~部门 *auditing department* / ~署 *auditing administration* / ~委员会 *audit committee* / ~员 *auditor* / ~长 *chief auditor* / ~制 *audit system*

【审校】① examine and revise; check and revise ② reviser

【审结】conclude an investigation:案子已经~。*The investigation about this case has been concluded.*

【审看】examine carefully; look closely into; scrutinize

【审理】【律】try; hear: ~案件 *try (or hear) a case* / ~民事纠纷 *adjudicate civil disputes*

【审美】appreciation of beauty; appreciation of the beautiful: ~标准 *aesthetic standards* / ~能力 *aesthetic judgement* /~观 *aesthetic conceptions; aesthetic perspective; aesthetic standards*

【审判】put on trial; try: ~工作 *administration of trial* / ~程序 *judicial procedure* / ~权 *judicial authority; jurisdiction* / ~机关 *judicial organ* / ~员 *judge; judicial officer* / ~长 *presiding judge*

【审批】examine and approve:报请上级~。*Submit to the higher authorities for examination and approval.*

【审片】review of a film or TV programmes by the censor

【审评】examine and evaluate

【审慎】cautious; careful; prudent: ~地进行 *proceeding with great circumspection* /我们要~地考虑问题。*We should think over the matter carefully.*

【审视】look at sb or sth attentively; look closely at; examine closely:老师~着座位上的同学们。*The teacher looked around carefully the students on their seats.*

【审题】examine carefully (before answer a question or writing an article); consider carefully

【审问】interrogate; question:法官正在~那名嫌疑犯。*The judge is interrogating the suspect.*

【审讯】【律】① hearing:被告家属在~时没有旁听。*The defendant's family were not present at the hearing.* ② interrogate; try: ~犯人 *interrogate a prisoner*

【审验】examine and verify: ~驾驶执照 *examine the drivers' license*

【审议】consideration; deliberation; discussion; review: ~提案 *make an examination of the proposal* / ~机构 *deliberative body* / ~法律草案 *submit the draft law to the deputies for examination and approval*

【审阅】examine carefully and critically; check and approve: ~手稿 *go over the manuscript*

婶 ① wife of father's younger brother; aunt:大~ *first aunt* ② form of address for a woman about one's mother's age; auntie; aunt:李大~ *aunt Li*

【婶母】wife of father's younger brother; aunt

【婶婶】[方] wife of father younger brother; aunt

【婶子】[口] wife of father's younger brother; aunt

shèn

肾【生理】kidney: ~功能试验 *kidney function test* / ~功能衰竭 *renal failure; kidney failure*

【肾病】【医】nephrosis; nephropathy: ~综合症 *nephrotic syndrome*

【肾积水】【医】hydronephrosis

【肾结石】【医】kidney stone; renal calculus

【肾亏】renal weakness; general weakness of the kidney

【肾囊】【中医】scrotum

【肾气】kidney *qi*

【肾衰竭】【医】kidney failure; renal failure

【肾炎】nephritis

【肾移植】kidney transplant; renal transplant

【肾盂】【生理】renal pelvis: ~炎 *pyelitis*

【肾脏】kidney

甚[1] ① very; most; extremely: ~高兴 *extremely happy* /对于这件事我知之~少。*I knew little about this matter.* ② more than:国际政治局势恶化,日~一日。*The international political situation was getting worse and worse.*

甚[2] [方] what:你姓~名谁? *Who are you?*

【甚为】very; most; extremely: ~关切 *be most concerned* / ~不安 *feel very upset*

【甚嚣尘上】raise a riotous clamour; cause a clamour

【甚至】(go) so far as to; so much so that; even

渗 seep; ooze; leak: ~着油的烤面包片 *toast oozing with oil* /从墙壁~出的水 *water seeping through the wall* /雨水~进了房间。*The rain is leaking in the room.*

【渗出液】【医】exudate

【渗沟】sewer

【渗井】seepage pit

【渗流】seep; ooze
【渗漏】seepage; leakage: ~损失 *seepage loss*
【渗滤】【化】percolation; filtration
【渗入】① permeate; seep into: 油已~土里。*The oil has permeated the soil.* ② penetrate; infiltrate: 烟已~室内。*The smoke penetrated into the room.*
【渗碳】【冶】carburization; cementation: ~钢 *carburized steel* / ~剂 *carburizer; carburization material*
【渗透】①【物】osmosis: 若肾功能衰退,可通过~作用使血液净化。*Blood can be cleaned by osmosis if one's kidneys have failed.* ② permeate; seep: 她的衣服~了雨水。*Her clothes were soaked in the rain.* ③ infiltrate: 文化~ *culture infiltration* / 思想~ *ideological infiltration* / ~经济 *economic infiltration* / ~剂 *penetration; penetrating agent* / ~率 *penetration coefficient* / ~平衡 *osmotic equilibrium* / ~速度 *seepage speed or velocity* / ~性 *permeability* / ~战术 *infiltration tactics*

蜃 【动】big clam; clam ① illusion ② mirage

慎 careful; prudent; cautious: 谨~ *prudent; careful; cautious* / 不~ *not careful; carelessly*
【慎密】careful and cautions; cautious and meticulous
【慎重】cautious; careful; prudent; scrupulous: ~行事 *act with discretion* / 我们说话需要~。*We should speak with great care.*

shēng

升[1] ① climb; go up; hoist; rise: 太阳从东方~起。*The sun rises from the east.* ② promote; elevate: 连~三级 *be promoted to a position three levels higher* / 最近他爸爸又高~了。*Recently his father was promoted to a higher position again.*

升[2] ① litre: 四~油 *four litres of oil* ② *sheng*, a unit of dry measure for grain (=1 litre) ③ measure
【升调】rising tune; rising tone
【升官】be promoted; move up: ~发财 *win-promotion and get rich*
【升华】① sublimate: ~为蒸汽 *be sublimated to steam* ② raising of things to a higher level; distillation
【升级】① go up; promote ② escalate
【升降】rise and fall; go up and down
【升幂】【数】ascending power; increasing power
【升旗】hoist or raise a flag: ~仪式 *flag-raising ceremony*
【升迁】be transferred and promoted
【升天】① die; ascend heaven ② go a up into the sky
【升温】rise in temperature
【升学】go to a school of a higher grade; enter a higher school: ~率 *proportion of students entering schools of a higher grade*
【升压】step up; boost
【升值】【经】(upward) revalue; appreciate

生[1] ① give birth to; deliver; bear: ~了一个男孩子 *be delivered of a baby boy* / ~育 *give birth to; beget; bear* / 她昨天~了一个孩子。*She gave birth to a child yesterday.* ② grow: ~根 *strike root; take root* / 水稻的~长期 *growth (or growing) period of rice* ③ livelihood; living: 改善人民~活 *improve people's livelihood* / 维持~计 *eke out a living; make (both) ends meet* ④ existence; life: ~存权 *right of existence; right of life* ⑤ have; get; cause; give rise to: 今年冬天他~了冻疮。*He had chilblains this winter.* ⑥ living; alive: 各种各样的~物 *all kinds of living things* ⑦ light (a fire): ~火做饭 *light a fire to prepare a meal* / ~炉子 *light a stove* ⑧ (Shēng) a surname

生[2] ① raw; uncooked: ~肉 *raw meat* / ~鱼 *raw meat* ② unripe; immature: 一个~得不能吃的苹果 *an apple too green to eat* / ~枣 *unripe jujube* ③ unprocessed; crude; raw; unrefined: ~铁 *pig iron* / ~石膏 *plaster stone* ④ unfamiliar; new; strange; unacquainted: ~词 *new word* / ~人 *stranger* ⑤ stiff; unnatural; mechanical: 他态度~硬。*He was stiff in manner.* ⑥ very: ~疼 *very painful* / ~怕 *for fear that; so as not to*

生[3] ① student; pupil: 师~ *teachers and students* / 学~运动 *student movement* / 学~时代 *school days* ② male character in traditional opera: 小~ *the role of young men*
【生搬硬套】apply mechanically or follow blindly in disregard of specific conditions; copy or apply mechanically
【生编】fabricate: 她提出的缺席理由显然是~的。*The reason she gave for her absence was obviously fabricated.*
【生变】bring trouble in the wake; trouble arises
【生病】fall ill
【生不逢时】born out of one's time; born at the wrong time
【生财】amass wealth; develop financial resources; make money: ~有道 *have the knack of making money; be good at making money; know how to make money*
【生菜】① romaine; romaine lettuce; cos lettuce; lettuce ② row vegetable
【生产】① manufacture; make; produce: ~设备 *production equipment* / ~成本 *cost of production* / ~方式 *mode of production* / 农业~ *agricultural production* / ~工具 *tool of production* / ~潜力 *productive potentialities; latent productive capacity* / ~关系 *relations of production* / ~过剩 *overproduction* / ~建设兵团 *production and construction corps* / ~劳动 *productive labour* / ~力 *productive forces* / ~率 *productivity* / 劳动~率 *labour productivity* / ~手段 *means of production* / ~线 *production line* / ~要素 *essential factors of production* / ~责任制 *production responsibility system* / ~指标 *production target* / ~资本 *productive cap-*

ital; production capital / ~资料 means of production / ~总值 total output value ② give birth to a child:她~了。She has had a baby.

【生辰】birthday

【生成】① come into being; produce; form; generate:这种物质是由几种液体混合~的。This substance is formed from a mixture of liquids. ② inborn; be gifted with; by nature:他~一副奴才相。He was born with servile behaviour.

【生成物】【化】resultant; product

【生词】new and unfamiliar words

【生凑】mechanically put together; arbitrarily dish up (unrelated facts); round up

【生存】subsist; exist; survive; live: ~竞争 struggle for existence / ~空间 living space / ~斗争 struggle for survival / ~权 right of existence; right to subsistence; right to life / ~环境 living environment / ~能力 viability

【生动】graphic; vivid; vital; lively:小说文笔~。The novel is written in a lively style.

【生动活泼】lively; vivid and vigorous; vivacious: ~的旋律 a lively melody

【生端】[书] provoke incidents

【生而知之】have inborn knowledge; be born wise

【生分】estranged; cause to become unfriendly to sb; not as close as before:他们~了。They are estranged.

【生俘】capture (alive); take prisoner

【生父】one's own father: ~母 biological parents

【生根】take root; put down roots

【生花妙笔】brilliant pen; brilliant style of writing; gifted pen

【生化】biochemistry: ~氧化 biochemical oxidation

【生还】survive; come back alive; return alive:只有1人~。There was only one survived.

【生活】① life:日常~ daily life /经济~ economic life /乡村~ rural life ② live:过平静的~ live a peaceful life /过独身~ live a bachelor ③ livelihood: ~门路 a chance to make a living / ~用品 articles for daily use /改善人民~ improve people's livelihood / ~幸福 live in blissful happiness; live happily ⑤ [方] work (used to refer to industrial, agricultural and handicraft work):勤勤恳恳~ do one's manual labour diligently / ~必需品 daily necessities; necessaries of life / ~补助 subsidy for living expenses; extra allowance for living expenses / ~待遇 material benefits / ~方式 life style; way of life / ~费 living expenses; cost of living; allowance / ~福利 welfare benefits; welfare / ~环境 surroundings; environment / ~经验 life experience / ~垃圾 consumer waste / ~来源 source of income / ~能力 viability / ~水平 living standard / ~条件 living conditions / ~习惯 habits and customs / ~周期(生物) life cycle / ~资料 means of subsistence; consumer goods / ~作风 behaviour; conduct; life style / ~救济 relief; hardship relief assistance

【生火】light a fire; make a fire

【生机】① lease of life; hope of life; hope of success:一线~ a gleam of hope; off chance of survival ② life; vitality; ~盎然 vibrant with life; full of life; overflowing with vigour

【生计】means of livelihood; livelihood; living:维持~ make (both) ends meet; eke out a living /另谋~ try to find some other means of livelihood

【生姜】[口] ginger

【生就】be born with; be endowed with; be gifted with: ~一副牛脾气 be born pigheaded; be born stubborn / ~一张利嘴 have the gift of a sharp tongue; have the gift of the gab

【生客】unfamiliar guest; stranger

【生恐】be very much afraid; fear greatly; lest: ~生病 afraid of falling ill

【生拉硬拽】① drag one against one's will ② draw a forced analogy; make a farfetched comparison

【生来】from birth; from childhood

【生老病死】birth, age, illness and death — the lot of man

【生冷】raw, cold food; uncooked or cold food:忌食~ avoid eating anything raw or cold

【生离死别】part for ever; part never to meet again; final separation

【生理】physiology: ~缺陷 physiological deficiency; physiological defect / ~反应 physiological reaction / ~现象 physiological phenomenon / ~学 physiology / ~盐水 physiological saline; normal saline

【生力军】① fresh and combat-worthy troops; fresh reinforcements ② new force; new activists; new blood:科技战线上的一支~ a vital new force on the science and technology front

【生料】raw material

【生灵】① [书] the people ② life; living thing:万物~ all kinds of living things on the earth

【生灵涂炭】common people are plunged into the abyss of untold suffering

【生龙活虎】brimming with energy; bursting with energy; full of vim and vigour

【生路】① means of livelihood:另谋~ seek some other means of livelihood; try to find another job ② way out:我们必须杀出一条~。We must fight our way out of the encirclement.

【生闷气】sulk; be pettish

【生命】life:他很悲哀,他的政治~就要结束了。He was very sad for his political life was going to end.

【生母】one's own other

【生怕】fear greatly; for fear that; be very much afraid; so as not to:他~父母会离开他。He was very much afraid that his parents would leave him alone.

【生僻】(of words, expressions, etc.) uncommon; obscure; rare

【生平】① all one's life:那位将军的~事迹感动了我们每一个人。All of us were moved by the capital's life story. ② ever since one's birth.

【生气】① be angry; be furious; take offence:因为没人送礼物,他又~了。He was angry again be-

cause nobody gave presents to him. ② life; vim; vitality: ~勃勃 *full of vitality*
【生前】during one's lifetime; before one's death
【生趣】joy of life; pleasure of life
【生人】① be born:她是1980年的~。*She was born in* 1980. ② stranger
【生日】birthday:祝你~快乐。*Happy birthday to you.*
【生身父母】give birth to; one's own parents
【生事】make trouble; foment disturbance:造谣~ *spread rumours and making troubles*
【生手】new hand; green hand; new to a job
【生疏】① unfamiliar:她是新来的雇员,业务~。*She was a new employee and unfamiliar in business.* ② out of practice; rusty ③ not as close as before
【生死】① life and death: ~未卜 *be poised between life and death* ② share weal and woe
【生态】ecology; organism's biological and life habits; modes of organic life and their environment: ~环境 *ecological environment* / ~工程 *eco-engineering*
【生物】living beings; living things; organisms:微~ *micro-organism* / ~工程 *biotechnology* / ~环境 *biological environment* / ~技术 *biotechnology*; *biological engineering* / ~圈 *biosphere* / ~学 *biology* / ~钟 *biological clock*; *living clock* / ~周期 *biological periodicity*
【生息】① bear interest ②[书] live; exist ③ grow; multiply; procreate; propagate:休养~ *recuperate and multiply*
【生肖】any of the names of 12 symbolic animals (rat, ox, tiger, rabbit, dragon, snake, horse, sheep, monkey, rooster, dog and pig), used to symbolize the year in which a person is born
【生效】come into force; take effect
【生性】one's nature; natural disposition
【生锈】rust; get rusty:窗户已经~了。*The window has got rusty.*
【生涯】career; life
【生意】(shēngyì) life and vitality; flourishing growth; tendency to grow: ~盎然 *full of life*
【生意】(shēngyi) business; deal; trade: ~经 *knack of doing business*; *business expertise* / ~人 *businessman*
【生硬】① not smooth; unnatural; crude ② rigid; stiff:他对我们态度~。*He is stiff in manner to us.*
【生育】give birth to; beget; bear
【生造】coin (words and expressions)
【生长】① grow: ~期 *growth period* ② grow up; be bred up; be brought up
【生殖】reproduction: ~器 *reproductive organs* /无性~ *asexual reproduction* /有性~ *sexual reproduction*
【生字】new words: ~表 *list of new words*
【生男】sister's son; nephew

声 ① sound; voice; noise:雨~ *sound of rain* / 请小~说话。*Please speak in a low voice.* ② fame; reputation:坏名~ *ill fame* /失去~望 *lost one's reputation* ③ the initial of a Chinese syllable: ~母 *the initial of a syllable* ④ tone:四~ *four tones in classical and modern Chinese* ⑤ [量] for sounds:我听到了一~杜鹃叫。*I heard a voice of the cuckoo.*
【声辩】argue; just; explain away:你不应该想方设法为自己~。*You shouldn't attempt to justify yourself.*
【声波】【物】sound wave; acoustic wave: ~记录仪 *voice printer*
【声部】part (in concert music):音乐分大提琴、小提琴、钢琴三个~。*The cello, violin and piano constitute the three musical part.*
【声场】sound (acoustic) field
【声称】claim; profess; state:他~自己无辜。*He asserted that he was innocent.*
【声带】①【生理】vocal cords ② (of a film) sound track
【声道】sound track; sound channel:单~ *single sound track* /双~ *double sound track*
【声调】① tone; voice note ②【语】the tone of Chinese characters
【声东击西】make a feint to the east and attack in the west
【声光】fame; prestige
【声抗】【物】acoustic reactance
【声控】sound-controlled; sound-activated; audio-controlled
【声浪】①【物】sound (acoustic) wave ② voice; clamour:复仇的~ *a clamour for revenge*
【声泪俱下】speaking while tears are streaming down
【声门】【生理】glottis
【声名】reputation; fame: ~鹊起 *rapid rise in fame* / ~狼藉 *have a bad name*; *be notorious*; *fall into disrepute*
【声明】① declare; announce:正式~ officially state; officially announce ② statement; declaration:联合~ *joint statement*
【声母】【语】initial of a syllable
【声囊】【动】vocal sac
【声能】【物】acoustic energy; sound-energy: ~学 *sonics*
【声谱】【物】sound spectrum: ~仪 *sound spectrograph*
【声气】information; message:互通~ *keep in contact with each other*; *keep in touch with each other*; *exchange information*
【声强】【物】sound intensity
【声情并茂】(of a singer) sing in a good voice and with much expression; be remarkable for one's voice and expression
【声色】① voice and countenance:不动~ *stay calm and collected*; *maintain one's composure* ② women and songs:他迷恋~。*He is fond of women and unhealthy music.* /你不应该沉溺于~。*You shouldn't wallow in sensual pleasure.*
【声色俱厉】be stern in voice and countenance
【声势】prestige and power; influence; impetus;

momentum；～浩大 *great in strength and momentum*；*gigantic in scale*；*powerful and dynamic* / ～浩大的游行 *huge and grand parade*

【声嘶力竭】be hoarse and exhausted；shout oneself blue

【声速】【物】velocity and sound；speed of sound

【声讨】denounce；condemn：愤怒～ *indignantly denounce* / ～会 *denunciation meeting* / 他们一致～虐待老人的行为。*They all condemn cruelly to the aged.*

【声望】popularity；prestige；reputation：～好的旅馆 *a hotel of good repute* / 失去（恢复）声望 *lose (regain) prestige*

【声威】fame；prestige；renown：～大震 *gain resounding fame*；*gain great fame and high prestige*

【声息】① information：互通～ *keep in contact with each other* ②（often used in the negative）sound；noise：没有一点～。*Not a sound was heard.*

【声响】sound；noise：她听到外面有一种奇怪的～。*She heard a strange sound outside.* / 我们听到咯噔咯噔的～。*We heard a rattling noise.*

【声像】【物】sound image

【声学】acoustics：几何～ *geometrical acoustics*；*ray acoustics* / 建筑～ *architectural acoustics* / ～工程 *acoustical engineering*

【声言】profess；declare；claim；state；assert：她～自己清白，谁也不相信。*Nobody believed her claim that she was to be innocent.*

【声音】sound；voice：～识别系统 *sound recognition system*

【声誉】fame；prestige；reputation；honour：在社会上很有～ *enjoy prestige in the community* / 毁坏某人的～ *ruin sb's reputation* / 博得～ *make a reputation (for oneself)* / ～鹊起 *quickly become known*；*gain a fast-growing reputation*

【声援】show support for；express support for；support

【声源】【物】sound event

【声乐】【音】vocal music

【声韵】rhyme and tone of words；sound；voice：～学 *phonology*

【声张】(usu. used in the negative) make public；reveal：拒绝～自己的地址。*Refuse to disclose one's address.*

【声障】【物】sound barrier；sonic barrier

牲 ① domestic animal ② animal sacrifice；offering of an ox，sheep，pig，etc. as a sacrifice：三～ *three sacrificial animals*

【牲畜】livestock；domestic

【牲口】draught animal；beast of burden

笙 *sheng*，a reed pipe wind instrument

shéng

绳 ① rope；cord；string；cable：钢～ *steel cable* ② restrict；restrain；punish ③［书］continue；carry on ④（Shéng）a surname

【绳索】rope；thick cord

【绳之以法】punish sb in accordance with the law；bring to justice；prosecute and punish according to law

【绳子】cord；rope；string

shěng

省[1] ① economize；save；be frugal：我们最好过简单的日子，能～就～。*We'd better lead a simple life and economize wherever possible.* ② omit；delete；leave out

省[2] ① province：～长 *governor of a province* ② capital of a province
see also xǐng

【省城】provincial capital

【省吃俭用】save money on food and expenses；live frugally；be thrifty

【省力】save effort；save labour

【省略】leave out；omit；delete：～号 *ellipsis*；*suspension points*；*ellipsis dots*

【省钱】save money

【省事】save trouble；make things easy；simplify matters

【省委】provincial party committee

【省心】save anxiety；save worry

【省优】superior quality product of a province

【省油灯】［方］lamp that does not burn much oil；oil — saving lamp-person who causes the least trouble

shèng

圣 ① holy；sacred：～地 *Holy Land*；*sacred place* ② master；sage：诗～ *poet of genius* ③ saint ④ emperor：面～ *face one's majesty* ⑤【宗】holy：朝～ *pilgrimage* / ～父、～子、～灵 *Father, Son and Holy Spirit*

【圣餐】【宗】Communion；Holy Communion；Eucharist；the Lord's Supper

【圣诞】① Christmas（the birthday of Jesus Christ）② birthday of Confucius：～节 *Christmas Day* / ～前夜 *Christmas Eve* / ～卡 *Christmas card* / ～树 *Christmas tree*

【圣公会】【宗】Anglican Church；Church of England

【圣火】holy fire；sacred fire

【圣洁】holy and pure

【圣经】holy Bible；the Bible；Holy Writ；Holy Scriptures

【圣明】august wisdom

【圣母】① female deity；goddess ② Catholicism Christianity the virgin Mary；Madonna

【圣人】① sage；wise man ② Your Majesty

【圣上】your Majesty

【圣徒】【宗】saint

【圣贤】stages and men of virtue
【圣谕】imperial decree
【圣战】holy war; jihad; crusade
【圣旨】imperial edict
胜[1] ① victory; success:乘～前进 *advance on the crest of a victory* ② win; defeat:以少～多 *use a small force to defeat a large one; defeat sb who is superior in number* ③ surpass; be better than; be superior to ④ superb; be fascinating
胜[2] be equal to; be up to; can bear:数不～数 *be too numerous to count*
【胜败】victory or defeat; success or failure; win or lose: ～乃兵家常事。*For a military commander, winning or losing a battle is a common occurrence.*
【胜地】famous scenic spot
【胜负】victory or defeat; win or lose; success or failure
【胜过】excel; surpass; be better than; be superior to
【胜局】victory; success
【胜利】① victory; success; triumph:我们赢得了最后的～。*We won the last victory.* ② attain the goal as planned
【胜券】confidence in victory:稳操～ *be certain of victory*
【胜似】be better than; superior to: ～兄弟 *be dearer than one's own brothers*
【胜诉】win a lawsuit
【胜算】[书] stratagem which ensures success; tactic that enables one to prevail over one's opponent
【胜仗】victory; victorious battle; triumph:上个月那些战士们又打了一次～。*Last month the soldiers won a battle again.*
盛 ① thriving; flourishing; prosperous ② aggressive; energetic; vigorous: 年轻气～ *young and aggressive* ③ grand; magnificent; solemn ④ rich; sumptuous ⑤ profound ⑥ popular; extensive; common ⑦ greatly; deeply ⑧ (Shèng) a surname
see also chéng
【盛产】abound in; rich in; team with
【盛传】by on everyone's lips; be widely rumoured; be widely known; spread far and wide:这个村庄里～着一个美丽的传说。*A beautiful tale is on everyone's lips in the village.*
【盛大】grand; majestic; magnificent:昨天我们学校举行了～的仪式欢迎他的到来。*Yesterday our school held a grand ceremony to welcome his coming.*
【盛典】grand ceremony; great occasion
【盛会】distinguished gathering; grand meeting; grand assembly
【盛开】be in full bloom; flourish:学校门口的鲜花～了。*The flowers at the gate of school are blooming now.*
【盛况】spectacular affair; spectacular event; grand occasion
【盛名】high fame; great reputation:久负～ *have long enjoyed a great reputation.*
【盛怒】angry; rage; fury
【盛气凌人】arrogant; domineering; overbearing; with overweening airs
【盛情】great kindness; boundless generosity; kind hospitality: ～难却 *would be ungracious of me not to accept the kindness*
【盛世】flourishing age; time of prosperity; heyday
【盛事】grand occasion; great event:乐坛～ *grand occasion in music*
【盛衰】prosperity and decline; rise and fall; up and down; wax and wane
【盛夏】midsummer; the height of summer; peak of summer
【盛行】popular; be in vogue; be current: ～一时 *in vogue for a time*
【盛宴】grand banquet; sumptuous dinner
【盛意】generosity; great kindness; magnanimity
【盛誉】great renown; high reputation:中国在世界各国中享有很高的～。*China has high reputation in the whole world.*
【盛装】splendid attire; rich dress:她身着～参加了朋友的婚礼。*With splendid attire, she attended the wedding ceremony of her friends.*
剩 leftover; surplus; remnant: ～饭 *leftover foods*
【剩下】be left; remain; stay
【剩余】surplus; remainder: ～货物 *surplus goods* / ～价值 *surplus value*

shī

尸 corpse; dead body; remains
【尸骸】skeleton
【尸体】corpse; cadaver; carcass; dead body:她准备死后把～捐献了。*She is ready to donate her remains after she dies.*
失 ① suffer loss of; lose:个人得～ *personal gains or losses* ② lose hold of; miss; let shift:坐～良机 *miss a good opportunity* ③ get lost ④ fail to achieve one's end:他所做的一切令我们大～所望。*What he had done made us greatly disappointed.* ⑤ deviate from the normal ⑥ break; go back on ⑦ mishap; defect; error
【失败】① be defeated; lost ② fail: ～是成功之母。*Failure is the mother of success.*
【失策】① miscalculation; wrong tactics ② be ill-advised; be unwise
【失常】abnormal; odd; not normal:她的儿子精神～了。*Her son was not in his right mind.*
【失宠】be out of favour; lose favour; be in disfavour
【失聪】become deaf
【失措】loss one's head; lose one's presence of mind; be at a loss:惊慌～ *be frightened out of one's senses*
【失道寡助】an unjust cause finds scant support

【失地】lost territory·收复～ *recover lost territory*

【失掉】① lose:他太生气了,以至于～了理智。*He was too angry to lose his mind.* ② miss; let slip

【失和】fail to get along well; become estranged

【失衡】lose balance

【失魂落魄】be panic-stricken; be scared out of one's wits

【失敬】slow inadequacy; be sorry; excuse me for my lack of manners

【失控】get out of control; out of hand; runaway

【失礼】① commit a breach of etiquette; impoliteness; discourtesy ② excuse me for any impropriety, lack of manners, etc.

【失利】be defeated; suffer a setback

【失恋】be disappointed in love; be jilted

【失灵】out of order; not work properly

【失落】lose; drop: ～感 *sense of loss*

【失眠】sleeplessness; (suffer from) insomnia

【失明】lose one's sight; be unable to see; go blind:他的左眼～了。*He lost the sight of his left eye.*

【失陪】take leave ahead of others

【失去】lost; forfeit:去年那位老人～了她唯一的女儿。*Last year the old man lost her only daughter.*

【失散】be scattered

【失色】① lose colour; be discoloured:年久～ *discoloured with the passage of time* ② turn pale

【失身】(of a woman) lose one's chastity; lose one's virginity

【失声】lose one's voice; burst out: ～痛哭 *be choked with tears; cry oneself hoarse*

【失事】have an accident

【失手】① lose control of one's hand; make a slip of the hand; accidentally drop ② loss or defeat; suffer defeat in competition

【失守】be take; (ot a city, etc); be lost:那座重要的城市已经～了。*The important city was lost to the enemy.*

【失算】miscalculate; misjudge; misread

【失态】lose control of oneself; be ill-mannered in one's bahaviour; forget oneself

【失调】① imbalance; dislocation:供求～ imbalance of supply and demand ② lack of proper care and rest ③ maladjustment:频率～ *maladjustment of frequency*

【失望】lose hope; lose confidence; be disappointed:她儿子上个周末没有回家,她～极了。*She was very disappointed that her son didn't come back last weekend.*

【失误】error; fault; mistake

【失效】① lose efficacy; lose effectiveness; cease to be effective:过期～ *cease to be effective after the specified date* ② (of a treaty, agreement, etc.) be no longer in force; be invalidated

【失信】break one's promise; go back on one's word:不要～于朋友。*Don't break faith with your friends.*

【失学】be unable to go to school; cannot afford to go to school; be obliged to discontinue one's studies

【失言】make an indiscreet remark; make a slip of the tongue

【失意】be disappointed; be frustrated; have one's aspirations

【失约】fail to keep an appointment:因为没赶上汽车,所以～了。*I failed to keep your appointment for missing buses.*

【失职】negligence of one's duty; dereliction of duty

【失主】owner of the lost property:我们终于找到了～,并把钱包还给了他。*At last we found the owner, and gave his wallet to him.*

【失踪】be missing; disappear:听说那个～的孩子又回来了。*I heard that the missing child came back again.*

【失足】① lose one's footing; miss one's step; slip ～落水 *slip and fall into the water* ② take a wrong step in life:社会有责任挽救～的青少年。*The society has responsibilities to reform juvenile delinquents.*

师[1] ① teacher; master; tutor:良～益友 *good teacher and helpful friend* ② model; guide; example ③ courtesy title for a Buddhist monk:法～ *master* ④ of one's master or teacher ⑤ person skilled in a certain trade ⑥ learn; follow: ～其所长 *learn from sb's strong points* ⑦ (Shī) a surname

师[2] ① division:步兵～ *infantry division* ② troops; army

【师表】person of exemplary virtue; paragon of virtue and learning

【师部】division headquarters

【师弟】① male junior fellow apprentice ② son of one's master (younger than oneself) ③ father's pupil (younger than oneself) ④ teacher and pupil

【师范】① teacher-training; normal school: ～大学 *normal university* ② model to be followed

【师傅】① master worker ② master skilled in any trade, business or art

【师姐】① female senior fellow apprentice ② daughter of one's master (older than oneself) ③ father's female apprentice (older than oneself)

【师妹】① female junior fellow apprentice ② daughter of one's master (younger than oneself) ③ father's female apprentice (younger than oneself)

【师母】wife of one's teacher or master

【师生】teach and student

【师徒】master and apprentice; teacher and student

【师兄】① male senior fellow apprentice ② son of one's master (older than oneself) ③ father's male apprentice (older than oneself)

【师友】teachers and friends

【师资】teaching staff; teachers; persons qualified to teach

诗 poetry; verse; poem:抒情～ *lyric poetry* / 叙事～ *narrative poetry* / 史～ *epic* / 散文～ *poem in prose*

【诗歌】poems and songs; poetry

【诗集】poetry anthology; collection of poems
【诗经】The Book of Songs, or Classic of Poetry, China's first ancient poem collection
【诗句】verse; line:那个孩子已经写了很多~。*The child has written a lot verses.*
【诗篇】① poem ② epic; inspiring story:壮丽~ *a magnificent epic*
【诗情画意】poetic beauty; quality suggestive of poetry; poetic charm
【诗人】poet
【诗圣】sage poet; poet among poets:人们尊唐朝的杜甫为~。*Du Fu of the Tang Dynasty was the sage poet.*
【诗史】① history of poetry:中国~ *history of Chinese poetry* ② poems reflecting the times and thus having historical significance
【诗意】poetic flavour; poetic quality; poetic sentiment

虱 louse

【虱子】louse:那个小孩太脏了,头上长了~。*The little child was so dirty that he had lice in his hair.*

狮 lion

【狮子】line

施 ① execute; carry out; put into effect:软硬兼~ *use both soft and hard tactics* /略~小技 *hatch a little scheme* ② exert; exercise; impose:不要再给他~加压力了。*Don't exert pressure on him.* ③ bestow; grant; hand out ④ use; apply:~肥 *apply fertilizer* ⑤ (Shī) a surname

【施放】let off; discharge; fire: ~毒气 *discharge poisonous gas*
【施肥】spread manure; apply fertilizer
【施工】carry out construction; carry out large repairs:他们需要的房间正在~。*The rooms they required are under construction.*
【施加】exert; inflict; bring to bear on
【施行】① put into force; carry out; execute ② perform; effect
【施用】use; apply

湿 wet; damp; humid; moist

【湿度】humidity; moisture: ~表 *moisture meter*
【湿乎乎】damp; moist; wet
【湿淋淋】drenched; dripping wet; soaking wet
【湿气】① moisture; dampness ②【中医】eczema; fungus infection of hand or foot
【湿润】damp; moist:面对他们的关心他的眼泪~了。*His eyes moistened at their care.*
【湿透】wet through; drenched; soaked

嘘 used to stop sb from doing sth or to drive sb or sth away: ~,有人过来了。*Hush! Somebody is coming.*
see also xū

shí

十 ① ten:老师给学生们~本书。*The teacher gave his students ten books.* ② highest; topmost: ~成 100 *per cent* / ~分 100 *per cent*; *complete*

【十二月】① December ② twelfth month of the lunar year; twelfth moon
【十二指肠】【生理】duodenum
【十分】fully; extremely; most; very: ~感谢你的帮助。*Thank you very much for your help.*
【十佳】ten best: ~运动员 *the top-ten athletes* / ~影片 *ten best films*
【十诫】【宗】ten commandments; Decalogue
【十进制】【数】decimal system; decimal scale
【十六进制】sexadecimal system; sexadecimal scale
【十拿九稳】ninety per cent sure; practically certain; in the bag; as good as steeled:她是个好学生,~能通过这次考试。*She is a good student and almost certain to pass this examination.*
【十年寒窗】ten year's study at a cold window — a student's long years of hard study
【十年九不遇】not once in ten years; be seldom seen; very rare
【十年树木,百年树人】it takes ten years to grow trees, but a hundred to cultivate people
【十全十美】be perfect in every way; be the acme of perfection; be the paragon of excellence; leave nothing to be desired
【十死一生】in a very critical or precarious situation
【十万火急】posthaste; most urgent:他有~的情况报告。*He has the extra-urgent matter to report.*
【十一】October 1, National Day of the people's Republic of China
【十一月】① November ② eleventh month of the lunar year; tenth moon
【十字架】cross; crucifix:不要给自己背上沉重的~。*Don't take up heavy cross on yourself.*
【十足】① 100 per cent; pure ② full:他神气~地来到教室。*He put on grand airs to enter the classroom.*

什 ① ten ② assorted; varied: ~家什 *home utensils and furniture*
see also shén

【什物】odds and ends; articles for everyday use; sundries

石 ① stone; rock; pebble: ~墙 *stone wall* ② stone inscription ③ stone needle used in ancient times to cure diseases ④ (Shí) a surname
see also dàn

【石碑】stone tablet; stele:他为自己的父亲立了~。*He erected a stone for his father.*
【石壁】rock cliff; precipice
【石沉大海】like a stone dropped into the sea — disappear for ever; never to be seen or heard of again

【石雕】stone carving; stone sculpture; carved stone 在学校门口有一座~像。*There is a stone statue before the school.*
【石墩】carved block of stone used as a stool or seat
【石膏】gypsum; plaster stone; plaster cast: ~夹板 *plaster splint*
【石拱桥】stone arch bridge
【石灰】lime:生~ *quick lime* /熟~ *slaked lime* / ~岩 *limestone*
【石窟】rock cave; grotto: ~画 *cave painting* /云冈~ *Yungang Grottoes* /龙门~ *Longmen Grottoes*
【石块】stone block; piece of stone
【石料】stone; rock:她家买了很多~,准备盖房子。*Her family bought many stones to build her house.*
【石林】stone Forest
【石榴】【植】pomegranate (Punica granatum)
【石墨】graphite
【石磨】millstone
【石器】stone implement; stone artifact; stone vessel; stoneware: ~时代 *Stone Age*
【石头】stone; rock:到现在他们家还是~房子。*Their house is made of stone until now.*
【石盐】rock salt; halite
【石油】oil; petroleum: ~勘探 *petroleum prospecting* /液化~气 *liquefied petroleum gas(LPG)* / ~输出国组织 *Organization of Petroleum Exporting Countries(OPEC)*
【石柱】①【地】stone pillar, formed when a stalactite joins a stalagmite in a cave ② stele
【石子】cobble; cobblestone; pebble

时 ① times; days; a long period of time:生逢其~ *be born at the right time* ② fixed time ③ current; present ④ fashion:那个小姑娘穿得比较入~。*The little girl dressed in vogue.* ⑤ one of the 12 periods into which the day was divided in ancient times. ⑥ hour; time of day; o'clock:下午~ *at three o'clock in the afternoon* ⑦ chance; opportune moment; opportunity ⑧ now and then; now... now...; sometimes... sometimes...: ~快~慢 *sometimes fast, sometimes slow* ⑨【语】tense:过去~ *past tense* /现在~ *present tense* ⑩ (Shí) a surname
【时弊】ill of the times; social veils of the day
【时不可失】don't let slip an opportunity: ~,机不再来。*Opportunity knocks only once.*
【时不时】from time to time; every now and then; often
【时差】① time difference between places belonging to different time zones ②【天】equation of time
【时常】often; frequently; again and again
【时辰】① time for sth; right time ② one of the 12 two-hour periods into which the day was traditionally divided before the introduction of western chronology
【时代】① times; age; era; epoch: ~潮流 *trend of the times* ② period in one's life; years:我们很想念大学~的同学。*All of us missed our classmates in college years.*
【时而】sometimes; from time to time ② now... now...; sometimes... sometimes
【时光】① time ② years; days; times
【时候】① (a point in) time; moment:正在那~,他爸爸走过来了。*At that time, his father was coming.* ② (the duration of) time
【时机】opportunity; opportune moment; chance
【时间】① (the duration of) time:你是怎样安排你的业余~的? *How do you arrange your spare time?* ② (the concept of) time
【时节】① season:秋收~到了,我不得不回家了。*The season for autumn harvest is coming, and I have to come back to my hometown.* ② time
【时局】current political situation
【时刻】① a point of time; hour; occasion ② always; at all times; constantly
【时髦】fashionable; latest; stylish; in vogue
【时期】period; stage; a particular period
【时尚】fashion; vogue; fad
【时时】often; constantly; again and again
【时事】current affairs; current events:我们同学中的几个人经常在一起讨论国际~。*Several students among our classmates often discuss current international affairs together.*
【时势】current situation; prevailing circumstances; trend of the times; the way things are going:顺应~ *move with the times* / ~造英雄。*The times produce their heroes.*
【时速】speed per hour; hourly speed:最高~ *maximum speed per hour*
【时态】【语】tense
【时务】current affair; current situation; prevalent circumstances; trend of the times
【时下】at present; right now
【时效】① effectiveness for a given period of time ②【律】prescription; limitation:诉讼~ *limitation of actions* ③【冶】ageing
【时兴】fashionable; popular; in vogue
【时宜】what is appropriate to the occasion
【时运】luck; fortune: ~不济 *have bad luck* / ~亨通 *have all the luck*
【时针】① hands of a clock or watch ② hour hand
【时装】① fashionable dress; latest fashions: ~表演 *fashion show* / ~设计师 *fashion designer* / ~展览 *fashion exhibition* ② modern clothing

识 ① know:不~字 *unable to read a single character* ② knowledge; learning:常~ *common sense*
【识别】distinguish; discern; identify; spot:他擅长指纹~工作。*He is good at fingerprint identification.*
【识货】be knowledgeable; be able to tell good from bad; know what's what
【识破】penetrate; see sb as sb really is; see though:老师马上~了那个学生的诡计。*The teacher saw through his student's conspiracy at once.*
【识趣】behave sensibly in a delicate situation; be judicious; be tactful:她一点也不~。*She is not*

tactful at all.

【识时务者为俊杰】a wise man submits to circumstances; those who know to objective necessity are wise people; whosoever understands the times is a great man; a person is wise who understands the signs of the times

【识相】[方] be sensible, be tactful; showing good sense: 你最好～点,这里已经没有机会给你了。*You'd better be more sensible and there is no chance for you.*

【识字】learn to read; become literate: 她三岁时,妈妈就开始教她读书～了。*Her mother began to teach her read and write when she was only three years old.*

实 ① solid; full: ～心球 *solid ball* ② real; true; actual; sincere: 真心～意 *truly and wholeheartedly* ③ reality; actuality; fact: 名副其～ *in mane but not in fact* ④ fruit; seed

【实词】【语】notional word; full word

【实地】① on-the-spot; field: 他决定去上海～调查。*He decided to go to Shanghai to carry out on-the-spot investigations.*

【实干】do solid work: ～家 *man of action*

【实话】truth: ～实说 *speak the plain truth*

【实惠】① real benefit; material gain: 你想从中间取得～是不可能的。*It's impossible that you want to really benefit from it.* ② practical; solid; substantial

【实际】① reality; actual practice: 理想和～相结合 *unity of theory and practice* ② real; true; actual: ～成本 *actual cost* ③ practical; realistic: ～行动 *practical action*

【实践】① implement; carry out; live up to; put into practice ② practice: ～是检验真理的唯一标准。*Practice is the sole criterion for testing truth.*

【实据】substantial evidence; actual proof

【实况】what is actually happening: ～转播 *live broadcast*

【实力】strength; power: 国防～ *national defence capabilities*

【实例】example; concrete

【实录】faithful record; factual record

【实情】actual state of affairs; real situation; truth: 请你把～告诉老师。*Please tell the truth to your teacher.*

【实权】real power

【实施】put into effect; enforce; implement: 李教授负责该项目的～。*Professor Li is responsible for the execution of the programme.*

【实事】① practical things; fact ② deeds; practical work; solid work

【实数】①【数】real number ② actual amount or number

【实说】tell the truth; speak frankly

【实体】①【哲】substance: ～形式 *substantial form* ②【律】entity: 政治～ *political entity*

【实物】① material object; real object: 今年开始学校决定采取～教学。*The school decided to adopt object lessons from this year.* ② in kind ③【物】matter

【实习】practice; fieldwork; exercise one's skill in: 毕业～ *graduation field work*

【实现】realize; achieve; bring about

【实效】actual effect; substantial benefit: 注重～ *emphasize practical results*

【实习】① sincere; honest ② solid

【实行】put into practice; carry out; implement; put into effect: ～税收政策 *put into effect the policy of tax*

【实验】experiment; test: 昨天我们在课上做了～。*We did an experiment in class yesterday.*

【实业】industry and commerce; a large-scale in factory; business: ～银行 *industrial bank* / ～救国 *save the nation through industrial development*

【实用】practical; functional: ～主义 *pragmatism*

【实在】(shízài) ① true; real; honest; practical: 那个老头是一个～的人。*The old man is an honest and truly dependable man.* ② in fact; in reality ③【哲】reality

【实在】(shízai) well done; done in real earnest

【实战】actual combat; actual fighting: ～演习 *combat exercise with live ammunition*

【实质】essence; gist; substance: 我们必须抓住问题的～。*We must master the matters of substance.*

拾[1] ① pick up; collect; gather: ～柴火 *gather crop stalks; collect firewood* ② clean; put in order; tidy up

拾[2] ten (used for the numeral to avoid mistakes or alterations)

【拾掇】① tidy up; clean up; put in order ② fix; mend; repair ③ punish; settle with; take to task

【拾金不昧】return money found; not pocket the money me picks up

【拾取】collect; gather; pick up

【拾物】lost article found

食 ① eat: 多～些水果。*Eat more fruits.* ② have one's meal: 废寝忘～ *forget food and sleep* ③ live on: 他只有十六岁,但已经自～其力了。*He was only sixteen, but he had lived by his own labour.* ④ food; meal: 那个小姑娘喜欢吃零～,不喜欢吃主～。*The little girl likes eating between-meal nibbles and dislikes eating staple food.* ⑤ edible: ～用油 *edible oil* ⑥ eclipse: 日～ *solar eclipse* / 月～ *lunar eclipse*

【食不下咽】unable to eat or swallow — be heavy-hearted

【食管】【生理】gullet; esophagus: ～癌 *cancer of the esophagus* / ～炎 *esophagitis*

【食客】① customer of a restaurant ② person sponging on an aristocrat; hanger-on of an aristocrat: 在旧社会,有钱人家经常养大量的～。*In old society, richers used to keep large numbers of hangers-on.*

【食粮】grain; food: 精神～ *nourishment for the mind*

【食品】food; foodstuff; provisions: 速冻～ *fast-frozen food* / 保健～ *health food*

【食谱】cookbook; recipe; menu: 她妈妈经常按照～

则做。*Her mother often cooks following a recipe.*
【食宿】board and lodging
【食堂】dining room; mess hall; canteen:学生～ *canteen for students* /我们经常在～吃饭。*We often go to the dining hall.*
【食物】eatables; edibles; food; victuals: ～链 *food chain*; *food cycle* / ～中毒 *food poisoning*
【食言】eat one's word; go back on one's word; break one's promise:他不可能～的。*It's impossible that he goes back on his promise.*
【食盐】table salt; salt
【食用】① eat; consume; used for food ② edible: ～植物油 *edible vegetable oil*
【食欲】appetite:他的儿子最近老是～不振。*His son has a poor appetite recently.*
【食指】index finger; forefinger

蚀 ① lose; erode; corrode ② eclipse
【蚀本】lose one's capital; lose money in business

shǐ

史 ① history:近代～ *modern history* /现代～ *contemporary history* /通～ *general history* ② official historian in ancient China; official:御～ *imperial censor* ③ (Shǐ) a surname
【史册】historical records; annals; history
【史官】official historian; historiographer
【史记】*Shi Ji or Historical Records*, by Si Maqian, of the western Han Dynasty
【史料】historical materials; historical data:为了写论文她收集了很多～。*She gathered historical data and materials for her paper.*
【史诗】epic; event
【史实】historical fact:她的小说里加入了很多～资料。*Her novel was added a lot of historical facts.*
【史书】history; historical records
【史无前例】without precedent in history; unprecedented; unparalleled: ～的盛典 *ceremony without precedent in history*
【史学】science of history; historiography: ～家 *historian*; *historiographer*

矢[1] arrow

矢[2] take an oath; vow; swear

矢[3] excrement; faces
【矢口否认】flatly disavow
【矢志不渝】vow to adhere unswervingly to one's chosen course; pledge steadfast devotion to a cause

使[1] ① send; have; tell sb to do sth ② use; employ; exert; apply ③ make; cause; enable ④ if; supposing

使[2] envoy; emissary; messenger:大～ *ambassador* /特～ *special envoy*
【使不得】① cannot be used; useless; unserviceable ② undesirable; impermissible; must not be done
【使出】use; exert; expend:他～全部的招数来表演。*He played his whole card to act.*
【使馆】diplomatic mission; embassy: ～区 *diplomatic quarter*
【使坏】be up to mischief; play a dirty trick:他竟然往我身上～。*He plays a dirty trick on me.*
【使唤】① order about; order around:他总是喜欢～别人。*He always likes ordering about other people.* ② use; handle; manage
【使节】diplomatic envoy; envoy:各国驻华～ *diplomatic envoys to China*; *heads of diplomatic missions in China*
【使劲】exert all one's strength; make efforts
【使命】mission
【使团】diplomatic mission; diplomatic corps
【使用】use; make use of; employ; apply; resort to: ～价值 *use value* /他～科学知识帮助别人。*He uses scientific knowledge to help other people.*
【使者】emissary; envoy; messenger

始 ① begin; commence; start:自～至终 *from beginning to end* ②［书］only then; not... until
【始创】initiate; originate; pioneer
【始料】original expectations: ～所及 *within one's expectations*
【始末】beginning and end; start to finish; whole story:我们开始调查该事故的～。*We began to investigate what the accident was all about.*
【始终】throughout; from beginning to end; from start to finish:这个星期他～都和我在一起。*He stayed with me from beginning to end in this week.*
【始终如一】constant; unchanging

驶 ① speed; go quickly:飞～而去 *speed by* ② drive; ride; sail

屎 ① dung; faeces; excrement; droppings; stool:马～ *horse dung* ② secretion (of the eye, ear, etc.):耳～ *earwax*
【屎壳郎】［方］dung beetle

shì

士 ① soldier; armyman; serviceman:战～ *soldier* ② scholar ③ noncommissioned officer:上～ *sergeant first class* /中～ *sergeant* /下～ *corporal* ④ person trained in a specified field ⑤ (commendable or praiseworthy) person:烈～ *martyr* /义～ *high-minded* /壮～ *hero*; *warrior* ⑥ social stratum between senior officials and the common people in ancient China ⑦ bodyguard, one of the pieces in Chinese chess ⑧ (Shì) a surname
【士兵】rank-and-file soldier; privates; rank and file
【士气】spirit; morale:我们必须保持旺盛的～同非典型性肺炎作斗争。*We must keep our high spirit to*

fight with SARS.

【士卒】soldiers; privates:身先～ *fight at the head of his man*; *lead the charge*

氏 ① family name; surname ② used after famous persons such as scientists, inventors, etc.:华～表 *Fahrenheit thermometer* ④［书］one's kinsfolk

【氏族】clan: ～社会 *clan society*

示 show; notify; produce; instruct:出入校园要出～你的证明。*When you go in or out of school, you must produce your certificate.*

【示范】demonstrate; set an example; show:请李明同学给大家作一个～。*Please Li Ming gave us a demonstration.*

【示人】show sth to others; let others have a look at sth:她有一个非常漂亮的项链,但从不～。*She has a very beautiful necklace, but she never shows it to others.*

【示弱】give the impression of weakness; show signs of weakness; take sth lying down

【示威】① demonstrate; hold a demonstration: ～游行 *demonstration*; *parade*; *march* / ～群众 *demonstrators*

【示意】hint; gesture; motion; signal:老师～我读课文。*The teacher motioned me to read the text.*

【示意图】① sketch map:交通～ *transport map* ②【机】schematic diagram; schematic drawing

【示众】publicly expose; punish before the public

世 ① life; lifetime:生生～～ *from generation to generation* / 一生一～ *all one's life* ② generation:三～同堂 *three generation under one roof* ③ from generation to generation:我们家和李叔叔家是～交。*There is long-standing friendship between Uncle Li and my family.* ④ used in terms of address among old family friends: ～叔 *younger friend of one's father* ⑤ age; era; time:乱～ *troubled times*; *turbulent years* / 盛～ *age of prosperity* ⑥ world; society:很多美丽的图片将公之于～。*A lot of beautiful pictures will be revealed to the public.* ⑦【地】epoch ⑧ (Shì) a surname

【世仇】① family feud; vendetta ② ancient enemy; sworn enemy

【世传】be handed down from generation to generation; be known for generations:他不敢相信老师竟把～秘方给了他。*He couldn't believe that his teacher sent the secret recipe handed down through generations to him.*

【世代】① years; ages; long period of time ② generation after generation: ～相传 *pass on from generation to generation*

【世道】manners and morals of the time; ways of the world

【世故】(shìgù) ways of the world:他只是个小孩子,不懂人情～。*He is only a little child, and inexperience in life.*

【世故】(shìgu) worldly-wise; shrewd; crafty:你是一个～的人。*You are quite a smooth character.*

【世纪】century: ～末 *end of the century*

【世家】noble family; aristocratic family; old and well-known family

【世交】① long-standing friendship spanning two or more generations ② old family friends

【世界】① world:美妙～ *wonderful world* / ～冠军 *world champion* ②【宗】universe:大千～ *boundless universe* ③ all over the world:这个消息很快传遍了整个～。*The news spread all over the world quickly.*

【世人】common people; people at large

【世上】in the world; on earth: ～无难事,只怕有心人。*Nothing in the world is difficult for one who sets his mind on it.*

【世事】affairs of the world

【世俗】① customs and traditions; social conventions; common views:你怎么有如此的～之见。*How you have so common views.* ② secular; worldly

【世态】ways of the world

【世外桃源】land of Peach Blossoms — an imaginary ideal world heaven of peace; beautiful retreat

【世袭】hereditary: ～财产 *hereditary property* / ～爵位 *hereditary title of nobility* / ～制度 *hereditary system*

仕 ① be an official; hold an official post:学而优则～。*A good scholar will make an official.*

【仕宦】be an official:她爷爷出生在一个～之家。*Her grandfather was born in an official's family.*

【仕途】［书］official career

市 ① market:鱼～ *fish market* / 早～ *morning market* ② buying and selling; business transaction ③ administrative units ④ city; municipality: ～中心 *the heart of the city*; *city centre*

【市场】market; marketplace; bazaar: ～行情 *market quotation* / ～价格 *market price* / ～经济 *market economy*

【市郊】suburb; outskirts:我们家在上海的～。*Our family live in the suburban district of Shanghai.*

【市面】market; market conditions; business situation

【市民】urban residents; urban inhabitants; townspeople

【市区】city proper; downtown area; urban district

【市容】appearance of a city:济南的～比过去更漂亮了。*The appearance of Jinan is more beautiful than before.*

【市委】municipal Party committee: ～书记 *secretary of the municipal Party committee*

【市长】mayor:我听说～参观了咱们公司。*I heard that the mayor had visited our company.*

【市政】municipal administration: ～工程 *municipal works*; *municipal engineering*

式 ① type; style; fashion:中～ *Chinese style* / 西～ *Western style* ② form; model; pattern ③ ceremony; celebration; ritual:开幕～和闭幕～他都参加了。*He attended both opening ceremony and closing ceremony.*

【式样】style; type; design; model: ～新颖 *novel*

style

似

see also sì

【似的】used after a noun, a pronoun, or a verb to indicate similarity

事 ① matter; affair; thing; business:家~和国~都很重要。*Both family affairs and affairs of state are important.* ② accident; trouble; difficulty:他的儿子又闹~了。*Her son made trouble again.* ③ job; work; task ④ involvement; responsibility ⑤［书］attend upon; wait upon; serve ⑥ go in for; be engaged in ⑦ way; means; measure

【事半功倍】half the work with twice the result; get twice the result with half the effort

【事倍功半】twice the work with half the result; get half the result with twice the effort

【事变】① incident ② emergency; exigency; eventuality ③ course of events

【事端】incident; disturbance; undesirable event

【事故】accident; mishap:意外~ *unforeseen accident*

【事后】after the event; afterwards: ~诸葛亮 *wise after the event*

【事迹】dead; merit; achievement:我们听说过他的英雄~。*We heard his heroic exploits.*

【事假】leave of absence; compassionate leave:昨天她儿子不舒服,她不得不请了两天~。*Yesterday her son didn't feel well, and she had to ask for two days leave of absence.*

【事件】event; particular event; incident

【事理】reason; sense; logic

【事例】example; instance:他举了几个~来证明他是个英雄。*He gave us several examples to prove that he was a hero.*

【事情】① affair; matter; business; question:那个孩子不得不说出~的真相。*The little child had to say out the truth of the matter.* ② work; occupation:他在他爸爸的公司里找了个~。*He got a job in his father's company.*

【事实】fact:与~不符 *not tally with reality* / ~胜于雄辩。*Facts speak louder than words.*

【事实上】in fact; really; as a matter of fact; actually: ~昨天他没去学校。*Yesterday he didn't go to school actually.*

【事态】state of affairs; developments; situation

【事务】① affair; work; routine:他在办公室处理一些日常~。*He often deals with daily affairs in his office.* ② general affairs: ~科 *general affairs section*

【事物】thing; object; reality:客观~ *objective reality* / 任何~都有自己的发展规律。*Everything has its own law of the development of things.*

【事项】item; matter; point

【事业】① career; cause; task; undertaking:教育~ *education career* ② institution:公共~ *public utilities* / ~单位 *public institution*

【事宜】arrangements; relevant matters; matters concerned:几位老师在办公室讨论考试的相关~。*Several teachers went to the office to discuss matters concerning examination.*

【事由】① origin of an incident; particulars of a matter; specifics of a matter

【事与愿违】things run counter to one's wishes; things turn out contrary to one's wishes

【事在人为】all success depends on human effort; human effort is the decisive factor

势 ① force; influence; power; strength:趋炎附~ *play up to those in power* ② momentum; tendency:以排山倒海之~ *with the momentum of an avalanche* ③ outward appearance of a nature object:水~汹涌 *turbulent flow of water* ④ circumstances; state of affairs; situation:大~所趋 *trend of the time* ⑤ sign; gesture:他作了个手~让我们进来。*He made a sign with his hand to let us come in.* ⑥ male genitals

【势必】be bound to; be certain to; certainly will

【势不可挡】irresistible; overwhelming

【势不两立】mutually exclusive; irreconcilable

【势单力薄】not enough manpower and resources; small in number and meagre in strength

【势均力敌】be evenly matched in strength; match each other in strength

【势力】force; influence; power: ~范围 *sphere of influence* / 进步~ *progressive forces*

【势利】snobbish: ~眼 *snobbish attitude*

【势能】【物】potential energy

【势如破竹】be like splitting bamboo; carry all before one

【势头】impetus; momentum; situation

【势在必行】be imperative; become unavoidable:学校改革,~。*It is imperative to carry out school reforms.*

侍 serve; wait upon; attend on

【侍从】attendants; retinue

【侍奉】serve; support and wait upon; attend upon; look after

【侍候】wait upon; take care of; look after

【侍弄】attend (crops, livestock, poultry, etc.); repair; fix

【侍者】attendant; servant; waiter:饭店~ *waiter*

饰 ① adorn; dress up; cover up; polish; hide:粉~太平 *gloss over* ② decorations; ornaments:她的丈夫买了很多首~给她。*Her husband bought a lot of women's personal ornaments for her.* ③ play the role; act the part of a dramatic character

【饰品】head ornaments; jewels

【饰物】① jewelry; articles for personal adornment ② decorations

【饰演】act; play the part of:他在《红楼梦》中~贾宝玉。*He plays the role of Jia Baoyu in A Dream of Red Mansions.*

试 ① attempt; test; try: ~一下我的自行车怎么样? *How about trying my bicycle?* ② examination; test:口~ *oral examination* /笔~ *written*

examination / 初 ~ *preliminary examination* / 复 ~ *final examination*
【试播】trial broadcast; trial telecast
【试点】① conduct tests as selected points; launch a pilot project; make experiments ② place where an experiment is made; experimental unit
【试管】【化】test tube: ~婴儿 *test-tube baby*
【试卷】examination paper; test paper: 李老师昨天批改了~。*Yesterday teacher Li went over the examination papers.*
【试生产】trial production
【试探】probe; explore; find out: 他的父亲来到学校~事情的虚实。*His father came to school to try to find out the truth.*
【试题】examination questions; test questions
【试问】may we ask; we should like to ask; it may well be asked
【试行】try out
【试演】trial performance
【试验】experiment; test; trial: ~田 *experimental field*
【试用】try out; on probation: ~期 *probationary period* / ~品 *trial products*
【试纸】test paper

视 ① look; look at; view ② regard; look upon; treat ③ examine; inspect; watch
【视差】【物】visual error; parallax
【视察】① inspect: ~团 *inspection team* / 上周她爸爸~基层去了。*Last week her father inspected the units at the grass-roots level.* ② examine; look carefully at
【视觉】【生理】vision; visual sense; sense of sight: 她总说她的~很敏锐。*She always says that she has an acute sense of sight.*
【视力】sight; power of vision; eyesight: 我们必须从小开始保护~。*We must protect our eyesight when we were a child.*
【视频】【物】video frequency
【视听】seeing and hearing; what one sees and hears; personal observation; mental horizons: ~中心 *audio-visual centre*
【视图】view
【视网膜】【生理】retina: ~脱落 *detached retina*; *retinal detachment* / ~炎 *retinitis*
【视为】regard as: 我把他~我的知己。*I regard him as a bosom friend.*
【视线】① line of vision; line of sight: 你挡住我们的~了。*You obstructed my view.* ② attention
【视野】field of vision; field of view: 开拓~ *enlarge one's horizons*

柿 persimmon
【柿饼】dried persimmon
【柿子】① persimmon tree ② persimmon
【柿子椒】sweet bell pepper

拭 wipe away; wipe; remove
【拭目以待】wait and see; look forward to: 你的学生能否通过这次考试,让我们~。*We shall wait and see if your students can pass the examination.*

是[1] ① correct; right; true: 实事求~ *seek truth from facts* ②［书］justify; praise; uphold: 口~心非 *say one thing and mean another* ③ yes; right: ~的,我帮你复印这些资料。*Yes, I can help you copy these materials.* ④ (Shì) a surname

是[2] this; that

是[3] ① used like "be" before nouns or pronouns to identify, describe or amplify the subject ② used with 的 to indicate classification ③ used to indicate existence: 他跑进屋里,浑身~汗。*He rushed into the room with sweat all over.* ④ used in between two identical nouns or verbs in two or more similar patterns to indicate distinction ⑤ used to indicate concession ⑥ used at the beginning of a sentence for the scale of emphasis ⑦ used before a noun to indicate each and everyone of the kind ⑧ used before a noun to indicate fitness or suitability ⑨ used in an alternative and negative question ⑩ pronounced emphatically to indicate certainty
【是非】① right and wrong; truth and falsehood: 谁又能够说明~呢? *Who can explain the right and wrong?* ② quarrel; dispute; trouble: 搬弄~ *tell tales* / 他总是挑拨~。*He always foments discord.*
【是否】if; whether; whether or not: 我不知道周末你~能来。*I don't know if you can come on this weekend.*
【是味儿】［口］① have the right flavour; suit one's taste; delicious: 他所做的食物很~。*What he cooked is very delicious.*

适[1] ① appropriate; fit; proper; suitable: 艾丽斯穿绿衣服看上去很合~。*Green looks very becoming on Iris.* ② right; opportune

适[2] ① go; follow; move towards: 无所~从 *be at a loss what to do* ②［书］(of a woman) get married; marry
【适当】appropriate; proper; right; suitable
【适得其反】be just the opposite; run counter to one's desire
【适度】appropriate; proper; to a moderate degree
【适合】suit; fit; befit
【适可而止】stop before going too far; know when or where to stop; not overdo it
【适量】just the right amount; an appropriate quantity
【适龄】of the right age: ~儿童都有权利上学。*Children of school age all have rights to go to school.*
【适时】in good time; at the right moment; timely; seasonable
【适销】salable; have a ready market: ~对路 *salable and in good demand; fit for sale*
【适宜】suitable; appropriate; proper; fit: 气候~ *genial climate*
【适应】suit; adapt to; adjust to; conform to: 我们刚搬到这儿,要慢慢~环境。*We have just been*

here, and adapt myself to circumstances.
【适用】suitable; applicable: ～性 *applicability*
【适者生存】survival of the fittest
【适中】① proper; appropriate; moderate ② well situated

恃 rely on; depend on; count on
【恃强凌弱】play the bully; use one's strength to bully the weak

室 ① room: 阅览～ *reading room* / 资料～ *reference room* ② office; administrative subdivision: 医务～ *clinic* / 财务～ *finance office* ③ shop (in a hotel, department store, etc.) ④ wife: 他是个有妻～的人。*He is a married man.* ⑤ family: 皇～ *royal family*
【室内】indoor; interior
【室外】outdoor; outside: 他经常做一些～活动。*He often does some outdoor activities.*

逝 ① pass: 时光飞～。*The time flies.* ② die; pass away
【逝世】be dead; die; pass away

舐 [书] lick
【舐犊情深】parental love; deep affection towards one's children

弑 murder: ～君 *murder one's sovereign; commit regicide*

释 ① explain; expound; elucidate: 我找不到书上的注～。*I can't find the explanatory notes of the book.* ② clean up; dispel; remove ③ let go; be relieved of; set free
【释放】① release; set from: 由于表现好,他被提前～了。*He was released before his sentence expires, because he actually perfectly.* ②【物】release
【释怀】vanish; disappear; dismiss from one's mind
【释然】feel relieved; feel at ease
【释手】let go; relax the hold
【释疑】clear up doubts; dispel doubts; explain difficult points
【释义】explain the meaning (of a word, sentence, etc.)

嗜 be addicted to; have a liking for; take to
【嗜好】addiction; hobby; habit: 他是个好同志,没有什么不良～。*He is a good man and has no harmful habit.*

誓 ① swear; pledge; vow; take an oath: 海～山盟 *lover's vow to be true to each other forever* ② oath; solemn promise; vow
【誓词】oath; pledge; vow
【誓师】① really to pledge resolution before going to war ② take a mass pledge: 昨天他们召开～大会,誓死保卫祖国。*Yesterday, they hold a meeting to pledge mass to fight to the death in defending their country.*
【誓言】oath; pledge

shi

匙 key: 把钥～给我。*Give the key to me.*

see also chí

shōu

收 ① bring in; put in proper place; collect: 他从那个村庄～了好多钱。*He collected a lot of money from the village.* ② accept; recover; retrieve: ～回 *take back* ③ charge: 分文不～ *without charging a single cent; free of charge* ④ gather in; harvest; reap: 丰～的季节到了。*The harvest season is coming.* ⑤ receive ⑥ control; restrain ⑦ arrest; take into custody; put in jail ⑧ bring to an end; stop: 天晚了,我们该～摊了。*It's too late; we may as well call it a day now.*
【收兵】① withdraw troops; call off a battle ② bring to an end
【收藏】collect; store up: 他喜欢～一些旧邮票。*He likes collecting some old stamps.*
【收场】① end up; stop; wind up ② ending; conclusion: 我们相信她不会有好的～。*I believe that she would come to no good end.*
【收成】harvest; crop
【收到】get; achieve; obtain; receive: 我们很快～了她的回信。*We got her letter very quickly.*
【收发】① receive and dispatch: ～信件 *receive and dispatch letters* / ～报 *receive and transmit telegrams* / ～室 *office for incoming and outgoing mail*
【收费】charge; collect fees; pay: ～电话 *pay phone*
【收复】recover; regain; recapture: ～失地 *recover lost territory*
【收割】gather in; harvest; reap: ～机 *harvester; reaper*
【收工】stop work for the day; knock off; pick up: 今天我们很早就～了。*We stopped work for this day very early.*
【收购】buy; purchase: ～站 *purchasing station or centre*
【收回】① take back; recover; recall; regain; call in: 1997年中国～了香港的主权。*In 1997, China regained sovereignty of Hong Kong.* ② countermand; rescind; withdraw
【收获】harvest; reap; gather in the crops
【收集】bring together; collect; gather
【收件人】addressee; consignee
【收缴】① take over; capture; confiscate: 战士们～了敌人的武器。*The soldiers captured the enemy's arms.* ② collect; levy: ～税款 *levy taxes*
【收进】include; incorporate
【收据】receipt: 请把～给我们看一下。*Please show the receipt to us.*

S

【收看】watch(TV); look in: ~率 *audience ratings*
【收款机】cash register
【收款人】payee
【收揽】① draw over to one's side; win over: ~民心 *try to win the support of the people*; *buy popular support* ② bring under control; keep in one's grasp
【收敛】① weaken; disappear; diminish ② show restraint; restraint oneself ③【医】shrink; astringent: ~剂 *astringent* ④【数】convergence
【收留】take in; have sb in one's care; undertake the care of
【收录】① enlist; employ; recruit ② collect; include ③ receive and record
【收买】① purchase; buy: 昨天他~了很多旧报纸。*He bought many old newspapers yesterday.* ② bribe; buy off; buy over; buy up: ~人心 *buy popular support*
【收盘】【经】closing quotation (on the exchange, etc.): ~价 *closing price*; *closing quotation*
【收票员】ticket collector: 那个孩子的妈妈是一名~。*The child's mother is a ticket collector.*
【收起】① pick up; pack up ② stop; cut out; give up
【收讫】received in full; payment received; paid: 现金~ *cash paid*
【收清】receive in full
【收取】get payment; collect; receive: ~支票 *collect cheque*
【收容】take in and provide for; accept; house: ~所 *collecting post* / ~难民 *house refugees*
【收入】① income; earnings; proceeds; revenue: 毛~ *gross income* /净~ *net income* /财政~ *state revenue* / ~分配 *income distribution* ② take in; include; incorporate
【收视率】(of TV program) rating; viewing rate
【收拾】① put in order; tidy up; clear away; get ready: 她每天都~房间。*She tidies up her room every day.* ② repair; mend; fix; pack: ~行李 *pack one's luggage* ③ settle with; punish: 他太坏了,迟早会被~的。*He is too bad and will be punished one day.* ④ get rid of; eliminate
【收缩】① contract; shrink; reduce: 这件衣服洗后会~。*The clothes shrink when they are washed.* ② draw back; tighten up; concentrate one's forces; cut: ~支出 *cut expenses* ③【生理】systole: ~期 (*of the heart*) *systole*
【收摊儿】pack up the stall-wind up the day's business; wind up a day's business; wind up a day's business
【收听】listen: 今天上午我们班~了足球的实况广播。*This morning our class listened to the live broadcast of football.*
【收尾】① final phase; bring to a conclusion ② ending
【收效】yield results; produce an effect; bear fruit: ~甚微 *produce very little effect* / ~明显 *produce notable results*
【收心】① get into the frame of mind for work or study; concentrate on more serious things ② have a change of heart; convert to a different view
【收信人】recipient; addressee
【收押】detain; take into custody.
【收养】adopt; take in and bring up; take into one's family: ~法 *law of adoption* / ~人 *adopter*
【收益】income; profit; proceeds; gains; returns; earnings: ~率 *rate of return*; *earning rate*
【收音】① radio reception: ~机 *radio set* ② acoustics
【收载】include and record
【收账】① enter into accounts; charge to an account ② collect debts; collect payment of bills
【收支】income and expenses; revenue and expenditure: ~平衡 *balance of revenue and expenditure* / ~逆差 *unfavourable balance of payments*; *balance of payments deficit*
【收治】① admit for treatment; accept for treatment: 这个医院已经~了很多非典病人。*A lot of SARS patients have been admitted into the hospital.* ②[书] arrest and punish

shǒu

手 ① hand: 举~ *put up one's hand(s)*; *rise one's hand(s)* ② hold in one's hand; possess ③ handy; easy to carry ④ in person ⑤ ability; stratagem: 大显身~ *give full play to one's abilities* ⑥ expert of some occupation ⑦[量] of skill or proficiency
【手背】back of a hand
【手笔】① sb's writing, calligraphy or painting; hand ② literary or artistic sk ill ③ style
【手臂】① arm ② reliable helper; aide; assistant
【手表】watch; wrist watch
【手册】① handbook; manual: 旅游~ *tourist guide* ② record book; workbook
【手抄】copy by hand; handwrite; handwritten: ~本 *handwritten copy*
【手电筒】electric torch; flashlight; torch light
【手动】hand; hand-operated: ~装置 *hand-gear*
【手段】① means; measure; method; way ② trick; artifice: 耍~ *play tricks* ③ skill; ability
【手法】① skill; technique: 艺术表现~ *means of artistic expression* ② trick; artifice
【手风琴】accordion
【手工】① handwork ② by hand: ~操作 *operated by hand*
【手工业】handicraft industry; handicraft
【手工艺】handicraft art or skill; handicraft: ~品 *articles of handicraft art*
【手机】mobile phone; cellular phone
【手疾眼快】quick of eye and deft of hand; sharp-sighted and neat-handed
【手迹】original calligraphic work
【手脚】① movement of limbs; motion: 那个孩子~特别勤快。*The little child is very quick and industrious.* ②[方] trick: 背后弄~ *play dirty*

tricks on the sly

【手紧】tightfisted; stingy; short of money

【手劲儿】strength of the hand; grip

【手巾】① towel: ~架 *towel rack* /他给了我一块湿~。*He gave me a wet towel.* ②［方］handkerchief

【手绢】handkerchief

【手铐】handcuffs

【手拉手】hand in hand

【手榴弹】hand grenade; grenade

【手忙脚乱】in a rush; in a flurry; in a in a great bustle; be thrown into confusion

【手帕】handkerchief

【手气】luck at gambling, etc.: 今天他~很好。*Luck is with her today.*

【手枪】pistol; handgun: ~射程 *pistol shot* / ~射击场 *pistol range*

【手巧】handy with needlework; skillful with one's hands; nimble-fingered; dexterous; deft: 她是一个心灵~的姑娘。*She is a clever and deft girl.*

【手软】lack firmness; soft-hearted; irresolute when firmness is needed

【手刹车】hand brake

【手生】lack practice and skill; out of practice

【手势】gesture; sign; signal: ~语言 *sign language* /老师打了个~让我们大声朗读课文。*The teacher signed to us to read the text aloud.*

【手术】surgical operation: ~台 *operating table* /腹腔~ *abdominal operation* / ~室 *operating room*

【手松】free with one's money; free-handed; liberal; openhanded

【手套】gloves; mittens: 棉~ *cotton* /棒球~ *baseball gloves* /拳击~ *boxing gloves*

【手提】① portables; hand: ~电脑 *portable computer* / ~行李 *hand luggage* ② carry with one's hand

【手头】① at hand; on hand: 我~还有事,不得不离开了。*I have to leave now for I have something to do on hand.* ② one's financial condition at the moment ③ writing or other abilities

【手腕】① wrist ② artifice; trick; finesse; stratagem: 耍~ *play tricks* /外交~ *diplomatic finesse*; *diplomatic skill*

【手无寸铁】bare-banded; unarmed; defenceless; without any weapon in one's hand

【手舞足蹈】dance for joy: 他高兴得有点~了。*He was so happy that he can't help dancing for joy.*

【手下】① under; under the leadership of ② at hand ③ one's financial condition: 最近他~不宽裕。*Recently he was short of money.* ④ at the hands of sb

【手相】palmistry; lines of the palm by which palmists tell one's fortune: ~术 *palmistry* /看~ *read the palm*; *practise palmistry*

【手写】write personally; write by hand; handwritten: ~体 *handwritten form*

【手心】① centre of the palm ② range of one's control

【手续】procedure; formalities: 办~ *go through formalities* / ~齐全 *all formalities gone through*

【手痒】① one's fingers itch ② have an itch to do sth

【手摇】operated by hand; motivated by hand: ~发电机 *hand generator*

【手艺】craftsmanship; workmanship; skill; trade; handicraft: ~人 *craftsman*

【手淫】masturbation; self-abuse

【手印】① thumbprint; fingerprint: 他不得不在纸上按下~。*He had to put his thumbprint on the paper.* ② impression of the hand; hand-print

【手掌】palm: ~心 *centre of the palm*

【手杖】walking stick; cane

【手纸】toilet paper; tissue

【手指】finger: ~甲 *fingernail* / ~尖 *fingertip*

【手镯】bracelet: 我结婚时,妈妈送我一对~。*My mother gave me a pair of bracelets when I married.*

【手足】① hand and foot; limbs ② brothers: 那两个小孩情同~。*The two children close like brothers.*

守 ① defend; garrison; guard; keep: 防~阵地 *hold or defend one's position* ② keep watch; look after: 留~办公室 *stay behind in the office to look after things* ③ observe; abide by; adhere: 遵~交规 *observe traffic rules* ④ next to; near; by the side of

【守财奴】miser; skinflint; tightwad

【守法】abide by the law; observe by the law; be law-abiding: 遵纪~ *observe discipline and abide by the law*

【守寡】remain a widow; live in widowhood

【守恒】【物】conservation: ~定律 *conservation law*

【守候】① wait for; await; expect ② watch over; look after: 在医院里,她~了生病的母亲一个星期。*She watched over her sick mother.*

【守护】defend; guard; protect: ~神 *guardian angel*

【守活寡】be a grass window; married woman living by herself away from her husband for a long time

【守旧】① stick to old ways; be conservative; adhere to past practices: 她那么年轻,却很~。*She is so young, but she sticks to old ways.* ② backcloth; backdrop

【守口如瓶】keep one's mouth shut; have one's lips sealed; be tight-mouthed

【守灵】stand as guards at the bier; keep vigil beside the coffin

【守门】① be on duty at the door; stand guard at the gate: ~人 *doorkeeper* / ~员 *goalkeeper* ②【体】keep goal

【守身如玉】maintain one's integrity like a piece of flawless jade; keep oneself as pure as jade-preserve one's honour; keep one's reputation as spotless as jade.

【守时】be punctual; be on time

【守岁】stay up all night on New Year's Eve

【守望】keep watch: ~台 *watchtower*

【守卫】keep safe; guard; defend: ~边疆 *defend national borders*

【守孝】observe a period of mourning for one's deceased parent
【守信】keep one's word; be trustworthy：他说话比较～。*He is reliable in his words.*
【守夜】spend the night on watch; keep watch at night
【守约】① keep a promise; stick by contract; abide by an agreement ② keep an appointment
【守则】rules; regulations：学生～ *rules and regulations for students*
【守职】stick to one's duty; be duty-conscious; stand fast at one's post; be faithful in the discharge of one's duties
【守株待兔】stand by a tree stump waiting for a hare to dash itself against it trust to chance and strokes of luck

首[1] ① head：翘～ *raise one's head and look* ② first; foremost; supreme：他们班又荣登榜～了。*Their class came out first in the list of successful candidates again.* ③ head; leader; boss; chief：罪魁祸～ *chief culprit*; *ring leader* ④ bring charges against sb：他妈妈劝服他去自～了。*His mother persuaded him to surrender oneself.* ⑤ first of ⑥（Shǒu）a surname

首[2] ［量］used for poems and songs

【首播】broadcast by TV or radio for the first time
【首创】originate; initiate; invent; pioneer
【首次】first; for the first time：他是～去大城市。*He is the first time to go to so big city.*
【首当其冲】be the first to be affected（by a disaster etc.）; bear the brunt
【首都】capital（of a country）
【首发式】ceremony celebrating the first publication of a book; inaugural ceremony for launching a publication
【首犯】arch-criminal; chief criminal; principal culprit
【首富】wealthiest family in the locality; richest person
【首功】first-class merit
【首届】first session; first：～毕业生 *first graduates of the school*
【首领】①［书］head and neck ② chieftain; leader; head
【首脑】head; leader：她父亲是一位政府～。*His father is a head of government.*
【首屈一指】be second to none; come first on the list; come out first; rank first
【首任】first to be appointed to an office
【首饰】jewellery; head ornaments：～盒 *jewellery box*
【首尾】① head and tail; first and last; beginning and end：～相连 *with head and tail linked together* ② from beginning to end; from start to finish
【首位】first place; first priority：你是个学生，必须把学习放在～。*You are a student and must put study in the first place.*
【首席】① seat of honour ② chief：～法官 *chief judge* /～执行官 *chief executive officer*（*CEO*）
【首先】① first; before all others ② in the first place; above all; fist of all
【首相】prime minister; premier
【首演】first performance; premiere
【首要】① of the first importance; primary; first：～条件 *primary condition* ② leader; chief：政府～ *government leaders*
【首映式】premiere; ceremony for the first show
【首战】first battle; first game：她告诉我们在这次考试中～告捷。*She told us that she won the first game in this examination.*
【首长】senior officer; senior official; leading cadre
【首座】seat of honour（at a banquet）② senior monk in a Buddhist sanctuary

shòu

寿 ① long life; old age; longevity：福～双全 *enjoy both fortune and longevity* ② life; age：短～ *short life* /长～ *long life* /高～ *long life*; *your venerable age* ③ birthday：祝～ *congratulate sb on one's birthday* ④（prepared before one's death）for burial ⑤（Shòu）a surname
【寿比南山，福如东海】may you live to be as old as southern mountain and may your happiness be as deep as the Eastern Sea
【寿辰】birthday（of an elderly person）：明天就是奶奶的八十～了。*Tomorrow it will be grandmother's birthday of eighty.*
【寿礼】birthday present
【寿命】life span; life; lifetime
【寿桃】① birthday peaches offered as a birthday present ② peach-shaped birthday cake
【寿险】life insurance
【寿星】① god of longevity ② elderly person whose birthday is being celebrated
【寿筵】birthday feast; birthday party
【寿衣】cerements; graveclothes; shroud
【寿终正寝】die of old age; die a natural death

受 ① accept; receive：接～礼物 *accept a gift* ② suffer; sustain; be subjected to：她因没父亲～到歧视。*She is subjected to discrimination for no father.* ③ stand; endure; bear; tolerate：我～不了它。*I can't stand it.* ④［方］pleasant; agreeable
【受不了】cannot stand; cannot bear
【受潮】get moist; become damp：又下雨了，衣服有点～。*It's raining again and clothes become damp.*
【受宠】be in one's favour; receive a favour：～若惊 *receive a favour with joy and surprise*
【受挫】be foiled; be defeated; suffer a setback
【受罚】be fined; be punished
【受粉】【植】be pollinated
【受害】be affected; be afflicted; fall victim：～者 *sufferer*

【受寒】catch a chill; catch cold
【受贿】accept bribes; take bribes
【受惠】receive benefits; benefit by: ~国 *beneficiary country*
【受惊】frightened; scared; startled
【受精】be fertilized; be inseminated: 体内~ *internal fertilization* / 体外~ *external fertilization* / ~卵 *fertilized egg*
【受看】① feel proud; be honoured ② good-looking; good to look at
【受苦】suffer; have a rough time: ~受难 *lead a life of hardships and sufferings*
【受累】(shòulěi) get involved on account of sb else; be implicated or incriminated on account of sb else: 他是个好人,不忍心别人~。*He is a kind man and can't bear to implicate others on his account.*
【受累】(shòulèi) be put to much trouble; cause inconvenience to
【受理】① accept and handle ②【律】accept and hear a case: ~案件 *accept and hear a case*
【受命】receive instructions or assignment
【受难】suffer calamities or disasters; be in distress
【受骗】be deceived; be cheated; be taken in
【受聘】① accept betrothal gifts ② accept invitation to take a job
【受气】be bullied; be made to suffer
【受穷】suffer from poverty; be poverty-stricken
【受权】be authorized; be empowered: 领导~他来处理该事故。*He was empowered to handle the accident.*
【受热】① be exposed to heat; be heated: 物体~膨胀。*When matter is heated, it expands.* ② *be affected by the heat; have heatstroke*
【受辱】be insulted; be mortified; be humiliated
【受伤】be injured; be wounded: 昨天他的腿~了。*His leg was injured yesterday.*
【受审】be on trial; be tried; stand trial
【受托】be entrusted; be charged; be commissioned: ~人 *trustee; fiduciary*
【受洗】【宗】be baptized; receive baptism
【受刑】be tortured; be put to torture
【受益】benefit from; profit by: ~人 *beneficiary*
【受用】(shòuyòng) enjoy; benefit from; profit by: ~美餐 *enjoy delicious food*
【受用】(shòuyong) feel comfortable
【受灾】be hit by a natural calamity; be disaster-stricken: ~地区 *disaster area*
【受之无愧】deserve sth; accept with a good conscience; be worthy of sth
【受之有愧】not deserve sth; be unworthy of sth
【受制】be controlled; be under control; suffer hardships: 我不想~于人。*I don't want to be under sb's control.*
【受阻】be obstructed; be hindered; be blocked; meet with obstruction
【受罪】suffer hardships; endure rough conditions; have a hard time

狩 [书] hunting(esp. in winter)
【狩猎】hunting; venery

授 ① award; confer; present; give; vest: 去年他被~予硕士学位。*He was conferred a master degree.* ② teach; tell; instruct: 函~ *teach by correspondence*
【授精】insemination: 人工~ *artificial insemination*
【授课】give lessons; give lectures: 今天上午,李教授将为我们~。*Professor Li will give lecture to us.*
【授命】① give one's life; lay down one's life ② give orders; authorize
【授权】empower; authorize; delegate power to: ~书 *letter of authorization*
【授人以柄】give sb a handle: 他太没礼貌,经常~。*He is impolite and often gives people a handle against himself.*
【授予】award; confer

售 ① sell; be on sale: 此书只零~出卖。*The books sell by retail.* ② carry out
【售后服务】after-sale service; service after sale; customer service
【售货】sell goods; vend goods: ~机 *vending machine* / ~员 *salesman; salesclerk*
【售价】selling price; price
【售卖】sell
【售票处】ticket seller; booking office; box office
【售票口】wicket; ticket window: 我们在~等他吧! *Let's wait for him at the ticket window.*
【售票员】ticket seller; booking office clerk

兽 ① beast; brute; animal: 猛~ *beast of prey* ② beastly; bestial: 衣冠禽~ *beast in human shape*
【兽行】brutal act; brutality; bestial behaviour
【兽性】brutish nature; brutality; beast in a man
【兽医】veterinary surgeon; veterinarian; vet: ~站 *veterinary station*
【兽欲】animal or bestial lust: 发泄~ *let off one's bestial lust*

瘦 ① think; slim; emaciated: 干~ *skinny; bony* / 面黄肌~ *sallow and emaciated* / 她长得很清~。*She is very thin.* ② lean: ~肉 *lean meat* ③ tight; fitting to closely ④ not fertile; poor; barren
【瘦长】long and thin; tall and thin; lanky
【瘦高挑儿】[方] tall and slender figure
【瘦骨嶙峋】all skin and bones; be thin and bony; be a bag of bones
【瘦弱】thin and weak; frail: 她长得比较~。*She looks like a little think and weak.*
【瘦小】thin and small
【瘦削】very thin; bony; gaunt; emaciated

shū

书 ① write; record: 罄竹难~ *too numerous to record* ② style of calligraphy; script: 隶~ *official script* / 楷~ *regular script* / 草~ *characters executed swiftly and with strokes flowing together* / 行~ *running hand* ③ letter ④ book: 工具~ *reference book* ⑤ document; official paper

【书包】satchel; schoolbag
【书本】back of a book; spine：他只懂得～知识。*He only knows book knowledge.*
【书呆子】bookworm; pedant
【书单】book list
【书店】bookshop; bookstore：昨天我去～买了几本书。*I went to the bookstore to buy several books.*
【书法】penmanship; calligraphy：～家 *calligrapher* / ～比赛 *calligraphy contest*
【书房】study
【书稿】manuscript; (of writings) script
【书画】painting and calligraphy：她父亲喜爱～。*Her father likes painting and calligraphy.*
【书籍】books; literature; works：他从小就喜欢看文学～。*He liked reading literary works when he was a child.*
【书记】secretary：总～ *general secretary* /团委～ *secretary of the League committee* /党委～ *secretary of the Party committee*
【书架】bookshelf; bookrack
【书卷气】bookishness; polished; cultured
【书刊】books and periodicals
【书面】written; in writing：～语 *written language*
【书目】① booklist; title catalogue ② various kinds of popular entertainment
【书皮】book cover; jacket; cover：她妈妈给她的～漂亮极了。*The book cover her mother given is so beautiful.*
【书签】① bookmark ② title label pasted on the cover of a Chinese-style thread bound book
【书商】bookseller
【书社】①［旧］book club of men of letters ② publishing house
【书生】intellectual; scholar：他看起来像个白面～。*He looks like a pale intellectual man.*
【书摊】bookstall; bookstand
【书亭】book-kiosk; bookstall
【书童】page boy; boy servant of a scholar
【书香门第】scholar-gentry family; literary family; family having a noted scholar or scholars
【书信】letter; written message; correspondence：请与我们互通～，告诉你们的情况。*Please keep up a correspondence and tell us your situation.*
【书院】［旧］academy of classical learning
【书札】［书］correspondence; letters
【书展】book exhibition; book fair：今年的～将在下个周六举行。*The book exhibition of this year will be held on next Saturday.*
【书证】written examples; written evidence (that supports facts in a case)

抒 ① convey; express：各～己见 *each airs his own views* ② relieve; alleviate
【抒发】convey; express; give voice to：她的这篇文章～了她的爱国热情。*Her article expresses the ardent patriotism of the poet.*
【抒情】express one's emotion; convey one's emotion; lyric：～诗 *lyric poetry*

枢 ① hinge; pivot：户～ *door-hinge* ② hub; centre：神经～ *nerve centre*
【枢纽】key; hub; axis; pivot：交通～ *hub of communications*

叔 ① father's younger brother; uncle：那边带眼睛的人是我四～。*The man with glasses is my uncle No. 4.* ② form of address for a man about one's father's age ③ husband's younger brother：小～子 *husband's younger brother* / ～嫂 *brother-in-law and sister-in law*
【叔伯】relationship between cousins of the same grandfather or great-grandfather
【叔父】father's younger brother; uncle
【叔叔】①［口］father's younger brother; uncle ② uncle (child's form of address for any young man one generation one's senior)

殊 ① different; divergent：他俩地位比较悬～。*The two have a little different position.* ② outstanding; special; remarkable; unusual：特～材料 *particular material* ③［书］exceedingly; extremely; really; very much ④［书］break off; cut off
【殊不知】who knows that... (contrary to what others say); little imagine; hardly expect (contrary who one oneself has thought)
【殊荣】unusual honour; special honour：获此～ *win exceptional honour*
【殊途同归】reach the same goal by different routes; all roads lead to Rome

倏 ［书］swiftly
【倏地】swiftly; suddenly：～一下到了春天。*Spring has come suddenly.*

梳 ① comb：木～ *wooden comb* ② comb sb's hair, etc.
【梳辫子】① braid one's hair; ② plait one's hair
【梳理】①【纺】carding ② comb; dress
【梳头】comb one's hair：早晨起来她先给女儿～。*Every morning she combs her daughter's hair when she gets up.*
【梳洗】wash and dress
【梳妆】dress and make up：～打扮 *make oneself up* / ～台 *dressing table*

淑 fair; graceful; pretty; pure; virtuous
【淑女】fair maiden; noble lady; virtuous woman

舒 ① relax; stretch; unfold ②［书］easy; leisurely ③ (Shū) a surname
【舒畅】relaxed; happy; entirely free from worry：他最近心情很～。*Recently he has ease of mind.*
【舒服】① pleasant; comfortable ② be well
【舒缓】① slow; unhurried; leisurely ② relaxed; gentle
【舒筋活血】【中医】relax the muscles and stimulate the blood circulation
【舒适】cosy; easy; comfortable; snug：她结婚了，过着～的生活。*She married and lived a comfortable life.*
【舒坦】comfortable; carefree：她爸爸一看到她心里就不～。*Her father feels very uncomfortable as soon as he sees her.*

【舒心】comfortable；happy；contented

【舒展】① unfold；smooth out ② limber up；stretch：～筋骨 *stretch one's limbs* ③ comfortable；at ease

疏 ① dredge（a river，etc.）② thin；sparse scattered；loose ③ distant ④ not familiar with：人地生～ *be unfamiliar with the place and the people* ⑤ negligent；careless ⑥ scanty；inadequate ⑦（Shū）a surname

【疏导】① dredge：～河流 *dredge a river* ② direct；regulate；remove obstructions；relieve：～交通 *relieve traffic congestion*

【疏忽】neglect；carelessness；oversight

【疏漏】careless omission；slip；oversight；negligence：在我的工作中有不少～。*There are a lot of oversights in my work.*

【疏浅】① crude and shallow：才学～ *of limited scholar* ②（of relationship）distant

【疏散】① sparse；scattered；dispersed ② evacuate；disperse

【疏松】① loose；puffy：土质～ *porous soil* ② loosen：～土壤 *loosen the soil*

【疏通】① dredge；remove obstacles from ② mediate between two parties

【疏远】drift apart；alienate；become estranged：我们俩吵架后，关系越来越～了。*After we quarrelled，we become more and more estranged.*

输¹ ① transport；transmit；convey：她们的苹果～往全国各地。*Their apples are carried to all over the whole country.* ②［书］make a gift；donate；contribute money

输² be beaten；lose；suffer defeat：昨天他～掉了所有的钱。*He lost all his money at gambling yesterday.*

【输出】① send out ② export：劳务～ *export of labour*；*export of services* / ～港 *port of export* ③ output；emit：～功率 *output power*

【输家】loser in a game；loser in a gamble

【输精管】【生理】seminal duct；spermatic duct；deferent duct

【输卵管】【生理】oviduct；Fallopian tube

【输尿管】【生理】ureter

【输入】① bring in ② introduce；import ③【电】computer input：～字段 *input field*

【输送】send；convey；carry；transport：～带 *conveyer belt* / 他们把鸡蛋～到大城市。*They transport eggs to big cities.*

【输血】① blood transfusion ② give aid and support；give sb a shot in the arm；shore up

【输氧】oxygen therapy

【输液】infusion

【输赢】victory or defeat；gain or loss：～不是最重要的。*Victory or defeat is not the most important.*

【输泵】fuel delivery pump

【输油管】petroleum pipeline；oil line

蔬 vegetables

【蔬菜】vegetables；greens；greenstuff

shú

秫 （Chinese）sorghum；kaoliang

【秫秸】kaoliang stalk；sorghum stalk

【秫米】husked sorghum

孰 ［书］① who；which：～是～非 *which is right and which is wrong* ② what：是可忍，～不可忍？*If this can be tolerated，what cannot?*

塾 ［旧］private school；family school：私～ *old-style private*

赎 ① redeem；ransom：～身 *redeem oneself* ② atone for（a crime）

【赎金】ransom money；ransom

【赎买】buy back；buy out；redeem：～政策 *buying out policy*

【赎刑】【律】buy freedom from punishment by law in ancient China

【赎罪】atone for one's crime：他给了她家好多钱来～。*He gave a lot of money to her family to atone for his crime.*

熟 ① ripe：一年三～ *three crops a year* ② cooked；done：饭～了，我们可以吃饭了。*The food is done；we can have a dinner.* ③ processed；wrought：～铜 *wrought copper* ④ familiar；well known；well acquainted：她看起来很～，好像在哪里见过她。*She looks like familiar and it seems that we have seen her in some place.* ⑤ skilled；practised；experienced；versed in：～手 *practised hand* ⑥ deeply；profoundly；thoroughly：我们都睡得很～，没有发觉她进屋了。*All of us slept deeply and didn't notice she had entered the room.*

【熟读】read carefully over and over again

【熟记】memorize；learn by rote；commit to memory

【熟客】frequent visitor

【熟练】skilled；expert；practised；proficient：～工 *skilled worker*

【熟路】familiar route；beaten track：熟门～ *familiar road and familiar door-things that one knows well*

【熟能生巧】practice makes perfect；skill comes from practice；the more you practise，the more you improve

【熟人】acquaintance；friend：我们都是老～了，不必客气。*We are old friends；there is no need to stand on ceremony.*

【熟石灰】slaked lime

【熟食】cooked food；prepared food

【熟视无睹】pay no attention to a familiar sight；pay no heed to；turn a blind eye to；ignore

【熟识】know well；be well acquainted；be conversant with：因为他离开这儿很长时间，所以现在已经不太～这儿的风俗习惯。*He is not familiar with the customs here because he left for a very long time.*

【熟手】old hand；practised hand

【熟睡】sleep soundly；be sound asleep；be fast asleep

【熟思】ponder deeply; mull over; consider carefully; deliberate; give serious thought to

【熟悉】know sth or sb well; be well acquainted with

【熟知】know very well; know intimately

shǔ

暑 summer heat; hot weather: 酷~ *intense heat of the summer*

【暑假】summer; summer vacation

【暑气】heat; summer heat

【暑天】hottest days of the year; dog days

【暑瘟】【中医】febrile diseases in summer, including encephalitis B, dysentery, malignant malaria, etc.

属 ① category: 金~ *metal* / 非金~ *nonmetal* ②【生】genus ③ come within one's jurisdiction: 所~单位 *subordinate units* ④ belong to; be part of: 那些水果~于我。*The fruits belong to me.* ⑤ family members; dependants: 直系亲~ *direct dependants* ⑥ be: 他所说的情况~实。*What he said proved to be true.* ⑦ be born in the year of

see also zhǔ

【属地】possession; dependency; colony

【属下】subordinates

【属相】any of the 12 symbolic animals used to denote the year of one's birth

【属性】attribute; property

【属于】belong to; be party of: 所有的这些钱都~大家。*All of the money will belong to all of us.*

署[1] ① government office; office: 海关总~ *customs head office; customs bureau* ② arrange; prepare; make arrangements for ③ act as deputy

署[2] sign; affix one's name to

【署名】sign; affix one's name to; put one's signature to: ~文章 *signed article*

【署长】head of an administrative bureau

蜀 ① another name for Sichuan Province ② name of a state in the Zhou Dynasty, located in the Chengdu area of Sichuan

【蜀汉】kingdom of Shu Han (221—263), one of the Three Kingdoms

【蜀绣】Sichuan embroidery

鼠 mouse; rat: 胆小如~ *as timid as a mouse*

【鼠标】mouse

【鼠窜】away like frightened rats; scurry away; scamper off like a rat: 狼狈~ *flee in panic like a rat*

【鼠害】damage caused by rats; a plague of rats

【鼠夹】mousetrap

【鼠疫】plague

数 ① count: 那个孩子特别聪明,能从一~到一百了。*The little child was very clever and can count from 1 to 100.* ② be reckoned as exceptionally; be particularly conspicuous by comparison ③ enumerate

see also shù; shuò

【数不胜数】countless; innumerable: 北京的名胜~。*There are so many scenic spots to be counted.*

【数不过来】countless; to many to be counted

【数不清】countless; incalculable; innumerable; too numerous to count: 听说他们家有~的钱。*It's heard that they had incalculable money.*

【数不着】not count as outstanding, important, etc.

【数得着】be counted among the best

【数九寒天】days after the Winter Solstice-Coldest days of the year

【数落】① rebuke; reprove; reproach; scold sb by enumerating his wrongdoings: 因为功课不好,昨天妈妈~了我一顿。*Yesterday my mother gave me a good scolding for my poor lessons.* ② enumerate; list; cite one example after another

【数数儿】count; reckon: 他只有两岁,却会~了。*He is only two years old, but he knows how to count.*

【数一数二】count as one of the best; rank very high; be among the very best

薯 potato; yam: 白~ *sweet potato* / 红~ *sweet potato* / 马铃~ *potato*

曙 [书] dawn; daybreak; break of day

【曙光】dawn; daylight; first light of morning

shù

术 ① art; skill; craft; technique: 不学无~ *have neither learning nor skill* ② method; tactics; trick: 我们看透了他的骗~。*We have seen through his deceitful trick.*

【术语】technical terms; terminology: 医用~ *medical terminology* / 政治~ *political terms*

戍 defend; garrison

【戍守】garrison; guard: ~边疆 *garrison the frontiers*

束 ① bind; bundle up; tie ② beam ③ control; restrain ④ [量] bundle; bunch; sheaf ⑤ (Shù) a surname

【束缚】bind up; fetter; shackle; tie; hinder: 旧制度~了经济的发展。*The old system hindered the economical development.*

【束身藏拙】hide one's inadequacy by keeping quiet

【束手】be helpless; have one's hands tied; be at one's wits' end: ~就擒 *allow oneself to be caught without putting up a fight* / ~无策 *be at a loss what to do*

【束手待毙】sit idly by waiting for destruction: 我们不能~。*We should not resign ourselves to fate.*

【束之高阁】lay aside on a high shelf

述 state; relate; narrate; recount: ~怀 *pour out one's feeling; unburden one's heart*

【述评】commentary; review: 记者~ *commentary by correspondent* / 经济~ *economic review*

【述说】state; recount, narrate
【述职】report on one's work; report
树 ① tree ② plant; cultivate:十年~木,百年~人。*It takes ten years to grow trees, but a hundred years to cultivate people.* ③ establish; set up; hold up ④ (Shù) a surname
【树碑立传】build up sb's prestige by and overdose of praise
【树杈】crotch of a tree
【树丛】grove; thicket; shrubbery
【树大招风】tall tree catches the wind — a person in a high position is liable to be attacked
【树袋熊】【动】koala
【树倒猢狲散】when the tree falls the monkeys scatter-when an influential person falls from power, his hangers-on disperse; a sinking ship is deserted by rats
【树敌】make enemy; arouse hostility
【树墩】tree stump; stump
【树干】tree trunk; trunk
【树高千丈,叶落归根】a tree may grow ten thousand feet high, but its leaves fall back to the roots-a person residing away from home eventually returns to his native soil; one who lives long in an alien and wished to return and be buried in one's hometown
【树冠】crown (of a tree)
【树胶】gum of a tree
【树立】build up; establish; set up:大家必须~战胜疾病的信心。*All of us should establish confidence to win disease.*
【树凉儿】cool shade of a tree
【树林】woods; grove
【树苗】sapling
【树木】trees generally: ~学 *dendrology* / ~栽培 *arboriculture*
【树皮】bark
【树梢】treetop; tip of a tree
【树身】tree trunk
【树叶】tree leaves
【树欲静而风不止】the tree may crave calm, but the wind will not drop-all things take their own course regardless of one's will; things will not occur as one wishes
【树枝】branch; twig
【树脂】resin:环氧~*epoxy resin*
【树种】① varieties of trees ② seeds of trees
【树桩】① stump of a tree ② dwarf tree
【树籽】seeds of trees
竖[1] ① vertical; upright; straight up; perpendicular: ~线 *vertical line* ② stand; set upright; erect ③ vertical stroke(in Chinese characters)
竖[2] [书] young servant
【竖笛】【音】recorder
【竖井】【矿】shaft
【竖立】erect; raise; stand
【竖起】hold up; stand up; erect; turn up:他高兴地~拇指表扬他的儿子。*He held up his thumb in approval for praising his son happily.*
【竖琴】【音】harp
【竖子】[书] ① lad; boy ② [贬] fellow; bloke
恕 ① forgive; pardon; excuse; allow for:请宽~我的错误。*Please forgive my false.* ② consideration for others; forbearance (as advocated by Confucius) ③ excuse me; beg your pardon: ~不奉陪 *excuse me for not keeping you company*
【恕不奉陪】excuse me for not keeping you company
【恕难从命】forgive me for not complying with your wishes
【恕罪】pardon an offence; forgive a sin
庶[1] ① multitudinous; myriad ② [书] common people; the multitude
庶[2] [旧] of or by the concubine (as distinguished from the wife)
庶[3] [书] so as to; in order to; so that
【庶民】common people; the multitude; the populace; man in the street
【庶子】son of a concubine
【庶族】(in feudal society) clan of commoners
数 ① number; figure ②【数】number:常~ *constant* /奇~ *odd number* /偶~ *even number* ③【语】number:单~ *singular number* /复~ *plural number* ④ fate; destiny ⑤ sever; a few: ~年以后,我们又相见了。*We met again a few years later.* ⑥ used before certain numerals to indicate an approximate number
see also shǔ; shuò
【数词】【语】numeral
【数额】number; a definite amount
【数据】data:预算~ *budget data* /~处理 *data processing* /~记录 *data logging*
【数控】numerical control(NC); digital control: ~设备 *numerical control equipment*
【数量】quantity; amount; volume
【数码】numeral; amount; digital: ~摄像机 *digital video camera* / ~照相机 *digital camera*
【数目】number; amount; sum
【数学】mathematics:应用~ *applied mathematics*
【数值】【数】numerical value
【数字】① numeral; figure; digit:阿拉伯~ *Arabic numerals* / ~显示 *digital display* ② numerical symbol ③ quantity; amount
墅 villa:最近他爸爸在上海买了一套别~。*His father bought a villa in Shanghai recently.*
漱 gargle; rinse(the mouth):你最好每天都洗~。*You'd better wash your face and rinse your mouth everyday.*
【漱口】gargle; rinse the mouth

shuā

刷[1] ① brush:牙~ *toothbrush* /鞋~ *shoe brush* ② scrub; clean; daub ③ expel; discharge; eliminate

刷[2] [象]swish; rustle

see also shuà

【刷洗】scrub; scour; clean:昨天他把门~完了。*He scrubbed the door yesterday.*

【刷新】renovate; refurbish; surpass

【刷牙】brush one's teeth

【刷子】brush; scrub

shuǎ

耍 ①[方] play ② juggle with; manipulate; perform: ~狮子 *perform lion dance* ③ make a show; give play to; behave: ~派头 *make a show of importance* ④ play with ⑤ (Shuǎ) a surname

【耍把戏】① give an acrobatic performance; perform juggling feats ② play tricks:没有必要给我~。*It's no use to play tricks on me.*

【耍猴儿】① put on a monkey show ② make fun of sb

【耍花招】① display showy movements in (wushu); show off one's cleverness or skill ② play tricks; get up to tricks; resort to deception

【耍赖】act in a brazen manner; act shamelessly

【耍流氓】act indecently; behave like a hoodlum; take liberties with women

【耍脾气】get into a huff; be in a fit of the sulks; be in a touchy mood; put on a show of bad temper:她经常和她丈夫~。*She often puts on a show of bad temper to her husband.*

【耍贫嘴】[方] be loquacious; be garrulous; shoot off one's mouth

【耍笑】① have fun; joke ② make fun of; pull sb's legs; play a joke on

【耍心眼儿】make use of one's petty cleverness to gain profit; exercise one's wits for personal gain; pull a smart trick:那个小孩总是跟他妈妈~。*The little child always pulls smart tricks with her mother.*

【耍嘴皮子】① talk glibly; show off one's eloquence; be a slick talker ② mere empty talk; play lip service

shuà

刷 [方] select; pick

see also shuā

【刷白】[方] white; pale; ashen:看到老师走过来,吓得她脸色~。*On seeing her teacher coming, she turned pale with fear.*

shuāi

衰 decline; wane:年老体~ *aged and frail*

【衰败】decline; wane; fall into disrepair; be at a low ebb

【衰变】【物】decay; disintegrate

【衰减】① weaken; diminish; fail; worsen ②【物】decay; attenuate

【衰竭】exhaustion; prostration:呼吸~ *prostration of breathing*

【衰老】old and feeble; aged:奶奶的身体~了。*My granny is old and feeble.*

【衰落】decline; deteriorate; go downhill

【衰弱】① frail; feeble; weak ② flag; decline in vigour

【衰退】decline; fail; physically deteriorate:最近他的体力有点~。*Recently he declined in physical strength.*

【衰亡】decline and fall; become feeble and die; become extinct

【衰谢】past bloom; thinning out; withered:公园里的花已经~了。*The flowers in the park are withered.*

摔 ① fall; tumble; lose one's balance:小孩从自行车上~了下来。*The kid tumbled off the bicycle.* ② crash; hurtle down; plunge:把瓶子猛~在墙上 *crash a bottle against the wall* ③ fall and break ④ throw; cast; hurl; fling ⑤ beat; knock

【摔打】① beat; knock; strike:把脚上的泥~掉了再进屋。*Knock the dirt and then come in.* ② temper oneself by roughing it; rough it

【摔跟头】① tumble; go head over heels; trip and fall ② come a cropper; make a blunder

【摔跤】① tumble; slip and fall ② come a cropper; fall into an error; ③【体】wrestling: ~运动员 *wrestler*

shuǎi

甩 ① swing; sway; wave; move backward and forward:他习惯~胳膊。*He is used to swing his arms.* ② throw; fling; hurl; toss:把东西~给某人 *toss things to sb* ③ leave sb behind; throw off

【甩掉】cast off; get rid of; shake off; throw off: ~包袱,继续前进。*Cast off the burden and go ahead.*

【甩卖】sell at a reduced price; markdown sale; dump:清仓大~ *clearance sale; rummage sale* / 商店正在~,我们一块去看看吧! *The goods in the shopping are selling at a reduced price; Let's go and see.*

【甩手】① swing one's arms ② refuse to do; throw up; wash one's hand

shuài

帅[1] ① commander in chief:挂~ *take command* ② (Shuài) a surname

帅[2] handsome; good-looking: 她的男朋友真~啊! *How handsome her boyfriend is.*
【帅气】handsome; elegant; graceful
【帅印】seal of a commander in chief
率[1] ① lead; command: ~师南下 *lead one's troops south* ② [书] follow; conform; comply
率[2] ① impetuous; hasty; rash ② frank; forthright; straightforward; outspoken ③ [书] generally; usually
see also lǜ
【率领】head; lead; command
【率先】be the first to do sth; take the lead in doing sth: 他~走出了教室。*He was the first to go out of classroom.*
【率真】honest and sincere; forthright and sincere
【率真】frank and straightforward

shuān

闩 door bolt; latch; beam used to bar a door: 门~ *door bolt*
拴 ① tie; bind; fasten; latch ② be bogged down
【拴绑】bind up; tie up
栓 ① bolt; plug: 消火~ *fire plug* ② rifle bolt ③ stopper; cork
【栓子】embolus

shuàn

涮 ① rinse: 把床单~一~ *rinse the sheet* ② scald thin slices of meat in boiling water ③ [方] fool; deceive; trick
【涮锅子】instant-boil slices of meat and vegetables in a chafing dish
【涮羊肉】instant boiled mutton; dip-boiled mutton slices

shuāng

双 ① two; twin; both; dual ② even: ~号 *even-numbered* ③ double; twofold: ~份 *double portion* ④ [量] pair: 一~手 *a pair of hands* ⑤ (Shuāng) a surname
【双胞胎】twins
【双边】bilateral: ~协定 *bilateral agreement* / ~贸易 *bilateral trade*
【双层】double-deck; double-layered
【双重】double; dual; twofold; both: ~标准 *double standard* / ~国籍 *dual nationality*
【双方】both sides; both parties; two parties; two sides
【双管齐下】paint a picture with two brushes at the same time-work along both lines; paint with a brush in each hand-work along two lines; do two things simultaneously
【双簧】two man comic show in which the front man does the acting while the one hiding behind him does the speaking
【双面】two-sided; double-edged; reversible
【双亲】both parents; father and mother
【双曲线】【数】hyperbola
【双全】enjoy a double blessing; possess both of two complementary qualities: 智勇~ *endowed with both wisdom and courage*
【双手】both hands
【双双】in pairs; both
【双喜】double happiness: ~临门。*Two happy events occur at the same time.*
【双向】two-way; bidirectional; bilateral: ~开关 *two-way switch* / ~选择 *two-way selection*
【双薪】double pay: 今年年底,我们会发~。*At the end of the this year, we will be got double pay.*
【双语】bilingual: ~教学 *bilingual teaching*
【双元音】【语】diphthong
【双月刊】bimonthly
霜 ① frost: 今天早晨下~了。*There was a frost in the morning.* ② frostlike powder ③ white; silver; hoar
【霜冻】frost
【霜花】① frostwork ② (soft) rime
【霜降】① Frost's Descent — the 18th of the 24 solar terms ② day marking such a seasonal division point, usu. falling on the 23rd or 24th of October ③ period lasting from such a seasonal point till the next one
【霜期】【气】frost season
【霜叶】red leaves; autumn maple leaves
孀 widow
【孀妇】[书] widow
【孀居】be a widow; live in widowhood

shuǎng

爽[1] ① bright; clear; crisp: 秋高气~ *fine clear autumn day* ② frank; straightforward; forthright ③ feel well: 人逢喜事精神~。*Morale soars in happy times.*
爽[2] make a mistake; deviate: 屡试不~ *prove effective after repeated trials*
【爽口】tasty and refreshing
【爽快】① happy; feel god; refreshed ② frank; forthright; straightforward
【爽朗】① bright and clear. ② frank and cheerful; hearty: 她们不时爆发出阵阵~的笑声。*They burst out peals of hearty laughter.*
【爽身粉】talcum powder
【爽约】[书] fail to keep an engagement; break an appointment: 你又~了。*You broke our appointment again.*
【爽直】frank; open; straightforward: 他为人~。*He is open and straightforward.*

S

shuǐ

水 ① water:一杯~ *a glass of water* ② river; water:我们家乡到处都是青山绿~。*There are green hills and clear water in our hometown.* ③ liquid ④ additional cost; extra income:油~ *extra income and benefits* ⑤ times of washing; washing of a garment ⑥ (Shuǐ) a surname

【水坝】dam

【水泵】water pump

【水表】water meter:今天李先生来查~了。*Mr. Li came to read the water meter today.*

【水兵】sailor; seaman; bluejacket

【水波】wave; ripple

【水彩】watercolour:~画 *watercolour painting* / ~纸 *watercolour paper*

【水草】① water and grass; pasture and water ② water plants

【水产】aquatic product:~业 *aquatic products industry; fishery*

【水池】pond; pool; cistern:我们家门前有一个~。*There is a pond before our door.*

【水袋】water bag

【水到渠成】where water flows, a channel is formed-when conditions are ripe, success is assured

【水稻】paddy (rice); rice

【水电】① water and electricity:~费 *charges for water and electricity* ② hydropower; hydroelectricity:~站 *hydropower station*

【水粉画】painting gouache

【水分】① moisture content:吸收~ *absorb moisture* ② exaggeration; overstatement

【水沟】ditch; drain; gutter:工人们在学校门口挖了很多~。*The workers dig many ditches at the gate of the school.*

【水垢】scale; incrustation

【水管】① water pipe ②【生理】aqueduct

【水果】fruit:小时候,我最爱吃~糖了。*I liked eating fruit drops best when I was a child.*

【水壶】① kettle ② canteen ③ watering can

【水花】① water spray; foam ②［方］water pox; chicken pox

【水火】① fire and water-two things diametrically opposed to each other; mutual contrariety:~不相容 *be absolutely irreconcilable as fire and water* ② extreme misery

【水货】smuggled good:那家商店专门经营从美国转来的~。*The shop managed in goods smuggled in America.*

【水饺】boiled dumplings

【水晶】crystal; rock crystal:~宫 *the Crystal Palace* / ~玻璃 *crystal glass*

【水井】water well; well

【水坑】puddle; pool; water hole

【水库】reservoir

【水力】waterpower; hydraulic power:~发电站 *hydroelectric station* / ~资源 *waterpower resources*

【水利】① water conservancy:最近,他们单位建造了许多~设施。*Recently, their unit built many water conservancy facilities.* ② irrigation works; water conservancy project

【水量】flow of water; volume of water

【水灵】① (of fruit, greens, etc.) fresh and juicy:你送来的水果真~啊。*The fruits you have given are very fresh and juicy.* ② (of appearance) bright and beautiful; spirited and pretty

【水流】① rivers; streams; waters ② current; flow

【水龙头】water tap; faucet; bibcock

【水陆】① land and water:~联运 *water-land transshipment* / ~交通线 *land and water communication* ② delicacies from land and sea

【水路】waterway; water route

【水落石出】when the water subsides the rocks emerge-the whole thing comes to light; the truth is fully revealed

【水面】① surface of the water ② water area; area of waters

【水墨画】painting ink and wash; wash painting:那个外国人很喜欢中国的~。*The foreigner likes Chinese ink and wash.*

【水能载舟,亦能覆舟】while the waters can bear the boat, they can also sink it — a warning to the ruler to pay attention to popular feelings

【水泥】cement:~厂 *cement plant* / ~墙 *cement wall*

【水牛】(water) buffalo

【水暖】① device of heating by radiator; hot water central heating system ② water supply and heating; general term for tap water and heating facilities

【水疱】blister

【水瓢】(gourd) water ladle

【水平】① level:~距离 *horizontal distance* ② standard; level

【水汽】moisture; steam; vapour

【水枪】① giant; water pistol ② fire-fighting device

【水渠】ditch; canal; water channel

【水溶液】【化】aqueous solution

【水乳交融】as well blended as milk and water-complete compatibility; perfect harmony

【水上】on or above water

【水深火热】deep water and scorching fire-abyss of suffering; extreme misery; dire distress

【水师】［旧］navy; waterborne forces

【水手】seaman; sailor

【水塔】water tower

【水獭】【动】otter

【水塘】pool; pond:~里的花盛开了。*The flowers in the pond are in full bloom.*

【水田】paddy field; paddy

【水桶】pail; bucket

【水土】① water and soil ② natural environment and climate:他刚来这儿,有点~不服。*He is a newcomer and unaccustomed to the climate of a new place.*

【水汪汪】① full of water; very wet; covered water ②（of children's or young women's eyes）bright and intelligent

【水位】water level; water table; groundwater level

【水系】river system; hydrographic net：黄河～ *Yellow River system*

【水下】underwater; undersea：～油井 *underwater well*

【水仙】【植】narcissus

【水线】waterline

【水乡】region of rivers and lakes

【水箱】water tank

【水泄不通】be very crowded; be packed with people; not even a drop of water could trickle through

【水性】① skill in swimming; ability in swimming：那个小姑娘精于～。*The little girl is good at swimming.* ② depth, velocity of flow and other characteristics of a river, lake, etc.

【水性杨花】（of women）fickle and lascivious; of easy virtue; of loose morals

【水锈】① scale; incrustation：他帮妈妈把～除掉了。*He helped his mother remove the scale.* ② water stain（in water vessels）

【水压】hydraulic pressure; water pressure

【水银】【化】mercury; quicksilver：～柱 *mercury column*

【水印】watermark; watercolour block printing

【水域】body water; mass water; water area

【水源】① source of a river; headwaters; waterhead ② water source

【水运】water transport：～费 *water transport fees*

【水灾】flood; inundation

【水藻】algae

【水闸】sluice; watergate：李先生的工作是负责开启～。*Mr. Li is responsible for lifting the sluice.*

【水战】battle on water; fighting on the water

【水涨船高】when the river rises the boat goes up

【水质】water quality：～监测 *water quality surveillance*

【水中捞月】fish for the moon in the water-make impractical or vain efforts

【水肿】oedema; dropsy

【水珠】drop of water

【水准】level; standard; horizontal plane

【水渍】water stain：～险 *with particular average*（*WPA*）

shuì

说 try to persuade or bring round：游～ *go around drumming up support for one's views; peddle an idea*

see also shuō

税 ① tax; duty; revenue：所得～ *income tax* / 印花～ *stamp tax* / 增值～ *value added tax*（*VAT*）

【税金】tax dues

【税款】tax payment; taxation; tax

【税率】rate of taxation; tax rate

【税目】tax items; taxable items

【税收】tax revenue：我想了解一些你们国家的～政策。*I want to know some tax policies of your country.*

【税务】taxation：～局 *tax bureau*

【税种】categories of taxes; items of taxation

睡 sleep：那个孩子正在～觉。*The little child is sleeping now.*

【睡袋】sleeping bag

【睡觉】sleep

【睡裤】pajama trousers

【睡莲】【植】water lily

【睡梦】sleep; dream; slumber

【睡眠】sleep：他的～严重不足。*He is insufficient sleep heavily.*

【睡眼惺忪】sleepy-eyed; eyes still heavy with sleep; eyes still fogged with sleep

【睡衣】night clothes; pajamas

【睡椅】reclining chair; sling chair; deck chair

【睡意】sleepiness; drowsiness

shǔn

吮 suck：他的儿子总是～手指头。*His son always sucks fingers.*

shùn

顺 ① in the same direction as; along with：今天骑车～风，我们很快来到了学校。*Riding with the wind, we came to school quickly.* ② along; follow ③ arrange; put in order; sort out ④ suitable; agreeable ⑤ in good luck; successfully：他又度过了不～的一年。*He spent an unlucky year again.* ⑥ in sequence ⑦ obey; yield to; act in submission to：百依百～ *be docile and obedient* ⑧（Shùn）a surname

【顺便】incidentally; in passing; in addition to what one is already doing, without much extra effort

【顺差】favourable balance; surplus：贸易～ *favourable balance of trade*

【顺产】【医】natural labour

【顺畅】smooth; unhindered

【顺次】in order; successively; in proper sequence：咱们根据年龄大小～进教室。*We enter the classroom one by one in order of age.*

【顺从】comply with; be obedient to; obey; submit; yield to：我不喜欢他老是～别人的意愿。*I dislike that he always complies with what other person's want.*

【顺当】smoothly; harmoniously; without a hitch：她～地通过了这次考试。*She passed the examination smoothly.*

【顺道】on the way; direct route

【顺耳】pleasing to the ear

S

【顺访】visit on the way; stop over; visit conveniently

【顺风】have a favourable wind; have a tail wind; get before the wind:一路~。*Have a pleasant journey.*

【顺服】obey; submit; be docile; yield

【顺竿儿爬】take one's cue from sb and say everything to please him; readily fall in with other people's wishes

【顺境】easy circumstances; favourable circumstances

【顺口】① read smoothly ② say offhandedly; speak casually ③［方］be palatable; suit one's taste

【顺口溜】doggerel; jingle:小孩子们经常朗诵一些~。*Children often read doggerel verse.*

【顺理成章】(of a statement, argument, etc.) logical; well reasoned; coherent

【顺利】smoothly; successfully; favourably; without a hitch

【顺势】① take advantage of an opportunity; take advantage of an opening ② conveniently; in passing

【顺手】① easily; smoothly; without difficulty; without a hitch ② conveniently; without extra trouble:你去商店时~帮我买些糖果。*Please help me buy some candies when you go shopping.* ③ handy; convenient and easy to handle ④ do sth as a natural sequence; in passing

【顺手牵羊】lead off a goat in passing-pick up sth on the sly; take sth by stealth; walk off with sth

【顺受】live with; accept sth as it is; submit to circumstances:逆来~ *meekly submit to oppression, maltreatment, etc.*

【顺水】downstream; with the current; with the stream

【顺藤摸瓜】follow the vine to get the melon-track down sb or sth by following clues

【顺心】be happy; satisfactory

【顺序】① sequence; order ② in proper order; in turn; in succession

【顺延】postpone

【顺眼】pleasing to look at; pleasing to the eye:她看起来很不~。*She looks offensive to the eye.*

【顺应】conform to; comply with; follow: ~民心 *follow the wishes of the people*

舜 Shun, name of a legendary sage monarch in ancient China

瞬 wink; twinkling

【瞬间】in the twinkling of an eye: ~功夫我们就找不到她了。*We can't find her in the twinkling of an eye.*

【瞬时】① shortly ②【物】instant; instantaneous: ~速度 *instantaneous velocity*

【瞬息万变】change rapidly; undergo a myriad of changes in an instant; fast changing; change rapidly

shuō

说 ① speak; say; talk:他能~一口流利的英语。*He can speak English smoothly.* ② give an explanation; explain:为什么不把这些~给他听呢? *Why not explain the entire thing to him?* ③ theory; doctrine; views:日心~ *heliocentric theory* ④ introduce; act as matchmaker:他媳妇是我给~的。*I introduced his wife to him.* ⑤ scold; criticise ⑥ hint; indicate; refer to
see also shuì

【说不得】① unspeakable; unmentionable; too shocking to say ② scandalous; not know how to put it ③［方］have nothing to say; have to comply with

【说不定】perhaps; maybe: ~她已经结婚了。*Maybe she has already married.*

【说不清】unable to explain clearly; cannot explain sth clearly

【说长道短】gossip; comment on other people's merits and demerits

【说唱】genre of popular entertainment consisting mainly of talking and singing such as comic dialogue, etc.

【说穿】expose; disclose

【说大话】brag; boast; talk big; blow one's own horn

【说到底】at bottom; in reality; in the final analysis; in the last analysis: ~你还是不爱我。*In the final analysis, you still didn't love me.*

【说道】① say; tell ② discuss; talk over ③［方］what lies behind sth; reason; cause

【说定】decide; settle; agree on:结婚的事就这么~了。*Our marriage is as good as settled.*

【说法】(shuō fǎ) expound Buddhist doctrine; expound Buddhist teachings

【说法】(shuō fa) ① way of saying a thing; wording; formulation:咱们换个~来解释它吧! *Let's explain it in another way.* ② statement; argument; view

【说服】persuade; convince; bring round; talk sb over; prevail on:最后我们~了他离开学校。*Finally, we persuaded him to leave the school.*

【说好】reach an agreement; come to an understanding

【说和】make peace between; mediate a settlement; compose a quarrel

【说话】① speak; talk; say:我们喜欢和那位老奶奶~。*We like to talk with the old granny.* ② chat; chit-chat ③ gossip; censure ④ in a minute; right away

【说教】①【宗】deliver a sermon; preach ② preachify

【说开】① explain:把事情给他~了,或许他就不生气了。*Maybe he is not angry any more if you explain it to him.* ② (of words, phrases, idioms, etc.) become current

【说客】① persuasive talker, person good at persuasion ② lobbyist; person often sent to win sb over or enlist his support through persuasion
【说理】① argue; reason thing out ② listen to reason; be reasonable; be sensible
【说明】① explain; illustrate：举例～ *illustrate by examples* ② explanation; directions; caption ③ prove; show
【说破】reveal; disclose; tell what sth really is
【说情】plead for mercy for sb; put in a good word for
【说三道四】make irresponsible remarks; gossip
【说啥】whatever one may say：～他也会离开这儿的。*He will leave here whatever you may say.*
【说是】it is said; they say：～公司要搬到另一个城市了。*They said the company would move to another city.*
【说书】storytelling
【说头儿】① something to talk about：这个故事还有个～呢。*There is still something to be said about this story.*
【说妥】come to an agreement
【说闲话】① gossip; complain; grumble：以后最好你不来我这里，免得别人～。*You'd better not come here so that we'll not give anyone cause for complaint.* ② chat; prattle; casually about
【说笑】talking and laughing
【说一不二】always keep one's promise; mean what one says; stand by one's word
【说着玩儿】joking; not serious in what one says

shuò

烁 bright; brilliant; shining
硕 big; large
【硕大】huge; enormous
【硕果】rich fruits; great achievements; tremendous achievements
【硕士】master：～学位 *master's degree* /文学～ *master of Arts* /理学～ *master of Science*
数 ［书］often; frequently; repeatedly
see also shǔ; shù
【数脉】【中医】rapid pulse (of more than 90 beats per minute)

sī

司 ① take charge of; operate; manage：各～其事。*Every man plays his own part.* ② department (under a ministry); official ③ (Sī) a surname
【司法】administration of justice; judicature：～部 *ministry of justice*
【司机】drive; chauffeur：他没想到他能当一名火车～。*He can't believe that he can become a engine driver.*
【司空见惯】common occurrence; common sight
【司令】commander; commanding officer
【司仪】master of ceremonies
丝 ① silk：真～*pure silk*; 100% *silk* ② one ten-thousandth of certain units of measure ③ anything threadlike ④ unit of weight ⑤ unit of length (=0.0033 millimetres)
【丝绸】silk; silk cloth：～之路 *silk Road*
【丝带】silk ribbon; silk braid; silk sash
【丝瓜】towel gourd; sponge gourd; dishcloth gourd：他妈妈在院子里种了很多～。*His mother plants lots of towel gourds in their yard.*
【丝毫】(usu. used in the negative) slightest amount or degree; at all; least bit：你所说的没有～意义。*What you said is completely meaningless.*
【丝绵】silk floss; silk wadding
【丝袜】silk stockings; silk socks
【丝绒】silk thread (for sewing) silk yarn
【丝织品】① silk fabrics ② silk knitwear
私 ① personal; private：隐～ *private matters* ② selfish：他说自己是一个大公无～的人。*He said he was a selfless man.* ③ secret; private; stealthy ④ illegal; unlawful
【私奔】elope
【私藏】① private collection; private property ② keep or possess illegally
【私产】private property; personal possession
【私仇】personal enmity; personal grudge
【私党】personal clique; personal faction
【私底下】in private; in secret
【私房】(sīfáng) private housing; private building; private residence
【私房】(sīfang) ① private savings：我私底下攒了一些～钱。*I save several private savings in secret.* ② secret; confidential
【私访】visit secretly; inspect in disguise; go incognito among the people to make investigations
【私愤】personal grudge; personal spite
【私活】moonlighting; private job：他在工作时间干了不少～。*He has done lots of private jobs during his work time.*
【私货】contraband goods; smuggled goods
【私交】personal friendship
【私立】private; privately run：～学校 *private school*
【私利】private interests; selfish interests; personal gain
【私了】settle in private; settle out of court; compound：最后那件事故～了。*At last the accident was settled in private.*
【私囊】one's own purse：中饱～ *fill one's own purse; line one's pockets; feather one's nest*
【私念】selfish motives; selfish ideas
【私情】personal friendship; personal sentiments; secret love
【私人】① private ② personal：不要计较～恩恩怨怨。*Don't care about personal friendships and enmi-*

S

ties. ③ personal friend relative
【私生活】private life
【私生子】bastard; illegitimate child; child born out of wedlock
【私事】private affairs; personal matters:上班时间不要干自己的～。*Don't do private affairs on work time.*
【私塾】old-style tutorial school
【私通】① have secret communication with; collude secretly with ② illicit intercourse; adultery
【私吞】embezzle; misappropriate
【私下】in private; in secret .
【私心】① heart; innermost being ② selfish motives; selfishness: ～杂念 *selfish ideas and personal considerations*
【私刑】illegal punishment or torture lamented out by a kangaroo court
【私营】privately run; privately operated; privately owned: ～企业 *private enterprise* / ～经济 *the private sector of the economy*
【私有】privately owned; private: ～财产 *private property* / ～观念 *private ownership mentality* / 生产资料～制 *private ownership of the means of production*
【私欲】selfish desire:为了满足自己的～,他把我们都骗了。*He cheated all of us in order to satisfy his selfish desires.*
【私章】personal seal; signet:刻～ *carve a personal seal*
【私自】privately; secretly; on the sly; without permission:为了见到妈妈,她从学校～跑了出来。*In order to see her mother, she ran out of the school without permission.*

思 ① consider; ponder; deliberate; think:深～熟虑 *give careful consideration to* ② think of; long for; miss ③ hope; desire; wish ④ train of thought; thinking ⑤ (Sī) a surname
【思潮】① trend of thought; current of thought; ideological trend:新～ *new trend of thought* ② (surging) thoughts: ～起伏 *disquieting thoughts surging in one's mind*
【思过】make an introspection into one's faults; ponder over one's mistakes; feel remorse
【思考】think deeply; ponder over; consider:让我～一下再给你答复。*Let me think it deeply and then give you a reply.*
【思恋】think fondly of ; remember of fondly; long for:爷爷年纪大的时候非常～故乡。*My grandpa thought fondly of his hometown when he was very old.*
【思量】① consider; turn sth over in one's mind ② [方] miss; thing of; long for
【思路】train of thought; line of thinking
【思念】think of; miss
【思前想后】think over again and again; mull over: 关于文章的问题,她～,还是没有定下来。*She thought over again and again on the article, and didn't decide how to choose.*
【思索】think deeply; ponder; reflect
【思维】① thought; thinking:逻辑～ *logical thinking* ② think; consider; weigh
【思贤若渴】(of a ruler) long for the assistance of wise men; be eager to enlist able people
【思乡】be homesick; miss one's hometown
【思想】① thought; thinking; ideology: ～方法 *way of thinking* / ～斗争 *ideological struggle* / ～检查 *check on one's thinking* / ～教育 *ideological education* / ～认识 *ideological understanding* / ～修养 *ideological cultivation* / ～政治工作 *ideological and political work* /端正～、工作和生活作风 *straighten out the style of one's thinking, work and life* ② idea ③ consider; think of
【思绪】① train of thought; line of thinking:整理～ *sort out one's thoughts* / 吵闹声打断了我的～。*The noise interrupted my train of thought.* ② feeling; mood

斯 ① [书] this; here:生于～,长于～ *be born and bred here* ② [书] then; thus ③ (sī) a surname
【斯德哥尔摩】Stockholm, capital of Sweden
【斯文】(sīwén) ① culture; learning: ～扫地 *learning and refinement are swept into the dust* ② learned person; scholar:他总是说自己是个～的人。*He always says he is a learned person.*
【斯文】(sīwen) refined; gentle

厮 1 ① male servant ② fellow; guy

厮 2 each other; together
【厮打】grapple; come to blows; exchange blows; tussle
【厮混】① be together; love together; fool around with sb:他俩老是～在一起。*The two men always are together.* ② mix
【厮杀】fight at close quarters; engage in hand-to-hand combat
【厮守】keep together; stay with each other

撕 tear; rend; rip
【撕毁】tear up; scrape:一怒之下,他～了他们的照片。*In his anger he tore up their photo.*
【撕票】(of kidnappers) kill a hostage
【撕破】tear; rip
【撕破脸】quarrel openly

嘶 ① (of horses) neigh ② hoarse:声～力竭 *hoarse and exhausted* ③ whistle
【嘶喊】shout; yell
【嘶叫】neigh; shriek
【嘶哑】hoarse:他说了一天话,嗓子都～了。*He talked all the day and shouted himself hoarse.*

sǐ

死 ① die; be dead; cease to live:半～不活 *half dead, half alive* ② to the death ③ adamantly; determinedly; unyieldingly ④ very; extremely ⑤ deadly; irreconcilable; ⑥ fixed; inflexible: ～工资

fixed salary ⑦ closed; impassable

【死板】rigid; inflexible; stiff; unpliant: 他是个~的人。*He is an inflexible person.*

【死不瞑目】not close one's eyes when one dies — die with a grievance or everlasting regret; not rest easy in one's grave

【死沉沉】① heavy as lead; very heavy; extremely heavy ② still as death; very quiet; silent as the grave ③ glum; sullen: 她脸上~的。*She looks glum.*

【死党】sworn followers; sworn supporter; diehard followers

【死敌】deadly enemy; implacable foe; mortal enemy

【死读书】study mechanically; read without thinking; rely on book learning rather than practical experience

【死对头】deadly enemy; deadly foe; irreconcilable opponent

【死光】① death ray ② all die

【死海】dead Sea

【死胡同】blind alley; dead end; impasse

【死缓】【律】death sentence with a two-year reprieve and forced labour; stay of execution

【死活】① life or death; fate; lot ②［口］anyway; simply

【死记硬背】learn by rote; memorize mechanically

【死角】①【军】dead angle; dead space; blind angle ② spot or corner as yet untouched by a trend, political movement, etc.

【死结】fast knot

【死里逃生】be out of the jaws of death; escape by the skin of one's teeth; have a narrow escape

【死路】blind alley; dead end; road to ruin

【死马当作活马医】doctor a dead horse as if it were still alive-make every possible effort; make a last attempt to save a hopeless situation

【死命】① death: 我们不敢相信他把他的好朋友制于~。*We can't believe that he sent his good friend to his doom.* ② desperately; recklessly

【死难】die in an accident or a political incident

【死皮赖脸】thick-skinned, utterly shameless; brazen and unreasonable

【死期】time of death; day of doom

【死气沉沉】lifeless; spiritless

【死囚】condemned prisoner; convict sentenced to death; convict awaiting execution

【死去活来】half dead, half alive; hovering between life and death; more dead than alive

【死人】① dead body; corpse ② devil; lazy-bones

【死神】god in charge of deaths-death

【死尸】corpse; dead body

【死守】① defend to the death; defend to the last: 他就这样~着教室,不肯离开。*He defended the classroom to the last, and didn't leave.*

【死水】stagnant water; standing water: 心如~ *with one's mind as settled as standing water*

【死胎】【医】stillborn foetus

【死亡】death; doom; extinction: ~率 *death rate* / ~线 *verge of death*

【死无对证】the dead cannot bear witness; dead men tell no tales; totally devoid of evidence

【死心】drop the idea forever; have no more illusions about the matter

【死心塌地】be dead set; be hell-bent; completely; with all one's heart

【死心眼】① stubborn; mulish; as obstinate as a mule: 他是一个~的孩子。*He is a stubborn child.* ② person with one-track mind

【死刑】【律】death penalty; death sentence; capital punishment

【死讯】new of sb's death: 听到妈妈的~,她禁不住大哭起来。*On hearing the news of her mother's death, she can't help crying.*

【死因】cause of death: 没有人知道他的~。*Nobody knows his cause of death.*

【死者】the dead; the deceased; the departed

【死罪】① capital offence; capital crime ② please pardon me

sì

巳 the sixth of the twelve Earthly Branches

【巳时】the period of the day from 9 a. m. to 11 a. m.

四 ① four: 教室里只有~把椅子。*There are only four chairs in the classroom.* ②（Sì）a surname

【四边形】quadrangle; quadrilateral: 平行~ *parallelogram*

【四不像】①【动】David's deer ② nondescript; neither fish nor fowl

【四处】all around; everywhere; in all directions; far and near

【四方】① four directions（north, south, east and west）; all sides; all quarters: 为了聚集资金,他奔走~。*To collect funds, he ran hither and thither.* ② square; cubic

【四分五裂】fall apart; be rent asunder; be all split up; disintegrate

【四海】four seas-whole country; whole world: ~之内皆兄弟。*All men are brothers within the four seas.*

【四害】four pests（rats, bedbugs）flies and mosquitoes

【四环素】【药】tetracycline: ~软膏 *tetracycline ointment*

【四季】four seasons: ~如春 *like spring all the year round* / ~中你最喜欢哪个季节? *Which one do you like best among four seasons?*

【四脚朝天】fall on one's back; fall backwards with one's hands and legs in the air

【四邻】one's close neighbourhood

【四面】four sides; all sides: ~八方 *all directions; all around* / 我的家乡~环山。*My hometown is surrounded by hills.*

【四面楚歌】be exposed to attack on all sides; be

utterly isolated

【四平八稳】well balanced; stable and dependable

【四书】four Books, the four mayor Confucian classics: The Great Learning《大学》, The Doctrine of the Mean《中庸》, The Analects of Confucius《论语》and Mencius《孟子》

【四维】① four basic virtues (of Confucian ethics: propriety, justice, integrity and honour ②［书］southeast, northeast, southwest and northwest ③【中医】four limbs; arms and legs ④ four dimensions: ~空间 *four dimensional space* / ~几何学 *four dimensional geometry*

【四项基本原则】four cardinal principles, adherence to the socialist road, the people's democratic dictatorship, the leadership of the communist party, and Marxism-Leninism and Mao Zedong Thought)

【四月】① April: ~末,我要出差去北京。*I will be on business to Beijing at the end of April.* ② fourth month of the lunar year

【四肢】four limbs; arms and legs: 他~健全,却什么也不会干。*He is sound in body, but cannot do anything.*

【四周】all around; all sides

【四座】all the people present: 语惊~ *words that startle all present*

寺 temple: 你去过少林~吗? *Have you gone the Shaolin Temple?*

【寺庙】temple

似 ① similar; look like; approximate ② look; seem; appear ③ indicating superiority

see also shì

【似曾相识】seen to be familiar; seem to have met before

【似乎】as if; it seems that; seemingly: 看起来她~是对的。*It looks as if he is right.*

【似是而非】apparently right but actually wrong; apparently true but actually false; specious; plausible

【似水流年】time passes as swiftly as flowing water; youth will not endure

伺 keep watch; await; observe

see also cì

【伺机】watch for one's chance

饲 ① raise; breed; bear ② forage; fodder; feed

【饲草】forage grass

【饲料】forage; feed; fodder: ~加工厂 *plant-processing plant* / ~作物 *forage crop*

【饲养】raise; rear

驷 team of four horses; horse

肆[1] wanton: 大~挥霍 *wantonly squander*

肆[2] four (used for the numeral 四 on cheques, etc. to avoid mistakes or alternations)

肆[3] shop

【肆口】talk without restraint (in scolding, abusing, etc.): ~大骂 *let loose a torrent of abuse*

【肆虐】indulge in wanton massacre; wreak havoc

【肆无忌惮】reckless and unbridled; unscrupulous

【肆行】wanton; unbridled

【肆意】wantonly; recklessly; willfully: ~破坏他国领土完整 *wantonly encroach upon the territorial integrity of another country*

嗣 ① succeed; inherit ② heir; descendant

【嗣位】succeed to the throne

sōng

松[1] ① pine ②(Sōng) a surname

松[2] ① not firm; loose; slack ② loosen; relax; relieve: ~了一口气 *heave a sigh of relief* ③ not hard up; well off ④ soft; light and flaky; fluffy: ~~的土质 *soft sand* ⑤ untie; unfasten; release ⑥ dried meat floss, dried minced meat

【松绑】① untie a person: 给你弟弟~。*Please untie your young brother.* ② relax restrictions

【松弛】① limp; slack; loose ② lax; not strict

【松动】① become less crowded ② not hard up ③ become loose; become flexible

【松劲】relax one's efforts; loosen up; slacken off: 考试前不要~。*Don't relax efforts before examination.*

【松口】① relax one's bite and release what is held; let go the bite ② be less unyielding; be less intransigent; soften; relent

【松快】① at ease; feel relieved: 考试完他心情~极了。*He has ease of mind after examination.* ② less crowded ③ relax: 太累了,我们一块~一下吧! *It's too tired; Let's relax ourselves together.*

【松气】relax one's efforts; slacken

【松软】① soft; loose; spongy: ~的棉花 *spongy cotton* ② weak; feeble: 下班后他感觉身体~极了。*He felt feeble after work.*

【松散】(sōngsǎn) ① loose; nor firm or compact ② inattentive; wandering

【松散】(sōngsan) relax; ease up

【松手】loosen one's grip; hold less tight; let go

【松鼠】squirrel

【松树】pine tree; pine

【松松垮垮】① not solid or compact ② lax and undisciplined; slack and perfunctory

【松闲】idle; not busy; unoccupied: 最近他挺~的。*He is not busy recently.*

【松懈】① lax; slack: 千万不要学习~。*Don't be laxity in your study.* ② weak-willed; undisciplined: 戒备~ *lax security* ③ uncoordinated; cool and indifferent

【松脂】rosin; pine gum

【松子】① pine nut ②［方］pine nut kernels

sóng

㞞 ① seminal fluid; semen ② weak and incompetent; good-for-nothing

【㞞包】good-for-nothing：你真是这么～。*You are really good-for-nothing.*

sǒng

怂 ［书］frightened; alarmed and panicky

【怂恿】abet; incite; instigate：他～我放弃这次机会。*He instigated me to give up the chance.*

耸 ① towering; high; lofty：高～入云 *tower into the clouds* ② alarm; attract

【耸肩】shrug one's shoulders

【耸立】tower aloft; rise high

【耸人听闻】deliberately exaggerate so as to create a sensation

【耸听】blow things up so as to create a sensation：危言～ *startling statement creates a sensation*

悚 ［书］terrified; horrified

【悚然】terrified; horrified; terror-stricken

sòng

讼 ① bring a case to court：诉～ *lawsuit* ② dispute; argue

【讼案】case in court; lawsuit

【讼事】lawsuit; litigation

宋 ① the song Dynasty（960—1279）②（Sòng）a surname

【宋词】poetry of the Song Dynasty：他小时候就能背诵好多～了。*He could recite many poetries of the Song Dynasty when he was a little child.*

送 ① carry; deliver; send：把书给我～过来吧！*Please send the book to me.* ② give as a present; offer ③ see sb off or out; accompany

【送别】see sb off：昨天他在机场～了好朋友。*He saw his good friend off at airport.*

【送还】give back; return; send back

【送货】deliver goods：～上门 *deliver goods to the doorstep of a customer*

【送客】give a visitor out

【送礼】give presents; present a gift to sb; send gifts：为了通过这次考试，他给老师～了。*He gave presents to his teacher in order to pass the examination.*

【送命】lose one's life; get killed; go to one's doom; die

【送亲】escort the bride to the bridegroom's home or the wedding party

【送人情】① deliberately do sb a good turn to curry one's favour; do favours at no great cost to oneself ② make a gift of sth

【送丧】attend a funeral; take part in a funeral procession

【送上门】deliver sth to the doorsteps

【送信儿】［口］send word; go and tell; convey a message

【送行】① see sb off; bid sb farewell; wish sb bon voyage：你离开北京时我一定给你～。*I must see you off when you leave Beijing.* ② give a send-off party

【送终】attend upon a dying parent or other senior member of one's family; arrange for the burial of a deceased parent or elder relative：养老～ *provide for and attend upon the old*

诵 ① read aloud; chant; declaim：吟～ *recite; chant* ② recite：朗～诗歌 *recite poems* ③ state; narrate

【诵读】read aloud; chant：请再～一遍课文。*Please read aloud the text again.*

颂 ① praise; extol; acclaim; laud：歌～ *sing the praises of* ② express good wishes ③ one of the three sections in paean; eulogy

【颂歌】song; paean; song

【颂扬】eulogize; extol; laud

sōu

搜 ① look for; collect; gather：～集邮票 *collect stamps* ② search：～查房间 *search the room*

【搜捕】track down and arrest; search and arrest

【搜查】search; ransack; rummage：～证 *search warrant*

【搜肠刮肚】think very hard; rack one's brains; cudgel one's brains

【搜刮】extort; forcibly seize; rob

【搜集】collect; gather; solicit; hunt high and low for

【搜救】search-and rescue

【搜身】search the person; make a body search; search by passing the hands over the body

【搜索】search for; hunt for; scout around：他们正在～那个失踪的孩子。*They are searching for the losing child.*

【搜寻】seek; search for; look for

嗖 ［象］whiz

馊 sour; spoiled：饭～了。*The food has spoiled.*

【馊主意】rotten idea; lousy idea：谁想出来的～？*Who thought out the rotten idea?*

艘 ［量］of ships：三～船 *three ships*

sǒu

叟 old man：童～无欺 *not cheating even children and old people*

sòu

嗽 cough:干~ *dry cough*

sū

苏[1] 【植】perilla; beefsteak plant

苏[2] threads hanging down:流~ *tassel*

苏[3] come to; become conscious; revive

苏[4] ① soviet ② short for Soviet Union of USSR (1922-1991)

苏[5] ① short for Suzhou ② short for Jiangsu Province ③ (Sū) a surname

【苏打】soda: ~饼干 *soda biscuit*

【苏丹】① sultan ② the Sudan: ~人 *Sudanese* / ~语 *Sudanic*

【苏格兰】Scotland

【苏醒】revive; come to; come round; regain consciousness:她~后禁不住哭了。*She cried after she regained consciousness.*

酥 ① crisp; fluffy; crunchy: ~糖 *crunchy candy* ② shortbread; shortcake: 牛角~ *horn-shaped shortcake* / 芝麻~ *sesame shortbread* / 杏仁~ *almond shortbread* ③ limp; frail; weak

【酥脆】crisp

【酥麻】limp and numb; weak:全身~ *feel weak all over*

【酥软】limp; soft; weak

【酥松】loose; porous

【酥胸】soft and fair-skinned breasts of a woman

【酥油】butter: ~茶 *buttered tea*

sú

俗 ① custom; convention; practice:民~ *folk custom* ② common; popular ③ boorish vulgar ④ lay

【俗不可耐】unbearably vulgar; hopelessly boorish

【俗话】common saying; popular saying; proverb

【俗气】vulgar; inelegant; in poor taste:她看起来有点~。*She looks a little vulgar.*

【俗人】① layman (as distinguished from a clergyman) ② vagaries; vulgar person; philistine:我就是~一个。*I am a vulgar person.*

【俗套】conventional etiquette; convention; stereotype:不落~ *conform to no conventional pattern*

【俗务】chores; routine business; everyday matters

【俗物】unrefined person or thing; vulgar person; vulgarian

【俗语】common saying; folk adage

sù

夙 [书] ① early in the morning ② old; long-standing: ~仇 *enemy of long standing*

【夙愿】long-cherish wish:告诉我们你的~吧! *Please tell us your long-cherish wish.*

诉 ① tell; relate; narrate; inform:陈~理由 *narrate a reason* ② complain; speak out who is on one's mind:倾~ *pour to (one's worries; grievances, etc.)* ③ accuse; sue:控~书 *written accusation* /起~ *sue; prosecute*

【诉苦】complain; vent one's grievances; pour out one's woes:我没有其他朋友,只有向你~了。*I have no other friends and have to vent my grievances to you.*

【诉说】tell; recount; give an account of:她含着眼泪向我们~了事故的经过。*She gave an account of how the accident happed with tears.*

【诉讼】【律】lawsuit; accusation; litigation:民事~ *civil lawsuit* /刑事~ *criminal lawsuit*

【诉状】【律】plaint; indictment; petition:他代爷爷写了~。*He wrote out the plaint for his grandfather.*

肃 ① respect; esteem: ~然 *respectful* ② solemn; sombre ③ eliminate; eradicate; clean up: ~反 *elimination of counter revolutionaries*

【肃静】solemn silence

【肃立】stand as a mark of respect; rise respectfully

【肃穆】① solemn and quiet; grave ② respectful and genial:他神情看上去庄重~。*He looks respectful and genial.*

【肃清】eliminate; clean up; root out:我们一定能~敌人所有的据点。*We surely can clean up all the enemy strongholds.*

【肃然起敬】be filled with deep veneration; be held in profound respect

素 ① white; unbleached and undyed: ~服 *white clothing* ② plain; simple; quiet: ~色的花 *plain flowers* ③ vegetable:四荤二~ *four meat dishes and two vegetable dishes* ④ native: ~性 *one's natural instincts* ⑤ basic element ⑥ usually; always; habitually

【素不相识】not be acquainted with each other; do not know at all; have never met

【素材】source material of art and literature:为了写小说,他去乡下收集~了。*In order to write novels, he went to countryside for collecting source materials.*

【素菜】vegetable dish

【素餐】① vegetarian meal ② be a vegetarian ③ [书] eat the bread of idleness; get one's pay without doing any work

【素淡】plain; quiet

【素服】plain white clothes

【素净】plain and neat; quiet:她买了一套~的衣服。*She bought a plain clothes.*

【素昧平生】have never met before; have never made sb's acquaintance

【素描】① sketch ② literary sketch

【素食】① vegetarian diet: 他喜欢吃～。*He likes eating vegetarian diets.* ② be a vegetarian: ～者 *a vegetarian*
【素雅】simple but elegant; plain and in good taste
【素养】accomplishment; attainment; qualities: 文学～ *literary attainments* /艺术～ *artistic accomplishment*
【素质】① quality; character: ～教育 *quality-oriented education* ②【心】diathesis
速[1] ① fast; rapid; quick: ～胜 *quick victory* ② speed; tempo: 全～ *full speed*
速[2] [书] invite: 不～之客 *uninvited guest*
【速成】achieve by quick methods; attain a goal in a much shorter time than usual; gain a quick mastery of a course or subject: ～班 *accelerated course*
【速冻】quick-freeze: ～食品 *quick-frozen food*
【速递】deliver directly and rapidly; send out by express mail: ～公司 *express mail company*
【速度】①【物】speed; velocity: 初～ *initial velocity* /加～ *acceleration* /匀～ *uniform velocity* ②【音】tempo ③ rate; pace; tempo; speed
【速记】shorthand; stenography: ～打字机 *stenograph* / ～员 *stenographer*
【速率】speed; rate
【速溶】instant: 她喜欢喝～咖啡。*She likes drinking instant coffee.*
【速胜】quick victory
【速效】quick results; quick acting: ～药 *medicine that produces quick results; quick-acting medicine*
【速写】① sketch; rough, quickly made drawing ② written sketch
宿[1] ① stay overnight; put up for the night: 留～ *put up a guest for the night* ② (Sù) a surname
宿[2] long-standing; old ③
see also xiǔ; xiù
【宿仇】long-standing enmity; old grievance; feud
【宿将】veteran general: 他爷爷是一位久经沙场的～。*His grandfather was a battle-tested veteran general.*
【宿命论】【哲】fatalism
【宿舍】dormitory; hostel; living quarters: 两年前她在单身～住。*She was in living quarters for unmarried staff two years ago.*
【宿营】camp; pitch a tent; take up quarters
【宿怨】old grudge; old score
【宿愿】long cherished wish
【宿主】host
粟 ① foxtail millet; millet ② (Sù) a surname
【粟米】[方] maize; corn
塑 ① model; mould; sculpture: 雕～ *carve and mould* ② plastic
【塑封】plastic-coated: ～文件夹 *plastic-coated documents folder*
【塑料】plastic: ～薄膜 *plastic film* / ～雨衣 *plastic raincoat* / ～袋 *plastic bag*
【塑像】statue: 在学校门口有座英雄的～。*There is a statue of a hero at the gate of school.*
【塑性】【物】plasticity: ～化 *plastification* / ～指数 *plasticity index*
【塑造】① model; mould ② create; portray
溯 ① go up the stream ② track back; recollect; recall
【溯源】trace to the source
簌
【簌簌】① rustle: 风铃随风～而响。*The wind bells are rustling in the wind.* ② streaming down

suān

酸[1] ①【化】acid: 盐～ *hydrochloric acid* /硝～ *nitric acid* ② sour; vinegary ③ sick at heart; feel sad; grieved ④ miserable; of impoverished pedantic scholars in the old days
酸[2] ache; prickling sensation: 腰～背疼 *have a backache; have a pain in the back*
【酸菜】pickled vegetables; Chinese cabbage; Chinese sauerkraut
【酸楚】grieved; painful; distressed: 没有通过这次考试，他心里感到有点～。*He felt a little grieved because he didn't pass the examination.*
【酸碱度】pH value
【酸苦】grieved; bitter; miserable
【酸辣酱】chutney, an Indian condiment made of fruits or vegetables, vinegar, spices, sugar, etc.
【酸辣汤】vinegar-pepper soup; hot and sour soup
【酸溜溜】① sour taste; sour smell ② aching ③ sad; mournful ④ pedantic; priggish
【酸梅】smoked plum: ～汤 *sweet-sour plum juice*
【酸奶】yogurt; sour milk
【酸涩】① sour and puckery ② fell sore in the eyes; sad; grieved
【酸甜苦辣】sour, sweet, bitter, hot-joys and sorrow of life; vicissitudes of life
【酸痛】ache: 回来以后，他感觉浑身～。*After coming back, he felt ache all over.*
【酸味】tart flavour; acidity
【酸性】acidity; acidness: ～反应 *acid reaction*
【酸雨】acid rain; acid precipitation
【酸枣】wild jujube: ～树 *wild jujube tree*
【酸值】【化】acid value; acid number

suàn

蒜 ① garlic: 一头～ *a head of garlic* /糖～ *garlic in syrup* ② bulb of this plant
【蒜瓣儿】garlic clove
【蒜黄】blanched garlic leaves
【蒜苗】garlic pedicel; garlic shoot
【蒜泥】mashed garlic
【蒜头】head of garlic; bulb of garlic
算 ① calculate; estimate; reckon: 计～生产成本 *reckon the cost of production* ② count; include; figure in: 运费～在账内。*The freight is in-*

S

cluded in the account. ③ plan; calculate; figure:打～明天出发。*We're planning to start tomorrow.* ④ think; guess; suppose:猜～某事 *make a guess at sth* ⑤ regard as; take for:今天不～太冷。*I don't think it is too cold today.* ⑥ carry weight; be effective:那可不～数。*That doesn't count.* ⑦ let it be; come ⑧ due to; in the end

【算法】【数】algorithm; way of calculation:谁能想出这道题的简便～? *Who can think out simple calculation of this problem?*

【算卦】practise divination; tell sb fortune or divine by using the Eight Trigrams

【算计】① calculate; figure; reckon ② consider; plan; think ③ estimate ④ scheme; intrigue; plot:别老想着～别人。*Don't always think to plot against others.*

【算旧账】settle an old account or score

【算命】fortune-telling: ～先生 *fortune-teller*

【算盘】① abacus:打～ *use an abacus* ② design; scheme

【算式】mathematical formula or equation

【算是】at last:我～见到你了。*At last I saw you.*

【算术】arithmetic: ～平均值 *arithmetic mean*

【算数】count; hold; stand; carry weight

【算账】① do accounts; work out accounts; balance the books; make out bills ② square a accounts with sb; get even with

suī

尿 urine

see also niào

虽 though; although; even if; even though

【虽然】though; although:他～很富裕,但是很少花钱。*Although he is very rich, he costs few money.*

【虽说】though; although: ～你是她姐姐,但也不该打她。*You cannot beat her, though you are her elder sister.*

【虽死犹生】live on in spirit; still live in the hearts of the people though dead

suí

绥 ① peaceful ② pacify; bring peace to

【绥靖】pacify; appease: ～政策 *appeasement policy*

隋 ① (sui) dynasty(58-618) ② (Suí) a surname

随 ① follow:紧～ *follow closely* /尾～ *follow at sb's heels; tail behind* ② come along with; adapt to; comply with ③ let (sb do as he likes): ～你怎样选择,我都会为你祝福。*No matter what you choose, I will bless you.* ④ along with ⑤ [方] look like; be similar, resemble

【随笔】① informal essay; familiar essay ② jottings; short notes

【随便】① at one's pleasure; at one's convenience; at one's discretion ② casual; random; informal; free:爸爸让我～谈谈我的想法。*My father lets me make some random thoughts.* ③ at will; at random; without consideration ④ any; anyhow; no matter

【随波逐流】go with the stream; drift with the tide or current

【随处】everywhere; anywhere:不能把它～乱扔。*Don't throw it away anywhere.*

【随从】① accompany or follow (one's superior); go along with; attend ② entourage; suite; retinue

【随大流】drift with the st ream; follow the herd

【随地】anywhere; everywhere; all over the places

【随访】① accompany (one's superior) on a visit: ～人员 *accompanying person* ② follow up a case by regular visits to or correspondence with a patient

【随和】amiable; obliging; easygoing

【随后】soon after; soon afterwards; right away:你们先走吧!我们～就到。*You go first; we will be there right away.*

【随机应变】be resourceful; act according to circumstances; do as the changing circumstances demand; suit one's actions to changing conditions

【随军】follow the army; go along with an army: ～家属 *camp family; families of officers accompanying the army*

【随口】speak thoughtlessly; speak casually; blurt out

【随身】carry on one's person; take with one

【随时】① at any time; at all times; whenever:无论碰到什么事情,～来找我。*Come to me whatever you meet.* ② whenever necessary

【随手】conveniently; immediately; without extra trouble:请～关灯。*Please turn the light off.*

【随俗】comply with convention; do as everybody else does:入乡～。*When in Rome, do as the Romans do.*

【随同】accompany; be accompanying; go with

【随心】① follow one's inclinations; have one's own way ② find sth satisfactory

【随行】① accompany sb on a trip ② suite; entourage; retinue

【随意】at will; as one please ; freely:在我家里请～。*Make yourselves at your own home.*

【随遇而安】fell at home wherever one is; take the world as one finds it; be able to adapt oneself to different circumstances

【随员】① staff members of a delegation; entourage ② diplomacy attache: ～领事 *diplomacy attache consul*

【随葬】be buried with the de ad: ～品 *funerary objects; burial articles*

【随着】following; along with; in pace with: ～时间的推移,我们越来越喜欢他。*At time going on, we like him more and more.*

suǐ

髓 marrow

【髓细胞】【医】myelocyte

suì

岁 ① year: ~岁 *the end of a year* ②［量］year: 你知道那个小姑娘几~了吗? *Do you know how old the little girl is?* ③ age: 虚~ *nominal age* / 足~ *real age* ④［书］the ⑤［书］year's harvest

【岁出】state expenditure in a fiscal year

【岁初】beginning of the year

【岁数】age; years: 照顾好您自己, 你已经是上了~的人了。*Take care of yourself; you are getting in years.*

【岁月】years; time: ~无情。*Time is inexorable.* / ~不等人。*Time and tide wait for no man.*

祟 ① evil spirit; ghost ② haunt and plague; act like an evil spirit: 作~ *exercise an evil influence on*

遂 ① gratify; fulfil; satisfy ② succeed: 未~ *fail to materialize*

【遂心】after one's own heart; to one's liking: ~所欲 *do as one likes*

【遂意】to one's liking; as one wishes

【遂愿】achieve what one wishes; have one's with fulfilled

碎 ① break to pieces: 那些盘子被打~了。*The plates were smashed to pieces.* ② break; broken; fragmentary; scattered

【碎布】cloth waste; macerated fabric

【碎花】fine and dense flower pattern: ~布 *cotton print in a fine and dense flower pattern*

【碎尸万段】cut up sb's body to thousands of pieces

【碎石】【建】crushed stone; broken stones: ~路 *broken stone road*

隧 ［书］tunnel

【隧道】tunnel: 海底~ *seabed tunnel*

穗 ① ear of grain; spike: 谷~ *ear of cereal* / 麦~ *ear of wheat* ② tassel ③（Suì）a surname

【穗状花序】【植】spike

【穗子】① ear of grain ② tassel; fringe

sūn

孙 ① grandson; son's son ② generations below that of the grandchild: 玄~ *great-grandson* ③ relative belonging to grandchild's generation: 我是他的外~。*I'm his grandson.* ④ second growth of plants ⑤（Sūn）a surname

【孙女】granddaughter: ~婿 *granddaughter's husband; grandson-in-law*

【孙媳妇】grandson's wife; granddaughter-in-law

【孙子】grandson: 听说他的~病得很重。*It's heard that his grandson was ill heavily.*

sǔn

损 ① lose; decrease; diminish: 遭受重大~失 *suffer heavy losses* ② harm; injure; damage: ~毁 *destroy; damage* ③［方］mean; shabby; vicious ④ biting; caustic: ~某人 *hurt sb with mean words; ridicule*

【损害】harm; injury; damage; impair: ~健康 *impair one's health*

【损耗】① consumption; loss; wear and tear ②【经】wastage; spoilage

【损坏】damage; destroy; break: 昨天他不小心~了计算机。*He damaged the computer with careless yesterday.*

【损人利己】harm others to benefit oneself; benefit oneself at the expense of others

【损伤】① harm; damage; injure ② loss

【损失】lose: 为了找回那些失去的孩子, 他们~了大量的人力和物力。*In order to find the losing child, they lost lot of materials and human resources.*

【损益】① increase and decrease ② profit and loss; gains and losses: ~表 *profit and loss account*

笋 bamboo shoot

【笋瓜】【植】winter squash

【笋尖】tender tips of bamboo shoots

suō

唆 abet; instigate

【唆弄】incite; instigate: ~是非 *sow discord*

【唆使】instigate; abet

梭 shuttle

【梭子】① weaver's shuttle ② cartridge clip ③［量］(of ammunition) clip: 请给我一~。*Please fire a whole clip at me.*

蓑 alpine rush or palm bark rain cape

【蓑衣】alpine rush or palm bark rain cape

缩 ① become smaller; contract; shrink: 热胀冷~ *expand with heat and contract with cold* ② draw back; recoil; withdraw

【缩编】reduce the staff; cut down the staff

【缩脖子】pull in one's neck; shrink back; draw back one's neck-draw back

【缩尺】reduced scale; scale: ~图 *scale drawing*

【缩短】shorten; cut down; cut short; reduce: ~距离 *reduce the distance*

【缩减】reduce; retrench; cut: ~开支 *cut back on*

spending
【缩略语】abbreviation; abbreviated expression
【缩手缩脚】① shrink with cold ② be over cautious; timid
【缩水】(of cloth through wetting) shrink
【缩头缩脑】① shrink from responsibility; recoil; flinch ② be timid; be fainthearted
【缩小】reduce; lessen; shrink; narrow:你必须努力学才能～我们之间的差距。*You must study hard to narrow the gap between us.*
【缩写】① abbreviation ② abridge: ～本 *abridged version*
【缩印】reprint books in a reduced format: ～机 *reduction printer*
【缩影】epitome; miniature
【缩语】abbreviation; abbreviated expression

suǒ

所 ① place:住～ *dwelling place* ② used as a name of an institution or other organization ③ [量] of house, school, buildings, etc.:三～学校 *three schools* ④ used together with 为 or 被, to indicate passive construction ⑤ (Suǒ) a surname
【所得】income; earnings; gains: ～税 *income tax*
【所属】① what is subordinate to one or under one's command ② what one belongs to or is affiliated with
【所谓】① what is called; what is known as ② so-called
【所向披靡】(of troops) carry all before one; be irresistible
【所以】① so; therefore; the reason ② used in set phrases as an object ③ that's why ④ [口] that's just the reason; that's just the point
【所以然】the whys and wherefores; the reason why:知其然而不知～ *know the how but not the why; know what is done but not why it is done*
【所有】① own; belong to: ～权 *ownership* /这家家具属于我～。*The furniture belongs to me.* ② possessions:那位老人倾其～来资助她上学。*The old man gave everything in his possession to help her study.*
【所有制】system of ownership; ownership; proprietary rights:生产资料～ *the system of ownership of the means of production*
【所在】① place; location; site ② where:这就是我们来这儿的原因～。*That's the reason why we come here.*
【所长】head of an office, institute, etc.
【所致】the caused by; be the result of
【所作所为】one's behaviour; one's conduct; what one had done:我一点都不喜欢她的～。*I didn't like her usually behaviour at all.*

索[1] ① large rope; large chain:铁～桥 *chain bridge* ② (Suǒ) a surname

索[2] ① look for; search:村民们还在搜～那个失踪的小孩。*The villagers are still searching for the losing child.* ② ask; demand: ～价 *ask a price*

索[3] all along; all by oneself; solitary; dull
【索道】cableway; ropeway:我们坐～登上了泰山。*We reached Mountain Tai By the cableway.*
【索贿】extort bribes
【索马里】Somalia: ～人 *Somali* / ～语 *Somali*
【索赔】claim damages; claim an indemnity: ～人 *claimant* / ～条款 *claim clause* / ～通知 *notice of claim* / ～委员会 *claims board*
【索求】demand; claim; seek:你～的太多了。*You ask for too much.*
【索取】ask for; exact; extort; demand: ～报酬 *ask for payment*
【索然】insipid; uninterested; dull; depressed in low spirit: ～寡味 *flat and insipid; dull and dry*
【索性】just; may as well; simply
【索要】ask for; claim; demand
【索引】index:目录～ *catalogue index* /笔画～ *index of strokes of Chinese characters*

唢
【唢呐】suona horn, a woodwind instrument

琐 ① trivial; insignificant; petty:繁～ *loaded down with trivia details* ② humble; lowly
【琐事】trifles; trivial matters
【琐碎】trifling; trivial:他不愿处理这些～的事情。*He didn't want to deal with these trivialities.*
【琐细】trifling; trivial
【琐杂】petty and involved; trifling; trivial

锁 ① lock:门～ *door lock* ② lock up: ～上自行车他就进屋了。*He entered the room after locking the bicycle.* ③ sth which resembles a lock ④ chains:枷～ *chains; yoke* ⑤ lockstitch: ～花边 *lockstitch a lace*
【锁匙】[方] key
【锁定】locking
【锁骨】【生理】clavicle; collarbone
【锁国】close the country to the outside world:闭关～ *close the country to international intercourse*
【锁匠】locksmith:年轻时他是个～。*He was a locksmith when he was young.*
【锁紧】locking
【锁链】① chain ② shackles; fetters; yoke:思想～ *the yoke of one's mind*
【锁眼】lock hole

T

tā

他 ① he or him; male person mentioned earlier or being observed now: ～俩 *the two of them* /瞧啊! ～在爬栅栏。*Look! He is climbing the fence.* /我比～高。*I am taller than him.* ② (male or female) person: 每个人都有～自己的特长。*Everyone has his or her own special skill.* ③ be a meaningless mock object: 亲～一口 *have a kiss* /咱们喝～几杯去。*Let's go and have a few drinks.* ④ [书] other; another; some other: 别无～求 *have no other demand* /留作～用 *reserve for other uses* /此人已～调。*The person has been transferred to another unit.* ⑤ express emphasis

【他动词】【语】transitive verb

【他妈的】damn; fucking; hell; shit; blast it: ～! 我的钢笔丢了。*Damn! I'm lost my pen.* /去～。*To hell with it.* / ～! 我没赶上火车。*Shit! I've missed the train.*

【他们】they or them; people mentioned earlier or being observed now: ～仨 *the three of them* / ～自己 *themselves* / ～的 *their* / ～单位 *their unit*

【他人】another person; other people; others: ～暗中相助 *secret help from others*

【他日】[书] some other time or day; some day; later on: 以备～之用 *set aside for future use* / ～再来看望。*I'll meet you again later on.*

【他杀】【律】homicide

【他山之石可以攻玉】a stone from other hills may serve to polish the jade of this one — advice from others may help one overcome one's shortcomings

【他乡】a place far away from home; an alien land; a strange land: ～遇故知 *run into an old friend in a distant land* / ～做客 *live in a strange land* /久在异国～ *live long in an alien land*

它 it; animal or thing mentioned earlier or being observed now: ～的 *its* / ～自己 *itself* /这杯水你喝了～。*Drink up this glass of water.* /詹妮捡起桌上的书,把～放回书架上。*Jenny picked up the book from the table and put it back on the shelf.*

【它们】they or them; plural of animal or thing: ～的 *their* / ～自己 *their selves*

她 she or her; female person mentioned earlier or being observed now: ～的 *her* / ～自己 *herself* /我姐姐个子很高, ～能够得到那个最高的架子。*My sister's very tall and can reach the top shelf.*

【她们】they or them; female person plural: ～的 *their* / ～自己 *themselves*

趿

【趿拉】wear shoes with the backs turned in; wear shoes as slippers: 别～着鞋走路。*Don't use your shoes as slippers.* /父亲～着鞋散步去了。*Father went for a walk with the backs of his shoes turned in.*

【趿拉板儿】[方] wooden slippers; clogs

【趿拉儿】[方] slippers: 皮～ *leather slippers* /草～ *straw slippers*

塌 ① collapse; cave in; crumble down; fall down: 楼梯突然倒～。*The staircase suddenly collapsed.* /发洪水的时候～了几座桥。*Several bridges fell down during the flood.* ② sink; subside: ～鼻子 *snub nose* /伊娃病了好久,两腮都～下去了。*Eva's cheeks were sunken after her long illness.* ③ calm down; ease; get down: ～下心去 *set one's mind at ease* / ～下心来,认真把作业写完。*Get down to finish your homework in earnest.*

【塌方】collapse; cave in; landslide; landslip: 河岸因暴雨～了。*There was a landslide in the river bank owing to the rainstorm.*

【塌架】① collapse; topple down; crumble ② fall from power

【塌落】fall down; cave in: 阳台～了,打在地上。*The balcony caved in on the ground.*

【塌实】① steady and sure; dependable; stable; steadfast: 工作～ *be steadfast in one's work* /她学习上～肯干。*She is steady and hard in her study.* ② free from anxiety; at ease; feel secure: 睡得很～ *have a good and sound sleep*

【塌台】fall from power; down and out: ～将军 *deposed general* / ～经理 *downfallen manager*

【塌陷】sink; cave in; subside: 屋顶在积雪的重压下而～。*The roof caved in under the weight of the snow.* /这座电影院的地基～了。*The foundations of this cinema have subsided.*

【塌心】settle down; calm down: 乔治什么都不能～。*George cannot set his mind to anything.*

溻 [方] become soaked with sweat; soak: 屋里太热,我的衬衣都～湿了。*It was too hot in the room and my shirt became soaked with sweat.*

tǎ

塔 ① Buddhist pagoda; pagoda: 千年～ *the millennium tower* / 佛～ *Buddhist pagoda* /舍利

～ *stupa* ② tower:铁～ *iron tower* /灯～ *lighthouse; beacon* /伦敦～ *the Tower of London* /金字～ *pyramid* /纪念～ *monument* /炮～ *gun turret* /小山上有一座白色的～。*A white tower stands on the hill.* ③【化】column; tower:氧化～ *oxidizing column* /提纯～ *purifying column* /蒸馏～ *distillation tower* ④(Tǎ) a surname

【塔车】【电】tower wagon
【塔吊】tower crane
【塔灰】[方] cobwebs and dirt under a ceiling
【塔吉克斯坦】Tadzhikistan: ～人 *Tajik*
【塔林】① pagoda forest, tombs of Buddhist monks near a temple ② Tallinn, capital of Estonia
【塔楼】① tower building ② turret
【塔轮】【机】cone pulley; stepped pulley
【塔桥】tower bridge
【塔什干】Tashkent, capital of Uzbekistan
【塔式】tower-type: ～锅炉 *updraft boiler* / ～建筑 *tower building* / ～起重机 *tower crane*
【塔钟】tower clock

獭 【动】otter:水～ (*common*) *otter* /海～ *sea otter* /旱～ *marmot*

tà

拓 make rubbings from inscriptions, pictures, etc. on stone tablets or bronze vessels:金石～片 *rubbings of ancient bronze and stone carvings*
see also tuò

【拓本】books of rubbings
【拓片】rubbing (from a stone tablet or bronze vessel)
【拓印】【印】rubbing

沓 [书] crowded; repeated:重～ *repeated* /杂～ *numerous and disorderly* /纷至～来 *come thick and fast* /拖～的行为 *dilatory behaviors*
see also dá

【沓乱】be cluttered; be disorderly: ～的灌木丛 *disorderly bush* /他的房间总是～不堪。*His room is always in a clutter.*
【沓杂】numerous and disorderly
【沓至】come thick and fast; keep pouring in:贵宾～ *distinguished guest come in a continuous stream* /公园游人～。*The travellers keep pouring in the park.*

挞 [书] whip; lash; flog: ～罚 *punishment by whipping* /他鞭～狮子。*He lashed the lion with the whip.*

【挞伐】[书] send armed forces to suppress; send a punitive expedition against

嗒 [书] be frustrated; depressed

【嗒然】[书] dejected; despondent; disheartened
【嗒丧】in low spirit; dejected

榻 long, narrow and low bed; couch:病～ *sick bed* /竹～ *bamboo bed* /藤～ *rattan couch* /卧～ *couch* /同～而卧 *sleep in the same bed* / 卧～之侧,岂容他人鼾睡。*How can one put up with people snoring at one's bedside — no person would tolerate other encroaching on his own preserve.*

踏 ① step on; set foot on; tread:脚～实地 *stand on solid ground* / ～上新的征程 *set foot on new journey* /请勿践～花草。*Keep off the flowers and plants.* /他～上月台。*He stepped onto the platform.* /他～着轻快的步伐走回家。*He went home with brisk steps.* ② go to the spot (to make an investigation or survey)

【踏板】① footboard; footplate; treadle; footrest:自行车～ *treadle of a bicycle* / ～踏得快 *pedal fast* ② footstool for resting the feet on when sitting in a chair ③ springboard for long-jump or high-jump ④【音】pedal:钢琴的强音～ *the loud pedal on a piano* /弱音～ *soft pedal*
【踏步】① march in place; mark time: ～不前 *remain where one is* ②[方] a flight of steps
【踏春】go hiking in spring; go sightseeing in spring
【踏凳】[方] footstool
【踏歌】singing accompanied by dancing; stamp feet to beat time
【踏勘】① make an on-the-spot survey ② make a personal investigation on the scene
【踏看】go to the spot to make a survey; make an on-site survey:军长亲临阵地～。*The army commander went to the forward position to make a survey.*
【踏破铁鞋无觅处,得来全不费功夫】you can wear out iron shoes in fruitless searching, and yet by a lucky chance you may find the lost thing without even looking for it; fancy finding by sheer luck what one has searched for far and wide
【踏青】go for an outing in early spring
【踏雪】walk in the snow
【踏月】walk in the moonlight
【踏足】set foot: ～社会 *set foot in society* / ～政坛 *set foot in political circles*

tāi

胎[1] ① foetus; embryo:娘～ *mother's womb* /胚～ *embryo* /胚～的 *of or like a foetus; embryonic* /胚～学家 *embryologist* /流产的胚～ *an aborted embryo* /祸～ *root of the trouble* /怀～ *be pregnant* ② birth; farrow:头～ *first baby* /一～生下十只小猪 *ten piglets at one farrow* / 她生下双胞～。*She gave birth to twins.* /这是第五～了。*This is the fifth birth.* ③ padding; stuffing; wadding:棉花～ *cotton padding of a quilt* ④ roughcast:泥～的金刚 *Buddha's warrior of clay roughcast*

胎[2] tyre:自行车～ *a bicycle tyre* /备用轮～ *a spare tyre* /爆了的轮～ *a burst tyre* /瘪了的轮～ *a flat tyre* /穿了孔的轮～ *a punctured tyre* /你的轮～磨损得很厉害。*Your tyres are badly worn.*

【胎动】quickening; movement of the foetus which can be felt by the mother
【胎儿】foetus; embryo: ～石化 *calcified foetus* / ～学 *fetology* /刚刚发育的～ *an embryonic foetus* /

她像~一样蜷曲起四肢。She curled up her legs and arms into a foetal position.
【胎记】birthmark
【胎教】foetal training; prenatal education; prenatal influences
【胎具】mold; model; matrix
【胎里富】innate rich guy; one who is born rich
【胎里坏】a born villain; innate bad guy
【胎毛】foetal hair; lanugo
【胎膜】【生理】fetal membrane
【胎盘】【生理】placenta: ~结构 *placentation* / ~炎 *placentitis*
【胎气】nausea; vomiting and oedema of legs during pregnancy
【胎生】【动】viviparity; be viviparous: ~动物 *vivipara* / ~学 *embryology* / 狗是一种~哺乳动物。*Dog is a kind of viviparous mammal.*
【胎位】【医】position of a foetus; presentation: ~不正 *foetus in a wrong position* / ~正常 *normal presentation*
【胎痣】birthmark
【胎座】【植】placenta

tái

台[1] ① platform; stage; terrace: 钻井平~ *drilling platform* / 站~ *platform* / 月~ *railway platform* / 舞~ *stage; arena* / 亭~楼阁 *pavilions* / 主席~ *rostrum; platform* ② tower: 烽火~ *beacon tower* / 塔~ *control tower* / 炮~ *fort; battery* / 瞭望~ *watch tower; lookout* ③ stand; support: 灯~ *lamp stand* / 烛~ *candlestick* / 镜~ *dressing table* ④ anything shaped like a platform, etc.: 窗~ *window sill* / 阳~ *balcony* / 柜~ *counter* ⑤ station; service: 广播电~ *broadcasting station* / 电视~ *television broadcasting station* / 查号~ *special telephone service* ⑥ table; desk: 写字~ *writing desk* / 工作~ *work bench* / 乒乓球~ *ping-pong table* ⑦【量】used of (a stage performance or a machine): 一~打字机 *a typewriter*
台[2] you; your: 兄~ *you* / ~鉴 *for your inspection (used after the name in a letter)*
台[3] short for Taiwan
【台班】work done by a machine in a working day
【台办】short for Taiwan Affairs Office of the State Council
【台胞】compatriots in or from Taiwan: 海外~ *Taiwan compatriots abroad* / ~联谊会 *the sodality of Taiwan compatriots*
【台刨】【机】bench plane
【台本】a stage playscript; a playscript with stage directions
【台标】station logo: 电视台~ *TV station logo* / 这个~很好看。*This station logo is nice.*
【台布】table cloth
【台步】gait; stage walk
【台秤】platform scale; platform balance; counter scale
【台词】actor's lines: 对~ *practice lines on each other* / 他在院子里背~。*He is reciting his lines in the yard.*
【台灯】desk lamp; table lamp; reading lamp
【台地】【地】platform; tableland; mesa
【台风】①【气】typhoon: 强~ *violent typhoon* / ~眼 *typhoon eyes* ② stage manners; actor's demeanor on the stage: ~稳健 *a calm and steady stage demeanor*
【台甫】[书] your personal name in honour: 您尊姓~? *May I know your name?*
【台虎钳】【机】bench vice
【台基】base of a structure aboveground
【台阶】① flight of steps; steps leading up to a house ② chance to extricate oneself from a predicament: 自己找个~下吧。*Find an out for yourself.* ③ bench: ~熔岩 *bench lava*
【台锯】【机】bench saw
【台历】a desk calendar
【台面】①【电】mesa: ~型晶体管 *mesa transistor* ② aboveboard; in public: ~上的话 *remark in public* / 你的话能拿到~上说吗? *Can you make public what you've told me just now?* ③ [方] winnings and losses (in gambling)
【台钳】【机】bench clamp
【台球】billiards; billiard ball
【台扇】desk fan
【台商】Taiwan businessman
【台上】in power; holding an official position
【台式电脑】desk computer
【台属】family members of Taiwan compatriots
【台湾】Taiwan province: ~海峡 *Taiwan strait* / ~岛 *Taiwan Island*
【台下】out of power; out of office
【台钟】[方] desk clock
【台柱子】leading member; pillar; soul member; mainstay
【台资】investment from Taiwan; Taiwan capital
【台子】① platform; stage: 戏~ *stage* ② table; tennis table; ping-pong table
【台钻】【机】bench drill
苔 【植】liverwort; moss; lichen
【苔藓】moss; lichen: ~丛生 *overgrown with moss* / ~植物 *bryophyte* / ~动物 *bryozoan; polyzoan*
【苔原】【地】tundra
抬 ① lift; raise: ~腿 *raise one's legs* / ~胳臂 *raise one's arms* / ~高嗓门 *raise one's voice* / ~头挺胸 *raise one's head and throw out one's chest* / 他把出价~高到500元。*He raised his offer to 500 yuan.* ② carry; move: ~担架 *carry a stretcher* ③ argue for the sake of arguing
【抬爱】favor and take good care of: 多谢~。*Many thanks for your favour and kindness.*
【抬称】huge steelyard worked by three people, with two lifting the steelyard on a shoulder pole and the third adjusting the weight

【抬杠】① argue for the sake of arguing; quarrel; wrangle:朋友之间～是常事。*Arguing and bickering is quite common between friends.* ②［旧］carry a coffin on stout status

【抬高】raise; enhance; heighten: ～租金 *raise the rent* / ～物价 *raise commodity prices* / ～身份 *enhance one's status* / ～声誉 *raise one's reputation*

【抬价】raise prices; force up prices; hike up prices

【抬肩】half the circumference of the sleeve where it joins the shoulder

【抬轿子】① carry sb In a sedan chair ② flatter; fawn on; boost

【抬举】① lift ② praise sb; favour sb; promote sb: 不识～ *not know how to appreciate favours*

【抬升】rise

【抬手】① raise one's hand ② be generous; make an exception in sb's favour; forgive

【抬头】① raise one's head: ～一看 *look up* / ～见喜 *raise head and see bliss* / ～挺胸 *chin up and chest out* ② rise; look up; gain ground:今年你休想～。*Don't imagine that you can rise again in this year.* ③ (on receipts, bills, etc.) name of the buyer, payee or space for filling in such a name

【抬头不见低头见】see each other in frequent; see much of each other

【抬头纹】wrinkles on one's forehead

炱 soot:煤～ *coal soot* /烟～ *soot* /松～ *pine soot*

鲐 【动】chub mackerel

tài

太 ① highest; greatest; remotest: ～古代 *the Archean* ② great; most senior: ～夫人 *mother of another person* / ～老伯 *great uncle* ③ over; too; very; extremely; quite:不～满意 *not very satisfactory* /这个苹果～大了。*This apple is too big.* /这些小说～有意思了。*These novels are extremely interesting.* /他不～愿意留在城里。*He is hesitant about staying in the town.*

【太白星】【天】Venus; Vesper

【太仓一粟】a grain of millet in the barn; a drop in the ocean:这点粮食对布莱尔来说不过是～。*This grain is just peanuts to Blair.*

【太阿】name of a famous sharp sword; power: ～在握 *hold the sword in one's hand*; *wield state power* / ～倒持 *hold the sword by the blade*; *surrender one's power to another at one's own peril*

【太妃】imperial concubine of the deceased emperor

【太妃糖】toffee; taffy

【太公】［方］great-grand father

【太古】remote past; remote antiquity

【太后】mother of an emperor; empress dowager; queen mother

【太皇太后】grandmother of emperor

【太极】quintessence of the universe; supreme Ultimate; the Absolute: ～图 *Diagram of the Supreme Ultimate* / ～拳 *Taijiquan, a kind of traditional Chinese shadow boxing*

【太监】(court) eunuch

【太空】space; firmament: ～旅行 *space travel* / ～船 *space ship* / ～时代 *space age* / ～站 *space station* / ～探险 *venture into space* / ～病 *space sickness* / ～人 *spaceman* / ～探测器 *deep-space probe* / ～梭 *space shuttle* / ～服 *spacesuit* /他是第一个在外～漫步的人。*He was the first man to walk in outer space.*

【太庙】the Imperial Ancestral Temple

【太平】peace and tranquility; having good social order and without war: ～盛世 *times of peace and prosperity* /天下～ *universal peace and tranquility* / ～车 *a heavy cart with four wheels* /时局不～。*The situation is far from tranquil.*

【太平间】mortuary; morgue; reposing room

【太平门】emergency exit; exit (of building, etc.)

【太平鸟】【动】waxwing

【太平梯】fire escape

【太平天国】the Taiping Heavenly Kingdom, established by Hong Xiuquan and his followers

【太平无事】all is well; everything is all right

【太平洋】the Pacific (ocean)

【太婆】［方］great-grandmother

【太甚】too far; be extreme:牢骚～ *have so many complaints* /欺人～。*That's going too far.*

【太师椅】an old-fashioned wooden armchair

【太岁】① Taisui, an ancient name for the Jupiter ② Taisui, the God of the year or the earth: ～头上动土 *break ground where Taisui presides* ③ a nickname for local tyrant or bully:花花～ *the King of Lechers*

【太太】① Mrs.; Madame:张～ *Mrs. Zhang*; *Madame Zhang* ② wife:我～和李～中学时是同学。*My wife and Mrs. Li were classmates in middle school.* ③［方］great-grandparents

【太息】heave a deep sigh:抚卷～ *heave a deep sigh while reading*

【太虚】［书］the great void; the heaven: ～幻景 *great void*; *a state of visionary and emptiness*

【太学】the imperial college

【太阳】① sun: ～光 *sunshine*; *sun's rays*; *sunlight* / ～偏西。*The sun slanted to the west.* ② sunshine; sunlight:晒～ *bask in the sun* / ～常数 *solar constant* / ～灯 *sunlamp*; *sunlight lamp* / ～电池 *solar cell* / ～地儿 *sunny spot* / ～风 *solar wind* / ～辐射 *solar radiation* / ～光谱 *solar spectrum* / ～黑子 *sunspot* / ～活动周 *solar cycle* / ～历 *solar calendar* / ～帆 *solar sail* / ～活动 *solar activity* / ～镜 *sunglasses* / ～炉 *solar furnace* / ～帽 *sun helmet* / ～年 *solar year* / ～系 *solar system* / ～灶 *solar cooker* / ～探测器 *solar probe* /今天～很好。*It's a sunny day.*

【太阳能】solar energy: ～发电 *solar electric power generation* / ～加热器 *solar collector* / ～电话 *solar telephone*

【太阳穴】temples of head

【太爷】① grandfather, grandpa ②［方］great-grandfather
【太医】① imperial physicians ②［方］doctor; medical man
【太阴】①［方］the moon ②【天】lunar: ～周 *lunar cycle* / ～历 *lunar calendar* / ～年 *lunar year*
【太子】prince; crown prince

汰 discard; eliminate: ～遣归故里 *discharge and send sb to his hometown* / 裁～冗员 *lay off surplus personnel* / 优胜劣～ *survival of the fittest* / 淘～ *eliminate; discard*

态 ① form; appearance; condition: 姿～ *posture* / 形～ *shape* / 状～ *state; situation* / 神～ *expression; manner* ②【语】voice: 主动语～ *active voice* / 被动语～ *passive voice* ③【物】state: 固～ *solid state* / 液～ *liquid state* / 气～ *gaseous state*
【态度】① manner; bearing; mien; expression: ～大方 *have an easy manner* / ～恶劣 *behave badly* / ～和蔼 *be kind* / ～冷淡 *have an indifferent attitude* / ～激烈 *a violent attitude* / 他今天～很好。*He is in good manner today.* ② attitude; approach: 工作～扎实 *have a down-to-earth approach towards one's work* / 劳动～ *attitude towards labour* / 她工作～非常积极。*She shows a very positive attitude to her work.* / 别用这种～对我,小伙子! *Don't take that attitude with me, young man!*
【态势】situation; state; condition: 战略～ *strategic situation* / 经济～ *economic condition* / 军事～ *military posture*

泰 ① safe; peaceful; healthy: 国～民安 *the country is prosperous and the people live in peace* / 身体康～ *in good health* ② extreme; most
【泰斗】mount Tai and the North Star (respectful epithet for a person of distinction): 京剧～ *the foremost actor of Beijing opera* / 画坛～ *leading painter*
【泰国】Thailand: ～人 *Thailander; Thai* / ～语 *Thai (language)*
【泰和】be peaceful and harmonious: 天下～ *peace and harmony throughout the country*
【泰然】be calm; be composed; be self-possessed: ～处之 *bear sth with equanimity* / ～自若 *behave with perfect composure; self-possessed*
【泰山】① Mount Tai ② father-in-law ③ symbol of great weight or import: 有眼不识～ *have eyes but fail to see Mount Tai* / 重如～,轻如鸿毛 *be as weighty as Mount Tai or as light as a feather* / ～压顶 *bear down on one with the weight of Mount Tai* / ～压卵 *like Mount Tai crushing an egg-with overwhelmingly superior force*
【泰晤士报】the Times, a kind of British newspapers
【泰晤士河】Thames, river of southern England flowing through Landon

tān

坍 collapse; fall down; cave in; tumble down: 那个旧谷仓已经快～了。*The old barn was practically tumbling down.*
【坍方】cave in; landslip; collapse
【坍架】collapse; crumble down; tumble down
【坍圮】［书］cave in; collapse; fall down
【坍塌】cave in; landslide; fall into ruin: 老房子～了。*The old house fell down.* / 麦垛～。*The stock of wheat crumpled.*
【坍台】［方］① fail; collapse; fold: 他的企业～了。*His enterprise collapsed.* ② fall into disgrace; lose face: 当众～。*Losing face in public.*
【坍陷】cave in; sink; subside: 路面～ *road surface cave in* / 地层～。*The stratum has sunk.*

贪 ① corrupt; accept bribes; practise graft: ～官污吏 *corrupt officials* / ～图功名 *be greedy for honour and fame* / 倡廉肃～ *promote honest and clean government and eliminate corruption* ② desire for; greedy: ～吃～喝 *be greedy for food and drink* / 起早～黑 *work hard from dawn to dusk* / ～食 *excessive desire for food* ③ covet; hanker after; pine after: ～小便宜 *covet small gains* / ～名图利 *pine after fame and money*
【贪杯】excessive desire for drinking; be too fond of drinks: 他一向很～。*He is too fond of drinks.* / 不要～。*Don't drink too much.*
【贪财】greedy for money; excessive and selfish desire for wealth; be a money-grubber: ～害命 *commit murder for money* / ～好色 *lust for money and woman*
【贪大求全】concentrate on grandiose projects; go after the grandiose
【贪得无厌】be insatiably avaricious; be inordinately greedy
【贪多嚼不烂】bite off more than one can chew
【贪官污吏】corrupt officials; venal officials
【贪贿】corruption and taking bribes
【贪婪】avaricious; greedy; rapacious: ～的目光 *greedy eyes* / 充满～和嫉妒 *consumed with greed and envy* / 巴克利是一个～的吸血鬼。*Barclay is a greedy blood-sucker.*
【贪恋】cling to; reluctant to leave; hate to give up: ～舒适的生活 *be reluctant to give up ease and comfort* / ～小家庭 *cling to one's own family* / ～女色 *be crazy about women*
【贪求】covet; seek; hanker after: ～富贵 *hanker after wealth and position* / ～权力 *be greedy for power*
【贪便宜】eager to get things on the cheap; keen on gaining petty advantages
【贪色】crazy about woman; be a womanize; indulge in sex
【贪生怕死】care for nothing but saving one's skin; mortally afraid of death; cling to life instead of braving death

【贪天之功】arrogate to oneself the merits of others; claim credit for other people's achievements; take credit for the achievements of others

【贪图】hanker after; greedy for; covet: ~安逸 *hanker after an ease and comfort life* / ~小利 *be greedy for small gains; seek trifling advantages* / ~口腹 *pamper one's appetite*

【贪玩】be crazy about play; be too fond of play

【贪污】embezzle; corrupt; graft: ~行贿 *take graft; commit bribery* / ~受贿 *embezzle money and engage in corrupt practices* / ~渎职 *corrupt and negligent about one's duties* / ~盗窃 *engage in graft and theft; embezzlement and theft* / ~腐化 *graft and corruption* / ~犯 *grafter* / ~分子 *embezzler*

【贪小失大】covet a little and lose a lot; penny-wise and pound-foolish

【贪心】① greed; avarice; rapacity ② greedy; avaricious; insatiable; voracious: ~不足 *insatiably greedy*

【贪欲】covetous desire greed

【贪赃】take bribes; practise graft: ~枉法 *take bribes and bend the law* / ~受贿 *practise graft and take bribes*

【贪占】embezzle: ~别人的东西 *embezzle other people's property*

【贪嘴】be too greedy for food; be gluttonous: ~的小男孩 *a greedy little boy*

摊 ① share; take a share in: 分~费用 *share the cost* / 男孩子们平均分~蛋糕。*The boys shared the cake equally.* ② spread out; unfold: ~开地图 *unfold a map* / 桌子上~着好几本书。*Quite a few books were spread out on the desk.* ③ vendor's stand; booth; stall: 菜~儿 *vegetable stall* / 书~儿 *bookstand* / 练~儿 *manage a booth* / 水果~ *fruit stall* ④ befall; happen to: 倒霉的事全让我给~上了。*Bad luck always befalls me.* ⑤ fry batter in a thin layer: ~煎饼 *make pancakes* ⑥［量］: 一~泥儿 *a mud puddle* / 一~血 *a pool of blood*

【摊车】vendor's stand and cart

【摊点】stand; booth: 夜市~ *night market booth* / 小吃~ *food booth*

【摊贩】street pedlar: 无照~ *unlicensed street pedlar*

【摊开】spread out: ~双手 *spread out one's hand*

【摊还】amortization

【摊牌】① lay one's cards on the table ② show one's cards; seek a showdown: 资方正在就非法罢工问题与工会~。*Management are seeking a showdown with the issue of illegal strikes.*

【摊派】allot; share out; apportion: ~任务 *apportion tasks* / 合理~ *rational allotment* / ~费用 *apportioned charges*

【摊市】open-air market; stall quarters

【摊手】loose one's grip; let go

【摊售】sell in a booth

【摊位】booth; stall; stand

【摊销】【经】amortization

【摊子】① vendor's stand; stall: 旧货~ *junk booth* / 菜~ *vegetable stall* ② an organization; set up: ~铺得太大。*Do things on too large a scale.*

滩 ① beach; sands: 海~ *beach; sea beach* / 沙~ *sands; sand bank* / 河~地 *flood land; floodplain* / 在沙~上做日光浴的度假者 *holiday-makers sunbathing on the beach* ② shoal: 险~ *dangerous shoal* / 暗~ *hidden shoal* / ~多水急 *with many shoals and rapids*

【滩头】sand bank; sand beach: ~阵地 *beach position* / ~堡 *beachhead*

【滩涂】low beach; low land

瘫 be paralyzed: 吓~了 *be paralyzed with fright* / 他~了两年了。*He's been paralyzed for two years.*

【瘫痪】① be paralytic: 他右腿~步履维艰。*The paralysis affects his right leg and he can only walk with difficulty.* ② break down; paralyze: 在台风袭击下，那里的交通运输全部陷于~。*When the typhoon struck, transport there was at a total standstill.* / 网络~了。*The Internet does not work any more.*

【瘫痪于地】sink helplessly to the ground

【瘫软】be weak and limp: 双腿~ *feel weak at the knees* / 听到妈妈去世的消息他浑身都~了。*On hearing the death of his mother, he collapsed.*

【瘫子】paralytic

【瘫坐】sit as if paralyzed: ~一旁 *sit on the side as if paralyzed*

tán

坛[1] ① altar: 日~ *altar to the sun* / 天~ *temple of heaven* ② a raised plot of land for planting flowers; terrace: 花~ *raised flower bed* ③ platform; forum: 讲~ *speaker's platform* ④ circles; world: 影~ *movie world* / 体~ *sports world* / 诗~ *poetry circles*

坛[2] ① earthen jar; jug: 醋~ *vinegar jug* / 酒~ *wine jar* ②［量］: 一~酒 *a jar of wine* / 三~醋 *three jugs of vinegar*

【坛坛罐罐】pots and pans; household goods: 地上摆满了~。*The floor is stacked with pots and pans.*

【坛子】earthen jar; jug

昙 be cloudy; overcast

【昙花】【植】broad-leaved epiphyllum (*epiphyllum oxypetalum*)

【昙花一现】flower briefly as the brood-leaved epiphyllum; be a flash in the pan

谈 ① talk; chat; discuss: ~闲天 *make conversation; chat* / ~言微中 *make one's point implicitly* / ~家常 *engage in small talk* / 高~阔论 *talk volubly or bombastically* / 健~ *have a good talk* / 洽~ *hold talks; negotiate* / 我们好好~~。*Let's have a good talk.* ② talk; tale; story: 奇~ *strange talk; fantastic tale* / 无稽之~ *fantastic talk; sheer nonsense* / 老生常~ *platitude*

【谈不到】out of the question; far from being: 他～是个优等生。*He is far from being an excellent student.*
【谈不来】not get along well; not hit it off
【谈到】speak of; mention; talk about: 他从未～你。*He never speaks of you.*
【谈得到】consider
【谈得来】get along well
【谈锋】volubility; eloquence: ～甚健 *talk volubly; have the gift of the gab* / ～犀利 *incisive in conversation*
【谈古说今】talk over past and present; discourse at random of things past and present
【谈何容易】easy to talk, difficult to achieve; easier said than done
【谈虎色变】turn pale at the mention of a tiger; turn pale when speaking of sth terrifying
【谈话】① have a talk; chat; discuss ② talk; statement: 书面～ *a written statement*
【谈家常】chitchat; talk about small things: 两人一见面就～。*The two started chatting as soon as they met.*
【谈论】discuss; talk about: ～天下大事 *discuss world events* / ～工作 *discuss sth about work*
【谈判】negotiate; hold talks: 和平～ *negotiate for peace* / 贸易～ *trade negotiations* / ～桌 *conference table* / ～心理 *psychology of negotiation* / ～语言 *negotiating language*
【谈情说爱】bill and coo; be courting; talk love
【谈天】chitchat; make conversation: ～说地 *talk everything; gossip and chat*
【谈吐】style of conversation; style of talk: ～文雅 *talk in polite and cultivated language* / ～不俗 *talk in good taste* / ～幽默 *talk with a sense of humor* / ～笨拙 *do not shine in conversation*
【谈笑】chat and laugh: ～风生 *talk and laugh cheerfully; joke and chat freely* / ～自若 *talk and laugh as usual; be completely at ease* / ～如前 *talk and laugh together precisely as in days gone by* / ～封侯 *obtain a high rank easily* / ～戏谑 *chat and jest*
【谈心】have a heart-to-heart talk
【谈兴】mood of talking: 他们～正浓。*They are having an animated conversation.*
【谈资】talk's matter; subject of a conversation: 茶余饭后的～ *the subject of chatting at one's leisure*

弹 ① spring; leap; bounce: 球从篮板上～回来。*The ball rebounded from the backboard.* ② flick; flip: ～烟灰 *flick the ash off a cigarette* ③ fluff; tease: ～棉花 *fluff cotton (with a bow)* ④ shoot; send forth: ～石子 *shoot pebbles with a catapult* ⑤ play; pluck: ～钢琴 *play the piano* / 对牛～琴 *play the lute to a cow-talk over sb's head* ⑥ accuse; impeach; lash out at: 讥～ *lash out at* ⑦ elastic; springy: ～簧门 *swing door* / ～性塑料 *resilient plastic* / ～性极限 *elastic limit*
see also dàn
【弹拨】play; pluck: ～乐器 *plucking string instrument*
【弹唱】plucking and singing: ～自如 *play and sing as one pleases*
【弹劾】censure; impeach: ～总统 *impeach the President*
【弹簧】spring: ～秤 *spring balance* / ～床 *spring bed* / ～锁 *spring lock*
【弹泪】pour tears; shed tears
【弹力】elastic force; elasticity; resilience; spring: ～尼龙 *elastic nylon* / ～袜 *stretch socks* / ～极限 ～ *elastic limit*
【弹球】glass beads; play marbles
【弹射】① launch; shoot off; send forth; eject ② [书] pick faults and criticize; censure: ～利弊 *pick faults* / ～座椅 *ejection seat* / ～座舱 *ejection capsule*
【弹跳】jump up; bounce: ～力 *jumping capacity* / ～板 *springboard*
【弹涂鱼】【动】mudskipper
【弹性】① elasticity; resilience; spring: 球的～符合标准。*The balls reach the specifications for bounce.* ② elastic; flexible: ～模量 *modulus of elasticity* / ～外交 *elastic or flexible diplomacy* / ～上班时间 *flexible hours of work* / 这些规定是有～的。*These regulations are elastic.*
【弹压】suppress; quell; subdue: ～学生运动 *suppress a student movement*
【弹指】a snap of fingers: ～光阴 *time zipping by* / ～之间 *in a flash; in an instant*
【弹奏】pluck; play: ～乐曲 *play music*

覃 [书] deep: ～思 *deep in thought*

痰 sputum; spittle; saliva: 咳～ *cough out phlegm* / 吐～ *spit*
【痰盂】spittoon; cuspidor
【痰郁】【中医】phlegm stasis in the body

潭 ① deep pool; pond: 水～ *a water pond* / 龙～虎穴 *dragon's pool and tiger's den; a danger spot* ② [方] pit; depression: 泥～ *mire; morass*
【潭第】[书] your house
【潭府】[书] ① abyss ② your house

檀 ① wingceltis ② (Tán) a surname
【檀板】【音】hardwood clappers
【檀香】【植】white sandalwood; sandalwood: ～木 *sandalwood* / ～扇 *sandalwood fan* / ～皂 *sandal soap*
【檀香山】Honolulu

tǎn

忐
【忐忑】be disturbed; be perturbed: 心情～ *feel disturbed* / ～不安 *uneasy; be upset; be restless*

坦 ① level; smooth: 地面～平 *level ground* / 平～ *level; smooth* ② calm; ease; composed: 雪中～步 *walk at a leisurely pace in the snow* / 舒～ *comfortable* ③ frank; open

T

【坦白】① be honest; be frank; be candid: ~地说 *frankly speaking*; *be honest with you* /襟怀~ *honest and above board* / ~地说,我不能同意你。*To be frank with you, I cannot agree with you.* ② confess; admit; own up:她~是她偷了它。*She confessed that she had stolen it.* / ~从宽,抗拒从严。*Be lenient to those who confess their crimes and severe to those who do not.*
【坦诚】frank and sincere; candid and sincere: ~相见 *be frank and honest towards each other*; *treat sb openly* / ~相处 *live frankly*
【坦荡】① broad and level ② magnanimous; big-hearted:胸怀~ *largeness of mind*; *open-hearted and above board*
【坦噶尼喀】Tanganyika, continental part of Tanzania
【坦噶尼喀湖】lake Tanganyika, world's longest freshwater lake, in east Africa
【坦怀】frank; candid: ~待人 *be frank with others*
【坦克】tank: ~手 *tankman* /空降~ *airborne tank* / ~兵 *panzer or tank forces*
【坦然】calm; ease; composed: ~对答 *reply calmly and confidently* / ~无惧 *calm and fearless* / ~自若 *calm and confident*; *completely at ease*
【坦桑尼亚】Tanzania: ~人 *Tanzanian*
【坦率】honest; frank; candid: ~直言 *state frankly* /双方~地交换了意见。*The two sides had a frank exchange of views.*
【坦途】level road; highway; easy path:视若~ *regard as an easy path* /科学上没有~。*There is no easy path in science.*
【坦言】speak candidly; say frankly: ~优劣 *say frankly which is better*
【坦挚】be candid and sincere; be frank and open: 汤姆对我的评价十分~。*Tom was quite candid and sincere in judging me.*

袒 ① be uncovered; be stripped to the waist; be unbuttoned: ~露手臂 *expose one's arms* / ~腹 *leave one's belly uncovered* ② shield; shelter:偏~ *give unprincipled support to*; *be partial to*
【袒护】give unprincipled support to; shield: ~一方 *be partial to one side* /你别~他。*Don't make excuses for him.*
【袒露】expose; reveal; uncover: ~心曲 *reveal one's inner thoughts*
【袒胸露背】expose one's neck and shoulders; bare one's chest and expose one's arms

毯 blanket; carpet; rug:毛~ *woolen blanket* / 地~ *rug*; *carpet* /壁~ *tapestry* /线~ *cotton blanket*
【毯子】rug; blanket

tàn

叹 ① sigh:望洋兴~ *lament one's smallness before the vast ocean*; *bemoan one's inadequacy before a great task* / ~号 *exclamation mark* (!) /悲~ *sigh mournfully* /长~一声 *heave a deep sigh* ② exclaim in admiration; praise: ~美 *highly praise*; *gasp in admiration* / ~为奇观 *admire and praise sth as a wonderful achievement* /赞~不已 *be full of praise*
【叹词】【语】interjection; exclamation
【叹服】express admiration sincerely; gasp in admiration:令人~ *compel admiration*
【叹绝】admire as unique or superb
【叹气】sigh; heave a sigh:唉声~ *sigh in despair*
【叹赏】admire; highly praise: ~不止 *admire without end*
【叹为观止】acclaim (a work of art, etc.) as the best
【叹息】sigh; heave a sigh
【叹惜】sigh with regret; lament

炭 ① charcoal; carbon:煤~ *coal* /木~ *charcoal* /骨~ *animal charcoal* /烧~ *make charcoal* /泥~ *peat* ②[方] coal:挖~ *dig coal*
【炭笔】crayon; charcoal pencil
【炭化】carbonize
【炭画】【美】charcoal drawing; charcoal: ~铅笔 *carbon pencil*
【炭火】charcoal fire
【炭精】① charcoal products ② artificial charcoal and graphite: ~棒 *carbon rod* / ~灯 *arc lamp*; *arc light*
【炭疽】【医】anthrax: ~病 *anthracnose*
【炭坑】[方] coal pit; charcoal kiln
【炭盆】charcoal brazier
【炭窑】charcoal

探 ① explore; sound out; prospect: ~险家 *explorer* / ~测气球 *sounding balloon* / ~查敌情 *gather intelligence about the enemy* /试~ *sound out* /勘~ *exploration* /钻~ *drilling* ② visit; call on: ~监 *visit a prisoner* ③ stretch forward; crane:行车时不要~身窗外。*Don't lean out of the window while the bus is in motion.* ④ scout; spy; detective:敌~ *enemy scout* /密~ *secret agent* /侦~ *detective*
【探案】survey a case: ~小说 *detective story* /密林~ *survey a case in dense wood*
【探宝】hunt for treasure; prospect for mineral deposits:海底~ *explore the deep sea resources*
【探病】call on a patient
【探测】make a survey; probe; detect: ~器 *sounder*; *probe*; *detector* / ~对方用意 *sound the other party out* / ~海底情况 *survey the seabed*
【探查】look over; scout; reconnoiter
【探察】observe; survey; watch: ~地形 *survey the terrain* / ~民情 *survey the feelings of people*
【探访】① seek; search: ~新闻 *seek news story* ② visit; call on: ~亲友 *call on one's relatives and friends*
【探风】inquiry about sb or sth; seek for information
【探戈】tango (a transliteration): ~舞曲 *tango music*
【探家】go home; make a brief trip home
【探监】pay a visit to a prisoner

【探井】① prospect pit; exploring shaft ② test well; exploratory well
【探究】look into; inquiry thoroughly; probe: ～案子发生的原因 *look into the causes of a case* /彻底～ *probe a matter to the bottom*
【探看】① visit; call on: ～病人 *visit a sick person* ② look about; watch; observe: 四处～ *look around*
【探空】sounding; air sounding: ～气球 *sounding balloon* / ～火箭 *rocket sounder; sounding rocket* / ～仪 *sonde* / ～研究 *research on air sounding*
【探口气】find out one's opinions; sound sb out
【探矿】prospect; sound
【探雷】detect a mine; locate a mine: ～器 *mine detector*
【探路】try to find out the way; explore the way
【探明】① find out; gain a clear understanding: ～来访者的用意 *try to find out what the visitor has come for* ② verify; ascertain: ～的石油储量 *ascertained deposit of oilfield*
【探囊取物】as easy as picking one's own pocket; like duck soup
【探亲】visit one's family; visit one's relatives: ～假 *home leave* /劳伦斯回故乡～访友去了。*Lawrence returned to his homeland to visit his relatives and friends.*
【探求】seek; find out; search for: 努力～ *strive to seek* / ～真理 *search for the truth* / ～光明 *seek brilliant future*
【探身】lean forward; bend over: ～窗外 *lean out of a window*
【探视】visit; call on: ～病人 *call on a patient* / ～时间 *visiting hours (in a hospital)* / ～犯罪嫌疑人 *call on a suspect*
【探索】explore; seek; find out: ～宇宙的奥妙 *explore the secrets of the universe* / ～战争的原因 *probe the causes of war* / ～真理 *seek truth*
【探讨】inquire; investigate; probe: ～事故的原因 *investigate the reason of an accident* / ～问题的答案 *inquire a solution to the problem*
【探听】inquire into; fish for; sound out: ～别人的私事 *inquire about other people's private affairs* / ～失踪儿童的下落 *inquire about the whereabouts of missing child*
【探头】crane one's neck; poke out one's head: ～探脑 *crane one's neck to watch; poke out one's head to peek at* / ～张望 *crane one's neck and look around*
【探望】① look around; have a glance: 四处～ *look all around* ② pay a visit; call on: 回乡～亲友 *return to one's home to visit relatives and friends*
【探问】① inquiry about; ask; question: ～敌人的兵力部署情况 *inquire out the deployment of the enemy troop* / ～新机器的效能 *inquire about the efficiency of the new machine* ② inquire after; visit: 她～那病人。*He inquired after the patient.*
【探悉】know; learn; find out: 从有关方面～ *learn from those concerned* /从老板那里～ *know from one's boss*
【探险】venture; explore: ～队 *exploring party; exploring team* /北极～者 *an Arctic explorer*
【探寻】search for; seek for; look for
【探询】inquiry about; ask
【探幽】[书] probe into profound truth: ～事物的本质 *probe into the essence of things* ② seek for beautiful scenery: ～览胜 *visit beautiful places*
【探鱼仪】fish-detector; fish-finder
【探照灯】searchlight
【探针】【医】probe; probing pin
【探知】learn; get to know
【探子】① scout; spy ② thin tube used to extract samples of food grains, etc.

碳 【化】carbon (C)
【碳棒】【电】carbon rod; crayon
【碳酐】【化】carbonic anhydride
【碳钢】【冶】carbon steel: 低～ *low carbon steel* /高～ *high carbon steel*
【碳化】carbonize: ～钙 *calcium carbide* / ～硅 *silicon carbide* / ～物 *carbide* / ～作用 *carbonization*
【碳精】pure carbon: ～棒 *carbon rod* / ～电极 *carbon electrode; baked carbon*
【碳氢化合物】hydrocarbon
【碳刷】【电】carbon brush
【碳水化合物】【化】carbohydrate
【碳丝】【电】carbon filament: ～灯 *carbon lamp*
【碳素钢】carbon steel
【碳酸】carbonic acid: ～同化作用 *carbonic acid assimilation* / ～钙 *calcium carbonate* / ～钠 *sodium carbonate; soda* / ～气 *carbon dioxide; choke damp* / ～氢钠 *sodium bicarbonate; baking soda* / ～盐 *carbonate*

tāng

汤 ① hot water; boiling water: 扬～止沸 *try to stop water from boiling by skimming it off and pouring it back; apply a palliative* /温～浸种 *hot water treatment of seeds* /赴～蹈火 *go through fire and water* ② hot springs: ～泉 *a hot spring* /小～山 *Little Hot Spring Hill* ③ soup; broth: 鸡～ *chicken soup* /肉～ *broth* /姜～ *ginger tea* /豆腐～ *soybean soap*
see also shāng
【汤包】steamed dumplings filled with minced meat and gravy
【汤池】① impregnable defense work ② hot-water bathing pool
【汤匙】tablespoon; soupspoon
【汤罐】hot-water pitcher
【汤锅】① butcher's cauldron in a slaughterhouse ② slaughterhouse
【汤壶】hot-water bottle
【汤剂】【中医】decoction of herbal medicine; herb soup
【汤料】soup stock
【汤面】noodles in soup

【汤泉沐浴】bathe in a hot spring
【汤勺】soup ladle
【汤水】①［方］hot water ② water in which sth has been boiled
【汤碗】soup bowl
【汤药】【中医】decoction of medicinal ingredients
【汤圆】dumplings made of glutinous rice flour served in soup：豆沙～ *dumplings with sweet bean meal filling*

táng

唐 ① the Tang Dynasty (618～907)：～诗 *tang poetry* /～律 *laws of the Tang Dynasty* ②（Táng）a surname
【唐花】hothouse flower
【唐人街】china town
【唐三彩】【考】tri-coloured glazed pottery of the Tang Dynasty; Tang tricolour
【唐突】［书］① be rude; be offensive; be too blunt：～古人 *profane an ancient sage* /～而入 *break in abruptly* ② pass oneself off as; pass sth off as
【唐装】Chinese costume
堂 ① hall or room for a specific purpose：登～入室 *pass through the hall into the inner room — reach a higher level in one's studies or official career* /人民大会～ *the Great Hall of the People* /食～ *dining hall* /礼～ *auditorium* ② the main room of a house：大～*lobby (of a hotel)* ③ court of law：大～之上 *in the court* /过～ *be tried* ④ relations between cousins：～兄弟 *male cousins* ⑤［量］：四～课 *four classes*
【堂而皇之】in state; in grand style; be openly and legally
【堂鼓】a barrel-shaped drum
【堂倌】waiter
【堂皇】magnificent; grand; splendid：～的房子 *a splendid house*
【堂上】① one's parents：～健在。*My parents are still living and in good health.* ② courtroom; courthouse ③ a term of address to magistrates or judges
【堂堂】① dignified; impressive：相貌～ *impressive-looking* ② having high aspirations and boldness of vision：～男子汉 *man worthy of the name; real man* ③ imposing; awe-inspiring; formidable：～大国 *a great and powerful nation*
【堂堂正正】① be fair and square; impressive in personal appearance：～，举止不俗 *impressive-looking and good-mannered* ② open and aboveboard：为官～ *be an upright official*
【堂屋】① the central room of the main wing ② the principal wing of a courtyard house
塘 ① dike; embankment：烂泥～*a muddy pond* /河～ *river embankment* /海～ *seawall* ② pool; pond：池～ *pool; pond* /苇～ *reed pond* /鱼～ *fish pond* ③ hot-water bathing pool：澡～ *bath-house* ④［方］stove chamber：火～ *stove-chamber of blazing coal*
【塘肥】pond sludge used as manure
【塘鳢】【动】sleeper
【塘泥】pond sludge; silt in a pond
【塘堰】small reservoir
搪[1] ① ward out; keep out; prevent from：～雨 *keep out the rain* /～风 *keep out the wind* /～寒 *keep out the cold* /～饥 *allay one's hunger* ② stall off; evade; shirk：～帐 *put off a creditor* /～差事 *perform a duty perfunctorily*
搪[2] spread over; daub：～炉子 *line a stove with clay*
【搪瓷】enamel：～碗 *enamel bowl* /～锅 *enamel pot* /～器皿 *enamelware* /～钢板 *enameled pressed steel*
【搪塞】perform perfunctorily; shirk：～事 *do sth perfunctorily*
樘 【建】door or window frame：门～ *door frame* /窗～ *window frame*
膛 ① chest; thorax：枪～ *bore (of a gun)* /开～ *cut its chest* /这鹅的～肥。*The goose has a plump breast.* ② chamber; an enclosed space：炉～ *chamber of a stove*
【膛式炉】【冶】hearth furnace
【膛线】【军】rifling
镗 【机】bore
【镗床】【机】boring machine; boring lathe; borer：坐标～ *jig boring machine*
【镗刀】【机】boring cutter; boring tool
【镗孔】【机】bore hole; boring
糖 ① candy; sweets; sweetmeats：泡泡～ *bubblegum* /水果～ *fruit drops* /一袋～ *a bag of sweets* /软～ *soft drops* /吃块～ *have a candy* ② sugar：白～ *sugar* /红～ *brown sugar* /方～ *cube sugar; lump sugar* /冰～ *crystal sugar; rock candy* ③ a kind of organic compound：果～ *fructose* /葡萄～ *glucose* /乳～ *milk sugar*
【糖包】steamed bun stuffed with sugar
【糖厂】sugar refinery
【糖醋】sweet and sour; sugar and vinegar：～排骨 *sweet and sour spareribs* /～鱼 *sweet and sour fish*
【糖果】sweets; candy; sweetmeats
【糖葫芦】sugar-coated haws on a stick
【糖姜】sugared ginger
【糖浆】① medicinal syrup：咳嗽～ *cough syrup* ② syrup：果味～ *fruit syrup* /金色餐用～ *golden syrup*
【糖料作物】【农】sugar crop
【糖萝卜】①［口］beet ②［方］preserved carrot
【糖蜜】molasses; treacle
【糖尿病】diabetes：～患者 *diabetic*
【糖人】sugar doll; sugar figure
【糖三角】triangular steamed bun stuffed with sugar
【糖食】sweet food; sweetmeats
【糖水】syrup：～橘子 *tangerines in syrup* /～苹果 *apples in syrup*
【糖蒜】garlic in syrup; sweetened garlic

【糖稀】thin malt sugar; maltose
【糖衣】sugar-coating: ~炮弹 *sugarcoated bullet* / 这种药片有~。*These pills are sugarcoated.*
【糖饴】maltose; malt sugar
【糖纸】wrapping paper for sweets; candy wraps

螳 mantis
【螳臂挡车】acting just like a mantis trying to stop a chariot — overrate oneself and try to hold back an overwhelmingly superior force
【螳螂】【动】mantis: ~捕蝉,黄雀在后。*The mantis seizes the cicada, not knowing the oriole behind-covet gains ahead, unaware of danger behind.*

tǎng

倘 if; on condition that; supposing; in case: ~有不测 *in case of accidents* / ~你肯多给钱,我就留下。*I'll only stay if you offer me more money.*
【倘或】[书] if; in case; supposing
【倘来之物】an undeserved gain; windfall
【倘若】if; on condition that; supposing
【倘使】if; on condition that; in case
【倘有不测】in the event of an accident; if anything untoward happen

淌 shed; pour out; drip: ~血 *shed blood* / ~口水 *slaver; slobber* / 伤口~血 *blood trickled from the wound* / ~泪 *shed tears* / 身体上的汗珠直往下~。*Sweat was dripping from his body.*

躺 lie; recline; rest: 仰~ *lie on one's back; lie supine* / ~下歇歇 *lie down and rest a while* / 一乞丐~在地上。*A beggar lies across on the ground.*
【躺倒】lie down: ~不干 *stay in bed and refuse to shoulder duties any longer*
【躺柜】a long low box with a lid on top; chest
【躺椅】deck chair; sling chair

tàng

烫 ① scald; burn: 让火~着了 *be scalded by fire* / 他嘴上~了个疤。*His mouth got a scar through being burnt.* ② iron; press: ~衬衣 *iron shirts* ③ warm; heat up in hot water: ~酒 *heat wine* / ~澡 *take a hot bath* / ~脚 *bathe one's feet in hot water* ④ perm: 她头发刚~过。*She just got her hair permed.* ⑤ very hot; scalding; steaming hot: 这杯水真~! *This glass of water is boiling hot.*
【烫发】perm; have one's hair permed
【烫花】branded flowers
【烫金】【印】gild; bronze: 布面~ *cloth gilt* / ~封面 *gilt cover* / ~机 *gilding press; bronzing machine*
【烫蜡】polish with melted wax; wax: ~地板 *waxed floor* / ~打光 *waxing and polishing* / 给家具~ *wax one's furniture*
【烫面】dough made with boiling water: ~饺子 *dumplings made of dough prepared with boiling water* / ~条 *noodle made of dough prepared with boiling water*
【烫伤】【医】scalding
【烫手】① burn the hand: 热得~ *so hot that it burns one's hand* ② thorny; troublesome; knotty: 这事有些~。*This is a sticky business.*
【烫头】have a permanent wave; perm

趟 ① [量] used of a trip or a single trip of a vehicle: 明天还有一~从北京来的车。*There will be another bus from Beijing.* ② used of a street or things arranged in a row: 一~街 *a street* / 两~树 *two rows of trees* ③ sth that is going on: 艾丽斯跟不上~。*Iris logged behind.*

tāo

叨 be favored with; gain the benefit of

see also dāo
【叨光】much obliged to you
【叨教】thank a lot for your advice
【叨扰】thank you for your hospitality

涛 large wave; billow: 江~滚滚 *rolling waves of the river* / 如波~汹涌的 *billowy* / 波~汹涌 *surging waves* / 林~ *soughing of the wind through a forest*

绦 silk ribbon; silk braid
【绦虫】【动】tapeworm; cestode; taenia: ~类 *cestode*
【绦子】silk ribbon; silk braid

掏 ① take out; draw out; fish out: ~钥匙 *draw one's keys* / ~手枪 *draw a pistol* / ~鸟窝 *take young birds or eggs out of a nest* / ~耳朵 *pick one's ears* / 他的钱包被~了。*His wallet was stolen.* / 这电影是他~的钱。*He treated us to the cinema.* ② hollow out; scoop out; dig: 在墙上~个洞 *make a hole in the wall* / ~防空洞 *dig air-raid shelter*
【掏槽】cutting
【掏底】find out the bottom line; survey the real intention or situation
【掏灰】[方] dig coal: ~的小工 *unskilled coal-digger*
【掏心】open one's heart: 说句~的话,杰西卡是个相当不错的人。*Frankly, Jessica is quite good person.*
【掏腰包】①[口] pay a bill; foot a bill: 下次我~。*The next meal is on me.* ② pick sb's pocket: 我的腰包被掏了。*My pocket was picked.*

滔 inundate; flood: 波浪~天 *waves running high*
【滔滔】① torrential; surging: ~洪水 *surging flood* ② be a constant flow of words; be a flow of eloquence

【滔滔不绝】pour out words in a flood：～地讲 *make a speech on and on in a flow of eloquence*

【滔天】①（of billows，etc.）dash to the skies；rush to the skies：白浪～ *whitecaps running high* ② heinous；monstrous：～大祸 *a terrible disaster* / ～大罪 *monstrous crimes*；*heinous crimes*；*towering crimes* / 罪恶～ *commit towering crimes*

韬 ［书］① sheath；bow case；close-fitting cover ② hide；conceal：～迹 *lie low*；*hide one's light* ③ art of war；military strategy

【韬笔】［书］write no more；let the pen idle：钳口～ *hold one's tongue and writing nothing*

【韬光养晦】hide one's capacities and bide one's time

【韬晦】［书］conceal one's true features or intention；lie low：～隐居 *hide one's light and live in seclusion*

【韬略】military strategy：～过人 *excel in military strategy*

饕 ［书］be greedy or gluttonous for money or food

【饕戾】［书］be greedily fierce and perverse

táo

逃 ① run away；fly away；escape；flee：这贼～掉了。*The thief has escaped.* / 鸟～掉了。*The bird has flown away.* / 敌人溃败而～。*The enemy were defeated and fled in disorder.* ② evade；dodge；shirk；escape：罪责难～ *can not shirk responsibility for the crime* / 难～法网 *be unable to escape from the punishment of law*

【逃奔】run away to；flee：～异乡 *run away to an alien land* / ～美国 *flee to the United States*

【逃避】escape；shun；shirk：～责任 *shirk responsibility* / ～现实 *shun reality* / ～困难 *dodge a difficulty* / ～社会 *shun society*

【逃兵】① army deserter；deserter ② person who escapes from difficulty：在学习中不能当～。*One should not shrink from difficulty in one's study.* / 那个～被杀了。*The deserter was killed.*

【逃窜】escape in panic；flee in disorder：狼狈～ *flee helter-skelter*

【逃遁】flee；run away；evade

【逃犯】escaped criminal；convict：通缉～ *order the arrest of a criminal at large* / 追击～ *pursue and attack a convict*

【逃荒】flee from famine；be away from a famine-stricken area

【逃汇】evade foreign exchange control；illegal dealings in foreign currency

【逃婚】flee from an arranged marriage

【逃课】play truant；cut class

【逃命】flee or fly for one's life

【逃难】run away from a calamity；be a refugee

【逃匿】escape and hide；go into hiding

【逃跑】escape；take to one's heels；take flight

【逃票】get a free-ride；steal rides

【逃散】be separated in flight：寻找～的弟妹 *look for one's brother and sister separated in flight* / 敌人～了。*The enemy fled in utter confusion.*

【逃生】flee for one's life；escape with one's life：死里～ *barely escape with one's life*；*have a narrow escape* / 虎口～ *be saved from the tiger's mouth*；*be snatched from the jaws of death*

【逃税】dodge taxes：～漏税 *tax evasion* / ～人 *tax dodger*

【逃脱】succeed in escaping；get clear of；free oneself from；cast off：半路～ *make one's escape on the way* / ～罪责 *shake off one's responsibility for an offence* / 罪犯无法～。*The criminal found no refuge.*

【逃亡】become a fugitive；run away from home；go into exile

【逃学】play truant；cut class

【逃逸】［书］abscond；run away；flee：～速度 *escape velocity* / 格雷斯从监狱～了。*Grace fled from prison.*

【逃债】avoid creditors；dodge debts

【逃之夭夭】decamp；show a clean pair of heels；slip away

【逃走】flee；run away；take flight

【逃罪】escape from the law；escape responsibility for offence

桃 ① peach：～李满天涯 *one's students is all over the world — have numerous pupils* / 投～报李 *give a plum in return for a peach*；*return gift for gift* ② a peach-shaped thing：棉～ *cotton boll* ③ walnut：胡～ *walnut* / 胡～树 *walnut tree* / 胡～木 *walnut wood*

【桃脯】preserved peach

【桃红】pink

【桃红柳绿】pink peach flowers and green willow；a beautiful spring scene

【桃花】peach blossom：～粉 *rouge* / ～米 *inferior rice*

【桃花心木】mahogany

【桃花雪】snow when the peaches blossom；spring snow

【桃花汛】spring flood

【桃花鱼】minnow

【桃花运】① a man's luck in love；romance：走～ *be lucky in love affairs* ② be good lucky

【桃李】peaches and plums；one's pupils and disciples：～满天下 *have pupils everywhere* / ～盈门 *a whole house of peaches and plums-many disciples*

【桃李不言，下自成蹊】peaches and plums do not have to talk，yet the world beats a path to them

【桃仁】①【药】peach kernel ② walnut meat；shelled walnut

【桃腮杏眼】rosy cheeks and almond eyes-fair feminine faces

【桃色】① pink ② illicit love and sex：～案件 *legal cases involving love and sex* / ～新闻 *newspaper reports of illicit love stories*

【桃树】peach（tree）

【桃子】peach

陶[1] ① pottery; earthenware: 坯 ~ *greenware* /彩 ~ *painted pottery* /黑 ~ *black pottery* ② make pottery ③ nurture; cultivate: 熏 ~ *nurture; have a gradual uplifting influence on* ④ (Táo) a surname

陶[2] be contented; be happy: ~情养性 *please oneself and be happy*

【陶瓷】pottery and porcelain; ceramics: ~工 *potter* / ~业 *ceramic industry; ceramics* / ~片 *potsherd* / ~学 *ceramics*

【陶管】【建】earthenware pipe

【陶匠】potter

【陶钧】[书] ① potter's wheel ② train (talents): ~之力 *efforts to cultivate people's mind*

【陶器】pottery; earthenware

【陶然】happy and content; happy and carefree

【陶塑】pottery figure; pottery statue

【陶陶】happy; carefree; drunk

【陶土】potter's clay; pottery clay

【陶文】【考】inscription on pottery

【陶冶】① make pottery and smelt metal ② exert a favourable influence on; mould: ~性情 *refine a person's temperament*

【陶俑】【考】pottery figurine; terracotta figurine

【陶铸】[书] ① mould; form; cast ② educate; cultivate; train: ~人才 *train talented persons*

【陶醉】feel intoxicated; revel in; take great delight in: 安妮特的眼睛使我~。*Annette's eyes made me feel intoxicated.* /他正~在春光美景之中。*He is reveling in the beauty of spring.*

萄 grapes: ~酒 *grape wine* / ~糖 *grape sugar*

淘[1] ① wash in a pan or basket: ~沙 *wash sand* / ~米 *wash rice* /沙里~金 *pan out gold* ② [方] seek or buy a second-hand thing: ~旧书 *buy used books* ③ clean out; dredge: ~阴沟 *clean out a sewer* / ~井 *dredge a well*

淘[2] ① tax (a person's energy): ② [方] naughty; mischievous: 这女孩特~气。*The girl is very naughty.*

【淘换】look for; seek; try to gain

【淘金】panning; pan out gold: ~热 *gold rush* / ~盘 *a gold pan*

【淘气】① naughty; mischievous; disobedient: 爱~ *be fond of pranks* / ~鬼 *a mischievous imp* /他是一个~的孩子。*He's a terribly naughty child.* ② [方] lose one's temper; get angry

【淘沙拣金】wash the sand for gold; choose or search for the very best

【淘神】[口] trying; bother some: ~费力 *worrying the mind and wasting energy* /乔伊是一个令人~的人。*Joy is a trying person to deal with.* /小号字看起来很~。*Small print is trying to the eyes.*

【淘汰】① eliminate through selection or competition; be sifted out: ~出去 *clean it out* / ~法 *concentration* / ~赛 *elimination series* ② die out; be obsolete: 这种汽车已经~了。*This kind of car is already obsolete.*

tǎo

讨 ① fight; send armed forces to suppress; go on a punitive expedition: 东征西~ *fight east and west* ② denounce; decry: 声~ *denounce* ③ demand; beg for: 去跟老张~点墨汁。*Go and ask Lao Zhang for some Chinese ink.* ④ marry; get married: ~老婆 *take a wife* ⑤ incur; court: 自~没趣儿 *court a rebuff for oneself* ⑥ discuss; study; discourse: 商~ *discuss* /研~ *study and discuss*

【讨伐】send armed forces to suppress; send a punitive expedition against

【讨饭】beg for food; be a beggar

【讨好】① fawn on; curry favour with; ingratiate oneself with: ~领导 *curry favour with the leadership* /韦尔斯总是~女人。*Welles always fawns on women.* ② be rewarded with a fruitful result; get good result: 费力不~ *put in much hard work, but get very little result*

【讨还】ask for the return of sth; get sth back: ~欠债 *get one's debt repaid* / ~血债 *make sb pay for his bloody crimes* /年底农民工~了工资。*The farmers got their salary paid at the end of year.*

【讨价】name a price; demand a price: ~还价 *bargain; haggle* /漫天~ *ask an exorbitant price*

【讨教】consult; ask for advice

【讨论】have a discuss; talk over: ~问题 *discuss an issue* / ~会 *discussion; symposium* / ~要点 *key points for discussion*

【讨便宜】look for a bargain; get the cheap; seek undue advantage

【讨巧】choose the easy way out; act art fully to get what one wants

【讨情】intercede for sb; beg for a favour; plead for sb: ~告饶 *beg for pardon* /向某人~宽恕 *plead (with sb) for mercy*

【讨饶】beg for mercy; ask for pardon: 一再~ *ask again and again for forgiveness*

【讨扰】thanks for your hospitality

【讨生活】make a living; drift along

【讨嫌】annoying; disagreeable; bothersome

【讨厌】① disagreeable; annoying; disgusting: ~的天气 *abominable weather* /真~,我把钥匙落在家里了。*Oh bother! I've left my key at home.* ② hard to deal with; troublesome; nasty ③ hate; dislike; be disgusted with: 谁都~维拉。*Everybody is disgusted by Vera's behaviour.*

【讨债】ask for the payment of a debt; demand repayment of a loan

【讨债鬼】① a child who dies young ② person who squanders the money of his family

tào

套 ① sheath; cover; sleeve; slipcover: 枕~ *pillowcase; pillow slip* /书~ *slipcase* /椅~ *slip-*

T

cover for a chair /手～ *glove* /外～ *overcoat* ② cover with; slip over; put a cover over: ～上一件大衣 *slip a coat on* ③ that which covers: ～袖 *oversleeves* / ～鞋 *overshoes* ④ interlock; overlap: 环环相～ *one ring linked with another*; *a closely linked succession* ⑤ the bend of a river or curve in a river or curve in a mountain range: 河～ *the Great Bend of Huanghe River* ⑥ put a ring; round; tie: 用绳子～一只狼 *catch a wolf with a lasso* ⑦ harness (a draught animal); hitch up (a draught animal to a cart): 让雷恩来～这匹骡子。*Let Wren hitch up this mule.* ⑧ copy; imitate: ～公式 *apply a formal* ⑨ illegally purchase: ～汇 *illegal procurement of foreign exchange* ⑩ coax a secret out of sb; sound out; try to find out: 拿话～他 *coax the secret out of him* / ～口供 *trick the accused into confession* ⑪ try to get one's friendship: ～交情 *try to establish friendship* ⑫ [方] cotton padding; batting: 棉花～ *cotton wadding* /被～ *quilt padding* ⑬ [方] put cotton, silk wadding, etc. into bedclothes and sew up ⑭ traces; harness: 牲口～ *animal harness* ⑮ knot; loop; noose: 双～结 *double knot* /拴个～儿 *make a loop* /活～儿 *slipknot*; *running knot* ⑯ convention; formula: 俗～ *conventionalities*; *stereotype* /老～ *the same old stuff* ⑰ set; suit; suite: 成～的书 *complete set of books* ⑱ use the tap or screw die to cut a thread

【套版】【印】① register ② process plate; colour plate

【套包】collar for a horse

【套裁】cut out a piece of cloth in a way with the minimum material to make two or more articles of clothing

【套菜】semi-finished dish

【套餐】set meal

【套车】hitch up an animal to a cart: 我去～。*I'll go and get the cart ready.*

【套房】① small room opening off another; inner room ② apartment; suite: 总统～ *presidential suite* /两居室的～ *a two-room flat*

【套服】suit; clothes: 毛料～ *suit of woolen clothes* /三件一套的～ *a three-piece suit* /男～ *a man's* /女～ *a woman's*

【套购】illegally procure; arbitrage; fraudulently purchase: ～外汇 *illegally procure foreign exchange* /～车票 *fraudulently purchase ticket*

【套话】① polite expressions; conventionality ② empty talk; empty speech

【套环】【机】lantern ring

【套换】gain or buy sth by illegal means: ～外汇 *get foreign currency through illegal channels* / ～邮票 *get stamps through illegal ways*

【套汇】① procure foreign exchange illegally: ～汇率 *arbitrage rate* ② engage in arbitrage; arbitrage: ～商 *arbitrageur* / ～账户 *arbitrage account*

【套间】① apartment; flat ② inner room; small room opening off another

【套交情】try to get in good with sb

【套近乎】try to chum up with sb; cotton up to sb; try to form ties with

【套裤】trouser legs worn over one's trousers; leggings

【套马】① lasso a horse ② hitch up a horse to a cart

【套曲】【音】divertimento

【套取】gain illegally

【套裙】woman's suit including a skirt

【套衫】pullover: 女～ *woman's pullover* /男～ *man's pullover*

【套绳】① lasso; noose ② harness; hitch up

【套数】① cycle of songs in a traditional opera ② series of skills and tricks ③ conventional remark; conventionality

【套索】lasso; noose

【套套】[方] method; ways: 老～ *old stuff*

【套筒】【机】sleeve; bush; thimble: ～扳手 *box spanner* /汽缸～ *cylinder sleeve*; *cylinder bush*

【套头交易】hedging

【套间】sound out; try to find out

【套鞋】overshoes

【套印】【印】① chromatography: 彩色～ *process printing* / ～本 *chromatograph edition*

【套用】copy; apply mechanically

【套语】① polite expressions; conventionalities ② conventional remark; empty formula

【套轴】【机】sleeve spindle

【套子】① sheath; cover; slipcover: 剑～ *sword's sheath* /沙发～ *slipcover for a sofa* ② empty remark; conventional formula: 俗～ *conventional pattern* ③ cotton wadding; batting: 棉花～ *cotton padding* ④ trap; snare: 我不会去钻他的～。*I couldn't walk into his trap.*

tè

特[1] ① special; particular; unusual; extraordinary: 工作～努力 *work hard* /奇～ *peculiar*; *quaint* /能力～强 *unusually capable* /他对烤面包有一套独～的方法。*He has a special way of baking bread.* ② especially; for a special purpose: 他～为此事而来。*He's come for this purpose especially.* /这是～别为你准备的。*This is especially for you.* ③ secret agent; spy: 敌～ *enemy agent*

特[2] [书] mere; but; only: 此～雕虫小技耳。*This is mere insignificant skill.*

【特别】① exceptional; special; peculiar; particular; extraordinary: ～重要的事情 *a matter of particular importance* /无～原因 *for no special reason* ② in particular; specially; specifically: 我～想看那部电影。*I particularly want to see that film.* ③ for a special purpose; specially: 他临走时～地去向女主人道谢。*He made a point of thanking his hostess before he left the party.* ④ unusually; uncommonly; extraordinarily: 个子～小 *of an unusually short in figure* / ～法 *special law* / ～会议 *special meeting* / ～监护病房 *intensive care unit*

(ICU) / ~快车 express train; special express / ~提款权 special drawing right (SDR) / ~条款 special clause / ~行政区 special administrative region / ~许可证 special license

【特产】special local products; specialty:北方~ specialties of the north / 土~ special local products

【特长】speciality; special skill; strong point:游泳是他的~。Swimming is his strong point.

【特此】hereby:~函告。You're hereby informed by the letter.

【特大】exceptionally big; very large; extra large; the most:~喜讯 excellent news / ~干旱 the worst drought

【特等】special grade; ace; top class:~舱 stateroom / ~奖 special award / 丹皮尔是一个~司机。Dampier is a driver in top class.

【特地】specially; for a special purpose:~前来拜访 come specially to visit

【特点】characteristic; unique feature; trait:事物的~ the distinctive features of a thing / 生理~ physiological characteristics

【特定】① specially appointed; specially assigned:~的人选 a person specially appointed for a post ② given; specific; particular:~的条件 given conditions / ~期限 definite term / ~的使命 specially assigned mission

【特工】spy; secret service:~人员 special agent; secret service personnel / 美国~ a American spy

【特供】special supply

【特护】① special-nursing:~病房 special-nursing ward ② special nurse:这个~叫伊丽莎白。The special nurse is Elizabeth.

【特惠】indulgence; preferential:~关税 preferential import tariffs / ~条款 preferential clause / ~待遇 preferential treatment

【特级】special grade; superfine:~糖 superfine sugar

【特急】extra urgent:~电报 extra urgent telegram

【特辑】① special number of a periodical ② special collection of short films

【特技】① stunt; trick:~飞行 stunt flying / ~跳伞 trick parachuting ② film special efforts

【特价】a bargain price; a low price:~出售 sell at a bargain price / ~柜台 bargain counter

【特警】special police; special policeman

【特刊】special issue:国庆~ special National Day Issue

【特快】① express:~邮件 express mail / ~业务的范围 the items of express (or urgent) business ② special express; express train

【特困户】destitute household

【特立独行】think and act independently; not drift with the tide:~的小说家 novelist with an independent mind

【特例】special case

【特洛伊】Troy:~战争 Trojan War / ~木马 Trojan horse

【特命全权大使】ambassador extraordinary and plenipotentiary

【特命全权公使】envoy extraordinary and minister plenipotentiary

【特派】specially appointed; specially employed:~员 special commissioner / ~记者 special correspondent; accredited journalist / ~大使 envoy extraordinary

【特遣部队】task force

【特区】special zone:经济~ special economic zone (SEZ)

【特权】privilege; special right:~阶层 privileged stratum / 外交~ diplomatic privileges / ~地位 privileged position

【特色】characteristic; unique feature:民族~ distinctive national features

【特设】ad hoc:~委员会 ad hoc committee / ~机构 ad hoc organ

【特赦】special pardon; special amnesty:~令 decree of special pardon

【特使】envoy extraordinary; ambassador extraordinary

【特殊】especial; exceptional; particular; more than usual:~情况 especial case / ~材料 particular material / ~现象 unusual phenomenon / ~教育 special education for the handicapped / ~化 become privileged

【特务】① special task or duties:~连 special task company ② special agent; spy:~机关 secret service / ~组织 spy organization / ~活动 espionage

【特效】specially good effect; special efficacy:~药 specific drug; specific; effective cure

【特写】① feature article or story; feature:报纸~ a feature in newspaper ② film close-up:~镜头 close-up shot

【特性】specific characteristic; specific property; specific feature

【特许】permit in particular:~证书 special permit; letters patent / ~公司 chartered company / ~经营商店 franchise store / ~权 chartered right; franchise

【特压】【化】extreme pressure:~添加剂 extreme pressure additive

【特邀】specially invite:~代表 specially invited representative / ~来宾 specially invited guests

【特异】① excellent; superfine; very good; extraordinary:成绩~ an excellent record ② peculiar; distinctive; unusual:~功能 extraordinary powers

【特有】peculiar; characteristic; used or practiced only by sb or sth

【特约】engage by special arrangement:~稿 special publication / ~评论员 special commentator / ~维修店 special repair shop / ~记者 special correspondent / ~演员 special actor

【特征】characteristic; feature; trait:中国的地理~是什么? What are the geographical features of China?

【特指】refer in particular to

【特制】specially made

【特种】special kind; particular type:~兵 special

T

troops / ～工艺 *special arts and crafts* / ～战争 *special warfare* / ～出版物 *special publications* (*SP*) / ～合金钢 *special alloy steel* / ～邮票 *special stamp*

【特装本】【印】edition binding

téng

疼 ① ache; hurt; have a pain: ～痛难忍 *have a unbearable pain* / 背～ *have a backache* / 胃～ *have a stomachache* / 牙～ *have a toothache* / 我头～。*My head aches.* / 我浑身～痛。*My body was all aches and pains.* ② love clearly; dote on; show much fondness for sb: 克米特十分～爱孙女。*Kermit dotes on his grandchildren.*

【疼爱】adore; be very food of: 过分～ *dote on* / 他特别～儿子。*He is very food of his son.*

【疼痛】ache; pain; hurt; soreness: ～的叫喊 *a cry of pain* / 他胸部～。*He has an ache in the chest.*

【疼惜】love tenderly; love dearly and take pity on

腾 ① gallop; go at a gallop; jump; bound: 热血沸～ *burning with righteous indignation*; *one's blood boils* / 欢～ *great rejoicing*; *jubilation* / ～身而过 *jump over sth* / 万马奔～ *ten thousand horses galloping ahead* / 万众欢～ *the people dance for joy* ② soar; rise; shoot up: 浓烟升～ *billows of thick smoke rising* ③ make room; release; vacate: ～出自己的位子 *vacate one's seat* ④ used after a verb denoting repeated action: 倒～ *do sth over and over again*

【腾达】① rise; ascend; skyrocket ② rise high; climb up; soar aloft: 飞黄～ *get rapid promotion*; *be successful in one's official career*

【腾飞】① fly rapidly; soar ② progress rapidly; take-off make rapid advance: 经济～ *rapid economic development*; *take-off* / 祖国在～。*Our country is developing rapidly.*

【腾空】soar; skyrocket; go up high in the air rapidly; rise high into the air: 那架喷气式飞机～而起。*The jet soared into the air.* / 凯歌～云霄。*Songs of victory soar to the skies.*

【腾挪】① divert; transfer (funds, etc.) to other use ② vacate; move sth to make room: ～房子 *vacate a house*

【腾迁】vacate and move elsewhere

【腾闪】dodge; evade: ～不及 *be too late to dodge*

【腾腾】steaming; seething: 雾气～ *hazy with mist* / 烈焰～ *raging flames* / 杀气～ *murderous-looking*

【腾越】jump over; leap; spring

【腾云驾雾】① ride the clouds and mount the mist ② feel giddy or dizzy: 他听爱因斯坦的报告感觉如～一般。*He felt totally dizzy when he attended an Einstein's lecture.*

誊 transcribe; copy sth in writing; make a written copy of sth: 她草草做了些笔记，然后～写在练习本上。*She jotted down a few notes, and later transcribed them into an exercise book.* / 他在～一篇报告。*He's copying out a report.*

【誊录】transcribe by hand; copy sth in writing: ～文稿 *copy out a manuscript*

【誊清】make a clean copy of: ～稿 *a clean copy*

【誊写】copy out; transcribe (by hand): ～出信函的复本 *copy out a letter* / ～版 *stencil* / ～蜡纸 *stencil paper* / ～油墨 *stencil ink* / ～信件 *copy out a letter*

【誊印社】mimeograph service

藤 ① vine: 冬瓜～ *wax gourd vine* / 顺～摸瓜 *follow the vine to get the melon-track sth or sb down by following clues* ② cane; rattan: ～箱 *rattan trunk* / ～椅 *cane chair*; *rattan chair*

【藤本植物】【植】liana; vine

【藤牌】cane shield; rattan shield

【藤条】rattan

【藤蔓】vine: 葡萄～ *grapevines* / 黄瓜～ *cucumber vine*

tī

剔 ① clean with a pointed instrument; pick out and reject; throw away; pick: ～眉毛 *pull eyebrows* / ～指甲 *clean the fingernails* / ～牙缝儿 *pick one's teeth* / ～骨头 *pick the bones* / 挑～ *nit-pick*; *be hypercritical* / 把烂苹果～出去。*Pick out the rotten apples.* ② rising stroke (in Chinese characters)

【剔除】remove; throw away; get rid of: ～错字病句 *get rid of misprints and ungrammatical sentences.* / ～杂草 *get rid of weeds* / 这本书我们吸取精华，～糟粕。*We should absorb the essence and reject the dross in this book.*

【剔透】bright and limpid; transparent: 晶莹～ *sparkling ling bright* / 玲珑～ *beautifully wrought*

梯 ① ladder; stairs; steps: 楼～ *staircase* / 自动扶～ *escalator* / 电～ *lift*; *elevator* / 三十级的～子 *a ladder of thirty steps* ② shaped like a staircase; terraced

【梯次队形】【军】echelon formation

【梯度】【物】gradient

【梯队】①【军】echelon formation; echelon ② echelon of successor; rank in an organization

【梯恩梯】【化】trinitrotoluene (TNT): ～当量 *TNT equivalent*

【梯级】① stair; step: 陡的～ *a steep stair* / 登～ *ascend a stairs* / 一段～ *a pair* (*or flight*) *of stairs* ② terraced water conservancy project or works

【梯己】① private money; private savings ② intimate; confidential: ～话 *words said in confidence*

【梯田】【农】terraced fields; terrace

【梯形】【数】trapezoid; trapezium: ～翼 *trapezoidal wing*; *tapered airfoil*

【梯子】ladder; step ladder

锑 【化】antimony; stibium (SB): ～合金 *antimony alloy* / ～铜矿 *horsfordite* / ～中毒 *stibialism*; *antimony poisoning*

踢 kick; hit with the foot; play (football): ~足球 *play football* / ~进一个球 *kick (or score) a goal* /他在墙上~了个洞。*He kicked a hole in the wall.* /他把石头~进河里了。*He kicked the rock into the river.* /安娜~我。*Anna kicked me.*

【踢脚板】【建】skirting board

【踢踏舞】step dance; tap dance

tí

提 ① carry (in one's hand with the arm down); fetch: 手~包 *hand-bag* / 手~电话 *cellular phone*; *mobile phone* /我去~壶水来。*I'm going to fetch a kettle of water.* ② lift; promote; move upward; raise: 把他~到领导岗位上去 *promote him to a position of leadership* ③ advance; shift a date; move to an earlier time ④ put forward; suggest; raise: ~方案 *suggest plans* / ~条件 *put forward conditions* ⑤ draw out; withdraw; extract: ~款 *draw money* /我到车站~行李去。*I'm going to collect my luggage at the station.* ⑥ summon; take out; bring out from prison under escort: ~犯人 *take out a convict from prison* ⑦ mention; speak about; refer to: 重~旧事 *recall a past event*; *bring up an old score* ⑧ dipper; ladle: 油~ *oil-dipper* /醋~*vinegar-dipper* ⑨ rising stroke (in Chinese characters)
see also dī

【提案】motion; formal proposal; draft resolution: 建设性的~ *constructive proposal* / ~国 *sponsor country* / ~审查委员会 *motions examination committee* / ~被否决了。*The motion was rejected.* / ~通过了。*The motion was rejected.*

【提拔】promote; raise: 破格~ *break a rule to promote sb* /彼特工作很努力,很快便获得~。*Peter worked hard and was soon promoted.*

【提包】bag; handbag; valise

【提笔】take up one's pen; start writing

【提倡】advocate; encourage; recommend; promote: ~计划生育 *advocate family planning* / ~说普通话 *promote the use of mandarin* / ~俭省节约 *advocate frugality* / ~消费 *advocate consumption* / ~国货 *promote domestic products*

【提成】draw a percentage; deduct a percentage; take a cut: ~额 *unit* /按合同~ *deduct a percentage of money according to a contract*

【提出】put forward; pose; raise; offer a proposal: ~异议 *make an objection* / ~建议 *put forward a proposal* / ~抗议 *lodge a protest* / ~警告 *give a warning* / ~辞职 *tender one's resignation*

【提纯】purify; refine: ~器 *purifier* / ~复壮 *purify and rejuvenate* / ~金属 *refine a metal*

【提词】prompt: 幕后~ *prompt behind the scenes* / ~人 *prompter*

【提单】bill of lading (B/L): 直达~ *direct bill of lading* /联运~ *through bill of lading*

【提兜】handbag; bag; shopping bag

【提督】provincial or military commander in imperial China: 水师~ *naval commander*

【提法】the manner of presentation; wording; the way sth is put: 这是个新的~。*This is a new formulation.* /这只是个~问题。*This is just a matter of wording.*

【提干】① promote sb to a higher position ② make sb an official: 他不久前~,当了排长。*He was promoted to be a platoon leader not long ago.*

【提纲】outline; statement of the main facts or points: 写讲演~ *make an outline for a lecture* /发言~ *outline for a speech*

【提高】increase raise; boost; heighten; improve; enhance: ~警惕 *raise one's vigilance* / ~经济效益 *increase economic efficiency* / ~水位 *raise the water level* / ~认识 *deepen one's understanding* / ~收入 *augment one's income*

【提供】supply; provide; offer; furnish: ~资金 *fund*; *finance* / ~援助 *give aid*; *provide assistance* / ~优质服务 *offer quality service* / ~贷款 *offer a loan*

【提行】【印】begin a new line: ~另起 *start another line*

【提盒】tiered box (for carrying pastry, etc.)

【提花】jacquard weave: ~织机 *jacquard loom*

【提货】pick up goods; fetch delivery of goods: 到车站~ *pick up goods at the station* / ~通知 *cargo delivery notice*

【提及】mention; speak of; talk about

【提级】promote; advance sb to a higher rank

【提价】increase prices; mark up: ~商品 *goods sold at raised prices* / ~过高 *excessive price increase*

【提交】submit sth to; give sth to; refer to: 向指导老师~论文 *submit an essay to one's tutor* /向委员会~计划呈请批准 *submit plans to the council for approval*

【提款】draw money from a bank; withdraw; take out: ~单 *withdrawal ticket* / 我们公司已经收到~通知了。*Our company has received the advice of drawing.*

【提篮】hand basket

【提炼】refine; purify; abstract: ~率 *rate of extraction* /从矿石中~金属 *extract metal from ore*

【提留】retain a percentage; deduct a portion from the whole

【提名】nominate: ~奖 *nomination* / ~人 *nominator* / ~委员会 *nomination committee*

【提起】① refer to; speak of; mention ② raise; arouse; brace up ③ initiate; institute: ~公诉 *initiate a public prosecution*

【提前】advance; move to an earlier time; move up; do sth in advance: ~完成任务 *accomplish a task ahead of time* / ~偿付 *prepayment* / ~量 *lead*

【提挈】[书] ① lead; take with one; marshal ② guide and support; give guidance and help to: ~后辈 *give guidance and help to younger people*

【提亲】make a proposal of marriage alliance

T

【提琴】【音】violin family:大～*violoncello*/小～*violin*/中～*viola*/低音～*double bass*

【提请】submit to; ask for; propose: ～辩论 *make a motion for debate* / ～大会批准 *submit to the congress for approval* / ～董事会审批 *submit a proposal to the board of directors for deliberation and approval*

【提取】① pick up; collect; take: ～存款 *withdraw a bank deposit* ② extract; abstract; recover: 从谷物中～酒精 *distil alcohol from grain* / ～器 *extractor* / ～塔 *extraction column*

【提神】refresh; revive; give a lift; invigorate: 喝茶能～*refresh oneself with a cup of tea* / ～健脑 *refresh oneself and invigorate the function of the brain*

【提审】① bring (a suspect, etc.) before the court; bring to trial; fetch (a detainee) for interrogation: ～罪犯 bring a criminal before the court ②【律】review

【提升】① raise; promote: ～他当经理 *promote him to be a manager* ② hoist; lift; elevate: ～机 *hoist; elevator* / ～设施 *elevating facilities*

【提示】prompt; help by suggesting the words; point out: ～要点 *point out the main points* / 阅读～*reading guide* / 演员需要不时给予～。*The actor needed an occasional prompt.*

【提说】[方] speak of; mention; talk about

【提味】make appetizing; make flavourful; render palatable

【提问】ask a question; put a question; quiz: ～方式 *ways to ask questions* / 当场～*ask questions on the spot*

【提线木偶】marionette

【提箱】suitcase

【提携】① lead (sb) by the hand ② guide and support; give guidance and help to

【提心】worry; concern

【提心吊胆】live in constant fear; pull up one's socks; be always on tenterhooks

【提醒】remind; inform sb of a fact; call attention to; alert; warn: 还需要我再次～你吗? *Do I have to remind you yet again?* / ～我回那封信。*Remind me to answer that letter.*

【提选】choose; pick; select: ～耐旱品种 *select drought-resistant varieties*

【提讯】bring (a convict, etc.) before the court; bring to trial; fetch for interrogation

【提要】abstract; summary; main points: 小说～*abstract of a novel* / 内容～*capsule summary*

【提议】① make a proposal; suggest; move; offer for consideration: ～人 *proposer* / 我～为我们的将来干杯。*I should like to proposer a toast to our future.* ② proposal; motion: 缔结和平条约新条款的～*the proposal of new terms for a peace treaty*

【提早】move to an earlier time; be earlier than planned or expected; do (sth) ahead of time: ～出发 *set out earlier than planned* / 灾难～降临了。*Disaster is upon us earlier than expected.*

【提制】gain through refining; refine; distil; abstract

啼

① cry; weep loudly; wail: 鸣～(*of birds*) *crow; warble* / 哀～*cry with despair; in agony* / 哭哭～～*weep and wail* ② crow; caw; howl: 月落乌～。*The crows caw when the moon goes down.*

【啼号】cry loudly; howl; wail

【啼饥号寒】cry from hunger and cold; howl for being hungry and cry for feeling cold

【啼叫】① (of birds and beasts) howl; crow ② [方] cry weep

【啼哭】cry; weep; wail: 女儿在妈妈怀里大声～。*The daughter cried loudly in his mother's lap.*

【啼鸣】(of birds) crow; tweet; warble

【啼笑皆非】not to know whether to laugh or cry; be able neither to cry nor to laugh

题

① topic; title; subject; title: 难～*thorny problem; poser* / 习～*exercise* / 问～*question; problem; issue* / 小标～*subtitle* / 讨论～*top for discussion* ② write; inscribe: ～诗一首 *inscribe a poem* / ～照 *sign one's photo* / ～跋 *preface and postscript; short annotations on a scroll of painting or handwriting*

【题材】topic; subject; theme: 城市～*theme on the town scene* / ～范围 *range of subjects*

【题词】① write an inscription ② inscription; dedication ③ foreword

【题花】title design

【题记】① preface ② short remarks at the beginning of an article; summary

【题解】① explanatory notes on the title or background of a book ② answer or key to exercises or problems

【题库】test question bank

【题名】① inscribe one's name; autograph: ～留念 *give one's autograph as a memento* ② title or name of (a book, poem etc.)

【题目】① subject; title; topic: 开会的～*topic of the meeting* / 小说的～*title of the novel* / 辩论的～*subject for a debate* ② exercise problems; examination questions

【题签】① write the title of a book on a label to be stuck on the cover ② label with the title of a book on it

【题外话】digression; passage, etc. in which one digresses

【题写】write; inscribe

【题旨】① meaning of the title of an article ② theme of a literary work

【题字】① write an inscription; inscribe ② inscription; autograph: 书上有作者亲笔～。*The book is autographed by the author.*

醍

【醍醐】[古] clarified butter; finest cream; supreme truth

【醍醐灌顶】feel refreshed suddenly; be filled with wisdom; be enlightened

蹄 hoof; trotters (esp. as food): 牛～ *ox's trotters* / 马～ *horse's hoofs* / 马不停～ *without any rest* / 猪 *pig's trotters*

【蹄筋】tendons of beef, mutton or pork: 红烧～ *tendons stewed in soy sauce*

【蹄膀】[方] upper part of a leg of pork

【蹄铁】【冶】horseshoe: ～钢 *horseshoe bar*

【蹄行磁铁】【电】horseshoe magnet

【蹄子】① [口] hoof ② [方] leg of pork ③ [旧] (used of a woman) bitch

tǐ

体 ① part of the body; body; limb: 魂不附～ *feel as if one's soul has left one's body* / 人～ *human body* / 遗～ *remains* / 肢～ *limb* / 五～投地 *be on all fours* ② substance; state of a substance: 固～ *solid* / 液～ *liquid* / 气～ *gas* / 天～ *celestial body* / 集～ *collective* / 个～ *individual* / 本～ *thing-in-itself*; *noumenon* ③ typeface; style; form: 文～ *type of writing*; *literary style* / 字～ *style of calligraphy*; *form of a written character* ④ system; regime: 政～ *system of government* / 国～ *state system* ⑤【语】aspect (of a verb): 进行～ *progressive aspect* / 完成～ *perfect aspect* ⑥ personally do or experience sth; put oneself in another's position: 身～力行 *earnestly practise what one preaches*

【体表】① body surface: ～面积 *body surface area* / ～温度 *temperature of body surface* ② body thermometer

【体裁】style or form of literature; genre

【体操】gymnastics: 自由～ *free exercise* / 艺术～ *artistic gymnastics* / ～运动员 *gymnast* / ～服 *gym suit* / ～器械 *gymnastic apparatus*

【体察】experience and observe; understand and sympathize: 虚心～情况 *be ready to look into matters with an open mind*; *not be prejudiced in sizing up situations*

【体罚】physical or corporal punishment: ～学生 *punish students physically*

【体格】① physique; constitution; general appearance and size of a person's body: 发育匀称的～ *a well-developed physique* / 健壮的～ *a fine physique* / ～检查 *health check-up*; *physical examination*; *physical* ② figure; build; bodily form

【体会】① know from experience; realize; feel: 他深深～到健康的重要。*He deeply felt the importance of the health.* ② knowledge; understanding: 深有～ *have an intimate knowledge of sth*

【体积】volume; bulk; size: ～大 *bulky* / 容器的～ *the volume of a container* / ～膨胀 *volume expansion*

【体检】physical examination; physical

【体力】physical (or bodily) strength; physical power; stamina: ～充沛 *be full of physical strength* / 增强～ *build up one's strength* / ～劳动 *physical labour* / ～话 *physical work*

【体例】stylistic rules and layout; style: 今天你一定要把～说明写完。*You must finish the mote to the style today.*

【体谅】understand; make allowances for

【体貌】figure and features; general physical appearance: ～端正 *have a regular appearance*

【体面】① dignity; face; prestige: 维持～ *keep up appearance* / 有失～ *lose one's dignity*; *be a loss of face* ② honorable; creditable; respectable: 不～的行为 *disgraceful* (*or disreputable*) *conduct* ③ good-looking; handsome; smart: 长得～ *have good looks*

【体能】physical strength; stamina: ～训练 *training of physical strength*

【体魄】[书] physique; build; constitution: 强壮的～ *powerful physique*; *vigorous health*

【体腔】【生理】body cavity; coelom: ～管 *coelomoduct* / ～动物 *coelomate*

【体式】① type of characters or letters ② [书] style of literary works; genre

【体视】【物】stereo: ～显微镜 *stereomicroscope* / ～摄影机 *stereo camera*

【体态】posture; carriage; bearing: ～轻盈 *have a graceful carriage*

【体坛】sports world; sports circles: 约翰的哥哥是一名～新秀。*Johns's elder brother is a new sports star.*

【体贴】considerate; care for; show consideration: ～妻子 *show one's wife every consideration* / ～入微 *look after with great care*; *care for with great solicitude*

【体统】propriety; decorum; decency: 有失～ *be disgraceful*; *be against decorum* / 成何～! *What impropriety or how disgraceful!*

【体外受精】external fertilization

【体委】short for commission for physical culture and sports; sports commission

【体位】posture; position

【体温】(body) temperature: 量～ *take one's temperature* / ～过低 *hypothermia* / ～计 (*clinical*) *thermometer*

【体无完肤】① be beaten black and blue: 他被打得～。*He was beaten black and blue.* ② be thoroughly refuted; be torn to pieces

【体系】system; setup

【体现】embody; manifest; incarnate; express visible form to (ideas, feelings, etc.): 在我看来,他本身～了战士应有的一切优秀品质。*To me he embodies all the best qualities of a soldier.*

【体形】bodily form; physical shape; build

【体型】type of build or figure

【体恤】show understanding and sympathy for; show solicitude for; concern oneself

【体恤衫】T-shirt

【体验】experience; have experience of; feel; learn from practice: ～生活 *observe and learn from real life* / ～痛苦 *experience pain* / 他从未～过真正的情绪低落。*I've ever experienced real depression.*

【体液】body fluid; humor

【体育】【体】① physical culture; physical education: ~锻炼 *physical training* / ~教材 *PE teaching material* ② sports: ~爱好者 *sports fan; sports enthusiast* / ~记者 *sports writer* / ~新闻编辑 *sports-editor* / ~节目广播 *sportscast* / ~节目主持人 *sports caster* / ~场 *stadium* / ~界 *the world of sport* / ~节目 *a sports programme* / ~疗法 *physical exercise therapy* / ~道德 *sportsmanship*

【体征】【医】pathological bodily sign

【体制】system (of organization); set-up; structure: 管理~ *managerial system*

【体制改革】structural reform; reform of system; restructuring: 经济~ *economic restructuring* / 政治~ *political structural reform* / 教育~ *structural reform of education* / ~委员会 *commission for structural reform*

【体质】physique; constitution; build: 增强~ *build up health* / ~人类学 *physical anthropology*

【体重】(body) weight: ~增加 *put on weight; gain weight* / ~不足 *under weight* / ~减轻 *lose weight* / ~过重 *overweight* / 那两个男孩~相同。*The two boys are the same weight.*

T

tì

屉 ① food steamer with several trays; steamer tray: ~帽 *lid (or cover) of a steamer* ② [方] drawer: 五~柜 *five-drawer chest*

【屉子】① (one of) a set of removable trays (in furniture or a utensil) ② [方] drawer

剃 shave: ~胡子 *shave oneself; have a shave*

【剃刀】razor

【剃刀鲸】blue whale

【剃度】【宗】tonsure: ~出家 *be tonsured*

【剃光头】① have one's head shaved ② score no points; lay an egg: 我们队给对方~了, 3 比 0。*Our team blanked the other, three to zero.*

【剃头】① have one's head shaved: ~刀 *shaver* ② have one's hair cut; have a haircut: ~师傅 *barber*

【剃须膏】shaving cream

倜

【倜傥】[书] elegant; handsome; free and easy: ~不群 *unconventional and aloof; a handsome dandy* / ~不羁 *untrammeled and romantic in character* / 风流~ *unconventional and romantic; casual and elegant bearing*

涕 ① tears: ~哭 *weep bitterly* / 痛哭流~ *cry and shed bitter tears; weep bitter tears of remorse* / 破~为笑 *turn tears into smiles; turn from grief to joy* ② mucus of the nose; snivel

【涕泪】① tears: ~纵横 *with tears streaming down one's face* ② tears and snivel: ~交流。*Tears and snivel fall down at the same time.*

【涕零】shed tears; weep tears: 痛哭~ *wail; cry bitterly; weep bitterly* / 感激~ *be moved to tears of gratitude*

【涕泣】[书] weep; be in tears

【涕泗】[书] tears and snivel: ~交流 *have tears and snivel flowing down together* / ~滂沱 *a flood of tears; tears and mucus run abundantly down one's face*

惕 cautious; watchful: 警~ *be on the alert; watch out*

替[1] ① replace; take the place of; substitute for; displace: 季节更~ *alternate of season; change of season* / 这个会我来不了, 我让助手~我出席。*I can't attend the meeting, but I'll send my assistant in my stead.* ② for; on behalf of; instead of: ~人受罪 *suffer for sb else*

替[2] [书] decline; fall: 百年兴~ *vicissitudes of a century*

【替班】work instead of sb: ~司机 *replacement driver*

【替补】substitute for; take the place of: ~人员 *replacement staff*

【替代】replace; supersede; take the place of; displace: 杂草越来越多, 有~其他植物之势。*Weeds tend to displace other plants*

【替工】① work as a replacement: ~记录 *replacement record* ② temporary substitute (worker)

【替古人担忧】worry about the ancients; waste one's energy by worrying needlessly

【替换】provide a substitute for; take the place of; replace: ~材料 *alternate* / 带上一套~的衣服。*Take a change of clothes with you.*

【替角儿】understudy

【替身】① substitute; displacement; replacement; stand-in: 当~ *serve as a replacement* ② scapegoat; fall guy: ~演员 *stunt man; stunt woman*

【替死鬼】[口] fall guy; scapegoat; whipping boy

【替天行道】act for God and perform moral acts; carry out the heavenly wishes; enforce justice on behalf of Heaven

【替罪羊】scapegoat; fall guy: 没想到我倒成了他的~。*I had never thought that I would become his scapegoat.*

嚏 [书] sneeze: ~喷 *sneeze*

tiān

天 ① sky; heaven: 蓝~ *blue sky* / 明朗的~ *clear sky* / 九重~ *ninth Heaven; highest of heavens* / 满~星斗 *star-studded sky* ② day: 昨~ *yesterday* / 大白~ *in broad daylight* ③ a period of time in a day; time of day: 五更~ *around four in the morning* / 正午~ *high noon* ④ season: 夏~ *summer* / 冷~ *cold days; cold season* ⑤ weather: 下雪~ *snowy weather* / 下雨~ *wet (or rainy) weather* ⑥ inborn; innate; natural: 先~ *congenital; priori; inborn* ⑦ nature: 人定胜~。*Man will conquer nature.* ⑧ heaven; god: 上~保佑。*May*

God be with me or God helps me ⑨ Heaven; paradise: 归~ *go to heaven*; *die* ⑩ overhead: ~桥 *overhead walkway*

【天崩地裂】heaven fall and earth rend; violent political or social up heavily

【天边】horizon; ends of the earth; remotest places: 远在~,近在眼前 *seemingly far away, actually close at hand*

【天兵】troops from heaven; invincible army

【天不怕,地不怕】fear neither heaven nor earth; fear nothing at all; nothing daunted

【天不负人】Heaven always rewards the faithful; all for the best

【天才】genius; talent; gift; endowment: 艺术~ *artistic genius*; *gift for art* / 音乐~ *musical talent* / ~论 *the theory of innate genius* / 画坛~ *master in painting*

【天蚕】【动】giant silkworm; wild silkworm

【天长地久】as long as the world lasts; enduring as the universe: 友谊~ *everlasting friendship*; *eternal friendship*

【天长日久】for a long time; for many, many years to come

【天车】【机】overhead traveling crane; shop traveler: ~滑道 *crane runway*

【天成佳偶】perfect match made by heaven; a godsend marriage

【天秤座】【天】libra; the Balance

【天窗】【建】skylight

【天赐】bestowed by heaven; sent by God: ~良机 *a godsend opportunity* / ~我也! *This is indeed a godsend!*

【天从人愿】God willing; heaven accords with human wishes; by the grace of God

【天大】extremely big; as large as the heavens: ~的好事 *excellent thing*; *wonderful*; *wonderful luck* / ~的面子 *mark of special favour* / ~的笑话 *colossal absurdity*

【天道】① way of heaven; objective laws; manifestations of God's will: 上逆~,下违人常 *run counter to the ways of both Heaven and man*; *be grossly unjust* ② weather: 看看~,好像要下雪了。*It looks like snow.*

【天敌】【生】natural enemy

【天底】【天】nadir

【天底下】[口] under heaven; on earth; in the world: ~哪有这种道理! *Nobody on earth would reason that way or how preposterous!*

【天地】① heaven and earth; world; universe: ~万物 *all creatures in the universe*; *everything in the world* ② field of activity; scope of operation; world: 儿童~ *children's world* / 每个人都有自己的~。*Everyone lives in his own circle.* ③ wretched situation; plight

【天地不容】can not be tolerated by heaven and earth; heaven forbid; a towering crime that neither god nor men can forgive

【天地良心】in my soul of souls; from the bottom of my heart; in all farness

【天地头】【印】top and bottom margins of a page; upper and lower margins of a page

【天帝】lord of Heaven

【天顶】【天】zenith

【天鹅】swan; cygnus: 小~ *cygnet* / ~绒毛 *swansdown* / ~绒 *velvet*

【天鹅座】【天】cygnus; northern cross

【天蛾】【动】sphingid; hawkmoth

【天翻地覆】turn the whole world upside down; heaven and earth have been overturned; earth-shaking: ~的变化 *earth-shaking changes*

【天方夜谭】① Arabian Nights Entertainments; the Thousand and One Nights ② cock-and-bull story; most fantastic tale

【天分】gift; talent; special endowments: ~高 *be gifted*; *be talented*

【天府之国】(usu. referring to Sichuan Province) Nature's storehouse; land of abundance

【天赋】① inborn; innate; endowed by nature; inherent ② natural gift; talent; endowments: ~人权论 *the theory of natural rights*

【天干】ten Heavenly Stems, used as serial numbers and also in combination with the twelve Earthly Branches to designate years, months, days and hours

【天罡】the Big Dipper; plough

【天高地厚】① high as heaven; deep as earth (of kindness, friendship etc.): ~的友情 *profound friendship* ② complexity of things; immensity of the universe: 小小年纪竟不知~。*You are so young and don't know the complexity of things.*

【天高皇帝远】the sky is high and the emperor far away; justice is tardy; law and government are far from here

【天高气爽】the sky is high and the air is crisp; a fine breezy day with clear skies

【天各一方】(of a family or friends) be far apart from each other; be scattered to different corners of the earth

【天公】the lord of Heaven; god; weather: ~真是不作美。*The weather is not too good.*

【天公地道】be fair and justice; be fully justifiable; absolutely fair

【天宫】heavenly palace

【天沟】【建】gutter

【天国】①【宗】the kingdom of heaven ② utopia; paradise: 人间~ *paradise on earth*

【天寒地冻】the weather is cold and the ground is frozen; be freezing: ~的天气 *icy weather*

【天河】Milky Way; Galaxy

【天黑】① deepening dusk; evening: ~了,妈妈有点担心儿子了。*It's dark*; *the mother worried about her son.* ② dark; dim

【天候】weather: 全~战机 *all-weather fighter*

【天花】【医】smallpox: ~病毒 *pox virus*

【天花板】ceiling

【天花乱坠】flowers cascading from the sky; give an extravagantly colourful description: 吹得~ *give an exaggerated account of sth*; *shoot one's mouth*

T

off
【天皇】① Son of Heaven; emperor ② emperor of Japan; mikado; tenno
【天昏地暗】① a murky sky over a dark earth; gloomy above and dark below ② be in a state of chaos and darkness ③ awfully; terribly; like hell
【天机】① nature's mystery; important secret: 一语道破了~ *lay bare the truth with one remark* ② God's design; secret: ~不可泄露。*God's design must not be revealed to mortal ears or one must not give away a heavenly secret.*
【天极】【天】celestial pole: ~仪 *polar telescope*
【天际】[书] horizon: ~星光闪耀。*The stars were twinkling over the horizon*
【天假良缘】Chance of a lifetime; heaven-sent opportunity
【天经地义】universally accepted principle; perfectly justified
【天井】① courtyard; patio; small yard ② uncovered skylight ③ raise: 通风~ *air raise*
【天空】sky; heavens
【天籁】[书] sounds of nature
【天蓝】sky blue; azure
【天狼星】【天】sirius
【天朗气清】clear sky and fresh air
【天理】① nature's justice: ~难容 *intolerable injustice* / ~良心 *the course of nature and one's conscience* ② heavenly principles; feudal ethics as propounded by the Song Confucians
【天良】conscience: ~发现 *stung by conscience; the conscience is revealed*
【天亮】daybreak; dawn: ~以前 *before daybreak*
【天伦】[书] natural bonds and ethical relationships between members of a family: ~之乐 *family happiness*
【天罗地网】nets above and snares below; a waiting trap; an escape-proof net: 布下~ *spread a dragnet from which there is no escape; cast an escape-proof net*
【天马行空】a heavenly steed soaring across the skies; vigorous and unconstrained in style
【天明】daybreak; dawn
【天命】god's will; fate; mandate of heaven; destiny
【天幕】① canopy of the heavens; sky ② backdrop (of a stage)
【天南地北】① far apart; poles apart: 整天~,他越发想念妻子。*Living far apart, he missed his wife very much.* ② all over the country; different parts of the country; different places: 来自~ *come from all over the country* ③ discursive; rambling: ~地闲谈 *chat about everything under the sun*
【天年】① natural span of life; one's allotted span; one's natural life: 尽其~ *die a natural death; live one's full span* ② [方] the year's harvest ③ [方] times; years; age; era
【天怒人怨】the wrath of God and the anger of men; widespread indignation and discontent
【天女】female deva; heavenly maiden: ~散花。*The heavenly maids scatter blossoms.*
【天棚】①【建】ceiling ② awning or canopy, usu. Made of reed matting and bamboo poles
【天平】balance; scales: 分析~ *analytical balance*
【天气】① weather: ~图 *weather map; synoptic chart* / ~形势预报 *weather prognostics* / ~学 *synoptic meteorology* / ~预报 *weather forecast* / ~要变。*The weather is changing.*
【天堑】natural moat; chasm: 长江~ *the natural moat of the Changjiang River*
【天桥】① overline bridge; overpass; platform bridge ②【体】bridge
【天穹】vault of heaven: ~如盖。*The firmament looks like a canopy.*
【天球】【天】celestial sphere: ~赤道 *celestial equator* / ~仪 *celestial globe* / ~子午圈 *celestial meridian* / ~坐标 *celestial coordinates*
【天然】natural: ~珍珠 *natural pearl* / ~色 *natural tint* / ~堤 *natural levee* / ~免疫 *innate immunity; natural immunity* / ~牧地 *natural pasture*
【天然气】natural gas: 干~ *dry gas; poor gas* / 湿~ *wet gas; rich gas* / ~回注 *gas injection*
【天壤之别】great difference as between heaven and earth; a wide difference; an immeasurably vast difference
【天日】sky and sunlight; the light of day: 重见~ *look again upon the light of day; regain freedom*
【天若有情天亦老】if Heaven has feelings, Heaven will become aged too
【天色】colour of the sky; time of the day; weather: ~突变。*The weather suddenly changed.* / ~已晚。*The sky is faintly light with the dawn.*
【天神】god; deity
【天生】inborn; inherent; innate born: ~的艺术家 *born artist*
【天生桥】【地】natural bridge
【天时】① weather; climate; season: ~不顺,久旱无雨。*The weather has been abnormal as there has been long-drawn-out drought.* ② timeliness; opportunity; chance: ~,地利,人和 *favourable climatic, geographical and human conditions*
【天使】angel
【天书】① book from heaven; heavenly immortal ② abstruse or illegible writing: 对我来说,这本书就跟~一样难懂。*This book is all Greek to me.*
【天数】predestination; fate; tragedy
【天塌地陷】① heaven falls and earth crumbles; the collapse of heaven and earth ② serious; grave; critical
【天坛】temple of Heaven (in Beijing)
【天堂】heaven; paradise: ~的召唤 *call from heaven* /人间~ *paradise on earth*
【天梯】tall ladder; scaling-ladder
【天体】【天】celestial body; star: ~力学 *celestial mechanics* / ~物理学 *astrophysics* / ~起源学 *cosmogony* / ~照相仪 *astrograph* / ~生物学 *astrobiology*
【天天】every day; daily: 老师告诉我们最好~读报。

Our teacher told us we'd better read newspaper every day. /好好学习，～向上。*Study well and make progress every day.*

【天条】① laws of heaven ② Heaven's commandments

【天庭】① middle of the forehead ② used in fairy tales and myths

【天头】top or upper margin of a page

【天外】① beyond the highest heavens; in the outer space; extraterrestrial ② highest and farthest place; sky of skies

【天王】① heavenly king-emperor：～老子 *emperor* ② god; deity

【天王星】【天】uranus

【天网恢恢，疏而不漏】heaven's vengeance is slow but sure; justice has a long arm; the net of heaven has large meshes, but it lets nothing through

【天威】[书] heavenly power; heavenly might; power of the emperor

【天文】【天】astronomy：～观测 *astronomical observation* / ～常数 *astronomical constant* / ～单位 *astronomical unit* / ～导航 *astronavigation; celestial navigation* / ～馆 *planetarium* / ～气象学 *astrometeorology* / ～台 (*astronomical*) *observatory* / ～照相术 *astrophotography* / ～制导 *celestial guidance* / ～时 *astronomical time* / ～数字 *astronomical* / ～望远镜 *astronomical telescope*

【天文学】astronomy：空间～ *space astronomy* /航海～ *nautical astronomy* /球面～ *spherical astronomy* /射电～ *radio astronomy* /恒星～ *stellar astronomy* /～家 *astronomer*

【天无二日，国无二主】only one supreme ruler in a country, as there is only one sun in Heaven

【天无绝人之路】Heaven always gives a man a way out; Heaven never cuts off a man's means

【天下】① land under heaven; world：～大乱 *turmoil under heaven; big upheaval throughout the world* / ～大势 *historical trends; the momentum of history* / ～太平 *peace reigns over the land; all is at peace* / ～大治 *great order across the country; the world was set in good order* / ～无敌 *all-conquering; invincible* / ～无双 *unique; matchless; peerless* / ～没有不散的宴席 *even the finest feast must break up at last; all good things must come to an end* / ～第一 *No. 1 in the world; the best in all the land* / ～奇闻 *most fantastic tale; very strange story* / ～为公 *the world belongs to everyone* / ～无难事，只怕有心人。*All difficulties on earth can te overcome if men but give their minds to it.* / ～乌鸦一般黑。*All crows under the sun are black or Evil people are bad all over the world.* ② rule; domination：打～坐～ *conquer and rule the country*

【天仙】① goddess ② fairy maiden; beauty：貌如～ *as beautiful as a goddess*

【天险】natural barrier; natural obstacle：跨越～ *fly over a natural barrier; cross natural barrier with lightning speed*

【天线】aerial; antenna：室外～ *outside antenna* / ～接头 *antenna terminal* / ～接线 *antenna connection* / ～反射器 *antenna reflector*

【天象】① astronomical phenomena; celestial phenomena：观～是一件很高兴的事情。*It's very pleasure to observe astronomical phenomena.* ② changes of wind and cloud

【天象仪】planetarium

【天晓得】[口] God or heaven knows：～什么时候他会来。*God knows when he will come.*

【天性】natural instincts; nature：父子～ *natural bonds between father and son* / ～聪明 *be intelligent by nature*

【天幸】providential escape; close call：绝处逢生，实乃～。*It was really providential luck for him to survive the desperate situation.*

【天旋地转】heaven and earth seem to be spinning round; be very dizzy：那个病人只觉得～，然后就什么都不知道了。*The patient felt as if the sky and earth were spinning round, and could know nothing.*

【天涯】world's end; remote regions; remotest corner of the earth：～海角 *end of the earth; uttermost ends of the earth* / ～咫尺。*It is but a small world.* /海内存知己，～若比邻。*A bosom friend afar brings a distant land near.*

【天衣无缝】be completely like nature; seamless heavenly robe; flawless：他落笔缜密，～。*His writing was meticulous and flawless.*

【天意】god's will; the will of heaven：～不能违背。*God's will is inviolable.*

【天有不测风云】in nature there are unexpected storms; sth unexpected may happen any time; a sudden storm may arise at any moment：～，人有旦夕祸福。*Sudden storms spring up in nature and men's fortunes may change overnight or storms gather without warning and bad luck befalls men overnight.*

【天宇】① sky; heaven：欢呼声响彻～。*The applause rang through the skies.* ② world; country

【天渊】[书] sky and sea; heaven and hell; high heaven and deep sea：～之别 *as different as heaven and hell; vast difference*

【天灾】natural calamity; natural disaster：～人祸 *natural and man-made calamities; natural disaster and human foe*

【天葬】celestial burial (by which bodies are exposed to birds of prey)

【天造地设】made by nature; be a heaven-made (place); ideal：～的一对夫妇 *ideal couple*

【天真】innocent; simple and unaffected; childish; naive：～可爱 *simple and lovely* / ～烂漫 *innocent and artless; simple and unaffected* /他待人处事太～了。*He was too simple minded in dealing with people.*

【天之骄子】God's favored one; an unusually lucky person; one especially blessed by Heaven

【天知道】God (or heaven) knows; nobody knows

【天职】bounden duty; mission; vocation：保卫国家是军人的～。*Safeguarding the country is a soldier's bounden duty.*

【天轴】①【机】line shaft ②【天】celestial axis

【天诛地灭】be destroyed by heaven and earth; stand condemned by God

【天主教】Catholicism: 罗马～会 *Roman Catholic Church* / ～徒 *Catholic* / ～堂 *Catholic church; Catholic chapel*

【天姿】① natural appearance or look ②［书］natural gift; natural endowments

【天资】talent; natural gift; endowments: ～过人 *unusual talent*

【天姿国色】surpassing beauty; reigning beauty; matchless beauty

【天子】son of heaven; the emperor

【天尊】celestial worthy (the title of some deities in the Taoist pantheon)

【天作之合】a match made in Heaven; a union made by Heaven

添 ① add; increase: ～油加醋 *garble a story by adding trimmings to it* / ～柴 *add firewood to the fire; put in more firewood* / ～饭 *get more rice (to eat); serve more rice* / ～了白发 *grow greyer* /给你们～麻烦了。*Sorry to have troubled you.* ②［方］have a baby: 李阿姨夫妇新～了个儿子。*Aunt Li couple had a son recently.*

【添补】replenish; get further supply of (sth)

【添彩】add honour to; add glory to; do credit to

【添丁】［旧］have a baby (esp. a boy) born into the family: ～之喜 *happy occasion of having a baby boy born into the family*

【添堵】increase one's vexations; be a bother

【添加】increase; add: ～法 *additive process*

【添乱】increase the confusion; add to the trouble

【添设】set up more; increase

【添箱】［旧］① add to the dowry; give wedding presents to the bride ② wedding presents or money given to the bride

【添加剂】【化】additive

【添枝加叶】add details of a story; add colour and emphasis to (a narration); embellish (a story)

【添置】add to one's possessions; buy: ～家具 *buy more furniture*

【添砖加瓦】add bricks and tiles to; work together to build; do one's bit: 为祖国的发展～ *do what little one can for the development of one's country*

tián

田 ① field; cropland; farmland; (cultivated) land: 耕～ *plough a field* /稻～ *paddy field; paddy* /在～间干活 *working in the fields* /一片好麦～ *a fine field of wheat* ② area from which minerals, etc. are obtained: 煤～ *coal fields* /油～ *oil field* ③ (Tián) a surname

【田鳖】【动】giant water bug; fish killer

【田产】land property; estate

【田地】① field; cropland; farmland ② wretched situation; plight

【田凫】【动】lapwing

【田赋】［旧］land tax

【田埂】ridge; low bank of earth between fields: 修～ *build ridges in the fields*

【田鸡】【动】frog

【田家】farmhouse; farmer's family

【田间】field; farm: ～持水量 *field capacity* / ～劳动 *field labour; farm work* / ～管理 *field management*

【田径】【体】track and field; sports performed on a track or on a field; athletics: ～队 *track and field meet* / ～全能运动 *all-round athletics* / ～赛 *track and field meet* / ～项目 *track and field event* / ～运动 *track and field; athletics* / ～选手 *track-and-field competitor*

【田猎】［书］go hunting; sport of chasing and killing foxes with dogs while on horseback

【田鹨】【动】paddy-field pipit

【田螺】【动】river snail

【田亩】land; cropland; fields

【田纳西】Tennessee, state in central southeastern United States

【田契】title deed for land; land deed

【田赛】【体】field-events

【田舍】［书］① land and house ② farmhouse ③ farming family: ～郎 *young farmer; farm boy*

【田鼠】vole; field mouse or rat: 普通～ *field vole*

【田野】field; farmland; the country: 广阔的～ *vast field; vast expanse of farmland* / ～工作 *field work* /我们走在～上。*We travelled across country.*

【田园】fields and gardens; countryside: ～生活 *idyllic life* / ～风光 *rural scenery* / ～诗 *pastoral poetry* / ～诗人 *pastoral poet*

【田庄】country estate

【田租】farm rent

恬 ［书］① quiet; tranquil; peaceful: ～淡的环境 *tranquil surroundings* / ～然自若 *calm and collected; unperturbed and nonchalant* / ～和 *quiet and gentle* ② be indifferent; remain unruffled: ～不为意 *not care at all; be indifferent (or nonchalant)*

【恬不知耻】be lost to shame; have no sense of shame; devoid of all sense of shame: 约翰真是个～的家伙，他竟然冲他妈妈大嚷。*John was really a shameless person; he shouted at his mother.*

【恬淡】indifferent to fame or gain; quiet in mind with few desires: ～一生 *seek neither fame nor wealth all one's life* / ～的生活 *quiet life*

【恬静】quiet; peaceful; serene; tranquil: ～舒适的环境 *peaceful and pleasant environment*

【恬美】quiet and charming; peaceful and beautiful

【恬谧】［书］quiet; peaceful; serene; tranquil: ～的夜晚 *serene (or tranquil) night*

【恬然】unperturbed; unruffled; calm; nonchalant

【恬适】［书］quiet and comfortable; tranquil and ease

钿 ① coin: 铜～ *copper coin* ② money: 多少～? *How much is it?* ③ fund; sum of money

甜 ① sweet; honeyed: ~酒 *sweet wine* /这块糕太~了。*This cake is much too sweet.* ② (of sleep) sound: 昨天晚上,我睡得很~。*I had a sound sleep last night.*

【甜不唧】sweetish; slightly sweet
【甜菜】① beet; sugar beet ② beetroot
【甜点】sweets; dessert; sweet snacks; sweet pastry
【甜津津】pleasantly sweet
【甜瓜】muskmelon
【甜美】① sweet; luscious: 这桃~多汁。*These peaches are juicy and sweet.* ② pleasant; refreshing: ~的爱情 *tender love*
【甜蜜】sweet; happy; pleasant: ~的微笑 *sweet smile* / ~的生活 *happy life* / ~蜜 *sweet*
【甜面酱】sweet sauce made of fermented flour
【甜腻腻】overly sweet; sweet and cloying
【甜品】sweet meats
【甜软】sweet and soft
【甜润】sweet and mellow; sweet and pleasant
【甜食】sweets; sweet food; dessert; sweetmeats
【甜爽】sweet and refreshing
【甜水】① sweet water; fresh water: ~井 *fresh water well* ② sugar water; happiness; comfort
【甜睡】sleep soundly; have a refreshing sleep; be fast asleep
【甜丝丝】① pleasant sweet; sweet: ~的苹果 *sweet apple* /这个菜~儿的。*This dish is sweet and delicious.* ② pleased; gratified; happy: 看到妈妈,我感觉心里~的。*On seeing my mother, I felt quite pleased.*
【甜酸儿】tartly sweet
【甜头】① sweet taste; pleasant flavour ② benefit; sop; good: 尝到成功的~ *taste the sweet of success*
【甜味】sweet taste: 这水有点~。*The water has a sweet taste.*
【甜言蜜语】honeyed words; honey-sweet words; sugarplum

填 ① fill; stuff; stop up: 用沙子把洞~满 *fill a hole with sand* /我得把墙上的那条裂缝~好。*I must fill that crack in the wall.* /那空缺已有人~上了。*The vacancy has already been filled.* ② fill in; fill out; write: ~写申请表格 *fill in an application form* /名字~错了。*Wrong name was filled in.*

【填报】fill out a form and submit it to the leadership or higher authorities: 每月~项目进度 *make a monthly progress report on a programme*
【填补】fill (a vacancy, gap, etc.); make up (a deficit): ~空白 *fill in a gap* / ~亏空 *make up a deficit* /这个空缺由他来~。*He is to fill the position.*
【填充】① fill in the blanks (in a test paper) ② fill up; stuff: ~作用 *filling effect* / ~物 *filler*; *packing material* / ~塔 *packed column or tower*
【填方】【建】fill: ~断面 *fill section*
【填房】① marry a widower ② woman who marries a widower: 给人作~ *become the wife of widower*; *marry a widower*
【填空】① fill in the blanks (in a test paper) ② fill a vacant position; fill a vacancy: ~补缺 *fill vacancies and supply deficiencies*
【填料】【机】packing; filling; filler; padding: ~函 *gland box*; *stuffing box* /塑料~ *plastic packing*
【填密】【机】packing; densification: 液压~ *hydraulic packing* / ~片 *sheet packing*
【填平】fill and level up: ~弹坑 *fill up bomb craters* /把沟~ *fill up a gully*
【填塞】stop up; fill up; block up: ~心灵上的空虚 *fill a spiritual vacuum*
【填写】fill in; fill out; write: ~表格 *fill in a form*
【填鸭】① force-feed a duck; cram ② a force-fed duck: ~式教学法 *cramming or force-feeding method of teaching*
【填字游戏】crossword puzzle

tiǎn

腆 ① sumptuous; rich; plentiful ②【方】protrude; stick out; bulge: ~着肚子 *stick out one's stomach*

舔 lick; lap: 他~手指。*He licked his fingers.* /猫在~自己的毛。*The cat was licking its fur.* /他把小勺~干净了。*He licked the spoon clean.*

【舔犊情深】affectionate toward one's children

tiāo

挑[1] ① choose; select; pick out: ~选礼物 *select a gift* /任~任选 *take your choice* / ~上谁来参与这项比赛? *Who has been selected to take part in the competition?* /把那筐西红柿~一~。*Pick over that basket of tomatoes.* ② find (fault); nit-pick; be fastidious: ~毛病 *find fault*; *pick holes* /他讲的话你就别~错儿了。*Stop picking holes in what he said.*

挑[1] ① carry on the shoulder with a pole; shoulder; put (sth) on one's shoulders: ~着一担菜 *carrying two baskets of vegetables on a shoulder pole* / ~起总经理的责任 *shoulder the duties of general manager* ② carrying pole with its loads; load carried on a shoulder pole: 杂货~儿 *two baskets of sundry goods carried on a shoulder pole* ③【量】(for a load carried on a shoulder): 两~水 *two buckets of water carried on a shoulder pole* see also tiǎo

【挑刺儿】【方】find fault; pick holes; nit-pick: 爱~的人 *captious person*
【挑肥拣瘦】pick the fat and choose the thin; choose whichever is to one's advantage; be choosy
【挑拣】choose; pick; pick and choose: 把发霉的花生~出来。*Pick out the rotten peanuts.*
【挑脚】carry luggage or goods for a fee; work as a porter
【挑礼】fussy about etiquette; reproach sb with a

faux pas
【挑三拣四】pick and choose; be very particular in (one's food, etc.); be choosy
【挑食】be particular about what one eats; be very choosy about what one eats:他从不~。*He is never choosy about food.*
【挑剔】be nit-picking; find fault in a petty way; be too critical:无可~ *beyond criticism*; *faultless*
【挑选】choose; select; pick out; opt for:从架子上~贺卡 *select a card from the rack* /~地毯 *choose a carpet* /细心~ *choose carefully* /我们得从五位候选人中~新经理。*We have to choose a new manager from a short-list of five candidates.*
【挑眼】[方] find fault; be hypercritical (about etiquette, etc.)
【挑字眼儿】find fault with the wording; quibble; be fastidious about choice of words:女儿说的不对,你别~。*What your daughter is not right; you don't get hung up on her choice of words.*
【挑子】carry pole with its load; load carried on a shoulder pole

tiáo

条 ① twig:柳~儿 *willow twig* /路边的大树长出了很多枝~。*The big trees grow many branches and twigs.* ② strip; slip; long narrow piece or area:一张纸~ *a strip of paper* /面~ *noodles* ③ note:便~ *brief information note* /经理不在,请给他留个~吧。*The manger is out; Will you leave a note for him please?* ④ stripe; streak:有红色~纹的白桌布 *a white table-cloth with red stripes* /带~纹的料子 *striped material* ⑤ item; article:律~ *articles of a regulation* ⑥ order:井井有~ *in perfect order*
【条案】long narrow table
【条播】【农】drilling:~机 *seed drill*; *drill* /~沟 *drill furrow* /~栽培 *drill culture* /~法 *drilling method*
【条材】【冶】bar stock
【条陈】① present item by item; state point by point ② [旧] written proposal to the superior
【条凳】bench
【条分缕析】analyze point by point; make a fine analysis
【条幅】vertically-hung scroll; wall scroll:草书~ *scroll of cursive- hand calligraphy* /帮我把这幅~卷起来。*Please help me roll up this scroll.*
【条钢】bar iron; bar steel
【条规】rules; regulations; restrictions:防火~ *fire regulations* /防洪~ *flood regulations*
【条几】long narrow table
【条件】① condition; term; circumstance:生活~ *living conditions* /贸易~ *terms of trade* ② require; prerequisite; qualification; precondition; 入学~ *entrance requirement* /先决~ *prerequisite*; *precondition* /有~地同意 *agree with qualifications* ③ situation; state; condition:他身体~很好。*He is in excellent condition physically.*
【条块】vertical and horizontal cines of leadership, management, control, or coordination: ~分割 *create barriers between central ministries and local governments*
【条款】clause; article; provision; term:法律~ *legal provision* /契约的~和条件 *the terms and conditions of lease* /合同中列有~,禁止承租人转租。*There is a clause in the contract-forbidding tenants to sublet.*
【条理】proper arrangement; good order; orderliness; method: ~不清 *badly organized*; *disorderly* /有~的头脑 *an orderly mind*
【条例】rules; regulations; conditions; ordinances; 组织~ *organizational rules* /工会~ *rules and regulations of labour unions*
【条令】【军】regulations:内务~ *routine service regulations*
【条码】bar code; (U. S.) Universal Product Code (UPC)
【条目】① clauses and sub clauses (in a formal document) ② entry (in a dictionary):这词典有十四万多~。*This dictionary has over* 140,000 *entries.*
【条绒】corduroy
【条石】rectangular stone slab
【条鳎】【动】striped sole
【条条框框】restrictions and fetters; regulations and restrictions; rules and regulations:打破~的束缚 *break down the trammels of outmoded conventions*
【条文】article; clause; provision: ~范例 *standard clause* /这个文件包括许多~。*This document includes many articles.*
【条纹】stripe; streak: ~衬衫 *streaky shirt*; *striped shirt* / ~布 *striped cloth*; *stripe*
【条形】linear: ~导线 *strip conductor*
【条形码】bar code: ~标识 *bar code label*
【条锈病】【农】stripe rust; yellow rust
【条约】treaty; pact; covenant:边界~ *boundary treaty* /友好合作~ *treaty of friendship and cooperation* /和平~ *peace treaty* /订立~ *conclude a treaty* /不平等~ *unequal treaty* / ~法 *law of treaties*; *law derived from treaty obligations*
【条子】① strip:布~ *strip of cloth* ② brief informal note:给发言人递~ *pass a note to the speak* ③ [方] gold bar

迢
【迢迢】far away; remote:千里~ *from a thousand li away*; *from afar*

调[1] ① suit well; be harmonious; be propitious: 风~雨顺 *good weather for crops*; *propitious weather* /最近汤姆的饮食失~了。*Recently Tom don't fit in perfectly by an irregular food-style.* ② mix; adjust; regulate; change: ~工资 *adjust wages* / ~房子 *change accommodations* / ~酒 *mix a drink*

调[1] ① mediate; reconcile; arbitrate: ~争端 *arbitrate a dispute* ② tease; provoke; tantalize;

dally：～戏妇女 *take liberties with a woman* ③ incite；abet；instigate；sow discord：～唆两家不和 *drive a wedge between the two families*
see also diào

【调处】mediate；reconcile；arbitrate：～冲突 *mediate in hostilities* / ～争端 *arbitrate a dispute*；*act as mediator*

【调挡】【机】gear shift

【调房】adjust housing；housing exchange

【调幅】【电】amplitude modulation（AM）：～广播 *AM broadcast* / ～干扰 *AM jamming*

【调羹】spoon

【调和】① harmonious；propitious；well-matched：色彩～ *harmonious colours* / 雨水～ *well-distributed rainfall* ② harmonize；blend；mix；regulate：～肝脾 *harmonize the liver and spleen* ③ mediate；reconcile；arbitrate：～各种利害冲突 *reconcile various conflicting interests* ④ compromise；make concessions：不可～的斗争 *uncompromising struggle* ⑤【数】harmonic：～比 *harmonic ratio* / ～方程 *harmonic equation*

【调和漆】mixed paint；ready-mixed paint：磁性～ *mixed varnish paint*

【调护】nurse；look after a patient during convalescence：病人需要特别～。*The patient needs special care during his convalescence.*

【调级】adjust a wage scale；raise sb's salary or wage

【调剂】① make up a prescription；fill a prescription ② adjust；regulate；enliven：～生活 *enliven one's life* / ～商品供应 *regulate the supply of commodities* / 自我～ *self-adjustment*

【调价】raise prices；modify prices；readjust prices

【调减】adjust and reduce

【调浆】【纺】size mixing

【调焦】【摄】focusing：～镜头 *focusing lens*

【调教】① teach；train；discipline；guide：～淘气的孩子 *discipline mischievous children* ② tame；train；domesticate；break in：～劣马 *tame a vicious horse*

【调节】adjust；regulate：～水流 *regulate the flow of water* / 市场～ *market regulation* / ～货币流通 *regulate money supply* / ～器 *regulator*；*adjuster*；*controller* / ～税 *regulatory tax*

【调解】mediate；make peace；patch up：～合同纠纷 *arbitrate a quarrel over a contract* / ～分歧 *iron out differences* / ～人 *mediator*；*peacemaker*

【调经】【中医】regulate menstrual function；regulate menstruation

【调侃】ridicule；jeer at；scoff；mock；banter：善于～ *be good at banter* / 你就喜欢～别人。*You likes scoffing at others.*

【调控】regulate；control；direct：宏观～ *macro-control* / ～手段 *controlling mechanism*

【调理】① nurse；recuperate：精心～ *nurse with great care* ② take care of；look after：～伙食 *take care of one's diet* ③ discipline；train；teach；tame：～警犬 *train police dogs* ④［方］make fun of；tease；fool：～老实人 *tease an honest guy* ⑤ opsonize：～素 *opsonin*

【调料】condiment；seasoning；flavoring

【调弄】① make fun of；tease；provoke；take liberties：～妇女 *dally with a woman* ② arrange；adjust；fix：～钟表 *tinkering at clocks and watches* ③ instigate；stir up：～是非 *stir up trouble*

【调配】mix；blend：～颜色 *mix colors*

【调皮】① naughty；mischievous；troublesome：他是个～的孩子。*He is a naughty child.* ② unruly；tricky；skittish ③ insincere；scheming：～捣蛋 *mischievous*；*making trouble*

【调频】【电】① adjust frequency or output ② frequency modulation（FM）：～广播 *FM broadcast* / ～电台 *FM radio station*

【调情】flirt；tease；dally

【调色】mix colours；tone：～板 *palette* / ～刀 *palette-knife* / ～剂 *toner*

【调试】①【电】debug：～程序 *debugging programme* ② trial run；preliminary or shakedown test

【调速器】【机】governor；speed controller

【调唆】incite；stir up；abet：～别人犯罪 *abet others in crime*

【调停】mediate；intervene；reconcile：～争端 *intervene in a dispute* / ～纠纷 *adjust disorder* / ～者 *intervener*

【调味】flavour；season：～品 *seasoning*；*flavouring*；*condiment*

【调戏】take liberties with；dally；assail with obscenities：～妇女 *take liberties with a woman*

【调弦】tune a stringed instrument

【调笑】make fun of；tease；jeer at；poke fun at：相互～ *poke fun at each other*

【调协】coordinate；adjust；harmonize；concerted

【调谐】① harmonious；propitious：上下～ *harmonious relations between the leader and the led* ② tune；resonate：～旋钮 *tuning knob* / ～电路 *tuned circuit*

【调谑】make fun of；poke fun at；tease

【调压】adjust pressure；regulate voltage：～变压器 *regulating transformer* / ～器 *pressure regulator*；*voltage regulator*

【调养】take good care of oneself；build up one's heath by rest and by taking nourishing food；nurse back to health：～身体 *nurse one's body*

【调音】【音】tune：为钢琴～ *tune a piano*

【调匀】mix well；blend evenly

【调整】adjust；regulate；readjust；modify：～供求关系 *regulate supply and demand* / ～计划 *revise a plan* / ～作息时间 *make changes in the work schedule* / ～杆 *adjusting rod* / ～器 *adjuster*

【调治】recuperate under medical treatment

【调制】① mix；concoct：～涂料 *mix paint* ②【电】modulation：～器 *modulator* ③ blend and make；mix and make：～鸡尾酒 *prepare a cocktail* / ～药丸 *blend and make medicinal pills*

【调制解调器】modulator-demodulator；modem

笤

【笤帚】whisk broom; small broom

tiǎo

挑 ① pick or push with a pole or stick; raise; hold up: ~大拇指 *hold up one's thumb* (*in approval*) / ~眉毛 *raise one's eyebrows* / ~着灯笼 *hold a lantern on a stick* / ~帘子 *raise the curtain* ② poke; pick; prick: ~刺 *pick out a splinter* / ~火 *poke a fire* / ~破水泡 *prick a blister with a needle* ③ stir up; instigate; foment: ~拨是非 *stir up trouble*; *sow discord* ④ rising stroke (in Chinese characters)
see also tiāo

【挑拨】stir up; foment; incite; sow discord: ~兄弟不和 *sow discord between the brothers*; *set the brothers against each other* / ~离间 *sow dissension*; *incite one against the other*

【挑大梁】play a key role; shoulder the main responsibility; be a mainstay: 青年工人~。*The younger workers are the mainstay now.*

【挑灯】① trim or pick the lampwick; raise the wick of an oil lamp ② hang a lamp from a pole; raise a lantern: ~夜战 *work late into the night*

【挑动】provoke; foment; stir up; incite: ~好奇心 *arouse one's curiosity* / ~内战 *provoke civil war*

【挑逗】provoke; tease; tantalize; take liberties with: ~动物 *tease animal* / ~寻衅 *pick a quarrel* / ~妇女 *dally with a women*

【挑花】cross-stitch work

【挑明】bring into the open; let it all out; lay bare: ~关系 *lay bare their relationship*

【挑弄】① stir up; provoke ② play tricks on; lease

【挑起】provoke; stir up; incite: ~冲突 *provoke a conflict*

【挑事】[口] sow discord; stir up trouble

【挑唆】incite; abet; instigate; stir up: 她人不怎么样,总是在背地里~别人。*She is not good and always stirs up trouble behind the scenes.*

【挑头】be the first; take the lead

【挑衅】provoke: ~者 *provocateur* / ~行为 *provocative act*

【挑战】① throw down the gauntlet; challenge to battle: 发出~ *issue a challenge* / 接受~ *accept a challenge* ② challenge to a contest: 富有~的工作 *a challenging job* / ~者 *challenger* / ~书 *letter of challenge*; *challenge* / ~者号 (*US*) *challenger* (*space shuttle*)

tiào

眺 look into the distance from a high place: 远~ *look far into the distance*

【眺台】gazebo

【眺望】look into the distance from a high place: ~远景 *gaze at the distant view*

跳 ① jump; leap; bounce; spring; hop: ~伞 *a parachute jump* / ~起来 *jump into the air* / ~过一条沟 *leap over a ditch* / ~出窗户 *jump out of a window* / ~到地上 *jump onto the ground* ② beat; pulsate; move up and down: 他的心脏还在~。*His heart is still beating.* / 她听到那消息心突突直~。*Her heart jumped when she heard the news.* ③ skip; make omission: ~过两行 *skip two lines* / ~针 (*in knitting*) *drop stitches*

【跳班】(of pupils) skip a grade

【跳板】① gangplank; gangway ② springboard; diving board: 三米~ *three-metre springboard* / ~跳水 *springboard diving*

【跳槽】① (of stable-kept livestock) go to another trough for fodder ② job-hop; throw up one job for another: ~做老师 *drop one's occupation to go in for a teacher*

【跳弹】【军】ricochet: ~轰炸 *ricochet bombing*; *skip bombing*

【跳动】beat; pulsate; move up and down: 她的心脏停止了~。*Her heart ceased to pulsate.*

【跳房子】hopscotch; a children's game

【跳发球】【体】jump-serving

【跳高】【体】high jump: 撑杆~ *pole vault*; *pole jump* / ~运动员 *high jumper*

【跳行】① skip a line (in reading or transcribing) ② start a new line ③ change to a new occupation

【跳级】(of pupils) skip a grade

【跳脚】stamp one's foot: 气得~ *stamp with rage*

【跳进黄河也洗不清】even if one jumped into the Yellow River, one could not wash oneself clean; find it hard to clear oneself (of a charge)

【跳井】drown oneself in a well: ~自杀 *jump into a well to commit suicide*

【跳栏】【体】hurdle race; the hurdles: ~运动员 *hurdler*

【跳雷】【军】bounding mine

【跳梁小丑】buffoon; clown; contemptible scoundrel

【跳楼】jump from a building to commit suicide: ~价 *distress price* / ~货 *distress merchandise*

【跳马】【体】① vaulting horse ② horse-vaulting

【跳皮筋儿】rubber band skipping; skipping and dancing over a chain of rubber bands

【跳棋】Chinese checkers; Chinese draughts; halma

【跳球】【体】jump ball

【跳伞】① parachute; bail out: ~门 *bailout door* ②【体】parachute jumping: ~运动员 *parachutist*; *parachuter* / ~区 *parachute drop zone* / ~塔 *parachute tower*

【跳绳】rope skipping; jump rope: 几个小孩在院子里~。*A few little kids were skipping ropes in the yard.*

【跳虱】[方] flea

【跳鼠】【动】jerboa

【跳水】【体】diving: 向前(后)~ *front* (*back*) *dive* / ~池 *diving pool* / ~运动 *fancy diving*; *diving* / ~运动员 *diver* / ~表演 *diving exhibition*

【跳台】diving tower; diving platform: ~滑雪 *sky*

jumping

【跳台跳水】【体】platform diving; high diving: 高难度~ *variety high diving*

【跳舞】① dance (as a performance) ② go to the ball: ~厅 *dancing hall* / 女士们都穿晚礼服去~了。*The ladies were all dressed in long gowns for the ball.*

【跳箱】【体】① box horse; vaulting box ② jump over the box horse

【跳鞋】(spiked) jumping shoes

【跳远】【体】long jump; broad jump: 三级~ *hop, step and jump*

【跳跃】jump; leap; hop; spring: ~前进 *leap forward* / ~运动 *jumping exercise*

【跳蚤】flea: ~市场 *flea market; swap market*

【跳闸】【电】trip; tripping: 过载~ *overload tripping; circuit breaker* / 自动~ *automatic tripping* / ~开关 *trip switch* / ~装置 *trip gear*

tiē

帖 ① pliant; obedient; submissive; servile: 俯首~耳 *be all obedience; be servile* ② well-settled; proper; secure ③ (Tiē) a surname

see also tiě; tiè

【帖服】[书] be docile and obedient; be submissive

贴 ① paste; stick; attach; adhere: 张~告示 *paste up a notice* / ~邮票 *stick on a stamp* / 剪~ *clip and paste* / ~布告 *put up a bulletin* / 在行李上~标签 *label one's luggage* / ~上胶布 *stick on a piece of adhesive tape* / 她把图片~在剪贴本上。*She pasted the pictures into a scrapbook.* ② cling to; stay close to; attach to; stick to: 紧~身体的连衣裙 *a dress that clings to the body* / ~着耳朵小声说 *murmur in sb's ear* ③ subsidize; help (out) financially: 爸爸每月~我 10 块钱。*My father helps me out by giving me 10 yuan each month.* ④ subsidies; allowance: 房~ *housing allowance* ⑤ [量] for medicated plaster: 一~膏药 *a piece of medicated plaster*

【贴边】① be connected with; be involved in: 说话不~ *make irrelevant remarks* ② hem; edge (of a garment): 有~的窗帘 *hemmed curtain*

【贴标签】① label ② (of comments or criticism) slap on a label without making a concrete analysis: ~机 *labeler; labelling machine*

【贴饼子】① bake corn or millet cakes on a pan ② baked corn; millet cakes

【贴补】① subsidize; help (out) financially: ~家用 *help pay family expenses* ② cover daily needs or expenses by drawing on one's savings

【贴兜】patch pocket

【贴花】【纺】applique

【贴画】① pinup picture; poster ② picture on a match box

【贴换】trade-in; trade sth in: ~一辆自行车要多少钱? *How much do I have to pay if I trade in my old bicycle for a new one?*

【贴己】① intimate; confidential; close: 汤姆有很多~的朋友。*Tom has many bosom friends.* ② [方] private savings; pin money

【贴金】① gild; cover with gold leaf ② touch up; prettify: ~漆 *gold size* / 他尽往自己脸上~。*He always puts feathers in his cap.*

【贴近】① keep close to; nestle up against: ~耳边低语 *whisper in sb's ear* ② intimate; close; confidential: ~的人 *trusted fellow; confident*

【贴脸】【建】wooden strip or board used to seal up the space between a window-frame and a wall

【贴面】face; facing: ~砖 *face brick; face tile; furring brick*

【贴面舞】cheek-to-cheek dancing

【贴切】suitable; proper; fitting; well-put; apt: ~的表达方式 *apt expression* / ~的引语 *an apt quotation*

【贴身】① next to the skin: ~内衣 *underwear; underclothes* ② fit well; be suitable: 他裁的衣服穿着很~。*The clothes he cut out fit well.* ③ personal; constantly accompanying: ~丫环 *personal maid* / ~警卫 *personal bodyguard*

【贴水】① pay an agio ② agio; currency exchange

【贴题】relevant; to the topic; pertinent: 小说写得很~。*The novel is very pertinent.*

【贴息】① pay a discount when cashing a promissory note ② interest so deduced; discount

【贴现】discount on (a promissory note): ~利息 *discount interest* / ~率 *discount rate* / ~市场 *discount market* / ~银行 *discount bank* / ~经纪人 *discount broker*

【贴心】intimate; close: ~朋友 *close friend; confidential friend* / 有什么~的话告诉我。*Please tell me if you have words spoken in confidence.*

tiě

帖 ① invitation; card: 发出宴会请~ *send out invitations to a party* / 请~ *an invitation card* ② note; card: 庚~ *age card* / 字~儿 *brief note* / 谢~ *card of thanks; thank-you note* ③ [量] used of Chinese herbal medicine: 几~草药 *a few doses of herbal medicine*

see also tiē; tiè

【帖子】① invitation ② note; card

铁 ①【化】iron; ferrum (Fe): ~锅 *iron pot* / 生~ *pig iron; cast iron* / 钢~ *iron and steel* / 废~ *scrap iron* / 熟~ *wrought iron* ② arms; weapon: 手无寸~ *completely unarmed; barehanded* ③ hard or strong as iron: ~一般地坚硬 *as hard as iron* ④ harsh; cruel; firm: ~汉 *a man of iron* / 有钢~般的意志 *have an iron will* / 施以~腕 *impose an iron rule* ⑤ unalterable; unchangeable; indisputable: ~的事实 *hard fact; ironclad evidence* / ~的纪律 *iron discipline* ⑥ stern; serious; severe; solemn: ~着脸 *look stern* ⑦ [口] close; intimate ⑧ resolve; determine: ~了心 *be unshakable in one's determination* ⑨

(Tiě) a surname

【铁案如山】a case demonstrated with conclusive and irrefutable evidence; an ironclad case

【铁板】iron plate; sheet iron

【铁板钉钉】be very sure; be absolutely certain; no two ways about it

【铁板块】be a monolithic whole; be a monolithic bloc

【铁笔】① cutting tool used in carving seals, etc. ② stylus for cutting stencils; stencil pen

【铁箅子】① grate (of a stove) ② gridiron; grill

【铁壁铜墙】iron walls and brass partitions; stronghold; impregnable fortress

【铁饼】① discus throw ② discus

【铁蚕豆】roasted broad bean

【铁杵磨成针】grind an iron pestle into a needle; long, persistent practice makes perfect; perseverance will prevail: 只要功夫深, ~。*So long as one works hard enough at it, even an iron pestle can be ground down to a needle or persistent effort leads to success.*

【铁窗】① window with grating ② prison bars; prison: ~生涯 *life behind bars*; *prison life*

【铁磁】【物】ferromagnetic: ~半导体 *ferromagnetic semi-conductor* / ~体 *ferromagnet* / ~共振 *ferromagnetic resonance* / ~性 *ferromagnetism*

【铁打】ironclad; steady; solid; unshakable: ~的汉子 *a sturdy man*

【铁道】railway; railroad: 地下~ *underground (railway)*; *subway* / 高架~ *aerial railway* / ~兵 *railway corps* / ~炮兵 *railway artillery* / ~部 *ministry of railways*

【铁定】ironclad; unchangeable; fixed: ~的事实 *unalterable fact*

【铁饭碗】iron rice bowl; secure job

【铁杆儿】① reliable; loyal: ~卫士 *loyal guards* ② stubborn; inveterate; dyed-in-the-wool ③ surefire; of guaranteed high yield

【铁哥们】[口] sworn friend; faithful pal

【铁工】① ironwork ② ironworker; blacksmith

【铁公鸡】iron cock; miser; stingy person: 他是个一毛不拔的~。*He is such a miser that no one could get a penny from him.*

【铁箍】iron hoop

【铁骨铮铮】firm and unyielding; staunch and unyielding

【铁管】iron pipe; iron tube

【铁轨】rails; tracks

【铁柜】iron or steel chest; strongbox

【铁合金】【冶】ferroalloy; iron alloy

【铁黑】【化】① iron oxide black ② iron black

【铁红】【化】iron oxide red

【铁花】ornamental work of iron; iron openwork

【铁画】iron picture: ~银钩 (*of calligraphy*) *vigorous and powerful*

【铁环】iron hoop: 滚~ *roll a hoop*; *play with a hoop*

【铁黄】iron oxide yellow

【铁灰】iron-grey; dark grey

【铁活】ironwork

【铁甲】① mail; armor: ~战袍 *coat of mail* / ~虫 *army weevil* ②【军】armor for vessels, vehicles, etc.: ~舰 *ironclad warship*; *ironclad*

【铁将军】door lock: 昨天你家~把门。*Your door locked fast yesterday.*

【铁匠】blacksmith; ironsmith: ~铺 *smithy*; *blacksmith's shop*

【铁脚板】iron soles; toughened feet

【铁军】iron army; invincible army

【铁铠】mail; armour

【铁矿】① iron ore: ~石 *iron ore*; *ironstone* ② iron mine: 富~ *high-grade iron mine*

【铁链】iron chain; shackles

【铁路】railway; railroad: 高架~ *aerial railway*; *elevated railroad* / ~运输 *railway transportation*; *rail transport* / ~路基 *railway bed* / ~网 *railway network* / ~道口 *railway crossing* / ~岔线 *railway siding* / ~干线 *trunk railway* / ~公路两用桥 (*railway and highway*) *combined or dual-use bridge* / ~线 *railway line*

【铁马】iron-clad or armored horses; strong mounted forces

【铁门】① iron gate ② grille

【铁面无私】be just and stern to sb; unmoved by personal appeals; impartial and incorruptible

【铁娘子】iron lady

【铁鸟】airplane; aeroplane

【铁牛】iron ox; tractor

【铁皮】iron sheet: 白~ *galvanized iron* / 黑~ *black sheet iron* / 洋~ *tinplate*

【铁骑】[书] cavalry; armored horses: 五千~ five thousand cavalrymen

【铁器】ironware: ~加工 *ironware processing* / ~时代 *the Iron Age*

【铁锹】spade; shovel

【铁青】livid; ashen; like ashes in colour; bluish-grey: 气得脸色~ *turn livid with rage*

【铁拳】iron fist; powerful fist; powerful striking force

【铁人】iron man; person of exceptional physical and moral strength

【铁纱】wire gauze; wire cloth

【铁砂】① iron sand ② shot (in a shotgun cartridge); pellets

【铁石心肠】have a rocky heart; be ironhearted; unmoved by feeling; be heartless

【铁树】【植】sago cycas (Cycas revolute)

【铁树开花】iron tree in blossom; sth seldom seen or hardly possible

【铁水】liquid iron; molten iron

【铁丝】iron wire: ~网 *wire netting*; *wire meshes*; *wire entanglement* / ~筐 *iron wire basket*

【铁素体】【冶】ferrite: ~铸铁 *ferrite cast iron*

【铁算盘】iron abacus; meticulous calculation; competent accountant; shrewd person

【铁索】iron chain; iron pagoda: ~吊车 *cable car* / ~桥 *chain bridge*

【铁塔】① iron tower; iron pagoda: 埃菲尔~ *Eiffel*

Tower ②【电】pylon; transmission tower: ~天线 pylon antenna mast antenna
【铁蹄】iron heel; cruel oppression; tyrannical rule
【铁桶】metal pail; metal bucket; metal drum: ~合围 *tightly encircled*
【铁腕】iron hand: ~统治 *strong rule; ruled by an iron hand*
【铁锹】shovel; spade
【铁屑】iron filings; iron chippings and shavings
【铁心】① be unshakable; be very determined; steel one's heart: 他~要上大学。*He has made up his mind to go to college.* ②【电】(iron) core: ~线圈 *iron core coil; magnet coil*
【铁锈】(iron) rust
【铁血】be iron-willed and ready to sacrifice oneself
【铁陨石】iron meteorite
【铁砧】anvil
【铁铮铮】firm as iron; staunch: ~的男人 *man of iron will*
【铁证】ironclad proof; irrefutable evidence: ~如山 *a mass of incontrovertible proof; irrefutable evidence*
【铁中铮铮】the finest of metals; a distinguished person

tiè

帖 book containing models of handwriting or painting for learners to copy: 字~ *calligraphy models* / 临~ *copy a model of calligraphy*
see also tiē; tiě

tīng

厅 ① hall: 休息~ *lounge; foyer* / 市政~ *the Town Hall* / 门~ *entrance hall* / 舞~ *dance hall; ballroom* / 餐~ *dining hall; restaurant* / 客~ *drawing room; living room* / 音乐~ *concert hall* ② office ③ government department at the provincial level: 水利~ *water conservancy department* / 教育~ *education department* / 农业~ *agricultural department* / ~长 *head of department (under a provincial government)*
【厅堂】hall; chamber

听[1] ① listen; hear; pay attention; overhear: 收~电台广播 *listen to a radio broadcast* / 她爱偷~别人闲谈。*She loves listening to other people's gossip.* / 她~觉不灵。*She can't hear very well.* / 我~说他病了。*I heard he was ill.* / 有人~见他在呻吟。*He was heard to groan.* ② take heed of; obey: ~从命令 *obey orders* / 不~劝告 *turn a deaf ear to advice* / ~医生的话吧。*Take heed of your doctor's advice.* / 你应该多~人劝。*You should be more heedful of advice.* ③ administer; manager: 兼~万事 *take care of many things simultaneously*

听[2] ① allow; let: 她~凭思绪徘徊。*She allowed her mind to wander.* / 悉~尊便。*Do whatever you like.* ②［方］tin; can: 三~咖啡 *three tins of coffee* / 六~啤酒 *six cans of beer*
【听便】please yourself; do as you like; do one pleases: 去留~。*You may go or stay as you please.*
【听差】［旧］manservant; footman; office attendant
【听从】obey; follow; listen to; accept; heed: ~吩咐 *be at sb's beck and call; do sb's bidding* / ~指挥 *obey orders* / ~劝告 *follow sb's advice* / ~教诲 *heed sb's instruction*
【听道】【生理】auditory canal
【听断】［书］try a case; hear a case
【听而不闻】listen but hear not; turn a deaf ear to; pay no attention to hear
【听风是雨】hear the wind and mistake it for the rain; be oversensitive; be credulous
【听骨】【生理】ear bones
【听候】wait for (a decision, settlement, etc.); be ready to do sth; be pending: ~分配 *wait for one's job assignment* / ~调遣 *be ready to do sb's bidding*
【听话】be willing to obey; be obedient; do what one is told to do: ~的孩子 *obedient children* / 他的狗很~。*His dog is very obedient.*
【听话儿】wait for a reply
【听见】hear: 我~有人笑。*I heard someone laughing.*
【听讲】listen to a talk; attend a lecture: 专心~ *listen to a lecture attentively*
【听觉】hearing; ability to hear: ~受损 *sb's hearing is impaired* / 她的~不灵。*Her hearing is poor.*
【听课】listen to a lecture; attend a class; sit in on a class
【听力】① hearing ability: 丧失~ lose one's hearing ② aural or listening comprehension (in language teaching)
【听命】take orders from; be at sb's command; follow one's orders: 甘心~ *resign oneself to take orders*
【听凭】allow; let sb do as one please
【听其言,观其行】listen to what one says and look at what one does; judge people by their deeds, not just by their words
【听其自然】leave the matter as it is; let things rip; let things take their natural course
【听取】listen to; hear: ~汇报 *hear reports* / 作为一个领导,你要经常~群众的意见。*You'd better listen to the opinions of the masses as a leader.*
【听任】［书］allow; let (sb do as one pleases): ~自流 *let things drift* / ~命运的摆布 *resign oneself to one's fate*
【听神经】【生理】auditory (or acoustic) nerve
【听说】① be told; hear of: ~那是部好电影。*I've heard that is a good film.* / ~你唱得好极了。*I hear you sing very well.* ② be obedient; heed what an elder or superior says
【听天由命】resign oneself to one's fate; bow to fate; trust to luck
【听筒】① (telephone) receiver ② headphone;

earphone ③【医】stethoscope
【听头儿】worth listening to
【听闻】what one hears; hearing
【听戏】go to the opera
【听写】dictation:三段英语~文字 *three English dictation*
【听信】① wait for information ② believe what one hears; believe ~~一面之词 *believe one-sided stories*
【听诊】【医】auscultation: ~器 *stethoscope*
【听政】hold court; administer affairs of state: ~会 *hearing*
【听之任之】let matters drift; let one have one's own way; let things go hang:对这种不良工作作风,我们不能~。*We cannot shut our eyes to such bad style of work.*
【听众】audience; listeners: ~来信 *letters from audience; listeners' letters*
【听装】tinned; canned: ~饼干 *canned biscuits* / ~咖啡 *tinned coffee*

烃 【化】hydrocarbon:开链~ *open chain hydrocarbon* / 闭链~ *closed chain hydrocarbon*
【烃气】【化】hydrocarbon gas

tíng

廷 court of a monarch; court of a feudal ruler; seat of a monarchical government:明~ *the Ming government* / 朝~ *royal court; imperial government* / 宫~ *palace; royal court*
【廷试】highest imperial examination presided over by the emperor (held in the imperial palace)
【廷杖】flogging with a big stick at court (a punishment in ancient China)

亭 ① pavilion:湖心~ *pavilion in the middle of a lake; mid-lake pavilion* / 八角~ *octagonal pavilion* ② stall; booth; kiosk:电话~ *telephone booth* / 邮~ *postal kiosk* / 书~ *book-stall*
【亭亭如盖】(of a tree) standing tall with a canopy of leaves
【亭亭玉立】(of a girl or tree) stand gracefully erect; be slim and graceful
【亭子】pavilion; kiosk; gazebo

庭 ① hall ② front courtyard; front yard:前~后院 *front courtyard and back garden* ③ law court:开~ *open a court session* / 出~ *appear in court* / 民~ *civil court*
【庭审】try; interrogate: ~日 *court day*
【庭训】[书] paternal instruction; parental admonitions
【庭园】flower garden; grounds
【庭院】courtyard: ~经济 *courtyard economy*
【庭长】president of a law court; presiding judge

停¹ ① stop; cease; come to a halt; pause:风~了。*The wind has stopped.* /钟~了。*The clock stopped.* /机器出了毛病,工作便~顿下来。*Work came to a halt when the machine broke down.* ② stop over; stay:在飞往中东途中在罗马~留两天。*Stop over in Rome for two days route for the Middle East.* /我在西安~了五天。*I stopped over at Xian for five days.* ③ (of cars) be parked; (of ships) lie at anchor; (of a dead body or coffin) be placed:禁止~车。*No parking.* ④ be ready; settle well: ~妥 *be all set; be in order*

停² part (of a total); portion
【停摆】(of a pendulum) come to a standstill; stop:钟~了。*The clock has stopped.*
【停办】stop a business; cease working; close down:这所学校现已~了。*The school has closed down.*
【停表】stopwatch
【停泊】berth; moor; anchor:寻找安全的~地 *find a safe berth* / ~处 *berth; dock* / ~费 *anchorage dues* / ~权 *right of anchorage* /班轮中午到达~地。*The liner berthed at midday.*
【停产】stop production: ~待料 *stop production to wait for raw materials* /下周工厂~整顿。*The factory will stop production to strengthen discipline next week.*
【停车】① park; stop (a vehicle) in a place for a time: ~场 *car park; parking lot or area* /这条街不准~。*You can't park in this street.* ② stop; pull up:每站~五分钟。*There is a five-minute stop at every station.* ③ (of a machine) stall; stop working: ~维修 *stop a machine for maintenance*
【停当】ready; fully prepared; in a fit state; settled:你的饭已准备~。*Your dinner is ready.*
【停电】① cut off the power supply; have a power failure ② power cut; power failure; blackout
【停顿】① halt; pause; stop temporarily:他们稍作~,然后继续上路。*After a short pause, they continued walking.* /学习~不前。*The study stagnated.* ② pause (in speaking)
【停放】park (a vehicle); place (a dead body or coffin):汽车~在哪儿? *Where can we park the car?*
【停飞】require or force (an aircraft) to stay on the ground; ground:因今天有雾,伦敦机场的所有飞机都被迫~。*All aircrafts at London Airport were grounded by fog today.*
【停工】stop work; shut down: ~待料 *work being held up for lack of material*
【停航】suspend air or shipping service
【停火】cease fire; stop shooting: ~协议 *cease-fire agreement* /长官命令士兵~。*The officer ordered his men to cease-fire.*
【停机】① (of a film, TV play, etc.) finish shooting ② (of an airplane) park ③ (of a computer) halt; stop calculation
【停机坪】aircraft parking area; parking apron
【停建】suspend construction: ~项目 *suspend project*
【停刊】stop publication; cease; suspend publication
【停靠】berth; moor; stop:火车~在8号站台。*The train stopped at platform No. 8.*

【停课】suspend classes; stop classes:那天学校~了。*Classes were suspended that day.*
【停灵】place a coffin in a temporary shelter before burial; rest the coffin temporarily
【停留】stay; remain; stop over; not depart:他在办公室~到很晚。*He stayed late at the office.*
【停留时间】retention period
【停球】【体】stop the ball
【停赛】①(of a match or sports meet) stop; halt ② be temporarily disqualified from contests: ~一年 *be disqualified from contests for one year*
【停食】【中医】gastric disorder; indigestion
【停水】cut off the water supply; cut off the water; be no water:今天全城~。*The whole city will be no water supply today.*
【停妥】be well arranged; be good in order; be all set:事情已商议~了。*The matter has been discussed and satisfactorily arranged.*
【停歇】① stop working; suspend a business; close down ② rest; stop for a rest:同学们在路边~。*The students rested on the roadside.*
【停薪留职】retain one's position without pay; obtain an indefinite leave of absence from one's work unit
【停学】drop out of school; stop going to school; suspend from school:因病~ *drop out of school because of illness*
【停业】① stop work; suspend a business; close temporarily:修理内部,暂时~。*Close temporarily for repairs.* ② close down; go out of business; wind up a business: ~甩卖 *closing sale*
【停战】stop fighting; cease fire; be armistice; truce: ~条约 *truce agreement*; *armistice* / ~谈判 *armistice talks (or negotiations)*
【停职】suspend sb from his duties; be relieved of one's post: ~检查 *be temporarily relieved of one's post and asked to make self-criticism*
【停止】stop; end; cease; halt; suspend: ~操作 *stop operation* / ~供应 *cut off the supply* / ~敌对行动 *cease hostilities*
【停滞】stagnate; bog down; become suck and unable to make progress:经济~。*The economy is stagnate.*
【停滞不前】remain stagnate; stand still; be bogged down:工作~。*There is no progress in the work.*

霆 thunderbolt:雷~ *thunderclap*; *thunderbolt*; *thunder-like rage*

tǐng

挺[1] ① straighten up; stick out; protrude; jut out:笔~的西装 *well-pressed wester-style clothes* / ~胸 *throw out one's chest*; *square one's shoulders* / ~起腰杆 *straighten one's back*; *straighten up* ② endure; bear; stand; hold out:太累了,我们都有点~不住了。*We were so tired that we could not hold out any more.* ③ hard and straight; erect; stiff:直~地站着 *stand still and stiff* ④ outstanding; striking; extraordinary ⑤ very; rather; quite: ~好 *very good* / ~和气的老人 *very kind old man*

挺[2] [量] used of machine guns:一~机关枪 *a machine gun*

【挺拔】① tall and straight; towering: ~的白杨 *tall, straight poplars* ② forceful; powerful:笔力~ *forceful strokes in handwriting*
【挺杆】【机】tappet:阀门~ *valve tappet* / ~扳手 *tappet wrench*
【挺进】(of troops) boldly drive on; thrust into; push forward:向前~ *press onward*
【挺举】【体】clean and jerk
【挺立】stand upright; stand erect; stand stiff:昂首~ *stand erect with one's chin up*
【挺身】straighten one's back; stand up; throw oneself forward: ~而出 *step forward bravely*; *come forward courageously* / ~反抗 *stand up and fight*; *rise in furious resistance*
【挺尸】lie stiff and sleep like a dead body; lie sleeping like a corpse
【挺胸突肚】stick out one's chest; stretch the chest and expand the belly
【挺秀】tall and graceful; elegant; towering
【挺直】straighten up; hold erect

铤 [书] (walk or run) quickly

【铤而走险】rush into danger; take a risk; become reckless in desperation; make a reckless move

艇 ① (light) boat; skiff:舰~ *naval ships and boat*; *naval vessels* /游~ *yacht*; *pleasure boat* /汽~ *steamboat* ② (light) naval vessel:潜水~ *submarine* /登陆~ *landing craft*

tōng

通 ① open; through:那条胡同是~的。*That is a through alley.* /水管是~的。*The water pipe is not blocked.* ② open up or clear out by poking or jabbing: ~炉子 *give the fire a poke*; *poke the fire* / ~下水道 *clear out a sewer* ③ lead to; go to; head for:条条大路~罗马。*All roads lead to Rome.* ④ connect; link; communicate; exchange:互~情报 *exchange information* /这些地道都是~着的。*These tunnels open into each other.* ⑤ tell; notify; inform:互~消息 *keep each other informed* / ~个电话 *give sb a ring*; *call sb up* ⑥ know; understand; comprehend; master:李明~四国语言。*Li Ming knows four languages.* ⑦ expert; authority; past master:万事~ *know-all*; *versatile person* ⑧ logical; correct; coherent:文字不~ *ungrammatical and incoherent writing* ⑨ general; common; ordinary: ~称 *a general term* ⑩ all; total; whole: ~共 *altogether*; *in all* / ~观全局 *take an overall view of the situation* ⑪(Tōng) a surname
【通报】① circulate a notice or dispatch; cite or announce in a dispatch or circular: ~批评 *circulate*

a notice of criticism ② circular; dispatch; notice:关于情况的～ *a circular on the situation* ③ bulletin; journal:《化学～》*Chemical Journal* /《科学～》*Science Bulletin* ④ inform; report:这个新情况要立刻向全国～。*The new development must be reported immediately to the whole country.*

【通便剂】【医】laxative; cathartic

【通禀】report to one's superior

【通病】common failing; common fault; prevalent problem:旧体制的～ *common defect of the old mechanism*

【通才】versatile person; universal genius; generalist; all-rounder:他是个难得的～。*He is a rare all-rounder.*

【通常】① general; usual; normal; common; ordinary: ～的做法 *usual practice* /请给我来一份我～要的饮料。*I'll have my usual drink.* ② usually; normally; ordinarily; most often:他～到得早。*He's usually early.*

【通畅】① unobstructed; smooth; clear; free:大便～*regular bowel movement* /血液循环～ *free circulation of blood* /干渠～。*The main canal is clear.* ② smooth; fluent:文笔～ *smooth writing*

【通车】① (of a railway or highway) be open to traffic; be commissioned:这条铁路两年内～。*The railway will be open to traffic within two years.* ② have (vehicle) traffic; have transport service:本线不～。*Service on this route is suspended.*

【通称】① be generally called; be generally known as:汞～水银。*Mercury is generally called quicksilver.* ② general term; common name

【通达】be understanding; be sensible; be reasonable: ～之士 *person of good sense* /见解～ *hold sensible views*; *show good sense*

【通道】① passage; passageway; narrow way through sth; thoroughfare:鼻腔～ *the nasal passages* /运输～ *transport thoroughfare* ② channel: ～程序 *channel program* / ～脉冲 *channel pulse*

【通敌】collude (or collaborate) with the enemy; work for the enemy (in secret): ～叛国 *collude with the enemy and betray one's country*

【通电】① set up an electric circuit; electrify; energize: ～的铁丝网 *electrified* (*or live*) *wire entanglements* ② issue a circular telegram; publish an open telegram: ～全国 *publish an open telegram to the nation* ③ circular or open telegram:发出～ *issue a open telegram*; *send a circular telegram*

【通牒】diplomatic note:最后～ *ultimatum*

【通都大邑】large city; metropolis

【通读】① read over or through; read from cover to cover: ～所有文章 *read the articles through* ② understand; comprehend; grasp well

【通断开关】【电】on-and-off switch; on-off switch

【通兑】circulate; exchange; cash

【通分】【数】reduction of fractions to a common denominator

【通风】① ventilate; air; let air into (a room, etc.):使煤矿坑道～ *ventilate the galleries of a coal-mine* / ～设备 *ventilation* (*equipment or installation*); *ventilator* / ～口 *ventilator*; *air vent*; *vent* /这个～设备出故障了。*The ventilation isn't working.* ② be well ventilated:我的办公室～很好。*My office is well ventilated.* ③ divulge information; tip off; furnish secret information:有人给他～报信。*Someone have tipped him off.*

【通告】① notify; announce; inform; make sth known publicly ② notice; announcement; circular:发出～ *give public notice* /王室成员降生的～已向全国广播。*The announcement of the royal birth was broadcast to the nation.*

【通共】in all; overall; altogether; as a total:我们～十二个人吃饭。*There were twelve of us in all for dinner.*

【通过】① pass; move forward; go past; traverse; cross: ～哨卡 *pass a sentry* / ～检查站 *pass check point* /她驾驶测验没～。*She has not passed her driving test yet.* ② accept; carry; pass; approve:议会～了该法案。*Parliament passed the bill.* /这部戏一定不能～审查这一关。*This play will never pass the censors.* ③ ask the consent or approval of ④ by; through; by way of: ～合法手段 *by legal means*

【通航】be open to navigation or air traffic:直接～ *direct air service*; *direct shipping service* / ～水域 *navigable waters*

【通红】very red; crimson; blush; red through and through:女孩的脸冻得～。*The girl's face was bright red from the cold.*

【通话】① converse; communicate ② communicate by telephone: ～计时器 *peg count meter* / ～时间 *air time*

【通婚】intermarry; be (or become) related by marriage

【通货】【经】currency; current money:硬～ *hard currency* / ～紧缩 *deflation* /自由～ *convertible currency* / ～贬值 *depreciation of currency* / ～膨胀 *inflation* / ～膨胀率 *rate of inflation*

【通缉】order the arrest of a criminal at large; list as wanted; put on the wanted list: ～名单 *wanted list* / ～布告 *wanted poster*

【通奸】commit adultery; fornicate

【通经】【中医】① stimulate the menstrual flow (by emmenagogues or acupuncture) ② be well versed in Confucian Classics

【通栏标题】banner headline; banner

【通览】read through; look at as a whole: ～全文 *read through the article*

【通力】put in a concerted effort; make a united effort; pitch in for sth together: ～合作 *give full co-operation to*; *fully cooperate*; *make a united effort*

【通例】① general rule; usual practice:星期天休息是学校的～。*It's a general rule that schools close on Sundays.* ②［书］universal principle; general law

【通亮】brightly lit; well-illuminated:照得～的房间 *a brightly lit room*

【通量】【物】flux: 中子~ a flux of neutrons

【通令】① issue a general order; public a circular order: ~全国 *issue a general order to the whole nation* ② circular order; general order

【通路】① thoroughfare; passage; passageway; route: 这是连接两个国家的唯一~。*This is the only passage way between the two countries.* ② channel; way; path

【通论】① well-rounded argument; convincing idea; convincing thesis ② general survey:《地震学~》*General Seismology*

【通脉】【中医】① promote blood circulation by invigorating vital energy ② promote lactation

【通名】① introduce oneself; announce one's name ② general term; common name

【通明】brightly lit; well-illuminated; be ablaze: 灯火~ *be ablaze with lights; be brightly lit*

【通年】throughout year; all the year round: ~辛劳 *toil throughout the year*

【通盘】overall; general; all-round; comprehensive: ~计划 *overall planning*

【通票】through ticket

【通铺】wide bed for several people

【通气】① ventilate; air; aerate: ~性差 *poorly ventilated* / ~孔 *air vent; vent* ② touch or communicate with each other; keep each other informed: 他们互不~。*They are out of touch with each other.*

【通窍】understand things; be sensible; be reasonable

【通情】be understanding; be reasonable; be sensible; be able to show tolerance of: ~的父母亲 *an understanding parents* / ~达理 *showing good sense; understanding; sympathy towards other's feelings and views*

【通权达变】be capable of versatility; do as necessity demands; not bound by old rules

【通融】① get around regulations to accommodate sb; make an exception in sb's favour ② accommodate sb with a short-term loan: 你能不能~100块钱? *Could you lend me one hundred yuan as a favour?*

【通商】(of nations) have trade relations: 订立~条约 *conclude a trade treaty* / ~口岸 *trading port; open port*

【通身】the whole body; all over: ~是汗 *sweat all over* / ~是伤 *be covered with wounds*

【通史】comprehensive history; general history: 世界~ *general history of the world*

【通式】【化】general formula

【通顺】smooth; coherent; clear

【通俗】popular; simple; common: ~易懂 *easy to understand* / ~文学 *popular literature* / ~化 *popularize* / ~歌星 *pop star*

【通体】whole body; entire mass; all over the body

【通天】① exceedingly high or great: ~的本事 *exceptional ability* ② direct access to the highest authorities

【通条】① (stove) poker or stick ② cleaning rod (for a gun)

【通通】all; wholly; entirely; completely; totally: 把所有的酒~都喝光。*Take all of the wine.* /这些~是你的。*This is all yours.*

【通途】thoroughfare; main street; major road; flat and smooth way: 天堑变~ *a deep chasm turn into a thoroughfare; turn a natural barrier into a thoroughfare*

【通宵】all night; whole night; throughout the night: 玩牌玩个~ *make a night of playing cards* / ~达旦 *all night till dawn; all through the night*

【通晓】understand; have a good command of; be proficient in: ~音律 *be proficient in musicology* / ~英国文学 *be well versed in English literature*

【通心粉】macaroni

【通信】① communicate by letter; correspond: ~录 *address book* / ~保密 *communication security* / ~兵 *signal corps; signalman* / ~处 *mailing address* / ~鸽 *homing pigeon; carrier pigeon* / ~连 *signal company* / ~联络 *signal communication; communication and liaison* / ~犬 *messenger dog* / ~枢纽 *signal (or communication) centre* / ~卫星 *communications satellite; telecommunication satellite* / ~员 *messenger; orderly* /他经常跟我~。*He often writes to me.* ② telecommunication: 数字~ *digital communication* / ~工程 *communication project; communication engineering*

【通行】① pass through; go through: 自由~ *can pass freely; have free passage* / ~能力 *traffic capacity* / ~费 *toll* / ~证 *pass; permit* / ~权 *right of way* /道路十分拥挤,汽车无法~。*The road was so crowded that cars were unable to pass.* ② current; common; general: 全国~的办法 *common practice throughout the country*

【通性】common character; generality; general quality

【通讯】① communication: 无线电~ *radio communication* / ~线路 *communication line* /激光~ *laser communication* / ~录 *address book* / ~社 *newsagency; news service* ② news report; newsletter; reportage: 人物~ *feature article about outstanding figures* /新华社~ *Xinhua dispatches* / ~文学 *reportage*

【通用】① current; in common use; general; common: ~软件 *common software* / ~程序 *common programme* / ~语种 *commonly used languages* / ~货币 *current money* / ~机械厂 *universal machine works* / ~件 *universal part; standardized part* ② interchangeable: 这两个词可以~。*These two words are interchangeable.*

【通用汽车公司】(US) General Motors Corporation (GM)

【通邮】be accessible by postal communication

【通则】general rule: 民法~ *general rules of civil law*

【通知】① notify; inform; keep informed; make sb know: 有事随时~我。*Keep me informed of what happens.* /他~我们说他要辞职。*He notified us*

T

that he was going to leave. ② notice; circular; notification; message: 书面～ *written message* /发出～ *dispatch a notice* / ～书 *notice*; *advice note*

tóng

同 ① same; equal; identical; alike; similar: ～事物 *the same thing* /异～ *similarities and differences* /混～ *confuse*; *mix up* ② be the same as; be similar to; be alike: ～上所言 *as mentioned above* /视～路人 *regard as a stranger* ③ together; in common: 一～前往 *go together* / 陪～ *accompany* / ～进退 *advance and withdraw together* ④ with: ～父母住 *live with one's parents* / ～专家意见计划 *discuss the plans with an expert* ⑤ as... as; like; as: 他～他父亲一样高。*He is as tall as his father.* /今天的工作～往常一样。*Today's work is the same as before.* ⑥ and; as well as; in addition to: 黄油～面包 *bread and butter* /老师～学生 *teachers and students*

T

【同案】involved in the same law case: ～犯 *companion in crime*; *accomplice*

【同班】① be in the same class: 他们现在是～同学。*They are in the same class now.* ② classmate: 大学时,他们是～。*They were classmates at college.*

【同伴】companion; playmate: 小时候的～ *childhood companion*

【同胞】① born of the same parents: ～兄妹 *full brothers and sisters* ② fellow countryman; compatriot: 海外～ *overseas compatriots*

【同辈】of the same generation; peer: 在～人内 *within one generation*

【同病相怜】similarly afflicted people pity each other; those who have the same complaint sympathize with each other; fellow suffers sympathize with one another

【同步】①【物】synchronism: 载波～ *carrier synchronization* ② synchronize; coordinate in time or progress; be in step with; keep simultaneous: ～增长 *grow in step with*; *grow in pace with* / ～电动机 *synchronous* / ～卫星 *synchronous satellite*; *geostationary satellite*

【同仇敌忾】have the same enemy and hatred; share a bitter hatred of the enemy

【同窗】① study in the same school or class: ～之谊 *friendship between fellow students* ② schoolmate or classmate: ～相聚 *class reunion*

【同床共枕】share the same bed and the same pillow; sleep on the same couch; be bedfellows or sex partners

【同床异梦】sleep in the same bed but dream different dreams; be strange bedfellows; hide different purposes behind the semblance of accord

【同党】① belong to the same party or organization ② member of the same party or organization; confederate; accomplice

【同道】① take the same route; travel together: 两人～上学。*The two of them went to school together.* ② people sharing the same idea; people having a common goal: 我们是事业上的～。*We work for the same cause.* ③ people of the same trade or occupation

【同等】of the same class; on an equal basis: ～就业机会 *equal employment opportunity* / ～学历 *the same educational level* / ～地位 *equal in status*; *on an equal footing*

【同恶相济】aid and abet each other in wrongdoings; evildoers collude with each other; conspire with someone in illegal acts

【同犯】partner in a crime; confederate; accessory; accomplice

【同房】① share a room; be roommates ② (of husband and wife) sleep together; have sexual intercourse ③ of the same branch of a family: ～兄弟 *brothers of the same family branch*

【同分异构体】【化】isomer

【同甘共苦】share joys and hardships; share happiness and sufferings; go through thick and thin together: 两位～的老朋友 *two old friends who have been through thick and thin together*

【同感】same feeling; same impression; consensus: 颇有～ *feel very much the same* / ～反应 *consensual reaction*

【同庚】of the same age

【同工同酬】receive the same pay as others doing the same work; get the same pay for the same job; gain equal pay for equal work

【同归于尽】die together; end up in ruin together; perish together: 他与敌人～。*He died together with the enemy.*

【同行】① be of the same trade or occupation: 原来你们是～啊。*So you are of the same trade.* ② people of the same trade or occupation: ～是冤家。*People of the same occupation are enemies.*

【同呼吸,共命运】share a common fate; identity oneself with sb; throw in one's lot with sb

【同化】assimilate (ethnic groups, etc.): ～政策 *the policy of national assimilation* (*as pursued by reactionary rulers*) / ～作用 *assimilation* / ～效应 *assimilation effect* /邻近～ *proximate assimilation* / ～率 *assimilability*

【同伙】① work together; collude (in doing evil): ～打劫 *loot in collusion* ② partner; confederate; accomplice; fellow gangster: 他有几个～。*He has several fellows.*

【同居】① live together ② cohabit: 他们～了三年才结婚。*They were cohabiting for three years before their marriage.*

【同类】of the same kind; similar: ～事物 *similar matters* / ～项 *similar terms* / ～色 *similar colours*

【同僚】[旧] colleague; fellow official

【同龄】of the same age; contemporary: 我们是～人。*We are the same age.*

【同流合污】join in their evildoings; play a part in their vile actions; join with the vicious

【同路】go the same way; travel the same way; take the same route: ～人 *fellow traveller* / ～远行 *go with sb on a long journey*

【同盟】① allied; joint: ~军 *allied forces; allies* / ~条约 *treaty of alliance* ② alliance; league: 与邻国结成~ *enter into an alliance with a neighboring state* / ~罢工 *joint strike* / ~条约 *pact of alliance*

【同盟国】① ally; allied nations ② (in World War Ⅰ) the central powers ③ (in World War Ⅱ) the Allies

【同名】of the same title or name: ~同姓 *namesake*

【同谋】① conspire; make secret plans: 他们~颠覆政府。*They conspired to overthrow the government.* ② confederate; accomplice: 他的~ *his confederates in the crime* / ~犯 *accessory*

【同母异父】born of the same mother but a different father: ~兄弟 *half-brother*

【同年】① same year: 他们~上学。*They started school in the same year.* ②[方] of the same age ③[旧] candidates who passed the imperial examinations in the same year

【同期】① corresponding period ② same time (in school, etc.): 我和他~毕业。*I graduated the same time as he.*

【同衾共枕】share the same quilt and the same pillow; sleep together; have sexual intercourse

【同情】sympathize; feel or express sympathy: ~心 *sympathy; compassion; fellow feeling* / 我很~你。*I sympathize with you.*

【同仁】colleague

【同日而语】be mentioned in the same breath; put on the same par

【同上】ditto; idem

【同生死,共患难】go through fire and water together; share weal and woe; share difficulties and hardships

【同声】① in chorus; in unison; with the same voice: ~歌颂 *sing the praises in unison* / ~呼喊 *shout in chorus* ② speak at the same time; speak simultaneously: ~传译 *simultaneous interpretation*

【同声相应,同气相求】have spiritual affinity; people of an inclination fall into the same group; like attracts like

【同时】① at the same time; simultaneously; meanwhile; in the meantime: ~发生 *happen at the same time; coincide* / ~输入输出 *simultaneous input and output* ② moreover; besides; in addition; furthermore; as well as

【同事】① work together; work in the same unit: 我们~已经多年。*We've worked together for years.* ② colleague; fellow worker: 在工作中不少~帮助过我。*Many colleagues help me a lot in my work.*

【同室操戈】fight against one's own men; family members drawing swords on each other; internal strife; internecine fight

【同岁】of the same age

【同榻】[书] sleep in the same bed; share a bed

【同位角】【数】corresponding angles

【同位素】【化】isotope: 放射性~ *radioisotope* / ~扫描器 *radioisotope scanner* / ~治疗 *isotope therapy* / ~量 *isotopic mass*

【同位语】【语】appositive

【同屋】share a room; be a roommate

【同系物】【化】homologue

【同乡】fellow villager; fellow townsman; fellow provincial: ~会 *association of fellow provincials or townsmen*

【同心】① concentric; having the same centre; homocentric: ~圆 *concentric circles* / ~度 *concentricity* / ~阀 *concentric valve* ② with one heart; of like mind and spirit: ~同德 *be of one heart and one mind; do sth whole heartedly with sb* / ~协力 *unite in concerted effort; have one heart to help each other*

【同行】travel together; go together

【同性】① of the same sex of the same nature or character; like: ~电 *like electricity* / ~极 *like pole*

【同性恋】homosexuality; homosexual: ~者 *homosexual* / 女~者 *lesbian* / 男~者 *gay*

【同姓】of the same surname

【同学】① study in the same school; be a schoolmate of sb: 他们~多年。*They studied in the same school for many years.* ② fellow student; schoolmate: 同班~ *classmate* / 新~ *new schoolmate; freshman* ③ form of address used in speaking to a student

【同学录】schoolmates' address book

【同样】same; similar; equal; alike: ~的方法 *the same method* / ~尺寸的衬衣 *shirts of the same size*

【同业】① the same trade or business ② person of the same trade or business

【同一】① the same; the identical: 这是我们去年住过的~间房间。*This is the identical room we stayed in last year.* ② identity; unity: ~律 *law of identity* / ~性 *identity*

【同义词】synonym

【同意】agree; consent; permit; approve; allow: 他~将这个计划付诸实施。*He gave his consent for the project to get under way.* / 法官~了我的要求。*The judge allowed my claim.*

【同音词】【语】homonym; homophone

【同余】【数】congruence: ~数 *congruent numbers*

【同志】comrade: 李~ *comrade Li* / ~关系 *comradeship* / ~般的劝告 *comradely advice*

【同种】of the same race

【同舟共济】cross a river in the same boat; pull together; share with sb in trouble

【同轴】【电】coaxial: ~圈 *coaxial circles* / ~电路 *coaxial circuit* / ~电缆 *coaxial cable*

【同宗】of the same clan or lineage; having common ancestry: ~兄弟 *cousins of the same clan*

【同族】① of the same clan; having common ancestry ② of the same race

彤

[书] red: 红~~ *bright red*

【彤云】[书] ① red clouds ② dark clouds: 严冬天

气，~密布。*The winter sky was darkly clouded.*

桐 【植】① paulownia ② tung tree; tung oil tree ③ phoenix tree

【桐油】tung oil: ~树 *tung tree*

铜 【化】copper (Cu): 紫~ *red copper* / 黄~ *brass* / 青~ *bronze* / 白~ *copper-nickel alloy* / ~号 *brass trumpet*

【铜氨液】cuprammonia

【铜板】copper coin; copper

【铜版】【印】copperplate: ~画 *copperplate etching (or engraving); copperplate* / ~印刷 *copperplate printing* / ~印刷机 *copperplate press; etching press* / ~纸 *art (printing) paper*

【铜币】copper coin; copper

【铜鼓】bronze drum

【铜管乐】music played by a brass band

【铜管乐队】brass band

【铜壶滴漏】【考】copper clepsydra

【铜匠】coppersmith

【铜筋铁骨】brass muscles and iron bones; strong and solid body; robust

【铜镜】bronze mirror

【铜绿】【化】verdigris

【铜模】【印】matrix; copper mould: ~雕刻机 *matrix cutting machine*

【铜牌】【体】bronze medal; bronze: ~得主 *bronze medal winner; bronze medallist*

【铜器】bronze ware; brass ware; copper ware: ~时代 *the Bronze Age*

【铜钱】copper cash; copper coin

【铜墙铁壁】a wall of bronze or iron; iron bastions; an impregnable fortress

【铜丝】copper wire

【铜像】bronze statue

【铜臭】the stink of money; profits-before-everything mentality: 满身~ *stinking with money; filthy rich*

【铜元】copper coin; copper

【铜子儿】[口] coin; copper

童 ① child; boy or girl: 六岁的儿~ *a child of six* / 儿~演员 *a child actor* / ~年 *childhood* / 学~ *schoolboy* / 报~ *newspaper boy* ② virgin; unmarried: ~男 *virgin boy* / ~女 *maiden; virgin* ③ page; page boy; boy servant: 家~ *page-boy* ④ bare; bald; barren: ~枯 *dried up and barren; bleak and desolate*

【童便】【中医】boy's urine; urine of boys under twelve

【童工】child labourer; child labour

【童话】children's story; fairy tales; nursery story: ~故事 *fairy tale* / ~世界 *world in children's stories; wonderland*

【童伶】child actor or actress

【童男】virgin girl; under-age girl

【童年】childhood: ~的快乐 *the joys of childhood* / ~的回忆 *childhood memories*

【童女】virgin girl; under-age girl

【童仆】[书] houseboy; manservants; servants

【童趣】children's interest; childish delight; innocent playfulness: 饶有~ *interesting in a childish way; full of childish playfulness*

【童山】bare hills: ~秃岭 *bare hills and mountains*

【童声】child's voice: ~合唱 *children's chorus*

【童叟无欺】be honest with all customs; neither old nor young cheated

【童心】children's hearted; childlike playful: ~未泯 *retain a childlike heart; retain childish disposition*

【童星】child star

【童颜鹤发】have white hair and a rosy complexion; look youthful in old age

【童养媳】child bride; child daughter-in-law

【童谣】children's folk rhyme; nursery song

【童贞】virginity (esp. of a woman); chastity

【童真】childlike naivety; child simplicity; innocence

【童稚】① child ② child's naivety; innocence

【童装】children's wear; children's clothing; children's garment

【童子】boy; lad

【童子鸡】[方] young chicken; broiler; cockerel

【童子军】scout: 女~ *girl guide; girl scout*

酮 【化】ketone: ~胺 *ketoamine* / ~酸 *ketonic acid*

【酮体】【生化】ketone body; acetone body

瞳 pupil (of the eye)

【瞳孔】【生理】pupil: ~放大 *have one's pupils dilated; mydriasis* / ~缩小 *myosis*

tǒng

统[1] ① interconnected system; genealogy: 血~ *blood relationship; genealogy* ② tube-shaped part of an article of clothing, etc.: 长~靴 *high boots* ③ all; together; wholly; entirely: ~算起来,有六人没回来。*Altogether, six people are still in outside.*

统[2] ① lead; command; control: ~兵打仗 *lead soldiers into battle* ② gather into one; unite: 由你来~管 *be under your overall leadership* ③ 【地】series: 更新~ *Pleistocene series*

【统舱】steerage (passenger accommodation): ~客票 *steerage ticket* / 坐~ *go steerage*

【统称】① be called by a joint name; be grouped together under a generic or common name ② general term; general name; general designation

【统筹】make overall plans; plan as a whole; take the whole situation into account; give overall consideration: ~安排 *make overall arrangements* / ~全局 *take the whole situation into account* / ~规划 *plan as a whole* / ~兼顾,全面安排 *make overall plans and take all factors into consideration* / ~医疗 *subsidized medical care under a coordinated plan; cooperative medical care*

【统共】altogether; in all; including everything; as a total: 你~欠我 68.03 美元。*You owe me $68.*

03 altogether.

【统购统销】state monopoly for purchase and marketing (of grain, cotton, etc.); unified purchase and sale by the state

【统计】① statistics: 以～数字表明的证据 *statistical evidence* / ～资料 *statistical data* / ～地图 *statistical map* / ～力学 *statistical mechanics* / ～数字 *statistical figures; statistics* / ～图表 *statistical graph* / ～学 *statistics* / ～推断 *statistical inference* / ～员 *statistician* / 你看到最新的人口～资料了吗? *Have you seen the latest statistics on population?* ② add up; count: ～选票 *count the votes* / 人口～ *vital statistics; census*

【统考】uniform or unified examination

【统领】① command; lead; control: ～各路人马 *lead a joint force* ② commander; leader

【统配】state controlled allocation; unified distribution: ～物资 *state allocated goods*

【统铺】wide bed for a number of people

【统属】subordination: ～关系 *relationship of subordination*

【统帅】① command; lead ② commander; commander-in-chief: 三军～ *commander of the armed forces*

【统率】command; lead: ～三军 *command the country's armed forces*

【统统】all; entirely; completely

【统辖】have under one's control; govern; exercise; control over

【统销】unified marketing: ～粮 *grain marketed only by the state*

【统一】① unify; make uniform; form into a single unit; unite: ～行动 *seek unity of action; act in unison* ② unified; unitary; centralized: ～领导 *unified leadership* / ～价格 *uniform prices* / ～管理 *uniform management* / ～经营 *unified or centralized management* / ～税 *flat tax; consolidated tax* / ～体 *entity; unity* / ～性 *unity* / ～战线 *united front*

【统战】united front: ～部 *United Front Work Department* / ～政策 *united front policy*

【统治】rule; control; dominate: 殖民～ *colonial rule* / ～者 *ruler* / ～阶级 *ruling class* / 占～地位 *occupy dominant position*

【统制】control: 经济～ *economic control* / 外汇～ *foreign exchange control*

捅 ① poke; jab; stab: ～火 *poke the fire* / 他被～死了。*He was stabbed to death.* ② nudge; touch; push: 他用胳膊肘～了我一下。*He gave me a nudge.* ③ disclose; leak; let out; reveal a secret; make sth known: 谁把秘密给～出去了? *Who gave away the secret?*

【捅娄子】[口] make a mess of sth; get into trouble; make a blunder; blunder: 警方～抓错了人。*The police blundered badly by arresting the wrong man.*

桶 bucket; tub; pail; keg; barrel: 小～啤酒 *keg beer* / 一～水 *a pail of water* / 水～ *water pail* / 汽油～ *petrol drum* / 火药～ *powder keg* / 饭～ *rice bucket; fat-head*

筒 ① section of thick bamboo: 竹～ *thick bamboo tube* ② thick tube-shaped object: 笔～ *brush pot* / 邮～ *pillar-box; mailbox* / 气～ *inflator; bicycle pump* / 电～ *torch; flashlight* ③ tube-shaped part of clothing or accessories: 袜～儿 *leg of a stocking* / 长～靴 *long boots*

【筒管】【纺】bobbin: ～丝 *bobbin filament*

【筒裤】straight-legged trousers

【筒裙】straight skirt

【筒状花】【植】tubular flower

【筒子】tube or tube-shaped object: 枪～ *barrel of a gun*

【筒子楼】building design characterized by a long corridor running the length of the building with rooms on both sides

tòng

恸 [书] ① deep sorrow; grief; agony: 悲～ *grieved; sorrowful* / 大～ *weep bitterly; wail* ② cry one's heart out; wail; weep bitterly

【恸哭】cry one's eye out; weep bitterly; wail with grief

痛 ① ache; pain; hurt: 牙～ *have a toothache* / 胃～ *have a stomachache* / 背～ *have a backache* / 我的手很～。*My hand hurts badly.* ② sadness; grief; sorrow: 悲～欲绝 *be stricken with infinite sorrow; grieve deeply* ③ deeply; sharply; bitterly; extremely

【痛不欲生】grieve to the extent of wishing to die; be so grieved as to wish one were dead; extremely sorrowful

【痛陈】make a strong statement; express in strong terms; present in energetic terms: ～百姓疾苦 *give an accusing account of the people's sufferings*

【痛斥】denounce sharply; refute thoroughly; attack bitterly: 在大会上,中国共产党～卖国贼。*In the meeting, the Party denounced traitors scathingly.*

【痛楚】pain; anguish; suffering; distress: 她向我倾诉她内心的～。*She poured out her innermost sufferings to me.*

【痛处】sore spot; tender spot

【痛打】beat hard; belabor; give a good thrashing

【痛定思痛】recall past pain; think over the reason after this bitter lesson; bring home the lessons painfully learned

【痛风】【医】gout

【痛改前非】correct one's errors completely; rectify one's errors thoroughly; repent thoroughly of one's misdeeds; sincerely mend one's way

【痛感】① keenly feel; be keenly aware of (of sth): ～自己知识不足 *keenly feel one's lack of knowledge* ② sense of pain: 失去～ *lose the sense of pain*

【痛恨】hate bitterly; utterly loathe; detest; feed a deep hatred: ～在心 *cherish bitter hatred in the mind* / ～不已 *harbour endless hatred* / 万般～ *de-*

test in every possible way

【痛悔】regret deeply; repent bitterly; be filled with remorse: ~前非 *regret one's mistakes deeply*

【痛击】strike relentless blows; deal a severe blow; deliver a telling blow: ~侵略者 *strike a telling blow at the aggressors*

【痛歼】wipe out; annihilate; destroy completely: 他们~了入侵的敌人。*They annihilated the invaders.*

【痛经】【医】dysmenorrhoea

【痛觉】【生理】sense of pain

【痛哭】wail; cry one's eye out; weep bitterly: ~流涕 *cry and shed bitter tears; shed tears over some loss* / ~欲绝 *cry one's heart out* / 大声~ *cry loudly and bitterly* / 为过去的错误~是没有用的。*There is no use wailing over mistakes made in the past.*

【痛苦】pain; suffering; distress; agony: 万分~ *be very distressing* / 那受伤的人~之极。*The wounded man was in agony.*

【痛快】① happy; joyful; delighted; gratified: 感到从未有过的~ *be filled with joy as never before* / 图一时的~ *seek momentary gratification* ② to one's heart content; to one's great satisfaction: 玩得~ *have a wonderful time* / 吃个~ *eat to one's heart content* ③ frank and direct; straightforward; forthright: 他说话很~。*He speaks simply and directly.*

【痛快淋漓】unrestrained and forceful; impassioned and forceful; smooth and clean; with great eloquence

【痛骂】scold severely; curse roundly; rebuke sharply; tell off scathingly

【痛切】with great agony; with intense sorrow; most sorrowfully; keenly: ~感到自己的不足 *feel one's deficiency keenly*

【痛诉】speak painfully; give a bitter account; pour our with grief

【痛惜】regret deeply; feel sorrow about; deplore; feel remorse for: 大家都很~他的死。*His death was regretted by all.*

【痛心】pained; distressed; saddened: 深感~ *be deep grieved; feel deep regret*

【痛心疾首】heartache and headache; resent deeply; deplore greatly

【痛痒】① hardships; sufferings; difficulties: 关心老百姓的~ *be concerned with the hardships of the common people* ② importance; consequence: 无关~ *be of no importance; be of little account* / ~相关 *share a common lot; care for one another's comfort and happiness*

【痛饮】drink to one's great satisfaction; drink one's fill: 为胜利~ *drink to victory; toast victory* / 为成功~ *drink to success*

【痛责】scold bitterly; rebuke severely; castigate

tōu

偷 ① steal; pilfer; take dishonestly; pinch: ~文物 *steal cultural relics* / ~东西是不对的。*It's wrong to steal.* ② thief; pilferer; burglar; pickpocket: 惯~ *hardened thief* ③ find (time); take (time) off: ~闲睡上几分钟 *steal a few minutes' sleep* / ~点功夫学外语 *find time to learn a foreign language* ④ drift along; muddle along ~安 *seek temporary ease* ⑤ stealthily; secretly; on the sly: 从镜中~看某人一眼 *steal a glance at sb in the mirror*

【偷安】seek temporary peace: 苟且~ *live in a fool's paradise; seek only temporary ease and comfort*

【偷盗】steal; pilfer; filch: ~汽车 *steal cars*

【偷渡】slip out of a blockade in a water area; stealthily cross (a blockaded river, etc.): ~入境 *steal into a country; enter a country illegally* / ~出境 *steal off a country; leave a country illegally*

【偷工减料】use inferior materials and do shoddy work; cheat in work and cut down on materials; scamp work and stint material; jerry-build

【偷汉子】have a secret lover; commit adultery; have illicit relations with a man

【偷换】replace secretly; substitute surreptitiously: ~概念 *distort a concept*

【偷鸡不成蚀把米】try to steal a chicken only to end up losing the rice; go for wool and come back shorn

【偷鸡摸狗】① steal; pilfer; pinch ② (of a man) have illicit love affairs with woman

【偷奸取巧】resort opportunism to serve oneself; be opportunistic

【偷看】peep; peek; peer; steal a glance: ~某人的日记 *peek at sb's diary* / 隔着窗户~ *have a peep through the window*

【偷空】find (time); take (time) off; snatch a moment: ~打个盹 *snatch a doze*

【偷懒】be lazy; loaf on the job: 这孩子学习总~。*The boy is always lazy in his studies.*

【偷垒】(in baseball and softball) steal a base; steal

【偷梁换柱】steal the beams and pillars and replace them with rotten timbers; perpetrate a fraud

【偷漏】evade (taxes): ~税款 *evade taxes*

【偷跑】【体】jump the gun; run away secretly

【偷窃】steal; pilfer; filch

【偷情】carry on a clandestine love affair; have a secret love affair

【偷生】cling to life; drag out an ignoble existence

【偷税】evade taxes: ~漏税 *tax evasions*

【偷天换日】steal the sky and change the sun; perpetrate a gigantic fraud; play a sly trick

【偷听】eavesdrop; listen in stealthily: ~讨论 *eavesdropping on the discussion*

【偷偷】stealthily; secretly; on the sly; furtively: ～溜出宿舍 *sneak out of one's dormitory* / ～告诉他 *tell him on the quiet*
【偷偷摸摸】in a sneak way; covertly; surreptitiously; stealthily
【偷袭】attack stealthily; raid on the sly: ～敌营 *launch a surprise attack on an enemy camp*
【偷闲】① find time; take time off; snatch a moment of leisure: 忙里～ *snatch a little leisure from a busy life* ②［方］loaf on the job; be idle; be lazy
【偷眼】steal a glance; look secretly; take a furtive glance: ～看人 *steal a look at sb*
【偷营】make a surprise attack on an enemy camp; raid an enemy camp
【偷越】cross illegally; slip through; run a blockade stealthily: ～国境 *illegally cross a national border*
【偷嘴】take food on the quiet

tóu

头 ① head: 我～痛。*My head aches.* ② hair; hairstyle: 洗～ *wash one's hair* / 染～ *dye one's hair* ③ top; tip; end: 村西～ *the west end of a village* / 笔～ *tip of a pen* / 坟～ *grave mound* ④ beginning; end: 开个好～ *make a good beginning* / 万事起～难。*Beginning is always difficult.* ⑤ remnant; leftover; end: 布～儿 *leftover of a bolt of cloth* / 烟～儿 *cigarette end* ⑥ chief; head; leader; boss: 工～ *foreman* / 办公室的～儿 *head of an office* ⑦ side; aspect: 两～讨好 *try to please both sides* ⑧ number one; first: ～回 *for the first time* ⑨ first: ～半场比赛 *the first half of a game* / ～两排位子 *the two front rows of seats* ⑩ previous; last: ～月 *last month* ⑪ leading: ～羊 *bellwether* ⑫ used with domestic animals; used with garlic: 两～骡子 *two mules* / 一～蒜 *a bulb of garlic* ⑬ noun suffix (a) used with a noun: 骨～ *bone* / 石～ *stone* (b) used with a verb: 想～ *sth worth thinking about*; *idea* (c) used with an adjective: 苦～儿 *foretaste of bitterness*; *hardship* ⑭ suffix of a noun of locality: 前～ *front* / 后～ *behind*; *rear*; *back*
【头版】front page (of a newspaper): ～头条 *headline news on the front page*; *banner headline*
【头半天】forenoon; morning
【头彩】first prize in a lottery: 中了个～ *win first prize in a lottery*
【头筹】first; championship: 拔取～ *win the championship*
【头寸】【经】① money market; money supply ② cash; liquidity: ～缺 *run short of cash*
【头灯】head lamp
【头等】first-class; first-rate: ～舱 *first-class cabin* / ～奖 *first prize* / ～人才 *first-rate personnel*; *most talented person*
【头等大事】a task of prime importance; a thing of the first importance; major event
【头顶】top of the head; crow of the head
【头发】hair: ～卡子 *hairpin* / ～定型喷剂 *hairspray*
【头盖骨】【生理】cranium; skull
【头功】first contribution; greatest service; highest merit: 立了～ *win a first-class merit citation*
【头号】① number one; size one; the greatest: ～新闻 *headline news* ② first-rate; top-grade: ～面粉 *top-grade flour*
【头花】headdress flower
【头昏】dizzy; confused; giddy: ～眼花 *feel one's head swimming and one's eyes misting*; *feel dizzy* / ～脑胀 *feel one's head swimming*; *feel giddy* / 我觉得～。*I feel dizzy.*
【头奖】first prize: 在运动会中得～ *win the first prize in a sports meet*
【头角】talent; brilliance; great ability: 崭露～ *make a brilliant show of one's talent* / ～峥嵘 *outstanding*; *very promising*
【头巾】scarf; kerchief
【头盔】(steel) helmet
【头里】① in front; ahead: 他处处走在～ *He takes the lead in everything.* ② in advance; beforehand: 我先把丑话说在～。*Let me make this blunt word in advance.* ③ ago; before: 五年～ *five years ago*
【头脸】① head and face ② face; features; appearance ③ reputation; prestige; dignity
【头领】leader; head; chief; commander: 义军～ *leader of the righteous army*
【头颅】head
【头鲈鱼】silver-spotted grunt
【头面人物】big shot; bigwig; magnate; prominent figure
【头名】number one; the first; the best; first place: ～状元 *number one successful scholar*
【头目】head of a gang; ringleader; chieftain: 大～ *ringleader* / 小～ *sub-group leader in a gang*
【头脑】① mind; brains: ～简单 *simple-minded* / 有～ *have plenty of brains*; *be resourceful* / ～清楚 *clearheaded*; *sober-minded* ② main threads; clue: 摸不着～ *can not make head or tail of sth* ③［口］chief; chieftain; head; leader
【头年】① first year ② last year; previous year; year before
【头皮】① scalp: ～针 *scalp acupuncture* ② dandruff; scurf: ～多 *having plenty of dandruff* / 去～ *cure dandruff*
【头破血流】head broken and bleeding; be badly battered; be black and blue; be thoroughly beaten
【头纱】gauze kerchief
【头生】① firstborn ② first birth ③ firstborn child; first child
【头虱】head louse
【头式】hair style; hairdo; coiffure
【头饰】head ornament
【头水】① top-quality; first-rate; top-notch: ～货 *first-rate goods* ② (of articles and utensils) first use ③ (of clothes) first washing

T

【头胎】firstborn
【头套】actor's headgear; wig:戴～ *wear a wig*
【头疼】(have a) headache
【头疼脑热】headache and slight fever; be in a fever; slight illness
【头条新闻】front-page headline; top story of the newspaper; headline news:这起事故成了报纸上的～。*The accident made front-page headline in the press.*
【头痛】(have a headache): ～得厉害 *have a bad headache*
【头痛医头,脚痛医脚】treat the head when the head aches, treat the foot when the foot hurts; treat the symptoms but not the disease; take stopgap measures; prescribe mere palliatives
【头头是道】closely reasoned and well argued; appear impressive; clear and logical:别看他说得～,其实他在撒谎。*What he said was clear and logical; in fact he was lying.*
【头衔】title:光荣的～ *glorious title* /世界冠军的～ *world championship*
【头像】head portrait; head sculpture:青铜～ *head sculpture in bronze*
【头屑】dandruff; scurf:去～香波 *shampoo that will cure dandruff; shampoo for scurf*
【头绪】main threads (of sth complicated); due:毫无～ *have no clues to follow; be in a complete mess* /～太多 *have so many things to attend to*
【头雁】lead wild goose
【头羊】bellwether; lead sheep; lead goat
【头油】hair oil; pomade
【头晕】dizzy; giddy; fainting
【头针疗法】【中医】head-acupuncture therapy
【头重脚轻】one's head was heavy and one's feet light; top-heavy and unsteady; dizzy:他病刚好,有些～的。*He has just recovered from illness and still feels heavy-headed.*
【头子】[贬] chieftain; chief; boss:土匪～ *bandit chief*
【头足动物】cephalopod

投 ① throw; toss; fling; hurl: ～球 *throw a ball* /他～掷很好。*He throws well.* ② put in; drop:把信～进邮筒 *drop a letter into the pillar-box* ③ throw oneself into (a river, well, etc. to commit suicide): ～河 *throw oneself into a river* ④ project; cast; throw:树在草坪上～下长长的影子。*The trees throw long shadows across the lawn.* /阳光从窗外～进来。*The sun shone through the windows.* ⑤ send; deliver; dispatch ⑥ enter; join; go to: ～军 *join the army* ⑦ fit in with; agree with; cater to: ～其所好 *cater to sb's tastes*

【投案】give oneself up (or surrender oneself) to the police: ～自首 *surrender oneself to the police department*
【投保】insure; buy insurance; take out an insurance policy:人寿～ *buy life insurance* / ～单 *insurance policy* / ～人 *applicant; policy holder* / ～方 *insured party;(insurance) policy holder*
【投奔】go to (a friend or a place) for shelter: ～亲友 *go to one's relatives and friends for help*
【投笔从戎】give up the pen for the sword; throw down the pen and join the army; throw one's pen and enter the army
【投标】bid for (a contract); enter a bid; submit a tender:公开～ *public tender; open tender*
【投镖】① dart; dart throwing ② throw a dart
【投产】go into operation; put into production; commission:工厂即将～。*The plant will soon go into operation.*
【投诚】(of enemy troops, rebels, bandits, etc.) surrender; come over; cross over:向人民～ *cross over to the side of the people*
【投弹】① drop a bomb; cast bomb; bomb ② throw a hand grenade: ～训练 *training in grenade-throwing* / ～高度 *release altitude* / ～角 *dropping angle* / ～器 *bomb rack control; bomb release mechanism* / ～手 *bombardier; grenadier*
【投敌】go over to the enemy; defect to the enemy
【投递】deliver; send: ～信件 *deliver letters* /无法～的信 *dead letter* / ～员 *postman; letter carrier; mailman*
【投放】① throw in; put in:向水里～鱼饵 *put bait into the pond* ② put (money) into circulation; put (goods) on the market; invest:他们生产的食品已～市场。*The food they produced has been put on market.*
【投稿】send; contribute (to a newspaper or magazine); submit a piece of writing for publication:向报纸～ *send a contribution to a newspaper* / ～人 *contributor* /欢迎～。*Contributions are welcome.*
【投合】① agree with; get along; fit in with; be congenial to ② cater to: ～大众口味 *cater to the public taste*
【投河】throw oneself into the river; drown oneself in the river
【投机】① be congenial; be agreeable:话不～半句多。*Even one word is too much when the conversation gets disagreeable.* ② speculate; profiteer; seek private gain by hook or by crook: ～买卖 *speculation* / ～商 *speculator* /做石油股票的～买卖 *speculate in oil shares*
【投寄】send; post; deliver; mail: ～信件 *mail a letter; post a letter* / ～包裹 *send a parcel by post*
【投井】throw oneself into a well; drown oneself in a well
【投考】sign up for an examination: ～不中 *fail an entrance examination*
【投靠】go and seek sb's patronage; go and seek refuge with sb: ～敌人 *throw in one's lot with the enemy; sell out to the enemy*
【投篮】【体】shoot (a basketball):近距离～ *close-in shot* /远距离～ *long shot* /跳起～ *jump up and shoot* /钩手～ *hook shot* / ～不中 *miss the basket*
【投票】vote; cast a vote; record a vote: ～总数 *the vote* / ～权 *the vote* /无记名～ *vote by ballot* / ～赞成 *vote for* / ～反对 *vote against* / ～日 *polling*

day / ～箱 *ballot box* / ～站 *polling booth*

【投其所好】cater to sb's wishes; cater to sb's tastes; hit on what one likes

【投枪】javelin; (throwing) spear

【投亲】go and seek refuge with relatives; go and live with relatives; seek shelter with relatives and friends

【投入】① be absorbed in; be engrossed in; do sth with concentration: 他学习不甚～。*He isn't quite engrossed in his study.* ② throw into; put into: ～生产 *put into production*; *go into operation* / ～使用 *put to use*; *commission* ③ investment; input: 现金～ *input n cash* / 教育～ *input into education* / ～产出关系 *input-output relationship*

【投射】① throw; cast; fling; hurl ② project; cast: 把眼光～到来访者身上 *cast one's eyes on the visitor* / 树影～在窗户上。*The tree cast its shadow on the window.*

【投身】throw oneself into; plunge into; dedicate; join: ～科学 *dedicate oneself to science*

【投生】① be reincarnated in a new body; be reborn ② seek a livelihood away from one's home

【投师】seek instruction from a master; go and become the disciple of a master: ～学艺 *learn skill from a master*

【投石问路】throw a stone to clear the road; send out a trial balloon; sound out

【投手】【体】pitcher: ～犯规 *balk*

【投售】sell on the market

【投鼠忌器】hesitate to pelt a rat for fear of smashing the vase beside it; hold back from taking action against an evildoer for fear of involving good people

【投诉】complain; appeal: 顾客～ *customer complaints*

【投宿】put up for the night; seek temporary lodging: ～客栈 *put up at an inn for the night*

【投胎】be reincarnated; reborn

【投桃报李】give a plum in return for a peach; return present for present; exchange gifts between friends; return a favor with a favor

【投纬】【纺】picking

【投降】surrender; capitulate; give oneself up to: ～派 *capitulators* / ～主义 *capitulationism*

【投药】① medicate; prescribe: ～量 *dosage* ② apply poison: ～灭鼠 *poison rats*

【投医】seek medical advice; go to a doctor; see a doctor: ～求药 *seek medical treatment*

【投影】projection; shadow: 极～ *polar projection* / ～几何学 *projection geometry* / ～图 *projection drawing*

【投缘】fit in with; find each other congenial; hit it off: 两人一见面就很～。*The two of them hit it off as soon as they met.*

【投掷】throw; hurl; cast; fling: ～铁饼 *throw a discus*

【投置】throw into; put into; join

【投注】throw (energy, etc.) into; devote to; dedicate: 把全部精力～到教育事业中 *throw all one's energies into educational work*

【投资】① invest, put in; make an investment: ～建厂 *invest to build a factory*; *invest in a factory* / ～办学 *make an investment in education* ② money or fund invested; investment; input: 国家～ *state investment* / ～效益 *returns on an investment* / 智力～ *investment in education* / ～保护 *investment protection* / ～场所 *outlet for investment* / ～额 *amount of capital invested* / ～公司 *investment company* / ～法 *investment law* / ～环境 *investment environment*; *investment climate* / ～人 *investor* / ～基金 *investment fund* / ～市场 *investment market* / ～信托公司 *investment trust* / ～收益 *income from investment*

tòu

透 ① penetrate; make through; pass through; seep through: ～水 *leaky* / 不～水 *waterproof* / 大雨湿～了她的裙子。*The heavy rain had penetrated right through her skirt.* ② tell secretly; tip off; leak; reveal a secret: ～消息 *tell sb news on the quiet* / ～出一点风声 *drop a hint or two* ③ appear; show; look; reveal: 白里～红 *white touched with red* / 小伙子～着机灵。*The boy has a smart look.* ④ completely; fully; to the extreme; thoroughly; clearly: 恨～了 *hate bitterly* / 糟～了 *extremely bad*

【透彻】penetrating; thoroughgoing; thorough: ～的分析 *penetrating analysis* / 有～的了解 *have a thorough understanding*

【透底】give the bottom line; reveal the exact details; tell the inside story: 向报界～ *release inside information to the press* / 向球迷～ *release the exact details to the ball fans*

【透顶】［贬］thoroughly; extremely; absolutely; downright; out-and-out: 愚蠢～ *downright stupidity* / 腐败～ *extremely corrupt*; *rotten to the core*

【透风】① let in air; aerate; ventilate: 开窗～。*Open the windows to let in fresh air.* / 这门关不严，有点～。*This door doesn't fit very tightly and the wind blows through.* ② dry in the air; air ③ leak; let out; reveal a secret: 他事先向经理～了。*He let out anything to his manager.*

【透骨】① chill one to the bone; pierce to the bone; be biting; be piercing: 冷风吹来～寒。*The cold wind chills one to the bone.* ② penetrating; deep; through; profound: 看得～ *see through*; *have a keen observation*

【透汗】good sweat; profuse sweat

【透话】hint; leak; give a hint; tip off: 他～下月来北京。*He hinted that he will be Beijing next month.*

【透镜】【物】lens: 凹～ *concave lens* / 凸～ *convex lens* / 分光～ *beam-splitting lens*

【透亮】① very bright; transparent ② perfectly clear; completely obvious

【透漏】divulge; leak; reveal: ～机密 *let out a se-*

cret

【透露】divulge; let out; tell secretly disclose: ~真相 *reveal the truth* / ~计划 *divulge the plan*

【透明】transparent; diaphanous: ~液体 *transparent liquid* / 半~ *translucent* / 不~ *opaque* / ~衣服 *see-through dress* / ~度 *transparency*; *diaphaneity* / ~漆 *celluloid paint*; *clear lacquer* / ~纸 *cellophane paper*; *cellophane* / ~塑料 *transparent plastic*

【透辟】penetrating; incisive; thoroughgoing; sharp: ~的分析 *penetrating analysis* / 讲解~ *explain penetratingly*

【透平机】turbine

【透气】① ventilate; air; let in air; aerate: 不~的房间 *stuffy room* / 打开窗子透~。*Open the windows and let some air in.* ② breathe freely ③ leak; let out; inform; tip off; drop a hint: 这件事千万不要给他~。*We should not let him know of the matter.*

【透气薄膜】breathable film

【透气性】【纺】(air) permeability

【透热性】【物】diathermancy

【透射】① pass through; penetrate: 月光从窗口~进来。*The moon shone in through the window.* ② transmission: 定向~ *regular transmission* / ~比 *transmittance* / ~率 *transmissivity*

【透视】① perspective: 三点~ *three-point perspective* / ~图 *perspective drawing* ②【医】fluoroscopy; roentgenoscopy; x-ray examination ③ see through; see clearly

【透水层】【地】previous bed; permeable stratum

【透心凉】① penetrating coolness; chill through; chill to the marrow; chill to the bone: 冷风吹了我个~。*The cold wind chilled me to the bone.* ② bitterly disappointed; thoroughly disillusioned

【透信】leak; disclose information; tip off; drop a hint: 有什么事情,提前~给我。*You'd better let me know if there is any news.*

【透雨】saturating or soaking rain; soaker: 树苗需要场~。*The saplings need a soaking rain.*

【透支】① overdraw; make an overdraft; be overdrawn: 巨额~的账户 *a heavily overdrawn account* / ~安排 *an overdraft arrangement* ② overspend; have a deficit; expenditure exceeds revenue ③ draw one's salary in advance: ~薪金 *anticipate one's pay*

tū

凸 protruding; raised; bulging; convex: ~花银瓶 *a silver vase with a raised floral design* / ~面 *convex* / 凹~不平 *rough and uneven*

【凸岸】【地】convex bank

【凸版】relief printing plate: ~印刷 *letterpress*; *relief printing* / ~纸 *relief printing paper*

【凸窗】bay window

【凸轮】【机】cam: 推动~ *actuating cam* / ~轴 *cam shaft*

【凸面镜】【物】convex mirror

【凸透镜】【物】convex lens

【凸缘】【机】flange: 环状~ *collar flange* / ~型钢 *flanged section*

秃 ① bald; bare; barren: 荒山~岭 *barren hills* / 光~的轮胎 *bald tyres* / 光~~的景象 *a bald landscape* / 头顶全~的 *bald as a coot* ② blunt; without a point: 铅笔~了。*The pencil is blunt.* ③ incomplete; deficient; unsatisfactory

【秃笔】bald writing brush; poor writing ability; low skill at composition

【秃顶】① become bald; bald: 他25岁就~了。*He was already balding at the age of 25.* ② bald head

【秃鹫】(cinereous) vulture

【秃头】① bareheaded; hatless ② baldhead; shaven head ③ baldheaded man; baldy

【秃子】① baldhead; baldpate ②［方］favus of the scalp

突 ① dash forward; rush; charge; sprint: 狼奔豕~ *run like a wolf and rush like a boar* / 骑兵~入敌人阵地。*The cavalry charged into enemy positions.* ② projecting; sticking out: ~兀的山石 *towering crags* ③ suddenly; abruptly; unexpectedly; all of a sudden: 气温~变。*The temperature suddenly dropped.*

【突变】① sudden veer; abrupt change: 事态~ *abrupt change in the situation* ②【哲】leap ③ mutation: 隐性~ *recessive mutation* / ~体 *mutant*

【突出】① projecting; protruding; prominent; sticking out: 眼球~ *bug-eyed* / 悬崖~ *projecting cliffs* ② charge out of; break through: ~重围 *break through a tight encirclement* ③ outstanding; salient; prominent: ~的成绩 *outstanding achievements* / 表现~ *be an outstanding example* / ~部 *salient* ④ stress; highlight; emphasize: ~重点 *stress the main point*

【突飞猛进】make a spurt of progress; make remarkable progress; advance by leaps and bounds: 学习发展~ *forge ahead in one's study*

【突击】① attack suddenly; assault: ~敌阵 *make a sudden and violent attack on the enemy positions* / ~点 *point of assault* / ~队 *shock team*; *shock brigade* / ~手 *shock worker* / ~战术 *shock tactics* ② concentrate effort to finish a job; make a rush; do a crash job

【突尼斯】① Tunisia: ~人 *Tunisian* ② Tunis, capital of Tunisia

【突破】① break through; make or effort a breakthrough: ~地区 *area of penetration or breakthrough* / ~点 *breakthrough point* / ~口 *breach*; *gap* ② surmount; break; top: ~难关 *overcome a difficulty*; *break the back of a tough job* ③ (in football, etc.) break through a defense

【突起】① break out; appear suddenly; come to the fore suddenly: 战事~。*Hostilities broke out.* / 险象~。*Dangers appear suddenly.* ② protrude; rise high; tower

【突然】sudden; abrupt; unexpected; all of a sudden：~的决定 a sudden decision / ~痛哭起来 burst into tears / ~袭击 surprise attack; sudden onslaught / 灯~都灭了。Suddenly the lights went out.

【突如其来】come suddenly; happen unexpectedly; appear all of a sudden; arrive unexpectedly

【突突】[象]：汽车~地驶入村庄。The truck chugged its way into the village.

【突围】break through an encirclement：~脱险 break through a ring of encirclement to safety

【突兀】① lofty; towering; protruding：高峰~。A peak thrusts itself towards the sky. ② sudden; abrupt; unexpected

【突袭】surprise attack; shock attack：~敌营 launch a surprise attack on an enemy camp

【突现】appear suddenly; emerge unexpectedly

tú

图 ① picture; drawing; map; diagram; chart：地~ map / 挂~ hanging chart / 绘~ draw a picture / 构~ composition of a picture / 示意~ sketch-map / 草~ (rough) sketch; draft / 蓝~ blueprint / 制~ make a drawing ② scheme; plan; attempt：另有所~ have another plan ③ intention; intent：良~ good intention / 宏~大略 great plan and broad strategy ④ pursue; seek; covet; desire：只~享受 pursue pleasure solely / ~一时痛快 seek momentary satisfaction ⑤ [书] draw; paint：绘~ draw sb's picture

【图案】pattern; design：格子~ checked pattern / ~设计 pattern design / 圆点~ polka dots / 有~的壁纸 patterned wallpaper / ~操 callisthenic performance forming patterns

【图板】drawing board

【图版】【印】plate (for printing photos, maps, illustrations etc.)

【图报】try to return sb's kindness; try to repay sb's kindness

【图表】chart; diagram; graph：统计~ statistical chart / 绘制~ draw a chart

【图财害命】murder for money

【图钉】drawing pin; thumbtack

【图符】【电】icon

【图画】drawing; picture; painting：~书 picture-book / ~文字 picture writing / ~纸 drawing paper

【图鉴】illustrated or pictorial handbook：《中草药~》Pictorial Handbook of Chinese Medical Herbs

【图解】① diagram; graph; figure; illustration：黑白~ black and white diagram ②【数】graphic solution：~法 graphic method

【图景】view; prospect; scene：一幅壮丽的~ a magnificent prospect / 田园生活的~ idyllic scenery

【图卷】picture scroll：历史~ panorama of history

【图例】legend (of a map, etc.); key

【图谋】plot; plan; attempt; conspire：plot an uprising：~不轨 scheme sedition

【图片】picture; photograph; photo：~说明 caption / ~展览 photo exhibition / 上周末，我和妈妈一起看了~展览。My mother and I went to see photo exhibition last weekend.

【图谱】a collection of illustrative plates; atlas：植物~ floral atlas

【图穷匕现】come to open hostilities after subterfuges fail; when the map was spread out, a stiletto was exposed; an attempt frustrated by its exposure

【图书】books：~资料 books and reference materials / ~阅览室 reading room / 英文~ books in English

【图书馆】library：~馆长 librarian (in charge of a library) / ~学 library science

【图文并茂】(of publications) both pictures and texts are excellent

【图文传真】fax; facsimile transmission

【图像】image; picture; pattern：~处理 image processing / ~修复 image restoration / ~识别 pattern recognition / ~传输 image transmission

【图形】graph; figure; geometric figure：绘制~ draw a picture / ~识别 pattern recognition / ~用户界面 graphical user interface (GUI)

【图样】pattern; draft; design; drawing：加工~ processing draft

【图章】seal; stamp：塑料~ plastic stamp

【图纸】blueprint; drawing：施工~ working drawing / 工程~ blueprint for a project

荼 [古] ① bitter edible plant ② white flower of reeds, etc.

【荼毒】[书] torment; afflict with great suffering; cause suffering：~生灵 cause suffering to the people; plunge the people into the depths of suffering

徒[1] ① apprentice; pupil; disciple：门~ pupil; disciple ② follower; believe：信~ believe; devotee ③ [贬] clique; member：纳粹党~ member of the Nazi Party ④ [贬] person; fellow：好事之~ busybody / 无耻之~ a shameless person / 赌~ gambler / 匪~ bandit / 叛~ renegade ⑤ (prison) sentence; imprisonment：~刑 sentence

徒[2] ① on foot：~涉 wade through; ford ② empty; bare：~手 bare-handed; unarmed ③ merely; only：~具形式 be a mere formality ④ in vain; for nothing：~费唇舌 simply to cost toil and work / ~劳无益 work in vain ⑤ (Tú) a surname

【徒步】on foot：~旅行 travel on foot

【徒弟】apprentice; disciple

【徒费唇舌】waste one's breath; waste one's words

【徒工】apprentice

【徒唤奈何】cry to no avail; utter bootless cries; regret in vain

【徒劳】work in vain; come to naught; end in smoke; make a futile effort：~无益 vain labour with no profit

【徒劳往返】make a futile journey; make a trip in vain

【徒劳无功】make useless trouble; make a futile effort; work to no avail; make a vain attempt

【徒然】① futile; vainly; with no result; uselessly: ～浪费时间 *waste one's time* ② merely; only; simply

【徒手】bare-handed; unarmed: ～搏斗 *fight bare-handed* / ～操 *free-standing exercises*

【徒孙】disciple's disciple; pupil's pupil

【徒刑】【律】imprisonment; sentence: 有期～ *specified (prison) sentence* / 无期～ *life imprisonment*

【徒有虚名】enjoy undeserved fame; possess an empty name; be only in name; have an unearned reputation: 她不过～罢了。*She simply has an unearned reputation.*

【徒长】【农】excessive growth (of branches and leaves); spindling

【徒子徒孙】disciples and followers; hangers-on and their spawn

途 way; road; path; journey: ～经 *by way of* / ～中 *on the way* / 长～ *long distance* / 沿～ *along the road* / 旅～ *journey*

【途程】road; way; route; course: 旅游的～ *course of travel*

【途经】by way of; via: 他们～伦敦去法国。*They are travelling to France by way of London.*

【途径】way; method; channel; path

涂 ① spread on; apply; put (a substance) on (a surface); smear; paint: 把黄油～在面包上 *spread butter on bread* / 把胶水～在墙上 *spread glue on wall* / ～漆 *apply a coat of paint; paint* ② scribble; scrawl; daub: 别在纸上乱～。*Don't scribble on the paper.* ③ blot out; cross out; erase: ～掉几个字 *cross out a few words* ④ sea shoal; shallows: 围～造田 *reclaim land from the sea* ⑤ mud; slush: 生灵～炭。*Living souls are in mud and charcoal.* ⑥ (Tú) a surname

【涂层】coat; coating; layer of paint: 减磨～ *friction coat* / ～材料 *coating; enamel*

【涂改】alter; change; modify; correct: ～液 *correction fluid* / 随意～ *change at random* / ～无效 *invalid if altered*

【涂画】scribble; scrawl; smear over; daub; paint without skill

【涂料】paint; coating: 耐火～ *refractory coating* / 透气～ *paint that can breathe*

【涂抹】① paint; smear ② scribble; scrawl: 胡乱～ *scribble aimlessly*

【涂片】【医】smear: 血～ *blood smear*

【涂饰】① cover with paint, lacquer, color wash, etc. ② daub (plaster, etc.) on a wall; whitewash: ～墙壁 *whitewash a wall*

【涂刷】paint with a brush; apply paint with a brush

【涂炭】①［书］mud and ashes; utter misery; misery and suffering ② make (people) suffer: ～百姓 *wreak havoc among the people*

【涂写】scribble; scrawl; doodle: 禁止～! *No scribbling!* / 不要在墙乱～。*Don't scribble on the wall.*

【涂鸦】［谦］poor handwriting; chicken tracks; graffiti: ～之作 *my poor handwriting*

【涂泽】［书］gloss over; cover up; apply cosmetics; whitewash

【涂脂抹粉】paint in glowing colors; put on powder and rough; apply cosmetics; apply facial make-up; prettify: 为自己～ *try to whitewash oneself*

屠 ① slaughter (animals for food); kill; butcher: ～牛宰羊 *butcher cows and sheep* ② massacre; butcher; slaughter: 大量～杀动物 *kill animals in large numbers*

【屠场】slaughterhouse; abattoir

【屠刀】butcher's knife: 放下～,立地成佛 *lay down the cleaver and become a Buddha*

【屠夫】butcher; ruthless ruler

【屠户】butcher or butcher's

【屠龙之技】the skilled — art of slaughtering dragons; useless skill

【屠戮】［书］massacre; butcher; slaughter; kill indiscriminately

【屠杀】massacre; butcher; slaughter; kill indiscriminately: 对无辜平民的～ *the slaughter of innocent civilians*

【屠宰】butcher; slaughter: ～牲畜 *slaughter animals; butcher fat stock* / ～场 *slaughterhouse* / ～税 *tax on slaughtering animals*

tǔ

土 ① soil; earth; dust: ～坷垃 *a lump of earth; clod* / 沃～ *fertile soil* / 瘠～ *poor soil* / 粘～ *clay soil* / 领～ *territory* / 尘～ *dust* / 用～把种子盖上 *cover seeds with earth* / 家具上有尘～。*The furniture was covered in dust.* ② land; ground; soil; territory: 国～ *country's territory; land* / 疆～ *territory* ③ local; home-made; indigenous: ～办法 *indigenous methods* / ～方子 *handed-down recipe; home remedy* ④ local; native: 奶奶说的是很～的家乡话。*My granny speaks with a broad native accent.* ⑤ rustic; unrefined; crude; unenlightened ⑥ opium: 烟～ *opium*

【土坝】【水】earth dam; earth-filled dam

【土包子】［贬］clodhopper; (country) bumpkin; crude guy; yokel

【土豹】【动】buzzard

【土崩瓦解】crumble; fall apart; be disintegrated; collapse

【土鳖】【动】ground beetle

【土拨鼠】【动】marmot

【土布】hand-woven cloth; hand-loomed cloth; home-spun cloth

【土产】① local product; native product: ～商店 *local produce store* / 经销～ *distribute local products* ② produce locally

【土地】① territory; area: ～辽阔 *a vast territory* ② local god of the land; village god: ～庙 *a tiny temple housing the village god* ③ soil; land; ground: 农用～ *farming* / 可耕～ *arable land* / ～法 *land law; agrarian law* / ～分红 *dividend on land shares* / ～改革 *land reform* / ～使用费 *land*

use charge / ~使用权 land-use right / ~税 land tax / ~征用 expropriation of land / ~证 land certificate / ~制度 land system
【土豆】[口] potato
【土耳其】Turkey: ~人 Turk / ~语 Turkish (language)
【土法】indigenous method; local method; traditional way: ~治病 treat an illness with a folk recipe
【土方】① cubic meter of earth ② earthwork: ~工程 earthwork ③【中医】folk recipe; home remedy; folk prescriptions: 那位医生收集了很多~。The doctor collected folk prescriptions.
【土房】adobe house
【土匪】bandit; brigand
【土豪】local tyrant; local despot: ~劣绅 local tyrant and evil gentry
【土话】local dialect
【土皇帝】local despot; local tyrant
【土黄】sallow; yellowish; color of loess: ~色的纸 yellowish brown paper
【土货】local product; native produce: 从家乡带回来几样~ bring from the hometown a few local products
【土老冒儿】[口] yokel; bumpkin; simple-minded country person; clodhopper
【土里土气】rustic; uncouth; countrified; cloddish
【土路】dirt road
【土霉素】terramycin; oxytetracycline
【土木】building; construction: 大兴~ go in for large-scale construction / ~工程 civil engineering
【土坯】sun-dried mud brick; adobe
【土气】① rustic style; cloddish manner; uncouth bearing ② rustic; uncouth; countrified
【土丘】mound; hillock
【土壤】soil: ~学 soil science; pedology
【土生土长】locally born and bred; born and raised in the locality: ~的作家 native writer
【土石方】cubic meter of earth and stone: ~量 earth and stone work
【土司】① system of appointing national minority hereditary headmen in the Yuan, Ming and Qing Dynasties ② such a headman; chieftain
【土特产】local speciality; local specialty
【土头土脑】rustic; cloddish; hillbilly
【土豚】【动】earth pig; aardvark
【土温】【农】soil temperature
【土星】【天】Saturn: ~光环 Saturn's rings
【土腥气】smell of soil; earthen taste
【土洋并举】use both modern and indigenous methods; employ both simple and sophisticated methods
【土洋结合】combine indigenous methods with modern ones; integrate traditional with modern methods
【土音】local accent: 那个农民说话一口的~。The farmer spoke with a strong local accent.
【土语】local dialect; local or colloquial expression
【土葬】burial in the ground; burial
【土造】make with local method; produce with indigenous method: ~手榴弹 grenades of local make
【土政策】local policies; regulations of a locality
【土质】the quality and composition of the soil; soil texture; soil property: ~肥沃 fertile soil
【土冢】grave mound
【土著】original inhabitant; aboriginal; aborigine
【土专家】local expert; self-taught expert
【土族】the Tu nationality

吐 ① spit; send out; put forth; emit: ~鱼刺 spit out a fishbone / 蚕~丝。Silkworms spin silk. ② say; tell; pour out: 谈~ conversation manner / ~真情 unbosom oneself; tell the truth / ~怨气 vent one's grievances
see also tù
【吐刚茹柔】avoid the strong and bully the weak
【吐故纳新】get rid of the stale and take in the fresh; exhale the old and inhale the new
【吐口】① tell the truth ② say in approval ③ put forward a claim; make a demand
【吐苦水】pour out one's grievances: 向同学~ pour out bitterness to one's classmate
【吐露】tell; unbosom; reveal: ~真情 unbosom oneself; tell the truth / ~心扉 pour out one's heart; unbosom oneself
【吐气】① exhale freely; be elated; feel elated and exultant: 扬眉~ exhale freely and expand the eye brows; feel proud and happy ②【语】aspirated: ~音 aspirated sound
【吐弃】spurn; discard; cast aside: 那个叛徒遭到了万人~。The traitor was spurned by the people.
【吐舌头】stick out one's tongue; put out one's tongue
【吐穗】【农】earing (up); heading (of cereal plants)
【吐痰】spit; expectorate
【吐絮】【农】opening of bolls; boll opening
【吐字】enunciate; articulate; pronounce: 那个孩子太小了,~还不清楚。The child was too small to enunciate clearly.

钍【化】thorium (Th)

tù

吐 ① vomit; eject; retch; throw up: 呕~声 the noise of vomiting / ~血 vomit blood ② give up unwillingly; disgorge: ~退赃款 return stolen money
see also tǔ
【吐酒石】【药】tartar emetic
【吐沫】saliva; spit; spittle: 满口~ foaming with saliva
【吐血】spitting blood; vomiting blood; haematemesis
【吐泻】vomiting and diarrhoea
【吐赃】disgorge ill-gotten gains

兔 hare; rabbit; bunny

【兔唇】【医】harelip; cleft lip

【兔毫】writing brush made of rabbit's hair

【兔死狗烹】when all hares are killed, the hounds are stewed and eaten; trusted aides are eliminated when they have outlived their usefulness

【兔死狐悲】the fox is sad at the death of a hare; feel sad for the loss of one's kind; like feels for like: ~,物伤其类。*The fox mourns over the death of the hare or like mourns over the death of like.*

【兔脱】[书] run away like a hare; flee; escape:走私者侥幸~。*The smuggler made a narrow escape.*

【兔崽子】brat; bastard

【兔子】hare; rabbit

【兔子不吃窝边草】rabbits don't eat the grass by their burrows; villains don't harm his next door neighbours

【兔子尾巴长不了】[贬] the tail of a rabbit can't be long; one's good times don't last long

tuān

湍 ①(of a current) rapid; ② rapids; rushing waters:急~ *rushing current*

【湍急】rapid; torrential; swift:水流~。*The current is swift.* /战士们跳进了~的江水。*The soldiers jumped into swift flow of the river.*

【湍流】①[书] swift current; rushing waters; torrent; rapids: ~滚下。*The torrents of water roll down.* ②【物】turbulent flow; turbulence

tuán

团 ① round; circular; roundish: ~脸 *round face* / ~~坐下 *sit down in a circle* ② sth shaped like a ball; dumpling:汤~ *boiled rice dumplings* /棉花~儿 *cotton ball* ③ roll into a ball; roll:把绳子绕成~ *roll the rope into a ball* ④ unite; conglomerate; assemble: ~结 *unite* ⑤ group; society; circle; organization:剧~ *drama troupe* /马戏~ *circus* /代表~ *delegation; mission* ⑥【军】regiment: ~参谋长 *regimental chief of staff* ⑦ political organization for teenagers ⑧ [量] ball; lump:一~绒线 *a ball of wool* /一~面 *a lump of dough*

【团拜】mass greetings; mass congratulations:参加~ *participate in mutual greetings in a group*

【团队】group; corps; team: ~协作精神 *teamwork spirit*

【团粉】cooking starch

【团伙】gang; ring; band; clique:打击犯罪~ *crack down on criminal gangs*

【团结】unite; rally: ~一致 *unite as one* / ~友爱 *unity and fraternity* / ~就是力量。*Unity is strength.*

【团聚】① reunite; gather again:合家~ *family reunion* /令人感动的~ *emotional reunions* ② gather; assemble:一队警察~在街头。*A team of policemen gathered on the street.*

【团课】league class; league lecture

【团粒】【农】granule: ~结构 *granular structure*

【团脐】① abdomen of a female crab ② female crab

【团体】team; group; society; organization:群众~ *mass organization* /社会~ *social organization* /学术~ *academic society* / ~保险 *group insurance* / ~操 *group calisthenics* / ~冠军 *team title* / ~票 *group ticket* / ~项目 *team event* / ~赛 *team competition*

【团团】round and round; all round: ~转 *pace about in an agitated state of mind* / ~围住 *surround completely; encircle* / ~簇簇 *in a cluster or swarm*

【团鱼】soft-shelled turtle

【团员】① member of a group or delegation:访问团~ *member of a visiting group* ② member of the Communist Youth League of China; league member:你的~证收到了吗? *Have you received your league member card?*

【团圆】① reunite; be reunion: ~饭 *family reunion dinner* /夫妻~ *reunion of husband and wife* /父母与失散的孩子~了。*Parents were reunited with their lost children.* ② round:这女孩儿长了个~脸。*The girl has a round face.*

【团圆节】mid-Autumn Festival; moon Festival; family Reunion Festival

【团长】【军】① regimental commander ② head of a troupe; chief of a delegation

【团子】dumpling:糯米~ *dumpling made of glutinous rice*

【团坐】sit in a circle:围炉~ *sit around a fire*

tuī

推 ① push; shove; thrust: ~车 *push a cart* / ~铅球 *shot put; put the shot* /把石头~进河里 *shove the stone into the river* /阿切尔把窗~开了。*Archer pushed the window open.* ② turn a mill or grindstone; grind: ~点白面 *grind some wheat into flour* ③ cut; pare; plane; mow: ~头 *have a haircut* /用刨子~光 *make smooth with a plane; plane* ④ push forward; promote; apply: ~动工作 *push the work forward* ⑤ infer; deduce; conclude ⑥ push away; shirk; shift:把责任~给某人 *shift the responsibility on to sb* / ~来~去 *each pushes sth away to the other; give the runaround* ⑦ put off; delay; postpone:往后~几天 *postpone for a few days* ⑧ elect; choose; recommend: ~贤让能 *recommend the worthy and make way for the talented* / ~他担任小组长 *elect him group leader; choose him to be group leader* ⑨ hold in esteem; praise highly: ~重 *hold in esteem* ⑩ decline; yield; give: ~梨让枣 *decline*

the pears and jujubes
【推刨】[方] plane
【推本溯源】trace the origin; detect the reason; ascertain the cause
【推波助澜】help intensify the strength of billows and waves; make a stormy sea stormier; fan the fire; increase troubles
【推测】infer; guess; conjecture:据~ *by inference* /~后果 *calculate the effect*
【推陈出新】bring forth the new through the old; weed through the old to let the new grow
【推诚相见】deal with sb on good faith; open one's heart to sb
【推迟】put off; postpone; defer; delay:把会议~到下个月开 *put off the meeting till next month*
【推斥】【物】repulsion: ~力 *repulsive force*
【推崇】hold in esteem; praise highly: ~备至 *admire sb very much*; *have the greatest esteem for*
【推出】introduce; present; promote; initiate:他们在会议上~了改革方案。*They introduced a reform programme in the meeting.*
【推辞】refuse; decline; turn down; derive: ~宴请 *decline an invitation to dinner*
【推戴】[书] support sb assuming leadership:那位老教授受广大老师的~。*The old professor enjoys the support of the teachers.*
【推挡】【体】half volley with push
【推导】deduce; derive (sth from sth); conclude
【推倒】① push over; overturn; topple:把他~了 *push him over*; *shove him to the ground* ② repudiate; cancel; reserve; overturn; overthrow: ~重来 *start all over again* / ~旧体制 *overthrow an old system*
【推定】① elect; choose:大家~他当总经理。*He was chosen by general consensus to the general manager.* ② conjecture; deduce; infer; conclude ③【律】constructive: ~欺诈 *constructive fraud*
【推动】push forward; promote; propel; give impetus to: ~生产力的发展 *promote the development of productive forces* / ~工作 *push the work forward*
【推断】infer; deduce; arrive at by reasoning:根据有关事实~ *draw inferences based on relevant facts* / ~出的明显结论是她无罪。*It is an obvious deduction that she is innocent.*
【推度】infer; conjecture; guess:妄加~ *make improper inferences* /我们私底下~她可能要离开公司了。*We conjecture in private she may leave the company.*
【推而广之】by an extension of this logic; by an logical extension of this point; likewise; in the same way
【推翻】① overturn; overthrow; topple; undo: ~军政权 *overturn the military regime* ② repudiate; cancel; reserve: ~错误的答案 *reserve a wrong answer* / ~原方案 *abolish the original plan*
【推杆】【机】push rod; pusher; pusher bar; pushover
【推故】give a pretext; find a reason; make an excuse
【推广】popularize; spread; extend: ~个人计算机的使用 *popularize the use of personal computers*
【推及】spread to; extend by analogy; extend
【推己及人】consider others in one's own place; extend one's own feelings to others; place oneself in another's place; be considerate
【推挤】① push; shove; push and shove:他把她~到了一边。*He shoved her out of the way.* ②[书] push out; squeeze out; elbow out
【推荐】recommend; praise sb as suitable for a post: ~信 *letter of recommendation*
【推进】① push on; carry forward; promote; advance ②【军】move forward; push; drive:前锋部队迅速~。*The vanguard troops pushed forward rapidly.* ③【物】propel; thrust: ~功率 *thrust power* / ~系数 *propulsive coefficient* / ~剂 *propellant* / ~力 *propulsive force*; *driving power* / ~器 *propeller* / ~舱 *propulsion module*
【推究】examine; study: ~成因 *examine the contributing factors*
【推举】① choose; elect:同学们一致~他到大会发言。*The students chose him to speak on their behalf at the meeting.* ②【体】clean and press; press: ~一百公斤 *press* 100 *kilograms*
【推理】【逻】inference; reasoning; ratiocination; deduction:间接~ *indirect reasoning* / ~小说 *ratiocinative novel* /演绎~ *deduction*
【推力】① thrust; propulsion: 发动机~ *engine thrust* / ~载荷 *thrust load* ② driving force; incentive
【推论】inference; deduction; corollary; conclusion:由~得出的证据 *inferential proof* /令人叹服的~ *deduction which compels admiration*
【推磨】turn a millstone
【推拿】【中医】massage
【推敲】weigh; deliberate: ~词句 *weigh one's words* /经得起~ *can stand close scrutiny*
【推求】find out; inquire into; study; ascertain: ~地震的原因 *inquire into the causes of earthquake*
【推却】refuse; decline; turn down:每个成员都不能~。*Every member should not decline with any excuses.* / 不要总是找借口~我们。*Don't turn down us with an excuse.*
【推让】decline; yield; submit:你先走吧! 不要相互~了。*You go first*; *Don't submit to one another.*
【推人犯规】【体】pushing
【推三阻四】make excuse s and put obstacles in the way
【推说】①[方] offer as an excuse (for not doing sth); plead ② infer; deduce: ~其意 *infer its meaning*
【推算】calculate; estimate; reckon: 我~大约需要100元。*I reckon it will cost about* 100 *yuan.*
【推涛作浪】make a stormy sea stormier; make trouble; create disturbances
【推头】[口] ① have a haircut ② cut sb's hair (with clippers)

【推土机】bulldozer
【推推搡搡】push and shove
【推托】offer as an excuse (for not doing sth); plead
【推脱】evade; dodge; shirk
【推挽】①[书] recommend; introduce ②【电】push-pull: ~电路 *push-pull circuit* / ~晶体管 *push-pull transistor*
【推诿】shift blame onto others; pass the buck; shirk: ~于人 *shift responsibility onto others*
【推问】question; investigate; cross-examine; interrogate; inquire
【推想】imagine; guess; conjecture; reckon: 不难~玛丽肯定又病了。*It's not hard to imagine Mary must be sick again.*
【推销】promote sales; sell; peddle: ~商品 *promote the sale of goods* / 廉价~ *sell at a low price* / ~员 *salesman*
【推销术】salesmanship; selling techniques
【推卸】shirk; evade; avoid; shift off: ~责任,委过于人 *shirk responsibility and shift the blame onto others*
【推心置腹】treat a person with sincerity; have a heart-to-heart talk with sb; repose full confidence in sb: 我们昨晚~地交换意见。*We had a confidential exchange of views last night.*
【推行】carry out; practice; introduce; perform: ~新制度 *introduce a new system* / ~新方案 *carry out new plans*
【推选】elect; choose: ~代表 *choose representatives*
【推移】①(of time) elapse; pass; go ②(of a situation, etc.) develop; evolve: 时局的~ *developments in current affairs*
【推知】infer; reckon; deduce
【推重】regard highly; hold in esteem
【推子】[口] hair-clippers; clippers

tuí

颓 ① ruined; dilapidated; decayed; collapsed: ~垣断壁 *crumbling walls and dilapidated houses* ② declining; decadent: 衰~ *weak and declining* ③ dejected; dispirited; discouraged: ~丧的表情 *dispirited expression*
【颓败】decline; decay; corrupt
【颓废】dejected; dispirited; depressed; decadent: ~的情绪 *decadent sentiments* / ~的生活 *dissipated life* / ~派 *decadent school*
【颓风】degenerate manners; depraved customs; corrupt morals
【颓坏】ruined; collapsed; decayed
【颓靡】dejected; crestfallen; decadent: ~之音 *decadent music*
【颓然】[书] dejected; disappointed: 自从汤姆生病以后他就一直~不振。*Tom became dejected and listless since he was ill.*
【颓丧】dejected; listless; dispirited; demoralized
【颓势】declining tendency; decadent trend
【颓唐】dejected; dispirited; depressed
【颓朽】rotten; decayed; ruined
【颓运】[书] adversity; misfortune; declining luck

tuǐ

腿 ① leg: 前~ *foreleg* /大~ *thigh* /小~ *shank; calf* / ~酸 *have stiff legs* /罗圈腿 *bowlegs; bandy legs* ② leg like support; leg: 桌子~ *legs of table* ③ ham
【腿肚子】[口] calf (of the leg)
【腿脚】legs and feet; ability to walk: ~有病 *have ailing legs and feet* / ~利落 *walking briskly* /我母亲~不方便,不能和我一起去商店了。*My mother has difficulty walking and can't go shopping with me.*
【腿快】quick-footed; swift-footed
【腿懒】reluctant to move around; disinclined to move about; lazy about paying visits
【腿勤】tireless in running about; like to move around
【腿腕子】ankle

tuì

退 ① retreat; move back; back up: 进~两难 *difficult to advance or retreat* / ~一步说 *even if that is so; even so* / ~而求其次 *have to take the second best* /我们后~了100米。*We retreated one hundred metres.* ② withdraw; remove; cause to move back: ~保 *withdraw one's guaranty* /把子弹~出来 *remove a cartridge from the breech of a gun; unload a gun* ③ decline; recede; decrease ④ retire; quit; adjourn: ~归林下 *retire from public life* ⑤ return; give back; refund: 空瓶不~。*Empty bottles are not refundable.* ⑥ cancel; break off; retreat: ~掉订货 *cancel an order*
【退避】withdraw and keep off; get out of the way; yield: ~再三 *yield (to sb) time and again*
【退避三舍】retreat about thirty miles as a condition for peace; keep at arm's length; keep three marches distant from sb
【退兵】① retreat; withdraw: 传令~ *order a retreat* ② force the enemy to retreat; repulse; repel: ~之计 *plan for repulsing the enemy*
【退步】① lag or fall behind; relapse; retrogress; backslide: 这学期我女儿的功课~了。*My daughter fell behind in her study in this period.* ② make a concession; give in; give way ③ room for manoeuvre; leeway
【退场】leave; exit; withdraw; march out: 领导先~。*The leaders march out first.*
【退潮】ebb tide; ebb: ~时分 *ebb time*
【退出】withdraw from; quit; leave; resign: ~组织 *withdraw from an organization* / ~会场 *walk out of a meeting*
【退磁】【物】demagnetize

【退党】quit a political party
【退敌】repulse the enemy; force the enemy to retreat
【退格键】【电】backspace key
【退耕】let lie fallow; stop cultivating (land): ~还林 *let cultivated land revert to woodland*
【退关】(of an exporter, etc.) cancel a declaration (of goods already cleared by customs)
【退化】①【生】degeneration; retrogradation: 机能~ *function retrogradation* ② degenerate; deteriorate; retrograde; retrogress ③ worsen; become worse: 老师素质~ *worsening quality of teachers*
【退还】return; give back: ~公物 *return public property* / 请把空瓶全部~。*Please return all empties.*
【退换】exchange a purchase; refund; exchange: 衣服售出,概不~。*Clothes sold are not returnable.*
【退回】① return; send back; give back: ~押金 *return a deposit* / ~余款 *return the balance* / 我把那封信原封~了。*I returned the letter unopened.* ② go or turn back: 原路~ *go back along the route one took*
【退婚】cancel an engagement
【退火】【冶】annealing: ~钢 *annealed steel*
【退伙】①［旧］withdraw from an underworld gang ② cancel an arrangement to eat at a mess; withdraw from a mess
【退货】return goods (or merchandise): ~报告 *return sales report*
【退居】① retreat; retire; withdraw: ~二线 *retreat to the second line of work* / ~幕后 *retire backstage* ② drop; go down; decline: 该厂产品已~最后一位。*The products of that factory have dropped to last place.*
【退路】① route or line of retreat: 切断敌军~ *cut off the enemy's retreat* ② room for manoeuvre; leeway: 留个~ *leave some leeway; keep another option open*
【退赔】return what one has unlawfully taken or pay compensation for it
【退票】① return a ticket; cancel a reservation; get a refund for a ticket: ~处 *ticket-refund window* ② returned ticket: 等~ *look for a returned ticket*
【退钱】refund; reimburse; pay back: 这衣服如果不合适,商店管~。*If the clothes do not wear well, the shop will refund your money.*
【退亲】break off an engagement
【退却】①【军】retreat; withdraw: 暂时的~ *temporary retreat* ② hang back; shrink back; flinch: ~不前 *flinch and not press forward*
【退让】① step aside; step back; keep out of the way: ~不及 *have no chance to get out of the way* ② make a concession; yield; give in: 稍作~ *give in a little* / 在原则问题上从不~ *never make concessions on matters of principle*
【退色】fade: 越洗越~ *fade with each washing*
【退烧】bring down or allay a fever; (of a person's temperature) come down: 打针~ *have an injection to bring down the fever* / ~药 *antipyretic*
【退守】retreat and defend; withdraw and stand on the defensive
【退税】【经】drawback; tax refund; tax rebate
【退缩】shrink back; flinch; cower; withdraw: ~不前 *withdraw from advancing*
【退庭】adjourn; withdraw from the court
【退团】withdraw from a youth league; give up league membership
【退位】give up the throne; abdicate: ~让贤 *give up the throne in favour of a better qualified person*
【退伍】retire or be discharged from active military service; be demobilized; leave the army: 光荣~ *leave the army with honour* / 彼特带着极大的荣誉~返乡了。*Peter left the army with great honour returned to his native village.*
【退席】*leave a banquet or a meeting; walk out*: 有事提前~ *quit half way for some urgent business*
【退闲】go into retirement and live an idle life
【退省】［书］self-examination; introspection; self-questioning
【退休】retire; go into retirement: ~职工 *retired workers and staff* / 提前~ *retire before the retirement age* / ~金 *retirement pay; pension* / ~人员 *retiree; retired personnel*
【退学】leave school; drop out; discontinue one's schooling: 因为家里贫穷,他~了。*He had to drop out of school door to poor family.*
【退役】① retire from active military service; leave the army: ~老兵 *an old ex-serviceman* ② be taken out of service; decommission: ~战斗机 *a decommissioned fighter* ③ (esp. of athletes) retire
【退赃】return ill-gotten gains; disgorge illegal gains
【退职】resign from office; be discharged from one's work; quit working: ~报告 *application for resignation* / ~金 *severance pay; dismissal pay; retirement pay*
【退走】retreat; withdraw

蜕 ① slough off; exuviate; moult ② exuviae; slough
【蜕变】① change qualitatively; transmute; degenerate ②【物】decay
【蜕化】① slough off; exuviate ② degenerate: ~变质 *degenerate* / ~变质分子 *degenerate*
【蜕皮】【动】slough; cast off a skin; ecdysis; exuviate

褪 ① take off (clothes); shed (feathers): 冬天来了,小鸟们都已经~毛了。*The winter has come and the birds have shed their feather down.* ② (of colour) fade
see also tùn
【褪色】fade

tūn

吞 ① swallow; make a swallowing motion; devour: 狼~虎咽地吃东西 *gulp one's food* / 一口气~下 *at a gulp* ② possess; annex: 独~ *take ex-*

clusive possession of
【吞并】annex; take possession of; take over: ~邻国 *annex a neighbouring state*
【吞吃】① gulp down; swallow up ② embezzle; misappropriate: ~公款 *misappropriate public money*
【吞金】swallow gold(to commit suicide)
【吞灭】conquer and annex; gobble up
【吞没】① embezzle; misappropriate; take (sb else's money) wrongly ② swallow up; envelop; submerge; engulf:被波涛~的小船 *a boat engulfed in the waves*
【吞声】[书] swallow the voice; gulp down one's sobs; suppress one's sobs
【吞食】swallow; gulp down; devour:大鱼~小鱼。*Big fish devour small fish.*
【吞蚀】① embezzle; misappropriate; swallow up ② corrode; erode
【吞噬】swallow up; devour; engulf:大火~了大片森林。*Fire devoured a huge area of forest.*
【吞吐】① swallow and spit; take in and send out in large quantities; (of a port, etc.) handle: ~货物 *handle cargoes* / ~量 *handling capacity*(*of a harbour*); *volume of freight handled* / ~港 *port*; *harbour* ② hesitate in speech; hum and ha
【吞吞吐吐】mutter and mumble; mince one's words; stumble over one's words; hesitate in speech:有话就说,不要~。*Please say out; no humming and hawing.*
【吞咽】swallow; gulp
【吞云吐雾】swallow clouds and blow out fog; smoke opium; blow clouds
【吞占】① invade and occupy; take possession of; usurp: ~别人的财产 *usurp sb else's property* ② embezzle; misappropriate

tún

屯 ① gather; collect; store up: ~粮 *store up grain* ② station(troops); quarter (troops): 驻~ *be stationed*: ③ village(often used in village names):皇姑~ *Huanggu Village*
【屯兵】station troops; quarter troops
【屯集】gather; assemble; collect
【屯聚】assemble; gather together; concentrate: ~兵马 *assemble military forces*
【屯垦】station troops to open up wasteland
【屯田】have garrison troops or peasants open up wasteland and grow food grain; a policy introduced in the Han Dynasty
【屯扎】station(troops); quarter (troops)
【屯驻】station; quarter; garrison
囤 store up; hoard; collect: ~粮 *hoard grain* / ~货 *hoard goods*
see also dùn
【囤积】store up (grain); hoard(for speculation); corner (the market): ~食物 *store up food* / ~居奇 *store up foods for a good bargain*; *hoard and corner* /在饥荒时期~食物的人受到了惩罚。*People found hoarding food during famine were punished.*
【囤聚】collect and store; gather and store; store
臀 buttocks; rump
【臀部】buttocks: ~受伤 *wounded in the buttocks*
【臀尖】pork rump
【臀鳍】【动】anal fin
【臀围】hipline

tùn

褪 ① slip out of sth:一下子~下连衣裙 *slip out of a dress* ②[方] keep or hide in the sleeve: ~着手 *keep one's hands in the sleeves*
see also tuì
【褪去】take off; put off; slip off: ~鞋子 *put one's shoes off*
【褪套儿】① break loose; free oneself; get oneself free:那只小猫~跑了。*The little cat broke loose and ran away.* ② shake off responsibility:这事你别想~。*You can't shake off responsibility.*

tuō

托[1] ① hold up; hold in the palm; support with the hand or palm:两手~腮 *cup one's chin in one's hand* ② sth serving as a support:枪~ *the stock of the rifle* ③ set off
托[2] ① ask; entrust; beg:这事就~给我吧。*Leave the matter to me.* ② serve as a foil; set off:烘~ (*in painting*) *add shading around an object to make it stand out*; *set off* ③ plead; give as a pretext: ~病 *plead illness* ④ count upon; rely on; owe to: ~庇 *rely upon one's elder or an influential person for protection* ⑤ nursery:全~ *boarding nursery*
【托板】【建】fascia
【托庇】rely upon one's elder or an influential person for protection; be under sb's protection
【托病】plead illness; on pretext of illness: ~不去 *beg off on account of illness*
【托辞】① find a pretext; make an excuse; use a subterfuge: ~谢绝 *decline on some pretext* ② pretext; excuse; subterfuge:我们不去参加聚会得找个~才是。*We will have to find a pretext for not going to the party.*
【托大】① give oneself airs; be self-important; be presumptuous ② careless; negligent
【托儿】[口] a partner of a street pedlar or shopkeeper who pretends to be a customer and lures people into buying; salesperson's decoy
【托儿所】nursery; kindergarten; childcare centre
【托福】① thanks to you:托您的福,我们全家都好。*We are all very well, thank you.* ② (transliteration) TOEFL(Test of English as a Foreign Lan-

guage）：~考试 *TOEFL test*

【托付】entrust；trust sb to take charge of sth or sb；commit sth to sb's care：我把这项工作~给助手。*I entrusted my assistant with the task.*

【托孤】entrust one's orphan to sb's care

【托故】find a pretext；make an excuse；give a reason：~离开 *leave a banquet（or a meeting）on a pretext*

【托管】trusteeship：~国 *trustee state*；*trustee* / ~领土 *trustee territory* / ~地 *trust territory* / ~理事会 *trusteeship council*

【托灰板】【建】hawk

【托架】【机】bracket：发动机~ *engine bracket* / 角形~ *angle bracket*

【托门子】gain one's end through pull；look for ways to enlist an influential person's help；seek the good offices of sb

【托梦】（of the ghost of one's kith and kin）appear in one's dream and a request

【托名】do sth in sb else's name；use sb else's name

【托盘】tray

【托人情】gain one's end through pull；seek the good offices of sb；ask an influential person to help arrange sth

【托身】① find a place to live in；look for shelter ② make a living；seek a living

【托生】reincarnation；reborn；transmigration

【托收】collection：~款项 *items sent for collection*

【托叶】【植】stipule

【托运】consign for shipment；check：~行李 *check one's baggage* / ~单 *booking note* / ~人 *consigner* / ~物 *consignment*

【托嘱】entrust；beg

【托子】base；support；stand

拖 ① pull；drag；tug；draw；haul：~后腿 *be a drag on sb* / 我们把倒下的树从路边~走。*We dragged the fallen tree clear of the road.* ② delay；drag on；postpone；go on too long：这事还要~多久？*How much longer is this going to drag on?* ③ drag behind one；trial behind one：~着个尾巴 *trial a tail behind one* / ~了一屁股债 *be weighed down with debt*；*be deep in debt*

【拖把】mop；swab

【拖车】trailer

【拖船】① tugboat；tug；towboat ② lighter；pinnace

【拖带】① tract；pull；drag；haul ② be burdened with：受家庭的~ *be burdened with one's family*

【拖儿带女】be burdened by children；have family burden

【拖后腿】hinder sb；hold sb back；impede sb：安德森老是拖别人后腿。*Anderson always holds others back.*

【拖家带口】have a family to take care of；be burdened with a family

【拖拉】dilatory；slow；sluggish：布洛姆学习从不~。*Blom never puts off his study.*

【拖拉机】tractor：手扶~ *walking tractor* / ~站 *tractor station* / ~手 *tractor driver*

【拖累】① encumber；be tied down；be a burden on：~家庭 *be a burden to one's family* ② implicate；involve：~他人 *involve others into trouble*

【拖泥带水】be dragged through mud and water；do things sloppily；be messy：蒙妮卡办事老是~。*Monica is always slovenly handling matters.*

【拖欠】fail to pay；be behind in payment；be in arrears：~税款 *be in arrears with tax payment*

【拖三拉四】put off one's work with all sorts of excuses；procrastinate by one pretext or another；give the runaround

【拖沓】dilatory；slow；sluggish；laggard：学风~ *dilatory style of study*

【拖堂】（of a teacher）not dismiss the class on time；drag on the class：英语老师经常~。*The English teacher often drags on the class.*

【拖尾巴】① hinder；impede；be a drag ② leave sth undone；leave loose ends：你最好把作业完成，不要~。*You'd better finish your homework today, without leaving any loose ends.*

【拖鞋】slippers

【拖延】delay；postpone；put off：~时间 *play for time* / 一再~ *put off again and again* / ~战术 *delaying tactics*

【拖曳】pull；draw；tug；tow

【拖油瓶】［贬］①（of a woman）remarry and bring children of her previous marriage ② such children

【拖债】be behind in payment；be in arrears with one's debt；default on debt：他从不~。*He never defaults on debts.*

脱 ① lose；shed；come off；let fall：鹿有些种类能~换鹿角。*Some kinds of deer shed their horns.* / 他的头发几乎~光。*He has lost most of his hair.* ② take off；put off；slip out of；cast off：~帽 *take off one's hat* ③ escape from；free oneself from ④ miss out；elide；omit：这一行里~了三个字。*Three characters are missing in this line.* ⑤［书］neglect；slight；flippant：轻~ *flippant* ⑥［书］supposing；in case ⑦（Tuō）a surname

【脱靶】miss the target in shooting practice

【脱班】be late for work；（of a bus, train, etc.）be behind schedule：地铁~了。*The subway is behind the schedule.*

【脱产】be released from one's regular work；be released from production：半~ *be released from production for half the time* / ~学习 *be released from work to study*

【脱出】get out of；veer from；deviate from；break away

【脱发】【医】loss of hair；alopecia：因病~ *lose hair owing to illness*

【脱肛】【医】prolapse of the anus

【脱稿】complete a manuscript：~日期 *date for completing a manuscript*

【脱钩】unhook；cut ties

【脱轨】derail：电车~了。*The streetcar was derailed.*

【脱滑】shirk work; avoid doing one's duty; act in slick way; sneak away:他临阵~了。*He sneaked away at a critical juncture.*
【脱货】be short in supply; be out of stock; sold out:这种药暂时~。*This medicine is temporarily out of stock.*
【脱缰之马】a run away horse; uncontrollable; like a horse without a bridle; running wild
【脱胶】① come unglued; come unstuck; come apart ②【化】degum
【脱节】be split; come apart; be disjointed; be out of line
【脱臼】【医】dislocation
【脱空】① come to naught; abort; fail; fall through:他的希望~了。*His hope failed to attain his hope.* ②［方］tell a lie; lie; resort a deception
【脱口成章】slip out of the mouth and become an essay; speak beautifully
【脱口而出】escape one's lips; speak without forethought; blurt out
【脱蜡】【油】dewaxing
【脱离】cut oneself from; break away from; separate oneself from; be apart from: ~群众 *cut oneself off from the masses* / ~苦海 *be rid of this trouble some life* / ~险境 *be out of danger*
【脱离速度】【航】second cosmic velocity
【脱磷】【化】dephosphorize
【脱硫】【化】desulphurize; sweeten: ~原油 *sweet crude*
【脱漏】be left out; omit; miss; drop: ~一针 *drop a stitch* (*in knitting*)
【脱落】drop; come off; fall away; shed:头发~*lose one's hair* / 牙齿~*lose one's tooth* /墙纸~了。*The wall paper peeled off.*
【脱盲】become literate; learn to read and write; wipe out illiteracy
【脱毛】① lose hair or feathers; moult; shed:这只狗春天~了。*The dog has shed in spring.* ② depilate: ~作用 *depilation*
【脱帽】take off or raise one's hat (in respect): ~默哀 *bare one's head and mourn in silence*
【脱模】【冶】drawing of patterns in silence
【脱贫】get rid of poverty; shake off poverty; become rich become prosperous:他们村的很多人早已~致富了。*Many people in their village have got ride of poverty and become rich.*
【脱期】(of a periodical) fail to come out on time; miss the deadline; delay:一再~ *miss the deadline again and again*
【脱氢】【化】dehydrogenation
【脱色】① decolour; decolourize: ~工艺 *decolourizing technology* ② fade
【脱身】escape from; get away; free oneself from; extricate oneself:这周末她的事情太多,一时不能~。*This weekend she has so much to do that she just can't get away.*
【脱手】① slip out of the hand; let slip: 手机~掉到地上。*The mobile phone slipped from his hand and fell to the floor.* ② dispose of; get off one's hand; sell; get rid of:这些衣服不好~。*These clothes are difficult to dispose of.*
【脱水】①【医】deprivation or loss of body fluids; dehydration: ~症状 *symptoms of dehydration* ②【化】dehydration; dewatering: ~蔬菜 *dehydrated vegetables*
【脱俗】free from vulgarity; refined
【脱榫】be out of joint; have a loose joint
【脱胎】① emerge from the womb of; be born out of; develop out of; derive from:这个神话故事~于民间传说。*This fairy story has been developed out of a folk story.* ② process of making bodiless lacquer water: ~漆器 *bodiless lacquerware* / ~瓷 *bodiless chinaware*
【脱胎换骨】be reborn; thoroughly remould oneself; cast off one's old self and take on a new self
【脱逃】escape; run away; get away; flee
【脱兔】［书］a fleeing hare; fast speed
【脱位】【医】dislocation
【脱险】escape from danger; become safe; be out of danger:她病重,但现已~。*She was very ill, but is now out of danger.*
【脱销】be in short supply; be out of stock:这本书~了。*The book is sold out.*
【脱卸】shirk one's duties, etc.; shake off; evade: 事情已经发生了,谁也~不了罪责。*The thing has happened; nobody can shirk responsibility for an offence.*
【脱氧】【化】deoxidate; deoxidize: ~核糖 *deoxyribose* / ~核糖核酸 *deoxyribonucleic acid* (*DNA*)
【脱衣舞】striptease
【脱颖而出】become eminent; come into the open; make one's way:那个小姑娘在聚会中~。*The little girl had come into prominence in the party.*
【脱症】【中医】exhaustion of vital energies at the critical stage of an illness; exhaustion syndrome
【脱脂】defat; degrease: ~剂 *degreasing agent* / ~棉 *absorbent cotton* / ~牛奶 *skim milk*; *nonfat milk* / ~纱布 *absorbent gauze*

tuó

驮 carry or bear on the back:这头驴能~五袋粮食。*This donkey can carry five sacks of grain.*
【驮畜】pack animal
【驮筐】pannier
【驮马】pack horse
see also duò

陀 ［书］hill; hillock
【陀螺】(spinning) top:抽~ *whip a top*
【陀螺罗盘】gyrocompass
【陀螺仪】【航】gyroscope; gyro

坨 ① (of food made of flour) stick together:饺子~了。*These dumplings are sticking together.* ② lump; heap
【坨子】lump; heap:泥~子 *lump of mud*; *clod*

沱 ①［方］a small bay in a river ② (of tears) stream down like rain

【坨茶】a bowl shaped compressed mass of tea leaves

驼 ① camel：双峰～ *bactrian camel*；*camel* ② hunchbacked；humpbacked：老爷爷的背～了。*The grandpa's back has become bent.*

【驼背】① hunchbacked；humpbacked ② hunchback；humpback

【驼峰】① hump（of a camel）②【交】hump：～调车场 *hump yard*

【驼铃】camel bell

【驼鹿】【动】elk；moose

【驼绒】① camel's hair：～毛线 *camel wool* ② camel's hair cloth

【驼色】colour of camel's hair；light tan

【驼子】［口］hunchback；humpback

柁 【建】girder

鸵 ostrich

【鸵鸟】【动】ostrich

tuǒ

妥 ① appropriate；sound；proper；suitable：请～为保存。*Please look after it carefully.* ② ready；settled；finished；resolved：事已办～。*The matter has been settled.*

【妥当】appropriate；proper；sound：把工作安排～ *make arrangements for the work*

【妥靠】dependable；reliable；trustworthy：他一定是那个～的人选。*He must be the reliable candidate.*

【妥善】proper；suitable；well arranged；appropriate：～处理 *handle properly* / 关于明天的会议，你一定～安排。*You should make an appropriate arrangement about the meeting next day.*

【妥帖】appropriate；proper；fitting：办事～ *manage things properly*

【妥协】compromise；come to terms；give up；make concessions：达成～ *reach a compromise* / 资方在与工人的谈判中做出了～。*Employers made concessions to the workers in negotiations.*

椭 ellipse

【椭率】【数】ellipticity

【椭面】【数】ellipsoid

【椭球】ellipsoid：～体 *spheroid*；*ellipsoid*

【椭圆】【数】ellipse：～轨道 *elliptical orbit* / ～截面 *oval cross section* / ～体 *ellipsoid* / ～星云 *elliptical nebula* / ～柱面 *elliptic cylinder* / ～锥面 *elliptic cone*

tuò

拓 open up；develop；reclaim：开～边远地区 *open up the border regions*
see also tà

【拓地】［书］extend or expand territory：～千里 *expand the territory far and wide by thousands of li*

【拓荒】reclaim wasteland；open up virgin soil：～者 *pioneer*；*trailblazer*

【拓宽】widen；broaden；extend：～业务 *extend one's business*

【拓落】① frustrated；disappointed ② broad；vast；extensive

【拓展】extend；expand；spread：他负责～市场的工作。*He takes charge of expanding market.*

唾 ① saliva；spittle；spit ② spit

【唾骂】spit on and curse；spurn；revile

【唾沫】saliva；spittle；spit：～星子 *sprays from coughs*

【唾弃】spurn；contemn；cast aside：在历史上，秦桧永远被世人所～。*Qin Hui was contemned by the people in history.*

【唾手可得】get with hands down；acquire a thing easily；extremely easy to obtain

【唾液】saliva；spittle：～腺 *salivary gland*

W

wā

挖 ① dig; grub; excavate: ~洞 *dig (or excavate) a hole* / ~土豆 *grub for potatoes* / ~煤 *dig coal* / ~泥塘 *scoop up sludge from a pond* / ~掘古墓群 *excavate an ancient burial site* ② explore; probe: 从书中~掘事实 *dig facts from books* ③ [方] scratch; claw

【挖补】mend by replacing a damaged place

【挖槽机】【机】groover

【挖兜】inset pocket

【挖方】【建】excavation (of earth or stone); cubage of excavation

【挖沟机】ditcher; trencher

【挖角儿】[口] undermine; lure away a important person

【挖掘】excavate; dig; unearth: 考古~ *an archaeological excavation* / ~古董 *excavate antiques*

【挖掘机】excavator; navvy: 斗式~ *bucket excavator* / 步行式~ *walking excavator* / 液压~ *hydraulic excavator*

【挖空心思】rack one's brains; cudgel one's brains; think hard

【挖苦】whip; speak sarcastically; disparage sb by innuendoes; taunt: 请不要再~我。*Please don't taunt me any more.*

【挖潜】tap or exploit the latent power (or potentialities)

【挖墙脚】cut the ground from under sb's feet; undermine the foundation

【挖肉补疮】cut out a piece of flesh to patch a boil; rob one's belly to cover one's back

【挖腰包】foot a bill; pay out of one's own purse

哇 [象] descriptive of sb's cries or vomit: ~地一声哭出来 *burst out crying* ② [书] decadent; licentious: 淫~之音 *sex music*
see also wa

【哇啦】hullabaloo (sound of crying); din; uproar: 不要~了。*Don't make so many dins.*

【哇哇】① cry; caw ② sweet words

洼 ① low-lying; concave; hollow: ~地 *low-lying land* ② depression: 水~儿 *water-logged depression*

【洼地】hollow; trough; depression; low-lying land

【洼下】low-lying

【洼陷】① be sunken; low-lying ② deep hole

蛙 frog: 青~ *frog* / 牛~ *bullfrog*

【蛙卵】frog-spawn

【蛙人】frogman

【蛙泳】breaststroke

wá

娃 ① baby; child: 男~儿 *baby boy* ② [方] newborn; animal: 鸡~ *chick* / 狗~ *puppy*

【娃娃】baby; child

【娃娃床】crib; cot; child's bed

【娃娃亲】arranged marriage when very young

【娃娃鱼】giant salamander

wǎ

瓦[1] ① earthenware; tile: 水泥~ *cement tile* / 屋脊~ *hanging tile* ② made of baked clay

瓦[2] 【电】watt

see also wà

【瓦房】house with tile roof

【瓦工】① bricklaying; tiling or plastering ② bricklayer; tiler; plasterer

【瓦棺】earthen coffin

【瓦罐】① earthenware pitcher; crock ② earthen jar

【瓦匠】bricklayer; tiler; plasterer

【瓦解】disintegrate; collapse; crumble; break up; fall apart: ~敌军 *crumble the enemy forces*

【瓦块】fractions of tiles; broken tiles

【瓦蓝】bright blue

【瓦楞】① rows of tiles on a roof ② corrugated: ~纸 *corrugated paper*

【瓦砾】debris; rubble

【瓦亮】polished; shiny; very bright: ~的晴天 *very bright day*

【瓦坯】unbaked tile

【瓦圈】rim (bicycle wheel, car wheel, etc.)

【瓦全】drag out an ignoble existence

【瓦舍】① tile-roofed house ② amusement park or market

【瓦时】【电】watt-hour

【瓦斯】gas: ~爆炸 *gas explosion* / ~弹 *gas bomb*

【瓦特】【电】watt: 有效~ *true watt*

【瓦窑】tile kiln

wà

瓦 cover (a roof) with tiles; tile
see also wǎ

【瓦刀】bricklayer's cleaver; trowel

袜 hose; socks; stocking

【袜带】suspenders; garters
【袜底儿】sole of a sock
【袜口】welt
【袜套】ankle socks
【袜筒】boot; leg of a stocking
【袜子】socks; hose; stockings

wa

哇 be used after a word ending phonetically in *u* or *ao*: 你真好~! *You are so kind!* / 多好~! *Wonderful!*
see also wā

wāi

歪 ① askew; inclined; slanting: 你的帽子~了。*Your hat is not erect.* ② crooked; devious; evil; underhand: ~点子 *evil ideas* / ~主意 *devil's advice* ③ take a nap or rest by lying down on one side: 他刚刚~下。*He just laid down.* ④ domineering; bossy; ruthless: 他在家很~的。*He is domineering at home.*

【歪才】① devious ability ② be proficient at the Eclectics
【歪词儿】unreasonable words; defamatory talk
【歪打正着】hit the mark by a fluke; fault on the right side
【歪道】① evil ideas: 不要想~。*Don't think of dirty trick.* ② depraved ways: 走~ *lead a depraved way*
【歪风】unhealthy trend; evil wind; noxious influence; bad tendency: 制止~ *put down the bad tendency*
【歪理】false reasoning; sophistry
【歪门邪道】crooked ways; dishonest practice; under-counter business
【歪扭】askew; crooked; twisted
【歪七扭八】crooked; twisted: 那个受伤的人~地走路。*The wounded man staggered along.*
【歪曲】① distort; misrepresent; twist: ~事实 *distort the facts* / ~某人的意见 *twist one's opinion* ② crooked; askew; aslant: 身体~ *distorted body*
【歪诗】doggerel; inelegant verses; verses written by oneself
【歪歪倒倒】① unsteady; shaky: 这个餐桌~的。*This table is unsteady.* ② irregular; uneven: 他的字看起来~。*His handwriting looks irregular.*
【歪歪扭扭】crooked; askew; be shapeless and twisted
【歪斜】inclined; slanting; aslant; crooked

wǎi

崴 ① (of mountain valley) rugged ② sprain; twist: 把脚~了 *sprain one's ankle*
see also wēi

wài

外[1] ① outside; outer: ~衣 *outer garments* / 宇宙(~层)空间 *outer space* / 门~ *outside the door* ② other (than one's own): ~乡 *another part of the country* ③ surface; face; outside appearance: 面部~表 *appearance of the face* ④ foreign; external: 对~开放 *open to the outside world* ⑤ (relatives) of one's mother, sisters or daughters: ~女 *sister's daughter* ⑥ beyond; outside besides: 预算~的开支 *extra-budgetary expenditure* ⑦ unofficial: ~传

外[2] role of an elderly man

【外办】foreign affairs office; foreign relations office
【外邦】foreign countries
【外币】foreign currency: ~兑换处 *foreign currency exchange section*
【外边】① outside: 去~喝一杯如何? *Would you like go out for a drink?* ② a place other than where one lives or works: 她的丈夫在~工作。*Her husband works somewhere away from home.* ③ exterior; outer: 柱子~涂上了一层油漆。*The pillar is painted with a layer of painting.*
【外表】① appearance; exterior: 事物的~ *the exterior of things* ② face; surface; border: ~光滑 *smooth surface*
【外宾】① foreign guest; foreign visitor
【外部】① outside external: ~条件 *external conditions* ② outside: ~形状 *exterior shape*
【外埠】towns or cities other than where one is
【外财】extra income; found money; bonanza
【外侧】outside; outer flank
【外层】out; out-field
【外层大气】outer atmosphere
【外差】heterodyne: ~频率 *heterodyne frequency*
【外场】① outfield: ~手 *outfielder* ② forestage: ~椅 *front-stage chair* ③ used to socializing and grandeur: 她是个~人儿,人头挺广。*She's a good mixer and has a large circle of acquaintances.*
【外钞】foreign currency
【外臣】① (in ancient China) minister from a foreign state ② vassal state ③ local officials
【外出】① go out ② go to other parts of the country (on business)
【外串】be a guest performer

【外带】① out cover (of a tyre): 你的车~有问题。*Something is wrong with your car's tyre.* ② besides; as well; in addition: 这个人其貌不扬,还~有些口吃。*The man is plain; in addition, he speaks with a slight stutter.*
【外待】treat as stranger
【外道】stand on ceremony; over polite
【外敌】foreign enemy
【外地】parts of the country other than where one is: 他工作在~。*He works in another city.*
【外电】dispatches from foreign news agencies: 据~报道 *according to report from foreign news agencies*
【外调】① transfer (materials or personnel) to other localities ② investigation mission outside the city or town
【外耳】【医】① outer ear ② external ear
【外放】(officials of central government) be sent to be local officials
【外感】【医】affection by exogenous pathogenic factors; diseases caused by external factors
【外公】[方] (maternal) grandfather
【外功】① external work ② exercises to benefit the muscles and bones
【外观】outward appearance; exterior: 这座大楼~很美。*This is a fine-looking building.*
【外国】foreign country: ~朋友 *foreign friend* / ~语 *foreign language* / ~驻华机构 *foreign institutions in China*
【外行】① lay; uninitiated ② layman; nonprofessional: 对于建筑,我是~。*I'm a layman of architecture.*
【外号】nickname
【外话】[方] utterances made as if by a stranger
【外汇】foreign exchange: ~收入 *foreign exchange earnings (or revenue)* / ~交易 *foreign exchange transactions* / ~储备 *foreign exchange reserve* / ~政策 *foreign exchange policy* / ~牌价 *foreign exchange quotations* / ~资产 *foreign exchange assets*
【外活】assignments from outside; processing work
【外籍】foreign nationality
【外加】superaddition; extra; more plus
【外家】① family of grandmother and grandfather on mother's side ② extra family ③ women in extra families ④ married woman's parent's home; wife's maiden home
【外间】① outer room ② the external world; outside circle
【外交】diplomacy; foreign affairs: ~部 *Ministry of Foreign Affairs* / ~官 *diplomat* / ~人员 *diplomatic personnel* / ~学院 *Foreign Affairs College* / ~大臣 *Foreign Secretary (in Britain)* / ~代表 *diplomatic agent (or representative)* / ~法 *diplomatic law* / ~辞令 *diplomatic language (or parlance)* / ~程序 *diplomatic procedure* / ~惯例 *diplomatic practice* / ~礼节 *diplomatic protocol (or etiquette)* / ~签证 *diplomatic visa* / ~使团 *diplomatic mission* / ~语言 *diplomatese; diplomatic language* / ~政策 *foreign policy* / ~途径 *diplomatic channel*
【外角】【数】exterior angle
【外教】foreign teacher
【外接圆】【数】circumscribed circle; circumcircle
【外界】external world; outside world view; scene shot on location: ~舆论 *public opinion* / ~因素促使他辞职。*Outside factors influenced him to resign.*
【外借】lent out: 内部资料不~。*Intramural datum books are not for lending.*
【外景】exterior view; outdoor scene: 在拍~ *be on location* / 真实~ *original location*
【外径】outside diameter; external diameter: 齿轮~ *exterior shot* / ~千分尺 *outside micrometer*
【外舅】father-in-law; wife's father
【外科】surgical department; surgery: 临床~ *clinical surgery* / 癌症通常需要~手术。*Cancer usually requires surgery.*
【外壳】outer covering; hull; shell: 摄像机~ *camera housing* / 传声器~ *microphone housing* / 热水瓶~ *outer casing of a thermos flask*
【外快】extra income; windfall: 捞~ *wangle extra income; make an extra penny*
【外来】families transferring from other places: ~的援助 *outside help* / ~词 *an exotic word* / ~干涉 *foreign interference* / ~侵略者 *foreign aggressor*
【外力】① external force ② outside force or power; outside or external influence: ~的援助 *extraneous aid*
【外流】drain; outflow: 资源~ *resource outflow* / 人才~ *brain drain* / ~河 *river that flows into the sea*
【外路】from other parts of country: ~人 *stranger; person from another place* / ~客商 *merchants from other cities*
【外露】① appear; reveal; show: 凶相~ *look most ferocious; display all one's ferocity* ②【地】outcropping: ~层 *outlier*
【外卖】take out; take away; carry-out
【外贸】foreign trade: ~部 *ministry of foreign trade* / ~经营权 *power to engage in foreign trade* / ~中心 *foreign trade centres* / ~仲裁 *foreign trade arbitration*
【外貌】appearance; looks; outward appearance; external appearance: 岁月明显地改变了他的~。*Age has made a pronounced change in his appearance.*
【外面】① outward appearance: 这盒子~是蓝色的。*The box was blue outside.* ② outside; out: ~很暗。*It was dark outside.*
【外婆】[方] (maternal) grandmother
【外戚】relatives of a king or an emperor on the side of his mother or wife
【外企】foreign enterprise
【外欠】① money that is owed by others ② extra debt
【外强中干】strong in appearance but weak in reality; be tough outside but brittle inside
【外侨】foreign national: ~身份 *alienism*
【外切】circumscribed; externally tangent: ~型 *circumscribed figure* / ~多边形 *circumscribed poly-*

gon
【外亲】① wife's or mother's relatives ② close in appearance
【外勤】① work done outside the office or in the field：～人员 *field staff* ② field personnel；fieldworker
【外倾】【心理】extroversion
【外圈】【体】outer lane；outside lane
【外人】① stranger，stranger in blood：别客气，大家都不是～。*Do not stand on ceremony；there are no strangers.* ② foreigner；alien
【外任】（in ancient time）be a local official
【外柔内刚】soft outside but hard inside — outwardly yielding but inwardly firm
【外伤】injury；wound；disease caused by exogenous pathogenic factors：～病 *traumatism* / ～性休克 *traumatic shock* / ～学 *traumatology*
【外商】foreign businessmen；foreign merchant：～独资企业 *exclusively foreign-owned enterprises；sole foreign invested enterprises*
【外生殖器】【生理】external genital organs
【外省】provinces other than where one lives
【外甥】① nephew；sister's son ② grandson
【外甥女】① niece；sister's daughter ② granddaughter
【外史】unofficial history；informal history
【外事】foreign affairs；external affairs：～部门 *foreign affairs department* / ～办公室 *office of foreign affairs* / ～活动 *public functions concerning foreigners* / ～局 *bureau of foreign affairs*
【外室】kept woman or mistress
【外手】（when driving a vehicle or operating a machine）the right-hand side
【外孙】daughter's son；grandson
【外孙女】granddaughter；daughter's daughter
【外胎】outer cover（of a tyre）；tyre
【外逃】flee to some other place；flee to a foreign country：～分子 *deserter；escapee* / ～出境 *run out of the country*
【外套】① overcoat；topcoat ② loose coat；outer garment
【外头】outside；out：夏天我常在～睡。*In summer I often sleep outdoors.*
【外围】periphery：～视野 *peripheral field* / ～防线 *outside defence line* / ～设备 *peripheral equipment* / ～组织 *peripheral organization* / 在人群～移动比较容易。*It was easier to move about on the fringe of the crowd.*
【外文】foreign language：～出版物 *foreign language publications*
【外屋】outer room
【外侮】foreign aggression；external aggression：～内患 *foreign invasion and domestic turbulence*
【外务】① matters outside one's job ② foreign affairs；external affairs：～大臣 *minister of foreign affairs* / ～省 *Ministry of Foreign Affairs*
【外县】counties other than where one lives
【外线】① outside line；outside connections：～不通 *can not make outside connections* ②【军】exterior lines：～作战 *fighting on exterior lines*
【外乡】some other place；another part of the country：宁娶邻家女，不娶～人。*Better wed over the mixer than over the moor.*
【外向】① extroversion ② export-oriented：～型经济 *export-oriented economy*
【外销】for sale abroad or in another part of the country：～产品 *product for export；product for sale in other parts of the country*
【外心】① unfaithful intentions（of husband or wife）②【数】circumcentre
【外星人】the people in other celestial bodies — no knowledge about social status；extraterrestrial being（ET）
【外形】appearance；external form；contour
【外性】（people）not of the same surname
【外延】【逻】denotation；extension
【外衣】① coat；jacket；outer garment：一件漂亮的丝绸长～ *a beautiful silk gown* ② semblance；appearance；garb
【外溢】outflow；spill：废水～ *overflow of waste water*
【外因】①【中医】exopathic factor ②【哲】cause
【外阴】【生理】cunnus；vulva：～炎 *vulvitis* / ～搔痒 *pruritus vulvae*
【外用】【药】external use or application：此药只供～，不可内服。*This medicine is for external use only，not for drinking.*
【外语】foreign language
【外域】foreign land
【外遇】have an affair；extramarital relations：他怀疑自己的妻子有～。*He suspects that his wife is carrying on with another man.*
【外圆内方】velvet glove；be smooth on the surface，but firm at heart
【外援】foreign aid；external assistance；outside help
【外运】transport out to other places or countries：内地蔬菜～ *transport vegetable out of backland*
【外在】extrinsic；external：～力量 *external force* / ～因素 *external factor* / ～性 *externalism* / ～论 *externalism*
【外债】external debt；loans from foreign countries
【外长】foreign minister
【外罩】outer garment；overall；dustcoat
【外痔】external piles；external hemorrhoids
【外传】①［旧］commentaries on the Confucian classics ② unauthorized biography；unofficial biography
【外资】foreign capital：引进～ *foreign capital introduction* / ～企业 *foreign enterprise*
【外族】① people not of the same clan：～敌人 *enemy from another clan* ② foreigner ③ other nationalities
【外祖父】maternal grandfather
【外祖母】maternal grandmother；grandma

wān

弯 ① curved; roundabout; tortuous: 月儿~~照九州。*The earth is bathed in the silvery rays of the crescent moon.* ② bend; flex; make curved: ~着腰系鞋带 *bend over to tie shoestring* /~铁丝 *bend a piece of wire* ③ turn; curve: 路在这里急转~。*The road bends sharply here.*

【弯刀】tulwar

【弯度】curvature; camber

【弯弓】draw a bowl; bend a bow

【弯路】① crooked road; tortuous path ② roundabout way; detour: 少走~ *avoid detours* /前面有段~。*There are a lot of twists and turns in the road a head.*

【弯曲】crooked; curved; meandering; winding; zigzag: 冲击~ *impact bending* /道路的~处 *a bend in the road* /~强度 *flexural strength* /~试验 *bending test* /~应力 *bending stress*

【弯头】bight bend; elbow: 直角~ *quarter bend* /蛇形~ *snake bend* /~螺丝刀 *offset screwdriver*

【弯腰】stoop; bend down: 他~往桌下看。*He stooped to look under the table.*

【弯子】bend; sled pole; curve

剜 cut out; gouge out: 把桃子烂的地方~掉。*Scoop out the rotten part of the peach.*

湾 ① bend in a stream: 河~ *river bend* ② bay; gulf: 港~ *estuary* /波斯~ *the Persian Gulf* ③ cast anchor; moor: 把船~在岸边。*Moor the boat against the shore beacon.*

【湾泊】anchor; moor

蜿 wriggle; meander; wind; zigzag; serpentine

【蜿蜒】wriggle; twist: ~的河道 *the serpentine course of the river* /这条蛇在草里~爬行。*The snake wriggled through the grass.*

豌

【豌豆】pea: 宽叶香~ *everlastingpea* /~黄 *pea flour cake* /~香 *pea weevil*

wán

丸 ① anything like a small ball; pellet: 泥~ *mud ball* ② pill; bolus: 每服两~ *take two pills each time*

【丸剂】pill

【丸药】pill of Chinese medicine; bolus of Chinese medicine

【丸子】① ball; round mass of food ② pill or bolus (pill) of Chinese medicine

纨 pure white and fine silk

【纨绔】sons of the rich: ~子弟 *profligate son of rich parents*

【纨扇】round fan with framed gauze

完 ① run up; use up: 水快喝~了。*We have run out of water.* ② whole; entire: 体无~肤 *have cuts and bruises all over the body* ③ complete; be over; end; finish: 我已经做~了作业。*I have finished my homework.* ④ pay: 税款早已~清。*The tax has been paid long since.* ⑤ (Wán) a surname

【完备】leave nothing to be desired; complete; perfect: ~的设施 *have all necessary facilities* /资料~ *have complete date* /手续~ *have completed all the formalities*

【完毕】finish; complete; end; be over: 课程尚未~。*The course still remains unfinished.* /一切准备~。*All is ready.*

【完璧归赵】return a thing intact to the owner; return the jade to its state of Zhao

【完成】accomplish; completes; be through; finish with: ~使命 *accomplish one's mission* /我已经~了我的工作。*I have carried out my work.*

【完蛋】be sunk; be all over with; be done for; be finished; be going to the dogs: 如果你工作不改进,你就~了。*If your work doesn't improve it will be curtains for you.*

【完稿】complete the manuscript; finish a piece of writing

【完工】complete a project; finish doing sth: 隧道按时~。*The tunnel ahead was completed on schedule.*

【完好】sound; in tact; whole; in good condition: 物归原主,~无损 *intact to its rightful owner*

【完婚】(of a man) get married

【完结】complete; end; finish; close: 事情并没有~。*This is not the end of the matter.*

【完了】come to end; be over

【完满】satisfactory; successful: 运动会~的结束了。*The athletic meeting came to a satisfactory close.*

【完美】perfect; consummate: ~的计划 *a perfect plan*

【完全】① complete; whole: 他的试卷没有回答~。*He did not hand in a full test paper.* ② completely; full; entirely; wholly; up to the hilt; hook; line and sinker: ~错误 *entirely wrong* /~不同 *totally dissimilar* /~变态 *complete metamorphosis* /~燃烧 *complete combustion* /~叶 *complete leaf* /我~忘记了它。*I clean forgot about it.* /我的看法~相反。*My view is clean contrary.*

【完人】paragon; perfect man: 人无~。*No man is perfect.*

【完善】① perfect; consummate: 设备~ *very well equipped* ② make perfect; improve: ~工作计划 *perfect the schedule of the work*

【完胜】thoroughly defeat

【完事】complete; end; finish; be over: 忙到傍晚才~ *not finished until dusk*

【完税】pay taxes

【完整】complete; integrated whole; comprehensive: 领土~ *territorial integrity* /主权~ *full sovereignty* /这是一个~的故事。*This is a complete story.*

玩[1] ① play; have fun; joke: ～的开心 *have a good time* ② engage in some kinds of sports or recreational activities: ～国际象棋 *play chess* ③ use; employ; resort to: ～花招 *resort to craft manoeuvres*

玩[2] ① trifle with; toy with; treat lightly: ～物丧志 *denigrate one's ambition by playing tricks on others* ② enjoy; appreciate; find pleasure in: 凭栏～月 *lean against the balustrades admiring the moon* ③ object for appreciation; curio: 古～ *curio; antique*

【玩法】trifle with law

【玩忽】neglect; trifle with: ～职守 *malpractice; dereliction of duty* /别～职责。*Don't forget your duties.*

【玩花招】play tricks

【玩话】joking words; words said in jest: 他说的不是～。*What he said is not joking words.*

【玩火】play with fire; risk or do people harm: ～自焚 *whoever plays with fire will perish by fire or he who plays with fire will get burned*

【玩具】toy; plaything: ～士兵 *a toy soldier* /～火车 *toy train* /～熊 *teddy bear* /～商店 *toyshop*

【玩乐】disport; have fun; amuse oneself

【玩弄】① play with; juggle with: ～词藻 *go in for rhetoric; juggle with words; play on words* ② tamper; resort to; engage in: ～权术 *play politics* ③ trifle with; dally with: ～女性 *dally with women*

【玩偶】doll; toy figurine

【玩儿不转】[口] can find no way out; cannot manage

【玩儿坏】play a dirty trick

【玩儿命】gamble with one's life: ～的工作 *work like hell*

【玩儿完】[口] the jig is up: 他的诡计～了。*The jig is up for his trick.*

【玩赏】enjoy; take delight (pleasure) in; appreciate: 他养一只狗供～。*He keeps a dog as a pet.*

【玩世不恭】be cynical; live in defiance of conventions

【玩手腕】play politics; play tricks

【玩耍】play; have fun; amuse oneself: 孩子们在院子里～。*The children were at play in the yard.*

【玩味】ponder; ruminate; savor: 这封信的内容很值得～。*The content of this letter is well worth pondering.*

【玩物】playthings; toy: ～丧志 *riding a hobby saps one's will to make progress; excessive attention to trivia saps the will*

【玩狎】dally with; treat without respect

【玩笑】joke; jest: 他只是开～罢了。*He is only joking.*

【玩兴】in the mood for playing

【玩意儿】① toy; plaything ② things; creature: 这个奇妙的～能用吗? *Does this contraption work?*

顽 ① stupid; foolish person; diehards ② insensate; persistent: 刁～ *sly and perverse* ③ naughty; mischievous

【顽敌】enemy; inveterate foe; stubborn enemy

【顽钝】① dull and obtuse; thickheaded: 质性～ *dull and obtuse by nature* ② blunt; not sharp: ～的斧子 *blunt axe* ③ lacking in integrity; unprincipled

【顽梗】obstinate; perverse

【顽固】① headstrong; obstinate; stubborn: 老～ *mulish old man* ② bitterly opposed to change or progress; bigoted; diehard: ～不化 *incorrigibly stubborn* /～派 *the diehards*

【顽疾】chronic and stubborn disease

【顽抗】stubbornly resist: 负隅～ *fight stubbornly with one's back to the wall*

【顽劣】stubborn and disobedient; naughty and unruly

【顽皮】mischievous; naughty: ～的孩子 *a naughty child*

【顽强】indomitable; staunch; steadfast: ～的革命精神 *a tenacious revolutionary spirit* /他继续～的努力。*He resumed his dogged effort.*

【顽石】monolith; hard rock; insensate stone: ～点头(*be so persuasive as to make*) *the insensate stone nod in agreement*

【顽童】urchin; naughty child

【顽症】persistent ailment; chronic and stubborn disease

wǎn

宛[1] ① circuitous; tortuous; winding ② (Wǎn) a surname

宛[2] as if: 音容～在 *as if the person were still alive*

【宛然】as if; as though: ～在目 *as if in front of eyes*

【宛如】as if; just like; as though: 温顺得～羔羊 *be as meek as a lamb*

【宛若】as if; just like: ～天仙 *as beautiful as a fairy maiden*

挽 ① draw; pull: ～弓 *draw a bow* ② roll up; coil up: ～起窗帘 *roll up the curtain* ③ reverse: 力～狂澜 *make vigorous efforts to turn the tide* ④ lament sb's death ⑤ tow: ～车 *tow a vehicle*

【挽词】elegiac words; memorial speech

【挽歌】dirge; elegy

【挽回】① retrieve; redeem ② recover; take back: ～名誉 *redeem one's reputation* /～败局 *retrieve a defeat* /～面子 *save face* /～损失 *retrieve a loss*

【挽救】remedy; rescue; save: ～病人的生命 *save the patient's life* /～失足青年 *make great efforts to reform juvenile delinquents*

【挽联】elegiac couplet

【挽留】persuade sb to stay; detain; return: 真心～ *sincerely urge sb to stay on*

【挽诗】elegiac poem

【挽幛】large elegiac scroll

莞 smiling

W

【莞尔】smile：～一笑 *give a winsome smile*

晚 ① evening; night：从早到～ *from morning till night* ② old age; one's later years：岁～ *evening of one's life* ③ late; far on in time：大器～成 *great minds mature late* /起的～ *get up late* ④ younger; junior：～妹 *your humble younger sister* ⑤【地】upper; neo-：～古生代 *Neopaleozoic*

【晚安】good evening; good night

【晚班】night shift：上～ *be on night shift*

【晚报】evening paper

【晚辈】younger; one's juniors; younger generation

【晚餐】supper; dinner

【晚场】evening show; evening performance

【晚车】night train

【晚春】late spring

【晚稻】late rice

【晚点】(of a train, ship, etc.) late; behind schedule time：飞机～了。*The plane was behind time.*

【晚饭】supper; dinner：我们坐下来吃了一顿丰盛的～。*We sat down to a good supper.*

【晚会】evening entertainment; evening gathering; evening reception：音乐～ *a music evening* /学校～ *school evening party*

【晚婚】marry at a mature age; late marriage：提倡～ *encourage late marriage*

【晚间】at night; (in the) evening：～新闻 *evening news*

【晚节】integrity in one's later years：保持～ *maintain one's integrity till the end of one's life*

【晚景】① evening scene：乡村的～ *the evening scene of the village* ② one's circumstances in old age：～凄凉 *lead a miserable and dreary life in old age*

【晚课】(of Buddhist monks) chant scriptures in the evening

【晚礼服】evening dress; evening clothes：去参加校长举行的晚会，必须穿上～。*People had to wear formal evening dress to go to the schoolmaster's party.*

【晚恋】be in love at a mature age

【晚年】old age; one's evening (later, remaining) years：精力充沛的～ *green old age*

【晚娘】[方] stepmother

【晚期】later period：～作品 *sb's later works* /～癌症 *terminal cancer*

【晚秋】① late autumn; late in the autumn：时近～ *approaching late autumn* ② late-autumn crops：～作物 *late-autumn crops*

【晚上】evening; night：我们整个～都在一起。*We stayed overnight together.*

【晚生】your pupil; junior

【晚熟】late-maturing：～品种 *late-maturing variety*

【晚霜】late frost

【晚霞】afterglow; sunset clouds; sunset glow

【晚香玉】【植】tuberose

【晚宴】evening banquet; dinner party

【晚育】late bear; late childbirth

【晚照】evening glow; sunset glow

惋 sigh; heave sign

【惋伤】sigh mournfully; lament

【惋叹】sign mournfully or regretfully

【惋惜】feel sorry (for sb or about sth); sympathize with：我不能接受你盛情的邀请，非常～。*Much to my regret, I'm unable to accept your kind invitation.*

婉 ① mild; tactful; restrained ② gentle：和～ *gentle; kind* ③ graceful; beautiful

【婉辞】① tactful expressions; gentle words ② politely refuse

【婉丽】beautiful; mild and exquisite：文章清新～。*The article is fresh and graceful.*

【婉顺】(of women) gentle and agreeable; meek：性格～ *have a mild disposition*

【婉谢】graciously decline; politely refuse

【婉言】gentle words; tactful expressions：～谢绝 *politely refuse; graciously decline* /～劝阻 *gently persuade*

【婉约】subtle and restrained：～其辞 *use restrained language*

【婉转】① mild and indirect; tactful：措辞～ *put it tactfully* ② sweet and agreeable：歌声～ *sweet singing*

绾 tie; coil up; roll up：把头发～起来 *coil one's hair*

碗 ① bowl：铁饭～ *iron rice-bowl; secure job* ② bowl-like object：活塞(橡)皮～ *rubber piston cup*

【碗柜】cupboard; closet

【碗盏】bowls and dishes; crockery

wàn

万 ① ten thousand ② myriad; multitudinous：～里长空 *boundless sky* /一本～利 *bring a ten-thousand-fold profit* ③ absolutely; certainly：～无此理 *cannot be true under any circumstances*

【万安】① surefire：～之计 *completely safe plan* ② rest assured; extremely

【万般】① all the different kinds：～皆下品，唯有读书高。*To be a scholar is to be at the top of society while all other careers are inferior.* ② utterly; extremely：～无奈 *have on alternative whatsoever; have no choice but*

【万变不离其宗】change ten thousand times without departing from the original aim or stand; remain the same despite all apparent changes

【万不得已】out of absolute necessity; have no alternative; the only thing possible; as a last resort：不到～，董事长不会亲自出马。*The board chairman won't take up the matter himself unless he absolutely has no choice.*

【万代】through unnumbered ages：～千秋 *throughout the ages*

【万端】multifarious; innumerable：变化～ *multifari-*

W

ous changer

【万恶】be absolutely vicious; extremely evil: ~之源 *the source of all evil*

【万方】① all places ② incomparably; extremely: 仪态~ *graceful in all aspects*

【万分】extremely; very much: ~激动 *be very excited* / ~热情 *be exceedingly enthusiastic* / ~悲痛 *be overwhelmed by grief* / ~抱歉 *be extremely sorry*

【万夫莫当】full of valor and vigor; more than a match for ten thousand men

【万福】[旧] salutation of women; curtsy

【万感】all kinds of feelings

【万古】through the ages; forever; eternally: ~长青 *remain fresh forever* / ~流芳 *leave a good name that will live forever; be remembered throughout the ages*

【万贯】wealthy; ten million cash: ~家财 *be worth millions* / 腰缠~ *be a millionaire; have pots of money*

【万户侯】dukes or princes under an emperor

【万花筒】kaleidoscope

【万机】numerous affairs of state: 日理~ *attend to numerous affairs of state every day*

【万家灯火】a myriad twinkling lights (of a city)

【万箭穿心】greatly distressed

【万劫不复】beyond redemption; be doomed eternally

【万金油】① *Tiger Balm* (for treating headaches, scalds and other minor ailments) ② Jack of all trades and master of none

【万钧】ten thousand *jun* — very heavy; very powerful: 雷霆~ *as powerful as a thunderbolt*

【万籁】all kinds of sounds: ~俱寂 *a great depth of stillness; all fretful stirrings of the world now hush; all in quiet and still*

【万类】all things on earth

【万里长城】the Great Wall

【万里长征】① Long Trip ② the long march of twenty-five thousand li (made by China Red Army)

【万里无云】cloudless

【万灵节】All Souls' Day, usu. on 2 November

【万缕千丝】countless ties

【万隆】Bandung, city in western Java, Indonesia: ~会议 *the Bandung Conference*

【万马奔腾】ten thousand horses galloping ahead

【万马齐喑】ten thousand horses standing mute

【万目睽睽】with everybody watching; all eyes centre on sth

【万难】① extremely difficult; very difficult: ~更改 *leave no room for modifications* / ~同意 *can by no means agree* ② all difficulties: 排出~ *surmount all difficulties*

【万能】① omnipotent; all-powerful ② universal; be able to do anything: ~台式铣床 *universal bench mill* / ~胶 *all-purpose adhesive* / ~老虎钳 *universal vice* / ~机械手 *general-purpose manipulator* / ~钥匙 *master-key*

【万年】ten thousand years; all ages; eternity: 遗臭~ *leave a bad name for all eternity* / ~历 *perpetual calendar*

【万念俱灰】be utterly disheartened; be tired of earthly life with all ambitious blasted and all hopes dashed to pieces

【万千】multifarious; myriad: 他思绪~。*Many thoughts passed through his mind.*

【万全】perfectly sound; surefire: ~之策 *a completely safe plan*

【万儿八千】ten thousand or nearly ten thousand; ten thousand or a little less

【万人坑】a pit of ten thousand corpses — a mass grave

【万人空巷】the whole town turns out (to welcome sb or celebrate some event)

【万世】all ages; thousands of generations: ~流芳 *leave a good name in history* / ~师表 *model for all ages*

【万事】all things; everything: ~如意 *legalize all one's wishes* / ~不求人 *never turn to anybody for help* / ~大吉 *everything is just fine; all is well and propitious* / ~亨通 *everything goes well* / ~具备,只欠东风 *everything else is ready, all that is needed is fair wind* / ~开头难 *getting things started is always difficult* / ~通 *know-it-all*

【万寿无疆】(wish sb) a long life

【万水千山】ten thousand crags and torrents

【万死】die ten thousand deaths: 罪该~ *deserve to die ten thousand deaths* / ~不辞 *willing to risk any danger to do one's duty*

【万岁】① long live: 世界和平~! *Long live world peaces!* ② Your Majesty; emperor

【万万】① absolutely: 我~没有想到。*This idea never occurred to me.* ② hundred million: 千千~ *thousands and tens of thousands*

【万无一失】no danger of anything going wrong; infallible; surefire; be perfectly safe; cannot possibly go wrong

【万物】universe; all things on earth: 人为~之灵。*Man is the wisest of all creatures on earth.*

【万向】universal: ~连结器 *joint coupling* / ~阀 *universal valve*

【万象】every phenomenon on earth; all manifestations of nature: ~更新 *all things take on a new aspect; everything looks fresh and gay*

【万幸】very lucky; be very fortunate; by sheer luck: 他在撞车中没撞死真是~。*It's a marvel that he wasn't killed in the car crash.*

【万一】① one ten-thousandth; very small portion: 笔墨不能形容其~。*It simply beggars description.* ② just in case: ~失败, 我还要试一试。*If I should fail I would try again.* ③ contingency; eventuality: 不怕一万,就怕~。*One should always prepare for the worst even if it is unlikely to happen.* ④ what if: ~他不来呢? *What if he doesn't come?*

【万有引力】universal gravitation; gravitational attraction: ~定律 *the law of universal gravitation*

【万丈】lofty or bottomless: ~光芒 *shine with boundless radiance* / ~高楼平地起。*A tall build-*

ing has to rise from the ground. /风暴在海面上掀起～波涛。The storm heaved the sea into mountainous waves.

【万众】millions of people; the multitude: ～一心 millions of people all of one mind /～欢腾庆祝胜利 signalize a victory by public rejoicing

【万状】in all manifestation; in every way: 惊恐～ be extremely frightened /危险～ be in great danger

【万紫千红】riot of colour; blaze of colour: 百花齐放,～。Flowers of all sorts are blooming in a riot of colour.

腕 wrist

【腕骨】carpus; carpal bone

【腕力】wrist power

【腕下垂】wristdrop

【腕子】wrist: 扳～ wrist-wrestling

【腕足动物】brachiopod

蔓 tendrilled vine: 顺～摸瓜 follow the vine to get the melon — track down sb or sth by following clues

see also mán; màn

wāng

汪[1] ①(of water) deep and wide ② collect; gather; accumulate: 眼里～着泪水 eyes brimming with tears ③ puddle; pond ④［量］use for liquid: 一～清水 a puddle of clear water ⑤ (Wāng) a surname

汪[2] bark; bow-wow

【汪汪】① profuse (tears) ② vast (water) ③ barking noise

【汪洋】① a vast expanse of water; boundless: ～大海 the boundless ocean; vast oceanic expanses ② broadminded: ～浩博 broadminded and knowledgeable /～自肆 a vast expanse of water-opening heart

wáng

亡 ① flee; escape; run away ② lose; be lost: 消～ wither away; die out /名存实～ cease to exist except in name ③ die; perish: 家破人～ with one's family broken up, some gone away, some dead ④ conquer; fall; subjugate: 兴～ rise and fall (of a country) ⑤ deceased; dead: ～妻 deceased wife /～友 deceased friend

【亡故】die; pass away; perish; decease

【亡国】① subjugate a nation; let a state perish ② a destroyed country: ～奴 conquered people; colonial slave; slave of a foreign nation

【亡魂】soul of the dead: ～丧胆 lose one's soul and bravery /～失魄 have no peace of mind

【亡灵】the soul of the dead; dead soul: 日本每年举行一次～节。A Festival for the Dead is held once a year in Japan.

【亡命】① flee; go into exile; seek refuge ② desperate: ～之徒 desperado; daredevil

【亡羊补牢】mend the fold after a sheep is lost; shut the stable when the horse is stolen: ～,犹未为晚。It is not too late to mend the fold even after the sheep are lost.

王 ① emperor; monarch: 帝～ king; emperor /女～ queen ② duck; prince: ～妃 princess ③ head; chief: 占山为～ occupy a hill to act as a lord ④ champion; best or strongest of its king ⑤ first or largest of its kind: 猴～ monkey king /蜂～ queen bee ⑥ senior; grand: ～父 grandfather /～母 grandmother ⑦ (Wáng) a surname

【王朝】① dynasty ② imperial court; royal court: 封建～ feudal dynasties

【王储】crown prince

【王法】the law of the land; the law

【王府】a prince's residence

【王公】princes and dukes; the high rank of nobility: ～大臣 princes, dukes and ministers /～贵族 the nobility

【王宫】a royal palace; imperial palace

【王冠】imperial crown; royal crown

【王国】① kingdom ② domain; realm: 文学艺术～ the realm of literature and art

【王侯】the nobility; princes and marquises

【王后】queen; queen consort: 红桃～ the queen of the hearts

【王老五】single man

【王牌】trump card; ace: ～军 elite troops; ace fighting units /～飞行员 ace pilot

【王权】regale; royally

【王室】① royal family: ～宗亲 relative of a royal family /～成员 a member of the royal family ② royal or imperial court

【王孙】prince's descendant; offspring of the nobility: ～公子 descendent of a noble family

【王位】throne; crown: 继承～ succeed to the throne /篡夺～ usurp the throne

【王子】king's son prince; noble sons: ～犯法,与庶民同罪。If a prince violates the law, he must be punished like an ordinary person.

【王族】blood royal; imperial kinsmen; royal lineage

wǎng

网 ① net: 结～ mesh a net /撒～ cast a net ② network: 交通～ network of transport /商业～ business network ③ catch with a net: ～鱼 net a fish /～鸟儿 net birds ④ cover or enclose as with a net: 眼里～着红丝 have a bloodshot eyes ⑤ internet: ～上采购 shopping on Internet

【网吧】internet buff; web enthusiast

【网点】the point of network: 服务～ network of service centres

【网兜】string bag

【网格】【建】lattice: 六边形～ hexagonal mesh

【网巾】hairnet
【网开一面】leave one side of the net open — give sb a way out; be lenient
【网篮】a basket with netting on top
【网罗】① a net for catching fish or birds; trap ② enlist the services of: ～人才 *enlist able men* /～死党 *scrape together one's sworn followers*
【网络】① network; system: 有源～ *active electric network* /组合～ *combinational network* /补偿～ *compensating network* /局部～ *localized network* ② network; web: ～分析 *network analysis* /～服务器 *network server* /～冲浪 *surfing the net* /～管理 *network management* /～文化 *cyberculture*
【网迷】web fun
【网球】① tennis: 草地～ *lawn tennis* /硬地～ *hard court tennis* /～拍 *tennis racket* /～场 *tennis court* ② tennis ball
【网上冲浪】surf the Internet
【网上购物】E-shopping; online transaction
【网坛】tennis circle
【网页】web page
【网友】cyber acquaintance
【网站】web site
【网址】web site
【网状脉】netted veins; reticulated veins: ～叶 *net-veined leaf*

枉 ① crooked; warped: 矫～过正 *straighten the crooked to excess* ② evil; wicked; vicious: ～杀无辜 *kill an innocent person* ③ in vain; to no avail: 不～此行。*This trip was not made in vain.* ④ treat unjustly; wrong: 不要冤～无辜。*Don not treat innocent unjustly.*
【枉担虚名】have an undeserved reputation
【枉道】① make a detour; go by a roundabout route ② curry favor by crooked means
【枉断】try a case unjustly
【枉法】pervert the law
【枉费】waste; be of no avail; try in vain: ～唇舌 *waste one's breath* /～工夫 *waste one's time and spirit* /～心机 *rack one's brains without results; scheme without avail* /反动政府～心机地企图削弱这场抗议运动。*The reactionary government tried vainly to take the steam out of the protest movement.*
【枉顾】I am honored by your visit
【枉然】in vain; futile: 和敌人讲理是～。*It is no use to argue with enemies.*
【枉死】be wronged and driven to death: ～鬼 *wronged souls*
【枉自】in vain; for nothing

罔 ① deceive ② no; not: 对对方的论点置若～闻 *to give short shrift to an opponent argument*
【罔知所措】be at a loss what to do

往 ① depart (head, leave, start) for; go to somewhere: 寒来暑～ *as summer goes and winter comes* ② in the direction of; towards: 这船是开～哪儿去的? *Where is ship bound?* ③ former; past: 一如既～ *as always; as in the past*
【往常】habitually in the past; as one used to do formerly: 他和～一样,很早就起了床。*As usual, he gets up early.*
【往返】go there and back; journey to and fro; move back and forth: 我想要张～票。*I would like a return ticket.*
【往复】① move back and forth; reciprocate: ～式蒸汽泵 *reciprocating steam pump* /～运动 *reciprocating engine* /循环～ *repeat itself in cycles* ② contact; intercourse: 书信～ *exchange of correspondence; written communications*
【往后】from now on; in the future: ～我会更加努力学习的。*I will study more hard in future.*
【往还】contact; intercourse; dealings: 经常有书信～ *write to each other regularly*
【往来】① come and go ② contact; exchange; dealings: 财务～ *financial transaction accounts* /贸易～ *have trade contacts*
【往年】(in) former years: 和～不同 *different from previous years*
【往前】before; formerly; in the past: 让我们～走。*Let us walk along.*
【往日】(in) former days; in bygone days: ～无仇,今日无冤。*We had no enmity against each other before, nor have we today.*
【往事】history; the past; past events: ～如烟。*The past has vanished like smoke.* /那老年人爱谈～。*The old man was reminiscent.*
【往往】often; frequently: 母亲～是家庭生活的中心人物。*The mother is often the pivot of family life.*
【往昔】yesterday; in former times: 一如～ *as in the past*

惘 feel frustrated; be in a trance
【惘然】frustrated; feel disappointed

wàng

妄 ① absurd; preposterous: 狂～ *crankiness* ② rash; unrestrained: ～作主张 *make a presumptuous* /～加评论 *make improper comments*
【妄称】make improper claim; be so presumptuous as to call oneself
【妄动】rash action; impulsive (reckless, ill-considered) action
【妄断】jump to conclusion; rush into a conclusion:
【妄念】wild fancy; improper thought: 他对那个古董动了～。*He takes a wild fancy to that antique.*
【妄求】inappropriate request; presumptuous demand
【妄取】presumptuously take
【妄说】talk nonsense: 无知～,不足为信。*This is the remark of an ignoramus, not to be taken seriously.*
【妄图】inappropriate request; try in vain: 杀人犯～贿赂法官宣判他无罪。*The official took bribes from those who wanted favours.*
【妄为】commit all kinds of outrages: 胆大～ *be reckless and act wildly*

W

【妄下雌黄】 blasphemous talk; make deceitful statements (unfounded charges)
【妄想】① entertain an extravagant hope: ~谋杀领袖 *vainly hope to murder the leader* ② vain hope; wishful thinking
【妄语】tell lies; wild talk; rant: 痴人~ *ranting rigmarole* / 出家人不打~。*Buddhist monks are not supposed to tell lies.*
【妄自菲薄】 belittle oneself; improperly belittle oneself; unduly humble oneself
【妄自尊大】self-conceited; lump large; play the peacock: 少年得志可能导致~。*Early success may lead to megalomania.*

忘 neglect; trifle with; idle; forget: 全面遗~ *general amnesia* / 别~了通知我。*Don not forget to inform me.*
【忘本】forget one's class origin; forget one's bitter past: 生活富裕了不能~。*One should not forget one's past sufferings when one becomes well off.*
【忘掉】forget; dismiss from one's mind; let slip from one's mind: ~过去 *forget the past*
【忘恩负义】forgetful; turn on one's friend; kick away the ladder; be devoid of all gratitude: 儿子的~伤了她的心。*She was saddened by her son's ingratitude.*
【忘乎所以】forget oneself; make one swellheaded: 兴之所至, ~ *be carried away by one's impulse; let one's jest get the better of oneself*
【忘怀】forget; dismiss from one's mind; no longer worry about: 当时的情景我久久不能~。*For a long time afterwards I could no get the scene out of my mind.*
【忘记】① forget: 她~寄这封信了。*She forgot to post the letter.* ② overlook; neglect: 不要~你的责任。*Don not neglect your duties.*
【忘年交】 friendship between generations; good friends despite great difference in age
【忘情】① be unruffled by emotion; be indifferent: 难以~ *remain sentimentally attached* ② let oneself go: ~的跳舞 *let oneself go and dance lustily*
【忘却】forget: 一个~的朋友 *a forgotten friend in one's past*
【忘我】oblivious of oneself; selfless: ~的歌唱 *singing untiringly*
【忘形】be beside oneself; have one's head turned; do not control oneself: 他因胜利而得意~。*He was swollen by victory.*
【忘性】forgetfulness: ~严重 *have a seriously poor memory*

旺 prosperous; flourishing; vigorous: 人畜两~。*Both men and livestock are flourishing.* / 过去两年一直是公司的兴~时期。*The last two years have been a good season for the company.*
【旺炽】roaring; blazing: 火焰~。*The fire was blazing.*
【旺季】peak period; busy season; rush season: 旅游~ *busy tourist season*
【旺盛】exuberant; flourishing; vigorous: 创造力~的头脑 *vigorous mind*
【旺销】flourishing; sell well: ~商品 *goods that have a ready market*
【旺月】busy month (in business)

望[1] ① look or gaze into the distance; look a head: 登高~远 *ascend high and look far ahead* ② carry on; visit: 拜~ *call to pay one's respects* ③ expect; hope: ~速归 *hope to be back soon* ④ reputation; prestige: 声~ *fame* / 德高~重 *be of noble character and high prestige* ⑤ towards: ~西走 *go westwards* ⑥ resentment; enmity: 怨~ *bear a grudge against sb* ⑦ (Wàng) a surname

望[2] the 15th day of a lunar month 'approaching; almost: 我爷爷已经是~九十的人了。*My granddad is approaching ninety.*
【望尘莫及】fall far behind; be too inferior to bear comparison
【望穿秋水】look forward with impatient expectancy; keep gazing anxiously till one's eyes are strained
【望断】look as far as the eye can reach
【望而却步】shrink back at the sight of (sth dangerous or difficult); flinch: 我们想提出帮助他, 但是他那种凶狠瞪视的目光使我们~。*We wanted to offer help, but the fierce glared on his face stopped us.*
【望而生畏】be terrified (awed) at the sight: 研究室主任是个令人~的老教授。*The head of the research section was a formidable old professor.*
【望风】be on the lookout (while conducting secret activities); keep watch
【望风而逃】flee at the mere sight of the oncoming force; flee at sight: 匪徒~。*The banditti fled pell-mell before policemen.*
【望风披靡】flee pell-mell at the mere sight of the oncoming force; flee helter-skelter at the mere sight
【望梅止渴】quench one's thirst by thinking of plums; feed on fancies
【望门】old and well-known family; distinguished or prominent family: 出身~ *come from a prominent family*
【望文生义】take the words too literally; interpret without real understanding
【望闻问切】【中医】watch, hear, ask and touch — a diagnosis method
【望眼欲穿】gaze anxiously till one's eyes are overstrained; bore one's eyes through by gazing anxiously; eagerly look forward to meeting a dear one
【望洋兴叹】lament one's littleness before the vast ocean — bemoan one's inadequacy in the face of a great task
【望远镜】telescope: 天文~ *astronomical telescope* / 电子~ *electronic telescope* / 红外~ *infrared telescope* / 夜视~ *night-vision telescope* / 反射~ *reflecting telescope*
【望子成龙】expect one's son to be talent; hope one's son will turn out a dragon

【望族】distinguished family; well-established family; prominent family

wēi

危 ① danger; peril: 趁人之~ *take advantage of sb's predicament* ② endanger; jeopardize; imperil ③ dying: 垂~ *be critically ill* ④ proper; upright: ~崖 *a precipitous cliff* ⑤ upright; precipitous; sheer ⑥ twelfth of the twenty-eight constellations in ancient astronomy ⑦ (Wēi) a surname

【危殆】in great danger; in jeopardy; in a critical condition: 情况~ *in a precarious situation* / 病情~ *be dangerously ill*

【危地马拉】Guatemala: ~人 *Guatemalan*

【危笃】be critically ill; on the point of death

【危房】buildings that are ready to collapse; unsafe buildings

【危害】harm; undermine; impair; endanger; jeopardize: 生态~ *ecological hazard* / 噪声~ *noise hazard* / 辐射~ *radiation hazard* / ~健康 *be detrimental to health* / ~国家安全 *be detrimental to national security* / ~人民利益 *damage the interests of the people*

【危机】crisis; crash: 政治~ *a political crisis* / 经济~ *an economic crisis* / 信任~ *crisis of confidence* / 金融~ *financial crisis* / 结构~ *structural crisis*

【危及】endanger; jeopardize: 城里被污染的空气正严重地~居民的健康。*The polluted air in the city is badly endangering the health of the residents.*

【危急】critical; in imminent danger; in a desperate situation: ~关头 *critical juncture* / ~存亡之秋 *at a most critical moment or time* / 伤势~。*The wound may be fatal.*

【危境】dangerous situation; advanced age

【危局】a dangerous situation; critical situation: 挽救~ *save a dangerous situation*

【危难】danger and disaster; dangerous and difficulty: ~之中见真情。*A friend in deed is a friend indeed.*

【危如累卵】in a precarious situation; as precarious as a pile of eggs

【危途】dangerous road or part

【危亡】in peril; be at stake: 民族~的关键时刻 *when the nation's existence is in peril; when the fate of the nation hangs in the balance*

【危险】dangerous; perilous: 失火的~ *a risk of fire* / 不顾~ *defy dangers* / 脱离~ *out of danger* / ~信号 *danger signal* / ~因素 *hazardous factor* / 病人已经脱离~了。*The patient was out of danger.*

【危言耸听】alarmist talk; have a thread; exaggerate things to scare the mass: 言过其实,有~之嫌。*It is an overstatement aimed probably at producing a sensational effect.*

【危在旦夕】be in deadly danger; on the verge of death (destruction): 生命~。*Death is expected at any moment.*

【危重】critically ill

【危坐】site bolt upright; sit properly: 正襟~ *straighten one's dress and sit bolt up right*

【委蛇】comply with; yield to: 虚与~ *pretend politeness and compliance*
see also wěi

威 ① impressive; strength; might; power: 军~ *military prowess; might of an army* / 扬我国~ *demonstrate out national might* ② fear; shock

【威逼】threaten by force; intimidate; bully: ~利诱 *alternate intimidation and bribery; use both coercion and cajolery*

【威风】① power and prestige ② awe-inspiring: ~凛凛 *majestic-looking; with great dignity; awe-inspiring* / ~扫地 *with energy shred of one's prestige swept away*

【威吓】intimidate; bully: 我们不怕~。*We fear no intimidation.*

【威力】power; formidable force: ~无比 *have matchless power* / 舆论的~ *the tremendous force of public opinion*

【威厉】powerful and stern

【威猛】powerful and bold

【威名】fame based on great strength or military exploits; prestige; renown: ~扬天下 *one's fame spread far and wide*

【威尼斯】Venice, city of northeast Italy built on numerous islands linked by canals and bridges

【威迫】coerce: ~利诱 *alternate intimidation and bribery*

【威慑】deterrence; terrorize with military force: ~政策 *deterrent policy* / ~力量 *deterrent power*

【威士忌】whiskey

【威望】prestige: 国际~ *international prestige*

【威武】① mighty; impressive: ~雄壮 *full of power and grandeur* ② might; power: ~不屈 *not to be subdued by force; no force can bend us*

【威胁】threaten; endanger; imperil: ~世界和平 *imperil world peace* / 人民正受到战争的~。*The people are being menaced by the threat of war.*

【威信】prestige; high repute; credit; popular trust: ~扫地 *with every shred of prestige swept away*

【威严】① dignified; stately; power and influence: 一位~的老妇人 *a stately old lady* ② awe prestige: 保持~ *keep up one's prestige*

【威仪】impressive and dignified manner: ~凛然 *awe-inspiring dignified bearing*

【威震天下】win resounding fame throughout the country

逶

【逶迤】winding; meandering: 群山~ *meandering mountain range*

偎 lean close to; snuggle up to: ~依在一起 *snuggle together*

【偎抱】hug; cuddle: 母亲~着自己的孩子。*The mother cuddled his child.*
【偎依】snuggle up to; lean close to: 孩子~在母亲怀里。*The child snuggled into its mother's arms.*

葳

【葳蕤】luxuriant; lush: 合欢树~盛开。*Silk trees are in lush blossom.*

崴

see also wǎi
【崴嵬】[书] (of mountains) lofty and towering

微 ① minute; tiny: 稍~ *a little*; *a bit* /轻~ *slight* /相差甚~。*The difference is slight.* ② one millionth part ③ decline: 式~ *on the decline* ④ elegant; exquisite
【微安】microampere: ~计 *microammeter*
【微波】ripple; microwave: ~炉 *micro-wave oven* / ~通信 *microwave communication*
【微薄】meagre; scanty; shabby: ~的收入 *meager income* /尽我们~的力量 *exert what little strength one has*
【微不足道】unworthy; negligible; trifling; be knee-high to a grasshopper: ~的成就 *an insignificant achievement* / ~的损失 *a trivial loss*
【微程序】【电】microprogram: ~设计 *microprogramming*
【微处理机】microprocessor
【微词】veiled criticism; complain: 同学们对他颇有~。*The students complained about him a lot in private.*
【微电脑】microcomputer; microprocessor
【微雕】miniature
【微法拉】【电】microfarad
【微分】【数】differential: 数字~ *digital differentiation* /间接~ *indirect differentiation* / ~学 *differential calculus* / ~几何 *differential geometry* / ~器 *differentiator*
【微服】(of officials) wear plain-clothes: ~私访 *travel incognito*
【微观】microscopic: ~经济理论 *microeconomic theory* / ~经济学 *microeconomics* / ~世界 *microworld* / ~物理学 *microphysics* / ~现象 *microphenomenon*
【微乎其微】very little; next to nothing: ~的兴趣 *glimmerings of interest* / ~的机会 *glimmerings of chance*
【微火】slow fire; gentle heat
【微机】【电】microcomputer
【微积分】【数】differential and integral; infinitesimal calculus: 复变~ *complex calculus*
【微贱】lowly; humble: 出身~ *be of humble origin*
【微粒】【物】corpuscle; infinitesimal particle; fallout: 胶体~ *colloidal particle* /遗传~ *hereditary particle* /金属~ *metal particle*
【微量】trace; micro-: ~分析 *microanalysis* / ~化学 *microchemistry* / ~元素 *trace element*
【微茫】hazy; blurred: 月色~ *dim moonlight* / ~的烛光 *faint candle lighting*
【微米】micron
【微妙】delicate; subtle; tricky: ~的主题 *a delicate subject*
【微末】trifling; insignificant: ~的功劳 *an insignificant contribution*
【微气象学】micrometeorology
【微热】【医】low fever
【微弱】faint; feeble; thin; weak; slim: ~的声音 *a faint sound* / ~的光 *a feeble light*
【微生物】microorganism; bacterium; microbe: 好氧~ *aerobic organisms* /水生~ *aquatic micro organism* / ~学 *microbiology*
【微调】fine tuning; trimming: ~开关 *inching switch*
【微微】① slight; faint: 一盏小灯笼在黑暗中~闪光。*A little lantern blinked in the darkness.* ② micromicro-; pico-
【微细】very small; tiny: ~结构 *minute structure* / ~差异 *fine difference*
【微小】small; little: ~的影响 *little influence* / ~的损失 *minor loss* / ~的希望 *slender hopes*
【微笑】smile: sweet smile: 她看见我时露出~。*She smiled when she saw me.* /他~以示同意。*He smiled his consent.*
【微型】mini-; miniature: ~电视 *microtelevision* / ~电路 *microcircuit* / ~照相机 *microcamera*
【微言大义】sublime words with deep meaning
【微恙】slight illness; indisposition
【微震】① slight shock ② microseism

煨 ① roast in fresh cinders ② cook over a slow fire; stew: ~鸡腿 *stewed drumstick*
【煨热】very intimate

巍 towering; soaring; lofty

【巍峨】towering; majestic; lofty: ~的山峰 *eminent peaks*
【巍然】towering; lofty; imposing: ~屹立 *stand lofty and form*
【巍巍】towering; majestic: ~昆仑 *towering Kunlun Mountains*

wéi

为[1] ① do; act; make: 尽力而~ *do one's best* /敢作敢~ *be decisive and bold in action* ② act as; serve as: 民以食为~。*The first and foremost need of the people is food.* /有诗~证。*A poem testifies to that.* ③ expect; hope ④ become; turn: 化险~夷 *turn danger into safety* ⑤ be; mean; take: 一星期~七天。*One week consists of seven days.*

为[2] ① used in a passive sentence: ~学生而爱戴 *be loved and respected by the students* ② used in a rhetorical question with: 何以家~? *What need have I of a home?* ③ used after an adjective to form an adverb: 广~流传 *spread far and wide* ④ used after an adverb for emphasis: 极~痛苦 *extremely anguish*
see also wèi

【为非作歹】do evil things; perpetrate outrages; commit crimes: 欺压百姓, ~ *ride roughshod over the people and commit all sorts of crimes*

【为富不仁】be rich and cruel; be heartless rich; muck and money go together

【为害】do harm; cause damage

【为患】bring about disaster: 洪水 ~ *be scourged by floods* /人满 ~ *be burdened with over-population*

【为难】① feel awkward; be in a quandary; feel embarrassed: 我左右 ~,不知是做数学还是写英语。*I am in a dilemma whether to do maths or English.* ② make things difficult for: 故意 ~ *deliberately make things difficult of sb*

【为期】(to be completed) by a definite date: 以半年 ~ *not to exceed half a year* /运动会 ~ 两天。*The gymkhana is scheduled to last two days.*

【为人】behave; conduct oneself: ~ 师表 *be worthy of the name of the teacher; be a paragon of virtue and learning* / ~ 正派 *be a decent man*

【为生】make a living: 以画画 ~ *make a living by drawing*

【为时】too (early, soon, late, etc.): ~ 过早 *too early; be too soon*

【为首】headed by; stand at the head of; in the foreground: 以某某 ~ 的内阁 *an administration captained by so-and-so*

【为数】amount to; number: 这个专门调查小组的成员 ~ 不多。*Members of the special investigation group are few in number.*

【为所欲为】do as one pleases; do whatever one likes; have one's own way: 他始终是 ~ 的。*He will have his own way all the time.*

【为伍】associate with: 与恐怖分子 ~ *associate with terrorists*

【为限】not exceed; be within the limit of: 时间以一周 ~。*The time shall not exceed a week.*

【为止】up to; till: 到目前 ~ 还没有人登上火星。*As yet, no man has set foot on Mars.*

【为重】attach great importance to; treasure; stress: 以大局 ~ *set store by the overall interests* /以人民利益 ~ *value the interests of the people above everything else*

【为主】rely mainly on; give priority to; give first place to: 以自力更生 ~ *rely mainly on oneself* /以自学 ~ *learn mainly by oneself*

圩 dyke; embankment; depression: 筑 ~ *build a dike*

【圩堤】embankment on the low-lying land

【圩田】low-lying paddy fields surrounded with dykes

【圩子】protective embankments surrounding low-lying fields

违 ① disobey; violate: 阳奉阴 ~ *overtly agree but covertly oppose* ② part with; leave: 久 ~ *not have seen sb for a long time*

【违碍】taboo; prohibition

【违拗】disobey; defy

【违背】against the grain; transgress; infringe; violate: ~ 良心 *go against* / ~ 协议 *violate an agreement* / ~ 道德标准 *run counter to the norms of morality* / ~ 诺言 *go back on one's word* / ~ 历史事实 *be contrary to the historical facts*

【违法】break the law; be illegal: ~ 行为 *illegal activity* / ~ 分子 *law-breaker* /有法可依, ~ 必究。*Laws must be obeyed and offenders prosecuted.* /偷东西是 ~ 的。*It is illegal to steal things.*

【违反】break; violate; transgress: ~ 契约 *in breach of contract* / ~ 纪律 *breach of discipline* / ~ 协议 *breach an agreement* / ~ 交通规则 *violate traffic regulations* /你们公司 ~ 了合同。*Your company is in breach of the contract.*

【违犯】violate; infringe; act contrary to: ~ 交通信号 *violation of signal*

【违纪】breach the principle

【违禁】violate a ban: 进口 ~ 品 *contraband of import* / ~ 贸易 *illicit trade*

【违抗】disobey; defy; be contrary to: ~ 命令 *disobedience to the command* / ~ 领导 *defy the higher-ups*

【违例】disobey practice; break rules (in sports game)

【违令】disobey orders; insubordination

【违逆】disobey; violate

【违误】disobey orders and cause delay: 立即完成, 不得 ~。*This is to be finished without delay.*

【违心】against one's will; contrary to one's convictions: ~ 之言 *assertion against one's own conscience*

【违约】① break a contract; violate a treaty; break off an engagement: ~ 责任 *liability for breach of contract* ② break one's promise; go back on one's words

【违章】violate (break) rules and regulations: 夜晚行车不开灯是 ~ 的。*It is an offense to drive a car at night without lights.*

围 ① enclose; surround; encompass; surround: ~ 而歼之 *besiege and annihilate* ② all round; around: 地球 ~ 绕太阳转。*The earth goes round the sun.* ③ measurement of certain parts of body: 胸 ~ *chest measurement* /三 ~ (*of women*) *measurements* ④ [量] (a) hand span: 柱大十 ~ *a pillar of ten arm spans around*

【围脖儿】muffler; scarf

【围捕】surround and seize; round up: ~ 凶手 *hunt down the muderer*

【围场】exclosure; hunting ground

【围城】① encircle a city; lay siege to a city ② besieged city

【围堵】besiege and intercept

【围攻】besiege; lay siege to; jointly attack sb: 警察局惨遭 ~。*The police station was terribly mobbed.*

【围观】surround to watch; look on: ~ 的人群 *a crowd of onlookers*

【围护】go along with sb to guard him

【围击】besiege; surround and attack

【围歼】surround and annihilate; encircle and wipe out

W

【围剿】encircle and annihilate; encircle and suppress

【围巾】muffler; scarf：你外出的话要围好～。*Mind you wrap up well if you go out.*

【围垦】(build dykes to) reclaim land from marshes; enclose tideland for cultivation

【围困】hem in; pin down; bottle up; invest; besiege：特洛伊城被希腊人～了十年。*Troy was besieged by the Greeks for ten years.*

【围栏】fencing：狗跳过了～。*The dog made a leap over the fence.*

【围猎】surround; close in and hunt

【围拢】close; crowd around

【围棋】go; Chinese draught; a game played with black and white pieces on a board of 361 crosses

【围墙】wall; enclosure

【围裙】apron; pinafore

【围绕】beset; around; round; centre on; revolve round

【围网】purse seine; purse net：～渔船 *purse seiner*; *purse boat*

【围岩】country rock; surrounding rock

【围堰】cofferdam; coffer

【围子】① defensive wall surrounding a village：墙～ *village stockade* ② curtain：床～ *bed curtain*

【围嘴儿】bib

【围坐】sit around; sit in a circle

桅 mast：船～ *mast*

【桅顶】① masthead light; range light ② barn lantern

【桅顶】masthead

【桅杆】mast

【桅楼】roundtop

【桅樯】mast

唯 only; alone

see also wěi

【唯美主义】aestheticism

【唯我主义】solipsism

【唯物论】materialism

【唯物主义】materialism

【唯心论】idealism

【唯心主义】idealism

帷 curtain

【帷幕】heavy curtain：防水～ *water-tightness curtain*

【帷幄】army tent：运筹～，决胜千里。*Strategies devised in the command tent will ensure victory in the far-away battlefield.*

【帷子】curtain：窗～ *window curtain*

惟[1] ① only; solely：～一无二 *only one* ② but; only that：～你是问。*You will be held personally responsible.*

惟[2] used before a year, month or day

惟[3] thinking; thought; idea

【惟独】only; alone：他没有什么才华，～画画不错。*He has almost no other talent than drawing.*

【惟恐】for fear that; lest：～天下大乱 *desire to see the world plunged into turmoil*; *crave nothing short of nationwide chaos*

【惟利是图】be intent on nothing but profit; be bent solely on profit; put profit making first; have an eye on he brain chance：～的奸商 *profiteer bent solely on profit*

【惟命是从】do as one is told; do as one is told; be absolutely obedient：对领导～ *be absolutely obedient to one's superior*

【惟其】precisely because; since

【惟我独尊】overweening; be terribly conceited; lording it over all others

【惟一】only; sole：～人选 *only candidate* /～选择 *no other alternative* /～出路 *the only way out* /～机会 *the only chance*

【惟有】only; alone：～斗争，才能胜利。*Struggle, and struggle alone, can ensure victory.*

维[1] ① bind; tie up; hold together ② keep; maintain; safeguard; uphold ③ dimension：思～空间 *four-dimensional space* ④ (Wéi) a surname

维[2] thought; thinking

【维持】maintain; protect; preserve：～和平 *preserve peace* /～生命 *keep alive* /～治安 *keep the pace* /警察的职责之一是～公共秩序。*It is one of the duties of the police to preserve public order.*

【维护】stick up for; maintain; assert：～权利 *to uphold a right* /～社会公德 *uphold civic virtues* /～国家的主权和独立 *defend national sovereignty and independence* /～民族尊严 *vindicate national honour* /～安定团结 *maintain unity and stability*

【惟妙惟肖】remarkably true to life; hit off; be absolutely lifelike：～的雕塑 *absolutely lifelike sculpture*

【维生】support oneself or one's family; make a living：他以打猎～。*He made a living by cynegetics.*

【维生素】vitamin：～过多症 *hypervitaminosis* /～缺乏症 *vitamin-deficiency*; *avitaminosis*

【维数】dimension; dimensionality：～论 *dimension theory*

【维他命】old name for (vitamin)

【维新】reform; modernization：百日～ *hundred Days of Reform* /～运动 *reform movement*

【维修】maintain; keep in repair：～工 *maintenance man* /故障～ *breakdown maintenance* /现场～ *field maintenance* /日常～ *ordinary maintenance* /～手册 *servicing manual* /～汽车 *service a car*

【维也纳】Vienna

wěi

伟 ① tall; gigantic: 魁～ *gigantic in stature* ② grand; magnificent: 雄～ *magnificent*

【伟岸】gigantic in stature: 身材～ *of great height and powerful build*

【伟大】great; greatness; lofty: 贝多芬是一位～的音乐家。*Beethoven was a great musician.*

【伟哥】Viagra, US brand name of medicine for sexual importance or erective dysfunction

【伟观】great wonder

【伟绩】great feats; great exploit; brilliant achievements: 著名英雄的丰功～ *the exploits of the famous heroes*

【伟人】great person; great man: 历史上的～ *the great names of history*

【伟业】great cause

伪 ① false; counterfeit; fake: 虚～ *hypocritical* ② puppet; collaborationist: ～政府 *illegitimate government* / ～政权 *puppet regime*

【伪币】① counterfeit money; spurious coin ② money issued by a puppet government

【伪钞】counterfeit (or forged) bank note

【伪经】forged scriptures

【伪军】puppet army or soldier

【伪君子】hypocrite: 装～ *play the hypocrite*

【伪劣】false and inferior: ～药品 *counterfeit and shoddy merchandise*

【伪善】hypocritical: ～的表情 *hypocritical expression*

【伪饰】false embellish; affectation

【伪书】ancient books of dubious authenticity; false document; fake document

【伪造】forge; falsify; counterfeit; fabricate: ～账目 *doctor accounts* / ～公章 *falsify a public seal* / ～文件 *spurious document* / ～现场 *simulate a scene* / ～品 *counterfeit*; *fake* / ～罪 *forgery* / 这封信是～品。*This letter is a forgery.*

【伪证】perjury; false evidence: 证人作了～。*The witness perjured himself.*

【伪装】① pretend; disguise: ～进步 *pretend to be progressive* / ～中立 *feign neutrality* ② mask; camouflage; disguise: 军车被～起来了。*The military vehicles were camouflaged.* ③ camouflage: ～工事 *camouflage works* / 天然～ *natural camouflage* / 人工～ *artificial camouflage* / 迷彩～ *colour camouflage*

【伪足】pseudopodium

苇 reed

【苇箔】reed matting

【苇丛】reed marshes

【苇塘】reed pond

【苇席】reed mat

【苇子】reed

尾 ① tail: 猪～ *pigtail* ② the sixth of the twenty-eight constellations into which the celestial sphere was divided in ancient Chinese astronomy (consisting of nine stars in the shape of a hook in Scorpio) ③ end: 首～相连 *join end to end* ④ remaining part; remnant: 扫～工程 *final phase of a project* ⑤ [量] used for fish: 几百～鱼 *hundreds of fish*

【尾巴】① tail: 麻雀竖起～。*The sparrow perked up its tail.* ② tail-like part: 彗星～ *tail of a comet* ③ appendage; servile adherent ④ a person shadowing sb; remaining part: 除掉～ *get rid of the tail*

【尾灯】taillight; tail lamp; stern light; backup light

【尾骨】coccyx; tailbone

【尾击】attack from the back; attack from the rear

【尾期】the last period; final phase

【尾气】tail gas

【尾声】① coda ② epilogue; come to an end; end: 故事的～ *epilogue of the tale*

【尾数】mantissa; odd amount in addition to the round number

【尾水】tail water

【尾随】tail behind; tag along after; follow at sb's heels: 警察一直在～着他。*The police has been tailing him.*

【尾翼】empennage; tail surface (of a aircraft)

【尾音】end sound; last or end syllable

【尾追】in hot pursuit; hot on the trail: ～不舍 *in hot pursuit of sb*

【尾韵】end rhyme

【尾子】① final phase or end ② odd amount in addition to the round number (usually of a credit balance)

【尾座】tailstock

纬 ① weave weft ② latitude

【纬编】weft knitting: ～针织物 *weft-knit fabric*

【纬度】latitude: 地心～ *geocentric latitude* / 高～ *high latitude* / 地形～ *topographical latitude*

【纬线】① weft ② parallel: 三十八度～ *the 38th parallel*

委1 ① entrust; delegate; appoint: ～以要职 *appoint sb to an important post* ② throw away; cast aside ③ shift; shirk ④ committee: 县～ *county Party committee* / 政～ *political commissar* / 常～ *standing committee*; *member of a standing committee*

委2 actually; definitely

委3 indirect; circuitous; roundabout

委4 ① accumulate; gather ② end

委5 listless; depressed; dejected

see also wēi

【委顿】tired; weary; exhausted

【委过】shift: ～于人 *put the blame on sb else*; *be undecided*

【委决不下】indecisive; wavering; hesitate to make

a decision
【委令】certificate of appointment
【委命】① entrust sb with life ② submit to the will of Heaven
【委靡】listless; dispirited; dejected and apathetic: 精神~ *listless; dispirited and inert* /~不振 *dejected; at one's worst; be in low spirits*
【委内瑞拉】Venezuela: ~人 *Venezuelan*
【委派】appoint; dispatch; send
【委培】sponsored training: ~生 *student who is sponsored by an organization*
【委弃】discard; abandon: ~不顾 *cast aside as useless* /~恶习 *get rid of one's bad downhill*
【委曲】① winding; tortuous ② the beginning and the end
【委曲求全】compromise out of consideration for the general interest; make concessions to achieve one's purpose; stoop to compromise
【委屈】① feel wronged; nurse a grievance; be misunderstood: 倾吐心中的~ *pour out one's grievances* ② put sb to great inconvenience: 对不起, ~你了。*Sorry to have made you go through all this.*
【委任】appoint; mandate: ~状 *a power letter of attorney* /~书 *certificate of appointment* /~统治 *mandate* /~行为 *act of commission* /~代理 *agency by mandate*
【委身】[书] submit to; give oneself to: ~事人 *stoop to serve sb*
【委实】indeed; really: ~如此。*That is what it is.* /他~去世了。*He really died.*
【委托】trust; entrust: ~人 *trustor* /~书 *trust instrument* /~销售 *sales on commission* /~责任 *fiduciary duty* /他把心爱的小狗~给朋友看管。*He entrusted his lovely little dog to the care of a friend.* /这件事情就~你了。*I leave the matter to you.*
【委婉】mild and roundabout; suavely; politely
【委员】committee member; member of a committee: 女~ *committee woman* /中央~ *member of the Central Committee* /~长 *chairman of a committee* /常务~ *standing committee* /市政~ *city council*
【委员会】commission; board; council; committee; panel: 学术常务~ *academic standing committee* /仲裁~ *appeal committee* /教育~ *educational committee* /~由七人组成。*The committee comprises seven people.*
【委罪】put the blame on sb else

诿

shirk; entrust; trust; implicate; tire; trouble: 推~ *shift responsibility onto others*
【诿过】put the blame on sb else
【诿卸】shirk; dodge: ~责任 *shirk responsibility*

娓

【娓娓】tirelessly: ~不倦 *talk tirelessly* /~动听 *charming; talk with eloquence*

萎

wither; wilt; decline; weaken
【萎黄】① withered and yellow: ~的叶子 *withered and yellow leaves* /~病 *chlorosis* ② wan and sallow; chlorosis: 面色~ *haggard have dropped*
【萎落】① wither and fall: 庄稼~ *withered emblement* ② decline; on the wane: 国力~。*The national power declined.*
【萎靡】listless; dejected; in low spirits
【萎蔫】wilting
【萎缩】① wither; shrivel; shrink ② dejected; listless: 神情~ *in low spirits; dispirited* ③ sag; contract: 生产~, 民生凋敝。*Production sagged and life was hard.* ④【医】*atrophy*: 脂肪~ *adipose atrophy* /机能性~ *functional atrophy* /视网膜~ *atrophy of the retina*
【萎谢】wither; wilt; fade: 秋风萧瑟, 草木~。*The autumn wind is soughing and the plants have all withered.*

唯

see also wéi
【唯唯诺诺】be a yes-man; be subservient: 在父亲面前~ *be a yes-man before one's father*

猥

① numerous; multifarious: ~杂 *miscellaneous* ② obscene; base; salacious; indecent: 贪~ *greedy and base*
【猥鄙】base and mean; despicable: ~小人 *mean and despicable person*
【猥辞】obscene language; salacious words
【猥贱】lowly; base and humble
【猥劣】abject; base; despicable: ~手段 *mean trick*
【猥琐】wretched; dreadful: ~的小偷 *a wretched thief*
【猥亵】① indecent assault ② obscene; salacious: 这本书中~不当的部分已删去。*This book has been bowdlerized.*

wèi

卫

defend; guard; protect: 警~连 *the guard company* /保家~国 *protect our homes and defend our country*
【卫兵】guard; bodyguard
【卫城】acropolis
【卫道】defend traditional moral principles: ~士 *apologist; champion*
【卫队】squad of bodyguards; armed escorts: 海岸警~巡逻船 *coast guard patrol cutter*
【卫护】protect; guard: ~祖国的边疆 *guard the border land of motherland*
【卫冕】continue to be the champion; maintain one's coronet
【卫生】hygiene; sanitation; health: 个人~ *personal hygiene* /环境~ *environmental sanitation* /家庭~ *domestic hygiene* /生理~ *physical hygiene* /~知识 *hygienic knowledge* /~队 *medical unit* /~间 *toilet; WC* /~巾 *feminine napkin* /~裤 *sweat pants* /~设备 *sanitary facilities or equipment* /~学 *hygiene* /~纸 *toilet paper*

【卫士】bodyguard; guard; escort:英国国王的~ *yeoman of the (royal) guard*

【卫戍】garrison:人民要求政府派军队~沿海城镇。*The people ask that the government garrisons the coastal towns.*

【卫星】【天】① satellite; moons:月球是地球的~。*The moon is a satellite of the earth.* ② man-made (artificial) satellite:发射人造~ *launch an artificial a man -made satellite* /测绘~ *cartographic satellite* /同步~ *geostationary satellite* /载人~ *inhabited satellite* /导航~ *navigational satellite* /摄影侦察~ *photoreconnaissance satellite* /无线电转播~ *radio relay satellite* /侦察~ *reconnaissance satellite* /科研~ *research satellite* /运载~ *vehicle satellite* /~云图 *satellite cloud picture* /~电视 *television programs transmitted by satellite* ③ central: ~城 *satellite town* /~国 *satellite state*

为 ① be on the side of; help ② on behalf of; for the benefit of ③ for the purpose of; for the sake of: ~了生存 *for existence* /他~了好玩才学习英语的。*He's learning English for the fun of it.* ④ to:此物请不要~外人道。*Please say nothing of this to other people.* ⑤ because; for; on account of: ~什么如此沮丧? *Why get so depression?*
see also wéi

【为此】by this; in this connection; for this purpose; to this end:他的妻子是个通情达理的人,~他引以为豪。*He is proud that his wife is amenable to reason.*

【为国捐躯】give up or sacrifice one's life for one's country; die for one's country:

【为何】why; for what reason:你~不再来看我们呢? *How come you never visit us any more?*

【为虎作伥】help a villain do evil; play the jackal to the lion; hold a candle to the devil

【为了】for the sake of; in order to; for the reason that: ~他们所有的人 *for all their sakes* /~老交情 *for old friend's sake*

【为民除害】rid the people of an evil; rid the people of a scourge

【为民请命】plead in the name of the people:打着~的幌子 *pose as a spokesperson of the people*

【为什么】why; why is it that:你~这样做? *Why did you do it?* /你知道他~迟到吗? *Do you know why he was late?*

未[1] ① not; yet: 意犹~尽 *have not given full expression to one's views* ② not; no: ~知可否 *not know whether sth can be done*

未[2] the eighth of the twelve Earthly Branches

【未必】may not; not necessarily:老师的观点~正确。*The teacher viewpoint is not necessarily correct.*

【未便】find it hard to; be not in a position to: ~多说 *not advisable to say more* /~声张 *find it inappropriate to make sth public*

【未卜先知】foresee, have foresight; know without consulting the oracle — have foresight

【未曾】have not; never: ~听说 *something unheard of*

【未尝】① have not; did not:他一天~吃东西。*He ate nothing the whole day.* ② use before a negative word, in making a guarded assertion:这样的解释也~不可。*Such an interpretation is by no means impossible.*

【未成年】not yet of age; under age: ~人 *minor*

【未定】undecided; uncertain; undefined:归期~。*The date of return is not yet fixed.* /局势~。*The situation is still uncertain.*

【未敢苟同】beg to differ; can not agree:他的观点我~。*I could hardly agree with his viewpoint.*

【未婚】unmarried; single: ~妻 *one's intended wife* /~夫 *one's intended husband* /~母亲 *single mother*

【未及】① too late; not enough time:妈妈~说完,孩子们就跑开了。*The child had run away before their mother finished his word.* ② have not reached or touched:你说的只是事情的表面,而~实质。*What you have said touches only the surface of things, not their essence.*

【未竟】incomplete; unfulfilled: ~之志 *an unfulfilled ambition*

【未决】unsettled; outstanding:胜负~。*The outcome of the battle is not yet decided.*

【未可】cannot; must not: 前途~限量 *have a brilliant future* /~厚非 *be not altogether inexcusable; give no cause for much criticism* /~乐观 *give no cause for optimism*

【未刻】period of the day from 1 p.m. to 3 p.m.

【未来】① future; tomorrow: ~冲击 *future shock* /我们的~难以预测。*Our future seems very uncertain.* ② coming; approaching: ~的一年 *the coming year* /~派 *futurism* /~学 *futurology*

【未老先衰】prematurely senile; be decrepit before one's age

【未了】unfinished; outstanding: ~的心愿 *an unfulfilled wish* /~工作 *unfinished work*

【未免】① rather; be a bit too; really:你的顾虑~多了些。*You are perhaps a little overcautious.* ② would naturally; unavoidably:当众训斥,~使他难堪。*He would be very much embarrassed if he were to be scolded in public.*

【未能】fail to; can not: ~完成 *fail to accomplish* /~免俗 *be unable to rise above the convention; can not but follow conventional practice*

【未然】take preventive measures

【未时】period of the day from 1 p.m. to 3 p.m.

【未遂】not accomplished; abortive: 自杀~ *a would-be suicide* /谋杀~ *an attempt at murder* /~罪 *an attempt at an offense*

【未完】unfinished: ~待续 *to be continued*

【未详】unknown:死因~的裁决 *an open verdict*

【未雨绸缪】repair the house before it rains; don't have thy cloak to make when it begins to rain

【未知量】unknown quantity

【未知数】① unknown number ② unknown; uncertain:这个工作会不会按时完成还是一个~。*It is still uncertain whether this task can be accomplished on time.*

位 ①place; seat:岗～ *one's post* /各就各～。*On your marks!* ②position; rank; status:爵～ *rank of nobility* /学～ *degree* ③throne:即～ *come to the throne* /退～ *give up the throne* ④【数】place; figure; digit:个～ *unit's place* /十～ *ten's place* ⑤[量] used in deferential reference to people:诸～女士先生 *Ladies and Gentlemen* ⑥【电】bit ⑦(Wèi) a surname

【位次】①precedence; seating arrangement ②rank

【位分】position; social status

【位移】【物】translocation; displacement:绝对～ *absolute displacement* /角～ *angular displacement* /水平～ *horizontal displacement* /相对～ *relative displacement*

【位置】①seat; site; location:装配～ *fitting position* /初始～ *initial position* /对称～ *symmetrical position* /这只碗的合适～是在架子上。*The right place for the bowl is on the shelf.* ②place; position:占有重要～ *hold an important position*

【位子】seat; place; position:我坐的～很好。*I had a very good seat.*

味 ①taste; flavour:风～儿 *local (or special) flavour* /辣味儿 *taste peppery* ②smell fragrant:香～儿 *a sweet smell* ③interest; relish:韵～ *lingering charm* /说得津津有～ *talk with great relish* ④dishes; food:山珍海～ *delicacies from land and sea* ⑤distinguish the flavour of:耐人寻～ *afford food for thought* ⑥[量] for ingredients of a Chinese medicine prescription

【味道】taste; flavour:这茶的～很香。*This tea tastes sweet.* /这汤有鸡的～。*This soup tastes of chicken.*

【味感】taste

【味精】monosodium glutamate; gourmet powder

【味觉】taste; gustatory sensation

【味同嚼蜡】it is like chewing wax-insipid; as dry as sawdust

畏 ①fear; dread:大无～的精神 *fearless spirit* ②admire:后生可～! *What an admirable young man!*

【畏避】avoid sth out of fear; flinch from; recoil from:～事实 *recoil from fact*

【畏怖】fear; dread:心怀～ *be in fear*

【畏服】be obedient with fear

【畏忌】have scruples; fear; dread

【畏惧】fear; dread:无所～ *be fearless*

【畏难】be afraid of difficulty:～情绪 *fear of difficulty*

【畏怯】timid; cowardly; chickenhearted

【畏首畏尾】be full of misgivings; be frightened all over

【畏缩】recoil in fear; shrink:因怕痛而～ *to flinch at pain*

【畏缩不前】recoil in fear; hang back in face of danger; hesitate to press forward:

【畏途】a dangerous road; a perilous undertaking

【畏罪】dread punishment for one's crime:～自杀 *commit suicide for fear of punishment* /～潜逃 *abscond to avoid punishment*

胃 ①stomach ②seventeenth of the twenty-eight constellations in ancient Chinese astronomy

【胃癌】cancer of stomach; gastric carcinoma

【胃病】gastric diseases; stomach trouble

【胃肠炎】gastroenteritis

【胃出血】gastrorrhagia; gastric bleeding

【胃穿孔】gastric perforation; stomach perforation

【胃大弯】greater curvature of the stomach

【胃口】①appetite:他的～好。*He has a good appetite.* ②liking:这个不合我的～兴趣。*It goes against my stomach.* ③[喻] ambition; appetite

【胃溃疡】gastric ulcer

【胃酸】hydrochloric acid in gastric juice:～过多 *hyperchlorhydria; hyperacidity* /～过少 *hypochlorhydria; hypoacidity*

【胃痛】stomachache; gastralgia

【胃下垂】ptosis of the stomach; gastroptosis

【胃腺】【生理】gastric gland

【胃炎】gastritis

【胃液】【生理】gastric juice

谓 ①tell; say:或～ *someone says* ②call name; mean:何～"非典"? *What is meant about SARS?*

【谓语】【语】predicate

尉 ①a military rank (above the rank of warrant officer and below that of major):少～ *second lieutenant* ②junior officer:太～ *imperial minister in charge of military affairs* ③(Wèi) a surname

喂 ①hello; hey:～!有人吗? *Hello! Is anybody there?* ②feed

【喂草】grass-feed

【喂食】feed; oral administration:～器 *feeding trough*

【喂养】feed; keep; raise:～鸽子 *keep pigeons*

猬 hedgehog

【猬集】as numerous as the spines of a hedgehog

蔚 ①luxuriant; grand ;magnificent ②colourful

【蔚蓝】azure; sky blue:～的天空 *a bright blue sky*

【蔚然】a flourishing; grand; exuberant

【蔚然成风】become common practice which prevails throughout; grow into a general trend:早操锻炼～。*Doing morning exercise is the order of the day.*

【蔚为大观】present a splendid sight; afford a magnificent view sight:展出的新式车辆,～。*There is a splendid array of the new cars on display.*

慰 ①console; soothe; comfort:安～ *console and comfort* /聊以自～ *take as a consolation* ②feel received:快～ *be relieved*

【慰安】comfort; solace:自我～ *solace oneself*

【慰安妇】comfort woman — Asian women enforced to satisfy the sexual desire of Japanese soldiers during World War Ⅱ

【慰抚】comfort; console; soothe
【慰藉】comfort; consolation
【慰劳】express sympathy and solicitude for; express regards to; extend one's best wishes to
【慰留】persuade sb to stay
【慰勉】comfort and encourage:好言～ *give well-intentioned consolation and encouragement*
【慰问】extend one's regards to; show gratitude and appreciation: ～信 *a letter of sympathy* /～团 *group sent to convey regards and appreciation* /～军烈属 *convey greetings to the people of disaster-stricken areas*
【慰唁】express sympathy for; condole with sb
【慰悦】comfortable and glad

魏 ① the Wei Dynasty ② the Kingdom of Wei (220-265) ③ (Wèi) a surname
【魏碑】tablet inscriptions of the Northern Dynasties (386-581)

wēn

温 ① warm; lukewarm: ～水 *lukewarm water* ② temperature:气～ *atmospheric temperature* ③ warm up; heat up: ～酒 *warm up the wine* ④ gentle; meek; tender ⑤ review; revise:重～旧梦 *revive an old dream*
【温饱】have enough food and clothing; dress warmly and eat one's fill:不足～的工资 *starvation wages* /～问题 *problem of (adequate) food and clothing* /～型 *just having enough to eat and wear*
【温差】difference in temperature; range of temperature: 昼夜～ *difference in temperature between day and night* /～电偶 *thermoelectric couple* /～电 *thermoelectricity* /～电池 *thermoelectric cell*
【温床】①【农】hotbed ②［喻］breeding ground: 现代城市是现代文明的窗口,同时又是犯罪的～。*Modern cities are a window of modern civilization and, at the same time, a hotbed of crime.*
【温存】① gentle; kind: 性格～ *temperamentally gentle and considerate* ② be attentive; give tender attention
【温带】temperate zone: ～气候 *temperate climate* /～雨林 *temperate rainforest*
【温度】temperature: 绝对～ *absolute temperature* /室内～ *indoor temperature*
【温度计】thermometer: 空气～ *air thermometer* /酒精～ *alcohol thermometer* /干球～ *dry-bulb thermometer* /电阻～ *electric resistance thermometer* /压力式～ *manometric thermometer* /水银～ *mercury thermometer* /半导体～ *semi-conductor thermometer* /摄氏～ *centigrade thermometer*
【温故知新】gain new insights through restudying old material
【温和】① gentle and kind: 气候～ *a temperate climate* ② temperate; mild: 性情～ *genial disposition* /语气～ *mild tone* /～派 *moderates*
【温厚】gentle and kind; good natured
【温乎乎】neither cold nor hot; fairly warm: ～的汤 *warm soup*
【温乎】lukewarm: 水还有些～。*The water is still warm.*
【温和】lukewarm; warm: 米饭还～呢。*The rice is still warm.*
【温静】gentle and quiet
【温良】gentle and kindhearted
【温暖】sense the warmth; warm: ～而舒适的小房子 *a cozy little house* /天气～ *warm weather*
【温情】① tender feeling ② too softhearted: ～脉脉 *full of tenderness* /～主义 *undue leniency or soft-heartedness*
【温泉】thermal spring; hot spring
【温柔】gentle and soft: 她脸上～的表情 *a tender expression on her face*
【温润】① gentle; kindly: 性格～ *of a gentle disposition* ② warm and humid: 气候～ *a temperate and moist climate*
【温室】greenhouse; hothouse; conservatory; glasshouse: ～气体 *greenhouse gas* /～效应 *greenhouse effect; gradual warming of earth's atmosphere said to be caused by increased carbon dioxide in the air*
【温淑】(of women) gentle and kindhearted
【温顺】meek; docile; tame: 性情～如小羊 *as meek as a lamb*
【温汤】① lukewarm water ② hot spring: ～浸种 *hot water treatment of seeds*
【温文】gentle; mild: ～有礼 *mild and courteous* /～尔雅 *gentle and cultivated; be cultured and refined*
【温习】review; brush up; revise: 我必须重新～法文。*I must brush up my French.*
【温馨】gentle and fragrant; warm; be softly fragrant: ～的情意 *warm friendship*
【温驯】tame; docile; meek: ～的小狗 *a docile little dog*
【温雅】gentle and graceful: ～的学者 *a gentle and elegant scholar*

瘟 ① acute communicable disease: 鸡～ *chick pest* ② dull; insipid; vapid
【瘟病】seasonal febrile diseases
【瘟神】god of plague
【瘟疫】pestilence: 当时～正在该城流行。*Pestilence was then prevailing in that city.*

wén

文 ① character; inscription; writing: 甲骨～ *"oracle bone" inscriptions (of the Shang Dynasty)* ② language: 德～ *German* ③ literary composition; article; writing: 公～ *official document* ④ literary or classical language: 半～半白 *half literary and half vernacular* ⑤ culture; civilization ⑥ formal ritual: 繁～缛节 *unnecessary and overelaborate formalities* ⑦ civilian; civil: ～职 *civil service* ⑧ gentle; mild; refined ⑨ used to certain natural phenomena: 天～学 *astronomy* ⑩ cover up; paint over; explain away: ~过 *gloss over one's fault* ⑪ [量] unit of ancient coins: 一~钱 *a cent* / 一~不值 *not worth a farthing* ⑫ tattoo: ~了右手 *have one's right hand tabooed* ⑬ (Wén) a surname

【文案】① official documents and letters ② people in charge of official documents and letters; clerk

【文本】version; text: 外部~ *external text*

【文笔】style of writing: 他是一位~流畅的作家。*He is a writer of fluency.*

【文不对题】irrelevant to the subject; be way off the beam; fly off at a tangent:

【文才】literary talent; aptitude for writing

【文采】① rich and bright colours ② literary talent and grace: 我的父亲很有~。*My father is a man of literary.*

【文昌鱼】【动】amphioxus; lancelet

【文辞】diction language: ~华丽 *flowery language*

【文斗】verbal struggle; struggle by reasoning:

【文法】① grammar: 特征~ *characteristic grammar* / 正规~ *regular grammar* ② decree

【文房】① [书] study ② [旧] department in charge of official documents and correspondence: ~四宝 *the four treasures of the study (writing brush, ink stick, ink slab and paper)*

【文风】style of writing: ~朴实 *a simple style of writing*

【文稿】manuscript; draft: 修改得一塌糊涂的~ *a copy disfigured by numerous corrections*

【文工团】song and dance ensemble; art troupe

【文官】civil official; civil servant; civil service

【文过饰非】cover up one's errors by excuses; conceal faults and glass over wrongs: 这话是用来~的。*This language serves to disguise and obscure.*

【文豪】literary giant; eminent writer; great writer: 莎士比亚是个~。*Shakespeare is a classic.*

【文化】① culture; civilization; literacy: 古代~ *ancient culture* / 外国~ *alien culture* / 黑人~ *black culture* / 通俗~ *popular culture* / 传统~ *traditional culture* / ~交流 *cultural exchanges* / ~遗产 *cultural heritage* / ~遗址 *a site of ancient cultural remains* ②【考】ancient culture or civilization: 玛雅~ *Maya Culture* ③ education; schooling; literacy: ~事业 *cultural establishments* / ~程度 *cultural level* / ~宫 *palace of culture* / ~馆 *cultural centre* / ~市场 *cultural market* / ~教养 *education and upbringing* / ~课 *literacy class* / ~部 *Ministry of Culture* / ~人 *intellectual; man of letters*

【文火】soft fire; slow fire; gentle heat: ~熬汤。*Use a slow fire to stew soup.*

【文集】collected works

【文件】① documents; papers; instruments: 机密~ *classified document* / ~袋 *documents pouch* / 磁盘~ *files on disk* / 索引~ *index file* / 玛丽小姐, 请把这份~归档。*Please file this paper away, Miss Mary.* ② articles: 纲领性~ *programmatic document*

【文教】culture and education; article and education: ~事业 *cultural and educational work* / ~部门 *cultural and educational institutions*

【文经武纬】a man of both literary and military capacity

【文静】gentle and quiet: 我的邻居是个~的小伙子。*My neighbour is a quiet young fellow.*

【文具】writing materials; stationery: ~盒 *a stationery case*

【文科】liberal arts; the humanities: ~大学 *liberal arts university; university of science*

【文库】a series of books issued in a single format by a publisher; library

【文莱】Brunei

【文理】unity and coherence in writing; pattern: ~不通 *illogical and ungrammatical* / ~通顺 *have unity and coherence; make smooth reading*

【文联】literacy federation

【文脉】unity and coherence in writing

【文盲】analphabet; illiterate person: 扫除~ *wipe out illiteracy* / 职业上的~ *functional illiteracy*

【文庙】Confucian temple

【文名】the fame of being good at writing; literary fame

【文明】① civilization; culture: 物质~ *material civilization* / 精神~ *spiritual civilization* / 城市~ *city civilization* ② civilized; civil: ~古国 *country with an ancient civilization* / ~社会 *civilized society* / ~礼貌 *decorum; manners* / ~棍 *walking stick* / ~戏 *early form of spoken drama*

【文墨】① literacy; writing: 粗通~ *barely know the rudiments of writing* ② of mental labour

【文痞】literary prostitute

【文凭】diploma: 大学~ *a college diploma*

【文气】(wénqì) force or cohesion of writing

【文气】(wénqi) [方] gentle and reserved: 你家儿子~的很呀。*Your son has very gentle and smooth manners.*

【文契】testament; deed; contract

【文情】literary grace and affection: ~并茂 *beautiful in both sentiment and expression*

【文人】man of letters; scholar: ~学者 *literary scholars* / ~相轻 *scholars tend to look down upon each other* / ~墨客 *literati* / 无聊~ *boring scribbler* / ~无行 *men of letters are lacking in moral character*

【文如其人】the writing mirrors the writer; style is an index of the mind; the style is the man himself

【文弱】gentle and frail-looking: ~书生 *a frail scholar*

【文身】tattoo

【文史】literature and history: ~资料 *historical accounts of past events*

【文士】man of letters

【文饰】① refine; polish ② cover up (one's mistake): ~过失 *cover up the defect*

【文书】① document; official despatch ② copy clerk

【文思】the thread of ideas in writing; train of

thoughts in writing; merits and moral: ~敏捷 *have a ready pen*
【文坛】the literary world; the world of letters
【文体】① style; literary form; type of writing ② recreation and sports: ~活动 *recreational and sports activities*
【文武兼备】be well versed in both polite betters and martial arts
【文武全才】a man of both civil and military ability
【文武双全】be well versed in both polite letters and martial arts
【文物】cultural relic; cultural treasures: 国家~局 *State Bureau for the Preservation of Cultural and Historical Relics*
【文献】document; literature: 历史~ *a historical document*
【文选】selected works; literary selections:《邓小平~》*Selected Works of Deng Xiaoping*
【文学】literature: 大众~ *light literature* /英国~ *English literature* /世界~ *world literature* / ~家 *writer; man of letters* / ~遗产 *literary heritage* / ~流派 *schools of literature* /当代~ *contemporary literary* / ~批评 *literary criticism* / ~作品 *literature; literary works*
【文雅】refined; cultured; elegant; polished: 举止~ *refined in manner*
【文言】the literary Chinese: ~文 *classical style of writing*
【文艺】literature and art: ~作品 *literary and artistic works* / ~复兴 *Renaissance* / ~节目 *programme of entertainment* / ~界 *literary and art circles* / ~思潮 *trend of thought in art and literature* / ~座谈会 *forum on art and literature* / ~会演 *theatrical festival* / ~批评 *art and literary criticism* / ~学 *study of art and literary* / ~语言 *language of art and literary*
【文友】literary friend
【文苑】literary world
【文摘】digest; abstract; piece: 作者~ *author abstract* /科技~ *science abstract*
【文章】① article; essay ② literary works; writings ③ hidden meaning: 她写了一篇题为《我的爸爸》的~。*She wrote an essay on My Father.*
【文职】civilian post: ~机构 *civil service* /她在政府~机关工作。*She works in the civil service.*
【文治】achievements in culture and education: ~武功 *cultural and military achievements*
【文质彬彬】gentle; combination of elegance end plainness; suave: ~的小伙子 *quiet scholarly young chap*
【文绉绉】genteel: 说话~的 *speak in a genteel manner*
【文字】① characters; script; writing: 象形~ *hieroglyphic writing* /楔形~ *cuneiform writing* ② written language: ~宣传 *written propaganda* ③ writing: ~简练 *written in a concise style* / ~处理机 *word processor* / ~方程 *literal equation* / ~改革 *reform of a writing system* / ~学 *philology* / ~游戏 *play on words; juggle with terms*
【文字狱】literary inquisition; imprisonment or execution of an author for writing sth considered offensive by the imperial court
【文宗】person whose writing is followed by all: 百代~ *long established master writer*

纹 pattern of silk fabrics; vein; grain

【纹理】lines; veins: 这块大理石的~很漂亮。*The marble has a very beautiful grain.*
【纹路】lines; grain
【纹丝不动】absolutely still: 没有风，红旗~。*There was not a breath of wind and the red flag was perfect still.*
【纹银】fine silver; silver ingot: ~十两 *ten taels of sterling silver*
【纹章】arm

闻 ① hear: 百~不如一见 *seeing for oneself is a hundred times better than hearing form others* ② news; story: ~自由 *freedom of the press* ③ smell: ~起来不错。*It smells good.* ④ repute; reputation: 秽~ *ill repute* ⑤ unknown; famous

【闻达】illustrious and influential; well-known: 不求~ *seek no fame*
【闻风而动】immediately respond to a call; act without delay upon hearing sth; go into action without delay
【闻风丧胆】become terror-stricken of the news; become panic-stricken at the news: 我军向前挺进，敌人~。*The enemies were scared to death on hearing the news of our advance.*
【闻过则喜】feel happy when told of one's errors; be glad when told of one's own errors
【闻鸡起舞】rise at cockcrow and practice martial arts — exert oneself to the utmost for a worthy cause
【闻见】① smell: 我~了花香。*I smelt the fragrance of a flower.* ② hear: ~风就要防备雨。*You'd better be prepared for the rain when you hear the wind blowing.*
【闻名】① well-known; hear of one's fame: 世界~ *world famous* ② be familiar with sb's name; know sb by repute
【闻所未闻】unheard-of; have never even heard of: 老和尚给我讲述了一些~奇事。*The old monk told me a lot of things I had never heard before.*
【闻悉】hear; be informed; come to one's knowledge: ~他的死亡消息，我十分难过。*On hearing the news of his death, I came into deep sorrow.*
【闻讯】get the news of: ~赶来 *rush over after hearing the news*

蚊 mosquito

【蚊虫】mosquito
【蚊香】mosquito-repellent incense
【蚊帐】mosquito net; mosquito curtain: ~砂 *mosquito netting*
【蚊子】mosquito

W

wěn

刎 cut one's throat

【刎颈之交】friends sworn to death; tested friends: 结为~ *become devoted friends*

吻 ① lips: 接~ *buss; osculate* ② a animal's mouth ③ kiss: 她~别他们。*She kissed them good-bye.*

【吻合】① coincide; accord with; agree with; be identical: 看法~ *have identical opinion* ② anastomose: ~术 *anastomosis*

紊 disordered; confused: 工作有条不~的人 *a systematic(al) worker*

【紊流】turbulence; turbulent flow

【紊乱】disorder; confusion; chaos: 秩序~ *in a state of turmoil* / 心律~ *arrhythmia* / 内分泌~ *internal secretion disorder*

稳 ① steady; firm: 步履不太~ *not very steady on one's leg* ② calm; stain; sedate: 他这个人很~。*He is very calm and self-possessed.* ③ sure; certain: 十拿九~ *quite sure* ④ stabilize; calm; put at ease: ~住情绪 *stabilize your emotion*

【稳步】with steady steps; steadily: ~前进 *tread a steady course; steer a steady course*

【稳操胜券】have full assurance of success: 我们肯定赢,这场比赛我们是~。*We're sure to win; the match is in the bag.*

【稳产】stable yield: ~高田 *land with high, stable yields*

【稳当】① reliable; secure; safe: ~的办法 *a reliable method* ② steady; stable

【稳定】① stable; firm; steady: 社会~ *social stability* / 局势~ *situation stability* ② steady; stabilize: ~物价 *stabilize prices* / ~情绪 *set sb's mind at rest* / ~度 *stability* / ~剂 *stabilizer* / ~流 *stable current* / ~平衡 *stable equilibrium* / ~装置 *stabilization plant*

【稳固】① firm; stable: ~的政权 *stable government* / ~的职业 *stable job* ② stabilize; consolidate: ~经济基础 *consolidate the economic foundation*

【稳获】be sure to get

【稳健】firm; steady: ~的政治家 *moderate politicians*

【稳拿】be sure to get or to do: 他~金牌。*He is a sure-fire gold medallist.*

【稳如泰山】as stable as Mount Tai

【稳妥】safe; reliable: ~的策略 *a safe strategy*

【稳压器】manostat; voltage regulator

【稳扎稳打】go ahead steadily and strike sure blows; go about things steadily: ~,沉着应战。*Move ahead steadily and meet the challenge calmly.*

【稳重】sedate; earnest; staid; steady: 他为人处事十分~。*He bears himself utmost discretion.*

【稳坐钓鱼台】take a tense situation calmly; sit leisurely in a fishing boat despite the storm

wèn

问 ① seek; ask; inquire: 明知故~ *ask a question when one already has the answer* / 所答非所~ *give a irrelevant answer to a question* ② ask after; inquire after: ~候他的健康 *inquire after his health* ③ interrogate; examine: 盘~ *cross-question* / ~口供 *interrogate someone* ④ hold responsible; intervene: 惟你是~。*I'll hold you responsible for it.* ⑤ from: 我想~你借些钱。*I will ask you to lend me some money.* ⑥ (Wèn) a surname

【问安】pay one's respects (usu. to elders); wish one's elders good health: 我向老爷爷~。*I wish granddad good health.*

【问案】try a case; hear a case

【问卜】divine; consult fortune tellers

【问长问短】take the trouble to make detailed inquiries; ask about this and that: 儿子一会来,母亲就~。*As soon as her son came back, she asked all kinds of questions about him.*

【问答】questions and answers: ~时间 *time for questions and answers*

【问鼎】① intend to seize power; have monarchic ambitions: ~之心 *have the ambition to seize state power* ② try to win the first prize: ~冠军 *win the championship*

【问寒问暖】ask after sb's health with deep concern

【问好】send one's regards to; say hello to: 请向她和她的家人~。*Give my greetings to her and her family.*

【问号】① question mark; interrogation point ② unknown factor; unsolved problem: 她是否适应这个工作是个~。*There's a question mark about her suitability for the job.*

【问候】send one's regards to; extend greetings to: 打电话去~ *give someone a ring of greetings*

【问话】inquire; ask; question: 领导要找你~。*The leader wants to ask you some questions.*

【问津】make inquiries; have interest in: 价格高得令人不敢~。*The price is prohibitive.*

【问卷】questionnaire: ~调查 *investigation by questionnaire*

【问难】query and argue again and again; test with difficult questions

【问世】be published; come out: 自从电脑~以来人们的消息灵通得多了。*People are much better informed since the advent of the computer.*

【问事】① inquire: ~处 *inquiry office; information desk* ② bother about something; be in charge: 退休后,他已不在~。*After retirement, he is no longer concern with works.*

【问题】① question; issue; problem; matters: 解决~ *solve a problem* / 律师问了证人几个~。*The lawyer put several questions to the witness.* ② trouble; difficulty; mishap: 上次比赛,差点出了

~。We nearly ran into trouble last match.

【问心无愧】have a clear conscience; feel no qualms upon self-examination: 他~。*He had a clear conscience.* /只要~,旁人的指责可一笑置之。*A clear conscience laughs at false accusation.*

【问询】ask about; ask; inquire

【问讯】inquire; ask: 详情请向~台询问。*For particulars, apply to the information desk.*

【问斩】behead; decapitate

【问罪】denounce; condemn

wēng

翁 ① old man: 亿万富~ *mega millionaire* ② father ③ father-in-law

【翁姑】mother-in-law; woman's parents-in-law

【翁婿】father-in-law and son-in-law

【翁仲】stone image in front of a grave

嗡 buzz; hum; drone: 机器的~~声 *the whirring of the machinery*

【嗡嗡】buzz; hum; drone: 我的脑袋~响。*My brain was in buzz.*

wèng

瓮 ① urn; earthen jar ② (Wèng) a surname

【瓮声瓮气】in a low, muffled voice

【瓮中之鳖】be bottled up like a turtle trapped in a jar; be hopeless like a rat in a hole

【瓮中捉鳖】have full assurance to get go after an easy prey as one who catches a turtle in a jar; be sure of success

wō

莴

【莴苣】lettuce

【莴笋】asparagus; lettuce

倭 [旧] Japan

【倭瓜】[方] pumpkin; cushaw

【倭寇】【史】Japanese pirates (operating in Chinese coastal waters from the 14th century to the 16th century)

涡 eddy; dimple: 旋~ *eddies of water*; *vortex*

【涡虫】【动】turbellarian worm

【涡流】① eddy current; vortex flow ② eddy; whirling fluid

【涡轮】worm gear; worm wheel; snail wheel: ~发电机 *turbine generator* /~喷气飞机 *turbojet* /风力~机 *wind turbine*

【涡旋】eddy; vortex: 大气~ *atmosphere vortex*

喔 (of cock) crow

窝 ① nest: 马蜂~ *hornet's nest* ② lair; den; haunt: 贼~ *thieves' den* ③ a hollow part of the human body; pit: 酒~儿 *dimple* ④ place or space occupied ⑤ harbour; shelter ⑥ bend: 把铁丝~成鸟笼。*Bend the wire into a birdcage.* ⑦ [量] litter; brood: 一~小鸡 *a brood of ducklings* ⑧ hold in; check ⑨ huddle up; curl up; stay still

【窝憋】① unhappy; feel frustrated: 没有按时完成任务,心里老觉得~得慌。*I can not help feeling exasperated as the task has not be accomplished on time.* ② narrow; poky: 这个房间太~了。*This room is too cramped.*

【窝藏】conceal; harbour; shelter: ~罪犯是犯法的。*Harbouring criminals is an offense in law.*

【窝匪】shelter bandit

【窝风】unventilated; lacking fresh air

【窝火】choke with resentment; simmering with rage: ~了一肚子火 *be simmering with rage*

【窝儿里横】be imperious in one's family only

【窝囊】① feel vexed; be annoyed: 心里实在~ *feel helplessly vexed* ② stupid; cowardly: ~废 *good-for-nothing*; *worthless wretch*

【窝棚】hut; shack; shanty; shed

【窝气】be forced to bottle up one's anger

【窝窝头】steamed corn bread

【窝心】feel vexed; feel irritated: 那件事情想起来就~。*I have a gnawing pain whenever I think of the incident.*

【窝赃】harbour stolen goods

【窝主】a person who harbours criminals; loot or contraband goods

蜗 snail

【蜗居】humble abode; live in humble abode

【蜗牛】snail

【蜗行】snail-paced; walk at a snail's gallop

【蜗旋】revolve; helix; spiral; wind: 阶梯绕着中间的石柱~而上。*The stairs spiraled round the central pillar.*

wǒ

我 ① I; me; my: ~的习惯 *my custom* ② we; us; our: ~国 *our homeland* ③ one; anyone: 大家你一言~一语地说开了。*With everyone joining in, people started talking among themselves.* ④ self: 忘~工作 *work selflessly*

【我辈】we; us

【我们】① we; us ② [口] I; me; my

【我行我素】persist in one's old wags; live by one's own definitions; stick to one's old way of doing things; the dogs bark, but the caravan goes on: ~,独断独行 *be a law to oneself*

wò

沃 ① fertile; rich:肥～的土地 *fertile land* ② irrigate; poor(water):～田 *irrigate farmland* ③ (Wò) a surname
【沃壤】fertile soil; rich soil
【沃饶】fertile; rich and abundant
【沃土】fertile soil; rich soil
【沃野】fertile land:～千里 *vast rich fields*

卧 ① lie:仰～ *lie on one's back* ② crouch; sit ③ for sleeping in ④ get babies to lie down
【卧病】be confined to bed; fall sick; be laid up with illness:～在床 *be ill in bed*
【卧舱】sleeping cabin
【卧车】① sleeping car; parlor car; pullman car ② sedan; parlor car:特等～ *drawing room car*
【卧床】①[方] bed ② stay in bed:～不起 *be very ill; be critically ill* /听他的劝告,我～休息。*On his advice I am staying in bed.*
【卧倒】drop to the ground; take a lying-down position:第一声警报一响我们就迅速～。*Alarmed at the first sound, we hit the dirt.*
【卧底】thieves act from inside; serve as a planted agent
【卧房】bedroom
【卧轨】lie on the rail (to stop the train or commit suicide)
【卧具】bedding
【卧铺】sleeping berth; couchette
【卧室】bedroom
【卧榻】[书] bed
【卧薪尝胆】stoop to conquer; firm resolve in danger to wipe out a national humiliation
【卧姿】【体】prone position

握 ① grasp; grip; hold:～刀 *hold a knife* ② have; possess:～有大权 *wield great power*
【握别】shake hands at parting:～以来,已逾半年。*It is more than half a year since we parted.*
【握力】the power of gripping; grip:～器 *spring-grip dumb-bells*
【握手】handshake; clasp hands:～言欢 *hold hands and converse cheerfully* /两人～。*The two men shook hands.*

斡 revolve; gyrate; rotate
【斡旋】① mediate; use one's good office to:～纠纷 *mediate a dissension* /居中～ *mediate between the two parties* ② turn back

龌
【龌龊】① dirty; filthy:～的房间 *dirty room* ② mean; despicable base; sordid:卑鄙～ *mean and sordid* ③ narrow-minded; petty

wū

乌 ① crow ② black; dark ③ young silkworm ④ (Wū) a surname
【乌沉沉】dark; black:～的天空 *dark sky*
【乌龟】tortoise:～壳 *tortoiseshell*
【乌合之众】mob; motley crowd; sheep without shepherd; disorderly band:一群各怀己见的～ *a medley of different ideas*
【乌黑】raven; jet-black; pitch-black
【乌呼】alas
【乌克兰】Ukraine:～人 *Ukrainian* /～语 *Ukrainian*
【乌拉尔山脉】Ural Mountains
【乌拉圭】Uruguay:～人 *Uruguayan*
【乌亮】glossy black:～的眼睛 *glossy black skin*
【乌溜溜】dark and liquid:～的一双大眼睛 *sparking, big black eyes*
【乌龙茶】oolong tea
【乌梅】smoke plum; dark plum
【乌木】ebony
【乌七八糟】in a terrible mess; horrible mess; great disorder; rubbish; garbage:满脑袋都是些～的东西。*Your head is in a terrible clutter.*
【乌纱帽】① black gauze cap ②[喻] official position:丢了～ *be dismissed from office*
【乌涂】①(of water) not hot but not cold ② beating about the bush
【乌托邦】Utopia
【乌鸦】crow
【乌烟瘴气】foul atmosphere; pandemonium reigns thorough:到处都是～ *a foul atmosphere everywhere*
【乌有】nothing; naught:化为～ *scatter to the four wind*
【乌鱼】snakehead
【乌云】① black clouds; dark clouds:天空～密布,我们看得出快来暴风雨了。*The sky clouded over; we could see there was going to be rainstorm.* ②[喻] sinister situation:战争的～ *dark clouds of war*
【乌枣】smoked jujube; black jujube
【乌贼】cuttlefish
【乌兹别克斯坦】Uzbekistan

污 ① dirt; filth:血～ *bloodiness* ② dirty; filthy; foul ③ corrupt; dishonest:贪官～吏 *malfeasant* ④ defile; smear; vilify:玷～ *sully; smirch*
【污点】stain; black mark; blemish; smirch; spot:一个人品行上的～ *a blot on one's character*
【污垢】dirt; filth
【污痕】filthy mark
【污秽】filthy; foul
【污蔑】① smear; calumniate; malign; slander ② defile; sully; tarnish
【污泥】sludge; mire; mud:活性～ *activated sludge*
【污染】contaminate; pollute:水～ *aquatic pollution*

/大气～air(borne) pollution /农业～agricultural pollution /工业～industrial pollution /噪声～noise pollution /视觉～visual pollution /～气象学～pollution meteorology /～生物学 pollution biology /～物 contaminant /～源 source of pollution
【污辱】① humiliate; insult ② defile sully
【污水】foul water; slop; sewage: ～净化 *sewage purification* /城市～ *municipal sewage* /生活～ *domestic sewage* /～处理 *sewage disposal* /～灌溉 *sewage irrigation* /～排放标准 *sewage discharge standard*
【污水坑】cesspit
【污损】dirty and destroy; damage: ～某人的名声 *defile one's repute*
【污浊】dirty; muddy; foul: ～的河流 *muddy river*
【污渍】stain; greasy filth

巫 shaman; witch
【巫婆】witch; sorceress
【巫师】doctor; wizard; sorcerer
【巫术】witchcraft; black art; sorcery
【巫医】witch doctor; medicine man

呜 toot; hoot; zoom: 那辆大汽车一路～～地开了过去。*The big car purred along the road.*
【呜呼】① alas; alack ② die: 一命～ *give up the ghost; kick the bucket*
【呜呼哀哉】① alas ② dead and gone; all is lost
【呜咽】① sob; whimper: 生病的孩子～地哭了。*The sick child whimpered.* ② (of wind, stream, stringed instrument, etc.) mourn; wail; weep

钨 tungsten; wolfram (w)
【钨钢】wolfram steel; tungsten steel
【钨砂】tungsten ore
【钨丝】tungsten filament: ～灯 *tungsten lamp*

诬 accuse; falsely; slander
【诬谤】slander; smear
【诬告】frame; false accusation; trump up a charge against: ～案件 *trumped-up case; frame-up*
【诬害】injure by spreading false reports about; false reports about
【诬控】bring a false charge against; trump up a charge against
【诬赖】falsely incriminate: ～好人 *incriminate innocent people*
【诬蔑】slander; vilify; smear; malign; besmirch; heap abuse on; mud slinging
【诬陷】frame-up; frame a case against sb: 他被真正的罪犯所～,结果成了罪恶与不公正的牺牲品。*He was framed by the real criminals and became the victim of the evil and injustice.*
【诬指】bring a false charge against

屋 ① house: 草～ *thatched house* ② room: 里～ *inner room* /外～ *outer room*
【屋场】[方] hamlet; village
【屋顶】roof; housetop: ～花园 *roof garden*
【屋脊】ridge of a roof
【屋架】roof truss
【屋面】【建】roofing
【屋舍】house; building
【屋檐】eaves
【屋子】room: 她怒冲冲地离开了～。*She flounced out of the house.*

wú

无 ① not have; be without; have nothing or nil: 一～所有 *have nothing at all* /学～止境。*There is no limit to learning.* ② not un-: ～足轻重 *insignificant; negligible* ③ *regardless of; irrespective of; on matter whether*: 国～大小,一律平等。*All nations, big or small, are equal.* ④ do not; must not
【无比】incomparable; unparalleled; matchless: ～的幸福 *height of happiness* /～的优越性 *incomparable superiority* /～的幸福 *furiously indignant*
【无边】borderless; vast: 黑暗～的天空 *the dark immense of air* /～落木萧萧下。*Ceaselessly, rustling leaves are falling.*
【无边无际】boundless; vast; limitless: ～的黑暗 *limitless darkness* /～大草原 *a vast expanse of llano*
【无柄叶】【植】sessile leaf
【无病呻吟】adopt a sentimental pose; make a fuss about an imaginary illness
【无补】of no avail; of no avail; do not help matter: 空言～画饼不能充饥。*Mere words will not fill a bushel.*
【无不】without exception; invariably: ～为之感动。*None were unmoved.*
【无产阶级】proletariat: ～先锋队 *the proletarian vanguard* /～专政 *proletarian dictatorship*
【无产者】proletarian: 全世界～,联合起来! *Workers of the word, unite!*
【无常】① variable; changeable; impermanence: 出尔反尔,反复～ *blow hot and cold (about)* ② pass away; die: 一旦～,如何是好? *When death comes, how can I do?*
【无偿】gratuitous; free; gratis: 提供～经济援助 *render economic assistance gratis; give free economic aid* /～服务 *service without remuneration*
【无成】achieve nothing; unfulfilled: 一事～ *accomplish nothing*
【无耻】cheekiness; brazen; impudent; shameless: ～诡计 *a barefaced trick* /～之徒 *a person with no sense of shame*
【无出其右】matchless; be unexcelled by no one; have nothing superior to; unequalled
【无从】have no way (of doing sth); be not in a position to: ～下手 *not know where to start* /那个小偷的陈述～证明。*The statement of the thief is not susceptible of proof.*
【无道】*be without principles; brutal; cruel; tyrannical*: ～的昏君 *an brutal emperor*
【无敌】unmatched; unconquerable; invincible: ～的军队 *an unbeaten army* /～于天下 *unmatched*

W

anywhere in the world

【无底洞】bottomless abyss; bottomless cavern: 战争把许多英雄吞进了它的～。*The war swallowed up many heroes into its maw.*

【无地自容】can find no place to hide oneself for shame; feel too ashamed to show one's face: 面对老师的斥责我感到～。*I stood abashed at teacher's rebuke.*

【无的放矢】shoot at random; discharge one's pistol in the air; shoot an arrow without a target: 训导要有针对性，不要～。*Education should have an aim; it shouldn't be undirected.*

【无动于衷】emotionless; unconcerned; unmoved; untouched; turn a deal ear to: 当朋友遇到困难的时候，我们不能～。*We can not remain indifferent when our friends are in difficulty.*

【无独有偶】it is not unique; do not come singly, but in pairs

【无毒不丈夫】ruthlessness is the mark of a truly great man

【无度】immoderate; excessive: 挥霍～ *squander wantonly* / 荒淫～ *excessive debauchery*

【无端】unprovoked; for no reason at all: ～的恐惧 *idle fears* / ～生事 *willfully make trouble*

【无恶不作】stop at nothing in doing evil; do not shrink from any crimes; stop at no evil: 除谋杀外，他们～。*They would commit every crime short of murder.*

【无法】unable; no way; no means of; incapable: ～履行 *unable to fulfill* / 你可以把马牵到水边，但你～强迫它饮水。*You can take a horse to water, but you cannot make him drink.*

【无法无天】without law and order; defy all laws; become absolutely lawless; run wild: ～的匪徒 *a lawless, ungovernable mobster*

【无方】in the wrong way; do not know how; not in the proper way: 经营～ *mismanage*

【无妨】there's no harm; may as well; might as well: 但说～。*Feel free to speak without apprehension.*

【无非】nothing but; only; no more than; simply: 他所说的～是老生常谈而已。*What he has said is a mere commonplace.*

【无风】calm; windless

【无风不起浪】there are no waves without wind; there is no smoke without fire

【无干】have nothing to do with: 这事与你～。*It is none of your business.*

【无根据】unfounded; groundless; without foundation

【无功受禄】get a reward without deserving it; one without merit receives emoluments

【无辜】① harmless; innocent: ～百姓 *innocent people* / ～的难民 *innocent refugee* ② an innocent person

【无故】without cause or reason: ～旷课 *stay away from school* / ～打人 *strike people without provocation*

【无关】have nothing to do with: 故事里与正题～的情节 *extraneous events in a story* / ～紧要 *neither here nor there* / ～痛痒 *matter of no consequence; superficial*

【无官一身轻】happy is the man who is relieved of his official duties

【无害】harmless; inoffensive; innocuous

【无后】without male offspring; without issue

【无花果】【植】fig

【无华】simple and unadorned: 文章朴实～ *written in a simple style*

【无机】【化】inorganic: ～化学 *inorganic chemistry* / ～物 *inorganic matter* / ～盐 *inorganic salts*

【无稽之谈】fantastic talk; baseless gossip; sheer nonsense; story made out of the whole cloth: 这种～不可信。*Such nonsense is not worth believing.*

【无及】it's too late (to do): 追悔～ *too late to repent*

【无疾而终】come to an eventual end

【无几】① very few; hardly ②［书］not long afterwards; soon after: 屈指可数，寥寥～ *can be counted on the fingers of one hand*

【无计可施】be at one's wits' end; at the end of one's rope

【无际】boundless; infinite: 一望～ *stretch as far as the eye can see*

【无济于事】of no avail; will not mend matters: 事到如今，后悔也～。*It is useless regretting at this late time.*

【无价之宝】priceless treasure; invaluable asset

【无坚不摧】be all-conquering; carry all before one

【无间】① very close to each other; do not keep anything from each other: 这对小两口亲密～。*The young couple are very close to each other.* ② continuously; without interruption: 勤学苦练，寒暑～。*Study diligently and practice hard all the year round.* ③ unable to distinguish; make no difference

【无疆】endless; limitless; boundless

【无节制】incontinency

【无尽无休】ceaseless; endless; incessant: ～的灾难 *endless disaster*

【无精打采】dispirited; downcast: 不要遇到困难就～。*Do not feel listless if you are in trouble.*

【无拘无束】be free and easy; unrestrained: ～地各抒己见 *express one's views freely*

【无菌】【生】germ-free; aseptic: ～隔离室 *germ-free isolation unit* / ～培养基 *axenic culture medium*

【无可比拟】unrivalled; unparalleled; unmatched: ～的优惠条件 *incomparable advantages*

【无可非议】blameless; beyond reproach; above criticism: 他的做法～。*What he has done is beyond reproach.*

【无可厚非】give no cause for much criticism

【无可讳言】undeniable; past dispute; there is no denying the fact: 这些都是～的证据。*All these are undeniable evidence.*

【无可奈何】helpless; have no alternative; have no way out; be utterly hopeless: ～花落去 *flowers will die, do what one may*

【无可无不可】not care one way or the other:对原则问题不应采取~的态度。*One should not take an indifferent attitude towards questions of principle.*

【无可争辩】indisputable; unquestionable; incontestable:~的能力 *undeniable ability*

【无可置疑】indubitable; unquestionable:~的事实 *incontrovertible facts*

【无孔不入】(of odours, ideas, etc.) be all-pervasive; make one's way into every nook and coners; seize every opportunity to do evil

【无愧】feel no qualms; be worthy of; have a clear conscience:他问心~。*He had a clear conscience.* /问心~,高枕无忧。*A good conscience is a constant feast.*

【无赖】① shamelessly ② naughty; mischievous:一群~ *a group of rowdies*

【无礼】rude; impolite; insolent

【无理】① unreasonable; outrageous; unwarranted; unjustifiable: ~挑衅 *unjustifiable provocation* / ~要求 *unreasonable demand* / ~指责 *unwarranted accusations* ②【数】irrational: ~数 *irrational number* / ~方程 *irrational equation* / ~根 *irrational root* / ~函数 *irrational function*

【无力】① beyond one's power; unable; incapable feel weak:病愈后他感到虚弱~。*He felt weak after illness.* ② powerless; feel weak; incapable; unable:这个任务我~完成。*It is not in my power to accomplish this task.*

【无量】① boundless; limitless; measureless ② numerous

【无聊】① bored; dull ② silly; senseless: ~的故事 *senseless tales*

【无虑】① more or less ② worry about nothing; consider about nothing

【无论】① no matter what ② don't say: ~用哪一种方法做,结果都相同。*It has the same result, whichever way you do it.*

【无论如何】however; in any case; whatever happens; right or wrong; anyway; anyhow: ~,我今天要完成这件事。*Anyhow I must finish this job today.*

【无米之炊】a meal without rice — impossible for lacking the most essentials; make bricks without straw:巧妇难为~。*One cannot make a silk purse out of a sow's ear.*

【无名】① anonymous; nameless:一座~墓 *a nameless grave* ② indefinable; indescribable:我为~的恐慌所控制。*I was seized by a nameless horror.*

【无名氏】anonymous people; anonymous person

【无名小卒】nowhere; nobody

【无名英雄】unknown hero; unsung hero: ~英雄纪念碑 *monument to the unknown warriors*

【无奈】① have no choice; cannot help but:出于~,我只得同意。*I had no alternative but to agree.* ② however; but; unfortunately: ~,他不了解我的难处。*Unfortunately he cannot understand my difficulty.*

【无能】disablement; inept; incapable:缺乏决断是~的表现。*Indecisiveness is a sign of incompetence.*

【无能为力】powerless; can do nothing about it:这件事,我~。*That is beyond my power.*

【无能之辈】impotent persons

【无期徒刑】be sentenced for life; life imprisonment:该凶犯被判~。*The murderer received a life sentence.*

【无奇不有】nothing is too strange in the world; there is no lack of strange things

【无牵无挂】have no cares; free from worldly

【无前】① invincible; unconquerable; unmatched:一往~ *press forward with indomitable courage* ② unprecedented:成绩~ *unprecedented achievement*

【无巧不成书】it is coincidence that makes a story:真是~。说曹操,曹操到。*What a coincidence! Talk of the devil, and here he is now.*

【无情】① ruthlessly ② mercilessly; heartless; inexorable: ~的打击 *a merciless blow* / ~的事实 *harsh reality* /法律是~的。*Law is inexorable.*

【无穷】infinite; boundless; endless; interminable: ~的差距 *boundless difference* / ~的忧虑 *endless worries*

【无穷大】infinitely great quantity; infinity

【无穷尽】inexhaustible

【无穷小】infinitesimal; infinitely small quantity

【无缺】intact; complete

【无人不知】to a proverb; there is no one but knows it

【无人问津】have no bidders; be nobody's business; nobody cares to ask sth; not be attended to by anybody:这个领域几乎~。*Almost no one seems to have taken any interest in this field.*

【无日】① every day: ~不在思念中 *have always been in one's thoughts* ② before long; soon

【无伤大雅】have only unimportant defects and do not affect the whole; involves no major principle and do not matter much:有时他虽然有些粗鲁,但~。*Sometimes he is clownery, but that does not matter much.*

【无上】the highest; supreme; paramount: ~的荣耀 *the highest glory* / ~的权威 *supreme authority*

【无神论】atheism: ~者 *atheist*

【无声】silent; noiseless: ~手枪 *pistol with a silencer* / ~即同意。*Silence gives consent.*

【无声无息】unknown; obscure:不甘心~地过一辈子 *not to want to remain obscure in life*

【无绳电话】cordless phone

【无师自通】learn sth without teacher; learn sth by oneself

【无时无刻】constantly; at all times; never for a moment:我们~不想念你。*You are in our minds all the time.*

【无视】overlook; ignore: ~别国主权 *disregard the sovereignty* / ~敌人的恐吓 *ignore the enemy's threat* / ~法纪 *defy law and discipline*

【无事不登三宝殿】would not go to sb's place except on business, for help, etc.; only goes to the temple when one is trouble

W

【无事忙】busy with unimportant matter; bustle about without accomplishing

【无事生非】make trouble out of nothing; be deliberately provocative:真是~! *What a fuss about nothing!*

【无殊】have no difference; just the same

【无数】① countless; numberless; innumerable: ~的敌人 *countless enemies* ② be uncertain; do not know for certain:任务是否会及时完成,我心中~。*I am not too sure whether I can accomplish that task in time.*

【无双】alone; matchless; unparalleled:盖世~ *absolutely unrivalled*

【无霜】frostless: ~期 *frost-free period*

【无水】【化】anhydrous: ~酒精 *absolute alcohol* / ~溶剂 *anhydrous solvent* / ~酸 *anhydrous acid*

【无私】selflessness; disinterested: ~无畏 *be selfless and fearless*

【无私有弊】be vulnerable to suspicion even without corrupt practice in a troubled place

【无损】① unaffected; be harmless:争吵~于任务的完成。*Dispute is not detrimental to the accomplishment of task.* ② undamaged; intact:完好~ *remain intact*

【无所不能】omnipotent; very capable:琴棋书画,~ *be equally adept in music, chess, calligraphy, and painting*

【无所不为】stop at nothing; do all manner of evil:叛逆者杀人放火,~。*Killing and burning, the traitors stopped at nothing.*

【无所不在】omnipresent; ubiquitous

【无所不知】be omniscient; know everything

【无所不至】① penetrate everywhere; pervade:妈妈对儿子的关怀,~。*Mother takes care of her son practically everywhere.* ② spare no pains (to de evil); stop at nothing:威胁利诱,~ *use intimidation, bribery and every other means*

【无所忌讳】has nothing to fear

【无所事事】be occupied with nothing; be at loose ends; idle away one's time; have nothing to do:游手好闲,终日~ *fool around all day without doing a stroke of decent work*

【无所适从】not know what course to take

【无所畏惧】fearless; dauntless; bold

【无所谓】① indifferent; it does not matter if:有些事情是~对错的。*Some things cannot be designated as right or wrong.* ② care nothing; be indifferent:参不参加,我~。*I don't really care whether attend or not.*

【无所用心】not give serious thought to anything

【无所作为】be in a state of inertia; attempt nothing and accomplish nothing

【无题】no title: ~诗 *poem without a title*

【无条件】unconditional; unreserved; with no strings attached: ~投降 *unconditional surrender* / ~服从 *unconditional obedience* / ~反射 *unconditioned reflex*

【无头案】a case without any clues; an unsolved mystery

【无土栽培】【农】soil-less cultivation

【无往不利】be ever-successful; carry all before one; all water runs to one's mill:拥有了丰富的知识,就会~。*In possession of abundance knowledge you will succeed wherever you go.*

【无往不胜】ever-victorious; be invincible at all times

【无望】hopeless; impossible:这消息使和平~。*The news brings little promise of peace.*

【无微不至】in every possible way; meticulously:现在大多数国家的儿童受到~的关怀。*The children have the best of care in most of the countries now.*

【无为】do nothing; letting things take their own course:清静~ *living in seclusion and doing nothing* / ~而治 *govern by noninterference*

【无味】① tasteless; unpalatable: ~的食物 *bland food* / 食之~,弃之可惜。*It is unappetizing and yet one would hesitate to throw it away.* ② dull; uninteresting; insipid:枯燥~ *dry as dust* / 平淡~ *flat and uninteresting*

【无畏】fearless:大~的革命精神 *dauntless revolutionary spirit*

【无谓】meaningless; pointless; senseless: ~的牺牲 *a meaningless sacrifice* / ~的争吵 *a pointless quarrel*

【无物】empty; without content:言之~ *empty talk* / 空洞~ *devoid of content*

【无误】all correct; no mistake:准确~ *accurate and correct* / 核查~ *checked and found correct*

【无隙可乘】no crack to get in by; no chink in sb's armour; no loophole to exploit; no weakness to take advantage of

【无暇】have no time to; too busy: ~过问 *have no time to attend to it* / ~理会 *too busy to attend*

【无瑕】immaculate; flawless:完美~ *flawless* / 白璧~ *flawless white jade*

【无限】infinite; immeasurable; boundless limitless: ~自由 *absolute liberty* / ~忠诚 *absolute loyalty* / ~愤慨 *unbridled indignation*

【无限期】indefinite duration: ~罢工 *a strike of indefinite duration* / ~休学 *suspend one's schooling indefinitely*

【无限制】unrestricted; unbridled; unlimited

【无线电】radio; wireless:拍发~报 *to send a message by radio* / 通过~收听音乐 *listen to music by radio* / ~传真 *radiophotography* / ~导航 *radio navigation* / ~发射机 *radio transmitter* / ~干扰 *radio jamming* / ~跟踪 *radio tracking* / ~电话 *radiotelephone* / ~收音机 *radio receiver* / ~通信 *radio communication; wireless communication* / ~侦察 *radio reconnaissance; reconnaissance by radio*

【无效】vitiation; null and void; invalid; of no avail:医治~ *fail to respond to medical treatment* / 宣布决议~ *declare a decision invalid* / ~劳动 *fruitless labour; labour lost*

【无邪】unaffected; innocent

【无懈可击】leaving no room for criticism; unassailable; invulnerable:他的非凡厨艺,~。*His ex-*

traordinary cuisine is unassailable.

【无心】① not be in the mood for: ~恋战 have no desire to continue fighting / ~工作 in no mood to work ② inadvertently; unwittingly: ~的过失 unwitting defect

【无行】villainous; immoral in conduct

【无形】invisible; imperceptibly: ~贸易 invisible trade / ~资本 incorporeal capital / ~损耗 invisible or intangible depreciation

【无形之中】virtually; imperceptibly: ~,我们成了合作伙伴。Imperceptibly, the relationship between us became symbiosis.

【无性】without sex or sex organs; asexual: ~繁殖 vegetative propagation / ~生殖 asexual reproduction / ~世代 asexual generation / ~杂交 asexual hybridization

【无休止】ceaseless; endless: ~的谈论衣服 endless tattle about dress

【无须】need not; not have to: ~顾虑 need not worry

【无涯】boundless; infinite: ~的沙漠 endless desert

【无烟区】smokeless zone

【无言以对】have nothing to say in reply; no know what to say in reply

【无恙】safe; good health; well; secure:安然~ safe and sound /上次我们相见后你一定~。I trust everything has been getting on well with you since we met last time.

【无业】① jobless; be out of work ② propertyless: ~游民 vagrant; deadbeat

【无依无靠】have no one to depend on; be helpless: ~的流浪汉 a helpless vagrant

【无遗】without residue; nothing left:暴露~ be thoroughly exposed

【无疑】beyond doubt; sure; certain; doubtless; undoubtedly:她~是家里最聪明的女孩子。She is easily the cleverest girl in the family.

【无已】① ceaseless; no end of:夸奖~ cry up again and again ② have to; have no choice but

【无以复加】the last word; be in the extreme; in the extreme: 荒唐到了~的地步 absurd in the extreme

【无异】the same as; be tantamount to differ in no way from:这件复制品几乎与原著~。The reproduction is almost as good as the original.

【无益】be no good; useless; unprofitable: ~的争论 a barren argument

【无意】① have no intention of (doing sth); not be inclined: ~参与 have no intention to participate in / ~退出 have no intention to exit ② by chance; not deliberately; unwittingly: ~发现一个古墓 discover a tumulus by accident

【无意识】unconscious: ~的动作 unconscious movements

【无垠】oceanic; vast; boundless:一望~的沙漠 a boundless desert

【无影无踪】vanish without a trace; disappear completely:他逃得~。He got clear away.

【无庸】need not: ~的证据 undoubtedly evidence

【无用】feckless; of no use; useless

【无忧无虑】be free from care; carefree; worriless: 很少人是~的。Few people are free from care.

【无余】completely; nothing left:一览~ take in everything at one glance

【无与伦比】incomparable; unique; without parallel: ~的功绩 unique achievement / ~的文物 incomparable cultural relic

【无源之水,无本之木】(like) water without a source, or a tree without roots

【无原则】involving no principle: ~的纠纷 dispute over trivial matter

【无缘】① without luck by which people are brought together: ~相识 be destined not to make sb's acquaintance ② have no way of (doing sth)

【无缘无故】uncalled-for; without reason or cause; for no reason at all: ~的争吵 get into dispute for no reason at all

【无援】unsupported; without aid or support:孤立~ be isolated and cut off from support

【无韵诗】blank verse

【无照】without a licence: ~驾驶 driving without a licence

【无政府主义】① anarchism ② undisciplined behaviour or idea

【无知】unacquaintance; ignorant: ~的人开导更~的人 the blind leading the blind /对某事全然~ sheer ignorance of sth

【无止境】unending; have no limits; know no end: 学~。There's no end to learning.

【无中生有】make sth out of nothing; be purely fabricated; be fictitious: ~的谣言 fabricated rumour

【无着落】without assured source:事业~ have one's business unassured

【无资格】disablement

【无足轻重】insignificant; of little moment; small-time: ~的人物 a nonentity / ~的比赛 match of little consequence

【无阻】without hindrance; unblocked: 风雨~ regardless of the weather

【无罪】be not guilty; a innocent: 该囚犯被宣告~。The prisoner was cleared.

毋 not; no: ~因小失大。Do not try to save a little at the expense of a lot.

【毋宁】rather... (than):他~死而决不受侮辱。He will die before he shall disgrace himself.

【毋庸】need not

芜 ① be overgrown with weeds ② (of writings) mixed and disorderly

【芜秽】overgrown with weeds; be unattended:荒凉~ desolate and overgrown with weeds

【芜菁】turnip

【芜杂】mixed and disorderly; jumbled

吾 I or me; we or us: 一日三省~身。I examine myself three times a day.

【吾辈】we; us

【吾人】[书] we; us

梧

【梧桐】Chinese parasol (tree); phoenix tree

蜈 centipede

【蜈蚣】【动】centipede

鼯

【鼯鼠】【动】flying squirrel

wǔ

五 five: ～官 *five senses* / ～行 *the five elements*

【五保】the five guarantees in Chinese rural areas, namely, food, clothing, medical care, housing and burial expenses: ～户 *household (of infirm and childless old people) enjoying the five guarantees*

【五彩】① multicoloured: ～缤纷 *be gandy with primary colours; colour; colourful* ② the five colours (blue, yellow, red, white and black)

【五大三粗】strapping; tall and stalwart

【五毒】the five poisonous creatures of scorpion, viper, centipede, house lizard and toad: ～俱全 *addicted to drinking, smoking, etc.*

【五更】① the five periods of the night ② before dawn; the fifth watch just before dawn: 起～,睡半夜 *retire at midnight and rise before dawn*

【五谷】the five cereals of rice, two kinds of millet ,wheat and leans: ～丰登 *horn of abundance*

【五官】① facial features; ② five sense organs of ears, eyes, lips, nose and tongue: 端正的～ *regular features*

【五光十色】painted; multicolored; of all hues and colours

【五湖四海】all corners of the land; all parts of the country: 来自～的英雄 *heroes from all over the country*

【五花八门】of a wide variety; multifarious; kaleidoscopic

【五花大绑】have one's hands and arms tied behind one's back; bind the criminal hand and foot with ropes

【五花肉】streaky pork

【五荤】the five vegetables with a peculiar smell

【五讲四美】Five stresses and Four points of Beauty

【五角大楼】Pentagon Building (headquarters of the US Department of Defence)

【五角星】pentacle; five-pointed star

【五金】hardware; five metals of gold, silver, copper, iron and tin: ～器具 *hardware*

【五经】the Five Classics — *The Book of Changes* (易), *Collection of Ancient Texts* [书], *The Books of Songs* (诗), *The Rites* (礼), *and The Spring and Autumn Annals* (春秋)

【五律】an eight-line poem with five characters to a line and a strict tonal pattern and rhyme scheme

【五马分尸】tear a body limb from limb; cruel punishment of dismembering the criminal's body by five horses

【五色】five colours of blue, yellow, red, white and black

【五体投地】adulate; prostrate oneself before sb in admiration: 对某人～ *prostrate oneself before sb*

【五味】the five flavour (sour, bitter, sweet, pungent and salty)

【五线谱】staff; stave; score

【五星红旗】Five-Star Red Flag; national flag of the People's Republic of China

【五行】① five elements (metal, wood, water, fire and earth) ② the five constant virtues: ～相克。*The five elements subdue one another.*

【五颜六色】of various colours; with all colours of rainbow; multicolored; colourful: 金刚石在阳光下放出～的光芒。*The diamond stone is with every hue under the sun.*

【五音】① the five notes of the ancient Chinese five-tone scale ② the five initial consonants (of Chinese syllables)

【五脏】five internal organs — heart, liver, spleen, lungs and kidneys

【五指】five fingers — thumb, index finger, middle finger, third or ring finger and little finger: 伸手不见～ *so dark that you can't see your own fingers*

【五洲】the five continents; all over the world

【五子棋】gobang

午 ① noon; midday ② the seventh of the twelve Earthly Branches

【午安】good-afternoon

【午餐】lunch; midday meal: ～肉 *luncheon*

【午饭】lunch; midday meal

【午后】afternoon

【午间】at noon; midday: ～新闻 *midday news*

【午觉】afternoon nap; siesta

【午门】front gate

【午前】in the morning; before noon

【午时】the period of the day from 11 a. m. to 1 p. m.

【午睡】① siesta; afternoon nap; noontime snooze ② take or have a nap after lunch

【午休】noon break; mid-day rest

【午宴】feast at noon; luncheon

【午夜】midnight

伍 ① basic five-man unit of the army in ancient China; army: 他应征入～。*He answered the call to arms.* ② company ③ five ④ (Wǔ) a surname

忤 ① unfilial ② on bad terms; uncongenial

【忤逆】disobedient (to one's parents): ～不孝 *filial impiety*

妩

【妩媚】lovely; charming: ～的女人 *a woman of great charm*

武 1 ① military; of military strength: ～力 *military strength; force* / 核～器 *nuclear weapon* ② (of) martial arts ③ bold and powerful; valiant, fierce; 威 ~ *valiant and majestic* ④ (Wǔ) a surname

武[2] footstep

【武打】 acrobatic fighting in Chinese operas or dances

【武旦】 actress playing a martial role

【武斗】 resort to violence; struggle by force of coercion; debate conducted by coercion

【武断】 arbitrary decision; subjective assertion; with high hand: ~的解释 *an arbitrary interpretation*

【武夫】 ① a brave and strong man ② man of valour: 一介 ~ *mere soldier*

【武工】 skill in acrobatics in Chinese operas: ~队 *armed working team*

【武功】 military accomplishments

【武官】 ① military attach ② officer: ~处 *military attache's office*

【武将】 military officer; general

【武警】 armed police

【武举】 military successful candidate in the imperial provincial examination

【武力】 ① violent force ② military force; armed might: 诉诸 ~ *resort to force* / ~侵占 *take by force*

【武林】 martial arts circles: ~高手 *master of martial arts*

【武器】 weapon; implements of warfare; military hardware: 常规 ~ *conventional weapon* / 激光 ~ *laser weapon* / 生物 ~ *biological weapon* / 辐射 ~ *radiation weapon* / 毒气 ~ *gas weapon* / ~交易 *arms deal*; *arms trade*

【武人】 soldier; army man

【武生】【戏】 man playing martial role

【武士】 ① samurai ② palace guards ③ man of prowess

【武术】 wushu, martial arts such as shadowboxing, swordplay, etc.: ~大师 *wushu master*; *master of martial arts* / ~表演 *wushu performance*; *martial arts show*

【武侠】 a person adept in martial arts and given to chivalrous conduct (in olden times): ~小说 *tales of roving knights*; *swordsman fiction*

【武艺】 ① skill in wushu ② martial arts

【武装】 ① arm ② arms; military equipment; battle outfit ③ equip (or supply) with arms: ~起来, 对付危险 *arm oneself against danger* / ~部队 *armed forces* / ~冲突 *armed clash* / ~斗争 *armed struggle* / ~干涉 *armed intervention* / ~力量 *armed power*; *armed forces* / ~警察 *armed police* / ~起义 *armed uprising* / ~侵略 *armed aggression*

侮 insult; humiliate; bully

【侮骂】 abuse; call names

【侮蔑】 despise; show disdain; look down on

【侮辱】 insult; subject sb to indignity; humiliate

捂 seal; cover; muffle: ~住某人的嘴巴 *cover one's mouse with one's hand* / ~汗 *be heavily dressed in order to sweat*

【捂盖子】 cover up the truth

【捂捂盖盖】 keep from being known or seen: 男子汉从不 ~。*A man never covers up his mistake.*

舞 ① dance: 歌 ~ *song and dance* / 芭蕾 ~ *ballet* / 交际 ~ *ballroom dancing*; *social dancing* ② move about as if in a dance; dance: 眉飞色 ~ *(with) dancing eyes and radiant face* / 手 ~ 足蹈 *dance for joy* ③ dance with sth in one's hand: ~剑 *perform swordplay* ④ flourish; wave; brandish: 张牙 ~ 爪 *bare fangs and show paws* / 树叶迎风飘 ~。*The leaves were dancing in the wind.* ⑤ culture; civilization ⑥ play with: ~文弄墨 *show off one's literary skill*; *juggle with words*

【舞伴】 dancing partner

【舞弊】 engage in embezzlement; corrupt practices; fraudulent practice: 徇私 ~ *fraudulence (or cheating) for selfish purposes*

【舞步】 dancing step: 炫目 ~ *dazzle dancing step*

【舞场】 dance hall; ballroom

【舞池】 dance pool

【舞蹈】 dance: 古典 ~ *classical dance* / ~设计 *choreography* / ~音乐 *dance music*

【舞动】 brandish; wave

【舞会】 ball; dancing party; dance: 化妆 ~ *fancy dress ball*

【舞技】 dancing skill

【舞剧】 dance drama; ballet

【舞迷】 dance fan; habitual dancer

【舞弄】 ① make fun of; dupe ② brandish; wave; brandish: ~刀枪 *brandish swords and spears*

【舞女】 ① dancing girl; dance-hostess

【舞曲】 dance music; dance

【舞台】 stage; arena: ~效果 *stage effect* / ~生涯 *stage career* / ~艺术 *stagecraft* / ~设计 *stage design* / ~监督 *stage manager (or director)*; *stage* / 登上政治 ~ *come on the stage* / 国际 ~ *international arena* / 历史 ~ *stage of history*; *historical stage*

【舞厅】 dance hall; ballroom

【舞文弄墨】 engage in phrase-mongering

【舞艺】 dancing skill

【舞姿】 a dancer's movements and postures

wù

兀 ① rising to a height; lofty; towering ② (of a hill) barren bald

【兀傲】 ① proud ② haughty

【兀立】 stand upright

【兀然】 ① towering; suddenly ② dazed ③ still

【兀突】 unexpected

勿 (usu. used in imperative sentences) no; not; never: 请 ~ 停车。*No Parking.* / 请 ~ 喧哗。*Be quiet, please.*

【勿忘草】 forget-me-not (Myosotis sylvatica)

【勿以恶小而为之,勿以善小而不为】 do not engage in evil even if it is small; do not fail to do good even if it is small

戊 the fifth of the ten Heavenly Stems

务 ① task; affair; business ② apply oneself to; be engaged in; go in for ③ outpost of a tax office (now used as part of a place name) ④ must; be sure to: ~请莅临指导。*You are cordially invited to come and give guidance.* / ~必完成这件任务。*Be sure to finish the important task.*

【务必】must; be sure to; should: 你~按时完成作业。*You must finish your homework in time.*

【务工】① be engaged in industry or project ② throw in labour force

【务农】be engaged in agriculture; go in for agriculture; be a farmer

【务求】be sure to require; must: 此事~妥善解决。*We must find a satisfactory solution to the problem.*

【务实】① try to be practical ② discuss concrete matters: ~的领导 *a pragmatically-inclined leader*

【务使】make sure; see to it that: ~孩子们得到足够的食物。*Make sure that every child has enough food.*

【务须】must; should

坞 ① depressed area ② a fortified building; castle

物 ① thing; creature; material ② outside world as distinct from oneself; people other than oneself ③ content; essence

【物产】product; produce

【物归原主】return sth to its rightful owner; render unto Caesar the things which are Caesar's-Bible

【物换星移】change of the seasons; things change with the passing of years

【物极必反】things will develop in the opposite direction when they become extreme; no extreme will hold long

【物价】commodity price: 调整~ *adjust prices* / 稳定~ *stabilize prices* / 哄抬~ *jack up prices* / ~失控 *prices get out of control* / ~上涨 *inflation of price* / ~政策 *pricing policy* / ~指数 *price index*

【物件】object; article

【物尽其用】make the best use of every person and thing; let all things serve their proper purposes

【物竞天择】survival of the fittest in natural selection

【物镜】【物】objective lens

【物理】①［书］innate laws of things ② physics: 应用~ *applied physics* / ~变化 *physical change* / ~化学 *physical chemistry* / ~疗法 *physical therapy* / ~性质 *physical diagnosis*

【物理学】physics: 低温~ *low temperature physics* / 地球~ *geophysics* / 高能~ *high energy physics* / 理论~ *theoretical physics* / 天体~ *astrophysics* / 应用~ *applied physics* / 原子~ *atomic physics* / ~家 *physicist*

【物力】material resources; material: 节约人力~ *use manpower and material resources sparingly*

【物美价廉】of excellent quality and reasonable price; cheap and fine

【物料】goods and materials

【物品】article; goods: 贵重~ *valuables* / 廉价~ *cheap goods* / 免税~ *duty-free articles* / 私人~ *personal belongings* / 违禁~ *contraband* / 自用~ *personal effects*

【物情】① principle ② human feelings ③ popular feeling

【物色】① look for; choose; seek out ② scenery ③ odds and ends

【物态】【物】state of matter

【物体】object; substance; body: 悬浮~ *suspending body* / 液态~ *liquid substance*

【物外】［书］above or outside worldly things

【物物交换】barter

【物像】① reflection; image ② visible phenomena

【物业】real estate; property: ~管理 *property management*

【物以类聚】things of one kind come together; like draws to like the world over; birds of a feather flock together

【物欲】desire for material wealth; human desire; material desire

【物证】material evidence

【物质】① objective reality; matter; substance: ~形态有三种:气体、液体和固体。*All matter has one of three forms: gas, liquid and solid.* ② material: ~不灭定律 *the law of conservation of matter* / ~财富 *material wealth* / ~刺激 *material incentive* / ~鼓励 *material reward* / ~基础 *material base* / ~生活 *material life* / ~条件 *material wealth* / ~世界 *the material world* / ~文明 *material civilization* / ~享受 *material comforts* / ~资料 *material goods*

【物种】【生】species

【物主】owner of lost property

【物资】goods and materials: ~调度 *distribution of materials* / ~管理 *handling of goods and materials* / ~循环利用 *the recycle of materials* / ~交流 *interflow of commodities* / ~运输 *transportation of materials*

误 ① wrong; mistake; error: 失~ *fire into the wrong flock* ② miss; delay: ~了航班 *miss the scheduled flight* / 磨刀不~砍柴工。*Deliberating is not delaying.* ③ harm; damage: 聪明反被聪明~。*Clever people may fall victim to their own cleverness.* ④ by mistake; accidentally: ~认 *take someone for*

【误差】mistake; error: 累计~ *accumulated error* / 绝对~ *absolute error* / 平均~ *mean error* / 系统~ *system error* / ~不超过百万分之一秒 *with a tolerance of less than one second of a million*

【误场】absent on the stage; miss a performance

【误车】① (of cars) behind schedule; be delayed ② miss the train or the bus

【误传】misrepresent

【误打误撞】accidentally

【误导】mislead; lead astray

【误点】behind schedule; late; behind time:火车~了。*The train is overdue.*
【误工】① delay one's work ② be absent or late for work; loss of working time
【误国】do harm to one's country
【误会】mistake; misunderstand; misconstrue:他对这事有~。*He is under a delusion in this matter.*
【误解】① misunderstand; misread:有被~的可能 *open to misconstruction* ② misunderstanding:消除~ *clear up a misunderstanding*
【误期】delay; miss the deadline:你的试验~了。*Your experiment is behind schedule.*
【误人子弟】lead young people astray; mislead and harm the young people
【误杀】manslaughter
【误伤】accidentally injure
【误事】cause delay in work of business; spoil matters
【误听】wrongly believe what one hears
【误信】believe by mistake
【误用】misapply
【误诊】① make a wrong diagnosis ② delay the diagnosis

恶 ① dislike; loathe; detest; hate ② aversion:个人好~ *one's likes and dislikes*
see also ě; è
【恶寒】aversion to cold

悟 realize; become aware; awaken:执迷不~ *obstinately stick to a wrong course* / ~出一个好主意 *realize a good idea*
【悟彻】comprehend completely; awake to the truth
【悟道】grasp the truth
【悟解】comprehend; grasp; understand
【悟性】understanding; comprehension

晤 meet; encounter; interview
【晤见】meet with; interview
【晤面】meet; see; interview
【晤商】meet and discuss
【晤谈】meet and talk

焐 warm up:先~~手,再吃晚饭。*Warm up your hand before you have the dinner.*

雾 ① fog; mist:烟~ *smog* / 大~ *heavy fog* ② fine spray:喷~器 *sprayer*
【雾霭】frog; mist; vapour
【雾标】frog buoy
【雾沉沉】heavy fog; covered by mist or fog:天气~的,我几乎什么都看不到。*It was very foggy; I can hardly see anything.*
【雾滴】droplet
【雾化】atomize aerosolize: ~器 *atomizer*
【雾里看花】have a blurred vision; admire the flowers while it is foggy
【雾茫茫】foggy; misty; hazy:道路~的,我不得不慢速开车。*The road was covered in thick mist, so I have to drove slowly.*
【雾气】vapour; mist; fog
【雾腾腾】heavy foggy:浴室里~的。*There was surging fog all around the bathroom.*

X

xī

夕 ① evening; night: 只争朝~ *seize the day, seize the hour; seize every second* ② sunset dusk: 朝令~改 *issue an order in the morning and rescind it in the evening — make changes in policy at will*

【夕辉】evening twilight; slanting rays of setting sun; brilliance of the sunset; sunlight at dusk

【夕暮】dusk; sunset; at nightfall

【夕烟】evening mist; mist: 袅袅~上升。*Evening smoke curled upward.*

【夕阳】setting sun: ~产业 *sunset industry; fading industry* / ~阳市场 *declining market; sunset market* / ~无限好, 只是近黄昏。*The setting sun was infinite lovely; only the dusk was too near.*

【夕照】evening glow; glow of the setting sun; reflected light s of sunset

兮 ①[书] express admiration: 归去来~。*Oh, come away home.* ② particle of pause (used in ancient poetry); still (used in eulogies): 风萧萧~易水寒。*Wind soughs and signs while the water in the Yishui River chills.*

西 ① west: 太阳从东边升起, 从~边落下。*The sun rises in the east and sets in the west.* ② the West; European; American; the occident

【西班牙】Spain: ~人 *Spaniard; Spanish; Spanish* / ~语 *Spanish* / ~内战 *Spanish Civil War* (1936-1939)

【西半球】Western Hemisphere

【西北】① northwest ② northwest China; the Northwest

【西北风】northwest wind

【西伯利亚】Siberia

【西部】the west; the western part: 教堂坐落在村~。*The church stands in the west of this village.*

【西餐】Western-style food; European meals; western food

【西点】① Western style pastries (dessert) ② West Point: ~军校毕业生 *West pointer*

【西方】① west: 日落~。*The sun sets in the west.* ② the West; the Occident: ~国家 *Western countries* ③ heaven; Buddhist paradise

【西风】① west wind; wester: 秋天常刮~。*The prevailing westerlies blow in autumn.* ② Western culture; West style; influences, customs, ways, etc. of the West: ~东渐。*The Western ways was extending to the East.* ③ decadent forces; decaying influences

【西风带】【地】westerlies

【西服】Western clothes; European or American attire; western suit: ~料 *suiting (for Western suit)*

【西宫】the imperial concubines; lesser wife of the King or emperor

【西瓜】watermelon: ~籽 *watermelon seeds*

【西海岸】western coast; the Western Coast of the United States

【西汉】Western Han Dynasty; earlier Han Dynasty

【西红柿】tomato

【西湖】West Lake, name of various lakes in a number of provinces, the most famous one is at Hangzhou

【西葫芦】【植】pumpkin; summer squash

【西化】westernize; westernization

【西经】【地】west longitude

【西南】southwest ② South West China

【西南风】southwest wind; southwesterly

【西晒】(of houses, rooms, etc.) facing west and exposed to the intensive heat of the afternoon sun

【西施】① name of a famous belle in the late Spring and Autumn Period ② beauty; belle; beautiful woman

【西式】Western-style; occidental style: ~糕点 *Western-style pastry*

【西太后】Empress Dowager Cixi, who ruled China as a regent toward the end of the 19th century

【西天】【宗】① India ② heaven; western Paradise

【西行】go west; travel west-ward: 孩子们沿河~。*The children went west along the river.*

【西学】Western learning (term used in the late Qing Dynasty for Western natural and social sciences)

【西雅图】Seattle, an American part and industrial city

【西亚】West Asia

【西洋】① the West; Western: ~文化 *Western culture* ② (a term used in the Yuan and Ming Dynasties) Western Seas i. e. seas and lands west of the South China Sea (west of longitude 1100E): 郑和七下~。*Zhenghe was seven voyages to the Western Seas* (1406—1433).

【西洋画】Western painting

【西洋镜】① peep show ② trickery; tricks; hanky-panky: 警察拆穿了骗子的~。*The policeman striped off the swindler's mask.*

【西洋人】Westerner

【西洋参】【药】American ginseng, panax quinquefolium
【西洋文学】Western literature
【西药】Western medicines
【西药房】pharmacy; pharmaceutical store
【西医】Western medicines; doctor practicing Western medicine
【西印度群岛】the West Indies, group of islands largely in the Caribbean Sea, extending from the coast of Florida in north America to that of Venezuela in south America
【西语】Western language
【西乐】Western music; European or American music:这个孩子喜欢~。*The kid likes to listen Western music.*
【西藏】Xizang; Tibet
【西藏自治区】the Tibet Autonomous Region
【西装】Western suit; western-style clothes

吸 ① inhale; draw; breathe in; respire:人类每天都要~新鲜空气。*The mankind need breathe in fresh air every day.* ② absorb; imbibe; suck up:海绵~收水分。*Sponge absorbs water.* ③ absorb; attract; draw to oneself:你感到她对你有~引力吗? *Do you feel attracted to her*? ④ absorb; digest:~取精华,剔除糟粕 *absorb essence and discard dross*
【吸尘器】vacuum clean; vacuum
【吸虫】fluke; trematode:肺~ *lung fluke* /~病 *distomiasis*; *trematodiasis*
【吸毒】drug addiction; be addicted to narcotics; freak-out; hit the pipe; smoke opium: ~者 *drug addict*; *drugger*; *druggy*; *junky*
【吸附】【化】absorption; absorb: ~汽油 *absorption gasoline* /~剂 *absorbent*; *absorbing agent*; *absorbing material* /~器 *absorber* /~水 *absorbed water* /~率 *absorption rate*
【吸根】【植】sucker; haustorium
【吸管】pipette; straw; suction pipe; sucker
【吸力】① attraction ②【物】gravitation: 地心~ *force of gravity*
【吸力计】suction gauge
【吸溜】[方] slurp:冻得直~ *be slurping with cold*
【吸盘】①【动】sucking disks; sucker ②【机】suction cup
【吸气】inhale: ~! 吐气! *Inhale! Exhale!*
【吸取】absorb; inhale; draw; assimilate: ~教训 *draw a lesson*; *learn a lesson* /那聪明的学生把老师所能教他的知识都~了。*The clever student absorbed all the knowledge his teachers could give him.* /种子从土壤中~水分。*Seeds suck to water from the soil.*
【吸热】absorption of heat
【吸入】① breathe in ② suction
【吸湿】moisture absorption; moisture-absorbing: ~剂 *absorbent*; *moisture absorbent*; *hygroscopic agent* /~性 *hygroscopic*; *moisture absorbency*
【吸食】suck; take in
【吸收】① absorb; take in; inhale; draw; imbibe; suck up; assimilate: ~知识 *absorb knowledge* /~营养 *suck up nutriment* ② recruit; enlist; admit; enrol; receive:她刚被团支部~为新成员。*She has just enlisted as a new member by the Communist Youth League branch.*
【吸收率】absorptivity
【吸吮】suckle; absorb
【吸筒】suction tube
【吸血鬼】vampire; blood-sucker; leech
【吸烟】smoke; smoking: ~有害健康。*Smoking is bad for your health.*
【吸引】attract; draw; fascinate; charm:孩子们被猴子所~。*Children were fascinated by the monkey.*

汐 night tide; evening tide; tide during the night:潮~ *tide*

希[1] hope; expect; wish; desire; long: ~望新年快乐! *Wish happy New Year*! /我~望明天下雪。*I hope it would snow tomorrow.*

希[2] ① rare; strange; precious; valuable: ~世珍宝 *rare treasure* ② uncommon: ~客 *uncommon guest*
【希伯来语】Hebrew (language)
【希贵】rare and precious; valuable
【希冀】[书] desire; wish; yearn for; expect; anticipate; aspire after:她~儿子将来能成为工程师。*She anticipated her son becoming an engineer.*
【希腊】Greece: ~语 *Greek* /~人 *Greek* /~文化 *Greek culture* /~教会 *Greek Orthodox church*
【希慕】long for; be desirous of:她~虚荣。*She was desirous of vanity.*
【希求】① hope to get: ~大家原谅 *hope to get pardon from all of us* ② wish; hope; expectation; anticipation:我们满足他的~。*We met his expectations.*
【希图】hope and scheme for; attempt to; try to
【希望】① hope; wish; expect: ~你生日快乐! *Wish you happy birthday*! /我们~每周都能见到你。*We hope to meet you every week.* ② hope; expectation; anticipation:所有的~都落空了。*All hope is gone.* ③ person or thing that is likely to bring success:儿子是他唯一的~。*His son is his only hope.*

昔 ① bygone; past; of old; former; previous: 今~ *present past*; *yesterday and today* /今~对比 *contrast the past with the present* /今非~比。*There is no comparing the present with the past.* ② a night; an evening:他通~不寐。*He couldn't sleep all night.*
【昔年】[书] bygone years; former years; the past
【昔人】the ancient people; people of the past; past generation
【昔日】past days; former times; in the olden days (or times):非典以后,村子又恢复了~的宁静。*The village regained its old still after SARS.*
【昔时】former times; (in) the olden days; past days:她是我~旧友,请像对我一样地关照她。*Please take care of her as much as you can, be-*

cause she is my old friend of mine.

【昔岁】last year; previous year

【昔者】[书] ① former times; past days; ancient times ② yesterday

析 ① split; rip or break apart; divide; separate:分崩离~*disintegrate*; *come apart* ② analyse; dissect; interpret:剖~*dissect*; *analyse*

【析出】①【化】separate out ② analyse; dissect

【析居】live separately

【析疑】explain a doubt; resolve a doubt; clear up a doubtful point; clarify an uncertainty:朱丽叶请老师为孩子们~解难。*Juliet invited teachers to explain the children's doubts.*

【析义】interpret the meaning (of a word):给出这词的~。*Please explain what this word means.*

唏 ①[书] sigh; sob ② express surprise

【唏嘘】sigh; sob: ~,作业终于做完了。*Hun! I had finally my homework.*

牺 [书] sacrifice; beast of uniform colour used for sacrifice

【牺牲】① a beast slaughtered for sacrifice; sacrifice; immolation ② give up; sacrifice; immolate; lay down one's life death:母亲会为了孩子~自己的生活。*A mother will sacrifice her life for her children.* ③ sacrifice oneself ④ expense; lay down one's life; die a martyr's death:他为国家~了。*He gave his life as a sacrifice for his country.*

【牺牲品】sacrifice; victim; sacrifice lamb prey:她是这场官司的~。*She was the victim of lawsuit.*

【牺尊】【考】wooden wine cup shaped like a cattle; ox-shaped drinking vessel

息 ① breath; pant: 窒~ *suffocate*; *choke* ② news; message:互通声~ *keep each other tidings* ③ end; stop; cease:风止雨~。*The wind stopped and the rain ended.* ④ rest; break:按时作~ *work and rest according to the timetable* ⑤ grow; breed; multiply:休养生~ *rest and improve strength* ⑥ interest (on money):无~贷款 *an interest-free loan* ⑦[书] one's own children ⑧ sigh:他叹~道:希望如此吧。*He said with a sigh: I wish so.* ⑨ calm down; get rid of; go out

【息兵】stop fighting; end hostilities; end hostilities; cease fire:偃鼓~ *call off the army maneuvers*; *cease or stop all military activities and lie low*

【息肩】① lay down the burden; put down one's burden; be relieved of a responsibility ② stay; dwell; stop:世界之大,无地~。*There is no place for dwelling in the world.*

【息怒】let one's anger cool off; clam one's anger; cease to be angry:请您~。*Please clam your anger.*

【息事宁人】① patch up a quarrel and reconcile the parties concerned; pour oil on troubled water ② give way to avoid trouble; settle one's disputes and bring about clam: 我们应~。*We should make concessions to avoid trouble.*

【息讼】end a lawsuit; stop litigation

【息息相关】be closely linked; be closely bound up; have much in common with:他们之间~。*They have much in common with each other.*

【息心】①[方] feel relieved; be at ease; set one's heart at rest:听说他没事啦,大家都~了。*All of us set our hearts at rest news that he had no worry.* ②[书] get rid of sundry ideas; dispel distracting thoughts (from one's mind): ~读书 *dispel distracting thoughts in studies*

【息影】retire from public life; live in retirement; go into seclusion

【息战】stop fighting; cease fire; end hostilities

【息止】stop; cease; end:地球永不~地转动。*The turn of the earth can't stop.*

奚 ①[书] why; how; what; which: ~可? *How can ?* ② servant: ~奴 *boy servant* ③ (Xī) surname

【奚落】laugh at; make a fool of; taunt; jeer at; scoff at; ridicule:不要~她,她受不了这样的~。*Don't jeer at her*; *she can't bear such ridicule.*

硒 【化】selenium(Se), non-metallic element

【硒电池】【化】selenium cell; selenium photocell; selenium conductive photocell

【硒鼓】【机】selenium-coated drum

【硒化物】【化】selenide

【硒酸】【化】selenic acid: ~盐 *selenate*

【硒中毒】【医】selenosis

悉[1] ① all; entirely; total; whole:文中错字,~以改正。*Please correct all the misspellings in the write.*

悉[2] know; understand; learn; be informed:来信收~。*Your letter has been received.* /据~,他离开了上海。*It is informed that he left Shanghai.*

【悉力】all one's strength ; might and main; do one's utmost: ~合作 *collaborate with all one's strength*

【悉尼】Sydney, the largest city of Australia

【悉数】① all; the entire sum: ~归公 *hand in everything to the public* ② enumerate in full detail; explain each point clearly

【悉听尊便】please:你去不去~。*Do just as you please.*

【悉心】with the entire mind; exercise the greatest care:护士~照料那个病人。*The nurse takes care for the patient.*

烯 ①【化】alkene ② the colour of fire

【烯醇】【化】enol

【烯烃】【化】alkene

淅 [书] wash rice

【淅沥】[象] rustle of falling leaves or rain; patter

【淅飒】[象] whistling (of wind, rain and snow); patter; rustle

惜 ① value highly; cherish; treasure:比尔非常珍~汤姆的友谊。*Bill values Tom's friend-*

ship. ② have pity on; regret; fell sorry for sh (sth):我们为她的离世感到惋~。*We felt sorry for her death.* ③ spare; grudge; stint:他不~冒险来救我。*He spared not for risk to help me.*

【惜别】be reluctant to part company; say goodbay; hate to see sb go; find it hard to take leave (of sb)

【惜寸阴】cherish or treasure every minute; harness one's time; be careful not to waste even a moment

【惜福】cherish one's good fortune; refrain from leading an excessively comfortable life; make sparing use of one's wealth; not waste when one has plenty

【惜老怜贫】pity the aged and the poor; care for the aged and sympathize with the poor; have compassion for the old and the poor: ~是中华民族的传统美德。*To take care of the aged and sympathize with the poor is traditional virtue of the Chinese nation.*

【惜力】be sparing of one's energy; contribute one's labour very reluctantly:他工作从不~。*He never spares himself in work.*

【惜怜】love and care for; pity; regret:他对女人充满~体贴。*He is filled with compassion for women.*

【惜墨如金】regard one's ink as if it were gold; grudge ink as if it were gold-reluctant (to write or paint):那位画师真是~。*That painter is really reluctant to paint.*

【惜玉怜香】be tender to the fair sex; be tender toward pretty girls:这样的人亦有~之情。*Such a man being boorish is tender toward pretty girls too.*

晰 clear; distinct; explicit:一张清~的照片 *a clear photograph*

稀 ① rare; scarce; unusual; uncommon:物以~为贵。*A thing is valuable if it is scarce.* ② thin (liquids, etc.); sparse: ~落 *sparse*; *scattered* / 叶少枝~ *few leaves and sparse branches* ③ watery; diluted:稀饭太~啦。*The porridge is too watery.* ④ very; extremely

【稀巴烂】smashed to pieces; broken to bits:那花瓶被砸得~。*The vase was smashed to pieces.*

【稀薄】rare; thin: ~空气 *thin air*

【稀饭】congee; gruel; porridge

【稀贵】rare and valuable

【稀罕】① rare; uncommon; unusual; scarce:一枚~的邮票 *a rare stamp* ② care; value; hold preciously:我们不~他的帮助。*We don't hold his help preciously.* ③ rare thing or sight; rarity:他从南方带回几条金鱼,让孩子们看~儿。*He brought back several goldfishes from the south as rare sight which the kids enjoy watching.*

【稀糊烂】① completely mashed; like paste; reduce to pulp; reduced to a paste:苹果捣得~。*Apples were reduced to a pulp.* ② completely crushed or routed:把对手打得~。*Rout antagonist completely.* ③ hard pressed; tired; weary; fatigue; toilsome:作业太多把学生们忙得~。*The assignment was so much that the students would be terribly busy.*

【稀货】rare commodity; scarcity; scare goods

【稀客】rare guest; rare visitor

【稀拉】① sparse; few and far between ②[方] careless; sloppy:他是一个~的人。*He is a sloppy man.*

【稀烂】completely; mashed; pulpy:鸡肉炖得~。*Chicken was cooked to a paste.*

【稀朗】(as of light or stars) a few scattered but bright:星光~ *a few scattered but bright stars*

【稀里呼噜】①[象] slurp; snore; stertorous sound ② be confused; casual; careless

【稀里糊涂】① not understanding; not knowing what one is about; at sea; ② careless; casual; thoughtless:任何人工作都不能~。*Anyone must never be thoughtless in the work.*

【稀里哗啦】①[象](in disorder, completely smashed) patter; crash; shore ② be smashed to pieces; be broke to bits

【稀奇】rare; peculiar; strange; curious

【稀溶液】【化】diluted element

【稀少】few; little; rare; scarce; hardly any

【稀世】rare on earth; precious

【稀释】dilute; attenuate:加水~酒 *dilute wine with water*

【稀疏】scattered; dispersed; thin; sparse:天空晨星~。*There were a few morning stars in the sky.*

【稀松】① lax; not strict; no good ② irrelevant; unimportant; trifling:别把那些~小事放在心上。*Don't take such irrelevant matters to your mind.* ③ poor; sloppy:这把椅子活儿做得太~。*The quality of this chair is just too poor.* ④ thin; loose:刚下过雨,土壤变~了。*The soil is loose and thin after it has just rained.*

【稀酸】【化】diluted acid

【稀碎】broken into pieces; smashed to bits:杯子被扔在地上,摔个~。*The cup was thrown on the ground, and broken to pieces.*

【稀土】rare earth: ~矿 *rare-earth mine of rare* / ~元素 *rare-earth element* / ~金属 *rare-earth metal*

【稀稀拉拉】① sparse; scattered:大厅里~地坐着几个观众。*There were scattered crowds in the hall.* ② sloppy; poorly organized:今天的会开得~。*Today 's meeting was poorly organized.*

翕 [书] ① amiable; compliant; submit to; docile ② close; draw together; fold; furl

【翕动】[书] open and close alternately:我看到他的嘴唇~,但什么也听不到。*I saw his lips keep moving but heard nothing.*

【翕合】join together; put together

犀 ① rhinoceros ② sharp; solid; strong

【犀角】rhinoceros horn

【犀利】sharp; incisive; trenchant; keen: ~的目光 *sharp sightedness* / 文笔~ *have a trenchant pen*

【犀牛】rhinoceros

皙 ① fair-skinned; white:她皮肤白~。*Her skin is very white.* ② bright

锡[1] ①【化】stannum (Sn); tin ② monk's cane

锡[2] grant; bestow:~福 *grant happiness*

【锡箔】tinfoil; tinfoil paper

【锡罐】can; tin; tin can

【锡焊料】【冶】tin solder

【锡合金】【冶】tin alloy

【锡匠】tinsmith

【锡婚】tin wedding anniversary-10th wedding anniversary

【锡器】tinware

【锡酸】【化】stannic acid

【锡纸】tinfoil; silver paper

傒 [书] ① wait for; expect ② narrow path; shortcut

【傒待】expect; look forward to:那些学生在~老师。*Those students were waiting for their teacher.*

溪 stream; brook; rivulet:小~潺潺 *babbling stream*

【溪谷】valley; dale; canyon; gorge

【溪间】mountain stream; mountain brook:森林中有一条蜿蜒的~。*There is a winding stream in the forest.*

【溪流】stream; brook; rivulet

熙 [书] ① brightness; light ② peaceful and happy; calm quiet placid ③ prosperous; booming; flourishing ④ gay; lovely; pleasant

【熙和】①[书] content and happy ② warm; genial:~的阳光 *genial sunshine*

【熙攘】bustling with activity; restless:大街上~的尽是人。*The pavement was filled with jostling crowds.*

【熙熙攘攘】restless; bustle about; coming and going busily:几乎每条街道上都是车马如云,行人~。*Almost every street is a sea of carriages and pedestrians.*

蜥 lizard; cabrite

【蜥甲】lizard beetle

【蜥蜴】lizard; cabrite

熄 ① extinguish; put out; turn off; turn out:请把灯~了。*Please turn off the light.* ② quash; destroy; obliterate; wither away; come to an end

【熄灯】turn out or put out the light; switch off the light:请你离开房间时~。*Please switch off the light when you leave the room.*

【熄火】① flame out; stop working; go dead:发动机~啦。*The engine stopped working.* ② extinguish; put out:~后,炉膛内依然很热。*The fire was extinguished, but it was hot in the stove.*

【熄灭】① extinguish; wink out ② go out; put out:灯~了。*The lights turned out.*

嘻 [书] ① (in literary text) an interjection of grief or surprise ②[象] sound of laughing happily

【嘻里呼噜】[象] sound of snoring or slurping (as when gulping down porridge)

【嘻嘻哈哈】laughing and joking; laughing merrily; joy; light-hearted; laughing and talk happily:一阵~的声音从门外传来。*A sound of laughing and joking came from outside the door.* ② not serious; happy-go-lucky; careless:千万别~! *Don't be careless!*

【嘻笑】giggle; titter:他~着表示欣赏我愚蠢的笑话。*He giggled his appreciation of my silly joke.*

膝 knee:左~ *the left knee* /屈~ *drop on one's knees*

【膝盖】knee; kneecap; patella:水深及~。*The water was knee-deep.*

【膝盖骨】kneecap; kneepan; patella

【膝关节】knee joint

嬉 [书] play; sport; have fun; frolic:业精于勤,荒于~。*Learning is perfected through diligence and lapses by neglect.*

【嬉闹】romp; laughing and joking; frolic:一群孩子在~。*A group of kids were romped together.*

【嬉皮士】hippie; hippy

【嬉皮笑脸】grin cheekily; smile and grimacing; grim cheekily; smile and grimace; be comically cheerful

【嬉耍】play; have fun; amuse oneself:孩子们在岸边~。*Children were playing on the bank.*

【嬉戏】[书] play; sport; frolic; make merry; gambol:孩子们赤脚在沙滩上~。*Children were gamboling bare-footed on the sand.*

【嬉笑】be laughing and playing; laugh and play; a mischievous smile

【嬉怡】[书] happy; cheerful; blissful:孩子脸上带着~的微笑。*The kid always smiles cheerfully on her face.*

【嬉游】play; sport:孩子们喜欢在河边~。*Children enjoy sporting by the river.*

熹 [书] ① dawn; daylight; daybreak; faint; sunlight ② giving out faint light ③ brightness

【熹微】(of morning sunlight) faint; dim; vague; pale

窸

【窸窣】rustle:我听见草丛中有东西~移动。*I hear sth rusting through the thick grass.*

蹊 [书] ① path; footpath ② trample; tread

see also qī

【蹊径】narrow path; way; footpath; shortcut:另辟~ *blaze another method; seek a different way*

蟋

【蟋蟀】【动】cricket

徯 quarrel; brawl

豀 ① stream; creek; brook ② valley; gorge

【豀谷】[书] mountain valley

【豀壑】[书] ravine; gully; valley

【豀刻】[书] caustic; petty; cutting

曦 [书] sunshine; sunlight (usu. in early morning):晨～下的森林显得安静而美丽。*The forest in the early morning sunshine appears calm and beautiful.*

【曦光】sunlight in early morning

巇 ① a crack ② hazardous of a mountain path

【巇险】① precipitous and difficult to ascend ② full of danger and hardship

xí

习 ① fly frequently ② review; practise; exercise; learn ③ be used to:她已～惯早上去户外活动。*She gets used to go out of the door every morning.* ④ habit; custom ⑤ trusted follower ⑥ often ⑦ (Xí) a surname

【习惯】① habit; custom; practice:他养成了早起的～。*He formed the habit of getting up early.* ② get used to; be accustomed to:他已～早上去公园锻炼。*He gets used to exercise in the park every morning.*

【习惯成自然】habit is second nature; habit makes things natural

【习惯法】consuetudinary law; common law; customary law

【习好】habit; hobby; liking ; addiction: ～吃甜点 *have a liking for sweets*

【习见】be commonly seen; often or frequently seen:种花侍草是人们所～的。*It is commonly seen to plant flower and grass.*

【习气】bad habit or custom; bad practice:官僚～ *bureaucratism; officialism*

【习染】[书] ① fall into a bad habit; contract a bad habit; get into evil ways ② bad habit

【习尚】custom; fashion:尊老爱幼是我们民族的优良～。*It is excellent custom of our nation to respect old people and love children.*

【习俗】custom; convention; practice:本地～ *local custom*

【习题】exercises; sum

【习习】breezy; blowing gently; refreshing:微风～。*Breezee is blowing gently.*

【习性】temperament; dispositions; habit and characteristics:某些动物有趋光～。*Some animals' characteristics are attracted to light.*

【习以成性】deeply ingrained into one's nature

【习以为常】be accustomed to sth; fall into a habit; be in the habit of:这小孩说谎已～了。*The kid was fallen into the habit of telling lies.*

【习艺】learn a skill or trade:他已～多年。*He has already learnt the skill to many years.*

【习用】use as a habit; habitually use; be in the habit of using

【习字】learn calligraphy; practise penmanship

【习字帖】copybook; calligraphy model

【习作】① do exercises in compositions; learn to do ② exercise in composition:这是他早年的～。*That picture is his early drawing.*

席 ① mat:草～ *straw* ② seat; place:就～ *take one's seat* ③ banquet; feast; seat:坐～ *attend a banquet* ④ post; seat in parliament:执政党在议会中有200～位。*The Party in power has 200 seats in legislature.* ⑤ sail ⑥ [量]: 一～话 *a talk* ⑦ (Xí) a surname

【席次】order of seats; seating arrangement; one's place among the seats arranged:请按～就座。*Please take your place among the seats arranged.*

【席地】on the ground or floor: ～而坐 *sit on the ground*

【席间】at a feast; during a banquet

【席卷】carry everything with one; roll up like a mat; sweep across; engulf; conquer: ～而去 *leave nothing behind or take everything away*

【席梦思】spring mattress

【席面】① banquet feast; the food ② presented at dinner

【席棚】mat shed; mat boarding

【席位】seat (at a conference, in a legislative assembly, etc.):这些是领导的～。*These are the seats for leaders.*

袭 ① graveclothes ② surname ③ [量] a suit; a set:一～新装 *a suit of new clothes* ④【动】follow the pattern off; carry on as before; take by surprise; raid; assail ⑤ plagiarize; appropriate:他抄～别人的文章。*He plagiarized other's article.* ⑥ raid; attack

【袭夺】① take or attack by surprise ②【地】(of rivers) capture

【袭封】inherit a little (from one's forefathers)

【袭击】raid; surprise; make a surprise attack on; attack by surprise

【袭取】① take by surprise; surprise: ～敌人的营地 *take enemy camp by surprise* ② take over

【袭扰】harass; make harassing attacks:游击队不断～敌人。*Guerrilla forces harassed the enemy.*

【袭用】take over

【袭占】attack and capture; attack and take by surprise:我们～敌人的军事基地。*We attacked and took an enemy station by surprise.*

媳 daughter-in-law: 翁 ～ *father-in-law and daughter-in-law*

【媳妇】① son's wife ② wife ③ married woman ④ young woman

檄 ① call to arms (in ancient times); official proclamation (denouncing a usurper, traitor, etc.): ～文 *war proclamation* ② condemn; denounce

【檄文】official public declaration; addressed to

junior officer and people, (usu. writing on bamboo slip) call to war; call summons to arms; manifesto listing the crimes of a tyrant

xǐ

洗 ① wash; rinse; bathe; clean; clear: 饭前～手。*Please wash your hands clean before each meal.* ②【宗】*baptize*: 受～礼入基督教 *be baptize into the Christian faith* ③ redress; right; remedy: ～冤 *clear oneself of a false charge* ④ clear away; eliminate: 清～ *purge* ⑤ develop (a film): 冲～照片 *print photos* ⑥ erase (a recording): 他的讲话录音被～掉啦。*That recording of his speech has been erased.* ⑦ shuffle: ～牌 *shuffle the playing cards* ⑧ kill and loot; sack: ～城 *massacre all inhabitants* ⑨ small vessel or tray for washing brushes

【洗布机】【纺】cloth washing machine

【洗槽】【化】washing tank; sink

【洗肠】intestinal lavage

【洗尘】give a welcome dinner (for someone arriving after a long trip): 今晚我们设宴为他～。*We'll give an informal dinner to welcome him tonight.*

【洗荡】wash clean; wash away; purify

【洗涤】wash; cleanse; rinse: ～粉 *washing powder* /经过大雨的～, 庄稼显得格外绿。*The crops appeared especially green through washed by rain.*

【洗耳恭听】listen respectfully; lend an attentive ear; be all ears; be very attentive to hear: 说吧, 我～。*go ahead! I listen respectfully.*

【洗发剂】shampoo

【洗脚礼】【宗】washing of feet; foot-washing

【洗劫】sack everything; loot; sack; ransack; rifle: 匪徒～了这个村子。*The bandits sacked everything in the village.*

【洗洁净】liquid detergent

【洗矿】ore wash: ～机 *ore washer*

【洗礼】baptism; cleaning flames; severe test: 伊拉克饱受战争的～。*Iraq received much baptism of war.*

【洗礼堂】【宗】baptistery

【洗脸盆】wash bowl; washbasin

【洗练】(as of literary writings) neat; succinct; terse; concise; laconic

【洗毛】【纺】scouring

【洗毛机】【纺】wool-scouring machine; wool-washing machine

【洗煤】coal washing

【洗煤厂】coal washery

【洗煤机】coal washer

【洗面膏】cleansing cream for the face

【洗脑】brainwash; indoctrinate

【洗牌】shuffle playing cards

【洗片】develop (a film); process (a film)

【洗钱】launder money; money laundering (i. e. transferring money obtained, etc. so as to disguise its source)

【洗染店】laundering and dyeing shop; cleaners and dyers

【洗手】① wash one's hands: 饭前～ *wash one's hands before the meal* ② stop doing evil and reform oneself: ～不干 *have none of washing one's hands of sth*; *stop doing evil* ③ go to the lavatory

【洗手间】lavatory; toilet; washroom; bathroom; water closet

【洗漱】wash one's face and rinse one's mouth

【洗刷】① scrub; clean: 地板需要好好地～一下。*The floor needs a good scrub.* ② wash off; clear oneself of; remove: ～不清 *unable to vindicate oneself*

【洗涮】wash and rinse: 他将蔬菜在河里～干净。*He gave the vegetables a thorough rinse in the river.*

【洗头】wash one's hair; shampoo; have one's hair washed

【洗碗碟机】dishwasher; dish-washing machine

【洗胃】【医】gastric lavage

【洗雪】wipe out; redress; revenge; vindicate: ～杀父之仇 *revenge one's father's murder*

【洗眼】wash eyes; wash attentively: ～杯 *eyecup* /～剂 *collyrium*; *eyewash*

【洗衣】wash clothes; do one's washing: ～店 *laundry shop*; *washhouse*; *dry cleaner*

【洗印】develop and print; process: ～机(*film*) *processor*

【洗浴】take a bath

【洗澡】have a bath; bath: ～盆 *bathtub* /～间 *bathroom*; *bathhouse*

【洗濯】wash; rinse; cleanse: 她在溪水中～衣服。*She washed clothes in a stream.*

徙 ① move from one place to another; migrate; remove; shift; change ②[书] be transferred to another post

【徙边】[书] move prisoners to the border areas; banish prisoners to a border region

【徙居】move house; change one's residence; move; migrate: 老人～他乡。*The old man migrated to another country.*

【徙倚】irresolution; indecision; linger; loiter, pace up and down

喜 ① happy; delightful; joyful: 欢天～地 *be highly delighted* ② happy event: ～怒不形于色 *expressionless* ③ be expressionless ④ be fond of: 她有～啦。*She was pregnant.* ⑤ joy: 充满欢～ *be full with joy* ⑥ be prone to; require; agree with ⑦ be prone to; require; agree with: 大部分植物～光。*Almost of plants prone to sunlight.*

【喜爱】like; love; be fond of: 她～交际。*She is sociable.*

【喜报】bulletin announcing glad tidings; report of good news

【喜报神】harbinger of good news

【喜冲冲】look exhilarated; be in a joyful mood; be radiant joy: 他～地冲到门外。*He rushed out of* the door with happiness on his face beyond.

【喜出望外】happy beyond expectations; be pleasantly surprised; joy over unexpected good luck; unexpected joy:他听到这个消息~。*He was unexpected joy to hear the news.*

【喜从天降】happiness comes from heaven; godsend; windfall

【喜封】packet of gift money; money given by the family celebrating some happy events:姑娘们每个人都得到一份~。*Each of the girls received a packet of gift money.*

【喜好】be fond of; like; be keen on; love:他非常~种花。*He likes to plant flowers.*

【喜欢】① like; love; be fond of; be keen on:她非常讨老师的~。*She wins her teacher's favour.* ② happy; delighted

【喜酒】wedding feast; win drunk at wedding feast:汤姆今天晚上请我们喝他的~。*Tom will invite us to his wedding feast tonight.*

【喜剧】comedy: ~演员 *comedian*

【喜乐】joy; happiness; delight; gladness: ~之事 *happy news*; *good news*

【喜马拉雅山】the Himalayas, is the highest mountain in the world

【喜脉】【中医】pulse beat showing symptoms of pregnancy

【喜眉笑眼】bearing with joy; very happy; one's eyes and brows twinkling with delight; all smiles

【喜娘】[旧] woman serving as bride's attendant; bridesmaid

【喜怒哀乐】pleasure, anger, sorrow and joy — the passions:比尔是一个~不形于色的人。*Bill is expressionless.*

【喜怒无常】subject to changing moods; volatile; capricious; mercurial:他的老板~。*His boss is volatile.*

【喜期】wedding day

【喜气】cheerful look or expression; joy or jubilation festive mood

【喜气洋洋】full of joy; radiant with happiness; jubilant; joyful atmosphere; festival mood; cheerful look:这幅画上有许多~的人物。*There are many radiant figures in the painting.*

【喜钱】money distributed on happy occasions:他把~分送给人们。*He distributed money on happy occasions to the people.*

【喜庆】① joyous; jubilant:在今天这个~的日子,每个人的脸上都洋溢着笑容。*Today is a joyous day, every face overflows with smiles.* ② happy occasions; calling for celebration

【喜鹊】【动】magpie

【喜人】gratifying; heartening; satisfactory:他在学业上取得了~的成绩。*He achieved satisfactory school marks.*

【喜容】① happy look; joyful expression:他面带~。*There is happy look on his face.* ② [旧] portrait

【喜色】pleased look; happy expression

【喜丧】funeral of an elder

【喜上眉梢】be radiant with joy; beam of delight

【喜事】happy event; occasion for joy; joyous occasion; pleasant tidings:人逢~精神爽。*A joyous occasion brings happiness to people.*

【喜堂】wedding hall:婚礼将在~进行。*The marriage will take place in the wedding hall.*

【喜糖】happy -sweets

【喜帖】wedding invitation; invitation card for wedding celebration

【喜慰】be pleased; be happy

【喜闻乐见】love; love to see and hear:这是一种~的文艺形式。*It's literary loved by the people.*

【喜相】[方] amiable expression; pleasant look

【喜笑颜开】cheerful; ear-to-ear grin; beam with pleasure; be wreathed:当小强答应帮他时,他立刻~。*He beamed with pleasure at once when Xiaoqiang promised to help him.*

【喜新厌旧】like the new and dislike the old; love the new and loathe the old — usu. referring to love affairs:她丈夫是个~的人。*Her husband loves the new and loathes the old.*

【喜形于色】look pleased; have an expression and delight; be radiant with joy:史密斯看到这个消息时~。*Smith was radiant with joy when he saw the news.*

【喜幸】[书] happy; delight; joyful: ~之事 *joyful occasion*

【喜讯】happy news; good news; glad tidings

【喜洋洋】beaming with pleasure or satisfaction; radiant; beam of delight

【喜吟吟】joyful; pleased; happy:看她~的样子,必定有什么好事。*We judged from her joyful expression that she must have good news for herself.*

【喜盈盈】happy; pleased

【喜雨】timely rain; seasonable rain; spell of welcome rain

【喜悦】joy; delight; gratification:他考入名牌大学,他的父母大为~。*As he passed the entrance examination of a famous university, his parents were greatly delightful.*

【喜跃】jump for joy

【喜滋滋】joyful; looking pleased; feeling happy

禧 happiness; blessings; auspiciousness; jubilation:恭贺新~! *Happy New Year*!

xì

戏 ① play; sport; toy; have fun:小鸭在水里嬉~。*Dusks were playing in the water.* ② jest; have fun; make fun; joke with ③ drama; play; show; opera:我们看~去。*let's go to the drama.*

【戏本】script of a play; text for a play or an opera

【戏场】[旧] theatre; opera house; hall for performance

【戏称】① call sb jokingly:人们~她为女巫。*People joking call her a witch.* ② joking nickname

【戏词】actor's lines; the words of actor's part

【戏单】programme of a play; playbill
【戏法】jugglery; trick; magic; sleight of hand: ~多数人会变,巧妙各不相同。*Most people can practice magic but each has himself tricks.*
【戏剧】① drama; play; theater:现代~ *modern drama* /献身~ *devote to the theater* ② text or script for a play
【戏剧家】dramatist; dramaturge
【戏剧界】playdom; drama circles
【戏剧文学】dramatic literature
【戏剧性】dramatic
【戏乐】make merry; have fun; amuse oneself; play
【戏路】ability to act different types of characters:她~很宽,能演各种各样的角色。*She is a versatile actress, able to play various actor.*
【戏弄】play a trick on; tease; kid; make fun of; play a prank on:不要~那孩子。*Don't make fun of the child.*
【戏评】dramatic criticism; dramatic review; theatrical review
【戏情】plot or scenario of a play
【戏曲】drama; play; theatrical composition; traditional opera
【戏耍】① play tricks on; make fun of; merry making ② play; amuse oneself
【戏台】stage
【戏谈】humorous; playful comments
【戏文】① southern drama ② traditional opera; drama; theatrical writing
【戏侮】insult sb by making fun of; insult; play a trick on sb
【戏谑】joke; witticism; pleasantry; jest; fun:我爸爸擅长~,常引得人们开怀大笑。*My father is good at joking and always makes people laugh cheerfully.*
【戏匣子】[方] radio; gramophone
【戏言】joke witticism; jest: 军中无~。*No joke is allowed in the army.*
【戏眼】most interesting part of a play
【戏衣】stage costume; theater costume
【戏园子】[旧] playhouse; theater
【戏院】theater; movie house
【戏照】photograph of a person in stage costume
【戏装】stage costume; theatrical costume
【戏子】[贬] drama player; actor or actress

系[1] ①[书] be:他~中国人。*He is Chinese.*

系[2] ① department; faculty:英文~ *English department* ② bind; belong to; attach to; connect with ③ relate to; rely on:成败所~ *success or failure relies on this* ④ tie up and carry; fasten and pull up; fasten and lower down ⑤ tie; fasten; tether: ~扣 *fasten buttons* ⑥ relation; line; series; system:友好关~ *the friendly relation* ⑦【地】system:泥盆~ *devonian* ⑧ be concerned; feel solicitous ⑨ take into custody or gaol; arrest:囚~ *imprison; incarcerate*
see also jì

【系绊】trammels; fetters; yoke:不要为琐事~。*Don't be yoke with trivialities.* .
【系带】① ribbon ② tie-tie ③ lace
【系缚】[书] tie; fasten; bind up
【系累】① burden; encumbrance ② fetter; yoke; tie; take into custody
【系恋】be attached to; be reluctant to leave:他~着他的女友。*He was attached to his girlfriend.*
【系列】series; sets: ~产品 *products series*
【系数】【数】coefficient:摩擦~ *coefficient of friction*
【系统】① system; set up:操作~ *operating system* ② systematic: ~研究 *systematically study*

细 ① tiny; small; little ② thin; slender; slim: ~线 *thin lines* ③ narrow; thin: ~流 *narrow river* ④ in small particles; fine: 面粉磨得很~。*The flour has been ground very fine.* ⑤ petty; trifling; minute; tiny:他每天作一些~琐的工作。*He does petty work everyday.* ⑥ (of one's voice) thin and soft; sharp; shrill ⑦ precise; exquisite; delicate; fine; superb:一套做工很~的衣服 *a suit of clothes exquisite* ⑧ careful; detailed: ~瞻景状 *look carefully at the views* ⑨ [方] young; little: ~妹 *little girl* ⑩ tender; delicate: ~皮嫩肉 *tender sink*

【细胞】cell:红~ *red blood cell* / ~分裂 *cell division; mitosis*
【细胞学】cytology
【细部】details (of drawing); minute parts
【细菜】fine vegetables
【细长】① tall and slender; be long and thin; slim:她身材~。*She is tall and slim figure.* /那有一条~的绳子。*There is a long and thin rope.*
【细底】ins and outs; exact circumstance
【细度】fineness: ~指数 *fineness index*
【细高挑儿】tall and slender figure
【细工】① fine workmanship ② delicate work:带有~银饰的匣子 *box with fine silver decorations*
【细故】trivial matter; triviality; trifle:他性格开朗,从不计较~。*He is sanguine not to mind trifle.*
【细活】skilled work; job requiring fine workmanship or meticulous care
【细火】slow fire; soft fire
【细嚼慢咽】swallow slowly the food after chewing it well eat one's meal slowly
【细节】details; minutiae; particulars:不忽略一个~ *not to afford to neglect any details*
【细究】probe into a matter; get to the bottom of a matter; examine or study into all details
【细菌】bacterium; germ: ~学 *bacteriology* / ~武器 *bacteriological weapon; germ weapon* / ~战 *bacteriological or germ warfare*
【细粮】fine grains; flour and rice
【细脉】①【中医】thready pulse ② joint vein
【细毛】fine; soft fur
【细蒙蒙】drizzly; misty: ~的春雨 *drizzly spring rain*
【细密】① close; fine:质地~ *be of close texture* ② careful; cautions; detailed; meticulous:考虑~

think meticulous of sth
【细描】(as in literature) minute description
【细磨】【机】fine grinding; finish grinding
【细目】detailed catalogue; specific items
【细嫩】fine; delicate; tender
【细腻】① fine and delicate; fine and smooth ② (in writing, dramas, etc.) minute; superb: 文笔～ *minute writing* ③［方］be careful
【细皮嫩肉】fine sink and soft flesh
【细巧】dainty; delicate; exquisite; fine; ingenious: ～的手工 *fine handwork*
【细柔】soft and delicate; gentle and slender
【细软】① jewelry, expensive clothing and other valuables ② slender and soft: ～的柳枝 *slender and soft weeping willow branches*
【细润】fine and smooth; fine: ～的皮肤 *fine and smooth skin*
【细弱】slim and fragile; thin and delicate
【细纱】【纺】spun yarn: ～纱 *spinning frame* / ～车间 *spinning workroom or shop*
【细声细气】in a gentle and quiet voice; soft-spoken in a soft voice
【细瘦】thinnish
【细水长流】① economize to avoid running short ② go about sth little by little without a letup
【细说】① run on ②［书］calumny; gossip; garbled story
【细碎】in small and broken bits; in fine scraps
【细琐】petty; trivial; trifle
【细谈】talk in detail; go into every minute; point in a conversation; run on
【细微】fine; humble; minute; slight; subtle; tiny: ～差别 *minute different; nuance*
【细味】［书］think carefully; think over; study carefully; reflect
【细小】little; petty; tiny; thin; trivial; very small
【细心】attentive; careful; cautions; meticulous: ～倾听 *listen attentive to*
【细伢子】［方］child; kid
【细腰】① slender waist ② slim waisted wasp
【细雨】drizzle; fine rain; misty rain: ～斜风 *inclining breeze and misty rain*
【细语】speak gently; whisper: 她说话总是轻声～。*She always speaks softly.*
【细则】detailed rules and regulations: 实施～ *rules and regulations for enforcing*
【细账】itemized account; detailed account: 关于收入来源的～ *break down the sources of one's income*
【细致】① fine and delicate; exquisite ② careful and thorough; precise; meticulous

隙 ① crack; fissure; crevice; chink; rift: 把门留点缝～ *leave the door open a crack* / 岩石裂～ *fissure in the rock* ② spare time; leisure; gap; internal ③ grudge; discord; dislike; dispute; quarrel; complaint; rift: 我与你并没有嫌～。*I owed you no discord.* ④ loophole; opportunity: 无～可乘 *there is no loophole to take advantage of*
【隙地】vacant lot or space; uncultivated land or place: 房子四周的～ *vacant tracts around a house*
【隙缝】chink; crack
【隙罅】［书］crack; crevice; fissure: 杯子上有条～。*There was a crack in the glass.*

xiā

呷 ［方］sip; drink: ～了一口咖啡 *take a sip of coffee; sip up one's coffee*

虾 shrimp: 油焖大～ *braised prawns*

【虾兵蟹将】shrimp soldier and crab generals — ineffective followers; numerous underlings
【虾干】dried prawns; dried shrimps
【虾酱】salty shrimp paste
【虾米】① dried shrimps ② small shrimp
【虾皮】dried small shrimps
【虾仁】shelled fresh shrimps; shrimp meat
【虾油】shrimp sauce
【虾子】shrimp roe: ～酱 *shrimp roe paste*

瞎 ① blind; blindly: 她天生就是一个～子。*She has been blind from birth.* ② reckless; heedless; rash: ～操心! *There are no grounds for anxiety.* ③ fail to detonate or explode; misfire; go dud: 炮弹～火啦。*The shell went dud.* ④［方］(as of seeds) fail to bud ⑤ become tangled ⑥［方］waste; spoil
【瞎掰】① work to no avail; work in vain; make a futile effort; waste one's effort ② talk nonsense; talk groundlessly; telling lies: 别听他～。*Don't hear his telling lies.*
【瞎扯】talk recklessly; tell lies; speak nonsense; talk rubbish waffle
【瞎吹】brag wildly; make wild boasts: 他总是～，但一无所成。*He always talked big, but never amounted to anything.*
【瞎点子】wild notion; impractical idea
【瞎胡勒】［方］talk groundlessly; speak groundlessly; talk rubbish: 他的讲演全是～。*His speech was all rot.*
【瞎话】untruth; lies; nonsensical remark: 对脸说～ *tell barefaced lies*
【瞎混】muddle along
【瞎火】fail to detonate or explode; be a dud; misfire
【瞎聊】converse at random; talk nonsense; chat idly; engage in chitchat: 走吧，别～啦。*Go ahead! Don't chat idly.*
【瞎忙】mess about; be busy for nothing; be all fuss and feathers: 他一天到晚～。*He has been busy for nothing from morning tonight.*
【瞎猫逮住死耗子】a blind cat caught a dead rat — by lucky hit
【瞎蒙】wild guess; stumble across sth
【瞎摸合眼】grasp in the dark; not seeing clearly where one's is going: ～的，我看不清。*I can hardly see clearly in the dark.*
【瞎闹】act senselessly; make nonsense; cause

meaningless trouble; fool around: 别~,快往前走。*Go ahead, quickly and don't mess.*
【瞎炮】dud; unexploded shell
【瞎三话四】[方] reckless talk; talk rubbish; says who
【瞎说】speak groundlessly; talk nonsense; wild talk
【瞎说八道】talk through one's hat; tell lies; talk rubbish; says who: 我证实他是~。*I tested that he talked rubbish.*
【瞎眼】blind: 怪我当初~了,给你那么多钱。*It was all my fault; I was so blind that I gave you so much money.*
【瞎指挥】command at whim; mess things up by giving wrong orders
【瞎诌】[方] speak groundlessly; spin a yarn; make up a wild story; talk irresponsibly
【瞎抓】grasp anything within reach without knowing what to do with if; spend a lot of energy without much achievement do things without a plan
【瞎字不识】illiterate; unable to read a single word
【瞎子】① blind person ② [方] blind seed
【瞎子点灯白费蜡】lighting a candle for a blind person — sheer waste
【瞎子摸象】a blindman feels an elephant — be unable to learn the whole; the blind men and the elephant
【瞎子摸鱼】a blindman gropes for fishes — act blindly or heedlessly
【瞎琢磨】torment

xiá

匣 ① small box or case ② coffin ③ collect in casket; lock
【匣子】① small box or case ② coffin
侠 ① knight-errant; person adept in martial arts and dedicated to helping the poor and weak; the man who fights rather than submit to injustice. ② chivalry; knight-errantry: ~义之士 *man of honour and gallantry*
【侠骨】[书] *chivalrous frame of mind*
【侠客】[书] chivalrous person; knight-errant; person adept in martial arts and given to chivalrous conduct
【侠气】chivalry; knight-errantry; heroic spirit
【侠士】practised swordsman; gallant person; knight-errant
【侠义】knight-errant; chivalrous; having a strong sense of justice: ~心肠 *chivalrous temperament*
狎 be improperly familiar with; indulge in flirtations or intimacies: ~近 *take liberties with*
【狎妓】visit a brothel; visit house of ill fame; have fun with a prostitute
【狎客】prostitute's customer; client at brothel
【狎昵】be improperly familiar with: 和他们~出游。*Have a trip to be improperly familiar with them.*
【狎亵】slight; be disrespectfully familiar
柙 ① wooden cage or box; formerly also used for felons ② look up; escort
峡 gorge: ~谷 *canyon*
【峡谷】【地】canyon; dale; valley
【峡江】cove
【峡口】【地】narrows
【峡湾】【地】fiord
狭 narrow; small and less
【狭隘】① narrow: 不要和如此~的人打交道。*Don't make dealings with so illiberal person.*
【狭长】long and narrow
【狭路相逢】come into unavoidable confrontation; meet face on a narrow path
【狭小】scrimpy; cramped; narrow and small: 他试图走出~的圈子。*He tried to step out of the marrow circle.*
【狭斜】[书] lane where prostitutes live crook; red-light district
【狭义】narrow sense
【狭窄】① narrow; cramped: ~的河流 *narrow river* ② little; narrow and limited: 心胸~ *insular*
遐 [书] ① distant; far; remote: 亚洲的~区 *the remotest past of Asia* ② lasting; durable; long: ~祉 *lasting blessings* / ~福 *enduring blessing or happiness* ③ abandon; cast off; die down; vanish: ~终 *forever*
【遐迩】far and near; near and distant
【遐迩闻名】be well-known far-and-near; enjoy great renown: 他~。*He was famous in the far and near.*
【遐思】day-dream; wild and fanciful thoughts: 他沉浸在~之中。*He was deeply in his day-dreams.*
【遐想】reverie; daydream; remote thoughts: 春天总带给人们无限的~。*Spring always brings people on wild and fanciful thoughts.*
瑕 a flaw; spot; blemish in piece of jade; defect; fault; error; short-coming: ~瑜 *good and bad points* / 白璧无~ *a piece of white jade without tiny flaw*
【瑕不掩瑜】one flaw cannot obscure the splendour of the jade — the defects can't outweigh the merits
【瑕疵】flaw; defect; blemish: 那宝石上有~。*There are flaws in the precious stone.*
【瑕玷】[书] flaws; defects; stains; taints
暇 free time; spare moment; leisure: ~刻 *a free moment* / ~时 *spare time*
【暇日】free day; day of leisure; spare time: ~孩子们时常去爬山。*The children often spend free day on mountain-climbing.*
【暇逸】[书] be leisurely; relaxation; relax; idle: 我们不可耽于~。*We mustn't indulge in relaxation.*
辖 ① govern; administer; manage ② imperial bodyguard ③ press from both sides: 为左右所~,进退两难 *press form both sides and stand up a*

gum tree

【辖区】area under one's jurisdiction; magistracy

【辖制】govern; control; check; restrain; rule

霞 coloured low-hanging clouds; rosy clouds:晚~ *evening rosy clouds*

【霞光】rays of morning or evening sunlight

【霞帔】embroidered scarf for woman of noble rank in ancient times; beautiful dancing dress:凤冠~ *the headgear and dress for a bride in ancient times*

黠 [书] cunning; crafty; sly; smart; clever:狡~ *guileful; sly*

【黠慧】crafty and intelligent

xià

下[1] ① put down ② lay:树木被暴风雨击中倒~。*Trees laid flat by heavy rainstorms.* ③ fall ④ descend; go down; get off:太阳慢慢落~西山。*The sun slowly descends over western mountain.*

下[2] ① issue; deliver; send: ~通知 *server notice* ② go (down) to: ~基层 *go to the grass roots* ③ exit; leave: ~岗 *leave position* ④ put in; cast: ~注 *lay bets* ⑤ play (games): ~棋 *play chess* ⑥ take away; take off; unload; dismantle:他的枪被~了。*His gun was taken away.* ⑦ form (an opinion); draw (a conclusion): ~结论 *draw a conclusion* ⑧ apply; use ⑨ capture; seize; take:红军连~敌人三城。*The Red Army captured three cities in succession.* ⑩ finish; leave off; be over: ~课。*Class is over.* ⑪ less than; at least:我找他不~十次。*I looked for him no less than ten times.* ⑫ give in; yield:相持不~ *neither side would give in it*

下[3] ① below; under; underneath; down:零~ *below zero* /控制之~ *under the control* ② lower; inferior; poor: ~策 *poor idea* / ~唇 *lower lip* ③ next; later:下~ *next time* ④ down:向~走 *walk down* ⑤ used in collocations indicating a particular time or season:节~ *during a holiday* /眼~ *at present; right now* ⑥ used after a numeral to indicate orientation or position:两~都同意,这事就算成啦。*If both sides were willing it would be success.* ⑦ used after a verb, indicate downward motion:他在床上躺~睡着啦。*He went to sleep in the bed.* ⑧ indicate room or space:这房间能容~100人。*The room can be held one hundred people.* ⑨ indicate completion or consequence of an action:定~锦囊妙计 *work out a wise plan* /写~锦绣文章 *write out an embroidered piece of literature*

【下巴】lower jaw; chin

【下巴颏儿】[口] chin

【下摆】lower hem (of a gown, jacket or shirt)

【下拜】bow; kneel down; bend the knee; make obeisance to:她希望每个人都对她~。*She expects everyone to bend the knee to her.*

【下班】come or go off work; knock off; return from work:从星期一到星期五我们都是17点~。*From Monday to Friday, we return from work at 17:00.*

【下板儿】[方] take off door-and window-shutters — open shop:杂货铺怎么十点还不~? *Why hasn't the grocery opened?*

【下半辈子】latter half of one's life; the rest of one's life

【下半场】second half (of a game)

【下半旗】fly a flag at half-mast:毛泽东逝世时,全国~致哀。*When Mao Zedong was died, we flew a flag at half-mast as a sign of mourning in our country.*

【下半身】below the waist; lower part of the body

【下半时】second half (of a game)

【下半天】afternoon; last half day

【下半夜】the time after midnight; wee hours; latter half of the night

【下辈】① next generation; future generation; offspring ② younger generation of a family ③ humble person

【下辈子】next life; next incarnation:就是到~也忘不了您。*I won't forget you even in next life.*

【下本儿】invest

【下笔】put pen to paper; start writing: ~千言,离题万里。*To write quickly but stray from the theme.*

【下笔成章】write quickly and skillfully; have literary acumen; write an essay at on go:他才思敏捷, ~。*He has a facile imagination and great literary acumen.*

【下不为例】not to be taken as a precedent; not to be repeated just this once; must not do it again

【下不来】① embarrassed; feel awkward:你这样做是故意让他面子上~。*You do so, he felt embarrassed at your doing such things.* ② can't go down

【下不来台】① be put on the spot; put sb in an awkward position:我要叫他~。*I won't put him in an awkward.* ② can not bring to a conclusion

【下部】① underpart; lower part; latter half ② lower part of the body; below the waist

【下操】① have drills:同学们每天早上起来就去~。*The students have drills in every morning.* ② finish drilling:同学们刚~,正在教室里早读。*The students have just finished drilling and are reading in the classroom.*

【下策】bad plan; bad policy; unwise decision; worst option or alternative

【下层】bower levels; lower strata; low-ranking; substory

【下茶】[书] send a gift of tea as a token of betrothal; present betrothal gifts

【下场】①【体】leave the playing field; exit:在上半场他就被罚~了。*He was punished to leave the playing field in the first half of the match.* ② conclusion; end:为非作歹的人绝没有好~。*Those who do evil will certainly come to no good end.*

【下场门】exit; the left side of the stage

【下场头】［方］end; fate

【下车伊始】take office; the moment when one gets off the official carriage; as soon as the moment one takes up one's official post

【下沉】go under; sink; subside; submerge：太阳已～，黑夜即将来临。*The sun is setting in west, night is getting.*

【下乘】①【宗】Hinayana ② (as of arts and literature) mediocrity; of poor quality：～之作 *inferior work*

【下处】one's temporary lodging during a trip; lodging for the night

【下船】① go ashore; disembark ②［方］go aboard ship; embark; get into a boat

【下垂】① fall; hand down; drop; let down：她的头发～。*Her hair is falling.* ② sag：这根绳子中间～。*The rope sags the middle.* ③【医】prolapse; ptosis：胃～ *gastroptosis*

【下存】(of a sum) remain after deduction：这笔款～数额还有七千元。*The balance of this account is 7000 yuan.*

【下达】send down; transmit or release to lower levels：～命令 *issue an order to lower levels*

【下蛋】lay eggs

【下道】［口］lowly; off-colour; near or close to the bone

【下得去】［方］① (usu. used in the negative or interrogative) feel at ease; bear：你这样对待孩子们，心里～吗？*You treat the children badly; Don't you feel at ease?* ② tolerable; passable; not too bad

【下等】① low-grade; poor; inferior：～舱 *cheap cabin* ② mean; depraved：他可不是一个～的老师。*He is no mean teacher.*

【下等人】persons of lower social status; lower orders

【下地】① go to the fields：～干活 *go to work in the fields* ② leave a sickbed; get out of bed：他已经能～走路啦。*He can have gotten out of bed.* ③［方］(of a baby) be born ④ infertile field：这是一块～。*This is the infertile field.*

【下店】put up at an inn; stay at hotel for the night：～投宿 *stay at hotel for the night*

【下调】transfer to a lower-level work unit

【下跌】fall; drop; go down; depreciate：股票～ *stock prices fall*

【下定义】define

【下毒】put poison into; poison

【下毒手】lay violent hands on (someone); strike a vicious blow：自己的妈妈，她也下得了毒手？*Would she go so far as to lay murderous hand on her own mother?*

【下颚】lower jaw; mandible; maxilla

【下凡】descend to earth from heaven：神仙～ *immortals descend to earth from heaven*

【下饭】go with rice：如果你不喜欢这些菜，拿什么～？*If you don't like these dishes, what are you going to have with rice?*

【下方】① below; underneath; lower part：桌子～埋有宝石。*There are precious stones under the table.* ② (in contrast to heaven) earth

【下房】servant's room; servant's quarters

【下放】① transfer to a lower level：他把权力～。*He transferred his power to a lower level.* ② send to work at the grass-roots level or to do manual labour in the countryside or in a factory：他被～到农村。*He was sent to work in the countryside.*

【下放干部】cadre sent to work at the grass-roots level or to do manual labour in the countryside or in a factory

【下风】① leeward; downwind：工厂在城市的～处。*The factory is situated on the downwind of the city.* ② inferior position; disadvantageous position; at a disadvantage：甘拜～ *candidly admit defeat; willing to take an inferior position*

【下浮】drop; decrease; float downward：价格～ *prices drop*

【下腹部】underbelly; weak or vulnerable part (of a place, plan, etc.)

【下岗】① come or go off sentry duty：那个工人～啦。*The worker came off sentry duty.* ② (as of a technician of worker) be removed from a post; be made redundant; be laid off

【下岗分流】lay off workers and reposition redundant personnel

【下功夫】put in time and energy; take pains; exert oneself; devote much time and energy to a task：如果想学好一门外语就要～。*If you want to learn a foreign language, you must put in much effort to study.*

【下跪】kneel down; be on bended knees; go down on one's knees：～祈祷 *kneel in prayer*

【下锅】put (rice, vegetable, etc.) into the cooking pan：等米～ *wait for rice to cook*

【下海】① go to sea; put out to sea：～捕鱼 *go fishing on the sea* / ～游泳 *go swimming in the sea* ② (of an amateur) turn career performer：～经商 *turn career performer on business* ③ be driven to prostitution：她因为生活所迫，～啦。*She was driven to prostitution because of her poverty.*

【下怀】one's heart's desire; one's concern：正中～ *be exactly what one wants*

【下回】① next chapter; next session ② next time

【下级】① lower level：～服从上级。*The lower level must obey higher organization.* ② subordinate：帮助～解决问题 *help subordinate to solve the problems in the work*

【下家】① next turn：轮～出牌啦。*It's time for the next person to play.* ②［方］my humble horse

【下家伙】［口］use weapons：亲兄弟怎能在街上～对打？*How could blood brother use weapons to cach other in the street?*

【下嫁】［旧］a noble lady marries a humble man

【下贱】①［旧］low; humble ② degrading; mean;

low-down; obscene

【下降】descend; decline; decrease; drop in; fall; go down: 价格～ *price fall*

【下脚】① get foothold; plant one's foot ② leftover bits and pieces; leftovers

【下脚料】tailings; leftover bits and piece (from processed industrial material)

【下街】go to the street: ～的也有发财的。*Some people made a fortune as going into the street.*

【下劲】work hard at; make a effort; strain oneself

【下井投石】throw stones at one who has fallen in a well; hit a man when he is down

【下酒】① go with wine: 来盘牛肉～。*Bring me a dish of beef to go with wine.* ② go well with wine: 准备几样～的菜。*Please prepare some dishes that go well with wine.*

【下酒菜】dish that goes well with wine

【下课】dismiss class; finish class; class is over: 十点～ *dismiss class at 10:00.*

【下口】eat: 包子太烫，无法～。*The steamed stuffed bun was too hot to eat.*

【下筷】apply one's chopsticks to the food — start eating help oneself: 不要客气，大家～吧。*Please start eating.*

【下款】signature at the end of a letter

【下来】(xiàlai) ① come down: 他～视察工作。*He came to inspect the work.* ② unwind: 他从机器上～就倒地睡着啦。*He fell down to sleep as soon as he left the machine.* ③ end: 一年～ *the end of year* ④ become ripe: 玉米一时还难～。*The maize will not become ripe for a sort while.*

【下来】(xialai) ① used after an adjective to indicate in creasing degree: 天色暗～了，风渐渐停了。*After it got darker, the wind stopped gradually.* ② used after a verb to indicate a downward direction or a movement from far to near: 上级派～的任务 *the tasks assigned by the higher authorities*

【下里巴人】① simple and crude folk songs ② popular literature or art

【下力】enforce; exert oneself; make effort; put forth strength: 他们为了达标，～苦干。*They worked hard in order to reach the standard.*

【下联】second line of a couplet

【下列】listed below; following: ～句子 *the following sentences*

【下令】① direct; give orders: 军官～缓行。*The officer directed his men to advance slowly.*

【下流】① lower reaches: 长江～ *lower reaches of the Changjiang river* ② sexy pornographic; low; nasty; mean: 有些报纸对演员作～的攻击。*Some newspapers made a scurrilous attack on the actors.* ③ [旧] of low or inferior rank

【下落】① fall; drop; descend: 食品价格～了。*The price of food has fallen.* ② where about

【下马】① get off a horse; dismount: 我为了减轻负担宁愿～。*I would rather dismount in order to ease horse's load.* ② discontinue (a project, etc.); abandon; give up: 那个工程～了。*That project has been discontinued.*

【下马威】warn against insubordination by enforcing strict disciplinary action when on first takes office — deal a head-on blow at the first encounter: 给他一个～ *show him one's strength right at the beginning*

【下毛毛雨】① drizzle: 天正～。*It's drizzling.* ② break (some bad news) little by little; criticize or scold gently

【下面】① cook noodles: 我很饿，快给我～。*I am angry, please cook noodles for me.* ② below; under; underneath; beneath: 地板～有老鼠。*There is a rat underneath the floor.* ③ next; following: 请记住～几点。*Please bear in mind the following points.* ④ lower level; subordinate: 倾听～的意见 *listen to the views of subordinates*

【下奶】promote secretion of milk; stimulate lactation

【下皮】【生理】hypodermis

【下品】inferior; low-grade

【下聘】give bride-price; present betrothal gifts

【下坡】① [方] go to the fields: ～干活 *go to fields to do farm work.* ② downgrade: 山的～ *downhill to the hill* ③ go down a slope; go downhill: 学习上稍有放松，成绩就走～。*If you don't study hard, your grades will go down.*

【下坡路】① downhill path; downhill journey; descending road ② decline; deteriorate

【下铺】lower berth or bunk

【下棋】play chess; have a game of chess: 我喜欢～。*I like to have a game of chess.*

【下气】① in a humble voice ②【医】break wind

【下欠】① still owing; outstanding: ～五十 *with fifty yuan still owing* ② sun still owing: ～全部还清。*The debt has been fully paid up.*

【下情】① situation at the lower levels: ～上达 *feeling or wishes of masses* ② [谦] my situation; my circumstances; my state of mind

【下丘脑】【生理】hypothalamus

【下去】(xiàqù) go down; descend; get off: ～看看，谁在喊。*Go downstairs and see who is shouting.*

【下去】(xiàqu) ① on (used after a verb to indicate a continuation): 你这样干～，会累坏的。*If you go on working like this, you'll crack up.* ② used after a verb to indicate a descending motion or going away from near to a far: 把领头闹事的带～。*Take the leader of the trouble-markers away!* ③ used after an adjective to indicate an increasing degree: 这个病人的情况一天天坏～。*This patient is getting worse and worse.*

【下人】① servant ② [方] children or grandchildren

【下三烂】① mean; dirty; low ② despicable good-for-nothing ③ cheap prostitute: 你可以打听打听，她不是～。*Go and find out for yourself! she is no cheap prostitute.*

【下山】① go down the hill: 我陪妹妹一起～去。*I went down the hill with my sister.* ② (of the sun) set:太阳~时,我们回家去。*We came back when the sun was setting.*

【下晌】[方] afternoon

【下梢】① end:木棍的~ *the end of the wooden stick* ② (often used in the early vernacular) ending; outcome:他作恶多端,落了个死无葬身之地的~。*He committed so many crimes that he came to a bad end.*

【下身】① lower part of the body ② privates; private parts; genital

【下神】(of witches) pretend to speak or act for gods or immortals

【下士】sergeant; junior seaman; petty officer:他是一个~。*He is a sergeant.*

【下市】① off season ② close shop:这家铺子早早就~了。*The shop closed early.*

【下世】① die; pass away:先父去年~。*My father died last year.* ② late generations; next life; next incarnation; future world

【下手】① put one's hand to; start; begin; set about:不知从何~ *have no idea where to start* ② [口] assistant; helper:打~ *act as an assistant* ③ right-hand seat:坐在主人的~ *sit on host's right-hand seat* ④ commit a crime; kill ⑤ third hand:在这方面,他是一个~。*In the way, he is a third hand.*

【下属】subordinate:关心~ *be concerned about one's subordinates*

【下水】(xiàshuǐ) ① launch; move into the water; enter the water:那艘新船~了。*That ship was launched.* ② (of textiles, fabrics, etc.) be soaked in water ③ fall into evil ways; engage in evildoing ④ downriver; downstream:我们如果乘~船,很快就能到达那里。*If we take a boat down river, we will arrive there quickly.*

【下水】(xiàshui) (cooked as food) offal; entrails; viscera; internal organs of animals

【下水道】sewers; drain

【下死劲】do one's utmost; with might and main; with all one's might:科学家~攻克了这个难题。*The scientist did his utmost to overcome the problem.*

【下宿】[方] put up for the night; stay at hotel for the night; get accommodation

【下榻】[书] stay; find accommodation; take up abode; lodge at:他们~于建国饭店。*They stayed at Jianguo Hotel.*

【下台】① step down from the stage or platform:他~来与观众握手。*He stepped down from the platform and held hands of the spectators.* ② fall out of power; leave office; fall:他被赶~。*He was driven out of office.* ③ get out of a predicament or an embarrassing situation:他没法~了。*He was unable to get out of a predicament.*

【下台阶】back down with good grace; extricate oneself:他给自己找了个~。*He extricated himself from a predicament.*

【下体】[书] ① lower part of the body ② genital ③ root and stem

【下田】go to the fields:~干活 *go to the fields to work*

【下调】lower the price; reduce

【下帖】send out invitations; deliver an invitation card:为某事~请某人 *deliver an invitation card for sb to do sth*

【下同】(often used in notes or brackets) similarly hereinafter; same below

【下网】off-line

【下文】① what following in the passage; later in an article or book ② later development; result; sequel:怎么没~了? *How come there has been no result?*

【下问】learn from one's inferiors:不耻~ *not feel a shamed to ask and learn from those who are less learned than oneself*

【下午】afternoon

【下弦】①【天】last quarter:月~ *moon at the last quarter*

【下限】lower limit; prescribed minimum; floor:文章字数~为1000字。*The article should be more than one thousand words.*

【下陷】settle; sink; subside; cave in

【下乡】go to the countryside; rusticate:爸爸十三岁那年就~了。*My father went to the countryside when I was thirteen years old.*

【下泻】① flow:我们要整治河道以利水流~。*We must regulate canal in order to flow water.* ② (of price, etc.) drop sharply; fall steeply; plummet:钢材价格正一路~。*Steel price was dropping sharply.* ③ have diarrhea; loose bowels

【下泄】flow or drain; rush downward

【下行】① down ② downriver; downstream:~船 *downriver boat* ③ (of a document) be issued to the lower levels

【下学】let out; finish school:同学们一~,马上就回家啦。*The students went home as soon as they finished school.*

【下旬】the last or the third ten-day period of a month

【下咽】swallow; gulp down:如此东西,实在难以~。*Such coarse food was really too difficult to swallow.*

【下药】① prescribe medicine:这个大夫能够对症~。*The doctor is able to prescribe medicine.* ② put in poison:他~害死他的妻子。*He put in poison to kill his wife.*

【下野】(of a ruler) retire from the political arena; quit from official posts; fall from power:他~之后,出洋考察。*He went abroad on a study tour after falling from power.*

【下夜】patrol at night; go on night patrol:今晚他~巡逻。*He should patrol at tonight.*

【下议院】Lower house; Lower Chamber; (UK) House of commons

【下意识】subconsciousness:他~地抓住我的手。*He subconsciously held my hands.*

【下游】① lower reaches (of a river); down stream:他被激流冲到~。*He was swept down stream by the rush of the current.* ② backward position; lagging behind ③ downstream
【下狱】be thrown into prison; be put behind bars; be imprisoned:他被捕~。*He was sent to prison.*
【下雨】rain
【下载】download
【下葬】bury; inter:他母亲昨日~了。*His mother was buried yesterday.*
【下账】enter into the account:有几笔款子需要~。*Several sums of money need be entered into the account book.*
【下诏】issue a imperial editor order: ~退位 *issue an imperial edict of abdication*
【下肢】【生理】lower limbs; legs: ~瘫痪。*Legs are paralyzed.*
【下中农】lower-middle-peasant
【下种】sow (seeds):农夫在春天~。*The farmer sows seeds in spring.*
【下注】put stake; stake a wager; lay a wager; wager:我愿对这条狗~100元。*I'm ready to wager 100 yuan on the dog.*
【下坠】① fall; drop; go down; sag:飞机燃烧着~。*The plane burning was falling.* ②【医】straining (at stool); tenesmus
【下钻】run the drilling tool into a well: ~速度 *running speed*
【下作】① low; nasty; low; obscene; mean:无耻~的做法 *brazen, low-down action* ②[方] greedy; gluttonous; ravenous ③[方] assistant; helper:打~ *act as a helper*

吓 intimidate; frighten; scare; startle; terrify:困难~不倒我们。*Difficulties don't frighten us.*
see also hè
【吓唬】bluff; frighten; scare intimidate:别~某人 *don't frighten sb*
【吓人】① frighten people:巫师专门装鬼弄神~。*The wizard specially mystified to frighten people.* /真是~的场面。*This really was a horrible sight.*

夏[1] summer: ~日 *summer days*

夏[2] ① the Xia Dynasty (2205-1782 B. C.) ② (Xià) a surname
【夏播】summer sowing
【夏锄】summer hoeing ; hoeing fields in summer
【夏候鸟】summer resident or bird
【夏季】summer
【夏历】lunar calendar; traditional Chinese calendar
【夏粮】grain crops harvested in summer; summer grain crops
【夏令】① summer; summer time ② summer weather
【夏令时】summer time (ST); daylight saving time
【夏日】① summer ② summer sun: ~炎炎 *blazing summer sun*
【夏收】① summer harvest ② summer harvesting
【夏熟】ripen in summer; summer maturing: ~作物 *summer maturing crops*
【夏天】summer
【夏娃】Eve, the first woman, according to the Bible
【夏威夷】Hawaii, a state of the US comprising a chain of islands in north pacific: ~人 *Hawaiian*
【夏衣】summer clothing; summer wear
【夏耘】[书] summer hoeing
【夏种】summer sowing: ~作物 *summer sowing crops or crops sown in summer*
【夏装】summer dress

厦 tall building; edifice
see also shà
【厦门】Xiamen or Amoy, a port city in Fujian Province

罅 [书] chink; cleft; crack; fissure; flaw; rift:石~ *a crack in a rock*
【罅缝】[书] fissure; cleft; crack; chink; rift
【罅漏】[书] crevice; deficiency; flaw; fault; loophole; short-coming; gap:亚伯拉罕长得~。*Abraham is elegant in an other-worldly way.*
【罅隙】[书] crack; cleft; fissure; flaw; rift

xiān

仙 immortal; fairy
【仙风道骨】be elegant in an other-worldly way
【仙姑】① fairy; immortal lady; celestial being ② woman taoist, sorceress
【仙鹤】① red-crowned crane; stork ② (as a divine bird) crane
【仙家】① divine abode ② immortal; fairy; celestial being
【仙界】land of the divine; paradise; fairy land
【仙境】a place of exquisite natural beauty
【仙居】divine abode
【仙女】fairy; young woman of divine; fairy maiden; beauty
【仙人】immortal; celestial being:请~给我指点迷津。*I ask an immortal for me what I should do.*
【仙逝】die; pass away:家父昨晚~。*My father died last night.*
【仙童】fairy messenger boy
【仙姿】fairylike look or figure; ethereal beauty
【仙子】① fairy; woman of immortal; fairy maiden:玫瑰~ *Rose Fairy* ② immortal; celestial being

先 ① first; foremost before; earlier:他首~发言。*He spoke first.* /他比我~到这里。*He arrived here earlier than I did.* ② older generation; ancestry:祖~ *ancestors* ③ late; deceased: ~总统 *late president* ④ earlier on; before:这里的环境比~前好多啦。*The environment here is much better than before.* ⑤ advance:争~恐后 *rush off to pioneer the front* ⑥ (Xiān) a surname

【先辈】① elder generation ② ancestors; forefathers; forerunners; seniors: 我们要牢记~的遗训。*We must bear in mind the teaching of our ancestors.*
【先妣】[书] late or deceased mother
【先鞭】be the first; take the lead; get ahead; take precedence
【先导】① lead the way; be in the van: ~部队首先出发了。*The army which led the way started out at first.* ② model; master; teacher: 他是我们学习的~。*He is the model whom we learn to.* ③ guide; forerunner; precursor: 失败常常是成功的~。*Failure is often the precursor of success.*
【先帝】late emperor; previous emperor: ~遗诏 *the previous imperial edict*
【先睹为快】watch before the voice; consider it a pleasure to be among the first to read
【先锋】harbinger; pioneer; forerunner; vanguard; van
【先锋队】vanguard: 工人阶级的~ *the vanguard of working class*
【先夫】late husband
【先父】late father
【先公后私】subordinate one's personal interests to public interests: 共产党员理所应当~。*The member of the Communist Party ought to put public interests before his personal interests.*
【先河】forerunner; source that is: 开创历史研究的~ *break a path for studies of history events*
【先后】① the order of things placed; early and late; from first to last: 工作都要干,但要有个~。*All the works should be done, but they must be taken up in priority order.* ② ins and outs of an incident; one after another: 我~到过那里五次。*I have been there five times.*
【先机】decisive occasion; opportunity of vital importance to the future
【先见之明】foresight; prophetic vision; ability to discern what is coming: 好像参谋长对任何事都有~。*The chief staff looks like to have foresight on anything.*
【先进】① advanced: ~技术 *advanced technology* ② advanced individual
【先决】prerequisite: ~条件 *precondition; antecedent condition*
【先觉】prophet; person of foresight: 穆罕默德是穆斯林的~。*Mohammed is the prophet of the Muslims.*
【先君】[书] late or deceased father
【先来后到】first come, first served; in order of arrival: 凡事都要有个~。*There is precedence in order of arrival in everything we do.*
【先礼后兵】diplomacy before the use of force; take strong measures only after courteous one's fail: 我们主张~。*We advocate words before blows.*
【先例】precedent; example: 在中国建设社会主义,我们无~可循。*In China, building socialism, we have no precedent to go by.*
【先烈】martyr: 革命~ *the martyrs of revolution*
【先令】① shilling (British and other) ② schilling (Austrian)
【先民】[书] ① ancient people ② ancient sages
【先母】late or deceased mother
【先农坛】Altar of the God of agriculture, Beijing
【先期】earlier on; in advance: 代表团的部分成员已~到达。*The part members of deputation arrived here in advance.*
【先前】before; earlier; previously: 这孩子比~高多啦。*The kid is much taller than before.*
【先遣】be sent in advance; advanced troops: ~队 *advance team*
【先秦】before Qin Dynasty; pre-Qin, the Spring and Autumn Period and the Warring States Period, 770-221B. C.
【先驱】pioneer; forerunner; leader
【先人】① ancestor; forefather: 他们的~都住在这个小村。*Their ancestors lived in the small village.* ② late father
【先人后己】put others before oneself: 作为一个共产党员我必须~。*As a communist, I must put myself interests behind the people's interests.*
【先入为主】first impressions are the strongest; be prejudged or preoccupied
【先入之见】preconceived idea or notion; preconception: 法官不应有~。*A judge must be free from prejudice.*
【先声】herald; first signs; harbinger
【先声夺人】forestall one's opponent by a show of strength; with an impressive start; overawe others by displaying one's strength
【先生】① teacher: 听~授课 *listen to the teacher* ② mister (Mr.): 王~ *Mr. Wang* ③ [方] doctor ④ husband (used together with personal pronouns)
【先世】forefather; ancestry; forebear
【先是】formerly; at first; originally: 这块土地~为私人所有,但现在归国家。*This land was formerly owned privately, but now it belongs to the Nation.*
【先天】① congenital; inbred; inborn by birth: ~畸形 *congenital disfiguration* / ~性心脏病 *the congenital heart disease* ②【哲】a priori; innate
【先天不足】be congenitally deficient; inborn deficiency inherited weakness: 这孩子~。*The child was congenitally deficient.*
【先头】① ahead in advance; in front of: 走在~ *walk in ahead* ② in advance, before; formerly; previously: 他~来过这儿。*He has come here before.* ③ van; vanguard: ~部队 *vanguard*
【先王】deceased emperors in former times
【先下手为强】catch the ball before the bound; who strikes first prevails; he who strikes first gains the upper hand
【先贤】wise men; scholars of the past; late sages
【先小人后君子】specify terms clearly at first and use a good deal of courtesy later
【先行】① go ahead of the rest; start off before the others; precede ② in advance; beforehand: ~通

知 *let sb know in advance* ③ antecedence; precession: ~词 *antecedent* ④ commander of an advance unit

【先行者】pioneer; vanguard; forerunner: 纪念伟大的革命~孙中山先生。*Let's pay tribute to great revolutionary forerunner, Dr. Sun Zhongshan.*

【先斩后奏】execute the criminal first and report to the emperor afterwards — act first and report afterwards; take action before reporting to one's superior: 你可以~。*You can act first and report afterwards.*

【先兆】omen; indication; sign; portent: 狂风是暴雨的~。*A evident wind is an indication of an impendings.*

【先哲】great thinker of the past

【先知】① person of foresight; prescience: 人类的~ *those with foresight among human being* ②【宗】prophet

【先知先觉】① person of foresight ② have foresight

【先祖】[书] ① deceased grandfather ② ancestry

纤 delicate; fine; minute; slender; tiny: 她身材~细。*She has a delicate figure.*
see also qiàn

【纤长】slender and long: 女人~的手指 *long and slender fingers of woman*

【纤尘】fine dust

【纤尘不染】without a speck of dust; be spotlessly clean; maintain one's original integrity: 当领导多年,他两袖清风,~。*Although he has been in leader for many years, he remains untainted with evil thoughts.*

【纤毫】finest hairs; minutest details or particles; very little: ~不爽 *be extremely accurate*

【纤美】slender and beautiful; delicate and pretty: 她玉手~。*She has slender and beautiful hands.*

【纤密】fine-woven; detailed; meticulous

【纤巧】delicate; exquisite: 漂亮女孩都有~的手。*The good girl has delicate hands.*

【纤柔】delicate and soft

【纤弱】fragile; delicate; thin and weak: 她身体~。*She was in thin and weak health.*

【纤手】delicate hands

【纤瘦】thin and small; slender and delicate; slim and fragile

【纤微】infinitesimal; microscopic; minute; tiny

【纤维】fiber; staple: 人造~ *man-make fiber* / ~板 *fiberboard* / ~玻璃 *fibreglass* / ~植物 *fibre plant*

【纤悉】[书] know thoroughly; be familiar with every detail of: ~无遗 *no detail escapes notice; no omission*

【纤细】fine; tiny; minute; slim; very thin

【纤纤】[书] ① delicate; fine; minute ② sharp; thin: ~细故 *trivial affairs*

【纤小】fine; little; trivial; tiny: ~轻盈 *little and graceful*

【纤屑】[书] details; piddling; trivial: 不要整日谈论~之事! *Don't talk trivial all day* !

【纤秀】fine and elegant

【纤腰】slender waist of a woman

【纤指】woman's slender fingers

掀 ① lift with the hands; raise; open up; turn over: ~帘进屋 *lift the door curtain and enter the room* ② cause; convulse; expose; reveal; rise; rock; stir; stir up: ~人老底 *reveal one's past*

【掀动】① lift; raise; instigate: 微风~起她的头发。*The breeze lifted her hair.* ② start; unleash; launch; stir up: ~战争 *start a war*

【掀风鼓浪】stir up an upheaval; cause unrest; make trouble: 别听那些人~。*Don't hear those stir up an upheaval.*

【掀起】① lift; raise ② surge: 大海~巨浪。*Large waves surged on the sea.* ③ launch; set off; start: ~新的辩论 *set off a new debate*

【掀腾】stir; overturn; convulse

【掀涌】be turbulent; seethe: 波浪~ *turbulent waves*

酰 【化】acyl

【酰胺】【化】amides: ~酶 *amidase* ~水解酶 *amidohydrolase*

【酰化】【化】acylate

【酰基】【化】acyl

锨 shovel; spade: 木~ *wooden winnowing shovel*

鲜 ① fresh; new: 新~水果 *fresh fruits* ② bright-coloured; bright; gaily-coloured: ~艳的花朵 *bright-coloured flower* ③ clear: 空气~新 *clear air* ④ delicious; tasty: 这汤很~。*This soup is delicious.* ⑤ special: 她的行动作风就是~,和别人不一样。*Her action was special and different from other's.* ⑥ live fish; aquatic food: 海~ *seafood* ⑦ fresh food; delicious food ⑧ (Xiān) a surname
see also xiǎn

【鲜脆】fresh and brittle

【鲜果】fresh fruit

【鲜红】bright-red; scarlet: ~的太阳东边升起。*The red sun rises from eastern.*

【鲜花】fresh flower; flowers

【鲜货】fresh fruit or vegetables; fresh aquatic foods

【鲜活】① vivid; lively: ~的商品 *perishable commodities* /这夹克的颜色很~。*The jacket is bright-coloured.*

【鲜丽】fresh and beautiful: 衣着~ *wear in bright-coloured dresses*

【鲜亮】①[方] fresh; be bright and shining: ~的绿色 *bright-green* ② pretty; beautiful: 那姑娘看起来很~。*That girl looks like pretty.*

【鲜灵】[方] fresh and tender: 花浇过水之后,显得更~。*After being watered, the flowers looked all the more fresh.*

【鲜美】① delicious; tasty: 味道~ *delicious taste* ② [书] fresh and beautiful: 牧场上有~的青草。*There is fresh and good pasture in a stock farm.*

【鲜明】① brilliant; bright; shiny: 色彩~ *brilliant colour* ② unequivocal; well-define; clear-cut;

sharp; distinct: ~的立场 *definite stand*

【鲜嫩】crisp; fresh and tender: ~的蔬菜 *fresh vegetable*

【鲜浓】rich and gaudy; bright and rich in colour: 色泽~ *bright and rich in colour*

【鲜润】fresh and smooth; fresh and moist

【鲜甜】fresh and sweet; sweet and delicious

【鲜血】blood

【鲜妍】vivid; bright-coloured; bright and beautiful

【鲜艳】bright-coloured; gaily-coloured: ~的彩虹 *bright and beautiful rainbow*

骞 [书] (of birds) fly

xián

闲 ① idle; unoccupied; free; spare; not busy: ~来垂钓 *spend free time on going fishing* ② not in use; vacant; unoccupied: ~屋 *unoccupied house* ~职 *job with little work* ③ informal; irrelevant; random; idle: 多管~事 *muddle in what is none of your business* ④ leisure; spare time

【闲笔】digression; irrelevant words in writing

【闲步】roam at leisure; saunter; stroll without a destination

【闲不住】keep oneself busy; unable to remain idle: 他总是~。*He refused to stay idle.*

【闲常】[方] usually; ordinary; in general: 他~在家看电视。*He usually watches TV at home.*

【闲扯】chat; chit-chat; babble chat: 下午与他~一番。*I had a chat with him at afternoon.*

【闲荡】saunter; stroll; idle; loaf; loiter: 顺着乡村街道~ *stroll along the countryside street*

【闲房】unoccupied house; vacant room

【闲工夫】spare time; leisure: 我没有~与你一起去看戏。*I have no free time to go to the theater with you.*

【闲逛】saunter; loiter; stroll; loaf; gad about: 大多数女人喜欢在街上~。*Most of women like to stroll along the street.*

【闲汉】bum; vagrant; idler; loafer; jobless person

【闲花野草】① weeds and wild flowers ② women of easy virtue; prostitutes: 她要求丈夫勿沾~。*She demands her husband mustn't get involved with promiscuous women.*

【闲话】① digression; cackle; gossip; random: 他太爱说~。*He was too fond of gossip.* ② complaint: 别让他们有说咱们~的机会。*We mustn't give them cause for complaint.* ③ [书] talk casually about; chat about; engage in idle talk

【闲寂】[书] deserted and quiet; unoccupied and still

【闲静】quiet; undisturbed; peaceful and calm in mind-without desires: 让我~一会儿。*Let me enjoy a little quiet.*

【闲居】stay at home idly; lead a placid life: 她喜欢~独处。*She enjoys living idly and alone.*

【闲空】free time; leisure; spare time

【闲聊】chat; have a gossip: 我曾和他~过。*I had a gossip with him.* /我隔着花园篱笆同邻居愉快地~。*I had a good gossip with a neighbour over the garden fence.*

【闲磨牙】chit-chat; babble

【闲篇】[方] gossip: 别介意, 那都是~。*Don't mind your heart; that is mere gossip.*

【闲气】anger about trifles; uncalled-for abuse: 他们就是因为这件琐事, 生了不少~。*They got a good deal of anger about such a trifle.*

【闲弃】abandon; unoccupied; unused: 耕地长期被~。*Cultivated land has been unused for a long time.*

【闲钱】[口] spare cash; spare money

【闲情逸致】leisurely and carefree mood; cultivated pleasures of a leisurely life

【闲人】① unoccupied person; idler: 他是一个大~。*He is an unoccupied.* ② persons not concerned: ~免进。*No admittance except on business.*

【闲散】① free and at leisure ② unused; idle: ~资金 *idle capital*

【闲时】free time; leisure

【闲事】① a matter that does not concern one; other people's business: 别多管~。*Don't mind other people's business.* ② unimportant matter; trifle: 我很忙, 没有工夫管这等~。*I was busy, and had no time to do such trifles.*

【闲是闲非】idle talk; chit-chat; idle gossip

【闲适】leisurely and comfortable; easy and carefree; quiet and comfortable: ~的心情 *quiet and comfortable mood*

【闲书】light reading; book for whiling away time as novel, etc.: 看~ *do light reading; read for amusement*

【闲谈】chat; tinkle; yatter; gossip; chit-chat: 终日~无所事事 *chit-chat all day with doing nothing*

【闲田】vacant field

【闲庭】quiet courtyard: 胜似~信步 *look like strolling in a quiet, tranquil garden*

【闲玩】play at leisurely manner: 孩子们喜欢在沙滩上~。*The children like to play at leisure manner on sands.*

【闲文】irrelevant words; digression

【闲暇】free time; spare time; leisure: 我一直都很忙, 没有~去玩。*I am always busy, and have no leisure for playing.*

【闲心】leisurely mood; easy mood: 我没有~管这事。*I am too busy to think about such matters.*

【闲言碎语】① sarcastic remarks; gossips; digressions ② groundless talk; nonsense: 她是一个长舌妇, 喜欢在背地里散布~。*She was a gossip, and was fond of talebearing behind sb back.*

【闲逸】[书] leisurely and comfortable; carefree: ~的生活 *carefree and comfortable life*

【闲游】saunter; stroll; loaf; gad: 他在外~了一天, 什么也没干。*He had sauntered for whole day and had nothing to do.*

【闲员】surplus personnel; redundant staff: 由于煤的需要量减少,很多矿工可能成为~。*With the decreasing demand for coal many miners may become redundant staff.*
【闲云野鹤】floating clouds and wild cranes — person who have a quietness and comfortableness of a secluded life
【闲杂】without fixed duties; irrelevant: ~人员 *people without fixed duties; miscellaneous personnel*
【闲职】job with little work; unoccupied post; sinecure
【闲置】leave unused; knock about; let sth lie idle; gather dust; set aside: 车间里有许多~的机器。*There are many idle machines in the workshop.*
【闲坐】sit idly and enjoy one's leisure: 他在家~。*He sat idle at home.*

贤 ① able; capable; good; talented; worthy; versatile; virtuous: ~臣能士 *virtuous and capable ministers* ② wise man; versatile mind; able and virtuous person: 见~思齐 *try to do as well as a versatile mind when one sees one* ③ term of respectful address to another, a polite express to you and your brother
【贤才】capable and virtuous person; man of great capability: 他是个难得的~。*He is a rare talent.*
【贤达】prominent personage; wise and virtuous; worthy
【贤德】① benevolence; virtue ② virtuous: ~女人 *kind lady*
【贤弟】my dear brother; term of respectful address to a male friend who is younger than oneself
【贤惠】virtuous and kind; good and wise; kind-hearted: 他老婆很~。*His wife is virtuous and intelligent.*
【贤良】[书] ① be able and virtuous ② able and virtuous man: 择~而用 *choose the virtuous to employ*
【贤妹】my dear sister; a term of respect for one's younger sister or woman younger than oneself
【贤明】① capable and wise; able and virtuous: ~的君主 *wise and able king* ② capable and virtuous man; sage; elite: 另请~ *engage sb of capabilities*
【贤内助】good wife; better half: 她是大家公认的~。*She is good wife by public.*
【贤能】① able and virtuous ② talented person
【贤妻】① virtuous wife; good wife; understanding wife ② dear wife
【贤妻良母】dutiful wife and loving mother; virtuous wife and worthy mother: 谁都知道她是位~。*Everyone know that she is an understanding wife and loving mother.*
【贤人】virtuous and talented person; worthy man; wise man
【贤士】person of high moral standing; wise man
【贤淑】usu. said of woman virtuous and kind; kind-hearted
【贤哲】person outstanding in virtue and learning; wise man
【贤侄】worthy nephew, a polite term for one's nephew or the son of one's friend

弦 ① bowstring: 箭在~不得不发。*The arrow is on the low; it must be shot.* ② string of a musical instrument ③ spring (of a watch, etc.) strings ④【数】hypotenuse ⑤【中医】tight ⑥ chord
【弦脉】【中医】tight; taut pulse
【弦歌】sing to the accompaniment of stringed instruments
【弦外之意】over tones; implication; implied meaning; connotations: 他这番话有~。*There are overtones in his words.*
【弦乐队】【音】string orchestra; string band
【弦乐器】【音】stringed instrument
【弦柱】the neck of a stringed instrument

咸[1] ① all: 老少~宜 *be good for old and young alike* ② (Xián) a surname

咸[2] salted; salty: 菜太~。*The dish lacks too salt.*
【咸不唧儿】saltish: 这水~的。*The water is saltish.*
【咸海】Aral Sea; inland sea east of the Caspian Sea between Kazakhstan and Uzbekistan
【咸津津】somewhat salty; brackish
【咸肉】salted meat; bacon
【咸涩】salty and bitter: ~的泪 *salty and bitter tears*
【咸水】salt water; brackish water
【咸丝丝】slightly salty; brackish
【咸盐】[方] slat

涎 saliva: 垂~ *drool; crave*
【涎皮赖脸】shameless; brazen-faced; cheekily: 谁都讨厌他那~相。*Everybody disliked his brazen behaviour.*
【涎石】【医】sialolith: ~病 *salivolithiasis*
【涎着脸】[方] behave in shameless or brazen-faced way

娴 [书] ① refined; graceful; elegant: ~慧 *graceful and fine* / ~雅的举止 *elegant manners* ② be skillful at; have the knock at: ~于辞令 *be skilled in speech*
【娴静】gentle and refined; demure; quiet and serious: 她是一个~的女孩。*She is a demure girl.*
【娴淑】refined and kind: 她举止端庄~。*She is refined and dignified in manners.*
【娴熟】adept; consummate; dexterous; expert; skilled; well-versed: 他在足球上表现了~的技巧。*He is skill at soccer.*
【娴习】be well-versed in; be skill in; be adept at: 他~新闻写作。*He is skilled in news writing.*
【娴雅】cultured; elegant; polished; refined: ~斯文 *elegant and cultured*

衔[1] ① hold in the mouth of earth in their bills ② cherish; bear ③ accept (instruction or order) ④ connect; link

衔[2] rank

【衔接】link to; connect with; join:由一条运河～的两个城镇。*Two towns linked by a canal.*

【衔头】title:他的～是什么 *What is his official title?*

【衔冤】a bitter sense of injustice; suffer a wrong:窦娥～而死。*Dou'er died with her name unlearned.*

舷

【舷边】gunwale; gunnel

【舷窗】porthole; scuttle

【舷门】gangway

【舷梯】① accommodation ladder; gangway ② ramp (of a plane)

痫 【医】癫～ *epilepsy*

【痫症】epilepsy

嫌 ① suspicion:涉～ *be under suspicion* ② ill will; grudge; hatred:他用～恶的目光看着那女人。*He looked at the woman with hatred.* ③ suspect; dislike; disgust

【嫌猜】dislike and suspicion:消释～ *clear up dislike and suspicion*

【嫌烦】not want to take the trouble; regard as too much bother; consider troublesome

【嫌忌】[书] reject; suspect; be suspicious and jealous:鲍勃对任何人都～。*Bob suspects everybody.*

【嫌怕】[方] dislike; fear; be afraid of

【嫌弃】dislike and shun; cold-shoulder; dislike and avoid; give up in disgust:不要～犯有过错的学生。*Don't dislike and avoid the student who has made mistakes.*

【嫌恶】abhor; loathe; detest; dislike; hate; loathe:我～那人。*I loathe that man.*

【嫌隙】animosity; enmity; ill feeling; old grudge:～冰消 *ill feeling thawed like ice.*

【嫌厌】dislike; loathe; detest

【嫌疑】suspicion; suspect

【嫌疑分子】suspect

【嫌怨】hatred; grudge; resentment; enmity; ill will:我从不引起～。*I have never stirred up enmity.*

【嫌憎】loathe; hate; dislike

xiǎn

显 ① apparent; clear; evident; manifest; noticeable; obvious; self-evident:明～ *conspicuous* ② display; expose; make known; manifest; show:～示某人的才干 *show one's talent* ③ well-known; renowned; high-positioned; eminent:权势～赫 *powerful influence*

【显摆】[方] show off; reveal; boast:这个年轻女子喜欢～自己。*The young lady likes to show off herself.*

【显出】appear; display; reveal; show; give evidence:～他的无知 *display his ignorance*

【显达】attain high office; be famous and powerful; be illustrious and influential

【显得】look; appear; seem:房子如此装修,～有格调多啦。*Decorated the way it is, the house looks much more stylish.*

【显而易见】apparently; clearly; evidently; obviously; as plain as daylight:这对我们大家是～的。*It was apparent to all of us.*

【显贵】① of high position; influential ② highest-tone; bigwig:结交～ *associate with eminent personages*

【显赫】celebrated; glorious; illustrious; influential; outstanding; mighty; powerful:位居～*occupy an eminent position*

【显见】obvious; plain; self-evident; apparent

【显灵】divine manifestation; theophany; make a supernatural appearance or otherwise; make its presence

【显亮】bright; conspicuous; striking:那架钢琴就放在房中最～的地方。*The piano is put on the most conspicuous spot of the room.*

【显露】appear; become visible; manifest; show; reveal; unveil: ～头角 *show one's promise* /她没有～出很想嫁给他的样子。*She doesn't manifest much desire to marry him.*

【显明】clear; evident; obvious; distinct; marked; manifest:那两姐妹之间的差异很～。*The contrast between the two sisters is remarkable.*

【显目】eye-catching; conspicuous; manifest; eye appeal; showy:红花在绿叶的陪衬下格外～。*Red flowers are extremely manifest among the green leaves.*

【显能】show off one's ability

【显亲扬名】make one's family illustrious by achieving fame

【显然】in evidence; obvious; clear

【显山露水】[方] attract attention by dis playing one's talent or skill (usu. used in the negative):刘芳不～就把这事给办了。*Liufang had such thing done without making the least fuss about it.*

【显身手】display one's talent or skill; show one's talent or skill:大～ *cut a brilliant figure*

【显圣】make evident a divine presence or power felt

【显示】show; display; demonstrate; manifest: ～出某人的智慧 *demonstrate one's intelligence*

【显现】appear; manifest oneself; reveal oneself; emerge; show

【显效】① show effect:我用了几次这药,一点也不～。*I have taken several medicine, and shown no effect.* ② apparent effect; conspicuous results:～明显。*There has been very much apparent effect.*

【显形】show one's (true) colours; appear in human form

【显眼】conspicuous; showy:布告贴在～的地方。

The notice was glued in conspicuous place.

【显扬】①［书］cite; commend; praise; acclaim; make known ② famous：他名声～，远近皆知。*He was well-known far and near.*

【显要】① influential figure ② powerful and influential; high and mighty

【显耀】① show off; vaunt ② be famous for one's fame and influence; wield power and prestige

【显证】［书］clear proof：这是他学习刻苦的～。*This is a clear proof that he hard studied.*

【显著】conspicuous; notable; striking; marked; outstanding; remarkable：～的进步 *marked progress*

【显祖】one's forebears

险 ①（of terrain, etc.）dangerous; perilous; high-abrupt：山高路～ *high-abrupt mountain and perilous road* ② defence fortification; defence works; place difficult of access（such as narrow pass, swift river）：长江天～ *natural pattier of the Changjiang river* ③ danger risk; imperil jeopardize; hazard ④ nearly; almost; by a hair's breadth ⑤ be rugged and rough; risk; imperil：探索活火山是非常危～的。*It is the most risky to go and examine inactive volcano.*

【险隘】strategic pass; place difficult of access; defile

【险地】① dangerous place; dangerous situation; perilous plight：身处～ *put oneself into a dangerous situation* ② strategic position; easily defended terrain

【险毒】sinister and venomous; treacherous and vicious：用心～ *have a sinister and pernicious intention*

【险厄】［书］① danger place; place difficult of access; easily defended position ② evil dangerous; perilous; hazardous：～境地 *perilous situation*

【险恶】① dangerous; parlous; ominous; treacherous：病情～*ominous state of illness* ② sinister; vicious; malicious; devious; diabolic：他居心～。*He had sinister intentions.*

【险峰】perilous peak（of a mountain）：无限风光在～ *dwells infinite beauty on perilous peaks*

【险工】dangerous task; perilous construction or engineering project

【险固】［书］strategic and impregnable; difficult of access and easily defended

【险关】strategic pass

【险急】extremely urgent; critical：病情～ *critical illness*

【险峻】① dangerous steep; precipitous：～的群山 *high-abrupt mountains* ② dangerous; severe：形势～。*The situation was fraught with danger or critical.*

【险僻】parlous and out-of-the-way：～的山路 *dangerous and out-of-the way mountain path*

【险峭】precipitous; dangerously steep：～的山峰 *giddy peak*

【险情】dangerous condition; dangerous situation; danger：～频发 *dangerous situation was high-frequent*

【险球】（mostly in football）near miss：救出～ *make a save*

【险胜】edge out; win by a narrow margin：他们～这场比赛。*They won the game by a narrow margin.*

【险滩】dangerous rapids（shoals）; nick point

【险象】dangerous phenomenon; dangerous sign or symptom：～环生 *be dangerous lurking on all sides; dangerous sign appear one after another*

【险些】almost; nearly; narrowly：她～摔进水里。*She nearly fell in the water.*

【险性】dangerous; perilous：～事故 *perilous accident*

【险要】（of place）strategic and capable of being easily defended：～之地 *location of strategic importance and easy defence*

【险语】sensational remarks; startling remarks; difficult and rare words（of classical poetry）

【险诈】sinister and crafty; sinister and sly：为人～ *sinister and crafty by nature*

【险兆】dangerous omen; evil omen; harbinger of danger

【险症】dangerous illness or disease：他专治～。*He specialized dangerous illness.*

【险阻】（of roads）dangers and difficulties

鲜 little rare：～为人知 *be little known*

see also xiān

xiàn

县 county town

【县城】county town; county seat

【县份】county：偏远～ *remote counties*

【县令】county magistrate

【县长】head of a county; county magistrate

【县志】county annals; general records of a county：按～记载 *according to county records*

现 ① present; now; current; modern; existing：她是～今最红的电影明星之一。*She is nowadays one of the most popular film stars.* ② as the occasion arises; extempore; impromptu; in time of need：～学～用 *learn while one uses* / ～编～唱 *make up a song as one sings* ③ available; ready; on hand：～货 *stock goods; goods on hand; spots* ④ cash; ready money ⑤ appear; emerge; reveal; show：母亲脸上～出一丝笑容。*A faint smile appeared on my mother's face.* ⑥ actual：～实情况 *actual conditions or facts*

【现场】① scene（of an incident or crime）：警察匆忙赶到发案～。*The police hurried to the scene of the crime.* ② spot; site：～表演 *live show* / ～采访 *spot coverage*

【现钞】cash

X

【现成】on hand; ready; ready-made: ~的衣服 *ready-made clothes*

【现成饭】food ready for the table; unearned gain: 他总是吃~。*He always eats whatever is ready.*

【现成话】kibitzer's comments

【现丑】make a fool of oneself; bring shame on oneself; show oneself up; show one's immature skills: 当众~ *make a fool of oneself in public*

【现出】show; reveal

【现存】in stock; on hand; available; extant: ~版本 *extant edition* / ~物资 *goods and materials in stock*

【现大洋】[口] silver dollar

【现代】① modern times; contemporary age; present: 从古代到~ *from the ancient time up to the present age* / ~人 *the people living in modern times* ② modern; present-day; present world; current: ~经济管理 *modern economic management*

【现汇】spot exchange: ~汇率 *spot exchange rate*

【现货】【经】stock goods; goods on hand; spots: ~交易 *spot transactions*

【现今】nowadays; at present; now; in these days; at the moment

【现金】① ready money; cash: 支付~ *pay cash for* ② cash reserve in a bank: 库存~ *cash in treasury*

【现局】present situation; current state of affairs; nowadays aspect

【现刻】[方] right now; at the present moment

【现款】cash; ready money: ~交易市场 *cash market*

【现露】appear; come into view; reveal; unveil show

【现年】present age: 她~五岁。*She is now five.*

【现期】current; at the very moment

【现钱】[口] ready money; cash

【现任】① present position, job or employment; incumbent: ~校长以前是主任。*The present principal used to be a head of an office.* ② at present hold the office of

【现如今】[方] nowadays; at present; now

【现身说法】act as an example to others; give a demonstration in person; use one's own experience as an object lesson

【现时】now; at present

【现实】① reality; actuality; things as they are: 客观~ *objective reality* ② practical pragmatic; real; actual; factual: ~生活 *real life*

【现世】① this world; this life: ~与彼世 *this life and the other life* ② be disgraced; bring shame on oneself; lose face: 丢人~ *be discredited*

【现势】present situation; current situation

【现象】appearance; phenomena

【现行】① existing; presently valid; in force: 维护~政策 *maintain the existing policies* ② (of a criminal) active

【现形】betray oneself; reveal one's true colours form, character, etc.

【现眼】be embarrassed; cut a sorry figure; lose face; make a scene; make a spectacle of oneself: 他在众人面前丢人~。*He made a fool of himself in public.*

【现役】active service; active duty: ~军人 *serviceman*

【现有】have on hand; available; existing: 在~情况下,食物不可能便宜。*Food will not be cheaper under existing conditions.*

【现在】nowadays, at present; today; for the time being

【现职】present job; current post or position

【现状】current situation; present state of affairs: 大部分人安于~。*Most people are content with things as they are.*

限 ① bounds; limits; restriction; 能力有~。*Power are limited.* /字数不~。*There is no restriction on the number of words.* ② allow; limit; prescribe; restrict: 我们必须~制开销不超过我们经济能力的范围。*We must limit the expense to what we can afford.* ③ [书] doorsill; threshold: 门~ *doorsill*

【限定】confine; limit; prescribe a limit to; specify; restrict: 与会者~为三十人。*Participation in the meeting will be limit to thirty.*

【限产】cut or limit production: ~压库促销 *limit production and stockpile and promote marketing.*

【限度】limit; limitation; degree: 我们的忍耐是有~的。*There is a limit to our patience.*

【限额】limit; quota; the maximum or minimum number or amount allowed: 达到~ *reach the full quota*

【限价】limited price of a certain commodity; price control; price fixed under a government specified ceiling: ~供应 *supply to prices control*

【限界】limits; bounds; boundary: 那超出了人类知识的~。*It is beyond the bounds of human knowledge.*

【限量】① limits; limitation; boundary ② restrict; set measure to; set the bounds to; limit the quantity: ~供应 *set measure to supply*

【限令】① order sb to do sth within a certain time: 他们~她二十四小时内离境。*They order her to leave the country within* 24 *hours.* ② orders to be executed within certain time: ~放宽 *extend the time limit*

【限期】① deadline; time limit; within a definite time ② fix or set a definite time limit; prescribe a deadline: ~完成 *finish within a definite time*

【限速】speed limit

【限位】【机】spacing: ~开关 *limit inheritance*

【限于】due to; be limited to; confine: ~篇幅,来稿不能一一登载。*Owing to the limitation of space, it is impossible to publish all the manuscripts we've received.*

【限制】confine; restrict; limit; quota system; restriction: 他~自己每天只抽一支烟。*He limited himself to smoke a cigarette per day.*

线 ① thread; string, wire, line: 电话～ *telephone wires* ②【数】line: 直～ *straight line* ③ ray; sth shaped like a line or thread: X光 *X-ray* ④ line; route: 设计路～ *plan a route for* ⑤ line ⑥ boundary; dividing line: 分界～ *a boundary between this land and that land* ⑦ clue; lead thread: 生命～ *life line* ⑧［量］: 一～希望 *a ray of hope*

【线板】thread-wound board: 接～ *socket board*

【线电压】line voltage

【线段】【数】line segment

【线规】【机】wire gauge

【线积分】【数】line integral

【线路】line; route; circuit; wire; track

【线圈】coil

【线人】inner connection; informer; spy

【线绳】cotton rope

【线速度】linear velocity

【线索】clue; lead; thread

【线毯】cotton blanket

【线条】①【美】line: 粗～ *broad-brush* ② lines; figure; out-line: 她的～很美。*She has graceful lines.*

【线头】① end of a thread ② odd piece of thread: 接～ *join two pieces of thread together*

【线性】【数】linear: ～代数 *linear algebra* / ～方程 *linear equation*

【线衣】cotton knitwear; cotton-knit sweater

【线闸】cable brake (of bike); calipers brake

【线轴儿】reel for thread; spool of thread; bobbin

宪 ①［书］decree; rule; statute; law ② constitution: ～法草案 *draft constitution* ③ reference to superior: ～官 *officer*

【宪兵】military police; gendarmes: ～奉命维持治安。*The military policemen were ordered to keep public security.*

【宪法】constitution; charter; constitutional law: ～条文 *constitutional provisions*

【宪警】gendarmes and police

【宪令】［书］laws and ordinances

【宪章】charter; laws and institution: 联合国～ *Untied Nations Charter*

【宪政】constitutional government; constitutional rule: 维护～ *defend constitutional government*

陷 ① pit, snare; trap: 设～ *take in a trap* ② bog down; sink to; fall down; submerge; stick: 卡车～在泥淖中动弹不得。*The truck was bogged down in the mud.* ③ sink; cave in; collapse: 凹～的双颊 *hollow cheek* ④ beguile; entrap; frame (up); harm another with trumped-up charges; set up: 他被人～害了。*He has been farmed.* ⑤ be crushed; fall; be captured; be taken: 他死于城～的那天。*He died on the day the city fell.* ⑥ defect; deficiency; flaw: 缺～ *shortcoming*

【陷害】frame (up); snare; set up; another with a trumped-up charge, slander, etc.; make a false charge against: 这完全是～,我根本没做那件事。*This is purely a frame-up; I never did that.*

【陷阱】pitfall, snare, trap: 格伦布置了一个～。*Glen laid a snare.*

【陷坑】① pit; snare; trap ② hollow; cave

【陷落】① sink; submerge; cave in: 地基～10厘米。*The foundations have cave in ten centimeters.* ② sink into; land (oneself) in; be caught in: 奥德丽～于绝望之中。*Audrey landed herself in hopelessness.* ③ be lost (to the enemy); be taken in; be captured by the enemy: 那个城市～敌人手中。*That city was lost to the enemy.*

【陷没】① sink; be submerged; be lost ② be lost; be captured (by the enemy)

【陷入】sink into; fall into; be entrapped; land (oneself) in; come to; get bogged down in: 他～失望之中。*He was lost in despair.*

【陷入僵局】come to a deadlock; end in a stalemate

【陷身】land oneself in; be caught in: ～囹圄 *find oneself in prison; be put in jail*

【陷阵】break enemy ranks; take an enemy position: 冲锋～ *make a frontal attack; charge the enemy lines; charge and shatter enemy positions*

馅 ① stuffing; filling ② the ins and outs: 事情露～。*The ins and outs were uncovered.*

【馅饼】meat pie

【馅子】［方］① stuffing; filling: 拌～ *prepare filling* ② sth middle inside; catch; implied meaning

羡 ① admire; covet; envy; be jealous of ② surplus; spare: ～款 *spare cash*

【羡妒】admire and envy; be jealous of: 令人～的成功 *success arousing both admiration and envy*

【羡慕】admire; envy; covet; one's heart warms toward sh: 安娜很～我有这样的好爸爸。*Anna envies me my good father.*

【羡叹】admiring exclamation

献 ① sacrifice; offer present; dedicate; forward; donate: 他捐～基金给那所大学。*He donated funds to that university.* ② display; show; stage; flatter: ～一个节目 *perform a programme*

【献宝】① present a treasure ② offer a valuable piece of advice or one's valuable experience: 经理提倡职工～,提出改造公司的意见。*The manager advocates workers offering their valuable advice for the renovation of company.* ③ show off what one treasures

【献策】① offer a plan, scheme, etc.; advise: 献计～ *offer scheme and advice* ② plan; advice: 国王欣然接受他的～。*The king took his suggestions quite cheerfully.*

【献谄】ingratiate oneself with sb

【献丑】［谦］show one's poor skill or talent; make a fool of oneself: 一定要我唱,我只好～了。*If you insist that I must sing, I have to make a fool of myself and sing.*

【献词】congratulatory message; dedication; dedication speech: 开幕～ *congratulator message on the opening ceremony*

【献花】present fresh flowers; lay a wreath:向英雄~ *present flowers to the heroes*
【献计】offer advice for adoption; make suggestion:无人~解决此事。*Nobody could make suggestion about this question.*
【献技】display one's feat; stage a performance of special skills or feat:布伦达到国外~去了。*Brenda went abroad to perform feats.*
【献媚】doll up; ingratiate oneself with sb: ~取宠 *curry favour with sb*
【献纳】① [书] make suggestions; offer opinion; offer advice ② contribute; offer as a tribute; present: ~食品与衣物救济灾民 *contribute food and clothes for the relief of the afflicted people*
【献颂】present flags or pennants
【献勤】curry favour; ingratiate oneself
【献身】devote oneself to; dedicate oneself to; lay down one's life for: ~社会 *devote oneself to social work*
【献演】perform (on stage): ~的节目 *performance*
【献议】[书] offer advice or suggestion
【献艺】show one's skill
【献殷勤】curry favour; ingratiate oneself; pay one's addresses:向女孩子~ *show attentions on the girl*
【献拙】[书] show my incompetence; show my poor skill

腺 gland:唾液~ *salivary gland*

【腺癌】【医】adenocarcinoma
【腺垂体】【生理】adenohypophysis

xiāng

乡 ① country; countryside; rural area; village; township ② native place; home village or town; birthplace ③ township government ④ an unreal delightful country

【乡巴佬儿】[贬] bumpkin; country bumpkin; clodhopper; hayseed; mossback; rube
【乡愁】nostalgia; homesickness
【乡村】country; countryside; village; rural area: ~教育 *rural education* / ~音乐 *country music* / 我喜欢~的宁静。*I like the tranquility in the country.*
【乡丁】[旧] gatekeeper or runner for a township office
【乡间】village; country:我喜欢住在~。*I like living in the country.*
【乡佬儿】country bumpkin
【乡里】① village or small town (where one's family have long lived): ~乡气 *stupid-looking; foolish and clumsy* ② fellow villager or townsman
【乡邻】① villager; fellow townsman ② person from same rural neighbourhood
【乡民】[旧] country folk: ~社会 *peasant society*
【乡僻】remote; far from town; out-of-the-way
【乡气】rustic; uncouth; rude
【乡亲】① person from one's native village or town; fellow villager or townsman ② local people; villagers folks
【乡情】provincialism; affection for one's hometown or village
【乡人】① country folk; villagers ② person from the same village, town, or province; fellow countryman
【乡绅】country gentleman; squire
【乡塾】private school in a village; private rural school; private village school
【乡思】homesickness
【乡俗】country custom; folk custom; folkway; local customs of one's native place; rural custom
【乡谈】dialects of one's native place; local dialects
【乡土】native land; native soil; home village: ~艺术 *local art* / ~文学 *local-colour literature; native literature*
【乡下】[口] village; country; countryside
【乡下人】① country folk; villager; out-of-towner; country cousin ② provincials
【乡音】accent of one's native place; local dialect
【乡友】fellow villager or townsman; friend from the same village or area
【乡愿】[书] conformist hypocrite
【乡长】head of a township or village
【乡镇】villages and towns; small towns: ~企业 *township business; rural enterprise*

相[1] ① each other; one another; mutually; reciprocal:素不~识 *not to know each other* ② used to indicate an action one side does to the other:有事~告 *have sth to tell sb* ③ substance ④ (Xiāng) a surname

相[2] see and evaluate in person; choose for oneself or for sb close to oneself: ~看 *take a look*
see also xiàng

【相爱】love each other; be in love with each other
【相安无事】lived in peace with each other; coexist without trouble:他们这种关系虽不是很好,倒也~。*Although their relation isn't good but they live in peace with each other.*
【相帮】help; aid:兄弟之间需要~。*Brothers need help each other.*
【相悖】be at variance or adds with; act counter to:你所做的与医生的指示~。*What you have done is contrary to the doctor's orders.*
【相比】compare (with); contrast:那两姐妹~有极显著的差别。*There is a remarkable contrast between the two sisters.* /作为一个作家,他无法与曹雪芹~。*He can't compare with Cao Xueqin as a writer.*
【相差】differ:两者~悬殊,无法相比。*There is no comparison between the two.* /今天的气温与昨天的相比,~很大。*There is great difference in the temperature between today and yesterday.*
【相称】(xiāngchèn) match fit; suit:这条裤子跟我的年龄不~。*The trousers doesn't suit a person of*

my age.

【相称】(xiangchēng) all each other

【相成】complement each other; be complimentary in action

【相承】pass on; inherit:一脉～ *derived from the same origin*

【相持】confront each other with neither side yielding; be locked in a stalemate:谈判进入～。*The talks come to deadlocked.*

【相持不下】be at a stalemate; neither side yields to the other:谈判一直处于～的阶段。*The negotiation has been at a stalemate.*

【相处】get along ; live together; spend time together:尽管我们～的时间不长,但我们已经是好朋友了。*We have not lived together long, but we have become very good friend each other.*

【相传】① be transmitted; it is said that . . . ; legend has it that ② pass on; hand down:这颗钻戒是他们家世代～的宝贝。*The diamond ring was the treasure handed down from generation to generation in his family.*

【相待】treat:请别把我当成小孩子～。*Please don't treat me as a child.*

【相当】① match; balance; correspond to; be equivalent to; be equal to ② becoming; suitable; fit; appropriate: ～的人选 *person suitably selected* ③ quite; fairly; considerably: ～清静 *be very quiet* ④ enough: ～多 *much(many) enough*

【相得】be friendly; be harmonious; get on well

【相得益彰】each gains in appearance from the presence of the other; each complements the other; each supplements and enriches the other:红花配上绿叶,真是～,恰到好处。*Red flower complement green leaves so well that they form a perfect picture.*

【相等】equal; equivalent:能力～ *equal in ability*

【相抵】① offset; cancel each others; counter balance:谈论～ *the arguments cancel each other* ② conflict with each other; go against each other: ～减项 *offsetting deductions*

【相对】①[书] opposite; face to face: ～而坐 *sit face to face* ② opposite to each other:针锋～ *stand in sharp opposition* ③ relative:静止是～的。*Stillness is relative.* ④ corresponding:一切的权利都带着～的责任。*All rights carry with them corresponding responsibilities.* ⑤ relatively; comparatively

【相对论】【物】theory of relativity; relativity:广义～ *general theory of relativity*

【相烦】trouble someone with request; ask for a favor bother sb:以个人琐事～ *trouble me about one's own unimportant business*

【相反】① opposed; opposite; contrary: ～的结果 *opposite result* / ～词 *antonym* ② on the contrary; just the opposite:你想我支持你的这种观点,～,我不赞成。*You expect me to support your view , on the contrary, I don't agree to it.*

【相仿】alike; more or less the same; similar:内容～ *similar in contents* / 年龄～ *about the same age*

【相逢】meet each other; come across; run into:狭路～ *meet on the narrow road*

【相符】conform to; agree with; correspond to; match; tally:他的话与事实～。*His words tallied with the facts.*

【相辅相成】supplement each other; complement each other; reciprocity and complement

【相干】① related; be concerned with; have to do with:这两个问题互不～。*The two problems are not related to each other.* ②【物】coherence: ～效应 *coherence effect*

【相干性】【物】coherence

【相告】tell; pass information; inform

【相隔】be separated by; be apart; be at a distance of:从我们上次来到现在～不过两年,但景色已经发生了很大的变化。*It is only a distance of two years since our last visit here, but the scenery has greatly changed.*

【相关】① related; connected; interrelated:公共卫生与国民健康密切～。*Public health has a direct bearing on the citizens health.* ②【数】correlation: ～图 *correlogram*

【相好】① be on friendly term; be friends ② intimate friend; good friend; close friend ③ lover; sweetheart ④ have an illicit love affair

【相互】each other; mutual; reciprocal; one another:讨论会增进了～的了解。*The discussion meeting promoted mutual understanding.*

【相会】meet together; meet each other; rendezvous:你知道他们约好在何处～吗? *Do you know where they made an appointment to meet?*

【相继】in succession; one after another:代表们～发言。*The representatives spoke in succession.*

【相间】alternate with; spaced on-between

【相见恨晚】regret having not met earlier; regret not to have known sb before:我感觉和他～。*I felt regret for not being able to meet him earlier.*

【相交】① intersect; cross:这条路与主要街道～。*The road intersects main streets.* ② make friends with each other; be come associated with each other

【相接】connect with; link to:两个城镇有铁路～。*The two towns are connected by a railway.*

【相近】① near; similar:我们在音乐方面爱好～。*We have similar tastes in music.* /金子和黄铜在颜色上～。*Gold is similar in colour to brass.* ② approximate; close; closely; be similar to:他的叙述与事实～。*His statement approximates to the true.*

【相敬如宾】treat each other with respect (of husband and wife); respect each other as to a guest; treat each other as if the other is a guest

【相救】come to sb's help; try to save sb; rescue sb from danger; help out of difficult

【相距】apart; at a distance of; away from; distance between two points:两人～一米。*There is a distance of one metre between two persons.*

【相聚】assemble; meet together
【相看】① look at each other ② regard; treat ③ appraise each other
【相克】mutually destructive; be ill-matched
【相礼】① help in presiding over a wedding, funeral, etc. ② assistant to a Master of Ceremonies
【相连】connected; joined; linked:两地有公路～。*The two places are linked by a road.*
【相邻】adjoin; border on:公园与湖滨～。*The park borders on the shore of the lake.*
【相骂】call each other; abuse each other; trade insults: ～无好言,相打无好拳。*There are no fine words in quarrels and no weak blows in fights.*
【相瞒】hide sth from sb:实不～ *tell you the truth*
【相陪】accompany; keep company with sb; in company (with):哈罗德留在家里与儿子～。*Harold stayed at home to keep his son company.*
【相配】fit; go well with; match well; be well match:他们是很～的一对夫妻。*They are a well-match couple.*
【相扑】【体】① wrestling with each other ② Japanese sumo wrestling
【相期】expect of each other; look forward: ～不久相见 *expect to meet each other sooner*
【相契】[书] be in accord; be good friends:我们两人～多年。*The two of us have been good friends for many years.*
【相强】force; compel; impose:基思不想去,～也没有用。*If Keith didn't want to go, it is no use to force him to do.*
【相切】【数】be tangent to
【相亲】① (of a boy or girl) see and size up a prospective mate; have a traditional blind date before engagement ② be deeply attached to each other
【相亲相爱】be kind to each other and love each other; be affectionate to each other
【相去】differ; be apart: ～甚远 *be poles apart; be widely separated*
【相劝】persuade; offer advice; try to bring round: 好言～*offer sb well-meaning advice*
【相让】① make concessions; give in:各不～ *neither would give in* ② defer to each other politely
【相扰】① disturb; interfere ② trouble you ; bother you
【相认】① be acquainted with each other:我根本没和他～。*I wasn't acquainted with him at all.* ② recognize; identify:父女～ *father and daughter identifying each other*
【相容】① be compatible with; tolerate each other ②【数】compatible; consistent: ～方程 *consistent equation* / ～性 *compatibility*
【相濡以沫】help and comfort each other in time of adversity or crisis; help and comfort each other in humble circumstances
【相若】[书] similar; alike:他们相貌～。*They are similar in appearance.*
【相商】consult; exchange views:我们有要事和他～,你先走吧。*You can walk away; we have sth important to consult with him.*
【相涉】have to do with; be concerned with; related:这两件事毫不～。*The two events are not at all connected each other.*
【相识】① be acquainted with each other; know each other:素不～ *not know each other* ② acquaintance; friend:旧～ *former acquaintance*
【相视】look at each other: ～而笑 *look at each other and smile*
【相熟】[方] be acquainted; know each other
【相率】one after another; in succession; leading one another
【相思】① yearning between lovers; lovesickness:单～*one-sided love; unrequited love* ② pine for each other; miss each other; be in love with each other
【相思病】lovesickness
【相似】resemble; be similar; be alike: ～多边形 *similar polygons* / ～词 *synonym*
【相送】see out; see part of the way
【相随】follow at sb's heels; follow; accompany:执手～ *follow sb by holding his hand; go hand in hand with sb*
【相提并论】(often used in the negative) mention in the same breath; group together; place on a par; mentioned and discussed as related things:这是不能～的两件事。*These are two things which cannot be mentioned and discussed as related things.*
【相通】communicate with each other; be interlinked; be connected or linked:息息～ *be closely linked; have much in common with*
【相同】① identical; in common; same ② alike; similar
【相投】① be congenial or compatible; agree with each other ② go and seek refuge with sb
【相托】entrust
【相违】disagree; differ; go against
【相像】assimilate with; resemble; be much the same; be similar; be alike
【相信】believe; trust; be convinced; have faith in; place reliance on; put one's trust in
【相形】by contrast; by comparison
【相形见绌】prove definitely inferior by contrast; not sustain comparison (with sth); pale (into insignificance) by comparison; be outshone
【相形失色】seem pallid by comparison; compare unfavourably; pale into insignificance
【相沿】① through long usage; following the old tradition ② pass down from generation to generation without change
【相沿成习】become a custom through long usage; have come down from the past and become customary
【相依】depend on each other; be mutually dependent; be interdependent:唇齿～ *be as closely related to each other as lips and teeth*

【相依为命】depend on each other for survival; rely upon each other for life
【相宜】advisable; appropriate; fitting; proper; suitable:你在舞会上这样穿不~。*You such dress on that party was not suitable.*
【相异】differ; be dissimilar
【相迎】greet; welcome; meet:笑脸~ *greet with smile on one's face*
【相应】corresponding; relevant; pertinent; appropriate:随着经济发展,对环境的保护也要采取~对策。*With the development of economic, relevant measures should be taken to protect the environment.*
【相映】set each other off; form a contrast
【相映成趣】set each other off and forma pleasant contrast; form an interesting or delightful contrast
【相与】① get along with; get on with:他是个极难~的人。*He is extremely difficult ot get along with.* ② with each other; mutually; together ③[旧] close friend
【相遇】meet each other; come across; encounter
【相约】agree (on sth); make an appointment; reach an agreement
【相悦】love each other; be happy with each other
【相赠】present to sb; give as a gift
【相知】① be well acquainted with each other; be on intimate terms; know each other well:我们~甚深。*We have known each other so well for a long time.* ② bosom friend; great friend
【相中】take a fancy to; settle on; choose
【相助】help; assist;; coordinate
【相撞】collide; crash
【相左】[书] ① fail to meet each other ② disagree; fail to see eye to eye

香 ① aromatic; fragrant; scented; sweet-smelling ② appetizing; delicious; palatable:饭热菜~ *appetizing and hot food* ③ with relish; with good appetite ④ (sleep) soundly:她睡得正~。*She is deeply sleeping.* ⑤ in vogue; popular; welcome ⑥ perfume; scent; spice ⑦ incense; joss stick ⑧[方] kiss ⑨ used as a complimentary attribute, esp. of women in traditional literature:怜~惜玉 *have a tender heart for the fair sex* ⑩ (Xiāng) a surname
【香槟酒】champagne, a white sparkling wine from Champagne, France
【香波】(transliteration) shampoo
【香饽饽】[口] sweet-smelling pie — popular or much desired person or thing; sweetie-pie
【香菜】coriander; cilantro
【香肠】sausage
【香巢】cohabiting place; house of ill fame
【香橙】orange
【香袋】sachet (for perfume, etc.); small perfume bag
【香粉】face powder; cosmetic powder
【香干】smoked bean curd
【香港】Hong Kong: ~特别行政区 *Hong Kong Special Administrative Region (HKSAR)*
【香菇】*xianggu* mushroom, a kind of edible mushroom grown on wooden logs
【香闺】(used in traditional literature) private room of a girl; boudoir: ~恬静。*A girl's private room is tranquil.*
【香瓜】muskmelon; cantaloupe:这~的味道很美。*This muskmelon is delicious.*
【香蒿】sweet wormwood
【香灰】incense ash
【香火】① joss sticks and candles burning at a temple-devotees of a temple: ~不绝 *endless stream of pilgrims* ② person who looks after incense and candles at a temple; temple attendant ③ ceremony to burn incense for one's family line: ~断了 *be unable to continue the ceremony to burn incense for one's family line discontinued; have no male heir* ④ burning joss stick; burning incense
【香蕉】banana: ~皮 *banana peelings*
【香精】essence
【香客】pilgrim
【香料】① perfume ② spice
【香炉】incense burner; censer
【香囊】perfume (spice) bag; perfume pouch; sachet; incense bag
【香柠檬】bergamot
【香喷喷】① sweet-smelling; fragrant ② delicious; savoury; appetizing
【香片】scented tea
【香气】sweet smell; pleasant scent; fragrance; aroma:玫瑰花~宜人。*These roses have delightful fragrance.*
【香钱】cash contributions by visitors to a temple; incense money — gift to a temple and its monks; donation to a temple
【香色】① fragrance and colour ② dark brown
【香山】Fragrant Hill, west of Beijing
【香水】perfume; scent
【香水梨】a kind of sweet, juicy pear
【香酥鸡】crisp-fried chicken
【香甜】① bouquet; fragrant and sweet ② (sleep) soundly
【香味】bouquet; sweet smell; fragrance; scent
【香烟】① incense smoke ② cigarette: ~摊 *cigarette booth*
【香艳】(of poetry or other writing) flowery; sensual; voluptuous; sexy: ~故事 *love story; novel of romantic love*
【香油】sesame oil
【香皂】perfumed soap; scented soap; toilet soap
【香脂】① balm; balsam ② face cream
【香纸】incense and paper (resembling coins or banknotes) burnt as offerings to the dead
【香烛】joss sticks and candles (burned when offering sacrifices to gods or ancestors)

厢 ① eastern or western gallery ② wing; wing-room: ~房 *side room* ③ carriage; compartment; box:戏院的包~ *box in the theater* ④ areas just outside a city gate; vicinity or outskirts of a city ⑤ (often used in the early vernacular) side

【厢房】wing; wing-room

湘 ① Xiangjiang River (in Hunan Province) ② alternative name for Hunan Province

【湘妃竹】mottled bamboo; speckled bamboo.

【湘剧】Hunan opera

【湘帘】bamboo curtain made of speckled bamboo

【湘绣】Hunan embroidery

【湘竹】speckled bamboo

箱 ① box; case; chest; trunk ② box-like thing; compartment ③[量]: 一~苹果 *a box of apples*

【箱底】① bottom of a chest or case ② one's store of valuables; nest-egg: ~很薄 have a few of values

【箱子】box; case; chest; trunk

镶 ① fill in mount; inlay; set (jewels, etc.): ~有银饰的盒子 *the box inlaid with silver* ② edge; border; hem; bordered; rim; provide with a rim: 女人的手帕~有花边。*A woman's handkerchief has a lace border.* ③ name of an ancient weapon

【镶板】【建】panel

【镶边】border; edge; hem; rim

【镶工】craftsman engaged in fixing insets on jewelry

【镶嵌】inlay; mount; set (jewels, etc.): 家具上有~的图案。*There was an inlaid design in a piece of furniture.*

【镶牙】sow a tooth; fill in an artificial tooth

xiáng

详 ① complete; detail; minute: 我~细说明了情况。*I gave particulars of situation.* ② explain in detail; elaborate; interpret: ~解 *explain in detail* ③ clear; know clearly: 作者的生卒年月不~。*The author's dates are unknown.* ④ lucky

【详备】detailed and complete; exhaustive: 资料~。*The dates were exhaustive.*

【详尽】detailed and complete; exhaustive; thorough: 此问题已经做了详尽的调查。*The problem has been studied detailedly.*

【详略】detailed and brief; whether sth should be detailed or brief; how detailed sth should be; where sth should be detailed and where brief: 写文章要~得当。*Writing must be just right complete.*

【详密】detailed and comprehensive; elaborate; scrupulous; meticulous: 研拟~的计划 *draw up a detailed and comprehensive plan*

【详明】detailed and clear: 书中有~的注释。*There are full and very clear annotations in the book.*

【详情】details; detailed information; specifics; particulars: ~见报 *details to follow*

【详实】detailed and accurate; full and accurate: ~的报道 *full and accurate report*

【详图】detail (drawing)

【详文】[旧] official document or report to one's superiors

【详悉】① know in detail; know clearly ② detailed and exhaustive

【详细】detailed; exhaustive; minute: 请说~一点。*Please give me a minute description.*

【详注】annotate fully; copious notice; provide full notes or detailed annotations

降 ① surrender; capitulate; show the white flag: 我们宁死不~。*We would rather die than surrender.* ② subdue; conquer; vanquish; tame *see also* jiàng

【降敌】① surrender to the enemy ② conquer the enemy

【降伏】be bring to terms; conquer subdue; overpower; vanquish; tame: 他~了一头牛。*He broke in a wild ox.*

【降服】yield; surrender: 敌人被我们~了。*The enemies yielded to us.*

【降龙伏虎】subdue the dragon and tame the tiger — conquer natural forces; overcome powerful adversaries

【降旗】white flag; flag of signifying capitulation

祥 ① auspicious; propitious; promising; lucky ② (Xiáng) a surname

【祥和】① auspicious and peaceful: ~的新年 *lucky new year* ② kind; gentle; benign

【祥瑞】auspicious sign; propitious omen

【祥云】(as in mythology) auspicious cloud (ridden by a deity)

【祥兆】good omen

翔 circle in the air; fly

【翔贵】[书] (of prices) soar

【翔实】be full and accurate; detailed and thorough

xiǎng

享 enjoy; share

【享福】enjoy a life of pleasure; be in clover; live in ease and comfort; have a blessing

【享乐】enjoy or lead a life of pleasure; indulge in creature comforts

【享年】die at or live to the age of: 弗兰克不幸因病昨日去世,~七十八。*Frank died of illness yesterday at age of seventy-eight.*

【享受】① enjoy; indulge oneself in (some pleasant pursuit) ② enjoyment; treat

【享用】enjoy the use of; enjoy

【享有】enjoy (rights, fame, prestige, etc.): 在全世界~盛名 *be well-known in the world*

【享誉】enjoy famc; be renowned: ~歌坛 *be renowned vocal circle*

响 ① echo; resound ② sound; ring; beat; fire: 电话铃正~着。*The telephone is ringing.*

③ loud; noisy·坦克的声音太～了。*The tank is too loud.* ④ sound; noise: ～声 *sound*

【响板】castanets

【响鼻】(of a mule, horse, etc.) snort

【响鞭】① crack a whip; a loud whip: ～阵阵 *a fitful loud whip* ②［方］firecracker

【响彻】resound; reverberate

【响脆】loud and crisp

【响当当】① loud; clang ② so good as to pass the stiffest test; worthy of the name; outstanding; thoroughbred: 罗宾是一个～的汉子。*Robin is a excellent man.*

【响动】sound of sth astir; noise: 课堂上,除了老师的粉笔在黑板上写字的吱吱声,一点～也没有。*There was no sound of anything tumultuous besides squeak of the teacher writing on the blackboard in the classroom.*

【响度】loudness; volume

【响雷】① thunder: 天～了。*It was thunder.* ② loud thunderclap

【响亮】loud and clear; ringing; sonorous: ～的歌声 *a resounding singing*

【响头】kowtow (with one's forehead knocking against the ground and thus making a sound)

【响音】【语】resonant, i. e. vowels such as a, e, o or sonorants such as m, n, l; (sometimes) sonorant

【响应】answer; echo in support; respond; reply: ～党的号召 *respond to Party 's call*

饷 ①［书］entertain (with food and drink): ～宾 *entertain guests with food* ②［旧］(usu. of soldiers, policemen, etc.) pay: 领～ *get pay*

【饷遗】［书］present (a gift); offer (a present): ～不继 *The rations of soldier's discontinued*

【饷银】［旧］army provisions; serviceman's pay

想 ① think; reflect; mull over: 让我～～。*Let me think it over.* ② suppose; consider; think; reckon: 我～他已经走啦。*I suppose he has gone.* ③ want; would like; feel like (doing sth); intend to: 我～要那本书。*I want to get that book.* ④ remember with longing; pine for; miss: 我非常～你。*I miss you very much.*

【想必】presumably; most probably; most likely: ～鲁道夫不知道这件事。*Rudolf most likely knows this.*

【想不到】do not expect; fancy; unexpectedly: 真是～的事。*It is something quite unexpected.*

【想不开】take things too seriously; take a matter to heart; be unable to take a resigned attitude: 别为这些小事～。*Don't take a matter to heart.*

【想出】think out; think up

【想出来】think up; work out; devise

【想当然】assume as a matter of course; take for granted: 什么事都不能～。*Nothing is taken for granted.*

【想到】think of; call to mind; (idea, etc.) occur to one

【想得到】(often used in a rhetorical question) think; guess; imagine; expect: 谁～会出此问题。*None can think there is such problems.*

【想得开】not take to heart; take things easy; try to look on the bright side of things

【想法】idea; opinion; view

【想方设法】do everything possible; use all means; move heaven and earth; try everything possible; try by hook or by crook

【想家】be homesick; be nostalgic

【想见】see; infer; gather: 从这件事上我们能～诺拉的为人。*We imagine what Nora was like from this.*

【想开】take things easy; not take sth to heart; not take things too hard

【想来】it may be assumed that; presumably; supposedly; in my guess: ～真是后悔。*When I come to think of it, I really feel sorry.*

【想来想去】give sth a good deal of thought; turn sth over and over in one's mind

【想念】recall with longing; long to see again; yearn for; miss

【想起】recall; remember; think of; call to mind

【想入非非】neurotic; indulge in fantasy; allow one's fancy to run wild; entertain a wild hope; have maggots in one's head: 露西亚喜欢～,却一事无成。*Lucia liked to build castles in the air, but never succeeded in anything.*

【想通】straighten out one's thinking; think through; think out; become convinced: 只要能～,他就会积极配合。*Once he has become convinced, he is able to coordinate.*

【想头】［口］① idea; notion ② hope

【想象】①【心】imagination ② imagine; envisage; fancy; visualize: 纯～的世界 *a world of mere fancy* / 你能～出琳达是一个贼吗? *Can you imagine Linda as a thief?*

【想象力】imaginative power; imaginative faculty; imagination

【想着】bear in mind; not forget; keep in mind

xiàng

向[1] ① face; face to: 转身～着我。*Turn round and face me.* ② direction; trend: 趋～死亡 *deathward* ③ close to; near; approaching ④ take sb's part; be partial to ⑤ to; toward ⑥ (Xiàng) a surname

向[2] always; all along

【向背】be for or against; support or opposition

【向导】① act as a guide; show sb the way ② guide

【向光性】【生】phototropism

【向后】towards the back; with the back first; backwards

【向火】［方］warm oneself by a fire

【向来】always; all along; invariably: ～都是他出主意。*He always makes the decisions.*

【向例】according to custom; convention; usual practice
【向量】【数】vector: ～分析 *vector analysis*
【向前】① towards the front; forward; onward; ahead ② go forward
【向日】[书] bygone days; former days; in the past
【向日葵】【植】sunflower
【向上】① upward; up ② move forward; advance; improve; turn upward
【向上爬】① climb up ② [喻] be intent on personal advancement; climb up the social ladder: 奥利维亚结交权贵,一心一意～。*Olivia climbs up the social ladder through taking up with influential officials.*
【向水性】【生】hydrotropism
【向酸性】【生】oxytropism
【向往】look forward to
【向下】downward; down
【向斜】【地】syncline
【向心】centripetal; towards the centre
【向性】【生】tropism
【向学】be resolved to pursue one's studies
【向阳】be exposed to the sun; face the sun; face south
【向阳花】sunflower
【向右】towards the right: ～,走! *By the right flank, march!*
【向隅而泣】be left to grieve in the cold; grieve out in the cold; weep all alone in a corner
【向着】① turn towards; face ② [口] take sb's part; side with; favour
【向左】towards the left: ～转 *turn the left!*

项[1] ① nape; back of the neck ② (Xiàng) a surname

项[2] ① [量] item; subparagraph, used of itemized things: 一～十分重要的工作 *an item important work* ② sum (of money) ③【数】term: 常数～ *constant term* / 同类～ *like term*

【项背】one's back and neck
【项背相望】walk one after another in close succession; walk in Indian file
【项链】necklace
【项目】item; project: 建设性的～ *constructive project*

巷 narrow street; lane; alley

see also hàng

【巷口】entrance to lane; either end of a lane
【巷陌】alley; streets and lanes
【巷尾】end of a lane
【巷议】street gossip; talk of the town: 街谈～ *town talk*
【巷战】street combat; street fighting; house-to-house fighting
【巷子】[方] lane; alleyway: 我妈妈就住在这条～里。*My mother lives in the lane.*

相[1] ① looks; countenance; examine the appearance and judge: ～马 *look at a horse to judge its worth* ② appearance of things; facies: 一副可怜～ *a pitiful appearance* ③ bearing; carriage; posture ④ phase position ⑤ phase: 周～ *stage in a circle* ⑥ form; image; picture: ～片 *photo* ⑦ state of element; phase state: 气～ *gas phase*; *gaseous phase* ⑧ look at and appraise; examine the physiognomy of; physiognomies: ～面 *tell sb's fortune by reading one's face*

相[2] ① assist; help: ～夫教子 *help the husband and teach the children* ② chief minister; prime minister; chancellor ③ minister in some countries: 外～ *foreign minister* ④ minister, one of the pieces in Chinese chess ⑤ [旧] attendant; master of ceremonies; usher: 傧～ *bridesmaid*
see also xiāng

【相变】【物】phase change; phase transition; phase transformation
【相册】photo album
【相衬】【物】phase contrast
【相机】① watch for an opportunity; bide one's time ② camera
【相角】① photo corner ②【数】phase angle
【相控阵】【无】phased array: ～雷达 *phased-array radar*
【相貌】appearance; bearing; countenance; facial features; looks: ～堂堂 *have a dignified appearance*
【相片儿】[口] photo; photograph
【相片】photograph; photo
【相平衡】【物】phase balance
【相声】【戏】comic dialogue; crosstalk
【相时而动】wait for the right moment; beat a graceful retreat
【相士】fortune-teller; physiognomist
【相手】tell sb's future by reading the lines on the palm of his or her hand: ～术 *palmistry*
【相术】physiognomy: ～精深 *one's physiognomy is profound*
【相态】【物】phase state
【相位】phase; phase position: ～差显微镜 *phase microscope*
【相序】【电】phase sequence: ～继电器 *phase-reversal relay*; *phase sequence relay*
【相移】【物】phase shift
【相纸】printing paper; photographic paper

象[1] ① elephant ② elephant, one of the pieces in Chinese chess

象[2] ① appearance; look; shape; image: 庄严气～ *dignified atmosphere* ② imitate; mimic

【象鼻】trunk; proboscis
【象棋】chess
【象限】【数】quadrant
【象限仪】【天】quadrant
【象形】【语】pictographic characters or pictographs, one of the six categories of Chinese characters: ～文字 *pictograph*; *hieroglyph*; *hiero-*

glyphics; glyph
【象牙】elephant tusk; ivory
【象牙塔】ivory tower — aloofness from practical life; separation from the harsh realities of ordinary life
【象眼儿】[方] rhombus; lozenge
【象征】① symbolize; signalize; signify; stand for ② symbol; sign; emblem; token: 狮子是勇敢的~。*The lion is the symbol of bravery.*
【象征性】as a token; symbolic; emblematic

像 ① likeness of sb; portrait; statue; picture: ~片 *photograph* ②【物】image: 实~ *real image* ③ be alike; resemble; take after; look like; be similar ④ look as if; appear; seem: 洛娜好像有心事。*Lorna seemed to be laden with anxiety.* ⑤ such as; for example; for example; for instance ⑥ as; like
【像话】reasonable; appropriate; proper; right (usu. used in the negative or in a rhetorical question): 梅西这人真不~。*Maisie really is not reasonable.*
【像回事儿】just like the real thing; in a decent manner; for real
【像框】frame
【像模像样】decent; presentable; up to the mark; respectable; proper: 她的书法活儿还挺~的。*Her handwriting is quite presentable.*
【像频】【电】picture frequency: ~调制 *image modulation*
【像散】【物】astigmatism: ~镜 *astigmatoscope*
【像样】be up to the mark; not bad; presentable; decent: 这家厂子连一台~的机器都没有。*There isn't even a decant machine in this factory.*
【像章】badge or button with sb's likeness on it

橡 ① oak; chestnut oak ② rubber tree
【橡虫】oak worm
【橡浆】rubber latex
【橡胶】rubber: ~乳汁 *latex* / ~树 *rubber tree*
【橡皮】① rubber: 我要些~筋。*I want some rubber bands.* ② eraser; rubber: 这支铅笔有~。*The pencil has a rubber.*
【橡树】oak
【橡子】acorn

xiāo

肖 ① small; tiny ② decline; die out; exterminate; perish ③ (Xiāo) a surname
see also xiào

枭 ① owl; legendary bird said to eat its own mother: ~鸟 *owl* ② [书] fierce and brave ③ chief; chieftain; ringleader ④ [旧] salt smuggler ⑤ [书] hang (severed heads)
【枭将】[书] brave general; brave leader of troops
【枭首】[旧] behead; cut sb's head; decapitate a person and hang up his head — a kind of capital punishment in former times
【枭首示众】behead and put before the public; cut off sb's head and hang it up as a warning to all
【枭雄】[书] fierce and ambitious person of the time (or age); formidable man: 张作霖是一代~。*Zhang Zuolin was a formidable man in his time.*

削 ① pare or peel with a knife; scrape; whittle: 他让我给他~铅笔。*He let me sharpen a pencil for him.* ②【体】cut; chop
【削尖脑袋】[贬] try hard to squeeze in; worm one's way in
【削面】paring knife
【削皮刀】paring knife
【削皮器】parer; peeler
【削球】(in pingpong) chop; cut

骁 [书] ① valiant; valorous; brave ② a powerful horse
【骁悍】[书] brave and fierce; valiant and strong; vigorous and valiant
【骁健】[书] valiant and robust
【骁将】[书] valiant general
【骁骑】[书] brave and fierce cavalryman; valiant cavalry; well-trained cavalryman
【骁勇】[书] brave; courageous; valiant: ~善战 *be good at fighting and braving*

逍
【逍遥】free and unfettered; carefree:
【逍遥自在】take life easy; be leisurely and carefree

消 ① disappear; die out; vanish; melt: 烟~云散 *disappear (vanish) like mist and smoke; turn to dust and ashes* ② eliminate; dispel; reduce; remove ③ pass the time in a leisurely way; idle away (the time) ④ need; require; take: 我来回只~三天。*I spend only three days on getting there and back.*
【消沉】dejected; downhearted; low spirits; depressed: 意志~ *mulligrubs*
【消愁】allay cares; dispel worries; divert oneself from care: 借酒~愁更愁 *drawn one's worries by drinking, but one become more worry*
【消除】clear up; eliminate; dispel; get rid of; ease: ~异己 *get rid of different view* / ~误会 *clear up a misunderstanding*
【消磁】degaussing; demagnetization; field discharge: ~电路 *degaussing circuit*
【消导】【中医】cure indigestion: ~药 *digestant*
【消毒】① disinfect; sterilize; pasteurize ② decontaminate; dispel pernicious: 埃里克患过肺结核后,他所住的房子曾彻底~过。*The house, which Eric had lived in was thoroughly disinfected after he had pulmonary tuberculosis.*
【消乏】① deplete; expend; use up: 所有的本钱都被~掉了。*All the capital has been used.* ② be impoverished; decline (in wealth and position): 家道~ *decline in wealth and position* ③ exhausted; tired out
【消防】fire fighting; fire control; fire prevention;

prevention and extinction of fire：~车 *fire engine or truck* / ~站 *fire station*

【消费】consume：~水平 *consumptive level* / ~基金 *fund for consumption*；*consumption fund* / ~结构 *consumption pattern*

【消耗】① consume；use up：~品 *expendables*；*consumables* ② expend；deplete；wear down：~体力 *deplete fleshly strength* ③（often used in the early vernacular）news；mail；message：那个孩子离开后~全无。*Nothing has been heard of him since the child left.*

【消化】① digest：这些食物难~。*This foods are digested difficultly.* ②［喻］digest；absorb；take in

【消化不良】indigestion；dyspepsia：~症 *dyspeptic symptom*

【消火器】fire extinguisher

【消火栓】fire hydrant；fire cock

【消极】① negative：~影响 *negative influence* / ~的态度 *pessimistic attitude* ② passive；inactive；lethargic：~怠工 *go slow*；*slow down*；*slack in one's work*

【消减】decrease；lessen；abate；reduce

【消解】get rid of；clear up；dispel；remove

【消灭】① perish；die out；become extinct ② annihilate；destroy；exterminate；eradicate；wipe out：~害虫 *annihilate injurious insect*

【消磨】① wear down；fritter away；blunt ② while away；fool away；idle away：~时间 *while away time*；*kill time*；*pass the time*

【消气】allay one's anger；cool down；calm down；be mollified

【消遣】① relax oneself；while away the time：打牌~*play cards as a pastime* ② pastime；distraction：看书是戈登唯一的~。*Reading became Gordon's only distraction.*

【消去】【数】cancellation；elimination：~法 *elimination method*

【消融】thaw；melt；ablate：冰雪~，万物复苏。*All things wake up during thawed the ice and melted the snow.*

【消散】scatter and disappear；dissipate；vanish

【消色】achromatism；decoloration：~指示器 *achromatic indicator*

【消失】die out；pass out of sight；disappear；vanish；fade away

【消石灰】hydrated lime

【消食】digest；help digestion

【消逝】die away；elapse；fade away；vanish：音乐慢慢~了。*The music slowly died away.*

【消释】①［书］melt；thaw ② clear up；remove；dispel

【消受】①（often used in the negative）enjoy ② endure；bear；sustain；stand：我无法~他。*I can't endure him.*

【消瘦】become thin；become emaciated；become skinny；be wasted：长期生病使兰斯看起来~不堪。*Lance looks like to be skinny for a long illness.*

【消暑】① take a summer holiday ② relieve summer heat；drive away summer heat

【消损】① wear and tear ② erode；fritter away；decrease；wear down

【消停】［方］① quiet；peaceful；stable；steady ② pause；stop；have a rest

【消退】decrease；fade away；disappear bit by bit；gradually vanish

【消亡】wither away；die out；be extinct

【消息】① news；information；report：~报道 *news report* ② tidings；news：你有诺曼的~吗？*Do you know news about Norman?*

【消夏】relieve summer heat；take a summer holiday；spend the summer at leisure

【消闲】① kill leisure time；idle away the hours ② at leisure；carefree

【消歇】［书］become extinct；stop；disappear；die away；subside：暴风雨已~。*The storm has subsided.*

【消协】consumers' association

【消炎】【医】diminish or allay inflammation：~止痛 *diminish inflammation and stop one's pain* / ~片 *sulfaguanidine table*；*anti-inflammation pill*

【消夜】［方］① midnight snack ② have a midnight snack

【消音】noise elimination or reduction

【消隐】① disappear；hide ②【电】blank；blackout：~部件 *blackout unit*

【消灾降福】ward off disasters and bring good luck；avert calamities and bring blessings

【消长】① growth and decline；rise and fall；wax and wane ② change

【消痔术】【医】hemorrhoidolysis

【消肿】【医】① subsidence of a swelling；detumescence；reducing or removing a swelling ② remove or reduce a swelling

【消字灵】eraser；eradicator；ink eradicator

宵

① night ② the first half of the night（from night-fall to midnight）③ silk ④ snack

【宵遁】［书］flee under the cover of night：~而去 *flee under the cover of night*

【宵禁】curfew：实行~ *impose a curfew*

【宵行】［书］go out at night；make a night journey：秉烛~ *take an evening stroll with a lantern*

【宵衣旰食】getting up before dawn and eating late；rise before dawn and eat after dusk — busy with state affairs；diligent in discharging official duties

绡

［书］① raw silk ② fabric made of unprocessed or raw silk

【绡头】silk ribbon for binding the hair；silk hair-ribbon

萧

① desolate；dreary ② free and easy

【萧墙】［书］screen wall inside the gate of a Chinese house：祸起~ *trouble breaks out at home*

【萧然】［书］① desolate；lonely ② empty；vacant

【萧飒】[书] desolate; bleak
【萧瑟】① rustle in the air; sough:秋风~ *autumn wind rustling in the air* ② bleak; melancholy; desolate
【萧森】[书] ① withered; wizened; bleak ② dreary and desolate
【萧疏】① desolate; bleak ② be sparse but graceful; be thinly scattered
【萧条】① desolate; bleak ②【经】depression; sluggish; slump: ~期 *slack time*
【萧闲】[书] ① leisurely and at ease ② lonely and silent
【萧萧】①[象] sound of wind soughing or of horses neighing ② sough; whistle ③ (of hair) white and sparse

硝 ① nitre ② taw; tan
【硝化】【化】nitrify
【硝化火药】【化】nitro-powder; nitro-explosive
【硝基】【化】nitro-: ~苯 *nitrobenzene*
【硝基甲烷】【化】nitromethane
【硝石】【化】nitre; saltpetre
【硝酸】【化】hydrogen nitrate; nitric acid: 亚~ *nitrous acid* / ~铵 *ammonium nitrate*
【硝烟】smoke of gunpowder: ~弥漫的战场 *battleground with smoking of gunpowder*
【硝盐】earth salt

销[1] ① melt (metal): ~银 *melt silver* ② cancel; annul; cross out: 注~ *cancel*; *write off* ③ put on sale; sell; market: 展~ *exhibit for sale* ④ pay out; expend; spend: 花~ *cost*

销[2] ① pin: 螺栓~ *dowel of bolt* ② fasten with a latch
【销案】close a case
【销差】report mission accomplished; report to one's superior upon the end of a mission
【销场】[方] demand; market
【销户口】cancel one's residence registration
【销毁】destroy by melting or burning; destroy: 嫌疑犯已经~了罪证。*The suspect has destroyed incriminating evidence.*
【销魂】be overwhelmed with sorrow or joy; enraptured; feel transported; be extremely happy and satisfied
【销货】goods; merchandise sales: ~部 *sales department* / ~单 *sales slip*
【销价】selling price; market value; sale price
【销假】begin work anew after vacation; report back after leave of absence
【销量】sales volume
【销路】sale; market; market conditions outlet: 夏天皮衣~不好。*There is a poor sale for fur clothings in summer.*
【销声匿迹】occultation; keep silent and lie low; disappear from the scene; go into hiding; stay in oblivion
【销售】market; sell: ~代理商 *selling agent*
【销行】sell; be on sale; be sold; be marketed: 这家书店已经~了一百万册现代汉英辞典。*The book store has sold a million copies of the Modern Chinese English Dictionary.*
【销赃】【律】① disposal of stolen goods or spoils ② destroy the stolen goods
【销账】cancel or remove from an account; write or cross off an account; cancel debts

潇 ① [书] (of water) deep and clear ② sound of wind and rain beating or driving
【潇洒】natural and elegant; free and unconventional; light-hearted; negligent; unconventional
【潇潇】① whistling and pattering: 风雨~ *whistling of wind and pattering of rain* ② drizzly

霄 ① graupel ② clouds; sky; heaven: 九~云外 *beyond the highest heavens*
【霄汉】[书] sky; firmament; heaven: 气冲~ *spirit soaring to the firmament*; *be in a towering rage*

嚣 noisy; loud; hubbub; din
【嚣闹】noisy; clamorous; bustling with noise and excitement
【嚣杂】noisy confusion; commotion
【嚣张】arrogant; blatantly; clamorously; rampant; insolent; aggressive: ~一时 *run rampant for a time*

xiáo

淆 confuse and disorder; mix
【淆惑】[书] confuse; befuddle; bewilder
【淆乱】① confuse; befuddle: 他散布谣言~视听。*He spread rumors to mislead the pubic.* ② disturb; confound: ~本末 *confound the means with the end*
【淆杂】mix; mingle; be miscellaneous

xiǎo

小 ① small; little; tiny; minor: ~错 *minor fault* ② for a short while; for a little time: ~别胜新婚。*A brief parting is as sweet as a honeymoon.* ③ a little; a bit; slightly: ~胜一筹 *a little bit better* ④ a little less than; almost ⑤ youngest: ~儿子 *youngest son* ⑥ young children; little ones: 动物也知道保护他们的老~。*Animals know to protect their elder and younger yet.* ⑦ lesser or minor wife; concubine: 娶~ *take to minor wife* ⑧ [谦] I; my; me: ~的胆小,不敢和他打。*I dare not beat him because of being timid.* ⑨ used before a surname to refer to a young person, or before a given name to refer to a child
【小矮凳】low stool
【小把戏】[方] child
【小白菜】variety of Chinese cabbage
【小白脸儿】[贬] good-looking young men; hand-

some young man with effeminate features
【小百货】small light-industrial or handicraft products of daily use; small articles of daily use; sundries
【小班】① small class (of 15 students or less) ② bottom class in a kindergarten
【小半】less than half; lesser or smaller part: 与会者不及~。*Attendees were less than half.*
【小报】small-sized newspaper; mosquito paper; tabloid; tab
【小辈】younger member of a family, profession, etc.; junior
【小本经营】run a small business; do business in a small way; business with a small capital
【小臂】forearm
【小便】① urinate; pass water; pee; piss ② urine; urination ③ penis; vulva
【小辫子】① short braid; pigtail: 她梳着~。*She wears her hair in short braid.* ② mistake or shortcoming that may be exploited by others; handle: 皮特喜欢抓别人的~。*Peter enjoys seizing on sb's mistake or shortcoming.*
【小标题】subheading; subhead; subtitle
【小冰川】glacieret
【小不点儿】[方] ① very small; tiny ② tiny tot; brat
【小布】narrow home-spun cloth
【小步】【军】half-step march
【小材大用】give great responsibility to a man of common ability; man of little ability in a high position
【小菜】① plain dish; pickled vegetables; side dish (such as pickles, fried peanuts, cold meats, etc. usu. to go with wine); hors d'oeuvres ② easy job; no big deal ③ [方] meat, fish or vegetable dishes as distinguished from rice, or other staples
【小册子】booklet; brochure; pamphlet; tract
【小差】① feel better; be lighten ② (of soldiers) desert
【小产】miscarriage; abortion; (of animals) slink: 朱利安为自己的~感到悲伤。*Julian was sad for her spontaneous abortion.*
【小肠】【生理】small intestine
【小肠串气】[口] hernia
【小抄儿】[口] crib; note for cheating in the exam; note brought in stealthily at examination
【小潮】neap (tide)
【小炒】individually stir-fried dish (cooked usually in a small wok as against food prepared in a big pot); a la carte dish
【小车】① wheelbarrow; handbarrow; handcart; pushcart ② sedan(car)
【小乘】【宗】Little Vehicle; Hinayana; Theravada
【小吃】① small and cheap dishes (in a restaurant) ② snacks; refreshments ③ cold dish; hors d'oeuvre
【小吃部】snack bar
【小丑】① clown; buffoon: 他扮演~。*He played a clown.* ② person who likes to poke fun at others; sport ③ villain; mean person; rascal
【小丑跳梁】contemptible wretch busy stirring up trouble; petty thieves going on the rampage
【小葱】① shallot; scallion; spring onion: 小葱拌豆腐 *complete innocent (of the charge)* ② young onion; tender shallot
【小聪明】[贬] be sharp-witted but pretty-minded; cleverness in trivial matters; petty shrewdness; petty trick: 保罗总是耍~。*Paul is always as clever in a small way.*
【小打小闹】(do sth) in dribs and drabs; on a small scale; in a piecemeal manner
【小大人儿】adultly; child behaving like an adult; demure child
【小旦】(Chinese opera) young female character
【小刀】① small sword or knife ② pocket knife
【小岛】small island; islet: 我不知道这~的名字。*I don't know the name of the islet.*
【小道】① path; trail ② unorthodox; heterodox; lowly ③ grapevine; bush telegraph
【小的】① little ones; young children: 利奥要那个~。*Leo wants the little ones.* ② [旧] used by commoners or yeoman runners when speaking to officials, I; me; my
【小弟】① youngest brother; little brother; kid brother ② [谦] used among friends, I or me ③ young male servant or young waiter: 他在那个酒吧当~。*He works as young waiter in that bar.*
【小调】① popular tune; ditty; folk song ②【音】minor key
【小动作】petty and mean actión; little trick; manoeuvre
【小豆】red bean
【小肚鸡肠】petty-minded; narrow-minded
【小肚子】[口] region below the navel; underbelly; lower abdomen
【小额】small sum or amount
【小恩小惠】bread and circuses; economic bait; petty favours; small favours
【小儿】① children; infant ② [谦] my son
【小儿疾病】children's disease; pediatric disease
【小儿科】①【医】pediatrics department ② kid's stuff; easy mark; petty stuff
【小儿麻痹症】【医】infantile paralysis; poliomyelitis; polio: ~使那个小孩成为跛子。*Polio made the child a cripple.*
【小二】young waiter in wineshop or hotel; boy
【小贩】badger; hawker; pedlar; stall holders; vendor
【小房】① small room or house ② lesser wife; concubine
【小费】gratuity; tip
【小斧】hatchet
【小腹】underbelly; lower abdomen
【小嘎】[方] child; kid
【小个子】little chap; small fellow

【小工】bull cook; unskilled labourer
【小姑儿】① husband's young sister; sister-in-law ② one's youngest paternal aunt
【小姑独处】young woman living on her own; girl not yet married; remain a spinster; single young woman:到现在埃伦还是~。*Ellen remains a spinster till today.*
【小鼓】side drum; snare drum
【小褂】Chinese style shirt
【小广播】① gossip; rumour; grapevine; hearsay ② spreading of hearsay information; spread rumours; town talk
【小鬼】① little devil that runs errands for the King of Hell; imp; goblin ② (term of endearment in addressing a child) little devil; mischievous boy; puck
【小孩儿】[口] ① child; kid ② sons and daughters, usu. those who have not yet grown up; children
【小号】① small-size (as distinct from medium and large sizes) ② my store; our store ③ trumpet; clarion ④ [方] single-person prison cell; single cell; small jail
【小猴子】(playful term for a naughty boy) little monkey
【小户】① family of limited means and without powerful connections; ordinary family ② small family
【小花脸】clown; buffoon (in Chinese opera)
【小话儿】[方] ① gossip ② words of intercession
【小黄鱼】little yellow croaker
【小活儿】add job; extra work; miscellaneous work
【小伙子】[口] young man; lad; young fellow; youngster
【小鸡儿】① chick ② little cock (referring to a small boy's penis)
【小计】subtotal
【小家碧玉】beautiful young lady in a small family; daughter of a humble family; pretty girl of humble birth
【小家伙】small thing; kiddy; toddler; baby
【小家子】person of humble birth; humble or lowly family; vulgar and lower-class person
【小家子气】unease or nervousness in public characteristic of people of low birth; petty or vulgar behaviour; narrow-mindedness; awkward
【小件】small article; small item
【小将】① young general ② [喻] young militant; young pathbreaker
【小脚】bound feet (of women in former times)
【小节】① small matter; trifle ②【音】bar; measure
【小劫】minor suffering; small disaster; minor misfortune
【小结】① brief sum-up; interim summary; preliminary summary; summary:做个~ *make a summary* ② make a summary; summarize:对上月工作~一下 *summarize briefly the work of last month* ③【医】nodule
【小解】urinate; pass water; make water
【小姐】① [旧] young lady ② (respectful term of address for a young woman) miss
【小金库】unit-owned exchequer; small exchequer" — funds or accounts owned by a subsidiary unit in violation of fiscal regulations
【小襟】smaller or inner piece on the right side of a Chinese garment which buttons on the right
【小径】① pathway; small path; trail ② (of a log) minor diameter; small in diameter
【小九九】① a pithy formula of multiplication; multiplication table for the abacus ② [喻] calculation; scheming:他心中的~比谁都多。*He has more calculations than others.*
【小舅子】[口] wife's younger brother; brother-in-law
【小开】① [方] son of a boss; son of a capitalist ② rich young boy or man; rich young dandy
【小楷】① regular script in small characters (as used in Chinese calligraphy exercises) ②【印】lowercase (letter)
【小看】belittle; look down upon; make light of; think little of; underrate; slight
【小康】comfortably off; comparatively well-off; moderately well off:她出身~家庭。*She came from a well-to-do family.*
【小考】minor examination; quiz
【小老婆】concubine
【小老头】prematurely old man
【小两口】[口] young couple:~吵架不久就言归于好。*Young couples have made up their quarrel sooner.*
【小量】a little amount; small dose
【小龙虾】crayfish; crawfish
【小萝卜】radish
【小萝卜头】① [方] kid child; small boy ② person of no importance; nobody; small potato; small fry
【小锣】small gong
【小买卖】small business
【小麦】wheat
【小卖】① (as in a restaurant) ready food; small dish ② do small business
【小卖部】① small shop attached to a hotel, school, factory, theatre, etc. (selling cigarettes, confectionery, etc.); retail section or department; store ② buffet; snack counter
【小猫熊】lesser panda
【小毛头】[方] infant; baby; child
【小帽】skullcap
【小门小户】poor and humble family
【小米】millet
【小名】baptismal name; pet name for a child; childhood name
【小命儿】life
【小拇哥儿】[方] little finger
【小拇指】[口] little finger
【小年】① lunar year of which the last month has 29 days ② preliminary Eve — (holiday which falls

on the 23rd or 24th of the 12th month of the lunar year when people offer sacrifices to the kitchen god) ③【农】off-year

【小年青儿】youngster; stripling

【小年夜】① night before the Eve of the Lunar New Year ② 23rd or 24th of the 12th month of the lunar year

【小妞儿】[口] little girl; young girl

【小农】small peasant or farmer: ~意识 *small peasant's consciousness*

【小女】[谦] my daughter

【小跑】[口] trot; jog; run

【小朋友】children (term of address used by an adult to a child)

【小便宜】trivial gain; petty advantage

【小品】short; simple literary or artistic creation; essay; skit; sketch: ~文 *familiar essay*; *essay*; *vignette*

【小气】① stingy; miserly; niggardly; mean ② [方] narrow-minded; petty

【小气鬼】miser; niggard; skinflint; penny pincher; scraper

【小器】① small household utensil ② stingy; mean; niggardly; narrow-minded: 他很~。*He is narrow-minded.*

【小憩】rest for a little while

【小钱】① inferior copper coin; coin ② small sum of money; petty cash ③[旧] small bribe

【小瞧】[方] look down upon; be slighting ; belittle

【小巧】small and nimble; small and skilful; small and ingenious

【小巧玲珑】① (said of a decorative item) small and exquisite: ~的玩具 *small and exquisite toy* ② small, trim and lovely; petite: 她长得~。*She is petite.*

【小青年】young people around twenty; youngsters; youth

【小秋】① [书] early autumn ② minor autumn harvest or crop

【小球】【体】sports using smaller balls, such as table tennis, badminton, etc.

【小区】plot; estate: 工业~ *an industrial estate*

【小曲儿】ditty; popular tune: 你会哼这首~吗? *Can you sing this tune?*

【小觑】despise; slight

【小圈子】① small circle or set of people; narrow confining environment or surroundings ② small coterie; clique; tightly knit clique

【小儿】[方] ① babyhood; childhood ② infant boy; baby boy

【小人】① [旧] person of low position; (used by such a person to refer to himself) your humble servant — I, me ② base or vile person; mean person; villain ③ [方] son or daughter; child; kid ④ [方] boy; kid; child

【小人得志】small man swelled with success; villains holding sway

【小人儿】[方] (as a loving term of addressing a minor) lad; lass; laddie

【小人儿书】[口] picture-story book; comics

【小人物】nobody; cipher; nonentity; no man; unimportant person; small potato

【小商品】small commodity

【小生】① young man's role ② [旧] (used by a young scholar to refer to himself) I; me ③ young

【小生产】small production; small-scale production; small commodity production

【小生产者】small producer

【小时】hour

【小时工】① worker paid by the hour ② maid or laborer paid by the hour, to come and clean up the apartment once a week

【小时候】[口] as a child; in childhood; early youth: 他们从~就是好朋友。*They have been good friends since childhood.*

【小食】① [方] snack ② between-meal nibbles

【小市民】① urban petty bourgeois ② philistine

【小事】small or petty thing; trifle; minor matter

【小试锋芒】display only a small part of one's talent; manifest a little of one's skill; make a casual demonstration of one's capability; show the tip of the iceberg

【小手小脚】① mean; miserly; stingy; niggardly ② lacking boldness; timid; cowardly

【小叔子】[口] husband's younger brother; brother-in-law

【小数】①【数】decimal number; decimal fraction; decimal ② small (in) number; small sum

【小数点】decimal point; radix point

【小睡】catnap; nap; doze

【小说】novel; fiction story

【小说家】novelist; fiction-writer; storywriter

【小算盘】selfish calculations; petty niggling

【小摊贩】street pedlar; vendor

【小摊儿】vendor's booth; stall; stand

【小提琴】violin; fiddle: ~手 *violinist* /首席~手 *concertmaster*; *concertmeister*

【小题大做】make a fuss over a trifle; make a mountain out of a molehill; make much of a trifle; use a hammer to swat a fly; have a tempest in a teacup: 这未免有点~。*This is making a mountain out of a molehill.*

【小蹄子】[旧] abusive term for maidservant; bitch

【小天地】little world; small world; limit sphere

【小帖儿】[方] card with the horoscope of a boy or girl sent as a proposal for betrothal

【小艇】small boat; skiff; dinghy

【小偷】burglar; petty thief; sneak thief; pilferer; pickpocket: 昨夜~闯进劳拉的房间。*Burglars broke into Laura's room last night.*

【小偷小摸】petty theft; pilfering

【小腿】shank: ~肚 *calf*

【小娃娃】kid; baby; toddler: 这~很逗人。*This little child is cute.*

【小玩意儿】① knickknack; trinket; bauble ② pet-

ty skill
【小巫见大巫】be like a small sorcerer in the presence of a great one — feel dwarfed; pale into insignificance by comparison; the moon is not seen when the sun shines：他的书法与名家一比简直就是～。*There is no comparison between his handwriting and the famous'.*
【小屋】cottage; cabin; lodge
【小戏】operetta; short item of performance
【小巷】by-lane; alley
【小小说】miniature story (usu. about 1,000 words long)
【小写】① ordinary form of a Chinese numeral ② small letter
【小心】watch out for; take care; be careful; be cautious：～火烛！*Guard against fire!* /一个～的人不会相信没有证据的事。*A cautious man doesn't believe things without proof.*
【小心谨慎】be careful; be cautious; mind one's p's and q's
【小心眼儿】① narrow-minded; petty; extremely ② petty calculation; petty scheming
【小心翼翼】with utmost care; with extreme caution; gingerly; on tiptoe; very timidly：他～地工作。*He did his job with extreme caution.*
【小行星】【天】asteroid; minor planet; planetoid
【小型】small; small-scale; miniature
【小性儿】［方］petty anger; childish temper; petulance
【小兄弟】little brother; young member of a group, faction or gang
【小学】① primary school; elementary school ② Little Learning (the study of the etymology, semantics and phonology of classical Chinese); philological studies
【小学生】(primary school) pupil; schoolboy or schoolgirl
【小扬琴】cimbalom
【小样】①【印】galley proof ②［方］model; sample (product) ③［方］small-minded; petty
【小幺儿】young servant; page boy
【小姨儿】① wife's younger sister; sister-in-law ② youngest of maternal aunts
【小姨子】［口］wife's younger sister; sister-in-law
【小意思】①［谦］small token (of kindly feelings); small gift; souvenir; keepsake：这点儿～送给你作个纪念。*This is just a small token for you.* ② not worth mentioning; insignificant; negligible
【小引】introductory note; foreword：那本字典有一序文而不是～。*That dictionary has a preface, not a forward.*
【小语种】minor language; ethnic minority language
【小月】① solar month of 30 days ② lunar month of 29 days ③ miscarriage; abortion
【小灶】① the best mess; special mess (as for high-ranking officials) ② special treatment or privilege
【小侄】［谦］① my nephew (used when speaking to others) ② your nephew — I or me (used when speaking to people of one's father's generation)
【小住】stay for a short while; sojourn：他～旅馆。*He sojourns at an inn.*
【小注】footnotes; fine notes between vertical lines of a book (usu. written in two lines)
【小传】brief biography; biographical sketch; profile：他问我如何写～。*He asked me how to write profile.*
【小酌】［书］drinks with snacks; a few drinks：他～了一下。*He took to a little drink.*
【小资产者】petty bourgeois; small proprietor：他们属于～。*They belong to petty bourgeois.*
【小子】［书］① youngster; teenager ②［旧］term of address used by seniors to juniors ③［旧］name by which the elder calls the younger ④［口］boy; guy ⑤［贬］bloke; fellow; chap
【小字】① small character ② childhood name
【小字辈】youngster; younger generation
【小卒】① pawn; private ② nobody; cipher; man of no consequence：无名～ *nobody; nowhere*
【小组】group：～讨论 *a group discussion*
【小坐】sit for a short while

晓 ① dawn; daybreak：天破～。*It is dawn.* ② morning：～日 *the morning sun* ③ know; understand：我～得这件事。*I know the thing.* ④ tell; let sb know：～字 *notice; official proclamation; bulletin*
【晓畅】① be well versed in; have a good command of ② (of writings) clear and fluent; readable：行文～ *write in a clear and fluent style*
【晓得】know; be aware of：不～玛丽是否在这里。*I don't know if Mary is here or not.*
【晓风残月】morning breeze and waning moon
【晓示】announce; tell explicitly; notify：他被～立即出发。*He was told to start at once.*
【晓事】sensible; intelligent; understanding
【晓悟】［书］① understand; realize ② clever; bright
【晓以利害】explain to sb where his or her interests lie; warn sb of the possible consequences

xiào

孝 ① dutiful; filial piety ② mourning period ③ mourning dress ④ (Xiào) a surname
【孝道】① Confucian doctrine of filial piety; code of supporting and waiting on one's parents; filial piety：尽～ *do one's filial piety to parents* ②［口］show filial obedience to one's parents; be filial and loving：孩子们都很～。*Children are filial and loving.*
【孝服】① mourning dress or garment ②［旧］mourning period
【孝敬】① be obedient and respectful to; show filial piety and respect：他～父母。*He is obedient and*

respectful to his parents. ② give presents (to one's elders or superiors):这是我～您的。*This is the present I give you.*

【孝顺】show filial obedience; show filial piety

【孝堂】hall or parlour in which the coffin (of one's parent) is laid

【孝心】filial love; filial piety; love for and devotion to one's parents; love toward parents

【孝行】filial behaviour or conduct

【孝衣】mourning dress; mourning garment; mourning apparel

【孝子】① filial or dutiful son ② bereaved son; son in mourning

【孝子贤孙】worthy progeny; true son

肖 resemble; be similar (to); be like

see also xiāo

【肖像】portrait; portraiture

校[1] school; college; university

校[2] field officer:少～ *major*

see also jiào

【校办工厂】factory attached to a school; school-run factory

【校办农场】farm attached to school; school-run farm

【校车】school bus

【校风】ethos of a school; school spirit

【校服】school uniform

【校歌】school song; college song; alma Mater

【校规】school regulations; school rules

【校花】[旧] campus queen; school belle; the prettiest girl student

【校徽】school badge

【校际】interschool; intercollegiate:～交流 *interschool exchange*

【校刊】college journal; school magazine

【校历】school calendar

【校旗】school flag

【校庆】anniversary of the founding of a school or college

【校容】appearance or look of a school

【校舍】schoolhouse; school building

【校外】outside school; after school; extramural; extracurricular:～辅导员 *guest counsellor for school children's activities*

【校务】affairs of a school

【校训】school motto; phrasal school regulations:要牢牢记住我们的～。*Please remember our school motto in your heart.*

【校医】school doctor

【校友】alumnus; alumna

【校园】campus; school yard:～歌曲 *campus song*

【校长】(primary or secondary school) schoolmaster; headmaster; principal; (university or college) president; chancellor

【校址】location of a school or college

哮 ① heavy breathing; wheeze; cough ② roar; howl; yell; cry

【哮喘】have (a fit of) asthma; cough and gasp for breath

笑 ① smile; grin; titter; laugh:破涕为～ *smile through tears* ② ridicule; laugh at; deride:贻～大方 *make a laughingstock of oneself before experts* ③ joke; make fun of ④ [喻] flow; open:百花～ *flowers open*

【笑柄】butt; laughing stock; joke:琼的声明成为人们的～。*Joan's declaration has become a laughing stock.*

【笑不合口】laugh so much that one cannot close the mouth; keep on laughing

【笑不可抑】double up with laughter; split one's sides; roll with laughter

【笑不唧儿】[方] smiling; all smiles:露西好像没不高兴的时候,整天～的。*Lucy is always smiling as if he has joyless nothing let him unhappy.*

【笑场】(actor's or entertainer's) undue laughter during performance

【笑掉大牙】be utterly ridiculous; burst out laughing over the absurdity of sth; (make people) laugh their heads off

【笑哈哈】laugh heartily

【笑呵呵】all smiles; laughing heartily; happy and gay

【笑话】① joke; jest; pleasantry:有趣的～ *good joke* ② laugh at; deride; ridicule:别～我的表演。*Don't laugh at my performance.* ③ deserving to be laughed at; ridiculous; absurd:～,我能在乎你们? *It is ridiculous; can I care about you?*

【笑剧】farce

【笑里藏刀】cover the dagger with smile; smile of treachery; iron hand in a velvet glove; velvet paws hide sharp claws; hide a dagger in a smile — with murderous intent behind one's smiles

【笑脸】smiling face; beaming face:我们对他～相迎。*We greeted him with a smiling face.*

【笑料】laughing stock; joke

【笑咧咧】grin; smile broadly

【笑林】book of jokes; collection of popular jokes

【笑骂】① deride and taunt:～由人 *let others say what they like* ② twit teasingly; rally

【笑貌】smiling expression:音容～ *voice and smiling expressions; one's voice and expression*

【笑眯眯】be all smiles; be wreathed in smiles; beaming; smilingly; with a smile on one's face

【笑面虎】wicked person wearing a hypocritical smile; wolf at heart but lamb in appearance; smiling tiger — an outwardly kind but inwardly cruel person:小心,埃里卡是个～。*Be careful! Erica is a smiling tiger.*

【笑纳】[套] kindly accept this small gift as a token of my respect:小小礼物,请～。*Please accept this small gift of my mine.*

【笑容】happy expression; smiling expression; smile:看到他的儿子,他面露愉快的～。*There was a pleasant smile on his face when he saw his son.*

【笑容可掬】be radiant with smiles; show pleasant smiles; wear a charming or captivating smile

【笑声】laugh; laughter: 一阵～从那边传过来。*A sound of laughing came from there.*

【笑谈】① object of ridicule; laughing stock; butt ② joke; jest ③ laugh over; joke; jest: 学生们常在一起～天下事。*The students often get together and laugh over worldly affairs.*

【笑微微】smiling

【笑纹】laugh limes

【笑嘻嘻】be all smiles; look very happy

【笑星】laughing star

【笑颜】smiling face

【笑靥】[书] ① dimple ② smiling face

【笑一笑,十年少】smiles make one young

【笑吟吟】smiling happy

【笑盈盈】smiling

【笑语】talk and smile; talk and laugh; cheerful talk: 欢声～ *cheerful chatting and laughing*

【笑逐颜开】beam with smiles; be all smiles; be wreathed in smiles: 看到爸爸她～。*She was wreathed in smiles on seeing her father.*

效[1] effect; efficiency; function; result: 行之有～ *effective*

效[2] imitate; follow suit; follow the example of: 东施～颦 *blind imitation with ludicrous affection; play the ape*

效[3] present; devote to; render (service); offer one's services: 报～祖国 *render service to repay nation*

【效法】follow the example of; pattern or model oneself on; learn from; emulate

【效仿】imitate; copy; follow the example of

【效果】① effect; result ② sound and lighting effects

【效劳】work for; serve: 为学校～ *offer one's services for school*

【效力】① render one's service to; serve ② effect; force; avail

【效率】productivity; efficiency

【效命】go all out to serve (one's country, etc.); be ready to die for (a consequence, etc.)

【效能】efficacy; effectiveness; efficiency; efficaciousness; usefulness; potency

【效颦】copy blindly; imitate servility; play the ape

【效死】be ready to give one's life (for a cause); do one's utmost; render service at the cost of one's life

【效验】desired result; direct effect; intended effect

【效益】result; benefit; profit: ～工资 *efficiency-related wages*

【效应】① (physical or chemical) effect ② effect; result: 法拉第～ *Michael Faraday effect*

【效用】effectiveness; utility; usefulness: ～论 *utility theory* /充分发挥～ *make full use of sth*

【效忠】pledge loyalty to; dedicate oneself to

啸 ① (of people) whistle: 一个落魄的电影明星仰天长～。*A frustrated film star howled noise in the open air.* ② (of birds or animals) scream; roar; howl ③ sound of some natural phenomena ④ whirring; buzzing; hissing; whizzing

【啸歌】keep whistling and singing; keep whistling songs

【啸呼】keep whistling and shouting

【啸叫】scream; whistle

【啸聚】[书] band together; call; gang up

【啸聚山林】(of bandits, etc.) form a band and take to one another and gather together

【啸鸣】① whistle; scream; whizz ② roaring; howling

【啸声】whistle; hiss

xiē

些 ① (used to indicate an indefinite quantity) a few; some ② (used after an adjective as a modifier of degree) a little; a bit; rather; somewhat: 他有～钱。*He has a little money.*

【些个】some; a little; a few

【些微】slightly; a trifle; a little; a bit: 夜风有～凉意。*The night wind is slightly cold.*

【些小】① a little; a bit ② small amount; small

【些许】a little; a bit: 没有必要为取得～成绩而沾沾自喜。*It is unnecessary you are pleased with yourself a little progress.*

楔 ① wedge; peg ② drive (a wedge, etc.): 他在墙上～钉子。*He is driving a nail into a wall.*

【楔子】① wedge ② (wooden or bamboo) peg ③ prologue or interlude in Yuan Dynasty drama ④ prologue or prelude in a novel

歇 ① rest; take a rest: 你太累了,先～会吧! *You are so tired; have a good rest first.* ② stop (work, etc.); knock off: 上床～息 *go to bed* ④ [方] a short time; a little while; a moment: 过一～儿你再来拿这本书。*You come to take the book after a little while.*

【歇班】be off duty; have time off: 明天该我～。*I should have time off tomorrow.*

【歇乏】take a rest or break

【歇工】① quit or stop work; knock off ② (of an enterprise) close down; (of a project) be suspended

【歇后语】two-part allegorical saying (of which the first part, always stated, is descriptive, while the second part, often unstated, carries the mes-

sage, e. g.)
【歇火】【航】burn-out
【歇脚】take a load off one's feet — take a break while walking; stop on the way for a rest
【歇凉】[方] relax in a cool place; enjoy the cool
【歇气】stop for a breather; take a break: 坐下来歇~。*Sit down and take a break.*
【歇憩】have a rest
【歇晌】take a midday nap or rest; have a doze at noon
【歇手】stop doing sth; stop working; break off
【歇斯底里】①【医】(transliteration) hysteria ② morbidly emotional; hysterical: ~地叫 *scream hysterically*
【歇宿】put up for the night; make an overnight stop; stay the night
【歇窝】[方] (as fo hens, duck, etc.) stop laying eggs (due to hot or cold weather)
【歇息】① have a rest; rest for a while: 我们~一会儿再干。*We rest for a while, then go on doing something.* ② go to sleep; put up for the night
【歇闲】[方] take a break from work; have a rest
【歇心】① set one's mind at rest; be relaxed in one's mind; be free from care and worry ② give up trying; drop an idea: 米兰达遭到好几次回绝,但仍不~。*Miranda has suffered several but he gives up trying yet.*
【歇业】go out of business; close a business; close down
【歇夜】put up for the night; stay overnight
【歇枝】unfruitful year (s); (as of fruit trees) bear less fruit; have a lean year: 今年的果树~,结果很少。*It is a unfruitful year for the fruit tree; there is a little of fruit in it this year.*
【歇止】stop; halt: 地球永不~地运动。*The earth never stops turning around.*

蝎 scorpion: ~毒 *scorpion venom*; *buthotoxin*
【蝎虎】①[方] terrible; formidable ② gecko; house lizard
【蝎子】scorpion

xié

协 ① harmony; concord; coordination ② joint; concerted; common: 齐心~力 *pull together*; *make concerted effort* ③ aid; assist: ~助 *provide help to*; *give assistance*; *lend a helping hand*
【协定】① agreement; convention; accord: 贸易~ *trade agreement* ② reach an agreement (on sth); agree on
【协和】harmonize; be consonant with; concert
【协和音】【音】consonance
【协会】① association; society: 消费者~ *consumers' association* ② meet
【协理】① assist in the management (of an enterprise, etc.); assist ② assistant manager
【协理员】【军】political assistant (of the PLA)
【协力】concur; combine efforts; join in a common effort: 同心~ *make concerted efforts*
【协领】(during the Qing Dynasty) brigade commander
【协商】consult; discuss; talk things over
【协调】coordinate; systematize; harmonize
【协同】work in concert or coordination; cooperate with: ~作战 *fight in coordination*
【协议】① agree; consult ② protocol
【协约】① negotiate ② agreement; convention; entente: 签订~ *sign an agreement*
【协约国】Entente countries (during World War)
【协助】aid; assist; help
【协奏曲】【音】concerto: 钢琴~ *piano concerto* / 管弦乐~ *orchestral music concerto*
【协作】cooperation; collaboration: 我们必须充分发扬~精神。*We must give full play to the spirit of cooperation.*

邪 ① evil; heresy: 歪门~道 *crooked ways*; *dishonest practice*; *under-counter business* ② irregular; abnormal; strange ③【中医】unhealthy environmental influence that causes disease; miasma ④ evil spirits that bring disasters: 驱~ *exorcise evil spirits*
【邪财】[方] ill-gotten gains
【邪道】evil ways; depraved life: 不走~ *don't take to evil ways*
【邪恶】evil; wicked; sinister; vicious: ~势力 *evil forces*
【邪乎】[口] ① abnormal; extraordinary; extreme ② excessive; strange; fantastic
【邪门儿】[方] ① abnormal; weird; strange; odd ② evil ways; crooked practices; vice
【邪门歪道】crooked ways or means; dishonest practices or methods; evil or illegal doings; under-counter business
【邪魔】evil spirit; devil; demon
【邪念】wicked idea; evil thought or idea; wicked or lascivious intention
【邪僻】[书] evil; perverse
【邪气】① perverse trend; evil influence; bad practice: 歪风~ *gust of evil winds*; *perverse trends*; *evil trends*; *evil winds and noxious influences* ②【中医】evil *qi* that causes various diseases
【邪术】witchcraft; black magic; sorcery
【邪说】heretical ideas; heresy; fallacy: 异端~ *heretical belief*; *unorthodox opinion*
【邪祟】evil spirit
【邪行】① wicked act; evil deed ②[贬] abnormal; especially; extraordinary; extreme

胁 ① flank; the upper part of side of the human body from the armpit to the waist ② compel; coerce; force
【胁逼】coerce; force; threaten
【胁持】① seize on both sides by the arms ② hold under duress; abduct
【胁从】be an accomplice under duress: ~分子 *ac-*

complice under duress
【胁迫】coerce; force; intimidate
【胁制】hold under duress; abduct
挟 ① hold under the arm: 莫妮卡进来的时候~着包。*Monica came into holding bag under the arm.* ② coerce; compel; force sb to submit or yield ③ bear; harbour (resentment, etc.)
【挟持】① seize sb (on both sides) by the arms ② abduct; coerce; hold under duress; kidnap
【挟仇】harbour a grudge or rancour: ~陷害 *frame sb be cause of a grudge one bears against him*
【挟带】carry or bring along forcibly: 风~着沙砾扑面而来。*The wind was blowing on the face with the sand and grit that was carrying along.*
【挟恨】nurse intense hatred
【挟天子以令诸侯】have the emperor under one's thumb and order the dukes about in his name
【挟嫌】[书] harbour or bear a grudge: ~报复 *retaliate against sb*
【挟怨】nurse a grudge; bear ill will
【挟制】take advantage of sb's weakness to enforce obedience; force sb to do one's bidding; have sb under one's thumb: 被人~ *be forced to do one's bidding*
偕 together with; accompanied by; in the company of: 邓肯~夫人前往南京。*Duncan went to Nanjing accompanied by his wife.*
【偕老】(of husband and wife) grow old together: 白头~ enjoy together /与民~ *enjoy with the common people*
【偕同】accompanied by; together with; along with: ~客人参观 *accompany guests on a visit*
【偕行】①[书] walk together ② coexist; stand together
斜 oblique; slanting; tilted; askew
【斜边】①【数】hypotenuse ②【机】bevel edge: ~凿 *bevel chisel*
【斜长石】plagioclase
【斜度】degree of inclination; gradient; slope
【斜对面】diagonally from; across from
【斜风细雨】gentle breeze and drizzling rain
【斜高】【数】slant height
【斜晖】[书] sun rays at dusk; slanting rays of the sun
【斜角】①【数】oblique angle ②【机】bevel angle
【斜角规】bevel square
【斜拉桥】stayed-cable bridge
【斜路】wrong path
【斜率】【数】slope
【斜面】①【数】inclined plane ②【机】oblique plane; bevel (face)
【斜睨】squint; look sideways
【斜坡】slope
【斜切面】【数】oblique section
【斜射】① slant; shine sideways or slantwise: 阳光~过来。*The sunshine slanted here.* ②【军】oblique fire
【斜视】①【医】strabismus ② look sideways; cast a sidelong glance; look askance: 目不~ *not look askance*
【斜视图】【机】oblique drawing
【斜体字】【印】italics
【斜透视】【机】oblique perspective
【斜纹】twill (weave); drill
【斜线】oblique line
【斜眼】①【医】strabismus ② squint-eye; cross-eyes ③ squint-eyed or cross-eyed person
【斜阳】setting sun
【斜轧】【冶】skew rolling
【斜照】① shine slantwise: 夕阳~。*The setting sun shines slantwise.* ② setting sun
【斜轴线】【数】oblique axis
谐 ① harmony; accord: 大自然的色彩非常~调。*The colour in nature is very much harmony.* ② come to an agreement; agree with; settle ③ humorous: 埃德温是一个诙~的人。*Edwin is a humorist.*
【谐波】【物】harmonic wave; harmonic component: ~检波器 *harmonic detector*
【谐和】harmonious; congenial; concordant
【谐美】(of words, etc.) concordant and melodious
【谐频】【电】harmonic frequency
【谐趣】① humour; humorous delight: ~横生 *be fraught with humour* ② harmonious and interesting
【谐调】harmonious; well-balanced
【谐婉】harmonic and mild; harmonious and gentle
【谐戏】[书] joke; make a humorous joke; poke fun (at sb) n a humorous way
【谐音】① homophonic; homonymic ② euphony; harmony of sound
【谐振】【物】resonance; syntony
颉 ①[书] (of birds) fly upwards; soar ② (Xié) a surname
携 ① carry; take or bring along ② take or hold by the hand
【携带】① carry; take; bring along ② guide and support
【携家带口】bring all one's family; be burdened by one's family
【携离】[书] betray; rebel
【携手】① hand in hand: ~同行 *walk hand in hand* ② cooperate; work together: ~合作 *work together; cooperate*
鞋 shoes
【鞋帮】upper of a shoe
【鞋带】shoelace; shoestring
【鞋底】tread; sole of a shoe: ~前掌 *hale sole*
【鞋垫】shoe-pad; insole
【鞋钉】spike (as of a track shoe); hobnail (for mending a shoe)
【鞋粉】shoe powder
【鞋跟】heel of a shoe
【鞋匠】shoemaker; cobbler

【鞋扣】shoe button; shoe buckle
【鞋里】shoe lining
【鞋刷】shoe brush
【鞋样】shoe pattern; outline of a shoe's upper and sole
【鞋油】shoe polish or cream

撷 ①［书］pick; pluck: 采～ *pick*; *gather*; *collect*
【撷取】pick; pluck; select
【撷英】［书］select the very best

xiě

写 ① write: ～下你的地址 *write down your address* ② compose; write: 布鲁斯每天都～日记。*Bruce keeps a diary everyday.* ③ describe; portray; depict: ～人物 *depict character* ④ paint; draw; sketch: ～生 *paint from life*
【写本】hand-copied book; hand-written copy; manuscript; transcript
【写法】① method of writing ② style of calligraphy
【写稿】write for; contribute: 巴里年老以后,过着以～为生的生活。*Barry wrote for a living when he was old.*
【写景】depict or describe scenery
【写生】paint or draw from life or nature: 人物～ *portrait from life*
【写生簿】sketch-block; sketch-book
【写实】write or paint realistically: ～的笔法 *realistic way of writing*
【写意】freehand brushwork aimed at catching the spirit of the object and expressing the author's impression or mood
【写照】① portray; characterize ② depiction; picture: 这篇文章是我们生活的真实～。*The article is authentic depiction of our life.*
【写真】① paint or portray a person; draw a portrait ② describe sth as it is ③ portrait
【写作】writing: ～技巧 *writing technique* / ～班子 *writing group*

血
see also xuè
【血肠】blood sausage
【血道子】welt; wale
【血豆腐】(cooked as food) blood curd
【血糊糊】covered or smeared with blood; bloody
【血淋淋】① dripping with blood; bloody ② cruel; atrocious: 亚当得到了～的教训。*Adam got a lesson paid for in blood.*
【血丝】trace of blood
【血晕】bruise

xiè

泄 ① let out; discharge; deflate; release: 水～不通 *be so jammed as to be impassable* ② divulge; let out; leak; disclose ③ give vent to; vent: 发～ *give vent to*; *let off*
【泄底】reveal or expose what is at the bottom of sth; divulge the bottom line
【泄愤】give vent to one's resentment or spite
【泄恨】give vent to one's resentment or hatred
【泄劲】lose heart; feel discouraged; lose momentum
【泄漏】① (of gases or liquids) leak; discharge ② divulge; give away; let out
【泄露】① get out; let out; disclose; reveal: ～秘密 *let out a secret* ② leak
【泄密】divulge or leak a secret; disclose confidential information; let out a secret
【泄气】① lose heart; feel frustrated; be disheartened ②［口］pathetic; piteous
【泄泻】【中医】loose bowels; diarrhoea

泻 ① flow swiftly; rush down; pour out: 一～千里 *rush down a thousand li* ② loose bowels; diarrhoea; (as in cattle) scour: 上吐下～ *suffer from vomiting and diarrhoea* ③【中医】purge; quench: ～火 *purge (the body of) pathogenic fire*; *quench pathogenic fire*
【泻肚】loose bowels; diarrhoea; scour
【泻根属】【植】bryony
【泻湖】【地】lagoon
【泻药】laxative; cathartic; purgative

卸 ① unload; discharge: ～车 *unload a vehicle* ② remove; take off ③ unhitch; unharness (draught animals, etc.) ④ remove; strip; dismantle: 拆～ *disassemble*; *dismount* ⑤ lay down; shirk: ～过 *shirk one's responsibility for an error* ⑥ fall: ～帆 *fall down sail*
【卸岸价格】landed price (at a place of import or delivery)
【卸包袱】unload a parcel -be rid of one's burden
【卸车】debus; unload; unload goods from a vehicle
【卸担子】lay down a burden
【卸货】unload or discharge cargo; unload
【卸甲归田】remove one's armour and go back to farm; be demobilized and return to civilian life
【卸肩】remove one's burden; shirk one's responsibility
【卸任】be relieved of one's office
【卸压】【机】pressure relief: ～阀 *pressure relief valve*
【卸责】off-load responsibility (onto others); shirk responsibility; pass the buck
【卸职】be relieved of one's post or office
【卸妆】remove one's make-up; take off one's formal dress and ornaments: 他下台后就开始～。*He started to take off his formal dress and ornaments as soon as he stepped down stage.*
【卸装】remove one's stage make-up and costume

屑 ① bits; scraps; fragments; crumbs: 头～ *scurf* ② trifling; trivial ③ (mostly used in the negative) deign; consider worthwhile
【屑屑】trifling; trivial; of little value: ～小事 *petty*

matter

械 ① tool; device; instrument: 器~ *apparatus; equipment* ② weapon; arms: 缴~投降 *lay down one's arms* ③［书］fetters; shackles: ~系 *put fetters on sb*

【械斗】fight with weapons (as between groups of people)

亵 ① treat with irreverence; slight; be disrespectful ② lewd; obscene; indecent: 猥~ *be lewd*

【亵渎】blaspheme; desecrate; profane; pollute

【亵慢】treat lightly; show disrespect; slight: 对工作不能有~之心。*One should not treat lightly one's work.*

【亵昵】be improperly familiar with

【亵玩】dally (with women)

【亵尊】［书］lower oneself (to do sth); condescend

谢 ① thank ② make an apology; apologize ③ decline; refuse ④ (of flowers, leaves, etc.) fall; wither ⑤ (Xiè) a surname

【谢病】［书］excuse oneself on grounds of illness; beg off

【谢词】thank-you speech

【谢顶】get thin on top; be balding

【谢恩】thank (an emperor, a monarch, etc.) for a favour

【谢绝】decline; refuse or decline with thanks

【谢客】① close one's door to guests ② express thanks to guests; thank visitors or guests for their company

【谢礼】gift in token of one's gratitude; gift of thanks

【谢幕】answer or respond to a curtain call

【谢却】decline or refuse politely: 我~了他的邀请。*I declined politely his invitation.*

【谢世】［书］depart this life; pass away; die: 自从爸爸~之后,母亲变得不怎么爱说笑了。*My mother was not fond of laughing since my father died.*

【谢天谢地】thank God; thank heaven; count oneself lucky: ~,你总算回来啦。*Thank God; you finally come back home.*

【谢帖】note of thanks; thank-you note

【谢谢】thanks; thank you

【谢意】credit; gratitude; thankfulness: 聊表~ *as a token of my gratitude*

【谢罪】apologize for an offence; offer an apology: 改天登门~ *call at sb's house to offer an apology another day*

塮 ［方］compost made from decomposed animal manure

解[1] get the point; get wise to (sth); be clear about; see

解[2] ［旧］acrobatic performance, especially on horseback

解[3] Lake Xie, in Shanxi Province ② (Xiè) a surname
see also jiě; jiè

榭 pavilion or house on a terrace: 亭台楼~ *pavilions, terraces, and towers*

邂

【邂逅】［书］meet by chance; run into

懈 slack; lax; remiss: 坚持不~ *be unremitting; keep on doing sth*

【懈弛】slack; lax

【懈怠】slack; sluggish; careless: 查尔斯工作从不~。*Charles has never been careless about his work.*

【懈惰】lax and idle; sluggish

【懈劲】slacken one's efforts; slack off; be disheartened: 别~,下次再试。*Don't slack off; try again next time.*

【懈气】relax or slacken one's efforts; slacken off

【懈意】sign of laxness; sign of slackening

蟹 crab: 虾兵~将 *ineffective troops*

【蟹粉】［方］crab meat (eaten as food)

xīn

心 ① heart ② heart; mind; feeling; moral nature or character; intention: ~不在焉 *absence of mind; absent-mindedness* ③ heart; centre; core: 菜~ *heart of a cabbage* ④ fifth of the 28 constellations in ancient Chinese astronomy

【心爱】love; treasure; cherish

【心安】feel at ease; have a good or easy conscience; comfort

【心安理得】feel at ease and justified; have a good or easy conscience; have no qualms of conscience

【心病】① mental anguish; worry; anxiety ② sore point; secret trouble ③ heart diseases

【心博】【生理】heartbeat

【心不在焉】absent-minded; inattentive; be preoccupied with sth else; one's mind is not on what one is doing

【心裁】mental plan; conception; idea; notion: 别出~ *try to be differcnt; adopt an original approach*

【心肠】① intention; mind; heart ② feeling; emotion; heart ③ state of mind; mood; inclination

【心潮】tidal surge of emotion; surging thoughts and emotions

【心潮澎湃】one's emotions and thoughts surge like the tide; one's mind is flooded with emotions and thoughts; feel an upsurge of emotions

【心驰神往】feel excited; let one's thought fly to; yearn after (a place) as if one's mind were already there; be so excited by sth as to take mental possession of it

【心慈面软】soft of heart and considerate of face; soft-hearted and lenient

【心粗】thoughtless and flighty

【心存芥蒂】nurse a grievance; bear a grudge
【心胆】① heart and gall ② guts; courage
【心荡神驰】be thrilled; be distracted (with rapture, excitement, etc.); go into ecstasies or raptures
【心得】what one has learned from work, study, etc.
【心底】① bottom of heart; heart of hearts ②[方] intention; intent
【心地】① mind; character; nature ② state of mind; mood
【心电图】【医】electrocardiogram
【心动】① heartbeat: ~过速 *tachycardia* ② have one's mind perturbed; have one's desire or enthusiasm aroused; be tempted; be stirred
【心窦】【生理】cardiac sinus
【心毒】with poison in one's heart; callous-hearted; evil-minded; malicious; cruel: 罗莎琳是一个~的人。*Rosalyn is very cruel.*
【心耳】【生理】auricle
【心烦】troubled; vexed; perturbed
【心烦意乱】be confused and worried; be terribly upset; be restless and disquieted
【心房】①【生理】atrium (of the heart) ② heart; mind
【心扉】[书] door of one's heart -heart; mind; thought
【心服】be genuinely convinced; acknowledge sincerely; admire from the bottom of one's heart
【心服口服】be wholly convinced; be won round completely
【心浮】flighty and impatient, the lad could not sit sown to his work
【心腹】① trusted; reliable ② trusted subordinate or follower; henchman ③ secret; confidential: 说~话 *confide in sb*; *tell sb the in strict confidence*; *exchange confidences*
【心肝】① sense of right and wrong; conscience ② darling
【心高】have high aspirations; cherish great ambitions; be lofty-minded
【心高气傲】ambitious and aggressive; proud and arrogant
【心寒】[方] be bitterly disappointed; be disenchanted
【心黑】① evil; venomous ② greedy; predatory
【心狠】ruthless; merciless
【心狠手辣】cruel and evil; vicious and merciless
【心花】① happy mood; joy ②[方] state of mind; mood
【心花怒放】burst with joy; be ecstatic; be elated
【心怀】① harbour; cherish; bear; entertain: ~不满 *grouch* ② feeling; mood; intention ③ nature; state of mind
【心怀鬼胎】cherish sinister motives; have evil designs
【心怀叵测】harbour sinister or malicious motives; cherish evil designs; have some dirty trick up one's sleeve
【心慌】① be flustered; be jittery; get nervous ②[方] (of the heart) palpitate
【心慌意乱】be fidgety and flustered; be alarmed and confused; be all in a flutter
【心灰意懒】be disheartened or downhearted; be dispirited; lose heart completely
【心魂】mind; state of mind; composure
【心活】be indecisive; be easily led; be pliable
【心机】thinking; calculating; scheming: 费尽~ *rack one's brains in scheming*
【心肌】【生理】cardiac muscle; myocardium
【心急】impatient; anxious; short-tempered: ~如焚 *be nervous with worry*; *be burning with impatience*
【心计】calculation; cunning; planning
【心迹】true state of mind; true motives or feeling; heart: 表明~ *make clear one's heart*
【心悸】①【医】palpitation ②[书] fright; fear; dread
【心尖】①【生理】apex of the heart; apex cordis ② in the recess of one's mind; heart of hearts ③[方] best-loved one; darling
【心间】in mind; at heart: 牢记~ *bear in mind*
【心焦】anxious; troubled; worried
【心绞痛】【医】angina pectoris
【心劲】① thought; idea; mind: 员工们的~都一样, 都希望把这件事做好。*All the staff wish do well it.* ② mental capabilities; brains: 别看他人小, 可很有~。*Young as he is, he is really smart.* ③ spirit; zeal; drive
【心惊胆战】tremble with fear; shake with fright; be panic-stricken; have one's heart in one's boot
【心惊肉跳】be filled with apprehension; feel nervous and jumpy; shake in one's boots
【心净】free from worries; be completely at ease
【心境】state or frame of mind; mental state; mood: ~闲适 *be in a relaxed, tranquil mood*
【心静】calm; composed: ~如水 *one's heart is as calm as still water*
【心疚】[书] feel distressed and uneasy; feel compunction or guilty conscience
【心坎】① pit of the stomach ② bottoms of one's heart
【心口】pit of the stomach: ~痛 *pain in the pit of the stomach*; *heartburn*
【心口不一】say one thing and mean another; say what one does not think; be hypocritical
【心口如一】say what one thinks; be frank and unreserved; speak one's mind
【心宽】be broad-minded; take things easy: ~体胖 *when the mind is at ease, the body grows healthy*; *be carefree and well-nourished*; *be fit and happy*
【心旷神怡】relaxed and happy; carefree and joyous; refreshed in mind and heart
【心劳】mental effort; laboured thought
【心理】psychology; mentality: ~障碍 *psychological obstruction* / ~分析 *psychoanalysis* / ~咨询 *psy-*

chological consultation
【心力】mental and physical efforts
【心力交瘁】be exhausted both mentally and physically
【心力衰竭】【医】heart failure
【心里】① in the heart ② in the mind; at heart
【心里话】what is on one's mind; one's innermost thoughts and feelings;说句～,我们不同意这样做。*To be honest, We don't agree on doing so.*
【心里美】a kind of radish with green shin and sweet purplish-red flesh
【心连心】heart linked to heart
【心灵】① clever; astute; intelligent; quick-witted: ～手巧 *have a lively mind and a quick hand*; *be clever and handy*; *be quick-witted and nimble-fingered* ② heart; soul; mind: ～美 *noble character*
【心领】① understand; comprehend ② express one's thanks:你的好意我～啦。*I appreciate your kindness.*
【心领神会】understand tacitly; readily take a hint or cue
【心路】① wit; intelligence: 斗～ *fight a battle of wits* ② breadth of mind; mindedness; tolerance ③ intention; design; motive ④ way of thinking; state of mind; train of thought
【心律】【医】rhythm of the heart
【心律不齐】【医】arrhythmia
【心率】【医】heart rate
【心乱如麻】have one's mind as confused as a tangled skein; be utterly confused and disconcerted; have one's mind in a tangle
【心满意足】be perfectly content; be completely satisfied
【心明眼亮】be sharp-eyed and clear-headed; be discerning; can tell right from wrong; see and think clearly
【心目】① vision (mental or physical); mind's eye ② mind; view:海伦是人们～中的英雄。*Helen is a hero in the eyes of people.*
【心念】cherished wish; aspiration; idea
【心平气和】even-tempered and good-humoured; unruffled; calm
【心魄】heart; soul; mind
【心气】① motive; intention:他～很高。*He has a high goal.* ② ambition; aspiration ③ mood; state of mind:这几天,妻子～不顺。*My wife has been in a bad mood these days.* ④ breadth of minded; tolerance
【心窍】aperture of the heart as a thinking organ; capacity for clear thinking:财迷～ *be possessed by a lust for money*
【心切】anxiety (to do sth); over-eagerness:他求胜～。*He was anxious to win.*
【心情】frame or state of mind; mood; spirit: ～舒畅 *enjoy ease of mind*
【心曲】[书] ① innermost being; mind ② what is on one's mind
【心如刀割】one's heart contracts in pain as if stabbed by a knife; one feels as if a knife were piecing one's heart; be cut to the quick
【心如死灰】one's heart is as dead as ashes — completely disheartened; hopelessly apathetic
【心如铁石】have a heart of stone; be firm; be determined
【心软】be soft-hearted; tender-hearted; lenient
【心上人】person of one's heart; lover; sweetheart
【心上】in one's heart; at heart
【心身】① mind and body ②【医】psychosomatic
【心神】① thought and energy ② state of mind; mind:最近乔治似乎有什么心事,整日～恍惚。*Georgie recently seemed to have sth weighing on his mind, looked like to be absent-minded all days.*
【心神不定】anxious and distracted
【心声】inner voice; heartfelt wish; aspiration; thinking:言为～ *words are the voice of the mind*; *what the heart thinks the tongue speaks*
【心盛】be in high spirits; be full of energy
【心事】sth weighing on one's mind; load on one's mind; preoccupation; worry
【心室】【生理】ventricle
【心术】①[贬] intention; design:罗杰～不正。*Roger has harbour evil designs.* ② calculation; scheming
【心思】① idea; thought; mind ② thinking:挖空～ *rack one's brains* ③ state of mind or mood for doing sth:我没～干任何事。*I am no mood for anything.*
【心酸】be sorrowful; feel sad:为往事感到～ *feel sad for past events*
【心算】mental arithmetic; mental calculation; doing sums in one's head
【心髓】innermost being; heart of hearts
【心碎】heartbroken:罗伊有一个令人～的过去。*Roy has a heartbreaking past.*
【心态】psychology; mentality; mental attitude
【心膛】[方] breadth of mind; view of life
【心疼】① love dearly; love:珍妮很～丈夫。*Jane loves dearly her husband.* ② feel painful; feel sorry; be tormented; be distressed
【心跳】palpitation
【心痛】painful; distressed
【心头】mind; heart: 往事涌上～。*Past events surged to his mind.*
【心头肉】darling of one's heart; best loved one; most treasured possession
【心窝儿】[口] pit of the stomach; heart of hearts: 他的话说到我～里去啦。*His words struck a chord in my heart.*
【心弦】heartstrings: 动人～ *pull at one's heartstrings*; *move one's heart*
【心想】think: ～事成 *get what one's long for*
【心心念念】keep thinking of or about; long for
【心心相印】have heart-to-heart communion with each other; share the same feeling; have mutual

love and affinity; be kindred spirit
【心性】disposition; temper or temperament; nature
【心胸】① deep in one's heart; at heart; im one's mind ② breadth of mind: ~豁达 *have a generous heart* ③ aspiration; ambition
【心虚】① afraid of being found out; with a guilty conscience; nervous: 做贼~ *have a guilty conscience* ② lacking in self-confidence; timorous; diffident
【心绪】state of mind; mood: ~不佳 *in a bad mood*; *in low spirits*
【心绪不宁】in a disturbed state of mind; flustered; in a flutter
【心血】painstaking care or effort: ~来潮 *be seized by a whim*
【心眼儿】① heart; mind: 我打~喜欢露西。*I like Lucy with my heart.* ② intention; heart: 波林~很好。*Pauline has a heart of gold.* ③ intelligence; wit: 缺~ *be slow-witted* ④ baseless doubts; unfounded misgivings ⑤ breadth or narrowness of mind; tolerance
【心痒】itch for; have an itch for
【心仪】[书] admire in one's heart
【心意】① regard; kindly feelings; gratitude or hospitality ② meaning; aim; intention
【心硬】hard-hearted; heartless; callous; unfeeling; stony-hearted
【心有灵犀一点通】hearts which beat in unison are linked; lovers' hearts are closely linked; strike a chord in sb's heart
【心有余而力不足】be more than willing, but lack the power (to do sth); be unable to do what one wants very much to; one's ability falls short of one's wish; the spirits is willing, but the flesh is weak
【心有余悸】one's heart still flutters with fear; have a lingering fear; the memory (of sth etc.) still haunts one
【心猿意马】restless and whimsical; fanciful and fickle; unsettled in mind; in several minds
【心愿】cherished desire; wisher dream
【心悦诚服】admire from the bottom of one's heart; be completely convinced; submit willingly
【心杂音】【医】heart murmur
【心脏】①【生理】heart: ~停跳 *cardiac arrest* ② centre; heart
【心脏病】heart disease; cardiopathy
【心脏移植】heart transplant
【心窄】have a one-track mind; be narrow-minded
【心照】understand each other without speaking a word; have a tacit understanding; have quick or keen apprehension
【心照不宣】understand each other without speaking a word; have a tacit mutual understanding; consider it unnecessary to say any more
【心直口快】be frank and outspoken; speak one's mind without any hesitation; be plain-spoken and straightforward; say what one thinks without much deliberation
【心志】will; meaning; resolve; determination
【心智】intelligence; wisdom: 我们愿为我们的国家献出自己全部的~和力量。*We'd like to devote all our wisdom and energy for our country.*
【心中】at heart; in one's heart; on one's mind: 最近他好像~有事。*He has something in his heart recently.*
【心中无数】have no clear idea (of the situation, etc.); not know one's own mind; not know what is what
【心中有数】have a clear idea (of the situation, etc.); know one's own mind; know what's what
【心重】take things too hard; be oversensitive
【心拙口笨】dull-witted and slow-tongued
【心醉】be charmed; be enchanted; be bewitched; be fascinated: 这里的美景令他~。*The beautiful scenery fascinates him here.*

芯 rush pith
see also xìn
【芯片】【电】microchip; chip: ~制造商 *chip manufacturer*

辛 ① hot (in taste, flavor, etc.); pungent ② arduous; difficult; hard; laborious; hard work; toil: 千~万苦 *innumerable trials and hardships* ③ painful; sad: ~酸 *misery* ④ acrid: ~辣地讽刺 *acrid remarks*; *bitter irony* ⑤ the eighth of the ten Heavenly Stems ⑥ (Xīn) a surname
【辛亥革命】Revolution of 1911, led by Dr. Sun Yat-sen, which overthrew the Qing Dynasty
【辛苦】① hard; toilsome; laborious: 大家一路上~了。*Everybody has a toilsome trip.* ② (formula for asking sb to do sth) go to trouble; take pains: 这事别人办不好,只得~你一下啦。*The thing can't be done by others, you have to go to trouble.*
【辛辣】pungent; bitter; incisive: ~的语言 *sharp language*; *acid remarks*
【辛劳】toil; pains
【辛勤】industrious; assiduous; hardworking
【辛酸】① sad; bitter; painful; miserable: ~的回忆 *sad memories* ②【化】caprylic acid

欣 glad; happy; elated; joyful: ~喜若狂 *jump out of one's skin*; *be wild with joy*
【欣快】happy; blissful; euphoric
【欣慕】admire; adore: ~不已 *be filled with admiration*
【欣然】[书] joyfully; gladly; with pleasure: ~同意 *readily agree*
【欣赏】① enjoy; admire: ~大自然的美景 *enjoy the beautiful scene of nature* ② appreciate; like: 自我~ *self-appreciation*; *self-glorification*
【欣慰】gratified; satisfied
【欣悉】[书] be glad to learn or hear
【欣喜】glad; elated; joyful; happy: ~雀跃 *dance with joy* / ~若狂 *rejoice*; *delight*; *exult*; *be wild with joy*

【欣羡】[书] admire: 不已 be filled with admiration
【欣欣】① happily; gladly ② luxuriant; exuberant; flourishing
【欣欣向荣】thriving; flourish prosperous; affluent; grow luxuriantly: 各行各业~。*Every trade is prosperous.*
【欣愉】joy; delight; happiness
【欣悦】delight; pleasure; joy
锌 【化】zinc(Zn)
【锌白】【化】zinc white
【锌锭】【冶】zinc pig
新¹ ① new; occurring for the time; fresh; modern: ~品种 *new variety* ② renewed; improved; new; neo-: 耳目一~ *find everything new and fresh; refreshing* /悔过自~ *repent and make a fresh start* ③ just begun; unused; new: ~钢笔 *new pen* ④ sth new; new thing; new people: 推陈出~ *put forth new ideas; weed through the old to bring for the new* ⑤ newly or recently married ⑥ newly; just: 这本是我~买的字典。*This is a dictionary I have just bought.*
新² ① name of dynasty founded by WangMang, AD8-23 ② short for Xinjiang Uygur Autonomous Region
【新兵】new recruit; recruit
【新茶】newly-picked tea; fresh tea
【新潮】① new trend or tendency ② modish; fashionable; avant-garde: ~服装 *modish clothing*
【新陈代谢】①【生】metabolism ② the new superseding the old
【新仇旧恨】old scores and new; new hatred piled on old; scores both old and new
【新春】10 or 20 days following the Lunar New Year's Day: ~佳节 *happy occasion of the Spring Festival*
【新词】new word; new expression; neologism
【新法】① new law ② new method
【新房】bridal chamber; wedding chamber
【新干线】Shinkansen Line, Japanese high-speed railway line connection Todyo and Fukuoka
【新官上任三把火】a new official applies strict measures; a new official introduces a rash of changes; a new broom sweeps clean
【新欢】new sweetheart
【新婚】newly-married: ~燕尔 *just happily-married*
【新记录】new record: 创造~ *create new record*
【新纪元】new era; new epoch
【新加坡】Singapore: ~人 *Singaporean*
【新疆维吾尔自治区】Xinjiang Uygur Autonomous Region, established in 1955
【新教】【宗】protestantism: ~徒 *protestant*
【新旧约全书】【宗】old and New Testaments
【新居】new home; new residence; new housing
【新郎】bridegroom
【新郎官】[口] bridegroom
【新老交替】succession of the older by the younger generation; replacement of the old by the new
【新历】new style; solar calendar (in contrast with the lunar calendar); gregorian calendar (in contrast with the Julian calendar)
【新年】New Year: ~贺词 *New Year message*
【新娘】bride
【新派】new style; modern style
【新篇章】new page; new chapter
【新瓶装旧酒】old wine in a new bottle — same old stuff with a new label
【新奇】new and strange; novel
【新人】① people of a new type ② new personality; new talent ③ new recruit ④ reformed person
【新任】① newly-appointed: ~的所长 *newly-appointed superintendent* ② new appointment; new post: 他已有~。*He has got a new post.*
【新生】① newborn; newly born: ~力量 *new power* ② new life; rebirth: 重获~ *receive a new lease of life* ③ new student; freshman: 招生~ *enrol new students*
【新生儿】newborn (baby); neonate
【新生事物】newly emerging thing; new thing
【新诗】(in contrast with classical poetry) verse written in the vernacular; new poetry
【新石器时代】Neolithic Age; new Stone Age: ~文化 *Neolithic culture*
【新式】new type; new-style; modern; up-to-date: ~服装 *clothing of the latest fashion*
【新手】new hand; raw recruit; novice; rookie
【新书】① new book ② book to be published or just off the press
【新四军】New Fourth Army, led by the Chinese Communist Party during the War of Resistance Against Japan, 1937—1945
【新体】new-style; modern; vernacular: 徐志摩擅长写~诗。*Xu Zhimo is good at writing new-style poet.*
【新闻】① news: 国际~ *international news* /~处 *information office or service* ② sth new; hearsay; rumour
【新西兰】New Zealand: ~人 *New Zealander*
【新希伯来语】New Hebrew
【新媳妇儿】[口] bride
【新鲜】① fresh: ~水果 *fresh fruit* ② new; original; novel; strange: ~事 *adventure*
【新兴】new and developing; newly emerging; rising; burgeoning: ~行业 *emergent industry*
【新星】①【天】nova ② [喻] new star; rising star: 歌坛~ *new singing star*
【新型】new style; new type; new pattern
【新秀】up-and-coming youngster; rising star: 文坛~ *promising young writer*
【新意】new idea or meaning; originality
【新颖】new; original; novel: 这篇文章构思~。*There is original conception in the article.*
【新址】new address; new site; new location
【新妆】① (of woman) new look after make-up; new appearance ② (woman's) new style; new

X

fashion
【新装】new clothes
【新作】new literary or artistic work: 名家 ~ *new works by well-known authors*
歆 [书] envy; admire; adore
【歆慕】[书] admire; envy
【歆羡】[书] envy; admire; long for
薪 ① firewood; fuel; faggot: 釜底抽 ~ *take away the firewood from under the cauldron*; (*fig*) *take a drastic measure to deal with a situation* ② salary: 升职加 ~ *have got a promotion and increase salary*
【薪俸】salary; pay; remuneration
【薪金】pay; salary
【薪水】salary; pay
【薪饷】pay (to the military and police) and supply (such as clothing, boots, etc.)
【薪资】salary; pay; wage: ~不丰 *modest pay*
馨 [书] strong and pervasive fragrance: 如兰之 ~ *as fragrant as an orchid* / 温 ~ *be softly fragrant*
【馨香】[书] ① fragrance; aroma ② smell of burning incense

xìn

芯 core: 灯 ~ *lampwick*; *wick*
see also xīn
【芯子】① fuse; wick ② forked tongue (of a snake)
信[1] ① honest; sincere; true; sure: ~誓旦旦 *vow solemnly* ② confidence; faith; trust; reputation: 失 ~ *break faith* ③ believe; trust: 偏听偏 ~ *be biased*; *heed and trust only one side* ④ keep one's word; keep one's credit ⑤ embrace; believe in; profess faith in: ~奉天主教 *believe in catholicism* ⑥ oath of alliance ⑦ messenger ⑧ message; information; new: 杳无音 ~ *disappear without a trace*; *no news have been received for a long time*; *have never been heard of since* ⑨ letter; mail: 写 ~ *write letter* ⑩ pledge; evidence; sign; token: 印 ~ *official*
信[2] ① conveniently; at well; at random: ~步 *walk aimlessly* ② certainly ③ arsenic: 红 ~ *red arsenic*
【信笔】write at random; write freely; scribble along
【信标】【航】beacon: ~灯 *beacon light*
【信步】walk aimlessly; stroll; roam
【信不过】not trust; distrust
【信差】[旧] ① messenger or courier for official documents and mail ② postman
【信从】believe, trust, or follow without doubt: 盲目 ~ *trust blindly*
【信得过】have faith or confidence in; trust
【信访】letters and visits (by the people, usu. airing complaints or making suggestions); correspondence and visitation (by the public)
【信封】envelope
【信奉】believe in; profess
【信服】have implicit faith in; accept completely; be convinced
【信鸽】carrier pigeon; homing pigeon; homer
【信函】letter; mail; correspondence
【信号】① sign; signal: ~灯 *signal lamp* ②【电】signal: ~失真 *signal distortion*
【信汇】mail transfer (M /T); postal money order; letter transfer
【信笺】letter paper; writing paper
【信件】letter; mail
【信教】profess or believe in a religion; be religious
【信口】blurt out one's thoughts: ~雌黄 *make irresponsible remarks*; *random talk*
【信赖】trust; believe in; have faith in
【信念】faith; belief; conviction
【信女】woman believe; devotee: 善男 ~ *devotee men and women*; *pious men and woman*; *Buddhist laymen and laywomen*
【信任】trust; confidence
【信实】① trustworthy; honest; dependable: 米歇尔待人 ~。*Michelle is honest towards people.* ② authentic; reliable
【信使】courier; messenger; emissary
【信誓旦旦】pledge or promise in all sincerity and seriousness; vow solemnly
【信手拈来】have (words, material, etc.) at one's fingertips and writhe with facility
【信守】keep faith; abide by; stick to: ~诺言 *keep faith*; *be as good as one's word*
【信条】article of creed or faith; precept; tenet
【信筒】pillar-box; mailbox
【信徒】believer; disciple; follower; devotee
【信托】① trust; entrust ②【经】trust: ~公司 *trust company*
【信物】authenticating object; token of pledge; keepsake
【信息】① information: ~中心 *information centre* ② news; message; word
【信箱】① post box; mail box ② post-office box (POB) ③ letter box
【信心】confidence; faith: 我们有 ~ 完成这项工作。*We are confident of accomplishing the work.*
【信仰】belief; conviction; faith: 中国人民有 ~ 自由。*Chinese have freedom of conviction.*
【信仰危机】crisis in belief or conviction; credibility crisis
【信以为真】take as valid; accept as true
【信义】good faith; honour: 重 ~, 守合同 *act in good faith*, *observe contract*
【信用】① credibility; credit; honour: 诺拉是一个讲

～的人。Nora is a man of honour ② credit：～贷款 *loan on credit* ③［书］trust and appoint

【信誉】prestige；credit；reputation：国际～ *international prestige*

【信约】covenant；pledge

【信札】letters

【信真】take sth as true

【信纸】letter paper；writing paper

衅 quarrel；row；dispute：挑～ *provocation* /寻～闹事 *throw down the gage*；*pick a quarrel*

【衅端】［书］cause for a quarrel or dispute

xīng

兴 ① be popular；get up；flourish；prevail；rise；thrive：～亡 *rise and fall* /～旺发达 *be prospering* ② encourage；foster promote ③ begin；start；found：百废俱～ *full-scale construction is under way* ④［方］allow；let；permit：不～胡说 *not permit to drivel* ⑤［方］probably；maybe；perhaps：远处那个女的～许是纳塔莎。*The woman in distance is probably Natasha.*
see also xìng

【兴办】set up；start；initiate：～工厂 *set up a factory*

【兴废】［书］rise and fall；wax and wane

【兴奋】① excited；elated ②【生理】excition

【兴风作浪】make waves；raise the devil；stir up or make trouble；fan the flames of disorder

【兴复】revive；rejuvenate：～故国 *revive one's native country*

【兴国】make a country prosperous；rejuvenate a nation：科教～ *invigorate a country through science and education*

【兴建】erect；build；construct：集资～工厂 *raise funds to build a factory*

【兴隆】prosperous；thriving；flourishing；brisk：生意～ *brisk one's business*

【兴起】① rise；spring up；be on the upsurge ②［书］spring to action（on stimulus）：闻风～ *spring to action upon hearing the news*

【兴盛】prosperous；thriving；flourishing；in the ascendant

【兴师】［书］raise；mobilize or send an army

【兴师动众】move troops about and stir up the people；mobilize an army and rally the people — drag in a great number or people（to do sth）

【兴师问罪】bring or lead an army to punish sb for one's crime；send a punitive expedition denounce sb publicly for his crimes；send a punitive force against

【兴时】fashionable；in vogue；all the rage

【兴衰】prosperity and adversity；rise and fall

【兴叹】［书］lament（one's inadequacy，etc.）

【兴旺】prosperous；flourishing；thriving；on the upgrade

【兴修】start construction（on a large project）；build：～水利 *start construction on irrigation works*

【兴许】［方］maybe；perhaps；probably

【兴学】set up schools（to promote education）

星 ① star ② any heavenly body：恒～ *fixed star* /行～ *planet* ③ bit；piece；particle：零～ *piecemeal*；*scrappy scattered*；*sporadic*；*tiny bit* ④ marks（resembling asterisks）on the arm of a steelyard indicating jin and its fractions：秤～ *the brass marks on the beam of a steel-yard* ⑤ famous performer；star：影～ *film star* ⑥ twenty -fifth of the 28 constellations in ancient astronomy ⑦ class：～级宾馆 *high-class hotel* ⑧（Xīng）a surname

【星表】【天】star catalogue；star chart

【星辰】stars；constellations：日月～ *sun*，*moon and stars*

【星点】［方］little bit；tiny bit：一年来我没有弗雷达半～消息。*I have nothing of Freda for one year.*

【星斗】stars：满天～ *star studded sky*；*starriness*

【星光】starlight：～灿烂 *the stars is shining*

【星河】Milky Way

【星火】① spot fire；spark ② shooting star；meteor

【星火燎原】a single spark can start a prairie fire

【星级】star，used in the ranking of hotels：五～饭店 *five-star hotel*

【星际】interplanetary；interstellar：～旅行 *interplanetary flight or travel*；*space travel*

【星空】starlit night sky；starry sky

【星期】① week：每～两次 *twice per week* ② used in combinations with 日，一，二，三，四，五，六 ③ Sunday

【星期天】Sunday

【星球】celestial or heavenly body

【星球大战】Star Wars — alternative name for Strategic Defense Initiative（SDI）initiated by US President Ronald Reagan（in office 1981-1989）

【星术】astrology

【星速】with meteoric speed；in the greatest hurry

【星体】【天】celestial or heavenly body；planet

【星条旗】① Stars and Stripes，US national flag ② Star-Spangled Banner，US national anthem

【星图】【天】star atlas；star chart；star map

【星相】astrology；horoscope

【星象】configuration and movement of the stars as basis for astrology

【星星】① tiny spots；a bit ②［口］star

【星星点点】a bit；tiny spots：草地上～地开着一些小白花。*There are blooming little white flowers on the grassplot.*

【星夜】① at night ② by night；on a starlit night

【星移斗转】passage of time；the stars change their posts in the sky

【星移物换】the stars move and things change — change of the seasons

【星云】【天】nebula

【星占术】astrology；horoscope

【星座】【天】constellation

猩 orangutan

【猩红】scarlet; bloodred

【猩猩】【动】orangutan

惺 [书] ① intelligent; clever; smart ② awake; come to one's senses; be sober; understand

【惺忪】(of eyes) not yet fully open on waking up; bleary -eyed: 睡眼~ *eyes still heavy with sleep*; *sleepy eyes*

【惺惺】①[书] wide a wake; sober ② clever; intelligent; smart; wise ③ hypocritical; unctuous

腥 ① raw meat or fish (as food) ② having the smell of fish, seafood, etc.; (fishy) odour

【腥臭】stinking smell as of rotten fish; reek; stench: 死鱼有股~味。*Dead fishes have a rancid rank.*

【腥风血雨】foul wind and rain of blood; reactionary reign of terror

【腥秽】foul and filthy; smelly and dirty

【腥气】fishy; fish-smell, seafood, etc.; rank smell; stinking

【腥臊】smell of fish and urine; stench; rancid, foul smell

【腥味儿】strong smell of fish; fishy odor; rank smell

xíng

刑 ① punishment; torture: 死~ *death sentence*; *death penalty*; *execution* ② punish torture ③ go on a punitive expedition: ~罚敌人 *go on a punitive expedition to enemy* ④ instrument of torture: 用~ *resort to torture*

【刑场】execution ground

【刑罚】penalty; punishment; torture

【刑法】① penal law; criminal code ② corporal punishment; torture

【刑具】instruments of torture or punishment; handcuffs and fetters

【刑律】criminal law

【刑期】【律】term of imprisonment; prison term: 希拉里被判~五年,快释放了。*Hilary was punished five-prison term, and is almost released now.*

【刑辱】[书] humiliating torture

【刑事】【律】criminal; penal: ~案件 *penal case* / ~处分 *criminal sanction* / ~拘留 *criminal detention or custody*

【刑释】be released after serving one's sentence

【刑堂】[旧] torture chamber

【刑讯】interrogate by torture; inquisition by torture

【刑杖】rod or bunch of sticks used in ancient times as instrument of torture

【刑种】forms of penalty

行 ① walk; go: 步~ *walk on foot* ② go on a tour; travel: 出~ *go out* ③ sail; drive: ~船 *sail boat* ④ operate: 医生对她施~了肺部手术。*The doctor operated on her lung.* ⑤ flow: ~云流水 *floating clouds and flowing water — natural and smooth writing* ⑥ be current; be popular; be in vogue: ~歌曲 *popular song* ⑦ pour ⑧ apply; use: ~使权利: *use one's right* ⑨ do; act; practise; implement; exercise: 量力而~ *do what is within one's capability* ⑩ distance; road; journey: 千里之~,始于足下。*A thousand-li road begins with the first step.* ⑪ running script: ~书 *running hand* ⑫ five elements ⑬ action; conduct; manner: ~为举止 *action* ⑭ conduct; 品~端正 *be on the straight* ⑮ all right; ok ⑯ (Xíng) a surname

see also háng

【行不通】unworkable; impracticable

【行车】drive (a vehicle): ~执照 *driver's license*

【行成】[书] seek a peaceful solution to a dispute; seek or negotiate peace

【行程】① route or distance of travel ② course; process: 在历史发展的~中 *in the course of history development* ③【机】stroke; throw

【行驰】drive; run: 小汽车~在宽广的马路上。*The car is running on wide road.*

【行船】sail; navigate

【行刺】assassinate: ~敌人 *try to assassinate one's enemy*

【行得通】workable; practicable

【行动】① move or get about; take action: 他可以下床~了。*He can move out of bed.* ② act; operate; move; action; operation: 军事~ *the army's operations*

【行方便】make things easy (for sb); be accommodating; do a favour

【行房】(as between husband and wife) sexual intercourse; sex; love-making

【行好】act charitably; be merciful; do a favour; forgive

【行贿】offer a bribe; resort to bribery; grease sb's palm

【行迹】movements; whereabouts; tracks; traces

【行奸】commit adultery

【行检】① [书] moral conduct or character: 无~ *without character* ② luggage inspection; baggage check

【行将】[书] soon; about to; on the point of: 他~到达这里。*He was about to arrive here.*

【行将就木】be drawing near the coffin — be fast approaching death; be near one's death; have one foot in the grave; one's days are numbered

【行脚僧】itinerant monk

【行劫】commit robbery: ~杀人 *kill to rob*

【行进】advance; march

【行经】①【生理】menstruate ② go by or through

【行径】[贬] act; action; move: 丑恶~ *hideous action*

【行酒】serve a round or drinks

【行军】march: ~床 *camp bed*; *camp cot*

【行客】passers-by; traveller

【行乐】[书] amuse oneself; indulge in merry making
【行礼】① greet; salute: 举手~ *raise one's hand in salute* ② [方] give a gift or present
【行李】baggage; luggage: ~寄存处 *left-luggage office; checkroom*
【行旅】traveller; wayfarer
【行囊】[书] travelling baggage
【行骗】cheat; swindle; practise deception
【行聘】[旧] give betrothal gifts; present gifts to consummate a betrothal
【行期】date of departure
【行乞】beg; beg one's bread; go begging: 以~为生 *beg for life*
【行窃】commit theft; steal
【行人】pedestrian
【行色】state of mind at departure; circumstances or style of departure: ~匆匆 *set out on one's journey in a great hurry; in a hurry to go on a trip*
【行善】do good deeds or works; be charitable: 他乐于~。*He takes pleasure in doing good deeds.*
【行赏】present awards; bestow rewards: 论功~ *award people according to their contributions*
【行尸走肉】walking corpse; zombies; utterly worthless person
【行时】(of a thing) be fashionable; be in vogue; (of a person) be in the ascendant
【行食】① [书] loaf about ② walk after a meal to help digestion
【行使】exercise; perform; use
【行驶】(of a vehicle, ship, etc.) go; drive; ply; travel
【行世】see the world; become popular
【行事】① behave or conduct oneself ② do things; act
【行书】running hand (in Chinese calligraphy); running script
【行水】[书] ① flowing water ② (of boats and ships) ply the waters; sail; navigate ③ work in flood control ④ inspect the water; inspect a flood
【行头】① actor's costumes and paraphernalia ② [谑] clothing
【行为】act; behaviour; conduct: ~不轨 *conspiratorial act; act against law* / ~规范 *code of conduct*
【行文】① style or manner of writing: ~流畅 *write fluently* ② (of a government office) send an official communication (to other organizations)
【行息】pay interest at a given rate
【行销】be on sale: ~全国 *be on sale in the whole country*
【行星】【天】planet
【行刑】carry ort a death sentence; execute: ~人员 *executioner*
【行凶】commit physical assault or murder; commit acts of violence
【行医】practise medicine (usu. on one's own)
【行者】① [书] traveller ②【宗】unshaven monk
【行政】administration; executive: ~部门 *administrative department* / ~处分 *administrative sanction; disciplinary sanction* / ~法规 *administrative statute*
【行政区】① administrative area or region: 香港特别~ *Hong Kong Special Administrative Region* ② administrative division
【行之有效】effective; effectual: ~的措施 *effectual measures*
【行舟】sail (a boat): 学如逆水~,不进则退。*Learning is like sailing against the current, you either forge ahead or fall back.*
【行装】outfit for a journey; travelling gear; baggage; luggage
【行踪】whereabouts; vestiges; track; trace
【行走】① walk; go ② [旧] be appointed to a government department with all the privileges but no specific duties of the post

形 ① appearance; form; shape: 图~ *map; figure* ② body; entity: 无~ *invisible; intangible; imperceptible* ③ appearance; seem; look: 喜~于色 *light up with pleasure; look very pleased* ④ terrain ⑤ situation: ~势分析 *analyse of situation* ⑥ mold ⑦ contrast; comparison
【形变】【物】deformation: ~效应 *deformation effect*
【形成】form; take shape; shape up: 他已经~早起的习惯。*He has formed the habit of getting up early.*
【形迹】① a person's movements and look or expression: ~可疑 *of suspicious appearance; look suspicious* ② sign; trace; mark: 有~可寻 *have some signs to follow* ③ etiquette; formality: 在日常生活中没有时间拘~。*There's no time for formality in everyday life.*
【形貌】form and appearance: ~特征 *characteristic of from*
【形容】① [书] look; appearance; countenance ② describe
【形容词】【语】adjective
【形色】① appearance and expression; look ② image and color
【形式】form; mode; shape: 以书面的~把意见表达出来 *deliver oneself of opinion in writing*
【形势】① terrain; topography: ~险要 *strategically advantageous topography* ② condition; state of affairs; situation; circumstances
【形势逼人】the situation calls for prompt action; the situation is getting better and better
【形似】be similar in form or appearance; be alike look
【形态】① form; shape; state pattern: 意识~ *ideology* ②【语】morphology: ~学 *morphology* / 生物的~ *morphology of organisms*
【形体】① body; shape of a person's body; figure; physique: 优美的~ *graceful figure* ② form and structure: 汉字的~特点 *form and structure of Chinese characters*
【形相】form and shape; appearance; look
【形象】① image; form; figure; object: 莫里斯在镜

X

子里看到他自己的～。*Morris saw himself image in the mirror.* ② literary or artistic image; imagery:艺术～ *artistic image* / ～塑造 *image-building* ③ expressive; graphic; vivid: ～的比喻 *vivid figure of words*

【形形色色】of every colour and hue; of many varieties of all shades of all forms: ～的人物 *people of every colour and hue*

【形影相吊】body and shadow comforting each other — extremely lonely

【形影相随】always together as body and shadow; inseparable:她们是～的好朋友。*They are close friends being always together as body and shadow.*

【形状】appearance; countenance; form; shape

型 ① mold:木～ *wooden mold* ② model; type; variety; pattern:血～ *blood group*

【型板】【机】template; templet

【型材】【冶】section bar; section material; sections

【型钢】【冶】rolled-steel section; section steel; shape (steel)

【型号】model; type

xǐng

省 ① examine oneself critically; introspect ② visit (sep. one's parents or elders): ～亲 *mothering; pay a visit to one's parents or elders* ③ come to realize; become conscious or aware:发人深～ *set people thinking; provide much food for thought*

see also shěng

【省察】examine oneself critically; examine one's thought and conduct; make self-scrutiny

【省墓】[书] pay homage at one's parents' or elders' tombs

【省视】call upon; pay a visit to:领导多次去家中～病中的王工程师。*The leader has visited engineer Wang in her home many times.*

【省事】be sagacious; be perceptive:这孩子很～。*The child is so perceptive.*

【省悟】[书] wake up to reality

醒 ① come round; regain consciousness; sober up:今宵酒～何处。*Where will you sober up tonight.* ② be clear in mind; be awake; wake up ③ recover: 春天来啦,万物苏～。*Spring coming, all things on earth recover.* ④ [方] know; understand ⑤ clear; obvious ⑥ keep dough (after mixing) till water and flour are well mixed: ～面 *the dough becomes soft and even*

【醒盹儿】wake up from a nap; become awake

【醒豁】clear; explicit; obvious:这个故事寓意～。*The moral of the story is clear.*

【醒酒】dispel or counter the effect of alcohol; sober up

【醒觉】awaken; become aware of; come to realize: 当罗德里克听说因工作效率低而被革职时,才猛然～。*It was a rude awakening when Roderick was told that he was to be dismissed for inefficiency.*

【醒木】small wooden block used by storyteller to strike the table before him to draw the audience's attention

【醒目】attract attention; be conspicuous; be striking ; catch the eyes

【醒世】arouse the public; rock the world: ～篇 *article to awaken the public*

【醒睡】sleep lightly and keep alert:今晚风大,你要小心～。*You must keep alert tonight, because of strong wind.*

【醒悟】be aware of; come to realize the truth; come to see the truth ; wake up to reality

【醒眼】[方] ① striking (to the eye); obvious; eye- catching; conspicuous:这套衣服很～。*The suit of clothe looks brighter in colour.* ② perceptive; sagacious

xìng

兴 ① excitement; interest; mood to do sth:乘～而来 *come while one is in high spirits; come on an impulse* ② metaphor:比～的手法 *figuration*

see also xīng

【兴冲冲】in high spirits; with joy and excitement; excitedly:西蒙～地跑进屋。*Simon rushed into the room in high spirits.*

【兴高采烈】jubilant; in great delight; in high spirits; with great joy

【兴趣】interest

【兴头】① enthusiasm; zest; keen interest: ～十足 *be over-flowing with zest at the moment* ② [方] be delighted; be elated

【兴味】interest; relish:饶有～ *be full of interest; be greatly interested*

【兴味索然】be fed up; have lost all interest

【兴致】interest; agreeable mood

【兴致勃勃】be full of interest; be in high spirits; be greatly elated; feel a surge of exhilaration

杏 【植】apricot

【杏脯】sun-dried or preserved sweetened apricot

【杏核儿】apricot stone

【杏黄】apricot yellow; apricot (colour)

【杏仁】apricot kernel; almond: ～露 *drink with almond flavour; almond drink*

【杏眼】(of a woman) almond eyes; pretty eyes

【杏子】[方] apricot

幸 ① good fortune; happiness; lucky: ～运 *chance* ② rejoice; be happy ③ [书] favour: 得～ *win favour* ④ I hope; I trust ⑤ (of emperor) visit:巡～江南 *come south of the Yangtze on an imperial tour of inspection* ⑥ fortunately; luckily:侥～心理 *luckily mentality* ⑦ (Xìng) a surname

【幸臣】[贬] favourite at court; favoured court official

【幸存】(fortunately) survive: ~者 *survivor*
【幸而】luckily; fortunately
【幸福】① happiness; welfare; well-being ② happy; blissful: ~的孩子 *blissful kid*
【幸会】be lucky enough to meet; have the honour to meet: 久闻大名,今日得以~。*I have heard a lot about you; I am lucky enough to meet you till today.*
【幸进】[书] lucky or fortunate promotion
【幸亏】fortunately; luckily: 出来时~带了伞,要不咱们就得淋雨啦。*Fortunately, we carried umbrellas; otherwise, we would be caught in rain.*
【幸免】escape by sheer luck; have a narrow escape; be a close call or shave
【幸巧】luckily; fortunately; just as well
【幸事】good fortune; blessing: 你没有跟着他去那儿,真是~。*Luckily, you haven't gone there with him.*
【幸运】① good fortune; unexpected luck ② fortunate; very gratifying
【幸运儿】fortune's favourite; lucky fellow; lucky dog
【幸灾乐祸】take pleasure in or gloat over others' misfortune; revel in sb's discomfiture; be glad when sb is in difficulty; show malicious joy: 朋友有难,斯科特却~。*Scott was glad when his friend was in difficulty.*

性 ① character; disposition; inclination; nature: 习~ *habit* ② characteristic; property; quality ③ noun-forming suffix used to express ideology, emotion, etc.: 纪律~ *sense of discipline* ④ noun-forming suffix used to denote a category: 必然~ *inevitability* ⑤ sex: ~生活 *sexual life* ⑥ sexual distinction; gender: 女~ *feminine; female* ⑦【语】gender: 中~名词 *neutral noun* ⑧ heart: ~地善良 *kind hearted*

【性爱】sexual love
【性本能】sexual instinct
【性变态】(sexual) perversion
【性别】sexual distinction; sex: ~歧视 *sexism; sexual discrimination*
【性病】【医】venereal disease or VD
【性感】sex appeal; sexiness
【性高潮】【生理】orgasm
【性格】character; disposition; nature; temperament
【性功能障碍】【医】sexual dysfunction
【性饥渴】sex-starved
【性激素】【生化】sex hormone
【性急】impatient; impetuous; short -tempered
【性交】coitus; love-making; sexual intercourse; sex: 与人~ *make love with sb*
【性教育】sex education
【性解放】sexual liberation
【性命】life
【性能】function (of a machine, etc.); performance; property
【性器官】【生理】sexual organs; genitals
【性情】disposition; temperament; temper
【性骚扰】sex harassment
【性卫生】sex hygiene
【性心理学】sex psychology
【性行为】sex act; sexual behaviour or activity
【性学】sexology
【性欲】sexual desire or urge
【性知识】sex knowledge
【性质】quality; nature; property; character
【性自由】sexual freedom
【性子】① temper: 托比真是一个急~。*Toby is so hot-tempered.* ② strength; potency: 这咖啡的~真厉害。*The coffee is very powerful.*

姓 family name; surname; clan name

【姓名】surname and given name; full name
【姓氏】surname

悻

【悻然】disgruntled; piqued; put out; enraged
【悻悻】angry; enraged; resentful

xiōng

凶 ① inauspicious; unlucky; ominous ② crop failure; famine ③ fierce; menacing; diabolical: 他爸爸很~。*His father is fierce.* ④ terrible; violent; fearful ⑤ act of violence; murder ⑥ evildoer; criminal; murderer: 帮~ *accomplice; accessory* ⑦ [方] efficient; effective; tough

【凶案】murder (case); homicide
【凶暴】brutally fierce; ferocious
【凶残】① savage and cruel; brutal and ruthless ② [书] savage and cruel person
【凶毒】ferocious and brutal; vicious
【凶多吉少】bode ill rather than well; be faced with a precarious situation; be fraught with grim possibilities
【凶恶】fierce; vicious; ferocious
【凶犯】killer; murderer
【凶服】[书] mourning garb
【凶悍】ferocious and tough
【凶耗】news of sb's death
【凶狠】① fierce and malicious; ferocious and ruthless ② forceful; vigorous: ~的狗 *forceful dog* / 他打球扣杀~。*He smash forcefully.*
【凶荒】complete crop failure; famine: ~年月 *famine years*
【凶狂】fierce and frenzied; fierce and ruthless: 沃伦喜欢逞~。*Warren likes playing the bully.*
【凶戾】cruel and fierce; ruthless and tyrannical
【凶猛】fierce; violent; ferocious: ~的豹子 *fierce panther*
【凶器】lethal weapon; tool or weapon for criminal purposes
【凶杀】homicide; murder
【凶身】[书] killer; murderer; homicide

X

【凶神】demon; monster; fiend: ~恶煞 *devil; evil spirit; fiend*
【凶事】unlucky events such as death, burial, etc.
【凶手】assassin; assailant; killer; murderer
【凶徒】cut-throat; ruffian; thug
【凶顽】fierce and stubborn
【凶险】① in a very dangerous state; precarious; critical ② ferocious and sinister; fiendish and insidious
【凶相】ferocious features; fierce look: ~毕露 *look thoroughly ferocious; be ferocity itself*
【凶信】news of sb's death
【凶宅】haunted house; unlucky abode
【凶兆】ill omen; evil boding: 昨天夜里威廉做了个噩梦,他认为是个~。*Last night william had a bad dream, which he believed to be an ill omen.*

兄 ① elder brother ② elder male relative of one's own generation: 堂~ *elder male cousin* ③ courteous form of address between men: 老~ *familiar form of address between male friends*
【兄弟】① brothers; brethren ② fraternal; brotherly: ~单位 *brotherly units* ③ younger brother ④ familiar form of address for a man younger than oneself ⑤[谦] your humble servant: ~我在此向各位道谢啦。*Now, I would like to express my thanks to all of you hereon.*
【兄长】① elder brother ② respectful form of address for an elder than oneself

匈
【匈奴】Xiongnu or Hum, ancient nomadic people living in the north of China
【匈牙利】Hungary: ~人 *Hungarian*

汹 tumult
【汹汹】[书] ① sound of roaring waves ② violent; fierce; truculent: 气势~ *get up on one's hind legs* ③[书] turbulent; tumultuous
【汹涌】surging; tempestuous; turbulent
【汹涌澎湃】raging; turbulent; tempestuous: 黄河的浪涛~。*The tempestuous waves of the Yellow River keep surging ahead.*

胸 ① bosom; chest: 挺~而立 *throw a chest* ② mind; heart: 心~狭窄 *narrow-hearted*
【胸靶】【军】chest silhouette
【胸部】chest; thorax: ~手术 *thorax operation*
【胸大肌】【生理】pectoris or pectoralis major; greater pectoral muscle
【胸骨】【生理】breastbone; sternum
【胸花】corsage; chest pin
【胸怀】① have in mind; cherish: ~祖国 *bear the interest of motherland in mind* ② heart; mind: 敞开~ *bare one's chest*
【胸甲】breastplate; cuirass
【胸襟】① heart; mind; breadth of mind: ~狭窄 *small-minded; parochial* ② mood; state of mind: 杰克对未来有乐观的~。*Jake is optimistic about his future.* ③ upper front part of a jacket: ~上贴着一张纸条。*There was a piece of paper on the chest.*
【胸卡】name tag; identification badge
【胸坎】pit of the stomach
【胸口】pit of the stomach; chest
【胸脯】chest; bust; breast
【胸腔】pectoral cavity; thoracic cavity: ~镜 *thoracoscope*
【胸膛】chest
【胸围】①(of human body) chest measurement; bust ②【林】circumference of a tree trunk taken at 1.3 metres above the ground
【胸无城府】artless; of no sophistication; simple and candid
【胸无点墨】completely illiterate; uneducated; unlearned; unlettered
【胸臆】feelings; sentiments: 在埃玛的文章中,她直抒~。*In Emma's articles, she expressed her feelings in a straightforward manner.*
【胸有成竹】have a card up one's sleeve; have a well-thought-out plan, stratagem, etc. in mind
【胸章】badge
【胸罩】brassiere; bra
【胸针】brooch
【胸中有数】have a good idea of how things stand; have full confidence; know what's what; know fairly well: 珍妮弗能不能解决这个问题,我~。*I know fairly well if Jennifer is able to solve the problems.*
【胸椎】【生理】thoracic vertebra

xióng

雄 ① male: ~鸡 *cock; rooster* ② commanding; grand; imposing; majestic ③ mighty; powerful; virile ④ person or state having great power and influence
【雄辩】① convincing argument; eloquence; declamation; fluency: 事实胜于~。*I would rather believe the fact than declamation.* ② eloquently; convincingly: ~家 *eloquent speaker; orator*
【雄兵】powerful army
【雄才大略】of great talent and bold vision; (statesman or general) of rare gifts and grand strategy
【雄飞】strive for a higher level of achievement
【雄风】①[书] strong wind; gale ② heroic carriage; bold or gallant appearance
【雄蜂】【动】male bee; drone
【雄关】impregnable pass
【雄豪】① talented person; hero ② sublime; magnificent
【雄厚】rich; huge; solid; abundant: 莱斯利有~的资金支持。*Lesley has abundant funds to support him.*
【雄花】【植】male flower; staminate flower
【雄浑】forceful; powerful; vigorous and firm: ~苍劲 *bold and vigorous*

【雄激素】【生化】androgenic hormone; androgen
【雄健】powerful; robust; virile; vigorous
【雄杰】① gifted; talented ② outstanding talent; person of great ability
【雄劲】brawny; powerful; robust; sturdy
【雄赳赳】valiantly; gallantly
【雄踞】be positioned majestically
【雄峻】magnificent and steep: 挺拔～的山峰 *mighty and imposing peaks*
【雄丽】imposing and beautiful; sublime
【雄奇】imposing and extraordinary
【雄师】powerful army
【雄狮】male lion
【雄图】lofty aspiration; great ambition; great design; grandiose plan
【雄威】① powerful and stately ② bravery; courage; valour: 一展我军～ *display the valour of our army*
【雄伟】① grand; imposing; magnificent ② tall and strong: 尼尔有～的身材。*Neil is tall and sturdy.*
【雄文】powerful writing; great works; masterpiece
【雄武】martial; gallant; valiant; valorous
【雄心】noble ambition; lofty aspiration
【雄性】male; masculine
【雄蚁】【动】male ant
【雄壮】① full of power and grandeur; imposing magnificent; majestic ② stalwart; robust
【雄姿】majestic appearance; valiant carriage; heroic posture

熊[1] ① bear: 北极～ *polar bear* ② (Xióng) a surname

熊[2] ①［方］abuse; rebuke; upbraid; scold: 我把杯子摔了,哥哥～了我。*My elder brother scolded me when I dropped the cup.* ② impotent; timid faint-hearted: ～包 *useless person; worthless wretch*

【熊包】chicken-heart; good-for-nothing; useless person; worthless wretch
【熊胆】gall of bear used as medicine
【熊蜂】bumblebee; humble-bee
【熊猴】【动】Assamese macaque
【熊猫】panda
【熊市】bear market, (stock) market with falling prices
【熊心豹胆】heart of a bear and gall of a leopard — very bold
【熊腰虎背】bear's waist and tiger's back — man of sturdy build; thick powerful back and shoulders
【熊掌】bear's paw served as a rare delicacy

xiū

休[1] ① cease; end; stop: 喋喋不～ *talk garrulously* ② rest; repose: 轮～ *rest in turn* ③［旧］divorce one's wife and send her home: ～妻 *divorce and send one's wife away* ④ don't: ～要无礼! *Don't insult!*

休[2]［书］good fortune; rejoicing

【休班】［方］have a day off
【休怪】don't blame
【休会】adjourn; recess: 他们不得不暂时～。*They had to adjourn the meeting for the time being.*
【休假】have a holiday; take a vacation: 带薪～ *holiday with pay; pay vacation*
【休刊】(of newspapers or magazines) cease to publish; stop publication; suspend publication
【休克】【医】shock: 中毒性～ *toxic shock* / 过敏性～ *allergic or anaphylactic shock*
【休伦湖】Lake Huron, one of the five Great Lakes of North America
【休眠】【生物】dormancy; hibernate: ～火山 *dormant volcano*
【休戚相关】be bound together by common cause; solidarity
【休戚与共】share weal and woe; stand or stay together through thick and thin
【休憩】have or take a rest; rest
【休书】［旧］letter by a husband unilaterally announcing his decision to divorce his wife
【休息】have or take a rest; rest: ～室 *anteroom; lobby; lounge*
【休闲】① be not working; have leisure; spend or beguile one's leisure ②【农】lie fallow: ～地 *fallow land*
【休闲鞋】leisure shoe
【休闲服】leisure clothing; leisure wear
【休想】don't think (you can do sth, etc.); don't imagine (that it's possible); stop dreaming
【休学】suspend one's schooling without losing one's status as a student; be temporarily absent from school; suspend schooling
【休养】① recuperate; convalesce ② (of economy) recover; rehabilitate; revitalize
【休养生息】(of a nation) recuperate and multiply; rest and build up strength; rest and regenerate; rehabilitate
【休养所】rest home; sanatorium
【休业】① suspend business; be closed down ② end; wind up
【休战】armistice; ceasefire; truce: 现在两家处于～状态。*The two sides are under ceasefire.*
【休整】(of troops) rest and reorganize
【休止】cease; end; stop
【休止符】【音】rest

咻［书］make a din

【咻咻】［象］① used for the sound of breathing: 发出～的鼻息 *breath noisily* ② used to describe the cry of some birds and animals: 小鸭～。*The ducklings were cheeping.*

修[1] ① embellish; decorate; adorn ② repair; mend; fix ③ write; compile ④ study; learn; cultivate: 必～课 *required course* ⑤ revise; amend: ～改文章 *revise article* ⑥ try to attain immortality through self-cultivation, etc. ⑦ build; construct; put in order; administer: ～路 *build road* ⑧ trim; pare; prune: ～指甲 *trim one's fingernails* ⑨ revisionism ⑩ (Xiū) a surname

修[2] [书] long; tall and slim: ～长的身材 *tall and slim figure*

【修补】① mend; patch up; repair; revamp: 这衣服不值得再～啦。*The clothing is not worth patching up.* ②【医】repair: ～合成 *repair synthesis*

【修长】tall and slim; slender

【修船厂】shipyard; dockyard

【修辞】【语】figure of speech; rhetoric

【修道士】【宗】monk

【修道院】【宗】monastery (for man)

【修订】revise; amend: ～一份合同 *amend a contract*

【修订本】revised edition: 教材～ *revised edition of teaching material*

【修短】[书] length: 这件裙子～适度。*Neither too long nor too short, the skirt fits me perfectly.*

【修复】① recondition; repair; renovate; restore: ～古建筑 *restore old-building* ②【医】repair

【修改】alter; amend; modify; revise: ～宪法 *amend or revise a constitution*

【修盖】build (houses)

【修函】[书] write a letter

【修好】①[书] promote friendly relations between states; reconciliation; rapprochement ②[方] do good; do good works: ～积德 *do good deeds to win Heaven's favour*

【修剪】① clip; manicure; prune; trim: ～苹果树 *prune apple trees* ② film editing; montage

【修建】build; construct; erect; put up: ～立交桥 *construct an cloverleaf junction*

【修脚】pedicure

【修理】① fix; mend; overhaul; repair ② prune; trim; pare: ～花枝 *prune the flowers* ③[方] punish: 哈里请别人～了她一顿。*Harry invited other person to teach her a lesson.*

【修理厂】repair shop; fix-it-shop

【修炼】【宗】give oneself up to austere religious discipline

【修女】【宗】(of the Roman Catholic and Greek Orthodox churches) nun; sister: ～院 *nunnery*; *convent*

【修配】make repairs and supply replacements; repair: ～工 *repairman*; *mechanic*

【修葺】fix; renovate; repair: 此建筑亟待～。*The building badly needs repair.*

【修桥补路】build bridges and repair roads

【修润】(of writing) polish; touch up

【修缮】renovate; refurbish; repair

【修身】cultivate one's mind or moral character: ～洁行 *cultivate one's moral character and perfect one's moral integrity*

【修史】[书] write or compile history: 直笔～ *give a truthful account of history*

【修士】【宗】(of the Roman Catholic and Greek Orthodox churches) monk; brother; cleric

【修饰】① adorn; decorate; embellish; ornament ②【语】polish (a piece of writing); modify; qualify ③ make up and dress up: 见男朋友之前，奥德丽精心～打扮了一番。*Audrey spent quite a while making up and dressing up before she met her boyfriend.*

【修书】[书] ① compile a book ② writer a letter

【修伟】[书] tall and strong: 他身材～。*He is tall and strong figure.*

【修学】study; research

【修养】① mastery; understanding: 文学～ *literary taste* ② self-cultivation: 他有很好的～。*He is cultured and well-behaved.*

【修业】study at school: ～证书 *courses taken*; *transcript of course work*

【修造】① build as well as repair ② build; construct

【修整】① repair and maintain; recondition ② prune; trim ③【机】trim; dress; shave; true: ～机 *dressing machine*

【修正】① amend; correct; modify; revise: ～错误 *revise one's mistakes* ② adulterate; revise

【修枝】【农】prune; trim: ～剪 *pruning scissors or shears*

【修治】dredge; repair and regulate: ～大坝 *dredge a river course*

【修竹】tall and slender bamboos

【修筑】build; construct; erect; put up: ～机场 *construct an airport*

羞 ① bashful; coy; shy: 怕～ *be shy* ② embarrass; shame: 她～于见人。*She was ashamed of calling on others.* ③ shame; mortification; disgrace: 不知～ *be shameless*; *shame on you* ④ feel ashamed: ～与为友 *feel ashamed to have such a friend*

【羞惭】be ashamed; feel ill at ease from shame

【羞耻】sense of shame; shame

【羞答答】bashful; coy; diffident; shy: 少女～的样子很可爱。*Maidenly coyness is very lovely.*

【羞愤】ashamed and indignant

【羞口】feel embarrassed to say; feel it hard to speak up

【羞愧】abashed; ashamed; discomfited: 贾斯廷对昨天的不好表现感到很～。*Justin behaved badly yesterday and he is ashamed of himself now.*

【羞明】【医】photophobia

【羞赧】[书] blush: 使人感到～ *cause sb to blush*

【羞恼】be annoyed or angry from shame

【羞怩】coy; embarrassed; shy

【羞怯】coy; sheepish; shy; timid: 她很～。*She is timid.*

【羞人】feel embarrassed or awkward: 这种～的事传出去，别人会耻笑的。*Such shameful stories made public, people can laugh at me.*

【羞辱】① disgrace; dishonour; humiliation; shame ② make people feel ashamed; humiliate

【羞臊】ashamed; shameful

【羞涩】bashful; diffident; embarrassed; shy: 埃米莉是一个～的姑娘。*Emily is a shy girl.*
【羞恶】[书] feel ashamed of and disgusted at sth or sb

xiǔ

朽 ①(mostly of wood) rotten; decayed: 永垂不～ *be immortal; eternal glory to; will endure forever* ② senile: 老～ *old and useless*
【朽败】decayed; rotten
【朽腐】rotten: 棺椁～。*The coffin is rotten.*
【朽迈】[书] old and weak; senile; decrepit
【朽木】rotten wood or tree; punk; worthless person: ～不可雕也。*As decayed wood cannot be carved so you can never help a good-for-nothing fellow.*

宿 [量] used to count nights: 在外呆了一～ *stay at outside for one night*
see also sù; xiù

xiù

秀[1] (of grain crops) put forth ears and flowers: ～穗 *put forth ears*
秀[1] ① beautiful; elegant; fine; pretty and delicate: 眉清目～ *have delicate features; be good-looking* ② clever; intelligent; smart: ～外慧中 *be both beautiful and intelligent* ③ excellent; superb: 在学校里艾琳是一个很优～的学生。*Irene is an excellent student in school.* ④ excellent person; outstanding talent: 新起之～ *up-and-coming youngster; promising young person*
【秀才】① *xiucai*, who passed the imperial examination at the county level in the Ming and Qing dynasties ② scholar; skilful writer
【秀而不实】flowering but bearing no fruit — outwardly beautiful but inwardly empty
【秀发】beautiful hair
【秀慧】elegant and intelligent; graceful and intelligent
【秀俊】beautiful; handsome; personable: 仪容～ *handsome look*
【秀丽】beautiful; pretty: 风景～ *beautiful scenery*
【秀美】delicate; elegant; graceful
【秀媚】pretty and charming; pretty and lovely
【秀气】① delicate; elegant; fine; graceful: 艾丽斯眉眼长得很～。*Iris has graceful eyes and brows.* ② (of speech and manners) refined; gentle; urbane: 谈吐～ *speak in a refined manner* ③ superb: 这个饰品做工精细,样子也很～。*The accouterment is both well-made and exquisite in form.*
【秀润】beautiful and sleek; pretty and smooth
【秀色】beautiful scenery or good looks; prettiness; beauty: ～迷人 *enchanting beauty*
【秀色可餐】feast to the eye; beauty to feast one's eyes on
【秀挺】outstanding; out of the common run; beautiful and forceful: ～的书法 *beautiful and forceful hand*
【秀外慧中】(of woman) be attractive in appearance and intelligent within; be endowed with both beauty and intelligence; be both pretty and bright
【秀雅】beautiful and elegant; graceful
【秀异】distinguished; extremely outstanding: 保罗是这群孩子中最～的。*Paul is the most extremely outstanding among the children.*

臭 odour; smell: 乳～未干 *sucking; young and inexperienced*

袖 ① sleeve: 最后马丁生气了,并且拂～而去。*At last Martin was very angry and went off in a huff.* ② tuck or hide inside the sleeve: 拂～而立 *stand there tuck one's hands in one's sleeves*
【袖标】armband; badge worn on the sleeve
【袖箍】armband
【袖管】① sleeve ② [方] cuff (of a sleeve); wristband
【袖口】cuff; wristband
【袖扣】cuff links; sleeve buttons
【袖笼】muffs
【袖手旁观】look on (or stand by) with folded arms; stand by unconcerned; remain an indifferent spectator: 同学们有难,我们不能～。*We can't look on with folded arms when our classmates were in danger.*
【袖筒】sleeve
【袖头】[方] cuff
【袖章】armband; brassard; sleeve badge
【袖珍】pocket- size; pocket; miniature: ～字典 *pocket dictionary*
【袖子】sleeve

溴 【化】bromine (Br)
【溴化氢】hydrogen bromide (HBr)
【溴化物】bromide
【溴化银】silver bromide
【溴水】bromine water

绣 ① embroider: 刺～ *embroider* ② embroidery: 苏～ *Suzhou embroidery*
【绣墩】ceramic stool with an embroidered cover
【绣房】[旧] young girl's bedroom; young lady's bedchamber; boudoir
【绣阁】[旧] young girl's bedroom; lady's private quarters; boudoir
【绣工】① embroidery worker ② embroidery (work)
【绣花】embroider; do embroidery: ～针 *embroidery needle*
【绣花枕头】① pillow with an embroidered case ② outwardly attractive but useless person
【绣画】embroidered picture
【绣货】embroidered works; embroideries
【绣球】ball made of rolled colored silk; ball made of strips of silk

【绣像】① tapestry or embroidered portrait：人物～ *personal embroidered portraits* ② exquisitely drawn portrait

【绣鞋】embroidered shoes (for woman)

宿 [古] constellation：二十八～ *twenty-eight constellation*
see also sù；xiǔ

锈 ① rust：不～钢 *stainless steel* ② become rusty：这把锁已经生～了。*The lack has become rusty.* ③【农】rust disease

【锈斑】①（of metals）rust spot；rust stain：盒子上生～了。*Rust spots appeared on the box.* ②（of crops）rust spots；russet

【锈病】【农】rust；rust disease：小麦～ *wheat rust*

【锈色】rust；rusty colour

【锈蚀】（of metals）rust out；be corroded by rust；be rust -eaten：铁易～。*Iron corrodes easily.*

嗅 scent；smell；sniff：～来～去 *scent about*；*smell around*

【嗅觉】sense of smell；scent；olfaction：～器官 *olfactory organ*

xū

戌 ① the eleventh of the twelve Earthly Branches ② the period of the day from 7 p. m. to 9 p. m.

【戌时】period of the day from 7 p. m. to 9 p. m.

吁 [书] ① sigh：长～短叹 *moan and groan*；*sighs and groans* ② express surprise
see also yū

【吁吁】[象] used to describe sound of breathing；当米奇到达小山顶时，他气喘～。*Mitch was panting when he reached the top of the hill.*

须[1] have to；must：天黑了，我必～得回家。*It is dark；I have to go home.*

须[2] wait for；await

须[3] ① beard；mustache：留～ *grow one's a beard* ②【动】palpus；feeler；tassel：花～ *pistil*；*stamen*／触～ *cirrus*

【须根】【植】fibrous root；fiber

【须鲸】【动】fin whale；finback；baleen whale；bone whale；whalebone whale

【须眉】[书] ① beard and eyebrows ② man：巾帼不让～。*Women are equal with men.*

【须知】① points for attention；guide；notice：观众～ *notice to audience* ② one should know that；it must be understood that；it must be borne in mind that

胥 ① [书] petty official：老～ *elder petty official* ② [书] all；each and every ③（Xū）a surname

【胥吏】[书] petty official

虚 ① emptiness；void：避实就～ *avoid the enemy's main forces and strike the weak point* ② empty；unoccupied；void vacant：～位以待 *reserve a seat for sb* ③ cowardly；diffident；wanting in self-confidence；timid：迈尔斯觉得有点心～。*Miles felt a little diffident.* ④ futile；in vain：不～此行 *have a worthy trip* ⑤ deceitful；sham；false；nominal：弄～作假 *finagle*；*practise fraud*；*employ trickery* ⑥ humble；modest；unassuming ⑦ feeble；debilitated；weak；be in poor health：体～ *be weak physically* ⑧ guiding principles；theory：～实并举 *pay attention to both theory and practical work*

【虚报】① make a false report；make a false declaration；report untruthfully：～成绩 *cook one's achievements* ② false return；misstatement

【虚词】【语】empty word；function word；form word

【虚辞】[书] boastful words；exaggeration；empty words

【虚度】spend (time) in vain；idle away；waste：～光阴 *be idle and silly*；*fool along*；*loaf about doing nothing*

【虚浮】impractical；shallow：作风～ *have a superficial style of work*

【虚根】【数】imaginary root

【虚构】concoct；fabricate；make up：凭空～ *out-and-out fabrication*；*sheer myth*

【虚汗】abnormal sweating due to general debility；deficiency sweat

【虚华】florid；empty show；false embellishment；ostentation

【虚话】empty talk；false allegation；uninformed statement

【虚怀若谷】have a mind as open as a valley；be of a receptive mind；be extremely open-minded；be very modest；have a receptive mind as a hollow mountain arouses echoes

【虚幻】illusory；imaginary；unreal

【虚晃】feint；deceptive movement

【虚火】【中医】fire of deficiency type；deficiency of fire

【虚假】false；hypocritical；sham：～现象 *sham phenomenon*

【虚价】【经】nominal price

【虚焦点】【物】virtual focus

【虚惊】false alarm：一场～ *a bout of alarm*

【虚空】empty；hollow；void

【虚夸】exaggerative；pompous；bombastic；boastful：～风 *boastful custom*

【虚脉】【中医】feeble pulse

【虚名】undeserved reputation；inflated reputation；false fame：徒有～ *unwarranted reputation*

【虚拟】① suppositional；hypothetical；subjunctive：～语气 *subjunctive mood* ② invented；assumed；fictitious：～人物 *fictitious figures*

【虚胖】puffiness

【虚飘飘】light；drift about；fluffy；unsteady：～的脚步 *unsteady on one's legs*

【虚情假意】false display of affection；hypocritical show of friendship；pretence of friendship

【虚荣】vanity
【虚弱】① be in poor health; frail; week; feeble; debilitated ② (of national strength, military force, etc.) weak; debilitated; feeble
【虚设】existing in name only; nominal; titular
【虚声】① undeserved reputation ② false show of strength
【虚实】① falsehood versus reality ② false or true - actual situation (as of the opposing side); things as they are
【虚数】①【数】imaginary number ② unreliable figure or statistics
【虚岁】nominal age (age of a person reckoned by the traditional method, who is considered one year old at birth and adds a year each lunar new year)
【虚脱】【医】collapse; heat exhaustion; prostration
【虚妄】unfounded; fabricated; concocted; invented
【虚伪】deceitful; false; hypocritical; sham: ~的民主 *sham democracy*
【虚位移】【物】virtual displacement
【虚位以待】leave a seat vacant for sb; reserve a seat for sb
【虚无】nihility; emptiness; nothingness: ~缥缈 *purely imaginary; ethereal; fanciful; illusory*
【虚线】① dotted line; line of dashes ②【数】imaginary line
【虚像】【物】virtual image
【虚心】open-minded; humble; unassuming; modest: ~求教 *modestly ask for advice*
【虚虚实实】combination of the true and the false; feints and ambushes
【虚言】empty words or talk; false statement; unfounded remarks
【虚掩】unlocked or unlatched; open; not buttoned
【虚有其表】look impressive but lack real worth; be striking only in appearance
【虚造】fabricate or invent out of thin air; forge

需 ① need; demand; require; want; ask for: 书本是学习所~之物。*Books are things wanted for learning.* ② should; ought to; inevitable: 孩子们有困难,我们~要去帮助他们。*We ought to help the children when they are in difficult.* ③ necessaries; needs: 不时之~ *untimely needs; sth which may be needed any time*
【需量】demand (as a quantity): 果品的~很大,我们一时无法满足。*The demand for different kinds of fruits is too big to meet for a short while.*
【需求】demand; need; requirement: 市场~ *market demand*
【需要】① call for; demand; require; want: 那边的情况~我到场。*The situation there requires that I should be present.* ② needs; necessities; requisition: 业务教育要尽量满足市场~。*Vocational education should to meet the needs of market.*

嘘 ① breathe out slowly: ~气 *exhale slowly* ② utter a sigh; sigh ③ (of cooking fire, steam, etc.) come into contact with; scald; sear; burn ④[方] sh, hush; ~,小声点! *Sh, lower your voice.* ⑤[方] hiss; boo; *give a Bronx cheer*
see also shī
【嘘寒问暖】ask after sb's needs; inquire after sb's health; inquire after sb's well-being; be solicitous about sb's health; give sb one's thoughtful attention; show great concern for sb
【嘘唏】[书] sob

xú

徐 ①[书] slowly; gently: 清风~~ *refreshing breeze blow slowly* ② (Xú) a surname
【徐步】[书] walk slowly or leisurely; stroll
【徐缓】slowly; gradually
【徐娘半老】Xuniang, beautiful lady past her prime; middle-aged woman
【徐徐】[书] slowly; gently

xǔ

许[1] ① praise; commend: 赞~ *praise; approve especially by superior* ② make a promise; promise ③ betroth; be betrothed to ④ allow; permit; consent ⑤ perhaps; probably; maybe
许[2] ① express extent or amount: 些~ *a bit; a little* ②[书] about; approximately: 年三十~ *about thirty years old*
许[3] [书] place: 何~人? *Where are you from?* ② (Xǔ) a surname
【许多】many; much; great deal of; lots of; large numbers of: 他有~朋友。*He has many friends.*
【许久】for a long time; for ages
【许可】allow; approve; permit: ~证 *licence; permit*
【许诺】make a promise; promise; pledge
【许配】(of an arranged marriage) betroth a girl
【许亲】accept a proposal of marriage
【许身】[书] resolve to do sth; dedicate oneself to
【许愿】① make a vow (to a god); make a resolution (to oneself): 多丽丝曾经~说要嫁给我。*Doris has made a wish to marry with me.* ② promise sb a reward

诩 [书] brag; boast; blow one's own horn: 自~ *brag; boast; praise oneself*

栩
【栩栩】vivid; lively; lifelike
【栩栩如生】lifelike; lively; spirited; vivid

xù

旭 [书] brilliance of the rising sun: ~日东升 *sun rising in the eastern sky-symbol of youth*

and vigour
【旭日】rising sun
序[1] ① order; sequence: 顺～ *order*; *sequence* ② [书] arrange in order; order ③ initial; opening introductory ④ preface: 作～ *write preface for*
序[2] ① [古] east-west wall of a hall ② wing-room: 东～ *east wing* ③ locally school in ancient times
【序跋】preface and postscript
【序次】① order; sequence ② [书] (of books) arrange in serial order; lay out in proper order
【序号】serial number; sequence number
【序列】① order; alignment; array: ～战斗 *battle array*; *battle order* ②【数】sequence: ～分析 *sequence analysis*; *sequential analysis* ③ put in order
【序论】(of works) introductory chapter; introduction; preface and review
【序目】(of books) preface and table of contents
【序幕】① opening scene in a play; prologue; prelude ② [喻] prologue or prelude to major events
【序曲】①【音】overture; prelude ② prelude
【序数】ordinal number; ordinal: ～词 *ordinal number*
【序文】preface; foreword
【序言】preface; foreword
叙 ① talk; chitchat; chat: 和老同学～旧是一件非常高兴的事情。*It's very good to talk about old days with former classmates.* ② give an account of; narrate; tell; recount; relate: 自～ *account of oneself*; *autobiographic note* ③ assess; evaluate; appraise: ～奖 *appraise sb's service and reward it* ④ preface ⑤ order; sequence ⑥ arrange in order; order
【叙别】have a farewell talk; bid farewell to sb
【叙功】[书] rate or assess sb's services: ～行赏 *award people according to their contributions*; *decide awards on the basis of services rendered*
【叙话】chat; talk
【叙旧】talk about the past or old days; reminisce about old days
【叙利亚】Syria: ～人 *Syrian*
【叙事】narrate; relate; recount: 这篇报道～生动。*There is a graphic narration in the news report.*
【叙述】narrate; recount; relate
【叙说】tell; relate; narrate
【叙谈】talk; chat; chitchat
恤 ① [书] worry; misgiving; apprehension ② pity; favor; sympathize; commiserate ③ give relief; help out; compensate: 抚～ *comfort and compensate a bereaved family or a disabled person* ④ obsequies: ～典 *obsequies*
【恤衫】[方] shirt
畜 raise (domestic animals); breed; rear: ～牧 *rear livestock*; *animal husbandry*
see also chù
【畜产】livestock or animal products: ～进出口 *import and export of livestock products*
【畜产品】animal product; livestock or poultry; animal husbandry; stock farming
【畜牧场】animal farm; livestock or stock farm
【畜牧区】pastoral area
【畜牧业】animal husbandry; livestock husbandry; livestock farming: 内蒙古今年准备大力发展～。*Inner Mongolia are ready to develop animal husbandry this year.*
【畜养】raise (domestic animals)
酗
【酗酒】be given to heavy drinking; indulge in excessive drinking; be alcoholic: ～成性 *become alcoholic*; *be given to alcoholism*
勖 [书] encourage
【勖励】[书] encourage; inspire: 霍华德～她努力学习。*Howard encouraged her to study hard.*
【勖勉】[书] encourage; inspire
绪 ① head of thread; beginning of matter ② [书] remaining; remnants ③ mental or emotional state; mood: 思～ *feeling*; *thinking* ④ [书] task; cause; enterprise; undertaking ⑤ (Xù) a surname
【绪论】(of works) introduction; forward; preface
续 ① continuous; successive; one after another: 时断时～ *intermittence on and off* ② continue; resume; extend: 连～不断 *be around-the-clock* ③ add; increase; supply more: 埃娃负责给客人～茶。*Ava is responsible for adding more tea.*
【续编】continuation (of a book)
【续貂】[谦] join a dog tail to a sable — make an unworthy continuation of a great work; write a wretched sequel to a fine work
【续订】renew one's subscription
【续集】continuation (of a book); sequel
【续假】extend one's leave of absence; extend leave
【续借】renew; renew a library book
【续篇】continuation or sequel (to a book or story)
【续聘】continue to engage sb; continue the employment of sb
【续娶】remarry after the death of one's wife
【续弦】① remarry after the death of one's wife ② second wife (after the death of one's first wife)
【续约】renew a treaty or contract
絮[1] ① (cotton) wadding; padding: ～被子 *wadding for a quilt* ② [古] coarse silk floss ③ sth resembling cotton: 柳～ *willow catkins* ④ wad or pad with cotton: ～棉衣 *wad one's clothes*
絮[2] ① long-winded; loquacious; talkative; garrulous ② [方] be bored with; be sick of; be fed up with
【絮被】[方] quilt wadded with cotton; wadded quilt
【絮叨】long-winded; garrulous; windy; wordy: 老太太～地讲着自己的经历。*The old woman talked tediously about her experience.*
【絮烦】be tired or bored (by monotonous repetition

of sth). 曼迪总重复那几句话，我们都听得～。*All of us became tired of listening to the same old words Mandy always repeated.*
【絮聒】① long-winded; chattering ② trouble (other people); bother
【絮棉】cotton for wadding
【絮说】talk garrulously; chatter; nag: 他来到这儿就～个没完。*He keeps on nagging when he comes here.*
【絮絮】be garrulous; talk endlessly
【絮语】[书] ① prattle on and on; incessantly chatter ② garrulous talk; endless chatter
【絮嘴】nag; be chatty; chatter; talk garrulously: 她是个爱～的人。*She is fond of talking garrulously.*

婿 ① son-in-law ② husband

蓄 ① accumulate; store up; save up: 储～ *deposit*; *saving* ② cause to grow; grow: ～发 *grow a hair* ③ harbour; cherish; entertain (ideas); hold in store; keep in mind
【蓄藏】save and store; lay up; lay in
【蓄电池】storage cell; storage battery; accumulator
【蓄洪】【水】store floodwater: ～量 *water storage capacity*
【蓄积】store up; storage; accumulate
【蓄谋】plan in advance; premeditate: ～已久 *plan in advance for a long time*
【蓄能】energy storage
【蓄热】thermal storage; accumulation of heat
【蓄水】impound; retain or store water: ～池 *cistern*; *reservoir*; *catch basin* / ～工程 *water storage project*
【蓄养】① store up; build up; accumulate ② rear; raise
【蓄意】premeditated; calculated; deliberate: ～挑衅 *pick a fight with sb*

煦 [书] warm; balmy: 和～春风 *warm spring breeze*
【煦暖】warm
【煦煦】① warm: ～的阳光使孩子们很舒服。*The warm sunshine makes the children very comfortable.* ② [书] happy and harmonious

xuān

轩¹ ① [书] high; lofty ② (Xuān) a surname

轩¹ ① small room or veranda with windows; open corridor or pavilion: 茶～ *tea room* ② [古] high-fronted, curtained carriage: 乘～ *ride in a curtained carriage* ③ [书] window or door: ～帘 *curtain*; *door drape*
【轩昂】① dignified; impressive; imposing: 器宇～ *be of dignified bearing*; *have an impressive presence* ② [书] tall and big
【轩豁】① bright and airy; open and spacious ② optimistic; sanguine; hopeful
【轩眉】[书] expand the eyebrows; raised eyebrows
【轩然大波】big, crushing wave; great disturbance; mighty uproar
【轩尾】cock the tail; strut like rooster
【轩轩自得】self-satisfied; complacent; perky; perked up
【轩辕】surname of the Yellow Emperor, legendary first Chinese ancestor

宣 ① announce; declare; proclaim; promulgate: 教授上课不能照本～科。*Professors can't read a text item by item.* ② summon into the presence of the emperor by an imperial edict: ～召 *summon sb into the presence of the emperor by an imperial edict*; *summon to court* ③ drain; draw off (liquids) ④ propagandize: ～传 *spread propagandize* ⑤ (Xuān) a surname
【宣布】announce; pronounce; declare; proclaim: 机长～飞机就要着陆了。*The captain announced that the plane was going to land.*
【宣称】assert; declare; claim; profess
【宣传】① publicize; disseminate; propagandize; propagate: 新闻～ *press publicity* ② propaganda: 政治～ *political propaganda*
【宣读】read out (in public); announce
【宣告】declare; announce; proclaim: 政府～一项法令。*The government proclaims a law.*
【宣讲】explain and publicize; preach: ～政策 *preach policy*
【宣教】propaganda and education; publicity and education: ～工作 *publicity and education*
【宣明】proclaim or declare clearly; announce explicitly: 马特向我～的他的观点。*Matt made known his viewpoint to me.*
【宣判】【律】pronounce judgement; deliver judgement; give decision in a case
【宣示】express in public; make known publicly
【宣誓】take or swear an oath; make a vow; make a pledge: ～入党 *take an oath to join the Party*
【宣泄】① drain off; lead off (liquids) ② blaze; get sth off one's chest; reveal: ～不满 *give vent to one's dissatisfaction* ③ [书] reveal; let out: 这是我们的秘密，不得～向外。*This is our secret; Don't let it out.*
【宣言】① declaration; proclamation; pronouncement; manifesto: 共产党～ *communist Manifesto* ② proclaim; declare; state
【宣扬】publicize; propagate; advocate; advertise
【宣战】① declare or proclaim war ② battle; fight a battle; wage a struggle against
【宣战书】declaration of war
【宣旨】[书] issue or publicly read an imperial edict; announce an imperial edict
【宣纸】*Xuan* paper, a high quality rice paper made in Xuancheng(宣城) or Jingxian(泾县) of Anhui Province, esp. good for traditional Chinese painting and calligraphy

喧 noisy; clamorous; uproarious

X

【喧宾夺主】a presumptuous guest usurps the host's role; the secondary supercedes the primary; a noisy guest steals the host's thunder
【喧哗】① noisy; full of confused noise; uproarious ② uproar; hubbub: 请不要大声～。*Please don't clamour!*
【喧叫】cry out loudly; shout; yell
【喧闹】noise and disturbance; din; bustle; racket: ～的场所 *bustling place*
【喧嚷】clamour; cries; hubbub; din; racket
【喧扰】noise and disturbance; racket; tumult
【喧声】hubbub of voices; confused and loud talking; uproar
【喧腾】noise and excitement; uproar
【喧天】fill the air with resounding noise: 锣鼓～ *a deafening sound of beating the gongs and drums; great din of gongs and drums*
【喧嚣】① noisy; clamorous: 这座城镇是一个～的地方。*This town is a noisy city.* ② noise; din; clamour: 城市的～ *the din of the city*
【喧笑】chatting and laughing loudly
【喧啸】whistle violently; boom; thunder: ～的浪涛 *roaring sea waves*
【喧杂】(of noise) loud and confused
【喧噪】loud shout; commotion

暄[1] [书] warmth (of the sun): 寒～ *exchange of conventional greetings*

暄[2] [方] fluffy; soft: ～土 *soft soil*

【暄风】warm, gentle wind; spring breeze
【暄和】soft; downy; loose
【暄暖】warm
【暄气】summer heat; sweltering heat

xuán

玄 ① black; dark ② mystic; profound; subtle; abstruse; far ③ mysterious; far-fetched; unreliable; incredible: 我不相信路易丝,她说得太～了。*I didn't believe Louise for her pretty tall story.* ④ the ninth moon of the lunar calendar

【玄奥】abstruse; profound; recondite: 学识～ *great erudition*
【玄根】①【宗】mysterious root of all things ②【宗】natural endowment
【玄乎】[口] unreliable; inscrutable; mysterious; subtle
【玄机】①【宗】(of Taoists) profound theory; mysteries of the universe ② abstruse plot; profound secret; ingenious principle of action; mysterious principles
【玄教】Taoism
【玄理】① abstruse principles; profound theories ② theories advocated by a philosophical sect in the Wei and Jin dynasties
【玄秘】mystery; occult
【玄妙】mysteriously wonderful; abstruse: 这件事情真是太～莫测了。*It's too mysterious to comprehend.*
【玄孙】great-great-grandson
【玄想】fantasy; fancy; illusion
【玄学】① *Xuanxue* or Dark Learning, a metaphysical sect in the Wei and Jin dynasties that tried to integrate Taoism with Confucian doctrine ② metaphysics

悬[1] ① hang; suspend; fly: ～在半空 *suspend in midair* ② announce openly; make known to the public: ～赏 *offer (post) a reward* ③ raise; lift ④ unresolved; unsettled; outstanding: ～案 *unsettled law case* ⑤ feel worried or anxious; be solicitous ⑥ imagine ⑦ far apart

悬[2] [方] dangerous; precarious; perilous: 真～, 差点错过这次出差的机会。*It's really dangerous to miss this chance for business.*

【悬案】① unsettled law case ② outstanding issue; unsettled question
【悬揣】guess; conjecture; suppose; surmise: 私下～ *surmise in private*
【悬垂】(of objects) hang down; overhang
【悬灯结彩】hang up lanterns and festoons; decorate with lanterns and coloured streamers
【悬吊】suspend; dangle; hang in midair; be held in midair; overhang
【悬断】deduce without foundation; conjecture; speculate
【悬而未决】outstanding; unsettled
【悬浮】①【化】suspension: ～剂 *suspending agent* ② float; suspend: 一张纸～在半空中。*A piece of paper is floating in the midair.*
【悬隔】be far apart; be widely separated
【悬钩子】【植】raspberry
【悬挂】① hang; suspend; fly ② (of a motor vehicle) suspension: 前～ *front suspension*
【悬河】① aboveground river; hanging river ② [书] waterfall ③ be very eloquent; talk glibly; utter a torrent of words
【悬乎】[方] dangerous; unsafe; perilous
【悬空】① hang in air; suspend in midair: ～作业 *work in midair* ② divorced from reality; uncertain; unsettled
【悬跨】【建】suspended span
【悬梁】hang oneself from a beam
【悬虑】worry; care; miss
【悬念】① [书] be concerned or worried about; think of (sb in absence) ② audience involvement in a film or play; reader involvement in a piece of literature; suspense
【悬赏】offer a reward; post a reward
【悬殊】far apart; vast difference; great disparity; wide gap
【悬梯】hanging ladder
【悬系】feel anxious about; be worried about; miss: 出门在外,迈克～妻儿。*Mike was worried about his wife and son when he was away from home.*
【悬想】conjecture; fancy; imagine

【悬心】feel anxious, be worried about; be consumed by worry and anxious

【悬崖】overhanging or steep cliff; precipice: ~绝壁 *sheer precipices and overhanging rocks; cliffs and precipices*

【悬崖勒马】rein in at the brink of the precipice — wake up to and escape disaster at eht last moment; pull back before it is too late.

旋 ① revolve; circle; spin; wheel: 天~地转 *feel as if heaven and earth were spinning round; feel faint and dizzy as if the sky and earth were spinning round; feel one's head swim* ② return; go back; come back ③ part of the scalp where the hair is whorled ④ [书] soon; quickly: ~即 *at once*

【旋背】[书] turn round; face about

【旋笛】siren

【旋归】[书] return home

【旋回】① hover; circle ②【地】cycle: ~构造 *tectonic cycle*

【旋即】shortly; soon afterwards; immediately; at once

【旋卷】whirl round; hover over

【旋律】【音】melody: 欢快的~ *cheerful melody*

【旋梯】winding stairs

【旋舞】dance round; hover: 姑娘们在花丛中~。*The girls are dancing round among flowers.*

【旋压】【机】rotary extrusion; spinning: ~机床 *spinning lathe*

【旋转】revolve; rotate; whirl; spin: 地球绕太阳~。*The earth rotates round the sun.*

【旋子】circle; whirl

漩 whirlpool

璇 [书] beautiful jade; fine jade

xuǎn

选 ① pick and choose; select ② elect: 总统~举 *presidential election* ③ those who are elected or chosen: 最佳人~ *best candidate* ④ selections; anthology

【选拔】select; choose; scout

【选拔赛】【体】tryout; qualifying trial; selective trials

【选编】① compile ② selections; selected works; anthology; collection

【选播】selective broadcast; broadcast of elected items

【选材】① choose qualified personnel ② select (suitable) material

【选场】selected scene

【选调】select and transfer; transfer selected people (usu. for promotion): ~技术出色的人到这个实验工作 *select a outstanding person of technical personnel and transfer them to the lab*

【选定】make a decision after careful selection; make a choice of sth; pick on sb

【选读】① read selectively; select and read ② selected readings

【选段】selections; selected passages or parts

【选购】pick out and buy; choose; selective purchasing

【选集】selected works or writings; selections; anthology

【选举】elect: 差额~ *competitive election*

【选刊】① select and publish ② edition of selected articles; selections

【选矿】ore dressing; mineral separation; beneficiation: ~厂 *ore dressing plant; concentration plant*

【选留】select and retain; select and remain

【选录】select and include; selected writings

【选民】(individually) voter; elector; (collectively) constituency; electorate: ~榜 *list of eligible voters* / ~证 *elector's certificate; voter registration card*

【选派】designate select; select and send; detail

【选配】① select and provide; match: 精心~的花束 *well selected bunch of flowers* ② cross-breeding: ~率 *rate of cross-breeding*

【选票】ballot; vote

【选聘】select and employ; select and engage

【选区】electoral or election district; electoral ward; constituency

【选曲】selected songs or tunes

【选取】select; choose

【选任】select and appoint

【选手】athlete selected for a sports meet; player; contestant: 优秀~ *topnotch player; top-ranking athlete*

【选送】select and recommend: ~新学生 *select and recommend new students*

【选题】① select or choose a topic; choose a subject ② chosen or selected subject: 根据~定计划。*Draw a plan according to the selected subject.*

【选修】take as an elective course: ~英文 *take English as an elective course* / ~课 *elective course; optional course; elective*

【选样】sampling; sample

【选用】select and use; choose and apply

【选育】【农】seed selection; breeding

【选择】choose; pick; opt; select: 自然~ *natural selection*

【选种】【农】seed selection

【选中】choose; decide on; select

【选准】make the right choice: ~方向 *make the right choice of direction*

晅 [书] ① bright; brilliant ② dry in the sun

烜 [书] grand; magnificent; of great renown and influence

【烜赫】be famous and influential: ~一时 *have great renown and influence for a time*

癣 tinea; ringworm: 脚～ *tinea pedis*; *athlete's foot*

【癣疥之疾】only a skin complaint; some slight ailment

xuàn

昡 ［书］sunshine; sunlight

炫 ［书］① daze; dazzle; blaze ② show off; display

【炫惑】［书］confuse sb with exaggerated words; mislead people by exaggeration or ostentation: 格伦因受到西方生活方式的～而出国。*Glen went abroad because that he was beguiled by West life styles.*

【炫目】dazzling: 华丽～ *brilliant splendour*

【炫弄】show off; parade; flaunt; vaunt: 吉姆懂得～自己的技巧。*Jim knows how to show off his skill.*

【炫示】make a show of; show off; display

【炫耀】① bright; shine; illuminate ② flaunt; vaunt

绚 gorgeous;(of colour) prismatic; effulgent

【绚烂】brilliant; gorgeous; splendid: ～多彩 *bright and colourful*; *riot of colour*; *gorgeous*

【绚丽】bright and colourful; florid; gorgeous; magnificent

眩 ① dizzy; giddy; vertiginous ②［书］dazzled; bewildered

【眩惑】be misled; be bewildered; indulge in

【眩目】dazzle; blind; daze: ～的阳光 *dazzling sunlight*

【眩晕】① dizziness; giddiness ②【医】vertigo: ～症 *vertigo*

铉 hook-like instrument to carry an ancient tripod by catching its rings or ears

旋1 ① whirl ② turn on a lathe; lathe; pare: ～土豆皮 *peel a potato* ③ copper plate (for making sheets of bean-starch jelly) ④ hot water container for warming wine

旋2 at the time when sth is needed; at the last moment: ～吃～做 *cook for immediate consumption*

【旋床】【机】(turning) lathe

【旋风】whirl; whirlwind; cyclone

【旋工】turner

渲 wash (a piece of drawing paper) with watercolours

【渲染】① apply colours to a drawing ② play up; exaggerate; overdo; pile it on: 大肆～ *hype with a lot of publicity*

楦 ① (shoe) last;(hat) block: 鞋～ *last*; *shoe last* ② shape with a last or block: ～帽 *block a hat* ③［方］stuff; fill up: 这张床里～满了棉絮，因此很柔软。*The bed was stuffed with cotton so it was very soft.*

【楦子】① shoe last; shoe tree ② hat block

xuē

削 scrape; pare; whittle; cut

【削壁】precipice; cliff

【削牍】［书］writing on bamboo strips in ancient times

【削发】shave one's hair; shave one's head (to become a monk or nun); take the tonsure: ～为尼 *shave one's hair to become a nun*

【削价】cut prices; lower the price; reduce the price

【削肩】drooping or sloping shoulders

【削减】cut (down); reduce; slash; whittle down: ～开支 *cut expenditure*

【削木为兵】sharpen wooden poles and use them as weapons; use sharpened wooden poles as weapons

【削平】［书］suppress; wipe out; eliminate; put down: ～叛乱 *put down the rebellion*

【削弱】cripple; impair; weaken; sap; enfeeble: ～敌人的势力 *weaken enemy's forces*

【削瘦】very thin; lank: 他颀长～。*He has a lanky figure.*

【削正】［书］point out mistakes (in poems or writings) so that they can be corrected: 敬请您～。*Please oblige me with your valuable comments.*

【削职】be dismissed from office

【削足适履】cut the feet to fit the shoes — mechanically copy regardless of specific conditions; act in a procrustean manner

靴 boots: 皮～ *leather boots*

【靴筒】bootleg

【靴子】boots

xué

穴 ① cave; hole ② den; lair; nest ③ grave; bomb: 墓～ *coffin pit* ④【中医】acupuncture point

【穴处】［书］① live in caves ② shallow or superficial learning

【穴位】① acupuncture point ② location of a coffin pit

学 ① learn; study: ～知识 *learn knowledge* ② imitate; copy: ～鸡叫 *mimic the crowing of the cock* ③ learning; knowledge; scholarship: 博～多才 *be of great learning and great ability* ④ subject of study: 哲～ *philosophy* / 文～ *literature* ⑤ school; college: 小～ *primary school* / 中～ *middle school* / 大～ *college*; *university*

【学报】learned journal; university journal

【学步】①（usu. of babies）learn to walk ② feel one's way along：邯郸～ *imitate others slavishly and lose one's own individuality*
【学部】① the Imperial Educational Ministry of the Qing Dynasty ② academic committee（sometimes translated as scientific division）of the Chinese Academy of Sciences
【学潮】campus upheaval；student strike：闹～ *go in for student strike*
【学而不厌】be never tired of reading；be insatiable learning；have an unquenchable desire to learn
【学费】① school fee；tuition fee；tuition ② education expenses；schooling
【学分】credit：～制 *credit system*
【学风】style of study；academic atmosphere：～严谨 *meticulous and rigorous academic discipline*
【学府】institution of higher learning；seat of learning
【学工】apprentice
【学贯古今】well versed in the learning of both ancient and modern times
【学棍】tyrant in the field of education
【学海】① persevere in one's studies ② sea of learning；academic studies：～波澜 *play an outstanding role in the literary or academic world*
【学好】learn from good example；emulate good
【学坏】follow bad example；pick up bad habits
【学会】learn；grasp；master
【学籍】one's status as a student；one's name on the school roll：保留～ *keep sb on the school roll*；*retain one's a status as a student*
【学界】educational circles
【学究】① scholar ② pedant：老～ *pedantic schoolmaster*；*old pedant*
【学科】① branch of learning；field of study ② course；discipline；subject：专业～ *specialized course* ③ knowledge course
【学力】knowledge；educational level；academic attainments：同等～ *same educational level*
【学历】educational background；record of formal schooling；record of education
【学联】federation of students' unions
【学龄】school age
【学路】① ways of education ② range of study：伦尼～基础扎实，很有发展前途。*Lenny has a bright future before him because he has extensive knowledge.*
【学名】① one's registered name at school；one's formal name used at school ② scientific name
【学年】academic or school year
【学派】school of thought；school
【学期】school term；term；semester：～教育 *preschool education*
【学区】school district
【学人】scholar；learned person
【学舌】① mechanically repeat other people's words；parrot ②［口］loose-tongued；gossipy
【学生】① student；pupil：～票 *ticket at student discount* / ～证 *student's identity card*；*student card* ② disciple；follower ③［方］male child；boy
【学识】learning；knowledge；erudition；scholarly attainments：～过人 outstrip others in knowledge
【学时】class hour；period
【学士】① scholar：文人～ *scholar*；*men of letters* ② bachelor
【学塾】old-style private school
【学术】learning；science：～研究 *academic research* ～领域 *sphere（or realm）of learning*
【学术界】academic community；academic circles；academic world；academia
【学说】theory；doctrine；teaching
【学堂】［方］school
【学童】young pupil；school child
【学徒】① serve one's apprenticeship ② apprentice；trainee：当某人的～ *be apprentice to sb*
【学位】degree；academic degree：硕士～ *master's degree* / 博士～ *Ph. D. degree*
【学问】① branch of learning ② knowledge；scholarship；scholarly attainments
【学无止境】knowledge know no bounds；there is no limit to knowledge
【学习】① study；learn：～英语 *learn English* ② learn from；follow the example of；emulate：我们一定要向他～。*We must learn from him.*
【学校】school；educational institution：马修已经去了～。*Matthew has gone to school.*
【学行】scholarly attainments and moral conduct
【学兄】one's former schoolmate
【学业】one's studies；school work
【学艺】① learn an artistic；learn a trade；learn a skill ② knowledge and expertise；learning and skill：这个学期，劳伦斯在～上有了明显的提高。*In this period, Laurence has made great progress in his knowledge and skill.*
【学友】classmate；fellow alumnus；schoolmate
【学员】（college）student；trainee
【学院】college；academy；institute：军事～ *military academy* / 工商～ *school of business*
【学长】① one's former schoolmate ②［旧］head of a branch of learning in college
【学者】scholar；learned man；man of learning：～风范 *demeanour of a scholar*；*style of a scholar*；*scholar's elegant carriage*
【学制】arrangements for schooling；educational system；school system：～四年 *four-year's schooling*
【学子】［书］student；scholar：莘莘～ *great number of disciples*；*numerous students*

踅 pace up and down；walk to and fro；turn back half way：～来～去 *walk to and from*
【踅摸】［口］look for

噱 ［方］laugh：发～ *make one laugh*；*excite laughter*；*raise a laugh*
see also jué
【噱头】［方］① words or acts meant to amuse people or to elicit laughter：一些演员总靠～来迎合观

众。*Some actors always please the audience with amusing tricks.* ② tricks; gimmicks：约瑟夫爱耍～。*Joseph is fond of playing tricks.* ③ funny; farcical

xuě

雪[1] ① snow：冰～ *ice and snow* ② snow-like：～白 *snow-white* ③（Xuě）a surname

雪[2] wipe out（a humiliation, disgrace, etc.）; avenge（a wrong）

【雪白】as white as snow; snow-white：～的皮肤 *fair skin; fair complexion*

【雪板】【体】shi：昨天我买了一副～。*I bought a pair of skis yesterday.*

【雪暴】snowstorm; blizzard

【雪崩】①（snow）avalanche：～气浪 *avalanche wind* ②【电】（Townsend）avalanche

【雪铲】snow-shovel

【雪耻】avenge an insult; wipe out a humiliation

【雪堆】snow drift; snowbank

【雪恨】avenge; wreak vengeance; revenge：报仇～ *revenge*

【雪花】snowflake

【雪茄】cigar

【雪亮】bright as snow; shiny; sharp

【雪量】【气】snowfall：～计 *snow gauge*

【雪片】snowflake

【雪橇】sled; sledge; sleigh

【雪青】lilac（colour）

【雪球】snowball

【雪雀】【动】snow finch

【雪人】① human-like figure made of snow; snowman：姑娘们一起在院子里堆～。*The girls were making a snowman in the yard.* ② human-like primate believed to live in Tibet or other frigid areas in China; abominable snowman; Bigfoot

【雪山】snow-capped mountain

【雪上加霜】snow plus frost — add to the miseries of sb who is already unfortunate enough; rub salt into sb's wounds

【雪水】newly-melted snow; snow-broth

【雪线】【地】snow line

【雪压】snow pressure

【雪雁】snow goose; wavey

【雪原】snowfield：火车在～上奔驰。*The train was galloping in the snowfield.*

【雪杖】【体】ski pole; ski stick

【雪中送炭】send charcoal in snowy weather — provide timely help; bring comfort to those in trouble

xuè

血 ① blood：鲜～ *fresh blood* ② related by blood：～亲 *blood relation; consanguinity* ③ ardour; courage; zeal ④ menstruation; period *see also* xiě

【血癌】blood cancer; leukemia

【血案】homicide or murder case

【血斑】bloodstain：床单上有～。*There is some caked blood on the sheet.*

【血本】original capital; principal：父母为了孩子上学不恤～。*Parents are willing to do things at any cost for study of their child.*

【血崩】【中医】flooding

【血沉】【医】erythrocyte sedimentation rate（ESR）：～试验 *sedimentation test*

【血仇】debt of blood; blood feud; vendetta：报～ *avenge a blood feud; settle a debt of blood* / 因为金钱问题，戈弗雷与亨利结下了～。*Godfrey started a blood feud with Henry for money.*

【血管】【生理】blood vessel; vascellum; vessel

【血海】sea of blood

【血海深仇】huge debt of blood; intense and inveterate hatred

【血汗】blood and sweat; sweat of one's brow：～钱 *money earned by onerous toil; hard-earned money*

【血红】splattering blood

【血迹】bloodstain：～斑斑 *be bloodstained; all covered with bloodstains*

【血祭】sacrificial offering of animal blood

【血浆】【生理】（blood）plasma

【血口】blood-dripping mouth

【血口喷人】curse and slander; maliciously attack; make unfounded and malicious attacks; venomously slander：你不要～。*Don't make malicious attacks to other people.*

【血库】【医】blood bank

【血块】half-solid lump formed from blood; blood clot

【血亏】【中医】anaemia; severe deficiency of blood

【血泪】blood and tears; tears of blood

【血流】blood flow; bloodstream

【血路】path crimson with blood：杀出一条～ *break through an encirclement after bloody fighting*

【血脉】①【中医】blood circulation ② blood relationship

【血泊】pool of blood; bloodbath：莱斯特被发现躺在～中。*Lester was found to welter in blood.*

【血气】① animal spirits; sap; vitality; vigour ② courage and rectitude：雨果是个～青年。*Hugo is a courageous and upright young man.*

【血气方刚】full of sap or mettle; of hot blood

【血亲】blood relations; consanguinity：～关系 *blood ties; relation by blood; relationship by consanguinity*

【血清】【生理】serum：～白蛋白 *serum albumin* / ～肝炎抗原 *serum hepatitis antigen（SHA）*

【血球】【生理】blood cell; blood corpuscle

【血染沙场】shed one's blood on the battlefield; lay down one's life in battle

【血刃】bloodstained blade of knife

【血肉】① blood and muscle ② extremely close relationship

【血肉横飞】blood and flesh flying in all directions

【血肉模糊】badly mauled：伊凡被那些人打得～。*Ivan was mangled almost out of recognition*

【血肉相连】as close as flesh and blood：全国人民～。*The people all over the world are as close as flesh and blood.*

【血肉之躯】human body；flesh and blood；mortal flesh

【血色】redness of the skin；colour：我们发现洛娜时，她已面无～。*Lorna had little colour in her cheeks when we found her.*

【血书】letter written in one's own blood

【血水】thin and watery blood

【血糖】【医】blood sugar：～高 *hyperglycemia* /～低 *hypoglycemia*

【血统】blood relationship；blood lineage

【血污】bloodstain

【血洗】drench in bloodbath；blood purge；massacre；slaughter：敌人～了这个小村。*The enemy slaughtered all the people in the village.*

【血细胞】blood cell：～计数 *blood count*

【血小板】【生理】(blood) platelet

【血腥】reeking of blood；bloody；bloodthirsty；sanguinary：～味 *smell of blood*

【血型】【生理】blood group；blood type：～分类 *blood grouping*

【血性】upright and courageous：～男儿 *brave and righteous man*

【血虚】【中医】blood deficiency and its resultant pathological changes

【血循环】【生理】blood circulation

【血压】【生理】blood pressure：高～ *high blood pressure*；*hypertension* /低～ *low blood pressure*；*hypotension*

【血压计】【医】sphygmomanometer

【血样】blood sample or specimen

【血液】①【生理】blood：～循环 *blood circulation* ② fresh blood；lifeline；backbone force：为党输送新鲜～。*Infuse fresh blood into the Party.*

【血衣】bloodstained garment；blood-shirt

【血印】bloodstain

【血雨腥风】foul wind and rain of blood — reactionary reign of terror

【血缘】ties of blood；consanguinity；relationship by birth

【血债】debt of blood

【血债累累】have heavy blood debts；have a mountain of blood debts；commit a string of murders

【血战】① bloody battle；extremely fierce battle ② wage desperate struggle：为了祖国，我们一定～到底。*We will fight to the last drop of our blood for motherland.*

【血脂】blood fat

【血肿】【医】haematoma

【血渍】bloodstain：弗朗基洗去衣服上的～。*Frankie washed the bloodstain off her clothes.*

谑 [书] joke；banter；tease；jest：戏～ *banter*；*tease*

【谑而不虐】tease without embarrassing

xūn

勋 ① meritorious service；exploit；merit；achievement ② medal；decoration：授～ *confer orders or medals*

【勋臣】official who has rendered meritorious service

【勋绩】meritorious service；outstanding contribution；remarkable achievements：盖世～ *peerless meritorious service*

【勋爵】① feudal title of nobility conferred for meritorious service ② (UK) lord

【勋业】[书] meritorious service；great achievement

【勋章】medal；decoration：米切尔又被授予了一块～。*Mitchell was awarded with a medal again.*

埙 ancient Chinese wind instrument, made of porcelain with one to six holes and shaped like an egg

熏 ① smoke；fumigate：烟火把墙壁～黑了。*Lighting fires blackened the wall.* ② treat (meat, fish, etc.) with smoke；smoke：～牛肉 *smoked beef* ③ pleasantly warm；genial

see also xùn

【熏干】dry smoked beancurd

【熏笼】bamboo or wire net over a brazier for scenting clothing or drying laundry

【熏炉】brazier used for scenting clothing or warming oneself；censer

【熏沐】burn incense and take a bath — a ritual for showing respect for the supernatural forces

【熏染】exert a gradual；corrupting in fluence on；be corrupted by

【熏肉】smoked meat or pork

【熏陶】exert a gradual, uplifting influence on；foster；nurture；cultivate：莫里斯从小受到良好的艺术～，画技很好。*Maurice's skill in painting is very good since he has been exerted with fine artistic taste as a child.*

【熏天】overwhelming

【熏鱼】smoked fish

【熏制】smoke；fumigate (sth with jasmine, etc.)；cure (meat, etc.) by smoke：奥斯卡喜欢吃～的食品。*Oscar like eating smoked food.*

薰 [书] a kind of sweet grass；aroma；fragrance

【薰剂】fumigant

醺 drunk：醉～～ *as drunk as a fiddler*；*dead drunk*；*tight*

xún

旬 ① period of ten days：五月下～ *last ten-day period of May* /中～ *second ten days of a month* ② period of ten years in an old person's age：祖父年近七～。*My grandfather is close upon seventy.*

【旬刊】publication appearing once every ten days

【旬日】［书］ten days：～为期 *with a time limit of ten days*

寻[1] ancient measure of length, equal to about eight chi

寻[2] try to find; look for; search; seek：又到了～亲访友的时候了。*It's time to call on relatives and friends.*

【寻查】look for; search for：四处～ *look here and there for*

【寻常】ordinary; common; normal; usual：～百姓 *common folk; man in the street*

【寻短见】try to commit suicide

【寻访】look for; try to find; inquire about

【寻根】① trace sth to its source; get to the bottom of things ② find the roots of one's family

【寻根究底】get to the bottom of things; inquire deeply into; trace sth to its root

【寻呼】beep-page; bleep：～机 *beep pager; beeper; bleeper*

【寻花问柳】① enjoy the spring scenery; run around ② be on the racket; visit brothels; go whoring

【寻欢作乐】go to town; gather life's roses; paint the lover red; seek pleasure and make merry; indulge in sensual pleasures; sow one's wild oats

【寻机】［书］look for an opening or opportunity：～闹事 *look for an opportunity to cause a trouble*

【寻究】probe into; investigate thoroughly; pursue

【寻开心】［方］make fun of; joke

【寻觅】try to find; seek; look for

【寻摸】［口］look for; seek：柯克在黑暗中～钱包。*Kirk looked for her wallet in the dark.*

【寻求】explore; go in quest of; pursue; seek; search for：为了～合作伙伴，罗德里克又一次去了北京。*Roderick went to Beijing again in order to seek partners.*

【寻声】try to locate (sth or sb) by following the sound：～追去 *chase sb by following one's sound*

【寻事】seek a quarrel; pick a fight

【寻死】commit suicide; try to kill oneself; try to commit suicide

【寻死觅活】(so agonizing as to) threaten to die; threaten to commit suicide

【寻思】① meditate; ponder; reflect; contemplate; think sth over：你～一下这样做是不是对。*You meditate carefully if it is right you do so.* ②［方］plan; think of：我～这事好久啦。*I have thought of the thing for long time.*

【寻索】① look for; pursue; search for; seek：在山上～某人的踪迹 *look for one's whereabouts in the mountain* ② search for; probe into; explore：～解决的方案 *search a scheme for solving the problem*

【寻味】chew sth over; ruminate; mull over; think over

【寻问】look for; inquire; explore; seek：他来～那件事的有关情况。*He came to seek about the matter.*

【寻隙】① pick a quarrel; find fault with sb (to provoke an argument) ② seek an opportunity; try to find a loophole

【寻衅】bite the thumb at; pick a quarrel; provoke：～滋事 *kick up a row and make trouble*

【寻找】look for; search for; seek; pursue：雷蒙德在努力～出差的借口。*Raymond is trying his best to seek an excuse for business.*

巡 ① patrol; inspect：南～ *inspection tour to the south* ②［量］round of drinks

【巡捕】① retinue of a provincial governor in the Qing Dynasty ② police or policeman (in former foreign concessions)：～房 *police station (in former foreign concessions)*

【巡查】go on a tour of inspection; make one's rounds

【巡察】make an inspection tour

【巡风】keep watch; watch：他派我到大门口～。*He sent me to keep watch at the gate.*

【巡官】police inspector

【巡航】cruise：～速度 *cruising speed* / ～导弹 *cruise missile*

【巡回】tour; go the rounds; make a circuit of：～辅导 *mobile coaching*

【巡警】①［旧］policeman ② patrolling police or policeman

【巡礼】① visit a sacred land; make a pilgrimage ② visit; tour; sightseeing

【巡逻】go on patrol; patrol：～队 *patrol party; patrol* / ～护卫舰 *patrol escort; patrol craft*

【巡哨】(of a small security detachment) go on patrol

【巡视】① make an inspection tour; tour ② look around

【巡行】go on a circuit; make one's rounds; patrol

【巡洋舰】【军】cruiser：～导弹 *guided missile cruiser*

【巡夜】make night patrol

【巡弋】(of warships) cruise; ply the waters

【巡游】① saunter; stroll ② patrol：警察在监狱四周～。*The policemen are patrolling around the jail.*

【巡展】exhibition tour; roving exhibition

【巡诊】(of a doctor) make a round of visits

询 ask; consult; inquire：～问 *ask; inquire* / 咨～ *consult; seek advice from*

【询查】make inquiries; inquire and seek：～原因 *inquire and seek reason*

【询问】ask; inquire; enquire; question：～处 *inquiry office*

峋 ① (of mountain rocks, cliffs, etc.) jagged; rugged; craggy ② (of a person) bony; thin

洵 ［书］really; truly; indeed

循 abide by; act in accordance with; follow

【循分】[书] act according to one's duties

【循规蹈矩】act with directions; follow the usual rules and regulations; conform to convention; follow accepted customs and practices; observe rules and follow orders docilely; toe the line: 马克做事~。*Mark does everything by rule.*

【循环】circulate; circle; cycle: 良性~ *virtuous circle* / 血在人体内~。*Blood circulates in the human body.*

【循例】follow the usual practice; follow a precedent; act in accordance with precedents

【循序】in proper order or sequence: ~处理 *sequential processing*

【循序渐进】advance gradually in due order; follow in proper sequence and make steady progress; follow in order and advance step by step; proceed in an orderly and gradual way

【循循善诱】be good at giving systematic guidance; be methodical in imparting knowledge; lead the students skillfully by orderly method; teach with skill and patience and admits of no impetuosity: 老师~地指导我们做功课。*Our teacher guided us in our studies patiently and systematically.*

xùn

训 ① lecture; instruct; teach: 教~ *lesson; moral* ② teachings; precept; maxim: 古~ *ancient maxim* / 校~ *school motto; phrasal school regulations* ③ drill; train: 你参加过计算机培~吗? *Do you take part in the training of computer?* ④ example; model; paragon; standard ⑤ explanation of words

【训斥】berate; dress down; get down; rebuke; reprimand; scold: 我再也不敢晚回家了,否则妈妈又会~我。*I daren't be late home again or I will get told off by my mother.*

【训词】admonition; exhortation; instructions: 我讨厌听卢克的~。*I dislike hearing Luke's exhortations for me.*

【训导】admonish; advise; guide; lesson; teach: ~处 *an office of the dean of students*

【训话】give an admonitory talk to subordinates: 教官正在对士兵~。*The instructor is giving an admonitory talk to soldiers.*

【训诲】[书] instruction; teaching

【训诫】① admonish; advise; sermonize: 警察~他不可开快车。*The policeman admonished him not to drive too fast.* ②【律】rebuke; reprimand

【训练】drill; train: 专业~ *professional training* / 军事~ *military drill* / ~有素的船员 *a well-drilled crew*

【训令】directive; orders; command; injunction; instructions

【训勉】instruct and encourage; exhort and encourage: 将军~他的部下好好打仗。*The general exhorted his men to fight well.*

【训示】instructions to subordinates; orders

【训释】explain; interpret: ~字义 *explain the meaning of a word*

【训诱】[书] instruct and guide: 杰伦特善于对学生们进行~。*Geraint is good at instructing and guiding to his students.*

【训喻】[书] instruct; teach

【训责】admonish and reprimand; instruct and denounce

汛 ① seasonal flood or high water: 防~ *flood control* ② season when fish schools emerge; fishing season: 黄鱼~ *yellow croaker season*

【汛期】【水】floodtime; flood season; high-water season

【汛情】flood situation; water level in flood season

讯 ① ask; inquire: 问~ *ask after; greet; send one's respects to* ② interrogate; call sb to account; question ③ message; dispatch; news: 通~社 *news agency*

【讯号】① signal sent by electro-magnetic wave ② signal

【讯实】be proved true by trial; confirm through interrogation

【讯问】① ask about; inquire ②【律】interrogate; question

迅 fast; swift

【迅步】[书] walk fast; hurry

【迅风】swift wind; gale

【迅急】very fast; at high speed; in a flash

【迅疾】swiftly; rapidly

【迅捷】fast; rapid agile; quick: 动作~ *agile in movement*

【迅雷不及掩耳】sudden; as sudden as lightening; sudden peal of thunder leaves no time for covering ears

【迅猛】impetuous; sudden and violent: ~发展 *develope rapidly*

【迅速】fast; quick; rapid; swift: 为了知道丈夫的病情,艾达~地跑到了医院看他。*Ida rushed to the hospital quickly in order to know her husband's illness.*

驯 ① tame and docile; gentle; obedient ② tame; domesticate: ~兽者 *animals tamer*

【驯服】① docile; meek; tame; tractable ② tame; subdue; break in; domesticate: ~野兽 *tame beast*

【驯和】goo-natured; gentle; mild: 这男孩性情~。*The boy has a gentle spirit.*

【驯化】acclimatization; domestication; domestication; taming

【驯良】tractable; docile; obedient; tame; gentle: 性情~的马 *tame and gentle horse*

【驯鹿】reindeer

【驯顺】submissive; tame and docile: 格洛丽亚骑着一匹~的马。*Gloria rides a docile mare.*

X

【驯养】raise and train (animals); domesticate

徇 ① comply with; give in to; submit to; yield to ② [书] declare to the public; announce publicly

【徇情】[书] act dishonestly out of personal considerations: ~枉法 *bend the law for benefit of one's relatives or friends*

【徇私】profit oneself; favoritism; act wrongly out of considerations for one's personal interests

逊 ① abdicate ② unassuming; modest ③ [书] inferior

【逊色】be inferior to

【逊位】[书] abdicate (one's throne)

殉 ① be buried alive with the dead ② sacrifice one's life for; die for: 以身~职 *die at one's post*

【殉道】die for a right cause or one's ideals; die a martyr: ~者 *martyr*

【殉国】die for one's country; give one's life for the country: 尼基的爸爸在战争中以身~了。*Nicky's father laid down his life for his country in the war.*

【殉教】martyr; sacrifice one's life for a religious cause

【殉节】① die in loyalty to one's country ② [旧] (of a woman) commit suicide after her husband's death ③ (of a woman) commit suicide to defend her chastity

【殉难】die for a just cause; die a martyr; be killed during some disaster: 去年他爸爸为国~了。*His father died for his country last year.*

【殉情】die or commit suicide for love; give one's life for the sake of love: ~者 *martyrs to love*

【殉死】① be buried alive with the dead ② commit suicide in order to follow the deceased to the grave

【殉葬】be buried alive with the dead: ~品 *grave goods; funerary object; sacrificial object; sacrifice*

【殉职】die at one's post; die in line of duty; die a martyr at one's post; die in time of duty; die in the course of performing one's duty; die on one's job: 亨利因公~了。*Henry died at his post.*

熏 [方] be poisoned or suffocated by coal gas

see also xūn

Y

yā

丫 ① bifurcation; fork:枝~ *branch; twig* ② [方] little girl

【丫杈】① crotch; fork ② forked; ramified

【丫环】slave girl; servant girl; maid

【丫头】① girl ② slave girl

压 ① press; crush; weigh down; push down: ~死 *die under pressure* / ~扁 *press flat; flatten* / ~平 *press flat* / ~塌 *collapse under pressure* /这盒子怕~。*This box won't stand much weight.* /那件事重重地~在他的心头。*The matter weighed heavily on his mind.* ② keep under control; control; hold back; repress:强~怒火 *try hard to control one's anger* / ~低嗓门 *lower one's voice; speak under one's breath* / ~住咳嗽 *hold back a cough* ③ bring pressure to bear on; intimidate; daunt; force:以势~人 *coerce people with one's power* /泰山~顶志不移 *not change one's mind even if Mount Tai topples overhead; not give in to any pressure or difficulty* ④ approach; be getting near:太阳~山了。*The setting sun was touching the hilltop.* ⑤ surpass; exceed:技~群芳 *have incomparable skills* ⑥ pigeonhole; shelve:这些邮包被~了不少时间。*These parcels have been pigeonholed for quite some time.* ⑦ risk (money, etc.) on; stake:在那个大热门(如赌马中的某匹马)上~五英镑 *stake five pounds on the favourite* ⑧ pressure:电~ *voltage* /水~ *hydraulic pressure* /血~ *blood pressure*
see also yà

【压场】① have a situation (an audience, a meeting, etc) well under one's control:压不住场 *unable to keep the situation under control* ② serve as the last item and usually the climax of a theatrical performance; serve as the grand finale: ~戏 *grand finale of a theatrical performance*

【压秤】① be relatively heavy per unit volume:棉花不~。*Cotton doesn't weigh much.* ② deliberately under-weigh sth (in order to underpay the seller)

【压倒】overwhelm; overpower; prevail over: ~多数 *an overwhelming majority* /困难压不倒我们。*No difficulty can overwhelm us.*

【压得住】able to keep under control: ~阵脚 *able to keep the troops in battle array; able to hold the line* / ~邪气 *keep unhealthy trends under control*

【压低】bring down; lower; reduce; abate: ~声音 *lower one's voice* / ~价格 *bring down the price*

【压底】serve as the last resort; be at the bottom of

【压电】【物】piezoelectricity; piezoelectric: ~材料 *piezoelectric* / ~晶体 *piezoelectric crystal; piezocrystal* / ~效应 *piezoelectric effect*

【压顶】① (in architecture) coping: ~石 *copingstone; the grand finale* ② (figuratively) press down from above:乌云~ *dark clouds were bearing down; threatening clouds were gathering* / ~之势 *an overwhelming force*

【压锻】【冶】press forging

【压队】bring up the rear and supervise

【压服】force sb to submit; bring sb to his knees: ~解决不了思想问题。*Ideological problems cannot be solved by coercion.*

【压焊】【冶】push welding; pressure welding

【压花】emboss: ~玻璃 *pattern glass*

【压挤】【机】extrusion: ~成形 *extrusion moulding*

【压价】force prices down; demand a lower price

【压惊】help sb get over a shock

【压境】press on to the border:大兵~。*Massed enemy troops are bearing down upon the border.*

【压库】① overstock ② reduce stock:限产~ *limit production and reduce stock*

【压力】①【物】pressure:大气~ *atmospheric pressure* /外界~ *ambient pressure* / ~锅 *pressure cooker* / ~计 *pressure gauge; manometer* ② strong or oppressive influence; pressure; strain:在很大~下工作 *work at high pressure* /对某人施加(使之做某事) ~ *bring pressure to bear on sb (to do sth)* /在舆论的~下 *under the pressure of public opinion* /减轻~ *ease (or lighten) the pressure (strain)* /社会~ *social pressure*

【压路机】road roller; roller

【压平】flatten; even; smooth:把路~ *even the road; roll the road* /把弄皱的纸~ *flatten crumpled paper*

【压迫】① oppress; repress: ~者 *oppressor* / ~阶级 *oppressor class* /哪里有~,哪里有反抗 *where there is oppression there is resistance* / ~弱小民族 *oppress small and weak nations* ② constriction:胸部有~感 *feel a constriction in the chest* /腿被~得麻木了。*My leg goes numb because of constriction.*

【压气】① calm sb's anger; placate ② compress or inject air: ~机 *compressor machine; compressor*

【压强】【物】intensity of pressure; pressure: ~计 *pressure gauge*

【压实】compaction; ramming

【压岁钱】money given to children as a lunar New Year gift:今年春节他得了许多~。*This Spring*

Festival he got a lot of gift money.
【压碎】【矿】crush：～机 *crusher*
【压缩】① compress；compact；condense：～比 *compression ratio* /～空气 *compressed air* /～饼干 *ship biscuit or bread*；*pilot biscuit or bread*；*hardtack* ② reduce；condense；cut down on：～开支 *pare down or cut down expenses* /将长篇报告～为摘要 *condense a long report into a brief summary* /～机 *compressor*/空气～机 *air compressor*
【压弯】bend（with the weight of sth）；weigh down
【压抑】① constrain；restrain；depress；hold back；hold in：～同学们的积极性 *restrain the enthusiasm of the students* /精神～ *feel oppressed* /～不住心头的哀思 *unable to contain one's grief* /那孩子的感情一直受到～。*The child's affections were kept under continual restraint.* ② oppressive；stifling：气氛～ *stifling atmosphere*
【压印】【印】stamp；impression
【压载舱】ballast tank
【压榨】① press；squeeze：～葡萄汁 *squeeze juice from grapes* /～机 *squeezer*；*mangle* ② exploit；oppress；squeeze：在工厂中受到残酷～的童工 *child labour ruthlessly exploited in factories*
【压阵】① bring up the rear：他～掩护大家脱险。*He brought up the rear to cover the others' escape from danger.* ② keep order；keep under control：压不住阵 *unable to keep the situation under control* /上自习时，老师在教室～。*When the pupils were studying in the classroom, the teacher was present to keep order.*
【压制】① suppress；stifle；repress；hold back：～人才 *suppress talented people* /～新生力量 *hold back new rising forces* /～怒火 *repress*（*or hold back*）*one's anger* /那独裁者竭力～一切批评他的言论。*The dictator tried to suppress all criticism of him.* ②【机】pressing：～纤维板 *pressed fiberboard* /～板 *pressboard*
【压轴戏】last and best item on a theatrical program；grand finale
【压铸】【冶】die-casting；die-cast：～模 *compression mould*

呀 ①（indicating surprise）ah；oh：哎～，多可怕～！*Oh, how horrible!* ②［象］creak：～的一声门开了。*The gate squeaked open or the gate opened with a creak.*

押[1] ① give as security；mortgage；pawn；pledge：以某物为～ *give sth as a security* /典～ *pawn* /他用房产～款创业。*He mortgaged his house to start a business.* ② detain；take into custody：被拘～ *be held in custody* /在～犯 *criminal in custody* /把他～下去！*Take him away!* /他被保安人员～起来了。*He has been detained by the security personnel.* ③ accompany as an escort；escort：～送 *escort*；*send under escort*

押[2] signature；mark made on a written statement in place of signature：画～ *sign*；*mark*（*a document*）*in place of a signature*
【押差】① take on the task of escort ② person entrusted with the task of escort
【押车】escort a vehicle（in transport）
【押当】pawn
【押队】bring up the rear
【押汇】loan secured from a bank by an exporter with the waybill as mortgage
【押解】send（a criminal or captive）away under escort；escort：～出境 *deport under escort* /～犯人去工地 *escort prisoners to the site*
【押金】deposit；security：退还～ *return the deposit*
【押送】① take a prisoner of captive to a place under escort ② escort（goods）in transport
【押尾】sign or mark in place of signature at the end of a written document
【押运】escort goods in transportation
【押韵】rhyme：～诗 *rhymed verse* / 这首诗不～。*This poem has no rhyme.*
【押租】rent deposit

鸦 crow
【鸦默雀静】even crows and sparrows are quiet — utter silence：葬礼～，气氛异常严肃。*Silence reigned in the funeral, and the atmosphere was heavy and solemn.*
【鸦片】opium：吸～ *smoke opium* /戒～ *give up opium-smoking* /～鬼 *opium addict* /～馆 *opium den*
【鸦片战争】Opium War（Britain's war of aggression against China, 1840-1842）：第二次～ *second Opium War*（*launched by Britain and France against China*, 1856—1860）
【鸦雀无声】not even a crow or sparrow can be heard — silence reigns：他一开口，教室里立刻～。*The students became quiet the moment he began to speak.*

哑
【哑哑】① croak；caw（of a crow）②（of babies）babble

桠 fork（of a tree）
【桠杈】① fork（of a tree）；branch；crotch ② forked；crotched；ramified
【桠枝】branch；twig

鸭 duck：公～ *drake* /母～ *duck* /一群～ *a flock of ducks* /～掌 *duck's foot or web* /～舌帽 *peaked cap*
【鸭蛋】egg of duck：～脸 *oval face* /～青 *pale blue*
【鸭黄】① tender yellow ②［方］duckling
【鸭绒】duck's down；eiderdown：～手套 *eiderdown gloves* / ～被 *eiderdown quilt*；*duck's down quilt* /～睡袋 *down sleeping-bag* /～背心 *eiderdown waistcoat* /～枕心 *down pillow*
【鸭行鹅步】walk slowly and unsteadily like a duck or goose；waddle
【鸭子】［口］duck：放～ *tend ducks* /～叫声 *quack* /～肉 *duck meat*
【鸭子儿】duck's egg
【鸭嘴笔】drawing pen；ruling pen
【鸭嘴兽】platypus；duckbill；duck mole

yá

牙 ① tooth:以～还～ *a tooth for a tooth; paying sb back in his own coin* /假～ *an artificial tooth* /拔～ *extract a tooth; have a tooth pulled out* /虎～ *pointed tooth* /刷～ *brush one's teeth* /补～ *have one's teeth filled* /镶～ *fix a false tooth; have a denture made* ② ivory: ～筷 *ivory chopsticks* ③ sth shaped like a tooth:轮～ *cog*

【牙白】creamy white; ivory

【牙本质】【生理】dentine

【牙槽】【生理】socket of tooth: ～炎 *dentoalveolitis*

【牙碜】①(of food) gritty ②(of language) vulgar; coarse; jarring

【牙齿】tooth: ～浮动 *looseness of tooth* /～打颤。*One's teeth are chattering.*

【牙床】①【生理】gum ② ivory-inlaid bed

【牙雕】ivory carving

【牙粉】tooth power

【牙缝】slit between the teeth:剔～ *prick one's teeth* /从～里省钱 *squeeze money out of one's tight food budget* /剩下的食物还不够填～。*There was almost no food left.*

【牙缸】glass or mug for tooth-cleaning; tooth glass

【牙膏】toothpaste

【牙垢】tartar; dental calculus

【牙关】mandibular joint; maxillary joint: 咬紧～ *grit one's teeth* /～紧闭 *lockjaw*

【牙冠】【生理】crown of a tooth; dental crown

【牙慧】remarks made by others:拾人～ *pick up remarks made by other people and pass them off as a sample of one's own wit; repeat what sb else has said; parrot sb else*

【牙祭】an unusually good meal with meat dishes:打～ *have a special treat*

【牙具】things for teeth-clearing and mouth-rinsing

【牙科】【医】(department of) dentistry: ～诊所 *dental clinic* /～技师 *dental technician* /～学 *dentistry* /～医生 *dentist; dental surgeon*

【牙口】① age of a draught animal as shown by the number of its teeth:这匹骡子～太老。*Just look at the number of its teeth; this mule is too old.* ② condition of an old person's teeth:老头儿的～还好。*The old man's teeth are still in good condition.*

【牙买加】Jamaica: ～人 *Jamaican*

【牙签】① toothpick: ～筒 *toothpick-holder* ②[书] ivory bookmark

【牙色】light yellow similar to ivory; creamy white

【牙刷】toothbrush

【牙髓】【生理】dental pulp: ～炎 *pulpitis*

【牙痛】toothache

【牙牙】[象](of babies) babble: ～学语 *begin to babble; babble out first speech sounds; learn to speak* /小孩开始～了。*The kid began to babble.*

【牙医】dentist

【牙龈】【生理】gingiva; gum: ～出血 *bleeding gum* /～炎 *gingivitis* /～萎缩 *gingival atrophy*

【牙质】① made of ivory: ～的石头 *ivory stone* ②【生理】dentine

【牙子】①[口] serrated edge ②[旧] middleman

伢 [方] child; kid

【伢崽】[方] child; kid

【伢子】[方] child; kid

芽 ① bud; sprout; shoot:麦～ *malt* /豆～ *bean sprout* /幼～ *young shoot* /抽～ *put forth buds* ② sth resembling a bud or sprout:肉～ *granulation*

【芽孢】【生】gemma (of a fungus); spore

【芽变】【植】bud mutation

【芽茶】young tea leaves; bud-tea

【芽豆】sprouted broad bean

【芽体】【生】gem; sprout; bud; gemmule

【芽眼】【植】eye (of a potato)

蚜 aphid; aphis; plant louse

【蚜虫】plant louse; aphid; aphis:棉～ *cotton aphid* /叶上有许多～。*There are many aphids on the leaves.*

崖 ① precipice; cliff; crag:山～ *cliff* /悬～ *steep cliff; precipice* ② limit; bound; boundary

【崖岸】① high and steep cliff or embankment ②[书] supercilious and difficult of approach

【崖壁】precipice; cliff; escarpment

【崖刻】inscriptions (engraved) on a cliff

【崖略】general sketch; rough idea; outline

涯 ① shore; bank ② margin; bound; limit:无～的学海 *boundless sea of learning* /无边无～ *boundless* /天～海角 *remotest corners of the earth; end of the earth*

【涯岸】embankment

【涯际】limit; bound; boundary:漫无～的大海 *boundless ocean; vast expanse of water*

睚 [书] corner of the eye

【睚眦】① angry stare ② petty grievance

【睚眦必报】seek revenge for the smallest grievance — be utterly narrow-minded and revengeful

衙 government office in feudal China:县～ *feudal government office of a county*

【衙门】government office in feudal China: ～作风 *bureaucratic style of work*

【衙内】① officials as imperial guard ②[旧] son of high officials

【衙役】government office in feudal China

yǎ

哑 ① incapable of speech; mute; dumb:先天性聋～ *congenitally deaf-mute; deaf and dumb from birth* ②(of voice) hoarse; husky:他把嗓子喊～了。*He shouted himself hoarse.* ③(of artillery shell or bullet) ineffective

【哑巴】dumb person; mute:吃~亏 *swallow one's grievances in silence; be compelled to keep one's grievances to oneself*

【哑场】awkward silence during a meeting or discussion

【哑火】① dud ② (of a person) quiet

【哑剧】dumb show; mime

【哑口无言】be left without an argument; be tongue-tied; be rendered speechless

【哑铃】【体】dumbbell

【哑谜】puzzling remark; enigma; riddle:猜~ *solve a riddle*

【哑默悄声】[方] ① quiet; still; silent:院子里~,一个人也没有。*The yard was quiet without a single soul.* ② whisper

【哑然】① [书] quiet; still; silent: ~无声。*Silence reigns.* ② be struck dumb with amazement, ③ sound of laughing; laugh: ~失笑 *be unable to suppress a laugh*

【哑语】sign language; dactylology:打~ *communicate with the aid of dactylology*

【哑子】[方] mute

雅[1] ① refined; polished; elegant:高~ *refined; elegant* /古~ *of classic elegance* /文~ *cultured; polished; refined* /无伤大~ *not deviating much from propriety; harmless* /不登大~之堂 *not appeal to refined taste* ② [书] standard; proper; correct; orthodox: ~音 *refined music; standard pronunciation* /~儒 *orthodox Confucian scholar* ③ one of the three genres of The Book of Songs

雅[2] [书] ① acquaintance; friendship:无一日之~ *not have the pleasure of knowing sb* ② usually; customarily; often:子所~言 *what Confucius often talked about* ③ very much; indeed: ~以为美 *consider sth very beautiful*

【雅爱】be fond of; have a liking for: ~丹青 *be keen on paining*

【雅淡】simple and in good taste; quietly elegant: ~的色调 *quiet and delicate colour*

【雅典】Athens, capital of Greece: ~人 *Athenian*

【雅尔塔】Yalta, port city on the Black Sea in the Ukraine: ~会议 *Yalta Conference* /~协定 *Yalta Agreement* (1945)

【雅观】(often used in the negative) refined (in manner, etc.); tasteful:很不~ *most unseemly; rather unsightly* /他的衣服看起很不~。*His clothes look rather unsightly.*

【雅号】① your elegant name (often used to refer to other people's names deferentially) ② (humorously) nickname

【雅加达】Jakarta, capital of Indonesia

【雅静】① tasteful and quiet:庭院~。*There is an atmosphere of refined beauty and elegant quietness in the garden.* ② gentle and quiet: ~的姑娘 *gentle girl*

【雅量】① magnanimity; generosity; large-mindedness:有~接受批评 *be broad-minded enough to accept to criticisms* ② great capacity for liquor

【雅趣】elegant taste; refined pleasure

【雅士】refined scholar; person of refined tastes:文人~ *refined men of letters*

【雅俗共赏】(of a work of art or literature) suit both refined and popular tastes; both the refined and vulgar can appreciate:一部~的好电影 *a good film to the taste of both intellectuals and ordinary readers*

【雅兴】aesthetic mood; refined interest:无此~ *be in no mood for such things* /~不浅 *have a really keen interest in sth*

【雅言】[书] ① standard language ② worthy opinion; good advice

【雅意】① noble sentiments ② your kindness; your opinion

【雅致】refined; elegant; tasteful:陈设~ *tastefully furnished*

【雅座】private room (in a restaurant, etc.):隔壁房间设有~。*Private rooms are available next door.*

yà

轧[1] ① flatten with a roller; roll; run over:被公共汽车~伤 *get run over and get injured by a bus* /~路 *roll a road* /~棉花 *gin cotton* /~碎 *crush to pieces* ② squeeze out; push out:内部倾~ *engage in internal strife*

轧[2] [象](of a machine) click:机器~~的嘈杂声 *the clicking of machine*
see also zhá

【轧场】① thresh grain on a threshing ground with a stone roller ② level a threshing floor with a stoner roller
see also zhá

【轧道机】road roller

【轧花】【纺】cotton ginning: ~厂 *cotton ginning mill* /~机 *cotton gin*

亚[1] ① inferior; second:不~于人 *second to none; not inferior to anyone* /他的才学不~于他父亲。*He is by no means inferior to his father in intelligence and learning.* ② sub-: ~科 *subfamily* /~属 *subgenus* /~种 *subspecies* ③ of lower (atomic) valence

亚[2] short for Asia:东南~ *southeast Asia* /欧~大陆 *Eurasia*

【亚当】Adam, the first man according to the Bible

【亚丁湾】Gulf of Aden, between the Red Sea and the Arabian Sea

【亚得里亚海】Adriatic Sea

【亚基因】【生】sub-gene

【亚军】second place (in a sports contest); runner-up:他得了~。*He finished in second place.*

【亚里士多德】Aristotle (384-322BC), Greek philosopher and scientist

【亚硫酸】【化】sulphurous acid

【亚美尼亚】Armenia: ~人 *Armenian* /~语 *Armenia (language)*

【亚热带】【地】subtropical zone; subtropics; semitropics: ~雨林 *subtropical rain forest; warm tem-*

perate rain forest
【亚太】Asia-Pacific：～地区 *Asia Pacific region* / ～经济合作会议 *Asia-Pacific Economic Cooperation (APEC)* / ～论坛 *the forum of Asia Pacific region*
【亚铁】【化】ferrous：氧化～ *ferrous oxide* / 氯化～ *ferrous chloride*
【亚文化】subculture
【亚硝酸】【化】nitrous acid
【亚音速】【物】subsonic speed：～飞机 *subsonic aircraft* / ～火箭 *subsonic rocket*
【亚运村】Asian Games Village (now a housing neighborhood in Beijing)
【亚运会】Asian Games
【亚种】subspecies
【亚洲】Asia：～人 *Asian* / ～基金会（US）*Asian Foundation* / ～开发银行 *Asian Development Bank (ADB)*

压
see also yā
【压板】[方] seesaw; teeter board; teeter-totter
【压根儿】(mainly used in the negative) from the start; ever; simply; at all：她～就没有钱。*She has no money at all.*

讶 [书] be surprised; be astonished; be amazed：惊～ *shocked*; *stunned*; *surprised*
【讶然】be astonished：～失色 *turn ashen with shock*

氩 【化】argon

ya

呀 used in place of 啊 when the preceding word ends in sound ɑ, e, i, o or ü：你在干什么～？*What are you doing there?* / 快来～。*Come here, quick!* / 他～，还在睡觉呢。*He is still sleeping now.*

yān

咽 【生理】pharynx
see also yàn
【咽鼓管】【生理】eustachian tube
【咽喉】①【生理】pharynx and larynx; throat：～炎 *sore throat* ② strategic (or vital) passage; key junction：～要道 *strategic (or vital) passage*; *key junction*
【咽炎】pharyngitis

恹
【恹恹】[书] weak and weary through illness; rundown：～欲睡 *feel weak and sleepy* / ～一息 *critically ill with a little breath*; *at one's last gasp*

殷 [书] blackish red; dark red
see also yīn
【殷红】blackish red; dark red：～的血迹 *blackish red bloodstains* / ～的鸡冠花 *the dark red cockscomb*

胭
【胭脂】rouge：往脸上擦～ *rouge one's cheeks*

烟 ① smoke：狼～ *smoke signals* / 浓～滚滚 *billows of smoke* ② mist; vapour：云～ *mist and cloud* / 轻～在树梢缭绕。*Mist is curling around the treetop.* ③ (of eyes) be irritated by smoke：屋里～得我睁不开眼了。*I couldn't even open my eyes for the smoke in the room.* ④ cigarette or pipe tobacco：烤～ *flue-cured tobacco* / 香～ *cigarette* / 雪茄～ *cigar* / 一条～ *a carton of cigarettes* / 戒～ *give up smoking* / 请勿吸～！*No smoking.* ⑤ opium：禁～ *ban opium*
【烟霭】[书] mist and cloud
【烟波】mist-covered waters：～浩渺 *vast expanse of misty waters* / ～浩渺 *vast expanse of mist covered waters*
【烟草】tobacco：～行业 *tobacco industry*
【烟尘】① smoke and dust：～弥漫（*of a place*）*be enveloped in smoke and dust* ② [古] beacon-fire and dust in the battlefield
【烟囱】chimney; funnel; stovepipe
【烟袋】a long-stemmed pipe or a water pipe：～杆儿 *the stem of a pipe* / ～荷包 *tobacco pouch* / ～嘴儿 *the mouth-piece of a long-stemmed pipe*
【烟道】flue; chimney; stack
【烟蒂】cigarette end; butt; stub
【烟斗】(tobacco) pipe
【烟鬼】① opium addict ② heavy smoker; chain smoker
【烟锅】pipe bowl
【烟海】[书] vast sea of fog - huge and voluminous：浩如～ *tremendous amount of*; *voluminous*
【烟盒】cigarette case
【烟花】①[书] a lovely spring scene ②[旧] prostitute; prostitution：～女 *prostitute* / ～巷 *red-light district* ③ fireworks：～爆竹 *fireworks*
【烟灰】tobacco or cigarette ash：～缸 *ashtray*
【烟火】① smoke and fire：严禁～。*Smoking is strictly forbidden.* ② cooked food：不食人间～ *do not eat cooked food*; *live the life in immortal* ③ fireworks
【烟火食】cooked food
【烟晶】【地】smoky quartz; smoky topaz
【烟具】smoking paraphernalia; smoking set
【烟卷儿】[口] cigarette
【烟煤】bituminous coal; soft coal; pit coal
【烟民】smokers; tobacco users
【烟幕】smokescreen：～弹 *smoke shell bomb*; *smoke screen* / 他的话只是一个～。*His words were only a smokescreen.*
【烟屁股】[口] cigarette end (or stub)
【烟枪】opium pipe
【烟圈】smoke ring
【烟色】dark brown
【烟丝】cut tobacco; pipe tobacco
【烟筒】chimney; funnel; stovepipe

【烟头】cigarette end(or stub,stump)
【烟土】crude opium
【烟雾】smoke,mist,or vapour; a mixture of smoke and vapour: ~弥漫 *full of smoke*; *covered by smoke* /~笼罩着伦敦。*A heavy smog is hovering low over London.*
【烟消云散】vanish like smoke and disperse like clouds — completely vanish:一天的不快一下子~了。*All the displeasures of the day vanished completely.*
【烟熏火燎】smoke and burn:我嗓子~地难受,快给我点饮料。*My throat is burning; get me some drink please.*
【烟叶】tobacco leaf; leaf tobacco
【烟瘾】a craving for opium; a craving for tobacco:他~可大了。*He's a heavy smoker or he smokes like a chimney.* /他~发了。*He's dying for a smoke.*
【烟油子】tobacco tar; cigarette tar
【烟雨】misty rain
【烟云】smoke,mists and clouds
【烟柱】a column of smoke
【烟嘴儿】cigarette holder
焉 [书] ① here; this:心不在~ *with one's attention elsewhere*; *absent-minded* ② how; why:不入虎穴,~得虎子? *How can you catch tiger cubs without entering the tiger lair?* /~能不去? *How could I possibly not go?*
阉 ① castrate; spay: ~鸡 *capon* /~牛 *bullock*; *steer* /~猪 *barrow*; *hog* ② eunuch
【阉割】① castrate or spay ② deprive a theory of its essence; emasculate
【阉人】castrated person; eunuch
淹 ① flood; submerge; inundate:洪水~了整个城市。*The flood submerged the whole city.* ② be tingling from sweat ③ [书] delay; tarry: ~思 *slow in thinking* ④ [书] wide; extensive: ~通古今 *be thoroughly acquainted with the ancient and the modern*
【淹灌】【农】basin irrigation
【淹蹇】① [书] be frustrated:宦途~ *have a disappointing official career* ② delay; hold up
【淹埋】cover up; bury:整个城市被淤泥~了。*The whole city was buried in mud.*
【淹没】submerge; flood; inundate; drown:村子被洪水~。*The village was inundated by flood.*
【淹死】be drowned
腌 preserve in salt, sugar, etc.; pickle; salt: ~菜 *pickled vegetables*; *pickles* /~鱼 *salted fish* /~肉 *salted meat*; *bacon*
【腌泡】marinate; marinade
【腌制】make by pickling or salting: ~酱菜 *make pickles*
【腌渍】preserve in brine, vinegar, etc.; pickle: ~黄瓜 *pickle cucumbers*
湮 [书] ① fall into oblivion; bury in oblivion ② silt up
【湮灭】bury in oblivion; annihilate; disappear
【湮没】① fall into oblivion; be neglected; be forgotten ②【物】annihilation: ~反应 *annihilation reaction* /~辐射 *annihilation radiation* /~光子 *annihilation photon*
嫣 [书] handsome; beautiful
【嫣红】bright red:姹紫~ (*of flowers*) *very colorful and beautiful*
【嫣然】[书] beautiful; sweet: ~一笑 *give a charming* (*or winsome*) *smile*
燕 ① one of the warring states of the Eastern Zhou dynasty ② northern Hebei province
see also yàn
【燕京】old name for Beijing

yán

延 ① prolong; extend; protract:蔓~ *spread* /绵~不断 *stretch long and unbroken* ② postpone; delay:舞会遇雨顺~。*In case of rain the party will be postponed till the first fine day.* ③ [书] engage (a teacher, adviser, etc.); send for: ~医 *send for a doctor*
【延挨】delay; stall: ~时日 *play for time*; *stall* (*for time*)
【延长】lengthen; prolong; renew; extend: ~期限 *extend the deadline* /~有效期两周 *validity renewed for another 2 weeks* /~寿命 *prolong one's life* /~时间 *extra period* /~线 *extension* (*or extended*) *line* /会议~了三天。*The conference was prolonged for three more days.*
【延迟】① delay; defer; postpone:运动会时间~了。*The sports meeting have been postponed* (*or deferred*). ②【电】time delay; delay: ~电路 *delay circuit* /~失真 *delay distortion*
【延宕】procrastinate; delay; keep putting off
【延搁】delay; procrastinate
【延缓】delay; postpone; put off: ~工作进度 *retard the progress of work* /~衰老 *postpone ageing*
【延揽】[书] enlist the services of; recruit: ~人才 *enlist the services of able people* /~新选手 *recruit new players*
【延年益寿】(of tonics, etc.) prolong life; conduce to longevity
【延聘】[书] engage; invite (sb to do sth in a particular capacity): ~某人为总经理 *engage sb as the general manager*
【延期】extend; postpone; defer; put off:办理~签证手续 *have one's visa extended* /~付款 *defer payment* /比赛因雨~。*The game was put off on account of rain.* /~审理 *postponement of the hearing* /~交货 *back order*
【延请】[书] invite (sb to do a particular job); engage
【延伸】extend; stretch; elongate: ~火力 *creeping fire*; *lift fire* /~率 *percentage elongation* /道路一直~到海边。*The road stretches right to the coast.*
【延时】【电】delay: ~摄影 *time-lapse photography*
【延寿】lengthen (or prolong) one's life

【延髓】【生理】medulla oblongata
【延误】incur loss through delay: ~时机 *miss an opportunity because of a delay* /~时日 *lose time*
【延性】【物】ductility
【延续】continue; go on; last: ~性 *continuity* /旱情~了半年之久。*The drought lasted for as long as six months.*
【延展】stretch; extend

严 ① tight: 戒备森~。*Tight security is in force.* /把门关~。*Shut the door tight.* ② strict; stern; rigorous: 高标准, ~要求 *high standards and strict demands* /~加管束 *bring under strict discipline* /纪律要~。*Be strict in discipline.* ③ heavy; severe; acute; extreme: ~寒 *severe cold* ④[书] used to refer to one's father: 家~ *my father*

【严办】deal with severely; punish with severity: 依法~ *punish strictly according to law*
【严惩】punish severely: ~犯罪分子 *punish the criminal severely* /~不贷 *punish without mercy; punish with severity*
【严词】strong terms; stern words: ~谴责 *denounce in strong terms; sternly condemn* /~拒绝 *give a stern rebuff; sternly refuse* /~驳斥 *sternly refute*
【严打】crackdown on crime; take severe measures against illegal and criminal activities: ~斗争 *campaign to crackdown on crime*
【严冬】a severe winter
【严防】be on full alert for; take strict precautions against
【严父】stern father; father: ~慈母 *stern father and compassionate mother* /在孩子面前他是一位~。*He is a stern father before his children.*
【严格】① strict; rigorous; rigid; stringent: ~说来 *strictly speaking* /老师对我们要求很~。*Our teacher is very strict with us.* ② rigorously enforce; regulate strictly: ~组织纪律 *rigidly enforce the discipline of the organization*
【严固】tight and consolidated: 防守~ *have a solid and impregnable defense*
【严寒】icy cold; severe cold
【严谨】① rigorous; meticulous; careful and precise: ~的科学态度 *a rigorous scientific approach* /为人~ *careful and prudent by nature* ② compact; well-knit: 文章结构~。*The essay is well-knit.*
【严禁】strictly forbid (or prohibit): ~吸烟。*Smoking is strictly prohibited.* /~酒后开车。*Drunk driving is strictly prohibited.*
【严峻】stern; severe; rigorous; grim: 对登山者耐力的~考验 *a severe test of climbers' stamina* /形势~ *grave situation*
【严酷】① harsh; bitter; grim: ~的环境 *harsh circumstances* /~的现实 *harsh reality* /~的教训 *a bitter lesson* ② cruel; ruthless: ~的剥削 *cruel exploitation*
【严冷】① cold and stern: 不要板着~的面孔。*Don't put on a cold, stern expression.* ② bitter cold: ~的天气 *bitter cold weather*
【严厉】stern; severe: 目光~ *stern look* /~的措施 *severe (or stringent) measures* /~申斥 *skin sb alive*
【严令】give strict orders: ~禁止走私 *issue strict orders to prohibit smuggling*
【严密】① tight; close: ~的封锁 *tight blockade* /~监视 *put under close surveillance; keep close watch over* /~防范 *take strict precautions against* ② compact; well-knit: 这种汽车构造~。*This kind of car is compact in construction.* /这篇故事结构~。*This story is well-knit.* ③ make compact; tighten
【严明】① strict and impartial: 赏罚~ *be strict and impartial in meting out rewards and punishments* /纪律~ *observe strict discipline; be highly disciplined* ② strictly enforce (discipline): ~军纪 *enforce and maintain strict military discipline* /~考试纪律 *enforce the discipline of examination*
【严声】(speak) in a stern voice: ~喝问 *shout a questions in a stern voice* /~厉色 *stern in voice and countenance*
【严师】a strict teacher: ~出高徒 *a strict teacher produces outstanding students; capable students are trained by exacting teacher masters* /~诤友 *strict teacher and outspoken friend* /在大学里他是一位~。*He is a strict teacher in the university.*
【严实】[方] ① tight; close: 她的嘴~着呢! *She has tight lips.* ② (hide) safely: 把东西藏~ *hide sth in very safe place*
【严守】① observe strictly: ~纪律 *observe strict discipline* /~合同 *abide by a contract faithfully* ② guard closely: ~国家机密 *strictly guard state secrets*
【严丝合缝】fit together perfectly; join tightly; dovetail
【严肃】① (of style, manner, etc.) serious; solemn; earnest: ~认真 *serious and conscientious* ② (of expression, atmosphere, etc.) stern; grave; serious; solemn: 神情~ *look serious or grave* ③ strictly enforce: ~法纪 *strictly enforce law and discipline* /~处理 *deal with strictly*
【严刑】cruel torture: ~拷打 *subject sb to severe torture; cruelly beat up*
【严以律己,宽以待人】be strict with oneself and lenient towards others
【严阵以待】be in full battle array; stand in combat readiness
【严整】① (usu. of troops) in neat formation; under strict discipline: 阵容~。*The battle array is in neat formation.* /军容~。*The troops are in gallant array.* ② meticulous: 治家~ *manage the family in a meticulous manner.*
【严正】solemn and just; serious and principled; stern: ~声明 *solemnly state or declare* /提出~抗议 *lodge a stern protest (with sb against sth)*
【严重】serious; grave; critical: ~后果 *serious (or grave) consequences* /~错误 *grieve mistake; blunder* /病情~ *be seriously ill* /感到~不安 *be deeply concerned*

言 ① speech; word: 留~ *leave a message; leave one's comments* / 发~ *make a speech* / 格~ *maxim* / ~听计从 *always follow sb's advice; act upon whatever sb says* / 有~在先 *let it clearly understood beforehand* ② character; word: 七~诗 *poem with seven characters in a line* / 下笔千~ *write a thousand words at a stroke; wield a facile pen* ③ say; talk; speak: 不~而喻 *it goes without saying* / ~不及义 *talk trivialities; never talk about anything serious* / 换~之 *in other words* / 妙不可~ *too wonderful for words; beyond words*

【言必信,行必果】promise must be kept and action must be resolute; be true in words and resolute in action

【言不尽意】I should like to say more (but I must bring my letter to a close now)

【言不由衷】speak insincerely; speak with one's tongue in one's cheek

【言差语错】mistakes or slips in speaking

【言传】explain or express in words: 只可意会,不可~ *only to be sensed, not explained* / ~身教 *teach by personal example as well as verbal instruction; teach by precept and example*

【言辞】words; speech; remark: 不善~ *be not good at expressing oneself* / ~恳切 *be sincere in what one says; speak earnestly* / ~激烈 *sharp criticism*

【言定】decide; agree

【言而无信】fail to keep faith; go back on one's word

【言而有信】be true to one's word; be as good as one's word

【言归于好】make it up (with sb); restore to friendship; become reconciled

【言归正传】come back to our story; to return to the subject

【言过其实】exaggerate; overstate

【言和】make peace; become reconciled; bury the hatchet: 握手~ *shake hands and make it up* / 同某人~ *be reconciled with sb*

【言简意赅】concise and comprehensive; brief and to the point; compendious

【言教】teach by word of mouth; give verbal directions: 身教胜于~。*Example is better than precept.*

【言近旨远】simple words but with deep meaning; plain remarks of profound meaning

【言路】channels through which criticisms and suggestions may be communicated to the authorities: 堵塞~ *stifle criticisms and suggestions* / 广开~ *provide more and better means for people to air their views*

【言论】opinion on public affairs; expression of one's political views; speech: ~自由 *freedom of speech* / 在人民内部实行~自由 *practise freedom of speech among the people*

【言情】(of works) romantic; sentimental: ~片 *film with a romantic story; sentimental movie* / ~小说 *a romantic or sentimental novel*

【言三语四】make irresponsible remarks; gossip

【言声儿】utter a sound or a word

【言说】put into words; say

【言谈】the way one speaks or what he says: ~举止 *speech and deportment* / ~得体 *speak in appropriate term*

【言外之意】meaning behind what is openly said or stated; implication: 体会其~ *read between the lines* / 我明白他的~,这事老师也有责任。*I'm quite aware of the overtones of what he was saying: the teacher should also be responsible.*

【言为心声】words are the voice of the mind; speech is the picture of the mind; what the heart thinks the tongue speaks

【言行】words and deeds; statements and actions: ~不一 *the deeds do not match the words* / ~一致 *suit one's actions to one's words; be as good as one's words*

【言犹在耳】the words still ring (or reverberate) in one's ears

【言有尽而意无穷】there is an end to the words but not to their meaning

【言语】① spoken language; speech ②[方] speak; talk; answer: 不明白的话就~一声。*Please let me know if you can't understand.*

【言责】① a subject's responsibility of offering advice to the ruler ② responsibility for what one says

【言者无心,听者有意】a casual remark sounds significant to a suspicious listener; while the speaker is careless, a hearer is attentive

【言者无罪,闻者足戒】blame not the speaker but be warned by his words

【言之成理】speak in a rational and convincing way; sound reasonable

【言之无物】(of speech or writing) be devoid of substance; be mere verbiage; hollow

【言之有据】speak on good grounds or with convincing proof

【言之凿凿】say sth with certainty

【言重】overstate; exaggerate

妍 [书] beautiful; enchanting: 群芳争~。*Flowers are vying with each other in beauty.*

【妍丽】beautiful: 色彩~ *beautiful colours* / 她的裙子很~。*Her skirt is very beautiful.*

【妍艳】bright-coloured and beautiful; gorgeous: 花朵~ *gorgeous flowers* / 云朵~ *beautiful cloud*

岩 ① rock: 花岗~ *granite* ② cliff; crag

【岩岸】【地】rocky coast

【岩壁】【地】crag; cliff

【岩层】rock stratum; rock formation

【岩洞】grotto

【岩画】rock painting; cliff carving

【岩浆】【地】magma

【岩羚羊】【动】chamois

【岩溶】【地】karst: ~地貌 *karst features; karst topography*

【岩石】rock: ~力学 *rock mechanics* / ~圈 *lithosphere* / ~学 *petrology* / 这里的~都很硬。*All* rocks here are hard.

【岩心】【地】(drill) core: ~回收率 *core recovery* / ~样品 *core sample*

【岩穴】cavern; cave

【岩崖】cliff

【岩盐】rock salt; halite

炎 ① scorching; burning hot: ~热的季节 *a torrid (or scorching) season* ② inflammation: 发~ *inflammation* / 消~ *counteract inflammation* ③ power; influence: 趋~附势 *be snobbish*

【炎旱】extremely hot and dry: ~的六月天 *a hot and dry days in June*

【炎凉】hot and cold, referring to different attitudes towards people of different fortune: 世态~ *the world as it is, fawning on the influential and snubbing the less fortunate*

【炎热】(of weather) scorching; blazing; burning hot: ~的天气 *the scorching weather*

【炎暑】hot summer; sweltering summer days; dog days

【炎夏】a torrid (or scorching) summer

【炎炎】scorching; sweltering; blazing: 烈日~ *the scorching sun*

【炎症】inflammation

沿 ① along: ~湖滨散步 *take a stroll along the lake* / ~街长着一排大树。*Big trees line the street.* ② follow or conform to (a tradition, pattern, etc.): 世代相~ *be handed down from generation to generation* ③ trim (with tape, ribbon, etc.): ~鞋口 *trim the top of a shoe* ④ edge; border: 缸~儿 *the brim of a jar* / 河~ *riverside*

【沿岸】along the bank or coast; littoral or riparian: 黄河~城市 *cities along the Yellow River* / 地中海~国家 *the littoral countries of the Mediterranean*

【沿边儿】trim (with tape, ribbon, etc.); braid: 用丝绸在裙子上~ *trim the skirt with a silk*

【沿革】the course of change and development; evolution

【沿海】along the coast; coastal; littoral: ~公路 *coastal road* / ~大坝 *coastal dam* / ~城市 *coastal cities* / ~岛屿 *offshore islands* / ~地区 *coastal areas; coastland*

【沿江】along the river (esp. the Yangtze)

【沿例】follow the usual practice; follow the established precedents

【沿路】along the road; on the way

【沿途】on the way; throughout a journey

【沿袭】carry on as before; follow: ~陈规 *follow convention* / ~老政策 *follow the old policy*

【沿线】along the line (i. e. a railway, highway, air or shipping line): 公路~ *along the highway* / 铁路~ *along the railway*

【沿用】continue to use (an old method, etc.): 这条规矩一直~下来。*This rule is still in use.*

研 ① grind; pestle: ~墨 *rub an ink stick on an ink slab (to prepare ink for brush writing)* ② study; research: 科~ *scientific research* / 钻~ *study assiduously; probe into*

【研读】study carefully: ~剧本 *study the play script carefully* / ~报告 *study the report carefully*

【研究】① study; research: ~客观规律 *study the objective principle* / 学术~ *academic study* / ~成果 *fruit of one's study* / ~工作者 *research worker* / ~生 *postgraduate (student); graduate student* / ~生院 *graduate school* / ~所 *research institute* / ~员 *research fellow; full professor* / ~院 *research institute; graduate school* ② consider; discuss; deliberate: 这些问题正在~。*These matters are under consideration.* / 我们认真~再给你答复。*We'll give you a reply after careful consideration.*

【研磨】【机】① grind; pestle ② abrade; polish: ~粉 *abrasive powder* / ~器 *abrader*

【研拟】discuss and formulate; develop

【研讨】deliberate; study and discuss: ~会 *symposium; seminar* / ~班 *research class*

【研习】study

【研修】engage in research and advanced studies

【研制】① research and manufacture; research and develop: ~新产品 *develop new product* ② prepare medicinal powder by pestling

盐 salt: 粗~ *crude salt* / 细~ *refined salt* / 酸式~ *acid salt* / 碱式~ *basic salt* / 岩~ *rock salt* / 海~ *sea salt*

【盐巴】[方] table salt; salt

【盐层】salt deposit; salt bed

【盐厂】saltern; saltworks

【盐池】salt pond

【盐分】salt content

【盐罐】saltcellar; saltshaker

【盐湖】salt lake

【盐花】① a little salt; a pinch of salt ② [方] salt frosting

【盐碱地】saline-alkali land

【盐井】salt well; brine pit

【盐矿】salt mine

【盐浓度】salinity

【盐瓶】saltcellar; saltshaker

【盐霜】salt efflorescence

【盐水】salt solution; brine: ~输液 *saline infusion* / ~选种 *seed sorting by salt water* / ~浴 *bathe in salt water*

【盐水鸭】salted duck

【盐酸】【化】hydrochloric acid

【盐滩】a beach for making sea salt

【盐田】salt pan

【盐土】【农】solonchak; saline soil

【盐析】【化】salt out: ~效应 *salting-out effect*

【盐业】salt industry

【盐液】saline solution (medical)

【盐渍土】【农】salinized soil

阎 [书] the entrance to a lane

【阎罗】【宗】Yama, King of Hell

【阎王】① Yama, King of Hell: ~爷 *Yama, king of Hell* / 活~ *a living King of Hell; a devil incarnate* / 见~ *kick the bucket; die* ② an extremely cruel and violent person: ~殿 *the Palace of the King of Hell*

筵 ①［书］bamboo mat spread on the floor for people to sit on ② feast; banquet：婚～ *a wedding feast* /寿～ *birthday feast*

【筵席】① seats arranged around a table at a banquet ② feast; banquet /庆功～ *a victory celebrating feast*

颜 ① face; countenance; look：强作欢～ *force oneself to look happy* /笑逐～开 *face wreathed in smiles* ② face; decency：无～见人 *not have the face to appear in public*; *be too ashamed to see anyone* /厚～无耻 *brazen and shameless* ③ colour; dye：五～六色 *colourful*; *of various colours*

【颜料】pigment; coloring：天然～ *natural pigments* /合成～ *artificial pigments*

【颜面】① face ② face; decency：～扫地 *lose face altogether*; *be thoroughly discredited* /最后大家都顾全了～。*Everyone saved his face at last.*

【颜色】① colour：～单调 *dull in colour* /～失真 *cross-colour* ②［书］countenance; facial expression：～憔悴 *haggard look* ③［口］look worn or action taken to warn or punish sb ④ pigment or dyestuff

檐 ① eaves：屋～ *eaves of a house* ② ledge; brim：帽～ *visor of a cap*; *brim of a hat*

【檐沟】【建】eaves gutter

【檐子】［口］eaves

yǎn

奄 ① cover; include; overspread ② all of a sudden; suddenly

【奄忽】［书］suddenly; all of a sudden; all at once：蜡烛～熄灭。*The candle suddenly died out.*

【奄奄】breathing feebly：～一息 *at one's last gasp*; *on the verge of death*

俨 ［书］① majestic; solemn; dignified ② just as; like

【俨然】［书］① solemn; dignified：望之～ *look dignified* ② neatly arranged：大楼～ *buildings set out in neat order* ③ just like

【俨如】just like

衍[1] ①［书］spread out; develop; amplify ② redundant; superfluous

衍[2] ① low-lying flatland：广～沃野 *a broad expanse of fertile flatland* ② marsh; swamp; bog

【衍变】develop; evolve

【衍射】【物】diffraction：～角 *diffraction angle* /～线 *diffracted ray*

【衍生】① derive ～物 *derivative* /～蛋白 *derived protein* ② evolve; produce

【衍续】flourish and continue

掩 ① cover; hide; conceal：～面而过 *pass by holding one's face* /～口而笑 *hide one's smile* /迅雷不及～耳 *as swift as a sudden clap of thunder* /～着怀 *cover one's breast*（*with coat unbuttoned*）②［方］get squeezed when closing a door, etc. ③ close; shut：～卷 *close a book* /虚～着门 *with the door left unlocked or unlatched* ④［书］launch a surprise attack：～袭 *launch a surprise attack*

【掩蔽】screen; camouflage; shelter cover：～目标 *cover up the object*; *keep from sight* /～物 *hide*; *screen*

【掩藏】hide; conceal; cover up

【掩耳盗铃】plug one's ears while stealing a bell; bury one's head in the sand like an ostrich; practice self-deception

【掩盖】① cover; overspread：沙子～着田野。*The fields were covered with sands.* ② conceal; cover up; conceal：极力～内心的高兴 *try hard to keep back one's happiness* /～罪行 *cover up a crime* /谎言～不了事实。*Lies cannot cover up the facts.*

【掩护】screen; shield; cover：～主力部队登陆 *cover the landing of the main force* /～部队 *covering force* /～火力 *covering fire* /大家都生你的气，我也没法为你打～。*Everyone is angry with you, and I can't screen you.*

【掩埋】bury

【掩泣】weep with one's face covered cover by one's hand

【掩人耳目】deceive the public; hoodwink people

【掩杀】［书］make a surprise attack; pounce on

【掩饰】cover up（faults, mistakes, etc.）; gloss over; conceal：～错误 *gloss over*（*or cover up*）*one's mistakes* /～窘态 *smooth over one's embarrassment* /～真实的意图 *conceal one's true intentions* /她毫不～对他的不满。*She has taken an undisguised resentment to him.*

【掩体】【军】blindage; bunker

【掩星】【天】occultation（of stars）：月～ *lunar occultation*

【掩映】set off（one another）：新楼翠竹交相～。*The new buildings and green bamboos set each other off.*

眼 ① eye：两～无神 *with dull eyes*/ 亲～所见 *see with one's own eyes* ② look; glance：瞥了他一～ *shoot a glance at him* ③ a small hole; aperture：泉～ *mouth of a spring* /针～ *eye of a needle* /网～ *mesh of a net* ④ key point; crux：节骨～ *critical juncture* ⑤ trap ⑥ an unaccented beat in traditional Chinese music：一板三～ *one accented beat and three unaccented beats in a bar* ⑦［量］used of a well or cave-dwelling：一～井 *a well*

【眼巴巴】① looking on with eager eyes;（expecting）eagerly and anxiously ② helplessly（when watching sth unpleasant happen）：他～地看着洪水淹没了整座城市。*He helplessly watched the flood inundate the whole city.*

【眼不见，心不烦】what the eye doesn't see, the heart doesn't grieve for

【眼馋】covet; eye covetously; envy

【眼瞅着】［方］① see sth happen ② soon; in no time

【眼底】① eye ground; funds ② in one's eyes; in sight：～检查 *funduscopy* /登山而望，全村景色尽

收～。*The top of the hill commands a panoramic view of the village.*
【眼底下】① right before one's eyes ② at the moment
【眼点】eyespot (of a protozoan); stigma
【眼福】the good fortune of seeing sth rare or wonderful: ～不浅 *be lucky enough to see sth* /饱～ *feast one's eyes on sth*
【眼高手低】have sharp eyes in criticizing others but clumsy hand in doing sth oneself; be fastidious but incompetent; have high goal but puny ability
【眼观六路,耳听八方】have sharp eyes and keen ears; be observant and alert; have one's eyes and ears open
【眼光】① eye: 恶毒的～ *an evil eye* /避开众人的～ *escape public gaze* ② sight; foresight; insight; vision: ～敏锐 *sharp sighted; sharp eyed* /～无神 *dull look* / ～远大 *far-sighted* /～短浅 *shortsighted* /政治～ *political foresight* /历史～ *historical perspective* ③ way of looking at things; viewpoint; out look
【眼红】① covet; be envious; be jealous ② eyes burning with fury; be furious: 仇人相见,分外～。*When enemies come face to face, their eyes burn with fury.*
【眼花】have dim eyesight; have blurred vision: 耳不聋眼不花 *(of an old person) be neither hard of hearing nor dim-sighted* /使人～的灯光 *dazzling lights* /～缭乱 *dazzled by looking at many things*
【眼疾手快】quick of eye and deft of hand
【眼尖】be sharp-eyed; have sharp eyes; have keen sight
【眼睑】【生理】eyelid
【眼见】soon; in no time: ～就要到秋天了。*It will be autumn here in no time.*
【眼见得】[方] (of sth unpleasant) be evident: 老人～不行了。*It's clear that the old man won't pull through.*
【眼角】corner of the eye; canthus
【眼睫毛】eyelash
【眼界】field of vision (or view); outlook: ～不广 *have a narrow outlook* /开阔～ *broaden one's outlook (or horizons)*
【眼镜】eyeglasses; glasses; spectacles: 一付近视～ *a pair of spectacles for nearsighted person* /戴～ *wear glasses* /～架 *rims (of spectacles); spectacles frame* /～蛇 *cobra*
【眼睛】eye: ～花 *daze* /眯起～ *narrow one's eyes* /眨～ *blink one's eyes*
【眼看】① soon; in a moment: 大雪～就要来了。*The snow is to start any moment.* ② watch helplessly; look on passively
【眼科】(department of) ophthalmology: ～学 *ophthalmology* /～医生 *oculist; ophthalmologist; eye-doctor* /～医院 *hospital of ophthalmology*
【眼快】be sharp-eyed; have sharp eyes; have keen sight
【眼眶】① eye socket; eyehole; orbit: ～里含着热泪 *with tears in one's eyes* ② rim of the eye: ～发黑 *have livid rings round one's eyes*
【眼泪】tears: 流～ *shed tears* /～汪汪 *having eyes damped with tears; tearful* /～哭干 *cry until one has no more tears to shed* /～如雨。*One's tears fell like rain.*
【眼力】① eyesight; vision: ～好(差) *have good (poor) eyesight* ② judgement; discrimination: 他～过人。*He's a man of excellent judgement.*
【眼里】in one's eyes; in one's view: ～有活 *see where there's work to be done; know where one can be of use* /同学们根本不把这点困难放在～。*The students think nothing of a difficulty like that.*
【眼帘】[书] eyes: 映入～ *come into view; greet the eye*
【眼量】perceptiveness
【眼明手快】quick of eye and deft of hand; sharp-eyed and deft-handed
【眼泡】upper eyelid: ～儿浮肿 *swollen eyes*
【眼皮】eyelid: 双～ *double-edged eyelid* /～底下 *under one's eye; under one's nose*
【眼皮子】① eyelid ② outlook; view: ～子高 *ambitious; conceited; hard to please* /～子浅 *short-sighted; shallow*
【眼前】① before one's eyes: ～之欢 *pleasure of the moment* /～亏 *trouble right before the eyes* /我们～是一片森林。*Before our eyes was a forest.* ② at the moment; at present; now: 只顾～利益 *think only of the immediate interests* /成功就在～。*Success is at hand.*
【眼球】eyeball
【眼圈】① eye socket; orbit: ～红 *verge of tears* ② rim of the eye /黑～ *livid rings round one's eyes*
【眼热】[口] cast covetous eyes at sth; eye sth covetously
【眼色】① a hint given with the eyes; a meaningful glance; wink: 使～ *tip sb the wink; wink at sb* /看某人的～行事 *take one's cue from sb* ② ability to act according to circumstances
【眼神】① expression in one's eyes: 她眼睛里露出悲伤的～。*A light of grief came into her eyes.* ② [方] eyesight: ～不好 *have poor eyesight*
【眼生】look unfamiliar
【眼屎】[方] gum (in the eyes)
【眼熟】look familiar: 这女孩看着很～。*The girl looks familiar.*
【眼跳】twitching of the eyelid
【眼窝】eye socket; eyehole, orbit
【眼下】at the moment; at present; now: ～正是春节,你怎么能离开呢? *It is Spring Festival at present; how can you leave now?*
【眼线】① eye-line: 描～ *paint eye-line; line the eyes* /～笔 *eye-liner* ② informer; snitch; scout
【眼药】medicament for the eyes; eyedrops: ～水 *eyedrops* /点～ *put drops in the eyes*
【眼影】eye-shadow
【眼晕】feel dizzy (owing to defective vision)
【眼罩儿】① eyeshade ② blinkers (fir a horse, donkey, etc.)
【眼睁睁】looking on helplessly or unfeelingly

【眼中钉,肉中刺】thorn in the flesh and sting in the eye
【眼中无人】haughty; having no respect for anyone; proud as a peacock
【眼珠子】① eyeball ② the apple of sb's eye
【眼拙】[套] used to indicate that the speaker forgets whether he has met sb before
偃 [书] ① fall on one's back; lie down: ~卧 *lie on one's back* ② cease; desist; stop: ~息 *rest; stop; cease*
【偃旗息鼓】① lower the banners and muffle the drums — cease all activities; roll up all banners and silence the drums ② be on a secret (and silent) march
【偃武修文】desist from military activities and encourage culture and education; abandon military career and be engaged in learning; give up the sword for the pen
演 ① develop; evolve ② deduce; elaborate: 推~ *deduce* ③ drill; practice: 操~ *drill; exercise* ④ perform; play; act; stage: ~电影 *show a film* /公~ *put on a public performance* /他~过周恩来。*He once played the part of Zhou Enlai.*
【演变】develop; evolve; change: 从猿到人的~ *evolution from ape to man* /局势的~ *development of the situation*
【演播】televise or broadcast performances: ~室 *television studio; studio* /~设备 *broadcast installation*
【演唱】sing(in a performance); act a part Beijing or provincial opera: ~京剧 *act in Beijing opera* /~会 *concert for singing or Chinese opera* /~豫剧 *act Henan opera*
【演出】perform; show; put on (a show): 登台~ *appear on the stage* /首场~ *first performance; first show* /~单位 *producer* /巡回~ *performance tour* /~开始。*The performance begins.*
【演化】① develop; evolve ② evolution
【演技】acting; stage performance: ~精湛 *excellent acting*/~一般 *ordinary acting*
【演讲】give a lecture; make or deliver a speech: ~比赛 *speech contest* /~人 *speaker; lecture* /~术 *elocution*
【演进】gradual progress; evolution
【演练】drill; practice: ~场 *drill ground* /~大厅 *drill hall*
【演示】demonstrate: ~法 *demonstration method*
【演说】deliver a speech; make an address: ~词 *text of a speech* /~术 *oratory; elocution*
【演算】perform mathematical calculations
【演替】succession: 植物的~ *succession of plants* /生命的~ *succession of life*
【演习】manoeuvre; exercise; drill; practice: 军事~ *military manoeuvre; war exercise* /防空~ *air defense exercise* /实弹~ *live ammunition manoeuvres* /消防~ *fire-fighting exercise*
【演戏】① put on a play; act in a play ② playact
【演义】historical novel; historical romance:《三国~》*The Romance of the Three Kingdoms*
【演艺】performing arts
【演绎】deduce; deduction; apriori: ~法 *the deductive method; deduction* /~性 *apriority* /~推理 *apriorism* /~主义 *deductivism*
【演员】actor or actress; performer; player: 戏曲~ *opera actor or actress* /哑剧~ *mime actor or actress* /电影~ *film (or movie) actor or actress* /相声~ *cross-talk performer* /喜剧~ *comedian* /舞蹈~ *dancer* /杂技~ *acrobat* /~表 *the cast*
【演奏】play a musical instrument in a performance; give an instrument performance: ~钢琴 *play the piano* /精湛的~ *excellent performance* /~家 *accomplished performer*

yàn

厌 ① be satisfied: be insatiably greedy: 贪得无~ *inordinately greedy* ② be fed up with; be bored with; be tired of: 吃~了 *be sick of eating sth* /看~了 *have seen more than enough of sth* ③ detest; be disgusted with; dislike: 喜新~旧 *love the new and loathe the old; be fickle in affection* /每个人都讨~她。*Everybody hates her.*
【厌烦】be sick of; be bored with: 感到~ *feel bored* /对什么事都~ *be tired of everything*
【厌恨】bitterly detest; loath; abhor
【厌倦】be weary of; be tired of: ~人世 *weary with human life* /~学习 *be weary of learning* /~婚姻 *be tired of marriage*
【厌腻】be bored with; be tired of; be fed up with: ~流言蜚语 *be tired of gossip; be fed up with rumors*
【厌弃】detest and reject; detest; loathe
【厌食】loss of appetite: ~症 *anorexia*
【厌世】be world-weary; be pessimistic
【厌恶】detest; abhor; abominate; be disgusted with: ~疗法 *an aversion therapy* /他的言辞实在令人~。*His words are simply disgusting.*
【厌学】be weary of studying
【厌战】be weary of war; be war-weary: ~情绪 *war-weariness*
砚 ① inkstone ② [旧] fellow student; classmate
【砚耕】make a living by writing
【砚台】inkstone
咽 swallow; devour: 狼吞虎~ *wolf down one's food; devour ravenously* /细嚼慢~ *chew carefully and swallow slowly* ~不下这口气 *unable to swallow an insult*
see also yān
【咽气】breathe one's last; die
彦 man of virtue and ability
【彦士】man of virtue and ability
艳 ① bright; fresh and attractive gorgeous; colourful; gaudy ② amorous; romantic: ~事 *love affair* ③ [书] admire; envy
【艳福】a man's good fortune in love affairs: 我们老

板很有～。*My boss has a lot of good fortune in love affairs.*

【艳红】bright red; scarlet: ～的阳光 *scarlet sunshine*

【艳丽】bright-coloured and beautiful; gorgeous: ～夺目 *of dazzling beauty* / 词藻～ *flowery diction*

【艳情】amorous; erotic: ～小说 *love novel*; *erotic fiction*

【艳如桃李】(of a woman) as beautiful as peach and plum blossoms — very beautiful: ～, 冷若冰霜 (*of a woman*) *as beautiful as peach and plum blossoms, but as cold as frost and ice*

【艳诗】erotic poetry

【艳史】love story; erotic adventures

【艳羡】[书] admire immensely; envy

【艳阳】① radiant sun ② bright sunny skies; bright spring day: ～天 *bright spring day*; *bright sunny skies*

晏 ① behind time; late: ～起 *get up late* ② ease and comfort ③ a surname

【晏驾】[旧] (of an emperor) pass away

唁 extend condolence

【唁电】telegraph or cable of condolence; message of condolence

【唁函】letter of condolence

宴 ① entertain at a banquet; fete: ～客 *entertain guests at a banquet*; *give a banquet* ② feast; banquet: 盛～ *a grand banquet*; *a magnificent feast* / 婚～ *wedding* (*or marriage*) *feast* ③ ease and comfort

【宴会】a banquet; feast; dinner party: 答谢～ *reciprocal banquet* / 欢迎～ *welcome banquet*

【宴请】entertain (to dinner); fete: ～贵宾 *entertain distinguished guests* / 当她们结婚时, ～了很多宾客。*They entertained lots of distinguished guests when they married.*

【宴席】banquet; feast

验 ① examine; check; test: 考～ *test*; *trial* / ～货 *check goods* / ～尿 *test the urine* / ～护照 *examine a passport* ② prove effective; produce the expected result: 屡试屡～ *prove successful in every test* / 应～ (*of prediction*) *come true* / 灵～ efficacious; effective; right; accurate ③ intended effect; desired result

【验钞机】a machine for checking paper money for counterfeits

【验方】proved recipe

【验关】customs examination

【验光】optometry

【验核】check; verify

【验讫】checked; examined

【验枪】inspect arms

【验尸】【律】postmortem; autopsy: ～官 *coroner*

【验收】check and accept; check before acceptance; check upon delivery: 逐项～ *check item by item before acceptance* / ～试验 *acceptance test* / ～合格证 *acceptance certificate* / ～质量标准 *acceptable quality level* / 你见到～单了吗? *Have you seen the receipt?*

【验算】【数】check computation

【验血】blood test

【验证】test and verify: ～理论 *test a theory* / ～荷载 *proof load* / ～实验 *demonstration test*

谚 proverb; saying; adage; saw

【谚语】proverb; saying; adage; saw

堰 weir; dam; barrage

【堰坝式水电站】barrage power station

【堰塞湖】barrier lake

雁 wild goose; goose

【雁过拔毛】pluck up feathers of the wild goose whenever it passes by — take advantage of every opportunity to benefits oneself

【雁行成行】wild geese fly in orderly formation — used to refer to brothers

【雁杳鱼沉】without news or letters

【雁影纷飞】separation of brothers

【雁阵】formation of wild geese in flight

焰 flame; blaze: 烈～ *blazing* (*or raging*) *flames*

【焰火】fireworks

【焰色反应】flame reaction

酽 (of tea, etc.) thick; strong: 你给我的那杯茶太～了。*The tea you gave me is too strong.*

餍 ① have enough food; be satiated ② satisfy; gratify

【餍足】[书] (of people's desire) be satisfied

燕 swallow: 一群飞～ *a flock of swallows* / 一～不成夏。*One swallow does not make a summer.*

see also yān

【燕巢幕上】a swallow nesting on a canopy — precarious; be in a very precarious situation; be in great peril

【燕好】[书] (of husband and wife) be very fond of each other; be happily married: 百年～ *remain a devoted couple to the end of their lives*

【燕麦】【植】oats

【燕鸥】【动】tern

【燕雀】brambling bramble finch

【燕雀安知鸿鹄之志】how could a sparrow understand the ambitions of a swan — how can a common man read the mind of a great man

【燕雀处堂】swallows and sparrows nesting in a hall, unmindful of the spreading fire — unaware of one's danger

【燕尾服】swallowtail; swallow-tailed coat; tailcoat

【燕窝】edible bird's nest

【燕语莺声】scene of spring with birds chirping merrily — the soft and charming voices of girls

【燕子】swallow

赝 [书] counterfeit; fake; spurious

【赝本】spurious edition or copy

【赝币】［书］counterfeit coin
【赝品】art forgery

yāng

央[1] entreat; beg; earnestly ask: ～人帮忙 *entreat sb for help*; *ask a favour of sb* / ～人说情 *ask sb to speak on one's behalf*; *ask sb to put in a word for someone*

央[2] ［书］end; finish: 夜未～。*The night is not yet spent.*

央[3] centre; in the middle

【央告】beg; plead; implore

【央求】beg; plead; implore: ～宽恕 *beseech for forgiveness*; *beg for mercy* / 那个小孩～妈妈,让他出去玩会儿。*The little child begged her mother for going out to play.*

【央托】entreat sb to do sth; entrust

泱

【泱泱】［书］① (of waters) vast ② grand; great; magnificent; glorious: ～大国 *a great and proud country*; *great and impressive country*

殃 ① calamity; disaster; misfortune: 遭～ *suffer (or meet with) disaster* ② bring disaster to: 祸国～民 *bring calamity to the country and the people*

【殃及】bring disaster to: ～无辜 *involve the innocent in the trouble*; *trouble involves the innocent people*

【殃及池鱼】bring disaster to the fish in the moat — bring disaster to the innocent people; misfortune befalls the fish in the moat: 城门失火,～。*When the city gate catches fire, the fish in the moat made victims — innocent people nearby get hurt when there is a trouble.*

秧 ① seedling; sprout: 树～ *tree seedling* / 黄瓜～儿 *cucumber sprout* ② rice seedling: 插～ *transplant rice seedlings* / 育～ *grow (or raise) rice seedlings* ③ vine: 白薯～ *sweet potato vine* / 瓜～ *melon (or squash) vine* ④ young; fry: 鱼～ *young fish*; *fry* / 猪～ *piglet*

【秧歌】yangge (dance), a popular dance: 扭～ *do the yangge*

【秧鸡】water rail

【秧龄】the length of time rice seedlings grow in seedling beds until they are transplanted

【秧苗】rice shoot; rice seedling

【秧田】rice seedling bed

【秧子】type or sort of person: 奴才～ *flunkey*; *lackey* / 她从小就是个病～。*She was a sick person when she was young.*

yáng

扬[1] ① raise; hoist: ～手 *raise one's hand* / ～帆 *hoist a sail*; *lift a sail* / ～鞭催马 *flourish the whip to urge on the horse*; *whip one's horse on* ② throw up and scatter; winnow: ～谷去糠 *winnow the chaff from the grain* ③ spread; make known: 宣～ *propagate*; *publicize* / 颂～ *extol*; *laud* / 发～ *develop*; *carry on*

扬[2] ① Yangzhou city in Jiangsu Province ② (Yáng) a surname

【扬长避短】make best use of the advantages and bypass the disadvantage; show one's strong points and hide one's weaknesses; maximize favourable factors and minimize unfavourable ones

【扬长补短】foster one's strengths to make up for one's weaknesses

【扬长而去】stalk off; swagger off

【扬场】【农】winnowing ～机 winnowing machine; winnower

【扬程】【水】lift: 高～ *high lift* / 高～水泵 *high-lift pump* / 高～抽水站 *high-lift pumping station*

【扬帆】［书］hoist the sails; set sail

【扬眉吐气】feel proud and elated

【扬名】make a name for oneself; become famous: ～天下 *become world-famous*; *become known throughout the country*

【扬弃】①【哲】sublate; develop what is useful and discard what is not ② discard; abandon

【扬琴】dulcimer

【扬清激浊】bring in fresh, clean water and drain away the mud-eradicate evil and usher in good

【扬声】① raise one's voice ② make public; disclose ③［书］make a name for oneself; become famous

【扬声器】loudspeaker

【扬水】pump up water: ～泵 *lift pump* / ～站 *pumping station*

【扬汤止沸】try to stop water from boiling by skimming it off and pouring it back — half solution; ineffective measure; apply a palliative

【扬言】threaten (to take action); boast

【扬扬】with great satisfaction; triumphantly; complacently: ～得意 *be immensely proud with oneself*; *look triumphant* / ～自得 *be very pleased with oneself*; *be complacent*

【扬誉】become famous; make a name for oneself: ～全球 *become world-famous*

【扬子鳄】【动】Chinese alligator

羊 sheep: 公～ *ram* / 绵～ *sheep* / 母～ *ewe* / 山～ *goat* / 小～ *lamb* / ～叫 *baa*; *bleat* / 一群～ *a flock of sheep* / 放～ *graze sheep*

【羊肠】sheep's intestine or gut: ～线 *catgut (suture)* / ～小道 *a narrow winding trail*; *a meandering footpath*

【羊齿】【植】bracken; fern

【羊肚儿手巾】［方］towel

【羊羔】lamb
【羊倌】shepherd
【羊毫】writing brush made of goat's hair
【羊角】ram's horn：~锤 *claw hammer* / ~面包 *croissant*; *crescent-shaped roll*
【羊角风】epilepsy
【羊圈】sheepfold; sheep pen; sheep cot
【羊毛】sheep's wool; wool; fleece：剪~ *shear a sheep* / ~衫 *woolen sweater*; *cardigan* / ~套衫 *pullover* / ~袜 *woolen socks or stockings* / ~脂 *lanolin*; *wool fat*
【羊毛出在羊身上】after all, the wool still comes from the sheep's back; benefits come, after all, from a price one has paid; in the long run, whatever you're given, you pay for it
【羊膜】【生理】amnion
【羊排】mutton chop; lamb chop
【羊皮】sheepskin：~手套 *sheepskin glove* / ~纸 *parchment*
【羊群里头出骆驼】stand out like a camel in a flock of sheep
【羊绒】cashmere：~衫 *cashmere sweater*
【羊肉】mutton：~串 *mutton cubes roasted on a skewer*; *shish kebab*; *shashlik*
【羊水】amniotic fluid
【羊驼】alpaca：~毛 *alpaca fibre*
【羊质虎皮】a sheep in a tiger's skin — outwardly strong, inwardly weak

阳 ① the sun：骄~似火 *a scorching sun beating down* / 灿烂的朝~ *bright rising sun* / 夕~ *the setting sun* / 向~的房子 *a house exposed to the sun* ② south of a hill or north of a river ③ (in Chinese philosophy, medicine, etc.) yang, the masculine or positive principle in nature：三~开泰 *three yang make it very positive* ④ male genitals ⑤ in relief; convex ⑥ open; overt ⑦ belonging to this world; concerned with living beings ⑧【物】positive：~电荷 *positive charges* ⑨ (Yáng) a surname
【阳春】spring (season)：~白雪 *Spring Snow* (*melodies of the elite in the State of Chu*) *highbrow art and literature* / ~三月 *third lunar month in late spring* / ~面 *noodles in a simple sauce*
【阳电】positive electricity
【阳刚】masculine; manly; virile：~之气 *masculinity*; *manliness*; *virility* / ~之美 *the beauty of masculine vigor*
【阳奉阴违】comply in appearance but oppose in heart; comply in public but oppose in private
【阳沟】open drain; ditch
【阳关道】a broad highway; a broad road; thoroughfare：你走你的~，我过我的独木桥。*You take the open road*; *I'll cross the log bridge — you go your way*, *I'll go mine.*
【阳光】sunlight; sunshine; sunbeam
【阳极】【电】positive pole; positive electrode; anode：~板 *positive plate* / ~栅 *anode grid* / ~射线 *positive ray*
【阳间】this (human) world
【阳离子】【物】positive ion; cation
【阳历】① solar calendar ② the Gregorian calendar
【阳平】rising tone (the second of the four tones in modern standard Chinese pronunciation)
【阳畦】【农】seed bed with windbreaks; cold bed
【阳伞】parasol; sunshade
【阳世】this world; human world
【阳台】balcony; veranda
【阳痿】【医】sexual impotence
【阳性】①【医】positive：~反应 *positive reaction* ②【语】masculine gender
【阳虚】【中医】deficiency of yang; lack of vital energy

杨 ① poplar ② a surname
【杨柳】① poplar and willow ② willow
【杨梅】red bayberry; fruits of red bayberry
【杨树】poplar
【杨枝鱼】pipefish

旸 ［书］① sunrise ② fine; sunny
【旸谷】［书］place where the sun was said to rise in ancient books

佯 pretend; feign; sham：~死 *feign death*; *play dead* / 他太聪明了，~作什么也不知道。*He was so clever that he pretended to know nothing.*
【佯嗔】pretend to be angry or displeased
【佯称】claim or allege falsely; lie; feign
【佯狂】［书］feign madness; pretend to be mad
【佯言】［书］allege falsely; tell lies; lie; pretend：~不知情 *pretend ignorance*
【佯装】［书］pretend; feign：~惊诧 *pretend to be surprised* / 他~没有看到任何人，马上离开了。*He pretended to see nobody*, *and went away.*

疡 ① sore ② ulcer

洋¹ ① vast; multitudinous：汪~大海 *boundless sea* ② foreign：~腔怪调 *exotic accent*; *outlandish way of talking* / 留~ *study abroad* / 崇~媚外 *warship and have blind faith in foreign things* / ~房 *wes-style house* ③ modern：~办法 *modern methods*

洋² ① ocean：太平~ *the Pacific Ocean* / 四大~ *the four oceans* ② silver dollar or coin
【洋白菜】cabbage
【洋博士】foreign-trained Ph. D
【洋财】an unexpected big fortune; windfall
【洋菜】agar
【洋场】metropolis infested with foreign adventures
【洋车】①［口］rickshaw：拉~ *pull a rickshaw* / 拉~的 *rickshaw man* ②［方］bicycle
【洋瓷】enamel：~器皿 *enamelware*
【洋葱】onion
【洋地黄】digitalis (a Chinese medicine)
【洋服】western-style clothes
【洋鬼子】foreign devil (a derogatory term mainly used in pre-liberation China for foreign invaders)
【洋行】foreign firm (in pre-liberation China)

Y

【洋灰】cement
【洋火】[口] matches
【洋货】foreign goods; imported goods
【洋气】① foreign flavour; western style ② foreign; outlandish; stylish
【洋钱】[口] silver dollar
【洋人】foreigner; outlander
【洋娃娃】(Western-style) doll
【洋为中用】make foreign things serve China; adapt foreign things for Chinese use
【洋务】management of foreign affairs in the late Qing Dynasty: ~运动 *Westernization Movement*
【洋相】used in the set phrase: 出~ *make a spectacle of sb; make an exhibition of sb* /他今天真是~百出。*He really made a spectacle of himself today.*
【洋洋】① numerous; copious: ~万言 *run to ten thousand words; a flood of words, be very lengthy* /~洒洒 *(of an article or talk) fluent and copious; voluminous; of great length* /~大观 *an impressive array of; a great and impressive sight* ② complacent; self-satisfied: ~得意 *proud and happy* /~自得 *be self-satisfied; be complacent*
【洋溢】be permeated with; brim with: ~着友好的感情 *be permeated with a friendly feeling* /热情~的讲话 *a speech brimming with warm feeling*
【洋装】① western style clothes ② western way of bookbinding

烊 [方] melt; dissolve

yǎng

仰 ① face upward: 前俯后~ *bend forwards and backwards* /~着睡 *sleep on one's back* /~头 *raise one's head; raise one's eyes* ② admire; respect; look up to: 瞻~ *pay one's respect to* /敬~ *revere; venerate* /信~ *believe in* ③ rely on ④ respectfully ⑤ (Yǎng) a surname
【仰八叉】[口] (fall) on one's back: 摔了个~ *fell flat on one's back*
【仰角】[数] angle of elevation
【仰面】face upward
【仰慕】admire; look up to; hold in high esteem: ~大作 *look up to your great works* /~英雄 *admire hero* /人们很~他的人品。*People admire his character very much.*
【仰视】look up: ~天空 *look up at the sky*
【仰首】[书] raise one's head : ~伸眉 *hold one's head high and smooth out one's eyebrow — feeling proud and elated*
【仰天】look up to heaven
【仰望】① look up at: ~星空 *look up at the starlit sky* ② [书] respectfully seek guidance or help from; look up to
【仰卧】lie on one's back; lie supine: ~起坐 *sit-ups*
【仰屋兴叹】look up at the ceiling and lament — be at the end of one's wits
【仰泳】[体] backstroke
【仰仗】count on; rely on; look to sb for support

养 ① support; provide for ② raise; keep; grow: ~鸭 *raise ducks* /~鸟 *keep pet birds* /她在家里~了很多花。*She grows many flowers in her home.* ③ give birth to: 她女儿~了个儿子。*Her daughter gave birth to a boy.* ④ form; acquire; cultivate ⑤ nourish; rest; convalesce; recuperate one's health; heal: ~伤 *take rest and nourishment to heal a wound* /疗~ *recuperate; convalesce* /调~ *be nursed back to health* ⑥ let (one's hair) grow ⑦ maintain; keep in good repair ⑧ refine; cultivate ⑨ foster; adoptive: ~父(母) *foster father (mother)* /~子(女) *adopted son (daughter)*
【养兵】maintain or keep an army: ~千日,用兵一时 *maintain an army for a thousand days for an hour's service; armies are to be maintained for years but used for a single day*
【养病】take rest and nourishment to regain one's health; recuperate: 他去海边~了。*He went to the seaside to recuperate.*
【养蚕】rearing of silkworm; sericulture; silkworm breeding
【养地】increase soil fertility (by fertilization, crop rotation, etc.)
【养儿防老】bring up children for one's old age; children are reared to be a support in old age
【养分】nutrient
【养蜂】raise or keep bees; engage in apiculture: ~场 *apiary; bee farm* /~业 *apiculture; beekeeping*
【养汉】(of a woman) commit adultery
【养护】① maintain; conserve: 道路~ *road maintenance* /设备~ *equipment maintenance* /生物资源~ *conservation of living resources* ② curing: 混凝土~ *concrete curing*
【养活】[口] ① support; feed ② raise (animals): 他家~了只狗。*His family raises a dog.* ③ give birth to: ~孩子 *have a baby*
【养鸡场】chicken run; chicken farm
【养家活口】support one's family
【养精蓄锐】conserve energy and build up strength; get oneself well-prepared; conserve one's strength for
【养老】① provide for the aged ② live out one's life in retirement: ~保险 *endowment insurance* /~金 *old-age pension* /~送终 *look after one's parents in their old age and give them a proper burial after they die* /~院 *home for the old*
【养廉】[书] (of government officials) cultivate honesty and integrity
【养料】nutriment; nourishment
【养路】maintain a road or railway: ~费 *road toll; road maintenance expense*
【养马场】horse ranch
【养伤】nurse one's injuries or wounds
【养神】rest to attain mental tranquility; repose: 闭目~ *sit in repose with one's eyes closed*
【养生】care for life; conserve one's vital powers;

preserve one's health; keep in good health: ～之道 *way to stay healthy*; *way to maintain good health*
【养性】cultivate one's nature
【养鱼】fish-framing; fish culture: ～池 *fishpond* / ～业 *fish-raising industry*
【养育】bring up; rear: ～子女 *bring up children*
【养殖】breed or cultivate (aquatics): ～海带 *cultivate kelp* / 淡水～ *freshwater aquiculture* / ～珍珠 *cultured pearl*
【养殖业】breeding industry; fish-breeding or poultry raising; aquiculture
【养尊处优】enjoy a high position and a life of ease and comfort; revel in a high position and indulge in comfort; live in clover

氧 oxygen

【氧吧】oxygen bar (for oxygen therapy)
【氧合作用】【生理】oxygenation
【氧化】【化】oxidize; oxidate: ～作用 *oxidation* / ～态 *oxidation state*; *oxidation number* / ～铁 *ferric oxide* / ～物 *oxide*
【氧气】oxygen: ～炼钢 *oxygen steel making* / ～袋 *oxygen bag* / ～面具 *oxygen mask* / ～瓶 *oxygen cylinder* / ～枪 *oxygen lance* / ～罩 *oxygen mask*

痒 itch; tickle: 搔到～处 *scratch where it itches — hit the nail on the head* / 无关痛～ *irrelevant*; *of no consequence*

【痒痒】[口] itch; tickle

yàng

怏

【怏然】[书] ① unhappy; gloomy ② self-important; arrogant
【怏怏】disgruntled; sullen: ～不乐 *disgruntled*; *depressed*; *sad and gloomy* / ～度日 *mope time away* / ～而归 *return in a very melancholy mood*; *come back sadly*

样 ① pattern; appearance; shape: 花～ *pattern* / 模～ *appearance*; *pattern* / 式～ *design*; *style* ② sample; model; pattern: 货～ *sample good*; *sample* / 鞋～ *shoe pattern* / 取～化验 *take a sample for examination and test* ③ [量] kind; type; variety: 两～礼物 *two kinds of presents* / 请你把那几～东西给我拿来。*Please fetch several things for me.* ④ trend; situation: 看～天儿要下雨了. *It looks like rain.*

【样板】① sample plate ② templet ③ model; example: ～戏 (*a term used during the Cultural Revolution*) *model Beijing opera*
【样本】① sample book ② sample; specimen
【样稿】sample manuscript or typescript
【样机】【航】① prototype ② sample machine
【样件】sample
【样款】pattern; style; sample
【样片】(of a film) rushes; work print; (of TV programme) pilot film; sample film
【样品】sample (product); specimen
【样式】pattern; type; style; form: ～典雅 *an elegant style*
【样书】sample book; specimen book
【样图】master drawing
【样样】every kind; each and every; all: ～都会 *can do everything*; *be good at every thing* / ～照办 *follow sb in every detail* / ～想懂～稀松。*Jack of all trades and master of none.*
【样张】【印】specimen page
【样子】① appearance; shape ② manner; air ③ sample; model; pattern: 衣服～ *clothes pattern* / 不要介意, 做出～来给大家看看! *Don't mind it and set an example for us!* ④ [口] tendency; likelihood; inclination

恙 [书] ailment; illness: 安然无～ *safe and sound* / 偶染微～ *feel slightly indisposed*

【恙虫】【动】tsutsugamushi mite
【恙螨】chigger; scrub mite; harvest mite

漾 ① ripple: 荡～ *ripple*; *undulate* ② brim over; overflow: 桶里的水直往外～。*The water in the bucket is full to brim over.*

【漾动】ripple; flutter;
【漾奶】(of a baby) throw up milk
【漾漾】rippling; full of ripples

yāo

幺 ① one (used orally for the numeral "一") ② [方] youngest: ～叔 *youngest uncle* / 在家里她是个～妹。*She is a youngest sister in her family.* ③ [书] small; thin: ～小 *small*; *petite* ④ (Yāo) a surname

【幺蛾子】[方] trick; mischief; wicked idea
【幺麽】[书] small; petty; little: ～小丑 *insignificant wretch*

夭[1] die young

夭[2] [书] luxuriant; exuberant

【夭矫】[书] twisted and robust
【夭殇】[书] die young
【夭寿】die young; short-lived
【夭亡】die young
【夭折】① die young ② stop half way; come to a premature end: 试验中途～了。*The test stopped half way.*

吆 bawl; shout; cry out

【吆喊】cry out; call
【吆喝】① cry out; call; shout: 他一～, 大家都跑了。*Everybody ran away at his call.* ② cry one's wares: 沿街～叫卖 *cry out for customers along the street* ③ loudly urge on (an animal)
【吆唤】cry out; call

约 [口] weigh in a balance (or on a scale): 给我～几斤苹果。*Weigh me several jīn of apples.*

妖 ① monster; goblin; demon; evil sprat: 照~镜 *monster-revealing mirror* / 降~伏魔 *vanquish demons and monsters* / 兴~作怪 *stir up troubles* ② evil and fraudulent ③ coquettish; seductive ④ [书] beautiful; charming

【妖道】Taoist sorcerer or witch

【妖风】evil wind; noxious trend

【妖怪】monster; bogy; goblin; demon

【妖精】① evil spirit; demon ② seductress; siren

【妖里妖气】seductive; sexy: 打扮得~的 *be seductively dressed*

【妖媚】seductively charming; bewitching; sexy

【妖魔】evil spirit; demon: ~鬼怪 *demons and ghosts; monsters of every description; all forces of evil*

【妖孽】[书] ① person or event associated with evil or misfortune ② evildoer ③ evil spirit; demon

【妖娆】[书] enchanting; fascinating; bewitching

【妖人】sorcerer; enchanter

【妖声妖气】coquettish; bewitching; witchery; sexy in an evil way

【妖术】sorcery; witchcraft; black art

【妖妄】fantastic; absurd; weird: 不要相信它,都是一些~之说。*Don't believe it; what they said was fallacy.*

【妖物】evil spirit; monster

【妖言】heresy; fallacy: ~惑众 *delude people with fabulous stories; spread fallacies to deceive people*

【妖艳】pretty and coquettish

【妖冶】pretty and flirtatious

要 ① demand; ask: ② force; compel; coerce ③ a surname

see also yào

【要求】① ask; demand; require; claim; call for: ~增加工资 *demand a raise in pay* / ~发言 *ask to be heard; ask for the floor* / 严格~自己 *be strict with oneself; set high standard for oneself* / ~赔偿损失 *claim compensation for one's loss* ② requirement; demand; claim: 质量~ *quality requirements* / 合理的~ *reasonable request* / 领土~ *territorial claims* / 提出~ *make a demand; present a request* / 满足~ *fulfill the requirements* / 符合~ *conform the requirements* / 答应~ *grant a demand*

【要挟】coerce; put pressure on; threaten: 受到绑架者的~ *be blackmailed by the kidnappers* / 以死相~ *threaten sb with death* / 对小国进行武力~ *coerce small nations with force*

腰 ① waist; the small of the back: 齐~深 *waist-deep; up to the waist* / 弯~ *bend down; stoop* / ~酸腿疼 *aching back and legs* / 扭了~ *sprain one's back muscles* / 两手叉~ *with one's hands on one's hips; akimbo* / 拦~抱住 *seize sb round the middle* ② waist (of a garment): 裤~ *waist of trousers* ③ pocket: 我告诉你,我~里还有些钱。*I told you that I still got some money in my pocket.* ④ middle: 半山~ *halfway up the mountain* ⑤ (Yāo) a surname

【腰板儿】① back: 直起~ *straighten one's back* ② physique; build

【腰包】purse; pocket: 他接受贿赂肥了自己的~。*He lined his purse by taking bribes.* / 你们今天吃饭谁掏的~? *Who paid for your dinner today?*

【腰部】waist; the small of the back

【腰缠万贯】be very rich

【腰带】belt; girdle; waistband

【腰杆子】① back: 挺起~ *straighten one's back — be confident and unafraid* ②backing; support: ~硬 *have strong backing; have powerful support*

【腰鼓】waist drum: ~舞 *waist drum dance*

【腰果】cashew nut; cashew: ~树 *cashew (tree)* / ~仁 *cashew nut*

【腰花】scalloped pork; lamb kidneys: 炒~ *stir fried kidneys*

【腰身】waistline; waist; waist measurement: ~细 *have a slender waist* / 胖得~都没了 *too fat to have no waist*

【腰酸背痛】have a sore waist and an aching back be aching all over

【腰痛】【医】lumbago

【腰围】① waistline; waist measurement ② girdle

【腰眼】either side of the small of the back

【腰斩】① cutting sb in half at the waist ② cut sth in half

【腰肢】waist: ~纤细 *have a slim waist*

【腰椎】【生理】lumbar vertebra: ~穿刺 *lumbar puncture*

【腰子】[口] kidney

邀 ① invite; ask; request: 我~请了几个亲戚周末来我们家参观。*I ask some relatives over for visiting my home on weekend.* ② gain; seek: ~准 *seek approval; ask for permission* ③ intercept: 举兵~讨 *send troops on an intercept mission*

【邀宠】try to win sb's favour; curry favour with sb

【邀功】[书] take credit for someone else's achievements: ~请赏 *take credit and seek rewards for someone else's achievements*

【邀集】invite to meet together; call together: ~有关人士讨论下一步局势。*People concerned are invited here to discuss the future situation.*

【邀买人心】buy popular support; court popularity

【邀请】invite: 应某人的~ *at sb's invitation* / 接受~ *accept an invitation* / ~国 *host country* / ~赛 *invitational tournament* / ~信 *letter of invitation*

【邀赏】ask to be rewarded for service rendered

yáo

尧 ① Yao, a legendary monarch and model for all rulers in ancient China ② (Yáo) surname

【尧舜】Yao and Shun, legendary sage kings in ancient China; ancient sages

【尧天舜日】the days of Yao and Shun — the golden age of remote antiquity; times of peace and prosperity; good old days

肴 meat and fish dishes: 佳~ *delicious dishes* / 酒~ *wine and dishes* / 菜~ *vegetable and*

meat dishes

【肴肉】cured pork; salted meat

【肴馔】[书] sumptuous courses at a meal

窑 ① kiln: 砖瓦~ *brick kiln* / 石灰~ *limekiln* ② pit: 小煤~ *small coal pit* ③ cave dwelling ④ [方] brothel

【窑洞】cave dwelling

【窑姐儿】[方] prostitute

【窑子】[方] brothel

谣 ① ballad; rhyme: 童~ *children's rhyme* / 他喜欢听民~。*He likes listening popular verse.* ② rumour: 你又造~了。*You start a rumour again.*

【谣传】① rumour; hearsay ② it is rumoured that; according to hearsay

【谣俗】[书] customs and habits; folkways

【谣言】rumour; unfounded report; gossip: 散布~ *spread (or circulate) rumours* / 老师正在追查~的来源。*The teacher is tracing the rumour to its source.*

摇 shake; waver; rock; sway: ~船 *row a boat; scull a boat* / ~铃 *ring a bell* / ~扇子 *wave a fan* / 动~人心 *sway the minds of men*

【摇摆】sway; swing; vacillate: ~不定 *swing to and fro; chop and change; vacillate* / 左右~ *vacillate now to the left, now to the right* / ~舞 *swing; rock and all rock* / ~乐 *swing; swing music*

【摇臂】【机】rocker arm: ~轴 *rocker shaft* / ~钻床 *radial drilling machine*

【摇床】【矿】table

【摇唇鼓舌】flap one's lips and beat one's tongue — speak evil of others; engage in loose talk (to stir up trouble)

【摇荡】rock; sway

【摇动】① wave; shake: ~花束 *wave the bouquets* ② sway; rock

【摇滚乐】rock and roll; rock (music)

【摇撼】give a violent shake to; shake to the root; rock: 大风怒吼, ~着屋顶。*The roaring wind rattled the window violently.*

【摇晃】rock; sway; shake: 树影~ *swaying shadow of trees* / 这床有点~。*The bed is a bit rickety (or shaky).*

【摇奖】lottery

【摇篮】cradle: ~曲 *cradle-song; lullaby* / 东方文明的~ *the cradle of Eastern Civilization* / 扼杀在~中 *strangle sth in the cradle*

【摇旗呐喊】wave flags and shout battle cries; drum up support; bang the drum for sb

【摇钱树】a legendary tree that sheds coins when shaken; money tree; a ready source of money

【摇纱机】【纺】reeling frame

【摇身一变】[贬] give oneself a shake and change into another form; suddenly change one's identity

【摇手】① shake one's hand in admonition of disapproval ② handle

【摇头】shake one's head

【摇头摆尾】shake the head and wag the tail — assume an air of complacency

【摇头晃脑】wag one's head — look pleased with oneself; assume an air of self-approbation or self-satisfaction

【摇尾乞怜】[贬] wag the tail ingratiatingly; beg like a dog for mercy

【摇摇欲坠】tottering; crumbling; on the verge of collapse: ~的老房子 *tottering old house* / ~的政府 *crumbling government*

【摇曳】flicker; sway: 灯光~。*The light is flickering.*

【摇椅】rocking chair

遥 [书] distant; remote; far: 路~知马力。*Distance tests a horse's stamina.*

【遥测】remote monitoring; telemetering: 空间~ *space telemetry* / ~计 *telemeter* / ~器 *remote detector* / ~术 *telemetry* / ~温度计 *telethermometer* / ~地震学 *teleseismology*

【遥感】【电】remote sensing: 红外~ *infrared remote sensing* / ~仪器 *remote sensing instrument* / ~卫星 *remote sensing satellite*

【遥控】remote control; telecontrol: ~机器人 *teleoperator* / ~开关 *teleswitch* / ~器 *remote controller* / ~车 *remote-control car* / ~力学 *telemechanics*

【遥望】look into the distance; look far ahead: ~星空 *look up into the star-studded sky*

【遥相呼应】echo each other at a distance; chime in from afar; coordinate with each other from afar

【遥想】① recall; recollect; reminisce: ~当年 *reminisce about the good old days* ② think of the future; envisage

【遥遥】① far away; a long way off: ~相对 *stand fart facing each other* / ~领先 *be far ahead; hold a safe lead* / ~无期 *far away and not within the foreseeable future* ② remote; far into the future

【遥远】distant; remote; faraway: ~的年代 *remote past* / 路途~ *a long journey; a long way to go*

【遥瞻】[书] look far: ~未来 *look far into the future*

瑶 [书] ① precious jade: 琼~ *fine jade* ② precious; wonderful

【瑶池】Jasper Lake, a legendary place where a fair queen lives

【瑶琴】fiddle inlaid with jade

【瑶族】Yao nationality

yǎo

杳 [书] too far away to be accessible:

【杳渺】[书] remote and deep

【杳然】[书] totally silent; without a trace

【杳无音信】there has been no news whatsoever about sb; no word has come from someone

【杳无踪迹】disappear without a trace; vanish

咬 ① bite; snap at; gnaw: ~~牙干下去 *go at it with set (or clenched) teeth* / 爱叫的狗不~人。*Barking dogs seldom bite.* ② grip; bite ③ (of a dog) bark ④ incriminate another person (usu. innocent) when blamed or interrogated：反～一口 *make a countercharge against one's accuser* / 不要～好人。*Don't implicate the innocent.* ⑤ [方] corrode (metals); irritate (the skin) ⑥ pronounce; articulate; enunciate：～字清楚 *enunciate clearly* ⑦ follow closely; close in; advance on ⑧ be fastidious (about the use of words)

【咬耳朵】[口] whisper in sb's ear; whisper

【咬紧牙关】grit (or clench) one's teeth; be determined; endure with dogged will：他～等待着结果。*He gritted his teeth and waited the result.*

【咬啮】gnaw：悔恨正～着她的心。*Regrets were gnawing at her heart.*

【咬舌儿】① lisp ② lisper

【咬文嚼字】pay excessive attention to wording

【咬牙】① grit (or clench, gnash) one's teeth (out of indignation or agony)：恨得直～ *gnash one's teeth in hatred* / ～切齿 *gnash one's teeth* ② grind one's teeth (in sleep)

【咬住】① bite into; grip with one's teeth ② grip; take firm hold of; refuse to let go of：紧紧～敌人 *be close at the heel of the enemy*

【咬字儿】pronounce; articulate：～清楚 *clear articulation or enunciation*

舀 ladle out; spoon up; scoop up：～水 *ladle out water*

【舀子】dipper; ladle; scoop

窈 [书] ① deep; profound ② dim

【窈冥】① deep; profound ② dim; dusky

【窈窕】[书] ① (of a woman) gentle and graceful：～淑女 *graceful fair maiden* / 他妻子的身材～。*Her wife has a graceful figure.* ② (of a place or landscape) deep and quiet; secluded：山涧～ *deep mountain stream*

yào

药 ① medicine; drug; remedy：西～ *western medicine* / 中～ *traditional Chinese medicine* / 草～ *herbal medicine* / 特效～ *specific medicine* / 丸～ *pill of Chinese medicine* / 汤～ *decoction of medicinal ingredients* / 膏～ *plaster* / 补～ *tonic* / 安眠～ *sleeping pill* / 止疼～ *pain killer* / 退热～ *antipyretic* / 服～ *take medicine* / 开～ *prescribe a medicine* / 配～ *(of a pharmacist) make up a prescription* / 抓～ *have a prescription filled* ② certain chemicals：火～ *gun-power* / 炸～ *explosive*; *dynamite* / 农～ *farm chemical*; *pesticide*; *insecticide* / 耗子～ *rat-poison* / 杀虫～ *insecticide*; *pesticide* ③ [书] cure with medicine：不可救～ *incurable*; *beyond cure*; *incorrigible* ④ kill with poison：～死人 *kill a man with poison*

【药补】build up one's health by taking tonic

【药材】medicinal materials; crude drugs

【药草】medicinal herbs

【药茶】herb tea; medicated tea

【药厂】pharmaceutical factory or plant

【药单】(medical) prescription

【药典】pharmacopoeia

【药店】drugstore; chemist's shop; pharmacy

【药方】prescription：医生给她开了个～。*The doctor wrote out a prescription.*

【药房】① drugstore; chemist's shop; pharmacy ② hospital pharmacy; dispensary

【药费】expenses for medicine

【药粉】(medicinal) powder

【药膏】plaster; ointment; salve

【药罐子】① a pot for decocting herbal medicine ② a chronic patient

【药害】environmental damage caused by improper use of insecticides

【药剂】medicament; drug：～师 *pharmacist*; *chemist*; *druggist* / ～学 *pharmaceutics*; *pharmacy*

【药检】drug test

【药劲儿】efficacy of a drug (or medicine)

【药酒】medicinal liquor

【药具】medical instrument

【药力】efficacy of a drag; efficacy of medicine：～没有发作。*The drug is not taking effect.*

【药棉】absorbent cotton

【药捻子】a slender roll of medicated paper of gauze; medical wick

【药农】a peasant who cultivates or collects medicinal herbs; medicinal herb grower or collector; herbalist

【药片】(medicinal) tablet

【药品】medicines and chemical reagents

【药瓶】medicine bottle

【药铺】herbal medicine shop

【药签】swab

【药膳】medicated food; food cooked with medicinal herbs

【药水】① liquid medicine; medicinal liquid ② lotion

【药丸】pill：大～ *bolus*

【药味】① herbal medicines in a prescription ② flavour of a drug

【药物】pharmaceuticals; medicament; medicines; drugs：～过敏 *drug allergy* / ～牙膏 *medicated toothpaste* / ～中毒 *drug poisoning*

【药箱】medical kit; medicine chest：急救～ *first-aid kit*

【药效】efficacy of a drug (or medicine)

【药性】property of a medicine：～平和 *mild medicine* / ～猛 *strong medicine*

【药学】pharmacy

【药引子】【中医】an ingredient added to enhance the efficacy of a dose of medicine; a medical supplement

【药皂】medicated soap

【药渣】dregs of a decoction

要[1] ① important; essential：～事 *an important matter (or affair)* / 主～ *principal*; *prime* / 首～ *first and foremost* / 紧～ *imperative*; *urgent* / 险～ *of strategic importance* ② main points; essentials：搞～abstract /明天把细～交给我。*Please give the outline to me tomorrow.*

要²① want；desire；need；ask for；like to keep：～财不～命 *want property than life* /这本我还～呢，你不能拿走。*I want to keep this book，you cannot take it away.* /他只～了碗面。*He ordered only a bowl of noodle.* ② ask（or want）sb to do sth：她～我替她捎个口信。*She wants me to take a message for her.* /我妈～我早点回去。*My mother told me to go back early.* ③ want to；wish to：这位同学～见你。*This student wishes to see you.* ④ must；should；have to：我～不～打扫完房间再走？*Shall I have the room cleaned before I leave？* /过马路时～当心。*You must be careful while crossing the street.* /我们～按医生说的做。*We should act on the doctor's advice.* ⑤ shall；will；be going to：春节就～到了。*The Spring Festival is drawing near.* /可怜的公主～死了。*The poor princess was dying.* ⑥ need；take：到那儿～一个多小时呢。*It will take more than one hour to get there.* ⑦ used to indicate an estimate in comparisons：新车～比旧车强多了。*The new car is far superior to the old one.* /上海～比那个城市大的多。*Shanghai is much bigger than that city.*

要³① if；suppose；in case：你～不能来，就给我说一声。*If you cannot come，please let me know it.* /他～不来怎么办？*What if he doesn't come？* ② either… or：～不就去教室，～不就去看电影，别再犹豫了。*We go either to the classroom or to the cinema；Don't hesitate any more.*

see also yāo

【要隘】strategic pass

【要案】important case

【要不】① otherwise；or else；or：我得马上走，～就迟到了。*I have to leave at once or I'll be late.* ② either... or...

【要不得】be no good；be intolerable：这种行为～。*Such acts are not to be tolerated.*

【要不是】if it were not for；but for；without：～你帮忙，我们的活儿现在还干不完呢。*If it were not for your help，we wouldn't have finished our work.* /～搭你的车，我今天肯定迟到了。*I would have been late today but for your lift.*

【要冲】communications centre（or hub）：军事～ *strategic point* /交通的～ *communications hub*

【要道】thoroughfare；main artery；arterial highway：交通～ *important line of communication*；*vital communication line*

【要得】[方] good；fine；desirable

【要地】important place；strategic point：军事～ *a place of strategic importance*

【要点】① main points；essentials；gist：讲话的～ *the gist of a speech* ② key stronghold：战略～ *strategic point*

【要犯】an important or principal criminal

【要饭】beg（for food or money）：～的 *beggar*

【要害】①（of one's body）vital part：～部位 *vital part（or organ）* /击中～ *hit home* ②[喻] crucial point；strategic point：～部门 *key department* /地处～ *be located at a strategic point*

【要好】① be on good terms；be close friends：我们俩从小就很～。*The two of us have been close friends since childhood.* ② be eager to improve oneself；try hard to make progress

【要价】ask a price；charge：漫天～ *demand an exorbitant price*；*ask too much* /～还价 *bargain*；*dicker*；*haggle*

【要件】① an important document ② an important condition

【要津】①[书] ferry of strategic importance；important communication hub ② key post

【要紧】① important；essential：～事儿 *urgent thing*；*matter of vital importance* ② be critical；be serious；matter：他的伤～吗？*Is his wound serious？* ③[方] be in a hurry to；be anxious to：我～去上班，得马上走。*I'm in a hurry to go to work，so I must be off now.*

【要诀】essential secret of success；important tricks of the trade；knack

【要脸】be keen on face-saving；care much about one's reputation：不～ *shameless*；*impudent*

【要领】① main points；gist：他讲话不得～。*He failed to grasp the knack.* ② basic requirement；knack；essentials（of an exercise in military or athletic training）：掌握～ *grasp the essentials*

【要略】outline；summary

【要么】or；either... or...：他～是喝醉了，～是疯了。*He must be either drunk or mad.* /这会儿我很忙，～我晚上去见你？*I'm very busy at this moment，how about seeing you this evening？*

【要面子】be keen on face-saying；be anxious to preserve one's reputation

【要命】① kill；drive sb to his death：心脏病要了他的命。*Heart disease killed him or he died of cancer.* /这活儿真～！*This work is really killing！* ② extremely；awfully；terribly：急得～ *worried to death* /胆小得～ *timid as a rabbit* /渴得～ *terribly thirsty* /热得～ *awfully hot* ③ a nuisance：真～，公共汽车又晚点了。*What an awful nuisance；the bus is late again.*

【要强】be eager to excel

【要人】very important person（VIP）；important personage

【要塞】fort；fortress；fortification：～区 *garrison area*

【要事】an important matter

【要是】[口] if；suppose；in case：～你母亲不同意怎么办？*What if your mother doesn't agree？* /～你愿意，我们一起去。*We can go together if you feel like it.*

【要死】① want to die；be going to die；be dying ② to an extreme degree；extremely，awfully：气得～ *be furious* /饿得～ *extremely hungry*

【要素】essential factor；key element

【要闻】important news；front-page story

【要务】important affair

【要员】important official

【要账】demand payment of a debt; press payment of a loan

【要职】an important post: 身居~ *hold an important post*

【要子】① rope made of wheat or rice straw, used to bundle up wheat or rice ② string used to bale

钥

see also yuè

【钥匙】key: 一串~ *a bunch of keys* /万能~ *master key* /配~ *have a key made to fit a lock* /~孔 *keyhole* /~环 *key ring*

鹞 ① harrier ② sparrow hawk

【鹞鹰】sparrow hawk

【鹞子】① sparrow hawk: ~翻身 *do a somersault*; *tumble* ② [方] kite: 放~ *fly a kite*

耀 ① shine, illuminate; dazzle: 照~ *shine on*; *illuminate* ② boast of; show off; laud: 夸~ *boast about*; *make a show of*; *vaunt* ③ glow; brilliance: 光~ *brilliance* ④ glory; honour; credit: 荣~ *honour*

【耀斑】【天】solar flare

【耀武扬威】make a big show of one's strength; swagger around; show one's prowess before others

【耀眼】dazzling: ~的车灯 *dazzling headlights* /~的红玫瑰 *bright red roses*

yē

耶

【耶和华】【宗】Jehovah, name of God in the Old Testament

【耶路撒冷】Jerusalem, holy city for both Islam and Judaism, now capital claimed by both Israel and Palestine

【耶稣】Jesus; Jesus Christ

掖 tuck in; tick up; thrust in between: 把钱~在兜里 *tuck a money into the pocket* /腰里~把枪 *with a pistol in one's belt* /~~藏藏 *clandestinely*; *trying to cover up* /把衬衣下摆~进裤腰里 *tuck one's shirt into one's trousers*

see also yè

椰 coconut palm; coconut tree

【椰壳】coconut husk: ~纤维 *coir fibre*; *coir*

【椰奶】coconut milk

【椰仁】coconut kernel; coconut meat: ~干 *desiccated coconut*; *copra*

【椰蓉】fine coconut mash (used as a filling for cakes): ~月饼 *moon cake* (*with coconut mash as a filling*)

【椰丝】shredded coconut meat

【椰油】coconut oil; coconut butter

【椰汁】coconut milk

【椰枣】① date palm ② palm date

【椰子】① coconut palm; coconut tree; coco ② coconut (the fruit): ~肉 *coconut meat* /~糖 *coconut candy* /~汁 *coconut milk*

噎 ① choke: 因~废食 *give up eating for fearing of choking* /被食物~着 *be choked by one's food*; *choke over one's food* ② [方] render sb speechless by saying sth blunt or rude; choke off: 他说话时总是~人。*He's always contradicting others when talking.*

yé

爷 ① [方] father: ~娘 *father and mother* ② [方] grandfather ③ a respectful form of address for a man of the older generation: 李~ *uncle Li* /大~ *uncle* ④[旧] (a form of address for an official or rich man) sir; master; lord: 老~ *sir*; *master*; *lord* /少~ *young master of* (*the house*) ⑤ a form of address for god used by worshippers: 老天~ *Heaven*; *God* /阎王~ *Yama, King of Hell*

【爷儿】[口] used to refer to a senior man of a family together with one or more juniors (often followed by numerals); father and son; uncle and nephew; grandfather and grandson: ~俩都在。*Both father and son were present.*

【爷儿们】[口] men of two or more generations: 老少~ *all the men, both old and young*

【爷们】[方] ① man or men folk ② husband

【爷们儿】[方] man or men folk:: ~儿家敢作敢当。*A man should have the courage to take the responsibility for what he does.*

【爷爷】[口] ① (paternal) grandfather ② used as a respectful form of address for any old man: 老~ *grandpa* /张~ *grandpa Zhang*

耶 [书] ① used to indicate the interrogative: 是~非~? *Is it or isn't it? or Yes or no?* ② father

揶

【揶揄】[书] ridicule; mock; deride: 以~的口吻讲话 *talk in a tone of mockery* /微笑中带着一丝~ *a smile with a trace of derision*

yě

也[1] [书] ① used at the end of a sentence indicating an explanation or a judgement: 师者,所以传道授业解惑~。*A teacher is one who propagates the doctrines of ancient sages, passes on knowledge and help to clear up the doubts.* /是不为~,非不能~。*This is a case of choosing not to, not of being unable to.* ② used to pose a question: 何~? *How is that? or Why so?* ③ used to indicate a pause in a sentence: 地之相去~,千里有余。*The place is a thousand li away.* ④ used to indicate exclamation: 何其毒~! *How pernicious!*

也² ① also; too; as well; either: 我～会说法语。*I can also speak French.* /长大了，我～想当个医生。*When I'm growing up, I want to become a doctor too.* ② (used in pairs) as well as; both ... and ...: 教室里有读书的，～有闲聊的。*In the classroom some of the students are reading, some are chatting.* /我哥哥会踢足球，～会打篮球。*My brother can play football as well as basketball.* ③ (used in pairs) either... or...; whether... or...: 你给我打电话～行，写信～行。*It doesn't matter whether you call me up or write to me.* ④ used to indicate concession: 即使失败一百次，我～不灰心。*I'll never lose my heart even if I should fail one hundred times.* ⑤ used in a hesitant or guarded statement: 他这儿～还不错。*He is not bad.* ⑥ used for emphasis, often before a negative expression: 只要有决心，什么困难～不怕。*There is no insurmountable difficulty before a determined mind.* /他病得一点～不想吃。*He is so ill that he doesn't feel like eating anything.*

【也罢】① (indicating tolerance or resignation) well; all right: 你学习忙，不去～，我自己去。*All right, I'll go myself since your study is too busy to go.* ② (used in pairs) whether... or...; no matter whether: 刮风～，下雪～，那对老夫妇都坚持晨练。*The old couples keep up his exercises whether it's blowing or snowing.* /你来～，不来～，反正我们可以自己干。*It makes no difference whether you come or not, we can do it by ourselves.*

【也好】① it may not be a bad idea; may as well: 说明一下～，以免大家误会。*To avoid any misunderstanding, you'd better give them an explanation.* ② (reduplicated) whether... or...; no matter whether: 警察～，保安～，他们都不了解这里发生的情况。*Nether policemen nor security personnel know what is happening here.*

【也门】Yemen: ～人 *Yemeni*

【也许】perhaps; probably; maybe: 他～来，～不来。*He may or may not come.*

【也…也…】① both... and..; either... or... ② no matter (whether, who, etc.)

冶¹ ① smelt (metal) ② (Yě) a surname

冶² (of a woman) coquettishly or seductively dressed: 妖～ *coquettish; seductive*

【冶炼】smelt: ～操作 *smelting operation* /～厂 *smeltery; smelting plant* /～过程 *smelting process* /～炉 *smelting furnace* /～时间 *duration of heat*

野 ① open country; wild land: 旷～ *open country; wilderness* /田～ *open field* /沃～千里 *a vast expense of fertile land* /漫山遍～ *all over the hills and plains* ② limit; boundary: 视～ *scope of vision* ③ not in power; out of office: 在～党 *a party not in power* /下～ *be forced to relinquish the power* ⑤ wild; uncultivated; undomesticated: ～花 *wild flowers* /～狗 *homeless dogs* /～猪 *boar; wild boar* ⑥ rude; rough: 撒～ *behave rudely* /说话太～ *use coarse language; speak rudely* /举止粗～ *behave boorishly* ⑦ unrestrained; abandoned; unruly

【野菜】edible wild herbs

【野餐】picnic

【野草】weeds: ～丛生 *be overgrown with weeds* /～闲花 *weeds and wild flowers; mistress; prostitute*

【野传】【体】(of baseball or basketball) wild throw

【野炊】cook in the open air

【野地】wild country; wilderness

【野果】wild fruit

【野汉子】lover (esp. of a married woman): 养～ *support a man with whom she carries on an affair*

【野合】[书] have illicit sexual relations

【野火】prairie fire; bush fire: ～烧不尽，春风吹又生。*Even a prairie fire cannot destroy the grass, it grows again when the spring breeze blows or no prairie fire can burn the grass utterly, the spring wind blows it back to life.*

【野鸡】①pheasant ② streetwalker; street girl

【野景】country view; wild scenery

【野菊花】mother chrysanthemum

【野驴】Asiatic wild ass; kiang

【野马】wild horse; untamed horse; mustang; bronco

【野蛮】① uncivilized; barbarian; savage: ～的习俗 *savage customs* /你真是一个～人。*You are really a savage.* ② barbarous; cruel; brutal: 举止～ *be ill-mannered* /～行为 *barbarous act*

【野猫】① wildcat ② stray cat ③ [方] hare

【野牛】wild ox ; buffalo

【野趣】pastoral appeal; idyllic taste

【野人】savage; barbarian

【野生】wild; undomesticated; uncultivated; feral: ～植物 *wild plant* /～动物 *wildlife* /有些草处于～状态。*Those grass are in a wild state.*

【野食儿】① animals' food picked up in the wilds ② [喻] extra irregular income

【野史】unofficial history

【野兽】wild beast; wild animal

【野兔】hare

【野外】open country; field; outdoor: ～作业 *field operation* /～活动 *outdoor activities; outdoors* /～工作 *fieldwork* /～运动 *field sports*

【野味】game(for food): 打～ *go to hunt wild game*

【野心】audacious ambition; wild ambition; careerism: 侵略～ *aggressive ambitions* /～勃勃 *be overwhelmingly ambitious; be obsessed with ambition* /称霸世界的～ *ambition for world domination* /篡权的～ *ambition for usurping power* /～不死 *cling to one's ambitious design* /～家 *careerist* /～狼 *a vicious wolf; a person of evil ambitions*

【野性】wild nature; unruliness: ～难驯 *untamable; the wild nature is hard to tame* /～十足 *untamable; untamed*

【野营】camp; bivouac: 出外～ *go camping* /～训练 *camp and field training* /～者 *camper* /他们非常喜欢～。*They are fond of camping.*

【野战】field operations: ～电话机 *camp telephone* /～军 *field army* /～仓库 *field depot* /～工事 *fieldwork* /～炮 *fieldpiece; field gun* /～医院 *field hospital*

【野种】bastard

yè

业[1] line of business; trade; industry: 工商～ *industry and commerce* / 保险～ *insurance business* / 旅游～ *tourism; tourist industry* / 饮食～ *catering trade* / 畜牧～ *livestock industry* / 工农～ *industry and agriculture* ② occupation; profession; employment; job: 就～ *employment* / 失～ *be unemployed; be out of a job* / 转～ (*of an armyman*) *be transferred to civilian work* / 安居乐～ *live in peace and work contentedly* ③ course of study: 修～ *study in a school* / 毕～ *graduate; finish schooling* / 肄～ *study in school without graduation* / 结～ *complete a course of study* ④ cause; enterprise: 伟～ *great cause; exploit* / 基～ *foundation; base* / 守～ *maintain what has been achieved by one's forefathers* ⑤ estate; property: 家～ *family property* ⑥【宗】karma; deed; action ⑦ engage in; go in for: ～农 *engage in farming*

业[2] already; before now: ～已病故 *already died of illness* / ～已核实 *have already been verified*

【业报】【宗】retribution for sins

【业海】【宗】sea of sin, iniquity

【业绩】outstanding achievement: 光辉的～ *glorious achievements* / 值得称颂的～ *praiseworthy achievements*

【业界】business circles

【业经】already: ～批准 *have been approved*

【业精于勤】mastery of a subject comes from diligence; efficiency comes from diligence

【业务】vocational work; professional work; business: ～差 *be incompetent for one's job* / 懂～ *know the business; know the ropes* / 钻研～ *diligently study one's profession* / 恢复正常～ *resume normal business* / ～范围 *scope of business* / ～能力 *professional competence* / ～素质 *professional skill* / ～学习 *vocational study* / ～知识 *professional knowledge* / ～班子 *professional team; business team* / ～挂帅 *professional work comes first* / ～尖子 *top-notch professional*

【业余】① spare time; leisure: ～爱好 *hobby* / ～教育 *spare-time education* / ～学校 *spare-time school* ② non-professional; amateur: ～演员 *amateur actor or actress* / ～运动员 *amateur athlete* / ～剧团 *an amateur theatrical troupe*

【业主】owner (of an enterprise or estate); proprietor

叶[1] ① leaf; foliage: 红花绿～ *red flowers and green leaves* / 秋～ *autumn foliage* ② leaf-like thing: 一～扁舟 *a small boat* / 百～窗 *shutter; blind* / 肺～ *lobe of the lung* ③ page; leave

叶[2] part of a historical period: 末～ *the end (of a century or dynasty)* / 十九世纪中～ *(in) the middle of the 19th century*

【叶柄】petiole; leafstalk

【叶公好龙】Lord Ye's love of dragons — profess love of what one really fears

【叶绿素】chlorophyll

【叶绿体】chloroplast

【叶轮】impeller; vane wheel: ～泵 *vane pump*

【叶落归根】the falling leaves settle on the roots — a person residing away from his ancestral home finally returns to it

【叶落知秋】when the leaves fall we know that autumn is here

【叶脉】leaf vein

【叶片】①【植】leaf blade ②【机】vane: ～泵 *vane pump* / ～式压缩机 *vane compressor*

【叶鞘】leaf sheath

【叶肉】mesophyll

【叶酸】folic acid; folacin

【叶芽】leaf bud

【叶子】① leaf ②［方］playing cards ③［方］tea leaves

页 ① leaf; sheet: 散～ *loose leaf* / 活～本 *loose leaf notebook* ② page: 插～ *inset; insert* / 扉～ *title page* / 打开新的一～ *open up a new chapter*

【页边】margin

【页码】page number

【页心】【印】type page

【页岩】【地】shale

曳 drag; haul; tug; tow: 长裙～地 *dress long enough to drag along the ground*

【曳白】［书］hand in a blank paper examination

【曳扯】［方］bring up; raise

【曳光弹】【军】tracer bullet or shell; tracer

【曳力】【物】drag force

夜 ① night; nighttime; evening: ～里 *at night* / 熬～ *stay up late* / 守～ *keep watch at night* / 新婚之～ *wedding night* / 每当～深人静的时候，她更加思念她的丈夫。*She missed her husband in the dead of night.* ②［方］get or grow dark; evening falls

【夜班】nightshift

【夜半】midnight

【夜不安枕】toss and turn all the night

【夜不闭户】doors are not bolted at night; robbery was rare, and people can always leave their doors open; honesty prevails throughout

【夜不成寐】lie awake all night; toss and turn all night

【夜餐】midnight snack

【夜长梦多】a long night is fraught with dreams along; delay means trouble

【夜场】evening show; evening performance

【夜车】① night train ② night work; night train: 开～ *work at night*

【夜工】night work; night job: 打～ *work at night; do a night job*

【夜光杯】a luminous wine glass

【夜间】at night: ～行军 *march by night; night march* / ～施工 *carry on construction work at night* / ～照明 *night illumination*

【夜景】night scene; nocturnal sight

【夜课】evening class
【夜空】the night sky
【夜阑人静】in the dead of night; in the still of the night
【夜郎自大】ludicrous conceit of the King of Yelang — parochial arrogance; conceit stemming from pure ignorance parochial arrogance
【夜里】at night
【夜盲】nyctalopia; night blindness
【夜猫子】［方］① owl ② a person who likes staying up late; night owl
【夜明珠】legendary luminous pearl
【夜幕】gathering darkness; night: ～降临。*Night has fallen.*
【夜尿症】enuresis; bed-wetting
【夜勤】night duty
【夜曲】nocturne: 小～ *serenade*
【夜色】night scene; darkness; dusk; the dim light of night: 趁着～ *under cover of night; by moonlight* / ～苍茫 *gathering dusk*
【夜生活】night life
【夜市】night market
【夜视仪】【军】night vision device (or instrument)
【夜晚】night
【夜袭】night attack (or raid)
【夜宵】food (or refreshments) taken late at night; midnight snack
【夜校】night or evening school
【夜行】① walk at night; travel by night ② night flight or navigation: ～军 *night march*
【夜夜】every night
【夜以继日】day and night
【夜莺】nightingale
【夜鹰】nighthawk; goatsucker
【夜游神】the legendary god on patrol at night; a person who is up and about at night; night owl
【夜战】① night fighting ② work at night
【夜总会】nightclub

咽 (of sound) obstructed and therefore low: 哽～ *choke with sobs* / 喇叭声～ *muffled sound of a horn*
【咽泣】choke with sobs
【咽哑】hoarse: 声音～ *have a hoarse voice*

烨 ① firelight; sunlight ② (of light) brilliant; bright: ～～雷电 *blasting thunder and glaring lightning*

掖 support sb by the arm; support; help; assist; promote: 扶～ *help; support* / 奖～ *reward and promote*
see also yē

液 liquid; fluid; juice: 体～ *body fluid* / 唾～ *saliva* / 血～ *blood*
【液肥】liquid manure or fertilizer
【液化】liquate; liquefy: ～器 *liquefier* / ～石油气 *liquefied petroleum gas (LPG)* / ～天然气 *liquefied natural gas (LNG)*
【液化气】liquefied natural gas (LNG): ～罐 *gas bottle*
【液晶】liquid crystal: ～显示 *liquid crystal display (LCD)* / ～电视 *liquid crystal T V*
【液冷】【机】liquid cooling (or cooled): ～式内燃机 liquid cooled engine
【液力】【机】hydraulic: ～变速箱 *hydraulic transmission box* / ～传动 *hydraulic power* / ～制动器 *hydraulic brake*
【液态】liquid state; liquid condition: ～合金 *liquid alloy* / ～空气 *liquid air*
【液体】liquid: ～电容 *liquid condenser* / ～比重计 *hydrometer* / ～镜 *liquid mirror* / ～燃料 *liquid fuel* / ～绝缘体 *liquid insulator*
【液压】hydraulic pressure: ～传递 *hydraulic transmission* / ～泵 *hydraulic pump* / ～表 *hydraulic pressure gauge* / ～传动装置 *hydraulic transmission device* / ～机 *hydraulic press*

谒 ［书］call on (a superior or an elder person); pay one's respects to; pay homage to: 进～ *call on (a superior)*
【谒拜】pay a formal visit
【谒见】call on (a superior or a senior in the clan hierarchy); have an audience with
【谒陵】pay homage at sb's mausoleum

腋 ①【生理】axilla; armpit ②【植】axil
【腋臭】underarm odour
【腋毛】armpit hair
【腋窝】armpit
【腋芽】【植】axillary bud

yī

一 ① one: ～个 *one; a; an* / 孤身～人 *all by oneself* ② same: ～码事 *the same thing* ③ another, also ④ whole; all; entire: 忙了～年 *be busy the whole year* / ～屋子的人 *all the people in the room* / 焕然～新 *take on an entirely new look; look brand-new* ⑤ concentrated; whole hearted: 专心～意 *single-minded; concentrated* ⑥ used between reduplicated verbs indicating the action is just for once or of short duration: 看～看 *take a look* / 笑～笑 *give a smile* / 歇～歇 *have a rest* ⑦ used between a verb and a verbal measure: 瞧～眼 *take a look* / 咳～声 *give a cough* / 她爸爸打了她～巴掌。*Her father gave her a slap.* ⑧ used either before a verb or a verbal classifier to indicate the action leads to a result: ～跳跳了过去 *get over in one jump* / 他～脚把门踢开了。/*He forced the door open with a kick.* ⑨ once; as soon as: ～见不忘 *Once seen, never forgotten.* / 天～亮，他们就出发了。*They started out at dawn.* / 你～回来就会明白了。*You will be clear about it as soon as you are back.* ⑩［书］used for emphasis: ～似瓮中捉鳖 *be as easy as catching a turtle in a jar* / ～何速也！*How fast it is!*
【一把好手】past master; good hand
【一把手】① a party to an undertaking; a member; a hand ② a good hand; a very capable person: 你妻子可是里里外外～。*Your wife is adept at every-*

Y

thing she does, both inside and outside the house. ③ leading official in an institution; head, chief

【一把抓】① take everything into one's own hands; attend to everything oneself ② try to tackle all problems at once regardless of their relative importance

【一败涂地】fail completely; suffer a crushing defeat; be routed:由于缺乏充分准备,他们队在联赛中~。*Having not been well prepared, their team was thoroughly defeated in the league match.*

【一班人】members of a squad — a small body of people working together

【一般】① same as; just like; as . . . as. . . : ~重 *of the same weight* / ~长 *of the same length* / 钢铁~的意志 *iron will* / 火车飞~地驰去。*The train flashed past like lightning.* ② general; ordinary; common: ~情况 *ordinary circumstances* / ~规律 *general rule; universal law* / ~来说 *generally speaking* / 这篇文章写得很~。*There is nothing striking about this article.* / 下午我~呆在家。*I usually stay at home in the afternoon.*

【一般化】generalization

【一般见识】lower oneself to the same level as sb:不必跟他这种人~! *Don't debase yourself by arguing with the likes of him.* / 别和小孩子~。*Don't behave like a child.*

【一斑】one spot on a leopard — a small but typical part of the whole or of many similar things:管中窥豹,可见~ *look at one spot on a leopard and you can visualize the whole thing or you can conjure up the whole thing through seeing a part of it*

【一板一眼】following a prescribed (or set) pattern in speech or action; meticulous and methodical

【一板正经】in all seriousness; in dead earnest

【一半】one half; half; in part: ~以上 *more than half* / 不到~ *less than half*

【一…半…】used with synonyms words or related words meaning not much or many or not a long time:天一时半刻下不了。*It will not rain very soon.* / 我只听到一句半句的。*What I heard was very fragmentary.*

【一半天】[口] in a day or two

【一报还一报】retribution paid out in kind; an eye for an eye, a tooth for a tooth

【一辈子】all one's life; throughout one's life; as long as one lives:我~也忘不了。*I won't forget it as long as I live.* / 妈妈享了~的福。*My mother lives in lifelong ease and comfort.*

【一本正经】in all seriousness; in dead earnest:显出~的样子 *put on an air of a serious manner; look prim and proper*

【一鼻孔出气】[贬] breathe through the same nostrils; sing the same tune; collude with one another

【一笔勾销】write off at one stroke; cancel:旧账~ *cancel all old debts*

【一臂之力】a helping hand:助我~ *lend me a hand*

【一边】① one side; side: ② either side ③ indicating two actions taking place at the same time:姑娘们~走,~唱着歌儿。*The girls sang as they walked along.*

【一边倒】① lean to one side; side with sb without reservation; be partial to ② be far superior; enjoy overwhelming superiority

【一表人才】a man of striking appearance

【一并】along with all the others; all; in the lump: ~考虑 *be considered together with sb or sth else* / ~告知 *inform sb of sth along with other matters*

【一波三折】full of twists and turns; with ups and downs; with unexpected changes

【一波未平,一波又起】hardly has one wave subsided when another rises — one trouble follows another

【一…不…】① used respectively before two verbs indicating that the action or condition is unchangeable once it takes place or is established: 一病不起 *take to one's bed and never leave it again; fall ill and fail to recover* / 一去不返 *gone never to return* / 一蹶不振 *never be able to recover after a setback* / 一借不还 *borrow sth but never return it* ② used respectively before a noun and a verb for emphasis or hyperbole:一字不漏 *without missing a single word* / 一丁不识 *not knowing a single word* / 一文不花 *spend not a single penny*

【一步登天】reach the sky in a single bound — attain the highest level in one step; have a sudden rise in life

【一步一个脚印】every step leaves its print — work steadily and make solid progress

【一差二错】a possible mistake or mishap:万一有个~ *just in case there is a slip somewhere; just in case of accident* / 谁办事也难保不出个~。*Nobody can be entirely free from making mistakes.*

【一刹那】in an instant; in a split second

【一场春梦】a fond dream in spring — evanescent happiness

【一场空】all in vain; futile

【一场秋雨一场寒】a spell of autumn rain, and a spell of cold; the weather gets colder with each autumn rain

【一唱百和】when one starts singing, the others join in — meet with general approval

【一唱一和】sing a duet; sing the same tune; echo each other

【一朝天子一朝臣】every new sovereign brings his own courtiers — a new chief brings in his own aides

【一尘不染】① (of environment) not soiled or stained by a speck of dust; spotlessly clean:屋里~。*The room is spotlessly clean.* ② (of person) pure-minded; pure-hearted

【一成不变】immutable and frozen; unalterable:没有~的规则。*There is no hard and fast rule.*

【一筹莫展】can find no way out; be at one's wits' end; be at the end of one's tether

【一触即发】may break out at any moment; be on the verge of breaking out:武装冲突有~之势。*Armed conflict may break out at any moment.*

【一触即溃】collapse at the first encounter

【一传】【体】first pass：～手 *first passer*
【一传十,十传百】(of news) spread from one person to ten, and from ten to a hundred — pass quickly from mouth to mouth; get around quickly
【一锤定音】set the tune with one beat of the gong — say the final word; make the last decision
【一锤子买卖】"once for all" deal：我们不做～。*We don't do once for-all deal.*
【一次】once：不只～ *more than once* /～付清 *pay in one lump sum* /我只去过～。*I've been there only once.*
【一次方程】【数】linear equation
【一次函数】【数】linear function
【一次能源】primary energy
【一次性】once only：～补助 *a lump-sum grant* /～筷子 *disposable chopsticks* /～注射器 *disposable syringes* /～尿布 *a disposable nappy*
【一蹴而就】reach the goal in one step; accomplish one's aim in one move; succeed overnight
【一寸光阴一寸金】an inch of time is an inch of gold; time is money; time is precious
【一搭】[方] together; at the same place
【一搭两用】one thing with two uses; dual-purpose article
【一打】a dozen
【一大早儿】[口] early in the morning：他～就上学去了。*He went to school early in the morning.*
【一代】① a dynasty：② an era; epoch; the present age：～英豪 *outstanding figures of the times* ③ a generation; life-time：年轻的～ *the young generation*
【一带】the area around a particular place：他是这～出名的医生。*He is one of the most famous doctors around here.*
【一旦】① in a single day; in a very short time：毁于～ *be destroyed in one day* ② some; day; once：相处多年,～分开,怎么能不想念呢? *Having been together for many years they can't bear to part from each other.*
【一刀两断】sever at one blow — make a clean break
【一刀切】cut it even at one stroke — make every thing rigidly uniform; impose uniformity in all cases; prescribe a single solution for all problems
【一道】① together; side by side; along with：咱们～走吧。*Let's go together.* /他和几个朋友～来的。*He came along with some friends.* ② a; one：～数学题 *a math problem* /～闪电 *a streak of lightening*
【一得之功】an occasional, minor success：不要沾沾自喜于～。*Don't feel self-satisfied over just a minor success.*
【一得之见】[谦] point of view; opinion; understanding
【一得之愚】[谦] my humble opinion：～,仅供参考。*This is my humble opinion, for what it's worth.*
【一等】first-class; first-rate; top-grade; top-notch：～品 *top-quality product* /～奖 *first prize* /～舱 *first class cabin* /～功 *Merit Citation First Class*
【一等兵】(US Army) private first class; (UK Army) lance corporal; (US Navy) seaman first class; (UK Navy) leading seaman; (US Air Force) airman first class; (UK Air Force) senior aircrafts man; (US Marine Corps) marine first class; (UK Marine Corps) marine first class
【一点儿】① a bit; a little：请你再吃～。*Please have a little more.* ② very small; very little：～也不累 *not feel the least bit tired* /～都不知道 *have not the faintest idea* /～意见都没有 *have no objection at all*
【一点一滴】every little bit：从～的小事做起 *start from working on small matters* /～地积累经验 *accumulate experience little by little*
【一丁点儿】[方] a wee bit; a tiny bit
【一定】① fixed; specified; definite; regular：在～的时间内完成工程项目 *complete the construction project within a fixed time* ② definitely; inevitably; necessarily：这些报纸他不～都读过。*He might not have read all these newspaper.* ③ be bound to; be sure to; firmly; resolutely：他～要今天走。*He is determined to leave today.* /今天～会下雨。*It's bound to rain today.* /他们～会赢的。*The are certain to win.* ③ given; particular; certain：在～意义上 *in a certain sense* /在～程度上 *to a certain degree* /在～条件下 *under given conditions* ④ proper; fair; due：达到～水平 *reach a fairly high level* /给于～的重视 *attach due importance to* /你的话也有～的道理。*You have a point there.*
【一定之规】① a fixed pattern; a set rule ② fixed idea or way to do sth; one's own way
【一动】easily frequently; at every turn：她～就哭。*She cries easily.*
【一动不如一静】better be still than stir; to stay put is better than to move
【一肚子】filled with; full of：～委屈 *full of grievances* /～坏水 *plenty of sinister ideas* /～牢骚 *full of complaint*
【一度】① once：一年～ *once a year; yearly; annually* ② on one occasion; for a time：局势～失控。*The situation was once out of control.* /他～失业。*He was out of work on one occasion.*
【一端】① one aspect (or side) of the matter：各执～ *each sticking to his own argument* ② one end (of sth)
【一…而】used respectively before two verbs indicating that one action follows another as an immediate result：一闪而过 *pass in a flash* /一怒而去 *go away in a temper; leave in anger* /一饮而尽 *empty the glass at one gulp* /一跃而下 *jump down at one bound*
【一而再,再而三】again and again; time and again; repeatedly
【一二】one or two; just a few; just a little：略知～ *know a little about; have some idea about* /邀请～知己 *invite a few close friends*
【一…二…】each used before a morpheme of some

disyllabic adjectives, verbs, etc, for emphasis: 一清二楚 *crystal clear* /如有一差二错 *if there should be an error or mishap* /一来二去两人成了情人。*They met each other for several times and became lovers.*

【一发】① all the more; even more ② together; along with all the others

【一帆风顺】plain or smooth sailing; successful career: 祝~,旅途平安。*Wish you a smooth and safe journey.*

【一反常态】depart from one's normal behaviour; act out of character

【一方有难,八方支援】when one place is in trouble, help comes from all quarters

【一方面】① on the one hand... on the other hand...; for one thing..., for another... ② one side or aspect

【一飞冲天】make astonishing achievements; do sth amazing

【一分耕耘,一分收获】the more ploughing and weeding, the better the crop; no pain; no gain

【一分钱一分货】the higher the price, the better the quality of the goods; what price, what goods

【一分为二】one divides into two; there are two sides to everything

【一夫当关,万夫莫开】if one man guards the pass, ten thousand men cannot break it open; one man can hold out against ten thousand at a strategic pass

【一概】one and all; without exception; totally: ~拒绝 *reject without exception* /~排斥 *totally exclude* /~没收 *confiscate everything* /具体情况我~不知。*I know nothing whatever about the situation.*

【一概而论】all alike; lump together: 不能~ *not to be lumped together; must not generalize about sth*

【一干】all those involved: ~人犯 *all the suspects and criminals involved in the case*

【一干二净】thoroughly; completely: 吃个~ *eat up all the food* /打扫得~ *sweep spotlessly clean* /推脱得~ *try to absolve oneself of all wrong things*

【一竿子到底】carry (a task or directive) right down to the grass-roots level; carry sth through to the end

【一个巴掌拍不响】one hand alone can't clap; it takes two to make a quarrel

【一个劲儿】continuously; persistently; without stopping: 雨~地下。*It kept on raining.*

【一个萝卜一个坑】one radish, one hole; each has his own task, and nobody is dispensable; steady and reliable

【一个心眼儿】① with one's heart set on sth; devotedly; be of one mind ② stubborn; obstinate

【一共】altogether; in all: 班上~多少人? *How many people are there in the class altogether?*

【一股劲儿】without a break; at one go; at a stretch: ~地干 *do sth without a break*

【一股脑儿】[方] completely; all; lock, stock and barrel; root and branch: 把要讲的话~都倒出来了 *pour out all one wants to say at once*

【一鼓作气】do sth at one go; get sth done in one sustained effort

【一官半职】some official post or other; minor official post

【一贯】consistently; persistently; steadily; all along: ~努力 *word hard unfailingly* /~政策 *consistent policy*

【一棍子打死】knock sb down at one stroke; finish off with one blow; completely negate: 他生活中有过失,但不能~。*It's true that he has made some errors in his life, but we must not write him off as totally worthless.*

【一锅端】① eliminate or wipe out completely ② bring everything out; speak out without reservation

【一锅粥】a pot of porridge — a shambles; a complete mess; all in a muddle: 乱成~ *be all muddled up; in a mess; in total confusion*

【一国两制】one country, two systems

【一国三公】a state with three rulers — a divided leadership

【一哄而起】(of a group of people) be roused to precipitate action

【一哄而散】break up in a hubbub; scatter in a rush

【一呼百应】hundreds respond to a single call

【一环扣一环】one ring linked with another — closely linked

【一晃】(yīhuǎng) in a flash: 他在屋里~就不见了。*He disappeared quickly in the room.*

【一晃】(yīhuàng) (of time) pass in a flash: ~几年又过去了。*Several years passed in a flash.*

【一挥而就】flourish the pen and it's done; finish a piece of writing or a painting at one go

【一回事】① one and the same (thing): 他们所说的是~。*They were talking about the same thing.* ② one thing: 嘴上说说是~,行动又是~。*While talking is one thing, getting things done is quite another.*

【一会儿】① a little while: 咱们歇~。*Let's rest fore while.* ② in a moment; presently: 我~就去上学了。*I'll be going to school in a moment.* /我~就回来。*I'll be back in a moment.* ③ used before each pair of antonyms, indicating alternating circumstances: 天气~晴~阴。*The weather is now clear, now cloudy.*

【一己】oneself: ~之私 *one's own selfish interests* /~之见 *personal point of view*

【一技之长】proficiency in a particular line (or field); professional skill; specialty

【一家之言】a distinctive point of view or theory; particular school of thought: ~,仅供参考。*As one view, this is only for your information.*

【一家子】① a family ② the whole family

【一见倾心】fall in love at first sight

【一见如故】feel like old friends at the first meeting; take to each other immediately

【一见钟情】fall in love at first sight

【一箭双雕】hit two hawks with one arrow; kill two

birds with one stone

【一箭之仇】the wrong of an arrow shot — a loss or defeat to be avenged

【一箭之地】as far as the arrow flies; stone's distance; not far:他家离公园不过~。*He lives only a short distance from the park.*

【一经】as soon as; once

【一径】straight; directly; straightaway:他进了家门~走进自己的卧室。*As soon as he entered the house, he went straight into his own bedroom.*

【一…就…】(of two things closely linked in sequence of time) no sooner... than...; the moment...; as soon as; at once:我一到就写信给你。*I'll write to you as soon as I arrive there.*

【一举】one action; one stroke; at the first try; at one fell swoop;achieve instant

【一举两得】gain two ends at once; kill two birds with one stone

【一举一动】every act and every move; every action:密切监视他的~。*Keep a close watch at his every move.*

【一句话】in a word; in short

【一决雌雄】fight it out; fight to see who is the stronger; wage a decisive battle

【一蹶不振】collapse after a single setback; be unable to recover after one defeat or failure

【一俊遮百丑】a beautiful appearance covers up many defects and deficiencies

【一刻千金】one minute or moment is worth a thousand pieces of gold; time is precious; value every minute

【一口】① a mouthful; a bite:吸~气 *draw a breath* /咬~ *take a bite* ② a manner of speech:讲~流利的英语 *speak fluent English* ③ with certainty; readily; flatly:~断定 *arbitrarily assert; allege* / ~答应 *readily agree; readily promise* /~回绝 *flatly refuse*

【一口吃不成胖子】no one grows fat on just one mouthful; nothing can be accomplished with one single effort

【一口气】① one breath:只要我还有~,我就不会停止工作。*As long as there's a breath left in me, I will not stop my work.* ② in one breath; without a break; at one go; at a stretch:~干完 *finish the work at one go* /~爬到山顶 *climb to the top of the mountain without pausing to rest*

【一口咬定】state categorically; assert emphatically; insist:他~当时他不在家里。*He insisted that he was not at the home.*

【一口钟】[方] mantle, cape; cloak

【一块儿】① at the same place:两个人在~上学。*The two of them study at the same school.* ② together:我们~回家吧。*Let's go home together.*

【一块石头落地】have a load off one's mind; the mind is at last set at rest; feel relieved

【一来二去】in the course of contacts

【一览】general survey; bird's — eye view; overview:~表 *table; schedule*

【一览无余】take in everything at a glance

【一揽子】wholesale; package:~建议 *package proposal* /~交易 *package deal* /~裁军措施 *package of disarmament measures*

【一劳永逸】by one supreme effort gain lasting repose; settle a matter once and for all; achieve a permanent solution

【一力】do one's best; make every effort; do all one can:~成全 *do one's best to help sb to achieve his aim* /~举荐 *do all one can to recommend sb*

【一连】in a row; in succession; running:~五次夺冠 *win championship five times in row* / ~下了五天雨。*It rained for five days running.*

【一连串】a succession of; a series of; a string of: a chain of:~的谎言 *a string of lies* /~问题 *a series of questions* /~灾祸的 *a succession of disasters*

【一连气儿】[方] in a row; in succession; running

【一了百了】all troubles end when the main trouble ends; death ends all one's troubles; death pays all one's debts

【一鳞半爪】odd bits; fragments:~的情况 *odd bits (or scraps) of information*

【一流】① a kind; the same kind ② first-class; first-rate; top-notch:~作家 *a first-class writer* / ~作品 *a first-rate work*

【一溜儿】[方] ① a row:~十个座位 *a row of ten seats* ② neighbourhood; vicinity:这~原来是一片树林。*There used to be a stretch of woods around here.* ③ in a burst or fit:他~小跑来到屋里。*He came running into the house.*

【一溜风】like a gust of wind —(run) very quickly

【一溜歪斜】[方](walk, etc.) unsteadily in a zigzag

【一溜烟】(run away) very quickly

【一路】① all the way; throughout the journey:~上说说笑笑 *chat cheerfully all the way* /~领先 *take the lead all the way* /~平安 *have a pleasant journey; have a good trip; bon voyage* /~顺风 *plain sailing; pleasant journey* /~保重。*Take care of yourself on the journey.* ② of the same kind:~货色 *the same sort of stuff; one of a kind; birds of a feather* ③ go the same way; take the same route:他们是~的。*They are going the same way.* ④ single file:成~纵队齐步走 *march (in) single file* ⑤ [方] continuously:股市~上扬。*The prices kept rising in the stock market.*

【一律】① same; alike; uniform:千篇~ *all following the same pattern* ② all; without exception:所有商品~八折 *a flat discount rate of 20% for all the goods* /在法律面前人人~平等。*All citizens are equal before the law.*

【一落千丈】drop a thousand zhang in one fall — suffer a disastrous decline; have a big comedown:信誉~ *disastrous decline of one's reputation*

【一抹平】① the same; equal:要按劳付酬,不能~。*Distribution should be set according to work; they shouldn't be uniform.* ② level; smooth:这座山山顶~。*The top of the mountain is very level.*

【一麻黑】pitch-dark; completely dark:地窖里～,什么也看不见。*It was pitch-dark in the cellar and nothing is visible.*

【一马当先】gallop at the head — take the lead; be in the forefront:他在抗洪抢险中处处都是～。*He took the lead in whatever work while fighting against the flood.*

【一马平川】a wide expanse of flat land; a wide stretch of flat country

【一脉相承】come down in one continuous line; can be traced to the same origin; be in direct line of descent (or succession)

【一毛不拔】unwilling to give up even a hair; very stingy; miserly

【一面】① one side:这种布～光～毛。*This kind of cloth is smooth on one side and coarse on the other.* ② one aspect; one field:独当～ *be solely responsible for one section (or department)* /问题的～ *one aspect of the question* ③ at the same time; simultaneously:～跳,～唱 *sing while dance* ④ [书] have met once before:～之词 *the statement of only one of the parties* /～之交 *have met only once; be casually acquainted*

【一鸣惊人】amaze the world with a single brilliant feat; set the Thames on fire

【一命归天】die; quit this world; pass away

【一命呜呼】die; kick the bucket; bite; give up the ghost

【一模一样】exactly alike; very image; as like as two peas

【一目了然】see clearly at a glance; be as plain as one's nose on sb's face

【一目十行】take in ten lines at a glance — read very rapidly

【一男半女】a son or a daughter; a child or two

【一年半载】in a year or so; in about a year

【一年到头】throughout the year; all the year round

【一年生】【植】annual:～植物 *annual plant; annual*

【一年四季】during the four seasons of the year; throughout the year; all the year round:山顶～被冰雪覆盖。*The top of the mountain is covered with snow all year round.*

【一年之计在于春】the work for the year has to be planned well in the spring; the whole year's work depends on a good start in spring

【一念之差】a wrong decision made in a moment of weakness; a momentary slip with serious consequences

【一诺千金】a promise worth a thousand pieces of gold; solemn promise

【一拍即合】hit it off readily; chime in easily

【一盘棋】① a game of chess ② overall situation

【一盘散沙】a sheet or heap of loose sand; a state of disunity or disarray

【一旁】one side:他站在～看热闹。*He stood by watching the fun.*

【一片】① [量] used to describe object, landscape, sound; feeling or mood, etc:～面包 *a slice of bread* /～火海 *a sea of flame* /～汪洋 *a vast expense of water* /～丹心 *a loyal heart* /～碧绿 *a scene of greenness* ② whole; entirety

【一瞥】① a quick glance:她向他投去会心的～。*She cast him a understanding glance.* ② a glimpse; a brief survey (often used as a title)

【一贫如洗】penniless; utterly destitute; as poor as a church mouse

【一品】① (of officials in feudal China) the highest in rank; first class; top-grade:～官 *top-rank official* ② [书] one kind:此～牡丹 *this kind of peony*

【一瓶子不响,半瓶子晃荡】the half-filled bottle sloshes, but the full bottle makes no sound — the dabbler in knowledge chatters away, the wise man stays silent; he who knows least boasts most

【一暴十寒】have one day's sun and then ten days' cold; work hard for one day and do nothing for ten; work by fits and starts

【一齐】at the same time; simultaneously; in unison:～动手 *go into action one and all* /～高呼 *shout in unison* /～努力 *make a concerted effort*

【一起】① in the same place:～工作 *work in the same place* ② together; in company:他儿子不跟他～走。*His son won't go along with him.* ③ [方] altogether; in all ④ [方] the same gang or group:他们是～的。*They are of the same group.*

【一气】① at one go; at a stretch; without break:他～跑了20里。*He walked 20 li at a stretch.* ② [贬] of the same gang; hand in glove:串通～ *work hand in glove; collude* ③ [贬] spell; fit:瞎闹～ *raise hell; kick up a row*

【一气呵成】① (of an essay) form a coherent whole; make smooth reading ② accomplish sth at one go; carry sth through without stopping:我们～完成了任务。*We completed our task at one go.*

【一气之下】in a fit of pique; in an outburst of anger

【一千零一夜】The Thousand and One Nights or Arabian Nights Entertainments, a collection of fairy stories and romances originally written in Arabic

【一钱不值】not worth a penny; utterly worthless; load of rubbish; mere trash:把那个人贬得～ *condemn the man as not worth*

【一钱如命】regard a penny as precious as life — extremely stingy; niggardly; miser

【一腔】have one's heart filled with:～热情 *be filled with enthusiasm* /甘洒～热血 *be willing to sacrifice one's life*

【一窍不通】know nothing about; have no knowledge of; be completely ignorant of:我对绘画艺术是～的。*I don't know anything about drawing.*

【一切】all; every:采取～手段 *take every measure* /想尽～办法 *try every means possible*

【一清二白】① perfectly clear ② clean

【一清二楚】very clear; distinct; as clear as day

【一清如水】as clear as water — honest and upright

【一清早】in early morning

【一穷二白】poor and blank

【一丘之貉】[贬] jackals from the same lair; birds of a feather; tarred with the same brush

【一去不复返】gone for ever; gone never to return; never to be found again:苦日子已经~了。*The hard and miserable life have gone forever.*

【一犬吠影,百犬吠声】one dog barks at a shadow, and a hundred dogs join in — blindly follow suit

【一人做事一人当】a man should be responsible for his actions; a man must bear the consequences of his own acts:我~。*I will take full responsibility for what I have done.*

【一日夫妻百日恩】one night of love is worth a hundred days of affection; a day together as husband and wife means devotion for the rest of their life

【一日千里】a thousand li a day-at a tremendous pace; with giant strides; by leaps and bounds

【一如既往】just as in the past; as usual; as before; as always:我们将~为明天而奋斗 *We will, as always, work for the future.*

【一扫而光】make a clean sweep of; clear off; finish off; get rid of sth lock and barrel

【一色】① of the same colour ② of the same type; uniform

【一霎】in an instant; in a moment: ~间 *in a flash* / ~时 *in a flash*

【一闪念】a fleeting thought

【一晌】[口] ① a period of time; a little while ② a period of time

【一上来】at first; at the beginning: 那个小伙子~就劲头十足。*The young fellow is full of enthusiasm from the very beginning.*

【一身】① the whole body; all over the body ② a suit: ~新衣服 *a new suit of clothes* ③ a single person:独自~ *solitary; all alone* / ~是胆 *one's whole body is all pluck-know no fear; be absolutely fearless*

【一审】【律】first instance

【一生】all one's life; throughout one's life: ~一世 *all one's life; throughout one's life*

【一声不响】not say a word; not utter a sound

【一失足成千古恨】one false step brings everlasting grief; a single slip may cause lasting sorrow; a moment's error can bring a lifelong regret

【一时】① a period of time ② for a short while; temporary momentary: ~的多数 *a temporary majority* ③ (used in pairs) now..., now...; one moment..., the next

【一世】① all one's life; a lifetime ② age; era; times

【一式】of the same form: ~两份 *in duplicate* / ~三份 *in triplicate*

【一事无成】accomplish nothing; get nowhere

【一视同仁】treat all alike without discrimination; make no exception

【一手】① skill; proficiency; expertise:露~ *show off one's skill* /业务上有~ *be proficient in one's own line, know one's stuff* ②trick; move:他这~真毒辣! *What a vicious trick he played!* ③ single-handed; all by oneself; all alone:这场争论是他~挑起的。*The argument was all started by him.* /婚礼是由他~操办的。*The wedding was arranged al by him.*

【一手包办】keep everything in one's own hands; take everything on oneself

【一手遮天】shut out the heavens with one hand; hide the truth from the masses; pull the wool over the eye of the public

【一瞬】an instant; a flash; twinkling of an eye: ~即逝 *vanish in a flash; be transitory*

【一丝不苟】neglect no detail; be scrupulous about every detail; be conscientious and meticulous

【一丝不挂】not have a stitch on; be stark-naked; be in one's birthday suit

【一丝一毫】a tiny bit; an iota; a trace:没有~的差别 *without the least difference*

【一塌糊涂】in a real muddle; messy; in an awful or terrible state:争吵得~ *kick up a terrible row* / 输得~ *suffer a overwhelming defeat* /他把事情弄得~。*He has made a mess of the job.*

【一潭死水】a pool of stagnant water; a stagnant or lifeless condition

【一体】① an organic or integral whole:融成~ *merge into an organic whole* / ~化 *integration* / ~化区域合作 *integrated regional cooperation* ② all people concerned; everyone: ~周知 *It's hereby notified to all concerned that*

【一天】① a day: ~服三次药 *take the medicine three times a day* ② one day (in the past): ~,他告诉妻子自己得了癌症。*One day he told his wife that he had a cancer.* ③ [方] the whole day; all (the) day; from morning till night ④ daytime:他整整忙了~一夜。*He was kept busy throughout the day and the night.*

【一天到晚】from morning till night; from dawn to dusk; all day long: ~都是忙 *be busy from dawn till dusk*

【一条道儿跑到黑】follow one road until it's dark — cling stubbornly to one course; be pigheaded

【一条龙】① one continuous line:等待就餐的学生排成了~。*There was a long line of students waiting for eating.* ② a connected sequence; a coordinated process

【一条心】be of one heart and one mind; be at one: 众人~,黄土变成金。*If we're all of one heart and one mind, we can change clay into gold.* /全班上下~。*All students in this class are of one mind.*

【一通百通】master one and you'll master a hundred; sort this one out you'll sort out all the rest

【一同】together; at the same time and place; in company: ~欢度春节 *celebrate the Spring Festival together* / ~出发 *set out together*

【一统】unify (a country):大~ *a unified domain; whole empire under one ruler* / ~天下 *unify the whole country; dominated the whole world*

【一头】① a head:儿子高我~。*My son is a head taller than I am.* /这个女人总觉得自己高人~。*The lady always feel superior to others.* ② one end; one side; one aspect:顾了这～,顾不了那～ *cannot attend both sides(or all aspects) at once* /桌子的～坐着母亲,另～坐着女儿。*The mother was sitting at one end of the table and the daughter at the other.* ③ suddenly; headlong:冷不防～撞见他 *rush headlong into him* ④ at the same time; simultaneously:他～说,～朝门口走。*So saying, he made for the door.* ⑤ be on the same side; belong to the same group ⑥［方］together; with each other

【一吐为快】cannot rest until one has one's say; have a view one must air

【一团和气】keep on good terms with everyone (at the expense of principle); keep on the right side of everyone; curry favor with people all around

【一团漆黑】pitch-dark; utterly hopeless:屋里～。*It's pitch-dark in the room.* /不能把我们的将来说成～。*We must not paint a black picture of our future.*

【一团糟】a complete mess; a chaotic state:你把工作搞得～。*You've made a mess of your job.* /屋子里～。*The room was in chaos.*

【一碗水端平】hold a bowl of water level — be impartial

【一网打尽】catch the whole lot in a dragnet; round up the whole gang at one fell swoop; make a clean sweep

【一往情深】be deeply attached; be passionately devoted; be head over heels in love

【一往无前】press forward with an indomitable will: ～的献身精神 *an indomitable spirit of dedication*

【一望无际】stretch as far as the eye can see; stretch to the horizon; there is a boundless stretch before one: ～的大草原 *a boundless stretch of grassland* /～的原野 *a vast expense of open country*

【一味】stubbornly; persistently; blindly: ～迁就 *make endless concessions; make one concession after another* /～强调客观条件 *put unjust emphasis on objective conditions*

【一文不名】not have a penny to one's name; be penniless

【一文不值】not worth a penny; utterly worthless

【一问三不知】say "I don't know" to every question — not know a thing; be completely in the dark

【一窝蜂】(of a crowd of people) like a swarm of bees:同学们～拥向教室门口。*The students swarmed towards the door of classroom.*

【一无可取】have nothing to recommend one; be without a single merit:这家宾馆儿除了价钱便宜之外,～之处。*This hotel has nothing to recommend it except that it's cheap.*

【一无是处】without a single redeeming virtue or quality; devoid of any merit

【一无所长】have no special skill

【一无所有】not own a thing in the world; possess nothing; not have a thing to one's name

【一无所知】know nothing about; not have the least inkling of be absolutely ignorant of:对这件事我真的是～。*I'm absolutely ignorant of it.*

【一五一十】(narrate) systematically and in full detail; from first to last:她把事故～地都给母亲讲了。*She told her mother the whole accident exactly as it had happened.*

【一物降一物】there is always one thing to conquer another; everything has its superior

【一误再误】① make one error after another; keep on making mistakes ② make things worse by repeated delays

【一息尚存】so long as one still has a breath left; till one breathe one's last

【一席话】what one says during a conversation:听君～,胜读十年书。*I profit more from one conversation with you than from ten years of reading.* /老师的～,对我很有启发。*What my teacher said is quite enlightening.*

【一系列】a series of: ～的事件 *a whole train of events* /～措施 *a series of measures* /～观点 *a whole string of views* /～事实 *a host of facts*

【一下】① used after a verb, indicating an act or action:看～ *have a look* /等～ *wait a minute* /试～ *have a try* /拍～他的头 *give him a pat on the head* ② in a short while; all at once; all of a sudden:天～晴了。*It cleared up all of a sudden.* /请等～,别挂上。*Will you please hold the line a minute?* /这天气,～冷,～热。*Look at this weather; it's cold one moment and hot the next.* /话题～转到他的婚事上去了。*The topic of the conversation was soon changed to his marriage.*

【一线】① a ray of; a gleam of: ～生机 *a gleam of hope in despair* /～阳光 *a ray of sunlight* /～微光 *a glimmer of light* ② war front; front line: ～战场 *front line battle field* /～工人 *worker at the production line* /他申请到～作战。*He applied for permission to fight at the front line.*

【一向】① earlier on; lately:你这～可好? *How have you been since I saw you last?* ② consistently, always; all along:我～不喜欢她。*I've never liked her.*

【一小撮】a handful of; a small number of: ～恐怖分子 *a handful of terrorists*

【一笑置之】dismiss with a laugh (or smile); laugh off

【一小儿】［方］from childhood; as a child:他～就聪明。*He has been clever ever since he was a child.*

【一些】① a number or amount of; a few; a little; certain; some:他去过～地方,见过～世面。*He's been to quite a few places and has seen some of the world.* /再给我～。*Please give me some more.* /有～问题我还不明白。*There are a few questions that still puzzle me.* ② tiny bit; little; few:家里可吃的水果就这～。*That's all the fruits left for the family.* ③ used after an adjective, a verb or verbal phrase to indicate a slight change in degree: 大声～! *Speak louder, please!* /多拿～。*Take more.* /说话客气～! *Be polite when speaking!*

【一泻千里】① (of a river) rush down a thousand li

— flow down powerfully ② (of a writer's style) unrestrained and fluent; bold and flowing

【一心】① wholeheartedly; heart and soul: ~扑在工作上 *devote oneself wholeheartedly to work* / ~为人民 *serve the people heart and soul* / ~想上大学 *be bent on going to college* ② of one mind; with one heart: 万众~ *millions of people are of one mind* / ~一德 *be of one heart and one mind; be dedicated to the same cause* / ~一意 *heart and soul; whole-heartedly*

【一新】entirely new; brand new: 大楼整修~。*The building looks completely new after repairs.*

【一星半点】a tiny bit; a very small amount: 不能有~差错。*There mustn't be the slightest slip.*

【一行】a group traveling together; party; team: 代表团~十五人 *the fifteen-person delegation* / 总统及其~ *the President and accompanying officials*

【一宿】[口] one night: ~没合眼 *not sleep a wink the whole night*

【一言不发】not say (or utter) a word; remain silent: 他一整天都~。*He remained silent the whole day.*

【一言既出,驷马难追】a word once spoken cannot be taken back even by a team of four horses-what is said cannot be unsaid: 男子汉做事~。*A real man never goes back on his words.*

【一言难尽】it's hard to explain in a few words; it's a long story

【一言堂】① [旧] (sign hung in a shop) fixed prices; no bargaining ② what I say goes; one person alone has the say; one person lays down the law: ~作风 *dictatorial style of work*

【一言为定】that's settled then; keep one's word: 我们~,决不反悔。*We will keep our word and never go back on it.*

【一言以蔽之】to sum up in a word; in short

【一氧化碳】carbon monoxide

【一氧化物】monoxide

【一样】the same; alike; equally; as... as...: 像海~深 *as deep as sea* / ~地聪明 *be equally bright* / 谁去都~。*It won't make any difference who goes.*

【一叶障目,不见泰山】a single leaf before the eye shuts out Mount Tai — partial or superficial phenomenon interferes with the understanding of the essence of things

【一叶知秋】the falling of one leaf heralds the autumn; a small sign can indicate a great trend

【一夜夫妻百夜恩】husband and wife for one night, love lingers on for a hundred nights

【一一】one by one; one after another: ~检查 *examine one by one* / ~解释 *explain one by one* / ~记在心里 *remember every detail*

【一……一……】① used with two nouns of similar kind (a) indicating the whole of: 一生一世 *one's whole life; all one's life* (b) *indicating each; every; single*: 一言一行 *every word and deed* / 一兵一卒 *every soldier* / 一草一木 *every tree and every grass* ② used with two verbs similar in meaning, indicating the continuance of the actions: 一惊一乍 *fuss and fluster* / 一瘸一拐 *limp along* / 一蹦一跳 *skip and hop* ③ used with two verbs contrasting in meaning, indicating the coordination or alternation of the two actions: 一问一答 *one asks and the other answers* / 一推一拉 *push and pull* / 一起一落 *rise one moment and fall down the other* ④ used with two words opposite in meaning, indicating opposition or contrast: 一前一后 *one in front, one following* / 一东一西 *one east, one west; poles apart* / 一高一矮 *one tall, one short*

【一衣带水】a narrow strip of water: ~的邻邦 *close neighbors separated by only a strip of water*

【一意孤行】cling obstinately to one's course; act willfully; insist on having one's own way

【一应】all; everything: ~工具 *all the tools* / ~花销 *all the expenses*

【一应俱全】everything needed is there

【一拥而上】① rush up in a crowd; gather around at once ② rush at sth in confusion; make no distinction between the important and trivial

【一隅】a corner: ~之地 *a very small area* / ~之见 *a very narrow (or limited) view*

【一语道破】lay bare the truth with one remark; hit the nail on the head: ~其中奥秘 *lay bare the secret of sth with one remark*

【一语破的】hit the mark with a single comment

【一语双关】a single phrase with a double meaning; pun

【一元方程】equation with one unknown

【一元化】centralized; unified: 实行~的领导 *exercise unified (or centralized) leadership* / ~化的体制 *unified system*

【一月】January

【一再】time and again; again and again; repeatedly: ~表示感谢 *express one's gratitude again and again* / ~声明 *state repeatedly*

【一…再…】used before the same replicated verb, indicating the repetition of the action: 一错再错 *keep on making mistakes* / 一拖再拖 *postpone again and again*

【一早】[口] ① early in the morning: 后天~ *first thing the day after tomorrow* / 他~就出去了。*He went out early in the morning.* ② [方] at first; in the beginning

【一张一弛】tension alternating with relaxation

【一着不慎,满盘皆输】one careless move loses the whole game; one wrong move spoils the entire game

【一朝】① in one day: ~覆亡 *collapse (or be toppled) in one short day* / ~之忿 *momentary anger* ② once: ~出错,悔恨一辈子。*A moment's error can bring a lifelong regret.*

【一朝被蛇咬,十年怕井绳】once bitten by a snake, one shies at coiled rope for ten years; once bitten, twice shy; a burnt child dreads the fire

【一朝一夕】in one morning or evening; in one day: 非~之功 *not the work of a single day*

【一针见血】draw blood with the first prick of a needle — get to the truth with a single pertinent remark; hit the nail on the head; hit or strike home: ~地讲出问题的症结所在 *point out sharply where the crucial cause of the problem exist* / 这些批评~。*Those criticism hit home.*

【一枕黄粱】golden Millet Dream — a brief dream or delusion of grandeur

【一阵】① a burst; a fit; a peal: ~掌声 *a burst of applause* / ~咳嗽 *a fit (or spasm) of coughing* / ~枪声 *a burst of gunfire* ② a period of time; a spell / 她这~工作很忙。*She has been busy with work these days.*

【一阵风】① a gust of wind ② like a whirlwind; very quickly: 同学们~冲了上去。*The classmates rushed forward like a whirlwind.* ③ transient; brief; of short duration

【一知半解】have a smattering of knowledge; have scanty or half-baked knowledge: 对学习不能满足于~。*We should not feel satisfied with little learning.*

【一直】① straight: ~走 *go straight ahead; keep straight on* / ~往东走 *go straight towards the east* ② continuously; all along; always; all the way: 我们~都是好朋友。*We have been good friends all along.*

【一纸空文】a mere scrap of paper: 这个结论只不过是~。*The conclusion is nothing but a mere scrap of paper.*

【一致】showing no difference; identical; unanimous; consistent: 言行~ *be as good as one's words* / 观点~ *hold identical views; be of the same view* / 步调~ *march in step; act in unison* / 官兵~ *unity between officers and men* / ~行动 *concerted action* / 双方~认为 *both sides agree (that...)*

【一掷千金】stake a thousand pieces of gold on one throw (of dice, etc); spend one's money wastefully and extravagantly; throw away money like dirt; spend money like water

【一专多能】expert in one thing and good at many

【一准】[口] sure; surely; certainly: 明儿我~来。*I'm sure to come tomorrow.*

【一字褒贬】one word clearly expressing praise or censure; a strict, deliberate choice of words

【一字儿】in a row; in a line: 摆开~长蛇阵 *draw up in single-line formation; string out in a long line*

【一字千金】each word worth a thousand pieces of gold; excellent literary work or calligraphy

【一字一板】(speak) unhurriedly and clearly: 他开始~地读起来。*He began to read deliberately.*

【一字之师】one's single-correction teacher

【一总】① altogether; all told; in all: ~来了二十个人。*There came about twenty people altogether.* ② all: 这些活~交给我吧。*Leave all the work to me.*

伊 [书] he or she

【伊甸园】[宗] Garden of Eden; paradise

【伊拉克】Iraq: ~人 *Iraqi*

【伊朗】Iran: ~人 *Iranian*

【伊人】[书] that person (esp. a woman)

【伊始】beginning: 上任~ *upon assuming office* / 新年~ *at the beginning of the New Year*

【伊斯兰教】Islam; Islamism: ~国家 *Islamic country* / ~历 *the Moslem Calendar* / ~徒 *Moslem; Muslimism*

衣 ① clothing; clothes; garment: 内~ *underclothes; underwear* / 毛~ *sweater; woolen sweater* / 大~ *overcoat* / 量体裁~ *cut the garment according to the figure — act according to actual circumstances* / 到了更~的时间的。*It's time to change clothes.* ② coating; covering: 糖~ *sugars coating* / 琴~ *piano cover* ③ afterbirth: 胞~ *afterbirth* ④ (Yī) a surname

【衣胞】(human) afterbirth

【衣钵】a Buddhist monk's mantle and alms bowl which he hands down to his disciple; legacy: 继承~ *inherit the mantle of sb*

【衣不蔽体】be dressed in rags; have nothing but rags on one's back

【衣不解带】cannot take off one's clothes and have a proper sleep because of pressure of work

【衣橱】wardrobe

【衣兜】pocket

【衣服】clothing; clothes

【衣钩】clothes hook

【衣冠】hat and clothes; dress: ~不整 *be sloppily dressed* / ~禽兽 *a beast in human attire; brute* / ~冢 *a tomb containing hat, clothes or other personal effects of the deceased, whose remains are either missing or buried elsewhere* / 每天他都穿得~楚楚。*Everyday he is immaculately dressed.*

【衣柜】wardrobe

【衣架】① coat hanger; clothes-rack ② clothes tree; clothes stand ③ stature; figure: ~饭囊 *clothes-horse and food bag — worthless person; good for nothing*

【衣襟】the one or two pieces making up the front of a Chinese jacket

【衣锦还乡】go back to one's old home in silken robes — return home after acquiring wealth and honour

【衣料】material for clothing; dress material

【衣领】collar

【衣帽架】clothes tree; clothes stand

【衣帽间】cloakroom

【衣衾】closes and quilts (esp. used for burying the dead)

【衣衫】clothes: ~不整 *not properly dressed* / ~褴褛 *shabbily dressed; out at elbows; in rags*

【衣裳】[口] clothing; clothes

【衣食父母】people on whom one relies for living

【衣食住行】food, clothing, shelter and transportation — basic necessities of life

【衣食足而知荣辱】when food and clothing are enough, men have a sense of honour and shame

【衣饰】dress and personal adornment; dress: ~华丽 *be gorgeously dressed*

【衣物】clothing and other articles of daily use; personal effects
【衣箱】trunk; suitcase
【衣装】① dress; attire ② clothes and luggage
【衣着】clothing, headgear and footwear: ～整洁 *be neatly dressed* / ～朴素 *be plainly dressed*
医 ① doctor (of medicine); medical practitioner: 内科～生 *physician* / 中～ *doctor of traditional Chinese medicine; practitioner of traditional Chinese medicine* / 西～ *doctor trained in Western medicine* / 牙～ *dentist* / 兽～ *veterinarian; vet* / 法～ *legal medical expert* / 神～ *highly skilled doctor quack* / 延～诊治 *call in a doctor for treatment* / 缺～少药 *be short of doctors and medicine* ② medical science; medical service; medicine: 行～ *practice medicine* / 中西～结合 *combine traditional Chinese and Western medicine* / 她女儿是学～的。*Her daughter studies medicine.* ③ cure; treat; get timely medical care: 讳疾忌～ *hide one's illness for fear of treatment*
【医道】medical expertise; knowledge; physician's skill: 听说你爸爸是一位～高明的医生。*I heard that your father was a highly skilled doctor.*
【医德】medical ethics: ～高尚 *exemplary medical ethics*
【医风】style of work, medical practice
【医护】give medical treatment and nursing
【医经】ancient Chinese medical classics
【医科】medical courses in general; medicine: ～大学 *medical university*
【医理】principles of medical science; medical knowledge
【医疗】medical treatment: ～机构 *medical establishment or institution* / ～器械 *medical apparatus and instruments* / ～事故 *unskillful and faulty medical or surgical treatment; malpractice* / ～队 *medical team* / ～站 *medical station; health centre*
【医生】doctor; medical man: 内科～ *physician* / 外科～ *surgeon* / 牙～ *dentist* / 儿～ *pediatrician* / 眼～ *oculist* / 实习～ *intern* / 主治～ *doctor in charge* / 住院～ *resident doctor* / 值班～ *doctor on duty*
【医师】(qualified) doctor
【医士】practitioner with secondary medical school education; medical assistant
【医书】medical book
【医术】medical skill; art of healing: ～精湛 *consummate medical skill*
【医务】medical matters: ～工作者 *medical worker* / ～人员 *medical personnel (or staff, workers)*; *public health worker* / ～室 *grass-roots health clinic, often small and equipped with basic facilities*
【医学】medical science; medicine: ～硕士 *master of medicine* / ～界 *medical circle* / ～文献 *medical literature* / ～遗产 *medical heritage* / ～科学院 *academy of medical sciences*
【医药】medicine: ～常识 *general medical knowledge* / 由谁来支付～费? *Who will pay the medical expenses?*
【医院】hospital: 儿童～ *children's hospital* / 综合性～ *general hospital* / 中～ *hospital of Chinese medicine* / 附属～ *affiliated or attached hospital* / 专科～ *specialized hospital*
【医治】cure; treat; heal: 得到及时～ *receive timely treatment* / ～无效 *fail to respond to medical treatment* / ～精神创伤 *heal mental wounds or emotional trauma*
【医嘱】doctor's advice (or orders)
【医助】assistant doctor (in the army)
依 ① depend on; rely on; count on: 无～无靠 *have nobody to depend on* / 相～为命 *depend on each other for existence* ② comply with; obey; yield to ③ according to; judging by
【依傍】① depend on; rely on ② imitate; model oneself on: ～前人 *emulate one's predecessors*
【依此类推】the rest may be inferred; and so on and so forth
【依次】in proper order; successively; one after another: ～入座 *take the seats in proper order* / ～发言 *speak in turn*
【依从】comply with; yield to: ～长辈 *comply with one's senior*
【依存】depend on sb or sth for existence: 相互～ *be interdependent*
【依法】① according to fixed rule: ～炮制 *prepare herbal medicine by the prescribed method — follow a set pattern; follow suit* ② according to law; in conformity with legal provisions; in accordance with the law: ～惩办 *punish according to law; deal with in accordance with the law; bring to justice*
【依附】depend on; attach oneself to; become an appendage to: ～权贵 *attach oneself to bigwigs* / ～他人 *attach oneself to sb*
【依借】use; turn to advantage; draw on
【依旧】as before; as usual; still: 他的房间陈设～。*His room is furnished as it was before.* / 都半夜了，他～在灯下看书。*It's almost midnight, and he was still reading by the light.*
【依据】① according to; in the light of on the basis of; judging by: ～上述意见 *in accordance with the above views* / ～先例 *act in the light of the precedents* / ～法律 *according the law* ② basis; foundation: 提供科学～ *provide scientific basis for sth* / 毫无～ *utterly baseless (or groundless)*
【依靠】① rely on; depend on: ～自己的力量 *depend on one's own strength* / ～群众 *rely on the masses* ② something to fall back on; support; backing: 生活有～ *have one's livelihood assured* / 寻找～ *seek support*
【依赖】rely on; be dependent on: ～别人 *be dependent on others* / ～性 *dependence*
【依恋】be reluctant to leave; feel regret at parting from: ～故乡的一草一木 *be attached to every tree and bush in one's hometown* / ～之情 *attachment; devotion*
【依然】still; as before: ～有效 *still hold good; remain valid* / ～如故 *remain as before; remain the same*

【依山傍水】at the foot of a hill and beside a stream
【依随】agree to; yield to; comply with
【依托】① rely on; depend on: ~权贵 *count on one's powerful connections* ② support; prop; backing
【依偎】snuggle up to; lean close to
【依稀】vaguely; dimly
【依循】follow; abide by
【依样画葫芦】draw a gourd according to the model — copy mechanically
【依依】①［书］(of branch or twig) frail and gentle, swaying in the wind ② reluctant to part: ~惜别 *part reluctantly from; bid farewell to each other reluctantly* / ~不舍 *be reluctant to part; cannot bear to part*
【依允】assent; consent: 点头~ *nod assent*
【依仗】count on; depend on; rely on: ~权势 *rely on one's power and position; count on one's powerful connections.*
【依照】according to; in accordance with; in the light of: ~情况而定 *decide as circumstances require* / ~法律行事 *act according to the law* / ~上级指示 *according to the directives of higher authorities*

咿

【咿唔】［象］the sound of reading aloud
【咿呀】①［象］squeak; creak ② prattle; babble: ~学语的小孩 *a babbling baby*

铱【化】iridium (Ir)

【铱金笔】iridium-point pen
【铱星】iridium satellite

壹 one (used for the numeral — on cheques, banknotes, etc. to avoid mistakes or alterations)

揖［书］(make a) bow with hands clasped

【揖别】［书］bid farewell by bowing with hands clasped
【揖让】［书］bowing with two hands clasped and giving precedence to the other, a form of courtesy between guest and host in ancient times

噫 ①［书］alas ② why; how come: ~, 他今天怎么没来? *How don't he come here today?*

yí

仪[1] ① appearance; bearing: ~态大方 *easy and unaffected manners* / 威~ *dignified hearing* ② ceremony; rite; protocol: 礼~ *courtesy; protocol* / 司~ *master of ceremonies* ③ present; gift: 贺~ *present for wedding, birthday, etc.* ④ admire; yearn for; look forward to: 哥哥对那个漂亮的姑娘心~已久。*My elder brother has long admired the pretty lady.*

仪[2] apparatus; instrument: 地球~ (*terrestrial*) *globe* / 地震~ *seismograph*

【仪表】① appearance; bearing: ~不凡 *have striking appearance* / ~堂堂 *dignified in appearance; impressive looking; imposing* / 注意~ *be careful about one's deportment* ② meter: 飞机~ *aeroplane meters* / ~厂 *instrument and meter plant*
【仪器】instrument; apparatus: 实验~ *experimental instrument* / 精密~ *precision instrument* / 光学~ *optical instrument* / ~厂 *instrument plant* / ~制造工业 *instrument-making industry*
【仪容】looks; appearance: ~俊秀 *handsome appearance* / ~文雅 *gentle appearance*
【仪式】ceremony; rite; function: 宗教~ *religious rites* / 签字~ *signing ceremony* / 奠基~ *foundation stone laying ceremony* / 受降 *the ceremony of accepting a surrender*
【仪态】［书］bearing; deportment; posture: ~万千 (*of a beauty*) *appear in all her glory or splendour*
【仪仗】① weapons carried by guards of honour at state ceremonies or welcoming ceremony for a foreign guests ② flags, weapons, etc. carried by the guards when the emperor or high officials went out in ancient times: ~队 *guard of honour; honour guard*

夷[1] ①［书］smooth; safe: 化险为~ *turn danger into safety* ② raze; level (to the ground): ~为平地 *level to the ground; raze* ③ exterminate; wipe out: ~族 *extermination of an entire family*

夷[2] his name for ancient tribes in the east of China; barbarism: 四~ *all the ethnic minorities around China* (*in ancient times*) ②［旧］foreign country; foreigner: ~人 *foreigners*

【夷灭】annihilate; exterminate
【夷平】level to the ground; raze

饴 maltose, malt sugar: 甘之如~ *enjoy sth bitter as if it were as sweet as malt sugar; gladly endure hardship* / 高粱~ *sorghum candy*

【饴糖】maltose; malt sugar

怡［书］happy; joyful; cheerful: 神情~然 *looking relaxed and happy* / 心旷神~ *feel relaxed and happy; be in a cheerful mood*

【怡和】［书］amiable; genial; happy
【怡然】happy and contented
【怡然自得】be happy and pleased with oneself; feel a glow of happiness
【怡神】［书］soothe the spirit: ~养性 *cultivate one's temperament and nourish; nourish one's nature*
【怡悦】happy; joyous

宜 ① suitable; appropriate; fitting: 老幼咸~ *good for both young and old* / 因地制~ *suit measures to local conditions* / 不合时~ *be out of keeping with the times* ② should; ought to: 讲演~短不~长。*A short speech is preferable to a long one.* ③ with no doubt ④ (Yí) a surname

【宜人】pleasant; delightful
【宜于】be good for; be suitable for: 这种土壤~种苹果。*This kind of soil is good for growing apples.*

贻［书］① make a gift of sth; present: 馈~ *present a gift* ② bequeath; leave behind; hand down: ~害终生 *bring ruin on one's entire life*

【贻害】leave a legacy of trouble to: ~无穷 *entail untold harm; cause no end of trouble*
【贻患】sow seeds of disaster; leave a legacy of trouble
【贻人口实】provide one's critic with a handle; give occasion for ridicule
【贻误】affect adversely; bungle; miss: ~战机 *bungle the chance of winning a battle; forfeit a chance for combat* / ~农时 *miss the farming season* / ~终身 *bring ruin upon one's whole life*
【贻笑大方】make a laughing stock of oneself before experts; incur the ridicule of experts; display one's incompetence before an expert and make a fool of oneself

姨 ① mother's sister; maternal aunt; aunt ② wife's sister; sister-in-law: 小~子 *one's wife's younger sister*
【姨表】maternal cousin; cousinship: ~兄弟 *male maternal cousins* / ~姐妹 *female maternal cousins* / ~亲 *maternal relatives*
【姨夫】the husband of mother's sister (or one's maternal aunt); uncle
【姨姥姥】sister of one's maternal grandmother; great-aunt
【姨妈】[口] (married) maternal aunt; aunt
【姨母】(married) maternal aunt; aunt
【姨奶奶】① sister of one's paternal grandmother; great-aunt ② [口] concubine
【姨娘】① [旧] a term of address for father's concubine ② [方] (married) maternal aunt; aunt
【姨太太】[口] concubine

胰 pancreas
【胰岛】pancreas islet: ~瘤 *insulinoma* / ~素 *insulin*
【胰淀粉酶】【生化】amylopsin
【胰腺】pancreas: ~炎 *pancreatitis*
【胰液】pancreatic juice
【胰皂】[方] soap
【胰子】① [口] pancreas (of pigs, sheep, etc.) ② [方] soap

移 ① move; remove; shift: 位~(物) *displacement* / 转~ *shift; transfer; divert* / 迁~ *remove; migrate; relocate* / 把桌子~到那边去 *move the table over there* ② change; alter; transform: 坚定不~ *firm and unshakable; unswerving* / 潜~默化 *imperceptibly influence* / 献身革命志不~ *dedicate oneself to the revolution with unshakable will* / 转~视线 *distract sb's attention*
【移调】【音】transposition: ~乐器 *transposing instrument*
【移动】① move; shift: ~电话 *cellular telephone; mobile phone* / ~电台 *mobile station* ②【机】move; travel: 我不会使用这台~电动机。*I can't use this travel motor.*
【移动交换中心】mobile switching centre (MSC)
【移防】(of troops) be shifted elsewhere for garrison duty
【移风易俗】change prevailing habits and customs; transform established social traditions
【移花接木】① graft one twig on another; graft ② stealthily substitute one thing for another; surreptitiously replace
【移交】① turn over; transfer; hand over: 那个案件已经~给中级法院审理了。*The case had been transferred to an intermediate court.* ② hand over one's job to a successor
【移居】move or change one's residence; migrate: ~国外 *emigrate to a foreign country*
【移苗】transplant seedlings
【移民】① migrate; emigrate or immigrate: 三峡~工程 *relocation projects of Three Gorge area* ② emigrant or immigrant: ~点 *settlement* / ~法 *immigration laws* / ~签证 *immigrant visa* / ~局 *immigration service (or office)*
【移情】① change one's interest or affection: ~山水 *become interested in mountains and rivers* / 他是个容易~别恋的人。*He is easy to shift his affection to another person.* ② empathize; transfer: ~作用 *empathy*
【移送】turn over (suspects, legal files, etc.) to
【移山倒海】move mountains and drain seas; make tremendous efforts to conquer nature; transform nature
【移时】[书] after a short while
【移位】【电】shift: ~寄存器 *shift register*
【移徙】move; migrate; change one's residence
【移项】【数】transposition
【移栽】【农】transplant
【移植】① transplant: ~秧苗 *transplant seedlings* ②【医】transplant; graft: 心脏~ *heart transplanting* / 皮肤~ *skin graft*

遗 ① lose ② sth lost: 路不拾~ *no one pockets anything found on the road* ③ omit; forget: 拾~补阙 *make good omissions and shortcoming* / 补~ *addendum* ④ leave behind; keep back; not give: 不~余力 *spare no efforts* / 养虎~患 *to rear a tiger is to court calamity; appeasement brings disaster* ⑤ leave behind at one's death; bequeath; hand down ⑥ involuntary discharge of urine, etc: 梦~ *nocturnal emission; wet dream*
【遗案】unsolved case
【遗笔】writings left behind by the deceased
【遗产】legacy; inheritance; heritage: 继承~ *bequeath (inherit) a legacy* / 历史~ *a legacy of history* / 文化~ *cultural heritage* / ~税 *inheritance tax; succession duty*
【遗臭万年】leave a stink for ten thousand years; go down in history as a byword for infamy; earn eternal notoriety
【遗传】【生理】heredity; inheritance: 隐性~ *recessive inheritance* / 显性~ *dominant inheritance* / ~特征 *hereditary feature; heredity* / ~病 *hereditary disease* / ~工程 *genetic engineering* / ~基因 *hereditary genes* / ~密码 *genetic code* / ~信息 *hereditary (or genetic) information* / ~学 *genetics* / ~学家 *geneticist* / ~因子 *genetic factor*
【遗存】① leave over; hand down: 这些化石~至今

已百万余年。*These fossils have been in existence for over a million years.* ② things left over from ancient times; remains; legacy:恐龙的化石～ *the fossil remains of a dinosaur*

【遗毒】baneful legacy; harmful tradition; pernicious influence

【遗范】model of one's predecessors

【遗风】tradition or customs left over from the past

【遗腹子】a posthumous child

【遗稿】a manuscript left unpublished by the author at his death; a posthumous manuscript

【遗骸】remains (of the dead):烈士～ *the remains of the martyrs* /士兵～ *the remains of soldiers*

【遗害】leave harm behind: ～后人 *do harm to later generations*

【遗憾】① regret; pity:这是他终生的～。*This is his lifelong regret.* ② regret; deplore:很～,她不能来。*It is very sorry she won't be able to come.*

【遗恨】eternal regret; remorse

【遗祸】leave harm behind; do harm to sb: ～子孙 *do harm to later generations*

【遗迹】historical ruins; remains; traces; vestiges: 古代村落的～ *the remains of ancient villages* /古代文明的～ *vestiges of an ancient civilization*

【遗教】teachings and works left behind by one after one's death

【遗精】(seminal) emission

【遗老】① a surviving adherent of a former dynasty; an old fogy; an old diehard ②[书] old people who have witnessed big social changes

【遗留】leave over; hand down: ～的痕迹 *surviving traces* /过去～下来的问题 *problem left over by history* /多年～下来的弊病 *long-standing abuse*

【遗漏】omit; leave out; fail to do sth:重大～ *an important omission*

【遗命】last will; dying words

【遗尿】【医】enuresis; bed-wetting

【遗篇】writings left behind by the deceased

【遗弃】① abandon; forsake or desert one's relatives that one should support or foster: ～妻儿 *forsake one's wife and children* /被～的女婴 *an abandoned baby girl* ② leave behind; cast away; abandon:敌人～大批辎重。*The enemy abandoned (or left behind) large quantities of supplies.*

【遗容】① the looks of the deceased:瞻仰～ *pay one's respects to the remains of sb* ② a portrait of the deceased

【遗少】a young adherent of an overthrown dynasty; a young diehard

【遗失】lose: ～声明 *lost property notice* /～的孩子 *a lost kid*

【遗事】① incidents of past ages ② deeds of those now dead

【遗书】① surviving works; posthumous works; collected writings published after the author's death ② a letter or note left by one immediately before death or suicide ③[书] books that have been lost

【遗孀】widow; relict

【遗体】remains (of the dead):向～告别 *pay one's last respects to the remains of the deceased* /向～鞠躬 *bow to the remains of the died*

【遗忘】forget; slip one's memory:被～角落 *a forgotten corner* /～症 *amnesia aphasia*

【遗物】things left behind by the deceased; relic:死者的～ *personal effects of the died*

【遗像】a portrait or photo of the deceased

【遗训】teachings of the deceased

【遗言】words of the deceased; (a person's) last words

【遗业】① work or cause left unfinished by one's predecessor or ancestor:继承先人～ *carry on where one's ancestor left off* ② property left by the deceased; legacy

【遗愿】unfulfilled wish of the deceased; last wish: 实现英雄的～ *realize or fulfill the last wish of the hero*

【遗赠】bequeath; give(one's belongings or property to donated persons or institutions) upon one's death

【遗照】photos of the deceased

【遗址】ruins; relics:古城～ *the site of an ancient city* /村落～ *the site of a village*

【遗志】unfulfilled wish; work leftover by the deceased:继承先烈～ *carry out the behest of the martyrs; continue the work left by the martyrs*

【遗嘱】testament; will; dying Words:立～ *make (or draw up) a will* /未立～ *in testate; will-less* /～检验 *probate(a will)* /～赠与 *gift by will* /～执行人 *executor(of a will)* /修改～ *revise one's will*

【遗著】posthumous work (of an author)

【遗作】unpublished work of a deceased person; posthumous work

颐[1] [书] chin or cheek

颐[2] [书] keep fit; take good care of one's health; preserve: ～神养性 *preserve one's vital energy*

【颐和园】the Summer Palace (in Beijing)

【颐养】[书] keep fit; take good care of oneself

【颐养天年】take good care of oneself so as to enjoy one's natural span of life

【颐指气使】order people about by gestures; be extremely arrogant

疑 ① doubt; disbelieve; suspect:将信将～ *half-believing, half-doubting; not quite convinced* /形迹可～ *of suspicious appearance* /无可置～ *beyond doubt; undoubtedly* /深信不～ *unquestioningly believe; not have the slightest doubt* ② doubtful; uncertain:存～ *leave the question open* /析～ *explain doubtful points*

【疑案】a doubtful (or disputed) case; an open question; mystery

【疑兵】troops deployed to mislead the enemy; deceptive deployment (of soldiers)

【疑病】【医】hypochondriasis; hypochondria: ～患者 *hypochondriac*

【疑点】doubtful or questionable point; an uncertain (or unclear) point: 这个事故还有几个[illegible]。*There are still a few questionable points in the accident.*

【疑窦】[书] cause for suspicion; doubtful point; suspicion: ~丛生 *full of suspicions* / 顿生~ *suddenly feel suspicious*

【疑惑】feel uncertain; not be convinced: ~不解 *feel puzzled; have doubts*

【疑忌】be suspicious; distrust: 心怀~ *be suspicious* / 不要~你的同学。*Don't distrust and have misgivings about your classmates.*

【疑惧】apprehensions; misgivings

【疑虑】misgivings; uncertainties; doubts: 心存~ *have doubts in one's mind* / 消除心中的~ *clear one's mind of doubt; free sb from doubts and misgivings*

【疑难】difficult; knotty; thorny: ~病症 *difficult and complicated cases (of illness)* / ~问题 *difficult problem*

【疑念】suspicions; doubts

【疑神疑鬼】be terribly suspicious; be even afraid of one's own shadow

【疑似】partly certain and partly uncertain; doubtful: ~之词 *ambiguous words*

【疑团】doubts and suspicions: ~顿释。*The suspicions were cleared up at once.*

【疑问】query; question; doubt: 毫无~ *doubtless; without a doubt; without question* / ~句 *interrogative sentence*

【疑心】suspicion: 起~ *become suspicious* / ~病 *a suspicious frame of mind; paranoia* / ~生暗鬼 *suspicions create grotesque fears*

【疑义】doubt; doubtful point: 毫无~ *no doubt*

【疑云】misgivings or suspicions clouding one's mind; doubt: 驱散~ *dispel suspicion*

【疑阵】deceptive battle array to mislead the enemy; stratagem

彝1 ①【考】wine vessel ② [书] law; rule

彝2 Yi nationality, distributed over Yunnan, Sichuan, and Guangdong provinces

yǐ

乙1 ① the second of the ten Heavenly Stems ② (Yǐ) a surname

乙2 ① second: ~等 *second class; second grade; class B* ② used for an unspecified person or thing: 甲方和~方 *the first party and the second party* / 甲队和~队 *team A and team B*

乙3 often a mark or sign

【乙胺】【化】ethylamine; aminoethane

【乙苯】【化】ethylbenzene; phenylethane

【乙醇】【化】ethyl alcohol; ethanol; alcohol

【乙醚】【化】ether

【乙脑】meningitis B

【乙醛】【化】acetic aldehyde; acetaldehyde

【乙炔】【化】acetylene; ethyne: ~焊 *acetylene welding* / ~灯 *acetylene burner*

【乙烷】【化】ethane

【乙烯】【化】ethylene

【乙烯基】【化】vinyl

【乙型超声波】B-mode ultrasound

【乙型肝炎】【医】hepatitis B

【乙种射线】【物】beta ray

已 ① cease; stop; end: 争论不~ *argue endlessly* / 冲突不~ *endless conflict* / 感叹不~ *keep sighing* ② already: 他~经起床了。*He has got up already.* ③ [书] afterwards: ~而悔之 *regret later on* ④ [书] too; excessively

【已而】[书] soon; before long; then; afterwards

【已故】deceased; late

【已极】to the utmost; in the extreme: 狂妄~ *extremely arrogant* / 糊涂~ *what an idiot; height of folly*

【已经】already: 孩子~上学去了。*The child has gone to school.*

【已然】① already ② be already so; have long been the case: 与其补救于~,不如防患于未然。*Prevention is better than cure.*

【已往】before; previously; in the past

【已知数】【数】known number

以1 ① with; by means of; use.: ~诚相待 *treat people with all sincerity* / ~理服人 *convince people by reasoning* / ~我之长,攻敌之短 *utilize our strong points to attack the enemy's weak points* / ~大局为重 *set store by the overall situation* / ~工补农 *supplement agriculture with the development of industry* ② according to: 物~类聚 *birds of a feather flock together* / ~此类推 *on the analogy of this* / ~姓氏笔画为序 *in order of the number of strokes of one's surname* ③ because of: 不~人废言,不~言举人。*You cannot reject a saying because the speaker is what or who he is, nor can you promote a person by what he says only.* ④ in order to; so as to: ~示区别 *so as to distinguish this from other cases* / ~博一笑 *in order to illicit a smile; so as to amuse sb* / 坐~待旦 *sit to wait for daybreak* / ~应急需 *in order to answer an urgent need* ⑤ [书] at (a certain time); on (a fixed date): 余~三月一日返。*I returned on March the first.* ⑥ used before words of locality to indicate the limits of time, place, direction or number: 两点~前 *before two o'clock* / 一个月~内 *within one month* / 三十岁~下 *below 30 years old*

以2 [书] and; as well as

【以暴易暴】replace one tyranny or despotic rule by another

【以便】so that; in order to; so as to; for the purpose of: 请大家提前做好准备,~明天一早动身。*Please make preparations in advance in order to start early tomorrow.*

【以不变应万变】cope with all changes by remaining unchanged — deal with a volatile situation by sticking to a fixed principle

【以此为戒】take this as a lesson; take warning from

this

【以大欺小】the strong bullies the weak

【以德报怨】return good for evil; repay evil good; requite ingratitude with kindness

【以点带面】fan out from point to area; use the experience of selected units to promote work in the entire area

【以毒攻毒】combat poison with poison; use poison as an antidote for poison

【以讹传讹】incorrectly relay an erroneous message; pass on errors (stories, rumors); spread false news

【以耳代目】rely upon hearsay instead of seeing for oneself; believe in what others said without making personal investigation

【以防万一】be prepared for all contingencies; be ready for any eventuality:也许他不会来,不过你还是过去看看吧,~。*He may not come, but you'd better go to have a look just in case.*

【以攻为守】use attack as a means of defense; attack in order to defend

【以古非今】use the past to attack; disparage the present by extolling the past

【以寡敌众】pit few against many; fight against all the odds

【以观后效】(lighten a punishment and) see if the offender mends his way

【以后】after; afterwards; later; since:从今(那)~ *from now (then) on* /毕业~ *after graduation* /从那~,我再也没来过这里。*I've never come back again since then.*

【以及】as well as; along with; and:中国~全世界 *Chine as well as the rest of the world*

【以己度人】judge others by oneself; measure others' corn with one's own bushel

【以假乱真】mix the false with the true; mix the spurious with the genuine

【以来】since:长期~ *for a long time past* /二年~,他妻子一个人待在家里。*His wife stayed home by herself in the past two years.*

【以泪洗面】have a tearful face; swim with tears

【以礼相待】treat sb with due respect

【以理服人】convince by reasoning

【以力服人】force people to submit; dominate others by force

【以貌取人】judge people solely by their appearances

【以免】in order to avoid or prevent; so as not to; lest:~被人看见 *lest one should be seen*

【以内】within; less than; inside:会场~ *inside the meeting hall* /五百字~的文章 *article not exceeding 500 words*

【以期】in the hope of

【以其人之道,还治其人之身】deal with a man as he deals with you; pay sb back in his own coin; give sb a dose of his own medicine

【以前】before; ago; previously:~,我去过他家。*I have been his home before.*

【以强凌弱】oppress the weak by sheer strength

【以求】in the hope of; in an attempt to:~自保 *in the hope of protecting oneself* /~相安无事 *in order to live peaceful with each other*

【以屈求伸】bend in order to straighten up; retreat in order to advance; make concessions to gain advantages

【以权谋私】seek personal gain by abusing one's position and authority; abuse power for personal gain

【以色列】Israel

【以上】① more than; over; above:一百人~ *over (or more than) one hundred people* ② the above; the foregoing; the above-mentioned:我完全同意你~所谈的观点。*I fully agree with what you have said.* /对于~几点请予以特别重视。*Please pay special attention to the above mentioned points.*

【以身试法】defy or challenge the law personally

【以身相许】(of a girl) pledge to marry sb

【以身殉国】lay down one's life for one's country; die a martyr in the service of one's country

【以身殉职】die at one's post:去年,她爸爸不幸~。*Last year, her father died at his post, to our great sorrow.*

【以身作则】set a good example with one's own conduct; set a personal example

【以退为进】retreat in order to advance; make concessions in order to gain advantages

【以外】beyond; outside; other than; except:除你~,所有人昨天都去了。*Everyone went there yesterday except you.*

【以往】before; formerly; in the past:~生活经验 *one's previous life experience* /突击队改变了~的战术。*The shock team has changed the tactics it formerly used.*

【以为】think; believe; consider:我还~是她呢。*I thought it was her.* /我们~当务之急是提高学生素质。*We consider it a task of priority to improve the quality of students.*

【以…为…】take... as...; regard... as...; consider... to be...:以他为榜样 *take him as one's role model; model oneself upon him* /以助人为乐 *regard it as a pleasure to help other* /这是不以人的意志为转移的客观规律。*It is objective law independent of man's will.*

【以文会友】make friends through the exchange of writings

【以下】① below; under:零度~ *below zero; subzero* /20 岁~的青年 *young people under the age of twenty* ② the following; hereafter:~是具体的行动计划。*The following is a detailed plan of action.* /~就来谈谈具体办法。*Now I'm coming to the concrete measures.*

【以销定产】plan production according to sales

【以小人之心,度君子之腹】a mean man always uses his own yardstick to measure the mind of the great; gauge the heart of gentleman with one's own mean measure

【以眼还眼,以牙还牙】an eye for an eye and a tooth

for a tooth; paying sb back in his own coin
【以一当十】pit one against ten; work efficiently
【以逸待劳】wait at one's ease for an exhausted enemy; be rested and ready to meet a tired out enemy or opponent
【以怨报德】return evil for good; repay good with evil; requite kindness with ingratitude; bite the hand that feeds one
【以正视听】in order to ensure a correct understanding of the facts
【以至】① down to; up to: 功效提高几倍~十几倍。*The efficiency has grown by several times and even by more than a dozen times.* ② to such an extent as to...; so...that...: 他工作非常专心,~连饭都忘了吃了。*He was so absorbed in his work that he even forgot his meals.*
【以致】(usu. referring to bad results) so that; with the result that; consequently; as a result
【以资】as; as a means of: ~证明 *in testimony thereof; this is to certify that* / ~鼓励 *as an encouragement* / ~参考 *as a reference*

迤 go or extend towards

【迤逦】winding; tortuous; meandering: 队伍沿着山道~而行。*The troops meandered along the mountain path.*

蚁 ant: 工~ *worker ant; ergate* / 白~ *termite*

【蚁巢】ant nest
【蚁封】mound of earth heaped by ants outside their nest; ant hill
【蚁后】ant queen
【蚁丘】ant hill

倚 ① lean on or against; rest on or against: ~在情人的臂上 *lean on one's lover's arm* / ~树而立 *stand leaning against a tree* ② rely on; count on; depend on: ~势欺人 *abuse one's power to bully other* ③ [书] biased; partial: 不偏不~ *unbiased; impartial*

【倚官仗势】rely on one's power and position; count on one's powerful connections
【倚靠】① lean on or against; rest on or against ② rely on ; depend on; count on
【倚老卖老】show self-importance for being old; flaunt one's seniority
【倚强凌弱】the strong bullying the weak
【倚偎】lean on or against affectionately; nestle against: 女孩紧紧~在男朋友身旁。*The girl nestled against his boyfriend.*
【倚音】【音】appoggiatura
【倚仗】rely on; count on: ~权势 *rely on one's power and position; count on one's powerful connections*
【倚重】rely heavily on sb's service

椅 chair: 轮~ *wheelchair* / 躺~ *deck chair* / 藤~ *cane chair; rattan chair* / 转~ *revolving chair*

【椅背】the back of a chair
【椅披】decorative chair cover usu. made of silk and satin
【椅套】slipcover for a chair
【椅子】chair

旖

【旖旎】[书] charming and gentle; enchanting: 春色~ *charming scenery of spring*

yì

亿 a hundred million

【亿万】hundreds of millions; millions upon millions: ~人民 *hundreds of millions of people; the people in their hundreds of millions* / ~富翁 *billionaire; multimillionaire* / ~年 *billions of years; time without end*

义[1] ① justice; righteousness: 背信弃~ *break faith; commit perfidy* / 见利忘~ *forget all moral principles at the sight of person gains* / 仗~直言 *speak out to uphold justice* / 仗~疏财 *distribute wealth for a just cause* / 多行不~必自毙。*Those who indulge in evildoing are bound to come to no good end.* ② friendly feeling or affection involved in human ties or relationship: 无情无~ *cold and ungrateful* / 忘恩负~ *ingratitude* ③ righteous; equitable; just ④ adopted; adoptive: ~子(女) *adopted son (daughter)* / ~父(母) *adoptive father (mother)* ⑤ artificial; false: ~发 *false hair*

义[2] meaning; significance: 望文生~ *interpret the meaning of a word or sentence superficially* / 断章取~ *quote out of context*

【义兵】a righteous army: 举~ *raise an army to fight for a just cause*
【义不容辞】be duty-bounds have an bounden duty
【义齿】false tooth; artificial tooth
【义愤】righteous indignation; moral indignation: 激起~ *rouse righteous indignation* / ~填膺 *be filled with righteous indignation*
【义举】magnanimous act undertaken for the public good; righteous undertaking
【义捐】donations for public welfare: ~门诊 *free consultations* / ~粮食 *donation of grain*
【义理】① reason and good sense ② argumentation (of a speech or essay) ③【哲】universal truth
【义卖】sale of goods (usually at much higher prices) for charity or other worthy causes; (charity) bazaar
【义旗】the banner of an army fighting a just war; banner of righteousness: 举~ *raise the banner of righteousness; rise against injustice*
【义气】① code of brotherhood; personal loyalty: 讲~ *be loyal (to one's friends)* / 哥儿们~ *code of brotherhood; chumminess* ② ready to help (one's friends); loyal (to one's friends)
【义犬】a faithful dog
【义师】an army fighting a just war; a righteous ar-

my：兴～ *raise an army to fight for a just cause*

【义士】a high -minded or chivalrous person; a person who upholds the cause of justice; a upright man

【义无反顾】honour permits no turning back; be duty-bound not to turn back：在抗日战争中许多青年人以身报国，～。*In the anti-Japanese war, many young people dedicated themselves to their mother land without the least reservation.*

【义务】① duty; obligation：公民的基本权利与～ *the fundamental rights and duties of citizens* / 条约规定的～ *treaty obligations* ② volunteer; voluntary：～演出 *voluntary performance* / ～兵 *compulsory serviceman* / ～兵役制 *compulsory military service; conscription* / ～教育 *compulsory education* / ～劳动 *voluntary labour*

【义项】item of an entry (in a dictionary)

【义形于色】with righteous indignation written on one's face; filled with righteous anger

【义演】benefit performance

【义勇军】army of volunteers; volunteers：～进行曲 *March of the Volunteers (the national anthem of the People's Republic of China)*

【义诊】free medical consultation; benefit outpatient service

【义正词严】speak out sternly out of a sense of justice; speak in all seriousness

【义肢】【医】artificial limb

艺 ① skill; technique：工～ / 技～ *technical skill* / 手～ *craftsmanship; workmanship* / 多才多～ *be of many gifts; be talented* ② art：文～ *art and literature*

【艺高人胆大】boldness of execution stems from superb skill; great skill engenders bravery

【艺妓】geisha (in Japan)

【艺林】the world of art; art circles

【艺龄】length of sb's stage career

【艺名】stage name (of an actor or actress)

【艺人】① actor or entertainer (in traditional Chinese drama, storytelling, acrobatics, etc.)：相声～ *comic dialogue performer* / 杂技～ *acrobat* / 说书～ *storyteller* ② artisan; handicraftsman

【艺术】① art：民间～ *folk art* / ～标准 *artistic criterion* / ～风格 *artistic style* / ～技巧 *artistry; craftsmanship* / ～形式 *artistic form; forms of art* / ～造诣 *artistic attainments* / 为～而～ *art for art's sake* / ～家 *artist* / ～节 *Arts Festival* / ～界 *art circles* / ～品 *work of art* / ～体操 *artistic or rhythmic gymnastics* / ～团 *art ensemble; art troupe* / ～性 *artistic quality; artistry* / ～造型 *artistic design* / ～指导 *art director* ② skill; art; craft：教学～ *teaching skill; art of teaching* / 领导～ *art of leadership* ③ artistic; tasteful; stylish：这个房间布置得很～。*The room is tastefully furnished.*

【艺坛】art circles：～新秀 *a new star in art circles*

【艺苑】the realm of art and literature; art and literary circles：～奇葩 *superb works of art*

刈 [书] mow; cut down：～草 *mow grass* / ～麦 *cut wheat*

【刈草机】mowing machine; mower

【刈除】cut off; root out; eradicate：～杂草 *root out weeds* / ～不良习惯 *eradicate bad habit*

忆 recall; recollect remember：～往事 *recall the past* / 记～犹新 *remain fresh in one's memory*

【忆苦思甜】recall the sorrows of the past and savoir the joys of the present; tell of one's sufferings in the old society and one's happiness in the new; contrast past misery with present happiness

【忆念】miss; think of：～老朋友 *cherish the memory of one's old friends*

【忆述】recall and relate

【忆昔抚今】recall the past and compare it with the present; reflect on the past in the light of the present

【忆想】recall; recollect call to mint：～往事 *recollect the past*

议 ① opinion; view; proposal：建～ *suggestion; advice* / 协～ *agreement* / 异～ *disagreement; dissenting opinion* ② discuss; exchange views on; talk over：从长计～ *take one's time in coming to decision; think sth over carefully* / 现在我们就来～一～这件事。*Lets discuss the matter now.* ③ comment; remark; debate：无可非～ *indisputable; irreproachable*

【议案】proposal; bill; motion

【议程】agenda; order of business：会议～ *the agenda of a meeting* / 列入～ *place on or include in the agenda*

【议定】reach a decision through consultation; agree on：～条款 *agreed provisions*

【议而不决】discuss sth without reaching a decision; have a fruitless discussion

【议购】buy at negotiated prices

【议和】negotiate peace; carry on peace negotiations：～未成，战端又起。*War broke out again after the peace negotiation failed.*

【议会】parliament; congress; legislative assembly：召开～ *convene a parliament* / 在～中占多数席位 *hold a majority in the parliament*

【议价】① negotiate a price ② negotiated price

【议决】resolve after deliberation; pass a resolution

【议论】comment; talk; discuss：大发～ *speak at great length* / ～纷纷 *give rise to much discussion; be widely discussed*

【议事】discuss official business：请告诉他～规则。*Please tell him rules of procedure or debate.*

【议题】subject under discussion; topic for discussion

【议席】seat in a legislative assembly or parliament

【议销】sell at negotiated prices

【议员】member of a legislative assembly; assemblyman; (in UK) Member of Parliament (M P); (in US) congressman or Congresswoman

【议院】legislative assembly; parliament; congress

【议长】speaker (of a legislative body); president：众议院～ *speaker of the (US) house of Represent-*

atives
【议政】discuss governmental affairs
屹 ［书］towering like a mountain peak
【屹立】stand towering like a giant
【屹然】towering; majestic: ～不动 *stand firm and erect*
亦 ［书］also; too; as well as:反之～然 *and the reveres is also true; and vice versa* / ～工～农 *be both worker and peasant* / ～复如是。*It is also the same.*
【亦步亦趋】ape sb at every step; imitate sb's every move; blindly follow suit
【亦庄亦谐】serious and comical at the same time; seriocomic; solemn and witty
异 ① different; not the same:同母～父 *uterine; born of the same mother but not the same father* / 求同存～ *seek common ground while reserving differences* ② strange; unusual; extraordinary; bizarre:优～ *excellent; outstanding* / 奇才～能 *extraordinary talents and abilities* ③ other; another: ～地 *a strange land* / ～日 *some other day* ④ surprise:诧～ *be surprised* / 骇～ *be appalled; be chocked* / 深以为～。*It strikes me as very strange.* ⑤ separate; part:离～ *divorce*
【异邦】a foreign country:他和妻子不得不漂泊在～。*He and his wife had to lead a wandering life in a foreign country.*
【异步】【物】asynchronous
【异才】exceptional talent or ability
【异彩】extraordinary splendour; radiant brilliance: 大放～ *blossom in radiant brilliance* / ～纷呈 *in varied colourful splendour*
【异常】① unusual; abnormal: ～现象 *abnormal phenomena* / 神色～ *not be one's usual self* ② extremely; exceedingly; particularly: ～危险 *extremely dangerous* / 凶猛～ *be extremely ferocious* / 小姑娘～聪明可爱。*The little girl is exceptionally clever and lovable.*
【异常期】anomalistic period
【异词】dissenting words; disagreement; objection
【异地】a place far away from home
【异读】variant pronunciation
【异端】unorthodox belief; heterodoxy; heresy: ～邪说 *heresies; unorthodox opinions*
【异国】a foreign country (or land): ～他乡 *alien land* / 流落～ *wander destitute in a foreign country* / ～情调 *exotic flavour; the exotic*
【异乎寻常】unusual; extraordinary: ～的冷 *extraordinarily cold* / ～地热心 *unusually enthusiastic*
【异花传粉】【植】cross pollination
【异花受精】【植】allogamy; cross fertilization
【异化】① alienate ②【哲】alienation ③【语】dissimilation
【异化作用】【生】dissimilation
【异己】dissident alien:在工作中他总是排除～。*In his work he always excludes those who hold different views.*
【异教】paganism; heathenism: ～徒 *pagan; heathen*
【异军突起】a new force suddenly coming to the fore
【异口同声】with one voice; in unison:同学们～地赞成。*All the students consented with one voice.*
【异类】①［旧］people not of the same ethnic group ② a different class or species (of plants or animals)
【异曲同工】different tunes sung with equal skill; different approaches but equally satisfactory in results; achieve the same goal through different means
【异人】①［旧］unusual person ; immortal ② another people
【异兽】strange animals; rare animals:珍禽～ *rare birds and animals*
【异说】① dissenting views; different views ② absurd remarks
【异体】① variant of a word: ～字 *a variant form of a Chinese character* ② not belonging to the same body or individual: ～受精 *allogamy; cross-fertilization*
【异同】① similarities and differences ②［书］*objection; dissent*
【异外】unusually; exceptionally: ～舒畅 *feel unusually happy*
【异味】① rare delicacy ② a peculiar smell; strong odor
【异物】① foreign matter; a foreign body: 食管～ *a foreign body in the esophagus* ②［书］a dead person; ghost: 化为～ *turn into dead body* ③ a rare object
【异乡】a foreign land; a strange land
【异香】peculiar fragrance
【异想天开】indulge in the wildest fantasy; have a most fantastic idea: 休要～。*Don't indulge in fantasies.*
【异心】infidelity; disloyalty:怀有～ *harbour disloyalty*
【异性】① the opposite sex ② different in nature: ～电互相吸引 *unlike electric charges attract each other*
【异言】［书］dissenting words:关于这个问题大家并无～。*Every one raise no objection about this question.*
【异样】① difference:她的神色有些～。*She looks a bit odd.* ② unusual; peculiar; odd: ～的沉着 *unusually calm* / ～的感觉 *unusual feeling*
【异议】objection; dissent:提出～ *raise an objection; take exception to; challenge* / 不持～ *raise no objection*
【异域】① a foreign county ② other than one's native place
【异族】a different race or nation: ～通婚 *mixed marriages* / ～入侵 *be invaded by a different nation*
抑[1] press down; restrain; repress; curb: ～恶扬善 *suppress the bad and eulogize the good* / 感到压～ *feel depressed* / ～价 *keep down the prices* / ～扬顿挫 *with a rising and falling rhythm; mod-*

ulation in tone

抑[2] [书] ① or: 马欤, ~骡欤? *Is it a horse being or is it a mule*? ② but ③ but also; moreover

【抑或】 or: 不知他们是赞成, ~是反对。*It is not clear whether they are for or against it.*

【抑强扶弱】 curb the strong and help the weak; restrain the powerful and help the weak

【抑且】 [书] also; moreover; furthermore

【抑扬】 (of sound) rise and fall; modulate

【抑郁】 despondent; depressed; gloomy; feeling low: ~不平 *feel disgruntled* / ~症 *depression* / 心情~ *feel gloomy*

【抑止】 hold back; check; restrain: ~不住自己的眼泪 *can't hold back one's tears* / ~住心中的怒火 *restrain one's fury*

【抑制】 ① restrain; control; check: ~自己的喜悦 *restrain one's happiness* ② inhibition: ~神经 *inhibitory nerve*

呓 talk in one's sleep: 梦~ *talk in one's sleep*; *somniloquy*

【呓语】 ① talk in one's sleep ② delirious utterances; crazy talk; ravings: 狂人~ *ravings of a madman* / 痴人~ *ravings of a idiot*

邑 ① town; city: 都~ *capital city* / 通都大~ *big city*; *metropolis* ② [古] county

佚

【佚失】 scattered and lost

【佚事】 anecdote

役 ① labour; service: 劳~ *forced labour* ② military service: 现~ *active service* / 退~ *retire from military service* ③ servant: 差~ *runner or bailiff in a feudal Yamen* / 仆~ *servant*; *flunkey* / 杂~ *odd-jobs man* (*in office*, *school*, *etc.*) ④ battle; campaign ④ use; work

【役畜】 draught animal; beast of burden

【役龄】 ① enlistment age; conscription age ② years of military service

【役使】 work (domestic animal); use: ~耕牛犁地 *plough the fields with farm oxen*

译 translate; interpret: 口~ *oral translation* / 笔~ *written translation* / 直~ *literal translation* / 意~ *free translation* / 古文今~ *translate ancient Chinese prose into contemporary Chinese* / ~成密码 *encipher*; *encode* / 破~密码 *crack a code* / 翻~电码 *decipher*; *decode*

【译本】 translated version (of a book); translation

【译笔】 quality or style of a translation

【译电】 ① encode or encipher a telegram ② decode or decipher a telegram

【译稿】 manuscript of a translation

【译码】 decode; decipher: ~器 *decoder*; *decipherer*

【译名】 translated term or name

【译文】 translated text; translation

【译音】 transliteration

【译员】 interpreter

【译者】 translator

【译制】 dub: ~片 *a dubbed film* / 用英语~中国影片 *Chinese films in English*

【译注】 translate and annotate: ~古籍 *translate and annotate ancient books*

【译著】 works of translation

【译作】 translated works

易[1] easy: 来之不~ *be not easily won*; *be hard-earned* / 简便~行 *be simple and easy to apply* / 显而~见 *obviously*; *evidently* / ~涝地区 *areas liable to water logging* ② amiable: 平~近人 *amiable and easy of access*

易[2] ① change: 埋名~性 *conceal one's identity and change one's name* / 移风~俗 *change prevailing habits and custom* / 数~寒暑。*Several years have passed.* ② exchange: 以物~物 *barter* / 贸~ *trade* / 交~ *transaction*; *deal*

【易爆物】 explosive substance

【易感者】【医】 susceptible person; susceptible

【易货】 barter: ~汇兑 *barter exchange* / ~经济 *barter economy* / ~贸易 *barter trade* / ~贸易制 *barter system* / ~协定 *an agreement on the exchange of commodities*; *barter agreement*

【易经】 yi Jing or The Book of Changes, one of Confucius classics

【易拉罐】 pop-top or ring-pull can

【易燃物】 combustibles; inflammables

【易熔】 fusible: ~点 *eutectic point* / ~合金 *fusible alloy*

【易如反掌】 as easy as turning one's hand over; as easy as falling off a log; piece of cake

【易手】 change hands

【易性癖】 transsexualism

【易于】 be easy to: 这个案子~处理。*This case is easy to manage.*

【易帜】 [书] change the flag of an army or country; change one's principles or allegiance

诣 ① call on (sb one respects); visit: ~请指教 *call on sb for advice* ② (academic or technical) attainments: 造~颇深 *highly scholarly attainments*

驿 [旧] post station now used mainly as part of place names

【驿道】 post road

【驿舍】 pothouse

【驿使】 courier (traveling on a post road)

【驿站】 [旧] post station; courier station: 络~不绝 *in and endless stream*

绎 [书] unravel; sort out: 演~ *deduction*

轶

【轶材】 [书] outstanding talents

【轶事】 anecdote; celebrities and their anecdote

疫 epidemic disease; pestilence: 防~ *epidemic prevention* / 免~ *immunity* (*from disease*) / 瘟~ *plague*

【疫病】 epidemic disease: 防止~蔓延 *prevent an epidemic disease from spreading*

【疫苗】【医】 vaccine

【疫情】 information about and appraisal of an epidemic; epidemic situation: 报告~ *report epidemic* disease / ~通报 bulletin of epidemic situation

【疫区】epidemic-stricken area

弈 ①[书] weiqi, a game played with black and white pieces on a board of 361 crosses ② play chess: 对~ *play chess against each other* / 搏~ *be locked in a fierce contest (in chess games)* / ~者举棋不定。*The chess player is hesitant over the next move.*

【弈林】chess circles; community of chess players: ~高手 *a master chess player*

【弈棋】play chess

奕 [书] grand; great; magnificent

【奕奕】① grand; magnificent ② radiating power and vitality: 神采~ *glowing with health and vitality* / ~的眼神 *clear and sparkling eyes*

益1 ① benefit; profit; advantage: 有~无害 *do good more than harm* / 受~不浅 *benefit a lot from; derive much benefit from* / 开卷有~。*It is always rewarding to start reading.* ② beneficial; helpful: 良师~友 *good teacher and helpful friend*

益2 increase; add to: ~智 *enhance intelligence* / 延年~寿 *prolong life* ② all the more; increasingly; still more: 精~求精 *always endeavor to do better; strive for perfection*

【益虫】beneficial insect

【益处】benefit; profit; good

【益鸟】beneficial bird

【益友】helpful friend; friend and mentor

悒 [书] sad; worried: ~~不乐 *feel depressed; mope*

【悒闷】[书] depressed; dejected; in low spirits

【悒郁】[书] depressed; despondent; gloomy

谊 friendship: 情~ *friendly feeling* / 师生之~ *friendly relationship between teacher and student* / 战友之~ *comradeship-in-arms*

逸 ① ease; rest; leisure: 好~恶劳 *love ease and hate work* / 一劳永~ *get sth done once and for all* / 有劳有~ *alternate work with rest* ② escape; flee; run away: 逃~ *escape* ③ be lost: ~书 *ancient works no longer extant* ④ excel: 有~群之才 *one whose talents excel all others*

【逸乐】comfort and pleasure

【逸趣】refined interests or taste

【逸散】escape; lose; disperse

【逸史】unofficial history

【逸闻】anecdote; hearsay

【逸致】a carefree mood

翌 [书] immediately following in time; next: ~日 *next day* / ~年 *next year*

肄 study

【肄业】study in school or at college (usu. indicating without finishing one's education): 大学~ *study at college (without graduation)*

裔 [书] ① descendants; posterity: 华~美国人 *American of Chinese descent (or origin); Chinese American* ② a distant land; a remote region: 四~ *far distant land in all directions*

【裔孙】[书] remote descendants

意 ① meaning; idea; thought: 说明来~ *explain the intention of coming* / 言简~赅 *simple ideas expressed succinctly* / 言不尽~ *the words fail to convey the meaning* ② wish; desire; intention: 随~ *as one pleases* / 任~ *willfully* / 称心如~ *to one's heart's content* / 怀有恶~ *harbour evil intention* ③ anticipate; expect: 出其不~ *catch sb unprepared; take sb by surprise* ④ suggestion; hint; trace: 颇有秋~ *make one feel that autumn has set in* / 醉~ *feeling getting drunk; tipsy* / 春~盎然。*Spring is in the air.*

【意会】understand what is implied; perceive by intuition; sense: 只可~,不可言传 *can be sensed, but not explained in words*

【意见】① idea; view; opinion; suggestion: 交换~ *exchange ideas (or views)* / 建设性~ *constructive ideas* ② objection; differing opinion; complaint: ~薄 *visitors' book; customers' book* / ~箱 *suggestion box* / 我对她很有~。*I have a lot of complaints about her.* / 有~当面提。*Those who have differing opinions should air their views openly.*

【意境】artistic mood or conception

【意料】anticipate; expect: ~中 *as expected* / 出乎~ *beyond one's expectation; unexpected; surprising*

【意念】idea; thought

【意气】① will and spirit; how one feels and thinks: ~高昂 *high-spirited* / ~风发 *high-spirited and vigorous; daring and energetic* / ~轩昂 *have an imposing appearance and brim with vigor and vitality* ② temperament: ~相投 *be alike in temperament; see eye to eye* ③ personal feelings (or prejudice): 爱闹~ *one is liable to be swayed by personal feeling* / ~之争 *a dispute caused by personal feelings* / ~用事 *act on impulse; abandon oneself to emotions; be swayed by personal feelings*

【意识】① consciousness; awareness: 思想~ *ideology* / 爱国~ *patriotism; patriotic feelings* / 法律~ *law awareness* / 宗教~ *religious consciousness* ② be conscious (or aware) of; awake to; realize: 他~到自己的责任了。*He is conscious of his responsibilities.*

【意识流】stream of consciousness

【意识形态】【哲】ideology

【意思】① meaning; idea; implication: 会议的中心~ *the central idea of a conference* / 他说这话是什么~? *What is the meaning of his word?* ② opinion; wish; view; desire: 他还没有要走的~。*He is not ready to leave yet.* ③ a token of affection, appreciation, gratitude, etc. ④ suggestion; hint; trace: 天有点要下雪的~。*It looks like snow.* / 他们两个是不是有点儿~? *Do they two have a fancy to each other?* ⑤ interest; fun: 这部电影没~。*The film is boring.* / 他这个人没~。*He's dull.* ⑥ express appreciation, gratitude, etc.: 老师要走了,咱们送她一只钢笔~~。*Our teacher is leaving; let's give her a pen as a token of our friend-*

ship.

【意态】mien; demeanor; bearing: ~自若 *appear calm and of ease*

【意图】intention; intent:领会领导~ *understand the intentions of the leaders*

【意外】① unexpected; unforeseen: ~收获 *unexpected gains* ② accident; mishap:以免发生~ *so as to avoid accidents*

【意外风险】emergency risk

【意味】① meaning; significance; implication: ~深长 *having deep meaning; pregnant with meaning; of profound significance* /他谈话的时候表情~深长。*He was talking with a look of deep significance.* ② interest; overtone; flavour:威胁~ *threatening overtone* /这散文大有诗的~。*This prose has much poetic flavour.*

【意味着】signify; mean; imply:他不吭声就~反对。*His silence means against.*

【意下】① in the mind; in the heart ② opinion; idea; view:老同学~如何? *What do you think of it, classmate?*

【意象】images; imagery

【意兴】interest; enthusiasm: ~索然 *have lost all interest in sth* /~勃勃 *be highly enthusiastic in high spirit* /~未尽 *have unceasing enthusiasm in sth*

【意想】imagine; expect: ~不到的事情 *unexpected matter*

【意向】intention: ~书 *letter of intent* /对手~不明。*The opponent's intentions are not clear.*

【意译】free translation

【意义】meaning; significance; sense:具有政治~的事件 *an event of politic significance* /~深远 *have a profound significance*

【意欲】intend to; want to:他~离婚。*He intends to divorce.*

【意愿】wish; desire; aspiration:表达同学的~ *express the wishes of the students*

【意蕴】meaning; implication

【意在笔先】have an idea in the mind before starting painting or writing

【意在言外】the meaning is implied; there is more than meets the eye

【意旨】intention; wish; will:秉承上司的~ *in compliance with one's superior's wish*

【意志】will; willpower; determination:坚强的~ *strong will; iron determination* /~消沉 *be in broken spirits; be depressed* /锻炼~ *temper one's willpower* /不以人的~为转移 *independent of man's will* /~薄弱 *weak-willed*

【意中人】the person one is in love with; person of one's heart; the beloved one

溢 ① overflow; spill:江水四~。*The river overflowed.* /都市的夜景流光~彩。*The night of this metropolis is colourful and brilliant.* /花香四~。*The fragrance of flowers permeated the air.* ② excessive; exaggerated: ~誉 *excessive praise*

【溢出】spill over; overflow

【溢额】surplus: ~部分 *surplus share*

【溢价】premium pricing: ~发行股票 *float (or issue) stocks at a premium* /债券~ *bond premium*

【溢流】overflow; brim over: ~坝 *water conservancy overfull dam; spillway dam* /~孔 *overfull hole*

【溢美】[书] overpraise; laud to the sky: ~之辞 *excessive praise*

【溢于言表】(of feelings) show clearly in one's words and manner

缢 [书] hang:自~ *hang oneself* /~杀 *strangle to death; kill by strangling*

毅 firm; resolute; staunch:坚~ *firm and staunch* /刚~ *fortitude*

【毅力】willpower; will; stamina; tenacity:锻炼~ *temper one's willpower* /百折不回的~ *indomitable will*

【毅然】resolutely; firmly; determinedly: ~决然 *resolutely; determinedly*

熠 [书] glistening; bright: ~耀 *dazzling; brilliant*

臆 ① chest:胸~ *thoughts; one's feeling; heart* ② subjectively

【臆测】conjecture; surmise; guess

【臆断】form a subjective judgement; assume

【臆度】[书] conjecture; surmise; guess

【臆见】a subjective view

【臆说】assumption; supposition

【臆造】fabricate (a story, reason, etc.); invent

翼 ① the wings of a bird, an insect, etc.:羽~ *wing* /如虎添~ *like a tiger that has grown wings with might redoubled* /不~而飞 *disappear without a trace; vanish into thin air* /比~双飞 *fly side by side* ② the wings of an aeroplane:机~ *wing of an aeroplane* ③ flank; side:两~阵地 *two flanks of the front* ④ the twenty-seventh of the twenty-eight constellations in ancient Chinese astronomy ⑤ [书] assist (a ruler): ~助 *render assistance (to a ruler)*

【翼蔽】[书] shield; protect; screen

【翼侧】【军】flank: ~攻击 *a flank attack* /~迂回 *outflank* /~运动 *a flank movement*

【翼翅】wing

【翼护】shield sb with one's own body

【翼型】【航】wing section; aerofoil

【翼翼】[书] ① in a grave and cautious manner:小心~ *with exceptional caution; carefully* ② in neat formation; in orderly array ③ thriving; flourish; numerous

镱 【化】ytterbium (yb)

yīn

因 ① [书] follow; carry on: ~循守旧 *stick to old way; follow the beaten track* ② [书] in accordance with; in the light of; on the basis of: ~病下药 *prescribe for a patient according to the symptoms* ③ cause; reason:诱~ *cause* /前~后果 *cause and effect; whys and hows* /内~ *internal*

factor / 外 ~ external factor / ④ because; due to; as a result of: ~事请假 ask for affair leave / ~公牺牲 die while on duty; die at one's post / 运动会~故延期。The sports meeting has been postponed for some reason.

【因材施教】teach students according to their aptitude; suit the instruction to the one's level

【因此】so; therefore; for this reason; consequently

【因次】【物】dimension: ~分析 dimensional analysis / ~公式 dimensional formula

【因地制宜】act according to circumstances; suit measures to local conditions: 按~的原则 in line with local conditions

【因而】thus; as a result; therefore

【因果】① cause and effect: ~关系 causality / ~倒置 invert cause and effect; put cart before the horse / ~律 the law of cause and effect; the law of causality(or causation) ②【宗】karma; preordained fate; destiny: ~报应 retribution; karma

【因祸得福】derive gain from misfortune; profit by adversity

【因陋就简】make do with whatever is available; do things simply and thriftily: 工厂设备是不够理想,但我们只好~。The device in our factory isn't perfect, but we must make do.

【因明】a system of Hindu logic

【因人成事】depend on others for success; achieve sth with help of others

【因人而异】vary with each individual; differ from person to person: 李大夫用药总能~。Doctor Li is always able to prescribe appropriate medicine for different people.

【因人制宜】do what is suited to each individual; take measures suited to each person

【因时制宜】do what is suited to the occasion; suit measures to the changing circumstances

【因式】factor: ~分解 factoring; factor analysis

【因势利导】adroitly guide action according to circumstances: ~夺取胜利 make the best use of the situation and guide the struggle to victory

【因数】【数】factor: ~分解 factorization into factors; factorization

【因素】factor; element; component: 积极~ positive factors / 不利~ unfavourable factors

【因特网】Internet

【因为】① because: ~我没发牢骚,人们就以为我满足了。Just because I don't complain, people think I'm satisfied. ② because of; on account of; owing to: 他走得慢是~腿有毛病。He walked slowly because of his bad leg.

【因袭】follow (old custom, methods, rules, etc.); copy: ~前人 follow in the footsteps of one's predecessors / ~古制 copy the ancient system

【因小失大】try to save a little only to lose a lot; be penny wise and pound foolish

【因循】① follow (old customs, etc.); stay in the same old rut: ~旧习 follow the old customs ② procrastinate; delay: ~延误 procrastinate until it is too late

【因噎废食】give up eating for fear of choking — refrain from doing sth necessary for fear of a slight risk; throw out the baby with the bathwater: 不能改革中出了点问题就~。We should not abandon our efforts in the reform because of a few minor setbacks.

【因由】reason; cause; origin: 不问~ regardless of the cause / 事情的~ the whys and wherefores of the matter

【因缘】①【宗】principal and subsidiary causes; cause ② predestined relationship: 这也是我们前世结下的~。This relationship between us is decided by fate.

阴

① the feminine or negative principle in nature (as opposed to Yang in Chinese philosophy) ② the moon: 太~ moon ③ (of weather) overcast; cloudy; gloom: 天~了。The sky is overcast. ④ north of a hill or south of a river / 山~ north of a hill ⑤ shade: 树~ shade of a tree / 背~儿的地方 shady spot / 背~处 shady spot ⑥ the back side: 碑~ the back of a stone tablet ⑦ in intaglio ⑧ private parts (esp. of the female) ⑨ hidden; secret; underhand: 阳奉~违 say nice things to a person's face but play tricks behind his back ⑩ sinister; perfidious; foul: 这小伙真~。This guy is very treacherous. ⑪ of the nether world; of ghosts ⑫【物】negative: ~射线 negative ray

【阴暗】dark; gloomy: ~的色调 gloomy colour; depressing colour / 脸色~ a glum face / ~的房间 dingy or dim room / ~面 the dark (or seamy) side of things; unhealthy things in life

【阴部】【生理】private parts; genitals;

【阴沉】cloudy; overcast; gloomy: ~的天空 a sombre sky

【阴唇】【生理】labia (of the vulva)

【阴错阳差】a mistake or error due to a strange combination of circumstances; accidental mistake or error

【阴道】【生理】vagina: ~炎 vaginitis

【阴德】good deeds to the credit of the doer in the nether world; hidden acts of merit

【阴电】negative electricity

【阴毒】insidious; treacherous and vicious; sinister: ~的女人 a insidious woman

【阴风】① a cold wind ② an ill (or evil) wind

【阴功】sinister energy

【阴沟】sewer; covered drain

【阴河】underground river

【阴黑】dark and gloomy; sombre

【阴魂】ghost; spirit: ~不散 the ghost lingers on; the evil influence remains / 使~消失 lay a ghost/ 使~出现 raise a ghost

【阴极】【物】negative pole; negative electrode; cathode: 冷~ cold cathode / ~射线 cathode ray

【阴间】the nether world; the Hades

【阴茎】【生理】penis: ~勃起 penile erection / 男人

Y

的～ *the penis of a man*

【阴冷】①(of weather) gloomy and cold; raw: ～的冬日 *a cold and gloomy winter day* ② sombre; glum: 脸色～ *be grim-faced*; *look sombre* /～的性格 *of a cold and glum nature*

【阴离子】【物】negative ion; anion

【阴历】lunar calendar; the traditional Chinese calendar: ～三月 *the third month of the lunar year*

【阴凉】① shady and cool: ～处 *a cool, dark place* ② cool shade; shady and cool spot

【阴霾】haze

【阴毛】【生理】pubes; pubic hair

【阴面】the shady or northern side; the back side

【阴谋】① conspire; plot; scheme: ～陷害某人 *conspire to frame sb* /～复辟 *plot to restore the old order* /～篡权 *scheme to usurp power* ② conspiracy; plot; underhand scheme: ～诡计 *schemes and intrigue* /政变～ *a coup plot* /外交～ *a diplomatic intrigue* /～家 *schemer*; *intriguer*; *conspirator* /不让他们的～得逞 *not let them succeed in their evil design*

【阴森】gloomy; ghastly: ～的树林 *a deep, dark forest* /～的古庙 *gruesome- looking old temple*

【阴盛阳衰】①【中医】Yin rises while Yang declines; the preponderance of Yin impairs the Yang ② the Yang forces recede in favour of the Yin forces ; the female being stronger and more powerful, or more numerous than the male

【阴湿】dark and damp

【阴私】shameful secret; skeleton in cupboard

【阴损】① insidious and acrimonious; sly and sarcastic: 说话～ *speak with vicious and biting sarcasm* ② secretly do harm to

【阴天】an overcast sky; a cloudy day

【阴文】characters or designs cut in intaglio; intaglio

【阴险】sinister; insidious; treacherous: ～毒辣 *sinister and ruthless* /居心～ *have a sinister motive* /为人～狡猾 *be crafty and treacherous*

【阴笑】a sinister smile: 脸上露出一丝～。*A sinister smile crept over one's face.*

【阴性】①【医】negative: ～反应 *negative reaction* ②【语】feminine gender

【阴虚】【中医】deficiency of yin, with thirst, constipation, irritability, etc. as symptoms main

【阴阳怪气】①(of a person's manner of speaking) mystifying; enigmatic; deliberately ambiguous ② eccentric; queer; cynical: 他这个人～的。*He's a queer chap.*

【阴阳家】① geomancer ② the Yin-Yang School or School of negative and positive (in the Warring States Period, 475-221 B. C.)

【阴一套,阳一套】act one way in public and another in private; be engaged in double-dealing

【阴翳】[书] ① shaded or hidden by foliage ② covered with luxuriant foliage

【阴影】shadow: 树木的～ *shadows of trees* /一场悲剧的～正笼罩着这个家庭。*The shadow of tragedy is ganging over the family.*

【阴雨】overcast and rainy: ～连绵 *cloudy and drizzly for days on end*

【阴郁】gloomy; dismal; depressed: 她总是脸色～。*She always looks sad and gloomy.*

【阴云】dark clouds: ～密布。*The sky is overcast or the sky is covered with dark clouds.*

【阴宅】grave; tomb

【阴着儿】[方] treacherous act; insidious trick

茵 mattress: 绿草如～ *a carpet of green grass*

【茵茵】lush; luxuriant: 芳草～ *fragrant grass growing lush and long* /绿～的稻田 *a lush green rice paddy*

荫 shade (of tree): 在阴凉的树～下 *under the cool shade of the trees* /绿树成～。*Green leafy trees make shade.*

see also yìn

【荫蔽】① shade; cover: 在树丛中的～之中 *within the shadow of the grove* ② be shaded or hidden as by foliage: 在灌木丛里～起来 *hide out in the bushes*; *hide among the bushes* /小屋～在森林之中。*The shed lies hidden among the forest.*

【荫棚】① shed over saplings, etc. ② shed that provides shade (in hot days)

【荫翳】①【中医】corneal opacity; nebula ② shed; shadow (of trees): 树木～的湖边 *lake banks shaded by trees* ③ rich foliage: 桃李～ *peach and plums trees with luxuriant foliage*

音 ① sound: 乐～ *musical sound* /噪～ *noise* /口～ *accent* ② musical sound; note; tone: 纯～ *pure or simple tone* /复～ *complex tone* ③ news; tidings: 静候佳～ *wait patiently for the good news* ④ syllable: 双～字 *disyllabic word*

【音爆】【航】sonic boom

【音标】【语】phonetic symbol; phonetic transcription

【音波】sound wave

【音叉】tuning fork

【音长】sound wave

【音程】【音】musical interval

【音带】audiotape

【音调】tone; pitch: ～低沉 *a full and deep voice* /降低～ *lower the pitch* /～失真 *tonal distortion*

【音读】pronunciation (of a Chinese character)

【音符】【音】note

【音高】【音】pitch

【音阶】【音】scale

【音节】【语】syllable: 单～词 *single syllable word* /多～词 *polysyllable* /～表 *syllabary* /～文字 *syllabic language*

【音控开关】voice-operated switch

【音量】volume (of sound): ～控制 *volume control* /～开关 *volume switch*

【音律】【音】temperament

【音名】【音】musical alphabet

【音频】【物】audio frequency: ～电话 *tone telephone* /～调制 *voice modulation* /～放大器 *audio frequency amplifier* /～振荡器 *audio oscillator*

【音强】intensity of sound

【音容】［书］voice and look of sb：～宛在 *one can recall sb's voice and look as if sb were still alive* /她的～笑貌，历历在目。*Her lovely voice and happy countenance still fresh in our's memory.*
【音色】tone；colour；timbre
【音素】【语】phoneme
【音速】【物】speed of sound；sound velocity
【音位】【语】phoneme：～文字 *phonemic language* /～学 *phonemics*
【音箱】speaker；loudspeaker；amplifier
【音响】① sound；acoustics：～效果 *sound effects；acoustics* /～师 *sound engineer* ② hi-fi stereo component system；hi-fi system
【音像】audio and video：～出版社 *audio-video publishing house* /～制品 *audio-video product*
【音信】mail；message；news：互通～ *communicate with each other；be in correspondence with each other*
【音译】transliterate ；translate words of one language into another by similar sound
【音域】【音】range；compass；gamut
【音乐】music：古典～ *classical music* /流行～ *popular music；pop* /乡村～ *country music* /～电视 *music TV(MTV)* /～会 *concert* /～家 *musician* /～疗法 *music therapy* /～片 *musical(film)* /～厅 *concert hall* /～学 *musicology* /～学院 *conservatory (of music)；music school* /～茶座 *music tea house* /～节 *musical festival* /～剧 *musical comedy*
【音韵】① harmonious sounds；meter and rhyme of poems and other literary writings ② sound，rhyme and tone of Chinese character
【音障】sound barrier；sonic barrier
【音质】① tone colour ② tone quality (of musical instrument) ③ acoustic fidelity (of radio，recording，etc.)
【音准】【音】tone accuracy

洇 (of ink) spread and sink in：～色 *diffusion or running of colouring matter* /这种纸写字容易～。*Ink blots this paper or ink runs on this paper.*

姻 ① marriage：婚～ *marriage* /联～ *connect by marriage* ② relation by marriage：～兄 *brother-in-law*
【姻亲】relation by marriage：～关系 *relationship by marriage；affinity* /他们两家是～。*Their two were connected by marriage.*
【姻缘】happy fate which brings lovers together：美满～ *a happy marriage；conjugal felicity* /悲惨～ *a tragic marriage；a bitter marriage*

殷[1] ［书］① abundant；rich：海内～商 *well-known merchant* ② eager；ardent：期望甚～ *cherish high hopes* ③ hospitable：招待甚～ *offer cordial hospitality*

殷[2] ① Yin Dynasty，the later period of the Shang Dynasty ② a surname
see also yān
【殷富】wealthy；wealthy
【殷切】ardent；eager；earnest：～的期望 *ardent expectations* /～教诲 *sincere teaching*
【殷勤】eagerly attentive；solicitous：～接待 *show solicitous hospitality* /～地端茶倒水 *bring in tea immediately with eager attentiveness* /一个劲地向某人献～ *do everything to please sb；shower attention upon sb*
【殷实】well-off；substantial；well-to-do：～之家 *a well-off family* /家道～ *family of substance*
【殷殷】ardent；sincere：～期望 *entertain ardent hopes* /～嘱咐 *exhort sincerely*

喑 ［书］① hoarse；husky：～不能语 *have lost one's voice* ② silent；mute：万马齐～ *ten thousand horses stand mute*

yín

吟 ① chant；intone；recite：～诗作画 *recite or compose poetry and do brush-work* /仰天长～ *chant loud and long to the sky* ② song (as a type of classical poetry) ③ the cry of certain animals or insects：猿～ *monkeys squealing* /蝉～ *cicada's* /虎啸龙～ *roar of dragons and tigers*
【吟唱】sing；chant；recite
【吟风弄月】sing of the moon and the wind — write sentimental verse
【吟诵】chant；recite：～唐诗 *recite a Tang poem* /～周恩来诗 *chant Zhou Enlai's poems*
【吟味】intone with relish；recite with appreciation：他～了这篇小说一整天。*He recited the novel a whole day with appreciation.*
【吟咏】recite (poetry) with a cadence；chant

垠 ［书］boundary；limit：一望无～ *stretch beyond the horizon；stretch as far as the eye can see*

银 ① silver (Ag)：～币 *silver coin* /～项链 *silver necklace* /～质奖章 *silver medal* /镀了～ *be coated with sliver；be silver-coated* ② relating to currency or money：收～台 *cashier's desk* /库中无～。*There is no money in the bank.* ③ silver-coloured：～色的月光 *silvery moon* /红地～字 *silver characters on a red background*
【银白】silvery white
【银杯】silver cup
【银锭】silver ingot
【银耳】tremella (Tremella fuciformis)
【银发】white hair；silver hair：满头～ *silver-haired*
【银根】【经】money；money market：～紧缩 *tight money policy；restrict growth of money supply*
【银行】bank：～账户 *bank account* /～存款 *bank deposit* /～储备金 *bank reserve* /储蓄～ *savings bank* /外汇指定～ *authorized bank for dealing in foreign exchange* /～贷款 *bank advance；bank loan* /～存折 *bankbook* /～汇款 *bank remittance* /～承兑 *banker's acceptance* ～家 *banker* /～贷款 *inter-bank loan* /～利率 *bank rate* /～信贷 *bank credit*
【银河】【天】milky Way：～系 *Milky Way system；the Galaxy* /～星团 *galactic cluster*

【银狐】silver fox
【银灰】silver gray
【银婚】silver wedding
【银匠】silversmith
【银两】silver (used as currency)
【银亮】bright and shinny like silver
【银幕】(motion-picture) screen; projection screen
【银牌】silver medal
【银票】(in former times) silver draft (a form of paper money)
【银屏】① silver screen (of motion picture or television) ② television; television circles: ~之花 *film or TV star*
【银器】silverware
【银钱】money
【银鼠】【动】snow weasel
【银条】silver bar
【银屑病】psoriasis
【银杏】【植】ginkgo
【银元】silver dollar
【银针】acupuncture needle
【银质奖】silver medal
【银装】snow cover: ~草地。*The grass land was covered with snow.*
【银子】silver; money

淫 ① excessive: ~雨成涝。*Excessive rains caused a flood.* ② wanton; wallow; indulge: 骄奢~逸 *wallowing in luxury and pleasure* ③ adulterous; licentious; lewd: 卖~ *prostitution* / 奸~ *rape*; *ravish* / 万恶~为首。*Lewdness is the worst of all vices.* ④ obscene; pornographic: ~书 *pornographic books* (*or publications*) / ~画 *obscene pictures* / ~话 *obscene language*; *dirty words*
【淫荡】loose in morals; lascivious; licentious; lewd
【淫风】wanton customs; lascivious practices
【淫妇】a wanton woman; adulteress
【淫棍】satyr; rake; wolf
【淫秽】obscene; salacious; bawdy: ~书刊 *pornographic literature*
【淫乐】indulging in carnal pleasure; sexual indulgence
【淫乱】(sexually) promiscuous; licentious
【淫靡】① obscene; decadent: ~的音乐 *obscene or decadent music* ② extravagant; showy and luxurious: 风气~。*Extravagance has become a common practice.*
【淫威】abuse of power; despotic power: 慑于权贵的~ *be cowed by the despotic power of bigwigs* / 施~ *abuse one's power*; *ride roughshod over others*
【淫猥】obscene; salacious
【淫邪】obscene and wicked; lewd and vicious
【淫亵】obscene; salacious; sexually harassing
【淫刑】[书] ① mete out excessive punishments ② excessive punishments
【淫雨】excessive rains
【淫欲】sexual desire; lust

寅 the third of the twelve Earthly Branches
【寅吃卯粮】eat next year's food; anticipate one's income
【寅时】period of the day from 3 a. m. to 5 a. m.

龈 gum; gingiva: 牙~ *gum*

yǐn

引 ① draw; stretch: ~出结论 *draw a conclusion* / 这烟囱~风不畅。*The chimney does not draw well.* / ~弓。*Draw a bow.* ② lead; guide: ~路人 *guide* / ~兵南下 *lead the army southward* / ~黄入津 *divert the water of the Yellow River to Tianjin* ③ leave ④ stretch out ⑤ induce; attract; draw: ~火 *kindle a fire* / 抛砖~玉 *cast a stone to get jade*; *say a few opening words to induce others to come up with valuable opinion* / 勾~ *lure*; *seduce* ⑥ cause; arouse; trigger; set off: 他的歌~得大家笑起来。*His song set everybody laughing.* ⑦ quote; cite: ~某人的话 *quote sb* / 旁证博~ *quote copiously from all available sources* / ~书为证 *cite a book as proof* / ~以为耻 *regard as a shame*
【引爆】ignite; detonate: ~装置 *igniter*
【引产】induced labour
【引出】draw forth; lead to; result in: ~错误的结论 *draw forth wrong conclusions*
【引导】guide; lead
【引逗】tantalize; tease; lure; entice
【引渡】① lead across (a river etc.): ~迷津 *lead sb out of confusion* ②【律】extradite: ~罪犯 *extradite a criminal*
【引而不发】draw the bow but not release the arrow — enlighten people through guidance; be skillful at guidance or control
【引发】initiate; set off; give rise to; arouse; trigger off: 那个事件~了一场战争。*The incident touched off* (*or sparked off*) *a war.*
【引吭高歌】sing at the top of one's voice; sing heartily
【引航】pilotage: ~员 *pilot*
【引号】quotation marks: 双~ *double quotation marks* / 单~ *single quotation marks*
【引河】① irrigation channel ② diversion canal
【引火】light a fire; kindle a fire; ignite: ~烧身 *draw fire against oneself — bring trouble on oneself* / ~线 *fuse*
【引见】present (a person) to another; introduce: 他把我~给经理。*He presented me to the manager.*
【引荐】recommend (a person)
【引进】① recommend (a person) ② introduce from elsewhere; import; absorb: ~新的蔬菜品种 *introduce new varieties of vegetable* / ~技术装备 *import technology and equipment* / ~生产线 *import assembly line*

【引经据典】quote the classics; quote authoritative works
【引颈】crane one's neck
【引咎】[书] hold oneself responsible for a serious mistake; take the blame: ~辞职 *admit one's mistakes and resign* / ~自杀 *take the blame and suicide*
【引狼入室】invite a wolf into the house — open the door to a dangerous foe
【引力】【物】gravitation; gravitational force; attraction:地心~ *earth gravitation* / 万有~ *universal gravitation* / 核~ *nuclear attraction* / ~场 *gravitational field*
【引领】① [书] crane one's neck to look afar — eagerly await: ~而望 *crane one's neck to see; eagerly look forward to* ② guide; lead; take
【引流】【医】drainage: ~物 *drain* / ~术 *drainage* / ~管 *drainage tube*
【引路】lead the way
【引起】give rise to; touch off; bring about; generate: ~争论 *set off a debate* / ~反感 *arouse antipathy* / ~麻烦 *give rise to trouble* / ~连锁反应 *set off a chain reaction* / ~公愤 *arouse public indignation*
【引桥】【交】bridge approach
【引擎】engine: ~盖 *bonnet; hood* / 喷气~ *a jet engine* / 蒸汽~ *a steam engine*
【引燃管】ignitron
【引人入胜】fascinating; enchanting; bewitching:把杂志办得~ *make the magazine interesting and absorbing*
【引人注目】noticeable; conspicuous; eye-catching: ~的成绩 *conspicuous achievement* / ~的变化 *spectacular changes*
【引入】lead into; draw into; introduce from elsewhere: ~圈套 *lure into a trap; ensnare* / ~新选手 *introduce new players* / ~歧途 *mislead ; lead sb astray*
【引申】extend (the meaning of a word or phrase): ~义 *extended meaning* / 词义的比喻~义 *figurative extension of the meaning of words*
【引首】raise one's head; crane one's neck
【引述】quote sb's words; quote from sb's speech
【引水】① pilot a ship (through difficult waters, or into or out of a harbour) ② draw or channel water: ~灌田 *channel water into the fields* / ~上山 *draw water up a hill* / ~工程 *flood diversion works or projcet* / ~员 *pilot (of a ship)* / ~入京 *draw water to Beijing*
【引头】take the lead; be the first to do sth
【引退】retire from office; resign
【引线】① fuse; detonator ② go-between ③ [方] sewing needle ④【电】lead-in(wire)
【引信】detonator; fuse:触发~ *contact fuse* / 延期~ *delay fuse* / 安全~ *safety fuse* / 火药~ *a detonating cord or fuse*
【引言】foreword; introduction
【引以为耻】regard it as a disgrace; consider it shameful
【引以为憾】deem it regrettable
【引以为鉴】take warning from it
【引以为戒】draw a lesson (from a mistake, etc.); take warning from
【引以为荣】regard it as an honour; take it as an honour
【引用】① quote; cite ② recommend; appoint
【引诱】lure; entice; seduce: ~日本鬼子进入伏击圈 *lure the Japanese invaders into a trap* / 经不起甜言蜜语的~ *submit to or fall victim to cajolery*
【引玉之砖】[谦] a brick cast to attract jade — brief commonplace remarks offered to stimulate and bring forth valuable opinion
【引证】quote or cite as proof or evidence: 多方~ *quote extensively to support one's argument*
【引种】introduce a new breed or strain
【引子】①【中医】an added ingredient (to enhance the efficacy of medicines) ② (of speech or writing) introductory remarks; introduction ③ introductory part of some music ④ opening lines of an actor or actress
【引座】usher: ~员 *usher*

饮 ① drink; drink wine or other liquor: ~凉水 *drink cool water* / ~茶 *drink tea* / ~酒 *drink wine or liquor* / 一~而尽 *drink it down in one gulp; gulp down* ② sth to drink; drink: 冷~ *cold drinks; ice drinks* ③ keep in the heart; nurse: ~辱 *nurse humiliation; bury one's humiliation deep* ④【中医】a decoction of Chinese medicine to be taken cold
see also yìn
【饮弹】[书] be hit by a bullet: ~身亡 *be killed by a bullet*
【饮恨】[书] nurse a grievance; bury one's hatred deep in one's heart: ~终身 *harbour hatred all one's life* / ~吞声 *swallow one's resentment and choke back one's sobs; endure insults and injuries* / ~而死 *die with hatred in one's heart*
【饮料】beverage; drink (esp. a soft drink)
【饮泣】[书] weep in silence
【饮食】food and drink; diet;给小孩规定~ *put a kid on a diet* / ~卫生 *dietetic hygiene* / ~店 *eating house; cafe; snack bar* / ~业 *the catering trade*
【饮水】drinking water; potable water: ~器 *drinking bowl; drinker*
【饮水思源】when you drink water, think of its source — bear in mind where one's happiness comes from
【饮水不忘掘井人】when you drink the water think of those who dug the well
【饮用水】drinking water; potable water
【饮誉】win praise; enjoy fame or popularity: ~全球 *be popular all over the world; win worldwide fame*
【饮鸩止渴】drink poison to quench thirst — seek temporary relief regardless of the consequences
【饮子】decoction of Chinese medicine to taken cold

Y

隐 ① hide from view; conceal: ~入深山 *hide in remote mountains* / ~入树丛 *hide in the woods or bushes* / ~名埋姓 *conceal one's name and surname*; *keep one's identity hidden* ② latent; dormant; lurking: ~欲 *latent desire* / ~恨 *lurking resentment* ③ secret; privacy: 难言之~ *sth embarrassing to mention*; *unspeakable personal secret*

【隐蔽】conceal; take cover: ~的活动 *covert activities* / ~阵地 *covered position* / ~的敌人 *hidden enemies* / 以~的方式进行 *do sth under cover*

【隐蔽色】cryptic colour (or coloration)

【隐藏】hide; conceal; remain under cover: ~证据 *conceal evidence* / ~罪犯 *screen offenders* / ~在暗处 *lurk in the shadows*

【隐恶扬善】cover up sb's faults and publicize his merits; conceal faults of others and praise his good deeds

【隐伏】lie concealed (or hidden); lie low; lurk: ~着的危险 *lurking danger* / 解放后,这个特务隐名改姓~了下来。*After liberation, the spy changed his name and lay low.*

【隐睾】【生理】cryptorchid: ~症 *cryptorchidism*

【隐含】imply; contain vaguely

【隐函数】【数】implicit function

【隐患】hidden trouble; lurking danger; snake in the grass: 留下~ *leave behind a hidden danger*; *leave a landmine* / 彻底消除~ *remove a hidden peril for good* / 火灾~ *a hidden fire danger*

【隐讳】avoid mentioning; cover up: 不要~自己的缺点。*One should not gloss over one's shortcomings.*

【隐晦】obscure; veiled; indistinct; ambiguous: 语意~ *be couched in ambiguous terms* / ~曲折 (*of a statement*) *veiled and roundabout* / 对某人~某事 *conceal sth from sb*

【隐疾】unmentionable disease

【隐居】live in seclusion; withdraw from society and live in solitude; be a hermit: ~田园 *dwell in seclusion in the countryside*; *retire to county hermitage*

【隐君子】retired scholar; dope addict; dope

【隐瞒】conceal; hide; hold back; cover up: ~错误 *conceal one's mistakes* / ~事实 *withhold the truth*; *keep the lid over sth*

【隐秘】① concealed; hidden: ~的藏身处 *a secret hiding place* / ~之事 *a secret* ② secret: 内心的~ *bosom secret* / 探听别人的~ *try to find out sb's secret*; *pry a secret out of sb*

【隐没】hide behind; disappear

【隐匿】[书] conceal; hide; go into hiding; lie low: ~逃犯 *hide an escaped convict* / ~罪证 *conceal criminal evidence*

【隐情】facts or reason one wishes to hide; secrets

【隐然】dimly; faintly; implicitly: ~可见 *dimly visible* / ~可闻 *faintly audible*

【隐忍】bear patiently; endure silently; forbear: ~不言 *forbear from speaking*; *bite one's tongue*

【隐射】insinuate; hint; imply

【隐身草】a person or thing acting as cover; blind; cover

【隐身术】disappearing act; vanishing act

【隐士】recluse; hermit

【隐私】one's secrets; personal secret; privacy: ~权 *rights of privacy*; *privacy* / 尊重别人的~。*Privacy should be respected.*

【隐痛】① secret anguish; pain endured silently ② dull pain

【隐退】① recede; fade away; disappear ② go and live in seclusion; retire from political life

【隐现】be now visible, now invisible; be dimly visible; flicker: 远处灯光~。*Lights were flickering in the distance.*

【隐形飞机】stealth aircraft

【隐形轰炸机】stealth bomber

【隐形收入】invisible income; off-payroll income

【隐形眼镜】contact lens

【隐性】recessiveness: ~基因 *recessive gene* / ~性状 *recessive character* / ~遗传 *recessive inheritance*

【隐性失业】recessive unemployment

【隐隐】indistinct; faint; dull: ~的雷声 *a distant roll of thunder* / ~可见 *be faintly visible* / ~作痛 *feel a dull pain*

【隐忧】secret worry or anxiety

【隐语】① enigmatic language; insinuating language; riddle ② argot; cant

【隐喻】metaphor

【隐约】indistinct; faint; dim; vague: ~可见 *faintly visible* / ~其词 *use ambiguous langue*; *speak or write in equivocal terms*; *be evasive*

【隐衷】feelings one wishes to keep to oneself; inner feeling

瘾 ① addiction; habitual craving: 吸毒成~ *be addicted to drugs* / 打牌上~了 *become addicted to card playing* / 有酒~ *have a craving for alcoholic drink* ② strong interest; passion: 跳舞上~ *have a passion for dancing* / 有车~ *have a passion for driving* / 他看电视看上~了。*He's crazy about TV.*

【瘾君子】① dope addict; doper ② heavy smoker; chain smoker

【瘾头儿】[口] addiction; strong interest; obsession

yìn

印 ① seal; stamp; chop: 盖~ *affix a seal*; *stamp a seal* / 钢~ *embossing seal*; *steel seal* / 私~ *personal seal* ② mark; trace; print: 脚~ *fingerprint* / 指~ *footprint* / 烙~ *brand* ③ print; engrave: ~书 *print books* / ~名片 *print name card* / 深深~在记忆里 *be engraved on one's mind* ② tally; conform: 心心相~ *have mutual affinity*; *be mutually attracted*

【印版】printing plate; form

【印本】printed copy; printed book

【印次】【印】impression

【印第安人】American Indian; red Indian; Indian

【印地语】Hindi
【印度】India：～教 *Hinduism* /～人 *Indian* /～洋 *the Indian Ocean*
【印度尼西亚】Indonesia：～人 *Indonesian* /～语 *Indonesian(language)*
【印度支那】Indo-China：～半岛 *the Indo-Chinese Peninsula; Indo-China Peninsula*
【印发】print and distribute; tribute leaflets
【印盒】seal box
【印痕】mark; trace
【印花】①【纺】printing：～丝绸 *printed silk* /～布 *printed calico; printed cotton fabric; prints* /～厂 *printworks* /～机 *printing machine* ② revenue stamp; stamp：帖～ *pay stamp tax* /～税 *stamp tax; stamp duty*
【印记】①［旧］seal; stamp; chop ② the impression of a seal; trace; mark：鲜红的～ *the red impression of a seal* ③ impress or stamp on one's mind
【印迹】trace; mark; vestige; stain
【印加】Inca：～人 *Inca*
【印鉴】a specimen seal impression for checking when marking payments
【印泥】red ink paste used for seals
【印染】【纺】printing and dyeing (of textiles)：～厂 *printing and dyeing mill*
【印数】【印】the number of copies of a book printed at one impression; impression
【印刷】printing：第三次～ *third impression (or printing)* /立体～ *stereoscopic printing; three-dimensional printing* /三色版～ *three-colour half-tone* /～厂 *printing house* /～错误 *misprint; typographic error* /～工人 *printing worker; printer* /～品 *printed matter* /～术 *art of printing; printing* /～体 *block letter; print hand* /～纸 *printing paper* /～机 *printing machine; press*
【印台】ink pad; stamp pad
【印玺】imperial seal
【印相纸】photographic paper
【印象】impression：深刻的～ *a deep impression* /模糊 *vague impression* /～派 *impressionist school; impressionist* /～主义 *impressionism*
【印行】print and distribute; publish
【印油】stamp-pad ink
【印张】【印】printed sheet
【印章】seal; signet; stamp
【印证】① confirm; corroborate; verify：他的话有待～。*His statement is yet to be confirmed.* ② sth that confirms, verifies, or corroborates

饮 water (an animal)：～牲口 *water draught animal* /这头马～过了。*The horse has been watered.*
see also yǐn

荫 ① shady; damp and chilly：这座朝北的老房子屋里很～。*This old house with a northern exposure is very damp and chilly.* ②［书］shelter; protect ③ (of a feudal ruler) confer privileges on sb's descendants in consideration of his distinguished service
see also yīn
【荫庇】protection by one's elders or ancestors

yīng

应1 ① answer; respond; reply：喊孩子不～。*I called my child, but he didn't answer.* ② agree; (to do sth); promise; accept

应2 should; ought to：～当没有差错 *there should no mistake* /理～如此 *this is as it should be* /～享受的权利 *a right one is entitled to* /～尽的义务 *one's bounden duty* /～给予奖励 *merit consideration* /发现错误～立即纠正。*When a mistake discovered, it should be corrected at once.*
see also yìng
【应当】should; ought to：这样做～不～？*It should be done this way, shouldn't we?*
【应得】deserve; merit; be due (to sb)：～荣誉 *well-deserved honour* /～的报酬 *a due reward* /～的惩罚 *a deserved punishment*
【应分】what one should do; part of one's job：帮助群众是干部～的事。*It's part of the duty as cadres to help the masses.*
【应付】payable; due：～票据 *note (or bill) payable* /～账款 *account payable* /～利息 *interest due; interest in the red* /～押款 *mortgage payable*
【应该】should; ought to; must：你～了解。*You ought to understand.* /教师～对学生有耐心。*Teachers ought to be patient with students.*
【应届毕业生】graduating students or pupils; this year's graduates
【应名儿】① serve as titular head; lend one's name ② only in name; nominally
【应声儿】［口］answer; respond
【应收】receivable：～税款 *tax receivable* /～押款 *mortgage receivable* /～账款 *account receivable; debt receivable* /～利息 *interest in black; interest receivable*
【应税商品】taxable good; dutiable commodity
【应许】① agree to do sth; promise：他～的事情一定会办。*He will certainly do whatever he promises to.* ② permit; allow：谁～他把计算机搬走的？*Who gave him permission to take the computer away?*
【应有】due; proper; deserved：发挥领导～的作用 *play the leader's proper role* /做出～的贡献 *make a due contribution* /受到～的谴责 *receive due condemnation; be duly censured* /～尽有 *have everything that one could wish for* /做出～的努力 *take a due effort*
【应允】assent; consent：点头～ *nod assent; nod approval*

英1 ①［书］flower; petal; bloom：遍地落～ *fallen petals everywhere* ② hero; outstanding person：群～聚集 *galaxy of talented people* /精～ *people with distinguished accomplishments; elite*

英2 Britain; England：大～帝国 *British Empire*

【英镑】pound sterling：～结存 *sterling balance* / ～区 *the sterling area*
【英才】a person of outstanding ability; a person of superior talents
【英尺】foot (a measure)
【英寸】inch
【英吨】long ton
【英国】Britain; England：～护照 *British passport* / ～文学 *English literature* / ～国民 *British national* / ～臣民 *British subject* / ～人 *the British; Englishman or Englishwoman*
【英豪】heroes; outstanding figures
【英魂】spirit of the brave departed which still command our respect：烈士～永存。*The martyrs are immortal.*
【英吉利海峡】the English Channel
【英杰】heroes; outstanding figures
【英俊】① eminently talented; brilliant; ② handsome and spirited; good-looking and bright：～少年 *a handsome young man* / 相貌～ *handsome appearance; good looks*
【英里】mile
【英联邦】the British Commonwealth (of Nations)
【英烈】① courageous and unyielding; indomitable ② martyr who died heroically ③ [书] outstanding exploits
【英灵】① spirit of the brave departed; spirit of a martyr：告慰～ *console the spirit of the martyr* ② [书] a person of outstanding talent and ability
【英名】illustrious name
【英明】wise; sagacious; brilliant：～决策 *wise decision* / ～远见 *wisdom and foresight; sagacity and farsightedness* / ～的领导 *a sagacious leader*
【英模】heroes and model workers：～事迹 *exemplary deeds of heroes and model workers* / ～报告会 *a public lecture of model people*
【英亩】acre
【英年】youthful years; youth; prime of life
【英气】heroic sprit; dashing spirit：～勃勃 *full of heroic spirit* / 同敌人血战到底的～ *have the dashing spirit to fight the enemy to the last drop of one's blood*
【英文】English (language)
【英武】[书] of soldierly (or martial) bearing
【英雄】① hero：女～ *heroine* / 盖世～ *matchless or peerless hero* / ～本色 *action or conduct befitting a hero* / ～所见略同 *heroes share the same thought; great minds think alike* / ～无用武之地 *a hero with no place to display his prowess; have no chance to put one's abilities to good use* / 儿女情长，英雄气短。*The spirit of a hero is overshadowed by the love between man and woman.* ② heroic：～气概 *heroic spirit; intrepidity*
【英勇】heroic; valiant; brave; gallant：～无比 *showing unparalleled heroism* / ～善战 *brave and skilful in battle*
【英语】English (language)：英国～ *British English* / 美国～ *American English* / ～国家 *English-speaking countries* / ～水平测验 *English Proficiency Test (EPT)*
【英制】British system of weights and measures
【英姿】heroic bearing：～焕发 *dashing; audacious and spirited* / ～飒爽 *valorous and heroic in bearing; bright and brave*

莺

warbler; oriole
【莺歌燕舞】orioles sing and swallows dart — the joy of spring; a scene of prosperity; excellent situation
【莺声燕语】like the trilling of an oriole and the song of a swallow — the sweet, delicate voice of a woman

婴

1 baby; infant：产一女～ *give birth to a girl baby* / 男～ *a boy baby*

婴

2 [书] touch; contract; surround; entangle：～疾 *contract a disease* / ～城固守 *fortify the city to beef up its defense*
【婴儿】baby; infant：～车 *pram; baby carriage; stroller; pushchair* / ～床 *crib; cot; cradle* / ～死亡率 *infant mortality*
【婴孩】baby; infant
【婴幼儿】infants and pre-school children

嘤

[象] trill; chirp
【嘤鸣】① (of birds) trill; chirp; sing ② [书] empathy between friends
【嘤泣】sob quietly
【嘤嘤】[象] chirp; low and soft sound：鸟鸣～ *birds chirping continuously* / ～啜泣 *sobbing quietly*

罂

[书] small- mouthed jar
【罂粟】【植】poppy：～花 *poppy flower* / ～壳 *poppy capsule or shell*
【罂子桐】tung oil tree

缨

① tassel：红～枪 *red-tasseled spear* ② sth shaped like a tassel：萝卜～儿 *radish leaves* ③ ribbon
【缨帽】red-tasseled official hat worn by officials of the Qing Dynasty
【缨子】① ornamental tassels ② sth shaped like a tassel：萝卜～ *radish leaves*

樱

① cherry ② oriental cherry
【樱唇】cherry lips (ruby lips of a pretty woman)
【樱花】oriental cherry; cherry blossom：日本～ *Japanese flowering cherry* / ～开了。*The cherries are blooming.*
【樱桃】cherry

鹦

【鹦鹉】parrot：长尾～ *parakeet* / 虎皮～ *budgerigar* / ～螺 *nautilus* / ～学舌 *repeat the words like a parrot; parrot*
【鹦嘴鱼】parrot fish

膺

1 [书] chest; breast：抚～长叹 *have a long sigh with one's hand on one's chest* / 义愤填～ *be filled with righteous indignation*

膺 ① [书] ① bear; shoulder; receive: 荣～要职 *be honoured to assume a post of great responsibility* ② send a punitive expedition against; attack

【膺惩】[书] attack and punish; send a punitive expedition against: ～国贼 *punish the traitors of the nation*

【膺赏】be awarded a prize

【膺选】be elected; be selected

鹰 hawk; eagle: 雄～展翅 *powerful hawk spreading its wings*

【鹰鼻鹞眼】hawk-nosed and eagle-eyed; sinister-and fierce-looking

【鹰钩鼻子】aquiline nose

【鹰犬】falcons and hounds — lackeys; hired thugs; running dogs

【鹰爪毛儿】a kind of curly sheep's wool

yíng

迎 ① meet; greet; welcome; receive: 逢～ *make up to; fawn on* / 远～ *go over a long distance to meet sb* / ～来送往 *receive and see off guests* / 喜～新年 *joyously usher in the New Year* ② go or move towards; meet face to face: ～着困难上 *meet difficulties head-on*

【迎宾】receive a visitor; meet or welcome a guest: ～曲 *a tune of welcome* / ～员 *doorman*

【迎风】① facing (or against) the wind: ～而立 *stand against the wind* / ～展翅 *fly against the wind* ② down the wind; with the wind: 红旗～招展。*Red flags fluttered in the breeze.*

【迎合】cater to; pander to: 百般～老板 *curry favour with one's boss sedulously*

【迎候】await the arrival of

【迎击】meet (an approaching enemy) head-on; attack head-on

【迎接】receive; meet; welcome; greet: ～新的挑战 *meet a new challenge* / ～外宾 *welcome foreign guests*

【迎面】head-on; in one's face; face to face: 大雪～扑来 *heavy snow blows in one's face* / 只见他正～走来。*I saw him coming up to me.*

【迎亲】[旧] send a party to meet the bride at the bride's home and escort her to the bridegroom's home for the wedding

【迎娶】marry a woman

【迎刃而解】(of a bamboo) splits all the way down as it meets the edge of the knife —(of a problem) be readily solved

【迎头】head-on; straight; directly: ～赶上 *try hard to catch up* / ～痛击 *knock sb on the head; give a head-on blow*

【迎新】① see the New Year in; welcome the arrival of a new year: 辞旧～ *ring out the old year and ring in the new* ② welcome new arrivals: ～晚会 *a welcome party in honour of the newcomers*

【迎战】meet (an approaching enemy) head-on

荧 [书] ① glimmering; shimmering; dim ② dazzled; perplexed

【荧光】【物】fluorescence; fluorescent light: ～灯 *fluorescent lamp* / ～粉 *fluorescent powder* / ～镜 *fluoroscope* / ～屏 *fluorescent screen; screen (of a television, monitor, etc.)* / ～管 *fluorescent tube*

【荧惑】①[书] bewilder; confuse: ～人心 *confuse people's minds* / ～观众 *bewilder the audience* ② [古] Mars

【荧幕】TV screen

【荧屏】① fluorescent screen; screen (of a television, monitor, etc.) ② television

【荧荧】(of stars, lights, etc.) gleaming; twinkling; glimmering: 众星～ *sparkling stars* / 一灯～。*A light is glimmering.*

盈 ① fill; pack; throng: 车马～门 *one's gateway is thronged with horses and carriages — the house is honoured with rich and distinguished guests* / 热泪～眶 *one's eyes brimming with tears* ② surplus; gain

【盈亏】① profit and loss: 自负～ *(of an enterprise) assume sole responsibility for its own profits and losses* ② the waxing and waning of the moon: 月有～。*The moon waxes and wanes.*

【盈利】make a profit: ～能力 *profitability*

【盈千累万】thousands upon thousands; myriad; numerous

【盈盈】① clear; lucid: 草叶上露珠～。*The grass leaves glistened with dewdrops.* ② engaging; enchanting: ～顾盼 *enchanting gaze* ③ brimming over: 喜气～ *brimming over with joy* ④ agile; lithe; graceful: ～起舞 *dance lithely*

【盈余】surplus; profit: 略有～ *make a small profit* / 对外贸易～ *foreign trade surplus*

莹 [书] ① jade-like stone ② lustrous and transparent: 晶～ *as clear as crystal*

【莹白】shining and white

【莹澈】lustrous and transparent; sparkling and crystal

【莹洁】shining and clean

萤 firefly; glowworm

【萤火】glowworm's light

【萤火虫】firefly; glowworm

【萤石】【矿】fluorite; fluorspar

营[1] seek; pursue: ～私舞弊 *engage in fraud for selfish ends* / 无求无～ *seek nothing for oneself* ② operate; run; manage: 私～ *privately-run; privately-owned* / 合～ *jointly-run; jointly-operated*

营[2] ① camp; barracks: 安～扎寨 *pitch a camp; camp* / 军～ *army barracks* ② battalion: ～部 *battalion headquarters* / ～教导员 *battalion political instructor*

【营巢】(of birds) build a nest; nest

【营地】campsite; camping ground / 宿～ *camping site; temporary quarters for soldiers*

【营房】barracks

【营火】campfire: ～会 *campfire party; campfire*

【营建】construct; build

【营救】succour; rescue; save
【营垒】① barracks and the enclosing ② camp; bloc:两个对立的～ *two opposing blocs* /反动～ *reactionary camp* /革命～ *revolutionary camp*
【营利】seek or pursue profits
【营盘】[旧] military camp; barracks
【营生】(yíngshēng) earn a living; make a living:靠打鱼～ *earn a living as a fisherman*
【营生】(yíngsheng)[方] line of business; occupation; job:他什么～都干过。*He has done all kinds of jobs.*
【营私】seek private gain; feather one's nest:结党～ *form a clique for selfish purpose*
【营销】marketing: ～员 *salesman* /～管理 *marketing management* /～学 *marketing*
【营养】nutrition; nourishment; aliment: ～学 *nutriology* /富于～ *nourishing*; *nutritious* /～不良 *malnutrition* /～过度 *over nutrition* /～钵 *nutritive bowel* /～级 *strophic level* /～价值 *nutritive* (*or nutritional*) *value* /～链 *food chain* /～品 *nutriment* /～师 *dietitian*; *nutritionist* /～霜 *nourishing cream* /～素 *nutrient*
【营业】do business:暂停～ *business temporarily suspended* /照常～ *business as usual* /～收入 *business income* (*or earnings*, *receipts*) /～范围 *scope of business operation* /～项目 *business items* /～执照 *business license* /～额 *turnover*; *volume of business* /～时间 *business hours* /～税 *business tax*; *transactions tax* /～员 *shop employees*; *shop assistant* /～时间 *business time*
【营员】participant in a summer or winter camp
【营运】operation (of vehicles, ships, airliners, etc.)
【营造】① construct; build: ～房屋 *construct houses* /～工事 *build positions* /～铁路 *build railways* ② plant trees; afforest: ～防风林 *plant windbreak forests*
【营寨】[旧] military camp; barracks
【营长】battalion commander
【营帐】tent:支起～ *pitch a tent* /～破了。*The tent was broken.*

萦 [书] entangle; encompass:魂牵梦～ *miss very much* /琐事～身 *be preoccupied with trivialities*; *get bogged down in petty matters*
【萦怀】occupy one's mind
【萦回】hover; linger
【萦念】think of; long for; be concerned about:回到日夜～的故乡 *return to one's sorely missed hometown*
【萦绕】hover; linger

楹 principal columns (or pillars) of a hall
【楹联】couplet written on a scroll and hung on the pillars of a hall

蝇 fly; housefly:灭～ *wipe out flies* /蚊～ *mosquitoes and flies*
【蝇虎】a kind of spider that feeds on flies
【蝇拍】flyswatter; fly flap
【蝇头】small as the head of a fly; tiny: ～小楷 *very small handwritten characters* /～小利 *petty profit* /～小子 *a little tiny boy*
【蝇子】[口] fly; housefly

赢 ① win; beat; defeat:这场足球谁～了? *Who won the football game?* /他下棋～了我。*He beat me at chess* ② gain (profit)
【赢得】win; gain; earn: ～独立 *win independence* /～观众的掌声 *draw applause from the audience* /～别人的尊重 *earn respect from others*
【赢家】winner
【赢利】profit; gain

yǐng

颖 ①【植】glume; grain husk ② tip (of a writing brush); point:锋～ *sharp point* ③ clever:聪～ *clever*
【颖果】【植】caryopsis
【颖慧】[书] (of a teenager) clever; bright; intelligent
【颖悟】[书] (of a teenager) clever; bright

影 ① shadow:人～ *the shadow of a human figure* /阴～ *shadow* /树～ *the shadow of a tree* ② reflection; image:倒～ *inverted image* ③ trace; sign; vague impression:消失得无～无踪 *vanish without a trace* ④ photograph; picture:留～ *take a photo as a reminder of one's visit to a place* /摄～ *take pictures* ⑤ film; movie: ～星 *film star* /～迷 *film fan* ⑥ [方] hide; cover; conceal:小孩～在妈妈身后。*The kid hid on the back of his mother.*
【影壁】① screen wall (facing the gate inside or outside a traditional Chinese courtyard) ② a wall with carved murals
【影带】videotape of a TV programme, film, etc.
【影帝】king of the silver screen; most popular male movie star
【影碟】VCR disk; videodisc
【影后】movie queen; most popular female movie star
【影剧院】theatre, cinemas, opera-houses, etc.
【影片儿】[口] film; movie; picture:故事～ *feature film* /国产～ *home-made film* /香港～ *Hong Kong made film*
【影评】film review
【影射】allude to; hint obliquely at; insinuate
【影视】film and television: ～明星 *a film and TV star* /～界 *film and TV circles* /～文化 *film and TV culture*
【影坛】film (or movie) circles; filmdom: ～人物 *a figure in film circles* /～生涯 *career in film circles* /退出～ *withdraw from filmland*
【影戏】① leather-silhouette show; shadow play ② [方] film; movie
【影响】① affect; influence: ～质量 *impair the quality* /～工作 *interfere with one's work* /～生产进度 *hold up the production* /文艺对人们的思想有很大的～。*Literature and art have a great influence on*

people's ideology /吸烟～健康。*Smoking affects health.* ② influence; effect; impact:产生重大～ *exert a significant influence; produce a great impact* /消除不良～ *eliminate or remove bad effects* ③ hearsay; gossip: ～之谈 *talk based on hearsay*

【影像】① portrait; picture ② figure; features ③ image: ～清晰 *clear image* / ～模糊 *blurred image*

【影业】film-making industry

【影印】【印】 photomechanical printing; photo printing; photo-offset process: ～本 *photo-offset copy; facsimile* /～件 *photocopy* /～照相机 *process camera* /～制版 *photomechanical process*

【影影绰绰】vague; dim; indistinct

【影院】cinema; movie theatre

【影展】① photo exhibition ② film exhibition

【影子】① shadow: ～内阁 *shadow cabinet* ② reflection; image ③ trace; sign; vague impression

瘿 ①【中医】goitre ②【植】gall

【瘿虫】gall insect

yìng

应 ① answer; respond; reply; echo:善于回～ *be good at repartee; always have ready response* /我按了铃，却没有人～门。*I rang the bell, but there is no answer.* /大厅中回～着他的歌声。*The hall echoed back his song.* ② comply with; grant:以～急需 *in order to fill an urgent need* /有求必～ *grant every request* /～邀访问美国 *visit America on invitation* ③ suit; conform to; accord with ④ deal with; cope with:从容～敌 *meet the enemy calmly*

see also ying

【应变】① meet an emergency or contingency: ～措施 *emergency measure* /随机～ *act according to circumstances; suit one's actions to changing conditions* ②【物】strain: ～硬化 *strain hardening* / ～规 *strain gauge* / ～计 *strain meter* / ～率 *strain rate*

【应标】respond to offer of tender

【应承】agree; promise:她～我立即处理这件事。*She promised me to attend to the matter promptly.*

【应酬】① socialize, entertain, treat with courtesy: ～不开 *have too many social engagements on one's hands* / ～几句 *exchange a few polite words* / ～函 *courtesy letter* ② a social engagement:明天我晚上有个～。*I will take part in a dinner party tomorrow.*

【应从】assent to; agree to; consent:他～了这件事。*He agreed to do this matter.*

【应答】reply; answer:从容～ *answer calmly* / ～如流 *reply readily and fluently*

【应电流】induced current

【应对】① reply; answer:他从容～每个问题。*He was calm and answered every question.* ②【电】 answer; answer back; respond: ～器 *responder* / ～台 *answering board*

【应付】① deal with; cope with:准备～突发事件 *get prepared against possible emergencies* /自如 *handle the situation with ease; be equal to the occasion* /这个女孩很难～。*The girl is really very difficult to deal with.* ② do sth perfunctorily: ～事儿 *go through the motions* /不要采取～的态度。*Don't take a perfunctory attitude.* ③ make do; serve as a makeshift:这工作我一个人还可以～。*I can somehow manage the job by myself.*

【应合】echo; respond in concert with

【应机】take an opportunity that rises; suit the situation

【应急】meet an urgent need; meet an emergency (or contingency): ～措施 *emergency measure* / ～灯 *emergency light* / ～电源 *emergency power supply* / ～计划 *contingency plan; crash program*/ ～机场 *an emergency airport* / ～会议 *an emergency meeting*

【应接不暇】have more visitors or business than one can attend to:前来参观的人太多,我们实在有点～了。*We could hardly attend to so many people coming to visit us.*

【应景】do sth for the occasion; act for the sake of politeness, formality, expediency, etc.; go through the motions: ～果品 *seasonal fruits* / ～文章 *occasional article*

【应考】take (or sit for) an entrance examination: ～的人不多。*Few people sat for the examination.*

【应力】【物】stress

【应募】respond to a call for recruits; enlist; enroll

【应诺】agree (to do sth); promise; undertake

【应聘】accept an offer of employment. . 她～到政府部门工作。*She accepted a post in a government office.*

【应声】right at the sound of sth: ～虫 *yesman; echo* /枪声一响,敌兵～而倒。*The enemy soldier fell at the report of the shotgun.* /小姑娘～而至。*The little girl appeared right on the call.*

【应时】① seasonable; in season: ～货品 *seasonable goods* / ～瓜果 *fruits of the season* /黄瓜正～。*Cucumbers are in season.* ② at once; immediately: ～而动 *act promptly according to circumstances* ③［方］at the appointed time

【应试】sit for or take an examination: ～教育 *examination-oriented education* / ～条件 *the requirement of examination*

【应诉】【律】respond to a charge; self-defense by the accused

【应许】promise; agree; permit

【应选】be a candidate for election; be an election candidate; run for election

【应验】come true; be confirmed; be fulfilled:他的预言～了。*His predictions have come true.*

【应邀】at sb's invitation; on invitation: ～来访 *come to visit on invitation*

【应用】① apply; use; employ:把知识～于实践 *apply knowledge to practice* / ～先进技术 employ advanced technology ② applied: ～化学 *applied chemistry* / ～数学 *applied mathematics* / ～程序

application program / ~科学 *applied science* / ~软件 *application software* / ~文 *practical writing* / ~语言学 *applied linguistics* / ~物理 *applied physics*

【应运而生】arise at the right moment; emerge as the times demand

【应战】① meet an enemy attack:沉着~ *meet the attack calmly* / 匆忙~ *meet the attack hastily* ② accept or take up a challenge: ~书 *letter accepting a challenge*

【应招】respond to a call for recruits or candidates; enlist

【应召】[书] respond to a call or summons: ~女郎 *call girl; prostitute* / ~先生 *call boy gigolo*

【应诏】do sth in response to an imperial decree

【应诊】(of a doctor) see patients

【应征】① be recruited; enlist; join up: ~参军 *be recruited into the army* ② respond to a call for contributions (to a publication): ~的稿件 *solicited contributions; contributions to a periodical, etc. at the editor's public invitation*

映 ① reflect; mirror; shine:反~ *reflect* / 朝霞~在海面上。*The glory of the dawn is mirrored on the sea.* ② project a film:首~ *the first showing*

【映衬】① set off: 在这件毛衣的~下,她眼睛的蓝色显得更漂亮了。*That jumper sets off the blue of her eyes.* ② antithesis

【映山红】【植】azalea

【映射】shine upon; cast light upon:阳光~在河面上。*The sun shines upon the river.*

【映托】set off; serve as a foil to

【映现】appear before one's eyes; come into view

【映照】shine upon; cast light upon

硬 ① hard; solid; stiff; tough: ~塑料 *hard plastic* / 软磨~泡 *alternate use of soft and tough tactics* / 坚~ *solid* / 僵~ *rigid; inflexible* / ~领子 *a stiff collar* / ~刷子 *a stiff brush* ② strong; firm; tough; obstinate:说话口气~ *speak in very tough tone* / 欺软怕~ *bully the weak and fear the strong* ③ manage to do sth with difficulty: ~充好汉 *act the hero* / 生搬~套 *copy mechanically* ④ good (quality); able (person):货色~ *goods of high quality* / 牌子~ *a trademark of high standing; a prestigious trademark* / 功夫~ *masterly skill*

【硬邦邦】very hard; very stiff; clumsy

【硬包装】① hard packaging ② hard packaging material, such as tinplate can glass bottle, etc.

【硬币】① coin; hard cash; specie:一壹分的~ *a one-fen piece or coin* ② hard currency

【硬撑】manage to do sth with difficulty ; force oneself to do sth:有困难不要~。*Don's force yourself to treat when face knotty problems.*

【硬道理】inescapable truth; established truth:发展是~。*Development is top priority.*

【硬顶】① resist stubbornly; strongly oppose; stand firmly against:对不合理的要求就要~。*One must stand firmly against unreasonable requirement.* ② retort or talk back rudely:你对老师怎么老这样~? *How could you be so boorish as to talk back to your teacher?*

【硬度】①【物】hardness ② hardness of water

【硬腭】【生理】hard palate

【硬功夫】great proficiency; masterly skill

【硬骨头】① hard bone; person of indomitable will ② hard nut ; difficult task:啃~ *crack a hard nut; work at a difficult task*

【硬骨鱼】bony fish

【硬汉】a dauntless, unyielding man; a man of iron will

【硬化】①【医】hardening:血管~ *vascular sclerosis* / 动脉~ *arteriosclerosis* ②【机】harden: 时效~ *age hardening* ③ (of ideas) become rigid or inflexible:思想~ *rigid mind; petrified thinking* / 肝~ *cirrhosis (of the liver)*

【硬环境】infrastructure

【硬件】① hardware ② machinery; and other equipment used in production, scientific research or business operation

【硬结】① indurate; harden ②【医】scleroma

【硬拷贝】【电】hard copy

【硬科学】hard science

【硬朗】① hale and hearty:老太太身子骨还挺~。*The old lady is still going strong.* ② (of statements) forceful

【硬煤】hard coal; anthracite

【硬面】unleavened dough; stiff dough

【硬木】hardwood: ~家具 *hardwood furniture* / ~床 *hardwood bed*

【硬盘】【电】hard magnetic disk

【硬碰硬】① confront the tough with toughness; meet force with force ② (of a job) demanding solid, painstaking work or real skill:改革可是~的事。*Innovation is an extremely difficult matter.*

【硬拼】fight recklessly; act in a foolhardy manner

【硬气】[方] ① tough; firm; unyielding:为人~ *unyielding in nature* ② have no qualms; feel justified

【硬砂岩】【地】greywacke

【硬是】①[方] actually; just; simply:妈妈嘱咐他在家休息,可他~不听。*The mother advised him to stay at home, but he just wouldn't listen.* / 他~不认错。*He just would not admit his fault.* ② despite all (difficulties, etc.); still:工程十分艰难,可我们~按时完成了任务。*We finished the project on schedule despite great difficulties.*

【硬实】①[方] strong; sturdy; robust ② hard:石头摸着很~。*The stone is hard to touch.*

【硬水】hard water

【硬说】stubbornly insist; obstinately assert; allege:她~自己漂亮。*She insisted that she was beautiful.*

【硬挺】① endure with all one's will; hold out with all one's might:老太太~过了这场灾难。*The old lady succeeded in pulling through the disaster.* / 那个学生生了病,还~到底了。*In spite of the student's illness, he stuck it out.* ② rigid; stiff

【硬通货】hard currency
【硬卧】sleeping carriage with hard berths; hard sleeping berths
【硬席】hard seats or berths (on a train): ~卧铺 *hard sleeping berth*
【硬橡胶】hard rubber; ebonite; vulcanite
【硬性】rigid; stiff; inflexible: ~规定 *hard and fast (or rigid) rules* / ~摊派 *mandatory apportionment*
【硬玉】jadeite
【硬仗】tough battle; formidable task: 我喜欢打~。*I like fight a hard battle.*
【硬着头皮】toughen one's scalp — brace oneself; force oneself to do sth against one's will: ~顶住 *brace oneself and bear it; stick it out; tough it out* / 他~把那笔钱还了。*He forced himself to repay the money.*
【硬着心肠】toughen one's heart; force oneself to discard tender feelings; steel oneself
【硬纸板】hardboard; cardboard
【硬指标】mandatory quota or criterion; inflexible target, goal, requirement
【硬质合金】【冶】hard alloy; hard metal: ~刀具 *hard alloy cutter; hard metal tool* / ~钻头 *hard alloy bit; hard metal bit (or drill)*
【硬质塑料】【化】rigid plastics: 半~ *semirigid plastics*
【硬着陆】①【航】hard-land ②【经】hard landing
【硬座】hard seat

yō

哟 used to express slight astonishment or surprise, sometimes with a tone of light-hearted joking: ~,是你呀! *Oh! It's you!*
see also yo

yo

哟 ① used at the end of a sentence to urge sb: 快点来~! *Come over here, quick!* / 用力拉~! *Heave ho!* ② (used as a syllable filler in a song): 太阳一出~,满山红。*The sun is rising and shining all over the mountain.*
see also yō

yōng

佣 ① hire; employ: 雇~ *hire a labourer* ② servant: 女~ *woman servant; maid* / 男~ *man servant*
see also yòng
【佣妇】woman servant; maid
【佣工】hired labourer; , servant: 室外~ *an outdoor servant*
【佣人】servant; maid: 室内~ *an indoor servant*

拥 ① hold in one's arms; embrace; hug: 把妻子紧紧~在怀里 *hug the wife tightly* ② surround; wrap around: 女孩~被而坐。*The girl sat wrapped in a quilt.* ③ crowd; throng; swarm: 一~而上 *throng forward* / 教室一开,同学一窝蜂似的往里~。*The students swarmed in as soon as the classroom opened.* ④ support; uphold: 军爱民,民~军。*The army cherishes the people and the people support the army.* ⑤ [书] have; possess; boast: ~兵自重 *build up one's power by dint of one's army; assume importance by raising an army* / ~书万卷 *possess a large collection of books*
【拥抱】embrace; hug; hold in one's arms: 他们互相热情~。*They embraced each other warmly.*
【拥戴】support; hold in esteem: 受到老百姓的~ *enjoy the support of the common people*
【拥护】support; uphold; endorse: 我们~这个决定。*We endorse this decision.*
【拥挤】① be crowded; be packed: 屋里很~。*The room was very crowded.* ② push and squeeze: 不要~! *Don't push!*
【拥进】(of people) crowd into; swarm into
【拥军优属】(of civilians) support the army and give preferential treatment to families of revolutionary armymen and martyrs
【拥塞】jam; congest: 道路~。*Roads are congested.*
【拥有】possess; have; own; boast: ~核武器 *possess nuclear weapons* / ~丰富的矿藏 *have rich mineral resources; abound in mineral resources* / 尼泊尔~世界上最高的十六座山峰中的十二座。*Nepal boasts of twelve of the world's sixteen highest peaks.*
【拥政爱民】(of the army) support the government and cherish the people

庸[1] ① commonplace; mediocre; ordinary: 中~之道 *doctrine of the mean; golden mean* / 凡~ *ordinary; dull* / 平~之辈 *person of mediocre calibre; mediocrity* ② inferior; second-rate; incompetent: 昏~ *fatuous; muddle-headed*

庸[2] [书] (used in the negative) need: 无~讳言 *no need for reticence* / 无~赘述。*There is needed to go into unnecessary details.*
【庸才】[书] a mediocre person; mediocrity
【庸常】commonplace; ordinary; mediocre: ~之人 *a person of ordinary ability*
【庸夫】a person of average ability; mediocrity
【庸劣】inferior; low-grade
【庸碌】mediocre and unambitious
【庸人】a mediocre person: ~自扰 *worry about imagined troubles; seek trouble*
【庸俗】vulgar; philistine; low: 趣味~ *have vulgar (or unrefined) tastes* / ~化 *vulgarize; debase* / ~不堪 *philistine*
【庸医】quack; charlatan: ~杀人不用刀。*A charlatan doesn't kill with a knife.*

雍 [书] harmony
【雍和】harmony
【雍容】natural, graceful and poised: 仪态~ *a dignified bearing* / ~大雅 *display poise and refine-*

ment / ~华贵 (*of a woman*) *elegant and poised*; *stately*

慵 [书] weary; lethargic; languid

【慵惰】[书] lazy; languid

【慵倦】tired and sleepy

【慵懒】[书] sluggish; indolent; lethargic

壅 [书] ① stop up; obstruct; bar ② heap soil or fertilizer over and around the roots (of plants and trees): ~肥 *heap fertilizer around the roots* / ~土 *hilling*

【壅塞】clog up; jam; congest: 水道~。*The waterway is blocked up.*

臃 [书] swollen

【臃肿】① too fat to move: 冬天孩子们穿得太~。*The kids are encumbered by too giant clothes in winter.* ② overstaffed; bloated: 机构~ *overstaffed organizations*

yǒng

永 perpetually; forever; for all time; always: ~生难忘 *not forget as long as one lives* / ~恒的真理 *everlasting truth* / ~葆青春 *always keep one's spirit young*; *keep alive the fervour of youth* / ~不反悔 *will never go back on one's words*

【永别】part never to meet again; part forever; be separated by death: 老人和我们~了。*The old man parted from us forever.*

【永垂不朽】live forever; be immortal: 人民英雄~! *Immortal are the people's heroes!*

【永磁】【物】permanent magnetism: ~发电机 *magneto*; *permanent-magnet generator* / ~体 *permanent magnet*

【永冻层】【地】permafrost

【永恒】eternal; perpetual; everlasting: ~运动 *perpetual motion* / ~的等待 *an eternity of waiting*

【永久】permanent; perpetual; everlasting; forever: ~磁铁 *permanent magnet* / ~船闸 *permanent ship lock* / ~资格 *perpetual qualifications* / ~冻土 *permafrost* / ~和平 *perpetual* (*or everlasting*) *peace* / ~会员 *permanent member* / ~性居民身份证 *permanent identity card* / ~雪线 *firm snow line* / ~中立 *permanent neutrality* / ~主权 *permanent sovereignty*

【永诀】[书] part forever; be separated by death

【永生】① eternal life; immortality ② all one's life; lifelong; forever: ~的追求 *life-long pursuit*

【永生永世】for ever and ever; timeless

【永世】forever; always: ~难忘 *will never forget* / ~长存 *live for ever and ever*; *be everlasting* / ~铭记 *remember forever*

【永远】always; forever; ever: ~忠于自己的党 *be forever loyal to one's party* / ~结束战争 *end a war once and for all*

【永志不忘】will forever bear in mind; will always cherish the memory of sb or sth

咏 ① chant; intone; recite: 吟~ *recite* (*a poem*) / 歌~ *sing* ② express or narrate in poetic form: 《~雪》*Ode to the Snow* / 歌以~志 *chant a poem to express one's aspirations*

【咏唱】chant; sing

【咏怀】express one's sentiments and aspirations in poetic form: ~散文 *prose which reveals one's innermost feelings*

【咏叹】intone; chant; sing: 反复~ *sing sth repeatedly* / ~调 *aria*; *operatic solo*

【咏赞】sing the praises of; praise

泳 swim: 蝶~ *butterfly* / 侧~ *sidestroke* / 潜~ *underwater swimming* / 仰~ *backstroke* / 蛙~ *breaststroke*

【泳道】swimming lane

【泳坛】swimming circles

【泳装】swim suit; swim wear; beach wear

俑 wooden or earthen human figure buried with the dead in ancient times; tomb figure; figurine: 陶~ *pottery figurine* / 兵马~ *terracotta warriors and horses*

勇 ① brave; valiant; courageous; dauntless: ~武过人 *surpass others in valour* / 勤劳~敢 *brave and industrious* / 奋~杀敌 *fight the enemy bravely* / 骁~无比 *exceptionally valiant* / 智~双全 *have both wisdom and courage* / 越战越~ *one's courage mounts as the battle progresses* ② temporary recruits in times of war during Qing Dynasty: 散兵游~ *stragglers and disbanded soldiers*

【勇敢】brave; courageous; valorous: ~的战士 *a brave soldier* / 机智~ *resourceful and brave*

【勇猛】bold and powerful; full of valour and vigour

【勇气】courage; nerve; gut; mettle: 鼓起~ *pick up or muster one's courage* / 失去~ *lose the nerve*

【勇士】a brave and strong man; warrior

【勇往直前】march forward courageously; advance bravely

【勇武】valiant; valorous

【勇毅】brave and strong-willed; courageous and resolute

【勇于】be brave in; be bold in; have the courage to; dare to: ~承担重任 *be bold in shouldering heavy responsibilities* / ~发表不同意见 *dare to air differing views*

涌 ① gush; pour; surge: 心潮~动 *surging emotions* / 风起云~ *wind rising and clouds scudding* / 泪如泉~ *tears welling up in one's eyes* / 鲜血喷~而出。*Blood gushes out of one's body.* ② rise; spring; well; emerge: 水上~出一轮红日。*A red sun rose above the water.* / 多少仇恨~上心头。*Memories of hatred welled up in my mind.*

【涌潮】raging tide; tidal bore

【涌动】surge; stream; billow

【涌进】pour or swarm into; surge ahead: 同学们从各个角落~大厅。*The students poured into the hall from all corners.*

【涌浪】surging waves

【涌流】flow rapidly; pour; gush

【涌现】spring up; come to the fore: 百万富翁不断~。*The millionaires are constantly emerging.*
【涌溢】gush out; overflow

蛹 pupa; chrysalis: 蚕~ *silkworm chrysalis* / 蝶~ *chrysalis*

踊 leap up; jump up: 跛者不~。*A cripple cannot leap.*
【踊跃】① leap; jump: ~欢呼 *leap and cheer* ② vying with one another; eagerly; enthusiastically: ~参加 *participate enthusiastically* / 大家~购买股票。*People purchased stocks enthusiastically.*

yòng

用 ① use; utilize; employ; apply: ~水洗 *wash with water* / 大材小~ *large material put to small use — talent wasted on a petty job* / ~手拿 *take with one's hand* / ~火烤 *bake over the fire* / ~剪子剪 *cut with scissors* / 你会~筷子吗? *Can you use chopsticks?* ② (usually used in the negative) need: 不~开电视。*There's no need to turn on the TV.* / 不~着急。*Don't worry.* / 不~麻烦! *Don't bother, please.* / 不~哭。*Don't cry, please.* ③ eat; drink: 请~茶。*Won't you have some tea, please.* / 请~饭! *Please help yourself!* ④ expenses; spending; outlay: 家~ *family expenses* / 零~钱 *pocket money; spending money* ⑤ usefulness; use: 有~ *useful* / 没~ *useless; worthless* / 功~ *function* / 作~ *part; role* ⑥ [书] hence; therefore: ~特函达。*Hence the present letter.*
【用兵】use military forces; resort to arms: 连年~ *fight wars for years on end* / 善于~ *be well versed in the art of war* / ~如神 *direct military operations with miraculous skill; be a superb military commander*
【用不了】① have more than is needed: 把~的书丢掉。*Discard the unnecessary books.* ② less than: ~三天, 他们就和好了。*They will be on good terms again in less than three days.*
【用不着】① not need; have no use for: 天气晴朗, ~这些伞。*It is clear; there is no use for the umbrellas.* ② there is no need to; it is not worthwhile to: ~为这些小事烦恼。*There's no need to be bothered by such trifling.* / ~为我担心。*You needn't worry about me.*
【用材林】【林】commercial forest; timber forest
【用场】use; application: 有~ *be useful* / 派上大~ *be turned to good account* / 派上新~ *be put to new uses*
【用出来】[口] ① use; exert: 他把所有的钱~了。*He used up all his money.* ② become easier to handle with use; be broken in
【用处】use; good; utility: 说了不干有什么~? *What is the good of talking without doing?* / 赶快记住这个词, 将来会有~。*Remember this word right away; it may come in handy.*
【用得了】need that much or many: 他要用这么多钢笔, ~吗? *Do he need all that pens?* / 这点儿活儿~三天吗? *Can such a work take you three days?*
【用得着】① need; require; find sth useful; need: 这些东西以后也许~。*These things may be useful later.* ② there is need to; it is necessary to; it is worthwhile to: ~他亲自来吗? *Is it necessary to for him to come in person?*
【用度】expenditure; expense; outlay: 他家人口多, ~大。*He has a big family and many expenses.*
【用法】use; usage: ~说明 *directions for use* / 学习词典的~ *learn how to use a dictionary*
【用非所长】what one is doing is not one's strong point
【用非所学】what one is doing has nothing to do with one's training
【用费】expense; cost; charge
【用工】recruit and use (workers): ~制度 *the system of recruitment* / ~岗位 *the post of recruitment*
【用工夫】make every effort; exert oneself; work hard
【用功】hardworking; diligent; studious: ~考试 *be studious; be diligent in one's examination*
【用户】consumer; user: 征求~意见 *ask for consumers' opinions* / 电话~ *telephone subscriber* / ~电报 *telex* / ~手册 *user's manual* / ~指南 *user's guide* / ~手机 *mobile phone subscriber*
【用户终端】*user terminal*
【用劲】exert oneself ; put forth one's strength
【用具】utensil; apparatus; appliance: 炊事~ *kitchen (or cooking) utensils* / 消防~ *fire-fighting apparatus* / 救生~ *lifesaving equipment* / 狩猎~ *hunting gear* / 避孕~ *contraceptives*
【用力】exert oneself; put forth one's strength: ~推门 *give the door a hard push* / ~喊叫 *shout at the top of one's voice* / ~过度 *overexert oneself*
【用品】articles for use: 生活~ *articles for daily use; daily necessities* / 办公~ *things for office* / 卫生~ *things for cleaning use; stationery*
【用人】① employ people; make use of personnel: ~制度 *the system of personnel placement* ② need hands: 工厂正是~的时候。*Now there is a growing need for qualified workers in the factory.*
【用人】servant; maid: 女~ *woman servant; maid*: 男~ *man servant*
【用上】be made use of; be put to use: 这些工具今天还都~了。*All these tool proved useful today.*
【用事】① act: 感情~ *be swayed by one's feeling; act rashly* ② [书] be in power ③ [书] make literary allusions
【用途】use; application; purpose: ~很广 *have many uses; be widely used* / ~少 *have fewer uses*
【用武】① use force; resort to arms ② prove oneself; display one's abilities or talents: 没有~之地。*There's no scope for one's abilities.*
【用项】items of expenditure; expenditures
【用心】① diligently; attentively: ~读书 *concentrate on one's studies; study diligently* / ~听讲 *listen attentively to a lecture* / ~思索 *think hard* / ~训练 *train hard* ② motive; intention: ~险恶

have vicious intentions; *harbour sinister motives* / 别有～ *have ulterior motives* / ～良苦 *have cudgeled one's brains*; *have expended much care and thought on sth*

【用刑】put sb to torture; torture

【用以】in order to; so as to; for the purpose of

【用意】intention; purpose: 她～何在? *what is her up to*? / 我这样做的～, 只是想帮助他一下。*I did all that just to give him some help.*

【用印】affix an official seal (to a document); seal (a document)

【用语】① choice of words; wording: ～精当。*The choice of words is exact and concise.* ② phraseology; term: 商业～ *commercial phraseology* / 外交～ *diplomatic language* / 书面～ *written phraseology*

佣 commission

see also yōng

【佣金】commission; brokerage; middleman's fee: ～优厚 *handsome commission*

yōu

优[1] ① excellent; good: ～异的成绩 *outstanding achievement* / 品学兼～ *excel in both scholarship and moral fibre* / 择～录取 *enroll the cream of the candidates* ② [书] adequate; plentiful; affluent ③ give preferential treatment; favor: 拥～军属 *support the army and give preferential treatment to army dependants* / ～待俘虏 *give special consideration to the prisoners of war*

优[2] actor or actress: 一代名～ *actor or actress famous in his or her own time*

【优待】give preferential, favoured or special treatment: ～儿童 *give special consideration to children* / 学生半价～票 *special half-price tickets for students* / 种种～ *perks and privileges*

【优等】top-notch; first-rate; excellent: ～生 *top-notch students*

【优点】merit; strong point; advantage; virtue: 发扬～ *give full play to one's strength* / 学习其他同学的～ *learn from the strong points of other students*

【优抚】give special care to disabled servicemen, and to family members of revolutionary martyrs and servicemen: ～对象 *the people who need special care*

【优厚】munificent; liberal; favourable: 收入～ *handsome income* / 福利～ *favourable fringe benefits*

【优弧】【数】major arc

【优化】optimize: ～产业结构 *optimize the industrial structure* / ～组合 *optimization grouping or regrouping* / ～学习方法 *optimize learning method* / ～旅行路线 *optimize the route of a journey*

【优惠】preferential; favourable: ～贷款 *loan on favourable terms*; *soft loan* / ～待遇 *preferential treatment*; *favoured treatment* / ～券 *coupon* / ～关税协定 *preferential tariff agreement* / ～国 *favoured nation* / ～价格 *favoured price* / ～权 *preferential rights* / ～条件 *favourable terms*; *concessional terms* / ～条款 *preferential clause* / ～政策 *preferential policy*

【优价】① favourable prices ; low prices ② good prices: 优质～ *good price for good quality* / 大米卖了～。*The rice was sold at good price.*

【优良】fine; good: 学业～ *do well in one's school work*

【优劣】good and bad; superior and inferior

【优伶】[旧] actor or actress

【优美】graceful; fine; exquisite: 风景～ *beautiful scenery* / 姿态～ *graceful postures* / 音色～ *melodious tune* / ～的曲线 *graceful curve*

【优柔】[书] ① leisurely, unhurried: ～不迫 (*do sth*) *in a leisurely and unhurried manner* ② [书] gentle; amiable ③ irresolute; hesitant: ～寡断 *irresolute and hesitant*; *indecisive*

【优生】giving birth to healthy children; healthy birth: ～学 *eugenics* / ～优育 *giving birth to healthy babies and bringing them up in a sound way*; *healthy birth and healthy care*

【优胜】winning; superior; excellent: ～奖 *wining prize* / ～者 *winner*; *champion* / ～队 *wining team*

【优胜劣汰】survival of the fittest: 物竞天择, ～。*Nature selects and the fittest survives.*

【优势】superiority; advantage; dominant position: 保持～ *maintain one's dominant position* / 兵力～ *superior force* / 空中～ *air supremacy* / 占～ *gain the upper hand* / ～专业 *superior specialities*

【优先】have priority; take precedence: ～发展教育 *give priority to the development of education* / 必须～回答的一个问题 *a question which claims precedence over all others*; *a top priority* / ～股 *preference shares*; *preferred shares* / ～权 *priority*; *preference* / ～债权人 *preferential creditor*

【优秀】outstanding; excellent; splendid; fine; : 成绩～ *excellent academic results or marks* / ～人才 *talented persons* / ～作品 (*literary or artistic*) *works of excellence* / ～小说 *novels of excellence* / ～学员 *excellent students*

【优雅】graceful; elegant; in good taste: 举止～ *elegant manners*; *graceful manners* / 房间布置得十分～。*The room was furnished with elegance and taste.*

【优异】excellent; outstanding; exceedingly good: 在工作中取得～成绩 *make outstanding contributions in one's work*

【优游】[书] leisurely and carefree: 我们不能～时光。*We must not pass out time in carefree leisure.*

【优裕】affluent; abundant: 生活～ *be well-off*; *be well-to-do*; *live in affluence* / 家境～ *come from a wealthy family*

【优遇】give special treatment; treat well: 以示～ *so as to show special consideration for sb* / ～有加 *give sb exceedingly good treatment* / ～外宾 *give special treatment to the foreign guests*

【优越】superior; advantageous; favourable: ～的社

~制度 *superior social system* / ~条件 *excellent conditions* / ~感 *sense of superiority*; *superiority complex* / ~性 *superiority*; *advantage*

【优哉游哉】[书] living a life of ease and leisure; leisurely and carefree; leisurely and unhurried

【优质】high (or top) quality; high grade; top-notch: ~产品 *quality product* / ~服务 *top-notch service* / ~小麦 *quality wheat*

忧 ① worry about; concern oneself about; be worried; be anxious: ~患意识 *sense of anxiety about lagging behind* / 担~ *worry about* / 杞人~天。*The man of Qi worries in case the sky should fall — worry about imagined troubles.* ② sorrow; anxiety; concern; care: 分~ *share sb's worries and burdens* / 无~无虑 *carefree*; *free from all anxieties* / 人无远虑, 必有近~。*Sorrow will come knocking at your door if you have no long-term plans.*

【忧愁】worried; sad; depressed

【忧烦】worried; vexed; dejected

【忧愤】worried and indignant

【忧国忧民】be concerned about one's country and one's people

【忧患】suffering; misery; hardship

【忧惧】worried and apprehensive

【忧虑】① be worried; be anxious; be concerned: 为孩子的前途~ *worry about one's children's future* ② worry; anxiety: 无穷的~ *endless worries*

【忧闷】depressed; feeling low; weighed down with cares

【忧戚】[书] distressed; weighed down with sorrow; laden with grief

【忧容】worried look

【忧伤】distressed; weighed down with sorrow

【忧思】① be worried; be anxious ② troubled thoughts

【忧心】[书] ① worried; concerned ② troubled heart; worry; anxiety: ~忡忡 *heavy-hearted*; *care-laden*; *weighed down with anxieties* / ~如焚 *burning with anxiety*; *extremely worried*

【忧悒】[书] anxious and disturbed

【忧郁】melancholy; heavyhearted; dejected: ~症 *melancholia*

呦 used to express surprise, astonishment, etc.: ~! 你怎么这么漂亮! *Hey! How beautiful you are!*

【呦呦】[书] the cry of a deer

幽 ① deep and remote; secluded; dim: 清~ *quiet and remote* / ~林 *a secluded wood* ② secret; hidden ③ quiet; tranquil; serene ④ imprison; place in confinement ⑤ of the nether world: ~魂 *ghost*; *spectre* ⑥ an ancient administrative district covering parts of present Hebei and Liaoning provinces

【幽暗】dim; dark; gloomy: ~的角落 *a dark corner* / ~的灯光 *dim light*

【幽闭】① incarcerate; put under house arrest ② confine oneself indoors; shut oneself up

【幽愤】hidden resentment

【幽会】a secret meeting of lovers; a lovers' rendezvous; tryst

【幽寂】secluded and quiet; lonely

【幽禁】put under house arrest; imprison

【幽静】quiet and secluded; peaceful: 湖边环境很~。*It's rather peaceful and secluded around the lake.*

【幽居】① live as a hermit; live in seclusion ② quiet and tranquil abode

【幽兰】[书] orchid

【幽蓝】dull blue

【幽灵】ghost; specter; spirit

【幽美】secluded and beautiful: ~的树林 *a secluded and beautiful forest*

【幽门】【生理】pylorus

【幽冥】① dark; gloomy; sombre ② the nether world

【幽默】(transliteration) humour: ~感 *sense of humour* / ~大师 *humorist* / 黑色~ *black humour* / ~曲 *humoresque*

【幽期】a secret meeting of lovers; tryst

【幽情】exquisite feelings

【幽趣】the delightful serenity of seclusion

【幽深】(of forests, palaces, etc.) deep and serene; deep and tranquil: 庭院~ *deep and quiet courtyard*

【幽思】① be lost in reverie; muse; meditate ② deep contemplation; melancholy brooding

【幽香】a delicate (or faint) fragrance: 茉莉~四溢。*The delicate fragrance of the jasmine permeates everywhere.*

【幽雅】(of a place) quiet and tastefully laid out; quiet and tranquil: 办公室陈设~。*The office is tastefully furnished.*

【幽幽】① (of light or sound) faint; feeble; weak: ~饮泣 *sob quietly* / 气息~ *feeble breath* ② [书] looming in the distance: ~南山。*The southern mountain looms in the distance.*

【幽远】deep and serene; profound; remote: 意境~ *be of profound implications*

【幽怨】hidden bitterness (of a young woman thwarted in love)

悠1 ① long; far; remote in time or space ② leisurely

悠2 [口] swing; sway: ~荡荡 *floating about*; *swinging to and fro* / 小姑娘在秋千上~来~去。*The little girl was swaying back and forth on the swing.*

【悠长】long; long-drawn out: ~的岁月 *long years* / ~的路 *a long road*

【悠荡】swing (to and fro); sway (back and forth)

【悠久】long; long-standing; age-old: 历史~ *have a long history* / ~的文化传统 *a cultural tradition of long standing* / ~的文明 *a civilization of long history*

【悠然】*carefree and leisurely*: ~神往 *one's thoughts turn to things distant* / ~自得 *be carefree and content* / 神态~ *look carefree and at ease*

【悠闲】leisurely and carefree: ~自在 *leisurely and*

carefree /他总是~地转来转去。*He always turns around leisurely.*

【悠扬】(of music, etc.) rising and failing; melodious; in harmony: ~的歌声 *melodious singing* / ~的小提琴声 *sweet violin music*

【悠悠】① long; infinite; remote: ~寒冬 *the long cold winter* / ~长夜。*The night seemed to drag.* ② leisurely; unhurried: 慢~地走着 *be walking at a leisurely pace* / 慢~地讲话 *be talking unhurried* ③ numerous; myriad; a multitude of: ~万事 *myriads of events* ④ [书] absurd; preposterous: ~之谈 *absurd remarks*

【悠悠忽忽】① loitering languidly; lounging around ② be in a trance

【悠远】① a long time ago; long ago; distant: ~的经历 an experience of the distant past / ~的往事 *events of the distant past* ② far; remote; distant: ~的故乡 *far away homeland*

【悠着】[方] take things easy; take it easy

yóu

尤[1] ① remarkable; conspicuous; outstanding: 选~ *pick out the best* / 拔~ *select and promote those of outstanding ability* / ~异的成绩 *excellent achievement* ② particularly; especially: ~妙 *even better; all the better* / 云南鲜花繁多, ~以茶花著称。*Yunnan province abounds with flowers, especially camellia.*

尤[2] ① fault; error; wrongdoing: 以儆效~ *so as to warn others not to follow the example of the wrongdoer* ② have a grudge against; blame: 我们不能整天怨天~人。*We should nit blame every person and everything bat ourselves all time.*

【尤其】especially; particularly: 我喜欢体育, ~喜欢球类。*I love sports, especially ball games.* / 北方风沙大, ~是在春天。*In the north it is especially windy and dusty, especially in spring.*

【尤甚】more so; especially

【尤物】[书] extraordinary or extraordinary thing or people; rarity; a woman of great beauty

由 ① cause; reason; grounds: 问清事~ *gain a clear idea of whole story* / 因~ *cause* / 理~ *reason; grounds* / 来~ *cause; origin* ② because of; owing to; due to ③ pass through; go by way of: 必~之路 *path or road one must take; only way* ④ follow; obey: 身不~己 *do sth in spite of oneself; lose control over oneself* / 来不来~你 *come here it or not* ④ by; through; via: ~正门出去。*Exit by the front door.* ⑤ for(sb); by(sb); to(sb): 这顿饭~我做东。*The dinner is on me.* / 这件事~他处理吧。*Leave it to him.* / 班长~他来担任。*It is for him to be the monitor.* ⑥ by means of: ~此可知 *know from this; tell by this* ⑦ (starting) from: ~西到东 *from east to west* / ~点到面 *spread over a whole area from one point* / ~下而上 *from bottom to top; from the lower level upward; from below* / ~简及繁 *from the simple to the complex* / ~近及远 *from the near to the distant*

【由表及里】from the outside to the inside; from the surface to the centre

【由不得】① not be up to sb to decide; be beyond the control of ② cannot help; cannot but: ~不信 *can not help believing it* / 很多孩子~一起哭了起来。*The kids couldn't help crying.*

【由此】from this; therefore; hence; as a result: ~入内。*This way in. or Entrance.* / ~看来 *judging from this; in view of this* / ~及彼 *from one to the other; from this to that* / ~可见 *thus it can be seen; hence one can see that; that proves*

【由来】① origin; source; cause: 事故的~ *the origin of the accident* ② up to now; so far: ~已久 *longstanding; time-honoured; of long duration*

【由浅入深】from the easy to the difficult; from the elementary to the profound

【由头】pretext; excuse: 拿不出~ *fail to find a pretext*

【由于】① owing to; thanks to; because of; due to; on the grounds of: ~健康关系 *on health grounds* / ~各种原因 *for various reasons* ② because; since

【由衷】from the bottom of one's heart; sincere; heartfelt: ~的感谢 *one's heartfelt thanks* / ~之言 *words from the bottom of one's heart; sincere words* / 言不~ *insincere words*

邮 ① post; mail: 你的文章~出去了吗? *Has your article been posted?* ② postal; mail ③ stamps: 集~ *collect stamps; go in for philately*

【邮包】postal parcel; parcel: ~保险 *parcel post insurance*

【邮编】post code; zip code

【邮差】[旧] postman

【邮车】mail car; postal car

【邮船】ocean liner; liner; packet ship

【邮戳】postmark

【邮袋】mailbag; postbag; (mail) pouch

【邮递】① send by post (or mail): ~员 *postman; mailman* ② postal or mail delivery

【邮电】post and telecommunications: ~服务 *postal and telecommunication service* / ~局 *post and telecommunications office*

【邮费】postage

【邮购】buy or purchase by mail postal order; mail-order: ~部 *mail-order department*

【邮汇】remit by post

【邮寄】send by post; post: ~包裹 *send packet by post*

【邮件】postal matter; post; mail: 挂号~ *registered post* / 航空~ *air mail* / 快递~ *express mail* / 普通~ *ordinary mail* / ~服务器 *mail server*

【邮局】post office

【邮路】postal (or mail) route: 不通~ *not served by a mail route*

【邮票】postage stamp; stamp: 纪念~ *commemorative stamps* / 特种~ *special stamps*

【邮亭】postal kiosk

【邮筒】pillar-box; postbox; mailbox

【邮箱】postbox; mailbox

【邮展】philatelic exhibition; stamp exhibition

【邮政】postal service: ～包裹 *postal parcel* / ～编码 *postcode*; *zip code* / ～储蓄 *postal savings deposit* / ～汇票 *postal money order*; *postal order* / ～局 *post office* / ～信箱 *post-office box*(*POB*)

【邮资】postage: ～不足 *postage underpaid*; *postage due* / ～已付 *postage paid*; *postpaid*

犹 [书] ① just as; like: ～缘木而求鱼 *like climbing up trees to look for fish* ② still; even: ～未定夺 *still undecided*; *not decided yet* / 言～在耳 *sb's words still ringing in one's ears* / 困兽～斗。*Even a cornered animal will fight.*

【犹大】【宗】Judas Iscariot, one of the 12 Apostles, who betrayed Christ for 30 pieces of silver

【犹且】[书] still, yet: 他～做不到，何况我。*Even he cannot do it, let alone me.*

【犹然】still; just as before; as if

【犹如】just as; like; as if: 二人～姐妹一般。*The two of them treat each other like sisters.*

【犹太人】Jew; Jewish people

【犹太教】Judaism: ～教徒 *Judaist Jew* / ～教堂 *synagogue*

【犹疑】hesitate; waver: ～不定 *hesitate*; *be of two minds*

【犹豫】hesitate; be irresolute; vacillate: ～不决 *remain undecided*; *waver* / ～观望 *watch in hesitation* / 毫不～ *without hesitation*

油 ① oil; fat; grease; petroleum: 菜籽～ *rapeseed oil* / 花生～ *peanut oil* / 猪～ *pork fat*; *lark* / 汽～ *petrol*; *gasoline*; *gas* / 加～站 *gas station* / ～枯灯灭 *when the oil gives out, the lamp expire* — (*of a person*) *die* ② apply tung oil, varnish, or paint: ～门窗 *paint the doors and windows* ③ be stained with oil or grease: 你脸上～了一大块儿。*Your face has got a big oil stains on it.* ④ greasy; oily; glib; slick: 这炖肉太～了。*The stewed pork is too greasy.* / 这个人～极了。*That chap is much too slippery*(*or tricky*).

【油泵】【机】oil pump

【油饼】① soya bean or peanut dregs after oil has been extracted; oilcake ② deep-fried dough cake

【油驳】oil barge

【油布】oilcloth; oilskin; tarpaulin

【油彩】greasepaint; paint

【油菜】① rape : ～籽 *rapeseed* ② green rape: 炒～ *fry green rape*

【油藏】oil deposit; oil pool

【油槽】oil reservoir; oil bath; oil trough: ～车 *petrol tanker*

【油层】oil reservoir; oil layer; oil horizon

【油茶】①【植】tea-oil tree; oil-tea camellia ② gruel of sweetened, fried flour: ～面儿 *flour fried in beef fat with sugar and sesame*

【油船】oil tanker; tanker; oil carrier

【油灯】oil lamp

【油坊】oil mill

【油橄榄】【植】olive

【油膏】【医】ointment

【油垢】greasy filth; greasy dirt: 满手～ *greasy hands*

【油管】① oil pipe: 铺设～ *lay oil pipes* ② oil tube: 你能测量出～的深度吗? *Can you measure the tubing depth?*

【油罐】oil tank; storage tank

【油光】glossy; shiny; varnished: ～碧绿的树叶 *shiny green leaves*

【油耗】oil consumption: 降低～ *bring down or reduce the oil consumption*

【油黑】glossy black; jet-black: 她的头发～发亮。*Her hair is glossy black.*

【油乎乎】oily; greasy: ～的工作服 *greasy working overalls* / 那个孩子的手～的。*The hands of the child are smeared with lil.*

【油壶】oilcan; oiler

【油葫芦】【动】a kind of field cricket

【油花儿】drops of oil on the surface of soup; blobs of oil

【油滑】slippery; foxy; slick

【油画】oil painting: ～色 *oil colours*; *oils* / 你会画～吗? *Can you paint in oils?*

【油灰】【建】*putty*

【油鸡】【动】cochin

【油迹】oil stains; grease spots: ～斑斑 *covered with grease spots*

【油井】oil well: 钻一口～ *drill*(*or bore*) *an oil well*

【油锯】chain saw

【油库】oil depot; oil house; tank farm

【油矿】① oil deposit ② oilfield

【油亮】(often reduplicated) glossy; shiny

【油料】oil-bearing seed; oilseed: ～作物 *oil bearing crops*; *oil crops*

【油绿】glossy dark green

【油轮】oil tanker; tanker; oil carrier

【油码头】oil jetty; oil wharf; tanker terminal

【油麦】【植】naked or raw oats

【油毛毡】【建】asphalt felt

【油门】① throttle ② [口] accelerator: 他踩了～溜了。*He stepped on the accelerator and went away.*

【油焖】braise: ～茄子 *braised eggplant slices*

【油苗】oil seepage

【油墨】printing ink: 快干～ *quick setting ink*

【油腻】① greasy; fatty; oily ② greasy food; fatty food; oily food

【油盘】food tray

【油票】① cooking oil coupon ② gasoline coupon

【油漆】① paint ② cover with paint; paint: ～匠 *painter*

【油气】【油】associated gas: ～比 *oil-gas ratio* / ～界面 *the interface of oil and gas*

【油枪】【机】oil gun

【油腔滑调】glib; unctuous: 说话～ *talk unctuously*

【油然】① spontaneously; involuntarily: ～而生 (*of feelings*) *rise of itself* ② densely; profusely

【油润】shinny and smooth; glossy

【油色】oil colours

【油砂】【油】oil sand

【油石】【机】oilstone(for sharpening cutting tools)

【油刷】cover with paint or varnish; paint: 他自己

把门~了。*He painted the door by himself.*
【油水】① grease; oil:这个肉~太大。*This meat is too greasy.* ② profit; profit
【油酥】short; crisp; flaky
【油酸】【化】oleic acid
【油田】oilfield: ~开发 *oilfield development* (*or exploitation*)
【油条】deep-fried twisted dough sticks
【油桶】oil drum
【油头粉面】sleek-haired and creamy-faced — heavily made-up; dressy or foppish
【油头滑脑】slick; smooth; oily:汤姆看起来像个~的家伙。*Tom looks like a shifty-looking fellow.*
【油汪汪】① dripping with oil; full of grease ② glossy; shiny
【油位】【机】oil level: ~表 *oil(level) gauge*
【油污】greasy dirt or filth:他满身~地回到了家。*He went home with greasy dirt all over him.*
【油箱】fuel tank
【油香】cakes made of mixed flour, water and salt fried in sesame oil for Moslems
【油星】oil blobs
【油性】oiliness; greasiness
【油压】oil pressure
【油烟】lampblack; soot
【油页岩】oil-shale
【油衣】[方] raincoat made of oilcloth; oilskins; slicker
【油印】mimeograph: ~机 *mimeograph* / ~蜡纸 *stencil; stencil paper*
【油油】[书] ① glossy; shiny ② flowing smoothly and incessantly ③ luxuriant and dense
【油浴】【化】oil bath
【油渣】① dregs of fat ② oil residue
【油毡】asphalt felt
【油脂】oil; fat
【油纸】oilpaper: ~伞 *oil-paper umbrella*
【油子】① black sticky substance; gunk ② [方] foxy old hand:你真是一个老~。*You are really a foxy old fellow.*
【油棕】【植】oil palm
【油嘴】① glib; sleek; unctuous: ~滑舌 *glib-tongued* ② glib talker ③ spray nozzle; spray head

柚

see also yòu
【柚木】teak; teakwood

铀

uranium(U):天然~ *native uranium* / ~矿石 *uranium ore*
【铀棒】uranium bar
【铀弹】U-bomb

鱿

【鱿鱼】squid

游

① swim: ~过河(一英里) *swim a river (mile)* /鱼会~水。*Fish can swim.* ② rove around; stroll; travel; tour:周~世界 *travel all over the world* ③ [书] associate with:交~甚广 *have a wide range of acquaintances* ④ moving about; roving; floating ⑤ part of a river; reach:中上~ *middle and upper reaches (of a river)*
【游伴】travel companion
【游标】【机】venire
【游程】① distance of swimming ② journey; trip travel ③ travel programme; itinerary
【游船】pleasure boat
【游春】go on a spring outing
【游荡】① loaf about; loiter; wander:他没事可做,整天在外~。*He has nothing to do and wanders all day long.* ② stroll; saunter ③ float
【游动】① move about; go from place to place:鱼在水里来回~。*The fish is swimming to and fro in the water.* ② mobile; moving; roving: ~探照灯 *mobile floodlight*
【游逛】go sightseeing; stroll about
【游魂】a wandering ghost
【游击】guerrilla warfare: ~队 *guerrilla forces; a guerrilla detachment* / ~战 *guerrilla war; guerrilla warfare*
【游记】travel notes; travels
【游街】parade sb through the streets; walk through the streets at the head of a parade: ~示众 *parade sb through the streets to expose him before the public*
【游客】visitor; tourist; excursionist; sightseer
【游览】go sightseeing; tour; visit: ~车 *tourist coach; tour bus* / ~地 *place for sightseeing; tourist resort* / ~区 *tourist area* / ~图 *tourist map*
【游廊】covered corridor; veranda
【游乐】amusement; recreation: ~场所 *places of recreation* / ~园 *amusement park; pleasure ground (or garden)*: ~车 *fun vehicle*
【游离】① dissociate; drift away ②【化】free: ~酸 *free acid* / ~状态 *free state* / ~基 *free radical*
【游历】travel for pleasure; travel; tour: ~甚广 *have traveled extensively*
【游猎】go on a hunting trip
【游民】tramp; vagrant; vagabond
【游目骋怀】look as far as one's eyes can see and give free rein to one's thoughts and feelings
【游牧】move about in search of pasture
【游人】visitor; sightseer; tourist: ~如织 *throngs of visitors*
【游刃有余】handle a butcher's cleaver with skill — do a job with skill and ease; be more than equal to a task
【游山玩水】wander about to enjoy the beauty of nature; tour various scenic spots
【游手好闲】idle about; loaf:他弟弟整天~,不务正业。*His younger brother idles about and does no decent work.*
【游水】swim
【游说】go about selling an idea; go about drumming up support ; go canvassing
【游丝】① gossamer ②【机】balance spring; hairspring
【游艇】yacht; pleasure-boat

【游玩】① amuse oneself; play ② go sightseeing; stroll about
【游戏】① pastime; game:做~ *play games* / ~规则 *rules of game* / ~机 *video game player* / 同学们和老师一起玩~。*The students and teachers played games together.* ② play; have fun:孩子们在校园里~。*The children are playing in the school yard.*
【游侠】(in former times) roving brave; knight-errant
【游行】① wander about; roam; rove ② parade; march; demonstration
【游兴】interest in going on an excursion or sightseeing
【游移】① move back and forth ② (of attitude, policy, etc.) waver; vacillate; wobble: ~不定 *keep on vacillating; hesitant* / ~于两者之间 *waver between the two*
【游弋】① move on water ② cruise; patrol:在海上~ *cruise on the sea*
【游艺】entertainment; recreation: ~室 *recreation room*
【游泳】① swim:去~ *go for a swim; go swimming* ② swimming: ~比赛 *swimming contest* / ~健将 *first-rate swimmer* / ~池 *swimming pool* / ~馆 *natatorium* / ~裤 *bathing or swimming trunks* / ~帽 *bathing or swimming cap* / ~衣 *swimsuit; swimming suit; bathing suit*
【游园】① visit a garden or park:昨天王老师带着我们~去了。*Yesterday teacher Wang showed us around a park.* ② mass celebrations in parks: ~会 *garden gathering; garden party*
【游资】idle fund; idle money; floating capital
【游子】[书] a man who has been away from home for a long time:海外~ *overseas Chinese*
【游踪】the whereabouts of a traveler: ~无定 *travel from place to place without a fixed plan or route*

yǒu

友 ① friend:良师益~ *good teacher and helpful friend* ② friendly; be close to
【友爱】friendly affection; fraternal love:姐妹二人甚是~。*The two sisters love each other affectionately.*
【友邦】friendly nation; friendly country
【友好】① close friend; friend:生前~ *friends of the deceased* ② friendly; amicable: ~人士 *friendly personage* / 在诚挚~的气氛中会谈 *hold a talk in a sincere and amicable atmosphere* / ~城市 *cities of friendship; sister cities* / ~邀请赛 *friendship invitational tournament* / ~代表团 *goodwill mission*
【友军】friendly forces
【友邻】friendly neighbours; good neighbours
【友情】friendly sentiments; friendship
【友人】friend:国际~ *foreign friend*
【友善】[书] friendly; amicable; genial
【友谊】friendship:深厚的~ *profound friendship* / 建立~ *build (or forge) ties of friendship* / 牢不可破的~ *unbreakable friendship* / ~赛 *friendly match or contest*

有 ① have; own; possess:他~个弟弟,两个妹妹。*He has one younger brother and two younger sisters.* ② there is; exist:从前~一个贫苦的农夫,他~四个儿子。*There once lived a poor farmer who had four sons.* / 没~理由去。*There is no reason to go.* ③ used in making a rough estimate:河~6米多宽。*The river is more than 6 metres wide.* / 他~没有你这么高? *Is he as tall as you?* ④ used to indicate sth that takes place or appears ⑤ used to indicate ample amount: ~前途 *be promising* / ~经验 *be experienced* / 他出门~些日子了。*He has been away from home for quite some time.* ⑥ used in a general sense, similar to the meaning of "某" ⑦ used before people, time, or place to indicate a part: ~人赞成,~人反对。*Some say yes, some say no.* ⑧ used before certain verbs to form polite formulae
【有碍】hinder; obstruct; affect adversely: ~交通 *hinder traffic* / ~风化 *adversely affect morals and manners* / ~卫生 *be bad for public sanitation* / ~观瞻 *be unpleasant to look at; offend the eye; be an eyesore*
【有板有眼】rhythmical; measured; orderly
【有备无患】where there is precaution, there is no danger; preparedness averts peril; be prepared
【有鼻子有眼儿】with every detail vividly described; be vivid and dramatic; life like
【有产阶级】propertied class
【有偿】with compensation; compensated; paid: ~技术转让 *compensated transfer of technology* / ~服务 *paid services* / ~使用 *paid use* / ~劳动 *paid labour*
【有成】[书] achieve success; succeed
【有错必纠】every wrong will be righted
【有待】remain (to be done); await: ~解决 *remain to be solved* / ~证明 *have yet to be proved* / ~研究 *await research*
【有道】have attained the way; uphold truth and principle; be just and sagacious
【有得】have learned sth; have gained some knowledge:学习~ *have profited from one's studies*
【有的】some
【有的是】have plenty of; be in abundance; there's no lack of:我~钱。*I have plenty of money.*
【有底】know how things stand and feel confident of handling them; be fully prepared for what is coming:你这么明白,我心里就~了。*After your explanation I now know how things stand and feel confident.*
【有的放矢】shoot the arrow at the target — have a definite object in view; do sth with a definite purpose in mind
【有点儿】① some; a little; small amount of:我手里还~食物。*I still have some food.* ② somewhat; rather; a bit
【有法必依】ensure that laws are observed; ensure

that laws be observed: ～,执法必严,违法必究。*Laws must be observed and strictly enforced and lawbreakers must be brought to justice.*

【有法不依】laws are ignored

【有法可依】there are laws to go by

【有方】with the proper method; in the right way:还是他指导～。*It was him who gave proper guidance.*

【有分量】weighty; significant

【有份儿】have a share; take a part in:功劳～,责任无干 *take a share of the credit but none of the responsibility* /人人～ *everyone has a share of it*

【有福同享 有祸同当】share joys and sorrow; share weal and woe; stick together through thick and thin

【有感】thoughts or reflections on sth (usu. used in the title of a literary sketch)

【有功】① have made great contributions; have performed meritorious service ②【电】active

【有关】① have something to do with; bear on; relate to; concern: ～全局 *have a bearing on the situation as a whole* /～当局 *authorities concerned; relevant authorities* /～方面 *the parties concerned* /～规定 *pertinent regulations* ② concerning; regarding

【有光】① glazed: ～纸 *glazed paper* ②【纺】bright: ～人造丝 *bright rayon*

【有轨电车】tramcar; streetcar

【有鬼】there's something fishy; have a guilty conscience:这里面一定～。*There's something fishy about it.* /我想他心里～。*I thought he must get a guilty conscience.*

【有过之无不及】go even farther than; outdo; surpass

【有害】harmful; pernicious; detrimental: 对身体健康～ *be harmful (or detrimental) to one's health* /～的影响 *pernicious effects*

【有会子】[口] quite a long while; quite some time:他出去可～啦! *He's been out for quite a while.*

【有机】①【化】organic: ～酸 *organic acid* /～盐 *organic salt* /～肥料 *organic fertilizer; manure* /～耕作 *organic farming* /～合成 *organic synthesis* /～化合物 *organic chemical compound* /～化学 *organic chemistry* /～染料 *organic dyestuff* /～体 *organism* /～物 *organic matter* /～物质 *organic substance* ② organic; intrinsic: ～组成部分 *a component part* /事物间的～关系 *intrinsic relationship between things*

【有机可乘】there's an opportunity to take advantage of; there's a loophole that can be used

【有禁不止】disregard prohibitions; ignore an interdiction

【有节】with restrain; having a sense of proportion

【有劲】① have great physical strength② with keen interest

【有救】can be saved, cured or remedied:不要担心,这病～了! *Don't worry; we've found a cure for the disease.*

【有口皆碑】win universal commendation; be universally acclaimed

【有口难辩】find it hard to defend or vindicate oneself

【有口难言】cannot bring oneself to mention sth; find it hard or embarrassing to bring up a matter; be unable to speak out

【有口无心】be sharp-tongued but mean no malice

【有愧】feel qualms about sth; have a guilty conscience:问心～ *have a guilty conscience*

【有来有往】give-and-take; be reciprocal

【有赖】rely on; depend on; rest on:要实现这项改革～于大家共同努力。*The success of the innovation depends on the concerted efforts of all of us.*

【有劳】polite formula used to ask others to do sth or thank others for having done sth: ～您代我捎个话儿。*May I trouble you to take a message for me?*

【有了】[口] ① (as an exclamation) I've got it! ② be pregnant

【有理】① reasonable; justified:妈妈讲的～。*What my mother said is reasonable.* ②【数】rational: ～分式 *rational fraction* /～函数 *rational function* /～式 *rational expression* /～数 *rational number*

【有理无情】① stick to the principle and disregard personal feelings ② for no apparent reason; without rhyme or reason

【有理走遍天下,无理寸步难行】with justice on your side; you can go anywhere; without it; you can't take a step

【有力】strong; powerful; forceful; mighty:进行～反击 *give a powerful rebuff* /提供～的证据 *advance convincing proof* / ～无处使 *have no outlet for one's surplus energy* /简短～ *terse and forceful* /爸爸在工作上给了我～的帮助。*My father gave me effective help on my work.*

【有利】advantageous; beneficial; favourable: ～地形 *favourable terrain* /～时机 *opportune time* /～可图 *have good prospects of profit; stand to gain; be profitable* /～无弊 *have all the advantages and not a single disadvantage; be advantageous in every respect* /～有弊 *have advantages as well as disadvantages; have both merits and demerits*

【有例在先】there is a precedent for that

【有脸】have face; have prestige

【有两下子】[口] have real skill; know one's stuff: 想不到他还真～,竟然把问题给解决了。*He really knows the ropes; to our surprise solved the difficulties.*

【有零】(used after round numbers) odd:五十～ *fifty odd* /一百～ *just over a hundred*

【有令不行,有禁不止】disobey orders and defy prohibitions

【有眉目】begin to take shape; begin to see light

【有门儿】[口] ① find the beginning of a solution; be hopeful ② get the hang

【有名】well-known; famous; celebrated

【有名无实】in name but not in reality; in name only; merely nominal

【有名有姓】identifiable by both given name and

surname — of established identity; of some repute

【有目共睹】be obvious to all; be as clear as day; be there for all to see：他们取得的成绩是～。*Their achievements are there for all to see.*

【有盼头】have hope for; become hopeful

【有凭有据】fully substantiated; well-documented

【有谱儿】know what is what; have confidence：做事儿～ *do things with confidence; know what one is doing*

【有期徒刑】【律】fixed-term imprisonment：被判～七年 *be sentenced to seven years' imprisonment*

【有其父，必有其子】like father, like son

【有气】be or get angry; take offence

【有气儿】be breathing：他还～，快叫救护车。*He's still breathing; call an ambulance, quick.*

【有气无力】feeble; weak; faint; listless：说话～ *speak in a faint (or feeble) voice*

【有钱】rich; wealthy：～能使鬼推磨 *with money you can make the devil turn the millstone; money makes the mare go; money talks*

【有情】be in love; be feeling：～人 *lovers* /～人终成眷属 *lovers are destined to be married; jack shall have Jill, all shall be well* /～有义 *true and loyal; affectionate and true*

【有请】a polite formula used to express the host's desire to see the guest

【有求必应】respond to every plea; grant whatever is requested

【有求于人】need sb's help; ask a favour of sb

【有去无还】gone never to return; gone forever

【有趣】interesting; fascinating; amusing：～的故事 *an interesting story*

【有染】［书］have illicit sexual relations

【有扰】［套］thanks for your hospitality

【有人家儿】(of a girl) be engaged：那个漂亮的小姑娘早就～。*The pretty girl is already engaged.*

【有日子】① for quite a few days; for days：咱们～没见面了。*We haven't seen each other for quite some time.* ② have fixed a date：你出差～了吧？*Have you fixed the date for business?*

【有如】just like; as if; as though

【有辱】be a discredit or disgrace (to sb)

【有色】coloured：戴着～眼镜看事情 *look at things through coloured spectacles — take a distorted view* /～金属 *nonferrous metal* /～人种 *coloured race*

【有伤】be destructive; harmful to; offend against：～风化 *be harmful to the morals; offend against decency*

【有身】be pregnant; be with child; be expecting

【有神】① be miraculous：下笔如～ *write as if with magic power* ② full of vigour

【有神论】theism：～者 *theist*

【有生】① ever since one's birth：～第一次 *the first time in one's life* ② while still alive

【有生力量】① effective strength ② troops; army

【有生之年】one's remaining years：他希望能在～看到儿子结婚。*He hopes he can live to see the marriage of his son.*

【有声】having sound：～读物 *audio-book* /～图书馆 *audio-library* /～片 *sound film, talkie*

【有声有色】full of sound and colour; vivid and dramatic

【有失身份】beneath one's dignity

【有识】［书］have vision; be far-sighted：～之士 *person with breadth of vision; man of insight* /有胆～ *have both courage and vision; be courageous and far-sighted*

【有时】sometimes; at times; from time to time：周末我～去拜访老同学。*I visit my old classmates sometimes.*

【有史以来】since the beginning or dawn of history; throughout history

【有始无终】start sth but fail to carry it through

【有始有终】carry sth through; manage sth from beginning to the end

【有事】① have a job; be employed ② be occupied; be busy ③ have sth untoward happen; meet with an accident; get into trouble ④ have sth on one's mind; worry

【有恃无恐】fear nothing with a strong backing; feel secure in the knowledge that one has strong backing; emboldened by sb's support

【有数】① know exactly how things stand; have a definite idea of what one's doing：不要着急，怎么做我心里～。*Don't worry; I know what I'm doing.* ② not many; only a few

【有说有笑】talk and laugh：几个姑娘～地在那儿聊天。*Several girls are chatting and laughing merrily together.*

【有所】to some extent; somewhat：～保留 *have reservations* /～增加 *increased to some extent* /我的学习～进步。*There has been some progress in my study.*

【有所不为而后可以有所为】you must leave some things undone if you want to get others done; refrain from doing some things in order to be able to do other things

【有条不紊】in an orderly way; methodically; systematically

【有条有理】methodical; systematic; orderly

【有头无尾】have a beginning but no end; leave sth unfinished; give up sth halfway

【有头有脸】enjoy prestige; command respect

【有头有尾】have a beginning and an end

【有望】hopeful

【有为】promising; full of promise /年轻～ *young and promising*

【有味儿】① (of food) be tasty; be delicious：这个汤挺～的。*This soup is quite delicious.* ② (*of food*) *smell bad; be off*：这个菜～了，不能吃了。*This dish has gone off we can't eat it.* ③ be interesting; be meaningful：这本书越读越～。*The more you read this book, the more meaningful you find it.*

【有…无…】① used to indicate that there is the former but not the latter ② used to indicate that with the former, there is no need for the latter

【有息】interest-bearing：～账户 *interest-bearing account*

【有喜】［口］be pregnant; be expecting; be in the family way

【有戏】［方］likely; hopeful：这次工作还～。*There is still hope in the work.*

【有隙】①［书］bear a grudge ② there is a loophole：～可乘 *there is a crack to squeeze through — there is a loophole to exploit*

【有闲】have leisure

【有限】① limited; finite：～公司 *limited company; limited-liability company* /～花序 *definite inflorescence* /～级数 *finite progression; finite series* /～战争 *limited war* ② not many; not high in degree：数量～ *limited in number; not many* /学识～ *have little learning* /能力～ *be incompetent*

【有线】wired：～通讯 *wire communication* /～传真 *wire photo* /～电报 *line telegraphy* /～电话 *wire telephony; electrophone* /～电视 *close-circuit television; cable television* /～广播 *wire or wired broadcasting; rediffusion on wire*

【有效】efficacious; effective; valid：～功率 *effective power; useful power* /～荷载 *useful load* /～库容 *effective storage* /～期 *term (or period) of validity; time of efficacy* /～射程 *effective range*

【有些】① some; part：～孩子在看书，～孩子在游戏。*Some children were reading, some were playing games.* ② somewhat; to some extent; rather：～失望 *be rather disappointed* /我对工作～不满意。I am somewhat dissatisfied.

【有心】① have a mind to; set one's mind on; intend to：～人 *a person who sets his mind on doing sth useful; a person with high aspirations and determination; an observant and conscientious person* ② intentionally, purposely：我可不是～为难你。*I didn't purposely make things difficult for you.*

【有形】tangible; visible; physical：～贸易 *visible trade* /～损耗 *material loss* /～资本 *material capital; physical capital* /～资产 *tangible assets; tangibles*

【有幸】be lucky to; have the luck or pleasure：我们～再次相会。*We are happy to meet again.*

【有性】【生】sexual：～孢子 *sexual spore* /～生殖 *sexual reproduction; zoogamy* /～杂交 *sexual hybridization*

【有血有肉】(of descriptions in literary works) lifelike; true to life; vivid：小说的主人公塑造得～。*The portrayal of the hero in the novel is lifelike.* /这篇报道～。*This news report is full of vivid details.*

【有言在先】make clear beforehand; forewarn

【有眼不识泰山】have eyes but not see Mount Tai — fail to recognize a person of eminence in his presence：我真是～！*I'm sorry for failing to recognize your eminence.*

【有眼无珠】have eyes but no pupils — have eyes but fail to see; be ignorant; see sth without knowing it

【有一搭没一搭】［口］① trying to engage sb in small talk; conversing for the sake of conversing ② not essential; not indispensable

【有一说一】speak the whole truth; call a spade a spade; speak one's conscience

【有一分热，发一分光】give as much light as the fuel can produce — do one's utmost

【有益】profitable; beneficial; useful：～于健康 *be good for one's health* /做出～的贡献 *make valuable contributions*

【有意】① have a mind to; be inclined (or disposed) to：我真的是～帮助你。*I am really to help you.* ② intentionally; deliberately; purposely：～歪曲事实真相 *deliberately distort the actual state of affair* /～刁难 *make things difficult for sb on purpose* ③ be sexually attracted; take a fancy to：谁都看得出来她对你～。*Everyone can see that she is attracted to you.*

【有意识】consciously：不要对他大声嚷了，他已经～地改变他自己了。*Don't shout at him; he has made conscious efforts to change himself.*

【有意思】① significant; meaningful ② interesting; enjoyable

【有意无意】wittingly or unwittingly; consciously or unconsciously; either by accident or design

【有影没影】groundless; unfounded：～的话 *groundless gossip*

【有勇无谋】have valour but lack strategy; be brave but not resourceful; be foolhardy

【有…有…】① used separately before two nouns or verbs opposite or contrastive in meaning for the sake of emphasis：有利有弊 *have both advantages and disadvantages* /有借有还 *borrow and return* ② used separately before two nouns or verbs with the same or similar meaning to indicate that both are present：他说的有声有色。*He spoke full of sound and colour.*

【有余】① have a surplus：绰绰～ *more than enough; enough and to spare* ② odd：那妇人三十～。*The lady is over thirty.*

【有缘】be fated; be predestined; have a bond; have an affinity for：你我今天能在这里重逢，也算～。*It seems to be our happy fate to meet each other again.*

【有缘千里来相会】people living far apart will meet if they are destined to：～，无缘对面不相逢。*If fated, people come together though a thousand li apart. If not, they miss each other though they meet face to face.*

【有则改之，无则加勉】correct mistakes if you have made any and guard against them if you have not

【有增无已】ever-increasing; ever-growing; ever-expanding

【有朝一日】some day; one day; if there is one day when

【有职无权】hold a post but have no real power or authority; be a figurehead

【有志者事竟成】where there's a will there's a way

【有志之士】a person of noble aspirations
【有种】[口] have guts; be plucky; be gritty: ~的站出来! *Let anyone who has guts step forward!*
【有助于】contribute to; be conducive to; help: 这次访问~增进我们的友谊。*This visit has contributed to our friendship.*
【有滋有味】① tasty; delicious: 饭做得~。*The meal is delicious.* ② with relish or enjoyment: 他正看书看得~。*He is absorbed in his reading.*
【有嘴无心】be sharp-tongued but mean no malice; be tactless
【有罪】be guilty of a crime; be guilty

莠 ①【植】green bristle grass ②[书] bad; vicious; undesirable: 良~不齐 *The good and the bad are intermingled.*

黝 black; dark

【黝黑】dark; swarthy: 皮肤~ *dark skin* / 由于长时间在外面, 他的胳膊晒得~。*He is with sunburnt arms for being outside for long time.*

yòu

又 ① (used for an actual action) again; repeatedly: 看了~看 *look at sth again and again* / 说了~说 *speak repeatedly; keep on speaking* / 你~迟到了。*You are late again.* ② also; in addition; furthermore ③ used to indicate that an odd number is added to a whole number ④ used often in parallel to indicate two contrary actions or ideas ⑤ used in a negative statement or a rhetorical question for emphasis: 这儿事情~不多, 我可以自己做。*There is not much things; I can do them by myself.* ⑥ (reduplicated, with verbs or adjectives) both... and...; not only... but also: 她很漂亮, ~很聪明, 真是个幸运儿。*She is a luck girl; she is not only pretty, but also clever.*
【又红又专】both red and expert; both socialist minded and professionally proficient; both politically conscious and professionally competent
【又惊又喜】be both startled and delighted; be pleasantly surprised
【又名】also called; alias; also known as
【又想当婊子, 又想立牌坊】lead the life of a whore and want a monument put up to one's chastity

右 ① the right side; the right: 到商店后请向~拐。*Please turn right when you reach to the store.* ② west③ the right side as the side of precedence: 无出其~ *second to none* / 虽然他还小, 但职位却位居他哥哥之~。*He is young, but he holds a post higher than that of his elder brother.* ④ conservative; the Right: 思想太~ *too far to the right in thinking* ⑤ uphold
【右边锋】【体】outside right; right wing
【右边】the right (or right-hand) side; the right
【右侧】right side
【右舵】right standard rudder; right rudder
【右锋】【体】right forward
【右后卫】【体】right back
【右面】the right (or right-hand) side; the right
【右内锋】【体】inside right
【右派】① the Right; the right wing; rightist ② bourgeois rightist
【右前轮】off-front wheel (of a car)
【右前卫】【体】right halfback; right half
【右倾】right deviation: ~思想 *Right-deviationist thinking* / ~机会主义 *Right opportunism*
【右手】① the right hand ② right-hand side
【右首】the right-hand side; the right
【右舷】starboard (of a ship)
【右翼】①【军】right wing; right flank ② the right wing; the Right: 他爸爸是一个~分子。*His father is a rightist.*

幼 ① young; under age: 请原谅她的年~无知。*Please forgive her young and ignorant.* ② children; the young: 扶老携~ *bring along the old and the young* / 尊老爱~ *respect the old and care for the young*
【幼虫】【动】larva
【幼雏】young bird; baby bird; nestling
【幼儿】child; infant: ~师范 *school for teachers of preschool children* / ~教育 *preschool education* / ~园 *kindergarten; nursery school; infant school*
【幼发拉底河】Euphrates, a river of southwest Asia
【幼龄林】【林】young growth
【幼苗】seedling; sapling
【幼嫩】① small and young; tender; delicate ② immature; naive; not mature
【幼年】childhood; infancy
【幼女】a young girl
【幼弱】young in years; small and weak
【幼时】early childhood
【幼体】the young; larva
【幼童】young child
【幼小】young and small; immature: 不要伤害她~的心灵。*Don't hurt her immature mind.*
【幼芽】young shoot; bud
【幼稚】① young; juvenile; infantile: ~工业 *infant industry* ② childish; puerile; naive: ~的想法 *naive ideas*
【幼稚病】①【心理】infantilism ② infantile disorder
【幼株】young plant; seed plant
【幼子】youngest son; young son; baby son

佑 help; protect; bless; defend: ~贤辅德 *help the virtuous* / 上帝保~我! *God bless me!*
【佑护】protect; bless
【佑助】help; aid; assist

柚 ① Rangoon teak; Burma teak ② fruit of Rangoon teak; shaddock; pomelo
see also yóu
【柚子】shaddock; pomelo

囿 ① animal farm; enclosure; park ② limit; hamper
【囿于成见】be blinded by prejudice; be biased

诱 ① guide; lead; induce: 她是一个好老师，擅长循循善~。*She is a good teacher, and good at giving systematic guidance.* ② lure; seduce; entice: ~人犯罪 *induce*

【诱逼】cajole and coerce; entice and threat

【诱导】① guide; lead; induce: 李阿姨善于~孩子看书和学习。*Aunt Li is good at guiding her children in their reading and studying.* ②【物】induction: ~分解 *induced decomposition* / ~作用 *induction* / ~反应 *induced reaction*

【诱敌深入】lure the enemy in deep

【诱饵】bait: 用金钱作~ *use money as bait*

【诱供】trap a person into a confession; coax a person to make a confession

【诱拐】abduct; carry off (a woman) by fraud; kidnap(a child)

【诱惑】① entice; tempt; lure ② attract; captivate

【诱奸】entice sb to have unlawful sexual intercourse; seduce

【诱骗】inveigle; cajole; trap; trick

【诱人】alluring; fascinating; captivating; enchanting: ~的景色 *captivating or enchanting scenery*

【诱杀】trap and kill; lure to destruction

【诱使】trick into; inveigle into; lure into

【诱降】lure into surrender

【诱胁】cajole and coerce

【诱因】cause(of an illness); immediate cause

【诱致】lead to; cause; result in: ~违法乱纪 *lead to the violation of law and discipline* / 金钱~他走上了堕落。*Money led to his degeneration.*

釉 glaze: 青~瓷器 (*white*) *blue glazed porcelain*

【釉彩玻璃】enameled glass

【釉工】glazer

【釉面砖】【建】glazed tile

【釉陶】glazed pottery

【釉质】【生理】enamel: ~龋 *enamel caries* / ~冠 *enamel cap*

【釉子】glaze

鼬 【动】weasel: 黄~ *yellow weasel*

【鼬獾】ferret badger

yū

—

迂 ① go round; wind one's way; detour: ~道访问 *make a detour to call on sb* ② clinging to outworn rules and ideas; pedantic: 她妈妈有点~。*Her mother is a little pedantic.*

【迂夫子】pedant

【迂腐】stubbornly clinging to outworn rules and ideas; pedantic: ~之谈 *pedantic views* / 你真是一位~的老学究。*You are really an old pedant.*

【迂缓】slow in movement; sluggish; dilatory

【迂回】① circuitous; tortuous; roundabout: ~前进 *advance in a roundabout way* ②【军】outflank: 向敌人左侧~ *outflank the enemy on the left* / ~曲折 *full of twists and turns; circuitous; tortuous* / ~战术 *outflanking tactics*

【迂阔】high-sounding and impracticable

【迂论】impractical or pedantic views

【迂曲】tortuous; winding: ~的山路 *a tortuous mountain path*

【迂儒】a pedantic scholar; pedant

【迂拙】impractical and foolish

吁 ［象］a call to an animal to stop; whoa

see also xū

纡 ① tortuous; winding ②［书］tie; bind

【纡徐】slow in action; dilatory

淤 ① silt up ② silt; sediment; mud: 沟~ *drainage silt* / 河~ *river mud; alluvium* ③ stasis: 活血化~ *reduce stasis and improve blood circulation* ④ overflow; spilt

【淤地】silted up land; alluvial plain: ~坝 *silt arrester; silt dam*

【淤淀】silt; deposition: 河身~。*The river is silted up.*

【淤灌】【农】warping

【淤积】silt up; deposit: 仇恨~在心头。*Hatred was pent up in his heart.*

【淤泥】silt; sludge; ooze

【淤塞】silt up; be blocked or choked with silt: 航道~。*The waterway is blocked with silt.*

【淤血】【医】extravasated blood

【淤滞】①(of a river, etc.) be retarded by silt; silt up ②【中医】stasis (of blood or other bodily fluids): 静脉~ *venous stasis* / 尿~ *urinary stasis* / 肠~ *colon stasis*

yú

于[1] ① (indicating time or place) in; on; at: 你的来信~三月三日收到。*I got your letter on 3 March.* ② (indicating the direction of action) to; towards; onto; on: 求助~人 *turn to sb for help* / 热衷~集邮 *be keen on stamp collecting* / 嫁祸~人 *shift the blame onto others* / 让位~人 *give place to others; make room for others* / 那对夫妇已经习惯~这种平静的生活。*The couples are used to the quiet life.* ③ with regard to; concerning; to ④ (indicating beginning or origin) from; out of: 出~自愿 *of one's free will; of one's own accord* / 出~好心 *out of good will* ⑤ (indicating comparison) than: 不少~八百人 *no less than* 800 *people* / 为人民而死，重~泰山。*It's weightier than Mount Tai to die for the people.* ⑥ (used in the passive voice to indicate the doer of an action) by ⑦ used as a suffix after a verb or adjective: 这件礼物是属~我的。*The gift belongs to me.* ⑧ (Yú) a surname

【于今】① up to the present; by now; since ② nowadays today; now

【于是】so; then; hence

【于心不忍】not have the heart to; can't bear to

【于心无愧】have a clear conscience; feel no prick of conscience

【于心有愧】have a guilty conscience; have something on one's conscience; feel ashamed

余1［书］① I; me; my: ～老矣。*I'm old.* ②（Yú）a surname

余2 ① surplus; spare; remaining; left: ～粮 *surplus grain* /自给有～ *more than self-supporting* /落日～辉 *afterglow of a setting sun* ② more than; odd; over: 他们结婚四十年有～。*They married more than forty years.* ③ beyond; after: 工作之～ *after working hours; after work* /给我们说说你有什么业～爱好。*Please tell us your hobby.*

【余波】aftermath; repercussions

【余存】balance; remainder

【余党】remnants of an overthrown clique remaining cohorts: 匪帮～ *remnants of the bandit bang*

【余地】leeway; margin; latitude: 还有商量的～。*There is still room for discussion.* /没有回旋的～ *No space for manoeuvre.* /没有思考的～。*There is no latitude for giving the matter further consideration.*

【余毒】residual poison; pernicious vestige; evil influence:

【余额】① vacancy yet to be filled ② remaining sum; balance

【余割】【数】cosecant

【余函数】【数】complementary function

【余晖】last rays of the setting sun; sunset glow

【余悸】lingering fear

【余角】complementary angle

【余烬】ashes; embers

【余款】remaining money; money left; balance

【余量】① remnant; leftover ②【机】allowance

【余年】one's remaining years

【余孽】remaining evil element; leftover evil: 封建～ *dregs of feudalism*

【余怒未息】be still angry; be still fuming; one's angry lingers on

【余切】【数】cotangent

【余缺】surplus and deficiency

【余热】① surplus heat; waste heat ②［喻］energy of retirees: 爷爷虽然退休了,但他仍发挥～为社会做贡献。*My grandpa still makes continued contributions to the society in his retirement.*

【余生】① the remainder of one's life; one's remaining years: 安度～ *live through one's remaining years in peace* ② survival (after a disaster)

【余矢】【数】conversed sine

【余数】【数】remainder

【余头】［口］remainder; change

【余威】remaining prestige or influence

【余味】agreeable aftertaste; pleasant impression: ～无穷 *leave a lasting and pleasant impression or aftertaste*

【余隙】① remaining space; gap ②【机】clearance

【余暇】spare time; leisure time; leisure

【余下】remaining: ～的钱 *the remaining sum* /～的朋友 *the rest of the friends; the other friends*

【余弦】【数】cosine: ～定律 *the cosine law*

【余兴】① lingering interest ② entertainment after a meeting or a dinner party

【余因子】【数】complementary divisor

【余音】lingering sound (of music or singing): ～绕梁 *the music lingering around the beams; the music lingering in the air long after the performance*

【余勇可贾】have strength yet to spare; still have plenty of mettle to show

【余韵】remaining grace: 真想不到,这个老太太～不减当年啊。*We can't believe that the old lady was as graceful as ever.*

【余震】【地】aftershock

鱼 fish: 黄花～ *yellow croaker* /鲤～ *common carp* /鲫～ *crucian carp* /草～ *grass carp; Chinese ide* /武昌～ *blunt-snout* /桂～ *mandarin fish* /鲈～ *perch* /鳗～ *sea eel* /鳝～ *fresh-water eel* /银～ *whitebait* /墨～ *cuttlefish* /比目～ *turbot; flat fish* /带～ *hairtail; cutlass fish* /沙丁～ *sardine* /鲨～ *shark* / 钓～ *going fish* /养～ *fish-culture; pisciculture* /～塘 *fish pond*

【鱼白】① fish sperm; milt ② the whitish colour of a fish's belly — grey dawn

【鱼鳔】air bladder; fish-sound

【鱼叉】fish spear; fish fork

【鱼池】fish pond

【鱼翅】shark's fin (a delicacy)

【鱼虫】water flea

【鱼唇】shark's lip

【鱼刺】fishbone: 剔掉～ *bone a fish* /小孩子容易被～卡住。*Little children are easy to have a fishbone in their throat.*

【鱼大水小】a big fish in shallow water — ponderous apparatus without sufficient resources for maintenance

【鱼肚】fish maw (as food): ～白 *the whitish colour of a fish's belly; pale; greyish white*

【鱼饵】(fish) bait

【鱼粉】fish meal

【鱼肝油】cod-liver oil

【鱼竿】fishing rod

【鱼缸】fish bowl; fish jar; fish tank

【鱼钩】fishhook

【鱼贯】one following the other; in single file: ～而入 *enter in single file; file in* /～而行 *move in single line*

【鱼胶】① fish glue ②［方］air bladder; swim bladder

【鱼具】fishing tackle (or gear)

【鱼雷】torpedo: ～艇 *torpedo boat; patrol torpedo boat*

【鱼鳞】fish scale; scale: 刮去～ *scale a fish; scrape the scales off a fish* /～坑 *pits arranged like fish scales, dug on mountain slopes for holding water or planting trees; fish-scale pits*

【鱼龙】【考】ichthyosaur

【鱼龙混杂】dragons and fishes jumbled together; good and bad people mixed up; thread and

thrum; the genuine being mixed with false
【鱼篓】bamboo fish hamper; creel
【鱼露】fish sauce
【鱼卵】(fish) roe
【鱼米之乡】a land of fish and rice; a land of milk and honey; a well-watered place where fish and rice are abundant
【鱼苗】(fish) fry
【鱼目混珠】pass off fish eyes as pearls; pass off the sham as the genuine
【鱼片】sliced fish meat
【鱼漂】cork on a fishing line; bob; float
【鱼鳍】fin
【鱼群】a shoal of fish
【鱼肉】① the flesh of fish ② fish and meat ③ cut up like fish and meat; cruelly oppress; victimize: ~百姓 *cruelly oppress and exploit the common people*
【鱼水】fish and water; intimacy; interdependence: ~情 *relationship between fish and water*; *fish-water relationship* / ~情深 *as close as fish and water*
【鱼死网破】either the fish dies or the net gets torn — a life-and-death struggle; end up in common ruin
【鱼丸子】fish ball
【鱼尾号】boldface square brackets
【鱼尾纹】crow's feet: 妈妈的眼角已有几道明显的~。*At the corners of my mother's eyes the crow's feet are quite noticeable.*
【鱼香肉丝】fish-flavoured shredded pork
【鱼秧子】fingerling
【鱼鹰】osprey; sea eagle; erne; fish hawk; cormorant
【鱼油】fish oil
【鱼跃】① jump or leap of a fish: ~龙门 *a fish leaping over the dragon gate — pass a competitive examination* / 海阔任~,天空凭鸟飞。*The fish swims merrily in the vast sea; the bird soars freely in the broad sky.* ② fish dive(as in volleyball)
【鱼闸】fish lock
【鱼种】fingerling; fish breed

竽 an ancient Chinese windpipe (made of a number of reed pipes blown through a single mouth pipe): 滥~充数 *pretend to play the yu in order to make up the number*; *put in an appearance just to swell the total*; *hold an office though unequal to the task*

俞 ① used in classical Chinese to indicate permission ② (Yú) a surname
【俞允】[书] permit; allow

谀 [书] fawn on; curry favor; flatter: 阿~奉承 *flatter and toady*
【谀辞】flattering remarks; flattery

娱 ① give pleasure to; amuse; entertain: 聊以自~ *just to amuse oneself* ② joy; pleasure; amusement
【娱乐】amusement; entertainment; recreation: ~场所 *public place of entertainment* / ~活动 *recreational activities*; *recreation* / ~室 *recreation room* / 我们全家都喜欢看~片。*All my family like watching TV programme for entertainment.*
【娱悦】please; make happy; give pleasure

渔 ① fishing; fishery ② take sth one is not entitled to
【渔叉】gaff; harpoon; fish spear; fish fork
【渔场】fishing ground; fishery
【渔船】fishing boat
【渔村】fishing village
【渔夫】fisherman
【渔港】fishing port(or harbour)
【渔歌】fisherman's song
【渔钩】fishhook
【渔鼓】① percussion instrument made of bamboo and leather, used to accompany the chanting of folk tales: ~道情 *chanting of folk tales to the accompaniment of a bamboo percussion instrument* ②【戏】folk tales sung to the accompaniment of a fisherman's drum
【渔火】lights on fishing boats
【渔家】fishing household: ~姑娘 *a fisherman's daughter*
【渔具】fishing tackle(or gear)
【渔利】① reap unfair gains; profit at others' expense: 从中~ *exploit a situation to benefit oneself* ② easy gains; spoils
【渔猎】① fishing and hunting: 他叔叔做~工作。*His uncle goes in for fishing and hunting.* ② [书] plunder; grab ③ [书] hanker after; pursue: 他空闲时~女色。*He seeks carnal pleasure in his spare time*
【渔轮】fishing vessel or ship
【渔民】fisherman; fisherfolk
【渔区】fishing zone
【渔人】fisherman: ~之利 *the fisherman's gains*; *profit reaped by a third party* / 坐收~ *wait quietly to profit from a fight between other people*
【渔网】fishnet; fishing net
【渔翁】elderly old fisherman
【渔汛】fishing season
【渔业】fishery: ~区 *fishing zone* / ~资源 *fishery resources*
【渔舟】fishing boat; fisher

隅 ① corner; nook: 墙~ (*in the*) *the corner* / 向~而泣 *weep all alone in a corner* ② an outlying place; border: 海~ *seaboard*

揄 [书] raise; tow; draw
【揄扬】[书] ① praise ② propagate; publicize; advocate

逾 ① exceed; go beyond: 年~花甲 *be over sixty years of age* / 年~古稀 *get on over seventy* / 你的借款已经~额了。*Your loan has exceeded the allowed amount.* ② [书] even more: 悲痛~甚 *become even more grieved*
【逾常】out of the ordinary; unusual: 听到那个好消息,同学们欣喜~。*On hearing the good news, the students are overjoyed.*
【逾分】excessive; undue: ~的要求 *excessive de-*

mandr
【逾恒】[书] out of the common; unusual: 勤奋~ *be exceedingly diligent*
【逾期】exceed the time limit; be overdue: 他借的书~了还没有还。*He failed to return the books after expected time.*
【逾限】exceed the time limit; be overdue
【逾越】exceed; go beyond: ~界限 *go beyond the limit; go out of bounds*
【逾越节】【宗】passover — a holiday in memory of the escape of the Jews from Egypt
腴 ① fat; plump: 体态丰~ *plump; fat* ② fertile: 膏~之地 *fertile land*
渝[1] (of one's attitude or feeling) change: 她对丈夫忠贞不~。*She remains loyal to her husband.*
渝[2] another name for Chongqing
愉 pleased; happy; joyful; cheerful: 面有不~之色 *wear an annoyed expression; look displeased*
【愉快】happy; joyful; cheerful: ~的微笑 *a happy smile* / ~的心情 *a merry heart* / 过得很~ *have a very good time* / 祝你假日~。*I hope you'll have a pleasant holiday.*
【愉乐】happy; joyful; cheerful
【愉悦】joyful; cheerful; delighted: 最近她的心情~。*She is with a joyful heart recently.*
瑜 ① fine jade; gem ② splendour or lustre of gems; virtues; good points
【瑜珈】yoga
榆 elm
【榆荚】elm fruit
【榆钱儿】[口] elm seeds; elm fruit
【榆树】elm tree; elm
虞 ① suppose; expect; predict: 以备不~ *just in case of an unforeseen emergency* ② anxiety; worry ③ deceive; cheat; fool: 尔~我诈 *each trying to cheat the other* ④ (Yú) a surname
【虞美人】【植】corn poppy
愚 ① foolish; stupid; doltish: 那个孩子有点~笨。*The child is a little stupid.* ② make a fool of; fool ③ [谦] humble: ~以为不然。*I beg to differ.*
【愚笨】foolish; stupid; clumsy
【愚不可及】couldn't be more foolish; be hopelessly stupid; impossibly dim-witted
【愚蠢】stupid; foolish; silly: ~想法 *silly idea* / ~的行为 *foolish act*
【愚钝】slow-witted; stupid
【愚公移山】like the Foolish old Man who removed the mountain — with dogged perseverance
【愚见】[谦] in my humble opinion
【愚昧】ignorant; benighted; foolish: ~无知 *benighted; unenlightened; ignorant*
【愚民】① ignorant people ② try to keep the people in ignorance; practice obscurantism: ~政策 *policy of keeping the people in ignorance; obscurantist policy; obscurantism*
【愚弄】deceive; hoodwink; make a fool of; dupe
【愚人】fool; simpleton: ~节 *All Fools' Day (April 1); April Fool's (or Fools') day*
【愚妄】ignorant but arrogant; stupid but conceited
【愚者千虑,必有一得】even a fool occasionally hits on a good idea
【愚忠】blind loyalty or devotion
【愚拙】stupid and clumsy; foolish
舆[1] [书] ① carriage; cart; coach ② the part of a carriage for passengers or goods ③ palanquin; palankeen; sedan chair
舆[2] [书] land; area; territory
舆[3] public; popular
【舆论】public opinion: ~工具 *mass media; the media* / ~界 *the media; press circles* / ~导向 *spin control*
【舆情】public sentiment; popular feelings

yǔ

与[1] ① give; offer; grant: 把这支笔赠~你。*Give you this pen.* ② [书] get along with; be in friendly contact with ③ praise; commend; support; assist ④ [书] wait for; await
与[2] ① with; against: ~人合作 *cooperate with others* ② and; together with: 批评~自我批评 *criticism and self-criticism*
【与共】together: 生死~ *share a common destiny; go through thick and thin together* / 荣辱~ *share (in) honour or disgrace*
【与君一席话,胜读十年书】one evening's conversation with you is worth more than ten years' study
【与其】rather than for to go by boat than by train
【与日俱增】grow with each passing day; increase daily: 他的声望~。*His reputation rises with each passing day.*
【与世长辞】[书] depart from the world for ever; pass away; die
【与世沉浮】drift with the tide; follow the general trend; go with the flow
【与世无争】hold oneself aloof from the world; stand aloof from worldly strife
【与众不同】out of the ordinary; different from the common run; unconventional: ~的见解 *opinion different from the rest*
予 give; grant; bestow; award: 免~起诉 *exempt sb from indictment*
【予夺】[书] ① give or strip off; bestow or deprive of: 生杀~ *hold absolute power over sb's life* ② commend or disparage; laud or belittle
【予人口实】give cause for gossip; give sb a handle
【予以】give; grant; bestow: ~表扬 *commend sb; give praise to sb* / ~便利 *provide facilities (for sb)* / ~解释 *throw some light on*

屿 small island; islet:岛~ *island and islets*; *islands*

伛 [书] ① bend ② bow (to show respect)

【伛偻】[书] ① be hunchbacked:她已经成了一位~的老人。*She has became hunchbacked old man.* ② bow to show respect

宇 ① eaves; house:庙~ *temple* /屋~ *house*; *building* ② space; universe; world:名扬~内 *be renowned the world over* ③ [书] bearing; manner:气~轩昂 *have an impressive bearing*; *have a dignified appearance* ④ (Yǔ) a surname

【宇航】space navigation; astronavigation: ~服 *space suit* /~学 *astronautics* /~员 *astronaut*; *spaceman*

【宇宙】① universe; cosmos: ~飞船 *spaceship*; *spacecraft* /~飞行 *space flight*; *space travel* /~飞行员 *astronaut*; *spaceman*; *cosmonaut* /~服 *spacesuit* /~航行 *space flight*; *space travel* /~航行学 *astronautics*; *cosmonautics* /~航行员 *astronaut*; *spaceman*; *cosmonaut* /~火箭 *space rocket* /~空间 *cosmic space*; *outer space* /~射线 *cosmic rays*; *cosmic radiation* /~生物学 *exobiology* /~速度 *cosmic velocity or speed* /~学 *cosmology* /~站 *space station* ② world: ~观 *world view*; *world outlook*

羽[1] ① feather; plume: ~翎 *plume* ② (of birds, etc.) wing ③ [量] used of birds

羽[2] a note of classical Chinese 5 — tone scale, similar to 6 of the numbered musical notation

【羽翅】wing:煽动~ *flap the wings*

【羽毛】① feather; plume ~丰满 *full-fledged*; *mature* /~球 *badminton*; *shuttlecock* /~扇 *feather fan* /~未丰 *unfledged*; *young and immature*; *inexperienced*

【羽绒】fine, soft feather; down; eiderdown

【羽纱】camlet

【羽扇】feather fan: ~纶巾 *feather fan and head scarf — image of a wise counselor or strategist*

【羽坛】badminton circles

【羽衣】① plumage ② [书] feather clothing ③ Taoist robe Taoist priest

【羽翼】① wing ② assistant; supporter; support

雨 rain:春~ *spring rain* /大~ *heavy rain* /毛毛~ *drizzle* /~夹雪 *sleet* /倾盆大~ *pouring rain*; *raining cats and dogs*; *rain coming down in buckets* /暴~ *torrential rain*; *downpour* /暴风~ *storm*; *tempest* /雷~ *thunderstorm* /阵~ *shower*

【雨布】waterproof cloth; rainwear

【雨层云】【气】nimbostratus

【雨带】rain belt

【雨滴】raindrop

【雨点】raindrop

【雨刮器】windscreen or windshield wiper (of a car)

【雨过天晴】the sun shines again after the rain; the rain passes off and the sky clears up; after gloom comes brightness

【雨果】Victor-Marie Hugo (1802-1885), French poet, novelist, dramatist and central figure of the Romantic Movement in France

【雨后春笋】spring up like bamboo shoots after a spring rain; grow or shoot up like mushrooms

【雨季】rainy season; monsoon (season)

【雨具】rain gear (umbrella, raincoat, etc.)

【雨量】【气】rainfall; precipitation: ~过多 *excess rain* /~分布图 *hyetograph* /~计 *udometer*; *rain gauge*; *hyetometer* /~学 *hyetology* /~站 *precipitation station*; *rainfall station*

【雨林】rainforest

【雨露】① rain and dew ② favour; bounty; grace

【雨帽】rain cap; rain hat

【雨幕】curtain of rain; rain streak; blinding rain

【雨棚】【建】canopy

【雨披】[方] rain cape

【雨情】rainfall

【雨区】rain field; rain area

【雨伞】umbrella

【雨势】force or intensity of the rain

【雨水】① rainwater; rainfall; rain ② rain water — the 2nd of the 24 solar terms ③ day marking such a seasonal division point

【雨丝】drizzle; very light rain

【雨蛙】tree frog; tree toad

【雨雾】misty rain: ~茫茫 *vast blur in the misty rain*

【雨鞋】rain shoes; rubber boots; rubbers; galoshes

【雨靴】rain boots; rubber boots; rubbers

【雨衣】raincoat; rain cape; waterproof:把~递给我。*Please give me my raincoat.*

【雨意】signs of approaching rain

【雨云】【气】nimbus; rain cloud

【雨珠】raindrop

禹 ① legendary leader who led the people in conquering floods and succeeded Shun (舜) as ruler:夏~ *the founder of the Xia Dynasty* (*as his son founded the Xia Dynasty*) ② (Yǔ) a surname

【禹贡】classic work of Chinese geography completed in the Warring States Period

【禹域】[书] territories of China

语 ① language; tongue; word:汉~ *Chinese* (*language*) /世界~ *esperanto* /口~ *spoken language*; *colloquial speech* /成~ *idiom* /谚~ *proverb* /古~ *classic or ancient language* /冷言冷~ *ironical remarks*; *sarcastic comments* ② say; speak:低~ *whisper* /自言自~ *talk to oneself* /那个小女孩说话柔声细~。*The little girl speaks in a soft, low voice.* ③ nonlinguistic means of communicating ideas; sign; signal:手~ *sign language*; *dactylology* ④ speak; saying

【语病】faulty wording or formulation

【语不惊人死不休】not cease racking one's brain until one finds the most catching turn of phrase

【语词】words and phrases

【语调】【语】intonation; voice: ~低沉 *speak in a deep low voice*

【语法】grammar
【语感】an instinctive feel for the language
【语汇】vocabulary:汉语的~是极其丰富的。*Chinese has a very rich vocabulary.*
【语惊四座】the words startle all present
【语境】① language environments; speech environment ②【语】context
【语句】sentence:~通顺 *smooth and clear language*
【语料】linguistic material:~库 *corpus*
【语流】flow of speech
【语录】recorded utterance; quotation:毛主席~ *quotations from Chairman Mao*
【语妙天下】speak or write with sparkling wit
【语气】① tone; manner of speaking:~友好 *a friendly tone* ②【语】mood:陈述~ *indicative mood* /祈使~ *imperative mood* /~助词 *auxiliary word that indicates one's mood or manner of speaking; tonal adjunct*
【语塞】unable to utter a word (due to excitement, anger, etc.); tongue-tied
【语失】make an indiscreet remark; make a slip of tongue
【语素】【语】morpheme
【语态】【语】voice:主动(被动)~ *active (passive) voice*
【语体】【语】type of writing; variety of language; style:口语~ *colloquialism* /科学~ *scientific style of writing*
【语体文】prose written in the vernacular
【语文】① Chinese (as a subject of study):~课 *Chinese (as a course)* ② language:~水平 *language proficiency* ③ language and literature
【语无伦次】speak incoherently or illogically; speak in a confused way
【语系】【语】family of languages; language family
【语序】【语】word order
【语言】language:~科学 *linguistic science* /~粗野 *in coarse language* /~简练 *in concise language* /官方~ *official language*
【语言学】linguistics:宏观~ *macrolinguistics* /微观~ *microlinguistics*
【语义】meaning of a word; semantic meaning:~学 *semantics* /~家 *semanticist* /~扩展 *semantic extension*
【语意】meaning of a remark:~深长 (*of one's remarks*) *very meaningful*
【语种】kind of language; language variety
【语重心长】sincere words and earnest wishes; (say sth) in all earnestness:~的教诲 *sincere instructions*

庾 [书] open-air barn:~积 *store grain outdoors*

瘐

【瘐死】[书] die of cold and hunger in jail:~狱中 *die of illness in prison*

yù

与 take part in; participate in:他参~了制订计划。*He took part in making plans.*
【与会】participate in a conference; attend a meeting:~国 *country (or state) represented at a conference* /~者 *participant; conferee*
【与闻】have the knowledge of an insider; be let into (a secret, etc.)

玉 ① jade; jade-like stone:碧~ *jasper* /青~ *sapphire* /汉白~ *white marble* /金~良缘 *happy marriage* ② pure; fair; handsome; beautiful:~颜 *beautiful features* /~容 *fair looks* ③ your:~照 *your picture* /~言 *your words* /听说您~体欠安。*I heard that you were in bad health.* ④ (Yù) a surname
【玉帛】[书] jade objects and silk fabrics (used as state gifts in ancient China):她们两个最后化干戈为~,成了好朋友。*They tow turned hostility into friendship and became good friends.*
【玉成】kindly help make a success of; assist sb in accomplishing a task:~其事 *kindly help make it a success*
【玉带】jade belt
【玉雕】jade carving; jade sculpture:~作品 *jade work (or article)*
【玉佛】jade statue of Buddha
【玉钩】① jade book ② crescent moon
【玉皇大帝】jade Emperor of the supreme deity of Taoism
【玉洁】as pure and clean as jade:冰清~ *as pure as jade and as clear as ice; pure and noble*
【玉兰】【植】magnolia
【玉立】① graceful (carriage):亭亭~ *have a graceful carriage; be fair, slim and graceful* ② [书] moral integrity; steadfast to principles
【玉米】maize; Indian corn; corn:~秆 *cornstalk* /~粉 *cornmeal; corn flour* /~面 *maize flour; maize meal; cornmeal* /~心 *corncob; cob* /~粥 *maize gruel; corn porridge*
【玉女】Jade Maiden:金童~ *Golden Boy and Jade Maiden — attendants of the Taoist immortals*
【玉盘】① jade plate, tray, etc. ②[喻] moon
【玉佩】jade pendant
【玉器】jade article or object; jadeware
【玉人】①[书] jade sculptor or carver ② carved jade figurine ③[书] beautiful woman
【玉容】[书] (of women) beautiful features; fair complexion
【玉色】jade green; light bluish green
【玉石】jade:~俱焚 *jade and stone burned together; everything destroyed, be it jade or stone; destruction of good and bad alike* /这个桌子是~的。*This table is made of jade.*
【玉手】jade hands — slender white hands (of a beauty)
【玉碎】be like a broken piece of jade — die in glo-

ry：宁为～，不为瓦全。*I would rather die than surrender*

【玉体】① your（his，her，etc.）health：最近公主～欠安。*The princess was ill recently.* ② beautiful body of a woman

【玉兔】［书］the Jade Hare — moon

【玉玺】imperial jade seal

【玉液】good wine

【玉宇】① beautiful palace for God：她想住在～琼楼里面。*She wishes that she would live in magnificent buildings.* ② universe

【玉簪】① jade hairpin ②【植】fragrant plantain lily

驭 ① drive（a carriage）②［书］command；master

【驭手】soldier in charge of pack animals；driver of a military pack train

芋 ① taro ② similar tuber crop：洋～ *potato* / 山～ *sweet potato*

【芋头】①【植】taro；dasheen：在旧社会，他们拿～当饭吃。*They lived on taro in old days.* ②［方］sweet potato

妪 ［书］old woman；old lady：老～ *old lady*

郁[1] ① strongly fragrant ②（Yù）a surname

郁[2] ①（of plants）lush；luxuriant ②（of mood）gloomy；depressed：抑～ *be depressed*；*be in low spirit*

【郁葱】exuberant；luxuriant；verdant：房子的前面是～的树林。*There are exuberant woods before houses.*

【郁愤】sorrow and indignation

【郁馥】［书］rich fragrance；intense perfume：香气～ *heavy perfume*；*strong scent*

【郁积】smoldering；pent up

【郁金】root-tuber of aromatic turmeric（Curcuma aromatic）

【郁金香】【植】tulip

【郁闷】gloomy；depressed：心情～ *feel depressed*

【郁怒】sulky；full of pent-up indignation

【郁然】① gloomy；sorrowful；worried：她爸爸～成疾，不久后就死去了。*Her father became ill from worries and died soon.* ②［书］（of trees，etc.）profuse；luxuriant

【郁热】sultry；stuffy；sweltering

【郁血】【医】stagnation of the blood；venous stasis

【郁抑】constrained；depressed；gloomy：～的神情 *depressed look*

【郁悒】［书］dejected；depressed：神情～ *look gloomy*

【郁郁】［书］① elegant；refined ② strongly fragrant：青草～。*The green grass are emitting strong fragrance.* ③（of plants）lush and green；luxuriant：～葱葱的密林 *lush and green forest* ④ gloomy；depressed：～寡欢 *depressed and unhappy* / ～而死 *die from sorrow* / ～不乐 *depressed*；*melancholy*；*sad*

【郁滞】【中医】stasis

育 ① give birth to；bear：节～ *birth control* ② rear；raise；bring up；cultivate；grow：～婴 *raise babies* / ～花 *cultivate flowers* ③ educate：德～ *moral education* / 智～ *intellectual education*

【育才】cultivate talent；educate people

【育肥】fatten

【育林】afforest

【育龄】childbearing age：～妇女 *women of childbearing age*

【育苗】【农】grow seedlings：～区 *nursery garden*

【育人】educate；cultivate or foster talent

【育秧】【农】raise rice seedlings

【育养】① bring up；rear：是姑姑把他～成人的。*It is his aunt that brought him up.* ② breed

【育婴堂】orphanage；foundling hospital

【育种】【农】breeding

狱 ① prison；jail：入～ *be put in prison*；*be imprisoned* / 越～ *escape from prison*；*break prison* ② lawsuit；case：冤～ *unjust charge*；*unjust verdict*

【狱警】prison guard

【狱吏】prison warder or wardress；prison warden；jailer

峪 ravine；valley：嘉～关 *Jayuguan*（*a pass of the Great Wall*）

钰 ［书］treasure

浴 have a bath；bathe：日光～ *sunbath* / 海水～ *sea bathing*

【浴场】outdoor bathing place：海滨～ *bathing beach* / 这真是一个天然的～啊。*This is a natural bathing place.*

【浴池】① common bathing pool ② public bathhouse；public bath

【浴缸】bathtub；bath

【浴巾】bath towel

【浴具】bathroom facilities

【浴盆】bathtub：你去商店时，帮我买个～。*Please help me buy a bathtub when you go shopping.*

【浴室】bathroom；shower room：男～ *men's bathroom* / 女～ *women's bathroom*

【浴堂】bathroom；shower room

【浴血】bathed in blood；bloody；sanguinary：～沙场 *fight in a sanguinary battle* / ～奋战 *fight a bloody war*

【浴衣】bathrobe；bathing-wrap；bathing-gown

【浴皂】toilet soap

【浴罩】plastic bathtub cover；bath hood

预[1] in advance；beforehand：～约 *make an appointment*

预[2] take part in：干～ *interfere*

【预报】forecast；prediction：地震～ *earthquake forecast*；*earthquake prediction* / 你今天听天气～了吗？*Have you heard today's weather forecast?*

【预备】prepare；get ready：～考试 *prepare for an examination* / ～饭 *get a meal ready* / ～党员 *probationary Party member* / ～队 *reserve force*；*reserves* / ～会议 *preparatory meeting* / ～金 *reserve fund* / ~军 *reserve army; reserves* / ~期 *probationary period* / ~役 *reserve duty* (*or service*) / 各就各位！~！跑！*Ready! Get set! Go!*

【预卜】augur; foretell; predict：他能~凶吉。*He can foretell one's fate.*

【预测】predict; foresee; forecast：~日食 *calculate an eclipse of the sun* / 市场~ *market prediction*

【预产期】【医】expected date of childbirth

【预订】reserve (in advance); place an order for subscribe; book：~机票 *book an air ticket* / ~杂志 *subscribe to a magazine* / 我帮他~了明天的火车票。*I help him book a train ticket for tomorrow.*

【预定】fix or arrange in advance; predetermine; schedule

【预断】predict; anticipate; prejudge

【预防】take precautions against; guard against; prevent：~接种 *preventive inoculation* / ~拘留 *preventive detention*

【预付】payment in advance：~房租 *pay rent in advance* / ~款项 *prepayments*

【预感】① have a premonition ② premonition; presentiment：不详的~ *an ominous presentiment*

【预告】① announce in advance; herald ② advance notice：电视~ *TV announcements*

【预购】place an order or purchase in advance：李经理~了机票。*Manager Li bought an air ticket in advance.*

【预计】calculate in advance; estimate; anticipate：~一年内可完成这个工作。*It is estimated that the work will finish in a year.*

【预见】① foresee; foretell; predict：~到的困难 *foreseen difficulties* ② foresight; prevision：缺乏~ *lack foresight* / 科学的~ *scientific previsions*

【预警】forewarning; early warning：~系统 *early-warning system* / ~飞机 *early warning plane*

【预科】preparatory course：大学~ *preparatory school; preschool*

【预料】expect; predict; anticipate：出乎~ *beyond all expectations* / 真是难以~接下来会发生什么事情。*It's hard to predict what will happen.*

【预谋】plan beforehand; prearrange

【预期】expect; envision; anticipate

【预赛】【体】preliminary contest; preliminary; trial match：你知道~的结果了吗？*Do you know the preliminary results?*

【预审】antecedent trial; preliminary hearing：~法官 *investigating magistrate* / ~庭 *preliminary hearing court*

【预示】betoken; foretell; forebode：~大风暴的来临 *forebode a big storm*

【预收】collect or take advance payment：~货款 *advances in sales* / ~定金 *collect a deposit*

【预算】budget：国家~ *state budget* / 地方~ *local government budget*

【预习】preview

【预先】beforehand; in advance; pre

【预想】anticipate; expect：~结果 *potential result* / ~不到的后果 *unexpected consequences* / 不像~的那样顺利 *not as smooth as anticipated*

【预选】① proceedings of selecting candidates before election, straw vote ②【体】preliminary

【预言】prophesy; predict; foretell

【预演】(of a show) preview：这些节目正式演出前要~一场。*A preview of those programme should be given before its premiere.*

【预约】make an appointment：今天下午，他~了一个客户。*He makes an appointment to see one of his customers.*

【预早】[方] in advance; beforehand; preparations in advance

【预兆】omen; portent; sign; foreshadow; presage：不祥的~ *bad omen* / 胜利的~ *a harbinger for victory*

【预支】pay or get in advance：~费用 *prepaid expenses* / 她已经申请了~她的工资。*She has asked for an advance of this month's salary.*

【预知】know in advance; foresee

【预制】prefabricate; precast：~构件 *precast unit; prefabricated components or parts*

【预祝】congratulate beforehand; wish：~成功！*Wish you success!*

域 ① land within certain boundaries; territory; region：地~辽阔 *vast territory* ② domain; sphere; range

【域名】domain name

【域外】outside the country

【域中】inside the country

欲 ① desire; longing; wish：食~ *appetite; desire for food* / 求知~ *thirst for knowledge* ② desire; want; wish：畅所~言 *pour out all that one wants to say; speech one's mind freely* / ~哭无泪 *with no tears to shed even though one is in deep sorrow* / 己所不~勿施与人。*Do not do to others what you would not have them do to you.* ③ be about to; be just going to; be on the point of：东方~晓。*Dawn is breaking.*

【欲罢不能】try to stop but cannot; be unable to stop even though one wants to; can't refrain forgoing on

【欲盖弥彰】the more one tries to hide, the more one is exposed; the harder one tries to conceal a thing, the more it attracts attention; try to cover up a misdeed, only to make it more conspicuous

【欲海】【宗】ocean of desire

【欲壑难填】greed is a valley that can never be filled; greed is hard to satisfy; the gully is hard to fill up, avarice knows no bounds

【欲火】strong desire; carnal lust

【欲念】desire; wish; drive

【欲擒故纵】leave sb at large the better to apprehend him; allow sb more latitude first to keep tighter rein on him later; play cat and mouse with sb

【欲求】desires and requests

【欲速则不达】more haste, less speed; the faster one tries to finish, the longer it seems to take him; haste makes waste; haste does not bring success

【欲望】desire; lust; wish：受~驱使 *be stung with*

desire / 对那个小姑娘,他充满了~。*He is filled with lust to the girl.*

【欲言又止】about to speak but speak nothing; hold back the words which sprang to one's lips

阈 [书] doorsill; threshold; limits: 视~ *visual range; visual threshold*

谕 (of superiors or seniors) decree; instruct; order: 面~ *give orders personally; instruct face to face* / 圣~ *imperial edict*

【谕告】[书] (of superiors or seniors) announce by edict; notify in a decree; tell

【谕令】[书] order

【谕示】[书] instruct

【谕旨】[书] imperial edict

遇 ① meet; encounter: 不期而~ *meet by chance; chance encounter* / 途中~雨 *be caught in the rain halfway* ② treat; receive: 待~ *treatment; remuneration; pay* / 他给岳母的待~不薄。*He treats his mother-in-law very generously.* ③ chance; opportunity: 机~ *opportunity* ④ (Yù) a surname

【遇刺】be attacked by an assassin

【遇到】meet; run into; come across: 上学的路上,我~到我的老师。*I met my teacher on my way to school.*

【遇害】be murdered

【遇见】meet; run into; come across

【遇救】be rescued; be saved

【遇难】① be killed in an accident; be murdered ② be in trouble

【遇事】when anything crops up; when confronted with a problem: ~谨慎 *be prudent when confronted with a problem* / 他那么小,竟然能~不惊。*He is so small, but he is calm in times of difficulties.*

【遇事生风】make trouble at every opportunity; sow discord wherever possible

【遇险】meet with a mishap; be in danger; be in distress

【遇缘】by chance; as luck would have it; by a lucky coincidence

喻 ① explain; tell; inform ② understand; know ③ analogy; figure of speech: 比~ *analogy* / 明~ *simile* / 暗~ *metaphor* ④ (Yù) a surname

【喻世】admonish the people

【喻义】allegorical or metaphorical meaning

御 ① drive; ride: ~马 *ride a horse* ② [旧] control; dominate ③ resist; keep out; ward off: 防~ *defend* / 抵~ *resist* / 天太冷了,~~寒吧! *It's very cold; please keep out cold.* ④ related to the emperor or king; imperial

【御宝】imperial seal

【御笔】emperor's brush — handwriting or painting of the emperor

【御赐】bestowed by the emperor

【御花园】imperial garden

【御驾】his majesty's carriage: ~亲征 *His majesty personally led the expedition*

【御览】for the emperor's inspection

【御林军】palace guards; imperial armed forces

【御膳】food for the emperor: ~房 *imperial kitchen*

【御玺】imperial seal; (UK) privy seal

【御医】imperial physician

【御用】① employed by the emperor; court physician: ~药品 *medicine for the use of his majesty* ② hired; in the pay of: ~文人 *hired scribbler; hack writer*

【御苑】imperial garden

【御制】made by order of his majesty

寓 ① reside; live ② imply; contain ③ residence; dwelling; abode: 公~大楼 *apartment building*

【寓处】residence; abode; house; dwelling place

【寓邸】residence or mansion (of a high official)

【寓居】live or make one's home in: 她奶奶晚年~日本。*He granny lived in Japan in her late life.*

【寓舍】dwelling place; house one lives in

【寓所】residence; dwelling

【寓言】parable; allegory; fable: 那个孩子喜欢读~故事。*The child likes reading fable story.*

【寓意】implied meaning; moral; message: ~深刻 *have a profound moral*

裕 ① abundant; plentiful; ample; rich: 充~ *plentiful; ample* / 他出生在富~的家庭中。*He wsa born from a rich family.* ② [书] enrich; make affluent: 富国~民 *enrich the nation and the people* ③ (Yù) a surname

【裕仁天皇】Hirohito (1901—1989), 124th emperor of Japan (1926—1989)

【裕如】① needing little effort; effortlessly with ease: 应付~ *handle the situation with ease* ② plentiful; abundant; affluent: 生活~ *well-to-do life*

粥 [书] give birth to (a child); bear

see also zhōu

愈1 ① be cured; heal; recover: 痊~ *be fully recovered; fully recover from an illness* / 汤姆已经病~出院了。*Tom has left hospital after recovery.* ② be better than

愈2 (used in duplicates) the more... the more; more and more; increasingly: ~早~好。*The sooner the better.*

【愈发】more; all the more; even more: 她变得~沮丧了。*She became even more depressed.*

【愈合】[医] heal up

【愈加】increasingly; even more; all the more: 比以前~好了 *even better than before* / 变得~麻烦了 *become increasingly troublesome*

【愈演愈烈】become increasingly intense; grow even more violent; go from bad to worse: 争吵~。*The quarrel is escalating.*

【愈益】increasingly; even more

誉 ① reputation; renown; fame: 美~ *good reputation* / 载~而归 *return home with honour* ② praise; eulogize; commend

【誉满全球】of world renown; world-famous: 我们的衣服的样式~。*The styles of our clothes enjoy a high reputation all over the world.*

熨

see also yùn

【熨帖】①(of wording) appropriate; fitting; proper ② calm; peaceful quiet:听了妈妈的一番话,我心里感到十分~。*Having heard mother's words, I felt very much at ease.* ③[方] comfortable; well ④[方] settled; well-done:这事办得真~! *You did a good job!*

豫[1] [书]① pleased; happy glad:面有不~之色 *look displeased* ② comfort contentment

豫[2] another name for Henan

【豫剧】Henan Opera (a local opera popular in Henan and parts of Shanxi and Shaanxi)

yuān

鸢 【动】kite; hawk

【鸢尾】【植】iris

鸳 mandarin duck

【鸳鸯】① mandarin duck: ~戏水 *mandarin ducks playing on water* ② loving couple

【鸳鸯房】mandarin duck room or apartment

【鸳鸯座】love seat (in a cinema, etc.)

冤 ① wrong; grievance; injustice:不白之~ *be wrongly accused* /伸~ *redress a grievance; right a wrong* /沉~ *long-standing injustice* /她丈夫是含~而死的。*Her husband died of unjust treatment.* ② hatred; enmity; feud:结~ *become enemies; incur hatred of; start a feud* ③ not commensurate with the effort or money; not worthwhile; in vain:花~钱 *waste money; not get one's money's worth* ④[方] kid; fool; pull sb's leg:人们不会~枉你的。*People can't kid you.*

【冤案】a wrong verdict; an unjust case; injustice

【冤沉海底】the injustice will remain unrepressed forever

【冤仇】enmity; rancour; feud

【冤大头】blockhead in money matters; foolish spender; sucker

【冤愤】indignation at injustice

【冤魂】wronged person's ghost

【冤家】① enemy; foe:这两个人是生死~。*They are deadly enemies.* ② one's destined love; sweetheart or lover in a love-hate relationship:不是~不聚头。*Enemies and lovers are destined to meet.*

【冤假错案】cases in which people were unjustly, falsely, or wrongly charged or sentenced:平反~ *redress the wrongs done to people who were unjustly, falsely, or wrongfully accused and sentenced*

【冤苦】① injustice and suffering:他小的时候,吃了不少~。*He experienced a great deal of injustice and distress when he was young.* ② wrong; do sb an injustice

【冤孽】enmity and sin: ~深重 *steeped in enmity and sin*

【冤气】resentment at being wronged; indignation about un — just treatment; feeling against injustice:一肚子~ *feel strongly about the injustice; resent one's wrong deeply*

【冤情】true state or facts of an injustices

【冤屈】① wrong; treat unjustly ② wrongful treatment; injustice

【冤死】die from injustice

【冤枉】① unfair; unjust; wrong ② wrong; treat unjustly or unfairly: ~某人 *put sb in the wrong* /受~ *suffer wrongful treatment* ③ not worthwhile; not repaying the effort; in vain:花~时间 *spend time in vain* /~路 *vain trip; the unnecessary the long way one has travelled*

【冤狱】unjust charge or verdict; miscarriage of justice; frame-up

渊 deep waters; deep pool:天~之别 *difference between heaven and the earth; completely different* /深~ *deep pool; abyss* ② deep ③ (Yuān) a surname

【渊博】broad and profound; scholarly; erudite:学识~ *erudite; learned; scholarly*:他爷爷是一位~的学者。*His grandpa was an erudite scholar.*

【渊海】deep pool and vast sea — (of content) wide in range and great in depth

【渊默】[书] profound silence

【渊深】profound; deep

【渊识博学】profound knowledge and extensive learning

【渊源】origin; source: ~极深 *be closely connected* /历史~ *historical origin* /文明的~ *origin of civilization*

yuán

元[1] ① first; initial; primary:纪~ *beginning of an era; epoch, etc.* ② arch; chief; principal ③ basic; essential; fundamental ④ element ⑤ unit; component:单~ *unit; section; apartment*

元[2] unit of money:这件衣服花了我3~钱。*The coat cost me three yuan.*

元[3] ① Yuan Dynasty(1271—1368) ② (Yuán) a surname

【元宝】shoe-shaped gold or silver ingot used as money in feudal china

【元旦】New Year's Day: ~联欢会 *New Year's Day party*

【元古代】【地】protrusion Era

【元件】element; component; cell:电路~ *circuit component* /敏感~ *sensor*

【元老】founding member(of an organization); senior statesman

【元年】first year of an era or of the reign of an emperor

【元气】vitality; vigour:恢复~ *regain one's strength; recuperate one's strength* /他还年轻,~

比较旺。*He is very young and full of vigour.*
【元件】elements and parts
【元曲】Yuan opera, popular during the Yuan Dynasty: ~作家 *playwright of Yuan opera*
【元日】first day of the lunar year
【元戎】[书] chief or supreme commander; commanding general
【元首】①[书] monarch ② head of state; chief executive: 昨天,中国~访问了日本。*China's head of State visited Japan yesterday.*
【元帅】【军】marshal: 陆军~*field marshal* /英国皇家空军~ *marshal of the Royal Air Force* ②[古] supreme commander
【元素】① element; essential factor ②【化】element: 稀有~ *rare element* /~周期表 *periodical table of elements* / ~分析 *ultimate analysis* /~符号 *element symbol*
【元宵】① 15th night of the first lunar month: ~佳节 *Lantern Festival* ② sweet dumpling made of glutinous rice flour (originally for the Lantern Festival): 包~ *make rice dumplings* /在~节,同学们聚在一起煮~吃。*On Lantern Festival, all the students stayed together to boil rice dumplings.*
【元宵节】lantern Festival
【元凶】prime culprit; arch-criminal
【元勋】man of outstanding merit; founding father: 开国~ *founders of a state*
【元音】【语】vowel: ~字母 *vowel letter*
【元月】① January ② the first month of the lunar year; the first moon

园 ① an area of land for growing plants: 菜~ *vegetable garden* /葡萄~ *vineyard* /果~ *orchard* ② park; garden: 动物~ *zoological garden; zoo* /植物~ *botanical garden* /颐和~ *the Summer Palace*
【园地】① garden plot; plot ② field; scope: 绘画~ *scope of drawing*
【园丁】① gardener ② school teacher
【园林】garden; park
【园陵】cemetery; mausoleum
【园圃】garden
【园艺】horticulture; gardening: ~家 *horticulturist* /~学 *horticulture; gardening*
【园子】garden; plot plantation

员 ① person engaged in a certain field of activity: 演~ *actor; actress* /学~ *student; trainee* /销售~ *salesman* /我爸爸是一名教~。*My father is a teacher.* ② member: 少先队~ *member of the Chinese Young Pioneers; Young Pioneer* /共青团~ *member of the Communist Youth League of China; league member* /中共党~ *member of the Chinese Communist Party; party member* ③ [量]: 一~学生 *a valiant student*
【员工】staff personnel
【员外】①[古] ministry counselor ② rich landowner; landlord

垣 ① wall ② town; city

原[1] ① primary; initial; original; former: ~职 *former post* /~义 *original meaning* /~单位 *the organization one formerly belonged to* ② unprocessed; crude; raw

原[2] excuse; forgive; pardon: 情有可~ *excusable; pardonable*

原[3] ① plain; level and open country: 平~ *plain* /高~ *plateau* /大草~ *prairie; grassland* ② (Yuán) a surname
【原班人马】old cast; original team
【原版】original edition; in the original
【原本】① original manuscript; master copy ② the original ③ originally; formerly: 他~是个农民。*He was formerly a farmer.*
【原材料】raw and processed material
【原封】with the seal unbroken; intact: ~退回 *return sth unopened* /~不动 *be left intact; remain untouched*
【原稿】original manuscript; master copy
【原告】【律】plaintiff(for civil cases); prosecutor (for criminal cases): ~证人 *evidence for the prosecution*
【原级】【语】positive degree
【原籍】ancestral home; native place; native home
【原价】original price
【原件】① original manuscript; master copy ② the original
【原教旨主义】fundamentalism
【原来】① original; formerly: ~的目标 *the original goal* ② so; as it turns out to be: ~是他呀! *So it's him!*
【原来如此】so, that's how it is; I see
【原理】principle; theory; axiom; tenet: 根本~ *a cardinal principle* /普遍~ *universally applicable principle*
【原谅】excuse; forgive; pardon: 不能~的行为 *unpardonable behaviour*
【原料】raw material
【原貌】original state; original appearance
【原煤】raw coal
【原木】log
【原判】【律】original judgement; original sentence
【原配】first wife
【原任】① predecessor ② formerly hold the post of
【原审】【律】first trial
【原声带】original sound tape
【原始】① primary; original; firsthand: ~记录 *original record* ② primeval; primitive: ~人 *primitive man* /~社会 *primitive society* /~部落 *primitive tribe* /~状态 *state of nature* /~公社 *primitive society; primitive commune* /~积累 *primitive accumulation* /~森林 *primeval or virgin forest* /~主义 *primitivism*
【原诉】【律】original suit: 撤回~ *withdraw an original suit*
【原委】how a thing happened from beginning to end; the whole story; all the details
【原文】original text; master copy; the original
【原物】the original

【原先】① former; original:这和我们～的计划不一样。*It's different with our former plan.* ② formerly; originally; at first: ～我觉得英语很难学。*I found English very difficulty at first.*
【原线圈】primary coil
【原形】original shape; true features; true shape beneath the disguise
【原型】prototype; archetype; model
【原盐】crude salt
【原样】original look or state; original sample
【原义】primary meaning; original meaning:词的～ *primary meaning of a word*
【原意】meaning; original meaning or intention:曲解～ *distort the meaning* /我的～不是这样的。*This is not what I meant.*
【原因】cause; grounds; reason:主要～ *main reason*; *basic cause* /～和结果 *cause and effect* /由于这个～ *on this account*
【原由】cause; reason
【原油】crude oil ; crude:含硫～ *sour crude* /低硫～ *sweet crude* /优质～ *high quality crude* /～库 *crude oil storage*
【原原本本】the whole story; everything; as exact as it is; from first to last:她把事情的全部都～地告诉了我。*She told the whole story exactly as it happened.*
【原早】[方] in the past; before; originally:我～是老师。*I used to be a teacher.*
【原则】principle:坚持～ *stick (or adhere) to principle*; *live up to one's principles* /和平共处五项～ *the Five Principles of Peaceful Coexistence* /～上同意 *agree (or accept) in principle* /这是一个～问题。*This is a matter of principle.*
【原职】former post or job
【原址】former address; original site
【原主】original owner:物归～ *return sth to its owner*
【原著】original work; original
【原装】in the original package; unopened; intact
【原状】original state; previous condition:保持～ *remain in the original state*; *leave sth in the original state*; *leave sth intact* /她离开家的时,把东西都恢复了～。*She returned to the former state where she left home.*
【原子】atom:复合～ *compound atom*; *complex atom* /自由～ *free atom* /标记～ *labeled atom* /～弹头 *atomic warhead* /～辐射 *atomic radiation* /～结构 *atomic structure* /～动力 *atomic power* /～装置 *atomic device* /～尘 *atomic fallout* /～弹 *A-bomb*; *atom bomb*; *atomic bomb* /～反应堆 *atomic reactor*; *atomic pile* /～核 *atomic nucleus* /～键 *atomic bond* /～量 *atomic weight* /～论 *atomic theory*; *atomism* /～能 *atomic energy* /～能发电站 *atomic power station* /和平利用～能 *peaceful utilization of atomic energy*; *atomic energy for peaceful purposes* /国际～能机构 *International Atomic Energy Agency (IAEA)* /～炮 *atomic cannon or artillery* /～武器 *atomic weapon* /～物理学 *atomic physics* /～战争 *atomic war* /～质量 *atomic mass* /～钟 *atomic clock*

【原罪】【宗】original sin
【原作】the original; master or primary copy; original work

圆[1] ① round; circular ② tactful; satisfactory ③ ball-shaped:滚～ *round as a ball* ④【数】*circle*:半～ *semicircle* /椭～ *ellipse*; *oval* /同心～ *concentric circle* /内切～ *inscribed circle* /外接～ *circumscribed circle*; *circum circle.* ⑤ justify; make perfect or complete:好梦难～。*Good dreams seldom come true.*

圆[2] ① the monetary unit of China ② coin:银～ *silver dollar* /铜～ *copper coin* ③ (Yuán) a surname

【圆白菜】cabbage
【圆材】【林】round wood; log
【圆场】mediate; smooth things over; help to effect a compromise:打～ *mediate a dispute*; *smooth things over*
【圆成】help sb to achieve sth:他很聪明能～这件事。*He is so clever that he can help me out in this matter.*
【圆顶】dome
【圆嘟嘟】full and round; plump: ～的小脸 *chubby face* / ～的手 plump hands
【圆度】circular degree; roundness
【圆房】consummate a marriage (when a child daughter-in-law and her husband reached adulthood)
【圆坟】[旧] add fresh soil onto the grave three days after the burial
【圆骨碌】round; ball-like: ～的小眼睛 *a pair of small round eyes*
【圆鼓鼓】bulging; sticking out round; rounded
【圆规】compasses:一副～ *a pair of compasses*
【圆滚滚】very round; plump:不要吃太多了,你都成了～的小猪了。*Don't eat too much*; *you have become a plump piglet.*
【圆和】① mediate ② flexible; accommodating:办事～ *be flexible in handling business* ③ mellow and full
【圆乎乎】rather round; plump
【圆弧】【数】circular arc
【圆滑】smooth and wily; slick and sly
【圆谎】make a lie sound plausible; patch up a lie
【圆浑】[书] ① (as of voice) rich; round ② smooth and natural
【圆活】① flexible; not dull ② mellow and full:她说话的声音～。*She speaks with mellow and full voice.*
【圆寂】【宗】(of Baddish monks or nuns) die; pass away
【圆孔】circular aperture
【圆锯】【机】circular saw
【圆括号】parentheses; curves
【圆溜溜】good and round: ～的眼睛 *round eyes*
【圆满】satisfactory: ～成功 *complete success* /～的答复 *a satisfactory reply*
【圆梦】① oneiromancy; divination by interpretation of one's dream ② have one's dream realized or

fulfilled：三年以后，他终于～去了北京。*He realized his long-cherished desire to go to Beijing three years later.*

【圆盘】disc：～除草机 *disc weeder* /～耙 *disc harrow* /～犁 *disc plough*

【圆圈】circle；ring

【圆全】［方］satisfactory；thoughtful

【圆润】① mellow and full：他有一副～的好嗓音。*He has a sweet，melodious voice.* ②（of handwriting，etc.）fluent；smooth

【圆熟】① skilful；proficient；dexterous ② astute；tactful；flexible：处世～ *be astute in one's behavior*

【圆说】justify；speak in defense of；argue in favour of

【圆通】flexible；accommodating

【圆舞曲】waltz

【圆心】centre of a circle：～角 *central angle*

【圆形】round；circular：～建筑

【圆周】circumference；periphery：～角 *circumferential angle* /～接缝 *circumferential seam* /～率 *ratio of the circumference of a circle to its diameter* /～运动 *circular motion*

【圆珠笔】ball-point pen；ball pen

【圆柱】①【数】cylinder：～根 *cylindrical root* /～体 *cylinder* ② column；round post or pillar

【圆锥】circular cone；taper：～根 *conical root* /～花序 *panicle* /～曲线 *conic section* /～台 *frustum of a cone*

【圆桌】round table：～会议 *round-table conference* /～面 *round table top*

【圆子】［方］① dumpling（made of glutinous rice flour）② ball

援 ① pull by hand；hold：攀～ *climb up by holding on to sth* ② quote；cite：有例可～。*There is a precedent to quote.* ③ help；aid；assist；rescue：救～ *come to sb's rescue* /增～ *reinforce* /我们向他求～，但他没有给我们答复。*We asked for help，but he didn't give us answer.*

【援笔】［书］take up a pen

【援兵】reinforcements；relief troops

【援建】provide aid in construction

【援救】rescue；help；save；deliver from danger：～溺水儿童 *rescue a child from drowning*

【援军】reinforcements；relief troops：派出～ *dispatch reinforcements*

【援款】relief money or fund；financial assistance or aid

【援例】cite a precedent

【援手】［书］helping hand；help；assistance

【援外】aid a foreign country；give aid to a foreign country：～物资 *materials in aid of a foreign country* /～项目 *foreign aid project*

【援引】cite；invoke；quote

【援用】① quote；cite；invoke：～惯例 *cite a precedent* ② recommend for appointment：老板决定～有才能的人。*The boss decided to recommend the able and virtuous.*

【援助】help；support；aid；assist：国际～ *international support* /～受难者 *help victims* /经济～ *economic aid* /无私的～ *selfless assistance*

缘 ① reason：她总是无～无故地和丈夫生气。*She is always angry with her husband without reasons.* ② predestined relationship or affinity；happy fate or chance：姻～（*predestined*）*marriage* ③ rim；brink；edge；fringe：边～ *rim*；*edge* ④ along

【缘分】fate or chance that brings people together；predestined relationship：我和妻子真是有～。*My wife and I brought together by fate.*

【缘故】cause；reason；motive：出于那个～ *for that reason*

【缘何】［书］why：你～给她钱？*What's the reason for giving her money?*

【缘木求鱼】climb a tree to catch fish — cannot get blood from stone；do things by the wrong method；resort to fruitless approach；do the impossible

【缘起】① cause；origin ② exposition of the cause or origin of

【缘悭一面】never have the luck to meet sb

【缘由】reason

猿 ape：长臂～ *gibbon* /从～到人，这是一段漫长的历史过程。*It's a long history from ape to man.*

【猿猴】apes and monkeys

【猿人】ape-man

源 ① water source；fountainhead：泉～ *fountainhead* ② source；cause；root：电～ *power supply* /没有人知道他的病～。*No one knows the cause of his disease.* ③（Yuán）a surname

【源程序】【电】source program：～模块 *source module*

【源代码】【电】source code program

【源语言】【电】source language

【源源】in a steady stream；steadily；continuously：～而来 *come in a steady or an endless stream* /～不绝 *in an endless flow*；*continuously*；*incessantly*

【源远流长】① distant source and long stream ② of long standing；having a long history

辕 ① shafts（of a cart，palanquin，etc.）：驾～ *pull a cart* ②［旧］outer gate of a government office or barracks；government office

【辕马】shaft-horse；horse in the shafts

【辕门】outer gate of a government office or barracks

【辕子】shafts of a cart or palanquin：车～ *shafts of a cart*

yuǎn

远[1] ①（of time or space）far；distant；remote：～处 *far away place*；*distant point or place* /在不～的将来 *in the not too distant future* ②（of relationship）distant：～亲 *distant relatives* ③（of differences）by far：～不及 *far inferior to* /～～超过 *far exceed* ④ keep away from；keep at a distance：～离小人 *keep away from the mean and* *selfish characters* ⑤（Yuǎn）a surname

【远程】long-range；long-distance；remote：~导弹 *long-range missile* / ~火箭 *long-range rocket* / ~程序输入 *remote programme entry* / ~存取 *remote access* / ~导航 *long-distance navigation*

【远大】long-range；broad；lofty；ambitious：~的目标 *grand objective*；*great aim*

【远道】long way：她是我~来的好朋友。*She is one of my good friends who has come from afar.*

【远地点】【天】apogee

【远东】the Far East

【远渡】travel cross vast seas or oceans：~重洋，来到中国 *come to China from across the vast occan*

【远方】distant place

【远房】distantly related

【远隔】far apart

【远隔重洋】separated by vast oceans

【远古】remote antiquity；remote times：在~时代 *in remote antiquity*；*in ancient times*

【远海】open seas；distant sea waters

【远航】take a long voyage；sail to a distant place

【远话】sth said as if by an outsider：咱们不说~。*We should not talk like an outsider.*

【远见】foresight；far-sightedness；foresight；vision：没有~的人 *a man without vision* / 政治~ *political foresight*（*or vision*）

【远见卓识】foresight and sagacity；far-sightedness

【远郊】outer suburbs；the remote outskirt of a city：他家住在~。*He lives in the far outskirts.*

【远近】① far and near；everywhere：~驰名 *be known far and wide*；*be widely known* ② distance：不论~我们都要去拜访他。*We must visit him how far it is.*

【远景】① distant view ② long-range perspective；prospect：~规划 *a long range plan* / 为…提供很有希望的~ *offer a very promising prospect for* ③（of film）long shot

【远客】guest or visitor from afar

【远路】long journey；long way；detour：让他好好休息吧，他走了很长的~。*Let him have a good rest*；*he has taken a long journey.*

【远虑】foresight；long view

【远略】long-term strategy

【远门】① go on a distant journey ②（of family relationship）distant：~表亲 *distant cousin*

【远谋】long-term plans

【远年】many years ago；of long standing

【远期】at a specified future date；relating to the future；forward：请把那份~汇票递给我。*Please pass the time bill to me.*

【远亲】distant relative；remote kinfolk：那个小孩是我的一位~。*The little child is a distant relation of mine.*

【远亲不如近邻】a close neighbour means more than a distant relative；a distant relative is not as helpful as a near neighbour

【远日点】【天】aphelion

【远涉】cover a vast distance：当他爷爷很小的时候，就~重洋，离开了家乡。*His grandpa travelled across the high seas and left his hometown when he was very young.*

【远射程】long range：~炮 *long range gun* / ~武器 *standoff weapon*

【远摄镜头】①（in film）long shot ②（photography）telephoto lens

【远识】foresight；far-sightedness；vision

【远视】long sight；hyperopia：~眼镜 *spectacles for the long-sighted*

【远水解不了近渴】distant water cannot quench present thirst

【远水解不了近火】distant water cannot put out a nearby fire；a slow remedy cannot meet an urgency

【远台】【体】far from the table：~长抽 *long drive*；*off-table drive* / ~防守 *far-from-table defense*

【远眺】look far into the distance（esp. from a high place）

【远图】a long term plan

【远销】sell to faraway places：~海外 *sell sth abroad*

【远行】go on a long journey

【远扬】（of fame，reputation）spread far and wide；become known far and wide

【远洋】① ocean ② of the open sea beyond the littoral zone；oceanic：~航行 *oceangoing voyage* / ~货轮 *oceangoing freighter* / ~渔业 *deep-sea fishing*；*pelagic fishing* / ~捕鲸 *pelagic whaling* / ~客轮 *ocean liner* / ~通信 *transoceanic communication* / ~海军 *blue-sea navy*

【远游】travel far away；be on a distant journey：他经常~。*He is always on a distant journey.*

【远缘】distant：~类型 *distant form* / ~嫁接 *distant grafting* / ~杂交 *distant hybridization*

【远在天边，近在眼前】close at hand though seemingly far away

【远征】expedition：红军不怕~难，万水千山只等闲。*The Red Army fears not the trials of the Long March，holding light ten thousand crags and torrents.*

【远志】① lofty ideals；high aspirations：胸怀~ *cherish noble aspirations* ② Chinese narrow-leaved polygala；polygala-root

【远走高飞】soar high and fly far；flee to faraway places：昨天那对情侣~了。*The couple fled to faraway place yesterday.*

【远足】excursion；pleasure trip on foot；walking tour

【远祖】remote ancestor

yuàn

苑 ①［书］enclosed ground for growing trees，keeping animals，etc.；imperial garden；park：御~ *imperial garden* ②［书］centre（of art and literature，etc.）：艺~ *centre of the arts* ③（Yuán）a surname

【苑囿】animal farm or park

怨 ① resentment; hatred ② blame: 他妻子总是任劳任～。*His wife always works hard and is not upset by criticisms.*

【怨不得】① cannot blame: 刚才的事～你，是我脾气不好。*You are not to blame for what has happened; it was just my bad temper.* ② no wonder; so that's why

【怨仇】resentment; enmity; hatred; rancour

【怨敌】enemy; foe

【怨毒】[书] hatred; enmity; venom

【怨怼】[书] resentment; enmity hatred: 心存～ *bear (or have) a grudge; be resentful*

【怨愤】discontent; indignation: 农民们～不能平。*The farmers can hardly restrain their indignation.*

【怨怪】blame: 妈妈～我多嘴。*My mother blamed me for not keeping my mouth shut.*

【怨恨】① have a grudge against; hate: ～战争 *hate war* ② hatred; resentment: ～的语气 *tone of discontent (resentment, or hatred)*

【怨悔】regret remorsefully; repent

【怨懑】discontented and angry; hostile and resentful

【怨女】[书] girl pining for a husband; single woman long overdue for marriage

【怨偶】[书] unhappy couple

【怨气】grievance; complaint; resentment: 看到孩子们回来，他充满了～。*On seeing his children come back, he was full of complaints.*

【怨声载道】grumbling of the people are heard everywhere; voices of discontent of the people fill the streets; complaints are heard everywhere

【怨天尤人】grumble against the Heaven and lay the blame upon the other people; find fault with everyone and everything; blame everybody but oneself

【怨言】complaint; grumble: 从未发过一句～ *never utter a word of complaint for anybody or anything* /毫无～ *without a word of complaint*

院 ① yard; courtyard; compound: 居民～ *neighbourhood compound* /前～ *front yard* /后～儿 *back yard* /四合～儿 *compound with houses around a courtyard* ② designation for certain government institutions and public places: 国务～ *State Council* /法～ *law court* /医～ *hospital* ③ institute of higher learning; college: 全～师生员工 *all the staff and students of the college (or institute)* ④ hospital: 住～ *be admitted to hospital; be hospitalized* /出～ *be discharged from hospital* ⑤ (Yuàn) a surname

【院落】courtyard; yard; compound

【院墙】courtyard wall; wall surrounding a house

【院士】academician

【院校】colleges and universities: 高等～ *institutions of higher learning*

【院长】president

【院子】courtyard; yard; compound: ～里驯不出千里马，温室里长不出万年松。*A fiery steed is not trained in a courtyard, nor does a pine grow sturdy in a green house.*

垸 ① [方] protective embankment in a riverside or lakeside area; levee: 堤～ *dyke; embankment*

【垸子】(used in Hunan and Hubei provinces, etc.) protective embankment around houses and fields

愿 [书] honest and prudent: 诚～ *honest and sincere*

愿 ① wish; hope; desire: 夙～ *long-cherished wish* ② vow (made before Buddha or a god): 许～ *make a vow* /还～ *redeem a vow* ③ be willing; be glad: 心甘情～ *be most willing; be perfectly happy* ④ [书] be willing to do what little one can; wish to render one's service

【愿望】wish; hope; desire; intention: 说说你的～吧！*Please say out your wishes.*

【愿意】① be willing; be ready: 我～帮助你。*I'm ready (or willing) to help you.* ② wish; want; hope: 全家人都～我出国。*The whole family wishes me to go abroad.*

yuē

曰 ① [书] say: 子～："学而时习之。" *The Master said, "Review what you learn from time to time."* ② call; name: 美其名～ *describe sth euphemistically as; give sth the fine-sounding name of*

约 ① make an appointment; arrange; agree: 他们～好在公园门口见面。*They agreed to meet at the park gate.* ② ask or invite in advance; engage: 我～了一位同事吃晚饭。*I invited a colleague to dinner.* ③ pact; treaty; agreement; appointment ④ check; restrict; restrain: ～束 *restrain; bind* ⑤ economical; thrifty; frugal: 节～ *economize* ⑥ simple; brief; succinct ⑦ about; around; or so; approximately: 大～一年 *about a year* ⑧ reduce (a fraction)

【约旦】Jordan: ～人 *Jordanian*

【约定】agree; appoint; arrange: 我们～在学校门口见面。*We agreed to meet at the gate of the school.*

【约定俗成】established by popular usage; approved by the people through long social practice; accepted through common practice

【约法】provisional constitution

【约法三章】agree on a three-point law — make or agree on a few simple rules to be observed by all concerned

【约分】【数】reduction of a fraction

【约会】① date; appointment; arrangement ② make an appointment; make an arrangement to meet: ～在火车站碰头 *arrange to meet at the railway station*

【约集】call together; invite to meet together; gather

【约计】count roughly; come approximately to: 赢利～二百万元。*The profit came approximately to two million yuan.*

【约见】make an appointment: 要求～美国大使 *ask*

for (or request) an appointment with the American ambassador

【约略】① rough; approximate: ~的估计 *a rough estimate* ② vaguely; dimly: ~知道一些 *know sth about*

【约莫】about; roughly; or so: ~一小时光景 *about an hour; an hour or so*

【约期】① agree on a date or time; fix or set a date; appoint a time ② fixed date; time of appointment: 记住咱们的~。*Remember the appointed time, please.* ③ term or duration of a contract or agreement

【约请】invite: ~某人到家里来 *invite sb to one's house*

【约束】① keep within bounds; restrain; constrain; bind: ~力 *binding force* / ~自己的感情 *restrain one's feelings* / 自我~ *self-discipline* / 不受传统观念的~ *be bound by no traditional ideas* ② restriction; restraint

【约数】① approximate number ② divisor

【约谈】make an appointment to talk over sth; arrange talks or discussions

yuè

月 ① moon: 新~ *crescent* ② month: 五~上旬 *first ten days of May* ③ monthly: ~收入 *monthly income* / ~刊 *monthly* (*magazine*) ④ full-moon shaped; round

【月报】① monthly (magazine) ② monthly report: ~统计表 *monthly statistical report*

【月饼】moon cake: 中秋~饼 *moon cake for the Mid-autumn Festival*

【月份】month: 出生的~ *the month in which one is born*

【月俸】monthly salary or pay

【月工】worker employed by the month; monthly worker

【月宫】① legendary palace on the moon ② moon

【月光】① moonlight; moonshine; moonbeam: 暗淡的~ *pale moonlight* ② [方] moon

【月桂树】【植】laurel; bay tree

【月黑天】moonless night; first and last days of the lunar month

【月黑头】[方] moonless night; dark night

【月季】【植】Chinese rose: 盆栽~ *potted Chinese rose*

【月经】menstruation; menstrual flow; (monthly) period: ~不调 *menoxenia; irregular (or abnormal) menstruation* / ~周期 *menstrual cycle*

【月刊】monthly (magazine): 艺术~ *art monthly*

【月利】monthly interest

【月亮】moon: ~门儿 *moon -shaped gate; arch*

【月面】moon surface: ~测量学 *selenodesy* / ~发射 *lunar departure; lift-off from the moon* / ~旅行车 *lunar rover* / ~学 *selenography* (*the study of the physical features of the moon's surface*) / ~图 *selenograph*

【月末】end of a month: 上~ *at the end of last month*

【月偏食】partial lunar eclipse

【月票】monthly ticket: 通用~ *monthly ticket for all urban and suburban lines*

【月夜】: moonlit night; moonlight night

【月钱】monthly pocket money (given to one's family members, apprentices, etc.)

【月琴】four-stringed moon-shaped Chinese mandolin

【月球】【天】moon: ~背面 *far side of the moon* / ~内部 *lunar interior* / ~土壤 *lunar soil* / ~车 *moon buggy* / ~飞船 *moon rah; moon ship; lunar space rah* / ~舱 *lunar module* / ~探测 *moon exploration* / ~学 *selenology* / ~仪 *lunar globe or sphere*

【月全食】total lunar eclipse

【月色】moonlight: 今晚的~美极了。*How beautiful the moonlight is tonight.*

【月事】[书] menstrual period; menstruation

【月台】① platform where people could stay and enjoy the moon ② platform built before the main hall of a palace, with a flight of steps on each of the other three sides ③ railway platform

【月坛】Altar of the Moon, Beijing

【月息】monthly interest

【月薪】monthly pay; monthly salary

【月牙】crescent (moon); new moon

【月夜】moonlit night; moonlight night: 这是一个多么美好的~啊! *What a moonlight night!*

【月晕】lunar halo

【月终】month-end; end of month: 又到了~结算的时候了。*It's time to settle accounts at the end of a month again.*

【月子】① month of confinement after childbirth: 坐~ *be in confinement* ② time of confinement; confinement: ~病 *puerperal fever*

乐 ① music: 声~ *vocal music* / 器~ *instrumental music* / 管~ *wind instrument music* / 古典~ *classical music* / 民~ *folk music* ② a surname

see also lè

【乐池】orchestra pit; orchestra

【乐段】【音】period

【乐队】band orchestra: 民~ *ethnic instruments orchestra* / 铜管~ *brass band* / 管弦~ *orchestra* / 军~ *military band* / 交响~ *symphony orchestra* / ~指挥 *conductor; bandmaster*

【乐府】① official conservatory set up in the Han Dynasty for the collection of folk songs and ballads ② folk songs or ballad in the Han style: ~民歌 *folk songs in the Han style; Han-styled folk songs*

【乐感】musicality; musical feeling; tonal quality

【乐句】【音】phrase

【乐理】【音】music theory: 他教了我很多~知识。*He taught me much knowledge of music theory.*

【乐律】【音】temperament

【乐迷】music aficionado; music devotee

【乐谱】music score; sheet music; music: ~架 *music stand* /他不识~。*He can not read a music score.*
【乐器】musical instrument; instrument: 管弦~ *wind and stringed instruments* /铜管~ *brass instrument*
【乐曲】(musical) composition; (a piece of) music
【乐师】music player; musician
【乐坛】musical circles: 她爸爸誉满~。*Her father enjoys high prestige in the musical world.*
【乐团】① philharmonic society ② philharmonic orchestra: 军~ *brass band* /中央~ *Central Philharmonic Orchestra*
【乐舞】dance with music accompaniment
【乐音】musical sound; tone
【乐章】【音】movement

岳 ① high mountain: 五~ *the famous Five mountains in China* /东~ *mount Tai in East China* ② wife's parents and parental uncles: 叔~ *wife's uncle; uncle-in-law* ③ (Yuè) a surname
【岳父】wife's father; father-in-law
【岳母】wife's mother; mother-in-law

钥 key

see also yào

阅 ① read; go over; scan; peruse: ~报 *read newspapers* ② review; inspect: ~兵 *review troops* ③ experience; undergo; pass though
【阅兵】review or inspect troops: ~场 *parade ground* /~台 *stand for reviewing a military parade*
【阅读】read: 你喜欢~吗? *Do you like reading?*
【阅卷】read and score (examination) papers; grade (examination) papers
【阅览】read: ~室 *reading room*
【阅历】① see, hear or do for oneself: 他有丰富的~。*He has rich experience.* ② experience: ~有限 *limited experience* /增长~ *enrich one's experience; gain experience*
【阅世】[书] see the world: ~颇深 *be deeply experienced in worldly affairs*

悦 ① happy; glad; pleased; delighted ② please; delight: 取~于人 *try to please sb* ③ (Yuè) a surname
【悦耳】pleasing to the ear; sweet: ~的音乐 *sweet music*
【悦服】enthusiastically agree; heartily admire
【悦目】pleasing to the eye; attractive; good-looking

跃 jump; leap: 一~而起 *get up with a jump* /~上马背 *leap onto a horse* /欢呼雀~ *leap to one's feet and cheer*
【跃动】jump; move up and down
【跃进】take a leap; leap forward; jump: 今年的工业生产呈现出~的局面。*This year's industrial production has increased by leaps and bounds.*
【跃居】leap or jump to: ~全国首位 *leap to first in the country; leap to lead the country*
【跃马】spur the horse on
【跃迁】【物】transition: ~概率 *transition probability*
【跃然】appear vividly
【跃然纸上】show graphically in one's writing
【跃跃欲试】be burning with eagerness for; be eager to have a go; itch for action

越[1] ① get over; jump over; cross: ~高山 *cross high mountains* ② exceed; overstep; pass: ~出范围 *overstep the bounds; exceed limits* /老人年~七十。*The old man is over seventy.* ③ (of voice, emotion) be at a high pitch; vigorous: 歌声清~ *sing in a clarion voice* /激~ *intense; vehement; loud and strong* ④ [书] loot: 杀人~货 *kill a person and seize his belonging; rob and kill*

越[2] ① used in duplicates: ~战~强。*The more one fights, the stronger one grows.* /~多~要。*The more one has, the more one wants.* /~早~好 *The earlier, the better.* /天气~变~糟。*The weather is getting tougher and tougher.* ② used in "越来…越…" more and more: ~好 *become better and better* /~有希望 *become increasingly hopeful* /~放肆 *become more and more intemperate*

越[3] ① eastern part of Zhejiang Province ② (Yuè) a surname
【越冬】live through the winter: ~作物 *winter crop; over wintering crop*
【越发】all the more; the more; even more: ~使人高兴 *please sb all the more*
【越轨】exceed the bounds; transgress; go beyond the limits
【越过】cross; traverse; surmount; negotiate: ~障碍 *surmount obstacles* /~边境 *cross the border* /~高山大河 *negotiate high mountains and big rivers*
【越级】① skip a grade or rank: ~提拔 *promote sb more than one grade at one time* ② bypass the immediate leadership: ~上报 *bypass the immediate leadership and submit one's complaint to a higher level*
【越加】even more; still more; all the more: 她想的越多,心里就~难过。*The more she thought of it, the angrier she became.*
【越界】overstep the boundary; cross the border
【越境】cross the boundary line illegally; sneak in or out of a country: ~走私分子 *smuggler who sneaks in and out of a country*
【越南】Vietnam: ~人 *Vietnamese* /~战争 *Vietnam War* (1955-1975)
【越权】exceed one's powers; overstep one's authority
【越位】【体】(of football, ice hokey, etc.) offside
【越洋】transoceanic: ~通信 *transoceanic communication*
【越野】cross-country: ~滑雪 *cross-country skiing* /~赛车 *off road racing* /~行驶 *cross-country run* /~汽车 *cross-country vehicle; cross-country car* /~赛跑 *cross-country race*
【越狱】break prison; escape from prison
【越俎代庖】exceed one's duties and meddle in other's affairs; take sb else's job into one's own hands; do on behalf of another sth not in one's own line

粤 ① Guangdong and Guangxi ② another name for Guangdong
【粤菜】Guangdong dishes; Guangdong food
【粤剧】Guangdong opera

yūn

晕 ① dizzy; giddy faint: 他有点头~。*He felt a little faint.* ② swoon; faint; lose consciousness; pass out: ~过去 *faint; lose consciousness; swoon*
see also yùn
【晕倒】fall (down) in a faint; faint; pass out: 今天早晨,他妈妈~了。*His mother fainted this morning.*
【晕动】motion sickness
【晕乎】dizzy; giddy
【晕厥】【医】syncope
【晕头晕脑】dizzy; muddle-headed: 这几天累的我~的。*I'm so tired these days that I am in a daze.*
【晕头转向】muddled; confused and disorientated
【晕眩】feel dizzy
【晕晕乎乎】① dizzy; giddy muddle-headed; in a daze ② muddle-headed

yún

云[1] ① say ② auxiliary word in classical Chinese
云[2] ① cloud: 浮~ *floating cloud* / 乌~滚滚 *dark rolling cloud* ② short for Yunnan province
云[3] ① Yunnan province ② (Yún) a surname
【云霭】thin, floating cloud
【云鬓】[书] thick, beautiful hair (of women): 梳理~ *comb her hair*
【云彩】[口] cloud
【云层】cloud layer
【云滴】【气】droplet; cloud drop
【云顶】【气】cloud top
【云端】high in the clouds
【云朵】mass of clouds; cloud
【云海】sea of clouds
【云鬟】(of woman's hair) bun
【云集】come together from various places; gather; converge
【云际】[书] high in the clouds
【云量】【气】cloud amount; cloudiness
【云母】【矿】mica: ~板岩 *mica-slate* / ~片 *mica sheet; sheet mica*
【云霓】cloud and secondary rainbow
【云气】thin, floating clouds
【云雀】【动】skylark
【云散】① disperse; scatter: 亲戚都~在不同的地方。*All the relatives go away to different places.* ② disappear; vanish: 烟消~ *disappear like smoke and cloud; vanish*
【云山雾罩】① enveloped in (cloud and) mist; heavy with mist ② discursive; confusing
【云杉】【植】dragon spruce
【云梯】scaling ladder: 架~ *erect (or fix, or set up) a scaling ladder*
【云天】sky
【云图】【气】cloud atlas; cloud chart; cloud picture
【云团】【气】cloud cluster
【云雾】cloud and mist; mist
【云霞】rosy clouds; rose-tinted clouds; pink clouds
【云消雾散】the clouds melt and the mists disperse — cease to exist; vanish into thin air
【云霄】the skies: 响彻~ *resound to the skies*
【云烟】cloud and smoke; mist and smoke
【云翳】grey clouds: 他母亲脸上总罩着一层忧郁的~。*His mother always looks gloomy.*
【云涌】① clouds scud ② emerge in large numbers; spring up; come to the fore
【云游】(of a Buddhist monk or Taoist priest) roam; wander: 他常年~四方。*He roams from place to place all the year.*
【云雨】[书] sexual intercourse; love-making
【云云】[书] and so on; and so on and so forth; etc.
【云遮雾障】heavy with cloud and mist; mist-laden; be enveloped in mist

匀 ① even; equitable: 分得不~ *be not evenly divided* ② even up; divide evenly ③ spare take from sth and give to sb: 你能把其中一个~给我吗? *Can you spare one of them for me?* / 我工作太忙,~不出时间来读小说。*I am too busy with my work to spare any time for reading fiction.*
【匀称】symmetry; well-proportioned; well-balanced; even
【匀兑】spare; divide and share
【匀和】① even; steady: 那个孩子睡着了,呼吸~。*The child slept with steady breathing.* ② even up; equalize
【匀净】even; in proportion; uniform
【匀脸】rub powder and paint evenly on one's face; rouge and powder evenly on one's face
【匀溜】[口] of uniform size, thickness, or density
【匀染】【纺】level dyeing: ~剂 *leveling agent*
【匀实】[口] even; uniform; neat: 这衣服又细密又~。*The clothes are of close and even texture.*
【匀速运动】【物】uniform motion
【匀调】even; regular; in proportion
【匀停】[方] be moderate
【匀妥】even and proper; equitable; fair
【匀细】neat; even
【匀整】tidy; even and orderly; neat and well-spaced

芸 【植】rue
【芸豆】【植】kidney bean
【芸香】【植】rue
【芸芸】[书] many; large amounts of; numerous: ~众生 *all living creatures; all living things; all*

mortal beings; numerous living beings

耘 weed: 耕~ *plough and weed; cultivate* / 春耕夏~,秋收冬藏。*Plough in spring, weed in summer, harvest in autumn and store in winter.*

【耘锄】【农】hoe

【耘田】weed the fields

筠 [书] ① green bamboo skin ② bamboo

yǔn

允¹ consent; grant; allow; permit

允² fair; just; impartial: 公~ *fair; equitable*

【允差】permissible margin of error or disparity

【允承】agree or promise to do sth; undertake: ~一个问题 *undertake a question*

【允从】consent to; assent to; agree to

【允当】proper; suitable

【允诺】commit oneself to; promise; consent; undertake: 欣然~ *readily consent; willingly allow*

【允许】agree to; allow; permit: 只~少数几个人入内。*Only a few are allowed inside.*

【允准】approve; permit; allow

陨 fall from the sky or outer space

【陨落】(of a heavenly body, meteorite, etc.) fall from the sky or outer space

【陨灭】① fall from the sky (or outer space) and burn up ② die; be killed; perish

【陨石】【天】aerolite: ~雨 *meteorite shower*

【陨铁】【天】siderite; meteorite iron; iron meteorite

【陨星】【天】meteorite: ~学 *meteoritics*

【陨越】[书] fail; neglect one's duty

殒 perish; die; pass away

【殒灭】[书] die; perish; meet one's death

【殒命】[书] meet one's death; perish

yùn

孕 ① pregnant: 她那时已怀有六个月的身~。*She was six months pregnant.* ② pregnancy: 避~ *avoid pregnancy; contraception*

【孕畜】pregnant domestic animal

【孕妇】pregnant woman

【孕期】pregnancy; gestation

【孕穗】booting: ~期 *booting stage*

【孕吐】【医】vomiting during pregnancy; morning sickness

【孕育】be pregnant with; give birth to; breed: 马克思的思想~了共产主义。*Marx's ideas gave birth to communism.* / 失业常会~社会的不安定. *Unemployment often breeds social unrest.*

运¹ ① be in motion; move: ~行 *move; be in motion; function* ② transport; carry: 客~ *passenger transport* / 货~ *freight transport* / 水~ *water transport* / 空~ *air transport; airlift* ③ use; wield; utilize: ~笔巧妙 *wield a pen with miraculous skill*

运² luck; fate; fortune; destiny: 不走~ *be out of luck; have no luck* / 走桃花~ *be lucky in love affair*

【运笔】wield a pen in writing or painting; write or paint with a brush: 他擅长于书法,总是~如飞。*He is good at handwriting and always quick in writing.*

【运程】【交】haul

【运筹】devise strategies; draw up plans: ~管理 *operations management* / ~学 *operational research*

【运筹帷幄】devise strategies in a tent: ~之中,决胜千里之外 *plan strategies within a command tent and ensure victory on the battle front a thousand li away*

【运道】[方] luck; fortune

【运动】(yùndòng) ① motion; movement: 物质~ *motion of matter* / 曲线~ *curvilinear motion* / 机械~ *mechanical movement* ② sports; exercise; athletics: ~场 *sports ground; playground; stadium* / ~服装 *sportswear* / ~会 *sports meet; games* / ~健将 *master of sports* / ~量 *amount of (physical) exercises* / ~衫 *sports shirt* / ~神经 *nerve* / ~学 *kinematics* / ~医学 *sports medicine* / ~员 *sportsman; sportswoman; athlete; player* / ~战 *mobile war or warfare* / 田径~ *track and field sports; athletics* / 室内~ *indoor sports* / 户外~ *outdoor sports* / 散步是一种很好的~。*Walking is a very good sport.* ③ (political) movement; campaign: 学生的爱国~ *the students' patriotic movement*

【运动】(yùndong) arrange things through pull; canvas: 暗中~ *make secret arrangements*

【运费】transport expenses; freight; carriage; fare: ~免付 *carriage free* / ~已付 *freight paid* / ~表 *freight list* / ~率 *freight rate*

【运河】canal: 大~ *Grand Canal* / 苏伊士~ *Suez Canal* / ~税 *canal fees or tolls*

【运力】means of transport

【运量】freight volume; traffic

【运气】(yùnqì) (the art of) directing one's strength, through concentration to a part of the body: 小伙子运了~,然后猛地抓起铁桶。*The young man took a deep breath and, through an exertion of strength, grasped the metal bucket and lifted it high above his head.*

【运气】(yùnqi) ① fate; lot: 碰~ *try one's luck; take one's chance* ② lucky; fortunate: 他今天真~,买奖券中了奖。*He is lucky today, drawing a prize winning ticket in the lottery.*

【运球】【体】(in basketball or field hockey) dribble

【运神】[方] mull over; ponder; contemplate

【运输】transport; carriage; conveyance: ~船 *cargo ship; transports ship* / ~队 *transport team* / ~方式 *mode of transport* / ~工具 *means of trans-*

port; conveyance / ~公司 transport company / ~业 transport service; carrying trade; transport

【运输机】①【航】transport plane; air freighter ② conveyor

【运数】[书] fortune; destiny; lot:她已经没了~。*Her days numbered.*

【运送】transport; carry; ship; convey

【运算】【数】operation; calculation:快速~ *fast calculating* / ~微积分 *operational calculus* / ~误差 *arithmetic error*

【运腕】use one's wrist (so as to control the tip of brush)

【运销】transport and sale (of commodities)

【运行】move; be in motion; be in action; be in operation:火车现在正在~。*The train is in motion right now.*

【运营】① (of vehicles or ships) open to service; put into operation:他的公司已经投入~。*His company has put into commission.* ② operate; run; ply

【运用】utilize; apply; use; put into practice; wield:她爸爸~手中的权利,帮她办了不少事情。*Her father used his power to do a lot of things for her.*

【运用自如】use or handle very skillfully; have a perfect command of; use sth with ease:历史和艺术在他笔下~。*He is expert at history and art to good use.*

【运载】carry; deliver; convey:用车~货物 *carry good in a vehicle* / ~导弹 *mother missiles* / ~飞机 *mother aircraft* / ~工具 *launch vehicle; means of delivery; carrier* / ~火箭 *carrier rocket* / ~技术 *delivery technology*

【运转】① move in a circular orbit; revolve; turn round:行星绕着太阳~。*The planets revolve around the sun.* ② work; operate:机器~正常。*The machine is running well.*

【运作】function:经济~ *functioning of the economy*

晕 ① dizzy; giddy faint; sick:头~目眩 *have a giddy spell; be afflicted with vertigo* ② halo:日~ *solar halo* / 月~ *lunar halo* ③ haze or halo round some colour or light:看到她的男朋友,她的脸上泛起了红~。*On seeing her boyfriend, she blushed on her face.*
see also yūn

【晕舱】【航】space sickness; motion sickness

【晕场】(of students taking an exam or an actor giving a performance) be so nervous as to faint; have stage fright

【晕车】be carsick:她好~。*She is susceptible to carsickness.*

【晕船】be seasick

【晕高儿】[方] feel dizzy when climbing high

【晕机】be airsick

【晕针】be afflicted with vertigo when being given an injection or under acupuncture

酝 ① make wine ② wine

【酝酿】① ferment ② [喻] brew; ferment: ~起义 *ferment an uprising* / 脑子里~着一个计划 *a plan fermented in one's mind* ③ have a preliminary informal discussion; deliberate on: ~经理名单 *consider and talk over the list of manager*

愠 [书] angry; irritated

【愠怒】be inwardly angry

【愠色】gloomy countenance

韵 ① musical or agreeable sound ② rhyme:押~ *be in rhyme* ③ charm:她是一个很有风~的女人。*She is a graceful woman.*

【韵脚】the rhyming word that ends a line of verse; rhyme

【韵律】① metre in verse ② rules of rhyming; rhyme scheme

【韵母】【语】single or compound vowel of a Chinese syllable

【韵事】① literary or artistic pursuits, often with pretence to good taste and refinement ② romantic affair

【韵书】rhyming dictionary

【韵味】lingering charm; lasting appeal:他的唱腔很有~。*His singing has a special pleasing quality about it.*

【韵文】literary composition in rhyme; verse

【韵致】poise and charm

蕴 accumulate; hold in store; contain

【蕴藏】hold in store; contain: ~着丰富的石油资源 *be rich in oil resources* / ~在原子里面的能量 *energy stored in atomic nuclear*

【蕴涵】① contain ② implication

【蕴藉】[书] temperate and refined; cultured and restrained

熨 iron; press: ~衣服 *iron or press clothes*
see also yù

【熨斗】flatiron; iron

【熨衣板】ironing board

Z

zā

扎 ① fasten; tie; bind: ~辫子 *tie up one's plaits; plait one's hair; wear one's hair in plaits* / ~一根黄头带 *tie one's plait with a piece of yellow yarn* / 用皮带~腰 *tie a leather belt around one's waist* / 带子~得紧。*The string is tied tight.* ② [量] bundle: 一~票 *a bundle of tickets*
see also zhā; zhá

【扎把子】[方] ① bind in a bundle ② unite closely

【扎彩】hang up streamers or festoons

【扎筏子】[方] give vent to one's anger; vent one's spite on sb

【扎染】【纺】tie-dye: ~衣服 *tie-dyed clothes*

匝 [书] ① circle; circumference: 绕树四~ *circle a tree four times* ② surround; encircle; revolve around ③ dense; full; whole: 密密~~ *thick; dense*

【匝道】[书] ring road

【匝地】[书] everywhere; all over

咂 ① sip; suck: ~一口水 *take a suck of water* ② make clicks of one's lips (in admiration, praise, surprise, etc.): ~着嘴 *with a smack of the lips* ③ taste or savour carefully

【咂摸】[方] savour; taste: ~不懂 *beyond one's comprehension or understanding; fail to know the meaning of sth* / 我一直在~她的话是什么意思。*I have been turning her words in my mind and trying to figure out what the really mean.*

【咂嘴】make clicks; smack one's lips (of admiration, agreement, surprise, etc.): 他对我的话,~赞同。*He clicked his tongue in agreement with my words.*

【咂嘴弄舌】① greedy; envious ② self-satisfied

zá

杂 ① miscellaneous; sundry; mixed; diverse; varied: ~事儿 *miscellaneous affairs* / 公务繁~ *miscellaneous official duties* / ~而乱 *mixed and confused* / 人很~。*People are mixed here.* ② extra; irregular ③ mix; mingle; combine: 警察混~在人群中。*The policemen mingled with the crowd.* / 花园中~有几株小树。*There is a scattering of little trees in the garden.*

【杂拌儿】① assorted preserved fruits; mixed sweetmeats: ~糖 *assorted candies* ② mixture; miscellany; medley; hotchpotch or hodgepodge: 这个果园是个~,有苹果树,梨树,桃树,还有杏树。*The orchard is a miscellany of apples, pears, peaches and apricots.*

【杂草】weeds; rank grass

【杂处】(of people from different places) live in one place; live together

【杂凑】put together at random; jumble up; knock together: 这场节目是~起来的。*The performance was put together at random.*

【杂肥】subsidiary fertilizers; miscellaneous fertilizers, such as refuse from cities, etc.

【杂费】① miscellaneous expense; incidental expense; incidentals: 削减~开支 *reduce miscellaneous expenses* ② sundry fees; sundry charges; extras

【杂感】① random thoughts; sundry impressions; stray thoughts: 一点~ *a few random remarks* ② a type of literature that record such thoughts: ~集 *collection of random thoughts*

【杂烩】① a stew of various ingredients; mixed stew; hotchpotch: 荤~ *assorted meat delicacies* / 素~ *assorted vegetarian delicacies* / 炒~ *stir-fried mixed delicacies* ② mixture; miscellany; olio; medley

【杂活儿】odd jobs; sundry duties

【杂货】groceries; sundry goods: ~店 *grocery; sundry store; variety store; general store*

【杂记】① jottings; notes: 旅行~ *notes of a journey* ② miscellanies (as a type of literature): 西京~ *miscellany of the Western Capital*

【杂家】① the Eclectics, a school of thought flourishing at the end of the Warring States Period and the beginning of the Han Dynasty ② eclectic; jack-of-all-trades

【杂件】odds and ends; sundry goods: 日用~ *small articles of daily use*

【杂交】【生】hybridize; crossbreed; cross: 无性~ *vegetative (or asexual) hybridization* / 有性~ *sexual hybridization* / ~繁殖 *crossing; crossbreeding* / ~水稻 *hybrid rice* / ~玉米 *hybrid or crossbred maize*

【杂居】(of two or more nationalities or ethnic groups) live in one place: 多民族~地 *areas inhabited by many nationalities or ethnic groups* / 少数民族~地 *areas inhabited by several minority nationalities*

【杂粮】food grains other than wheat and rice; coarse cereals; coarse food grains (e.g. maize, sorghum, barley, oat, millet, etc.)

【杂乱】untidy; chaotic; confused; in a jumble; in a muddle; mired and disorderly: 书桌上的东西很～。*The things on the desk were all in a jumble.*
【杂乱无章】disorderly and unsystematic; jumbled; incoherent; chaotic: ～的议论 *random remarks*
【杂面】① flour made from various coarse cereals and beans ② noodles made from such flour
【杂木】【林】weed tree
【杂念】distracting thoughts; selfish considerations: 工作不能掺杂个人私心～。*One should not let personal considerations interfere with one's work.*
【杂牌】a less known and inferior brand: ～产品 *goods of an inferior brand* /～军 *miscellaneous troops; troops of miscellaneous allegiances* /这台电视是～的。*The TV set is of inferior quality.*
【杂品】sundry goods; groceries; odds and ends: 谁来清理这些～? *Who will sort out the odds and ends?*
【杂七杂八】mixed; assorted; miscellaneous; motley: ～的想法 *eclectic ideas* /屋里～堆得满满的。*The room is crammed with junk.*
【杂散】【物】stray: ～磁场 *stray magnetic field* / ～电流 *stray current*
【杂色】① variegated; motley: ～布料 *multi-coloured cloth; cloth of various colours* ② less known or inferior brand
【杂生】【植】intergrowth
【杂食】eating all kinds of things; omnivorous: ～动物 *omnivorous animal*
【杂事】trivial matters; sundry matters of daily life
【杂书】① non-essential books (not directly related to the subject of the imperial examination) ② books not directly pertaining to one's field of studies: 不要读一些～。*Don't read miscellaneous books.*
【杂耍】[旧] variety show; vaudeville
【杂税】miscellaneous levies; sundry taxes
【杂坛】acrobatics circles: ～新秀 *new stars in acrobatics*
【杂文】essay; satirical essay: ～家 *essayist*
【杂务】odd jobs; sundry duties
【杂音】① noise ②【电】static ③【医】murmur; souffle: 心脏～ *heart murmur*
【杂院儿】a compound occupied by many households
【杂志】① magazine: 买～ *buy a magazine* ② (usu. used as title of books) records; notes; miscellaneous notes: ～架 *magazine rack*
【杂质】① impurity: 将酒过滤除去其中～ *filter the win to remove its impurities* ②【化】foreign matter or substance
【杂种】①【生】hybrid; crossbreed: ～牛 *crossbred cattle* ② bastard; son of a bitch

砸 ① pound; tamp; crush: ～实地基 *tamp the foundations solid* /搬起石头～自己的脚 *pick up a stone only to drop it on one's own feet* ② break; smash; shatter: 杯子～了。*The glass is broken.* ③ [方] *fail; fall through; be bungled; foul up*: 在上次的考试中他又考～了。*He failed again in last examination.*
【砸饭碗】be fired; lose one's job; smash sb's rice bowl; dismiss sb from his job
【砸锅】[方] fail; fall through; be bungled; come a cropper
【砸锅卖铁】spend one's entire fortune; give a way all one has
【砸碎】break into pieces; smash; shatter

zǎ

咋 how; why; what: 你～这样? *How could you do things like that?*
see also zhā
【咋个】[方] how; why: 他的父亲～晓得? *How could his father know?*

zāi

灾 ① calamity; disaster: 天～ *natural disaster* ② personal misfortune; ill luck; mishap; adversity: 牢狱之～ *be in prison* /多～多难 *be dogged by misfortunes and mishaps* /没病～灾 *good health and good luck*
【灾害】calamity; disaster; misfortune
【灾患】calamity; disaster
【灾荒】famine due to crop failures; famine: 去年这里闹～。*Famine hit here last year.*
【灾祸】disaster; calamity; catastrophe; adversity
【灾民】victims of natural calamity; afflicted people
【灾难】suffering; calamity; disaster; catastrophe: ～深重 *long suffering; disaster-ridden*
【灾年】famine (or lean) year
【灾歉】crop failure due to natural disasters
【灾情】the condition of a disaster or the damage caused by a disaster: ～有所减轻。*The losses caused by the disaster have been mitigated.*
【灾区】disaster area; afflicted area: 旱～ *drought-stricken area* /水～ *flooded area*

哉 [书] ① indicating exclamation ② used together with an interrogative word to ask a question or make a retort: 有何难～? *What's so difficult about it?*

栽[1] ① plant; grow: ～水稻 *transplant rice seedlings* / ～松树 *plant pines* / ～花 *grow flowers* ② insert; plant; erect; stick in: ～牌子 *erect a sign* ③ force or impose sth on sb ④ young plant; seedling

栽[2] ① seeding tumble; topple; fall: ～跤 *trip and fall* ② set back; frustrate
【栽跟头】① tumble; fall; go head over heels ② suffer a setback; come a cropper: 他～后,才明白事理。*He saw sense until he came to grief.*
【栽培】① cultivate; grow: ～技术 *cultivation techniques* /玫瑰～ *the culture of roses* /谷物～ *cereals cultivation* ② foster; train; educate; instruct ③ help advance sb's career; patronize; support and

encourage: ~品种 *cultivar* / ~植物 *cultivated plant*

Z

【栽诬】falsely accuse; fabricate a charge against sb; slander: ~好人 *trump up a charge against an innocent person*

【栽秧】transplant seedings (of tomatoes or eggplant, etc.)

【栽养】plant and cultivate: ~树苗 *cultivate saplings*

【栽赃】① plant stolen or contraband goods on sb ② frame sb; fabricate a charge against sb

【栽植】plant; transplant; grow: ~机 *planting machine*

【栽种】plant; grow

zǎi

载[1] year: 三年五~ *three of five years*

载[2] put down in writing; record: 连~ *publish in instalments; serialize* / ~入书本 *record in books* / 报~ *according to press reports* / 契约~明 *be clearly stated in the treaty*
see also zài

【载入史册】be written into the annals of history; go down in history

宰[1] ① govern; rule; be in charge of; head: 主~自己的未来 *decide one's own future; have one's fate in his own hand* ② (in ancient times) government official

宰[2] ① slaughter; butcher: 屠~牲畜 *slaughter animals; butcher fat stock* ② [口] overcharge; fleece; soak; rip off: ~人 *rip off sb* / 挨~ *be made to pay much more for what one gets' be ripped off*

【宰割】invade, oppress and exploit; persecute

【宰杀】slaughter; butcher

【宰相】prime minister (in feudal China); chancellor

【宰相肚里能撑船】a prime minister's heart is big enough to pole a boat in — be large-minded; be broad minded

崽 ① son ② young man; young animal: 打工~ *young manual worker* ③ young animal; whelp: 猪~ *piglets*

【崽子】whelp; bastard; brat

zài

再 ① again; once more; further; another time: 我不能~吃了。*I can't eat any more.* ② to a greater extent or degree; more: 这事~好不过了。*It couldn't be better.* / ~冷的天也得去上学。*Even if it were colder, we should go to school.* / 这道题~简单不过了。*The problem is too simple.* ③ indicating the continuing of a situation in condition or suppositional clauses ④ indicating that one action takes place after the completion of another; then, only then: 做完运动~休息一下。*Have a rest after you do exercises.* ⑤ in addition; on top of that; still: 到场的有工人,农民,~就是明星。*Present at the meeting are workers, farmers and also stars.* ⑥ (followed by a negative expression) no matter how... still (not): 工作~难也得完成。*The work is to be done no matter how hard it is.*

【再版】① second edition ② [旧] reprint; second impression or printing

【再不】[口] or else; or; if not: 叫张明去,~小王也行。*Send Zhang Ming, or else Xiao Wang.*

【再次】once more; a second time; once again: ~发生事故 *the taking place of accidents one more time*

【再度】once more; one more time

【再分配】【经】redistribution

【再会】goodbye; see you again

【再婚】remarry; marry again

【再嫁】(of a woman) remarry

【再见】good-bye; see you again

【再接再厉】make persistent efforts; continue to exert oneself; advance from strength to strength: 只有~,才能取得更好的成绩。*Only can we work ceaselessly and unremittingly, we will achieve still better results.*

【再就业】re-employment; find jobs again; be re-employed

【再起】recurrence; resurgence; return; revival: ~事端 *the recurrence of disturbances*

【再三】over and over again; time and again; again and again; repeatedly: 他~要求留下来。*He wants to stay here again and again.*

【再审】① review ②【律】retrial

【再生】① revive; rise again; be a second so and so: 他手艺巧得如同他师傅~。*His carpentry is so exquisite that he is really like his teacher.* ②【生】regeneration ③ reprocess; recycle; regenerate: ~能源 *renewable source of energy* / ~橡胶 *reclaimed or regenerated rubber*

【再生】【经】reproduction

【再说】put off until some time later; not consider or tackle a problem until some other time: 这事过几天~。*Let's put the matter aside for a few days.* / 等找到合适的人~。*Wait until suitable person has been found.* ② what's more; besides; moreover: 现在去超市购物太晚了,~我也不熟悉路。*It's too late to go to the supermarket shopping; besides, I don't quite know the way.*

【再贴现】【经】rediscount

【再投资】【经】reinvest; plough back

【再现】(of a past event) reappear; be reproduced: 离别时的情景生动地~在银幕上。*The parting scene reappeared vividly on the screen.*

【再造】① give sb a new lease of life ② restore lost limbs or any other body part important made from macro-molecular materials: 手指~技术 *finger restructuring technique*

【再者】[书] what is more; further more; besides

在 ① exist; be alive:我父母都还健在。*My parents are both living and in robust health.* ② be at, in or an (a place):我今晚~家。*I am at home tonight.* /书~桌子上。*The book is on the desk.* ③ depend on; rest with:来不来~她自己。*It's up to her whether she will come or not.* /事~人为。*Human effort is the decisive factor.* /贵~坚持。*The most important thing is perseverance.* ④ remain:~校学生 *in-school student* /~职员工 *staff and workers on the regular payroll* ⑤ join or belong to an organization; be a member of an organization:她~外交部工作。*She works with Ministry of Foreign Affairs.* ⑥ be on the job or at the post ⑦ at, in, or on (a place or time); indicating time, place, condition, scope, etc.:~光天化日之下 *in broad daylight* /~最后时刻 *at the eleventh hour* /~此期间 *during this period* ⑧ indicating an action in progress:我~做作业。*I'm doing my homework.* /你~干什么? *What are you doing?*

【在案】be on record

【在编】(of personnel) be on the permanent staff; be on the regular payroll

【在场】be on the scene; be on the spot; be present:当时他不~。*He wasn't there at the time.*

【在岗】be at one's post; on duty; employed

【在行】be expert at sth; know the ropers; be a professional:我对烹调很~。*I know a lot about cooking.* /他打篮球~。*He is good at playing basketball.*

【在乎】① depend on; rest with:去不去~你自己。*It's up to you whether you go or not.* ② lie in; consist in:要办好事情,~心齐。*Success depends on unity of purpose.* ③ (usu. used in the negative) care about; bother about; mind; take to heart:满不~ *couldn't care less*; *not care a bit* /你~这种事吗? *Do you mind such kind of things?*

【在即】near at hand; shortly; soon:寒假~。*The winter vacation is near at hand.* /节目开幕~。*The performance will be held shortly.*

【在家】① be at home; be in:今晚我~。*I'll be in tonight.* ② have not renounced the family and become a layman:~办公 *telecommuting*

【在建】under construction

【在劫难逃】it is impossible to escape one's doom; what is destined cannot be avoided; if you're doomed; you're doomed; there's no escape

【在理】reasonable; sensible; right

【在内】included; including:所有同学,我~,都要参加晚会。*All the students, including me, should take part in the ball.*

【在世】be living; be above ground:人生~应有所作为。*One should accomplish something worthwhile in one's life-time.*

【在所不辞】will not decline under any circumstances; will not hesitate to

【在所难免】can hardly be avoided; be unavoidable:由于时间有限,错误~。*There are bound to be errors in the essay which time is limited.*

【在逃】【律】has escaped; be at large:~犯 *escaped criminal*; *criminal at large*; *fugitive*

【在天之灵】soul of the deceased resting in heaven (said when thinking fondly of a dead person)

【在外】① be away; be out:出门~ *be away from home* ② apart from; excluding; not including

【在望】① be visible; be in sight; come in view ② will soon materialize; be in sight; be round the corner

【在位】① be on the throne; reign ② be at one's post; be on the job

【在握】be in one's hands; be within one's grasp; be quite certain; be under one's control

【在先】① formerly; in the past; before ② in advance; beforehand

【在线】【电】on-line:~服务网 *on-line service network*

【在押】【律】be under detention; be in custody; be in prison:~犯 *criminal in custody*; *prisoner*

【在野】be out of office; be on opposition:~党 *a party not in office*; *opposition party*

【在意】(usu. used in the negative) take notice of; care about; pay attention to; mind:他从不~金钱。*He won't take such trifles on money.*

【在业】employed; having a job:~人口 *the working population*

【在于】① depend on; rest with; be deter mined by ② lie in; consist in

【在职】be on the job; be employed; be at one's post:~人员 *people in employment* /~期间 *during one's tenure of office* /~干部 *cadres at their posts*; *cadres at work*

【在座】be present (at a meeting, banquet; etc.); participate in:~的客人 *guests present here*

载¹ ① bring; carry; be loaded with ② be filled with ③ (Zài) a surname

载² [书] and; at the same time; moreover:~歌~舞 *festively singing and dancing*

see also zǎi

【载波】carrier wave; carrier:~电流 *carrier current* /~电话 *carrier telephone*

【载歌载舞】singing and dancing joyously; festively singing and dancing

【载荷】load

【载货】carry cargo; carry freight:~卡车 *lorry*; *truck* /~容积 *cargo carrying capacity*

【载客】carry passengers

【载人】【航】manned:~飞行器 *manned vehicle*

【载体】*carrier*; *vehicle*; *medium*:数据~ *data carrier*

【载途】① passage; transit ② be filled with

【载誉】be highly acclaimed; win great honour:同学们~归来。*The students came back with flying honour.*

【载运】carry; ship; transport

【载重】load; carrying capacity:~量 *loading capacity* /~线 *load line*

Z

zān

簪 ① hairpin：玉～ *jade hairpin* ② wear in one's hair：～花 *wear flowers in one's hair*

【簪子】hair clasp；hairpin

zán

咱 ① we or us (including both the speaker and the person or person spoken to)：～爸～妈 *our parents* ②［方］I or me：～不明白。*I don't understand.*

【咱们】① we or us (including both the speaker and the person or persons spoken to)：～要相互帮助。*We must help each other.* ② I or me：～说话只会直来直去。*I can only put this bluntly.* ③［方］you：～从哪来？*Where are you from?*

zǎn

攒 accumulate；hoard；save；collect：～钱 *save (or scrape) up money* / 积～ *save (or collect) bit by bit*

see also cuán

趱 ①［旧］hurry (or rush) through：紧～一程 *rush through one part of the journey* ② urge；hasten；press：～马向前 *spur a horse on or urge on a horse*

zàn

暂 ① of short duration；transient；brief：巴克利的一生是短～而光荣的。*Barclay's life was short but glorious.* ② temporarily；for the moment；for the time being：～别 *temporary separation* / 学习～告一段落。*The study has been brought to a temporary close.*

【暂定】arranged for the time being；tentative；provisional：～办法 *provisional measures*；*tentative measure*

【暂缓】put off；postpone；defer；suspend：～执行 *put off carrying out* / ～出行 *postpone one's trip* / ～决定 *defer (or put off) making a decision*

【暂且】temporarily；for the time being；for the moment：工作～告一段落。*Let's stop the work temporarily.*

【暂缺】① (of a post) be left vacant temporarily ② (of a commodity) be out of stock at the moment

【暂时】① temporary；transient ② temporarily；for the time being；for the moment：我～去不了。*I can't go right away.* / 他～不能给你回复。*He is not able to answer you right now.*

【暂停】① suspend；discontinue：～付款 *suspend payment* ②【体】sports time-out

【暂行】provisional；interim；temporary：～条例 *provisional regulations* / ～法规 *provisional rules and decrees* / ～办法 *temporary measures*

錾 ① engrave on gold or silver；carve ② engraving tool；chisel；graver

【錾刀】(engraver's) burin；graver

【錾子】chisel (for cutting stone)；cold chisel

赞 ① support；favour；assist：～和 *agree with*；*approve of* ② praise；commend：～慕 *admire* / ～佩 *esteem*；*admire* ③ eulogy：像～ *an inscription eulogizing the subject of a portrait*

【赞比西河】Zambezi River, an African river flowing through Angola, Zambia and Mozambique to the Indian Ocean

【赞比亚】Zambia：～人 *Zambian*

【赞不绝口】be profuse in praise；be full of praise；praise unceasingly

【赞成】① approve of；favour；agree with；assent：我不～你的意见。*I don't agree with you.* / 她完全～。*She is all for it.* / 老师最不～学生这样做。*Teachers don't like the way the students do it at all.* ②［书］help accomplish：～票 *affirmative vote*

【赞歌】song of praise；paean；hymn：她给我们唱了一曲友谊的～。*She sang the praise of friendship.*

【赞美】praise；eulogize；extol：～诗 *hymn*；*psalm*；*chant* / 他的勤奋受到同学的～。*He was praised for his diligence by his classmates.*

【赞赏】think highly of；appreciate；admire

【赞颂】extol；eulogize；sing the praise of；laud

【赞叹】gasp in (or with) admiration；highly praise；marvel at：画家高超的技巧令人～。*People gasped with admiration at the superb skill of the artist.*

【赞同】approve of；agree with；accept；endorse：他～这次我们的行动。*He did approve of our action.*

【赞许】speak favourable of；praise；commend：他的脸上露出了～的微笑。*The approving smiles appear his face.*

【赞扬】speak highly of；pay tribute to；praise；commend：～孩子的进步 *praise the children for their progress* / 您的成绩值得～。*Your success deserves commendation.*

【赞语】words of praise；praise

【赞誉】praise；acclaim；commend；approve：饭后的优质服务受到客人的～。*The hotel's fine service has won the commendation of guests.*

【赞助】support；assistance；aid

zāng

赃 ① stolen goods；booty；spoils；loot：窝～ *harbour stolen goods*；*conceal booty* ② bribes；embezzled money or goods：贪～枉法 *take bribes and bend the law*；*pervert justice for a bribe*

【赃官】a corrupt official; dishonest official
【赃款】stolen money; accepted bribes; illicit money: 退还 ~ *return the bribes*
【赃物】① stolen goods; booty; loot; spoils ② bribes; embezzled money or goods
脏 dirty; filthy; unclean: 别把新衣服弄 ~ 了。*Don't dirty your new clothes.*
see also zàng
【脏话】dirty word; obscene (or dirty, foul) language; obscenities; four-letter word: 说 ~ *talk dirty; use filthy and dirty words* / 满口 ~ *foul-mouthed*
【脏乱】dirty and disorderly; untidy; dirty and messy
【脏钱】[口] ill-gotten money; illegal or immoral earnings; filthy money
【脏土】rubbish; garbage; dirt; dust
【脏污】① dirty; filthy: ~ 的手 *dirty hands* / ~ 的想法 *dirty idea* ② stain; soil: 我骂他还嫌 ~ 了我的嘴呢。*Talking dirty to him I shall only be fouling myself.*
【脏字】obscene word; swearword; dirty word; rude word: 他说话总是带 ~。*He always speaks in abusive terms.*

zàng

脏 internal organs of the body, such as the heart, liver, spleen, lungs and kidneys; viscera: 心 ~ *heart* / 肝 ~ *liver*
see also zāng
【脏器】internal organs of the body; viscera
葬 bury; inter; consign to the grave: 安 ~ *bury (the dead)*
【葬礼】*funeral (or burial) rives, funeral*
【葬身】*be buried*: ~ 大海 *lose one's life in the sea; be drowned* / 死无 ~ 之地 *die without a burial place — come to a bad end*
【葬送】ruin; wreck; spell an end to: ~ 了前程 *ruin one's future (or prospects, or career)* / 她哥哥 ~ 了她一生幸福。*Her elder brother condemned her unhappy marriage life.*
【葬仪】funeral; funeral rites
藏1 ① storing place; depository: 发掘宝 ~ *unearth buried treasure; tap mineral resources* ② Buddhist or Taoist scriptures
藏2 ① Xizang (or Tibet) Autonomous Region: ~ 南地区 *southern Tibet* ② the Zang ethnic group
see also cáng
【藏蓝】purplish blue
【藏青】dark blue
【藏语】Tibetan language

zāo

遭1 meet with (disaster, misfortune, etc.); sustain; suffer: ~ 遇敌人 *meet with the enemy* / ~ 险 *run into danger* / 屡 ~ 挫折 *suffer repeated setbacks*
遭2 ① round: 用绳子绕两 ~ *wind the string around twice* ② time; turn: 这是他头一 ~ 在生人面前讲话。*It is the first time he has ever spoken before strangers.*
【遭到】suffer; meet with; encounter; sustain: 他 ~ 了妻子的拒绝。*He was turned down by his wife.*
【遭劫】meet with catastrophe; come face to face with calamity
【遭难】meet with misfortune; suffer disaster
【遭遇】① meet with; encounter; run up against; come across: ~ 不幸 *meet with misfortune; have hard luck* ② (bitter) experience; (hapless) fate; (hard) lot
【遭灾】be hit by a natural calamity; suffer disaster
【遭罪】endure hardships, tortures, rough conditions, etc.; have a hard time; suffer
糟 ① distillers' grains; grains ② be pickled with grains or in wine: ~ 鱼 *pickled fish; fish pickled with grains or in wine* ③ rotten; poor; worn out: 他爸爸的健康状况很 ~。*His father is in very poor health condition.* ④ in a wretched state; in a mess: 你把事情搞 ~ 了。*You have made a mess of the matter.* / ~ 了, 迟到了。*Oh, blast! We are late.*
【糟糕】[口] how terrible; what bad luck; too bad: 真 ~, 电视机坏了。*What bad luck; the TV set is out of work.*
【糟践】[方] ① waste; damage; ruin; spoil: ~ 粮食 *waste grain* ② insult; trample on; ravage: ~ 人 *insult sb* ③ violate (a woman); rape; ravage
【糟糠】distillers' grains, husks, chaff, etc. — things used by the poor to allay hunger
【糟糠之妻】the wife of one's "chaff and husks" days; woman married to a man before he became prosperous; wife who shared her husband's hard lot
【糟粕】waste matter; dross; dregs
【糟蹋】① waste; ruin; spoil; damage: ~ 光阴 *idle away one's time* ② insult; trample on; ravage; ride roughshod over: 不能随便 ~ 人。*Don't insult the others in such dreadful terms.* ③ violate (a woman); rape; ravish
【糟心】vexed; annoyed; dejected; depressed: 这样的结果真是 ~。*We are really vexed the result has turned out this way.*

záo

凿1 ① chisel: 冷 ~ *a cold chisel* ② cut a hole; bore a hole; chisel; dig: ~ 个窟窿 *bore a hole*

凿[2]［书］certain; sure; authentic; irrefutable

【凿井】① dig (or sink, bore) a well ②【矿】shaft sinking; pit sinking: 冻结法～ *freeze sinking*

【凿空】［书］forced; farfetched; implausible: ～之谈 *irrelevant talk*

【凿岩】【矿】(rock) drilling: ～机 *rock drill*

【凿子】chisel

zǎo

早 ① (early) morning: 今天～上我起晚了。*I got up very late this morning.* ② long time ago; as early as; for a long time: 我～就想和你聊天了。*I have wanted to have a chat with you.* ③ early, in advance; beforehand: ～睡～起 *go to bed early and get up early; early to bed and early to rise* / ～知如此,我就不来了。*If I'd known this before I would not have come here.* / 他～两年就出国了。*He has gone abroad two years before.* / 会议开始还～呢。*It's still quite a while before the film starts.*

【早安】good morning

【早班】morning shift: 上～ *be on the morning shift*

【早餐】breakfast

【早操】morning exercises

【早茶】morning tea

【早产】【医】premature delivery

【早场】morning show (at a cinema, theatre, etc.)

【早车】morning train or coach

【早晨】(early) morning

【早春】early spring; early in spring

【早稻】early (season) rice

【早点】(light) breakfast

【早饭】breakfast

【早婚】marry too early: ～在某些国家仍然存在。*It is still exists in some countries to get married at an early age.*

【早年】① many years ago; in the past ② in one's early years

【早期】early stage; early phase; early days; initial stage: ～作品 *sb's early works*

【早起】get up early; rise early

【早秋】early autumn; early in autumn

【早日】at an early date; early; soon: ～竣工 *complete the project as soon as possible* / 请～答复。*Your early reply is requested.*

【早上】(early) morning: ～好。*Good morning.*

【早市】① morning market; morning fair ② morning business; morning business transactions: 本店～供应豆浆。*We sell soya-bean milk in the morning.*

【早熟】①【生理】precocity: ～的小孩 *a precocious child* ② early-ripe; early-maturing: ～品种 *early-maturing variety* / ～玉米 *early-maturing maize*

【早衰】【医】premature senility or decrepitude; early ageing

【早霜】early frost

【早退】leave earlier than one should; leave early

【早晚】① morning and evening: ～各服两丸 *take two pills in the morning and two in the evening* ② sooner or later; one of these days: 他～要吃大亏。*One of these days he will come a cropper.* ③ time ④［方］some time in the future; some day; some future time: 我～要去北京。*I'll go to Beijing some day.*

【早先】previously; before; in the past; formerly: 我～听说过这事儿。*I've heard of this matter before.*

【早泄】【医】premature ejaculation

【早已】for a long period of time; long ago; for a long time: 我～忘记过去的事了。*I've forgotten the entire thing in the past.*

【早早儿】as early as possible; well in advance: 要做的活,就～办。*Having to do it we do it as soon as possible.*

枣 jujube; (Chinese) date

【枣红】purplish red; claret

【枣泥】jujube paste

【枣树】jujube tree

蚤 flea

澡 bath

【澡盆】bathtub

【澡堂】public baths; bathhouse

【澡塘】common bathing pool (in a bathhouse)

藻 ① algae: 蓝～ *blue green algae* ② aquatic plants ③ literary embellishment: 辞～ *ornate diction* / 华丽的词～ *flowery language*

【藻井】【建】sunk panel; caisson ceiling; coffer

【藻类植物】algae

zào

皂 ① black: 青红～白 *black and white; right and wrong* / ～鞋 *black shoes* / ～衣 *black coat* ②［旧］yamen runner; office boy ③ soap: 香～ *toilet soap* / 药～ *medicated soap*

【皂白】black and white — right and wrong: 不分青红～ *make no distinction between right and wrong*

【皂片】soap flakes

灶 ① kitchen range; cooking stove: 炉～ *cooking range; kitchen range* ② kitchen; mess; canteen; cafeteria: 学生～ *students' cafeteria or canteen*

【灶间】［方］kitchen

【灶具】［方］cooking utensils

【灶神】kitchen god; god of the hearth

【灶台】the top of a kitchen range

【灶头】［方］kitchen range; cooking stove

造[1] ① make; build; construct; create: 制～纠纷 *sow dissension; create trouble* / ～假象 *put up a false front* / ～舆论 *create (or prepare) public opinion* / ～花名册 *compile a register (of names)*

② invent; cook up; concoct; fabricate: ~假账 *cook accounts*

造² ① one of the two parties to a legal agreement or in a lawsuit ②【律】one of the two parties to a legal agreement or in a lawsuit: 两~ *both parties* ③［方］crop: 早~ *early crops* / 一年三~ *three crops a year*

造³ ① go to; arrive at; reach: 他的书法在当时可以说登峰~极。*His handwriting attained a level never known at that time.* ② achievements; accomplishments; success: 她是个~诣很深的专家。*She is an expert of great attainments.* ③ train; educate; cultivate: 出国深~ *pursue advanced studies abroad*

【造币厂】mint

【造成】create; cause; give rise to; bring about; result in

【造船】shipbuilding: ~厂 *shipyard; dockyard* / ~工业 *shipbuilding industry*

【造次】① hurried; hasty: ~之间 *in a hurry; in a moment of haste* ② rash; impetuous; imprudent: 不可~。*Don't be rash.*

【造反】rise in rebellion; rebel; mutiny; revolt

【造访】［书］pay a visit; call on: 登门~ *call at sb's house; pay sb a visit*

【造福】bring benefit to; do good for: ~后代 *benefit posterity (or future generations)* / ~人民 *work for the well-being of the people*

【造化】［书］① the creator; Nature; Creation: ~是公正的。*Nature is fair.* ② good luck; good fortune: 看他的~了。*It depends on his luck.*

【造假】manufacture fake products; forge; counterfeit

【造价】cost (of construction or manufacture): 这座建筑物质量好, ~低。*This building is of good quality and low cost.*

【造就】① create; bring up; train: ~人才 *train competent personnel* / ~良好的社会风气 *foster high standard of social conduct* ② achievements; attainments (usu. of young people)

【造句】make a sentence: 学习~ *learn to make sentences*

【造林】afforestation: ~面积 *afforested area; area under afforestation*

【造孽】【宗】do evil; commit a sin

【造物】the divine force that created the universe; Nature: ~主 *God; the Creator*

【造型】① modelling; mould-making: 这些艺术品~优美。*These art objects are beautifully shaped.* ② model; mould; form: ~独特 *unique in shape* ③【机】moulding: 干砂~ *dry sand moulding*

【造谣】cook up a story; spread a rumour: ~是不道德的。*It's shameful to spread rumours.*

【造诣】(academic or artistic) achievements: 文学~高 *of high literary attain meats* / 有~的歌唱家 *an accomplished singer*

【造纸】papermaking: ~厂 *paper mill* / ~工业 *papermaking industry* / ~机 *paper machine* / ~术 *papermaking technology*

【造作】① make, manufacture ② affected; artificial

噪 ① (of birds, insects, etc.) chirp: 虫~ *the chirping of insects* ② make noise; make an uproar; clamour: 人声~杂 *a hubbub of voice* / 汽车的~声 *the noise of car* ③ become well known: 名~一时 *be enormously popular for a time*

【噪闹】noisy; noise; racket; din

【噪嚷】cry; shout; hubbub: 再别~了! *Don't shouting any more!*

【噪音】noise; din: ~干扰 *noise jamming* / ~污染 *noise pollution*

燥 dry: 干~ *dry; arid*

【燥裂】crack from dryness; chap: 皮肤~ *chapped skin*

【燥热】hot and dry

躁 rash; impetuous; restless; impulsive: 戒骄戒~ *guard against arrogance and rashness* / 烦~ *irritable; agitated*

【躁动】move restlessly; be jittery; keep moving up and down

【躁急】restless; uneasy; irritable; rash; impetuous

【躁狂】【医】mania: ~者 *a maniac*

zé

则¹ ① standard; norm; gauge; criterion: 行为准~ *code of conduct* / 外交准~ *diplomatic norms* ② rule; decree; regulation: 交通规~ *traffic regulations* ③［书］imitate; follow; take as a model ④ (for news, writing, etc.) piece; item: 一~新闻 *an item of news* / 寓言三~ *three fables*

则² ［书］① indicating cause, condition, etc.: 欲速~不达。*More haste, less speed.* / 不战~已, 战~必胜。*Fight no battle unless victory is sure.* ② indicating concession, contrast, etc.: 好~好, 但不可行。*Your method is good, but it is difficult to carry out.* ③ used together with 一, 二, 三 to enumerate causes or reasons: 今天我不能去了。一~没准备好, 二~发高烧了。*I can't go there today; for one thing I don't prepare well, for another is I've caught a high fever.*

责 ① duty; responsibility; obligation: 爱护草坪, 人人有~。*It is everybody's duty to take good care of the grassland.* ② demand; exact; require ③ question closely; call sb to account; interrogate ④ reproach; criticize; blame; censure ⑤ punish

【责备】reproach; blame; reprove; take sb to task: ~的眼光 *a look of reproach*

【责编】editor-in-charge; executive editor

【责成】instruct; charge; order; enjoin: 经理~她培训新来的员工。*The manager instructed her to train the new employees.*

【责打】punish be beating

【责罚】punish; penalize

【责怪】blame; reproach: 这事不该~孩子。*The child should not be blamed for this.*

Z

【责令】order; instruct; charge; enjoin:被～停业 *be instructed to stop business.*

【责骂】scold; rebuke; dress down; reprove:挨～ *get a good scolding*

【责难】censure; blame; reproach:受到公开～ *receive a public censure*

【责任】① duty; obligation; responsibility:～重大 *have a grave responsibility* ② responsibility for a faculty or wrong; blame:追究～ *ascertain where the responsibility lies* / 推卸～ *shirk responsibility; shift the blame onto others* / ～保险 *liability insurance* / ～感 *sense of responsibility* (*or duty*) / ～事故 *accident due to negligence; accident involving criminal or civil liability* / ～田 *responsibility field* / ～限额 *liability limit*

【责问】call sb to account; ask reprovingly

【责无旁贷】be duty-bound; be one's unshirkable responsibility

【责怨】blame; reproach; complain:父亲的语气有些～。*Father spoke in a somewhat reproachful tone.*

择 select; choose; opt for; pick:良禽～木 *a good bird chooses the branch it perches on — a wise man chooses the right master to serve under* / ～友 *choose friends* / 不～手段 *by hook or by crook; unscrupulously* / ～日成婚 *fix a wedding date*
see also zhái

【择吉】select an auspicious (or lucky) day (for a marriage, funeral, etc.):～开张 *choose an auspicious day to start a business*

【择交】choose friends:一定要慎重～朋友。*You must be cautious in choosing your friends.*

【择偶】choose one's spouse

【择期】choose or fix a date:～完婚 *select a day for the marriage ceremony*

【择善而从】choose and embrace what is good

【择业】choose an occupation; select a job:～权 *right to choose one's calling* / 自行～ *select a job for oneself; choose one's job*

【择优】select the superior or the best:～录取 *enroll* (*or employ*) *on the basis of competitive selection*

泽 ① pool; pond; swamp:沼～ *marsh; swamp* / 水乡～国 *a region of rivers and lakes* ② luster (of metals, pearls, etc.):光～ *lustre; gloss; sheen* ③ [书] favour; beneficence; largeness ④ wet; moist; damp

【泽国】① flooded area ② land that abounds in lakes and rivers

啧 click of the tongue

【啧啧】① click of the tongue; chatter ② [书] chirping

【啧啧称赞】click the tongue in admiration

zè

仄[1] narrow

仄[2] uneasy; disturbed

【仄声】【语】oblique tone

zéi

贼[1] ① thief; burglar:窃～ *burglar; thief* / ～巢 *thieves' den* / ～赃 *stolen goods; loot; booty* ② traitor; enemy:认～作父 *take one's enemy for one's father; regard one's foe as kith and kin* / 卖国～ *traitor* ③ crooked; wicked; evil; furtive:～溜溜 *shifty-eyed; furtive* ④ crafty; sly; cunning; wily; deceitful:这个骗子很～。*The cheat is very crafty.*

贼[2] [方] (used to show disapproval or abnormality) extremely; exceedingly; disagreeable:～热 *terribly hot* / ～便宜 *extremely cheap*

【贼船】pirate ship:上～ *board the pirate ship — join a criminal gang; go astray*

【贼喊捉贼】a thief crying "stop thief"

【贼眉鼠眼】wear a thievish expression; thievish-looking; shifty-eyed

【贼死】[方] extremely; utterly; exceedingly:累个～ *be tired out; be dog-tired; be totally exhausted*

【贼头贼脑】thievish; stealthy; furtive

【贼窝】thieves' den; family of thieves

【贼心】evil designs; evil intentions:～不死 *refuse to give up one's evil designs*

【贼眼】shifty eyes; furtive glance

【贼子】[书] traitor; one who harms the country and oppresses the people

zěn

怎 [口] why; how; what:你～不去上课? *Why didn't you go to school?*

【怎么】① used to inquire about nature, condition, cause, etc.:我～不知道? *How come I never knew it?* / 你～学会钢琴的? *How did you learn to play piano?* ② used to indicate nature, condition or manner in general:这事该～办就～办。*Handled the matter the way it should be handled.* ③ used in the negative as an understatement which usually means not very, not much, not quite:质量不～好。*That's not very high quality.* ④ used at the beginning of a sentence to indicate surprise, usu. followed by a pause:～，你没来上课? *What? Didn't you go to school?* / ～，你想赖账? *What? You want to deny your debt?*

【怎么得了】where will it all end; what a terrible mess it is; this is one hell of a mess

【怎么样】① how; what:你能把我～? *What can you do to me?* / 后来～? *What happened in the end?* ② what's like; how are things; what do you think:坐车去～? *What about going by bus?* / 再来杯牛奶～? *How about another cup of tea?* ③ in a certain way; in any way; no matter how ④ euphemistic formula used in the negative：这支歌不～。*The song isn't up to much.* /他做饭不～。*He's not much of a cooker.*

【怎么看】① what to do；what：我们下课后踢足球，你～？*We'll play football after class；what about you*？② no matter what；whatever：～都可以。*It'll be all right whatever it is.* /我想～就～。*I'll do as I please.*

【怎样】① how，what：你～做作业的？*How did you do your homework*？/这只瓶子～？*What about this bottle*？② in a certain way；in any way：我爱～就～。*I do what I want.*

zèn

谮［书］falsely charge；slander；calumniate；defame：～言 *calumny*；*defamation*

zēng

曾 relationship between great-grandchildren and great-grandparents
see also céng

【曾孙】great-grandson

【曾孙女】great-granddaughter

【曾祖】（paternal）great-grandfather

【曾祖母】（paternal）great-grandmother

增 increase；gain；add；enhance：今年产量～加了很多。*The output increased sharply this year.*

【增白】【化】brighten：～剂 *brightening agent*；*brightener* /～霜 *fair complexion cream*

【增补】augment；supplement；increase：书的品种有所～。*There are a greater variety of books in the store.*

【增补本】an enlarged edition

【增产】increase production：～节约 *increase production and practise economy*

【增订】revise and enlarge（a book）：～本 *a revise and enlarged edition*

【增多】grow in number or quantity；increase：摩天大楼日益～。*There are more and more skyscrapers.*

【增防】【军】strengthen defences；fortify the defences；strengthen the garrison

【增幅】increasing range；growing rate：今年五月份，电视机出口～达到20%。*The export of televisions this May grow at a rate of* 20%.

【增高】① get higher；rise；increase；heighten：现在的楼房比以前～了。*The buildings now get higher than before.* ② raise；make higher；heighten；increase：～房间温度 *raise the temperature of the room*

【增股】【经】rights issue

【增光】add lustre to；do credit to；add to the prestige of：为中国人民～ *do credit to Chinese people*

【增加】increase；raise；add；augment：～工资 *get a raise in pay* /～财富 *multiply one's wealth* /～困难 *add to the difficulties*；*multiply the difficulties* /～体重 *put on weight*；*grow heavier* /～抵抗力 *build up one's resistance to disease*

【增减】increase and decrease；fluctuate

【增进】enhance；promote；further；improve：～交流 *promote exchanges*

【增刊】supplement（to a newspaper or periodical）；supplementary issue

【增量】① increase：投资～ *investment increase* ②【数】increment；incremental quantity：～计算 *increment computer* /～数字记录器 *incremental digital recorder* /～法 *reinforcement method*

【增强】strengthen；heighten；enhance：～战斗力 *strengthen fighting capacity* /～团结 *strengthen unity*；*close one's ranks* /～体质 *build up one's health*

【增色】add colour to；add beauty to：这首曲子给今晚的节目～不少。*The music adds beauty to the programme tonight.*

【增删】additions and deletions

【增设】add；set up more（departments，etc.）：～新专业 *establish a new subject*；*offer a new subject*

【增收】increase one's income；increase revenue：～节支 *raise revenues and cut expenditures*

【增添】add；increase；augment：～设备 *get additional equipment*

【增效剂】【化】synergist

【增页】text or pictures added to a periodical

【增益】① increase；raise；add ②【电】gain：分贝～ *decibel gain*

【增盈】increase profit or profitability：～目标 *increased profits*

【增援】【军】reinforce：～前线 *send reinforcements to the battlefront*

【增长】increase；rise；grow；enhance：经济～ *economic growth* /～见闻 *enrich one's experience*

【增支】increase expenditure

【增值】①【经】appreciate；appreciation：美元～ *appreciation of us dollar* ②【经】rise or increase in value；add value；increment ③［喻］increase in value：知识～ *the rise in the value of knowledge*

【增殖】①【医】hyperplasia；proliferation；multiplication：细胞～ *proliferation of cells* ② breed；reproduce；multiply；propagate

【增砖添瓦】① add bricks and tiles（to the construction of a building）②［喻］make whatever contribution one can（to a cause）

【增资】increase salary：～幅度 *the range of pay raise*

憎 hate；loathe；detest

【憎恨】hate；detest：因为金钱关系，他～他爸爸。*He hated his father for money.*

【憎恶】detest，abhor；loathe；abominate：我～破坏公物的行为。*I detest the action of destroying public property.*

【憎厌】dislike；be disgusted with

Z

zèng

锃 [方] (of utensils, etc.) polished

【锃亮】[方] shiny; polished

赠 give as a present; send as a gift: 临别～言 *words of advice at parting; parting advice* / 互～礼物 *exchange gifts; present each other with gifts*

【赠别】present a friend with gifts, poems, etc. at parting; see a friend off

【赠答】present each other with gifts, poems, etc.

【赠品】(complimentary) gifts; giveaway: 在商店里她得到了很多～。*She got a lot of gifts in the store.*

【赠券】gift coupons

【赠书】① present sb with a book ② complimentary copy

【赠送】give (or present) as a gift: ～锦旗 *present sb with a silk banner* / ～仪式 *presentation ceremony*

【赠言】words of advice or encourage meat given to a friend at parting

【赠予】present to; donate to

【赠阅】(of a book, periodical, etc.) given free by the publisher

zhā

扎 prick; needle into: 身上被～了一刀 *be stabbed in the body* ②[方] plunge into; dive into; get into: ～到人堆里 *dash into the crowd* / 他整天～在书堆里。*He buried himself in books all day.* ③ (of troops) be stationed; be quartered
see also zā; zhá

【扎堆儿】[方] get together; gather around: ～聊天 *get together to chat*

【扎耳朵眼儿】[口] grate or jar on the ear; piece the earlobe (in order to wear earrings)

【扎根】take root; strike root: ～边疆 *settle in the border areas* / ～群众 *take root among the masses*

【扎花】[方] embroider

【扎猛子】[方] swim with the head kept submerged in water; dive

【扎实】① sturdy; strong; robust ② solid; sound; down-to-earth: 工作很～ *do a solid job* / ～的理论基础 *firm grounding in theory*

【扎手】① prick the hand: 仙人掌有刺，当心～。*The cactus is thorny; take care lest they prick your hands.* ② difficult to handle; thorny; ticklish: 这事真～。*The matter is really a hard nut to crack.*

【扎眼】① dazzling; loud; garish; offending to the eye: ～的颜色 garish colour; colour unpleasant to the eye ② offensively conspicuous; very showy

【扎伊尔】Zaire: ～人 *Zairian*

【扎寨】pitch a camp; camp

【扎针】give or have an acupuncture treatment: 在医院～ *have acupuncture treatment in hospital*

咋
see also zǎ

【咋呼】[方] ① shout blusteringly, cry out loudly ② show off; make a fuss; make a display: 到处～ *try to show off everywhere* / 什么事儿他都爱～。*He's rather fussy about anything.*

喳 ①[旧] yes, sir — formerly used by an inferior to a superior ② chatter; chirp: 麻雀～～叫。*Sparrows are chattering.*

渣 ① dregs; slag; residue; sediment: 人～ *social trash; dregs* / 沉～ *dregs* / 炉～ *cinder; slag* / 豆～ *soya-bean residue* ② broken bits: 碎玻璃～儿 *bits of broken glass*

【渣车】【冶】slag car or wagon

【渣坑】【冶】hunch pit

【渣块】【冶】slag block

【渣炉】【冶】slag hearth

【渣煤】【冶】dross coal

【渣土】【矿】dirt with waste residue

【渣油】residual oil; residuum: ～路 *residual-oil road*

【渣滓】① dregs; sediment; residue ② broken bits: 桌子上有很多点心～。*There are lots of cake crumbs on the table.*

zhá

扎
see also zā; zhā

【扎挣】[方] struggle to maintain; move with difficulty

札 ① thin pieces of wood used for writing on in ancient china ②[书] letter: 读书～记 *reading notes* / 信～ *letter*

【札记】reading notes or commentary

轧 roll (steel)
see also yà

【轧钢】steel rolling: ～工人 *steel rolling worker; roller* / ～厂 *steel rolling mill*

闸 ① floodgate; sluice; sluice gate: 船～ *(ship) lock* ② brake ③[口] electric switch: 扳～ *operate a switch; switch on or off* ④ dam up a stream, river, etc.: ～住河水 *dam up the river*

【闸盒】fuse box:

【闸门】① water gate; sluice gate ② (ship) lock gate ③【机】throttle valve

【闸瓦】【机】brake shoe

炸 ① fry in deep fat or oil; deep-fry: ～花生 *fried peanuts* / ～鸡蛋 *fried egg* / ～油饼 *deep-fried dough cake* ②[方] scald (as a way of cooking); dip in boiling water
see also zhà

【炸酱】fried bean sauce

Z

【炸土豆条】chips, French fries

铡 ① hand hay cutter; fodder chopper ② cut up with a hay cutter: ~草 *chop hay*

【铡草机】hay cutter; chaff cutter; chaff slicer; straw breaker

【铡刀】hand hay (or straw) cutter; fodder chopper; straw chopper

zhǎ

拃 ① span ② [量]span:这块布有三~宽。*The cloth is three spans wide.*

眨 blink; wink; hat (the eyes):眼睛一~ *blink (one's eyes)* /那个调皮的孩子朝我~眼。*The naughty boy are twinkling at me.*

【眨巴】[方] blink:他吃惊地朝我~着眼睛。*He is blinking at me in surprise.*

【眨眼】very short time; wink; twinkle:一~的工夫 *in the twinkling of an eye*

砟 tiny fragment of stone, coal, etc.:炉灰~儿 *cinder*

【砟子】tiny fragment of stone, coal, etc.

zhà

乍 ① first; for the first time; at first: ~一听 *at first hearing* /~一看 *at first glance* /初来~到 *be a newcomer; be a new arrival* ② suddenly; abruptly; all of a sudden:天气~冷~热。*The temperature changes abruptly.* ③ spread; extend; open out

【乍暖还寒】after a short warm spell, it's turned cold again.

诈 ① cheat; swindle; deceive: 欺~ *cheat; swindle* /讹~ *blackmail* /~人钱财 *cheat (or swindle) people out of their money; get money by fraud* ② pretend; feign; fake: ~死 *feign death; play death (or possum)* /~病 *feign illness; pretend sickness; malinger* /~败 *feign defeat* ③ bluff sb into giving information; feel out

【诈病】malinger; malingering

【诈唬】bluff; bluster

【诈骗】defraud; swindle; trick into: ~犯 *swindler*

【诈降】pretend to surrender; feign surrender

【诈语】lie; deceit; falsehood; fabrication

栅 railings; paling; bars; palisade: 木~ *paling; palisade* /铁~ *iron railings; metal rails; iron bars* /炉~ *grate* /监狱被~栏围着。*The prison is surrounded by fences.*
see also shān

【栅栏】① railings; paling; bars; fence fails ② boom: ~网 *boom nets*

炸 ① explode; break; burst:飞机~了。*The plane has burst.* /轮胎~了。*The tyre blew out.* ② blow up; blast; bomb:轰~海上目标 *bomb targets on the sea* / ~碉堡 *blow up the blockhouse* ③ [口] fly into rage; explode with anger; flare up ④ [方] scamper; scurry away; flee in terror
see also zhá

【炸弹】bomb: ~坑 *bomb-crater; crater*

【炸锅】① oil spattering when food is fried ② [喻] get excited; and angry; lose one's temper:听到这一坏消息,全家立刻~了。*The whole family was instantly in an uproar at the bad news.*

【炸雷】[方] a clap of thunder

【炸窝】[方] (of a crowd of people) be thrown into confusion; be in disarray:敌人一下子~了。*The enemy was thrown into great confusion instantly.*

【炸响】explode; make cracking noise:鞭子甩得~ *crack the whip*

【炸药】explosive (charges); dynamite: ~包 *pack (or satchel) of dynamite; explosive package; satchel charges*

蚱

【蚱蜢】grasshopper

榨 ① press; extract; squeeze out:残酷压~ *ruthless exploitation* / ~干血汗 *wring every ounce of swear and blood out of sb* /~橘子 *squeeze juice from an orange* ② a press for extracting juice, oil, etc.

【榨菜】① mustard tuber ② hot pickled mustard tuber

【榨取】① press; extract; squeeze: ~果汁 *squeeze juice out of some kind of fruit* ② extort; squeeze: 他从那个小女孩那里~了很多钱。*He extorted much money from the little girl.*

【榨油】extract oil: ~机 *oil press*

【榨汁机】juicer

zhāi

斋[1] ① abstain from meat, wine, etc.:开~ *break one's fast* ② vegetarian diet adopted for religious reasons:吃~ *be a vegetarian for religious reason* ③ give alms (to a monk)

斋[2] room or building

【斋饭】food that monks obtained by begging

【斋果】[方] oblation; sacrificial offering

【斋戒】abstain from meat, wine, etc. (when offering sacrifices to gods or ancestors); fast: ~节 *Ramadan; the fast of Ramadan* /~日 *fast day*

【斋期】fast days; fast; Lent

【斋日】fast day

【斋堂】dining room at a temple

【斋月】【宗】Ramadan; 9th month of the Muslim year

摘 ① pick; pluck; take off; remove: ~棉花 *pick cotton* / ~花 *pluck flowers* /~苹果 *pick apples* /~眼镜 *take off one's glasses* ② select; make extracts from; pick out ③ borrow money when in urgent need: ~几个钱救急 *borrow some money to meet an urgent need*

Z

【摘报】make a summary report: ~工作计划 *submit a summary report of the working-plan*
【摘编】① select and edit; make extracts ② extracts
【摘抄】① take passages; make extracts; extract; cull; expert ② extracts; excerpts: 日记 ~ *pages from a diary*
【摘除】【医】excise; remove: ~ 肿瘤 *excise a tumour*
【摘登】publish excerpts of sth: 报纸~了代表的发言。*The paper carried excerpts of the delegates.*
【摘发】publish excerpts of sth: ~大会发言 *publish extracts of speeches given at a conference*
【摘桂】take the crown; win the title
【摘记】① take notes: ~讲话要点 *take down the gist of a speech* ② extracts; excepts
【摘借】borrow money when in urgent need
【摘录】① take passages; make extracts; extract ② extracts; excerpts: 报刊 ~ *excerpts from newspaper articles*
【摘取】① obtain; get: ~银牌 *win a silver medal* ② quote; select; choose: ~自己需要的材料 *select materials one wants*
【摘桃子】① pick peaches ②［喻］steal the fruit of other's labour
【摘要】① make a summary; make an abstract: ~记录 *jot down the main points* ② summary; abstract: 社论 ~ *the summary of an editorial*
【摘译】① translate selected passage ② translations of selected passages
【摘引】quote

zhái

宅 residence; house; dwelling
【宅第】a large house; mansion
【宅基】the foundations of a house; the site of a house
【宅门】① gate of an old-style big house or a mansion ② family living in such a mansion
【宅院】a house with a courtyard; house
【宅子】［口］residence; house

择 *see also* zé
【择不开】① unable to disentangle or undo; impossible to unravel; past disentanglement ② cannot get away from; cannot tear oneself away from: 他的爸爸病了以后,他一点时间也~了。*He had no time to spare since his father was sick.*
【择菜】trim vegetables for cooking

zhǎi

窄 ① narrow: ~道 *narrow path* ② petty; narrow; small-minded: ~心眼儿 *narrow-minded; petty; oversensitive* ③ hard up; badly off; on the rocks: 他父亲死后,日子过得挺~。*He was very hard up after his father died.*
【窄小】narrow and small; narrow: ~的房屋 *a small house*

zhài

债 debt: 举~筹资 *debt financing* / 负~ *be in debt; get into debt* / 借~ *borrow money* / 外~ *external debt* / 三角~ *debt chains*
【债户】debtor
【债款】loan
【债权】【律】creditor's rights: ~国 *creditor nation* / ~人 *creditor; lender*
【债券】bond; debenture: ~持有者 *bond holder* / ~担保人 *bond underwriter* / ~发行 *the issuance of debentures* / ~价格 *bond price* / ~交易 *bond exchange* / ~投资 *bond investment* / ~溢价 *bond premium*
【债台高筑】be heavily in debt; be up to one's ears in debt; be head over heels in debt; be debt-ridden
【债务】debt; liabilities: ~公司 *debtor corporation* / ~国 *debtor nation* / ~咨询 *debt counseling*
【债主】creditor: ~权益 *creditor's equity*

寨 ① stockade; fence: 鹿~ *abatis* ② stockaded village; fenced hamlet: 村~相望 *neighbouring villages within sight of each other* ③［旧］camp ④ mountain stronghold
【寨主】(in former times) brigand chief
【寨子】stockaded village

zhān

占 practise divination; divine
see also zhàn
【占卜】practise divination; divine
【占卦】divine by means of the Eight Diagrams
【占课】divine by tossing coins
【占梦】divination by interpreting dreams; necromancy
【占星】divine by astrology; cast a horoscope: ~家 *astrology*

沾 ① moisten; wet; soak: ~满泪痕 *be blotted with tears* ② be stained with; be soiled with: ~污了脚 *soil one's feet* / ~水 *get wet* / ~油 *stained with grease* ③ touch ④ get sth out of association with sb or sth; benefit from some sort of relationship: 他喜欢~点小便宜。*He likes getting a bargain.*
【沾边】① touch on (upon) only lightly: 这案子与戈顿一点儿不~。*Gorton had nothing at all to do with the case.* ② be close to what is should be; be relevant; be pertinent: 你的话一点也不~。*Your remarks are completely off the mark.*
【沾光】benefit from association with sb or sth; cash

in on one's connection with sb; gain from the support or influence of sb:我们工厂每周办舞会,附近居民都~。*The residents in the neighbourhood benefit from the parties which our factory weekly holds.*
【沾亲】be somewhat related
【沾亲带故】be related somehow or other; have ties of kinship or friendship
【沾染】be infected with; be contaminated by; be tainted with; contract: ~恶习 *contract bad habits*
【沾惹】provoke; incur
【沾手】① touch with one's hands:这脏东西最好别~。*We'd better not touch such kind of dirties.* ② have a hand in; interfere:你不必~。*You need not intervene in this matter.*
【沾沾自喜】feel complacent; be pleased with oneself:不能有一点成功就~。*Don't be complacent over accidental success.*

毡 felt: ~帽 *felt hat* /~靴 *felt boots*

【毡条】[方] felt rug; felt
【毡子】felt; felt rug; felt blanket

粘 glue; stick; paste:把两块布~在一起 *glue the two pieces of cloth together*
see also nián
【粘连】①【医】adhesion:他和这事有~。*He has something to do with the matter.*
【粘贴】paste; glue; stick: ~布告 *put up a notice*

谵 [书] rave; be delirious; rant

【谵妄】【医】delirium
【谵语】[书] delirious speech; wild talk; ranting and raving; ravings

瞻 look up or forward

【瞻顾】[书] look ahead and behind
【瞻念】look to; think of; look ahead:作为他的父亲,你必须~他的前途。*You must look ahead to the future as his father.*
【瞻前顾后】① think over carefully; weigh the pros and cons ② be over-cautious and indecisive; hesitate
【瞻赏】enjoy the sight of
【瞻望】look forward; look far ahead:放眼~ *look far ahead*
【瞻仰】look at with reverence; pay tribute to: ~遗容 *pay respects to sb's remains*

zhǎn

斩 slay; chop; cut; kill:我们必须~断敌人的魔爪。*We must cut off the enemy's talons.*
【斩草除根】cut the weeds and dig up the roots — destroy root and branch; stamp out the source of trouble
【斩除】root out; wipe out
【斩钉截铁】resolute and decisive; categorical; final
【斩尽杀绝】kill all; wipe out; exterminate; go to extremes
【斩首】behead; decapitate

盏 ① a small cup:酒~ *a small wine cup* ② [量] (for lamps):一~花灯 *a festival lantern*

展 ① open up; spread out; unfold; unfurl; stretch:舒~眉头 *smooth one's brows* /她总是愁眉不~。*She always wears a worried frown.* ② put to good use; give free play to; display:大~宏图 *carry out a great plan* /施~才华 *display one's talents* ③ postpone; extend; prolong; put off ④ exhibition; show
【展播】a special TV programme; run (on TV, as in a festival)
【展翅】unfold the wings; get ready for flight:那个孩子想~高飞。*The child wish he could soar to great heights.*
【展出】put on display; be on show or view; display; exhibit:公开~ *make a public exhibition* /手工艺品~ *handicrafts exhibition* /巡回~ *itinerant exhibition*
【展地】site of an exhibition
【展馆】exhibition centre; exhibition hall
【展柜】showcase; display window
【展读】open (a book or a letter) and read
【展缓】postpone; extend; prolong; put off:婚期不得~。*The wedding is not to be extended.*
【展开】① spread out; unfold; open up; roll out: ~地毯 *roll out the carpet* ② launch; unfold; develop; carry out; set off: ~攻势 *mount an offensive* /我们的工作已经全面~。*Our job is now in full swing.*
【展览】put on display; exhibit; show:农业~ *agricultural exhibition* /花卉~ *flower show* /时装~ *fashion show* /~室 *exhibition room; showroom*
【展廊】exhibition gallery
【展露】reveal; show; become visible; appear:他~笑容。*A smile appeared on his face.*
【展卖】exhibit for sale
【展品】exhibit; item on display
【展评】display and appraise; exhibit and compare: ~会 *exhibition and appraisal meeting*
【展期】① extend a time limit; postpone:运动会~举办。*The sport-meeting is been postponed (or put off).* ② *duration of an exhibition; exhibition period*
【展区】*exhibition area; place of exhibition*
【展示】*show; reveal; lay bare; put on display:* ~样品 *put sample products on display*
【展室】exhibition room; showroom
【展台】showcase; booth; display counter
【展望】① look into the distance; look to the future; look ahead: ~未来 *look forward to the future* ② fore cast; prospect; vista
【展现】unfold before one's eyes; emerge; show; appear:过去美好的回忆~在我眼前。*The beautiful memories in the past time appeared to my eyes.*
【展销】display and sell (goods): ~会 *commodities fair*

【展映】film festival：新片～ *hold a new film festival*

崭 ①［书］towering (over); rise high ②［方］fine; superb; swell

【崭露头角】(of a young person) begin to distinguish oneself; display one's brilliant talents; cut a striking figure

【崭新】brand-new; completely new：～的制服 *a brand-new tunic suit*

搌 wipe or dab (with a soft dry object) to sop up liquid：快～一～墨水。*Blot up the ink quickly.*

【搌布】dishcloth; dish towel

辗

【辗转】① pass through many hands or places ② toss about (in bed); toss and turn：～反侧 *toss about (in bed)*

zhàn

占 ① take possession of; occupy; seize; take：～压 *occupy and keep long in stock* / ～据优势 *have the advantage* / ～座位 *occupy seats* ② constitute; hold; make up; form：～绝对优势 *hold an overwhelming advantage; hold all trumps* / ～第一位 *take the first place; rank first*
see also zhān

【占地】(of a garden, building, etc.) cover an area of：这座超市～5000平方米。*The supermarket covers an area of 5,000 square metres.*

【占据】occupy; hold; siege

【占理】be reasonable; make sense; be sensible; be right：他的话一点儿不～。*He's not right at all.*

【占领】capture; occupy; seize; take：～制高点 *capture a commanding point* / 军事～ *military occupation* / ～区 *occupied area* / ～国 *occupation power* / ～军 *occupation army*

【占便宜】① gain extra advantage by unfair means; profit at other people's expense：别总想处处～。*Don't always try to take everything of others.* ② have the edge over; be advantageous; be favourable：个子高的人打篮球～。*Tall man has an advantage in playing basketball.*

【占上风】get the upper hand; win an advantage; turn the tables on; prevail

【占先】go before; take the lead; get ahead of; take precedence：他在跑步比赛中总是～。*He always takes the lead in the races.*

【占线】the line is busy or engaged：～通道 *active channel*

【占小便宜】gain petty advantages; make small gains at other's expense; secure small advantages at other people's expense

【占用】occupy and use; take up (time)

【占有】① own; possess; have：～资金 *own funds* ② occupy; hold：～重要地位 *occupy an important place in sth*

栈 ① warehouse ② inn ③ shed; pen; fold：羊～ *sheep pen; sheepfold* / 马～ *stable*

【栈道】a plank road built along the face of a cliff by means of wooden brackets

【栈房】① warehouse; storehouse ②［方］inn

【栈桥】landing stage (at a port); loading bridge (at a railway station)

战¹ ① war; warfare; battle; fight：宣～ *declare war* / 挑～ *challenge to fight* ② fight; battle：为和平而～ *fight for peace* / ～死沙场 *die on the battlefield* ③ (Zhàn) a surname

战² shiver; tremble; shake; shudder

【战败】① be defeated; lose (a battle or war); suffer a defeat; be vanquished：他的部队～了。*His troops were defeated.* ② defeat; vanquish; beat; triumph over：～国 *vanquished (or defeated) nation*

【战备】war preparedness; combat readiness; war preparations：～状态 *combat readiness*

【战场】battle field; battleground; battle front：欧洲～ *European theatre* / 开辟新～ *open another front* / 东北～ *the Northeast theatre*

【战车】war chariot

【战船】man-of-war; war ship; naval vessel

【战地】battlefield; battleground; combat zone：～指挥部 *field headquarters* / ～记者 *war correspondent*

【战斗】① fight; battle; combat; action：艰苦的～ *a hard-fought battle* / 进行～ *go into battle; engage in a battle* ② militant; fighting：～英雄 *combat hero*

【战端】the beginning of a war：挑起～ *provoke a war*

【战法】strategies and tactics of war; ways of operation

【战犯】war criminal

【战俘】prisoner of war (P. O. W.)：～营 *prisoner-of-war camp* / ～收容所 *prisoner-of-war collecting post*

【战歌】battle song; fighting song

【战功】meritorious military service; outstanding military exploit; great feats in war; battle achievement：立～ *distinguish oneself on the battlefield*

【战鼓】war drum; battle drum

【战国】Warring States (475—221BC)

【战果】results of battle; fruits of victory; combat success：扩大～ *exploit the victory (or success)*

【战壕】trench; entrenchment

【战后】postwar

【战火】flames of war：～蔓延。*The flames of war are spreading.*

【战祸】disaster of war

【战机】① opportunity for combat：失去～ *lose the opportunity to win a battle* ② secret in formation about military actions; military secret ③ fighter plane; fighter

【战绩】military success (or exploits, feats); combat gains; combat achievements

【战舰】warship; war vessel
【战将】warrior; skillful high-ranking military officer; able general
【战局】war situation：扭转～ *turn the tables on the enemy*
【战况】situation on the battlefield; progress of a battle
【战利品】spoils of war; captured equipment; war trophies (or booty)
【战栗】tremble; shiver; shudder; shake：四肢～ *tremble in every limb*
【战乱】chaos caused by war; war turmoil
【战略】strategy：全球～ *global strategy* /～转移 *strategic shift* /～部署 *strategist*
【战马】battle steed; war-horse
【战幕】curtain on war, sport games, etc.：揭开～ *lift the war curtain-start a war or a match*
【战袍】(in former times) war robe; soldier's garb
【战前】prewar：～准备 *prewar preparations; preparations for a war* /～动员 *mobilization before a battle*
【战区】war zone; theatre of operations; theatre of war
【战胜】defeat; triumph over; vanquish; conquer：～敌人 *defeat (or vanquish) the enemy*
【战时】wartime：～内阁 *wartime cabinet*
【战史】military history; war history
【战士】① soldier; man：解放军～ *a PLA soldier* /老～ *veteran soldier* ② champion; warrior; fighter：国际主义～ *champion of internationalism*
【战事】war; battle; hostilities：～再起 *war broke out again.*
【战书】written challenge to war; letter of challenge：下～ *deliver a letter of challenge*
【战术】(military) tactics
【战死】die (or be killed) in battle
【战位】【军】battle station：进入～ *get into the action position*
【战无不胜】all-conquering; ever-victorious; always triumphant; invincible
【战线】battle line; battlefront; front; action front：思想～ *ideological front* /前方～ *fighting front*
【战役】campaign; battle：三大～ *three Great campaigns* /～指挥员 *commander of a campaign*
【战鹰】fighting eagle (pet name for a fighter plane)
【战友】comrade-in-arms; battle companion：～情谊 *comradeship-in-arms* /老～ *old-time comrade-in-arms*
【战战兢兢】trembling with fear; with fear and trepidation; gingerly：人们～地听他讲话。*People were listening to him with great fear.*
【战争】war; warfare：敌方挑起了～。*The enemy provoked the war.*

站[1] ① stand; be on one's feet; take a stand; get up：往前～！*Stand forth!*

站[2] ① stop; halt：车还没～稳。*The bus has not come to a full stop yet.* ② station; stop：公共汽车～ *bus stop* /终点～ *terminal; terminus* ③ station or centre for rendering certain services：文化～ *cultural centre* /供应～ *supply centre*

【站不住脚】unable to stand one's ground; cannot be justified; impossible to defend
【站得高,看得远】stand high and see far ahead; have foresight; be far-sighted
【站队】line up; fall in; stand in line
【站岗】stand or mount guard; stand sentry; be on sentry duty; stand sentinel：昨晚是他～。*It's he who was on sentry duty yesterday.*
【站柜台】serve as a shop assistant; serve behind the counter (as a shop assistant)
【站立】stand; rise; be on one's feet
【站票】ticket for standing room; standing ticket：～观众 *standee*
【站哨】[方] stand (or mount) guard; be on sentry duty; stand sentry
【站台】platform (in a railway station)：～票 *platform ticket*
【站位】court position; playing position
【站稳】① come to a stop ② stand firm; take a firm stand：～脚跟 *get a firm foothold*
【站长】head of a station, centre, etc.：气象站～ *head of the meteorological station*
【站住】① come to a stop; stop; halt：～,否则要开枪了。*Halt, or I'll shoot.* ② stand firmly on one's feet; keep one's footing：他脚抖得站不住。*With his legs trembling he could not keep his feet.* ③ stand or hold one's ground; consolidate one's position ④ hold water; be valid; be tenable：这种说法站不住。*The statement holds water.*
【站住脚】① stop; halt; stop moving：风太大,人都站不住脚了。*The wind was so strong that one could hardly keep one's feet.* ② be so busy that one cannot stand still at all ③ keep or hold one's ground; consolidate one's position：他终于在单位～了。*He finally gained a footing in his workshop.* ④ hold water; be tenable; be valid：你说的话能～。*What you have said are valid.*

绽 split; tear; burst：破～ *flaw; weak point*

【绽放】(of flowers) come into bloom; break into blossom; burst forth
【绽裂】split open; break; burst open：她的衣服～了,露出雪白的棉花。*Her clothes bolls have burst open in a riot of white.*
【绽露】show; appear; become visible

湛 ① profound; deep; thorough：精～ *superb; consummate* ② crystal clear; limpid：清～ *limpid*

【湛蓝】(of the sky, the sea, a lake etc.) azure blue; azure：～的天空 *clear blue sky; azure skies*
【湛清】limpid; clear：～的湖水 *a limpid lake*

颤 tremble; shiver; shudder; shake

see also chàn

【颤栗】shake; tremble; shiver; shudder

蘸 dip in (ink, sauce, etc.)：～蓝墨水 *dip in blue ink* /大葱～酱 *scallions dipped in thick*

sauce
【蘸火】【冶】quenching

zhāng

张 ① open; spread; stretch; draw: ~嘴 *open one's mouth* / ~开翅膀 *spread the wings* / ~网捕鱼 *spread a net to fish* / 一~一弛 *tension alternates with relaxation* ② lay on; display: set out: 铺~浪费 *extravagant and wasteful* ③ magnify; amplify; exaggerate ④ look; glance ⑤ (of a shop) start business; set up: 开~ *open a business* ⑥ [量]: 两~报纸 *two pieces of newspaper* / 一~床 *one bed* / 一~笑脸 *a smiling face* / 一~利嘴 *a sharp tongue* ⑦ one of the twenty-eight constellations
【张榜】put up a notice; post a notice
【张灯结彩】hang up lanterns and silk festoons; be decorated with lanterns and coloured streamers; be decked with lanterns and bunting
【张帆】set sails; make sail
【张挂】hang up
【张冠李戴】put Zhang's hat on Li's head — attribute sth to the wrong person; confuse one thing with another; get things mixed up
【张皇】[书] alarmed; scared; flurried; flustered: ~失措 *be in a flurry of alarm*; *lose one's head*; *get into panic*
【张家长,李家短】gossip; idle talk
【张口结舌】be agape and tongue-tied; be at a loss for words; be unable to say anything
【张狂】rampant; insolent; arrogant; impudent
【张力】【物】① tension; tensible force ② pulling force
【张量】【数】tensor
【张罗】① take care of; get busy about; attend to: ~家务 *manage household affairs* ② raise (funds); get together (money, etc.): ~一笔钱 *collect a sum of money* ③ greet and entertain (guests); wait on (customers, etc.); attend to (customers, etc.): ~客人 *look after guests*
【张目】① open one's eyes wide: ~注视 *gaze at sth with wide-open eyes* ② inflate sb's arrogance
【张贴】put up (a notice, poster, etc.): ~广告 *put up an advertisement* / ~通告 *post a notice* / ~海报 *put up posters* / 此处禁止~。*Post no bills here.*
【张望】① peep (through a crack, etc.); ② look around: 抬头~ *raise one's head and look around*
【张牙舞爪】bare fangs and brandish claws — make threatening gestures; be arrogant and ferocious; engage in sabre rattling
【张扬】make widely known; come out into the open; make public; publicize
【张嘴】① open one's mouth (to say sth): 他正要~就被人打断了。*He was cut in when he was on the point of saying something.* ② request a loan; ask for a favour: 我不好意思~。*I am embarrassed to ask for a favour.*

章¹ ① chapter; section; division: 全书共十五~。*The whole book has fifteen chapters.* ② clauses and subclasses ③ order; orderliness ④ rules; regulations; charter; constitution ⑤ seal; signet; stamp: 刻~ *engrave a seal* / 私~ *personal seal* ⑥ (Zhāng) a surname

章² badge; medal; insignia

【章程】① rules; regulations; constitution: 学生~ *student regulations* ②[方] solution; way: 这事怎么办,我心里有~。*I was sure of what is the best way to go about it.*
【章法】① presentation of ideas in a piece of writing; art of composition: 不拘~ *with no regard for the logical presentation of ideas* / 这篇文章毫无~。*The essay is short of unity and coherence.* ② orderly ways
【章节】chapters and sections; chapters
【章句】① chapters, sections, sentences and phrases in ancient writings ② syntactic and semantic analysis of ancient writings; philological study
【章鱼】octopus

獐 river deer

【獐子】river deer

彰 ① clear; evident; conspicuous; obvious ② make known; display; commend

樟 camphor tree

【樟木】camphor wood
【樟脑】camphor
【樟脑油】camphor oil
【樟树】camphor tree

蟑

【蟑螂】cockroach; roach

zhǎng

长¹ ① older; elder; senior: 年~ *be a senior* / 罗伯特~我 3 岁。*Robert is three years elder than I am.* ② eldest; oldest: ~兄 *eldest brother* / ~房~孙 *eldest son's eldest son* ③ chief; head; leader ④ (Zhǎng) a surname

长² ① grow; develop: 苹果~得很好! *The apple trees are growing very well.* ② come into being; spring up; form: 他~牙了。*He is teething.* / 柳树~叶了。*The willow leaves are coming out.* ③ acquire; enhance; increase; boost: ~见识 *increase one's knowledge*; *gain experience* / ~信心 *boost one's confidence*
see also cháng

【长辈】senior member of a family; elder; senior
【长膘】(of a domestic animal) get fat; put on flesh; flesh out; fatten
【长大】grow up; be brought up: 他在知识分子家庭~。*He was brought up in an intellectual's fami-*

ly.
【长房】the eldest branch of a family (i. e. that of the eldest son)
【长官】[旧] senior officer or official; commaʌding officer
【长进】progress; improvement
【长者】① [书] elder people ② (a respectful term of address for an old monk) elder ③ (of Judaism and Christianity) local religious leader; elder
【长肉】put on flesh; fill out; get fatter: 他最近又长了几斤肉。*He has put on quite some weight lately.*
【长势】the way a crop is growing; growth: 禾苗~喜人。*The seedlings of cereal crops are coming along fine.*
【长孙】① eldest son's eldest son ② eldest grand son
【长相】[口] looks; feature; appearance; countenance: ~好 *be good-looking* / 从~上看,她有三十岁了。*She looks like a woman of thirty.*
【长者】① elder; senior ② venerable elder
【长子】eldest son: ~继承权 (*right of*) *primogeniture*; *birthright*

涨 (of water, prices, etc.) rise; go up

see also zhàng
【涨潮】rising tide; flood tide
【涨幅】(of prices, etc.) range, extent or rate of rise; rise
【涨价】rise in price; hike a price
【涨落】(of water, prices, etc.) rise and fall; fluctuate: 价格~ *fluctuations of prices*
【涨水】(of a river) rise; go up; (of price) rise

掌 ① palm: 击~为号 *signal by clapping hands* / 鼓~ *clap one's hands*; *applaud* ② the bottom of certain animal's feet; pad; sole: 熊~ *bear's paw* ③ shoe sole or heel: 鞋后~ *heel of a shoe* ④ horseshoe: 这匹马昨天刚钉~。*The horse was just be shod yesterday.* ⑤ strike with the palm of the hand; slap ⑥ hold in one's hand; take charge of; control; wield ⑦ [方] mend the sole of a shoe: 他会~鞋。*He can mend the sole of a shoe.* ⑧ [方] add; put in (salt, oil, act.): ~醋 *add a bit of vinegar* ⑨ [方] used in the same way as 把: ~门关上。*Close the door.*
【掌厨】be the chief cook; be in charge of cooking: 他在一家饭店~。*He is a chief at a restaurant.*
【掌火】① hold a lamp in one's hand ② light an oil lamp
【掌舵】① be at the helm; operate the rudder; take the tiller ② helmsman; steersman
【掌故】anecdotes; tales
【掌管】be in charge of; run; administer: ~财政 *administer finances* / ~两个车间 *take charge of two workshops*
【掌柜】① shopkeeper; manager (of a shop) ② [方] husband
【掌权】hold power; wield power; exercise control
【掌上明珠】a pearl in the palm-a beloved daughter; apple of one's eyes: 小女儿是他的~。*The young daughter is the apple of his eyes.*
【掌勺儿】be the chef: 今天他~。*Today he is to do the cooking.*
【掌声】clapping; applause: 长时间的~ *prolonged applause*
【掌握】① grasp; master; learn thoroughly; know well: ~技术 *master techniques* / ~规律 *learn the rules thoroughly* ② have in hand; take charge of; control: ~方向盘 *be at the wheel* (*or helm*) / ~主动 *take the initiative* / 她决定自己~自己的命运。*She decided to take her destiny into her own hands.*
【掌心】① the centre (or hollow) of the palm ② control; influence: 孙悟空跳不出如来佛的~。*Monkey King cannot jump out of Buddha's palm — be unable to escape.*
【掌印】keep the seal — take control; be in power
【掌嘴】slap sb's face; box sb's ears

zhàng

丈[1] ① [量] zhang, a unit of length / = $3\frac{1}{3}$ metres ② measure (land): 清~ *make an exact measurement of the land*

丈[2] ① senior; elder ② husband (used in certain kinship terms): 岳~ *wife's father*; *father-in-law*
【丈夫】① man ② husband
【丈量】measure (land): ~土地 *take the dimensions of a field*
【丈人】wife's father; father-in-law

仗[1] ① [书] weaponry; weapons; arms: 明火执~ *carry torches and weapon* (*in a robbery*) — *do evil openly* ② battle; war; fight: 胜~ *win a battle*; *triumph over* / 败~ *lost battle*; *defeat*

仗[2] ① hold (a weapon): ~剑 *hold a sword* ② rely on; depend on; be on the strength of: 仰~ *rely on*; *look to sb for backing*
【仗势欺人】abuse one's power and bully people; play the bully on the strength of one's powerful connections or position; take advantage of one's own ob sb else's power to bully people
【仗恃】rely on (an advantage); depend on
【仗义】① [书] uphold justice ② be loyal (to one's friends)
【仗义疏财】be generous in helping the poor on needy
【仗义执言】speak out to uphold justice

杖 ① cane; stick: 拐~ *walking stick* ② rod or staff used for a specific purpose: 权~ *staff of authority as carried by political or religious leader* ③ flogging with a stick (a punishment in ancient China)

帐 curtain; canopy; tent
【帐幕】tent
【帐篷】tent: 搭~ *pitch a tent* / 拆~ *strike a tent*

Z

【帐子】① bed-curtain ② mosquito net

账 ① account: 流水～ *day-to-day account*; *current account* /记～ *keep accounts* /算～ *figure out the account* /赊～ *buy sth on credit* ② account book: 两本～ *two account books* ③ debt; bill: 欠～ *owe a debt* /还～ *repay a debt*

【账册】account book

【账单】bill; check; account: 凭～报销 *reimbursement may be claimed on handing in the bills*

【账房】[书] ① accountant's office ② accountant

【账号】account number

【账户】account: 开～ *open on account with* (*or in*) *a bank*

【账款】funds on account; credit

【账面】as shown in an account book; items of an account: ～价值 *book value* /～净值 *net book value* /～利润 *book profit* /～损失 *book loss* /～盈余 *book surplus* /～余额 *book balance* /～债务 *book debt*

【账目】items of an account; accounts

胀 ① grow in size; expand; distend: 热～冷缩 *expend with heat and contract with cold* ② swell; be bloated

涨 ① swell after absorbing water, etc.: 海带发～了。*The kelps swelled up after being soaked.* ② (of the head) be swelled by a rush of blood; redden: 因发怒而脸～红 *be red with anger* /露西气得～红了脸。*Lucy's face flushed* (*red*) *with anger.* /谢丽尔的脸～红到脖子根了。*Sherrill flushed* (*up*) *to the root of her hair.* ③ (of weights and measures, etc.) be more, longer, etc. than expected: 上周西尼尔钱花～了。*Last week Senior spent more than he got or Senior couldn't make ends meet last week.*

see also zhǎng

障 ① hinder; impede; obstruct: ～碍赛跑 *obstacle race*; *steeplechase* / 路～ *barricade*; *roadblock* ② barrier; block; screen: 路～ *roadblock*; *barricade* /屏～ *protective screen*

【障碍】① hinder; block; obstruct: ～物 *obstacle*; *barrier*; *entanglement*; *hindrance* ② obstacle; obstruction; barrier; impediment

【障蔽】block; obstruct; shut out

【障眼法】cover-up; camouflage; disguise: 玩～ *throw dust into people's eyes*

【障子】a barrier made of reeds, sorghum stalks or closely planted shrubs; hedge

幛 a large, oblong sheet of silk with on inscription presented at a wedding, birthday or funeral

【幛子】large, oblong sheet of silk with an appropriate message attached, presented at a birthday, wedding or funeral

嶂 a screen-like mountain peak: 层峦叠～ *peaks rising one upon another*

瘴 miasma

【瘴疠】communicable subtropical diseases, such as pemicious malaria, etc.

【瘴气】miasma

zhāo

招[1] ① beckon; gesture: 格林～手要我进去。*Green beckoned me in.* /老师一～手,我们都向他跑去。*We rushed over to him when the teacher beckoned.* ② recruit; enlist; enroll; engage: ～临时工 *recruit temporary workers* ③ attract; invite; incur; court: ～蚊子 *attract mosquitoes* /～人嫌 *incur odium* ④ offend; provoke; tease ⑤ [方] infect; be contagious; be catching ⑥ (Zhāo) a surname

招[2] ① confess; admit; own up: 他～供了。*He has confessed.* ② a move in chess

【招安】(of feudal rulers) after amnesty to rebels and enlist their service: 接受～ *accept amnesty and pledge loyalty to the ruler*

【招标】invite tenders (or bid, public bidding): ～制 *completive-bidding system*

【招兵】recruit soldiers; raise troops ～买马 *recruit men and buy horses — raise or enlarge an army*; *recruit personnel*; *recruit followers*

【招财进宝】let riches and treasures come into the house

【招待】receive (guests); entertain; serve (customers); offer hospitality: ～费 *entertainment allowance or expenses* /～券 *complimentary ticket* /～所 *guest house*; *hostel*

【招待会】reception: 参加～ *attend a reception*

【招风】catch the wind — attract too much attention and invite trouble: 树大～ *a tall tree catches the wind — a person in a high position is liable to be attached*

【招蜂引蝶】attract bees and butterflies — flirt with men; be flirtatious

【招干】recruit cadres: ～条件 *qualifications for recruitment*

【招工】advertise for workers; recruit workers ～提干 *recruit workers and promote personnel*

【招供】confess one's crime; confess

【招股】raise capital by floating shares

【招雇】recruit; employ

【招呼】① call; shout: ～人们过来 *call the people to come over* ② hail; greet; say hello to: 亲切地～ *greet cordially* ③ notify; tell; ask: ～他去医院。*Tell him to go to the hospital.* ④ take care of; look after; attend to: ～小孩 *take good care of the children* ⑤ [方] watch; mind; take care: 天气冷,别～感冒了。*It is cold; take care not to catch a cold.*

【招幌】shop sign (formerly signs and emblems denoting certain trades, e. g. barbershop, blacksmith, wins merchant, grain merchant, etc.)

【招魂】call back the spirit of the dead; revive

【招集】call together; convene

【招架】ward off blows; hold one's own
【招考】give public notice of entrance examination; employ by examination; admit (students, applicants, tec.) by examination
【招揽】solicit (customers or business); canvass; attract: ~买卖 *canvass business orders*; *drum up trade* /~顾客 *attract customers*
【招领】announce the finding of lost property: 失物~ *found* (*as in notice*) /拾物~处 *Lost and Found*
【招募】recruit; enlist; enroll
【招纳】[书] recruit; seek and admit: ~贤士 *recruit men of worth*
【招女婿】take a man into the family as a son-in-law; have the groom move into the bride's house after marriage
【招牌】shop sign; signboard: 打着人道主义的~ *in the name of humanitarianism* /不要打着老师的~吓唬我们。*Don't frightened us in the name of teachers.*
【招聘】① engage by public notice; invite applications for a job; advertise for (a secretary, teacher, etc.): ~老师 *advertise for teachers*
【招亲】marry into and live with one's bride's family
【招请】① hire help ② invite; take in: ~帮工 *take in helpers*
【招惹】① provoke; incur; court; invite: ~麻烦 *court trouble*; *bring trouble* ② [方] tears; annoy provoke: 别~这人。*Don't provoke the fellow.*
【招认】confess one's crime; plead guilty
【招商】invite outside investments
【招生】enroll new students; recruit students: ~制度 *enrollment system*; *admission system* /~简章 *school admission brochure*
【招事】bring trouble on oneself; invite trouble
【招收】enroll; recruit; take in: ~技术人员 *recruit skilled workers*
【招手】move one's hand as a signal; beckon; wave: ~致意 *wave one's greetings*; *wave back in acknowledgement* /他~要我出去一下。*He beckoned me out.*
【招贴】poster; placard; bill
【招贤】① Summon men of worth to serve their country ② call he able to service
【招降】(all on or summon) sb to surrender
【招训】recruit and train: ~公车司机 *recruit and train bus driver*
【招眼】be eye-catching; attract people's attention; be ostentatious
【招摇】act ostentatiously; show off: ~撞骗 *swindle and bluff*; *bluff one's way around*; *brow beat and swindle*
【招引】draw; attract; induce: ~人围观 *draw a crowd of on lookers*
【招展】flutter; wave; move to and fro: 红旗迎风~。*Red flags fluttered in the breeze.*
【招致】① recruit; seek and employ ② bring about; lead to; result in
【招租】(house) for rent; ask for lodgers; attract lodgers; to let: 房屋~! *Room to let.*

昭 ① clear, obvious, evident: 罪恶~彰 *have committed flagrant crimes* ② [书] show; demonstrate: ~告 *proclaim*; *publicly declare*
【昭布】make known to the public; explicitly declare; clearly proclaim
【昭然】clear; obvious; manifest: ~若揭 *all too obvious*; *abundantly clear*
【昭示】make dear to all; declare publicly: ~后世 *make it dear to the posterity*
【昭雪】exonerate; rehabilitate; redress: 沉冤得以~。*The gross injustice was redressed.*
【昭彰】clear; evident; obvious; manifest
【昭著】clear; evident; manifest; obvious: 臭名~ *of ill repute*; *notorious*

着 ① a move in chess: 高~ *a clever move* /走错一~ *make a false move*; *take a wrong step* ② trick; device; move: 别耍花~儿。*Don't play tricks.* /他实在冷~了。*He is at his wits' end.* ③ [方] put in; add: ~点儿醋 *add a bit vinegar* ④ all right; O. K.: ~,就这么办。*Okay, do it that way.*
see also zháo; zhe; zhuó

朝 ① early morning; dawn; morning: ~霞 *rosy clouds of dawn*; *morning glow* ② day: 明~ *tomorrow*
see also cháo
【朝不保夕】not know in the morning what may happen in the evening; be in a critical condition; be in a precarious state
【朝发夕至】start at dawn and arrive at dusk — a short journey
【朝令夕改】issue an order in the morning and rescind it in the evening; make unpredictable change in policy
【朝露】[书] morning dew — short lived; ephemeral; transitory
【朝气】youthful spirit; vigour; vitality: 充满~ *be full of vitality* /~蓬勃 *be bursting with youthful spirit*
【朝三暮四】blow hot and cold; play fast and loose
【朝思暮想】yearn day and night; long day and night; pine for sth: 他对她~。*He thought about her from dawn to dusk.*
【朝夕】① morning and evening; day and night; every day; daily; constantly: ~相处 *be constantly together*; *be closely associated* ② very short time; shortly
【朝阳】the rising sun; the morning sun: ~工业 *sunrise industry*

zháo

着 ① touch; contact; come in contact with: 别让小孩~凉水。*Do not let the child touch the cold water.* ② be affected by (cold, etc.); be troubled with; suffer; feel ③ be ignited; be lit; burn: 森林~火了。*The forest was on fire.* /炉子点~了。*The stove is lit.* /干柴一点就~。*Firewood is highly in flammable.* ④ [方] fall asleep：昨天晚上她上床就～了。*She fell asleep as soon as she lain down on her bed last night.* ⑤ (used as a complement to another verb) hitting the mark; succeeding in：这次被他说～了。*This time he really hit the mail on the head.*

see also zhāo; zhe; zhuó

【着边】be close to what it should be; be relevant

【着风】be chilled by the wind, become unwell through being in a draught

【着慌】panic; feel alarmed; become flustered ar jittery; get nervous：孩子丢了，全家都～了。*The whole family was thrown into a panic because of the lost child.*

【着火】catch fire; be on fire; be in flames

【着急】get excited; feel anxious：干～ *be anxious but unable to do anything about it* /瞎～ *worry to no purpose* /别～！*Take it easy*!

【着凉】catch cold; catch a chill：当心～。*Be careful not to catch cold.*

【着忙】① be in a hurry or rush：别～，还赶得上火车。*Don't be in such a rush; we still can catch the train.*

【着迷】be fascinated; be enchanted; be captivated：他对唱歌很～。*He is crazy about singing very much.* /小孩容易对电视～。*The children are easily glued to the television.*

【着魔】be bewitched; be entranced; be possessed：他～似的看着远方。*He looked into the distance like a man possessed.*

【着色】coloration：～玻璃 *stained glass*；*pigmented glass* /～橡胶 *tinted rubber*

zhǎo

爪 claw; talon

see also zhuǎ

【爪哇】Java, the 4th largest island of Indonesia：～人 *Javanese*

【爪牙】talons and fangs — flunkeys; underlings; lackeys

找 ① look for; hunt for; try to find; seek：寻～失物 *look for lost articles* / ～东西 *look for sth* /～机会 *look for an opportunity* /～原因 *find out the cause* /～答案 *try to find the answer* ② want to see; call on; approach; ask for：有人～小李。*Someone wants to see Xiao Li.* /后天来～你。*I am to call on you the day after tomorrow.* ③ give change：这是～给你的钱。*Here is your change.* /售货员～给他二十元钱。*The shop assistant gave her 20 yuan change.* /不用～了。*Keep the change, please.*

【找不开】have no small change for (money of a higher denomination)：没零钱，～了。*No small change for your note.*

【找不自在】[口] ask for trouble; borrow trouble; bring trouble upon oneself：和他吵架，是～。*You are borrowing trouble if you quarrel with him.*

【找茬儿】find fault; pick holes; pick a quarrel; nitpick：故意～ *deliberately pick a quarrel*

【找对象】look for a partner in marriage

【找麻烦】look for trouble; cause sb trouble; ask for trouble：他总给别人～。*He always causes people so much trouble.*

【找婆家】look for a husband：她今年三十岁了，可还不急着～。*She is thirty years old, but still not want to get married.*

【找齐】① make uniform; even up; balance ② make up deficiency; make complete：先给他一部分，等有零钱了，再～。*I'll pay you part of the money at first and the balance will be paid on when I have some change.*

【找钱】give change：他还等着～。*He is still waiting to be given change.*

【找事】① look (or hunt) for a job; seek employment ② pick a quarrel

【找死】court death：过马路不看车，想～啊！*Why not watch out for the passing vehicles when crossing the road; you are trying to kill yourself, aren't you?*

【找头】change (from money paid)：给你～。*Here is your change.*

【找寻】① look for; seek; try to find ② [方] find fault with; pick holes; embarrass; pick on：他总是～人。*He is always finding fault with others.*

沼 marital pond：池～ *pond*；*pool*

【沼气】marsh gas; firedamp; methane; sewage gas; bio-gas：～池 *methane-generating pit*；*methane tank*

【沼泽】marsh; swamp; bog：～地 *marshland*；*swamp land* /～土 *bog soil*

zhào

召[1] call together; gather; convene; summon：感～ *move and inspire*；*impel*

召[2] (usu. used in place names) temple; monastery

【召唤】call; summon (usu.)：时代在～我们。*The times is calling us.*

【召回】recall：～大使 *recall an ambassador*

【召集】call together; convene; assemble：～会议 *call (or convene) a conference*

【召见】① call in (a subordinate) officially ② diplomacy common can envoy to an interview

【召开】hold; convene; convoke：～学术会议 *hold a symposium*

兆[1] ① sign; omen：先～ *omen*；*sign*；*indication* ② portend; foretell ③ (Zhào) a surname

兆[2] 【数】million; trillion

【兆赫】megahertz (MHZ)

【兆头】sign; omen; portent：凶～ *ill omen* /好(坏)～ *a good (bad) omen* /这是个吉祥的～。*That's a propitious sign.*

【兆位】megabit (Mb)

【兆字节】megabyte

诏 ［书］① instruct; admonish; warn; exhort ② imperial edict

【诏令】order issued by an emperor; imperial edict

【诏书】imperial edict

笊

【笊篱】a bamboo, wicker or wire strainer

照 ① shine; radiate; light up; illuminate：阳光普～ *the sun illuminates every corner of the land* /日～ *sunshine* /光～ *illumination* /拿手电～路 *light the way with a torch* ② reflect; mirror：～镜子 *look in the mirror* /湖面～出了树的倒影。*The lake reflected clearly the images of the trees.* ③ take a picture (or photograph); photograph; film; shoot：这些相片～得很好。*The pictures are well taken.* ④ take care of; look after ⑤ notify; inform：关～一声 *notify sb; let sb know* ⑥ contrast; compare ⑦ understand; make out：心～不宣 *have a tacit understanding* ⑧ photograph; picture：半身～ *half-length photo* ⑨ licence; permit：车～ *licence of a car* /牌～ *licence plate; numberplate; licence tag* ⑩ in the direction of; towards：～左边看 *look in the left* /～着马路走。*Go towards the road.* ⑪ according to; in accordance with; in conformity with：～我看，他在骗人。*It seems to me that he is lying.*

【照搬】indiscriminately imitate; mechanically copy：盲目地～ *follow sth blindly* /～别人的经验 *copy indiscriminately the experience of others*

【照办】act accordingly; act in accordance with; act upon; conform to; comply with; follow：这事无法～。*The matter cannot be handled the way you have proposed.*

【照本宣科】repeat what the book says; read entirely from the text; echo what the book says

【照常】as usual：～工作 *work as usual* /～营业 *business as usual* /比赛～进行。*The match will be played as planned.*

【照抄】copy word for word; copy verbatim：～不误 *copy without fail*

【照登】publish sth as it is (i. e without alterations)

【照发】① issue as before; be paid as usual ② approve for distribution (used for notices or circulars submitted for approval)

【照顾】① give consideration to; show consideration for; make allowances for; take into account：～个人的实际需要 *consider the individual's actual needs* /～他的困难 *give consideration to his difficulties* ② look after; care for; attend to ③ keep an eye on; look after：你～一下行李。*Please keep an eye on the luggage.* ④ (of customer) patronize; shop at

【照管】look after; care for; be in charge of; tend：～机器 *tend a machine*

【照葫芦画瓢】draw a dipper with a gourd as model-ape; repeat; imitate; copy

【照会】① present (or deliver, address) a note to (a government) ② note：递交～ *present a note* /交换～ *exchange notes* /正式～ *formal note; official note*

【照价】according to the cost or set price：～赔偿 *compensate according to the cost*

【照旧】as before; as usual; as of off old：开会程序～。*The meeting procedure remains unchanged.*

【照看】look after; attend to; keep an eye on; care for：～小孩 *attend to the children* /～行李 *keep an eye on they luggage*

【照理】① according to reason; in the ordinary course of events; normally：～他该去上班了。*Normally, he should go to work by now.* ②［方］look after; attend to

【照例】as a role; in general as usual; usually：晚会～安排在周末。*The ball is usually arranged in the weekends.*

【照料】care for; attend to; take care of：虽然她还小，却把家里～得挺好。*Although only a little girl, she manages her house very well.*

【照临】shine on; illuminate; light up：月光～大地。*The moonlight lit up the land.*

【照面】① (mostly in the negative) put in an appearance; show up; turn up; meet：从不～ *never show up* ② encounter; run into; come across：打个～ *come face to face with sb; run into sb*

【照明】illumination; lighting：舞台～ *stage illumination* /～设备 *lighting installation* /～电路 *lighting circuit*

【照片】photograph; picture：彩色～ *colour photograph* /洗～ *develop a film*

【照射】shine; illuminate; irradiate; light up：激光～ *irradiate with laser rays*

【照实】according to facts：～说。*Tell the truth.*

【照说】ordinarily; as a rule; generally：～你应该早点儿做出这道题的。*You should have worked out the problem earlier.*

【照相】take a picture (or photograph); photograph 他想～。*He wants to have a picture taken.*

【照相机】camera：全景～ *panoramic camera* /傻瓜～ *foolproof camera* /小型～ *miniature camera* /折叠式～ *folding camera* /制版～ *process camera*

【照样】① after a patter or model：～复制 *reproduce from the original* ② in the same old way; as before; as usual; all the same：下雨比赛～进行。*The game will proceed in the same way no matter if it rains.*

【照耀】shine; illuminate; irradiate：阳光～大地。*The sun is shining over the land.*

【照应】① coordinate; correlate：前后～ *be well organized* ② look after; take care of：～周到 *look after thoughtfully*

【照章】according to rules and regulations：～办事 *act according to the rules*

【照直】① (go) straight on; (walk) straight ahead：沿街～走。*Go along the street.* ② straightforward; direct; blunt; point-blank

【照准】① (used in official documents) request granted ② aim at：～靶心射击。*Shoot at the bull's-eye.*

Z

罩 ① cover; envelop; overspread; wrap: 笼~ *envelop; shroud* / 他毛衣外~着一件蓝布褂儿 *He wore a blue dustcoat over his sweater.* ② cover; shade; hood; casing: 灯~ *lampshade* / 保险~ *protecting casing* ③ a bamboo fish trap ④ a bamboo chicken coop ⑤ outer garment; dust-robe; dust-gown; overall

【罩棚】an awning over a gateway or a courtyard

肇 [书] ① start; commence; initiate; begin ② cause (trouble, etc.); lead to

【肇端】[书] beginning; origin

【肇祸】cause trouble; cause an accident

【肇始】[书] start; commence; initiate; begin

【肇事】make trouble; stir up a disturbance: ~者 *a person who has created a disturbance; trouble-maker*

zhē

折 [口] ① roll over; turn over and over: 昨晚格雷斯~到河里了。*Grace fell into the river last night.* ② pour back and forth between two containers

see also shé; zhé

【折跟头】turn a somersault; loop the loop

【折腾】[口] ① turn from side to side; toss about; toss and turn: 他~了一晚上才睡着。*He tossed about in the bed all night before he got to sleep.* ② do sth over and over again; fool around with; mess with: 他整天没事瞎~。*He is fooling around all day.* ③ cause physical or mental suffering; get sb down; torment ④ spend freely; squander: ~钱财 *squander money*

蜇 ① (of bees, wasps, etc.) prick with a sting; sting: 蜜蜂也~人。*The bee also stings people.* ② smart; sting

遮 ① hide from view; cover; screen; conceal: 乌云~天。*Dark clouds blotted out the sky.* / 树木~住了月亮。*The moon was hidden by trees.* ② block; obstruct; impede; hinder: ~道 *block the way* ③ keep out; cover up; cloak: ~风挡雨 *keep out wind and rain* / ~人耳目 *throw dust in people's eyes; hoodwink (or fool) the public*

【遮蔽】① hide from view; cover; screen; conceal ② obstruct; block; shelter: ~视线 *obstruct the view* ③【军】defilade: ~物 *defilade* / ~阵地 *defiladed position*

【遮藏】hide; cover up; keep out of sight; conceal

【遮丑】hide one's shame; cover up one's defect; gloss over one's blemishes; screen one's fault

【遮挡】① shelter from; keep out; cover: ~风沙 *keep out wind and dust* ② a shelter; a cover

【遮盖】① cover; overspread: 马路被大雪~。*The roads were all covered by snow.* ② hide; conceal; cover up: ~矛盾 *conceal contradictions* / ~缺点 *hide one's weaknesses*

【遮拦】block; obstruct; impede

【遮天盖地】① (of wind; rain; sand, etc.) ② blot out the sky and cover up the earth ② (of a group of people) be enormous in number

【遮羞】hush up a scandal; cover up one's embarrassment

【遮掩】① cover; envelop; block; overspread ② cover up; hide; conceal; gloss over

【遮阳】sunshade

【遮阴】shelter from heat or light; shade: ~的树 *a shade tree*

zhé

折[1] ① break; snap; fracture: 啪的一下~断树枝 *snap off a twig* / ~成两截 *snap sth in half* / ~断腿 *fracture (or break) one's leg* ② suffer the loss of; lose; deprived of ③ bend; twist; turn: 曲~ *twists and turns* ④ turn back; change direction: 他半路又~了回去。*He turned back after he walked halfway.* ⑤ be convinced; be filled with admiration; be won over: 心~ *be deeply convinced; be filled with heartfelt admiration* ⑥ convert into; amount to; change to: ~价 *convert into money; evaluate in terms of money* ⑦ fold: ~衬衣 *fold a shirt* ⑧ discount; rebate: 打六~ *give 40% discount; charge 60% of the full price* ⑨ turning stroke (in Chinese characters)

折[2] book or booklet used for keeping accounts, etc.; folder

see also shé; zhē

【折半】reduce (a price) by half; give 50% discount

【折变】[方] sell off (one's property)

【折尺】folding rule

【折叠】fold: ~好报纸 *fold up the newspaper*

【折兑】exchange (gold or silver) for money; convert

【折返】return; turn back

【折服】① subdue; bring into submission; convince: ~对手 *beat one's rival; subdue one's opponent* ② be convinced; be filled with admiration; win over: 使人~ *be fully convinced; compel admiration*

【折光】(of water, glass, etc.) refract light

【折合】convert into; amount

【折回】turn back (half way)

【折价】convert into money; evaluate in terms of money: ~赔偿 *pay compensation at the market price*

【折扣】discount; rebate: 这已经是~价了。*This is the discounted price.*

【折磨】cause physical or mental suffering; torment: 嫉妒的~ *suffer severely from the anguish of jealousy*

【折扇】folding fan

【折射】【物】refraction: ~角 *angle of refraction; refraction angle* / ~率 *index of refraction; refraction power* / ~望远镜 *refracting telescope* / ~线 *refracted ray*

【折实】① reckon the actual amount after a discount ② adjust payment in accordance with the price index of certain commodities
【折寿】reduce one's lifetime because of having or getting more than one deserves
【折算】convert：用外汇～ *convert into foreign exchange* /～率 *conversion rate*
【折线】【数】broken line
【折腰】bend one's back-bow; cringe
【折页】【印】folding：～机 *folding machine*
【折纸】paper folding
【折子】booklet in accordion form with a slipcase, used for keeping accounts, etc.
【折子戏】highlights from operas

哲 ① wise; sagacious; intelligent：富兰克林的话很有～理。*What Franklin said is philosophical.* ② wise man; sage：历代先～ *sages through the ages*
【哲理】philosophical theory; philosophy：富于～ *teeming with philosophical wisdom*
【哲人】［书］sage; philosopher
【哲学】philosophy：～家 *philosopher* /～理论 *philosophical theory*; *philosophical thinking*

蛰 ［书］hibernate：惊～ *waking of Insects* (*3rd solar term*)
【蛰伏】【动】dormancy; hibernation
【蛰居】［书］live in seclusion or solitude：～斗室 *cloister oneself in one's little room*

谪 ［书］①（as a punishment in feudal china）relegate a high official to a minor post in a remote border town; banish from the court; exile：汉森去年被贬～了。*Hansen was relegated to a secondary position last year.* ②（of an immortal, etc.）be banished from Heaven ③ blame; rebuke
【谪居】（of officials in former times）live in banishment

辙 ① the track of a wheel; rut; groove：车～ *rut* /如出一～ *be exactly the same*; *be no different from each other* ② direction of traffic ③ rhyme（of a song, poetic drama, etc.）④［方］way; idea; with
【辙叉】frog
【辙口】rhyme（of a song, poetic drama, etc.）
【辙乱旗靡】crisscross chariot tracks and drooping banners — flee in disarray

zhě

者 ①（used after a verb or adjective, or verb or adjective phrase to indicate a class of person or things）one or those who; the thing or things which：作～ *writer*; *author* /读～ *reader* /劳动～ ② follower of a doctrine, etc.; -ist：社会主义～ *socialist* ③ the former（latter）：两～ *take two things*; *these two persons* ④［书］indicating a rhetorical pause

锗 【化】germanium（Ge）

赭 reddish brown; burnt ochre
【赭石】ochre（a mineral）

褶 pleat; crease; fold; wrinkle：百～裙 *pleated skirt*
【褶皱】①【地】fold：～作用 *folding* /～山 *folded mountain* ② wrinkle（in the skin）
【褶子】① pleat：这件衣服上有～。*The clothes has pleats.* ② crease; fold; wrinkle：烫平～。*Iron out the wrinkles.* ③ wrinkle（on the face）

zhè

这 ① this; these：～张桌子旧了。*This table is old.* ② now; then：你～是要做什么？*What do you want then?*
【这儿】① here ② now; then
【这边】this side; here; this way：请～走。*This way please.*
【这次】this time; present; current：～会议 *the present session* /～运动会 *the current sports meeting*
【这等】like this; so; such; such kind of
【这番】this; these
【这个】① this one; this ②［口］（used before a verb or adjective to give force to it）so; such ③（repeated to show hesitation）：～，～，我想不起来了。*Ah...ah, I can't remember.*
【这号人】［方］this kind of person; people of this sort：～真少！*There won't be many this kind of person.*
【这会儿】［口］now; at the moment; at present; just now：他～正在睡觉。*He is sleeping at the moment.*
【这里】over here; here：我们～人很多。*We have many people here.*
【这么】so; such; this way; like this：他～说。*So he says.*
【这么点儿】such a tiny bit：就～路，很快就到了。*It is so close; we can walk there in a short time.*
【这么样】so; such; like this; this way：他总～办事吗？*Does he always do things like this?*
【这么着】like this; this way; so
【这样】so; such; like this; this way：一会儿～，一会儿那样，到底你要什么？*Now one way, now another, what on earth do you want?*
【这样那样】this or that; of kind or another; all kinds of this：由于～的原因，他又迟到了。*He was late again for an reason.*
【这早晚儿】① so late：～了，别出去了！*It's too late to go out.* ② now; at the moment; at present：怎么～了还不起床？*Why not get up now?*

蔗 sugarcane
【蔗农】sugarcane grower
【蔗糖】①【化】sucrose：～蜜 *cane molasses* ②

cane sugar

鹧

【鹧鸪】【动】Chinese francolin; partridge

zhe

着 ① be doing: 窗户开~呢。*The windows are open.* /他正听~歌呢。*He is listening to the radio now.* ② used to indicate a state: 桌上放~很多碗。*There are a lot of bowls on the desk.* ③ used to give forth to a verb or adjective: 听~。*Just listen.* /小心~点儿。*Be careful.* ④ used in forming a preposition: 朝~ *towards* /顺~ *along*
see also zhāo; zháo; zhuó

zhēn

贞[1] loyal; faithful

贞[2] (of women) chastity

【贞操】① chastity or virginity ② loyalty; moral integrity

【贞节】① loyalty; constancy ② chastity or virginity

【贞洁】chaste and undefiled

【贞烈】(of a woman) would rather die than lose one's chastity.

【贞女】a chaste girl; virgin

【贞淑】[书] chaste and gentle

针 ① needle: 磁~ *a magnetic needle* /罗盘~ *a compass needle* /毛线~ *knitting needle* ② stitch: 在毛衣上缝两~ *sew (or put) a couple of stitches in one's sweater* /他手上的伤口缝了五~。*The cut in his hand was closed with five stitches.* ③ anything like a needle: 松~ *pine needle* /表~ *(watch) hand; indicator; pointer* ④ injection; shot: 打~ *give or have a injection* ⑤ acupuncture

【针鼻儿】the eye of a needle

【针布】【纺】card clothing

【针对】① be directed against; be aimed at; be targeted on ② in the light of; in accordance with; in connection with

【针锋相对】tit for tat; measure for measure; in direct opposition to: 进行~的斗争 *wage a tit-for-tat struggle against*

【针箍】[方] thimble

【针剂】【药】injection

【针尖】the point of a needle; pinpoint

【针脚】stitch: ~细密 *short stitches*

【针筒】syringe

【针头】【医】syringe needle

【针线】needlework: ~活儿 *needlework; sewing; stitching* /学~ *learn how to do needlework* /~包 *sewing kit*

【针眼】① the eye of a needle ② pinprick ③【医】sty

【针叶树】conifer; coniferous tree; softwood

【针织】knitting: ~机 *knitting machine* /~品 *knit goods; knitwear; hosiery; knitting*

【针锥】[方] awl

侦 detect; scout; investigate; explore

【侦办】investigate and handle a case

【侦查】【律】investigate (a crime)

【侦察】【军】reconnoitre; scout: 敌后~ *reconnoitre the enemy read* /~排 *scout platoon* /~兵 *scout* /~部队 *reconnaissance troops; scouting force* /~机 *reconnaissance plane; scout* /~卫星 *reconnaissance satellite* /~员 *scout*

【侦获】capture after investigation (criminal, etc.); investigate and crack: ~赃物 *hunt for and seize a batch of stolen goods*

【侦缉】track down and arrest

【侦破】investigate and crack; break (a criminal case); detect; solve: ~案件 *solve case; crack a criminal case*

【侦探】① do detective work ② detective; spy: ~小说 *detective story; detective fiction; criminal novel*

【侦听】monitor; intercept: ~器 *detectaphone; monitor* /~台 *intercept station*

【侦讯】investigate and interrogate

珍 ① treasure; riches ② precious; valuable; rare; treasured ③ value highly; treasure; set great store by

【珍爱】treasure; love dearly; bc very food of; cherish

【珍宝】jewellery; riches; treasure: 她们家有许多~。*There are lots of treasures in her family.*

【珍本】rare edition; rare book

【珍藏】collect (rare books; art treasures, etc.)

【珍贵】valuable; precious; rare: ~药材 *valuable ingredients of traditional Chinese medicine* /~的古籍 *rare ancient books* /人才最~。*Talents are most precious.*

【珍品】treasure; curiosity; curio: 艺术~ *art treasure*

【珍奇】rare: ~动物 *rare animals*

【珍禽异兽】rare birds and animals

【珍赏】treasure and delight in (curios, etc.); highly value and appreciate

【珍视】value; prize; cherish; treasure: ~今天的幸福生活 *cherish today's happy life*

【珍惜】treasure; value; cherish: ~时间 *value one's time* /~友谊 *treasure friendship*

【珍稀】rare and precious: ~动物 *rare animals* /~濒危物种 *rare and endangered species*

【珍重】① prize; cherish; treasure; value highly: ~权利 *value one's right* ② take good care of yourself; look after yourself: 请~! *Take good care of yourself, please.*

【珍珠】pearl: ~贝 *earl shell; pearl oyster*

胗 gizzard: 鸡~儿 *chicken's gizzard*

【胗肝儿】gizzard and liver (esp. chicken's or duck's)

真 ① true; real; factual; genuine: 此话当~? *Is it really true?* ② clear; unmistakable: 你听得~么? *Can you hear clearly?* ③ really; truly; indeed: 天气~好。*It's really fine.* / 你~聪明。*You are really bright.*

【真才实学】real ability and learning; genuine; knowledge or competence: 这些老教师大多具有~。*These senior teachers are persons of real learning.*

【真诚】sincere; genuine; true; earnest; honest: ~的心意 *sincerity* / ~的友谊 *true friendship* / 他的~感动了在场的人。*His earnestness touched everyone present.*

【真传】essence of a craft or knowledge imparted by a master

【真刀真枪】real swords and spears — the real thing: 重要的是不要空谈,要~地干。*The most important is to stop empty talk and get down to brass tacks.*

【真谛】true essence; true meaning: 人生的~ *the true meaning of life*

【真分数】【数】proper fraction

【真格的】[方] real; true; serious: 说~,我不知道。*To tell the truth, I don't know.*

【真话】the truth: 把~告诉我。*Please tell me the truth.*

【真迹】authentic work (of painting or calligraphy)

【真金不怕火炼】true gold fears no fire — a good anvil does not fear the hammer; a person of integrity can stand severe tests

【真菌】fungus

【真空】【物】vacuum: ~过滤 *vacuum filtration* / 完全~ *perfect vacuum* / 未尽~ *partial vacuum* / ~吸尘器 *vacuum cleaner* / ~压铸 *vacuum die casting* / ~包装 *vacuum packing* / ~泵 *pick-up pump*; *vacuum pump* / ~地带 *no man's land* / ~度 *vacuity*; *degree of vacuum*

【真理】truth: 普遍~ *universal truth* / 坚持~ *uphold the truth*

【真面目】true features; true colours; true face: 认清其~ *see sb in his true colours*; *know sb for what he is*

【真命】sent by God or Heaven: ~天子 *Son of Heaven*; *emperor*

【真皮】①【生理】derma; corium ② real or genuine leather; true leather

【真凭实据】genuine evidence; hard evidence; conclusive proof

【真枪实弹】real guns and bullets; live ammunition

【真切】① distinct; clear; graphic: 看得~ *see clearly* ② sincere; genuine: 情意~ *genuine feeling*

【真情】① the real (or true) situation; the facts; the actual state of affairs; truth ② true feelings; real sentiment: ~流露 *a revelation of one's true feelings*

【真确】① authentic; true; genuine; real ② clear; distinct; plain

【真实】true; real; authentic; actual: ~地址 *real address* / ~记录 *authentic records* / ~感 *sense of reality* / ~性 *authenticity*; *truthfulness*; *factuality*

【真是】(used in a complaint) indeed; really: ~!这雨下不停了。*What a shame! The rain just doesn't stop!* / 你也~,下这点雨就不去上班了。*You are the limit; just because of a bit of rain you won't go to work.*

【真相】the real (or true) situation; the actual state of affairs; facts; truth; the real (or actual) facts: 揭露~ *reveal (or disclose) the truth* / 掩盖~ *cover up the matter* / 了解事实~ *find out the facts*; *clarify the truth of the matter*

【真心】heartfelt; wholehearted; true; sincere: ~相爱 *be truly in love (with each other)* / ~拥护 *give whole-hearted support to* / ~话 *sincere words* / 说~话 *speak from the bottom of one's heart* / 妈妈说的是~话。*Your mother was speaking her mind.*

【真真假假】the true mingled with the false; a mixture of truth and falsehood

【真正】① genuine; true; real: ~的朋友 *a true friend* / ~的人民公仆 *faithful servant of the people* ② really; truly; genuinely: 这个家伙~不简单。*The fellow is truly remarkable.*

【真知】genuine (or real) knowledge; knowledge: ~灼见 *real knowledge and deep understanding*; *profound insight*; *penetrating judgement*

【真挚】sincere; cordial; genuine: ~话语 *cordial remarks* / ~的感情 *genuine feelings* / ~的态度 *sincere (or earnest) attitude*

【真主】【宗】allah

砧 hammering block; anvil: 锻~ *smith anvil*

【砧板】chopping block

【砧子】[口] hammering block; anvil

斟 pour (tea or wine): 自~自饮 *help oneself to the wine*

【斟酌】turn over in one's mind; consider; deliberate: ~字句 *weigh one's words* / ~损益 *make alterations after due consideration* / 请~后再告诉我你的决定。*Please tell me your decision after considering carefully again and again.*

甄 [书] discriminate; distinguish; examine; draw a distinction

【甄拔】select; choose: ~人才 *select qualified people*

【甄别】① examine and distinguish; screen; discriminate ② test and assess; reexamine a case

【甄选】select

榛 【植】① hazel ② hazelnut; filbert

【榛鸡】hazel grouse

【榛莽】[书] luxuriant vegetation

【榛子】① hazel ② hazelnut

箴 ① [书] advise; exhort; admonish ② a type of didactic literary composition

【箴言】[书] admonition; exhortation; maxim

臻 [书] ① attain (a high level); become better: 他的想法日~成熟。*His idea is becoming*

Z

more and mature. ② arrive; reach; come

zhěn

诊 examine (a patient)

【诊病】make a diagnosis; diagnose a disease
【诊察】examine (a patient)
【诊断】diagnose:物理~ *physical diagnosis* /医生~他的病是肺炎。*The doctor diagnosed his illness as pneumonia.*
【诊疗】make a diagnosis and give treatment: ~器械 *medical instruments*
【诊脉】feel the pulse
【诊室】consulting room
【诊所】① clinic; dispensary:私人~ *private clinic* ② a small hospital
【诊台】diagnostic table; examination table
【诊治】make a diagnosis and give treatment

枕 ① pillow:一对绣花~头 *a pair of embroidered pillows* ②【机】block:转~ *swivel block* ③ rest and head on:小孩~在妈妈肩上睡着了。*The child fell asleep on her mother's shoulder.*

【枕戈待旦】wait for daybreak with one's head pillowed on one's weapon; maintain combat readiness; be on the alert
【枕巾】a towel used to cover a pillow
【枕木】railway sleeper; tie
【枕套】pillowcase; pillowslip
【枕头】pillow: ~箱 *a box in the bedroom used to keep valuables*
【枕席】①[书] bed ② a mat used to cover a pillow; pillow mat
【枕心】pillow (without the pillowcase)

疹 rash

【疹子】[口] measles

缜

【缜密】careful; deliberate; detailed; meticulous: ~的计划 *a deliberate (or carefully thought-out) plan* /文思~ *meticulously written*

zhèn

阵[1] ① battle array; battle formation:矩~ *matrix* /方~ *phalanx; square array* ② position; front; front lines:敌~ *enemy position* /上~ *go into battle; play in a game*

阵[2] ① a period of time; some time:他来了有一~儿。*He has been here for sometime.* ②[量] short period; spell: ~~狂风 *gusts of winds* /一~两 *a spatter of rain* /~大笑 *a fit (or burst) of laughter* /一~欢呼 *a burst of cheers* /一~咳嗽 *a fit (or spasm) of coughing*

【阵地】position; front:坚守~ *hold one's ground; hold fast to one's position* /~攻击 *positional attack (defence)*
【阵法】tactical disposition or deployment of troops
【阵风】a gust of wind
【阵脚】① front line ② position; condition; situation; circumstances:乱了~ *be thrown into confusion*
【阵列】【数】array: ~处理机 *array processor*
【阵容】① battle array; battle formation ② lineup: ~强大 *have a strong lineup*
【阵势】① battle array; battle formation; a disposition of combat forces:摆开~ *deploy the ranks in battle array* ② situation; condition; circumstances; scene
【阵痛】①【医】labour pains; throes (of childbirth); birth pangs ② growing pains; problems and discomfort caused by social dislocation as a result of rapid change
【阵图】a system of battle formations:八~ *the Eightfold Maze*
【阵亡】be killed in action; fall in battle
【阵线】front; ranks; alignment:民主~ *alignment of democratic forces* /民族统一~ *national united front*
【阵型】formation
【阵雪】snow shower
【阵营】a group of people who pursue a common interest; camp:民主~ *a democratic camp*
【阵雨】shower

鸩 ① a legendary bird with poisonous feathers ②[书] poisoned wine ③ kill with poisoned wine

【鸩毒】[书] poisoned wine
【鸩酒】poisoned wine

振 ① shake; flutter; flap: ~笔直书 *wield one's pen furiously; write with flying strokes* ② rise with force and spirit; brace up; boost: ~作起来 *cheer (or brace) up* ③ vibrate:共~ *resonance*

【振笔直书】write with flying strokes; wield one's pen furiously
【振臂】raise one's arm: ~高呼 *raise one's arm and shout*
【振翅高飞】flutter and soar high
【振荡】①【物】vibrate ②【电】oscillate:本机~ *local oscillation* /~放电 *oscillatory discharge* /~电路 *oscillating circuit* /~管 *oscillator valve* /~器 *oscillator*
【振动】【物】vibration:简频~ *simple harmonic vibration* /~频率 *vibration frequency*
【振奋】① rouse oneself; rise with force and spirit; be inspired with enthusiasm; be high-spirited:听到那个好消息,大家精神~。*On hearing the good news, all of us are in high spirits.* ② inspire; stimulate; encourage: ~士气 *boost (or raise) the morale (of the troops)* /~人心 *inspire people; fill people with enthusiasm*
【振幅】【物】amplitude (of vibration):脉冲~ *pulse amplitude* /~畸变 *amplitude distortion*
【振聋发聩】rouse the deaf, enlighten the benighted:您说的话真是~啊。*What you have said*

would make a deaf man hear and a blind man see.

【振兴】develop vigorously; promote; vitalize:大力~农业 *vigorously develop agriculture* /~社会主义道德 *promote socialist morality*

【振振有词】speak plausibly and volubly (in self-justification); speak-glibly (to justify oneself)

【振作】pull oneself together; bestir oneself; display vigour; exert oneself: ~精神 *bestir oneself; brace (or cheer) up* /~情绪 *buoy up one's spirits*

朕[1] I, the sovereign; we (used by an emperor to refer to himself)

朕[2] [书] sign; omen

【朕兆】[书] sign; omen; portent

赈 relieve; aid; bring relief to

【赈济】relieve; aid: ~灾民 *relieve the people in stricken areas; aid the victims*

【赈款】relief fund or money

【赈灾】relieve the people in stricken or disaster areas

震 ① shake; shock; vibrate; quake:地~ *earthquake* ② greatly excited; shocked; deeply astonished: ~惊 *astonished; taken aback* ③ one of the Eight Trigrams

【震波】【地】scismic wave; earthquake wave: ~图 *seismogram*

【震颤】tremble; quiver; vibrate

【震荡】shake; shock; quake; vibrate; reverberate:社会~ *social upheaval*

【震动】① shake; quake; tremble; quiver:炮声~了整个山谷。*The thunder of guns quiver berated throughout the whole valley.* ② shock (people); astonish; stir; excite:他逝世的噩耗~了全国。*The sad news of his death shocked the whole nation.*

【震耳欲聋】deafening; thunderous: ~的掌声 *the deafening applause*

【震感】sensation of vibration and quaking; seism aesthesia:这次地震百里之外都有~。*The earthquake was felt a hundred miles away.*

【震撼】shake; shock; vibrate; stir; touch

【震级】magnitude (of an earthquake)

【震惊】shock; stun; amaze; astonish

【震怒】be enraged; be furious

【震情】situation after an earthquake; condition of an earthquake

【震慑】awe; frighten; scare; intimidate

【震天动地】shake heaven and earth:团结起来的力量可以~。*The strength of getting together can shake heaven and earth.*

【震音】【音】tremolo

【震源】focus (of an earthquake)

镇 ① press down; force down; keep down; ease: ~压暴乱 *put down a riot* / ~痛作用 *relieve the pain* ② calm; tranquil; at ease; stable:保持~静 *keep cool; keep one's head* ③ guard; garrison ④ cool with cold water or ice:冰~橘子汁 *iced apple juice* ⑤ garrison post ⑥ town; township ⑦ a relatively large trading centre ⑧ (Zhèn) a surname

【镇定】① calm; cool; composed; unruffled; collected: ~自若 *be perfectly calm and collected; be in possession of oneself* /神色~ *be calm and collected; show composure and presence of mind* ② calm down: ~自己 *calm oneself down*

【镇服】force sb into submission; bring sb to his knees; intimidate sb into surrender

【镇静】① calm; cool; composed; collected:面容~ *keep one's countenance* /保持~ *keep calm* ② calm down

【镇守】guard or garrison (a strategically important place)

【镇痛】① ease pain; relieve pain ②【医】analgesia: ~效果 *analgesic effect*

【镇压】① suppress; repress; put down; quell: ~叛乱 *put down (or suppress) a rebellion* ② execute (a criminal):依法~ *put down according to law* ③【农】rolling; compacting; tamping

【镇长】town head

【镇派】paperweight

【镇住】bring sb to submission; keep sb under control; reduce sb to submission; subdue:我们被老师的话~了。*We were put ourselves in our teacher's place.*

zhēng

正 the first month of the lunar year; the first moon

see also zhèng

【正旦】[书] the lunar New Year's Day

【正月】the first month of the lunar year; the first moon: ~初三 *third (day) of first lunar month*

争 ① contend; vie; strive; compete: ~权 *contend for power* /不~一日之短长 *not strive for temporary superiority* /明~暗斗 *open quarrels and secret wrangles* ② argue; dispute; wrangle:你们不要再~了。*You'd better stop bickering.*

【争霸】contend (or struggle) for hegemony; scramble or strive for supremacy: ~世界 *strive to dominate the world*

【争辩】argue; dispute; debate; contend:无休止的~ *an endless debate* /面对事实,他不再~了。*Faced with facts, he did not argue any longer.*

【争吵】quarrel; wrangle; squabble; bicker:无谓的~ *a pointless quarrel* /不停的~ *an endless bickering* /激烈的~ *fierce (or bitter) wrangling*

【争宠】vie (with each other) for sb's favour; strive for sb's favour

【争斗】① fight; struggle ② contend; oppose

【争端】dispute; conflict; controversial issue; controversy:国际~ *an international dispute* /世界~ *a border dispute* /引起~ *give rise to a dispute* /挑起~ *provoke a dispute* /解决~ *settle a dispute*

Z

【争夺】struggle for; enter into rivalry with sb over sth; vie with sb for sth: ~遗产 *contend for the legacy* / ~权力 *vie for power* / ~市场 *scramble for markets*

【争分夺秒】race (or work) against time; make every minute and second count; seize every minute and second

【争风吃醋】be jealous (of a rival in love); fight for the affections of a man or woman

【争锋】fight for mastery; strive for a decisive victory; fight to see who is the winner

【争购】① hectic buying ② snap up (goods)

【争光】win honour (or glory) for; do credit to: 为祖国~ *win honour for one's homeland*; *do credit to one's motherland*

【争脸】try to win credit or honour

【争论】controversy; dispute; debate; contention: 激烈的~ *heated argument*

【争鸣】contend (over academic issues)

【争气】try to make a good showing; try to win credit for; try to bring credit to: 给父母~ *bring credit to parents*

【争抢】fight for; scramble for; contend for

【争取】strive for; fight for; win over; make every effort to achieve: ~胜利 *fight for victory*

【争胜】compete for first place

【争先】try to be the first to do sth; try to get ahead of the others; strive to be the first to do: ~恐后 *strive to be the first and fear to lag behind*; *vie with each other for the lead*; *fall over each other*

【争雄】contend for supremacy (or hegemony)

【争议】dispute; debate; controversy: 该问题没有什么~。*The problem is beyond dispute.*

【争执】disagree; dispute; stick to one's position (or guns); take issue with: ~不下 *each holds on to his position*; *each sticks to his guns*; *each sticks top his own stand*

征[1] ① go on a journey: 踏上~程 *set off a journey* ② go on an expedition (or a campaign): 南~北战 *campaign all across the county*; *fight north and south*

征[2] ① levy (troops); call up; draft; recruit ② levy (taxes); collect; impose; extort ③ ask for; solicit

征[3] ① evidence; proof: 有史料可~。*There are historical documents as proof.* ② sign; portent; phenomenon

【征兵】conscription; draft; call-up; recruitment: ~年龄 *conscription age*; *age for enlistment* / ~制 *universal military service*; *conscription system*

【征尘】dust settling on one during an expedition or a journey

【征程】journey; march

【征答】question and answer game: 有奖~比赛 *question and answer competition with prizes*

【征调】requisition; draft; call up: ~救灾粮 *call up relief grain*

【征伐】go on a punitive expedition

【征帆】[书] a boat or ship on a long voyage

【征服】conquer; vanquish; subjugate: 精彩的节目~了观众朋友。*The wonderful programme captivated the audience.*

【征稿】solicit contributions (to a magazine, journal, etc.)

【征购】requisition by purchase: ~棉花 *cotton purchase by the state* / ~任务 *state purchase quotas* / ~派购 *purchase (grain or other agricultural products) by the state on fixed quota*

【征管】levy (or collect) and administer (taxes)

【征候】sign; indication

【征婚】seek a marriage partner: ~启事 *lonely hearts ad*

【征集】① solicitor seek publicly; gather or collect through public channels: ~意见 *solicit suggestions* / ~文物 *collect historical relics* ② draft; call up; recruit; requisition: ~新兵 *draft (or recruit) soldiers* /战时~ *wartime draft*

【征粮】impose grain levies; collect farm taxes in kind; collect grain taxes

【征募】enlist; recruit

【征求】seek; ask for; invite: ~专家的意见 *seek (or solicit) criticisms from the specialists* / ~顾客的看法 *ask for customers' comments* / ~意见本 *trial edition*

【征收】levy; collect; impose; charge: ~进口税 *impose import duties*

【征税】levy (or collect) taxes; taxation: ~标准 *standards for taxation* / ~货物 *dutiable goods*

【征讨】go on a punitive expedition

【征途】journey; the road to be travelled: 艰险的~ *a hard (or perilous) journey* /我们已经踏上了~。*We have started on a journey.*

【征文】solicit articles or essays on a chosen subject: ~启事 *a notice soliciting articles or essays for a special*

【征询】seek the opinion of; consult

【征引】quote; cite; mention as an example

【征用】take over for use; commandeer; requisition: ~农具 *requisition farm tools*

【征战】go on an expedition or a campaign; go out to battle

【征召】① call up; enlist; draft; recruit; conscript: ~入伍 *enlist in the army* ② [书] appoint sb to an office; place sb in an official position

【征兆】sign; omen; portent; indication: 下雨的~ *indications of an impending earthquake*

怔 error-stricken; panicked; terrified

see also zhèng

挣

see also zhèng

【挣扎】struggle; battle: 垂死~ *last-ditch struggle*; *death-bed struggle*

峥

【峥嵘】① lofty and steep; towering; soaring: ~的山峰 *soaring (mountain) peaks* ② outstanding;

remarkable; extraordinary: ~岁月 *memorable years* (*of one's life*); *eventful years*

狰

【狰狞】sinister; hideous; ferocious; savage

症 【中医】lump in the abdomen

see also zhèng

【症结】crux; crucial cause; core: 这个问题的~究竟在哪儿? *Where on earth does the crux of the problem lie?*

睁 open (the eyes): 半~眼睛 *with one's eyes half open*

【睁眼瞎】a blind person with his (or her) eyes open- an illiterate

【睁一只眼,闭一只眼】turn a blind eye to sth; keep one eye closed; wink at sth

蒸 ① evaporate: 云~霞蔚 (*of scenery*) *magnificent* ② steam: ~米饭 *steam rice* / ~包子 *put the stuffed buns in the steamer*

【蒸饼】steamed cake

【蒸发】evaporate: 水加热会~。*Heat will evaporate water.*

【蒸饺】steamed dumpling

【蒸烤】scorch; roast: 烈日~ *scorching sun*

【蒸馏】【物】distillation: 常压~ *atmospheric distillation* / 真空~ *vacuum distillation* / ~器 *distiller*; *retort* / ~水 *distilled water*

【蒸笼】① steamer (used to steam food) ② (of room, etc.) very hot and sultry

【蒸馍】[方] steamed bun

【蒸气】vapour: 水~ *aqueous vapour*

【蒸汽】steam: ~发生器 *steam generator* / ~供暖 *steam heating* / ~锅炉 *steam boiler* / ~机车 *steam locomotive* / ~轮机 *steam turbine* / ~动力 *steam power* / ~机 *steam engine* / ~机船 *steam boat* / ~浴 *sauna*; *steam bath* / ~脱脂 *vapour degreasing* / ~学 *atmology*

【蒸腾】(of steam) rising: 热气~ *steaming* / ~作用 *transpiration*

【蒸蒸日上】prosper day by day; make rapid progress; be developing fast; be thriving

【蒸煮器】boiler; digester

zhěng

拯 save; rescue; free: ~民于水火之中 *deliver the people from an abyss of misery*

【拯救】save; rescue; deliver; preserve: ~被奴役的人们 *free the enslaved*

整 ① whole; complete; full; entire; total: 三点~ *three o'clock sharp* / ~天 *whole day*; *all day long* / 一~年 *a full year* / 两年~ *two solid years* ② in good order; neat; tidy; orderly: 仪容不~ *untidy in one's appearance* ③ put in order; rectify; straighten: 你去~一~床铺。*Go and tidy up your bed.* ④ repair; mend; fix; renovate: 修~ *fix*; *repair* ⑤ make sb suffer; punish; castigate; fix ⑥ [方] make; do; work: 我也不知道咋~的。*I don't know how it happened.*

【整备】reorganize and outfit (troops)

【整编】reorganize (troops); restructure

【整除】【数】consolidate the Party organization

【整点】【数】integral point

【整队】dress the ranks; get (or bring) the ranks into orderly alignment; line up: ~队待发 *dress the ranks and wait to set out* / ~进入会场 *file into the meeting hall*

【整顿】rectify; consolidate; reorganize; strengthen: ~规章制度 *strengthen rules and regulations*; *reestablish rules and regulations* / ~党风 *rectify the working style of the Party*

【整风】rectify incorrect style of work or thinking: ~运动 *rectification movement*

【整复】restore; restitution; renovate: ~外科 *reparative surgery*; *plastic surgery*

【整个】whole; entire; full: ~工作 *the entire work* / ~国家 *the whole nation* (*or state*) / ~来说 *generally speaking*; *by and large*; *on the whole*

【整合】①【地】conformity ② integrate; consolidate; unify; unite

【整洁】clean and tidy; orderly; neat; trim: ~的街道 *clean streets* / 衣着~ *be neatly dressed*

【整理】put in order; straighten out; tidy up; sort out; arrange: ~笔记 *arrange one's notes* / ~抽屉 *sort out things in the drawer*

【整流】【电】rectification: ~管 *rectifier tube* / ~器 *rectifier*

【整齐】① in good order; meat; tidy: 步调~ *keep in step* ② even; regular; level: ~的稻田 *even rice field* / ~牙齿 *regular teeth* / ~的阵容 *a well-balanced lineup*

【整人】make sb suffer; fix sb

【整容】① tide oneself up (i. e. have a hair cut, a shave, etc.) ② face-lift: ~术 *cosmetic operation*; *face-lifting*

【整数】①【数】integer; whole number ② round number; round figure

【整肃】[书] ① serious; strict; rigid: 军容~ *serious appearance and bearing of the soldiers* ② rectify; consolidate; put in order:

【整套】a whole (or complete) set of: ~家具 *a whole set* (*or suit*) *of furniture* / ~理论 *sum total of theories*

【整体】whole; entirety; totality: 进行~规划 *make an overall plan* / ~观念 *the concept of viewing the situation as a whole*

【整天】the whole day; all day; all day long: 干了五~ *work for five whole days*

【整形】【医】plastic: ~手术 *plastic operation* / ~外科 *plastic surgery*; *plastics*

【整修】rebuild; renovate; recondition

【整枝】【农】prune (off or down); train (a plant): 给树~ *prune the branches of trees*

【整治】① renovate; repair; recondition; dredge (a river, etc.): ~旧房 *renovate old houses* / ~河道 *recondition o river* ② punish; fix; make to suffer

Z

③ fix the black sheep ④ do; work at; perform: ~库房 *put the ware house in order*

【整装】get one's things ready (for a journey); pack one's things (for a journey): ~待发 *all packed up and ready to set out* / ~待命 *in full battle array awaiting orders*

zhèng

正 ① straight; upright; perpendicular: ~前方 *straight ahead* /这幅画挂得不~。*The picture on the wall is not straight.* ② situated in the middle; main: ~门 *main entrance* ③ punctually; sharp; on time:七点~ *at seven o'clock sharp* ④ obverse; front:衣服的~面 *the right side of the clothes* ⑤ upright; impartial; honest:清~廉明 *be clean and upright* ⑥ correct; right; proper:走~道儿 *follow the correct path* ⑦ (of colour, flavour, etc.) pure; right: ~蓝 *pure blue* /味~ *the right flavour* ⑧regular; standard; normal: ~楷 *regular script* ⑨ chief; prime; principal: ~副主席 *president and deputy president* ⑩ (of figures, designs, etc.) regular: ~六边形 *regular hexagon* ⑪【数】positive; plus ⑫【物】positive; plus: ~电 *positive electricity* ⑬ rectify; straighten; set right; put straight:把帽子~一~ *put one's hat straight* ⑭ make right; correct ⑮ just; right; exactly; precisely: ~中下怀 *precisely to one's liking* /你给我的衣服尺寸~合适。*The clothes you given is just the right size.* ⑯ be doing:他~听收音机呢。*He is listening to the radio.*

see also zhēng

【正版】(of a product) genuine

【正本】① reserved copy (of a library book) ② original (of a document):

【正比】direct proportion; direct ratio: ~例 *direct proportion*

【正步】【军】parade step; goose step: ~走! *Parade step, march!*

【正餐】① lunch or supper ② dinner

【正册】regular register

【正常】normal; regular; usual: ~交往 *regular contact* /~的生活水平 *average living standard* / ~化 *normalize*

【止大】upright; honest; aboveboard; fair and square: ~光明 *open and aboveboard*; *frank and honest*; *just and honourable*

【正当】(zhèngdāng) just when; just the time for; just as: ~春天来临 *just when spring is coming*

【正当】(zhèngdàng) ① proper; appropriate; lawful; legitimate: ~权益 *legitimate rights and interest* / ~要求 *just* (*or rightful*) *claim* (*or demand*) ② (of behaviour, etc.) correct; proper / ~防卫 *legitimate defence*; *justified defence*

【正道】① the right way or (course); the correct path:走~ *follow the right path* ② truth; law:人间~是沧桑。*It the truth of the world that all things are changing.*

【正点】(of trains, ships, planes, etc.) on schedule; on time; punctually; at the expected time: ~到达 *arrive on time*

【正殿】main hall (in a place or temple)

【正法】execute (a criminal)

【正反】positive and negative

【正方】square: ~盒子 *a square box*

【正割】【数】secant

【正宫】① empress's palace ② empress

【正规】regular; standard; proper: ~部队 *regular troops*; *regulars* / ~化 *regularize*; *standardize*; *be put on a regular basis* / ~军 *regular army* / ~学校 *regular school* / ~教育 *proper education*; *regular education* / ~战 *regular warfare*

【正轨】the right track; the correct path:走上~ *get on to the right track*

【正果】【宗】the right fruit — the proper consequence of a regulated life in this world; attain consummation and become a Buddha

【正好】① (of time, position, size, number, degree, etc.) just right:这件毛衣他穿~。*The sweater fits him nicely.* ② happen to; chance to; as it happen:我~听到。*I happened to hear of that.*

【正号】【数】positive sign; plus sign

【正话】① serious words or talk ② what one really means; original meaning; real intention

【正极】【电】positive electrode; positive pole; anode: ~板 *positive plate*

【正经】① decent; respectable; honest: ~人 *a decent person* ② serious; proper; right: ~事儿 *serious affairs* /说~的 *talk business* ③ formal; standard: ~货 *standard goods* ④ [方] really; truly; indeed; very much so

【正剧】serious drama; serious play

【正楷】(in Chinese calligraphy) regular script

【正理】correct principle; valid reason; truth; the right thing to do

【正路】the correct path; the right way

【正门】front door (or gate); main entrance

【正面】① front; frontage; face; facade: ~进攻 *frontal attack* / ~火力 *frontal fire* ② the obverse side; the right side:硬币的~ *the obverse side of a coin* /分不清~反面 *can not tell the right* (*or obverse*) *side from the wrong* (*or reverse*) *side* ③ positive: ~教育 *educate by positive measures or examples*; *positive education* ④ directly; openly: ~人物 *positive character*; *hero* /有意见请~提。*Please express your views openly.*

【正派】upright; honest; decent; just: ~人家 *an honest family* /他为人~。*He is honest and upright.*

【正品】quality products (or goods); certified products (or goods)

【正气】① healthy trend or atmosphere; probity; moral spirit:扶植~ *foster healthy trends* ② vital energy

【正巧】① happen to; chance to; as it happens;

have the luck to：～我带钱了。*It to happened that I caught some money with me.* ② just in time；in the nick of time；just at the right moment：你来得～，我们刚做好晚饭。*You've come just in time；we've just cooked supper.*

【正切】【数】tangent

【正确】correct；right；proper；sound：～方针 *sound policy* / ～地引导 *guide properly* / ～性 *correctness；soundness；validity*

【正人君子】gentleman；a man of honour；a man of integrity

【正史】history books written in biographical style

【正式】formal；official；regular：～职业 *regular occupation* / ～警告 *formal warning* / ～党员 *full member of the Party；full party member* / ～访问 *official visit；formal visit* / ～会谈 *formal talks；formal negotiations* / ～记录 *official records；formal minutes (of meeting)* / ～声明 *official statement* / ～文本 *official text*

【正视】look squarely at；face squarely；face up to：～现实 *face reality；look reality in the face*

【正事】one's proper business

【正室】① legal wife（as contrasted with concubine）② ［书］the wife's eldest son

【正数】【数】positive number

【正题】subject or topic of a talk or essay：转入～ *come to the subject*

【正体】① standardized form of Chinese characters ② block letter

【正统】① legitimism ② orthodox：～思想 *orthodox ideas* / ～派 *orthodox party or school*

【正文】main body（of a book，etc.）；text

【正屋】principal rooms（in a courtyard，usu. facing south）

【正午】high noon；midday

【正误】correct（typographical）errors：～表 *errata；corrigenda*

【正眼】look straight；look sb or sth in the face；look squarely at：他从不～看人。*He never looks squarely at people.*

【正业】regular occupation；proper duties；decent work

【正义】① justice：主持～ *uphold justice* / 为～而战 *fight for justice* ② just；righteous：～的事业 *a just cause* / ～的斗争 *a just struggle* / ～的举动 *a just action* ③（of words）correct meaning；proper meaning：～感 *a sense of what is right；a sense of justice (or righteousness)*

【正音】① correct one's pronunciation ② standard pronunciation

【正院儿】main courtyard

【正在】in the process of；in the course of；be doing：他～喝咖啡。*He's drinking coffee.*

【正直】honest；upright；fair

【正职】①（of a unit）principal；chief ② main occupation or profession；full-time job

【正中】right in the middle or centre：桌子～ *right in the middle of the table*

【正传】main story；subject itself；subject under discussion

【正宗】① orthodox school ② authentic：～川菜 *authentic Sichuan-style dishes*

【正座】central seats that directly face the stage；stalls

证 ① testify to；prove；demonstrate：求～ *seek to prove* ② evidence；proof；testimony：物～ *material evidence；exhibit* ③ certificate；card

【证词】testimony

【证婚人】chief witness at a wedding ceremony

【证监会】Securities Supervision Commission

【证件】credentials；papers；certificate

【证据】evidence；proof；testimony：搜集～ *collect evidence* / 掌握～ *have evidence in one's hands*

【证明】① prove；testify；bear out；uphold：这件事已经由实践～是对的。*The thing has been verified through practice.* ② certificate；identification；testimonial；papers：～文件 *certificate；testimonial*

【证券】bond；security；negotiable securities：～持有人 *fund holder* / ～代理 *securities business on commission* / ～公司 *securities company* / ～行 *securities house；bond house* / ～交易 *securities trading；dealings in securities* / ～交易所 *stock exchange；securities；exchange* / ～交易委员会 *stock exchange committee* / ～交易指数 *stock exchange index* / ～经纪人 *bill broker；stock broker* / ～经纪业 *stock brokerage* / ～融资 *securities finance* / ～商 *stock jobber；securities dealer* / ～市场 *securities market；stock market*

【证实】confirm；verify；establish；bear out：有待～ *remain to be confirmed*

【证书】certificate；testimonial；credentials：发毕业～ *grant sb a diploma* / 领取合格～ *receive a quality certificate (or certification of inspection)*

【证物】【律】exhibit（produced in court as evidence）

【证言】testimony

郑 one of the warring states

【郑重】serious；solemn；earnest；grave：～宣布 *solemnly declare* / ～其事 *seriously；in earnest* / 他～地向我道了歉。*He said sorry to me in a earnest tone.*

怔 ［方］stare blankly；be in a daze；be in a trance：听到那个坏消息，她立刻～住了。*Hearing that bad news she was stunned at once.* see also zhēng

【怔神儿】［方］stare blankly；be in a daze

诤 ［书］criticize one's faults frankly；admonish；expostulate；remonstrate

【诤言】［书］forthright admonition；frank criticism

【诤友】［书］a friend who will give forthright admonition

政 ① politics；government；political affairs：参～议～ *participate in the deliberation and administration of state affairs* ② certain administrative aspects of government：民～机关 *civil administration organ* / 总～治部 *the General Political*

Z

Department ③ affairs of a family or an organization

【政策】policy：～教育 *education in policy*

【政党】political party；party

【政敌】political opponent（or foe）

【政法】politics and law：～学院 *institute of political science and law*

【政府】government：～部门 *government departments or authorities* /～官员 *government official* /～机构 *government apparatus* /～机关 *government bodies*（*or organizations*）/～首脑 *head of government* /～代表 *government representative* /～发言人 *government spokesperson* /～公文 *government documents*

【政纲】political programme；platform

【政工】① political work：～员 *people engaged in political work*；*political worker* /～组 *political work office or section* ② cadres responsible for political work；political cadre

【政绩】achievements in one's official career

【政见】political view：持不同～者 *dissidents* /持不同～ *hold different political views*

【政界】political circles；government circles

【政局】political situation；political scene：～动荡 *turbulent political scene*

【政客】politician；demagogue

【政权】① political power；state power；regime：巩固～ *consolidate political power* ② state organs

【政坛】political arena

【政体】form of government；system of government

【政治】politics：～舞台 *political arena*（*or stage*，*scene*）/～态度 *political attitude* /～信仰 *political conviction*（*or belief*）/～气候 *political climate* /～避难 *political refuge*；*political asylum* /～部 *political department* /～犯 *political offender*；*political prisoner* /～经济学 *political economy* /～局 *the Political Bureau* /～面目 *political affiliation or background* /～权利 *political rights* /～社会学 *political sociology* /～思想工作 *political and ideological work* /～委员 *political commissar*（*of a PLA regiment and above*）/～协理员 *political assistant*（*of a PLA regiment and above*）/～协商会议 *political consultative conference* /～资本 *political capital*

挣[1] struggle to get free；try to throw off：～脱枷锁 *throw off the shackles*

挣[2] get by one's labour；earn；make：～钱糊口 *earn*（*or make*）*a living* /他去年～得挺多。*He made*（*or earned*）*much money last year.*

see also zhēng

【挣命】struggle to save one's life

【挣钱】earn（or make）money

症 disease；illness；malady

see also zhēng

【症候】① disease ② symptom

【症状】symptom：临床～ *clinical symptoms* /早期～ *early*（*or incipient*）*symptoms* /晚期～ *terminal symptoms*

铮［方］dazzling；shining；polished：他把玻璃擦得～亮。*He made the windows very polished.*

zhī

之1 ①［书］go to

之2 ① used in place of an objective noun or pronoun：将～如何？*How to deal with it？* /为～感动 *be moved for sth* ② used in certain set phrases without actual reference：总～ *to sum up*；*in short*；*in a word* /久而久～ *with the passage of time* /我们三个人我最高个，张次～，李又次～。*Of the three of us，I am the tallest，Zhang is shorter，and Li is shortest.* ③ this or that：～二人又如何？*What about these two men？*

之3 ① used to connect the modifier and the word modified：意料～中 *as was expected* ② used between the subject and the predicate to express subordination

【之后】later；after；afterwards；there after：从那～他再没给我写过信。*He hasn't written to me since then.*

【之乎者也】literary jargon；pedantic terms；pedantries；archaisms：那个小男孩竟然满口～，令人发笑。*The little boy mouthed so many pedantic terms that people could not help laughing.*

【之前】ago；before；prior to：两年～ *two years ago* /天黑～ *before dark*

支1 ① prop up；put up；set up：～帐篷 *put up a tent* /两手～着头 *rest one's head in both hands* ② protrude；raise；pick up：～着耳朵听 *prick up one's ears* ③ support；sustain；bear；stand：体力不～ *too tired to go on doing sth*；*too weak physically to stand it* /乐不可～ *overwhelmed with joy* ④ send away；put sb off；order about：别～别人了，自己干吧！*Don't send anyone else*；*better do it yourself* ⑤ pay out or draw（money）：预～ *get pay in advance* /开～ *expense* ⑥（Zhī）a surname

支2 ① branch；off shoot：分～机构 *branch institution* /邮政～局 *branch post office* ② for long，thin，inflexible objects：一～烟 *a cigarette*

支3 ①（for troops，fleets；etc.）：一～军队 *an army contingent* /一～舰队 *a fleet* ②（for songs on musical compositions）：～民歌 *a folk song* ③（for the size or quality of yarn）count：两百～纱 200 *count yarn*

【支边】support the border areas；go and help with the development of the border regions

【支部】① branch of political parties or organizations ② branch of the Chinese Communist Party or the Chinese Communist Youth League：～大会 *general membership meeting of the branch* /～书记 *branch secretary*

【支撑】① prop up；sustain；support；hold up：所有柱子～着整个庙宇。*All the posts sustain the tem-*

ple. ②【建】strut; brace: ~点 *strong point*; *centre of resistance*
【支持】① sustain; hold out; bear: 他快~不住了。*He couldn't bear up any longer.* ② support; back; stand by; be in favour of: 他认为对的,他就~。*He stands up for what he thinks is right.*
【支出】① pay (money); expend; spend; disburse ② expense; expenditure; outlay; disbursement: 教育~ *expenditure on education*
【支点】【物】fulcrum
【支队】detachment: 独立~ *independent detachment*
【支付】pay (money); defray: ~房租 *pay rent* / ~水电费 *pay for electricity and water* / 现金~ *payment in cash*; *cash payment* / ~手段 *means of payment*
【支行】sub-branch (of a bank)
【支架】support; stand; trestle: 自行车~ *prop stand of bicycle*
【支离】① fragmented; broken; disconnected; disorganized ② (of writing) trivial and jumbled; incoherent: ~破碎 *torn to pieces*; *broken up*; *fragmented*; *shattered*
【支流】① tributary; affluent; branch: 长江~ *the branch of Changjiang River* ② minor aspects; minor current; nonessentials: 主流和~ *essentials and nonessential*
【支配】① allocate; budget; arrange; dispose: 合理~自己的时间 *arrange one's time properly*; *make good use of one's time* ② control; dominate; govern; determine: 受人~ *be controlled by others*
【支票】cheque; check: ~兑现 *cash a cheque* / 空头~ *rubber cheque*
【支气管】bronchus: ~性气喘 *bronchial asthma* / ~炎 *bronchitis*
【支前】support the front
【支渠】branch (irrigation) canal
【支取】draw (money); receive: 我来~我这个月的工资。*I come to draw my payment of this month.*
【支使】① order about; boss about: 别总~人。*Don't always order people about.* ② send away; put sb off
【支书】secretary of a Party or League branch; branch secretary
【支吾】prevaricate; equivocate; hum and haw; hedge
【支线】branch line; feeder (line): 铁路~ *feeder railway* / 公路~ *feeder highway*
【支援】support; aid; assist; help: ~灾区 *give aid (or send relief) to disaster areas* / ~部队 *support unit*; *supporting troops*
【支柱】① pillar; prop: 矿用~ *pit prop* ②[喻] pillar; mainstay: 他是家庭~。*He is the mainstay of the family.*

只 ① single; one only; isolated: ②[量] for one of a pair: 两~鸟 *two birds* / 两~眼睛 *two eyes*
see also zhǐ
【只身】alone; all by oneself; solitarily: ~在外 *be alone and far away from home*
【只言片语】a word or two; a few isolated words and phrases: 只留下~ *leave behind just a single word*

汁 juice: 果~ *fruit juice* / 乳~ *milk*
【汁水】[方] juice: 这种番茄~很多。*The tomato is juicy.*
【汁液】juice

芝
【芝加哥】Chicago
【芝麻】① sesame ② sesame seed: ~酱 *sesame paste* / ~油 *sesame oil*

吱 a creaking sound: ~~作响的竹椅 *creaky bamboo chair*

枝 ① branch: ~蔓 *branches and tendrils* / ~接 *scion grafting* / ~柯 *branches of a tree* / ~条 *twig*; *branches* / 树~ *tree branches* ② for flowers with stems intact: 一~梨花 *a spray of pearl blossoms* ③ for stick-like things: 一~步枪 *a rifle* / 三~铅笔 *three pencils* / 两~鱼竿 *two fishing rods*
【枝杈】branch; twig
【枝节】① branches and knots-side issue; minor matters: ~问题 *a side issue*; *trifle*; *trivial matter* ② complication; unexpected difficulties
【枝头】on a branch
【枝桠】branch; twig
【枝叶】① branches and leaves ② nonessentials; trifles; minor details
【枝子】branch; twig

知 ① know; realize; be aware of: 我不~道。*I don't know.* ② inform; notify; tell; learn: 发出通~ *send out a notice* ③ administer; be in charge of ④ knowledge; learning
【知彼知己,百战不殆】know the enemy and know yourself, and you can fight a hundred battles without danger of fear
【知道】know; realize; the aware of; wise up (to): 我不~到底发生了什么。*I didn't know what happened on earth.*
【知底】know the inside story; be in the know
【知法犯法】know the law but break it; deliberately flout the law; knowingly violate the law
【知根知底】know sb's background; know sb through and through
【知过必改】always correct one's error when one becomes aware of it
【知会】[口] tell orally; notify orally
【知己】① intimate; understanding; on intimate terms: 我们俩说了很多~话。*We have heart-to-heart talks.* ② bosom friend
【知交】bosom or intimate friend; alter ego; second self: 他是我的~。*He is my second self.*
【知觉】①【心理】perception ② consciousness: 失去~ *lose consciousness*; *pass out*
【知了】cicada
【知名】well-know; famous; renowned; noted; celebrated: ~人士 *a well-known (or noted) personage*; *celebrity*; *a public figure*: ~度 *popularity*
【知命】[书] ① know the will of Heaven; under-

stand the decree of Heaven：～安身 *be contented with one's lot* ② fifty years of age；fifty years old

【知难而进】press forward despite difficulties；advance in the face of difficulties；take or seize the bull by the horns

【知难而退】beat a retreat in the face of difficulties；shrink back from difficulties；shy away from difficulties

【知其不可而为之】know it's no use；but keep on doing it；do what one knows is impossible

【知其一,不知其二】know only one aspect of a thing；have a one-side view；see only one side of the picture

【知情】① be in the know；know the inside story；have inside information：～不报 *fail to report what one knows of a case* ② feel grateful to sb；appreciate the kindness：你对我很好，我很～。*You are so kind to me, and I'm grateful to your kindness.*

【知趣】be sensible；be tactful；behave properly in a delicate situation；show good sense：他一点也不～！*He has no idea how to behave!*

【知识】knowledge；intellectual：～渊博 *have a wide range of knowledge；be knowledgeable；be learned；be erudite* / 书本～ *book learning* / ～产业 *knowledge industry* / ～经济 *knowledge economy* / ～就是力量 *knowledge is power* / ～密集型产业 *knowledge intensive industry*

【知识分子】intellectual；the intelligentsia；educated person

【知悉】know；learn of；be informed of：～详情 *be informed of the details of the matter*

【知县】[旧]（in former times）county magistrate

【知晓】know；be aware of；understand

【知心】intimate；understanding；heart-to-heart：～人 *a intimate friend；confidant* / ～话 *intimate words；words from the heart；heart-go-heart talk*

【知音】a friend keenly appreciative of one's talents；an understanding friend；a bosom friend；alter ego

【知遇】have found a patron or superior appreciative of one's ability：～之恩 *a debt of gratitude for sb's recognition and appreciation*

【知子莫若父】no one knows a son better than his father.

【知足】be content with one's lot：～常乐 *happy is he who is content；contentment is happiness*

肢

limb

【肢体】① limbs ② limbs and trunk

【肢障】physical disability；handicap（of the limbs）

织

① weave：纺～ *spinning and weaving* ② knit：～围巾 *knit a scar*

【织补】darning；invisible mending

【织布】weave cloth；weave

【织物】fabric：机织～ *woven fabric*

【织造】weaving：～厂 *weaving mill*

【织针】knitting needle

栀

【栀子】【植】cape jasmine

脂

① fat；grease；tallow；resin：松～ *resin；pine resin* ② rouge

【脂肪】fat：动物～ *animal fat* / 植物～ *vegetable fat*

【脂粉】rouge and powder；cosmetic：略施～ *apply a light make-up* / ～气 *womanlike ways；womanliness*

蜘

【蜘蛛】spider：～网 *spider's web；cobweb*

zhí

执

① hold；grasp；grip：～手相望 *look at each other hand in hand* ② take charge of；control；manage；direct：～掌政权 *hold the reins of government* ③ stick to adhere to；persist in：偏～ *stubbornly biased* / 各～一词。*Different people tell different stories.* ④ carry out；execute ⑤［书］catch；seize；capture ⑥ written acknowledgement

【执棒】hold the baton；conduct music：这次会议由他来～。*He is the conductor of the meeting.*

【执笔】write；do the actual writing；put on paper：这封信由他亲自～。*He wrote the letter himself.*

【执鞭】［书］① hold the horse whip-be sb's driver ② hold the teacher's pointer-be a teacher

【执导】direct a film or a play

【执法】enforce laws and decrees；execute the law：～不阿 *impartial in executing the law；uphold justice* / ～不公 *denial of（or miscarriage）justice* / ～犯法 *violation of the law by law-executors* / ～如山 *enforce the law strictly；uphold the law firmly*

【执管】be in charge of；manage；administer

【执教】be a teacher；teach：他在复旦大学～。*He is teaching at Fudan University.*

【执迷不悟】obstinately stick to a wrong source；be perverse；refuse to mend one's ways；refuse to come to one's senses

【执拗】stubborn；pigheaded；willful；self-willed

【执勤】（of soldiers，policemen，etc.）be on duty

【执行】① carry out；execute；implement；perform：～任务 *perform a task* / ～命令 *execute an order* / ～纪律 *enforce discipline* / ～独立自主的外交政策 *pursue（or implement，follow）an independent foreign policy* ② execute：～机构 *executive body* / ～秘书 *executive secretary* / ～员 *marshal* / ～主席 *executive（or presiding）chairman*

【执意】be determined to；persist in：～不从 *stubbornly refuse to comply with*

【执掌】be in control of；wield；control：～财权 *have control over financial matters*

【执照】license；permit：驾驶～ *driver's license；driving permit*

【执政】be in power；be in office；wield state power；be at the helm of state：～党 *the party in pow-*

Z

er or office; *the ruling or governing party*

【执著】persistent; persevering: ~地追求理想 *persevere in the pursuit of one's goal*

直 ① straight: 笔~的马路 *the straight road* ② upright; vertical; perpendicular: 笔~地站着 *stand* (*or hold oneself*) *upright* ③ just; upright ④ candid; frank; straight forward: ~言不讳 *speak plainly*; *call a spade a spade* ⑤ straighten: ~起身来 *straighten up* ⑥ vertical stroke (in Chinese characters) ⑦ directly; straight: 沿着街一~走 *go straight a head along the street* / ~达火车站 *go directly to the railway station* ⑧continuously: 伤口~流血。*Blood was continuously oozing out of the cut.* ⑨ just; simply; exactly: 待我~如自己的孩子 *treat me just like a child of her own*

【直白】① say plainly; tell straight; be frank and honest: 请~告诉我到底发生了什么。*Please tell me straight what happened.* ② boring; flat: ~的演讲 *boring speech*

【直播】①【农】direct seeding ② live broadcast by a TV or radio station; broadcast live: 现场~排球赛 *make a live broadcast of a volleyball match*

【直布罗陀】Gibraltar, a fortified town at the southern tip of the Iberian peninsula on the strait of Gibraltar: ~海峡 *the Strait of Gibraltar*

【直肠】【生理】rectum

【直肠子】① straightforward; downright; forthright ② a straightforward person

【直尺】straightedge; ruler

【直达】through; nonstop; direct: ~车 *express*; *through train or through bus*

【直捣】drive straight on to; press straight on to: ~匪窝 *press straight on to the bandits' den*

【直到】① until: 我们~昨晚才出发。*We didn't set out until last night.* ② up to: ~现在我们还没有出发。*We haven't set out up to now.*

【直观】directly perceived through the senses; audio-visual: ~教学 *abject teaching*

【直航】nonstop flight; direct route; fly non-stop: ~北京 *straight flights to Beijing*

【直角】【数】right angle: ~尺 *square* / ~三角形 *right or right-angled triangle*

【直接】direct; straight; immediate: ~联系 *direct contact* / ~成本 *direct cost* / ~会晤 *meet sb in person* / ~宾语 *direct object* / ~经验 *direct experience* / ~起飞 *rolling take-off*; *rolling start*; *follow-through take off* / ~染料 *direct dyes* / ~税 *direct tax* / ~推理 *immediate reasoning* / ~着陆 *straight-in landing*

【直截】straightforward; blunt; point-blank: ~了当 *straightforward*; *blunt*; *point-blank*; *flat and plain*

【直径】【数】diameter: 大~ *major diameter* / 小~ *minor diameter*

【直觉】【心理】intuition

【直来直去】frank and outspoken; blunt; frank; candid

【直流电】direct current

【直露】forthright; explicit

【直朴】upright and simply; honest and sincere; forthright and uncomplicated: 他为人~, 心地善良。*He is honest, sincere and kindhearted.*

【直抒己见】state one's views frankly; be plain-spoken

【直属】directly under; directly subordinate or affiliated: ~外交部 *be directly affiliated to the Foreign Ministry*

【直率】outspoken; candid; straightforward; frank: ~的批评 *candid criticism*

【直爽】frank; candid; outspoken; straightforward: 性格~ *forthright in character*

【直挺挺】straight and stiff; bolt upright: ~地坐着 *sit blot upright*

【直投】deliver directly

【直系亲属】directly-related members of one's family-parents, spouse and children

【直销】direct sale

【直辖】directly under the jurisdiction of: ~市 *municipality directly under the central Government*

【直线】① straight line: 两点之间~距离最短。*A straight line is the shortest distance between two points.* ② linear; rectilinear; direct: ~飞行 *rectilinear* (*or straight*) *flight* ③ steep; rising and falling sharply: 物价~上升。*Commodity prices have shot up.*

【直心眼儿】[口] open; frank; straightforward

【直性子】① straightforward; downright; blunt; forthright ② a straightforward person

【直言】speak bluntly; state candidly or outright: 恕我~。*Excuse me for speaking bluntly.*

【直译】*word-for-word translation*; *literal translation*

【直至】① *until*: 再接再厉, ~胜利。*Make repeated efforts till victory is assured* ② up to: ~此时 *up to how*

侄 brother's son; nephew

【侄女】brother's daughter; niece

【侄女婿】husband of brother's daughter; niece's husband

【侄孙】brother's grandson; grandnephew

【侄孙女】brother's granddaughter; grandniece

【侄媳妇】wife of brother's son; nephew's wife

【侄子】brother's son; nephew

值 ① price; value ②【数】value ③ be worth; be worth while: 这衣服买得~。*The clothes are worth the price.* / 不~一提。*It's not worth mentioning.* ④ happen to; chance to: ~此国难当头之时 *at the time of national crisis* / 他来旅游时, 正~我外出。*I happened to be out when he came to tour.* ⑤ be on duty; take one's turn at sth

【值班】be on duty or shift: ~员 *person on duty* / 昨天谁~? *Who was on duty yesterday?*

【值不当】[方] not be worthwhile

【值得】be worth; merit; deserve: ~买 *be worth buying* / ~赞许 *deserve commendation*; *be praiseworthy* / ~怀疑 *be open to doubt* / ~仔细考虑

Z

warrant careful consideration

【值钱】worth much; valuable; costly; expensive: 这古董~。*This antique is worth a great deal.*

【值勤】be on duty; be on point duty: ~交通警 *policeman on point duty* / ~人员 *personnel on duty*

【值日】be on duty for the day; be one's turn to be on duty: ~表 *duty roster* / ~生 *student on duty*

【值守】guard; watch over

【值夜】on night-duty; on the night watch

职 ① duty; job: 忠于~守 *be devoted to one's duty* / 各司其~ *each does his or her duty* ② post; position; office: 保罗担任公司会计一~。*Paul holds the position as accountant for the firm.* ③ manage; direct

【职称】professional title (such as engineer, professor, lecture, academician, etc.): 高级~ *senior professional titles* / 技术~ *technical titles* / ~改革 *the reform in professional titles* / ~评定 *the evaluation of professional title*

【职代会】meeting of employee representatives; employees' representatives conference: 举行~ *hold a meeting of employee representatives*

【职分】① bounden duty ② official post; position

【职工】① staff and workers; workers and staff members ② [旧] workers; labour: ~代表大会 *the congress of workers and staff*

【职级】rank

【职能】function: 政府~ *function of a government*: 商品~ *functions of commodities* / ~部门 *functional department (in government)* / ~机构 *functional institution*

【职权】powers or authority of office; functions and powers: 滥用~ *abuse one's authority of office* / ~范围 *limits or scope of one's functions and powers*; *terms of reference*

【职守】post; duty: 擅离~ *leave one's post without permission*

【职位】position; post

【职务】post; position; duty; job: 履行~ *do (or perform) one's duties* / ~工资 *wages related to specific work posts*; *pay according to one's post*

【职业】occupation; profession; vocation; calling: 各种~的人 *people of all occupations* / ~教育 *vocational education* / ~特权 *professional privilege* / ~道德 *professional ethics* / ~妇女 *career woman* / ~高中 *vocational high school* / ~介绍所 *job centre*; *career service centre*; *employment agency* / ~团体 *professional organization* / ~外交官 *career diplomat* / ~学校 *vocational school* / ~运动员 *professional athlete*; *professional*

【职员】office worker; staff member; functionary

【职责】duty; obligation; responsibility: ~范围 *scope of official duty* / 应尽的~ *bounden duty* / 神圣的~ *sacred duty*

【职掌】[书] ① be in charge of; take charge of: ~政务 *be in charge of state affairs* ② duty; charge

植 ① plant; grow: 种~水稻 *plant rice* / ~被类型 *vegetation form* / 密~ *close planting* ② set up; establish: 扶~ *foster*; *prop up*

【植被】【植】vegetation

【植根】① take root ② lay a solid basis

【植苗】plant seedlings; transplant saplings

【植皮】【医】skin grafting

【植树】tree planting: ~造林 *afforestation*

【植物】plant; flora; vegetable: ~保护 *plant (or crop) protection* / ~病害 *plant disease* / ~检疫 *plant quarantine* / ~胶 *vegetable gum or glue* / ~净化 *plant purification* / ~化石 *phytolite*; *phytolith* / ~化学 *phytochemistry*; *vegetable chemistry* / ~人 *vegetable* / ~纤维 *vegetable fibre* / ~学 *botany* / ~学家 *botanist* / ~园 *botanical garden*

殖 breed; multiply; propagate

【殖民】establish a colony; colonize: ~统治 *colonial role* / ~战争 *colonialist war*

zhǐ

止 ① stop; halt; cease; desist: ~痒 *stop or relieve itching* / ~痛 *relieve pain* ② close; end: 从五号到八号~ *from the 5th to 8th* ③ only; sole: 不~一次 *not just once*; *more than once*

【止步】halt; stop; go no further / ~不前 *halt*; *stand still* / 游人~ *no visitors*; *out of bounds*; *off limits*

【止付】【经】banking stop payment

【止境】end; limit; boundary: 学无~。*There is no end to learning.*

【止咳】relieve a cough: ~糖浆 *cough syrup*

【止渴】quench or satisfy one's thirst

【止痛】relieve pain; stop pain: ~药 *anodyne*; *painkiller*; *analgesic*

【止血】stop bleeding; stanch bleeding: ~带 *tourniquet*

只 only; just merely: 他~有一个建议。*He has just one suggestion.* / 全班~一个女生。*There is only one girl in the class.* / 这不~是个法律问题。*It is not merely a question of law.*
see also zhī

【只不过】only; just; merely; nothing but: 这~是个笑话,别太认真了。*Take it easy! It's nothing but a joke.* / 我~是太累了,没别的。*I'm only very tired; that's all.*

【只得】have no choice but to; be compelled to; have to; be obliged to: 没有车,我们~步行过去。*As there was no car, we had no alternative but to get there by foot.* / 天下大雨,运动会~延期举行。*It is raining heavily; the sports game had to be put off.*

【只顾】① be absorbed in: 他~学习,把吃饭的事都忘了。*He was so engrossed in his study that he forgot all about the dinner.* ② pay attention only to; care only for: 不要~自己。*Don't just think of yourself.*

【只管】by all means; feel free to: 你~干下去,经费

的事由我来管。*Go ahead by all means. I shall take care of the funding.* /有什么想法~说。*Please feel free to show what you think.*

【只好】cannot but; have to; be forced to

【只见树木,不见森林】be unable to see the woods for the trees

【只可意会,不可言传】can be sensed, but not explained in words; can be apprehended but not expressed; can be felt, but beyond description

【只是】① merely; only; just; nothing but:这~托词。*It's merely a pretext.* /他~有点好奇而已。*He was just being a little curious.* ② but; except that; only:我想离开,~父母不让走。*I want to leave, only my parents don't let me go.*

【只要】so long as; provided; if only: ~肯下功夫,就一定能成功。*Anyone can succeed as long as he makes an effort.*

【只有】① only; alone: ~这个办法了。*There is no other alternative.* ② have to; be forced to:你~早点儿起才赶得上车。*You have to get up earlier to catch the bus.*

【只争朝夕】sized the day, seize the hour; seize every minute; race against time

旨[1] tasty; delicious; delicious; delectable

旨[2] ① purpose; aim: ~提高英语口语 *aim at improve one's Spoken-English* ② intension; wish; decree:圣~ *imperial edict or decree*

【旨趣】[书] purport; objective; intent

【旨意】decree; order:奉领导的~行事 *act on the orders of the leader*

址 location; site; ground

纸 ① paper:草~ *rough straw paper* ②[量] (for letters documents, etc.):一~家书 *a letter from home*

【纸版】【印】paper mould; paper matrix

【纸币】paper money; paper currency; (bank) note:不兑现~ *fiat money*

【纸浆】paper pulp; pulp: ~板 *pulp board* /~厂 *pulp mill* /~原材 *pulpwood* /~制造机 *macerator*

【纸巾】paper towel; towel

【纸老虎】paper tiger (used to refer to sth or sb that is outwardly strong but inwardly weak)

【纸钱】paper made to resemble money and burned as an offering to the dead

【纸张】paper; sheets of paper

指 ① finger:小~ *little finger* /大拇~ *thumb* /弹~之间 *during the snapping of the fingers; in an instant* ② fingerbreadth; digit:一~宽的 *a strip of paper one fingerbreadth wide* ③ point at; point to; show the direction of:时针~向四点。*The hour hand points to four.* /他朝那个房间~了~。*He pointed his finger at the room* ④ indicate; point out; refer to: ~出不足 *point out one's shortcomings* /特~ *refer in particular to* /暗~ *hint at* ⑤ depend on; count on; rely on:别~着别人帮你完成任务。*Don't count on others to help you finish your work.* ⑥ (of hair) stand; bristle:发~ *make one's blood boil*

【指标】target; index:质量~ *quality index*

【指不定】[方] perhaps; maybe; not sure:你别等她了,他~来不来呢。*Don't wait for her; maybe she won't come.*

【指出】point out; lay one's finger on:他~了我的弱点。*He pointed out my weak spot.*

【指导】guide; direct; instruct

【指点】① give directions (or pointers, advice):经他一~,我茅塞顿开。*I'm enlightened by his advice.* ② gossip about sb's faults; point one's (or the) finger at; pick on

【指定】appoint; assign; name: ~继承人 *designated heir* /~代理人 *authorized agent* /在~的地点集合 *assemble at the appointed meeting place*

【指腹为婚】an antenatal (or prenatal) betrothal

【指画】① point at; point to ② finger drawing (or painting)

【指环】(finger) ring

【指挥】① command; direct; conduct: ~交通 *direct traffic* /~乐队 *conduct an orchestra* ② commander; director; conductor ③ conductor: ~部 *command post; headquarters* /~舱 *space command module* /~车 *command car* /~刀 *officer's sword* /~官 *commanding officers; commander*

【指甲】nail:手~ *fingernail* /脚~ *toenail* /~刀 *nail clippers* /~盖儿 *nail* /~花 *garden balsam* /~油 *nail polish*

【指教】give advice or comments

【指靠】depend on; rely on; look to; count on:他~你的帮助。*He looks to you for help.*

【指控】accuse; charge: ~他收贿。*He's charged with taking bribes.*

【指明】indicate clearly; point out; show clearly; demonstrate: ~出路 *point the way out* /~两者的质量差别 *show clearly the quality-difference between the two*

【指南】guide; guidebook

【指南针】compass

【指派】appoint; assign; designate; name: ~代表 *name delegates*

【指认】point out; identify; recognize; point out and affirm: ~边界 *identify a boundary line*

【指日可待】can be realized very soon; be just round the corner:胜利~。*Victory is just round the corner.*

【指桑骂槐】abuse the locust when they mean mulberry — point at one but abuse another; make oblique accusations

【指使】instigate; incite; put sb up to sth; stir up:受人~ *act on sb's instigation; act as sb's cat's-paw*

【指示】① indicate; point out; show: ~前进的方向 *indicate the direction of advance* ② instruct; direct: ~部队立即出发 *instruct the troops to set out at once* ③ instruction; directive; order:下达~ *give (or issue) instructions* /~代词 *demonstrative pronoun* /~灯 *pilot lamp (or light); indicator lamp* /~功率 *indicated power* /~剂 *indicator* /

~器 *indicator* / ~植物 *indicator plant*

【指手划脚】① make gestures; gesticulate: ~地高谈阔论 *talk volubly with dramatic gestures* ② make indiscreet remarks or criticisms this and condemn that; carp and cavil

【指数】①【数】exponent ② index number; index: 综合~ *composite index* / 生活费~ *cost of living index*

【指头】① finger ② toe

【指头肚儿】[方] finger cushion; face of the fingertip

【指望】① look to; count on ② prospect; hope

【指纹】① loops and whorls on a finger ② fingerprint: ~鉴定 *fingerprint identification*

【指向】① directional: ~天线 *directional antenna* / ~植物 *compass plant* ② point to: ~天空 *point to the sky* ③ direction that is being pointed to

【指引】point (the way); guide; show; lead: ~航向 *chart the course* / 一位老人~我们走出森林。*An old man showed us the way out of the forest.*

【指印】fingerprint; finger mark: 按~ *make a fingerprint*

【指责】censure; criticize; find fault with; reproach: 横加~ *make unwarranted charges* / 受到公众~ *be subject to the censure of the public; receive a public censure*

【指针】① needle; indicator; pointer ② guiding principle; guide: 发展教育事业的~ *as a guide for the development of education* ③ pressing with a finger (on an acupuncture point)

【指正】① point out and correct mistakes ② make a comment or criticism: 请予~。*Please remedy our errors.*

咫 [量] an ancient measure of length, equal to 8 cun (寸)

【咫尺】[书] very close or near: ~之间 *only a short distance; very close; close at hand*

【咫尺天涯】so near and yet so far-see little of each other though living close together

趾 ① toe ② foot

【趾高气扬】strut about and give oneself airs; be swollen with arrogance; be on one's high horse: 他~,目中无人。*He is on his high horse and looked down his nose at everybody.*

【趾骨】phalanx; metatarsus; metatarsal bones

【趾甲】toenail

酯 【化】ester

【酯化】【化】esterify

【酯酶】esterase

zhì

至 ①[书] arrive; reach: 人迹罕~ *without human trace; untraversed* / 女孩飘然而~。*The girl sailed in gracefully.* ② to; until: 截~本月底 *up to the end of this month* ③[书] extremely; most; very: 感激之~ *be deeply grateful; be very much obliged*

【至宝】priceless treasure; most valuable treasure

【至诚】① complete sincerity: 出于~ *in all sincerity; from the bottom of one's heart* ② sincere; straightforward: ~的友人 *a sincere friend*

【至迟】at (the) latest; no later than: 会议~星期五举行。*We will hold the meeting no later than Friday.*

【至此】up to this point; at this stage: 事已~,没有别的办法了。*Things have gone too far be remedied.*

【至多】at (the) most; not more than: 她~二十岁。*She is at most in her twenties.* / 他~呆两天。*He will stay here two days at most.*

【至高无上】highest; supreme; paramount: ~的权力 *supreme power (or authority)* / ~的领袖 *a paramount*

【至关紧要】most important; imperative; of the utmost importance

【至好】most intimate friend; best friend; bosom friend

【至极】extremely; exceedingly; to the utmost point

【至交】most intimate friend; best friend

【至今】up to now; to this day; so far; to date: 他~仍未结婚。*To date he has not gotten married.*

【至亲】next of kin; closed relative; close kin: 骨肉~ *kinfolk; close kin; one's own flesh and blood* / ~好友 *close relatives and good friends*

【至情】true feelings; heartfelt; emotion

【至上】supreme; the highest: 顾客~ *customers (or patrons) first*

【至少】at (the) least: ~可以说,他没尽力。*He didn't try his best, to say the least.* / 他~六十岁了。*He's at least sixty.*

【至死】unto death; till death; to the end of one's life: ~不屈 *not yield even unto death* / ~不渝 *will never change until death*

【至言】profound words; pertinent remarks

【至友】most intimate friend; best friend

【至于】① as for; as to: ~他,就让他自己解决吧! *As for him, let he solve the problem himself.* ② go so far as to; go to such an extent: 你要是早点儿准备,何~通过不了考试。*If you had prepared a litter earlier, how could you fail the examination?* / 他不~去偷东西吧? *He wouldn't go so far as to steal.*

志[1] ① will; aspiration; ambition; ideal: ~士仁人 *people with high aspirations* / 少年得~ *realize one's ambition* ② (Zhì) a surname

志[2] ascertain the weight, length, size, etc.

志[3] ① remember; keep in mind: 永~不忘 *will forever be imprinted on one's mind* ② records; annals: 县~ *annals of a county* / 墓~铭 *epitaph* ③ mark; sign

【志大才疏】have lofty aspirations but little talent

【志气】aspiration; ambition; ideal: 有~ *have high aspirations*

【志趣】aspiration and interest; inclination; bent; interest: ～相投 *have similar inclinations*

【志士】person of firm resolve; person of ideals and integrity: 爱国～ *noble-minded patriots*

【志同道合】cherish the same ideals and follow the same path; have a common goal; be devoted to a common cause; be of like mind: 他们是一对～的好友。*They are a couple of like mind friends.*

【志喜】serve as congratulation or celebration

【志向】aspiration; ideal; dream; ambition: 他年轻时就立下救国图强的～。*He has made up his mind to struggle for the salvation and prosperity of the nation in his youth.*

【志愿】① aspiration; wish; ideal ② volunteer; do sth of one's own free will: ～兵 *volunteer* (*soldier*) / ～书 *application form* / ～军 *volunteers; people who volunteer to fight in another country*

【志在必得】be determined to win; be bent on winning

帜 [书] flag; banner; streamer

制 ① make; manufacture: 精心～作 *make with meticulous care* / 定～ *have sth made to order* ② work out; formulate; draw up: ～定计划 *formulate a plan* ③ restrict; check; control ④ system

【制版】【印】plate making: 平版～ *lithographic plate making*

【制备】【化】preparation

【制币】standard national currency: ～厂 *mint*

【制表】① draw up a form or list ② statistics tabulation

【制裁】sanction; punish: 实行～ *impose sanctions against sb*

【制成品】finished products; manufactured goods; manufactures

【制导】guide; control and guide: 雷达～ *radar guidance* / 激光～武器 *laser-guided weapon*

【制订】work (or map) out; formulate: ～第五个五年计划 *draw up the fifth Five-year plan*

【制定】lay down; draw up; formulate; draft; enact; make: ～政策 *formulate a policy* / ～计划 *work out a plan* / ～法律 *make laws*

【制动】apply the brake; brake: ～火箭 *retrorocket* / ～距离 *transportation braking* (*or stopping*) *distance* / ～器 *brake* / ～闸 *damper brake*

【制度】① system; institution: 社会～ *social system; social order* / 教育～ *system of education* ② rules; regulations: 遵守～ *abide by the rules*

【制伏】subdue; check; bring under control; over power: ～风沙 *check wind and sand* / ～强盗 *subdue the robber*

【制服】uniform: ～呢 *uniform coating* (*or suiting*)

【制高点】commanding elevation (or point, ground, height)

【制革】process hides; tan: ～厂 *tannery* / ～工人 *tanner*

【制海权】mastery of the seas; command of the sea

【制空权】【军】control of the air; air domination

【制冷】refrigerate: ～循环 *refrigeration cycle* / ～剂 *refrigerant*

【制片】produce (a film): ～厂 *a film studio* / ～人 *producer*

【制品】products; goods; wares: 乳～ *dairy products* / 黄麻～ *jute goods*

【制胜】get the upper hand of; subdue; defeat: 出奇～ *defeat one's opponent by a surprise move*

【制糖】refine sugar: ～厂 *sugar refinery*

【制图】charting; map-making; drafting: ～员 *cartographer; draftsman* / ～学 *cartography; graphics*

【制宪】draw up a constitution

【制药】pharmacy: ～厂 *pharmaceutical factory*

【制约】restrict; condition; restrain; limit: 受历史条件～ *be limited by historical conditions*

【制造】① make; manufacture; produce: ～飞机 *make aircraft*; ② engineer; create; foment: ～事端 *engineer an incident* / ～分裂 *foment splits* / ～矛盾 *sour dissension* / ～舆论 *shape* (*or mould*) *public opinion*

【制止】check; curb; prevent; stop; ban: ～通货膨胀 *check* (*or halt*) *inflation* / ～黑市交易 *ban the black market* / ～侵略战争 *stop aggression* / ～流沙 *curb shifting sand*

【制作】make; manufacture: 精心～ *make with meticulous care* (*or elaborate workmanship*)

质¹ ① nature; essence; character ② quality: 劣～ *low-quality* / 优～ *high-quality* / ～优价廉 *high quality and low price* ③ matter; substance: 铁～器具 *ironware* ④ [书] pledge: 以此为～ *with this as a pledge* ⑤ simple; plain; natural: ～言之 *to put it bluntly*

质² question; ask

质³ [书] pawn

【质地】① quality of a material; texture; grain: ～精美 *of superb* (*or exquisite*) *texture* ② character; traits; disposition

【质点】【物】particle

【质感】(of works of art) sense of reality; real: 不同的物体相不同的～。*The various objects have various senses of reality.*

【质检】quality testing; quality inspection; quality control: 工人人员对产品进行严格的～。*The workers have exercised strict control over the quality of the products.*

【质量】① quality: ～好 *of high quality* / ～差 *of poor quality; inferior* ②【物】mass: 相对论～ *relativistic mass* / ～标准 *quality specification* / ～第一 *quality first* / ～控制 *quality control* / ～守恒 *conservation of mass*

【质料】material: ～很好 *quality material*

【质朴】simply and unadorned; unaffected; plain; natural: 为人忠厚～ *be simply and kindhearted; be unsophisticated*

【质数】【数】prime number

【质问】question; interrogate; put to question: 提出

~ *bring sb to account*
【质询】inquire about; ask for explanation; address inquiries to
【质疑】call in question; query; question
【质因数】【数】prime (number) factor

炙 broil; roast; grill
【炙烤】scorch; broil; grill:火热的太阳~着路人。*The passersby are being broiled in the scorching sun.*
【炙晒】expose to the not sun
【炙热】scorching not; burning hot: ~的太阳 *broiling sun; scorching sun*
【炙手可热】if you stretch out your hand you feel the heat — extreme arrogance of the very powerful people; the imperative manner of a person with power

治 ① rule; govern; administer; manage: 统~阶级 *ruling class* /高压统~ *high-handed rule* /人~ *rule by man* (*as distinct from rule by law*) /法~ *rule of law* ② treat (a disease); heal; cure: 救~ *treat and cure*; *bring a patient out of danger* ③ control; harness (a river): ~淮 *harness the Huai River* ④ wipe out (injurious insects); eliminate; stamp out: ~害虫 *eliminate pests* ⑤ punish: ~一~坏蛋。*Let's teach that skunk a lesson.* ⑥ study; research; pursue one's studies: ~史 *specialize in history* ⑦ order; peace; stability ⑧ [旧] seat of a local government
【治安】public order; public security; law and order: 维持~ *maintain public order* /扰乱社会~ *disturb peace and order*
【治保】public security work: ~办公室 *security department*
【治病救人】cure the sickness to save the patient; help sb mend his or her way
【治国】govern (or administer) a country; manage state affairs: ~安民 *run the country well and give the people peace and security*
【治家】manage the household
【治理】① administer; govern; rule; administer a country; run a state ② (of nature) harness; tame; bring under control; put in order: ~河流 *harness a river; bring a river under control*
【治疗】treat; cure: 住院~ *be hospitalized* /隔离~ *treat sb in quarantine*
【治丧】make funeral arrangements; arrange a funeral: ~委员会 *funeral committee*
【治沙】sand control
【治水】harness rivers; regulate rivers and water courses; prevent floods by water control
【治学】pursue scholarly work; do scholarly research; purse one's studies: 严谨~精神 *meticulous* (*or rigorous*) *scholarship*
【治愈率】【医】cure rate
【治罪】bring to justice; punish sb (for a crime)

栉 ① comb: 手执巾~ *hove the towel and comb in hand* ② comb (hair): ~发 *comb one's hair*
【栉风沐雨】be combed by the wind and washed by the rain-travel or work in the open despite wind and rain
【栉比鳞次】(of buildings) be close together like comb teeth and fish scales
【栉沐】[书] comb and wash

峙 [书] stand erect; tower: 两军对~ *Tow opposing armies confront each other.*
【峙立】stand towering

桎 [书] fetters
【桎梏】[书] fetter and handcuffs; shackles; chains

挚 earnest; heartfelt; sincere
【挚爱】true love, sincere love; deep love, profound and sincere love
【挚诚】earnest, heartfelt; sincere: 我被他的~感动。*I was touched by his sincerity.*
【挚切】earnest, sincere, cordial, wholehearted
【挚情】deep emotion or feeling
【挚深】genuine; true
【挚意】① sincerely; genuinely ② sincere wish: 他~要求见您。*He sincerely wants to see you.*
【挚友】bosom friend; chose friend; intimate friend

致[1] ① send; extend; deliver make: ~信 *send* (*sb*) *a letter* /~欢迎词 *deliver a welcoming speech* /~以热烈的祝贺 *extend warm congregations* ② devote; concentrate ③ cause; incur; bring about; result in; lead to: ~死 *cause death or die* /她不听建议,导~多人死亡。*She refused to head other's suggestions, which result in many people's death.* ④ achieve; attain; apply: 学以~用 *study sth in order to apply it*

致[2] manner or style that engages attention or arouses interest; interest: 兴~ *interest, mood to enjoy* /情~ *temperament and interest*

致[3] fine; delicate; exquisite
【致哀】pay one's respects to the dead: 向烈士~ *pay one's respects to the martyrs*
【致癌】cause (or produce) cancer; be carcinogenic
【致病】cause a disease
【致残】cause disability or become disabled; be crippled: 他因飞机失事~。*He became disabled after a flight accident.*
【致辞】make (or deliver) an address (or a speech)
【致富】acquire wealth; become rich; make a fortune: 劳动~ *become rich by doing honest labour* (*through sweat and toil*) /发家~ *build up family fortunes*
【致函】write a letter to
【致敬】salute; pay homage to; pay one's respects to pay tribute to
【致力】be devoted to; work for
【致命】mortal; fatal deadly, causing death.
【致使】cause; result in; lead to

【致死】lethal, deadly, cause death or die: ~的原因 *cause of death*
【致谢】express one's thanks (to)
【致意】send (give) one's regards; present one's compliments: 向朋友代为~。*Please give my best wishes to my friends.*
秩 ① order ②［书］decade ③ official rank in feudal times; official salary
【秩序】order, sequence: 工作~ *sequence of work* / 守~ *observe order*
掷 cast; fling; hurl; throw: 投~ *throw*; *fling* / 抛~ *throw*; *cast* / ~手榴弹 *throw a grenade* / 一~千金 *spend money like water*
【掷还】please return (to the writer, etc.)
【掷弃】cast aside /away; abandon; throwaway
【掷扔】throw; cast: 他将球~出很远。*He threw the ball a great distance.*
【掷铁饼】discus throw
痔 haemorrhoids; piles
【痔疮】haemorrhoids; piles
【痔漏】【医】anal fistula
窒 ［书］block, obstruct, stop up
【窒闷】close; stuffy
【窒热】oppressive; stuffy
【窒息】choke; stifle; suffocate
蛭 leech
【蛭石】vermiculite (a mineral)
智 intelligence; resourcefulness; wisdom; wit
【智残人】mentally handicapped
【智齿】wisdom tooth
【智慧】intelligence, sagacity, wisdom
【智力】intelligence, intellect: ~测验 *intelligence test* / ~衰退 *intellectual deterioration* / ~开发 *tap (or develop) intellectual resources* / ~结构 *structure of talent in an institution*
【智利】Chile: ~人 *Chilean*
【智略】wisdom and resourcefulness
【智谋】resourcefulness, wit: 这个人很有~。*The man is full of good ideas.*
【智能】intellectual power; intellectual ability intellect and ability: ~人工 *artificial intelligence*
【智巧】brains and tact
【智穷才尽】at the end of one's resources; at the end of one's tether, at one's wits' end
【智取】take, capture (a fort, town, etc.) by stratagem
【智商】intelligence quotient (IQ): 他儿子的~可不低。*The IQ of his son is not low.*
【智能双全】be both intelligent and courageous be both brave and resourceful
【智育】intellectual education; intellectual development mental development
【智障】【医】person afflicted with a mental deficiency

痣 mole: 胎~ *birthmark* /他腿上有一颗痣。*He has a mole on his leg.*
滞 stagnant; sluggish
【滞呆】dull, dim-witted: 两眼~ *with a dull look in one's eyes, with lackluster eyes*
【滞洪】flood detention; slow down flood waters: ~区 *detention basin*; *retarding basin*; *area for flood dispersal*
【滞后】①【物】hysteresis ② lag behind; delay
【滞缓】slow; tardy; torpid; sluggish: 迈着~的步子 *walk with slow steps*
【滞留】be held up; be detained; (of ship, vehicle, etc.) wait on demurrage
【滞纳金】fine for delaying payment; fine for paying
【滞塞】block; clog; obstructed; impeded; be held up: 交通~。*The traffic is held up.*
【滞销】unmarketable
【滞胀】stagflation
置 ① place; put; set: 安~于案头 *be placed on one's desk* ② set up; establish; from; install: 设~新机构 *establish news organ.* ③ buy; purchase: ~一套衣服 *buy a suit*
【置办】buy, purchase: ~家具 *buy furniture* / ~嫁妆 *buy a dowry*
【置备】purchase (equipment, furniture, implement, etc.)
【置产】buy property, purchase real estate
【置放】place, put, lay up
【置换】displacement, replacement, substitution
【置买】buy purchase.
【置评】(usu. used in the negative) comment on; make comments; discuss: 不予~ *give no comment*
【置若罔闻】turn a deaf ear to; pay no heed to, ignore: 他对父母的忠告~。*He turned a deaf ear to the advice of his parents.*
【置身】get involved; place oneself; stay: 一个好的领导总是~于群众当中。*A good leader always places himself in the middle of the masses.*
【置身事外】stay aloof from the affair, take no part in the business, refuse to be drown into the matter
【置信】(usu. used in the negative) believe, trust: 不可~ *not to be believed*; *unbelievable*; *incredible*
【置疑】(usu. used in the negative) doubt
【置之不顾】pay no heed to; ignore; leave out of account disregard
【置之不理】brush aside; close one's eyes to; pay no attention to, ignore
【置之度外】disregard; have no regard for; give no thought to: 把生死~ *face death with equanimity*
【置之脑后】ignore and forget, dismiss from one's mind
雉 pheasant
【雉鸠】turtledove
稚 childish, young

【稚虫】【动】naiad
【稚嫩】① young and tender：~的心灵 *an innocent heart* ② immature
【稚气】childishness
【稚弱】childish and tender：~的身体 *a tender body*
【稚拙】unsophisticated, uncomplicated：~的造型 *simple shape*
【稚子】(innocent) child

zhōng

中 ① centre; middle：教室的正当~ *right in the middle of the classroom* ② China ③ among; amid; amidst; in：半空~ *in midair* ④ middle; mid ⑤ medium, intermediate：~号 *medium size* ⑥ mean, impartial, between two extremes：适~ *moderate* ⑦ intermediary ⑧in the process of ⑨ fit for; good for; suitable for：不~看 *no good, good for nothing* ⑩［方］okay; all right
see also zhòng
【中波】medium wave
【中不溜儿】［口］medium; middling; fair to middling
【中部】middle part; central section
【中餐】Chinese food; Chinese cuisine; Chinese meal
【中草药】Chinese herbal medicine
【中层】① middle-level：~干部 *middle-level cadres*/他爸爸属于~管理人员。*His father belongs to middle management.*
【中产阶级】middle bourgeoisie; middle class
【中场】【体】midfield
【中成药】Prepared Chinese medicine (ready-made product of pharmaceutical factories through mass production according to scientific prescriptions)
【中档】medium quality at middling price：~货 *good of middling grade*
【中等】① medium; moderate; middling; average：~身材 *of medium height* /~城市 *medium-sized city* ② (of education) secondary：~教育 *secondary school education* /~师范学校 *secondary normal school* /~专科学校 *secondary specialized school* /~职业学校 *secondary vocational school* /~技术学校 *secondary technical school*
【中东】the Middle East
【中短波】intermediate wave; medium-short wave
【中断】break off; hold up; interrupt; suspend; discontinue：~判断 *break off the negotiations (or talks)*
【中队】detachment：交通~ *detachment of traffic police*
【中非】central Africa
【中锋】【体】(of football, etc.) centre forward
【中共中央】the central committee of the communist Party of China：~政治局 *the Political Bureau of the Central Committee of the Chinese Communist Party*
【中国】china：~大陆 *China's mainland* /~共产主义青年团 *the Communist Youth League of China*
【中级】intermediate; middle rank; middle level：~人民法院 *intermediate people's court* /~职称 *academic (or professional) titles of middle rank*
【中间】① between, among：他是几个人中最聪明的一个。*He is the brightest among these persons.* ② centre; middle：~道路 *middle road* /~阶层 *intermediate strata* /~分子 *middle (or intermediate) element*
【中坚】backbone, hard core; nucleus; mainstay：~分子 *backbone elements* /社会~ *pillar of society*
【中介】intermediary; medium：~人 *broker; matchmaker; intermediary; medium* /起~作用 *be an intermediary*
【中看】be pleasant to the eye, look nice：~不中用 *be pleasant to the eye but not to the use*
【中立】neutrality：保持~ *keep neutrality; remain neutral* /~主义 *neutralism*
【中流】midstream
【中流砥柱】mainstay; tower of strength; a firm rock in midstream
【中落】(of family fortunes) ebb; decline; sink：家道~ *the family is on the decline.*
【中美洲】Central America
【中年】middle age：~人 *a middle-age person*
【中期】metaphase; middle period：~审查 *midterm review* /二十世纪~ *mid 20th century*
【中秋节】the Mid-Autumn Festival (15th day of the 8th lunar month)
【中世纪】Middle Ages
【中式】Chinese style：~服装 *Chinese style clothing*
【中枢】centre：交通~ *communication hub* /神经~ *nerve centre* /~神经系统 *central nervous system*
【中听】pleasant to the ear; to one's liking; agreeable to the hearer：她觉得这句话很~。*She found these words very agreeable.*
【中途】halfway, midway：~停顿 *stop halfway*
【中外】china and foreign countries; at home and abroad：~合作企业 *a Chinese-foreign cooperative venture*
【中微子】【物】neutrino
【中文】the Chinese (written) language; Chinese：~书刊 *books and magazines in Chinese*
【中午】noon; midday：正~ *high noon*
【中西】Chinese and Western：~合璧 *Chinese and Western styles combined*
【中心】① middle; centre; heart; core; hub; central position：小镇~ *in the centre of the town* ② main key：~人物 *key figure* /研究~ *research centre*
【中型】medium, medium-sized; medium-duty; medium-scales; medium-type：~字典 *a medium-sized dictionary*
【中性】① neutral：~土 *neutral soil* ②【语】neuter：~名词 *neuter noun*
【中学】middle school; high school; secondary school：初级~ *junior middle school* /高级~ *senior middle school*
【中间】the middle ten days of a month：本月~ *the*

middle of this month

【中央】① centre; middle: 湖~ *at the centre of the lake* ② highest leading body (of a state, party, etc): 团~ *the central committee of the Youth League* / ~处理器 *central processing unit (CPU)* / ~机构 *central organs and institutions* / ~纪律检查委员会 *the Central Commission for Discipline Inspection* / ~军事委员会 *the Central Military Commission* / ~人民广播电台 *Central People's Broadcasting station of china (CPBS)*

【中药】traditional Chinese medicine: ~店 *Chinese pharmacy*

【中叶】middle period: 十九世纪~ *the middle of the 19th century*

【中医】① traditional Chinese medical science ② doctor of traditional Chinese medicine: ~学院 *college of traditional Chinese medicine* / ~研究院 *academy of traditional Chinese medicine*

【中用】(used in the negative) of use, useful

【中游】① middle reaches (of a river) ② the state of being middling

【中雨】moderate rain

【中止】break off, cut short, discontinue, suspend: ~订货 *suspend an order for goods* / ~谈判 *suspend (or break off) negotiations* / ~发行 *discontinue publishing*

【中指】middle finger

【中转】【交】change trains: ~站 *transfer station*

【中子】neutron: ~弹 *neutron bomb* / ~源 *neutron source* / ~反应堆 *neutron reactor*

忠 devoted, faithful, loyal, staunch honest

【忠臣】loyal court official

【忠诚】loyal faithful staunch, sincere: 玛丽是我的一名~朋友。*Mary is one of my loyal friend.*

【忠告】① admonish; exhort; sincerely advise ② exhortation; sincerely advice; advice

【忠厚】sincere and kindhearted; honest and tolerant

【忠君爱国】be loyal to the sovereign and faithful to the country

【忠实】loyal true trustworthy, faithful: ~信徒 *a faithful follower* / ~原著 *true to the original*

【忠顺】loyal and obedient: ~仆人 *a willing servant*

【忠孝】loyalty and filial piety

【忠心】dedication; devotion; loyalty: 表~ *express one's loyalty*; *pledge one's loyalty* / ~耿耿 *loyal and devoted*; *most faithful and steadfast*

【忠言】earnest exhortation; sincere advice: ~逆耳 *golden words offend the ear*; *candid advice grates on the ear*; *good advice jars on the ear*

【忠义】loyal and staunch; faithful and righteous

【忠勇】faithful and courageous; loyal and brave.

【忠于】true to; faithful to; devoted to; loyal to; steadfast in the performance of duty

【忠贞】loyal and steadfast: ~不渝 *unswervingly loyal*

终 ① close; end; finish ② die: 他七十而~。*He died at the age of 70.* ③ eventually, ultimately after all in the end ④ all; entire; fully; whole: ~年 *whole year*

【终场】① end of a performance, game or show ② [旧] final session in an examination

【终点】① destination; terminal point: 旅途的~ *end of a journey* ②【体】finish: ~线 *finishing line*; *terminal cine*; *finishing tape*

【终点站】terminal; terminus

【终端】terminal: ~电缆 *terminal cable*

【终归】eventually; finally; after all; in the end: 这个孩子~会记忆起发生的一切。*This child will forgive what had happened eventually.*

【终极】ultimate; final: ~目标 *final aim*; *ultimate goal*

【终结】end; final stage

【终究】eventually; all in all after all; in the end: 他有很多坏习惯, 但他~是个孩子。*He has many bad habits, but all in all he is a child.*

【终局】end; result; outcome

【终老】spend one's remaining years of one's life

【终了】end (of a period): 学期~ *the end of the term*

【终年】① throughout the year; (all) the year around: ~积雪的山 *mountains covered with snow all the year round* ② the age at which one dies He died at the seventy

【终曲】【音】finale

【终日】all day; all day long

【终身】lifelong; all one's life; throughout one's life: ~大事 *a great event in one's life (usu. referring to marriage) event of life long significance*

【终审】【律】final judgement; last instance: ~法院 *court of last instance* / ~权 *power of final adjudication*

【终生】all one's life; all one's lifetime: ~事业 *one's lifework* / ~难忘的教训 *a lesson for life*

【终席】come to a close; end of a banquet or meeting: 没等~, 他就哭了起来。*Before the dinner party ended, he cried loudly.*

【终于】eventually, finally; at (long) last; in the end: 他~成功了。*he succeeded at last.*

【终止】① ut an end to; stop; terminate; end: ~日期 *closing date*; *expiry date* / ~合同 *terminate a contract* ② annulment; abrogation; termination ③【音】cadence

钟[1] ① bell: 铜~ *bronze bell* ② clock: 电子~ *electric clock* / 挂~ *wall clock* ③ time (as measured. in hours and minutes): 六点~ *six o'clock* / 五分~ *five minutes*

钟[1] ① concentrate (one's affections etc.) ② (Zhōng) a surname

【钟爱】cherish; love dearly; dote on (a child)

【钟摆】pendulum (of a clock)

【钟表】timepiece; clocks and watches

【钟点】① time for something to be done or to happen: 还没到~。*It's not time yet.* ② hour: 我等了半个~车。*I've been waiting for bus half an hour.*

【钟楼】① clock tower ② belfry; bell tower

【钟情】be deeply in love; be captivated

【钟头】[口] hour：两个～*two hours*

衷 heart; inner feelings

【衷肠】[书] heartfelt remarks; words right from one's heart：畅叙～*heart-to-heart talk; pour to one's heart*

【衷情】[书] heartfelt feelings; inner feelings：那对恋人正在互诉～。*The lovers are opening their hearts to each other.*

【衷曲】[书] heartfelt emotion, inner feelings：倾吐～*pour out one's heart*

【衷心】heartfelt; cordial; wholehearted：～感谢你们的努力。*For your noble effort, I thank you from my bottom of my heart.*

zhǒng

肿 swell; be swollen：她的脸～了。*Her face is swollen.* / ～消了。*The swelling has subsided.*

【肿瘤】tumour：良性～*benign tumour* / 恶性～*malignant tumour; cancer* / ～医院 *tumour hospital*

【肿胀】① swelling ②【中医】edema and abdominal distension

种 ①【生】species：外地品～*exotic species* / 本地品～*endemic species* ② race ③ breed; seed; strain：稻～*rice seeds* / 麦～*wheat seeds* ④ grit; guts; nerve; pluck ⑤ kind; sort; style; type：这～方法 *this kind of method* / 裤子有许多～。*There are pants in difference styles.* ⑥ (Zhǒng) a surname

see also zhòng

【种类】category, kind, type, varied

【种种】all sorts (or kinds) of; various

【种子】① seed：～植物 *seed plants* / ～处理 *seed treatment* / ～测定 *seed testing* ②【体】seed; seeded player：被列为～选手 *be seeded*

【种族】race：～隔离 *racial segregation* / ～灭绝 *genocide* / ～歧视 *racial discrimination* / ～清洗 *ethnic cleansing*

踵 ①[书] heel ② call in person：～门相告 *call in person to pass the news* ③ follow close behind; follow on sb's heels

【踵趾相接】follow in sb's footsteps; on after another arrive in quick succession

【踵至】[书] arrive on the heels of another; come immediately after another

zhòng

中 ① hit; be just right; fit exactly：命～*hit the target* ② fall into; sustain; suffer be hit by; be affected by：～埋伏 *fall into an ambush*

see also zhōng

【中标】get or win the tender or bid; be chosen to be the tender (of a bid)

【中彩】win a prize in a lottery; draw a prize wing ticket in a lottery

【中弹】be hit (or struck) by a bullet; get shot

【中毒】① poisoning; toxicosis ② be poisoned (usu. accidentally)：煤气～*gas poisoning*

【中风】suffer from a stroke of apoplexy; be seized with apoplexy：他爷爷死于～。*His grandpa died of apoplexy.*

【中计】be taken in; fall into a trap; play into sb's hand's be ensnared

【中奖】get the winning number in a lottery-attached deposit

【中肯】①(of remarks) sincere and pertinent; to the point; apropos：她说的话很～。*What she have said are sincere and pertinent.* ②【物】critical：～质量 *critical mass*

【中签】be the lucky number (in drawing lost, etc)

【中伤】calumniate; malign; slander; vilify

【中暑】① suffer heatstroke (or sunstroke); be affected by the heat ② heatstroke; sunstroke; fever; headache, etc. cause by exposure to strong sunlight

【中选】be chosen; be opted for; be selected.

【中意】be to one's liking; be to one's taste; catch the fancy of：这几张挂毯我都～。*None of these rugs is to my liking.*

仲 ① middle; inter mediate ② the second month of the three moths in a season ③ second oldest brother

【仲春】second month of spring; mid-spring

【仲夏】second month of summer; mid-summer

【仲秋】second month of autumn; mid-autumn

【仲冬】second month of winter; mid-winter

众 ① many, numerous ② crowd; multitude

【众多】many; numerous; multitudinous

【众寡悬殊】wide gap or great disparity in numerical strength

【众口铄金】public clamour can confound right and wrong

【众口一词】unanimously; with one voice

【众目睽睽】with everybody watching; with all eyes centred on sth or sb; in the public eye

【众叛亲离】be opposed by the masses and deserted by one's followers; be utterly isolated; with the masses rising in rebellion and one's friends deserting

【众生】all living creatures

【众说纷纭】opinions differ greatly; opinions are widely divided; opinions vary

【众所周知】s it well known; as everyone knows; it is common knowledge that：由于～的原因 *for reasons known to all*

【众望所归】command public respect and support; enjoy popular confidence of trust

【众志成城】unity of will is an impregnable stronghold; unity is the path to victory, unity is strength

种 cultivate; grow; plant; sow：～蔬菜 *grow vegetables* / 这里每年都可以～水稻。*The pad-*

dy fields here yield two crops year.
see also zhǒng
【种地】go in for farming, till (or cultivate) land
【种瓜得瓜,种豆得豆】plant melons and you get melons, sow beans and you get beans — as you sow, so will you reap
【种花】① cultivate (or grow) flowers; grow cotton
【种田】do farm work; farm; till (or cultivate the land)
【种养】cultivate; grow: ~玫瑰 *grow rose*
【种因】[书] do things that will entail grave consequences sow the seed (of later clash, suffering, etc.)
【种植】cultivate; plant; grow: ~园 *plantation*

重 ① weight: 举~ *weight-lifting* / 净~ *net weight* / 毛~ *gross weight* ② heavy; important; weighty: 铁比木头~。*Iron is weightier than wood.* ③ considerable in amount or value ④ deep; heavy; serious: 口音~ *a marked* (*or heavy*) *accent* / 私心很~ *extremely selfish* ⑤ discreet; prudent ⑥ attach importance to; lay stress on; set store by
see also chóng
【重办】severely punish (a criminal)
【重兵】huge forces; a large number of troops: ~压境 *be heavily pressed by huge forces*
【重臣】[书] high court officials; minister (of a monarchy) holding an important post or shouldering heavy responsibilities
【重酬】① generously or liberally reward ② a high or handsome reward
【重创】maul (heavily); inflict heavy losses (or casualties) on
【重大】great; major; significant; tremendous; weighty: ~问题 *vital problem* / ~损失 *heavy* (*or grievous*) *losses* / ~嫌疑犯 *main suspect*
【重担】great responsibility; difficult task; heave burden: 挑~ *shoulder heavy burdens* (*or responsibility*)
【重地】important place which is out of bounds to the general public: 机房~,闲人免进。*Machine in operation; no Admittance.*
【重点】①【物】weight ② emphasis; key; focal point; stress: ~突出 *make a key points stand out* / ~项目 *major project* / 今天~讨论降低成本问题。*We'll for us our discussion today on cutting costs; our discussion today will centre on cutting costs.*
【重读】【语】stress: ~音节 *stressed syllable* / 非~音节 *unstressed syllable*
【重罚】severe punishment: 对多次不改者予以~ *severely punish repeated offenders*
【重犯】major criminal
【重负】heavy burden; heavy load
【重工业】heavy industry
【重荷】grave responsibility; heavy burden
【重话】biting remarks; harsh words; hard words: 我们两个从没说过~。*Both of us have never a harsh word.*
【重奖】give or offer rich or ample rewards
【重金】a huge sum of money: ~收买 *buy over sb with a high sum of money*
【重金属】【化】heavy metal
【重力】【物】gravity; gravitational force: ~场 *gravitational field* / ~秤 *gravity balance*
【重利】① high or exorbitant interest; ② huge profit
【重量】weight: ~证明书 *weight certificate; surveyor's report on weight*
【重量级】【体】heavyweight
【重男轻女】① value men and belittle women; ② prefer sons to daughters preference of boys to girls
【重炮】heavy artillery; heavy artillery piece; heavy gun
【重任】important task; heavy responsibility: 肩负~ *hold a position of important tasks*
【重伤】a severe injury: 受~ *receive or sustain serious wound*
【重赏】a rich or handsome reward: ~之下,必有勇夫 *a big reward will make the brave come forward*
【重视】pay attention to; attach important to; lay stress on; think highly of; take sth seriously; value: ~教育 *attach important to education*
【重听】hard of hearing: 你说话响点,爸爸有点~。*You have to raise your voice for grandfather is hard of hearing.*
【重头】① traditional opera involving much singing and action ② important part of an activity: ~作品 *significant work*
【重托】great trust
【重望】① good reputation; great fame; high renown. ② great expectation; high hopes
【重武器】heavy weapons
【重心】①【物】centre of gravity ② heart; core; focus ③【数】median point
【重刑】heavy sentence; heavy penalty; cruel corporal; severe punishment
【重型】heavy; heavy-duty: ~机床 *heavy-duty machine tool*
【重压】heavy (or strong) pressure; heavy load; heavy strain: 承担生活的~ *be under heavy burden of life* / 树枝经不起雷的~终于折断了。*Weighed down by snow, the twig broke off in the end.*
【重要】essential; important; major; significant: ~任务 *vital task; important mission* / ~原则 *cardinal principle* / ~政策 *essential policy* / ~人物 *important figure; prominent personage; VIP* / ~关头 *critical juncture* / ~因素 *key factor* / ~性 *importance; significance*
【重音】①【语】accent; stress: 单词~ *word stress* / 句子~ *sentence stress* / 主~ *primary accent* / 次~ *secondary accent* / ~符号 *accent; stress mark* ②【音】accent
【重用】assign sb to a key post; put sb in an important position: 受到~ *have been employed at high levels*
【重镇】place of strategic importance 军事~ *a strategic post*

Z

【重子】【物】baryon
【重罪】【律】felony; serious crime; heavy offence

zhōu

舟 [书] boat:一叶扁~ *a small (or light) boat*
【舟车】[书] ① vessel and vehicle; boat and carriage ② journey; travel
【舟楫】[书] vessels
【舟子】[书] boatman
州 ①【历】an administrative division in former times ② (autonomous) prefecture ③ (us) state
诌 fabricate (tales, etc); make up
周[1] ① circuit; circumference; periphery; perimeter:绕房子一~ *make (or do) a circuit of the city wall* /月亮绕地球一~大约一个月。*It makes a moon about one month finish a circuit around the earth.* ② circle; make a circuit; move in a circular course ③ all; whole ④ considerate; attentive ⑤ week:下~ *next week* ⑥ cycle
周[2] help out; assist; relieve
周[3] ① Zhou Dynasty (c. 11th century-256 BC) ② Northern Zhou of the Northern Dynasties (557-581) ③ Later Zhou of the Five Dynasties (951-960) ④ (Zhōu) a surname
【周报】weekly; a weekly newspaper or periodical
【周边】①【机】periphery; ② neighboring
【周长】circumference; girth; perimeter
【周到】attentive and satisfactory, considerable; solicitous, thoughtful:他们向我们提供了~的服务。*They offered excellent service for us.*
【周济】relieve; help out
【周刊】weekly; a weekly publication (a magazine, a supplement to the newspaper, etc.)
【周率】【物】frequency
【周密】careful; thorough; well-conceived: ~推理和分析 *a thorough investigation and a detailed analysis*
【周末】weekend
【周年】anniversary
【周期】cycle; period:短~ *short cycles* /~表 *periodic table* /~律 *periodic law*
【周全】① comprehensive; circumspect; through:计划~ *plan to the last detail* ② assist; help sb attain his aim
【周身】all over the body; the whole body: ~疼痛 *ache all over*
【周岁】one full year of life; exactly one year
【周围】about; (a) round:环视~ *look about (or around)* /~环境 *surroundings; environment*
【周详】careful; complete; comprehensive; detailed; thorough:考虑~ *give careful consideration to* /~的报告 *exhaustive report*
【周旋】① circle; spiral; circle around; wheel ② fraternize; socialize; mix with other people: ~于客商之间 *move in the business community* ③ engage; contend with; deal with:长期与敌人~ *fight with the enemy for a long time*
【周游】travel or journey around: ~各地 *travel to many places* /~世界 *travel around the world*
【周遭】around; round; the surrounding area: ~寂静无声。*It was very quiet all round.*
【周章】[书] ① scared; terrified: ~失措 *be flurried out of one's wits* ② effort; pains, trouble:煞费~ *take great pains; go to a lot of trouble; spare no effort*
【周折】trouble; setbacks; twists and turns:颇费~ *a great deal of bother* /几经~ *after repeated setbacks*
【周知】everybody knows or make known to all; make sth public
【周转】①【经】turnover:资本~ *capital turnover* /资金~不灵 *slow turnover of funds* /~资金 *working fund; revolving fund; circulation fund* /~率 *turnover rate* ② have adequate to meet the need:因为学生增加,教室~不开。*We are short of classroom as there are too many students now.*
洲 ① continent ② sandbar; islet in a river
【洲际】intercontinental: ~导弹 *intercontinental missile*
粥 gruel; congee; porridge:麦片~ *oatmeal porridge* /小米~ *millet gruel*
see also yù
【粥少僧多】many monks and little gruel — not enough to go around

zhóu

妯
【妯娌】wives of brothers; sister-in-law
轴 ① axle; shaft:车~ *car (or bicycle) axle; axle* ② axis; pivot ③ rod; roller; spool ④ [量]:一~线 *a spool of thread* /几~山水画 *a scroll painting of scenery*
【轴承】【机】bearing: ~钢 *bearing steel* /~衬 *bearing bush* /滚珠~ *ball bearing*
【轴对称】【数】axial symmetry
【轴距】wheel base (of a vehicle)
【轴线】①【机】axis:垂直~ *normal axis* ② spool cotton; spool thread
【轴向】【机】axial: ~运动 *axial motion* /~剖面 *axial section*
【轴心】①【机】axle centre ② axis
【轴子】① roller (for a scroll of calligraphy or painting) ② (tuning) peg (or pin); peg (of a stringed instrument)

zhǒu

肘 elbow

【肘窝】crook of the arm

【肘腋】[书] elbow and armpit-close hand

【肘子】① elbow ② upper part of a leg of pork

帚 broom

zhòu

咒 ① incantation：念～ *chant incantation* ② curse；damn；swear：不要～我。*Don't curse me.*

【咒骂】abuse；curse；swear；revile；utter curses against

【咒语】incantation

宙 time (conceived as past，present and future)：宇～ *cosmos*；*universe*

绉 crape；crepe

【绉布】cotton crepe；crepe

【绉纱】crape

昼 daylight；daytime；day

【昼伏夜出】hide by day and come out by night

【昼夜】day and night；all the time；around the clock：～看守 *keep watch round the clock*

皱 crease；crumple；wrinkly：这料子易～。*This material crumples easily.* /衣服～的厉害。*This jacket is full of creases.* /别把纸弄～了。*Don't crumple the paper.*

【皱眉头】frown；knit (or contract) one's brows：他～沉思。*His brow furrowed in deep thought.*

【皱纹】creases；lines；wrinkles：眼角的～ *crow's-feet*

【皱褶】crease；fold；rumple；wrinkle

【皱皱巴巴】crumpled；rumpled；wrinkled；full of wrinkles：她总穿着那身～的衣服。*She is always seen in that rumpled suit.*

骤 ① (of a horse) trot ② abrupt；sudden：气温～降。*The temperature suddenly dropped.* /枪声～起。*There was a burst of gunfire.*

【骤然】abruptly；suddenly；all of a sudden：～一惊 *with a start*；*be startled*；*be stupefied*

zhū

朱 ① vermilion；bright red：～颜 *peach and cream complexion*；*peach blossom face of a beauty* ② cinnabar

【朱古力】chocolate

【朱红】bright red；vermilion

【朱鹮】【动】red ibis

【朱门】vermilion gates-red-lacquered gates of wealthy people mansions：酒肉臭，路有冻死骨。*Behind the red doors meat and wine go to waste while out on the road lie the bones of the frozen.*

【朱墨】① red and black：～套印 *printed in red and black* ② ink made of cinnabar；vermilion ink

【朱批】remarks written in red with a brush

【朱砂】cinnabar

侏 [书] short and small

【侏儒】dwarf；midget；pygmy

诛 [书] ① put (a criminal) to death；execute ② condemn；punish：人人得而～之。*Everybody has the right to punish.*

【诛戮】[书] kill，slaughter；put to death

【诛心之论】exposure of sb's ulterior motives；penetrating criticism.

珠 ① pearl ② bead：汗～ *beads of sweat* /算盘～ *beads on an abacus*

【珠蚌】mussel；nacre；pearl oyster；pearl shell

【珠宝】pearls jewels；jewelry：～店 *a jeweller's (shop)*

【珠翠】pearls and jade；ornaments made with pearls and jade

【珠光宝气】be adorned with brilliant jewels and pearls bedecked with jewels；be richly bejewelled

【珠联璧合】strings of pearls and girdles of jade — a perfect pair；a happy combination

【珠算】calculation with an abacus；reckoning by the abacus

【珠圆玉润】round as pearls and smooth as jade — excellent singing or polished writing

【珠子】① bead ② pearl

株 ① stump；stem of a plant；trunk of a tree ② individual plant；plant ③ [量] of plants and trees：三～梨树 *three pear trees*

【株距】【农】spacing in the rows

【株连】incriminate；implicate

诸 all；numerous；various：～研究领域 *the various research fields* /学院中～老师 *all the teachers of the department*

【诸多】[书] (used for abstract things) a good deal；a lot of；lots of plenty of：～不便 *great inconvenience*；*a lot of trouble*

【诸侯】ducks or princes under an emperor

【诸君】(used in addressing a group of people) ladies and gentlemen；you

【诸如】such as；for example

【诸如此类】things like that；and suchlike；and all that；and what hot；and so on；and so forth

【诸事】everything；all mutter：～顺利！*Wish you every success！*

【诸位】(used in addressing a group of people) ladies and gentlemen；you：～老师谁有兴趣？*Is there any teacher present interested in this？*

铢 [量] an ancient unit of weight，equal to 1/24 *liang*

【铢积寸累】accumulate little by little or bit by bit；

build up gradually

【铢两悉称】be exactly equal in weight or quality; carry the same weight

猪 hog; pig; swine:小～ *piglet* /母～ *sow*; 公～ *boar*

【猪场】piggery; pig farm

【猪肚】poke tripe

【猪肝】pork liver

【猪倌】swineherd

【猪猡】[方] pig; swine

【猪排】pork chop

【猪肉】pork

【猪舍】pig (or hog) house

【猪食】pig wash; swill; pig feed:

【猪蹄】pig's trotters

【猪腿】ham; leg of pork

【猪瘟】hog cholera; swine fever

【猪窝】pigsty:这个房间像～一样脏。*This room is as dirty as a pigsty.*

【猪血】peg's blood; coagulated pig's blood used as a food

【猪腰子】pork kidney

【猪油】lard

【猪鬃】(hog) bristles

蛛 spider

【蛛丝马迹】the thread of a spider and the trail of a horse-chase; traces; tracks:找出～ *find a clue*

zhú

竹 bamboo: ～林 *bamboo forest*; *groves of bamboo*: ～篓 *bamboo basket or bamboo crate*

【竹板】bamboo clappers

【竹编】bamboo woven articles

【竹材】bamboo used as lumber:用～代替木材 *substitute bamboo for wood*

【竹雕】bamboo carving

【竹筏】bamboo raft

【竹简】bamboo slip (used for writing on in ancient times)

【竹篮打水一场空】all in vain; draw water with a bamboo basket — achieve nothing

【竹帘】bamboo screen or curtain

【竹排】bamboo raft

【竹器】articles made of bamboo

【竹笋】bamboo shoots

【竹筒】a thick bamboo tube

【竹席】bamboo-strip mat

【竹椅】bamboo chair

【竹子】bamboo

逐 ① chase; pursue; seek: 追～猎物 *pursue one's prey* /追～名利 *hanker after fame and gain* ② expel; oust: ～出门外 *drive out of the door* ③ one by one; in turn: ～日 *day by day* /～项 *item by item*

【逐步】progressively; step by step; gradually: 我们～来解决问题。*We will settle the problems step by step.*

【逐处】everywhere; in all places

【逐个】one after another; one by one: ～解决 *solve the problem one after another*

【逐渐】gradually; by degree; steadily:天气～变暖。*It's getting warmer and warmer.*

【逐客令】order for guests to leave:下～ *show sb the door*

【逐年】year by year; year after year; with every passing years

【逐日】day by day; every day; daily

【逐条】item by item; point by point; article by article:他～解释给我们听。*He explained point by point to us.*

【逐一】one by one:他～介绍客人。*He introduced the guests one by one.*

【逐字】verbatim; word by word; in exactly the same words: ～校对 *proofread word by word*

【逐字逐句】word by word and sentence by sentence; word by word; literally: ～翻译 *literal translation*; *word-for-word translation*

烛 ① candle: 香～ *joss sticks and candles* ② [书] illuminate; height up; make bright with bright.

【烛光】【物】candle; candlepower

【烛台】candlestick

【烛心】candlewick

zhǔ

主 ① lust:宾～ *host and guest* ② owner; master; lord: ～仆 *master and man*; *master and servant* /一家之～ *head of a family* ③ person or party concerned:她快三十了,也该找个～了。*She is about thirty and it's time she looked for a husband.* ④ Lord, God; the Master ⑤ Allah ⑥ [方] trunk card (in poker) ⑦ main; primary: ～教练 *principal coach* ⑧manage; direct; be in charge of; preside over ⑨ indicate; signify; foretell ⑩ advocate; favour; hold a definite view about sth:力～放弃这个方法 *strongly advocate give up this way*

【主板】mainboard; motherboard

【主办】direct; sponsor; be under the auspices of: ～单位 *sponsor* /这个比赛由上海～。*This competition will be sponsored by Shanghai.*

【主笔】[旧] ① editor in chief ② chief commentator

【主编】① chief editor or compiler editor on chief ② supervise the publication of (for guests of honour) seat for the guest of honour

【主裁判】chief reference; head reference

【主菜单】【电】main menu

【主持】① direct; manage; take charge (or care) of ② chair; preside over; host: ～会议 *chair the meeting*; *preside over a meeting* ③ champion; hold; uphold; stand for: ～公道 *uphold justice*; *stand for fair play*

【主持人】compere; host; hostess; interviewer;

moderator; anchorperson; anchorman

【主厨】① chef; chief cook; person in charge of the cooking at a hotel, canteen, etc. ② do the cooking, be the chef

【主次】primary and secondary; major and minor: ~不分 *confuse the principal with the secondary* / 学习要分清~。*We must differentiate what is primary from what is secondary in our study.*

【主从】principal and subordinate: ~关系 *subordination*

【主刀】【医】① operator ② operating surgeon; perform an operation: 这个年轻医生~。*This young surgeon perform the operation.*

【主导】dominant; guiding; leading; ruling: 占~地位 *occupy the leading position*; *hold sway* / ~思想 *dominant ideology ruling ideas*

【主动】① take the initiative; do sth of one's own accord: 争取~ *try to gain the initiative*; *contend for the initiative* ②【机】driving: ~轴 *driving spindle*; *driving shaft* / ~齿轮 *driving gear*

【主动脉】aorta

【主队】【体】home team; host team

【主伐】【林】final felling (or cutting)

【主犯】【律】prime culprit; principle criminal (or offender); principle: ~和从犯 *principal and accessories in a crime*

【主峰】the highest peak in a mountain range.

【主妇】hostess; housewife

【主干】①【植】trunk; ② backbone; mainstay

【主攻】【军】main attack: ~部队 *main attack force* / ~方向 *main direction of attack*

【主顾】client; customer

【主观】subjective: ~愿望 *wishful thinking*; *subjective desire* / ~努力 *subjective efforts* / ~能动性 *subjective initiative*; *conscious activity* / ~唯心主义 *subjective idealism*

【主管】① be responsible for; be in charge of: ~教育 *be in charge of education* / ~机关 *responsible institutions*; *competent authorities* ② person in charge: 他是这个部门的~。*He is the person in charge of the department.*

【主和】advocate peace; be for a peaceful settlement: ~派 *peace party*

【主机】①【机】main engine; main processor ②【军】leader; lead plane ③【电】main body of a computer (compared with display and peripherals) ④【电】host computer.

【主见】ideas or thoughts of one's own; definite view; one's own judgement: 没有~ *have no definite views of one's own*

【主讲】give lectures; lecture on; be the speaker

【主将】【军】chief commander; commanding general

【主教】bishop

【主句】【语】main (or principal) clause

【主角】lead; leading role; protagonist; star part: 在电影中扮演~ *play the lead in the film*

【主考】① be in charge of examination ② chief examiner (in a school, etc.)

【主考官】official in charge of an imperial examination; chief examiner

【主客】① host and guest ② guest of honour

【主课】major; main; course; main subject

【主力】main force; main body or strength of an army: ~舰 *battleship*; *capital ship* / ~军 *main (or principal) force* / ~兵团 *main formations* / ~队员 *top players of a team*

【主粮】staple food grain

【主流】① mainstream; trunk stream; essential aspect: 历史~ *the mainstream of history* ② main trend; essential or main aspect: ~和支流 *the principal and secondary aspects*

【主楼】main building in a complex

【主谋】① head a conspiracy; be the chief plotter ②【律】chief instigator; chief plotter

【主脑】① centre of operation; control centre; ② head; chief; leader

【主权】sovereignty; sovereign rights: 国家~ *a sovereign state*

【主人】① host: 女~ *hostess* ② master ③ owner: 房子的~ *the owner of the house*

【主人公】leading character in a novel etc.; hero or heroine; protagonist

【主人翁】master (of one's country, society, etc.): 有一种~感 *have a sense of being the master of one's own affairs*

【主任】chairman; chief; director; head: 车间~ *workshop director* / 副~ *deputy director* / 教研室~ *chief of teaching and research section*

【主食】principal food; staple food

【主事】be in charge of; take charge

【主题】motif; leitmotiv; subject; theme: 作品的~ *motif of a literary work* / ~歌 *theme song*

【主体】① main body; main (or principal) part: ~工程 *principal part*; *principal part of a project* / 以老年人为~的队伍 *a team composed of mainly of old people* ②【哲】subject

【主谓句】【语】subject-predicate sentence

【主席】① chairman (of a meeting): 担当~ *be in the chair*; *chair (or preside over) a meeting*; *take the chair* ② chairman or president (of an organization or a state)

【主席台】platform; rostrum: 登上~ *go up to the rostrum*

【主线】thread (of a novel, etc)

【主心骨】① backbone; chief support; mainstay; pillar: 他是这个团体的~。*He is the mainstay of this team.* ② a definite view; one's own judgement: 他是个没~的人。*He has no judgement of his own.*

【主刑】【律】principal penalty

【主凶】principal; principal; murderer; principal assassin

【主修】① major; specialize (in a subject): ~科目 *main subjects* ② be responsible for the repair or overhaul (of a machine)

【主旋律】main melody; theme; top melody

【主演】play (or act) the leading role (in a play or

film); star:她～了三部电影。*She starred in three films.*

【主要】chief; main; major; principal: ～原因 *main reasons* /～矛盾 *principal contradiction* /～因素 *main factor*

【主页】【电】home page

【主意】① idea; plan; way:想出好～ *hit upon a good idea* /出～ *give advice* ② decision; definite view; judgement:拿定～ *make up one's mind; make a decision* /拿不定～ *be in two minds (about sth); hesitate* /改变～ *change one's mind*

【主因】major cause; main reason

【主语】【语】subject

【主宰】control; dominate; dictate; decide; govern:她为不能～自己的命运而哭泣。*She cried because she can't decide her own destiny.*

【主战】advocate war; favour the use of force.

【主张】① advocate; hold; maintain; favour; stand for: ～改革 *favour reforms* /～和平 *advocate peace* ② view; position; proposition; stand:我同意你的～。*I am for your proposal.* /那是我国的一贯～。*That has been our country's consistent stand.*

【主政】head the government:新市长很快将上任～。*The new major will assume office soon.*

【主旨】gist; purport; substance:文章～ *the gist of the article* /～演讲 *keynote speech*

【主治】【医】indications: ～医生 *doctor in charge of a case*

【主轴】【机】spindle; main shaft

【主子】boss; master

拄 lean on (a stick, etc.): ～杖而行 *walk with a stick*

煮 boil; cook; stew: ～鸡蛋 *boil eggs or boiled eggs* /～饭 *cook rice*

【煮呢】【纺】potting

属 [书] ① join; connect; combine: ～文 *compose a piece of prose writing* ② centre (one's attention, etc) upon fix (one's mind) on *see also* shǔ

嘱 advise; exhort; enjoin; urge

【嘱咐】enjoin; exhort; tell:再三～ *exhort again and again; din sth into sb* /性别～ *departure injunction* /～某人注意身体 *tell sb to pay attention to health*

【嘱托】entrust; ask:受朋友～ *be at the request of sb's friends* /他～我办事。*He entrusted me with the task.*

瞩 gaze; look steadily; fasten one's look on

【瞩目】[书] fix one's eyes on; focus one's attention upon:受世界～ *attract worldwide attention*

【瞩望】[书] ① earnestly expect; look forward to: ～已久 *have been eagerly looking forward to sth for a long time* ② gaze at; have a steady look at; look long and steadily upon

zhù

伫 [书] stand for a long while

助 aid; assist; help give help to: ～一臂之力 *lend (or give) sb a helping hand* /～消化 *aid digestion*

【助产】midwifery /～士 *midwife*

【助词】auxiliary word

【助攻】【军】holding (or secondary) attack: ～部队 *holding element*

【助教】assistant professor (of a college faulty)

【助理】assistant: ～工程师 *assistant engineer*

【助力】help; assistance; aid; a helping hand

【助跑】【体】approach; run-up

【助燃】【化】combustion-supporting

【助人为乐】find it a pleasure to help others; take pleasure in helping others

【助手】aide; assistant; helper

【助听器】audiphone; deaf-aid; hearing aid

【助兴】add to the fun; make things more lively; liven things up

【助战】① bolster sb's morale ② assist in fighting

【助长】[贬] abet; encourage; foment; foster: ～他的惰性 *encourage his laziness* /～不正之风 *encourage the evil trends*

住 ① dwell; live; reside; stay:我～在上海。*I live in Shanghai.* /我家对面没人～。*Nobody lives in the room opposite mine.* ② end; cease; stop:风～了。*The wind drops.* ③ to a stop:拿～了。*Hold tight.*

【住处】accommodation; dwelling; lodging; residence quarters:固定～ *fixed abode* /你找到～了吗? *Have you found accommodation?*

【住房】lodgings; housing: ～问题 *accommodation* /～制度改革 *housing system reform* /～面积 *floor space* /～商品化 *commercialization of housing*

【住户】household; resident:这幢楼里有 12 家～。*There are twelve households in this building.*

【住家】① (of one's family) live; reside in:他的～在城里。*He lives with his family in town.* ② household; resident

【住口】keep quiet; stop talking; shut up:快～ *cut it out!*

【住声】hold one's tongue; stop talking, laughing or crying

【住手】stay one's hand; stop(doing sth)

【住宿】accommodate; get accommodation; put up; stay:安排～ *find lodgings (or arrange accommodation) for sb* /你们～在我家。*Put you up in my family.*

【住所】abode; domicile; residence; dwelling place

【住校】(of a student) board at school

【住院】be in hospital; be hospitalized: ～病人 *in-patient* /～部 *in-patient department* /～处 *admission office (in a hospital)* /～费 *hospitalization expenses*

【住宅】dwelling, resident: ~小区 *dwelling districts*; *resident quarters* / ~设计 *housing design* / ~保险 *residence insurance*

【住址】address

【住嘴】stop talking:她闲聊起来不能~。*She would keep on when she were chatting.*

贮 keep; save; store; lay aside: ~粮备荒 *store grain against a lean year*; *store away grain against famine*

【贮藏】store up; lay in: ~蔬菜 *store vegetables*

【贮存】store; keep in storage: ~期 *storage time*

【贮蓄】① conserve; lay up; store up ② storage or savings:他没有~。*He is not a saving man.*

【贮运】storage; shipping; transportation

注¹ ① fill; pour ② concentrate; fix ③ stakes (in gambling) ④ for deals or sums of money: 一~钱 *a sum of money*

注² ① annotate; explain with notes ② record; register ③ notes: ~用小字表示。*The notes are to be in small type.*

【注册】① register ② log-in: ~商标 *registered trademark* / ~证书 *registration certificate* / ~处 *registrar's office*

【注定】be destined; be doomed; be fated:命中~ *predestined*; *decreed by fate* / ~要灭亡 *be doomed to destruction*

【注解】① annotate; explain with notes ② (explanatory) note, annotation

【注明】label; give dear indication of:这种药未~日期。*This medicine is undated.*

【注目】gaze at; have a steady look at; fix one's eyes on

【注入】① pour into; empty into:长江~东海。*The Changjiang River empties into the East China Sea.* ② petroleum injection: ~井 *injection well*

【注射】【医】inject: ~器 *injector*; *syringe* / ~针头 *syringe needle*

【注视】closely watch; gaze at; look attentively at: 目不转睛地~ *look intently at*

【注释】annotation; explanatory note:附有~ *annotated plays*

【注水】petroleum water flooding

【注文】notes; explanatory notes

【注销】cancel; write off; annul: ~登记 *nullify the registration* / ~欠款 *write off the debt* /把借条~ *cancel a written acknowledgement of a loan*; *cancel an I. O. U.*

【注意】be careful about; pay attention to; take note of: ~广度 *attention span* / ~事项 *points for attention*; *matters needing attention* /我没~他是否来开会了。*I didn't notice whether he was at the meeting.*

【注音】phonetic notation

【注重】attach importance to; lay stress on; pay attention to

驻 ① halt; stay; stop: ~足观赏 *stop to enjoy the beautiful sight* ② be posted; be stationed: ~外机构 *in situations stationed abroad*

【驻地】① place where troops, fieldworkers etc are stationed:勘探队~ *encampment of prospecting team* ② seat (of a local administrative organ)

【驻防】garrison; be on garrison duty; defend with or as a garrison: ~部队 *garrison (troops)*

【驻军】① station troops; base troops ② garrison troops; garrison

【驻守】defend, garrison

【驻屯】(of troops) be stationed; be quartered

【驻颜】[书] remain youthful looks: ~有术 *be able to presence men's youthful looks*; *poses the secret of preserving youthful looks*

【驻扎】(of troops) be stationed; be quartered

【驻足】halt; stop; go no father; make a temporary stay: ~观看 *stop to watch*

柱 ① column; pillar; post; upright:房~ *pillars of a house* ② sth shaped like a column: 水~ *pillar of water*, *water column* ③【数】cylinder

【柱石】[喻] mainstay; pillar

【柱子】post; pillar

【柱座】plinth; column base

祝 express good wishes; wish: ~你生日快乐! *Happy birthday to you!* / ~你一路顺风! *Have a pleasant journey!*

【祝词】① congratulatory speech (at ceremony, etc); congratulation ② prayers at sacrificial rites in ancient times

【祝福】blessing; benediction: ~你! *Blessing on you.*

【祝贺】congratulate:致以节日的~ *extend holiday greetings*

【祝酒】toast; drink a toast:致~辞 *propose a toast* / 向贵宾们~ *toast the guests* /答谢~ *respond (or reply) to a toast*

【祝寿】congratulate (an elderly person) on his or her birthday

【祝愿】wish:致以良好~ *with best wish*

著 ① marked; outstanding:这个月阿尔文有了显~进步。*Alvin has made marked progress in this month.* ② display; prove; show:颇~成效 *prove rather effective* ③ write; compose: ~书 *write books* ④ book, work:新~ *sb's latest work*

【著称】celebrate, famous:北京以长城~全世。*Beijing is world-famous for its Great Wall.*

【著名】celebrated; famous; noted; well-known: ~特产 *famous product* / ~论断 *a celebrated thesis* / ~风景区 *well-known scenic spot* / ~学者 *noted scholar*

【著书立说】produce scholarly works, write books to expound a theory

【著述】① compile; write:埋头~ *be engrossed in the writing and compilation of scholarly works* ② book; work:主要~ *major works* / ~等身 *one's works piled up to one's own height-be a prolific writer*

【著作】① book; work; writings:医学~ *medical literature* ② write:那个作家一生~很多。*The writer wrote many books during his lifetime.*

蛀 ① moth or any other insect that eats books, clothes wood, etc. ② (of moths, etc.) eat;

bore through

【蛀齿】decayed tooth; dental caries

【蛀虫】insect that eats books, clothes or wood; moth; borer

铸 cast, found: ~钱 *coin money* / 铜~的古钟 *bronze bell*

【铸币】coin; specie: ~权 *mintage*

【铸成大错】[书] make a serious blunder; commit a gross error; stupendous mistake

【铸错】commit blunders; make grave mistakes

【铸钢】cast steel

【铸工】① foundry work ② founder; founder worker: ~车间 *foundry (shop)* / ~鼓风机 *foundry fan*

【铸件】cast; casting; founding: 冷硬~ *chill or chilled casting*

【铸铁】① iron casting ② casting iron

【铸造】casting; founding: ~厂 *foundry* / ~车间 *foundry (shop) casting shop*

【铸字】【印】typecasting; typefounding: ~工人 *typefounder* / ~机 *typecasting machine; caster*

筑 build; construct: 修~公路 *construct a road*

【筑巢】① build nest ② build infrastructure

zhuā

抓 ① grab; clutch; seize: ~要点 *grasp the main points* / ~机会 *seize a good opportunity* / ~一把糖 *take a handful of sweets* ② scratch ③ arrest, catch: ~小偷 *catch a thief* ④ stress; lay stress on; pay special attention to: ~本质 *stress he essence* / ~苗头 *watch out for the first signs* ⑤ take charge of; responsible for: 她~生产方面。*He is in charge of production.*

【抓捕】apprehend; arrest; catch: 因抢劫商店而被~ *be arrested for robbing a shop*

【抓耳挠腮】scratch one's head; tweak one's ears and scratch one's cheeks (as a sign of anxiety or delight)

【抓工夫】find time (to do sth); make good use of one's time

【抓好】do a good job of; make great efforts to: 你要~学习。*You must do a good job of learning.*

【抓获】capture; catch (a criminal, etc); seize

【抓紧】grasp firmly; lose no time in doing sth; pay close attention to: ~有利时机 *seize (or grasp) a golden opportunity* / ~时间 *make the best use of one's time*

【抓挠】[方] ① scratch: ~几下就不痒了。*Scratch and it won't itch any more.* ② mess about; make a mess of sth; muddle things up ③ fight; exchange blows; come to blows ④ prepare sth hastily: 一下子来了这么多学生, 老师怕~不了吧! *With so many students here all of a sudden for studying, I wonder how a teacher can hustle them up.* ⑤ sth one can use or sth and sb one can rely on: 丈夫在世时, 她还有个~。*If her husband were still live, she would have someone to fall back on.* ⑥ way to handle a problem; solution to a difficulty, etc.: 事前要充分考虑, 以免没了~。*Think it over well beforehand so as to be prepared for all eventualities.*

【抓拍】① take a candid photograph (or picture); take a snapshot of ② a candid photograph (or picture); candid

【抓破】damage or injure by clawing or scratching: ~脸 *come out clawing and scratching; scratch each other's face-offend sb openly; quarrel openly*

【抓人】apprehend; arrest sb; take sb into custody

【抓瞎】[口] be in a rush and muddle; be thrown off balance; find oneself at a loss

【抓住】① grip; catch (or seize) hold of: ~要害 *scratch where it itches* ② catch; capture: ~个小偷 *catch a thief* ③ grip one's attention: 这部电影~了观众的心。*This film gripped the attention of the audience.*

【抓壮丁】press-gang able-bodied men

zhuǎ

爪 claw; talon

see also zhǎo

【爪儿】[口] ① paw of small animal ② foot of a utensil: 这种锅有3个~。*This pan stands on three pans.*

【爪子】[口] claw; paw; talon: 鹰~ *an eagles' talons* / 鸡~ *chicken's feet* / 猫~ *cats' paws*

zhuāi

拽 [方] cast; hurl; fling; throw: 把书~给我。*Throw the book to me.*

see also zhuài

zhuǎi

跩 [方] waddle 鸭子一~一~的走路。*Ducks waddle.*

zhuài

拽 drag; haul; pull: ~住不放 *catch hold of sb or sth and not let go* / 生拉硬~ *drag sb along against his will*

see also zhuāi

zhuān

专 ① special; focused on one thing; for a particular person, occasion, purpose, etc.: ~业技术 *professional skill* ② monopolize: ~制者 *despot; autocrat*

【专案】case; special case for investigation: ~组

special group for handling a special case / ～人员 *person engaged in the examination of a case* / ～材料 *dossier; material relating to a special case*

【专长】special skill or knowledge; specialty; expertise: 学有～ *be expert in a special field of study* / 发挥～ *give full play to one's professional knowledge or skill*

【专场】special performance; show intended for a limited audience: 杂技～ *acrobatic show*

【专车】a special train or car

【专诚】specially; for a particular purpose: ～拜访 *pay a special visit to sb*

【专程】special trip: 她～来机场迎接贵宾。*She made a special trip to airport to welcome the honoured guests.*

【专断】act peremptorily; make arbitrary decisions.

【专访】exclusive interview on a specific topic

【专攻】specialize in

【专柜】special counter in shop (for specific products)

【专号】special issue (of a periodical): 研究～ *special issue on studies*

【专横】domineering; imperious; peremptory: ～跋扈 *imperious and despotic; arrogant and domineering*

【专机】① special plane; ② private plane

【专家】expert; specialist: 医学～ *expert in medicine* / 眼科～ *eye specialist; ophthalmologist* / ～门诊 *outpatient consultation by a specialist* / ～系统 *expert system*

【专刊】① special issue or column ② monograph: 政治学～ *monograph on politics*

【专科】① specialized subject; specialty; special field of study ② vocational training school; college for professional training

【专款】special fund

【专栏】special column: ～作家 *columnist*

【专利】patent: 申请～ *apply for a patent; patent application* / ～法 *patent law* / ～局 *patent office* / ～品 *patent; patent article* / ～权 *patent; patent right*

【专卖】monopoly; exclusive possession of the trade in some commodity: ～店 *franchised store; exclusive agency*

【专门】special; specialized: ～研究政治学 *specialize in politics* / ～机构 *special organ; special agency* / ～人才 *specialized personnel* / ～人民法院 *special people's court*

【专权】monopolize power; arrogate all powers to oneself

【专人】person specially assigned for a task or job: 这项工作由～负责。*Someone has been put in charge of public relations.*

【专属】exclusive: ～经济区 *exclusive economic zone* / ～渔区 *exclusive fishery right* / ～主权 *exclusive sovereignty*

【专题】special subject; special topic: ～报告 *lecture on a special topic; special coverage* / ～研究 *monographic study* / ～研讨会 *symposium* / ～著作 *monograph; treatise*

【专线】① special railway line ② special telephone line; leased line; private line

【专项】assigned (to a use); dedicated: ～训练 *specialized training; training in special field*

【专心】be absorbed; concentrate one's attention; be engrossed

【专修】specialize in: ～经济学 *specialize in economics* / ～科目 *special course; training course*

【专业】① special field of study; specialty; discipline; specialized subject: 这所大学设了 30 个～。*This university has 30 specialties.* ② special line; specialized trade or profession: 提供～服务 *after professional service* / ～队伍 *professional contingent*

【专一】concentrated; single-minded: ～的爱情 *be faithful in love* / 心思～ *with concentrated attention*

【专营】monopoly under exclusive government control; exclusive sale rights

【专用】for a special purpose; special: ～电话 *telephone for special use* / ～贷款 *loan for a special purpose*

【专有】related to a particular person or thing: ～名词 *nomenclature; technical term*

【专员】① (administrative) commissioner; assistant director: 行政～ *administrative commissioner* / ～公署 *commissioner's office* ② person specially assigned for a job

【专政】dictatorship: ～机关 *organ of dictatorship*

【专职】① sole duty; special duty ②full-time: 他是一名～志愿者。*He is a full-time volunteer.*

【专制】① autocracy ② autocratic; despotic: ～君主 *autocrat* / ～政体 *autocracy* / ～政府 *autocratic movement*

【专注】be absorbed in; concentrate one's attention on; devote one's mind to; focus on

【专著】a book on a special subject; monograph; treatise: 这是本政治学～。*This is a book about politics.*

砖 ① brick: ～墙 *brick wall* / 砌～ *lay bricks* / ～房 *brick house* ② brick-like thing; sth shaped like a brick

【砖厂】brickfield; brickyard

【砖坯】unfired brick

【砖头】[方] brick

【砖窑】brickkiln

zhuǎn

转 ① change; shift; transform; turn: 多云～小雨 *change from cloudy to drizzle; cloudy to drizzle* / ～弱为强 *transform (or grow) from weak to strong* / 晴～多云 *change from fine to cloudy; clear to cloudy* / 向右～ *turn to the right; right turn* / 他～过头与我打招呼。*He greeted me over his shoulder.* ② forward; transfer; pass on: ～交给他 *pass sth on to him*
see also zhuàn

【转包】contract out to sb else the contracted project (cor GPT) one has undertaken; subcontract: 这

个工程队~了这项工程。*This construction brigade has sub-contracted this project.*

【转败为胜】turn defeat into victory

【转变】change; transform: ~态度 *change one's attitude lor out look* / ~立场 *shift one's ground; change one's stand* / 经过多次谈话,他终于~的思想。*He changed his ideology after repeated talking.*

【转播】relay (a radio or TV broadcast): ~台 *relay station* / 实况~ *televise sth live*

【转产】change the line of production; (of an enterprise, etc.) switch to the manufacture of another line of products

【转达】convey; communicate; forward; pass on: ~问候 *give sb one's regards*

【转道】via; go by way of; make a detour

【转递】transmit; pass on

【转调】【音】① modulation ② transfer; transfer from one unit to another: 他办了人事~手续。*He went through transfer procedures.*

【转动】move; turn; turn around: ~手臂 *move one's arm* / ~眼睛 *goggle (or roll; rotate) one's eyes*

【转发】transmit; dispatch: ~到各个国家 *to be transmitted to all the countries*

【转干】(of a workers) be promoted to the position of a cadre

【转岗】change jobs; transfer (or switch) to another job

【转港】route through one part to another

【转告】convey; transmit; pass on a message

【转行】change fobs; change profession: 他由老师~经商。*He became a businessman after teaching.*

【转化】change, transform; turn

【转换】charge; switch; transform: ~话题 *switch the conversation to another subject; change the subject of conversation* / ~频道 *switch to another channel*

【转机】① a favourable turn; a turn for the better: 他的事情有了~。*His situation has taken a turn for the better.* ② change plane

【转嫁】① remarry; (a woman) marry again ② shift; transfer: ~罪责 *lay the blame upon sb else*

【转交】transmit; pass on; send (in) care of: ~信件 *Address letters care of somebody.*

【转接器】adapter

【转口】transit: ~贸易 *switch trade; transit trade*

【转脸】① turn one's face ② in no time; in an instant; in the twinkling of an eye: 小孩~不见了。*The child disappeared in a wink.*

【转录】copy; record; make a recording of another recording

【转念】reconsider and change one's opinion: 他~一想,忍住没谈话。*He did not speak when he though better of it.*

【转让】transfer; make over; transfer he ownership of: ~技术 *technology transfer*

【转入】change over to; shift to; switch to: ~正常 *return to normal* / ~地下 *go underground*

【转身】(of a person) turn round; face about

【转生】【宗】reincarnation; transmigration

【转手】① (ask sb to) pass on: 这封信由他~交给我。*This letter gave me through him.* ② sell what one has bought

【转述】report; relate sth as told by another: 我~老师的话。*I am reporting what he said.*

【转瞬】in a flash; in an instant; in the twinkling of an eye: 他~即到。*He arrived in the twinkling of an eye.*

【转送】① pass on; transmit on ② make a present of what one has been given

【转体】【体】turn; twist: ~动作 *rotational movement* / ~跳 *turning leap; turning jump* / ~三周 *triple turn*

【转托】ask someone else to do what is asked of one: 我~我朋友替你办了。*I've asked my friends to do it for you.*

【转弯】turn a corner; make a turn: 向右~ *turn right* / 教室在~口处。*The classroom is just right around the corner.*

【转弯抹角】① zigzag; full of twists and turns: 这条路~很难走。*The road is full of twists and turns, which makes heavy going.* ② beat about the bush; speak in a roundabout t way: 她说话总~。*She speaks always in a roundabout way.*

【转弯子】① speak in a roundabout way; beat about the rush ② change one's position or get one's thinking straightened out

【转危为安】pull through a crisis; turn changer into safety

【转向】① change direction ② change one's political stand

【转型】transformation; change the mode of production: 经济~ *economy in transformation*

【转学】(of a student) transfer to another school: ~生 *transfer student*

【转眼】soon; in an instant; in a trice; in the twinkling of an eye: ~间,一年过去了。*A year passed before we knew it.*

【转业】① (of an armyman) be transferred to civilian work: ~军人 *armyman transferred to civilian work* ② (of laid-off worker) transfer to a new occupation; move to a new area

【转移】① divert; shift; transfer: ~目标 *distract people's attention from sth or sb* / ~兵力 *shift forces* / ~重点 *shift focus on to sth or sb* ② change; transform

【转院】(of a patient) transfer from one hospital to another

【转运】① have a turn or change of luck; luck turns in one's favour ② transfer; transship; transport: ~站 *transfer post*/ ~公司 *transport company*

【转载】reprint sth that has been published else where; reprint: ~权 *right of reprint*

【转赠】make a present of what one has been given

【转战】fight in one place after another

【转账】transfer accounts: ~凭单 *transfer document* / ~支票 *check only for account*

【转折】① turn or shift in the course of events: 戏剧

性的 ~ *dramatic turn* ② transition (of an essay)
【转折点】turning point
【转正】① (of a probationary member of the communist Party of China) become a full member after completion of the probationary period ② become a regular work
【转租】sublease; sublet

zhuàn

传 ① commentaries on classics: 名不见经 ~ *be a mere nobody; be not well known* ② biography:《马克思 ~》*Marx biography* / 评 ~ *critical biography* ③ story or novel
see also chuán
【传记】biography
【传略】brief biography; biographical sketch
转 ① spin; turn; rotate; revolve: 他绕着操场 ~ 了两圈。*He walked twice around the playground.* ② revolution
see also zhuǎn
【转笔刀】pencil sharpener
【转动】spin; revolve; rotate; turn: 顺时针 ~ *clockwise rotation*
【转炉】【冶】converter: ~ 钢 *converter steel*
【转门】revolving door
【转盘】① turntable (as of a record player) ② sports giant stride ③ petroleum rotary table
【转速】rotational speed: ~ 计 *tachometer*
【转向】get lost; lose one's bearings; be confused
【转椅】revolving chair; swivel chair
【转悠】[口] ① turn; roll; move from side to side: 他盯着那个女孩,眼珠直 ~。*He rolled his eyes at that girl.* ② saunter; stroll; take a leisurely walk: 爷爷每天在街上 ~ 一小时。*Grandfather strolls around the street one hour every day.*
【转轴】axle
【转转】[口] go for a stroll; take a short walk: 他陪客人在超市里 ~。*He showed guests round the supermarket.*
赚 ① gain; make a profit: 他净 ~ 了两千元。*He netted* 2,000 *yuan.* ② [方] earn (money) ③ [口] profit
【赚钱】make a profit; make money: ~ 生意 *profitable business*
【赚头】[口] profit
撰 compose; write: 他从去年开始为杂志 ~ 稿。*He wrote articles for a magazine.*
【撰述】① compile; write ② book; work
【撰写】write; compose (usu. a short articles)
【撰著】compose; write
篆 ① seal character (a style of Chinese calligraphy) ② seal inscribe in such style: ~ 额 *write seal characters on the top of a tablet*
【篆刻】seal cutting
【篆书】seal character (a style of Chinese calligraphy, often used on seals)

zhuāng

妆 ① make up; apply make up; wear makeup: 梳 ~ 打扮 *deck oneself out; be dress up; dress smartly* / 浓 ~ 艳抹 *richly attired and heavily made-up* ② woman's personal adornments ③ trousseau; dowry
【妆扮】attire; deck out; dress up
【妆饰】① adorn; deck out; dress up ② make up
【妆梳】make up and dress up
【妆台】dressing table
庄[1] ① village ② manor ③ a place of business: 饭 ~ (*big*) *restaurant* ④ (in gambling) person who holds the bank; banker: 谁做 ~? *Who is banking?*
庄[2] grave; serious; solemn; sober
【庄户】peasant household: ~ 人家 *peasant family*
【庄家】banker (in a gambling game)
【庄稼】crops: 种 ~ *plant (or grow) crops* / 收 ~ *harvest (or get in) crops* / ~ 汉 *farmer; peasant* / ~ 活 *farm work* / ~ 人 *peasant farmer*
【庄严】dignified; stately; solemn: 神情 ~ *grave expression* / ~ 声明 *solemnly declare* / ~ 场面 *a grand occasion*
【庄园】manor
【庄重】grave; sedate; serious; solemn: 语气 ~ *in a solemn tone*
【庄子】[口] village; hamlet
桩 pile; post; stake: 桥 ~ *bridge stake* / 打 ~ *drive piles*
【桩子】pile; stake
装[1] ① attire; deck; act; dress up; play the part (or role) of: 女扮男 ~ *woman in man's disguise* ② outfit; clothing; dress; suit: 学生 ~ *students' uniform* / 西 ~ *western style suit* / 时 ~ *fashionable dress* ③ luggage; outfit for a journey ④ pretend; feign; make believe: 不懂 ~ 懂 *pretend to know what you don't know*
装[2] ① load; fill; hold; pack: ~ 箱 *put sth in a crate; pack a box* ② assemble; fit; install: ~ 保险锁 *fit a safety lock* ③ binding; bookbinding: ~ 订成册 *bind in a volume*
【装扮】① attire; deck out; dress up ② disguise: ~ 新娘 *dress up the bride* / ~ 房间 *deck out the room*
【装备】① equip; fit out ② equipment; outfit; installation: 全套野营 ~ *complete outfit for going a camping*
【装病】malinger; feign illness; pretend sickness
【装舱】stow the hold (with cargo)
【装点】deck; decorate; dress: ~ 大厅。*The hall was decorated.*
【装船】shipment: 抓紧 ~ *speed up the shipment*
【装订】bookbinding; binding: 布面 ~ *clothbound* / 硬面 ~ *hardbound* / ~ 工人 *bookbinder* / ~ 机 *binding machine* / ~ 车间 *bindery; bookbindery*

Z

【装疯卖傻】feign madness and act like an idiot
【装糊涂】feign ignorance; play the tool; pretend not to know
【装潢】① dress; mount (a picture, etc.) ② decoration; mounting; packaging: ~门面 *do window dressing; keep up appearance; put up a facade*
【装货】load (cargo): ~单 *loading list; shipping order* / ~港 *part of loading; port of shipment*
【装甲】armoured: ~兵 *armoured force (or troops)* / ~车 *armoured car; armoured vehicle*
【装假】feign; make believe; pretend
【装殓】dress and lay a corpse in a coffin
【装料】① feed (a machine) ②【冶】charging; loading
【装聋作哑】feign ignorance; pretend to be deaf and dumb
【装门面】keep up appearance; maintain an outward show; put up a front
【装模作样】attitudinize; be affected; behave in an affected way put on an act
【装配】assemble; fit together: ~工 *assembler; fitter* / ~车间 *assembly shop; fitting shop* / ~线 *assembly line* / ~件 *assembly parts*
【装腔】be artificial; behave affectedly
【装傻】act dumb; pretend not to know; pretend to be naive or stupid
【装神弄鬼】purposely make a mystery of simple things
【装饰】adorn; deck; decorate; ornament: ~布 *upholstery fabrics* / ~艺术 *art deco* / ~品 *ornament*
【装束】① attire; dress ②［书］pack up
【装睡】pretend sleep; sham sleep
【装死】sham dead; feign death
【装蒜】［口］pretend no to know ; feign ignorance
【装相】put on an act; pretend
【装卸】① load and unload: ~之物 *load and unload good* / 文明~ *careful loading and unloading* ② assemble and disassemble.
【装运】ship; load and transport: ~货物 *ship cargo*
【装载】loading: ~量 *loading capacity*
【装帧】binding and layout (of a book, magazine, etc.)
【装置】① equip; fit; install: ~仪器 *install instrument* ② device; installation; plant; unit: 防护~ *protective equipment* / 威震~ *damping device*
【装作】disguise as; pretend to be: ~教师 *disguise oneself as a teacher*

zhuàng

壮 ① strong; robust: 他的身体很健~。*He has a strong physique.* ② grand; magnificent: 胸怀~志 *entertain great ambitions* ③ make better; strengthen; improve: ~声势 *enhance fame and influence; lend impetus and strength*
【壮大】① expand; strengthen; grow in strength: 经济实力~ *increase or enhance the economic power* ② bulky; thick and strong: 四肢~ *have thick and strong arms and legs; strong limbs*
【壮胆】boost one's courage; build up sb's courage
【壮丁】［旧］able-bodied man
【壮观】grand spectacle; magnificent sight
【壮举】heroic undertaking; magnificent feat: 史无前例的~ *an unparalleled feat*
【壮阔】grand; grandiose; magnificent; vast
【壮劳力】① strong labour power ② able-bodied adult
【壮丽】glorious; magnificent; majestic; splendid: ~的山河 *a land of glories* / ~事业 *glorious undertaking*
【壮烈】brave; heroic: ~牺牲 *die a hero's death give one's life heroically*
【壮美】magnificent; majestic
【壮年】prime of life; the more robust years of a person's life (between thirty and fifty)
【壮士】brave man; hero; heroic man; warrior
【壮实】robust; sturdy: ~的年轻人 *a sturdy young man*
【壮伟】grand; lofty; magnifying: ~的山峰 *lofty mountain peak*
【壮志】great aspiration; lofty ideal: ~凌云 *with high (or soaring) aspirations* / ~未酬 *with one's lofty aspirations unrealized*

状 ① form; shape: 形~不同 *of different forms* ② condition, state ③ account; record ④ plaint; write complaint ⑤ certificate
【状词】indictment; plaint; written complaint
【状况】condition; state; state of affairs: 他的~并不好。*He is in bad condition.*
【状态】condition; state; state of affairs: 心理~ *psychology; state of mind* / 落后~ *backward state*
【状语】【语】adverbial; adverbial modifier
【状元】① Number One Scholar; title conferred on the one who came first in the highest imperial examination ② the very best (in any field): 养鸡~ *a champion chicken-raiser*
【状子】［口］plaint; indictment; written complaint

撞 ① crash; collide; bump against; run into: ~墙 *bump into a wall* / ~开门 *ram the door open* ② bump into; run into; meet by chance: 昨天我~见李老师了。*I ran across Mrs Li yesterday.* ③ barge; dash; rush: 横冲直~ *barge around; dash about badly* ④ try; probe; take one's chance: 他们来北京~运气了。*They came to Beijing to try their luck.*
【撞车】① collision of vehicles ② clash of opinions or interests ③［口］(of meeting, etc.) clash
【撞击】ram; strike; dash against: 波浪~着船帮。*The breakers dashed on the side of the ship.*
【撞见】catch sb in the act; meet or discover by chance; run across
【撞锁】① spring lock ②［口］find sb that is not in: 我顺道拜访你,却~了。*I stopped by your last night nd found the door locked.*

Z

zhuī

追 ① chase (or run) after; pursue; catch up with: ～上同学 *catch up with his students* ② court (a woman): 福克在～求那姑娘。*Focke is paying court to the girl.* ③ trace; look into; get to the bottom of: ～根究底 *get to the bottom of sth* ④ see; go after ⑤ recall; reminisce: 抚今～昔 *contemplate the present and recall the past* ⑥ act posthumously; retroactively

【追本溯源】get to the root of the matter; trace to its source

【追逼】① purse closely (a fleeing army) ② press for (repayment); extort (a confession)

【追兵】pursuing troops

【追补】remedy; make good; make up: 不可～的失败 *an irretrievable failure*

【追捕】pursue and capture: ～杀人犯 *pursue and capture murderer*

【追查】investigate; trace; find out: ～死亡原因 *investigate (or look into) the cause of her death*

【追悼】mourn over a person's death: ～会 *memorial meeting*

【追访】make a follow-up visit

【追赶】pursue; run after; quicken one's pace to catch up: ～时尚潮流 *follow the trend*

【追根】get to the root of sth

【追怀】recall; reminisce; call to mind: ～往事 *call to mind of one's past*

【追回】recover: ～赃款 *recover stolen money*

【追悔】regret; repent; remorse: ～莫及 *too late to repent*

【追击】pursue and attack; follow up: ～敌人 *pursue and attack the enemy* / ～战 *warfare of pursuit and attack*

【追加】add to (the original amount): ～保险 *supplementary insurance* / ～条款 *rider clause*

【追歼】pursue and wipe out: ～逃敌 *pursue and wipe out the fleeing enemy*

【追剿】pursue and wipe out: ～队 *pursuit detachment*

【追缴】① demand payment (of tax arrears, etc.): ～税款 *demand tax arrears* ② recover: ～赃物 *recover stolen property*

【追究】investigate; find out; look into: ～责任 *investigate responsibility*; *find out who is to blame for sth*

【追名逐利】seek (or be after) fame and wealth

【追求】① pursue; seek ② court (a woman); woo

【追认】① recognize retroactively; subsequently confirm or enclose: ～一项决议 *subsequently endorse a resolution*; ② admit or confirm

【追述】tell about the past; relate; recount

【追溯】date from; trace back to: 这件事可以～到很久以前。*This thing goes back to a long time ago.*

【追随】follow: ～者 *adherent*; *follower*; *following*

【追讨】demand payment of an old debt

【追问】examine minutely; make a detailed inquiring; question closely

【追寻】pursue; search; track down

【追忆】recall; recollect; look back

【追赃】make sb disgorge the spoils; order the return of stolen money or goods; recover stolen money or goods

【追赠】confer posthumously (a title)

【追债】claim repayment of a debt

【追逐】① chase; pursue ② seek; quest: ～利润 *seek profits*

【追踪】trace; track; follow the trail of

椎 vertebra

【椎骨】vertebra

锥 ① awl ② anything shaped like an awl ③【数】cone ④ drill; bore: ～孔 *make a hole with an awl*

【锥度】① coning; taper: ～规 *taper gauge* ② taper ratio

【锥面】①【数】conical surface ② pyramidal face

【锥形】cone; pyramid; taper; conical contour

【锥子】awl

zhuì

坠 ① drop; fall; tumble: 直升机～入海中。*The helicopter fell into the sea.* ② weigh down: 苹果把树枝～弯了。*The apples weighed the twigs down.* ③ weight; a hanging object

【坠地】[书] (of a child) be born

【坠毁】(of a plane, etc.) fall and break; crash: 飞机～在山里。*The plane crashed in the mountains.*

【坠楼】jump off building (to kill oneself)

【坠落】drop; fall

【坠子】[方] ① weight; plummet; pendant ② ear pendant

缀 ① mend; sew; stitch: ～扣子 *sew buttons on to sth* ② compose; write; put words together correctly: ～字成文 *put words together to make a sentence and sentences together to make an essay* ③ decorate; embellish

【缀文】compose an essay; write a composition

惴 [书] anxious and fearful

【惴惴不安】[书] be alarmed; be anxious and fearful; be on tenterhooks

赘 ① redundant; superfluous; tautological: ～瘤 *anything useless*; *redundancy*; *superfluity* ② (of a man) go to live in the house hold of one's in-laws on getting married; (of the bride's parents) gain a son-in-law in such a manner: 入～女婿 *man who comes to live with the family of his parents-in-law* ③ [方] be burdensome; be cumbersome: 这群孩子太～人了。*Those children are really burdensome.*

【赘词】redundancy; superfluous words

【赘述】give unnecessary details; say more than is needed：你最好一一～。*You'd better go into details.*
【赘婿】a son-in-law who lives in the home of his wife's parents
【赘言】① give unnecessary details; say more than needed：不再～。*No more need be said.* ② redundancy; superfluous words

zhūn

谆 earnest; sincere：～嘱 *advise* (*or enjoin*) *earnestly*
【谆谆】earnest and ceaseless：～教导 *earnestly instruct*

zhǔn

准[1] allow; approve; grant; permit：～假一周 *grant sb one week's leave*
准[2] ① follow; in accordance with ② criterion; norm; standard：以此为～ *take this as the standard* ③ accurate; exact：时间很～。*The watch keeps good time.*
【准保】certainly; for sure：他～会准时到达。*He'll guarantee arrive on time.*
【准备】① prepare; get ready：～阶段 *preparatory stage* / ～材料 *prepare materials* ② intend; plan; think：他～去海边度假。*He intends to go to beach for the holidays.*
【准话】definite information：什么时候过来，你给个～。*Tell me when you come here.*
【准确】accurate; exact; precise
【准绳】criterion; yardstick
【准时】punctual; on schedule; on time：～到达 *arrive on time* / ～出发 *take off at the scheduled time*
【准头】[口] accuracy (in speech, marksmanship, etc.)
【准信】definite and accurate information or answer：你什么时候出发，给我个～。*Please let me know in advance exactly when you start out.*
【准行】[口] it's a sure-fire success：这事找他～。*It's a sure-fire success if you ask him.*
【准许】allow; permit
【准予】approve; grant; permit：～放行 *allow sb to pass* / ～休假 *grant a leave*
【准则】criterion; norm; standard：行为～ *social norms* / 国际法的起码～ *elementary requirements of international law* / 道德～ *moral code; morality*

zhuō

拙 ① awkward; clumsy; dull：手～ *be all thumbs* / ～于言辞 *inarticulate; be clumsy in expressing oneself* ② my
【拙笨】clumsy：口齿～ *inarticulate be clumsy of speech*
【拙见】my (humble) opinion
【拙劣】clumsy; inferior：～手法 *clumsy trick; inferior tactics* / ～表演 *a clumsy* (*or poor*) *performance; a bad show* / 文笔～ *bad* (*or poor*) *writing*
【拙朴】simple (or plain) and unadorned
【拙著】my (poor) writing; my (poor) work
【拙嘴笨腮】inarticulate; clumsy-tongued
【拙作】my (poor) writing, painting, etc.; my (poor) work
捉 ① clutch; grab; grasp; hold：～住他 *grab at him* ② catch; capture：～贼！*Stop thief.* / 猫～老鼠。*The cat caught a rat.*
【捉刀】ghostwrite; write (an article, etc) for sb else：～者 *ghostwriter*
【捉奸】catch adulterers in the act
【捉迷藏】① hide-and-seek; blindman's buff ② be tricky and evasive; play hide-and-seek
【捉摸】(usu. used in the negative) ascertain; fathom; predict：～不定 *elusive; difficult to ascertain*
【捉拿】arrest; catch：～凶手 *arrest a murderer* / ～归案 *arrest and bring the criminal to justice*
【捉弄】tease; make fun of; play tricks on
桌 desk; table
【桌布】tablecloth
【桌面】tabletop; to of a table;
【桌面上】aboveboard; in public; on the table：我们最好把问题拿到～来谈。*We'd better place problems on the table.*
【桌子】desk; table

zhuó

灼 ① burn; scorch：真知～见 *real knowledge and deep insight; wise judgement* ② bright; luminous
【灼急】anxious：过去～ *be too anxious* / ～的表情 *worried look*
【灼见】penetrating view; profound view
【灼烤】bake; burn; scorch：受到烈日的～ *exposed to the blazing sun*
【灼亮】bright; shining：～灯光 *bright lamplight*
【灼热】scorching hot
【灼然】fairly clear; quite obvious：～无疑 *unquestionable indisputable* / ～可见 *perfectly obvious; abundantly clear*
【灼伤】(of fire, acid, etc.) burn
【灼灼】[书] brilliant; shining：目光～ *with keen, sparkling eyes*
茁 thriving
【茁壮】healthy and strong; sturdy：孩子们～成长。*The children grew up healthy and strong.*
卓 ① stand upright：～立于东方 *stand upright in the east* ② eminent; outstanding：远见～识 *foresight and sagacity*

【卓尔不群】stand head and shoulders above all others, be preeminent; be outstanding
【卓见】brilliant idea; excellent opinion
【卓绝】extreme; of the highest degree; outstanding; unsurpassed: 英勇～的斗争 *extremely brave struggle*
【卓然】outstanding; remarkable; splendid: 他们取得了～的成绩。*They achieved outstanding results.*
【卓识】sagacity; judicious judgement
【卓异】outstanding; preeminent; unique; out of the ordinary
【卓有成效】very fruitful; highly effective: ～改革 *fruitful reform*
【卓越】brilliant; outstanding; remarkable: ～才能 *superior ability* / ～科学家 *a brilliant scientist*
【卓著】distinguished; eminent; outstanding: 这位市长政绩～。*This mayor achieved outstanding service in his political career.*

浊 ① muddy; turbid: ～水 *turbid water* / ～流 *muddy stream* ② deep and thick ③ chaotic; confused; disorderly
【浊酒】unstrained wine or liquor
【浊气】foul smell
【浊物】ignoramus; absurd creature; insensitive creature
【浊音】【语】voiced sound

酌 ① drink; pour out (wine): 独～ *drink alone* ② consider; think over; use one's discretion: 字斟句～ *weigh one's words* / ～字答复 *favour us with a reply* ③ a meal with wine
【酌办】act according to one's judgement; do as one thinks fit; act as one's decision
【酌量】consider; deliberate; use one's judgement: 由你来～购买食物。*Buy food at your discretion.*
【酌情】exercise discretion in the light of the circumstances take into consideration the circumstances, use one's discretion: ～处理 *settle a matter as one sees fit*
【酌予】grant (a subsidy, etc) according to the conditions of the grantee: ～补助 *give some financial assistance*

啄 peck: 小鸡～来。*The chicks peck at the rice.*
【啄木鸟】woodpecker

着1 ① wear (clothes): 吃～不愁 *need not worry about food and clothing* ② touch; come into contact with: 水太深,摸不～底。*The water is too deep to touch its bottom.* ③ attach; apply; use ④ whereabouts; assured source: 生活无～ *have one's livelihood unassured*

着2 ① send; dispatch: 你马上～人去工地。*Send someone to the site right away.* ② used in official documents, expressing peremptory tone
see also zhāo; zháo; zhe
【着笔】begin to write or paint; put (or set) pen to paper: 难以～ *find it difficult to put it in writing*
【着力】exert oneself; put forth effort: ～描写 *take great pains to describe sb or sth*; *concentrate one's efforts on depicting sb*
【着陆】land; touch down: ～舱 *space landing module* / 飞机即将～。*The plane is going to touch down.*
【着落】① whereabouts: 丢失的钱包已有～。*The missing wallet has been found.* ② assured source: 这项任务仍无～。*We still don't know where to find the task.* ③ fall to sb; rest with sb ④ [旧] settle: ～停当 *all set*; *settled*
【着墨】apply ink to paper-write or paint: ～不多 *sketchily described or painted*
【着色】colour; put colour on: ～法 *colouring*
【着实】① indeed; really: 这个生日晚会,他～用了心思。*He really put in a lot of time preparing for this birthday party.* ② severely: ～说了他一顿 *reprove him sharply*
【着手】put one's hand to; sent about
【着想】consider (the interests of sb or sth): 为你～。*It's for your good.*
【着眼】have sth in mind; see (or view) from angle of: ～点 *focus of attention*; *starting point*; *object in mind*
【着意】act with care and effort; take pains: ～准备 *take great pains with the preparation for*
【着重】emphasize; stress: 他～谈了这个问题。*He addressed this question in some detail or he dwelled on this subject at some length.*
【着装】① put on; wear ② clothing, head gear and footwear

琢 carve; chisel: ～玉石 *cut and polish the jade* / 用翡翠～成装饰品 *carved agate ornaments*
【琢磨】① carve and polish (jade) ② (of literary works) polish; refine

镯 bracelet: 玉～ *jade bracelet*
【镯子】bracelet: 金～ *gold bracelet*

zī

吱 ① (of mice) squeak ② (of small birds) chirp; peep
【吱声】make a sound; utter sth: 他一声也不～。*He doesn't utter a word.*

孜
【孜孜】diligent; hardworking; industrious: ～以求 *diligently strive after*; *assiduously seek*
【孜孜不倦】assiduously; diligently; indefatigably

咨 consult; take counsel
【咨文】① [旧] official communication (between government offices of equal rank) ② message; report delivered by the head of a government on affairs of state: 预算～ *budget message* / 总统～ *presidential message*
【咨询】consult; hold counsel with; seek advice from: ～机关 *advisory body* / 提供～服务 *provide consulting service* / 技术～ *technical consultation* /

~委员会 *consultative committee*

Z

姿

【姿容】appearance; looks: ~俏丽 *attractive*; *pretty*; *good-looking*

【姿色】(of a woman) good looks: ~出众 *extraordinary beauty*

【姿势】gesture; posture: ~优美 *have a graceful carriage* /站立的~ *standing posture*

【姿态】① carriage; posture:不同的~的塑像 *figures in various postures* ② attitude; pose; gesture:保持低~ *maintain* (*or cut*) *a low profile*

资1 ① money; expenses: 捐~ *contribute funds to* /工~ *salary*; *pay*; *wages* / 筹~*fund raising* ② help; support; subsidize ③ provide; supply; serve: ~助 *aid financially*; *subsidize* ④ (Zī) a surname

资2 ① natural ability; endowment qualifications: 天~过人 *unusual talent* ② record of service

【资本】① capital: ~投入 *capital input* / ~输出 *export of capital* / ~周转 *turnover of capital* ② sth to capitalize on: 捞政治~ *gain political capital* / ~市场 *capital market* / ~原物 *capital goods* / ~家 *capitalist* / 垄断~*monopoly capital* /官僚~ *bureaucrat-capital* /固定~ *fixed capital* / 流动~ *circulating capital*; *working capital* / ~市场 *capital market*

【资本主义】capitalism: ~社会 *capitalist society* / ~制度 *capitalist system* / ~道路 *the capitalist road* /国家垄断~ *state monopoly capitalism* / ~生产方式 *capitalist mode of production*

【资财】assets; capital and goods:清点~ *make an inventory of the assets*

【资产】① property ② capital; capital fund ③【经】assets:无形~ *intangible assets* / ~冻结 *freezing of assets* / ~负债表 *balance sheet*; *statement of assets and liabilities*

【资产阶级】the bourgeoisie; the capitalist class: ~革命 *bourgeois revolution*: ~思想 *bourgeois ideology* / ~分手 *bourgeois element* / ~世界观 *bourgeois world outlook*

【资方】capital; those representing capital: ~人员 *capitalists and their representatives* / ~代理人 *agent of a capitalist*

【资费】expenses

【资格】① qualifications:必要的~ *requisite qualifications*; ② seniority: ~审查委员会 *credentials committee* / ~证书 *credentials*

【资金】capital; fund: ~市场 *capital market* / ~积累 *accumulation of funds* / ~外流 *capital outflow* / ~短缺 *shortage of funds*

【资力】financial strength: ~雄厚 *be financially powerful have a large capital*

【资历】qualifications; record of service: ~缺乏 *lack in qualifications and experience*

【资料】① means ② data; material: ~处理 *data processing* / ~室 *reference room* /参考~ *reference material* /搜集~ *collect data*; *gather material*

【资深】senior

【资信】capital and credit

【资讯】data; information (used in Taiwan):交换~ *exchange data and information*

【资源】resources; natural resources: ~丰富 *abound* (*or be rich*) *in natural resources* / ~共享 *resource sharing*; *share of resources*/ ~开发 *resources development* / ~优势 *resource advantages*

【资质】natural endowments; aptitude

孳 multiply; propagate

【孳生】breed; multiply; propagate: ~蚊蝇 *breed flies and mosquitoes*

滋1 ① grow; multiply ② more ③ flavour; taste

滋2 [方] *burst*; *spurt*:杯子裂了,水~外流。*Water is spurting from the crack in the cup.*

【滋补】nourishing; nutritious: ~食品 *nourishment*; *nourishing food* /苹果~功效很强。*Apples have a good tonic effect.*

【滋润】① moist: ~大地 *moist soil* ② moisten: ~皮肤 *soften* (*or moisten*) *one's skin* ③ comfortable; well-off:他们回到家乡后,过着很~的生活。*The led a very comfortable life after they returned hometown.*

【滋生】① breed; multiply; propagate ② cause; create; provoke

【滋身】make (or stir up) trouble

【滋味】flavour; taste:听到那个坏消息,他心里很不是~。*On hearing the bad news, he felt bad.*

【滋养】① nourish: ~身体 *be nourishing* ② nutriment:吸收~ *assimilate nutriment* / ~品 *nutriment nourishment*; *nourishing food*

【滋阳】【中医】method of treating yin deficiency by reinforcing body fluid and nourishing the blood

【滋育】breed; grow; multiply 太阳~着万物生长。*The sun gives life to all things on earth.*

【滋长】develop; grow

锱 [量] an ancient unit of weight; equal to one fourth of a liang

【锱铢必较】dispute over every detail; haggle over every penny

龇 [口] bare; show

【龇牙咧嘴】① look fierce; show one's teeth ② grimace (with pain); contort one's face (in agony)

zǐ

子1 ① son; child:父~ *father and son* /独生~ *only son* ② person③ ancient title of respect for a learned or virtuous man: 夫~ *master* ④ seed: 结~ *go to seed*; *bear seed* /没~ *seedless* ⑤ egg ⑥ sth small and hard ⑦ copper; copper coin:不值一个~儿 *not worth a copper* /没有一个~儿 *penniless* ⑧ viscount

子2 used for sth long and thin

子[3] [书] you

子[4] small; tender; young

【子菜单】【电】submenu

【子丑寅卯】the first four of the twelve Earthly Branches-in an orderly way; systematically:他半天也没说出个～来。*He failed to come out with a coherent story.*

【子弹】cartridge; bullet: ～带 *bandoleer; cartridge belt* / ～箱 *cartridge box* /步枪～ *rifle bullet*

【子弟】juniors; children; sons and younger brothers:职工～ *children of the workers and staff* (*of a factory, etc.*) / ～兵 *army made up of the sons of the people*

【子房】【植】ovary

【子公司】subsidiary; subsidiary company

【子宫】uterus; womb: ～颈 *cervix* (*of womb*)

【子母】① son and mother ② of similar relationship like a son and mother: ～扣 *snap fastener; popper*

【子女】children; offspring; sons and daughters

【子嗣】son; male offspring

【子孙】descendants; children and grandchildren: ～后代 *coming generations; descendants; posterity* / ～满堂 (*of a person*) *be blessed with many children*

【子午仪】meridian instrument

【子叶】【植】cotyledon

【子夜】midnight

仔 young

【仔畜】young animal; newborn animal

【仔鸡】chick

【仔密】(of knitwear) close-knitted; (of textiles) close-woven

【仔细】① attentive; careful: ～研究 *pore over* ② be careful; look out ③ [方] frugal; economical:日子过得～ *be frugal of one's expenses*

【仔猪】piglet

姊 elder sister; sister

【姊妹】elder ad younger sisters: ～花 *the two sisters* / ～城 *sister city* / ～篇 *companion volume*

籽 seed

紫 purple; violet

【紫菜】【植】laver

【紫丁香】(early) lilac

【紫红】purplish red

【紫花】pale reddish brown: ～布 *nankeen* (*a kind of coarse cloth*)

【紫荆花】bauhinia flower:香港行政特区的区徽是～。*The bauhinia flower is the emblem of the Hong Kong Special Administrative Region.*

【紫禁城】the Forbidden City (in Beijing)

【紫羚羊】bongo

【紫罗兰】violet; common stock

【紫萍】duckweed

【紫杉】【植】(Japanese) yew

【紫石英】amethyst

【紫藤】【植】Chinese wistaria

【紫外线】ultraviolet ray: ～灯 *ultraviolet lamp*

【紫薇】【植】crape myrtle

【紫竹】black bamboo

zì

自[1] ① self; oneself; one's own:他不得不独～回家。*He had to go home by himself.* ② certainly; naturally; of course: ～当如此。*It should be so as a matter of course.*

自[2] from; since: ～此以后 *from then on; since then* / ～即日起生效 *become effective* (*as*) *from this date; with effect from* / ～古至今 *from ancient times to now* / ～左至右 *from left to right*

【自爱】regard for oneself; self-respect

【自傲】① arrogant; conceited; ② be proud of; take pride in

【自拔】free oneself (from pain or evildoing); extricate oneself

【自白】make clear one's meaning or position; vindicate oneself: ～书 *a written confession*

【自暴自弃】give oneself up as hopeless; have no urge to make progress be resigned to one's backwardness

【自卑】be self-abased; feel oneself inferior: ～感 *a sense of inferiority; inferiority complex*

【自备】provide for oneself: ～家具 *bring one's own furniture*

【自变数】【数】independent variable

【自便】as one pleases; at one's convenience:请～。*Please do as you like.*

【自不量力】overestimate one's strength or oneself; not know one's own limitations

【自裁】[书] commit suicide; take one's own life

【自惭】feel ashamed: ～形秽 *have a sense of inferiority feel unworthy* (*of others' company*)

【自测】self-test; test oneself

【自嘲】laugh at oneself

【自称】call oneself; claim to be; profess 他～不了解。*He professed ignorance.* /他～是她的男友。*He claimed to be her boy-friend.*

【自成一家】have a style of one's own; have a unique style (in calligraphy, painting, sculpture etc.)

【自出心裁】make a new departure; think up an original idea

【自吹自擂】crack oneself up; blow one's own trumpet or horn

【自从】from; since: ～他回来后便一直保持沉默。*He always kept silent since he came back.*

【自大】arrogant; self-important; conceited: ～狂 *megalomania*

【自得】complacent; contented; self-satisfied:悠然～ *be free and contented* / ～其乐 *derive pleasure from sth*

【自动】① voluntary; of one's own accord: ~加入 *participate voluntarily* ② automatic; automated: ~报价系统 *automated quotation system* / ~补胎 *tubeless seal tire* / ~除霜系统 *automatic defrosting system* / ~取款机 *automatically teller machine* (*ATM*) / ~传呼 *auto call* / ~电话 *automatic telephone* / ~售货机 *vending machine*; *slot machine* (*in Britain*) *automatic answer* / ~诊断程序 *automated conversion routine*

【自动挡】(car) automatic gearshift; automatic transmission

【自动扶梯】escalator

【自动化】automate: ~过程 *automation process*

【自渎】[书] masturbation; self-abuse

【自发】spontaneous: ~罢工 *wildcat strike* / ~的积极性 *automatic enthusiasm*

【自费】at one's own expense: ~出版 *vanity publication* / ~生 *fee-paying student* /她决定~旅行。*She decided to travel at her expense.*

【自焚】burn oneself to death

【自封】① proclaim oneself: ~为艺术家 *proclaim oneself an artist* ② confine oneself; isolate oneself

【自负】① be conceited; think highly of oneself ② be responsible for one's own action: ~盈亏 (*of an enterprise*) *assume sole responsibility for its profits or losses*

【自甘堕落】abandon oneself to vice; wallow in degeneration

【自高自大】arrogant; conceited; self-important

【自告奋勇】volunteer (to do sth difficult); offer to undertake (a difficult or dangerous task): 他~当导游。*He volunteered to act as a guider.*

【自个儿】[方] oneself; by oneself: 不要只想着~。*Don't be so selfish.* /我~做。*I'll do this myself.*

【自顾不暇】be busy enough with one's own affairs; be unable even to fend for oneself

【自豪】be proud of sth; have a proper sense of pride or dignity

【自花传粉】self-pollination

【自画像】self-portrait

【自毁】【军】self-destruction: ~装置 *destructor*

【自己】① oneself: ~动手 *use one's own hands*; *do it yourself* (*DIY*) ② referring to the person mentioned earlier in the sentence: 我~觉得能做。*I felt what I can do.* ③ own; close related: ~家人 *one's own family*

【自己人】one of us; people on one's own side: 都是~不要担心。*Don't worry; they are among friends.*

【自给】self-sufficient; self-supporting: ~经济 *self-supporting economy* / ~率 *degree of self-sufficiency*

【自家】[方] one or oneself: ~家具 *one's own furniture*

【自家人】[方] one of us; people on one's own side

【自荐】offer one's services; recommend oneself for a job

【自尽】commit suicide; take one's own life

【自净】self-purification

【自疚】have qualms of conscience; feel compunction

【自咎】blame oneself; rebuke oneself

【自救】save oneself; provide for and help oneself: 团结~ *unite for self-preservation* /生产~ *provide for and help oneself by engaging in production*

【自居】consider oneself to be; call oneself; poses: 以老资格~ *flaunt one's seniority*

【自决】self-determination: ~权 *right to self-determination*

【自觉】① realize; be aware of; be conscious (usu used in the negative): 他不~地读出了声。*He read it aloud without realizing it.* ② conscious; on one's own initiative: ~遵守纪律 *observe discipline conscientiously* / ~性 *level of political consciousness* / ~自愿 *voluntarily*; *willing*; *of one's own free will*

【自绝】alienate oneself: ~于人民 *alienate oneself from the people*

【自掘坟墓】dig one's own grave; work for one's own destruction

【自控】① automatic control ② self-control

【自夸】crack oneself up; sing one's own praises

【自愧不如】feel ashamed of one's inferiority

【自拉自唱】accompany one's own singing — do everything by oneself

【自来水】running water; tap water

【自理】provide for oneself; take care of oneself: 费用~ *pay one's own expenses* /伙食~ *make one's own eating arrangements*

【自力】depend on one's own strength; rely on oneself

【自力更生】regeneration (or reconstruction) through one's own efforts self-reliance

【自立】support oneself; earn one's own living: 他们从18岁时开始~了。*They were self-supporting when they were 18.*

【自量】rate one's ability: 不知~ *fail to take a proper measure of oneself*; *overrate one's abilities*

【自流】① (of water, etc) flow automatically; flow by itself ② (of a person) do as one pleases; (of a thing) drift along; let people act as one please: ~灌溉 *gravity irrigation* / ~井 *artesian well*

【自留】reserve sth for one's own use: ~地 *family plot*; *private plot* / ~畜 *privately owned livestock*

【自律】exercise self-discipline; self-management: 自尊和~ *self-respect and self-discipline*

【自卖自夸】praise one's own wares; blow one's own trumpet — indulge in self-glorification

【自满】self-satisfied

【自明】self-evident; obvious 道理~ *the principle involved is obvious*

【自鸣得意】be very pleased with oneself; preen oneself; show self-satisfaction

【自命清高】profess to be above worldly considerations

【自命】consider oneself; regard oneself as: ~不凡

consider oneself no ordinary being; *think no end of oneself*

【自谋出路】find one's own means of livelihood

【自谋职业】search for a job oneself; seek a job on one's own

【自欺欺人】self-deception; deceiving oneself as well as others: ~的借口 *self-deceiving excuse*

【自弃】give oneself up as hopeless; lose self-confidence and have no urge to make progress

【自谦】be modest; be self-effacing

【自强不息】strive to become stronger constantly; work hard to improve oneself

【自轻自贱】belittle oneself; demean oneself; lack self-confidence and self-respect

【自取灭亡】court (or invite) destruction; take the road to one's doom

【自取其咎】bring blame on oneself: 不要管他,他这是~。*Don't care about him*; *he asked for it.*

【自然】① nature; natural world: ~条件 *natural conditions* /征服~ *conquer nature* ② natural: 表情~ *look natural* ③ naturally; in ordinary course of events: 你到时~明白。*You'll understand in due course.* ④ naturally; of course: ~保护区 *nature reserve* / ~辩证法 *dialectics of nature*/ ~村 *natural village*/ ~博物馆 *museum of natural history* / ~规律 *nature law* / ~地理 *physical geography* / ~键盘 *natural key board* / ~金属 *native metal* / ~经济 *natural economy* / ~类群(生物) *natural group* / ~死亡 *natural death*

【自然而然】automatically; naturally; spontaneously; of oneself: 他~地喜欢上学。*He loves school naturally.*

【自然】natural; at ease; free from affectation: 态度~ *be at ease*

【自燃】【化】spontaneous combustion (or ignition)

【自认】accept as unavoidable; resign oneself to

【自如】[书] freely; smoothly; with ease: 应付~ *handle situation with ease* /动作~ *move about freely*

【自若】[书] composed; calm and at ease; self-possessed: 神志~ *appear composed* /泰然~ *behave with perfect composure*

【自杀】commit suicide; take one's own life

【自伤】self-injury; self-inflicted wound

【自上而下】from above to below; from top to bottom: ~的计划 *plans issued from top to bottom*

【自身】self; oneself: ~物质利益 *one's own material benefits* /你已经是~难保了,不要管别人了。*Don't care about others*; *you couldn't even protect yourself.*

【自生自灭】take its course; (of a thing) emerge of itself and perish of itself

【自食其果】eat one's own bitter fruit — reap what one has sown

【自食其力】support oneself by one's own labour; earn one's own bread: ~的劳动者 *working people earning their own living*

【自食其言】break one's promise; break faith with sb; go back one one's word

【自始至终】from start to finish; from beginning to end

【自视】consider or imagine oneself: ~过高 *be self-important think highly of oneself*

【自恃】① over confident ② [书] capitalize on; count on; rely on: ~有后台 *count on sb's backing* / ~其功 *capitalize on one's achievements*

【自是】naturally; of course

【自首】① confess one's crime; give oneself up; (of a criminal) surrender oneself ② surrender to the enemy: ~书 *confession*

【自述】an account in one's own words

【自私】selfish

【自私自利】selfish: 出于~的动机 act from selfish motives

【自讨苦吃】ask for trouble; bring trouble upon oneself

【自投罗网】bite the hook; cast oneself into the net; leap at the bait; walk right into the trap

【自卫】defend oneself; self-defence: ~原则 *principle of self-defence* / ~战争 *war of self-defence* / ~反击 *fight* (*or strike*) *back in self-defence* / ~军 *self-defence corps*

【自慰】① console oneself ② masturbate

【自刎】cut one's throat commit suicide by cutting onc's throat

【自问】① ask oneself; examine oneself ② reach a conclusion after weighing a matter: 我~已经尽力帮助他了。*I believe I've done my best to help him.*

【自我】(used before disyllabic verbs) self; oneself: ~安慰 *self-consolation* / ~暗示 *self-suggestion* / ~暴露 *self-exposure* / ~辩解 *self-justification* / ~催眠 *autohypnosis* / ~观察 *self-observation* / ~检查 *self-examination* / ~教育 *self-education* / ~批评 *self-criticism* / ~介绍 *introduce oneself* / ~牺牲 *self-sacrifice*

【自习】study by oneself in scheduled time

【自下而上】from below

【自相矛盾】contradict oneself; be self-contradictory

【自小】since childhood

【自新】turn over a new leaf

【自信】confident; self-confident: 缺乏~ *lack confidence in oneself*

【自行】① by oneself: ~安排 *arrange by oneself* ② of oneself; of one's own accord; voluntarily: ~到来 *come of itself* ③ proper motion

【自行车】bicycle; bike: 骑~ *ride a bicycle* / ~赛 *cycling*; *cycle racing*

【自省】examine oneself; examine one's ability etc.

【自诩】[书] brag; crack oneself up; praise oneself

【自序】① preface; author's preface ② autobiographic note; brief account of oneself

【自选】【体】free; optional: ~动作 *optional exercise* / ~市场 *supermarket*

【自学】teach oneself; study independently; study on one's own: ~成长 *be self-taught* / ~课本 *teach-yourself books*

Z

【自寻烦恼】bring vexation on oneself; worry about needlessly

【自言自语】talk to oneself; soliloquize; think aloud

【自以为是】be self-opinionated; consider oneself (always) in the right

【自缢】[书] hang oneself

【自用】①[书] self-opinionated; self-willed:刚愎~ *bigoted opinionated* ② for private use; personal:~之物 *personal belongings; personal effects*

【自由】① freedom; liberty:言论~ *freedom of speech* ②【哲】freedom ③ free; unrest rained:~讨论 *have a free exchange of views* / ~电子 *free electron* / ~兑换 *convertibility* / ~泛滥 (*of erroneous ideas etc*) *spread unchecked; run wild* / ~放任 *let people do what they like* / ~放任主义 *laissez-faire* / ~港 *free port* / ~化 *liberalize* / ~汇率 *free exchange rate* / ~竞争 *free competition* / ~价格 *free price*/ ~恋爱 *free courtship* / ~贸易 *free trade* / ~诗 *free verse* / ~市场 *open /free market* / ~体操 *free exercise* / ~王国 *realm of freedom* / ~泳 *freestyle crawl* / ~主义 *liberalism* / ~资本主义 *non-monopoly* / ~自在 *leisurely and carefree*

【自娱】amuse oneself; please oneself

【自圆其说】justify oneself; make one's statement valid:不能~ *cannot offer a tenable argument*

【自怨自艾】repent; be full of remorse

【自愿】voluntary; of one's own accord:出于~ *on a voluntary basis*

【自在】(zì zài) unrestrained; free:过~日子 *lead a free and easy life*

【自在】(zì zai) comfortable; at ease:身体有些不~ *not be quite oneself*

【自责】blame oneself; reprove oneself

【自找】ask for it; suffer from one's own actions:不要总是~麻烦。*Don't always look for trouble.*

【自知之明】knowledge of oneself:人贵有~ *a man's virtues lies in taking a proper measure of himself*

【自治】autonomy; self-government:~条例 *regulations on the exercise of autonomy* / ~机关 *organ of self-government* / ~领 *dominion* / ~区 *autonomous region* / ~权 *autonomy* / ~县 *autonomous country* / ~州 *autonomous prefecture*

【自制】① made by oneself:这种玩具是他~的。*This toy is made by himself.* ② self-control:最后那个孩子失去了~,和老师吵了起来。*At last the child lose self-restraint and quarrelled with his teacher.*

【自重】① conduct oneself with dignity; be self-possessed ② dead weight

【自主】act on one's own; decide for oneself; keep the initiative in one's own hands:~经营 *be independent in management*

【自主权】power to make one's own decisions

【自助餐厅】cafeteria

【自传】autobiography

【自转】【天】rotation:~轴 *axis of rotation*

【自尊】proper pride; self-esteem; self-respect

【自作自受】stew in one's own juice; suffer from one's own actions

【自作聪明】think oneself clever; try to be smart

【自作多情】proffer a love or affection which is not reciprocated

【自作主张】act on one's own; decide for oneself

字 ① word; character:~义 *meaning of a word* ② pronunciation (of a word):表达~~清楚 *express every word clearly* ③ printing type; style of handwriting:黑体~ *boldface type* ④ scripts; writings:收藏~画 *collect scripts and paintings* ⑤ receipt

【字标】slogan written in large characters

【字典】character dictionary:~纸 *bible paper*

【字调】【语】tones of Chinese characters

【字段】【电】field:~名 *field name*

【字幅】horizontal or vertical scroll of calligraphy

【字符】character

【字号】font size; type size; word size

【字盒】【印】mould

【字画】calligraphy and painting

【字汇】glossary; lexicon; writing

【字迹】handwriting:~工整 *neat writing*

【字节】byte

【字据】written pledge

【字库】① word bank ② font bank; font collection

【字里行间】by implication; between the lines:从~可以感受到他对你的鼓励。*You'll find his courage between the lines.*

【字谜】a riddle about a character or word

【字面】literal:~意义 *literal meaning*

【字模】【印】(type) matrix 冲压~ *punched matrix*

【字母】letter; letters of an alphabet

【字幕】captions (of films; videos, etc.); subtitles:中文~ *Chinese subtitles*

【字体】① script; typeface; form of a write or printed character ② style of calligraphy ③【电】font; typeface

【字条】not; brief note:他留给你一张~。*He left you a note.*

【字眼】diction; wording:玩弄~ *play with words*

【字样】① model of written characters ② printed or written words

【字斟句酌】weigh every word

恣 ① be self-indulgent; throw off all restraint ② at ease; comfortable

【恣情】① as much as one likes:~欢笑 *laugh heartily* ② arbitrary; willful; wanton:~放纵 *indulge in passions and run wild*

【恣行无忌】be wilful and unscrupulously in action; act recklessly

【恣意】reckless; unbridled; unscrupulous; wilful:~妄为 *behave unscrupulously*;

渍 ① ret; soak; steep:衣服被汗水~黄了。*The clothes have yellowed with sweat.* ② be soiled (with grease, etc.):衣服上~了许多油子。*The coat is caked with tar.* ③ water logging; floodwater on low-lying land:防洪排~ *prevention of water logging and drainage of flood water* ④[方] stain; sludge:油~ *oil sludge* /汗~ *sweat stains*

【渍染】dye：血污～ *be soiled with blood*；*blood-stained*
【渍水】accumulated water

zōng

宗 ① ancestor：老祖～ *forefather*；*ancestor* ② clan：～法 *patrician clan system* ③ faction；school；sect：正～。*orthodox school* ④ aim；principal aim；purpose：开～明义 *make clear the theme and purpose from the very beginning* ⑤ model；great master ⑥（in academic or artistic work）model on ⑦（Zōng）a surname
【宗祠】ancestral ball（or temple）
【宗教】religion：～信仰 *religious belief* / ～仪式 *religious rites*；*ritual* / ～自由 *freedom*（*or liberty*）*of religion*；*religious freedom* / ～事业 *religious undertaking* / ～法庭 *the Inquisition*（*in European history*）/ ～改革 *the Reformation*；*religious reform*
【宗庙】ancestral temple（or shrine）of a ruling house
【宗派】sect；faction：～斗争 *factional strife* / ～活动 *sectarian actives* / ～主义 *factionalism sectarianism*
【宗谱】genealogy；genealogical tree；family tree
【宗亲】clansmen；members of the same clan
【宗师】master of great learning and integrity
【宗室】① imperial（or royal）clan ② imperial（or royal）clansman
【宗仰】［书］hold in esteem：远近～ *be held in esteem far and near*
【宗主国】suzerain（state）；metropolitan state
【宗主权】suzerainty
【宗族】① clansman ② patriarchal clan

综 sum up；put together：～上所述 *to sum up*
【综观】make a comprehensive survey：～全局 *take a look at the overall situation*
【综合】① summarize：synthesize：～考虑。*This has to be taken as a whole.* ② synthetical；comprehensive；composite；multiple：～保险 *comprehensive insurance* / ～报道 *news roundup*；*comprehensive*（*or composite*）*dispatch* / ～报告 *comprehensive report*；*summing-up report* / ～病征 *syndrome* / ～大学 *university* / ～服务 *comprehension service* / ～规划 *unified plan* / ～考察 *comprehensive survey* / ～利用 *comprehensive utilization*；*multipurpose use* / ～平衡 *overall balance* / ～性工厂 *multiple-producing factory* / ～银行 *universal bank* / ～指数 *composite index* / ～治理 *tackle a problem in comprehensive way*
【综计】add up；sun up：全文～5千字。*The essay has 5,000 words altogether.*
【综括】sum up：～起来 *to state succinctly*；*to sum up*
【综述】summarize；sum up：一周～ *round up of the weeks news*

棕 ① palm ② coir；palm fibre
【棕黑】dark brown
【棕红】reddish brown
【棕黄】pale brown
【棕榈】palm：～油 *palm butter*；*palm oil*
【棕毛】palm fibre：～蓑衣 *palm rain cape*
【棕色】brown：～土地 *brown soil*
【棕绳】coir rope
【棕熊】brow bear
【棕衣】palm-bark rain cape

踪 footprint；trace；track
【踪迹】trace；track：他消失的没了～。*He disappeared without any trace.*
【踪影】（usu. used in the negative）trace；shadow；sign：我目送他直到不见～。*I gazed after him until he was out of sight.*

鬃 hair on the neck of a pig，horse，etc.：马～ *horse's mane*
【鬃刷】bristle brush

zǒng

总 ① assemble；put together；sum up：～起来说你做得不错。*To sum up you have done a good job.* ② general；overall；total：～成本 *overall cost* / ～趋势 *general trend* / ～根源 *root cause* ③ chief；general；head：～头目 *chief boss* ④ always；invariably：我～是7：00起床。*I always get up at 7：00.* ⑤ eventually；anyway；after all；sooner or later：你～有一天会成功。*You'll become accomplished one day.* / 他～是你老师。*But after all，he is your teacher.* / 你～会理解的。*You'll understand it sooner or later.* ⑥ certainly；probably；surely：你～该给你朋友一个解释。*You should at any rate give your friend an explanation.*
【总罢工】general strike
【总编辑】editor in chief
【总部】general headquarters
【总裁】director-general（of a political party）；president（of a company）；governor（of a bank）
【总参谋部】the Headquarters of the General staff
【总参谋长】chief of the general staff
【总产值】total output value；gross output value
【总代理】general agent
【总得】be bound to；must；have to：他～说几句。*He's bound to say something.* / 你～答应他的条件 *You should have got to grant his request.*
【总店】main store（of a business）
【总动员】general mobilization
【总督】governor；viceroy；governor-general
【总额】total：工资～ *payroll*；*total wages*
【总而言之】in a world；in brief；in short；to make a long story short：～，今天他不来了。*In a word，he won't come today.*
【总方针】general principle；general policy：教育～

the general policy of education
【总纲】general principles; general programme:宪法~ *general principles of the constitution*
【总工程师】chief engineer
【总工会】federation of trade unions:中华全国~ *all-China Federation of Trade Unions*
【总公司】head office (of a corporation)
【总攻】【军】general offensive
【总供给】aggregate supply
【总共】altogether; in all; in the aggregate
【总管】① take overall responsibility ②[旧] butler; steward
【总归】anyway; eventually; after all:问题~可以解决。*This problem will eventually be solved.*
【总行】head office (of a bank)
【总和】sum; total; sum total:半年产量~ *output of half year taken as a whole*
【总后方】rear area (in wartime)
【总后勤部】the General Logistics Department
【总汇】① confluence; aggregate; concourse:力量的~ *aggregation of strength* ②(of streams) come or flow together:几条河~入长江。*These rivers flow into the Changjiang river together.*
【总机】① switchboard; telephone exchange ② operator
【总计】①【数】grand total ② total; amount to; add up to:观众~二万人。*The audience totaled* 2,0000.
【总监】chief inspector; inspector general
【总角】[书] a child's hair twisted in a knot-childhood:~之交 *childhood friend*
【总结】① summarize; sum up:~经验 *sum up one's experience* ② summary; summing-up:作~ *make a summary* / ~报告 *summary (or final, concluding) report* / ~会 *summing-up meeting*
【总经销】exclusive distribution
【总括】sum up
【总揽】assume overall responsibility; take on everything:~大权 *exercise overall authority*
【总理】premier; prime minister:国务院~ *the Premier of the State Council* / 副~ *vice-premier of the State Council*
【总量】aggregate; total supply and demand:~调控 *control of total supply and demand* / ~平衡 *overall balance*
【总领事】consul general:~馆 *consulate general*
【总路线】general line
【总论】introduction (at the beginning of a book)
【总平面图】general table of contents; catalogue
【总评】general comment; overall appraisal
【总设计师】chief architect
【总书记】general secretary; secretary-general
【总数】total; sum total
【总司令】commander-in-chief
【总司令部】general headquarters
【总算】① finally; at long last:雨~停了。*The rain stilled down at last.* ② considering everything; on the whole; all things considered:对这个孩子而言,画的~还可以。*For a child's printing, it's quite good.*
【总体】total; overall:~规划 *overall plan* / ~设计 *master design* / ~水平 *overall quality level* / ~战略 *total strategy* / ~外交 *total diplomacy*
【总统】president (of a republic):~府 *presidential palace* / ~选举 *presidential election* / ~制 *presidential system*
【总务】① general affairs ② person in charge of general affairs:~处 *general affairs department* / ~科 *general affairs section* / ~司 *general service department*
【总则】general rules; general principles
【总闸门】master gate; petroleum master valve
【总长】① cabinet minister ②[口] chief of the general staff
【总账】general leader; general account
【总账单】master bill
【总政治部】to General Political Department
【总之】① in brief; in a word; in short:~,他是个好孩子。*In a word, he is a good child.* ② anyway; anyhow:准确方向我记不清了,~,他家在这条街上。*I can't remember the exact direction; anyway, his family is somewhere in this street.*
【总支】general branch
【总值】total (or gross) value:进(出)口~ *gross import (export) value* / 国民生产~ *gross national product (GNP)*
【总指挥】① commander in chief ② general director
【总指挥部】general headquarters
【总装】assemble a machine; final assembly

zòng

纵1 ① from north to south or vice versa ② vertical; lengthwise; longitudinal
纵2 ① release; set free ③ indulge; let loose; let oneself go ③ jump into the air; jump up:他向上一~,把球投给队友。*He jumped up and shot the ball to his teammate.*
纵3 [书] even if; even though:~死不悔 *even to the end of one's life refuse to repent*
【纵波】【物】longitudinal wave
【纵步】① stride:~向前 *stride forward* ② jump; bound; leap
【纵队】① column; file:一路~ *single file; column of files* ② a military unit during the War of Liberation, equivalent to an army
【纵观】make a general survey:~全局 *make a general survey of the situation*
【纵贯】pass through from north to south or from south to north:公路~两省的铁路。*Road passes through two provinces.*
【纵横】① in length and breadth; vertically and horizontally:~交错的高速公路 *crisscross of highways* ② freely; with great ease; fluently:笔意~ *write with great ease* ③ sweep over; march over unhindered
【纵横驰骋】(of an army) move about freely and

quickly; sweep through the length and breadth of：人类在科学领域中 。*The length and breadth of the whole realm of science is open for human beings to explore and conquer.*

【纵横交错】crisscross：～高速公路 *crisscross of highways*

【纵火】commit arson; set on fire：～犯 *arsonist*

【纵酒】drink to excess

【纵览】scan：～群书 *read extensively*

【纵论】have a wide-ranging discussion; talk freely：～天下大事 *talk freely about world events*

【纵目】look far ahead; look as far as the eye can see

【纵剖面】vertical section

【纵情】as much as one likes; to one's heart content：～歌唱 *sing to one's heart content; sing heartily*

【纵然】even if; even though：～可能失败，我们也要干到底。*We will stick to the end even if it maybe fail.*

【纵容】connive; wink at; indulge

【纵身】jump; leap：～上马 *leap onto a horse* / ～一跳 *jump up*

【纵深】【军】depth：向～发展 *develop in depth*

【纵声】at the top of one's voice：～歌唱 *sing lustily*

【纵使】even if; even though

【纵谈】talk freely：～时事 *talk freely about current affairs*

【纵眺】look as far as one's eyes can see：～景色 *scan the scenery*

【纵向】lengthwise, longitudinal; vertical：～结合 *vertical integration*

【纵欲】indulge in sensual pleasures; give way to one's carnal desires

【纵恣】［书］self-indulgent; undisciplined; wanton

【纵坐标】【数】ordinate

粽

【粽子】a pyramid-shaped dumpling made of glutinous rice wrapped in bamboo or reed leaves (eaten during the Dragon Boat Festival)

zǒu

走

① go; walk：～进教室 *go into the classroom* / ～一条新路 / *break new paths* / ～向门 *make for the door* ② run; move：钟不～了。*The clock has stopped.* / 该你～这步棋。*It's your turn to make a money.* ③ leave; go away：～开！*Clear off! Move away!* / 他把书拿～了. *He took the book away.* ④ call on; visit：他俩～得很近。*They often visit each other.* ⑤ from; through：请～这扇门！*Please go in through this door.* ⑥ escape; leak; let out：气漏～了。*The air is escaping.* ⑦ lose the original shape; depart from the original：衣服～样了。*The dress is no longer the shape it used to be.*

【走步】【体】walking

【走村串寨】go from village to village

【走道】① sidewalk; pavement; ② footpath; path; walk

【走道儿】［口］walk

【走调】out of tune：你唱歌又～。*Your singing got out of tune again.*

【走动】① stretch one's legs ② walk about：来回～ *walk go and from* ③ socialize; visit each other：他家亲戚过年才～。*They and their relatives call on each other only on festive occasions.*

【走读】attend a day school：～生 *day student; non-resident student*

【走访】① interview; have an interview with：老师～了这个学生的家长。*The teacher interviewed this student's parents.* ② go and see; pay a visit to：～亲友 *visit relatives and friends*

【走钢丝】① wire walking ② take risks：你这样做是在～。*The way you did it was nothing short of tightrope walking.*

【走狗】running dog; lackey; flunkey; stooge; servile follower

【走红】have good luck; be in luck

【走后门】get in by the back door get sth done through pull; secure advantages through influence

【走火】① sparking ② (of firearms) discharge accidentally：他的枪～了。*His rifle went off accidentally.* ③ go too far in what one says; put sth too strongly ④ catch fire; be on fire：房子～了。*The rooms is on fire.*

【走廊】corridor; passage passageway

【走漏】① divulge; leak out：～消息 *leak information; divulge a secret* / 是谁～了消息？*Who leaked information?* ② smuggling and tax evasion

【走路】① walk; go on foot：我们～去公园。*We went to the park by foot.* ② leave; go away

【走马观花】look at flowers while riding a horse gain a shallow understanding from a fleeting glance

【走马上任】go to one's post; take up (or assume) office

【走门路】solicit help from potential backers; gain one's end through pull

【走南闯北】journey north and south; travel widely

【走俏】(of goods) sell well; be in great demand

【走亲戚】call on relatives

【走人】［口］leave; go away：卷铺盖～ *tell him to pack up and quit*

【走色】lose colour; fade; discolour：这条裤子一洗就～了. *The pants discoloured after only one wash.*

【走神】(of one's attention) wander; be absent-minded：他看书～了. *He was absent-minded while he was reading.*

【走失】① be lost; be missing; wander away：孩子～了。*The child got lost on the way.* ② lose; fail to keep

【走势】tendency：产品价格～下降。*This products tend to fall.*

【走私】smuggle：～货 *smuggled goods*

Z

【走题】(of a speech, etc) digress from the subject; stray from the point
【走投无路】be in an impasses:穷困潦倒~ *be down-and-out and have no place to turn* /最后他被逼得~了。*He was driven to the wall at last.*
【走味儿】lose flavour:食品~了。*The food lost its flavour.*
【走下坡路】be on the decline; go downhill
【走向】① run; trend:东西~ *from east to west* ②【地】strike:~断层 *strike fault* ③ head for; move towards be on the way to:~反面 *change into one's opposite* /~死亡 *go down to one's doom*
【走相】become deformed
【走形式】go through the motions; do sth as a mere formality
【走穴】[口] moonlight:这歌星~发财了。*The singer made a fortune by moonlighting.*
【走眼】see wrong; mistake for
【走样】be out of form; lose shape; deviate from the original model:衣服被洗~了。*This dress was washed out of form.*
【走一步,看一步】go about cautiously; proceed without the plan or with caution
【走运】have good luck; be in luck:祝你~! *Good luck!*
【走着瞧】wait and see:咱们~! *We'll see.*
【走走】① take a stroll ② come or go in a general sense
【走卒】pawn; lackey; stooge; cat's-paw
【走嘴】let slip an inadvertent remark; blurt sth out:是她妈妈~了。*It was her mother who blurted the secret out.*

zòu

奏 ① play; perform; strike up:~国歌 *play the national anthem* ② achieve; produce
【奏捷】score a success; win a battle:~归来 *return in triumph*
【奏鸣曲】【音】sonata:~式 *sonata form*
【奏效】be successful; get the desired result; prove effective:这种药很快会~。*The medicine proved quite effective.* /这个方法~了 *This method worked.*
【奏乐】play music; strike up a tune

揍 ①[口] beat, hit, strike 挨~ *get a thrashing* ②[方] break; smash:把玻璃~碎了 *break the glass*

zū

租 ① charter; hire; rent:~三间房 *rent three rooms* / ~一架飞机 *charter a plane* ② lease; let out; rent out:这个房间已~给别人了。*The room has been leased out.* ③ rent ④ land tax
【租船】chartering:~代理 *chartering agent* /~契约 *charter; charter party* /~市场 *chartering market*
【租佃】(of a landlord) rent out land to tenants:~关系 *tenancy relationship* /~制度 *tenancy system*
【租户】① leaseholder; lessee; tenant ② hirer
【租价】rent; rental
【租界】concession; settlement
【租借】lease; hire; rent:~地 *leasehold; leased territory*
【租金】rent; rental
【租赁】hire; lease; rent:~合同 *contract for lease* /~经营 *leasing business* /~业 *leasing trade*
【租让】lease
【租书处】book rental
【租税】land tax and other levies
【租用】hire; rent, take on lease:~礼堂 *hire a hall* /~人 *leaseholder; hirer; leaser; tenant*
【租约】lease:短期~ *short term tenancy*
【租债】debt and rent

zú

足[1] ① foot; leg:~不出户 *stay indoors; never go out of one's room* ② leg (of certain utensils)

足[1] ① ample; enough; sufficient:赚~了钱 *make plenty of money* ② fully; as much as:这个行李~有十斤。*This suitcase weighs a full ten jin.* ③ enough; sufficiently:无~挂齿 *not worth mentioning*
【足本】an unabridged version (of a novel, etc)
【足赤】pure gold; solid gold
【足够】ample; enough; sufficient:~估计 *take full account*
【足迹】footmark; footprint; track
【足金】pure gold; solid gold
【足球】① football; soccer:踢~ *play football (or soccer)* ② football:英式~ *soccer; association football* /~队 *football team; eleven* /~迷 *football fan* /~运动员 *footballer*
【足色】(of gold or silver) of standard purity
【足坛】the football world:~劲旅 *a strong football team*
【足下】a polite form of address between friends:~愿意帮忙吗? *Would you like to help me?*
【足以】ample; enough; sufficient:这个证据~证明问题。*This evident is enough to elucidate the matter.*
【足银】pure silver
【足月】(of a foetus) born after the normal period of gestation; mature
【足智多谋】wise and resourceful; wise and full of strategies

卒[1] ① private; soldier ② servant ③ pawn; one of the pieces in Chinese chess

卒[2] ① finish; end:有始有~ *begin well and end well* ② dire:病~ *die of illness* ③ finally; at last;
【卒岁】[书] get through the year:聊以~ *just to tide over the year*
【卒业】[书] graduate; finish a course of study

【卒子】① rank-and-file soldier ② pawn, one of the pieces in Chinese chess

族 ① clan: 贵~ *noble* ② a death penalty in ancient China, imposed on an offender and his whole family; or even the families of his mother and wife ③ race; nationality ④ a class or group of things or people with common features

【族类】the same clan (tribe, nation)

【族权】clan authority (or power)

【族人】clansman

【族长】the head of a clan; clan elder

zǔ

诅 [书] curse; swear; wish sb evil

【诅骂】abuse; curse; revile; swear

【诅咒】curse; imprecate; swear; wish sb evil

阻 block; hinder; obstruct

【阻碍】block; hinder; impede: ~交通 *block (or hold up) the traffic*

【阻车】traffic jam; hold up traffic

【阻挡】obstruct; resist; stop; stem: ~犯规 *blocking*

【阻隔】【军】block; check: ~战 *blocking action*

【阻截】bar the way; stop ; obstruct

【阻抗】impedance: 反射~ *reflected impedance* / ~匹配 *impedance matching*

【阻拦】obstruct; bar the way; stop: 他决心做这个工作，父母不好~。*His parents thought it better not to stop him as he was determined to do this job.*

【阻力】① obstruction; hindrance; resistance: 改革的~ *resistance to reform* ②【物】drag; resistance; pullback: ~系数 *drag coefficient*

【阻挠】obstruct; put a spoke in sb's wheel; thwart; stand in the way: 百般~ *create all sorts of obstacles*

【阻尼】【物】damping: ~振荡 *damped oscillation* / ~器 *damper*

【阻塞】clog; block; obstruct: 交通~了。*The traffic is held up.*

【阻援】【军】hold off enemy reinforcements

【阻止】prevent; stop; hold back; stop: 没有人能~他离开家。*No one can stop him leave home.*

组 ① form; organize ② group ③ battery; set; series: 两~发电机 *two generators* / 两~电池 *two batteries* / 一~镜头 *a series of shots*

【组办】run; organize: ~比赛 *organize a competition*

【组编】fit together; compile; edit: ~一套资料 *compile a set of issues*

【组成】compose; form; make up consist of: 我们班由60个同学~。*Our class consists sixty students.*

【组成部分】component; ingredient; component part

【组阁】form (or set up, organize) a cabinet

【组合】① compose; combine; constitute; make up ② association; combination ③【数】combination: ~柜 *composite cabinet* / ~机床 *combination lathe* / ~家具 *component furniture* / ~理论 *combinatorial theory* / ~体 *assembly*

【组画】a series of paintings

【组件】module; package

【组建】form; establish; set up: ~剧团 *setup a theatre group*

【组接】film editing; film montage

【组台】organize a performance

【组团】organize a performance group: 三十个老教师~旅行。*Thirty old teachers are organizing travel groups.*

【组织】① form; organize: ~团队 *form a team* ② organization organized system / ~条例 *organic rules* / ~委员会 *organizing committee* ③【纺】weave: 平信~ *plain weave* / 密~ *tight weave* ④【生理】tissue: 神经~ *nerve tissue* / ~关系 *membership credentials* / ~生活 *regular activities of an organization* / ~学 *histology* / ~行为学 *organizational behaviorism* / ~液 *tissue fluid*

【组装】assemble; put together

祖 ① grandfather ② ancestor: 先~ *ancestor* ③ founder (of a craft, religious sect, etc.); originator

【祖辈】ancestor; ancestry; forefathers

【祖传】hand down from one's forefathers

【祖坟】ancestral grave

【祖父】grandfather

【祖国】homeland; motherland; fatherland; native land

【祖籍】ancestral home; original family home; the land of one's ancestors

【祖居】① ancestral home ② be a native of; have one's ancestral home at

【祖母】(paternal) grandmother

【祖上】ancestors; forbears; forefathers

【祖师】① the founder of a school of learning, a craft etc ② the founder of a sect of Buddhism or Taoism

【祖孙】grandparent and grandchild

【祖先】ancestors; ancestry; forbears; forefathers

【祖宗】ancestry; forbears; forefathers

【祖祖辈辈】from generation to generation; for generations: 他家~是农民。*His family has been farmers for generations.*

zhān

钻 ① bore; drill: ~孔 *drill a hole* / ~木取火 *drill wood to make fire* ② get into; go through; make one's way into: 飞机从云层中~出来。*The plane broke through the clouds.* ③ dig into; make a thorough study of: ~业务 *dig into one's job*
see also zuàn

【钻劲】studiousness; application to studies: 他工作

上有股～。*He is a man of great perseverance.*

【钻空子】exploit an advantage; take advantage of loopholes:不要让小偷～。*Don't let the thief exploit this loophole.*

【钻圈】jumping (or plunging) through hoops

【钻探】(exploration) drilling: ～工 *driller* /～机 *drilling machine* /～设备 *drilling equipment*

【钻心】① unbearable:他手上的伤口疼的～。*He was seized with sharp pains in his hand cut.* ② infiltrate; sneak in

【钻研】dig into; study intensively: ～技术 *perfect one's skill*

躜 ① jump up ② dash forward:老鹰～云而上。*The hawk darted up through the clouds.*

zuǎn

纂 ①[书] compile; edit ② compile a dictionary

【纂修】compile; edit

zuàn

钻 ① auger; drill:电～ *electric drill* /手摇～ *hand drill* ② diamond; jewel:十九～的手表 *a 19-jewel watch* ③ bore; drill: ～个眼 *bore a hole*

see also zuān

【钻床】driller; drill machine

【钻机】(drilling) rig; drilling machine

【钻戒】diamond ring

【钻井】well drilling:海洋～ *offshore drilling* /～船 *oil rig* /～队 *drilling crew* /～工人 *driller* /～记录 *drill log*

【钻具】drilling tool; drilling rig

【钻模】【机】(drill) jig: 分度～ *indexing jig*

【钻石】① diamond ② jewel (used in a watch)

【钻塔】derrick; boring tower

【钻挺】drill collar

【钻头】aiguille; bit (of a drill): 装上～ *brace a bit* /卸下～ *break out a bit*

【钻压】bit pressure; bit weight

攥 hold; grip; grasp: ～着一把斧子 *hold an axe in one's hand* /～紧拳头 *clench one's fist*

zuǐ

嘴 ① mouth:请闭上你的～。*Keep your mouth shut please.* ② anything shaped or functioning like a mouth:瓶～儿 *the mouth of a bottle*

【嘴巴】① mouth ②[口](usu. used in):打～ *slap sb's in the face box sb's ears*

【嘴笨】clumsy of speech; inarticulate

【嘴不饶人】fond of making sarcastic remarks

【嘴馋】greedy; voracious; fond of good food

【嘴唇】lip:上(下)～ *the upper (lower) lip*

【嘴乖】(of children) talking sweetly; clever and pleasant when speaking to elders:她～招人喜爱。*The little girl was a darling to everyone around, talking so sweetly!*

【嘴尖】① sharp-tongued; pungent in speech ② have a keen sense of taste; particular about fond:这个孩子～。*Child is rather choosy about food and eats only what suits his taste.*

【嘴角】corners of the mouth

【嘴紧】closemouthed; tight-lipped

【嘴快】have a loose tongue:她～。*She has a rather loosen-tongued.*

【嘴懒】not inclined to talk much

【嘴脸】face; features; countenance:他一副丑恶～。*The look on his face is disgusting.*

【嘴皮子】[口] lip: 他不只是耍耍～,而是很有诚意。*He is not sweet-talking; he is sincere.*

【嘴贫】garrulous; loquacious

【嘴勤】chatty; fond of talking

【嘴软】afraid to speak out

【嘴上没毛,力事不牢】a man too young to grow a beard is not dependable; a man with downy lips is bound to make slips

【嘴松】have a loose tongue:性直～ *have a candid nature and a loose tongue*

【嘴碎】garrulous; loquacious; talkative

【嘴甜】ingratiating in speech; smooth-tongued;

【嘴严】closemouthed; tight-lipped

【嘴硬】stubborn and reluctant to admit mistakes or defeats

【嘴直】plainspoken; outspoken

zuì

最 ① most: ～能表明问题 *can best illustrate the point* /～优先考虑 *top priority* ② farthest to or nearest (a place): ～下层 *at the very bottom* /～南边 *farthest to the South*

【最初】first; initial; earliest: ～几天 *on the first few days* /～印象 *first impressions*

【最低】lowest; minimum: ～工资 *subsistence wages*

【最多】maximum; most; at most:她～一天完成30个玩具。*She makes a maximum of thirty toys a day.* /这个学校～时有600名学生。*The school's enrollment at its height reached* 600.

【最高】highest; tallest; supreme: ～法院 *supreme court* /～权威 *supreme authority* /～点 *statistics peak* /～年产量 *peak annual output* /～权力 *supreme power* /～速度 *maximum speed* /～限额 *ceiling* /～限价 *ceiling price*

【最高级】① highest; summit: ～会谈 *top-level talks; summit talks* ②【语】the superlative degree: ～会议 *summit meeting*

【最好】① best; first-rate: ～等级 *highest grade* /～方法 *best method* ② had better: 你～听听同学的建议。*You'd better hear your classmates' suggestions.*

【最后】last; final; ultimate: ～冲刺 *final spurt* /～

条款 *final provisions* / ~议定书 *final protocol*

【最佳】① best; top: ~口译人员 *top-notch interpreter* ②【物】optimum: ~数 *optimum number*

【最近】① lately; recently; of late: ~消息 *recent news* ② soon; in the near future: ~我准备去休假。*I'll have a holiday soon.*

【最少】minimum; least; at least: ~付出 *least expense*

【最新】latest; up-to-date: ~产品 *latest product*; *newest product* / ~技术 *up-to-date technology*

【最终】final; ultimate: ~目的 *ultimate aim* / ~消费者 *ultimate consumer* / ~用户 *final user*

罪 ① crime; guilt: 犯~ *commit a crime* / 受贿~ *crimes of accepting bribes* ② blame; fault ② blame; fault ③ suffering; hardship pain

【罪案】case; details of a criminal case;

【罪不容诛】be guilty of crimes for which even death is insufficient punishment; even death cannot atone for the offence

【罪大恶极】be guilty of the most heinous crimes

【罪恶】crime; evil; guilt

【罪恶昭彰】have committed flagrant crimes

【罪犯】culprit; criminal; offender

【罪该万死】be guilty of a crime for which one deserves to die ten thousand deaths; be guilty of a crime for which even death cannot atone

【罪过】① fault; offence; sin; ② thanks, but it is really too much of an honour

【罪魁】chief criminal (of culprit, offender)

【罪名】accusation; charge: 网罗~ *frame a case against sb*

【罪孽】sin; fault; wrongdoing that brings retribution

【罪人】guilty person; offender; sinner: 历史的~ *person condemned by history*

【罪行】crime; guilt; offence: 滔天~ *towering crimes* / ~较轻 *minor offence*

【罪有应得】one deserves one's punishment

【罪责】responsibility for one's offence: 推卸~ *shirk responsibility for an offence*

【罪证】evidence of a crime; proof of one's guilt

【罪状】charges in an indictment; facts about a crime

醉 ① drunk; intoxicated; inebriated: 喝~ *be tipsy* ② (of some kind of food) steeped in liquor; liquor-saturated: ~蟹 *liquor-saturated crab*

【醉鬼】drunkard; inebriate; soak; sot

【醉汉】drunkard; drunken man

【醉酒】drunk; intoxicated: ~的人 *an intoxicated person*

【醉拳】drunken boxing

【醉生梦死】lead a befuddled life; dream one's life away

【醉翁之意不在酒】the drinker's heart is not in the cup — have other things in mind; have ulterior motives

【醉心】be wrapped up in; be preoccupied with: ~金钱 *be infatuated with fortune* / ~于技术研究 *be engrossed in technical research*

【醉醺醺】drunk; sottish

【醉眼】[书] eyes showing the effects of drink: ~朦胧 *drunken and bleary-eyed*

【醉意】signs or feeling of getting drunk: 她喝多了，已有几分~了。*She drunk so much and was a bit tipsy.*

zūn

尊 ① senior; of a senior generation; elder ② your: 令~ *your father* / ~姓大名? *May I know your name?* ③ respect; honour; venerate ④[量]: 一~银雕像 *a silver figure*

【尊称】① honorific title; address sb respectfully: 张老是人们对他的~。*The venerable Zhang is an honorific way that people address him.*

【尊崇】revere; venerate; worship

【尊府】① your residence ②[书] your father

【尊贵】honourable; respected; respectable: ~的老人 *an honoured guest*

【尊驾】you: 恭候~光临! *Your presence is cordially requested!*

【尊敬】esteem; honour; respect: ~师长 *honour the elders and teachers* / ~的来宾们 *distinguished guests*

【尊容】sb's looks or appearance

【尊师爱生】respect the teacher and cherish the student; students respect teachers and teachers cherish students

【尊师重道】honour the teacher and revere his teaching

【尊严】dignity; honour; integrity: 国家的~ *national dignity* / 维护做人的~ *guard the human dignity*

【尊重】① esteem; respect; value: ~老师 *respect teachers* / ~生命 *cherish life* / ~知识和人才 *esteem knowledge and talent* ② dignified; serious; proper: 请你放~些! *Behave yourself, please!*

遵 follow; obey; abide by: ~纪守法 *observe law and discipline* / ~令而行 *according to orders*

【遵办】do as ordered; act in compliance with instructions

【遵从】comply with; defer to; follow: ~朋友劝告 *follow the advice of friends*

【遵命】obey your command; comply with your wish

【遵守】abide by; comply with; observe: ~交通规则 *observe traffic rules* / ~契约 *abide by the contract*

【遵循】abide by; adhere to; follow: ~方针政策 *pursue policy* / ~原则 *follow the principle.*

【遵照】obey; act in accordance with comply with; conform to: ~惯例 *according to the established practice* / ~社会习俗 *conform to the customs of society*

Z

zuō

作 workshop：石～ *stonemasons' workshop* / 洗衣～ *cleaner's; laundry*
see also zuò

【作坊】workshop：纺织品～ *workshop for making textiles*

zuó

昨 ① yesterday ② the past

【昨日】yesterday

【昨天】yesterday：～我们拜访了他爸爸。*We visited his father yesterday.*

【昨晚】yesterday evening; last night

【昨夜】last night; yesterday evening

琢

【琢磨】ponder; think over; turn over in one's mind：反复～ *turn sth over and over in one's mind* / ～出办法 *figure out a way*

zuǒ

左 ① the left side; the left：向～转 *turn left* ② the left ③ heretical; queer; unorthodox ④ incorrect; wrong：他说～了。*What he said is incorrect.* ⑤ contrary; different opposite

【左膀右臂】right-hand man; a capable assistant

【左边锋】【体】outside left; left wing

【左边】the left; the left side：房子～是花园。*There is a park on the left of the house.*

【左不过】① anyhow; anyway; in any event ② justly; merely; only：我没什么，～有点不舒服。*Nothing serious; just a little uncomfortable.*

【左舵】left standard rudder; left rudder：～十五度 *port fifteen degrees!*

【左锋】【体】left forward

【左顾右盼】look around; glance right and left：他～走在街上。*He looked around while walking in the street.*

【左后卫】【体】left back

【左邻】nearby; around the corner; in the neighbourbood：我住在～。*I live nearby.*

【左轮】revolver

【左面】the left side; the left

【左内锋】【体】inside left

【左派】① the left; the left wing：～政党 *parties of the left* ② leftist

【左撇子】lefty; left-handed person

【左前卫】【体】left half; left halfback

【左倾】① left-leaning; progressive; inclined towards the revolution ② "left" deviation：～机会主义 *"left" opportunism*

【左手】the left hand

【左首】the left; the left-hand side：她丈夫坐在她～。*Her husband sat on her left.*

【左思右想】think over from different angles; turn sth over in one's mind：她～不得其解。*She thought this thing over and over again but failed to understand it.*

【左翼】①【军】left wing; left flank ② the left; the left wing：～分子 *leftist; left-winger*

【左右】① the left and right sides：～摇摆 *waver between the left and right* ② (used after a numeral) about; or so：两点～ *around two o'clock* / 六十元 *about sixty yuan* / 三天～ *three days or so* / 15个女孩～ *fifteen girls* ③ control; master：为人所～ *fall under sb's influence; be controlled by sb* ④ attendants; retinue; those in close attendance ⑤ [方] anyhow, anyway; in any case; in any event

【左右逢源】① be able to achieve success one way or another ② gain advantage from both sides

【左右手】a capable assistant

【左右为难】in a dilemma

佐 ① assistant ② assist

撮 [量] (for hair) tuft：一～白毛 *a tuft of white hair*

【撮子】[口] tuft (of hair)：一～头发 *a tuft of hair*

zuò

作 ① grow; rise; get up：请你振～起来。*You must bestir yourself, please.* ② compose; write：写～ *write* / ～诗 *compose a poem* / ～画 *paint a picture.* ③ prevent; affect：装模～样 *put on an act; behave affectedly* ④ regard as; take sb or sth for ⑤ feel; have ⑥ work; writings：成功之～ *a successful work*
see also zuō

【作案】carry out criminal activates; commit a crime or an offence：那个小偷～时被捕。*The thief was caught in the act.*

【作罢】drop; cancel; relinquish; give up：由于他住院，这事只好～。*Since he was in hospital, the matter had to be dropped.*

【作保】be sb's guarantor; go bail for sb; sponsor sb

【作弊】cheat; indulge in corrupt practices; practise fraud

【作别】[书] bid farewell; take one's leave; say adieu：与兄弟～ *take leave of one's brothers*

【作词】write words (for a song)：由李先生～ *words by Mr. Li*

【作答】answer

【作对】① oppose; be antagonistic to; set oneself against：他总是和我～。*He always sets himself against me.* ② join in a marriage; pair off in marriage：成双～ *in pairs*

【作恶】① do evil：～多端 *do all kinds of evil* ② [书] gloomy; melancholy

【作法】① practice; course of action; doing things: 惯常的～ *usual way of doing things* ② technique of writing: 文章～ *art of composition* ③ exercise magic

【作废】be annulled; be invalidated; become invalid: 过期～ *become invalid upon expiration* / 宣布合同～ *declare the contract null and void*

【作风】style; style of work; way: 杜绝不良～ *put an end to a bad style*

【作古】[书] pass away; die

【作怪】stir up trouble; make mischief

【作家】author; writer: 多产～ *a prolific writer* / ～协会 *the writers' union*

【作假】① counterfeit; falsify; adulterate ② cheat; play tricks ③ be unnatural; behave affectedly

【作价】evaluate; fix a price for sth: 旧首饰～变卖 *sell old jewelry at a reduced price*

【作奸犯科】commit offences against law and discipline; perpetrate crimes in defiance of the law

【作茧自缚】get enmeshed in a web of one's own spinning; spin a cocoon around oneself

【作践】① spoil; ruin; waste: ～东西 *spoil things* ② run sb down; disparage

【作乐】enjoy oneself; have a good time; make merry

【作料】condiments; seasoning

【作乱】incite a revolt

【作难】[书] ① feel awkward; feel embarrassed ② make things difficult for sb

【作孽】do evil

【作弄】tease; make a fool of; play a trick on; poke fun at

【作呕】feel like vomiting; feel sick; be overcome by nausea

【作陪】be invited to keep the chief guest company at a banquet; help entertain the guest of honour

【作品】works (of literature and art)

【作情】[方] ① admire ② send gifts ③ mediate; arbitrate ④ feel grateful to sb ⑤ strike a pose; make a pretence

【作曲】① compose; write music: 他十二岁第一次～。*He began to compose when he was* 12 *years old.* ② write music (for a song): ～家 *composer*

【作死色】get angry; show signs of anger

【作死】seek death; court trouble; take the road to ruin

【作速】hasten; lose no time: 你的事情我们一定～处理。*We will deal with your matter as soon as possible.*

【作祟】① (of ghosts, spirits, etc.) haunt ② cause trouble, make mischief: 对金钱的欲望在～。*All this trouble is caused by the lust for fortune.*

【作痛】ache; have a pain

【作为】① action; conduct; deed: 好的～ *good deed* ② achievement: 有所～ *be able to display one's talent and do well in life* ③ scope for one's abilities or talents ④ look on as; regard as; take as: 以他经验～借鉴 *make use of his experience for reference* ⑤ as; in the capacity, character, or role of: ～父亲，你得给你儿子一些建议。*As your son's father, you should give him some advice.*

【作文】① (of students) write a composition ② composition

【作物】crop: 经济～ *cash (or money) crops* / 低产～ *low-yielding crop*

【作息】work and rest: 按时～ *work and rest according to schedule* / ～时间表 *daily schedule; timetable*

【作响】make a sound: 树叶沙沙～。*The leaves rustled in the wind.*

【作业】① school assignment: 做～ *do one's assignment* ② operation; production; task; work: ～进度 *progress of operation*

【作揖】make a bow with hands folded in front

【作用】① act on; affect: 社会环境的～ *affected by a social environment* ② action; function: 光合～ *photosynthesis* / ～与反～ *action and reaction* ③ effect: 起～ *be effective* / 不起～ *have no effect on sb* ④ purpose; intention; motive

【作用力】【物】acting force

【作战】conduct operation; do battle; fight: 英勇～ *fight heroically* / ～部队 *combat troops* / ～部署 *operational preparations* / ～地图 *battle map* / ～方案 *battle plan* / ～方法 *method of fighting* / ～方式 *mode of operations* / ～方针 *operational principles* / ～基地 *operational base* / ～命令 *combat order* / ～区域 *theatre of war* / ～指挥部 *operational headquarters*

【作者】author; writer: 请回答谁是这本书的～。*Please answer me who is the author of this book.*

【作证】① be used as proof or evidence ② testify; bear witness; give evidence: 传某人～ *call sb to witness*

坐 ① sit: ～一会儿 *sit for a while* ② travel by (or on) (bus, train, plane etc): ～汽车 *ride on a bus* / ～电梯下楼 *go down by life* ③ (of a building) have its back towards: 这间房子～南朝北。*This house faces south.* ④ put (a pan, pot, kettle, etc.) on a fire: 把壶～上 *put the kettle on (the fire)* ⑤ (of a building) say; sink; subside: 这个建筑向后～了。*This building is beginning to slope backwards.* ⑥ (of rifles, guns, etc.) kick back; recoil ⑦ bear; fruit ⑧ be punished

【坐标】【数】coordinate: ～轴 *coordinate axis*

【坐班】have office hours

【坐不下】(of a vehicle, table, room, etc.) have not enough seats for (a certain number of people); cannot seat

【坐不住】fidgety; restless; cannot sit still: 他总是～。*He simply can't sit still for any length of time.*

【坐禅】【宗】sit in meditation

【坐吃山空】remain idle and eat away a whole fortune; spend without earning

【坐得住】can sit still: 他～很适合办公室工作。*He who has the patience to stay behind an office desk is suitable for this job.*

Z

【坐等】sit back and wait：~时机 *sit tight and wait for an opportunity*
【坐定】①［书］sit down；be seated ② be destined
【坐而论道】be a phrase-monger；sit back and indulge in empty talk
【坐骨】【生理】ischium：~神经 *ischial nerve*；*sciatic nerve*
【坐江山】rule the country
【坐井观天】look at the sky from the bottom of a well — have a very narrow view
【坐牢】be imprisoned；be jn jail：他儿子出生的时候，他正在~呢。*He was doing time when his son was born.*
【坐冷板凳】be kept waiting for an assignment；hold an unimportant post and be ignored
【坐立不安】be on tenterhooks；be fidgety；be restless whether sitting or standing：你跑哪儿去了，害得我~。*Where did you go? I became quite restless from anxiety.*
【坐落】be situated；be located；be established：我们家~在山脚下。*Our house is located at the foot of a hill.*
【坐山雕】【动】cinereous vulture
【坐山观虎斗】sit on top of the mountain to watch the tigers fight — watch in safety while others fight，and reap the spoils when both sides are exhausted
【坐失】take no action and lose（a good chance）：~良机 *let slip a golden opportunity*
【坐视】sit by and watch
【坐收渔利】reap third party profit；profit from other's tussle
【坐卧不安】be agitated；be on tenterhooks；unable to sit or sleep at ease
【坐席】① dinner seat ② take one's seat at a banquet table；attend a banquet：她邀请我们今天晚上去她家~。*She invited us to dinner this evening.*
【坐享其成】sit idle and enjoy the fruits of others' work；reap where one has not sown
【坐以待毙】await one's doom；sit still waiting for death；resign oneself to death
【坐月子】［口］lying-in；confinement in childbirth
【坐镇】assume personal command；（of a commander）personally attend to garrison duty
【坐庄】① be a resident buyer of a business firm ② be the banker or dealer（in a gambling game）

座 ① place；seat：这个大厅有2000个~。*This hall seats* 2000. ② base；stand：塑像~儿 *pedestal base* ③【天】constellation ④ used of large and solid thing：一~大楼 *a skyscraper* / 一~大理石像 *a status in marble*
【座舱】① cabin ②（of a fighter）cockpit
【座号】seat number
【座机】sb's private plane
【座谈会】forum；informal discussion；symposium
【座谈】have an informal discussion
【座位】① seat；chair；a thing to sit on：让她坐在~上。*Bring her a seat.* ② place；seat：别忘了给老师留两个~。*Don't forget to reserve two seats for teachers.*
【座右铭】maxim；motto
【座钟】desk clock

做 ① do；make；manufacture；produce：~衣服 *make clothes* ② cook；prepare：~菜 *cook a dish* ③ act；do；engage in：~零活儿 *do odd jobs* / 从小事~起 *start with little things* ④ be；become：~翻译 *act as an interpreter* / ~厨师 *become a cooker* ⑤ compose；write：~诗一首 *write a poem* ⑥ hold a home celebration ⑦ be used as；serve as：草可以~造纸材料。*Glass may be used as one of the row material for paper.* ⑧form or contract a relationship：他想和你~朋友。*He wants to make friends with you.*
【做爱】make love
【做伴】keep sb company
【做操】do exercises；do gymnastics
【做大】［旧］give oneself airs；put on airs；assume airs
【做到】accomplish；achieve：说到~ *be true to one's promise*
【做东】act as host to sb；host sb；play the host：这次我~。*This is my treat.*
【做法】practice；method of work；way of doing or making a thing：惯常~ *habitual practice*
【做饭】do the cooking prepare a meal
【做工】① work；do manual work：她在工厂做~。*She works in a factory.* ② charge for the making of sth：这件衬衫~二十元。*The charge for the tailoring of this suit was twenty yuan.* ③ workmanship：~低劣 *of poor workmanship*
【做官】be an official；hold an official position
【做鬼】get up to mischief；play an underhand game
【做好人】try to get along with everyone（often at the expense of principle）；try to be a good fellow
【做活儿】do manual labour；work：整天~ *toil all today*
【做绝】leave no room for manoeuvre；allow no latitude：不要把事情~了。*Don't push things to the extreme.*
【做客】be a guest：欢迎来我家~。*You are welcome to my house.*
【做礼拜】be at church；go to church
【做买卖】carry on trade；do business：~的人 *businessman*；*merchant*；*trader*
【做满月】celebrate a baby's birth when he is one month old
【做媒】be a matchmaker（or go-between）
【做梦】① dream ② have a dream
【做亲】① become related by marriage ② get married
【做人】① conduct oneself；behave：懂的~处事的道理 *know how to conduct oneself in society* ② be an upright person
【做生意】be engaged in trade；do business
【做事】① do work；do a deed；handle affairs；act：她~一直认真负责。*She is conscientious in everything she does.* ② work；have a job

Z

【做寿】celebrate the birthday (usu. of elderly people); give a birthday party

【做文章】① make an issue of sth; make a fuss about sth ② write a composition:抓住这件小事她大~。*She made a fuss about a trifling matter.*

【做戏】① act in a play; put on a play ② play; act; pretend

【做学问】do research; engage in scholarship; do academic work

【做样子】make a show; do sth for the sake of appearance

【做一天和尚撞一天钟】go on tolling the bell as long as one is a monk do the least that is expected of one; take a passive attitude towards one's work

【做贼心虚】have a guilty conscience:他们的表情暴露了他们~。*Their appearances revealed their own guilty conscience.*

【做主】① decide; take the responsibility for a decision ② support; back up

【做针线】sew; do needlework

【做作】affected; artificial; unnatural:她的表演太~。*Her acting is overdone.*

附录一　世界各国家、地区、首都(或首府)及货币名称表

Appendix 1　Countries, Regions, Capitals and Currencies

国家、地区 Country, Region	简称 Abbreviation	首都、首府 Capital	货币 Currency	地理位置 Location
阿尔巴尼亚共和国 the Republic of Albania	Albania	地拉那 Tirana	列克 Lek	欧洲 Europe
阿尔及利亚民主人民共和国 the Democratic People's Republic of Algeria	Algiria	阿尔及尔 Algiers	阿尔及利亚第纳尔 Algerian Dinar (Ad)	非洲 Africa
阿富汗伊斯兰国 the Islamic State of Afghanistan	Afghanistan	喀布尔 Kabul	阿富汗尼 Afghani (Af)	亚洲 Asia
阿根廷共和国 the Republic of Argentina	Argentina	布宜诺斯艾利斯 Buenos Aires	比索 Peso	美洲 Americas
阿拉伯埃及共和国 the Arab Republic of Egypt	Egypt	开罗 Cairo	埃及镑 Egyptian Pound	非洲 Africa
阿拉伯联合酋长国 the United Arab Emirates	the United Arab Emirates	阿布扎比 Abu Dhabi	迪拉姆 Dirham (Dh)	亚洲 Asia
阿拉伯叙利亚共和国 the Syrian Arab Republic	Syrian	大马士革 Damascus	叙利亚镑 Syrian Pound	亚洲 Asia
阿鲁巴(荷) Aruba (Dutch)	Aruba	奥兰也斯特德 Oranjestad	阿鲁巴弗罗林 Aruban Florin (AFl)	美洲 Americas
阿曼苏丹国 the Sultanate of Oman	Oman	马斯喀特 Muscat	阿曼里亚尔 Rial Omani (RO)	亚洲 Asia
阿塞拜疆共和国 Azerbaijani Republic	Azerbaijani	巴库 Baku	马纳特 Manat	亚洲 Asia
埃塞俄比亚联邦民主共和国 the Federal Democratic Republic of Ethiopia	Ethiopia	亚的斯亚贝巴 Addis Ababa	比尔 Birr	非洲 Africa
爱尔兰共和国 the Republic of Ireland (Eire)	Ireland	都柏林 Dublin	爱尔兰镑 Irish Pound (I£)	欧洲 Europe
爱沙尼亚共和国 the Republic of Estonia	Estonia	塔林 Tallinn	爱沙尼亚克朗 Estonian Kroom	欧洲 Europe
安道尔公国 the Principality of Andorra	Andorra	安道尔城 Andorra la Vella	西班牙比塞塔和法国法郎 Spanish Peseta & Franc	欧洲 Europe
安哥拉共和国 the Republic of Angola	Angola	罗安达 Luanda	新宽扎 New Kwanza	非洲 Africa
安圭拉(英) Anguilla (UK)	Anguilla	瓦利 Valley	东加勒比元 East Caribbean Dollar(EC $)	美洲 Americas
安提瓜和巴布达 Antigua and Barbuda	Antigua and Barbuda	圣约翰 St. John's	东加勒比元 East Caribbean Dollar(EC $)	美洲 Americas
奥地利共和国 the Republic of Austria	Austria	维也纳 Vienna	奥地利先令 Austrian Schilling	欧洲 Europe
澳大利亚联邦 the Commonwealth of Australia	Australia	堪培拉 Canberra	澳大利亚元 Australian Dollar($A)	大洋洲及 太平洋岛屿 Oceania and the Pacific Islands
巴巴多斯 Barbados	Barbados	布里奇敦 Bridgetown	巴巴多斯元 Barbados Dollar	美洲 Americas
巴布亚新几内亚独立国 the Independent State of Papua New Guinea	Papua New Guinea	莫尔兹比港 Port Moresby	基纳 Kina (K)	大洋洲及 太平洋岛屿 Oceania and the Pacific Islands
巴哈马联邦 the Commonwealth of the Bahamas	the Bahamas	拿骚 Nassau	巴哈巴元 Bahamian Dollar(B $)	美洲 Americas
巴基斯坦伊斯兰共和国 the Islamic Republic of Pakistan	Pakistan	伊斯兰堡 Islamabad	巴基斯坦卢比 Pakistan Rupee	亚洲 Asia
巴拉圭共和国 the Republic of Paraguay	Paraguay	亚松森 Asuncion	瓜拉尼 Guarani (G)	美洲 Americas
巴勒斯坦 Palestine	Palestine	耶路撒冷* Jerusalem		亚洲 Asia
巴林国 the State of Bahrain	Bahrain	麦纳麦 Manama	巴林第纳尔 Bahrain Dinar (BD)	亚洲 Asia
巴拿马共和国 the Republic of Panama	Panama	巴拿马城 Panama City	巴波亚 Balboa (B)	美洲 Americas

国家、地区 Country, Region	简称 Abbreviation	首都、首府 Capital	货币 Currency	地理位置 Location
巴西联邦共和国 the Federative Republic of Brazil	Brazil	巴西利亚 Brasilia	雷亚尔 Real	美洲 Americas
白俄罗斯共和国 the Republic of Belarus	Belarus	明斯克 Minsk	白俄罗斯卢布 Belarus Rouble	欧洲 Europe
百慕大群岛(英) the Bermuda Islands (UK)	Bermuda	哈密尔顿 Hamilton	百慕大元 Bermuda Dollar (B $)	美洲 Americas
保加利亚共和国 the Republic of Bulgaria	Bulgaria	索菲亚 Sofia	列弗 Lev	欧洲 Europe
贝宁共和国 the Republic of Benin	Benin	波多诺伏 Porto_Novo	非洲法郎 African Franc (FA)	非洲 Africa
比利时王国 the Kingdom of Belgium	Belgium	布鲁塞尔 Brussels	比利时法郎 Franc Belge (FB)	欧洲 Europe
秘鲁共和国 the Republic of Peru	Peru	利马 Lima	新索尔 New Sol	美洲 Americas
冰岛共和国 the Republic of Iceland	Iceland	雷克雅未克 Reykjavik	冰岛克朗 Icelandic Krona (IKr)	欧洲 Europe
波多黎各自由邦(美) the Commonwealth of Puerto Rico (US)	Puerto Rico	圣胡安 San Juan	美元 US Dollar ($)	美洲 Americas
波兰共和国 the Republic of Poland	Poland	华沙 Warsaw	兹罗提 Zloty (ZL)	欧洲 Europe
波斯尼亚和黑塞哥维那共和国 the Republic of Bosnia and Herzegovina	Bosnia and Herzegovina	萨拉热窝 Sarajevo	第纳尔 Dinar	欧洲 Europe
玻利维亚共和国 the Republic of Bolivia	Bolivia	苏克雷 Sucre	玻利维亚诺 Boliviano (B)	美洲 Americas
伯利兹 Belize	Belize	贝尔莫潘 Belmopan	伯利兹元 Belizean Dollar (BZ $)	美洲 Americas
博茨瓦纳共和国 the Republic of Botswana	Botswana	哈博罗内 Gaborone	普拉 Pula (P)	非洲 Africa
不丹王国 the Kingdom of Bhutan	Bhutan	廷布 Thimphu	努尔特鲁姆 Ngultrum (Nu)	亚洲 Asia
布基纳法索 Burkina Faso	Burkina Faso	瓦加杜古 Ouagadougou	非洲法郎 African Franc	非洲 Africa
布隆迪共和国 the Republic of Burundi	布琼布拉 Bujumbura	布隆迪法郎 Burundi Franc (Fbu)	非洲 Africa	Burundi
朝鲜民主主义人民共和国 the Democratic People's Republic of Korea	Korea	平壤 Pyongyang	朝鲜元 Won	亚洲 Asia
赤道几内亚共和国 the Republic of Equatorial Guinea	Equatorial Guinea	马拉博 Malabo	非洲法郎 African Franc (FA)	非洲 Africa
大不列颠及北爱尔兰联合王国 the United Kingdom of Great Britain and Northern Ireland	U. K.	伦敦 London	英镑 Pound Sterling (£)	欧洲 Europe
大韩民国 the Republic of Korea	South Korea	汉城 Seoul	韩元 Won	亚洲 Asia
丹麦王国 the Kindom of Denmark	Denmark	哥本哈根 Copenhagen	丹麦克朗 Danish Krone (DKr)	欧洲 Europe
德意志联邦共和国 the Federal Republic of Germany	Germany	柏林 Bermin	德意志马克 Deutsche Mark (DM)	欧洲 Europe
东萨摩亚(美) Eastern Samoa (US)	Eastern Samoa	帕果帕果 Pago_Pago	美元 US Dollar	大洋洲及太平洋岛屿 Oceania and the Pacific Islands
多哥共和国 the Republic of Togo	Togo	洛美 Lomé	非洲法郎 African Franc (FA)	非洲 Africa
多米尼加共和国 the Dominican Republic	Dominica	圣多明各 Santo Domingo	比索 Peso	美洲 Americas
多米尼克联邦 the Commonwealth of Dominica	the Dominican Republic	罗索 Roseau	东加勒比元 East Caribbean Dollar(EC $)	美洲 Americas
俄罗斯联邦 the Russian Federation	Russia	莫斯科 Moscow	卢布 Rouble (Ruble)	欧洲 Europe
厄瓜多尔共和国 the Republic of Ecuador	Ecuador	基多 Quito	苏克雷 Sucre	美洲 Americas
厄立特里亚国 Eritrea	Eritrea	阿斯马拉 Asmara	比尔 Birr	非洲 Africa

国家、地区 Country, Region	简称 Abbreviation	首都、首府 Capital	货币 Currency	地理位置 Location
法兰西共和国 the Republic of France	France	巴黎 Paris	法郎 Franc	欧洲 Europe
法属波利尼西亚 French Polynesia	French Polynesia	帕皮提 Papeete	太平洋法郎 Pacific Franc	大洋洲及太平洋岛屿 Oceania and the Pacific Islands
梵蒂冈城国 the Vatican City State	Vatican	梵蒂冈城 the Vatican City	意大利里拉 Italian Lira	欧洲 Europe
菲律宾共和国 the Republic of the Philippines	Philippines	马尼拉 Manila	菲律宾比索 Philippine Peso	亚洲 Asia
斐济群岛共和国 the Republic of the Fiji Islands	Fiji	苏瓦 Suva	斐济元 Fiji Dollar（$ F）	大洋洲及太平洋岛屿 Oceania and the Pacific Islands
芬兰共和国 the Republic of Finland	Finland	赫尔辛基 Helsinki	芬兰马克 Finnish Markka（FIM）	欧洲 Europe
佛得角共和国 the Republic of Cape Verde	Cape Verde	普拉亚 Praia	埃斯库多 Escudo（Esc）	非洲 Africa
冈比亚共和国 the Republic of Gambia	Gambia	班珠尔 Banjul	达拉西 Dalasi	非洲 Africa
刚果共和国 the Republic of the Congo	Congo	布拉柴维尔 Brazzaville	非洲法郎 African Franc（FA）	非洲 Africa
刚果民主共和国 the Democratic Republic of Congo	Co	金沙萨 Kinshasa	刚果法郎 Congolese Franc	非洲 Africa
哥伦比亚共和国 the Republic of Colombia	Colombia	圣菲波哥大 Santa Fe Bogota	比索 Peso	美洲 Americas
哥斯达黎加共和国 the Republic of Costa Rica	Costa Rica	圣何塞 San José	科朗 Colón	美洲 Americas
格林纳达 Grenada	圣乔治 St. George's	东加勒比元 East Caribbean Dollar（EC $）	美洲 Americas	美洲 Americas
格陵兰(丹) Greenland（Danish）	Greeland	戈德堆普 Godthaab	丹麦克朗 Danish Krone（DKr）	欧洲 Europe
格鲁吉亚共和国 the Republic of Georgia	Georgia	第比里斯 Tbilisi	拉里 Lari	亚洲 Asia
古巴共和国 the Republic of Cuba	Cuba	哈瓦那 La Havana	比索 Peso	美洲 Americas
瓜德罗普(法) Guadeloupe（French）	Guadeloupe	巴斯特尔 Basse_Terre	法国法郎 French Franc	美洲 Americas
关岛(美) Guam（US）	Guam	阿加尼亚 Agana	美元 US Dollar	大洋洲及太平洋岛屿 Oceania and the Pacific Islands
圭亚那(法) Guyana（French）	French Guiana	卡宴 Cayenne	法国法郎 French Franc	美洲 Americas
圭亚那合作共和国 the Cooperative Republic of Guyana	Guyana	乔治敦 Georgetown	圭亚那元 Guyana Dollar	美洲 Americas
哈萨克斯坦共和国 the Republic of Kazakhstan	Kazakhstan	阿斯塔纳 Astana	坚戈 Tanga	亚洲 Asia
海地共和国 the Republic of Haiti	Haiti	太子港 Port_au_Prince	古德 Gourde	美洲 Americas
荷兰王国 the Kingdom of the Netherlands	the Netherlands	阿姆斯特丹 Amsterdam	荷兰盾 Guilder or Florin（Fl）	欧洲 Europe
荷属安的列斯 Netherlands Antilles	Netherlands Antilles	威廉斯塔德 Willemstad	荷属安的列斯盾 Netherlands Antilles Guilder or Florin	美洲 Americas
洪都拉斯共和国 the Republic of Honduras	Honduras	特古西加尔巴 Tegucigalpa	伦皮拉 Lempira	美洲 Americas
基里巴斯共和国 the Republic of Kiribati	Kiribati	塔拉瓦 Tarawa	澳大利亚元 Australian Dollar（$A）	大洋洲及太平洋岛屿 Oceania and the Pacific Islands
吉布提共和国 the Republic of Djibouti	Djibouti	吉布提市 Djibouti	吉布提法郎 Djibouti Franc（DF）	非洲 Africa
吉尔吉斯共和国 Kyrghyz Republic	Kyrghyz	比什凯克 Bishkek	索姆 Som	亚洲 Asia

国家、地区 Country, Region	简称 Abbreviation	首都、首府 Capital	货币 Currency	地理位置 Location
几内亚比绍共和国 the Republic of Guinea_Bissau	Guinea-Bissau	比绍 Bissau	比索 Peso	非洲 Africa
几内亚共和国 the Republic of Guinea	Guinea	科纳克里 Conakry	几内亚法郎 Guinea Franc (GF)	非洲 Africa
加拿大 Canada	Canada	渥太华 Ottawa	加拿大元 Canadian Dollar (C $)	美洲 Americas
加纳共和国 the Republic of Ghana	Ghana	阿克拉 Accra	塞迪 Cedi	非洲 Africa
加蓬共和国 the Republic of Gabon	Gabon	利伯维尔 Libreville	非洲法郎 African Franc (FA)	非洲 Africa
柬埔寨王国 the Kingdom of Cambodia	Cambodia	金边 Phnom Penh	瑞尔 Riel	亚洲 Asia
捷克共和国 the Czech Republic	Czech	布拉格 Prague	捷克克朗 Czech Crown	欧洲 Europe
津巴布韦共和国 the Republic of Zimbabwe	Zimbabwe	哈拉雷 Harare	津巴布韦元 Zimbabwe Dollar (Z $)	非洲 Africa
喀麦隆共和国 the Republic of Cameroon	Cameroon	雅温得 Yaoundé	非洲法郎 African Franc (FA)	非洲 Africa
卡塔尔国 the State of Qatar	Qatar	多哈 Doha	卡塔尔里亚尔 Qatar Riyal (QR)	亚洲 Asia
开曼群岛(英) Cayman Islands (UK)	Cayman Islands	乔治敦 Georgetown	开曼元 Cayman Dollar	美洲 Americas
科摩罗伊斯兰联邦共和国 the Islamic Federal Republic of Comoros	the Comoros	莫罗尼 Moroni	科摩罗法郎 Comoros Franc	非洲 Africa
科特迪瓦共和国 the Republic of Cote d'Ivoire	Cote d'Ivoire	亚穆苏克罗 Yamoussoukro	非洲法郎 African Franc (FA)	非洲 Africa
科威特国 the State of Kuwait	Kuwait	科威特城 Kuwait City	科威特第纳尔 Kuwait Dinar (KD)	亚洲 Asia
克罗地亚共和国 the Republic of Croatia	Croatia	萨格勒布 Zagreb	库纳 Kuna	欧洲 Europe
肯尼亚共和国 the Republic of Kenya	Kenya	内罗毕 Nairobi	肯尼亚镑 Kenya Pound (K£)	非洲 Africa
库克群岛(新) the Cook Islands (New Zealand)	the Cook Islands	阿瓦鲁阿 Avarua	新西兰元 New Zealand Dollar($NZ)	大洋洲及 太平洋岛屿 Oceania and the Pacific Islands
拉脱维亚共和国 the Republic of Latvia	Latvia	里加 Riga	拉特 Lat	欧洲 Europe
莱索托王国 the Kingdom of Lesotho	Lesotho	马塞卢 Maseru	洛蒂 Loti	非洲 Africa
老挝人民民主共和国 the Lao Peopleś Democratic Republic	Laos	贝鲁特 Beirut	黎巴嫩镑 Lebanese Pound(£ L)	亚洲 Asia
黎巴嫩共和国 the Rpublic of Lebanon	Lebanon	贝鲁特 Beirut	黎巴嫩镑 Lebanese Pound (£ L)	亚洲 Asia
立陶宛共和国 the Republic of Lithuania	Lithuania	维尔纽斯 Vilnius	利塔斯 Litas (Lt)	欧洲 Europe
利比里亚共和国 the Republic of Liberia	Liberia	蒙罗维亚 Monrovia	利比里亚元 Liberian Dollar (L $)	非洲 Africa
列支敦士登公国 the Principality of Liechtenstein	Liechtenstein	瓦杜兹 Vaduz	瑞士法郎 Swiss Franc (SF)	欧洲 Europe
留尼汪岛 Réunion	Réunion	圣旦尼 Saint_Denis	法国法郎 French Franc	非洲 Africa
卢森堡大公国 the Grand Duchy of Luxembourg	Luxembourg	卢森堡 Luxembourg	卢森堡法郎 Franc Luxembourgeois	欧洲 Europe
卢旺达共和国 the Republic of Rwanda	Rwanda	基加利 Kigali	卢旺达法郎 Rwanda Franc	非洲 Africa
罗马尼亚 Romania	Romania	布加勒斯特 Bucharest	摩尔多瓦列伊 Moldovian Leu	欧洲 Europe
马达加斯加共和国 the Republic of Madagascar	Madagascar	塔那那利佛 Antananarivo	马达加斯加法郎 Madagascar Franc	非洲 Africa
马尔代夫共和国 the Rpublic of Maldives	Maldives	马累 Male	拉菲亚 Rufiyaa	亚洲 Asia
马耳他共和国 the Republic of Malta	Malta	瓦莱塔 Valletta	马耳他里拉 Malta Lira (LM)	欧洲 Europe

国家、地区 Country, Region	简称 Abbreviation	首都、首府 Capital	货币 Currency	地理位置 Location
马拉维共和国 the Republic of Malawi	Malawi	利隆圭 Lilongwe	马拉维克瓦查 Malawi Kwacha(K)	非洲 Africa
马来西亚 Malaysia	Malaysia	吉隆坡 Kuala Lumpur	林吉特 Ringgit	亚洲 Asia
马里共和国 the Republic of Mali	Mali	巴马科 Bamako	非洲法郎 African Franc (FA)	非洲 Africa
马其顿共和国 the Republic of Macedonia	Macedonia	斯科普里 Skopje	代纳尔 Denar	欧洲 Europe
马绍尔群岛共和国 the Republic of the Marshall Islands	Marshall	马朱罗 Majuro	美元 US Dollar	大洋洲及 太平洋岛屿 Oceania and the Pacific Islands
马提尼克(法) Martinique (French)	Martinique	法兰西堡 Fort_de_France	法国法郎 French Franc	美洲 Americas
马约特岛(法) Mayotte (French)	Mayotte	扎乌兹 Dzaoudzi	法国法郎 French Franc	非洲 Africa
毛里求斯共和国 the Republic of Mauritius	Mauritius	路易港 Port Louis	毛里求斯卢比 Mauritius Rupee	非洲 Africa
毛里塔尼亚伊斯兰共和国 the Islamic Republic of Mauritania	Mauritiania	努瓦克肖特 Nouakchott	乌吉亚 Ouguiya	非洲 Africa
美利坚合众国 the United States of America	U. S. A.	华盛顿特区 Washington D. C.	美元 US Dollar (US $)	美洲 Americas
美属维尔京群岛 the Virgin Islands of the United States	the virgin Islands of the United States	夏洛特阿马利亚 Charlotte Amalie	美元 US Dollar	美洲 Americas
蒙古国 the State of Mongolia	Mongolia	乌兰巴托 Ulan Bator	图格里克 Tugrik	亚洲 Asia
蒙特塞拉特(英) Montserrat (UK)	Montserrat	普利茅斯 Plymouth	东加勒比元 East Caribbean Dollar	美洲 Americas
孟加拉人民共和国 the People's Republic of Bangladesh	Bangladesh	达卡 Dhaka	塔卡 Taka	亚洲 Asia
密克罗尼西亚联邦 the Federated States of Micronesia	Micronesia	波纳佩 Ponape	美元 US Dollar	大洋洲及 太平洋岛屿 Oceania and the Pacific Islands
缅甸联邦 the Union of Myanmar	Myanmar	仰光 Yangon	缅元 Kyat	亚洲 Asia
摩尔多瓦共和国 the Republic of Moldova	Moldova	基希讷乌 Kishinev	摩尔多瓦列伊 Moldovian Leu	欧洲 Europe
摩洛哥王国 the Kingdom of Morocco	Morocco	拉巴特 Rabat	迪拉姆 Dirham	非洲 Africa
摩纳哥公国 the Principality of Monaco	Monaco	摩纳哥 Monaco_Ville	法国法郎 French Franc	欧洲 Europe
莫桑比克共和国 the Republic of Mozambique	Mozambique	马普托 Maputo	梅蒂卡尔 Metical	非洲 Africa
墨西哥合众国 the United States of Mexico	Mexico	墨西哥城 Mexico City	比索 Peso	美洲 Americas
纳米比亚共和国 the Republic of Namibia	Namibia	温得和克 Windhoek	纳米比亚元 Namibia Dollar	非洲 Africa
南非共和国 the Republic of South Africa	South Africa	比勒陀利亚 Pretoria	兰特 Rand (R)	非洲 Africa
南斯拉夫联盟共和国 the Federal Republic of Yugoslavia	Yugoslavia	贝尔格莱德 Belgrade	第纳尔 Dinar	欧洲 Europe
瑙鲁共和国 the Republic of Nauru	Nauru	亚伦区 Yaren District	澳大利亚元 Australian Dollar($ A)	大洋洲及 太平洋岛屿 Oceania and the Pacific Islands
尼泊尔王国 the Kingdom of Nepal	Nepal	加德满都 Kathmandu	尼泊尔卢比 Nepalese Rupee (NR)	亚洲 Asia
尼加拉瓜共和国 the Republic of Nicaragua	Nicaragua	马那瓜 Managua	科多巴 Córdoba	美洲 Americas
尼日尔共和国 the Republic of Niger	Niger	尼亚美 Niamey	非洲法郎 African Franc (FA)	非洲 Africa
尼日利亚联邦共和国 the Federal Republic of Nigeria	Nigeria	阿布贾 Abuja	奈拉 Naira (N)	非洲 Africa

国家、地区 Country, Region	简称 Abbreviation	首都、首府 Capital	货币 Currency	地理位置 Location
纽埃(新) Nieu (New Zealand)	Niue Island	阿洛菲 Alofi	新西兰元 New Zealand Dollar($ NZ)	大洋洲及 太平洋岛屿 Oceania and the Pacific Islands
挪威王国 the Kingdom of Norway	Norway	奥斯陆 Oslo	挪威克朗 Norwegian Krone	欧洲 Europe
诺福克岛(澳) Norfolk Island (Australian)	Norfolk Isalnd	金斯敦 Kingstown	澳元 Australian Dollar($ A)	大洋洲及 太平洋岛屿 Oceania and the Pacific Islands
帕劳共和国 the Republic of Palau	Palau	科罗尔 Koror	美元 US Dollar	大洋洲及 太平洋岛屿 Oceania and the Pacific Islands
葡萄牙共和国 the Portuguese Republic	Portugal	里斯本 Lisbon	埃斯库多 Escudo	欧洲 Europe
日本国 Japan	Japan	东京 Tokyo	日元 Yen	亚洲 Asia
瑞典王国 the Kingdom of Sweden	Sweden	斯德哥尔摩 Stockholm	瑞典克朗 Swedish Krona	欧洲 Europe
瑞士联邦 the Confederation of Switzerland	Switzerland	伯尔尼 Bern(e)	瑞士法郎 Swiss Franc	欧洲 Europe
萨尔瓦多共和国 the Republic of El Salvador	El Salvador	圣萨尔瓦多 San Salvador	科郎 Colón	美洲 Americas
萨摩亚独立国 the Independent State of Samoa	Somoa	阿皮亚 Apia	塔拉 Tala	大洋洲及 太平洋岛屿 Oceania and the Pacific Islands
塞拉利昂共和国 the Republic of Sierra Leone	Sierra Leone	弗里敦 Freetown	利昂 Leone (L)	非洲 Africa
塞内加尔共和国 the Republic of Senegal	Sierra Leone	达喀尔 Dakar	非洲法郎 African Franc (FA)	非洲 Africa
塞浦路斯共和国 the Republic of Cyprus	Cyprus	尼科西亚 Nicosia	塞浦路斯镑 Cyprus Pound (Cyprus £)	亚洲 Asia
塞舌尔共和国 the Republic of Seychelles	Seychelles	维多利亚 Victoria	塞舌尔卢比 Seychelles Rupee	非洲 Africa
沙特阿拉伯王国 the Kingdom of Saudi Arabia	Saudi Arabia	利雅得 Riyadh	沙特里亚尔 Saudi Riyal	亚洲 Asia
圣多美和普林西比民主共和国 the Democratic Republic of So Tomé Principe	São Tomé and Principe	圣多美 Sao Tomé	多布拉 Dobra (Db)	非洲 Africa
圣卢西亚 St. Lucia	St. Lucia	卡斯特里 Castries	东加勒比元 East Caribbean Dollar (EC)	美洲 Americas
圣马力诺共和国 the Republic of San Marino	San Marino	圣马力诺 San Marino	意大利里拉 Italian Lira	欧洲 Europe
斯里兰卡民主社会主义共和国 the Democratic Socialist Republic of Sri Lanka	Sri Lanka	科伦坡 Colombo	斯里兰卡卢比 Sri Lanka Rupee	亚洲 Asia
斯洛伐克共和国 the Slovak Republic	Slouak	布拉迪斯拉发 Bratislava	克朗 Slovak Crown	欧洲 Europe
斯洛文尼亚共和国 the Republic of Slovenia	Slovenia	卢布尔雅那 Ljubljana	托拉尔 Tolar	欧洲 Europe
斯威士兰王国 the Kingdom of Swaziland	Swaziland	姆巴巴纳 Mbabane	埃马兰吉尼 Emalangeni	非洲 Africa
苏丹共和国 the Republic of Sudan	Sudan	喀土穆 Khartoum	苏丹镑 Sudanese Pound	非洲 Africa
苏里南共和国 the Republic of Suriname	Suriname	帕拉马里博 Paramaribo	苏里南盾或弗罗林 Surinam Guilder or Florin	美洲 Americas
所罗门群岛 Solomon Islands	Solomon Islands	霍尼亚拉 Honiara	所罗门群岛元 Solomon Dollar	大洋洲及 太平洋岛屿 Oceania and the Pacific Islands
索马里共和国 the Somali Republic	Somalia	摩加迪沙 Mogadishu	索马里先令 Somali Shilling (So. Sh.)	非洲 Africa
塔吉克斯坦共和国 the Republic of Tadzhikistan	Tadzhikistan	杜尚别 Dushanbe	塔吉克卢布 Tajik Rouble (Ruble)	亚洲 Asia
泰王国 the Kingdom of Thailand	Thailand	曼谷 Bangkok	铢 Baht	亚洲 Asia

国家、地区 Country, Region	简称 Abbreviation	首都、首府 Capital	货币 Currency	地理位置 Location
坦桑尼亚联合共和国 the United Republic of Tanzania	Tanzania	达累斯萨拉姆 Dar es Salaam	坦桑尼亚先令 Tanzania Shilling	非洲 Africa
汤加王国 the Kingdom of Tonga	Tonga	努库阿洛法 Nukualofa	潘加 Pa'anga	大洋洲及 太平洋岛屿 Oceania and the Pacific Islands
特立尼达和多巴哥共和国 the Republic of Trinidad & Tobago	Trinidad & Tobago	西班牙港 Port of Spain	特立尼达和多巴哥元 Trinidad & Tobago Dollar	美洲 Americas
突尼斯共和国 the Republic of Tunisia	Tunisia	突尼斯 Tunis	突尼斯第纳尔 Tunisian Dinar (TD)	非洲 Africa
图瓦卢 Tuvalu	Tuvalu	富纳富提 Funafuti	澳元和图瓦卢硬币 Australian or Tuvaluan Dollars	大洋洲及 太平洋岛屿 Oceania and the Pacific Islands
土耳其共和国 the Republic of Turkey	Turkey	安卡拉 Ankara	土耳其里拉 Turkish Lira (TL)	亚洲 Asia
土库曼斯坦 Turmenistan	Turkmenistan	阿什哈巴德 Ashkhabad	马纳特 Manat	亚洲 Asia
瓦利斯和富图纳群岛(法) Wallis and Futuna Islands (French)	Wallis and Futuna	马塔乌图 Mata_Utu	太平洋法郎 Pacific Franc	大洋洲及 太平洋岛屿 Oceania and the Pacific Islands
瓦努阿图共和国 the Republic of Vanuatu	Vanuatu	维拉港 Port Vila	瓦图 Vatu	大洋洲及 太平洋岛屿 Oceania and the Pacific Islands
危地马拉共和国 the Republic of Guatemala	Guatemala	危地马拉城 Guatemala City	格查尔 Quetzal	美洲 Americas
委内瑞拉共和国 the Republic of Venezuela	Venezuela	加拉加斯 Caracas	玻利瓦尔 Bolivar	美洲 Americas
文莱达鲁萨兰国 Negara Brunei Darussalam	Brunei	斯里巴加湾市 Bandar Seri Begawan	文莱元 Brunei Dollar (Br $)	亚洲 Asia
乌干达共和国 the Republic of Uganda	Uganda	坎帕拉 Kampala	乌干达先令 Uganda Shilling	非洲 Africa
乌克兰 Ukraine	Ukraine	基辅 Kyiv (Kiev)	格里夫纳 Hryyina	欧洲 Europe
乌拉圭东岸共和国 the Oriental Republic of Uruguay	Uruguay	蒙得维的亚 Montevideo	新比索 New Peso	美洲 Americas
乌兹别克斯坦共和国 the Republic of Uzbekistan	Uzbekistan	塔什干 Tashkent	苏姆 Sum	亚洲 Asia
西班牙王国 the Kingdom of Spain	Spain	马德里 Madrid	比塞塔 Peseta	欧洲 Europe
希腊共和国 the Hellenic Republic (or the Republic of Greece)	Greece	雅典 Athens	德拉克马 Drachma	欧洲 Europe
锡金 Sikkim	Sikkim	甘托克 Gangtok	印度卢比 Indian Rupee	亚洲 Asia
新加坡共和国 the Republic of Singapore	Singapore	新加坡城 Singapore City	新加坡元 Singapore Dollar (S $)	亚洲 Asia
新喀里多尼亚(法) New Caledonia (French)	New Caledonia	努美阿 Noumea	太平洋法郎 Pacific Franc	大洋洲及 太平洋岛屿 Oceania and the Pacific Islands
新西兰 New Zealand	New Zealand	惠灵顿 Wellington	新西兰元 New Zealand Dollar($NZ)	大洋洲及 太平洋岛屿 Oceania and the Pacific Islands
匈牙利共和国 the Republic of Hungary	Hungary	布达佩斯 Budapest	福林 Forint	欧洲 Europe
牙买加 Jamaica	Jamaica	金斯敦 Kingstown	牙买加元 Jamaican Dollar(J $)	美洲 Americas
亚美尼亚共和国 the Republic of Armenia	Armenia	埃里温 Yerevan	德拉姆 Dram	亚洲 Asia
也门共和国 the Republic of Yemen	Yemen	萨那 Sana'a	里亚尔 Rial	亚洲 Asia

国家、地区 **Country, Region**	简称 **Abbreviation**	首都、首府 **Capital**	货币 **Currency**	地理位置 **Location**
伊拉克共和国 the Republic of Iraq	Iraq	巴格达 Baghdad	伊拉克第纳尔 Iraqi Dinar (ID)	亚洲 Asia
伊朗伊斯兰共和国 the Islamic Republic of Iran	Iran	德黑兰 Tehran	里亚尔 Rial	亚洲 Asia
以色列国 the State of Israel	Israel	耶路撒冷* Jerusalem	谢克尔 Shekel	亚洲 Asia
意大利共和国 the Italian Republic	Italy	罗马 Rome	里拉 Lira	欧洲 Europe
印度共和国 the Republic of India	India	新德里 New Delhi	卢比 Rupee	亚洲 Asia
印度尼西亚共和国 the Republic of Indonesia	Indonesia	雅加达 Jakarta	印尼盾 Indonesia Rupiah (Rp)	亚洲 Asia
约旦哈希姆王国 the Hashemite Kingdom of Jordan	Jordan	安曼 Amman	约旦第纳尔 Jordanian Dinar (JD)	亚洲 Asia
越南社会主义共和国 the Socialist Republic of Viet Nam	Viet Nam	河内 Hanoi	越盾 Dong	亚洲 Asia
赞比亚共和国 the Republic of Zambia	Zambia	卢萨卡 Lusaka	克瓦查 Kwacha	非洲 Africa
乍得共和国 the Republic of Chad	Chad	恩贾梅纳 N'Djamena	非洲法郎 African Franc (FA)	非洲 Africa
智利共和国 the Republic of Chile	Chile	圣地亚哥 Santiago	比索 Peso	美洲 Americas
中非共和国 the Central African Republic	the Central African Republic	班吉 Bangui	非洲法郎 African Franc (FA)	美洲 Americas
中华人民共和国 the People's Republic of China	China	北京 Beijing	人民币元 Renminbi Yuan (RMB)	亚洲 Asia

*巴、以有争议。Disputed by Palestine and Israel.

附录二 世界主要城市时差

Appendix 2 Time Difference in World City

世界主要城市与北京时差表
[说明：+表示早于北京时间；-表示迟于北京时间]

ASIA 亚洲	
城 市(国家)	与北京时差
Abadan 阿巴丹 [伊朗]	-4:30
Abu Dhabi 阿布扎比[阿联酋]	-4
Aden 亚丁 [也门]	-5
Amman 安曼 [约旦]	-6
Ankara 安卡拉 [土耳其]	-6
Baghdad 巴格达 [伊拉克]	-5
Baku 巴库 [阿塞拜疆]	-6
Bandar Seri Begawan 斯里巴加湾港 [文莱]	0
Bangkok 曼谷 [泰国]	-1
Beirut 贝鲁特 [黎巴嫩]	-6
Bombay 孟买 [印度]	-2:30
Calcutta 加尔各答 [印度]	-2:30
Colombo 科伦坡 [斯里兰卡]	-2:30
Damascus 大马士革 [叙利亚]	-6
Dhaka 达卡 [孟加拉]	-2
Djakarta 雅加达 [印度尼西亚]	-1
Guangzhou 广州 [中国]	0
Hanoi 河内 [越南]	-1
Hong Kong 中国香港	0
Irkutsk 伊尔库次克[俄罗斯]	0
Islamabad 伊斯兰堡 [巴基斯坦]	-3
Jerusalem 耶路撒冷 [巴勒斯坦]	-6
Karachi 卡拉奇 [巴基斯坦]	-3
Katmandu 加德满都 [尼泊尔]	-2:30
Kuala Lumpur 吉隆坡 [马来西亚]	0
Kuwait 科威特 [科威特]	-5
Kyoto 京都 [日本]	+1
Macao 澳门地区	0

Manila 马尼拉［菲律宾］	0
Mecca 麦加［沙特］	−5
Nagasaki 长崎［日本］	+1
New Delhi 新德里［印度］	−2:30
Osaka 大阪［日本］	+1
Phnom Penh 金边［柬埔寨］	−1
Pyongyang 平壤［朝鲜］	+1
Rangoon 仰光［缅甸］	−1:30
Rawalpindi 拉瓦尔品第［巴基斯坦］	−3
Seoul 汉城［南朝鲜］	+1
Shanghai 上海［中国］	0
Singapore 新加坡［新加坡］	0
Taibei 台北［中国］	0
Tehran 德黑兰［伊朗］	−4:30
Tokyo 东京［日本］	+1
Ulan Bator 乌兰巴托［蒙古］	0
Yokohama 横滨［日本］	+1

EUROPE 欧洲

城　市(国家)	与北京时差
Aberdeen 阿伯丁［英国］	−8
Amsterdam 阿姆斯特丹［荷兰］	−7
Antwerp 安特卫普［比利时］	−7
Athens 雅典［希腊］	−6
Belfast 贝尔法斯特［英国］	−8
Belgrade 贝尔格莱德［南斯拉夫］	−7
Berlin 柏林［德国］	−7
Birmingham 伯明翰［英国］	−8
Bonn 波恩［德国］	−7
Brussels 布鲁塞尔［比利时］	−7
Bucharest 布加勒斯特［罗马尼亚］	−6
Budapest 布达佩斯［匈牙利］	−7
Constantsa 康斯坦萨［罗马尼亚］	−6
Copenhagen 哥本哈根［丹麦］	−7
Dublin 都柏林［爱尔兰］	−8
Edinburgh 爱丁堡［英国］	−8

Frankfurt 法兰克福［德国］	−7
Gdansk 格但斯克［波兰］	−7
Geneva 日内瓦［瑞士］	−7
Genoa 热那亚［意大利］	−7
Gibraltar 直布罗陀［英国殖民地］	−7
Glasgow 格拉斯哥［英国］	−8
Hamburg 汉堡［德国］	−7
Helsinki 赫尔辛基［芬兰］	−6
Istanbul 伊斯坦布尔［土耳其］	−6
Kiev 基辅［乌克兰］	−5
Leeds 利兹［英国］	−8
Leipzig 莱比锡［德国］	−7
Lisbon 里斯本［葡萄牙］	−8
Liverpool 利物浦［英国］	−8
London 伦敦［英国］	−8
Madrid 马德里［西班牙］	−7
Manchester 曼彻斯特［英国］	−8
Marseilles 马塞［法国］	−7
Milan 米兰［意大利］	−7
Moscow 莫斯科［俄罗斯］	−5
Munich 慕尼黑［德国］	−7
Murmansk 摩尔曼斯克［俄罗斯］	−5
Odessa 敖德萨［乌克兰］	−5
Oslo 奥斯陆［挪威］	−7
Paris 巴黎［法国］	−7
Prague 布拉格［捷克］	−7
Reykjavik 雷克雅未克［冰岛］	−8
Rome 罗马［意大利］	−7
Rotterdam 鹿特丹［荷兰］	−7
St. Petersburg 圣彼得堡［俄罗斯］	−5
Sofia 索非亚［保加利亚］	−6
Stockholm 斯德哥尔摩［瑞典］	−7
Tirana 地拉那［阿尔巴尼亚］	−7
Vatican 梵蒂冈［罗马教廷所在地］	−7
Venice 威尼斯［意大利］	−7

Vienna 维也纳［奥地利］	–7
Warsaw 华沙［波兰］	–7
Zurich 苏黎世［瑞士］	–7
AMERICA 美洲	
城　市(国家)	与北京时差
Anchorage 安克雷奇［美国］	–17
Asuncion 亚松森［巴拉圭］	–12
Atlanta 亚特兰大［美国］	–13
Baltimore 巴尔的摩［美国］	–13
Bogota 波哥大［哥伦比亚］	–13
Boston 波士顿［美国］	–13
Brasilia 巴西利亚［巴西］	–11
Buenos Aires 布宜诺斯艾利斯［阿根廷］	–11
Caracas 加拉加斯［委内瑞拉］	–12
Chicago 芝加哥［美国］	–14
Churchill 丘吉尔港［加拿大］	–14
Colon 科隆［巴拿马］	–13
Dallas 达拉斯［美国］	–14
Denver 丹佛［美国］	–15
Detroit 底特律［美国］	–13
Edmonton 埃德蒙顿［加拿大］	–15
Havana 哈瓦那［古巴］	–13
Houston 休斯敦［美国］	–14
Kingston 金斯敦［牙买加］	–13
La Paz 拉巴斯［玻利维亚］	–12
Las Vegas 拉斯韦加斯［美国］	–16
Lima 利马［秘鲁］	–13
Los Angeles 洛杉矶［美国］	–16
Mexico City 墨西哥城［墨西哥］	–14
Miami 迈阿密［美国］	–13
Montevideo 蒙得维的亚［乌拉圭］	–11
Montreal 蒙特利尔［加拿大］	–13
New Orleans 新奥尔良［美国］	–14
New York 纽约［美国］	–13
Ottawa 渥太华［加拿大］	–13

Panama 巴拿马城［巴拿马］	−13
Paramaribo 帕拉马里博［苏里南］	−11
Philadelphia 费城［美国］	−13
Pittsburgh 匹兹堡［美国］	−13
Port－of－Spain 西班牙港［特立尼达和多巴哥］	−12
Quebec 魁北克［加拿大］	−13
Ria de Janeiro 里约热内卢［巴西］	−11
saint Louis 圣路易斯［美国］	−14
Salt Lake City 盐湖城［美国］	−15
San Diego 圣迭戈［美国］	−16
San Francisco 旧金山(圣弗兰西斯科)［美国］	−16
San Juan 圣胡安［波多黎各］	−12
Santiago 圣地亚哥［智利］	−12
Seattle 西雅图［美国］	−16
Toronto 多伦多［加拿大］	−13
Vancouver 温哥华［加拿大］	−16
Washington, D. C. 华盛顿［美国］	−13
Winnipeg 温尼伯［加拿大］	−14

AFRICA 非洲

城　市(国家)	与北京时差
Abidjan 阿比让［科特迪瓦］	−8
Addis Ababa 亚的斯亚贝巴［埃塞俄比亚］	−5
Alexandria 亚历山大［埃及］	−6
Algiers 阿尔及尔［阿尔及利亚］	−7
Bamako 巴马科［马里］	−8
Beira 贝拉［莫桑比克］	−6
Brazzaville 布拉柴维尔［刚果］	−7
Cairo 开罗［埃及］	−6
Cape Town 开普敦［南非］	−6
Dakar 达喀尔［塞内加尔］	−8
Dar el Beida 达尔贝达(卡萨布兰卡)［摩洛哥］	−8
Dar es Salaam 达累斯萨拉姆［坦桑尼亚］	−5
Djibouti 吉布提［吉布提］	−5
Douala 杜阿拉［喀麦隆］	−7
Durban 德班［南非］	−6

Gaborone 哈博罗内［博茨瓦纳］	−6
Johannesburg 约翰内斯堡［南非］	−6
Kampala 坎帕拉［乌干达］	−5
Kano 卡诺［尼日利亚］	−7
Khartoum 喀土穆［苏丹］	−6
Kinshasa 金沙萨［民主刚果］	−7
Lagos 拉各斯［尼日利亚］	−7
Las Palmas 拉斯帕耳马斯［加那利群岛］	−8
Luanda 罗安达［安哥拉］	−7
Lusaka 卢萨卡［赞比亚］	−6
Maputo 马普托［莫桑比克］	−6
Mogadishu 摩加迪沙［索马里］	−5
Mombasa 蒙巴萨［肯尼亚］	−5
Monrovia 蒙罗维亚［利比里亚］	−8
Nairobi 内罗毕［肯尼亚］	−5
Ndjamena 恩贾梅纳［乍得］	−7
Niamey 尼亚美［尼日尔］	−8
Nouakchott 努瓦克肖特［毛里塔尼亚］	−8
Port Louis 路易港［毛里求斯］	−4
Pretoria 比勒陀利亚［南非］	−6
Rabat 拉巴特［摩洛哥］	−8
São Tome 圣多美［圣多美和普林西比］	−8
Tananarive 塔那那利佛［马达加斯加］	−5
Tripoli 的黎波里［利比亚］	−6
Tunis 突尼斯［突尼斯］	−7
Windhoek 温得和克［纳米比亚］	−6
OCEANIA AND PACIFIC LSLANDS 大洋洲及太平洋岛屿	
城　市(国家)	**与北京时差**
Agana 阿加尼亚［关岛］	+2
Apia 阿皮亚［西萨摩亚］	−19
Auckland 奥克兰［新西兰］	+4
Brisbane 布里斯班［澳大利亚］	+2
Canberra 堪培拉［澳大利亚］	+2
Hobart 霍巴特［澳大利亚］	+2
Honolulu 火奴鲁鲁(檀香山)［美国］	−18

Melbourne 墨尔本［澳大利亚］	+2
Noumea 努美阿［法属新喀里多尼亚］	+3
Papeete 帕皮提［法属波利尼西亚］	−18
Perth 佩思［澳大利亚］	0
Port Moresby 莫尔兹比港［巴布亚新几内亚］	+2
Suva 苏瓦［斐济］	+4
Sydney 悉尼［澳大利亚］	+2
Wellington 惠灵顿［新西兰］	+4

附录三 联合国组织

Appendix 3 The United Nations

联合国主要机构
Principal Organs of the United Nations

中文名称 Name in Chinese	中文简称 Chinese Abbreviation	英文名称 Name in English	英文简称 English Abbreviation
联合国大会	联大	General Assembly	GA
安全理事会	安理会	Security Council	SC
经济及社会理事会	经社理事会	Economic and Social Council	ECOSOC
托管理事会		Trusteeship Council	
国际法院		International Court of Justice	
秘书处		Secretariat	

联合国的组织及专门机构
Organizations and Specialized Agencies under the United Nations

中文名称 Name in Chinese	中文简称 Chinese Abbreviation	英文名称 Name in English	英文简称 English Abbreviation
国际电信联盟	国际电联	International Telecommunication Union	ITU
国际复兴开发银行（世界银行）	复兴开发银行；世行	International Bank for Reconstruction and Development (World Bank)	IBRD
国际海事组织	海事组织	International Maritime Organization	IMO
国际货币基金组织	货币基金	International Monetary Fund	IMF
国际金融公司		International Finance Corporation	IFC
国际开发协会		International Development Association	IDA
国际劳工组织	劳工组织	International Labour Organization	ILO
国际民用航空组织	民航组织	International Civil Aviation Organization	ICAO
联合国教育、科学及文化组织	教科文组织	United Nations Educational, Scientific and Cultural Organization	UNESCO
联合国粮食及农业组织	粮农组织	Food and Agriculture Organization of the United Nations	FAO
世界气象组织	气象组织	World Meteorological Organization	WMO
世界卫生组织	卫生组织	World Health Organization	WHO
万国邮政联盟	万国邮联	Universal Postal Union	UPU
国际麻醉品管理局		International Narcotics Control Board	INCB
国际农业发展基金	农发基金	International Fund for Agricultural Development	IFAD
国际提高妇女地位研究所		International Research and Training Institute for the Advancement of Women	
联合国巴勒斯坦和解委员会		United Nations Conciliation Commission for Palestine	UNCCP
联合国巴勒斯坦难民救济组织		United Nations Relief for Palestine Refugees	UNRPR
联合国裁军会议		United Nations Conference on Disarmament	UNCD
联合国裁军审议委员会		United Nations Disarmament Commission	UNDC
联合国裁军中心		United Nations Center for Disarmament	

中文名称 Name in Chinese	中文简称 Chinese Abbreviation	英文名称 Name in English	英文简称 English Abbreviation
联合国大学		United Nations University	UNU
联合国地区经济委员会		United Nations Regional Economic Commission	
联合国儿童基金会		United Nations Children Fund	UNICEF
联合国非殖民化特别委员会		United Nations Special Committee on Decolonization	
联合国非洲经济委员会		United Nations Economic Commission for Africa	UNECA
联合国妇女地位委员会		United Nations Commission on the Status of Women	
联合国工业发展组织	工发组织	United Nations Industrial Development Organization	UNIDO
联合国脱离接触观察员部队		United Nations Disengagement Observer Force	UNDOF
联合国国际法委员会		United Nations International Law Commission	UNILC
联合国国际贸易法委员会		United Nations Commission on International Trade Law	UNCITRAL
联合国国际刑事管辖问题委员会		United Nations Committee on International Criminal Jurisdiction	
联合国环境规划署	环境署	United Nations Environment Programme	UNEP
联合国环境基金		United Nations Environment Fund	UNEF
联合国环境与发展大会	环发大会	United Nations Conference on Environment and Development	UNCED
联合国货币金融会议		United Nations Monetary and Financial Conference	
联合国禁毒中心		United Nations Fund for Drug Abuse Control	UNFDAC
联合国经济发展特别基金		Special United Nations´Fund for Economic Development	SUNFED
联合国经济发展总署		United Nations Economic Development Administration	UNEDA
联合国经济合作行动计划署		United Nations Action Programme for Economic Cooperation	
联合国开发公司		United Nations Development Corporation	UNDC
联合国救灾协调专员办事处		Office of United Nations Disaster Relief Co-ordinator	UNDRO
联合国开发计划署	开发署	United Nations Development Programme	UNDP
联合国跨国公司委员会		United Nations Economic Commission on Transnational Corporations	
联合国跨国公司中心		United Nations Centre on Transnational Corporations	UNCTC
联合国拉丁美洲经济委员会		United Nations Economic Commission for Latin America	UNECLA
联合国麻醉品管制署	禁毒署	United Nations International Drug Control Programme	UNIDCP
联合国贸易促进中心		Trade Promotion Centre of the United Nations	UNTPC
联合国贸易和发展会议	贸发会议	United Nations Conference on Trade and Development	UNCTAD
联合国贸易与发展理事会		United Nations Trade and Development Board	UNTDB

中文名称 Name in Chinese	中文简称 Chinese Abbreviation	英文名称 Name in English	英文简称 English Abbreviation
联合国难民事务高级专员办事处		Office of the United Nations High Commissioner for Refugees	UNHCR
联合国区域发展中心		United Nations Centre for Regional Development	UNCRD
联合国人口活动基金	人口基金	United Nations Fund for Population Activities	UNFPA
联合国人口奖委员会		Committee for the United Nations Population Award	
联合国人口委员会		Population Commission of the United Nations	
联合国人类环境会议		United Nations Conference on the Human Environment	
联合国人类住区会议		United Nations Conference on Human Settlement	
联合国人类住区中心		Centre for Human Settlements	HABITAT
联合国人权委员会		United Nations Commission on Human Rights	
联合国人权中心		United Nations Centre for Human Rights	
联合国善后救济总署	救济总署	United Nations Relief and Rehabilitation Administration	UNRRA
联合国社会发展和人道主义事务中心		United Nations Centre for Social Development and Humanitarian Affairs	UNCSDHA
联合国社会发展首脑会议		World Summit for Social Development	Social Summit
联合国社会发展研究所		United Nations Research Institute for Social Development	UNRISD
联合国特别基金		United Nations Special Fund	
联合国停战监督组织		United Nations Truce Supervision Organization	UNTSO
联合国统计局		United Nations Statistical Office	
联合国宪章问题委员会		Committee on the Charter of the United Nations	
联合国协会世界联合会		World Federation of United Nations Associations	WFUNA
联合国行政法庭		United Nations Administrative Tribunal	
联合国行政和预算问题咨询委员会		UN Advisory Committee on Administrative and Budgetary Questions	UNACABQ
联合国训练研究所	训研所	United Nations Institute for Training and Research	UNITAR
联合国亚洲及太平洋经济和社会委员会	亚太经社委员会	United Nations Economic and Social Commission for Asia and the Pacific	ESCAP
联合国印度巴基斯坦委员会		United Nations Commission for India and Pakistan	UNCIP
联合国预防和控制犯罪委员会		United Nations Committee on Crime Prevention and Control	
联合国殖民主义问题特别委员会		United Nations Special Committee on Colonialism	
联合国周转基金		United Nations Revolving Fund	
联合国资本开发基金		United Nations Capital Development Fund	UNCDF
世界粮食理事会	粮食理事会	World Food Council	WFC
世界知识产权组织		World Intellectual Property Organization	WIPO

附录四 中国历史年代简表

Appendix 4 A Brief Chinese Chronology

夏 Xia Dynasty			C. 2100—C. 1600 B. C.
商 Shang Dynasty			C. 1600—C. 1100 B. C.
周 Zhou Dynasty	西周 Western Zhou Dynasty		1100—771 B. C.
	东周 Eastern Zhou Dynasty	春秋 Spring and Autumn	770—476 B. C.
		战国 Warring States	475—221 B. C.
秦 Qin Dynasty			221—206 B. C.
汉 Han Dynasty	西汉 Western Han		206 B. C.—25 A. D.
	东汉 Eastern Han		25—220 A. D.
三国 Three Kingdoms	魏 Wei		220—265
	蜀汉 Shu Han		221—263
	吴 Wu		222—280
西晋 Western Jin Dynasty			265—316
东晋 Eastern Jin Dynasty			317—420
南北朝 Northern and Southern Dynasties	南朝 Southern Dynasties	宋 Song	420—479
		齐 Qi	479—502
		梁 Liang	502—557
		陈 Chen	557—589
	北朝 Northern Dynasties	北魏 Northern Wei	386—534
		东魏 Eastern Wei	534—550
南北朝 Northern and Southern Dynasties	北朝 Northern Dynasties	北齐 Northern Qi	550—577
		西魏 Western Wei	535—556
		北周 Northern Zhou	557—581
隋 Sui Dynasty			581—618
唐 Tang Dynasty			618—907
五代 Five Dynasties	后梁 Later Liang		907—923
	后唐 Later Tang		923—936
	后晋 Later Jin		936—946
	后汉 Later Han		947—950
	后周 Later Zhou		951—960
宋 Song Dynasty	北宋 Northern Song Dynasty		960—1127
	南宋 Southern Song Dynasty		1127—1279
辽 Liao Dynasty			916—1125
金 Jin Dynasty			1115—1234
元 Yuan Dynasty			1279—1368
明 Ming Dynasty			1368—1644
清 Qing Dynasty			1644—1911
中华民国 Republic of China			1912—1949
中华人民共和国 People's Republic of China			1949—

附录五　中国各族人民

Appendix 5　Ethnic Groups in China

中　文 in Chinese	英　文 in English	中　文 in Chinese	英　文 in English
阿昌族	Achang	傈僳族	Lisu
白　族	Bai	珞巴族	Lhoba
保安族	Bonan	满　族	Manchu
布朗族	Blang	毛南族	Maonan
布依族	Bouyei	门巴族	Monba
朝鲜族	Korean	蒙古族	Mongol
达斡尔族	Daur	苗　族	Miao
傣　族	Dai	仫佬族	Mulam
德昂族	De'ang	纳西族	Naxi
东乡族	Dongxiang	怒　族	Nu
侗　族	Dong	普米族	Primi
独龙族	Derung	羌　族	Qiang
俄罗斯族	Russian	撒拉族	Salar
鄂伦春族	Oroqen	畲　族	She
鄂温克族	Ewenki	水　族	Sui
高山族	Gaoshan	塔吉克族	Tajik
仡佬族	Gelao	塔塔尔族	Tatar
哈尼族	Hani	土　族	Tu
哈萨克族	Kazak	土家族	Tujia
汉　族	Han	佤　族	Va
赫哲族	Hezhen	维吾尔族	Uygur
回　族	Hui	乌孜别克族	Uzbek
基诺族	Jino	锡伯族	Xibe
京　族	Gin	彝　族	Yi
景颇族	Jingpo	瑶　族	Yao
柯尔克孜族	Kirgiz	裕固族	Yugur
拉祜族	Lahu	藏　族	Tibetan
黎　族	Li	壮　族	Zhuang

附录六 中国、英国、美国军衔表

Appendix 6 Ranks in the Chinese, US and UK Armed Forces

陆军 Army

中国军衔 Rank in Chinese Armed Forces	美国军衔 Rank in US Armed Forces	英国军衔 Rank in UK Armed Forces
	General of the Army(五星上将)	Field Marshal(陆军元帅)
一级上将* General, First Class		
上将 General	General	General
中将 Lieutenant General	Lieutenant General	Lieutenant General
少将 Major General	Major General	Major General
	Brigadier General(准将)	Brigadier(准将)
大校 Senior Colonel		
上校 Colonel	Colonel	Colonel
中校 Lieutenant Colonel	Lieutenant Colonel	Lieutenant Colonel
少校 Major	Major	Major
上尉 Captain	Captain	Captain
中尉 First Lieutenant	First Lieutenant	Lieutenant
少尉 Second Lieutenant	Second Lieutenant**	Second Lieutenant**
军士长 Master Sergeant	Command Sergeant Major**	
专业军士 Specialist Sergeant		
上士 Sergeant, First Class	Staff Sergeant	Staff Sergeant
中士 Sergeant	Sergeant	Sergeant
下士 Corporal	Corporal	Corporal
上等兵 Private, First Class	Private, First Class (一等兵)	Lance Corporal (一等兵)
列 兵 Private	Private(二等兵) Basic Private(三等兵)	Private(二等兵) Recruit(新兵)

* 1955 年中国首次颁布军官军衔时,还包括元帅(Marshal)、大将(Senior General)和大尉(Senior Captain),但无一级上将。

** 英美军制少尉以下设有准尉(Warrant Officer, etc.),而美国军士长在 Command Sergeant Major 以下还有数级,均与中国军衔不对应,此处略去。空、海军也有此种情况,从略。

海军 Navy

中国军衔 **Rank in Chinese Armed Forces**	美国军衔 **Rank in US Armed Forces**	英国军衔 **Rank in UK Armed Forces**
-	Fleet Admiral （五星上将）	Admiral of the Fleet （海军元帅）
一级上将 * Admiral, First Class		
上　将 Admiral	Admiral	Admiral
中　将 Vice Admiral	Vice Admiral	Vice Admiral
少　将 Rear Admiral	Rear Admiral	Rear Admiral
	Commodore （准将）	Commodore （准将）
大　校 Senior Captain		
上　校 Captain	Captain	Captain
中　校 Commander	Commander	Commander
少　校 Lieutenant Commander	Lieutenant Commander	Lieutenant Commander
上　尉 Lieutenant	Lieutenant	Lieutenant
中　尉 Lieutenant, Junior Grade	Lieutenant, Junior Grade	Sub-Lieutenant
少　尉 Ensign	Ensign	Acting Sub-Lieutenant
军士长 Chief Petty Officer	Master Chief Petty Officer	Fleet Chief Petty Officer （舰队上士）
专业军士 Specialist Petty Officer		
上　士 Petty Officer, First Class	Petty Officer, First Class	Chief Petty Officer
中　士 Petty Officer, second Class	Petty Officer, second Class	Petty Officer, First Class
下　士 Petty Officer, Third Class	Petty Officer, Third Class	Petty Officer, Second Class
上等兵 Seaman, First Class	Seaman, First Class （一等兵）	Leading Seaman（上等水兵） Able Seaman（一等水兵）
列　兵 Seaman, Second Class	Seaman Apprentice（二等兵） Seaman Recruit（三等兵）	Ordinary Seaman（二等水兵） Junior Seaman（新兵）

* 1955 年中国首次颁布军衔时还包括海军大将（Senior Admiral）、海军大尉（Senior Lieutenant），但无一级上将。

空军 Air Force

中国军衔 Rank in Chinese Armed Forces	美国军衔 Rank in US Armed Forces	英国军衔 Rank in UK Armed Forces
	General of the Air Force （五星上将）	Marshal of the Royal Air Force （皇家空军元帅）
一级上将 * General, First Class		
上 将 General	General	Air Chief Marshal
中 将 Lieutenant General	Lieutenant General	Air Marshal
少 将 Major General	Major General	Air Vice Marshal
	Brigadier General（准将）	Air Commodore（准将）
大 校 Senior Colonel		
上 校 Colonel	Colonel	Group Captain
中 校 Lieutenant Colonel	Lieutenant Colonel	Wing Commander
少 校 Major	Major	Squadron Leader
上 尉 Captain	Captain	Flight Lieutenant
中 尉 First Lieutenant	First Lieutenant	Flying Officer
少 尉 Second Lieutenant	Second Lieutenant	Pilot Officer
军士长 Master Sergeant	Chief Master Sergeant	
专业军士 Specialist Sergeant		Technician * * （技术军士）
上 士 Technical Sergeant	Technical Sergeant	Flight Sergeant
中 士 Staff Sergeant	Staff Sergeant	Sergeant
下 士 Sergeant	Sergeant	Corporal
上等兵 Airman, First Class	Airman, First Class （一等兵）	Senior Aircraftsman （一等兵）
列 兵 Airman, Second Class	Airman, Second Class（二等兵） Airman Basic（三等兵）	Leading Aircraftsman（二等兵） Aircraftsman（新兵）

* 1955 年中国首次颁布军衔时无一级上将，而有空军大尉（Senior Captain）。

* * 英空军中技术军士有两级：总技术军士（Chief Technician），在上士之下，中士之上；初级技术军士（Junior Technician）则在下士之下，上等兵之上。

附录七　中国度量衡

Appendix 7　China's Weights and Measures

（中国采用公制为度量衡法定单位。
China follows the metric system for weights and measures.）

(一)长度单位表 Units of Linear Measure

公制 metric system	符号 symbol	市制 traditional Chinese system	英制 British system
千米(公里) (kilometre) =1000 米	km	2 市里(*li*)	0.6214 英里(mile)
米(公尺) (metre) =10 分米	m	3 市尺(*chi*)	3.2808 英尺(foot; ft); 1.0936 码(yard; yd)
分米(公寸) (decimetre) =0.1 米	dm	3 市寸(*cun*)	0.32808 英尺(foot; ft); 0.10936 码(yard; yd)
厘米(公分) (centimetre) =0.01 米	cm	3 市分(*fen*)	0.3937 英寸(inch; in)
毫米(公厘) (millimetre) =0.001 米	mm	3 市厘(*li*)	
微米(公微) (micrometre; micron) $=10^{-6}$米	μm		
纳米 (nanometre) = millionth m $=10^{-9}$米	nm		

注:1 海里(nautical mile; nmi) =1.85 公里 =3.704 市里 =1.15 英里

(二)面积单位表 Units of Area Measure

公制 metric system	符号 symbol	市制 traditional Chinese system	英美制 British-American system
平方千米 (平方公里) (Square kilometre)	km^2	4 平方公里(*li*²) 1500 市亩(*mu*)	0.3861 平方英里(sq mi; mi^2); 100 公顷(hectare; ha); 247.1 英亩(acre)
平方米 (square metre) =100 平方分米	m^2	9 平方市尺(*chi*²)	10.7639 平方英尺(sq ft; ft^2); 1.1960 平方码(sq yd; yd^2)
平方分米 (square decimetre) =0.01 平方米 =100 平方厘米	dm^2	0.09 平方市尺(*chi*²)	0.107639 平方英尺(sq ft; ft^2); 0.01196 平方码(sq yd; yd^2)
平方厘米 (square centimetre) =0.0001 平方米 =0.01 平方分米 =100 平方毫米	cm^2		
平方毫米 (square millimetre)	mm^2		
公顷(hectare) =100 公亩(are) =10000 平方米	ha	15 亩(*mu*)	2.47 英亩(acre)

注:1 亩(*mu*)=60 平方丈(*zhang*²)=0.1644 英亩(acre)=0.0667 公顷(hectare; ha)

(三)体积单位表 Units of Cubic Measure

公制 metric system	符号 symbol	市制 traditional Chinese system	英美制 British-American system
立方米 (cubic metre) =1000 立方分米	m^3	27 立方市尺(*chi*³)	35.3147 立方英尺(cubic foot; ft^3) 1.308 立方码(cubic yard; yd^3)
立方分米 (cubic decimetre) =0.001 立方米 =1000 立方厘米	dm^3	0.027 立方市尺(*chi*³)	0.0353147 立方英尺(ft^3); 0.001308 立方码(yd^3)
立方厘米 (cubic centimetre) =0.000001 立方米 =0.001 立方分米 =1000 立方毫米	cm^3		
立米毫米 (cubic millimetre) =0.001 立方厘米	mm^3		

(四)容积单位表 Units of Capacity Measure

公制 metric system	符号 symbol	市制 traditional Chinese system	英美制 British-American system
升(liter) =10 分升	L(l)	1 市升(*sheng*)	1. 7598 品脱(pint) 0. 22 加仑(gallon, UK)
分升(decilitre) =0. 1 升 =10 厘升	dL(dl)	1 市合(*ge*)	0. 17598 品脱(pint) 0. 022 加仑(gallon, UK)
厘升(centilitre) =0. 01 升 =10 毫升	cL(cl)		
毫升(millilitre); 西西(cc) =0. 001 升	mL(ml)		

(五)重量单位表 Units of Weight

公制 metric system	符号 symbol	市制 traditional Chinese system	英美制 British-American system
吨(metric ton; tonne) =1000 公斤	t	2000 市斤(*jin*)	0. 9842 长吨(long ton, UK); 1. 1023 短吨(short ton, US)
千克(公斤) (kilogramme) =1000 克	kg	2 市斤(*jin*)	2. 2046 磅(pound)
克(gram) =10 分克	g	2 市分	15. 4324 格令(grain) 0. 035 盎司(ounce; oz)
分克(decigram) =0. 0001 千克 =0. 1 克	dg		
厘克(centigram) =0. 00001 千克 =0. 1 分克	cg		
毫克(milligram) =0. 000001 千克 =0. 1 厘克	mg		

(六)英美制计量单位换算表
Conversion Tables from the British-American to the Metrical & Traditional Chinese System

1. 长度单位 Units of Length

1 英里(mi) = 1.609 千米(公里)(km) = 3.218 市里(*li*) = 0.869 海里(nmi)
1 码(yd) = 3 英尺(ft; foot) = 0.9144 米 = 2.7432 市尺(*chi*)
1 英尺(ft) = 0.305 米(m) = 0.914 市尺(*chi*)

2. 面积单位 Units of Area

1 英亩(acre) = 6.070 市亩(*mu*) = 0.405 公顷(ha)
1 平方码(yd^2) = 0.8361 平方公尺(m^2)
1 平方英尺(ft^2) = 0.835 平方市尺(chi^2) = 0.0939 平方公尺(m^2)

3. 重量单位 Units of Weight

1 磅(pound) = 0.45359 千克(公斤)(kg) = 0.90719 市斤(*jin*)
长吨(long ton) = 1016.05 千克(公斤)(kg) = 2032.09 市斤(*jin*)
短吨(short ton) = 907.185 千克(公斤)(kg) = 1814.37 市斤(*jin*)

4. 容量单位 Units of Capacity Measure

1 加仑(gallon, UK) = 4 夸脱(quart) = 8 品脱(pint) = 4.5461 升(L) = 4.5461 市升(*sheng*)
1 品脱(pint, US) = 0.10409 加仑(gal) = 0.5 夸脱(quart) = 0.47317 升(L) = 0.47317 市升(*sheng*)

附录八 二十四节气

Appendix 8 The Twenty-Four Seasonal Division Points

	节气名、序 **Order and Name of Seasonal Division Point**	太阳到达黄经(度) **Sun's Position at Ecliptic**	节气的公历日期 **Date on Gregorian Calendar**
春季 spring	1. 立春 Beginning of Spring	315°	4 or 5 February
	2. 雨水 Rain Water	330°	19 or 20 February
	3. 惊蛰 Waking of Insects	345°	6 or 5 March
	4. 春分 Vernal Equinox	0°	21 or 20 March
	5. 清明 Pure Brightness	15°	5 or 6 April
	6. 谷雨 Grain Rain	30°	20 or 21 April
夏季 summer	7. 立夏 Beginning of Summer	45°	6 or 5 May
	8. 小满 Grain Budding	60°	21 or 22 May
	9. 芒种 Grain in Ear	75°	6 or 7 June
	10. 夏至 Summer Solstice	90°	22 or 21 June
	11. 小暑 Slight Heat	105°	7 or 8 July
	12. 大暑 Great Heat	120°	23 or 24 July
秋季 autumn	13. 立秋 Beginning of Autumn	135°	8 or 7 August
	14. 处暑 Limit of Heat	150°	23 or 24 August
	15. 白露 White Dew	165°	8 or 7 September
	16. 秋分 Autumnal Equinox	180°	23 or 24 September
	17. 寒露 Cold Dew	195°	8 or 9 October
	18. 霜降 Frost's Descent	210°	24 or 23 October
冬季 winter	19. 立冬 Beginning of Winter	225°	8 or 7 November
	20. 小雪 Slight Snow	240°	23 or 22 November
	21. 大雪 Great Snow	255°	7 or 8 December
	22. 冬至 Winter Solstice	270°	22 or 23 December
	23. 小寒 Slight Cold	285°	6 or 5 January
	24. 大寒 Great Cold	300°	20 or 21 January

附录九 天干地支

Appendix 9 Heavenly Stems and Earthly Branches

天 干(*tiangan*) Heavenly Stem	相应元素 Corresponding Element	相应星宿 Corresponding Star
甲(*jia*) Heavenly Stem One	木 wood	木星 Jupiter
乙(*yi*) Heavenly Stem Two		
丙(*bing*) Heavenly Stem Three	火 fire	火星 Mars
丁(*ding*) Heavenly Stem Four		
戊(*wu*) Heavenly Stem Five	土 earth	土星 Saturn
已(*ji*) Heavenly Stem Six		
庚(*geng*) Heavenly Stem Seven	金 metal	金星 Venus
辛(*xin*) Heavenly Stem Eight		
壬(*ren*) Heavenly Stem Nine	水 water	水星 Mercury
癸(*gui*) Heavenly Stem Ten		

地 支(*dizhi*) Earthly Branch	生 肖 Symbolic Animal	相应时间 Corresponding Hours
子(*zi*) Earthly Branch One	鼠 Rat	11:00 p. m. -1:00 a. m.
丑(*chou*) Earthly Branch Two	牛 Ox	1:00-3:00 a. m.
寅(*yin*) Earthly Branch Three	虎 Tiger	3:00-5:00 a. m.
卯(*mao*) Earthly Branch Four	兔 Rabbit	5:00-7:00 a. m.
辰(*chen*) Earthly Branch Five	龙 Dragon	7:00-9:00 a. m.
巳(*si*) Earthly Branch Six	蛇 Snake	9:00-11:00 a. m.
午(*wu*) Earthly Branch Seven	马 Horse	11:00 a. m. -1:00 p. m.
未(*wei*) Earthly Branch Eight	羊 Sheep	1:00-3:00 p. m.
申(*shen*) Earthly Branch Nine	猴 Monkey	3:00-5:00 p. m.
酉(*you*) Earthly Branch Ten	鸡 Rooster	5:00-7:00 p. m.
戌(*xu*) Earthly Branch Eleven	狗 Dog	7:00-9:00 p. m.
亥(*hai*) Earthly Branch Twelve	猪 Pig	9:00-11:00 p. m.

附录十 中国法定假日和主要传统节日

Appendix 10 Official Holidays and Traditional Festivals

法定假日 Official Holidays

元旦	New Year's Day (1 January,1 day off)
春节	Spring Festival(*or* Chinese New Year's Day,1st of the first lunar month,3 days off)
国际劳动妇女节	Internatioal Working Women's Day (8 March,1/2 day off for women)
国际劳动节	International Labour Day (1 May,3 days off)
中国青年节	Chinese Youth Day (4 May,1/2 day off for youths of and above 14)
国际儿童节	International Children's Day (1 June,1 day off for those below 14)
中国人民解放军建军节	Army Day (Anniversary of the Founding of the Chinese People's Liberation Army,1 August,1/2 day off for those in active service)
国庆节	National Day (1 October,3 days off)

传统节日 Traditional Festivals

春节	Spring Festival(*or* Chinese New Year's Day,1st of the first lunar month,3 days off)
元宵节	Lantern Festival (15th of the first lunar month,marking the end of Chinese New Year celebrations with a display of colourful lanterns and eating of *yuanxiao*)
清明节	Pure Brightness Festival (marking the 5th seasonal division point and usually falling on the 5th or 6th of April, a traditional festival for commemorating the dead)
端午节	Dragon Boat Festival (5th of the fifth lunar month,celebrated by eating *zongzi* and holding dragon boat races)
中秋节	Mid-Autumn Festival (15th of the eighth lunar month,a traditional festival for family reunion , celebrated by eating moon cakes and enjoying the full moon)
重阳节	Double Ninth Festival (9th of the ninth lunar month, celebrated by climbing heights to enjoy nature and honouring elderly people)

附录 11 奥运会常用语

Appendix 11 The Everyday Expressions of Olympic

国际奥林匹克委员会　International Olympic Committee
国际奥委会总部　the headquarters of the IOC
奥林匹克运动会　Olympic Games;Olympics;Olympiad
冬季奥林匹克运动会　Olympic Winter Games
夏季奥林匹克运动会　Olympic Summer Games
奥运会年　Olympic year
奥运会日程安排　Olympic schedule
奥运会前的预选赛　Olympic Qualification
奥运会选拔赛　Olympic trial
奥运会比赛项目　Olympic event
奥运会城　Olympic city
奥运会金牌　Olympic gold medal
奥运会杯　Olympic cup
奥运会圣火　Olympic flame
奥运会火炬　Olympic torch
奥运会宣誓词　Olympic Oath
奥运会会旗　The Olympic flag
奥运会主会场　Olympic stadium
奥运会官方吉祥物　Official Olympic mascots
奥运会主题歌　Olympic theme song
奥运会会歌　The Olympic anthem
奥运会官方永久会歌　the official Olympic anthem
奥运会奖状　Olympic diploma of merit
奥运会秩序册　Olympic programme
参加奥运会选手　Olympian

附录十二 化学元素表

Appendix 12 A Table of Chemical Elements

元素 Element		符号 Symbol	原子序数 Atomic Number	原子量 Atomic Weight
actinium	锕	Ac	89	227
aluminium	铝	Al	13	26.9815
americium	镅	Am	95	243
antimony	锑	Sb	51	121.76
argentum	银	Ag	47	107.868
argon	氩	Ar	18	39.948
arsenic	砷	As	33	74.922
astatine	砹	At	85	210
barium	钡	Ba	56	137.33
berkelium	锫	Bk	97	247
beryllium	铍	Be	4	9.012
bismuth	铋	Bi	83	208.98
bohrium	铍	Bh	107	264
boron	硼	B	5	10.81
bromine	溴	Br	35	79.904
cadmium	镉	Cd	48	112.41
caesium	铯	Cs	55	132.905
calcium	钙	Ca	20	40.08
californium	锎	Cf	98	251
carbon	碳	C	6	12.011
cerium	铈	Ce	58	140.12
chlorine	氯	Cl	17	35.453
chromium	铬	Cr	24	51.996
cobalt	钴	Co	27	58.933
copper	铜	Cu	29	63.546
curium	锔	Cm	96	247
darmstadtium	钛	Ds	110	269
dubnium	钳	Db	105	262
dysprosium	镝	Dy	66	162.50
einsteinium	锿	Es	99	252
erbium	铒	Er	68	167.26
europium	铕	Eu	63	151.96
fermium	镄	Fm	100	257
ferrum	铁	Fe	26	55.845
fluorine	氟	F	9	18.9984
francium	钫	Fr	87	223
gadolinium	钆	Gd	64	157.25
gallium	镓	Ga	31	69.72
germanium	锗	Ge	32	72.64
gold	金	Au	79	196.967
hafnium	铪	Hf	72	178.49
hassium	镙	Hs	108	265
helium	氦	He	2	4.0026

元素 Element		符号 Symbol	原子序数 Atomic Number	原子量 Atomic Weight
holmium	钬	Ho	67	164.930
hydrargyrum	汞	Hg	80	200.59
hydrogen	氢	H	1	1.008
indium	铟	In	49	114.82
iodium	碘	I	53	126.9045
iridium	铱	Ir	77	192.22
kalium	钾	K	19	39.10
kryptonum	氪	Kr	36	83.80
lanthanum	镧	La	57	138.9055
lawrencium	铹	Lr	103	260
lithium	锂	Li	3	6.941
lutetium	镥	Lu	71	174.97
magnesium	镁	Mg	12	24.305
manganum	锰	Mn	25	54.938
meitnerium	鿏	Mt	109	268
mendelevium	钔	Md	101	258
molybdaenum	钼	Mo	42	95.94
natrium	钠	Na	11	22.9898
neodymium	钕	Nd	60	144.24
neonum	氖	Ne	10	20.18
neptunium	镎	Np	93	237
niccolum	镍	Ni	28	58.69
niobium	铌	Nb	41	92.906
nitrogenium	氮	N	7	14.0067
nobelium	锘	No	102	259
osmium	锇	Os	76	190.2
oxygenium	氧	O	8	15.9994
palladium	钯	Pd	46	106.4
phosphorum	磷	P	15	30.9738
platinum	铂	Pt	78	195.08
plumbum	铅	Pb	82	207.2
plutonium	钚	Pu	94	239.244
polonium	钋	Po	84	209.2
praseodymium	镨	Pr	59	140.9077
promethium	钷	Pm	61	147
protactinium	镤	Pa	91	231.0359
radium	镭	Ra	88	226.0254
radon	氡	Rn	86	222
rhenium	铼	Re	75	186.2
rhodium	铑	Rh	45	102.9055
rubidium	铷	Rb	37	85.47
rutherfordium	𬬻	Rf	104	261
ruthenium	钌	Ru	44	101.07
samarium	钐	Sm	62	150.36
scandium	钪	Sc	21	44.956
seaborgium	𬭳	Sg	106	263
selenium	硒	Se	34	78.96

元素 Element		符号 Symbol	原子序数 Atomic Number	原子量 Atomic Weight
silicium	硅	Si	14	28.086
stannum	锡	Sn	50	118.71
strontium	锶	Sr	38	87.62
sulphur	硫	S	16	32.065
tantalum	钽	Ta	73	180.948
technetium	锝	Tc	43	97.99
tellurium	碲	Te	52	127.60
terbium	铽	Tb	65	158.9253
thallium	铊	Tl	81	204.38
thorium	钍	Th	90	232.038
thulium	铥	Tm	69	168.934
titanium	钛	Ti	22	47.90
uranium	铀	U	92	238.0289
vanadium	钒	V	23	50.9414
wolfram	钨	W	74	183.85
xenonum	氙	Xe	54	131.30
ytterbium	镱	Yb	70	173.04
yttrium	钇	Y	39	88.9059
zincum	锌	Zn	30	65.39
zirconium	锆	Zr	40	91.22